Pocket Oxford German Dictionary

Third Edition

German → English
English → German

Chief Editors
M. Clark
O. Thyen

OXFORD UNIVERSITY PRESS

OXFORD
UNIVERSITY PRESS

Great Clarendon Street, Oxford OX2 6DP

Oxford University Press is a department of the University of Oxford.
It furthers the University's objective of excellence in research, scholarship,
and education by publishing worldwide in

Oxford New York
Auckland Cape Town Dar es Salaam Hong Kong Karachi
Kuala Lumpur Madrid Melbourne Mexico City Nairobi
New Delhi Shanghai Taipei Toronto

With offices in
Argentina Austria Brazil Chile Czech Republic France Greece
Guatemala Hungary Italy Japan Poland Portugal Singapore
South Korea Switzerland Thailand Turkey Ukraine Vietnam

Published in the United States
by Oxford University Press Inc., New York

First edition published 1992
Revised edition published 1997
Second edition published 2000
Revised second edition published 2003
Third edition published 2006
Revised 2008

British Library Cataloguing in Publication Data
Data available

Library of Congress Cataloging in Publication Data
Data available

Designed by Information Design Unit, Newport Pagnell
Typeset in Nimrod, Arial and Meta by Tradespools
Printed in Great Britain by Clays Ltd, Bungay, Suffolk

ISBN 978-0-19-954748-7

1

Preface

This new edition of the *Pocket Oxford German Dictionary* has been enlarged and updated to take account of new vocabulary and recent developments in German, with the needs of both the general and school user in mind. New words and phrases reflect scientific and technological innovations as well as changes in politics, culture, and society. Reforms to the spelling of German ratified by the governments of Germany, Austria, and Switzerland in 1996 have been fully incorporated and are clearly signposted.

Combining the authority of the *Oxford German Dictionary* with the convenience of a smaller format and quick-access layout, this easy-to-use pocket dictionary is the ideal reference tool for all those requiring quick and reliable answers to their translation questions. It provides clear guidance on selecting the most appropriate translation, numerous examples to help with problems of usage and construction, and precise information on grammar, style, and pronunciation. All grammatical terms used are explained in a glossary at the back of the dictionary.

New features of the dictionary include an expanded and updated A–Z of life and culture, giving essential encyclopedic and cultural information about contemporary Germany and German-speaking countries, and a practical guide to letter-writing in German, including sample letters, e-mails, and CVs, with practical tips about key differences between German and English letter styles and layout, and a new section on text messaging.

Designed to meet the needs of a wide range of users, from the student at intermediate level and above to the enthusiastic traveller and business professional, the *Pocket Oxford German Dictionary* is an invaluable practical resource for learners of modern, idiomatic German.

Michael Clark
Oxford University Press

Editors and contributors

Editors
Michael Clark
Olaf Thyen
Werner Scholze-Stubenrecht
Magdalena Seubel
Bernadette Mohan
Robin Sawers
Gunhild Prowe

Data input
Susan Wilkin
Anne McConnell
Anna Cotgreave

A–Z of German culture
Calendar of traditions, festivals, and holidays
Ella Associates
Valerie Grundy
Eva Vennebusch
Neil Morris
Roswitha Morris
Penelope Isaac

Summary of German Grammar
Nicholas Rollin
Marie-Louise Wasmeier

Inhalt / Contents

Als Markenzeichen geschützte Wörter / Note on Proprietary Status

Namen und Kennzeichen, die als Marken bekannt sind und entsprechenden Schutz genießen, sind durch die Zeichen ® oder Ⓦⓩ gekennzeichnet. Handelsnamen ohne Markencharakter sind nicht gekennzeichnet. Aus dem Fehlen der Zeichen ® oder Ⓦⓩ darf im Einzelfall nicht geschlossen werden, dass ein Name oder Zeichen frei ist. Eine Haftung für ein etwaiges Fehlen der Zeichen ® oder Ⓦⓩ wird ausgeschlossen.

This dictionary includes some words which have, or are asserted to have, proprietary status as trade marks or otherwise. Their inclusion does not imply that they have acquired for legal purposes a non-proprietary or general significance, nor any other judgement concerning their legal status. In cases where the editorial staff have some evidence that a word has proprietary status, this is indicated in the entry for that word by the abbreviation ® or Ⓦⓩ, but no judgement concerning the legal status of such words is made or implied thereby.

Erläuterungen zum deutsch-englischen Text / Key to German-English Entries

Stichwort — **Bịld·schirm** *der* (Ferns., Informationst.) screen
Headword

Bịldschirm-: ~gerät *das* VDU; visual display unit; **~schoner** *der;* ~~s, ~~ (DV) screen saver — **Kompositablock. Eine Tilde ersetzt jeweils den gemeinsamen ersten Bestandteil der Komposita**
Compound block with a swung dash representing the first element of each compound

Die Ausspracheangaben (in IPA-Lautschrift) stehen unmittelbar hinter dem Stichwort (s.S.xi) — **Blues** /blu:s/ *der;* ~, ~: blues *pl.*
Pronunciation is shown in IPA immediately after the headword (see p. xi)

dar|bieten (geh.) *unr. tr. V.* (aufführen, vortragen) perform; ... — **Ein senkrechter Strich nach dem ersten Bestandteil eines zusammengesetzten Verbs zeigt an, dass es sich um eine unfeste Zusammensetzung handelt**
A vertical bar indicates that a compound verb is separable

Ein unter einen Vokal gesetzter waagerechter Strich zeigt die Länge des Vokals und in mehrsilbigen Wörtern zugleich die Betonung der betreffenden Silbe an — **darüber** *Adv.* **(a)** over it/them; ~ **stehen** (fig.) be above such things
An underline indicates a long vowel, stressed in words of more than one syllable

darụm *Adv.* **(a)** [a]round it/them; ... — **Ein unter einen Vokal gesetzter Punkt zeigt die Kürze des Vokals und in mehrsilbigen Wörtern zugleich die Betonung der betreffenden Silbe an**
An underdot indicates a short vowel, stressed in words of more than one syllable

Ein hochgestellter Stern vor einem Stichwort zeigt an, dass es sich um eine alte, nicht mehr gültige Schreibung handelt — **dạss**, ***dạß** *Konj.* **(a)** that; ...
An asterisk indicates an old spelling

Erst·aufführung *die* première — **Kompositionsfuge**
Dot marking the juncture of the elements of a compound

Grammatische Gliederungspunkte und Wortartangaben — **erstklassig** **1** *Adj.* first-class **2** *adv.* superbly
Grammatical categories and parts of speech

Die Formen des Genitivs und des Plurals eines Substantivs
Genitive and plural forms of a noun

Falter *der;* **~s, ~** (Nacht~) moth; (Tag~) butterfly

fliehen /'fli:ən/ *unr. itr. V.;* ***mit sein*** flee (**vor** + *Dat.* from); ...

Der Hinweis *mit sein* zeigt an, dass das betreffende Verb die Perfekttempora mit dem Hilfsverb *sein* bildet
mit sein indicates that a verb is conjugated with the auxiliary verb *sein* in its perfect tenses

Unregelmäßige Steigerungsformen eines Adjektivs
Irregular comparative and superlative forms of an adjective

fromm; **~er** *od.* **frömmer, ~st...** *od.* **frömmst...** [1] *Adj.* pious, devout ‹*person*›;

Gehässigkeit *die;* **~, ~en (a)** (Wesen) spitefulness;
(b) (Äußerung) spiteful remark

Semantische Gliederungspunkte und Bedeutungsindikatoren
Sense categories and indicators

Stilistische Kennzeichnungen
Style labels

happig *Adj.* (ugs.) **~e Preise** fancy prices (coll.)

Haube *die;* **~, ~n (a)** bonnet; (einer Krankenschwester) cap;
(b) (Kfz-W.) bonnet (Brit.); hood (Amer.)

heuer *Adv.* (südd., österr., schweiz.) this year

Angaben zur räumlichen Zuordnung
Regional labels

Bereichsangaben
Subject labels

Icon /'ai:kən/ *das;* **~s, ~s** (DV) icon

Immun·schwäche *die* (Med.) immunodeficiency; immune deficiency

knallen [1] *itr. V.* **(a)** ‹*shot*› ring out; ‹*firework*› go bang; ‹*cork*› pop; ‹*door*› slam; ‹*whip, rifle*› crack;

knapp [1] *Adj.* **(a)** meagre; narrow ‹*victory, lead*›; narrow, bare ‹*majority*›;

Kollokatoren (Wörter, mit denen zusammen das Stichwort häufig vorkommt) als Hilfe zur Auswahl der für den jeweiligen Kontext passenden Übersetzung
Collocators—words often used with the headword, shown to help select the correct translation for each context

Beispiele (jeweils mit einer Tilde an Stelle des Stichworts)
Examples (with a swung dash representing the headword)

machen [1] *tr. V.* **(a)** make; **aus Plastik/Holz** *usw.* **gemacht** made of plastic/wood *etc.;* **sich** (*Dat.*) **etw. ~ lassen** have sth. made; ...

Omi *die;* **~, ~s** ▶ OMA

Ein Pfeil verweist auf ein bedeutungsgleiches anderes Stichwort
An arrow directs the user to another headword with the same meaning

Mit *s. auch* wird auf ein Stichwort verwiesen, unter dem noch zusätzliche Informationen zu finden sind
s. auch directs the user to another headword where additional information can be found

Samstag *der;* **~[e]s, ~e** Saturday; *s. auch* DIENSTAG

Key to English-German Entries / Erläuterungen zum englisch-deutschen Text

Headword Stichwort

barber /ˈbɑːbə(r)/ *n.* [Herren]friseur, *der;* **~'s shop** (Brit.) Friseursalon, *der*
barbiturate /bɑːˈbɪtjʊrət/ *n.* (Chem.) Barbiturat, *das*

bar: ~chart *n.* Stabdiagramm, *das;* **~code** *n.* Strichcode, *der*

Compound block with a swung dash representing the first element of each compound Kompositablock. Eine Tilde ersetzt jeweils den gemeinsamen ersten Bestandteil der Komposita

Each phrasal verb is entered on a new line immediately following the entry for the first element Die *Phrasal Verbs* folgen, jedes auf einer neuen Zeile, direkt auf den Eintrag zu ihrem Grundverb

bear[2] **1** *v.t.*, **bore** /bɔː(r)/, **borne** /bɔːn/ …
■ **bear 'out** *v.t.* (fig.) bestätigen ‹*Bericht, Erklärung*›; **~ sb. out** jmdm. Recht geben.
■ **'bear with** *v.t.* Nachsicht haben mit

bemused /bɪˈmjuːzd/ *adj.* verwirrt

Pronunciation shown in IPA (see p. xiii). Ausspracheangaben (in IPA-Lautschrift) (s. S. xiii)

Stress mark, showing stress on the following syllable Betonungszeichen vor der betonten Silbe

'bin liner *n.* Müllbeutel, *der*

cart /kɑːt/ **1** *n.* Wagen, *der* **2** *v.t.* (coll.) schleppen

Grammatical categories and parts of speech Grammatische Gliederungspunkte und Wortartangaben

Irregular tenses of a verb Unregelmäßige Verbformen

choose /tʃuːz/ **1** *v.t.*, **chose** /tʃəʊz/, **chosen** /ˈtʃəʊzn/ **(a)** wählen

dub /dʌb/ *v.t.*, **-bb-** (Cinemat.) synchronisieren

Doubling of a final consonant of a verb before -ed *or* -ing Verdoppelung des Endkonsonanten eines Verbs vor -ed *oder* -ing

Irregular comparative and superlative forms of an adjective Unregelmäßige Steigerungsformen eines Adjektivs

good /gʊd/ **1** *adj.*, **better** /ˈbetə(r)/, **best** /best/ **(a)** gut; günstig ‹*Gelegenheit, Angebot*›; …

groom /gruːm, grʊm/ **1** *n.* **(a)** (stable boy) Stallbursche, *der*
(b) (bride~) Bräutigam, *der*

Sense categories and sense indicators Semantische Gliederungspunkte und Bedeutungs-indikatoren

Subject labels Bereichsangaben

HTML *abbr.* (Comp.) **hypertext markup language** HTML
immobilizer /ɪˈməʊbɪlaɪzə(r)/ *n.* (Motor Veh.) Wegfahrsperre, *die*

Key to English-German entries

Style labels
Stilistische Kennzeichnungen

jam-packed *adj.* (coll.) knallvoll (ugs.), proppenvoll (ugs.) (**with** von)

loch /lɒx, lɒk/ *n.* (Scot.) See, *der*

Medicare /'medɪkeə(r)/ *n.* (Amer.) *[bundes]staatliches Krankenversicherungssystem für Personen über 65 Jahre*

Regional labels
Angaben zur räumlichen Zuordnung

Collocators —words often used with the headword, shown to help select the correct translation for each context.
Kollokatoren (Wörter, mit denen zusammen das Stichwort häufig vorkommt) als Hilfe zur Auswahl der für den jeweiligen Kontext passenden Übersetzung

oppress /ə'pres/ *v.t.* unterdrücken; (fig.) ‹*Gefühl:*› bedrücken

oppressive /ə'presɪv/ *adj.* repressiv; (fig.) bedrückend ‹*Ängste, Atmosphäre*›; (hot and close) drückend ‹*Wetter, Klima, Tag*›

price /praɪs/ *n.* (lit. or fig.) Preis, *der;* **at a ~ of** zum Preis von; **what is the ~ of this?** was kostet das?; **at/not at any ~:** um jeden/keinen Preis

Examples (with a swung dash representing the headword)
Beispiele (jeweils mit einer Tilde an Stelle des Stichworts)

An arrow directs the user to another headword with the same meaning
Ein Pfeil verweist auf ein bedeutungsgleiches anderes Stichwort

sitcom /'sɪtkɒm/ (coll.) ▶ SITUATION COMEDY

Sunday /'sʌndeɪ, 'sʌndɪ/ *n.* Sonntag, *der;* **~ opening** die sonntägliche Öffnung; **~ trading** sonntägliche Ladenöffnung; *see also* FRIDAY

***see also* directs the user to another headword where additional information can be found**
Mit *see also* wird auf ein Stichwort verwiesen, unter dem noch zusätzliche Informationen zu finden sind

Phonetic symbols used in transcriptions of German words

Phonetic information given in the German-English section

The pronunciation of German is largely regular, and phonetic transcriptions have only been given where additional help is needed. In all other cases only the position of the stressed syllable and the length of the vowel in that syllable are shown: a long vowel is indicated by an underline, e.g. **Ma̱ß**, a short vowel by a dot placed underneath, e.g. **Mạsse**.

a	*hạt*	hat
aː	*Ba̱hn*	baːn
ɐ	*O̱ber*	ˈoːbɐ
ɐ̯	*U̱hr*	uːɐ̯
ɑ̃	*Ensemble*	ɑ̃ˈsɑ̃ːbl̩
ɑ̃ː	*Abonnement*	abɔnəˈmɑ̃ː
a͜i	*we̱i̱t*	va͜it
a͜u	*Ha̱u̱t*	ha͜ut
b	*Bạll*	bal
ç	*ịch*	ɪç
d	*dạnn*	dan
d͜ʒ	*Gịn*	d͜ʒɪn
e	*ega̱l*	eˈgaːl
eː	*Be̱e̱t*	beːt
ɛ	*mạ̈sten*	ˈmɛstn̩
ɛː	*wählen*	ˈvɛːlən
ɛ̃	*Mạnnequin*	ˈmanəkɛ̃
ɛ̃ː	*Cousin*	kuˈzɛ̃ː
ə	*Na̱se*	ˈnaːzə
f	*Fạß*	fas
g	*Gạst*	gast
h	*hạt*	hat
i	*vita̱l*	viˈtaːl
iː	*vi̱e̱l*	fiːl
i̯	*Stu̱die*	ˈʃtuːdi̯ə
ɪ	*Bịrke*	ˈbɪrkə
j	*ja̱*	jaː
k	*kạlt*	kalt
l	*Lạst*	last
l̩	*Na̱bel*	ˈnaːbl̩

m	*Mạst*	mast
n	*Na̲ht*	naːt
n̩	*baden*	'baːdn̩
ŋ	*lạng*	laŋ
o	*Mora̲l*	mo'raːl
oː	*Bo̲o̲t*	boːt
o̯	*loya̲l*	lo̯a'jaːl
õ	*Fondue*	fõ'dyː
õː	*Fond*	fõː
ɔ	*Pọst*	pɔst
ø	*Ökono̲m*	øko'noːm
øː	*Ö̲l*	øːl
œ	*gọ̈ttlich*	'gœtlɪç
œ̃	*Parfum*	par'fœ̃ː
ɔ͜y	*He̲u̲*	hɔ͜y
p	*Pạkt*	pakt
p͜f	*Pfa̲hl*	p͜faːl
r	*Rạst*	rast
s	*Hạst*	hast
ʃ	*scha̲l*	ʃaːl
t	*Ta̲l*	taːl
t͜s	*Za̲hl*	t͜saːl
t͜ʃ	*Mạtsch*	mat͜ʃ
u	*kulạnt*	ku'lant
uː	*Hu̲t*	huːt
u̯	*aktuẹll*	ak'tu̯ɛl
ʊ	*Pụlt*	pʊlt
v	*wạs*	vas
x	*Bạch*	bax
y	*Physi̲k*	fy'ziːk
yː	*Rü̲be*	'ryːbə
y̆	*Nuance*	'ny̆ãːsə
ʏ	*Fụ̈lle*	'fʏlə
z	*Ha̲se*	'haːzə
ʒ	*Geni̲e̲*	ʒe'niː

|	Glottal stop, e.g. beạchten /bə|axtn̩/
ː	Length sign, indicating that the preceding vowel is long, e.g. Chrom /kroːm/
~	Indicates a nasal vowel, e.g. Fond /fõː/
'	Stress mark, immediately preceding a stressed syllable, e.g. Ballon /ba'lɔn/

Die für das Englische verwendeten Zeichen der Lautschrift

ɑ	*barb*	bɑːb
ɑ̃ː	*séance*	'seɪɑ̃s
æ	*fat*	fæt
æ̃	*lingerie*	'læ̃ʒərɪ
aɪ	*fine*	faɪn
aʊ	*now*	naʊ
b	*bat*	bæt
d	*dog*	dɒg
dʒ	*jam*	dʒæm
e	*met*	met
eɪ	*fate*	feɪt
eə	*fairy*	'feərɪ
əʊ	*goat*	gəʊt
ə	*ago*	ə'gəʊ
ɜː	*fur*	fɜː(r)
f	*fat*	fæt
g	*good*	gʊd
h	*hat*	hæt
ɪ	*bit, lately*	bɪt, 'leɪtlɪ
ɪə	*nearly*	'nɪəlɪ
iː	*meet*	miːt
j	*yet*	jet
k	*kit*	kɪt
l	*lot*	lɒt
m	*mat*	mæt
n	*not*	nɒt
ŋ	*sing*	sɪŋ
ɒ	*got*	gɒt
ɔː	*paw*	pɔː
ɔɪ	*boil*	bɔɪl
p	*pet*	pet
r	*rat*	ræt
s	*sip*	sɪp
ʃ	*ship*	ʃɪp
t	*tip*	tɪp
tʃ	*chin*	tʃɪn
θ	*thin*	θɪn
ð	*the*	ðə
uː	*boot*	buːt
ʊ	*book*	bʊk
ʊə	*tourist*	'tʊərɪst
ʌ	*dug*	dʌg
v	*van*	væn
w	*win*	wɪn
x	*loch*	lɒx
z	*zip*	zɪp
ʒ	*vision*	'vɪʒn
ː	Längezeichen, bezeichnet Länge des unmittelbar davor stehenden Vokals, z. B. boot /buːt/	
'	Betonung, steht unmittelbar vor einer betonten Silbe, z. B. ago /ə'gəʊ/	
(r)	Ein „r" in runden Klammern wird nur gesprochen, wenn im Textzusammenhang ein Vokal unmittelbar folgt, z. B. pare /peə(r)/; pare away /peər ə'weɪ/	

German spellings in this dictionary

German spellings in this dictionary are in accordance with the reforms ratified by the governments of Germany, Austria, and Switzerland in July 1996 and in force since August 1998. Key points of the reforms are summarized below. In cases of doubt the editors have followed *Duden—Rechtschreibung der deutschen Sprache*, twenty-first edition, 1996.

To help the user who may not yet be familiar with the reforms, the German-English section of the dictionary gives both the new spellings and the old versions which became 'invalid' in 2005. The old spellings are marked with an asterisk and are cross-referred where necessary to the new. For example, the translations of the compound verb *wiedererkennen* will no longer be found at this headword, since under the new spelling rules the word vanishes from the language. Instead they are covered by two phrases at the entry for *wieder: jemanden/etwas wieder erkennen* (in the form *jmdn./etw. ~ erkennen*) and *er war kaum wieder zu erkennen* (in the form *er war kaum ~ zu erkennen*). Similarly, the translations of the adjective previously written *belemmert* will be found at the new entry for the headword *belämmert*.

In a number of cases, however, implementing the new spelling rules has meant that just some, but not all, uses of a word have had to be transferred from one entry to another. In these cases the headword is not marked with an asterisk, but the entry is provided with a cross-reference to where the transferred information is now to be found. So, for example, the user who consults the entry for *leid* looking for a translation of the phrase previously written *jemandem leid tun* will find a cross-reference to the entry for the noun *Leid*, since according to the new spelling rules the word is written with a capital *L* in this expression. The headword *leid* itself is not marked with an asterisk, since it continues to exist in its own right as an adjective.

The following summary lists the most important changes:

1 The ß character The ß character, which is generally replaced in Switzerland by a double s, is retained in Germany and Austria, but is only be written after a long vowel (as in Fuß, Füße) and after a diphthong (as in Strauß, Sträuße).

Fluß, Baß, keß, läßt, Nußknacker become: *Fluss, Bass, kess, lässt, Nussknacker*

2 Nominalized adjectives Nominalized adjectives is written with a capital even in set phrases.

sein Schäfchen ins trockene bringen, im trüben fischen, im allgemeinen become: *sein Schäfchen ins Trockene bringen, im Trüben fischen, im Allgemeinen*

3 Words from the same word family In certain cases the spelling of words belonging to the same family have been made uniform.

numerieren, überschwenglich become: *nummerieren* (like Nummer), *überschwänglich* (being related to Überschwang)

4 The same consonant repeated three times When the same consonant repeated three times occurs in compounds, all three are written even when a vowel follows.

Brennessel, Schiffahrt become: *Brennnessel, Schifffahrt* (exceptions are dennoch, Drittel, Mittag)

5 Verb, adjective and participle compounds Verb, adjective and participle compounds are written more frequently than previously in two words.

spazierengehen, radfahren, ernstgemeint, erdölexportierend become: *spazieren gehen, Rad fahren, ernst gemeint, Erdöl exportierend*

6 Compounds containing numbers in figures Compounds containing numbers in figures are now written with a hyphen.

24karätig, 8pfünder become: *24-karätig, 8-Pfünder*

7 The division of words containing st st is treated like a normal combination of consonants and is no longer be indivisible.

Ha-stig, Ki-ste become: *has-tig, Kis-te*

8 The division of words containing ck The combination ck is not be divided and goes on to the next line.

Bäk-ker, schik-ken become: *Bä-cker, schi-cken*

9 The division of foreign words Compound foreign words which are hardly recognized as such today may be divided by syllables, without regard to their original components.

He-li-ko-pter (from the Greek helix and pteron) may also be written: *He-li-kop-ter*

10 The comma before und Where two complete clauses are connected by *und* a comma is no longer obligatory.

Karl war in Schwierigkeiten, und niemand konnte ihm helfen. may also be written: *Karl war in Schwierigkeiten und niemand konnte ihm helfen.*

11 The comma with infinitives and participles Even longer clauses containing an infinitive or participle do not have to be divided off with a comma.

Er begann sofort, das neue Buch zu lesen. Ungläubig den Kopf schüttelnd, verließ er das Zimmer. may also be written: *Er begann sofort das neue Buch zu lesen. Ungläubig den Kopf schüttelnd verließ er das Zimmer.*

Abkürzungen / Abbreviations

anderes, andere	**a.**	other, others
ähnliches, ähnliche	**ä.**	similar
Abkürzung	**abbr.**	abbreviation
Abkürzung	**Abk.**	abbreviation
absolut	**abs.**	absolute
adjektivisch	**adj.**	adjective, adjectival
Adjektiv	**Adj.**	adjective
Verwaltungssprache	**Admin.**	Administration, Administrative
adverbial	**adv.**	adverb, adverbial
Adverb	**Adv.**	adverb
Flugwesen	**Aeronaut.**	Aeronautics
Landwirtschaft	**Agric.**	Agriculture
Akkusativ	**Akk.**	accusative
Amerika	**Amer.**	American, America
amerikanisch	**amerik.**	American
Amtssprache	**Amtsspr.**	official language
Anatomie	**Anat.**	Anatomy
Anthropologie	**Anthrop.**	Anthropology
veraltet	**arch.**	archaic
Archäologie	**Archaeol.**	Archaeology
Architektur	**Archit.**	Architecture
Artikel	**art.**	article
Astrologie	**Astrol.**	Astrology
Astronomie	**Astron.**	Astronomy
Raumfahrt	**Astronaut.**	Astronautics
Altes Testament	**A. T.**	Old Testament
attributiv	**attr., attrib.**	attributive
Australien	**Austral.**	Australian, Australia
Bauwesen	**Bauw.**	Construction
Bergmannssprache	**Bergmannsspr.**	Mining terminology
besonders	**bes.**	especially
Bezeichnung	**Bez.**	name
biblisch	**bibl.**	biblical
Biologie	**Biol.**	Biology
Buchführung	**Bookk.**	Bookkeeping
Börsenwesen	**Börsenw.**	Stock Market
Botanik	**Bot.**	Botany
Bundesrepublik Deutschland	**BRD**	Federal Republic of Germany
britisch, Großbritannien	**Brit.**	British, Britain
britisch	**brit.**	British
Bruchzahl	**Bruchz.**	fraction
Buchführung	**Buchf.**	Bookkeeping
Buchwesen	**Buchw.**	Book Trade
Chemie	**Chem.**	Chemistry
chemisch	**chem.**	chemical
Kindersprache	**child lang.**	child language
christlich	**christl.**	Christian
Kinematographie	**Cinemat.**	Cinematography
umgangssprachlich	**coll.**	colloquial
Kollektivum	**collect.**	collective
Kombination	**comb.**	combination
Handel, Handels-	**Commerc.**	Commerce, Commercial
elektronische Datenverarbeitung	**Comp.**	Computing
Komparativ, komparativ	**compar.**	comparative
Konditional, konditional	**condit.**	conditional
Konjunktion	**conj.**	conjunction
Dativ	**Dat.**	dative
Deutsche Demokratische Republik	**DDR**	German Democratic Republic
bestimmt	**def.**	definite
Deklination	**Dekl.**	declension
Demonstrativpronomen	**Demonstrativpron.**	demonstrative pronoun
Zahnmedizin	**Dent.**	Dentistry
abwertend	**derog.**	derogatory
das heißt	**d. h.**	that is [to say]
Dialekt	**dial.**	dialect
dichterisch	**dichter.**	poetic
Damenschneiderei	**Dressm.**	Dressmaking
Druckwesen	**Druckw.**	Printing
deutsch	**dt.**	German
Datenverarbeitung	**DV**	Data Processing
kirchlich	**Eccl.**	Ecclesiastical
Ökologie	**Ecol.**	Ecology
Ökonomik	**Econ.**	Economics
Bildungswesen	**Educ.**	Education
ehemals, ehemalig	**ehem.**	former, formerly
Eisenbahn	**Eisenb.**	Railways
Elektrizität	**Electr.**	Electricity
Elektrotechnik	**Elektrot.**	Electrical Engineering
elektrisch	**elektr.**	electrical
elliptisch	**ellipt.**	elliptical
emphatisch	**emphat.**	emphatic
besonders	**esp.**	especially
etwas	**etw.**	something
euphemistisch	**euphem.**	euphemistic
evangelisch	**ev.**	Evangelical
ausdrückend	**expr.**	expressing

Abkürzungen / Abbreviations

fachsprachlich	**fachspr.**	technical
familiär	**fam.**	familiar
feminin	**fem.**	feminine
Fernsehen	**Ferns.**	Television
Fernsprechwesen	**Fernspr.**	Telephony
figurativ	**fig.**	figurative
Finanzwesen	**Finanzw.**	Finance
Flugwesen	**Flugw.**	Aeronautics
Fußball	**Footb.**	Football
Forstwesen	**Forstw.**	Forestry
Fotografie	**Fot.**	Photography
Gastronomie	**Gastr.**	Gastronomy
gehoben	**geh.**	elevated
Genitiv	**Gen.**	genitive
Geographie	**Geog.**	Geography
Geologie	**Geol.**	Geology
Geometrie	**Geom.**	Geometry
Handarbeit	**Handarb.**	Handicraft
Heraldik	**Her.**	Heraldry
Hilfsverb	**Hilfsv.**	auxiliary verb
historisch	**hist.**	historical
Geschichte, historisch	**Hist.**	History, historical
Hochschulwesen	**Hochschulw.**	Higher Education
Gartenbau	**Hort.**	Horticultural
Imperativ, imperativisch	**imper.**	imperative
unpersönlich	**impers.**	impersonal
unbestimmt	**indef.**	indefinite
Indefinitpronomen	**Indefinit-pron.**	indefinite pronoun
Indeklinabel	**Indekl.**	indeclinable
Indikativ	**Indik.**	indicative
Infinitiv	**Inf.**	infinitive
Interjektion	**Interj., int.**	interjection
interrogativ	**interrog.**	interrogative
intransitiv	**intr.**	intransitive
irisch, Irland	**Ir.**	Irish, Ireland
ironisch	**iron.**	ironical
Jägersprache	**Jägerspr.**	hunting language
jemand	**jmd.**	somebody
jemandem	**jmdm.**	somebody
jemanden	**jmdn.**	somebody
jemandes	**jmds.**	somebody
scherzhaft	**joc.**	jocular
Journalismus	**Journ.**	Journalism
Jugendsprache	**Jugendspr.**	young people's language
juristisch	**jur.**	legal
Kardinalzahl	**Kardinalz.**	cardinal number
katholisch	**kath.**	Catholic
Kaufmannssprache	**Kaufmannsspr.**	business language
Kraftfahrzeugwesen	**Kfz-W.**	Motor Vehicles
Kindersprache	**Kinderspr.**	child language
Kochkunst	**Kochk.**	Cookery
Komparativ	**Komp.**	Comparative
Konjunktion	**Konj.**	conjunction
landschaftlich	**landsch.**	regional
Landwirtschaft	**Landw.**	Agriculture
Linguistik	**Ling.**	Linguistics
wortwörtlich	**lit.**	literal
Literatur	**Lit.**	Literature
Literaturwissenschaft	**Literaturw.**	Literary Studies
Luftfahrt	**Luftf.**	Aeronautics
mittelalterlich	**ma.**	medieval
Mittelalter	**MA**	Middle Ages
marxistisch	**marx.**	Marxist
maskulin	**masc.**	masculine
Mathematik	**Math.**	Mathematics
Maschinenbau	**Mech. Engin.**	Mechanical Engineering
Medizin	**Med.**	Medicine
Meereskunde	**Meeresk.**	oceanography
Meteorologie	**Met.**	Meteorology
Metallurgie	**Metall.**	Metallurgy
Metallbearbeitung	**Metallbearb.**	Metalwork
Metallbearbeitung	**Metalw.**	Metalwork
Meteorologie	**Meteorol.**	Meteorology
Militär	**Mil., Milit.**	Military
modifizierend	**mod.**	modifying
Modalverb	**Modalv.**	modal verb
Kraftfahrzeugwesen	**Motor Veh.**	Motor Vehicles
Musik	**Mus.**	Music
Mythologie	**Mythol.**	Mythology
Substantiv	**n.**	noun
Seemannssprache	**Naut.**	Nautical
negativ	**neg.**	negative
Nominativ	**Nom.**	nominative
norddeutsch	**nordd.**	North German
nordostdeutsch	**nordostd.**	North-East German
Substantive	**ns.** *(English)*	nouns
nationalsozialistisch	**ns.** *(Deutsch)*	National Socialist
Neues Testament	**N. T.**	New Testament
Kernphysik	**Nucl. Phys.**	Nuclear Physics
ohne; oben	**o.**	without; above
Objekt	**obj.**	object
oder	**od.**	or
Ordinalzahl	**Ordinalz.**	ordinal number
Ornithologie	**Ornith.**	Ornithology
österreichisch	**österr.**	Austrian
Papierdeutsch	**Papierdt.**	officialese
Parlament	**Parl.**	Parliament
Partizip	**Part.**	participle

Abkürzungen / Abbreviations

Passiv	pass.	passive
Perfekt	Perf.	perfect
Person	Pers.	person
Philosophie	Philos.	Philosophy
Fotografie	Photog.	Photography
Phrase(n)	phr(s).	Phrase(s)
Physik	Phys.	Physics
Physiologie	Physiol.	Physiology
Plural	Pl., pl.	plural
Plusquamperfekt	Plusq.	pluperfect
dichterisch	poet.	poetical
Politik	Polit.	Politics
possessiv, Possessiv-	poss.	possessive
nachgestellt	postpos.	postpositive
Postwesen	Postw.	Post Office
zweites Partizip	p.p.	past participle
prädikativ	präd.	predicative
Präposition	Präp.	preposition
Präsens	Präs.	present
Präteritum	Prät.	preterite
prädikativ	pred.	predicative
Präfix	pref.	prefix
Präposition	prep.	preposition
Präsens	pres.	present
erstes Partizip	pres. p.	present participle
Eigenname	pr. n.	proper noun
Pronomen	Pron., pron.	pronoun
sprichwörtlich	prov.	proverbial
Psychologie	Psych.	Psychology
Präteritum	p.t.	past tense
Warenzeichen	®	Registered Trade Mark
Eisenbahn	Railw.	Railways
Raumfahrt	Raumf.	Space Travel
römisch-katholische Kirche	RC Ch.	Roman Catholic Church
Rechtssprache	Rechtsspr.	legal terminology
Rechtswesen	Rechtsw.	Law
reflexiv	refl.	reflexive
regelmäßig	regelm.	regular
relativ	rel.	relative
Religion	Rel.	Religion
Relativpronomen	Relativpron.	relative pronoun
römisch	röm.	Roman
römisch-katholisch	röm-kath.	Roman Catholic
Rundfunk	Rundf.	Radio
siehe	s.	see
Seite	S.	page
jemand	sb.	somebody
Schule	Sch.	School
scherzhaft	scherzh.	jocular
Schülersprache	Schülerspr.	school slang
schweizerisch	schweiz.	Swiss
Wissenschaft	Sci.	Science
schottisch	Scot.	Scottish, Scotland
Schulwesen	Schulw.	School System
Seemannssprache	Seemannsspr.	Nautical
Seewesen	Seew.	maritime affairs
Singular	Sg., sing.	singular
salopp	sl.	slang
siehe oben	s. o.	see above
Soziologie	Sociol.	Sociology
Soldatensprache	Soldatenspr.	army slang
Soziologie	Soziol.	Sociology
spöttisch	spött.	derisive
Sprichwort	Spr.	proverb
Sprachwissenschaft	Sprachw.	Linguistics
Börsenwesen	St. Exch.	Stock Exchange
Steuerwesen	Steuerw.	Taxation
etwas	sth.	something
Studentensprache	Studentenspr.	student slang
siehe unten	s. u.	see below
Subjekt	Subj.	subject
substantivisch; substantiviert	subst.	nominal; nominalized
Substantiv	Subst.	noun
süddeutsch	südd.	South German
südwestdeutsch	südwestd.	South-West German
Suffix	suf.	suffix
Superlativ	Sup., superl.	superlative
Landvermessung	Surv.	Surveying
Symbol	symb.	symbol
fachsprachlich	tech.	technical
Fernsprechwesen	Teleph.	Telephony
Fernsehen	Telev.	Television
Textilwesen	Textilw.	Textiles
Theologie	Theol.	Theology
Tiermedizin	Tiermed.	Veterinary Medicine
transitiv	tr.	transitive
Trennung	Trenn.	division
und	u.	and
und Ähnliches	u. Ä.	and similar
umgangssprachlich	ugs.	colloquial
unbestimmt	unbest.	indefinite
Universität	Univ.	University
unpersönlich	unpers.	impersonal
unregelmäßig	unr.	irregular
gewöhnlich	usu.	usually
und so weiter	usw.	et cetera
von	v.	of
Verb	V.	verb
Hilfsverb	v. aux.	auxiliary verb

Abkürzungen / Abbreviations

veraltet; veraltend	**veralt.**	obsolete; obsolescent
Verhaltensforschung	**Verhaltensf.**	Behavioural Research
verhüllend	**verhüll.**	euphemistic
Verkehrswesen	**Verkehrsw.**	Transport
Versicherungswesen	**Versicherungsw.**	Insurance
Tiermedizin	**Vet. Med.**	Veterinary Medicine
vergleiche	**vgl.**	compare
intransitives Verb	**v. i.**	intransitive verb
Verkleinerungsform	**Vkl.**	diminutive
Völkerkunde	**Völkerk.**	Ethnology
volkstümlich	**volkst.**	popular, vernacular
reflexives Verb	**v. refl.**	reflexive verb
transitives Verb	**v. t.**	transitive verb
transitives und intransitives Verb	**v. t. & i.**	transitive and intransitive verb
vulgär	**vulg.**	vulgar
Werbesprache	**Werbespr.**	advertising jargon
westdeutsch	**westd.**	western German
Wirtschaft	**Wirtsch.**	Commerce and Industry
Wissenschaft	**Wissensch.**	Science
Warenzeichen	**Wz.**	Registered Trade Mark
Zahnmedizin	**Zahnmed.**	Dentistry
zum Beispiel	**z. B.**	for example
Zeitungswesen	**Zeitungsw.**	Newspaper Industry
Zoologie	**Zool.**	Zoology
Zusammensetzung	**Zus.**	compound
Zusammenschreibung	**Zusschr.**	writing as one word

Aa

a, A /aː/ *das;* ~, ~ **(a)** (Buchstabe) a/A; **das A und O** (fig.) the essential thing/things (*Gen.* for); **von A bis Z** (fig. ugs.) from beginning to end
(b) (Musik) [key of] A

a *Abk.* = **Ar**

à /a/ *Präp. mit Nom., Akk.* (Kaufmannsspr.) **zehn Marken à 0,56 Euro** ten stamps at 0·56 euro each

A *Abk.* = **Autobahn** ≈ M

Aal *der;* ~[e]s, ~e eel; ~ **grün** (Kochk.) green eels; stewed eels

aalen *refl. V.* (ugs.) stretch out

aal·glatt (abwertend) 1 *Adj.* slippery; ~ **sein** be as slippery as an eel
2 *adv.* smoothly

Aas *das;* ~es, ~e *od.* **Äser** **(a)** *Pl.* ~e carrion *no art.*; (Kadaver) [rotting] carcass
(b) *Pl.* **Äser** (salopp abwertend) swine; (anerkennend) devil

ab 1 *Präp. mit Dat.* **(a)** from; **ab 1980** as from 1980; **ab Werk** (Kaufmannsspr.) ex works; **ab Frankfurt fliegen** fly from Frankfurt
(b) ([Rang]folge) from ... on[wards]; **ab 20 Euro** from 20 euros [upwards]
2 *Adv.* **(a)** (weg) off; away; **[an etw.** (*Dat.*)**] ab sein** (ugs.: sich [von etw.] gelöst haben) have come off [sth.]
(b) (ugs.: Aufforderung) off; away; **ab nach Hause** get off home
(c) Gewehr ab! (milit. Kommando) order arms!
(d) ab und zu *od.* **an** now and then

ab|ändern *tr. V.* alter; amend ‹*text*›

Ab·änderung *die* alteration; (eines Textes) amendment

ab|arbeiten *tr. V.* work for ‹*meal*›; work off ‹*debt, amount*›

Ab·art *die* variety

ab·artig *Adj.* deviant; abnormal

Ab·artigkeit *die;* ~, ~en abnormality; deviancy

Abb. *Abk.* = **Abbildung** Fig.

Ab·bau *der* **(a)** dismantling; (von Zelten, Lagern) striking
(b) ▶ ABBAUEN C: cutback (*Gen.* in); pruning; reduction
(c) (Bergbau) mining; (von Stein) quarrying

ab|bauen *tr. V.* **(a)** dismantle; strike ‹*tent, camp*›
(b) (beseitigen) gradually remove; break down ‹*prejudices, inhibitions*›
(c) (verringern) cut back ‹*staff*›; prune ‹*jobs*›; reduce ‹*wages*›
(d) (Bergbau) mine; quarry ‹*stone*›

ab|beißen 1 *unr. tr. V.* bite off
2 *unr. itr. V.* have a bite

ab|bekommen *unr. tr. V.* **(a)** get
(b) einen Schlag/ein paar Kratzer ~: get hit/get a few scratches; **etwas** ~ (getroffen werden) be hit; (verletzt werden) be hurt
(c) (los-, herunterbekommen) get ‹*paint, lid, chain*› off

ab|berufen *unr. tr. V.* recall ‹*ambassador, envoy*› (**aus, von** from)

ab|bestellen *tr. V.* cancel

ab|bezahlen *tr. V.* pay off

ab|biegen *unr. itr. V.; mit sein* turn off; **links/rechts** ~: turn [off] left/right

Abbieger *der;* ~s, ~, **Abbiegerin** *die;* ~, ~nen (Verkehrsw.) motorist/cyclist/car *etc.* turning off

Ab·bild *das* (eines Menschen) likeness; (eines Gegenstandes) copy; (fig.) portrayal

ab|bilden *tr. V.* copy; reproduce ‹*object, picture*›; depict ‹*person, landscape*›; (fig.) portray

Abbildung *die* illustration

ab|binden *unr. tr. V.* **(a)** (losbinden) untie; undo
(b) (abschnüren) put a tourniquet on ‹*artery, arm, leg, etc.*›; tie ‹*umbilical cord*›

ab|blasen *unr. tr. V.* (ugs.) call off

ab|blättern *itr. V.; mit sein* flake off

ab|blenden *tr., itr. V.* black out; dip (Brit.), dim (Amer.) ‹*headlights*›; **bei Gegenverkehr frühzeitig** ~: dip *or* (Amer.) dim one's headlights promptly when there is oncoming traffic

ab|blitzen *itr. V.; mit sein* (ugs.) **sie ließ alle Verehrer** ~: she gave all her admirers the brush-off

ab|brausen *tr. V.* ▶ ABDUSCHEN

ab|brechen 1 *unr. tr. V.* **(a)** break off; break ‹*needle, pencil*›
(b) (zerlegen) strike ‹*tent, camp*›
(c) (abreißen) demolish, pull down ‹*building*›
(d) (beenden) break off ‹*negotiations, [diplomatic] relations, discussion, activity*›; (vorzeitig) cut short ‹*conversation, holiday, activity*›
(e) (DV) cancel
2 *unr. itr. V.* **(a)** *mit sein* break [off]
(b) (aufhören) break off

ab|bremsen 1 *tr. V.* **(a)** brake
(b) retard ‹*motion*›
2 *itr. V.* brake

ab|brennen 1 *unr. itr. V.; mit sein* **(a)** be burned down; **das Haus ist abgebrannt** the house has burned down
(b) ‹*fuse*› burn away; ‹*candle*› burn down
2 *unr. tr. V.* **(a)** let off ‹*firework*›
(b) burn down ‹*building*›

a

ab|bringen *unr. tr. V.* **jmdn. davon ∼, etw. zu tun** dissuade sb. from doing sth; **jmdn. vom Kurs ∼:** make sb. change course

ab|bröckeln *itr. V.; mit sein* (auch fig.) crumble away

Ab·bruch *der* **(a)** (Abriss) demolition; pulling down
(b) (Beendigung) breaking-off; (einer Schwangerschaft) termination
(c) einer Sache (*Dat.*) **[keinen] ∼ tun** do [no] harm to sth.

ab|buchen *tr. V.* ‹*bank*› debit (**von** to); ‹*creditor*› claim by direct debit (**von** to); **etw. ∼ lassen** (durch die Bank) pay sth. by standing order; (durch Gläubiger) pay sth. by direct debit

ab|bügeln *tr. V.* (ugs.) reject, brush aside ‹*warning, question, criticism*›; rebuff ‹*person*›

ab|bürsten *tr. V.* **(a)** brush off
(b) (säubern) brush ‹*garment*›

ab|büßen *tr. V.* serve [out] ‹*prison sentence*›

Abc /a(:)be(:)ˈtse:/ *das;* ∼ (auch fig.) ABC

Abc-Schütze *der,* **Abc-Schützin** *die* child just starting school

ab|dampfen *itr. V.; mit sein* (ugs.: abfahren) set off

ab|danken *itr. V.* ‹*ruler*› abdicate; ‹*government, minister*› resign

Abdankung *die;* **∼, ∼en** ▶ ABDANKEN: abdication; resignation

ab|decken *tr. V.* **(a)** open up; ‹*gale*› take the roof/roofs off ‹*house*›, take the tiles off ‹*roof*›
(b) (herunternehmen, -reißen) take off
(c) (abräumen) clear ‹*table*›; clear away ‹*dishes*›
(d) (schützen) cover ‹*person*›

ab|dichten *tr. V.* seal

ab|drängen *tr. V.* push away

ab|drehen 1 *tr. V.* **(a)** (ausschalten) turn off; **den Hahn ∼** (fig.) turn off the supply
(b) (abtrennen) twist off
2 *itr. V.; meist mit sein* turn off

Ab·druck *der; Pl.* **Abdrücke** mark; (Fuß∼) footprint; (Wachs∼) impression; (Gips∼) cast

ab|drücken 1 *itr. V.* pull the trigger; shoot
2 *tr. V.* (zudrücken) constrict

ab|dunkeln *tr. V.* darken ‹*room*›; dim ‹*light*›

ab|duschen *tr. V.* **sich/jmdn. [warm] ∼:** take/give sb. a [hot] shower

ab|düsen *itr. V.* (ugs.) zoom off

***abend** ▶ ABEND A

Abend *der;* **∼s, ∼e** evening; **guten ∼!** good evening; **am [frühen/späten] ∼:** [early/late] in the evening; **heute/morgen/gestern ∼:** this/tomorrow/yesterday evening; **zu ∼ essen** have dinner; (allgemeiner) have one's evening meal; **ein bunter ∼:** a social [evening]

abend-, Abend-: ∼akademie *die* evening school; **∼anzug** *der* evening suit; **∼blatt** *das* evening [news]paper; **∼brot** *das* supper; **∼dämmerung** *die* [evening] twilight; **∼essen** *das* dinner; **∼füllend** *Adj.* occupying a whole evening *postpos., not pred.;* **ein ∼füllendes Programm** a full evening's programme; **∼gymnasium** *das* night school, evening classes *pl.* (*leading to the 'Abitur'*); **∼kasse** *die* box office (*open on the evening of the performance*); **∼kleid** *das* evening dress; **∼kurs[us]** *der* evening class

Abend·land *das;* **∼[e]s** West

abendlich *Adj.* evening; ‹*quiet, coolness*› of the evening

Abend-: ∼mahl *das* (Rel.) Communion; (N.T.) Last Supper; **∼programm** *das* evening programmes *pl.;* **∼rot** *das* red glow of the sunset sky

abends *Adv.* in the evenings; **um sechs Uhr ∼:** at six o'clock in the evening

Abend-: ∼schule *die* night school; **∼sonne** *die* evening sun; **∼stern** *der* evening star; **∼stunde** *die* evening hour; **in den frühen/späten ∼stunden** early/late in the evening; **∼vorstellung** *die* evening performance; **∼zeitung** *die* ▶ ∼BLATT

Abenteuer *das;* **∼s, ∼ (a)** (auch fig.) adventure
(b) (Unternehmen) venture
(c) (Liebesaffäre) affair

abenteuerlich *Adj.* **(a)** (riskant) risky
(b) (bizarr) bizarre

Abenteuer-: ∼lust *die* thirst for adventure; **∼roman** *der* adventure novel

Abenteurer *der;* **∼s, ∼:** adventurer

Abenteurerin *die;* **∼, ∼nen** adventuress

aber 1 *Konj.* but
2 *Partikel* **∼ ja/nein!** why, yes/no! **∼ natürlich!** but of course!; **du bist ∼ groß!** aren't you tall!

Aber·glaube[n] *der* superstition

aber·gläubisch *Adj.* superstitious

abermals *Adv.* once again; once more

Abf. *Abk.* = **Abfahrt** dep.

ab|fahren 1 *unr. itr. V.; mit sein* **(a)** (wegfahren) leave; **wo fährt der Zug nach Paris ab?** where does the Paris train leave from?
(b) (hinunterfahren) drive down; (Skisport) ski down
(c) (salopp: sich begeistern) **auf jmdn./etw. [voll] ∼:** be mad about sb./sth.
(d) (salopp: abgewiesen werden) **jmdn. ∼ lassen** tell sb. where he/she can go (sl.)
2 *unr. tr. V.* **(a)** (abtransportieren) take away
(b) (abnutzen) wear out; **abgefahrene Reifen** worn tyres

Ab·fahrt *die* **(a)** departure
(b) (Skisport) descent; (Strecke) run

Abfahrts-: ∼lauf *der* (Skisport) downhill [racing]; **∼läufer** *der,* **∼läuferin** *die*

---

*old spelling - see note on page xiv

(Skisport) downhill racer; **~rennen** *das* (Skisport) downhill [racing]; **~zeit** *die* time of departure; departure time

Ab·fall *der* (Küchen~ o Ä.) rubbish, (Amer.) trash *no indef. art., no pl.;* (Fleisch~) offal *no indef. art., no pl.;* (Industrie~) waste *no indef. art.;* (auf der Straße) litter *no indef. art., no pl.*

Abfall: ~beseitigung *die* refuse disposal; (industriell) waste disposal; **~eimer** *der* rubbish bin; trash can (Amer.); (auf der Straße) litter bin; trash can (Amer.)

ab|fallen *unr. itr. V.; mit sein* **(a)** fall off
(b) (abschüssig sein) ‹*land, road, etc.*› drop away, slope
(c) (übrigbleiben) be left [over]; **für dich wird [dabei] auch etwas ~:** you'll get something out of it too
(d) von jmdm. ~: leave sb.; **vom Glauben ~:** desert the faith

ab·fällig [1] *Adj.* disparaging
[2] *adv.* **sich ~ über jmdn. äußern** make disparaging remarks about sb.

Abfall-: ~produkt *das* (auch fig.) by-product; (Sekundärstoff) secondary product; **~vermeidung** *die* waste avoidance

ab|fangen *unr. tr. V.* **(a)** catch; intercept ‹*agent, message, aircraft*›
(b) repel ‹*charge, assault*›; ward off ‹*blow, attack*›

ab|färben *itr. V.* **(a)** ‹*colour, garment, etc.*› run
(b) auf jmdn./etw. ~ (fig.) rub off on sb./sth.

ab|fassen *tr. V.* write ‹*report, letter, etc.*›; draw up ‹*will*›

ab|fegen *tr. V.* **(a)** brush off; **etw. von etw. ~:** brush sth. off sth.
(b) (säubern) **etw. ~:** brush sth. clean

ab|feiern *tr. V.* use up ‹*excess hours worked*› (*by taking time off*)

ab|fertigen *tr. V.* dispatch ‹*mail*›; deal with ‹*applicant*›; handle ‹*passengers*›; serve ‹*customer*›; clear ‹*ship*› for sailing; clear ‹*aircraft*› for take-off; clear ‹*lorry*› for departure

ab|feuern *tr. V.* fire

ab|finden [1] *unr. tr. V.* **jmdn. mit etw. ~:** compensate sb. with sth.; **seine Gläubiger ~:** settle with one's creditors
[2] *unr. refl. V.* **sich ~:** resign oneself; **sich ~ mit** come to terms with; learn to live with ‹*noise, heat*›

Abfindung *die;* ~, **~en** settlement; **eine ~ in Höhe von ... zahlen** make a settlement of ...

Abfindungs·summe *die* ▶ ABFINDUNG

ab|flauen *itr. V.; mit sein* die down; subside; ‹*interest, conversation*› flag; ‹*business*› become slack; ‹*noise*› abate

ab|fliegen *unr. itr. V.; mit sein* leave

ab|fließen *unr. itr. V.; mit sein* flow off

Ab·flug *der* departure

Abflug·zeit *die* departure time

Ab·fluss, *Ab·fluß *der* drain; (Rohr) drainpipe; (für Abwasser) waste pipe

Ab·folge *die* sequence; **die ~ der Jahreszeiten** the cycle of the seasons

ab|fotografieren *tr. V.* take pictures of

ab|fragen *tr. V.* test; **jmdn.** *od.* **jmdm. die Vokabeln ~:** test sb. on his/her vocabulary

Abfuhr *die;* ~, **~en (a)** removal
(b) jmdm. eine ~ erteilen (fig. ugs.) rebuff sb.

ab|führen [1] *tr. V.* **(a)** (nach Festnahme) take away
(b) (zahlen) pay out
(c) (abbringen) take away
[2] *itr. V.* (für Stuhlgang sorgen) be a laxative

Abführ·mittel *das* laxative

ab|füllen *tr. V.* (in Flaschen) bottle; (in Dosen) can

Ab·gabe *die* **(a)** handing in; (eines Briefes, Pakets, Telegramms) delivery; (eines Gesuchs, Antrags) submission
(b) (Steuer, Gebühr) tax; (auf Produkte) duty
(c) (Ausstrahlung) release; emission
(d) (Sport: Abspiel) pass

Ab·gang *der* **(a)** leaving; departure; (Abfahrt) departure; (Theater) exit
(b) (jmd., der ausscheidet) departure; (Schule) leaver
(c) (bes. Amtsspr.: Todesfall) death
(d) (Turnen) dismount

Ab·gas *das* exhaust

Abgas·katalysator *der* (Kfz-W.) catalytic converter

abgearbeitet *Adj.* work-worn ‹*hands*›

ab|geben [1] *unr. tr. V.* **(a)** (aushändigen) hand over; deliver ‹*letter, parcel, telegram*›; hand in, submit ‹*application*›; hand in ‹*school work*›; **den Mantel in der Garderobe ~:** leave one's coat in the cloakroom
(b) *auch itr.* **jmdm. [etwas] von etw. ~:** let sb. have some of sth.
(c) (abfeuern) fire
[2] *unr. refl. V.* **sich mit jmdm./etw. ~:** spend time on sb./sth.; (geringschätzig) waste one's time on sb./sth.

ab·gebrannt *Adj.* (ugs.) broke (coll.)

abgebrüht *Adj.* (ugs.) hardened

ab·gedroschen *Adj.* (ugs.) hackneyed

ab·gegriffen *Adj.* battered

ab|gehen *unr. itr. V.; mit sein* **(a)** (sich entfernen) leave; (Theater) exit
(b) (ausscheiden) leave
(c) (abfahren) ‹*train, ship, bus*› leave, depart
(d) (abgeschickt werden) ‹*message, letter*› be sent [off]
(e) (abzweigen) branch off
(f) (sich lösen) come off

abgehetzt *Adj.* exhausted

ab·gelegen *Adj.* remote; (einsam) isolated; out-of-the-way ‹*district*›

abgemagert *Adj.* emaciated; wasted

ab·geneigt *Adj.* averse (*Dat.* to); **[nicht] ~ sein, etw. zu tun** [not] be averse to doing sth.

a

Abgeordnete *der/die; adj. Dekl.* member [of parliament]; (z.B. in Frankreich) deputy
ab·gerissen *Adj.* ragged
ab·geschieden *Adj.* secluded; (abgelegen) isolated
ab·geschlagen *Adj.* (Sport) [well] beaten
ab·geschlossen *Adj.* secluded
ab·geschnitten *Adj.* isolated; **von der Außenwelt ~:** cut off from the outside world
ab·gesehen *Adv.* **~ von** apart from; **~ davon, dass ...** apart from the fact that ...
ab·gespannt *Adj.* weary; exhausted
ab·gestanden *Adj.* flat
ab·gestorben *Adj.* dead ‹*branch, tree*›; numb ‹*fingers, legs, etc.*›
ab·getreten *Adj.* worn down
abgewetzt *Adj.* well-worn; battered ‹*case etc.*›
ab|gewöhnen *tr. V.:* **jmdm. etw. ~:** make sb. give up sth.; **sich** (*Dat.*) **etw. ~:** give up sth.
ab|gießen *unr. tr. V.* pour away ‹*liquid*›; drain ‹*potatoes*›
abgöttisch *Adj.* idolatrous
ab|grenzen *tr. V.* **(a)** bound; **etw. gegen** *od.* **von etw. ~:** separate sth. from sth.
(b) (unterscheiden) distinguish
Ab·grund *der* abyss; chasm; (Abhang) precipice
ab|hacken *tr. V.* chop off; **jmdm. die Hand** *usw.* **~:** chop sb.'s hand *etc.* off
ab|haken *tr. V.* tick off; check off (Amer.)
ab|halten *unr. tr. V.* **(a) jmdn./etw. [von jmdm./etw.] ~:** keep sb./sth. off [sb./sth.]
(b) jmdn. davon ~, etw. zu tun stop sb. doing sth.
(c) (durchführen) hold ‹*elections, meeting, referendum*›
ab|handeln *tr. V.* **(a) jmdm. etw. ~:** do a deal with sb. for sth.
(b) (darstellen) deal with
abhanden *Adv.* **~ kommen** get lost; go astray; **etw. kommt jmdm. ~:** sb. loses sth.
Ab·handlung *die* treatise (**über** + *Akk.* on)
Ab·hang *der* slope; incline
ab|hängen¹ *unr. itr. V.* **von jmdm./etw. ~:** depend on sb./sth.
ab|hängen² [1] *tr. V.* **(a)** take down
(b) (abkuppeln) uncouple
(c) (ugs.) shake off ‹*pursuer, competitor*›
[2] *itr. V.* (den Hörer auflegen) hang up
abhängig *Adj.* dependent (**von on**); (süchtig) addicted (**von** to); **von jmdm./etw. ~ sein** depend on sb./sth.
Abhängige *der/die; adj. Dekl.* (Rechtspr.) dependant; (Untergebene) subordinate
Abhängigkeit *die; ~, ~en* dependence; (Sucht) addiction
Abhängigkeits·verhältnis *das* relationship of dependence (**zu** on)

*alte Schreibung - vgl. Hinweis auf S. xiv

ab|härten *tr. V.* harden
ab|hauen [1] *unr. tr. V.* **(a)** *Prät.* **haute ab** knock off
(b) *Prät.* **hieb** (geh.) *od.* **haute ab** (mit Schwert, Axt usw.) chop off
[2] *unr. itr. V.; mit sein; Prät.* **haute ab** (salopp) beat it (coll.)
ab|heben [1] *unr. tr. V.* **(a)** lift off ‹*lid, cover, etc.*›; **[den Hörer] ~:** answer [the telephone]
(b) (von einem Konto) withdraw ‹*money*›
[2] *unr. itr. V.* ‹*balloon*› rise; ‹*aircraft, bird*› take off; ‹*rocket*› lift off
[3] *unr. refl. V.* stand out (**von** against)
ab|heften *tr. V.* file
ab|hetzen *refl. V.* rush [around]; *s. auch* ABGEHETZT
Ab·hilfe *die* action to improve matters; **~ schaffen** put things right
ab|holen *tr. V.* collect, pick up ‹*parcel, book, tickets, etc.*›; pick up ‹*person*›
ab|hören *tr. V.* **(a) jmdm.** *od.* **jmdn. Vokabeln ~:** test sb.'s vocabulary [orally]; **das Einmaleins ~:** ask questions on the multiplication tables
(b) tap ‹*telephone conversation, telephone*›; bug (coll.) ‹*conversation, premises*›; **jmdn. ~:** tap sb.'s telephone
abhör·sicher *Adj.* bug-proof (coll.); tap-proof ‹*telephone*›
Abi *das; ~s, ~s* (Schülerspr.), **Abitur** *das; ~s, ~e* Abitur (*school-leaving examination at grammar school needed for entry to higher education*); ≈ A levels (Brit.)
Abiturient *der; ~en, ~en,* **Abiturientin** *die; ~, ~nen sb. who is taking/has passed the 'Abitur'*
ab|jagen *tr. V.* **jmdm. etw. ~:** finally get sth. away from sb.
Abk. *Abk.* = **Abkürzung** abbr.
ab|kapseln *tr. V.* encapsulate; **sich gegen die Umwelt ~** (fig.) isolate oneself from one's surroundings
ab|kaufen *tr. V.* **jmdm. etw. ~:** buy sth. from sb.
Ab·klatsch *der* (abwertend) pale imitation; poor copy
ab|klopfen *tr. V.* **(a)** knock off
(b) (säubern) knock the dirt/snow/crumbs *etc.* off
(c) (untersuchen) tap
ab|knallen *tr. V.* (salopp) shoot down; gun down
ab|knicken [1] *tr. V.* snap off
[2] *itr. V.; mit sein* snap
ab|kochen *tr. V.* boil
ab|kommen *unr. itr. V.; mit sein* **(a) vom Weg ~:** lose one's way; **vom Kurs ~:** go off course; **von der Fahrbahn ~:** leave the road; **vom Thema ~:** stray from the topic
(b) von einem Plan ~: abandon a plan
Ab·kommen *das; ~s, ~:* agreement
abkömmlich *Adj.* free; available

ab|können *unr. tr. V.* (nordd.: mögen) stand; (vertragen) take

ab|kratzen 1 *tr. V.* **(a)** (mit den Fingern) scratch off; (mit einem Werkzeug) scrape off
(b) (säubern) scrape [clean]
2 *itr. V.; mit sein* (derb) snuff it (sl.)

ab|kriegen *tr. V.* (ugs.) ▶ ABBEKOMMEN

ab|kühlen 1 *tr. V.* cool down
2 *itr., refl. V.; itr. meist mit sein* cool down

Ab·kühlung *die* cooling

ab|kupfern *tr. V.* (ugs.) copy mechanically (**bei** from)

ab|kürzen *tr., itr. V.* **(a)** (räumlich) shorten; **den Weg ~**: take a shorter route
(b) (zeitlich) cut short
(c) (kürzer schreiben) abbreviate (**mit** to)

Abkürzung *die* **(a)** (Weg) short cut
(b) (Wort) abbreviation

ab|küssen *tr. V.* cover with kisses

ab|laden *unr. tr., itr. V.* unload

Ab·lage *die* **(a)** storage place
(b) (Raum) storage room
(c) (Bürow.) filing

ab|lagern *tr. V.* deposit

ab|lassen 1 *unr. tr. V.* let out (**aus** of); let off ‹*steam*›
2 *unr. itr. V.* **(a) von jmdm./etw. ~**: leave sb./sth. alone
(b) von etw. ~ (etw. aufgeben) give sth. up

Ab·lauf *der* **(a)** (Verlauf) course; (einer Veranstaltung) passing off
(b) (Ende) **nach ~ eines Jahres** after a year; **nach ~ einer Frist** at the end of a period of time

ab|laufen *unr. itr. V.; mit sein* **(a)** flow away; (aus einem Behälter) run out
(b) (verlaufen) pass off
(c) ‹*alarm clock*› run down; ‹*parking meter*› expire
(d) ‹*period, contract, passport*› expire

ab|lecken *tr. V.* **(a)** lick off
(b) (säubern) lick clean

ab|legen 1 *tr. V.* **(a)** lay *or* put down
(b) (Bürow.) file
(c) stop wearing ‹*clothes*›
(d) give up ‹*habit*›; lose ‹*shyness*›
(e) swear ‹*oath*›; sit ‹*examination*›; make ‹*confession*›
2 *tr., itr. V.* take off; **möchten Sie ~?** would you like to take your coat off?
3 *itr. V.* **[vom Kai] ~**: cast off

Ableger *der;* **~s, ~**: layer; (Steckling) cutting

ab|lehnen *tr. V.* **(a)** decline; decline, turn down ‹*money, invitation, position*›; reject ‹*suggestion, applicant*›
(b) (missbilligen) disapprove of

Ablehnung *die;* **~, ~en** **(a)** rejection
(b) (Missbilligung) disapproval

ab|leiten *tr. V.* **(a)** divert
(b) (herleiten) **etw. aus/von etw. ~**: derive sth. from sth.

Ab·leitung *die* derivation

ab|lenken *tr. V.* **(a)** deflect
(b) jmdn. von etw. ~: distract sb. from sth.
(c) (zerstreuen) divert; **sich ~**: amuse oneself

Ab·lenkung *die* ▶ ABLENKEN: deflection; distraction; diversion

Ablenkungs·manöver *das* diversion[ary tactic]

ab|lesen *unr. tr. V.* **(a)** read ‹*speech, lecture*›; **werden Sie frei sprechen oder ~?** will you be talking from notes or reading your speech?
(b) read ‹*gas meter, thermometer, etc.*›; check ‹*time, speed, temperature*›
(c) (erkennen) see

ab|lichten *tr. V.* **(a)** (fotokopieren) photocopy
(b) (fotografieren) take a photograph of

Ab·lichtung *die* **(a)** (das Fotografieren) photographing; (das Fotokopieren) photocopying
(b) (Fotokopie) photocopy

ab|liefern *tr., itr. V.* hand in; deliver ‹*goods*›

ab|lösen 1 *tr. V.* **(a) etw. [von etw.] ~**: get sth. off [sth.]
(b) jmdn. ~: relieve sb.; **sich** *od.* **einander ~**: take turns
2 *refl. V.* **sich [von etw.] ~**: come off [sth.]

Ab·lösung *die* (eines Postens) changing; **ich schicke Ihnen jemanden zur ~**: I'll send someone to relieve you

ab|machen *tr. V.* **(a)** (ugs.) take off; take down ‹*sign, rope*›
(b) (vereinbaren) agree

Abmachung *die;* **~, ~en** agreement

ab|magern *itr. V.; mit sein* become thin; (absichtlich) slim

Abmagerungs·kur *die* reducing diet

ab|marschieren *itr. V.; mit sein* depart; (Milit.) march off

ab|melden *tr. V.* **(a) sich/jmdn. ~**: report that one/sb. is leaving
(b) (Umzug melden) *notify the authorities that one is moving from an address;*
(c) ein Auto ~: cancel a car's registration
(d) (DV) ▶ AUSLOGGEN

Ab·meldung *die* **(a)** (beim Weggehen) report that one is leaving
(b) (beim Umzug) *registration of a move with the authorities at one's old address;*
(c) ~ eines Autos cancellation of a car's registration

Ab·messung *die* (Dimension) dimension; measurement

ab|montieren *tr. V.* take off ‹*part*›; dismantle ‹*machine, equipment*›

ab|mühen *refl. V.* toil; **sie mühte sich mit dem schweren Koffer ab** she struggled with the heavy suitcase

ab|murksen *tr. V.* (salopp) do in (sl.)

Abnahme *die;* **~, ~n** **(a)** (das Entfernen) removal
(b) (Verminderung) decrease

a

ab|nehmen 1 *unr. tr. V.* **(a)** (entfernen) take off; take down ‹*picture, curtain, lamp*›
(b) **jmdm. den Koffer ~**: take sb.'s suitcase; **jmdm. eine Arbeit ~**: save sb. a job
(c) **jmdm. ein Versprechen/einen Eid ~**: make sb. give a promise/swear an oath
(d) (prüfen) inspect and approve; test and pass ‹*vehicle*›
(e) **jmdm. etw. ~** (wegnehmen) take sth. off sb.
(f) (beim Telefon) answer ‹*telephone*›; pick up ‹*receiver*›
(g) (Handarb.) decrease
(h) **das nehme ich dir/ihm** *usw.* **nicht ab** I won't buy that (coll.)
2 *unr. itr. V.* **(a)** (Gewicht verlieren) lose weight
(b) (sich verringern) decrease; drop; ‹*attention, interest*› flag; ‹*brightness*› diminish; **wir haben ~den Mond** there is a waning moon
(c) (beim Telefon) answer the telephone

Ab·neigung *die* dislike (**gegen** for)

ab|nutzen, (landsch.:) **ab|nützen** *tr., refl. V.* wear out; **abgenutzt** worn

Abonnement /abɔnəˈmã:/ *das;* **~s, ~s** subscription (*Gen.* to)

Abonnent *der;* **~en, ~en, Abonnentin** *die;* **~, ~nen** subscriber (+ *Gen.* to); (Theater, Oper) season ticket holder

abonnieren *tr. V.* subscribe to

Ab·ordnung *die* delegation

ab|packen *tr. V.* pack; wrap ‹*bread*›; **abgepacktes Obst/abgepackte Fleischportionen** packaged fruit/pieces of meat

ab|passen *tr. V.* **(a)** (abwarten) wait for
(b) (aufhalten) catch

ab|pausen *tr. V.* trace

ab|pfeifen (Sport) 1 *itr. V.* blow the whistle
2 *tr. V.* [blow the whistle to] stop

Ab·pfiff *der* (Sport) final whistle; (Halbzeit~) half-time whistle

ab|pflücken *tr. V.* pick

ab|plagen *refl. V.* slave away

ab|prallen *itr. V.; mit sein* rebound; ‹*bullet, missile*› ricochet

Ab·produkt *das* waste product

ab|putzen *tr. V.* (ugs.); **(a)** wipe off
(b) (säubern) wipe; **jmdm./sich das Gesicht ~**: clean sb.'s/one's face

ab|quälen *refl. V.* **sich [mit etw.] ~**: struggle [with sth.]

ab|rackern *refl. V.* (ugs.) flog oneself to death (coll.)

ab|rasieren *tr. V.* shave off

ab|raten *unr. itr. V.* **jmdm. von etw. ~**: advise sb. against sth.

ab|räumen *tr. V.* **(a)** clear away
(b) (leer machen) clear ‹*table*›

ab|rechnen 1 *itr. V.* cash up; **mit jmdm. ~** (fig.) call sb. to account
2 *tr. V.* **die Kasse ~**: reckon up the till; **seine Spesen ~**: claim one's expenses

Ab·rechnung *die* **(a)** cashing up *no art.;* (Aufstellung) statement
(b) (fig.: Vergeltung) reckoning

Ab·rede *die* **(a)** arrangement; agreement
(b) **etw. in ~ stellen** deny sth.

ab|regen *refl. V.* (ugs.) calm down; **reg dich ab!** cool it! (coll.); calm down!

ab|reiben *unr. tr. V.* **(a)** rub off
(b) (säubern) rub

Ab·reise *die* departure (**nach** for); **bei meiner ~**: when I left/leave

ab|reisen *itr. V.; mit sein* leave (**nach** for)

ab|reißen 1 *unr. tr. V.* **(a)** tear off; tear down ‹*poster, notice*›; pull off ‹*button*›
(b) (niederreißen) demolish, pull down ‹*building*›
2 *unr. itr. V.; mit sein* **(a)** fly off; ‹*shoelace*› break off
(b) (aufhören) come to an end; ‹*connection, contact*› be broken off

ab|richten *tr. V.* train

Ab·riss, *Ab·riß *der* **(a)** ▶ ABREISSEN 1B: demolition; pulling down
(b) (knappe Darstellung) outline

ab|rollen 1 *tr. V.* unwind
2 *itr. V.; mit sein* unwind [itself]

ab|rücken 1 *tr. V.* (wegschieben) move away
2 *itr. V.; mit sein* move away

Ab·ruf *der:* **auf ~**: on call; (DV) in retrievable form

ab|rufen *unr. tr. V.* summon; call

ab|runden *tr. V.* **(a)** (auch fig.) round off
(b) round ‹*figure*› up/down (**auf** + **Akk.** to); **etw. nach oben/unten ~**: round sth. up/down

abrupt 1 *Adj.* abrupt
2 *adv.* abruptly

ab|rüsten *itr., tr. V.* disarm

Ab·rüstung *die;* **~**: disarmament

ab|rutschen *itr. V.; mit sein* **(a)** slip
(b) (nach unten rutschen) slide down

Abs. *Abk.* **(a)** = **Absender;**
(b) = **Absatz**

ABS *Abk.* = **Antiblockiersystem** ABS

Ab·sage *die* (auf eine Einladung) refusal; (auf eine Bewerbung) rejection

ab|sagen 1 *tr. V.* cancel; withdraw ‹*participation*›
2 *itr. V.* **jmdm. ~**: tell sb. one cannot come

ab|sägen *tr. V.* saw off

Ab·satz *der* **(a)** (am Schuh) heel
(b) (Textunterbrechung) break
(c) (Textabschnitt) paragraph
(d) (Kaufmannsspr.) sales *pl.*

Absatz-: **~chance** *die* (Kaufmannsspr.) sales prospect; **~förderung** *die* (Kaufmannsspr.) sales promotion; **~markt** *der* (Kaufmannsspr.) market; **~steigerung** *die* (Kaufmannsspr.) increase in sales

---

*old spelling - see note on page xiv

ab|saufen *unr. itr. V.; mit sein* (ugs.) ‹*engine, car*› flood

ab|saugen *tr. V.* **(a)** suck away
(b) (säubern) hoover (Brit.)

ab|schaben *tr. V.* **(a)** scrape off
(b) (säubern) scrape [clean]

ab|schaffen *tr. V.* **(a)** (beseitigen) abolish ‹*capital punishment, regulation, customs duty, institution*›; repeal ‹*law*›; put an end to ‹*injustice, abuse*›
(b) (weggeben) get rid of

Ab·schaffung *die* abolition; (von Gesetzen) repeal; (von Unrecht, Missstand) ending

ab|schalten *tr., itr. V.* switch off; shut down ‹*power station*›

abschätzig 1 *Adj.* derogatory
2 *adv.* derogatorily

Ab·scheu *der;* **~s** detestation; abhorrence

abscheulich 1 *Adj.* **(a)** disgusting ‹*smell, taste*›; repulsive ‹*sight*›
(b) (verwerflich) disgraceful ‹*behaviour*›; abominable ‹*crime*›
2 *adv.* disgracefully

ab|schicken *tr. V.* send [off]

ab|schieben *unr. tr. V.* **(a)** push away
(b) (abwälzen) shift ‹*responsibility, blame*›
(c) (außer Landes bringen) deport

Ab·schiebung *die* (Rechtsw.) deportation

Abschiebungs·haft *die* (Rechtsw.) detention prior to deportation

Abschied *der;* **~[e]s, ~e** parting (**von** from); farewell (**von** to); **~ nehmen** take one's leave (**von** of)

Abschieds-: ~brief *der* farewell letter; **~geschenk** *das* parting gift; **~gruß** *der* goodbye; farewell

ab|schießen *unr. tr. V.* **(a)** shoot down ‹*aeroplane*›
(b) fire ‹*arrow*›; launch ‹*spacecraft*›
(c) (töten) take

ab|schirmen *tr. V.* **(a)** (schützen) shield
(b) (fernhalten) screen off ‹*light, radiation*›

ab|schlachten *tr. V.* slaughter

Ab·schlag *der* **(a)** (Kaufmannsspr.) discount
(b) (Teilzahlung) interim payment; (Vorschuss) advance
(c) (Fußball) goalkeeper's kick out

ab|schlagen 1 *unr. tr. V.* **(a)** knock off; (mit dem Beil, Schwert usw.) chop off
(b) (ablehnen) refuse
(c) (abwehren) beat off
2 *unr. itr. V.* (Fußball) kick the ball out

ab|schleifen *unr. tr. V.* (von Holz) sand off; (von Metall, Glas usw.) grind off

Abschlepp·dienst *der* breakdown recovery service; tow[ing] service (Amer.)

ab|schleppen tow away; take ‹*ship*› in tow; **ein Auto zur Werkstatt ~:** tow a car to the garage

Abschlepp-: ~seil *das* tow rope; (aus Draht) towing cable; **~stange** *die* tow bar; **~wagen** *der* breakdown vehicle; tow truck (Amer.); (der Polizei) tow-away vehicle

ab|schließen 1 *unr. tr. V.* **(a)** *auch itr.* (zuschließen) lock ‹*door, gate, cupboard*›; lock [up] ‹*house, flat, room, park*›
(b) (verschließen) seal; **etw. luftdicht ~:** seal sth. hermetically
(c) (begrenzen) border
(d) (zum Abschluss bringen) conclude; **sein Studium ~:** finish one's studies; **Bewerber mit abgeschlossenem Universitätsstudium** applicants with a degree
(e) (vereinbaren) strike ‹*bargain, deal*›; make ‹*purchase*›; enter into ‹*agreement*›
2 *unr. itr. V.* (aufhören, enden) end; **~d sagte er ...:** in conclusion he said ...

Ab·schluss, *Ab·schluß *der* **(a)** (Verschluss) seal
(b) (Beendigung) conclusion; end
(c) (eines Geschäfts, Vertrags) conclusion

Abschluss-, *Abschluß-: ~ball *der* final dance; **~prüfung** *die* **(a)** (Schulw.) leaving *or* (Amer.) final examination; (Hochschulw.) final examination; finals *pl.;* **(b)** (Wirtsch.) audit

ab|schmecken *tr. V.* **(a)** (kosten) taste; try
(b) (würzen) season

ab|schmieren *tr. V.* (Technik) grease

ab|schminken *tr. V.* **jmdn./sich ~:** remove sb.'s/one's make-up

ab|schmirgeln *tr. V.* rub off with emery; (mit Sandpapier) sand off

ab|schnallen *tr. V.* unfasten

ab|schneiden 1 *unr. tr. V.* **(a)** (auch fig.: isolieren) cut off; cut down ‹*sth. hanging*›; **etw. von etw. ~:** cut sth. off sth.; **sich** (*Dat.*) **eine Scheibe Brot ~:** cut oneself a slice of bread
(b) (kürzer schneiden) cut
(c) jmdm. den Weg ~: take a short cut to get ahead of sb.
2 *unr. itr. V.* **bei etw. gut/schlecht ~:** do well/badly in sth.

Ab·schnitt *der* **(a)** (Kapitel) section
(b) (Zeitspanne) phase
(c) (Teil eines Formulars) [detachable] portion

ab|schrauben *tr. V.* unscrew [and remove]

ab|schrecken *tr. V.* **(a)** deter
(b) (fernhalten) scare off
(c) (Kochk.) pour cold water over

Abschreckung *die;* **~, ~en** deterrence; (Mittel zur Abschreckung) deterrent

ab|schreiben 1 *unr. tr. V.* **(a)** copy out; **etw. bei** *od.* **von jmdm. ~** (in der Schule) copy sth. off sb.; (als Plagiator) plagiarize sth. from sb.
(b) (Wirtsch.) amortize
2 *unr. itr. V.* **bei** *od.* **von jmdm. ~** (in der Schule) copy off sb.; (als Plagiator) copy from sb.

Ab·schreibung *die* (Wirtsch.) amortization

Ab·schrift *die* copy

ab|schürfen *tr. V.* graze

Ab·schuss, *Ab·schuß *der* **(a)** (eines Flugzeugs) shooting down ···›

(b) (von Geschossen) firing; (eines Raumschiffs) launching

ạbschüssig *Adj.* downward sloping ‹*land*›

ạb|schütteln *tr. V.* shake off; (herunterschütteln) shake down

ạb|schwächen 1 *tr. V.* **(a)** (mildern) tone down ‹*statement, criticism*›
(b) (verringern) lessen ‹*effect, impression*›; cushion ‹*blow, impact*›
2 *refl. V.* ‹*interest, demand*› wane

Ạbschwächung *die;* ~ **(a)** (Milderung) toning down
(b) (eines Aufpralls, Stoßes usw.) cushioning

ạb|schweifen *itr. V.; mit sein* digress

Ạbschweifung *die;* ~, **~en** digression

ạb|schwören *unr. itr. V.* **dem Teufel/seinem Glauben ~:** renounce the Devil/one's faith; **dem Alkohol/Laster ~:** forswear alcohol/vice

ạbsehbar *Adj.* foreseeable; **in ~er Zeit** within the foreseeable future

ạb|sehen 1 *unr. tr. V.* **(a)** (voraussehen) predict; foresee ‹*event*›
(b) es auf etw. (*Akk.*) **abgesehen haben** be after sth.; **er hat es darauf abgesehen, uns zu ärgern** he's out to annoy us; **der Chef hat es auf ihn abgesehen** the boss has got it in for him
2 *unr. itr. V.* **(a) von etw. ~** (etw. nicht beachten) leave aside sth.; *s. auch* ABGESEHEN;
(b) von etw. ~ (auf etw. verzichten) refrain from sth

ạb|seilen 1 *tr. V.* lower [with a rope]
2 *refl. V.* (Bergsteigen) abseil

***ạb|sein** ▶ AB 2A

ạbseits 1 *Präp. mit Gen.* away from
2 *Adv.* **(a)** far away
(b) (Ballspiele) **~ sein** *od.* **stehen** be offside

Ạbseits *das;* ~, ~: **das war ein klares ~:** that was clearly offside

ạb|senden *unr. od. regelm. tr. V.* dispatch

Ạb·sender *der,* **Ạb·senderin** *die;* ~, **~nen** sender; (Anschrift) sender's address

ạb|setzen 1 *tr. V.* **(a)** take off ‹*hat, glasses, etc.*›
(b) (hinstellen) put down ‹*bag, suitcase*›
(c) (aussteigen lassen) **jmdn. ~** (im öffentlichen Verkehr) put sb. down; let sb. out (Amer.); (im privaten Verkehr) drop sb. [off]
(d) remove ‹*chancellor, judge*› from office; depose ‹*king, emperor*›
2 *refl. V.* **(a)** (sich ablagern) be deposited
(b) (flüchten) get away

Ạbsetzung *die;* ~, **~en** ▶ ABSETZEN 1D: removal; deposition

ạb|sichern 1 *tr. V.* make safe
2 *refl. V.* safeguard oneself

Ạb·sicht *die* intention; **etw. mit ~ tun** do sth. intentionally; **etw. ohne** *od.* **nicht mit ~ tun** do sth. unintentionally

ab·sịchtlich 1 *Adj.* intentional; deliberate
2 *adv.* intentionally; deliberately

ạb|sinken *unr. itr. V.; mit sein* sink

absolut *Adj.* absolute

Absolutịsmus *der;* ~ (hist.) absolutism *no art.*

Absolvent /...'vɛnt/ *der;* **~en, ~en, Absolvẹntin** *die;* ~, **~nen** (einer Schule) one who has taken the leaving *or* (Amer.) final examination; (einer Akademie) graduate

absolvieren *tr. V.* complete

Absolvierung *die;* ~: completion

ab·sọnderlich *Adj.* strange; odd

ạb|sondern 1 *tr. V.* exude; (Physiol.) secrete
2 *refl. V.* isolate oneself

absorbieren *tr. V.* absorb

ạb|speisen *tr. V.* **jmdn. mit etw. ~:** fob sb. off with sth.

ạbspenstig *Adj.* **jmdm. etw. ~ machen** get sb. to part with sth.

ạb|sperren *tr. V.* seal off; close off

Ạb·spiel *das* (Ballspiele) passing

ạb|spielen 1 *tr. V.* **(a)** play ‹*record, tape*›
(b) vom Blatt ~: ‹*piece of music*› play at sight
(c) (Ballspiele) pass
2 *refl. V.* take place

Ạb·sprache *die* arrangement; **eine ~ treffen** make an arrangement

ạb|sprechen *unr. tr. V.* **(a) jmdm. etw. ~:** deny that sb. has sth.
(b) (vereinbaren) arrange

ạb|springen *unr. itr. V.; mit sein* jump off; (herunterspringen) jump down; **vom Fahrrad ~:** jump off one's bicycle

Ạb·sprung *der* take-off; (das Herunterspringen) jump

ạb|spülen 1 *tr. V.* **(a)** wash off
(b) (reinigen) rinse off; **sich** (*Dat.*) **die Hände** *usw.* **~:** rinse one's hands *etc.;* **das Geschirr ~** (bes. südd.) wash the dishes
2 *itr. V.* (bes. südd.) wash up

ạb|stammen *itr. V.* be descended (**von** from)

Ạbstammung *die;* ~, **~en** descent

Ạb·stand *der* **(a)** distance; **in 20 Meter ~:** at a distance of 20 metres
(b) (Unterschied) gap

ạb|stauben *tr., itr. V.* dust

Ạbstecher *der;* **~s**, ~: side trip

ạb|stehen *unr. itr. V.* ‹*hair*› stand up; ‹*pigtail*[*s*]› stick out; **~de Ohren** protruding ears

Ạb·steige *die;* ~, **~n** (ugs. abwertend) cheap and crummy hotel (coll. derog.)

ạb|steigen *unr. itr. V.; mit sein* **(a)** [**vom Pferd/Fahrrad**] **~:** get off [one's horse/bicycle]
(b) (abwärts gehen) go down

ạb|stellen *tr. V.* **(a)** put down
(b) (unterbringen) put; (parken) park
(c) (ausschalten, abdrehen) turn off

*alte Schreibung - vgl. Hinweis auf S. xiv

(d) (unterbinden) put a stop to

Abstell-: ~kammer *die,* **~raum** *der* lumber room

ab|stempeln *tr. V.* **(a)** frank ‹*letter*›; cancel ‹*stamp*›
(b) (fig.) label, brand (**zu, als** as)

ab|sterben *unr. itr. V.; mit sein* **(a)** [gradually] die
(b) (gefühllos werden) go numb

Abstieg *der;* **~[e]s, ~e (a)** descent
(b) (Niedergang) decline

ab|stimmen 1 *itr. V.* vote (**über** + *Akk.* on)
2 *tr. V.* **etw. mit jmdm. ~:** discuss and agree on sth. with sb.

Ab·stimmung *die* **(a)** vote; **während der ~:** during the voting
(b) (Absprache) agreement

abstinent /apsti'nɛnt/ *Adj.* teetotal; **~ sein** be a teetotaller

Abstinenz *die;* **~:** teetotalism

Abstinenzler *der;* **~s, ~, Abstinenzlerin** *die;* **~, ~nen** teetotaller

ab|stoppen 1 *tr. V.* halt; stop; check ‹*advance*›
2 *itr. V.* come to a halt; ‹*person*› stop

Ab·stoß *der* (Fußball) goal kick

ab|stoßen *unr. tr. V.* **(a)** push off
(b) (beschädigen) chip ‹*crockery, paintwork, plaster*›
(c) (verkaufen) sell off
(d) (anwidern) repel; put off

abstoßend *Adj.* repulsive

abstrakt /ap'strakt/ *Adj.* abstract

ab|streifen *tr. V.* pull off; strip off ‹*berries*›; **die Asche [von der Zigarette/Zigarre] ~:** remove the ash [from one's cigarette/cigar]

ab|streiten *unr. tr. V.* deny

Ab·strich *der* **(a)** (Med.) swab; **einen ~ machen** take a swab
(b) (Streichung, Kürzung) cut; **~e machen** make cuts (**an** + *Dat.* in)

ab|stumpfen *itr. V.; mit sein* **jmd. stumpft ab** (wird unsensibel) sb.'s mind becomes deadened

Ab·sturz *der* fall; (eines Flugzeugs) crash

ab|stürzen *itr. V.; mit sein* fall; ‹*aircraft, pilot, passenger*› crash

Absturz·ursache *die* cause of the crash

ab|stützen 1 *refl. V.* support oneself (**mit** on, **an** + *Dat.* against)
2 *tr. V.* support

ab|suchen *tr. V.* search (**nach** for)

absurd *Adj.* absurd

absurderweise *Adv.* absurdly enough

Absurdität *die;* **~, ~en** absurdity; (Ungereimtheit) inconsistency

Abszess, *Abszeß *der;* **Abszesses, Abszesse (a)** (Med.) abscess
(b) (Geschwür) ulcer

Abszisse *die;* **~, ~n** (Math.) abscissa

Abt *der;* **~[e]s, Äbte** abbot

Abt. *Abk.* = **Abteilung**

ab|tasten *tr. V.* **etw. ~:** feel sth. all over

ab|tauen 1 *itr. V.; mit sein* (eis-/schneefrei werden) become clear of ice/snow; ‹*refrigerator*› defrost
2 *tr. V.* melt; thaw; defrost ‹*refrigerator*›

Abtei *die;* **~, ~en** abbey

Abteil *das;* **~[e]s, ~e** compartment

Ab·teilung *die* department

Abteilungs·leiter *der,* **Abteilungs·leiterin** *die* head of department

ab|tippen *tr. V.* (ugs.) type out

Äbtissin *die;* **~, ~nen** abbess

ab|tönen *tr. V.* tint

ab|töten *tr. V.* destroy ‹*parasites, germs*›; deaden ‹*nerve, feeling*›

ab|tragen *unr. tr. V.* (abnutzen) wear out; **abgetragen** well worn

abträglich *Adj.* (geh.) **einer Sache** (*Dat.*) **~ sein** be detrimental to sth.

Ab·transport *der* ▶ ABTRANSPORTIEREN: taking away; removal

ab|transportieren *tr. V.* take away; remove ‹*dead, injured*›

ab|treiben 1 *unr. tr. V.* **(a)** carry away; **jmdn./ein Schiff vom Kurs ~:** drive sb./a ship off course
(b) abort ‹*foetus*›; **ein Kind ~ lassen** have an abortion
2 *unr. itr. V.; mit sein* be carried away; ‹*ship*› be driven off course

Abtreibung *die;* **~, ~en** abortion

ab|trennen *tr. V.* detach

ab|treten 1 *unr. tr. V.* **(a) sich** (*Dat.*) **die Füße/Schuhe ~:** wipe one's feet
(b) jmdm. etw. ~: let sb. have sth.
2 *unr. itr. V.; mit sein* **(a)** (Theater) exit; (fig.) make one's exit
(b) (zurücktreten) step down; ‹*monarch*› abdicate

Abtreter *der;* **~s, ~:** doormat

ab|trocknen *tr. V.* dry; **sich** (*Dat.*) **die Hände/die Tränen ~:** dry one's hands/tears

ab|tropfen *itr. V.; mit sein* drip off

abtrünnig *Adj.* (einer Partei) renegade; (einer Religion, Sekte) apostate; **der Kirche/dem Glauben ~ werden** desert the Church/the faith

ab|tun *unr. tr. V.* dismiss

ab|wägen *unr. od. regelm. tr., itr. V.* weigh up; **abgewogen** carefully weighted; balanced ‹*judgement*›

ab|wählen *tr. V.* vote out; drop ‹*school subject*›

ab|wandeln *tr. V.* adapt

ab|wandern *itr. V.; mit sein* migrate; (in ein anderes Land) emigrate

Abwanderung *die* migration; (in ein anderes Land) emigration

Ab·wandlung *die* adaptation

Ab·wärme *die* (Technik) waste heat

ab|warten [1] *itr. V.* wait; **sie warteten ab** they awaited events; **warte ab!** wait and see; (als Drohung) just you wait! [2] *tr. V.* wait for

abwärts *Adv.* downwards; (bergab) downhill; **den Fluss ~:** downstream

Abwärts·trend *der* downward trend

Abwasch *der;* **~[e]s** washing-up (Brit.); washing dishes (Amer.); **den ~ machen** do the washing-up/wash the dishes

abwaschbar *Adj.* washable

ab|waschen [1] *unr. tr. V.* **(a)** wash off **(b)** (reinigen) wash down; wash [up] ‹*dishes*› [2] *unr. itr. V.* wash up (Brit.); wash the dishes (Amer.)

Ab·wasser *das; Pl.* **Abwässer** sewage

Abwasser: ~aufbereitung *die;* **~~:** sewage treatment; **~kanal** *der* sewer

ab|watschen *tr. V.* (ugs.) lambaste (coll.)

ab|wechseln *refl., itr. V.* alternate; **wir wechselten uns ab** we took turns

abwechselnd *Adv.* alternately

Abwechslung *die;* **~, ~en** variety; (Wechsel) change; **zur ~:** for a change

Ab·weg *der:* **auf ~e kommen** *od.* **geraten** go astray

abwegig erroneous; false ‹*suspicion*›

Ab·wehr *die;* **~ (a)** repulsion; (von Schlägen) fending off; (Sport) clearance; clearing (Amer.) **(b)** (Sport: Hintermannschaft) defence

ab|wehren *tr. V.* **(a)** repulse; fend off ‹*blow*›; (Sport) clear ‹*ball, shot*› **(b)** avert ‹*danger, consequences*›

Abwehr: ~kraft *die* power of resistance; **~spieler** *der,* **~spielerin** *die* (Sport) defender

ab|weichen *unr. itr. V.; mit sein* **(a)** deviate **(b)** (sich unterscheiden) differ

Abweichung *die;* **~, ~en (a)** deviation **(b)** (Unterschied) difference

ab|weisen *unr. tr. V.* turn away; turn down ‹*applicant, suitor*›

abweisend *Adj.* cold ‹*look, tone of voice*›; **in ~em Ton** coldly

Ab·weisung *die:* ▶ ABWEISEN: turning away; turning down

ab|wenden [1] *unr. od. regelm. tr. V.* **(a)** turn away **(b)** *nur regelm.* (verhindern) avert [2] *unr. od. regelm. refl. V.* turn away

ab|werben *unr. tr. V.* lure away

ab|werfen [1] *unr. tr. V.* **(a)** drop; throw off ‹*clothing*›; jettison ‹*ballast*›; throw ‹*rider*› **(b)** (ins Spielfeld werfen) throw out ‹*ball*› **(c)** (einbringen) bring in; **Profit ~:** make a profit [2] *unr. itr. V.* (Sport) throw the ball out

ab|werten *tr., itr. V.* devalue

abwertend *Adj.* derogatory ‹*term*›

Ab·wertung *die* devaluation

abwesend *Adj.* absent

Abwesenheit *die;* **~:** absence

ab|wickeln *tr. V.* **(a)** unwind **(b)** (erledigen) deal with ‹*case*›; do ‹*business*›

Abwicklung *die;* **~, ~en** ▶ ABWICKELN 1B: dealing (*Gen.* with); doing

ab|wiegen *unr. tr. V.* weigh out; weigh ‹*single item*›

ab|wimmeln *tr. V.* (ugs.) get rid of

ab|winken *itr. V.* **uninteressiert ~:** wave it/them aside uninterestedly; **Skat dreschen bis zum Abwinken** (ugs.) play skat till you can't stand any more (coll.); **Champagner bis zum Abwinken** (ugs.) more champagne than you can drink

ab|wischen *tr. V.* **(a)** wipe away **(b)** (säubern) wipe

Ab·wurf *der* **(a)** dropping; (von Ballast) jettisoning **(b) beim ~ stolperte der Torwart** the goalkeeper stumbled as he threw the ball out

ab|zahlen *tr. V.* pay off ‹*debt, loan*›

ab|zählen *tr. V.* count

Ab·zahlung *die* paying off; **etw. auf ~ kaufen/verkaufen** buy/sell sth. on easy terms

Ab·zeichen *das* emblem; (Anstecknadel, Plakette) badge

ab|zeichnen [1] *tr. V.* **(a)** (kopieren) copy **(b)** (signieren) initial [2] *refl. V.* stand out; (fig.) begin to emerge

Abzieh·bild *das* transfer

ab|ziehen [1] *unr. tr. V.* **(a)** pull off; peel off ‹*skin*›; strip ‹*bed*› **(b)** (Fot.) make a print/prints of **(c)** (Milit., auch fig.) withdraw **(d)** (subtrahieren) subtract; take away; (abrechnen) deduct [2] *unr. itr. V.; mit sein* **(a)** (sich verflüchtigen) escape **(b)** (Milit.) withdraw

Ab·zug *der* **(a)** (an einer Schusswaffe) trigger **(b)** (Fot.) print **(c)** (Verminderung) deduction

abzüglich *Präp. mit Gen.* (Kaufmannsspr.) less

ab|zweigen [1] *itr. V.; mit sein* branch off [2] *tr. V.* put aside

Abzweigung *die;* **~, ~en** turn-off; (Gabelung) fork

ach *Interj.* **(a)** (betroffen, mitleidig) oh [dear] **(b)** (bedauernd, unwirsch) oh **(c)** (klagend) ah **(d)** (erstaunt) oh; **~, wirklich?** no, really?; **~, der!** oh, him! **(e) ~ so!** oh, I see; **~ was** *od.* **wo!** of course not

Achat *der;* **~[e]s, ~e** (Min.) agate

Achse *die;* **~, ~n (a)** (Rad~) axle **(b)** (Dreh~, Math., Astron.) axis

---

*old spelling - see note on page xiv

Achsel *die;* ~, ~**n** (Schulter) shoulder; (~höhle) armpit

Achsel-: ~**haare** *Pl.* armpit hair *sing.;* ~**höhle** *die* armpit

acht[1] *Kardinalz.* eight; **um ~ [Uhr]** at eight [o'clock]; **um halb ~:** at half past seven; **drei viertel ~, Viertel vor ~:** [a] quarter to eight; **es steht ~ zu ~/~ zu zwei** (Sport) the score is eight all/eight to two

acht[2]**: sie waren zu ~:** there were eight of them

acht... *Ordinalz.* eighth; **der ~e September** the eighth of September; **München, [den] 8. Mai 1984** Munich, 8 May 1984

Acht[1] *die;* ~, ~**en (a)** eight
(b) (Figur) figure eight
(c) (Verbiegung) buckle; **mein Rad hat eine ~:** my wheel is buckled

Acht[2]**: etw. außer ~ lassen** disregard sth.; **sich in ~ nehmen** be careful; **sich vor jmdm./etw. in ~ nehmen** be wary of sb./sth.; **auf jmdn./etw. ~ geben** take care of sb./sth.; **~ geben** be careful

Achte *der/die; adj. Dekl.* eighth

acht-, Acht-: ~**eck** *das* octagon; ~**eckig** *Adj.* octagonal; ~**einhalb** *Bruchz.* eight and a half

achtel *Bruchz.* eighth

Achtel *das* (schweiz. meist *der*); ~**s**, ~**:** eighth

Achtel·note *die* (Musik) quaver

achten [1] *tr. V.* respect
[2] *itr. V.* **auf etw.** (*Akk.*) **~:** pay heed to sth.

achtens *Adv.* eighthly

Achterbahn *die* roller coaster

acht·fach *Vervielfältigungsz.* eightfold; **die ~fache Menge** eight times the quantity; **~fach vergrößert/verkleinert** magnified/reduced eight times; **das Achtfache kosten** cost eight times as much

***acht|geben** ▸ ACHT[2]

acht-: ~**hundert** *Kardinalz.* eight hundred; ~**jährig** *Adj.* (8 Jahre alt) eight-year-old *attrib.;* eight years old *pred.;* (8 Jahre dauernd) eight-year *attrib.;* ~**köpfig** *Adj.* ‹*family, committee*› of eight

acht·los [1] *Adj.* heedless
[2] *adv.* heedlessly

Achtlosigkeit *die;* ~**:** heedlessness

acht-: ~**mal** *Adv.* eight times; ~**spurig** *Adj.* eight-lane ‹*road*›; eight-track ‹*cassette*›; ~**stellig** *Adj.* eight-figure *attrib.;* **~stellig sein** have eight figures; ~**stimmig** [1] *Adj.* eight-part *attrib.;* [2] *adv.* in eight parts; ~**stöckig** *Adj.* eight-storey *attrib.;* ~**tägig** *Adj.* (8 Tage alt) eight-day-old *attrib.;* (8 Tage dauernd) eight-day[-long] *attrib.;* ~**tausend** *Kardinalz.* eight thousand; ~**teilig** *Adj.* eight-piece ‹*tea service, tool set, etc.*›; eight-part ‹*series, serial*›

Achtung *die;* ~ **(a)** respect (**vor** + *Dat., Gen.* for)
(b) ~! watch out!; **~, fertig, los!** on your marks, get set, go!

acht·zehn *Kardinalz.* eighteen; **18 Uhr 33** 6.33p.m.; (auf der 24-Stunden-Uhr) 1833

achtzehn·jährig *Adj.* (18 Jahre alt) eighteen-year-old *attrib.;* eighteen years old *pred.;* (18 Jahre dauernd) eighteen-year *attrib.*

achtzig *Kardinalz.* eighty; **[mit] ~ [km/h] fahren** drive at *or* (coll.) do eighty [k.p.h.]; **über/etwa ~ [Jahre alt] sein** be over/about eighty [years old]; **mit ~ [Jahren]** at eighty [years of age]

achtzig·jährig *Adj.* (80 Jahre alt) eighty-year-old *attrib.;* eighty years old *pred.;* (80 Jahre dauernd) eighty-year *attrib.*

ächzen *itr. V.* groan

Acker *der;* ~**s, Äcker** field

Acker: ~**bau** *der* arable farming; ~**land** *das* farmland

A.D. *Abk.* = **Anno Domini** AD

ADAC *Abk.* = **Allgemeiner Deutscher Automobilclub**

Adams·apfel *der* (ugs.) Adam's apple

adäquat /at|ɛ'kva:t/ *Adj.* appropriate (*Dat.* to); suitable (*Dat.* for)

addieren [1] *tr. V.* add [up]
[2] *itr. V.* add

Addition *die;* ~, ~**en** addition

ade *Interj.* (veralt., landsch.) farewell (dated); bye (coll.); **jmdm. ~** *od.* **Ade sagen** bid farewell to sb.

Adel *der;* ~**s** nobility; **der niedere/hohe ~:** the lesser nobility/the aristocracy

adelig ▸ ADLIG

Adelige ▸ ADLIGE

adeln *tr. V.* **jmdn. ~:** give sb. a title; (in den hohen Adel erheben) raise sb. to the peerage

Adels-: ~**geschlecht** *das* noble family; ~**stand** *der* nobility; (hoher Adel) nobility; ~**titel** *der* title of nobility

Ader *die;* ~, ~**n (a)** blood vessel
(b) (Anlage, Begabung) streak
(c) (Bot., Geol.) vein
(d) (Elektrot.) core

adieu /a'di̯ø:/ *Interj.* (veralt.) adieu

Adjektiv *das;* ~**s**, ~**e** (Sprachw.) adjective

Adjutant *der;* ~**en**, ~**en**, **Adjutantin** *die;* ~, ~**nen** adjutant

Adler *der;* ~**s**, ~**:** eagle

adlig *Adj.* noble; **~ sein** be a noble [man/woman]

Adlige *der/die; adj. Dekl.* noble [man/woman]

Admiral *der;* ~**s**, ~**e** *od.* **Admiräle** admiral

adoptieren *tr. V.* adopt

Adoption *die;* ~, ~**en** adoption

Adoptiv-: ~**eltern** *Pl.* adoptive parents; ~**kind** *das* adopted child; ~**mutter** *die; Pl.* ~**mütter** adoptive mother; ~**sohn** *der* adoptive *or* adopted son; ~**tochter** *die* adoptive *or* adopted daughter; ~**vater** *der* adoptive father

a

Adressat *der;* **~en, ~en, Adressatin** *die;* **~, ~nen** addressee
Adress·buch, *Adreß·buch *das* directory
Adresse *die;* **~, ~n** address; **bei jmdm. an die falsche ~ kommen** *od.* **geraten** (fig. ugs.) come to the wrong address (fig.)
adressieren *tr. V.* address
adrett 1 *Adj.* smart
2 *adv.* smartly
Advent /at'vɛnt/ *der;* **~s (a)** Advent
(b) (Adventssonntag) Sunday in Advent
Advents-: ~kalender *der* Advent calendar; **~kranz** *der: garland of evergreens with four candles for the Sundays in Advent*
Adverb /at'vɛrp/ *das;* **~s, ~ien** (Sprachw.) adverb
adverbial (Sprachw.) 1 *Adj.* adverbial
2 *adv.* adverbially
Advokat /atvo'ka:t/ *der;* **~en, ~en, Advokatin** *die;* **~, ~nen** (österr., schweiz., sonst veralt.) lawyer; advocate (arch.)
Aero- /aero- *od.* ɛ:ro-/: **~gramm** *das* air[mail] letter; **~sol** *das;* **~~s, ~~e** aerosol
Affäre *die;* **~, ~n** affair; **sich aus der ~ ziehen** (ugs.) get out of it
Affe *der;* **~n, ~n (a)** monkey; (Menschen~) ape
(b) (salopp) (dummer Kerl) oaf; clot (Brit. coll.); (Geck) dandy
Affekt *der;* **~[e]s, ~e** emotion; **im ~:** in the heat of the moment
affektiert (abwertend) 1 *Adj.* affected
2 *adv.* affectedly
Affen·theater *das* (salopp) farce
Afghane /af'ga:nə/ *der;* **~n, ~n (a)** Afghan
(b) (Hund) Afghan hound
Afghanin *die;* **~, ~nen** Afghan
afghanisch *Adj.* Afghan
Afghanistan /af'ga:nɪsta:n/ *(das);* **~s** Afghanistan
Afrika *(das);* **~s** Africa
Afrikaner *der;* **~s, ~, Afrikanerin** *die;* **~, ~nen** African
afrikanisch *Adj.* African
After *der;* **~s, ~:** anus
AG *Abk.* **(a)** = **Aktiengesellschaft** PLC (Brit.); Ltd. (*private company*) (Brit.); Inc. (Amer.)
(b) = **Arbeitsgemeinschaft**
Agent *der;* **~en, ~en, Agentin** *die;* **~, ~nen** agent
Agentur *die;* **~, ~en** agency
Agentur·bericht *der,* **Agentur·meldung** *die* agency report
Aggregat *das;* **~[e]s, ~e** (Technik) unit; (Elektrot.) set
Aggregat·zustand *der* (Chemie) state

*alte Schreibung - vgl. Hinweis auf S. xiv

Aggression *die;* **~, ~en** aggression
aggressiv 1 *Adj.* aggressive
2 *adv.* aggressively
Aggressivität *die;* **~:** aggressiveness
Aggressor *der;* **~s, ~en, Aggressorin** *die;* **~, ~nen** aggressor
Agitation *die;* **~:** agitation
agitieren *itr. V.* agitate
Agrar·land *das* agrarian country
Ägypten *(das);* **~s** Egypt
Ägypter *der;* **~s, ~, Ägypterin** *die;* **~, ~nen** Egyptian
ägyptisch *Adj.* Egyptian
ah *Interj.* (verwundert) oh; (freudig, genießerisch) ah; (verstehend) oh; ah
äh /ɛ(:)/ *Interj.* **(a)** (angeekelt) ugh
(b) (stotternd) er; hum
aha /a'ha(:)/ *Interj.* (verstehend) oh[, I see]; (triumphierend) aha
Ahn *der;* **~[e]s,** *od.* **~en, ~en** (geh.), **Ahne** *der;* **~n, ~n** forebear; ancestor
ähneln *itr. V.* **jmdm. ~:** resemble *or* be like sb.; **jmdm. sehr/wenig ~:** strongly resemble *or* be very like sb./bear little resemblance to sb.; **einer Sache** (*Dat.*) **~:** be similar to sth.; be like sth.; **sich** (*Dat.*) **~:** resemble one another; be alike
ahnen *tr. V.* **(a)** (im Voraus fühlen) have a premonition of
(b) (vermuten) suspect; **das konnte ich doch nicht ~!** I had no way of knowing that
Ahnin *die;* **~, ~nen** ▶ AHN
ähnlich 1 *Adj.* similar; **jmdm. ~ sein** be like sb.; **~ wie** like
2 *adv.* similarly; ‹*answer, react*› in a similar way
3 *Präp. mit Dat.* like
Ähnlichkeit *die;* **~, ~en** similarity; **mit jmdm. ~ haben** be like sb.
Ahnung *die;* **~, ~en (a)** (Vorgefühl) premonition
(b) (ugs.: Kenntnisse) knowledge; **von etw. [viel] ~ haben** know [a lot] about sth.; **keine ~!** [I've] no idea
ahnungs·los *Adj.* (nichts ahnend) unsuspecting; (naiv, unwissend) naïve
Ahnungslosigkeit *die;* **~** (Naivität, Unschuld) naïvety; innocence; (Unwissenheit) naïvety
ahoi *Interj.* (Seemannsspr.) ahoy
Ahorn /'a:hɔrn/ *der;* **~s, ~e** maple
Ähre *die;* **~, ~n** ear
Aids /e:ts/ *das;* **~:** Aids
Aids-: ~kranke *der/die* person suffering from Aids; **~test** *der* Aids test
Airbag /'ɛ:ɐ̯bɛk/ *der;* **~s, ~s** (Kfz.-W.) air bag
Akademie *die;* **~, ~n** academy; (Bergbau, Forstw., Bauw.) school; college
Akademiker *der;* **~s, ~, Akademikerin** *die;* **~, ~nen** [university/college] graduate
akademisch 1 *Adj.* academic

a

2 *adv.* academically
Akazie /a'ka:tsi̯ə/ *die;* ~, ~**n** acacia
akklimatisieren *refl. V.* become *or* get acclimatized
Akkord *der;* ~[**e**]**s**, ~**e** (**a**) (Musik) chord (**b**) (Wirtsch.) (Arbeit) piecework; (Lohn) piecework pay *no indef. art., no pl.;* (Satz) piece rate
Akkordeon *das;* ~**s**, ~**s** accordion
Akku *der;* ~**s**, ~**s** (ugs.), **Akkumulator** *der;* ~**s**, ~**en** accumulator (Brit.); storage battery
akkurat 1 *Adj.* meticulous
2 *adv.* meticulously
Akkusativ *der;* ~**s**, ~**e** (Sprachw.) accusative [case]
Akkusativ·objekt *das* (Sprachw.) accusative *or* direct object
Akne *die;* ~, ~**n** (Med.) acne
Akribie /akri'bi:/ *die;* ~ (geh.) meticulousness; meticulous precision
akribisch /a'kri:bɪʃ/ 1 *Adj.* meticulous; meticulously precise
2 *adv.* meticulously; with meticulous precision
Akrobat *der;* ~**en**, ~**en** acrobat
Akrobatik *die;* ~: acrobatics *pl.*
Akrobatin *die;* ~, ~**nen** acrobat
akrobatisch *Adj.* acrobatic
Akt *der;* ~[**e**]**s**, ~**e** (**a**) (auch Theater, Zirkus-, Varieteeakt) act
(**b**) (Zeremonie) ceremony
(**c**) (Geschlechtsakt) sexual act
(**d**) (Kunst) nude
Akt-: ~**aufnahme** *die* nude photograph; ~**bild** *das* nude [picture]
Akte *die;* ~, ~**n** file
Akten-: ~**deckel** *der* folder; ~**koffer** *der* attaché case; ~**mappe** *die* briefcase; ~**notiz** *die* note [for the files]; ~**ordner** *der* file; ~**tasche** *die* briefcase; ~**zeichen** *das* reference
Akteur /ak'tø:ɐ̯/ *der;* ~**s**, ~**e**, **Akteurin** *die;* ~, ~**nen** person involved
Akt·foto *das* nude photo
Aktie /'akts:i̯ə/ *die;* ~, ~**n** (Wirtsch.) share; ~**n** shares (Brit.); stock (Amer.); **die ~n fallen/steigen** share *or* stock prices are falling/rising
Aktien-: ~**gesellschaft** *die* joint stock company; ~**kapital** *das* share capital; ~**mehrheit** *die* majority shareholding (*Gen.* in); ~**paket** *das* block of shares
Aktion *die;* ~, ~**en** (**a**) action *no indef. art.;* (militärisch) operation
(**b**) (Kampagne) campaign
Aktionär *der;* ~**s**, ~**e**, **Aktionärin** *die;* ~, ~**nen** shareholder
aktiv 1 *Adj.* (**a**) active
(**b**) (Milit.) serving *attrib.* ‹*officer, soldier*›
2 *adv.* actively
Aktiv *das;* ~**s**, ~**e** (Sprachw.) active
Aktive *der/die; adj. Dekl.* (Sport) participant
aktivieren *tr. V.* (**a**) mobilize ‹*party members, group, class, etc.*›; **den Kreislauf** ~: stimulate the circulation
(**b**) (DV) activate
Aktivität *die;* ~, ~**en** activity
Akt·modell *das* nude model
aktualisieren *tr. V.* update
Aktualität *die;* ~, ~**en** (**a**) (Gegenwartsbezug) relevance [to the present]
(**b**) (von Nachrichten usw.) topicality
aktuell *Adj.* topical; (gegenwärtig) current; (neu) up-to-the-minute; **eine ~e Sendung** (Ferns., Rundf.) a [news and] current affairs programme
Akupunktur *die;* ~, ~**en** (Med.) acupuncture
Akustik *die;* ~ (**a**) (Lehre vom Schall) acoustics *sing., no art.;*
(**b**) (Schallverhältnisse) acoustics *pl.*
akustisch 1 *Adj.* acoustic
2 *adv.* acoustically
akut *Adj.* (auch Med.) acute; pressing, urgent ‹*question, issue*›
AKW *Abk.* = **Atomkraftwerk**
Akzent *der;* ~[**e**]**s**, ~**e** (**a**) (Sprachw.) (Betonung) stress; (Betonungszeichen) accent
(**b**) (Sprachmelodie, Aussprache) accent
akzeptabel 1 *Adj.* acceptable
2 *adv.* acceptably
akzeptieren *tr. V.* accept
à la /ala/ (Gastr., ugs.) à la
Alabaster *der;* ~**s**, ~: alabaster
à la carte /ala'kart/ (Gastr.) à la carte
Alarm *der;* ~[**e**]**s**, ~**e** alarm; (Flieger~) air-raid warning; ~ **geben**/(fig. ugs.) **schlagen** raise the alarm; **blinder** ~: false alarm
alarm-, Alarm-: ~**anlage** *die* alarm system; ~**bereit** *Adj.* on alert *postpos.;* ~**bereitschaft** *die* alert
alarmieren *tr. V.* (**a**) alarm
(**b**) (zu Hilfe rufen) call [out] ‹*doctor, police, fire brigade, etc.*›
Alarm-: ~**sirene** *die* warning siren; ~**stufe** *die* alert stage
Albaner *der;* ~**s**, ~, **Albanerin** *die;* ~, ~**nen** Albanian
Albanien /al'ba:ni̯ən/ (*das*); ~**s** Albania
albanisch *Adj.* Albanian
Albatros *der;* ~, ~**se** (Zool.) albatross
Alben ▸ ALBUM
albern *Adj.* (**a**) silly; **sich ~ benehmen** act silly
(**b**) (ugs.: nebensächlich) silly; stupid
Albernheit *die;* ~, ~**en** silliness
Albino *der;* ~**s**, ~**s** albino
Alb·traum *der* nightmare
Album *das;* ~**s**, **Alben** album
Alge *die;* ~, ~**n** alga
Algebra /*österr.:* al'ge:bra/ *die;* ~: algebra
Algerien /al'ge:ri̯ən/ (*das*); ~**s** Algeria

a

Algerier *der;* **~s, ~, Algerierin** *die;* **~, ~nen** Algerian
algerisch *Adj.* Algerian
alias *Adv.* alias
Alibi *das;* **~s, ~s** alibi
Alkohol *der;* **~s, ~e** alcohol
alkohol-, Alkohol-: ~abhängig *Adj.* dependent on alcohol *postpos.;* **~abhängigkeit** *die* dependence on alcohol; alcohol dependence; **~ein·fluss,** ***~ein·fluß** *der,* **~ein·wirkung** *die* influence of alcohol *or* drink; **unter ~einfluss** *od.* **~einwirkung [stehen]** [be] under the influence of alcohol *or* drink; **~fahne** *die* smell of alcohol [on one's breath]; **eine ~fahne haben** smell of alcohol; **~frei** *Adj.* non-alcoholic
Alkoholiker *der;* **~s, ~, Alkoholikerin** *die;* **~, ~nen** alcoholic
alkoholisch *Adj.* alcoholic
Alkoholismus *der;* **~:** alcoholism *no art.*
alkohol-, Alkohol-: ~konsum *der* consumption of alcohol; **~missbrauch,** ***~mißbrauch** *der* alcohol abuse; **~sucht** *die* alcohol addiction; alcoholism; **~süchtig** *Adj.* addicted to alcohol *postpos.;* alcoholic; **~süchtige** *der/die; adj. Dekl.* alcoholic; **~sünder** *der,* **~sünderin** *die* (ugs.) drunk[en] driver; **~vergiftung** *die* alcohol[ic] poisoning
all *Indefinitpron. u. unbest. Zahlw.* [1] *attr.* (ganz, gesamt...) all; **~es andere/Weitere/Übrige** everything else; **~es Schöne** everything *or* all that is beautiful; **~es Gute!** all the best!; **wir/ihr/sie ~e** all of us/you/them; **~e Anwesenden** all those present; **~e Bewohner der Stadt** all the inhabitants of the town; **~e Jahre wieder** every year; **~e fünf Minuten/Meter** every five minutes/metres; **in ~er Ruhe** in peace and quiet
[2] *allein stehend* **(a) ~e** all; **~e, die ...:** all those who ...
(b) ~es (auf Sachen bezogen) everything; (auf Personen bezogen) everybody; **das ~es** all that; **trotz ~em** in spite of everything; **~es in ~em** all in all; **vor ~em** above all; **das ist ~es** that's all *or* (coll.) it; **ist das ~es?** is that all *or* (coll.) it?; **~es mal herhören!** (ugs.) listen everybody!; **~es aussteigen!** (ugs.) everyone out!; (vom Schaffner gesagt) all change!
All *das;* **~s** ▶ WELTALL
alle *Adj.* **~ sein** be all gone; **~ werden** run out
alle·dem *Pron.* **trotz ~:** in spite of *or* despite all that
Allee *die;* **~, ~n** avenue
allein [1] *Adj.* **(a)** (für sich) alone; on one's/its own; by oneself/itself; **ganz ~:** all on one's/its own
(b) (einsam) alone
[2] *adv.* (ohne Hilfe) by oneself/itself; on one's/its own; **etw. ~ tun** do sth. oneself; **von ~** (ugs.) by oneself/itself
[3] *Adv.* **(a)** (geh.: ausschließlich) alone
(b) [schon] ~ der Gedanke, [schon] der Gedanke ~: the mere thought [of it]
alleine (ugs.) ▶ ALLEIN 1A, 2, 3B
allein-, Allein-: *~erziehend *Adj.* single ‹*mother, father, parent*›; **~erziehende** *der/die; adj. Dekl.* single parent; **~gang** *der* (fig.) independent initiative; **im ~gang** off one's own bat
alleinig *Adj.* sole
***allein·stehend** *Adj.* ‹*person*› living alone; (ledig) single ‹*person*›
Alleinstehende *der/die; adj. Dekl.* person living alone; (Ledige[r]) single person
alle·mal *Adv.* (ugs.) any time (coll.); **was der kann, das kann ich doch ~:** anything he can do, I can do too; *s. auch* EIN[1] 1
allen·falls *Adv.* **(a)** (höchstens) at [the] most **(b)** (bestenfalls) at best
aller-: ~dings *Adv.* **(a)** (einschränkend) though; **es stimmt ~dings, dass ...:** it's true though that ...; **(b)** (zustimmend) [yes,] certainly; **das war ~dings Pech** that was bad luck, to be sure; **~erst...** *Adj.* **(a)** very first; **der/die/das ~erste** the very first; **(b)** (best...) very best
Allergen /alɛrˈgeːn/ *das;* **~s, ~e** (Med.) allergen
Allergie *die;* **~, ~n** (Med.) allergy
allergisch [1] *Adj.* (Med.) allergic (**gegen** to) [2] *adv.* **auf etw.** (*Akk.*) **~ reagieren** have an allergic reaction to sth
aller-, Aller-: ~größt... *Adj.* utmost ‹*trouble, care, etc.*›; biggest ‹*car, house, town, etc.*› of all; tallest ‹*person*› of all; **am ~größten sein** be [the] biggest/tallest of all; **~hand** *indekl. Adj.* (ugs.) **(a)** *attr.* all kinds *or* sorts of; **(b)** *allein stehend* all kinds *or* sorts of things; **das ist ~hand** (viel) that's a lot; **das ist ja ~hand!** that's just not on! (Brit. coll.); **~heiligen** *das;* **~~s** (bes. kath. Kirche) All Saints' Day; **~herzlichst** [1] *Adj.* warmest ‹*thanks, greetings, congratulations*›; most cordial ‹*reception, welcome, invitation*›; [2] most warmly; **~höchst...** [1] *Adj.* highest ‹*building, tree, etc.*› of all; [2] *adv.* **am ~höchsten** ‹*fly, jump, etc.*› the highest of all; **~höchstens** *Adv.* at the very most
allerlei *indekl. Adj.* all kinds *or* sorts of; *allein stehend* all kinds *or* sorts of things
Allerlei *das;* **~s, ~s** (Gemisch) pot-pourri; (Durcheinander) jumble
aller-: ~letzt... *Adj.* **(a)** very last; **(b)** (ugs. abwertend) most dreadful (coll.); **das ist das Allerletzte** that is the absolute limit; **~liebst...** [1] *Adj.* most favourite; **es wäre mir am ~liebsten** *od.* **das Allerliebste, wenn ...:** I should like it best of all if ...; [2] *adv.* **etw. am ~liebsten tun** like doing sth. best of all; **~meist...** [1] *Indefinitpron. u. unbest. Zahlw.* by far the most *attrib.;* **das ~meiste/am ~meisten** most of all/by far the most; [2] *Adv.* **am ~meisten** most of all;

*old spelling - see note on page xiv

~mindest... *Adj.* slightest; least; **das ~mindeste** the very least; **~nächst...** [1] *Adj.* very nearest *attrib.;* (Reihenfolge ausdrückend) very next *attrib.;* [2] *adv.* **am ~nächsten** nearest of all; **~neu[e]st...** *Adj.* very latest *attrib.;* **das Allerneu[e]ste** the very latest; **~schlimmst...** *Adj.* very worst *attrib.;* **~schönst...** [1] *Adj.* most beautiful *attrib.;* loveliest *attrib.;* (angenehmst...) very nicest *attrib.;* [2] *adv.* **er singt am ~schönsten** his singing is the most beautiful of all; **~seits** *Adv.* **guten Morgen ~seits!** good morning everyone

Allerwelts-: ~gesicht *das* nondescript face; **~wort** *das* hackneyed word

allerwenigst... [1] *Adj.* lest ... of all; *Pl.* fewest ... of all
[2] *adv.* **am ~wenigsten** least of all

alle·samt *Indefinitpron. u. unbest. Zahlw.* (ugs.) all [of you/us/them]; **wir ~:** we all

Alles·kleber *der* all-purpose adhesive

all·gemein [1] *Adj.* general; universal ‹*conscription, suffrage*›; **im ~en Interesse** in the common interest; **im Allgemein, *~en** in general
[2] *adv.* **(a)** generally; (ausnahmslos) universally; **es ist ~ bekannt, dass ...:** it is common knowledge that ...
(b) (unverbindlich) ‹*write, talk, discuss*› in general terms

Allgemein-: ~befinden *das* (Med.) general state of health; **~bildung** *die* general education

Allgemeinheit *die;* **~ (a)** generality **(b) die ~:** the general public

Allgemein-: ~medizin *die* general medicine; **~wohl** *das* public good

All·heilmittel *das* (auch fig.) cure-all; panacea

Alligator *der;* **~s, ~en** alligator

Alliierte *der; adj. Dekl.* ally; **die ~n** the Allies

all-: ~jährlich [1] *Adj.* annual; yearly; [2] *adv.* annually; every year; **~mächtig** *Adj.* all-powerful

all·mählich [1] *Adj.* gradual
[2] *adv.* gradually
[3] *Adv.* **wir sollten ~ gehen** it's time we got going

all-, All-: ~morgendlich [1] *Adj.* regular morning; [2] *adv.* every morning; **~seitig** [1] *Adj.* general; all-round, (Amer.) all-around *attrib.;* [2] *adv.* generally; **~seits** *Adv.* on all sides; **~tag** *der* **(a)** (Werktag) weekday; **(b)** (Einerlei) daily routine; **der graue ~:** the dull routine of everyday life; **~täglich** *Adj.* ordinary ‹*face, person, appearance, etc.*›; everyday ‹*topic, event, sight*›; commonplace ‹*remark*›; **ein nicht ~täglicher Anblick** a sight one doesn't see every day; **~tags** *Adv.* [on] weekdays; **~zu** *Adv.* all too; **~zu bald/früh** all too soon/early; **~zu lange/oft/sehr** too long/often/much; **~zu viel** too much; **nicht ~zu viele** not too many

***allzu·bald** *usw.* ▶ ALLZU

Alm *die;* **~, ~en** mountain pasture; Alpine pasture

Alm·hütte *die* Alpine hut

Almosen *das;* **~s, ~:** alms *pl.*

Alp *die;* **~, ~en** (bes. schweiz.) ▶ ALM

Alpaka *das;* **~s, ~s** alpaca

Alpen *Pl. die* **~:** the Alps

Alpen-: ~rose *die* rhododendron; **~veilchen** *das* cyclamen

Alpha *das;* **~[s], ~[s]** alpha

Alphabet *das;* **~[e]s, ~e** alphabet

alphabetisch [1] *Adj.* alphabetical
[2] *adv.* alphabetically

Alp·horn *das* alpenhorn

alpin *Adj.* Alpine

Alpinist *der;* **~en, ~en, Alpinistin** *die;* **~, ~nen** Alpinist

Alp·traum ▶ ALBTRAUM

als *Konj.* **(a)** (zeitlich) when; **damals, ~:** [in the days] when; **gerade ~:** just as
(b) (kausal) **um so mehr, ~: all the more since** *or* in that
(c) *Vergleichspartikel* **größer/älter/mehr/weniger ~:** bigger/older/more/less than; **anders ~ wir sein/leben** be different/live differently from us; **so viel/so weit ~ möglich** as much/as far as possible; **so bald/schnell ~ möglich** as soon/as quickly as possible; **~ [wenn od. ob]** (+ *Konjunktiv II*) as if; as though; **~ ob ich das nicht wüsste!** as if I didn't know
(d) ~ Rentner/Arzt as a pensioner/a doctor; **sich ~ wahr/Lüge erweisen** prove to be true/a lie

also [1] *Adv.* so; therefore
[2] *Partikel* **(a)** (das heißt) that is
(b) (nach Unterbrechung) well [then]
(c) (verstärkend) **na ~!** there you are[, you see]; **~ schön** well all right then

alt, älter, ältest... *Adj.* **(a)** old; **Alt und Jung** old and young; **seine ~en Eltern** his aged parents; **wie ~ bist du?** how old are you?; **mein älterer/ältester Bruder** my elder/eldest brother
(b) (nicht mehr frisch) old; **~es Brot** stale bread
(c) (vom letzten Jahr) old; **~e Äpfel/Kartoffeln** last year's apples/potatoes
(d) (langjährig) long-standing ‹*acquaintance*›
(e) (antik, klassisch) ancient
(f) (vertraut) old familiar ‹*streets, sights, etc.*›; **ganz der/die Alte sein** be just the same

Alt[1] *der;* **~s, ~e** (Musik) alto; (Frauenstimme) contralto; (im Chor) contraltos *pl.*

Alt[2] *das;* **~[s], ~:** *top fermented, dark beer*

Altar *der;* **~[e]s, Altäre** altar

alt-, Alt-: ~bau·wohnung *die* flat (Brit.) *or* (Amer.) apartment in an old building; **~bekannt** *Adj.* well-known; **~bier** *das* ▶ ALT[2]

a

Alte *der/die; adj. Dekl.* **(a)** (alter Mensch) old man/woman; *Pl.* old people
(b) (salopp) (Vater, Ehemann) old man (coll.); (Mutter, Ehefrau) old woman (coll.); (Chef) governor (coll.); (Chefin) boss (coll.); **die ~n** (Eltern) my/his *etc.* old man and old woman (coll.)
(c) *Pl.* (Tiereltern) parents

alt·ehrwürdig *Adj.* (geh.) venerable; time-honoured ‹*customs*›

Alt·englisch *das* Old English

Alten-: ~pfleger *der*, **~pflegerin** *die* geriatric nurse; **~tages·stätte** *die* old people's day centre

Alter *das; ~s, ~:* age; (hohes ~) old age; **im ~:** in one's old age; **im ~ von** at the age of

älter 1 ▸ ALT
2 *Adj.* (nicht mehr jung) elderly

altern *itr. V.; mit sein* age

alters-, Alters-: ~beschwerden *Pl.* complaints of old age; **~genosse** *der*, **~genossin** *die* contemporary; person/child of the same age; **meine ~genossen** my contemporaries; people of my age; **~gruppe** *die* age group; **~heim** *das* old people's home; old-age home (Amer.); **~rente** *die* old-age pension; **~ruhe·geld** *das* retirement pension; **~schwach** *Adj.* old and infirm ‹*person*›; old and weak ‹*animal*›; **~schwäche** *die* (bei Menschen) [old] age and infirmity; (bei Tieren) [old] age and weakness; **~starrsinn** *der* obstinacy of old age; **~stufe** *die* age; **~unterschied** *der* age difference; **~versorgung** *die* provision for one's old age; (System) pension scheme

Altertum *das; ~s* antiquity *no art.*

Älteste *der/die; adj. Dekl.* **(a)** (Dorf-, Vereins-, Kirchenälteste usw.) elder
(b) (Sohn, Tochter) eldest

alt-, Alt-: ~glas·behälter *der* bottle bank; **~griechisch** *das* classical *or* ancient Greek; **~hochdeutsch** *das* Old High German; **~klug; ~kluger, ~klugst...** 1 *Adj.* precocious; 2 *adv.* precociously; **~last** *die* (Ökologie) old, improperly disposed of harmful waste; (fig.) inherited problem

ältlich *Adj.* rather elderly

alt-, Alt-: ~metall *das* scrap metal; **~modisch** 1 *Adj.* old-fashioned; 2 *adv.* in an old-fashioned way; **~papier** *das* waste paper; **~rosa** *Adj.* old rose; **~stadt** *die* old [part of the] town; **~waren·händler** *der*, **~waren·händlerin** *die* second-hand dealer

Alu *das; ~s* (ugs.) aluminium

Alu·folie *die* aluminium foil

Aluminium *das; ~s* aluminium; aluminum (Amer.)

am *Präp. + Art.* **(a) = an dem;**
(b) Frankfurt am Main Frankfurt on [the] Main; **am Marktplatz** on the market square; **am Meer/Fluss** by the sea/on *or* by the river; **am Anfang/Ende** at the beginning/end; **am 19. November** on 19 November; **am schnellsten laufen** run [the] fastest; **am Verwelken sein** be wilting

Amalgam *das; ~s, ~e* (Chemie, auch fig.) amalgam

Amalgam·füllung *die* (Zahnmed.) amalgam filling

Amateur /ama'tøːɐ̯/ *der; ~s, ~e,* **Amateurin** *die; ~, ~nen* amateur

Amazonas *der; ~:* Amazon

Amboss, *Amboß *der;* **Ambosses, Ambosse** anvil

ambulant (Med.) 1 *Adj.* outpatient *attrib.;* 2 *adv.* **jmdn. ~ behandeln** give sb. outpatient treatment

Ambulanz *die; ~, ~en* **(a)** (in Kliniken) outpatient[s'] department
(b) (Krankenwagen) ambulance

Ameise *die; ~, ~n* ant

Ameisen-: ~bär *der* anteater; **~haufen** *der* anthill

amen *Adv.* amen

Amen *das; ~s, ~:* Amen

Amerika (*das*)*; ~s* America

Amerikaner *der; ~s, ~* **(a)** American
(b) (Gebäck) *small, flat iced cake*

Amerikanerin *die; ~, ~nen* American

amerikanisch *Adj.* American

Amino·säure *die* (Chemie) amino acid

Ammann *der; ~[e]s,* **Ammänner** (schweiz.) (Gemeinde-, Bezirksamman) ≈ mayor; (Landamman) cantonal president

Amme *die; ~, ~n* wet nurse

Amnestie /amnɛs'tiː/ *die; ~, ~n* amnesty

amnestieren *tr. V.* grant an amnesty to

Amöbe *die; ~, ~n* (Biol.) amoeba

Amok *der:* **~ laufen** run amok

Amok·läufer *der* madman

Amok·läuferin *die* madwoman

Ampel *die; ~, ~n* **(a)** traffic lights *pl.*
(b) (für Pflanzen) hanging flowerpot

Amphibie /am'fiːbi̯ə/ *die; ~, ~n* (Zool.) amphibian

Amphibien·fahrzeug *das* amphibious vehicle

Amphi·theater *das* amphitheatre

Ampulle *die; ~, ~n* (Med.) ampoule

Amputation *die; ~, ~en* (Med.) amputation

amputieren *tr. V.* amputate

Amsel *die; ~, ~n* blackbird

Amt *das; ~[e]s,* **Ämter (a)** (Stellung) post; position; (hohes politisches od. kirchliches ~) office; **im ~ sein** be in office
(b) (Aufgabe) task; job
(c) (Behörde) office
(d) (Fernsprechvermittlung) exchange

amtieren *itr. V.* **(a)** hold office

*alte Schreibung - vgl. Hinweis auf S. xiv

(b) (vorübergehend) act (**als** as)
amtlich [1] *Adj.* official; (ugs.: sicher) definite
[2] *adv.* officially
Amt·mann *der; Pl.* **...männer** *od.* **...leute, Amt·männin** *die;* **~, ~nen** *senior civil servant*
Amts-: ~anmaßung *die* (Rechtsw.) unauthorized assumption of authority; **~arzt** *der,* **~ärztin** *die* medical officer; **~eid** *der* oath of office; **~gericht** *das* local *or* district court; **~geschäfte** *Pl.* official duties; **~handlung** *die* official act *or* duty; **~leitung** *die* (Fernspr.) exchange line
Amulett *das;* **~[e]s, ~e** amulet; charm
amüsant [1] *Adj.* entertaining; amusing
[2] *adv.* in an entertaining *or* amusing way
amüsieren [1] *refl. V.* **(a)** (sich vergnügen) enjoy oneself; **sich mit jmdm. ~:** have fun *or* a good time with sb.
(b) (belustigt sein) be amused; **sich über jmdn./etw. ~:** find sb./sth. funny
[2] *tr. V.* amuse
an [1] *Präp. mit Dat.* **(a)** (räumlich) at; (auf) on; **Frankfurt an der Oder** Frankfurt on [the] Oder; **Tür an Tür** next door to one another; **an ... vorbei** past
(b) (zeitlich) on; **an jedem Sonntag** every Sunday; **an Ostern** (bes. südd.) at Easter
(c) arm/reich an Vitaminen low/rich in vitamins; **jmdn. an etw. erkennen** recognize sb. by sth.; **an etw. leiden** suffer from sth.; **an einer Krankheit sterben** die of a disease
(d) an [und für] sich actually
[2] *Präp. mit Akk.* **(a)** to; (auf, gegen) on
(b) an etw./jmdn. glauben believe in sth./sb.; **an etw. denken** think of sth.; **sich an etw. erinnern** remember sth.
[3] *Adv.* **(a)** (Verkehrsw.) **Köln an: 9.15** arriving Cologne 09.15
(b) (ugs.: in Betrieb) on; **die Waschmaschine/der Fernseher/das Licht/das Gas ist an** the washing machine/television/light/gas is on
(c) (ugs.: ungefähr) around; about; **an [die] 2 000 Euro** around *or* about 2,000 euros
Anabolikum *das;* **~s, Anabolika** (Med.) anabolic steroid
analog [1] *Adj.* **(a)** (gleichartig) analogous; **~ [zu] diesem Fall** analogous to this case
(b) (Technik, DV) analogue
[2] *adv.* **(a)** (gleichartig) analogously
(b) (Technik, DV) ‹*display, reproduce*› in analogue form
Analog-: ~rechner *der* (DV) analogue computer; **~uhr** *die* analogue clock; (Armbanduhr) analogue watch
Analphabet *der;* **~en, ~en, Analphabetin** *die;* **~, ~nen** illiterate [person]; **~ sein** be illiterate
Analyse *die;* **~, ~n** analysis
analysieren *tr. V.* analyse
Analyst *der;* **~en, ~en, Analystin,** *die;* **~, ~nen** (Börsenw.) analyst
analytisch [1] *Adj.* analytical
[2] *adv.* analytically
Ananas *die;* **~, ~** *od.* **~se** pineapple
Anarchie *die;* **~, ~n** anarchy
Anarchist *der;* **~en, ~en, Anarchistin** *die;* **~, ~nen** anarchist
Anästhesie *die;* **~, ~n** (Med.) anaesthesia
anästhesieren *tr. V.* (Med.) anaesthetize
Anästhesist *der;* **~en, ~en, Anästhesistin** *die;* **~, ~nen** (Med.) anaesthetist
Anatomie *die;* **~, ~n** anatomy
anatomisch *Adj.* anatomical
an|bahnen [1] *tr. V.* initiate ‹*negotiations, talks, process, etc.*›; develop ‹*relationship, connection*›
[2] *refl. V.* ‹*development*› be in the offing; ‹*friendship, relationship*› start to develop
an|bändeln *itr. V.* **mit jmdm. ~** (ugs.) get off with sb. (Brit. coll.); pick sb. up
An·bau *der; Pl.* **~ten (a)** building
(b) (Gebäude) extension
(c) (das Anpflanzen) growing
an|bauen [1] *tr. V.* **(a)** build on
(b) (anpflanzen) grow
[2] *itr. V.* (das Haus vergrößern) build an extension
an·bei *Adv.* (Amtsspr.) herewith; **Rückporto ~:** return postage enclosed
an|beißen [1] *unr. tr. V.* bite into; take a bite of
[2] *unr. itr. V.* (auch fig. ugs.) bite
an|belangen *tr. V.* **was mich/dies** *usw.* **anbelangt** as far as I am/this matter is *etc.* concerned
an|beten *tr. V.* (auch fig.) worship
An·betracht *der:* **in ~ einer Sache** (*Gen.*) in view of sth.
an|betreffen *unr. tr. V.* ▶ ANBELANGEN
an|betteln *tr. V.* **jmdn. ~:** beg from sb.; **jmdn. um etw. ~:** beg sb. for sth.
Anbetung *die;* **~, ~en** (auch fig.) worship
an|biedern *refl. V.* **sich [bei jmdm.] ~:** curry favour [with sb.]
an|bieten [1] *unr. tr. V.* offer; **jmdm. etw. ~:** offer sb. sth.
[2] *unr. refl. V.* **(a)** offer one's services; **sich ~, etw. zu tun** offer to do sth.
(b) (fig.) ‹*possibility, solution*› suggest itself
An·bieter *der,* **An·bieterin** *die* (Wirtsch.) supplier
an|binden *unr. tr. V.* tie [up] (**an** + *Dat. od. Akk.* to); tie up, moor ‹*boat*› (**an** + *Dat. od. Akk.* to); tether ‹*animal*› (**an** + *Dat. od. Akk.* to)
an|blasen *unr. tr. V.* **(a)** blow at
(b) (anfachen) blow on
An·blick *der* sight
an|blicken *tr. V.* look at
an|blinzeln *tr. V.* **(a)** blink at
(b) (zuzwinkern) wink at
an|brechen [1] *unr. tr. V.* **(a)** crack
(b) (öffnen) open

a

(c) (zu verbrauchen beginnen) break into ‹*supplies, reserves*›
2 *unr. itr. V.; mit sein* (geh.: beginnen) ‹*dawn, day*› break; ‹*age, epoch*› dawn

an|brennen **1** *unr. tr. V.* (anzünden) light
2 *unr. itr. V.; mit sein* burn

an|bringen *unr. tr. V.* **(a)** (befestigen) put up ‹*sign, aerial, curtain, plaque*› (**an** + *Dat.* on)
(b) (äußern) make ‹*request, complaint, comment*›
(c) (zeigen) demonstrate ‹*knowledge, experience*›
(d) (ugs.: herbeibringen) bring

An·bruch *der* (geh.: Beginn) dawn[ing]; **der ~ des Tages** daybreak

an|brüllen *tr. V.* (ugs.) bellow at

Andacht *die;* ~, ~**en** **(a)** (Sammlung) rapt attention; (im Gebet) silent worship *or* prayer
(b) (Gottesdienst) prayers *pl.*

andächtig **1** *Adj.* rapt; (ins Gebet versunken) devout
2 *adv.* with rapt attention; (ins Gebet versunken) devoutly

an|dauern *itr. V.* ‹*negotiations*› continue, go on; ‹*weather, rain*› last

andauernd **1** *Adj.* continual; constant
2 *adv.* continually; constantly

Anden *Pl. die* ~: the Andes

An·denken *das;* ~**s**, ~ **(a)** memory; **zum ~ an jmdn./etw.** to remind you/us *etc.* of sb./sth.
(b) (Erinnerungsstück) memento; (Reise~) souvenir

ander... *Indefinitpron.* **1** *attr.* **(a)** other; **ein ~er/eine ~e/ein ~es** another; **das Kleid gefällt mir nicht, haben Sie noch ~e/ein ~es?** I don't like that dress, do you have any others/another?; **jemand ~er** *od.* **~es** someone else; (in Fragen) anyone else; **niemand ~er** *od.* **~es** nobody else; **etwas ~es** something else; (in Fragen) anything else; **nichts ~es** nothing else; not anything else
(b) (verschieden) different
2 *allein stehend* **ein ~r/eine ~e:** another [one]; **nicht drängeln, einer nach dem ~n** don't push, one after the other; **ein ~er/eine ~e/ein ~es** another [one]; **ein[e]s nach dem ~[e]n** first things first; **ich will weder das eine noch das ~e** I don't want either

anderen·falls *Adv.* otherwise

anderer·seits *Adv.* on the other hand

ander·mal *Adv.* **ein ~:** another time

ändern **1** *tr. V.* change; alter; alter ‹*garment*›; change ‹*person*›
2 *refl. V.* change

andern·falls *Adv.* otherwise

anders *Adv.* **(a)** (verschieden) ‹*think, act, feel, do*› differently (**als** from *or* (esp. Brit) to); ‹*be, look, sound, taste*› different (**als** from *or* (esp. Brit.) to); **es war alles ganz ~:** it was all quite different
(b) (sonst) else; **niemand ~:** nobody else; **jemand ~:** someone else; (in Fragen) anyone else

anders-, Anders-: **~artig** *Adj.* different; **~farbig** *Adj.* different-coloured *attrib.;* of a different colour *postpos.;* **~gläubige** *der/die* person of a different religion; **~herum** *Adv.* the other way round *or* (Amer.) around; **~herum gehen/fahren** go/drive round *or* (Amer.) around the other way; **~wo** *Adv.* (ugs.) elsewhere; **~woher** *Adv.* (ugs.) from somewhere else; **~wohin** *Adv.* (ugs.) somewhere else

andert·halb *Bruchz.* one and a half; **~ Stunden** an hour and a half

Änderung *die;* ~, ~**en** change (*Gen.* in); alteration (*Gen.* to)

Änderungs·schneiderei *die* tailor's [that does alterations]

anderweitig **1** *Adj.* other
2 *adv.* in another way

an|deuten **1** *tr. V.* **(a)** (zu verstehen geben) hint
(b) (nicht vollständig ausführen) outline; (kurz erwähnen) indicate
2 *refl. V.* be indicated

An·deutung *die* hint

An·drang *der* crowd; (Gedränge) crush

andre... ▶ ANDER...

an|drehen *tr. V.* **(a)** (einschalten) turn on
(b) **jmdm. etw. ~** (ugs.) palm sb. off with sth.

andrer·seits *Adv.* on the other hand

an|drohen *tr. V.* **jmdm. etw. ~:** threaten sb. with sth

An·drohung *die* threat

an|drücken *tr. V.* press down

an|ecken *itr. V.; mit sein* **bei jmdm. ~** (fig. ugs.) rub sb. [up (Brit.)] the wrong way

an|eignen *refl. V.* **(a)** appropriate
(b) (lernen) acquire; learn

an·einander *Adv.* (zusammen) together; (nebeneinander) next to each other; next to one another; **~ denken** think of each other *or* one another; **~ vorbeigehen** pass each other *or* one another

***aneinander|binden** *usw.* ▶ ANEINANDER

Anekdote *die;* ~, ~**n** anecdote

an|ekeln *tr. V.* disgust

Anemone *die;* ~, ~**n** anemone

an|erkennen *unr. tr. V.* **(a)** recognize ‹*country, record, verdict, qualification, document*›; acknowledge ‹*debt*›; accept ‹*demand, bill, conditions, rules*›; allow ‹*claim, goal*›
(b) (nicht leugnen) acknowledge
(c) (würdigen) appreciate; respect ‹*viewpoint, opinion*›; **ein ~der Blick** an appreciative look

anerkennens·wert *Adj.* commendable

Anerkennung *die;* ~, ~**en** ▶ ANERKENNEN:
(a) recognition; acknowledgement; acceptance; allowance
(b) acknowledgement
(c) appreciation; respect (*Gen.* for)

---

*old spelling - see note on page xiv

an|fachen *tr. V.* fan; (fig.) arouse ‹*anger, curiosity, enthusiasm*›; inflame ‹*passion*›; stir up ‹*hatred*›; inspire ‹*hope*›; ferment ‹*discord, war*›

an|fahren 1 *unr. tr. V.* **(a)** run into; hit **(b)** (herbeifahren) deliver **(c)** (ansteuern) stop at ‹*village etc.*›; ‹*ship*› put in at ‹*port*› **(d)** (zurechtweisen) shout at 2 *unr. itr. V.; mit sein* **(a)** (starten) start off **(b)** **angefahren kommen** come driving/riding up

An·fahrt *die* **(a)** (das Anfahren) journey **(b)** (Weg) approach

Anfahrts·skizze *die* map showing directions

An·fall *der* attack; (epileptischer ~, fig.) fit; **einen ~ bekommen** *od.* (ugs.) **kriegen** have an attack/a fit

an·fallen 1 *unr. tr. V.* attack 2 *unr. itr V.; mit sein* ‹*costs*› be incurred; ‹*interest*› accrue; ‹*work*› come up

an·fällig *Adj.* ‹*person*› with a delicate constitution; ‹*machine*› susceptible to faults; **gegen** *od.* **für etw. ~ sein** be susceptible to sth.

An·fang *der* beginning; start; (erster Abschnitt) beginning; **am** *od.* **zu ~:** at first; **von ~ an** from the outset; **~ 1984/der Woche** *usw.* at the beginning of 1984/of the week *etc.*

an·fangen 1 *unr. itr. V.* **(a)** begin; start; **mit etw. ~:** start [on] sth.; **~, etw. zu tun** start to do sth. **(b)** (zu sprechen anfangen) begin; **von etw. ~:** start on about sth. **(c)** (eine Stelle antreten) start 2 *unr. tr. V.* **(a)** begin; start; (anbrechen) start **(b)** (machen) do

An·fänger *der;* **~s, ~, An·fängerin** *die;* **~, ~nen** beginner

anfänglich *Adj.* initial

anfangs *Adv.* at first; initially

Anfangs-: ~buchstabe *der* initial [letter]; **~stadium** *das* initial stage

an|fassen 1 *tr. V.* **(a)** (fassen, halten) take hold of **(b)** (berühren) touch **(c)** **jmdn. ~** (an der Hand nehmen) take sb.'s hand **(d)** (angehen) tackle ‹*problem, task, etc.*› **(e)** (behandeln) treat ‹*person*› 2 *itr. V.* **[mit] ~:** lend a hand

anfechtbar *Adj.:* ▸ ANFECHTEN A: disputable; contestable; challengeable

an|fechten *unr. tr. V.* **(a)** dispute ‹*statement, contract*›; contest ‹*will*›; challenge ‹*decision, law, opinion*› **(b)** (beunruhigen) trouble

an|fertigen *tr. V.* make

an|feuchten *tr. V.* moisten ‹*lips, stamp*›; dampen ‹*ironing, cloth, etc.*›

an|feuern *tr. V.* spur on

an|fixen *tr. V.* (Drogenjargon) **jmdn. ~:** get sb. shooting up for the first time (sl.); **von etw. angefixt sein** (fig.) be hooked on sth. (coll.)

an|flehen *tr. V.* beseech; implore

an|fliegen 1 *unr. itr. V.; mit sein* fly in; **angeflogen kommen** come flying in; **gegen den Wind ~:** fly into the wind 2 *unr. tr. V.* fly to ‹*city, country, airport*›

An·flug *der* **(a)** approach **(b)** (Hauch) hint **(c)** (Anwandlung) fit; **in einem ~ von Großzügigkeit** in a fit of generosity

an|fordern *tr. V.* ask for; order ‹*goods, materials*›; send for ‹*ambulance*›

An·forderung *die* **(a)** (das Anfordern) request (*Gen.* for) **(b)** (Anspruch) demand

An·frage *die* inquiry; (Parl.) question

an|fragen *itr. V.* inquire; ask

an|freunden *refl. V.* become friends

an|fügen *tr. V.* add

an|fühlen *refl. V.* feel

an|führen *tr. V.* **(a)** lead **(b)** (zitieren) quote **(c)** (nennen) give ‹*example, reason, details, proof*› **(d)** (ugs.: hereinlegen) have on (Brit. coll.); dupe

An·führer *der,* **An·führerin** *die* leader; (Rädelsführer) ringleader

An·führung *die* **(a)** (das Zitieren, Zitat) quotation **(b)** (Nennung) giving

Anführungs-: ~strich *der,* **~zeichen** *das* quotation mark

An·gabe *die* **(a)** (das Mitteilen) giving **(b)** (Information) piece of information; **~n** information *sing.;* **(c)** (Ballspiele) service; serve

an|geben 1 *unr. tr. V.* **(a)** give ‹*reason*›; declare ‹*income, dutiable goods*›; name ‹*witness*› **(b)** (bestimmen) set ‹*course, direction*›; **den Takt ~:** keep time 2 *unr. itr. V.* **(a)** (prahlen) boast; brag; (sich angeberisch benehmen) show off **(b)** (Ballspiele) serve

Angeber *der;* **~s, ~:** braggart

Angeberei *die;* **~:** showing-off

Angeberin *die;* **~, ~nen** ▸ ANGEBER

angeblich 1 *Adj.* alleged 2 *adv.* supposedly; allegedly

an·geboren *Adj.* innate ‹*characteristic*›; congenital ‹*disease*›

An·gebot *das* **(a)** offer **(b)** (Wirtsch.) supply; (Sortiment) range; **~ und Nachfrage** supply and demand **(c)** (Kaufmannsspr.: Sonder~) [special] offer; **im ~:** on [special] offer; **~ der Woche** bargain of the week

an·gebracht *Adj.* appropriate

a

an·gegriffen *Adj.* weakened ‹*health, stomach*›; strained ‹*nerves, voice*›

angeheitert *Adj.* tipsy

an|gehen 1 *unr. itr. V.; mit sein* **(a)** ‹*radio, light, heating*› come on; ‹*fire*› catch
(b) (anwachsen, wachsen) ‹*plant*› take root
(c) es mag noch ~: it's [just about] acceptable
(d) gegen etw./jmdn. ~: fight sth./sb.
2 *unr. tr. V.* **(a)** (angreifen) attack
(b) (in Angriff nehmen) tackle ‹*problem, difficulty*›; take ‹*fence, bend*›
(c) (bitten) ask (**um** for)
(d) (betreffen) concern; **das geht dich nichts an** it's none of your business

angehend *Adj.* budding; (zukünftig) prospective

an|gehören *itr. V.* **jmdm./einer Sache ~**: belong to sb./sth.; **der Regierung/einer Familie ~**: be a member of the government/a family

an·gehörig *Adj.* belonging (*Dat.* to)

Angehörige *der/die; adj. Dekl.* **(a)** (Verwandte) relative; relation
(b) (Mitglied) member

Angeklagte *der/die; adj. Dekl.* accused; defendant

Angel *die; ~, ~n* **(a)** fishing rod
(b) (Tür~, Fenster~ usw.) hinge; **etw. aus den ~n heben** (fig.) turn sth. upside down

An·gelegenheit *die* matter; (Aufgabe, Problem) affair

Angel·haken *der* fish hook

angeln 1 *tr. V.* (zu fangen suchen) fish for; (fangen) catch
2 *itr. V.* angle; fish

Angel·rute *die* fishing rod

Angel·sachse *der,* **Angel·sächsin** *die* Anglo-Saxon

Angel·schnur *die* fishing line

an·gemessen *Adj.* appropriate; reasonable, fair ‹*price, fee*›

an·genehm 1 *Adj.* pleasant; **~e Reise/Ruhe!** [have a] pleasant journey/have a good rest; **[sehr] ~!** delighted to meet you
2 *adv.* pleasantly

an·gesehen *Adj.* respected

angesichts *Präp. mit Gen.* (geh.) **(a)** in the face of
(b) (fig.: in Anbetracht) in view of

angespannt *Adj.* **(a)** close ‹*attention*›; taut ‹*nerves*›
(b) tense ‹*situation*›; tight ‹*market, economic situation*›

angestellt *Adj.* **bei jmdm. ~ sein** be employed by sb.; work for sb.

Angestellte *der/die; adj. Dekl.* [salaried] employee

Angestellten·gewerkschaft *die* white-collar union

an·getan *Adj.* **von jmdm./etw. ~ sein** be taken with sb./sth.

an·getrunken *Adj.* [slightly] drunk

an·gewiesen *Adj.* **auf jmdn./etw. ~ sein** have to rely on sb./sth.

an|gewöhnen *tr. V.* **jmdm. etw. ~**: get sb. used to sth.; **jmdm. ~, etw. zu tun** get sb. used to doing sth.; **sich** (*Dat.*) **etw. ~**: get into the habit of sth.; **[es] sich** (*Dat.*) **~, etw. zu tun** get into the habit of doing sth.

An·gewohnheit *die* habit

an|gleichen 1 *unr. tr. V.* **etw. einer Sache** (*Dat.*) *od.* **an etw.** (*Akk.*) **~**: bring sth. into line with sth.
2 *unr. refl. V.* **sich jmdm./einer Sache** *od.* **an jmdn./etw. ~**: become like sb./sth.

An·gleichung *die:* **die ~ der Löhne an die Preise** bringing wages into line with prices

Angler *der; ~s, ~,* **Anglerin** *die; ~, ~nen* angler

Anglikaner *der; ~s, ~,* **Anglikanerin** *die; ~, ~nen* Anglican

anglikanisch *Adj.* Anglican

Anglistik *die; ~*: English studies *pl., no art.*

Angola *(das); ~s* Angola

Angora-: ~katze *die* angora cat; **~wolle** *die* angora [wool]

an|greifen 1 *unr. tr. V.* **(a)** (auch fig.) attack
(b) (schwächen) affect ‹*health, heart, stomach, intestine, voice*›; weaken ‹*person*›
2 *unr. itr. V.* (auch fig.) attack

Angreifer *der; ~s, ~,* **Angreiferin** *die; ~, ~nen* (auch fig.) attacker

An·griff *der* **(a)** attack; **zum ~ blasen** (auch fig.) sound the attack
(b) etw. in ~ nehmen tackle sth.

angst *Adj.* **jmdm. ist/wird [es] ~ [und bange]** sb. is/becomes frightened

Angst *die; ~,* **Ängste (a)** (Furcht) fear; **~ bekommen** *od.* (ugs.) **kriegen** become frightened; **~ haben** be frightened (**vor** + *Dat.* of)
(b) (Sorge) anxiety; **~ haben** be anxious (**um** about); **keine ~, ich vergesse es schon nicht!** don't worry, I won't forget [it]!

ängstigen 1 *tr. V.* frighten; (beunruhigen) worry
2 *refl. V.* be frightened; (sich sorgen) worry

ängstlich 1 *Adj.* anxious
2 *adv.* anxiously

Ängstlichkeit *die; ~*: timidity

an|gucken *tr. V.* (ugs.) look at; **sich** (*Dat.*) **etw./jmdn. ~**: have a look at sth./sb.

an|gurten *tr. V.* strap in; **sich ~**: put on one's seat belt

an|haben *unr. tr. V.* **(a)** (ugs.: am Körper tragen) have on
(b) jmdm./einer Sache etwas ~ können be able to harm sb./sth.

an|halten 1 *unr. tr. V.* **(a)** stop
(b) (auffordern) urge

---

*alte Schreibung - vgl. Hinweis auf S. xiv

2 *unr. itr. V.* **(a)** stop
(b) (andauern) go on; last
anhaltend 1 *Adj.* constant; continuous
2 *adv.* constantly; continuously
An·halter *der* hitch-hiker; **per ~ fahren** hitch[-hike]
An·halterin *die* hitch-hiker
Anhalts·punkt *der* clue (**für** to); (für eine Vermutung) grounds *pl.*
an·hand 1 *Präp. mit Gen.* with the help of
2 *Adv.* **~ von** with the help of
An·hang *der* **(a)** (Buchw.) appendix
(b) (Anhängerschaft) following
(c) (Verwandtschaft) family
an|hängen 1 *tr. V.* **(a)** hang up (**an** + *Akk.* on)
(b) (ankuppeln) couple on (**an** + *Akk.* to); hitch up ‹*trailer*› (**an** + *Akk.* to)
(c) (anfügen) add (**an** + *Akk.* to)
(d) (ugs.: zuschreiben, anlasten) **jmdm. etw. ~** blame sb. for sth.; blame sth. on sb.; **er will mir nur was ~** he just wants to pin something on me
2 *refl. V.* **(a)** hang on (**an** + *Akk.* to)
(b) (ugs.: sich anschließen) **sich [an jmdn.** *od.* **bei jmdm.] ~:** tag along [with sb.]
An·hänger *der* **(a)** (Mensch) supporter
(b) (Wagen) trailer
(c) (Schmuckstück) pendant
(d) (Schildchen) tag
Anhängerin *die;* **~, ~nen** ▶ ANHÄNGER A
Anhängerschaft *die;* **~, ~en** supporters *pl.*
anhänglich *Adj.* devoted ‹*dog, friend*›
Anhänglichkeit *die;* **~:** devotion
an|hauchen *tr. V.* breathe on ‹*mirror, glasses*›; blow on ‹*fingers, hands*›
an|häufen *tr. V.* accumulate
Anhäufung *die* accumulation
an|heben *unr. tr. V.* **(a)** lift [up]
(b) (erhöhen) raise ‹*prices, wages, etc.*›
an|heften *tr. V.* attach ‹*label, list*›; put up ‹*sign, notice*›
anheim (geh.): **[es] jmdm. ~ stellen, etw. zu tun** leave it to sb. to do sth.
***anheim|stellen** ▶ ANHEIM
An·hieb *der:* **auf ~** (ugs.) straight off
an|himmeln *tr. V.* worship
An·höhe *die* rise
an|hören 1 *tr. V.* listen to; **sich** (*Dat.*) **jmdn./etw. ~:** listen to sb./sth.
2 *refl. V.* sound
animieren *tr. V.* encourage
Anis *der;* **~es** aniseed
Ank. *Abk.* = **Ankunft** arr.
An·kauf *der* purchase
an|kaufen *tr. V.* purchase; buy
Anker *der;* **~s, ~** anchor; **vor ~ gehen/liegen** drop anchor/lie at anchor; **~ werfen** drop anchor
ankern *itr. V.* **(a)** anchor
(b) (vor Anker liegen) be anchored

Anker·platz *der* anchorage
An·klage *die* **(a)** charge; **unter ~ stehen** have been charged (**wegen** with)
(b) (**~**vertretung) prosecution
Anklage·bank *die; Pl.* **Anklagebänke** dock; **auf der ~ sitzen** (auch fig.) be in the dock
an|klagen *tr. V.* **(a)** (Rechtsw.) charge (*Gen.*, **wegen** with); accuse
(b) (geh.: beschuldigen) accuse
An·kläger *der,* **An·klägerin** *die* prosecutor
an|klammern 1 *tr. V.* peg (Brit.), pin (Amer.) ‹*clothes, washing*› up; clip ‹*sheet etc.*›; (mit Heftklammern) staple ‹*sheet etc.*›
2 *refl. V.* **sich an jmdn./etw. ~:** cling to sb./sth.
An·klang *der:* **[bei jmdm.] ~ finden** meet with [sb.'s] approval
an|kleben 1 *tr. V.* stick up ‹*poster, etc.*›
2 *itr. V.; mit sein* stick
an|kleiden *tr. V.* (geh.) dress; **sich ~:** dress
an|klicken *tr. V.* (DV) click on
an|klopfen *itr. V.* knock
an|knüpfen 1 *tr. V.* **(a)** tie on (**an** + *Akk.* to)
(b) (beginnen) start up ‹*conversation*›; establish ‹*relations, business links*›; form ‹*relationship*›
2 *itr. V.* **an etw.** (*Akk.*) **~:** take sth. up; **ich knüpfe dort an, wo ...** I'll pick up where ...
an|kommen *unr. itr. V.; mit sein* **(a)** (eintreffen) arrive; **seid ihr gut angekommen?** did you arrive safely?
(b) **[bei jmdm.] [gut] ~** (fig. ugs.) go down [very] well [with sb.]
(c) **gegen jmdn./etw. ~:** be able to deal with sb./fight sth.
(d) *unpers.* **es kommt auf jmdn./etw. an** (jmd./etw. ist ausschlaggebend) it depends on sb./sth.; **es kommt auf etw.** (*Akk.*) **an** (etw. ist wichtig) sth. matters (*Dat.* to); **es kommt [ganz] darauf** *od.* **drauf an** (ugs.) it [all] depends
(e) *unpers.* **es darauf** *od.* **drauf ~ lassen** (ugs.) chance it; **es auf etw.** (*Akk.*) **~ lassen** [be prepared to] risk sth.
an|koppeln 1 *tr. V.* couple ‹*carriage*› up; hitch ‹*trailer*› up; dock ‹*spacecraft*›
2 *itr. V.* ‹*spacecraft*› dock
an|kreuzen *tr. V.* mark with a cross
an|kündigen 1 *tr. V.* announce
2 *refl. V.* announce itself
An·kündigung *die* announcement
Ankunft *die;* **~, Ankünfte** arrival; **„~"** 'arrivals'
Ankunfts-: ~halle *die* arrival[s] hall; **~tafel** *die* arrivals board
an|kuppeln *tr. V.* ▶ ANKOPPELN 1
an|kurbeln *tr. V.* **(a)** crank [up]
(b) (fig.) boost ‹*economy, production, etc.*›
Anl. *Abk.* = **Anlage** encl.
an|lächeln *tr. V.* smile at

a

an|lachen 1 *tr. V.* smile at
2 *refl. V.* **sich** (*Dat.*) **jmdn.** ~ (ugs.) get off with sb. (Brit. coll.); pick sb. up
An·lage *die* **(a)** (das Anlegen) (einer Kartei) establishment; (eines Parks, Gartens usw.) laying out; (eines Parkplatzes, Stausees) construction
(b) (Grünanlage) park; (um ein Schloss usw. herum) grounds *pl.;*
(c) (Einrichtung) facilities *pl.;* **militärische ~n** military installations
(d) (Werk) plant
(e) (Musikanlage usw.) system
(f) (Geldanlage) investment
(g) (Konzeption) conception; (Struktur) structure
(h) (Veranlagung) aptitude; (Neigung) tendency
(i) (Beilage zu einem Brief) enclosure
Anlage-: ~berater *der*, **~beraterin** *die* investment advisor; **~kapital** *das* investment capital
Anlass, *Anlaß *der;* **Anlasses, Anlässe (a)** cause (**zu** for); **etw. zum ~ nehmen, etw. zu tun** take sth. as an opportunity to do sth.; **aus aktuellem ~:** because of current events
(b) (Gelegenheit) occasion
an|lassen 1 *unr. tr. V.* **(a)** leave ‹*light, radio, heating, etc.*› on; leave ‹*engine*› running; leave ‹*candle*› burning
(b) keep ‹*coat, gloves, etc.*› on
(c) (in Gang setzen) start [up]
2 *unr. refl. V.* **sich gut/schlecht ~:** get off to a good/bad start
Anlasser *der;* **~s, ~:** starter
an·lässlich, *an·läßlich *Präp. mit Gen.* on the occasion of
An·lauf *der* **(a)** run-up; **[mehr] ~ nehmen** take [more of] a run-up
(b) (Versuch) attempt; **beim** *od.* **im ersten/dritten ~:** at the first/third attempt
an|laufen 1 *unr. itr. V.; mit sein* **(a)** **angelaufen kommen** come running along; (auf einen zu) come running up
(b) **gegen jmdn./etw. ~:** run at sb./sth.
(c) (Anlauf nehmen) take a run-up
(d) (zu laufen beginnen) ‹*engine*› start [up]; (fig.) ‹*film*› open; ‹*production, campaign, search*› start
(e) **rot/dunkel** *usw.* **~:** go *or* turn red/dark *etc.;*
(f) (beschlagen) mist up
2 *unr. tr. V.* put in at ‹*port*›
an|legen 1 *tr. V.* **(a)** put *or* lay ‹*domino, card*› [down] (**an** + *Akk.* next to); place, position ‹*ruler, protractor*› (**an** + *Akk.* on); put ‹*ladder*› up (**an** + *Akk.* against)
(b) **die Flügel/Ohren ~:** close its wings/lay its ears back; **die Arme ~:** put one's arms to one's sides
(c) (geh.: anziehen, umlegen) don
(d) (schaffen, erstellen) lay out ‹*town, garden, plantation, street*›; start ‹*file, album*›; compile ‹*statistics, index*›
(e) (investieren) invest
(f) (ausgeben) spend (**für** on)
(g) **es darauf ~, etw. zu tun** be determined to do sth.
2 *itr. V.* **(a)** (landen) moor
(b) (Kartenspiele) lay a card/cards
(c) (Domino) play [a domino/dominoes]
(d) (zielen) aim (**auf** + *Akk.* at)
3 *refl. V.* **sich mit jmdm. ~:** pick an argument with sb
Anlege-: ~platz *der* berth; **~steg** *der* jetty
an|lehnen 1 *tr. V.* **(a)** lean (**an** + *Akk. od. Dat.* against)
(b) leave ‹*door, window*› slightly open
2 *refl. V.* **sich [an jmdn.** *od.* **jmdm./etw.] ~:** lean [on sb./against sth.]
Anlehnung *die:* **in ~ an** (+ *Akk.*) in imitation of; following
Anleihe *die;* **~, ~n** (Finanzw.) bond
an|leiten *tr. V.* instruct
An·leitung *die* instructions *pl.*
an|lernen *tr. V.* train
an|liegen *unr. itr. V.* **(a)** ‹*pullover etc.*› fit tightly
(b) (ugs.: vorliegen) be on
An·liegen *das;* **~s, ~** (Bitte) request; (Angelegenheit) matter
anliegend *Adj.* **(a)** (angrenzend) adjacent
(b) (beiliegend) enclosed
Anlieger *der;* **~s, ~, Anliegerin** *die;* **~, ~nen** resident; **„~ frei“** 'access only'
an|locken *tr. V.* attract ‹*customers, tourists, etc.*›; lure ‹*bird, animal*›
an|lügen *tr. V.* lie to
an|machen *tr. V.* **(a)** put ‹*light, radio, heating*› on; light ‹*fire*›
(b) mix ‹*cement, plaster, paint, etc.*›; dress ‹*salad*›
(c) (ugs.: ansprechen) ‹*woman, girl*› give ‹*man, boy*› the come-on (coll.); ‹*man, boy*› chat ‹*woman, girl*› up (Brit. coll.)
(d) (ugs.: begeistern, erregen) get ‹*audience etc.*› going; **das macht mich ungeheuer/nicht an** it really turns me on (coll.)/does nothing for me (coll.)
(e) (provozieren) **mach mich nicht an!** leave me alone!
an|malen *tr. V.* paint
an|maßen *refl. V.* **sich** (*Dat.*) **etw. ~:** claim sth. [for oneself]
an·maßend 1 *Adj.* presumptuous; (arrogant) arrogant
2 *adv.* presumptuously; (arrogant) arrogantly
Anmaßung *die;* **~, ~en** presumption; (Arroganz) arrogance
Anmelde·formular *das* **(a)** application form
(b) (einer Meldebehörde) registration form
an|melden 1 *tr. V.* **(a)** (als Teilnehmer) enrol (**zu** for); **sich ~:** enrol (**zu** for)
(b) (melden, anzeigen) license ‹*radio, television*›; apply for ‹*patent*›; register ‹*domicile, change of address, car, trade mark*›; **sich ~:** register one's new address

*old spelling - see note on page xiv

(c) (ankündigen) announce; **sind Sie angemeldet?** do you have an appointment?; **sich beim Arzt ~:** make an appointment to see the doctor
(d) (geltend machen) express ‹*reservation, doubt, wish*›; put forward ‹*demand*›
[2] *refl V.* (DV) log on

An·meldung *die* **(a)** (zur Teilnahme) enrolment
(b) ▶ ANMELDEN B: licensing; application (*Gen.* for); registration
(c) (Ankündigung) announcement; (beim Arzt, Rechtsanwalt usw.) making an appointment

an|merken *tr. V.* **(a) jmdm. seinen Ärger/seine Verlegenheit** *usw.* **~:** notice that sb. is annoyed/embarrassed *etc.*; **man merkt ihm [nicht] an, dass er krank ist** you can[not] tell that he is ill; **sich nichts ~ lassen** not let it show
(b) (geh.: bemerken) note

Anmerkung *die;* **~, ~en (a)** (Fußnote) note
(b) (geh.: Bemerkung) comment

an|motzen *tr. V.* (ugs.) swear at

Anmut *die;* **~** (geh.) grace

an·mutig (geh.) [1] *Adj.* graceful ‹*girl, movement, dance*›; charming, delightful ‹*girl, smile, picture, landscape*›
[2] *adv.* ‹*move, dance*› gracefully; ‹*smile, greet*› charmingly

an|nähen *tr. V.* sew on

an|nähern [1] *refl. V.* get closer (*Dat.* to sth)
[2] *tr. V.* bring closer (*Dat.* to)

annähernd [1] *Adv.* almost; (ungefähr) approximately
[2] *adj.* approximate

Annahme *die;* **~, ~n (a)** (das Annehmen) acceptance
(b) (Vermutung) assumption; **in der ~, dass ...:** on the assumption that ...

annehmbar [1] *Adj.* **(a)** acceptable
(b) (recht gut) reasonable
[2] *adv.* reasonably [well]

an|nehmen *unr. tr. V.* **(a)** accept; take; accept ‹*alms, invitation, condition, help*›; take ‹*food, telephone call*›; accept, take up ‹*offer, challenge*›
(b) (Sport) take ‹*ball, pass, etc.*›
(c) (billigen) approve
(d) (aufnehmen) take on ‹*worker, patient, pupil*›
(e) (hinnehmen) accept ‹*fate, verdict, punishment*›
(f) (adoptieren) adopt
(g) (haften lassen) take ‹*dye, ink*›
(h) (sich aneignen) adopt ‹*habit, mannerism, name, attitude*›
(i) (bekommen) take on ‹*look, appearance, form, dimension*›
(j) (vermuten, voraussetzen) assume; **angenommen, [dass] ...:** assuming [that] ...

Annehmlichkeit *die;* **~, ~en** comfort; (Vorteil) advantage

annektieren *tr. V.* annex

Annektierung *die;* **~, ~en, Annexion** *die;* **~, ~en** annexation

Annonce /a'nõ:sə/ *die;* **~, ~n** advertisement; advert (Brit. coll.)

annoncieren *itr. V.* advertise

annullieren *tr. V.* annul

Annullierung *die;* **~, ~en** annulment

anonym [1] *Adj.* anonymous
[2] *adv.* anonymously

Anonymität *die;* **~:** anonymity

Anorak *der;* **~s, ~s** anorak

an|ordnen *tr. V.* **(a)** (arrangieren) arrange
(b) (befehlen) order

An·ordnung *die* ▶ ANORDNEN: **(a)** arrangement
(b) order

anorektisch /an|o'rɛktɪʃ/ *Adj.* anorexic

Anorexie /an|orɛ'ksi:/ *die;* **~** (Med.) anorexia

an·organisch *Adj.* inorganic

an|packen [1] *tr. V.* **(a)** (ugs.: anfassen) grab hold of
(b) (angehen) tackle
[2] *itr. V.* **[mit] ~** (ugs.: mithelfen) lend a hand

an|passen [1] *tr. V.* **(a)** (passend machen) fit
(b) (abstimmen) suit (*Dat.* to)
[2] *refl. V.* adapt [oneself] (*Dat.* to); ‹*animal*› adapt

Anpassung *die;* **~, ~en** adaptation (**an** + *Akk.* to)

anpassungs·fähig *Adj.* adaptable

an|pfeifen [1] *unr. tr. V.* **das Spiel/die zweite Halbzeit ~:** blow the whistle to start the game/the second half
[2] *unr. itr. V.* blow the whistle

An·pfiff *der* **(a)** (Sport) whistle for the start of play
(b) (salopp: Zurechtweisung) bawling-out (coll.)

an|pflanzen *tr. V.* **(a)** plant
(b) (anbauen) grow

an|pöbeln *tr. V.* (ugs.) abuse

an|prangern *tr. V.* denounce (**als** as)

an|preisen *unr. tr. V.* extol

An·probe *die* fitting

an|probieren *tr. V.* try on

an|rechnen *tr. V.* **(a)** count
(b) jmdm. etw. ~ (in Rechnung stellen) charge sb. for sth.

An·recht *das* right; **ein ~ auf etw.** (*Akk.*) **haben** be entitled to sth.

An·rede *die* form of address

an|reden *tr. V.* address

an|regen *tr. V.* **(a)** stimulate ‹*imagination, digestion*›; whet ‹*appetite*›
(b) (ermuntern) prompt; (vorschlagen) propose

anregend *Adj.* stimulating

An·regung *die* **(a)** ▶ ANREGEN A: stimulation; whetting
(b) (Denkanstoß) stimulus
(c) (Vorschlag) proposal

an|reichern [1] *tr. V.* enrich ⋯

a

2 *refl. V.* accumulate
An·reise *die* journey [there/here]
an|reisen *itr. V.; mit sein* travel there/here; **mit der Bahn ~:** go/come by train
An·reiz *der* incentive
an|rempeln *tr. V.* barge into; (absichtlich) jostle
Anrichte *die; ~, ~n* sideboard
an|richten *tr. V.* **(a)** arrange ‹*food*›; (servieren) serve
(b) cause ‹*disaster, confusion, devastation, etc.*›
anrüchig *Adj.* **(a)** disreputable
(b) (unanständig) indecent
an|rücken *itr. V.; mit sein* ‹*troops*› advance; ‹*firemen, police*› move in
An·ruf *der* call
Anruf·beantworter *der; ~s, ~:* [telephone] answering machine
an|rufen *unr. tr. V.* **(a)** call *or* shout to ‹*friend, passer-by*›; call ‹*sleeping person*›
(b) (geh.: angehen, bitten) appeal to ‹*person, court*› (**um** for); call upon ‹*God*›
(c) *auch itr.* (telefonisch ~) call
Anrufer *der; ~s, ~,* **Anruferin** *die; ~, ~nen* caller
an|rühren *tr. V.* **(a)** touch
(b) (bereiten) mix
ans *Präp. + Art.* **(a)** = **an das;**
(b) sich ~ Arbeiten machen set to work
An·sage *die* announcement
an|sagen *tr. V.* **(a)** announce
(b) (Kartenspiele) bid
Ansager *der; ~s, ~,* **Ansagerin** *die; ~, ~nen* (Radio, Fernsehen) announcer
an|sammeln 1 *tr. V.* accumulate; amass ‹*riches, treasure*›
2 *refl. V.* accumulate; (fig.) ‹*anger, excitement*› build up
An·sammlung *die* **(a)** collection
(b) (Auflauf) crowd
ansässig *Adj.* resident
An·satz *der* (erstes Zeichen, Beginn) beginnings *pl.*
an|schaffen *tr. V.* [**sich** (*Dat.*)] **etw. ~** get [oneself] sth.
An·schaffung *die* purchase
an|schalten *tr. V.* switch on
an|schauen *tr. V.* (bes. südd., österr., schweiz.) ▶ ANSEHEN
anschaulich 1 *Adj.* vivid
2 *adv.* vividly
Anschauung *die; ~, ~en* **(a)** (Wahrnehmung) experience
(b) (Auffassung) view
An·schein *der* appearance; **allem** *od.* **dem ~ nach** to all appearances
an·scheinend *Adv.* apparently
an|schieben *unr. tr. V.* push ‹*vehicle*›
an|schießen *unr. tr. V.* shoot and wound

*alte Schreibung - vgl. Hinweis auf S. xiv

An·schlag *der* **(a)** (Bekanntmachung) notice; (Plakat) poster
(b) (Attentat) assassination attempt; (auf ein Gebäude, einen Zug usw.) attack
(c) (Texterfassung) keystroke
(d) mit dem Gewehr im ~: with rifle/rifles levelled
an|schlagen *unr. tr. V.* **(a)** put up, ‹*notice, announcement, message*› (**an** + *Akk.* on)
(b) (beschädigen) chip
an|schließen 1 *unr. tr. V.* **(a)** connect (**an** + *Akk. od. Dat.* to); connect up ‹*electrical device*›
(b) (festschließen) lock, secure (**an** + *Dat. od. Akk.* to)
2 *unr. refl. V.* **sich jmdm./einer Sache ~:** join sb./sth.
An·schluss, *An·schluß *der* connection; **kein ~ unter dieser Nummer** number unobtainable
Anschluss-, *Anschluß-: ~kabel *das* connecting cable *or* (esp. Brit.) lead; **~zug** *der* connecting train
an|schnallen *tr. V.* put on ‹*skis, skates*›; **sich ~** (im Auto) put on one's seat belt; (im Flugzeug) fasten one's seat belt
an|schrauben *tr. V.* screw on (**an** + *Akk.* to)
An·schreiben *das* covering letter
an|schreien *unr. tr. V.* shout at
An·schrift *die* address
Anschuldigung *die; ~, ~en* accusation
an|schwärzen *tr. V.* (ugs.) **jmdn. ~** (in Misskredit bringen) blacken sb.'s name; (schlecht machen) run sb. down (**bei** to); (denunzieren) inform *or* (Brit. sl.) grass on sb. (**bei** to)
an|schwellen *unr. itr. V.; mit sein* **(a)** swell [up]; (fig.) swell; ‹*water, river*› rise
(b) (lauter werden) grow louder; ‹*noise*› rise
an|schwemmen *tr. V.* wash ashore
an|sehen *unr. tr. V.* **(a)** look at; watch ‹*television programme*›; see ‹*play, film*›; **jmdn. groß/böse ~:** stare at sb./give sb. an angry look; **hübsch** *usw.* **anzusehen sein** be pretty *etc.* to look at; **sieh [mal] [einer] an!** (ugs.) well, I never! (coll.)
(b) (erkennen) **man sieht ihm sein Alter nicht an** he does not look his age; **man sieht ihr die Strapazen an** she's showing the strain
(c) (zusehen bei) **etw. [mit] ~:** watch sth.; **das kann man doch nicht [mit] ~:** I/you can't just stand by and watch that
Ansehen *das; ~s* [high] standing
an·sehnlich *Adj.* **(a)** (beträchtlich) considerable
(b) (gut aussehend, stattlich) handsome
***an|sein** ▶ AN 3B
an|setzen *tr. V.* **(a)** (in die richtige Stellung bringen) position ‹*ladder, jack, drill, saw*›
(b) (anfügen) attach, put on (**an** + *Akk. od. Dat.* to)
(c) (festlegen) fix ‹*meeting etc.*› (**für, auf** + *Akk.* for); fix, set ‹*deadline, date, price*›

(d) (veranschlagen) estimate
(e) (anrühren) mix

An·sicht *die* **(a)** (Meinung) opinion; view; **meiner ~ nach** in my opinion *or* view
(b) (Bild) view

Ansichts·karte *die* picture postcard

an|spannen *tr. V.* **(a)** harness ‹*horse etc.*› (**an** + *Akk.* to); yoke up ‹*oxen*› (**an** + *Akk.* to); hitch up ‹*carriage, cart, etc.*› (**an** + *Akk.* to)
(b) (anstrengen) strain

An·spannung *die* strain

an|spielen *itr. V.* **auf jmdn./etw. ~:** allude to sb./sth.

Anspielung *die;* **~, ~en** allusion (**auf** + *Akk.* to); (verächtlich, böse) insinuation (**auf** + *Akk.* about)

Ansporn *der;* **~[e]s, ~e** incentive

an|spornen *tr. V.* spur on

An·sprache *die* speech; address

an|sprechen [1] *unr. tr. V.* **(a)** speak to
(b) (gefallen) appeal to
[2] *unr. itr. V.* (reagieren) respond (**auf** + *Akk.* to)

ansprechend [1] *Adj.* attractive; attractive, appealing ‹*personality*›
[2] *adv.* attractively

Ansprech·partner *der,* **Ansprech·partnerin** *die* contact

an|springen [1] *unr. itr. V.; mit sein* ‹*car, engine*› start
[2] *unr. tr. V.* jump up at

An·spruch *der* **(a)** claim; (Forderung) demand; **[keine] Ansprüche stellen** make [no] demands; **in ~ nehmen** take advantage of ‹*offer*›; exercise ‹*right*›; take up ‹*time*›; **[einen] ~/keinen ~ auf etw.** (*Akk.*) **haben** be/not be entitled to sth.
(b) (Anrecht) right

an·spruchs-: ~los [1] *Adj.* **(a)** (genügsam) undemanding; **(b)** (schlicht) unpretentious;
[2] *adv.* **(a)** (genügsam) undemandingly; ‹*live*› modestly; **(b)** (schlicht) unpretentiously;
~voll *Adj.* discriminating ‹*reader, audience, gourmet*›; (schwierig) demanding; ambitious ‹*subject*›

an|spucken *tr. V.* spit at

Anstalt *die;* **~, ~en** institution

An·stand *der* decency

anständig [1] *Adj.* decent; (ehrbar) respectable
[2] *adv.* decently; (ordentlich) properly

an|starren *tr. V.* stare at

an·statt *Konj.* **~ zu arbeiten/~, dass er arbeitet** instead of working

an|stecken [1] *tr. V.* **(a)** pin on ‹*badge, brooch*›; put on ‹*ring*›
(b) (infizieren, auch fig.) infect
[2] *itr. V.* be infectious

ansteckend *Adj.* infectious; (durch Berührung) contagious

Ansteckung *die;* **~, ~en** infection; (durch Berührung) contagion

Ansteckungs·gefahr *die* risk *or* danger of infection

an|stehen *unr. itr. V.* (Schlange stehen) queue [up], (Amer.) stand in line (**nach** for)

an·stelle [1] *Präp. mit Gen.* instead of
[2] *Adv.* **~ von** instead of

an|stellen [1] *refl. V.* queue [up], (Amer.) stand in line (**nach** for)
[2] *tr. V.* **(a)** (aufdrehen) turn on
(b) (einschalten) switch on
(c) (einstellen) employ

An·stellung *die* **(a)** employment
(b) (Stellung) job

Anstieg *der;* **~[e]s** rise, increase (+ *Gen.* in)

an|stiften *tr. V.* incite

An·stifter *der,* **An·stifterin** *die* instigator

An·stiftung *die* incitement

an|stimmen *tr. V.* start singing ‹*song*›; start playing ‹*piece of music*›; **ein Geschrei ~:** start shouting

An·stoß *der* **(a)** stimulus (**zu** for); **den [ersten] ~ zu etw. geben** initiate sth.
(b) ~ erregen cause offence (**bei** to); **[keinen] ~ an etw.** (*Dat.*) **nehmen** [not] object to sth.

an|stoßen [1] *unr. itr. V.* **(a)** *mit sein* **an etw.** (*Akk.*) **~:** bump into sth.
(b) [mit den Gläsern] ~: clink glasses; **auf jmdn./etw. ~:** drink to sb./sth.
[2] *unr. tr. V.* **jmdn./etw. ~:** give sb./sth. a push; **jmdn. aus Versehen ~:** knock into sb. inadvertently

anstößig [1] *Adj.* offensive
[2] *adv.* offensively

an|strahlen *tr. V.* **(a)** illuminate; (mit Scheinwerfer) floodlight
(b) (anblicken) beam at

an|streben *tr. V.* (geh.) aspire to; (mit großer Anstrengung) strive for

an|streichen *unr. tr. V.* **(a)** paint
(b) (markieren) mark

an|strengen [1] *refl. V.* make an effort; **sich mehr/sehr ~:** make more of an effort/a great effort
[2] *tr. V.* strain ‹*eyes, ears, voice*›; be a strain on ‹*person*›; **seine Fantasie ~:** exercise one's imagination

anstrengend *Adj.* (körperlich) strenuous; (geistig) demanding

Anstrengung *die;* **~, ~en (a)** effort; **große ~en machen, etw. zu tun** make every effort to do sth.
(b) (Strapaze) strain

An·strich *der* paint

An·sturm *der* rush (**auf** + *Akk.* to); (auf Banken, Waren) run (**auf** + *Akk.* on)

Antarktika (*das*)**; ~s** Antarctica

Antarktis *die;* **~:** Antarctic

antarktisch *Adj.* Antarctic

An·teil *der* share (**an** + *Dat.* of); **~ an etw.** (*Dat.*) **nehmen** take an interest in sth.

a

An·teilnahme *die;* ~ **(a)** interest (**an** + *Dat.* in)
(b) (Mitgefühl) sympathy (**an** + *Dat.* with)

Antenne *die;* ~, ~**n** aerial; antenna (Amer.)

Anthrax /'antraks/ *der;* ~ (Med.) anthrax

anti-, Anti- anti-

Anti·alkoholiker *der*, **Anti·alkoholikerin** *die* teetotaller

Antibiotikum *das;* ~**s, Antibiotika** (Med.) antibiotic

anti-, Anti-: ~**blockier·system** *das* (Kfz-W.) anti-lock braking system; ~**faschist** *der*, ~**faschistin** *die* anti-fascist; ~**faschistisch** *Adj.* anti-fascist

antik *Adj.* **(a)** classical
(b) (aus vergangenen Zeiten) antique ‹*furniture, fittings, etc.*›

Antike *die;* ~: classical antiquity *no art.*

Antilope *die;* ~, ~**n** antelope

Antipathie *die;* ~, ~**n** antipathy

Antiquariat antiquarian bookshop/ department; (mit neueren gebrauchten Büchern) second-hand bookshop/department

Antiquität *die;* ~, ~**en** antique

Antiviren·software *die* (DV) anti-virus software

Antlitz *das;* ~**es,** ~**e** (dichter., geh.) countenance (literary); face

Antrag *der;* ~**[e]s, Anträge (a)** application (**auf** + *Akk.* for); **einen** ~ **stellen** make an application
(b) (Formular) application form

Antrags·formular *das* application form

an|treffen *unr. tr. V.* find; (zufällig) come across

an|treiben *unr. tr. V.* **(a)** drive ‹*animals, column of prisoners*› on *or* along; (fig.) urge
(b) (in Bewegung setzen) drive; power ‹*ship, aircraft*›

an|treten [1] *unr. itr. V.; mit sein* **(a)** form up; (in Linie) line up; (Milit.) fall in
(b) (sich stellen) meet one's opponent; (als Mannschaft) line up; **gegen jmdn.** ~: meet sb./ line up against sb.
[2] *unr. tr. V.* start ‹*job, apprenticeship*›; take up ‹*position, appointment*›; set out on ‹*journey*›; begin ‹*prison sentence*›; come into ‹*inheritance*›

An·trieb *der* drive

An·tritt *der:* **vor** ~ **Ihres Urlaubs** before you go on holiday (Brit.) *or* (Amer.) vacation; **vor** ~ **der Reise** before setting out on the journey

an|tun *unr. tr. V.* **(a) jmdm. ein Leid** ~: hurt sb.; **jmdm. etwas Böses/ein Unrecht** ~: do sb. harm/an injustice
(b) jmd./etw. hat es jmdm. angetan sb. was taken with sb./sth.; *s. auch* ANGETAN

Antwort *die;* ~, ~**en (a)** answer; reply; **er gab mir keine** ~: he didn't answer [me] *or* reply
(b) (Reaktion) response

antworten *itr. V.* **(a)** answer; reply; **auf etw.** (*Akk.*) ~: answer sth.; reply to sth.; **jmdm.** ~: answer sb.; reply to sb.
(b) (reagieren) respond (**auf** + *Akk.* to)

an|vertrauen [1] *tr. V.* **jmdm. etw.** ~: entrust sb. with sth.; (fig.: mitteilen) confide sth. to sb.
[2] *refl. V.* **sich jmdm./einer Sache** ~: put one's trust in sb./sth.; **sich jmdm.** ~ (fig.: sich jmdm. mitteilen) confide in sb.

an|wachsen *unr. itr. V.; mit sein* **(a)** grow on
(b) (Wurzeln schlagen) take root
(c) (zunehmen) grow

Anwalt *der;* ~**[e]s, Anwälte, Anwältin** *die;* ~, ~**nen (a)** (Rechtsanwalt, -anwältin) lawyer; solicitor (Brit.); attorney (Amer.); (vor Gericht) barrister (Brit.); attorney[-at-law] (Amer.); advocate (Scot.)
(b) (Fürsprecher) advocate

An·wärter *der*, **An·wärterin** *die* candidate (**auf** + *Akk.* for); (Sport) contender (**auf** + *Akk.* for)

an|weisen *unr. tr. V.* instruct

An·weisung *die* instruction

an|wenden *unr. (auch regelm.) tr. V.* use, employ ‹*process, trick, method, violence, force*›; use ‹*medicine, money, time*›; apply ‹*rule, paragraph, proverb, etc.*› (**auf** + *Akk.* to)

Anwender *der;* ~**s,** ~ (DV) user

anwender·freundlich *Adj.* (bes. DV) user-friendly

Anwenderin *die;* ~, ~**nen** (DV) user

An·wendung *die* **(a)** ▶ ANWENDEN: use; employment; application
(b) (DV) application

An·wesen *das* property

anwesend *Adj.* present (**bei** at); **die Anwesenden** those present

Anwesenheit *die;* ~: presence

an|widern *tr. V.* nauseate

Anwohner *der;* ~**s,** ~, **Anwohnerin** *die;* ~, ~**nen** resident; **Parken nur für** ~ residents-only parking

An·zahl *die;* ~: number; **eine ganze** ~: a whole lot

an|zahlen *tr. V.* put down ‹*sum*› as a deposit (**auf** + *Akk.* on); (bei Ratenzahlung) make a down payment of ‹*sum*› (**auf** + *Akk.* on)

An·zahlung *die* deposit; (bei Ratenzahlung) down payment

An·zeichen *das* sign; indication

Anzeige *die;* ~, ~**n (a)** (Straf~) report
(b) (Inserat) advertisement
(c) (eines Instruments) display

an|zeigen *tr. V.* **(a)** (Strafanzeige erstatten) **jmdn./etw.** ~: report sb./sth. to the police/the authorities
(b) (zeigen) show; indicate; show ‹*time, date*›
(c) (DV) display

*old spelling - see note on page xiv

Anzeigen-: ~blatt *das* advertiser; **~teil** *der* advertisement section *or* pages *pl.*
an|ziehen *unr. tr. V.* **(a)** (auch fig.) attract
(b) draw up ‹*knees, feet, etc.*›
(c) tighten ‹*rope, wire, screw, knot, belt, etc.*›; put on ‹*handbrake*›
(d) (ankleiden) dress; **sich ~**: get dressed
(e) (anlegen) put on ‹*clothes*›
anziehend *Adj.* attractive
An·ziehung *die* attraction
Anziehungs·kraft *die* attractive force; (fig.) attraction
An·zug *der* **(a)** suit
(b) im ~ sein ‹*storm*› be approaching; ‹*fever, illness*› be coming on; ‹*enemy*› be advancing
anzüglich **1** *Adj.* insinuating ‹*remark, question*›
2 *adv.* in an insinuating way
Anzüglichkeit *die*; **~, ~en** **(a)** (Art) insinuating nature
(b) (Bemerkung) insinuating remark
an|zünden *tr. V.* light; set fire to ‹*building etc.*›
an|zweifeln *tr. V.* doubt; question
apart **1** *Adj.* individual *attrib.*;
2 *adv.* in an individual style
Apartheid *die;* **~**: apartheid *no art.*
Apartheit *die;* **~**: individuality
Apartment *das;* **~s, ~s** studio flat (Brit.); studio apartment (Amer.)
Apartment·haus *das* block of studio flats (Brit.) *or* (Amer.) studio apartments
Apathie *die;* **~, ~n** apathy
apathisch **1** *Adj.* apathetic
2 *adv.* apathetically
Aperitif /aperi'ti:f/ *der;* **~s, ~s** aperitif
Apfel *der;* **~s, Äpfel** apple
Apfel-: ~baum *der* apple tree; **~kuchen** *der* apple cake; (mit Äpfeln belegt) apple flan; **~mus** *das* apple purée; **~saft** *der* apple juice
Apfelsine *die;* **~, ~n** orange
Apfel-: ~strudel *der* apfelstrudel; **~wein** *der* cider
Apostel *der;* **~s, ~**: apostle
Apotheke *die;* **~, ~n** **(a)** chemist's [shop] (Brit.); drugstore (Amer.)
(b) (Hausapotheke) medicine cabinet; (Reise-, Bordapotheke) first-aid kit
Apotheker *der;* **~s, ~, Apothekerin** *die;* **~, ~nen** [dispensing] chemist (Brit.); druggist
App. *Abk.* = **Apparat** ext.
Apparat *der;* **~[e]s, ~e** **(a)** apparatus *no pl.*; (Haushaltsgerät) appliance; (kleiner) gadget
(b) (Radio) radio; (Fernseher) television; (Kamera) camera
(c) (Telefon) telephone; (Nebenstelle) extension; **am ~!** speaking!
(d) (Personen und Hilfsmittel) organization; (Verwaltungsapparat) system
Apparate·medizin *die* (oft abwertend) high-technology medicine
Appartement /apartə'mã:, (schweiz. auch:) -'mɛnt/ *das;* **~s, ~s** (schweiz. auch: **~e**) **(a)** ▶ APARTMENT;
(b) (Hotelsuite) suite
Appell *der;* **~s, ~e** **(a)** appeal (**zu** for, **an** + *Akk.* to)
(b) (Milit.) muster; (Anwesenheits~) roll-call
appellieren *itr. V.* appeal (**an** + *Akk.* to)
Appetit *der;* **~[e]s, ~e** appetite (**auf** + *Akk.* for); **guten ~!** enjoy your meal!
appetitlich *Adj.* **(a)** appetizing
(b) (sauber, ansprechend) attractive and hygienic
Appetit·losigkeit *die;* **~**: lack of appetite
applaudieren *itr. V.* applaud
Applaus *der;* **~es, ~e** applause
Aprikose *die;* **~, ~n** apricot
April *der;* **~[s], ~e** April; **der ~**: April
apropos /apro'po:/ *Adv.* apropos; by the way; incidentally
Aquädukt *der od. das;* **~[e]s, ~e** aqueduct
Aquarell *das;* **~s, ~e** watercolour [painting]
Aquarium *das;* **~s, Aquarien** aquarium
Äquator *der;* **~s** equator
Ar *das od. der;* **~s, ~e** are
Ära *die;* **~, Ären** era
Araber *der;* **~s, ~, Araberin** *die;* **~, ~nen** Arab
Arabien /a'ra:bi̯ən/ (*das*); **~s** Arabia
arabisch *Adj.* Arabian; Arabic ‹*language, numeral, literature, etc.*›
Arbeit *die;* **~, ~en** **(a)** work *no indef. art.*; **vor/nach der ~** (ugs.) before/after work
(b) (Produkt, Werk) work
(c) (Aufgabe) job
(d) (Klassenarbeit) test
arbeiten **1** *itr. V.* work
2 *tr. V.* (herstellen) make
Arbeiter *der;* **~s, ~, Arbeiterin** *die;* **~, ~nen** worker; (Bau~, Land~) labourer
Arbeiter-: ~kind *das* working-class child; **~klasse** *die* working class[es *pl.*]
Arbeiterschaft *die;* **~**: workers *pl.*
Arbeit·geber *der;* **~s, ~**: employer
Arbeitgeber·anteil *der* employer's contribution
Arbeit·geberin *die;* **~, ~nen** employer
Arbeitgeber·verband *der* employers' association *or* organization
Arbeitnehmer *der;* **~s, ~** employee
Arbeitnehmer·anteil *der* employee's contribution
Arbeitnehmerin *die;* **~, ~nen** employee
arbeits-, Arbeits-: ~amt *das* job centre (Brit.); **~anfang** *der* starting time [at work]; **~bedingungen** *Pl.* working conditions; **~beginn** *der* ▶ **~**ANFANG; **~belastung** *die* workload;

···>

a

~beschaffungs·maßnahme *die* job-creation measure; **~erlaubnis** *die* work permit; **~fähig** *Adj.* fit for work *postpos.;* (grundsätzlich) able to work *postpos.;* **~gang** *der* operation; **~genehmigung** *die* work permit; **~gericht** *das* industrial tribunal; **~kollege** *der*, **~kollegin** *die* (bei Arbeitern) workmate (Brit.); fellow worker; (bei Angestellten, Beamten) colleague; **~kraft** *die* **(a)** capacity for work; **(b)** (Mensch) worker; **~last** *die* burden of work; **~leben** *das* **(a)** (Berufstätigkeit) working life; **(b)** (Arbeitswelt) world of work; working life *no art.;* **~los** *Adj.* unemployed; **sich ~los melden** sign on [for the dole] (coll.;) **~lose** *der/die; adj. Dekl.* unemployed person/man/woman *etc.;* **die ~losen** the unemployed; **~losengeld** *das* (full-rate) earnings-related unemployment benefit; **~losenhilfe** *die* **(a)** (Geld) reduced-rate unemployment benefit; **(b)** (Institution) reduced-rate unemployment benefit system; **~losigkeit** *die;* **~~:** unemployment *no indef. art.;* **~mangel** *der* lack of work; **~markt** *der* labour market; **~platz** *der* **(a)** (Platz im Betrieb) workplace; **am ~platz** at one's workplace; **(b)** (~stätte) place of work; **den ~platz wechseln** change one's place of work; **(c)** (~verhältnis) job; **~scheu** *Adj.* work-shy; **~suchende** *der/die; adj. Dekl.* person/man/woman looking for work; **die ~suchenden** those looking for work: **~tag** *der* working day; **~teilung** *die* division of labour; **~unfähig** *Adj.* unfit for work *postpos.;* (grundsätzlich) unable to work *postpos.;* **~unfähigkeit** *die* ▶ ~UNFÄHIG: inability to work; unfitness for work; **~unfall** *der* industrial accident; **er hatte einen ~unfall** he had an accident at work; **~vermittlung** *die* **(a)** (Tätigkeit) arranging employment; **(b)** (Stelle) employment exchange; job centre (Brit.); (Firma) employment agency; **~vertrag** *der* contract of employment; **~zeit** *die* working hours *pl.;* **die tägliche ~zeit** the working day; **~zeit·konto** *das* flexitime work record; **~zimmer** *das* study

Archäologe *der;* **~n, ~n** archaeologist

Archäologie *die;* **~:** archaeology *no art.*

Archäologin *die;* **~, ~nen** archaeologist

archäologisch *Adj.* archaeological

Arche *die;* **~, ~n** ark; **die ~ Noah** Noah's Ark

Architekt *der;* **~en, ~en, Architektin** *die;* **~, ~nen** architect

Architektur *die;* **~** architecture

Archiv *das;* **~s, ~e** archives *pl.;* archive

Ären ▶ ÄRA

Arena *die;* **~, Arenen** arena; (Stierkampf~, Manege) ring

*alte Schreibung - vgl. Hinweis auf S. xiv

arg, ärger, ärgst... (geh., landsch.) [1] *Adj.* **(a)** (schlimm) bad; **im Argen liegen** be in a sorry state
(b) (unangenehm groß, stark) severe ‹*pain, hunger, shock, disappointment*›; serious ‹*error, dilemma*›; extreme ‹*embarrassment*›; gross ‹*exaggeration, injustice*›
[2] *adv.* (äußerst, sehr) extremely

Ärger *der;* **~s (a)** annoyance
(b) (Unannehmlichkeiten) trouble; **~ bekommen** get into trouble

ärgerlich [1] *Adj.* **(a)** annoyed
(b) (Ärger erregend) annoying
[2] *adv.* **(a)** with annoyance
(b) (Ärger erregend) annoyingly

ärgern [1] *tr. V.* **(a)** annoy
(b) (reizen) tease
[2] *refl. V.* **sich [über jmdn./etw.] ~:** be/get annoyed [at sb./about sth.]

Ärgernis *das;* **~ses, ~se** annoyance; (etw. Anstößiges) nuisance

arg-, Arg-: ~list *die* deceit; (Heimtücke) malice; **~listig** *Adj.* deceitful; (heimtückisch) malicious; **~los** [1] *Adj.* unsuspecting; [2] *adv.* unsuspectingly; **~losigkeit** *die;* **~~:** unsuspecting nature

ärgst... ▶ ARG

Argument *das;* **~[e]s, ~e** argument

Argumentation *die;* **~, ~en** argumentation

argumentieren *itr. V.* argue

Argwohn *der;* **~[e]s** suspicion

argwöhnisch (geh.) [1] *Adj.* suspicious
[2] *adv.* suspiciously

Arie /ˈaːri̯ə/ *die;* **~, ~n** aria

arisch *Adj.* (Völkerk., Sprachw., ns.) Aryan

Aristokrat *der;* **~en, ~en** aristocrat

Aristokratie *die;* **~, ~n** aristocracy

Aristokratin *die;* **~, ~nen** aristocrat

aristokratisch [1] *Adj.* aristocratic
[2] *adv.* aristocratically

arithmetisch [1] *Adj.* arithmetical
[2] *adv.* arithmetically

Arkade *die;* **~, ~n** arcade

Arktis *die;* **~:** Arctic

arktisch *Adj.* Arctic; (fig.) arctic

arm, ärmer, ärmst... *Adj.* poor; **Arm und Reich** (veralt.) rich and poor [alike]; **~ an Nährstoffen** poor in nutrients; **der/die Ärmste** *od.* **Arme** the poor man/boy/woman/girl

Arm *der;* **~[e]s, ~e** arm; **jmdm. [mit etw.] unter die ~e greifen** help sb. out [with sth.]; **ein Hemd mit halbem ~:** a short-sleeved shirt

Armaturen·brett *das* instrument panel; (im Kfz) dashboard

Arm-: ~band *das* bracelet; (Uhr~) strap; **~band·uhr** *die* wristwatch

Armee *die;* **~, ~n** (auch fig.) army

Ärmel *der;* **~s, ~:** sleeve; **[sich (*Dat.*)] etw. aus dem ~ schütteln** (ugs.) produce sth. just like that

Ärmel·kanal *der;* **~s** [English] Channel

ärmer ▶ ARM

ärmlich 1 *Adj.* cheap ‹*clothing*›; shabby ‹*flat, office*›; meagre ‹*meal*›
2 *adv.* cheaply ‹*furnished, dressed*›

arm·selig *Adj.* **(a)** miserable; pathetic ‹*result, figure*›; meagre ‹*meal, food*›; paltry ‹*return, salary, sum, fee*›
(b) (abwertend: erbärmlich) miserable

ärmst... ▶ ARM

Armut *die;* ~: poverty

Armuts: **~falle** *die* poverty trap; **~grenze** *die* poverty line

Aroma *das;* **~s, Aromen** (Duft) aroma; (Geschmack) flavour

aromatisch *Adj.* aromatic; distinctive ‹*taste*›; **~ duften** give off an aromatic fragrance

arrangieren /arã'zi:rən/ 1 *tr. V.* (geh., Musik) arrange
2 *refl. V.* **sich ~**: adapt; **sich mit jmdm. ~**: come to an accommodation with sb.

Arrest *der;* **~[e]s, ~e** detention

arrogant 1 *Adj.* arrogant
2 *adv.* arrogantly

Arroganz *die;* ~ arrogance

Arsch *der;* **~[e]s, Ärsche** (derb) **(a)** arse (Brit. coarse); ass (Amer. sl.); **leck mich am ~!** (fig.) piss off (sl.); **im ~ sein** (fig.) be buggered (coarse)
(b) (widerlicher Mensch) arsehole (Brit. coarse); asshole (Amer. coarse.)

Arsch·loch *das* (derb) ▶ ARSCH B

Art *die;* **~, ~en** **(a)** kind; sort; **Bücher aller ~**: all kinds *or* sorts of books; **[so] eine ~ ...**: a sort of ...; **aus der ~ schlagen** not be true to type; (in einer Familie) be different from all the rest of the family
(b) (Biol.) species
(c) (Wesen) nature; (Verhaltensweise) way; (gutes Benehmen) behaviour; **die feine englische ~** (ugs.) the proper way to behave
(d) (Weise) way; **auf diese ~**: in this way; **~ und Weise** way; (Kochk.) **nach ~ des Hauses** à la maison; **nach Schweizer ~**: Swiss style

arten-, Arten-: ~barriere *die,* **~grenze** *die* (Biol.) species barrier; **~reich** *Adj.* (Biol.) species-rich; **~reichtum** *der* (Biol.) species-richness; **~schutz** *der* protection of species; species protection

Arterie /ar'te:ri̯ə/ *die;* **~, ~n** artery

artig *Adj.* well-behaved; **sei ~**: be a good boy/girl/dog *etc.*

Artikel *der;* **~s, ~** **(a)** article
(b) (Ware) item

Artillerie *die;* **~, ~n** artillery

Artischocke *die;* **~, ~n** artichoke

Artist *der;* **~en, ~en, Artistin** *die;* **~, ~nen** [variety/circus] performer

Arznei *die;* **~, ~en** (veralt.), **Arznei·mittel** *das* medicine

Arzt *der;* **~es, Ärzte, Ärztin** *die;* **~, ~nen** doctor

Arzthelferin *die* doctor's receptionist

ärztlich 1 *Adj.* medical; **auf ~e Verordnung** on doctor's orders
2 *adv.* **sich ~ behandeln lassen** have medical treatment

***As** ▶ ASS

Asbest *der;* **~[e]s, ~e** asbestos

Asche *die;* **~, ~n** ash[es *pl.*]; (sterbliche Reste) ashes *pl.*

Aschen-: ~becher *der* ashtray; **~brödel** *das;* **~~s, ~~** (auch fig.) Cinderella

Ascher·mittwoch *der* Ash Wednesday

Äser ▶ AAS

Asiat *der;* **~en, ~en, Asiatin** *die;* **~, ~nen** Asian

asiatisch *Adj.* Asian

Asien /'a:zi̯ən/ *(das);* **~s** Asia

Asket *der;* **~en, ~en, Asketin** *die;* **~, ~nen** ascetic

asketisch 1 *Adj.* ascetic
2 *adv.* ascetically

asozial 1 *Adj.* asocial; (gegen die Gesellschaft gerichtet) antisocial
2 *adv.* asocially

Aspekt *der;* **~[e]s, ~e** aspect

Asphalt *der;* **~[e]s, ~e** asphalt

aß *1. u. 3. Pers. Sg. Prät. v.* ESSEN

Ass *das;* **~es, ~e** ace

Assistent *der,* **~en, ~en, Assistentin** *die;* **~, ~nen** assistant

Ast *der;* **~[e]s, Äste** branch; **sich** (*Dat.*) **einen ~ lachen** (ugs.) split one's sides [with laughter]

Aster *die;* **~, ~n** aster; (Herbstaster) Michaelmas daisy

ästhetisch 1 *Adj.* aesthetic
2 *adv.* aesthetically

Asthma *das;* **~s** asthma

ast·rein 1 *Adj.* (ugs.) (in Ordnung) on the level (coll.); (echt) genuine; (salopp: prima, toll) fantastic (coll.); great (coll.)
2 *adv.* (salopp: prima) fantastically (coll.)

Astrologe *der;* **~n, ~n** astrologer

Astrologie *die;* **~**: astrology *no art.*

Astrologin *die;* **~, ~nen** astrologer

Astronaut *der;* **~en, ~en, Astronautin** *die;* **~, ~nen** astronaut

Astronom *der;* **~en, ~en** astronomer

Astronomie *die;* **~**: astronomy *no art.*

Astronomin *die;* **~, ~nen** astronomer

astronomisch *Adj.* astronomical

Asyl *das;* **~s, ~e** **(a)** asylum
(b) (Obdachlosenheim) hostel

Asylant *der;* **~en, ~en, Asylantin** *die;* **~, ~nen** asylum seeker

Asylanten·heim *das* asylum seekers' hostel

Asyl-: ~antrag *der* application for asylum; **~bewerber** *der,* **bewerberin** ···>

a

die person seeking [political] asylum; **~bewerber·heim** *das* ▶ ASYLANTENHEIM; **~gesetz** *das* asylum law[s *pl.*]; **~missbrauch, *~mißbrauch** *der* misuse of asylum; **~recht** *das* (Rechtsw.) **(a)** right of [political] asylum; **(b)** (eines Staates) right to grant [political] asylum; **~werber** *der;* **~~s, ~~, ~werberin** *die;* **~~, ~~nen** (österr.) ▶ ~BEWERBER

Atelier /atəˈli̯eː/ *das;* **~s, ~s** studio

Atem *der;* **~s** breath; **außer ~ sein/geraten** be/get out of breath

atem-, Atem-: ~beraubend 1 *Adj.* breathtaking; 2 *adv.* breathtakingly; **~los** 1 *Adj.* breathless; 2 *adv.* breathlessly; **~pause** *die* breathing space; **~zug** *der* breath

Atheismus *der;* **~:** atheism *no art.*

Atheist *der;* **~en, ~en, Atheistin** *die;* **~, ~nen** atheist

atheistisch 1 *Adj.* atheistic 2 *adv.* atheistically

Athen *(das);* **~s** Athens

Äther *der;* **~s, ~:** ether

Äthiopien /ɛˈti̯oːpi̯ən/ *(das);* **~s** Ethiopia

Athlet *der;* **~en, ~en (a)** (Sportler) athlete **(b)** (ugs.: kräftiger Mann) muscleman

Athletin *die;* **~, ~nen** athlete

athletisch *Adj.* athletic

Atlanten ▶ ATLAS[1]

Atlantik *der;* **~s** Atlantic

atlantisch *Adj.* Atlantic; **der Atlantische Ozean** the Atlantic Ocean

Atlas *der;* **~** *od.* **~ses, Atlanten** *od.* **~se** atlas

atmen *itr., tr. V.* breathe

Atmosphäre /atmoˈsfɛːrə/ *die;* **~, ~n** (auch fig.) atmosphere

Atmung *die;* **~:** breathing

Atom *das;* **~s, ~e** atom

atomar *Adj.* atomic; (Atomwaffen betreffend) nuclear

atom-, Atom-: ~ausstieg *der* abandonment of nuclear power; **~bombe** *die* atom bomb; **~energie** *die* nuclear energy *no indef. art.;* **~kern** *der* atomic nucleus; **~kraft** *die* nuclear power *no indef. art.;* **~kraftwerk** *das* nuclear power station; **~krieg** *der* nuclear war; **~müll** *der* nuclear waste; **~physik** *die* nuclear physics *sing., no art.;* **~pilz** *der* mushroom cloud; **~reaktor** *der* nuclear reactor; **~strom** *der* (ugs.) electricity generated by nuclear power; **~waffe** *die* nuclear weapon; **~waffen·frei** *Adj.* nuclear-free; **~waffen·test** *der* nuclear [weapons] test; **~zeit·alter** *das* nuclear age

Attacke *die;* **~, ~n** (auch Med.) attack (**auf +** *Akk.* on)

Attentat *das;* **~[e]s, ~e** assassination attempt; (erfolgreich) assassination

Attentäter *der;* **~s, ~, Attentäterin** *die;* **~, ~nen** would-be assassin; (erfolgreich) assassin

Attest *das;* **~[e]s, ~e** medical certificate

Attraktion *die;* **~, ~en** attraction

attraktiv 1 *Adj.* attractive 2 *adv.* attractively

Attraktivität *die;* **~:** attractiveness

Attrappe *die;* **~, ~n** dummy

Attribut *das;* **~[e]s, ~e** attribute

ätzen 1 *tr. V.* etch 2 *itr. V.* corrode

ätzend 1 *Adj.* corrosive; (fig.) caustic ‹*wit, remark, criticism*›; pungent ‹*smell*› 2 *adv.* caustically ‹*ironic, critical*›

au *Interj.* **(a)** (bei Schmerz) ouch **(b)** (bei Überraschung, Begeisterung) oh

Aubergine /obɛrˈʒiːnə/ *die;* **~, ~n** aubergine (Brit.); eggplant

auch 1 *Adv.* **(a)** as well; too; also; **Klaus war ~ dabei** Klaus was there as well *or* too; Klaus was also there; **Ich gehe jetzt. – Ich ~:** I'm going now – So am I; **Mir ist warm. – Mir ~:** I feel warm – So do I; **das weiß ich ~ nicht** I don't know either **(b)** (sogar, selbst) even; **~ wenn, wenn ~:** even if
2 *Partikel* **(a) etwas anderes habe ich ~ nicht erwartet** I never expected anything else; **nun hör aber ~ zu!** now listen! **(b) bist du dir ~ im Klaren, was das bedeutet?** are you sure you understand what that means?; **bist du ~ glücklich?** are you truly happy?; **lügst du ~ nicht?** you're not lying, are you? **(c) wo …/wer …/was …** *usw.* **~:** wherever/whoever/whatever *etc.* …; **wie dem ~ sei** however that may be **(d) mag er ~ noch so klug sein** no matter how clever he is

Audienz *die;* **~, ~en** audience

Auditorium *das;* **~s, Auditorien (a)** (Hörsaal) auditorium **(b)** (Zuhörerschaft) audience

auf 1 *Präp. mit Dat.* **(a)** on; **~ See** at sea; **~ dem Baum** in the tree; **~ der Erde** on earth; **~ der Welt** in the world; **~ der Straße** in the street **(b)** at ‹*post office, town, hall, police station*›; **~ seinem Zimmer** (ugs.) in his room; **Geld ~ der Bank haben** have money in the bank; **~ der Schule/Uni** at school/university **(c)** at ‹*party, wedding*›; on ‹*course, trip, walk, holiday, tour*›
2 *Präp. mit Akk.* **(a)** on; **~ einen Berg steigen** climb up a mountain; **~ die Straße gehen** go [out] into the street **(b) ~ die Schule/Uni gehen** go to school/university; **~ einen Lehrgang gehen** go on a course **(c) ~ 10 km [Entfernung]** for [a distance of]

*old spelling - see note on page xiv

10 km; **wir näherten uns der Hütte [bis] ~ 30 m** we approached to within 30m of the hut
(d) ~ Jahre [hinaus] for years [to come]; **etw. ~ nächsten Mittwoch verschieben** postpone sth. until next Wednesday; **die Nacht von Sonntag ~ Montag** Sunday night; **das fällt ~ einen Montag** it falls on a Monday
(e) ~ diese Art und Weise in this way; **~ Deutsch** in German; **~ das Sorgfältigste** (geh.) most carefully
(f) ~ Wunsch on request; **~ meine Bitte** at my request; **~ Befehl** on command
(g) ein Teelöffel ~ einen Liter Wasser one teaspoon to one litre of water; **~ die Sekunde/den Millimeter [genau]** [precise] to the second/millimetre; **~ deine Gesundheit!** your health; **~ bald/morgen!** (bes. südd.) see you soon/tomorrow
3 *Adv.* **(a)** (aufgerichtet, aufgestanden) up; **~!** (steh/steht auf!) up you get!
(b) sie waren längst ~ und davon they had made off long before
(c) ~! (bes. südd.: los) come on; **~ gehts** off we go; **~ ins Schwimmbad!** come on, off to the swimming pool!
(d) ~ und ab (hin und her) up and down; to and fro
(e) Helm/Hut/Brille ~! helmet/hat/glasses on!
(f) (ugs.: geöffnet, offen) open; **Fenster/Mund ~!** open the window/your mouth!

auf|atmen *itr. V.* breathe a sigh of relief

auf|bahren *tr. V.* lay out; **aufgebahrt sein** lie in state

Auf·bau *der; ~[e]s, ~ten* **(a)** building
(b) (Struktur) structure
(c) *Pl.* (Schiffbau) superstructure *sing.*

auf|bauen *tr. V.* **(a)** erect ‹*hut, kiosk, podium*›; set up ‹*equipment, train set*›; build ‹*house, bridge*›; put up ‹*tent*›
(b) (hinstellen, arrangieren) lay *or* set out ‹*food, presents, etc.*›
(c) (fig.: schaffen) build ‹*state, economy, etc.*›; build up ‹*business, organization, army, spy network*›
(d) (fig.: strukturieren) structure

auf|bäumen *refl. V.* rear up; **sich gegen jmdn./etw. ~** (fig.) rise up against sb./sth.

auf|bessern *tr. V.* improve; increase ‹*pension, wages, etc.*›

auf|bewahren *tr. V.* keep; **etw. kühl ~:** store sth. in a cool place

Auf·bewahrung *die* keeping

auf|bieten *unr. tr. V.* exert ‹*strength, energy, will power, influence, authority*›; call on ‹*skill, wit, powers of persuasion or eloquence*›

auf|blasen *unr. tr. V.* blow up; inflate

auf|bleiben *unr. itr. V.; mit sein* **(a)** (geöffnet bleiben) stay open
(b) (nicht zu Bett gehen) stay up

auf|blenden *itr. V.* switch to full beam

auf|blicken *itr. V.* **(a)** look up; (kurz) glance up
(b) zu jmdm. ~ (fig.) look up to sb.

auf|blühen *itr. V.; mit sein* **(a)** come into bloom; ‹*bud*› open
(b) (fig.: aufleben) blossom [out]

auf|brauchen *tr. V.* use up

auf|brechen **1** *unr. tr. V.* break open ‹*lock, safe, box, crate, etc.*›; break into ‹*car*›; force [open] ‹*door*›
2 *unr. itr. V.; mit sein* **(a)** ‹*bud*› open; ‹*ice [sheet], surface, ground*› break up; ‹*wound*› open
(b) (losgehen, -fahren) set off

auf|bringen *unr. tr. V.* **(a)** find; raise ‹*money*›; (fig.) summon [up] ‹*strength, energy, courage*›; find ‹*patience*›
(b) (kreieren) start ‹*fashion, custom, rumour*›; introduce ‹*slogan, theory*›
(c) jmdn. ~: make sb. angry
(d) jmdn. gegen jmdn./etw. ~: set sb. against sb./sth.

Auf·bruch *der* departure

auf|brühen *tr. V.* brew [up]

auf|decken *tr. V.* **(a)** uncover
(b) (Kartenspiele) show
(c) (fig.) reveal; uncover; (enthüllen) expose

auf|drängen **1** *tr. V.* **jmdm. etw. ~:** force sth. on sb.
2 *refl. V.* **sich jmdm. ~:** force oneself on sb.

auf|drehen *tr. V.* **(a)** unscrew ‹*bottle cap, nut*›; undo ‹*screw*›; turn on ‹*tap, gas, water*›; open ‹*valve, bottle, vice*›
(b) (ugs.) turn up ‹*radio, record player, etc.*›

auf·dringlich **1** *Adj.* pushy (coll.) ‹*person*›; (fig.) insistent ‹*music, advertisement*›; pungent ‹*perfume, smell*›; loud ‹*colour, wallpaper*›
2 *adv.* ‹*behave*› pushily (coll.)

Aufdringlichkeit *die; ~* ▶ AUFDRINGLICH: pushiness (coll.); insistent manner; pungency

auf·einander *Adv.* **(a)** on top of one another; **~ prallen** crash into one another; collide; (fig.) ‹*opinions*› clash; **~ treffen** (fig.) meet
(b) ~ folgen follow one another; **~folgend** successive

Aufeinander·folge *die* sequence; **in rascher ~** in rapid *or* quick succession

***aufeinander|folgen** *usw.* ▶ AUFEINANDER

Aufenthalt *der; ~[e]s, ~e* **(a)** stay
(b) (Fahrtunterbrechung) stop

Aufenthalts-: ~erlaubnis *die* residence permit; **~raum** *der* (in einer Schule o. Ä.) common room (Brit.); (in einer Jugendherberge) day room; (in einem Betrieb o. Ä.) recreation room

auf|essen *unr. tr.* (*auch itr.*) *V.* eat up

auf|fahren **1** *unr. itr. V.; mit sein* **(a) auf ein anderes Fahrzeug ~** (aufprallen) drive into the back of another vehicle

⋯▸

a

(b) **auf den Vordermann zu dicht ~:** drive too close to the car in front
(c) (vorfahren) drive up
(d) (in Stellung gehen) move up [into position]
2 *unr. tr. V.* **(a)** (in Stellung bringen) move up
(b) (ugs.: auftischen) serve up

Auf·fahrt *die* **(a)** drive up
(b) (Weg) drive
(c) (Autobahnauffahrt) slip road (Brit.); access road (Amer.)
(d) (schweiz.) ▶ HIMMELFAHRT

Auffahr·unfall *der* rear-end collision

auf|fallen *unr. itr. V.; mit sein* stand out; **jmdm. fällt etw. auf** sb. notices sth.

auffallend **1** *Adj.* conspicuous; (eindrucksvoll, bemerkenswert) striking
2 *adv.* conspicuously; (eindrucksvoll, bemerkenswert) strikingly

auf·fällig **1** *Adj.* conspicuous; garish ‹*colour*›
2 *adv.* conspicuously

auf|fangen *unr. tr. V.* **(a)** catch
(b) (aufnehmen, sammeln) collect

Auffang·lager *das* reception camp

auf|fassen *tr. V.* grasp; **etw. als etw. ~:** regard sth. as sth.; **etw. persönlich/falsch ~:** take sth. personally/misunderstand sth.

Auf·fassung *die* (Ansicht) view; (Begriff) conception; **der ~ sein, dass ...:** take the view that ...

auffindbar *Adj.* findable

auf|finden *unr. tr. V.* find

auf|fordern *tr. V.* **jmdn. ~, etw. zu tun** call upon sb. to do sth.; (einladen, ermuntern) ask sb. to do sth.; **jmdn. [zum Tanz] ~:** ask sb. to dance

Auf·forderung *die* request; (nachdrücklicher) demand; (Einladung, Ermunterung) invitation

auf|forsten **1** *tr. V.* afforest; (wieder ~) reforest; **einen Wald ~:** restock a forest
2 *itr. V.* establish woods; (wieder ~) reestablish the woods

Aufforstung *die; ~, ~en* afforestation; (Wieder~) reforestation; **die ~ der Wälder** restocking the forests

auf|fressen *unr. tr. V.* (auch fig.) eat up

auf|frischen **1** *tr. V.* freshen up; brighten up ‹*colour, paintwork*›; renovate ‹*polish, furniture*›; (restaurieren) restore ‹*tapestry, fresco, etc.*›; (fig.) revive ‹*old memories*›; renew ‹*acquaintance, friendship*›; **seine Englischkenntnisse ~:** brush up one's [knowledge of] English
2 *itr. V.; auch mit sein* ‹*wind*› freshen

auf|führen **1** *tr. V.* **(a)** put on ‹*film*›; stage ‹*play, ballet, opera*›; perform ‹*piece of music*›
(b) (auflisten) list
2 *refl. V.* behave

Auf·führung *die* performance

Auf·gabe *die* **(a)** task
(b) (fig.: Zweck, Funktion) function
(c) (Schulw.) (Übung) exercise; (Prüfungs~) question; (Haus~) ▶ HAUSAUFGABE
(d) (Rechen~, Mathematik~) problem
(e) (Kapitulation) retirement; (im Schach) resignation; **jmdn. zur ~ zwingen** force sb. to retire/resign
(f) (das Aufgeben a) giving up
(g) (einer Postsendung) posting (Brit.); mailing (Amer.); (eines Telegramms) handing in; (einer Bestellung, einer Annonce) placing
(h) (von Gepäck) checking in

Aufgaben-: ~bereich *der,* **~gebiet** *das* area of responsibility

Auf·gang *der* **(a)** (eines Gestirns) rising
(b) (Treppe) stairs *pl.;* staircase; stairway; (in einem Bahnhof, zu einer Galerie, einer Tribüne) steps *pl.*

auf|geben **1** *unr. tr. V.* **(a)** give up; (Sport) retire from ‹*race, competition*›
(b) (übergeben, übermitteln) post (Brit.), mail ‹*letter, parcel*›; hand in, (telefonisch) phone in ‹*telegram*›; place ‹*advertisement, order*›; check ‹*luggage, baggage*› in
(c) (Schulw.: als Hausaufgabe) set (Brit.); assign (Amer.)
(d) **jmdm. ein Rätsel ~:** set (Brit.) *or* (Amer.) assign sb. a puzzle
2 *unr. itr. V.* give up; (im Sport) retire; (im Schach) resign

Auf·gebot *das* **(a)** contingent; **ein gewaltiges ~ an Polizisten/Fahrzeugen/Material** a huge force of police/array of vehicles/materials
(b) (zur Heirat) notice of an/the intended marriage; (kirchlich) banns *pl.*

auf|gehen *unr. itr. V.; mit sein* **(a)** rise
(b) (sich öffnen [lassen]) ‹*door, parachute, wound*› open; ‹*stage curtain*› go up; ‹*knot, button, zip, bandage, shoelace, stitching*› come undone; ‹*boil, pimple, blister*› burst; ‹*flower, bud*› open [up]
(c) (keimen) come up
(d) (aufgetrieben werden) ‹*dough, cake*› rise
(e) (Math.) ‹*calculation*› work out; ‹*equation*› come out
(f) **etw. geht jmdm. auf** sb. realizes sth.

auf|geilen *tr. V.* (salopp) **jmdn. [mit/durch etw.] ~:** get sb. randy [with sth.]; **sich [an etw. (*Dat.*)] ~:** get randy [with sth.]; (fig.) get worked up [about sth.]

aufgeklärt *Adj.* enlightened; **~ sein** (sexualkundlich) know the facts of life

auf·gelegt *Adj.* **gut/schlecht** *usw.* **~ sein** be in a good/bad *etc.* mood; **zu etw. ~ sein** be in the mood for sth.

auf·gelöst *Adj.* distraught ‹*person*›

aufgeregt **1** *Adj.* excited; (nervös, beunruhigt) agitated
2 *adv.* excitedly; (nervös, beunruhigt) agitatedly

auf·geschlossen *Adj.* open-minded (**gegenüber** as regards, about); (interessiert, empfänglich) receptive (*Dat.*, **für** to); (zugänglich) approachable

---

*alte Schreibung - vgl. Hinweis auf S. xiv

Auf·geschlossenheit *die* ▶ AUFGESCHLOSSEN: open-mindedness; receptiveness; approachableness

aufgeweckt *Adj.* bright

Aufgewecktheit *die;* ~: brightness

auf|gießen *unr. tr. V.* make ‹*coffee, tea*›

auf|gliedern *tr. V.* subdivide, break down (**in** + *Akk.* into)

Auf·gliederung *die* subdivision; breakdown

auf|greifen *unr. tr. V.* pick up

aufgrund *Präp. mit Gen.* on the basis *or* strength of; (wegen) because of

auf|haben (ugs.) **1** *unr. tr. V.* **(a)** (aufgesetzt haben) have on
(b) (geöffnet haben) have ‹*zip*› undone; have ‹*door, window, jacket, blouse*› open
2 *unr. itr. V.* ‹*shop, office*› be open

auf|halsen *tr. V.* (ugs.) **jmdm./sich etw. ~:** saddle sb./oneself with sth.; **sich** (*Dat.*) **etw. ~ lassen** get oneself saddled with sth.

auf|halten **1** *unr. tr. V.* **(a)** halt
(b) (stören) hold up
(c) (ugs.: geöffnet halten) hold ‹*sack, door, etc.*› open; **die Augen [und Ohren] ~:** keep one's eyes [and ears] open
2 *unr. refl. V.* **(a)** stay
(b) sich mit jmdm./etw. ~: spend [a long] time on sb./sth

auf|hängen **1** *tr. V.* **(a)** hang up; hang ‹*picture, curtains*›
(b) (erhängen) hang
2 *refl. V.* hang oneself

Aufhänger *der;* **~s, ~:** loop

auf|heben *unr. tr. V.* **(a)** pick up
(b) (aufbewahren) keep
(c) (abschaffen) abolish; repeal ‹*law*›; rescind ‹*order, instruction*›; cancel ‹*contract*›; lift ‹*ban, prohibition*›
(d) (ausgleichen) cancel out; neutralize ‹*effect*›

Aufheben *das;* **~s: viel ~[s]/kein ~ von jmdm./etw. machen** make a great fuss/not make any fuss about sb./sth.

Aufhebungs·vertrag *der* agreement to terminate a/the contract

auf|heitern **1** *tr. V.* cheer up
2 *refl. V.* ‹*weather*› brighten up

Aufheiterung *die;* **~, ~en** **(a)** (des Wetters) bright period
(b) (Erheiterung) cheering up

auf|hetzen *tr. V.* incite

auf|holen **1** *tr. V.* make up ‹*time, delay*›; pull back ‹*lead*›
2 *itr. V.* catch up; ‹*athlete, competitor*› make up ground

auf|horchen *itr. V.* prick up one's ears

auf|hören *itr. V.* stop; **[damit] ~, etw. zu tun** stop doing sth.

auf|kaufen *tr. V.* buy up

auf|klappen *tr. V.* open, fold open ‹*chair, table*›; open [up] ‹*suitcase, trunk*›; open ‹*book, knife*›

auf|klären **1** *tr. V.* **(a)** clear up ‹*matter, mystery, question, misunderstanding, error, confusion*›; solve ‹*crime, problem*›; explain ‹*event, incident, cause*›; resolve ‹*contradiction, disagreement*›
(b) (unterrichten) enlighten; **ein Kind ~** (sexualkundlich) tell a child the facts of life
2 *refl. V.* **(a)** ‹*misunderstanding, mystery*› be cleared up
(b) ‹*weather*› brighten [up]; ‹*sky*› brighten

Auf·klärung *die* ▶ AUFKLÄREN 1: **(a)** clearing up; solution; explanation; resolution
(b) enlightenment; **die ~ der Kinder** (über Sexualität) telling the children the facts of life

auf|kleben *tr. V.* stick on; (mit Kleister) paste on

Auf·kleber *der* sticker

auf|knöpfen *tr. V.* unbutton; undo

auf|kochen **1** *tr. V.* bring to the boil
2 *itr. V.; mit sein* come to the boil

auf|kommen *unr. itr. V.; mit sein* **(a)** ‹*wind*› spring up; ‹*storm, gale*› blow up; ‹*fog*› come down; ‹*rumour*› start; ‹*suspicion, doubt, feeling*› arise; ‹*fashion, style, invention*› come in; ‹*boredom*› set in; ‹*mood, atmosphere*› develop
(b) ~ für (bezahlen) bear ‹*costs*›; pay for ‹*damage*›; pay ‹*expenses*›; be liable for ‹*debts*›; stand ‹*loss*›
(c) ~ für (Verantwortung tragen für) be responsible for

auf|krempeln *tr. V.* roll up

auf|laden **1** *unr. tr. V.* **(a)** load (**auf** + *Akk.* on [to])
(b) jmdm. etw. ~ (ugs.) load sb. with sth.; (fig.) saddle sb. with sth.
(c) charge [up] ‹*battery*›
2 *unr. refl. V.* ‹*battery*› charge

Auf·lage *die* **(a)** (Buchw.) edition
(b) (Verpflichtung) condition

auflagen·stark *Adj.* high-circulation ‹*newspaper, magazine*›

auf|lassen *unr. tr. V.* (ugs.) **(a)** leave ‹*door, window, jacket, etc.*› open
(b) keep on ‹*hat, glasses, etc.*›

auf|lauern *itr. V.* **jmdm. ~:** lie in wait for sb.

Auf·lauf *der* **(a)** (Menschen~) crowd
(b) (Speise) soufflé

auf|leben *itr. V.; mit sein* revive; (fig.: wieder munter werden) come to life

auf|legen **1** *tr. V.* **(a)** put on; **den Hörer ~:** put down the receiver
(b) (Buchw.) publish
2 *itr. V.* (den Hörer auflegen) hang up

auf|lehnen *refl. V.* rebel

Auflehnung *die;* **~, ~en** rebellion

auf|leuchten *itr. V.; auch mit sein* light up; (für kurze Zeit) flash

auf|lockern *tr. V.* **(a)** loosen; break up ‹*soil*›
(b) (fig.) introduce some variety into ···›

a

‹landscape, lesson, lecture›; relieve ‹pattern, façade›; make ‹mood, atmosphere, evening› more relaxed

Auf·lockerung *die* **(a)** ▶ AUFLOCKERN A: loosening; breaking up
(b) **zur ~ der Stimmung/des Abends** to make the mood/evening more relaxed

auf|lösen [1] *tr. V.* dissolve; resolve ‹*difficulty, contradiction*›; solve ‹*puzzle, equation*›; break off ‹*engagement*›; cancel ‹*arrangement, contract, agreement*›; dissolve ‹*organization*›
[2] *refl. V.* dissolve (**in** + *Akk.* into); ‹*parliament*› dissolve itself; ‹*crowd, demonstration*› break up; ‹*fog, mist*› lift; (fig.) ‹*empire, social order*› disintegrate

Auf·lösung *die* **(a)** ▶ AUFLÖSEN 1: dissolving; resolution; solution; breaking off; cancellation; dissolution
(b) ▶ AUFLÖSEN 2: dissolving; breaking up lifting; disintegration

auf|machen [1] *tr. V.* **(a)** open; undo ‹*button, knot*›
(b) (ugs.: eröffnen) open [up] ‹*shop, business, etc.*›
[2] *itr. V.* **(a)** ‹*shop, office, etc.*› open
(b) (ugs.: die Tür öffnen) open the door; **jmdm. ~:** open the door to sb.
(c) (ugs.: eröffnet werden) ‹*shop, business*› open [up]

Aufmachung *die;* **~, ~en** presentation; (Kleidung) get-up

Aufmarsch·gebiet *das* (Milit.) deployment area

auf|marschieren *itr. V.; mit sein* assemble; (heranmarschieren) march up; **Truppen sind an der Grenze aufmarschiert** troops were deployed along the border

aufmerksam [1] *Adj.* **(a)** attentive; sharp ‹*eyes*›; **jmdn. auf jmdn./etw. ~ machen** draw sb.'s attention to sb./sth.; **auf jmdn./etw. ~ werden** become aware of sb./sth.; **~ werden** notice
(b) (höflich) attentive
[2] *adv.* attentively

Aufmerksamkeit *die;* **~, ~en (a)** attention
(b) (Höflichkeit) attentiveness
(c) (Geschenk) small gift

auf|motzen *tr. V.* (ugs.) tart up (Brit. coll.); doll up (coll.)

auf|muntern *tr. V.* **(a)** cheer up
(b) (beleben) liven up
(c) (ermutigen) encourage

Aufmunterung *die;* **~** ▶ AUFMUNTERN: cheering up; livening up; encouragement

Aufnahme *die;* **~, ~n (a)** ▶ AUFNEHMEN B: opening; establishment; taking up
(b) (Empfang) reception
(c) ▶ AUFNEHMEN D: admission (**in** + *Akk.* into)
(d) (Einschließung) inclusion
(e) (Finanzw.) raising
(f) (Aufzeichnung) taking down; (von Personalien, eines Diktats) taking [down]
(g) ▶ AUFNEHMEN K: taking: photographing; filming
(h) (Bild) shot
(i) (das Aufnehmen auf Tonträger, das Aufgenommene) recording
(j) (Anklang) reception; response (*Gen.* to)
(k) (Einverleibung, Absorption) absorption

aufnahme-, Aufnahme-: ~antrag *der* application for membership; **~fähig** *Adj.* receptive (**für** to); **ich bin nicht mehr ~fähig** I can't take any more in; **~fähigkeit** *die* receptivity (**für** to); ability to take things in; **~land** *das* host country

auf|nehmen *unr. tr. V.* **(a)** (aufheben) pick up; (fig.) take up ‹*idea, theme, etc.*›; **es mit jmdm./etw. ~/nicht ~ können** (fig.) be a/no match for sb./sth.
(b) (beginnen mit) open ‹*negotiations, talks*›; establish ‹*relations, contacts*›; take up ‹*studies, activity, occupation*›; start ‹*production, investigation*›
(c) (empfangen) receive; (beherbergen) take in
(d) (beitreten lassen) admit (**in** + *Akk.* to)
(e) (einschließen, verzeichnen) include
(f) (erfassen) take in ‹*impressions, information, etc.*›
(g) (absorbieren) absorb
(h) (Finanzw.) raise ‹*mortgage, money, loan*›
(i) (reagieren auf) receive
(j) (aufschreiben) take down; take [down] ‹*dictation, particulars*›
(k) (fotografieren) take ‹*picture*›; photograph, take a photograph of ‹*scene, subject*›; (filmen) film
(l) (auf Tonträger) record
(m) (auf Videoband) videotape; video

auf|opfern *refl. V.* devote oneself sacrificingly (**für** to)

aufopfernd [1] *Adj.* self-sacrificing
[2] *adv.* self-sacrificingly

auf|passen *itr. V.* **(a)** watch out; (konzentriert sein) pay attention; **pass mal auf!** (ugs.: hör mal zu!) now listen
(b) **auf jmdn./etw. ~:** keep an eye on sb./sth.

auf|platzen *itr. V.; mit sein* burst open; ‹*seam, cushion*› split open; ‹*wound*› open up

Auf·prall *der;* **~[e]s, ~e** impact

auf|prallen *itr. V.; mit sein* **auf etw.** (*Akk.*) **~:** hit sth.

Auf·preis *der* additional charge

auf|pumpen *tr. V.* pump up

auf|putschen *tr. V.* stimulate; arouse ‹*passions, urge*›

Aufputsch·mittel *das* stimulant

auf|räumen *tr., itr. V.* clear up

Aufräumungs·arbeiten *Pl.* clearance work *sing.*

auf·recht [1] *Adj.* (auch fig.) upright
[2] *adv.* ‹*walk, sit, hold oneself*› straight

aufrecht|erhalten *unr. tr. V.* maintain; keep up ‹*deception, fiction, contact, custom*›

---

*old spelling - see note on page xiv

auf|regen 1 *tr. V.* excite; (ärgern) annoy; irritate; (beunruhigen) agitate
2 *refl. V.* get worked up (**über** + *Akk.* about)

Auf·regung *die* excitement *no pl.;* (Beunruhigung) agitation *no pl.;* **jmdn. in ~ versetzen** make sb. excited/agitated

auf|reißen 1 *unr. tr. V.* **(a)** (öffnen) tear open; wrench open ‹*drawer*›; fling open ‹*door, window*›; **die Augen/den Mund ~:** open one's eyes/mouth wide
(b) (beschädigen) tear open; tear ‹*clothes*›; break up ‹*road, soil*›
2 *itr. V.; mit sein* ‹*clothes*› tear; ‹*seam*› split; ‹*wound*› open; ‹*cloud*› break up

auf|reizen *tr. V.* excite

auf·reizend 1 *Adj.* provocative
2 *adv.* provocatively

auf|richten 1 *tr. V.* erect; put up; **den Oberkörper ~:** raise one's upper body; **jmdn. [wieder] ~** (fig.) give fresh heart to sb.
2 *refl. V.* stand up [straight]; **sich an jmdm./etw. [wieder] ~** (fig.) take heart from sb./sth.

auf·richtig 1 *Adj.* sincere
2 *adv.* sincerely

Auf·richtigkeit *die* sincerity

auf|rücken *itr. V.; mit sein* move up

Auf·ruf *der* **(a)** call
(b) (Appell) appeal (**an** + *Akk.* to)

auf|rufen *unr. tr. V.* **(a)** call
(b) jmdn. ~, etw. zu tun call upon sb. to do sth.
(c) (Rechtsw.) appeal for ‹*witnesses*›

Aufruhr *der;* **~s, ~e (a)** (Widerstand) rebellion
(b) (Erregung) turmoil

aufrührerisch *Adj.* inflammatory

auf|rüsten *tr., itr. V.* **(a)** arm; **wieder ~:** rearm
(b) (DV) upgrade

Auf·rüstung *die* armament

aufs *Präp.* + *Art.* = **auf das**

auf|sagen *tr. V.* recite

auf|sammeln *tr. V.* gather up

aufsässig 1 *Adj.* recalcitrant
2 *adv.* recalcitrantly

Aufsässigkeit *die;* **~, ~en (a)** recalcitrance
(b) (Handlung) piece of recalcitrance

Auf·satz *der* (Text) essay

auf|saugen *unr.* (*auch regelm.*) *tr. V.* soak up; (fig.) absorb

auf|schieben *unr. tr. V.* postpone

Auf·schlag *der* **(a)** (Aufprall) impact
(b) (Preis~) surcharge
(c) (Ärmel~) cuff; (Hosen~) turn-up; (Revers) lapel
(d) (Tennis usw.) serve

auf|schlagen 1 *unr. itr. V.* **(a)** *mit sein* **auf etw.** (*Dat. od. Akk.*) **~:** hit sth.
(b) (teurer werden) ‹*price, rent, costs*› go up
(c) (Tennis usw.) serve
2 *unr. tr. V.* **(a)** (öffnen) crack ‹*nut, egg*› [open]; knock a hole in ‹*ice*›; **sich** (*Dat.*) **das Knie/den Kopf ~:** cut one's knee/head
(b) open ‹*book, newspaper, one's eyes*›; **schlagt Seite 15 auf!** turn to page 15
(c) turn up ‹*collar, sleeve, trouser leg*›
(d) (aufbauen) set up ‹*camp*›; pitch ‹*tent*›; put up ‹*bed, hut, scaffolding*›
(e) 5 % auf etw. (*Akk.*) **~:** put 5% on sth.

auf|schließen 1 *unr. tr. V.* unlock
2 *unr. itr. V.* **[jmdm.] ~:** unlock the door/gate *etc.* [for sb.]

Auf·schluss, *Auf·schluß *der* information *no pl.*

auf|schneiden 1 *unr. tr. V.* **(a)** cut open
(b) (zerteilen) cut
2 *unr. itr. V.* (ugs.: prahlen) boast (**mit** about)

Auf·schneider *der*, **Auf·schneiderin** *die* (ugs. abwertend) boaster; braggart

Auf·schnitt *der* [assorted] cold meats *pl.*/cheeses *pl.*

auf|schnüren *tr. V.* undo

auf|schrauben *tr. V.* unscrew; unscrew the top of ‹*bottle, jar, etc.*›

Auf·schrei *der* cry; (stärker) yell; (schriller) scream; **ein ~ der Empörung** *od.* **Entrüstung** (fig.) an outcry

auf|schreiben *unr. tr. V.* write down; **[sich** (*Dat.*)**] etw. ~:** make a note of sth.

auf|schreien *unr. itr. V.* cry out; (stärker) yell out; (schrill) scream

Auf·schrift *die* inscription

Auf·schub *der* postponement; **die Sache duldet keinen ~:** the matter brooks no delay

Auf·schwung *der* upturn (*Gen.* in)

Aufsehen *das;* **~s** stir; **[großes] ~ erregen** cause a [great] stir

Auf·seher *der*, **Auf·seherin** *die;* **~, ~nen** (im Gefängnis) warder (Brit.); [prison] guard (Amer.); (im Park) park-keeper; (im Museum, auf dem Parkplatz) attendant; (auf einem Gut, Sklavenaufseher) overseer

***auf|sein** ▶ AUF 3A, F

auf|setzen 1 *tr. V.* **(a)** put on
(b) (verfassen) draw up ‹*text*›
2 *refl. V.* sit up

Auf·sicht *die* supervision; (bei Prüfungen) invigilation (Brit.); proctoring (Amer.)

auf|spielen 1 *refl. V.* (ugs. abwertend: angeben) put on airs; **sich vor jmdm. ~:** show off in front of sb.
2 *itr. V.* **(a)** (musizieren) play; **zum Tanz ~:** play dance music
(b) (Sport) **groß/eindrucksvoll ~:** give a fine/impressive display

auf|springen *unr. itr. V.; mit sein* **(a)** jump up
(b) (hinaufspringen) jump on (**auf** + *Akk.* to)
(c) (rissig werden) crack

auf|stacheln *tr. V.* incite

Auf·stand *der* rebellion

auf·ständisch *Adj.* rebellious

a

auf|stehen *unr. itr. V.; mit sein* stand up; (aus dem Liegen) get up

auf|steigen *unr. itr. V.; mit sein* **(a)** (auf ein Fahrzeug) get on; **auf etw.** (*Akk.*) **∼**: get on [to] sth.
(b) (bergan steigen) climb
(c) (hochsteigen) ‹*sap, smoke, mist*› rise
(d) (beruflich, gesellschaftlich) rise (**zu** to); **zum Direktor ∼**: rise to be manager

auf|stellen 1 *tr. V.* **(a)** put up (**auf** + *Akk.* on); set up ‹*skittles*›; (postieren) post
(b) (aufrecht hinstellen) stand up
(c) (Sport) select, pick ‹*team, player*›
(d) (bilden) put together ‹*team of experts*›; raise ‹*army*›
(e) (nominieren) nominate; put up
2 *refl. V.* position oneself

Auf·stellung *die* **(a)** ▶ AUFSTELLEN 1A: putting up; setting up; posting
(b) ▶ AUFSTELLEN B: standing up
(c) ▶ AUFSTELLEN C: selection; picking
(d) ▶ AUFSTELLEN D: putting together; raising
(e) (Nominierung) nomination

Aufstieg *der;* **∼[e]s, ∼e (a)** climb
(b) ▶ AUFSTEIGEN D: rise

auf|stoßen 1 *unr. tr. V.* push open
2 *unr. itr. V.* belch; ‹*baby*› bring up wind

Auf·strich *der* spread

auf|stützen 1 *tr. V.* rest ‹*one's arms etc.*›
2 *refl. V.* support oneself; **die Arme auf etw.** (*Akk. od. Dat.*) **∼**: rest one's arms on sth.

auf|suchen *tr. V.* call on; go to ‹*doctor*›

Auf·takt *der* **(a)** (fig.) start
(b) (Musik) upbeat

auf|tauchen *itr. V.; mit sein* **(a)** surface
(b) (sichtbar werden) appear

auf|tauen 1 *tr. V.* thaw
2 *itr. V.; mit sein* (auch fig.) thaw

auf|teilen *tr. V.* **(a)** divide [up]
(b) (verteilen) share out

Auftrag *der;* **∼[e]s, Aufträge (a)** instructions *pl.;* **in jmds. ∼** (*Dat.*) on sb.'s instructions; (für jmdn.) on behalf of sb
(b) (Bestellung) order; (bei Künstlern, Architekten usw.) commission
(c) (Mission) task; (Aufgabe) job

auf|tragen *unr. tr. V.* **(a) jmdm. ∼, etw. zu tun** instruct sb. to do sth.
(b) (aufstreichen) put on ‹*paint, make-up, etc.*›

Auftrag·geber *der;* **∼s, ∼, Auftrag·geberin** *die;* **∼, ∼nen** client

auftrags-, Auftrags-: ∼buch *das* (Kaufmannsspr.) order book; **∼killer** *der,* **∼killerin** *die* contract killer

auf|treten *unr. itr. V.; mit sein* **(a)** tread
(b) (sich benehmen) behave
(c) (eine Vorstellung geben) appear; **als Zeuge/Kläger ∼**: appear as a witness/a plaintiff
(d) (auftauchen) ‹*problem, difficulty, difference of opinion*› arise; ‹*symptom, danger, pest*› appear

Auftreten *das;* **∼s** (Benehmen) manner

Auf·trieb *der* **(a)** (Physik) (statischer ∼) buoyancy; (dynamischer ∼) lift
(b) (fig.) impetus; **das hat ihm ∼/neuen ∼ gegeben** that has given him a lift/given him new impetus

Auf·tritt *der* **(a)** (Vorstellung) appearance
(b) (Theater: das Auftreten) entrance; (Szene) scene

auf|tun *unr. refl. V.* (geh.) open; (fig.) open up

auf|wachen *itr. V.; mit sein* wake up, awaken (**aus** from); (aus Ohnmacht, Narkose) come round (**aus** from)

auf|wachsen *unr. itr. V.; mit sein* grow up

Auf·wand *der;* **∼[e]s** cost; expense

aufwändig ▶ AUFWENDIG

Aufwands·entschädigung *die* expense allowance

auf|wärmen 1 *tr. V.* heat *or* warm up ‹*food*›
2 *refl. V.* warm oneself up

aufwärts *Adv.* upwards

Aufwärts·trend *der* upward trend

auf|wecken *tr. V.* wake [up]; waken

auf|weichen 1 *tr. V.* soften
2 *itr. V.; mit sein* become soft; soften up

auf|wenden *unr.* (*auch regelm.*) *tr. V.* use ‹*skill, influence*›; expend ‹*energy, resources*›; spend ‹*money, time*›; **viel Geld/seine ganze Freizeit für etw. ∼** spend a great deal of money/all one's spare time on sth.

auf·wendig 1 *Adj.* lavish; (kostspielig) costly; expensive
2 *adv.* lavishly; (kostspielig) expensively

Auf·wendung *die* **(a)** ▶ AUFWENDEN: using; expenditure; spending; **unter ∼ von etw.** by using/expending/spending sth.
(b) *Pl.* (Kosten) expenditure *sing.*

auf|wiegeln *tr. V.* incite; stir up

auf|wirbeln *tr. V.* swirl up

auf|wischen *tr. V.* **(a)** wipe *or* mop up
(b) (säubern) wipe ‹*floor*›; (mit Wasser) wash ‹*floor*›

auf|zählen *tr. V.* list

Auf·zählung *die* **(a)** listing
(b) (Liste) list

auf|zeichnen *tr. V.* **(a)** record
(b) (zeichnen) draw

Auf·zeichnung *die* record; (Film-, Tonaufzeichnung) recording; **∼en** (Notizen) notes

auf|ziehen 1 *unr. tr. V.* **(a)** pull open ‹*drawer*›; open, draw [back] ‹*curtains*›; undo ‹*zip*›
(b) wind up ‹*clock, toy, etc.*›
2 *unr. itr. V.; mit sein* come up; ‹*clouds, storm*› gather

Auf·zucht *die* raising; rearing

Auf·zug *der* **(a)** (Lift) lift (Brit.); elevator (Amer.)
(b) (abwertend: Aufmachung) get-up
(c) (Theater: Akt) act

Aug·apfel *der* eyeball

Auge *das;* **∼s, ∼n** eye; **gute/schlechte ∼n**

*alte Schreibung - vgl. Hinweis auf S. xiv

haben have good/poor eyesight; **auf einem ~ blind** blind in one eye; **da wird er ~n machen** (fig. ugs.) his eyes will pop out of his head; **ich traute meinen ~n nicht** (ugs.) I couldn't believe my eyes; **ein ~** *od.* **beide ~n zudrücken** (fig.) turn a blind eye; **jmdn./etw. nicht aus den ~n lassen** not take one's eyes off sb./sth.; **ins ~ gehen** (fig. ugs.) end in disaster; **unter vier ~n** (fig.) in private

augen; Augen-: ~arzt *der,* **~ärztin** *die* eye specialist; **~blick** */auch: --'-/ der* ▶ MOMENT[1]; **~blicklich** */auch: --'--/* [1] *Adj.* **(a)** (sofortig) immediate; **(b)** (gegenwärtig) present; [2] *adv.* **(a)** (sofort) at once; **(b)** (zurzeit) at the moment; **~braue** *die* eyebrow; **~farbe** *die* colour of one's eyes; **~klinik** *die* eye hospital; **~lid** *das* eyelid; **~maß** *das:* **ein gutes/schlechtes ~maß haben** have a good eye/no eye for distances; **~merk** *das:* **sein ~merk auf jmdn./etw. richten** *od.* **lenken** give one's attention to sb./sth.; **~optiker** *der,* **~optikerin** *die* ophthalmic optician

Augen·schein *der* (geh.) **(a)** (Eindruck) appearance; **dem ~ nach** by all appearances **(b)** (Betrachtung) inspection; **jmdn./etw. in ~ nehmen** have a close look at sb./sth.; give sb./sth. a close inspection

augen·scheinlich (geh.) [1] *Adj.* (scheinbar) apparent; evident; (sichtbar) obvious; evident
[2] *adv.* (scheinbar) apparently; evidently; (sichtbar) obviously; evidently

augen-, Augen-: ~weide *die* feast for the eyes; **~zeuge** *der,* **~zeugin** *die* eyewitness; **~zwinkernd** [1] *Adj.* tacit ‹*agreement*›; [2] *adv.* with a wink

August *der;* **~[e]s** *od.* **~, ~e** August

Auktion *die;* **~, ~en** auction

Aula *die;* **~, Aulen** *od.* **~s** hall

aus [1] *Präp. mit Dat.* **(a)** (aus dem Inneren von) out of
(b) (Herkunft, Quelle, Ausgangspunkt angebend, auch zeitlich) from; **~ Spanien/Köln** *usw.* from Spain/Cologne *etc.;*
(c) ~ der Mode/Übung sein be out of fashion/training
(d) (Grund, Ursache angebend) out of; **etw. ~ Erfahrung wissen** know sth. from experience; **~ Versehen** by mistake
(e) (bestehend ~) of; (hergestellt ~) made of; **~ etw. bestehen** consist of sth.
(f) ~ ihm ist ein guter Arzt geworden he made a good doctor
[2] *Adv.* **(a)** (ugs.: vorbei) over; **wann ist die Vorstellung ~?** what time does the performance end?; **die Schule ist ~** school is out; **~ jetzt!** that's enough
(b) (ausgeschaltet) off; (erloschen) out
(c) vom Fenster/obersten Stockwerk ~: from the window/top storey; **von mir ~** (ugs.) if you like; **von sich** (*Dat.*) **~:** of one's own accord

aus|atmen *itr., tr. V.* breathe out

aus|baden *tr. V.* (ugs.) carry *or* take the can for (Brit. coll.); take the rap for (coll.)

Aus·bau *der;* **~[e]s (a)** (Erweiterung) extension
(b) (Ausgestaltung) conversion (**zu** into)

aus|bauen *tr. V.* **(a)** (demontieren) remove (**aus** from)
(b) (erweitern) extend

Aus·beute *die* yield

aus|beuten *tr. V.* exploit

Ausbeutung *die;* **~, ~en** exploitation

aus|bilden *tr. V.* **(a)** train
(b) (entwickeln) develop

Aus·bildung *die* **(a)** training
(b) (Entwicklung) development

Aus·blick *der* view (**auf** + *Akk.* of)

aus|brechen *unr. itr. V., mit sein* **(a)** break out (**aus** of); (fig.) break free (**aus** from)
(b) jmdm. bricht der Schweiß aus sb. breaks into a sweat
(c) ‹*volcano*› erupt
(d) (beginnen) break out; ‹*crisis*› break
(e) in Gelächter/Weinen ~: burst out laughing/crying; **in Beifall/Tränen ~:** burst into applause/tears

aus|breiten [1] *tr. V.* spread; spread [out] ‹*map, cloth, sheet, etc.*›; open out ‹*fan, newspaper*›; (nebeneinander legen) spread out
[2] *refl. V.* spread

Aus·bruch *der* **(a)** (Flucht) escape (**aus** from)
(b) (Beginn) outbreak
(c) (Gefühlsausbruch) outburst
(d) (eines Vulkans) eruption

aus|brüten *tr. V.* hatch out; (im Brutkasten) incubate

aus|bürsten *tr. V.* brush out ‹*dust, dirt*› (**aus** of); brush ‹*clothes, upholstery, etc.*›

Aus·dauer *die* stamina

aus·dauernd *Adj.* with stamina *postpos.*

Ausdauer·training *das* stamina training

aus|dehnen [1] *tr. V.* **(a)** stretch; (fig.) extend (**auf** + *Akk.* to)
(b) (zeitlich) prolong
[2] *refl. V.* expand; (zeitlich) go on

Aus·dehnung *die* expansion; (fig.) extension; (zeitlich) prolongation

aus|denken *unr. refl. V.* **sich** (*Dat.*) **etw. ~:** think sth. up

aus|diskutieren *tr. V.* **etw. ~:** discuss sth. fully *or* thoroughly

Aus·druck *der; Pl.* **Ausdrücke** expression; (Terminus) term; **etw. zum ~ bringen** express sth.

aus|drucken *tr. V.* (Nachrichtenw., DV) print out

aus|drücken [1] *tr. V.* **(a)** (auspressen) squeeze ‹*juice*› out; squeeze [out] ‹*lemon, grape, orange, etc.*›; squeeze out ‹*sponge*›; squeeze ‹*boil, pimple*›
(b) stub out ‹*cigarette*›
(c) (mitteilen) express

···›

a

[2] *refl. V.* **(a)** express oneself
(b) (offenbar werden) be expressed

ausdrücklich /*od.* -ˈ--/ [1] *Adj.* express *attrib.* ‹*command, wish, etc.*›; explicit ‹*reservation*›
[2] *adv.* expressly; ‹*mention*› explicitly

ausdrucks-: ~los [1] *Adj.* expressionless; [2] *adv.* expressionlessly; **~voll** [1] *Adj.* expressive; [2] *adv.* expressively

aus·einander *Adv.* **(a)** (voneinander getrennt) apart; **etw. ~ schreiben** write sth. as separate words; **~ brechen** break up; **etw. ~ brechen** break sth. up; **~ gehen** part; ‹*crowd*› disperse; ‹*opinions, views*› differ; **zwei Dinge ~ halten** (unterscheiden) distinguish between two things; **ich kann die beiden Brüder nicht ~ halten** I cannot tell the two brothers apart; **etw. ~ nehmen** take sth. apart
(b) jmdm. etw. ~ setzen explain sth. to sb.; **sich mit jmdm. ~ setzen** have it out with sb.; **sich mit etw. ~ setzen** concern oneself with sth.

***auseinander|brechen** *usw.* ▶ AUSEINANDER

Auseinandersetzung *die;* **~, ~en (a)** (Streit) argument
(b) (Kampfhandlung) clash

Aus·fahrt *die* exit

Aus·fall *der* **(a)** (das Nichtstattfinden) cancellation
(b) (Einbuße, Verlust) loss
(c) (eines Motors) failure; (einer Maschine, eines Autos) breakdown

aus|fallen *unr. itr. V.; mit sein* **(a)** fall out
(b) (nicht stattfinden) be cancelled; **etw. ~ lassen** cancel sth.
(c) (ausscheiden) drop out
(d) (nicht mehr funktionieren) ‹*engine, brakes, signal*› fail; ‹*machine, car*› break down
(e) (ein bestimmtes Ergebnis zeigen) turn out

ausfallend *Adj.* **[gegen jmdn.] ~ sein/werden** be/become abusive [towards sb.]

Ausfall·straße *die* main road out of the/a town/city

aus·findig *Adv.* **jmdn./etw. ~ machen** find sb./sth.

Aus·flug *der* outing

Ausflügler *der;* **~s, ~, Ausflüglerin** *die;* **~, ~nen** day tripper; excursionist (Amer.)

Ausflugs-: ~dampfer *der* pleasure steamer; **~lokal** *das* restaurant/café catering for [day] trippers; **~verkehr** *der* (am Wochenende) weekend holiday traffic; (an Feiertagen) holiday traffic

aus|fragen *tr. V.* **jmdn. ~:** question sb., ask sb. questions (**nach, über** + *Akk.* about)

aus|fransen *itr. V.; mit sein* fray

Aus·fuhr *die;* **~, ~en** ▶ EXPORT

aus|führen *tr. V.* **(a)** (ausgehen mit) take ‹*person*› out
(b) (spazieren führen) take ‹*person, animal*› for a walk
(c) (exportieren) export
(d) (durchführen) carry out; (Sport) take ‹*penalty, free kick, corner*›

ausführlich /*auch:* -ˈ--/ [1] *Adj.* detailed; full
[2] *adv.* in detail

Ausfuhr·sperre *die* ▶ AUSFUHRVERBOT

Aus·führung *die* (Durchführung) carrying out; (Sport) taking

Ausfuhr·verbot *das* (Wirtsch.) export embargo

aus|füllen *tr. V.* **(a)** fill; fill in ‹*form, crossword puzzle*›
(b) (beanspruchen, einnehmen) take up ‹*space*›

Aus·gabe *die* **(a)** giving out; (von Essen) serving
(b) (Geldausgabe) item of expenditure; **~n** expenditure *sing.* (**für** on)
(c) (Edition) edition
(d) (DV) output

Ausgabe·gerät *das* (DV) output device

Aus·gang *der* **(a)** (Erlaubnis zum Ausgehen) time off; (von Soldaten) leave
(b) (Tür ins Freie) exit (*Gen.* from)
(c) (Anat.) outlet
(d) (Ende) end; (eines Romans, Films usw.) ending
(e) (Ergebnis) outcome; (eines Wettbewerbs) result; **ein Unfall mit tödlichem ~:** an accident with fatal consequences

Ausgangs-: ~punkt *der* starting point; **~sperre** *die* (bes. Milit.) (für Zivilisten) curfew; (für Soldaten) confinement to barracks; **[eine] ~sperre verhängen** impose a curfew/confine the soldiers/regiment *etc.* to barracks

aus|geben *unr. tr. V.* **(a)** give out; serve ‹*food, drinks*›
(b) (verbrauchen) spend ‹*money*› (**für** on)

ausgebucht *Adj.* booked up

ausgedehnt *Adj.* extensive

aus·gefallen *Adj.* unusual

Ausgeflippte *der/die; adj. Dekl.* (salopp) dropout (coll.)

ausgeglichen *Adj.* balanced; well-balanced ‹*person*›; equable ‹*climate*›

aus|gehen *unr. itr. V.; mit sein* **(a)** go out
(b) (fast aufgebraucht sein) run out
(c) (enden) end; **gut/schlecht ~:** turn out well/badly; ‹*story, film*› end happily/unhappily
(d) von jmdm./etw. ~: come from sb./sth.
(e) von etw. ~ (etw. zugrunde legen) take sth. as one's starting point; (etw. annehmen) assume sth.

aus·gelassen [1] *Adj.* exuberant ‹*mood, person*›; lively ‹*party, celebration*›; (wild) boisterous
[2] *adv.* exuberantly; (wild) boisterously

---

*old spelling - see note on page xiv

aus·gemacht *Adj.* **(a)** (beschlossen) agreed; **es ist [eine] ~e Sache, dass ...** it is an accepted fact that ...
(b) (vollkommen) complete; complete, utter ‹*nonsense*›; **eine ~e Dummheit** downright stupidity

aus·genommen *Konj.* except

ausgeprägt *Adj.* marked

ausgerechnet *Adv.* (*ugs.*) **~ heute/morgen** today/tomorrow of all days; **~ hier** here of all places; **~ Sie** you of all people

aus·geschlossen *Adj.* **das ist ~:** that is out of the question

aus·geschnitten *Adj.* low-cut ‹*dress, blouse, etc.*›

aus·gesprochen **1** *Adj.* definite, marked ‹*preference, inclination, resemblance*›; pronounced ‹*dislike*›; marked ‹*contrast*›; **~es Pech/Glück haben** be decidedly unlucky/lucky; **ein ~es Talent für etw.** a definite talent for sth.; **ein ~er Gegner von etw. sein** be a strong opponent of sth.
2 *adv.* (besonders) decidedly; downright ‹*stupid, ridiculous, ugly*›

aus·gestorben *Adj.* **[wie] ~:** deserted

aus·gewogen *Adj.* (ausgeglichen) balanced; [well-]balanced ‹*personality*›

Aus·gewogenheit *die;* **~:** balance

ausgezeichnet /*od.* '--'--/ **1** *Adj.* excellent; outstanding ‹*expert*›
2 *adv.* excellently

ausgiebig **1** *Adj.* substantial ‹*meal*›
2 *adv.* ‹*profit*› handsomely; ‹*read*› extensively; **von etw. ~ Gebrauch machen** make full use of sth.

aus|gießen *unr. tr. V.* **(a)** pour out (**aus** of)
(b) (leeren) empty

Ausgleich *der;* **~[e]s, ~e (a)** ▶ AUSGLEICHEN A: evening out; reconciliation
(b) (Schadensersatz) compensation; **als** *od.* **zum ~ für etw.** to make up for sth.

aus|gleichen *unr. tr. V.* **(a)** even out; reconcile ‹*differences of opinions, contradictions*›
(b) compensate for ‹*damage*›; make up for ‹*misfortune, lack*›; **etw. durch etw. ~:** make up for sth. with sth.; **sich ~:** balance out; (sich gegenseitig aufheben) cancel each other out

aus|graben *unr. tr. V.* dig up; (Archäol.) excavate

Aus·grabung *die* (Archäol.) excavation

Aus·guss, *Aus·guß *der* sink

aus|halten *unr. tr. V.* stand; bear; endure; withstand ‹*attack, load, pressure, test, wear and tear*›; **er konnte es zu Hause nicht mehr ~:** he couldn't stand it at home any more; **es ist nicht zum Aushalten** it is unbearable

aus|handeln *tr. V.* negotiate

aus|händigen *tr. V.* hand over

Aus·hang *der* notice; **einen ~ machen** put up a notice

aus|heben *unr. tr. V.* dig out ‹*earth etc.*›; dig ‹*trench, grave, etc.*›

aus|helfen *unr. itr. V.* help out; **jmdm. ~:** help sb. out (**mit, bei** with)

Aus·hilfe *die* **(a)** (das Aushelfen) help
(b) ▶ AUSHILFSKRAFT

aushilfs-, Aushilfs-: ~kraft *die* temporary worker; (in Läden, Gaststätten) temporary assistant; (Sekretärin) temporary secretary; temp (coll.); **~lehrer** *der,* **~lehrerin,** *die* supply teacher; **~weise** *adv.* on a temporary basis

aus|holen *itr. V.* **[mit dem Arm] ~:** draw back one's arm; (zum Schlag) raise one's arm

aus|kennen *unr. refl. V.* (an einem Ort usw.) know one's way around; (in einem Fach, einer Angelegenheit usw.) know what's what; **sie kennt sich in dieser Stadt aus** she knows her way around the town; **sich [gut] mit/in etw.** (*Dat.*) **~:** know [a lot] about sth.

Aus·klang *der* (geh.) end; **zum ~ des Festes** to end *or* close the festival

aus|kleiden *tr. V.* (geh.) undress; **sich ~:** undress

aus|klingen *unr. itr. V.; mit sein* end

aus|klopfen *tr. V.* **(a)** beat out (**aus** + *Dat.* of)
(b) (säubern) beat ‹*carpet*›; knock ‹*pipe*› out

aus|kochen *tr. V.* boil; (keimfrei machen) sterilize ‹*instruments etc.*› [in boiling water]

aus|kommen *unr. itr. V.; mit sein* **(a)** manage (**mit** on)
(b) mit jmdm. [gut] ~: get on [well] with sb.

Auskommen *das;* **~s** livelihood

Auskunft *die;* **~, Auskünfte (a)** piece of information; **Auskünfte** information *sing.;* **[jmdm. über etw.** (*Akk.*)**] ~ geben** give [sb.] information [about sth.]
(b) (Stelle) information desk/counter/office/centre *etc.;* (Fernspr.) directory enquiries *no art.* (Brit.); directory information *no art.* (Amer.)

Auskunftei *die;* **~, ~en** private detective agency; (Kredit~) credit reference agency

Auskunfts-: ~büro *das* information office; enquiry office (Brit.); **~schalter** *der* information counter; **~stelle** *die* information office

aus|kungeln *tr. V.* (ugs.) reach by wheeling and dealing

aus|kurieren *tr. V.* heal ‹*wound*› [completely]

aus|lachen *tr. V.* laugh at

aus|laden *unr. tr. V.* unload ‹*goods etc.*›

Aus·lage *die* **(a)** *Pl.* (Unkosten) expenses
(b) (ausgestellte Ware) item on display; **~n** goods on display

aus|lagern *tr. V.* **(a)** remove ‹*art treasures*› for safe-keeping
(b) relocate ‹*firm, activity*› (**nach** to); (an einen externen Dienstleister) outsource ‹*function, activity*›

Aus·land *das* foreign countries *pl.;* **im/ins ~:** abroad; **aus dem ~:** from abroad
Ausländer *der;* **~s, ~, Ausländerin** *die;* **~, ~nen** foreigner
ausländer·feindlich *Adj.* hostile to foreigners *postpos.*
ausländisch *Adj.* foreign
Auslands-: ~aufenthalt *der* stay abroad; **~gespräch** *das* (Fernspr.) international call; **~korrespondent** *der,* **~korrespondentin** *die* foreign correspondent; **~reise** *die* trip abroad
aus|lassen *unr. tr. V.* **(a)** (weglassen) leave out
(b) (versäumen) miss ‹*opportunity, chance, etc.*›
Auslauf *der* **(a) keinen/zu wenig ~ haben** have no/too little chance to run around outside
(b) (Raum) space to run around in
aus|laufen *unr. itr. V.; mit sein* **(a)** run out (**aus** of)
(b) (leer laufen) empty; ‹*egg*› run out
(c) (in See stechen) sail (**nach** for)
(d) (erlöschen) ‹*contract, agreement, etc.*› run out
Aus·läufer *der* **(a)** (Geogr.) foothill *usu. in pl.;*
(b) (Met.) (eines Hochs) ridge; (eines Tiefs) trough
aus|legen *tr. V.* **(a)** (hinlegen) lay out; display ‹*goods, exhibits*›
(b) etw. mit Fliesen/Teppichboden ~: tile/carpet sth.
(c) (leihen) lend
(d) (interpretieren) interpret; **etw. falsch ~:** misinterpret sth.
Auslegung *die;* **~, ~en** interpretation
aus|leihen *unr. tr. V.* ▶ LEIHEN
aus|liefern *tr. V.* **(a) jmdm. etw.** *od.* **etw. an jmdn. ~:** hand sth. over to sb.
(b) *auch itr.* (Kaufmannsspr.: liefern) deliver
Aus·lieferung *die* **(a)** (Übergabe) handing over; (an ein Land) extradition; **jmds. ~ fordern** demand that sb. be handed over/extradited
(b) (Kaufmannsspr.: Lieferung) delivery
Auslieferungs-: ~antrag *der* application for extradition; **~lager** *das* (Wirtsch.) distribution centre
aus|loggen *refl. V.* (DV) log off *or* out
aus|löschen *tr. V.* **(a)** extinguish
(b) (beseitigen) erase ‹*drawing, writing*›
aus|losen *tr. V.* **etw. ~:** draw lots for sth.
aus|lösen *tr. V.* **(a)** trigger ‹*mechanism, device, alarm, etc.*›; release ‹*camera shutter*›
(b) provoke ‹*discussion, anger, laughter, reaction, outrage, heart attack*›; cause ‹*sorrow, horror, surprise, disappointment, panic, war*›; excite, arouse ‹*interest, enthusiasm*›
Auslöser *der;* **~s, ~** (Fot.) shutter release

*alte Schreibung - vgl. Hinweis auf S. xiv

aus|machen *tr. V.* **(a)** (ugs.) put out ‹*light, fire, cigarette, candle*›; switch off ‹*television, radio, hi-fi*›; turn off ‹*gas*›
(b) (vereinbaren) agree [on]; **~, dass ...:** agree that ...
(c) (auszeichnen, kennzeichnen) make up
(d) wenig/nichts/viel ~: make little/no/a great difference
(e) das macht mir nichts aus I don't mind
Aus·maß *das* **(a)** (Größe) size
(b) (Grad) extent
aus|messen *unr. tr. V.* measure up
Aus·nahme *die;* **~, ~n** exception; **mit ~ von** with the exception of; **bei jmdm. eine ~ machen** make an exception in sb.'s case
Ausnahme-: ~erscheinung *die* exceptional phenomenon; **~zustand** *der* state of emergency
ausnahms-: ~los **1** *Adj.* unanimous ‹*approval, agreement*›; **2** *adv.* without exception; **~weise** *Adv.* by way of an exception; **Dürfen wir mitkommen? – Ausnahmsweise [ja]** May we come too? – Yes, just this once
aus|nehmen *unr. tr. V.* **(a)** gut ‹*fish, rabbit, chicken*›
(b) (ausschließen von) exclude; (gesondert behandeln) make an exception of
aus|nüchtern *tr., itr., refl. V.* sober up
Ausnüchterung *die;* **~, ~en** sobering up; **jmdn. zur ~ auf die Wache bringen** take sb. to the [police] station to sober up
Ausnüchterungs·zelle *die* drying-out cell
aus|nutzen, (bes. südd., österr.) **aus|nützen** *tr. V.* **(a)** take advantage of
(b) (ausbeuten) exploit
Aus·nutzung *die,* (bes. südd., österr.) **Ausnützung** *die;* **~:** use; (Ausbeutung) exploitation; **unter voller ~ einer Sache** (*Gen.*) making full use of sth.
aus|packen **1** *tr., itr. V.* unpack; (auswickeln) unwrap
2 *itr. V.* (ugs.) (Geheimnisse verraten) talk (coll.); squeal (sl.)
aus|pressen *tr. V.* squeeze out ‹*juice*›; squeeze ‹*orange, lemon*›; (keltern) press ‹*grapes etc.*›
aus|probieren *tr. V.* try out
Aus·puff *der* exhaust
Auspuffgase *Pl.* exhaust fumes *pl.*
aus|radieren *tr. V.* rub out; erase
aus|rangieren *tr. V.* (ugs.) throw out; discard; scrap ‹*vehicle, machine*›; **ausrangierte Fahrzeuge** scrap vehicles
aus|rasten *itr. V.; mit sein* (Technik) disengage; **er rastete aus, es rastete bei ihm aus** (fig. salopp) something snapped in him
aus|rauben *tr. V.* rob
aus|räuchern *tr. V.* (auch fig.) smoke out; fumigate ‹*room*›
aus|räumen **1** *tr. V.* **(a)** clear out (**aus** of)

(b) (fig.) clear up; dispel ‹*prejudice, suspicion, misgivings*›
2 *itr. V.* clear everything out

aus|rechnen *tr. V.* work out; **das kannst du dir leicht ~** (ugs.) you can easily work that out [for yourself]

Aus·rede *die* excuse

aus|reden **1** *itr. V.* finish [speaking]
2 *tr. V.* **jmdm. etw. ~:** talk sb. out of sth.

aus|reichen *itr. V.* be enough *or* sufficient (**zu** for)

ausreichend **1** *Adj.* sufficient; enough; (als Note) fair
2 *adv.* sufficiently

Aus·reise *die:* **jmdm. die ~ verweigern** refuse sb. permission to leave [the/a country], **vor/bei der ~:** before/when leaving the country

Ausreise·antrag *der* application to leave the country; application for an exit visa

aus|reißen **1** *unr. tr. V.* tear out; pull out ‹*plants, weeds*›
2 *unr. itr. V.; mit sein* **(a)** (sich lösen) come off
(b) (ugs.: weglaufen) run away (*Dat.* from)

aus|renken *tr. V.* dislocate

aus|richten *tr. V.* **(a) jmdm. etw. ~:** tell sb. sth.
(b) (einheitlich anordnen) line up
(c) (erreichen) achieve

aus|rollen *tr. V.* roll out

aus|rotten *tr. V.* eradicate

Aus·ruf *der* cry

aus|rufen *unr. tr. V.* **(a)** call out; **„Schön!", rief er aus** 'Lovely', he exclaimed
(b) (offiziell verkünden) proclaim; declare ‹*state of emergency*›
(c) (zum Kauf anbieten) cry

Ausrufe·zeichen *das* exclamation mark

aus|ruhen *refl., itr. V.* have a rest; **[sich] ein wenig/richtig ~:** rest a little/have a good rest; **ausgeruht sein** be rested

aus|rüsten *tr. V.* equip

Aus·rüstung *die* **(a)** equipping
(b) (Gegenstände) equipment *no pl.*

Ausrüstungs·gegenstand *der* item of equipment

aus|rutschen *itr. V.; mit sein* slip

aus|säen *tr.* (*auch itr.*) *V.* (auch fig.) sow

Aus·sage *die* statement

aussage-, Aussage-: ~kraft *die* meaningfulness; (Ausdruckskraft) expressiveness; **~kräftig** *Adj.* meaningful; (ausdruckskräftig) expressive

aus|sagen **1** *tr. V.* **(a)** say
(b) (vor Gericht, vor der Polizei) state; (unter Eid) testify
2 *itr. V.* make a statement; (unter Eid) testify

aus|saugen *regelm.* (*geh. auch unr.*) *tr. V.* **(a)** suck out (**aus** of); (leer saugen) suck dry
(b) (fig.: ausbeuten) **jmdn./etw. ~:** bleed sb./sth. [white]; **jmdn. bis aufs Blut** *od.* **Mark ~:** bleed sb. white

aus|schaben *tr. V.* **(a)** scrape out
(b) (Med.) remove; (mit der Kürette) curette

aus|schalten *tr. V.* **(a)** switch *or* turn off
(b) (fig.) eliminate; exclude ‹*emotion, influence*›; dismiss ‹*doubt, objection*›; shut out ‹*feeling, thought*›

Aus·schank *der;* **~[e]s** serving

Aus·schau *die:* **nach jmdm./etw. ~ halten** keep a lookout for sb./sth.

aus|schauen *itr. V.* **nach jmdm./etw. ~:** look out for sb./sth.

aus|scheiden **1** *unr. itr. V.; mit sein* **(a) aus etw. ~:** leave sth.; **aus dem Amt ~:** leave office
(b) (Sport) be eliminated
(c) diese Möglichkeit/dieser Kandidat scheidet aus this possibility/candidate has to be ruled out
2 *unr. tr. V.* (Physiol.) excrete ‹*waste*›; eliminate, expel ‹*poison*›; exude ‹*sweat*›

Aus·scheidung *die* **(a)** (Physiol.) ▶ AUSSCHEIDEN 2: excretion; elimination; expulsion; exudation; **~en** (Ausgeschiedenes) excreta
(b) (Sport) qualifier

aus|schenken *tr. V.* serve

aus|scheren *itr. V.; mit sein* pull out

aus|schildern *tr. V.* signpost

aus|schimpfen *tr. V.* **jmdn. ~:** tell sb. off

aus|schlachten *tr. V.* **(a)** (ugs.: brauchbare Teile ausbauen aus) cannibalize ‹*machine, vehicle*›; break ‹*vehicle*› for spares
(b) (ugs. abwertend: ausnutzen) exploit; **etw. politisch ~:** make political capital out of sth.

aus|schlafen **1** *unr. itr., refl. V.* have a good sleep
2 *unr. tr. V.* **seinen Rausch ~:** sleep off the effects of alcohol

Aus·schlag *der* **(a)** (Hautausschlag) rash
(b) (eines Zeigers, einer Waage) deflection; (eines Pendels) swing; **den ~ geben** (fig.) tip the scales (fig.)

aus|schlagen **1** *unr. tr. V.* **(a)** knock out
(b) (ablehnen) turn down
2 *unr. itr. V.* **(a)** ‹*horse*› kick
(b) ‹*needle, pointer*› be deflected, swing
(c) (sprießen) come out [in bud]

ausschlag·gebend *Adj.* decisive

aus|schließen *unr. tr. V.* **(a)** (ausstoßen) expel (**aus** from)
(b) (nicht teilnehmen lassen) exclude (**aus** from)
(c) (fig.) rule out ‹*possibility*›; **jeden Irrtum ~:** rule out all possibility of error
(d) (aussperren) lock out

aus·schließlich /od. '-'--, -'--/ **1** *Adj.* exclusive
2 *Adv.* exclusively
3 *Präp. mit Gen.* excluding

a

Ausschließlichkeit *die; ~:* exclusiveness

Aus·schluss, *Aus·schluß *der* exclusion (**von** from); (aus einer Gemeinschaft) expulsion (**aus** from); **unter ~ der Öffentlichkeit** with the public excluded; (Rechtsw.) in camera

aus|schmücken *tr. V.* deck out

aus|schneiden *unr. tr. V.* cut out; (DV) cut

Aus·schnitt *der* **(a)** (Zeitungsausschnitt) cutting; clipping
(b) (Halsausschnitt) neck; **ein tiefer ~:** a plunging neckline
(c) (Teil) part; (eines Textes) excerpt; (eines Films) clip; (Bildausschnitt) detail

aus|schreiben *unr. tr. V.* **(a)** (nicht abgekürzt schreiben) **etw. ~:** write sth. out in full
(b) (ausstellen) make out ‹*cheque, invoice, receipt*›
(c) (bekannt geben) call ‹*election, meeting*›; advertise ‹*flat, job*›; put ‹*supply order etc.*› out to tender

Aus·schreibung *die* ▶ AUSSCHREIBEN C: calling; advertisement; invitation to tender

Ausschreitungen *Pl.* acts of violence

Aus·schuss, *Aus·schuß *der* committee

aus|schütten *tr. V.* tip out ‹*water, sand, coal, etc.*›; (ausleeren) empty ‹*bucket, bowl, container*›

ausschweifend [1] *Adj.* wild ‹*imagination, emotion, hope, desire, orgy*›; extravagant ‹*idea*›; riotous, wild ‹*enjoyment*›; dissolute ‹*life, person*›
[2] *adv.* **~ leben** lead a dissolute life

Ausschweifung *die; ~, ~en* (im Genießen) dissolution

aus|sehen *unr. itr. V.* look (**wie** like); **so siehst du aus!** (ugs.) that's what you think!

Aussehen *das; ~s* appearance

***aus|sein** *unr. itr. V.; mit sein; nur im Inf. und Part. zusammengeschrieben* **(a)** ‹*play, film, war*› be over; **wann ist die Vorstellung aus?** what time does the performance end?; **die Schule ist aus** school is out
(b) ‹*fire, candle, etc.*› be out
(c) ‹*radio, light, etc.*› be off

außen *Adv.* outside; **die Vase ist ~ bemalt** the vase is painted on the outside; **das Fenster geht nach ~ auf** the window opens outwards; **von ~:** from the outside

außen-, Außen-: ~dienst *der:* **im ~dienst sein** *od.* **arbeiten, ~dienst machen** *od.* **haben** be working out of the office; ‹*salesman*› be on the road; **~handel** *der* foreign trade *no art.;* **~handels·bilanz** *die* balance of trade; **~minister** *der,* **~ministerin** *die* Foreign Minister; **~ministerium** *das* Foreign Ministry; **~politik** *die* foreign politics *sing.;* **~politisch** [1] *Adj.* ‹*question*› relating to foreign policy; [2] *adv.* as regards foreign policy; **~seite** *die* outside

Außenseiter *der; ~s, ~,* **Außenseiterin** *die; ~, ~nen* outsider

Außen: ~spiegel *der* exterior mirror; **~stände** *Pl.* outstanding debts *or* accounts; **~wand** *die* external *or* outside wall; **~welt** *die* outside world

außer [1] *Präp. mit Dat.* **(a)** (abgesehen von) apart from; aside from (Amer.)
(b) (außerhalb von) out of; **~ sich sein** be beside oneself (**vor** + *Dat.* with)
(c) (zusätzlich zu) in addition to
[2] *Präp. mit Akk.* **~ sich geraten** become beside oneself (**vor** + *Dat.* with)
[3] *Konj.* except

äußer... *Adj.* outer; outside ‹*pocket*›; outlying ‹*district, area*›; external ‹*injury, form, circumstances, cause, force*›; outward ‹*appearance, similarity, effect, etc.*›; foreign ‹*affairs*›

außer·dem /*auch:* --'-/ *Adv.* as well; (überdies) besides

Äußere *das; adj. Dekl.* [outward] appearance

außer-: ~ehelich [1] *Adj.* extra-marital; illegitimate ‹*child, birth*›; [2] *adv.* outside marriage; **~gewöhnlich** [1] *Adj.* **(a)** unusual; **(b)** (das Gewohnte übertreffend) exceptional; [2] *adv.* **(a)** unusually; **(b)** (sehr) exceptionally; **~halb** *Präp. mit Gen.* outside

äußerlich [1] *Adj.* external ‹*use, injury*›; outward ‹*appearance, calm, similarity, etc.*›
[2] *adv.: s. Adj.:* externally; outwardly

Äußerlichkeit *die; ~, ~en* formality; (Unwesentliches) minor point

äußern [1] *tr. V.* express, voice ‹*opinion, view, criticism, reservations, disapproval, doubt*›; express ‹*wish*›; voice ‹*suspicion*›
[2] *refl. V.* **(a) sich über etw.** (*Akk.*) **~:** give one's view on sth.
(b) ‹*illness*› manifest itself (**in** + *Dat.*, **durch** in)

außer-: ~ordentlich [1] *Adj.* **(a)** extraordinary; **(b)** (das Gewohnte übertreffend) exceptional; [2] *adv.* (sehr) exceptionally; extremely ‹*pleased, relieved*›; **~schulisch** *Adj.* outside the school *postpos.*

äußerst *Adv.* extremely

äußerst... *Adj.* **(a)** extreme
(b) (letztmöglich) latest possible ‹*date, deadline*›; (höchst...) highest ‹*price*›; (niedrigst...) lowest ‹*price*›
(c) (schlimmst...) worst

außerstande *Adv.* **~ sein, etw. zu tun** (nicht befähigt) be unable to do sth.; (nicht in der Lage) not be in a position to do sth.

Äußerung *die; ~, ~en* comment

aus|setzen [1] *tr. V.* **(a)** expose (*Dat.* to); **Belastungen ausgesetzt sein** be subject to strains

---

*old spelling - see note on page xiv

(b) (sich selbst überlassen) abandon ‹*baby, animal*›; (auf einer einsamen Insel) maroon
(c) an jmdm./etw. etwas auszusetzen haben find fault with sb./sth.
[2] *itr. V.* **(a)** (aufhören) stop; ‹*engine, machine*› cut out
(b) (pausieren) ‹*player*› miss a turn; **mit der Arbeit/dem Training [ein paar Wochen] ~:** stop work/training [for a few weeks]

Aus·sicht *die* **(a)** view (**auf** + *Akk.* of)
(b) (fig.) prospect; **~ auf etw.** (*Akk.*) **haben, etw. in ~ haben** have the prospect of sth.

aussichts-, Aussichts-: ~los [1] *Adj.* hopeless; [2] *adv.* hopelessly; **~losigkeit** *die; ~~:* hopelessness; **~punkt** *der* vantage point; **~reich** *Adj.* promising; **~turm** *der* lookout tower

Aus·siedler *der* (Auswanderer) emigrant; (Evakuierter) evacuee; (Umsiedler) resettled person

Aussiedler·heim *das* resettlement hostel (*for German nationals and ethnic Germans from Eastern europe*)

Aussiedlerin *die* ▶ AUSSIEDLER

aus|sortieren *tr. V.* sort out

aus|spannen *itr. V.* take *or* have a break

aus|sparen *tr. V.* leave ‹*line etc.*› blank; (fig.) leave out; omit

Aussparung *die; ~, ~en* **(a)** (das Aussparen) leaving blank
(b) (Stelle) gap

aus|sperren [1] *tr. V.* lock out; shut ‹*animal*› out
[2] *itr. V.* lock the workforce out

Aus·sperrung *die* lockout

aus|spielen *tr. V.* **(a)** *auch itr.* (Kartenspiel) lead
(b) jmdn./etw. gegen jmdn./etw. ~: play sb./sth. off against sb./sth.

Aus·sprache *die* **(a)** pronunciation
(b) (Gespräch) discussion

aus|sprechen [1] *unr. tr. V.* **(a)** pronounce
(b) (ausdrücken) express; voice ‹*suspicion, request*›
[2] *unr. refl. V.* **(a) sich lobend/missbilligend** *usw.* **über jmdn./etw. ~:** speak highly/disapprovingly of *etc.* sb./sth.
(b) (offen sprechen) say what's on one's mind; **sich bei jmdm. ~:** have a heart-to-heart talk with sb.
(c) (Strittiges klären) talk things out (**mit** with)
[3] *unr. itr. V.* (zu Ende sprechen) finish [speaking]

Aus·spruch *der* remark

aus|spucken [1] *itr. V.* spit
[2] *tr. V.* spit out

aus|spülen *tr. V.* rinse out

Aus·stand *der* strike

aus|statten /ˈauːsʃtatn̩/ *tr. V.* provide (**mit** with); (mit Gerät) equip; (mit Möbeln, Teppichen, Gardinen usw.) furnish

Ausstattung *die; ~, ~en* **(a)** ▶ AUSSTATTEN provision; equipping; furnishing
(b) (Ausrüstung) equipment; (Innenausstattung eines Autos) trim
(c) (Einrichtung) furnishings *pl.*

aus|stehen [1] *unr. itr. V.* **noch ~** ‹*debt*› be outstanding; ‹*decision*› be still to be taken; ‹*solution*› be still to be found
[2] *unr. tr. V.* **ich kann ihn/das nicht ~:** I can't stand him/it

aus|steigen *unr. itr. V.;* **(a)** *mit sein* get out; (aus einem Zug, Bus) get off
(b) (ugs.: sich nicht mehr beteiligen) **~ aus** opt out of; give up ‹*show business, job*›; leave ‹*project;*›
(c) (ugs.: der Gesellschaft den Rücken kehren) drop out

Aussteiger *der; ~s, ~,* **Aussteigerin** *die; ~, ~nen* (ugs.) dropout (coll.)

aus|stellen *tr. V.* **(a)** put on display; display; (im Museum, auf einer Messe) exhibit
(b) (ausfertigen) make out ‹*cheque, prescription, receipt, bill*›; issue ‹*visa, passport, certificate*›; **einen Scheck auf jmdn. ~:** make out a cheque to sb.
(c) (ugs.: ausschalten) switch off ‹*cooker, radio, heating, engine*›

Aus·stellung *die* **(a)** exhibition
(b) ▶ AUSSTELLEN B: making out; issuing

Ausstellungs-: ~gelände *das* exhibition site; **~katalog** *der* exhibition catalogue

aus|sterben *unr. itr. V.; mit sein* die out; ‹*species*› become extinct; **vom Aussterben bedroht sein** be threatened with extinction

Aus·steuer *die* trousseau (*consisting mainly of household linen*)

Ausstieg *der: ~[e]s, ~e* **(a)** exit
(b) (ugs.) opting out (**aus** of); **der ~ aus einem Projekt/aus der Atomenergie** leaving a project/abandoning nuclear energy

aus|stopfen *tr. V.* stuff

Aus·stoß *der* (Wirtsch.) output

aus|stoßen *unr. tr. V.* **(a)** expel; give off, emit ‹*gas, fumes, smoke*›
(b) give ‹*cry, whistle, laugh, sigh, etc.*›; let out ‹*cry, scream, yell*›; utter ‹*curse, threat, etc.*›

aus|strahlen [1] *tr. V.* **(a)** (auch fig.) radiate; ‹*lamp*› give out ‹*light*›
(b) (Rundf., Ferns.) broadcast
[2] *itr. V.* **(a)** radiate; ‹*light*› be given out; (fig.) ‹*pain*› spread
(b) auf jmdn./etw. ~ (fig.) communicate itself to sb./influence sth.

Aus·strahlung *die* (fig.) charisma

aus|strecken [1] *tr. V.* stretch out; put out ‹*feelers*›
[2] *refl. V.* stretch out

aus|streichen *unr. tr. V.* cross out

aus|strömen *itr. V.; mit sein* pour out; ‹*gas, steam*› escape

a

aus|suchen *tr. V.* choose; pick
Aus·tausch *der* **(a)** exchange; **im ~ für** *od.* **gegen** in exchange for
(b) (das Ersetzen) replacement (**gegen** with)
aus|tauschen *tr. V.* **(a)** exchange (**gegen** for)
(b) (ersetzen) replace (**gegen** with)
Austausch-: ~motor *der* replacement engine; **~schüler** *der,* **~schülerin** *die* exchange pupil *or* student
aus|teilen *tr. V.* distribute (**an** + *Akk.* to); (aushändigen) hand out ‹*books, post, etc.*› (**an** + *Akk.* to); give ‹*orders*›; deal [out] ‹*cards*›; give out ‹*marks, grades*›; serve ‹*food etc.*›
Auster *die;* **~, ~n** oyster
aus|tragen *unr. tr. V.* **(a)** deliver ‹*newspapers, post*›
(b) ‹*pregnant woman*› carry ‹*child*› to full term; (nicht abtreiben) have ‹*child*›
(c) (ausfechten) settle ‹*conflict, differences*›; fight out ‹*battle*›
Australien /au:s'tra:li̯ən/ (*das*)*;* **~s** Australia
Australier *der;* **~s, ~, Australierin** *die;* **~, ~nen** Australian
australisch *Adj.* Australian
aus|treiben *unr. tr. V.* **(a)** exorcize, cast out ‹*evil spirit, demon*›
(b) jmdm. etw. ~: cure sb. of sth.
aus|treten [1] *unr. tr. V.* **(a)** tread out ‹*spark, cigarette end*›; trample out ‹*fire*›
(b) (bahnen) tread out ‹*path*›
(c) wear out ‹*shoes*›
[2] *unr. itr. V.; mit sein* **(a)** (ugs.: zur Toilette gehen) pay a call (coll.)
(b) aus etw. ~ (ausscheiden) leave sth.
aus|trinken *tr. V.* drink up ‹*drink*›; finish ‹*glass, cup, etc.*›
Aus·tritt *der* leaving
aus|trocknen [1] *tr. V.* dry out; dry up ‹*river bed, marsh*›
[2] *itr. V.; mit sein* dry out; ‹*river bed, pond, etc.*› dry up; ‹*skin, hair*› become dry
aus|üben *tr. V.* practise ‹*art, craft*›; follow ‹*profession*›; carry on ‹*trade*›; do ‹*job*›; hold ‹*office*›; wield ‹*power, right, control*›
Aus·verkauf *der* sale
ausverkauft *Adj.* sold out
Aus·wahl *die* **(a)** choice
(b) (Sortiment) range; **viel/wenig ~ haben** have a wide/limited selection (**an** + *Dat.,* **von** of)
aus|wählen *tr. V.* choose (**aus** from)
Aus·wanderer *der,* **Aus·wanderin** *die* emigrant
aus|wandern *itr. V.; mit sein* emigrate
Aus·wanderung *die* emigration
auswärtig *Adj.* **(a)** non-local
(b) (das Ausland betreffend) foreign
auswärts *Adv.* **(a)** (nach außen) outwards
(b) (nicht zu Hause) ‹*sleep*› away from home; **~ essen** eat out
(c) (nicht am Ort) in another town; (Sport) away
Auswärts·spiel *das* (Sport) away match
aus|waschen *unr. tr. V.* wash out
aus|wechseln *tr. V.* **(a)** change (**gegen** + *Akk.* for)
(b) (ersetzen) replace (**gegen** with); (Sport) substitute ‹*player*›
Aus·weg *der* way out (**aus** of)
ausweg·los [1] *Adj.* hopeless
[2] *adv.* hopelessly
Ausweglosigkeit *die;* **~:** hopelessness
aus|weichen *unr. itr. V.; mit sein* get out of the way (*Dat.* of); (Platz machen) make way (*Dat.* for); **einem Schlag/Angriff ~:** dodge a blow/evade an attack; **dem Feind ~:** avoid [contact with] the enemy; **einer Frage ~:** evade a question; **eine ~de Antwort** an evasive answer
Ausweich·manöver *das* evasive manœuvre
aus|weinen *refl. V.* have a good cry; **sie hat sich bei mir darüber ausgeweint** (ugs.) she had a good cry on my shoulder about it
Ausweis *der;* **~es, ~e** card; (Personalausweis) identity card
aus|weisen [1] *unr. tr. V.* **(a)** expel (**aus** from)
(b) jmdn. als etw. ~: show that sb. is/was sth.
[2] *unr. refl. V.* prove *or* establish one's identity [by showing one's papers]; **können Sie sich ~?** do you have any means of identification?
Ausweis·papiere *Pl.* identity papers
Aus·weisung *die* expulsion (**aus** from)
aus|weiten *tr. V.* stretch
aus·wendig *Adv.* **etw. ~ können/lernen** know/learn sth. [off] by heart
aus|werfen *unr. tr. V.* **(a)** cast ‹*net, anchor, rope, line, etc.*›
(b) (herausschleudern) throw out ‹*sparks*›; ‹*volcano*› eject, spew out ‹*lava, ash, etc.*›; eject ‹*cartridge case*›
aus|werten *tr. V.* analyse and evaluate
Aus·wertung *die* analysis and evaluation
aus|wirken *refl. V.* have an effect (**auf** + *Akk.* on); **sich günstig ~:** have a favourable effect
Aus·wirkung *die* effect (**auf** + *Akk.* on)
Aus·wuchs *der* **(a)** (Wucherung) growth; excrescence (Med., Bot.)
(b) (fig.) unhealthy product; (Exzess) excess
aus|wuchten *tr. V.* (Technik) **die Räder ~:** balance the wheels
aus|zahlen [1] *tr. V.* **(a)** pay out ‹*money*›
(b) pay off ‹*employee, worker*›; buy out ‹*business partner*›
[2] *refl. V.* pay
aus|zählen *tr. V.* **(a)** count [up] ‹*votes etc.*›
(b) (Boxen) count out

---
*alte Schreibung - vgl. Hinweis auf S. xiv

aus|zeichnen *tr. V.* **(a)** (mit einem Preisschild) mark
(b) (ehren) honour

Aus·zeichnung *die* **(a)** (von Waren) marking
(b) (Ehrung) honouring; (Orden) decoration; (Preis) award

aus|ziehen [1] *unr. tr. V.* **(a)** pull out ‹*couch*›; extend ‹*table, tripod, etc.*›
(b) (ablegen) take off ‹*clothes*›
(c) (entkleiden) undress; **sich ~:** get undressed
[2] *unr. itr. V.; mit sein* move out (**aus** of)

Auszubildende *der/die; adj. Dekl.* (bes. Amtsspr.) trainee; (im Handwerk) apprentice

Aus·zug *der* **(a)** (das Ausziehen) move
(b) (Bankw.) statement
(c) (Textpassage) extract

auszugs·weise *Adv.* in extracts *or* excerpts; **etw. ~ lesen** read extracts from sth.

authentisch *Adj.* authentic

Autist *der;* **~en, ~en, Autistin** *die;* **~, ~nen** autistic

autistisch *Adj.* (Med.) autistic

Auto *das;* **~s, ~s** car; automobile (Amer.); **~ fahren** drive; (mitfahren) go in the car

auto-, Auto-: ~bahn *die* motorway (Brit.); expressway (Amer.); **~biografie** /-----'-/ *die* autobiography; **~biografisch** /----'--/ *Adj.* autobiographical; **~bombe** *die* car bomb; **~bus** *der* ▶ BUS; **~dieb** *der,* **~diebin** *die* car thief; **~fähre** *die* car ferry; **~fahren** *das;* **~~s** driving; motoring; **~fahrer** *der,* **~fahrerin** *die* [car] driver; **~fahrt** *die* drive; **~gramm** /--'-/ *das;* **~~s, ~~e** autograph; **~immun·erkrankung** *die* autoimmune disease; **~kino** *das* drive-in cinema

Automat *der;* **~en, ~en (a)** (Verkaufs~) [vending] machine; (Spiel~) slot machine
(b) (in der Produktion) robot

Automatik *die;* **~, ~en** automatic control mechanism; (Getriebeautomatik) automatic transmission

automatisch (auch fig.) [1] *Adj.* automatic [2] *adv.* automatically

automatisieren *tr. V.* automate

Automatisierung *die;* **~, ~en** automation

auto-, Auto-: ~mobil /---'-/ *das;* **~~s, ~~e** (geh.) motor car; automobile (Amer.); **~nom** /--'-/ [1] *Adj.* autonomous; [2] *adv.* autonomously; **~nomie** /---'-/ *die;* **~~, ~~n** autonomy; **~nummer** *die* [car] registration number; **~pilot** *der* (Flugw.) autopilot

Autopsie /autɔ'psi:/ *die;* **~, ~n** post mortem [examination]

Autor *der;* **~s, ~en** author

Auto-: ~radio *das* car radio; **~reifen** *der* car tyre; **~reise·zug** *der* Motorail train (Brit.); auto train (Amer.); **~reparatur** *die* car repair; repair to the/a car

Autorin *die;* **~, ~nen** authoress; author

autoritär *Adj.* authoritarian

Autorität *die;* **~, ~en** authority

Auto-: ~schalter *der* drive-in counter; **~schlange** *die* queue of cars; **~schlüssel** *der* car key; **~skooter** /-sku:tɐ/ *der;* **~~s, ~~:** dodgem; bumper car; **~stopp** *der* hitch-hiking; **per ~stopp fahren, ~stopp machen** hitch-hike; **~telefon** *das* car telephone; **~tür** *die* car door; **~unfall** *der* car accident; **~vermietung** *die* car rental firm; **~verwerter** *der,* **~verwerterin** *die* car breaker; **~verwertung** *die* car breaker's [yard]; **~wäsche** *die* car wash; **~werkstatt** *die* garage

Avocado /avo'ka:do/ *die;* **~, ~s** avocado [pear]

Axt *die;* **~, Äxte** axe

Azalee /ats:a'le:ə/ *die;* **~, ~n** azalea

Azubi *der;* **~s, ~s**/*die;* **~, ~s** (ugs.) ▶ AUSZUBILDENDE

B b

b, B /beː/ *das;* **~, ~ (a)** (Buchstabe) b/B **(b)** (Musik) [key of] B flat

B *Abk.* = **Bundesstraße** ≈ A (Brit.)

Baby /ˈbeːbi/ *das;* **~s, ~s** baby

Baby·sitter /ˈbeːbisɪtɐ/ *der;* **~s, ~; Baby·sitterin** *die;* **~, ~:** babysitter

Bach *der;* **~[e]s, Bäche (a)** stream; brook **(b)** (Rinnsal) stream [of water]

Back·blech *das* baking sheet

Back·bord *das* (Seew., Luftf.) port [side]

Backe *die;* **~, ~n** cheek

backen [1] *unr. itr. V.* bake [2] *unr. tr. V.* **(a)** bake **(b)** (bes. südd.) ▶ BRATEN

Backen·zahn *der* molar

Bäcker *der;* **~s, ~:** baker; **er ist ~:** he is a baker; **zum/beim ~:** to the/at the baker's

Bäckerei *die;* **~, ~en** baker's [shop]

Bäckerin *die;* **~, ~nen** baker

Back-: ~fisch *der* fried fish (*in breadcrumbs*); **~form** *die* baking tin (Brit.); baking pan (Amer.); **~hähnchen** *das,* **~hen** *das* (österr.), **~huhn** *das* fried chicken (*in breadcrumbs*); **~ofen** *der* oven; **~pulver** *das* baking powder; **~stein** *der* brick; **~waren** *Pl.* bread, cakes, and pastries

Bad *das;* **~[e]s, Bäder (a)** bath; (das Schwimmen) swim; (im Meer usw.) bathe; **ein ~ nehmen** (geh.) take a bath; (schwimmen) go for a swim; (im Meer usw.) bathe **(b)** (Badezimmer) bathroom; **ein Zimmer mit ~:** a room with [private] bath **(c)** (Schwimm~) [swimming] pool **(d)** (Heil~) spa; (See~) [seaside] resort

Bade-: ~anzug *der* bathing costume; **~hose** *die* bathing trunks *pl;* **~mantel** *der* dressing gown; bathrobe; **~meister** *der,* **~meisterin** *die* swimming-pool attendant; **~mütze** *die* bathing cap

baden [1] *itr. V.* **(a)** have a bath **(b)** (schwimmen) bathe; **~ gehen** go for a bathe [2] *tr. V.* bath ‹*child, patient, etc.*›; bathe ‹*wound, eye, etc.*›

Baden-Württemberg (*das*); **~s** Baden-Württemberg

Bäder ▶ BAD

Bade-: ~strand *der* bathing beach; **~tuch** *das; Pl.* **~tücher** bath towel; **~wanne** *die* bath[tub]; **~wasser** *das* bath water; **~zimmer** *das* bathroom

Badminton *das;* **~s** badminton

*old spelling - see note on page xiv

Bagatelle *die;* **~, ~n** trifle

Bagger *der;* **~s, ~:** excavator; (Schwimmbagger) dredger

Bagger·see *der* flooded gravel pit

Bahn *die;* **~, ~en (a)** (Weg) path **(b)** (Route) path; (eines Geschosses) trajectory **(c)** (Sport) track; (für Pferderennen) course (Brit.); track (Amer.); (für einzelne Teilnehmer) lane; (Kegel~) alley; (Bowling~) lane **(d)** (Eisen~) railways *pl.;* railroad (Amer.); (Zug) train; **jmdn. zur ~ bringen** take sb. to the station; **[mit der] ~ fahren** go by train **(e)** (Straßen~) tram; streetcar (Amer.)

bahn-, Bahn-: ~beamte *der,* **~beamtin** *die* railway *or* (Amer.) railroad official; **~brechend** *Adj.* pioneering; **~brecher** *der,* **~brecherin** *die;* **~~, ~~nen** pioneer; **~bus** *der* railway bus; **~damm** *der* railway embankment

bahnen *tr. V.* clear ‹*way, path*›; **jmdm./einer Sache einen Weg ~** (fig.) pave the way for sb./sth.

Bahn-: ~fahrt *die* train journey; **~hof** *der* [railway *or* (Amer.) railroad] station; **~reise** *die* train journey; **~schranke** *die* level crossing (Brit.) *or* (Amer.) grade crossing barrier/gate; **~steig** *der;* **~~[e]s, ~~e** [station] platform; **~übergang** *der* level crossing (Brit.); grade crossing (Amer.); **~verbindung** *die* train connection

Bahre *die;* **~, ~n (a)** (Trage) stretcher **(b)** (Totenbahre) bier

Baiser /bɛˈzeː/ *das;* **~s, ~s** meringue

Bajonett *das;* **~[e]s, ~e** bayonet

Bakterie /bakˈteːri̯ə/ *die;* **~, ~n** bacterium

Balance /baˈlaŋsə/ *die;* **~, ~n** balance

balancieren *itr., tr. V.; itr. mit sein* balance

bald *Adv.* **(a)** soon; (leicht, rasch) quickly; easily; **wirds ~?** get a move on, will you; **bis ~!** see you soon **(b)** (ugs.: fast) almost

Baldrian /ˈbaldriaːn/ *der;* **~s, ~e** valerian

Balkan /ˈbalkaːn/ *der;* **~s: der ~:** the Balkans *pl.;* (Gebirge) the Balkan Mountains *pl.* **auf dem ~:** in the Balkans

Balken *der;* **~s, ~:** beam

Balkon /balˈkɔŋ, balˈkoːn/ *der;* **~s, ~s** /balˈkɔŋs/ *od.* **~e** /balˈkoːnə/ **(a)** balcony **(b)** (im Theater, Kino) circle

Ball *der;* **~[e]s, Bälle (a)** ball; **~ spielen** play ball **(b)** (Fest) ball

Ballade *die;* **~, ~n** ballad

Ballast *der;* **~[e]s, ~e** ballast

Ballast·stoffe *Pl.* (Med.) roughage *sing.*
ballen [1] *tr. V.* clench ‹*fist*›
[2] *refl. V.* ‹*fist*› clench
Ballen *der;* ~**s,** ~ **(a)** (Packen) bale
(b) (Hand-, Fußballen) ball
Ballerina *die;* ~, **Ballerinen** ballerina
Ballett *das;* ~**[e]s,** ~**e** ballet
Ballett-: ~**schuh** *der* ballet shoe; ~**schule** *die* ballet school; ~**tänzer** *der,* ~**tänzerin** *die* ballet dancer
Ball-: ~**junge** *der* ballboy; ~**kleid** *das* ball gown
Ballon /ba'lɔŋ/ *der;* ~**s,** ~**s** balloon
Ball-: ~**saal** *der* ballroom; ~**spiel** *das* ball game; ~**spielen** *das;* ~~**s** playing ball *no art.*
Ballungs·gebiet *das* conurbation
Balsam *der;* ~**s,** ~**e** balsam; (fig.) balm
Balte *der;* ~**n,** ~**n, Baltin** *die;* ~, ~**nen** Balt
Baltikum *das;* ~**s** Baltic States *pl.*
baltisch *Adj.* Baltic
Bambus *der;* ~ *od.* ~**ses,** ~**se** bamboo
banal *Adj.* **(a)** banal
(b) (gewöhnlich) commonplace
Banane *die;* ~, ~**n** banana
Banause *der;* ~**n,** ~**n, Banausin** *die;* ~, ~**nen** (abwertend) philistine
band *1. u. 3. Pers. Sg. Prät. v.* BINDEN
Band¹ *das;* ~**[e]s, Bänder (a)** ribbon; (Haar~, Hut~) band; (Schürzen~) string
(b) (Klebe~, Isolier~, Ton~ usw.) tape; **etw. auf** ~ (*Akk.*) **aufnehmen** tape[-record] sth.
(c) ▶ FÖRDERBAND;
(d) ▶ FLIESSBAND;
(e) am laufenden ~ (ugs.) nonstop
(f) (Anat.) ligament
Band² *der;* ~**[e]s, Bände** /'bɛndə/ volume
Band³ /bɛnt/ *die;* ~, ~**s** band; (Beat~, Rock~ usw.) group
Bande¹ *die;* ~, ~**n (a)** gang
(b) (ugs.: Gruppe) mob (coll.)
Bande² *die;* ~, ~**n** (Sport) [perimeter] barrier; (mit Reklame) billboards *pl.;* (Billard) cushion
Banden-: ~**krieg** *der* gang war; ~**werbung** *die: advertising on hoardings around the perimeter of a football pitch etc.*
Bänder ▶ BAND¹
Bänder-: ~**riss,** *~**riß** *der* (Med.) torn ligament; ~**zerrung** *die* (Med.) pulled ligament
bändigen *tr. V.* tame ‹*animal*›; control ‹*person, anger, urge*›
Bandit *der;* ~**en,** ~**en** bandit
Band·scheibe *die* [intervertebral] disc
bang, bange; banger, bangst... *od.* **bänger, bängst...:** [1] *Adj.* afraid; scared; (besorgt) anxious; **mir ist/wurde** ~ **[zumute]** I am/became scared
[2] *adv.* anxiously
bangen *itr. V.* be anxious

Bank¹ *die;* ~, **Bänke** bench; (mit Lehne) bench seat; (Kirchen~) pew; **etw. auf die lange** ~ **schieben** (ugs.) put sth. off
Bank² *die;* ~, ~**en** bank
Bankett¹ *das;* ~**[e]s,** ~**e** banquet
Bankett² *das;* ~**[e]s,** ~**e** (an Straßen) shoulder; (unbefestigt) verge
Bank·geheimnis *das* (Wirtsch.) bankers' duty to maintain confidentiality
Bankier /baŋ'ki̯e:/ *der;* ~**s,** ~**s** banker
Bank-: ~**kauffrau** *die,* ~**kaufmann** *der* [qualified] bank/building society/stock market clerk; ~**konto** *das* bank account; ~**leit·zahl** *die* [bank] sort code; ~**note** *die* banknote; bill (Amer.); ~**raub** *der* bank robbery; ~**räuber** *der,* ~**räuberin** *die* bank robber
bankrott *Adj.* bankrupt; **Bankrott** *od.* *~ **gehen** go bankrupt
Bankrott *der;* ~**[e]s,** ~**e** bankruptcy; ~ **machen** go bankrupt; *s. auch* BANKROTT
Bankrott·erklärung *die* declaration of bankruptcy; (fig.) declaration of [one's own] failure
Bank-: ~**überfall** *der* bank raid; ~**verbindung** *die* particulars of one's bank account; ~**wesen** *das* banking system
Bann *der;* ~**[e]s** (fig. geh.) spell
bar [1] *Adj.* cash
[2] *adv.* in cash; **etw. [in]** ~ **bezahlen** pay for sth. in cash; pay cash for sth.
Bar *die;* ~, ~**s** bar
Bär *der;* ~**en,** ~**en** bear
Baracke *die;* ~, ~**n** hut
Barbar *der;* ~**en,** ~**en** barbarian
Barbarei *die;* ~, ~**en (a)** (Rohheit) barbarity
(b) (Kulturlosigkeit) barbarism *no indef. art.*
Barbarin *die;* ~, ~**nen** barbarian
barbarisch [1] *Adj.* **(a)** (roh) barbarous
(b) (unzivilisiert) barbaric
[2] *adv.* **(a)** (roh) barbarously
(b) (unzivilisiert) barbarically
Bar·dame *die* barmaid
bären-, Bären-: ~**dienst** *der:* **jmdm. einen** ~**dienst erweisen** do sb. a disservice; ~**hunger** *der* (ugs.) **einen** ~**hunger haben/ kriegen** be famished (coll.) *or* starving (coll.)/ get famished (coll.) *or* ravenous (coll.); ~**stark** *Adj.* as strong as an ox *postpos.*
Barett *das;* ~**[e]s,** ~**e** (eines Geistlichen) biretta; (eines Richters, Professors) cap; (Baskenmütze) beret
bar·fuß *indekl. Adj.; nicht attr.* barefooted; ~ **herumlaufen/gehen** run about/go barefoot
barg *1. u. 3. Pers. Sg. Prät. v.* BERGEN
bar-, Bar-: ~**geld** *das* cash; ~**geld·los** *Adj.* cashless; ~**hocker** *der* bar stool
Bariton /'ba(:)ritɔn/ *der;* ~**s,** ~**e** baritone
Barkasse *die;* ~, ~**n** launch
barmherzig (geh.) [1] *Adj.* merciful

[2] *adv.* mercifully
Barmherzigkeit *die;* ~ (geh.) mercy
Barock *das od. der;* ~[s] **(a)** baroque **(b)** (Zeit) baroque age
Baro·meter *das* barometer
Baron *der;* ~s, ~e baron; (als Anrede) [Herr] ~: ≈ my lord
Baronin *die;* ~, ~nen baroness; (als Anrede) [Frau] ~: ≈ my Lady
Barren *der;* ~s, ~ **(a)** (Gold~, Silber~ usw.) bar
(b) (Turngerät) parallel bars *pl.*
Barriere /ba'ri̯e:rə/ *die;* ~, ~n (auch fig.) barrier
Barrikade *die;* ~, ~n barricade
barsch [1] *Adj.* curt
[2] *adv.* curtly
Barsch *der;* ~[e]s, ~e perch
barst *1. u. 3. Pers. Sg. Prät. v.* BERSTEN
Bart *der;* ~[e]s, **Bärte (a)** beard; (Oberlippen~, Schnurr~) moustache
(b) (von Katzen, Mäusen, Robben) whiskers *pl.;*
(c) (am Schlüssel) bit
Barten·wal *der* (Zool.) whalebone whale
bärtig *Adj.* bearded
Bart·wuchs *der* growth of beard
Bar-: ~zahlung *die* cash payment; **~zahlungs·rabatt** *der* cash discount
Basalt *der;* ~[e]s, ~e basalt
Basar *der;* ~s, ~e bazaar
Basis *die;* ~, **Basen (a)** (Grundlage) basis
(b) (Math., Archit., Milit.) base
Baske *der;* ~n, ~n Basque
Basken-: ~land *das* Basque region; **~mütze** *die* beret
Baskin *die;* ~, ~nen Basque
Basket·ball /'ba(:)skət-/ *der* basketball
Bass, *Baß *der;* **Basses, Bässe** (Musik) **(a)** bass
(b) (Instrument) double bass
Bassin /ba'sɛ̃:/ *das;* ~s, ~s (Schwimmbecken) pool; (im Garten) pond
Bassist *der;* ~en, ~en (Musik) **(a)** (Sänger) bass
(b) (Instrumentalist) double-bass player; bassist; (in einer Rockband) bass guitarist
Bassistin *die;* ~, ~nen ▶ BASSIST B
Bast *der;* ~[e]s, ~e bast; (Raffia~) raffia
basta *Interj.* (ugs.) that's enough; **und damit ~!** and that's that!
Bastelei *die;* ~, ~en; **(a)** (Gegenstand) piece of handicraft work
(b) (ugs.: das Basteln) handicraft work
basteln [1] *tr. V.* make
[2] *itr. V.* make things [with one's hands]
Bastion *die;* ~, ~en bastion
bat *1. u. 3. Pers. Sg. Prät. v.* BITTEN
Bataillon /batal'jo:n/ *das;* ~s, ~e (Milit.) battalion

*alte Schreibung - vgl. Hinweis auf S. xiv

Batik *der;* ~s, ~en *od. die;* ~, ~en batik
Batist *der;* ~[e]s, ~e batiste
Batterie *die;* ~, ~n battery
batterie-, Batterie-: ~betrieb *der* battery operation; **~betrieben** *Adj.* battery-operated; **~huhn** *das* battery chicken; (Henne) battery hen
Batzen *der;* ~s, ~ (ugs.) **(a)** (Klumpen) lump
(b) (Menge) pile (coll.)
Bau[1] *der;* ~[e]s, ~ten **(a)** (Errichtung) building; **im ~ sein** be under construction
(b) (Gebäude) building
(c) auf dem ~ arbeiten (Bauarbeiter sein) be in the building trade
(d) (Struktur) structure
Bau[2] *der;* ~[e]s, ~e (Kaninchenbau) burrow; hole; (Fuchsbau) earth
Bau·arbeiten *Pl.* building work *sing.*
Bauch *der;* ~[e]s, **Bäuche** (auch fig.: von Schiffen, Flugzeugen) belly
bauchig *Adj.* bulbous
Bauch-: ~laden *der* vendor's tray; **~landung** *die* belly landing; **~nabel** *der* (ugs.) belly button (coll.); **~redner** *der,* **~rednerin** *die* ventriloquist; **~schmerzen** *Pl.* stomach ache *sing.;* **~speichel·drüse** *die* pancreas; **~tanz** *der* belly dance; **~tänzerin** *die* belly dancer; **~weh** *das* (ugs.) tummy ache (coll.); stomach ache
Bau·denkmal *das* architectural monument
bauen [1] *tr. V.* build
[2] *itr. V.* **(a)** build; **wir wollen ~:** we want to build a house; (bauen lassen) we want to have a house built
(b) auf jmdn./etw. ~ (fig.) rely on sb./sth.
Bauer[1] *der;* ~n, ~n **(a)** farmer; (mit niedrigem sozialem Status) peasant
(b) (Schachfigur) pawn
(c) (Kartenspiele) ▶ BUBE
Bauer[2] *das od. der;* ~s, ~: [bird]cage
Bäuerin *die;* ~, ~nen **(a)** ▶ BAUER[1] A: [lady] farmer; peasant [woman]
(b) (Frau eines Bauern) farmer's wife
bäuerlich *Adj.* farming *attrib.;* (ländlich) rural
Bauern-: ~haus *das* farmhouse; **~hof** *der* farm
bau-, Bau-: ~fällig *Adj.* ramshackle; unsafe ‹*roof, ceiling*›; **~fälligkeit** *die* bad state of dilapidation; badly dilapidated state; **~herr** *der,* **~herrin** *die* client (*for whom a house etc. is being built*); **~jahr** *das* year of construction; (bei Autos) year of manufacture; **~kasten** *der* construction set; (mit Holzklötzen) box of bricks; **~kasten·system** *das* unit construction system; **~klotz** *der* building brick; **~kran** *der* construction crane
baulich *Adj.* structural
Baum *der;* ~[e]s, **Bäume** tree
Bau-: ~markt *der* (Kaufhaus) DIY

hypermarket; ~**maschine** *die* piece of construction plant *or* machinery; ~**maschinen** construction plant *sing. or* machinery

Bäumchen *das;* ~**s,** ~ small tree

Bau·meister *der* (hist.) [architect and] master builder

baumeln *itr. V.* (ugs.) dangle (**an** + *Dat.* from)

Baum-: ~**schule** *die* tree nursery; ~**stamm** *der* tree trunk; ~**sterben** *das;* ~~**s,** ~~: dying-off of trees; ~**stumpf** *der* tree stump; ~**wolle** *die* cotton

Bau·platz *der* site for building

bäurisch (abwertend) 1 *Adj.* boorish 2 *adv.* boorishly

Bau·satz *der* kit

Bausch *der;* ~[e]**s,** ~**e** *od.* **Bäusche** (**a**) (Watte~) a wad (**b**) **etw. in** ~ **und Bogen verwerfen/verdammen** reject/condemn sth. wholesale

bauschen 1 *tr. V.* billow ‹*sail, curtains, etc.*› 2 *refl. V.* ‹*dress, sleeve*› puff out; (ungewollt) bunch up; (im Wind) ‹*curtain, flag, etc.*› billow [out]

bauschig *Adj.* puffed ‹*dress*›; baggy ‹*trousers*›

bau-, Bau-: ~**sparen** *itr. V.; nur Inf. gebr.* save with a building society; ~**sparkasse** *die* building society; ~**stein** *der* (**a**) building stone; (**b**) (Bestandteil) element; (Elektronik, DV) module; (**c**) (~klotz) building brick; ~**stelle** *die* building site; (beim Straßenbau) roadworks *pl.*; ~**stoff** *der* building material; ~**teil** *das* component

Bauten *Pl.:* ▶ BAU

Bau-: ~**unternehmer** *der,* ~**unternehmerin** *die* building contractor; ~**weise** *die* method of construction; ~**werk** *das* building; (Brücke, Staudamm) structure; ~**wirtschaft** *die* building *or* construction industry

Bayer *der;* ~**n,** ~**n** **Bayerin** *die;* ~, ~**nen** Bavarian

bay[e]risch *Adj.* Bavarian

Bayern (*das*); ~**s** Bavaria

Bazille *die;* ~, ~**n** (ugs.) ▶ BAZILLUS A

Bazillus *der;* ~, **Bazillen** (**a**) bacillus (**b**) (fig.) cancer

Bd. *Abk.* = **Band** Vol.

beabsichtigen *tr. V.* intend

beachten *tr. V.* (**a**) follow ‹*rule, regulations, instruction*›; heed, follow ‹*advice*›; obey ‹*traffic signs*›; observe ‹*formalities*› (**b**) (berücksichtigen) take account of; (achten auf) pay attention to

beachtlich 1 *Adj.* considerable 2 *adv.* considerably

Beachtung *die;* ~ (**a**) ▶ BEACHTEN A: following; heeding; obeying (**b**) (Berücksichtigung) consideration (**c**) (Aufmerksamkeit) attention

Beamte *der; adj. Dekl.* official; (Staats~) [permanent] civil servant; (Kommunal~) [established] local government officer; (Polizei~) [police] officer

Beamtin *die;* ~, ~**nen** ▶ BEAMTE

beängstigend *Adj.* worrying

beanspruchen *tr. V.* (**a**) claim; **etw.** ~ **können** be entitled to expect sth. (**b**) (ausnutzen) make use of ‹*person, equipment*›; take advantage of ‹*hospitality, services*› (**c**) (erfordern) demand ‹*energy, attention, stamina*›; take up ‹*time, space, etc.*›

Beanspruchung *die;* ~, ~**en** demands *pl.* (*Gen.* on); **die** ~ **durch den Beruf** the demands of his/her job

beanstanden *tr. V.* take exception to; (sich beklagen über) complain about

Beanstandung *die;* ~, ~**en** complaint

beantragen *tr. V.* apply for

beantworten *tr. V.* answer; reply to ‹*letter*›; return ‹*greeting*›

bearbeiten *tr. V.* (**a**) deal with; handle ‹*case*› (**b**) edit ‹*text, document*› (**c**) (adaptieren) adapt (**für** for)

Bearbeitung *die;* ~, ~**en** (**a**) **die** ~ **eines Antrags/eines Falles** *usw.* dealing with an application/handling a case *etc.;* (**b**) (Adaption) adaptation

beaufsichtigen *tr. V.* supervise; look after ‹*child*›

beauftragen *tr. V.* entrust

bebauen *tr. V.* build on; develop

bebaut *Adj.* **ein [dicht]** ~**es Gebiet** a densely built-up area; **ein** ~**es Gelände** a developed site

Bebauung *die;* ~, ~**en** (**a**) development (**b**) (Gebäude) buildings *pl.*

beben *itr. V.* shake

Beben *das;* ~**s,** ~ ▶ ERDBEBEN

bebildern *tr. V.* illustrate

Bebilderung *die;* ~, ~**en** illustrations *pl.*

Becher *der;* ~**s,** ~ (Glas~, Porzellan~) glass; tumbler; (Plastik~) beaker; cup; (Eis~) (aus Glas, Metall) sundae dish; (aus Pappe) tub; (Joghurt~) carton

Becken *das;* ~**s,** ~ (**a**) (Wasch~) basin; (Abwasch~) sink; (Toiletten~) pan (**b**) (Anat.) pelvis (**c**) *Pl.* (Musik) cymbals

bedacht *Adj.* **auf etw.** (*Akk.*) ~ **sein** be intent on sth.

bedächtig 1 *Adj.* (**a**) deliberate; measured ‹*steps, stride, speech*› (**b**) (besonnen) thoughtful; well-considered ‹*words*› 2 *adv.* (**a**) deliberately (**b**) (besonnen) thoughtfully

b

bedanken *refl. V.* say thank you; **sich bei jmdm. [für etw.] ~:** thank sb. [for sth.]

Bedarf *der;* **~[e]s** need (**an** + *Dat.* of); requirement (**an** + *Dat.* for); (Bedarfsmenge) needs *pl.;* requirements *pl.;* **bei ~:** if required

bedauerlich *Adj.* regrettable

bedauerlicher·weise *Adv.* regrettably

bedauern *tr., itr. V.* **(a)** feel sorry for; **sie lässt sich gerne ~:** she likes being pitied **(b)** (schade finden) regret; **ich bedaure sehr, dass ...:** I am very sorry that ...

Bedauern *das;* **~s** regret; **zu meinem ~:** to my regret

bedauerns·wert *Adj.* (geh.) unfortunate ‹*person*›

bedecken *tr. V.* cover

bedeckt *Adj.* overcast ‹*sky*›

bedenken *unr. tr. V.* **(a)** consider **(b)** (beachten) take into consideration

Bedenken *das;* **~s, ~** reservation (**gegen** about); **ohne ~:** without hesitation

bedenken·los [1] *Adj.* unhesitating; (skrupellos) unscrupulous [2] *adv.* without hesitation; (skrupellos) unscrupulously

bedenklich [1] *Adj.* **(a)** dubious ‹*methods, transactions, etc.*› **(b)** (bedrohlich) alarming [2] *adv.* alarmingly

Bedenk·zeit *die* time for reflection

bedeuten *tr. V.* **(a)** mean; **was soll das ~?** what does that mean? **(b)** (sein) represent; **das bedeutet ein Wagnis** that is being really daring

bedeutend [1] *Adj.* **(a)** significant; important **(b)** (groß) substantial; considerable ‹*success*› [2] *adv.* considerably

Bedeutung *die;* **~, ~en (a)** meaning **(b)** (Wichtigkeit) importance

bedeutungs-: ~los *Adj.* insignificant; **~voll** [1] *Adj.* **(a)** significant; **(b)** (viel sagend) meaningful; meaning ‹*look*›; [2] *adv.* meaningfully

bedienen [1] *tr. V.* **(a)** serve; **werden Sie schon bedient?** are you being served? **(b)** (handhaben) operate ‹*machine*› [2] *itr. V.* serve [3] *refl. V.* help oneself; **sich selbst ~** (im Geschäft, Restaurant usw.) serve oneself

Bedienstete *der/die; adj. Dekl.* (Amtsspr.) employee

Bedienung *die;* **~, ~en (a)** (das Bedienen) service; **~ inbegriffen** service included **(b)** (das Handhaben) operation **(c)** (Servierer[in]) waiter/waitress

Bedienungs·anleitung *die* operating instructions *pl.*

bedingen *tr. V.* cause

Bedingung *die;* **~, ~en** condition; **unter der ~, dass ...:** on condition that ...

bedingungs·los *Adj.* unconditional

bedrängen *tr. V.* **(a)** besiege ‹*town, fortress, person*›; put ‹*opposing player*› under pressure **(b)** (belästigen) pester

Bedrängnis *die;* **~, ~se** (geh.) (innere Not) distress; (wirtschaftliche Not) [great] difficulties *pl.;* **in ~ geraten/sein** get into/be in great difficulties *pl.*

bedrohen *tr. V.* threaten

bedrohlich [1] *Adj.* (Unheil verkündend) ominous; (gefährlich) dangerous [2] *adv.* (Unheil verkündend) ominously; (gefährlich) dangerously

Bedrohlichkeit *die;* **~:** dangerousness; (einer Krankheit usw.) dangerous nature

Bedrohung *die* threat (*Gen.* to)

bedrucken *tr. V.* print

bedrücken *tr. V.* depress

Beduine *der;* **~n, ~n, Beduinin** *die;* **~, ~nen** Bed[o]uin

bedürfen *unr. itr. V.* **jmds./einer Sache ~** (geh.) require *or* need sb./sth.

Bedürfnis *das;* **~ses, ~se** need (**nach** for); **das ~ haben, etw. zu tun** feel a need to do sth.

bedürfnislos *Adj.* ‹*person*› with few [material] needs; modest, simple ‹*life*›; **~ sein** have few [material] needs

Bedürfnislosigkeit *die;* **~:** lack of [material] needs

bedürftig *Adj.* needy

Beef·steak /'bi:f-/ *das* [beef]steak; **deutsches ~:** ≈ beefburger

beehren *tr. V.* (geh.) honour

beeiden *tr. V.* **~, dass ...:** swear [on oath] that ...; **eine Aussage ~:** swear to the truth of a statement

beeilen *refl. V.* hurry [up (coll.)]

beeindrucken *tr. V.* impress

beeindruckend *Adj.* impressive

beeinflussen *tr. V.* influence

Beeinflussung *die;* **~, ~en** influencing

beeinträchtigen *tr. V.* restrict ‹*sights, freedom*›; detract from ‹*pleasure, enjoyment, value*›; spoil ‹*appetite, good humour*›; impair ‹*quality, reactions, efficiency, vision, hearing*›; damage, harm ‹*sales, reputation*›

Beeinträchtigung *die;* **~, ~en** ▶ BEEINTRÄCHTIGEN: restriction; detracting (+ *Gen.* from); spoiling; impairment; damage (*Gen.* to)

beenden, beendigen *tr. V.* **(a)** end; finish ‹*piece of work etc.*›; complete ‹*studies*› **(b)** (DV) quit ‹*program*›

beengen *tr. V.* hinder, restrict ‹*movements*›; (fig.) restrict ‹*freedom [of action]*›; **beengt wohnen** live in cramped surroundings *or* conditions; **sich beengt fühlen** feel cramped

---

*old spelling - see note on page xiv

beerben *tr. V.* **jmdn. ~:** inherit sb.'s estate

beerdigen *tr. V.* bury

Beerdigung *die; ~, ~en* burial; (Trauerfeier) funeral

Beerdigungs·institut *das* [firm *sing.* of] undertakers *pl.*

Beere *die; ~, ~n* berry

Beet *das; ~[e]s, ~e* (Blumenbeet) bed; (Gemüsebeet) plot

befahrbar *Adj.* passable

befahren *unr. tr. V.* **(a)** drive on ‹*road*›; drive across ‹*bridge*›; use ‹*railway line*›; **die Straße ist stark/wenig ~:** the road is heavily/little used; **eine stark ~e Straße** a busy road
(b) sail ‹*sea*›; navigate, sail up/down ‹*river, canal*›

befallen *unr. tr. V.* **(a)** overcome; ‹*misfortune*› befall; **von Panik/Angst ~ werden** be seized with panic/fear
(b) ‹*pests*› attack

befangen [1] *Adj.* **(a)** self-conscious ‹*person*›
(b) (voreingenommen) biased
[2] *adv.* self-consciously

Befangenheit *die; ~* **(a)** self-consciousness
(b) (Voreingenommenheit) bias

befassen *refl. V.* **sich mit etw. ~:** occupy oneself with sth.; ‹*article, book*› deal with sth.; (etw. studieren) study sth.

Befehl *der; ~[e]s, ~e* **(a)** order
(b) den ~ über jmdn./etw. haben be in command of sb./sth.

befehlen [1] *unr. tr., itr. V.* order; (Milit.) order; **man befahl ihm zu warten** he was told to wait
[2] *unr. itr. V.* **über jmdn./etw. ~:** have command of *or* be in command of sb./sth.

Befehls·haber *der; ~s, ~* (Milit.) commander

befestigen *tr. V.* **(a)** fix; **etw. an der Wand ~:** fix sth. to the wall
(b) (haltbar machen) stabilize ‹*bank, embankment*›; make up ‹*road, path, etc.*›
(c) (sichern) fortify ‹*town etc.*›; strengthen ‹*border*›

Befestigung *die; ~, ~en* **(a)** fixing
(b) (Milit.) fortification

befeuchten *tr. V.* moisten; damp ‹*hair, cloth*›

befiehlst, befiehlt *2., 3. Pers. Sg. Präsens v.* BEFEHLEN

befinden *unr. refl. V.* be

Befinden *das; ~s* health; (eines Patienten) condition

befindlich *Adj.***(a)** to be found *postpos.*; **das in der Kasse ~e Geld** the money in the till
(b) (in einem Zustand) **die im Bau ~en Häuser** the houses [which are/were] under construction

Befindlichkeit *die; ~, ~en* (geh.) state

beflecken *tr. V.* stain

befohlen *2. Part. v.* BEFEHLEN

befolgen *tr. V.* follow, obey ‹*instruction, grammatical rule*›; obey, comply with ‹*law, regulation*›; follow ‹*advice, suggestion*›

Befolgung *die; ~* ▶ BEFOLGEN: following; obedience (*Gen.* to); compliance (*Gen.* with)

befördern *tr. V.* **(a)** carry; transport
(b) (aufrücken lassen) promote

Beförderung *die; ~, ~en* **(a)** carriage; transport; (von Personen) transport
(b) (das Aufrückenlassen) promotion

befragen *tr. V.* **(a)** question (**über** + *Akk.* about)
(b) (konsultieren) ask

Befragung *die; ~, ~en* **(a)** questioning
(b) (Konsultation) consultation
(c) (Umfrage) opinion poll

befreien [1] *tr. V.* **(a)** free; liberate ‹*country, people*› (**von** from)
(b) (freistellen) exempt (**von** from)
(c) jmdn. von Schmerzen ~: free sb. of pain
[2] *refl. V.* free oneself (**von** from)

Befreier *der,* **Befreierin** *die; ~, ~nen* liberator

Befreiung *die; ~* **(a)** ▶ BEFREIEN 1A: freeing; liberation
(b) (Freistellung) exemption
(c) die ~ von Schmerzen release from pain

befremden *tr. V.* **jmdn. ~:** put sb. off

Befremden *das; ~s* surprise and displeasure

befremdlich (geh.) [1] *Adj.* strange; odd
[2] *adv.* strangely

befreunden *refl. V.* ▶ ANFREUNDEN; **[gut** *od.* **eng] befreundet sein** be [good *or* close] friends (**mit** with)

befriedigen *tr. V.* **(a)** satisfy; gratify ‹*lust*›
(b) (ausfüllen) ‹*job, occupation, etc.*› fulfil
(c) (sexuell) satisfy; **sich [selbst] ~:** masturbate

befriedigend [1] *Adj.* satisfactory
[2] *adv.* satisfactorily

Befriedigung *die; ~* **(a)** ▶ BEFRIEDIGEN A: satisfaction; gratification
(b) (*Genugtuung*) satisfaction

befristet *Adj.* temporary ‹*visa*›; fixed-term ‹*ban, contract*›

befruchten *tr. V.* fertilize ‹*egg*›; pollinate ‹*flower*›; impregnate ‹*female*›; **ein Tier künstlich ~:** artificially inseminate an animal

Befruchtung *die; ~, ~en* ▶ BEFRUCHTEN: fertilization; pollination; impregnation; **künstliche ~:** artificial insemination

Befugnis *die; ~, ~se* authority

befühlen *tr. V.* feel

Befund *der* (bes. Med.) result[s *pl.*]

befürchten *tr. V.* fear; **ich befürchte, dass ...:** I am afraid that ...

befürworten *tr. V.* support

begabt *Adj.* talented; gifted; **hoch ~:** highly talented *or* gifted
Begabung *die; ~, ~en* talent; gift
begann *1. u. 3. Pers. Sg. Prät. v.* BEGINNEN
begatten *tr. V.* mate with; ‹*man*› copulate with; **sich ~:** mate; ‹*persons*› copulate
Begattung *die; ~, ~en* mating; (bei Menschen) copulation
begeben *unr. refl. V.* (geh.) proceed; make one's way; go; **sich zu Bett ~:** retire to bed; **sich an die Arbeit ~:** commence work
Begebenheit *die; ~, ~en* (geh.) event; occurrence
begegnen *itr. V.; mit sein* **jmdm. ~:** meet sb.; **sich** (*Dat.*) **~:** meet [each other]
Begegnung *die; ~, ~en* **(a)** meeting **(b)** (Sport) match
begehen *unr. tr. V.* **(a)** commit ‹*crime, adultery, indiscretion, sin, suicide, faux-pas, etc.*›; make ‹*mistake*›; **eine [furchtbare] Dummheit ~:** do something [really] stupid **(b)** (geh.: feiern) celebrate
begehren *tr. V.* desire
begehrens·wert *Adj.* desirable
begehrlich [1] *Adj.* greedy [2] *adv.* greedily
begehrt *Adj.* much sought-after
begeistern [1] *tr. V.* **jmdn. [für etw.] ~:** fire sb. with enthusiasm [for sth.] [2] *refl. V.* get enthusiastic (**für** about)
begeisternd *Adj.* rousing
begeistert [1] *Adj.* enthusiastic (**von** about) [2] *adv.* enthusiastically
Begeisterung *die; ~:* enthusiasm
begeisterungs-, Begeisterungs-: ~fähig *Adj.* ‹*children, people, etc.*› who are able to get enthusiastic *or* are capable of enthusiasm; **~fähigkeit** *die* capacity for enthusiasm; **~sturm** *der* storm of enthusiastic applause
Begierde *die; ~, ~n* desire (**nach** for)
begierig [1] *Adj.* eager [2] *adv.* eagerly
begießen *unr. tr. V.* water ‹*plants*›
Beginn *der; ~[e]s* beginning; **[gleich] zu ~:** [right] at the beginning
beginnen [1] *unr. itr. V.* start; begin; **mit dem Bau ~:** start *or* begin building; **dort beginnt der Wald** the forest starts there [2] *unr. tr. V.* start; begin; start ‹*argument*›; **~, etw. zu tun** start to do sth.
beglaubigen *tr. V.* certify
Beglaubigung *die; ~, ~en* certification
begleichen *unr. tr. V.* settle ‹*bill, debt*›; pay ‹*sum*›
Begleit·brief *der* covering *or* accompanying letter
begleiten *tr. V.* accompany; **jmdn. nach Hause ~:** see sb. home

*alte Schreibung - vgl. Hinweis auf S. xiv

Begleiter *der; ~s, ~,* **Begleiterin** *die; ~, ~nen* companion; (zum Schutz) escort; (Führer[in]) guide
Begleitung *die; ~, ~en* **(a) er bot uns seine ~ an** he offered to accompany us; **in ~ eines Erwachsenen** accompanied by an adult **(b)** (Musik) accompaniment
beglückwünschen *tr. V.* congratulate (**zu** on)
begnadet *Adj.* (geh.) divinely gifted
begnadigen *tr. V.* pardon; reprieve
Begnadigung *die; ~, ~en* reprieving; (Straferlass) pardon; reprieve
begnügen *refl. V.* content oneself
Begonie /be'go:ni̯ə/ *die; ~, ~n* begonia
begonnen *2. Part. v.* BEGINNEN
begraben *unr. tr. V.* bury
Begräbnis *das; ~ses, ~se* burial; (~feier) funeral
begreifen [1] *unr. tr. V.* understand; **er konnte nicht ~, was geschehen war** he could not grasp what had happened [2] *itr. V.* understand; **schnell** *od.* **leicht/langsam** *od.* **schwer ~:** be quick/slow on the uptake
begreiflich *Adj.* understandable
begrenzen *tr. V.* limit, restrict (**auf** + *Akk.* to)
Begriff *der* **(a)** concept; (Terminus) term **(b)** (Auffassung) idea; **sich** (*Dat.*) **keinen ~ von etw. machen können** not be able to imagine sth.; **ein/kein ~ sein** be/not be well known **(c) im ~ sein** *od.* **stehen, etw. zu tun** be about to do sth.
begriffs·stutzig *Adj.* (abwertend) obtuse
Begriffsstutzigkeit *die; ~* (abwertend) obtuseness
begründen *tr. V.* **(a)** give reasons for **(b)** (gründen) found; establish ‹*fame, reputation*›
Begründer *der; ~s, ~,* **Begründerin** *die; ~, ~nen* founder
begründet *Adj.* well-founded; reasonable ‹*demand, objection, complaint*›
Begründung *die; ~, ~en* reason[s]; **mit der ~, dass ...:** on the grounds that ...
begrüßen *tr. V.* **(a)** greet; ‹*hostess, host*› welcome **(b)** (fig.) welcome
Begrüßung *die; ~, ~en* greeting; (von Gästen) welcoming; (Zeremonie) welcome (*Gen.* for)
begünstigen *tr. V.* favour
Begünstigung *die; ~:* favouring
begutachten *tr. V.* **(a)** examine and report on **(b)** (ugs.) have a look at
Begutachtung *die; ~, ~en* examination
begütert *Adj.* wealthy
begütigen *tr. V.* placate
behaart *Adj.* hairy; **stark ~ sein** be covered with hair; **stark ~e Beine** very hairy legs

behäbig 1 *Adj.* slow and ponderous
2 *adv.* slowly and ponderously
behagen *itr. V.* **etw. behagt jmdm.** sb. likes sth.
Behagen *das;* **~s** pleasure
behaglich 1 *Adj.* comfortable
2 *adv.* comfortably
Behaglichkeit *die;* **~:** comfortableness
behalten *unr. tr. V.* **(a)** keep; **etw. für sich ~:** keep sth. to oneself
(b) (zurück~) be left with ‹*scar, defect, etc.*›
(c) (sich merken) remember
Behälter *der;* **~s, ~** container; (für Abfälle) receptacle
behämmert *Adj.* (salopp) ▶ BEKLOPPT
behänd, behände 1 *Adj.* (geschickt) deft; (flink) nimble
2 *adv. s. Adj.:* deftly; nimbly
behandeln *tr. V.* (auch Med.) treat; handle ‹*matter, machine, device*›; deal with ‹*subject, question etc.*›
Behandlung *die;* **~, ~en** treatment
behängen *tr. V.* hang
beharren *itr. V.* **auf etw.** (*Dat.*) **~** (etw. nicht aufgeben) persist in sth.; (auf etw. bestehen) insist on sth.
beharrlich 1 *Adj.* dogged
2 *adv.* doggedly
Beharrlichkeit *die;* **~:** doggedness
behauen *unr. tr. V.* hew
behaupten 1 *tr. V.* **(a)** maintain; assert; **~, jmd. zu sein/etw. zu wissen** claim to be sb./know sth.; **man behauptet** *od.* **es wird behauptet, dass ...:** it is said *or* claimed that ...
(b) (verteidigen) maintain ‹*position*›; retain ‹*record*›
2 *refl. V.* **(a)** assert oneself; (nicht untergehen) hold one's ground; (dableiben) survive
(b) (Sport) win through
Behauptung *die;* **~, ~en** assertion
Behausung *die;* **~, ~en** dwelling
beheben *unr. tr. V.* remove ‹*danger, difficulty*›; repair ‹*damage*›; remedy ‹*abuse, defect*›
Behebung *die;* **~, ~en** ▶ BEHEBEN: removal; repair; remedying
beheimatet *Adj.* **an einem Ort/in einem Land** *usw.* **~ sein** be native to a place/to a country *etc.*
beheizbar *Adj.* heatable; **eine ~e Heckscheibe** a heated rear window
beheizen *tr. V.* heat
behelfen *unr. refl. V.* make do
behelfs·mäßig 1 *Adj.* makeshift
2 *adv.* in a makeshift way
behelligen *tr. V.* bother; (zudringlich werden gegen) pester
***behend, *behende** ▶ BEHÄND, BEHÄNDE
beherbergen *tr. V.* accommodate
beherrschen 1 *tr. V.* **(a)** control; rule ‹*country, people*›
(b) (meistern) control ‹*vehicle, animal*›; be in control of ‹*situation*›
(c) (bestimmen, dominieren) dominate ‹*townscape, landscape, discussions*›
(d) (zügeln) control ‹*feelings*›; control, curb ‹*impatience*›
(e) (gut können) have mastered ‹*instrument, trade*›; have a good command of ‹*language*›
2 *refl. V.* control oneself
beherrscht 1 *Adj.* self-controlled
2 with self-control
Beherrschung *die;* **~ (a)** control; (eines Volks, Landes usw.) rule
(b) (das Meistern) control
(c) (Beherrschtheit) self-control
(d) (das Können) mastery
beherzigen *tr. V.* take ‹*sth.*› to heart
beherzt 1 *Adj.* spirited
2 *adv.* spiritedly
behilflich *Adj.* **[jmdm.] ~ sein** help [sb.] (**bei** with)
behindern *tr. V.* **(a)** hinder; impede ‹*movement*›; hold up ‹*traffic*›
(b) (Sport, Verkehrsw.) obstruct
behindert *Adj.* handicapped
Behinderte *der/die; adj. Dekl.* handicapped person; **die ~n** the handicapped; **WC für ~:** toilet for disabled persons
Behinderung *die;* **~, ~en (a)** hindrance
(b) (Sport, Verkehrsw.) obstruction
(c) (Gebrechen) handicap
Behörde *die;* **~, ~n** authority; (Amt, Abteilung) department
behördlich 1 *Adj.* official
2 *adv.* officially
behüten *tr. V.* protect (**vor** + *Dat.* from); (bewachen) guard
behutsam 1 *Adj.* careful
2 *adv.* carefully
bei *Präp. mit Dat.* **(a)** (nahe) near; (dicht an, neben) by; **wer steht da ~ ihm?** who is standing there with him?; **etw. ~ sich haben** have sth. with *or* on one; **sich ~ jmdm. entschuldigen** apologize to sb.
(b) (unter) among; **war heute ein Brief für mich ~ der Post?** was there a letter for me in the post today?
(c) (an) by; **jmdn. ~ der Hand nehmen** take sb. by the hand
(d) (im Wohn-/Lebens-/Arbeitsbereich von); **~ uns tut man das nicht** we don't do that; **~ mir [zu Hause]** at my house; **~ uns um die Ecke/gegenüber** round the corner from us/opposite us; **~ seinen Eltern leben** live with one's parents; **wir sind ~ ihr eingeladen** we have been invited to her house; **wir treffen uns ~ uns/Peter** we'll meet at our/Peter's place; **~ uns in der Firma** in our company; **~ Schmidt** (auf Briefen) c/o Schmidt; **~ einer Firma sein** be with a company; **~ jmdm./einem Verlag arbeiten** work for sb./a publishing house
(e) (im Bereich eines Vorgangs) at; **~ einer** ···›

Hochzeit/einem Empfang *usw.* be at a wedding/reception *etc.*; **~ einem Unfall** in an accident
(f) (im Werk von) **~ Goethe** in Goethe
(g) (im Falle von) in the case of; **wie ~ den Römern** as with the Romans; **~ der Hauskatze** in the domestic cat
(h) (modal) **~ Tag/Nacht** by day/night; **~ Tageslicht** by daylight; **~ Nebel** in fog
(i) (im Falle des Auftretens von) **„~ Nässe Schleudergefahr"** 'slippery when wet'
(j) (angesichts) with; **~ dieser Hitze** in this heat; **~ deinen guten Augen/ihrem Talent** with your good eyesight/her talent
(k) (trotz) **~ all seinem Engagement/seinen Bemühungen** in spite of *or* despite *or* for all his commitment/efforts

bei|behalten *unr. tr. V.* keep; retain; keep up ‹*custom, habit*›; keep to ‹*course, method*›; preserve, maintain ‹*way of life; attitude*›

bei|bringen *unr. tr. V.* **(a) jmdm. etw. ~:** teach sb. sth.
(b) (ugs.: mitteilen) **jmdm. ~, dass ...:** break it to sb. that ...
(c) (zufügen) **jmdm./sich etw. ~:** inflict sth. on sb./oneself

Beichte *die;* **~, ~n** confession *no def. art.*

beichten [1] *itr. V.* confess
[2] *tr. V.* (auch fig.) confess

Beicht-: ~stuhl *der* confessional; **~vater** *der* father confessor

beid... *Indefinitpron. u. Zahlw.* [1] *Pl.* **~e** both; (der/die/das eine oder der/die/das andere) either *sing.*; **die ~en** the two; **die/seine ~en Brüder** the/his two brothers; **die ~en ersten Strophen** the first two verses; **kennst du die ~en?** do you know those two?; **alle ~e** both of us/you/them; **ihr/euch ~e** you two; **ihr/euch ~e nicht** neither of you; **wir/uns ~e** the two of us/both of us; **er hat ~e Eltern verloren** he has lost both [his] parents; **mit ~en Händen** with both hands; **ich habe ~e gekannt** I knew both of them; **einer/eins von ~en** one of the two; **keiner/keins von ~en** neither [of them]
[2] *Neutr. Sg.*; **~es** both *pl.*; (das eine oder das andere) either; **~es ist möglich** either is possible; **ich glaube ~es/~es nicht** I believe both things/neither thing; **das ist ~es nicht richtig** neither of those is correct

beiderlei *indekl. Adj.* **~ Geschlechts** of both sexes

beider·seits [1] *Präp. mit Gen.* on both sides of
[2] *Adv.* on both sides

bei·einander *Adv.* together; **~ Trost suchen** seek comfort from each other

Bei·fahrer *der,* **Bei·fahrerin** *die* **(a)** passenger
(b) (berufsmäßig) co-driver; (im LKW) driver's mate

*old spelling - see note on page xiv

Beifahrer·sitz *der* passenger seat; (eines Motorrads) pillion

Bei·fall *der* **(a)** applause
(b) (Zustimmung) approval

bei·fällig [1] *Adj.* approving
[2] *adv.* approvingly

beige /be:ʃ/ *Adj.* beige

Beige /be:ʃ/ *das;* **~, ~** *od.* (ugs.) **~s** beige

Bei·geschmack *der:* **einen bitteren** *usw.* **~ haben** have a slightly bitter *etc.* taste [to it]

Bei·hilfe *die* **(a)** aid; (Zuschuss) allowance
(b) (Rechtsw.: Mithilfe) aiding and abetting

bei|kommen *unr. itr. V.*; *mit sein* **(a)** (gewachsen sein) **jmdm. ~:** get the better of sb.
(b) (bewältigen) **den Schwierigkeiten/der Unruhe/jmds. Sturheit ~:** overcome the difficulties/deal with the unrest/cope with sb.'s obstinacy

Beil *das;* **~[e]s, ~e** axe; (kleiner) hatchet

Bei·lage *die* **(a)** (Zeitungs~) supplement
(b) (zu Speisen) side dish; (Gemüse) vegetables *pl.*

bei·läufig [1] *Adj.* casual
[2] *adv.* casually

bei|legen *tr. V.* **(a)** enclose
(b) (schlichten) settle ‹*dispute etc.*›

Bei·leid *das* sympathy; **[mein] herzliches** *od.* **aufrichtiges ~!** please accept my sincere condolences

bei|liegen *unr. itr. V.* **einem Brief ~:** be enclosed with a letter

bei·liegend *Adj.* enclosed; **~ senden wir ...:** please find enclosed ...

beim *Präp. + Art.* **(a)** = **bei dem;**
(b) ~ Film sein be in films
(c) er will ~ Arbeiten nicht gestört werden he doesn't want to be disturbed when working; **~ Duschen sein** be taking a shower

bei|messen *unr. tr. V.* attach

Bein *das;* **~[e]s, ~e** leg; **jmdm. ein ~ stellen** trip sb.; (fig.) put *or* throw a spanner *or* (Amer.) a monkey wrench in sb.'s works; **wieder auf den ~en sein** be back on one's feet again

bei·nah[e] *Adv.* almost

Bei·name *der* epithet

Bein·bruch *der:* **das ist [doch] kein ~** (ugs.) it's not the end of the world

beinhalten *tr. V.* (Papierdt.) involve

-beinig *adj.* -legged

bei|pflichten *itr. V.* agree (*Dat.* with)

beirren *tr. V.* **sich durch nichts/von niemandem ~ lassen** not be deterred by anything/anybody

beisammen *Adv.* together

beisammen|haben *unr. tr. V.* **(a)** have got together
(b) er hat [sie] nicht alle beisammen (ugs.) he's not all there (coll.)

Beisammen·sein *das* get-together

Bei·schlaf *der* sexual intercourse

Bei·sein *das:* **in jmds. ~:** in the presence of sb. *or* in sb.'s presence
bei·seite *Adv.* aside
Beis[e]l *das;* **~s, ~** *od.* **~n** (österr.) pub (Brit.); bar (Amer.)
bei|setzen *tr. V.* lay to rest; inter ‹*ashes*›
Bei·setzung *die;* **~, ~en** funeral; burial
Bei·spiel *das* example (**für** of); **zum ~:** for example; **mit gutem ~ vorangehen** set a good example
beispielhaft *Adj.* exemplary
beispiel·los *Adj.* unparalleled
beispiels·weise *Adv.* for example
beißen [1] *unr. tr., itr. V.* (auch fig.) bite [2] *unr. refl. V.* (ugs.) ‹*colours, clothes*› clash
beißend *Adj.* biting ‹*cold*›; acrid ‹*smoke, fumes*›; sharp ‹*frost*›
Beiß·zange *die* ▶ KNEIFZANGE
Bei·stand *der* (geh.: Hilfe) aid
bei|stehen *unr. itr. V.* **jmdm. ~:** aid sb.
bei|steuern *tr. V.* contribute
Beitrag *der;* **~[e]s, Beiträge** contribution; (Versicherungsbeitrag) premium; (Mitgliedsbeitrag) subscription
bei|tragen *unr. tr., itr. V.* contribute (**zu** to)
bei|treten *unr. itr. V.; mit sein* join ‹*union, club, etc.*›; **einem Abkommen/Pakt** accede to ‹*pact, agreement*›
Bei·tritt *der* joining
Bei·wagen *der* sidecar
Bei·werk *das* accessories *pl.*
bei|wohnen *itr. V.* **einer Sache** (*Dat.*) **~** (geh.) be present at sth.
Beize *die;* **~, ~n** (Holzbearb.) [wood]stain
beizeiten *Adv.* in good time
beizen *tr. V.* (Holzbearb.) stain
bejahen /bəˈjaːən/ *tr. V.* **(a)** *auch itr.* answer ‹*sth.*› in the affirmative
(b) (gutheißen) approve of; **das Leben ~:** have a positive *or* an affirmative attitude to life
Bejahung *die;* **~, ~en (a)** affirmative reply
(b) (das Gutheißen) approval
bejammern *tr. V.* lament
bejubeln *tr. V.* cheer; acclaim
bekämpfen *tr. V.* **(a)** fight against
(b) combat ‹*disease, epidemic, pest, unemployment, crime, etc.*›
Bekämpfung *die;* **~ (a)** fight (*Gen.* against)
(b) ▶ BEKÄMPFEN B: combating
bekannt *Adj.* **(a)** well-known; **etw. ~ geben** announce sth.; **etw. ~ machen** announce sth.; (der Öffentlichkeit) make sth. public; **~ werden** become known; **es ist nichts davon ~:** nothing is known concerning it
(b) jmd./etw. ist jmdm. ~: sb. knows sb./sth.; **Darf ich ~ machen? Meine Eltern** may I introduce my parents?
Bekannte *der/die; adj. Dekl.* acquaintance
Bekannt·gabe *die;* **~:** announcement
***bekannt|geben** ▶ BEKANNT A
bekanntlich *Adv.* as is well known; **etw. ist ~ der Fall** sth. is known to be the case
***bekannt|machen** ▶ BEKANNT A
Bekannt·machung *die;* **~, ~en** announcement
Bekanntschaft *die;* **~, ~en** acquaintance
***bekannt|werden** ▶ BEKANNT A
bekehren [1] *tr. V.* convert [2] *refl. V.* become converted
Bekehrung *die;* **~, ~en** (auch fig.) conversion (**zu** to)
bekennen [1] *unr. tr. V.* **(a)** confess; **~, dass ...** admit that ...
(b) (Rel.) profess
[2] *refl. V.* **sich zum Islam ~:** profess Islam; **sich zu Buddha ~:** profess one's faith in Buddha; **sich zu seiner Schuld ~:** confess one's guilt; **sich schuldig/nicht schuldig ~:** confess/not confess one's guilt; (vor Gericht) plead guilty/not guilty
Bekenntnis *das;* **~ses, ~se (a)** confession
(b) (Eintreten) **ein ~ zum Frieden** a declaration for peace
(c) (Konfession) denomination
bekiffen *refl. V.* (ugs.) get stoned (sl.)
bekifft *Adj.* (ugs.) stoned
beklagen [1] *tr. V.* (geh.) **(a)** (betrauern) mourn
(b) (bedauern) lament
[2] *refl. V.* complain
bekleckern *tr. V.* (ugs.) **etw./sich [mit Soße** *usw.*] **~:** drop *or* spill sauce *etc.* down sth./oneself
bekleiden *tr. V.* **(a)** clothe; **mit etw. bekleidet sein** be wearing sth.
(b) (geh.: innehaben) occupy ‹*office, position*›
Bekleidung *die;* **~, ~en** clothing; clothes *pl.*
beklemmend *Adj.* oppressive
Beklemmung *die;* **~, ~en** oppressive feeling
beklommen *Adj.* uneasy; (stärker) apprehensive
bekloppt *Adj.* (salopp) barmy (Brit. coll.); loony (coll.)
beknackt *Adj.* (salopp) lousy (coll.); **ein ~er Typ** a berk (Brit. coll.); a jerk (coll.)
beknien *tr. V.* (ugs.) beg
bekommen [1] *unr. tr. V.* **(a)** get; get, receive ‹*money, letter, reply, news, orders*›; (erreichen) catch ‹*train, bus, flight*›; **was ~ Sie?** (im Geschäft) can I help you?; (im Lokal, Restaurant) what would you like?; **was ~ Sie [dafür]?** how much is that?; **Hunger/Durst ~:** get hungry/thirsty; **Angst/Mut ~:** become frightened/take heart; **er bekommt einen Bart** he's growing a beard; **sie bekommt eine** ⋯

Brust her breasts are developing; **Zähne ~:** ‹*baby*› teethe; **sie bekommt ein Kind** she's expecting a baby
(b) etw. durch die Tür/ins Auto ~: get sth. through the door/into the car
2 *unr. V.; in der Funktion eines Hilfsverbs zur Umschreibung des Passivs* get; **etw. geschenkt ~:** get [given] sth. *or* be given sth. as a present
3 *unr. itr. V.; mit sein* **jmdm. gut ~:** do sb. good; **jmdm. [gut] ~:** ‹*food, medicine*› agree with sb.; **wohl bekomms!** your [very good] health!

bekömmlich *Adj.* easily digestible

beköstigen *tr. V.* cater for

bekräftigen *tr. V.* reinforce ‹*statement*›; reaffirm ‹*promise*›

bekreuzigen *refl. V.* (kath. Kirche) cross oneself

bekriegen *tr. V.* wage war on; (fig.) fight; **sich ~:** be at war; (fig.) fight

bekümmern *tr. V.* **jmdn. ~:** cause sb. worry

bekümmert *Adj.* worried; (stärker) distressed

bekunden *tr. V.* express

belächeln *tr. V.* smile [pityingly/tolerantly *etc.*] at

beladen *unr. tr. V.* load ‹*ship*›; load [up] ‹*car, wagon*›; load up ‹*horse, donkey*›

Belag *der;* **~[e]s, Beläge (a)** coating
(b) (Fußbodenbelag) covering; (Straßenbelag) surface; (Bremsbelag) lining
(c) (von Kuchen, Scheibe Brot usw.) topping; (von Sandwiches) filling

belagern *tr. V.* (auch fig.) besiege

Belagerung *die;* **~, ~en** siege; (fig.) besieging

Belang *der;* **~[e]s, ~e (a) von/ohne ~ sein** be of importance/of no importance
(b) *Pl.* (Interessen) interests

belangen *tr. V.* (Rechtsw.) sue; (strafrechtlich) prosecute

belang·los *Adj.* (trivial) trivial; (unerheblich) of no importance (**für** for)

Belanglosigkeit *die;* **~, ~en** unimportance; (Trivialität) triviality

belassen *unr. tr. V.* leave

belastbar *Adj.* tough, resilient ‹*person*›; **seelisch/körperlich ~ sein** be emotionally/physically tough *or* resilient; be able to stand emotional/physical stress; **ein ~er Mitarbeiter** an employee who can work under pressure

Belastbarkeit *die;* **~, ~n** toughness; resilience; (von Mitarbeitern) ability to work under pressure

belasten *tr. V.* **(a) etw. ~:** put sth. under strain; (durch Gewicht) put weight on sth.
(b) (beeinträchtigen) pollute ‹*atmosphere*›; put pressure on ‹*environment*›
(c) (in Anspruch nehmen) burden (**mit** with)
(d) jmdn. ~ ‹*responsibility, guilt*› weigh upon sb.; ‹*thought*› weigh upon sb.'s mind
(e) (Rechtsw.) incriminate
(f) (Geldw.) **jmds. Konto mit 100 Euro ~:** debit sb.'s account with 100 euros

belästigen *tr. V.* bother; (sehr aufdringlich) pester; (sexuell) molest

Belästigung *die* ▶ BELÄSTIGEN: bothering; pestering; molestation

Belastung *die;* **~, ~en (a)** strain; (das Belasten) straining; (durch Gewicht) loading; (Last) load
(b) die ~ der Atmosphäre/Umwelt durch Schadstoffe the pollution of the atmosphere by harmful substances/the pressure on the environment caused by harmful substances
(c) (Bürde, Sorge) burden

Belastungs-: ~-EKG *das* (Med.) electrocardiogram after effort; **~zeuge** *der,* **~zeugin** *die* (Rechtsw.) witness for the prosecution

belaufen *unr. refl. V.* **sich auf ...** (*Akk.*) **~:** come to ...

belauschen *tr. V.* eavesdrop on

beleben **1** *tr. V.* enliven; stimulate ‹*economy*›
2 *refl. V.* ‹*market, economic activity*› revive, pick up

belebend **1** *Adj.* invigorating
2 *adv.* **~ wirken** have an invigorating effect

belebt *Adj.* busy ‹*street, crossing, town, etc.*›

Beleg *der;* **~[e]s, ~e** (Beweisstück) piece of [supporting] documentary evidence; (Quittung) receipt

belegen *tr. V.* **(a)** (Milit.: beschießen) bombard; (mit Bomben) attack
(b) (mit Belag versehen) cover ‹*floor*› (**mit** with); fill ‹*flan base, sandwich*›; top ‹*open sandwich*›; **eine Scheibe Brot mit Käse ~:** put some cheese on a slice of bread
(c) (in Besitz nehmen) occupy ‹*seat, room, etc.*›
(d) (Hochschulw.) enrol for ‹*seminar, lecture course*›
(e) den ersten/letzten Platz ~ (Sport) take first place/come last
(f) (nachweisen) prove; give a reference for ‹*quotation*›

Belegschaft *die;* **~, ~en** staff

belegt *Adj.* **(a) ein ~es Brot** an open *or* (Amer.) openface sandwich; (zugeklappt) a sandwich; **ein ~es Brötchen** a roll with topping; an open-face roll (Amer.); (zugeklappt) a filled roll; a sandwich roll (Amer.)
(b) (mit Belag bedeckt) furred ‹*tongue, tonsils*›
(c) (heiser) husky ‹*voice*›
(d) (nicht mehr frei) ‹*room, flat*› occupied

belehren *tr. V.* teach; instruct; (aufklären) enlighten; (informieren) inform; **ich lasse mich gern ~:** I'm quite willing to believe otherwise

Belehrung *die;* **~, ~en** instruction; (Zurechtweisung) lecture

beleibt *Adj.* (geh.) portly

---
*alte Schreibung - vgl. Hinweis auf S. xiv

beleidigen *tr. V.* insult
beleidigt *Adj.* insulted; (gekränkt) offended
Beleidigung *die;* ~, ~**en (a)** insult **(b)** (Rechtsw.) (schriftlich) libel; (mündlich) slander
belesen *Adj.* well-read
beleuchten *tr. V.* light up; light ‹*stairs, room, street, etc.*›
Beleuchtung *die;* ~, ~**en** lighting; (Anstrahlung) illumination
beleumdet *Adj.* **übel/gut ~ sein** have a bad/good reputation
Belgien /ˈbɛlgi̯ən/ *(das);* ~**s** Belgium
Belgier *der;* ~**s**, ~, **Belgierin** *die;* ~, ~**nen** Belgian
belgisch *Adj.* Belgian
belichten *tr. V.* (Fot.) expose; *itr.* **richtig/falsch/kurz ~:** use the right/wrong exposure/a short exposure time
Belichtung *die* (Fot.) exposure
Belieben *das;* ~**s: nach ~:** just as you/they *etc.* like
beliebig 1 *Adj.* any 2 *adv.* as you like/he likes *etc.*; **~ lange/viele** as long/many as you like/he likes *etc.*
beliebt *Adj.* popular; favourite *attrib.*
Beliebtheit *die;* ~: popularity
beliefern *tr. V.* supply
bellen *itr. V.* bark
Belletristik /bɛleˈtrɪstɪk/ *die;* ~: belles-lettres *pl.*
belohnen *tr. V.* reward ‹*person, thing*›
Belohnung *die;* ~, ~**en** reward
belüften *tr. V.* ventilate
Belüftung *die* ventilation
belügen *unr. tr. V.* lie to
belustigen *tr. V.* amuse
Belustigung *die;* ~, ~**en** amusement
bemächtigen *refl. V.* **sich jmds./einer Sache ~** (geh.) seize sb./sth.
bemalen *tr. V.* paint; (verzieren) decorate
bemängeln *tr. V.* find fault with
bemerkbar *Adj.* **sich ~ machen** attract attention; (erkennbar werden) become apparent; (spürbar werden) make itself felt
bemerken *tr. V.* **(a)** (wahrnehmen) notice; **ich wurde nicht bemerkt** I was unobserved **(b)** (äußern) remark
bemerkenswert 1 *Adj.* remarkable 2 *adv.* remarkably
Bemerkung *die;* ~, ~**en (a)** (Äußerung) remark; comment **(b)** (Notiz) note; (Anmerkung) comment
bemitleiden *tr. V.* pity; feel sorry for
bemitleidens·wert *Adj.* pitiable
bemogeln *tr. V.* (ugs.) cheat; diddle (Brit. coll.)
bemühen *refl. V.* make an effort; **sich ~, etw. zu tun** endeavour to do sth.; **sich um etw. ~:** try to obtain sth.; **sich um eine Stelle ~:** try to get a job; **sich um jmdn. ~** (kümmern) seek to help sb.
Bemühung *die;* ~, ~**en** effort
benachbart *Adj.* neighbouring *attrib.*
benachrichtigen *tr. V.* notify (**von** of)
Benachrichtigung *die;* ~, ~**en** notification
benachteiligen *tr. V.* put at a disadvantage; (diskriminieren) discriminate against; **die sozial benachteiligten Schichten** the underprivileged classes
Benachteiligte *der/die; adj. Dekl.* disadvantaged person; **die ~n** the disadvantaged; those at a disadvantage; **die sozial ~n** the underprivileged
benehmen *unr. refl. V.* behave
Benehmen *das;* ~**s** behaviour; **kein ~ haben** have no manners *pl.*
beneiden *tr. V.* envy; **jmdn. um etw. ~:** envy sb. sth.
beneidens·wert *Adj.* enviable
Benelux·länder *Pl.* Benelux countries
benennen *unr. tr. V.* name
Bengel *der;* ~**s**, ~ *od.* (nordd.) ~**s (a)** (abwertend: junger Bursche) young rascal **(b)** (fam.: kleiner Junge) little lad
benommen *Adj.* dazed; (durch Fieber, Alkohol) muzzy
benoten *tr. V.* mark (Brit.); grade (Amer.); **einen Test mit „gut" ~:** mark a test 'good' (Brit.); assign a grade of 'good' to a test (Amer.)
benötigen *tr. V.* need; require
benutzen *tr. V.* use
Benutzer *der;* ~**s**, ~: user
benutzer·freundlich *Adj.* user-friendly
Benutzerin *die;* ~, ~**nen** user
Benutzer·name *der* (DV) user name
Benutzung *die;* ~: use
Benzin *das;* ~**s** petrol (Brit.); gasoline (Amer.); gas (Amer. coll.); (Wasch~) benzine
Benzol *das;* ~**s**, ~**e** (Chemie) benzene
beobachten *tr. V.* observe; watch
Beobachter *der;* ~**s**, ~, **Beobachterin** *die;* ~, ~**nen** observer
Beobachtung *die;* ~, ~**en** observation
bepacken *tr. V.* load
bepfanden *tr. V.* charge a deposit on ‹*bottle etc.*›
bepflanzen *tr. V.* plant
bequem 1 *Adj.* **(a)** comfortable **(b)** (abwertend: träge) idle 2 *adv.* **(a)** comfortably **(b)** (leicht) easily
bequemen *refl. V.* **sich dazu ~, etw. zu tun** (geh.) condescend to do sth.
Bequemlichkeit *die;* ~ **(a)** comfort **(b)** (Trägheit) idleness
berappen *tr., itr. V.* (ugs.) ▶ BLECHEN
beraten 1 *unr. tr. V.* **(a)** advise; **jmdn. gut/schlecht ~:** give sb. good/bad advice **(b)** (besprechen) discuss ‹*plan, matter*› ··›

b

2 *unr. itr. V.* **über etw.** (*Akk.*) **~**: discuss sth.
3 *unr. refl. V.* **sich mit jmdm. ~, ob ...**: discuss with sb. whether ...

Berater *der;* **~s, ~, Beraterin** *die;* **~, ~nen** adviser

beratschlagen **1** *tr. V.* discuss
2 *itr. V.* **über etw.** (*Akk.*) **~**: discuss sth.

Beratung *die;* **~, ~en (a)** advice *no indef. art.;* (durch Arzt, Rechtsanwalt) consultation
(b) (Besprechung) discussion

berauben *tr. V.* (auch fig.) rob (*Gen.* of)

berauschen (geh.) **1** *tr. V.* (auch fig.) intoxicate
2 *refl. V.* become intoxicated (**an** + *Dat.* with)

Berber *der;* **~s, ~(a)** Berber
(b) (Teppich) Berber carpet/rug
(c) (Nichtsesshafter) tramp

Berberin *die;* **~, ~nen** ▶ BERBER A, C

berechenbar *Adj.* calculable; predictable ‹*behaviour*›

Berechenbarkeit *die;* **~**: calculability; (des Verhaltens) predictability

berechnen *tr. V.* **(a)** (auch fig.) calculate; predict ‹*behaviour, consequences*›
(b) (anrechnen) charge; **jmdm. 10 Euro für etw.** *od.* **jmdm. etw. mit 10 Euro ~**: charge sb. 10 euros for sth.; **jmdm. zu viel ~**: overcharge sb.

Berechnung *die;* **~, ~en (a)** calculation
(b) (Eigennutz) [calculating] self-interest

berechtigen *tr. V.* entitle; *itr.* **die Karte berechtigt zum Eintritt** the ticket entitles the bearer to admission

berechtigt *Adj.* **(a)** (gerechtfertigt) justified
(b) (befugt) authorized

Berechtigung *die;* **~, ~en (a)** (Befugnis) entitlement; (Recht) right
(b) (Rechtmäßigkeit) legitimacy

bereden *tr. V.* **(a)** (besprechen) discuss
(b) jmdn. ~, etw. zu tun talk sb. into doing sth.

beredsam *Adj.* eloquent

Beredsamkeit *die;* **~**: eloquence

beredt *Adj.* (auch fig.) eloquent

Bereich *der;* **~[e]s, ~e** area; **im privaten/staatlichen ~**: in the private/public sector

bereichern *refl. V.* get rich

Bereicherung *die;* **~, ~en (a)** money-making
(b) (Nutzen) valuable acquisition

bereifen *tr. V.* put tyres on ‹*car*›; put a tyre on ‹*wheel*›

Bereifung *die;* **~, ~en** [set *sing.* of] tyres *pl.*

bereinigen *tr. V.* clear up ‹*misunderstanding*›; settle, resolve ‹*dispute*›

bereisen *tr. V.* travel around *or* about; travel through ‹*towns*›; (beruflich) ‹*representative etc.*› cover ‹*area*›; **fremde Länder ~**: travel in foreign countries

bereit *Adj.* ready; **~ sein, etw. zu tun** be ready *or* willing to do sth.

bereiten *tr. V.* **(a)** prepare; make ‹*tea, coffee*›
(b) (verursachen) cause ‹*trouble, sorrow, difficulty, etc.*›

bereit-: ~|halten *unr. tr. V.* have ready; **~|legen** *tr. V.* lay out ready; **~|liegen** *unr. itr. V.* be ready

bereits *Adv.* already

Bereitschaft *die;* **~**: readiness; willingness

Bereitschafts·dienst *der:* **~ haben** ‹*doctor, nurse*› be on call; ‹*policeman, fireman*› be on standby duty; ‹*chemist's*› be on rota duty (*for dispensing outside normal hours*)

bereit-: ~|stehen *unr. itr. V.* be ready; **~|stellen** *tr. V.* place ready; get ready ‹*food, drinks*›; ready, make ‹*money, funds*› available; **~willig** **1** *Adj.* willing. **2** *adv.* readily

Bereitwilligkeit *die;* **~**: willingness

bereuen **1** *tr. V.* regret
2 *itr. V.* be sorry; (Rel.) repent

Berg *der;* **~[e]s, ~e (a)** hill; (im Hochgebirge) mountain
(b) (Haufen) huge pile; (von Akten, Abfall auch) mountain

berg-, Berg-: ~ab /-'-/ *Adv.* downhill; **~auf** /-'-/ *Adv.* uphill; **~bahn** *die* mountain railway; (Seilbahn) mountain cableway; **~bau** *der* mining

bergen *unr. tr. V.* **(a)** rescue, save ‹*person*›; salvage ‹*ship, cargo, belongings*›
(b) (geh.: enthalten) hold

Berg-: ~führer *der,* **~führerin** *die;* **~~, ~~nen** mountain guide; **~hütte** *die* mountain hut

bergig *Adj.* hilly; (mit hohen Bergen) mountainous

Berg-: ~kette *die* range *or* chain of mountains; mountain range *or* chain; **~kristall** *der* rock crystal; **~land** *das* hilly country *no indef. art.;* (mit hohen Bergen) mountainous country *no indef. art.;* **~mann** *der; Pl.* **~leute** miner; **~station** *die* top station; **~steigen** *das;* **~~s** mountaineering *no art.;* **~steiger** *der,* **~steigerin** *die;* **~~, ~~nen** mountaineer

Bergung *die;* **~, ~en (a)** rescue
(b) (von Schiffen, Gut) salvaging

Berg-: ~wacht *die* mountain rescue service; **~werk** *das* mine

Bericht *der;* **~[e]s, ~e** report

berichten *tr., itr. V.* report

Bericht-: ~erstatter *der;* **~~s, ~~, ~erstatterin** *die;* **~~, ~~nen** reporter; **~erstattung** *die* reporting *no indef. art.*

berichtigen *tr. V.* correct

*old spelling - see note on page xiv

Berichtigung *die;* **~, ~en** correction
berieseln *tr. V.* **(a)** (bewässern) irrigate **(b) sich ständig mit Musik ~ lassen** (ugs. abwertend) constantly have music on in the background
Berlin *(das);* **~s** Berlin
Berliner 1 *indekl. Adj.* Berlin 2 *der;* **~s, ~: (a)** Berliner **(b)** (Gebäck) [jam (Brit.) *or* (Amer.) jelly] doughnut
Berlinerin *die;* **~, ~nen** Berliner
berlinisch *Adj.* Berlin *attrib.*
Bern *(das);* **~s** Bern[e]
Bernhardiner *der;* **~s, ~:** St. Bernard [dog]
Bern·stein *der* amber
bersten *unr. itr. V.; mit sein* (geh.) ‹*ice*› break up; ‹*glass*› shatter [into pieces]; ‹*wall*› crack up
berüchtigt *Adj.* notorious **(wegen** for); (verrufen) disreputable
berücksichtigen *tr. V.* take into account; consider ‹*applicant, application, suggestion*›
Berücksichtigung *die;* **~: bei ~ aller Umstände** taking all the circumstances into account
Beruf *der;* **~[e]s, ~e** occupation; (akademischer) profession; (handwerklicher) trade; **was sind Sie von ~?** what do you do for a living?
berufen¹ 1 *unr. tr. V.* **(a)** (einsetzen) appoint **(b) berufe es nicht!** (ugs.) don't speak too soon! 2 *unr. refl. V.* **sich auf etw.** *(Akk.)* **~:** refer to sth.; **sich auf jmdn. ~:** quote *or* mention sb.'s name
berufen² *Adj.* **(a)** competent; **aus ~em Munde** from somebody qualified to speak **(b) sich dazu ~ fühlen, etw. zu tun** feel called to do sth.
beruflich 1 *Adj.* vocational ‹*training etc.*›; (bei akademischen Berufen) professional ‹*training etc.*› 2 *adv.* **~ erfolgreich sein** be successful in one's career; **sich ~ weiterbilden** undertake further job training
berufs-, Berufs-: ~akademie *die* vocational college **~ausbildung** *die* vocational training; **~aussichten** *Pl.* job prospects (*in a particular profession etc.*); **~berater** *der,* **~beraterin** *die* vocational adviser; **~beratung** *die* vocational guidance; **~bild** *das* outline of a/the profession/trade as a career; **~erfahrung** *die* [professional] experience; **~geheimnis** *das* professional secret; (Schweigepflicht) professional secrecy; **~krankheit** *die* occupational disease; **~leben** *das* working life; **~schule** *die* vocational school; **~soldat** *der,* **~soldatin** *die* regular soldier; **~sportler** *der* professional sportsman; **~sportlerin** *die* professional sportswoman; **~tätig** *Adj.* working *attrib.;* **~tätige** *der/die; adj. Dekl.* working person; **~tätige** *Pl.* working people; **~verkehr** *der* rush hour traffic
Berufung *die;* **~, ~en (a)** (für ein Amt) offer of an appointment **(auf, in, an** + *Akk.* to) **(b)** (innerer Auftrag) vocation **(c)** (das Sichberufen) **unter ~** *(Dat.)* **auf jmdn./etw.** referring *or* with reference to sb./sth. **(d)** (Rechtsw.: Einspruch) appeal; **~ einlegen** lodge an appeal
beruhen *itr. V.* **auf etw.** *(Dat.)* **~:** be based on sth.; **etw. auf sich ~ lassen** let sth. rest
beruhigen /bə'ruːɪgn̩/ 1 *tr. V.* calm [down]; pacify ‹*child, baby*›; salve ‹*conscience*›; (trösten) soothe; (von einer Sorge befreien) reassure 2 *refl. V.* ‹*person*› calm down; ‹*sea*› become calm
Beruhigung *die;* **~** ▶ BERUHIGEN 1: calming [down]; pacifying; salving; soothing; reassurance
Beruhigungs·mittel *das* tranquillizer
berühmt *Adj.* famous
berühmt-berüchtigt *Adj.* notorious
Berühmtheit *die;* **~, ~en (a)** (Ruhm) fame **(b)** (Mensch) celebrity
berühren *tr. V.* **(a)** touch; (fig.) touch on ‹*topic, issue. etc.*›; **sich ~:** touch **(b)** (beeindrucken) affect; **das berührt mich nicht** it's a matter of indifference to me
Berührung *die;* **~, ~en** touch; **mit jmdm./etw. in ~** *(Akk.)* **kommen** (auch fig.) come into contact with sb./sth.
besagen *tr. V.* say; (bedeuten) mean
besänftigen *tr. V.* calm [down]; pacify; calm, soothe ‹*temper*›
Besatz *der;* **~es, Besätze** (Borte) trimming *no indef. art.*
Besatzung *die;* **~, ~en (a)** (Mannschaft) crew **(b)** (Milit.: Verteidigungstruppe) garrison **(c)** (Milit.: Okkupationstruppen) occupying forces *pl.*
Besatzungs-: ~macht *die* occupying power; **~zone** *die* occupied zone
besaufen *unr. refl. V.* (salopp) get canned (Brit. sl.) *or* bombed (Amer. sl.)
Besäufnis *das;* **~ses, ~se** (salopp) booze-up (Brit. coll.): blast (Amer. coll.)
beschädigen *tr. V.* damage
Beschädigung *die;* **~, ~en (a)** damaging **(b)** (Schaden) damage
beschaffen¹ *tr. V.* obtain, get *(Dat.* for)
beschaffen² *Adj.* **so ~ sein, dass ...:** be such that ...
Beschaffenheit *die;* **~:** properties *pl.*
Beschaffung *die;* **~:** ▶ BESCHAFFEN: obtaining; getting
beschäftigen 1 *refl. V.* occupy oneself; ⋯>

b

sich viel mit Musik/den Kindern ~: devote a great deal of one's time to music/the children; **sehr beschäftigt sein** be very busy
2 *tr. V.* **(a)** (geistig in Anspruch nehmen) **jmdn. ~:** preoccupy sb.
(b) (angestellt haben) employ ‹*workers, staff*›
(c) (zu tun geben) occupy; **jmdn. mit etw. ~:** give sb. sth. to occupy him/her

Beschäftigte *der/die; adj. Dekl.* employee

Beschäftigung *die;* **~, ~en (a)** (Tätigkeit) activity
(b) (Anstellung, Stelle) job
(c) (mit einer Frage, einem Problem) consideration (**mit** of); (Studium) study (**mit** of)
(d) (von Arbeitskräften) employment

beschämen *tr. V.* shame

beschämend 1 *Adj.* **(a)** (schändlich) shameful
(b) (demütigend) humiliating
2 *adv.* shamefully

beschämt *Adj.* ashamed

Beschämung *die;* **~:** shame

beschatten *tr. V.* **(a)** (geh.) shade
(b) (überwachen) shadow

beschaulich 1 *Adj.* peaceful ‹*life, manner, etc.*›
2 *adv.* peacefully

Beschaulichkeit *die;* **~:** peacefulness

Bescheid *der;* **~[e]s, ~e (a)** (Auskunft) information; (Antwort) answer; reply; **jmdm. ~ geben** *od.* **sagen[, ob ...]** let sb. know or tell sb. [whether ...]; **sage bitte im Hotel ~, dass ...:** please let the hotel know that ...; **[über etw.** (*Akk.*)**] ~ wissen** know [about sth.]
(b) (Entscheidung) decision

bescheiden[1] 1 *unr. tr. V.* **jmdn./etw. abschlägig ~:** turn sb./sth. down
2 *unr. refl. V.* (geh.) be content

bescheiden[2] 1 *Adj.* modest
2 *adv.* modestly

Bescheidenheit *die;* **~:** modesty

bescheinigen *tr. V.* confirm ‹*sth.*› in writing

Bescheinigung *die;* **~, ~en** written confirmation *no indef. art.;* (Schein, Attest) certificate

bescheißen *unr. tr. V.* (derb) **jmdn. ~:** rip sb. off (coll.); screw sb. (coarse)

beschenken *tr. V.* give ‹*sb.*› a present/presents

bescheren *tr. V.* **jmdn. [mit etw.] ~:** give sb. [sth. as] a Christmas present/Christmas presents

Bescherung *die;* **~, ~en (a)** (zu Weihnachten) giving out of the Christmas presents
(b) das ist ja eine schöne ~ (ugs.) this is a pretty kettle of fish

bescheuert *Adj.* (salopp) **(a)** (verrückt) barmy (Brit. coll.); nuts (coll.)
(b) (unangenehm) stupid ‹*task, party, etc.*›

beschichten *tr. V.* (Technik) coat

Beschichtung *die;* **~, ~en** (Technik) coating

beschießen *unr. tr. V.* fire at; (mit Artillerie) bombard

beschimpfen *tr. V.* abuse; swear at

Beschimpfung *die;* **~, ~en** insult; **~en** abuse *sing.;* insults

beschissen *Adj.* (derb) lousy (coll.); shitty (coarse)

Beschlag *der;* **~[e]s, Beschläge (a)** fitting
(b) jmdn./etw. mit ~ belegen *od.* **in ~ nehmen** monopolize sb./sth.

beschlagen[1] 1 *unr. tr. V.* shoe ‹*horse*›
2 *unr. itr. V.; mit sein* ‹*window*› mist up (Brit.), fog up (Amer.); (durch Dampf) steam up

beschlagen[2] *Adj.* knowledgeable

Beschlagnahme *die;* **~, ~n** confiscation

beschlagnahmen *tr. V.* confiscate

Beschlagnahmung *die;* **~, ~en**
▶ BESCHLAGNAHME

beschleunigen 1 *tr. V.* accelerate; speed up ‹*work, delivery*›; quicken ‹*pace, step[s], pulse*›
2 *refl. V.* ‹*heart rate*› increase; ‹*pulse*› quicken
3 *itr. V.* ‹*driver, car, etc.*› accelerate

Beschleunigung *die;* **~, ~en**
▶ BESCHLEUNIGEN 1: acceleration; speeding up; quickening

beschließen *unr. tr. V.* **(a)** decide; pass ‹*law*›; **~, etw. zu tun** decide *or* resolve to do sth.
(b) (beenden) end

Beschluss, *Beschluß *der;* **Beschlusses, Beschlüsse** decision; (gemeinsam gefasst) resolution; **einen ~ fassen** come to a decision/pass a resolution

beschluss·fähig, *beschluß·fähig *Adj.* quorate

Beschluss·fähigkeit, *Beschluß·fähigkeit *die* presence of a quorum

beschmieren *tr. V.* **etw./sich ~:** get sth./oneself in a mess

beschmutzen *tr. V.* make ‹*sth.*› dirty

beschneiden *unr. tr. V.* **(a)** cut ‹*hedge*›; prune ‹*bush*›; cut back ‹*tree*›; **einem Vogel die Flügel ~:** clip a bird's wings
(b) (Med., Rel.) circumcise

Beschneidung *die;* **~, ~en (a)**
▶ BESCHNEIDEN A: cutting; pruning; cutting back
(b) (Med., Rel.) circumcision

beschnüffeln *tr. V.* sniff at

beschönigen *tr. V.* gloss over

beschränken 1 *tr. V.* restrict (**auf** + *Akk.* to)
2 *refl. V.* **sich auf etw.** (*Akk.*) **~:** restrict oneself to sth.

beschränkt 1 *Adj.* **(a)** (dumm) dull-witted
(b) (engstirnig) narrow-minded

*alte Schreibung - vgl. Hinweis auf S. xiv

2 *adv.* narrow-mindedly
Beschränktheit *die;* ~: **(a)** (Dummheit) lack of intelligence
(b) (Engstirnigkeit) narrow-mindedness
Beschränkung *die;* ~, ~**en** restriction
beschreiben *unr. tr. V.* **(a)** write on; (voll schreiben) write ‹*page, side, etc.*›
(b) (darstellen) describe
Beschreibung *die;* ~, ~**en** description
beschriften *tr. V.* label; inscribe ‹*stone*›; letter ‹*sign, label, etc.*›; (mit Adresse) address
beschuldigen *tr. V.* accuse (*Gen.* of)
Beschuldigte *der/die; adj. Dekl.* accused
Beschuldigung *die;* ~, ~**en** accusation
beschummeln *tr. V.* (ugs.) cheat; diddle (Brit. coll.)
Beschuss, *Beschuß *der;* **Beschusses** fire; **[heftig** *od.* **stark] unter ~ geraten/stehen** *od.* **liegen** (auch fig.) come/be under [heavy] fire
beschützen *tr. V.* protect (**vor** + *Dat.* from)
Beschützer *der;* ~**s**, ~, **Beschützerin** *die;* ~, ~**nen** protector
Beschwerde *die;* ~, ~**n** **(a)** complaint (**gegen, über** + *Akk.* about)
(b) *Pl.* (Schmerz) pain *sing.;* (Leiden) trouble *sing.*
beschweren 1 *refl. V.* complain (**über** + *Akk.*, **wegen** about); **sich bei jmdm. ~:** complain to sb.
2 *tr. V.* weight down
beschwerlich *Adj.* arduous; (ermüdend) exhausting
beschwichtigen *tr. V.* pacify; mollify ‹*anger etc.*›
Beschwichtigung *die;* ~, ~**en** pacification; (des Zorns usw.) mollification
beschwingt *Adj.* lively
beschwipst *Adj.* (ugs.) tipsy
beschwören *unr. tr. V.* **(a)** swear to; **~, dass ...:** swear that ...; **eine Aussage ~:** swear a statement on oath
(b) charm ‹*snake*›
(c) (erscheinen lassen) invoke ‹*spirit*›
(d) (bitten) implore
Beschwörung *die;* ~, ~**en** **(a)** (Zauberspruch) spell; incantation
(b) ▶ BESCHWÖREN C: invoking
(c) (Bitte) entreaty
beseitigen *tr. V.* remove; eliminate ‹*error, difficulty*›; dispose of ‹*rubbish*›
Beseitigung *die;* ~: ▶ BESEITIGEN: removal; elimination; disposal
Besen *der;* ~**s**, ~ broom; **ich fress einen ~, wenn das stimmt** (salopp) I'll eat my hat if that's right (coll.); **neue ~ kehren gut** (Spr.) a new broom sweeps clean (prov.)
besessen *Adj.* **(a)** possessed
(b) (fig.) obsessive ‹*gambler*›; **von einer Idee ~ sein** be obsessed with an idea
Besessenheit *die;* ~ **(a)** possession
(b) obsessiveness
besetzen *tr. V.* **(a)** (mit Pelz, Spitzen) edge; trim; **mit Perlen besetzt** set with pearls
(b) (belegen; auch Milit.: erobern) occupy
(c) (vergeben) fill ‹*post, position, role, etc.*›
besetzt *Adj.* occupied; ‹*table, seat*› taken *pred.;* (gefüllt) full; (Fernspr.) engaged; busy (Amer.)
Besetzung *die;* ~, ~**en** **(a)** (einer Stellung) filling
(b) (Film, Theater usw.) cast
(c) (Eroberung) occupation
besichtigen *tr. V.* see ‹*sights*›; see the sights of ‹*town*›; view ‹*house etc. for sale*›
Besichtigung *die;* ~, ~**en: zur ~ der Stadt/des Schlosses/der Wohnung** to see the sights of the town/to see the castle/to view the flat
besiedeln *tr. V.* settle
besiedelt *Adj.* **dicht/dünn ~:** densely/thinly populated
besiegen *tr. V.* defeat
besinnen *unr. refl. V.* **(a)** think it over
(b) sich [auf jmdn./etw.] ~: remember [sb./sth.]
Besinnung *die;* ~: consciousness; **die ~ verlieren** faint; **[wieder] zur ~ kommen** regain consciousness
besinnungs·los 1 *Adj.* unconscious
2 *adv.* mindlessly
Besinnungslosigkeit *die;* ~: unconsciousness *no art.*
Besitz *der* **(a)** property
(b) (das Besitzen) possession; **im ~ einer Sache** (*Gen.*) **sein** be in possession of sth.
Besitz·anspruch *der* claim to ownership
besitzen *unr. tr. V.* own; have ‹*quality, talent, etc.*›; (nachdrücklicher) possess
Besitzer *der;* ~**s**, ~, **Besitzerin** *die;* ~, ~**nen** owner
besoffen *Adj.* (salopp) canned (Brit. sl.); bombed (Amer. sl.)
Besoffene *der/die; adj. Dekl.* (salopp) drunk
besohlen *tr. V.* sole; **neu ~:** resole
besonder... *Adj.* special; **ein ~es Ereignis** an unusual *or* a special event; **keine ~e Leistung** no great achievement
Besonderheit *die;* ~, ~**en** special feature; (Eigenart) peculiarity
besonders 1 *Adv.* particularly
2 *Adj.; nicht attr.; nur verneint* (ugs.) **nicht ~ sein** be nothing special
besonnen 1 *Adj.* prudent
2 *adv.* prudently
Besonnenheit *die;* ~: prudence
besorgen *tr. V.* **(a)** get; (kaufen) buy
(b) (erledigen) take care of
Besorgnis *die;* ~, ~**se** concern
besorgt 1 *Adj.* concerned (**um** about)
2 *adv.* with concern
Besorgung *die;* ~, ~**en** purchase

bespitzeln *tr. V.* spy on
besprechen *unr. tr. V.* discuss; (rezensieren) review
Besprechung *die;* ~, ~**en** discussion; (Konferenz) meeting; (Rezension) review
bespritzen *tr. V.* **(a)** splash; (mit einem Wasserstrahl) spray
(b) (beschmutzen) bespatter
besprühen *tr. V.* spray
besser 1 *Adj.* **(a)** better; **umso ~:** so much the better
(b) (sozial höher gestellt) superior
2 *adv.* **[immer] alles ~ wissen** always know better; **es ~ haben** be better off; **es geht ihr ~:** she feels better; **~ gesagt** to be [more] precise
3 *Adv.* (lieber) **das lässt du ~ sein** *od.* (ugs.) **bleiben** you'd better not do that
***besser|gehen** ▸ BESSER 2
bessern 1 *refl. V.* improve; ‹*person*› mend one's ways
2 *tr. V.* improve; reform ‹*criminal*›
Besserung *die;* ~, ~**en** recovery; **gute ~!** get well soon
best... 1 *Adj.* **(a)** best; **bei ~er Gesundheit/Laune sein** be in the best of health/spirits *pl.;* **im ~en Falle** at best; **in den ~en Jahren, im ~en Alter** in one's prime; **~e Grüße an ...** (*Akk.*) best wishes to ...; **mit den ~en Grüßen** *od.* **Wünschen** with best wishes; (als Briefschluss) ≈ yours sincerely
(b) es ist *od.* **wäre das Beste, wenn ...:** it would be best if ...; **der/die/das nächste Beste ...:** the first ... one comes across; **einen Witz zum Besten geben** entertain [those present] with a joke; **das Beste vom Besten** the very best; **sein Bestes tun** do one's best; **zu deinem Besten** for your benefit
2 *adv.* **am ~en** best
3 *Adv.* **am ~en fährst du mit dem Zug** it would be best for you to go by train
Bestand *der;* ~, **Bestände (a)** existence, (Fort~) continued existence
(b) (Vorrat) stock (**an** + *Dat.* of)
bestanden *Adj.* **von** *od.* **mit etw. ~ sein** have sth. growing on it; **mit Tannen ~e Hügel** fir-covered hills
beständig 1 *Adj.* **(a)** constant
(b) (gleich bleibend) constant; steadfast ‹*person*›; settled ‹*weather*›
(c) (widerstandsfähig) resistant (**gegen** to)
2 *adv.* constantly
Beständigkeit *die;* ~ **(a)** steadfastness
(b) (Widerstandsfähigkeit) resistance (**gegen** to)
Bestand·teil *der* component
bestärken *tr. V.* confirm
bestätigen 1 *tr. V.* confirm; endorse ‹*document*›; acknowledge ‹*receipt*›
2 *refl. V.* be confirmed; ‹*rumour*› prove to be true

***old spelling - see note on page xiv**

Bestätigung *die;* ~, ~**en** confirmation; (des Empfangs) acknowledgement; (schriftlich) letter of confirmation
bestatten *tr. V.* (geh.) inter (formal); bury
Bestattung *die;* ~, ~**en** (geh.) interment (formal); burial; (Feierlichkeit) funeral
Bestattungs-: ~institut *das,* **~unternehmen** *das* [firm of] undertakers *pl. or* funeral directors *pl.;* funeral parlor (Amer.)
bestäuben *tr. V.* **(a)** dust
(b) (Biol.) pollinate
bestaunen *tr. V.* marvel at
bestechen *unr. tr. V.* bribe
bestechlich *Adj.* corruptible; open to bribery *postpos.*
Bestechung *die;* ~, ~**en** bribery *no indef. art.*
Bestechungs-: ~geld *das* bribe; **~versuch** *der* attempted bribery
Besteck *das;* ~**[e]s, ~e** cutlery setting; (ugs.: Gesamtheit der Bestecke) cutlery
bestehen 1 *unr. itr. V.* **(a)** exist; **es besteht [die] Aussicht/Gefahr, dass ...:** there is a prospect/danger that ...; **noch besteht die Hoffnung, dass ...:** there is still hope that ...; **~ bleiben** remain; ‹*regulation*› remain in force
(b) (fortdauern) survive; last
(c) aus etw. ~: consist of sth.; (hergestellt sein) be made of sth.
(d) auf etw. (*Dat.*) **~:** insist on sth.
2 *unr. tr. V.* pass ‹*test, examination*›
Bestehen *das;* ~**s** existence; **die Firma feiert ihr 10-jähriges ~:** the firm is celebrating its tenth anniversary
***bestehen|bleiben** ▸ BESTEHEN 1A
bestehend *Adj.* existing; current ‹*conditions*›
bestehlen *unr. tr. V.* rob
besteigen *unr. tr. V.* **(a)** climb; mount ‹*horse, bicycle*›; ascend ‹*throne*›
(b) board ‹*ship, aircraft*›; get on ‹*bus, train*›
Besteigung *die;* ~, ~**en** ascent
bestellen *tr. V.* **(a)** *auch itr.* order (**bei** from); **würden Sie mir bitte ein Taxi ~?** would you order me a taxi?
(b) (reservieren lassen) reserve ‹*tickets, table*›
(c) jmdn. [für 10 Uhr] zu sich ~: ask sb. to go/come to see one [at 10 o'clock]
(d) (ausrichten) **jmdm. etw. ~:** tell sb. sth.; **bestell deinem Mann schöne Grüße von mir** give your husband my regards
Bestellung *die;* ~, ~**en (a)** order
(b) (Reservierung) reservation
besten·falls *Adv.* at best
bestens *Adv.* extremely well
besteuern *tr. V.* tax
bestialisch 1 *Adj.* **(a)** bestial
(b) (ugs.: schrecklich) ghastly (coll.)
2 *adv.* **(a)** in a bestial manner
(b) (ugs.: schrecklich) awfully (coll.)
Bestialität *die;* ~: bestiality

besticken *tr. V.* embroider

Bestie /ˈbɛsti̯ə/ *die;* ~, ~**n** beast

bestimmen 1 *tr. V.* **(a)** (festsetzen) decide on; fix ‹*price, time, etc.*›
(b) (vorsehen) intend; **das ist für dich bestimmt** that is meant for you
(c) (identifizieren) identify; determine ‹*age, position*›; define ‹*meaning*›
(d) (prägen) determine the character of
2 *itr. V.* **(a)** make the decisions
(b) über jmdn. ~: tell sb. what to do; **[frei] über etw.** (*Akk.*) ~: do as one wishes with sth.

bestimmend 1 *Adj.* decisive
2 *adv.* decisively

bestimmt 1 *Adj.* **(a)** (speziell) particular; (gewiss) certain; (genau) definite
(b) (festgelegt) fixed; given ‹*quantity*›
(c) (Sprachw.) definite ‹*article etc.*›
(d) (entschieden) firm
2 *adv.* **(a)** (deutlich) clearly; (genau) precisely
(b) (entschieden) firmly
3 *Adv.* for certain; **du weißt es doch [ganz]** ~ **noch** I'm sure you must remember it; **ich habe das** ~ **liegen gelassen** I must have left it behind

Bestimmtheit *die;* ~: firmness; (im Auftreten) decisiveness

Bestimmung *die;* ~, ~**en (a)** (das Festsetzen) fixing
(b) (Vorschrift) regulation
(c) (Zweck) purpose
(d) ▶ BESTIMMEN 1c: identification; determination; definition
(e) (Sprachw.) modifier; **adverbiale** ~: adverbial qualification

best·möglich *Adj.* best possible

bestrafen *tr. V.* punish (**für, wegen** for); **es wird mit Gefängnis bestraft** it is punishable by imprisonment

Bestrafung *die;* ~, ~**en** punishment

bestrahlen *tr. V.* **(a)** illuminate; floodlight ‹*building*›
(b) (Med.) treat ‹*tumour, part of body*› using radiotherapy

Bestrahlung *die;* ~, ~**en** (Med.) radiation [treatment] *no indef. art.*

Bestreben *das;* ~**s** endeavour[s *pl.*]

bestrebt *Adj.*: ~ **sein, etw. zu tun** endeavour to do sth.

Bestrebung *die;* ~, ~**en** effort; (Versuch) attempt

bestreichen *unr. tr. V.* **A mit B** ~: spread B on A

bestreiten *unr. tr. V.* **(a)** dispute; (leugnen) deny
(b) (finanzieren) finance ‹*studies*›; pay for ‹*studies, sb.'s keep*›; meet ‹*costs, expenses*›
(c) (gestalten) carry ‹*programme, conversation, etc.*›

bestreuen *tr. V.* sprinkle

Bestseller /ˈbɛstzɛlɐ/ *der;* ~**s**, ~: best seller

bestürzend *Adj.* disturbing; (erschreckend) alarming

bestürzt 1 *Adj.* dismayed
2 *adv.* with dismay

Bestürzung *die;* ~: dismay

Besuch *der;* ~[e]**s**, ~**e (a)** visit (*Gen.*, **bei** to); **ein** ~ **bei jmdm.** a visit to sb.; (kurz) a call on sb.
(b) (Teilnahme) attendance (*Gen.* at)
(c) (Gast) visitor; (Gäste) visitors *pl.*; ~ **haben** have visitors/a visitor

besuchen *tr. V.* **(a)** visit; (weniger formell) go to see ‹*person*›; go to ‹*exhibition, theatre, museum, etc.*›; (zur Besichtigung) go to see ‹*church, exhibition, etc.*›
(b) die Schule/Universität ~: go to school/ university

Besucher *der;* ~**s**, ~, **Besucherin** *die;* ~, ~**nen** visitor

Besuchs-: ~**erlaubnis** *die* visiting permit; ~**zeit** *die* visiting time *or* hours *pl.*; **es ist keine** ~**zeit** it is not visiting time

besucht *Adj.* **gut/schlecht** ~: well/poorly attended ‹*lecture, performance, etc.*›; much/ little frequented ‹*restaurant etc.*›

Beta·blocker /-blɔkɐ/ *der;* ~**s**, ~ (Med.) betablocker

betagt *Adj.* (geh.) elderly

betasten *tr. V.* feel [with one's fingers]

betätigen 1 *refl. V.* occupy oneself; **sich politisch/körperlich** ~: engage in political/ physical activity
2 *tr. V.* operate ‹*lever, switch, flush, etc.*›; apply ‹*brake*›

Betätigung *die;* ~, ~**en: (a)** activity
(b) ▶ BETÄTIGEN 2: operation; application

betäuben *tr. V.* **(a)** (Med.) anaesthetize; deaden ‹*nerve*›; **jmdn. örtlich** ~: give sb. a local anaesthetic
(b) (unterdrücken) deaden ‹*pain*›; still ‹*unease, fear*›
(c) (benommen machen) daze; (mit einem Schlag) stun

Betäubung *die;* ~, ~**en: (a)** (Med.) anaesthetization; (Narkose) anaesthesia
(b) (Benommenheit) daze

Betäubungs·mittel *das* narcotic; (Med.) anaesthetic

beteiligen 1 *refl. V.* take part (**an** + *Dat.* in)
2 *tr. V.* **jmdn. [mit 10 %] an etw.** (*Dat.*) ~: give sb. a [10%] share of sth.

beteiligt *Adj.* **(a)** involved (**an** + *Dat.* in)
(b) (finanziell) **an einem Unternehmen/am Gewinn** ~ **sein** have a share in a business/ in the profit

Beteiligte *der/die; adj. Dekl.* person involved

Beteiligung *die;* ~, ~**en (a)** participation (**an** + *Dat.* in)
(b) (Anteil) share (**an** + *Dat.* in)

beten 1 *itr. V.* pray (**für, um** for)
2 *tr. V.* say ‹*prayer*›

beteuern *tr. V.* affirm; protest ‹*one's innocence*›

Beteuerung *die;* ~, **~en** ▸ BETEUERN: affirmation; protestation

Beton /be'tɔŋ, *bes. österr.:* be'to:n/ *der;* **~s, ~s** /-ɔŋs/ *od.* (bes. österr.:) **~e** /-o:nə/ concrete

betonen *tr. V.* **(a)** stress ‹*word, syllable*› **(b)** (hervorheben) emphasize

betonieren *tr. V.* concrete; surface ‹*road etc.*› with concrete

betont 1 *Adj.* **(a)** stressed **(b)** (bewusst) studied 2 *adv.* studiedly

Betonung *die;* ~, **~en (a)** stressing **(b)** (Akzent) stress; (Intonation) intonation **(c)** (Hervorhebung) emphasis

betören *tr. V.* (geh.) captivate

betr. *Abk.* = **betreffs, betrifft** re

Betr. *Abk.* = **Betreff** re

Betracht: **jmdn./etw. in ~ ziehen** consider sb./sth.; **jmdn./etw. außer ~ lassen** disregard sb./sth.

betrachten *tr. V.* **(a)** look at **(b) jmdn./etw. als etw. ~**: regard sb./sth. as sth. **(c)** (beurteilen) consider

Betrachter *der;* **~s, ~, Betrachterin** *die;* ~, **~nen** observer

beträchtlich 1 *Adj.* considerable 2 *adv.* considerably

Betrachtung *die;* ~, **~en (a)** contemplation; (Untersuchung) examination **(b)** (Überlegung) reflection

Betrachtungs·weise *die* way of looking at things; (Standpunkt) point of view

Betrag *der;* **~[e]s, Beträge** amount; **„~ dankend erhalten“** 'received with thanks'

betragen 1 *unr. itr. V.* be; (bei Geldsummen) come to; amount to 2 *unr. refl. V.* behave

Betragen *das;* **~s** behaviour

Betreff *der;* **~[e]s, ~e** (im Brief) heading

betreffen *unr. tr. V.* concern; ‹*new rule, change, etc.*› affect

betreffend *Adj.* concerning; **der ~e Sachbearbeiter** the person dealing with this matter; **in dem ~en Fall** in the case in question

betreffs *Präp. mit Gen.* (Amtsspr., Kaufmannsspr.) concerning

betreiben *unr. tr. V.* **(a)** proceed with, (energisch) press ahead with ‹*task, case, etc.*›; pursue ‹*policy, studies*›; carry on ‹*trade*›; go in for ‹*sport*› **(b)** run ‹*business, shop*› **(c)** (in Betrieb halten) operate

betreten[1] *unr. tr. V.* (hineintreten in) enter; (treten auf) step on to; (begehen) walk on ‹*carpet, grass, etc.*›; **„Betreten verboten“** 'Keep off'; (kein Eintritt) 'Keep out'

*alte Schreibung - vgl. Hinweis auf S. xiv

betreten[2] 1 *Adj.* embarrassed 2 *adv.* with embarrassment

betreuen *tr. V.* look after; care for ‹*invalid*›; supervise ‹*youth group*›; see to the needs of ‹*tourists, sportsmen*›

Betreuung *die;* ~: care *no indef. art.*

Betrieb *der;* **~[e]s, ~e (a)** business; (Firma) firm **(b)** (das In-Funktion-Sein) operation; **außer ~ sein** not operate; (wegen Störung) be out of order; **in/außer ~ setzen** start up/stop ‹*machine etc.*› **(c)** (ugs.: Treiben) bustle; (Verkehr) traffic; **es herrscht großer ~, es ist viel ~**: it's very busy

betrieblich *Adj.* firm's; company

Betriebs-: ~angehörige *der/die* employee; **~anleitung** *die,* **~anweisung** *die* operating instructions *pl.;* **~ausflug** *der* staff outing; **~ferien** *Pl.* firm's annual close-down *sing.;* **„Wegen ~ferien geschlossen“** 'closed for annual holidays'; **~klima** *das* working atmosphere; **~rat** *der* **(a)** works committee; **(b)** (Person) member of a/the works committee; **~rätin** *die* ▸ BETRIEBSRAT B; **~system** *das* (DV) operating system; **~versammlung** *die* meeting of the workforce; **~wirt** *der,* **~wirtin** *die* graduate in business management; **~wirtschaft** *die* business management

betrinken *unr. refl. V.* get drunk

betroffen 1 *Adj.* upset; (bestürzt) dismayed 2 *adv.* in dismay

Betroffenheit *die;* ~: dismay

betrüblich *Adj.* gloomy

betrübt 1 *Adj.* sad; gloomy ‹*face etc.*› 2 sadly; (schwermütig) gloomily

Betrug *der;* **~[e]s** deception; (Delikt) fraud

betrügen 1 *unr. tr. V.* deceive; be unfaithful to ‹*husband, wife*›; (Rechtsw.) defraud; (beim Spielen) cheat; **jmdn. um 100 Euro ~**: cheat *or* (coll.) do sb. out of 100 euros; (arglistig) swindle sb. out of 100 euros 2 *unr. itr. V.* cheat; (bei Geschäften) swindle people

Betrüger *der;* **~s, ~**: swindler; (Hochstapler) conman (coll.); (beim Spielen) cheat

Betrügerei *die;* ~, **~en** deception; (beim Spielen usw.) cheating; (bei Geschäften) swindling

Betrügerin *die;* ~, **~nen** swindler; (beim Spielen) cheat

betrunken *Adj.* drunken *attrib.;* drunk *pred.*

Betrunkene *der/die; adj. Dekl.* drunk

Bett *das;* **~[e]s, ~en (a)** bed; **ins** *od.* **zu ~ gehen** go to bed; **die Kinder ins ~ bringen** put the children to bed **(b)** (Feder~) duvet

Bett-: ~bezug *der* duvet cover; **~decke** *die* blanket; (gesteppt) quilt

Bettelei *die;* ~, **~en** begging *no art.*

betteln *itr. V.* beg (**um** for)
bett·lägerig *Adj.* bedridden
Bett·laken *das* sheet
Bett·lektüre *die* bedtime reading *no indef. art.*
Bettler *der;* **~s, ~, Bettlerin** *die;* **~, ~nen** beggar
bett-, Bett-: ~reif *Adj.* (ugs.) ready for bed *pred.;* **~ruhe** *die* bed rest; **~schwere** *die:* **die nötige** *od.* **notwendige ~schwere haben** (ugs.) be ready for one's bed; **~tuch** *das; Pl.* **~tücher** sheet; **~wäsche** *die* bedlinen; **~zeug** *das* (ugs.) bedclothes *pl.*
betucht *Adj.* (ugs.) well-heeled (coll.); well-off
betupfen *tr. V.* dab
Beuge *die;* **~, ~n** (Turnen) bend
beugen [1] *tr. V.* **(a)** bend; bow ‹*head*›
(b) (Sprachw.: flektieren) inflect ‹*word*›
[2] *refl. V.* **(a)** bend over; **sich nach vorn/hinten ~:** bend forwards/bend over backwards; **sich aus dem Fenster ~:** lean out of the window
(b) (sich fügen) give way
Beugung *die;* **~, ~en** (Sprachw.) inflexion
Beule *die;* **~, ~n** bump; (Vertiefung) dent
beulen *itr. V.* bulge
beunruhigen *tr., refl. V.* worry
beurlauben *tr. V.* **(a) jmdn. [für zwei Tage] ~:** give sb. [two days'] leave of absence
(b) (suspendieren) suspend
beurteilen *tr. V.* judge; assess ‹*situation etc.*›
Beurteilung *die;* **~, ~en (a)** judgement; (einer Lage usw.) assessment
(b) (Gutachten) assessment
Beute *die;* **~, ~n (a)** (Gestohlenes) haul; loot *no indef. art.;*
(b) (von Raubtieren) prey; (eines Jägers) bag
Beute·kunst *die* looted art
Beutel *der;* **~s, ~** bag; (kleiner, für Tabak usw.) pouch
bevölkern *tr. V.* populate
Bevölkerung *die;* **~, ~en** population; (Volk) people
Bevölkerungs-: ~dichte *die* population density; **~explosion** *die* population explosion; **~zunahme** *die,* **~zuwachs** *der* increase in population
bevollmächtigen *tr. V.* authorize
Bevollmächtigte *der/die; adj. Dekl.* authorized representative
bevor *Konj.* before; **~ du nicht unterschrieben hast** until you have signed
bevor·munden *tr. V.* **jmdn. ~:** impose one's will on sb.; **sie wollen sich nicht länger ~ lassen** they do not want to be dictated to any longer
bevor|stehen *unr. itr. V.* be near; **unmittelbar ~:** be imminent; **jmdm. steht etw. bevor** sth. is in store for sb.
bevorstehend *Adj.* forthcoming; **unmittelbar ~:** imminent
bevorzugen *tr. V.* **(a)** (vorziehen) prefer (**vor** + *Dat.* to)
(b) (begünstigen) favour; give preference *or* preferenzial treatment to (**vor** + *Dat.* over)
bevorzugt [1] *Adj.* favoured; (privilegiert) privileged; preferenzial ‹*treatment*›
[2] *adv.* **jmdn. ~ behandeln** give sb. preferential treatment
Bevorzugung *die;* **~, ~en** (Begünstigung) preferential treatment
bewachen *tr. V.* guard; **bewachter Parkplatz** car park with an attendant
Bewacher *der;* **~s, ~, Bewacherin** *die;* **~, ~nen** guard
Bewachung *die;* **~, ~en** guarding
bewaffnen [1] *tr. V.* arm
[2] *refl. V.* (auch fig.) arm oneself (**mit** with)
bewaffnet *Adj.* armed; **bis an die Zähne ~:** armed to the teeth
Bewaffnung *die;* **~, ~en (a)** arming
(b) (Waffen) weapons *pl.*
bewahren *tr. V.* **(a)** protect (**vor** + *Dat.* from)
(b) (erhalten) **seine Fassung ~:** retain one's composure; **Stillschweigen ~:** remain silent
bewähren *refl. V.* prove oneself/itself
bewährt *Adj.* proven ‹*method, design, etc.*›; well-tried ‹*recipe, cure*›; reliable ‹*worker*›
Bewährung *die;* **~, ~en** (Rechtsw.) probation
Bewährungs-: ~frist *die* (Rechtsw.) period of probation; **~helfer** *der,* **~helferin** *die* probation officer; **~zeit** *die* (Rechtsw.) probation period
bewaldet *Adj.* wooded
bewältigen *tr. V.* cope with; overcome ‹*difficulty, problem*›; cover ‹*distance*›
Bewältigung *die;* **~, ~en** ▶ BEWÄLTIGEN: coping with; overcoming; covering
bewandert *Adj.* well-versed
Bewandtnis *die;* **~, ~se: mit etw. hat es [s]eine eigene/besondere ~:** there's a [special] story behind sth.
bewässern *tr. V.* irrigate
Bewässerung *die;* **~, ~en** irrigation
bewegen[1] [1] *tr. V.* **(a)** move
(b) (ergreifen) move
(c) (innerlich beschäftigen) preoccupy
[2] *refl. V.* move
bewegen[2] *unr. tr. V.* **jmdn. dazu ~, etw. zu tun** ‹*thing*› induce sb. to do sth.; ‹*person*› prevail upon sb. to do sth.
Beweg·grund *der* motive
beweglich *Adj.* **(a)** movable; moving ‹*target*›
(b) (rege) agile ‹*mind*›
bewegt *Adj.* eventful; (unruhig) turbulent
Bewegung *die;* **~, ~en (a)** movement; (bes. Technik, Physik) motion
(b) (körperliche **~**) exercise

(c) (Ergriffenheit) emotion
(d) (Bestreben, Gruppe) movement

Bewegungs·freiheit *die* freedom of movement

bewegungslos *Adj.* motionless

Bewegungslosigkeit *die;* ~: motionlessness

beweiden *tr. V.* (Landw.) **(a)** graze the grass in ‹*garden etc.*›
(b) (als Weide nutzen) use ‹*meadow etc.*› as pasture

Beweis *der;* ~es, ~e proof (*Gen.*, **für** of); **belastende** ~e incriminating evidence

beweisbar *Adj.* provable

beweisen *unr. tr. V.* prove

Beweis-: ~**material** *das* evidence; ~**mittel** *das* (Rechtsw.) form of evidence; ~**stück** *das* piece of evidence; ~**stücke** evidence *sing.*

bewenden *unr. V.* **es bei** *od.* **mit etw.** ~ **lassen** content oneself with sth.

bewerben *unr. refl. V.* apply (**bei** to, **um** for)

Bewerber *der;* ~s, ~, **Bewerberin** *die;* ~, ~nen applicant

Bewerbung *die* application

Bewerbungs-: ~**bogen** *der* application form; ~**schreiben** *das* letter of application; ~**unterlagen** *Pl.* documents in support of an/the application

bewerfen *unr. tr. V.* **jmdn./etw. mit etw.** ~: throw sth. at sb./sth.

bewerkstelligen *tr. V.* pull off, manage ‹*deal, sale, etc.*›; **es** ~, **etw. zu tun** contrive *or* manage to do sth.

bewerten *tr. V.* assess; rate; (dem Geldwert nach) value (**mit** at)

Bewertung *die;* ~, ~en assessment; (dem Geldwert nach) valuation

bewilligen *tr. V.* grant

Bewilligung *die;* ~, ~en granting

bewirken *tr. V.* bring about; cause

bewirten *tr. V.* feed; **jmdn. mit etw.** ~: serve sb. sth.

bewirtschaften *tr. V.* **(a)** manage ‹*estate, farm, restaurant, business, etc.*›
(b) farm ‹*fields, land*›

Bewirtung *die;* ~, ~en provision of food and drink

bewog *1. u. 3. Pers. Sg. Prät. v.* BEWEGEN²

bewohnbar *Adj.* habitable

bewohnen *tr. V.* inhabit, live in ‹*house, area*›; live in ‹*room, flat*›

Bewohner *der;* ~s, ~, **Bewohnerin** *die;* ~, ~nen (eines Hauses, einer Wohnung) occupant; (einer Stadt, eines Gebietes) inhabitant

bewohnt *Adj.* occupied ‹*house etc.*›; inhabited ‹*area*›

bewölken *refl. V.* cloud over; become overcast

bewölkt *Adj.* cloudy; overcast

Bewölkung *die;* ~, ~en cloud [cover]

Bewunderer *der;* ~s, ~, **Bewunderin** *die;* ~, ~nen admirer

bewundern *tr. V.* admire (**wegen, für** for)

bewunderns·wert 1 *Adj.* admirable
2 *adv.* admirably

Bewunderung *die;* ~: admiration

bewusst, *bewußt 1 *Adj.* conscious ‹*reaction, behaviour, etc.*›; (absichtlich) deliberate ‹*lie, deception, attack, etc.*›; **etw. ist/wird jmdm.** ~: sb. is/becomes aware of sth.; sb. realizes sth.; **sich** (*Dat.*) **einer Sache** (*Gen.*) ~ **sein/werden** be/become aware of something
2 *adv.* consciously; (absichtlich) deliberately

bewusst·los, *bewußt·los *Adj.* unconscious

Bewusstlosigkeit, *Bewußtlosigkeit *die;* ~: unconsciousness

Bewusst·sein, *Bewußt·sein *das* **(a)** consciousness; **das** ~ **verlieren/wiedererlangen** lose/regain consciousness; **bei vollem** ~ **sein** be fully conscious
(b) (deutliches Wissen) awareness

bewusstseins-, *bewußtseins-, Bewusstseins-, *Bewußtseins-: ~**erweiternd** *Adj.* mind-expanding; psychedelic; ~**erweiterung** *die* expansion of consciousness; ~**trübung** *die* clouding *or* dimming of consciousness; ~**veränderung** *die* change of awareness

bezahlbar *Adj.* affordable

bezahlen 1 *tr. V.* pay ‹*person, bill, taxes, rent, amount*›; pay for ‹*goods etc.*›; **das macht sich bezahlt** it pays off
2 *itr. V.* pay; **ich möchte** ~ *od.* **bitte** ~: the bill *or* (Amer.) check please

Bezahl·fernsehen *das* pay television; pay TV

Bezahlung *die;* ~, ~en payment; (Lohn, Gehalt) pay

bezaubernd 1 *Adj.* enchanting
2 *adv.* enchantingly

bezeichnen *tr. V.* **(a) jmdn./sich/etw. als etw.** ~: call sb./oneself/sth. sth.
(b) (Name, Wort sein für) denote

bezeichnend *Adj.* characteristic (**für** of)

Bezeichnung *die;* ~, ~en **(a)** marking; (Angabe durch Zeichen) indication
(b) (Name) name

bezeugen *tr. V.* testify to

bezichtigen *tr. V.* accuse

beziehen 1 *unr. tr. V.* **(a)** cover ‹*seat, cushion, etc.*›; **die Betten frisch** ~: put clean sheets on the beds
(b) (einziehen in) move into ‹*house, office*›
(c) (Milit.) take up ‹*position, post*›
(d) (erhalten) obtain ‹*goods*›; take ‹*newspaper*›; draw ‹*pension, salary*›
(e) (in Beziehung setzen) apply (**auf** + *Akk.* to)
2 *unr. refl. V.* **(a) es/der Himmel bezieht sich** it/the sky is clouding over *or* becoming overcast

*old spelling - see note on page xiv

(b) **sich auf jmdn./etw. ~** (sich berufen auf) ‹*person, letter, etc.*› refer to sb./sth.; (betreffen) ‹*question, statement, etc.*› relate to sb./sth.; **wir ~ uns auf Ihr Schreiben vom 28. 8.** with reference to your letter of 28 August

Beziehung *die;* ~, ~**en** (a) relation; (Zusammenhang) connection (**zu** with); **zwischen A und B besteht keine/eine ~:** there is no/a connection between A and B (b) (Freundschaft, Liebes~) relationship (c) (Hinsicht) respect; **in mancher ~:** in many respects

beziehungs·weise *Konj.* and ... respectively; (oder) or

beziffern *tr. V.* estimate (**auf** + *Akk.* at); **den Schaden auf 3000 Euro ~:** estimate the damage at 3,000 euros

Bezirk *der;* ~[e]s, ~e district

***bezug** ▶ BEZUG D

Bezug *der* (a) (für Kissen usw.) cover; (für Polstermöbel) loose cover; slip cover (Amer.); (für Betten) duvet cover; (für Kopfkissen) pillowcase (b) (Erwerb) obtaining; (Kauf) purchase; **~ einer Zeitung** taking a newspaper (c) *Pl.* salary *sing.;* (d) (Papierdt.) **mit** *od.* **unter ~ auf etw.** (*Akk.*) with reference to sth.; **in ~ auf jmdn./etw.** regarding sb./sth.; **~ nehmend auf unser Telex** with reference to our telex

bezüglich *Präp. mit Gen.* regarding

bezwecken *tr. V.* aim to achieve

bezweifeln *tr. V.* doubt

bezwingen *unr. tr. V.* conquer ‹*enemy, mountain, pain, etc.*›; defeat ‹*opponent*›; capture ‹*fortress*›

BH /be:'ha:/ *der;* ~[s], ~[s] *Abk.* = **Büstenhalter** bra

Bibel *die;* ~, ~n (auch fig.) Bible

Biber *der;* ~s, ~: beaver

Bibliographie *die;* ~, ~n bibliography

bibliographisch *Adj.* bibliographical

Bibliothek *die;* ~, ~en library

Bibliothekar *der;* ~s, ~e, **Bibliothekarin** *die;* ~, ~nen librarian

biblisch *Adj.* biblical

Bidet /bi'de:/ *das;* ~s, ~s bidet

bieder *Adj.* unsophisticated; (langweilig) stolid; (treuherzig) trusting

biegen [1] *unr. tr. V.* bend [2] *unr. refl. V.* bend; (nachgeben) give [3] *unr. itr. V.; mit sein* turn

biegsam *Adj.* flexible; pliable ‹*material*›

Biegsamkeit *die;* ~ ▶ BIEGSAM: flexibility; pliability

Biegung *die;* ~, ~en bend

Biene *die;* ~, ~n bee

Bienen-: ~**honig** *der* bees' honey; ~**königin** *die* queen bee; ~**korb** *der* straw hive; ~**stock** *der* beehive

Bier *das;* ~[e]s, ~e beer

Bier-: ~**bauch** *der* (ugs. spött.) beer belly; ~**brauerei** *die* brewery; ~**deckel** *der* beer mat; ~**dose** *die* beer can; ~**fass**, ***~faß** *das* beer barrel; ~**flasche** *die* beer bottle; ~**garten** *der* beer garden; ~**glas** *das* beer glass; ~**kasten** *der* beer crate; ~**trinker** *der,* ~**trinkerin** *die* beer drinker; ~**zelt** *das* beer tent

Biest *das;* ~[e]s, ~er (ugs. abwertend) (a) (Tier, Gegenstand) wretched thing (b) (Mensch) wretch

bieten [1] *unr. tr. V.* (a) offer; put on ‹*programme etc.*›; provide ‹*shelter, guarantee, etc.*› (b) **ein schreckliches Bild ~:** present a terrible picture; **einen prächtigen Anblick ~:** be a splendid sight [2] *unr. refl. V.* **sich jmdm. ~:** present itself to sb. [3] *unr. itr. V.* bid

Bigamie *die;* ~: bigamy *no def. art.*

Bigamist *der;* ~en, ~en, **Bigamistin** *die;* ~, ~nen bigamist

Bikini *der;* ~s, ~s bikini

Bilanz *die;* ~, ~en (a) balance sheet (b) (Ergebnis) outcome; **~ ziehen** take stock

Bild *das;* ~[e]s, ~er (a) picture (b) (Anblick) sight (c) (Metapher) image

bilden [1] *tr. V.* (a) form (**aus** from); (modellieren) mould (**aus** from); **eine Gasse ~:** make a path; **sich** (*Dat.*) **ein Urteil ~:** form an opinion (b) (ansammeln) build up ‹*fund, capital*› (c) (darstellen) be ‹*exception etc.*› (d) (erziehen) educate [2] *refl. V.* (a) form (b) (lernen) educate oneself

bildend *Adj.* (a) **die ~e Kunst, die ~en Künste** the plastic arts *pl.* (*including painting and architecture*) (b) (belehrend) educational

Bilder-: ~**buch** *das* picture book (*for children*); ~**geschichte** *die* picture story; ~**rahmen** *der* picture frame; ~**rätsel** *das* picture puzzle; (Rebus) rebus

bild-, Bild: ~**hauer** *der* sculptor; ~**hauerin** *die;* ~~, ~~nen sculptress; ~**hübsch** *Adj.* really lovely; stunningly beautiful ‹*girl*›

bildlich [1] *Adj.* pictorial; (übertragen) figurative [2] *adv.* pictorially; (übertragen) figuratively

Bildnis /'bɪltnɪs/ *das;* ~ses, ~se portrait

Bild-: ~**qualität** *die* picture quality; ~**röhre** *die* (Ferns.) picture tube

Bild·schirm *der* (Ferns., Informationst.) screen

Bildschirm-: ~**gerät** *das* VDU; visual display unit; ~**schoner** *der;* ~~s, ~~ (DV) screen saver

bild-, Bild-: ~**schön** *Adj.* really lovely; stunningly beautiful ‹*girl, woman*›; ~**telefon** *das* video telephone

b

Bildung *die;* **~, ~en (a)** (Erziehung) education; (Kultur) culture
(b) (das Formen) formation

Bildungs-: ~lücke *die* gap in one's education; **~minister** *der,* **~ministerin** *die* minister of education; ≈ Secretary of State for Education (Brit.); **~wesen** *das* education system; **das ~wesen** education

Bild·unterschrift *die* caption

Billard /'bɪljart, *österr.:* bi'jaːɐ̯/ *das;* **~s, ~e** billiards

Billard-: ~kugel *die* billiard ball; **~stock** *der* billiard cue; **~tisch** *der* billiard table

Billett /bɪl'jɛt/ *das;* **~[e]s, ~e** *od.* **~s** (schweiz., veralt.) ticket

Billiarde *die;* **~, ~n** thousand million million; quadrillion (Amer.)

billig 1 *Adj.* **(a)** cheap
(b) (abwertend: primitiv) cheap ‹*trick*›; feeble ‹*excuse*›
2 *adv.* cheaply

Billig·angebot *das* special *or* cut-price offer

billigen *tr. V.* approve

Billig-: ~flug *der* cheap flight; **~flug·linie** *die* low-cost airline; **~lohn·land** *das* low-wage country

Billigung *die;* **~:** approval

Billion *die;* **~, ~en** trillion; million million

bimmeln *itr. V.* (ugs.) ring

bin *1. Pers. Sg. Präsens v.* SEIN[1]

binär *Adj.* binary

Binde *die;* **~, ~n (a)** (Verband) bandage; (Augenbinde) blindfold
(b) (Armbinde) armband

Binde-: ~gewebe *das* (Anat.) connective tissue; **~haut** *die* (Anat.) conjunctiva

binden *unr. tr. V.* **(a)** (auch fig.) tie; knot ‹*tie*›; make up ‹*wreath, bouquet*›; **jmdn. an sich** (*Akk.*) **~** (fig.) make sb. dependent on one
(b) (fesseln, festhalten, zusammenhalten, fig.: verpflichten, Buchw.) bind
(c) (Kochk.: legieren) thicken ‹*sauce*›

Binder *der;* **~s, ~** tie

Binde·strich *der* hyphen

Bind·faden *der* string

Bindung *die;* **~, ~en (a)** (Beziehung) relationship (**an** + *Akk.* to)
(b) (Verbundenheit) attachment (**an** + *Akk.* to)
(c) (Skibindung) binding

binnen *Präp. mit Dat. od.* (*geh.*) *Gen.* within

Binnenmarkt *der* (Wirtsch.) domestic *or* home market; **europäischer ~:** internal European market

Binsen·weisheit *die* truism

Bio- (ugs.) organic ‹*farmer, garden, vegetables, etc.*›

bio-, Bio-: ~abfall *der* biowaste; **~chemie** *die* biochemistry; **~graf** *der;* **~~en, ~~en** biographer; **~grafie** *die;* **~~, ~~n** biography; **~grafin** *die;* **~~, ~~nen** biographer; **~grafisch** *Adj.* biographical; **~loge** *der;* **~~n, ~~n** biologist; **~logie** *die;* **~~:** biology *no art.;* **~login** *der;* **~~, ~~nen** biologist; **~logisch** *Adj.* **(a)** biological; **(b)** (natürlich) natural ‹*medicine, cosmetic, etc.*›; **~masse** *die* biomass; **~müll** *der* biowaste; **~technologie** *die* biotechnology; **~terrorismus** *der* bioterrorism; **~top** *der od.* das; **~~s, ~~e** (Biol.) biotope; **~waffe** *die* biological weapon

Birke *die;* **~, ~n** birch [tree]; (Holz) birch[wood]

Birma (*das*); **~s** Burma

Birn·baum *der* pear tree

Birne *die;* **~, ~n (a)** pear
(b) (Glühlampe) [light]bulb
(c) (salopp: Kopf) nut (coll.)

bis 1 *Präp. mit Akk.* **(a)** (zeitlich) until; till; (die ganze Zeit über und bis zu einem bestimmten Zeitpunkt) up until; up till; (nicht später als) by
(b) (räumlich) to; **dieser Zug fährt nur ~ Offenburg** this train only goes as far as Offenburg; **~ 5000 Euro** up to 5,000 euros
(c) ~ auf (einschließlich) down to; (mit Ausnahme von) except for
2 *Adv.* **~ zu 6 Personen** up to six people
3 *Konj.* **(a)** (nebenordnend) to
(b) (unterordnend) until; till; (österr.: sobald) when

Bischof *der;* **~s, Bischöfe, Bischöfin** *die;* **~, ~nen** bishop

bischöflich *Adj.* episcopal

bi·sexuell 1 *Adj.* bisexual
2 *adv.* bisexually

bis·her *Adv.* up to now; (aber jetzt nicht mehr) until now; till now

bisherig *Adj.* (vorherig) previous; (momentan) present

Biskuit /bɪs'kviːt/ *das od. der;* **~[e]s, ~s** *od.* **~e (a)** sponge biscuit
(b) (**~**teig) sponge

bis·lang *Adv.:* ▶ BISHER

Bison *der;* **~s, ~s** bison

Biss, *Biß *der;* **Bisses, Bisse** bite

bisschen, *bißchen *indekl. Indefinitpron.* **(a)** *adj.* **ein ~ Geld/Wasser** a bit of *or* a little money/a drop of *or* a little water; **ein/kein ~ Angst haben** be a bit/not a bit frightened
(b) *adv.* **ein/kein ~:** a bit *or* a little/not a *or* one bit
(c) *subst.* **ein ~:** a bit; a little; (bei Flüssigkeiten) a drop; a little; **das/kein ~:** the little [bit]/not a *or* one bit

Bissen *der;* **~s, ~:** mouthful

bissig 1 *Adj.* **(a) ~ sein** ‹*dog*› bite; **ein ~er Hund** a dog that bites; **„Vorsicht, ~er Hund"** 'beware of the dog'
(b) cutting ‹*remark, tone, etc.*›
2 *adv.* ‹*say*› cuttingly

---

*alte Schreibung - vgl. Hinweis auf S. xiv

Bịss·wunde, *Bịß·wunde *die* bite
bịst *2. Pers. Sg. Präsens v.* SEIN[1]
Bistum /ˈbɪstu:m/ *das;* **~s, Bịstümer** bishopric; diocese
bis·weilen *Adv.* (geh.) from time to time
Bit /bɪt/ *das;* **~s, ~[s]** (DV) bit
bịtte **1** *Adv.* please
2 *Interj.* **(a)** (Bitte, Aufforderung) please; **zwei Tassen Tee, ~:** two cups of tea, please; **~[, nehmen Sie doch Platz]!** do take a seat; **Noch eine Tasse Tee? – [Ja] ~!** Another cup of tea? – Yes, please
(b) (Aufforderung, etw. entgegenzunehmen) **~ [schön** *od.* **sehr]!** there you are!
(c) (Ausdruck des Einverständnisses) **~ [gern]!** certainly; of course; **Entschuldigung! – Bitte!** [I'm] sorry! – That's all right!
(d) ~ [schön *od.* **sehr]!** (im Laden, Lokal) yes, please?
(e) [wie] ~? (Nachfrage) sorry
(f) Vielen Dank! – Bitte [schön *od.* **sehr]** Many thanks! – Not at all *or* you're welcome
Bịtte *die;* **~, ~n** request; (inständig) plea
bịtten *unr. tr. V.* **(a)** *auch itr.* ask **(um** for); **darf ich Sie um Feuer/ein Glas Wasser ~?** could I ask you for a light/a glass of water, please?
(b) (einladen) ask
bịtter **1** *Adj.* **(a)** bitter; plain ‹*chocolate*›
(b) (fig.) (verbittert) bitter
(c) (schmerzlich) bitter, painful, hard ‹*loss*›; hard ‹*time, fate, etc.*›; dire ‹*need*›; desperate ‹*poverty*›; grievous ‹*injustice, harm*›
2 *adv.* (sehr stark) desperately; ‹*regret*› bitterly
bịtter-: ~böse **1** *Adj.* furious; **2** *adv.* furiously; **~kạlt** *Adj.* bitterly cold
bịtterlich **1** *Adj.* slightly bitter ‹*taste*›
2 *adv.* (heftig) ‹*cry, complain, etc.*› bitterly
bịtter·süß *Adj.* (auch fig.) bitter-sweet
Bịtt·steller *der;* **~s, ~, Bịtt·stellerin** *die;* **~, ~nen** petitioner
Biwak *das;* **~s, ~s** (bes. Milit., Bergsteigen) bivouac
bizạrr **1** *Adj.* bizarre
2 *adv.* bizarrely
Bizeps *der;* **~[es], ~e** biceps
Blähung *die;* **~, ~en** flatulence *no art., no pl.*
Blamage /blaˈma:ʒə/ *die;* **~, ~n** disgrace
blamieren **1** *tr. V.* disgrace
2 *refl. V.* disgrace oneself; (sich lächerlich machen) make a fool of oneself
blạnk *Adj.* shiny
Blạnko-: ~scheck *der* (auch fig.) blank cheque; **~vollmacht** *die* (auch fig.) carte blanche
Bläschen /ˈblɛ:sçən/ *das;* **~s, ~ (a)** [small] bubble
(b) (in der Haut) [small] blister
Blase *die;* **~, ~n (a)** bubble
(b) (in der Haut) blister
(c) (Harn~) bladder
Blase·balg *der;* **~s, Blasebälge** bellows *pl.*
blasen **1** *unr. itr. V.* blow
2 *unr. tr. V.* **(a)** blow
(b) (spielen) play ‹*musical instrument, tune, melody, etc.*›
Bläser *der;* **~s, ~, Bläserin** *die;* **~, ~nen** (Musik) wind player
blasiert (abwertend) **1** *Adj.* blasé
2 *adv.* in a blasé way
Blas-: ~instrument *das* wind instrument; **~kapelle** *die* brass band; **~musik** *die* brass-band music
Blasphemie /blasfeˈmi:/ *die;* **~, ~n** blasphemy
Blas·rohr *das* blowpipe
blạss, *blạß **1** *Adj.* pale
2 *adv.* palely
Blạ̈sse *die;* **~:** paleness
Blạtt *das;* **~[e]s, Blätter (a)** (von Pflanzen) leaf
(b) (Papier) sheet
(c) (Buchseite usw.) page; **etw. vom ~ spielen** sight-read sth.
(d) (Zeitung) paper
(e) (Spielkarten) hand
(f) (am Werkzeug, Ruder) blade
Blạ̈ttchen *das;* **~s, ~ (a)** (von Pflanzen) [small] leaf
(b) (Papier) [small] sheet
blạ̈ttern *itr. V.* **in einem Buch ~:** leaf through a book
Blạ̈tter·teig *der* puff pastry
Blạtt-: ~gold *das* gold leaf; **~grün** *das* chlorophyll; **~laus** *die* aphid
blau *Adj.* blue; **ein ~er Fleck** a bruise; **~ sein** (fig. ugs.) be tight (coll.); **das Blaue vom Himmel herunterlügen** (ugs.) lie like anything
Blau *das;* **~s, ~** *od.* (ugs.:) **~s** blue
blau-, Blau-: ~äugig *Adj.* **(a)** blue-eyed; **(b)** (naiv) naive; **~beere** *die* bilberry; **~grau** *Adj.* blue-grey; **~grün** *Adj.* blue-green
bläulich *Adj.* bluish
blau-, Blau-: ~licht *das* flashing blue light; **~|machen** *itr. V.* (ugs.) skip work; **~mann** *der; Pl.* **~männer** (ugs.) boiler suit; **~säure** *die* (Chemie) prussic acid; **~stichig** *Adj.* (Fot.) with a blue cast *postpos., not pred.;* **~stichig sein** have a blue cast
Blazer /ˈble:zɐ/ *der;* **~s, ~:** blazer
Blẹch *das;* **~[e]s, ~e (a)** sheet metal; (Stück Blech) metal sheet
(b) (Back~) [baking] tray
Blẹch-: ~bläser *der*, **~bläserin** *die* brass player; **die ~bläser** (im Orchester) the brass [section] *sing;* **~büchse** *die*, **~dose** *die* tin
blẹchen *tr., itr. V.* (ugs.) cough up (coll.)
blẹchern **1** *Adj.* (metallisch klingend) tinny ‹*sound, voice*›
2 *adv.* tinnily
Blẹch-: ~musik *die* (abwertend) brass-band music; **~napf** *der* metal bowl

b

Blechner *der;* **~s, ~, Blechnerin** *die;* **~, ~nen** (südd.) ▶ KLEMPNER

Blech-: ~schaden *der* (Kfz-W.) damage *no indef. art.* to the bodywork; **~trommel** *die* tin drum

blecken *tr. V.* **die Zähne ~:** bare one's/its teeth

Blei *das;* **~[e]s, ~e** lead

Bleibe *die;* **~, ~n** place to stay

bleiben *unr. itr. V.; mit sein* **(a)** stay; remain; **~ Sie bitte am Apparat** hold the line please; **wo bleibt er so lange?** where has he got to?; **auf dem Weg ~:** keep to the path; **sitzen ~:** stay *or* remain sitting down *or* seated; **bei etw. ~** (fig.: an etw. festhalten) keep to sth.
(b) (übrig bleiben) be left; remain
(c) etw. ~ lassen give sth. a miss

bleibend *Adj.* lasting; permanent ‹*damage*›

***bleiben|lassen** ▶ BLEIBEN C

bleich *Adj.* pale

bleichen¹ *tr. V.* bleach

bleichen² *regelm., veralt. auch unr. itr. V.* become bleached

blei-, Blei-: ~frei *Adj.* unleaded ‹*fuel*›; **~kristall** *das* lead crystal; **~kugel** *die* lead ball; (Geschoss) lead bullet; **~schwer** *Adj.* heavy as lead *postpos.;* **~stift** *der* pencil; **mit ~stift** in pencil; **~stift·spitzer** *der* pencil sharpener

Blende *die;* **~, ~n (a)** (Lichtschutz) shade; (am Fenster) blind
(b) (Optik, Film, Fot.) diaphragm; (Blendenzahl) aperture setting

blenden 1 *tr. V.* **(a)** (auch fig.) dazzle
(b) (blind machen) blind
2 *itr. V.* ‹*light*› be dazzling

blendend 1 *Adj.* **es geht mir ~:** I feel wonderfully well
2 *adv.* **wir haben uns ~ amüsiert** we had a marvellous time

blich *1. u. 3. Pers. Sg. Prät. v.* BLEICHEN²

Blick *der;* **~[e]s, ~e (a)** look; (flüchtig) glance
(b) (Ausdruck) look in one's eyes; **mit misstrauischem ~:** with a suspicious look in one's eye
(c) (Aussicht) view; **ein Zimmer mit ~ aufs Meer** a room with a sea view
(d) (Urteil[skraft]) eye

blicken 1 *itr. V.* look; (flüchtig) glance
2 *tr. V.* **sich ~ lassen** put in an appearance

Blick-: ~fang *der* eye-catcher; **als ~fang dienen** serve to catch the eye; **~feld** *das* field of vision; **~kontakt** *der* eye contact; **~punkt** *der* view; **~winkel** *der* **(a)** angle of vision; **(b)** (fig.) point of view; viewpoint

blieb *1. u. 3. Pers. Sg. Prät. v.* BLEIBEN

blies *1. u. 3. Pers. Sg. Prät. v.* BLASEN

blind 1 *Adj.* **(a)** (auch fig.) blind; **~ werden** go blind
(b) (trübe) clouded ‹*glass*›
(c) ein ~er Passagier a stowaway
(d) ~er Alarm a false alarm
2 *adv.* **(a)** (ohne hinzusehen) without looking; (wahllos) blindly
(b) (unkritisch) ‹*trust*› implicitly; ‹*obey*› blindly

Blind-: ~bewerbung *die* unsolicited application; **~darm** *der* **(a)** caecum; **(b)** (volkst.: Wurmfortsatz) appendix

Blinde *der/die; adj. Dekl.* blind person; blind man/woman; **die ~n** the blind

Blinde·kuh: ~ spielen play blind man's buff

Blinden-: ~hund *der* guide dog; **~schrift** *die* Braille

Blindheit *die;* **~** (auch fig.) blindness

blindlings *Adv.* blindly; ‹*trust*› implicitly

blind-, Blind-: ~schleiche *die;* **~, ~n** slowworm; **~wütig** 1 *Adj.* raging ‹*anger, hatred, fury, etc.*›; wild ‹*rage*›; 2 *adv.* in a blind rage

blinken 1 *itr. V.* **(a)** ‹*light, glass, crystal*› flash; ‹*star*› twinkle; ‹*metal, fish*› gleam
(b) (Verkehrsw.) indicate
2 *tr. V.* flash

Blinker *der;* **~s, ~:** indicator [light]

Blink-: ~licht *das* **(a)** flashing light; **(b)** ▶ BLINKER; **~zeichen** *das* flashlight signal

blinzeln *itr. V.* blink; (mit einem Auge, um ein Zeichen zu geben) wink

Blitz *der;* **~es, ~e (a)** lightning *no indef. art.;* **ein ~:** a flash of lightning; **[schnell] wie der ~:** like lightning
(b) (Blitzlicht) flash

blitz-, Blitz-: ~ab·leiter *der* lightning conductor; **~artig** 1 *Adj.* lightning; 2 *adv.* like lightning; ‹*disappear*› in a flash; **~blank** *Adj.* (ugs.) **~blank [geputzt]** sparkling clean; brightly polished ‹*shoes*›

blitzeblank ▶ BLITZBLANK

blitzen *itr. V.* **(a)** *unpers.* **es blitzte** (einmal) there was a flash of lightning; (mehrmals) there was lightning
(b) (glänzen) ‹*light, glass, crystal*› flash; ‹*metal*› gleam

blitz-, Blitz-: ~gerät *das* flash [unit]; **~licht** *das* flash[light]; **~schnell** 1 *Adj.* lightning *attrib.;* **~schnell sein** be like lightning; 2 *adv.* like lightning; ‹*disappear*› in a flash; **~start** *der* lightning start

Block *der;* **~[e]s, Blöcke** *od.* **~s (a)** *Pl. nur* **Blöcke** (Brocken) block
(b) (Wohnblock) block
(c) *Pl. nur* **Blöcke** (Gruppierung von politischen Kräften, Staaten) bloc
(d) (Schreibblock) pad

Blockade *die;* **~, ~n** blockade

Block-: ~flöte *die* recorder; **~haus** *das,* **~hütte** *die* log cabin

blockieren *tr. V.* block; jam ‹*telephone line*›; halt ‹*traffic*›; lock ‹*wheel, machine, etc.*›

Block·schrift *die* block capitals *pl.*

blöd[e] (ugs.) 1 *Adj.* **(a)** (dumm) stupid; idiotic (coll.)

---

*old spelling - see note on page xiv

(b) (unangenehm) stupid
[2] *adv.* stupidly; idiotically (coll.)
Blödelei *die;* ~, **~en** silly joke
blödeln *itr. V.* make silly jokes
Blödheit *die;* ~, **~en** stupidity
blöd-, Blöd-: ~mann *der; Pl.* **~männer** (salopp) stupid idiot (coll.); **~sinn** *der* (ugs.) nonsense; **mach doch keinen ~sinn!** don't be stupid; **~sinnig** (ugs.) [1] *Adj.* idiotic (coll.); [2] *adv.* idiotically (coll.)
blöken *itr. V.* ‹*sheep*› bleat; ‹*cattle*› low
blond *Adj.* fair-haired, blond ‹*man, race*›; blonde ‹*woman*›; blond/blonde, fair ‹*hair*›
Blondine *die;* ~, **~n** blonde
bloß [1] *Adj.* **(a)** (nackt) naked
(b) (nichts als) mere ‹*words, promises, triviality, suspicion, etc.*›; **der ~e Gedanke daran** the mere thought of it
[2] *Adv.* (ugs.: nur) only
[3] *Partikel* **was hast du dir ~ dabei gedacht?** what on earth were you thinking of?
Blöße *die;* ~: **sich** (*Dat.*) **eine/keine ~ geben** show a/not show any weakness
bloß|stellen *tr. V.* show up; expose ‹*swindler, criminal, etc.*›
Blouson /blu'zõ:/ *das od. der;* **~s, ~s** blouson
blubbern *itr. V.* (ugs.) bubble
Bluejeans /'blu:dʒi:ns/ *Pl. od. die;* ~, ~: [blue] jeans *pl.*
Blues /blu:s/ *der;* ~, ~: blues *pl.*
Bluff *der;* **~s, ~s** bluff
bluffen *tr., itr. V.* bluff
blühen *itr. V.* **(a)** ‹*plant*› flower, be in flower *or* bloom; ‹*flower*› be in bloom, be out; ‹*tree*› be in blossom; **~de Gärten** gardens full of flowers
(b) (florieren) thrive
(c) (ugs.: bevorstehen) **jmdm. ~:** be in store for sb.; **das kann dir auch noch ~:** the same could happen to you
blühend *Adj.* **(a)** (frisch, gesund) glowing ‹*colour, complexion, etc.*›; radiant ‹*health*›
(b) (übertrieben) vivid ‹*imagination*›
Blümchen *das;* **~s,** ~: [little] flower
Blume *die;* ~, **~n** **(a)** flower
(b) (des Weines) bouquet
(c) (des Biers) head
blumen-, Blumen-: ~beet *das* flower bed; **~erde** *die* potting compost; **~geschäft** *das* florist's; **~geschmückt** *Adj.* flower-bedecked; adorned with flowers *postpos.;* **~kasten** *der* flower box; (vor einem Fenster) window box; **~kohl** *der* cauliflower; **~strauß** *der; Pl.* **~sträuße** bunch of flowers; (Bukett) bouquet of flowers; **~topf** *der* flowerpot; **~vase** *die* [flower] vase; **~zwiebel** *die* bulb
Bluse *die;* ~, **~n** blouse
Blut *das;* **~[e]s** blood
blut-, Blut-: ~arm *Adj.* (Med.) anaemic; **~armut** *die* (Med.) anaemia; **~bad** *das* bloodbath; **~bahn** *die* bloodstream; **~bank** *die; Pl.* **~~en** (Med.) blood bank; **~befleckt** *Adj.* bloodstained; **~beschmiert** *Adj.* smeared with blood *postpos.;* **~buche** *die* copper beech; **~druck** *der; Pl.* **~drücke** blood pressure
Blüte *die;* ~, **~n** **(a)** flower; bloom; (eines Baums) blossom; **~n treiben** flower; ‹*tree*› blossom
(b) (das Blühen) flowering; (Baumblüte) blossoming
Blut·egel *der;* **~s,** ~: leech
bluten *itr. V.* bleed (**aus** from)
blüten-, Blüten-: ~blatt *das* petal; **~honig** *der* blossom honey; **~staub** *der* pollen; **~weiß** *Adj.* sparkling white
Bluter *der;* **~s,** ~, **Bluterin** *die;* ~, **~nen** (Med.) haemophiliac
Blut·erguss, *Blut·erguß *der* haematoma; (blauer Fleck) bruise
Bluter·krankheit *die* haemophilia *no art.*
Blut-: ~fleck[en] *der* bloodstain; **~gefäß** *das* (Anat.) blood vessel; **~gerinnsel** *das;* **~~s, ~~** blood clot; **~gruppe** *die* blood group; **~hochdruck** *der* high blood pressure; **~hund** *der* bloodhound
blutig **(a)** bloody; **jmdn. ~ schlagen** beat sb. to a pulp
(b) (fig. ugs.: völlig) complete ‹*beginner, layman, etc.*›
blut-, Blut-: ~jung *Adj.* very young; **~konserve** *die* container of stored blood; **~konserven** stored blood; **~körperchen** *das;* **~~s, ~~:** blood corpuscle; **rote/weiße ~körperchen** red/white corpuscles; **~krebs** *der* leukaemia; **~kreislauf** *der* blood circulation; **~lache** *die* pool of blood; **~leer** *Adj.* bloodless; **~leere** *die* restricted blood supply; **~orange** *die* blood orange; **~plasma** *das* (Physiol.) blood plasma; **~probe** *die* **(a)** (~entnahme, ~untersuchung) blood test; **(b)** (kleine ~menge) blood sample; **~rache** *die* blood revenge; **~rot** *Adj.* blood-red; **~rünstig** [1] *Adj.* bloodthirsty; [2] *adv.* bloodthirstily; **~schande** *die* incest; **~spende** *die* (das Spenden) giving *no indef. art.* of blood; (~menge) blood donation; **~spender** *der;* **~spenderin** *die* blood donor; **~spur** *die* trail of blood; **~stillend** *Adj.* styptic
bluts-, Bluts-: ~tropfen *der* drop of blood; **~verwandt** *Adj.* related by blood *postpos.;* **~verwandtschaft** *die* blood relationship
Blut-: ~tat *die* (geh.) bloody deed; **~transfusion** *die* blood transfusion; **~übertragung** *die* blood transfusion
Blutung *die;* ~, **~en** **(a)** bleeding *no indef. art., no pl.;*
(b) (Regelblutung) period
blut-, Blut-: ~unterlaufen *Adj.* suffused with blood *postpos.;* bloodshot

‹eyes›; **~vergießen** *das;* **~~s** bloodshed; **~vergiftung** *die* blood poisoning *no indef. art., no pl.*; **~wurst** *die* black pudding; **~zucker·spiegel** *der* (Physiol.) blood-sugar level

Bö *die;* **~, ~en** gust [of wind]

Bob *der;* **~, ~s** bob[sleigh]

Bob-: ~bahn *die* bob[sleigh] run; **~fahrer** *der,* **~fahrerin** *die* bobber

Bock[1] *der;* **~[e]s, Böcke (a)** (Reh~, Kaninchen~) buck; (Ziegen~) billy goat; he-goat; (Schafs~) ram; **einen/keinen ~ auf etw.** (*Akk.*) **haben** (ugs.) fancy/not fancy sth.; **einen/keinen ~ haben, etw. zu tun** (ugs.) fancy/not fancy doing sth.
(b) (Gestell) trestle
(c) (Turngerät) buck

Bock[2] *das;* **~s** (Bier) bock [beer]

Bock·bier *das* bock [beer]

bocken *itr. V.* refuse to go on; (vor einer Hürde) refuse; (sich aufbäumen) buck

bockig [1] *Adj.* stubborn and awkward
[2] *adv.* stubbornly [and awkwardly]

Bocks·horn *das:* **sich ins ~ jagen lassen** (ugs.) let oneself be browbeaten

Bock-: ~springen *das;* **~~s** (Turnen) vaulting [over the buck]; **~wurst** *die* bockwurst

Boden *der;* **~s, Böden (a)** (Erd~) ground; (Fuß~) floor; **am ~ zerstört [sein]** (ugs.) [be] shattered (coll.); **bleiben wir doch auf dem ~ der Tatsachen** (fig.) let's stick to the facts
(b) (unterste Fläche) bottom; (Torten~) base
(c) (Dach~, Heu~) loft

boden-, Boden-: ~belag *der* floor-covering; **~ertrag** *der* crop yield; **~fläche** *die* land area; **~frost** *der* ground frost; **~kammer** *die* attic; **~los** *Adj.* **(a)** bottomless; **(b)** (ugs.: unerhört) incredible ‹*foolishness, meanness, etc.*›; **~nebel** *der* ground fog/mist; **~satz** *der* sediment; **~schätze** *Pl.* mineral resources

Boden·see *der;* **~s** Lake Constance

boden-, Boden-: ~ständig *Adj.* indigenous ‹*culture, population, etc.*›; **~turnen** *das* floor exercises *pl.*; **~welle** *die* bump

Bodybuilding /ˈbɔdibɪldɪŋ/ *das;* **~s** bodybuilding *no art.*

Böe *die;* **~, ~n** ▶ BÖ

bog *1. u. 3. Pers. Sg. Prät. v.* BIEGEN

Bogen *der;* **~s, ~,** (südd., österr.:) **Bögen (a)** curve; (Math.) arc
(b) (Archit.) arch
(c) (Waffe, Musik: Geigen~ usw.) bow
(d) (Papier~) sheet

bogen-, Bogen-: ~fenster *das* arched window; **~förmig** *Adj.* arched; **~schießen** *das;* **~~s** archery *no art.*

Boheme /boˈeːm/ *die;* **~:** bohemian society

Bohemien /boeˈmi̯ɛ̃ː/ *der;* **~s, ~s** bohemian

Bohle *die;* **~, ~n** [thick] plank

Böhnchen *das;* **~s, ~:** [small] bean

Bohne *die;* **~, ~n** bean; **nicht die ~** (ugs.) not one little bit

Bohnen-: ~eintopf *der* bean stew; **~kaffee** *der* real coffee; **~kraut** *das* savory; **~stange** *die* (auch ugs.: Mensch) beanpole; **~stroh** *das:* **dumm wie ~stroh** (ugs.) as thick as two short planks (coll.); **~suppe** *die* bean soup

bohnern *tr., itr. V.* polish

Bohner·wachs *das* floor polish

bohren [1] *tr. V.* **(a)** bore; (mit Bohrer, Bohrmaschine) drill, bore ‹*hole*›; sink ‹*well, shaft, pole, post etc.*› (**in** + *Akk.* into)
(b) (bearbeiten) drill ‹*wood, concrete, etc.*›
(c) (drücken in) poke (**in** + *Akk.* in[to])
[2] *itr. V.* **(a)** drill; **in der Nase ~:** pick one's nose; **nach Öl/Wasser** *usw.* **~:** drill for oil/water *etc.;*
(b) (ugs.: drängen, fragen) keep on
[3] *refl. V.* bore its way

bohrend *Adj.* **(a)** gnawing ‹*pain, hunger, remorse*›
(b) (hartnäckig) piercing ‹*look etc.*›; probing ‹*question*›

Bohrer *der;* **~s, ~** drill

Bohr-: ~insel *die* drilling rig; **~maschine** *die* drill; **~schrauber** *der* power drill/screwdriver; **~turm** *der* derrick

Bohrung *die;* **~, ~en** drill hole

böig *Adj.* gusty

Boiler /ˈbɔyːlɐ/ *der;* **~s, ~:** water heater

Boje *die;* **~, ~n** buoy

Bolivien /boˈliːvi̯ən/ (*das*)*;* **~s** Bolivia

Böller·schuss, *Böller·schuß *der* gun salute

Boll·werk *das* bulwark; (fig.) bulwark; bastion; stronghold

Bolschewik *der;* **~en, ~i,** (abwertend:) **~en, Bolschewikin** *die;* **~, ~nen** Bolshevik

Bolschewismus *der;* **~:** Bolshevism *no art.*

Bolschewist *der;* **~en, ~en, Bolschewistin** *die;* **~, ~nen** Bolshevist

bolschewistisch *Adj.* Bolshevik

bolzen (ugs.) *itr. V.* kick the ball about

Bolzen *der;* **~s, ~:** bolt

bombardieren *tr. V.* **(a)** bomb
(b) (fig. ugs.) bombard

Bombardierung *die;* **~, ~en (a)** (Milit.) bombing
(b) (fig. ugs.) bombardment

bombastisch [1] *Adj.* bombastic
[2] *adv.* bombastically

Bombe *die;* **~, ~n** bomb

bomben-, Bomben-: ~angriff *der* bomb attack; **~anschlag** *der* bomb attack; **~attentat** *das* bomb attack; **~drohung**

---

*alte Schreibung - vgl. Hinweis auf S. xiv

die bomb threat; ~**erfolg** *der* (ugs.) smash hit (coll.); ~**fest** *Adj.* (ugs.: unveränderbar) dead certain; ~**fest stehen** be dead certain; be a dead cert (Brit. coll.); ~**form** *die* (ugs.) top form; ~**sicher** *Adj.* (ugs.: gewiss) dead certain; **das ist eine ~sichere Sache** that's dead certain; that's a dead cert (Brit. coll.) *or* a sure thing (Amer.); ~**stimmung** *die* (ugs.) tremendous *or* fantastic atmosphere (coll.); ~**trichter** *der* bomb crater

Bomber *der;* ~**s,** ~: bomber

Bon /bɔŋ/ *der;* ~**s,** ~**s (a)** voucher; coupon **(b)** (Kassenzettel) receipt

Bonbon /bɔŋ'bɔŋ/ *der od.* (österr. nur) *das;* ~**s,** ~**s** sweet (Brit.); candy (Amer.); (fig.) treat

bongen *tr. V.* (ugs.) ring up; **gebongt sein** (ugs.) be fine; **ist gebongt!** (ugs.) fine!

Bongo *das;* ~**[s],** ~**s** *od. die;* ~, ~**s** bongo [drum]

Bonmot /bõ'mo:/ *das;* ~**s,** ~**s** bon mot

Bonze *der;* ~**n,** ~**n** bigwig (coll.)

Boom /bu:m/ *der;* ~**s,** ~**s** boom

Boot *das;* ~**[e]s,** ~**e** boat

Boots-: ~**fahrt** *die* boat trip; ~**haus** *das* boathouse; ~**steg** *der* landing stage; ~**verleih** *der* boat hire

Bord¹ *das;* ~**[e]s,** ~**e** shelf

Bord² *der;* ~**[e]s,** ~**e** (eines Schiffes) side; **an** ~: on board; **über** ~: overboard

Bordell *das;* ~**s,** ~**e** brothel

Bord·stein *der* kerb

Bordüre *die;* ~, ~**n** edging

borgen *tr. V.:* ▶ LEIHEN

Borke *die;* ~, ~**n** bark

Borken·käfer *der* bark beetle

borniert [1] *Adj.* bigoted
[2] *adv.* in a bigoted way

Börse *die;* ~, ~**n** stock market; (Gebäude) stock exchange

Börsen-: ~**krach** *der* stock market crash; ~**makler** *der* stockbroker

Borste *die;* ~, ~**n** bristle

borstig *Adj.* bristly

Borte *die;* ~, ~**n** braiding *no indef. art.;* edging *no indef. art.*

bös ▶ BÖSE

bös·artig [1] *Adj.* **(a)** (heimtückisch) malicious ‹*person, remark, etc.*›; vicious ‹*animal*›
(b) (Med.) malignant
[2] *adv.* maliciously

Bös·artigkeit *die;* ~ **(a)** maliciousness; (von Tieren) viciousness
(b) (Med.) malignancy

Böschung *die;* ~, ~**en** embankment

böse [1] *Adj.* **(a)** wicked; evil
(b) (übel) bad ‹*times, illness, dream, etc.*›; nasty ‹*experience, affair, situation, trick, surprise, etc.*›
(c) (ugs.) (wütend) mad (coll.); (verärgert) cross (coll.)
(d) (fam.: ungezogen) naughty
(e) (ugs.: arg) terrible (coll.) ‹*pain, fall, shock, disappointment, storm, etc.*›
[2] *adv.* **(a)** (übel) ‹*end*› badly; **es war doch nicht ~ gemeint** I didn't mean it nastily
(b) (ugs.) (wütend) angrily; (verärgert) crossly (coll.)
(c) (ugs.: sehr) terribly (coll.)

boshaft [1] *Adj.* malicious
[2] *adv.* maliciously

Boshaftigkeit *die;* ~, ~**en (a)** maliciousness
(b) (Bemerkung) malicious remark

Bosheit *die;* ~, ~**en (a)** malice
(b) (Bemerkung) malicious remark

Boss, *Boß *der;* **Bosses, Bosse** (ugs.) boss (coll.)

bös·willig [1] *Adj.* malicious; wilful ‹*desertion*›
[2] *adv.* maliciously; wilfully ‹*desert*›

Bös·willigkeit *die;* ~: malice; maliciousness

bot *1. u. 3. Pers. Sg. Prät. v.* BIETEN

Botanik *die;* ~: botany *no art.*

botanisch [1] *Adj.* botanical
[2] *adv.* botanically

Bötchen *das;* ~**s,** ~: little boat

Bote *der;* ~**n,** ~**n (a)** messenger
(b) (Laufbursche) errand boy

Botin *die;* ~, ~**nen** ▶ BOTE: **(a)** messenger
(b) errand girl

Botschaft *die;* ~, ~**en (a)** message
(b) (diplomatische Vertretung) embassy

Botschafter *der;* ~**s,** ~, **Botschafterin** *die;* ~, ~**nen** ambassador

Böttcher *der;* ~**s,** ~, **Böttcherin** *die;* ~, ~**nen** cooper

Bottich *der;* ~**s,** ~**e** tub

Bouillon /bul'jɔŋ/ *die;* ~, ~**s** bouillon

Boulevard /bulə'va:ɐ̯/ *der;* ~**s,** ~**s** boulevard

Boulevard-: ~**blatt** *das* ▶ BOULEVARDZEITUNG; ~**presse** *die* (abwertend) popular press; ~**stück** *das* (Theater) boulevard drama; ~**zeitung** *die* (abwertend) popular rag (derog.); tabloid

Bourgeoisie /burʒo̯a'zi:/ *die;* ~, ~**n** bourgeoisie

Boutique /bu'ti:k/ *die;* ~, ~**s** *od.* ~**n** boutique

Bowle /'bo:lə/ *die;* ~, ~**n** punch (*made of wine, champagne, sugar, and fruit or spices*)

bowlen /'boʊlən/ *itr. V.* bowl

Bowling /'boʊlɪŋ/ *das;* ~**s,** ~**s** [tenpin] bowling

Bowling·bahn *die* bowling alley

Box *die;* ~, ~**en (a)** box
(b) (Lautsprecher) speaker
(c) (Pferdebox) [loose] box
(d) (Motorsport) pit

boxen [1] *itr. V.* box; **gegen jmdn. ~:** fight sb.; box [against] sb.
[2] *tr. V.* punch

Boxer *der;* **~s, ~** (Sportler, Hund) boxer
Boxerin *die;* **~, ~nen** boxer
Box-: ~handschuh *der* boxing glove; **~kampf** *der* boxing match; (im Streit) fist fight; **~ring** *der* boxing ring; **~sport** *der* boxing *no art.*
Boy /bɔy:/ *der;* **~s, ~s** servant; (im Hotel) pageboy
Boykott /bɔy:'kɔt/ *der;* **~[e]s, ~s** boycott
boykottieren *tr. V.* boycott
brach¹ *1. u. 3. Pers. Sg. Prät. v.* BRECHEN
brach² *Adj.* fallow; (auf Dauer) uncultivated
Brachial·gewalt *die* brute force
Brach·land *das* fallow [land]; (auf Dauer) uncultivated land
brach|liegen *unr. itr. V.* (auch fig.) lie fallow; (auf Dauer) lie waste
brachte *1. u. 3. Pers. Sg. Prät. v.* BRINGEN
Branche /'brã:ʃə/ *die;* **~, ~n** [branch of] industry
Branchen·verzeichnis *das* classified directory; (Telefonbuch) Yellow Pages ® *pl.*
Brand *der;* **~[e]s, Brände** fire; **beim ~ der Scheune** when the barn caught fire; **etw. in ~ stecken** set fire to sth.
Brand·anschlag *der* arson attack (**auf** + *Akk.* on)
branden *itr. V.* (geh.) break
Branden·burg *(das);* **~s** Brandenburg
brand-, Brand-: ~marken *tr. V.* brand ‹*person*›; denounce ‹*thing*›; **~neu** *Adj.* (ugs.) brand-new; **~salbe** *die* ointment for burns; **~schaden** *der* fire damage *no pl., no indef. art.;* **~stelle** *die* burn; **~stifter** *der,* **~stifterin** *die* arsonist; **~stiftung** *die* arson
Brandung *die;* **~, ~en** surf
Brand·wunde *die* burn
brannte *1. u. 3. Pers. Sg. Prät. v.* BRENNEN
Brannt·wein *der* spirits *pl.;* (Sorte) spirit
Brasilianer *der;* **~s, ~, Brasilianerin** *die;* **~, ~nen** Brazilian
brasilianisch *Adj.* Brazilian
Brasilien /bra'zi:li̯ən/ *(das);* **~s** Brazil
brät *3. Pers. Sg. Präsens v.* BRATEN
Brat·apfel *der* baked apple
braten *unr. tr., itr. V.* fry; (im Backofen) roast
Braten *der;* **~s, ~ (a)** joint
(b) roast [meat] *no indef. art.*
Braten-: ~saft *der* meat juice[s *pl.*]; **~soße** *die* gravy
Brat-: ~fett *das* [cooking] fat; **~fisch** *der* fried fish; **~hähnchen** *das,* (südd., österr.) **~hendl** *das* roast chicken; (gegrillt) broiled chicken; **~hering** *der* fried herring; **~kartoffeln** *Pl.* fried potatoes; home fries (Amer.); **~pfanne** *die* frying pan; **~spieß** *der* spit; **~wurst** *die* [fried/grilled] sausage
Brauch *der;* **~[e]s, Bräuche** custom

brauchbar *Adj.* useful; (benutzbar) usable; wearable ‹*clothes*›
brauchen 1 *tr. V.* **(a)** (benötigen) need
(b) (aufwenden müssen) **mit dem Auto braucht er zehn Minuten** it takes him ten minutes by car; **wie lange brauchst du dafür?** how long will it take you?; (im Allgemeinen) how long does it take you?
(c) (benutzen, gebrauchen) use; **ich könnte es gut ~:** I could do with it
2 *mod. V.; 2. Part* **brauchen:** need; **du brauchst nicht zu helfen** there is no need [for you] to help; **du brauchst doch nicht gleich zu weinen** there's no need to start crying
Brauchtum /'brau:xtu:m/ *das;* **~s, Brauchtümer** custom
Braue *die;* **~, ~n** [eye]brow
brauen *tr. V.* brew
Brauerei *die;* **~, ~en** brewery
braun *Adj.* brown; **~ werden** (sonnengebräunt) get a tan; **~ gebrannt** [sun]-tanned
Braun *das;* **~s, ~,** (ugs.) **~s** brown
Braun·bär *der* brown bear
Bräune *die;* **~:** [sun]tan
bräunen *tr. V.* **(a)** tan; **sich ~:** get a tan
(b) (Kochk.) brown
braun-, Braun-: *~gebrannt ▶ BRAUN; **~kohle** *die* brown coal; lignite
bräunlich *Adj.* brownish
Bräunung *die;* **~, ~en** browning
Braus ▶ SAUS
Brause *die;* **~, ~n (a)** fizzy drink; (~pulver) sherbet
(b) (veralt.: Dusche) shower
brausen 1 *itr. V.* **(a)** ‹*wind, water, etc.*› roar
(b) (sich schnell bewegen) race
(c) *auch refl.:* ▶ DUSCHEN 1;
2 *tr. V.* ▶ DUSCHEN 2
Brause-: ~pulver *das* sherbet; **~tablette** *die* effervescent tablet
Braut *die;* **~, Bräute** bride
Bräutigam *der;* **~s, ~e** [bride]groom
Braut-: ~jungfer *die* bridesmaid; **~kleid** *das* wedding dress; **~paar** *das* bride and groom
brav 1 *Adj.* **(a)** (artig) good
(b) (redlich) honest
2 *adv.* **nun iss schön ~ deine Suppe** be a good boy/girl and eat up your soup
bravo /'bra:vo/ *Interj.* bravo
Bravo *das;* **~s, ~s** cheer
Bravo·ruf *der* cheer
BRD *Abk.* = **Bundesrepublik Deutschland** FRG
Brech-: ~bohne *die* green bean; **~eisen** *das* crowbar
brechen 1 *unr. tr. V.* **(a)** break; **sich** *(Dat.)* **den Arm/das Genick ~:** break one's arm/neck
(b) (ablenken) break ‹*waves*›; refract ‹*light*›

*old spelling - see note on page xiv

(c) (bezwingen) overcome ‹*resistance*›; break ‹*will, silence, record, blockade, etc.*›
(d) (nicht einhalten) break ‹*agreement, contract, promise, the law, etc.*›
(e) (ugs.: erbrechen) bring up
2 *unr. itr. V.* **(a)** *mit sein* break; **brechend voll sein** be full to bursting
(b) mit jmdm. ~: break with sb.
(c) *mit sein* **durch etw. ~:** break through sth.
(d) (ugs.: sich erbrechen) throw up
3 *unr. refl. V.* ‹*waves etc.*› break; ‹*rays etc.*› be refracted

Brecher *der;* **~s, ~:** breaker

Brech-: ~mittel *das* emetic; **~reiz** *der* nausea; **~stange** *die* crowbar

Bredouille /bre'dʊljə/ *die;* **~, ~n** (ugs.) **in der ~ sein** *od.* **sitzen** be in real trouble; **in die ~ kommen** get into real trouble

Brei *der;* **~[e]s, ~e** (Hafer~) porridge (Brit.), oatmeal (Amer.) *no indef. art.;* (Reis~) rice pudding; (Grieß~) semolina *no indef. art.*

breiig *Adj.* mushy

breit 1 *Adj.* **(a)** wide; broad, wide ‹*hips, face, shoulders, forehead, etc.*›; **etw. ~er machen** widen sth.; **die Beine ~ machen** open one's legs; **ein 5 cm ~er Saum** a hem 5 cm wide
(b) (groß) **die ~e Masse** the general public
(c) sich ~ machen take up room; (sich ausbreiten) be spreading
2 *adv.* **~ gebaut** sturdily built

Breit·band *das* (DV) broadband

breit·beinig 1 *Adj.* rolling ‹*gait*›
2 *adv.* with one's legs apart

Breite *die;* **~, ~n (a)** ▶ BREIT 1A: width; breadth
(b) (Geogr.) latitude

breiten (geh.) *tr., refl. V.* spread

Breiten-: ~grad *der* degree of latitude; parallel (~kreis); **~kreis** *der* parallel

breit-, Breit-: *~|machen ▶ BREIT 1C; **~schult[e]rig** *Adj.* broad-shouldered; **~seite** *die* long side; (eines Schiffes) side; **~|treten** *unr. tr. V.* (ugs. abwertend) go on about; **~wand** *die* (Kino) big screen

Bremen *(das);* **~s** Bremen

Brems-: ~backe *die* brake shoe; **~belag** *der* brake lining

Bremse¹ *die;* **~, ~n** brake

Bremse² *die;* **~, ~n** (Insekt) horsefly

bremsen *tr. V.* **(a)** *auch itr.* brake
(b) (fig.) slow down ‹*rate, development, production, etc.*›; restrict ‹*imports etc.*›

Brems-: ~klotz *der* brake pad; **~licht** *das* brake light; **~pedal** *das* brake pedal; **~spur** *die* skid mark; **~weg** *der* braking distance; **~zug** *der* brake cable

brenn·bar *Adj.* combustible

brennen 1 *unr. itr. V.* **(a)** burn; ‹*house etc.*› be on fire; **schnell/leicht ~:** catch fire quickly/easily; **es brennt!** fire!
(b) (glühen) be alight
(c) (leuchten) be on; **das Licht ~ lassen** leave the light on
(d) die Sonne brannte the sun was burning down
(e) (schmerzen) ‹*wound etc.*› sting; ‹*feet etc.*› be sore
(f) darauf ~, etw. zu tun be dying to do sth.
2 *unr. tr. V.* **(a)** burn ‹*hole, pattern, etc.*›; **einem Tier ein Zeichen ins Fell ~:** brand an animal
(b) (mit Hitze behandeln) fire ‹*porcelain etc.*›; distil ‹*spirits*›
(c) (rösten) roast ‹*coffee beans, almonds, etc.*›

brennend 1 *Adj.* (auch fig.) burning; lighted ‹*cigarette*›; urgent ‹*topic*›
2 *adv.* **es interessiert mich ~, ob ...:** I'm dying to know whether ...

Brenner *der;* **~s, ~:** burner

Brennerei *die;* **~, ~en** distillery

***Brennessel** *die;* **~, ~n** ▶ BRENNNESSEL

Brenn-: ~glas *das* burning glass; **~holz** *das* firewood; **~material** *das* fuel; **~nessel** *die* stinging nettle; **~ofen** *der* kiln; **~punkt** *der* focus; **~spiritus** *der* methylated spirits *pl.;* **~stoff** *der* fuel; **~weite** *die* (Optik) focal length

brenzlig *Adj.* **(a)** ‹*smell, taste, etc.*› of burning *not pred.;*
(b) (ugs.: gefährlich) dicey (coll.)

Bresche *die;* **~, ~n** gap; breach; **[für jmdn.] in die ~ springen** stand in [for sb.]

Brett *das;* **~[e]s, ~er** board; (lang und dick) plank; (Diele) floorboard; **schwarzes ~:** noticeboard; **ein ~ vor dem Kopf haben** (fig. ugs.) be thick

Bretter-: ~wand *die* wooden partition; **~zaun** *der* wooden fence

Brett·spiel *das* board game

Brezel *die;* **~, ~n** pretzel

Bridge /brɪtʃ:/ *das;* **~:** bridge

Brief *der;* **~[e]s, ~e** letter

Brief-: ~beschwerer *der;* **~~s, ~~:** paperweight; **~block** *der; Pl.* **~~s** *od.* **~blöcke** writing pad; **~bogen** *der* sheet of writing paper; **~freund** *der,* **~freundin** *die* penfriend; pen pal (coll.); **~freundschaft** *die* penfriendship; **~geheimnis** *das* privacy of the post; **~karte** *die* correspondence card; **~kasten** *der* **(a)** postbox; **(b)** (privat) letter box; **~kopf** *der* **(a)** letter heading; **(b)** (aufgedruckt) letterhead; **~kuvert** *das* (veralt.) ▶ ~UMSCHLAG

brieflich 1 *Adj.* written
2 *adv.* by letter

Brief·marke *die* [postage] stamp

Briefmarken-: ~album *das* stamp album; **~sammler** *der,* **~sammlerin** *die* stamp collector; **~sammlung** *die* stamp collection

Brief-: ~öffner *der* letter-opener; **~papier** *das* writing paper; **~partner** 

der, ~**partnerin** *die* penfriend; ~**schreiber** *der,* ~**schreiberin** *die* [letter-]writer; ~**tasche** *die* wallet; ~**taube** *die* carrier pigeon; ~**träger** *der* postman; letter-carrier (Amer.); ~**trägerin** *die* postwoman; [female] letter-carrier (Amer.); ~**umschlag** *der* envelope; ~**waage** *die* letter scales *pl.;* ~**wahl** *die* postal vote; ~**wechsel** *der* correspondence

Bries *das;* ~**es,** ~**e** (Kochk.) sweetbreads *pl.*

briet *1. u. 3. Pers. Sg. Prät. v.* BRATEN

Brigade *die;* ~, ~**n** (Milit.) brigade

Brikett *das;* ~**s,** ~**s** briquette

brillant /brɪl'jant/ [1] *Adj.* brilliant [2] *adv.* brilliantly

Brillant *der;* ~**en,** ~**en** brilliant

Brillant-: ~**ring** *der* (brilliant-cut) diamond ring; ~**schmuck** *der* (brilliant-cut) diamond jewellery

Brillanz /brɪl'jants:/ *die;* ~: brilliance

Brille *die;* ~, ~**n** **(a)** glasses *pl.;* spectacles *pl.;* **eine** ~: a pair of glasses *or* spectacles; **eine** ~ **tragen** wear glasses *or* spectacles **(b)** (ugs.: Klosettbrille) [lavatory] seat

Brillen-: ~**etui** *das,* ~**futteral** *das* glasses case; spectacle case; ~**glas** *das* [spectacle] lens; ~**schlange** *die* spectacled cobra; ~**träger** *der,* ~**trägerin** *die* person who wears glasses; ~**träger/-trägerin sein** wear glasses

Brimborium *das;* ~**s** (ugs. abwertend) hoo-ha (coll.)

bringen *unr. tr. V.* **(a)** (her~) bring; (hin~) take; **jmdm. Glück/Unglück** ~: bring sb. [good] luck/bad luck; **jmdm. eine Nachricht** ~: bring sb. news **(b)** (begleiten) take; **jmdn. nach Hause/zum Bahnhof** ~: take sb. home/to the station **(c) es zu etwas/nichts** ~: get somewhere/get nowhere **(d) jmdn. ins Gefängnis** ~ ‹*crime, misdeed*› land sb. in gaol; **jmdn. wieder auf den rechten Weg** ~ (fig.) get sb. back on the straight and narrow; **jmdn. zum Lachen/zur Verzweiflung** ~: make sb. laugh/drive sb. to despair; **jmdn. dazu** ~, **etw. zu tun** get sb. to do sth.; **etw. hinter sich** ~ (ugs.) get sth. over and done with **(e) jmdn. um seinen Besitz** ~: do sb. out of his property **(f)** (präsentieren) present; (veröffentlichen) publish; (senden) broadcast **(g) ein Opfer** ~: make a sacrifice **(h) einen großen Gewinn/hohe Zinsen** ~: make a large profit/earn high interest **(i) das bringt es mit sich, dass ...:** that means that ... **(j)** (verursachen) cause

brisant *Adj.* explosive

Brisanz *die;* ~: explosiveness

Brise *die;* ~, ~**n** breeze

Britannien *(das);* ~**s** Britain; (hist.) Britannia

Brite *der;* ~**n,** ~**n** Briton; **die** ~**n** the British; **er ist [kein]** ~: he is [not] British

Britin *die;* ~, ~**nen** Briton; British girl/ woman

britisch *Adj.* British; **die Britischen Inseln** the British Isles

bröckelig *Adj.* crumbly

bröckeln [1] *itr. V.* **(a)** crumble **(b)** *mit sein* **von der Wand** ~: crumble away from the wall [2] *tr. V.* crumble

Brocken *der;* ~**s,** ~ (von Brot) hunk; (von Fleisch) chunk; (von Lehm, Kohle, Erde) lump; **ein paar** ~ **Englisch** (fig.) a smattering of English

brodeln *itr. V.* bubble

Broiler /'brɔy:lɐ/ *der;* ~**s,** ~ (regional) ▶ BRATHÄHNCHEN

Brokat *der;* ~**[e]s,** ~**e** brocade

Brokkoli *der;* ~**s,** ~**[s]** broccoli

Brom·beere *die* blackberry

Bronchie /'brɔnçi̯ə/ *die;* ~, ~**n** bronchial tube

Bronchitis *die;* ~, bronchitis

Bronze /'brõ:sə/ *die;* ~: bronze

Bronze-: ~**medaille** *die* bronze medal; ~**zeit** *die* Bronze Age

Brosche *die;* ~, ~**n** brooch

Broschüre *die;* ~, ~**n** booklet

Brösel *der;* ~**s,** ~: breadcrumb

bröselig *Adj.* crumbly

bröseln *itr. V.* crumble

Brot *das;* ~**[e]s,** ~**e** bread *no pl., no indef. art.;* (Laib) loaf [of bread]; (Scheibe) slice [of bread]

Brot-: ~**aufstrich** *der* spread; ~**belag** *der* topping; (im zusammengeklappten Brot) filling

Brötchen *das;* ~**s,** ~: roll

Brot-: ~**erwerb** *der* way to earn a living; ~**korb** *der* bread basket; ~**laib** *der* loaf [of bread]; ~**messer** *das* bread knife; ~**rinde** *die* [bread] crust; ~**zeit** *die* (südd.) **(a)** (Pause) [tea/coffee/lunch] break; **(b)** (Vesper) snack; (Vesperbrot) sandwiches *pl.*

Browser /'braʊzɐ/ *der;* ~**s,** ~ (DV) browser

Bruch *der;* ~**[e]s, Brüche (a)** break; **in die Brüche gehen** (zerbrechen) get broken; (fig.) break up **(b)** (Med.: Knochen~) fracture; break **(c)** (Med.: Eingeweide~) hernia **(d)** (fig.) (eines Versprechens) breaking; (eines Abkommens, Gesetzes) violation **(e)** (Math.) fraction

brüchig *Adj.* **(a)** brittle ‹*rock, brickwork*› **(b)** (fig.) crumbling ‹*relationship, marriage, etc.*›

Bruch-: ~**landung** *die* crash-landing; ~**rechnen** *das* fractions *pl.;* ~**strich** *der* fraction line; ~**stück** *das* fragment; ~**teil** *der* fraction; **im** ~**teil einer Sekunde** in a split second

---

*alte Schreibung - vgl. Hinweis auf S. xiv

Brụcke *die;* ~, ~n **(a)** (auch: Kommandobrücke, Zahnmed., Bodenturnen, Ringen) bridge
(b) (Landungsbrücke) gangway
(c) (Teppich) rug

Brụcken-: **~bogen** *der* arch [of a/the bridge]; **~geländer** *das* parapet; **~kopf** *der* (Milit., auch fig.) bridgehead

Bruder *der;* ~s, **Brüder** brother

Brüderchen *das;* ~s, ~: little brother

brüderlich 1 *Adj.* brotherly
2 *adv.* in a brotherly way

Brüderlichkeit *die;* ~: brotherliness

Brüderschaft *die;* ~: **[mit jmdm.] ~ trinken** drink to close friendship [with sb.] (*agreeing to use the familiar 'du' form*)

Brühe *die;* ~, ~n **(a)** stock, (als Suppe) clear soup
(b) (ugs. abwertend) (Getränk) muck; (verschmutztes Wasser) filthy water

brühen *tr. V.* **(a)** blanch
(b) (auf~) brew, make ‹*tea*›; make ‹*coffee*›

brüh-, Brüh-: **~wạrm** *Adj.* **etw. ~warm weitererzählen** (ugs.) pass sth. on straight away; **~würfel** *der* stock cube

brüllen 1 *itr. V.* **(a)** ‹*bull, cow, etc.*› bellow; ‹*lion, tiger, etc.*› roar
(b) (ugs.) (schreien) roar; (weinen) howl
2 *tr. V.* yell

brụmmen *tr., itr. V.* **(a)** ‹*insect*› buzz; ‹*bear*› growl; ‹*engine etc.*› drone
(b) (unmelodisch singen) drone
(c) (mürrisch sprechen) mumble

Brụmmer *der;* ~s, ~ (ugs.) **(a)** (Fliege) bluebottle
(b) (LKW) heavy lorry (Brit.) *or* truck

brụmmig *Adj.* (ugs.) grumpy

Brụmm-: **~kreisel** *der* humming top; **~schädel** *der* (ugs.) thick head

brünẹtt *Adj.* dark-haired ‹*person*›; dark ‹*hair*›

Brünẹtte *die;* ~, ~n brunette

Brụnnen *der;* ~s, ~ **(a)** well
(b) (Springbrunnen) fountain

Brụnnen·kresse *die* watercress

Brụnst *die;* ~, **Brụ̈nste** (von männlichen Tieren) rut; (von weiblichen Tieren) heat

Brụnst·zeit *die* (bei männlichen Tieren) rutting season; (bei weiblichen Tieren) [season of] heat

brụ̈sk 1 *Adj.* brusque
2 *adv.* brusquely

brüskieren *tr. V.* offend; (stärker) insult; (schneiden) snub

Brụ̈ssel *(das);* ~s Brussels

Brụst *die;* ~, **Brụ̈ste** **(a)** chest
(b) (der Frau) breast
(c) (Hähnchen~) breast; (Rinder~) brisket
(d) (Brustschwimmen) breaststroke

brụ̈sten *refl. V.* **sich mit etw. ~:** boast about sth.

brụst-, Brụst-: **~kasten** (ugs.) chest; **~korb** *der* (Anat.) thorax (Anat.); **~krebs** *der* breast cancer; **~schwimmen** *unr. itr. V.; nur im Inf.* do [the] breaststroke; **~schwimmen** *das* breaststroke; **~tasche** *die* breast pocket

Brụ̈stung *die;* ~, ~en parapet; (Balkon~) balustrade

Brụst·warze *die* nipple

Brut *die;* ~, ~en **(a)** brooding
(b) (Jungtiere, auch fig. scherzh.: Kinder) brood

brutal 1 *Adj.* brutal; violent ‹*attack, programme, etc.*›; brute ‹*force, strength*›
2 *adv.* brutally

Brutalität *die;* ~, ~en **(a)** brutality
(b) (Handlung) act of brutality

brüten *itr. V.* **(a)** brood
(b) (grübeln) ponder (**über** + *Dat.* over);
brütend: **~ heiß:** (ugs.) boiling hot

Brüter *der;* ~s, ~ (Kernphysik) breeder

Brut-: **~kasten** *der* incubator; **~reaktor** *der* (Kernphysik) breeder reactor; **~stätte** *die* (auch fig.) breeding ground

brụtto *Adv.* gross

Brụtto-: **~einkommen** *das* gross income; **~gehalt** *das* gross salary; **~sozialprodukt** *das* (Wirtsch.) gross national product

brụtzeln 1 *itr. V.* sizzle
2 *tr. V.* (ugs.) fry [up]

BSE /beɛs'e:/ *die;* ~: BSE

Bub *der;* ~en, ~en (südd., österr., schweiz.) boy; lad

Bube *der;* ~n, ~n (Kartenspiele) jack; knave

Bubi *der;* ~s, ~s **(a)** [little] boy *or* lad
(b) (salopp: Schnösel) young lad

Buch *das;* ~[e]s, **Bücher** book; (Dreh~) script; **über etw.** (*Akk.*) **~ führen** keep a record of sth.

Buch-: **~besprechung** *die* book review; **~binder** *der,* **~binderin** *die;* ~~, ~~nen bookbinder; **~druck** *der* letterpress printing

Buche *die;* ~, ~n **(a)** beech [tree]
(b) (Holz) beech[wood]

Buch·ecker *die;* ~, ~n beech nut

buchen *tr. V.* **(a)** enter
(b) (vorbestellen) book

Bücher·brett *das* bookshelf

Bücherei *die;* ~, ~en library

Bücher-: **~regal** *das* bookshelves *pl.;* **~schrank** *der* bookcase; **~wurm** *der* (scherzh.) bookworm; **~verbrennung** *die* burning of books

Buch-: **~fink** *der* chaffinch; **~führung** *die* bookkeeping; **~halter** *der,* **~halterin** *die* bookkeeper; **~haltung** *die* **(a)** accountancy; **(b)** (Abteilung) accounts department; **~händler** *der,* **~händlerin** *die* bookseller; **~handlung** *die* bookshop; **~klub** *der* book club; **~laden** *der; Pl.* **~läden** ▶ ~HANDLUNG; **~messe** *die* book fair; **~rücken** *der* spine

Buchs·baum /ˈbʊks-/ *der* box [tree]
Buchse /ˈbʊksə/ *die;* **~, ~n (a)** (Elektrot.) socket
(b) (Technik) bush
Büchse /ˈbʏksə/ *die;* **~, ~n (a)** tin
(b) (ugs.: Sammel~) [collecting] box
(c) (Gewehr) rifle; (Schrot~) shotgun
Büchsen- ▶ DOSEN-
Buchstabe *der;* **~ns, ~n** letter; (Druckw.) character; **ein großer/kleiner ~:** a capital [letter]/small letter
buchstabieren *tr. V.* spell
buchstäblich *Adv.* literally
Bucht *die;* **~, ~en** bay
Buchung *die;* **~, ~en (a)** entry
(b) (Vorbestellung) booking
Buckel *der;* **~s, ~ (a)** hump; **einen ~ machen** ‹*cat*› arch its back; ‹*person*› hunch one's shoulders
(b) (ugs.: Rücken) back; **rutsch mir den ~ runter!** (salopp) get lost! (coll.)
buckeln *itr. V.* (ugs.) bow and scrape; **vor jmdm. ~:** kowtow to sb.
bücken *refl. V.* bend down
bucklig *Adj.* hunchbacked
Bucklige *der/die; adj. Dekl.* hunchback
Bückling[1] *der;* **~s, ~e** (ugs. scherzh.: Verbeugung) bow
Bückling[2] *der;* **~s, ~e** (Hering) bloater
buddeln *itr., tr. V.* (ugs.) dig
Buddha /ˈbʊda/ *der;* **~s, ~s** Buddha
Buddhismus *der;* **~:** Buddhism *no art.*
Buddhist *der;* **~en, ~en, Buddhistin** *die;* **~, ~nen** Buddhist
buddhistisch *Adj.* Buddhist *attrib.*
Bude *die;* **~, ~n (a)** kiosk; (Markt~) stall; (Jahrmarkts~) booth
(b) (Bau~) hut
(c) (ugs.) (Haus) dump (coll.); (Zimmer) room; digs *pl.* (Brit. coll.)
Budget /bʏˈdʒeː/ *das;* **~s, ~s** budget
Büfett *das;* **~[e]s, ~s** *od.* **~e (a)** sideboard
(b) (Schanktisch) bar
(c) (Verkaufstisch) counter
(d) kaltes ~: cold buffet
Büffel *der;* **~s, ~:** buffalo
büffeln (ugs.) **1** *itr. V.* swot (Brit. coll.); cram
2 *tr. V.* swot up (Brit. coll.); cram
Buffet /byˈfeː/ *das;* **~s, ~s** ▶ BÜFETT
Bug *der;* **~[e]s, ~e** *u.* **Büge** bow
Bügel *der;* **~s, ~ (a)** (Kleider~) hanger
(b) (Brillen~) earpiece
(c) (an einer Tasche, Geldbörse) frame
bügel-, Bügel-: ~brett *das* ironing board; **~eisen** *das* iron; **~falte** *die* [trouser] crease; **~frei** *Adj.* non-iron
bügeln *tr., itr. V.* iron
bugsieren /bʊˈksiːrən/ *tr. V.* (ugs.) shift; manœuvre; steer ‹*person*›

*old spelling - see note on page xiv

buh *Interj.* boo
Buh *das;* **~s, ~s** (ugs.) boo
buhen *itr. V.* (ugs.) boo
buhlen *itr. V.* (geh. abwertend) **um jmds. Gunst ~:** court sb.'s favour
Buh·mann *der* whipping boy
Buhne /ˈbuːnə/ *die;* **~, ~n** groyne
Bühne *die;* **~, ~n (a)** stage; **ein Stück auf die ~ bringen** put on *or* stage a play
(b) (Theater) theatre
bühnen-, Bühnen-: ~arbeiter *der,* **~arbeiterin** *die* stagehand; **~ausstattung** *die* stage set; **~bild** *das* [stage] set; **~bildner** *der;* **~~s, ~~, ~bildnerin** *die;* **~~, ~~nen** stage designer; **~reif** *Adj.* ‹*play etc.*› ready for the stage; ‹*imitation etc.*› worthy of the stage; dramatic ‹*entrance etc.*›
Buh·ruf *der* boo
buk *1. u. 3. Pers. Sg. Prät. v.* BACKEN
Bukett *das;* **~s, ~s** *od.* **~e** (geh.) bouquet
Bulette *die;* **~, ~n** (bes. berl.) rissole
Bulgare *der;* **~n, ~n** Bulgarian
Bulgarien /bʊlˈgaːri̯ən/ *(das);* **~s** Bulgaria
Bulgarin *die;* **~, ~nen** Bulgarian
bulgarisch *Adj.* Bulgarian
Bull-: ~auge *das* circular porthole; **~dogge** *die* bulldog; **~dozer** /-doːzɐ/ *der;* **~~s, ~~:** bulldozer
Bulle *der;* **~n, ~n (a)** bull
(b) (salopp: Polizist) cop (coll.)
Bullen·hitze *die* (ugs.) sweltering *or* boiling heat
Bulletin /bylˈtɛ̃ː/ *das;* **~s, ~s** bulletin
bullig 1 *Adj.* **(a)** beefy ‹*person, appearance, etc.*›; chunky ‹*car*›
(b) (drückend) sweltering ‹*heat*›
2 *adv.* **~ heiß** boiling hot
Bull·terrier *der* bull terrier
bum *Interj.* bang
Bumerang *der;* **~s, ~e** *od.* **~s** boomerang
Bummel *der;* **~s, ~ (a)** stroll (**durch** around)
(b) (durch Lokale) pub crawl (coll.)
Bummelei *die;* **~, ~en** (ugs.) **(a)** dawdling
(b) (Faulenzerei) loafing about
bummelig (ugs.) **1** *Adj.* **(a)** slow
(b) (nachlässig) slipshod
2 *adv.* **(a)** slowly
(b) (nachlässig) in a slipshod way
bummeln *itr. V.* **(a)** *mit sein* stroll (**durch** around); **durch die Kneipen ~:** go on a pub crawl (Brit. coll.)
(b) (trödeln) dawdle
(c) (faulenzen) laze about
bums *Interj.* bang
Bums *der;* **~es, ~e** (ugs.) bang; (dumpfer) thud
bumsen *itr. V.* (ugs.) **(a)** bang; (dumpfer) thump; *unpers.* **es bumste ganz furchtbar** there was a terrible bang/thud
(b) *mit sein* (stoßen) bang

Bund¹ *der;* ~[e]s, **Bünde (a)** (Vereinigung) association; (Bündnis, Pakt) alliance **(b)** (föderativer Staat) federation **(c)** (an Röcken, Hosen) waistband

Bund² *das;* ~[e]s, ~e bunch

Bündchen *das;* ~s, ~ band

Bündel *das;* ~s, ~ bundle

bündeln *tr. V.* bundle up ‹*newspapers, old clothes, rags, etc.*›; tie ‹*banknotes etc.*› into bundles/a bundle; tie ‹*flowers, radishes, carrots, etc.*› into bunches/a bunch; sheave ‹*straw, hay, etc.*›

Bundes- federal; (in Namen, Titeln) Federal

bundes-, Bundes-: ~bürger *der,* **~bürgerin** *die* (veralt.) West German citizen; **~deutsch** *Adj.* (veralt.) West German; **~ebene** *die:* **auf ~ebene** at federal *or* national level; **~gerichtshof** *der* Federal Supreme Court; **~kabinett** *das* Federal Cabinet; **~kanzler** *der* **(a)** Federal Chancellor; **(b)** (schweiz.) Chancellor of the Confederation; **~land** *das* [federal] state; (österr.) province; **~liga** *die* national division; **~minister** *der,* **~ministerin** *die* Federal Minister; **~ministerium** *das* Federal Ministry; **~präsident** *der,* **~präsidentin** *die* **(a)** [Federal] President; **(b)** (schweiz.) President of the Confederation; **~rat** *der* Bundesrat; **~regierung** *die* Federal Government; **~republik** *die* federal republic; **die ~republik Deutschland** The Federal Republic of Germany; **~straße** *die* federal highway; ≈ A road (Brit.); **~tag** *der* Bundestag

Bundestags-: ~abgeordnete *der/die* member of parliament; member of the Bundestag; **~präsident** *der,* **~präsidentin** *die* President of the Bundestag; **~wahl** *die* parliamentary *or* general election

bundes-, Bundes-: ~trainer *der,* **~trainerin** *die* national team manager; **~verfassungs·gericht** *das* Federal Constitutional Court; **~verwaltungs·gericht** *das* Supreme Administrative Court; **~wehr** *die* [Federal] Armed Forces *pl.;* **~weit** *Adj., adv.* nationwide

Bund-: ~falten *Pl.* pleats; **~falten·hose** *die* pleat[ed]-front trousers *pl.;* **~hose** *die* knee breeches

bündig [1] *Adj.* **(a)** succinct **(b)** (schlüssig) conclusive [2] *adv.* **(a)** succinctly **(b)** (schlüssig) conclusively

Bündnis *das;* ~ses, ~se alliance

Bungalow /ˈbʊŋgalo/ *der;* ~s, ~s bungalow

Bunker *der;* ~s, ~ **(a)** bunker **(b)** (Luftschutzbunker) air-raid shelter

bunt [1] *Adj.* **(a)** colourful; (farbig) coloured; **~e Farben/Kleidung** bright colours/brightly coloured clothes **(b)** (fig.) varied ‹*programme etc.*› [2] *adv.* **(a)** colourfully; **~ bemalt** brightly painted **(b)** (fig.) **ein ~ gemischtes Programm** a varied programme

bunt-, Bunt-: *~bemalt ▶ BUNT 2A; **~papier** *das* coloured paper; **~specht** *der* spotted woodpecker; **~stift** *der* coloured pencil/crayon

Bürde *die;* ~, ~n (geh.) weight; load

Burg *die;* ~, ~en **(a)** castle **(b)** (Strand~) wall of sand

Bürge *der;* ~n, ~n guarantor

bürgen *itr. V.* **(a) für jmdn./etw. ~:** vouch for sb./sth. **(b)** (fig.) guarantee

Bürger *der;* ~s, ~, **Bürgerin** *die;* ~, ~nen citizen

Bürger-: ~initiative *die* citizens' action group; **~krieg** *der* civil war

bürgerlich *Adj.* **(a)** (staats~) civil ‹*rights, marriage, etc.*›; civic ‹*duties*› **(b)** (dem Bürgertum zugehörig) middle-class; **die ~e Küche** good plain cooking **(c)** (Polit.) non-socialist; (nicht marxistisch) non-Marxist

bürger-, Bürger-: ~meister *der,* **~meisterin** *die* mayor; **~nah** *Adj.* which/who reflects the general public's interests *postpos., not pred.;* **~pflicht** *die* duty as a citizen; **~steig** *der;* ~~s, ~~e pavement (Brit.); sidewalk (Amer.)

Bürgertum /ˈ--tuːm/ *das;* ~s **(a)** middle class **(b)** (Großbürgertum) bourgeoisie

Bürgin *die;* ~, ~nen ▶ BÜRGE

Bürgschaft *die;* ~, ~en **(a)** guarantee **(b)** (Betrag) penalty

Büro *das;* ~s, ~s office

Büro-: ~angestellte *der/die* office worker; **~artikel** *der* item of office equipment; **~haus** *das* office block; **~klammer** *die* paper clip; **~kraft** *die* clerical worker

Bürokrat *der;* ~en, ~en bureaucrat

Bürokratie *die;* ~, ~n bureaucracy

Bürokratin *die;* ~, ~nen bureaucrat

bürokratisch [1] *Adj.* bureaucratic [2] *adv.* bureaucratically

Büro·technik *die* office technology

Bürschchen /ˈbʏrʃçən/ *das;* ~, ~: little fellow

Bursche *der;* ~n, ~n **(a)** boy; lad **(b)** (abwertend: Kerl) guy (coll.)

burschikos [1] *Adj.* **(a)** sporty ‹*look, clothes*›; [tom]boyish ‹*behaviour, girl, haircut*› **(b)** (ungezwungen) casual ‹*comment, behaviour, etc.*› [2] *adv.* **(a)** [tom]boyishly **(b)** (ungezwungen) in a colloquial way

Bürste *die;* ~, ~n brush

bürsten *tr. V.* brush

C

Bus *der;* **~ses, ~se** bus
Bus·bahnhof *der* bus station
Busch *der;* **~[e]s, Büsche** bush; **auf den ~ klopfen** (fig. ugs.) sound things out
Büschel *das;* **~s, ~:** tuft; (von Heu, Stroh) handful
Busen *der;* **~s, ~** bust
Bus-: ~fahrer *der,* **~fahrerin** *die* bus driver; **~haltestelle** *die* bus stop; **~linie** *die* bus route
Bussard *der;* **~s, ~e** buzzard
Buße *die;* **~, ~n** (Rel.) penance *no art.*
büßen 1 *tr. V.* **(a)** atone for **(b)** (fig.) pay for
2 *itr. V.* **(a) für etw. ~:** atone for sth. **(b)** (fig.) pay
Buß·geld *das* (Rechtsw.) fine
Buß- und Bettag *der* (ev. Kirche) Day of Prayer and Repentance (*Wednesday eleven days before the first Sunday in Advent*)
Büsten·halter *der* bra; brassière (formal)
Butan·gas *das* butane gas
Butt *der;* **~[e]s, ~e** flounder; butt
Bütten·papier *das* handmade paper (*with deckle edge*)
Butter *die;* **~:** butter; **es ist alles in ~** (ugs.) everything's fine
butter-, Butter-: ~berg *der* (ugs.) butter mountain; **~blume** *die* (Sumpfdotterblume) marsh marigold; (Hahnenfuß) buttercup; **~brot** *das* slice of bread and butter; (zugeklappt) sandwich; **~creme** *die* buttercream; **~milch** *die* buttermilk; **~weich** *Adj.* beautifully soft
b. w. *Abk.* = **bitte wenden** p.t.o.
Bypass /ˈbaipɑs/ *der;* **~es, Bypässe** (Med.) bypass
Byte /bait/ *das;* **~s, ~[s]** (DV) byte
bzw. *Abk.* = **beziehungsweise**

Cc

c, C /t͜seː/ *das;* **~, ~: (a)** (Buchstabe) c/C **(b)** (Musik) [key of] C
C *Abk.* = **Celsius** C
ca. *Abk.* = **cirka** c.
Café *das;* **~s, ~s** café
Cafeteria *die;* **~, ~s** cafeteria
cal *Abk.* = **[Gramm]kalorie** cal.
Callboy /ˈkɔːlbɔɪ/ *der;* **~s, ~s** call-boy
Callgirl /ˈkɔːlgəːl/ *das;* **~s, ~s** call girl
Camp /kɛmp/ *das;* **~s, ~s** camp
campen *itr. V.* camp
Camping *das;* **~s** camping
Camping-: ~bus *der* motor caravan; camper; **~kocher** *der* camping stove; **~platz** *der* campsite; campground (Amer.)
Cannabis /ˈkanabɪs/ *der;* **~:** cannabis
Cantilever·bremse /ˈkæntɪliːvɐ-/ *die* cantilever brake
Caravan /ˈka(ː)ravan/ *der;* **~s, ~s** (Wohnwagen) caravan; trailer (Amer.)
Cashflow /kæʃˈfloʊ/ *der;* **~s** (Wirtsch.) [gross] cash flow
Castor-: ~behälter *der* Castor container; Castor cask; **~transport** *der* Castor transport
Catcher /ˈkɛtʃɐ/ *der;* **~s, ~, Catcherin** *die;* **~, ~nen** all-in wrestler
Cayenne·pfeffer /kaˈjɛn-/ *der* cayenne [pepper]

*alte Schreibung - vgl. Hinweis auf S. xiv

CD /t͜seːˈdeː/ *die;* **~, ~s** CD
CD-Brenner *der;* **~s, ~** (DV) CD burner; CD writer
CD-ROM /t͜seːdeːˈrɔm/ *die;* **~, ~[s]** (DV) CD-ROM
CD-ROM-Laufwerk *das* (DV) CD-ROM drive
CD-Spieler /t͜seːˈdeː-/ *der* CD player
CDU *Abk.* = **Christlich-Demokratische Union [Deutschlands]** [German] Christian Democratic Party
C-Dur /ˈt͜seː-/ *das* C major
Cellist /tʃɛˈlɪst/ *der;* **~en, ~en, Cellistin** *die;* **~, ~nen** cellist
Cello /ˈtʃɛlo/ *das;* **~s, ~s** *od.* **Celli** cello
Celsius: 20 Grad ~: 20 degrees Celsius *or* centigrade
Cembalo /ˈtʃɛmbalo/ *das;* **~s, ~s** *od.* **Cembali** harpsichord
Cent *der;* **~[s], ~[s]** cent; **50 ~** 50 cents
Champagner /ʃamˈpanjɐ/ *der;* **~s, ~** champagne (from Champagne)
Champignon /ˈʃampɪnjɔn/ *der;* **~s, ~s** mushroom
Chance /ˈʃãːsə/ *die;* **~, ~n (a)** chance **(b)** *Pl.* (Aussichten) prospects; **[bei jmdm] ~n haben** stand a chance [with sb.]
Chancen·gleichheit *die* (Soziol.) equality *no art.* of opportunity

Chaos /'k.../ *das;* ~: chaos *no art.*

Chaot /ka'o:t/ *der;* **~en, ~en, Chaotin** *die;* **~, ~nen(a)** (Politik) anarchist (trying to undermine society)
(b) (salopp: unordentlicher Mensch) **ein [furchtbarer] ~ sein** be [terribly] disorganized

chaotisch 1 *Adj.* chaotic
2 *adv.* chaotically; **es geht ~ zu** there is chaos

Charakter /ka.../ *der;* **~s, ~e** /...'te:rə/ character

charakterisieren *tr. V.* characterize

charakteristisch *Adj.* characteristic (**für** of)

charakterlich 1 *Adj.* character *attrib.;*
2 *adv.* in [respect of] character

charakter·los *Adj.* unprincipled; (niederträchtig) despicable; (labil) spineless

Charisma /'ça:rɪsma/ *das;* **~s, Charismen** charisma

charismatisch /çarɪs'ma:tɪʃ/ *Adj.* charismatic

charmant /ʃar'mant/ 1 *Adj.* charming
2 *adv.* charmingly

Charme /ʃarm/ *der;* **~s** charm

Charter- /'tʃartɐ-/: **~flug** *der* charter flight; **~maschine** *die* chartered aircraft

Charts /tʃarts/ *Pl.* charts

Chassis /ʃa'si:/ *das;* ~ /ʃa'si:(s),/ ~ /ʃa'si:s/ chassis

chatten /'tʃɛtn̩/ *itr. V.* (DV Jargon) chat

Chauffeur /ʃɔ'fø:ɐ̯/ *der;* **~s, ~e, Chauffeurin** /ʃɔ'fø:rɪn/ *die;* **~, ~nen** driver; (privat angestellt) chauffeur

checken /'tʃɛkn̩/ *tr. V.* **(a)** (bes. Technik: kontrollieren) check; examine
(b) (salopp: begreifen) twig (coll.); (bemerken) spot; **ich habe das noch nicht gecheckt** I haven't got it yet

Check·liste *die* checklist; (Passagierliste) passenger list

Chef /ʃɛf/ *der;* **~s, ~s, Chefin** /'ʃɛfɪn/ *die;* **~, ~nen** (Leiter[in]) head; (der Polizei, des Generalstabs) chief; (einer Partei, Bande) leader; (Vorgesetzte[r]) superior; boss (coll.)

Chef-: ~koch *der,* **~köchin** *die* chef; head cook; **~sekretärin** *die* director's secretary

Chemie *die;* **~ (a)** chemistry *no art.;*
(b) (ugs.: Chemikalien) chemicals *pl.*

Chemikalie /çemi'ka:li̯ə/ *die;* **~, ~n** chemical

Chemiker *der;* **~s, ~, Chemikerin** *die;* **~, ~nen** (graduate) chemist

chemisch 1 *Adj.* chemical
2 *adv.* chemically

Chemo·therapie *die* (Med.) chemotherapy

Chicorée /'ʃikore/ *der;* **~s** *od. die;* **~:** chicory

Chiffon /'ʃɪfõ/ *der;* **~s, ~s** chiffon

Chiffre /'ʃɪfrə/ *die;* **~, ~n (a)** (Zeichen) symbol
(b) (Geheimzeichen) cipher
(c) (in Annoncen) box number

Chile /'tʃi:le, 'çi:lə/ *(das);* **~s** Chile

Chilene /tʃi'le:nə, çi'le:nə/ *der;* **~n, ~n, Chilenin** *die;* **~, ~nen** Chilean

chilenisch *Adj.* Chilean

Chili /'tʃi:li/ *der;* **~s, ~es (a)** *Pl.* (Schoten) chillies
(b) (Gewürz) chilli [powder]

China *(das);* **~s** China

Chinese *der;* **~n, ~n, Chinesin** *die;* **~, ~nen** Chinese

chinesisch *Adj.* Chinese

Chip /tʃɪp/ *der;* **~s, ~s (a)** (Spielmarke) chip
(b) (Kartoffel~) [potato] crisp (Brit.) *or* (Amer.) chip
(c) (Elektronik) [micro]chip

Chip·karte *die* smart card

Chirurg *der;* **~en, ~en** surgeon

Chirurgie *die;* **~, ~n (a)** surgery *no art.;*
(b) (Abteilung) surgical department; (Station) surgical ward

Chirurgin *die;* **~, ~nen** surgeon

chirurgisch 1 *Adj.* surgical
2 *adv.* surgically; by surgery

Chlor /k.../ *das;* **~s** chlorine

Chloroform /k.../ *das;* **~s** chloroform

Chlorophyll /k.../ *das;* **~s** chlorophyll

Cholera *die;* **~:** cholera

cholerisch *Adj.* irascible; choleric ‹*temperament*›

Cholesterin *das;* **~s** cholesterol

Chor *der;* **~[e]s, Chöre** /'kø:rə/ (auch Archit.) choir; (in Oper, Sinfonie, Theater; Komposition) chorus; **im ~ rufen** shout in chorus

Choral *der;* **~s, Choräle** (Kirchenlied) chorale

Choreograph /koreo'gra:f/ *der;* **~en, ~en** choreographer

Choreographie *die;* **~, ~n** choreography

Choreographin *die;* **~, ~nen** choreographer

choreographisch *Adj.* choreographic

Chose /'ʃo:zə/ *die;* **~, ~n** (ugs.) stuff; **die ganze ~:** the whole lot (coll.) *or* (coll.) shoot

Chow-Chow /tʃau̯ tʃau̯/ *der;* **~s, ~s** chow

Christ /k.../ *der;* **~en, ~en** Christian

Christ-: ~baum *der* (bes. südd.) Christmas tree; **~demokrat** *der,* **~demokratin** *die* (Politik) Christian Democrat

Christenheit *die;* **~:** Christendom *no art.*

Christentum *das;* **~s** Christianity *no art.;* (Glaube) Christian faith

Christin *die;* **~, ~nen** Christian

Christ·kind *das* Christ-child (*as bringer of Christmas gifts*)

christlich 1 *Adj.* Christian
2 *adv.* in a [truly] Christian spirit

Christ-: ~messe *die* (kath. Rel.) Christmas ⋯

Mass; **~mette** *die;* **~~, ~~n** (kath. Rel.) Christmas Mass; (ev. Rel.) midnight service [on Christmas Eve]; **~rose** *die* Christmas rose; **~stollen** *der* stollen; [German] Christmas loaf (*with candied fruit, almonds, etc.*)

Christus (*der*); ~ *od.* **Christi** Christ

Chrom /k.../ *das;* **~s** chromium

Chromosom /k.../ *das;* **~s, ~en** (Biol.) chromosome

Chromosomen·satz *der* (Biol.) chromosome set

Chronik /k.../ *die;* **~, ~en** chronicle

chronisch *Adj.* chronic

Chrysantheme /k.../ *die;* **~, ~n** chrysanthemum

City /'sɪti/ *die;* **~, ~s** city centre

clean /kli:n/ *Adj.* (ugs.) clean (coll.); **~ werden** come off drugs

clever /'klɛvɐ/ **1** *Adj.* (raffiniert) shrewd; (intelligent, geschickt) clever
2 *adv.: s. Adj.:* shrewdly; cleverly

Clique /'klɪkə/ *die;* **~, ~n (a)** (abwertend) clique
(b) (Freundeskreis) set; (größere Gruppe) crowd (coll.)

Clown /klau̯n/ *der;* **~s, ~s, Clownin** /'klau̯nɪn/ *die;* **~, ~nen** clown

Club ▶ KLUB

cm *Abk.* = **Zentimeter** cm.

Co. *Abk.* = **Compagnie** Co.

Coach /koʊtʃ/ *der;* **~s, ~s** (Sport) coach; (bes. Fußball: Trainer) manager

coachen /'koʊtʃn̩/ *tr., itr. V.* (Sport) coach; (Trainer sein) manage

Cockpit *das;* **~s, ~s** cockpit

Cocktail /'kɔkteɪl/ *der;* **~s, ~s** cocktail

Cognac Ⓦⓩ /'kɔnjak/ *der;* **~s, ~s** Cognac

Cola /'ko:la/ *das;* **~s, ~s** *od. die;* **~, ~s** (ugs.) Coke ®

Color- (Fot.) colour ‹*film, slide, etc.*›

Colt Ⓦⓩ *der;* **~s, ~s** Colt ® [revolver]

Comeback /kam'bɛk/ *das;* **~s, ~s** comeback; **ein ~ feiern** stage a comeback

Comic·heft *das* comic

Computer /kɔm'pju:tɐ/ *der;* **~s, ~:** computer

computer·gestützt *Adj.* computer-aided; computer-assisted

computerisieren *tr. V.* computerize ‹*data, system*›; (aufbereiten) make ‹*data*› computer-compatible

computer-, Computer-: ~raum *der* computer rooom; **~spiel** *das* computer game **~unterstützt** *Adj.* computer-aided; computer-assisted

Container /kɔn'te:nɐ/ *der;* **~s, ~:** container; (für Müll) [refuse] skip

cool /ku:l/ (ugs.) **1** *Adj.* cool; **~ bleiben** keep one's cool (coll.)
2 *adv.* coolly (coll.)

Cord *der;* **~[e]s, ~e** *od.* **~s** cord; (~samt) corduroy

Corned Beef /'kɔ:nd'bi:f/ *das;* **~s** corned beef

Couch /kau̯tʃ/ *die,* (schweiz. auch:) *der;* **~, ~es** sofa

Coup /ku:/ *der;* **~s, ~s** coup

Coupon /ku'põ:/ *der;* **~s, ~s** coupon; voucher

Courage /ku'ra:ʒə/ *die;* **~** (ugs.) courage

Cousin /ku'zɛ̃:/ *der;* **~s, ~s, Cousine** *die;* **~, ~n** cousin

Cover /'kavɐ/ *das;* **~s, ~s (a)** (von Illustrierten) cover
(b) (von Schallplatten) sleeve

covern /'kavɐn/ *tr. V.* cover ‹*song, record*›

Cowboy /'kau̯bɔy̯:/ *der;* **~s, ~s** cowboy

Credo ▶ KREDO

Creme /kre:m/ *die;* **~, ~s,** (schweiz.:) **~n** cream

CSU *Abk.* = **Christlich-Soziale Union** CSU

CT (Med.) *Abk.*
= **Computertomographie** CT

Curry /'kœri/ *das;* **~s, ~s** curry powder

Curry·wurst *die: sliced fried sausage sprinkled with curry powder and served with ketchup*

Cursor /'kə:sə/ *der;* **~s, ~s** (DV) cursor

Cyberspace /'sai̯bɐspeɪs/ *der;* **~** (DV) cyberspace

---

*old spelling - see note on page xiv

Dd

d, D /deː/ *das;* ~, ~ **(a)** (Buchstabe) d/D **(b)** (Musik) [key of] D

D *Abk.* = **Damen**

da 1 *Adv.* **(a)** (dort) there; **da draußen/drinnen/drüben/unten** out/in/over/down there; **da, wo** where **(b)** (hier) here **(c)** (zeitlich) then; (in dem Augenblick) at that moment **(d)** (deshalb) **der Zug war schon weg, da habe ich den Bus genommen** the train had already gone, so I took the bus **(e)** (ugs.: in diesem Fall) **da kann man nichts machen** there's nothing one can do about it **(f) da sein** (existieren) exist; (übrig sein) be left; (anwesend sein) be about *or* around; (im Haus, zu Hause sein) be in; (zu sprechen sein) be available; (angekommen, eingetroffen sein) have arrived; (fig.) ‹*case*› have occurred; ‹*moment*› have arrived; ‹*situation*› have arisen; **ich bin gleich wieder da** I'll be right *or* straight back 2 *Konj.* (weil) as; since

da·bei *Adv.* **(a)** with it/him/her/them; **nahe ~:** close by; **~ sein** (anwesend sein) be there; be present (**bei** at); (teilnehmen) take part (**bei** in) **(b)** (währenddessen) at the same time; (bei diesem Anlass) then; on that occasion; **die ~ entstehenden Kosten** the expense involved; **[gerade] ~ sein, etw. zu tun** be just doing sth. **(c)** (außerdem) **~ [auch]** what is more **(d)** (hinsichtlich dessen) about it/them; **was hast du dir denn ~ gedacht?** what 'were you thinking of?

dabei-: ~|bleiben *unr. itr. V.; mit sein* stay there; be there; **~|haben** *unr. tr. V.* have with one; ***~|sein** ▶ DABEI A, B; **~|stehen** *unr. itr. V.* stand there

da|bleiben *unr. itr. V.; mit sein* stay there; (hier bleiben) stay here

Dach *das;* **~[e]s, Dächer** roof

Dach-: ~antenne *die* roof aerial; **~boden** *der* loft; **auf dem ~boden** in the loft; **~decker** /-dɛkɐ/ *der;* **~~s, ~~,** **~deckerin** *die;* **~~, ~~nen** roofer; **~fenster** *das* skylight; (~gaube) dormer window; **~garten** *der* roof garden; **~gaube** *die* dormer window; **~gepäckträger** *der* (Kfz-W.) roof rack; **~geschoss, *~geschoß** *das* attic [storey]; **~kammer** *die* attic [room]; **~luke** *die* skylight; **~pappe** *die* roofing felt; **~rinne** *die* gutter

Dachs /daks/ *der;* **~es, ~e** badger

Dach·stuhl *der* roof truss

dachte *1. u. 3. Pers. Sg. Prät. v.* DENKEN

Dach-: ~terrasse *die* roof terrace; **~wohnung** *die* attic flat (Brit.) *or* (Amer.) apartment; **~ziegel** *der* roof tile; **~zimmer** *das* attic room

Dackel *der;* **~s, ~:** dachshund

da·durch *Adv.* **(a)** through it/them **(b)** (durch diesen Umstand) as a result; (durch dieses Mittel) by this [means]

da·für *Adv.* **(a)** for it/them; **~, dass ...** (wenn man berücksichtigt, dass) considering that ...; (damit) so that ...; **~ sorgen [, dass ...]** see to it [that ...] **(b) ~ sein** be in favour [of it]; **ein Beispiel ~ ist ...:** an example of this is ... **(c)** (als Gegenleistung) in return [for it]; (beim Tausch) in exchange; (stattdessen) instead **(d) etwas/nichts ~ können** be/not be responsible

***dafür|können** ▶ DAFÜR D

dagegen *Adv.* **(a)** against it/them; **etwas ~ haben** have sth. against it; **ich habe nichts ~:** I've no objection; **~ sein** be against it **(b)** (im Vergleich dazu) by *or* in comparison

da·heim *Adv.* (bes. südd., österr., schweiz.) **(a)** (zu Hause) at home; (*nach Präp.*) home **(b)** (in der Heimat) [back] home

da·her *Adv.* **(a)** from there **(b)** (durch diesen Umstand) hence **(c)** (deshalb) therefore; so

daher|kommen *unr. itr. V.* come along

da·hin **(a)** there **(b)** (fig.) **~ musste es kommen** it had to come to that **(c) bis ~:** to there; (zeitlich) until then **(d) ~ sein** be *or* have gone **(e)** (in diesem Sinne) **~ [gehend], dass ...:** to the effect that ...

da·hinten *Adv.* over there

da·hinter *Adv.* behind it/them; (folgend) after it/them

Dahlie /ˈdaːli̯ə/ *die;* **~, ~n** dahlia

da-: ~|lassen *unr. tr. V.* (ugs.) leave [there]; (hier lassen) leave here; **~|liegen** *unr. itr. V.* lie there

dalli *Adv.* (ugs.) [~] **~!** get a move on!

damalig *Adj.* at that *or* the time *postpos.*

damals *Adv.* at that time

Damast *der;* **~[e]s, ~e** damask

Dame *die;* **~, ~n** **(a)** (Frau) lady **(b)** (Schach, Kartenspiele) queen **(c)** (Spiel) draughts (Brit.); checkers (Amer.)

Damen-: ~binde *die* sanitary towel (Brit.) *or* (Amer.) napkin; **~friseur** *der,* ···>

~friseurin *die* ladies' hairdresser; **~rad** *das* lady's bicycle; **~toilette** *die* ladies' toilet

da·mit 1 *Adv.* **(a)** with it/them **(b)** (gleichzeitig) with that **(c)** (daher) thus 2 *Konj.* so that

dämlich (ugs. abwertend) 1 *Adj.* stupid 2 *adv.* stupidly

Damm *der;* **~[e]s, Dämme** embankment; levee (Amer.); (Deich) dike; (Stau~) dam

dämmern *itr. V.* **es dämmert** (morgens) it is getting light; (abends) it is getting dark

Dämmerung *die;* **~, ~en (a)** (Abend~) twilight; dusk **(b)** (Morgen~) dawn

Dämon *der;* **~s, ~en** /dɛˈmoːnən/ demon

dämonisch *Adj.* demonic

dämonisieren *tr. V.* demonize; portray as a demon/demons

Dampf *der;* **~[e]s, Dämpfe** steam *no pl., no indef. art.*

Dampf·bügel·eisen *das* steam iron

dampfen *itr. V.* steam **(vor** + *Dat.* with)

dämpfen *tr. V.* **(a)** (garen) steam ‹*fish, vegetables, potatoes*› **(b)** (mildern) muffle ‹*sound*›; cushion, absorb ‹*blow, impact, shock*›

Dampfer *der;* **~s, ~:** steamer

Dampf-: ~kochtopf *der* pressure cooker; **~maschine** *die* steam engine; **~nudel** *die* (südd., Kochk.) steamed yeast dumpling; **~walze** *die* steamroller

da·nach *Adv.* **(a)** (zeitlich) after it/that; then **(b)** (räumlich) after it/them **(c)** (entsprechend) in accordance with it/them

Däne *der;* **~n, ~n** Dane

da·neben *Adv.* **(a)** beside him/her/it/them *etc.;* **(b)** (im Vergleich dazu) in comparison

daneben-: ~|benehmen *unr. refl. V.* (ugs.) blot one's copybook (coll.); **~|gehen** *unr. itr. V.; mit sein* miss [the target]; **~|schießen** *unr. itr. V.* miss [the target]

Dänemark *(das);* **~s** Denmark

Dänin *die;* **~, ~nen** Dane; Danish woman/girl

dänisch *Adj.* Danish

dank *Präp. mit Dat. u. Gen.* thanks to

Dank *der;* **~[e]s** thanks *pl.;* **mit [vielem** *od.* **bestem] ~ zurück** thanks for the loan; (bes. geschrieben) returned with thanks!; **vielen/besten/herzlichen ~!** thank you very much

dankbar 1 *Adj.* grateful; (anerkennend) appreciative ‹*child, audience, etc.*›; **[jmdm.] für etw. ~ sein** be grateful [to sb.] for sth. 2 *adv.* gratefully

Dankbarkeit *die;* **~:** gratitude

danke *Höflichkeitsformel* thank you; (ablehnend) no, thank you; **~ schön/sehr/vielmals** thank you very much

danken 1 *itr. V.* (Dank aussprechen) thank; **ich danke Ihnen vielmals** thank you very much; **na, ich danke!** (ugs.) no, ˈthank you! 2 *tr. V.* **[aber bitte,] nichts zu ~:** don't mention it

Danke·schön *das;* **~s** thank-you

dann *Adv.* **(a)** then; **was ~?** what happens then?; **noch drei Tage, ~ ist Ostern** another three days and it will be Easter; **bis ~:** see you then; **~ und wann** now and then **(b)** (in diesem Falle) then; in that case; **~ will ich nicht weiter stören** in that case I won't disturb you any further; **[na,] ~ eben nicht!** in that case, forget it!; **nur ~, wenn ...:** only if ...

daran /daˈran/ *Adv.* **(a)** (an dieser/diese Stelle, an diesem/diesen Gegenstand) on it/them; **dicht ~:** close to it/them; **nahe ~ sein, etw. zu tun** be on the point of doing sth. **(b)** (hinsichtlich dieser Sache) about it/them; **~ ist nichts zu machen** there's nothing one can do about it; **kein Wort ~ ist wahr** not a word of it is true; **mir liegt viel ~:** it means a lot to me **(c) ich wäre beinahe ~ erstickt** I almost choked on it; **er ist ~ gestorben** he died of it

daran|setzen *tr. V.* devote ‹*energy etc.*› to it; summon up ‹*ambition*› for it; (aufs Spiel setzen) risk ‹*one's life, one's honour*› for it

darauf *Adv.* **(a)** on it/them; (oben ~) on top of it/them **(b) er hat ~ geschossen** he shot at it/them **(c)** (danach) after that; **ein Jahr ~/kurz ~ starb er** he died a year later/shortly afterwards; **~ folgend** following

darauf-: *~folgend ▶ DARAUF C; **~hin** /--ˈ-/ *Adv.* **(a)** thereupon; **(b)** (unter diesem Gesichtspunkt) with a view to this/that

daraus *Adv.* **(a)** from it/them; out of it/them **(b) mach dir nichts ~:** don't worry about it; **was ist ~ geworden?** what has become of it?

dar|bieten (geh.) *unr. tr. V.* (aufführen, vortragen) perform; **es wurden Gedichte und Lieder dargeboten** a recital of poems and songs was presented

Darbietung *die;* **~, ~en** (geh.) **(a)** presentation **(b)** (Aufführung) performance; (beim Varieté usw.) act

darf *1. u. 3. Pers. Sg. Präsens v.* DÜRFEN

darfst *2. Pers. Sg. Präsens v.* DÜRFEN

darin *Adv.* **(a)** in it/them **(b)** (in dieser Hinsicht) in that respect

dar|legen *tr. V.* explain; set forth ‹*reasons, facts*›

Darlehen *das;* **~s, ~:** loan; **ein ~ aufnehmen** get *or* raise a loan; **jmdm. ein ~ gewähren** give *or* grant sb. a loan

Darm *der;* **~[e]s, Därme** intestines *pl.;* bowels *pl.*

---

*alte Schreibung - vgl. Hinweis auf S. xiv

dar|stellen *tr. V.* **(a)** depict; portray; **etw. grafisch ~:** present sth. graphically
(b) (verkörpern) play; act
(c) (schildern) describe ‹*person, incident, etc.*›; present ‹*matter, argument*›
(d) (sein, bedeuten) represent

Darsteller *der;* **~s, ~:** actor

Darstellerin *die;* **~, ~nen** actress

Darstellung *die* **(a)** representation; (Schilderung) portrayal; (Bild) picture; **grafische/schematische ~:** diagram; (Graph) graph
(b) (Beschreibung, Bericht) description; account;
(c) (einer Theaterrolle) interpretation; **seine ~ des Mephisto** his portrayal *or* interpretation of Mephisto

darüber *Adv.* **(a)** over it/them; **~ stehen** (fig.) be above such things
(b) ~ hinaus in addition [to that]; (noch obendrein) what is more
(c) (über dieser/diese Angelegenheit) about it/ them
(d) (über diese Grenze, dieses Maß hinaus) over [that]

***darüber|stehen** ▶ DARÜBER A

darum *Adv.* **(a)** [a]round it/them
(b) (diesbezüglich) **ich sorge mich ~:** I worry about it
(c) /'--/ (deswegen) for that reason

darunter *Adv.* **(a)** (unter dem Genannten/das Genannte) under it/them
(b) (unter dieser Grenze, diesem Maß) less; **Bewerber im Alter von 40 Jahren und ~:** applicants aged 40 and under

das **1** *best. Art. Nom. u. Akk.* the
2 *Demonstrativpron.* **(a)** *attr.* **das Kind war es** it was 'that child
(b) *allein stehend* **das [da]** that one; **das [hier]** this one [here]
3 *Relativpron.* (Mensch) who; that; (Sache, Tier) which; that

***da|sein** ▶ DA 1F

Da·sein *das* existence

Daseins·berechtigung *die* right to exist; **das findet darin** *od.* **dadurch seine ~:** this justifies its existence

da|sitzen *unr. itr. V.* sit there

dasjenige ▶ DERJENIGE

dass, *daß *Konj.* **(a)** that; **entschuldigen Sie bitte, ~ ich mich verspätet habe** please forgive me for being late; **ich verstehe nicht, ~ sie ihn geheiratet hat** I don't understand why she married him
(b) (nach Pronominaladverbien o. Ä.) [the fact] that; **das liegt daran, ~ du nicht aufgepasst hast** that comes from your not paying attention
(c) (im Konsekutivsatz) that; **[so]~:** so that
(d) (im Finalsatz) so that
(e) (im Ausruf) **~ mir das passieren musste!** why did it have to [go and] happen to me!

dasselbe ▶ DERSELBE

da|stehen *unr. itr. V.* **(a)** stand there
(b) (fig.) **gut ~:** be in a good position; **[ganz] allein ~:** be [all] alone in the world

Datei /da'tai:/ *die;* **~, ~en** data file

Daten **1** ▶ DATUM
2 *Pl.* data

Daten-: ~autobahn *die* (DV) data highway; **~bank** *die; Pl.* **~~en** data bank; **~erfassung** *die* data collection *or* capture; **~schutz** *der* data protection *no def. art.;* **~träger** *der* data carrier; **~verarbeitung** *die* data processing *no def. art.*

datieren *tr. V.* date

Dativ *der;* **~s, ~e** (Sprachw.) dative [case]

Dativ·objekt *das* (Sprachw.) indirect object

Dattel *die;* **~, ~n** date

Dattel·palme *die* date palm

Datum *das;* **~s, Daten** date

Dauer *die;* **~ (a)** length; **für die ~ eines Jahres** *od.* **von einem Jahr** for a period of one year
(b) (Fortbestehen) **von ~ sein** last [long]; **auf die ~:** in the long run; **auf ~:** permanently

dauer-, Dauer-: ~auftrag *der* (Bankw.) standing order; **~haft** **1** *Adj.* **(a)** [long-]lasting ‹*peace, friendship, etc.*›; **(b)** (haltbar) durable; **2** *adv.* lastingly; **~karte** *die* season ticket; **~lauf** *der* jogging *no art.;* **ein ~lauf** a jog

dauern *itr. V.* last; ‹*job etc.*› take; **einen Moment, es dauert nicht lange** just a minute, it won't take long

dauernd **1** *Adj.*constant ‹*noise, interruptions, etc.*›; permanent ‹*institution*›
2 *adv.* constantly; **er kommt ~ zu spät** he keeps on arriving late

Dauer-: ~regen *der* continuous rain; **~stellung** *die* permanent position; **~welle** *die* perm; **~wurst** *die* smoked sausage (*with good keeping properties, esp. salami*); **~zustand** *der* permanent state [of affairs]; **zum ~zustand werden** become permanent *or* a permanent state

Daumen *der;* **~s, ~:** thumb

Daune *die;* **~, ~n** down [feather]; **~n** down *sing.*

davon *Adv.* **(a)** (von dieser Stelle entfernt, weg) from it/them; (von dort) from there; (mit Entfernungsangabe) away [from it/them]
(b) (hinsichtlich dieser Sache) about it/them
(c) (durch diese Angelegenheit verursacht) by it/ them; **das kommt ~!** (ugs.) [there you are,] that's what happens
(d) ich hätte gern ein halbes Pfund ~: I would like half a pound of that/those
(e) ~ kann man nicht leben you can't live on that

davon-: ~|fahren *unr. itr. V.; mit sein* leave; (mit dem Auto) drive off; (mit dem Fahrrad, Motorrad) ride off; **~|kommen** *unr. itr. V.; mit sein* get away; **~|laufen** *unr. itr. V.; mit sein* run away; **~|tragen** *unr. tr. V.* **(a)** ···

carry away; take away ‹*rubbish*›; **(b)** (geh.: erringen) gain ‹*a victory, fame*›; **(c)** (geh.: sich zuziehen) receive ‹*injuries*›

da·vor *Adv.* **(a)** in front of it/them; **~ liegen/stehen** *usw.* lie/stand *etc.* in front of it/them
(b) (zeitlich) before [it/them]

***davor|liegen** *usw.* ▶ DAVOR A

Dax *der; ~:* Dax [index]

da·zu *Adv.* **(a)** (zusätzlich zu dieser Sache) with it/them; (gleichzeitig) at the same time; (außerdem) what is more
(b) (diesbezüglich) about it/them
(c) (zu diesem Zweck) for it
(d) (zu diesem Ergebnis) to it; **~ reicht unser Geld nicht** we haven't enough money for that

dazu-: ~|geben *unr. tr. V.* add; **~|gehören** *tr. V.* belong to it/them; **~|kommen** *unr. itr. V.; mit sein* **(a)** (hinkommen) arrive; **(b)** (hinzukommen) **kommt noch etwas dazu?** is there anything else [you would like]?; **~ kommt, dass ...** (fig.) what's more, ...; on top of that ...; **~|rechnen** *tr. V.* add on; **~|tun** *unr. tr. V.* (ugs.) add

da·zwischen *Adv.* in between; between them; (darunter) among them

dazwischen-: ~|kommen *unr. itr. V.; mit sein* **(a) mit dem Finger ~kommen** get one's finger caught [in it]; **(b)** (es verhindern) prevent it; **es ist mir etwas ~gekommen** I had problems; **~|reden** *itr. V.* interrupt

DDR *Abk.* = **Deutsche Demokratische Republik** GDR; East Germany

Deal /di:l/ *der od. das; ~s, ~s* (salopp) deal

dealen /'di:lən/ *itr. V.* (ugs.) push drugs; **mit LSD ~:** push LSD

Dealer *der; ~s, ~,* **Dealerin** *die; ~, ~nen* (ugs.) pusher

Debatte *die; ~, ~n* debate (**über** + *Akk.* on); **zur ~ stehen** be under discussion

Debüt /de'by:/ *das; ~s, ~s* debut

Deck *das; ~[e]s, ~s* deck

Deck·bett *das* ▶ OBERBETT

Decke *die; ~, ~n* **(a)** (Tisch~) tablecloth
(b) (Woll~, Pferde~, fig.) blanket; (Reise~) rug
(c) (Zimmer~) ceiling

Deckel *der; ~s, ~* **(a)** lid; (auf Flaschen, Gläsern usw.) top; (Schacht~, Uhr~, Buch~ usw.) cover
(b) (Bier~) beer mat

decken [1] *tr. V.* **(a) etw. über etw.** (*Akk.*) **~:** spread sth. over sth.
(b) roof ‹*house*›; cover ‹*roof*›
(c) den Tisch ~: lay the table
(d) (schützen; Finanzw., Versicherungsw.) cover
(e) (befriedigen) meet ‹*need, demand*›
[2] *itr. V.* (den Tisch decken) lay the table

Deck·mantel *der* cover

***old spelling - see note on page xiv**

Deckung *die; ~, ~en* **(a)** (Schutz; auch fig.) cover (esp. Mil.); (Boxen) guard; (bes. Fußball) defence; **in ~ gehen** take cover
(b) (Befriedigung) meeting
(c) (Finanzw., Versicherungsw.) cover[ing]

deckungs·gleich *Adj.* (Geom.) congruent

defekt *Adj.* defective; faulty; **~ sein** have a defect; be faulty; (nicht funktionieren) not be working

Defekt *der; ~[e]s, ~e* defect, fault (**an** + *Dat.* in)

defensiv [1] *Adj.* defensive
[2] *adv.* defensively

Defensive *die; ~, ~n* defensive; **in der ~:** on the defensive; **die ~** (Sport) defensive play

definieren *tr. V.* define

Definition *die; ~, ~en* definition

definitiv [1] *Adj.* definitive
[2] *adv.* finally

Defizit *das; ~s, ~e* **(a)** deficit
(b) (Mangel) deficiency

deformieren *tr. V.* **(a)** (verformen) distort
(b) (entstellen) deform (also fig.)

deftig *Adj.* (ugs.) **(a)** [good] solid *attrib.* ‹*meal etc.*›; [nice] big ‹*sausage etc.*›
(b) (derb) crude, coarse ‹*joke, speech, etc.*›

Degen *der; ~s, ~* **(a)** (Waffe) [light] sword
(b) (Fechtsport) épée

degradieren *tr. V.* demote

Degradierung *die; ~, ~en* **(a)** (im Rang) demotion
(b) (Herabwürdigung) degradation; reduction (**zu** to the level of)

dehnbar *Adj.* **(a)** (elastisch) ‹*material etc.*› that stretches *not pred.*; elastic ‹*waistband etc.*›
(b) (fig.: vage) elastic; **das ist ein ~er Begriff** it's a loose concept

Dehnbarkeit *die; ~:* elasticity

dehnen *tr., refl. V.* stretch

Deich *der; ~[e]s, ~e* dike

Deichsel /'daiksḷ/ *die; ~, ~n* shaft

deichseln *tr. V.* (ugs.) fix

dein *Possessivpron.* your; **viele Grüße von ~em Emil** with best wishes, yours Emil; **das Buch dort, ist das ~[e]s?** that book over there, is it yours?; **du und die Deinen** (geh.) you and yours

deiner *Gen. des Personalpronomens* **du** (geh.) of you

deiner·seits *Adv.* (von deiner Seite) on your part; (auf deiner Seite) for your part

deinet·wegen *Adv.* because of you; (für dich) on your behalf; (dir zuliebe) for your sake

Dekade /de'ka:də/ *die; ~, ~n* decade

dekadent *Adj.* decadent

Dekadenz *die; ~:* decadence

deklamieren *tr., itr. V.* recite

Deklination *die; ~, ~en* (Sprachw.) declension

deklinieren *tr. V.* (Sprachw.) decline

dekodieren *tr. V.* (fachspr.) decode

Dekolleté /dekɔl'te:/ *das;* **~s, ~s** low[-cut] neckline; décolletage
Dekor *das;* **~s, ~s** *od.* **~e** decoration; (Muster) pattern
Dekorateur /dekora'tø:ɐ̯/ *der;* **~s, ~e, Dekorateurin** *die;* **~, ~nen** (Schaufenster~) window dresser; (von Innenräumen) interior designer
Dekoration *die;* **~, ~en** decorations *pl.;* (Schaufenster~) window display
dekorativ [1] *Adj.* decorative [2] *adv.* decoratively
dekorieren *tr. V.* decorate ‹*room etc.*›; dress ‹*shop window*›
Deko·stoff *der* furnishing fabric
Dekret *das;* **~[e]s, ~e** decree
Delegation *die;* **~, ~en** delegation
delegieren *tr. V.* **(a)** send as a delegate/as delegates
(b) delegate ‹*task etc.*› **(an** + *Akk.* to)
Delegierte *der/die; adj. Dekl.* delegate
Delfin ▶ DELPHIN
delikat *Adj.* **(a)** delicious; (fein) delicate ‹*bouquet, aroma*›
(b) (heikel) delicate
Delikatesse *die;* **~, ~n** delicacy
Delikt *das;* **~[e]s, ~e** offence
Delinquent *der;* **~en, ~en, Delinquentin** *die;* **~, ~nen** offender
Delirium *das;* **~s, Delirien** delirium
Delle *die;* **~, ~n** (ugs.) dent
Delphin *der;* **~s, ~e** dolphin
dem [1] *best. Art., Dat. Sg. v.* DER[1] 1 *u.* DAS 1: to the; (nach Präp.) the
[2] *Demonstrativpron., Dat. Sg. v.* DER[1] 2 *u.* DAS 2: **(a)** *attr.* that; **gib es dem Mann** give it to 'that man
(b) *allein stehend* **gib es nicht dem, sondern dem da!** don't give it to him, give it to that man/child *etc.;*
[3] *Relativpron., Dat. Sg. v.* DER[1] 3 *u.* DAS 3 (Person) that/whom; (Sache) that/which; **der Mann/das Kind, dem ich das Geld gab** the man/the child I gave the money to
Demagoge *der;* **~n, ~n, Demagogin** *die;* **~, ~nen** demagogue
demagogisch *Adj.* demagogic
Dementi *das;* **~s, ~s** denial
dementieren [1] *tr. V.* deny
[2] *itr. V.* deny it
dem-: ~entsprechend [1] *Adj.* appropriate; [2] *adv.* accordingly; (vor Adjektiven) correspondingly; **~gemäß** *Adv.* **(a)** (infolgedessen) consequently; **(b)** (entsprechend) accordingly; **~jenigen** ▶ DERJENIGE; **~nach** *Adv.* therefore; **~nächst** *Adv.* shortly
Demo *die;* **~, ~s** (ugs.) demo; **auf der ~:** at the demo
Demokrat *der;* **~en, ~en** democrat; (Parteimitglied) Democrat
Demokratie *die;* **~, ~n** democracy
Demokratin *die;* **~, ~nen** ▶ DEMOKRAT
demokratisch [1] *Adj.* democratic
[2] *adv.* democratically
demokratisieren *tr. V.* democratize
demolieren *tr. V.* wreck; smash up ‹*furniture*›
Demonstrant *der;* **~en, ~en, Demonstrantin** *die;* **~, ~nen** demonstrator
Demonstration *die;* **~, ~en** demonstration **(für** in support of, **gegen** against)
demonstrativ [1] *Adj.* **(a)** pointed
(b) (Sprachw.) demonstrative
[2] *adv.* pointedly
Demonstrativ·pronomen *das* (Sprachw.) demonstrative pronoun
demonstrieren [1] *itr. V.* demonstrate **(für** in support of, **gegen** against)
[2] *tr. V.* demonstrate
dem·selben ▶ DERSELBE
Demut *die;* **~:** humility
demütig [1] *Adj.* humble
[2] *adv.* humbly
demütigen [1] *tr. V.* humiliate
[2] *refl. V.* humble oneself
Demütigung *die;* **~, ~en** humiliation
dem·zufolge *Adv.* consequently
den¹ [1] *best. Art., Akk. Sg. v.* DER[1] 1: the
[2] *Demonstrativpron., Akk. Sg. v.* DER[1] 2: **(a)** *attr.* that; **ich meine den Mann** I mean 'that man
(b) *allein stehend* **ich meine den [da]** I mean 'that one
[3] *Relativpron., Akk. Sg. v.* DER[1] 3 (Person) that/whom; (Sache) that/which; **der Mann, den ich gesehen habe** the man that I saw
den² [1] *best. Art., Dat. Pl. v.* DER[1] 1, DIE[1] 1, DAS 1: the
[2] *Demonstrativpron. Dat. Pl. v.* DER[1] 2A, DIE[1] 2A, DAS 2A: those
denen [1] *Demonstrativpron., Dat. Pl. v.* DER[1] 2B, DIE[1] 2B, DAS 2B them; **gib es ~, nicht den anderen** give it to 'them, not to the others
[2] *Relativpron., Dat. Pl. v.* DER[1] 3, DIE[1] 3, DAS 3 (Personen) that/whom; (Sachen) that/which; **die Menschen, ~ wir Geld gegeben haben** the people to whom we gave money; **die Tiere, ~ er geholfen hat** the animals that he helped
denjenigen ▶ DERJENIGE
denkbar [1] *Adj.* conceivable
[2] *adv.* (sehr, äußerst) extremely
denken [1] *unr. itr. V.* think **(an** + *Akk.* of, **über** + *Akk.* about); **wie denkst du darüber?** what do you think about it?; what's your opinion of it?; **schlecht von jmdm. ~:** think badly of sb.; **denk daran, dass .../zu ...:** don't forget that .../to ...; **ich denke nicht daran!**

no way!; not on your life!; **ich denke nicht daran, das zu tun** I've no intention of doing that
2 *unr. tr. V.* think; **wer hätte das gedacht?** who would have thought it?; **eine gedachte Linie** an imaginary line
3 *unr. refl. V.* **(a)** (sich vorstellen) imagine **(b) sich** (*Dat.*) **bei etw. etwas ~:** mean something by sth.; **ich habe mir nichts [Böses] dabei gedacht** I didn't mean any harm [by it]

Denken *das;* **~s** thinking; (Denkweise) thought

Denker *der;* **~s, ~, Denkerin** *die;* **~, ~nen** thinker

denk·faul *Adj.* mentally lazy

Denk-: ~fehler *der* flaw in one's reasoning; **~mal** *das; Pl.* **~mäler** *od.* **~e** monument; memorial; **jmdm. ein ~ errichten** *od.* **setzen** erect *or* put up a memorial to sb.

Denkmal[s]·schutz *der* protection of historic monuments; **unter ~ stehen/stellen** be/put under a preservation order

denk-, Denk-: ~pause *die* pause for thought; **~sport·aufgabe** *die* brain teaser; **~vermögen** *das* ability to think [creatively]; **~würdig** *Adj.* memorable; **~zettel** *der* lesson

denn 1 *Konj.* **(a)** (kausal) for; because **(b)** (geh.: als) than
2 *Adv.* **es sei ~, ...:** unless ...
3 *Partikel* (in Fragesätzen) **wie geht es dir ~?** tell me, how are you?; **wie heißt du ~?** tell me your name; **warum ~ nicht?** why ever not?

dennoch *Adv.* nevertheless

denselben ▶ DERSELBE

Denunziant *der;* **~en, ~en, Denunziantin** *die;* **~, ~nen** informer; grass (sl.)

denunzieren *tr. V.* denounce; (bei der Polizei) inform against; grass on (sl.) (**bei** to)

Deo *das;* **~s, ~s, Deodorant** *das;* **~s, ~s** (auch:) **~e** deodorant

Deo·spray *das* deodorant spray

Deponie *die;* **~, ~n** tip (Brit.); dump

deponieren *tr. V.* put; (im Safe o. Ä.) deposit

Deportation *die;* **~, ~en** transportation; (ins Ausland) deportation

deportieren *tr. V.* transport; (ins Ausland) deport

Deportierte *der/die; adj. Dekl.* transportee; (ins Ausland) deportee

Depot /de'po:/ *das;* **~s, ~s (a)** depot; (Lagerhaus) warehouse; (für Möbel usw.) depository; (im Freien, für Munition o. Ä.) dump; (in einer Bank) strongroom; safe deposit **(b)** (hinterlegte Wertgegenstände) deposits *pl.*

Depp *der;* **~en** (auch:) **~s, ~en** (auch:) **~e** (bes. südd., österr., schweiz. abwertend) ▶ DUMMKOPF

*alte Schreibung - vgl. Hinweis auf S. xiv

Depression *die;* **~, ~en** depression

depressiv 1 *Adj.* depressive
2 *adv.* **~ veranlagt sein** have a tendency towards depression

deprimieren *tr. V.* depress

deprimierend *Adj.* depressing

deprimiert 1 *Adj.* depressed
2 *adv.* dejectedly

der¹ 1 *best. Art. Nom.* the; **der Tod** death; **der „Faust"** 'Faust'; **der Bodensee/Mount Everest** Lake Constance/Mount Everest; **der Iran/Sudan** Iran/the Sudan; **der Mensch/Mann ist ...:** man is .../men are ...
2 *Demonstrativpron.* **(a)** *attr.* that; **der Mann war es** it was 'that man **(b)** *allein stehend* he; **der war es** it was 'him; **der [da]** (Person) that man/boy; (Sache) that one; **der [hier]** (Person) this man/boy; (Sache) this one
3 *Relativpron.* (Person) who/that; (Sache) which/that; **der Mann, der da drüben entlanggeht** the man walking along over there
4 *Relativ- u. Demonstrativpron.* the one who

der² 1 *best. Art.* **(a)** *Gen. Sg. v.* DIE¹ 1: **der Hut der Frau** the woman's hat; **der Henkel der Tasse** the handle of the cup **(b)** *Dat. Sg. v.* DIE¹ 1 to the; (nach Präp.) the **(c)** *Gen. Pl. v.* DER¹ 1, DIE¹ 1, DAS 1: **das Haus der Freunde** our/their *etc.* friends' house; **das Bellen der Hunde** the barking of the dogs
2 *Demonstrativpron.* **(a)** *Gen. Sg. v.* DIE¹ 2: of the; of that **(b)** *Dat. Sg. v.* DIE¹ 2 *attr.* **der Frau [da/hier] gehört es** it belongs to that woman there/this woman here **(c)** *Gen. Pl. v.* DER¹ 2A, DIE¹ 2A, DAS 2A: of those
3 *Relativpron.; Dat. Sg. v.* DIE¹ 3: **die Frau, der ich es gegeben habe** the woman I gave it to; **die Katze, der er einen Tritt gab** the cat [that] he kicked

der·art *Adv.* so; **es hat lange nicht mehr ~ geregnet** it hasn't rained as hard as that for a long time; **sie hat ~ geschrien, dass ...:** she screamed so much that ...

der·artig 1 *Adj.* such
2 *adv.* ▶ DERART

derb 1 *Adj.* **(a)** tough ‹*material*›; stout, ‹*shoes*› **(b)** (kraftvoll, deftig) earthy ‹*scenes, humour*›
2 *adv.* **(a)** strongly ‹*made, woven, etc.*› **(b)** (kraftvoll, deftig) earthily

deren 1 *Relativpron.* **(a)** *Gen. Sg. v.* DIE¹ 3 (Personen) whose; (Sachen) of which **(b)** *Gen. Pl. v.* DER¹ 3, DIE¹ 3, DAS 3 (Personen) whose; (Sachen) **Maßnahmen, ~ Folgen wir noch nicht absehen können** measures, the consequences of which we cannot yet foresee
2 *Demonstrativpron.* **(a)** *Gen. Sg. v.* DIE¹ 2: **meine Tante, ihre Freundin und ~ Hund** my aunt, her friend and her dog

(b) *Gen. Pl. v.* DER[1] 2, DIE[1] 2, DAS 2: **meine Verwandten und ~ Kinder** my relatives and their children

derent-: ~wegen *Adv.* 1 *relativ* (Personen) because of whom; (Sachen) because of which; 2 *demonstrativ* because of them; **~willen** *Adv.* **um ~willen** (Personen) for whose sake; (Sachen) for the sake of which

derer *Demonstrativpron.; Gen. Pl. v.* DER[1] 2, DIE[1] 2, DAS 2 of those

der·gleichen *indekl. Demonstrativpron.* (a) *attr.* such; like that *postpos., not pred.;* (b) *allein stehend* that sort of thing

Derivat *das;* ~[e]s, ~e derivative

der·jenige, die·jenige, das·jenige *Demonstrativpron.* (a) *attr.* that; *Pl.* those (b) *allein stehend* that one; *Pl.* those

derlei *indekl. Demonstrativpron.:* ▶ DERGLEICHEN

der·maßen *Adv.* **~ schön** *usw.*, **dass ...:** so beautiful *etc.* that ...

derselbe, dieselbe, dasselbe *Demonstrativpron.* (a) *attr.* the same (b) *allein stehend* the same one; *Pl.* the same people; **er sagt immer dasselbe** he always says the same thing; **noch einmal dasselbe, bitte** (ugs.) [the] same again please

der·zeit *Adv.* at present

der·zeitig *Adj.* present; current

des 1 *best. Art.; Gen. Sg. v.* DER[1] 1, DAS 1: **die Mütze des Jungen** the boy's cap; **das Klingeln des Telefons** the ringing of the telephone
2 *Demonstrativpron.; Gen. Sg. v.* DER[1] 2, DAS 2: **er ist der Sohn des Mannes, der ...:** he's the son of the man who ...

Deserteur /dezɛr'tøːɐ̯/ *der;* ~s, ~e, **Deserteurin** /dezɛr'tøːrɪn/ *die;* ~, ~nen deserter

desertieren *itr. V.; mit sein* desert

des·gleichen *Adv.* likewise; **er ist Arzt, ~ sein Sohn** he is a doctor, as is his son

des·halb *Adv.* for that reason; **~ bin ich zu dir gekommen** that is why I came to you

Design /di'zai̯n/ *das;* ~s, ~s design

Designer /di'zai̯nɐ/ *der;* ~s, ~, **Designerin** *die;* ~, ~nen designer

Designer·droge /-'----/ *die;* ~, ~n designer drug

Desinfektion *die;* ~, ~nen disinfection

Desinfektions·mittel *das* disinfectant

desinfizieren *tr. V.* disinfect

Desinteresse *das;* ~s lack of interest

Despot /dɛs'poːt/ *der;* ~en, ~en, **Despotin** *die;* ~, ~nen despot; (fig. abwertend) tyrant

despotisch 1 *Adj.* despotic
2 *adv.* despotically

des·selben ▶ DERSELBE

dessen 1 *Relativpron.; Gen. Sg. v.* DER[1] 3, DAS 3 *attr.* (Person) whose; (Sache) of which
2 *Demonstrativpron.; Gen. Sg. v.* DER[1] 2, DAS 2: mein Onkel, sein Sohn und ~ Hund my uncle, his son, and 'his dog

Dessert /dɛ'seːɐ̯/ *das;* ~s, ~s dessert

Destille *die;* ~, ~n distillery

destillieren *tr. V.* (Chemie) distil

desto *Konj., vor Komp.* **je eher, ~ besser** the sooner the better

des·wegen *Adv.* ▶ DESHALB

Detail /de'tai̯/ *das;* ~s, ~s detail

detailliert 1 *Adj.* detailed
2 *adv.* in detail; **sehr ~:** in great detail

Detektiv *der;* ~s, ~e, **Detektivin** *die;* ~, ~nen [private] detective

Detonation *die;* ~, ~en detonation; explosion

detonieren *itr. V.; mit sein* detonate; explode

Deut keinen ~: not one bit

deuten 1 *itr. V.* point; **[mit dem Finger] auf jmdn./etw. ~:** point [one's finger] at sb./sth.
2 *tr. V.* interpret

deutlich 1 *Adj.* clear
2 *adv.* clearly

Deutlichkeit *die;* ~ (a) clarity (b) (Eindeutigkeit) clearness

deutsch 1 *Adj.* German; **Deutsche Mark** Deutschmark; German mark
2 *adv.* **Deutsch sprechen/schreiben** speak/write German

Deutsch *das;* ~[s] German; **gutes/fließend ~ sprechen** speak good/fluent German; **auf** *od.* **in ~:** in German; **auf [gut] ~** (ugs.) in plain English

Deutsche[1] *der/die; adj. Dekl.* German; **er ist ~r** he is German

Deutsche[2] *das; adj. Dekl.* **das ~:** German; **aus dem ~n/ins ~ übersetzen** translate from/into German

Deutschland *(das);* ~s Germany

deutsch-, Deutsch-: ~lehrer *der,* **~lehrerin** *die* German teacher; **~sprachig** *Adj.* (a) German-speaking; (b) German-language *attrib.;* **~unterricht** *der* German teaching; (Unterrichtsstunde) German lesson

Deutung *die;* ~, ~en interpretation

Devise *die;* ~, ~n motto

Devisen *Pl.* foreign currency *sing.*

Devisen-: ~börse *die* foreign exchange market; **~kurs** *der* exchange rate; rate of exchange

Dezember *der;* ~s, ~: December

dezent 1 *Adj.* quiet ‹*colour, pattern, suit*›; subdued ‹*lighting, music*›
2 *adv.* discreetly; ‹*dress*› unostentatiously

dezimal *Adj.* decimal

Dezimal-: ~system *das* decimal system; **~zahl** *die* decimal [number]

dezimieren *tr. V.* decimate

dgl. *Abk.* = **dergleichen, desgleichen**
d. h. *Abk.* = **das heißt** i.e.
Di. *Abk.* = **Dienstag** Tue[s].
Dia *das;* **~s, ~s** slide
Diabetes *der;* **~:** diabetes
Diabetiker *der;* **~s, ~, Diabetikerin** *die;* **~, ~nen** diabetic
Diagnose /dia'gno:zə/ *die;* **~, ~n** diagnosis
diagonal [1] *Adj.* diagonal
[2] *adv.* diagonally
Diagonale *die;* **~, ~n** diagonal
Diagramm *das* graph; (von Gegenständen) diagram
Dialekt *der;* **~[e]s, ~e** dialect
Dialog *der;* **~[e]s, ~e** dialogue
Dialog·fenster *das* (DV) dialogue box
Dialyse /dia'ly:zə/ *die;* **~, ~n** (Physik, Chemie, Med.) dialysis
Diamant *der;* **~en, ~en** diamond
***diät** ▶ DIÄT
Diät *die;* **~, ~en** diet; **eine ~ einhalten** keep to a diet; **~ essen** be on a diet; **~ kochen** cook according to a/one's diet
Diäten *Pl.* [parliamentary] allowance *sing.*
dich [1] *Akk. von* DU you
[2] *Akk. des Reflexivpron. der 2. Pers. Sg.* yourself
dicht [1] *Adj.* **(a)** thick; dense ‹*forest, hedge, crowd*›; heavy, dense ‹*traffic*›
(b) (undurchlässig) (für Luft) airtight; (für Wasser) watertight
[2] *adv.* **(a)** densely ‹*populated, wooded*›; **~ bebaut** heavily built up
(b) (undurchlässig) tightly
(c) *mit Präp.* (nahe) **~ neben** right next to
***dicht·bebaut** ▶ DICHT 2A
Dichte *die;* **~** (Physik, fig.) density
dichten [1] *itr. V.* write poetry
[2] *tr. V.* (verfassen) write; compose
Dichter *der;* **~s, ~:** poet; (Schriftsteller) writer; author
Dichterin *die;* **~, ~nen** poet[ess]; (Schriftstellerin) writer; author[ess]
dichterisch *Adj.* poetic; (schriftstellerisch) literary
dicht|machen *tr., itr. V.* (ugs.) shut; (endgültig) shut down
Dichtung¹ *die;* **~, ~en** seal; (am Hahn usw.) washer; (am Vergaser, Zylinder usw.) gasket
Dichtung² *die;* **~, ~en (a)** work of literature; (in Versform) poetic work; poem
(b) (Dichtkunst) literature; (in Versform) poetry
dick [1] *Adj.* **(a)** thick; stout ‹*tree*›; fat ‹*person, legs, etc.*›; swollen ‹*cheek, ankle, tonsils, etc.*›; **~ werden** get fat; **5 cm ~ sein** be 5 cm thick
(b) (ugs.) big ‹*mistake*›; hefty ‹*salary*›
[2] *adv.* thickly; **etw. ~ unterstreichen** underline sth. heavily; **sich ~ anziehen** wrap up warm[ly]; **etw. 5 cm ~ schneiden** cut sth. 5 cm. thick; **~ geschwollen** (ugs.) badly swollen
Dicke¹ *die;* **~:** thickness; (von Menschen, Körperteilen) fatness
Dicke² *der/die; adj. Dekl.* (ugs.) fatty (coll.)
dick·fellig (ugs.) *Adj.* thick-skinned
Dickfelligkeit *die;* **~** (ugs.) insensitivity
Dickicht /'dɪkɪçt/ *das;* **~[e]s, ~e** thicket
dick-, Dick-: ~kopf *der* (ugs.) mule (coll.); **ein ~kopf sein** be stubborn as a mule; **einen ~kopf haben** be pigheaded; **~köpfig** *Adj.* (ugs.) pigheaded; **~macher** *der* (ugs.) fattening food; **~milch** *die* sour milk
die¹ [1] *best. Art. Nom.* the; **die Helga** (ugs.) Helga; **die Frau/Menschheit** women *pl.*/mankind
[2] *Demonstrativpron.* **(a)** *attr.* **die Frau war es** it was 'that woman
(b) *allein stehend* she; **die war es** it was 'her; **die [da]** (Person) that woman/girl; (Sache) that one
[3] *Relativpron. Nom.* (Person) who; that; (Sache, Tier) which; that
[4] *Relativ- u. Demonstrativpron.* the one who
die² [1] *best. Art.* **(a)** *Akk. Sg. v.* DIE¹ 1 the; **ich sah die Frau** I saw the women
(b) *Nom. u. Akk. Pl. v.* DER¹ 1, DIE¹ 1, DAS 1: the
[2] *Demonstrativpron. Nom. u. Akk. Pl. v.* DER¹ 1, DIE¹ 1, DAS 1: *attr.* **ich meine die Männer, die ...** I mean those men who ...; *allein stehend* **ich meine die [da]** I mean 'them
[3] *Relativpron.* **(a)** *Akk. Sg. v.* DIE¹ 3 (Person) who; (Sache) that
(b) *Nom. u. Akk. Pl. v.* DER¹ 3, DIE¹ 3, DAS 3 (Personen) whom; (Sachen) which; **die Männer, die ich gesehen habe** the men I saw
Dieb *der;* **~[e]s, ~e** thief
Diebin *die;* **~, ~nen** [woman] thief
diebisch [1] *Adj.* **(a)** thieving
(b) (verstohlen) mischievous
[2] *adv.* mischievously
Diebstahl *der;* **~[e]s, Diebstähle** theft
die·jenige ▶ DERJENIGE
Diele *die;* **~, ~n** hall[way]
dienen *itr. V.* serve; **womit kann ich ~?** what can I do for you?
Diener *der;* **~s, ~:** servant; **einen ~ machen** (ugs.) bow; make a bow
Dienerin *die;* **~, ~nen** maid; servant
dienlich *Adj.* helpful
Dienst *der;* **~[e]s, ~e (a)** (Tätigkeit) work; (von Soldaten, Polizeibeamten, Krankenhauspersonal usw.) duty; **seinen ~ antreten** start work/go on duty; **~ haben** be at work/on duty; ‹*doctor*› be on call; ‹*chemist*› be open
(b) (Arbeitsverhältnis) post; **Major außer ~:** retired major
(c) (Tätigkeitsbereich) service; *s. auch* ÖFFENTLICH;
(d) (Hilfe) service

*old spelling - see note on page xiv

Diens·tag *der* Tuesday; **am ~:** on Tuesday; **~, der 1. Juni** Tuesday, 1 June; **er kommt ~:** he is coming on Tuesday; **ab nächsten ~:** from next Tuesday [onwards]; **~ in einer Woche** a week on Tuesday; **~ vor einer Woche** a week last Tuesday

diens·tags *Adv.* on Tuesday[s]

dienst-, Dienst-: ~bereit *Adj.* ‹*chemist*› open *pred.;* ‹*doctor*› on call; ‹*dentist*› on duty; **~bote** *der,* **~botin** *die* servant; **~eifrig** *Adj.* zealous; **~frei** *Adj.* free ‹*time*›; **~geheimnis** *das* **(a)** professional secret; (im Staatsdienst) official secret; **(b)** professional secrecy; (im Staatsdienst) official secrecy; **~grad** *der* (Milit.) rank; **~leister** *der;* **~~s, ~~, ~leisterin** *die;* **~~, ~~nen** (Firma, auch DV) service provider; **~leistung** *die* (auch Wirtsch.) service

Dienstleistungs-: ~branche *die* (Wirtsch.) **(a)** service industry; **(b)** ▶ ~SEKTOR; **~sektor** *der* (Wirtsch.) service sector

dienstlich [1] *Adj.* business ‹*call*›; (im Staatsdienst) official ‹*letter, call, etc.*› [2] *adv.* on business; (im Staatsdienst) on official business

Dienst-: ~reise *die* business trip; **~stelle** *die* office; **~wagen** *der* official car; (Geschäftswagen) company car; **~weg** *der* official channels *pl.;* **~zeit** *die* **(a)** period of service; **(b)** (tägliche Arbeitszeit) working hours *pl.*

dies ▶ DIESER

dies·bezüglich *adv.* regarding this

diese ▶ DIESER

Diesel *der;* **~s, ~:** diesel

die·selbe ▶ DERSELBE

Diesel·motor *der* diesel engine

dieser, diese, dieses, dies *Demonstrativpron.* **(a)** *attr.* this; *Pl.* these **(b)** *allein stehend* this one; *Pl.* these; **dies alles** all this; **dies und das,** (geh.) **dieses und jenes** this and that

diesig *Adj.* hazy

dies-: ~mal *Adv.* this time; **~seits** [1] *Präp. mit Gen.* on this side of; [2] *Adv.* **~seits von** on this side of

Dietrich *der;* **~s, ~e** picklock

diffamieren *tr. V.* defame

Diffamierung *die;* **~, ~en** defamation

Differential *usw.* ▶ DIFFERENZIAL *usw.*

Differenz *die;* **~, ~en** difference; (Meinungsverschiedenheit) difference [of opinion]

Differenzial /dɪfərɛnˈtsi̯a:l/ *das;* **~s, ~e** **(a)** (Math.) differential **(b)** (Technik) differential [gear]

Differenzial·rechnung *die* (Math.) differential calculus

differenziert *Adj.* complex; subtly differentiated ‹*methods, colours*›; sophisticated ‹*taste*›

diffus [1] *Adj.* **(a)** (Physik, Chemie) diffuse **(b)** (geh.) vague; vague and confused ‹*idea, statement, etc.*› [2] *adv.* in a vague and confused way

digital (DV) [1] *Adj.* digital [2] *adv.* digitally

Digital- digital ‹*clock, display, etc.*›

Digital·fernsehen *das* digital television

digitalisieren *tr. V.* (DV) digitalize

Digital·radio *das* digital radio

Diktat *das;* **~[e]s, ~e** dictation

Diktator *der;* **~s, ~en, Diktatorin** *die;* **~, ~nen** dictator

diktatorisch [1] *Adj.* dictatorial [2] *adv.* dictatorially

Diktatur *die;* **~, ~en** dictatorship

diktieren *tr. V.* dictate

Diktier·gerät *das* dictating machine

Dilemma *das;* **~s, ~s** dilemma

Dilettant /dileˈtant/ *der;* **~en, ~en, Dilettantin** *die;* **~, ~nen** dilettante

dilettantisch [1] *Adj.* dilettante; amateurish [2] *adv.* amateurishly

Dimension *die;* **~, ~en** (Physik, fig.) dimension

DIN /di:n/ *Abk.* = **Deutsche Industrie-Norm[en]** *German Industrial Standard[s];* DIN; **DIN-A4-Format** A4

Ding[1] *das;* **~[e]s, ~e** **(a)** thing **(b)** **nach Lage der ~e** the way things are; **persönliche/private ~e** personal/private matters; **ein ~ der Unmöglichkeit sein** be quite impossible; **vor allen ~en** above all **(c)** **guter ~e sein** (geh.) be in good spirits

Ding[2] *das;* **~[e]s, ~er** (ugs.) thing; **das ist ja ein ~!** that's really something

Dino *der;* **~s, ~s** (ugs.) dinosaur

Dino·saurier *der;* **~s, ~:** dinosaur

Diode *die;* **~, ~n** (Elektrot.) diode

Dioden·rücklicht *das* LED rear light

Dioxin *das;* **~s** (Chemie) dioxin

Diözese *die;* **~, ~n** diocese

Dipl.-Ing. *Abk.* = **Diplomingenieur** *academically qualified engineer*

Diplom *das;* **~s, ~e** ≈ [first] degree (*in a scientific or technical subject*); (für einen Handwerksberuf) diploma

Diplom- qualified

Diplomat *der;* **~en, ~en, Diplomatin** *die;* **~, ~nen** diplomat

diplomatisch [1] *Adj.* diplomatic [2] *adv.* diplomatically

dir [1] *Dat. von* DU to you; (nach Präp.) you; **Freunde von ~:** friends of yours [2] *Dat. des Reflexivpron. der 2. Pers. Sg.* yourself

direkt [1] *Adj.* direct [2] *adv.* straight; directly; **etw. ~ übertragen** broadcast sth. live

Direkt·flug *der* direct flight

d

d

Direktion *die;* ~, ~**en** management; (Büroräume) managers' offices *pl.*
Direktor *der;* ~**s**, ~**en**, **Direktorin** *die;* ~, ~**nen** director; (einer Schule) headmaster/ headmistress; (einer Strafanstalt) governor; (einer Abteilung) manager
Direkt·übertragung *die* live broadcast
Dirigent *der;* ~**en**, ~**en**, **Dirigentin** *die;* ~, ~**nen** conductor
dirigieren *tr. V.* **(a)** *auch itr.* conduct **(b)** (führen) steer
Disc·jockey /'dɪskdʒɔke/ *der* disc jockey
Disco /'dɪsko:/ *die;* ~, ~**s** disco
Diskette *die;* ~, ~**n** (DV) floppy disk
Disketten·laufwerk *das* (DV) [floppy-]disk drive
Diskont·satz *der* (Finanzw.) discount rate
Diskothek *die;* ~, ~**en** discothèque
Diskrepanz *die;* ~, ~**en** discrepancy
diskret 1 *Adj.* (vertraulich) confidential; (taktvoll) discreet; tactful
2 *adv.* (vertraulich) confidentially; (taktvoll) discreetly; tactfully
Diskretion *die;* ~ **(a)** (Verschwiegenheit, Takt) discretion
(b) (Unaufdringlichkeit) discreetness
diskriminieren *tr. V.* discriminate against
Diskriminierung *die;* ~, ~**en** discrimination
Diskussion *die;* ~, ~**en** discussion; **zur** ~ **stehen** be under discussion
Diskussions-: ~**beitrag** *der* contribution to a/the discussion; ~**leiter** *der* chair[man] [of the discussion]; ~**leiterin** *die* chair[woman] [of the discussion]
diskutieren 1 *itr. V.* **über etw.** (*Akk.*) ~: discuss sth.
2 *tr. V.* discuss
Disqualifikation *die;* ~, ~**en** (auch Sport) disqualification
disqualifizieren *tr. V.* disqualify
Distanz *die;* ~, ~**en** (auch fig.) distance
distanzieren *refl. V.* **sich von jmdm./etw.** ~ (fig.) dissociate oneself from sb./sth.
distanziert *Adj.* reserved
Distel *die;* ~, ~**n** thistle
Distel·fink *der* goldfinch
Disziplin *die;* ~, ~**en** discipline; (Selbstbeherrschung) [self-]discipline
disziplinieren 1 *tr. V.* discipline
2 *refl. V.* discipline oneself
diszipliniert 1 *Adj.* well-disciplined; (beherrscht) disciplined
2 *adv.* in a well-disciplined way; (beherrscht) in a disciplined way
divers... /di'vɛrs.../ *Adj.* various; (mehrer...) several
Dividende /divi'dɛndə/ *die;* ~, ~**n** (Wirtsch.) dividend

*alte Schreibung - vgl. Hinweis auf S. xiv

dividieren *tr. V.* divide
Division *die;* ~, ~**en** (auch Milit.) division
DM *Abk.* = **Deutsche Mark** DM
D-Mark /'de:-/ *die* Deutschmark
DNS *Abk.* (Chemie) = **Desoxyribonukleinsäure** DNA
Do. *Abk.* = **Donnerstag** Thur[s].
doch 1 *Konj.* but
2 *Adv.* **(a)** (jedoch) but
(b) (dennoch) all the same; still
(c) (geh.: nämlich) **wusste er** ~, **dass ...**: because he knew that ...
(d) (entgegen allen gegenteiligen Behauptungen, Annahmen) **er war also** ~ **der Mörder!** so he 'was the murderer!
(e) (ohnehin) in any case
3 *Interj.* **Das stimmt nicht. – Doch!** That's not right. – [Oh] yes it is!; **Hast du keinen Hunger? – Doch!** Aren't you hungry? – Yes [I am]!
4 *Partikel* **(a)** (Ungeduld ausdrückend) **pass** ~ **auf!** [oh] do be careful!; **das ist** ~ **nicht zu glauben** that's just incredible
(b) (Zweifel ausdrückend) **du hast** ~ **meinen Brief erhalten?** you did get my letter, didn't you?
(c) (Überraschung ausdrückend) **das ist** ~ **Karl!** there's Karl!
(d) (verstärkt Bejahung/Verneinung ausdrückend) **gewiss/sicher** ~: [why] certainly; of course; **ja** ~: [yes,] all right; **nicht** ~**!** (abwehrend) [no,] don't!
(e) (Wunsch verstärkend) **wäre es** ~ **...**: if only it were ...
Docht *der;* ~**[e]s**, ~**e** wick
Dock *das;* ~**s**, ~**s** dock
Dogge *die;* ~, ~**n**: **[deutsche]** ~: Great Dane
Dogma *das;* ~**s**, **Dogmen** (auch fig.) dogma
dogmatisch (Theol., auch fig.) *Adj.* dogmatic
Dohle *die;* ~, ~**n** jackdaw
Doktor *der;* ~**s**, ~**en** (auch ugs.: Arzt) doctor; (Titel) Doctor
Doktor·arbeit *die* doctoral thesis
Doktor·grad *der* doctorate; doctor's degree
Doktorin *die;* ~, ~**nen** ▶ DOKTOR
Doktor·titel *der* title of doctor
Doktrin *die;* ~, ~**en** doctrine
Dokument *das;* ~**[e]s**, ~**e** document
Dokumentar-: ~**bericht** *der* documentary report; ~**film** *der* documentary [film]
Dokumentation *die;* ~, ~**en (a)** documentation
(b) (Bericht) documentary report
dokumentieren *tr. V.* **(a)** document; (fig.) demonstrate
(b) (festhalten) record
Dolch *der;* ~**[e]s**, ~**e** dagger
Dolde *die;* ~, ~**n** (Bot.) umbel
doll (bes. nordd., salopp) 1 *Adj.* **(a)** (ungewöhnlich) incredible

(b) (großartig) great (coll.)
[2] *adv.* (a) (großartig) fantastically [well] (coll.)
(b) (sehr) ‹*hurt*› dreadfully (coll.), like mad

Dollar *der;* ~s, ~s dollar; **zwei** ~: two dollars

dolmetschen *itr. V.* act as interpreter

Dolmetscher *der;* ~s, ~, **Dolmetscherin** *die;* ~, ~nen interpreter

Dom *der;* ~[e]s, ~e cathedral

dominieren *itr. V.* dominate

dominikanisch *Adj.* Dominican; **die Dominikanische Republik** the Dominican Republic

Domino *das;* ~s, ~s (Spiel) dominoes *sing.*

Domizil *das;* ~s, ~e (geh.) domicile; residence

Dom·pfaff *der;* ~en *od.* ~s, ~en (Zool.) bullfinch

Dompteur /dɔmp'tøːɐ/ *der;* ~s, ~e, **Dompteurin** /dɔmp'tøːrɪn/ *die;* ~, ~nen, **Dompteuse** /dɔmp'tøːzə/ *die;* ~, ~n tamer

Donau *die;* ~: Danube

Donner *der;* ~s, ~: thunder

donnern *itr. V.* (a) (*unpers.*) thunder (b) (fig.) thunder; ‹*engine*› roar

Donners·tag *der* Thursday; *s. auch* DIENSTAG

donnerstags *Adv.* on Thursday[s]; *s. auch* DIENSTAGS

Donner·wetter *das* (ugs.) (a) (Krach) row (b) /'--'--/ **zum ~ [noch einmal]!** damn it!; ~! my word

doof (ugs.) [1] *Adj.* stupid; dumb (coll.) [2] *adv.* stupidly

Doping /'doːpɪŋ/ *das;* ~s (Sport) taking drugs

Doping·kontrolle *die* (Sport) drug[s] test

Doppel *das,* ~s, ~ (a) (Kopie) duplicate; copy (b) (Sport) doubles *sing. or pl.*

doppel-, Doppel-: **~bett** *das* double bed; **~bock** *das* extra-strong bock beer; **~decker** *der;* ~~s, ~~: biplane; **~deutig** /-dɔytɪç/ [1] *Adj.* (a) ambiguous; (b) (anzüglich) suggestive; [2] *adv.* (a) ambiguously; (b) (anzüglich) suggestively; **~fenster** *das* double-glazed window; **~gänger** *der;* ~~s, ~~, **~gängerin** *die;* ~~, ~~nen double; **~haus** *das* pair of semi-detached houses; **~haus·hälfte** *die* semi[-detached house]; **~kinn** *das* double chin; **~klick** *der;* ~~s, ~~s (DV) double click; **~moral** *die* double standards *pl.;* **~pass,** ***~paß** *der* (ugs.) **der ~pass** dual nationality *no art.;* **~punkt** *der* colon; **~stunde** *die* double period

doppelt [1] *Adj.* double; **die ~e Menge** twice the quantity; **mit ~er Kraft arbeiten** work with twice as much energy [2] *adv.* ~ **so groß/alt wie ...**: twice as large/ old as ...; **sich ~ anstrengen** try twice as hard

Doppelte *das; adj. Dekl.* **das ~ bezahlen** pay twice as much; pay double

Doppel-: **~tür** *die* double door; **~zentner** *der* 100 kilograms; **~zimmer** *das* double room

Dorf *das;* ~[e]s, **Dörfer** village; **auf dem ~**: in the country

Dorf-: **~bewohner** *der,* **~bewohnerin** *die* villager; **~depp** *der* (bes. südd., österr.) village idiot; **~trottel** *der* village idiot

Dorn *der;* ~[e]s, ~en thorn; **jmdm. ein ~ im Auge sein** annoy sb. intensely

dornig *Adj.* thorny

Dorn·röschen (*das*) the Sleeping Beauty

dörren *tr. V.* dry

Dörr-: **~fleisch** *das* (südd.) lean bacon; **~obst** *das* dried fruit

Dorsch *der;* ~[e]s, ~e cod

dort *Adv.* there; **~ bleiben** stay there; *s. auch* DA 1A

dort-: ***~|bleiben** ▶ DORT; **~her** *Adv.* **[von] ~her** from there; **~hin** *Adv.* there

dortig *Adj.* there

Dose *die;* ~, ~n (a) (Blech~) tin; (Pillen~) box; (Zucker~) bowl (b) (Konserven~) can; tin (Brit.); (Bier~) can

dösen *itr. V.* (ugs.) doze

Dosen-: **~bier** *das* canned beer; **~milch** *die* canned *or* (Brit.) tinned milk; **~öffner** *der* can-opener; tin-opener (Brit.); **~pfand** *das* deposit on [drink] cans

dosieren *tr. V.* **etw. ~**: measure out the required dose of sth.

Dosierung *die;* ~, ~en (a) measuring out; (das Zuführen) administering; (fig.) dispensing (b) ▶ DOSIS

Dosis *die;* ~, **Dosen** dose

Dossier /dɔ'si̯eː/ *das,* (veraltet:) *der;* ~s, ~s dossier

Dotcom /'dɔtkɔm/ *das;* ~s, ~ dot-com [company]

Dotter *der od. das;* ~s, ~: yolk

Dotter·blume *die* marsh marigold

doubeln /'duːbl̩n/ *tr. V.* stand in for ‹*actor*›; use a stand-in for ‹*scene*›; **sich ~ lassen** use *or* have a stand-in

Dozent *der;* ~en, ~en, **Dozentin** *die;* ~, ~nen lecturer (**für** in)

dpa *Abk.* = **Deutsche Presse-Agentur** German Press Agency

Dr. *Abk.* = **Doktor** Dr

Drache *der;* ~n, ~n (Myth.) dragon

Drachen *der;* ~s, ~ (a) kite (b) (Fluggerät) hang-glider

Draht *der;* ~[e]s, **Drähte** (a) wire (b) (Leitung) wire; (Telefonleitung) line; wire (c) (Telefonverbindung) line

draht-, Draht-: **~los** (Nachrichtenw.) [1] *Adj.* wireless; [2] *adv.* **etw. ~los** →

telegrafieren/übermitteln radio sth.; **~seil** *das* [steel] cable; **~seil·bahn** *die* cable railway; **~zieher** *der;* **~~s, ~~, ~zieherin** *die;* **~~, ~~nen** (fig.) wire puller

drall *Adj.* strapping ‹*girl*›; full, rounded ‹*cheeks, face, bottom*›

d

Drama *das;* **~s, Dramen** drama; (fig., ugs.) disaster

Dramatiker *der;* **~s, ~, Dramatikerin** *die;* **~, ~nen** dramatist

dramatisch [1] *Adj.* dramatic
[2] *adv.* dramatically

dramatisieren *tr. V.* dramatize

dramaturgisch *adj.* dramaturgical

dran *Adv.* (ugs.) **(a) häng das Schild ~!** put the sign up!
(b) arm ~ sein be in a bad way; **gut/schlecht ~ sein** be well off/badly off; **früh/spät ~ sein** be early/late; **ich bin ~:** it's my turn

dran|bleiben *unr. itr. V.; mit sein* (ugs.) (am Telefon) hang on (coll.)

drang *1. u. 3. Pers. Sg. Prät. v.* DRINGEN

Drang *der;* **~[e]s, Dränge** urge

dränge *1. u. 3. Pers. Sg. Konjunktiv II v.* DRINGEN

drängeln (ugs.) [1] *itr. V.* **(a)** push [and shove]
(b) (auf jmdn. einreden) go on (coll.)
[2] *tr. V.* **(a)** push; shove
(b) (einreden auf) go on at (coll.)
[3] *refl. V.* **sich nach vorn ~:** push one's way to the front

drängen [1] *itr. V.* **(a)** push
(b) die Zeit drängt time is pressing
[2] *tr. V.* **(a)** push
(b) (antreiben) press; urge
[3] *refl. V.* crowd

drangsalieren *tr. V.* (quälen) torment; (plagen) plague

dran-: ~|halten *unr. refl. V.* (ugs.) get a move on (coll.); **~|kommen** *unr. itr. V.; mit sein* (ugs.) have one's turn; **~|nehmen** *unr. tr. V.* (ugs.) (beim Friseur usw.) see to; (beim Arzt) see

drastisch [1] *Adj.* drastic ‹*measure, means*›
[2] *adv.* drastically; ‹*punish*› severely

drauf *Adv.* (ugs.) on it

drauf-, Drauf-: ~gänger *der;* **~~s, ~~, ~gängerin** *die;* **~~, ~~nen** daredevil; **~gängerisch** *Adj.* daring; **~|gehen** *unr. itr. V.; mit sein* (ugs.) **(a)** (umkommen) kick the bucket (coll.); **(b)** (verbraucht werden) go (**für** on); **~|zahlen** (ugs.) [1] *tr. V.* **noch etwas/50 Euro ~zahlen** fork out (coll.) *or* pay a bit more/an extra 50 euros; [2] *itr. V.* (Unkosten haben) **ich zahle dabei noch ~:** it's costing me money

draußen *Adv.* outside; **hier/da ~:** out here/there; **von/nach ~:** from outside/outside

Dreck *der;* **~[e]s (a)** (ugs.) dirt; (sehr viel) filth; (Schlamm) mud
(b) (salopp abwertend: Angelegenheit) **mach deinen ~ allein** do it yourself; **das geht dich einen [feuchten] ~ an** (salopp) none of your damned business (coll.)
(c) (salopp abwertend: Zeug) junk *no indef. art.*

Dreck·arbeit *die* (auch fig.) dirty work *no indef. art., no pl.*/dirty job

dreckig [1] *Adj.* **(a)** (ugs., auch fig.) dirty; (sehr schmutzig) filthy
(b) (salopp: unverschämt) cheeky
[2] *adv.* **(a) es geht ihm ~** (ugs.) he's in a bad way
(b) (salopp: unverschämt) cheekily

Dreck-: ~sau *die,* **~schwein** *das* (derb) filthy swine

Dreh *der;* **~s, ~s** (ugs.) **(a) den ~ heraushaben** have [got] the knack
(b) [so] um den ~: about that

Dreh-: ~arbeiten *Pl.* (Film) shooting *sing.* (zu of); **~bank** *die; Pl.* **~bänke** lathe; **~buch** *das* screenplay; [film] script

drehen [1] *tr. V.* **(a)** turn
(b) (formen) twist ‹*rope, thread*›; roll ‹*cigarette*›
(c) (Film) shoot ‹*scene*›; film ‹*report*›; make ‹*film*›
[2] *itr. V.* **(a)** ‹*car*› turn; ‹*wind*› change
(b) an etw. (*Dat.*) **~:** turn sth.
(c) (Film) shoot; film
[3] *refl. V.* **(a)** turn
(b) (ugs.: zum Gegenstand haben) **sich um etw. ~:** be about sth.

Dreh-: ~kreuz *das* turnstile; **~orgel** *die* barrel organ; **~ort** *der* (Film) location; **~restaurant** *das* revolving restaurant; **~stuhl** *der* swivel chair; **~tür** *die* revolving door

Drehung *die;* **~, ~en** turn; (um einen Mittelpunkt) revolution

Dreh-: ~zahl *die* revolutions *or* (coll.) revs (*esp. per minute*); **~zahl·messer** *der;* **~~s, ~~:** revolution counter; rev counter (coll.); tachometer

drei *Kardinalz.* three;

Drei *die;* **~, ~en** three; **eine ~ schreiben** (Schulw.) get a C

drei-, Drei-: ~eck *das* (Geom.) triangle; **~eckig** *Adj.* triangular; **~ein·halb** *Bruchz.* three and a half

Dreier *der;* **~s, ~** (ugs.) three

dreierlei *indekl. Adj.* **(a)** *attr.* three kinds *or* sorts of; three different
(b) *subst.* three [different] things

drei-, Drei-: ~fach *Vervielfältigungsz.* triple; **die ~fache Menge** three times the amount; **~fache** *das; adj. Dekl.* **das ~fache kosten** cost three times as much; **das ~fache von 3 ist 9** three times three is nine; **~faltigkeit** *die;* **~~** (christl. Rel.) Trinity; **~hundert** *Kardinalz.* three hundred; **~jährig** *Adj.* (3 Jahre alt) three-year-old *attrib.;* (3 Jahre dauernd) three-year *attrib.;*

*old spelling - see note on page xiv

~kampf *der* (Sport) triathlon; **~klang** *der* triad; **~köpfig** *Adj.* ‹*family, crew*› of three; **~mal** *Adv.* three times; **~malig** *Adj.* **eine ~malige Wiederholung** three repeats

drein (ugs.) ▶ DAREIN

drein-: ~|blicken, ~|schauen *itr. V.* look

drei-, Drei-: ~rad *das* tricycle; **~satz** *der* rule of three; **~seitig** *Adj.* three-sided ‹*figure*›; three-page ‹*letter, leaflet, etc.*›

dreißig *Kardinalz.* thirty; *s. auch* ACHTZIG

dreißigjährig *Adj.* (30 Jahre alt) thirty-year-old *attrib.;* (30 Jahre dauernd) thirty-year *attrib.*

dreißigst... *Ordinalz.* thirtieth

Dreißigstel *das;* **~s, ~:** thirtieth

dreist [1] *Adj.* brazen; barefaced ‹*lie*› [2] *adv.* brazenly

drei·stellig *Adj.* three-figure *attrib.*

Dreistigkeit *die;* **~, ~en (a)** brazenness **(b)** (Handlung) brazen act

drei-, Drei-: ~tausend *Kardinalz.* three thousand; **~teilig** *Adj.* three-part *attrib.;* three-piece *attrib.* ‹*suit*›; ***~viertel** ▶ VIERTEL; **~viertel·stunde** /---'--/ *die* three-quarters of an hour; **~viertel·takt** /-'---/ *der* three-four time; **~zehn** *Kardinalz.* thirteen; *s. auch* ACHTZEHN

Dresche *die;* **~** (salopp) walloping (coll.); thrashing

dreschen [1] *unr. tr. V.* **(a)** thresh **(b)** (salopp: schlagen) wallop (coll.); thrash [2] *unr. itr. V.* thresh

dressieren *tr. V.* train ‹*animal*›

Dressur *die;* **~, ~en** training

Drill *der;* **~[e]s** drilling; (Milit.) drill

drillen *tr. V.* (auch Milit.) drill

Drilling *der;* **~s, ~e** triplet

drin *Adv.* (ugs.) **(a)** in it **(b)** ▶ DRINNEN

dringen *unr. itr. V.* **(a)** *mit sein* **durch/in etw. ~:** penetrate sth. **(b)** *mit sein* **in jmdn. ~** (geh.) press sb. **(c) auf etw.** (*Akk.*) **~:** insist upon sth.

dringend [1] *Adj.* urgent; strong ‹*suspicion, advice*› [2] *adv.* urgently; ‹*advise, suspect*› strongly; **~ erforderlich** essential

dringlich [1] *Adj.* urgent [2] *adv.* urgently

Dringlichkeit *die;* **~:** urgency

drinnen *Adv.* inside; (im Haus) indoors; inside

dritt *in* **wir waren zu ~:** there were three of us

dritt... *Ordinalz.* third

Drittel *das,* (schweiz. meist *der*); **~s, ~:** third

dritteln *tr. V.* split *or* divide three ways

drittens *Adv.* thirdly

DRK *Abk.* = **Deutsches Rotes Kreuz** German Red Cross

Dr. med. *Abk.* = **doctor medicinae** MD

droben *Adv.* (südd., österr., sonst geh.) up there

Droge *die;* **~, ~n** drug

drogen-, Drogen-: ~abhängig *Adj.* addicted to drugs *postpos.;* **~abhängige** *der/die; adj. Dekl.* drug addict; **~abhängigkeit** *die* drug addiction; **~beratungs·stelle** *die* drug advice centre; **~gefährdet** *Adj.* at risk from drugs *postpos.;* **~handel** *der* drug trafficking; **~konsum** *der* drug-taking; **~konsument** *der,* **~konsumentin** *die* drug user; **~missbrauch,** ***~mißbrauch** *der* drug abuse; **~rausch** *der* [state of] drug intoxication; **etw. im ~rausch tun** do sth. while under the influence of drugs *or* while [high (coll.)] on drugs; **~süchtig** *Adj.* ▶ ~ABHÄNGIG; **~szene** *die* drug scene

Drogerie *die;* **~, ~n** chemist's [shop] (Brit.); drugstore (Amer.)

Drogist *der;* **~en, ~en, Drogistin** *die;* **~, ~nen** chemist (Brit.); druggist (Amer.)

drohen *itr., mod. V.* threaten; (bevorstehen) be threatening; **jmdm. droht etw.** sb. is threatened with sth.

drohend *Adj.* threatening; (bevorstehend) impending

Drohne *die;* **~, ~n** drone

dröhnen *itr. V.* boom; ‹*machine*› roar

Drohung *die;* **~, ~en** threat

drollig [1] *Adj.* funny; comical; (niedlich) sweet; cute (Amer.) [2] *adv.: s. Adj.:* comically; sweetly; cutely (Amer.)

Dromedar *das;* **~s, ~e** dromedary

Drops *der od. das;* **~, ~:** fruit *or* (Brit.) acid drop

drosch *1. u. 3. Pers. Sg. Prät. v.* DRESCHEN

Drossel *die;* **~, ~n** thrush

drosseln *tr. V.* **(a)** turn down ‹*heating, air conditioning*›; throttle back ‹*engine*› **(b)** (herabsetzen) reduce

Dr. phil. *Abk.* = **doctor philosophiae** Dr

drüben *Adv.* **dort** *od.* **da ~:** over there; **~ auf der anderen Seite** over on the other side

Druck[1] *der;* **~[e]s, Drücke (a)** (auch fig.) pressure **(b) ein ~ auf den Knopf** a touch of the button

Druck[2] *der;* **~[e]s, ~e (a)** printing; **in ~ gehen** go to press **(b)** (Produkt) print

Druck·buchstabe *der* printed letter

drucken *tr., itr. V.* print

drücken [1] *tr. V.* **(a)** press; press, push ‹*button*›; squeeze ‹*juice, pus*› **(aus** out of); **jmdm. die Hand ~:** squeeze sb.'s hand **(b)** (liebkosen) **jmdn. ~:** hug [and squeeze] sb. **(c)** ‹*shoe etc.*› pinch

⋯▸

(d) (herabsetzen) push down ‹*price, rate*›; depress ‹*sales*›; bring down ‹*standard*› **2** *itr. V.* **(a)** press; **auf den Knopf ~:** press *or* push the button; **„bitte ~":** 'push' **(b)** (Druck verursachen) ‹*shoe etc.*› pinch **3** *refl. V.* (ugs.: sich entziehen) shirk; **sich vor etw.** (*Dat.*) **~:** get out of sth.

drückend *Adj.* **(a)** heavy ‹*debt, taxes*›; serious ‹*worries*›; grinding ‹*poverty*› **(b)** (schwül) oppressive

Drucker *der;* **~s, ~:** printer

Druckerei *die;* **~, ~en** printing works; (Firma) printing house; printer's

Druckerin *die;* **~, ~nen** printer

druck-, Druck-: ~fehler *der* misprint; printer's error; **~knopf** *der* press stud (Brit.); snap fastener; **~luft** *die* compressed air; **~mittel** *das* means of bringing pressure to bear (**gegenüber** on); **~reif 1** *Adj.* ready for publication; (~fertig) ready for press; **2** *adv.* ‹*speak*› in a polished manner; **~sache** *die* (Postw.) printed matter; **~schrift** *die* **(a)** printed writing; **(b)** (Schriftart) type[face]; **(c)** (Schriftwerk) pamphlet

drum *Adv.* (ugs.) **(a)** ▸ DARUM; **(b)** [a]round; **alles** *od.* **das [ganze] Drum und Dran** (bei einer Mahlzeit) all the trimmings; (bei einer Feierlichkeit) all the palaver that goes with it (coll.)

Drum·herum *das;* **~s** everything that goes/went with it

drunter *Adv.* (ugs.) underneath; **es** *od.* **alles geht ~ und drüber** everything is topsy-turvy

Drüse *die;* **~, ~n** gland

Dschungel /ˈdʒʊŋl̩/ *der;* **~s, ~** (auch fig.) jungle

dt. *Abk.* = **deutsch** G.

Dtzd. *Abk.* = **Dutzend** doz.

du *Personalpron.; 2. Pers. Sg. Nom.* you; **Du zueinander sagen** use the familiar form in addressing one another; *s. auch* (*Gen.*) DEINER, (*Dat.*) DIR, (*Akk.*) DICH

Dübel *der;* **~s, ~:** plug

ducken 1 *refl. V.* duck **2** *itr. V.* (fig. abwertend) humble oneself (**vor** + *Dat.* before)

Duckmäuser *der;* **~s, ~, Duckmäuserin** *die;* **~, ~nen** (abwertend) moral coward

Duckmäusertum *das;* **~s** (abwertend) moral cowardice

Dudel·sack *der* bagpipes *pl.*

Duell *das;* **~s, ~e** duel

duellieren *refl. V.* fight a duel

Duett *das;* **~[e]s, ~e** (Musik) duet; **im ~ singen** sing a duet

Duft *der;* **~[e]s, Düfte** scent; (von Parfüm, Blumen) scent; fragrance; (von Kaffee usw.) aroma

duften *itr. V.* smell (**nach** of)

dulden *tr. V.* tolerate; put up with

duldsam 1 *Adj.* tolerant (**gegen** towards) **2** *adv.* tolerantly

Duma *die:* **die ~:** the Duma

dumm, dümmer, dümmst... 1 *Adj.* **(a)** stupid **(b)** (unvernünftig) foolish **(c)** (ugs.: töricht, albern) idiotic; silly **(d)** (ugs.: unangenehm) nasty ‹*feeling*›; annoying ‹*habit*›; **das wird mir jetzt zu ~** (ugs.) I've had enough of it **2** *adv.* (ugs.) idiotically

Dumme *der/die; adj. Dekl.* fool; **der/die ~ sein** (ugs.) be the loser

dummer·weise *Adv.* **(a)** unfortunately; (ärgerlicherweise) annoyingly **(b)** (törichterweise) foolishly

Dummheit *die;* **~, ~en (a)** stupidity **(b)** (unkluge Handlung) stupid thing

Dumm·kopf *der* (ugs.) nitwit (coll.)

dumpf 1 *Adj.* **(a)** dull ‹*thud, rumble of thunder*›; muffled ‹*sound, thump*› **(b)** (muffig) musty **(c)** (stumpfsinnig) dull **2** *adv.* **(a)** ‹*echo*› hollowly **(b)** (stumpfsinnig) apathetically

Dumping /ˈdampɪŋ/ *das;* **~s** (Wirtsch.) dumping

Dumping·preis *der* dumping price

Düne *die;* **~, ~n** dune

düngen 1 *tr. V.* fertilize ‹*soil, lawn*›; spread fertilizer on ‹*field*›; scatter fertilizer around ‹*plants*› **2** *itr. V.* **gut ~** ‹*substance*› be a good fertilizer

Dünger *der;* **~s, ~:** fertilizer

dunkel 1 *Adj.* (auch fig.) dark; (tief) deep ‹*voice, note*›; (undeutlich) vague **2** *adv.* **(a)** (tief) ‹*speak*› in a deep voice **(b)** (undeutlich) vaguely

Dünkel *der;* **~s** (geh.) arrogance; (Einbildung) conceit[edness]

dunkel-: ~blond *Adj.* light brown ‹*hair*›; ‹*person*› with light brown hair; **~häutig** *Adj.* dark-skinned

Dunkelheit *die;* **~:** darkness

Dunkel·kammer *die* darkroom

dunkeln *itr. V.* (*unpers.*) **es dunkelt** (geh.) it is growing dark

Dunkel·ziffer *die* number of unrecorded cases

dünn 1 *Adj.* thin; slim ‹*book*›; fine ‹*stocking*›; watery ‹*coffee, tea, beer*› **2** *adv.* thinly ‹*sliced, populated*›; lightly ‹*dressed*›

Dunst *der;* **~[e]s, Dünste (a)** haze; (Nebel) mist **(b)** (Geruch) smell

dünsten *tr. V.* steam ‹*fish, vegetables*›; braise ‹*meat*›; stew ‹*fruit*›

dunstig *Adj.* hazy

*alte Schreibung - vgl. Hinweis auf S. xiv

Duo *das;* **~s, ~s** (Musik) duet; (fig. scherzh.) duo; pair

Duplikat *das;* **~[e]s, ~e** duplicate

duplizieren *tr. V.* duplicate

Dur *das;* **~** (Musik) major [key]

durch 1 *Präp. mit Akk.* **(a)** (räumlich) through
(b) (modal) by; **~ Boten** by courier; **zehn [geteilt] ~ zwei** ten divided by two
2 *Adv.* **(a)** (hin~) **das ganze Jahr ~:** throughout the whole year
(b) (ugs.: vorbei) **es war 3 Uhr ~:** it was gone 3 o'clock
(c) ~ und ~ nass/überzeugt wet through [and through]/completely *or* totally convinced
(d) [durch etw.] ~ sein be through [sth.]
(e) ~ sein (abgefahren sein) ‹*train, bus, etc.*› have gone
(f) ~ sein (fertig sein) have finished; **durch etw. ~ sein** have got through sth.
(g) ~ sein ‹*cheese*› be ripe; ‹*meat*› be well done

durch|arbeiten 1 *tr. V.* work through
2 *itr. V.* work through; **die Nacht ~:** work through the night

durch·aus *Adv.* absolutely; perfectly, quite ‹*correct, possible, understandable*›; **das ist ~ richtig** that is entirely right; **~ nicht** by no means

durch|beißen *unr. tr. V.* bite through

durch|blättern *tr. V.* leaf through

Durch·blick *der* (ugs.) **den [absoluten] ~ haben** know [exactly] what's going on

durch|blicken *itr. V.* **(a)** look through; **durch etw. ~:** look through sth.
(b) ~ lassen, dass .../wie ...: hint that .../at how ...

Durch·blutung *die* flow of blood (+ *Gen.* to); [blood] circulation

Durchblutungs·störung *die* disturbance of the blood supply

durch|bohren[1] *tr. V.* drill through ‹*wall, plank*›; drill ‹*hole*›

durch·bohren[2] *tr. V.* pierce

durch|brechen[1] 1 *unr. tr. V.* **etw. ~:** break sth. in two
2 *unr. itr. V.; mit sein* **(a)** break in two
(b) (hervorkommen) ‹*sun*› break through
(c) (einbrechen) fall through ‹*ice, floor, etc.*›

durch·brechen[2] *unr. tr. V.* break through

durch|brennen *unr. itr. V.; mit sein* **(a)** ‹*heating coil, lightbulb*› burn out; ‹*fuse*› blow
(b) (ugs.: weglaufen) (von zu Hause) run away; (mit der Kasse, mit dem Geliebten/der Geliebten) run off

durch|bringen *unr. tr. V.* get through; (bei Wahlen) **jmdn. ~:** get sb. elected; **seine Familie/sich ~:** support one's family/oneself

Durch·bruch *der* (fig.) breakthrough

durch·dacht *Adj.* **ein wenig/gut ~er Plan** a badly/well thought-out plan; **nicht [genügend] ~ sein** not be sufficiently well thought-out

durch|drehen 1 *tr. V.* put ‹*meat*› through the mincer *or* (Amer.) grinder
2 *itr. V. auch mit sein* (ugs.) crack up (coll.)

durch|dringen[1] *unr. tr. V.; mit sein* ‹*rain, sun*› come through

durch·dringen[2] *unr. tr. V.* penetrate; **jmdn. ~** ‹*idea*› take hold of sb. [completely]

durch·einander *Adv.* **~ bringen** (+ *Akk.*) (in Unordnung bringen) get ‹*room, flat*› into a mess; get ‹*papers, file*› into a muddle; muddle up ‹*papers, file*›; (verwirren) confuse; (verwechseln) confuse ‹*names, etc*›; get ‹*names etc.*› mixed up; **~ sein** ‹*papers, desk, etc.*› be in a muddle; (verwirrt sein) be confused; (aufgeregt sein) be flustered

Durcheinander *das;* **~s (a)** muddle; mess
(b) (Wirrwarr) confusion

***durcheinander|bringen**
▶ DURCHEINANDER

durch|exerzieren *tr. V.* (ugs.) go through, practise ‹*rules, multiplication tables*›; rehearse ‹*situation*›

durch|fahren *unr. itr. V.; mit sein* **(a) [durch etw.] ~:** drive through [sth.]
(b) (nicht anhalten) go straight through; (mit dem Auto) drive straight through; **der Zug fährt [in H.] durch** the train doesn't stop [at H.]

Durch·fahrt *die* **(a) „~ verboten"** 'no entry except for access'; **auf der ~ sein** be passing through
(b) (Weg) thoroughfare; **„bitte [die] ~ freihalten"** 'please do not obstruct'

Durch·fall *der* diarrhoea *no art.*

durch|fallen *unr. itr. V.; mit sein* **(a)** fall through
(b) (ugs.: nicht bestehen) fail

durch|finden *unr. refl. V.* find one's way through

durchführbar *Adj.* practicable

Durchführbarkeit *die;* **~:** practicability;

durch|führen 1 *tr. V.* carry out; put into effect ‹*decision, programme*›; perform ‹*operation*›; hold ‹*meeting, election, examination*›
2 *itr. V.* **durch etw./unter etw.** (*Dat.*) **~** ‹*track, road*› go through/under sth.

Durch·führung *die* carrying out; (einer Operation) performing; (einer Versammlung, Wahl, Prüfung) holding; (eines Wettbewerbs) staging

Durch·gang *der* **(a)** passage[way]; **„kein ~", „~ verboten"** 'no thoroughfare'
(b) (Phase) stage; (einer Versuchsreihe) run; (Sport, Wahlen) round

Durchgangs-: ~straße *die* through road; **~verkehr** *der* through traffic

durch|geben *unr. tr. V.* announce ‹*news*›; ⋯

give ‹*results, weather report*›; **eine Meldung im Radio/Fernsehen ~**: make an announcement on the radio/on television

dụrch·gefroren *Adj.* frozen stiff; chilled to the bone

dụrch|gehen [1] *unr. itr. V.; mit sein* **(a)** [**durch etw.**] **~**: go *or* walk through [sth.] **(b)** (hindurchdringen) [**durch etw.**] **~**: ‹*rain, water*› come through [sth.] **(c)** (direkt zum Ziel führen) ‹*train etc.*› go [right] through (**bis** to); ‹*flight*› go direct **(d)** (andauern) go on (**bis zu** until) **(e)** (hingenommen werden) ‹*discrepancy*› be tolerated; ‹*mistake, discourtesy*› be allowed to pass; **jmdm. etw. ~ lassen** let sb. get away with sth. **(f)** ‹*horse*› bolt [2] *unr. tr. V.; mit sein* go through ‹*newspaper, text*›

dụrch·gehend [1] *Adj.* **(a)** continuous ‹*line, pattern, etc.*›; constantly recurring ‹*motif*› **(b)** (direkt) through *attrib.* ‹*train, carriage*›; direct ‹*flight, connection*› [2] *adv.* **~ geöffnet haben/bleiben** be/stay open all day

dụrchgeknallt *Adj.* (ugs.) crazy

dụrch·geschwitzt *Adj.* ‹*person*› soaked *or* bathed in sweat; ‹*clothes*› soaked with sweat; sweat-soaked *attrib.* ‹*clothes*›

dụrch|greifen *unr. itr. V.* [**hart**] **~**: take drastic measures *or* steps

dụrch|halten [1] *unr. itr. V.* hold out; (bei einer schwierigen Aufgabe) see it through [2] *unr. tr. V.* stand

dụrch|hängen *unr. itr. V.* sag

dụrch|kämmen *tr. V.* **(a)** comb ‹*hair*› through **(b)** (durchsuchen) comb ‹*area etc.*›

dụrch|kommen *unr. itr. V.; mit sein* **(a)** come through; (mit Mühe) get through **(b)** (ugs.: beim Telefonieren) get through **(c)** (durchgehen, -fahren usw.) **durch etw. ~**: come through sth. **(d)** (ugs.: überleben) pull through

dụrch|kreuzen[1] *tr. V.* cross out

durch·kreuzen[2] *tr. V.* (vereiteln) frustrate

dụrch|lassen *unr. tr. V.* **(a) jmdn.** [**durch etw.**] **~**: let sb. through [sth.] **(b)** (durchlässig sein) let ‹*light, water, etc.*› through

dụrchlässig *Adj.* permeable; (porös) porous; (undicht) leaky; ‹*raincoat, shoe*› that lets in water

Dụrch·lauf *der* (Sport, DV) run

dụrch|laufen[1] [1] *unr. itr. V.; mit sein* **(a)** [**durch etw.**] **~**: run through [sth.]; (durchrinnen) trickle through [sth.] **(b)** (passieren) ‹*runners*› run *or* pass through **(c)** (ohne Pause laufen) run without stopping [2] *unr. tr. V.* go through ‹*soles*›

durch·laufen[2] *unr. tr. V.* go through ‹*phase, stage*›

dụrchlaufend [1] *Adj.* continuous [2] *adv.* ‹*numbered, marked*› in sequence

dụrch|lesen *unr. tr. V.* **etw.** [**ganz**] **~**: read sth. [all the way] through

durch·leuchten *tr. V.* x-ray; (fig.) investigate ‹*case, matter, problem, etc.*› thoroughly

durch·lọ̈chern *tr. V.* make holes in

dụrch|machen (ugs.) [1] *tr. V.* **(a)** undergo ‹*change*›; complete ‹*training course*›; go through ‹*stage, phase*›; serve ‹*apprenticeship*› **(b)** (erleiden) go through **(c)** (durcharbeiten) work through ‹*lunch break etc.*› [2] *itr. V.* (durcharbeiten) work [right] through; (durchfeiern) celebrate all night/day *etc.*; keep going all night/day *etc.*

Dụrchmesser *der*; **~s, ~**: diameter

dụrch|nehmen *unr. tr. V.* (Schulw.: behandeln) do

dụrch|pauken *tr. V.* (ugs.) force through ‹*law, regulation, etc.*›

dụrch|peitschen *tr. V.* (ugs. abwertend) railroad ‹*law, application, etc.*› through

dụrch|probieren *tr. V.* taste ‹*wines, cakes, etc.*› one after another

durch·queren *tr. V.* cross; travel across ‹*country*›; ‹*train*› go through ‹*country*›

dụrch|rechnen *tr. V.* calculate ‹*costs etc.*› [down to the last penny]; check ‹*bill*› thoroughly

Dụrch·reise *die* journey through

dụrch|reisen *itr. V.; mit sein* travel through

Dụrchreise·visum *das* transit visa

dụrch|reißen [1] *unr. tr. V.* **etw. ~**: tear sth. in two *or* in half [2] *unr. itr. V.; mit sein* ‹*fabric, garment*› rip, tear; ‹*thread, rope*› snap [in two]

dụrch|rosten *itr. V.; mit sein* rust through

dụrchs *Präp. + Art.* = **durch das**

Dụrch·sage *die* announcement; (an eine bestimmte Person) message

durchschaubar *Adj.* transparent; **leicht ~**: easy to see through

durch·schauen *tr. V.* see through ‹*person, plan, etc.*›; see ‹*situation*› clearly

dụrch|schlafen *unr. itr. V.* sleep [right] through

Dụrch·schlag *der* **(a)** (Kopie) carbon [copy] **(b)** (Küchengerät) strainer

dụrch|schlagen *unr. tr. V.* **etw. ~**: chop sth. in two

dụrchschlagend *Adj.* resounding ‹*success*›; decisive ‹*effect, measures*›; conclusive ‹*evidence*›

dụrch|schneiden *unr. tr. V.* cut through

---

*old spelling - see note on page xiv

‹*thread, cable*›; cut ‹*ribbon, sheet of paper*› in two; cut ‹*throat, umbilical cord*›; **etw. in der Mitte ~:** cut sth. in half

Durch·schnitt *der* average; **im ~:** on average; **über/unter dem ~ liegen** be above/below average

durchschnittlich 1 *Adj.* **(a)** *nicht präd.* average ‹*growth, performance, output*› **(b)** (ugs.: nicht außergewöhnlich) ordinary ‹*life, person, etc.*› **(c)** (mittelmäßig) modest; ordinary ‹*appearance*› 2 *adv.* ‹*earn etc.*› on [an] average; **~ groß** of average height

Durchschnitts-: ~alter *das* average age; **~geschwindigkeit** *die* average speed; **~mensch** *der* average person; (Alltagsmensch) ordinary person; **~temperatur** *die* average temperature; **~wert** *der* average *or* mean value

Durch·schrift *die* carbon [copy]

durch|sehen 1 *unr. itr. V.* **[durch etw.] ~:** look through [sth.] 2 *unr. tr. V.* look through

***durch|sein** ▶ DURCH 2 D–G

durch|setzen 1 *tr. V.* carry through; achieve ‹*objective*›; enforce ‹*demand, claim*› 2 *refl. V.* assert oneself; ‹*idea etc.*› find *or* gain acceptance

Durch·sicht *die:* **nach ~ der Unterlagen** after looking *or* checking through the documents

durchsichtig *Adj.* (auch fig.) transparent

durch|sprechen *unr. tr. V.* talk ‹*matter etc.*› over; discuss ‹*matter etc.*› thoroughly

durch|stehen *unr. tr. V.* stand ‹*pace, boring job*›; come through ‹*difficult situation*›; get over ‹*illness*›

durch|stellen *tr. V.* put ‹*call*› through **(in** + *Akk.*, **auf** + *Akk.* to)

durch|streichen *unr. tr. V.* cross out; (in Formularen) delete

durch·suchen *tr. V.* search **(nach** for); search, scour ‹*area*› **(nach** for)

Durchsuchung *die;* **~, ~en** search

durch|treten *unr. tr. V.* press ‹*clutch pedal, brake pedal*› right down

durchtrieben (abwertend) 1 *Adj.* crafty; sly 2 *adv.* craftily; slyly

durch·wachsen *Adj.* **~er Speck** streaky bacon

Durch·wahl *die* **(a)** direct dialling; **mein Apparat hat keine ~:** I don't have an outside line **(b)** ▶ DURCHWAHLNUMMER

durch|wählen *itr. V.* **(a)** dial direct **(b)** (bei Nebenstellenanlagen) dial straight through

Durchwahl·nummer *die* number of the/one's direct line

durch|zählen *tr. V.* count; count up

durch|ziehen 1 *unr. tr. V.* **jmdn./etw. [durch etw.] ~:** pull sb./sth. through [sth.]; **ein Gummiband [durch etw.] ~:** draw an elastic through [sth.] 2 *unr. itr. V.; mit sein* pass through; ‹*soldiers*› march through

Durch·zug *der* draught

dürfen 1 *unr. Modalverb; 2. Part.* **dürfen: (a) etw. tun ~:** be allowed to do sth.; **darf ich rauchen?** may I smoke?; **was darf es sein?** can I help you? **(b)** *Konjunktiv II* + *Inf.* **das dürfte der Grund sein** that is probably the reason 2 *unr. tr., itr. V.* **er hat nicht gedurft** he was not allowed to

durfte *1. u. 3. Pers. Sg. Prät. v.* DÜRFEN

dürfte *1. u. 3. Pers. Sg. Konjunktiv II v.* DÜRFEN

dürr *Adj.* **(a)** withered; arid, barren ‹*ground, earth*› **(b)** (mager) scrawny

Dürre *die;* **~, ~n** drought

Durst *der;* **~[e]s** thirst; **~ haben** be thirsty; **ich habe ~ auf ein Bier** I could just drink a beer

durstig *Adj.* thirsty

durst-, Durst-: ~löscher *der* thirst-quencher; **~stillend** *Adj.* thirst-quenching; **~strecke** *die* lean period *or* time

Dusche *die;* **~, ~n** shower

duschen *itr., refl. V.* have a shower

Düse *die;* **~, ~n** (Technik) nozzle; (eines Vergasers) jet

Düsen-: ~flugzeug *das* jet aircraft; **~motor** *der* jet engine

düster 1 *Adj.* **(a)** dark; gloomy; dim ‹*light*› **(b)** (fig.) gloomy; sombre ‹*colour, music*› 2 *adv.* (fig.) gloomily

Dutzend *das;* **~s, ~e** dozen; **zwei ~:** two dozen

dutzend·weise *Adv.* in [their] dozens (coll.)

duzen *tr. V.* call ‹*sb.*› 'du' (*the familiar form of address*)

Duz·freund *der*, **Duz·freundin** *die* good friend (*whom one addresses with 'du'*)

dynamisch 1 *Adj.* (auch fig.) dynamic 2 *adv.* dynamically

Dynamit *das;* **~s** dynamite

Dynamo *der;* **~s, ~s** dynamo

Dynastie *die;* **~, ~n** dynasty

D-Zug /'de:-/ *der* express train

Ee

e, E /eː/ *das;* ~, ~ **(a)** (Buchstabe) e/E
(b) (Musik) [key of] E

Ebbe *die;* ~, ~**n** ebb tide; (Zustand) low tide; **es ist** ~: the tide is out

eben 1 *Adj.* **(a)** flat
(b) (glatt) level
2 *adv.* **(a)** (gerade jetzt) just
(b) (kurz) [for] a moment

Ebene *die,* ~, ~**n** **(a)** plain; **in der** ~: on the plain
(b) (Geom., Physik) plane
(c) (fig.) level

eben·falls *Adv.* likewise; as well; **danke,** ~: thank you, [and] [the] same to you

Eben·holz *das* ebony

eben·so *Adv.* **(a)** *mit Adjektiven, Adverbien* just as; **ich mag Erdbeeren** ~ **gern [wie...]** I like strawberries just as much [as ...]; ~ **gern würde ich an den Strand gehen** I would just as soon go to the beach; ~ **gut** just as well
(b) *mit Verben* in exactly the same way

***ebenso·gern** *usw.* ▶ EBENSO A

Eber *der;* ~**s,** ~: boar

Eber·esche *die* rowan; mountain ash

ebnen *tr. V.* level ‹*ground*›

Echo *das;* ~**s,** ~**s** echo

echt 1 *Adj.* **(a)** genuine; real ‹*love, friendship*›
(b) (typisch) real, typical
2 *adv.* **(a)** (ugs. verstärkend) really
(b) (typisch) typically

Eck *das;* ~**s,** ~**e** (südd., österr.:) ~**e** corner

Eck-: ~**ball** *der* (Sport) corner [kick/hit/throw]; **einen** ~**ball treten** take a corner; ~**bank** *die; Pl.* ~**bänke** corner seat

Ecke *die;* ~, ~**n** corner; **an der** ~: on *or* at the corner; **um die** ~: round the corner

eckig *Adj.* square; angular

Eck·zahn *der* canine tooth

edel *Adj.* **(a)** thoroughbred ‹*horse*›; species ‹*rose*›
(b) (großmütig) noble[-minded], high-minded ‹*person*›; noble ‹*thought, gesture, feelings, deed*›; honourable ‹*motive*›

Edel-: ~**metall** *das* precious metal; ~**nutte** *die* (salopp) high-class tart (sl.); ~**pilz·käse** *der* blue[-veined] cheese; ~**stahl** *der* stainless steel; ~**stein** *der* precious stone; gem[stone]

Edition *die;* ~, ~**en** edition

Edutainment /ɛdju'teɪnmənt/ *das;* ~**s** edutainment

*alte Schreibung - vgl. Hinweis auf S. xiv

EDV *Abk.* = **elektronische Datenverarbeitung** EDP

EEG *Abk.* = **Elektroenzephalogramm** EEG; **ein EEG machen lassen** have an EEG

Efeu *der;* ~**s** ivy

Effekt *der;* ~**[e]s,** ~**e** effect

effekt·voll *Adj.* effective; dramatic ‹*pause, gesture, entrance*›

EG *Abk.* **(a)** = **Europäische Gemeinschaft** EC
(b) = **Erdgeschoss**

egal *Adj.* (ugs.: einerlei) **es ist jmdm.** ~: it's all the same to sb.; **[ganz]** ~, **wie/wer** *usw.* ...: no matter how/who *etc.* ...

Egge *die;* ~, ~**n** harrow

E-Gitarre *die* electric guitar

Egoist *der;* ~**en,** ~**en, Egoistin** *die;* ~, ~**nen** egoist

egoistisch 1 *Adj.* egoistic[al]
2 *adv.* egoistically

ehe *Konj.* before

Ehe *die;* ~, ~**n** marriage

Ehe-: ~**bett** *das* marriage bed; (Doppelbett) double bed; ~**bruch** *der* adultery; ~**frau** *die* wife; (verheiratete Frau) married woman; ~**krach** *der* (ugs.) row; ~**leute** *Pl.* married couple

ehelich *Adj.* marital; matrimonial; conjugal ‹*rights, duties*›; legitimate ‹*child*›

ehemalig *Adj.* former

ehe-, Ehe-: ~**mann** *der; Pl.* ~**männer** husband; (verheirateter Mann) married man; ~**mündig** *Adj.* (Rechtsspr.) of marriageable age *postpos.;* ~**mündig sein** be of marriageable age *or* of an age to marry; ~**mündigkeit** *die* (Rechtsspr.) being of marriageable age; ~**paar** *das* married couple

eher *Adv.* **(a)** (früher) earlier; sooner
(b) (lieber) rather; sooner

Ehe-: ~**ring** *der* wedding ring; ~**scheidung** *die* divorce; ~**vertrag** *der* (Rechtsw.) marriage contract

Ehre *die;* ~, ~**n** honour; **jmdm.** ~ **antun** pay tribute to sb.

ehren *tr. V.* **(a)** honour; **Sehr geehrter Herr Müller!/Sehr geehrte Frau Müller!** Dear Herr Müller/Dear Frau Müller
(b) (Ehre machen) **deine Hilfsbereitschaft ehrt dich** your willingness to help does you credit

ehren-, Ehren-: ~**amt** *das* honorary position *or* post; ~**amtlich** 1 *Adj.*

honorary ‹*position, membership*›; voluntary ‹*help, worker*›; [2] *adv.* in an honorary capacity; (freiwillig) on a voluntary basis

ehrenhaft *Adj.* honourable

ehren-, Ehren-: ~rührig *Adj.* defamatory ‹*allegations*›; **~sache** *die:* **das ist ~sache** that is a point of honour; **~sache!** you can count on me!; **~voll** *Adj.* honourable; **~wert** *Adj.* (geh.) worthy; **~wort** *das; Pl.* **~~e: ~wort** [!/?] word of honour [!/?]

ehrerbietig *Adj.* (geh.) respectful

Ehr·furcht *die* reverence (**vor** + *Dat.* for)

ehrfürchtig *Adj.* reverent

ehr-, Ehr-: ~gefühl *das* sense of honour; **~geiz** *der* ambition; **~geizig** *Adj.* ambitious

ehrlich *Adj.* honest; genuine ‹*concern, desire, admiration*›; upright ‹*character*›

Ehrlichkeit *die;* ~ ▶ EHRLICH: honesty; genuineness; uprightness

ehr·los *Adj.* dishonourable

Ehrung *die;* **~, ~en: die ~ der Preisträger** the prize-giving (Brit.) *or* (Amer.) awards ceremony; **bei der ~ der Sieger** when the winners were awarded their medals/ trophies

ehr·würdig *Adj.* venerable

Ei *das;* **~[e]s, ~er** egg

Eiche *die;* **~, ~n** oak [tree]; (Holz) oak [wood]

Eichel *die;* **~, ~n** acorn

eichen *tr. V.* calibrate ‹*measuring instrument, thermometer*›; standardize ‹*weights, measures, containers, products*›; adjust ‹*weighing scales*›

Eich·hörnchen *das* squirrel

Eid *der;* **~[e]s, ~e** oath

Eidechse /ˈaiːdɛksə/ *die;* **~, ~n** lizard

eides·stattlich *Adj.* (Rechtsw.) **eine ~e Erklärung** a statutory declaration

Ei·dotter *der od. das* egg yolk

Eier-: ~becher *der* eggcup; **~kuchen** *der* pancake; (Omelett) omelette; **~likör** *der* egg flip; **~stock** *der* (Physiol., Zool.) ovary; **~uhr** *die* egg timer

Eifer *der;* **~s** eagerness

Eifer·sucht *die* jealousy (**auf** + *Akk.* of)

eifer·süchtig *Adj.* jealous (**auf** + *Akk.* of)

eifrig *Adj.* eager

Ei·gelb *das;* **~[e]s, ~e** egg yolk

eigen *Adj.* own; (selbstständig) separate

eigen-, Eigen-: ~art *die* (Wesensart) particular nature; (Zug) peculiarity; **eine ~art dieser Stadt** one of the characteristic features of this city; **~artig** *Adj.* peculiar; strange; odd; **~artigerweise** *Adv.* strangely [enough]; oddly [enough]; **~artigkeit** *die* peculiarity; strangeness; oddness; **~brötelei** *die;* **~~, ~~en** taking an [unduly] independent line; **~brötler** *der;* **~~s, ~~, ~brötlerin** *die;* **~~, ~~nen** loner; lone wolf; **~dynamik** *die* inherent dynamism; **~händig** [1] *Adj.* personal ‹*signature*›; holographic ‹*will, document*›; [2] *adv.* ‹*present, sign*› personally; **~heim** *das* house of one's own

Eigenheit *die;* **~, ~en** peculiarity

eigen-, Eigen-: ~initiative *die* initiative of one's own; **~lob** *das* self-praise; **~mächtig** *Adj.* unauthorized; **~name** *der* proper name; **~nützig** *Adj.* self-seeking; selfish ‹*motive*›

eigens *Adv.* specially

Eigenschaft *die;* **~, ~en** quality; characteristic; (von Sachen, Stoffen) property

Eigenschafts·wort *das; Pl.* **Eigenschaftswörter** adjective

eigen-, Eigen-: ~sinn *der* obstinacy; **~sinnig** *Adj.* obstinate; **~ständig** *Adj.* independent; **~ständigkeit** *die;* **~~:** independence

eigentlich [1] *Adj.* (wirklich) actual; real; (wahr) true; (ursprünglich) original

[2] *Adv.* actually

[3] *Partikel* **wie spät ist es ~?** tell me, what time is it?; **was willst du ~?** what exactly do you want?

Eigen·tor *das* (Ballspiele, fig.) own goal

Eigentum *das;* **~s** property; (einschließlich Geld usw.) assets *pl.*

Eigentümer *der;* **~s, ~:** owner; (Hotel~, Geschäfts~) proprietor

Eigentümerin *die;* **~, ~nen** owner; (Hotel~, Geschäfts~) proprietress; proprietor

Eigentums·wohnung *die* owner-occupied flat (Brit.); condominium apartment (Amer.)

eigen-, Eigen-: ~vorsorge private [pension] provision; **~willig** *Adj.* self-willed

eignen *refl. V.* be suitable

Eigner *der;* **~s, ~, Eignerin** *die;* **~, ~nen** owner

Eignung *die;* **~:** suitability; **seine ~ zum Fliegen** his aptitude for flying

Eignungs-: ~prüfung *die,* **~test** *der* aptitude test

Eil-: ~bote *der,* **~botin** *die* special messenger; **„durch** *od.* **per ~boten"** (veralt.) 'express'; **~brief** *der* express letter

Eile *die;* **~:** hurry; **in ~ sein** be in a hurry

eilen *itr. V.* **(a)** *mit sein* hurry; (besonders schnell) rush

(b) (dringend sein) be urgent; **„eilt!"** 'urgent'

eilig [1] *Adj.* **(a)** hurried; **es ~ haben** be in a hurry

(b) (dringend) urgent

[2] *adv.* hurriedly

Eil·zug *der* semi-fast train

Eimer *der;* **~s, ~:** bucket; (Milch~) pail; (Abfall~) bin; **ein ~ [voll] Wasser** a bucket of water; **im ~ sein** (salopp) be up the spout (coll.)

ein[1] [1] *Kardinalz.* one; **~ für alle Mal, *~ für allemal** once and for all
[2] *unbest. Art.* a/an
[3] *Indefinitpron.* ▶ IRGENDEIN A; *s. auch* EINER

ein[2] (elliptisch) **~ – aus** (an Schaltern) on – off

Einakter *der; ~s, ~:* one-act play

einander *reziprokes Pron.; Dat. u. Akk.* (geh.) each other; one another

ein|arbeiten *tr. V.* train ‹*employee*›

ein·armig *Adj.* one-armed

ein|äschern *tr. V.* cremate

ein|atmen *tr., itr. V.* breathe in

ein·äugig *Adj.* one-eyed

Ein·bahn·straße *die* one-way street

Ein·band *der; Pl.* **Einbände** binding

Ein·bau *der; Pl.* **~ten** fitting; (eines Motors) installation

ein|bauen *tr. V.* build in, fit; install ‹*engine, motor*›

Einbau·küche *die* fitted kitchen

ein·beinig *Adj.* one-legged

ein|berufen *unr. tr. V.* summon; call

Ein·berufung *die* **(a)** (das Einberufen) calling
(b) (zur Wehrpflicht) call-up; conscription; draft (Amer.)

Einbett·zimmer *das* single room

ein|beziehen *unr. tr. V.* include

ein|biegen *unr. itr. V.; mit sein* turn

ein|bilden *refl. V.* **(a) sich** (*Dat.*) **etw. ~:** imagine sth.
(b) (ugs.) **sich** (*Dat.*) **etwas ~:** be conceited (**auf** + *Akk.* about)

Ein·bildung *die* **(a)** imagination
(b) (falsche Vorstellung) fantasy
(c) (Hochmut) conceitedness

ein|binden *unr. tr. V.* bind ‹*book*›; **etw. neu ~:** rebind sth.

ein|blenden *tr. V.* (Rundf., Ferns., Film) insert

Ein·blick *der* **(a)** view; **~ in etw.** (*Akk.*) **haben** be able to see into sth.
(b) (Durchsicht) **jmdm. ~ in etw.** (*Akk.*) **gewähren** allow sb. to look at *or* examine sth.
(c) (Kenntnis) insight

ein|brechen *unr. itr. V.* **(a)** *mit haben od. sein* break in; **in eine Bank ~:** break into a bank; **bei jmdm. ~:** burgle sb.
(b) *mit sein* (einstürzen) ‹*roof, ceiling*› cave in
(c) *mit sein* (durchbrechen) fall through

Einbrecher *der; ~s, ~,* **Einbrecherin** *die; ~, ~nen* burglar

ein|bringen *unr. tr. V.* **(a)** bring in ‹*harvest*›
(b) (verschaffen) **Gewinn/Zinsen ~:** yield a profit/bring in interest; **jmdm. Ruhm ~:** bring sb. fame
(c) (Parl.: vorlegen) introduce ‹*bill*›
(d) invest ‹*capital, money*›

*old spelling - see note on page xiv

Ein·bruch *der* **(a)** burglary; **ein ~ in eine Bank** a break-in at a bank
(b) (das Einstürzen) collapse

einbürgern [1] *tr. V.* naturalize
[2] *refl. V.* ‹*custom, practice*› become established; ‹*person, plant, animal*› become naturalized

Einbürgerung *die; ~, ~en* naturalization

Ein·buße *die* loss

ein|büßen *tr. V.* lose; (durch eigene Schuld) forfeit

ein|checken *tr., itr. V.* (Flugw.) check in

ein|cremen *tr. V.* put cream on ‹*hands etc.*›; **sich ~:** put cream on

ein|dämmen *tr. V.* (fig.) check; stem

ein|decken [1] *refl. V.* stock up
[2] *tr. V.* (ugs.: überhäufen) **jmdn. mit Arbeit ~:** swamp sb. with work

Eindecker *der; ~s, ~* (Flugw.) monoplane

eindeutig *Adj.* clear

Eindeutigkeit *die; ~, ~en* clarity

ein|dringen *unr. itr. V.; mit sein* **in etw.** (*Akk.*) **~:** penetrate into sth.; ‹*bullet*› pierce sth.; (allmählich) ‹*water, sand, etc.*› seep into sth.

ein·dringlich *Adj.* urgent; impressive ‹*voice*›; forceful, powerful ‹*words*›

Eindringling *der; ~s, ~e* intruder

Ein·druck *der; Pl.* **Eindrücke** impression

ein|drücken *tr. V.* smash in ‹*mudguard, bumper*›; stave in ‹*side of ship*›; smash ‹*pier, column, support*›; break ‹*window*›; crush ‹*ribs*›; flatten ‹*nose*›

eindrucks·voll [1] *Adj.* impressive
[2] *adv.* impressively

eine ▶ EIN[1]

ein|ebnen *tr. V.* level

eineiig /ˈaiːn|aiːɪç/ *Adj.* identical ‹*twins*›

ein·ein·halb *Bruchz.* one and a half; **~ Stunden** an hour and a half

ein|engen *tr. V.* **(a) jmdn. ~:** restrict sb.'s movement[s]
(b) (fig.) restrict

einer, eine, eines, eins *Indefinitpron.* (man) one; (jemand) someone; somebody; (fragend, verneint) anyone; anybody; **kaum einer** hardly anybody; **ein[e]s ist sicher** one thing is for sure

Einer *der; ~s, ~* **(a)** (Math.) unit
(b) (Sport) single sculler; **im ~:** in the single sculls

einerlei *Adj.* **~, ob/wo/wer** *usw.* no matter whether/where/who *etc.*; **es ist ~:** it makes no difference

Einerlei *das; ~s* monotony

einerseits *Adv.* on the one hand

ein·fach [1] *Adj.* **(a)** simple
(b) (nicht mehrfach) single ‹*knot, ticket, journey*›
[2] *Partikel* simply; just

Einfachheit *die; ~:* simplicity

ein|fädeln [1] *tr. V.* thread (**in** + *Akk.* into)

[2] *refl. V.* (Verkehrsw.) filter in

ein|fahren [1] *unr. itr. V.; mit sein* come in; ‹*train*› pull in; **in den Bahnhof ~:** pull into the station
[2] *unr. tr. V.* **(a)** bring in ‹*harvest*›
(b) (beschädigen) knock down ‹*wall*›; smash in ‹*mudguard*›

Ein·fahrt *die* **(a)** (das Hineinfahren) entry; **Vorsicht bei der ~ des Zuges!** stand clear [of the edge of the platform], the train is approaching
(b) (Zufahrt) entrance; (Autobahn~) slip road; **„keine ~"** 'no entry'

Ein·fall *der* **(a)** (Idee) idea
(b) (Licht~) incidence (Optics)

ein|fallen *unr. itr. V.; mit sein* **(a) jmdm. ~:** occur to sb.; **was fällt dir denn ein!** what do you think you're doing?
(b) (in Erinnerung kommen) **ihr Name fällt mir nicht ein** I cannot think of her name; **plötzlich fiel ihr ein, dass ...:** suddenly she remembered that ...
(c) (von Licht) come in

einfalls-, Einfalls-: ~los *Adj.* unimaginative; lacking in ideas; **~losigkeit** *die; ~~:* unimaginativeness; lack of ideas; **~reich** *Adj.* imaginative; full of ideas; **~reichtum** *der* imaginativeness; wealth of ideas; **~tor** *das* gateway

Einfalt *die; ~:* simpleness; simple-mindedness

einfältig *Adj.* simple; naïve; naïve ‹*remarks*›

Ein·familien·haus *das* house (as opposed to block of flats etc.)

ein|fangen *unr. tr. V.* catch

ein|fassen *tr. V.* border; edge; frame ‹*picture*›; set ‹*gem*›; edge ‹*grave, lawn, etc.*›

Ein·fassung *die* ▶ EINFASSEN: border; edging; frame; setting

ein|fetten *tr. V.* grease; dubbin ‹*leather*›; **sich** (*Dat.*) **die Haut/Hände ~:** rub cream into one's skin/hands

ein|finden *unr. refl. V.* arrive; (sich treffen) meet; ‹*crowd*› gather

ein|fliegen *unr. tr. V.* fly in

ein|flößen *tr. V.* **(a) jmdm. Tee ~:** pour tea into sb.'s mouth
(b) (fig.) **jmdm. Angst ~:** put fear into sb.

Ein·fluss, *Ein·fluß *der* influence

einfluss-, *einfluß-, Einfluss-, *Einfluß-: ~bereich *der* sphere of influence; **~nahme**, *die; ~~:* exertion of influence (**auf** + *Akk.* on); **~reich** *Adj.* influential

ein·förmig *Adj.* monotonous

ein|frieren [1] *unr. itr. V.; mit sein* freeze; ‹*pipes*› freeze up
[2] *unr. tr. V.* **(a)** deep-freeze ‹*food*›
(b) (fig.) freeze

ein|fügen *tr. V.* **(a)** fit in; **etw. in etw.** (*Akk.*) **~:** fit sth. into sth.
(b) (DV) insert; paste

ein|fühlen *refl. V.* **sich in jmdn. ~:** empathize with sb.

einfühlsam *Adj.* understanding

Ein·fühlung *die; ~:* empathy (**in** + *Akk.* with)

Ein·fuhr *die; ~, ~en* ▶ IMPORT

ein|führen *tr. V.* **(a)** (als Neuerung) introduce ‹*fashion, method, technology*›
(b) (importieren) import

Einfuhr-: ~sperre *die,* **~stopp** *der* embargo *or* ban on imports

Ein·führung *die* introduction

Einfuhr·verbot *das* ▶ ~SPERRE

Ein·gabe *die* **(a)** (Gesuch) petition; (Beschwerde) complaint
(b) (DV) input

Eingabe-: ~gerät *das* (DV) input device; **~taste** *die* (DV) enter key

Ein·gang *der* entrance; **„kein ~"** 'no entry'

ein·gängig *Adj.* catchy

eingangs *Adv.* at the beginning *or* start

Eingangs-: ~halle *die* entrance hall; (eines Hotels, Theaters) foyer; **~tür** *die* (von Kaufhaus, Hotel usw.) [entrance] door; (von Wohnung, Haus usw.) front door

ein|geben *unr. tr. V.* (DV) input; **etw. in den Computer ~:** input sth. into the computer

ein·gebildet *Adj.* **(a)** imaginary ‹*illness*›
(b) (arrogant) conceited

Eingeborene *der/die; adj. Dekl.* (veralt.) native

ein·gefahren *Adj.* long-established; deep-rooted ‹*prejudice*›; **sich auf** *od.* **in ~en Bahnen** *od.* **Gleisen bewegen** go on in the same old way

ein|gehen [1] *unr. itr. V.; mit sein* **(a)** arrive
(b) (fig.) **in die Geschichte ~:** go down in history
(c) (schrumpfen) shrink
(d) auf eine Frage ~/nicht ~: go into *or* deal with/ignore a question; **auf jmdn. ~:** be responsive to sb.; **auf jmdn. nicht ~:** ignore sb.'s wishes
[2] *unr. tr. V.* enter into ‹*contract, matrimony*›; take ‹*risk*›; accept ‹*obligation*›

eingehend *Adj.* detailed

Ein·gemachte *das; adj. Dekl.* preserved fruit/vegetables

ein|gemeinden *tr. V.* incorporate ‹*village*› (**in** + *Akk.*, **nach** into)

ein·geschnappt *Adj.* (ugs.) huffy

Ein·geständnis *das* admission

ein|gestehen *unr. tr. V.* admit

Eingeweide *das; ~s, ~:* entrails *pl.*; innards *pl.*

ein|gewöhnen *refl. V.* get used to one's new surroundings

ein|gießen *unr. tr., itr. V.* pour in

ein|gliedern *tr. V.* integrate (**in** + *Akk.* into); incorporate ‹*village, company*› (**in** + *Akk.* into); (einordnen) include (**in** + *Akk.* in)

Ein·gliederung *die* ▶ EINGLIEDERN: integration; incorporation; inclusion

ein|graben *unr. tr. V.* bury (**in** + *Akk.* in); sink ‹*pile, pipe*› (**in** + *Akk.* into)

ein|gravieren *tr. V.* engrave (**in** + *Akk.* on)

ein|greifen *unr. itr. V.* intervene (**in** + *Akk.* in)

Ein·griff *der* **(a)** intervention (**in** + *Akk.* in) **(b)** (Med.) operation

ein|haken 1 *tr. V.* **(a)** (mit Haken befestigen) fasten
(b) **sich** ~: link arms
2 *refl. V.* **sich bei jmdm.** ~: link arms with sb.

Ein·halt *der:* **jmdm./einer Sache ~ gebieten** *od.* **tun** (geh.) halt sb./sth.

ein|halten 1 *unr. tr. V.* keep ‹*appointment*›; meet ‹*deadline, commitments*›; keep to ‹*diet, speed limit, agreement*›; observe ‹*regulation*›
2 *unr. itr. V.* (geh.) stop

ein·heimisch *Adj.* native; home *attrib.* ‹*team*›

Einheimische *der/die; adj. Dekl.* local

Einheit *die;* ~, ~**en** unity

einheitlich 1 *Adj.* unified; (unterschiedslos) uniform ‹*dress*›; standard ‹*procedure, practice*›
2 *adv.* ~ **gekleidet sein** be dressed the same

einhellig 1 *Adj.* unanimous
2 *adv.* unanimously

ein|holen 1 *tr. V.* **(a)** catch up with ‹*person, vehicle*›
(b) make up ‹*arrears, time*›
2 *itr. V.* (ugs.) ▶ EINKAUFEN 1

ein·hundert *Kardinalz.* ▶ HUNDERT

einig *Adj.* **sich** (*Dat.*) ~ **sein** be agreed; **sich** (*Dat.*) ~ **werden** reach agreement

einig... *Indefinitpron. u. unbest. Zahlwort* some; ~**e wenige** a few; ~**e Hundert** several hundred

einigen 1 *tr. V.* unite
2 *refl. V.* reach an agreement

einigermaßen *Adv.* somewhat

Einigkeit *die;* ~ **(a)** unity
(b) (Übereinstimmung) agreement

ein·jährig *Adj.* (ein Jahr alt) one-year-old *attrib.;* one year old *pred.;* (ein Jahr dauernd) one-year *attrib.*

Ein·kauf *der* **(a) Einkäufe machen** do some shopping
(b) (eingekaufte Ware) purchase
(c) (Abteilung) purchasing department

ein|kaufen 1 *itr. V.* shop; ~ **gehen** go shopping
2 *tr. V.* buy; purchase

---

*alte Schreibung - vgl. Hinweis auf S. xiv

Ein·käufer *der,* **Ein·käuferin** *die* buyer

Einkaufs-: ~bummel *der* [leisurely] shopping expedition; **~liste** *die* shopping list; **~preis** *der* (Kaufmannsspr.) wholesale price; **~tasche** *die* shopping bag; **~tüte** *die* shopping bag; **~zentrum** *das* shopping centre; **~zettel** *der* shopping list

ein|kehren *itr. V.; mit sein* stop; **in einem Wirtshaus** ~: stop at an inn

ein|klammern *tr. V.* **etw.** ~: put sth. in brackets; bracket sth.

Ein·klang *der* harmony; **in** *od.* **im ~ stehen** accord

ein|kleben *tr. V.* stick in

ein|kleiden *tr. V.* clothe

ein|klemmen *tr. V.* **(a)** (quetschen) catch **(b)** (fest einfügen) clamp

ein|kochen *tr. V.* preserve ‹*fruit etc.*›

Einkommen *das;* ~**s,** ~: income

Einkommen·steuer *die* income tax

ein|kreisen *tr. V.* **(a) etw.** ~: put a circle round sth.
(b) (umzingeln) surround

Einkünfte *Pl.* income *sing.;* **feste** ~: a regular income

ein|laden¹ *unr. tr. V.* load ‹*goods*›

ein|laden² *unr. tr. V.* invite ‹*person*› (**zu** for)

einladend *Adj.* inviting

Ein·ladung *die* invitation

Ein·lage *die* **(a)** (in Brief) enclosure
(b) (Kochk.) *vegetables, dumplings, etc. added to a clear soup;*
(c) (Schuh~) arch support
(d) (Programm~) interlude

ein|lagern *tr. V.* store; lay in ‹*stores*›

Einlass, *Einlaß *der;* **Einlasses, Einlässe** admission

ein|lassen *unr. tr. V.* **(a)** (hereinlassen) admit; let in
(b) (einfüllen) run ‹*water*›

Ein·lauf *der* (Med.) enema

ein|laufen 1 *unr. itr. V.; mit sein* **(a)** ‹*ship*› come in
(b) (kleiner werden) shrink
2 *unr. tr. V.* wear in ‹*shoes*›>

ein|leben *refl. V.* settle down>

ein|legen *tr. V.* **(a)** load ‹*film*›; engage ‹*gear*›
(b) (Kochk.) pickle

ein|leiten *tr. V.* **(a)** introduce
(b) induce ‹*birth*›
(c) lead in; **etw. in etw.** (*Akk.*) ~: lead sth. into sth.

Ein·leitung *die* **(a)** introduction
(b) (einer Geburt) induction

ein|leuchten *itr. V.* **jmdm.** ~: be clear to sb.

einleuchtend *Adj.* plausible

ein|liefern *tr. V.* take ‹*letter, person*› (**bei, in** + *Akk.* to)

Einlieger·wohnung *die* ≈ granny flat
ein|lösen *tr. V.* cash ‹*cheque*›
ein|machen *tr. V.* preserve ‹*fruit etc.*›; (in Gläser) bottle
einmal [1] *Adv.* **(a)** once; **noch ~ so groß** [**wie**] twice as big [as]; **etw. noch ~ tun** do sth. again
(b) /'-'-/ (später) one day; (früher) once; **es war ~ ...:** once upon a time there was ...
[2] *Partikel* **nicht ~:** not even; **wieder ~:** yet again
Einmal·eins *das;* ~: [multiplication] tables *pl.*
einmalig [1] *Adj.* **(a)** unique; one-off ‹*payment, purchase*›
(b) (ugs.) fantastic (coll.)
[2] *adv.* (ugs.) really fantastically (coll.)
Ein·marsch *der* **(a)** entry
(b) (Besetzung) invasion (**in** + *Akk.* of)
ein|marschieren *itr. V.; mit sein* march in
ein|massieren *tr. V.* massage *or* rub in
ein|mauern *tr. V.* **(a)** immure ‹*prisoner, traitor*›; wall in ‹*relic, treasure*›
(b) (ins Mauerwerk einfügen) **etw. in die Wand** *usw.* **~:** set sth. into the wall *etc.*
ein|mischen *refl. V.* interfere (**in** + *Akk.* in)
ein|motten *tr. V.* **etw. ~:** put sth. into mothballs; (fig.) mothball
Ein·mündung *die* (von Straßen) junction
einmütig [1] *Adj.* unanimous
[2] *adv.* unanimously
ein|nähen *tr. V.* sew in
Einnahme *die;* **~, ~n** **(a)** income; (Staats~) revenue; (Kassen~) takings *pl.;*
(b) (von Arzneimitteln) taking
(c) (einer Stadt, Burg) taking
Einnahme·quelle *die* source of income; (des Staates) source of revenue
ein|nehmen *unr. tr. V.* **(a)** take; (verdienen) earn
(b) (ausfüllen) take up ‹*amount of room*›
(c) (beeinflussen) **jmdn. für sich ~:** win sb. over
einnehmend *Adj.* winning ‹*manner*›; **ein ~es Wesen haben** (scherzh.) take everything one can get
Ein·öde *die* barren waste
ein|ölen *tr. V.* **(a)** (mit Öl einreiben) **sich/jmdn. ~:** put *or* rub oil on oneself/sb.
(b) (ölen) oil
ein|ordnen [1] *tr. V.* arrange; put in order
[2] *refl. V.* **(a)** (Verkehrsw.) get into the correct lane; **„~"** 'get in lane'
(b) (sich einfügen) fit in
ein|packen [1] *tr. V.* pack (**in** + *Akk.* in); (einwickeln) wrap [up]
[2] *itr. V.* (ugs.) **er kann ~:** he's had it (coll.)
ein|parken *tr., itr. V.* park
ein|pflanzen *tr. V.* **(a)** plant
(b) (Med., fig.) implant
ein|prägen *tr. V.* **(a)** stamp (**in** + *Akk.* into, on)
(b) (fig.) **sich** (*Dat.*) **etw. ~:** memorize sth.; **jmdm. etw. ~:** impress sth. on sb.
einprägsam *Adj.* easily remembered
ein|pudern *tr. V.* powder; **sich** (*Dat.*) **das Gesicht ~:** powder one's face
ein|rahmen *tr. V.* frame
ein|räumen *tr. V.* **(a)** put away
(b) (füllen) **seinen Schrank ~:** put one's things away in one's cupboard; **ein Zimmer ~:** put the furniture into a room
(c) (zugestehen) admit
ein|reden [1] *tr. V.* **jmdm. etw. ~:** talk sb. into believing sth.; **sich** (*Dat.*) **~, dass ...:** persuade oneself that ...
[2] *itr. V.* **auf jmdn. ~:** talk insistently to sb.
ein|regnen *refl. V.; unpers.* **es hat sich eingeregnet** it's begun to rain steadily
ein|reiben *unr. tr. V.* rub ‹*substance*› in; **etw. mit Öl ~:** rub oil into sth.
ein|reichen *tr. V.* submit; lodge ‹*complaint*›; tender ‹*resignation*›
ein|reihen [1] *refl. V.* **sich in etw.** (*Akk.*) **~:** join sth.
[2] *tr. V.* **jmdn. in eine Kategorie ~:** place sb. in a category
Einreiher *der;* **~s, ~:** single-breasted suit/jacket
Ein·reise *die* entry
Einreise·erlaubnis *die* entry permit
ein|reisen *itr. V.; mit sein* enter; **nach Schweden ~:** enter Sweden
ein|reißen [1] *unr. tr. V.* **(a)** pull down ‹*building*›
(b) (einen Riss machen in) tear; rip
[2] *unr. itr. V.; mit sein* tear; rip
ein|renken *tr. V.* **(a)** (Med.) set
(b) (ugs.: bereinigen) sort out
ein|richten [1] *refl. V.* **sich schön ~:** furnish one's home beautifully; **sich häuslich ~:** make oneself at home
[2] *tr. V.* furnish ‹*flat, house*›; fit out ‹*shop*›; equip ‹*laboratory*›
Ein·richtung *die* **(a)** furnishing
(b) (Mobiliar) furnishings *pl.*
ein|rollen [1] *tr. V.* roll up ‹*carpet etc.*›; put ‹*hair*› in curlers
[2] *itr. V.; mit sein* roll in
ein|rosten *itr. V.; mit sein* go rusty
ein|rücken [1] *itr. V.; mit sein* (einmarschieren) move in
[2] *tr. V.* indent ‹*line, heading, etc.*›
eins [1] *Kardinalz.* one; **es ist ~:** it is one o'clock; **~ zu null** one-nil; **~ zu ~:** one all; **„~, zwei, drei!"** 'ready, steady, go'
[2] *Adj.* **mir ist alles ~:** it's all the same to me
[3] *Indefinitpron.* ▶ IRGENDEIN A
Eins *die;* **~, ~en** **(a)** one
(b) (Schulnote) one; A
einsam *Adj.* **(a)** lonely ‹*person, decision*›
(b) (einzeln) solitary ‹*tree, wanderer*›

(c) (abgelegen) isolated
(d) (menschenleer) deserted

Einsamkeit *die;* **~** **(a)** loneliness
(b) (Alleinsein) solitude
(c) (Abgeschiedenheit) isolation

ein|sammeln *tr. V.* **(a)** (auflesen) pick up; gather up
(b) (sich aushändigen lassen) collect in; collect ‹*tickets*›

Ein·satz *der* **(a)** (aus Stoff) inset; (in Kochtopf, Nähkasten usw.) compartment
(b) (Betrag) stake
(c) (Gebrauch) use; (von Truppen) deployment

Einsatz-: ~befehl *der* order to go into action; **den ~befehl haben** have operational command; **~leiter** *der,* **~leiterin** *die* head of operations; **~wagen** *der* (der Polizei) police car; (der Feuerwehr) fire engine; (Notarztwagen) ambulance

ein|saugen *unr.* (*auch regelm.*) *tr. V.* suck in; breathe [in] ‹*fresh air*›

ein|schalten 1 *tr. V.* **(a)** switch on ‹*radio, TV, electricity, etc.*›
(b) (fig.) call in ‹*press, police, expert, etc.*›
2 *refl. V.* **(a)** switch [itself] on
(b) (eingreifen) intervene (**in** + *Akk.* in)

Einschalt·quote *die* (Rundf.) listening figures *pl.;* (Ferns.) viewing figures *pl.*

ein|schärfen *tr. V.* **jmdm. etw. ~:** impress sth. [up]on sb.

ein|schätzen *tr. V.* judge ‹*person*›; assess ‹*situation, income, damages*›; (schätzen) estimate

Ein·schätzung *die* ▸ EINSCHÄTZEN: judging; assessment; estimation

ein|schenken *tr., itr. V.* **(a)** (eingießen) pour [out]; **jmdm. etw. ~:** pour out sth. for sb.
(b) (füllen) fill [up] ‹*glass, cup*›

ein|scheren *itr. V.; mit sein* **auf eine Fahrspur ~:** get *or* move into a lane

ein|schicken *tr. V.* send in

ein|schieben *unr. tr. V.* **(a)** push in
(b) (einfügen) insert; put on ‹*trains, buses*›

ein|schiffen *tr., refl. V.* embark

einschl. *Abk.* = **einschließlich** incl.

ein|schlafen *unr. itr. V.; mit sein* **(a)** fall asleep
(b) (verhüll.: sterben) pass away
(c) (gefühllos werden) go to sleep

ein|schläfern *tr. V.* **(a) jmdn. ~:** send sb. to sleep, (betäuben) put sb. to sleep
(b) (schmerzlos töten) **ein Tier ~:** put an animal to sleep

einschläfernd 1 *Adj.* soporific
2 *adv.* **~ wirken** have a soporific effect

ein|schlagen 1 *unr. tr. V.* **(a)** knock in
(b) (zertrümmern) smash [in]
(c) (einwickeln) wrap up ‹*present*›; cover ‹*book*›
2 *unr. itr. V.* **(a)** ‹*bomb*› land; ‹*lightning*› strike
(b) auf jmdn./etw. ~: rain blows on sb./sth.

einschlägig 1 *Adj.* specialist ‹*journal, shop*›; relevant ‹*literature, passage*›
2 *adv.* **er ist ~ vorbestraft** he has previous convictions for a similar offence/similar offences

ein|schleichen *unr. refl. V.* steal in

ein|schließen *unr. tr. V.* **(a) etw. in etw.** (*Dat.*) **~:** lock sth. up [in sth.]; **jmdn./sich ~:** lock sb./oneself in
(b) (umgeben) surround

einschließlich 1 *Präp. mit Gen.* including; **~ der Unkosten** including expenses
2 *adv.* **bis ~ 30. Juni** up to and including 30 June

ein|schmeicheln *refl. V.* **sich bei jmdm. ~:** ingratiate oneself with sb.

ein|schmuggeln *tr. V.* smuggle in

ein|schneiden *unr. tr. V.* **(a)** make a cut in
(b) (einritzen) carve

einschneidend *Adj.* drastic

ein|schneien *itr. V.; mit sein* get snowed in

Ein·schnitt *der* cut

ein|schränken 1 *tr. V.* **(a)** reduce, curb ‹*expenditure, consumption*›
(b) (einengen) limit; restrict; **jmdn. in seinen Rechten ~:** limit *or* restrict sb.'s rights
2 *refl. V.* economize

Einschränkung *die;* **~, ~en (a)** restriction; limitation
(b) (Vorbehalt) reservation

ein|schrauben *tr. V.* screw in

ein|schreiben *unr. tr. V.* **(a)** (Postw.) register ‹*letter*›
(b) (eintragen) **sich/jmdn. ~:** enter one's/sb.'s name

Ein·schreiben *das* (Postw.) registered letter; **per ~:** by registered mail

ein|schreiten *unr. itr. V.* intervene

ein|schrumpfen *itr. V.; mit sein* shrivel up; (fig.) dwindle

ein|schüchtern *tr. V.* intimidate

ein|schulen *tr. V.* **eingeschult werden** start school

ein|sehen *unr. tr. V.* **(a)** (überblicken) see into
(b) (prüfend lesen) look at
(c) (erkennen) realize
(d) (begreifen) see

ein|seifen *tr. V.* lather

ein·seitig 1 *Adj.* **(a)** on one side *postpos.;*
(b) (tendenziös) one-sided
2 *adv.* **(a)** on one side
(b) (tendenziös) one-sidedly

ein|senden *unr.* (*auch regelm.*) *tr. V.* send [in]

*old spelling - see note on page xiv

Ein·sender *der*, **Ein·senderin** *die;* ~, ~**nen** sender; (bei einem Preisausschreiben) entrant

Einsende·schluss, ***Einsende·schluß** *der* closing date

ein|setzen 1 *tr. V.* **(a)** (hineinsetzen) put in **(b)** put on ‹*special train etc.*› **(c)** (ernennen) appoint **(d)** (in Aktion treten lassen) use **(e)** (aufs Spiel setzen) stake ‹*money*› **(f)** (riskieren) risk 2 *itr. V.* begin; ‹*storm*› break 3 *refl. V.* (sich engagieren) **ich werde mich dafür ~, dass ...**: I shall do what I can to see that ...; **sich nicht genug ~**: ‹*pupil*› be lacking application; ‹*minister*› be lacking in commitment

Ein·sicht *die* **(a)** view (**in** + *Akk.* into) **(b)** (Einblick) **~ in die Akten nehmen** take *or* have a look at the files **(c)** (Erkenntnis) insight

einsichtig *Adj.* **(a)** (verständnisvoll) understanding **(b)** (verständlich) comprehensible

Ein·siedler *der*, **Ein·siedlerin** *die* hermit

ein·silbig *Adj.* **(a)** monosyllabic ‹*word*› **(b)** (fig.) taciturn ‹*person*›

Einsilbigkeit *die;* ~ (fig.) taciturnity

ein|sinken *unr. itr. V.* sink in

ein|sitzen *unr. itr. V.* (Rechtsw.) serve a prison sentence; **er sitzt für drei Jahre ein** he is serving three years *or* a three-year sentence

Einsitzer *der;* ~**s**, ~: single-seater

einsitzig *Adj.* single-seater *attrib.*

ein|spannen *tr. V.* harness ‹*horse*›; put in ‹*paper*›: fix ‹*fabric*›; clamp ‹*work*›

ein|sparen *tr. V.* save

Einsparung *die;* ~, ~**en** saving (**an** + *Dat.* in); ~**en an Kosten/Energie/Material** savings *or* economies in costs/energy/materials

ein|speichern *tr. V.* (DV) feed in; input

ein|speisen *tr. V.* (Technik, DV) feed in

ein|sperren *tr. V.* lock up

einsprachig *Adj.* monolingual

ein|springen *unr. itr. V.; mit sein* stand in; (aushelfen) step in and help out

ein|spritzen *tr. V.* inject; **jmdm. etw. ~**: inject sb. with sth.

Einspritz·motor *der* fuel-injection engine

Ein·spruch *der* objection (**gegen** to)

einspurig 1 *Adj.* single-track ‹*road*› 2 *adv.* **die Autobahn ist nur ~ befahrbar** only one lane of the motorway is open

einst *Adv.* (geh.) once

ein|stampfen *tr. V.* pulp ‹*books*›

Ein·stand *der:* **seinen ~ geben** celebrate starting a new job

ein|stecken *tr. V.* **(a)** put in **(b)** (mitnehmen) put ‹*sth.*› in one's pocket/bag *etc.*

ein|stehen *unr. itr. V.* **für jmdn. ~**: vouch for sb.; **für etw. ~**: take responsibility for sth.

ein|steigen *unr. itr. V.; mit sein* **(a)** (in ein Fahrzeug) get in; **in ein Auto ~**: get into a car; **in den Bus ~**: get on the bus **(b)** (eindringen) climb in

einstellbar *Adj.* adjustable

ein|stellen 1 *tr. V.* **(a)** (einordnen) put away ‹*books etc.*› **(b)** (unterstellen) put in ‹*car, bicycle*› **(c)** (beschäftigen) take on ‹*workers*› **(d)** (regulieren) adjust **(e)** (beenden) stop; call off ‹*search, strike*› **(f)** (Sport) equal ‹*record*› 2 *refl. V.* **(a)** arrive **(b)** ‹*pain, worry*› begin; ‹*success*› come; ‹*symptoms, consequences*› appear **(c)** **sich auf etw.** (*Akk.*) **~**: prepare oneself for sth.; **sich schnell auf neue Situationen ~**: adjust quickly to new situations

ein·stellig *Adj.* single-figure *attrib.*

Ein·stellung *die* **(a)** (von Arbeitskräften) employment **(b)** (Regulierung) adjustment **(c)** (Beendigung) stopping **(d)** (Sport) **die ~ eines Rekordes** the equalling of a record **(e)** (Ansicht) attitude; **ihre politische/religiöse ~**: her political/religious views *pl.;* **(f)** (Film) take

Ein·stich *der* **(a)** insertion **(b)** (~stelle) puncture; prick

Ein·stieg *der;* ~[e]**s**, ~**e** (Eingang) entrance; (Tür) door/doors; **„kein ~“** 'exit only'

Einstiegs·droge *die* come-on drug

ein|stimmen 1 *itr. V.* join in 2 *tr. V.* **jmdn. auf etw.** (*Akk.*) **~**: get sb. in the [right] mood for sth.

einstimmig 1 *Adj.* **(a)** (Musik) for one voice **(b)** (einmütig) unanimous ‹*decision, vote*› 2 *adv.* **(a)** (Musik) in unison **(b)** (einmütig) unanimously

ein·stöckig *Adj.* single-storey *attrib.*

ein|stöpseln *tr. V.* plug in ‹*telephone, electrical device*›

Ein·strahlung *die* irradiation; (Sonnen~) insolation

ein|streichen *unr. tr. V.* (ugs.: für sich behalten) pocket ‹*money, winnings, etc.*›; (ugs. abwertend) rake in (coll.) ‹*money, profits, etc.*›

ein|studieren *tr. V.* rehearse

ein|stufen *tr. V.* classify; categorize

ein·stündig *Adj.* one-hour *attrib.*

ein|stürmen *itr. V.* **mit Fragen auf jmdn. ~**: besiege sb. with questions

Ein·sturz *der* collapse

ein|stürzen *itr. V.; mit sein* collapse

einst·weilen *Adv.* for the time being

eintägig *Adj.* one-day *attrib.*

Eintags·fliege *die* (Zool.) mayfly; (fig. ugs.) seven-day wonder

ein|tauchen 1 *tr. V.* dip; (untertauchen) immerse
2 *itr. V.; mit sein* dive in; ‹*submarine*› dive

ein|tauschen *tr. V.* exchange (**gegen** for)

ein·tausend *Kardinalz.*: ▶ TAUSEND

ein|teilen *tr. V.* **(a)** divide up; classify ‹*plants, species*›
(b) (disponieren, verplanen) organize

einteilig *Adj.* one-piece

ein|tippen *tr. V.* (in die Kasse) register; (in einen Rechner) key in

eintönig 1 *Adj.* monotonous
2 *adv.* monotonously

Eintönigkeit *die;* ~: monotony

Ein·topf *der* stew

Ein·tracht *die* harmony

ein·trächtig *Adj.* harmonious

Eintrag *der;* ~**[e]s, Einträge** entry

ein|tragen *unr. tr. V.* **(a)** enter
(b) (Amtsspr.) register

einträglich *Adj.* lucrative

ein|treffen *unr. itr. V.; mit sein* **(a)** arrive
(b) (verwirklicht werden) come true

ein|treiben *unr. tr. V.* collect ‹*taxes, debts*›; (durch Gerichtsverfahren) recover ‹*debts, money*›

Eintreibung *die;* ~, ~**en** (von Steuern, Schulden) collection; (durch Gerichtsverfahren) recovery

ein|treten 1 *unr. itr. V.; mit sein* **(a)** enter; **bitte, treten Sie ein!** please come in
(b) (Mitglied werden) **in einen Verein/einen Orden** ~: join a club/enter a religious order
(c) (Raumfahrt) enter
2 *unr. tr. V.* kick in ‹*door, window, etc.*›

ein|trichtern *tr. V.* (salopp) **jmdm. etw.** ~: drum sth. into sb.

Ein·tritt *der* **(a)** entry; entrance; **vor dem ~ in die Verhandlungen** (fig.) before entering into negotiations
(b) (Beitritt) **der ~ in einen Verein/einen Orden** joining a club/entering a religious order
(c) (von Raketen) entry
(d) (Zugang, Eintrittsgeld) admission
(e) (Beginn) onset; **~ der Dunkelheit** nightfall

Eintritts-: ~**geld** *das* admission fee; ~**karte** *die* admission ticket; ~**preis** *der* admission charge

ein|trocknen *itr. V.; mit sein* dry; ‹*water, toothpaste*› dry up; ‹*leather*› dry out; ‹*berry, fruit*› shrivel

ein|üben *tr. V.* practise

Ein·vernehmen *das;* ~**s** harmony; (Übereinstimmung) agreement

ein·vernehmlich (Amtsspr.) 1 *Adv.* conjointly
2 *adj.* conjoint

einverstanden *Adj.* **~ sein** agree; **mit jmdm./etw. ~ sein** approve of sb./sth.

Ein·verständnis *das* consent (**zu** to)

Ein·waage *die* (Kaufmannsspr.) contents *pl.*

ein|wachsen *unr. itr. V.; mit sein* grow into the flesh; **eingewachsen** ingrown ‹*toenail*›

Einwand *der;* ~**[e]s, Einwände** objection (**gegen** to)

Ein·wanderer *der,* **Ein·wanderin** *die* immigrant

ein|wandern *itr. V.; mit sein* immigrate (**in** + *Akk.* into)

Ein·wanderung *die* immigration

Einwanderungs-: ~**behörde** *die* immigration authorities *pl.;* ~**land** *das* country of immigration

einwand·frei 1 *Adj.* flawless; impeccable ‹*behaviour*›; indisputable ‹*proof*›
2 *adv.* flawlessly; ‹*behave*› impeccably; ‹*prove*› beyond question

ein|wechseln *tr. V.* **(a)** change ‹*money*›
(b) (Sport) substitute ‹*player*›

ein|wecken *tr. V.* preserve; bottle

Ein·weg-: ~**flasche** *die* non-returnable bottle; ~**pfand** *das* deposit on a/the disposable container; ~**spritze** *die* disposable [hypodermic] syringe; ~**verpackung** *die* disposable container

ein|weichen *tr. V.* soak

ein|weihen *tr. V.* open [officially] ‹*bridge, road*›; dedicate ‹*monument*›

Einweihung *die;* ~, ~**en** ▶ EINWEIHEN: [official] opening; dedication

ein|weisen *unr. tr. V.* **(a)** (in eine Tätigkeit) introduce
(b) (in ein Amt) install

ein|wenden *unr.* (*auch regelm.*) *tr. V.* **dagegen lässt sich vieles** ~: there is a lot to be said against that

ein|werfen *unr. tr. V.* **(a)** mail ‹*letter*›; insert ‹*coin*›
(b) smash ‹*window*›
(c) throw in ‹*ball*›
(d) (bemerken, sagen) throw in ‹*remark*›

ein|wickeln *tr. V.* wrap [up]

ein|willigen *itr. V.* agree (**in** + *Akk.* to)

Einwilligung *die;* ~, ~**en** agreement

ein|wirken **(a)** (beeinflussen) **auf jmdn.** ~: influence sb.
(b) (eine Wirkung ausüben) have an effect (**auf** + *Akk.* on)

Ein·wirkung *die* (Einfluss) influence; (Wirkung) effect

Einwohner *der;* ~**s**, ~, **Einwohnerin** *die;* ~, ~**nen** inhabitant

Einwohner·zahl *die* population

Ein·wurf *der* **(a)** insertion; (von Briefen) mailing
(b) (Ballspiele) throw-in
(c) (Bemerkung) interjection

Ein·zahl *die* singular

ein|zahlen *tr. V.* pay in; **Geld auf ein Konto** ~: pay money into an account

Ein·zahlung *die* payment

ein|zäunen *tr. V.* fence in; enclose

*alte Schreibung - vgl. Hinweis auf S. xiv

Einzäunung *die;* ~, ~**en** fencing-in
ein|zeichnen *tr. V.* draw *or* mark in
einzeilig *Adj.* one-line *attrib.*
Einzel *das;* ~**s**, ~ (Sport) singles *pl.*
Einzel-: ~**bett** *das* single bed; ~**fall** *der* **(a)** particular case; **(b)** (Ausnahme) isolated case; ~**gänger** *der;* ~~**s**, ~~, ~**gängerin** *die;* ~~, ~~**nen** loner; ~**haft** *die* solitary confinement;
Einzel·handel *der* retail trade
Einzelhandels·preis *der* retail price
Einzel·händler *der,* ~**händlerin** *die* retailer
Einzelheit *die;* ~, ~**en** **(a)** detail **(b)** (einzelner Umstand) particular
Einzel·kind *das* only child
Einzeller *der;* ~**s**, ~ (Biol.) unicellular organism
einzeln *Adj.* **(a)** (für sich allein) individual **(b)** (allein stehend) solitary ‹*building, tree*›; single ‹*lady, gentleman*› **(c)** ~**e** (wenige) a few; (einige) some **(d)** *substantivisch* **der/jeder Einzelne** the/each individual; **Einzelnes** (manches) some things *pl.;* **das Einzelne** the particular
Einzel-: ~**preis** *der* individual price; ~**teil** *das* individual part; ~**zelle** *die* single cell; ~**zimmer** *das* single room
ein|ziehen [1] *unr. tr. V.* **(a)** put in; thread in ‹*tape, elastic*› **(b)** (einholen) haul in ‹*net*› **(c)** (einatmen) breathe in ‹*scent, fresh air*›; inhale ‹*smoke*› **(d)** (einberufen) call up ‹*recruits*› **(e)** (beitreiben) collect [2] *unr. itr. V.; mit sein* **(a)** ‹*liquid*› soak in **(b)** (einkehren) enter **(c)** (in eine Wohnung) move in
einzig [1] *Adj.* only; **kein** ~**es Wort** not a single word [2] *adv.* **(a)** *intensivierend bei Adj.* extraordinarily **(b)** (ausschließlich) only; **das** ~ **Wahre** the only thing
einzig·artig [1] *Adj.* unique [2] *adv.* uniquely
Einzigartigkeit *die,* **Einzigkeit** *die* uniqueness
Ein·zug *der* **(a)** entry (**in** + *Akk.* into) **(b)** (in eine Wohnung) move
Einzugs·bereich *der* catchment area
Eis *das;* ~**es** **(a)** ice; ~ **laufen** ice-skate **(b)** (Speise~) ice cream; **ein** ~ **am Stiel** an ice lolly (Brit.) *or* (Amer.) ice pop
Eis-: ~**bahn** *die* ice rink; ~**bär** *der* polar bear; ~**becher** *der* ice cream sundae; ~**bein** *das* (Kochk.) knuckle of pork; ~**berg** *der* iceberg; ~**beutel** *der* ice bag; ~**blume** *die* frost flower; ~**bombe** *die* (Gastr.) bombe glacée; ~**brecher** *der* ice-breaker; ~**café** *das* ice cream parlour
Ei·schnee *der* stiffly beaten egg white
Eis·diele *die* ice cream parlour
Eisen *das;* ~**s**, ~: iron
Eisen·bahn *die* **(a)** railway; railroad (Amer.); **mit der** ~ **fahren** go by train **(b)** (Bahnstrecke) railway line; railroad track (Amer.)
Eisenbahn·abteil *das* railway *or* (Amer.) railroad compartment
Eisenbahner *der;* ~**s**, ~: railwayman; railway worker; railroader (Amer.)
Eisenbahnerin *die;* ~, ~**nen** railway worker
Eisenbahn·unglück *das* train crash
Eisen-: ~**erz** *das* iron ore; ~**kette** *die* iron chain; ~**ring** *der* iron ring; ~**stange** *die* iron bar; ~**waren** *Pl.* ironmongery *sing.;* ~**zeit** *die* Iron Age
eisern [1] *Adj.* (auch fig.) iron [2] *adv.* resolutely; ‹*save, train*› with iron determination; ~ **durchgreifen** take drastic measures
eis-, Eis-: ~**fach** *das* freezing compartment; ~**frei** *Adj.* ice-free; ~**gekühlt** *Adj.* iced; ~**glatt** *Adj.* **(a)** icy ‹*road*›; **(b)** /'-'-/ (ugs.) ‹*floor, steps*› as slippery as ice; ~**glätte** *die* black ice; ~**hockey** *das* ice hockey
eisig [1] *Adj.* **(a)** icy ‹*wind, cold*›; icy [cold] ‹*water*› **(b)** (fig.) frosty [2] *adv.* **(a)** ~ **kalt sein** be icy cold **(b)** (fig.) ‹*smile*› frostily
***eisig·kalt** *Adj.* ▶ EISKALT 1A
eis-, Eis-: ~**kaffee** *der* iced coffee; ~**kalt** [1] *Adj.* **(a)** ice-cold ‹*drink*›; freezing cold ‹*weather*›; **(b)** (gefühllos) icy; ice-cold ‹*look*›; [2] *adv.* **es lief mir** ~**kalt über den Rücken** a cold shiver went down my spine; ~**kunst·lauf** *der* figure skating; ~**kunst·läufer** *der,* ~**kunst·läuferin** *die* figure skater; ~**lauf** *der* ice skating; *~**|laufen** ▶ EIS A; ~**laufen** *das;* ~~**s** ice skating; ~**läufer** *der,* ~**läuferin** *die* ice skater
Ei·sprung *der* (Physiol.) ovulation
Eis-: ~**regen** *der* sleet; ~**schrank** *der* refrigerator; ~**sport** *der* ice sports *pl.;* ~**tanz** *der* (Sport) ice dancing; ~**waffel** *die* [ice cream] wafer; ~**wein** *der: wine made from grapes frozen on the vine;* ~**würfel** *der* ice cube; ~**zapfen** *der* icicle; ~**zeit** *die* ice age
eitel *Adj.* vain
Eitelkeit *die;* ~, ~**en** vanity
Eiter *der;* ~**s** pus
eitern *itr. V.* suppurate
eitrig *Adj.* suppurating
Ei·weiß *das;* ~**es**, ~**e** **(a)** egg white **(b)** (Protein) protein
eiweiß-: ~**arm** *Adj.* low-protein *attrib.;* low in protein *postpos.;* ~**reich** *Adj.* high-protein *attrib.;* rich in protein *postpos.*
Ejakulation *die;* ~, ~**en** (Physiol.) ejaculation

Ekel¹ *der;* **~s** revulsion; **[einen] ~ vor etw.** (*Dat.*) **haben** have a revulsion for sth.
Ekel² *das;* **~s, ~** (ugs. abwertend) horror; **er ist ein [altes] ~:** he is quite obnoxious
ekelhaft *Adj.* revolting ‹*sight*›; horrible ‹*weather, person*›
ekeln [1] *refl. V.* be disgusted; **sich vor etw.** (*Dat.*) **~:** find sth. repulsive
[2] *tr., itr. V.* (*unpers.*) **es ekelt mich** *od.* **mir ekelt davor** I find it revolting
eklig *Adj.* **(a)** ▶ EKELHAFT;
(b) (ugs.: gemein) nasty
Ekstase /ɛk'sta:zə/ *die;* **~, ~n** ecstasy
Ekzem *das;* **~s, ~e** (Med.) eczema
Elan *der;* **~s** zest; vigour
elastisch *Adj.* elasticated ‹*material*›; springy ‹*surface*›; supple ‹*person, body*›
Elastizität *die;* **~:** elasticity; (Federkraft) springiness; (Geschmeidigkeit) suppleness
Elch *der;* **~[e]s, ~e** elk; (in Nordamerika) moose
Elefant *der;* **~en, ~en** elephant
elegant [1] *Adj.* elegant
[2] *adv.* elegantly
Eleganz *die;* **~:** elegance
elektrifizieren *tr. V.* electrify
Elektrifizierung *die;* **~, ~en** electrification
Elektriker *der;* **~s, ~, Elektrikerin** *die;* **~, ~nen** electrician
elektrisch [1] *Adj.* electric; electrical ‹*resistance, wiring, system*›
[2] *adv.* **~ kochen** cook with electricity; **~ geladen sein** be electrically charged
elektrisieren [1] *tr. V.* (Med.) treat using electricity
[2] *refl. V.* get an electric shock
Elektrizität *die;* **~** electricity
Elektrizitäts·werk *das* power station
elektro-, Elektro-: ~artikel *der* electrical appliance; **~auto** *das* electric car; **~gerät** *das* electrical appliance; **~geschäft** *das* electrical shop *or* (Amer.) store; **~herd** *der* electric cooker; **~magnet** *der* electromagnet; **~magnetisch** [1] *Adj.* electromagnetic; [2] *adv.* electromagnetically; **~mobil** *das;* **~~s, ~~e** electric car; **~motor** *der* electric motor
Elektron *das;* **~s, ~en** /-'tro:nən/ electron
Elektronen-: ~[ge]hirn *das* (ugs.) electronic brain (coll.); **~hülle** *die* electron shell; **~rechner** *der* electronic computer
Elektronik *die;* **~ (a)** electronics *sing., no art.;*
(b) (Teile) electronics *pl.*
Elektronik·schrott *der* scrapped electrical appliances *pl.*
elektronisch [1] *Adj.* electronic
[2] *adv.* electronically

*old spelling - see note on page xiv

elektro-, Elektro-: ~rasierer *der* electric shaver; **~smog** *der* (Jargon) electronic smog; **~statisch** [1] *Adj.* electrostatic; [2] *adv.* electrostatically; **~technik** *die* electrical engineering *no art.;* **~techniker** *der,* **~technikerin** *die* **(a)** electronics engineer; **(b)** (Elektriker) electrician
Element *das;* **~[e]s, ~e** element
elementar *Adj.* **(a)** (grundlegend) fundamental
(b) (einfach) elementary ‹*knowledge*›
(c) (naturhaft) elemental ‹*force*›
Elementar·teilchen *das* (Physik) elementary particle
elend *Adj.* wretched; miserable
Elend *das;* **~s** misery
Elends-: ~quartier *das* slum [dwelling]; **~viertel** *das* slum area
elf *Kardinalz.* eleven
Elf *die;* **~, ~en (a)** eleven
(b) (Sport) team; side
Elfe *die;* **~, ~n** fairy
Elfen·bein *das* ivory
Elfenbein-: ~schnitzerei *die* ivory carving; **~turm** *der* (fig.) ivory tower
Elf·meter *der* (Fußball) penalty; **einen ~ schießen** take a penalty
Elfmeter·schießen *das;* **~s** (Fußball) **durch ~:** by *or* on penalties
eliminieren *tr. V.* eliminate
elitär *adj.* élitist; **ein ~es Bewusstsein** an élite-awareness
Elite *die;* **~, ~n** élite
Elite·truppe *die* (Milit.) élite *or* crack force
Ell·bogen *der; Pl.* **~:** elbow
Elle *die;* **~, ~n** (Anat.) ulna
Ellen·bogen *der; Pl.* **~:** ▶ ELLBOGEN
Ellipse *die;* **~, ~n** ellipse
Elsass, *Elsaß *das;* **~** *od.* **Elsasses** Alsace
Elster *die;* **~, ~n** magpie
elterlich *Adj.* parental
Eltern *Pl.* parents *pl.*
eltern-, Eltern-: ~abend *der* (Schulw.) parents' evening; **~bei·rat** *der* (Schulw.) parents' association; **~haus** *das* home; **~los** *Adj.* orphaned; **~teil** *der* parent; **~zeit** *die* [period of] parental leave
Email /e'mai:/ *das;* **~s, ~s, Emaille** /e'maljə/ *die;* **~, ~n** enamel
E-Mail /'i:meɪl/ *die;* **~, ~s** (DV) e-mail
Emanzipation *die;* **~, ~en** emancipation
emanzipieren *refl. V.* emancipate
emanzipiert *Adj.* emancipated; emancipated, liberated ‹*woman*›
Embargo *das;* **~s, ~s** embargo
Emblem *das;* **~s, ~e** emblem
Embryo *der;* **~s, ~nen** /-y'o:nən/ *od.* **~s** embryo
Embryonen·forschung *die* embryo research

Emigrant *der;* **~en, ~en, Emigrantin** *die;* **~, ~nen** emigrant; (Flüchtling) emigré
Emigration *die;* **~, ~en** (das Emigrieren) emigration
emigrieren *itr. V.; mit sein* emigrate
Emission (a) (Physik, Ökologie) emission
(b) (Ausgabe [von Briefmarken, Wertpapieren]) issue
emissions·arm *Adj.* low-emission; **~ sein** be low in emissions
Emotion *die;* **~, ~en** emotion
emotional [1] *Adj.* emotional; emotive ‹*topic, question*›
[2] *adv.* emotionally
Empfang *der;* **~[e]s, Empfänge** reception; (Entgegennahme) receipt
empfangen *unr. tr. V.* receive
Empfänger *der;* **~s, ~ (a)** recipient; (eines Briefs) addressee
(b) (Empfangsgerät) receiver
Empfängerin *die;* **~, ~nen** ▶ EMPFÄNGER A
empfänglich *Adj.* **(a)** receptive (**für** to)
(b) (beeinflussbar) susceptible
Empfänglichkeit *die;* **~ (a)** (Zugänglichkeit) receptivity, receptiveness (**für** to)
(b) (Beeinflussbarkeit) susceptibility (**für** to)
Empfängnis *die;* **~**: conception
Empfängnis·verhütung *die* contraception
empfangs-, Empfangs-: ~berechtigt *Adj.* authorized to receive payment/goods *postpos.;* **~chef** *der* head receptionist; **~dame** *die* receptionist; **~halle** *die* reception lobby
empfehlen [1] *unr. tr. V.* recommend
[2] *unr. refl. V.* **(a)** take one's leave
(b) *unpers.* **es empfiehlt sich, ... zu ...**: it's advisable to ...
empfehlens·wert *Adj.* **(a)** to be recommended *postpos.;* recommendable
(b) (ratsam) advisable
Empfehlung *die;* **~, ~en (a)** recommendation
(b) (Empfehlungsschreiben) letter of recommendation
empfiehl *Imperativ Sg. v.* EMPFEHLEN
empfiehlst *2. Pers. Sg. Präsens v.* EMPFEHLEN
empfiehlt *3. Pers. Sg. Präsens v.* EMPFEHLEN
empfinden *unr. tr. V.* **(a)** (wahrnehmen) feel
(b) (auffassen) **etw. als Beleidigung ~**: feel sth. to be an insult
Empfinden *das;* **~s** feeling; **für mein** *od.* **nach meinem ~**: to my mind
empfindlich [1] *Adj.* **(a)** sensitive; fast ‹*film*›
(b) (leicht beleidigt) sensitive
(c) (anfällig) **zart und ~**: delicate
(d) (spürbar) severe ‹*punishment, shortage*›
[2] *adv.* **~ auf etw.** (*Akk.*) **reagieren** (sensibel) be susceptible to sth.; (beleidigt) react oversensitively to sth.
Empfindlichkeit *die;* **~, ~en** ▶ EMPFINDLICH: sensitivity; severity; (eines Films) speed
empfindsam *Adj.* sensitive ‹*nature*›
Empfindung *die;* **~, ~en** (Gefühl) feeling
empfing *1. u. 3. Pers. Sg. Prät. v.* EMPFANGEN
empfohlen [1] *2. Part. v.* EMPFEHLEN;
[2] *Adj.* recommended
empirisch [1] *Adj.* empirical
[2] *adv.* empirically
empor *Adv.* (geh.) upwards
empören [1] *tr. V.* fill with indignation; outrage
[2] *refl. V.* become indignant *or* outraged
empörend *Adj.* outrageous
empört *Adj.* outraged
Empörung *die;* **~, ~en** outrage
emsig [1] *Adj.* industrious ‹*person*›; bustling ‹*activity*›
[2] *adv.* industriously
Emu *der;* **~s, ~s** (Zool.) emu
Ende *das;* **~s, ~n** end; **am ~ der Straße/Stadt** at the end of the road/town; **am/bis/gegen ~ des Monats** at/by/towards the end of the month; **~ April** at the end of April; **zu ~ sein** ‹*patience, war*› be at an end; ‹*school*› be over; ‹*film, game*› have finished; **~ gut, alles gut** all's well that ends well (prov.)
End·effekt *der* **im ~**: in the end; in the final analysis
enden *itr. V.* **(a)** end; ‹*programme*› finish
(b) in der Gosse ~: end up in the gutter; (dort sterben) die in the gutter
end-, End-: ~ergebnis *das* final result; **~gültig** [1] *Adj.* final ‹*consent, decision*›; conclusive ‹*evidence*›; [2] *adv.* **das ist ~gültig vorbei** that's all over and done with; **sich ~gültig trennen** separate for good; **~haltestelle** *die* terminus; **~kampf** *der* (Sport) final; (Milit.) final battle; **~lauf** *der* (Sport) final
endlich *Adv.* **(a)** (nach langer Zeit) at last
(b) (schließlich) in the end
end-, End-: ~los [1] *Adj.* **(a)** (ohne Ende) infinite; (ringförmig) continuous; **(b)** (nicht enden wollend) endless; interminable ‹*speech*›; [2] *adv.* **~los lange dauern** be interminably long; **~lösung** *die* (ns. verhüll.) Final Solution (*to the Jewish question*); **~resultat** *das* final result; **~runde** *die* (Sport) final; **~spiel** *das* (Sport) final; **~spurt** *der* (bes. Leichtathletik) final spurt; **~stadium** *das* final stage; (Med.) terminal stage; **~station** *die* terminus; **~summe** *die* [sum] total
Endung *die;* **~, ~en** (Sprachw.) ending
End-: ~verbraucher *der,* **~verbraucherin** *die* (Wirtsch.) consumer; ···

~ziffer *die* final number; **das Los mit der ~ziffer 4** the coupon with a number ending in 4

Energie *die;* ~, **~n** energy

energie-, Energie-: ~bewusst, ***~bewußt** *Adj.* energy-conscious; **~mix** *der* mix of energy sources; **~politik** *die* energy policy; **~quelle** *die* energy source; **~spar·lampe** *die* energy-saving lamp; **~verbrauch** *der* energy consumption; **~versorgung** *die* energy supply; **~wirtschaft** *die* energy sector

e

energisch 1 *Adj.* **(a)** energetic ‹*person*›; firm ‹*action*›
(b) forceful ‹*voice, words*›
2 *adv.* **(a)** energetically; **~ durchgreifen** take drastic action
(b) ‹*reject, say*› forcefully; ‹*stress*› emphatically; ‹*deny*› strenuously

eng /ɛŋ/ 1 *Adj.* **(a)** (schmal) narrow
(b) (dicht) close ‹*writing*›
(c) (fest anliegend) close-fitting
(d) (beschränkt) narrow
(e) (nahe) close ‹*friend*›
2 *adv.* **(a)** (dicht) **~ [zusammen]sitzen/stehen** sit/stand close together
(b) (fest anliegend) **~ anliegen/sitzen** fit closely
(c) (beschränkt) **etw. zu ~ auslegen** interpret sth. too narrowly
(d) (nahe) closely

Engagement /ãgaʒəˈmã:/ *das;* **~s, ~s**
(a) (Einsatz) involvement; **sein ~ für etw.** his commitment to sth.; **sein ~ gegen etw.** his committed stand against sth.
(b) (eines Künstlers) engagement

engagiert *Adj.* committed ‹*literature, film, director*›; **politisch/sozial ~ sein** be politically/socially committed *or* involved

Engagiertheit *die;* ~: commitment; involvement

Enge *die;* ~, **~n** confinement

Engel *der;* **~s,** ~: angel

eng·herzig *Adj.* petty

England *(das);* **~s** England

Engländer *der;* **~s,** ~: Englishman/English boy; **er ist ~:** he is English; **die ~:** the English

Engländerin *die;* ~, **~nen** Englishwoman/English girl; **sie ist ~:** she is English

englisch 1 *Adj.* English; **die ~e Sprache/Literatur** the English language/English literature
2 *adv.* **~ sprechen** speak English

Englisch *das;* **~[s]** English

englisch-, Englisch-: ~lehrer *der,* **~lehrerin** *die* English teacher; **~sprachig** *Adj.* **(a)** English-language ‹*book, magazine*›; **(b)** (Englisch sprechend) English-speaking ‹*population, country*›; **~unterricht** *der* English teaching; (Unterrichtsstunde) English lesson

***alte Schreibung - vgl. Hinweis auf S. xiv**

Eng·pass, ***Eng·paß** *der* **(a)** defile
(b) (fig.) bottleneck

eng·stirnig *Adj.* narrow-minded

Enkel *der;* **~s,** ~: grandson

Enkelin *die;* ~, **~nen** granddaughter

Enkel·kind *das* grandchild

enorm 1 *Adj.* enormous ‹*sum, costs*›; tremendous (coll.) ‹*effort*›; immense ‹*strain*›
2 *adv.* tremendously (coll.)

Ensemble /ãˈsã:bl̩/ *das;* ~, **~s** ensemble; (Theater~) company

entarten *itr. V.; mit sein* degenerate

entbehren *tr. V.* (verzichten auf) do without

entbehrlich *Adj.* dispensable

Entbehrung *die;* ~, **~en** privation

entbinden 1 *unr. tr. V.* **(a) jmdn. von einem Versprechen ~:** release sb. from a promise; **seines Amtes** *od.* **von seinem Amt entbunden werden** be relieved of [one's] office
(b) jmdn. ~ (Med.) deliver sb.'s baby
2 *unr. itr. V.* give birth

Entbindung *die* (Med.) delivery

Entbindungs·station *die* maternity ward

entblößen 1 *refl. V.* take one's clothes off; ‹*exhibitionist*› expose oneself
2 *tr. V.* uncover ‹*one's arm etc.*›

entdecken *tr. V.* **(a)** discover
(b) (ausfindig machen) **jmdn. ~:** find sb.; **etw. ~:** find *or* discover sth.

Entdecker *der;* **~s,** ~, **Entdeckerin** *die;* ~, **~nen** discoverer

Entdeckung *die;* ~, **~en** discovery

Ente *die;* ~, **~n** duck

entehren *tr. V.* dishonour; **~d** degrading

enteignen *tr. V.* expropriate

Enteignung *die;* ~, **~en** expropriation

enterben *tr. V.* disinherit

entern *tr., itr. V.* board ‹*ship*›

entfachen *tr. V.* (geh.) **(a)** kindle, light ‹*fire*›
(b) (fig.) provoke ‹*quarrel, argument*›; arouse ‹*passion, enthusiasm*›

entfallen *unr. itr. V.; mit sein* **(a)** (aus dem Gedächtnis) **es ist mir ~:** it escapes me
(b) (zugeteilt werden) **auf jmdn./etw. ~:** be allotted to sb./sth.
(c) (wegfallen) lapse

entfalten 1 *tr. V.* **(a)** open [up]; unfold ‹*map etc.*›
(b) (fig.) display ‹*ability, talent*›
2 *refl. V.* **(a)** open [up]
(b) (fig.) ‹*personality, talent, etc.*› develop

Entfaltung *die;* ~, **~en** (fig.) **(a)** (Entwicklung) development
(b) ▶ ENTFALTEN 1B: display

entfernen 1 *tr. V.* remove; take out ‹*tonsils etc.*›
2 *refl. V.* go away

entfernt 1 *Adj.* **(a)** (fern) remote; **das ist**

od. **liegt weit ~ von der Stadt** it is a long way from the town; **10 km/zwei Stunden ~:** 10 km/two hours away
(b) slight ‹*acquaintance*›; distant ‹*relation*›; slight ‹*resemblance*›
[2] *adv.* **(a)** (fern) remotely
(b) slightly ‹*acquainted*›; distantly ‹*related*›

Entfernung *die;* **~, ~en (a)** (Abstand) distance
(b) (das Beseitigen) removal

entfesseln *tr. V.* unleash

entflammen [1] *tr. V.* arouse ‹*enthusiasm etc*›
[2] *itr. V.; mit sein* flare up

entfliehen *unr. itr. V.; mit sein* escape; **jmdm. ~:** escape from sb.

entfremden [1] *tr. V.* **(a) etw. seinem Zweck ~:** use sth. for a different purpose
(b) (Philos., Soziol.) **entfremdet** alienated
[2] *refl. V.* **sich jmdm./einer Sache ~:** become estranged from sb./unfamiliar with sth.

Entfremdung *die;* **~, ~en** alienation; estrangement

entführen *tr. V.* kidnap ‹*child etc.*›; hijack ‹*plane, lorry, etc.*›

Entführer *der,* **Entführerin** *die* ▶ ENTFÜHREN: kidnapper; hijacker

Entführung *die* ▶ ENTFÜHREN: kidnapping; hijacking

entgegen [1] *Adv.* towards
[2] *Präp. mit Dat.* **~ meinem Wunsch** against my wishes; **~ dem Befehl** contrary to orders

entgegen-, Entgegen-: ~|bringen *unr. tr. V.* (fig.) show ‹*love, understanding*›; **~|fahren** *unr. itr. V.; mit sein* **jmdm. ~fahren** come/go to meet sb.; **~|gehen** *unr. itr. V.; mit sein* **(a) jmdm. ~gehen** go to meet sb.; **(b)** (fig.) be heading for ‹*catastrophe, hard times*›; **~gesetzt** [1] *Adj.* **(a)** (umgekehrt) opposite ‹*end, direction*›; **(b)** (gegensätzlich) opposing; [2] *adv.* **genau ~gesetzt handeln/denken** do/think exactly the opposite; **~|kommen** *unr. itr. V.; mit sein* **jmdm. ~kommen** come to meet sb.; (Zugeständnisse machen) be accommodating towards sb.; **~kommen** *das;* **~~s** cooperation; (Zugeständnis) concession; **~kommend** *Adj.* obliging; **~|nehmen** *unr. itr. V.* receive; **~|treten** *unr. itr. V.; mit sein* go/come up to; (fig.) stand up to ‹*difficulties*›

entgegnen *tr. V.* retort; reply

entgehen *unr. itr. V.; mit sein* **(a)** (entkommen) escape
(b) jmdm. entgeht etw. sb. misses sth.

entgeistert *Adj.* dumbfounded

Entgelt *das;* **~[e]s, ~e** payment; fee

entgiften *tr. V.* decontaminate ‹*substance etc.*›; detoxicate ‹*body etc.*›

entgleisen *itr. V.; mit sein* **(a)** be derailed
(b) (fig.) make a/some faux pas

entgräten *tr. V.* fillet

enthaaren *tr. V.* remove hair from

Enthaarungs·mittel *das* hair remover

enthalten¹ [1] *unr. tr. V.* contain
[2] *unr. refl. V.* **sich einer Sache** (*Gen.*) **~:** abstain from sth.; **sich der Stimme ~:** abstain

enthalten² *Adj.* **in etw.** (*Dat.*) **~ sein** be contained in sth.; **das ist im Preis ~:** that is included in the price

enthaltsam [1] *Adj.* abstemious; (sexuell) abstinent
[2] *adv.* **~ leben** live in abstinence

Enthaltsamkeit *die;* **~:** abstinence

Enthaltung *die;* **~, ~en** abstention

enthaupten *tr. V.* (geh.) behead

enthäuten *tr. V.* skin

entheben *unr. tr. V.* (geh.) relieve

enthemmt *Adj.* uninhibited

enthüllen *tr. V.* unveil ‹*monument etc.*›; reveal ‹*face, truth, secret*›

Enthüllung *die;* **~, ~en** ▶ ENTHÜLLEN: unveiling; revelation

Enthusiasmus /ɛntu'zi̯asmʊs/ *der;* **~:** enthusiasm

Enthusiast *der;* **~en, ~en, Enthusiastin** *die;* **~, ~nen** enthusiast

enthusiastisch [1] *Adj.* enthusiastic
[2] *adv.* enthusiastically

entkalken *tr. V.* decalcify

entkleiden *tr. V.* (geh.) **(a)** undress
(b) (berauben) strip

entkommen *unr. itr. V.; mit sein* escape

entkorken *tr. V.* uncork ‹*bottle*›

entkräften *tr. V.* **(a)** weaken; **völlig ~:** exhaust
(b) (fig.) refute ‹*argument etc.*›

Entkräftung *die;* **~, ~en (a)** debility; **völlige ~:** exhaustion
(b) (fig.) refutation

entladen [1] *unr. tr. V.* unload
[2] *unr. refl. V.* **(a)** ‹*storm*› break
(b) (fig.) ‹*anger etc.*› erupt; ‹*aggression etc.*› be released

entlang [1] *Präp. mit Akk. u. Dat.* along
[2] *Adv.* along; **hier/dort ~, bitte!** this/that way please!

entlang-: ~|fahren *unr. itr. V.; mit sein* **(a)** drive along; **(b)** (streichen) go along; **~|gehen** *unr. itr. V.; mit sein* ‹*person*› go *or* walk along; **~|laufen** *unr. itr. V.; mit sein* **(a)** walk/run along; **(b)** (verlaufen) go *or* run along

entlarven *tr. V.* expose

entlassen *unr. tr. V.* **(a)** (aus dem Gefängnis) release; (aus dem Krankenhaus, der Armee) discharge
(b) (aus einem Arbeitsverhältnis) dismiss; (wegen Arbeitsmangels) make redundant (Brit.); lay off

Entlassung *die;* **~, ~en** ▶ ENTLASSEN: release; discharge; dismissal; redundancy (Brit.); laying off

entlasten *tr. V.* **(a)** relieve ··›

(b) (Rechtsw.) exonerate ‹*defendant*›
Entlastung *die;* ~, ~**en (a)** relief **(b)** (Rechtsw.) exoneration; defence
entlaufen *unr. itr. V.; mit sein* run away; **ein ~er Sträfling/Sklave** an escaped convict/a runaway slave
entlausen *tr. V.* delouse
entledigen *refl. V.* **sich jmds./einer Sache** (*Gen.*) ~ (geh.) rid oneself of sb./sth.
entleeren *tr. V.* empty; evacuate ‹*bowels, bladder*›
entlegen *Adj.* remote
entleihen *unr. tr. V.* borrow
entlocken *tr. V.* (geh.) **jmdm. etw. ~:** elicit sth. from sb.
entlohnen *tr. V.* pay
Entlohnung *die;* ~, ~**en** payment; (Lohn) pay
entlüften *tr. V.* ventilate
Entlüfter *der;* ~**s**, ~: ventilator
entmachten *tr. V.* deprive of power
entmilitarisieren *tr. V.* demilitarize
entmündigen *tr. V.* incapacitate
Entmündigung *die;* ~, ~**en** incapacitation
entmutigen *tr. V.* discourage
Entnahme *die;* ~, ~**n** (von Wasser) drawing; (von Blut) extraction
Entnazifizierung *die;* ~, ~**en** denazification
entnehmen *unr. tr. V.* **(a) etw. [einer Sache** (*Dat.*)**] ~:** take sth. [from sth.] **(b)** (ersehen aus) gather (*Dat.* from)
entnervend *Adj.* nerve-racking
entnervt *Adj.* ~ **sein** be worn down; have reached *or* be at the end of one's tether; **er gab ~ auf** he had reached the end of his tether and gave up
entpuppen *refl. V.* **sich als etw./jmd. ~:** turn out to be sth./sb.
entrahmen *tr. V.* skim ‹*milk*›
entreißen *unr. tr. V.* **jmdm. etw. ~:** snatch sth. from sb.
entrichten *tr. V.* (Amtsspr.) pay ‹*fee*›
entrümpeln *tr. V.* clear out
Entrümpelung *die;* ~, ~**en** clear-out
entrüsten 1 *refl. V.* **sich [über etw.** (*Akk.*)**] ~:** be indignant [at *or* about sth.] 2 *tr. V.* (empören) **jmdn. ~:** make sb. indignant
Entrüstung *die;* ~, ~**en** indignation (**über** + *Akk.* at, about)
Entsafter *der;* ~**s**, ~: juice extractor
entsagen *itr. V.* **einer Sache** (*Dat.*) ~ (geh.) renounce sth.
Entsagung *die;* ~, ~**en** (geh.) renunciation
entschädigen *tr. V.* compensate (**für** for); **jmdn. für etw. ~** (fig.) make up for sth.

***old spelling** - see note on page xiv

Entschädigung *die;* ~, ~**en** compensation
entschärfen *tr. V.* defuse; tone down ‹*discussion, criticism*›
entscheiden 1 *unr. refl. V.* **(a)** decide **(b)** (*unpers.*) **morgen entscheidet es sich, ob ...:** I/we/you will know tomorrow whether ... 2 *unr. itr. V.* **über etw.** (*Akk.*) ~: settle sth. 3 *unr. tr. V.* decide on ‹*dispute*›; decide ‹*outcome, result*›
entscheidend 1 *Adj.* crucial; decisive ‹*action*› 2 *adv.* **jmdn./etw. ~ beeinflussen** have a decisive influence on sb./sth.
Entscheidung *die;* ~, ~**en** decision
entschieden 1 *Adj.* **(a)** (entschlossen) determined; resolute **(b)** (eindeutig) definite 2 *adv.* resolutely; **das geht ~ zu weit** that is going much too far
Entschiedenheit *die;* ~: decisiveness; **etw. mit ~ behaupten/verneinen** state/deny sth. categorically; **etw. mit ~ fordern** demand sth. emphatically
entschlafen *unr. itr. V.; mit sein* pass away
entschließen *unr. refl. V.* decide
Entschließung *die;* ~, ~**en** resolution
entschlossen *Adj.* determined
Entschlossenheit *die;* ~: determination
Entschluss, *Entschluß *der;* **Entschlusses, Entschlüsse** decision
entschlüsseln *tr. V.* decipher
entschuldigen 1 *refl. V.* apologize 2 *tr.* (*auch itr.*) *V.* excuse ‹*person*›; **sich ~ lassen** ask to be excused; **~ Sie [bitte]!** (bei Fragen, Bitten) excuse me; (bedauernd) I'm sorry
Entschuldigung *die;* ~, ~**en (a)** apology **(b)** (Grund) excuse **(c)** (Höflichkeitsformel) **~!** (bei Fragen, Bitten) excuse me; (bedauernd) [I'm] sorry
entschwinden *unr. itr. V.; mit sein* (geh.) disappear; vanish
entsetzen 1 *refl. V.* be horrified 2 *tr. V.* horrify; **über etw.** (*Akk.*) **entsetzt sein** be horrified by sth.
Entsetzen *das;* ~**s** horror
entsetzlich 1 *Adj.* **(a)** horrible ‹*accident, crime, etc.*› **(b)** (ugs.: stark) terrible ‹*thirst, hunger*› 2 *adv.* terribly (coll.)
entsinnen *unr. refl. V.* **sich jmds./einer Sache ~:** remember sb./sth.
entsorgen *tr. V.* (Amtsspr., Wirtsch.) dispose of ‹*waste etc.*›
Entsorgung *die;* ~, ~**en** (Amtsspr., Wirtsch.) waste disposal
entspannen 1 *tr. V.* relax 2 *refl. V.* **(a)** ‹*person*› relax **(b)** (fig.) ‹*situation, tension*› ease
Entspannung *die;* ~ **(a)** relaxation **(b)** (politisch) easing of tension; détente

Entspannungs·politik *die* policy of détente

entsprechen *unr. itr. V.* **(a)** (übereinstimmen mit) **einer Sache** (*Dat.*) **~:** correspond to sth.; **der Wahrheit/den Tatsachen ~:** be in accordance with the truth/the facts
(b) (nachkommen) **einem Wunsch ~:** comply with a request; **den Anforderungen ~:** meet the requirements

entsprechend [1] *Adj.* **(a)** corresponding; (angemessen) appropriate
(b) (dem~) in accordance *postpos.;*
[2] *adv.* **(a)** (angemessen) appropriately
(b) (dem~) accordingly
[3] *Präp. mit Dat.* in accordance with

entspringen *unr. itr. V.; mit sein* **(a)** ‹*river*› rise
(b) (entstehen aus) **einer Sache** (*Dat.*) **~:** spring from sth.

entstehen *unr. itr. V.; mit sein* **(a)** originate; ‹*quarrel, friendship, etc.*› arise
(b) (gebildet werden) be formed (**aus** from, **durch** by)
(c) (sich ergeben) occur; (als Folge) result

Entstehung *die;* **~:** origin

entsteinen *tr. V.* stone

entstellen *tr. V.* **(a)** disfigure
(b) (verfälschen) distort ‹*text, facts*›

Entstellung *die;* **~, ~en (a)** disfigurement
(b) (Verfälschung) distortion

entstören *tr. V.* (Elektrot.) suppress ‹*engine, electrical appliance*›

Entstörungs·stelle *die* fault repair service

enttarnen *tr. V.* uncover

enttäuschen *tr. V.* disappoint

enttäuschend *Adj.* disappointing

enttäuscht *Adj.* disappointed; dashed ‹*hopes*›

Enttäuschung *die;* **~, ~en** disappointment

entwachsen *unr. itr. V.; mit sein* **einer Sache** (*Dat.*) **~:** grow out of sth.

entwaffnen *tr. V.* (auch fig.) disarm

entwaffnend *Adj.* disarming

entwarnen *itr. V.* sound the all-clear

Entwarnung *die;* **~, ~en** all-clear

entwässern *tr. V.* drain

Entwässerung *die;* **~, ~en** drainage

entweder *Konj.:* **~ ... oder** either ... or

entweichen *unr. itr. V.; mit sein* escape

entwenden *tr. V.* (geh.) purloin

entwerfen *unr. tr. V.* design ‹*furniture, dress*›; draft ‹*novel etc.*›; draw up ‹*plans etc.*›

entwerten *tr. V.* **(a)** cancel ‹*ticket, postage stamp*›
(b) devalue ‹*currency*›

Entwerter *der;* **~s, ~:** ticket-cancelling machine

entwickeln [1] *refl. V.* develop
[2] *tr. V.* produce ‹*vapour, smell*›; display ‹*ability, characteristic*›; develop ‹*equipment, photograph, film*›; elaborate ‹*theory, ideas*›

Entwicklung *die;* **~, ~en (a)** development; (von Dämpfen usw.) production; **in der ~ sein** ‹*young person*› be adolescent
(b) (Darlegung) elaboration
(c) (Fot.) developing

Entwicklungs-: ~helfer *der,* **~helferin** *die* development aid worker; **~hilfe** *die* [development] aid; **~land** *das* developing country; **~politik** *die* development aid policy

entwirren *tr. V.* disentangle

entwischen *itr. V.; mit sein* (ugs.) get away

entwöhnen *tr. V.* wean

entwürdigend *Adj.* degrading

Entwurf *der;* **~, Entwürfe (a)** design
(b) (Konzept) draft

entwurzeln *tr. V.* uproot

entziehen [1] *unr. tr. V.* **(a)** take away
(b) (nicht zugestehen) withdraw
[2] *unr. refl. V.* **sich seinen Pflichten** (*Dat.*) **~:** evade one's duty; **das entzieht sich meiner Kontrolle** that is beyond my control

Entziehung *die;* **~, ~en (a)** withdrawal
(b) (Entziehungskur) withdrawal treatment *no indef. art.*

entziffern *tr. V.* decipher

entzückend *Adj.* delightful

entzückt *Adj.* delighted

Entzug *der;* **~[e]s** withdrawal

Entzugs·erscheinung *die* withdrawal symptom

entzündbar *Adj.* [in]flammable

entzünden [1] *tr. V.* light ‹*fire*›; strike ‹*match*›
[2] *refl. V.* **(a)** ignite
(b) (anschwellen) become inflamed

entzündlich *Adj.* **(a)** [in]flammable ‹*substance*›
(b) (Med.) inflammatory

Entzündung *die;* **~, ~en** inflammation

entzwei *Adj.* (geh.) in pieces

entzweien *refl. V.* fall out

entzwei|gehen *unr. itr. V.; mit sein* (geh.) break

Enzian *der;* **~s, ~e** gentian

Enzyklika *die;* **~, Enzykliken** encyclical

Enzyklopädie *die;* **~, ~n** encyclopaedia

enzyklopädisch *Adj.* encyclopaedic

Epen ▸ EPOS

Epidemie *die;* **~, ~n** epidemic

epigonal *Adj.* (geh.) ▸ EPIGONENHAFT

Epigone *der;* **~n, ~n** (geh.) imitator

epigonenhaft *Adj.* (geh.) imitative; unoriginal

Epigonin *die;* **~, ~nen** ▸ EPIGONE

Epik /'eːpɪk/ *die;* **~** (Literaturw.) epic poetry

Epilepsie *die;* ~, **~n** (Med.) epilepsy *no art.*
Epileptiker *der;* **~s, ~, Epileptikerin** *die;* **~, ~nen** epileptic
epileptisch *Adj.* epileptic
episch *Adj.* epic
Episode *die;* **~, ~n** episode
Epoche *die;* **~, ~n** epoch
Epos /'e:pɔs/ *das;* **~, Epen** epic [poem]; epos
er *Personalpron. 3. Pers. Sg. Nom. Mask.* he; (betont) him; (bei Dingen/Tieren) it; *s. auch* IHM; IHN; SEINER
erachten *tr. V.* (geh.) consider; **etw. als** *od.* **für seine Pflicht ~:** consider sth. [to be] one's duty
erarbeiten *tr. V.* work for
Erb·anlage *die* hereditary disposition
erbarmen *refl. V.* (geh.) take pity (*Gen.* on)
Erbarmen *das;* **~s** pity
erbärmlich [1] *Adj.* **(a)** (elend) wretched **(b)** (unzulänglich) pathetic **(c)** (abwertend: gemein) mean; wretched **(d)** (sehr groß) terrible ‹*hunger, fear, etc.*› [2] *adv.* terribly
erbauen [1] *tr. V.* **(a)** build **(b)** (geh.: erheben) uplift [2] *refl. V.* **sich an etw.** (*Dat.*) **~:** be uplifted by sth.
Erbauer *der;* **~s, ~, Erbauerin** *die;* **~, ~nen** architect
Erbe¹ *das;* **~s (a)** inheritance **(b)** (Vermächtnis) legacy
Erbe² *der;* **~n ~n** heir
erben *tr.* (*auch itr.*) *V.* inherit
erbetteln *tr. V.* get by begging
erbeuten *tr. V.* carry off, get away with ‹*valuables, prey, etc.*›; capture ‹*enemy plane, tank, etc.*›
Erb-: ~faktor *der* hereditary factor; **~folge** *die* succession; **~gut** *das* (Biol.) genetic make-up
Erbin *die;* **~, ~nen** heiress
erbitten *unr. tr. V.* (geh.) request
erbittern *tr. V.* enrage
erbittert [1] *Adj.* bitter [2] *adv.* **~ kämpfen** wage a bitter struggle
Erb·krankheit *die* hereditary disease
erblassen *itr. V.; mit sein* (geh.) turn pale; blanch (literary)
erbleichen *itr. V.; mit sein* (geh.) ▶ ERBLASSEN
erblich *Adj.* hereditary ‹*title, disease*›
erblicken *tr. V.* (geh.) catch sight of; (fig.) see
erblinden *itr. V.; mit sein* lose one's sight
erblühen *itr. V.; mit sein* (geh.) bloom; blossom
Erb·masse *die* (Biol.) genetic make-up
erbost *Adj.* furious
erbrechen [1] *unr. tr. V.* bring up ‹*food*› [2] *unr. itr., refl. V.* vomit
Erbrechen *das;* **~s** vomiting
erbringen *unr. tr. V.* produce
Erbschaft *die;* **~, ~en** inheritance
Erbschaft[s]·steuer *die* estate *or* death duties *pl.*
Erb-: ~schleicher *der;* **~~s, ~~** (abwertend) legacy hunter; **~schleicherei** *die;* **~~, ~~en** (abwertend) legacy hunting; **~schleicherin** *die;* **~~, ~~nen** ▶ ~SCHLEICHER
Erbse *die;* **~, ~n** pea
Erb-: ~stück *das* heirloom; **~sünde** *die* original sin; **~teil** *das* share of an/the inheritance
Erd-: ~achse *die* earth's axis; **~anziehung** *die* earth's gravitational pull; **~apfel** *der* (bes. österr.) ▶ KARTOFFEL; **~atmosphäre** *die* earth's atmosphere; **~beben** *das* earthquake; **~beere** *die* strawberry; **~boden** *der* ground; earth; **etw. dem ~boden gleichmachen** raze sth. to the ground
Erde *die;* **~, ~n (a)** (Erdreich) soil; earth **(b)** (fester Boden) ground **(c)** (Welt) earth; world **(d)** (Planet) Earth
erdenklich *Adj.* conceivable
Erd-: ~gas *das* natural gas; **~geschoss, *~geschoß** *das* ground floor; first floor (Amer.); **~kugel** *die* terrestrial globe; earth; **~kunde** *die* geography; **~magnetismus** *der* terrestrial magnetism; **~nuss, *~nuß** *die* peanut; **~oberfläche** *die* earth's surface; **~öl** *das* oil; **~öl exportierende Länder** oil-exporting countries
erdöl-, Erdöl-: *~exportierend ▶ ERDÖL; **~gewinnung** *die* oil production; **~leitung** *die* oil pipeline
erdrosseln *tr. V.* strangle
erdrücken *tr. V.* **(a)** crush **(b)** (fig.: belasten) overwhelm
erdrückend *Adj.* overwhelming; oppressive ‹*heat, silence*›
Erd-: ~rutsch *der* landslide; **~rutsch·sieg** *der* (Politik) landslide victory; **~teil** *der* continent
erdulden *tr. V.* endure ‹*sorrow, misfortune*›; tolerate ‹*insults*›; (über sich ergehen lassen) undergo
Erd-: ~umdrehung *die* rotation of the earth; **~umlauf·bahn** *die* orbit [of the earth]
ereifern *refl. V.* get excited
ereignen *refl. V.* happen; ‹*accident, mishap*› occur
Ereignis *das;* **~ses, ~se** event; occurrence
ereignis·reich *Adj.* eventful
Eremit *der;* **~en, ~en, Eremitin** *die;* **~, ~nen** hermit
ererbt *Adj.* inherited

*alte Schreibung - vgl. Hinweis auf S. xiv

erfahren[1] *unr. tr. V.* **(a)** find out; learn; (hören) hear
(b) (geh.: erleben) experience; (erleiden) suffer

erfahren[2] *Adj.* experienced

Erfahrung *die; ~, ~en* experience; **~en sammeln** gain experience *sing.*; **etw. in ~ bringen** discover sth.

erfahrungs·gemäß *Adv.* in our/my experience

erfassen *tr. V.* **(a)** (mitreißen) catch
(b) (begreifen) grasp ‹*situation, etc.*›
(c) (registrieren) record

Erfassung *die; ~, ~en* registration

erfinden *unr. tr. V.* invent; **das ist alles erfunden** it is pure fabrication

Erfinder *der; ~s, ~,* **Erfinderin** *die; ~, ~nen* **(a)** inventor
(b) (Urheber) creator

erfinderisch *Adj.* inventive; (schlau) resourceful

Erfindung *die; ~, ~en* invention

erflehen *tr. V.* (geh.) beg

Erfolg *der; ~[e]s, ~e* success; **keinen ~ haben** be unsuccessful

erfolgen *itr. V.; mit sein* take place; occur; **es erfolgte keine Reaktion** there was no reaction

erfolg-, Erfolg-: ~los [1] *Adj.* unsuccessful; [2] *adv.* unsuccessfully; **~losigkeit** *die; ~~:* lack of success; **~reich** [1] *Adj.* successful; [2] *adv.* successfully

Erfolgs·erlebnis *das* feeling of achievement

erfolg·versprechend *Adj.* promising

erforderlich *Adj.* required; necessary

erfordern *tr. V.* require; demand

erforschen *tr. V.* discover ‹*facts, causes, etc.*›; explore ‹*country*›

Erforschung *die; ~* research (+ *Gen.* into); (eines Landes usw.) exploration

erfreuen [1] *tr. V.* please
[2] *refl. V.* **sich an etw.** (*Dat.*) **~:** take pleasure in sth.

erfreulich *Adj.* pleasant

erfreulicherweise *Adv.* happily

erfrieren [1] *unr. itr. V.; mit sein* freeze to death; ‹*plant, harvest, etc.*› be damaged by frost
[2] *unr. refl. V.* **sich** (*Dat.*) **die Finger ~:** get frostbite in one's fingers

Erfrierung *die; ~, ~en* frostbite *no pl.*; **~en an den Händen/Füßen** frostbitten hands/feet

erfrischen [1] *tr.* (*auch itr.*) *V.* refresh
[2] *refl. V.* freshen oneself up

erfrischend (auch fig.) *Adj.* refreshing

Erfrischung *die; ~, ~en* (auch fig.) refreshment

Erfrischungs-: ~getränk *das* soft drink; **~raum** *der* refreshment room; **~tuch** *das; Pl.* **~tücher** tissue wipe; towelette

erfüllen [1] *tr. V.* grant ‹*wish, request*›; fulfil ‹*contract*›; carry out ‹*duty*›; meet ‹*condition*›
[2] *refl. V.* ‹*wish*› come true

Erfüllung *die:* **in ~ gehen** come true

erfunden *Adj.* fictional ‹*story*›

ergänzen *tr. V.* **(a)** (vervollständigen) complete; (erweitern) add to
(b) (hinzufügen) add ‹*remark*›

Ergänzung *die; ~, ~en* **(a)** (Vervollständigung) completion; (Erweiterung) enlargement
(b) (Zusatz) addition; (zu einem Gesetz) amendment

ergattern *tr. V.* (ugs.) manage to grab

ergaunern *tr. V.* get by underhand means

ergeben[1] [1] *unr. refl. V.* **(a) sich in etw.** (*Akk.*) **~:** submit to sth.
(b) (kapitulieren) surrender (*Dat.* to)
(c) (folgen, entstehen) arise (**aus** from)
[2] *unr. tr. V.* result in

ergeben[2] *Adj.* **(a)** (zugeneigt) devoted
(b) (resignierend) **mit ~er Miene** with an expression of resignation

Ergebnis *das; ~ses, ~se* result

ergebnis·los *Adj.* fruitless

ergehen *unr. refl. V.* **sich in etw.** (*Dat.*) **~:** indulge in sth.

ergiebig *Adj.* rich ‹*deposits, resources*›; fertile ‹*topic*›

Ergiebigkeit *die; ~* ▶ ERGIEBIG: richness; fertility

ergonomisch [1] *Adj.* ergonomic
[2] *adv.* ergonomically

ergötzen (geh.) [1] *tr. V.* enthrall
[2] *refl. V.* **sich an etw.** (*Dat.*) **~:** be delighted by sth.

ergrauen *itr. V.; mit sein* go grey

ergreifen *unr. tr. V.* **(a)** (greifen) grab
(b) (festnehmen) catch ‹*thief etc.*›
(c) (fig.: erfassen) seize
(d) (fig.: aufnehmen) take up ‹*career*›; take ‹*initiative, opportunity*›
(e) (fig.: bewegen) move

ergreifend *Adj.* moving

ergriffen *Adj.* moved

Ergriffenheit *die; ~:* **voller ~:** deeply moved

ergründen *tr. V.* ascertain; discover ‹*cause*›

Erguss, *Erguß *der* (geh. abwertend) outburst; **ein poetischer ~:** a poetic outpouring

erhaben *Adj.* solemn ‹*moment*›; awe-inspiring ‹*sight*›; sublime ‹*beauty*›; **über etw.** (*Akk.*) **~ sein** be above sth.

Erhalt *der; ~* (Amtsdt.) receipt

erhalten *unr. tr. V.* **(a)** receive ‹*letter, news, gift*›; be given ‹*order*›; get ‹*good mark, impression*›
(b) (bewahren) preserve ‹*town, building*›
erhältlich *Adj.* obtainable
Erhaltung *die;* ~: preservation; (des Friedens) maintenance
erhängen *tr. V.* hang
erhärten *tr. V.* strengthen ‹*suspicion, assumption*›; substantiate ‹*claim*›
erheben 1 *unr. tr. V.* **(a)** raise
(b) (verlangen) levy ‹*tax*›; charge ‹*fee*›
2 *unr. refl. V.* **(a)** rise
(b) (rebellieren) rise up (**gegen** against)
erhebend *Adj.* uplifting
erheblich 1 *Adj.* considerable
2 *adv.* considerably
Erhebung *die;* ~, ~**en** **(a)** (Anhöhe) elevation
(b) (Aufstand) uprising
(c) (Umfrage) survey
(d) (Einziehen) (von Steuern) levying; (von Gebühren) charging
erheitern *tr. V.* **jmdn.** ~: cheer sb. up
Erheiterung *die;* ~, ~**en** amusement
erhellen *tr. V.* light up
erhitzen 1 *tr. V.* heat ‹*liquid*›; **jmdn.** ~: make sb. hot
2 *refl. V.* heat up; ‹*person*› become hot
erhoffen *tr. V.* **sich** (*Dat.*) **viel/wenig von etw.** ~: expect a lot/little from sth.
erhöhen 1 *tr. V.* increase ‹*prices, productivity, etc.*›
2 *refl. V.* ‹*rent, prices*› rise
Erhöhung *die;* ~, ~**en** increase (*Gen.* in)
erholen *refl. V.* (auch fig.) recover (**von** from); (sich ausruhen) have a rest
erholsam *Adj.* restful
Erholung *die;* ~: ▶ ERHOLEN: recovery; rest; ~ **brauchen** need a rest
erholungs·bedürftig *Adj.* in need of a rest *postpos.*
Erholungs·urlaub *der* holiday for convalescence
erhören *tr. V.* (geh.) hear
Erika *die;* ~, ~**s** *od.* **Eriken** (Bot.) erica
erinnern 1 *refl. V.* **sich an jmdn./etw.** ~: remember sb./sth.; **sich [daran]** ~, **dass** ...: remember *or* recall that ...
2 *tr. V.* **jmdn. an etw./jmdn.** ~: remind sb. of sth./sb.
Erinnerung *die;* ~, ~**en** memory (**an** + *Akk.* of); **etw. [noch gut] in** ~ **haben** [still] remember sth. [well]; **zur** ~ **an jmdn./etw.** in memory of sb./sth.
Erinnerungs·lücke *die* gap in one's memory
erjagen *tr. V.* **(a)** catch
(b) (gewinnen) win ‹*fame*›; make ‹*money, fortune*›

erkalten *tr. V.; mit sein* cool
erkälten *refl. V.* catch cold
Erkältung *die;* ~, ~**en** cold
Erkältungs·krankheit *die* cold
erkämpfen *tr. V.* win; **den Sieg** ~: gain a victory
erkaufen *tr. V.* **(a)** (durch Opfer) win
(b) (durch Geld) buy
erkennbar *Adj.* recognizable; (sichtbar) visible
erkennen *unr. tr. V.* **(a)** recognize
(b) (deutlich sehen) make out
erkenntlich *Adj.* **(a)** **sich [für etw.]** ~ **zeigen** show one's appreciation for sth.
(b) ▶ ERKENNBAR
Erkenntnis *die;* ~, ~**se** discovery; **zu der** ~ **kommen, dass** ...: come to the realization that ...
Erkennungs-: ~**melodie** *die* (einer Sendung) theme music; (eines Senders) signature tune; ~**zeichen** *das* sign [to recognize sb. by]
Erker *der;* ~**s**, ~: bay window
Erker·fenster *das* bay window
erklärbar *Adj.* explicable
erklären 1 *tr. V.* **(a)** explain
(b) (mitteilen) state; declare
(c) **jmdn. für tot** ~: pronounce someone dead; **jmdn. zu etw.** ~: name sb. as sth
2 *refl. V.* **sich einverstanden/bereit** ~: declare oneself [to be] in agreement/willing
erklärlich *Adj.* understandable
erklärt *Adj.* declared
Erklärung *die;* ~, ~**en** **(a)** (Darlegung) explanation
(b) (Mitteilung) statement
erklimmen *unr. tr. V.* (geh.) climb
erklingen *unr. itr. V.; mit sein* ring out
erkranken *itr. V.; mit sein* become ill (**an** + *Dat.* with); **schwer erkrankt sein** be seriously ill
Erkrankung *die;* ~, ~**en** illness; (eines Körperteils) disease
erkunden *tr. V.* reconnoitre ‹*terrain*›
erkundigen *refl. V.* **sich nach jmdm./etw.** ~: ask after sb./enquire about sth.
Erkundigung *die;* ~, ~**en** enquiry
Erkundung *die;* ~, ~**en** (meist Milit.) reconnaissance
Erkundungs-: ~**fahrt** *die* exploratory trip; ~**flug** *der* reconnaissance flight
erlahmen *itr. V.; mit sein* tire; ‹*strength*› flag
erlangen *tr. V.* gain; obtain ‹*credit, visa*›; reach ‹*age*›
Erlass, *Erlaß *der;* **Erlasses, Erlasse** decree
erlassen *unr. tr. V.* **(a)** enact ‹*law*›; declare ‹*amnesty*›; issue ‹*warrant*›
(b) (verzichten auf) remit ‹*sentence*›
erlauben 1 *tr. V.* **(a)** allow
(b) (ermöglichen) permit

*old spelling - see note on page xiv

2 *refl. V.* **sich** (*Dat.*) **etw. ~:** permit oneself sth

Erlaubnis *die;* **~, ~se** permission; (Schriftstück) permit

erläutern *tr. V.* explain; comment on ‹*picture etc.*›; annotate ‹*text*›

Erläuterung *die* explanation

Erle *die;* **~, ~n** alder

erleben *tr. V.* experience; **etwas Schreckliches ~:** have a terrible experience; **er wird das nächste Jahr nicht mehr ~:** he won't see next year; **du kannst was ~!** (ugs.) you won't know what's hit you!

Erlebnis *das;* **~ses, ~se** experience

erledigen **1** *tr. V.* deal with ‹*task*›; settle ‹*matter*›; **ich muss noch einige Dinge erledigen** I must see to a few things; **sie hat alles pünktlich erledigt** she got everything done on time

2 *refl. V.* ‹*matter, problem*› resolve itself; **vieles erledigt sich von selbst** a lot of things sort them'selves out

erledigt *Adj.* closed ‹*case*›; (ugs.) worn out ‹*person*›

erlegen *tr. V.* shoot ‹*animal*›

erleichtern *tr. V.* **(a)** make easier
(b) (befreien) relieve

Erleichterung *die;* **~, ~en (a) zur ~ der Arbeit** to make the work easier
(b) (Befreiung) relief
(c) (Verbesserung, Milderung) alleviation

erleiden *unr. tr. V.* suffer

erlernbar *Adj.* learnable

erlernen *tr. V.* learn

erlesen *Adj.* superior ‹*wine*›; choice ‹*dish*›

erleuchten *tr. V.* **(a)** light
(b) (geh.: mit Klarheit erfüllen) inspire

Erleuchtung *die;* **~, ~en** inspiration

erliegen *unr. itr. V.; mit sein* succumb (*Dat.* to); **einem Irrtum ~:** be misled; **einer Krankheit** (*Dat.*) **~:** die from an illness

erlogen *Adj.* made up

Erlös *der;* **~es, ~e** proceeds *pl.*

erlöschen *unr. itr. V.; mit sein* ‹*fire*› go out; **ein erloschener Vulkan** an extinct volcano

erlösen *tr. V.* save, rescue **(von** from)

Erlöser *der;* **~s, ~ (a)** saviour
(b) (christl. Rel.) redeemer

Erlöserin *die;* **~, ~nen** ▶ ERLÖSER A

Erlösung *die;* **~, ~en** release **(von** from)

ermächtigen *tr. V.* authorize

Ermächtigung *die;* **~, ~en** authorization

ermahnen *tr. V.* admonish; tell (coll.); (warnen) warn

Ermahnung *die;* **~, ~en** admonition; (Warnung) warning

Ermang[e]lung *die;* **~: in ~** (+ *Gen.*) (geh.) in the absence of

ermäßigen *tr. V.* reduce

Ermäßigung *die;* **~, ~en** reduction

ermatten (geh.) **1** *itr. V.; mit sein* become exhausted
2 *tr. V.* exhaust, tire

ermessen *unr. tr. V.* estimate, gauge

Ermessen *das;* **~s** estimation

ermitteln **1** *tr. V.* ascertain ‹*facts*›; discover ‹*culprit, address*›; establish ‹*identity, origin*›; decide ‹*winner*›; calculate ‹*quota, rates, data*›
2 *itr. V.* (Rechtsw.) investigate

Ermittlung *die;* **~, ~en (a)** (das Ermitteln) ▶ ERMITTELN A: ascertainment; discovery; establishment
(b) (Untersuchung) investigation

ermöglichen *tr. V.* enable

ermorden *tr. V.* murder

Ermordung *die;* **~, ~en** murder

ermüden **1** *itr. V.; mit sein* tire
2 *tr. V.* tire; make tired

ermüdend *Adj.* tiring

Ermüdung *die;* **~, ~en** tiredness

ermuntern *tr. V.* encourage

ermunternd *Adj.* encouraging

ermutigen *tr. V.* encourage

Ermutigung *die;* **~, ~en** encouragement

ernähren **1** *tr. V.* **(a)** feed ‹*young, child*›
(b) (unterhalten) keep ‹*family, wife*›
2 *refl. V.* feed oneself

Ernährer *der;* **~s, ~, Ernährerin** *die;* **~, ~nen** breadwinner

Ernährung *die;* **~:** feeding; (Nahrung) diet

Ernährungs·wissenschaft *die* dietetics *sing., no art.*

ernennen *unr. tr. V.* appoint

Ernennung *die* appointment **(zu** as)

erneuerbar *Adj.* renewable; **~e Energien** renewable sources of energy

erneuern *tr. V.* **(a)** replace
(b) (wiederherstellen) renovate ‹*roof, building*›; (fig.) thoroughly reform ‹*system*›

Erneuerung *die;* **~, ~en (a)** replacement
(b) (Wiederherstellung) renovation

erneut **1** *Adj.* renewed
2 *adv.* once again

erniedrigen *tr. V.* humiliate

Erniedrigung *die;* **~, ~en** humiliation

ernst **1** *Adj.* **(a)** serious
(b) (aufrichtig) genuine ‹*intention, offer*›
(c) (gefahrvoll) serious ‹*injury*›; grave ‹*situation*›
2 *adv.* seriously; **jmdn./etw. ~ nehmen** take sb./sth. seriously; **~ gemeint** serious; sincere ‹*wish*›

Ernst *der;* **~[e]s (a)** seriousness; **das ist mein [voller] ~:** I mean that [quite] seriously; **etw. im ~ meinen** mean sth. seriously
(b) (Wirklichkeit) **daraus wurde [blutiger/bitterer] ~:** it became [deadly] serious; **der ~ des Lebens** the serious side of life

ernst-, Ernst-: ~fall *der:* **im ~fall** when the real thing happens; ***~gemeint** ⋯>

▶ ERNST 2; **~haft** 1 *Adj.* serious; 2 *adv.* seriously; **~haftigkeit** *die; ~~:* seriousness

ernstlich 1 *Adj.* **(a)** serious **(b)** (aufrichtig) genuine ‹*wish*› 2 *adv.* **(a)** seriously **(b)** (aufrichtig) genuinely ‹*sorry, repentant*›

Ernte *die; ~, ~n* **(a)** harvest **(b)** (Ertrag) crop; **die ~ einbringen** bring in the harvest

Ernte·dank·fest *das* harvest festival

ernten *tr. V.* harvest

ernüchtern *tr. V.* sober up; (fig.) bring down to earth; **~d** sobering

Ernüchterung *die; ~, ~en* (fig.) disillusionment

Eroberer *der; ~s, ~,* **Eroberin** *die; ~, ~nen* conqueror

erobern *tr. V.* **(a)** conquer; take ‹*town, fortress*› **(b)** seize ‹*power*›

Eroberung *die; ~, ~en* conquest; (einer Stadt, Festung) taking

eröffnen *tr. V.* **(a)** open; start ‹*business, practice*› **(b)** (mitteilen) **jmdm. etw. ~:** reveal sth. to sb. **(c) ein Testament ~:** read a will

Eröffnung *die; ~, ~en* **(a)** opening; (einer Sitzung) start **(b)** (Mitteilung) revelation **(c)** (Testaments~) reading

erogen *Adj.* erogenous ‹*zone*›

erörtern *tr. V.* discuss

Erörterung *die; ~, ~en* discussion

Eros·Center *das* [licensed] brothel; eros centre

Erosion *die; ~, ~en* erosion

Erotik *die; ~:* eroticism

erotisch *Adj.* erotic

Erpel *der; ~s, ~:* drake

erpicht *Adj. in* **auf etw.** (*Akk.*) **~ sein** be keen on sth.

erpressbar, *erpreßbar *Adj.* blackmailable; susceptible to blackmail *postpos.*

Erpressbarkeit, *Erpreßbarkeit *die; ~:* susceptibility to blackmail

erpressen *tr. V.* **(a)** (nötigen) blackmail **(b)** (erlangen) extort ‹*money etc.*›

Erpresser *der; ~s, ~,* **Erpresserin** *die; ~, ~nen* blackmailer

Erpressung *die; ~, ~en* blackmail *no indef. art.;* (von Geld, Geständnis) extortion

Erpressungs·versuch *der* blackmail attempt

erproben *tr. V.* test ‹*medicine*› (**an** + *Akk.* on)

Erprobung *die; ~, ~en* testing

erquickend *Adj.* (geh.) refreshing

erraten *unr. tr. V.* guess

errechnen *tr. V.* calculate

erregen 1 *tr. V.* **(a)** annoy **(b)** (sexuell) arouse **(c)** (verursachen) arouse 2 *refl. V.* get excited

erregend *Adj.* exciting; (sexuell) arousing

Erreger *der; ~s, ~* (Med.) pathogen

erregt *Adj.* excited; (sexuell) aroused

Erregung *die; ~, ~en* excitement

erreichbar *Adj.* **(a)** within reach *postpos.;* **(b) der Ort ist mit dem Zug ~:** the place can be reached by train

erreichen *tr. V.* **(a)** reach; **den Zug ~:** catch the train; **er ist telefonisch zu ~:** he can be contacted by telephone **(b)** (durchsetzen) achieve ‹*goal, aim*›

errichten *tr. V.* **(a)** build ‹*house, bridge, etc.*› **(b)** (aufstellen) erect

erringen *unr. tr. V.* gain ‹*victory*›; reach ‹*first etc. place*›

erröten *itr. V.; mit sein* blush

Errungenschaft *die; ~, ~en* achievement

Ersatz *der; ~es* **(a)** replacement **(b)** (Entschädigung) compensation

Ersatz-: ~frau *die* replacement; (Sport) substitute; **~kasse** *die* private health insurance company; **~mann** *der; Pl.* **~männer** *od.* **~leute** *die* replacement; (Sport) substitute; **~rad** *das* spare wheel; **~reifen** *der* spare tyre; **~spieler** *der,* **~spielerin** *die* (Sport) substitute [player]; **~teil** *das* (bes. Technik) spare part; spare (Brit.)

ersaufen *unr. itr. V.; mit sein* (salopp) drown

ersäufen *tr. V.* drown

erschaffen *unr. tr. V.* create

Erschaffung *die* creation

erschaudern *itr. V.; mit sein* (geh.) shudder (**bei** at)

erscheinen *unr. itr. V.; mit sein* ‹*book*› be published

Erscheinung *die; ~, ~en* **(a)** (Vorgang) phenomenon **(b)** (äußere Gestalt) appearance **(c)** (Vision) apparition; **eine ~ haben** see a vision

Erscheinungs-: ~bild *das* appearance; **~form** *die* manifestation; **~weise** *die* **die ~weise einer Zeitung** the frequency of publication of a newspaper; **wöchentliche/monatliche ~weise** weekly/monthly publication

erschießen *unr. tr. V.* shoot dead

Erschießung *die; ~, ~en* shooting

erschlaffen *itr. V.; mit sein* ‹*muscle, limb*› become limp; ‹*skin*› grow slack

erschlagen[1] *unr. tr. V.* strike dead; kill

erschlagen[2] *Adj.* (ugs.) **(a)** (erschöpft) worn out

*alte Schreibung - vgl. Hinweis auf S. xiv

(b) (verblüfft) **wie ~ sein** be flabbergasted (coll.) *or* thunderstruck

erschließen *unr. tr. V.* develop ‹*area, building land*›; tap ‹*resources*›

erschöpfen *tr. V.* exhaust

erschöpfend *Adj.* exhaustive

erschöpft *Adj.* exhausted

Erschöpfung *die;* **~, ~en** exhaustion

Erschöpfungs·zustand *der* state of exhaustion

erschrecken¹ *unr. itr. V.; mit sein* be startled; **vor etw.** (*Dat.*) *od.* **über etw.** (*Akk.*) **~:** be startled by sth.

erschrecken² *tr. V.* frighten; scare

erschrecken³ *unr. od. regelm. refl. V.* get a fright

erschreckend *Adj.* alarming

erschrocken [1] *2. Part. v.* ERSCHRECKEN¹; [2] *Adj.* frightened

erschüttern *tr. V.* (auch fig.) shake

erschütternd *Adj.* deeply distressing; deeply shocking ‹*conditions*›

Erschütterung *die;* **~, ~en** **(a)** vibration; (der Erde) tremor
(b) (Ergriffenheit) shock; (Trauer) distress

erschweren *tr. V.* **etw. ~:** make sth. more difficult

erschwerend [1] *Adj.* complicating ‹*factor*›
[2] *adv.* **es kommt ~ hinzu, dass er ...:** to make matters worse he ...

Erschwernis *die;* **~, ~se** difficulty

erschwinglich *Adj.* reasonable

ersehen *unr. tr. V.* see; **aus etw. zu ~ sein** be evident from sth.

ersetzen *tr. V.* **(a)** replace (**durch** by)
(b) (erstatten) reimburse ‹*expenses*›; **jmdm. einen Schaden ~:** compensate sb. for damages

Ersetzung *die;* **~, ~en** (von Kosten usw.) reimbursement; **die ~ von Schaden** compensation for damage

ersichtlich *Adj.* apparent

ersinnen *unr. tr. V.* (geh.) devise

erspähen *tr. V.* (geh.) espy (literary); catch sight of

ersparen *tr. V.* save

Ersparnis *die;* **~, ~se** saving

ersprießlich *Adj.* (geh.) fruitful ‹*contacts, collaboration*›

erst [1] *Adv.* **(a)** (zu~) first; **~ einmal** first [of all]
(b) (nicht eher als) **eben ~:** only just; **~ nächste Woche** not until next week; **er war ~ zufrieden, als ...:** he was not satisfied until ...
(c) (nicht mehr als) only
[2] *Partikel* **so was lese ich gar nicht ~:** I don't even start reading that sort of stuff

erst... *Ordinalz.* **(a)** first; **etw. das ~e Mal tun** do sth. for the first time; **am Ersten [des Monats]** on the first [of the month]; **als Erster/Erste etw. tun** be the first to do sth.
(b) (best...) **das ~e Hotel** the best hotel; **der/die Erste [der Klasse]** the top boy/girl [of the class]

erstarren *itr. V.; mit sein* ‹*jelly, plaster*› set; ‹*limbs, fingers*› grow stiff

erstatten *tr. V.* **(a)** reimburse ‹*expenses*›
(b) Anzeige gegen jmdn. ~: report sb. [to the police]

Erstattung *die;* **~, ~en** (von Kosten) reimbursement

Erst·aufführung *die* première

erstaunen *tr. V.* astonish

Erstaunen *das;* **~s** astonishment

erstaunlich [1] *Adj.* astonishing
[2] *adv.* astonishingly

erstaunlicher·weise *Adv.* astonishingly *or* amazingly [enough]

erstaunt *Adj.* astonished; amazed

Erst·ausgabe *die* first edition

erstechen *unr. tr. V.* stab [to death]

erstehen (geh.) [1] *unr. tr. V.* (kaufen) purchase
[2] *unr. itr. V.; mit sein* ‹*difficulties, problems*› arise

ersteigen *unr. tr. V.* climb

ersteigern *tr. V.* buy [at an auction]

erstellen *tr. V.* (Papierdt.) **(a)** (bauen) build
(b) (anfertigen) make ‹*assessment*›; draw up ‹*plan, report, list*›

***erste·mal** ▶ MAL¹

***ersten·mal** ▶ MAL¹

erstens *Adv.* firstly; in the first place

erster... *Adj.* the former

erst·geboren *Adj.* first-born

ersticken [1] *itr. V.; mit sein* suffocate; (sich verschlucken) choke
[2] *tr. V.* **(a)** (töten) suffocate
(b) smother ‹*flames*›

erstklassig [1] *Adj.* first-class
[2] *adv.* superbly

erstmals *Adv.* for the first time

erstrangig *Adj.* **(a)** first-class
(b) (vordringlich) of top priority *postpos.*

erstreben *tr. V.* strive for

erstrebens·wert *Adj.* ‹*ideals etc.*› worth striving for; desirable ‹*situation*›

erstrecken *refl. V.* **(a)** (sich ausdehnen) stretch
(b) (dauern) **sich über 10 Jahre ~:** carry on for 10 years

Erst·stimme *die* first vote

erstürmen *tr. V.* take by storm

ersuchen *tr. V.* (geh.) ask; **jmdn. ~, etw. zu tun** request sb. to do sth.

ertappen *tr. V.* catch ‹*thief, burglar*›

erteilen *tr. V.* give ‹*advice, information*›; give, grant ‹*permission*›

Erteilung *die;* ~, ~**en** giving; (einer Genehmigung) granting
ertönen *itr. V.; mit sein* sound
Ertrag *der;* ~**[e]s, Erträge (a)** yield **(b)** (Gewinn) return
ertragen *unr. tr. V.* bear
erträglich *Adj.* tolerable; bearable ‹*pain*›
ertrag·reich *Adj.* lucrative ‹*business*›; productive ‹*land, soil*›
ertränken *tr. V.* drown
ertrinken *unr. itr. V.; mit sein* be drowned; drown
erübrigen **1** *tr. V.* spare ‹*money, time*› **2** *refl. V.* be unnecessary
erwachen *itr. V.; mit sein* (geh.) awake
Erwachen *das;* ~**s** (auch fig.) awakening
erwachsen[1] *unr. itr. V.; mit sein* **(a)** grow (**aus** out of); ‹*rumour*› spread **(b)** (sich ergeben) ‹*difficulties, tasks*› arise
erwachsen[2] *Adj.* grown-up *attrib.;* ~ **sein** be grown up
Erwachsene *der/die; adj. Dekl.* adult; grown-up
erwägen *unr. tr. V.* consider
Erwägung *die;* ~, ~**en** consideration; **etw. in ~ ziehen** take sth. into consideration
erwählen *tr. V.* (geh.) choose
erwähnen *tr. V.* mention
erwähnens·wert *Adj.* worth mentioning *postpos.*
Erwähnung *die;* ~, ~**en** mention
erwärmen **1** *tr. V.* heat **2** *refl. V.* (warm werden) ‹*air, water*› warm up
Erwärmung *die;* ~: **eine ~ der Luft/des Wassers** an increase in air/water temperature; **bei ~ der Flüssigkeit** when the liquid is heated
erwarten *tr. V.* expect; **jmdn. am Bahnhof ~**: wait for sb. at the station
Erwartung *die;* ~, ~**en** expectation
erwartungs-: ~**gemäß** *Adv.* as expected; ~**voll** *Adj.* expectant
erwecken *tr. V.* **(a)** (auf~) wake **(b)** (erregen) arouse ‹*longing, pity*›
erweichen *tr. V.* soften
erweisen **1** *unr. tr. V.* **(a)** prove **(b)** (bezeigen) **jmdm. Achtung ~**: show respect to sb. **2** *unr. refl. V.* **sich als etw. ~**: prove to be sth.
erweitern **1** *tr. V.* widen ‹*river, road*›; expand ‹*library, business*›; enlarge ‹*collection*›; dilate ‹*pupil, blood vessel*› **2** *refl. V.* ‹*road, river*› widen; ‹*pupil, blood vessel*› dilate
Erweiterung *die;* ~, ~**en** ▶ ERWEITERN: widening; expansion; enlargement; dilation
Erwerb *der;* ~**[e]s (a)** (Aneignung) acquisition **(b)** (Kauf) purchase
erwerben *unr. tr. V.* **(a)** (verdienen) earn **(b)** (sich aneignen) gain **(c)** (kaufen) acquire
erwerbs-, Erwerbs-: ~**fähig** *Adj.* capable of gainful employment *postpos.;* able to work *postpos.;* ~**fähigkeit** *die* ability to work; ~**los** *Adj.:* ▶ ARBEITSLOS; ~**lose** *der/die; adj. Dekl.:* ▶ ARBEITSLOSE; ~**tätig** *Adj.* gainfully employed; ~**unfähig** *Adj.* incapable of gainful employment *postpos.;* unable to work *postpos.*
Erwerbung *die* acquisition; (Gekauftes) purchase
erwidern *tr. V.* **(a)** reply **(b)** (reagieren auf) return ‹*greeting, visit*›; reciprocate ‹*sb.'s feelings*›
Erwiderung *die;* ~, ~**en (a)** reply (**auf** + *Akk.* to) **(b)** ▶ ERWIDERN B: return; reciprocation
erwiesen *Adj.* proved; proven ‹*fact*›
erwiesener·maßen *Adv.* as has been proved
erwirken *tr. V.* obtain
erwirtschaften *tr. V.* **etw. ~**: obtain sth. by careful management
erwischen *tr. V.* (ugs.) **(a)** catch ‹*culprit, train, bus*› **(b)** (greifen) grab **(c)** (bekommen) manage to get **(d)** (*unpers.*) **es hat ihn erwischt** (ugs.) (er ist tot) he's bought it (sl.); (er ist krank) he's got it; (er ist verletzt) he's been hurt; (scherzh.: er ist verliebt) he's got it bad (coll.)
erwünscht *Adj.* wanted
erwürgen *tr. V.* strangle
Erz /ɛrts: *od.* e:ɐ̯ts:/ *das;* ~**es,** ~**e** ore
erzählen *tr.* (*auch itr.*) *V.* tell ‹*joke, story*›; **jmdm. etw. ~**: tell sb. sth.
Erzähler *der,* **Erzählerin** *die* storyteller; (Autor[in]) writer [of stories]; narrative writer
Erzählung *die;* ~, ~**en** narration; (Bericht) account; (Literaturw.) story
Erz-: ~**bischof** *der* archbishop; ~**bistum** *das,* ~**diözese** *die* archbishopric; archdiocese; ~**engel** *der* archangel
erzeugen *tr. V.* produce; generate ‹*electricity*›
Erzeuger *der;* ~**s,** ~ (Vater) father
Erzeugnis *das;* ~**ses,** ~**se** product
Erzeugung *die;* ~, ~**en** (von Lebensmitteln usw.) production; (von Industriewaren) manufacture; (Strom~) generation
Erz·feind *der,* **Erz·feindin** *die* arch enemy
erziehen *unr. tr. V.* bring up; (in der Schule) educate; **ein Kind zu Sauberkeit und Ordnung ~**: bring a child up to be clean and tidy
Erzieher *der;* ~**s,** ~, **Erzieherin** *die;* ~, ~**nen** educator; (Pädagoge) educationalist; (Lehrer) teacher
Erziehung *die;* ~, ~**en** upbringing; (Schul~) education

*old spelling - see note on page xiv

Erziehungs-: ~berechtigte *der/die; adj. Dekl.* parent or [legal] guardian; **~urlaub** *der* child-rearing leave

erzielen *tr. V.* reach ‹*agreement, compromise, speed*›; achieve ‹*result, effect*›; make ‹*profit*›; obtain ‹*price*›

erzürnen (geh.) *tr. V.* anger; (stärker) incense

erzwingen *unr. tr. V.* force

es *Personalpron.; 3. Pers. Sg. Nom. u. Akk. Neutr.* **(a)** (*s. auch Gen.* **seiner;** *Dat.* **ihm**) (Sache) it; (weibliche Person) she/her; (männliche Person) he/him
(b) *ohne Bezug auf ein bestimmtes Subst., mit unpers. konstruierten Verben, als formales Satzglied* it; **ich bin es** it's me; **wir sind traurig, ihr seid es auch** we are sad, and so are you; **es sei denn, [dass] ....** unless ...; **es ist genug!** that's enough; **es hat geklopft** there was a knock; **es klingelt** someone is ringing; **es wird schöner** the weather is improving; **es geht ihm gut/schlecht** he is well/unwell; **es wird gelacht** there is laughter; **es lässt sich aushalten** it is bearable; **er hat es gut** he has it good; **er meinte es gut** he meant well

Esche *die; ~, ~n* (Bot.) ash

Esel *der; ~s, ~* **(a)** donkey; ass
(b) (ugs.: Dummkopf) ass (coll.)

Esels-: ~brücke *die* (ugs.) mnemonic; **~ohr** *das* (ugs.: umgeknickte Stelle) dog-ear

Eskalation *die; ~, ~en* escalation

eskalieren *tr., itr. V.* escalate

Eskapade /ɛska'pa:də/ *die; ~, ~n* escapade; (Seitensprung) amorous adventure

Eskimo *der; ~[s], ~[s]* Eskimo

Eskimo·frau *die* Eskimo woman

Eskorte *die; ~, ~n* escort

eskortieren *tr. V.* escort

Espe *die; ~, ~n* aspen

Essay /'ɛse/ *der od. das; ~s, ~s* essay

essbar, *eßbar *Adj.* edible; **nicht ~:** inedible

essen *unr. tr., itr. V.* eat; **etw. gern ~:** like sth.; **sich satt ~:** eat one's fill; **gut ~:** have a good meal; (immer) eat well; **~ gehen** go out for a meal

Essen *das; ~s, ~* (Mahlzeit) meal; (Speise) food; **[das] ~ machen/kochen** get/cook the meal

Essen[s]-: ~marke *die* meal ticket; **~zeit** *die* mealtime

Essenz *die; ~, ~en* essence

Esser *der; ~s, ~,* **Esserin** *die; ~, ~nen:* **er ist ein schlechter Esser** he has a poor appetite

Essig *der; ~s, ~e* vinegar

Essig·gurke *die* pickled gherkin

Ess-, *Eß-: ~kastanie *die* sweet chestnut; **~löffel** *der* (Suppenlöffel) soup spoon; (für Nach-, Vorspeise) dessert spoon; **~stäbchen** *das* chopstick; **~teller** *der* dinner plate; **~tisch** *der* dining table; **~waren** *Pl.* food *sing.;* **~zimmer** *das* dining room

Establishment /ɪs'tɛblɪʃmənt/ *das; ~s, ~s* Establishment

Este *der; ~n, ~n,* **Estin** *die; ~, ~nen* Estonian

Est·land (*das*)*; ~s* Estonia

Estragon /'ɛstragɔn/ *der; ~s* tarragon

Estrich /'ɛstrɪç/ *der; ~s, ~e* composition floor

Eszett /ɛs'tsɛt/ *das; ~, ~* [the letter] ß

etablieren *tr. V.* establish; set up

etabliert *Adj.* established

Etablissement /etablɪs(ə)'mã:/ *das; ~s, ~s* establishment

Etage /e'ta:ʒə/ *die; ~, ~n* floor; storey

Etappe *die; ~, ~n* stage

Etat /e'ta:/ *der; ~s, ~s* budget

etepetete /e:təpe'te:tə/ *Adj.* (ugs.) fussy; finicky

Ethik *die; ~, ~en* **(a)** ethics *sing.;*
(b) (sittliche Normen) ethics *pl.*

ethisch *Adj.* ethical

ethnisch **1** *Adj.* ethnic; **~e Säuberung** ethnic cleansing
2 *adv.* ethnically

Etikett *das; ~[e]s, ~en od. ~e od. ~s* label

Etikette *die; ~, ~n* etiquette

Etiketten·schwindel *der* (abwertend) playing with names

etikettieren *tr. V.* label

etlich... *Indefinitpron. u. unbest. Zahlwort: Sg.* quite a lot of; *Pl.* quite a few

Etüde *die; ~, ~n* (Musik) étude

Etui /ɛt'vi:/ *das; ~s, ~s* case

etwa **1** *Adv.* **(a)** (ungefähr) about; **~ so groß wie ...:** about as large as ...; **~ so** roughly like this
(b) (beispielsweise) for example
2 *Partikel* **störe ich ~?** am I disturbing you at all?

etwaig... /'ɛtva(:)ɪg.../ *Adj.* possible

etwas *Indefinitpron.* **(a)** something; (fragend, verneinend) anything; **irgend~:** something
(b) (Bedeutsames) **aus ihm wird ~:** he'll make something of himself
(c) (ein Teil) some; (fragend, verneinend) any; **~ von dem Geld** some of the money
(d) (ein wenig) a little; **~ lauter/besser** a little louder/better

Etymologie *die; ~, ~n* etymology

EU *Abk.* = **Europäische Union** EU

euch **1** *Dat. u. Akk. Pl. des Personalpron.* **ihr** you
2 *Dat. u. Akk. Pl. des Reflexivpron. der 2. Pers. Pl.* yourselves

euer[1] *Possessivpron.* your; **Grüße von eu[e]rer Helga/eu[e]rem Hans** Best wishes, Yours, Helga/Hans

euer² *Gen. des Personalpron.* **ihr** (geh.) **wir werden ~ gedenken** we will remember you
Eule *die;* ~, ~n owl; **~n nach Athen tragen** carry coals to Newcastle
Eunuch *der;* ~en, ~en eunuch
Euphorie *die;* ~, ~n (bes. Med., Psych.) euphoria
euphorisch (bes. Med., Psych.) 1 *Adj.* euphoric
2 *adv.* euphorically
eure ▶ EUER¹
eurer·seits ▶ DEINERSEITS
euret·wegen *Adv.* ▶ DEINETWEGEN
Euro *der;* ~[s], ~[s] euro; **50 ~** 50 euros
Eurocheque /ˈɔyːroʃɛk/ *der;* ~s, ~s Eurocheque
Europa (*das*); ~s Europe
Europäer *der;* ~s, ~, **Europäerin** *die;* ~, ~nen European
europäisch *Adj.* European; **die Europäische Union** the European Union
Europa-: ~meister *der,* **~meisterin** *die* (Sport) European champion; **~meisterschaft** *die* (Sport) **(a)** (Wettbewerb) European Championship; **(b)** (Sieg) European title; **~parlament** *das* European Parliament; **~pokal** *der* (Sport) European cup; **~rat** *der* Council of Europe; **~straße** *die* European long-distance road
Euro-: ~scheck *der* ▶ EUROCHEQUE; **~zone** *die* eurozone
Euter *das od. der;* ~s, ~: udder
ev. *Abk.* = **evangelisch** ev.
e.V., E.V. *Abk.* = **eingetragener Verein**
evakuieren /evakuˈiːrən/ *tr. V.* evacuate
Evakuierung *die;* ~, ~en evacuation
evangelisch /evaŋˈgeːlɪʃ/ *Adj.* Protestant
Evangelium *das;* ~s, **Evangelien (a)** (auch fig.) gospel
(b) (christl. Rel.) Gospel
Event /iˈvɛnt/ *der od. das;* ~s, ~s event
Eventualität /evɛntu̯aliˈtɛːt/ *die;* ~, ~en eventuality; contingency
eventuell 1 *Adj.* possible
2 *adv.* possibly; perhaps
Evolution /evoluˈtsi̯oːn/ *die;* ~, ~en evolution
evtl. *Abk.* = **eventuell**
EWG *Abk.* = **Europäische Wirtschaftsgemeinschaft** EEC
ewig 1 *Adj.* eternal; (abwertend) never-ending
2 *adv.* eternally; for ever
Ewig·gestrige *der/die; adj. Dekl.* (abwertend) **ein ~r sein** be an old reactionary
Ewigkeit *die;* ~, ~en **(a)** eternity
(b) (ugs.) **es dauert eine ~:** it takes ages (coll.)
ex *Adv.* (ugs.) **etw. ex trinken** drink sth. down in one (coll.)

*alte Schreibung - vgl. Hinweis auf S. xiv

exakt *Adj.* exact; precise
Exaktheit *die;* ~: precision; exactness
Examen *das;* ~s, ~ *od.* **Examina** examination
exekutieren *tr. V.* **(a)** execute
(b) (österr.) ▶ PFÄNDEN
Exekution *die;* ~, ~en **(a)** execution
(b) (österr.) ▶ PFÄNDUNG
Exekutive *die;* ~, ~n (Rechtsw., Politik) executive
Exempel *das;* ~s, ~: example
Exemplar *das;* ~s, ~e specimen; (Buch, Zeitung usw.) copy
exemplarisch *Adj.* exemplary
exerzieren *tr., itr. V.* drill
Exhibitionist *der;* ~en, ~en, **Exhibitionistin** *die;* ~, ~nen (Psych., fig.) exhibitionist
exhibitionistisch (Psych.) 1 *Adj.* exhibitionist
2 *adv.* **er ist ~ veranlagt** he has exhibitionist tendencies
Exil *das;* ~s, ~e exile
exiliert *Adj.* exiled
Exil·regierung *die* government in exile
existentiell ▶ EXISTENZIELL
Existenz *die;* ~, ~en **(a)** existence
(b) (Lebensgrundlage) livelihood
(c) (Mensch) character
Existenz·grundlage *die* basis of one's livelihood
existenziell *Adj.* existential; **in etw.** (*Dat.*) **eine ~e Bedrohung sehen** see in sth. a threat to one's existence
Existenz-: ~kampf *der* struggle for existence; **~minimum** *das* subsistence level
existieren *itr. V.* exist
Exitus *der;* ~ (Med.) death
exkl. *Abk.* = **exklusiv[e]** excl.
exklusiv 1 *Adj.* exclusive
2 *adv.* exclusively
exklusive *Präp.* + *Gen.* exclusive of
Exklusiv·vertrag *der* exclusive contract
Exkommunikation *die;* ~, ~en excommunication
Exkursion *die;* ~, ~en study trip
exotisch 1 *Adj.* exotic
2 *adv.* exotically
expandieren *tr., itr. V.* expand
Expansion *die;* ~, ~en expansion
Expedition *die;* ~, ~en expedition
Experiment *das;* ~[e]s, ~e experiment
experimentell 1 *Adj.* experimental
2 *adv.* experimentally
experimentieren *itr. V.* experiment
Experte *der;* ~n, ~n, **Expertin** *die;* ~, ~nen expert (**für** in)
Experten·system *das* (DV) expert system
explizit 1 *Adj.* explicit
2 *adv.* ‹*describe, define*› explicitly

explodieren *itr. V.; mit sein* (auch fig.) explode; ‹*costs*› rocket
Explosion *die;* **~, ~en** explosion
explosiv [1] *Adj.* (auch fig.) explosive [2] *adv.* explosively
Exponent *der;* **~en, ~en** (Math.) exponent
exponiert *Adj.* exposed
Export[1] *der;* **~[e]s, ~e** export
Export[2] *das;* **~s, ~e** (Bier) export; **zwei ~:** two export
Export-: ~artikel *der* export; **~bier** *das* export beer
Exporteur /ɛkspɔr'tøːɐ̯/ *der;* **~s, ~e, Exporteurin** *die;* **~, ~nen** (Wirtsch.) exporter
Export-: ~firma *die* exporter; **~handel** *der* export trade
exportieren *tr., itr. V.* export
Express·gut, *Expreß·gut *das* express freight
Expressionismus *der;* **~:** expressionism *no art.*
expressionistisch *Adj.* expressionist
exquisit [1] *Adj.* exquisite [2] *adv.* exquisitely
extern *Adj.* external
extra *Adv.* **(a)** (gesondert) ‹*pay*› separately **(b)** (zusätzlich, besonders) extra **(c)** (eigens) especially
Extra *das;* **~s, ~s** extra
Extra·blatt *das* special edition
Extrakt *der;* **~[e]s, ~e** extract
extra·terrestrisch *Adj.* (Astron.) extraterrestrial
extravagant /-va'gant/ *Adj.* flamboyant; flamboyantly furnished ‹*flat*›
Extravaganz /-va'gants:/ *die;* **~, ~en** **(a)** flamboyance **(b)** *Pl.* **seine ~en** his flamboyance *sing.*
extravertiert /-vɛr'tiːɐ̯t/ *Adj.* (Psych.) extrovert[ed]
Extravertiertheit *die;* **~** (Psych.) extroversion
Extra·wurst *die* (fig. ugs.) **eine ~ bekommen** get special treatment *or* special favours
extrem *Adj.* extreme
Extrem *das;* **~s, ~e** extreme
Extrem·fall *der* extreme case
Extremismus *der;* **~:** extremism
Extremist *der;* **~en, ~en, Extremistin** *die;* **~, ~nen** extremist
extremistisch *Adj.* extremist
Extremität /ɛkstremi'tɛːt/ *die;* **~, ~en** **(a)** extremity **(b)** (das Extremsein) extremeness
Extrem-: ~sportart *die* extreme sport; **~wert** *der* (Math.) extremum
Exzellenz *die;* **~, ~en** Excellency
Exzentriker *der;* **~s, ~, Exzentrikerin** *die;* **~, ~nen** eccentric
exzentrisch [1] *Adj.* eccentric [2] *adv.* eccentrically
Exzess, *Exzeß *der;* **Exzesses, Exzesse** excess
exzessiv /ɛkstsɛ'siːf/ [1] *Adj.* excessive [2] *adv.* excessively

Ff

f, F /ɛf/ *das;* **~, ~ (a)** (Buchstabe) f/F **(b)** (Musik) [key of] F
f. *Abk.* = **folgend** f.
Fa. *Abk.* = **Firma**
Fabel *die;* **~, ~n** fable; (Kern einer Handlung) plot
fabelhaft [1] *Adj.* (ugs.: großartig) fantastic (coll.) [2] *adv.* (ugs.) fantastically (coll.)
Fabrik *die;* **~, ~en** factory
Fabrikant *der;* **~en, ~en** manufacturer
Fabrikat *das;* **~[e]s, ~e** product; (Marke) make
Fabrikation *die;* **~:** production
Fabrikations·fehler *der* manufacturing fault; factory fault
Fabrik-: ~besitzer *der,* **~besitzerin** *die* factory owner; **~direktor** *der,* **~direktorin** *die* works manager
fabrizieren *tr. V.* (ugs. abwertend) knock together (coll.)
fabulieren *itr. V.* invent stories; spin yarns
Fach *das;* **~[e]s, Fächer (a)** compartment; (für Post) pigeonhole **(b)** (Studien~, Unterrichts~) subject; (Wissensgebiet) field; (Berufszweig) trade; **ein Mann vom ~:** an expert
Fach-: ~arbeiter *der,* **~arbeiterin** *die* skilled worker; **~arzt** *der,* **~ärztin** *die* specialist (für in); **~bereich** *der* (Hochschulw.) faculty; school; (in der Schule) department
fächer·übergreifend *Adj.:* ▶ FACHÜBERGREIFEND

Fach-: ~frau *die* expert; **~geschäft** *das* specialist shop; **~hochschule** *die* college (*offering courses in a special subject*)

fachlich *Adj.* specialist ‹*knowledge, work*›; technical ‹*problem, explanation, experience*›

fach-, Fach-: ~mann *der; Pl.* **~männer** *od.* **~leute** expert; **~terminus** *der* specialist/technical term; **~übergreifend** [1] *Adj.* interdisciplinary ‹*teaching*›; [2] *adv.* ‹*think, argue*› along interdisciplinary lines; ‹*teach*› using interdisciplinary methods; **~werk** *das* (Bauweise) half-timbered construction; **~werk·haus** *das* half-timbered house; **~zeitschrift** *die* specialist/technical journal

Fackel *die;* ~, **~n** torch

fade *Adj.* insipid; **ein ~r Beigeschmack** (fig.) a flat aftertaste

Faden *der;* **~s, Fäden** thread; **ein ~:** a piece of thread

faden·scheinig *Adj.* threadbare; flimsy ‹*excuse*›

Fagott *das;* **~[e]s, ~e** bassoon

fähig *Adj.* **(a)** (begabt) able; capable **(b) zu etw. ~ sein** be capable of sth.

Fähigkeit *die;* ~, **~en (a)** ability; capability; **geistige ~en** intellectual faculties **(b)** (Imstandesein) ability (**zu** to)

fahl *Adj.* pale; pallid; wan ‹*light*›

fahnden *itr. V.* search (**nach** for)

Fahndung *die;* ~, **~en** search

Fahne *die;* ~, **~n** flag

Fahr·bahn *die* carriageway

Fähr·betrieb *der* ferry service; (von mehreren Fähren) ferry services *pl.*

Fähre *die;* ~, **~n** ferry

fahren [1] *unr. itr. V.; mit sein* **(a)** (als Fahrzeuglenker) drive; (mit dem Fahrrad, Motorrad usw.) ride
(b) (als Mitfahrer; mit öffentlichem Verkehrsmittel) go (**mit** by); (mit dem Aufzug/der Rolltreppe/der Seilbahn) take the lift (Brit.) *or* (Amer.) elevator/escalator/cable car; (per Anhalter) hitch-hike
(c) (reisen) go; **in Urlaub ~:** go on holiday
(d) (los~) go; leave
(e) ‹*motor vehicle, train, lift, cable car*› go; ‹*ship*› sail; **mein Auto fährt nicht** my car won't go
(f) (verkehren) ‹*train etc.*› run
(g) etw. ~ lassen (loslassen) let sth. go; (fig.: aufgeben) abandon sth.
[2] *unr. tr. V.* **(a)** (fortbewegen) drive ‹*car, lorry, train, etc.*›; ride ‹*bicycle, motor cycle*›
(b) 50/80 km/h ~: do 50/80 k.p.h.; **hier muss man 50 km/h ~:** you've got to keep to 50 k.p.h. here; sail ‹*boat*›; **Auto ~:** drive [a car]; **Kahn** *od.* **Boot/Kanu ~:** go boating/canoeing; **Ski ~:** ski; **U-Bahn ~:** ride on the underground (Brit.) *or* (Amer.) subway
(c) (befördern) take

*old spelling - see note on page xiv

Fahrenheit: 70 Grad ~: 70 degrees Fahrenheit

***fahren|lassen** ▸ FAHREN 1G

Fahrer *der;* **~s, ~:** driver

Fahrerflucht *die:* **wegen ~:** for failing to stop after [being involved in] an accident; **~ begehen** fail to stop after [being involved in] an accident

Fahrerin *die;* ~, **~nen** driver

Fahr-: ~gast *der* passenger; **~geld** *das* fare

fahrig *Adj.* nervous

fahr-, Fahr-: ~karte *die* ticket; **~karten·automat** *der* ticket machine; **~karten·schalter** *der* ticket window; **~lässig** [1] *Adj.* negligent ‹*behaviour*›; **~lässige Tötung/Körperverletzung** (Rechtsw.) causing death/injury through [culpable] negligence; [2] *adv.* negligently; **~lehrer** *der,* **~lehrerin** *die* driving instructor

Fähr·mann *der; Pl.* **Fährmänner** *od.* **Fährleute** ferryman

fahr-, Fahr-: ~plan *der* timetable; schedule (Amer.); **~plan·mäßig** [1] *Adj.* scheduled ‹*departure, arrival*›; [2] *adv.* ‹*depart, arrive*› according to schedule, on time; **~preis** *der* fare; **~prüfung** *die* driving test; **~rad** *das* bicycle; cycle; **mit dem ~rad fahren** cycle; ride a bicycle; **~rad·kurier** *der,* **~rad·kurierin** *die* bicycle *or* bike messenger; bicycle *or* bike courier; **~rad·ständer** *der* bicycle rack; **~schein** *der* ticket; **~schein·automat** *der* ticket machine; **~schein·entwerter** *der* ticket cancelling machine; **~schule** *die* driving school; **~spur** *die* traffic lane

fährst *2. Pers. Sg. Präsens v.* FAHREN

Fahr-: ~stuhl *der* lift (Brit.); elevator (Amer.); (für Lasten) hoist; **~stunde** *die* driving lesson

Fahrt *die;* ~, **~en (a)** journey; **freie ~ haben** have a clear run; (Schiffsreise) voyage; (kurze Reise, Ausflug) trip
(b) (Geschwindigkeit) **in voller ~:** at full speed

fährt *3. Pers. Sg. Präsens v.* FAHREN

Fährte *die* trail; **jmds. ~ verfolgen** track sb.

Fahrt·kosten *Pl.* (für öffentliche Verkehrsmittel) fare/fares; (für Autoreisen) travel costs

Fahr·treppe *die* escalator

Fahrt·richtung *die* direction; **in ~ parken** park in the direction of the traffic; **die ~ ändern** change direction

fahr·tüchtig *Adj.* ‹*driver*› fit to drive; ‹*vehicle*› roadworthy

Fahrt-: ~wind *der* airflow; **~ziel** *das* destination

Fahr-: ~wasser *das* shipping channel; fairway; **in ein gefährliches ~wasser geraten** (fig.) get on to dangerous ground; **~werk** *das* (Flugw.) undercarriage; **~zeit** *die* travelling time; **~zeug** *das* vehicle; (Luft~) aircraft; (Wasser~) vessel; **~zeug·papiere** *Pl.* vehicle documents *pl.*

fair /fɛ:ɐ̯/ 1 *Adj.* fair (**gegen** to)
2 *adv.* fairly
Fäkalien /fɛ:'ka:li̯ən/ *Pl.* faeces *pl.*
Fakten ▶ FAKTUM
faktisch 1 *Adj.* real; actual
2 *adv.* **das bedeutet ~ ...:** it means in effect ...
Faktor *der;* **~s, ~en** (auch Math.) factor
Faktum *das;* **~s, Fakten** fact
Fakultät *die;* **~, ~en** (Hochschulw.) faculty
Falke *der;* **~n, ~n** (auch Politik fig.) hawk
Fall *der;* **~[e]s, Fälle (a)** (Sturz) fall; **zu ~ kommen** have a fall; **jmdn. zu ~ bringen** (fig.) bring about sb.'s downfall
(b) (das Fallen) descent; **der freie ~:** free fall
(c) (Ereignis; Rechtsw., Med., Grammatik) case; (zu erwartender Umstand) eventuality; **es ist [nicht] der ~:** it is [not] the case; **gesetzt den ~:** assuming; **auf jeden ~, in jedem ~, auf alle Fälle** in any case; **auf keinen ~:** on no account
Falle *die;* **~, ~n** (auch fig.) trap
fallen *unr. itr. V.; mit sein* **(a)** fall; **jmdn./etw. ~ lassen** drop sb./sth.
(b) (hin~, stürzen) fall [over]; **über einen Stein ~:** trip over a stone
(c) ‹*prices, light, glance, choice*› fall; ‹*temperature, water level*› fall, drop; ‹*fever*› subside; ‹*shot*› be fired
(d) (im Kampf sterben) die; fall (literary)
fällen *tr. V.* **(a)** fell ‹*tree, timber*›
(b) ein Urteil ~ ‹*judge*› pass sentence; ‹*jury*› return a verdict
***fallen|lassen** ▶ FALLEN A
fällig *Adj.* due
Fall·obst *das* windfalls *pl.*
Fallout /fɔ:l'|aʊt/ *der;* **~s, ~s** (Kernphysik) fallout
falls *Konj.* **(a)** (wenn) if
(b) (für den Fall, dass) in case
Fall·schirm *der* parachute; **mit dem ~ abspringen** (im Notfall) parachute out; (als Sport) make a [parachute] jump
falsch 1 *Adj.* **(a)** (unecht, imitiert) false ‹*teeth, plait*›; imitation ‹*jewellery*›
(b) (gefälscht) forged; assumed ‹*name*›
(c) (irrig, fehlerhaft) wrong
2 *adv.* wrongly; **die Uhr geht ~:** the clock is wrong
fälschen *tr. V.* forge
Fälscher *der;* **~s, ~, Fälscherin** *die;* **~, ~nen** forger
Falschgeld *das* counterfeit money
fälschlich 1 *Adj.* false
2 *adv.* falsely
Falsch·meldung *die* false report
Fälschung *die;* **~, ~en** fake
Falt·blatt *das* leaflet; (in Zeitungen, Zeitschriften, Büchern) insert
Falte *die;* **~, ~n (a)** crease
(b) (im Stoff) fold; (mit scharfer Kante) pleat
(c) (Haut~) wrinkle
falten 1 *tr. V.* fold; **die Hände ~:** fold one's hands
2 *refl. V.* (auch Geol.) fold; ‹*skin*› become wrinkled
Falten·rock *der* pleated skirt
Falter *der;* **~s, ~** (Nacht~) moth; (Tag~) butterfly
faltig (a) *Adj.* ‹*clothes*› gathered [in folds]; wrinkled ‹*skin, hands*›
(b) (zerknittert) creased
-fältig *Adj., adv.* -fold
Falt·rad *das* folding bicycle
Falz *der;* **~es, ~e** fold
falzen *tr. V.* fold; seam
familiär *Adj.* **(a)** family ‹*problems, worries*›
(b) (zwanglos) familiar; informal
Familie /fa'mi:li̯ə/ *die;* **~, ~n** family; **~ Meyer** the Meyer family
Familien-: ~angehörige *der/die* member of the family; **~feier** *die* family party; **~grab** *das* family grave; **~leben** *das* family life; **~name** *der* surname; **~planung** *die* family planning *no art.;* **~stand** *der* marital status; **~vater** *der:* **~vater sein** be the father of a family; **ein guter ~vater** a good husband and father
Fan /fɛn/ *der;* **~s, ~s** fan
Fanatiker *der;* **~s, ~, Fanatikerin** *die;* **~, ~nen** fanatic; (religiös) fanatic; zealot
fanatisch 1 *Adj.* fanatical
2 *adv.* fanatically
fanatisieren *tr. V.* rouse to fanaticism; **der fanatisierte Mob** the fanatically excited mob
fand *1. u. 3. Pers. Sg. Prät. v.* FINDEN
Fanfare *die;* **~, ~n** (Signal) fanfare
Fang *der;* **~[e]s, Fänge (a)** (Tier~) trapping; (von Fischen) catching
(b) (Beute) bag; (von Fischen) catch
fangen 1 *unr. tr. V.* catch; capture ‹*fugitive etc.*›; **jmdn./ein Tier gefangen halten** hold sb. prisoner/keep an animal in captivity; **jmdn. gefangen nehmen** take sb. prisoner
2 *unr. refl. V.* **(a)** (in eine Falle geraten) be caught
(b) (wieder in die normale Lage kommen) **sich [gerade] noch ~:** [just] manage to steady oneself
Fang·frage *die* catch question
Fantasie *die;* **~, ~n (a)** imagination
(b) (Produkt der ~) fantasy
fantasie·los 1 *Adj.* unimaginative
2 *adv.* unimaginatively
Fantasielosigkeit *die;* **~:** lack of imagination; (Eintönigkeit) dullness
fantasieren *itr. V.* indulge in fantasies, fantasize (**von** about)
fantasievoll 1 *Adj.* imaginative
2 *adv.* imaginatively
fantastisch 1 *Adj.* **(a)** fantastic; ‹*idea*› divorced from reality
(b) (ugs.: großartig) fantastically (coll.)

Farb-: ~bild *das* (Foto) colour photo; **~dia** *das* colour slide; **~drucker** *der* (DV) colour printer

Farbe *die;* ~, **~n (a)** colour **(b)** (für Textilien) dye; (zum Malen, Anstreichen) paint; **~n mischen/auftragen** mix/apply paint

farb·echt *Adj.* colour-fast

färben 1 *tr. V.* dye 2 *refl. V.* change colour; **sich schwarz/rot** *usw.* **~:** turn black/red *etc.* 3 *itr. V.* (ugs.: ab~) ‹*material, blouse etc.*› run

-farben *Adj.* coloured

farben-, Farben-: ~blind *Adj.* colour-blind; **~froh** *Adj.* colourful; **~pracht** *die* colourful splendour; **~prächtig** *Adj.* vibrant with colour *postpos.*

Farb-: ~fernsehen *das* colour television; **~fernseher** *der* (ugs.) colour telly (coll.) *or* television; **~film** *der* colour film; **~foto** *das* colour photo

farbig 1 *Adj.* **(a)** coloured **(b)** (bunt, auch fig.) colourful 2 *adv.* colourfully

-farbig *Adj.* -coloured

Farbige *der/die; adj. Dekl.* coloured man/woman; *Pl.* coloured people

farblich 1 *Adj.* in colour *postpos.;* as regards colour *postpos;* 2 *adv.* **etw. ~ abstimmen** match sth. in colour

farb-, Farb-: ~los *Adj.* (auch fig.) colourless; clear ‹*varnish*›; neutral ‹*shoe polish*›; **~losigkeit** *die;* ~~ (auch fig.) colourlessness; **~stift** *der* coloured pencil; **~stoff** *der* **(a)** (Med., Biol.) pigment; **(b)** (für Textilien) dye; **(c)** (für Lebensmittel) colouring; **~ton** *der; Pl.* **~töne** shade; **~tupfen, ~tupfer** *der* spot of colour

Färbung *die;* ~, **~en** colouring

Farn *der;* **~[e]s, ~e, Farn·kraut** *das* fern

Fasan *der;* **~[e]s, ~e[n]** pheasant

Fasching *der;* **~s, ~e** *od.* **~s** [pre-Lent] carnival

Faschismus *der;* **~:** fascism *no art.*

Faschist *der;* **~en, ~en, Faschistin** *die;* **~, ~nen** fascist

faschistisch *Adj.* fascist

faseln *itr. V.* (ugs. abwertend) drivel

Faser *die;* **~, ~n** fibre

fasern *itr. V.* fray

Fass, *Faß *das;* **Fasses, Fässer** barrel; (Öl~) drum; (kleines Bier~) keg; (kleines Sherry~ usw.) cask; **Bier vom ~:** draught beer; **ein ~ ohne Boden** an endless drain on sb.'s resources

Fassade *die;* **~, ~n** façade

fassbar, *faßbar *Adj.* **(a)** tangible ‹*results*› **(b)** (verständlich) comprehensible

Fass·bier, *Faß·bier *das* draught beer; beer on draught

fassen 1 *tr. V.* **(a)** (greifen) grasp; take hold of **(b)** (festnehmen) catch ‹*thief, culprit*› **(c)** (aufnehmen können) ‹*hall, tank*› hold **(d)** (begreifen) **ich kann es nicht ~:** I cannot take it in **(e) einen Entschluss ~:** make *or* take a decision 2 *itr. V.* (greifen) **nach etw. ~:** reach for sth.; **in etw.** (*Akk.*) **~:** put one's hand in sth.

fasslich, *faßlich *Adj.* comprehensible

Fasson /fa'sõ:/ *die;* **~, ~s** style; shape

Fassung *die;* **~, ~en (a)** (Form) version **(b)** (Selbstbeherrschung) composure; **die ~ bewahren** keep one's composure; **die ~ verlieren** lose one's self-control; **jmdn. aus der ~ bringen** upset sb. **(c)** (für Glühlampen) holder

fassungs·los *Adj.* stunned

fast *Adv.* almost; nearly; **~ nie** hardly ever

fasten *itr. V.* fast

Fast·nacht *die* carnival; **~ feiern** celebrate Shrovetide *or* the carnival

Fastnachts-: ~brauch *der* Shrovetide custom; **~dienstag** *der* Shrove Tuesday; **~zug** *der* carnival procession

faszinieren *tr. V.* fascinate

faszinierend 1 *Adj.* fascinating 2 *adv.* fascinatingly

fatal *Adj.* **(a)** (peinlich, misslich) awkward **(b)** (verhängnisvoll) fatal

fauchen *itr. V.* ‹*cat*› hiss; ‹*tiger, person*› snarl

faul *Adj.* **(a)** (verdorben) rotten; bad ‹*food, tooth*›; foul ‹*water, air*› **(b)** (träge) lazy

Fäule *die;* **~:** foulness

faulen *itr. V.; meist mit sein* rot; ‹*water*› go foul; ‹*meat, fish*› go off

faulenzen *itr. V.* laze about; loaf about (derog.)

Faulenzer *der;* **~s, ~, Faulenzerin** *die;* **~, ~nen** idler; lazybones *sing.* (coll.)

Faulheit *die;* **~:** laziness

faulig *Adj.* stagnating ‹*water*›; **~ schmecken/riechen** taste/smell off

Fäulnis *die;* **~:** rottenness

Faul-: ~pelz *der* (fam.) lazybones *sing.* (coll.); **~tier** *das* **(a)** (Zool.) sloth; **(b)** (ugs.: Faulenzer[in]) ▶ ~PELZ

Fauna *die;* **~, Faunen** (Zool.) fauna

Faust *die;* **~, Fäuste** fist; **eine ~ machen** clench one's fist; **das passt wie die ~ aufs Auge** (ugs.) (passt nicht) that clashes horribly; (passt) that matches perfectly; **auf eigene ~:** on one's own initiative

Fäustchen *das;* **~s, ~: sich** (*Dat.*) **ins ~ lachen** laugh up one's sleeve

*alte Schreibung - vgl. Hinweis auf S. xiv

faust·dick *Adj.* as thick as a man's fist *postpos.;* (fig.) barefaced ‹*lie*›
Fäustling *der;* **~s, ~e** mitten
Faust·regel *die* rule of thumb
Favorit /favo'ri:t/ *der;* **~en, ~en, Favoritin** *die;* **~, ~nen** favourite
Fax *das;* **~, ~[e]** fax
Fax·anschluss, *Fax·anschluß *der* fax line
faxen *tr. V.* fax
Faxen *Pl.* (ugs.) fooling around
Fax-: ~gerät *das* fax machine; **~nachricht** *der* fax message; **~nummer** *die* fax number
Fazit *das;* **~s, ~s** *od.* **~e** result
FCKW *Abk.* = **Fluorchlorkohlenwasserstoff** CFC
FCKW-frei *Adj* CFC-free
FDP, F.D.P. *Abk.* = **Freie Demokratische Partei**
Feature /'fi:tʃɐ/ *das;* **~s, ~s** (Rundf., Ferns., Zeitungsw.) feature
Februar *der;* **~[s], ~e** February
fechten *unr. itr., tr. V.* fence
Fechter *der;* **~s, ~, Fechterin** *die;* **~, ~nen** fencer
Feder *die;* **~, ~n (a)** (Vogel~) feather **(b)** (zum Schreiben) nib **(c)** (Technik) spring
feder-, Feder-: ~ball *der* **(a)** (Spiel) badminton; **(b)** (Ball) shuttlecock; **~bett** *das* duvet (Brit.); stuffed quilt (Amer.); **~führend** *Adj.* in charge *postpos.;* **~halter** *der* fountain pen; **~leicht** *Adj.* ‹*person*› as light as a feather; featherweight ‹*object*›; **~lesen** *das:* **nicht viel ~lesen[s] mit jmdm./etw. machen** give sb./sth. short shrift
federn **1** *itr. V.* ‹*springboard, floor, etc.*› be springy **2** *tr. V.* (mit einer Federung versehen) spring; **das Bett ist gut gefedert** the bed is well-sprung
Federung *die;* **~, ~en** (Kfz-W.) suspension
Fee *die;* **~, ~n** fairy
Feedback /'fi:dbæk/ *das;* **~s, ~s** feedback
Fege·feuer *das* purgatory
fegen **1** *tr. V.* **(a)** (bes. nordd.: säubern) sweep **(b)** (schnell entfernen) brush **2** *itr. V.* sweep up
Fehde *die;* **~, ~n** feud
Fehde·hand·schuh *der* **jmdm. den ~ hinwerfen** throw down the gauntlet to sb.
fehl *Adv.* **~ am Platz[e] sein** be out of place
Fehl·anzeige *die:* **~!** (ugs.) no chance! (coll.)
fehlen *itr. V.* **(a)** (nicht vorhanden sein) **ihm fehlt das Geld** he has no money **(b)** (ausbleiben) be absent **(d)** (verschwunden sein) be missing; **in der Kasse fehlt Geld** money is missing from the till **(d)** (vermisst werden) **er/das wird mir ~:** I shall miss him/that **(e)** (erforderlich sein) be needed; **ihm ~ noch zwei Punkte zum Sieg** he needs only two points to win; **es fehlte nicht viel, und ich wäre eingeschlafen** I all but fell asleep **(f)** *unpers.* (mangeln) **es fehlt an Lehrern** there is a lack of teachers **(g)** (krank sein) **was fehlt Ihnen?** what seems to be the matter?; **fehlt dir etwas?** is there something wrong?
Fehl-: ~entscheidung *die* wrong decision; **~entwicklung** *die* abortive development
Fehler *der;* **~s, ~ (a)** (Irrtum) mistake, error; (Sport) fault **(b)** (schlechte Eigenschaft) fault
fehler·frei *Adj.* faultless
fehlerhaft *Adj.* faulty; defective; imperfect ‹*pronunciation*›
Fehler·quelle *die* source of error
fehl-, Fehl-: ~geburt *die* miscarriage; **~investition** *die* (bes. Wirtsch.) bad investment; **~planung** *die* [piece of] bad planning *no art.;* **~schlag** *der* failure; **~|schlagen** *unr. itr. V.; mit sein* fail; **~start** *der* (Leichtathletik) false start; **~tritt** *der* (fig. geh.) slip; **~urteil** *das* **(a)** (Rechtsw.) **ein ~urteil fällen** ‹*jury*› return a wrong verdict; ‹*judge*› pass a wrong judgement **(b)** (falsche Beurteilung) error of judgement; **~verhalten** *das* (fehlerhaftes Verhalten) incorrect conduct; **~zündung** *die* (Technik) misfire
Feier *die;* **~, ~n (a)** (Veranstaltung) party; (aus festlichem Anlass) celebration **(b)** (Zeremonie) ceremony
Feier·abend *der* (Arbeitsschluss) finishing time; **nach ~:** after work; **~ machen** finish work
feierlich **1** *Adj.* ceremonial ‹*act etc.*›; solemn ‹*silence*› **2** *adv.* solemnly; ceremoniously
Feierlichkeit *die;* **~, ~en (a)** solemnity **(b)** (Veranstaltung) celebration
feiern **1** *tr. V.* **(a)** celebrate ‹*birthday, wedding, etc.*› **(b)** acclaim ‹*artist, sportsman, etc.*› **2** *itr. V.* celebrate
Feier·tag *der* holiday; **ein gesetzlicher/kirchlicher ~:** a public holiday/religious festival
feig[e] **1** *Adj.* cowardly **2** *adv.* in a cowardly way
Feige *die;* **~, ~n** fig
Feigheit *die;* **~:** cowardice
Feigling *der;* **~s, ~e** coward
Feile *die;* **~, ~n** file
feilen *tr., itr. V.* file
feilschen *itr. V.* haggle **(um** over)

fein 1 *Adj.* **(a)** fine; finely-ground ‹*flour*›; finely-granulated ‹*sugar*›
(b) (hochwertig) high-quality ‹*fruit, soap, etc.*›; fine ‹*silver, gold*›; fancy ‹*cakes, pastries, etc.*›
(c) (ugs.: erfreulich) great (coll.)
(d) sich ~ machen (ugs.) dress up
2 *adv.* **~ [he]raus sein** (ugs.) be sitting pretty (coll.)

Feind *der;* **~[e]s, ~e, Feindin** *die;* **~, ~nen** enemy

feindlich 1 *Adj.* **(a)** hostile
(b) (Milit.) enemy ‹*attack, activity*›
2 *adv.* in a hostile manner

Feindschaft *die;* **~, ~en** enmity

feind·selig *Adj.* hostile

Feind·seligkeit *die;* **~, ~en** hostility; **~en** (Milit.) hostilities

Feinheit *die;* **~, ~en (a)** fineness; delicacy **(b)** (Nuance) subtlety

fein-, Fein-: ~kost·geschäft *das* delicatessen; ***~|machen** ▶ FEIN 1D; **~schmecker** *der;* **~~s, ~~, ~schmeckerin** *die;* **~~, ~~nen** gourmet; **~sinnig** *Adj.* sensitive and subtle; **~waschmittel** *das* mild detergent

feist *Adj.* (meist abwertend) fat

Feld *das;* **~[e]s, ~er (a)** field
(b) (Sport: Spiel~) pitch; field
(c) (auf Formularen) box; space; (auf Brettspielen) space; (auf dem Schachbrett) square
(d) (Tätigkeitsbereich) field; sphere

Feld-: ~herr *der* (veralt.) commander; **~marschall** *der* Field Marshal; **~salat** *der* corn salad; **~stecher** *der;* **~~s, ~~** binoculars *pl.;* **~versuch** *der* (Wissensch.) field experiment; **~webel** *der;* **~~s, ~~** (Milit.) sergeant; **~weg** *der* path; track; **~zug** *der* (Milit., fig.) campaign

Felge *die;* **~, ~n** [wheel] rim

Fell *das;* **~[e]s, ~e (a)** (Haarkleid) fur; (Pferde~, Hunde~, Katzen~) coat; (Schaf~) fleece
(b) (Material) fur
(c) (abgezogen) hide; **ein dickes ~ haben** (ugs.) be thick-skinned

Fels *der;* **~en, ~en** rock

Felsen *der;* **~s, ~:** rock; (an der Steilküste) cliff

felsen-, Felsen-: ~fest *Adj.* firm; unshakeable ‹*opinion, belief*›; **~küste** *die* rocky coast *or* coastline

felsig *Adj.* rocky

Fels-: ~spalte *die* crevice [in the rock]; **~wand** *die* rock face

feminin *Adj.* feminine

Feminismus *der;* **~:** feminism *no art.*

Feminist *der;* **~en, ~en, Feministin** *die;* **~, ~nen** feminist

Fenchel *der;* **~s** fennel

Fenster *das;* **~s, ~:** window

*old spelling - see note on page xiv

Fenster-: ~bank *die Pl.* **~bänke** window sill; **~laden** *der* [window] shutter; **~leder** *das* wash leather; **~platz** *der* window seat; **~putzer** *der;* **~~s, ~~, ~putzerin** *die;* **~~, ~~nen** window cleaner; **~rahmen** *der* window frame; **~scheibe** *die* window pane

Ferien /ˈfeːri̯ən/ *Pl.* holiday[s *pl.*] (Brit.); vacation (Amer.); **in die ~ fahren** go on holiday/vacation; **~ haben** have a *or* be on holiday/vacation

Ferien-: ~arbeit *die* vacation work; **eine ~arbeit** a vacation job; **~haus** *das* holiday house (Brit.); vacation house (Amer.); **~job** *der* vacation job; **~ort** *der* holiday resort (Brit.); vacation resort (Amer.); **~paradies** *das* holiday[maker's] paradise (Brit.); vacationer['s] paradise (Amer.); **~wohnung** *die* holiday flat *or* apartment (Brit.); vacation apartment (Amer.)

Ferkel *das;* **~s, ~:** piglet

fern 1 *Adj.* distant; **jmdn./etw. ~ halten** keep sb./sth. away
2 *adv.* **~ von der Heimat** far from home

fern-, Fern-: ~bedienung *die* remote control; **~|bleiben** *unr. itr. V.; mit sein* (geh.) stay away

Ferne *die;* **~, ~n** distance

ferner *Adv.* furthermore

fern-, Fern-: ~fahrer *der,* **~fahrerin** *die* long-distance lorry driver (Brit.) *or* (Amer.) trucker; **~flug** *der* long-distance *or* long-haul flight; **~gelenkt** *Adj.* remote-controlled; **~gespräch** *das* long-distance call; **~gesteuert** *Adj.* ▶ **~**GELENKT; **~glas** *das* binoculars *pl.;* ***~|halten** ▶ FERN 1; **~heizung** *die* district heating system; **~lenkung** *die* remote control; **~licht** *das* (Kfz-W.) full beam; **~melde·amt** *das* telephone exchange; **~ost: in/aus/nach ~ost** in/from/to the Far East; **~rohr** *das* telescope; **~ruf** *der* telephone number; **~schreiben** *das* telex [message]; **~schreiber** *der* telex [machine]

Fernseh-: ~antenne *die* television aerial (Brit.) *or* (Amer.) antenna; **~apparat** *der* television [set]; **~bericht** *der* television report; **~bild** *das* television picture

fern|sehen *unr. itr. V.* watch television

Fern·sehen *das;* **~s** television; **im ~:** on television

Fern·seher *der;* **~s, ~** (ugs.) telly (Brit. coll.); TV

Fernseh-: ~gebühren *Pl.* television licence fee; **~gerät** *das* television [set]; **~journalist** *der,* **~journalistin** *die* television reporter; **~kanal** *der* television channel; **~nachrichten** *Pl.* television news; **~programm** *das* **(a)** (Sendungen) television programmes *pl.;* **(b)** (Kanal) television channel; **(c)** (Blatt, Programmheft) television [programme] guide; **~publikum**

das viewing public; **~sender** *der* television transmitter; **~sendung** *die* television programme; **~serie** *die* television series; **~spiel** *das* television play; **~star** *der* television star; **~studio** *das* television studio; **~zuschauer** *der*, **~zuschauerin** *die* television viewer

Fern·sicht *die* (Aussicht) view; (gute Sicht) visibility

Fern·sprecher *der* telephone

Fernsprech-: ~gebühren *Pl.* telephone charges; **~teilnehmer** *der*, **~teilnehmerin** *die* telephone subscriber; telephone customer (Amer.)

Fern-: ~steuerung *die* (Technik) remote control; **~straße** *die* major road; **~studium** *das* correspondence course; ≈ Open University course (Brit.); **~unterricht** *der* correspondence courses *pl.*; **~verkehr** *der* long-distance traffic; **~zug** *der* long-distance train

Ferse *die;* **~, ~n** heel

fertig *Adj.* **(a)** finished ‹*manuscript, picture, etc.*›; **das Essen ist ~:** lunch/dinner *etc.* is ready; **[mit etw.] ~ sein/werden** have finished/finish [sth.]; **etw. ~ machen** finish sth.
(b) (bereit, verfügbar) ready (**zu, für** for)
(c) (ugs.: erschöpft) shattered (coll.); **jmdn. ~ machen** (erschöpfen) wear sb. out; (schikanieren) wear sb. down; (deprimieren) get sb. down
(d) etw. ~ bekommen *od.* **bringen** *od.* (ugs.) **kriegen** manage sth; **etw. ~ stellen** complete sth.

fertig-, Fertig-: ~bau *der; Pl.* **~~ten** prefabricated building; **~bauweise** *die* prefabricated construction; prefabrication; ***~|bringen** ▶ FERTIG D

fertigen *tr. V.* make

Fertig-: ~gericht *das* ready-to-serve meal; **~haus** *das* prefabricated house

Fertigkeit *die;* **~, ~en** skill

fertig-, Fertig-: *~|machen ▶ FERTIG A, C; ***~|stellen** ▶ FERTIG D; **~stellung** *die* completion

Fertigung *die;* **~:** production; manufacture

Fessel *die;* **~, ~n** fetter; shackle; (Kette) chain

fesseln *tr. V.* **(a)** tie up; **ans Bett/ans Haus/ an den Rollstuhl gefesselt sein** (fig.) be confined to [one's] bed/tied to the house/ confined to a wheelchair
(b) (faszinieren) ‹*book*› grip; ‹*work, person*› fascinate

fesselnd [1] *Adj.* compelling
[2] *adv.* compellingly

fest [1] *Adj.* **(a)** (nicht flüssig od. gasförmig) solid
(b) firm ‹*bandage*›; sound ‹*sleep*›; sturdy ‹*shoes*›; strong ‹*fabric*›; solid ‹*house, shell*›; steady ‹*voice*›; **der ~en Überzeugung sein, dass ...:** be of the firm opinion that ...
(c) (dauernd) permanent ‹*address*›; fixed ‹*income*›
[2] *adv.* **(a)** ‹*tie, grip*› tight[ly]
(b) (*ugs. auch* **~e**) ‹*work*› with a will; ‹*eat*› heartily; ‹*sleep*› soundly
(c) ‹*believe, be convinced*› firmly; **sich auf jmdn./etw. ~ verlassen** rely one hundred per cent on sb./sth.
(d) (endgültig) firmly; **etw. ~ vereinbaren** come to a firm arrangement about sth.
(e) (auf Dauer) permanently; **~ befreundet sein** be close friends; (als Paar) be going steady

Fest *das;* **~[e]s, ~e (a)** celebration; (Party) party
(b) (Feiertag) festival; **frohes ~!** happy Christmas/Easter!

fest-, Fest-: ~akt *der* ceremony; **~|binden** *unr. tr. V.* tie [up]; **~|bleiben** *unr. itr. V.; mit sein* stand firm; **~essen** *das* banquet; **~|fahren** *unr. itr., refl. V.* (itr. V. mit sein) get stuck; (fig.) get bogged down; **~|halten** [1] *unr. tr. V.* **(a)** (halten, packen) hold on to; **(b)** (nicht weiterleiten) withhold ‹*letter, parcel, etc.*›; **(c)** (verhaftet haben) hold, detain ‹*suspect*›; [2] *unr. refl. V.* **sich an jmdm./etw. ~halten** hold on to sb./sth.

festigen [1] *tr. V.* strengthen; consolidate ‹*position*›
[2] *refl. V.* ‹*friendship, ties*› become stronger

Festival /ˈfɛstivəl/ *das;* **~s, ~s** festival

fest-, Fest-: ~|kleben *tr., itr. V.; mit sein* stick (**an** + *Dat.* to); **~land** *das* (Kontinent) continent; (im Gegensatz zu den Inseln) mainland; **~|legen** *tr. V.* **(a)** fix ‹*time, deadline, price*›; arrange ‹*programme*›; **(b)** (verpflichten) **sich [auf etw.** (*Akk.*)**] ~legen [lassen]** commit oneself [to sth.]; **jmdn. [auf etw.** (*Akk.*)**] ~legen** tie sb. down [to sth.]

festlich [1] *Adj.* festive ‹*atmosphere*›; formal ‹*dress*›
[2] *adv.* festively; formally

fest-, Fest-: ~|machen *tr. V.* **(a)** (befestigen) fix; **(b)** (fest vereinbaren) arrange ‹*meeting etc.*›; **~|nageln** *tr. V.* **(a)** (befestigen) nail (**an** + *Dat.* to); **(b)** (ugs.: festlegen) **jmdn. [auf etw.** (*Akk.*)**] ~nageln** tie sb. down [to sth.]; **~nahme** *die;* **~~, ~~n** arrest; **bei seiner ~nahme** when he was/is arrested; **~|nehmen** *unr. tr. V.* arrest; **~platte** *die* (DV) fixed disk; **~rede** *die* speech; **~|schnallen** *tr. V.* tie (**an** + *Dat.* to); **~|sitzen** *unr. itr. V.* be stuck; **~|stehen** *unr. itr. V.* ‹*order, appointment, etc.*› have been fixed; ‹*decision*› be definite; ‹*fact*› be certain; **~|stellen** *tr. V.* **(a)** establish ‹*identity, age, facts*›; **(b)** (wahrnehmen) detect; diagnose ‹*illness*›; **~stellung** *die* **(a)** establishment; **(b)** (Wahrnehmung) realization; **die ~stellung machen, dass ...:** realize that ...

Fest·tag *der* holiday; (Ehrentag) special day

Festung *die;* **~, ~en** fortress

fest-, Fest-: ~zeit *die* holiday (Brit.) *or* (Amer.) vacation [period]; **~zelt** *das* marquee; **~|ziehen** *unr. tr. V.* pull tight

Fete *die;* **~, ~n** (ugs.) party

fẹtt [1] *Adj.* **(a)** fatty ‹*food*›; **~er Speck** fat bacon
(b) (sehr dick) fat
(c) (Druckw.) bold
[2] *adv.* **(a) ~ essen** eat fatty foods
(b) ~ gedruckt bold

Fẹtt *das;* ~[e]s, ~e fat; **~ ansetzen** ‹*animal*› fatten up; ‹*person*› put on weight

fẹtt-, Fẹtt-: ~arm *Adj.* low-fat ‹*food*›; low in fat *pred.;* **~auge** *das* speck of fat; **~creme** *die* enriched [skim] cream; **~druck** *der* bold type; **~fleck[en]** *der* grease mark; ***~gedruckt** ▶ FETT 2B; **~gehalt** *der* fat content

fẹttig *Adj.* greasy

fẹtt-, Fẹtt-: ~leibig *Adj.* obese; **~leibigkeit** *die;* ~~: obesity; **~näpfchen** *das:* **ins ~näpfchen treten** (scherzh.) put one's foot in it; **~polster** *das* subcutaneous fat *no indef. art.;* fat pad; **~reich** *Adj.* high-fat; **~säure** *die* (Chemie) fatty acid; **~wanst** *der* (salopp abwertend) fatso (coll.)

Fetus *der;* ~ *od.* **~ses, ~se** *od.* **Feten** (Med.) foetus

Fẹtzen *der;* ~s, ~: scrap

feucht *Adj.* damp; humid ‹*climate*›

feucht·fröhlich *Adj.* (ugs. scherzh.) merry ‹*company*›; boozy (coll.) ‹*evening*›

Feuchtigkeit *die* moisture

Feuchtigkeits·creme *die* (Kosmetik) moisturizing cream; moisturizer

feucht-: ~kạlt *Adj.* cold and damp; **~wạrm** *Adj.* muggy

feudal *Adj.* **(a)** feudal ‹*system*›
(b) aristocratic ‹*regiment etc.*›
(c) (ugs.: vornehm) plush ‹*hotel etc.*›

Feuer *das;* ~s, ~ **(a)** fire; **jmdm. ~ geben** give sb. a light
(b) (Brand) fire; blaze; ~! fire!
(c) (Milit.) **das ~ einstellen** cease fire

feuer-, Feuer-: ~alarm *der* fire alarm; **~eifer** *der* enthusiasm; zest; **~fest** *Adj.* heat-resistant ‹*dish, plate*›; fireproof ‹*material*›; **~gefährlich** *Adj.* [in]flammable; **~holz** *das* firewood; **~leiter** *die* (bei Häusern) fire escape; (beim ~wehrauto) [fireman's] ladder; **~löscher** *der;* ~~s, ~~: fire extinguisher; **~melder** *der;* ~~s, ~~: fire alarm

feuern [1] *tr. V.* **(a)** (ugs.: entlassen) fire (coll.); sack (coll.)
(b) (ugs.: schleudern, werfen) fling
[2] *itr. V.* (Milit.) fire (**auf** + *Akk.* at)

feuer-, Feuer-: ~rot *Adj.* fiery red; **~schlucker** *der,* **~schluckerin** *die;* ~~, ~~nen fire-eater; **~sirene** *die* fire siren; **~stein** *der* flint; **~versicherung** *die* fire insurance; **~waffe** *die* firearm; **~wehr** *die;* ~~, ~~en fire service; **~wehr·auto** *das* fire engine; **~wehr·mann** *der; Pl.* **~männer** *od.* **~leute** fireman; **~wehr·wagen** *der* fire engine; **~werk** *das* firework display; (~werkskörper) fireworks *pl.;* **~werks·körper** *der* firework; **~zeug** *das* lighter

Feuilleton /fœjə'tõ:/ *das;* ~s, ~s arts section

feurig *Adj.* fiery

ff. *Abk.* = **folgende [Seiten]** ff.

Ffm. *Abk.* = **Frankfurt am Main**

Fiaker /'fi̯akɐ/ *der;* ~s, ~ (österr.) cab

Fiạsko *das;* ~s, ~s fiasco

Fibel *die;* ~, ~n reader; primer

ficht /fɪçt/ *Imperativ Sg. u. 3. Pers. Sg. Präsens v.* FECHTEN

Fịchte *die;* ~, ~n spruce

fịcken *tr., itr. V.* (vulg.) fuck (coarse)

fick[e]rig *Adj.* (landsch.: nervös) nervous

fidel *Adj.* (ugs.) jolly

Fieber *das;* ~s [high] temperature; (über 38°C) fever; **~ haben** have a [high] temperature/a fever; **bei jmdm. ~ messen** take sb.'s temperature

fieber·frei *Adj.* ‹*person*› free from fever

fieberhaft *Adj.* feverish

fieberig *Adj.* feverish

fiebern *itr. V.* have a temperature

Fieber·thermometer *das* [clinical] thermometer

fiebrig *Adj.* feverish

Fiedel *die;* ~, ~n (veralt., scherzh.) fiddle

fiel *1. u. 3. Pers. Sg. Prät. v.* FALLEN

fiepen *itr. V.* ‹*dog*› whimper; ‹*bird*› cheep

fies [1] *Adj.* (ugs.) nasty ‹*person, character*›
[2] *adv.* in a nasty way

Figur *die;* ~, ~en **(a)** (einer Frau) figure; (eines Mannes) physique
(b) (Bildwerk) figure
(c) (geometrisches Gebilde) shape
(d) (Spielstein) piece
(e) (Persönlichkeit) figure
(f) (literarische Gestalt) character

fiktiv *Adj.* fictitious

Filet /fi'le:/ *das;* ~s, ~s fillet

Filiale *die;* ~, ~n branch

Filigran *das;* ~s, ~e filigree

Fịlm *der;* ~[e]s, ~e **(a)** (Fot.) film
(b) (Kino~) film; movie (Amer. coll.)

Fịlme·macher *der,* **Fịlme·macherin** *die* film-maker

fịlmen *tr., itr. V.* film

Fịlm-: ~festival *das* film festival; **~festspiele** *Pl.* film festival *sing.;* **~industrie** *die* film industry; **~kamera** *die* film camera; (Schmalfilmkamera) cine camera; **~kunst** *die* cinematic art; **~musik** *die* film music; (eines einzelnen ~s) theme music; **~plakat** *das* film poster; **~produzent** *der,* **~produzentin** *die* film producer; **~regisseur** *der,* **~regisseurin** *die* film director;

---
*alte Schreibung - vgl. Hinweis auf S. xiv

~schauspieler *der*, **~schauspielerin** *die* film actor; **~star** *der* film star

Filter *der*, **~s, ~:** filter

filtern *tr. V.* filter

Filter-: ~papier *das* filter paper; **~zigarette** *die* [filter-]tipped cigarette

Filz *der;* **~es, ~e** felt

filzen *tr. V.* (ugs.: durchsuchen) search ‹*room, car, etc.*›; frisk ‹*person*›

Filz·stift *der* felt-tip pen

Fimmel *der;* **~s, ~: einen ~ für etw. haben** (ugs. abwertend) have a thing about sth. (coll.)

Finale *das;* **~s, ~[s] (a)** (Sport) final **(b)** finale

Finalist *der;* **~en, ~en, Finalistin** *die;* **~, ~nen** (Sport) finalist

Finanz *die;* **~:** finance *no art.*

Finanz-: ~amt *das* **(a)** (Behörde) ≈ Inland Revenue; **(b)** (Gebäude) tax office; **~beamte** *der*, **~beamtin** *die* tax officer

Finanzen *Pl.* finances

finanziell /finan'tsi̯ɛl/ *Adj.* financial

finanzieren *tr. V.* finance

Finanzierung *die;* **~, ~en** financing

finanz-, Finanz-: ~kraft *die* financial strength; **~kräftig** *Adj.* financially powerful; **~lage** *die* financial situation; **~minister** *der*, **~ministerin** *die* minister of finance; **~politik** *die* (des Staates, eines Unternehmens) financial policy; (allgemeine) politics of finance

Findel·kind *das* foundling

finden *unr. tr. V.* **(a)** find **(b) Freunde ~:** make friends **(c)** (einschätzen, beurteilen) **etw. gut/richtig ~:** think sth. is good/right; **wie ~ Sie dieses Bild?** what do you think of this painting?

Finder *der;* **~s, ~:** finder

Finder·lohn *der* reward [for finding sth.]

findig *Adj.* resourceful

Findling *der;* **~s, ~e (a)** (Findelkind) foundling **(b)** (Geol.) erratic block

fing *1. u. 3. Pers. Sg. Prät. v.* FANGEN

Finger *der;* **~s, ~:** finger; **lange ~ machen** (ugs.) get itchy fingers

Finger-: ~abdruck *der* fingerprint; **~fertigkeit** *die* dexterity; **~handschuh** *der* glove [with fingers]; **~hut** *der* thimble; **~kuppe** *die* fingertip

fingern *itr. V.* fiddle; **an etw.** (*Dat.*) **~:** fiddle with sth.; **nach etw. ~:** fumble [around] for sth.

Finger-: ~nagel *der* fingernail; **~spitze** *die* fingertip; **~spitzen·gefühl** *das* feeling

fingieren *tr. V.* fake; **ein fingierter Name** a false name

Fink *der;* **~en, ~en** finch

Finne *der;* **~n, ~n, Finnin** *die;* **~, ~nen** Finn

finnisch *Adj.* Finnish

Finnland (*das*)*;* **~s** Finland

finster 1 *Adj.* dark; dimly-lit ‹*pub, district*› 2 *adv.* **jmdn. ~ ansehen** give sb. a black look

Finsternis *die;* **~, ~se** darkness; (auch bibl., fig.) dark

Finte *die;* **~, ~n** trick; **jmdn. durch eine ~ täuschen** deceive sb. by trickery

Firlefanz *der;* **~es** (ugs. abwertend) frippery; trumpery

firm *Adj.* **in etw.** (*Dat.*) **~ sein** be well up in sth.

Firma *die;* **~, Firmen** firm; company

Firmen-: ~inhaber *der*, **~inhaberin** *die* owner of the/a company; **~schild** *das* company's name plate; **~zeichen** *das* trademark

Firmung *die;* **~, ~en** confirmation

First *der;* **~[e]s, ~e** ridge

Fisch *der;* **~[e]s, ~e (a)** fish; **[fünf] ~e fangen** catch [five] fish; **kleine ~e** (fig.) small fry **(b)** (Astrol.) **die ~e** Pisces; **er ist [ein] ~:** he is a Piscean

fischen 1 *tr. V.* **(a)** fish for **(b)** (ugs.) **etw. aus etw. ~:** fish sth. out of sth. 2 *itr. V.* fish; **nach etw. ~:** fish for sth.

Fischer *der;* **~s, ~:** fisherman

Fischer-: ~boot *das* fishing boat; **~dorf** *das* fishing village

Fischerei *die;* **~:** fishing

Fischerin *die;* **~, ~nen** fisherwoman

Fisch-: ~fang *der:* **vom ~fang leben** make a/one's living by fishing; **auf ~fang gehen** go fishing; **~geschäft** *das* fishmonger's [shop] (Brit.); fish store (Amer.); **~grät[en]·muster** *das* (Textilw.) herringbone pattern; **~industrie** *die* fishing industry; **~konserve** *die* canned fish; **~kutter** *der* fishing trawler; **~stäbchen** *das* (Kochk.) fish finger; **~sterben** *das* death of the fish

Fiskus *der;* **~, Fisken** *od.* **~se** Government (*as managing the State finances*)

Fitness·zentrum *das* fitness centre

Fittich *der;* **~[e]s, ~e** (dichter.) wing

fix 1 *Adj.* (ugs.) quick; **ein ~er Bursche** a bright lad; **~ und fertig** quite finished; (völlig erschöpft) completely shattered (coll.) 2 *adv.* (ugs.) quickly; **mach ~!** hurry up!

fixen *itr. V.* (Drogenjargon) fix (sl.)

Fixer *der;* **~s, ~, Fixerin** *die;* **~, ~nen** (Drogenjargon) fixer

fixieren *tr. V.* **(a)** fix one's gaze on; **jmdn. scharf ~:** gaze sharply at sb. **(b)** (geh.: schriftlich niederlegen) take down

Fix·stern *der* (Astron.) fixed star

Fjord /fjɔrt/ *der;* **~[e]s, ~e** fiord

FKK /ɛf ka: 'ka:/ *Abk.* = **Freikörperkultur** nudism *no art.*; naturism *no art.*
FKK-Strand *der* nudist beach
flach *Adj.* **(a)** flat
(b) (niedrig) low
(c) (nicht tief) shallow ‹*water, dish*›
Fläche *die;* **~, ~n (a)** area
(b) (Ober~) surface
(c) (Geom.) area; (einer dreidimensionalen Figur) side
Flächen-: ~inhalt *der* area; **~maß** *das* unit of square measure; **~staat** *der* territorial state
flach, Flach-: ~|fallen *itr. V.; mit sein* (ugs.) ‹*trip*› fall through; ‹*event*› be cancelled; **~land** *das* lowland
Flachs *der;* **~es** flax
flachsen *itr. V.* **mit jmdm. ~** (ugs.) joke with sb.
Flach·zange *die* flat tongs *pl.*
flackern *itr. V.* flicker
Fladen *der;* **~s, ~:** *flat, round unleavened cake made with oat or barley flour*
Flagge *die;* **~, ~n** flag
flaggen *itr. V.* put out the flags
flambieren *tr. V.* (Kochk.) flambé
Flamme *die;* **~, ~n (a)** flame
(b) (Brennstelle) burner
Flanell *der;* **~s, ~e** flannel
flanieren *itr. V.; mit Richtungsangabe mit sein* stroll
Flanke *die;* **~, ~n (a)** (Weiche) flank
(b) (Ballspiele: Vorlage) centre
(c) (Teil des Spielfeldes) wing
Flasche *die;* **~, ~n** bottle; **eine ~ Wein** a bottle of wine; **dem Kind die ~ geben** feed the baby
Flaschen-: ~bier *das* bottled beer; **~öffner** *der* bottle-opener; **~post** *die* message in a/the bottle; **~zug** *der* block and tackle
flatterhaft *Adj.* fickle
flattern *itr. V.; mit Richtungsangabe mit sein* flutter
flau *Adj.* **(a)** slack ‹*breeze*›
(b) (leicht übel) queasy ‹*feeling*›
Flaum *der;* **~[e]s** fuzz
Flausch *der;* **~[e]s, ~e** brushed wool
flauschig *Adj.* fluffy
Flause *die;* **~, ~n;** *meist Pl.* (ugs.) **er hat nur ~n im Kopf** he can never think of anything sensible
Flaute *die;* **~, ~n (a)** (Seemannsspr.) calm
(b) (Kaufmannsspr.) fall[-off] in trade
Flechte *die;* **~, ~n (a)** (Bot.) lichen
(b) (Med.) eczema
flechten *unr. tr. V.* plait ‹*hair*›; weave ‹*basket, mat*›
Fleck *der;* **~[e]s, ~e (a)** stain
(b) (andersfarbige Stelle) patch
flecken *itr. V.* stain
flecken·los 1 *Adj.* spotless
2 *adv.* spotlessly
Fleck·entferner *der* stain *or* spot remover
fleckig *Adj.* stained; blotchy ‹*face, skin*›
Fleder·maus *die* bat
Flegel *der;* **~s, ~** (abwertend) lout
Flegelei *die;* **~, ~en** (abwertend) loutish behaviour
flegelhaft *Adj.* (abwertend) loutish
flegeln *refl. V.* (abwertend) **sich auf ein Sofa/in einen Sessel ~:** flop on to a sofa/into an armchair
flehen /'fle:ən/ *itr. V.* plead (**um** for)
Fleisch *das;* **~[e]s (a)** flesh; **~ fressend** (Biol.) carnivorous
(b) (Nahrungsmittel) meat
Fleisch·brühe *die* bouillon; consommé
Fleischer *der;* **~s, ~:** butcher
Fleischerei *die;* **~, ~en** butcher's shop
fleisch·fressend *Adj.* carnivorous
Fleisch·fresser *der* (Biol.) carnivore
fleischig *Adj.* plump ‹*hands, face*›; fleshy ‹*leaf, fruit*›
Fleisch-: ~käse *der;* **~~s, ~~:** meat loaf; **~klößchen** *das;* **~~s, ~~:** small meat ball; **~pastete** *die* (Kochk.) pâté; **~salat** *der* (Kochk.) meat salad; **~vergiftung** *die* food poisoning [from meat]; **~waren** *Pl.* meat products; **~wolf** *der* mincer; **~wunde** *die* flesh wound; **~wurst** *die* pork sausage
Fleiß *der;* **~es** hard work; (Eigenschaft) diligence
fleißig 1 *Adj.* hard-working
2 *adv.* hard; **~ lernen** learn as much as one can
flennen *itr. V.* (ugs.) blubber
fletschen *tr., itr. V.* **die Zähne** *od.* **mit den Zähnen ~:** bare one's teeth
Fleurop (Wz) /'flɔy:rɔp/ *die* Interflora ®
flexibel 1 *Adj.* flexible
2 *adv.* flexibly
flicht *Imperativ Sg. u. 3. Pers. Sg. Präsens v.* FLECHTEN
flicken *tr. V.* mend; repair ‹*engine, cable*›
Flicken *der;* **~s, ~:** patch
Flick-: ~werk *das* (abwertend) botched-up job; **~zeug** *das* repair kit
Flieder *der;* **~s, ~:** lilac
Fliege *die;* **~, ~n (a)** fly
(b) (Schleife) bow tie
fliegen 1 *unr. itr. V.; mit sein* **(a)** fly
(b) (ugs.: fallen) **vom Pferd/Fahrrad ~:** fall off a/the horse/bicycle
(c) (ugs.: entlassen werden) get the sack (coll.); **von der Schule ~:** be chucked out [of the school] (coll.)
2 *unr. tr. V.* fly

*old spelling - see note on page xiv

Fliegen-: ~draht *der* fly screen; **~fenster** *das* wire-mesh window; **~gewicht** *das* (Schwerathletik) flyweight; **~pilz** *der* fly agaric

Flieger *der;* **~s, ~**: pilot

Flieger·alarm *der* air-raid warning

Fliegerin *die;* **~, ~nen** pilot

fliegerisch *Adj.* aeronautical

fliehen /ˈfliːən/ *unr. itr. V.; mit sein* flee (**vor** + *Dat.* from); (aus dem Gefängnis usw.) escape (**aus** from); **ins Ausland/über die Grenze ~**: flee the country/escape over the border

Flieh·kraft *die* (Physik) centrifugal force

Fliese *die;* **~, ~n** tile

Fließ·band *das* conveyor belt; **am ~ arbeiten** *od.* (ugs.) **stehen** work on the assembly line

fließen *unr. itr. V.; mit sein* flow; **~des Wasser** running water; **eine Sprache ~d sprechen** speak a language fluently

Flimmer·kasten *der,* **Flimmer·kiste** *die* (ugs.) telly (coll.); box (coll.)

flimmern *itr. V.* shimmer

flink [1] *Adj.* nimble ‹*fingers*›; sharp ‹*eyes*›; quick ‹*hands*›
[2] *adv.* quickly

Flinkheit *die;* **~** ▶ FLINK 1: nimbleness; sharpness; quickness

Flinte *die;* **~, ~n** shotgun; **die ~ ins Korn werfen** (fig.) throw in the towel

Flirt *der;* **~s, ~s** flirtation

flirten *itr. V.* flirt

Flittchen *das;* **~s, ~** (ugs. abwertend) floozie

Flitter *der;* **~s** frippery; trumpery

Flitter·wochen *Pl.* honeymoon *sing.*

flitzen *itr. V.; mit sein* (ugs.) shoot; dart

Flitzer *der;* **~s, ~** (ugs.) sporty job (coll.)

floaten /ˈfloʊtn̩/ *tr., itr. V.* (Wirtsch.) float

flocht *1. u. 3. Pers. Sg. Prät. v.* FLECHTEN

Flocke *die;* **~, ~n** **(a)** flake
(b) (Staub~) piece of fluff

flockig *Adj.* fluffy

flog *1. u. 3. Pers. Sg. Prät. v.* FLIEGEN

floh *1. u. 3. Pers. Sg. Prät. v.* FLIEHEN

Floh *der;* **~[e]s, Flöhe** flea

Floh-: ~markt *der* flea market; **~zirkus** *der* flea circus

Flora *die;* **~, Floren** flora

Florett *das;* **~[e]s, ~e** foil

florieren *itr. V.* flourish

Florist *der;* **~en, ~en, Floristin** *die;* **~, ~nen** [qualified] flower arranger

Floskel *die;* **~, ~n** cliché

floss *1. u. 3. Pers. Sg. Prät. v.* FLIESSEN

Floß *das;* **~es, Flöße** raft

Flosse *die;* **~, ~n** **(a)** (Zool., Flugw.) fin
(b) (zum Tauchen) flipper

flößen *tr., itr. V.* float

Flößer *der;* **~s, ~**: raftsman

Flößerin *die;* **~, ~nen** raftswoman

Flöte *die;* **~, ~n** flute; (Block~) recorder

flöten [1] *itr. V.* ‹*bird*› flute; **~ gehen** (ugs.) ‹*money*› go down the drain; ‹*time*› be wasted
[2] *tr. V.* whistle

***flöten|gehen** ▶ FLÖTEN 1

flott [1] *Adj.* **(a)** (schwungvoll) lively
(b) (schick) smart
[2] *adv.* ‹*work*› quickly; ‹*dance, write*› in a lively manner; ‹*be dressed*› smartly

Flotte *die;* **~, ~n** fleet

flott|machen *tr. V.* refloat ‹*ship*›; get ‹*car*› back on the road

Flöz *das;* **~es, ~e** (Bergbau) seam

Fluch *der;* **~[e]s, Flüche** curse; oath

fluchen *itr. V.* curse; swear

Flucht *die;* **~**: flight

flucht·artig [1] *Adj.* hurried; hasty
[2] *adv.* hurriedly; hastily

flüchten [1] *itr. V.; mit sein* **vor jmdm./etw. ~**: flee from sb./sth.; **vor der Polizei ~**: run away from the police
[2] *refl. V.* take refuge

Flucht-: ~fahrzeug *das* getaway vehicle; **~helfer** *der,* **~helferin** *die* person who aids/aided an/the escape; **~hilfe** *die* aiding an escape

flüchtig [1] *Adj.* **(a)** fugitive
(b) cursory; superficial ‹*insight*›
[2] *adv.* **(a)** (oberflächlich) cursorily
(b) (eilig) hurriedly

Flüchtigkeit *die;* **~, ~en** cursoriness

Flüchtigkeits·fehler *der* slip

Flüchtling *der;* **~s, ~e** refugee

Flüchtlings-: ~elend *das* hardship among refugees; **~hilfe** *die* refugee relief; (Organisation) refugee relief agency; **~lager** *das* refugee camp; **~treck** *der* long stream of refugees

Flucht·weg *der* escape route

Flug *der;* **~[e]s, Flüge** flight

Flug-: ~bahn *die* trajectory; **~blatt** *das* pamphlet; leaflet

Flügel *der;* **~s, ~** **(a)** wing
(b) (Klavier) grand piano

Flügel·mutter *die; Pl.* **~n** wing nut

Flug·gast *der* [air] passenger

flügge *Adj.* fully-fledged

Flug-: ~gesellschaft *die* airline; **~hafen** *der* airport; **~hafen·steuer** *die* airport tax; **~linie** *die* **(a)** (Strecke) air route; **(b)** (Gesellschaft) airline; **~lotse** *der,* **~lotsin** *die* air traffic controller; **~platz** *der* airfield; **~schein** *der* air ticket; **~schreiber** *der* flight recorder; **~verbindung** *die* air connection; **~verkehr** *der* air traffic

Flug·zeug *das* aeroplane (Brit.); airplane (Amer.); aircraft

Flugzeug-: ~absturz *der* plane crash; **~entführer** *der,* **~entführerin** *die* ···>

[aircraft] hijacker; **~entführung** *die* [aircraft] hijack[ing]; **~katastrophe** *die* air disaster; **~träger** *der* aircraft carrier

Flunder *die;* ~, ~**n** flounder

flunkern *itr. V.* tell stories

Fluor *das;* ~**s** (Chemie) fluorine

Fluor·chlor·kohlen·wasserstoff *der* (Chemie) chlorofluorocarbon

Flur¹ *der;* ~**[e]s**, ~**e** (Korridor) corridor; (Diele) [entrance] hall; **im/auf dem** ~: in the corridor/hall

Flur² *die;* ~, ~**en** farmland *no indef. art.*

Fluss, *Fluß *der;* **Flusses, Flüsse** river; (fließende Bewegung) flow

fluss-, *fluß-, Fluss-, *Fluß-: ~**ab[wärts]** *Adv.* downstream; ~**auf[wärts]** *Adv.* upstream; ~**bett** *das* river bed

Flüsschen, *Flüßchen *das;* ~**s**, ~: small river

Fluss·diagramm *das* (DV, Arbeitswiss.) flow chart

flüssig [1] *Adj.* **(a)** liquid
(b) (fließend, geläufig) fluent
(c) einen Betrag ~ machen make a sum of money available
[2] *adv.* ‹*write, speak*› fluently

Flüssig·gas *das* liquid gas

Flüssigkeit *die;* ~, ~**en** **(a)** liquid; (auch Gas) fluid
(b) (Geläufigkeit) fluency

Flüssig·kristall·anzeige *die* (Technik) liquid crystal display

***flüssig|machen** ▸ FLÜSSIG 1C

Fluss·pferd, *Fluß·pferd *das* hippopotamus

flüstern *itr., tr. V.* whisper

Flut *die;* ~, ~**en** **(a)** tide
(b) (geh.: Wassermasse) flood

fluten *itr. V.; mit sein* (geh.) flood

Flut·licht *das* floodlight

focht *1. u. 3. Pers. Sg. Prät. v.* FECHTEN

Föderalismus *der;* ~: federalism *no art.*

föderalistisch *Adj.* federalist

Fohlen *das;* ~**s**, ~: foal

Föhn *der;* ~**[e]s**, ~**e** **(a)** föhn
(b) (Haartrockner) hair-drier

föhnen *tr. V.* blow-dry

Folge *die;* ~, ~**n** **(a)** (Auswirkung) consequence; (Ergebnis) consequence; result
(b) (Aufeinander~) succession; (zusammengehörend) sequence
(c) (Fortsetzung) (einer Sendung) episode; (eines Romans) instalment

Folge·erscheinung *die* consequence

folgen *itr. V.; mit sein* follow; **jmdm. im Amt/in der Regierung** ~: succeed sb. in office/in government; **auf etw.** (*Akk.*) ~: follow sth.; **aus etw.** ~: follow from sth.

folgend *Adj.* following; **der/die/das Folgende** the next in order; **im Folgenden** *od.* **in Folgendem** in [the course of] the following discussion/passage *etc.*

folgendermaßen *Adv.* as follows; (so) in the following way

folge·richtig [1] *Adj.* logical; consistent ‹*behaviour, action*›
[2] *adv.* logically; ‹*act, behave*› consistently

Folge·richtigkeit *die* (einer Entscheidung, Schlussfolgerung) logicality; (eines Verhaltens, einer Handlung) consistency

folgern [1] *tr. V.* **etw. aus etw.** ~: infer sth. from sth.
[2] *itr. V.* **richtig** ~: draw a/the correct conclusion

Folgerung *die;* ~, ~**en** conclusion

Folge·schaden *der* **(a)** damaging after-effects
(b) (Versicherungsw.) consequential damage

folglich *Adv.* consequently

folgsam [1] *Adj.* obedient
[2] *adv.* obediently

Folgsamkeit *die;* ~: obedience

Folie /ˈfoːli̯ə/ *die;* ~, ~**n** (Metall~) foil; (Plastik~) film

Folklore *die;* ~ **(a)** folklore
(b) (Musik) folk music

folkloristisch [1] *Adj.* folkloric
[2] *adv.* in a folkloric way

Folter *die;* ~, ~**n** torture; **jmdn. auf die ~ spannen** (fig.) keep sb. in an agony of suspense

Folterer *der;* ~**s**, ~, **Folterin** *die;* ~, ~**nen** torturer

foltern *tr. V.* torture; (fig.) torment

Folterung *die;* ~, ~**en** torture

Fön Ⓦⓩ *der;* ~**[e]s**, ~**e** hairdrier

Fond /fõ:/ *der;* ~**s**, ~**s** (geh.) back

Fonds /fõ:/ *der;* ~ /fõ:(s),/ ~ /fõ:s/ fund

Fondue /fõˈdy:/ *die;* ~, ~**s** *od. das;* ~**s**, ~**s** (Kochk.) fondue

***fönen** ▸ FÖHNEN

Fontäne *die;* ~, ~**n** jet; (Springbrunnen) fountain

forcieren /fɔrˈsiːrən/ *tr. V.* step up ‹*production*›; intensify ‹*efforts*›; push forward ‹*developments*›

Förderer *der;* ~**s**, ~: patron

Förderin *die;* ~, ~**nen** patroness

fordern *tr. V.* **(a)** demand
(b) (in Anspruch nehmen) make demands on

fördern *tr. V.* **(a)** promote; patronize, support ‹*artist, art*›; further ‹*investigation*›; foster ‹*talent, tendency*›; improve ‹*appetite*›; aid ‹*digestion, sleep*›
(b) (Bergbau, Technik) mine ‹*coal, ore*›; extract ‹*oil*›

Forderung *die;* ~, ~**en** **(a)** demand
(b) (Kaufmannsspr.) claim (**an** + *Akk.* against)

Förderung *die;* ~, ~**en** **(a)** ▸ FÖRDERN A: promotion; patronage; support; furthering; fostering; improvement; aiding

*alte Schreibung - vgl. Hinweis auf S. xiv

(b) (Bergbau, Technik) output; (das Fördern) mining; (von Erdöl) extraction

Forelle *die;* ~, **~n** trout

Form *die;* ~, **~en (a)** shape; **in ~ von Tabletten** in the form of tablets
(b) (bes. Sport: Verfassung) form; **in ~ sein** be on form
(c) (vorgeformtes Modell) mould; (Back~) baking tin
(d) (Darstellungs~, Umgangs~) form

formal [1] *Adj.* formal
[2] *adv.* formally

formalisieren *tr. V.* formalize

Formalität *die;* ~, **~en** formality

Format *das;* ~[e]s, **~e (a)** size; (Buch~, Papier~, Bild~) format
(b) (Persönlichkeit) stature

formatieren *tr. V.* (DV) format

formbar *Adj.* malleable

Form-: ~blatt *das* form; **~brief** *der* form letter

Formel *die;* ~, **~n** formula

formell *Adj.* formal

formen *tr. V.* **(a)** (gestalten) form; shape
(b) (bilden, prägen) mould, form ‹*character, personality*›

Form·fehler *der* irregularity

formieren *tr., refl. V.* form

förmlich [1] *Adj.* **(a)** formal
(b) (regelrecht) positive
[2] *adv.* **(a)** formally
(b) (geradezu) **sich ~ fürchten** be really afraid

form·los *Adj.* **(a)** informal
(b) (gestaltlos) shapeless

Form·sache *die* formality

Formular *das;* ~s, **~e** form

formulieren *tr. V.* formulate

Formulierung *die;* ~, **~en (a)** (das Formulieren) formulation; (eines Entwurfes, Gesetzes) drafting
(b) (formulierter Text) formulation

form·vollendet [1] *Adj.* perfectly executed ‹*pirouette, bow, etc.*›; ‹*poem*› perfect in form
[2] *adv.* faultlessly

forsch *Adj.* forceful

forschen *itr. V.* **(a) nach jmdm./etw. ~:** search *or* look for sb./sth.
(b) (als Wissenschaftler) research

Forscher *der;* ~s, **Forscherin** *die;* ~, **~nen** researcher

Forschung *die;* ~, **~en** research

Forschungs-: ~reaktor *der* research reactor; **~reisende** *der/die* explorer

Forst *der;* ~[e]s, **~e[n]** forest

Förster *der;* ~s, ~, **Försterin** *die;* ~, **~nen** forest warden

Forst·wirtschaft *die* forestry

Forsythie /fɔr'zytsi̯ə/ *die;* ~, **~n** forsythia

fort *Adv.* **(a)** ▶ WEG;
(b) (weiter) **und so ~:** and so on

fort-, Fort-: ~an /-'-/ *Adv.* from now/then on; **~bestand** *der* continuation; (eines Staates) continued existence; **~|bewegen** [1] *tr. V.* move; shift; [2] *refl. V.* move [along]; **~|bilden** *tr. V.* **sich/jmdn. ~bilden** continue one's/sb.'s education; **~bildung** *die* further education; (beruflich) further training; **~bildungs·kurs** *der* further education course; (beruflich) training course; **~|bleiben** *unr. itr. V.; mit sein* fail to come; **~|bringen** *unr. tr. V.:* ▶ WEGBRINGEN; **~dauer** *die* continuation; **~|dauern** *itr. V.* continue; **~|fahren** [1] *unr. itr. V.* **(a)** *mit sein* leave; **(b)** *auch mit sein* (weitermachen) continue; go on; [2] *unr. tr. V.* drive away; **~|führen** *tr. V.* **(a)** lead away; **(b)** (fortsetzen) continue; **~gang** *der* **(a)** departure (**aus** from); **(b)** (Weiterentwicklung) progress; **~|gehen** *unr. itr. V.; mit sein* leave; **geh ~!** go away!; **~geschritten** *Adj.* advanced; **~geschrittene** *der/die; adj. Dekl.* advanced student/player; **~|kommen** *unr. itr. V.; mit sein* ▶ WEGKOMMEN A, B; **~|laufen** *unr. itr. V.; mit sein* **(a)** ▶ WEGLAUFEN; **(b)** (sich ~setzen) continue; **~laufend** [1] *Adj.* continuous; [2] *adv.* continuously; **~|pflanzen** *refl. V.* **(a)** reproduce [oneself/itself]; **(b)** (sich verbreiten) ‹*idea, mood*› spread; ‹*sound, light*› travel; **~pflanzung** *die;* ~~: reproduction; **~|schaffen** *tr. V.* take away; **~|schreiben** *unr. tr. V.* update; (in die Zukunft) project forward; **~schreibung** *die* updating; (in die Zukunft) forward projection; **~|schreiten** *unr. itr. V.; mit sein* ‹*process*› continue; ‹*time*› move on; **~schritt** *der* progress; **~schritte** progress *sing.;* **ein ~schritt** a step forward; **~schrittlich** [1] *Adj.* progressive; [2] *adv.* progressively; **~schrittlichkeit** *die;* ~~: progressiveness; **~|setzen** [1] *tr. V.* continue; [2] *refl. V.* continue; **~setzung** *die;* ~~, **~~en (a)** (das ~setzen) continuation; **(b)** (anschließender Teil) instalment; **~setzungs·roman** *der* serial; serialized novel; **~|während** [1] *Adj.* continual; [2] *adv.* continually; **~|werfen** *unr. tr. V.:* ▶ WEGWERFEN

fossil *Adj.* fossilized; fossil *attrib.*

Foto *das;* ~s, **~s** photo; **~s machen** take photos

Foto-: ~album *das* photo album; **~apparat** *der* camera

fotogen *Adj.* photogenic

Foto·graf *der;* ~en, **~en** photographer

Fotografie *die;* ~, **~n (a)** photography *no art.*
(b) (Lichtbild) photograph

fotografieren *tr. V.* photograph; take a photograph/photographs of

Fotografin *die;* ~, **~nen** photographer

foto-, Foto-: ~kopie *die* photocopy; **~kopieren** *tr., itr. V.* photocopy; **~kopierer** *der* photocopier

Foto-: ~labor *das* photographic laboratory; **~modell** *das* photographic model

Foul /faul/ *das;* **~s, ~s** (Sport) foul (**an** + *Dat.* on)

Foul·spiel /'faʊl-/ *das* foul

Foyer /foa'je:/ *das;* **~s, ~s** foyer

FPÖ *Abk.* = **Freiheitliche Partei Österreichs**

Fr. *Abk.* **(a)** = **Franken** SFr.
(b) = **Frau;**
(c) = **Freitag** Fri.

Fracht *die;* **~, ~en** (Schiffs~, Luft~) cargo; freight; (Bahn~, LKW-~) goods *pl.;* freight

Fracht·brief *der* consignment note; waybill

Frachter *der;* **~s, ~:** freighter

Fracht-: ~gut *das* slow freight; slow goods *pl.;* **~schiff** *das* cargo ship

Frack *der;* **~[e]s, Fräcke** tails *pl.;* evening dress

Frage *die;* **~, ~n** question; (Angelegenheit) issue; **in ~:** ▶ INFRAGE

Fragebogen *der* questionnaire; (Formular) form

fragen [1] *tr., itr. V.* **(a)** ask
(b) (sich erkundigen) **nach etw. ~:** ask *or* inquire about sth.
(c) (nachfragen) ask for
[2] *refl. V.* **sich ~, ob ...:** wonder whether ...

Frage·zeichen *das* question mark

fraglich *Adj.* **(a)** doubtful
(b) (betreffend) in question *postpos.;* relevant

Fragment *das;* **~[e]s, ~e** fragment

frag·würdig *Adj.* **(a)** questionable
(b) (zwielichtig) dubious

Fragwürdigkeit *die;* **~, ~en**
(a) questionableness
(b) (Zwielichtigkeit) dubiousness

Fraktion *die;* **~, ~en** parliamentary party; (mit zwei Parteien) parliamentary coalition

Fraktions- (Parl.)**: ~führer** *der,* **~führerin** *die* leader of the parliamentary party/coalition; **~zwang** *der* obligation to vote in accordance with party policy

frank *Adv.* **~ und frei** frankly and openly; openly and honestly

Franken *der;* **~s ~:** [Swiss] franc

Frankfurter *die;* **~, ~** (Wurst) frankfurter

frankieren *tr. V.* frank

Frank·reich *(das);* **~s** France

Franse *die;* **~, ~n** strand [of a/the fringe]

Franzose *der;* **~n, ~n** Frenchman; **er ist ~:** he is French; **die ~n** the French

Französin *die;* **~, ~nen** Frenchwoman

französisch *Adj.* French

Französisch *das;* **~[s]** French

*old spelling - see note on page xiv

Fräse *die;* **~, ~n** (für Holz) moulding machine; (für Metall) milling machine

fraß *1. u. 3. Pers. Sg. Prät. v.* FRESSEN

Fraß *der;* **~es** (derb) muck

Fratze *die;* **~, ~n (a)** hideous face
(b) (ugs.: Grimasse) grimace

Frau *die;* **~, ~en (a)** woman
(b) (Ehe~) wife
(c) (Titel, Anrede) **~ Schulze** Mrs Schulze; (in Briefen) **Sehr geehrte ~ Schulze** Dear Madam; (bei persönlicher Bekanntschaft) Dear Mrs/Miss/Ms Schulze

Frauen-: ~arzt *der,* **~ärztin** *die* gynaecologist; **~bewegung** *die* women's movement; **~emanzipation** *die* female emancipation; women's emancipation; **~gefängnis** *das* women's prison; **~gruppe** *die* women's group; **~haus** *das* battered wives' refuge; **~klinik** *die* gynaecological hospital *or* clinic; **~misshandlung, *~mißhandlung** *die* abuse of women; **~recht** *das* women's right; **~rechtlerin** *die;* **~~, ~~nen** feminist; Women's Libber (coll.); **~zeitschrift** *die* women's magazine; **~zimmer** *das* (abwertend) female

Fräulein *das;* **~s, ~** (*ugs.* **~s**) **(a)** (junges ~) young lady; (ältliches ~) spinster
(b) (Titel, Anrede) **~ Mayer/Schulte** Miss Mayer/Schulte

fraulich [1] *Adj.* feminine
[2] *adv.* in a feminine way

frech [1] *Adj.* **(a)** impertinent; cheeky; barefaced ‹*lie*›
(b) (keck, kess) saucy
[2] *adv.* impertinently; cheekily

Frech·dachs *der* (ugs., meist scherzh.) cheeky little thing

Frechheit *die;* **~, ~en (a)** impertinence; cheek
(b) (Äußerung) impertinent *or* cheeky remark

frei [1] *Adj.* **(a)** (unabhängig) free
(b) (nicht angestellt) freelance
(c) (ungezwungen) free and easy
(d) (nicht mehr in Haft) free
(e) (offen) open; **im Freien sitzen/übernachten** sit out of doors/spend the night in the open; **ständig im Freien übernachten** sleep rough
(f) (unbesetzt) vacant; free
(g) (kostenlos) free ‹*food, admission*›
(h) (verfügbar) spare; free ‹*time*›
[2] *adv.* freely

frei-, Frei-: ~bad *das* open-air swimming pool; **~|bekommen** [1] *unr. itr. V.* (ugs.) get time off; [2] *unr. tr. V.* **jmdn./etw. ~bekommen** get sb./sth. released; **~beruflich** [1] *Adj.* self-employed; freelance; ‹*doctor, lawyer*› in private practice; [2] *adv.* **~beruflich tätig sein/arbeiten** work freelance/practise privately; **~betrag** *der* (Steuerw.) [tax] allowance; **~bier** *das* free beer

Freier *der;* **~s, ~** (veralt.) suitor

frei-, Frei-: ~exemplar *das* (Buch) free

copy; (Zeitung) free issue; **~frau** *die* baroness; **~gabe** *die* release; **~|geben** *unr. tr. V.* release; **~gebig** *Adj.* generous; open-handed; **~gebigkeit** *die; ~~:* generosity; open-handedness; **~gehege** *das* outdoor enclosure; **~gepäck** *das* baggage allowance; **~hafen** *der* free port; **~|halten** *unr. tr. V.* **(a)** treat; **(b)** (offen halten) keep ‹*entrance, roadway*› clear; **Einfahrt ~halten!** no parking in front of entrance; **~handels·zone** *die* free-trade zone; **~händig** *adv.* ‹*cycle*› without holding on

Freiheit *die; ~, ~en* **(a)** freedom; **~, Gleichheit, Brüderlichkeit** Liberty, Equality, Fraternity
(b) (Vorrecht) freedom; privilege

freiheitlich 1 *Adj.* liberal ‹*philosophy, conscience*›; **~ und demokratisch** free and democratic
2 *adv.* liberally

Freiheits-: ~beraubung *die* (jur.) wrongful detention; **~strafe** *die* (Rechtsw.) term of imprisonment; prison sentence

frei-, Frei-: ~herr *der* baron; **~karte** *die* complimentary ticket; **~|kaufen** *tr. V.* ransom ‹*hostage*›; buy the freedom of ‹*slave*›; **~|kommen** *unr. itr. V.* **aus dem Gefängnis ~kommen** be released from prison; **~körper·kultur** *die* nudism *no art.;* naturism *no art.;* **~land** *das* open ground; **~|lassen** *unr. tr. V.* set free; release; **~|legen** *tr. V.* uncover

freilich *Adv.* of course

Frei·licht-: ~bühne *die,* **~theater** *das* open-air theatre

frei-, Frei-: ~|machen 1 *refl. V.* (ugs.: frei nehmen) take time off; 2 *tr. V.* (Postw.) frank; **etw. mit 0,56 Euro ~machen** put a 0.56 euro stamp on sth.; **~marke** *die* postage stamp; **~mütig** 1 *Adj.* candid; frank; 2 *adv.* candidly; frankly; **~mütigkeit** *die; ~~:* candidness; frankness; **~schaffend** *Adj.* freelance; **~schärler** *der; ~~s, ~~,* **~schärlerin** *die; ~~, ~~nen* irregular [soldier]; **~|schwimmen** *unr. refl. V.* **sich ~schwimmen** pass the 15-minute swimming test; **~|sprechen** *unr. tr. V.* **(a)** (Rechtsw.) acquit; **(b)** (für unschuldig erklären) exonerate **(von** from); **~spruch** *der* (Rechtsw.) acquittal; **~|stellen** *tr. V.* **(a)** **jmdm. etw. ~stellen** leave sth. up to sb.; **(b)** (befreien) release ‹*person*›; **jmdn. vom Wehrdienst ~stellen** exempt sb. from military service; **~stoß** *der* (Fußball) free kick

Frei·tag *der* Friday; *s. auch* DIENSTAG *usw.*

freitags *Adv.* on Friday[s]; *s. auch* DIENSTAGS

frei-, Frei-: ~tod *der* (verhüll.) suicide *no art.;* **~treppe** *die* [flight of] steps; **~übung** *die; meist Pl.* (Sport) keep-fit exercise; **~wild** *das* fair game; **~willig** 1 *Adj.* voluntary ‹*decision*›; optional ‹*subject*›; 2 *adv.* voluntarily; **sich ~willig melden** volunteer; **~willige** *der/die; adj. Dekl.* volunteer; **~zeichen** *das* ringing tone;

Frei·zeit *die* spare time

Freizeit-: ~beschäftigung *die* hobby; leisure pursuit; **~gestaltung** *die* (Soziol., Päd.) leisure activity; **~park** *der* amusement park

frei-, Frei-: ~zügig *Adj.* **(a)** generous; **(b)** (gewagt, unmoralisch) risqué ‹*remark, film, dress*›; **~zügigkeit** *die; ~~* **(a)** generosity; **(b)** (freie Wahl des Wohnsitzes) freedom of domicile

fremd *Adj.* **(a)** foreign
(b) (nicht eigen) other people's; of others *postpos.;*
(c) (unbekannt) strange

fremd-, Fremd-: ~arbeiter *der,* **~arbeiterin** *die* (veralt., schweiz.) foreign worker; **~artig** *Adj.* strange

Fremde[1] *der/die; adj. Dekl.* **(a)** stranger
(b) (Ausländer) foreigner

Fremde[2] *die; ~* (geh.) **die ~:** foreign parts *pl.*

fremden-, Fremden-: ~feindlich *Adj.* xenophobic; hostile to strangers/ foreigners *postpos.;* **~feindlichkeit** *die* xenophobia; hostility towards foreigners; **~führer** *der,* **~führerin** *die* tourist guide; **~hass, *~haß** *der* xenophobia; hatred of foreigners; **~verkehr** *der* tourism *no art.;* **~zimmer** *das* room

fremd-, Fremd-: ~|gehen *unr. itr. V.; mit sein* (ugs.) be unfaithful; **~herrschaft** *die* foreign domination; **~ländisch** *Adj.* foreign; (exotisch) exotic

Fremdling *der; ~s, ~e* (veralt.) stranger

fremd-, Fremd-: ~sprache *die* foreign language; **~sprachen·assistent** *der,* **~sprachen·assistentin** *die* foreign-language assistant; **~sprachig** *Adj.* bilingual/multilingual ‹*staff, secretary*›; foreign ‹*literature*›; foreign-language ‹*edition, teaching*›; **~sprachlich** *Adj.* foreign-language ‹*teaching*›; foreign ‹*word*›; **~wort** *das; Pl.* **~wörter** foreign word

frenetisch 1 *Adj.* frenetic
2 *adv.* frenetically

Frequenz *die; ~, ~en* (Physik) frequency; (Med.: Puls~) rate

Fressalien /frɛˈsaːli̯ən/ *Pl.* (ugs. scherzh.) grub (coll.)

Fresse *die; ~, ~n* (derb) **(a)** (Mund) gob (sl.)
(b) (Gesicht) mug (coll.)

fressen 1 *unr. tr. V.* **(a)** ‹*animal*› eat; (sich ernähren von) feed on
(b) (ugs.: verschlingen) swallow up ‹*money, time, distance*›, drink ‹*petrol*›
(c) (zerstören) eat away
(d) (derb: von Menschen) guzzle
2 *unr. itr. V.* (von Tieren) feed; (derb: von Menschen) stuff one's face (sl.)

f

Fressen *das;* **~s (a)** (für Hunde, Katzen usw.) food; (für Vieh) feed
(b) (derb: Essen) grub (coll.)
Fresserei *die;* **~, ~en** (derb) guzzling
Freude *die;* **~, ~n** joy; (Vergnügen) pleasure; **~ an etw.** (*Dat.*) **haben** take pleasure in sth.
Freuden-: ~fest *das* celebration; **ein ~fest feiern** hold a celebration; **~haus** *das* house of pleasure; **~tag** *der* happy day
freudestrahlend *Adj.* beaming with joy;
freudig *Adj.* joyful; joyous ‹*heart*›; delightful ‹*surprise*›;
freud·los *Adj.* joyless;
freuen [1] *refl. V.* be glad (**über** + *Akk.* about); (froh sein) be happy; **sich auf etw.** (*Akk.*) **~**: look forward to sth.
[2] *tr. V.* please; **es freut mich, dass ...** I am pleased *or* glad that ...; **das hat ihn sehr gefreut** he was very pleased about it
Freund *der;* **~es, ~e (a)** friend
(b) (Verehrer, Geliebter) boyfriend
Freundes·kreis *der* circle of friends; **im engen ~**: among close friends
Freundin *die;* **~, ~nen (a)** friend
(b) (Geliebte) girlfriend; (älter) lady friend
freundlich [1] *Adj.* **(a)** kind ‹*face*›; friendly ‹*reception*›
(b) (angenehm) pleasant
(c) (freundschaftlich) friendly
[2] *adv.* **jmdm. ~ danken** thank sb. kindly
Freundlichkeit *die;* **~**: kindness
Freundschaft *die;* **~, ~en** friendship; **mit jmdm. ~ schließen** make friends with sb.
freundschaftlich [1] *Adj.* friendly
[2] *adv.* in a friendly way
Frevel /ˈfreːfl̩/ *der;* **~s, ~** (geh., veralt.) crime; outrage
frevelhaft (geh.) [1] *Adj.* wicked ‹*deed, rebellion, person*›; criminal ‹*stupidity*›
[2] *adv.* wickedly
Friede *der;* **~ns, ~n** (älter, geh.) ▸ FRIEDEN
Frieden *der;* **~s, ~**: peace
Friedens-: ~abkommen *das* peace agreement; (Friedensvertrag) peace treaty; **~bewegung** *die* peace movement; **~bruch** *der* violation of the peace; **~forschung** *die* peace studies *pl., no art.;* **~konferenz** *die* peace conference; **~nobelpreis** *der* Nobel Peace Prize; **~pfeife** *die* pipe of peace; **~richter** *der,* **~richterin** *die: lay magistrate dealing with minor offences;* ≈ Justice of the Peace; **~taube** *die* dove of peace; **~verhandlungen** *Pl.* peace negotiations; **~vertrag** *der* peace treaty; **~zeiten** *Pl.* peacetime *sing.*
fried·fertig *Adj.* peaceable ‹*person, character*›
Fried·fertigkeit *die;* **~**: peaceableness
Fried·hof *der* cemetery; (Kirchhof) graveyard
friedlich [1] *Adj.* peaceful
[2] *adv.* peacefully
Friedlichkeit *die;* **~**: peacefulness
fried·liebend *Adj.* peace-loving
frieren *unr. itr. V.* **(a)** be *or* feel cold
(b) *mit sein* (gefrieren) freeze
Frikadelle *die;* **~, ~n** rissole
frisch [1] *Adj.* fresh; new-laid ‹*egg*›; clean ‹*linen, underwear*›; wet ‹*paint*›
[2] *adv.* freshly
Frische *die;* **~** freshness; **geistige ~**: mental alertness; **körperliche ~**: physical fitness
Frisch-: ~fleisch *das* fresh meat; **~halte·beutel** *der* airtight bag; **~luft** *die* fresh air; **~milch** *die* fresh milk
Friseur /friˈzøːɐ̯/ *der;* **~s, ~e, Friseuse** /friˈzøːzə/ *die;* **~, ~n** hairdresser
frisieren *tr. V.* **jmdn./sich ~**: do sb.'s/one's hair; **sich ~ lassen** have one's hair done
friss, *friß *Imperativ Sg. v.* FRESSEN
frisst, *frißt *2. u. 3. Pers. Sg. Präsens v.* FRESSEN
Frist *die;* **~, ~en (a)** time; period; **die ~ verlängern** extend the deadline
(b) (begrenzter Aufschub) extension
frist-: ~gemäß, ~gerecht *Adj., adv.* within the specified time *postpos.;* (bei Anmeldung usw.) before the closing date *postpos.;* **~los** [1] *Adj.* instant; [2] *adv.* without notice
Frisur *die;* **~, ~en** hairstyle
fritieren *tr. V.* deep-fry
frivol /friˈvoːl/ *Adj.* **(a)** (schamlos) suggestive ‹*remark, picture, etc.*›; risqué ‹*joke*›; earthy ‹*man*›; flighty ‹*woman*›
(b) (leichtfertig) frivolous
froh *Adj.* **(a)** happy; cheerful ‹*person, mood*›; good ‹*news*›
(b) (ugs.: erleichtert) pleased, glad (**über** + *Akk.* about)
fröhlich *Adj.* cheerful; happy
Fröhlichkeit *die;* **~**: cheerfulness; (eines Festes, einer Feier) gaiety
Froh-: ~natur *die* cheerful person; **~sinn** *der* cheerfulness; gaiety
fromm; ~er *od.* **frömmer, ~st...** *od.* **frömmst...** [1] *Adj.* pious, devout ‹*person*›; devout ‹*Christian*›
[2] *adv.* piously
Frömmigkeit *die;* **~**: piety; devoutness
Fron·leichnam /froːn-/ (*das*); **~s** [the feast of] Corpus Christi
Front *die;* **~, ~en (a)** (Gebäude~) front; façade
(b) (Kampfgebiet) front [line]
frontal [1] *Adj.* head-on ‹*collision*›; frontal ‹*attack*›
[2] *adv.* ‹*collide*› head-on; ‹*attack*› from the front
Front·antrieb *der* (Kfz-W.) front-wheel drive
fror *1. u. 3. Pers. Sg. Prät. v.* FRIEREN

*alte Schreibung - vgl. Hinweis auf S. xiv

Frosch *der;* ~[e]s, **Frösche** frog
Frosch-: ~**mann** *der; Pl.* ~**männer** frogman; ~**perspektive** *die* worm's-eye view; ~**schenkel** *der* frog's leg
Frost *der;* ~[e]s, **Fröste** frost
Frostbeule *die* chilblain
frösteln *itr. V.* feel chilly
Frost·grenze *die* (Met.) 0° C isotherm; (Geol.) frost line
frostig 1 *Adj.* (auch fig.) frosty
2 *adv.* frostily
Frostigkeit *die;* ~: frostiness
Frost-: ~**schaden** *der* frost damage; ~**schutz·mittel** *das* **(a)** frost protection agent; **(b)** (Kfz-W.) antifreeze
Frottee *das* u. *der;* ~s, ~s terry towelling
Frottee·handtuch *das* terry towel
frottieren *tr. V.* rub; towel
frotzeln 1 *tr. V.* tease
2 *itr. V.* **über jmdn./etw.** ~: make fun of sb./sth.
Frucht *die;* ~, **Früchte** fruit
frucht·bar *Adj.* fertile; fruitful ‹*work, idea, etc.*›
Fruchtbarkeit *die;* ~: fertility; fruitfulness
Frucht·becher *der* fruit sundae
fruchten *tr. V.* **nichts** ~: be no use
fruchtig *Adj.* fruity
frucht·los *Adj.* fruitless, vain ‹*efforts*›
Frucht·losigkeit *die;* ~~: fruitlessness
Frucht-: ~**saft** *der* fruit juice; ~**wasser** *das; Pl.* ~**wässer** (Anat.) amniotic fluid; waters *pl.* (coll.)
früh 1 *Adj.* **(a)** early
(b) (vorzeitig) premature
2 *adv.* early; **heute** ~: this morning
früh·auf: **von** ~ from early childhood on[wards]
Frühaufsteher *der;* ~s, ~, **Frühaufsteherin** *die;* ~, ~**nen** early riser
Frühe *die;* ~: **in aller** ~: at the crack of dawn
früher 1 *Adj., nicht präd.* **(a)** (vergangen) earlier; former
(b) (ehemalig) former ‹*owner, occupant, friend*›
2 *adv.* formerly; ~ **war er ganz anders** he used to be quite different
Früh·erkennung *die* (Med.) early recognition
frühestens *Adv.* at the earliest
Früh·geburt *die* **(a)** premature birth
(b) (Kind) premature baby
Früh·jahr *das* spring
Frühjahrsmüdigkeit *die* springtime tiredness
Frühling *der;* ~s, ~e spring
Frühlings·anfang *der* first day of spring
früh-, Früh-: ~**reif** *Adj.* precocious ‹*child*›; ~**schoppen** *der* morning drink; (um Mittag) lunchtime drink; ~**sport** *der* early-morning exercise
Früh·stück *das;* ~s, ~e breakfast
frühstücken *itr. V.* have breakfast
Frühstücks-: ~**fernsehen** *das* breakfast television; ~**pause** *die* morning break; coffee break
früh-, Früh-: ~**warn·system** *das* early warning system; ~**zeitig** 1 *Adj.* early; (vorzeitig) premature; 2 *adv.* early; (vorzeitig) prematurely
Frustration *die;* ~, ~en (Psych.) frustration
frustrieren *tr. V.* frustrate
Fuchs *der;* ~es, **Füchse** fox
fuchsen *tr. V.* annoy; vex
fuchs·teufels·wild *Adj.* (ugs.) livid (coll.)
Fuchtel *die;* ~: **unter jmds.** ~ (ugs.) under sb.'s thumb
fuchteln *itr. V.* (ugs.) **mit etw.** ~: wave sth. about
Fuder *das;* ~s, ~: cartload
Fuge[1] *die;* ~, ~n joint; (Zwischenraum) gap
Fuge[2] *die;* ~, ~n (Musik) fugue
fügen 1 *tr. V.* place; set; **etw zu etw.** ~ (fig.) add sth. to sth.
2 *refl. V.* **(a)** (sich ein~) **sich in etw.** (*Akk.*) ~: fit into sth.
(b) (gehorchen) **sich** ~: fall into line
fügsam *Adj.* obedient
fühlbar *Adj.* noticeable
fühlen 1 *tr., itr. V.* feel
2 *refl. V.* **sich krank** ~: feel sick
Fühler *der;* ~s, ~: feeler; antenna
Fühlungnahme *die;* ~: initial contact
fuhr *1. u. 3. Pers. Sg. Prät. v.* FAHREN
Fuhre *die;* ~, ~n load
führen 1 *tr. V.* **(a)** lead; **jmdn. durch ein Haus/eine Stadt** ~: show sb. around a house/town; **durch das Programm führt [Sie] Klaus Frank** Klaus Frank will present the programme
(b) (verkaufen) stock, sell ‹*goods*›
(c) (durch~) **Gespräche/Verhandlungen** ~: hold conversations/negotiations; **eine glückliche Ehe** ~: be happily married
(d) (leiten) manage, run ‹*company, business, pub, etc.*›; lead ‹*party, country*›; command ‹*regiment*›
(e) (Amtsspr.) drive ‹*train, motor, vehicle*›
(f) (als Kennzeichnung, Bezeichnung haben) bear; **einen Titel/Künstlernamen** ~: have a title/use a stage name
(g) (angelegt haben) keep ‹*diary, list, file*›
(h) (registrieren) **jmdn. in einer Liste/Kartei** ~: have sb. on a list/on file
(i) (tragen) **etw. bei** *od.* **mit sich** ~: have sth. on one; **eine Waffe/einen Ausweis bei sich** ~: carry a weapon/a pass
2 *itr. V.* **(a)** lead
(b) (an der Spitze liegen) lead; be ahead

führend *Adj.* leading; high-ranking ‹*official*›; prominent ‹*position*›
Führer *der;* **~s, ~** **(a)** (Leiter) leader **(b)** (Fremdenführer, Buch) guide
Führerin *die;* **~, ~nen** ▶ FÜHRER
führer-, Führer-: ~los [1] *Adj.* leaderless; (ohne Lenker) driverless ‹*car*› [2] *adv.* ▶ 1: without a leader; without a driver; **~schein** *der* driving licence (Brit.); driver's license (Amer.); **~schein·entzug** *der* disqualification from driving; driving ban
Führung *die;* **~, ~en** **(a)** ▶ FÜHREN 1D: management; running; leadership; command **(b)** (Fremdenführung) guided tour **(c)** (führende Position) lead
Führungs-: ~kraft *die* manager; **~spitze** *die* (Politik) top leadership; (im Betrieb) top management; **~zeugnis** *das: document issued by police certifying that holder has no criminal record*
Fuhr-: ~unternehmer *der,* **~unternehmerin** *die* haulage contractor; **~werk** *das* cart
Fülle *die;* **~** **(a)** wealth; abundance **(b)** (Körper~) corpulence
füllen [1] *tr. V.* **(a)** fill; (Kochk.) stuff **(b)** (fig.) fill in ‹*gap, time*› [2] *refl. V.* (voll werden) fill [up]
Füller *der;* **~s, ~** (ugs.) [fountain] pen
Füll·federhalter *der* fountain pen
füllig *Adj.* corpulent, portly ‹*person*›; ample ‹*figure, bosom*›
Füllung *die;* **~, ~en** stuffing; (Kochk.; Zahnmed.) filling; (in Schokolade) centre
fummeln *itr. V.* (ugs.) **(a)** (fingern) fiddle **(b)** (erotisch) pet
Fund *der;* **~[e]s, ~e** (auch Archäol.) find
Fundament *das;* **~[e]s, ~e** **(a)** (Bauw.) foundations *pl.;* **(b)** (Basis) base; basis
fundamental *Adj.* fundamental
Fundamentalismus *der;* **~:** fundamentalism
Fundamentalist *der;* **~en, ~en, Fundamentalistin** *die;* **~, ~nen** fundamentalist
Fund-: ~büro *das* lost property office (Brit.); lost and found office (Amer.); **~grube** *die* treasure house
fundieren *tr. V.* underpin
fündig *Adj.* **~ sein** yield something; **~ werden** make a find; (bei Bohrungen) make a strike
Fund·ort *der* place *or* site where sth. is/was found
fünf *Kardinalz.* five
Fünf *die;* **~, ~en** five; (Schulnote) E
fünf-, Fünf-: ~eck *das;* pentagon; **~fach** *Vervielfältigungsz.* fivefold; **~fache** *das; adj. Dekl.* five times as much; **~hundert** *Kardinalz.* five hundred; **~kampf** *der* (Sport) pentathlon
Fünfling *der;* **~s, ~e** quintuplet; quin (coll.)
fünf-: ~mal *Adv.* five times; **~stellig** *Adj.* five-figure
fünft... *Ordinalz.* fifth
Fünf·tagewoche *die* five-day [working] week
fünf·tausend *Kardinalz.* five thousand
fünftel *Bruchz.* fifth
Fünftel *das* (schweiz. meist *der*); **~s, ~:** fifth
fünftens *Adv.* fifthly
fünf·zehn *Kardinalz.* fifteen
fünfzig *Kardinalz.* fifty
Fünfzig *die;* **~:** fifty
fünfziger *indekl. Adj.* **die Fünfzigerjahre** the fifties
Fünfziger *der;* **~s, ~** **(a)** (ugs.) fifty-pfennig piece/fifty-euro note *etc.* **(b)** (50-Jähriger) fifty-year-old
Fünfzig-: ~mark·schein *der* fifty-mark note; **~pfennig·stück** *das* fifty-pfennig piece
fünfzigst... *Ordinalz.* fiftieth
fungieren *itr. V.* **als etw. ~** ‹*person*› act as sth.; ‹*word etc.*› function as sth.
Funk *der;* **~s** radio
Funk·ausstellung *die* radio and television exhibition
Funke *der;* **~ns, ~n** (auch fig.) spark
funkeln *itr. V.* ‹*light, star*› twinkle; ‹*gold, diamonds*› glitter; ‹*eyes*› blaze
funken *tr. V.* radio; ‹*transmitter*› broadcast
Funker *der;* **~s, ~, Funkerin** *die;* **~, ~nen** radio operator
Funk-: ~gerät *das* radio set; (tragbar) walkie-talkie; **~haus** *das* broadcasting centre; **~kolleg** *das* radio-based [adult education] course; **~sprech·gerät** *das* radiophone; (tragbar) walkie-talkie; **~spruch** *der* radio signal; (Nachricht) radio message; **~station** *die,* **~stelle** *die* radio station; **~stille** *die* radio silence; **~streife** *die* [police] radio patrol; **~taxi** *das* radio taxi; **~telefon** *das* radio-telephone
Funktion *die;* **~, ~en** function
Funktionär *der;* **~s, ~e** official; functionary
funktionieren *itr. V.* work; function
funktions·tüchtig *Adj.* working; sound ‹*organ*›
Funk-: ~turm *der* radio tower; **~verbindung** *die* radio contact
Funzel *die;* **~, ~n** (ugs.) useless light
für *Präp. mit Akk.* for; **etw. ~ ungültig erklären** declare sth. invalid; *s. auch* WAS 1
Furche *die;* **~, ~n** **(a)** furrow **(b)** (Wagenspur) rut

---
*old spelling - see note on page xiv

Furcht *die;* **~**: fear; **~ vor jmdm./etw. haben** fear sb./sth.
furchtbar [1] *Adj.* **(a)** dreadful **(b)** (ugs.: unangenehm) terrible (coll.) [2] *adv.* (ugs.) terribly (coll.)
fürchten [1] *refl. V.* **sich [vor jmdm./etw.] ~**: be afraid *or* frightened [of sb./sth.] [2] *tr. V.* be afraid of; **ich fürchte, [dass] ...**: I'm afraid [that] ...
fürchterlich *Adj., adv.* ▶ FURCHTBAR
furcht·los [1] *Adj.* fearless [2] *adv.* fearlessly
furchtsam [1] *Adj.* timid [2] *adv.* timidly
für·einander *Adv.* for one another; for each other
Furie /'fu:ri̯ə/ *die;* **~, ~n** Fury
Furnier *das;* **~s, ~e** veneer
Für·sorge *die;* **~ (a)** care **(b)** (veralt.: Sozialhilfe) welfare **(c)** (veralt.: Sozialamt) social services *pl.*
für·sorglich [1] *Adj.* considerate [2] *adv.* considerately
Für·sprache *die* support
Für·sprecher *der,* **Für·sprecherin** *die* advocate
Fürst *der;* **~en, ~en** prince
Fürstentum *das;* **~s, Fürstentümer** principality
Fürstin *die;* **~, ~nen** princess
fürstlich [1] *Adj.* **(a)** royal **(b)** (fig.: üppig) lavish [2] *adv.* lavishly
Furt *die;* **~, ~en** ford
Furunkel *der od. das;* **~s, ~**: boil; furuncle
Für·wort *das; Pl.* **-wörter** pronoun
Furz *der;* **~es, Fürze** (derb) fart (coarse); **einen ~ lassen** let off a fart; **jeder ~** (fig.) the slightest thing
furzen *itr. V.* (derb) fart (coarse)
Fusion *die;* **~, ~en** amalgamation; (von Konzernen) merger
fusionieren *itr. V.* merge
Fuß *der;* **~es, Füße** foot; (einer Lampe, Säule) base; (von Möbeln) leg; **zu ~ gehen** go on foot; walk; **bei ~!** heel!; (fig.) **auf freiem ~ sein** be at large; **auf großem ~ leben** live in great style
Fuß·ball *der* **(a)** (Ballspiel) [Association] football **(b)** (Ball) football
Fußballer *der;* **~s, ~, Fußballerin** *die;* **~, ~nen** footballer
Fußball-: ~platz *der* football ground; (Spielfeld) football pitch; **~spiel** *das* **(a)** football match; **(b)** (Sportart) football *no art.;* **~spieler** *der,* **~spielerin** *die* football player
Fuß·boden *der* floor
Fußboden·heizung *die* underfloor heating
fußen *itr. V.* **auf etw.** (*Dat.*) **~**: be based on sth.
Fuß·ende *das* foot
Fußgänger *der;* **~s, ~, Fußgängerin** *die;* **~, ~nen** pedestrian
Fußgänger-: ~brücke *die* footbridge; **~übergang** *der,* **~überweg** *der* pedestrian crossing; **~unterführung** *die* pedestrian subway; **~zone** *die* pedestrian precinct
Fuß-: ~nagel *der* toenail; **~note** *die* footnote; **~stapfen** *der;* **~~s, ~~**: footprint; **~tritt** *der* kick; **~volk** *das* **(a)** (hist.) footmen *pl.;* **(b)** (abwertend: Untergeordnete) lower ranks *pl.;* **~weg** *der* footpath
futsch *Adj.* (salopp) **~ sein** have gone for a burton (Brit. coll.)
Futter[1] *das;* **~s** (Tiernahrung) feed; (für Pferde, Kühe) fodder
Futter[2] *das;* **~s, ~** (von Kleidungsstücken usw.) lining
Futteral *das;* **~s, ~e** case
Futter·mittel *das* animal food
füttern[1] *tr. V.* feed
füttern[2] *tr. V.* (mit Futter[2] ausstatten) line
Futter·pflanze *die* fodder plant; forage plant
Fütterung *die;* **~, ~en** feeding
Futur *das;* **~s, ~e** (Sprachw.) future [tense]
Fuzzi *der;* **~s, ~s** (salopp) bozo (sl.)

Gg

g, G /ge:/ *das;* ~, ~ **(a)** (Buchstabe) g/G **(b)** (Musik) [key of] G

g *Abk.* **(a)** = **Gramm** g **(b)** = **Groschen**

gab *1. u. 3. Pers. Sg. Prät. v.* GEBEN

Gabe *die;* ~, ~**n** **(a)** (geh.: Geschenk, Talent) gift **(b)** (Almosen, Spende) alms *pl.*

Gabel *die;* ~, ~**n** fork; (Telefon~) cradle

gabeln *refl. V.* fork

Gabel-: ~**schlüssel** *der* flat spanner; ~**stapler** *der;* ~~**s**, ~~: forklift truck

Gabelung *die;* ~, ~**en** fork

Gaben·tisch *der* gift table

gackern *itr. V.* **(a)** cluck **(b)** (ugs.: lachen) cackle

gaffen *itr. V.* (abwertend) gape; gawp (coll.)

Gaffer *der;* ~**s**, ~, **Gafferin** *die;* ~, ~**nen** gaper; starer

Gag /gɛk/ *der;* ~**s**, ~**s** **(a)** (Theater, Film) gag **(b)** (Besonderheit) gimmick

Gage /'ga:ʒə/ *die;* ~, ~**n** salary; (für einzelnen Auftritt) fee

gähnen *itr. V.* (auch fig.) yawn

Gala /'ga:la, *auch* 'gala/ *die;* ~: formal dress

galant [1] *Adj.* gallant; (amourös) amorous [2] *adv.* gallantly

Gala·vorstellung *die* gala performance

Galeere *die;* ~, ~**n** galley

Galerie *die;* ~, ~**n** gallery

Galgen *der* gallows *sing.*

Galgen-: ~**frist** *die* reprieve; ~**humor** *der* gallows humour

Galle *die;* ~, ~**n** **(a)** (Gallenblase) gall [bladder] **(b)** (Sekret) (bei Tieren) gall; (bei Menschen) bile

Galopp *der;* ~**s**, ~**s** *od.* ~**e** gallop

galoppieren *itr. V.; meist mit sein* gallop

galt *1. u. 3. Pers. Sg. Prät. v.* GELTEN

galvanisch /gal'va:nɪʃ/ *Adj.* galvanic

Gamasche *die;* ~, ~**n** gaiter; (bis zum Knöchel reichend) spat

Gambe *die;* ~, ~**n** (Musik) viola da gamba

Gamma·strahlen *Pl.* (Physik, Med.) gamma rays

gammelig *Adj.* (ugs.) **(a)** bad; rotten **(b)** (unordentlich) scruffy

gammeln *itr. V.* **(a)** (ugs.) go off **(b)** (nichts tun) loaf around; bum around (Amer. coll.)

Gammler *der;* ~**s**, ~, **Gammlerin** *die;* ~, ~**nen** (ugs.) dropout (coll.)

Gämse *die;* ~, ~**n** chamois

gang: ~ **und gäbe sein** be quite usual

Gang *der;* ~[**e**]**s**, **Gänge** **(a)** walk; gait **(b)** (Besorgung) errand **(c)** (Verlauf) course **(d)** (Technik) gear **(e)** (Flur) (in Zügen, Gebäuden usw.) corridor; (Verbindungs~) passage[way]; (im Theater, Kino, Flugzeug) aisle **(f)** (Kochk.) course

gangbar *Adj.* passable; (fig.) practicable

Gängel·band *das:* **jmdn. am** ~ **führen** keep sb. in leading reins

gängeln *tr. V.* (ugs.) **jmdn.** ~: boss sb. around

gang·genau *Adj.* accurate

Gang·genauigkeit *die* accuracy

gängig *Adj.* **(a)** (üblich) common; (aktuell) current **(b)** (leicht verkäuflich) popular

Gang·schaltung *die* (Technik) gear system; (Art) gear change

Gangway /'gæŋweɪ/ *die;* ~, ~**s** gangway

Ganove /ga'no:və/ *der;* ~**n**, ~**n** (ugs. abwertend) crook (coll.)

Gans *die;* ~, **Gänse** goose

Gänse-: ~**blümchen** *das* daisy; ~**braten** *der* roast goose; ~**füßchen** *das;* ~~**s**, ~~ (ugs.) ▶ ANFÜHRUNGSZEICHEN; ~**haut** *die* (fig.) gooseflesh; goose pimples *pl.;* ~**marsch** **im** ~**marsch** in single *or* Indian file

Gänserich *der;* ~**s**, ~**e** gander

ganz [1] *Adj.* **(a)** (gesamt) whole; entire; **den** ~**en Tag/das** ~**e Jahr** all day/year **(b)** (ugs.: alle) **die** ~**en Kinder/Leute/Gläser** *usw.* all the children/people/glasses *etc.;* **(c)** (vollständig) whole **(d)** (ugs.: ziemlich [groß]) **eine** ~**e Menge/ein** ~**er Haufen** quite a lot/quite a pile **(e)** (ugs.: unversehrt) intact; **etw. wieder** ~ **machen** mend sth. [2] *adv.* quite

Ganze *das; adj. Dekl.* **(a)** whole **(b)** (alles) **das** ~: the whole thing

gänzlich *Adv.* entirely

ganz-: ~**tägig** [1] *Adj.* all-day; **eine** ~**tägige Arbeit** a full-time job; [2] *adv.* all day; ~**tags** *Adv.* **arbeiten** work full-time

Ganztags-: ~**schule** *die* all-day school; (System) all-day schooling *no art.;* ~**stelle** *die* full-time job

gar[1] *Adj.* cooked; done *pred.*

gar[2] *Partikel* **(a)** (überhaupt) ~ **nicht** [**wahr**] not [true] at all; ~ **nichts** nothing at all; ~

*alte Schreibung - vgl. Hinweis auf S. xiv

niemand *od.* **keiner** nobody at all; **~ keines** not a single one; **~ kein Geld** no money at all
(b) (südd., österr., schweiz.: verstärkend) **~ zu** only too
(c) (geh.: sogar) even

Garage /ga'ra:ʒə/ *die;* **~, ~n** garage

Garagen-: ~firma *die* garage startup; **~wagen** *der* garaged car

Garant *der;* **~en, ~en** guarantor

Garantie *die;* **~, ~n** guarantee

Garantie·frist *die* guarantee period

garantieren 1 *tr. V.* guarantee 2 *itr. V.* **für etw. ~:** guarantee sth.

garantiert *Adv.* (ugs.) **wir kommen ~ zu spät** we're dead certain to arrive late (coll.)

Garantie·schein *der* guarantee [certificate]

Garantin *die;* **~, ~nen** guarantor

Garaus /'ga:ɐ̯|au:s/: **jmdm. den ~ machen** do sb. in (coll.)

Garbe *die;* **~, ~n (a)** sheaf
(b) (Geschoss~) burst of fire

Garde *die;* **~, ~n** guard

Garderobe *die;* **~, ~n (a)** wardrobe; clothes *pl.;*
(b) (Flur~) coat rack
(c) (im Theater usw.) cloakroom; checkroom (Amer.)

Garderoben·frau *die* cloakroom *or* (Amer.) checkroom attendant

Gardine *die;* **~, ~n (a)** net curtain
(b) (landsch., veralt.) curtain

Gardinen-: ~predigt *die* (ugs.) telling-off (coll.); (einer Ehefrau zu ihrem Mann) curtain lecture; **~stange** *die* curtain rail

garen *tr., itr. V.* cook

gären *regelm. (auch unr.) itr. V.* ferment; (fig.) seethe

Garn *das;* **~[e]s, ~e (a)** thread; (Näh~) cotton
(b) (Seew.) yarn

Garnele *die;* **~, ~n** shrimp

garnieren *tr. V.* **(a)** decorate
(b) (Gastr.) garnish

Garnison *die;* **~, ~en** garrison

Garnitur *die;* **~, ~en (a)** set; (Wäsche) set of [matching] underwear; (Möbel) suite
(b) (ugs.) **die erste/zweite ~:** the first/second-rate people *pl.*

garstig *Adj.* nasty; bad ‹*behaviour*›

Garstigkeit *die;* **~, ~en (a)** nastiness
(b) (Handlung) piece of nastiness

Gärtchen *das;* **~s, ~:** little garden

Garten *der;* **~s, Gärten** garden

Garten-: ~abfall *der* garden waste; **~abfälle** garden waste; **~arbeit** *die* gardening; **~bau** *der* horticulture; **~fest** *das* garden party; **~haus** *das* summer house; **~laube** *die* summerhouse; garden house; **~lokal** *das* beer garden; (Restaurant) open-air café; **~schau** *die* horticultural show; **~wirtschaft** *die* ▶ **~**LOKAL; **~zwerg** *der* **(a)** garden gnome; **(b)** (salopp abwertend) little runt

Gärtner *der;* **~s, ~:** gardener

Gärtnerei *die;* **~, ~en** nursery

Gärtnerin *die;* **~, ~nen** gardener

Gärung *die;* **~, ~en** fermentation

Gas *das;* **~es, ~e (a)** gas
(b) (Treibstoff) petrol (Brit.); gasoline (Amer.); gas (Amer. coll.); **~ wegnehmen** take one's foot off the accelerator; **~ geben** accelerate; put one's foot down (coll.)

gas-, Gas-: ~flasche *die* gas cylinder; (für einen Herd, Ofen) gas bottle; **~förmig** *Adj.* gaseous; **~hahn** *der* gas tap; **~herd** *der* gas cooker; **~kammer** *die* gas chamber; **~leitung** *die* gas pipe; (Hauptrohr) gas main; **~maske** *die* gas mask; **~pedal** *das* accelerator [pedal]; gas pedal (Amer.); **~pistole** *die* pistol that fires gas cartridges

Gasse *die;* **~, ~n** lane; (österr.) street

Gassen·junge *der* (abwertend) street urchin

Gast *der;* **~[e]s, Gäste (a)** guest
(b) (Besucher eines Lokals) patron
(c) (Besucher) visitor

Gast-: ~arbeiter, *der,* **~arbeiterin** *die* immigrant *or* guest worker; **~dozent** *der,* **~dozentin** *die* (Hochschulw.) visiting lecturer

Gäste-: ~buch *das* guest book; **~haus** *das* guest house; **~zimmer** *das* (privat) guest room; spare room; (im Hotel) room

gast-, Gast-: ~freundlich *Adj.* hospitable; **~freundlichkeit** *die,* **~freundschaft** *die* hospitality; **~geber** *der* host; **~geberin** *die* hostess; **~haus** *das,* **~hof** *der* inn

gastieren *itr. V.* give a guest performance

gastlich *Adj.* hospitable

Gastlichkeit *die;* **~:** hospitality

Gast·professor *der,* **Gast·professorin** *die* visiting professor

Gastronom *der;* **~en, ~en** restaurateur

Gastronomie *die;* **~:** catering *no art.;* (Gaststättengewerbe) restaurant trade

Gastronomin *die;* **~, ~nen** restaurateur

Gast-: ~spiel *das* guest performance; **~stätte** *die* public house; (Speiselokal) restaurant; **~wirt** *der* publican; landlord; (eines Restaurants) [restaurant] proprietor; (Pächter) restaurant manager; **~wirtin** *die* ▶ **~**WIRT: publican; landlady; [restaurant] proprietress *or* owner; restaurant manageress; **~wirtschaft** *die* ▶ **~**STÄTTE

Gas-: ~vergiftung *die* gas poisoning *no indef. art.;* **~versorgung** *die* gas supply; **~werk** *das* gasworks *sing.;* **~zähler** *der* gas meter

Gatte *der;* **~n, ~n** husband

Gatter *das;* **~s, ~ (a)** (Zaun) fence; (Lattenzaun) fence; paling

(b) (Tor) gate
Gattin *die;* ~, **~nen** (geh.) wife
Gattung *die;* ~, **~en (a)** kind; sort; (Kunst~) genre; form
(b) (Biol.) genus
GAU *der;* **~s, ~s** *Abk.* = **größter anzunehmender Unfall** MCA; maximum credible accident
Gaudi *das;* **~s** (bayr., österr.) *die;* ~ (ugs.) bit of fun
Gaukler *der;* **~s,** ~, **Gauklerin** *die;* ~, **~nen (a)** (veralt.: Taschenspieler[in]) itinerant entertainer
(b) (geh.: Betrüger[in]) charlatan
Gaul *der;* **~[e]s, Gäule** nag (derog.)
Gaumen *der;* **~s,** ~: palate
Gauner *der;* **~s,** ~ (abwertend) crook (coll.); rogue
Gaunerei *die;* ~, **~en** swindle
Gaunerin *die;* ~, **~nen** ▶ GAUNER
Gauner·sprache *die* thieves' cant *or* Latin
Gaze /'ga:zə/ *die;* ~, **~n** gauze
geachtet *Adj.* respected
Geäst *das;* **~[e]s** branches *pl.*
geb. *Abk.* **(a)** = **geboren;**
(b) = **geborene**
Gebäck *das;* **~[e]s, ~e** cakes and pastries *pl.;* (Kekse) biscuits *pl.;* (Törtchen) tarts *pl.*
gebacken *2. Part. v.* BACKEN
Gebälk *das;* **~[e]s, ~e** beams *pl.;* (Dach~) rafters *pl.*
gebar *1. u. 3. Pers. Sg. Prät. v.* GEBÄREN
Gebärde *die;* ~, **~n** gesture
gebärden *refl. V.* behave
gebären *unr. tr. V.* bear; give birth to; *s. auch* GEBOREN
gebär·fähig *Adj.* **Frauen im ~en Alter** women of child-bearing age.
Gebär·mutter *die; Pl.* **Gebärmütter** womb
Gebäude *das;* **~s,** ~ **(a)** building
(b) (Gefüge) structure
gebaut *Adj.* **gut ~ sein** have a good figure
Gebein *das;* **~[e]s, ~e** *Pl.* (geh.) bones *pl.;* (sterbliche Reste) [mortal] remains
Gebell *das;* **~[e]s** barking; (der Jagdhunde) baying
geben 1 *unr. tr. V.* give; **jmdm. die Hand ~:** shake sb.'s hand; **~ Sie mir bitte Herrn N.** please put me through to Mr N.; **Unterricht ~:** teach; **eins plus eins gibt zwei** one and one is *or* makes two; **etw. von sich ~:** utter sth.
2 *unr. tr. V. (unpers.)* **es gibt** there is/are; **heute gibts Fisch** we're having fish today; **morgen gibt es Schnee** it'll snow tomorrow
3 *unr. itr. V.* **(a)** (Karten austeilen) deal
(b) (Sport: aufschlagen) serve
4 *unr. refl. V.* **(a) sich [natürlich/steif] ~:** act *or* behave [naturally/stiffly]

*old spelling - see note on page xiv

(b) das gibt sich noch it will get better
Gebet *das;* **~[e]s, ~e** prayer
gebeten *2. Part. v.* BITTEN
Gebets-: ~mühle *die* prayer wheel; **~teppich** *der* (islam. Rel.) prayer mat
gebiert *3. Pers. Sg. Präsens v.* GEBÄREN
Gebiet *das;* **~[e]s, ~e** region; area; (Staats~) territory; (Bereich, Fach) field
gebieten (geh.) **(a)** command; order
(b) (erfordern) demand
Gebieter *der;* **~s,** ~ (veralt.) master
Gebieterin *die;* ~, **~nen** (veralt.) mistress
gebieterisch (geh.) *Adj.* imperious; (herrisch) domineering; peremptory ‹*tone*›
Gebiets·anspruch *der* territorial claim
Gebilde *das;* **~s,** ~: object; (Bauwerk) structure
gebildet *Adj.* educated
Gebimmel *das;* **~s** (ugs.) ringing; (von kleinen Glocken) tinkling
Gebirge *das;* **~s,** ~: mountain range; **im ~:** in the mountains
gebirgig *Adj.* mountainous
Gebiss, *Gebiß *das;* **Gebisses, Gebisse**
(a) set of teeth; teeth *pl.;*
(b) (Zahnersatz) denture; plate (coll.); (für beide Kiefer) dentures *pl.*
gebissen *2. Part. v.* BEISSEN
geblasen *2. Part. v.* BLASEN
geblichen *2. Part. v.* BLEICHEN
geblümt *Adj.* flowered
Geblüt *das;* **~[e]s** (geh.) blood
gebogen *2. Part. v.* BIEGEN
geboren 1 *2. Part. v.* GEBÄREN;
2 *Adj.* **blind/taub ~ sein** be born blind/deaf; **Frau Anna Schmitz ~e Meyer** Mrs Anna Schmitz née Meyer
geborgen 1 *2. Part. v.* BERGEN;
2 *Adj.* safe; secure
Geborgenheit *die;* ~: security
geborsten *2. Part. v.* BERSTEN
gebot *1. u. 3. Pers. Sg. Prät. v.* GEBIETEN
Gebot *das;* **~[e]s, ~e (a)** (Grundsatz) precept; **die Zehn ~e** (Rel.) the Ten Commandments
(b) (Vorschrift) regulation
geboten 1 *2. Part. v.* BIETEN, GEBIETEN;
2 *Adj.* (ratsam) advisable; (notwendig) necessary
Gebr. *Abk.* = **Gebrüder** Bros.
gebracht *2. Part. v.* BRINGEN
gebrannt *2. Part. v.* BRENNEN
gebraten *2. Part. v.* BRATEN
Gebrauch *der* **(a)** use
(b) (Brauch) custom
gebrauchen *tr. V.* use
gebräuchlich *Adj.* **(a)** normal; customary
(b) (häufig) common
gebrauchs-, Gebrauchs-: ~anweisung *die* instructions *pl.* [for

use]; **~fertig** *Adj.* ready for use *pred.;* **~gegenstand** *der* item of practical use; **~wert** *der* utility value

gebraucht *Adj.* second-hand; used ‹*car*›

Gebraucht·wagen *der* used car

Gebrechen *das;* **~s, ~** (geh.) affliction

gebrechlich *Adj.* infirm

Gebrechlichkeit *die;* **~**: infirmity

gebrochen 1 *2. Part. v.* BRECHEN;
2 *Adj.* **~es Englisch/Deutsch** broken English/German
3 *adv.* **~ Deutsch sprechen** speak broken German

Gebrüder *Pl.:* **die ~ Meyer** Meyer Brothers

Gebrüll *das;* **~[e]s** roaring

Gebrumm *das;* **~[e]s** (von Bären) growling; (von Flugzeugen, Bienen) droning; (von Insekten) buzz[ing]

gebückt *Adj.* **in ~er Haltung** bending forward

Gebühr *die;* **~, ~en** charge; (Maut) toll; (Anwalts~) fee

gebühren (geh.) *itr. V.* **jmdm. gebührt Achtung** *usw.* sb. deserves respect *etc.*

Gebühren·anzeiger *der* (Fernspr.) telephone meter

gebührend 1 *Adj.* fitting
2 *adv.* fittingly

gebühren-, Gebühren-: **~ermäßigung** *die* reduction of charges/ fees; **~frei** 1 *Adj.* free of charge *pred.;* 2 *adv.* free of charge; **~pflichtig** *Adj.* **eine ~pflichtige Verwarnung** a fine and a caution; **~vignette** *die* [Swiss] motorway fee sticker

gebunden 1 *2. Part. v.* BINDEN;
2 *Adj.* (verpflichtet) bound

Geburt *die;* **~, ~en** birth

Geburten-: **~kontrolle** *die* birth control; **~rate** *die* birth rate; **~ziffer** *die* birth rate

gebürtig *Adj.* **ein ~er Schwabe** a Swabian by birth

Geburts-: **~anzeige** *die* birth announcement; **~datum** *das* date of birth; **~haus** *das:* **das ~haus Beethovens** the house where Beethoven was born; Beethoven's birthplace; **~helfer** *der,* **~helferin** *die* (Arzt, Ärztin) obstetrician; **~hilfe** *die* (Med.) obstetrics *sing.;* (von einer Hebamme) midwifery; **~stadt** *die* native town/city; **~ort** *der* place of birth; **~tag** *der* birthday; **jmdm. zum ~tag gratulieren** wish sb. many happy returns of the day; **~ur·kunde** *die* birth certificate

Gebüsch *das;* **~[e]s, ~e** bushes *pl.*

gedacht *2. Part. v.* DENKEN, GEDENKEN

Gedächtnis *das;* **~ses, ~se** **(a)** memory
(b) (Andenken) memory

Gedächtnis-: **~lücke** *die* gap in one's memory; **~schwund** *der* loss of memory

gedämpft *Adj.* subdued ‹*mood*›; subdued, soft ‹*light*›; muffled ‹*sound*›

Gedanke *der;* **~ns, ~n** **(a)** thought; **der ~ an etw.** (*Akk.*) the thought of sth.
(b) *Pl.* (Meinung) ideas
(c) (Einfall) idea

gedanken-, Gedanken-: **~gang** *der* train of thought; **~gut** *das* thought; **christliches ~gut** Christian thought; **staatszersetzendes ~gut** subversive ideas *pl.;* **~los** 1 *Adj.* unconsidered; (zerstreut) absent-minded; 2 *adv.* without thinking; (zerstreut) absent-mindedly; **~losigkeit** *die;* **~~** (Zerstreutheit) absent-mindedness; (Unüberlegtheit) lack of thought; **~strich** *der* dash; **~verloren** *Adv.* lost in thought; **~voll** 1 *Adj.* pensive; 2 *adv.* pensively

gedanklich 1 *Adj.* intellectual
2 *adv.* intellectually

Gedärm *das;* **~[e]s, ~e** intestines *pl.;* bowels *pl.,* (eines Tieres) entrails *pl.*

Gedeck *das;* **~[e]s, ~e** **(a)** place setting; cover
(b) (Menü) set meal
(c) (Getränk) drink [with a cover charge]

gedeihen *unr. itr. V.; mit sein* **(a)** thrive; (wirtschaftlich) flourish; prosper
(b) (fortschreiten) progress

gedenken *unr. itr. V.* **(a)** **jmds./einer Sache ~** (geh.) remember sb./sth.; (in einer Feier) commemorate sb./sth.
(b) **etw. zu tun ~**: intend to do *or* doing sth.

Gedenk·stätte *die* memorial

Gedicht *das;* **~[e]s, ~e** poem

gediegen 1 *Adj.* solid ‹*furniture*›; sound ‹*piece of work*›
2 *adv.* **~ gebaut/verarbeitet** solidly built/ made

gedieh *1. u. 3. Pers. Sg. Prät. v.* GEDEIHEN

gediehen *2. Part. v.* GEDEIHEN

Gedränge *das;* **~s** **(a)** pushing and shoving; (Menge) crush; crowd
(b) **ins ~ kommen** *od.* **geraten** get into difficulties

gedroschen *2. Part. v.* DRESCHEN

gedrungen 1 *2. Part. v.* DRINGEN;
2 *Adj.* stocky; thickset

Geduld *die;* **~**: patience

gedulden *refl. V.* be patient; **~ Sie sich bitte ein paar Minuten** please be so good as to wait a few minutes

geduldig 1 *Adj.* patient
2 *adv.* patiently

Gedulds-: **~probe** *die* trial of one's patience; **~spiel** *das* puzzle

gedurft *2. Part. v.* DÜRFEN

geeignet *Adj.* suitable; (richtig) right

Gefahr *die;* **~, ~en** **(a)** danger; (Bedrohung) danger; threat (**für** to); **bei ~**: in case of emergency
(b) (Risiko) risk; **auf eigene ~**: at one's own risk

gefährden *tr. V.* endanger; jeopardize ‹*enterprise, success, position, etc.*›
gefährdet *Adj.* ‹*people, adolescents, etc.*› at risk *postpos.*
Gefährdung *die;* ~, ~**en (a)** endangering; (eines Unternehmens, einer Position usw.) jeopardizing
(b) (Gefahr) threat (+ *Gen.* to)
gefahren *2. Part. v.* FAHREN
gefährlich [1] *Adj.* dangerous; (gewagt) risky
[2] *adv.* dangerously
gefahr·los [1] *Adj.* safe
[2] *adv.* safely

g

Gefährt *das;* ~[e]**s**, ~**e** (geh.) vehicle
Gefährte *der;* ~**n**, ~**n**, **Gefährtin** *die;* ~, ~**nen** (geh.) companion; (Ehemann/Ehefrau) partner in life
Gefälle *das;* ~**s**, ~: slope; incline; (einer Straße) gradient
gefallen[1] *unr. itr. V.* **(a) das gefällt mir [gut]** I like it [a lot]
(b) sich (*Dat.*) **etw.** ~ **lassen** put up with sth.
gefallen[2] *2. Part. v.* FALLEN, GEFALLEN
Gefallen[1] *der;* ~**s**, ~: favour
Gefallen[2] *das;* ~**s** pleasure
Gefallene *der; adj. Dekl.* soldier killed in action; **die** ~**n** the fallen
Gefälle·strecke *die* incline
gefällig [1] *Adj.* **(a)** obliging; helpful
(b) (anziehend) pleasing; agreeable ‹*programme, behaviour*›
[2] *adv.* pleasingly; agreeably
Gefälligkeit *die;* ~, ~**en** favour
gefälligst *Adv.* (ugs.) kindly
gefangen *2. Part. v.* FANGEN
Gefangene *der/die; adj. Dekl.* prisoner
gefangen-: ***~|halten**, ***~|nehmen** ▶ FANGEN 1
Gefangenschaft *die;* ~, ~**en** captivity
Gefängnis *das;* ~**ses**, ~**se (a)** prison; gaol
(b) (Strafe) imprisonment
Gefängnis-: ~**strafe** *die* prison sentence; ~**wärter** *der,* ~**wärterin** *die* [prison] warder
Gefasel *das;* ~**s** (ugs. abwertend) twaddle (coll.); drivel (derog.)
Gefäß *das;* ~**es**, ~**e (a)** vessel; container
(b) (Anat.) vessel
gefasst, ***gefaßt** *Adj.* **(a)** calm; composed
(b) *in* **auf etw.** (*Akk.*) **[nicht]** ~ **sein** [not] be prepared for sth.
Gefecht *das;* ~[e]**s**, ~**e** battle
Gefieder *das;* ~**s**, ~: plumage; feathers *pl.*
gefiedert *Adj.* feathered
geflissentlich [1] *Adj.* deliberate
[2] *adv.* deliberately
geflochten *2. Part. v.* FLECHTEN
geflogen *2. Part. v.* FLIEGEN

*alte Schreibung - vgl. Hinweis auf S. xiv

geflohen *2. Part. v.* FLIEHEN
geflossen *2. Part. v.* FLIESSEN
Geflügel *das;* ~**s** poultry
Geflügel·schere *die* poultry shears *pl.*
geflügelt *Adj.* winged ‹*insect, seed*›; **ein** ~**es Wort** (fig.) a standard *or* familiar quotation
gefochten *2. Part. v.* FECHTEN
Gefolge *das;* ~**s**, ~: entourage
Gefolgschaft *die;* ~, ~**en: jmdm.** ~ **leisten** obey *or* follow sb.; give one's allegiance to sb.; **jmdm. die** ~ **verweigern** refuse to obey *or* follow sb.; refuse to give sb. one's allegiance
gefragt *Adj.* in great demand *postpos.;* sought-after
gefräßig *Adj.* (abwertend) greedy
Gefreite *der; adj. Dekl.* (Milit.) lance corporal (Brit.); private first class (Amer.); (Marine) able seaman; (Luftw.) aircraftman first class (Brit.); airman third class (Amer.)
gefressen *2. Part. v.* FRESSEN
gefrieren *unr. itr. V.; mit sein* freeze
gefrier-, Gefrier-: ~**fach** *das* freezing compartment; ~**punkt** *der* freezing point; ~**schrank** *der* freezer; ~**|trocknen** *tr. V.; meist im Inf. u. 2. Part.* freeze-dry; ~**truhe** *die* [chest] freezer
gefroren *2. Part. v.* FRIEREN, GEFRIEREN
gefrustet *Adj.* (ugs.) frustrated
Gefüge *das;* ~**s**, ~: structure
gefügig *Adj.* compliant; docile ‹*animal*›
Gefühl *das;* ~**s**, ~**e (a)** sensation; feeling
(b) (Gemütsverfassung) feeling
gefühl·los *Adj.* **(a)** numb
(b) (herzlos, kalt) unfeeling
gefühls-, Gefühls-: ~**betont** *Adj.* emotional; ~**duselei** *die;* ~~ (ugs. abwertend) mawkishness; ~**mäßig** *Adj.* emotional ‹*reaction*›; ‹*action*› based on emotion; ~**regung** *die* emotion
gefühl·voll [1] *Adj.* sensitive; (ausdrucksvoll) expressive
[2] *adv.* sensitively; expressively
gefüllt *2. Part. v.* FÜLLEN
gefunden *2. Part. v.* FINDEN; *s. auch* FRESSEN B
Gegacker *das;* ~**s (a)** (dauerndes Gackern) cackling
(b) (ugs.: Kichern) giggling
gegangen *2. Part. v.* GEHEN
gegeben *2. Part. v.* GEBEN
gegebenen·falls *Adv.* should the occasion arise
gegen *Präp. mit Akk.* **(a)** against; ~ **etw. stoßen** knock into sth.; **ein Mittel** ~ **Krebs** a cure for cancer; ~ **die Abmachung** contrary to the agreement
(b) ~ **Abend/Morgen** towards evening/dawn; ~ **vier Uhr** around 4 o'clock
(c) (im Vergleich zu) compared with

(d) (im Ausgleich für) for; **~ Quittung** against a receipt

Gegen-: ~angriff *der* counter-attack; **~argument** *das* counter-argument; **~besuch** *der* return visit

Gegend *die;* **~, ~en (a)** area **(b)** (Körperregion) region

Gegen-: ~darstellung *die:* **eine ~darstellung [der Sache]** an account [of the matter] from an opposing point of view; **~druck** *der* counter pressure

gegen·einander *Adv.* against each other *or* one another

gegen-, Gegen-: ~gewicht *das* counterweight; **ein ~gewicht zu** *od.* **gegen etw. bilden** (fig.) counterbalance sth.; **~gift** *das* antidote; **~kandidat** *der,* **~kandidatin** *die* opposing candidate; rival candidate; **~leistung** *die* service in return; **~mittel** *das* (gegen Gift) antidote; (gegen Krankheit) remedy; **~partei** *die* opposing side; other side; (Sport) opposing side *or* team; **~probe** *die* cross-check; **~satz** *der* **(a)** (Gegenteil) opposite; **im ~satz zu** in contrast to *or* with; unlike **(b)** (Widerspruch) conflict; **~sätzlich** *Adj.* conflicting; **~schlag** *der* counterstroke; **zum ~schlag ausholen** prepare to counter-attack *or* strike back; **~seite** *die* **(a)** (einer Straße, eines Flusses usw.) other side; far side; **(b)** ▶ ~PARTEI; **~seitig** [1] *Adj.* (wechselseitig) mutual; [2] *adv.* **sich ~seitig helfen/überbieten** help/outdo each other *or* one another; **~seitigkeit** *die;* **~~:** reciprocity; **auf ~seitigkeit** (*Dat.*) **beruhen** be mutual; **~spieler** *der,* **~spielerin** *die* opponent; (Sport) opposite number

Gegen·stand *der* object; (Thema) subject; topic

gegenständlich *Adj.* (Kunst) representational; (Philos.) objective

gegenstands·los *Adj.* **(a)** (hinfällig) invalid **(b)** (grundlos, unbegründet) unfounded ‹*accusation, complaint, jealousy*›; baseless ‹*fear*›

gegen-, Gegen-: ~stimme *die* vote against; **ohne ~stimme** unanimously; **~stück** *das* companion piece; (fig.) counterpart; **~teil** *das* opposite; **im ~teil** on the contrary; **~teilig** *Adj.* opposite; contrary; **~tor** *das* (Sport) goal for the other side

gegen·über *Präp. mit Dat.* **(a)** opposite **(b)** (in Bezug auf) **~ jmdm.** *od.* **jmdm. ~ freundlich sein** be kind to sb. **(c)** (im Vergleich zu) compared with

gegenüber-, Gegenüber-: ~|stehen *unr. itr. V.* **(a) jmdm./einer Sache ~stehen** stand facing sb./sth.; (fig.) face sb./sth.; **(b) jmdm./einer Sache feindlich/wohlwollend ~stehen** be ill/well disposed towards sb./sth.; **~|stellen** *tr. V.* confront; **~stellung** *die* **(a)** confrontation; **(b)** (Vergleich) comparison; **(c)** (zur Identifizierung) identification parade; **~|treten** *unr. itr. V.; mit sein* **jmdm./einer Sache ~treten** (auch fig.) face sb./sth.

Gegen·verkehr *der* oncoming traffic

Gegenwart *die;* **~ (a)** present **(b)** (Anwesenheit) presence **(c)** (Grammatik) present [tense]

gegenwärtig [1] *Adj.* present [2] *adv.* at present; at the moment

Gegen-: ~wehr *die* resistance; **~wert** *der* equivalent; **~wind** *der* head wind; **~zug** *der* (Brettspiele, fig.) countermove

gegessen *2. Part. v.* ESSEN

geglichen *2. Part. v.* GLEICHEN

geglitten *2. Part. v.* GLEITEN

Gegner *der;* **~s, ~, Gegnerin** *die;* **~, ~nen (a)** adversary; opponent **(b)** (Sport) opponent

gegnerisch *Adj.* opposing; opponents' ‹*goal*›

Gegnerschaft *die;* **~** (Einstellung) hostility; antagonism

gegolten *2. Part. v.* GELTEN

gegoren *2. Part. v.* GÄREN

gegossen *2. Part. v.* GIESSEN

gegriffen *2. Part. v.* GREIFEN

Gehabe *das;* **~s** (abwertend) affected behaviour; **ihr wichtigtuerisches ~:** her pompous behaviour

gehabt *Adj.* (ugs.: schon da gewesen) same old (coll.); usual; **wie ~:** as before

Gehalt[1] *der;* **~[e]s, ~e (a)** meaning **(b)** (Anteil) content

Gehalt[2] *das* (österr. auch: *der*); **~[e]s, Gehälter** salary

gehalten *2. Part. v.* HALTEN

Gehalts-: ~abrechnung *die* salary statement; payslip; **~empfänger** *der,* **~empfängerin** *die* salary earner; **~erhöhung** *die* salary increase; **~zettel** *der* salary slip

gehalt·voll *Adj.* nutritious ‹*food*›; ‹*novel, speech*› rich in substance

gehässig *Adj.* (abwertend) spiteful

Gehässigkeit *die;* **~, ~en (a)** (Wesen) spitefulness **(b)** (Äußerung) spiteful remark

gehauen *2. Part. v.* HAUEN

gehäuft *Adj.* **ein ~er Teelöffel/Esslöffel** a heaped teaspoon/tablespoon

Gehäuse *das;* **~s, ~** (einer Maschine) casing; housing; (einer Kamera, Uhr) case

geh·behindert *Adj.* able to walk only with difficulty *postpos.;* disabled

Gehege *das;* **~s, ~ (a)** (Jägerspr.) preserve; **jmdm. ins ~ kommen** (fig.) poach on sb.'s preserve; **sich** (*Dat.*) **[gegenseitig] ins ~ kommen** (fig.) encroach on each other's territory **(b)** (im Zoo) enclosure

geheim [1] *Adj.* **(a)** secret; **etw. ~ halten** keep sth. secret
(b) (mysteriös) mysterious
[2] *adv.* **~ abstimmen** vote by secret ballot

geheim-, Geheim-: ~agent *der,* **~agentin** *die* secret agent; **~dienst** *der* secret service; ***~|halten** ▶ GEHEIM 1A

Geheimnis *das;* **~ses, ~se** secret

Geheimnis·tuerei *die;* **~** (ugs.) secretiveness

geheimnis·voll *Adj.* mysterious

Geheim·nummer *die* **(a)** (Bankw.) personal identification number; PIN
(b) (Telefonnummer) ex-directory number; unlisted number (Amer.)

Geheim·zahl *die* ▶ GEHEIMNUMMER A

Geheiß *das:* **auf jmds. ~** (geh.) at sb.'s behest

gehen [1] *unr. itr. V.; mit sein* **(a)** walk; go; **über die Straße ~:** cross the street
(b) (sich irgendwohin begeben) go
(c) (regelmäßig besuchen) attend
(d) (weg~) go; leave
(e) (in Funktion sein) work; **meine Uhr geht falsch** my watch is wrong
(f) (möglich sein) **ja, das geht** yes, I/we can manage that; **das geht nicht** that can't be done
(g) (ugs.: gerade noch angehen) **Hast du gut geschlafen? – Es geht** Did you sleep well? – Not too bad
(h) (sich entwickeln) **der Laden/das Geschäft geht gut/gar nicht** the shop/business is doing well/not doing well at all; **es ist gut gegangen** it turned out well
(i) (*unpers.*) **wie geht es dir?** How are you?; **jmdm. geht es gut/schlecht** (gesundheitlich) sb. is well/not well; (geschäftlich) sb. is doing well/badly
(j) (*unpers.*) (sich um etw. handeln); **worum geht es hier?** what is this all about?
(k) **sich ~ lassen** (sich nicht beherrschen) lose control of oneself; (sich vernachlässigen) let oneself go
(l) (ein Liebespaar sein) **mit jmdm. ~:** go out with sb.
[2] *unr. tr. V.* (zurücklegen) **10 km ~:** walk 10 km

***gehen|lassen** ▶ GEHEN 1K

geheuer *Adj.* **(a)** **in diesem Gebäude ist es nicht ~:** this building is eerie
(b) **ihr war doch nicht [ganz] ~:** she felt [a little] uneasy
(c) **die Sache ist [mir] nicht ganz ~:** [I feel] there's something odd about this business

Gehilfe *der;* **~n, ~n, Gehilfin** *die;* **~, ~nen** assistant

Gehirn *das;* **~[e]s, ~e** brain

Gehirn-: ~erschütterung *die* concussion; **~schlag** *der* stroke; **~wäsche** *die* brainwashing *no indef. art.*

gehoben [1] *2. Part. v.* HEBEN;
[2] *Adj.* **(a)** higher; senior ‹*position*›
(b) (gewählt) elevated, refined

geholfen *2. Part. v.* HELFEN

Gehör *das;* **~[e]s** [sense of] hearing; **[etw.] nach dem ~ singen/spielen** sing/play [sth.] by ear; **das absolute ~** (Musik) absolute pitch

gehorchen *itr. V.* **jmdm. ~:** obey sb.

gehören [1] *itr. V.* **(a)** **jmdm. ~:** belong to sb.
(b) (Teil eines Ganzen sein) **zu jmds. Freunden/Aufgaben ~:** be one of sb.'s friends/part of sb.'s duties
(c) (passend sein) **dein Roller gehört nicht in die Küche!** your scooter does not belong in the kitchen!
(d) (nötig sein) **es hat viel Fleiß dazu gehört** it took a lot of hard work; **dazu gehört sehr viel** that takes a lot
[2] *refl. V.* (sich schicken) be fitting; **es gehört sich [nicht], … zu …:** it is [not] good manners to …

gehörig [1] *Adj.* **(a)** proper
(b) (ugs.: beträchtlich) **ein ~er Schrecken/eine ~e Portion Mut** a good fright/a good deal of courage
[2] *adv.* (ugs.: beträchtlich) **~ essen/trinken** eat/drink heartily

gehorsam *Adj.* obedient

Gehorsam *der;* **~s** obedience

Geh·steig *der;* **~[e]s, ~e** pavement (Brit.); sidewalk (Amer.)

Geht·nicht·mehr *das:* **bis zum ~** (salopp) ad nauseam

Gehupe *das;* **~s** honking; hooting

Geier *der;* **~s, ~:** vulture

Geige *die;* **~, ~n** violin

Geiger *der;* **~s, ~, Geigerin** *die;* **~, ~nen** violin player; violinist

Geiger·zähler *der* (Physik) Geiger counter

geil *Adj.* **(a)** (oft abwertend: sexuell erregt) randy; horny (sl.); (lüstern) lecherous
(b) (Jugendspr.) great (coll.); fabulous (coll.)

Geilheit *die;* **~** ▶ GEIL A randiness; horniness (sl.); lecherousness

Geisel *die;* **~, ~n** hostage

Geisel-: ~nahme *die;* **~~, ~~n** taking of hostages; **~nehmer** *der;* **~~s, ~~, ~nehmerin** *die;* **~~, ~~nen** terrorist/guerrilla *etc.* holding the hostages

Geißel *die;* **~, ~n** (hist., auch fig.) scourge

Geist *der;* **~[e]s, ~er** **(a)** (Verstand) mind
(b) (Scharfsinn) wit
(c) (innere Einstellung) spirit
(d) (denkender Mensch) mind; intellect; **ein großer/kleiner ~:** a great mind/a person of limited intellect
(e) (überirdisches Wesen) spirit; **der Heilige ~** (christl. Rel.) the Holy Ghost *or* Spirit
(f) (Gespenst) ghost

Geister-: ~bahn *die* ghost train; **~fahrer** *der;* **~fahrerin** *die: person driving on the wrong side of the road or the wrong carriageway*

*old spelling - see note on page xiv

geisterhaft *Adj.* ghostly; eerie ‹*atmosphere*›
Geister·hand *die:* **wie von** *od.* **durch ~:** as if by an invisible hand
geistes-, Geistes-: ~abwesend [1] *Adj.* absent-minded; [2] *adv.* absent-mindedly; **~blitz** *der* (ugs.) brainwave; **~gegenwart** *die* presence of mind; **~gegenwärtig** [1] *Adj.* quick-witted; [2] *adv.* with great presence of mind; **~krank** *Adj.* mentally ill; **~krankheit** *die* mental illness; **~wissenschaften** *Pl.* arts; humanities; **~wissenschaftler** *der*, **~wissenschaftlerin** *die* arts scholar; scholar in the humanities; **~zustand** *der* mental state
geistig [1] *Adj.* **(a)** intellectual; (Psych.) mental
(b) alcoholic ‹*drinks*›
[2] *adv.* intellectually; (Psych.) mentally
geistlich *Adj.* sacred ‹*song, music*›; religious ‹*order, book, writings*›
Geistliche *der; adj. Dekl.* clergyman
geist-, Geist-: ~los *Adj.* dim-witted; (trivial) trivial; **~losigkeit** *die;* **~~:** dim-wittedness; (Trivialität) triviality; **~reich** [1] *Adj.* witty; (klug) clever; [2] *adv.:* wittily; cleverly; **~tötend** *Adj.* soul-destroying ‹*work, job*›; stupefyingly boring ‹*chatter, drivel*›
Geiz *der;* **~es** meanness; (Knauserigkeit) miserliness
geizen *itr. V.* be mean
Geiz·hals *der* (abwertend) skinflint
geizig *Adj.* mean; (knauserig) miserly
gekannt *2. Part. v.* KENNEN
Gekicher *das;* **~s** giggling
geklungen *2. Part. v.* KLINGEN
geknickt *Adj.* (ugs.) dejected
gekniffen *2. Part. v.* KNEIFEN
gekommen *2. Part. v.* KOMMEN
gekonnt [1] *2. Part. v.* KÖNNEN; [2] *Adj.* accomplished; (hervorragend ausgeführt) masterly
gekrochen *2. Part. v.* KRIECHEN
gekünstelt [1] *Adj.* artificial
[2] *adv.* **er lächelte ~:** he gave a forced smile
Gelächter *das;* **~s, ~:** laughter
geladen *2. Part. v.* LADEN
Gelände *das;* **~s, ~ (a)** (Landschaft) ground; terrain
(b) (Grundstück) site; (von Schule, Krankenhaus usw.) grounds *pl.*
Geländer *das;* **~s, ~:** banisters *pl.;* handrail; (am Balkon, an einer Brücke) railing[s *pl.*]; (aus Stein) parapet
gelang *3. Pers. Sg. Prät. v.* GELINGEN
gelangen *itr. V.; mit sein* **an etw.** (*Akk.*)/**zu etw. ~:** reach sth.; (fig.) **zu Ansehen ~:** gain esteem
gelassen [1] *2. Part. v.* LASSEN; [2] *Adj.* calm; (gefasst) composed
Gelassenheit *die;* **~:** calmness; (Gefasstheit) composure
Gelatine /ʒela'ti:nə/ *die;* **~:** gelatine
gelaufen *2. Part. v.* LAUFEN
geläufig *Adj.* (vertraut) common ‹*expression, concept*›
gelaunt *Adj.* **gut ~:** cheerful; **schlecht ~:** bad-tempered; **gut/schlecht ~ sein** be in a good/bad mood
gelb *Adj.* yellow
Gelb *das;* **~s, ~** *od.* (ugs.) **~s** yellow
gelblich *Adj.* yellowish; yellowed ‹*paper*›; sallow ‹*skin*›
Gelb·sucht *die* (Med.) jaundice
Geld *das;* **~es, ~er** money; **großes ~:** large denominations *pl.;* **kleines/bares ~:** change/cash
geld-, Geld-: ~automat *der* cash dispenser; **~beutel** *der* (bes. südd.) purse; **~börse** *die* purse; **~buße** *die* fine; **~gier** *die* avarice; **~gierig** *Adj.* avaricious; **~institut** *das* financial institution; **~mangel** *der* lack of money; **~mittel** *Pl.* financial resources; **~preis** *der* cash prize; **~rück·gabe** *die* **(a) ~rückgabe verlangen** ask for one's money back; **Anspruch auf ~rückgabe haben** be entitled to one's money back; **(b)** (eines Automaten) coin return; **~schein** *der* banknote; bill (Amer.); **~schrank** *der* safe; **~schwierigkeiten** *Pl.* financial difficulties *or* straits; **~spende** *die* donation; contribution; **~strafe** *die* fine; **~stück** *das* coin; **~wechsel** *der* exchanging of money; **„~wechsel"** 'bureau de change'
Gelee /ʒe'le:/ *der od. das;* **~s, ~s** jelly
gelegen [1] *2. Part. v.* LIEGEN; [2] *Adj.* (passend) convenient
Gelegenheit *die;* **~, ~en** opportunity; (Anlass) occasion
Gelegenheits-: ~arbeit *die* casual work; **~kauf** *der* bargain
gelegentlich [1] *Adj.* occasional
[2] *adv.* occasionally
gelehrig *Adj.* ‹*child*› who is quick to learn; ‹*animal*› that is quick to learn
gelehrt *Adj.* learned
Gelehrte *der/die; adj. Dekl.* scholar
Geleit *das;* **~[e]s, ~e** (geh.) **sie bot uns ihr ~ an** she offered to accompany us
geleiten *tr. V.* (geh.) escort
Geleit·schutz *der* (Milit.) escort
Gelenk *das;* **~[e]s, ~e** joint
gelenkig [1] *Adj.* agile ‹*person*›; supple ‹*limb*›
[2] *adv.* agilely
Gelenkigkeit *die;* **~:** agility; (von Gliedmaßen) suppleness
gelernt *Adj.* qualified
gelesen *2. Part. v.* LESEN
Geliebte *der/die; adj. Dekl.* lover/mistress

geliefert *Adj.*: ~ **sein** (salopp) have had it (coll.)
geliehen *2. Part. v.* LEIHEN
gelind[e] [1] *Adj.* mild
[2] *adv.* mildly; **~e gesagt** to put it mildly
gelingen *unr. itr. V.; mit sein* succeed
Gelingen *das;* **~s** success
gelitten *2. Part. v.* LEIDEN
gellen *itr. V.* **(a)** (hell schallen) ring out
(b) (nachhallen) ring
geloben *tr. V.* (geh.) vow; **das Gelobte Land** the Promised Land
gelogen *2. Part. v.* LÜGEN
gelöst *Adj.* relaxed
gelten [1] *unr. itr. V.* **(a)** (gültig sein) be valid; ‹*banknote, coin*› be legal tender; ‹*law etc.*› be in force
(b) (angesehen werden) **als etw. ~:** be regarded as sth.
(c) (+ *Dat.*) (bestimmt sein für) be directed at
[2] *unr. tr. V.* **(a)** (wert sein) **sein Wort gilt viel/wenig** his word carries a lot of/little weight
(b) *unpers.* **es gilt, etw. zu tun** it is essential to do sth.
geltend: etw. ~ machen assert sth.
Geltung *die;* **~ (a)** validity; **für jmdn. ~ haben** apply to sb.
(b) (Wirkung) recognition; **zur ~ kommen** show to [its best] advantage
Geltungs·bedürfnis *das* need for recognition
gelungen [1] *2. Part. v.* GELINGEN;
[2] *Adj.* **(a)** (ugs.: spaßig) priceless
(b) (ansprechend) inspired
gemächlich /gəˈmɛ(ː)çlɪç/ [1] *Adj.* leisurely
[2] *adv.* in a leisurely manner
Gemächlichkeit *die;* **~:** leisureliness
gemacht: ein ~er Mann sein (ugs.) be a made man
Gemahl *der;* **~s, ~e** (geh.) consort; husband
Gemahlin *die;* **~, ~nen** (geh.) consort; wife
Gemälde *das;* **~s, ~:** painting
gemäß *Präp. + Dat.* in accordance with
gemäßigt *Adj.* moderate; qualified ‹*optimism*›; temperate ‹*climate*›
Gemecker[e] *das;* **~s (a)** (von Schafen, Ziegen) bleating
(b) (ugs. abwertend: Nörgelei) griping (coll.); grousing (coll.); moaning
gemein [1] *Adj.* **(a)** vulgar ‹*joke, expression*›; nasty ‹*person*›
(b) (niederträchtig) mean; dirty ‹*lie*›; mean ‹*trick*›
[2] *adv.* in a mean *or* nasty way
Gemeinde *die;* **~, ~n (a)** municipality; (Bewohner) community
(b) (Pfarr~) parish
(c) (versammelte Gottesdienstteilnehmer) congregation

*alte Schreibung - vgl. Hinweis auf S. xiv

Gemeinde-: ~rat *der* **(a)** (Gremium) local council; **(b)** (Mitglied) local councillor; **~rätin** *die* local councillor; **~schwester** *die* district nurse; **~verwaltung** *die* local administration
gemein·gefährlich *Adj.* dangerous to the public
Gemein·gut *das* (geh.) common property
Gemeinheit *die;* **~, ~en (a)** meanness
(b) (Handlung) mean trick
gemein·nützig *Adj.* serving the public good *postpos., not pred.;* (wohltätig) charitable
gemeinsam [1] *Adj.* **(a)** common ‹*interests, characteristics*›; mutual ‹*acquaintance, friend*›; joint ‹*property, account*›; shared ‹*experience*›; **~e Interessen/Merkmale haben** have interests/characteristics in common
(b) (miteinander unternommen) joint; **viel Gemeinsames haben** have a lot in common
[2] *adv.* together
Gemeinsamkeit *die;* **~, ~en** common feature
Gemeinschaft *die;* **~, ~en (a)** community
(b) (Verbundenheit) coexistence
gemeinschaftlich ▶ GEMEINSAM
gemein·verständlich *Adj.* generally comprehensible
Gemein·wohl *das* public good
gemessen [1] *2. Part. v.* MESSEN;
[2] *Adj.* (würdevoll) measured ‹*steps, tones, language*›; deliberate ‹*words, manner of speaking*›
Gemetzel *das;* **~s, ~:** massacre
gemieden *2. Part. v.* MEIDEN
Gemisch *das;* **~[e]s, ~e** mixture **(aus, von** of**)**
gemocht *2. Part. v.* MÖGEN
gemolken *2. Part. v.* MELKEN
***Gemse** ▶ GÄMSE
Gemurmel *das;* **~s** murmuring
Gemüse *das;* **~s, ~:** vegetables *pl.*
gemusst, * gemußt *2. Part. v.* MÜSSEN
Gemüt *das;* **~[e]s, ~er (a)** nature
(b) (Empfindungsvermögen) heart
(c) (Mensch) soul
gemütlich [1] *Adj.* snug; cosy; (bequem) comfortable; (ungezwungen) informal
[2] *adv.* cosily; (bequem) comfortably; **~ beisammensitzen** sit pleasantly together
Gemütlichkeit *die;* **~:** snugness; (Zwanglosigkeit) informality
gemüts-, Gemüts-: ~krank *Adj.* (Med., Psych.) emotionally disturbed; **~mensch** *der* (ugs.) even-tempered person
gemüt·voll *Adj.* warm-hearted; (empfindsam) sentimental
Gen *das;* **~s, ~e** (Biol.) gene
genannt *2. Part. v.* NENNEN
genas *1. u. 3. Pers. Sg. Prät. v.* GENESEN
genau [1] *Adj.* **(a)** (exakt) exact; precise

(b) (sorgfältig, gründlich) meticulous, ‹*person*›; careful ‹*study*›
2 *adv.* **(a)** exactly; precisely; **~ um 8⁰⁰** at 8 o'clock precisely
(b) (gerade, eben) just
(c) (als Verstärkung) just
(d) (als Zustimmung) exactly; precisely
(e) (sorgfältig) **~ arbeiten/etw. ~ durchdenken** work/think sth. out meticulously; **~ genommen** strictly speaking

***genau·genommen** ▶ GENAU 2E

Genauigkeit *die;* **~ (a)** (Exaktheit) exactness; precision; (einer Waage) accuracy
(b) (Sorgfalt) meticulousness

genau·so *Adv.* **(a)** *mit Adjektiven* just as
(b) *mit Verben* in exactly the same way; (in demselben Maße) just as much

genaustens *Adv.* **etw. ~ durchdenken/beachten** think sth. out/observe sth. most meticulously

Gendarm /ʒan'darm/ *der;* **~en, ~en** (österr., sonst veralt.) village *or* local policeman *or* constable

Gendarmerie /ʒandarmə'ri:/ *die;* **~, ~n** (österr., sonst veralt.) village *or* local constabulary

genehm *Adj.* **jmdm. ~ sein** (geh.) (jmdm. passen) be convenient to sb.; (jmdm. angenehm sein) be acceptable to sb.

genehmigen *tr. V.* approve ‹*plan, alterations, application*›; authorize ‹*stay*›; grant ‹*request*›; give permission for ‹*demonstration*›; **sich** (*Dat.*) **etw. ~** (ugs.) treat oneself to sth.

Genehmigung *die;* **~, ~en (a)** ▶ GENEHMIGEN; approval; authorization; granting; permission (*Gen.* for)
(b) (Schriftstück) permit; (Lizenz) licence

geneigt *Adj. in* **~ sein, etw. zu tun** be inclined to do sth.

General *der;* **~s, ~e** *od.* **Generäle** general

General-: ~direktor *der* chairman; president (Amer.); **~direktorin** *die* chairwoman; president (Amer.)

generalisieren *tr., itr. V.* generalize

Generalisierung *die;* **~, ~en** generalization

general-, General-: ~probe *die* (auch fig.) dress rehearsal; **~streik** *der* general strike; **~überholen** *tr. V.; nur im Inf. und 2. Part. gebr.* (bes. Technik) **etw. ~überholen** give sth. a general overhaul; **~vertreter** *der,* **~vertreterin** *die* general representative; **~vollmacht** *die* (Rechtsw.) full *or* unlimited power of attorney

Generation *die;* **~, ~en** generation

Generations·konflikt *der* generation gap

Generator *der;* **~s, ~en** generator

generell **1** *Adj.* general
2 *adv.* generally

genervt *Adj.* annoyed

genesen *unr. itr. V.; mit sein* (geh.) recover

Genesung *die;* **~, ~en** (geh.) recovery

genetisch (Biol.) *Adj.* genetic

Genf (*das*)*;* **~s** Geneva

Genfer **1** *der;* **~s, ~:** Genevese
2 *Adj.* Genevese; **der ~ See** Lake Geneva

Genferin *die;* **~, ~nen** Genevese

Gen·forschung *die* (Biol.) genetic research

genial *Adj.* brilliant

Genialität *die;* **~:** genius

Genick *das;* **~[e]s, ~e** back *or* nape of the neck

Genie /ʒe'ni:/ *das;* **~s, ~s** genius

genieren /ʒe'ni:rən/ *refl. V.* be embarrassed

genießbar *Adj.* (essbar) edible; (trinkbar) drinkable; **er ist heute nicht ~** (fig. ugs.) he is unbearable today

genießen *unr. tr. V.* enjoy

Genießer *der;* **~s, ~, Genießerin** *die;* **~, ~nen: er ist ein richtiger Genießer** he is a regular 'bon viveur'; **sie ist eine stille Genießerin** she enjoys life [to the full] in her own quiet way

genießerisch **1** *Adj.* appreciative
2 *adv.* appreciatively; ‹*drink, eat*› with relish

Genitale *das;* **~s, Genitalien** /geni'ta:li̯ən/,

Genital·organ *das* genital organ

Genitiv *der;* **~s, ~e** (Sprachw.) genitive [case]

Gen·manipulation *die* genetic manipulation

gen·manipuliert *Adj.* genetically engineered; genetically manipulated

Genom /ge'no:m/ *das;* **~s, ~e** (Biol.) genome

genommen *2. Part. v.* NEHMEN

genoss, *genoß *1. u. 3. Pers. Sg. Prät. v.* GENIEẞEN

Genosse *der;* **~n, ~n** comrade

genossen *2. Part. v.* GENIESSEN

Genossenschaft *die;* **~, ~en** cooperative

Genossin *die;* **~, ~nen** comrade

gen-, Gen-: ~technik *die* genetic engineering *no art.*; **~technisch** **1** *Adj.* genetic engineering ‹*techniques, research etc.*›; ‹*research, developments etc.*› in genetic engineering **2** *adv.* by genetic engineering; **~technisch verändert** genetically altered *or* modified; altered *or* modified by genetic engineering; **~technologie** *die* genetic engineering *no art.*

genug *Adv.* enough

genügen *itr. V.* **(a)** be enough
(b) einer Sache (*Dat.*) **~:** satisfy sth.

genügend **1** *Adj.* **(a)** enough
(b) (befriedigend) satisfactory
2 *adv.* enough

genügsam *Adj.* modest

Genugtuung /-tu:ʊŋ/ *die;* **~, ~en** satisfaction

Genus *das;* ~, **Genera** (Sprachw.) gender
Genuss, *Genuß *der;* **Genusses, Genüsse** (a) consumption
(b) (Wohlbehagen) **etw. mit ~ essen/lesen** eat sth. with relish/enjoy reading sth.
genüsslich, *genüßlich *Adv.* ‹*eat, drink*› with relish
gen·verändert *Adj.* genetically modified
Geograph *der;* **~en, ~en** geographer
Geographie *die;* ~: geography *no art.*
Geographin *die;* ~, **~nen** geographer
geographisch *Adj.* geographic[al]
Geologe *der;* **~n, ~n** geologist
Geologie *die;* ~: geology *no art.*
Geologin *die;* ~, **~nen** geologist
geologisch *Adj.* geological
Geometrie *die;* ~: geometry *no art.*
geometrisch *Adj.* geometric[al]
Gepäck *das;* **~[e]s** luggage (Brit.); baggage (Amer.); (am Flughafen) baggage
Gepäck-: ~annahme *die* **(a)** checking in the luggage/baggage; **(b)** (Schalter) [in-counter of the] luggage office (Brit.) *or* baggage office (Amer.); (zur Aufbewahrung) [in-counter of the] left-luggage office (Brit.) *or* checkroom (Amer.); (am Flughafen) baggage check-in; **~aufbewahrung** *die* left-luggage office (Brit.); checkroom (Amer.); (Schließfächer) luggage lockers (Brit.); baggage lockers (Amer.); **~ausgabe** *die* [out-counter of the] luggage office (Brit.) *or* (Amer.) baggage office; (zur Aufbewahrung) [out-counter of the] left-luggage office (Brit.) *or* (Amer.) checkroom; (am Flughafen) baggage reclaim; **~kontrolle** *die* baggage check; **~netz** *das* luggage rack (Brit.); baggage rack (Amer.); **~schalter** *der* ▸ ~ANNAHME B; **~schein** *der* luggage ticket (Brit.); baggage check (Amer.); **~träger** *der* **(a)** porter; **(b)** (am Fahrrad) carrier; rack
Gepard *der;* **~s, ~e** cheetah
gepfeffert *Adj.* (ugs.) steep (coll.) ‹*price, rent, etc.*›
Gepfeife *das;* **~s** (ugs. abwertend) [continuous, tuneless] whistling
gepfiffen *2. Part. v.* PFEIFEN
gepflegt *Adj.* **(a)** well-groomed; spruce ‹*appearance*›; neat ‹*clothing*›
(b) (hochwertig) choice ‹*food, drink*›
Gepflogenheit *die;* ~, **~en** (geh.) custom; (Gewohnheit) habit
Geplapper *das;* **~s** (ugs., oft abwertend) prattling
geplättet *Adj.* (salopp) flabbergasted
Gepolter *das;* **~s** clatter
gepriesen *2. Part. v.* PREISEN
Gequake *das;* **~s** (ugs.) croaking; (von Enten) quacking
Gequäke *das;* **~s** (ugs.) bawling
gequält *Adj.* forced ‹*smile, gaiety*›; pained ‹*expression*›

*old spelling - see note on page xiv

gequollen *2. Part. v.* QUELLEN
gerade [1] *Adj.* **(a)** straight; **etw. ~ biegen** bend sth. straight; straighten sth. [out]; **~ stehen** stand up straight
(b) (nicht schief) upright
(c) (aufrichtig) forthright; direct
(d) (Math.) even ‹*number*›
[2] *Adv.* just; (direkt) right
Gerade *die;* ~, **~n;** *auch adj. Dekl.* (Geom.) straight line
gerade-: ~aus *Adv.* straight ahead; **~|biegen** *unr. tr. V.* (ugs.: bereinigen) straighten out; **~heraus** /----'-/ (ugs.) *Adv.* **etw. ~heraus sagen** say sth. straight out; **~so** *Adv.* **~so groß/lang wie ...:** just as big/long as ...; **~|stehen** *unr. itr. V.* (fig.: einstehen) **für etw. ~stehen** accept responsibility for sth.; **~zu** *Adv.* really; (beinahe) almost
gerad-, Gerad-: ~linig [1] *Adj.* **(a)** straight; direct, lineal ‹*descent, descendant*›
(b) (aufrichtig) straightforward; [2] *adv.*
(a) ~linig verlaufen run in a straight line
(b) (aufrichtig) **~linig handeln/denken** be straightforward; **~linigkeit** *die;* ~~
(a) straightness; **(b)** (Aufrichtigkeit) straightforwardness
gerammelt *Adv.* **~ voll** (ugs.) [jam-]packed (coll.); packed out (coll.)
Geranie /ge'ra:ni̯ə/ *die;* ~, **~n** geranium
gerann *3. Pers. Sg. Prät. v.* GERINNEN
gerannt *2. Part. v.* RENNEN
gerät *3. Pers. Sg. Präsens v.* GERATEN[1]
Gerät *das;* **~[e]s, ~e (a)** piece of equipment; (Fernseher, Radio) set; (Garten~) tool
(b) (Turnen) piece of apparatus
geraten[1] *unr. itr. V.; mit sein* **(a)** (gelangen) get
(b) (werden) turn out; (gut ~) turn out well
geraten[2] [1] *2. Part. v.* RATEN, GERATEN[1]
[2] *Adj.* advisable
Geratewohl: aufs ~ (ugs.) ‹*select*› at random; **wir fuhren aufs ~ los** (ugs.) we went for a drive just to see where we ended up
geraum *Adj.* (geh.) considerable
geräumig *Adj.* spacious ‹*room*›; roomy ‹*cupboard etc.*›
Geräusch *das;* **~[e]s, ~e** sound; (unerwünscht) noise
geräusch-, Geräusch-: ~arm [1] *Adj.* quiet; [2] *adv.* quietly; **~los** [1] *Adj.* silent [2] *adv.* **(a)** silently; **(b)** (fig. ugs.) without [any] fuss; **~pegel** *der* noise level; **~voll** *Adj.* noisy
gerben *tr. V.* tan ‹*hides, skins*›
gerecht [1] *Adj.* just; (unparteiisch) fair
[2] *adv.* justly
gerechtfertigt *Adj.* justified
Gerechtigkeit *die;* ~: justice
Gerechtigkeits·sinn *der* sense of justice
Gerede *das;* **~s** (abwertend) **(a)** (ugs.) talk
(b) (Klatsch) gossip

geregelt *Adj.* regular, steady ‹*job*›
gereizt *Adj.* irritable
Gericht¹ *das;* **~[e]s, ~e** court; (Richter) bench; (Gebäude) court [house]; **das Jüngste ~** (Rel.) the Last Judgement
Gericht² *das;* **~[e]s, ~e** dish
gerichtlich 1 *Adj.* judicial; legal ‹*proceedings*›
2 *adv.* **jmdn. ~ verfolgen** take sb. to court
Gerichts-: ~hof *der* Court of Justice; **~kosten** *Pl.* legal costs; **~saal** *der* courtroom; **~verfahren** *das* legal proceedings *pl.*; **ein ~verfahren einleiten** institute legal *or* court proceedings; **ohne ~verfahren** without trial; **~vollzieher** *der;* **~~s, ~~**, **~vollzieherin** *die;* **~~, ~~nen** bailiff
gerieben *2. Part. v.* REIBEN
geriffelt *Adj.* corrugated ‹*surface, sheet metal*›; fluted ‹*column*›; ribbed ‹*glass*›
gering *Adj.* **(a)** low; little ‹*value*›; small ‹*quantity, amount*›; short ‹*distance, time*› **(b)** (unbedeutend) slight; minor ‹*role*›; **nicht im Geringsten** not in the slightest *or* least; **jmdn./etw. ~ achten** *od.* **schätzen** have a low opinion of *or* think very little of sb./sth.; **den Erfolg/Reichtümer ~ achten** *od.* **schätzen** set little store by success/riches
geringfügig 1 *Adj.* slight; minor ‹*alteration, injury*›; trivial ‹*amount, detail*›
2 *adv.* slightly
Geringfügigkeit *die;* **~, ~en** triviality
***gering|schätzen** ▶ GERING B
geringschätzig *Adj.* disdainful; disparaging ‹*remark*›
gerinnen *unr. itr. V.; mit sein* ‹*blood*› clot; ‹*milk*› curdle
Gerippe *das;* **~s, ~**: skeleton
gerippt *Adj.* ribbed; fluted ‹*glass, column*›
gerissen 1 *2. Part. v.* REISSEN;
2 *Adj.* (ugs.) crafty
geritten *2. Part. v.* REITEN
geritzt *Adj.* (salopp) **etw. ist ~**: sth. is [all] settled; **ist ~!** will do! (coll.)
Germane *der;* **~n, ~n**, **Germanin** *die;* **~, ~nen** (hist.) ancient German; Teuton
germanisch *Adj.* (auch fig.) Germanic; Teutonic
Germanistik *die;* **~**: German studies *pl.*, *no art.*
gern[e]; **lieber, am liebsten** *Adv.* **(a) etw. ~ tun** like *or* enjoy doing sth.; **er spielt lieber Tennis als Golf** he prefers playing tennis to golf; **etw. ~/am liebsten essen** like sth./like sth. best; **ja, ~/aber ~**: yes, of course; certainly!
(b) (durchaus) **das glaube ich ~**: I can well believe that
gerochen *2. Part. v.* RIECHEN
Geröll *das;* **~s, ~e** debris; (größer) boulders *pl.*
geronnen *2. Part. v.* RINNEN, GERINNEN
Gerste *die;* **~**: barley
Gersten·korn *das* (Med.) sty
Gerte *die;* **~, ~n** switch
Geruch *der;* **~[e]s, Gerüche** smell; (von Blumen) scent
Gerücht *das;* **~[e]s, ~e** rumour
gerufen *2. Part. v.* RUFEN
geruhsam 1 *Adj.* peaceful; leisurely ‹*stroll*›
2 *adv.* leisurely; quietly
Geruhsamkeit *die;* **~**: peacefulness; (eines Spaziergangs) leisureliness
Gerümpel *das;* **~s** junk
gerungen *2. Part. v.* RINGEN
Gerüst *das;* **~[e]s, ~e** scaffolding *no pl., no indef. art.*
gesamt *Adj.* whole; entire
gesamt-, Gesamt-: ~deutsch *Adj.* all-German; **~eindruck** *der* general impression
Gesamtheit *die:* **die ~ der Bevölkerung** the entire population
Gesamt-: ~schule *die* comprehensive [school]; **~werk** *das* œuvre; (Bücher) complete works *pl.*
gesandt *2. Part. v.* SENDEN
Gesandte *der/die; adj. Dekl.* envoy
Gesandtschaft *die;* **~, ~en** legation
Gesang *der;* **~[e]s, Gesänge (a)** singing **(b)** (Lied) song
Gesang-: ~buch *das* hymn book; **~verein** *der* choral society
Gesäß *das;* **~es, ~e** backside; buttocks *pl.*
geschaffen *2. Part. v.* SCHAFFEN 1
Geschäft *das;* **~[e]s, ~e (a)** business; (Transaktion) [business] deal; **mit jmdm. ~e/ein ~ machen** do business with sb./strike a bargain *or* do a deal with sb.; **ein gutes ~ machen** make a good profit
(b) (Laden) shop; store (Amer.)
Geschäfte·macher *der,* **Geschäfte·macherin** *die* (abwertend) profit-seeker
geschäftig *Adj.* bustling
geschäftlich 1 *Adj.* business *attrib.*
2 *adv.* on business
geschäfts-, Geschäfts-: ~bedingungen *Pl.* terms [and conditions] of trade; **~brief** *der* business letter; **~frau** *die* businesswoman; **~freund** *der,* **~freundin** *die* business associate; **~führer** *der* manager; (Vereinswesen) secretary; **~führerin** *die* ▶ ~FÜHRER: manageress; secretary; **~führung** *die* management; **~gebaren** *das* business *no art.*; business practices *pl.*; **~inhaber** *der,* **~inhaberin** *die* owner of the/a business; **~jahr** *das* financial year; **~kosten** *Pl.* **auf ~kosten** on expenses; **~lage** *die* [business] position; **~leitung** *die* ▶ ~FÜHRUNG; **~leute** ▶ ~MANN; **~mann** *der; Pl.* **~leute** businessman; ···›

~ordnung *die* standing orders *pl.;* (im Parlament) [rules *pl.* of] procedure; **~partner** *der,* **~partnerin** *die* business partner; **~reise** *die* business trip; **~schluss** *der* closing time; **~stelle** *die* branch; (einer Partei, eines Vereins) office; **~straße** *die* shopping street; **~tüchtig** *Adj.* able, ‹*businessman, landlord, etc.*›; **~viertel** *das* business quarter; (Einkaufszentrum) shopping district; **~wagen** *der* company car; **~zeit** *die* business hours *pl.;* (im Büro) office hours *pl.*

geschah *3. Pers. Sg. Prät. v.* GESCHEHEN

geschehen *unr. itr. V.; mit sein* happen; occur; (ausgeführt werden) be done; **jmdm. geschieht etw.** sth. happens to sb.

gescheit *Adj.* **(a)** (intelligent) clever **(b)** (ugs.: vernünftig) sensible

Gescheitheit *die;* ~: cleverness

Geschenk *das;* **~[e]s, ~e** present; gift

Geschenk-: ~artikel *der* gift; **~packung** *die* gift pack

Geschichte *die;* **~, ~n (a)** history **(b)** (Erzählung) story

geschichtlich *Adj.* **(a)** historical **(b)** (bedeutungsvoll) historic

Geschichts-: ~atlas *der* historical atlas; **~buch** *das* history book

Geschick[1] *das;* **~[e]s, ~e** (geh.) fate

Geschick[2] *das;* **~[e]s** skill

Geschicklichkeit *die;* ~: skilfulness; skill

geschickt [1] *Adj.* **(a)** skilful **(b)** (klug) clever; adroit
[2] *adv.* **(a)** (gewandt) skilfully **(b)** (klug) cleverly; adroitly

geschieden *2. Part. v.* SCHEIDEN

geschienen *2. Part. v.* SCHEINEN

Geschirr *das;* **~[e]s, ~e (a)** crockery; (benutzt) dishes *pl.;* **(b)** (für Zugtier) harness

Geschirr-: ~spül·maschine *die* dishwasher; **~tuch** *das; Pl.* **~tücher** tea towel; dish towel (Amer.)

geschissen *2. Part. v.* SCHEISSEN

geschlafen *2. Part. v.* SCHLAFEN

geschlagen *2. Part. v.* SCHLAGEN

Geschlecht *das;* **~[e]s, ~er (a)** sex **(b)** (*Generation*) generation **(c)** (Sippe) family **(d)** (Sprachw.) gender

geschlechtlich *Adj.* sexual

geschlechts-, Geschlechts-: ~akt *der* sex[ual] act; **~chromosom** *das* (Biol.) sex chromosome; **~krank** *Adj.* ‹*person*› suffering from VD; **~krankheit** *die* venereal disease; **~organ** *das* sex[ual] organ; genital organ; **~teil** *das* genitals *pl.;* **~verkehr** *der* sexual intercourse; **~wort** *das* ▸ ARTIKEL A

geschlichen *2. Part. v.* SCHLEICHEN

geschliffen [1] *2. Part. v.* SCHLEIFEN; [2] *Adj.* polished

geschlossen [1] *2. Part. v.* SCHLIESSEN; [2] *Adj.* united ‹*action, front*›; unified ‹*procedure*›; **eine ~e Ortschaft** a built-up area

Geschlossenheit *die;* ~: unity

geschlungen *2. Part. v.* SCHLINGEN

Geschmack *der;* **~[e]s, Geschmäcke** taste

geschmacklos [1] *Adj.* tasteless
[2] *adv.* tastelessly

Geschmacklosigkeit *die;* **~, ~en** lack of [good] taste; bad taste; (Äußerung) tasteless remark

Geschmack[s]·sache *die* **das ist ~:** that is a question *or* matter of taste

geschmack·voll [1] *Adj.* tasteful
[2] *adv.* tastefully

Geschmatze *das;* **~s** (ugs. abwertend) smacking one's lips *no art.;* (beim Essen) noisy eating *no art.*

Geschmeide *das;* **~s, ~** (geh.) jewellery *no pl.*

geschmeidig [1] *Adj.* **(a)** sleek ‹*hair, fur*›; soft ‹*leather, boots, skin*› **(b)** (gelenkig) supple ‹*fingers*›; lithe ‹*body, movement, person*›
[2] *adv.* (gelenkig) agilely

Geschmeidigkeit *die;* ~: ▸ GESCHMEIDIG 1: sleekness; suppleness; softness; litheness

geschmissen *2. Part. v.* SCHMEISSEN

geschmolzen *2. Part. v.* SCHMELZEN

Geschmuse *das;* **~s** (ugs.) cuddling; (eines Pärchens) kissing and cuddling

Geschnetzelte *das; adj. Dekl.: small, thin slices of meat* [*cooked in sauce*]

geschnitten *2. Part. v.* SCHNEIDEN

geschoben *2. Part. v.* SCHIEBEN

geschollen *2. Part. v.* SCHALLEN

gescholten *2. Part. v.* SCHELTEN

Geschöpf *das;* **~[e]s, ~e** creature

geschoren *2. Part. v.* SCHEREN

Geschoss[1], *Geschoß *das;* **Geschosses, Geschosse** projectile; (Kugel) bullet; (Rakete) missile

Geschoss[2], *Geschoß *das;* **Geschosses, Geschosse** floor; storey

geschossen *2. Part. v.* SCHIESSEN

geschraubt *Adj.* (ugs.) stilted

Geschrei *das;* **~s (a)** shouting; (von Verletzten, Tieren) screaming; screams *pl.;* **(b)** (ugs. fig) fuss

geschrieben *2. Part. v.* SCHREIBEN

geschrie[e]n *2. Part. v.* SCHREIEN

geschritten *2. Part. v.* SCHREITEN

geschunden *2. Part. v.* SCHINDEN

Geschütz *das;* **~es, ~e** [big] gun

Geschütz·feuer *das* artillery fire; shell fire

geschützt *Adj.* **(a)** sheltered

*alte Schreibung - vgl. Hinweis auf S. xiv

(b) (unter Naturschutz) protected
(c) ~er Geschlechtsverkehr sex with a condom

Geschwader *das;* ~s, ~ (Marine) squadron; (Luftwaffe) wing (Brit.); group (Amer.)

Geschwätz *das;* ~es (ugs. abwertend) prattling; (Klatsch) gossip

geschwätzig *Adj.* (abwertend) talkative

geschweige *Konj.* ~ [denn] let alone; never mind

geschwiegen *2. Part. v.* SCHWEIGEN

geschwind (bes. südd.) 1 *Adj.* swift; quick 2 *adv.* swiftly; quickly

Geschwindigkeit *die;* ~, ~en speed

Geschwindigkeits-: **~begrenzung** *die,* **~beschränkung** *die* speed limit

Geschwister *Pl.* brothers and sisters

geschwollen 1 *2. Part. v.* SCHWELLEN; 2 *Adj.* (a) swollen
(b) (fig. abwertend) pompous
3 *adv.* pompously

geschwommen *2. Part. v.* SCHWIMMEN

geschworen *2. Part. v.* SCHWÖREN

Geschworene *der/die; adj. Dekl.* juror

Geschwulst *die;* ~, Geschwülste tumour

geschwunden *2. Part. v.* SCHWINDEN

geschwungen 1 *2. Part. v.* SCHWINGEN; 2 *Adj.* curved

Geschwür *das;* ~s, ~e ulcer; (Furunkel) boil

gesehen *2. Part v.* SEHEN

Geseire *das;* ~s (ugs.) drivel

Geselle *der;* ~n, ~n journeyman; (Kerl) fellow

gesellen *refl. V.* sich zu jmdm. ~: join sb.

gesellig *Adj.* sociable; ein ~er Abend/~es Beisammensein a convivial evening/a friendly get-together

Geselligkeit *die;* ~: die ~ lieben enjoy [good] company

Gesellin *die;* ~, ~nen journeyman; journeywoman (rare)

Gesellschaft *die;* ~, ~en (a) society
(b) (Veranstaltung) party
(c) (Kreis von Menschen) group of people
(d) (Wirtschaft) company

Gesellschafter *der;* ~s, ~ (a) ein guter ~ sein be good company
(b) (Wirtsch.) partner; (Teilhaber) shareholder

Gesellschafterin *die;* ~, ~nen (a) [lady] companion
(b) (Wirtsch.) partner; (Teilhaberin) shareholder

gesellschaftlich *Adj.* social

gesellschafts-, Gesellschafts-: **~fähig** *Adj.* (auch fig.) socially acceptable; **~ordnung** *die* social order; **~reise** *die* group tour; **~schicht** *die* stratum of society; **~spiel** *das* party game

gesessen *2. Part. v.* SITZEN

Gesetz *das;* ~es, ~e (a) law; (geschrieben) statute
(b) (Regel) rule

gesetz-, Gesetz-: **~buch** *das* statute book; **~gebend** *Adj.* legislative; **~geber** *der* legislator; (Organ) legislature; **~gebung** *die;* ~: legislation

gesetzlich 1 *Adj.* legal; statutory ‹*holiday*›; lawful ‹*heir, claim*›
2 *adv.* legally

gesetz-, Gesetz-: **~los** *Adj.* lawless; **~losigkeit** *die;* ~~: lawlessness; **~mäßig** 1 *Adj.* (a) law-governed; ~mäßig sein be governed by *or* obey a [natural] law/[natural] laws; (b) (gesetzlich) legal; (rechtmäßig) lawful; 2 *adv.* in accordance with a [natural] law/[natural] laws; **~mäßigkeit** *die* (a) conformity to a [natural] law/[natural] laws; (b) (Gesetzlichkeit) legality; (Rechtmäßigkeit) lawfulness

gesetzt *Adj.* staid

Gesetztheit *die;* ~: staidness

gesetz·widrig *Adj.* illegal; unlawful

Gesetz·widrigkeit *die* illegality; unlawfulness

Gesicht *das;* ~[e]s, ~er face; (fig.) das ~ einer Stadt the appearance of a town

Gesichts-: **~ausdruck** *der* expression; look; **~creme** *die* face cream; **~punkt** *der* point of view; **~wasser** *das* face lotion; **~züge** *Pl.* features

Gesindel *das;* ~s (abwertend) rabble

gesinnt *Adj.* christlich/sozial ~ [sein] [be] Christian-minded/public-spirited; jmdm. freundlich ~ sein be well-disposed towards sb.

Gesinnung *die;* ~, ~en [basic] convictions *pl.;* [fundamental] beliefs *pl.*

gesinnungs-, Gesinnungs-: **~los** (abwertend) *Adj.* unprincipled; **~wandel** *der* change of attitude

gesittet *Adj.* well-behaved; well-mannered

gesogen *2. Part. v.* SAUGEN

gesondert 1 *Adj.* separate
2 *adv.* separately

gesonnen *Adj.* ~ sein, etw. zu tun feel disposed to do sth.

gesotten *2. Part. v.* SIEDEN

Gespann *das;* ~[e]s, ~e (a) (Zugtiere) team
(b) (Wagen) horse and carriage
(c) (Menschen) couple; pair

gespannt *Adj.* (a) eager; rapt ‹*attention*›; ~ zuhören listen with rapt attention
(b) tense ‹*situation, atmosphere*›; strained ‹*relationships*›

Gespenst *das;* ~[e]s, ~er (a) ghost
(b) (geh.: Gefahr) spectre

gespenstig, gespenstisch *Adj.* ghostly; eerie ‹*building, atmosphere*›

gespie[e]n *2. Part. v.* SPEIEN

gesponnen *2. Part. v.* SPINNEN

Gespött *das;* ~[e]s mockery; ridicule

Gespräch *das;* ~[e]s, ~e conversation; (Diskussion) discussion; (Telefon~) call (mit to)

gesprächig *Adj.* talkative
Gesprächs-: **~partner** *der,* **~partnerin** *die:* **wer war dein ~partner/ deine ~partnerin?** who were you talking to?; **~stoff** *der* topics *pl.* of conversation; **~thema** *das* topic of conversation
gesprochen *2. Part. v.* SPRECHEN
gesprossen *2. Part. v.* SPRIESSEN
gesprungen *2. Part. v.* SPRINGEN
Gespür *das;* **~s** feel
gest. *Abk.* = **gestorben** d.
Gestalt *die;* **~, ~en** **(a)** build **(b)** (Mensch, Persönlichkeit) figure **(c)** (in der Dichtung) character **(d)** (Form) form
gestalten *tr. V.* fashion; lay out ‹*public gardens*›; shape ‹*character, personality*›; arrange ‹*party, conference, etc.*›
Gestaltung *die;* **~, ~en** ▶ GESTALTEN: fashioning; laying out; arranging
gestand *1. u. 3. Pers. Sg. Prät. v.* GESTEHEN
gestanden [1] *2. Part. v.* STEHEN, GESTEHEN; [2] *Adj.* **ein ~er Mann** a grown man; **ein ~er Parlamentarier** an experienced *or* seasoned parliamentarian
geständig *Adj.:* **~ sein** have confessed
Geständnis *das;* **~ses, ~se** confession
Gestank *der;* **~[e]s** (abwertend) stench; stink
Gestapo *die;* **~** (ns.) Gestapo
gestatten [1] *tr., itr. V.* permit; allow; **~ Sie, dass ich ...:** may I ...? [2] *refl. V.* **sich** *(Dat.)* **etw. ~:** allow oneself sth.
Geste /ˈgɛstə, ˈgeːstə/ *die;* **~, ~n** (auch fig.) gesture
Gesteck *das;* **~[e]s, ~e** flower arrangement
gestehen *tr., itr. V.* confess
Gestein *das;* **~[e]s, ~e** rock
Gestell *das;* **~[e]s, ~e** **(a)** (für Weinflaschen) rack; (zum Wäschetrocknen) horse **(b)** (Unterbau) frame
gestern *Adv.* yesterday
gestiegen *2. Part. v.* STEIGEN
gestikulieren *itr. V.* gesticulate
Gestirn *das;* **~[e]s, ~e** star
gestochen [1] *2. Part. v.* STECHEN; [2] *Adj.* extremely neat ‹*handwriting*›
gestohlen *2. Part. v.* STEHLEN
Gestöhne *das;* **~s** groaning
gestorben *2. Part. v.* STERBEN
gestoßen *2. Part. v.* STOSSEN
Gestrampel *das;* **~s** (ugs.) kicking about; (beim Radfahren) pedalling
Gesträuch *das;* **~[e]s, ~e** shrubbery; bushes *pl.*
gestreift *Adj.* striped
gestrichen [1] *2. Part. v.* STREICHEN; [2] *Adj.* level ‹*measure*›

*old spelling - see note on page xiv

gestrig *Adj.* yesterday's
gestritten *2. Part. v.* STREITEN
Gestrüpp *das;* **~[e]s, ~e** undergrowth
gestunken *2. Part. v.* STINKEN
Gestüt *das;* **~[e]s, ~e** stud [farm]
Gesuch *das;* **~[e]s, ~e** request (**um** for); (Antrag) application (**um** for)
gesucht *Adj.* **(a)** [much] sought-after **(b)** (gekünstelt) laboured
gesund; **gesünder,** *seltener:* **~er, gesündest...,** *seltener:* **~est...** *Adj.* healthy; **wieder ~ werden** get better; **bleib ~!** look after yourself!
gesunden *itr. V.; mit sein* ‹*person*› recover
Gesundheit *die;* **~:** health; **~!** (ugs.) bless you!
gesundheitlich [1] *Adj.; nicht präd.* **~e Betreuung** health care; **sein ~er Zustand** [the state of] his health [2] *adv.* **wie geht es Ihnen ~?** how are you?
gesundheits-, Gesundheits-: **~amt** *das* [local] public health department; **~gefährdend** *Adj.* **~gefährdend sein** be a danger to health; **~gefährdende Bakterien/ Produkte** bacteria that are a danger to health/products that are a health risk; **~gefährdung** *die* risk to health; **~schädlich** *Adj.* detrimental to [one's] health *postpos.;* **~system** *das* health-care system; **~vorsorge** *die* health care; **~zeugnis** *das* certificate of health; **~zustand** *der* state of health
gesungen *2. Part. v.* SINGEN
gesunken *2. Part. v.* SINKEN
getan *2. Part. v.* TUN
Getöse *das;* **~s** [thunderous] roar; (von vielen Menschen) din
getragen *2. Part. v.* TRAGEN
Getränk *das;* **~[e]s, ~e** drink; beverage (formal)
getrauen *refl. V.* dare
Getreide *das;* **~s** grain
Getreide-: **~anbau** *der* growing of cereals; **~handel** *der* corn trade
getrennt [1] *Adj.* separate [2] *adv.* ‹*pay*› separately; ‹*sleep*› in separate rooms
getreten *2. Part. v.* TRETEN
getreu [1] *Adj.* (geh.) exact; faithful ‹*image*› [2] *adv.* (geh.) ‹*report, describe*› faithfully
Getriebe *das;* **~s, ~:** gears *pl.;* (in einer Maschine) gear system
getrieben *2. Part. v.* TREIBEN
getroffen *2. Part. v.* TREFFEN, TRIEFEN
getrogen *2. Part. v.* TRÜGEN
getrost [1] *Adj.* confident [2] *adv.* confidently; **du kannst es mir ~ glauben** you can take my word for it
getrunken *2. Part. v.* TRINKEN
Getto *das;* **~s, ~s** ghetto

Getue *das;* **~s** (ugs. abwertend) fuss (**um** about)
Getümmel *das;* **~s** tumult
geübt *Adj.* accomplished; practised ‹*eye, ear*›
Gewächs *das;* **~es, ~e** plant
gewachsen [1] *2. Part. v.* WACHSEN; [2] **jmdm./einer Sache ~ sein** be a match for sb./be equal to sth.
gewagt *Adj.* daring; (gefährlich) risky; (fast anstößig) risqué ‹*joke etc.*›
gewählt [1] *Adj.* refined [2] *adv.* in a refined manner
Gewähr *die;* **~:** guarantee; **keine ~ übernehmen** be unable to guarantee sth.
gewähren *tr. V.* grant; give ‹*pleasure, joy*›
gewähr·leisten *tr. V.* guarantee
Gewahrsam *der;* **~s (a)** (Obhut) safe-keeping
(b) (Haft) custody
Gewährs·mann *der; Pl.* **~männer** *od.* **~leute, Gewährs·person** *die* informant; source
Gewalt *die;* **~, ~en (a)** power
(b) (Willkür) force
(c) (körperliche Kraft) force; violence
gewalt-, Gewalt-: ~akt *der* act of violence; **~anwendung** *die* use of force *or* violence **~bereit** *Adj.* ‹*person*› prone to violence; ‹*group, organization*› prepared to resort to *or* use violence; **~bereitschaft** *die: s.* ~BEREIT: propensity to violence; willingness to resort to *or* use violence
Gewalten·teilung *die* separation of powers
gewaltig [1] *Adj.* **(a)** (immens) huge
(b) (imponierend) mighty, huge, massive ‹*building etc*›; monumental ‹*literary work etc.*›
[2] *adv.* (ugs.) very much
gewalt·los [1] *Adj.* non-violent [2] *adv.* without violence
Gewalt·losigkeit *die;* **~:** non-violence
gewaltsam [1] *Adj.* forcible ‹*expulsion*›; enforced ‹*separation*›; violent ‹*death*› [2] *adv.* forcibly
gewalt·tätig *Adj.* violent
Gewalt·tätigkeit *die* **(a)** (gewalttätige Art) violence
(b) ▶ GEWALTAKT
Gewand *das;* **~[e]s, Gewänder** (geh.) robe; gown
gewandt [1] *2. Part. v.* WENDEN; [2] *Adj.* skilful; (körperlich) agile [3] *adv.* skilfully; (körperlich) agilely
Gewandtheit *die;* **~:** ▶ GEWANDT 2: skill; skilfulness; agility
gewann *1. u. 3. Pers. Sg. Prät. v.* GEWINNEN
gewaschen *2. Part. v.* WASCHEN
Gewässer *das;* **~s, ~:** stretch of water
Gewebe *das;* **~s, ~ (a)** (Stoff) fabric
(b) (Med., Biol.) tissue
Gewehr *das;* **~[e]s, ~e** rifle; (Schrot~) shotgun
Geweih *das;* **~[e]s, ~e** antlers *pl.*
Gewerbe *das;* **~s, ~:** business; (Handel, Handwerk) trade
Gewerbe-: ~freiheit *die* right to carry on a business *or* trade; **~ordnung** *die* laws *pl.* governing trade and industry; **~schein** *der* licence to carry on a business *or* trade; **~treibende** *der/die; adj. Dekl.* tradesman/tradeswoman; **~zweig** *der* branch of trade
gewerblich [1] *Adj.* commercial; business *attrib.;* (industriell) industrial
[2] *adv.* **~ tätig sein** work
gewerbs·mäßig *Adj.* professional
Gewerkschaft *die;* **~, ~en** trade union
Gewerkschaft[l]er *der;* **~s, ~, Gewerkschaft[l]erin** *die;* **~, ~nen** trade unionist
gewerkschaftlich [1] *Adj.* [trade] union *attrib.;*
[2] *adv.* **~ organisiert sein** belong to a [trade] union
Gewerkschafts·funktionär *der,* **Gewerkschafts·funktionärin** *die* [trade] union official
gewesen *2. Part. v.* SEIN[1]
gewichen *2. Part. v.* WEICHEN
Gewicht *das;* **~[e]s, ~e** (auch fig.) weight; **[nicht] ins ~ fallen** be of [no] consequence
Gewicht·heben *das;* **~s** weightlifting
gewichtig *Adj.* weighty
Gewichts·klasse *die* (Sport) weight [division *or* class]
gewieft *Adj.* (ugs.) cunning
gewiesen *2. Part. v.* WEISEN
gewillt *Adj. in* **[nicht] ~ sein, etw. zu tun** be [un]willing to do sth.
Gewimmel *das;* **~s** throng; (von Insekten) teeming mass
Gewinde *das;* **~s, ~** (Technik) thread
Gewinn *der;* **~[e]s, ~e (a)** profit
(b) (Preis einer Lotterie) prize; (beim Spiel) winnings *pl.;*
(c) (Sieg) win
Gewinn·beteiligung *die* (Wirtsch.) profit sharing; (Betrag) profit-sharing bonus
gewinn·bringend *Adj.* lucrative
gewinnen [1] *unr. tr. V.* win; gain ‹*time, influence, validity, etc.*›
[2] *unr. itr. V.* win (**bei** at)
gewinnend *Adj.* winning
Gewinner *der;* **~s, ~, Gewinnerin** *die;* **~, ~nen** winner
Gewinn-: ~quote *die* share of prize money; **~spanne** *die* profit margin; **~sucht** *die* greed for profit
Gewinnung *die;* **~ (a)** (von Kohle, Erz usw.) mining; extraction; (von Öl) recovery; (von Metall aus Erz) extraction
(b) (Erzeugung) production
Gewinn·zahl *die* winning number
Gewirr *das;* **~[e]s (a)** tangle

(b) (Durcheinander) **ein ~ von Ästen** a maze of branches

gewiss, *gewiß 1 *Adj.* certain 2 *adv.* certainly

Gewissen *das;* **~s, ~:** conscience

gewissenhaft 1 *Adj.* conscientious 2 *adv.* conscientiously

gewissen·los *Adj.* unscrupulous

Gewissens·bisse *Pl.* pangs of conscience

gewissermaßen *Adv.* (sozusagen) as it were; (in gewissem Sinne) to a certain extent

Gewissheit, *Gewißheit *die;* **~, ~en** certainty

g

Gewitter *das;* **~s, ~:** thunderstorm

Gewitter·wolke *die* thundercloud

gewittrig *Adj.* thundery

gewitzt *Adj.* shrewd

gewoben *2. Part. v.* WEBEN

gewogen 1 *2. Part. v.* WIEGEN 2 *Adj.* (geh.) well disposed (+ *Dat.* towards)

gewöhnen 1 *tr. V.* **jmdn. an jmdn./etw. ~:** get sb. used to sb./sth.; accustom sb. to sb./sth. 2 *refl. V.* **sich an jmdn./etw. ~:** get used *or* get *or* become accustomed to sb./sth.; accustom oneself to sb./sth.

Gewohnheit *die;* **~, ~en** habit

gewohnheits-, Gewohnheits-: ~mäßig 1 *Adj.* habitual ‹*drinker etc.*›; automatic ‹*reaction etc.*›; 2 *adv.* (regelmäßig) habitually; **~mensch** *der* creature of habit; **~tier** *das* (scherzh.) creature of habit; **~trinker** *der,* **~trinkerin** *die* habitual drinker; **~verbrecher** *der,* **~verbrecherin** *die* (Rechtsw.) habitual criminal

gewöhnlich 1 *Adj.* **(a)** normal; ordinary **(b)** (gewohnt, üblich) usual **(c)** (abwertend: ordinär) common 2 *adv.* **(a) [für] ~:** usually; **wie ~:** as usual **(b)** (abwertend: ordinär) in a common way

gewohnt *Adj.* **(a)** usual **(b) etw.** (*Akk.*) **~ sein** be used to sth.

Gewölbe *das;* **~s, ~:** vault

gewonnen *2. Part. v.* GEWINNEN

geworben *2. Part. v.* WERBEN

geworfen *2. Part. v.* WERFEN

gewrungen *2. Part. v.* WRINGEN

Gewühl *das;* **~[e]s** milling crowd

gewunden *2. Part. v.* WINDEN

Gewürz *das;* **~es, ~e** spice; (würzende Zutat) seasoning

Gewürz-: ~gurke *die* pickled gherkin; **~nelke** *die* clove

gewusst, *gewußt *2. Part. v.* WISSEN

gez. *Abk.* = **gezeichnet** sgd.

Gezeit *die;* **~, ~en** tide

Gezerre *das;* **~s** wrangling

gezielt 1 *Adj.* specific ‹*questions, measures, etc.*›; deliberate ‹*insult, indiscretion*›; well-directed ‹*advertising campaign*› 2 *adv.* ‹*proceed, act*› purposefully

geziemen (geh. veralt.) 1 *itr. V.* **jmdm. [nicht] ~:** [ill] befit sb 2 *refl. V.* be proper; **sich für jmdn. ~:** befit sb.

geziert 1 *Adj.* (abwertend) affected 2 *adv.* (abwertend) affectedly

gezogen *2. Part. v.* ZIEHEN

Gezwitscher *das;* **~s** twittering

gezwungen 1 *2. Part. v.* ZWINGEN 2 *Adj.* forced

gezwungenermaßen *Adv.* of necessity

gib *Imperativ Sg. Präsens v.* GEBEN

gibst *2. Pers. Sg. Präsens v.* GEBEN

gibt *3. Pers. Sg. Präsens v.* GEBEN

Gicht *die;* **~:** gout

Giebel *der;* **~s, ~:** gable

Gier *die;* **~:** greed (**nach** for)

gierig 1 *Adj.* greedy 2 *adv.* greedily

gießen 1 *unr. tr. V.* **(a)** pour (**in** + *Akk.* into, **über** + *Akk.* over) **(b)** (verschütten) spill (**über** + *Akk.* over) **(c)** (begießen) water 2 *unpers.* (ugs.) pour [with rain]

Gießer *der;* **~s, ~:** caster

Gießerei *die;* **~, ~en** foundry

Gießerin *die;* **~, ~nen** caster

Gift *das;* **~[e]s, ~e** poison; (Schlangen~) venom

gift·grün *Adj.* garish green

giftig *Adj.* poisonous; venomous ‹*snake*›; toxic, poisonous ‹*substance, gas, chemical*›; (fig.) venomous

Gift-: ~mord *der* [murder by] poisoning; **~mörder** *der,* **~mörderin** *die* poisoner; **~müll** *der* toxic waste; **~pilz** *der* poisonous mushroom; [poisonous] toadstool; **~schlange** *die* venomous snake; **~schrank** *der* poison cabinet *or* cupboard; **~stachel** *der* poisonous sting; **~zahn** *der* poison fang

Gigant *der;* **~en, ~en** giant

gigantisch *Adj.* gigantic

Gilde *die;* **~, ~n** (hist.) guild

gilt *3. Pers. Sg. Präsens v.* GELTEN

Gimpel *der;* **~s, ~:** bullfinch

Gin /dʒɪn/ *der;* **~s, ~s** gin

ging *1. u. 3. Pers. Sg. Prät. v.* GEHEN

Ginster *der;* **~s, ~:** broom

Gipfel *der;* **~s, ~:** peak; (höchster Punkt des Berges) summit; (fig.) height

Gipfel·konferenz *die* summit conference

gipfeln *itr. V.* **in etw.** (*Dat.*) **~:** culminate in sth.

Gipfel·treffen *das* summit meeting

Gips *der;* **~es, ~e** plaster; gypsum (Chem.)

Gips·abdruck *der* plaster cast

*alte Schreibung - vgl. Hinweis auf S. xiv

gipsen *tr. V.* plaster; put ‹*leg, arm, etc.*› in plaster

Gips·verband *der* plaster cast

Giraffe *die;* ~, ~**n** giraffe

Girlande *die;* ~, ~**n** festoon

Giro /ˈʒiːro/ *das;* ~**s**, ~**s**, *österr. auch* **Giri** (Finanzw.) giro

Giro·konto *das* (Finanzw.) current account

gis, Gis *das;* ~, ~ (Musik) G sharp

Gischt *der;* ~[**e**]**s**, ~**e** *od.* **die;** ~, ~**en** spray

Gitarre *die;* ~, ~**n** guitar

Gitarrist *der;* ~**en**, ~**en**, **Gitarristin** *die;* ~, ~**nen** guitarist

Gitter *das;* ~**s**, ~: bars *pl.*; (vor Fenster-, Türöffnungen) grille; (in der Straßendecke, im Fußboden) grating; (Geländer) railing[s *pl.*]

Gitter·fenster *das* barred window

Glacé·hand·schuh /glaˈseː.../ *der* kid glove

Gladiole *die;* ~, ~**n** gladiolus

Glanz *der;* ~**es** **(a)** (von Licht, Sternen, Augen) brightness; (von Haar, Metall, Perlen, Leder usw.) lustre; sheen
(b) (der Jugend, Schönheit) radiance; (des Adels usw.) splendour

glänzen *itr. V.* **(a)** (Glanz ausstrahlen) shine; ‹*hair, metal, etc.*› gleam; ‹*elbows, trousers, etc.*› be shiny
(b) (Bewunderung erregen) shine (**bei** at)

glänzend (ugs.) [1] *Adj.* **(a)** shining; gleaming ‹*hair, metal, etc.*›; shiny ‹*elbows, trousers, etc.*›
(b) (bewundernswert) brilliant; splendid ‹*references, marks, results, etc.*›
[2] *adv.* ~ **mit jmdm. auskommen** get on very well with sb.; **es geht mir/uns** ~: I am/we are very well

glanz-, Glanz-: ~**leistung** *die* (auch iron.) brilliant performance; ~**los** *Adj.* dull; lacklustre; ~**nummer** *die* star turn; ~**voll** [1] *Adj.* brilliant; sparkling ‹*variety number*›; [2] *adv.* brilliantly

Glas *das;* ~**es**, **Gläser** **(a)** glass
(b) (Trinkgefäß) glass; **zwei** ~ *od.* **Gläser Wein** two glasses of wine
(c) (Behälter) jar

Glas: ~**bläser** *der,* **Glas·bläserin** *die* glass-blower; ~**container** *der* bottle bank

Gläschen *das;* ~**s**, ~ **(a)** [little] glass
(b) (kleines Gefäß) [little] [glass] jar

Glaser *der;* ~**s**, ~, **Glaserin** *die;* ~, ~**nen** glazier

gläsern *Adj.* glass

Glas·faser *die* glass fibre

glasieren *tr. V.* **(a)** glaze
(b) (Kochk.) ice; glaze ‹*meat*›

glasig *Adj.* **(a)** glassy
(b) (Kochk.) transparent

Glas·malerei *die* stained glass

Glasur *die;* ~, ~**en** **(a)** glaze
(b) (Kochk.) icing; (auf Fleisch) glaze

glatt [1] *Adj.* **(a)** smooth; (rutschig) slippery
(b) (ugs.: offensichtlich) downright ‹*lie*›; outright ‹*deception, fraud*›; flat ‹*refusal*›
[2] *adv.* **(a)** smoothly; ~ **gehen** (ugs.) go smoothly
(b) (ugs.: rückhaltlos) **jmdm. etw.** ~ **ins Gesicht sagen** tell sb. sth. straight to his/her face; ‹*reject, deny*› flatly

Glätte *die;* ~: smoothness; (Rutschigkeit) slipperiness

Glatt·eis *das* glaze; ice; (auf der Straße) black ice

glätten *tr. V.* smooth out ‹*piece of paper, etc.*›; smooth [down] ‹*feathers, fur, etc.*›; plane ‹*wood etc.*›

glatt-: *~|**gehen** ▶ GLATT 2A; ~**weg** *Adv.* (ugs.) **etw.** ~**weg ablehnen/ignorieren** turn sth. down flat/simply ignore sth.; **das ist** ~**weg erlogen/erfunden** that's a downright lie/that's pure invention

Glatze *die;* ~, ~**n** bald head; **eine** ~ **haben/bekommen** be/go bald

Glaube *der;* ~**ns** faith (**an** + *Akk.* in); (Überzeugung, Meinung) belief (**an** + *Akk.* in)

glauben [1] *tr. V.* **(a)** (meinen) think
(b) (für wahr halten) believe; **das glaube ich dir nicht** I don't believe you; **das glaubst du doch selbst nicht!** [surely] you can't be serious; **sie glaubt ihm jedes Wort** she believes every word he says; **ob du es glaubst oder nicht ...** believe it or not ...; **das ist doch kaum zu** ~ (ugs.) it's incredible
[2] *itr. V.* believe (**an** + *Akk.* in)

Glaubens-: ~**bekenntnis** *das* creed; ~**freiheit** *die* religious freedom; ~**krieg** *der* religious war; ~**sache** *die* (ugs.) matter of faith *or* belief

glaubhaft [1] *Adj.* credible
[2] *adv.* convincingly

gläubig [1] *Adj.* devout; (vertrauensvoll) trusting
[2] *adv.* devoutly; (vertrauensvoll) trustingly

Gläubige *der/die; adj. Dekl.* believer

Gläubiger *der;* ~**s**, ~: creditor

glaub·würdig [1] *Adj.* credible
[2] *adv.* convincingly

Glaubwürdigkeit *die;* ~: credibility

gleich [1] *Adj.* **(a)** (identisch, von derselben Art) same; ~ **bleiben** remain the same; ‹*speed, temperature, etc.*› remain constant; ~ **bleibend** constant, steady ‹*temperature, speed, etc.*›; (~berechtigt, ~wertig, Math.) equal
(b) (ugs.: gleichgültig) **es ist mir völlig** *od.* **ganz** ~: I couldn't care less (coll.); **ganz** ~, **wer anruft, ...:** no matter who calls, ...
[2] *adv.* **(a)** (übereinstimmend) ~ **groß/alt** *usw.* **sein** be the same height/age *etc.*; ~ **gut/schlecht** *usw.* equally good/bad *etc.*;
(b) (in derselben Weise) ~ **aufgebaut/gekleidet** having the same structure/wearing identical clothes
(c) (sofort) at once; straight away; (bald) in a moment ⇢

(d) (räumlich) right; just; **~ rechts/links** immediately on the right/left

gleich-, Gleich-: ~alt[e]rig /-alt(ə)rɪç/ *Adj.* of the same age (**mit** as); **~artig** [1] *Adj.* of the same kind *postpos.* (+ *Dat.* as); (sehr ähnlich) very similar (+ *Dat.* to); [2] *adv.* in the same way; **~berechtigt** *Adj.* having equal rights *postpos.*; **~berechtigte Partner** equal partners; **~berechtigung** *die* equal rights *pl.*; ***~|bleiben, ~bleibend** ▶ GLEICH 1A

gleichen *unr. itr. V.* **jmdm./einer Sache ~:** be like *or* resemble sb./sth.;

gleichermaßen *Adv.* equally

gleich-, Gleich-: ~falls *Adv.* (auch) also; (ebenfalls) likewise; **danke ~falls!** thank you, [and] the same to you; **~förmig** [1] *Adj.* **(a)** (einheitlich) uniform; **(b)** (monoton) monotonous; [2] *adv.* **(a)** (einheitlich) uniformly; **(b)** (monoton) monotonously; **~geschlechtlich** *Adj.* homosexual; **~gewicht** *das* balance; **~gewichts·störung** *die* disturbance of one's sense of balance; **~gültig** [1] *Adj.* indifferent (**gegenüber** towards); (belanglos) trivial; **das ist mir ~gültig** it's a matter of indifference to me; [2] *adv.* indifferently; **~gültigkeit** *die* indifference (**gegenüber** towards)

Gleichheit *die;* **~, ~en (a)** identity; (Ähnlichkeit) similarity **(b)** (gleiche Rechte) equality

Gleichheits·zeichen *das* equals sign

gleich-, Gleich-: ~|kommen *unr. itr. V.; mit sein* **(a)** (entsprechen) be tantamount to; **(b)** (die gleiche Leistung erreichen) **jmdm./einer Sache [an etw.** (*Dat.*)**] ~kommen** equal sb./sth. [in sth.]; **~|machen** *tr. V.* make equal; **~macherei** *die;* **~~, ~~en** (abwertend) levelling down (derog.); egalitarianism; **~mäßig** [1] *Adj.* regular ‹*interval, rhythm*›; uniform ‹*acceleration, distribution*›; even ‹*heat*›; [2] *adv.* ‹*breathe*› regularly; **etw. ~mäßig verteilen/auftragen** distribute sth. equally/apply sth. evenly; **~mut** *der* equanimity; **~mütig** [1] *Adj.* calm; composed; [2] *adv.* with equanimity; calmly; **~namig** *Adj.* **(a)** of the same name *postpos.*; **(b)** (Math.) **~namige Brüche** fractions with a common denominator; **Brüche ~namig machen** reduce fractions to a common denominator

Gleichnis *das;* **~ses, ~se** (Allegorie) allegory; (Parabel) parable

gleichsam *Adv.* (geh.) as it were

gleich-, Gleich-: ~|schalten *tr. V.* force into line; **~schenk[e]lig** *Adj.* (Math.) isosceles; **~schritt** *der* marching in step; **~seitig** *Adj.* (Math.) equilateral; **~|setzen** *tr. V.* equate; **~|stellen** *tr. V.* equate; **~strom** *der* (Elektrot.) direct current

Gleichung *die;* **~, ~en** equation

gleich-: ~wertig *Adj.* of the same value *postpos.*; **~wohl** /-'- *od.* '--/ *Adv.* nevertheless; **~zeitig** [1] *Adj.* simultaneous; [2] *adv.* at the same time

Gleis *das;* **~es, ~e** track; (Bahnsteig) platform; (einzelne Schiene) rail

gleiten *unr. itr. V.; mit sein* glide; ‹*hand*› slide

Gleit-: ~flug *der* glide; **~zeit** *die* flexitime; flexible working hours *Pl.*

Gletscher *der;* **~s, ~:** glacier

Gletscher·spalte *die* crevasse

glich *1. u. 3. Pers. Sg. Prät. v.* GLEICHEN

Glied *das;* **~[e]s, ~er (a)** limb; (Finger~, Zehen~) joint **(b)** (Ketten~, auch fig.) link **(c)** (Teil eines Ganzen) section; (Mitglied) member

gliedern [1] *tr. V.* structure; organize ‹*thoughts*› [2] *refl. V.* **sich in Gruppen/Abschnitte** *usw.* **~:** be divided into groups/sections *etc.*

Gliederung *die;* **~, ~en** structure

Glied-: ~maße /-ma:sə/ *die;* **~, ~n** limb; **~satz** *der* (Sprachw.) subordinate clause

glimmen *unr. od. regelm. itr. V.* glow

Glimm·stängel, *Glimm·stengel *der* (ugs. scherzh.) fag (coll.); ciggy (coll.)

glimpflich [1] *Adj.* **(a) der Unfall nahm ein ~es Ende** the accident turned out not to be too serious **(b)** (mild) lenient ‹*sentence, punishment*› [2] *adv.* **(a)** (ohne Schaden) **~ davonkommen** get off lightly **(b)** (mild) leniently

glitschig *Adj.* (ugs.) slippery

glitt *1. u. 3. Pers. Sg. Prät. v.* GLEITEN

glitzern *itr. V.* ‹*star*› twinkle; ‹*diamond, decorations*› sparkle; ‹*snow, eyes, tears*› glisten

global [1] *Adj.* **(a)** global; worldwide **(b)** (umfassend) all-round ‹*education*›; overall ‹*control, planning, etc.*› **(c)** (allgemein) general [2] *adv.* **(a)** worldwide **(b)** (umfassend) in overall terms **(c)** (allgemein) in general terms

globalisieren *tr. V.* globalize

Globalisierung *die;* **~, ~en** globalization

Globen ▶ GLOBUS

Globetrotter *der;* **~s, ~:** globetrotter

Globus *der;* **~** *od.* **~ses, Globen** globe

Glöckchen *das;* **~s, ~:** [little] bell

Glocke *die;* **~, ~n** bell

Glocken-: ~blume *die* (Bot.) campanula; **~rock** *der* widely flared skirt; **~spiel** *das* **(a)** carillon; (mit einer Uhr gekoppelt auch) chimes *pl.*; **(b)** (Instrument) glockenspiel

glomm *1. u. 3. Pers. Sg. Prät. v.* GLIMMEN

Glorien·schein /'glo:ri̯ən-/ *der* glory; (um den Kopf, fig.) halo

glorifizieren *tr. V.* glorify

Glorifizierung *die;* **~, ~en** glorification

glor·reich [1] *Adj.* glorious

*old spelling - see note on page xiv

2 *adv.* gloriously

Glossar *das;* **~s, ~e** glossary

Glosse *die;* **~, ~n** commentary; (spöttische Bemerkung) sneering comment

Glotze *die;* **~, ~n** (salopp) box (coll.); gogglebox (Brit. coll.)

glotzen *itr. V.* (abwertend) goggle; gawp (coll.)

Glotz·kiste *die* (salopp) box (coll.); gogglebox (Brit. coll.)

Glück *das;* **~[e]s (a)** luck; **[es ist] ein ~, dass ...:** it's lucky that ...; **[kein] ~ haben** be [un]lucky; **viel ~!** [the] best of luck!; **zum ~** *od.* **zu meinem/seinem** *usw.* **~:** luckily *or* fortunately [for me/him *etc.*]
(b) happiness

Glucke *die;* **~, ~n** brood hen

glücken *tr. V.; mit sein* succeed; **etw. glückt jmdm.** sb. is successful with sth.

gluckern *itr. V.* gurgle; glug

glücklich 1 *Adj.* **(a)** happy (**über** + *Akk.* about)
(b) (erfolgreich) lucky ‹*winner*›; successful ‹*outcome*›; safe ‹*journey*›
(c) (vorteilhaft) fortunate
2 *adv.* **(a)** (erfolgreich) successfully
(b) (vorteilhaft, zufrieden) happily ‹*chosen, married*›

glücklicher·weise *Adv.* fortunately; luckily

glück·selig 1 *Adj.* blissfully happy
2 *adv.* blissfully

Glück·seligkeit *die;* **~:** bliss

glucksen *itr. V.* **(a)** ▶ GLUCKERN;
(b) (lachen) chuckle

Glücks-: ~klee *der* four-leaf clover; **~pfennig** *der* lucky penny; **~pilz** *der* (ugs.) lucky devil (coll.)

Glück[s]·sache *die:* **das ist ~:** it's a matter of luck

Glücks·spiel *das* game of chance

glück·strahlend *Adj.* radiantly happy

Glücks·zahl *die* lucky number

Glück·wunsch *der* congratulations *pl.;* **herzlichen ~ zum Geburtstag!** happy birthday!

Glüh·birne *die* lightbulb

glühen *itr. V.* glow

glühend 1 *Adj.* red-hot ‹*metal etc.*›; blazing ‹*heat*›; ardent ‹*admirer etc.*›; passionate ‹*words, letter, etc.*›
2 *adv.* ‹*love*› passionately; ‹*admire*› ardently; **~ heiß** blazing hot

Glüh-: ~wein *der* mulled wine; **~würmchen** *das;* **~~s, ~~** (ugs.) (weiblich) glow-worm; (männlich) firefly

Glut *die;* **~, ~en (a)** embers *pl.;*
(b) (geh.: Leidenschaft) passion

glut·rot *Adj.* fiery red

Glyzerin *das;* **~s** glycerine

GmbH *Abk.* = **Gesellschaft mit beschränkter Haftung** ≈ plc, PLC

Gnade *die;* **~, ~n** (Gunst) favour; (Rel.) grace; (Milde) mercy

gnaden-, Gnaden-: ~brot *das:* **jmdm./einem Tier das ~brot geben** keep sb./an animal in his/her/its old age; **~frist** *die* reprieve; **~gesuch** *das* plea for clemency; **~los** (auch fig.) 1 *Adj.* merciless; 2 *adv.* mercilessly; **~losigkeit** *die;* **~~:** mercilessness; **~schuss**, ***~schuß** *der* coup de grâce (*by shooting*)

gnädig *Adj.* gracious; (glimpflich) lenient ‹*sentence etc.*›

Gnom *der;* **~en, ~en** gnome

Gockel *der;* **~s, ~** (bes. südd., sonst ugs. scherzh.) cock

Gold *das;* **~[e]s** gold

Gold·barren *der* gold bar

golden 1 *Adj.* (aus Gold) gold; (herrlich) golden ‹*days, memories, etc.*›
2 *adv.* like gold

Gold-: ~fisch *der* goldfish; **~füllung** *die* gold filling; **~grube** *die* (auch fig.) gold mine; **~hamster** *der* golden hamster

goldig *Adj.* sweet

gold-, Gold-: ~richtig (ugs.) *Adj.* absolutely right; **~schmied** *der,* **~schmiedin** *die* goldsmith; **~schnitt** *der* gilt; **~währung** *die* (Wirtsch.) currency tied to the gold standard

Golf¹ *der;* **~[e]s, ~e** gulf

Golf² *das;* **~s** (Sport) golf

Golf-: ~platz *der* golf course; **~schläger** *der* golf club; **~spieler** *der,* **~spielerin** *die* golfer; **~strom** *der* Gulf Stream

Gondel *die;* **~, ~n** gondola

gondeln *itr. V.; mit sein* (ugs.) **(a)** (mit einem Boot) cruise
(b) (reisen) travel around
(c) (herumfahren) cruise around

Gong *der;* **~s, ~s** gong

gongen *itr. V.* **es hat gegongt** the gong has sounded

gönnen *tr. V.* **jmdm. etw. ~:** not begrudge sb. sth.; **sich/jmdm. etw. ~:** allow oneself/sb. sth.

Gönner *der;* **~s, ~:** patron

gönnerhaft (abwertend) *Adj.* patronizing

Gönnerin *die;* **~, ~nen** patroness

gor *3. Pers. Sg. Prät. v.* GÄREN

Göre *die;* **~, ~n** (nordd., oft abwertend) kid (coll.)

Gorilla *der;* **~s, ~s** gorilla

goss, *goß *1. u. 3. Pers. Sg. Prät. v.* GIESSEN

Gosse *die;* **~, ~n** gutter

Gotik *die;* **~** (Stil) Gothic [style]; (Epoche) Gothic period

gotisch *Adj.* Gothic

Gott *der;* **~es, Götter (a)** God; **grüß [dich]** ⋯

~! (landsch.) hello!; **um ~es Willen** (bei Erschrecken) for God's sake; (bei einer Bitte) for heaven's sake
(b) (übermenschliches Wesen) god

Gottes-: ~dienst *der* service; **~haus** *das* (geh.) house of God; **~lästerung** *die* blasphemy

Gottheit *die;* ~, **~en** deity

Göttin *die;* ~, **~nen** goddess

göttlich [1] *Adj.* (auch fig.) divine
[2] *adv.* divinely

gott-, **Gott-: ~lob** *adv.* thank goodness; **~los** [1] *Adj.* **(a)** ungodly ‹*life etc.*›; impious ‹*words, speech, etc.*›; **(b)** (Gott leugnend) godless ‹*theory etc.*›; [2] *adv.* (verwerflich) irreverently; **~vater** *der* God the Father; **~verlassen** *Adj.* (ugs.: abseits) godforsaken; **~vertrauen** *das* trust in God

Götze *der;* **~n, ~n** (auch fig.) idol

Götzen-: ~bild *das* idol; **~diener** *der* idolater; **~dienerin** *die* idolatress

Gouverneur /guvɛr'nø:ɐ̯/ *der;* **~s, ~e** governor

Grab *das;* **~[e]s, Gräber** grave; **das Heilige ~**: the Holy Sepulchre; **das ~ des Unbekannten Soldaten** the tomb of the Unknown Warrior

graben *unr. tr., itr. V.* dig

Graben *der;* **~s, Gräben** ditch; (Schützen~) trench; (Festungs~) moat

Grab-: ~hügel *der* grave mound; **~kammer** *die* burial chamber; **~mal** *das; Pl.* **~mäler**, *geh.* **~male** monument; **~schändung** *die* desecration of a/the grave/of [the] graves

grabschen [1] *tr. V.* grab; snatch
[2] *itr. V.* **nach etw. ~**: grab at sth.

gräbst *2. Pers. Sg. Präsens v.* GRABEN

gräbt *3. Pers. Sg. Präsens v.* GRABEN

Grab·stein *der* gravestone

Grabung *die;* ~, **~en** (bes. Archäol.) excavation

Gracht *die;* ~, **~en** canal

Grad *der;* **~[e]s, ~e** degree; (Milit.) rank

grade (ugs.) ▶ GERADE

Grad·messer *der* gauge, yardstick (**für** of)

graduell [1] *Adj.* gradual; slight ‹*difference etc.*›
[2] *adv.* gradually; ‹*different*› in degree

graduiert *Adj.* graduate; **ein ~er Ingenieur** an engineering graduate

Graf *der;* **~en, ~en** count; (britischer ~) earl

Graffito *der od. das;* **~[s], Graffiti (a)** (Kunst) graffito
(b) *Pl.* (Kritzelei) graffiti

Grafik *die;* ~, **~en** graphic art[s *pl.*]; (Kunstwerk) graphic; (Druck) print

Grafiker *der;* **~s**, ~, **Grafikerin** *die;* ~, **~nen** [graphic] designer; (Künstler[in]) graphic artist

grafisch [1] *Adj.* graphic
[2] *adv.* graphically

Gräfin *die;* ~, **~nen** countess

Grafschaft *die;* ~, **~en (a)** count's land; (in Großbritannien) earldom
(b) (Verwaltungsbezirk) county

Gram *der;* **~[e]s** (geh.) grief; sorrow

grämen [1] *tr. V.* grieve
[2] *refl. V.* grieve (**über** + *Akk.*, **um** over)

Gramm *das;* **~s, ~e** gram

Grammatik *die;* ~, **~en** grammar

grammatisch [1] *Adj.* grammatical
[2] *adv.* grammatically

Grammophon (Wz) *das;* **~s, ~e** gramophone; phonograph (Amer.)

Granat *der;* **~[e]s, ~e** (Schmuckstein) garnet

Granat·apfel *der* pomegranate

Granate *die;* ~, **~n** shell; (Hand~) grenade

Granat·feuer *das* shellfire *no pl., no indef. art.*

grandios [1] *Adj.* magnificent
[2] *adv.* magnificently

Granit *der;* **~s, ~e** granite

grantig (südd., österr. ugs.) [1] *Adj.* bad-tempered
[2] *adv.* bad-temperedly

Grapefruit /'gre:pfru:t/ *die;* ~, **~s** grapefruit

Graph *der;* **~en, ~en** (Math., Naturw.) graph

Graphik *usw.:* ▶ GRAFIK *usw.*

Graphit *der;* **~s, ~e** graphite

Gras *das;* **~es, Gräser (a)** grass; **über etw.** (*Akk.*) **~ wachsen lassen** (ugs.) let the dust settle on sth.
(b) (Drogenjargon) grass (sl.)

grasen *itr. V.* graze

Gras-: ~halm *der* blade of grass; **~land** *das* grassland; **~narbe** *die* turf

grässlich, *gräßlich [1] *Adj.* **(a)** (abscheulich) horrible; terrible ‹*accident*›
(b) (ugs.: unangenehm) dreadful (coll.)
(c) (ugs.: sehr stark) terrible (coll.)
[2] *adv.* **(a)** (abscheulich) horribly; terribly
(b) (ugs.: unangenehm) terribly (coll.)
(c) (ugs.: sehr) terribly (coll.)

Grässlichkeit, *Gräßlichkeit *die;* ~, **~enz (a)** (Abscheulichkeit) horribleness; (eines Unfalls) terribleness
(b) (unangenehme Art) dreadfulness (coll.)

Grat *der;* **~[e]s, ~e** ridge

Gräte *die;* ~, **~n** [fish] bone

Gratifikation *die;* ~, **~en** bonus

gratinieren *tr. V.* (Gastr.) brown [the top of]; **gratinierter Blumenkohl** cauliflower au gratin

gratis *Adv.* free [of charge]; gratis

Gratis-: ~aktie *die* (Börsenw.) bonus share; **~muster** *das*, **~probe** *die* free sample

Grätsche *die;* ~, **~n** (Turnen) straddle; (Sprung) straddle vault

*alte Schreibung - vgl. Hinweis auf S. xiv

Gratulant *der;* **~en, ~en, Gratulantin** *die;* **~, ~nen** well-wisher

Gratulation *die;* **~, ~en** congratulations *pl.*

gratulieren *itr. V.* **jmdm. ~:** congratulate sb.; **jmdm. zum Geburtstag ~:** wish sb. many happy returns [of the day]

Grat·wanderung *die* ridge walk; (fig.) balancing act

grau *Adj.* grey; (trostlos) dreary; drab; **~ meliert** greying ‹*hair*›

Gräuel *der;* **~s, ~ (a) etw./jmd. ist jmdm. ein ~:** sb. loathes *or* detests sth./sb.
(b) (geh.) (~tat) atrocity

Gräuel·tat *die* atrocity

grauen¹ *itr. V.* (geh.) **der Morgen/der Tag graut** morning/day is breaking

grauen² *itr. V.* (*unpers.*) **ihm graut [es] davor/vor ihr** he dreads [the thought of] it/he's terrified of her

Grauen *das;* **~s, ~:** horror (**vor** + *Dat.* of)

grauen·haft [1] *Adj.* horrifying; (ugs.: sehr unangenehm) terrible (coll.)
[2] *adv.* horrifyingly; (ugs.: sehr unangenehm) terribly (coll.)

grauhaarig *Adj.* grey-haired

gräulich [1] *Adj.* **(a)** horrifying
(b) (unangenehm) awful
[2] *adv.* **(a)** horrifyingly
(b) (unangenehm) terribly

***grau·meliert** ▸ GRAU

Graupe *die;* **~, ~n (a)** grain of pearl barley
(b) *Pl.* (Gericht) pearl barley *sing.*

Graupel *die;* **~, ~n** soft hail pellet; **~n** soft hail; graupel

graupeln *itr. V.* (*unpers.*) **es graupelt** there's soft hail falling

grausam [1] *Adj.* **(a)** cruel
(b) (furchtbar) terrible; dreadful
[2] *adv.* **(a)** cruelly
(b) (furchtbar) terribly, dreadfully

Grausamkeit *die;* **~, ~en (a)** cruelty
(b) (Handlung) act of cruelty

grausen [1] *tr., itr. V.* (*unpers.*) **es grauste ihm** *od.* **ihn davor/vor ihr** he dreaded it/he was terrified of her
[2] *refl. V.* **sich vor etw./jmdm. ~:** dread sth./be terrified of sb.

Grausen *das;* **~s** horror

grausig *Adj., adv.* ▸ GRAUENHAFT

gravieren *tr. V.* engrave

gravierend *Adj.* serious, grave

Gravierung *die;* **~, ~en** engraving

Gravitation *die;* **~** (Physik, Astron.) gravitation

Gravur /gra'vu:ɐ̯/ *die;* **~, ~en** engraving

Grazie /'gra:tsi̯ə/ *die;* **~, ~n (a)** (Anmut) gracefulness
(b) (Myth.) Grace

greif·bar [1] *Adj.* **(a) in ~er Nähe** (fig.) within reach; **der Urlaub ist in ~e Nähe gerückt** (fig.) the holiday is just coming up [now]
(b) (deutlich) tangible; concrete
(c) (ugs.: verfügbar) available
[2] *adv.* **~ nahe** (fig.) within reach

greifen [1] *unr. tr. V.* **(a)** (ergreifen) take hold of; grasp; (rasch ~) seize
(b) (fangen) catch
[2] *unr. itr. V.* **(a) in/unter/hinter etw./sich** (*Akk.*) **~:** reach into/under/behind sth./one; **nach etw. ~:** reach for sth.; (hastig) make a grab for sth.
(b) (Technik) grip

Greis *der;* **~es, ~e** old man

Greisin *die;* **~, ~nen** old woman

grell [1] *Adj.* **(a)** (hell) glaring, ‹*light, sun, etc.*›
(b) (auffallend) garish ‹*colour etc.*›; loud ‹*dress, pattern, etc.*›
(c) (schrill) shrill, ‹*cry, voice, etc.*›
[2] *adv.* **(a)** (hell) with glaring brightness
(b) (auffallend) **gegen** *od.* **von etw. ~ abstechen** contrast sharply with sth.
(c) (schrill) shrilly

Gremium *das;* **~s, Gremien** committee

Grenze *die;* **~, ~n (a)** boundary; (Staats~) border; (gedachte Trennungslinie) borderline
(b) (fig.) limit

grenzen *itr. V.* **an etw.** (*Akk.*) **~:** border [on] sth.

grenzen·los [1] *Adj.* boundless; (fig.) boundless, unbounded ‹*joy, wonder, jealousy, grief, etc.*›; unlimited ‹*wealth, power*›; limitless ‹*patience, ambition*›; extreme ‹*tiredness, anger, foolishness*›
[2] *adv.* endlessly; (fig.) beyond all measure

Grenzen·losigkeit *die;* **~:** boundlessness

Grenz-: ~gänger *der;* **~~s, ~~, ~gängerin** *die;* **~~, ~~nen** [regular] commuter across the border *or* frontier; **~konflikt** *der* border *or* frontier conflict; **~land** *das* border *or* frontier area; **~posten** *der* border *or* frontier guard; **~stein** *der* boundary stone; **~übergang** *der* border crossing-point; **~übertritt** *der* crossing of the border; **der ungesetzliche ~übertritt** crossing the border illegally; **~verkehr** *der* [cross-]border traffic

Gretchen·frage *die* crucial question; sixty-four-thousand-dollar question (coll.)

***Greuel** ▸ GRÄUEL

***Greueltat** ▸ GRÄUELTAT

***greulich** ▸ GRÄULICH

Grieche *der;* **~n, ~n** Greek

Griechen·land (*das*)**;** **~s** Greece

griechisch [1] *Adj.* Greek
[2] *adv.* ‹*speak, write*› in Greek

Griechisch *das;* **~[s]** Greek *no art.*

Griechin *die;* **~, ~nen** Greek

griesgrämig [1] *Adj.* grumpy
[2] *adv.* in a grumpy manner

Grieß *der;* **~es, ~e** semolina

Grieß·brei *der* semolina
griff *1. u. 3. Pers. Sg. Prät. v.* GREIFEN
Griff *der;* **~[e]s, ~e (a)** grip; grasp
(b) (Knauf, Henkel) handle
griff·bereit *Adj.* ready to hand *postpos.*
Griffel *der;* **~s, ~:** slate pencil
griffig *Adj.* **(a)** (handlich) handy
(b) (gut greifend) that grips well *postpos., not pred.;* non-slip ‹*surface, floor*›
Grill *der;* **~s, ~s** grill; (Rost) barbecue
Grille *die;* **~, ~n (a)** cricket
(b) (sonderbarer Einfall) whim
grillen 1 *tr. V.* grill
2 *itr. V.* **im Garten ~:** have a barbecue in the garden
Grill·platz *der* barbecue area
Grimasse *die;* **~, ~n** grimace
grimmig 1 *Adj.* furious ‹*person*›; grim ‹*expression*›
2 *adv.* grimly
grinsen *itr. V.* grin; (höhnisch) smirk
Grippe *die;* **~, ~n (a)** influenza; flu (coll.)
(b) (volkst.: Erkältung) cold
Grips *der;* **~es** brains *pl.*
grob 1 *Adj.* **(a)** coarse; thick ‹*wire*›; rough ‹*work*›
(b) (ungefähr) rough
(c) (schwerwiegend) gross; flagrant ‹*lie*›
(d) (barsch) rude
2 *adv.* **(a)** coarsely
(b) (ungefähr) roughly
(c) (schwerwiegend) grossly
(d) (barsch) rudely
Grobheit *die;* **~, ~en (a)** rudeness
(b) (Äußerung) rude remark
Grobian *der;* **~[e]s, ~e** lout
Grog *der;* **~s, ~s** grog
groggy *Adj.* **(a)** (Boxen) groggy
(b) (ugs.: erschöpft) whacked [out] (coll.); all in (coll.)
grölen 1 *tr. V.* (ugs. abwertend) bawl [out]; roar, howl ‹*approval*›
2 *itr. V.* bawl
Groll *der;* **~[e]s** (geh.) rancour
grollen *itr. V.* (geh.) **(a) [mit] jmdm. ~:** bear a grudge against sb.
(b) ‹*thunder*› rumble
Grönland *(das);* **~s** Greenland
Gros /gro:/ *das;* **~** /gro:s/, **~** /gro:s/ bulk
Groschen *der;* **~s, ~ (a)** (österreichische Münze) groschen
(b) (ugs.: Zehnpfennigstück) ten-pfennig piece; (fig.) penny; cent (Amer.)
groß; größer, größt... 1 *Adj.* **(a)** big, large; great ‹*length, width, height*›; tall ‹*person*›; wide ‹*selection*›; **1m² ~:** 1m² in area; **im Großen und Ganzen** by and large
(b) (älter) big ‹*brother, sister*›; (erwachsen) grown-up
(c) (lange dauernd) long, lengthy
(d) intense ‹*heat, cold*›; high ‹*speed*›; great, major ‹*event, artist, work*›
2 *adv.* (ugs.: besonders) greatly; **~ geschrieben werden** (ugs.) be stressed; *s. auch* GROSSSCHREIBEN
groß-, Groß-: ~abnehmer *der,* **~abnehmerin** *die* bulk buyer *or* purchaser; **~aktionär** *der,* **~aktionärin** *die* (Wirtsch.) principal *or* major shareholder; **~artig** 1 *Adj.* magnificent; splendid; 2 *adv.* magnificently; splendidly; **~auftrag** *der* (Wirtsch.) large order
Großbritannien *(das);* **~s** the United Kingdom; [Great] Britain
Groß·buchstabe *der* capital [letter]
Größe *die;* **~, ~n** size; (Höhe, Körper~) height; (fig.) greatness; **die ~ der Katastrophe** the [full] extent of the catastrophe
Groß·eltern *Pl.* grandparents
Größen·ordnung *die* order [of magnitude]; **in einer ~ von einer Milliarde Euro** in the order of a thousand million *or* a billion euros
großen·teils *Adv.* largely; for the most part
Größen·wahn *der* delusions *pl.* of grandeur
größer ▶ GROSS
Groß-: ~fahndung *die* large-scale search; **~familie** *die* (Soziol.) extended family; (mehrere Kleinfamilien) composite family; **~handel** *der* wholesale trade; **~händler** *der,* **~händlerin** *die* wholesaler; **~industrielle** *der/die; adj. Dekl.* big industrialist
Grossist *der;* **~en, ~en, Grossistin** *die;* **~, ~nen** (Kaufmannsspr.) wholesaler
groß-, Groß-: ~macht *die* great power; **~maul** *das* (ugs. abwertend) bigmouth (coll.); **~mut** *die;* **~~:** generosity; **~mütig** *Adj.* generous; **~mutter** *die; Pl.* **~mütter** grandmother; **~rechner** *der* (DV) mainframe [computer]; **~reinemachen** *das;* **~~s** (ugs.) thorough cleaning; **~|schreiben** *unr. tr. V.* write ‹*word*› with a capital; *s. auch* GROSS 2; **~spurig** (abwertend) 1 *Adj.* boastful; (hochtrabend) pretentious; 2 *adv.* boastfully; (hochtrabend) pretentiously; **~stadt** *die* city; large town; **~städter** *der,* **~städterin** *die* city-dweller
größt... ▶ GROSS
Groß·teil *der* **(a)** (Hauptteil) major part
(b) (nicht unerheblicher Teil) large part
größten·teils *Adv.* for the most part
größt·möglich *Adj.* greatest possible
groß-, Groß-: ~|tun *unr. itr. V.* boast; **~unternehmen** *das* (Wirtsch.) large-scale enterprise; big concern; **~vater** *der* grandfather; **~verbraucher** *der,* **~verbraucherin** *die* bulk *or* large consumer; **~|ziehen** *unr. tr. V.* bring up;

*old spelling - see note on page xiv

raise; rear ‹*animal*›; ~**zügig** [1] *Adj.* generous; grand and spacious ‹*building, garden, etc.*›; [2] *adv.* generously; ~**zügigkeit** *die;* ~~: generosity

grotesk [1] *Adj.* grotesque [2] *adv.* grotesquely

Grotte *die;* ~, ~**n** grotto

grub *1. u. 3. Pers. Sg. Prät. v.* GRABEN

Grübchen *das;* ~**s**, ~: dimple

Grube *die;* ~, ~**n** pit; (Bergbau) mine

grübeln *itr. V.* ponder (**über** + *Dat.* on, over)

Gruben·arbeiter *der,* **Gruben·arbeiterin** *die* miner; mineworker

grüezi *Interj.* (schweiz.) hallo

Gruft *die;* ~, **Grüfte** vault; (in einer Kirche) crypt

grün *Adj.* green

Grün *das;* ~**s**, ~ *od.* (ugs.) ~**s** **(a)** green **(b)** (Pflanzen) greenery

Grün·anlage *die* green space; (Park) park

Grund *der;* ~[e]**s**, **Gründe** **(a)** ground; (eines Gewässers) bottom; **im** ~**e [genommen]** basically **(b)** (Ursache, Veranlassung) reason; **auf** ~: ▶ AUFGRUND

Grund-: ~**besitz** *der* **(a)** (Eigentum an Land) ownership of land; **(b)** (Land) land; ~**buch** *das* land register

gründen [1] *tr. V.* **(a)** found; set up, establish ‹*business*›; start [up] ‹*club*› **(b)** (aufbauen) base ‹*plan, theory, etc.*› (**auf** + *Akk.* on) [2] *itr. V.* **auf** *od.* **in etw.** (*Dat.*) ~: be based on sth. [3] *refl. V.* **sich auf etw.** (*Akk.*) ~: be based on sth.

Gründer *der;* ~**s**, ~, **Gründerin** *die;* ~, ~**nen** founder

Grund·erwerb[s]·steuer *die* (Steuerw.) land transfer tax

Grund·gesetz *das* Basic Law

grundieren *tr. V.* prime

Grundierung *die;* ~, ~**en** **(a)** (das Grundieren) priming **(b)** (erster Anstrich) priming coat

grund-, Grund-: ~**kenntnis** *die* basic knowledge *no pl.* (**in** + *Dat.* of); ~**lage** *die* basis; foundation

Grundlagen·forschung *die* basic research

grund·legend [1] *Adj.* fundamental, basic (**für** to); seminal ‹*idea, work*› [2] *adv.* fundamentally

gründlich [1] *Adj.* thorough [2] *adv.* thoroughly

Gründlichkeit *die;* ~: thoroughness

grund·los [1] *Adj.* groundless [2] *adv.* **sich** ~ **aufregen/ängstigen** be needlessly agitated/alarmed

Grund·nahrungsmittel *das* basic food[stuff]

Grün·donnerstag *der* Maundy Thursday

Grund-: ~**ordnung** *die* basic fundamental [constitutional] order; ~**prinzip** *das* fundamental principle; ~**recht** *das* basic *or* constitutional right; ~**riss**, *~**riß** *der* **(a)** (Bauw.) [ground] plan; **(b)** (Leitfaden) outline; ~**satz** *der* principle

grund·sätzlich [1] *Adj.* **(a)** fundamental ‹*difference, question, etc.*› **(b)** (aus Prinzip) ‹*opponent etc.*› on principle **(c)** (allgemein) ‹*agreement etc.*› in principle [2] *adv.* **(a)** fundamentally **(b)** (aus Prinzip) on principle **(c)** (allgemein) in principle

Grund-: ~**schule** *die* primary school; ~**stein** *der* foundation stone; ~**stein·legung** *die;* ~~, ~~**en** laying of the foundation stone; ~**stück** *das* plot [of land]

Gründung *die;* ~, ~**en** ▶ GRÜNDEN 1A: foundation; setting up; establishing; starting [up]

Grund-: ~**wasser** *das* (Geol.) ground water; ~**wortschatz** *der* (Sprachw.) basic vocabulary; ~**zug** *der* essential feature

Grüne[1] *das; adj. Dekl.* green; **im** ~**n/ins** ~: [out] in/into the country

Grüne[2] *der/die; adj. Dekl.* (Politik) member of the Green Party; **die** ~**n** the Greens

Grün-: ~**fläche** *die* green space; (im Park) lawn; ~**gürtel** *der* green belt; ~**land** *das* (Landw.) (Wiese) meadow land; (Weide) pastureland; ~**pflanze** *die* foliage plant; ~**schnabel** *der* (abwertend) [young] whippersnapper; (Neuling) greenhorn; ~**span** *der* verdigris; ~**streifen** *der* central reservation (*grassed and often with trees and bushes*)

grunzen *tr., itr. V.* grunt

Gruppe *die;* ~, ~**n** **(a)** group **(b)** (Klassifizierung) class; category

Gruppen-: ~**druck** *der* group pressure; ~**dynamik** *die* (Sozialpsych.) group dynamics *sing., no art.;* ~**leiter** *der,* ~**leiterin** *die* group leader; ~**reise** *die* (Touristik) group travel *no pl., no art.;* **eine** ~**reise nach London machen** travel to London with a group; ~**sieg** *der* (Sport) top place in the group

gruppieren [1] *tr. V.* arrange [2] *refl. V.* form a group/groups

Gruppierung *die;* ~, ~**en** grouping

gruselig *Adj.* eerie; creepy

gruseln [1] *tr., itr. V.* (*unpers.*) **es gruselt jmdn.** *od.* **jmdm.** sb.'s flesh creeps [2] *refl. V.* be frightened

Gruß *der;* ~**es**, **Grüße** **(a)** greeting; (Milit.) salute **(b)** (im Brief) **mit herzlichen Grüßen** [with] best wishes; **mit bestem** ~**/freundlichen Grüßen** yours sincerely

g

grüßen 1 *tr. V.* **(a)** greet; (Milit.) salute **(b)** (Grüße senden) **grüße deine Eltern [ganz herzlich] von mir** please give your parents my [kindest] regards; **grüß dich!** (ugs.) hello *or* (coll.) hi [there]! 2 *itr. V.* say hello; (Milit.) salute

Grütze *die;* ~, ~n groats *pl.;* **rote** ~: red fruit pudding (*made with fruit juice, fruit and cornflour, etc.*)

gucken *itr. V.* (ugs.) **(a)** look; (heimlich) peep **(b)** (hervorsehen) stick out **(c)** (dreinschauen) look

Guck·loch *das* spyhole

Guerilla /ge'rɪlja/ *die;* ~, ~s guerrilla war; (Einheit) guerrilla unit

Gulasch /'gʊlaʃ, 'gu:laʃ/ *das od. der;* ~[e]s, ~e *od.* ~s goulash

Gulden *der;* ~s, ~: guilder

gültig *Adj.* valid; current ‹*note, coin*›

Gültigkeit *die;* ~: validity; ~ **haben/erlangen** be/become valid

Gummi *der od. das;* ~s, ~[s] rubber

Gummi-: ~**band** *das* rubber *or* elastic band; (in Kleidung) elastic *no indef. art.;* ~**bärchen** *das;* ~~s, ~~: jelly baby; ~**baum** *der* rubber plant

gummieren *tr. V.* gum

Gummi-: ~**handschuh** *der* rubber glove; ~**knüppel** *der* [rubber] truncheon; ~**sohle** *die* rubber sole; ~**stiefel** *der* rubber boot; (für Regenwetter) wellington [boot] (Brit.)

Gunst *die;* ~ **(a)** favour; goodwill **(b) zu** ~**en** ▸ ZUGUNSTEN

günstig 1 *Adj.* favourable; propitious ‹*sign*›; auspicious ‹*moment*›; beneficial ‹*influence*›; good 2 *adv.* favourably; **etw.** ~ **beeinflussen** have *or* exert a beneficial influence on sth.

günstig[st]en·falls *Adv.* at best

Gurgel *die;* ~, ~n throat; **jmdm. die** ~ **zudrücken** throttle sb.

gurgeln *itr. V.* gargle

Gurke *die;* ~, ~n cucumber; (eingelegt) gherkin

gurren *itr. V.* (auch fig.) coo

Gurt *der;* ~[e]s, ~e strap; (im Auto, Flugzeug) [seat] belt

Gürtel *der;* ~s, ~: belt

Gürtel-: ~**linie** *die* waist[line]; **das war ein Schlag unter die** ~**linie** (fig. ugs.) that was hitting below the belt (fig. coll.); ~**reifen** *der* radial[-ply] tyre

Gurt·straffer *der;* ~s, ~ (Kfz.-W.) [seat-]belt tensioner

Guru *der;* ~s, ~s guru

GUS *Abk.* = **Gemeinschaft Unabhängiger Staaten** CIS

Guss, *Guß *der;* **Gusses, Güsse (a)** (das Gießen) casting **(b)** (ugs.: Regenschauer) downpour

Guss·eisen, *Guß·eisen, *das* cast iron

guss·eisern, *guß·eisern *Adj.* cast-iron

gut; besser, best... 1 *Adj.* good; fine ‹*wine*›; **ein** ~**es neues Jahr** a happy new year; ~ **tun** do good; **mir ist nicht** ~: I'm not feeling well; ~ **aussehend** good-looking; ~**en Appetit!** enjoy your lunch/dinner *etc.*!; **eine** ~**e Stunde [von hier]** a good hour [from here] 2 *adv.* **(a)** well; ~ **gemeint** well-meant; **so** ~ **wie nichts** next to nothing **(b)** (mühelos) easily; *s. auch* BESSER, BEST...

Gut *das;* ~[e]s, **Güter (a)** property; (Besitztum, auch fig.) possession **(b)** (landwirtschaftlicher Grundbesitz) estate **(c)** (Fracht~, Ware) item; **Güter** goods; (Fracht~) freight *sing.;* goods (Brit.)

gut-, Gut-: ~**achten** *das;* ~~s, ~~: [expert's] report; ~**artig** *Adj.* **(a)** good-natured; **(b)** (nicht gefährlich) benign; ~**artigkeit** *die* **(a)** good nature; goodnaturedness; **(b)** (Ungefährlichkeit) benignity; *~**aussehend** ▸ GUT 1; ~**bürgerlich** *Adj.* good middle-class; ~**bürgerliche Küche** good plain cooking; ~**dünken** *das;* ~~s discretion

Güte *die;* ~: goodness; kindness; (Qualität) quality

Gute·nacht·kuss, *Gute·nacht·kuß *der* goodnight kiss

Güter-: ~**abfertigung** *die* **(a)** (Abfertigung von Waren) dispatch of freight *or* (Brit.) goods; **(b)** (Annahmestelle) freight *or* (Brit.) goods office; ~**bahnhof** *der* freight depot; goods station (Brit.); ~**wagen** *der* goods wagon (Brit.); freight car (Amer.); ~**zug** *der* goods train (Brit.); freight train (Amer.)

gut-, Gut-: *~|**gehen** ▸ GEHEN H, I; *~**gelaunt** ▸ GELAUNT; *~**gemeint** ▸ GUT 2A; ~**gläubig** *Adj.* innocently trusting; ~**haben** *das;* ~~s, ~~: credit balance; ~|**heißen** *unr. tr. V.* approve of; ~**herzig** *Adj.* kind-hearted

gütig 1 *Adj.* kindly 2 *adv.* ~ **lächeln** give a kindly smile

gütlich *Adj.* amicable

gut-, Gut-: ~|**machen** *tr. V.* make good ‹*damage*›; put right ‹*omission, mistake, etc.*›; ~**mütig** *Adj.* good-natured; ~**mütigkeit** *die;* ~~: good nature

Guts·besitzer *der,* **Guts·besitzerin** *die* owner of a/the estate; landowner

gut-, Gut-: ~**schein** *der* voucher, coupon **(für, auf** + *Akk.* for); ~|**schreiben** *unr. tr. V.* credit; ~**schrift** *die* credit

Guts·hof *der* estate; manor

gut-: *~|**tun** ▸ GUT 1; ~**willig** 1 *Adj.* willing; (entgegenkommend) obliging; 2 *adv.* **etw.** ~**willig herausgeben/versprechen** hand sth. over voluntarily/promise sth. willingly

Gymnasium *das;* ~s, **Gymnasien** ≈ grammar school

---

*alte Schreibung - vgl. Hinweis auf S. xiv

Gymnastik *die;* **~**: physical exercises *pl.;* (Turnen) gymnastics *sing.*

Gynäkologe *der;* **~n, ~n, Gynäkologin** *die;* **~, ~nen** gynaecologist

h, H /ha:/ *das;* **~, ~(a)** (Buchstabe) h/H **(b)** (Musik) [key of] B

h *Abk.* **(a)** = **Uhr** hrs **(b)** = **Stunde** hr[s]

H *Abk.* **(a)** = **Herren; (b)** = **Haltestelle**

ha¹ /ha(:)/ *Interj.* **(a)** (Überraschung) ah **(b)** (Triumph) aha

ha² *Abk.* = **Hektar** ha

Haar *das;* **~[e]s, ~e** hair; **blonde ~e** *od.* **blondes ~ haben** have fair hair; (fig.) **~e auf den Zähnen haben** (ugs. scherzh.) be a tough customer; **um ein ~** (ugs.) very nearly

Haar-: ~ausfall *der* hair loss; **~bürste** *die* hairbrush; **~büschel** *das* tuft of hair

haaren *itr. V.* moult

Haares·breite *die:* **um ~**: by a hair's breadth

haar-, Haar-: ~festiger *der;* **~s, ~**: setting lotion; **~genau** (ugs.) [1] *Adj.* exact; [2] *adv.* exactly

haarig *Adj.* hairy

haar-, Haar-: ~klemme *die* hairgrip; **~nadel** *die* hairpin; **~nadel·kurve** *die* hairpin bend; **~schnitt** *der* haircut; (modisch) hairstyle; **~spalterei** *die;* **~~, ~~en** (abwertend) hair-splitting; **das ist doch ~spalterei** that's splitting hairs; **~spange** *die* hairslide; **~sträubend** *Adj.* **(a)** (grauenhaft) hair-raising; **(b)** (empörend) outrageous; shocking; **~teil** *das* hairpiece; **~waschmittel** *das* shampoo; **~wasser** *das* hair lotion

Habe *die;* **~** (geh.) possessions *pl.*

haben [1] *unr. tr. V.* have; have got; **heute ~ wir schönes Wetter** the weather is fine today; **es gut/schlecht/schwer ~**: have it good (coll.)/have a bad time [of it]/have a difficult time; **du hast zu gehorchen** you must obey; **das Jahr hat 12 Monate** there are 12 months in a year
[2] *refl. V.* (ugs.: sich aufregen) make a fuss
[3] *Hilfsverb* have; **ich habe/hatte ihn eben gesehen** I've/I'd just seen him; **er hat es gewusst** he knew it
[4] *mod. V.* **du hast zu gehorchen** you must obey; **er hat sich nicht einzumischen** he's not to interfere

Haben *das;* **~s, ~** (Kaufmannsspr.) credit

Habe·nichts *der;* **~, ~e** pauper

Haben-: ~seite *die* (Kaufmannsspr.) credit side; **~zinsen** *Pl.* interest *sing.* on deposits

Hab·gier *die* (abwertend) greed

hab·gierig [1] *Adj.* (abwertend) greedy [2] *adv.* greedily

Habicht *der;* **~s, ~e** hawk

Hab-: ~seligkeiten *Pl.* [meagre] belongings; **~sucht** *die;* (abwertend) greed; avarice

Hachse *die;* **~, ~n** (südd.) knuckle

Hack *das;* **~s** (ugs., bes. nordd.) mince

Hack·braten *der* meat loaf

Hacke¹ *die;* **~, ~n** hoe; (Pickel) pick[axe]

Hacke² *die;* **~, ~n** (bes. nordd. u. md.) heel

hacken [1] *itr. V.* **(a)** hoe **(b)** (picken) peck
[2] *tr. V.* **(a)** hoe ‹*garden, flower bed, etc.*› **(b)** (zerkleinern) chop; chop [up] ‹*meat, vegetables, etc.*›

Hacker *der;* **~s, ~, Hackerin** *die;* **~, ~nen** (DV-Jargon) hacker

hacke·zu *Adj.* (salopp) paralytic [drunk] (coll.)

Hack·fleisch *das* minced meat; mince

Häcksel *der od. das;* **~s** (Landw.) chaff

hadern *itr. V.* (geh.) **mit etw. ~**: be at odds with sth.

Hafen *der;* **~s, Häfen** harbour; port

Hafen-: ~arbeiter *der,* **~arbeiterin** *die* dock worker; docker; **~kneipe** *die* dockland pub (Brit.) *or* (Amer.) bar; **~rundfahrt** *die* trip round the harbour; **~stadt** *die* port; **~viertel** *das* dock area

Hafer *der;* **~s** oats *pl.*

Hafer-: ~brei *der* porridge; **~flocken** *Pl.* porridge oats

Haff *das;* **~[e]s, ~s** *od.* **~e** lagoon

-haft *Adj., adv.* -like

Haft *die;* **~ (a)** (Gewahrsam) custody; (aus politischen Gründen) detention **(b)** (Freiheitsstrafe) imprisonment

haftbar *Adj.* (bes. Rechtsspr.) **für etw. ~ sein** be liable for sth.

Haft·befehl *der* (Rechtsw.) warrant [of arrest]

haften¹ *itr. V.* stick (sich festsetzen) ‹*smell, dirt, etc.*›; cling (**an** + *Dat.* to); **~ bleiben** ···›

stick; (**an/auf** + *Dat.* to); ‹*smell, smoke*› cling (**an/auf** + *Dat.* to); (ugs.: im Gedächtnis bleiben) stick

haften² *itr. V.* **für jmdn./etw. ~:** be responsible for sb./liable for sth.; (Rechtsw., Wirtsch.) be liable

***haften|bleiben** ▶ HAFTEN¹

Häftling *der;* **~s, ~e** prisoner

Haft·pflicht *die* liability (**für** for)

Haftpflicht·versicherung *die* personal liability insurance; (für Autofahrer) third party insurance

Haft-: ~prüfung *die* (Rechtsw.) review of a/the remand in custody; **~schale** *die* contact lens; **~strafe** *die* (Rechtsspr. veralt.) prison sentence

Haftung *die;* **~, ~en** liability; **Gesellschaft mit [un]beschränkter ~:** [un]limited [liability] company

Hagebutte *die;* **~, ~n (a)** (Frucht) rose hip **(b)** (ugs.: Heckenrose) dog rose

Hagel *der;* **~s, ~** (auch fig.) hail

hageln *itr., tr. V.* (*unpers.*) hail

Hagel-: ~schaden *der* damage *no pl.* caused by hail; **~schauer** *der* [short] hailstorm; **~schlag** *der* hail

hager *Adj.* gaunt

haha /ha'ha(:)/ *Interj.* ha ha

Häher *der;* **~s, ~:** jay

Hahn¹ *der;* **~[e]s, Hähne** cock; (Wetter~) weathercock

Hahn² *der;* **~[e]s, Hähne,** *fachspr.:* **~en (a)** tap; faucet (Amer.) **(b)** (bei Waffen) hammer

Hähnchen *das;* **~s, ~:** chicken

Hahnen·fuß *der* buttercup

Hai *der;* **~s, ~e** shark

Häkchen *das;* **~s, ~ (a)** [small] hook **(b)** (Zeichen) mark; (beim Abhaken) tick

häkeln *tr., itr. V.* crochet

Häkel·nadel *die* crochet hook

haken **1** *tr. V.* hook (**an** + *Akk.* on to) **2** *itr. V.* (klemmen) be stuck

Haken *der;* **~s, ~ (a)** hook **(b)** (Zeichen) tick **(c)** (ugs.: Schwierigkeit) catch **(d)** (Boxen) hook

haken-, Haken-: ~förmig **1** *Adj.* hooked; hook-shaped; **2** *adv.* **~förmig gebogen** hooked; hook-shaped; **~kreuz** *das* swastika; **~nase** *die* hooked nose; hook nose

halb **1** *Adj. u. Bruchz.* half; **eine ~e Stunde/ein ~er Meter** half an hour/a metre; **zum ~en Preis** [at] half price; **~ Europa/die ~e Welt** half of Europe/half the world; **es ist ~ eins** it's half past twelve; **die ~e Wahrheit** half [of] the truth; **[noch] ein ~es Kind sein** be hardly more than a child **2** *adv.* **~ voll/leer** half-full/-empty; **~ offen** half-open; **~ angezogen** half dressed; **~ links/rechts** (Fußball) ‹*play*› [at] inside left/right

Halb·dunkel *das* semi-darkness

Halbe *der od. die od. das; adj. Dekl.* (ugs.) half litre (*of beer etc.*)

Halb·edelstein *der* (veralt.) semi-precious stone

halber *Präp. mit Gen.; nachgestellt* (wegen) on account of; (um ... willen) for the sake of

halb-, Halb-: ~finale *das* (Sport) semi-final; **~gar** *Adj.* half-cooked; **~gefror[e]ne** *das; adj. Dekl.* soft ice cream

Halbheit *die;* **~, ~en** (abwertend) half measure

halbieren *tr. V.* cut/tear ‹*object*› in half; halve ‹*amount, number*›

halb-, Halb-: ~insel *die* peninsula; **~jahr** *das* six months *pl.;* half year; **~jährlich** **1** *Adj.* six-monthly; **2** *adv.* every six months; **~kreis** *der* semicircle; **~kugel** *die* hemisphere; **~lang** *Adj.* mid-length ‹*hair*›; mid-calf length ‹*coat, dress, etc.*›; **~links** /-'-/ *Adv.* (Fußball) ‹*play*› [at] inside left; **~mast** *Adv.* at half-mast; **~mond** *der* **(a)** (Mond) half-moon; **(b)** (Figur) crescent; ***~offen** *Adj.:* ▶ HALB 2; **~pension** *die* half-board; **~rechts** /-'-/ *Adv.* (Fußball) ‹*play*› [at] inside right; **~schlaf** *der* light sleep; **im ~schlaf liegen** be half asleep; doze; **~schuh** *der* shoe; **~starke** *der; adj. Dekl.* (ugs. abwertend) [young] hooligan

halb·tags *Adv.* ‹*work*› part-time; (morgens/nachmittags) ‹*work*› [in the] mornings/afternoons

Halbtags-: ~arbeit *die,* **~beschäftigung** *die* part-time job; (morgens/nachmittags) morning/afternoon job; **~schule** *die* half-day school; **~stelle** *die* part-time job; (morgens/nachmittags) morning/afternoon job

halb-, Halb-: *~voll *Adj.:* ▶ HALB 2; **~wegs** *Adv.* to some extent; **~wüchsig** /-vy:ksıç/ *Adj.* adolescent; **~wüchsige** *der/die; adj. Dekl.* adolescent; **~zeit** *die* (bes. Fußball) **(a)** half; **(b)** (Pause) half-time; **~zeit·pause** *die* (Sport) half-time

Halde *die;* **~, ~n** (Bergbau) slag heap

half *1. u. 3. Pers. Sg. Prät. v.* HELFEN

Hälfte *die;* **~, ~n (a)** half **(b)** (ugs.: Teil) part

Halfter¹ *der od. das;* **~s, ~:** halter

Halfter² *die;* **~, ~n;** *auch das;* **~s, ~:** holster

Hall *der;* **~[e]s, ~e (a)** (geh.) reverberation **(b)** (Echo) echo

Halle *die;* **~, ~n** hall; (Fabrik~) shed; (Hotel~, Theater~) foyer

hallen *itr. V.* **(a)** reverberate; ‹*shot, bell, cry*› ring out **(b)** (widerhallen) echo

---

*old spelling - see note on page xiv

Hallen- indoor ‹*swimming pool, handball*›
Hallig *die;* **~, ~en** small low island (*particularly one of those off Schleswig-Holstein*)
hallo *Interj.* hello
Hallo *das;* **~s, ~s** cheering
Halluzination *die;* **~, ~en** hallucination
Halm *der;* **~[e]s, ~e** stalk; stem
Hals *der;* **~es, Hälse** neck; (Kehle) throat; **~ über Kopf** (ugs.) in a rush
hals-, Hals-: ~ab·schneider *der,* **~ab·schneiderin** *die* (ugs. abwertend) shark; **~band** *das* (für Tiere) collar; **~bruch** *der:* ▶ ~- UND BEINBRUCH; **~entzündung** *die* inflammation of the throat; **~kette** *die* necklace; **~-Nasen-Ohren-Arzt** *der,* **~-Nasen-Ohren-Ärztin** *die* ear, nose, and throat specialist; **~schlagader** *die* carotid [artery]; **~schmerzen** *Pl.* sore throat *sing.;* **~starrig** *Adj.* (abwertend) stubborn; obstinate; **~tuch** *das; Pl.* **~tücher** cravat; (des Cowboys) neckerchief; **~- und Beinbruch** *Interj.* (scherzh.) good luck; **~weh** *das* (ugs.) ▶ ~SCHMERZEN
halt *Interj.* stop
Halt *der;* **~[e]s, ~e (a)** hold
(b) (Stopp) stop; **~ machen** stop
haltbar *Adj.* **(a) ~ sein** ‹*food*› keep [well]; **~ bis 5. 3.** use by 5 March
(b) (nicht verschleißend) hard-wearing ‹*material, clothes*›
(c) (aufrechtzuerhalten) tenable ‹*hypothesis etc.*›
Haltbarkeit *die;* **~** (Strapazierfähigkeit) durability
Halte·bucht *die* (Verkehrsw.) lay-by (Brit.); turnout (Amer.)
halten [1] *unr. tr. V.* **(a)** (auch Milit.) hold; **die Hand vor den Mund ~:** put one's hand in front of one's mouth
(b) (Ballspiele) save ‹*shot, penalty, etc.*›
(c) (bewahren) keep; (beibehalten, aufrechterhalten) keep up ‹*speed etc.*›; maintain ‹*temperature, equilibrium*›
(d) (erfüllen) keep; **sein Wort/ein Versprechen ~:** keep one's word/a promise
(e) (besitzen, beschäftigen, beziehen) keep ‹*chickens etc.*›; take ‹*newspaper, magazine, etc.*›
(f) (einschätzen) **jmdn. für reich/ehrlich ~:** think sb. is rich/honest; **viel von jmdm. ~:** think a lot of sb.
(g) (ab~, veranstalten) give, ‹*speech, lecture*›
[2] *unr. itr. V.* **(a)** (stehen bleiben) stop
(b) (unverändert, an seinem Platz bleiben) last
(c) (Sport) save
(d) (beistehen) **zu jmdm. ~:** stand by sb.
[3] *unr. refl. V.* **(a)** (sich durchsetzen, behaupten) **wir werden uns/die Stadt wird sich nicht länger ~ können** we/the town won't be able to hold out much longer
(b) (sich bewähren) **sich gut ~:** do well
(c) (unverändert bleiben) ‹*weather, flowers, etc.*› last; ‹*milk, meat, etc.*› keep
(d) (Körperhaltung haben) **sich schlecht/gerade ~:** hold oneself badly/straight
(e) (bleiben) **sich auf den Beinen/im Sattel ~:** stay on one's feet/in the saddle; **sich links/rechts ~:** keep [to the] left/right; **sich an etw.** (*Akk.*) **~:** keep to sth.
Halte·punkt *der* stop
Halter *der;* **~s, ~ (a)** (Fahrzeug~) keeper
(b) (Tier~) owner
(c) (Vorrichtung) holder
Halterin *die;* **~, ~nen (a)** ▶ HALTER A: keeper
(b) ▶ HALTER B: owner
Halterung *die;* **~, ~en** support
Halte-: ~stelle *die* stop; **~verbot** *das* **(a)** „**~verbot**" 'no stopping'; **hier ist ~verbot** this is a no-stopping zone; **(b)** (Stelle) no-stopping zone; **~verbots·schild** *das* no-stopping sign
-haltig, (österr.) **-hältig: vitamin~/silber~** *usw.* containing vitamins/silver *etc. postpos., not pred.;* **vitamin~ sein** contain vitamins
halt-, Halt-: ~los *Adj.* **(a)** (labil) **~los sein** be a weak character; **ein ~loser Mensch** a weak character; **(b)** (unbegründet) unfounded; **~losigkeit** *die;* **~~ (a)** (Labilität) weakness of character; **(b)** (mangelnde Begründung) unfoundedness; ***~|machen** ▶ HALT B
Haltung *die;* **~, ~en (a)** (Körper~) posture
(b) (Pose) manner
(c) (Einstellung) attitude
(d) (Fassung) composure
Halunke *der;* **~n, ~n** scoundrel; villain
Hamburger *der;* **~s, ~** (Frikadelle) hamburger
hämisch [1] *Adj.* malicious
[2] *adv.* maliciously
Hammel *der;* **~s, ~ (a)** wether
(b) (Fleisch) mutton
Hammel·fleisch *das* mutton
Hammer *der;* **~s, Hämmer (a)** hammer; (Holz~) mallet; **~ und Sichel** hammer and sickle
(b) (Technik) ram
hämmern *itr., tr. V.* hammer
Hämorrhoiden /hɛmɔro'i:dn̩/ *Pl.* (Med.) haemorrhoids; piles
Hampel·mann *der* **(a)** jumping jack
(b) (ugs. abwertend) puppet
hampeln *itr. V.* (ugs.) jump about
Hamster *der;* **~s, ~:** hamster
hamstern *tr., itr. V.* **(a)** (horten) hoard
(b) (Lebensmittel tauschen) barter goods for [food]
Hand *die;* **~, Hände** hand; **eine ~ voll** a handful; **jmdm. die ~ geben** shake sb.'s hand; **~ und Fuß/weder ~ noch Fuß haben** (ugs.) make sense/no sense; **alle** *od.* **beide Hände damit voll haben, etw. zu tun** (ugs.) have one's hands full doing sth.; **die Hände in den Schoß legen** sit back and do nothing; **etw. aus der ~ geben** let sth. out of one's hands; **~ in ~ arbeiten** work hand in hand; ···

etw. zur ~ haben have sth. handy; **zu Händen [von] Herrn Müller** attention Herr Müller; **unter der ~** (fig.) on the quiet

Hand-: ~arbeit *die* **(a)** handicraft; **etw. in ~arbeit herstellen** make sth. by hand; **(b)** (Gegenstand) handmade article; **(c)** (Nadelarbeit) [piece of] needlework; **~ball** *der* handball; **~besen** *der* brush; **~betrieb** *der* manual operation; **~bewegung** *die* **(a)** movement of the hand; **(b)** (Geste) gesture; **~bremse** *die* handbrake; **~buch** *das* handbook; (technisches ~buch) manual

Händchen *das;* **~s, ~:** [little] hand

Hände ▶ HAND

Hände-: ~druck *der; Pl.* **~drücke** handshake; **~klatschen** *das;* **~~s** clapping

Handel *der;* **~s** trade; **~ treiben** trade; **~ treibend** trading ‹*nation*›

handeln [1] *itr. V.* **(a)** trade; deal
(b) (feilschen) haggle
(c) (agieren) act
(d) (sich verhalten) behave
(e) von etw. *od.* **über etw.** (*Akk.*) **~** ‹*book, film, etc.*› be about *or* deal with sth.
[2] *refl. V.* (*unpers.*) **es handelt sich um …:** it is a matter of …; (es dreht sich um) it's about …

handels-, Handels-: ~abkommen *das* trade agreement; **~bank** *die; Pl.* **~~en** merchant bank; **~bilanz** *die* **(a)** (eines Betriebes) balance sheet; **(b)** (eines Staates) balance of trade; **~einig, ~eins: mit jmdm. ~einig** *od.* **~eins werden/sein** agree/have agreed terms with sb.; **~flotte** *die* merchant fleet; **~gesellschaft** *die* company; **~kammer** *die:* ▶ INDUSTRIE- UND HANDELSKAMMER; **~klasse** *die* grade; **~marine** *die* merchant navy; **~partner** *der,* **~partnerin** *die* trading partner; **~register** *das* register of companies; **~schiff** *das* merchant ship; **~schule** *die* commercial college; **~straße** *die* (hist.) trade route; **~üblich** *Adj.* **~übliche Praktiken/Größen** standard business practices/standard [commercial] sizes; **~unternehmen** *das* trading concern; **~vertreter** *der,* **~vertreterin** *die* [sales] representative; travelling salesman/saleswoman; **~vertretung** *die* trade mission; **~zentrum** *das* trading centre

hände·ringend *Adv.* (ugs.: dringend) ‹*need*› urgently; ‹*search for sb./sth.*› desperately

hand-, Hand-: ~feger *der* brush; **~fest** *Adj.* **(a)** robust; sturdy; **(b)** substantial ‹*meal etc.*›; **(c)** solid ‹*proof*›; concrete ‹*suggestion*›; complete ‹*lie*›; well-founded ‹*argument*›; **~fläche** *die* palm [of one's/the hand]; flat of one's/the hand; **~gas** *das* (Kfz-W.) hand throttle; **~gearbeitet** *Adj.* handmade; **~gelenk** *das* wrist; **~gemenge** *das* fight; **~gepäck** *das* hand baggage; **~geschrieben** *Adj.* handwritten; **~granate** *die* hand grenade; **~greiflich** *Adj.* **(a)** (tätlich) **~greiflich werden** start using one's fists; **(b)** tangible ‹*success, advantage, proof, etc.*›; palpable ‹*contradiction, error*›; obvious ‹*fact*›; **~griff** *der* **(a) mit einem ~griff/wenigen ~griffen** in one movement/without much trouble; (schnell) in no time at all/next to no time; **(b)** (am Koffer, an einem Werkzeug) handle; **~habe** *die;* **~~, ~~n: eine [rechtliche] ~habe [gegen jmdn.]** a legal handle [against sb.]; **~haben** *tr. V.* **(a)** handle; operate ‹*device, machine*›; **(b)** (praktizieren) implement ‹*law etc.*›; **~habung** *die;* **~~, ~~en (a)** handling; (eines Gerätes, einer Maschine) operation; **(b)** (Durchführung) implementation

Handikap /ˈhɛndikɛp/ *das;* **~s, ~s** (auch Sport) handicap

handikapen /ˈhɛndikɛpn̩/ *tr. V.* handicap

Hand-: ~käse *der* (landsch.) *small, hand-formed curd cheese;* **~koffer** *der* [small] suitcase; **~kuss, *~kuß** *der* kiss on sb.'s hand; **~langer** *der;* **~~s, ~~,** (ungelernter Arbeiter) labourer; (abwertend) lackey; **~lauf** *der* handrail

Händler *der;* **~s, ~, Händlerin** *die;* **~, ~nen** trader

handlich *Adj.* handy; easily carried ‹*parcel, suitcase*›; easily portable ‹*television, camera*›

Handlung *die;* **~, ~en (a)** (Vorgehen) action; (Tat) act
(b) (Fabel) plot

handlungs-, Handlungs-: ~arm *Adj.* short on action *pred.;* **~fähig** *Adj.* able to act *pred.;* working *attrib.* ‹*majority*›; **~freiheit** *die* freedom of action; **~reisende** *der/die* ▶ HANDELSVERTRETER; **~weise** *die* conduct

hand-, Hand-: ~puppe *die* glove *or* hand puppet; **~schelle** *die* handcuff; **~schlag** *der* handshake; **~schrift** *die* handwriting; **~schriftlich** [1] *Adj.* handwritten; [2] *adv.* by hand; **~schuh** *der* glove; **~schuh·fach** *das* glove compartment; **~signiert** *Adj.* signed; **~spiegel** *der* hand mirror; **~stand** *der* (Turnen) handstand; **~tasche** *die* handbag; **~tuch** *das; Pl.* **-tücher** towel; **~umdrehen: im ~umdrehen** in no time at all; **~verlesen** *Adj.* hand-picked; ***~voll** ▶ HAND; **~wäsche** *die* washing by hand

Hand·werk *das* craft; (als Beruf) trade; **sein ~ kennen/beherrschen** know one's job

Handwerker *der;* **~s, ~:** tradesman

Handwerkerin *die;* **~, ~nen** tradeswoman;

handwerklich *Adj.* **ein ~er Beruf** a [skilled] trade

Handwerks·zeug *das* tools *pl.*

Handy /ˈhɛndi/ *das;* **~s, ~s** mobile [phone]

Handy·nummer *die* mobile number

Hand·zeichen *das* sign [with one's hand]; (eines Autofahrers) hand signal; (Abstimmung) show of hands

*alte Schreibung - vgl. Hinweis auf S. xiv

Hanf *der;* **~[e]s** hemp
Hang *der;* **~[e]s, Hänge** slope; (Neigung) tendency
Hänge-: ~brücke *die* suspension bridge; **~lampe** *die* pendant light; **~matte** *die* hammock
hängen¹ *unr. itr. V.; südd., österr., schweiz. mit sein* hang (**an** + *Dat.* from); (an einem Fahrzeug) be hitched (**an** + *Dat.* to); **[mit der Ärmel** *usw.* **an/in etw.** (*Dat.*) **~ bleiben** get one's sleeve *etc.* caught on/in sth.; **~ bleiben** (ugs.: haften) stick (**an/auf** + *Dat.*) to; (ugs.: verweilen) get stuck (coll.)
hängen² [1] *tr. V.* **(a)** hang (**in/über** + (*Akk.*) in/over; **an/auf** + *Akk.* on)
(b) (befestigen) hitch up (**an** + *Akk.* to); couple on ‹*railway carriage, etc.*› (**an** + *Akk.* to)
[2] *refl. V.* **(a) sich an etw.** (*Akk.*) **~:** hang on to sth.
(b) (sich festsetzen) cling (**an** + *Akk.* to)
***hängen|bleiben** ▸ HÄNGEN¹
hängend *Adj.* hanging
Hänge·schrank *der* wall cupboard
Hang·lage *die* hillside location
Hansaplast Ⓦⓩ *das;* **~[e]s** sticking plaster; Elastoplast ®
hänseln *tr. V.* tease
Hanse·stadt *die* Hanseatic city
Hantel *die;* **~, ~n** (Sport) (kurz) dumb-bell; (lang) barbell
hantieren *itr. V.* be busy
Häppchen *das;* **~s, ~ (a)** [small] morsel
(b) (Appetithappen) canapé
Happen *der;* **~s, ~:** morsel
happig *Adj.* (ugs.) **~e Preise** fancy prices (coll.)
Happyend, Happy-End /ˈhɛpiˈ|ɛnt/ *das;* **~[s], ~s** happy ending
Hardware /ˈhaːdwɛə/ *die;* **~, ~s** (DV) hardware
Harfe *die;* **~, ~n** harp
Harke *die;* **~, ~n** rake
harken *tr. V.* rake
harm·los [1] *Adj.* **(a)** (ungefährlich) harmless; slight ‹*injury, cold, etc.*›; mild ‹*illness*›; safe ‹*medicine, bend, road, etc.*›
(b) (arglos) innocent; harmless ‹*fun, pastime, etc.*›
[2] *adv.* **(a)** (ungefährlich) harmlessly
(b) (arglos) innocently
Harmlosigkeit *die;* **~ (a)** (Ungefährlichkeit) harmlessness; (einer Krankheit) mildness; (eines Medikamentes) safety
(b) (Arglosigkeit, harmloses Verhalten) innocence
Harmonie *die;* **~, ~n** (auch fig.) harmony
harmonieren *itr. V.* **(a)** harmonize
(b) (miteinander auskommen) get on well
Harmonika *die;* **~, ~s** *od.* **Harmoniken** harmonica
harmonisch [1] *Adj.* harmonious; (Musik) harmonic
[2] *adv.* harmoniously; (Musik) harmonically
harmonisieren *tr. V.* coordinate; **etw. mit etw. ~** (Wirtsch.) bring sth. into line with sth.
Harmonisierung *die;* **~, ~en** (Wirtsch.) harmonization
Harmonium *das;* **~s, Harmonien** harmonium
Harn *der;* **~[e]s, ~e** (Med.) urine
Harn·blase *die* bladder
Harnisch *der;* **~s, ~e** armour
Harpune *die;* **~, ~n** harpoon
harpunieren *tr. V.* harpoon
harren *itr. V.* (geh.) **jmds./einer Sache** *od.* **auf jmdn./etw. ~:** await sb./sth.
harsch [1] *Adj.* **(a)** (vereist) crusted
(b) (barsch) harsh
[2] *adv.* harshly
Harsch *der;* **~[e]s** crusted snow
hart; härter, härtest... [1] *Adj.* **(a)** hard; **~ gekocht** hard-boiled ‹*egg*›
(b) tough ‹*situation, job*›; harsh ‹*reality, truth*›
(c) (streng) harsh ‹*penalty, punishment, judgement*›; tough ‹*measure, law, course*›
(d) (rau) rough ‹*game, opponent*›
[2] *adv.* hard chair; **(a)** (mühevoll) ‹*work*› hard
(b) (streng) harshly
(c) (nahe) close (**an** + *Dat.* to)
Härte *die;* **~, ~n (a)** (auch Physik) hardness
(b) (Widerstandsfähigkeit) toughness
(c) (schwere Belastung) hardship
(d) (Strenge) harshness
(e) (Heftigkeit) (eines Aufpralls usw.) force; (eines Streits) violence
(f) (Rauheit) roughness
Härte·fall *der* **(a)** case of hardship
(b) (ugs.: Person) hardship case
härten *tr., itr. V.* harden
härter ▸ HART
härtest... ▸ HART
hart-, Hart-: *~gekocht ▸ HART 1A; **~geld** *das* coins *pl.;* **~gummi** *das* hard rubber; **~herzig** [1] *Adj.* hard-hearted [2] *adv.* hard-heartedly; **~herzigkeit** *die;* **~~:** hard-heartedness; **~käse** *der* hard cheese; **~näckig** [1] *Adj.* **(a)** (eigensinnig) obstinate; stubborn; **(b)** (ausdauernd) dogged [2] *adv.* **(a)** (eigensinnig) obstinately; stubbornly; **(b)** (ausdauernd) doggedly; **~näckigkeit** *die;* **~~ (a)** (Eigensinn) obstinacy; stubbornness; **(b)** (Ausdauer) doggedness
Härtung *die;* **~, ~en** hardening; (von Stahl auch) tempering
Hart·wurst *die* dry sausage
Harz *das;* **~es, ~e** resin
Harzer Käse *der;* **~ ~s, ~ ~:** Harz [Mountain] cheese
Haschee (Kochk.) *das;* **~s, ~s** hash
haschen¹ *tr. V.* (veralt.) catch
haschen² *itr. V.* (ugs.) smoke [hash] (coll.)
Häschen /ˈhɛːsçən/ *das;* **~s, ~s** bunny
Haschisch *das od. der;* **~[s]** hashish

Haschisch·rausch *der* [state of] hashish intoxication; **etw. im** *od.* **bei einem ~rausch tun** do sth. while under the effects of hashish *or* while [high (coll.)] on hashish

Hase *der;* **~n, ~n (a)** hare **(b)** (landsch.) ▶ KANINCHEN

Hasel·nuss, *Hasel·nuß *die* hazelnut

Hasen-: ~fuß *der* (spöttisch abwertend) coward; chicken (coll.); **~scharte** *die* (Med.) harelip

Haspel *die;* **~, ~n** (Technik) (für Garn) reel; (für ein Seil, Kabel) drum

Hass, *Haß *der;* **Hasses** hatred (**auf** + *Akk.*, **gegen** of, for)

hassen *tr., itr. V.* hate

hass·erfüllt, *haß·erfüllt *Adj.* filled with hatred *postpos.*

hässlich, *häßlich [1] *Adj.* **(a)** ugly **(b)** (gemein) nasty **(c)** (unangenehm) awful ‹*weather, cold, situation, etc.*› [2] *adv.* **(a)** ‹*dress*› unattractively **(b)** (gemein) nastily

Hässlichkeit, *Häßlichkeit *die;* **~, ~en (a)** (Aussehen) ugliness **(b)** (Gesinnung) nastiness

hast *2. Pers. Sg. Präsens v.* HABEN

Hast *die;* **~:** haste

hasten *itr. V.; mit sein* hurry

hastig [1] *Adj.* hasty; hurried [2] *adv.* hastily; hurriedly

hat *3. Pers. Sg. Präsens v.* HABEN

hätscheln *tr. V.* caress

hatschi *Interj.* atishoo

hatte *1. u. 3. Pers. Sg. Prät. v.* HABEN

hätte *1. u. 3. Pers. Sg. Konjunktiv II v.* HABEN

Haube *die;* **~, ~n (a)** bonnet; (einer Krankenschwester) cap **(b)** (Kfz-W.) bonnet (Brit.); hood (Amer.)

Hauch *der;* **~[e]s, ~e** (geh.) **(a)** (Atem, auch fig.) breath **(b)** (Luftzug) breath of wind **(c)** (leichter Duft) delicate smell **(d)** (dünne Schicht) [gossamer-]thin layer

hauch·dünn *Adj.* gossamer-thin ‹*material, dress*›; wafer-thin ‹*layer, slice, majority*›

hauchen *itr. V.* breathe (**gegen, auf** + *Akk.* on)

Haue *die;* **~, ~n (a)** (südd., österr.: Hacke) hoe **(b)** (ugs.: Prügel) a hiding (coll.)

hauen [1] *unr. tr. V.* **(a)** (ugs.: schlagen) belt; clobber (coll.) **(b)** (ugs.: auf einen Körperteil) belt (coll.); hit **(c)** (herstellen) carve ‹*figure, statue, etc.*› (**in** + *Akk.* in) [2] *unr. itr. V.* **(a)** (ugs.: prügeln) **er haut immer gleich** he's quick to hit out **(b)** (auf einen Körperteil) belt (coll.); hit **(c)** (ugs.: auf/gegen etw. schlagen) thump [3] *unr. refl. V.* (ugs.: sich prügeln) have a punch-up (coll.)

Hauer *der;* **~s, ~** (Jägerspr.) tusk; (fig.) fang

Haufen *der;* **~s, ~:** heap; pile; (Gruppe) bunch (coll.)

häufen [1] *tr. V.* heap, pile (**auf** + *Akk.* on to); (aufheben) hoard ‹*money, supplies*› [2] *refl. V.* (sich mehren) pile up

häufig [1] *Adj.* frequent [2] *adv.* frequently; often

Häufigkeit *die;* **~, ~en** frequency

Häufung *die;* **~, ~en** increasing frequency

Haupt *das;* **~[e]s, Häupter** (geh., auch fig.) head

haupt-, Haupt-: ~bahnhof *der* main station; **~beruflich** [1] *Adj.* **seine ~berufliche Tätigkeit** his main occupation; [2] *adv.* **er ist ~beruflich als Elektriker tätig** his main occupation is that of electrician; **~darsteller** *der* (Theater, Film) male lead; **~darstellerin** *die* (Theater, Film) female lead; **~eingang** *der* main entrance; **~einschalt·zeit** *die* peak *or* prime viewing time; **~fach** *das* major; **~figur** *die* main character; **~film** *der* main feature; **~gang** *der* **(a)** main corridor; **(b)** ▶ ~GERICHT; **~gebäude** *das* main building; **~gericht** *das* main course; **~gewinn** *der* first prize

Häuptling *der;* **~s, ~e** chief[tain]

haupt-, Haupt-: ~mahlzeit *die* main meal; **~mann** *der; Pl.* **~leute** (Milit.) captain; **~person** *die* central figure; **~postamt** *das* main post office; **~quartier** *das* (Milit., auch fig.) headquarters *sing. or pl.;* **~reise·zeit** *die* high season; peak [holiday] season; **~rolle** *die* main role; lead; **die ~rolle spielen** (fig.) play the leading role; **~sache** *die* main thing; **~sächlich** [1] *Adv.* mainly; principally; [2] *Adj.; nicht präd.* main; principal; **~saison** *die* high season; **~satz** *der* main clause; (allein stehend) sentence; **~schalter** *der* (Elektrot.) mains switch; **~schlagader** *die* aorta; **~schul·abschluss, *~schul·abschluß** *der* ≈ secondary school leaving certificate; **~schule** *die* ≈ secondary modern school; **~schüler** *der,* **~schülerin** *die* ≈ secondary modern school pupil; **~sitz** *der* head office; headquarters *pl.;* **~stadt** *die* capital [city]; **~städtisch** *Adj.* metropolitan; **~straße** *die* main street; **~thema** *das* main topic *or* theme; (Musik) main theme; **~verkehr** *der* bulk of the traffic

Hauptverkehrs-: ~straße *die* main road; **~zeit** *die* rush hour

Haupt-: ~versammlung *die* (Wirtsch.) shareholders' meeting; **~wache** *die* main police station; **~wort** *das* (Sprachw.) noun

hau ruck *Interj.* heave[-ho]

Haus *das;* **~es, Häuser (a)** house; (Amts-,

*old spelling - see note on page xiv

Firmengebäude usw.) building; (Heim) home; **nach ~e** home; **zu ~e** at home; **das erste ~ am Platze** the best hotel in the town
(b) ~ halten be economical

haus-, Haus-: ~angestellte *der/die* domestic servant; **~apotheke** *die* medicine cabinet; **~arbeit** *die* housework; (Schulw.) homework; **~arrest** *der* house arrest; **~arzt** *der,* **~ärztin** *die* family doctor; **~aufgabe** *die* homework; **~backen** 1 *Adj.* plain; unadventurous ‹*clothes*›; 2 *adv.* ‹*dress*› unadventurously; **~besetzer** *der;* **~~s, ~~, ~besetzerin** *die;* **~~, ~~nen** squatter; **~besitzer** *der* houseowner; (Vermieter) landlord; **~besitzerin** *die* houseowner; (Vermieterin) landlady; **~besuch** *der* house call; **~boot** *das* houseboat

Häuschen /ˈhɔyːsçən/ *das;* **~s, ~:** small house; **aus dem ~ sein** (ugs.) be over the moon (coll.)

hausen *itr. V.* **(a)** (ugs. abwertend) live
(b) (Verwüstungen anrichten) **[furchtbar] ~:** wreak havoc

Häuser·block *der* block [of houses]

haus-, Haus-: ~flur *der* hall[way]; (im Obergeschoss) landing; **~frau** *die* housewife; **~freund** *der* **(a)** friend of the family; **(b)** (verhüll.: Liebhaber) man friend (euphem.); **~freundin** *die* friend of the family; **~friedens·bruch** *der* (Rechtsw.) trespass; **~gebrauch** *der* domestic use; **das reicht für den ~gebrauch** (ugs.) it's good enough to get by (coll.); **~gehilfin** *die* [home] help; **~gemacht** *Adj.* home-made

Haus·halt *der* **(a)** household
(b) (Arbeit im ~) housekeeping; **jmdm. den ~ führen** keep house for sb.
(c) (Politik) budget

***haus|halten** ▸ HAUS B

Haushälterin *die;* **~, ~nen** housekeeper

Haushalts-: ~artikel *der* household article; **~debatte** *die* (Politik) budget debate; **~geld** *das* housekeeping money; **~jahr** *das* financial year; **~kasse** *die* housekeeping money; **~plan** *der* budget; **~waren** *Pl.* household goods

haus-, Haus-: ~herr *der* **(a)** (Familienoberhaupt) head of the household; **(b)** (als Gastgeber) host; **(c)** (Rechtsspr.) (Eigentümer) owner; (Mieter) occupier **~herrin** *die* **(a)** ▸ ~HERR A; **(b)** ▸ ~HERR B; **~hoch** 1 *Adj.* as high as a house; (fig.) overwhelming; 2 *adv.* (fig.) **~hoch gewinnen** win hands down

hausieren *itr. V.* **[mit etw.] ~:** hawk [sth.]; peddle [sth.]; **„Hausieren verboten"** 'no hawkers'

Hausierer *der;* **~s, ~, Hausiererin** *die;* **~, ~nen** pedlar; hawker

häuslich *Adj.* **(a)** domestic
(b) (das Zuhause liebend) home-loving

Hausmacher·art *die:* **nach ~:** home-made-style *attrib.*

Haus·mann *der: man who stays at home and does the housework;* (Ehemann) househusband

Hausmanns·kost *die* plain cooking

Haus-: ~marke *die* **(a)** house wine; **(b)** (ugs.: bevorzugtes Getränk) favourite tipple (coll.); **~meister** *der,* **~meisterin** *die* caretaker; **~mittel** *das* household remedy; **~musik** *die* music at home; **~nummer** *die* house number; **~ordnung** *die* house rules *pl.;* **~putz** *der* spring-clean; (regelmäßig) clean-out

Haus·rat *der* household goods *pl.*

Hausrat·versicherung *die* [household *or* home] contents insurance

Haus-: ~schlüssel *der* front-door key; house key; **~schuh** *der* slipper; **~segen** *der:* **bei ihnen hängt der ~segen schief** (ugs. scherzh.) they've been having a row

Haussuchung *die;* **~, ~en** house search

Haussuchungs·befehl *der* search warrant

Haus-: ~telefon *das* internal telephone; **~tier** *das* **(a)** pet; **(b)** (Nutztier) domestic animal; **~tür** *die* front door; **~verbot** *das* ban on entering the house/pub/restaurant *etc.;* **~verwalter** *der,* **~verwalterin** *die* manager [of the block]; **~wirt** *der* landlord; **~wirtin** *die* landlady; **~wirtschaft** *die* domestic science and home economics; **~zelt** *das* ridge tent

Haut *die;* **~, Häute** skin; **aus der ~ fahren** (ugs.) go up the wall (coll.)

Haut-: ~arzt *der,* **~ärztin** *die* skin specialist; **~ausschlag** *der* [skin] rash

häuten 1 *tr. V.* skin; flay
2 *refl. V.* shed its skin/their skins

haut-, Haut-: ~eng *Adj.* skintight; **~farbe** *die* [skin] colour; **~krankheit** *die* skin disease; **~krebs** *der* skin cancer

Häutung *die;* **~, ~en (a)** ▸ HÄUTEN 1: skinning; flaying
(b) (das Sichhäuten) **eine Eidechse bei der ~:** a lizard shedding its skin

Haxe *die;* **~, ~n** ▸ HACHSE

he *Interj.* (ugs.) hey

Heb·amme *die* midwife

Hebel *der;* **~s, ~:** lever

heben *unr. tr. V.* **(a)** lift; raise ‹*baton, camera, glass*›
(b) (verbessern) raise ‹*standard, level*›; increase ‹*turnover, self-confidence*›; improve ‹*mood*›; enhance ‹*standing*›; boost ‹*morale*›

hecheln[1] *itr. V.* (ugs. abwertend) gossip

hecheln[2] *itr. V.* pant [for breath]

Hecht *der;* **~[e]s, ~e** pike

Hecht·sprung *der* **(a)** (Turnen) Hecht vault
(b) (Schwimmen) racing dive; (vom Sprungturm) pike-dive

Heck *das;* **~[e]s, ~e** *od.* **~s** stern; (Flugzeug~) tail; (Auto~) rear

Heck·antrieb *der* (Kfz-W.) rear-wheel drive

Hecke *die;* ~, ~**n (a)** hedge
(b) (wild wachsend) thicket

Hecken-: ~**rose** *die* dogrose; ~**schütze** *der,* ~**schützin** *die* sniper

Heck·scheibe *die* rear window

Heer *das;* ~**[e]s,** ~**e** armed forces *pl.;* (für den Landkrieg, fig.) army

Hefe *die;* ~, ~**n** yeast

Hefe·teig *der* yeast dough

Heft[1] *das;* ~**[e]s,** ~**e** (geh.) haft; handle

Heft[2] *das;* ~**[e]s,** ~**e (a)** (bes. Schule) exercise book
(b) (Nummer einer Zeitschrift) issue

Heftchen *das;* ~**s,** ~: book [of tickets/stamps *etc.*]

heften 1 *tr. V.* **(a)** (mit einer Nadel) pin; (mit einer Klammer) clip; (mit Klebstoff) stick
(b) (Schneiderei) tack
(c) (Buchbinderei) stitch; (mit Klammern) staple
2 *refl. V.* **sich an jmds. Fersen** (*Akk.*) ~: stick hard on sb.'s heels

Hefter *der;* ~**s,** ~: [loose-leaf] file

heftig 1 *Adj.* violent; heavy ‹*rain, shower, blow*›; severe ‹*pain*›; ‹*person*› with a violent temper
2 *adv.* ‹*rain, snow, breathe*› heavily; ‹*hit*› hard; ‹*quarrel*› violently

Heftigkeit *die;* ~: ▶ HEFTIG 1: violence; heaviness; severity

Heft-: ~**klammer** staple; ~**pflaster** *das* sticking plaster; ~**zwecke** *die* ▶ REISSZWECKE

hegen *tr. V.* **(a)** (bes. Forstw., Jagdw.) look after, tend
(b) (geh.: umsorgen) look after
(c) (fig.) feel ‹*contempt, hatred, mistrust*›; cherish ‹*hope, wish, desire*›; harbour ‹*grudge, suspicion*›

Hehl *der od. das:* **kein[en]** ~ **aus etw. machen** make no secret of sth.

Hehler *der;* ~**s,** ~: receiver [of stolen goods]

Hehlerei *die;* ~, ~**en** (Rechtsw.) receiving [stolen goods] *no art.*

Hehlerin *die;* ~, ~**nen** ▶ HEHLER

Heide[1] *der;* ~**n,** ~**n** heathen

Heide[2] *die;* ~, ~**n** heath; (Landschaft) heathland

Heide-: ~**kraut** *das* heather; ~**land** *das* moorland; heathland

Heidel·beere *die* bilberry

Heidin *die;* ~, ~**nen** heathen

heidnisch *Adj.* heathen

heikel *Adj.* **(a)** (schwierig) delicate, ticklish ‹*matter, subject*›; ticklish tricky ‹*problem, question, situation*›
(b) (wählerisch) fussy (**in Bezug auf** + *Akk.* about)

heil *Adj.* (nicht entzwei) in one piece; **wieder** ~ **sein** ‹*injured part*› have healed [up]

Heil *das;* ~**s (a)** (Wohlergehen) benefit
(b) (Rel.) salvation

Heiland *der;* ~**[e]s,** ~**e** Saviour

Heil·anstalt *die* (Anstalt für Kranke od. Süchtige) sanatorium; (psychiatrische Klinik) mental hospital

heilbar *Adj.* curable

Heil·butt *der* halibut

heilen 1 *tr. V.* cure; heal ‹*wound*›
2 *itr. V.; mit sein* ‹*wound*› heal [up]; ‹*fracture*› mend

heil·froh *Adj.* very glad

heilig *Adj.* **(a)** holy; **die Heiligen Drei Könige** the Three Kings *or* Wise Men; the Magi; **die Heilige Schrift** the Holy Scriptures *pl.;* **der Heilige Abend** Christmas Eve
(b) (geh.: unantastbar) sacred ‹*right, tradition, cause, etc.*›

Heilig·abend *der* Christmas Eve

Heilige *der/die; adj. Dekl.* saint

heiligen *tr. V.* keep ‹*tradition, Sabbath, etc.*›; **der Zweck heiligt die Mittel** the end justifies the means

Heiligen·schein *der* gloriole; (um den Kopf) halo

Heiligkeit *die;* ~: holiness

Heiligtum *das;* ~**s, Heiligtümer** shrine

Heil-: ~**kraut** *das* medicinal herb; ~**mittel** *das* (auch fig.) remedy (**gegen** for); (Medikament) medicament; ~**praktiker** *der,* ~**praktikerin** *die* non-medical practitioner

heilsam *Adj.* salutary

Heils·armee *die* Salvation Army

Heilung *die;* ~, ~**en** (einer Wunde) healing; (von Krankheit, Kranken) curing

Heim *das;* ~**[e]s,** ~**e (a)** (Zuhause) home
(b) (Anstalt, Alters~) home; (für Obdachlose) hostel

Heim·arbeit *die* outwork

Heimat *die;* ~, ~**en (a)** (Ort) home; home town/village; (Land) home; homeland
(b) (Ursprungsland) natural habitat

Heimat-: ~**kunde** *die* local history, geography, and natural history; ~**land** *das* native land; (fig.) home

heimatlich *Adj.* native ‹*dialect*›; nostalgic ‹*emotions*›

heimat-, Heimat-: ~**los** *Adj.* homeless; ~**museum** *das* museum of local history; ~**ort** *der* home town/village; ~**stadt** *die* home town; ~**vertriebene** *der/die; adj. Dekl.* expellee [from his/her homeland]

heim-, Heim-: ~**|bringen** *unr. tr. V.* **(a) jmdn.** ~: take *or.* see sb. home; **(b)** bring home; ~**computer** *der* home computer; ~**|fahren** 1 *unr. itr. V.; mit sein* drive home; 2 *unr. tr. V.* drive home; ~**fahrt** *die* journey home; (mit dem Auto) drive home; ~**|gehen** *unr. itr. V.; mit sein* go home

heimisch *Adj.* (einheimisch) indigenous,

*alte Schreibung - vgl. Hinweis auf S. xiv

native ‹*plants, animals, etc.*› (**in** + *Dat.* to); domestic ‹*industry*›; **sich ~ fühlen** feel at home; **~ werden** [**in** (+ *Dat.*)] settle in[to]

heim-, Heim-: ~kehr *die; ~~*: return home; homecoming; **~|kehren** *itr. V.; mit sein* return home (**aus** from); **~|kommen** *unr. itr. V.; mit sein* come home

heimlich [1] *Adj.* secret [2] *adv.* secretly

Heimlichkeit *die; ~*, **~en** secret

heim-, Heim-: ~reise *die* journey home; **~spiel** *das* (Sport) home match *or* game; **~|suchen** *tr. V.* ‹*storm, earthquake, epidemic*› strike; ‹*disease*› afflict; ‹*nightmares, doubts*› plague; **~suchung** *die; ~~*, **~~en** affliction; visitation; **~tuckisch** [1] *Adj.* (bösartig) malicious, (fig.) insidious ‹*disease*›; [2] *adv.* maliciously; **~wärts** *Adv.* (nach Hause zu) home; (in Richtung Heimat) homeward[s]; **~weg** *der* way home; **~weh** *das* homesickness; **~weh haben** be homesick (**nach** for); **~|zahlen** *tr. V.* **jmdm. etw. ~zahlen** pay sb. back for sth.

Heinzel·männchen *das* brownie

Heirat *die; ~*, **~en** marriage

heiraten [1] *itr. V.* get married [2] *tr. V.* marry

Heirats-: ~antrag *der*: **jmdm. einen ~antrag machen** propose to sb.; **~anzeige** *die* announcement of a/the forthcoming marriage; **~schwindler** *der*, **~schwindlerin** *die*: *person who makes a spurious offer of marriage for purposes of fraud*

heiser [1] *Adj.* hoarse [2] *adv.* in a hoarse voice

Heiserkeit *die; ~*: hoarseness

heiß [1] *Adj.* hot; **jmdm. ist ~**: sb. feels hot; **etw. ~ machen** heat sth. up; heated ‹*debate, argument*›; fierce ‹*fight, battle*›; ardent ‹*wish, love*›; **ein ~es Thema** a controversial subject [2] *adv.* ‹*fight*› fiercely; ‹*love*› dearly; ‹*long*› fervently

heißen *unr. itr. V.* (den Namen tragen) be called; (bedeuten) mean; (lauten) ‹*saying*› go; (*unpers.*) **es heißt, dass ...**: they say that ...; **in dem Artikel heißt es ...**: in the article it says that ...

Heiß·luft *die* hot air

Heißluft·backofen *der* fan oven

heiter *Adj.* cheerful, happy ‹*person, nature*›; happy, merry ‹*laughter*›; fine ‹*weather, day*›

Heiterkeit *die; ~* **(a)** (Frohsinn) cheerfulness
(b) (Belustigung) merriment

heizbar *Adj.* heated

Heiz·decke *die* electric blanket

heizen [1] *itr. V.* have the heating on [2] *tr. V.* heat ‹*room etc.*›

Heizer *der; ~s, ~*, **Heizerin** *die; ~*, **~nen** stoker

Heiz-: ~kissen *das* heating pad; **~körper** *der* radiator; **~ofen** *der* stove; heater; **~platte** *die* hotplate

Heizung *die; ~*, **~en** **(a)** [central] heating *no pl., no indef. art.*;
(b) (ugs.: Heizkörper) radiator

Hektar *das od.* **der; ~s, ~e** hectare

Hektik *die; ~*: hectic rush; (des Lebens) hectic pace

hektisch *Adj.* hectic

Held *der; ~en, ~en* hero

heldenhaft [1] *Adj.* heroic [2] *adv.* heroically

Heldentum *das; ~s* heroism

Heldin *die; ~*, **~nen** heroine

helfen *unr. itr. V.* help; **jmdm.** [**bei etw.**] **~**: help sb. [with sth.]; (*unpers.*) **es hilft nichts** it's no use *or* good

Helfer *der; ~s, ~*, **Helferin** *die; ~*, **~nen** helper; (Mitarbeiter[in]) assistant; (eines Verbrechens) accomplice

Helikopter *der; ~s, ~*: helicopter

hell [1] *Adj.* **(a)** (von Licht erfüllt) light; well-lit ‹*stairs*›
(b) (klar) bright ‹*day, sky, etc.*›
(c) (viel Licht spendend) bright ‹*light, lamp, star, etc.*›
(d) (blass) light ‹*colour*›; fair ‹*skin, hair*›; light-coloured ‹*clothes*›
(e) (akustisch) high, clear ‹*sound, voice*›; ringing ‹*laugh*›
(f) (klug) bright
(g) (ugs.: absolut) sheer, utter ‹*madness, foolishness, despair*›
[2] *adv.* brightly

hell-: ~blau *Adj.* light blue; **~blond** *Adj.* very fair; light blonde

Helle *das; adj. Dekl.* ≈ lager

Heller *der; ~s, ~*: heller; **bis auf den letzten ~/bis auf ~ und Pfennig** (ugs.) down to the last penny *or* (Amer.) cent

hell-: ~grün *Adj.* light green; **~häutig** *Adj.* fair-skinned

Helligkeit *die; ~*, **~en** (auch Physik) brightness

hell-, Hell-: ~rot *Adj.* light red; **~sehen** *unr. itr. V.; nur im Inf.* **~sehen können** have second sight; **~seher** *der*, **~seherin** *die* clairvoyant; **~wach** *Adj.* wide awake

Helm *der; ~[e]s, ~e* helmet

Hemd *das; ~[e]s, ~en* shirt; (Unterhemd) [under]vest; undershirt

Hemds·ärmel *der* shirtsleeve

hemmen *tr. V.* **(a)** (verlangsamen) slow [down]
(b) (aufhalten) check; stem ‹*flow*›
(c) (beeinträchtigen) hinder

Hemmung *die; ~*, **~en** **(a)** (Gehemmtheit) inhibition
(b) (Bedenken) scruple

hemmungs·los [1] *Adj.* unrestrained [2] *adv.* unrestrainedly
Hendl *das;* **~s, ~[n]** (bayr., österr.) chicken; (Brathähnchen) [roast] chicken
Hengst *der;* **~[e]s, ~e** (Pferd) stallion
Henkel *der;* **~s, ~:** handle
Henker *der;* **~s, ~:** hangman; (Scharfrichter, auch fig.) executioner
Henne *die;* **~, ~n** hen
her /heːɐ̯/ *Adv.* **~ damit** give it to me; give it here (coll.); **vom Fenster ~:** from the window; **wo ist er ~?** where is he from?; **von ihrer Kindheit ~:** since childhood; **von der Konzeption ~:** as far as the basic design is concerned; **hinter jmdm.** (ugs.)/**etw. ~ sein** be after sb./sth.; **einen Monat/lange ~ sein** be a month/a long time ago; **es ist lange ~, dass wir...:** it is a long time since we...
herab *Adv.* down; **von oben ~** (fig.) condescendingly
herab-: ~|hängen *unr. itr. V.* hang [down] (**von** from); **~hängende Schultern** drooping shoulders; **~|lassen** [1] *unr. tr. V.* let down; lower; [2] *unr. refl. V.* (iron.: bereit sein) **sich ~lassen, etw. zu tun** condescend to do sth.; **~lassend** [1] *Adj.* condescending; patronizing (**zu** towards); [2] *adv.* condescendingly; patronizingly; **~|sehen** *unr. itr. V.* **auf jmdn. ~sehen** look down on sb.; **~|setzen** *tr. V.* **(a)** reduce; **(b)** (abwerten) belittle
heran *Adv.* **an etw.** (*Akk.*) **~:** right up to sth.
heran-, Heran-: ~|bilden *tr. V.* train [up]; (auf der Schule, Universität) educate; **~|bringen** *unr. tr. V.* **(a)** bring [up] (**an** + *Akk.*, **zu** to); **(b)** (vertraut machen) **jmdn. an etw.** (*Akk.*) **~bringen** introduce sb. to sth.; **~|fahren** *unr. itr. V.; mit sein* drive up (**an** + *Akk.* to); **~|kommen** *unr. itr. V.; mit sein* **an etw.** (*Akk.*) **~kommen** come near to sth.; (erreichen) reach sth.; (erwerben) obtain sth.; **~|reifen** *itr. V.; mit sein* ‹*fruit, crops*› ripen; **zur Frau ~reifen** mature into a woman; **~|treten** *unr. itr. V.; mit sein* (sich wenden) **an jmdn. ~treten** approach sb.; **~|wachsen** *unr. itr. V.; mit sein* grow up; **~wachsende** *der/die; adj. Dekl.* young person; **~|ziehen** *unr. tr. V.* pull over; pull up ‹*chair*›; **etw. zu sich ~ziehen** pull sth. towards one
herauf *Adv.* up
herauf-: ~|beschwören *tr. V.* **(a)** (verursachen) cause ‹*disaster, war, crisis*›; **(b)** (erinnern) evoke ‹*memories etc.*›; **~|kommen** *unr. itr. V.; mit sein* (nach oben kommen) come up; **~|setzen** *tr. V.* increase, put up ‹*prices, rents, interest rates, etc.*›
heraus *Adv.* **~ aus den Federn!/dem Bett!** rise and shine!/out of bed!
heraus-, Heraus-: ~|bekommen *unr. tr. V.* **(a)** (entfernen) get out (**aus** of); **(b)** (ugs.: lösen) work out ‹*problem, answer, etc.*›; solve ‹*puzzle*›; **(c)** (ermitteln) find out; **(d)** (als Wechselgeld bekommen) **5 Euro ~bekommen** get back 5 euros change; **ich bekomme noch 5 Euro ~:** I still have 5 euros [change] to come; **~|bringen** *unr. tr. V.* **(a)** (nach außen bringen) bring out (**aus** of); **(b)** (nach draußen begleiten) show out; **(c)** (veröffentlichen) bring out; (aufführen) put on, stage ‹*play*›; screen ‹*film*›; **(d)** (auf den Markt bringen) bring out; **(e)** (populär machen) make widely known; **~|fahren** [1] *unr. itr. V.; mit sein* **(a)** (nach außen fahren) **aus etw. ~fahren** drive/ride out of sth.; **(b)** (fahrend herauskommen) come out; [2] *unr. tr. V.* **den Wagen [aus dem Hof] ~fahren** drive the car out [of the yard]; **jmdn. ~fahren** drive sb. out (**zu** to); **~|finden** [1] *unr. tr. V.* find out; trace ‹*fault*›; [2] *unr. itr. V.* find one's way out (**aus** of); **~|fordern** [1] *tr. V.* **(a)** (auch Sport) challenge; **(b)** (heraufbeschwören) provoke ‹*person, resistance, etc.*›; invite ‹*criticism*›; court ‹*danger*›; [2] *itr. V.* **zu etw. ~fordern** provoke sth.; **~forderung** *die* (auch Sport) challenge; (Provokation) provocation; **~|geben** [1] *unr. tr. V.* **(a)** (aushändigen) hand over ‹*property, person, hostage, etc.*›; (zurückgeben) give back; **(b)** (als Wechselgeld zurückgeben) **5 Euro/zu viel ~geben** give 5 euros/too much change; **(c)** (veröffentlichen) publish; **(d)** issue ‹*stamp, coin, etc.*›; [2] *unr. itr. V.* give change; **~geber** *der;* **~~s, ~~, ~geberin** *die;* **~~, ~~nen** publisher; (Redakteur[in]) editor; **~|gehen** *unr. itr. V.; mit sein* **(a)** go out (**aus** of); **(b)** (sich entfernen lassen) ‹*stain etc.*› come out; **~|halten** *unr. refl. V.* keep out; **~|hängen** *tr. V.* hang out (**aus** of); **~|helfen** *unr. itr. V.* **jmdm. ~helfen** (auch fig.) help sb. out (**aus** of); **~|holen** *tr. V.* **(a)** (nach außen holen) bring out; **(b)** (ugs.: erwirken) win ‹*wage increase, advantage, etc.*›; **~|kommen** *unr. itr. V.; mit sein* **(a)** come out (**aus** of); **(b)** (erscheinen; ugs.: auf den Markt kommen, bekannt werden) come out; **~|nehmen** *unr. tr. V.* **(a)** take out (**aus** of); **(b)** (ugs.: entfernen) take out ‹*appendix, tonsils, tooth, etc.*›; **~|reden** *refl. V.* (ugs.) talk one's way out (**aus** of); **~|reißen** *unr. tr. V.* **(a)** tear out (**aus** of); pull up ‹*plant*›; **(b)** (aus der Umgebung, der Arbeit) tear away (**aus** from); **die Krankheit hat ihn aus der Arbeit ~gerissen** the illness has interrupted his work; **(c)** (Mängel ausgleichen) **den zunächst etwas langweiligen Abend ~reißen** rescue what had been rather a boring evening; **die Eins im Aufsatz reißt die Drei im Diktat heraus** the A for the essay makes up for the C in the dictation; **~|rutschen** *itr. V.; mit sein* (ugs.) ‹*remark etc.*› slip out; **~|stellen** *refl. V.* **es stellte sich ~, dass ...:** it turned out that ...; **~|suchen** *tr. V.* pick out; look out ‹*file*›
herb *Adj.* [slightly] sharp ‹*taste*›; dry ‹*wine*›; [slightly] sharp ‹*smell, perfume*›; bitter ‹*disappointment*›; severe ‹*face, features*›; austere ‹*beauty*›; harsh ‹*words, criticism*›

*old spelling - see note on page xiv

herbei-: ~|eilen *itr. V.; mit sein* hurry over; **~|laufen** *unr. itr. V.; mit sein* come running up

Herberge *die;* **~, ~n** (veralt.: Gasthaus) inn

Herbergs-: ~mutter *die; Pl.* **~mütter, ~vater** *der* warden [of the/a youth hostel]

her|bringen *unr. tr. V.* **etw. ~:** bring sth. [here]

Herbst *der;* **~[e]s, ~e** autumn; fall (Amer.); *s. auch* FRÜHLING

Herbst·anfang *der* beginning of autumn

herbstlich *Adj.* autumn *attrib.; autumnal*

Herd *der;* **~[e]s, ~e** cooker; (fig.) centre (*of disturbance/rebellion*)

Herde *die;* **~, ~n** herd

Herd·platte *die* hot-plate

herein-: ~|bitten *unr. tr. V.* **jmdn. ~ bitten** ask *or* invite sb. in; **~|brechen** *unr. itr. V.; mit sein* (geh.) ‹*night, evening, dusk*› fall; ‹*winter*› set in; ‹*storm*› strike, break; **~|bringen** *unr. tr. V.* bring in; **~|fallen** *unr. itr. V.; mit sein* (ugs.) be taken for a ride (coll.); be done (coll.); **~|kommen** *unr. itr. V.; mit sein* come in; **~|lassen** *unr. tr. V.* let in; **~|legen** *tr. V.* (ugs.) **jmdn. ~legen** take sb. for a ride (coll.) **(mit, bei** with); **~|platzen** *itr. V.; mit sein* (ugs.) burst in; **~|schneien** *unr. itr. V.; mit sein* (ugs.) turn up out of the blue (coll.)

her-, Her-: ~fahrt *die* journey here; **~|fallen** *unr. itr. V.; mit sein* **über jmdn. ~fallen** attack sb.; (gierig zu essen beginnen) **über etw.** (*Akk.*) **~fallen** fall upon sth.; **~gang** *der:* **der ~gang der Ereignisse** the sequence of events; **~|geben** *unr. tr. V.* hand over; (weggeben) give away; **~|gehen** *unr. itr. V.; mit sein* **neben/vor/hinter jmdm. ~gehen** walk along beside/in front of/ behind sb.; **~|haben** *unr. tr. V.* (ugs.) **wo hat er/sie das ~?** where did he/she get that from?; **~|halten** *unr. itr. V.* **~halten müssen [für jmdn./etw.]** be the one to suffer [for sb./sth.]; **~|hören** *itr. V.* listen

Hering *der;* **~s, ~e (a)** herring **(b)** (Zeltpflock) peg

her-: ~|kommen *unr. itr. V.; mit sein* come here; **~kömmlich** *Adj.* conventional; traditional ‹*custom*›

Herkunft *die;* **~, Herkünfte** origin

Herkunfts·land *das* country of origin

her-: ~|laufen *unr. itr. V.; mit sein* **vor/ hinter/neben jmdm. ~laufen** run [along] in front of/behind/alongside sb.; (nachlaufen) **hinter jmdm. ~laufen** run after sb.; (fig.) chase sb. up; **~|leiten** *tr., refl. V.* derive **(aus, von** from); **~|machen** (ugs.) *refl. V.* **sich über etw.** (*Akk.*) **~machen** get stuck into sth. (coll.)

Hermelin *der;* **~s, ~e** (Pelz) ermine

hermetisch [1] *Adj.* hermetic [2] *adv.* hermetically

Heroin *das;* **~s** heroin

Heroin·sucht *die* heroin addiction

heroin·süchtig *Adj.* addicted to heroin *postpos.*

Herr *der;* **~n, ~en (a)** (Mann) gentleman **(b)** (Titel, Anrede) **~ Schulze** Mr Schulze; **Sehr geehrter ~ Schulze!** Dear Sir; (bei persönlicher Bekanntschaft) Dear Mr Schulze; **meine ~en** gentlemen **(c)** (Gebieter) master

herren-, Herren-: ~ausstatter *der* [gentle]men's outfitter; **~los** *Adj.* abandoned ‹*car, luggage*›; stray ‹*dog, cat*›; **~salon** *der* men's hairdressing salon; **~schuh** *der* man's shoe; **~schuhe** men's shoes; **~toilette** *die* [gentle]men's toilet

Herr·gott *der;* **~s: der [liebe]/unser ~:** the Lord [God]; God

Herrgotts·frühe *die* **in aller ~:** at the crack of dawn

her|richten *tr. V.* (bereitmachen) get ‹*room, refreshments, etc.*› ready; arrange ‹*table*›; (in Ordnung bringen) renovate

Herrin *die;* **~, ~en** mistress

herrisch [1] *Adj.* overbearing; imperious [2] *adv.* imperiously

herrlich [1] *Adj.* marvellous; magnificent ‹*view, clothes*› [2] *adv.* marvellously

Herrlichkeit *die;* **~, ~en (a)** (Schönheit) magnificence; splendour **(b)** (herrliche Sache) marvellous thing

Herrschaft *die;* **~, ~en (a)** rule; (Macht) power **(b)** *Pl.* (Damen u. Herren) ladies and gentlemen

herrschen *itr. V.* rule; ‹*monarch*› reign, rule; **draußen ~ 30° Kälte** it's 30° below outside

Herrscher *der;* **~s, ~, Herrscherin** *die;* **~, ~nen** ruler

herrsch-, Herrsch-: ~sucht *die* thirst for power; (herrisches Wesen) domineering nature; **~süchtig** *Adj.* domineering

her-: ~|rühren *itr. V.* **von jmdm./etw. ~rühren** come from sb./stem from sth.; ***~|sein** ▸ HER; **~|stellen** *tr. V.* produce; manufacture; make

Hersteller *der;* **~s, ~, Herstellerin** *die;* **~, ~nen** producer

Her·stellung *die* production; manufacture

herüber *Adv.* over

herum *Adv.* **um ... ~** (Richtung) round; (Anordnung) around; **um Weihnachten ~:** around Christmas; **~ sein** (ugs.: vergangen sein, vorüber sein) have passed

herum-: ~|ärgern *refl. V.* (ugs.) **sich mit jmdm./etw. ~ärgern** keep getting annoyed with sb./sth.; **~|drehen** [1] *tr. V.* (ugs.) turn ‹*key*›; turn over ‹*coin, mattress, hand, etc.*› [2] *refl. V.* turn [a]round; **~|fahren** (ugs.) [1] *unr. itr. V.; mit sein* (sich plötzlich herumdrehen) spin round; [2] *unr. tr. V.* **jmdn. [in der Stadt] ~fahren** drive sb. around the town; **~|führen** [1] *tr. V.* **jmdn. [in der Stadt] ~führen** show sb. around the town; ⋯

2 *itr. V.* **um etw. ~führen** ‹*road etc.*› go round sth.; **~|gehen** *unr. itr. V.; mit sein* (vergehen) pass; **um etw. ~gehen** go round sth.; **etw. ~gehen lassen** circulate sth.; pass; **~|kommandieren** (ugs.) 1 *tr. V.* **jmdn. ~kommandieren** boss (coll.) *or* order sb. around *or* about; 2 *itr. V.* boss (coll.) *or* order people around *or* about; **~|kommen** *unr. itr. V.; mit sein* (ugs.) **(a)** (vermeiden können) **um etw. [nicht] ~kommen** [not] be able to get out of sth.; **(b)** (viel reisen) get around *or* about; **in der Welt ~kommen** see a lot of the world; **~|laufen** *unr. itr. V.; mit sein* **(a)** walk/(schneller) run around *or* about; **um etw. ~laufen** go round sth.; **(b)** (gekleidet sein) **wie ein Hippie ~laufen** go about looking like a hippie; **~|lungern** *itr. V.* (salopp) loaf around; **~|schlagen** *unr. refl. V.* (ugs.) **sich mit Problemen/Einwänden ~schlagen** grapple with problems/battle against objections; ***~|sein** ▶ HERUM; **~|sitzen** *unr. itr. V.* (ugs.) sit around *or* about; **~|sprechen** *unr. refl. V.* get around *or* about; **~|stöbern** *itr. V.* (ugs.) keep rummaging around *or* about (**in** + *Dat.* in); **~|treiben** *unr. refl. V.* (ugs. abwertend) **sich auf den Straßen/in Discos ~treiben** hang around the streets/in discos; **sich in der Welt ~treiben** roam about the world

herunter *Adv.* **(a)** (nach unten) down; **[körperlich] ~ sein** be in poor health **(b)** (fort) off; **~ vom Sofa!** [get] off the sofa!

herunter-: ~|bringen *unr. tr. V.* bring down; **~|fallen** *unr. itr. V.; mit sein* fall down; **vom Tisch/Stuhl ~fallen** fall off the table/chair; **~|gehen** *unr. itr. V.; mit sein* **(a)** come down; **(b)** (niedriger werden) ‹*temperature*› drop; ‹*prices*› come down, fall; **~gekommen** 1 *2. Part. v.* ~KOMMEN; 2 *Adj.* poor ‹*health*›; dilapidated ‹*building*›; run-down ‹*area*›; down and out ‹*person*›; **~|handeln** *tr. V.* (ugs.) **einen Preis ~handeln** beat down a price; **~|hängen** *unr. itr. V.* hang down; **~|hauen** *unr. tr. V.* (ugs.) **jmdm. eine ~hauen** give sb. a clout round the ear (coll.); **~|kommen** *unr. itr. V.; mit sein* **(a)** come down; **(b)** (ugs.: verfallen) go to the dogs (coll.); **~|lassen** *unr. tr. V.* lower; **~|schlucken** *tr. V.* swallow; ***~|sein** ▶ HERUNTER A; **~|spielen** *tr. V.* (ugs.) play down

hervor *Adv.* **aus … ~:** out of

hervor-: ~|heben *unr. tr. V.* stress; **~ragend** 1 *Adj.* outstanding[ly good]; 2 *adv.* **~ragend geschult** outstandingly well trained; **~ragend spielen/arbeiten** play/work outstandingly well; **~|tun** *unr. refl. V.* distinguish oneself; (wichtig tun) show off

Herz *das;* **~ens, ~en** heart; (Kartenspiel) hearts *pl.;* **von ~en kommen** come from the heart; **ein ~ für die Armen haben** feel for the poor; **ein ~ für Kinder haben** have a love of children; **schweren ~ens** with a heavy heart; **etw. auf dem ~en haben** have sth. on one's mind; **es nicht übers ~ bringen, etw. zu tun** not have the heart to do sth.; **sich** (*Dat.*) **etw. zu ~en nehmen** take sth. to heart

Herz-: ~an·fall *der* heart attack; **~beschwerden** *Pl.* heart trouble *sing.*

herzens-, Herzens-: ~gut /'--'-/ *Adj.* kind-hearted; **~lust** *die:* **nach ~lust** to one's heart's content

herzhaft 1 *Adj.* hearty; (nahrhaft) hearty ‹*meal*›; (von kräftigem Geschmack) tasty 2 *adv.* heartily; (nahrhaft) **er isst gern ~:** he likes to have a hearty meal

her|ziehen *unr. itr. V.; mit sein od. haben* (ugs.) **über jmdn./etw. ~:** run sb./sth. down

herzig 1 *Adj.* sweet; delightful 2 *adv.* sweetly; delightfully

herz-, Herz-: ~infarkt *der* heart attack; **~klappen·fehler** *der* (Med.) valvular defect *or* insufficiency; **~klopfen** *das;* **~~s: jmd. hat ~klopfen** sb.'s heart is pounding; **~krank** *Adj.* ‹*person*› with a heart condition; **~kranz·gefäß** *das* coronary vessel

herzlich 1 *Adj.* warm ‹*smile, reception*›; kind ‹*words, regards*›; (ehrlich gemeint) sincere; **~en Dank** many thanks 2 *adv.* warmly; (ehrlich gemeint) sincerely; ‹*congratulate*› heartily; **~ wenig** very *or* (coll.) precious little

Herzlichkeit *die;* **~:** warmth; kindness; (Aufrichtigkeit) sincerity

herz·los 1 *Adj.* heartless 2 *adv.* heartlessly

Herzog *der;* **~s, Herzöge** duke

Herzogin *die;* **~, ~nen** duchess

Herz·rhythmus·störung *die* (Med.) disturbance of the heart *or* cardiac rhythm

herz-, Herz-: ~schlag *der* heartbeat; (Herzversagen) heart failure; **~schmerz** *der* pain in the region of the heart; **~schrittmacher** *der* (Anat., Med.) [cardiac] pacemaker; **~transplantation** *die* (Med.) heart transplantation; **~zerreißend** 1 *Adj.* heart-rending; 2 *adv.* heart-rendingly

Hessen (*das*)*;* **~s** Hesse

hetero·sexuell *Adj.* heterosexual

Hetze *die;* **~ (a)** [mad] rush **(b)** (abwertend) smear campaign

hetzen 1 *tr. V.* **(a)** hunt **(b)** (antreiben) rush 2 *itr. V.* **(a)** (in großer Eile sein) rush **(b)** *mit sein* (hasten) rush; (rennen) dash; race

Hetz-: ~kampagne *die* (abwertend) smear campaign; (gegen eine Minderheit) hate campaign; **~rede** *die* (abwertend) inflammatory speech

Heu *das;* **~[e]s** hay

Heuchelei *die;* **~:** hypocrisy

heucheln 1 *itr. V.* be a hypocrite 2 *tr. V.* feign

*alte Schreibung - vgl. Hinweis auf S. xiv

Heuchler *der;* **~s, ~, Heuchlerin** *die;* **~, ~nen** hypocrite
heuchlerisch [1] *Adj.* hypocritical [2] *adv.* hypocritically
heuer *Adv.* (südd., österr., schweiz.) this year
Heuer *die;* **~, ~n** (Seemannsspr.) pay; wages *pl.*
Heu·ernte *die* **(a)** hay harvest **(b)** (Ertrag) hay crop
heulen *itr. V.* **(a)** howl; ‹*siren etc.*› wail **(b)** (ugs.: weinen) howl; bawl
Heurige *der; adj. Dekl.* (bes. österr.) **(a)** (Wein) new wine **(b)** (Weinlokal) inn with new wine on tap
Heu-: ~schnupfen *der* hay fever; **~schrecke** *die* grasshopper
heute *Adv.* today; **~ früh** early this morning; **~ Morgen/Abend** this morning/ evening; **~ Mittag** [at] midday today; **~ Nacht** tonight; (letzte Nacht) last night; **~ in einer Woche** a week [from] today; today week; **~ vor einer Woche** a week ago today
heutig *Adj.* **(a)** (von diesem Tag) today's; **der ~e Tag** today **(b)** (gegenwärtig) today's; of today *postpos.;* **in der ~en Zeit** nowadays
heut·zu·tage *Adv.* nowadays
Hexe *die;* **~, ~n** witch
hexen *itr. V.* work magic
Hexen·schuss, *Hexen·schuß *der* lumbago *no indef. art.*
Hexerei *die;* **~, ~en** witchcraft; (von Kunststücken usw.) magic
Hickhack *das od. der;* **~s, ~s** (ugs.) squabbling; bickering
hieb *1. u. 3. Pers. Sg. Prät. v.* HAUEN
Hieb *der;* **~[e]s, ~e (a)** (Schlag) blow; (mit der Peitsche) lash **(b)** *Pl.* (ugs.: Prügel) hiding *sing.*
hieb·fest *Adj.:* **hieb- und stichfest** watertight; cast-iron
hielt *1. u. 3. Pers. Sg. Prät. v.* HALTEN
hier *Adv.* **(a)** here; **[von] ~ oben/unten** [from] up/down here **(b)** (jetzt) now; **von ~ an** from now on
hieran *Adv.* here; **sich ~ festhalten** hold on to this; (fig.) **im Anschluss ~:** immediately after this
Hierarchie /hierar'çi:/ *die;* **~, ~n** hierarchy
hierauf *Adv.* **(a)** on here; (darauf) on this; **wir werden ~ zurückkommen** we'll come back to this **(b)** (danach) after that; then **(c)** (infolgedessen) whereupon
hieraus *Adv.* out of here; (aus dieser Tatsache, Quelle) from this
hier-: ~|behalten *unr. tr. V.* **jmdn./etw. ~behalten** keep sb./sth. here; **~bei** *Adv.* **(a)** (bei dieser Gelegenheit) **Diese Übung ist sehr schwierig. Man kann sich ~bei leicht verletzen.** This exercise is very difficult. You can easily injure yourself doing it; **(b)** (bei der erwähnten Sache) here; **~|bleiben** *unr. itr. V.; mit sein* stay here; **~durch** *Adv.* through here; (aufgrund dieser Sache) because of this; **~für** *Adv.* for this
hier·her *Adv.* here; **ich gehe bis ~ und nicht weiter** I'm going this far and no further; **~gehören** belong here; (hierfür wichtig sein) be relevant [here]; **~kommen** *mit sein* come here
hier·hin *Adv.* here; **bis ~:** up to here
hier-: ~in *Adv.* **(a)** (räumlich) in here; **(b)** in this; **~mit** *Adv.* with this/these; **~mit ist der Fall erledigt** that puts an end to the matter; **~nach** *Adv.* (anschließend) after that
Hieroglyphe /hiero.../ *die;* **~, ~n** hieroglyph
hier-: *~sein ▶ HIER A; **~über** *Adv.* **(a)** (über dem Erwähnten) above here; (über das Erwähnte) over here; **(b)** (das Erwähnte betreffend) about this/these; **~von** *Adv.* of this/these; **~zu** *Adv.* with this; (hinsichtlich dieser Sache) about this; **~zu gehört/gehören ...:** this includes/these include; **~zu reicht mein Geld nicht** I haven't got enough money for that; **~zu·lande** *Adv.* [here] in this country
hiesig *Adj.* local
hieß *1. u. 3. Pers. Sg. Prät. v.* HEISSEN
Hi-Fi-Anlage /'hai:fi-/ *die* hi-fi system
high /haɪ/ *Adj.* (ugs.) high (coll.)
Hightech-, High-Tech- /'hai'tɛk-/ high-tech
Hilfe *die;* **~, ~n (a)** help; (für Notleidende) aid; relief; **zu ~!** help! **(b)** (Hilfskraft) help; (im Geschäft) assistant
Hilfe-: ~leistung *die* help; **~ruf** *der* cry for help; **~stellung** *die* (Turnen) **jmdm. ~stellung geben** act as spotter for sb.
hilflos [1] *Adj.* helpless [2] *adv.* helplessly
Hilflosigkeit *die;* **~** helplessness
hilfs-, Hilfs-: ~bedürftig *Adj.* **(a)** (schwach) in need of help *postpos.;* **(b)** (notleidend) in need; needy; **~bereit** *Adj.* helpful; **~bereitschaft** *die* helpfulness; **~gelder** *Pl.* aid money *sing.;* **~kraft** *die* assistant; **~mittel** *das* aid; **~organisation** *die* aid *or* relief organization; **~programm** *das* aid *or* relief programme; **~verb** *das,* **~zeitwort** *das* (Sprachw.) auxiliary [verb]
Himalaja *der;* **~[s]: der/im ~:** the/in the Himalayas *pl.*
Him·beere *die* raspberry
Himmel *der;* **~s, ~** sky; (Rel.) heaven; **~ noch [ein]mal!** for Heaven's sake!
himmel-, Himmel-: ~bett *das* four-poster bed; **~blau** *Adj.* sky-blue; clear blue ‹*eyes*›; **~fahrt** *die* (Rel.) **(a) Christi/Mariä ~fahrt** the Ascension of Christ/the Assumption of the Virgin Mary; **(b)** (Festtag) **[Christi] ~:** Ascension Day *no art.*

Himmels-: ~richtung *die* point of the compass; **~schlüsselchen** *das; ~~s, ~~:* cowslip
himmel·weit *Adj.* enormous, vast ‹*difference*›
himmlisch *Adj.* (auch fig.) heavenly
hin *Adv.* **(a)** (räumlich) **zur Straße ~ liegen** face the road
(b) (zeitlich) **gegen Mittag ~:** towards midday
(c) (in Verbindungen) **nach außen ~:** outwardly; **auf meinen Rat ~:** on my advice; **auf seine Bitte ~:** at his request
(d) (in Wortpaaren) **~ und zurück** there and back; **einmal Köln ~ und zurück** a return [ticket] to Cologne; **~ und her** to and fro; back and forth; **~ und wieder** [every] now and then
(e) ~ sein (ugs.: verloren sein); be gone; (ugs.: nicht mehr brauchbar sein); have had it (coll.); ‹*car*› be a write-off; (salopp: tot sein) have snuffed it (sl.); **von jmdm./etw. ganz ~ sein** (ugs.: hingerissen sein) be mad about sb./bowled over by sth.
hinab *Adv.* ▶ HINUNTER
hinab|- ▶ HINUNTER-
hinauf *Adv.* up; **bis ~ zu** up to
hinauf-: ~|fahren *unr. itr. V.; mit sein* go up; (im Auto) drive up; (mit einem Motorrad) ride up; **~|gehen** *unr. itr. V.; mit sein* **(a)** (nach oben gehen) go up; **(b)** (nach oben führen) lead up; **(c)** (ugs.: steigen) ‹*prices, taxes, etc.*› go up; rise; **~|klettern** *itr. V.; mit sein* climb up; **~|steigen** *unr. itr. V.; mit sein* climb up; **~|ziehen** [1] *unr. tr. V.* pull up; [2] *unr. itr. V.; mit sein* move up; [3] *unr. refl. V.* (sich erstrecken) stretch up
hinaus *Adv.* **(a)** (räumlich) out
(b) (zeitlich) **auf Jahre ~:** for years to come
(c) (etw. überschreitend) **über etw.** (*Akk.*) **~:** in addition to sth.
(d) über etw. (*Akk.*) **~ sein** be past sth.
hinaus-: ~|bringen *unr. tr. V.* **jmdn./etw. ~bringen** see sb. out/take sth. out (**aus** of); **~|fahren** [1] *unr. itr. V.; mit sein* **aus etw. ~fahren** (mit dem Auto) drive out of sth.; (mit dem Zweirad) ride out of sth.; ‹*car, bus*› go out of sth.; ‹*train*› pull out of sth.; **zum Flugplatz ~fahren** drive out to the airport; [2] *unr. tr. V.* **jmdn./etw. ~fahren** drive sb./take sth. out; **~|fallen** *unr. itr. V.; mit sein* fall out (**aus** of); **~|finden** *unr. itr. V.* find one's way out (**aus** of); **~|gehen** *unr. itr. V.; mit sein* **(a)** go out (**aus** of); **(b)** (gerichtet sein) **das Zimmer geht zum Garten/nach Westen ~:** the room looks out on to the garden/faces west; **~|kommen** *unr. itr. V.; mit sein* come out (**aus** of); **~|laufen** *unr. itr. V.; mit sein* **(a)** run out (**aus** of); **(b)** (als Ergebnis haben) **auf etw.** (*Akk.*) **~laufen** lead to sth.; **~|sehen** *unr. itr. V.* look out; **zum Fenster ~sehen** look out of the window; ***~|sein** ▶ HINAUS D; **~|tragen** *unr. tr. V.* **jmdn./etw. ~tragen** carry sb./sth. out; **~|werfen** *unr. tr. V.* (auch ugs. fig.) throw out (**aus** of); **~|ziehen** [1] *unr. tr. V.* **(a)** (nach draußen ziehen) **jmdn./etw. ~ziehen** pull sb./sth. out (**aus** of); tow ‹*ship*› out; **(b)** (verzögern) put off; delay; [2] *unr. refl. V.* be delayed; **~|zögern** [1] *tr. V.* delay; [2] *refl. V.* be delayed
hin-, Hin-: ~blick *der:* **im** *od.* **in ~blick auf etw.** (*Akk.*) (wegen) in view of; (hinsichtlich) with regard to; **~|bringen** *unr. tr. V.* **jmdn./etw. ~bringen** take sb./sth. [there]; **~|denken** *unr. itr. V.* **wo denkst du hin?** (ugs.) whatever are you thinking of?
hinderlich *Adj.* **~ sein** get in the way
hindern *tr. V.* **(a)** (abhalten) **jmdn. ~:** stop sb. (**an** + *Dat.* from)
(b) (behindern) hinder
Hindernis *das; ~ses, ~se* obstacle
hin|deuten *itr. V.* **(a) auf jmdn./etw.** *od.* **zu jmdm./etw. ~:** point to sb./sth.
(b) auf etw. (*Akk.*) **~** (fig.) point to sth.
Hindu *der; ~[s], ~[s]* Hindu
Hinduismus *der; ~* Hinduism *no art.*
hin·durch *Adv.* **(a)** (räumlich) **durch den Wald ~:** through the wood
(b) (zeitlich) **das ganze Jahr ~:** throughout the year
hinein *Adv.* **(a)** (räumlich) in; **in etw.** (*Akk.*) **~:** into sth.
(b) (zeitlich) **bis in den Morgen/tief in die Nacht ~:** till morning/far into the night
hinein-: ~|bringen *unr. tr. V.* take in; **~|fahren** (mit dem Auto) drive in; (mit dem Zweirad) ride in; **in etw.** (*Akk.*) **~fahren** drive/ride into sth.; **~|fallen** *unr. itr. V.; mit sein* fall in; **in etw.** (*Akk.*) **~fallen** fall into sth.; **~|gehen** *unr. itr. V.; mit sein* go in; **in etw.** (*Akk.*) **~gehen** go into sth.; **~|gucken** *itr. V.* (ugs.) look in; **in etw.** (*Akk.*) **~gucken** look in[to] sth.; **~|kommen** *unr. itr. V.; mit sein* **(a)** come in; **in etw.** (*Akk.*) **~kommen** come into sth.; **(b)** (gelangen, auch fig.) get in; **in etw.** (*Akk.*) **~kommen** get into sth.; **~|reden** *itr. V.* **jmdm. in seine Angelegenheiten/Entscheidungen** *usw.* **~reden** interfere in sb.'s affairs/decisions *etc.;* **~|sehen** *unr. itr. V.* look in; **in etw.** (*Akk.*) **~sehen** look into sth.; **~|versetzen** *refl. V.* **sich in jmdn.** *od.* **jmds. Lage ~versetzen** put oneself in sb.'s position; **~|ziehen** *unr. tr. V.* **(a)** pull *or* draw in; **etw./jmdn. in etw.** (*Akk.*) **~ziehen** pull *or* draw sth./sb. into sth.;
(b) (verwickeln) **jmdn. in eine Angelegenheit/einen Streit/Skandal ~ziehen** drag sb. into an affair/a dispute/scandal
hin-, Hin-: ~|fahren [1] *unr. itr. V.; mit sein* go there; [2] *unr. tr. V.* **jmdn. ~fahren** drive sb. there; **~fahrt** *die* journey there; (Seereise) voyage out; **~|fallen** *unr. itr. V.; mit sein* **(a)** fall over; **(b) jmdm. fällt etw. ~:** sb. drops sth.; **etw. ~fallen lassen** drop sth.; **~fällig** *Adj.* **(a)** infirm; frail; **(b)** (ungültig) invalid; **~|fliegen** *unr. itr. V.; mit sein* fly there; **~flug** *der* outward flight
hing *1. u. 3. Pers. Sg. Prät. v.* HÄNGEN

*old spelling - see note on page xiv

Hin·gabe *die;* ~: devotion; (Eifer) dedication

Hingebung *die;* ~: devotion

hingebungs·voll [1] *Adj.* devoted [2] *adv.* devotedly; with devotion; ‹*listen*› with rapt attention; ‹*dance, play*› with abandon

hin·gegen *Konj., Adv.* (jedoch) however; (andererseits) on the other hand

hin-, Hin-: ~**|gehen** *unr. itr. V.; mit sein* **(a)** go [there]; **zu jmdm./etw. ~gehen** go to sb./sth.; **(b)** (verstreichen) ‹*time*› go by; ~**|halten** *unr. tr. V.* **(a)** hold out; **(b)** (warten lassen) **jmdn. ~halten** keep sb. waiting; ~**halte·taktik** *die* delaying tactics *pl.;* ~**|hören** *itr. V.* listen

hinken /ˈhɪŋkn̩/ *itr. V.* **(a)** walk with a limp
(b) *mit sein* (hinkend gehen) limp

hin-, Hin-: ~**|kommen** *unr. itr. V.; mit sein* **(a)** get there; **(b)** (an einen Ort gehören) go; belong; **(c)** (ugs.: stimmen) be right; ~**länglich** [1] *Adj.* sufficient; (angemessen) adequate; [2] *adv.* sufficiently; (angemessen) adequately; ~**|legen** [1] *tr. V.* put; (weglegen) put down; [2] *refl. V.* lie down; ~**reichend** [1] *Adj.* sufficient; (angemessen) adequate; [2] *adv.* sufficiently; (angemessen) adequately; ~**reise** *die* journey there; (mit dem Schiff) voyage out; ~**reißend** *Adj.* enchanting ‹*person, picture, view*›; captivating ‹*speaker, play*›; ~**|richten** *tr. V.* execute; ~**richtung** *die* execution

Hinrichtungs·kommando *das* firing squad

hin-, Hin-: ~**|sehen** *unr. itr. V.* look; *~**|sein** ▸ HIN E; ~**|setzen** [1] *tr. V.* put; [2] *refl. V.* sit down; ~**sicht** *die* **in gewisser ~sicht** in a way/in some respects *or* ways; **in jeder ~sicht** in every respect; **in finanzieller ~sicht** financially; ~**sichtlich** *Präp. mit Gen.* (Amtsspr.) with regard to; (in Anbetracht) in view of; ~**|stellen** [1] *tr. V.* put; put up ‹*building*›; (absetzen) put down; [2] *refl. V.* stand

hinten *Adv.* at the back; **sich ~ anstellen** join the back of the queue (Brit.) *or* (Amer.) line; **weiter ~:** further back; (in einem Buch) further on; **die Adresse steht ~ auf dem Brief** the address is on the back of the envelope; **nach ~ hinaus liegen/gehen** be at the back; **die anderen sind ganz weit ~:** the others are a long way back

hinter [1] *Präp. mit Dat.* behind; (nach) after; **3 km ~ der Grenze** 3 km beyond the frontier; **eine Prüfung ~ sich haben** (fig.) have got an examination over [and done] with; **viele Enttäuschungen/eine Krankheit ~ sich haben** have experienced many disappointments/have got over an illness [2] *Präp. mit Akk.* behind

hinter... *Adj.; nicht präd.* back

hinter-, Hinter-: ~**einander** *Adv.* **(a)** (räumlich) one behind the other; **(b)** (zeitlich) one after another *or* the other; ~**gedanke** *der* ulterior motive; ~**gehen** /--ˈ--/ *unr. tr. V.* deceive; ~**grund** *der* background; ~**grund·bericht** *der* background report; ~**gründig** [1] *Adj.* enigmatic; [2] *adv.* enigmatically; ~**grund·information** *die* item *or* piece of background information; ~**grundinformationen** [items *or* pieces of] background information *sing.;* ~**halt** *der* ambush; ~**hältig** [1] *Adj.* underhand; [2] *adv.* in an underhand manner; ~**her** *Adv.* (räumlich) behind; (nachher) afterwards; ~**hof** *der* courtyard; ~**land** *das* hinterland; (Milit.) back area; ~**lassen** /--ˈ--/ *unr. tr. V.* leave; ~**legen** /--ˈ--/ *tr. V.* deposit (**bei** with); ~**list** *die* guile; deceit; ~**listig** *Adj.* deceitful; ~**mann** *der* **(a)** person behind; **(b)** (Gewährsmann) [secret] informant

Hintern *der;* ~**s,** ~ (ugs.) backside; bottom

hinter-, Hinter-: ~**rad** *das* rear wheel; ~**sinn** *der* deeper meaning; ~**sinnig** *Adj.* ‹*remark, story, etc.*› with a deeper meaning; ~**teil** *das* backside; behind; ~**treffen** *das* (ugs.): **ins ~treffen geraten** *od.* **kommen** fall behind; ~**treiben** /--ˈ--/ *unr. tr. V.* foil ‹*plan*›; prevent ‹*marriage, promotion*›; block ‹*law, investigation, reform*›; ~**treppe** *die* back stairs *pl.;* ~**tür** *die* back door; ~**wäldler** *der;* ~~**s,** ~~ (spött.) backwoodsman; ~**wäldlerin** *die;* ~~, ~~**nen** backwoodswoman; ~**wäldlerisch** *Adj.* (spött.) backwoods *attrib.* ‹*views, attitudes, manners, etc.*›

hinüber *Adv.* over; across

Hin- und Rück·fahrt *die* journey there and back; round trip (Amer.)

hinunter *Adv.* down

hinunter-: ~**|fahren** [1] *unr. itr. V.; mit sein* go down; (mit dem Auto) drive down; (mit dem Fahrrad) ride down; [2] *unr. tr. V.* **jmdn./ein Auto/eine Ladung ~fahren** drive sb. down/drive a car down/take a load down; ~**|gehen** *unr. itr. V.; mit sein* go down; ‹*aircraft*› descend; ~**|klettern** *itr. V.; mit sein* climb down; ~**|reichen** [1] *tr. V.* hand down; [2] *itr. V.* (sich bis hinunter erstrecken) reach down (**bis auf** + *Akk.* to)

hin·weg *Adv.* **(a)** (geh.) ~ **mit dir!** away with you!
(b) **über etw. ~:** over sth.

Hin·weg *der* way there

hinweg-: ~**|gehen** *unr. itr. V.; mit sein* **über etw.** (*Akk.*) **~gehen** pass over sth.; ~**|kommen** *unr. itr. V.; mit sein* **über etw.** (*Akk.*) **~kommen** get over sth.; ~**|setzen** *refl. V.* **sich über etw.** (*Akk.*) **~setzen** ignore sth.

Hinweis /ˈhɪnvaiːs/ *der;* ~**es,** ~**e** hint; **unter ~ auf** (+ *Akk.*) with reference to

hin-: ~**|weisen** [1] *unr. itr. V.* **auf jmdn./etw. ~weisen** point to sb./sth.; [2] *unr. tr. V.* **jmdn. auf etw.** (*Akk.*) **~weisen** point sth. out to sb.; ~**weisend** *Adj.* (Grammatik) demonstrative; ~**|werfen** *unr. tr. V.* throw ···›

down; ~|**ziehen** [1] *unr. tr. V.* pull, draw (**zu** to, towards); [2] *unr. itr. V.; mit sein* (umziehen) move there; **wo ist sie ~gezogen?** where did she move to?; [3] *unr. refl. V.* **(a)** (sich erstrecken) drag on (**über** + *Akk.* for); **(b)** (sich verzögern) be delayed

hinzu-: ~|**fügen** *tr. V.* add; ~|**kommen** *unr. itr. V.; mit sein* **(a)** come along; **(b)** (hinzugefügt werden) **zu etw. ~kommen** be added to sth.; **es kommt noch ~, dass ...** (fig.) there is also the fact that ...; ~|**tun** *unr. tr. V.* (ugs.) add

Hiobs·botschaft *die* bad news

Hirn *das;* ~[e]s, ~e **(a)** brain **(b)** (Speise; ugs.: Verstand) brains *pl.*

Hirsch *der;* ~[e]s, ~e deer; (Rothirsch) red deer; (männlicher Rothirsch) stag; (Speise) venison

Hirse *die;* ~, ~n millet

Hirt *der;* ~en, ~en, **Hirte** *der;* ~n, ~n herdsman; (Schaf~) shepherd

Hirtin *die;* ~, ~nen shepherdess

hissen *tr. V.* hoist

historisch *Adj.* **(a)** historical **(b)** (geschichtlich bedeutungsvoll) historic

Hit *der;* ~[s], ~s (ugs.) hit

Hitler·jugend *die* Hitler Youth

Hit·parade *die* hit parade

Hitze *die;* ~: heat

hitze-, Hitze-: ~**beständig** *Adj.* heat-resistant; ~**frei** *Adj.* **~frei haben** have the rest of the day off [school/work] because of excessively hot weather; ~**periode** *die* hot spell; spell *or* period of hot weather; ~**welle** *die* heat wave

hitzig *Adj.* **(a)** hot-tempered **(b)** (erregt) heated ‹*discussion etc.*›

hitz-, Hitz-: ~**kopf** *der* hothead; ~**köpfig** *Adj.* hot-headed; ~**schlag** *der* heatstroke

HIV-: ~**-Anti·körper** *der* HIV antibody; ~**-Infektion** *die* HIV infection; ~**-infiziert** *Adj.* HIV-infected; ~**-kontaminiert** *Adj.* HIV-contaminated; ~**-positiv** *Adj.* HIV-positive; ~**-Test** *der* HIV test; ~**-verseucht** *Adj.* HIV-contaminated

hl *Abk.* = **Hektoliter** hl

H-Milch *die;* ~ long-life *or* UHT milk

HNO-Arzt *der*, **HNO-Ärztin** *die* ENT specialist

hob *1. u. 3. Pers. Sg. Prät. v.* HEBEN

Hobby *das;* ~s, ~s hobby

Hobel *der;* ~s, ~ **(a)** plane **(b)** (Küchengerät) [vegetable] slicer

Hobel·bank *die; Pl.* **Hobel·bänke** woodworker's bench

hobeln *tr., itr. V.* **(a)** plane **(b)** (schneiden) slice

hoch; höher, höchst... [1] *Adj.* high; tall ‹*tree, mast*›; long ‹*grass*›; deep ‹*snow, water*›; heavy ‹*fine*›; large ‹*sum, amount*›; severe, extensive ‹*damage*›; senior ‹*official, officer, post*›; high-level ‹*diplomacy, politics*›; **höchste Gefahr** extreme danger; **es ist höchste Zeit, dass ...**: it is high time that ...; **das hohe C** top C; **vier ~ zwei** (Math.) four to the power [of] two; four squared [2] *adv.* (in großer Höhe) high; (nach oben) up; (zahlenmäßig viel, sehr) highly; **~ begabt** highly gifted; **~ empfindlich** highly sensitive ‹*instrument, device, material, etc.*›; fast ‹*film*›; extremely delicate ‹*fabric*›; **~ gestellt** ‹*person*› in a high position; important ‹*person*›; **~ verschuldet/versichert** heavily in debt/insured for a large sum [of money]; **etw. ~ und heilig versprechen** promise sth. faithfully

Hoch *das;* ~s, ~s **(a)** (Hochruf) **ein [dreifaches] ~ auf jmdn. ausbringen** give three cheers for sb. **(b)** (Met.) high

Hoch·achtung *die* great respect

hochachtungs·voll *Adv.* (Briefschluss) yours faithfully

hoch-, Hoch-: ~**aktuell** *Adj.* highly topical; ~**amt** *das* (kath. Rel.) high mass; ~|**arbeiten** *refl. V.* work one's way up; ~**begabt** *Adj.* highly gifted; ~**betagt** *Adj.* aged; ~**betrieb** *der* (ugs.) **es herrschte ~betrieb im Geschäft** the shop was at its busiest; ~**blüte** *die* golden age; ~**burg** *die* stronghold; ~**deutsch** *Adj.* High German; ~**deutsch** *das*, ~**deutsche** *das* High German; ~**druck** *der; Pl.* ~**drücke** (Physik, Met.) high pressure; ***~empfindlich** ▶ HOCH 2; ~|**fahren** *unr. itr. V.; mit sein* **(a)** (ugs.) go up; (mit dem Auto) drive up; (mit dem Fahrrad, Motorrad) ride up; **(b)** (auffahren) start up; **aus dem Sessel ~fahren** start [up] from one's chair; **(c)** (aufbrausen) flare up; ~**finanz** *die;* ~~: high finance; ~**fliegend** *Adj.* ambitious; ~**form** *die* top form; ~**gebirge** *das* [high] mountains *pl.;* ~**gefühl** *das* [feeling of] elation; ~|**gehen** *unr. itr. V.; mit sein* (ugs.) go up; (zornig werden) blow one's top (coll.); explode; (explodieren) ‹*bomb, mine*› go off; ~**genuss**, ***~genuß** *der:* **ein ~genuss sein** be a real delight; ~**geschlossen** *Adj.* high-necked ‹*dress*›; ***~gestellt** ▶ HOCH 2; ~**glanz** *der:* **etw. auf ~glanz bringen** give sth. a high polish; (fig.) make sth. spick and span; ~**gradig** [1] *Adj.* extreme; [2] *adv.* extremely; ~|**halten** *unr. tr. V.* hold up; ~**haus** *das* high-rise building; ~|**heben** *unr. tr. V.* lift up; raise ‹*arm, leg, hand*›; ~**interessant** *Adj.* extremely interesting; ~**kant** *Adv.* (ugs.): **jmdn. ~kant hinauswerfen** chuck sb. out (coll.); throw sb. out on his/her ear (coll.); ~|**kommen** *unr. itr. V.; mit sein* (ugs.) come up; (vorwärts kommen) get on; ~**konjunktur** *die* (Wirtsch.) boom; **auf dem Automarkt herrscht ~konjunktur** the car market is booming;

---

*alte Schreibung - vgl. Hinweis auf S. xiv

~|**krempeln** *tr. V.* roll up; ~**land** *das* highlands *Pl.;* ~|**leben** *itr. V.* **jmdn./etw. ~leben lassen** cheer sb./sth.; **er lebe ~!** three cheers for him; ~**leistungs·sport** *der* top-level sport; ~**modern** *Adj.* ultra-modern; ~**mut** *der* arrogance; ~**mütig** *Adj.* arrogant; ~**näsig** *Adj.* (abwertend) stuck-up; ~|**nehmen** *unr. tr. V.* (ugs.: verspotten) **jmdn. ~nehmen** pull sb.'s leg; ~**ofen** *der* blast furnace; ~**prozentig** *Adj.* high-proof ‹*spirits*›; ~|**rechnen** project; ~**rechnung** *die* (Statistik) projection; ~**ruf** *der* cheer; ~**saison** *die* high season; ~|**schlagen** [1] *unr. tr. V.* turn up ‹*collar, brim*›; [2] *unr. itr. V.; mit sein* ‹*water, waves*› surge up; ‹*flames*› leap up; ~**schule** *die* college; (Universität) university; ~|**scrollen** (DV) *itr. u. tr. V.* scroll up

Hochsee·fischerei *die* deep-sea fishing *no art.*

hoch-, Hoch-: ~**sitz** *der* (Jägerspr.) raised hide; ~**sommer** *der* high summer; ~**spannung** *die* (Elektrot.) high voltage; ~|**spielen** *tr. V.* blow up

höchst *Adv.* extremely; most

höchst... ▸ HOCH

Hoch·stapler /-ʃtaːplɐ/ *der;* ~**s,** ~: confidence trickster; conman (coll.); (Aufschneider) fraud

höchsten·falls *Adv.* at [the] most *or* the outside; at the very most

höchstens *Adv.* at most; (bestenfalls) at best

Höchst-: ~**fall** *der:* **im ~fall** at [the] most; ~**form** *die* (bes. Sport) peak form; ~**geschwindigkeit** *die* top speed; (Geschwindigkeitsbegrenzung) speed limit

Hoch·stimmung *die* high spirits *pl.*

höchst-, Höchst-: ~**leistung** *die* supreme performance; (Ergebnis) supreme achievement; ~**maß** *das:* **ein ~maß an etw.** (*Dat.*) a very high degree of sth.; ~**persönlich** [1] *Adj.* personal; [2] *adv.* in person; ~**temperatur** *die* maximum *or* highest temperature; ~**wahrscheinlich** *Adv.* very probably; ~**wert** *der* maximum value

hoch-, Hoch-: ~**tour** *die:* **auf ~touren laufen** run at full speed; (intensiv betrieben werden) be in full swing; ~**trabend** (abwertend) [1] *Adj.* high-flown; [2] *adv.* in a high-flown manner; ~|**treiben** *unr. tr. V.* force up ‹*prices etc.*›; ~**verrat** *der* high treason; ~**wasser** *das* (Flut) high tide; (Überschwemmung) flood; ~**wertig** *Adj.* high-quality ‹*goods*›; highly nutritious ‹*food*›; ~**würden** *der;* ~~**[s]** (veralt.) Reverend Father

Hoch·zeit *die;* ~, ~**en** wedding

Hochzeits-: ~**feier** *die* wedding; ~**nacht** *die* wedding night; ~**reise** *die* honeymoon [trip]

Hocke *die;* ~, ~**n (a)** (Körperhaltung) squat; crouch **(b)** (Turnen) squat vault

hocken [1] *itr. V.* **(a)** *mit haben od. (südd.) sein* squat; crouch **(b)** *mit haben od. (südd.) sein* (ugs.: sich aufhalten) sit around [2] *refl. V.* crouch down

Hocker *der;* ~**s,** ~: stool

Höcker *der;* ~**s,** ~: hump; (auf der Nase) bump; (auf dem Schnabel) knob

Hockey /'hɔki/ *das;* ~**s** hockey

Hoden *der;* ~**s,** ~: testicle

Hoden·bruch *der* (Med.) scrotal hernia

Hof *der;* ~**[e]s, Höfe (a)** courtyard; (Schul~) playground; (Gefängnis~) [prison] yard **(b)** (Bauern~) farm **(c)** (Herrscher, Hofstaat) court

Hof·dame *die* lady of the court; (Begleiterin der Königin) lady-in-waiting

hof·fähig *Adj.* presentable at court *pred.*

hoffen [1] *tr. V.* hope [2] *itr. V.* hope; **auf etw.** (*Akk.*) ~: hope for sth.; (Vertrauen setzen auf) **auf jmdn./etw.** ~: put one's faith in sb./sth.

hoffentlich *Adv.* hopefully; ~! let's hope so

Hoffnung *die;* ~, ~**en** hope

hoffnungs-, Hoffnungs-: ~**los** [1] *Adj.* hopeless; despairing ‹*person*›; [2] *adv.* hopelessly; ~**losigkeit** *die;* ~~: despair; (der Lage) hopelessness; ~**voll** [1] *Adj.* **(a)** hopeful; full of hope *pred.;* **(b)** (erfolgversprechend) promising; [2] *adv.* **(a)** full of hope; **(b)** (erfolgversprechend) promisingly

höflich [1] *Adj.* polite [2] *adv.* politely

Höflichkeit *die;* ~: politeness

hoh... ▸ HOCH

Höhe /'høːə/ *die;* ~, ~**n** height; **etw. in die ~ heben** lift sth. up; **das ist ja die ~!** (fig. ugs.) that's the limit!

Hoheit *die;* ~, ~**en** sovereignty (**über** + *Akk.* over); **Seine/Ihre ~:** His/Your Highness

Hoheits-: ~**gebiet** *das* [sovereign] territory; ~**gewässer** *das* territorial waters

Höhen-: ~**angst** *die* fear of heights; ~**flug** *der* (fig.) flight; ~**lage** *die* altitude; ~**luft** *die* mountain air; ~**messer** *der* altimeter; ~**sonne** *die* (Med.) sun lamp; ~**unterschied** *der* difference in altitude; ~**zug** *der* (Geogr.) range of hills; (Bergkette) range of mountains; mountain range

Höhe·punkt *der* high point; (einer Veranstaltung) high spot; highlight; (einer Laufbahn, des Ruhms) peak; pinnacle; (Orgasmus; eines Stückes) climax

höher /'høːɐ/ ▸ HOCH

hohl *Adj.* hollow

Höhle *die;* ~, ~**n (a)** cave; (größer) cavern **(b)** (Tierbau) lair

Hohl-: **~maß** *das* measure of capacity; **~raum** *der* cavity; [hollow] space; **~spiegel** *der* concave mirror

Hohn *der;* **~[e]s** scorn; derision

höhnen (geh.) *itr. V.* jeer

höhnisch 1 *Adj.* scornful
2 *adv.* scornfully

Hokuspokus *der;* **~:** hocus-pocus; (abwertend: Drum und Dran) fuss

hold *Adj.* (dichter. veralt.) fair; lovely; lovely ‹*sight, smile*›

holen 1 *tr. V.* **(a)** fetch; get
(b) (ab~) fetch
(c) (ugs.: erlangen) get ‹*prize etc.*›; carry off ‹*medal, trophy, etc.*›
2 *refl. V.* (ugs.: sich zuziehen) catch; **sich** (*Dat.*) **[beim Baden] einen Schnupfen ~:** catch a cold [swimming]

Holland (*das*); **~s** Holland

Holländer *der;* **~s, ~:** Dutchman

Holländerin *die;* **~, ~nen** Dutchwoman

holländisch *Adj.* Dutch

Hölle *die;* **~, ~n** hell *no art.*

Höllen·lärm *der* (ugs.) diabolical noise *or* row (coll.)

höllisch 1 *Adj.* **(a)** infernal; ‹*spirits, torments*› of hell
(b) (ugs.: sehr groß) tremendous (coll.)
2 *adv.* (ugs.: sehr) hellishly (coll.)

Holm *der;* **~[e]s, ~e** (Turnen) bar

Holocaust *der;* **~[s]** Holocaust

holpern *itr. V. mit sein* (fahren) jolt; bump

holprig *Adj.* **(a)** bumpy; rough
(b) (stockend) halting ‹*speech*›; clumsy ‹*verses, style, language, etc.*›

Holunder *der;* **~s, ~:** elder

Holz *das;* **~es, Hölzer** wood; (Bau~, Tischler~) timber; wood

Holz-: **~bein** *das* wooden leg; **~bläser** *der,* **Holz·bläserin** *die* woodwind player

hölzern *Adj.* (auch fig.) wooden

holz-, Holz-: **~fäller** *der;* **~~s, ~~:** woodcutter; lumberjack (Amer.); **~frei** *Adj.* wood-free ‹*paper*›

holzig *Adj.* woody

Holz-: **~klotz** *der* block of wood; (als Spielzeug) wooden block; **~kohle** *die* charcoal; **~kopf** *der* (salopp abwertend) blockhead; **~pantoffel** *der* clog; **~scheit** *das* piece of wood; (Brenn~) piece of firewood; **~schnitt** *der* **(a)** (Technik) woodcutting *no art.;* **(b)** (Blatt) woodcut; **~schuh** *der* clog; **~stoß** *der* pile of wood; **~weg** *der:* **auf dem ~weg sein** be on the wrong track (fig.); **~wolle** *die* wood wool; **~wurm** *der* woodworm

homogen *Adj.* homogeneous

homöopathisch *Adj.* homoeopathic

Homo·sexualität *die;* **~:** homosexuality

homo·sexuell 1 *Adj.* homosexual
2 *adv.* **~ veranlagt sein** have homosexual tendencies

Honig *der;* **~s, ~e** honey

Honig·kuchen *der* honey cake

Honig·wabe *die* honeycomb

Honorar *das;* **~s, ~e** fee; (Autoren~) royalty

Honoratioren /honora'ts̯i̯o:rən/ *Pl.* notabilities

honorieren *tr. V.* **(a) jmdn. ~:** pay sb. [a/his/her fee]
(b) (würdigen) appreciate; (belohnen) reward

Hopfen *der;* **~s, ~:** hop; **bei ihm ist ~ und Malz verloren** (ugs.) he's a hopeless case

hopp *Interj.* quick; look sharp

hoppeln *itr. V.; mit sein* hop; (**über** + *Akk.* across, over)

hoppla *Interj.* oops; whoops

hopsen *itr. V.; mit sein* (ugs.) (springen) jump; (hüpfen) ‹*animal*› hop; ‹*child*› skip; ‹*ball*› bounce

Hopser *der;* **~s, ~** (ugs.) [little] jump

Hör·apparat *der* hearing aid

hörbar 1 *Adj.* audible
2 *adv.* audibly; (geräuschvoll) noisily

Hör·buch *das* audiobook

horchen *itr. V.* listen (**auf** + *Akk.* to); (heimlich zuhören) eavesdrop

Horde *die;* **~, ~n** horde; (von Halbstarken) mob

hören 1 *tr. V.* hear; (anhören) listen to
2 *itr. V.* hear; (zuhören) listen; **auf jmdn./jmds. Rat ~:** listen to sb./sb.'s advice

Hören·sagen *das:* **vom ~:** from hearsay

Hörer *der;* **~s, ~** **(a)** listener
(b) (Telefon~) receiver

Hörerin *die;* **~, ~nen** listener

Hörerschaft *die;* **~, ~en** audience

Hör-: **~fehler** *der* **(a) das war ein ~fehler** he/she *etc.* misheard; **(b)** (Schwerhörigkeit) hearing defect; **~funk** *der* radio; **im ~funk** on the radio; **~funk·sendung** *die* radio programme; **~gerät** *das* hearing aid

hörig *Adj.:* **jmdm. ~ sein** be submissively dependent on sb.; (sexuell) be sexually enslaved to sb.

Horizont *der;* **~[e]s, ~e** (auch Geol., fig.) horizon

horizontal 1 *Adj.* horizontal
2 *adv.* horizontally

Horizontale *die;* **~, ~n** **(a)** (Linie) horizontal line
(b) (Lage) **die ~:** the horizontal

Hormon *das;* **~s, ~e** hormone

Horn *das;* **~[e]s, Hörner** horn

Hörnchen *das;* **~s, ~** (Gebäck) croissant

Horn·haut *die* **(a)** callus; hard skin *no indef. art.;*
(b) (am Auge) cornea

Hornisse *die;* **~, ~n** hornet

Horoskop *das;* **~s, ~e** horoscope

*old spelling - see note on page xiv

horrend *Adj.* shocking (coll.), horrendous (coll.) ‹*price*›; colossal (coll.) ‹*sum, amount, rent*›

Hör·rohr *das* stethoscope

Horror *der;* ~s horror

Horror-: ~film *der* horror film; **~roman** *der* horror novel

Hör-: ~saal *der* lecture theatre *or* hall; **~spiel** *das* radio play

Horst *der;* ~[e]s, ~e eyrie

Hort *der;* ~[e]s, ~e ▶ KINDERHORT

horten *tr. V.* hoard; stockpile ‹*raw materials*›

Hortensie /hɔr'tɛnzi̯ə/ *die;* ~, ~n hydrangea

Hör·weite *die:* **in/außer ~weite** in/out of earshot

Höschen /'hø:sçən/ *das;* ~s, ~: trousers *pl.;* pair of trousers; (kurzes ~) shorts *pl.;* pair of shorts

Hose *die;* ~, ~n **(a)** trousers *pl.;* pants *pl.* (Amer.); (Unter~) pants *pl.;* (Freizeit~) slacks *pl.;* (Bund~) breeches *pl.;* (Reit~) riding breeches *pl.;* **eine ~:** a pair of trousers/ pants/slacks *etc.;*
(b) (fig.) **die ~n anhaben** (ugs.) wear the trousers; **die ~n runterlassen** (salopp) come clean (coll.); **in die ~[n] gehen** (salopp) be a [complete] flop (coll.); **es ist tote ~** (Jugendspr.) there's nothing doing (coll.)

Hosen-: ~anzug *der* trouser suit (Brit.); pant suit; **~matz** *der;* ~~es, ~~e *od.* **~mätze** (ugs. scherzh.) toddler; **~rock** *der* culottes *pl.;* **~tasche** *die* trouser pocket; pants pocket (Amer.); **~träger** *Pl.* braces; suspenders (Amer.); pair of braces/ suspenders

Hospital *das;* ~s, ~e *od.* **Hospitäler** hospital

Hospiz *das;* ~es, ~e hospice

Hostie /'hɔstḭə/ *die;* ~, ~n (christl. Rel.) host

Hotel *das;* ~s, ~s hotel

Hotel·bar *die* hotel bar

Hotel garni /- gar'ni:/ *das;* ~ ~, ~s ~s /- gar'ni:/ bed-and-breakfast hotel

Hotelier /hotɛ'li̯e:/ *der;* ~s, ~s hotelier

Hotline /'hɔtlaɪn/ *die;* ~, ~s hotline

hüben *Adv.* over here

hübsch 1 *Adj.* pretty; nice ‹*area, flat, voice, tune, etc.*›; nice-looking ‹*boy, person*›; **ein ~es Sümmchen** (ugs.) a tidy sum (coll.); a nice little sum; **das ist eine ~e Geschichte** (ugs. iron.) this is a fine *or* pretty kettle of fish (coll.)
2 *adv.* prettily; (ugs.: sehr) **~ kalt** perishing cold

Hub·schrauber *der;* ~s, ~: helicopter

Hubschrauber·lande·platz *der* heliport; (kleiner) helicopter pad; landing pad

huckepack *Adv.* **jmdn. ~ tragen** (ugs.) give sb. a piggyback

hudeln *itr. V.* (bes. südd., österr.) be sloppy (**bei** in)

Huf *der;* ~[e]s, ~e hoof

huf-, Huf-: ~eisen *das* horseshoe; **~eisen·förmig** 1 *Adj.* horseshoe-shaped; 2 *adv.* in [the shape of] a horseshoe; **~schmied** *der* farrier

Hüfte *die;* ~, ~n hip

Hüft-: ~gelenk *das* (Anat.) hip joint; **~gürtel** *der* girdle

Hügel *der;* ~s, ~ hill

hügelig *Adj.* hilly

Huhn *das;* ~[e]s, **Hühner** chicken; (Henne) chicken; hen

Hühnchen *das;* ~s, ~: small chicken; **mit jmdm. [noch] ein ~ zu rupfen haben** (ugs.) [still] have a bone to pick with sb.

Hühner-: ~auge *das* (am Fuß) corn; **~brühe** *die* chicken broth

hui /hui:/ *Interj.* whoosh

huldigen *itr. V.* **jmdm. ~:** pay tribute to sb.

Huldigung *die;* ~, ~en tribute

Hülle *die;* ~, ~n cover

hüllen *tr. V.* (geh.) wrap

Hülse *die;* ~, ~n **(a)** case
(b) (Bot.) pod

Hülsen·frucht *die* **(a)** (Frucht) fruit of a leguminous plant; **Hülsenfrüchte** pulse *sing.;* **(b)** (Pflanze) legume; leguminous plant

human *Adj.* humane

Humanismus *der;* ~: humanism; (Epoche) Humanism *no art.*

humanitär *Adj.* humanitarian

Humbug *der;* ~s (ugs.) humbug

Hummel *die;* ~, ~n bumble-bee

Hummer *der;* ~s, ~: lobster

Humor *der;* ~s humour; (Sinn für ~) sense of humour; **den ~ nicht verlieren** remain good-humoured

Humorist *der;* ~en, ~en, **Humoristin** *die;* ~, ~nen **(a)** (Autor[in]) humorist
(b) (Vortragskünstler[in]) comedian

humoristisch *Adj.* humorous

humor-: ~los *Adj.* humourless; **~losigkeit** *die;* ~~: humourlessness; lack of humour; **~voll** *Adj.* humorous

humpeln *itr. V.* **(a)** *auch mit sein* walk with a limp
(b) *mit sein* (sich ~d fortbewegen) limp

Hund *der;* ~es, ~e **(a)** dog; **auf den ~ kommen** (ugs.) go to the dogs (coll.); **vor die ~e gehen** (ugs.) go to the dogs (coll.); (sterben) kick the bucket (coll.)
(b) (abwertend) bastard (sl.)

hunde-, Hunde-: ~elend *Adj.* (ugs.) [really] wretched *or* awful; **~hütte** *die* [dog] kennel; **~kuchen** *der* dog biscuit; **~müde** *Adj.* (ugs.) dog tired; **~rasse** *die* breed of dog

hundert *Kardinalz.* **(a)** a *or* one hundred
(b) (ugs.: viele) hundreds of

Hundert[1] *das;* ~s, ~e hundred

Hundert² *die;* ~, ~**en** hundred
Hunderter *der;* ~**s**, ~ (ugs.) hundred-euro/-mark/-dollar *etc.* note
hundert·mal *Adv.* a hundred times; **auch wenn du dich ~ beschwerst** (ugs.) however much you complain
Hundert-: ~**mark·schein** *der* hundred-mark note; ~**meter·lauf** *der* (Leichtathletik) hundred metres *sing.*
hundert·prozentig 1 *Adj.* **(a)** [one-]hundred per cent *attrib.;*
(b) (ugs.: völlig) a hundred per cent
(c) (ugs.: ganz sicher) absolutely reliable
2 *adv.* (ugs.) **ich bin nicht ~ sicher** I'm not a hundred per cent sure
hundertst... /'hʊndɐtsːt.../ *Ordinalz.* hundredth
hundertstel /'hʊndɐtsːtl̩/ *Bruchz.* hundredth
Hundertstel *das* (schweiz. meist *der*); ~**s**, ~: hundredth
hundert·tausend *Kardinalz.* a *or* one hundred thousand
Hunde-: ~**scheiße** *die* (derb) dog shit (coarse); ~**steuer** *die* dog licence fee; ~**zwinger** *der* dog run
Hündin *die;* ~, ~**nen** bitch
Hüne *der;* ~**n**, ~**n** giant
Hünen·grab *das* megalithic tomb; (Hügelgrab) barrow
Hunger *der;* ~**s** **(a)** ~ **bekommen/haben** get/be hungry
(b) (geh.: Verlangen) hunger; (nach Ruhm, Macht) craving
Hunger·kur *die* starvation diet
hungern *itr. V.* go hungry; starve; **nach etw. ~:** (fig.) hunger for sth.
Hungers·not *die* famine
Hunger-: ~**streik** *der* hunger strike; ~**tuch** *das:* **am ~tuch nagen** (ugs. scherzh.) be on the breadline
hungrig *Adj.* (auch geh. fig.) hungry (**nach** for)
Hupe *die;* ~, ~**n** horn
hupen *itr. V.* sound one's horn; **dreimal ~:** hoot three times
hüpfen *itr. V.; mit sein* hop; ‹*ball*› bounce
Hürde *die;* ~, ~**n** hurdle
Hürden·lauf *der* (Leichtathletik) hurdling; (Wettbewerb) hurdles *pl.*
Hure *die;* ~, ~**n** (abwertend) whore
huren *itr. V.* (abwertend) whore
hurra *Interj.* hurray; hurrah; ~**/Hurra schreien** cheer
Hurra *das;* ~**s**, ~**s** cheer
hurtig 1 *Adj.* rapid
2 *adv.* quickly
huschen *itr. V.; mit sein* (lautlos u. leichtfüßig) ‹*person*› steal; (lautlos u. schnell) dart; ‹*mouse, lizard, etc.*› dart; ‹*smile*› flit; ‹*light*› flash; ‹*shadow*› slide quickly
hüsteln *itr. V.* give a slight cough
husten 1 *itr. V.* cough; (Husten haben) have a cough
2 *tr. V.* cough up ‹*blood, phlegm*›
Husten *der;* ~**s**, ~: cough
Husten-: ~**anfall** *der* coughing fit; fit of coughing; ~**bonbon** *das* cough drop; ~**reiz** *der* tickling in the throat; ~**saft** *der* cough mixture; ~**tropfen** *Pl.* cough drops
Hut¹ *der;* ~**es**, **Hüte** hat; (fig.) **da geht einem/mir der ~ hoch** (ugs.) it makes you/me mad (coll.); **das kann er sich** (*Dat.*) **an den ~ stecken** (ugs. abwertend) he can keep it (coll.)
Hut² *die;* ~ (geh.) keeping; care; **auf der ~ sein** be on one's guard
hüten 1 *tr. V.* look after; tend ‹*sheep, cattle*›
2 *refl. V.* be on one's guard
Hut·schnur *die:* **das geht mir über die ~** (ugs.) that's going too far
Hütte *die;* ~, ~**n** **(a)** hut; (ärmliches Haus) shack; hut
(b) (Eisen~) iron [and steel] works *sing. or pl.;*
(c) (Jagd~) [hunting] lodge
Hütten-: ~**käse** *der* cottage cheese; ~**schuh** *der* slipper sock
Hyäne *die;* ~, ~**n** hyena
Hyazinthe *die;* ~, ~**n** hyacinth
Hydrant *der;* ~**en**, ~**en** hydrant
Hydrat *das;* ~**[e]s**, ~**e** (Chemie) hydrate
Hydraulik *die;* ~ (Technik) **(a)** (Theorie) hydraulics *sing., no art.;*
(b) (Vorrichtungen) hydraulics *pl.*
hydraulisch (Technik) 1 *Adj.* hydraulic
2 *adv.* hydraulically
Hydro·kultur *die* (Gartenbau) hydroponics *sing.*
Hygiene *die;* ~ **(a)** (Gesundheitspflege) health care
(b) (Sauberkeit) hygiene
hygienisch 1 *Adj.* hygienic
2 *adv.* hygienically
Hymne /'hʏmnə/ *die;* ~, ~**n** hymn; (National~) national anthem
Hypnose *die;* ~, ~**n** hypnosis
hypnotisieren *tr. V.* hypnotize
Hypochonder /hypo'xɔndɐ/ *der;* ~**s**, ~, **Hypochonderin** *die;* ~, ~**nen** hypochondriac
hypochondrisch *Adj.* hypochondriac
Hypotenuse *die;* ~, ~**n** (Math.) hypotenuse
Hypothek *die;* ~, ~**en** (Bankw.) mortgage; (fig.) burden
Hypothese *die;* ~, ~**n** hypothesis
hypothetisch 1 *Adj.* hypothetical
2 *adv.* hypothetically
Hysterie *die;* ~, ~**n** hysteria
hysterisch 1 *Adj.* hysterical
2 *adv.* hysterically

*alte Schreibung - vgl. Hinweis auf S. xiv

Ii

i, I /iː/ *das;* ~, ~ i/I; **das Tüpfelchen** *od.* **der Punkt auf dem** ~ (fig.) the final touch

i *Interj.* ugh; **i bewahre, i wo** (ugs.) [good] heavens, no!

i.A. *Abk.* = **im Auftrag[e]** p.p.

IC *Abk.* = **Intercity** IC

ICE *Abk.* = **Intercityexpress[zug]** ICE

ich *Personalpron.; 1. Pers. Sg. Nom.* I; **immer** ~ (ugs.) [it's] always me; ~ **nicht** not me; **Menschen wie du und** ~: people like you and me; *s. auch (Gen.)* MEINER, *(Dat.)* MIR, *(Akk.)* MICH

Ich *das;* ~[s], ~[s] **(a)** self **(b)** (Psych.) ego

Ichform *die* first person

Icon /'aiːkən/ *das;* ~s, ~s (DV) icon

ideal [1] *Adj.* ideal [2] *adv.* ideally

Ideal *das;* ~s, ~e ideal

Ideal-: ~**bild** *das* ideal; ~**fall** *der* ideal case; ~**gewicht** *das* ideal weight

idealisieren *tr. V.* idealize

Idealismus *der;* ~ (auch Philos.) idealism

Idealist *der;* ~en, ~en, **Idealistin** *die;* ~, ~nen idealist

idealistisch (auch Philos.) [1] *Adj.* idealistic [2] *adv.* idealistically

Idee *die;* ~, ~n **(a)** idea **(b)** (ein bisschen) **eine** ~: a shade; **eine** ~ **[Salz/Pfeffer]** a touch [of salt/pepper]

ideell *Adj.* non-material; (geistig-seelisch) spiritual

ideen·los *Adj.* [completely] lacking in ideas *postpos.*

Identifikation /idɛntifika'tsi̯oːn/ *die;* ~, ~en (auch Psych.) identification

identifizieren [1] *tr. V.* identify [2] *refl. V.* (auch Psych.) **sich mit jmdm./etw.** ~: identify with sb./sth.

identisch *Adj.* identical

Identität *die;* ~: identity

Ideologe *der;* ~n, ~n ideologue

Ideologie *die;* ~, ~n /-iːən/ ideology

Ideologin *die;* ~, ~nen ideologue

ideologisch [1] *Adj.* ideological [2] *adv.* ideologically

Idiot *der;* ~en, ~en (auch ugs. abwertend) idiot

idioten-, Idioten-: ~**hügel** *der* (ugs. scherzh.) nursery slope; ~**sicher** *Adj.* (ugs. scherzh.) foolproof

Idiotie *die;* ~, ~n /-iːən/ **(a)** idiocy **(b)** (ugs. abwertend: Dummheit) madness

Idiotin *die;* ~, ~nen (auch ugs. abwertend) idiot

idiotisch [1] *Adj.* **(a)** (Psych.) severely subnormal **(b)** (ugs. abwertend) idiotic [2] *adv.* (auch ugs. abwertend) idiotically

Idol *das;* ~s, ~e (auch bild. Kunst) idol

Idyll *das;* ~s, ~e idyll

Idylle *die;* ~, ~n idyll

idyllisch *Adj.* idyllic

Igel *der;* ~s, ~: hedgehog

Iglu *der od. das;* ~s, ~s igloo

Ignoranz /ɪgno'rants:/ *die;* ~: ignorance

ignorieren *tr. V.* ignore

ihm *Dat. von* ER, ES: (bei männlichen Personen) him; (bei weiblichen Personen) her; (bei Dingen, Tieren) it; **gib es** ~: give it to him; give him it; **Freunde von** ~: friends of his

ihn *Akk. von* ER (bei männlichen Personen) him; (bei Dingen, Tieren) it

ihnen *Dat. von* SIE, *Pl.* them; **gib es** ~: give it to them; give them it; **Freunde von** ~: friends of theirs

Ihnen *Dat. von* SIE you; **ich habe es** ~ **gegeben** I gave it to you; **Freunde von** ~: friends of yours

ihr[1] /iːɐ̯/ *Dat. von* SIE, *Sg.* (bei Personen) her; (bei Dingen, Tieren) it

ihr[2], *Personalpron.; 2. Pers. Pl. Nom.* you

ihr[3] *Possessivpron.* **(a)** *Sg.* (einer Person) her; (eines Tieres, einer Sache) its **(b)** *Pl.* their

Ihr *Possessivpron.* (Anrede) your; ~ **Hans Meier** (Briefschluss) yours, Hans Meier; **welcher Mantel ist** ~**er?** which coat is yours?

ihrer **(a)** *Gen. von* SIE, *Sg.* (geh.) **wir gedachten** ~: we remembered her **(b)** *Gen. von* SIE, *Pl.* (geh.) **wir werden** ~ **gedenken** we will remember them; **es waren** ~ **zwölf** there were twelve of them

Ihrer *Gen. von* SIE (geh.) **wir werden** ~ **gedenken** we will remember you

ihrerseits *Adv.* for her/their part; (von ihr/ihnen) on her/their part

Ihrerseits *Adv.:* ▶ DEINERSEITS

ihres·gleichen *indekl. Pron.* people *pl.* like her/them; (abwertend) the likes of her/them

Ihres·gleichen *indekl. Pron.* people *pl.* like you; (abwertend) the likes of you

ihret·wegen *Adv.:* ▶ MEINETWEGEN: because of her/them; for her/their sake; about her/them; as far as she is/they are concerned

Ihret·wegen *Adv.:* ▶ DEINETWEGEN

Ikone *die;* ~, ~n icon

illegal [1] *Adj.* illegal
[2] *adv.* illegally
Illegalität *die;* ~, ~**en** illegality
illegitim *Adj.* (geh.) illegitimate
illuminieren *tr. V.* illuminate
Illusion *die;* ~, ~**en** illusion
illusorisch *Adj.* illusory; (zwecklos) pointless
Illustration *die;* ~, ~**en** illustration
illustrieren *tr. V.* illustrate
Illustrierte *die; adj. Dekl.* magazine
Iltis *der;* ~**ses,** ~**se** polecat; (Pelz) fitch
im *Präp. + Art.* **(a)** = **in dem;**
(b) (räumlich) in the; **im Theater** at the theatre; **im Fernsehen** on television; **im Bett** in bed
(c) (zeitlich) **im Mai** in May; **im letzten Jahr** last year; **im Alter von ...** at the age of ...
(d) (Verlauf) **etw. im Sitzen tun** do sth. [while] sitting down; **im Gehen sein** be going
Image /ˈɪmɪtʃ:/ *das;* ~**[s],** ~**s** image
imaginär *Adj.* (geh., Math.) imaginary
Imbiss, *Imbiß *der;* **Imbisses, Imbisse (a)** (kleine Mahlzeit) snack
(b) ▶ IMBISSSTUBE
Imbiss·stube, *Imbiß·stube *die* café
Imitation *die;* ~, ~**en** imitation
imitieren *tr. V.* imitate
Imker *der;* ~**s,** ~, **Imkerin** *die;* ~, ~**nen** bee-keeper
Immatrikulation *die;* ~, ~**en** (Hochschulw.) registration
immatrikulieren *tr., refl. V.* (Hochschulw.) register
immer *Adv.* **(a)** always; **schon** ~: always; ~ **wieder** time and time again; ~, **wenn** every time that
(b) immer + *Komp.:* ~ **dunkler** darker and darker; ~ **mehr** more and more
(c) (ugs.: jeweils) ~ **drei Stufen auf einmal** three steps at a time
(d) (auch) **wo/wer/wann/wie [auch]** ~: wherever/whoever/whenever/however
(e) (verstärkend) ~ **noch, noch** ~: still
(f) (ugs.: bei Aufforderung) ~ **geradeaus!** keep [going] straight on
immer-, Immer-: ~**fort** *Adv.* all the time; ~**grün** *Adj.* evergreen; ~**grün** *das* periwinkle; ~**hin** *Adv.* **(a)** (wenigstens) at any rate; **(b)** (trotz allem) all the same; **(c)** (schließlich) after all; ~**zu** *Adv.* (ugs.) the whole time
Immigrant *der;* ~**en,** ~**en, Immigrantin** *die;* ~, ~**nen** immigrant
Immigration *die;* ~, ~**en** immigration
immigrieren *itr. V.; mit sein* immigrate
Immobilien *Pl.* property *sing.;* real estate *sing.*
immun (a) (Med., fig.) immune (**gegen** to)
(b) (Rechtsspr.) ~ **sein** have immunity

*old spelling - see note on page xiv

Immunität *die;* ~, ~**en (a)** (Med.) immunity (**gegen** to)
(b) (Rechtsspr.) immunity (**gegen** from)
Immun-: ~**schwäche** *die* (Med.) immunodeficiency; immune deficiency; ~**therapie** *die* (Med.) immunotherapy; immune therapy
Imperativ *der;* ~**s,** ~**e (a)** (Sprachw.) imperative
(b) (Philos.) **[kategorischer]** ~: [categorical] imperative
Imperfekt *das;* ~**s,** ~**e** (Sprachw.) imperfect [tense]
Imperialismus *der;* ~: imperialism
imperialistisch *Adj.* imperialistic
Imperium *das;* ~**s, Imperien** (hist., fig.) empire
impfen *tr. V.* vaccinate; inoculate
Impf-: ~**pass, ***~**paß** *der* vaccination certificate; ~**stoff** *der* vaccine
Impfung *die;* ~, ~**en** vaccination
implantieren *tr. V.* (Med.) implant
imponieren *itr. V.* impress
imponierend [1] *Adj.* impressive
[2] *adv.* impressively
Imponier·gehabe *das* (Verhaltensf.) display; (fig.) showing off
Import *der;* ~**[e]s,** ~**e** import
Importeur /ɪmpɔrˈtøːɐ̯/ *der;* ~**s,** ~**e, Importeurin** *die;* ~, ~**nen** importer
importieren *tr., itr. V.* import
imposant [1] *Adj.* imposing; impressive ‹*achievement*›
[2] *adv.* imposingly
impotent *Adj.* impotent
Impotenz *die;* ~: impotence
imprägnieren *tr. V.* impregnate; (wasserdicht machen) waterproof
Improvisation *die;* ~, ~**en** improvisation
improvisieren *tr., itr. V.* improvise
Impuls *der;* ~**es,** ~**e** stimulus; (innere Regung) impulse
impulsiv [1] *Adj.* impulsive
[2] *adv.* impulsively
imstande *Adv.* ~ **sein, etw. zu tun** be able to do sth.
in[1] [1] *Präp. mit Dat.* (auf die Frage: wo?/wann?/wie?) in; **er hat** ~ **Tübingen studiert** he studied at Tübingen; *s. auch* IM;
[2] *Präp. mit Akk.* (auf die Frage: wohin?) into; *s. auch* INS
in[2] *Adj.:* ~ **sein** (ugs.) be in
In·anspruchnahme *die;* ~, ~**n** (starke Belastung) demands *pl.*
In·begriff *der* quintessence
inbegriffen *Adj.* included
In·betrieb·nahme *die;* ~, ~**n, In·betrieb·setzung** *die;* ~, ~**n** bringing into service
In·brunst *die;* ~ (geh.) fervour; (der Liebe) ardour

in·brünstig (geh.) 1 *Adj.* fervent; ardent ‹*love*›
2 *adv.* fervently; ‹*love*› ardently

in·dem *Konj.* **(a)** (während) while; (gerade als) as
(b) (dadurch, dass) ~ **man etw. tut** by doing sth.

Inder *der;* **~s, ~, Inderin** *die;* **~, ~nen** Indian

in·dessen 1 *Konj.* (geh.) **(a)** (während) while
(b) (wohingegen) whereas
2 *Adv.* **(a)** (inzwischen) meanwhile; in the mean time
(b) (jedoch) however

Index *der;* **~** *od.* **~es, ~e** *od.* **Indizes (a)** *Pl.* **~e** *od.* **Indizes** (Register) index
(b) *Pl.* **~e** (kath. Kirche) Index

Indianer *der;* **~s, ~:** [American] Indian

Indianer·häuptling *der* Indian chief

Indianerin *die;* **~, ~nen** [American] Indian

indianisch *Adj.* Indian

Indien /ˈɪndi̯ən/ *(das);* **~s** India

in·different *Adj.* indifferent

Indikativ *der;* **~s, ~e** /-iːvə/ (Sprachw.) indicative [mood]

Indikator *der;* **~s, ~en** (auch Chemie, Technik) indicator

in·direkt 1 *Adj.* indirect
2 *adv.* indirectly

indisch *Adj.* Indian

in·diskret *Adj.* indiscreet

In·diskretion *die;* **~, ~en** indiscretion

Individualist *der;* **~en, ~en, Individualistin** *die;* **~, ~nen** (geh.) individualist

Individualität *die;* **~, ~en** (geh.) **(a)** individuality
(b) (Persönlichkeit) personality

individuell 1 *Adj.* individual; private ‹*property, vehicle, etc.*›
2 *adv.* individually

Individuum *das;* **~s, Individuen** (auch Chemie, Biol.) individual

Indiz *das;* **~es, ~ien (a)** (Rechtsw.) piece of circumstantial evidence; **~ien** circumstantial evidence *sing.;*
(b) (Anzeichen) sign (**für** of)

Indizes ▸ INDEX

Indizien·beweis *der* (Rechtsw.) piece of circumstantial evidence; **~e** circumstantial evidence *sing.*

indoktrinieren *tr. V.* indoctrinate

Indonesien /ɪndoˈneːzi̯ən/ *(das);* **~s** Indonesia

Indonesier *der;* **~s, ~, Indonesierin** *die;* **~, ~nen** Indonesian

indonesisch *Adj.* Indonesian

industrialisieren *tr. V.* industrialize

Industrialisierung *die;* **~:** industrialization

Industrie *die;* **~, ~n** industry

Industrie-: ~betrieb *der* industrial firm; **~gebiet** *das* industrial area; **~kauffrau** *die,* **~kaufmann** *der: person with three years' business training employed on the business side of an industrial company*

industriell 1 *Adj.* industrial
2 *adv.* industrially

Industrielle *der/die; adj. Dekl.* industrialist

Industrie-: ~staat *der* industrial nation; **~stadt** *die* industrial town

Industrie- und Handels·kammer *die* Chamber of Industry and Commerce

Industriezweig *der* branch of industry

in·einander *Adv.* **~ greifen** mesh together (lit. or fig); **~ verliebt sein** be in love with each other *or* one another; **~ verschlungene Ornamente** intertwined decorations

***ineinander|greifen** ▸ INEINANDER

infam 1 *Adj.* disgraceful
2 *adv.* disgracefully

Infanterie *die;* **~, ~n** (Milit.) infantry

infantil (Psych., Med., sonst abwertend) 1 *Adj.* infantile
2 *adv.* in an infantile way

Infarkt *der;* **~[e]s, ~e** (Med.) infarction

Infekt *der;* **~[e]s, ~e** (Med.) infection

Infektion *die;* **~, ~en** (Med.) **(a)** (Ansteckung) infection
(b) (ugs.: Entzündung) inflammation

Infektions-: ~gefahr *die* (Med.) risk of infection; **~herd** *der* (Med.) seat of the/an infection; **~krankheit** *die* (Med.) infectious disease

Inferno *das;* **~s** (geh.) inferno

Infinitiv *der;* **~s, ~e** (Sprachw.) infinitive

infizieren 1 *tr. V.* infect
2 *refl. V.* become infected; **sich bei jmdm. ~:** be infected by sb.

in flagranti *Adv.* (geh.) in flagrante [delicto]

Inflation *die;* **~, ~en** (Wirtsch.) inflation; (Zeit der ~) period of inflation

inflationär *Adj.* inflationary

Inflations·rate *die* inflation rate; rate of inflation

in·folge 1 *Präp. + Gen.* as a result of
2 *Adv.* **~ von etw.** *(Dat.)* as a result of sth.

infolge·dessen *Adv.* consequently

Informatik *die;* **~:** computer science *no art.*

Informatiker *der;* **~s, ~, Informatikerin** *die;* **~, ~nen** computer scientist

Information *die;* **~, ~en (a)** information *no pl., no indef. art.* (**über** + *Akk.* about, on); **eine ~:** [a piece of] information
(b) (Büro) information bureau; (Stand) information desk

Informations-: ~büro *das* information ···

bureau *or* office; **~freiheit** *die* freedom of information; **~gesellschaft** *die* (Soziol.) information society; **~material** *das* informational literature; **~quelle** *die* source of information; **~vielfalt** *die* variety of information

informativ *Adj.* informative

informieren 1 *tr. V.* inform (**über** + *Akk.* about)
2 *refl. V.* inform oneself, find out (**über** + *Akk.* about)

in·frage: **~ kommen** be possible; **das kommt nicht ~** (ugs.) that is out of the question

Infra·rot *das* (Physik) infra-red radiation

Infra·struktur *die* infrastructure

Infusion *die; ~, ~en* (Med.) infusion

Ing. *Abk.* = **Ingenieur**

In·gebrauch·nahme *die; ~, ~n*: **vor ~ des Geräts** before operating the appliance

Ingenieur /ɪnʒeˈni̯øːɐ̯/ *der; ~s, ~e*, **Ingenieurin** *die; ~, ~nen* [qualified] engineer

Ingwer *der; ~s, ~*: ginger

Inhaber *der; ~s, ~*, **Inhaberin** *die; ~, ~nen* **(a)** holder
(b) (Besitzer) owner

inhaftieren *tr. V.* take into custody; detain

Inhaftierung *die; ~, ~en* detention

inhalieren *tr. V.* inhale

Inhalt *der; ~[e]s, ~e* **(a)** contents *pl.;*
(b) (einer Geschichte usw.) content
(c) (Flächen~) area; (Raum~) volume

inhaltlich 1 *Adj.* **an ~en Gesichtspunkten gemessen** from the point of view of content
2 *adv.* **~ ist der Aufsatz gut** the essay is good as regards content; **~ übereinstimmen** be the same in content

Inhalts-: **~angabe** *die* summary [of contents]; synopsis; (eines Films, Dramas) synopsis; **~verzeichnis** *das* table of contents; (auf einem Paket) list of contents

in·human *Adj.* **(a)** (unmenschlich) inhuman
(b) (rücksichtslos) inhumane

Initiale *die; ~, ~n* initial [letter]

Initiative *die; ~, ~n* initiative

Initiator *der; ~s, ~en*, **Initiatorin** *die; ~, ~nen* initiator; (einer Organisation) founder

Injektion *die; ~, ~en* (Med.) injection

injizieren *tr. V.* (Med.) inject

Inkarnation *die; ~, ~en* incarnation

inkl. *Abk.* = **inklusive** incl.

inklusive /ɪnkluˈziːvə/ 1 *Präp.* + *Gen.* (bes. Kaufmannsspr.) including
2 *Adv.* inclusive

inkognito *Adv.* (geh.) incognito

in·kompetent *Adj.* incompetent

In·kompetenz *die* incompetence

in·konsequent 1 *Adj.* inconsistent
2 *adv.* inconsistently

***alte Schreibung - vgl. Hinweis auf S. xiv**

In·konsequenz *die* inconsistency

in·korrekt 1 *Adj.* incorrect
2 *adv.* incorrectly

In·korrektheit *die; ~, ~en*
(a) (Fehlerhaftigkeit) incorrectness
(b) (Fehler) mistake

In·kraft·treten *das; ~s*: **mit [dem] ~ des Gesetzes** when the law comes/came into force

Inkubations·zeit *die; ~, ~en* (Med.) incubation period

In·land *das* **(a) im ~**: at home
(b) (Binnenland) interior; inland; **im/ins ~**: inland

inländisch *Adj.* domestic; home-produced ‹*goods*›

Inlands-: **~markt** *der* domestic market; **~porto** *das* inland postage

in·mitten 1 *Präp.* + *Gen.* (geh.) in the midst of
2 *Adv.* **~ von** in the midst of

inne|haben *unr. tr. V.* hold, occupy ‹*position*›; hold ‹*office*›

innen *Adv.* inside; (auf/an der Innenseite) on the inside

innen-, Innen-: **~architekt** *der*, **~architektin** *die* interior designer; **~aufnahme** *die* (Fot.) indoor photo[graph]; (Film) interior shot; **~einrichtung** *die* furnishings *pl.;* **~hof** *der* inner courtyard; **~leben** *das* **(a)** [inner] thoughts and feelings *pl.;* **(b)** (oft scherzh.: Ausstattung) inside; **~minister** *der*, **~ministerin** *die* Minister of the Interior; ≈ Home Secretary (Brit.); ≈ Secretary of the Interior (Amer.); **~ministerium** *das* Ministry of the Interior; ≈ Home Office (Brit.); ≈ Department of the Interior (Amer.); **~politik** *die* (eines Staates) home affairs *pl.;* (einer Regierung) domestic policy/policies *pl.;* **~politisch** ▶ ~POLITIK: 1 *Adj.* **~politische Fragen** matters of domestic policy; 2 *adv.* as regards home affairs/domestic policy; **~stadt** *die* town centre; downtown (Amer.); (einer Großstadt) city centre

inner... *Adj.* inner; (inländisch; Med.) internal; inside ‹*pocket, lane*›

Innere *das; adj. Dekl.* inside; (eines Gebäudes, Wagens, Schiffes) interior; inside; (eines Landes) interior

Innereien *Pl.* entrails; (Kochk.) offal *sing.*

inner·halb 1 *Präp.* + *Gen.* **(a)** within; **~ der Familie/Partei** (fig.) within the family/party
(b) (binnen) within; **~ einer Woche** within a week
2 *Adv.* **(a) ~ von** within
(b) (im Verlauf) **~ von zwei Jahren** within two years

innerlich 1 *Adj.* inner
2 *adv.* inwardly

innerst... *Adj.* innermost

Innerste *das; adj. Dekl.* innermost being

inne|wohnen *itr. V.* (geh.) **etw. wohnt jmdm./einer Sache ~:** sb./sth. possesses sth.
innig [1] *Adj.* deep ‹*affection, sympathy*›; fervent ‹*wish*›; intimate ‹*friendship*›; **mein ~ster Dank** my sincerest thanks
[2] *adv.* ‹*love*› with all one's heart
Innigkeit *die;* ~: depth; (einer Beziehung) intimacy
innovativ *Adj.* innovative
Innung /ˈɪnʊŋ/ *die;* ~, **~en** [trade] guild
in·offiziell [1] *Adj.* unofficial
[2] *adv.* unofficially
in puncto as regards
ins *Präp. + Art.* **(a)** = **in das**
(b) (räumlich) to the; **~ Bett gehen** go to bed
(c) ~ Schlendern geraten go into a skid
Insasse *der;* **~n, ~n, Insassin** *die,* ~, **~nen (a)** (Fahrgast) passenger
(b) (Bewohner[in]) inmate
ins·besond[e]re *Adv.* particularly; in particular
In·schrift *die* inscription
Insekt /ɪnˈzɛkt/ *das;* **~s, ~en** insect
Insel *die;* ~, **~n** island
Insel-: ~bewohner *der,* **~bewohnerin** *die* islander; **~gruppe** *die* group of islands; **~staat** *die* island state; **~welt** *die* islands *pl.*
Inserat *das;* **~[e]s, ~e** advertisement (*in a newspaper*)
Inserent *der;* **~en, ~en, Inserentin** *die;* ~, **~nen** advertiser
inserieren *itr. V.* advertise
ins·geheim *Adv.* secretly
ins·gesamt *Adv.* in all; altogether; (alles in allem) all in all
insofern [1] *Adv.* /ɪnˈzoːfɛrn/ (in dieser Hinsicht) to this extent; **~ als** in so far as
[2] *Konj.* /ɪnzoˈfɛrn/ (falls) provided [that]
Insolvenz·verfahren *das* insolvency proceedings *pl.*
insoweit [1] *adv.* /ɪnˈzoːvaiːt/ ▸ INSOFERN 1;
[2] *Konj.* /ɪnzoˈvaiːt/ ▸ INSOFERN 2
in spe /ɪn ˈspeː/ future *attrib.*; **mein Schwiegersohn ~ ~:** my future son-in-law
Inspektion *die;* ~, **~en** inspection; (Kfz-W.) service
Inspiration *die;* ~, **~en** inspiration
inspirieren *tr. V.* inspire
inspizieren *tr. V.* inspect
Installateur /ɪnstalaˈtøːɐ̯/ *der;* **~s, ~e, Installateurin** *die;* ~, **~nen** plumber; (Gas~) [gas] fitter; (Heizungs~) heating engineer; (Elektro~) electrician
Installation *die;* ~, **~en** installation; (Rohre) plumbing *no pl.*
installieren *tr. V.* install
in·stand *Adv.* **etw. ist gut/schlecht ~:** sth. is in good/poor condition; **etw. ~ halten** keep sth. in good condition; **etw. ~ setzen/bringen** repair sth.
Instand·haltung *die* maintenance
in·ständig [1] *Adj.* urgent
[2] *adv.* urgently
Instand·setzung *die;* ~, **~en** repair; (Renovierung) renovation
Instanz /ɪnˈstants:/ *die;* ~, **~en (a)** authority
(b) (Rechtsw.) **[die] erste/zweite/dritte ~:** the court of original jurisdiction/the appeal court/the court of final appeal; **durch alle ~en gehen** go through all the courts
Instinkt /ɪnˈstɪŋkt/ *der;* **~[e]s, ~e** instinct
instinktiv [1] *Adj.* instinctive
[2] *adv.* instinctively
Institut /ɪnstɪˈtuːt/ *das;* **~[e]s, ~e** institute
Institution *die;* ~, **~en** (auch fig.) institution
Instruktion /ɪnstrʊkˈtsi̯oːn/ *die;* ~, **~en** instruction
Instrument /ɪnstruˈmɛnt/ *das;* **~[e]s, ~e** instrument
instrumental (Musik) [1] *Adj.* instrumental
[2] *adv.* instrumentally
Insulin *das;* **~s** insulin
inszenieren *tr. V.* stage; put on; (Regie führen bei) direct; (fig.) (einfädeln) engineer; (organisieren) stage
Inszenierung *die;* ~, **~en** staging; (Regie) direction; (Aufführung) production
intakt *Adj.* **(a)** (unbeschädigt) intact
(b) (funktionsfähig) in [proper] working order *postpos.*; healthy ‹*economy*›
integer *Adj.* **eine integre Persönlichkeit** a person of integrity; **~ sein** be a person of integrity
Integral *das;* **~s, ~e** (Math.) integral
Integration *die;* ~, **~en** (auch Math.) integration
integrieren *tr. V.* integrate
Intellekt *der;* **~[e]s** intellect
intellektuell *Adj.* intellectual
Intellektuelle *der/die; adj. Dekl.* intellectual
intelligent [1] *Adj.* intelligent
[2] *adv.* intelligently
Intelligenz *die;* ~, **~en (a)** intelligence
(b) (Gesamtheit der Intellektuellen) intelligentsia
Intelligenz·quotient *der* intelligence quotient
Intendant *der;* **~en, ~en, Intendantin** *die;* ~, **~nen** (Theater) manager and artistic director; (Fernseh~, Rundfunk~) director general
Intensität *die;* ~: intensity
intensiv [1] *Adj.* (gründlich) intensive (kräftig) intense
[2] *adv.* intensively
intensivieren *tr. V.* intensify; increase ‹*exports*›; strengthen ‹*connections*›
Intensiv·station *die* intensive-care unit
interaktiv *Adj.* interactive
Intercityzug *der* inter-city train
interessant [1] *Adj.* interesting
[2] *adv.* **~ schreiben** write in an interesting way

interessanterweise *Adv.* interestingly enough

Interesse *das;* **~s, ~n** interest; **~ an jmdm./etw. haben** be interested in sb./sth.

interesse·halber *Adv.* out of interest

Interessen·gebiet *das* field of interest

Interessent *der;* **~en, ~en, Interessentin** *die;* **~, ~nen** interested person; (möglicher Käufer/mögliche Käuferin) potential buyer

Interessen·verband *der* [organized] interest group

Interessen·vertretung *die* **(a)** representation
(b) (Vertreter von Interessen) representative body

interessieren 1 *refl. V.* **sich für jmdn./etw. ~:** be interested in sb./sth.
2 *tr. V.* interest; **das interessiert mich nicht** I'm not interested [in it]

interessiert *Adj.* interested (**an** + *Dat.* in)

Interjektion *die;* **~, ~en** interjection

Inter-: ~kontinental·rakete *die* (Milit.) intercontinental ballistic missile; **~mezzo** *das;* **~~s, ~~s** *od.* **~mezzi** (Theat., Musik) intermezzo; (fig.) interlude; intermezzo

intern 1 *Adj.* internal
2 *adv.* internally

Internat *das;* **~[e]s, ~e** boarding school

inter-, Inter-: ~national 1 *Adj.* international; 2 *adv.* internationally; **~nationale** *die;* **~, ~n (a)** International; Internationale; **(b)** (Lied) Internationale

Internats-: ~schule *die* boarding school; **~schüler** *der,* **~schülerin** *die* boarding school pupil; boarder

Internet /'ɪntɐnɛt/ *das;* **~s** Internet; **im ~:** on the Internet

internet-, Internet: ~anbeiter *der,* **~anbeiterin** *die* (DV) Internet provider; **~anschluss** *der,* ***~anschluß** *der* Internet connection; connection to the Internet; **einen ~anschluss haben** be connected to the Internet; **~fähig** *Adj.* (DV) Internet-capable; Internet-enabled; **~seite** *die* (DV) Internet page; Web page

internieren *tr. V.* (Milit.) intern

Internierung *die;* **~, ~en** internment

Internist *der;* **~en, ~en, Internistin** *die;* **~, ~nen** (Med.) internist

Interpol *die;* **~:** Interpol *no art.*

Interpret *der;* **~en, ~en** interpreter (*of music, text, events, etc.*)

Interpretation *die;* **~, ~en** interpretation (*of music, text, events, etc.*)

interpretieren *tr. V.* interpret ‹*music, texts, events, etc.*›

Interpretin *die;* **~, ~nen** ▶ INTERPRET

Interpunktion *die;* **~** (Sprachw.) punctuation

*old spelling - see note on page xiv

Intervall /ɪntɐ'val/ *das;* **~s, ~e** (Musik, Math.) interval

intervenieren *itr. V.* (geh., Politik) intervene

Intervention *die;* **~, ~en** (geh., Politik) intervention; (Protest) representations *pl.*

Interview /ɪntɐ'vju:/ *das;* **~s, ~s** interview

interviewen /ɪntɐ'vju:ən/ *tr. V.* interview

Interviewer *der;* **~s, ~, Interviewerin** *die;* **~, ~nen** interviewer

intialisieren *tr. V.* (DV) initialize

intim *Adj.* intimate

Intimität *die;* **~, ~en** intimacy

Intim-: ~partner *der,* **~partnerin** *die* intimate partner; sexual partner; **~sphäre** *die* private life

in·tolerant *Adj.* intolerant

In·toleranz *die* intolerance (**gegenüber** of)

Intonation *die;* **~, ~en** intonation

Intranet *das* **~s, ~s** (DV) Intranet

in·transitiv 1 *Adj.* (Sprachw.) intransitive
2 *adv.* intransitively

intravenös (Med.) 1 *Adj.* intravenous
2 *adv.* intravenously

Intrige *die;* **~, ~n** intrigue

Intuition *die;* **~, ~en** intuition

intuitiv 1 *Adj.* intuitive
2 *adv.* intuitively

intus: **etw. ~ haben** (ugs.) (begriffen haben) have got sth. into one's head; (gegessen od. getrunken haben) have put sth. away (coll.)

Invalide *der; adj. Dekl.* invalid

Invasion *die;* **~, ~en** invasion

Inventar *das;* **~s, ~e** (einer Firma) fittings and equipment *pl.*; (eines Hauses, Büros) furnishings and fittings *pl.*

inventarisieren *tr. V.* inventory; draw up *or* make an inventory of

Inventur *die;* **~, ~en** stock-taking

investieren *tr., itr. V.* (auch fig.) invest (**in** + *Akk.* in)

Investition *die;* **~, ~en** investment

Investitions·güter *Pl.* (Wirtsch.) capital goods

Investor *der;* **~s, ~en** /-'to:rən/, **Investorin** *die;* **~, ~nen** (Wirtsch.) investor

in·wie·fern *Adv.* in what way; (bis zu welchem Grade) to what extent

in·wie·weit *Adv.* to what extent

In·zahlung·nahme *die;* **~, ~n** part exchange; trade in (Amer.)

Inzest *der;* **~[e]s, ~e** incest

In·zucht *die;* **~:** inbreeding

in·zwischen *Adv.* **(a)** (seither) in the meantime; since [then]
(b) (bis zu einem Zeitpunkt) (in der Gegenwart) by now; (in der Vergangenheit/Zukunft) by then
(c) (währenddessen) meanwhile

IOK *Abk.* **Internationales Olympisches Komitee** IOC

Ion /i̯:n/ *das;* **~s, ~en** (Physik, Chemie) ion

ionisieren *tr. V.* (Physik, Chemie) ionize

Iono·sphäre *die* ionosphere
Irak *(das);* **~s** *od. der;* **~[s]** Iraq
Iraker *der;* **~s, ~, Irakerin** *die;* **~, ~nen** Iraqi
irakisch Iraqi
Irak·krieg *der* Iraq War
Iran *(das);* **~s** *od. der;* **~[s]** Iran
Iraner *der;* **~s, ~, Iranerin** *die;* **~, ~nen** Iranian
iranisch *Adj.* Iranian
irden *Adj.* earthen[ware]
irdisch *Adj.* **(a)** earthly; worldly ‹*goods, pleasures, possessions*›
(b) (zur Erde gehörig) terrestrial; **das ~e Leben** life on earth
Ire *der;* **~n, ~n** Irishman
irgend *Adv.* **(a) ~ so ein Politiker** (ugs.) some politician [or other]; **~ so etwas** something like that
(b) (irgendwie) **wenn ~ möglich** if at all possible
irgend-: ~ein *Indefinitpron.* **(a)** *attr.* some; (fragend, verneinend) any; **(b)** *subst.* **~einer/~eine** someone; somebody; (fragend, verneinend) anyone; anybody; **~eines** *od.* (ugs.) **~eins** any one; **~einmal** *Adv.* sometime; **~etwas** something; (fragend, verneinend) anything; **~jemand** *Indefinitpron.* someone; somebody; (fragend, vereinend) anyone; anybody; **~wann** *Adv.* [at] some time [or other]; (zu jeder beliebigen Zeit) [at] any time; **~was** *Indefinitpron.* (ugs.) something [or other]; (fragend, verneinend) anything; **~welch** *Indefinitpron.* some; (fragend, verneinend) any; **~wer** *Indefinitpron.* (ugs.) somebody or other (coll.); (fragend, verneinend) anyone; anybody; **~wie** *Adv.* somehow; **~wo** *Adv.* somewhere; (fragend, verneinend) anywhere; **~woher** *Adv.* from somewhere; (fragend, verneinend) from anywhere; **~wohin** *Adv.* somewhere; (fragend, verneinend) anywhere
Irin *die;* **~, ~nen** Irishwoman
Iris *die;* **~, ~** (Bot., Anat.) iris
irisch *Adj.* Irish
Irland *(das);* **~s** Ireland
Ironie *die;* **~, ~n** irony
ironisch 1 *Adj.* ironic; ironical
2 *adv.* ironically
ir·rational 1 *Adj.* irrational
2 *adv.* irrationally
irre 1 *Adj.* **(a)** insane
(b) (salopp: faszinierend) amazing (coll.)
2 *adv.* (salopp) terribly (coll.)
Irre *der/die; adj. Dekl.* madman/madwoman; lunatic; (fig.) lunatic
irre-, Irre-: ~|führen *tr. V.* mislead; (täuschen) deceive; **~führung** *die:* **eine bewusste ~führung** a deliberate attempt to mislead; **~führung der Öffentlichkeit** misleading the public
ir·relevant *Adj.* irrelevant **(für** to)
irre|machen *tr. V.* disconcert; put off
irren 1 *refl. V.* be mistaken; **Sie haben sich in der Nummer geirrt** you've got the wrong number
2 *itr. V.* **(a) da ~ Sie** you are wrong there
(b) *mit sein* (ziellos umherstreifen) wander
Irren-: ~anstalt *die* (veralt. abwertend) mental home; **~haus** *das* (abwertend) [lunatic] asylum
ir·reparabel *Adj.* irreparable
Irr·fahrt *die* wandering
irriger·weise *Adv.* mistakenly
Irritation *die;* **~, ~en** irritation
irritieren *tr., itr. V.* **(a)** (verwirren) put off
(b) (stören) disturb
irr-, Irr-: ~licht *das* will o' the wisp; **~sinn** *der* **(a)** insanity; madness; **(b)** (ugs. abwertend) lunacy; **~sinnig** 1 *Adj.* **(a)** (geistig gestört) insane; mad; (absurd) idiotic; **(b)** (ugs.: extrem) terrible (coll.); terrific (coll.) ‹*speed, heat*›; 2 *adv.* (ugs.) terribly (coll.)
Irrtum *der;* **~s, Irrtümer** mistake; **~!** wrong!; **im ~ sein** be wrong *or* mistaken
irrtümlich 1 *Adj.* incorrect
2 *adv.* by mistake
Irr·weg *der* error; **diese Methode hat sich als ~ erwiesen** this method has proved to be wrong
Ischias *der od. das od. (Med.) die;* **~:** sciatica
Islam /ɪs'la:m *od.* 'ɪslam/ *der;* **~[s]** Islam
islamisch *Adj.* Islamic
Islamismus *der;* **~:** Islamic fundamentalism; Islamism
Islamist *der;* **~en, ~en, Islamistin** *die;* **~, ~nen** Islamic fundamentalist; Islamist
islamistisch *Adj.* Islamic fundamentalist; Islamist
Island *(das);* **~s** Iceland
Isländer *der;* **~s, ~, Isländerin** *die;* **~, ~nen** Icelander
isländisch *Adj.* Icelandic
Isolation *die;* **~, ~en** ▸ ISOLIERUNG
Isolator *der;* **~s, ~en** insulator
Isolier·band *das* insulating tape
isolieren *tr. V.* **(a)** isolate
(b) (Technik) insulate ‹*wiring, wall, etc.*›; lag ‹*boilers, pipes, etc.*›
Isolier·station *die* (Med.) isolation ward
Isolierung *die;* **~, ~en (a)** isolation
(b) (Technik) ▸ ISOLIEREN B: insulation; lagging
Isotop *das;* **~s, ~e** isotope
Israel /'ɪsrae:l/ *(das);* **~s** Israel
Israeli *der;* **~[s], ~[s]/***die;* **~, ~[s]** Israeli
israelisch *Adj.* Israeli
Israelit *der;* **~en, ~en, Israelitin** *die;* **~, ~nen** Israelite
israelitisch *Adj.* Israelite
iss, *iß *Imperativ Sg. v.* ESSEN
isst, *ißt *2. u. 3. Pers. Sg. Präsens v.* ESSEN

ist *3. Pers. Sg. Präsens v.* SEIN
Italien /i'ta:li̯ən/ *(das);* **~s** Italy
Italiener *der;* **~s, ~, Italienerin** *die;* **~, ~nen** Italian
italienisch *Adj.* Italian
I-Tüpfel[chen] *das;* **~s, ~:** final touch; **bis aufs [letzte] ~:** down to the last detail
i.V. *Abk.* = **in Vertretung**

Jj

j, J /jɔt, *österr.:* je:/ *das;* **~, ~:** j/J
ja 1 *Interj.* yes; (nachgestellt: nicht wahr?) won't you/doesn't it *etc.?*
2 *Partikel* **Sie wissen ja, dass ...:** you know, of course, that ...; **da seid ihr ja!** there you are!
Ja *das;* **~[s], ~[s]** yes; **mit ~ stimmen** vote yes
Jacht *die;* **~, ~en** yacht
Jacke *die;* **~, ~n** jacket; (gestrickt) cardigan
Jacken·kleid *das* dress and jacket combination
Jacket·krone /'dʒɛkɪt-/ *die* (Zahnmed.) jacket crown
Jackett /ʒa'kɛt/ *das;* **~s, ~s** jacket
Jade *die;* **~:** jade
Jagd *die;* **~, ~en (a) die ~:** shooting; hunting; **auf die ~ gehen** go hunting/shooting
(b) (Veranstaltung) shoot; (Hetzjagd) hunt
(c) (Verfolgung) hunt; (Verfolgungsjagd) chase; **auf jmdn./etw. ~ machen** hunt for sb./sth.
Jagd-: ~beute *die* bag; kill; **~bomber** *der* (Luftwaffe) fighter-bomber; **~flieger** *der,* **~fliegerin** *die* (Luftwaffe) fighter pilot; **~flugzeug** *das* (Luftwaffe) fighter aircraft; **~gewehr** *das* sporting gun; **~horn** *das* hunting horn; **~hund** *der* gun dog; **~hütte** *die* shooting box; **~revier** *das* preserve; shoot; **~schein** *der* game licence; **~wurst** *die* chasseur sausage; **~zeit** *die* open season
jagen 1 *tr. V.* **(a)** hunt ‹*game, fugitive, criminal, etc.*›; shoot ‹*game, game birds*›; (hetzen) chase ‹*fugitive, criminal, etc.*›
(b) (treiben) drive; **jmdn. aus dem Haus ~:** throw sb. out of the house
2 *itr. V.* (die Jagd ausüben) go shooting *or* hunting
Jäger *der;* **~s, ~: (a)** hunter
(b) (Milit.) rifleman
(c) (Soldatenspr.: Jagdflugzeug) fighter
Jäger·hut *der* huntsman's hat
Jägerin *die;* **~, ~nen** huntress
Jäger-: ~latein *das* (scherzh.) [hunter's] tall story/stories; **das ist das reinste ~latein** that's all wild exaggeration; **~rock** *der* hunting jacket; **~schnitzel** *das* (Kochk.) escalope chasseur
Jaguar *der;* **~s, ~e** jaguar
jäh 1 *Adj.* (geh.) **(a)** sudden; abrupt ‹*change, movement, stop*›; sudden, sharp ‹*pain*›
(b) (steil) steep; precipitous
2 *adv.* **(a)** ‹*change*› abruptly
(b) (steil) ‹*fall, drop*› steeply
jählings *Adv.* (geh.) **(a)** (plötzlich) ‹*change, end, stop*› suddenly, abruptly; ‹*die*› suddenly
(b) (steil) steeply
Jahr *das;* **~[e]s, ~e** year; **ein halbes ~:** six months; **im ~[e] 1908** in [the year] 1908; **er ist zwanzig ~e [alt]** he is twenty years old; **Kinder bis zu zwölf ~en** children up to the age of twelve; **zwischen den ~en** between Christmas and the New Year
jahr·aus *Adv.* **~, jahrein** year in, year out
jahre·lang 1 *Adj.* [many] years of; long-standing ‹*feud, friendship*›
2 *adv.* for [many] years
jähren *refl. V.* **heute jährt sich zum zehnten Mal, dass ...:** it is ten years ago today that ...
Jahres-: ~bilanz *die* (Wirtsch., Kaufmannsspr.) annual balance [of accounts]; (Dokument) annual balance sheet; **~einkommen** *das* annual income; **~ende** *das* end of the year; **~frist: in** *od.* **innerhalb** *od.* **binnen ~frist** within [a period of] a *or* one year; **~hälfte** *die:* **die erste/zweite ~hälfte** the first/secound half *or* six months of the year; **~karte** *die* yearly season ticket; **~tag** *der* anniversary; **~umsatz** *der* annual turnover; **~urlaub** *der* annual holiday *or* (formal) leave *or* (Amer.) vacation; **~wechsel** *der* turn of the year; **zum ~wechsel die besten Wünsche** best wishes for the New Year; **~zahl** *die* date; **~zeit** *die* season
Jahr·gang *der* **(a)** (Altersklasse) year; **der ~ 1900** those born in 1900
(b) (eines Weines) vintage
(c) (einer Zeitschrift) set [of issues] for a/the year
Jahr·hundert *das* century
Jahrhundert·wende *die* turn of the century
-jährig (a) (... Jahre alt) **ein elfjähriges Kind** an eleven-year-old child

*alte Schreibung - vgl. Hinweis auf S. xiv

(b) (... Jahre dauernd) ... year's/years'; **nach vierjähriger Vorbereitung** after four years' preparation; **mit dreijähriger Verspätung** three years late

jährlich 1 *Adj.*; annual; yearly 2 *adv.* annually; yearly; **zweimal ~**: twice a year

Jahr-: ~markt *der* fair; funfair; **~tausend** *das* thousand years; millennium; **~tausend·wende** *die* turn of the millennium; **~zehnt** *das* decade

jahrzehnte·lang 1 *Adj.*; *nicht präd.* decades of ‹*practice, experience, etc.*› 2 *adv.* for decades

Jäh·zorn *der* violent anger

jäh·zornig 1 *Adj.* violent-tempered 2 *adv.* in a blind rage

ja·ja *Part.* (ugs.) **(a)** (seufzend) **~[, so ist das Leben]** oh well[, that's life] **(b)** (ungeduldig) **~[, ich komme schon]**! all right, all right[, I'm coming]!

Jalousie /ʒalu'zi:/ *die;* **~, ~n** Venetian blind

Jamaika *(das);* **-s** Jamaica

Jamaikaner *der;* **~s, ~, Jamaikanerin** *die;* **~, ~nen** Jamaican

Jammer *der;* **~s** [mournful] wailing; (Elend) misery

jämmerlich 1 *Adj.* **(a)** pitiful **(b)** wretched ‹*appearance, existence, etc.*›; paltry, meagre ‹*quantity*› 2 *adv.* pitifully

jammern *itr. V.* wail; (sich beklagen) moan

jammer·schade *Adj.* (ugs.) **es ist ~, dass ...**: it's a crying shame that ...; **es ist ~ um ihn** it's a great pity about him

Janker *der;* **~s, ~** (südd., österr.) Alpine jacket

Januar *der;* **~[s], ~e** January

Japan *(das);* **~s** Japan

Japaner *der;* **~s, ~, Japanerin** *die;* **~, ~nen** Japanese

japanisch *Adj.* Japanese

japsen *itr. V.* (ugs.) pant

Jargon /jar'gõ:/ *der;* **~s, ~s** jargon

Jasmin *der;* **~s, ~e** jasmine

Ja·stimme *die* yes-vote

jäten *tr., itr. V.* weed; **Unkraut ~**: weed

Jauche *die;* **~, ~n** liquid manure

Jauche·grube *die* liquid-manure reservoir

jauchzen *itr. V.* cheer; **vor Freude ~**: shout for joy

Jauchzer *der;* **~s, ~**: cry of delight

jaulen *itr. V.* howl

Jause *die;* **~, ~n** (österr.) **(a)** snack; **eine ~ machen** have a snack **(b)** (Nachmittagskaffee) [afternoon] tea

ja·wohl *Part.* certainly

Ja·wort *das* consent; **jmdm. das ~ geben** consent to marry sb.

Jazz /dʒæz *od.* dʒɛs *od.* jats:/ *der;* **~**: jazz

jazzen /'dʒɛsn̩/ *od.* 'jatsn̩/ *itr. V.* play jazz

Jazzer /'dʒɛsɐ *od.* 'jats:ɐ/ *der;* **~s, ~, Jazzerin** *die;* **~, ~nen** jazz musician

Jazz-: ~keller *der* jazz cellar; **~tanz** *der* jazz dance

je[1] 1 *Adv.* **(a)** (jemals) ever; **mehr/besser denn je** more/better than ever **(b)** (jeweils) **je zehn Personen** ten people at a time; **sie kosten je 30 Euro** they cost 30 euros each **(c)** (entsprechend) **je nach Gewicht** according to weight 2 *Präp. mit Akk.* per; for each 3 *Konj.* **je länger, je lieber** the longer the better; **je nachdem** it all depends

je[2] *Interj.* **ach je, wie schade!** oh dear, what a shame!

Jeans /dʒi:nz/ *Pl. od. die;* **~, ~**: jeans *pl.*; denims *pl.*

jede ▶ JEDER

jeden·falls *Adv.* **(a)** in any case **(b)** (zumindest) at any rate

jeder, jede, jedes *Indefinitpron. u. unbest. Zahlwort* 1 *attr.* **(a)** (alle) every **(b)** (alle einzeln) each **(c)** (jeglicher) all 2 *allein stehend* **(a)** (alle) everyone; everybody **(b)** (alle einzeln) **jedes der Kinder** each of the children

jeder-: ~mann *Indefinitpron.* everyone; everybody; **~zeit** *Adv.* [at] any time

jedes ▶ JEDER

***jedes·mal** ▶ MAL[1]

je·doch *Konj., Adv.* however

je·her /*od.* '-'-/ *Adv.* **seit** *od.* **von ~**: always; since time immemorial

jemals *Adv.* ever

jemand *Indefinitpron.* someone; somebody; (fragend, verneinend) anyone; anybody

Jemen *(das);* **~s** *od.* **der; ~[s]** Yemen

jener, jene, jenes *Demonstrativpron.* (geh.) 1 *attr.* that; (im Pl.) those 2 *allein stehend* that one; (im Pl.) those

jenseits 1 *Präp. mit Gen.* on the other side of; (in größerer Entfernung) beyond 2 *Adv.* on the other side; **~ von** on the other side of

Jenseits *das;* **~**: hereafter; beyond

Jersey[1] /'dʒø:ɐ̯zi/ *der;* **~[s], ~s** (Textilind.) jersey

Jersey[2] *das;* **~s, ~s** (Sport: Trikot) jersey

Jesus *(der);* **Jesu** Jesus

Jet /dʒ:ɛt/ *der;* **~[s], ~s** jet; **mit einem ~ fliegen/reisen** fly/travel by jet

jetzig *Adj.* current

jetzt *Adv.* **(a)** just now; **bis ~**: up to now; **bis ~ noch nicht** not yet; **von ~ an** *od.* **ab** from now on[wards]; **erst ~** *od.* **~ erst** only just; **schon ~**: already **(b)** (heutzutage) now; nowadays

jeweilig *Adj.* **(a)** (in einem bestimmten Fall) particular
(b) (zu einer bestimmten Zeit) current; of the time *postpos., not pred.;*
(c) (zugehörig, zugewiesen) respective

jeweils *Adv.* **(a)** (jedesmal) **~ am ersten/letzten Mittwoch des Monats** on the first/last Wednesday of each month
(b) (zur Zeit) at the time

Jg. *Abk.* = **Jahrgang**

Jh. *Abk.* = **Jahrhundert** c.

JH *Abk.* = **Jugendherberge**

jiddisch /ˈjɪdɪʃ/ *Adj.* Yiddish

Job /dʒɔp/ *der;* **~s, ~s** (ugs.; auch DV) job

jobben /dʒɔbn̩/ *itr. V.* (ugs.) do a job/jobs

Job-: ~killer *der* destroyer of jobs; **~sharing** /ˈ-ʃɛərɪŋ/ *das;* **~~s** jobsharing

Joch *das;* **~[e]s, ~e** yoke

Jockei, Jockey /ˈdʒɔke *od.* ˈdʒɔki/ *der;* **~s, ~s** jockey

Jod *das;* **~[e]s** iodine

jodeln *itr., tr. V.* yodel

jod·haltig *Adj.* iodiferous

Joga *der od. das;* **~[s]** yoga

joggen /ˈdʒɔgn̩/ *itr. V.; mit Richtungsangabe mit sein* jog

Jogging·anzug *der* jogging suit

Joghurt /ˈjoːgʊrt/ *der od. das;* **~[s], ~[s]** yoghurt

Joghurt·becher *der* yoghurt pot (Brit.) *or* (Amer.) container

Johannis·beere *die* currant; **rote/weiße/schwarze ~n** redcurrants/white currants/blackcurrants

johlen *itr. V.* yell; (vor Wut) howl

Joint /dʒɔɪnt/ *der;* **~s, ~s** (ugs.) joint (sl.)

Jolle *die;* **~, ~n** keel-centreboard yawl

Jongleur /ʒɔŋˈløːɐ̯/ *der;* **~s, ~e, Jongleurin** *die;* **~, ~nen** juggler

jonglieren *tr., itr. V.* juggle

Joppe *die;* **~, ~n** heavy jacket

Jordanien *(das);* **~s** Jordan

Jordanier *der;* **~s, ~, Jordanierin** *die;* **~, ~nen** Jordanian

jordanisch *Adj.* Jordanian

Jot *das;* **~, ~:** j, J

Journalismus /ʒʊr.../ *der;* **~:** journalism *no art.*

Journalist *der;* **~en, ~en, Journalistin** *die;* **~, ~nen** journalist

journalistisch [1] *Adj.* journalistic; **eine ~e Ausbildung** a training in journalism
[2] *adv.* journalistically; **~ tätig sein** be a journalist

Joystick/ˈdʒɔystik/ *der;* **~s, ~s** (DV) joystick

jr. *Abk.* = **junior** Jr.

Jubel *der;* **~s** rejoicing; jubilation; (laut) cheering

Jubel·jahr *das* jubilee; **alle ~e [einmal]** once in a blue moon

jubeln *itr. V.* cheer; **über etw.** (*Akk.*) **~:** rejoice over sth.

Jubilar *der;* **~s, ~e** man celebrating his anniversary/birthday

Jubilarin *die;* **~, ~nen** woman celebrating her anniversary/birthday

Jubiläum *das;* **~s, Jubiläen** anniversary; (eines Monarchen) jubilee

jubilieren *itr. V.* (geh.) jubilate (literary); rejoice

juchzen *itr. V.* (ugs.) shout with glee

jucken [1] *tr., itr. V.* **(a) mir juckt die Haut** I itch; **es juckt mich hier** I've got an itch here
(b) (Juckreiz verursachen) irritate
[2] *tr. V.* (reizen, verlocken) **es juckt mich, das zu tun** I am itching to do it
[3] *refl. V.* (ugs.: sich kratzen) scratch

Juck·reiz *der* itch

Jude *der;* **~n, ~n** Jew

Juden: ~hass, *~haß *der* anti-Semitism; hatred of [the] Jews; **~stern** *der* (ns.) Star of David

Judentum *das;* **~s (a)** (Volk) Jewry; Jews *pl.;*
(b) (Kultur u. Religion) Judaism

Juden·verfolgung *die* persecution of [the] Jews

Jüdin *die;* **~, ~nen** Jewess

jüdisch *Adj.* Jewish

Judo *das;* **~[s]** judo *no art.*

Jugend *die;* **~ (a)** youth
(b) (Jugendliche) young people

jugend-, Jugend-: ~amt *das* youth office (*agency responsible for education and welfare of young people*); **~arbeitslosigkeit** *die* youth unemployment; **~arrest** *der* detention in a community home; **~bewegung** *die* (hist.) [German] youth Movement; **~buch** *das* book for young people; **~frei** *Adj.* ‹*film, book, etc.*› suitable for persons under 18; **nicht ~frei** ‹*film*› not U-certificate *pred.;* **~gefährdend** *Adj.* liable to have an undesirable influence on the moral development of young people *postpos.;* **~heim** *das* youth centre; **~herberge** *die* youth hostel; **~klub** *der* youth club; **~kriminalität** *die* juvenile delinquency

jugendlich *Adj.* **(a)** young ‹*offender, customer, etc.*›
(b) (für Jugendliche charakteristisch) youthful

Jugendliche *der/die; adj. Dekl.* young person; **die ~n** the young people

Jugend-: ~liebe *die* sweetheart of one's youth; **~schutz** *der* protection of young people; **~schutz·gesetz** *das* laws *pl.* protecting young people; **~sprache** *die* young people's language *no art.;* **~stil** *der* art nouveau; (in Deutschland) Jugendstil; **~strafanstalt** *die* detention centre;

*old spelling - see note on page xiv

~strafe *die* youth custody sentence; **~sünde** *die* youthful folly; **~zeit** *die* youth; **~zentrum** *das* youth centre
Jugo·slawe *der* Yugoslav
Jugo·slawien *(das); ~s* Yugoslavia
Jugo·slawin *die* Yugoslav
jugo·slawisch *Adj.* Yugoslav[ian]
Julei *der; ~[s], ~s* ▶ JULI
Juli *der; ~[s], ~s* July; *s. auch* APRIL
jung *Adj.;* **jünger, jüngst... (a)** young; new ‹*project, undertaking, sport, marriage, etc.*› **(b)** (letzt...) recent; **in jüngster Zeit** recently
Junge[1] *der; ~n, ~n od.* (ugs.) **Jung[en]s** boy
Junge[2] *das; adj. Dekl.* **ein ~s** one of the young; **~ kriegen** give birth to young
jungen *itr. V.* give birth; ‹*cat*› have kittens; ‹*dog*› have pups
jungenhaft *Adj.* boyish
jünger *Adj.* youngish; **sie ist noch ~:** she is still quite young; *s. auch* JUNG
Jünger *der; ~s, ~,* **Jüngerin** *die; ~, ~nen* follower
Jungfer *die; ~, ~n* (abwertend: ältere ledige Frau) spinster
Jungfern·fahrt *die* maiden voyage
Jungfern·häutchen *das; ~s, ~:* hymen
Jung·frau *die* **(a)** virgin
(b) (Astrol.) Virgo
jung·fräulich *Adj.* (geh., auch fig.) virgin
Jung·geselle *der* bachelor
Jung·gesellin *die* bachelor girl
Jüngling *der; ~s, ~e* (geh., spött.) youth; boy
jüngst *Adv.* (geh.) recently
jüngst... ▶ JUNG
Jüngste *der/die; adj. Dekl.* youngest [one]
Jung-: ~verheiratete *der/die; adj. Dekl.,* young married man/woman; **die ~verheirateten** the newly-weds; **~wähler** *der,* **~wählerin** *die* first-time voter
Juni *der; ~[s], ~s* June; *s. auch* APRIL
junior *indekl. Adj.; nach Personennamen* junior
Junior *der; ~s, ~en* **(a)** (oft scherzh.) junior (joc.)
(b) (Kaufmannsspr.) junior partner
Junior-: ~chef *der* owner's *or* (coll.) boss's son; **~chefin** *die* owner's *or* (coll.) boss's daughter
Juno *der; ~[s], ~s* ▶ JUNI
Junta /ˈxʊnta/ *die; ~,* **Junten** junta
Jura law *sing.; ~* **studieren** read Law
Jurist *der; ~en, ~en,* **Juristin** *die; ~, ~nen* lawyer; jurist
juristisch *Adj.* legal
Jury /ʒyˈriː/ *die; ~, ~s* **(a)** (Preisrichter) panel [of judges]; jury
(b) (Sachverständige) panel [of experts]
just *Adv.* (veralt., noch scherzh.) just; **~ in diesem Augenblick** just at that moment; at that very moment
justieren *tr. V.* adjust
Justierung *die; ~, ~en* adjustment
Justiz *die; ~:* justice; (Behörden) judiciary
Justiz-: ~irrtum *der* miscarriage of justice; **~minister** *der,* **~ministerin** *die* Minister of Justice; **~ministerium** *das* Ministry of Justice; **~mord** *der* judicial murder; **~vollzugs·anstalt** *die* (Amtsspr.) penal institution (formal); prison
Jute *die; ~:* jute
Jütland *(das); ~s* Jutland
Juwel *das od. der; ~s, ~en* piece of jewellery; (Edelstein) jewel
Juwelier /juvəˈliːɐ̯/ *der; ~s* jeweller
Juwelier·geschäft *das* jeweller's shop
Jux *der; ~es, ~e* (ugs.) joke

Kk

k, **K** /ka:/ *das;* ~, ~: k/K

Kabarett *das;* **~s, ~s** *od.* **~e (a)** satirical revue
(b) (Ensemble) cabaret act

Kabarettist *der;* **~en, ~en, Kabarettistin** *die;* **~, ~nen** revue performer

kabarettistisch *Adj.* [satirical] revue *attrib.;* **~e Szenen** scenes in the style of a [satirical] revue

kabbeln *refl. V.* (ugs.) bicker **(mit** with**)**

Kabel *das;* **~s, ~:** cable; (für kleineres Gerät) flex

Kabel·fernsehen *das* cable television

Kabeljau *der;* **~s, ~e** *od.* **~s** cod

kabellos 1 *Adj.* wireless
2 *adv.* ‹*communicate*› in wireless format; ‹*install*› without wires

Kabine *die;* **~, ~n (a)** cabin
(b) (Umkleideraum, abgeteilter Raum) cubicle
(c) (einer Seilbahn) [cable] car

Kabinett *das;* **~s, ~e** Cabinet

Kabrio *das;* **~s, ~s, Kabriolett** *das;* **~s, ~s** convertible

Kachel *die;* **~, ~n** [glazed] tile

kacheln *tr. V.* tile

Kachel·ofen *der* tiled stove

Kacke *die;* **~** (derb; auch fig.) shit (coarse); crap (coarse)

kacken *itr. V.* (derb) shit (coarse); crap (coarse)

Kadaver *der;* **~s, ~:** carcass

Kader *der od.* (schweiz.) *das;* **~s, ~ (a)** cadre
(b) (Sport) squad

Käfer *der;* **~s, ~:** beetle

Kaff *das;* **~s, ~s** *od.* **Käffer** (ugs. abwertend) dump (coll.)

Kaffee /'kafe *od.* (österr.) ka'fe:/ *der;* **~s, ~s**
(a) coffee
(b) (Nachmittags~) afternoon coffee; **~ trinken** have afternoon coffee

Kaffee-: ~kanne *die* coffee pot; **~kränzchen** *das* (veralt.) **(a)** (Zusammentreffen) coffee afternoon; **(b)** (Gruppe) coffee circle; **~maschine** *die* coffee maker; **~mühle** *die* coffee grinder; **~satz** *der* coffee grounds *pl.;* **~tante** *die* (ugs. scherzh.) coffee addict

Käfig *der;* **~s, ~e** cage

kahl *Adj.* **(a)** (ohne Haare) bald; **jmdn. ~ scheren** shave sb.'s head
(b) (ohne Grün, schmucklos) bare; **etw. ~ fressen** strip sth. bare

kahl-, Kahl-: ***~|fressen** ▶ KAHL B; **~köpfig** *Adj.* bald[-headed]; ***~|scheren** ▶ KAHL A; **~schlag** *der* **(a)** clear-felling *no indef. art.;* **(b)** (Waldfläche) clear-felled area

Kahn *der;* **~[e]s, Kähne (a)** (Ruder~) rowing boat; (Stech~) punt
(b) (Lastschiff) barge

Kai *der;* **~s, ~s** quay

Kaiser *der;* **~s, ~:** emperor

Kaiserin *die;* **~, ~nen** empress

Kaiser-: ~krone *die* imperial crown; **~reich** *das* empire; **~schnitt** *der* Caesarean section; **~wetter** *das* (scherzh.) glorious, sunny weather (*for an event*)

Kajüte *die;* **~, ~n** (Seemannsspr.) cabin

Kakao /ka'kau:/ *der;* **~s, ~s** cocoa; **jmdn./etw. durch den ~ ziehen** (ugs.) make fun of sb./sth.

Kakerlak *der;* **~s** *od.* **~en, ~en** cockroach

Kaktus *der;* **~, Kakteen** cactus

Kalauer *der;* **~s, ~:** corny joke (coll.); (Wortspiel) atrocious *or* (coll.) corny pun

Kalb *das;* **~[e]s, Kälber (a)** calf
(b) (ugs.: ~fleisch) veal

kalben *itr. V.* calve

Kalb·fleisch *das* veal

Kalbs-: ~braten *der* (Kochk.) roast veal *no indef. art.;* (Gericht) roast of veal; **~leder** *das* calfskin; **~schnitzel** *das* veal cutlet

Kalender *der;* **~s, ~:** calendar; (Taschen~) diary

Kalender-: ~jahr *das* calendar year; **~monat** *der* calendar month

Kali *das;* **~s, ~s** potash

Kaliber *das;* **~s, ~: (a)** (Technik, Waffenkunde) calibre
(b) (ugs., oft abwertend) sort; kind

Kalifornien /kali'fɔrni̯ən/ (*das*)*;* **~s** California

Kalium (Chemie) *das;* **~s** potassium

Kalk *der;* **~[e]s, ~e** calcium carbonate; (Baustoff) lime; quicklime

kalken *tr. V.* whitewash

Kalk-: ~mangel *der* calcium deficiency; **~stein** *der* limestone

Kalkül *das od.* **der; ~s, ~e** (geh.) calculation

Kalkulation *die;* **~, ~en** (auch Wirtsch.) calculation

kalkulieren *tr. V.* calculate ‹*cost, price*›; cost ‹*product, article*›

Kalorie *die;* **~, ~n** calorie

kalorien-, Kalorien-: ~arm 1 *Adj.*

---

*alte Schreibung - vgl. Hinweis auf S. xiv

low-calorie *attrib.;* **~arm sein** be low in calories; 2 *adv.* **~arm kochen** cook low-calorie meals; **~gehalt** *der* calorie content

kalt; kälter, kältest… 1 *Adj.* cold; frosty ‹*atmosphere, smile*›; **~ bleiben** (fig.) remain unmoved; **jmdn. ~ lassen** (ugs.) leave sb. unmoved; (nicht interessieren) leave sb. cold (coll.)
2 *adv.* **(a) ~ duschen** have a cold shower **Getränke/Sekt ~ stellen** cool drinks/chill champagne
(b) (nüchtern) coldly
(c) (abweisend, unfreundlich) frostily

kalt-, Kalt-: *~|bleiben ▶ KALT 1; **~blütig** 1 *Adj.* **(a)** cool-headed; **(b)** (abwertend: skrupellos) cold-blooded; 2 *adv.* **(a)** coolly; **(b)** (abwertend: skrupellos) cold-bloodedly; **~blütigkeit** *die;* **~~:** ▶ ~BLÜTIG A, B: cool-headedness; cold-bloodedness

Kälte *die;* ~ cold; (fig.) coldness

Kälte-: ~einbruch *der* (Met.) sudden onset of cold weather; **~grad** *der* degree of frost

kälter ▶ KALT

kältest… ▶ KALT

Kälte·welle *die* cold spell

kalt-, Kalt-: ~gepresst, *~gepreßt *Adj.* cold-pressed; **~herzig** *Adj.* cold-hearted; ***~lächelnd** *Adv.* (ugs. abwertend) **etw. ~lächelnd tun** take callous pleasure in doing sth.; ***~|lassen** ▶ KALT 1; **~|machen** *tr. V.* (salopp) **jmdn. ~machen** do sb. in (sl.); **~miete** *die* rent exclusive of heating; **~schale** *die: cold sweet soup made with fruit, beer, wine, or milk;* **~schnäuzig** (ugs.) 1 *Adj.* cold and insensitive; (frech) insolent; 2 *adv.* coldly and insensitively; (frech) insolently; **~stellen** *tr. V.* (ugs.) **jmdn. ~stellen** put sb. out of the way (coll. joc.)

kam *1. u. 3. Pers. Prät. v.* KOMMEN

Kambodscha *(das);* **~s** Cambodia

käme *1. u. 3. Pers. Konjunktiv II v.* KOMMEN

Kamel *das;* **~s, ~e** camel

Kamera *die;* **~, ~s** camera

Kamerad *der;* **~en, ~en, Kameradin** *die;* **~, ~nen** companion; (Freund[in]) friend; (Mitschüler[in]) mate; (Soldat[in]) comrade; (Sport) teammate

Kameradschaft *die;* **~:** comradeship

kameradschaftlich 1 *Adj.* comradely 2 *adv.* in a comradely way

Kamera-: ~frau *die* camerawoman; **~mann** *der Pl.;* **~männer** *od.* **~leute** cameraman; **~team** *das* camera crew

Kamerun /'kaməru:n/ *(das);* **~s** Cameroon; the Cameroons *pl.*

Kamille *die;* **~, ~n** camomile

Kamin *der, schweiz.: das;* **~s, ~e** fireplace

Kamin·feger *der,* **Kamin·fegerin** *die* (bes. südd.) ▶ SCHORNSTEINFEGER

Kamm *der;* **~[e]s, Kämme (a)** comb
(b) (bei Hühnern usw.) comb
(c) (Gebirgs~) ridge

kämmen *tr. V.* comb

Kammer *die;* **~, ~n (a)** storeroom
(b) (Biol., Med., Technik, Waffenkunde) chamber
(c) (Parl.) chamber

Kammer-: ~diener *der* (veralt.) valet; **~jäger** *der,* **~jägerin** *die* pest controller; **~musik** *die* chamber music; **~sänger** *der,* **~sängerin** *die: title awarded to singer of outstanding merit;* **~zofe** *die* (veralt.) lady's maid

Kamm·garn *das* worsted

Kampagne /kam'panjə/ *die;* **~, ~n** campaign

Kampf *der;* **~[e]s, Kämpfe (a)** (militärisch) battle (um for)
(b) (zwischen persönlichen Gegnern) fight; (fig.) struggle
(c) (Wett~) contest; (Boxen) contest; bout
(d) (Einsatz aller Mittel) fight (**um, für** for; **gegen** against)

kampf-, Kampf-: ~abstimmung *die* (Politik) crucial vote; **~bereit** *Adj.* ready to fight *postpos.;* ‹*army, troops*› ready for battle

kämpfen *itr. V.* **(a)** fight
(b) (Sport: sich messen) ‹*team*› play; ‹*wrestler, boxer*› fight

Kampfer *der;* **~s** camphor

Kämpfer *der;* **~s, ~, Kämpferin** *die;* **~, ~nen** fighter

kampf-, Kampf-: ~fähig *Adj.* ‹*troops*› fit for action; ‹*boxer etc.*› fit to fight; **~handlungen** *Pl.* fighting *sing.;* **~preis** *der* (Wirtsch.) cut price; **~richter** *der,* **~richterin** *die* (Sport) judge; **~unfähig** *Adj.* ‹*troops*› unfit for action; ‹*boxer etc.*› unfit to fight

kampieren *itr. V.* camp

Kanada *(das);* **~s** Canada

Kanadier /ka'na:di̯ɐ/ *der;* **~s, ~, Kanadierin** *die;* **~, ~nen** Canadian

kanadisch *Adj.* Canadian

Kanal *der;* **~s, Kanäle (a)** canal
(b) (Geogr.) **der ~:** the [English] Channel
(c) (für Abwässer) sewer
(d) (zur Entwässerung, Bewässerung) channel; (Graben) ditch
(e) (Rundf., Ferns., Weg der Information) channel

Kanalisation *die;* **~, ~en** sewerage system; sewers *pl.*

kanalisieren *tr. V.* **(a)** (lenken) channel ‹*energies, goods, etc.*›
(b) (schiffbar machen) canalize

Kanal·tunnel *der* Channel Tunnel

Kanaren *Pl.* Canaries

Kanarien·vogel /ka'na:ri̯ən-/ *der* canary

Kanarische Inseln *Pl.* Canary Islands

Kandare *die;* **~, ~n** curb bit; **jmdn. an die ~ nehmen** (fig.) take sb. in hand

Kandidat *der;* **~en, ~en, Kandidatin** *die;* **~, ~nen (a)** candidate
(b) (beim Quiz usw.) contestant

Kandidatur *die;* **~, ~en** candidature (**auf** + *Akk.* for)
kandidieren *itr. V.* stand [as a candidate] (**für** for)
kandieren *tr. V.* candy; **kandiert** crystallized ‹*orange, petal*›; glacé ‹*cherry, pear*›; candied ‹*peel*›
Kandis *der;* **~, Kandis·zucker** *der* rock candy
Känguru, ***Känguruh** *das;* **~s, ~s** kangaroo
Kaninchen *das;* **~s, ~:** rabbit
Kanister *der;* **~s, ~:** can; [metal/plastic] container
kann *1. u. 3. Pers. Sg. Präsens v.* KÖNNEN
Kännchen *das;* **~s, ~:** [small] pot; (für Milch) [small] jug
Kanne *die;* **~, ~n (a)** pot; (für Milch, Wein, Wasser) jug
(b) (Henkel~) can; (für Milch) pail; (beim Melken) churn
kannst *2. Pers. Sg. Präsens v.* KÖNNEN
kannte *1. u. 3. Pers. Sg. Prät. v.* KENNEN
Kanon *der;* **~s, ~s** canon
Kanone *die;* **~, ~n** cannon; (fig. ugs.: Könner) ace
Kantate *die;* **~, ~n** (Musik) cantata
Kante *die;* **~, ~n** edge
kantig *Adj.* square-cut ‹*timber, stone*›; rough-edged ‹*rock*›; angular ‹*face*›; square ‹*chin*›
Kantine *die;* **~, ~n** canteen
Kanton *der;* **~s, ~e** canton
kantonal [1] *Adj.* cantonal
[2] *adv.* on a cantonal basis
Kantor *der;* **~s, ~en** choirmaster and organist
Kantorin *die;* **~, ~nen** choirmistress and organist
Kanu *das;* **~s, ~s** canoe
Kanüle *die;* **~, ~n** (Med.) cannula
Kanzel *die;* **~, ~n (a)** pulpit
(b) (Flugw.) cockpit
Kanzlei *die;* **~, ~en (a)** (veralt.: Büro) office
(b) (Anwalts~) chambers *pl.* (*of barrister*); office (*of lawyer*)
Kanzler *der;* **~s, ~** chancellor
Kap *das;* **~s, ~s** cape
Kapazität *die;* **~, ~en (a)** capacity
(b) (Experte) expert
Kapelle *die;* **~, ~n (a)** (Archit.) chapel
(b) (Musik~) band; [light] orchestra
Kapell·meister *der,* **Kapell·meisterin** *die* bandmaster/-mistress; (im Orchester) conductor; (im Theater usw.) musical director
Kaper *die;* **~, ~n** caper *usu. in pl.*
kapern *tr. V.* **(a)** (hist.) capture
(b) (ugs.) **jmdn. [für etw.] ~:** rope sb. in[to sth.]
kapieren (ugs.) [1] *tr. V.* (ugs.) get (coll.)
[2] *itr. V.* **kapiert?** got it? (coll.)
Kapital *das;* **~s, ~e** *od.* **~ien (a)** capital
(b) (fig.) asset
Kapital·anlage *die* (Wirtsch.) capital investment
Kapitalismus *der;* **~:** capitalism *no art.*
Kapitalist *der;* **~en, ~en, Kapitalistin** *die;* **~, ~nen** capitalist
kapitalistisch *Adj.* capitalistic
Kapital·verbrechen *das* serious offence; (mit Todesstrafe bedroht) capital offence
Kapitän *der;* **~s, ~e, Kapitänin** *die;* **~, ~nen** captain
Kapitel *das;* **~s, ~:** chapter
Kapitulation *die;* **~, ~en** surrender; capitulation; **seine ~ erklären** admit defeat
kapitulieren *itr. V.* **(a)** surrender; capitulate
(b) (fig.: aufgeben) give up; **vor etw.** (*Dat.*) **~:** give up in the face of sth.
Kaplan *der;* **~s, Kapläne** (kath. Kirche) chaplain; (Hilfsgeistlicher) curate
Kappe *die;* **~, ~n** cap
kappen *tr. V.* **(a)** (Seemannsspr.) cut
(b) (beschneiden) cut back ‹*hedge etc.*›; (abschneiden) cut off ‹*branches etc.*›
Käppi *das;* **~s, ~s** garrison cap
Kapsel *die;* **~, ~n** capsule
Kapstadt (*das*); **~s** Cape Town
kaputt *Adj.* **(a)** broken; **das Telefon ist ~:** the phone is not working
(b) (ugs.: erschöpft) shattered (coll.)
kaputt-: ~|gehen *unr. itr. V.; mit sein* (ugs.) (entzweigehen) break; ‹*machine*› break down, (coll.) pack up; ‹*lightbulb*› go; (zerbrechen) be smashed; **~|lachen** *refl. V.* (ugs.) kill oneself [laughing] (coll.); **~|machen** (ugs.) [1] *tr. V.* break; spoil ‹*sth. made with effort*›; ruin ‹*clothes, furniture, etc.*›; finish ‹*person*› off; [2] *refl. V.* wear oneself out
Kapuze *die;* **~, ~n** hood; (bei Mönchen) cowl; hood
Kapuziner *der;* **~s, ~:** Capuchin [friar]
Karabiner *der;* **~s, ~:** carbine
Karaffe *die;* **~, ~n** carafe; (mit Glasstöpsel) decanter
Karambolage /karambo'la:ʒə/ *die;* **~, ~n** (ugs.) crash; collision
***Karamel** *usw.* ▶ KARAMELL *usw.*
Karamell *der* (*schweiz.: das*); **~s** caramel
Karamell·bonbon *der od. das* caramel [toffee]
Karat *das;* **~[e]s, ~e** carat
Karate *das;* **~[s]** karate
Karawane *die;* **~, ~n** caravan
Kardinal *der;* **~s, Kardinäle** (kath. Kirche) cardinal

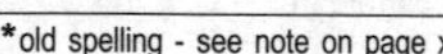
*old spelling - see note on page xiv

Kardinal-: **~fehler** *der* cardinal error; **~tugend** *die* cardinal virtue; **~zahl** *die* cardinal [number]

Karenz *die;* **~, ~en, Karenz·zeit** *die* waiting period

Kar·freitag *der* Good Friday

karg 1 *Adj.* meagre ‹*wages etc.*›; frugal ‹*meal etc.*›; poor ‹*light, accommodation*›; (wenig fruchtbar) barren
2 *adv.* **~ bemessen sein** ‹*helping*› be mingy (Brit. coll.); ‹*supply*› be scanty; **~ leben** live frugally

kärglich 1 *Adj.* meagre, poor ‹*wages etc.*›; poor ‹*light*›; frugal ‹*meal*›; scanty ‹*supply*›
2 *adv.* poorly ‹*lit, paid, rewarded*›

karibisch *Adj.* Caribbean

kariert *Adj.* check, checked ‹*material, pattern*›; check ‹*jacket etc.*›; squared ‹*paper*›

Karies /ˈkaːri̯ɛs/ *die;* **~:** caries

Karikatur *die;* **~, ~en** cartoon; (Porträt) caricature

Karikaturist *der;* **~en, ~en, Karikaturistin** *die;* **~, ~nen** cartoonist; (Porträtist) caricaturist

karikieren *tr. V.* caricature

kariös *Adj.* (Zahnmed.) carious

karitativ *Adj.* charitable

Karl /karl/ (*der*) Charles; **~ der Große** Charlemagne

Karneval /ˈkarnəval/ *der;* **~s, ~e** *od.* **~s** carnival; **~ feiern** join in the carnival festivities

karnevalistisch *Adj.* carnival *attrib.*

Karnevals-: **~kostüm** *das* carnival costume; **~verein** *der* carnival society; **~zug** *der* carnival procession

Karnickel *das;* **~s, ~** (landsch.) rabbit

Kärnten (*das*)*;* **~s** Carinthia

Karo *das;* **~s, ~s (a)** square; (auf der Spitze stehend) diamond
(b) (Karomuster) check
(c) (Kartenspiel: Farbe) diamonds *pl.;*
(d) (Kartenspiel: Karte) diamond

Karosse *die;* **~, ~n** [state] coach

Karosserie *die;* **~, ~n** bodywork

Karotte *die;* **~, ~n** small carrot

Karpaten *Pl.* Carpathians; Carpathian Mountains

Karpfen *der;* **~s, ~:** carp

Karre *die;* **~, ~n** (bes. nordd.) **(a)** ▶ KARREN;
(b) (abwertend: Fahrzeug) [old] heap (coll.)

Karree *das;* **~s, ~s: ums ~ gehen/fahren** walk/drive round the block

karren *tr. V.* **(a)** cart
(b) (salopp: mit einem Auto) run (coll.)

Karren *der;* **~s, ~** (bes. südd., österr.) cart; (zweirädrig) barrow

Karriere /kaˈri̯eːrə/ *die;* **~, ~n** career; **~ machen** make a [successful] career for oneself

Kärrner·arbeit *die* donkey work

Kar·samstag *der* Easter Saturday

Karte *die;* **~, ~n** card; (Speise~) menu; (Fahr~, Flug~, Eintritts~) ticket; (Land~) map; **alles auf eine ~ setzen** stake everything on one chance

Kartei *die;* **~, ~en** card file

Kartei-: **~karte** *die* file card; **~kasten** *der* file-card box

Kartell *das;* **~s, ~e** (Wirtsch., Politik) cartel

Kartell-: **~amt** *das: government body concerned with the control and supervision of cartels;* ≈ Monopolies and Mergers Commission (Brit.); **~gesetz** *das* law relating to cartels; ≈ monopolies law (Brit.)

Karten-: **~haus** *das* house of cards; **~spiel** *das* **(a)** (Spiel mit Karten) card game; **(b)** (Satz Spielkarten) pack *or* (Amer.) deck [of cards]; **~telefon** *das* cardphone; **~vorverkauf** *der* advance booking

Kartoffel *die;* **~, ~n** potato

Kartoffel-: **~brei** *der* mashed potatoes *pl.;* mash (coll.); **~chips** *Pl.* [potato] crisps (Brit.) *or* (Amer.) chips; **~käfer** *der* Colorado beetle; **~kloß** *der* potato dumpling; **~puffer** *der* potato pancake (*made from grated raw potatoes*); **~püree** *das:* ▶ ~BREI

Karton /karˈtɔŋ/ *der;* **~s, ~s (a)** (Pappe) card[board]
(b) (Schachtel) cardboard box

Karussell *das;* **~s, ~s** *od.* **~e** merry-go-round; carousel (Amer.); (kleineres) roundabout

Kar·woche *die* Holy Week

karzinogen *Adj.* (Med.) carcinogenic

Karzinom *das;* **~s, ~e** (Med.) carcinoma

kaschieren *tr. V.* conceal; hide; disguise ‹*fault*›

Kaschmir[1] (*das*)*;* **~s** Kashmir

Kaschmir[2] *der;* **~s, ~e** (Textilw.) cashmere

Käse *der;* **~s, ~:** cheese; (ugs. abwertend: Unsinn) rubbish

Käse-: **~blatt** *das* (salopp abwertend) rag; **~glocke** *die* cheese dome

Kaserne *die;* **~, ~n** barracks *sing. or pl.*

käse·weiß *Adj.* (ugs.) [as] white as a sheet

käsig *Adj.* (ugs.) pasty; pale

Kasino *das;* **~s, ~s (a)** (Spiel~) casino
(b) (Offiziers~) [officers'] mess
(c) (Speiseraum) canteen

Kasko·versicherung *die* (Voll~) comprehensive insurance; (Teil~) *insurance against theft, fire, or act of God*

Kasper *der;* **~s, ~:** ≈ Punch; (fig. ugs.) clown

Kasperl *das;* **~s, ~[n]** (österr.), **Kasperle** *das od.* **der; ~s, ~:** ▶ KASPER

Kasper-: **~puppe** *die* ≈ Punch and Judy puppet; **~theater** *das* ≈ Punch and Judy show; (Puppenbühne) ≈ Punch and Judy theatre

Kasse *die;* **~, ~n (a)** cash box; (Registrier~) till ···>

(b) (Ort zum Bezahlen) cash desk; (im Supermarkt) checkout; (in einer Bank) counter
(c) (Kassenraum) cashier's office
(d) (Theater~, Kino~) box office

Kasseler *das;* **~s** smoked loin of pork

Kassen-: ~arzt *der,* **~ärztin** *die: doctor who treats members of health insurance schemes;* **~bon** *der* sales slip; receipt; **~lage** *die* financial situation; **die ~lage der Firma** the state of the company's finances; **nach ~lage** as finances allow/allowed; **eine Rentenpolitik nach ~lage** a pensions policy dependent on what finances will allow; **~patient** *der,* **~patientin** *die: patient who is a member of a health insurance scheme;* **~wart** *der;* **~~s, ~~e, ~wartin** *die;* **~~, ~~nen** treasurer; **~zettel** *der:* ▶ ~BON

Kassette *die;* **~, ~n (a)** box; case
(b) (mit Büchern, Schallplatten) boxed set; (Tonband~, Film~) cassette

Kassetten-: ~deck *das* cassette deck; **~recorder, ~rekorder** *der;* **~~s, ~~:** cassette recorder

kassieren 1 *tr. V.* **(a)** collect
(b) (ugs.: wegnehmen) confiscate; take away ‹*driving licence*›
2 *itr. V.* **bei jmdm. ~:** give sb. his/her bill *or* (Amer.) check; (ohne Rechnung) settle up with sb.; **darf ich bei Ihnen ~?** would you like your bill?/can I settle up with you?

Kassierer *der;* **~s, ~, Kassiererin** *die;* **~, ~nen** cashier; (bei einem Verein) treasurer

Kastanie /kas'ta:ni̯ə/ *die;* **~, ~n** chestnut

kastanien·braun *Adj.* chestnut

Kästchen *das;* **~s, ~ (a)** small box
(b) (vorgedrucktes Quadrat) square; (auf Fragebögen) box

Kaste *die;* **~, ~n** caste

kasteien *refl. V.* **(a)** (als Bußübung) chastise oneself
(b) (sich Entbehrungen auferlegen) deny oneself

Kasteiung *die;* **~, ~en (a)** (als Bußübung) self-chastisement
(b) (Auferlegung von Entbehrungen) self-denial

Kastell *das;* **~s, ~e (a)** (hist.: röm. Lager) fort
(b) (Burg) castle

Kasten *der;* **~s, Kästen (a)** box; (für Flaschen) crate
(b) (ugs.: Briefkasten) postbox
(c) (ugs. abwertend) (Gebäude) barracks *sing. or pl.;* (Auto) heap (coll.); (fig. ugs.) **etw. auf dem ~ haben** have got it up top (coll.)

Kasten·brot *das* tin [loaf]

Kastration /kastra'ts:i̯o:n/ *die;* **~, ~en** castration

kastrieren *tr. V.* castrate

Kat *der;* **~s, ~s** (ugs.) ▶ KATALYSATOR B

Katalog *der;* **~[e]s, ~e** (auch fig.) catalogue

katalogisieren *tr. V.* catalogue

*alte Schreibung - vgl. Hinweis auf S. xiv

Katalysator *der;* **~s, ~en (a)** (Chemie, fig.) catalyst
(b) (Kfz-W.) catalytic converter

Katamaran *der od. das;* **~s, ~e** catamaran

katapultieren *tr. V.* (auch fig.) catapult; eject ‹*pilot*›

Katarrh /ka'tar/ *der;* **~s, ~e** (Med.) catarrh

katastrophal /katastro'fa:l/ 1 *Adj.* disastrous; (stärker) catastrophic
2 *adv.* disastrously; (stärker) catastrophically

Katastrophe /katas'tro:fə/ *die;* **~, ~n** (Unglück) disaster; (stärker, auch Literaturw.) catastrophe

Katastrophen-: ~alarm *der* disaster alert; **~gebiet** *das* disaster area; **~schutz** *der* (Organisation) emergency services *pl.;* (Maßnahmen) disaster procedures *pl.*

Kategorie *die;* **~, ~n** category

kategorisch 1 *Adj.* categorical
2 *adv.* categorically

Kater *der;* **~s, ~ (a)** tomcat
(b) (ugs.) hangover

Kathedrale *die;* **~, ~n** cathedral

Katholik *der;* **~en, ~en, Katholikin** *die;* **~, ~nen** [Roman] Catholic

katholisch *Adj.* [Roman] Catholic

Katholizismus *der;* **~:** [Roman] Catholicism *no art.*

Katz *die* **~ und Maus [mit jmdm.] spielen** (ugs.) play cat and mouse [with sb.]; **für die ~ sein** (salopp) be a waste of time

Kätzchen *das;* **~s, ~ (a)** little cat; pussy; (junge Katze) kitten
(b) *meist Pl.* catkin

Katze *die;* **~, ~n** cat

katzen-, Katzen-: ~auge *das* reflector; Cat's-eye ®; **~jammer** *der* **(a)** (Kater) hangover; **(b)** (fig.) mood of depression; **~musik** *die* (ugs. abwertend) terrible row (coll.); **~sprung** *der* stone's throw; **~wäsche** *die* (ugs.) **~wäsche machen** have a lick and a promise (coll.)

Kauderwelsch *das;* **~[s]** gibberish *no indef. art.*

kauen *tr., itr. V.* chew; **[die] Nägel ~:** bite one's nails

kauern *itr., refl. V.* crouch [down]; (ängstlich) cower

Kauf *der;* **~[e]s, Käufe (a)** (das Kaufen) buying; purchasing (formal)
(b) (das Gekaufte) purchase

kaufen 1 *tr. V.* buy; purchase
2 *itr. V.* (einkaufen) shop

Käufer *der;* **~s, ~, Käuferin** *die;* **~, ~nen** buyer; purchaser (formal)

Kauf-: ~frau *die* (Geschäftsfrau) businesswoman; (Händlerin) trader; **~haus** *das* department store; **~kraft** *die* (Wirtsch.) **(a)** (Wert des Geldes) purchasing power; **(b)** (Zahlungsfähigkeit) spending power

käuflich [1] *Adj.* **(a)** for sale *postpos.;* **(b)** (bestechlich) venal; **~ sein** be easily bought
[2] *adv.* **etw. ~ erwerben/erstehen** purchase sth.

Kauf·mann *der; Pl.* **Kaufleute (a)** (Geschäftsmann) businessman; (Händler) trader **(b)** (Besitzer) shopkeeper; (eines Lebensmittelladens) grocer

kaufmännisch *Adj.* commercial; business *attrib.*

Kauf-: ~preis *der* purchase price; **~vertrag** *der* contract of sale; (beim Hauskauf) title deed

Kau·gummi *der od. das;* **~s, ~s** chewing gum

Kaukasus *der;* **~:** the Caucasus

Kaulquappe *die;* **~, ~n** tadpole

kaum *Adv.* hardly; scarcely; **~ hatte er Platz genommen, als ...:** no sooner had he sat down than ...

kausal *Adj.* (geh., Sprachw.) causal

Kau·tabak *der* chewing tobacco

Kaution *die;* **~, ~en (a)** (bei Freilassung eines Gefangenen) bail
(b) (beim Mieten einer Wohnung) deposit

Kautschuk *der;* **~s, ~e** rubber

Kauz *der;* **~es, Käuze (a)** (Wald~) tawny owl; (Stein~) little owl
(b) (Sonderling) strange fellow; oddball (coll.)

Kavalier /kava'li:ɐ̯/ *der;* **~s, ~e** gentleman

Kavaliers·delikt *das* trifling offence

Kavallerie /kavalə'ri:/ *die;* **~, ~n** (Milit. hist.) cavalry

Kavallerist *der;* **~en, ~en** cavalryman

Kaviar /'ka:vi̯ar/ *der;* **~s, ~e** caviare

kcal *Abk.* = **Kilo[gramm]kalorie** kcal

keck [1] *Adj.* **(a)** cheeky; saucy (Brit.)
(b) (veralt.: verwegen) bold
(c) (flott) jaunty, pert ‹*hat etc.*›
[2] *adv.* **(a)** cheekily; saucily (Brit.)
(b) (veralt.: verwegen) boldly
(c) (flott) jauntily

Keckheit *die;* **~, ~en (a)** cheek; sauce (Brit.)
(b) (veralt.: Kühnheit) boldness

Kegel *der;* **~s, ~ (a)** cone
(b) (Spielfigur) skittle; (beim Bowling) pin

Kegel-: ~bahn *die* skittle alley; **~förmig** *Adj.* conical

kegeln [1] *itr. V.* play skittles *or* ninepins
[2] *tr. V.* **eine Partie ~:** play a game of skittles *or* ninepins; **eine Neun ~:** score a nine

Kehle *die;* **~, ~n** throat

Kehl·kopf *der* (Anat.) larynx

Kehlkopf·krebs *der* (Med.) cancer of the larynx

Kehre *die;* **~, ~n** sharp bend

kehren¹ [1] *tr. V.* turn
[2] *refl. V.* turn

kehren² [1] *itr. V.* (bes. südd.) sweep; do the sweeping
[2] *tr. V.* sweep; (mit einem Handfeger) brush

Kehricht *der od. das;* **~s** (schweiz.: Müll) refuse; garbage (Amer.)

Kehr·seite *die* **(a)** back; (einer Münze, Medaille) reverse; (scherzh.) (Gesäß) backside
(b) (nachteiliger Aspekt) drawback; disadvantage

kehrt|machen *itr. V.* (ugs.) turn [round and go] back

keifen *itr. V.* (abwertend) nag

Keil *der;* **~[e]s, ~e (a)** (zum Spalten) wedge
(b) (zum Festklemmen) chock; (unter einer Tür) wedge

keilen *refl. V.* (ugs.: sich prügeln) fight; scrap

Keiler *der;* **~s, ~** (Jägerspr.) wild boar

Keilerei *die;* **~, ~en** (ugs.) punch-up (coll.); fight

Keil-: ~riemen *der* (Technik) V-belt; **~schrift** *die* cuneiform script

Keim *der;* **~[e]s, ~e** (Bot.) shoot; (Biol.) embryo

Keim-: ~bahn *die* (Biol.) germ line; **~drüse** *die* (Zool., Med.) gonad

keimen *itr. V.* germinate; (fig.) ‹*hope*› stir

keim-, Keim-: ~frei *Adj.* germ-free; sterile; **~zelle** *die* nucleus

kein *Indefinitpron.* **(a)** no
(b) (ugs.: nicht ganz, nicht einmal) less than

kein... *Indefinitpron.* **~er/~e** nobody; no one; **~s von beiden** neither [of them]

keinerlei *indekl. Adj.* no ... what[so]ever

keines-: ~falls *Adv.* on no account; **~wegs** *Adv.* by no means

kein·mal *Adv.* not [even] once

Keks *der;* **~ od. ~es, ~ od. ~e** biscuit (Brit.); cookie (Amer.)

Kelch *der;* **~[e]s, ~e** goblet; (Rel.) chalice

Kelle *die;* **~, ~n (a)** ladle
(b) (Signalstab) signalling disc
(c) (Maurer~) trowel

Keller *der;* **~s, ~:** cellar; (~geschoss) basement

Keller·assel *die;* **~, ~n** woodlouse

Kellerei *die;* **~, ~en** winery; (Kellerräume) [wine] cellars *pl.*

Keller: ~geschoss, ***~geschoß** *das* basement; **~wohnung** *die* basement flat (Brit.) *or* (Amer.) apartment

Kellner *der;* **~s, ~:** waiter

Kellnerin *die;* **~, ~nen** waitress

kellnern *itr. V.* (ugs.) work as a waiter/waitress

Kelte *der;* **~n, ~n** Celt

Kelter *die;* **~, ~n** winepress

keltern *tr. V.* press ‹*grapes etc.*›

Keltin *die;* **~, ~nen** Celt

keltisch *Adj.* Celtic

Kenia *(das);* **~s** Kenya

Kenianer *der;* **~s, ~, Kenianerin** *die;* **~, ~nen** Kenyan

kennen *unr. tr. V.* know; **jmdn./etw. ~ lernen** get to know sb./sth.; **jmdn. ~ lernen** (jmdm. erstmals begegnen) meet sb.; **jmdn. als etw. ~ lernen** come to know sb. as sth.

Kenner *der;* **~s, ~:** expert (+ *Gen.* on); (von Wein, Speisen) connoisseur

Kenner·blick *der* expert eye; **mit ~:** with an expert eye

Kennerin *die;* **~, ~nen** ▶ KENNER

Kenn·marke *die* [police] identification badge; ≈ [police] warrant card *or* (Amer.) ID card

kenntlich *Adj.*: **~ sein** be recognizable (**an** by); **etw./jmdn. ~ machen** mark sth./make sb. [easily] identifiable

Kenntnis *die;* **~, ~se** knowledge

***kennen|lernen** ▶ KENNEN

Kenntnisnahme *die;* **~** (Papierdt.) **nach ~ der Akten** after giving the documents my/his *etc.* attention

kenntnis·reich *Adj.* well-informed; knowledgeable

kenn-, Kenn-: ~wort *das; Pl.* **~wörter** code word; (Parole) password; code word; **~zahl** *die* index; **~zeichen** *das* **(a)** sign; **(b)** (Erkennungszeichen) badge; (auf einem Behälter, einer Ware usw.) label; (am Fahrzeug) registration number; **~zeichnen** *tr. V.* **(a)** mark; label; mark ‹*way*›; **(b)** (charakterisieren) characterize; **~zeichnend** *Adj.* typical, characteristic (**für** of)

kentern *itr. V. mit sein* capsize

Keramik *die;* **~, ~en** ceramics *pl.;* pottery; (Gegenstand) piece of pottery

Kerbe *die;* **~, ~n** notch

Kerbel *der;* **~s** chervil

Kerb·holz *das:* **etwas auf dem ~ haben** (ugs.) have done a job (sl.)

Kerker *der;* **~s, ~** (hist.) dungeons *pl.;* (einzelne Zelle) dungeon

Kerl *der;* **~s, ~e** (*nordd., md. auch:* **~s**) (ugs.) fellow (coll.); bloke (Brit. coll.)

Kern *der;* **~[e]s, ~e** pip; (von Steinobst) stone; (von Nüssen usw.) kernel; (Atom~) nucleus; (fig.) **der ~ einer Sache** the heart of a matter; **der harte ~:** the hard core

kern-, Kern-: ~energie *die* nuclear energy *no art.;* **~gehäuse** *das* core; **~geschäft** *das* core business; **~gesund** *Adj.* fit as a fiddle *pred.*

kernig *Adj.* earthy ‹*language*›; forceful ‹*speech*›; pithy ‹*saying*›

kern-, Kern-: ~kraft *die* nuclear power; **~kraftwerk** *das* nuclear power station *or* plant; **~los** *Adj.* seedless; **~obst** *das* pomaceous fruit; **~physik** *die* nuclear physics *sing., no art.;* **~reaktor** *der* nuclear reactor; **~seife** *die* washing soap; **~spaltung** *die* (Physik) nuclear fission *no art.;* **~spin·tomographie** /ˈkɛrnspɪntomografiː/ *die;* **~~** (Med.) [nuclear] magnetic resonance imaging; **~waffe** *die* nuclear weapon; **~zeit** *die* core time

Kerze *die;* **~, ~n** candle

kerzen-, Kerzen-: ~gerade, (ugs.) **~grade** 1 *Adj.* dead straight; 2 *adv.* bolt upright; **~halter** *der* candle holder; **~leuchter** *der* candlestick; **~licht** *das* the light of a candle/of candles; **bei ~licht** by candlelight

kess, *keß 1 *Adj.* **(a)** pert; jaunty ‹*hat, dress, etc.*›
(b) (frech) cheeky
2 *adv.* **(a)** (flott) jauntily
(b) (frech) cheekily

Kessel *der;* **~s, ~ (a)** kettle; (zum Kochen) pot; (Wasch~) copper
(b) (Berg~) basin-shaped valley
(c) (Milit.) encircled area

Kessel-: ~stein *der* scale; **~treiben** *das* (Hetzkampagne) witch-hunt

Kette *die;* **~, ~n** chain; (Hals~) necklace; (von Ereignissen) string

ketten *tr. V.* chain (**an** + *Akk.* to)

Ketten-: ~hund *der* guard dog (*kept on a chain*); **~rauchen** *das;* **~~s** chain-smoking *no art.;* **~raucher** *der,* **~raucherin** *die* chain-smoker; **~säge** *die* chain saw; **~schaltung** *die* derailleur gears *pl.*

Ketzer *der;* **~s, ~** (auch fig.) heretic

Ketzerei *die;* **~, ~en** (auch fig.) heresy

Ketzerin *die;* **~, ~nen** ▶ KETZER

keuchen *itr. V.* gasp for breath

Keuch·husten *der* whooping cough *no art.*

Keule *die;* **~, ~n (a)** club
(b) (Kochk.) leg

keusch 1 *Adj.* chaste
2 *adv.* **~ leben** lead a chaste life

Keuschheit *die;* **~:** chastity

Kfz *Abk.* = **Kraftfahrzeug**

kg *Abk.* = **Kilogramm** kg

KG *Abk.* = **Kommanditgesellschaft**

kichern *itr. V.* giggle

kicken (ugs.) 1 *itr. V.* play football
2 *tr. V.* kick

kidnappen /ˈkɪtnɛpn̩/ *tr. V.* kidnap

Kidnapper *der;* **~s, ~, Kidnapperin** *die;* **~, ~nen** kidnapper

Kiebitz *der;* **~es, ~e** lapwing; peewit

Kiefer[1] *der;* **~s, ~:** jaw; (~knochen) jawbone

Kiefer[2] *die;* **~, ~n** pine[tree]

Kiefer·höhle *die* (Anat.) maxillary sinus

Kiefern·holz *das* pine [wood]

Kiel *der;* **~[e]s, ~e** keel

kiel·holen *tr. V.* (Seemannsspr.) keelhaul ‹*person*›

Kiel·wasser *das* wake

*old spelling - see note on page xiv

Kieme *die;* ~, ~n gill

Kien *der;* ~[e]s resinous wood

Kies *der;* ~es, ~e gravel; (auf dem Strand) shingle

Kiesel *der;* ~s, ~: pebble

Kiesel·stein *der* pebble

Kies-: ~**grube** *die* gravel pit; ~**weg** *der* gravel path

kiffen *itr. V.* (ugs.) smoke pot (sl.) *or* grass (sl.)

Kiffer *der;* ~s, ~, **Kifferin** *die;* ~, ~nen (ugs.) pothead (sl.)

kikeriki /kikəri'ki:/ *Interj.* (Kinderspr.) cock-a-doodle-doo

Killer *der;* ~s, ~, **Killerin** *die;* ~, ~nen (salopp) killer; (gegen Bezahlung) hit man

Kilo *das;* ~s, ~[s] kilo

Kilo·gramm *das* kilogram

Kilometer *der;* ~s, ~: kilometre

kilometer-, Kilometer-: ~**lang** [1] *Adj.* miles long *pred.;* [2] *adv.* for miles [and miles]; ~**stand** *der* mileage reading

Kilowatt·stunde *die* (Physik; bes. Elektrot.) kilowatt-hour

Kimme *die;* ~, ~n sighting notch

Kimono *der;* ~s, ~s kimono

Kind *das;* ~[e]s, ~er **(a)** child; **ein ~ erwarten** be expecting
(b) [~er,] ~er! my goodness!

Kinder-: ~**arzt** *der,* ~**ärztin** *die* paediatrician; ~**betreuung** *die* child care; ~**bett** *das* cot; (für größeres Kind) child's bed; ~**dorf** *das* children's village

Kinderei *die;* ~, ~en childishness *no indef. art., no pl.*

kinder-, Kinder-: ~**erziehung** *die* bringing up of children; ~**feindlich** *Adj.* hostile to children *pred.;* ~**freundlich** *Adj.* fond of children *pred.;* ‹*town, resort*› which caters for children; ‹*planning, policy*› which caters for the needs of children; ~**garten** *der* nursery school; ~**gärtnerin** *die* nusery-school teacher; ~**geld** *das* child benefit; ~**heilkunde** *die* paediatrics *sing., no art.;* ~**hort** *der* day home for schoolchildren; ~**krankheit** *die* **(a)** (Infektionskrankheit) children's disease *or* illness; **(b)** *Pl.* (fig.: Anfangsschwierigkeiten) teething troubles; ~**krippe** *die* crèche; day nursey; ~**lähmung** *die* poliomyelitis; ~**leicht** (ugs.) *Adj.* childishly simple; dead easy; **das ist ~leicht** it's kid's stuff (coll.); it's child's play; ~**lieb** *Adj.* fond of children *pred.;* ~**los** *Adj.* childless; ~**reich** *Adj.* with many children *postpos., not pred.;* ~**sterblichkeit** *die* child mortality; ~**stube** *die* **eine gute/schlechte ~stube gehabt haben** have been well/badly brought up; ~**tages·heim** *das,* ~**tages·stätte** *die* day nursery; crèche ~**teller** *der* (auf der Speisekarte) children's menu; ~**wagen** *der* pram (Brit.); baby carriage (Amer.); (Sportwagen) pushchair (Brit.); stroller (Amer.)

Kindes-: ~**alter** *das* childhood; ~**misshandlung**, *~**mißhandlung** *die* (Rechtsw.) child abuse

Kindheit *die;* ~: childhood

kindisch [1] *Adj.* childish, infantile; naïve ‹*ideas*›
[2] *adv.* childishly

kindlich [1] *Adj.* childlike
[2] *adv.* ‹*behave*› in a childlike way

Kinkerlitzchen *Pl.* (ugs.) trifles

Kinn *das;* ~[e]s, ~e chin

Kinn-: ~**haken** *der* hook to the chin; ~**lade** *die* jaw

Kino *das;* ~s, ~s cinema (Brit.); movie theater (Amer.)

Kino-: ~**gänger** *der;* ~~s, ~~, ~**gängerin** *die;* ~~, ~~nen cinema-goer (Brit.); movie-goer (Amer.); ~**karte** *die* cinema ticket (Brit.); movie ticket (Amer.)

Kiosk *der;* ~[e]s, ~e kiosk

Kippe[1] *die;* ~, ~n (ugs.) cigarette end; dog-end (coll.)

Kippe[2] *die;* ~, ~n **(a)** (Bergmannsspr.) slag heap
(b) etw. steht auf der ~ (fig.) it's touch and go with sth.; (etw. ist noch nicht entschieden) sth. hangs in the balance

kippen [1] *tr. V.* **(a)** tip [up]
(b) (ausschütten) tip [out]
(c) (ugs.: trinken) knock back (coll.); **einen ~:** have a quick one (coll.) *or* a drink
[2] *itr. V.; mit sein* tip over; ‹*top-heavy object*› topple over; ‹*person*› topple; ‹*boat*› overturn; ‹*car*› roll over

Kipp-: ~**fenster** *das* horizontally pivoted window; ~**schalter** *der* tumbler switch

Kirche *die;* ~, ~n church; **in die ~ gehen** go to church

Kirchen-: ~**fest** *das* church festival; ~**lied** *das* hymn; ~**musik** *die* church music; ~**steuer** *die* church tax

Kirch-: ~**gänger** *der;* ~~s, ~~, ~**gängerin** *die;* ~~, ~~nen churchgoer; ~**hof** *der* (veralt.) churchyard

kirchlich [1] *Adj.* ecclesiastical; church *attrib.* ‹*wedding, funeral*›
[2] *adv.* **~ getraut/begraben werden** have a church wedding/funeral

Kirch-: ~**turm** *der* [church] steeple; (ohne Turmspitze) church tower; ~**weih** *die;* ~~, ~~en fair (held on the anniversary of the consecration of a church)

Kirmes *die;* ~, **Kirmessen** (bes. md., niederd.) ▸ KIRCHWEIH

Kirsch·baum *der* cherry [tree]

Kirsche *die;* ~, ~n cherry

Kirsch-: ~**torte** *die* cherry gateau; (mit Tortenboden) cherry flan; ~**wasser** *das; Pl.* ~**wässer** kirsch

Kissen *das;* ~s, ~: cushion; (Kopf~) pillow

Kiste *die;* **~, ~n** box; (Truhe) chest; (Latten~) crate
Kita *die;* **~, ~s** day nursery; crèche
Kitsch *der;* **~[e]s** kitsch
kitschig *Adj.* kitschy
Kitt *der;* **~[e]s, ~e** putty; (für Porzellan, Kacheln usw.) cement
Kittchen *das;* **~s, ~** (ugs.) clink (sl.)
Kittel *der;* **~s, ~ (a)** overall; (eines Arztes usw.) white coat
(b) (hemdartige Bluse) smock
kitten *tr. V.* cement [together]
Kitz *das;* **~es, ~e** (Reh~) fawn; (Ziegen~, Gämsen~) kid
kitzeln *tr., itr. V.* tickle
kitzlig *Adj.* (auch fig.) ticklish
KKW *Abk.* = **Kernkraftwerk**
Klacks *der;* **~es, ~e** (ugs.) dollop (coll.); (~ Senf) dab; **etw. ist nur ein ~ [für jmdn.]** (fig.) sth. is no trouble at all [for sb.]
Kladde *die;* **~, ~n** rough book
Kladderadatsch *der;* **~[e]s, ~e** (ugs.) unholy mess (coll.)
klaffen *itr. V.* yawn; ‹*hole, wound*› gape
kläffen *itr. V.* (abwertend) yap
Kläffer *der;* **~s, ~** (ugs. abwertend) yapping dog; yapper
Klafter *der od. das;* **~s, ~** (Raummaß für Holz) cord
Klage *die;* **~, ~n (a)** (Äußerung der Trauer) lament
(b) (Beschwerde) complaint
(c) (Rechtsw.) action; (im Strafrecht) charge
klagen **1** *itr. V.* **(a)** (geh.: jammern) wail; (stöhnend) moan
(b) (sich beschweren) complain (**über** + *Akk.* about)
(c) (bei Gericht) take legal action
2 *tr. V.* **jmdm. sein Leid/seine Not ~:** pour out one's sorrows *pl.*/troubles *pl.*
Kläger *der;* **~s, ~, Klägerin** *die;* **~, ~nen** (im Zivilrecht) plaintiff; (im Strafrecht) prosecuting party; (bei einer Scheidung) petitioner
kläglich *Adj.* **(a)** (Mitleid erregend) pitiful
(b) (minderwertig) pathetic
(c) (erbärmlich) despicable ‹*behaviour, role, compromise*›; pathetic ‹*result, defeat*›
Klamauk *der;* **~s** (ugs. abwertend) fuss; (Lärm, Krach) row (coll.)
klamm *Adj.* **(a)** (feucht) cold and damp
(b) (steif) numb
Klammer *die;* **~, ~n** (Wäsche~) peg; (Haar~) [hair]grip; (Zahn~) brace; (Büro~) paper clip; (Heft~) staple; (Schriftzeichen) bracket
klammern **1** *refl. V.* **sich an jmdn./etw. ~** (auch fig.) cling to sb./sth.
2 *tr. V.* **(a) eine Wunde ~:** close a wound with a clip/clips
(b) (mit einer Büroklammer) clip; (mit einer Heftmaschine) staple; (mit Wäscheklammern) peg
Klamotten *Pl.* (salopp) (Kleidung) gear *sing.* (coll.); (Kram) stuff *sing.*
Klampfe *die;* **~, ~n** (volkst.: Gitarre) guitar
klang *1. u. 3. Pers. Sg. Prät. v.* KLINGEN
Klang *der;* **~[e]s, Klänge (a)** (Ton) sound
(b) (~farbe) tone
Klapp·bett *das* folding bed
Klappe *die;* **~, ~n (a)** [hinged] lid; (am LKW) tailgate; (seitlich) side gate; (am Kombiwagen) back; (am Ofen) [drop-]door
(b) (an Musikinstrumenten) key; (an einer Trompete) valve
(c) (Filmjargon) clapperboard
(d) (salopp: Mund) trap (sl.)
klappen **1** *tr. V.* **nach oben/unten ~:** turn up/down ‹*collar, hat brim*›; lift up/put down ‹*lid*›; **nach vorne/hinten ~:** tilt forward/back ‹*seat*›
2 *itr. V.* **(a)** ‹*door, shutter*› bang
(b) (stoßen) bang
(c) (ugs.: gelingen) work out all right
klapperig *Adj.* rickety
klappern *itr. V.* **(a)** rattle
(b) (ein Klappern erzeugen) make a clatter
Klapper·schlange *die* rattlesnake
Klapp·fahrrad *das* folding bicycle
klapprig *Adj.* rickety
Klapp-: ~sitz *der* tip-up seat; **~stuhl** *der* folding chair
Klaps *der;* **~es, ~e** (ugs.) smack; slap
Klaps·mühle *die* (salopp) loony bin (sl.)
klar **1** *Adj.* **(a)** clear; straight ‹*question, answer*›; **sich** (*Dat.*) **über etw.** (*Akk.*) **~ werden** realize sth.; **jmdm. ~ werden** become clear to sb.; **sich** (*Dat.*) **über etw.** (*Akk.*) **im Klaren sein** realize sth.; **etw. ~ machen** (ugs.) make sth. clear
(b) (fertig) ready
2 *adv.* clearly; **~ sehen** understand the matter
Klär·anlage *die* sewage treatment plant
Klare *der;* **~n, ~n** schnapps
klären **1** *tr. V.* **(a)** settle ‹*question, issue, matter*›; clarify ‹*situation*›; clear up ‹*case, affair, misunderstanding*›
(b) (reinigen) purify; treat ‹*effluent, sewage*›
2 *refl. V.* **(a)** ‹*situation*› become clear; ‹*question, issue, matter*› be settled
(b) (rein werden) ‹*liquid, sky*› clear; ‹*weather*› clear [up]
klar|gehen *unr. itr. V.; mit sein* (ugs.) go OK (coll.)
Klarheit *die;* **~:** clarity; **sich** (*Dat.*) **über etw.** (*Akk.*) **~ verschaffen** clarify sth.
Klarinette *die;* **~, ~n** clarinet
klar-: ~|machen *tr. V.* (Seemannsspr.) get ready; ***~|sehen** ▸ KLAR 2
klaro *Adj., Interj.* (ugs.) of course; it goes without saying; **~, dass ...:** it goes without saying that ...

*alte Schreibung - vgl. Hinweis auf S. xiv

Klarsicht·folie *die* transparent film

klar|stellen *tr. V.* clear up; clarify

Klar·text *der* (auch DV) clear text; **im ~text** (fig.) in plain language

Klärung *die; ~,* **~en (a)** clarification **(b)** (Reinigung) purification; (von Abwässern) treatment

***klar|werden** ▶ KLAR 1A

Klär·werk *das* sewage works *sing. or pl.*

klasse (ugs.) [1] *indekl. Adj.* great (coll.) [2] *adv.* marvellously

Klasse *die; ~,* **~n (a)** (Schul~) class; (Raum) classroom; (Stufe) year; grade (Amer.) **(b)** (Sport) league; (Boxen) division **(c)** (Fahrzeug~, Boots~, Qualitätsstufe) class; **das ist einsame** *od.* **ganz große ~!** (ugs.) that's [just] great (coll.) *or* marvellous!

klassen-, Klassen-: ~arbeit *die* (Schulw.) [written] class test; **~buch** *das* (Schulw.) *book recording details of pupils' attendance, behaviour, and of topics covered in each lesson;* ≈ [class] register; **~fahrt** *die* (Schulw.) class outing; **~gesellschaft** *die* (Soziol.) class society; **~kampf** *der* (marx.) class struggle; **~lehrer** *der,* **~lehrerin** *die* (Schulw.) class teacher; **~los** *Adj.* (Soziol.) classless; **~sprecher** *der,* **~sprecherin** *die* (Schulw.) class spokesman; **~treffen** *das* (Schulw.) class reunion; **~ziel** *das* (Schulw.) required standard (*for pupils in a particular class*); **~zimmer** *das* (Schulw.) classroom

klassifizieren *tr. V.* classify (**als** as)

Klassifizierung *die; ~,* **~en** classification

Klassik *die; ~* **(a)** (Antike) classical antiquity *no art.;* **(b)** (Zeit kultureller Höchstleistung) classical period

Klassiker *der;* **~s, ~, Klassikerin** *die;* **~, ~nen** classical writer/composer

klassisch *Adj.* classical; (vollendet, zeitlos; auch iron.) classic

Klassizismus *der; ~:* classicism

Klatsch *der;* **~[e]s, ~e (a)** (ugs. abwertend) gossip **(b)** (Geräusch) smack

Klatsch·base *die* (ugs. abwertend) gossip

klatschen *itr. V.* **(a)** *auch mit sein ‹waves, wet sails›* slap **(b)** (mit den Händen; applaudieren) clap **(c)** (schlagen) slap **(d)** (ugs. abwertend: reden) gossip (**über** + *Akk.* about)

klatschhaft *Adj.* gossipy; fond of gossip *pred.*

klatsch-, Klatsch-: ~mohn *der* corn poppy; **~nass**, ***~naß** *Adj.* (ugs.) sopping wet; dripping wet *‹hair›*; **~spalte** *die* (ugs. abwertend) gossip column

Klaue *die; ~,* **~n (a)** claw; (von Raubvögeln) talon; (salopp: Hand) mitt (coll.) **(b)** (salopp abwertend: Schrift) scrawl

klauen (ugs.) [1] *tr. V.* pinch (coll.); **jmdm. etw. ~:** pinch sth. from sb. [2] *itr. V.* pinch (coll.) things

Klause *die; ~,* **~n** hermitage; (Klosterzelle) cell

Klausel *die; ~,* **~n** clause; (Bedingung) condition; (Vorbehalt) proviso

Klausur *die; ~,* **~en** [examination] paper; (Examen) examination; **eine ~ schreiben** take a[n examination] paper/an examination

Klausur-: ~arbeit *die* [examination] paper; **~tagung** *die* private meeting

Klavier /kla'viːɐ̯/ *das;* **~s, ~e** piano

Klebe·folie *die* adhesive film

kleben [1] *itr. V.* **(a)** stick (**an** + *Dat.* to) **(b)** (ugs.: klebrig sein) be sticky (**von, vor** + *Dat.* with) [2] *tr. V.* **(a)** (befestigen) stick; (mit Klebstoff) glue; **jmdm. eine ~** (salopp) belt sb. one (coll.) **(b)** (reparieren) stick *or* glue *‹vase etc.›* back together

Kleber *der;* **~s, ~:** adhesive; glue

klebrig *Adj.* sticky

Kleb-: ~stoff *der* adhesive; glue; **~streifen** *der* adhesive *or* sticky tape

kleckern (ugs.) *itr. V.* make a mess

Klecks *der;* **~es, ~e (a)** stain; (nicht aufgesogen) blob; (Tintenfleck) [ink] blot **(b)** (ugs.: kleine Menge) spot; (von Senf, Mayonnaise) dab

klecksen *itr. V.* **(a)** make a stain/stains; (mit Tinte) make a blot/blots; *‹pen›* blot **(b)** (ugs. abwertend: schlecht malen) daub

Klee *der;* **~s** clover

Klee·blatt *das* cloverleaf

Kleid *das;* **~es, ~er (a)** dress **(b)** *Pl.* (Kleidung) clothes

kleiden [1] *refl. V.* dress [2] *tr. V.* **(a)** dress **(b)** (jmdm. stehen) suit

Kleider-: ~bügel *der* clothes hanger; coat hanger; **~bürste** *die* clothes brush; **~haken** *der* coat hook; **~schrank** *der* wardrobe; **~spende** *die* donation of [second-hand] clothes *or* clothing; **~ständer** *der* coat stand

kleidsam *Adj.* becoming

Kleidung *die; ~:* clothes *pl.*

Kleidungs·stück *das* garment

klein [1] *Adj.* **(a)** little; small; **er ist ~er als ich** he is shorter than me; **etw. ~ schneiden** cut sth. into small pieces; **Zwiebeln ~ schneiden/hacken** chop up onions [small] **(b)** (jung) little; **von ~ auf** from an early age **(c)** (von kurzer Dauer) little, short *‹while›*; short *‹walk, break, holiday›*; brief *‹moment›* **(d)** (von geringer Menge) small; low *‹price›*; **~es Geld haben** have some [small] change **(e)** (von geringem Ausmaß) small *‹party, gift›*; scant *‹attention›*; slight *‹cold, indisposition, mistake, irregularity›*; minor *‹event, error›* ⋯›

(f) (unbedeutend) lowly ‹*employee*›; minor ‹*official*›; ~ **anfangen** (ugs.) start off in a small way
[2] *adv.* **die Heizung ~/~er einstellen** turn the heating down low/lower; **ein Wort ~ schreiben** write a word with a small initial letter

klein-, Klein-: ~aktionär *der*, **~aktionärin** *die* (Wirtsch.) small shareholder; **~anzeige** *die* (Zeitungsw.) small *or* classified advertisement; **~asien** (*das*) Asia Minor; **~buchstabe** *der* small letter; **~bürger** *der*, **~bürgerin** *die* lower middle-class person; (abwertend: Spießbürger) petit bourgeois; **~bürgerlich** *Adj.* **(a)** (das Kleinbürgertum betreffend) lower middle-class; **(b)** (abwertend: spießbürgerlich) petit bourgeois

Kleine[1] *der; adj. Dekl.* **(a)** (kleiner Junge) little boy
(b) (ugs. Anrede) little man

Kleine[2] *die; adj. Dekl.* **(a)** (kleines Mädchen) little girl
(b) (ugs. Anrede) love; (abwertend) little madam

k

klein-, Klein-: ~familie *die* (Soziol.) nuclear family; **~geld** *das* [small] change; **~gläubig** *Adj.* sceptical

Kleinigkeit *die; ~, ~en* small thing; (Einzelheit) [small] detail; **ich habe noch eine ~ zu erledigen** I still have a small matter to attend to; **eine ~ essen** have a bite to eat; **eine ~ für jmdn. sein** be no trouble for sb.

klein-, Klein-: ~kind *das* small child; **~kram** *der* (ugs.) odds and ends *pl.*; (unbedeutende Dinge) trivial matters *pl.*; **~kredit** *der* (Bankw.) personal loan (*repayable within two years*); **~|kriegen** *tr. V.* (ugs.) **(a)** (zerkleinern) crush [to pieces]; **(b)** (zerstören) smash; break; **(c)** (aufbrauchen) get through; **(d) jmdn. ~kriegen** get sb. down (coll.); (durch Drohungen) intimidate sb.; (gefügig machen) bring sb. into line; **~kunst** *die* cabaret; **~laut** [1] *Adj.* subdued; (verlegen) sheepish; [2] *adv.* in a subdued fashion; (verlegen) sheepishly

kleinlich (abwertend) [1] *Adj.* pernickety; (ohne Großzügigkeit) mean; (engstirnig) small-minded; petty
[2] *adv.* meticulously

Kleinod *das; ~[e]s, ~e od. ~ien* (geh.) **(a)** (Schmuckstück) piece of jewellery; (Edelstein) jewel
(b) (Kostbarkeit) gem

klein-, Klein-: ~|rechnen *tr. V.* undercalculate; ***~|schneiden** ▸ KLEIN 1A; **~stadt** *die* small town; **~städter** *der*, **~städterin** *die* small-town dweller

Kleinste *der/die/das; adj. Dekl.* youngest boy/girl/child

klein|stellen *tr. V.* turn down [low]

Klein·wagen *der* small car

Kleister *der; ~s, ~:* paste

Klementine *die; ~, ~n* clementine

Klemme *die; ~, ~n* clip; **in der ~ sein** *od.* **sitzen** (ugs.) be in a fix (coll.)

klemmen [1] *tr. V.* **(a)** (befestigen) tuck **(b)** (quetschen) **sich** (*Dat.*) **den Fuß/die Hand ~:** get one's foot/hand caught *or* trapped
[2] *refl. V.* **sich hinter etw.** (*Akk.*) **~** (fig. ugs.) put some hard work into sth.
[3] *itr. V.* ‹*door, drawer, etc.*› stick

Klempner *der; ~s, ~,* **Klempnerin** *die; ~, ~nen* tinsmith; (Installateur[in]) plumber

Kleptomanie *die; ~* (Psych.) kleptomania *no art.*

klerikal *Adj.* (auch abwertend) clerical; church ‹*property*›

Klerus *der; ~:* clergy

Klette *die; ~, ~n* bur; (Pflanze) burdock

klettern *itr. V.; mit sein* (auch fig.) climb; **auf einen Baum ~:** climb a tree

Kletter·pflanze *die* creeper; (Bot.) climbing plant; climber

Klett·verschluss, *Klett·verschluß *der* Velcro ® fastening

klicken *itr. V.* click

Klient *der; ~en, ~en,* **Klientin** *die; ~, ~nen* client

Klima *das; ~s, ~s od.* **Klimate** climate

Klima·anlage *die* air conditioning *no indef. art.*

klimatisch *Adj.* climatic

klimatisieren *tr. V.* air-condition

Klima-: ~wandel *der* climate change; **~wechsel** *der* climate change; (Med.) change of climate

Klimm·zug *der* (Turnen) pull-up

klimpern [1] *itr. V.* jingle
[2] *tr. V.* (ugs. abwertend) plunk out ‹*tune etc.*›

Klinge *die; ~, ~n* blade

Klingel *die; ~, ~n* bell

Klingel-: ~beutel *der* offertory bag; collection bag; **~knopf** *der* bell push

klingeln *itr. V.* ring; ‹*alarm clock*› go off; **es klingelt** (an der Tür) there is a ring at the door; (Telefon) the telephone is ringing

Klingel·ton *der* ringtone

klingen *unr. itr. V.* sound; **die Glocken klangen** the bells were ringing

Klinik *die; ~, ~en* hospital; (spezialisiert) clinic

Klinke *die; ~, ~n* door handle

klipp *Adv.* **~ und klar** (ugs.) quite plainly

Klippe *die; ~, ~n* rock

klirren *itr. V.* clink; ‹*weapons in fight*› clash; ‹*window pane*› rattle; ‹*chains, spurs*› rattle; ‹*harness*› jingle

Klischee *das; ~s, ~s* cliché

klitsch·nass, *klitsch·naß *Adj.* (ugs.) sopping wet; (tropfnass) dripping wet

klitze·klein *Adj.* (ugs.) teeny[-weeny] (coll.)

*old spelling - see note on page xiv

Klo *das;* **~s, ~s** (ugs.) loo (Brit. coll.); john (Amer. coll.)

Kloake *die;* **~, ~n** cesspit; (Kanal) sewer

klobig *Adj.* heavy and clumsy[-looking] ‹*shoes, furniture*›; bulky ‹*figure*›; (plump) clumsy

Klon *der;* **~s, ~e** (Biol.) clone

klonen *tr. V.* clone

Klo·papier *das* (ugs.) loo paper (Brit. coll.); toilet paper

klopfen 1 *itr. V.* **(a)** (schlagen) knock **(b)** (pulsieren) ‹*heart*› beat; ‹*pulse*› throb 2 *tr. V.* beat ‹*carpet*›

Klöppel *der;* **~s, ~** (Glocken~) clapper

klöppeln *tr., itr. V.* **[etw.] ~:** make [sth. in] pillow lace

Klops *der;* **~es, ~e** (nordostd.) meat ball

Klosett *das;* **~s, ~s** *od.* **~e** lavatory

Kloß *der;* **~es, Klöße** dumpling; (Fleisch~) meat ball

Kloster *das;* **~s, Klöster** (Mönchs~) monastery; (Nonnen~) convent

Klotz *der;* **~es, Klötze** block [of wood]; (Stück eines Baumstamms) log

Klub *der;* **~s, ~s** club

Klub·sessel *der* club chair

Kluft[1] *die;* **~, ~en** (ugs.) gear (coll.); (Uniform) garb

Kluft[2] *die;* **~, Klüfte** (veralt.) (Spalte) cleft; (im Gletscher) crevasse; (Abgrund) chasm; (fig.) gulf

klug; **klüger, klügst...** *Adj.* clever; bright ‹*child, pupil*›; intelligent ‹*eyes*›; (vernünftig) wise; sound ‹*advice*›; (geschickt) shrewd ‹*politician, negotiator, question*›; astute ‹*businessman*›

Klugheit *die;* **~** ▶ KLUG: cleverness; brightness; intelligence; wisdom; soundness; shrewdness; astuteness

klumpen *itr. V.* go lumpy

Klumpen *der;* **~s, ~:** lump; **ein ~ Gold** a gold nugget

km *Abk.* = **Kilometer** km.

knabbern 1 *tr. V.* nibble 2 *itr. V.* **an etw.** (*Dat.*) **~:** nibble [at] sth.

Knabe *der;* **~n, ~n** (geh. veralt./südd., österr., schweiz.) boy; (ugs.: Bursche) chap (coll.)

knabenhaft 1 *Adj.* boyish 2 *adv.* boyishly

Knäcke·brot *das* crispbread; (Scheibe) slice of crispbread

knacken 1 *itr. V.* **(a)** ‹*bed, floor, etc.*› creak **(b)** *mit sein* (ugs.: zerbrechen) snap; ‹*window*› crack 2 *tr. V.* **(a)** crack ‹*nut, shell*› **(b)** (salopp: aufbrechen) crack ‹*safe*› [open]; break into ‹*car, bank, etc.*›

knackig *Adj.* **(a)** crisp **(b)** (ugs.: attraktiv) delectable

Knacks *der;* **~es, ~e** (ugs.) crack; (fig.: Defekt) **einen ~ bekommen** ‹*person*› have a breakdown; ‹*health*› suffer

Knall *der;* **~[e]s, ~e** bang

knallen 1 *itr. V.* **(a)** ‹*shot*› ring out; ‹*firework*› go bang; ‹*cork*› pop; ‹*door*› slam; ‹*whip, rifle*› crack; **mit der Tür ~:** slam the door **(b)** (ugs.: schießen) shoot, fire (**auf** + *Akk.* at) **(c)** (Ballspiele ugs.) **aufs Tor ~:** belt the ball/puck at the goal (coll.) 2 *tr. V.* **(a)** (ugs.) slam down; (werfen) sling (coll.) **(b)** (ugs.: schlagen) **jmdm. eine ~** (salopp) belt sb. one (coll.)

knall-: ~hart (ugs.) 1 *Adj.* very tough ‹*demands, measures, etc.*›; ‹*person*› as hard as nails; 2 *adv.* brutally; **gegen etw. ~hart vorgehen** take very tough action against sth.; **~rot** *Adj.* bright *or* vivid red; **sie wurde ~rot** she turned as red as a beetroot

knapp 1 *Adj.* **(a)** meagre; narrow ‹*victory, lead*›; narrow, bare ‹*majority*›; **die Vorräte wurden ~:** supplies ran short; **vor einer ~en Stunde** just under an hour ago **(b)** (eng) tight-fitting ‹*garment*›; (zu eng) tight ‹*garment*› **(c)** (kurz) terse ‹*reply, greeting*›; succinct ‹*description, account, report*› 2 *adv.* **(a) ~ bemessen sein** be meagre, ‹*time*› be limited; **~ gewinnen/verlieren** win/lose narrowly; **er ist ~ fünfzig** he is just this side of fifty **(b)** (eng) **~ sitzen** fit tightly; (zu eng) be a tight fit **(c)** (kurz) ‹*reply*› tersely; ‹*describe, summarize*› succinctly

Knappheit *die;* **~ (a)** (Mangel) shortage (**an** + *Dat.* of) **(b)** (Kürze) (einer Antwort, eines Grußes) terseness; (einer Beschreibung, eines Berichts) succinctness

Knarre *die;* **~, ~n** (salopp: Gewehr) shooting iron (coll.)

knarren *itr. V.* creak

Knast *der;* **~[e]s, Knäste** *od.* **~e** (ugs.) **(a)** (Strafe) bird (sl.); time **(b)** (Gefängnis) clink (sl.); prison

Knatsch *der;* **~[e]s** (ugs.: Ärger) trouble

knattern *itr. V.* clatter; ‹*sail*› flap; ‹*radio*› crackle

Knäuel *der od. das;* **~s, ~** ball; (wirres ~) tangle

Knauf *der;* **~[e]s, Knäufe** knob; (eines Schwertes, Dolches) pommel

knauserig *Adj.* (ugs. abwertend) stingy; tight-fisted

knausern *itr. V.* (ugs. abwertend) be stingy; skimp

knautschen (ugs.) 1 *tr. V.* crumple; crease ‹*dress*› 2 *itr. V.* ‹*dress, material*› crease

Knebel *der;* **~s, ~ (a)** gag **(b)** (Griff) toggle

knebeln *tr. V.* gag

Knecht *der;* **~[e]s, ~e** farm labourer

knechten *tr. V.* (geh.) reduce to slavery; enslave; (unterdrücken) oppress

Knechtschaft *die;* ~, **~en** (geh.) bondage; slavery

kneifen [1] *unr. tr., itr. V.* pinch
[2] *unr. itr. V.* **(a)** ‹*clothes*› be too tight
(b) (ugs.: sich drücken) chicken (coll.) out (**vor** + *Dat.* of)

Kneif·zange *die* pincers *pl.*

Kneipe *die;* ~, **~n** (ugs.) pub (Brit. coll.); bar (Amer.)

Kneipen·tour *die* (ugs.) pub crawl

kneippen *itr. V.* (ugs.) take a Kneipp cure

Kneipp·kur *die* Kneipp cure

kneten *tr. V.* **(a)** (bearbeiten) knead ‹*dough, muscles*›; work ‹*clay*›
(b) (formen) model ‹*figure*›

Knet·masse *die* Plasticine ®

Knick *der;* **~[e]s, ~e** sharp bend; (Falz) crease

knicken [1] *tr. V.* **(a)** (brechen) snap
(b) (falten) crease ‹*page, paper, etc.*›
[2] *itr. V.; mit sein* snap

knick[e]rig *Adj.* (ugs. abwertend) stingy

Knick[e]rigkeit *die;* ~ (ugs. abwertend) stinginess

Knicks *der;* **~es, ~e** curtsy

knicksen *itr. V.* curtsy (**vor** + *Dat.* to)

Knie *das;* **~s, ~** /'kni:(ə)/ **(a)** knee
(b) (Biegung) sharp bend

knie-, Knie-: ~beuge *die* knee bend; **~bund·hose** *die* knee breeches *pl.;* **~fall** *der:* **einen ~fall tun** *od.* **machen** (auch fig.) go down on one's knees (**vor** + *Dat.* before); **~kehle** *die* hollow of the knee

knien /'kni:(ə)n/ [1] *itr. V.* kneel
[2] *refl. V.* kneel [down]

Knie-: ~scheibe *die* kneecap; **~strumpf** *der* knee-length sock

Kniff *der;* **~[e]s, ~e (a)** pinch
(b) (Falte) crease
(c) (Kunstgriff) trick

knipsen *tr. V.* **(a)** (entwerten) clip; punch
(b) (fotografieren) take a snap[shot] of

Knirps *der;* **~es, ~e (a)** (Wz *Taschenschirm*) telescopic umbrella
(b) (ugs.: Junge) nipper (coll.)

knirschen *itr. V.* crunch; **mit den Zähnen ~:** grind one's teeth

knistern *itr. V.* rustle; ‹*wood, fire*› crackle

knittern *tr., itr. V.* crease; crumple

knobeln *itr. V.* (mit Würfeln) play dice

Knob·lauch *der* garlic

Knoblauch·zehe *die* clove of garlic

Knöchel *der;* **~s, ~:** ankle; (am Finger) knuckle

Knochen *der;* **~s, ~:** bone

knochen-, Knochen-: ~bau *der* bone structure; **~bruch** *der* fracture; **~hart** *Adj.* (ugs.) rock-hard; **~mark** *das* bone marrow

knochig *Adj.* bony

Knödel *der;* **~s, ~** (bes. südd., österr.) dumpling

Knöllchen *das;* **~s, ~** (ugs.: Strafzettel) [parking] ticket

Knolle *die;* ~, **~n** tuber

Knopf *der;* **~[e]s, Knöpfe** button; (Knauf) knob

knöpfen *tr. V.* button [up]

Knopf·loch *das* buttonhole

Knorpel *der;* **~s, ~** (Anat.) cartilage; (im Steak o. Ä.) gristle

knorrig *Adj.* gnarled

Knospe *die;* ~, **~n** bud

knospen *itr. V.* bud

knoten *tr. V.* knot

Knoten *der;* **~s, ~:** knot; (Haartracht) bun; knot; (Med.) lump

Knoten·punkt *der* junction; intersection

Know-how /noʊ'hau:/ *das;* **~[s]** know-how

knuffen *tr. V.* poke

Knüller *der;* **~s, ~** (ugs.) sensation; (Angebot, Verkaufsartikel) sensational offer

knüpfen *tr. V.* **(a)** tie (**an** + *Akk.* to); **Bedingungen an etw.** (*Akk.*) **~:** attach conditions to sth.
(b) (durch Knoten herstellen) knot; make ‹*net*›

Knüppel *der;* **~s, ~** cudgel; (Polizei~) truncheon

knüppel-, Knüppel-: ~dick *Adv.* (ugs.) **es kam ~dick** it was one disaster after the other; **~schaltung** *die* (Kfz-W.) floor[-type] gear change

knurren *itr. V.* **(a)** ‹*animal*› growl; (wütend) snarl; (fig.) ‹*stomach*› rumble
(b) (murren) grumble (**über** + *Akk.* about)

knusprig *Adj.* crisp; crusty ‹*bread, roll*›

knutschen (ugs.) [1] *tr. V.* smooch with (coll.); (sexuell berühren) pet; **sich ~:** smooch (coll.)/pet
[2] *itr. V.* smooch (coll.); (sich sexuell berühren) pet

k. o. /ka:'|o:/ *Adj.* **(a)** (Boxen) **jmdn. k. o. schlagen** knock sb. out
(b) (ugs.: übermüdet) all in (coll.)

koalieren *itr. V.* (Politik) form a coalition (**mit** with)

Koalition *die;* ~, **~en** coalition

Koax·kabel *das* (Technik Jargon) coax [cable]; coaxial cable

Kobalt *das;* **~s** (Chemie) cobalt

Kobold *der;* **~[e]s, ~e** goblin

Kobra *die;* ~, **~s** cobra

Koch *der;* **~[e]s, Köche** cook; (Küchenchef) chef

Koch·buch *das* cookery book (Brit.); cookbook (Amer.)

---

*alte Schreibung - vgl. Hinweis auf S. xiv

kochen 1 *tr. V.* **(a)** boil; (zubereiten) cook ‹*meal*›; make ‹*purée, jam*›; **Tee ~:** make some tea
(b) (waschen) boil
2 *itr. V.* **(a)** (Speisen zubereiten) cook
(b) (sieden) ‹*water, milk, etc.*› boil

Kocher *der;* **~s, ~** [small] stove; (Kochplatte) hotplate

Köcher *der;* **~s, ~** (für Pfeile) quiver

Koch·feld *das* ceramic hob

Köchin *die;* **~, ~nen** cook

Koch-: ~löffel *der* wooden spoon; **~nische** *die* kitchenette; **~salz** *das* common salt; **~topf** *der* [cooking] pot; **~wäsche** *die* washing that is to be boiled

Köder *der;* **~s, ~:** bait

ködern *tr. V.* lure

Koffein *das;* **~s** caffeine

koffein·frei *Adj.* decaffeinated

Koffer *der;* **~s, ~:** [suit]case

Koffer-: ~kuli *der* luggage trolley; **~radio** *das* portable radio; **~raum** *der* boot (Brit.); trunk (Amer.)

Kognak /'kɔnjak/ *der;* **~s, ~s** brandy; *s. auch* COGNAC

Kohl *der;* **~[e]s (a)** cabbage
(b) (ugs. abwertend: Unsinn) rubbish; rot (coll.)

Kohl·dampf *der* (salopp) **~ haben** be ravenously hungry

Kohle *die;* **~, ~n (a)** coal
(b) (salopp: Geld) dough (coll.)

Kohle·hydrat ▶ KOHLENHYDRAT

kohlen[1] *itr. V.* smoulder; ‹*wick*› smoke

kohlen[2] *itr. V.* (fam.) (lügen) tell fibs; (übertreiben) exaggerate

Kohlen-: ~dioxid, ~dioxyd /--'---/ *das* (Chemie) carbon dioxide; **~grube** *die* coal mine; **~händler** *der,* **~händlerin** *die* coal merchant; **~hydrat** *das* (Chemie) carbohydrate; **~monoxid, ~monoxyd** /--'---/ *das* (Chemie) carbon monoxide; **~säure** *die* carbonic acid; **~stoff** *der* carbon

Kohle·papier *das* carbon paper

Köhler *der;* **~s, ~:** charcoal burner

Kohle·zeichnung *die* charcoal drawing

Kohl-: ~kopf *der* [head of] cabbage; **~rübe** *die* swede

Koitus *der;* **~, Koitus** (geh.) sexual intercourse; coitus (formal)

Koje *die;* **~, ~n (a)** (Seemannsspr.) bunk; berth
(b) (Ausstellungsstand) stand
(c) (ugs. scherzh.: Bett) bed

Kokain *das;* **~s** cocaine

kokett 1 *Adj.* coquettish
2 *adv.* coquettishly

kokettieren *itr. V.* **mit etw. ~:** make much play with sth.

Kokos·nuss, *Kokos·nuß *die* coconut

Koks *der;* **~es** coke

Kolben *der;* **~s, ~ (a)** (Technik) piston
(b) (Chemie: Glas~) flask
(c) (Teil des Gewehrs) butt

Kolchose /kɔl'ço:zə/ *die;* **~, ~n** kolkhoz; Soviet collective farm

Kolibri *der;* **~s, ~s** hummingbird

Kolik *die;* **~, ~en** colic

Kollaborateur /kɔlabora'tø:ɐ̯/ *der;* **~s, ~e, Kollaborateurin** *die;* **~, ~nen** collaborator

Kollaps *der;* **~es, ~e** collapse

Kolleg *das;* **~s, ~s** lecture

Kollege *der;* **~n, ~n** colleague

kollegial 1 *Adj.* helpful and considerate
2 *adv.* ‹*act etc.*› like a good colleague/good colleagues

Kollegin *die;* **~, ~nen** colleague

Kollegium *das;* **~s, Kollegien (a)** (Gruppe) group; (unmittelbar zusammenarbeitend) team
(b) (Lehrkörper) [teaching] staff

Kollekte *die;* **~, ~n** collection

Kollektion *die;* **~, ~en** collection; (Sortiment) range

kollektiv 1 *Adj.* collective
2 *adv.* collectively

kollidieren *itr. V.* **(a)** *mit sein* collide
(b) (fig.) conflict

Kollier /kɔ'li̯e:/ *das;* **~s, ~s** necklace

Kollision *die;* **~, ~en** collision

Köln *(das);* **~s** Cologne

Kölner 1 *indekl. Adj.* Cologne *attrib.;* (in Köln) in Cologne *postpos., not pred;* ‹*suburb, archbishop, mayor, speciality*› of Cologne
2 *der;* **~s, ~:** inhabitant of Cologne; (von Geburt) native of Cologne

Kölnerin *die;* **~, ~nen** ▶ KÖLNER 2

Kolonialisierung *die;* **~, ~en** colonialization

Kolonialismus *der;* **~:** colonialism *no art.*

Kolonie *die;* **~, ~n** colony

kolonisieren *tr. V.* colonize

Kolonisierung *die;* **~, ~en** colonization

Kolonne *die;* **~, ~n** column

Koloss, *Koloß *der;* **Kolosses, Kolosse** (auch fig. ugs.) giant

kolossal 1 *Adj.* **(a)** colossal; gigantic
(b) (ugs.: sehr groß) tremendous (coll.); incredible (coll.) ‹*rubbish, nonsense*›
2 *adv.* (ugs.) tremendously (coll.)

Kolumbianer *der;* **~s, ~, Kolumbianerin** *die;* **~, ~nen** Colombian

Kolumbien /ko'lʊmbi̯ən/ *(das);* **~s** Colombia

Kombination *die;* **~, ~en (a)** combination
(b) (gedankliche Verknüpfung) deduction; piece of reasoning
(c) (Kleidungsstücke) ensemble; suit; (Herren~) suit

kombinieren 1 *tr. V.* combine
2 *itr. V.* deduce; reason

Kombi-: ~wagen *der* estate [car]; station wagon (Amer.); **~zange** *die* combination pliers *pl.*
Komet *der;* **~en, ~en** comet
Komfort /kɔm'foːɐ/ *der;* **~s** comfort
komfortabel 1 *Adj.* comfortable 2 *adv.* comfortably
Komik *die;* **~:** comic effect; (komisches Element) comic element
Komiker *der;* **~s, ~, Komikerin** *die* **~, ~en (a)** (Vortragskünstler[in]) comedian **(b)** (Darsteller[in]) comic actor
komisch *Adj.* **(a)** comical; funny **(b)** (seltsam) funny
Komitee *das;* **~s, ~s** committee
Komma *das;* **~s, ~s** *od.* **~ta** comma; (Math.) decimal point; **zwei ~ acht** two point eight
Kommandant *der;* **~en, ~en** (Milit.) commanding officer
Kommandeur /kɔman'døːɐ̯/ *der;* **~s, ~e** (Milit.) ▶ KOMMANDANT
kommandieren 1 *tr. V.* **(a)** command; be in command of; order ‹*retreat, advance*› **(b)** (ugs.) **jmdn. ~:** boss sb. about (coll.) 2 *itr. V.* (ugs.) boss people about (coll.)
Kommandit·gesellschaft *die* (Wirtsch.) limited partnership
Kommando *das;* **~s, ~s** command
Komma·stelle *die* decimal place; **auf die ~ [genau]** [correct] to the last decimal place; (fig.) ‹*know, calculate*› with complete accuracy
kommen *unr. itr. V.; mit sein* **(a)** come; **angelaufen ~:** come running along; (auf jmdn. zu) come running up **(b)** (gelangen, geraten) get; **unter ein Auto ~:** be knocked down by a car; **wie kommst du darauf?** what gives you that idea? **(c) ~ lassen** (bestellen) order ‹*taxi*›; **den Arzt/die Polizei ~ lassen** send for a doctor/the police **(d)** (aufgenommen werden) **zur Schule/aufs Gymnasium ~:** start school/grammar school **(e)** (auftauchen) ‹*seeds, plants*› come up; ‹*buds, flowers*› come out; ‹*teeth*› come through **(f)** (seinen festen Platz haben) go; belong; **in die Schublade ~:** go *or* belong in the drawer; (seinen Platz erhalten) **in die Mannschaft ~:** get into the team; **auf den ersten Platz ~:** go into first place **(g)** (Gelegenheit haben) **dazu ~, etw. zu tun** get round to doing sth. **(h)** (sich ereignen) come about; **wie kommt es, dass ...:** how is it that ... **(i)** (etw. erlangen) **zu Geld ~:** become wealthy; **zu Erfolg/Ruhm ~:** gain success/fame
kommend *Adj.* **(a)** (folgend) next; **in den ~en Jahren** in years to come **(b)** (mit großer Zukunft) **der ~e Mann/Meister** the coming man/future champion
Kommentar *der;* **~s, ~e** commentary; (Stellungnahme) comment; **kein ~!** no comment!

*old spelling - see note on page xiv

Kommentator *der;* **~s, ~en, Kommentatorin** *die;* **~, ~nen** commentator
kommentieren *tr. V.* **(a)** (erläutern) furnish with a commentary ‹*text, work*› **(b)** (Stellung nehmen zu) comment on
kommerziell 1 *Adj.* commercial 2 *adv.* commercially
Kommiss, *Kommiß *der;* **Kommisses** (Soldatenspr.) army
Kommissar *der;* **~s, ~e, Kommissarin** *die;* **~, ~nen (a)** (Beamter/Beamtin der Polizei) detective superintendent **(b)** (staatlicher Beauftragter/staatliche Beauftragte) commissioner
Kommission *die;* **~, ~en (a)** (Gremium) committee; (Prüfungs~) commission **(b) etw. in ~ nehmen/haben/geben** (Wirtsch.) take/have sth. on commission/give sth. to a dealer for sale on commission
Kommode *die;* **~, ~n** chest of drawers
kommunal *Adj.* local; (bei einer städtischen Gemeinde) municipal; local
Kommunal·wahl *die* local [government] elections *pl.*
Kommunikation *die;* **~, ~en** (Sprachw., Soziol.) communication
Kommunion *die;* **~, ~en** (kath. Kirche) [Holy] Communion
Kommuniqué /kɔmyni'keː/ *das;* **~s, ~s** communiqué
Kommunismus *der;* **~:** communism
Kommunist *der;* **~en, ~en, Kommunistin** *die;* **~, ~nen** communist
kommunistisch 1 *Adj.* communist 2 *adv.* Communist-‹*influenced, led, ruled, etc.*›
kommunizieren *itr. V.* **(a)** (geh.) communicate **(b)** (kath. Kirche) receive [Holy] Communion
Komödiant *der;* **~en, ~en, Komödiantin** *die;* **~, ~nen** (veralt.) actor/actress; player; (abwertend: Heuchler[in]) play-actor
Komödie /ko'møːdi̯ə/ *die;* **~, ~n** comedy; (Theater) comedy theatre
Kompagnon /kɔmpan'jõː/ *der;* **~s, ~s** (Wirtsch.) partner; associate
kompakt *Adj.* solid
Kompanie *die;* **~, ~n** company
Komparativ *der;* **~s, ~e** (Sprachw.) comparative
Kompass, *Kompaß *der;* **Kompasses, Kompasse** compass
kompatibel *Adj.* (Nachrichtenw., Sprachw.) compatible
Kompatibilität *die;* **~, ~en** compatibility
Kompensation *die;* **~, ~en** (Wirtsch., Physik, geh.) compensation
kompensieren *tr. V.* **etw. mit etw.** *od.* **durch etw. ~:** compensate for sth. by sth.
kompetent *Adj.* competent

Kompetenz *die;* ~, **~en** competence; (bes. Rechtsw.) authority
komplett 1 *Adj.* complete 2 *adv.* fully ‹*furnished, equipped*›; (ugs.: ganz und gar) completely
komplettieren *tr. V.* complete
Komplett·preis *der* all-inclusive price
komplex *Adj.* complex
Komplex *der;* **~es, ~e** (auch Psych.) complex
Komplexität *die;* ~: complexity
Komplikation *die;* ~, **~en** (auch Med.) complication
Kompliment *das;* **~[e]s, ~e** compliment
Komplize *der;* **~n, ~n** (abwertend) accomplice
komplizieren *tr. V.* complicate
kompliziert 1 *Adj.* complicated 2 *adv.* **~ aufgebaut sein** have a complicated *or* complex structure
Kompliziertheit *die;* ~: complexity; complicatedness
Komplizin *die;* ~, **~nen** ▶ KOMPLIZE
Komplott *das;* **~[e]s, ~e** plot; conspiracy
komponieren *tr., itr. V.* compose
Komponist *der;* **~en, ~en, Komponistin** *die;* ~, **~nen** composer
Komposition *die;* ~, **~en** composition
Kompost *der;* **~[e]s, ~e,** compost
Kompost·haufen *der* compost heap
kompostierbar *Adj.* compostable
kompostieren *tr. V.* compost
Kompott *das;* **~[e]s, ~e** stewed fruit; compote
Kompresse *die;* ~, **~n** (Med.) **(a)** (Umschlag) [wet] compress **(b)** (Mull) [gauze] pad
Kompression *die;* ~, **~en** (Physik, Technik, Med., DV) compression
Kompressor *der;* **~s, ~en** (Technik) compressor
komprimieren *tr. V.* (auch Physik, Technik, DV) compress
Kompromiss, *Kompromiß *der;* **Kompromisses, Kompromisse** compromise
kompromiss-, *kompromiß-, Kompromiss-, *Kompromiß-: ~bereit *Adj.* willing to compromise *pred.*; **~los** 1 *Adj.* uncompromising; 2 *adv.* uncompromisingly; **~vorschlag** *der* compromise proposal
kompromittieren *tr. V.* compromise
Kondensation *die;* ~, **~en** (Physik, Chemie) condensation
Kondensator *der;* **~s, ~en** (Elektrot.) capacitor
kondensieren *tr., itr. V.* (*itr. auch mit sein*) (Physik, Chemie) condense
Kondens-: ~milch *die* condensed milk; **~streifen** *der* condensation trail; **~wasser** *das* condensation
Kondition *die;* ~, **~en** condition; **eine gute/schlechte ~ haben** be/not be in good condition *or* shape; **keine ~ haben** be out of condition; (fig.) have no stamina
Konditional·satz *der* (Sprachw.) conditional clause
Konditions·training *das* fitness training
Konditor *der;* **~s, ~en** pastry cook
Konditorei *die;* ~, **~en** cake shop; (Lokal) café
kondolieren *itr. V.* offer one's condolences; **jmdm. [zu jmds. Tod] ~:** offer one's condolences to sb. [on sb.'s death]
Kondom *das od. der;* **~s, ~e** condom
Konfekt *das;* **~[e]s (a)** confectionery; sweets *pl.* (Brit.); candies *pl.* (Amer.) **(b)** (bes. südd., österr., schweiz.: Teegebäck) [small] fancy biscuits *pl.* (Brit.) *or* (Amer.) cookies *pl.*
Konfektion *die;* ~, **~en** ready-made garments *pl.*
Konferenz *die;* ~, **~en** conference; (Besprechung) meeting
konferieren *itr. V.* confer (**über** + *Akk.* on, about)
Konfession *die;* ~, **~en** denomination
konfessionell 1 *Adj.* denominational 2 *adv.* as regards denomination; **~ [un]gebunden sein** have [no] denominational ties
Konfetti *das;* **~[s]** confetti
Konfirmand *der;* **~en, ~en, Konfirmandin** *die;* ~, **~nen** (ev. Rel.) confirmand
Konfirmation *die;* ~, **~en** (ev. Rel.) confirmation
konfirmieren *tr. V.* (ev. Rel.) confirm
konfiszieren *tr. V.* (bes. Rechtsw.) confiscate
Konfitüre *die;* ~, **~n** jam
Konflikt *der;* **~[e]s, ~e** conflict
Konföderation *die;* ~, **~en** confederation
konform *Adj.* concurring *attrib.*; **~ gehen** be in agreement
Konformismus *der;* ~: conformism
Konformist *der;* **~en, ~en, Konformistin** *die;* ~, ~: conformist
konformistisch 1 *Adj.* conformist 2 *adv.* in a conformist way
Konfrontation *die;* ~, **~en** confrontation
konfrontieren *tr. V.* confront
konfus 1 *Adj.* confused 2 *adv.* in a confused fashion
Kongo[1] *der;* **~[s]** (Fluss) Congo
Kongo[2] (*das*); **~s** *od.* **der; ~[s]** (Staat) the Congo
Kongress, *Kongreß *der;* **Kongresses, Kongresse** congress; conference; **der ~** (USA): Congress
Kongress·halle, *Kongreß·halle *die* conference hall

k

König *der;* **~s, ~e** king

Königin *die;* **~, ~nen** queen

königlich 1 *Adj.* **(a)** royal **(b)** (vornehm) regal **(c)** (reichlich) princely ‹*gift, salary, wage*› 2 *adv.* ‹*pay*› handsomely; (ugs.: außerordentlich) ‹*enjoy oneself*› immensely (coll.)

König·reich *das* kingdom

Königs·haus *das* royal house

Königtum *das;* **~s, Königtümer (a)** (Monarchie) monarchy **(b)** (veralt.: Reich) kingdom

Konjugation *die;* **~, ~en** (Sprachw.) conjugation

konjugieren *tr. V.* (Sprachw.) conjugate

Konjunktion *die;* **~, ~en** (Sprachw.) conjunction

Konjunktiv *der;* **~s, ~e** (Sprachw.) subjunctive

Konjunktur *die;* **~, ~en** (Wirtsch.) **(a)** (wirtschaftliche Lage) [level of] economic activity; economy; (Tendenz) economic trend **(b)** (Hoch~) boom; (Aufschwung) upturn [in the economy]

konjunkturell *Adj.* economic

Konjunktur·politik *die* (Wirtsch.) measures *pl.* aimed at avoiding violent fluctuations in the economy

konkav (Optik) 1 *Adj.* concave 2 *adv.* concavely

konkret 1 *Adj.* concrete 2 *adv.* in concrete terms

konkretisieren *tr. V.* **etw. ~:** put sth. in concrete terms

Konkurrent *der;* **~en, ~en, Konkurrentin** *die;* **~, ~nen** (Sport, Wirtsch.) competitor

Konkurrenz *die;* **~, ~en** (Sport, Wirtsch.) competition

konkurrenz-, Konkurrenz-: ~fähig *Adj.* competitive; **~kampf** *der* competition; (zwischen zwei Menschen) rivalry

konkurrieren *itr. V.* compete

Konkurs *der;* **~es, ~e (a)** (Bankrott) bankruptcy; **~ machen** *od.* **in ~ gehen** go bankrupt **(b)** (gerichtliches Verfahren) bankruptcy proceedings *pl.*

können 1 *unr. Modalverb; 2. Part.* **können: (a)** be able to; **er kann gut reden/tanzen** he is a good talker/dancer; **ich kann nicht schlafen** I cannot *or* (coll.) can't sleep; **kann das explodieren?** could it explode?; **man kann nie wissen** you never know; **es kann sein, dass ...:** it could be that ...; **kann ich Ihnen helfen?** can I help you? **(b)** (Grund haben) **du kannst ganz ruhig sein** you don't have to worry; **das kann man wohl sagen!** you could well say that **(c)** (dürfen) **kann ich gehen?** can I go?; **~ wir mit[kommen]?** can we come too? 2 *unr. tr. V.* (beherrschen) know ‹*language*›; be able to play ‹*game*›; **sie kann das [gut]** she can do that [well]; **etw./nichts für etw. ~:** be/not be responsible for sth. 3 *unr. itr. V.* **(a)** (fähig sein) **er kann nicht anders** there's nothing else he can do; (es ist seine Art) he can't help it (coll.) **(b)** (Zeit haben) **ich kann heute nicht** I can't today (coll.) **(c)** (ugs.: Kraft haben) **kannst du noch [weiter]?** can you go on? **(d)** (ugs.: umgehen ~) **[gut] mit jmdm. ~:** get on [well] with sb.

Können *das;* **~s** ability

Könner *der;* **~s, ~, Könnerin** *die;* **~, ~nen** expert

konnte *1. u. 3. Pers. Sg. Prät. v.* KÖNNEN

könnte *1. u. 3. Pers. Sg. Konjunktiv II v.* KÖNNEN

Konsens·gespräch *das* (Politik) discussion aimed at reaching a consensus

konsequent 1 *Adj.* consistent; (folgerichtig) logical 2 *adv.* consistently; (folgerichtig) logically

Konsequenz *die;* **~, ~en (a)** (Folge) consequence **(b)** (Unbeirrbarkeit) determination

konservativ 1 *Adj.* conservative 2 *adv.* conservatively

Konservative *der/die; adj. Dekl.* conservative

Konservatorium *das;* **~s, Konservatorien** conservatoire; conservatory (Amer.)

Konserve *die;* **~, ~n (a)** (Büchse) can; tin (Brit.) **(b)** (konservierte Lebensmittel) preserved food; (in Dosen) canned *or* (Brit.) tinned food

Konserven-: ~büchse *die,* **~dose** *die* can; tin (Brit.)

konservieren *tr. V.* preserve; conserve ‹*work of art*›

Konservierung *die;* **~, ~en** preservation

Konservierungs·mittel *das* preservative

konsolidieren *tr. V.* consolidate

Konsolidierung *die;* **~, ~en** (Festigung) consolidation

Konsonant *der;* **~en, ~en** consonant

Konsortium *das;* **~s, Konsortien** (Wirtsch.) consortium

konspirativ /kɔnspira'ti:f/ *Adj.* conspiratorial

konstant /kɔn'stant/ 1 *Adj.* **(a)** constant **(b)** (beharrlich) persistent 2 *adv.* **(a)** constantly **(b)** (beharrlich) persistently

Konstellation /kɔnstɛla'ts̮i̯o:n/ *die;* **~, ~en (a)** (von Parteien usw.) grouping; (von Umständen) combination **(b)** (Astron., Astrol.) constellation

konstituieren /kɔnstitu'i:rən/ 1 *tr. V.* (gründen) constitute; set up 2 *refl. V.* be constituted

---

*alte Schreibung - vgl. Hinweis auf S. xiv

Konstitution /kɔnstitu'tsi̯o:n/ *die;* ~, **~en** constitution

konstruieren /kɔnstru'i:rən/ *tr. V.* **(a)** (entwerfen) design
(b) (aufbauen, Geom. Sprachw.) construct
(c) (abwertend) fabricate

Konstrukteur /kɔnstrʊk'tø:ɐ̯/ *der;* **~s, ~e, Konstrukteurin** *die;* ~, **~nen** designer; design engineer

Konstruktion /kɔnstrʊk'tsi̯o:n/ *die;* ~, **~en** **(a)** (Aufbau, Geom., Sprachw.) construction; (das Entwerfen) designing
(b) (Entwurf) design; (Bau) construction

konstruktiv [1] *Adj.* constructive
[2] *adv.* constructively

Konsul *der;* **~s, ~n** (Dipl., hist.) consul

Konsulat *das;* **~[e]s, ~e** (Dipl., hist.) consulate

Konsulin *die;* ~, **~nen** ▶ KONSUL

konsultieren *tr. V.* (auch fig.) consult

Konsum *der;* **~s** consumption

Konsument *der;* **~en, ~en, Konsumentin** *die;* ~, **~nen** consumer

Konsum·gesellschaft *die* consumer society

konsumieren *tr. V.* consume

Kontakt *der;* **~[e]s, ~e** contact; **mit** *od.* **zu jmdm. ~ haben/halten** be/remain in contact with sb.

kontakt-, Kontakt-: ~freudig *Adj.* sociable; **~linse** *die* contact lens; **~mann** *der; Pl.:* **~männer** *od.* **~leute** (Agent) contact; **~person** *die* (Med.) contact

Kontamination *die;* ~, **~en** contamination

kontaminieren *tr. V.* contaminate

Konten ▶ KONTO

kontern *tr., itr. V.* (Boxen, auch fig.) counter; (Ballspiele) counter-attack

Konter·revolution *die* counter-revolution

Kontinent *der;* **~[e]s, ~e** continent

kontinental *Adj.* continental

Kontingent *das;* **~[e]s, ~e** quota

kontinuierlich [1] *Adj.* steady
[2] *adv.* steadily

Kontinuität *die;* **~:** continuity

Konto *das;* **~s, Konten** *od.* **Konti** account; **ein laufendes ~:** a current account

Konto-: ~auszug *der* (Bankw.) [bank] statement; **~bewegung** *die* transaction; **~nummer** *die* account number

Kontor *das;* **~s, ~e** branch; (einer Reederei) office

Konto·stand *der* (Bankw.) balance; state of an/one's account

kontra [1] *Präp. mit Akk.* (Rechtsspr., auch fig.) versus
[2] *Adv.* against

Kontra *das;* **~s, ~s** (Kartenspiele) double; **jmdm. ~ geben** (fig. ugs.) flatly contradict sb.

Kontrahent *der;* **~en, ~en, Kontrahentin** *die;* ~, **~nen** adversary; opponent

konträr *Adj.* contrary; opposite

Kontrast *der;* **~[e]s, ~e** contrast

Kontroll·abschnitt *der* stub

Kontrolle *die;* ~, **~n** **(a)** (Überwachung) surveillance
(b) (Überprüfung) check; (bei Waren, bei Lebensmitteln) inspection
(c) (Herrschaft) control; **die ~ über etw.** (*Akk.*) **verlieren** lose control of sth.

Kontrolleur /kɔntrɔ'lø:ɐ̯/ *der;* **~s, ~e, Kontrolleurin** *die;* ~, **~nen** inspector

Kontroll·gang *der* tour of inspection; (eines Nachtwächters) round; (eines Polizisten) patrol

kontrollieren *tr. V.* **(a)** (überwachen) check; monitor
(b) (überprüfen) check; inspect ‹*goods, food*›
(c) (beherrschen) control

Kontrollturm *der* control tower

kontrovers [1] *Adj.* conflicting; (strittig) controversial
[2] *adv.* **sich ~ zu etw. äußern** express conflicting opinions on sth.

Kontroverse /kɔntro'vɛrzə/ *die;* ~, **~n** controversy (**um, über** + *Akk.* about)

Kontur *die;* ~, **~en** contour; outline

Konvention /kɔnvɛn'tsi̯o:n/ *die;* ~, **~en** convention

konventionell [1] *Adj.* **(a)** conventional
(b) (förmlich) formal
[2] *adv.* **(a)** conventionally
(b) (förmlich) formally

Konversation /kɔnvɛrza'tsi̯o:n/ *die;* ~, **~en** conversation

Konversations·lexikon *das* encyclopaedia

konvertieren [1] *itr. V.; auch mit sein* (Rel.) be converted
[2] *tr. V.* (Wirtsch., DV) convert

konvex /kɔn'vɛks/ (Optik) [1] *Adj.* convex
[2] *adv.* convexly

Konvoi /kɔn'vɔy/ *der;* **~s, ~s** (bes. Milit.) convoy

Konzentration *die;* ~, **~en** concentration

Konzentrations-: ~fähigkeit *die* ability to concentrate; **~lager** *das* (bes. ns.) concentration camp

konzentrieren *refl., tr. V.* concentrate; **sich auf etw.** (*Akk.*) **~:** concentrate on sth.

konzentriert [1] *Adj.* concentrated
[2] *adv.* with concentration

Konzept *das;* **~[e]s, ~e** **(a)** [rough] draft
(b) (Programm) programme; (Plan) plan

Konzern *der;* **~[e]s, ~e** (Wirtsch.) group [of companies]

Konzert *das;* **~[e]s, ~e** **(a)** (Komposition) concerto
(b) (Veranstaltung) concert

Konzert·saal *der* concert hall
Konzession *die;* ~, ~**en (a)** (Amtsspr.) licence
(b) (Zugeständnis) concession
Konzil *das;* ~**s**, ~**e** *od.* ~**ien** (kath. Kirche) council
konzipieren *tr. V.* draft; design ‹*device, car, etc.*›
Kooperation *die;* ~, ~**en** cooperation *no indef. art.*
kooperativ 1 *Adj.* cooperative
2 *adv.* cooperatively
kooperieren *tr. V.* cooperate
Koordinate *die;* ~, ~**n** coordinate
Koordinaten·system *das* (Math.) system of coordinates
koordinieren *tr. V.* coordinate
Kopenhagen (*das*)*;* ~**s** Copenhagen
Kopf *der;* ~**[e]s, Köpfe (a)** head; **ein** ~ **Salat** a lettuce; ~ **an** ~: shoulder to shoulder; (im Wettlauf) neck and neck; (fig.) ~ **stehen** (ugs.: überrascht sein) be bowled over; **nicht wissen, wo einem der** ~ **steht** not know whether one is coming or going; ~ **hoch!** chin up!; **den** ~ **hängen lassen** become disheartened
(b) (Person) person; **ein kluger/fähiger** ~ **sein** be a clever/able man/woman; **pro** ~: per head; **die führenden Köpfe der Wirtschaft** the leading minds in the field of economics
(c) (Wille) **seinen** ~ **durchsetzen** make sb. do what one wants
(d) (Verstand) mind; head; **sich** (*Dat.*) **den** ~ **zerbrechen** (ugs.) rack one's brains (**über** + *Akk.* over)
Kopf-: ~**bahnhof** *der* terminal station; ~**bedeckung** *die* headgear; **ohne** ~**bedeckung** without anything on one's head
Köpfchen *das;* ~**s**, ~: brains *pl.;* ~ **muss man haben** you've got to have it up here (coll.)
köpfen *tr. V.* **(a)** decapitate; (hinrichten) behead
(b) (Fußball) head
kopf-, Kopf-: ~**ende** *das* head end; ~**haut** *die* [skin of the] scalp; ~**hörer** *der* headphones *pl.;* ~**kissen** *das* pillow; ~**lastig** *Adj.* down by the head *pred.;* ~**los** 1 *Adj.* rash; (in Panik) panic-stricken; 2 *adv.* rashly; ~**los davonrennen** flee in panic; ~**rechnen** *itr. V.; nur im Inf. gebr.* do mental arithmetic; ~**rechnen** *das* mental arithmetic; ~**salat** *der* head lettuce; ~**schmerz** *der* headache; ~**schmerzen haben** have a headache *sing.;* ~**sprung** *der* header; ~**stand** *der* headstand; *~|**stehen** ▸ KOPF A; ~**stein·pflaster** *das* cobblestones *pl.;* ~**tuch** *das; Pl.* ~**tücher** headscarf; ~**weh** *das* (ugs.) headache; ~**weh haben** have a headache; ~**zerbrechen** *das;* ~**s: etw. bereitet** *od.* **macht jmdm.** ~**zerbrechen** sb. has to rack his/her brains about sth.; (etw. macht jmdm. Sorgen) sth. is a worry to sb.

*old spelling - see note on page xiv

Kopie *die;* ~, ~**n** copy; (Durchschrift) carbon copy; (Fotokopie) photocopy; (Fot., Film) print
kopieren *tr. V.* copy; (fotokopieren) photocopy; (Fot., Film) print
Kopierer *der;* ~**s**, ~: [photo]copier
Kopier·gerät *das* photocopier
Kopilot *der;* ~**en**, ~**en**, **Kopilotin** *die;* ~, ~**nen** (Flugw.) co-pilot
Koppel[1] *das;* ~**s**, ~, *österr.: die;* ~, ~**n** (Gürtel) [leather] belt (*as part of a uniform*)
Koppel[2] *die;* ~, ~**n** paddock
koppeln *tr. V.* couple (**an** + *Akk.* to); dock ‹*spacecraft*›
Koppelung ▸ KOPPLUNG
Kopplung *die;* ~, ~**en** coupling; (Raumf.) docking
kopulieren *itr. V.* copulate
Koralle *die;* ~, ~**n** coral
Koran *der;* ~**s**, ~**e** Koran
Korb *der;* ~**es, Körbe (a)** basket
(b) jmdm. einen ~ **geben** turn sb. down
Korb·ball *der* netball
Kord *der;* ~**[e]s (a)** corduroy; cord
(b) ▸ KORDSAMT
Kordel *die;* ~, ~**n** cord
Kord·samt *der* cord velvet
Korea (*das*)*;* ~**s** Korea
Koreaner *der;* ~**s**, ~, **Koreanerin** *die;* ~, ~**nen** Korean
koreanisch *Adj.* Korean
Korinthe *die;* ~, ~**n** currant
Kork *der;* ~**s**, ~**e** cork
Korken *der;* ~**s**, ~: cork
Korken·zieher *der;* ~**s**, ~: corkscrew
Korn[1] *das;* ~**[e]s, Körner (a)** (Frucht) grain; (Getreide~) grain [of corn]; (Pfeffer~) corn
(b) *o. Pl.* (Getreide) corn; grain
(c) (Salz~, Sand~) grain; (Hagel~) stone
Korn[2] *der;* ~**[e]s**, ~ (ugs.) corn schnapps; corn liquor (Amer.)
Korn·blume *die* cornflower
Körnchen *das;* ~**s**, ~: tiny grain; (von Sand usw.) [tiny] grain; granule
Körner ▸ KORN
Korn·feld *das* cornfield
körnig *Adj.* granular
Korona *die;* ~, **Koronen** crowd (coll.)
Körper *der;* ~**s**, ~: body
körper-, Körper-: ~**bau** *der* physique; ~**behindert** *Adj.* physically handicapped; ~**behinderte** *der/die* physically handicapped person; ~**behinderte** *Pl.* physically handicapped people; ~**geruch** *der* body odour; BO (coll.); ~**größe** *die* height
körperlich 1 *Adj.* physical
2 *adv.* physically
Körper·pflege *die* body care *no art.*

Körperschaft[s]·steuer *die* (Steuerw.) corporation tax

Körper-: ~spray *der od. das* deodorant spray; **~teil** *der* part of the/one's body; **~verletzung** *die* (Rechtsw.) bodily harm *no indef. art.*

Korps /ko:ɐ̯/ *das;* ~ /ko:ɐ̯(s),/ ~ /ko:ɐ̯s/ **(a)** (Milit.) corps
(b) (Studentenverbindung) student duelling society

korpulent *Adj.* corpulent

korrekt [1] *Adj.* correct
[2] *adv.* correctly

korrekter·weise *Adv.* to be [strictly] correct

Korrektheit *die;* ~: correctness

Korrektor *der;* **~s, ~en** /-'to:rən/, **Korrektorin** *die;* ~, **~nen** proof-reader

Korrektur *die;* ~, **~en** correction

Korrespondent *der;* **~en, ~en, Korrespondentin** *die;* ~, **~nen** correspondent

Korrespondenz *die;* ~, **~en** correspondence

korrespondieren *itr. V.* correspond (**mit** with)

Korridor *der;* **~s, ~e** corridor

korrigieren *tr. V.* correct; revise ‹*opinion, view*›

korrodieren *tr., itr. V.* (*itr. mit sein*) (bes. Chemie, Geol.) corrode

Korrosion *die;* ~, **~en** (auch Geol., Med.) corrosion

korrosions-, Korrosions-: ~beständig *Adj.*, **~fest** *Adj.* corrosion-resistant; **~schutz** *der* protection against corrosion

korrupt *Adj.* corrupt

Korruption *die;* ~, **~en** corruption

Korsett *das;* **~s, ~s** *od.* **~e** corset

Korsika (*das*); **~s** Corsica

Kortison *das;* **~s** (Med.) cortisone

koscher *Adj.* kosher

Kose-: ~form *die* familiar form; **~name** *der* pet name

Kosinus *der;* ~, ~ *od.* **~se** (Math.) cosine

Kosmetik *die;* ~ **(a)** beauty culture *no art.;*
(b) (fig.) cosmetic procedures *pl.*

Kosmetikerin *die;* ~, **~nen** cosmetician; beautician

Kosmetikum *das;* **~s, Kosmetika** cosmetic

kosmetisch [1] *Adj.* (auch fig.) cosmetic
[2] *adv.* **jmdn. ~ beraten** give sb. advice on beauty care; **sich ~ behandeln lassen** have beauty treatment

kosmisch *Adj.* cosmic ‹*ray, dust, etc.*›; space ‹*age, station, research, etc.*›; meteoric ‹*iron*›

Kosmos *der;* ~: cosmos

Kost *die;* ~: food; ~ **und Logis** board and lodging

kostbar [1] *Adj.* valuable; precious ‹*time*›
[2] *adv.* expensively ‹*dressed*›; luxuriously ‹*decorated*›

Kostbarkeit *die;* ~, **~en (a)** (Sache) treasure
(b) (Eigenschaft) value

kosten[1] [1] *tr. V.* taste; try
[2] *itr. V.* (probieren) have a taste

kosten[2] *tr. V.* **(a)** cost
(b) (erfordern) take; cost ‹*lives*›

Kosten *Pl.* cost *sing.;* costs; (Auslagen) expenses; (Rechtsw.) costs; **auf jmds. ~:** at sb.'s expense

kosten-, Kosten-: ~deckend *Adj.* that covers/cover [one's] costs *postpos., not pred.;* **~erstattung** *die* reimbursement of costs; **~los** [1] *Adj.* free; [2] *adv.* free of charge; **~pflichtig** (Rechtsw.) [1] *Adj.* **eine ~pflichtige Verwarnung** a fine and a caution; [2] *adv.* **eine Klage ~pflichtig abweisen** dismiss a case with costs; **ein Auto ~pflichtig abschleppen** tow a car away at the owner's expense; **~punkt** *der* (ugs.) **~punkt?** how much is it/are they?; **~punkt 25 Euro** it costs/they cost 25 euros; **~stelle** *die* (Wirtsch.) cost centre; **~vor·anschlag** *der* estimate

Kost·gänger *der;* **~s**, ~, **Kost·gängerin** *die;* ~, **~nen** (veralt.) boarder

köstlich [1] *Adj.* delicious; (unterhaltsam) delightful
[2] *adv.* ‹*taste*› delicious; **sich ~ amüsieren/unterhalten** enjoy oneself enormously (coll.)

Köstlichkeit *die;* ~, **~en** (Sache) delicacy

Kost·probe *die;* ~, **~n** taste

kost·spielig *Adj.* costly

Kostüm *das;* **~s, ~e (a)** suit
(b) (Theater~, Verkleidung) costume

kostümieren *tr. V.* dress up

Kot *der;* **~[e]s, ~e** excrement

Kotangens *der;* ~, ~ (Math.) cotangent

Kotelett /kɔt'lɛt/ *das;* **~s, ~s** chop; (vom Nacken) cutlet

Koteletten *Pl.* side whiskers

Köter *der;* **~s**, ~ (abwertend) cur

Kot·flügel *der* (Kfz-W.) wing

kotzen *itr. V.* (derb) puke (coarse)

KP *Abk.* = **Kommunistische Partei** CP

Krabbe *die;* ~, **~n (a)** (Zool.) crab
(b) (ugs.: Garnele) shrimp; (größer) prawn

krabbeln [1] *itr. V.; mit sein* crawl
[2] *tr. V.* (ugs.: kraulen) tickle

Krach *der;* **~[e]s, Kräche (a)** (Lärm) noise; row
(b) (lautes Geräusch) crash
(c) (ugs.: Streit) row

krachen [1] *itr. V.* **(a)** (Krach auslösen) ‹*thunder*› crash; ‹*shot*› ring out ···›

(b) *mit sein* (ugs.: bersten) ‹*ice*› crack; ‹*bed*› collapse
(c) *mit sein* (ugs.: mit Krach auftreffen) crash
[2] *refl. V.* (ugs.) row (coll.)

krächzen *itr. V.* ‹*raven, crow*› caw; ‹*parrot*› squawk; ‹*person*› croak

kraft *Präp. + Gen.* (Amtsspr.) ~ **[meines] Amtes** by virtue of my office; ~ **Gesetzes** by law

Kraft *die;* ~, **Kräfte** strength; (Wirksamkeit) power; (Physik) force; (Arbeits~) employee; **mit letzter** ~: with one's last ounce of strength; **aus eigener** ~: by one's own efforts; **mit vereinten Kräften werden wir …**: if we join forces *or* combine our efforts we will …; **außer** ~ **setzen** repeal ‹*law*›; countermand ‹*order*›; **außer** ~ **sein/treten** no longer be/cease to be in force; **in** ~ **treten/sein/bleiben** come into/be in/remain in force

Kraft-: ~**aufwand** *der* effort; ~**brühe** *die* strong meat broth; ~**fahrer** *der,* ~**fahrerin** *die* driver; motorist;

Kraft·fahrzeug *das* motor vehicle

Kraftfahrzeug-: ~**brief** *der* vehicle registration document; logbook (Brit.); ~**schein** *der* vehicle registration document; ~**steuer** *die* vehicle tax

kräftig [1] *Adj.* strong; vigorous ‹*plant, shoot*›; powerful, hefty ‹*blow, kick, etc.*›; nourishing ‹*soup, bread, meal, etc.*›
[2] *adv.* powerfully ‹*built*›; ‹*rain, snow*› heavily; ‹*eat*› heartily

kräftigen *tr. V.* ‹*holiday, air, etc.*› invigorate; ‹*food etc.*› fortify

kraft-, Kraft-: ~**meier** *der;* ~~s, ~~ (ugs.: abwertend) muscleman; ~**probe** *die* trial of strength; ~**rad** *das* (Amtsspr.) motorcycle; ~**stoff** *der* (Kfz-W.) fuel; ~**stoff·verbrauch** *der* fuel consumption; ~**voll** [1] *Adj.* powerful; [2] *adv.* powerfully; ~**wagen** *der* motor vehicle; ~**werk** *das* power station

Kragen *der;* ~s, ~, (südd., österr. u. schweiz. auch:) **Krägen** collar

Kragen·weite *die* collar size

Krähe /'krɛːə/ *die;* ~, ~n crow

krähen *itr. V.* (auch fig.) crow

Krähen·füße *Pl.* (ugs.) crow's feet

krakeelen *itr. V.* (ugs.) kick up a row (coll.)

krakeln *tr., itr. V.* (ugs.) scrawl

kraklig *Adj.* (ugs. abwertend) scrawly

Kralle *die;* ~, ~n claw

krallen [1] *refl. V.* **sich an etw.** (*Akk.*) ~ ‹*cat*› dig its claws into sth.; ‹*person*› clutch sth. [tightly]
[2] *tr. V.* (fest greifen) **die Finger in/um etw.** (*Akk.*) ~: dig one's fingers into sth./clutch sth. [tightly] with one's fingers

Kram *der;* ~[e]s (ugs.) **(a)** stuff; (Gerümpel) junk
(b) (Angelegenheit) affair

*alte Schreibung - vgl. Hinweis auf S. xiv

kramen [1] *itr. V.* **in etw.** (*Dat.*) ~: rummage about in sth.
[2] *tr. V.* (ugs.) **etw. aus etw.** ~: fish (coll.) sth. out of sth.

Krämer *der;* ~s, ~, **Krämerin** *die;* ~, ~**nen** grocer

Kram·laden *der* (ugs. abwertend) junk shop

Krampf *der;* ~[e]s, **Krämpfe (a)** cramp; (Zuckung) spasm
(b) painful strain; (sinnloses Tun) senseless waste of effort

Krampf·ader *die* varicose vein

krampfhaft [1] *Adj.* convulsive; (verbissen) desperate
[2] *adv.* convulsively; (verbissen) desperately

Kran *der;* ~[e]s, **Kräne (a)** crane
(b) (südwestd.: Wasserhahn) tap; faucet (Amer.)

Kranich *der;* ~s, ~e crane

krank; **kränker, kränkst…** *Adj.* ill *usu. pred.;* sick; bad ‹*leg, tooth*›; diseased ‹*plant, organ*›; (fig.) ailing ‹*economy, business*›; ~ **werden** be taken ill

Kranke *der/die; adj. Dekl.* sick man/woman; (Patient) patient

kränkeln *itr. V.* be in poor health

kränken *tr. V.* **jmdn.** ~: hurt sb. *or* sb.'s feelings

Kranken-: ~**geld** *das* sickness benefit; ~**gymnastik** *die* remedial *or* medical gymnastics *sing.;* physiotherapy; ~**gymnastin** *die;* ~~, ~~**nen** remedial gymnast; medical gymnast; physiotherapist; ~**haus** *das* hospital; ~**kasse** *die* health insurance scheme; (Körperschaft) health insurance institution; (privat) health insurance company; ~**pfleger** *der* male nurse; ~**schein** *der* health insurance certificate; ~**schwester** *die* nurse; ~**versicherung** *die* **(a)** (Versicherung) health insurance; **(b)** (Unternehmen) health insurance company; ~**wagen** *der* ambulance

kränker ▶ KRANK

krank|feiern *itr. V.* (ugs.) skive off work (coll.) [pretending to be ill]

krankhaft [1] *Adj.* pathological; morbid ‹*growth, state, swelling, etc.*›
[2] *adv.* pathologically; morbidly ‹*swollen, sensitive*›

Krankheit *die;* ~, ~en **(a)** illness; (bestimmte Art, von Pflanzen, Organen) disease
(b) (Zeit des Krankseins) illness

Krankheits·erreger *der* pathogen

kränklich *Adj.* ailing

krank|schreiben *tr. V.* give ‹*person*› a medical certificate

kränkst… ▶ KRANK

Kränkung *die;* ~, ~en: **eine** ~: an injury to one's/sb.'s feelings

Kranz *der;* ~es, **Kränze** wreath; garland; (auf einem Grab usw.) wreath

Kränzchen *das;* ~s, ~: coffee circle; coffee klatch (Amer.)

Krapfen *der;* **~s, ~**: doughnut
krass, *kraß 1 *Adj.* blatant ‹*case*›; flagrant ‹*injustice*›; stark ‹*contrast*›; complete ‹*contradiction*›; sharp ‹*difference*›; out-and-out ‹*egoist*›
2 *adv.* **sich ~ ausdrücken** put sth. bluntly; **sich von etw. ~ unterscheiden** be in stark contrast to sth
Krater *der;* **~s, ~**: crater
Kratz·bürste *die* (ugs. scherzh.) prickly so-and-so
kratzen 1 *tr. V.* scratch; (entfernen) scrape
2 *itr. V.* **(a)** scratch
(b) (jucken) itch
Kratzer *der;* **~s, ~** (ugs.) scratch
kratzig *Adj.* itchy ‹*material*›
Kraul *das;* **~s** (Sport) crawl
kraulen¹ 1 *itr. V.* do the crawl
2 *tr. V.; auch mit sein* **eine Strecke ~**: cover a distance using the crawl
kraulen² *tr. V.* **jmdm. das Kinn ~**: tickle sb. under the chin; **jmdn. in den Haaren ~**: run one's fingers through sb.'s hair
kraus *Adj.* creased ‹*skirt etc.*›; frizzy ‹*hair*›
Krause *die;* **~, ~n** (Kragen) ruff; (am Ärmel) ruffle
kräuseln 1 *tr. V.* ruffle ‹*water, surface*›; gather ‹*material etc.*›; frizz ‹*hair*›
2 *refl. V.* ‹*hair*› go frizzy; ‹*water*› ripple; ‹*smoke*› curl up
Kraut *das;* **~[e]s, Kräuter (a)** herb
(b) (bes. südd., österr.: Kohl) cabbage
Kraut·salat *der* coleslaw
Krawall *der;* **~s, ~e (a)** riot
(b) (ugs.: Lärm) row (coll.)
Krawatte *die;* **~, ~n** tie
kraxeln *itr. V.; mit sein* (bes. südd., österr. ugs.) climb; (mit Mühe) clamber
kreativ 1 *Adj.* creative
2 *adv.* **~ veranlagt sein** have a creative bent
Kreativität *die;* **~**: creativity
Kreatur *die;* **~, ~en** creature
Krebs *der;* **~es, ~e (a)** crustacean; (Fluss~) crayfish; (Krabbe) crab
(b) (Krankheit) cancer
(c) (Astrol.) Cancer; the Crab
krebs-, Krebs-: ~ erregend, ~erzeugend *Adj.* carcinogenic; **~forschung** *die* cancer research; **~geschwulst** *die* cancerous growth *or* tumour; **~geschwür** *das* (volkst.) cancerous ulcer; (fig. geh.) cancer; **~krank** *Adj.* **~krank sein** have cancer; **~rot** *Adj.* as red as a lobster *postpos.*
Kredit *der;* **~[e]s, ~e** credit; (Darlehen) loan
kredit-, Kredit-: ~institut *das* credit institution; **~karte** *die* credit card; **mit ~karte bezahlen** pay by credit card; **~nehmer** *der;* **~~s, ~~, ~nehmerin** *die;* **~~, ~~nen** borrower; **~würdig** *Adj.* (Finanzw.) creditworthy

Kreide *die;* **~, ~n** chalk
kreide·bleich *Adj.* as white as a sheet *postpos.*
Kreide·felsen *der* chalk cliff
kreieren /kre'i:rən/ *tr. V.* create
Kreis *der;* **~es, ~e** circle; (Verwaltungsbezirk) district; (Wahl~) ward
Kreis·bahn *die* orbit
kreischen *itr. V.* screech; ‹*door*› creak
Kreisel *der;* **~s, ~** (Kinderspielzeug) top; (ugs.: Kreisverkehr) roundabout
kreisen *itr. V.; auch mit sein* ‹*planet*› revolve (**um** around); ‹*satellite etc.*› orbit; ‹*aircraft, bird*› circle
kreis-, Kreis-: ~förmig *Adj.* circular; **~lauf** *der* (Physiol.) circulation; (der Natur, des Lebens usw.) cycle; **~lauf·störungen** *Pl.* (Med.) circulatory trouble *sing.*; **~rund** *Adj.* [perfectly] round; **~säge** *die* circular saw
Kreiß·saal *der* (Med.) delivery room
Kreis-: ~stadt *die* chief town of a/the district; **~verkehr** *der* roundabout
Krem *die;* **~, ~s** ▶ CREME
Krematorium *das;* **~s, Krematorien** crematorium
Krempe *die;* **~, ~n** brim
Krempel *der;* **~s** (ugs. abwertend) stuff; (Gerümpel) junk
krepieren *itr. V.; mit sein* (salopp) ‹*person*› snuff it (sl.)
Krepp *der;* **~s, ~s** *od.* **~e** crêpe
***Kreppapier** *das*, **Krepp·papier** *das* crêpe paper
Kresse *die;* **~, ~n** (Bot.) cress
Kreta *(das);* **~s** Crete
Kreuz *das;* **~es, ~e (a)** cross; (Kreuzzeichen) sign of the cross
(b) (Teil des Rückens) small of the back; **jmdn. aufs ~ legen** (salopp) take sb. for a ride (coll.)
(c) (Kartenspiel) (Farbe) clubs *pl.*; (Karte) club
(d) (Autobahn) interchange
(e) (Musik) sharp
kreuzen 1 *tr. V.* (auch Biol.) cross
2 *refl. V.* **(a)** (überschneiden) cross
(b) (zuwiderlaufen) clash (**mit** with)
3 *itr. V.; mit haben od. sein* (fahren) cruise
Kreuz-: ~fahrer *der* (hist.) crusader; **~fahrt** *die* cruise; **~feuer** *das* (Milit., auch fig.) crossfire; **~gang** *der* cloister
kreuzigen *tr. V.* crucify
Kreuzigung *die;* **~, ~en** crucifixion
Kreuz-: ~otter *die* adder; [common] viper; **~ritter** *der* (hist.) crusader; **~schlitz·schraube** *die* Phillips screw ®; **~schmerzen** *Pl.* pain *sing.* in the small of the back; **~spinne** *die* cross spider; garden spider
Kreuzung *die;* **~, ~en (a)** crossroads *sing.*
(b) (Biol.) crossing; cross-breeding; (Ergebnis) cross
kreuz-, Kreuz-: ~verhör *das* cross-

examination; **~weise** *Adv.* crosswise; **~wort·rätsel** *das* crossword [puzzle]; **~zug** *der* (hist., fig.) crusade

kribbelig *Adj.* (ugs.) (vor Ungeduld) fidgety; (nervös) edgy

kribbeln *itr. V.* (jucken) tickle; (prickeln) tingle

kriechen *unr. itr. V.* **(a)** *mit sein* ‹*insect, baby*› crawl; ‹*plant*› creep; ‹*person, animal*› creep, crawl
(b) *auch mit sein* (fig. abwertend) crawl (**vor** + *Dat.* to)

Kriecher *der;* **~s, ~, Kriecherin** *die;* **~, ~nen** (abwertend) crawler

Kriech·spur *die* (Verkehrsw.) crawler lane

Krieg *der;* **~[e]s, ~e** war; **~ führend** warring; belligerent

kriegen *tr. V.* (ugs.) get; (erreichen) catch ‹*train, bus, etc.*›

Krieger *der;* **~s, ~, Kriegerin** *die;* **~, ~nen** warrior

kriegerisch *Adj.* **(a)** (kampflustig) warlike **(b)** (militärisch) military; **eine ~e Auseinandersetzung** an armed conflict

***krieg·führend** ▶ KRIEG

kriegs-, Kriegs-: ~beil *das* tomahawk; **das ~beil begraben** (scherzh.) bury the hatchet; **~bemalung** *die* (Völkerk.) warpaint; **~beschädigt** *Adj.* war-disabled; **~beschädigte** *der/die; adj. Dekl.* war invalid; **~dienst** *der* **(a)** (im Krieg) active service; **(b)** (Wehrdienst) military service; **den ~dienst verweigern** be a conscientious objector; **~dienst·verweigerer** *der* conscientious objector; **~ende** *das* end of the war; **bei/vor ~ende** at/before the end of the war; **~erklärung** *die* declaration of war; **~gefangene** *der* prisoner of war; POW; **~gefangenschaft** *die* captivity; **~opfer** *das* war victim; **~schiff** *das* warship; **~verbrechen** *das* (Rechtsw.) war crime; **~verbrecher** *der,* **~verbrecherin** *die* war criminal; **~waise** *die* war orphan

Krimi *der;* **~[s], ~[s]** (ugs.) crime thriller

Kriminal·beamte *der,* **Kriminal·beamtin** *die* [plain-clothes] detective

kriminalisieren *tr. V.* **jmdn. ~:** make sb. turn to crime

kriminalistisch 1 *Adj.* ‹*methods, practice*› of criminalistics; ‹*abilities*› in the field of criminalistics
2 *adv.* ‹*proceed etc.*› using the methods of criminalistics

Kriminalität *die;* **~:** crime *no art.*

Kriminal-: ~polizei *die* criminal investigation department; **~roman** *der* crime novel; (mit Detektiv als Held) detective novel

kriminell 1 *Adj.* criminal
2 *adv.* **~ veranlagt sein** have criminal tendencies; **~ handeln** act illegally

Kriminelle *der/die; adj. Dekl.* criminal

Krimskrams *der;* **~[es]** (ugs.) stuff

Kringel *der;* **~s, ~** (Kreis) [small] ring; (Kritzelei) round squiggle; (Gebäck) [ring-shaped] biscuit

kringeln *refl. V.* curl [up]; ‹*hair*› go curly; **sich ~ [vor Lachen]** (ugs.) kill oneself [laughing] (coll.)

Kripo *die;* **~** (ugs.) **die ~:** ≈ the CID

Krippe *die;* **~, ~n (a)** (Futtertrog) manger; crib
(b) (Weihnachts~) model of a nativity scene
(c) (Kinder~) crèche

Krise *die;* **~, ~n** (auch Med.) crisis

kriseln *itr. V.* (*unpers.*) **es kriselt in ihrer Ehe/in der Partei** their marriage is in trouble/the party is in a state of crisis

Krisen-: ~gebiet *das* crisis area; **~herd** *der* trouble spot

Kristall[1] /krɪs'tal/ *der;* **~s, ~e** crystal

Kristall[2] *das;* **~s** crystal *no indef. art.*

Kristallisation *die;* **~, ~en** (bes. Chemie) crystallization

kristallisieren *itr. V.* (bes. Chemie) crystallize

Kriterium *das;* **~s, Kriterien** criterion

Kritik *die;* **~, ~en (a)** criticism *no indef. art.* (**an** + *Dat.* of); **an jmdm./etw. ~ üben** criticize sb./sth.
(b) (Besprechung) review

Kritiker *der;* **~s, ~, Kritikerin** *die;* **~, ~nen** critic

kritik·los 1 *Adj.* uncritical
2 *adv.* uncritically

kritisch 1 *Adj.* critical
2 *adv.* critically

kritisieren *tr. V.* criticize; review ‹*book, play, etc.*›

kritzeln 1 *itr. V.* (schreiben) scribble; (zeichnen) doodle
2 *tr. V.* scribble

Kroatien /kro'a:tsi̯ən/ (*das*)*;* **~s** Croatia

kroatisch *Adj.* Croatian

kroch *1. u. 3. Pers. Sg. Prät. v.* KRIECHEN

Krokant *der;* **~s** praline

Krokette *die;* **~, ~n** (Kochk.) croquette

Krokodil *das;* **~s, ~e** crocodile

Krokodils·tränen *Pl.* (ugs.) crocodile tears

Krokus *der;* **~, ~** *od.* **~se** crocus

Krone *die;* **~, ~n** crown; (eines Baumes) top; crown; (einer Welle) crest; **die ~ der Schöpfung** the pride of creation

krönen *tr. V.* (auch fig.) crown

Kronen·korken *der* crown cork

Kron-: ~juwelen *Pl.* Crown jewels;

---

*old spelling - see note on page xiv

~leuchter *der* chandelier; **~prinz** *der* crown prince; **~prinzessin** *die* crown princess

Krönung *die;* **~, ~en** coronation; (fig.) culmination

Kron·zeuge *der,* **Kron·zeugin** *die* (Rechtsw.) person who turns Queen's/King's evidence; **als ~ auftreten** turn Queen's/King's evidence

Kropf *der;* **~[e]s, Kröpfe** (Med.) goitre

Kröte *die;* **~, ~n (a)** toad **(b)** *Pl.* (salopp: Geld) **ein paar/eine ganze Menge ~n verdienen** earn a few bob (Brit. coll.)/a fair old whack (coll.)

Krücke *die;* **~, ~n** crutch

Krück·stock *der* walking stick

Krug *der;* **~[e]s, Krüge** jug; (größer) pitcher; (Bier~) mug

Krume *die;* **~, ~n** crumb

Krümel *der;* **~s, ~:** crumb

krümeln *itr. V.* **(a)** crumble **(b)** (Krümel machen) make crumbs

krumm 1 *Adj.* **(a)** bent ‹*nail, back*›; crooked ‹*stick, branch, etc.*›; bandy ‹*legs*›; **sich über etw.** (*Akk.*) **~ lachen** (ugs.) fall about laughing over sth. **(b)** (ugs.: unrechtmäßig) crooked **(c) etw. ~ nehmen** (ugs.) take sth. the wrong way 2 *adv.* crookedly

krümmen 1 *tr. V.* bend 2 *refl. V.* **(a)** (sich winden) writhe **(b)** (krumm verlaufen) ‹*road, path, river*› bend

krumm-: ***~|lachen** ▶ KRUMM 1A; ***~|nehmen** ▶ KRUMM 1C

Krümmung *die;* **~, ~en** bend

Krüppel *der;* **~s, ~:** cripple

Kruste *die;* **~, ~n** crust; (vom Braten) crisp

Kruzifix *das;* **~es, ~e** crucifix

Krypta *die;* **~, Krypten** (Archit.) crypt

Kuba *(das);* **~s** Cuba

Kubaner *der;* **~s, ~, Kubanerin** *die;* **~, ~nen** Cuban

Kübel *der;* **~s, ~:** pail

Kubik- cubic ‹*metre, foot, etc.*›

Küche *die;* **~, ~n** kitchen; (Einrichtung) kitchen furniture *no indef. art.;* (Kochk.) cooking; cuisine; **kalte/warme ~:** cold/hot food

Kuchen *der;* **~s, ~:** cake; (Obst~) flan; (Torte) gateau

Küchen-: **~abfälle** *Pl.* kitchen scraps; **~chef** *der,* **~chefin** *die* chef

Kuchen-: **~form** *die* cake tin; **~gabel** *die* pastry fork

Küchen-: **~gerät** *das* kitchen utensil; (als Kollektivum) kitchen utensils *pl.;* **~maschine** *die* food processor; **~meister** *der,* **~meisterin** *die* chef; **~messer** *das* kitchen knife; **~schabe** *die* cockroach; **~schrank** *der* kitchen cupboard; **~tisch** *der* kitchen table

Kuckuck *der;* **~s, ~e (a)** cuckoo; **zum ~ [noch mal]!** (salopp) for crying out loud! (coll.) **(b)** (scherzh.: Pfandsiegel) bailiff's seal (*placed on distrained goods*)

Kuckucks·uhr *die* cuckoo clock

Kufe *die;* **~, ~n** runner; (von Flugzeugen, Hubschraubern) skid

Kugel *die;* **~, ~n (a)** ball; (Geom.) sphere; (Kegeln) bowl; (beim Kugelstoßen) shot **(b)** (ugs.: Geschoss) bullet

Kugel·lager *das* (Technik) ball bearing

kugeln 1 *tr. V.* roll 2 *refl. V.* **sich [vor Lachen] ~** (ugs.) double *or* roll up [laughing]

kugel-, Kugel-: **~rund** /--'-/ *Adj.* round as a ball *postpos.;* (scherzh.: dick) rotund; tubby; **~schreiber** *der* ball pen; Biro ®; **~sicher** *Adj.* bulletproof; **~stoßen** *das;* **~~s** shot[-put]; (Disziplin) putting the shot *no art.*

Kuh *die;* **~, Kühe** cow

Kuh-: **~fladen** *der* cowpat; **~handel** *der* (ugs. abwertend) shady horse-trading *no indef. art.;* **ein ~handel** a bit of shady horse-trading; **~haut** *die:* **das geht auf keine ~haut** (fig. salopp) it's absolutely staggering

kühl 1 *Adj.* cool; **etw. ~ lagern** keep sth. in a cool place 2 *adv.* coolly

Kuhle *die;* **~, ~n** (ugs.) hollow

Kühle *die;* **~:** coolness

kühlen 1 *tr. V.* cool; chill ‹*wine*›; refrigerate ‹*food*› 2 *itr. V.* ‹*cold compress, ointment, breeze, etc.*› have a cooling effect

Kühler *der;* **~s, ~ (a)** (am Auto) radiator; (Kühlerhaube) bonnet (Brit.); hood (Amer.) **(b)** (Sekt~) ice bucket

Kühler·haube *die* bonnet (Brit.); hood (Amer.)

Kühl-: **~fach** *das* frozen food compartment; **~haus** *das* cold store; **~raum** *der* cold store; cold-storage room; **~schrank** *der* refrigerator; fridge (Brit. coll.); icebox (Amer.); **~truhe** *die* [chest] freezer; (im Lebensmittelgeschäft) freezer [cabinet]

Kühlung *die;* **~, ~en** cooling; (Vorrichtung) cooling system; (für Lebensmittel) refrigeration system

Kühl·wasser *das* cooling water

kühn 1 *Adj.* bold; (dreist) audacious 2 *adv.* boldly; (gewagt) daringly; (dreist) audaciously

Kühnheit *die;* **~:** boldness; (Gewagtheit) daringness; (Dreistigkeit) audacity

Kuh·stall *der* cowshed

Küken *das;* **~s, ~:** chick

kulant *Adj.* obliging; fair ‹*terms*›

Kulanz *die;* **~:** willingness to oblige

Kuli *der;* **~s, ~s (a)** coolie **(b)** (ugs.) ballpoint; Biro ®

kulinarisch *Adj.* culinary
Kulisse *die;* ~, ~n piece of scenery; flat; (Hintergrund) backdrop; **die ~n** the scenery *sing.*; **hinter den ~n** (fig.) behind the scenes
kullern (ugs.) *itr. V. mit sein* roll
Kult *der;* ~[e]s, ~e (auch fig.) cult
Kult·film *der* cult film
kultivieren *tr. V.* (auch fig.) cultivate
kultiviert 1 *Adj.* cultured; (vornehm) refined
2 *adv.* in a cultured manner; (vornehm) in a refined manner
Kultur *die;* ~, ~en **(a)** culture; (kultivierte Lebensart) refinement; **ein Mensch von ~:** a cultured person
(b) (Zivilisation, Lebensform) civilization
Kultur-: **~abkommen** *das* cultural agreement; **~austausch** *der* cultural exchange; **~beutel** *der* sponge bag (Brit.); toilet bag
kulturell 1 *Adj.* cultural
2 *adv.* culturally
Kultur-: **~film** *der* documentary film; **~geschichte** *die* history of civilization; (einer bestimmten Kultur) cultural history; **~politik** *die* cultural and educational policy
Kultus·minister *der,* **Kultus·ministerin** *die* minister for education and cultural affairs
Kümmel *der;* ~s, ~: caraway [seed]; (Branntwein) kümmel
Kummer *der;* ~s sorrow; grief; (Ärger, Sorgen) trouble; **~ um** *od.* **über jmdn.** grief for sb.; **jmdm. ~ machen** give sb. trouble
kümmerlich *Adj.* **(a)** (schwächlich) puny; stunted ‹*vegetation, plants*›
(b) (ärmlich) wretched; miserable
(c) (abwertend: gering) miserable; meagre ‹*knowledge, leftovers*›
kümmern 1 *refl. V.* **(a) sich um jmdn./etw. ~:** take care of sb./sth.
(b) (sich befassen mit) **sich nicht um Politik ~:** not be interested in politics
2 *tr. V.* concern
Kumpan *der;* ~s, ~e, **Kumpanin** *die;* ~, ~nen (ugs.) **(a)** pal (coll.); buddy (coll.)
(b) (abwertend: Mittäter[in]) accomplice
Kumpel *der;* ~s, ~ **(a)** (Bergmannsspr.) miner
(b) (salopp: Kamerad) pal (coll.); buddy (coll.)
Kumulus·wolke *die* (Met.) cumulus cloud
kündbar *Adj.* terminable ‹*contract*›; redeemable ‹*loan, mortgage*›
Kunde[1] *der;* ~n, ~n customer; (eines Architekten-, Anwaltbüros, einer Versicherung usw.) client
Kunde[2] *die;* ~ (geh.) tidings *pl.* (literary)
Kunden·dienst *der* service to customers; (Wartung) after-sales service
Kundgebung *die;* ~, ~en rally

*alte Schreibung - vgl. Hinweis auf S. xiv

kundig *Adj.* (kenntnisreich) knowledgeable; (sachverständig) expert
kündigen 1 *tr. V.* cancel ‹*subscription, membership*›; terminate ‹*contract, agreement*›; **seine Stellung ~:** hand in one's notice (**bei** to)
2 *unr. itr. V.* **(a)** (ein Mietverhältnis beenden) ‹*tenant*› give notice; **jmdm. ~** ‹*landlord*› give sb. notice to quit; **zum 1. Juli ~:** give notice for 1 July
(b) (ein Arbeitsverhältnis beenden) ‹*employee*› hand in one's notice (**bei** to); **jmdm. ~** ‹*employer*› give sb. his/her notice
Kündigung *die;* ~, ~en **(a)** (der Mitgliedschaft, eines Abonnements) cancellation; (eines Vertrags) termination
(b) (eines Arbeitsverhältnisses) **jmdm. die ~ aussprechen** give sb. his/her notice
Kündigungs-: **~frist** *die* period of notice; **~schutz** *der* protection against wrongful dismissal
Kundin *die;* ~, ~nen customer/client
Kundschaft *die;* ~, ~en ▶ KUNDE[1]: customers *pl.*; clientele
Kundschafter *der;* ~s, ~, **Kundschafterin** *die;* ~, ~nen scout
kund|tun (geh.) *unr. tr. V.* announce
künftig 1 *Adj.* future
2 *adv.* in future
Kunst *die;* ~, Künste **(a)** art; **die bildende ~, die bildenden Künste** the plastic arts *pl.*; **die schönen Künste** [the] fine arts
(b) (das Können) skill; **die ärztliche ~:** medical skill; **das ist keine ~!** (ugs.) there's nothing 'to it
kunst-, Kunst-: **~ausstellung** *die* art exhibition; **~buch** *das* art book; **~druck** *der; Pl.* ~~e **(a)** [fine] art print; **(b)** (Druckw.) fine-art printing; **~erzieher** *der,* **~erzieherin** *die* art teacher; **~faser** *die* synthetic fibre; **~führer** *der* guide to cultural and artistic monuments [of an/the area]; **~genuss**, ***~genuß** *der* enjoyment of art; (Ereignis) artistic treat; **~gerecht** 1 *Adj.* expert; 2 *adv.* expertly; **~geschichte** *die* art history; **~geschichtlich** 1 *Adj.* art historical ‹*studies, evidence, expertise*›; ‹*work*› on art history; 2 *adv.* **~ geschichtlich interessiert/versiert** interested/well versed in art history; **~gewerbe** *das* arts and crafts *pl.*; **~griff** *der* trick; dodge; **~halle** *die* art gallery; **~händler** *der,* **~händlerin** *die* [fine-]art dealer; **~handwerk** *das* craftwork; **~kritiker** *der,* **~kritikerin** *die* art critic; **~leder** imitation leather
Künstler *der;* ~s, ~, **Künstlerin** *die;* ~, ~nen **(a)** artist; (Zirkus~, Varietee~) artiste
(b) (Könner) genius (**in** + *Dat.* at)
künstlerisch 1 *Adj.* artistic
2 *adv.* artistically
Künstler·name *der* stage name
künstlich 1 *Adj.* **(a)** artificial

(b) (gezwungen) forced ‹*laugh, cheerfulness, etc.*›
[2] *adv.* artificially

kunst-, Kunst-: ~licht *das* artificial light; **~los** *Adj.* plain; **~postkarte** *die* art postcard; **~saal** *der* art room; **~sammler** *der*, **~sammlerin** *die* art collector; **~sammlung** *die* art collection; **~schatz** *der* art treasure; **~stoff** *der* synthetic material; plastic; **~stück** *das* trick; **das ist kein ~stück** (ugs.) it's no great feat; **~turnen** *das* gymnastics *sing.*; **~voll** [1] *Adj.* ornate and artistic; (kompliziert) elaborate; [2] *adv.* **(a)** ornately *or* elaborately and artistically; **(b)** (geschickt) skilfully; **~werk** *das* work of art

kunter·bunt [1] *Adj.* multi-coloured; (abwechslungsreich) varied; (ungeordnet) jumbled ‹*confusion, muddle, etc.*›
[2] *adv.* ‹*painted, printed*› in many colours; **~ durcheinander sein** be higgledy-piggledy

Kupfer *das;* **~s (a)** copper
(b) (~geschirr) copperware; (~geld) coppers *pl.*

Kupfer-: ~geld *das* coppers *pl.*; **~stich** *der* **(a)** copperplate engraving *no art.*; **(b)** (Blatt) copperplate print *or* engraving

Kuppe *die;* **~, ~n (a)** [rounded] hilltop
(b) (Finger~) tip; end

Kuppel *die;* **~, ~n** dome; (kleiner) cupola

Kuppelei *die;* **~:** procuring

kuppeln *itr. V.* operate the clutch

Kuppelung ▶ KUPPLUNG

Kuppler *der;* **~s, ~:** procurer

Kupplerin *die;* **~, ~nen** procuress

Kupplung *die;* **~, ~en (a)** (Kfz-W.) clutch
(b) (Technik: Vorrichtung zum Verbinden) coupling

Kur *die;* **~, ~en** [health] cure; (ohne Aufenthalt im Badeort) course of treatment

Kür *die;* **~, ~en** (Eiskunstlauf) free programme; (Turnen) optional exercises *pl.*

Kurbel *die;* **~, ~n** crank [handle]; (an Spieldosen, Grammophonen) winder; (an einem Brunnen) [winding] handle

kurbeln *tr. V.* **etw. nach oben/unten ~:** wind sth. up/down

Kurbel·welle *die* (Technik) crankshaft

Kürbis *der;* **~ses, ~se** pumpkin

Kurde *der;* **~n, ~n, Kurdin** *die;* **~, ~nen** Kurd

kurdisch *Adj.* Kurdish

Kur-: ~fürst *der* (hist.) Elector; **~gast** *der* visitor to a/the spa; (Patient) patient at a/the spa

Kurier *der;* **~s, ~e** courier

kurieren *tr. V.* (auch fig.) cure (**von** of)

Kurierin *die;* **~, ~nen** ▶ KURIER

kurios [1] *Adj.* curious
[2] *adv.* curiously; strangely; oddly

Kuriosität *die;* **~, ~en (a)** strangeness
(b) (Gegenstand) curiosity; curio

Kur-: ~konzert *das* concert [at a spa]; **~ort** *der* spa; **~pfuscher** *der*, **~pfuscherin** *die* (ugs. abwertend) quack

Kurs *der;* **~es, ~e (a)** (Richtung) course; **ein harter/weicher ~** (fig.) a hard/soft line
(b) (von Wertpapieren) price; (von Devisen) exchange rate; **der ~ des Dollars** the dollar rate
(c) (Lehrgang) course; (Teilnehmer) class

Kürschner *der;* **~s, ~, Kürschnerin** *die;* **~, ~nen** furrier

kursieren *itr. V.; auch mit sein* circulate

Kurs·teilnehmer *der*, **Kurs·teilnehmerin** *die* course participant

Kursus *der;* **~, Kurse** ▶ KURS

Kurs·wagen *der* (Eisenb.) through carriage

Kur·taxe *die;* visitors' tax (*at a spa*)

Kurve *die;* **~, ~n (a)** (einer Straße) bend
(b) (Geom.) curve
(c) (in der Statistik, Temperatur~ usw.) graph

kurven *itr. V.; mit sein* **(a)** ‹*aircraft*› circle; ‹*tanks etc.*› circle [round]
(b) (ugs.: fahren) drive around

kurven·reich *Adj.* winding; twisting

kurz; kürzer, kürzest... [1] *Adj.* short; (zeitlich; knapp) short, brief; quick ‹*look*›
[2] *adv.* **(a)** (zeitlich) briefly; (knapp) **~ gesagt** in a word
(b) (wenig) just; **~ vor/hinter der Kreuzung** just before/past the crossroads; **~ vor/nach Pfingsten** just before/after Whitsun

kurz-, Kurz-: ~arbeit *die* short-time working; **~ärm[e]lig** *Adj.* short-sleeved

Kürze *die;* **~ (a)** shortness
(b) (geringe Dauer) shortness; brevity; **in ~:** shortly
(c) (Knappheit) brevity

Kürzel *das;* **~s, ~:** shorthand symbol

kürzen *tr. V.* shorten; abridge ‹*article, book*›; cut ‹*pension, budget*›

kürzer ▶ KURZ

kurzer·hand *Adv.* without more ado

kürzest... ▶ KURZ

kurz-, Kurz-: ~fristig [1] *Adj.* **(a)** ‹*refusal, resignation, etc.*› at short notice; **(b)** (für kurze Zeit) short-term; [2] *adv.* **(a)** at short notice; **(b)** (für kurze Zeit) for a short time; (auf kurze Sicht) in the short term; (in kurzer Zeit) without delay; **~geschichte** *die* short story; **~haar·frisur** *die* bob; bobbed hairstyle; **~lebig** *Adj.* (auch fig.) short-lived; **~lebigkeit** *die;* **~~:** short-livedness

kürzlich *Adv.* recently; not long ago

kurz-, Kurz-: ~meldung *die* brief report; (während einer anderen Sendung) news flash; **~parker** *der;* **~~s, ~~, ~parkerin** *die;* **~~, ~~nen** short-stay (Brit.) *or* short-term parker; **~schluss, *~schluß** *der* (Elektrot.) short circuit; **~sichtig** (auch fig.) [1] *Adj.* short-sighted; [2] *adv.* short-sightedly; **~sichtigkeit** *die;* **~~** (auch fig.) short-sightedness

k

Kurzstrecken·rakete *die* short-range missile
Kürzung *die;* ~, ~**en** cut
kurz-, Kurz-: ~**waren** *Pl.* haberdashery *sing.* (Brit.); notions (Amer.); ~**welle** *die* (Physik, Rundf.) short wave; ~**weilig** *Adj.* entertaining; ~**zeitig** 1 *Adj.* brief; 2 *adv.* briefly
kuschelig *Adj.* cosy
kuscheln *refl. V.* **sich an jmdn. ~:** snuggle up to sb.
Kuschel·tier *das* cuddly toy
kuschen *itr. V.* knuckle under (**vor** + *Dat.* to)
Kusine *die;* ~, ~**n** ▶ COUSINE
Kuss, *Kuß *der;* **Kusses, Küsse** kiss
kuss·echt, *kuß·echt *Adj.* kissproof
küssen *tr., itr. V.* kiss
Kuss·hand, *Kuß·hand *die:* **jmdm. eine ~ zuwerfen** blow sb. a kiss; **mit ~** (ugs.) gladly
Küste *die;* ~, ~**n** coast
Küsten-: ~**linie** *die* coastline; ~**wache** *die* coastguard [service]
Küster *der;* ~**s**, ~, **Küsterin** *die;* ~, ~**nen** sexton
Kutsche *die;* ~, ~**n** coach
Kutscher *der;* ~**s**, ~, **Kutscherin** *die;* ~, ~**nen** coach driver
kutschieren 1 *itr. V.; mit sein* drive, ride [in a coach]
2 *tr. V.* **jmdn. ~:** drive sb. [in a coach]
Kutte *die;* ~, ~**n** [monk's/nun's] habit
Kutter *der;* ~**s**, ~: cutter
Kuvert /ku'veːɐ̯/ *das;* ~**s**, ~**s** envelope; (geh.: Gedeck) cover
Kuwait /ku'vaiːt/ *(das);* ~**s** Kuwait
Kybernetik *die;* ~: cybernetics *sing.*
Kybernetiker *der;* ~**s**, ~, **Kybernetikerin** *die;* ~, ~**nen** cybernetician; cyberneticist
kybernetisch *Adj.* cybernetic
KZ *Abk.* = **Konzentrationslager**
KZ-Häftling *der,* **KZler** *der;* ~**s**, ~, **KZlerin** *die;* ~, ~**nen** concentration-camp prisoner

Ll

l, L /ɛl/ *das;* ~, ~: l/L
l *Abk.* = **Liter** l.
Lab *das;* ~**[e]s**, ~**e** rennet
labberig *Adj.* (ugs. abwertend) **(a)** (fade) wishy-washy; ~ **schmecken** taste of nothing **(b)** (weich) floppy, limp ‹*material*›; floppy ‹*trousers, dress, etc.*›
laben (geh.) 1 *tr. V.* **jmdn. ~:** give sb. refreshment
2 *refl. V.* refresh oneself (**an** + *Dat.*, **mit** with)
labern *itr. V.* (ugs. abwertend) rabbit (Brit. coll.) *or* babble on
labil *Adj.* **(a)** (Med.) delicate ‹*constitution, health*›; poor ‹*circulation*›
(b) (auch Psych.) unstable ‹*person, character, situation, etc.*›
Labor *das;* ~**s**, ~**s**, *auch:* ~**e** laboratory
Laboratorium *das;* ~**s**, **Laboratorien** laboratory
Labor·test *der* laboratory test (**an** + *Dat.* of; **auf** + *Akk.* for)
Labyrinth *das;* ~**[e]s**, ~**e** maze; labyrinth
Lache¹ *die;* ~, ~**n** (ugs.) laugh
Lache² /'la(ː)xə/ *die;* ~, ~**n** puddle; (von Blut, Öl) pool

*old spelling - see note on page xiv

lächeln *itr. V.* smile (**über** + *Akk.* at)
Lächeln *das;* ~**s** smile
lachen 1 *itr. V.* laugh (**über** + *Akk.* at)
2 *tr. V.* **was gibt es denn zu ~?** what's so funny?
Lachen *das;* ~**s** laughter; **ein lautes ~:** a loud laugh
lächerlich 1 *Adj.* ridiculous; ludicrous ‹*argument, statement*›
2 *adv.* ridiculously
Lächerlichkeit *die;* ~: ridiculousness; (von Argumenten, Behauptungen usw.) ludicrousness
lachhaft *Adj.* ridiculous
Lachs *der;* ~**es**, ~**e** salmon
Lack *der;* ~**[e]s**, ~**e** varnish; (für Metall, Lackarbeiten) lacquer
lackieren *tr. V.* varnish; spray ‹*car*›
Lack·leder *das* patent leather
laden¹ 1 *unr. tr. V.* load; (Physik) charge
2 *unr. itr. V.* load [up]
laden² *unr. tr. V.* **(a)** (Rechtsspr.) summon **(b)** (geh.: einladen) invite
Laden *der;* ~**s**, **Läden** **(a)** shop; store (Amer.); **der ~ läuft** (ugs.) business is good **(b)** (Fensterladen) shutter
Laden-: ~**dieb** *der,* ~**diebin** *die* shoplifter; ~**diebstahl** *der* shoplifting;

~schluss, *~schluß *der* shop *or* (Amer.) store closing time; **~tisch** *der* [shop] counter

Lade-: ~rampe *die* loading ramp; **~raum** *der* (beim Auto) luggage space; (beim Flugzeug, Schiff) hold; (bei LKWs) payload space

lädieren *tr. V.* damage

lädst *2. Pers. Sg. Präsens v.* LADEN

lädt *3. Pers. Sg. Präsens v.* LADEN

Ladung *die;* ~, ~**en (a)** (Schiffs~, Flugzeug~) cargo; (eines LKW) load **(b)** (beim Sprengen, Schießen; Physik) charge **(c)** (Rechtsspr.: Vor~) summons *sing.*

lag *1. u. 3. Pers. Sg. Prät. v.* LIEGEN

Lage *die;* ~, ~**n (a)** situation; **eine gute ~ haben** be well situated **(b)** (Art des Liegens) position **(c)** (Situation) situation

Lage·plan *der* map of the area

Lager *das;* ~**s,** ~ **(a)** camp **(b)** storeroom; (in Geschäften, Betrieben) stockroom **(c)** (Warenbestand) stock

Lager-: ~bestand *der* (Wirtsch.) stock; **den ~bestand aufnehmen** do a stocktake; **~feuer** *das* campfire; **~halle** *die* warehouse

lagern 1 *tr. V.* **(a)** store **(b)** (hinlegen) lay down 2 *itr. V.* **(a)** camp **(b)** (liegen) lie; ‹*foodstuffs, medicines, etc.*› be kept

Lager-: ~platz *der* campsite; **~raum** storeroom; (im Geschäft, Betrieb) stockroom

Lagerung *die;* ~, ~**en** storage

Lagune *die;* ~, ~**n** lagoon

lahm *Adj.* **(a)** (gelähmt) lame; (ugs.: unbeweglich) stiff **(b)** (ugs.: unzureichend) lame ‹*excuse, explanation, etc.*› **(c)** (ugs. abwertend: matt) dreary

lahmen *itr. V.* be lame

lähmen *tr. V.* paralyse; (fig.) paralyse ‹*economy, industry*›; bring ‹*traffic*› to a standstill

Lähmung *die;* ~, ~**en** paralysis; (fig.) (der Wirtschaft, Industrie) paralysis; **zu einer ~ des Verkehrs führen** bring traffic to a standstill

Laib *der;* ~[e]**s,** ~**e** loaf; **ein [halber] ~ Brot** [half] a loaf of bread

Laich *der;* ~[e]**s,** ~**e** spawn

laichen *itr. V.* spawn

Laie *der;* ~**n,** ~**n** (Mann) layman; (Frau) laywoman

Lakai *der;* ~**en,** ~**en** lackey; liveried footman

Lake *die;* ~, ~**n** brine

Laken *das;* ~**s,** ~ (bes. nordd.) sheet

Lakritze *die;* ~, ~**n** liquorice

lallen *tr., itr. V.* ‹*baby*› babble; ‹*drunk/ drowsy person*› mumble

Lamelle *die;* ~, ~**n** (einer Jalousie) slat; (eines Heizkörpers) rib

lamentieren *itr. V.* (ugs.) moan (**über** + *Akk.* about)

Lametta *das;* ~**s** lametta

Lamm *das;* ~[e]**s, Lämmer** lamb

lamm-, Lamm-: ~fell *das* lambskin; **~fleisch** *das* lamb; **~fromm** 1 *Adj.* ‹*person*› as meek as a [little] lamb; 2 *adv.* ‹*answer*› like a lamb

Lämpchen *das;* ~**s,** ~: small *or* little light; **ein rotes ~:** a little red light

Lampe *die;* ~, ~**n** light; (Tisch~, Öl~, Signal~) lamp

Lampen-: ~fieber *das* stage fright; **~schirm** *der* [lamp]shade

Lampion /lam'pi̯ɔŋ/ *der;* ~**s,** ~**s** Chinese lantern

Land *das;* ~**es, Länder** *od.* (veralt.) ~**e (a)** land *no indef. art.;* (dörfliche Gegend) country *no indef. art.;* **an ~:** ashore; **auf dem ~ wohnen** live in the country **(b)** (Staat) country; **hier zu ~e** [here] in this country **(c)** (Bundesland) Land; state; (österr.) province

Land-: ~arbeiter *der,* **~arbeiterin** *die* agricultural worker; farm worker; **~bevölkerung** *die* rural population

Lande-: ~anflug *der* (Flugw.) [landing] approach; **~bahn** *die* (Flugw.) [landing] runway; **~erlaubnis** *die* (Flugw.) permission to land *no art.*

landen 1 *itr. V.; mit sein* **(a)** land; (ankommen) arrive **(b)** (ugs.: gelangen) land up 2 *tr. V.* **(a)** land ‹*aircraft, troops, passengers, fish, etc.*› **(b)** (ugs.: zustande bringen) pull off ‹*victory, coup*›; have ‹*smash hit*›

Ländereien *Pl.* estates

Länder-: ~kampf *der* (Sport) international match; **~spiel** *das* (Sport) international [match]

Landes-: ~innere *das* interior [of the country]; **~kunde** *die* regional studies *pl., no art.;* **~regierung** *die* government of a/ the Land/province; **~sprache** *die* language of the country

Lande·steg *der* landing stage; jetty

Landes-: ~tracht *die* national costume *or* dress; **~verrat** *der* (Rechtsw.) treason; **~währung** *die* currency of a/the country

land-, Land-: ~flucht *die* migration from the land *or* countryside [to the towns]; **~friedens·bruch** *der* (Rechtsw.) breach of the peace; **~gewinnung** *die* reclamation of land; **~haus** *das* country house; **~karte** *die* map; **~kreis** *der* district; **~läufig** *Adj.* widely accepted

ländlich *Adj.* rural; country *attrib.* ‹*life*›

Land-: ~luft *die* country air; **~mine** *die* landmine; **~plage** *die* (fig.) pest; nuisance; **~ratte** *die* (ugs.) landlubber

Landschaft *die;* ~, ~**en** landscape; (ländliche Gegend) countryside

landschaftlich [1] *Adj.* regional [2] *adv.* ~ **herrlich gelegen sein** be in a glorious natural setting; **die Umgebung der Stadt ist** ~ **sehr schön** the town is in *or* has a beautiful natural setting

Land·schul·heim *das* ▶ SCHULLANDHEIM

Lands-: ~**mann** *der; Pl.* ~**leute** fellow countryman; compatriot; ~**männin** *die;* ~~, ~~**nen** fellow countrywoman; compatriot

Land-: ~**straße** *die* country road; (im Gegensatz zur Autobahn) ordinary road; ~**streicher** *der;* ~~**s**, ~~, ~**streicherin** *die;* ~~, ~~**nen** tramp; ~**strich** *der* area; ~**tag** *der* Landtag; state parliament; (österr.) provincial parliament

Landung *die;* ~, ~**en** landing

Landungs·brücke *die* [floating] landing stage

land-, Land-: ~**weg** *der* overland route; **auf dem** ~**weg** overland; ~**wirt** *der,* ~**wirtin** *die* farmer; ~**wirtschaft** *die* agriculture *no art.;* farming *no art.;* ~**wirtschaftlich** [1] *Adj.* agricultural; [2] *adv.* ~**wirtschaftlich genutzt werden** be used for agricultural purposes; ~**zunge** *die* (Geogr.) tongue of land

lang; **länger, längst...** [1] *Adj.* long; (ugs.: groß) tall [2] *adv.* [for] a long time; **eine Sekunde/mehrere Stunden** ~: for a second/several hours

lang-: ~**ärm[e]lig** *Adj.* long-sleeved; ~**atmig** [1] *Adj.* long-winded; [2] *adv.* long-windedly; ‹*relate*› at great length

lange; **länger, am längsten** *Adv.* **(a)** a long time; **bist du schon** ~ **hier?** have you been here long?
(b) (bei weitem) **ich bin noch** ~ **nicht fertig** I'm nowhere near finished; **hier is es** ~ **nicht so schön** it isn't nearly as nice here

Länge *die;* ~, ~**n** length; (Geogr.) longitude

langen (ugs.) [1] *itr. V.* **(a)** be enough
(b) (greifen) reach (**in** + *Akk.* into; **auf** + *Akk.* on to; **nach** for)
[2] *tr. V.* **jmdm. eine** ~ (ugs.) give sb. a clout [around the ear] (coll.)

Längen·grad *der* (Geogr.) degree of longitude

länger [1] ▶ LANG, LANGE;
[2] *Adj.* **seit** ~**er Zeit** for quite some time

Lange·weile *die;* ~ *od.* **Langenweile** boredom; ~ **haben** be bored

lang-, Lang-: ~**fristig** [1] *Adj.* long-term; long-dated ‹*loan*›; [2] *adv.* on a long-term basis; ~**jährig** *Adj.* ‹*customer, friend*› of many years' standing; long-standing ‹*friendship*›; ~**jährige Erfahrung** many years of experience; ~**lauf** *der* (Skisport) cross-country; ~**lebig** *Adj.* long-lived ‹*animals, organisms*›; durable ‹*goods, materials*›

länglich *Adj.* oblong

lang-, Lang-: ~**mut** *die;* ~~: forbearance; ~**mütig** *Adj.* forbearing; ~**mütigkeit** *die;* ~~: forbearance

längs [1] *Präp.* + *Gen. od.* (*selten*) *Dat.* along [2] *Adv.*lengthways

Längs·achse *die* longitudinal axis

langsam [1] *Adj.* slow
[2] *adv.* **(a)** slowly; ~, **aber sicher** (ugs.) slowly but surely
(b) (allmählich) gradually

Lang-: ~**schläfer** *der,* ~**schläferin** *die* late riser; ~**spiel·platte** *die* long-playing record; LP

Längs·schnitt *der* longitudinal section

längst *Adv.* **(a)** (schon lange) a long time ago **(b)** (bei weitem) **hier ist es** ~ **nicht so schön** it isn't nearly as nice here

längst... ▶ LANG

längstens *Adv.* (ugs.) (höchstens) at [the] most; (spätestens) at the latest

Languste *die;* ~, ~**n** spiny lobster

lang-, Lang-: ~**weilen** [1] *tr. V.* bore; [2] *refl. V.* be bored; ~**weilig** [1] *Adj.* boring; dull ‹*place*›; [2] *adv.* boringly; ~**welle** *die* (Physik, Rundf.) long wave; ~**wierig** *Adj.* lengthy; prolonged ‹*search*›

Lanze *die;* ~, ~**n** lance; (zum Werfen) spear

Laos (*das*)*;* **Laos'** Laos

Laote *der;* ~**n**, ~**n**, **Laotin** *die;* ~, ~**nen** Laotian

lapidar [1] *Adj.* (kurz, aber wirkungsvoll) succinct; (knapp) terse
[2] *adv.* succinctly/tersely

Lappalie /la'pa:li̯ə/ *die;* ~, ~**n** trifle

Lappe *der;* ~**n**, ~**n** Lapp

Lappen *der;* ~**s**, ~: cloth; (Fetzen) rag; (Wasch~) flannel

Lappin *die;* ~, ~**nen** Lapp

läppisch *Adj.* silly

Lapp·land (*das*)*;* ~**s** Lapland

Laptop *der;* ~**s**, ~**s** (DV) laptop

Lärche *die;* ~, ~**n** larch

Lärm *der;* ~[**e**]**s** noise; (Krach) din; row (coll.)

Lärm·belästigung *die* disturbance caused by noise

lärmen *itr. V.* make a noise *or* (coll.) row

Lärm-: ~**pegel** *der* noise level; ~**schutz** *der* **(a)** protection against noise;
(b) (Vorrichtung) noise barrier; noise *or* sound insulation *no indef. art.;* ~**schutz·wand** *die* sound-insulating wall

Larve *die;* ~, ~**n** grub; larva

las *1. u. 3. Pers. Sg. Prät. v.* LESEN

lasch [1] *Adj.* limp ‹*handshake*›; feeble ‹*action, measure*›; lax ‹*upbringing*›
[2] *adv. s. Adj.:* limply; feebly; laxly

*alte Schreibung - vgl. Hinweis auf S. xiv

Lasche *die;* ~, ~n (Gürtel~) loop; (eines Briefumschlags) flap; (Schuh~) tongue

Laser /'leɪzə/ *der;* ~s, ~ (Physik) laser

Laser-: **~drucker** *der* (DV) laser printer; **~pointer** *der* (DV) laser pointer

lass, *laß *Imperativ Sg. v.* LASSEN

lassen 1 *unr. tr. V.* **(a)** *mit Inf.* + *Akk.* (*2. Part.* **lassen**) (veranlassen) **etw. tun/machen/bauen/waschen ~**: have *or* get sth. done/made/built/washed; **jmdn. warten ~**: keep sb. waiting; **jmdn. grüßen ~**: send one's regards to sb.; **jmdn. kommen/rufen ~**: send for sb.
(b) *mit Inf.* + *Akk.* (*2.Part.* **lassen**) (erlauben) **jmdn. etw. tun ~**: let sb. do sth.; allow sb. to do sth.
(c) (belassen) **jmdn. in Frieden ~**: leave sb. in peace
(d) (hinein~/heraus~) let *or* allow (**in** + *Akk.* into, **aus** out of)
(e) (unterlassen) stop
(f) (zurück~; bleiben ~) leave
(g) (überlassen) **jmdm. etw. ~**: let sb. have sth.
(h) (als Aufforderung) **lass/lasst uns gehen/fahren!** let's go!
(i) (verlieren) lose; (ausgeben) spend
2 *unr. refl. V.* **die Tür lässt sich leicht öffnen** the door opens easily; **das lässt sich nicht beweisen** it can't be proved
3 *unr. itr. V.* **(a)** (ugs.) **Lass mal. Ich mache das schon** Leave it. I'll do it
(b) (veranlassen) **ich lasse bitten** would you ask him/her/them to come in

lässig 1 *Adj.* casual
2 *adv.* casually

lässt, *läßt *3. Pers. Sg. Präsens v.* LASSEN

Last *die;* ~, ~en load; (Gewicht) weight; (Bürde) burden

lasten *itr. V.* be a burden; **auf jmdm./etw. ~**: weigh heavily [up]on sb./sth.

Laster[1] *der;* ~s, ~ (ugs.: Lkw) truck; lorry (Brit.)

Laster[2] *das;* ~s, ~: vice

lasterhaft *Adj.* (abwertend) depraved

lästern 1 *itr. V.* (abwertend) **über jmdn./etw. ~**: make malicious remarks about sb./sth.
2 *tr. V.* (veralt.) blaspheme against

lästig *Adj.* tiresome; troublesome ‹*illness, cough, etc.*›

Last-: **~schrift** *die* debit; **~wagen** *der* truck; lorry (Brit.)

Lasur *die;* ~, ~en varnish; (farbig) glaze

Latein *das;* ~s Latin

Latein·amerika (*das*) Latin America

lateinisch *Adj.* Latin

latent *Adj.* latent

Laterne *die;* ~, ~n **(a)** (Leuchte) lamp; lantern (Naut.)
(b) (Straßen~) street light

Laternen·pfahl *der* lamp post

Latrine *die;* ~, ~n latrine

latschen *itr. V.; mit sein* (salopp) trudge; (schlurfend) slouch

Latschen *der;* ~s, ~ (ugs.) old worn-out shoe/slipper

Latte *die;* ~, ~n **(a)** lath; (Zaun~) pale
(b) (Sport: Quer~ des Tores) [cross]bar
(c) (Leichtathletik) bar

Latten-: **~rost** *der* (auf dem Boden) duckboards *pl.;* (eines Bettes) slatted frame **~zaun** *der* paling fence

Latz *der;* ~es, **Lätze** bib

Lätzchen *das;* ~s, ~: bib

lau *Adj.* tepid, lukewarm ‹*water etc.*›; mild ‹*wind, air, evening, etc.*›

Laub *das;* ~[e]s leaves *pl.;* **dichtes ~**: thick foliage

Laub·baum *der* broad-leaved tree

Laube *die;* ~, ~n summer house; (überdeckter Sitzplatz) bower; arbour

Laub-: **~frosch** *der* tree frog; **~säge** *die* fretsaw; **~wald** *der* deciduous wood/forest

Lauch *der;* ~[e]s (Porree) leek

Lauer *die;* ~: **auf der ~ liegen** *od.* **sein** (ugs.) (jmdm. auflauern) lie in wait

lauern *itr. V.* (auch fig.) lurk

Lauf *der;* ~[e]s, **Läufe** **(a)** running
(b) (Sport: Wettrennen) heat
(c) (Ver~) course; **im ~[e] der Zeit** in the course of time; **im ~[e] der Jahre/des Tages** over the years/during the day
(d) (von Schusswaffen) barrel

Lauf·bahn *die* **(a)** (Werdegang) career
(b) (Leichtathletik) running track

laufen 1 *unr. itr. V.; mit sein* **(a)** run; (beim Eislauf) skate; (beim Ski~) ski; (gehen) go; (zu Fuß gehen) walk; **in** (*Akk.*)/**gegen etw. ~**: walk into sth.; **dauernd zum Arzt ~** (ugs.) keep running to the doctor
(b) (im Gang sein) ‹*machine*› be running; ‹*radio, television, etc.*› be on; (funktionieren) ‹*machine*› run; ‹*radio, television, etc.*› work
(c) (gelten) ‹*contract, agreement, engagement, etc.*› run
(d) (gespielt werden) ‹*programme, play, etc.*› be on
2 *unr. tr. u. itr. V.* **(a)** *mit sein* (zurücklegen) (zu Fuß) walk; (rennen) run
(b) *mit sein* (erzielen) **einen Rekord ~**: set up a record
(c) *mit haben od. sein* **Ski/Schlittschuh/Rollschuh ~**: ski/skate/roller-skate

laufend 1 *Adj.* **(a)** (ständig) regular ‹*interest, income*›; recurring ‹*costs*›
(b) (gegenwärtig) current ‹*issue, year, month, etc.*›
2 *adv.* constantly; ‹*increase*› steadily

Läufer *der;* ~s, ~ **(a)** (Sport) runner; (Handball; Fußball veralt.) halfback
(b) (Teppich) (*long narrow*) carpet

Läuferin *die;* ~, ~nen ▸ LÄUFER A

Lauf·feuer *das* brush fire; **wie ein ~**: like wildfire

Lauf-: **~masche** *die* ladder; **~pass,** ···

***~paß** *der:* **er hat seiner Freundin den ~pass gegeben** (ugs.) he finished with his girlfriend (coll.); **~schritt** *der:* **im ~schritt, marsch, marsch!** at the double, quick march!

läufst *2. Pers. Sg. Präsens v.* LAUFEN

Lauf·stall *der* playpen

läuft *3. Pers. Sg. Präsens v.* LAUFEN

Laufwerk *das* (Technik) mechanism; (DV) drive

Lauge *die; ~, ~n* **(a)** soapy water **(b)** (Chemie) alkaline solution

Laugen·brezel *die* (südd.) pretzel

Laune *die; ~, ~n* mood

launenhaft *Adj.* temperamental; (unberechenbar) capricious

launig witty

launisch *Adj.:* ▶ LAUNENHAFT

Laus *die; ~,* **Läuse** louse

Laus·bub *der* little rascal

Lausch·aktion *die,* **Lausch·angriff** *der* bugging operation (coll.)

lauschen *itr. V.* **(a)** (horchen) listen **(b)** (zuhören) listen [attentively]

Lauscher *der; ~s, ~,* **Lauscherin** *die; ~, ~nen* eavesdropper

lauschig *Adj.* cosy, snug ‹*corner*›

lausig [1] *Adj.* (ugs.) **(a)** (abwertend: unangenehm, schäbig) lousy (coll.); rotten (coll.) **(b)** (sehr groß) perishing (Brit. coll.), freezing ‹*cold*›; terrible (coll.) ‹*heat*›
[2] *adv.* terribly (coll.)

laut¹ [1] *Adj.* loud; (geräuschvoll) noisy
[2] *adv.* loudly; (geräuschvoll) noisily

laut² *Präp. + Gen. od. Dat.* (Amtsspr.) according to

Laut *der; ~[e]s, ~e* sound

Laute *die; ~, ~n* lute

lauten *itr. V.* ‹*answer, instruction, slogan*› be, run; ‹*letter, passage, etc.*› read, go; ‹*law*› state

läuten [1] *tr., itr. V.* ring; ‹*alarm clock*› go off
[2] *itr. V.* (bes. südd.: klingeln) ring; **es läutete** the bell rang *or* went (**zu** for)

lauter¹ *Adj.* (geh.) honourable ‹*person, intentions, etc.*›; honest ‹*truth*›

lauter² *indekl. Adj.* nothing but; sheer ‹*nonsense, joy, etc.*›

läutern *tr. V.* (geh.) reform ‹*character*›; purify ‹*soul*›

Läuterung *die; ~, ~en* (geh.) reformation; (der Seele) purification

laut·hals *Adv.* at the top of one's voice; **~ lachen** roar with laughter

lautlich [1] *Adj.* phonetic
[2] *adv.* phonetically

laut-, Laut-: ~los [1] *Adj.* silent; soundless; (wortlos) silent; [2] *adv.* silently; soundlessly; **~schrift** *die* (Phon.) phonetic alphabet; (Umschrift) phonetic transcription; **~sprecher** *der* loudspeaker; (einer Stereoanlage usw.) speaker; **~stark** [1] *Adj.* loud; vociferous, loud ‹*protest*›; [2] *adv.* loudly; ‹*protest*› vociferously; **~stärke** *die* volume

lau·warm *Adj.* lukewarm

Lava *die; ~,* **Laven** (Geol.) lava

Lavendel *der; ~s, ~:* lavender

Lawine *die; ~, ~n* (auch fig.) avalanche; **eine ~ von Protesten** (fig.) a storm of protest

Lawinen·gefahr *die* danger of avalanches

lax [1] *Adj.* lax
[2] *adv.* laxly

Laxheit *die; ~:* laxness; laxity

Layout /leɪˈaʊt/ *das; ~s, ~s* (Druckw., Elektronik) layout

Lazarett *das; ~[e]s, ~e* military hospital

Lead·sänger /ˈliːt-/ *der,* **Lead·sängerin** *die* lead singer

leasen /ˈliːzn̩/ *tr. V.* rent; (für längere Zeit mieten) lease ‹*car etc.*›

leben *itr. V.* live; (lebendig sein) be alive; **leb[e] wohl!** farewell!; **von seiner Rente/seinem Gehalt ~:** live on one's pension/salary

Leben *das; ~s, ~* **(a)** life; **das ~:** life; **sich** (*Dat.*) **das ~ nehmen** take one's [own] life; **am ~ sein/bleiben** be/stay alive; **ums ~ kommen** lose one's life
(b) (Betriebsamkeit) **auf dem Markt herrschte ein reges ~:** the market was bustling with activity; **das ~ auf der Straße** the comings and goings in the street

lebend *Adj.* living; live ‹*animal*›

lebendig [1] *Adj.* living; (lebhaft) lively
[2] *adv.* (lebhaft) in a lively way

Lebendigkeit *die; ~:* liveliness

lebens-, Lebens-: ~abend *der* (geh.) evening of one's life (literary); **~art** *die* **(a)** way of life; **(b)** (Umgangsformen) manners *pl.;* **~aufgabe** *die* life's work; **~bejahend** *Adj.* ‹*person*› with a positive attitude to life; **~bereich** *der* area of life; **~dauer** *die* lifespan; **~ende** *das* end [of one's life]; **~erinnerungen** *Pl.* memories of one's life; (aufgezeichnet) memoirs; **~erwartung** *die* life expectancy; **~fähig** *Adj.* (auch fig.) viable; **~freude** *die* zest for life; **~froh** *Adj.* full of zest for life *postpos.;* **~gefahr** *die* mortal danger; **„Achtung, ~gefahr!"** 'danger'; **~gefährlich** [1] *Adj.* highly dangerous; critical ‹*injury*›; [2] *adv.* critically ‹*injured, ill*›; **~gefährte** *der,* **~gefährtin** *die* (geh.) companion through life (literary); **~geister** *Pl.* **jmds. ~geister [wieder] wecken** put new life into sb.; **~groß** *Adj.* life-size; **~größe** *die:* **eine Statue in ~größe** a life-size statue

Lebens·haltung *die* cost of living

Lebenshaltungs-: ~index *der* (Wirtsch.) cost-of-living index; **~kosten** *Pl.* cost of living *sing.*

lebens-, Lebens-: ~jahr *das* year of [one's] life; **~kraft** *die* vitality;

*old spelling - see note on page xiv

~künstler *der,* **~künstlerin** *die:* **ein [echter/wahrer] ~künstler** a person who always knows how to make the best of things; **~lage** *die* situation [in life]; **~lang** [1] *Adj.* lifelong; [2] *adv.* all one's life; **~länglich** [1] *Adj.* **~länglicher Freiheitsentzug** life imprisonment; [2] *adv.* **jmdn. ~länglich gefangen halten** keep sb. imprisoned for life; **~lauf** *der* curriculum vitae; c.v.; **~licht** *das* (geh.) flame of life (literary); **jmdm. das ~licht ausblasen** *od.* **auspusten** (ugs.) send sb. to kingdom come (coll.); **~lustig** *Adj.* ‹*person*› full of the joys of life

Lebens·mittel *das* food[stuff]; **~** *Pl.* food *sing.*

Lebensmittel-: ~abteilung *die* food department; **~geschäft** *das* food shop; **~vergiftung** *die* food poisoning

lebens-, Lebens-: ~müde *Adj.* weary of life *pred.;* **~notwendig** *Adj.* essential; **~raum** *der* **(a)** (Umkreis) lebensraum; **(b)** (Biol.) ▶ BIOTOP; **~retter** *der,* **~retterin** *die* rescuer; **~standard** *der* standard of living; **~unterhalt** *der:* **seinen ~unterhalt verdienen/bestreiten** earn one's living/ support oneself; **~versicherung** *die* life insurance; **~wandel** *der* way of life; **~weg** *der* [journey through] life; **~weise** *die* way of life; **~zeichen** *das* sign of life; **~zeit** *die* life[span]; **auf ~zeit** for life

Leber *die;* **~, ~n** liver

Leber-: ~fleck *der* liver spot; **~käse** *der: meat loaf made with mincemeat,* [*minced liver,*] *eggs, and spices;* **~tran** *der* fish-liver oil; (des Kabeljaus) cod-liver oil; **~wurst** *die* liver sausage; **~zirrhose** *die* (Med.) cirrhosis of the liver

Lebe-: ~wesen *das* living being; **~wohl** /--'--/ *das;* **~~[e]s, ~~** *od.* **~~e** (geh.) farewell

lebhaft [1] *Adj.* **(a)** lively; busy ‹*traffic*›; brisk ‹*business*›
(b) (deutlich) vivid ‹*idea, picture, etc.*›
(c) (kräftig) bright ‹*colour*›; vigorous ‹*applause, opposition*›
[2] *adv.* **(a)** in a lively way
(b) (deutlich) vividly
(c) (kräftig) brightly ‹*coloured*›

leb-, Leb-: ~kuchen *der* ≈ gingerbread; **~los** *Adj.* lifeless; **~zeiten** *Pl.* **bei** *od.* **zu jmds. ~zeiten** during sb.'s lifetime

lechzen *itr. V.* (geh.) **nach einem Trunk ~:** long for a drink; **nach Rache** *usw.* **~:** thirst for revenge *etc.*

leck *Adj.* leaky; **~ sein** leak

Leck *das;* **~[e]s, ~s** leak

lecken[1] [1] *tr. V.* lick
[2] *itr. V.* **an etw.** (*Dat.*) **~:** lick sth.

lecken[2] *itr. V.* (leck sein) leak

lecker *Adj.* tasty ‹*meal*›; delicious ‹*cake etc.*›; good ‹*smell, taste*›

Lecker·bissen *der* delicacy; **ein musikalischer ~** (fig.) a musical treat

Leckerei *die;* **~, ~en** (ugs.) dainty; (Süßigkeit) sweet [meat]

led. *Abk.* = **ledig**

Leder *das;* **~s, ~:** leather

Leder-: ~handschuh *der* leather glove; **~hose** *die* leather shorts *pl.;* lederhosen *pl.;* (lang) leather trousers; **~jacke** *die* leather jacket; **~riemen** *der* [leather] strap; **~waren** *Pl.* leather goods

ledig *Adj.* single; **eine ~e Mutter** an unmarried mother

Ledige *der/die; adj. Dekl.* single person

lediglich *Adj.* merely

leer *Adj.* empty; clean ‹*sheet of paper*›; **~ stehend** empty, unoccupied

Leere *die;* **~** (auch fig.) emptiness

leeren *tr., refl. V.* empty

leer-, Leer-: ~gefegt *Adj.* deserted ‹*street, town*›; **wie ~gefegt** deserted; **~lauf** *der* **im ~lauf den Berg hinunterfahren** ‹*driver*› coast down the hill in neutral; ‹*cyclist*› freewheel down the hill; ***~stehend** ▶ LEER; **~taste** *die* space bar

Leerung *die;* **~, ~en** emptying; (von Briefkästen) collection

Lefze *die;* **~, ~n** lip

legal [1] *Adj.* legal
[2] *adv.* legally

legalisieren *tr. V.* legalize

Legalisierung *die:* **~, ~en** legalization

Legalität *die;* **~:** legality

legen [1] *tr. V.* **(a)** lay [down]
(b) (verlegen) lay ‹*pipe, cable, carpet, tiles, etc.*›
[2] *tr., itr. V.* ‹*hen*› lay
[3] *refl. V.* **(a)** lie down
(b) (nachlassen) die down; abate; ‹*enthusiasm*› wear off, subside

legendär *Adj.* legendary

Legende *die;* **~, ~n** legend

leger /le'ʒeːɐ̯/ [1] *Adj.* casual
[2] *adv.* casually

legieren *tr. V.* alloy

Legierung *die;* **~, ~en** alloy

Legislative *die;* **~, ~n** (Politik) legislature

Legislatur·periode *die* legislative period

legitim *Adj.* legitimate

Legitimation *die;* **~, ~en (a)** legitimation
(b) (Ausweis) proof of identity

legitimieren [1] *tr. V.* **(a)** (rechtfertigen) justify
(b) (bevollmächtigen) authorize
(c) (für legitim erklären) legitimize ‹*child, relationship*›
[2] *refl. V.* show proof of one's identity

Legitimität *die;* **~:** legitimacy

Lehm *der;* **~s** loam; (Ton) clay

l

Lehne *die;* ~, ~**n** (Rücken~) back; (Arm~) arm

lehnen [1] *tr., refl. V.* lean (**an** + *Akk.*, **gegen** against)
[2] *itr. V.* be leaning (**an** + *Dat.* against)

Lehn-: ~**stuhl** *der* armchair; ~**wort** *das; Pl.* ~**wörter** loanword

Lehr-: ~**auftrag** *der* lectureship; ~**buch** *das* textbook

Lehre *die;* ~, ~**n** **(a)** apprenticeship
(b) (Weltanschauung) doctrine
(c) (Theorie, Wissenschaft) theory
(d) (Erfahrung) lesson

lehren *tr., itr. V.* teach

Lehrer *der;* ~**s**, ~ (auch fig.) teacher; (Ausbilder) instructor

Lehrer-: ~**ausbildung** *die* teacher training *no art.;* ~**ausflug** *die* staff outing

Lehrerin *die;* ~, ~**nen** teacher

Lehrer-: ~**kollegium** *das* teaching staff; faculty (Amer.); ~**konferenz** *das* staff meeting; ~**zimmer** *das* staffroom

Lehr-: ~**gang** *der* course (**für, in** + *Dat.* in); ~**jahr** *das* year as an apprentice; ~**körper** *der* (Amtsspr.) teaching staff; faculty (Amer.)

Lehrling *der;* ~**s**, ~**e** apprentice; (in kaufmännischen Berufen) trainee

lehr-, Lehr-: ~**plan** *der* (Schulw.) syllabus; (Gesamtlehrgang) curriculum; ~**reich** *Adj.* informative; ~**stelle** *die* apprenticeship; (in kaufmännischen Berufen) trainee post; ~**stoff** *der* (Schulw.) syllabus

Leib *der;* ~**[e]s**, ~**er** (geh.) body; **mit ~ und Seele Arzt/Krankenschwester** *usw.* **sein** be a dedicated doctor/nurse *etc.;* **mit ~ und Seele dabei sein** put one's whole heart into it

Leibes-: ~**übungen** *Pl.* (Schulw.) physical education *sing.;* PE; ~**visitation** *die;* ~~, ~~**en** body search

Leib·gericht *das* favourite dish

leibhaftig *Adj.* in person *postpos.;* (echt) real

leiblich *Adj.* physical ‹*well-being*›; (blutsverwandt) real

Leib-: ~**schmerzen** *Pl.* abdominal pain *sing.;* ~**wächter** *der,* ~**wächterin** *die* bodyguard

Leiche *die;* ~, ~**n** [dead] body; corpse

Leichen *der* hearse

leichen-, Leichen-: ~**blass**, *~**blaß** *Adj.* deathly pale; ~**schau·haus** *das* morgue; ~**wagen** *der* hearse

Leichnam *der;* ~**s**, ~**e** (geh.) body

leicht [1] *Adj.* light; lightweight ‹*suit, material*›; easy ‹*task, question, job, etc.*›; slight ‹*accent, illness, wound, doubt, etc.*›; mild ‹*cigar, cigarette*›; ~ **fallen** be easy; **das fällt mir ~:** it's easy for me; **jmdm./sich etw. ~ machen** make sth. easy for sb./oneself; **etw. ~ nehmen** make light of sth.
[2] *adv.* lightly ‹*built*›; (einfach, schnell, spielend) easily; (geringfügig) slightly; ~ **verletzt** slightly injured

leicht-, Leicht-: ~**athletik** *die* [track and field] athletics *sing.;* *~**fallen** ▸ LEICHT 1; ~**fertig** [1] *Adj.* careless ‹*behaviour, person*›; rash ‹*promise*›; ill-considered, slapdash ‹*plan*›; [2] *adv.* carelessly; ~**gläubig** *Adj.* gullible

Leichtigkeit *die;* ~ (geringes Gewicht) lightness; (Mühelosigkeit) ease

leicht-, Leicht-: *~|**machen** ▸ LEICHT 1; *~|**nehmen** ▸ LEICHT 1; ~**sinn** *der* carelessness *no indef. art.;* (mit Gefahr verbunden) recklessness *no indef. art.;* ~**sinnig** [1] *Adj.* careless; (sich, andere gefährdend) reckless; (fahrlässig) negligent; [2] *adv.* carelessly; (gefährlich) recklessly; ‹*promise*› rashly; ~**sinniger·weise** *Adv.* carelessly; (gefährlicherweise) recklessly; ‹*promise*› rashly; *~**verletzt** ▸ LEICHT 2

leid *Adj.* **etw./jmdn. ~ sein/werden** (ugs.) be/get fed up with sth./sb. (coll.); *s. auch* LEID[2]

Leid[1] *das;* ~**[e]s** **(a)** (Schmerz) suffering; (Kummer) grief; sorrow
(b) (Unrecht) wrong; (Böses) harm

Leid[2]: **es tut mir ~, [dass]...:** I'm sorry [that]...; **er tut mir ~:** I feel sorry for him

leiden [1] *unr. itr. V.* suffer (**an, unter** + *Dat.* from)
[2] *unr. tr. V.* **(a) jmdn. [gut] ~ können** *od.* **mögen** like sb.
(b) (geh.: ertragen müssen) suffer ‹*hunger, thirst, etc.*›

Leiden *das;* ~**s**, ~ **(a)** (Krankheit) illness; (Gebrechen) complaint
(b) (Qual) suffering

leidend *Adj.* **(a)** (krank) ailing
(b) (schmerzvoll) strained ‹*voice*›; martyred ‹*expression*›

Leidenschaft *die;* ~, ~**en** passion (**zu, für** for)

leidenschaftlich [1] *Adj.* passionate; vehement ‹*protest*›
[2] *adv.* passionately; (eifrig) dedicatedly; **etw. ~ gern tun** adore doing sth.

Leidens·genosse *der,* **Leidens·genossin** *die* fellow sufferer

leider *Adv.* unfortunately

leidig *Adj.* tiresome

leidlich *Adj.* reasonable

Leid·tragende *der/die; adj. Dekl.* victim

Leier *die;* ~, ~**n** lyre

leihen *unr. tr. V.* **(a) jmdm. etw. ~:** lend sb. sth.
(b) (entleihen) borrow

Leih-: ~**gabe** *die* loan (*Gen.* from); ~**gebühr** *die* hire *or* (Amer.) rental charge; (bei Büchern) borrowing fee; ~**haus** *das* pawnbroker's; pawnshop; ~**mutter** *die; Pl.* ~**mütter** surrogate mother; ~**wagen** *der* hire *or* (Amer.) rental car

Leim *der;* ~**[e]s** glue

*alte Schreibung - vgl. Hinweis auf S. xiv

leimen *tr. V.* glue (**an** + *Akk.* to)
Leine *die;* ~, ~**n** rope; (Wäsche~, Angel~) line; (Hunde~) lead (esp. Brit.); leash; ~ **ziehen** (ugs.) clear off
leinen *Adj.* linen ‹*tablecloth, sheet, etc.*›
Leinen *das;* ~**s** **(a)** (Gewebe) linen
(b) (Buchw.) cloth
Leinen·band *der* cloth-bound volume
Lein·wand *die* **(a)** linen; (grob) canvas
(b) (des Malers) canvas
(c) (für Filme und Dias) screen
leise [1] *Adj.* **(a)** quiet; soft ‹*steps, music, etc.*›
(b) (leicht) faint; slight; slight, gentle ‹*touch*›
[2] *adv.* **(a)** quietly
(b) (leicht; kaum merklich) slightly; ‹*touch, rain*› gently
Leiste *die;* ~, ~**n** strip; (Holz~) batten; (profiliert) moulding
leisten [1] *tr. V.* do ‹*work*›; (schaffen) achieve ‹*a lot, nothing*›; **jmdm. Hilfe** ~: help sb.
[2] *refl. V.* (ugs.) **sich** (*Dat.*) **etw.** ~: treat oneself to sth.; **sich** (*Dat.*) **etw.** **[nicht]** ~ **können** [not] be able to afford sth.
Leisten·bruch *der* rupture
Leistung *die;* ~, ~**en** **(a)** (Qualität bzw. Quantität der Arbeit) performance
(b) (Errungenschaft) achievement; (im Sport) performance
(c) (Leistungsvermögen, Physik: Arbeits~) power
(d) (Zahlung, Zuwendung) payment; (Versicherungsw.) benefit
(e) (Dienst~) service
leistungs-, Leistungs-: ~**druck** *der* (bei Arbeitnehmern) pressure to work harder; (bei Sportlern, Schülern) pressure to achieve *or* to do well; ~**fähig** *Adj.* capable ‹*person*›; (körperlich) able-bodied; ~**gesellschaft** *die* competitive society; ~**prinzip** *das* competitive principle; ~**sport** *der* competitive sport *no art.*
Leit·artikel *der* (Zeitungsw.) leading article; leader
leiten *tr. V.* **(a)** (anführen) lead; head; be head of ‹*school*›; (verantwortlich sein für) be in charge of ‹*project, expedition, etc.*›; manage ‹*factory, enterprise*›; (den Vorsitz führen bei) chair; conduct ‹*orchestra, choir*›; ~**der Angestellter** manager
(b) (begleiten, führen) lead
(c) (lenken) direct; route ‹*traffic*›; (um~) divert
Leiter¹ *der;* ~**s**, ~: leader; (einer Abteilung) head; (eines Instituts) director; (einer Schule) head teacher; headmaster (Brit.); principal (esp. Amer.); (Vorsitzender) chair[man]
Leiter² *die;* ~, ~**n** ladder
Leiterin *die;* ~, ~**nen** ▶ LEITER¹; (einer Schule) head teacher; headmistress (Brit.); principal (esp. Amer.)
Leit-: ~**motiv** *das* (Musik, Literaturw., fig.) **(a)** leitmotiv; **(b)** (Leitgedanke) dominant *or* central theme; ~**planke** *die* crash barrier; guardrail (Amer.)
Leitung *die;* ~, ~**en** **(a)** ▶ LEITEN A: leading; heading; being in charge; management; chairing
(b) (einer Expedition usw.) leadership; (Verantwortung) responsibility (*Gen.* for); (eines Betriebes, Unternehmens) management; (einer Sitzung, Diskussion) chairmanship
(c) (leitende Personen) management; (einer Schule) head and senior staff
(d) (Rohr~) pipe; (Haupt~) main
(e) (Draht, Kabel) cable; (für ein Gerät) lead
(f) (Telefon~) line
Leitungs·wasser *das* tap water
Leit·zins[satz] *der* (Finanzw.) discount rate; ≈ base rate
Lektion /lɛk'tsi̯oːn/ *die;* ~, ~**en** lesson
Lektor *der;* ~**s**, ~**en** **(a)** (Hochschulw.) *junior university teacher in charge of practical or supplementary classes etc.;*
(b) (im Verlag) [publisher's] editor
Lektüre *die;* ~, ~**n** **(a)** reading
(b) (Lesestoff) reading [matter]
Lende *die;* ~, ~**n** loin
Lenden-: ~**gegend** *die* loins *pl.;* lumbar region (Anat.); ~**schurz** *der* loincloth; ~**wirbel** *der* (Anat.) lumbar vertebra
lenken *tr. V.* **(a)** *auch itr.* steer; be at the controls of ‹*aircraft*›; guide ‹*missile*›; (fahren) drive ‹*car etc.*›
(b) direct ‹*thoughts etc.*› (**auf** + *Akk.* to); turn ‹*attention*› (**auf** + *Akk.* to)
(c) (kontrollieren) control ‹*person, press, economy*›; govern ‹*state*›
Lenker *der;* ~**s**, ~ **(a)** handlebars *pl.;*
(b) (Fahrer) driver
Lenkerin *die;* ~, ~**nen** ▶ LENKER B
Lenk-: ~**rad** *das* steering wheel; ~**rad·schloss**, *~**rad·schloß** *das* (Kfz-W.) steering [wheel] lock; ~**stange** *die* handlebars *pl.*
Lenz *der;* ~**es**, ~**e** (dichter. veralt.) spring
Leopard *der;* ~**en**, ~**en** leopard
Lepra *die;* ~: leprosy *no art.*
Lerche *die;* ~, ~**n** lark
lernen [1] *itr. V.* study; (als Lehrling) train
[2] *tr. V.* learn (**aus** from)
lesbar *Adj.* legible; (klar) lucid ‹*style*›; (verständlich) comprehensible
Lesbe *die;* ~, ~**n** (ugs.) lesbian
Lesbierin /'lɛsbi̯ərɪn/ *die;* ~, ~**nen** lesbian
lesbisch *Adj.* Lesbian
Lese-: ~**brille** *die* reading glasses *pl.;* ~**buch** *das* reader
lesen¹ *unr. tr., itr. V.* read
lesen² *unr. tr. V.* **(a)** pick ‹*grapes, berries, fruit*›; gather ‹*firewood*›; **Ähren** ~: glean [ears of corn]
(b) (aussondern) pick over
Leser *der;* ~**s**, ~: reader

Leserbrief *der* reader's letter; **~e** readers' letters; **„~e"** (Zeitungsrubrik) 'Letters to the editor'
Leserin *die;* **~, ~nen** reader
Leserkreis *der* readership
leserlich [1] *Adj.* legible
[2] *adv.* legibly
Lese·zeichen *das* bookmark
Lesung *die;* **~, ~en** reading
Lette *der;* **~n, ~n, Lettin** *die;* **~, ~nen** Latvian
lettisch *Adj.* Latvian; Lettish ‹*language*›
Lett·land (*das*)*;* **~s** Latvia
Letzt: zu guter ~: in the end
letzt... *Adj.* last; **~en Endes** in the end; (äußerst...) ultimate; (neuest...) latest ‹*news*›
***letzte·mal**: ▶ MAL[1]
***letzen·mal**: ▶ MAL[1]
letzter... *Adj.* latter
letztlich *Adv.* ultimately; in the end
Leucht·diode *die* light-emitting diode; LED
Leuchte *die;* **~, ~n** light
leuchten *itr. V.* **(a)** ‹*moon, sun, star, etc.*› be shining; ‹*fire, face*› glow
(b) shine a/the light; **jmdm. ~:** light the way for sb.
leuchtend *Adj.* **(a)** shining ‹*eyes*›; brilliant ‹*colours*›; bright ‹*blue, red, etc.*›
(b) (großartig) shining ‹*example*›
Leuchter *der;* **~s, ~:** candelabrum; (für eine Kerze) candlestick
Leucht-: ~farbe *die* luminous paint; **~kugel** *die* flare; **~reklame** *die* neon sign; **~stoff·lampe** *die* fluorescent light *or* lamp; **~turm** *der* lighthouse; **~ziffer·blatt** *das* luminous dial
leugnen [1] *tr. V.* deny
[2] *itr. V.* deny it
Leukämie *die;* **~, ~n** (Med.) leukaemia
Leumund *der;* **~[e]s** (geh.) reputation
Leute *Pl.* people; **die reichen/alten ~:** the rich/the old
Leutnant *der;* **~s, ~s** second lieutenant
leut·selig [1] *Adj.* affable
[2] *adv.* affably
Lexikon *das;* **~s, Lexika** *od.* **Lexiken** encyclopaedia (*Gen.*, **für** of)
Libanese *der;* **~n, ~n, Libanesin** *die;* **~, ~nen** Lebanese
Libanon (*das*) *od. der;* **~s** Lebanon
Libelle *die;* **~, ~n** dragonfly
liberal [1] *Adj.* liberal
[2] *adv.* liberally
Liberale *der/die; adj. Dekl.* liberal
liberalisieren *tr. V.* liberalize; relax ‹*import controls*›
Libero *der;* **~s, ~s** (Fußball) sweeper

*old spelling - see note on page xiv

Libyen (*das*)*;* **~s** Libya
libysch *Adj.* Libyan
licht *Adj.* **(a)** light
(b) (dünn bewachsen) sparse; thin
Licht *das;* **~[e]s, ~er (a)** light
(b) (elektrisches) light
(c) *Pl. auch* **~e** (Kerze) candle
licht-, Licht-: ~bild *das* [small] photograph (*for passport etc.*); **~empfindlich** *Adj.* sensitive to light
lichten[1] [1] *tr. V.* thin out ‹*trees etc.*›
[2] *refl. V.* ‹*trees*› thin out; ‹*hair*› grow thin; ‹*fog, mist*› lift
lichten[2] *tr. V.* (Seemannsspr.) **den/die Anker ~:** weigh anchor
lichterloh [1] *Adj.* blazing ‹*fire*›; leaping ‹*flames*›
[2] *adv.* **~ brennen** be blazing fiercely
Lichter·meer *das* sea of lights
Licht-: ~hupe *die* headlight flasher; **~jahr** *das* (Astron.) light year; **~kegel** *der* beam; **~maschine** *die* (Kfz-W.) (mit Gleichstrom) dynamo; (mit Wechselstrom) alternator; generator (esp. Amer.); **~reklame** *die* neon sign; **~schalter** *der* light switch; **~schranke** *die* photoelectric beam; **~schutz·faktor** *der* protection factor (*against sunburn*)
Lichtung *die;* **~, ~en** clearing
Lid *das;* **~[e]s, ~er** eyelid
lieb [1] *Adj.* **(a)** (liebevoll) kind ‹*words, gesture*›
(b) (liebenswert) likeable; nice; (stärker) lovable ‹*child, girl, pet*›; **~ aussehen** look sweet *or* (Amer.) cute
(c) (artig) good ‹*child, dog*›
(d) (geschätzt) dear; **sein liebstes Spielzeug** his favourite toy; **~er Hans/~e Else!** (am Briefanfang) dear Hans/Else
(e) (angenehm) welcome; **es wäre mir ~/~er, wenn ...:** I should be glad/should prefer it if ...
(f) jmdn. ~ haben love sb.; (gern haben) be fond of sb.
[2] *adv.* **(a)** (liebenswert) kindly
(b) (artig) nicely
Liebe *die;* **~, ~n (a)** love; **~ zu jmdm./zu etw.** love for sb./of sth.; **aus ~ [zu jmdm.]** for love [of sb.]; **tu mir die ~ und ...:** do me a favour and ...; **mit ~:** lovingly; with loving care
(b) (ugs.: geliebter Mensch) love
Liebelei *die;* **~, ~en** flirtation
lieben [1] *tr. V.* **(a) jmdn. ~:** love sb.; (sexuell) make love to sb.; **sich ~:** be in love; (sexuell) make love
(b) etw. ~: be fond of sth.; (stärker) love sth.
[2] *itr. V.* be in love
liebend *Adv.* **etw. ~ gern tun** [simply] love doing sth.
liebens·würdig *Adj.* kind; charming ‹*smile*›
lieber *Adv.* **(a)** ▶ GERN;

(b) better; **lass das ~:** better not do that

Liebes-: ~brief *der* love letter; **~paar** *das* courting couple; **~roman** *der* romantic novel

liebe·voll [1] *Adj.* loving *attrib.* ‹*care*›; affectionate ‹*embrace, gesture, person*› [2] *adv.* lovingly; affectionately; (mit Sorgfalt) lovingly

***lieb|haben** ▶ LIEB 1F

Liebhaber *der;* **~s, ~ (a)** lover **(b)** (Interessierter, Anhänger) enthusiast (*Gen.* for); (Sammler) collector

Liebhaberei *die;* **~, ~:** hobby

Liebhaberin *die;* **~, ~nen** ▶ LIEBHABER

lieblich [1] *Adj.* charming; (angenehm) sweet ‹*scent, sound*› [2] *adv.* sweetly; (angenehm) pleasingly

Liebling *der;* **~s, ~e** (bes. als Anrede) darling; (bevorzugte Person) favourite

Lieblings- favourite

lieb·los [1] *Adj.* loveless [2] *adv.* **(a)** without affection **(b)** (ohne Sorgfalt) without proper care

liebsten: **am ~:** ▶ GERN

Liechtenstein *(das);* **~s** Liechtenstein

Lied *das;* **~[e]s, ~er** song

liederlich *Adj.* slovenly; messy ‹*hairstyle, person*›

Lieder-: ~macher *der;* **~~s, ~~, ~macherin** *die;* **~~, ~~nen** singer-songwriter

lief *1. u. 3. Pers. Sg. Prät. v.* LAUFEN

Lieferant *der;* **~en, ~en, Lieferantin** *die;* **~, ~nen** supplier

lieferbar *Adj.* available; (vorrätig) in stock

Liefer·bedingungen *Pl.* terms of delivery

liefern *tr. V.* **(a)** (bringen) deliver (**an** + *Akk.* to); (zur Verfügung stellen) supply **(b)** (hervorbringen) produce; provide ‹*eggs, honey, examples, raw material, etc.*›

Liefer-: ~schein *der* delivery note; **~termin** *der* delivery date

Lieferung *die;* **~, ~en** delivery

Liefer-: ~wagen *der* [delivery] van; **~zeit** *die* delivery time

Liege *die;* **~, ~n** daybed; (zum Ausklappen) bed settee; (als Gartenmöbel) sunlounger

liegen *unr. itr. V.* lie; ‹*person*› be lying down; (sich befinden) be; ‹*object*› be [lying]; ‹*town, house, etc.*› be [situated]; **im Bett ~:** lie in bed; **~ bleiben** (liegen gelassen werden) stay; be left; (vergessen werden) be left behind; (unerledigt bleiben) be left undone; (nicht aufstehen) stay [lying]; **[im Bett] ~ bleiben** stay in bed; **etw. ~ lassen** leave sth.; (vergessen) leave sth. [behind]; (unerledigt lassen) leave sth. undone; **einen Brief ~ lassen** (nicht abschicken) leave a letter unposted; (nicht öffnen) leave a letter unopened; **das liegt an ihm** *od.* **bei ihm** it is up to him; (ist seine Schuld) it is his fault; **es liegt mir nicht** it doesn't suit me; (es spricht mich nicht an) it doesn't appeal to me; (ich mag es nicht) I don't like it; **daran liegt ihm viel/wenig/nichts** he sets great/little/no store by that

liegen-: *~|bleiben ▶ LIEGEN; ***~|lassen** ▶ LIEGEN

Liege-: ~stuhl *der* deckchair; **~stütz** *der;* **~~es, ~~e** press-up; **~wagen** *der* couchette car; **~wiese** *die* sunbathing lawn

lieh *1. u. 3. Pers. Sg. Prät. v.* LEIHEN

lies *Imperativ Sg. v.* LESEN

ließ *1. u. 3. Pers. Sg. Prät. v.* LASSEN

liest *3. Pers. Sg. Präsens v.* LESEN

Lift *der;* **~[e]s, ~e** *od.* **~s (a)** lift (Brit.); elevator (Amer.) **(b)** *Pl.:* **~e** (Ski~, Sessel~) lift

Liga *die;* **~, Ligen** league; (Sport) division

Likör *der;* **~s, ~e** liqueur

lila *indekl. Adj.* mauve; (dunkel~) purple

Lila *das;* **~s, ~** *od.* (ugs.) **~s** mauve; (Dunkel~) purple

Lilie /ˈliːli̯ə/ *die;* **~, ~n** lily

Liliputaner *der;* **~s, ~, Liliputanerin** *die;* **~, ~nen** dwarf

Limit *das;* **~s, ~s** limit

Limo *die, auch: das;* **~, ~[s]** (ugs.) fizzy drink

Limonade *die;* **~, ~n** fizzy drink; (Zitronen~) lemonade

Limousine *die;* **~, ~n** [large] saloon (Brit.) *or* (Amer.) sedan

Linde *die;* **~, ~n** lime [tree]

lindern *tr. V.* relieve ‹*suffering, pain*›; slake ‹*thirst*›

Lineal *das;* **~s, ~e** ruler

Linie /ˈliːni̯ə/ *die;* **~, ~n** line; (Verkehrsstrecke) route; **die ~ 12** (Verkehrsw.) the number 12; **auf die [schlanke] ~ achten** (ugs. scherzh.) watch one's figure; **auf der ganzen ~** (fig.) all along the line

linien-, Linien-: ~bus *der* regular bus; **~flug** *der* scheduled flight; **~richter** *der,* **~richterin** *die* (Fußball usw.) linesman; (Tennis) line judge; (Rugby) touch judge; **~treu** [1] *Adj.* loyal to the party line *postpos.;* [2] *adv.* ‹*act*› in accordance with the party line

linieren, liniieren *tr. V.* rule

link... *Adj.* **(a)** left **(b)** (innen, nicht sichtbar) wrong, reverse ‹*side*› **(c)** (in der Politik) left-wing

linkisch [1] *Adj.* awkward [2] *adv.* awkwardly

links *Adv.* on the left; (Politik) on the left wing

links-, Links-: ~abbieger *der,* **~abbiegerin** *die* (Verkehrsw.) motorist/cyclist/car *etc.* turning left; **~außen** *der;* **~~, ~~** (Ballspiele) left wing; outside left; **~extremist** *der,* **~extremistin** *die* ⋯

(Politik) left-wing extremist; **~händer** *der;* **~~s, ~~, ~händerin** *die;* **~~, ~~nen** left-hander; **~kurve** *die* left-hand bend; **~radikal** (Politik) 1 *Adj.* radical left-wing; 2 *adv.* **eine ~radikal orientierte Gruppe** a group with a radical left-wing orientation; **~radikale** *der/die* left-wing radical; **~radikalismus** *der* left-wing radicalism; **~verkehr** *der* driving *no art.* on the left

Linoleum *das;* **~s** linoleum; lino

Linse *die;* **~, ~n (a)** (Bot., Kochk.) lentil **(b)** (Med., Optik) lens

Lippe *die;* **~, ~n** lip

Lippen·stift *der* lipstick

liquid *Adj.* (Wirtsch.) liquid ‹*funds, resources*›; solvent ‹*business*›

liquidieren (verhüll.: töten; Wirtsch.) liquidate

lispeln *itr. V.* lisp

Lissabon *(das);* **~s** Lisbon

List *die;* **~, ~en (a)** [cunning] trick **(b)** (listige Art) cunning

Liste *die;* **~, ~n** list; **schwarze ~:** blacklist

listig 1 *Adj.* cunning; crafty 2 *adv.* cunningly; craftily

Litauen *(das);* **~s** Lithuania

Litauer *der;* **~s, ~, Litauerin** *die;* **~, ~nen** Lithuanian

litauisch *Adj.* Lithuanian

Liter *der, auch: das;* **~s, ~:** litre

literarisch *Adj.* literary

Literatur *die;* **~, ~en** literature

Literatur-: ~geschichte *die* literary history; history of literature; **~verzeichnis** *das* list of references

liter·weise *Adv.* by the litre; in litres

Litfaß·säule *die* advertising column

Lithografie, Lithographie *die;* **~, ~n** (Druck) lithograph

litt *1. u. 3. Pers. Sg. Prät. v.* LEIDEN

Litze *die;* **~, ~n** braid

live /laiːf/ (Rundf., Ferns.); 1 *Adj.* live 2 *adv.* live; **in dieser Sendung wird nur ~ gesungen** in this programme all the singing is live

Live-: ~sendung, *~-Sendung *die* (Rundf., Ferns.) live programme; **~übertragung** *die* (Rundf., Ferns.) live broadcast

Lizenz *die;* **~, ~en** licence

Lizenz·gebühr *die* licence fee; (Verlagsw.) royalty

Lkw, LKW /ɛlkaːˈveː/ *der;* **~[s], ~[s]** *Abk.* = **Lastkraftwagen** truck; lorry (Brit.)

Lob *das;* **~[e]s, ~e** praise *no indef. art.*

Lobby /ˈlɔbi/ *die;* **~, ~s** *od.* **Lobbies** lobby

loben *tr. V.* praise

lobens·wert 1 *Adj.* praiseworthy; laudable; commendable 2 *adv.* laudably; commendably

*alte Schreibung - vgl. Hinweis auf S. xiv

löblich *Adj.* commendable

Lob·lied *das* song of praise

Loch *das;* **~[e]s, Löcher** hole

lochen *tr. V.* punch holes/a hole in; punch ‹*ticket*›

Locher *der;* **~s, ~:** punch

löcherig *Adj.* full of holes *pred.*

Locke *die;* **~, ~n** curl

locken *tr. V.* **(a)** lure **(b)** (reizen) tempt

Locken·wickler *der* [hair] curler

locker 1 *Adj.* loose; (entspannt) relaxed ‹*position, muscles*›; slack ‹*rope, rein*›; (fig.) relax ‹*regulation, law, etc.*› 2 *adv.* **~ sitzen** ‹*tooth, screw, nail*› be loose; (entspannt, ungezwungen) loosely

locker|lassen *unr. itr. V.* (ugs.) **nicht ~:** not give up

lockern 1 *tr. V.* loosen; slacken [off] ‹*rope etc.*›; relax ‹*muscles, limbs*› 2 *refl. V.* ‹*brick, tooth, etc.*› work itself loose; ‹*person*› loosen up

Lockerung *die;* **~, ~en (a)** loosening; (fig.: von Bestimmung, Gesetz usw.) relaxation **(b)** (Entspannung) loosening up; relaxation

lockig *Adj.* curly

Lock·vogel *der* decoy

Loden·mantel *der* loden coat

Löffel *der;* **~s, ~:** spoon; (als Maßangabe) spoonful; (Jägerspr.) ear

löffeln *tr. V.* spoon [up]

log *1. u. 3. Pers. Sg. Prät. v.* LÜGEN

Logarithmus *der;* **~, Logarithmen** (Math.) logarithm; log

Loge /ˈloːʒə/ *die;* **~, ~n** box

logieren *itr. V.* (veralt.) stay

Logik *die;* **~:** logic

logisch 1 *Adj.* logical 2 *adv.* logically

logischer·weise *Adv.* logically; (selbstverständlich) naturally

logo *Adj.* (salopp) **[ist doch] ~!** you bet! (coll.); of course!

Lohn *der;* **~[e]s, Löhne (a)** wage[s *pl.*]; pay *no indef. art., no pl.* **(b)** (Belohnung) reward

Lohn·büro *das* payroll office

lohnen 1 *refl., itr. V.* be worth it 2 *tr. V.* be worth

lohnend *Adj.* rewarding

Lohn·steuer *die* income tax

Lohn-: ~steuer·karte *die* income-tax card; **~streifen** *der* payslip; **~tüte** *die* pay packet (Brit.); wage packet

lokal *Adj.* local

Lokal *das;* **~s, ~e** pub (Brit. coll.); bar (Amer.); (Speise~) restaurant

Lokalität *die;* **~, ~en** locality

Lokal-: ~blatt *das* local paper; **~patriotismus** *der* local patriotism;

~teil *der* (Zeitungsw.) local section; **~termin** *der* (Rechtsspr.) visit to the scene [of the crime]

Lok·führer *der*, **Lok·führerin** *die:* ▶ LOKOMOTIVFÜHRER

Lokomotive /lokomo'ti:və/ *die;* **~, ~n** locomotive

Lokomotiv·führer *der*, **Lokomotiv·führerin** *die* engine driver (Brit.); engineer (Amer.)

Lokus *der;* **~** *od.* **~ses, ~** *od.* **~se** (salopp) loo (Brit. coll.); john (Amer. coll.)

London *(das);* **~s** London

Londoner [1] *indekl. Adj.* London [2] *der;* **~s, ~:** Londoner

Londonerin *die;* **~, ~nen** Londoner

Lorbeer *der;* **~s, ~en (a)** laurel **(b)** (Gewürz) bayleaf

Lore *die;* **~, ~n** car; (kleiner) tub

los [1] *Adj.* **(a)** (gelöst, ab) off **(b) es ist etwas ~:** there is something going on **(c) jmdn./etw. ~ sein** be rid of sb./sth. [2] *Adv.* (als Aufforderung) come on!

Los *das;* **~es, ~e (a)** lot **(b)** (Lotterie~) ticket

Lösch·blatt *das* piece of blotting paper

löschen *tr. V.* **(a)** put out; extinguish; **seinen Durst ~** (fig.) quench one's thirst **(b)** (tilgen) delete ‹*entry*›; erase ‹*recording, memory, etc.*›

Lösch-: ~fahrzeug *das* fire engine; **~papier** *das* blotting paper

lose [1] *Adj.* loose [2] *adv.* loosely

Löse·geld *das* ransom

losen *itr. V.* draw lots (**um** for)

lösen [1] *tr. V.* **(a)** remove ‹*stamp, wallpaper*›; **etw. von etw. ~:** remove sth. from sth. **(b)** (lockern) undo ‹*screw, belt, tie*› **(c)** (klären) solve; resolve ‹*contradiction, conflict*› **(d)** (annullieren) break off ‹*engagement*›; cancel ‹*contract*›; sever ‹*relationship*› **(e)** (kaufen) buy, obtain ‹*ticket*› [2] *refl. V.* **(a)** (lose werden) come off; (sich lockern) ‹*wallpaper, plaster*› come off; ‹*packing, screw*› come loose **(b)** (sich klären) ‹*puzzle, problem*› be solved **(c)** (sich auflösen) dissolve

los-: ~|fahren *unr. itr. V.; mit sein* set off; (wegfahren) move off; **~|gehen** *unr. itr. V.; mit sein* **(a)** (aufbrechen) set off; **(b)** (ugs.: beginnen) start; **(c)** (ugs.: abgehen) ‹*button, handle, etc.*› come off; **~|kommen** *unr. itr. V.; mit sein* (ugs.) **(a)** get away; **(b)** (freikommen) get free; **~|lassen** *unr. tr. V.* **(a)** (nicht festhalten) let go of; **(b)** (freilassen) let ‹*person, animal*› go; **~|legen** *itr. V.* (ugs.) get going

löslich *Adj.* soluble

Löslichkeit *die;* **~:** solubility

los|machen *tr. V.* (ugs.) let ‹*animal*› loose; untie ‹*string, line, rope*›; unhitch ‹*trailer*›

Los·nummer *die* [lottery-]ticket number

los-: ~|reißen *unr. refl. V.* break free *or* loose; **~|sagen** *refl. V.* **sich von jmdm./etw. ~sagen** break with sb./sth.; **~|schlagen** *unr. itr. V.* (bes. Milit.) attack; launch one's attack

Löss, *Löß *der;* **Lösses, Lösse** (Geol.) loess

Losung *die;* **~, ~en** slogan; (Milit.: Kennwort) password

Lösung *die;* **~, ~en (a)** solution (*Gen.*, **für** to) **(b)** ▶ LÖSEN 1D: breaking off; cancellation; severing

los|werden *unr. tr. V.; mit sein* get rid of

Lot *das;* **~[e]s, ~e** plumb [bob]; **[nicht] im ~ sein** be [out of] plumb

löten *tr. V.* solder

Lotion *die;* **~, ~en** lotion

Löt·kolben *der* soldering iron

lot·recht [1] *Adj.* perpendicular; vertical [2] *adv.* perpendicularly; vertically

Lotse *der;* **~n, ~n** (Seew.) pilot

lotsen *tr. V.* guide

Lotsin *die* ▶ LOTSE

Lotterie *die;* **~, ~n** lottery

Lotto *das;* **~s, ~s** national lottery

Lotto-: ~schein *der* national-lottery coupon; **~zahlen** *Pl.* winning national-lottery numbers

Löt·zinn *das* [tin-lead] solder

Löwe *der;* **~n, ~n (a)** lion **(b)** (Astrol.) Leo; the Lion

Löwen-: ~anteil *der* lion's share; **~mäulchen** *das;* **~~s, ~~:** snapdragon; **~zahn** *der* dandelion

Löwin *die;* **~, ~nen** lioness

loyal /loa'ja:l/ [1] *Adj.* loyal [2] *adv.* loyally

Loyalität *die;* **~:** loyalty

LP /ɛl'pe:/ *die;* **~, ~[s]** *Abk.* = **Langspielplatte** LP

LSD /ɛl|ɛs'de:/ *das;* **~[s]** LSD

Luchs *der;* **~es, ~e** lynx

Lücke *die;* **~, ~n** gap

lücken-, Lücken-: ~büßer *der*, **~~s, ~~, ~büßerin** *die;* **~~, ~~nen** (ugs.) stopgap; **~haft** *Adj.* sketchy; **~los** *Adj.* complete

lud *1. u. 3. Pers. Sg. Prät. v.* LADEN

Luder *das;* **~s, ~** (salopp) so-and-so (coll.)

Luft *die;* **~, Lüfte** air; **an die frische ~ gehen** get out in[to] the fresh air; **die ~ anhalten** hold one's breath; **tief ~ holen** take a deep breath; **in die ~ gehen** (fig. ugs.) blow one's top (coll.)

luft-, Luft-: ~angriff *der* (Milit.) air raid; **~ballon** *der* balloon; **~brücke** *die* airlift; **~dicht** *Adj.* airtight; **~druck** *der* **(a)** (Physik) air pressure; **(b)** (Druckwelle) blast

lụ̈ften 1 *tr. V.* **(a)** air ‹*room, clothes, etc.*› **(b)** raise ‹*hat*› **(c)** disclose ‹*secret*› 2 *itr. V.* air the room/house *etc*

lụft-, Lụft-: ~fahrt *die* aviation *no art.;* **~feuchtigkeit** *die* [atmospheric] humidity; **~gekühlt** *Adj.* air-cooled; **~getrocknet** *Adj.* air-dried; **~gewehr** *das* air rifle; airgun

lụftig *Adj.* airy ‹*room, building, etc.*›; light ‹*clothes*›

Lụft·kissen·boot *das* hovercraft

lụft-, Lụft-: ~leer *Adj.* **ein ~leerer Raum** a vacuum; **~linie** *die* **1000 km ~linie** 1,000 km. as the crow flies; **~loch** *das* air hole; **~matratze** *die* airbed; air mattress; Lilo ®; **~pirat** *der,* **~piratin** *die* [aircraft] hijacker; **~post** *die* airmail; **etw. per** *od.* **mit ~post schicken** send sth. [by] airmail; **~pumpe** *die* air pump; (für Fahrrad) [bicycle] pump; **~röhre** *die* (Anat.) windpipe; **~schiff** *das* airship; **~schloss,** ***~schloß** *das* castle in the air; **~schutz** *der* air-raid protection *no art.;* **~schutz·bunker, ~schutz·keller, ~schutz·raum** *der* air-raid shelter; **~verschmutzung** *die* air pollution; **~waffe** *die* air force; **~zug** *der* [gentle] breeze; (in Zimmern, Gebäuden) draught

Lü̲ge *die;* **~, ~n** lie

lü̲gen *itr., tr. V.* lie; **das ist gelogen!** that's a lie!

Lü̲gner *der;* **~s, ~, Lü̲gnerin** *die;* **~, ~nen** liar

Lu̲ke *die;* **~, ~n** (Dach~) skylight; (bei Schiffen) hatch; (Keller~) trapdoor

lukrati̲v 1 *Adj.* lucrative 2 *adv.* lucratively

Lụ̈mmel *der;* **~s, ~:** lout; (ugs., fam.: Bengel) rascal

Lụmp *der;* **~en, ~en** scoundrel

lụmpen (ugs.) *tr. V.* **sich nicht ~ lassen** splash out (coll.)

Lụmpen *der;* **~s, ~** rag

Lụmpen-: ~sammler *die* rag-and-bone man; **~sammlerin** *die* rag-and-bone woman

Lụnge *die;* **~, ~n** lungs *pl.*

Lụngen-: ~entzündung *die* pneumonia *no indef. art.;* **~krebs** *der* lung cancer; **~zug** *der* inhalation

Lụnte *die;* **~, ~n** fuse; match

Lu̲pe *die;* **~, ~n** magnifying glass

Lụrch *der;* **~[e]s, ~e** amphibian

Lụst *die;* **~ (a) ~ haben, etw. zu tun** feel like doing sth. **(b)** (Vergnügen) pleasure; joy

lụstig 1 *Adj.* **(a)** merry; jolly; enjoyable ‹*time*› **(b)** (komisch) funny 2 *adv.* **(a)** merrily **(b)** (komisch) funnily

lụst-, Lụst-: ~los 1 *Adj.* listless; 2 *adv.* listlessly; **~spiel** *das* comedy

lụtherisch *Adj.* Lutheran

lụtschen 1 *tr. V.* suck 2 *itr. V.* suck; **an etw.** (*Dat.*) **~:** suck sth.

Lụxemburg (*das*)*;* **~s** Luxembourg

luxuriö̲s 1 *Adj.* luxurious 2 *adv.* luxuriously

Lụxus *der;* **~:** luxury

Lỵmphe *die;* **~, ~n** lymph

Lỵmph·knoten *der* lymph node

lỵnchen *tr. V.* lynch

Ly̲rik *die;* **~:** lyric poetry

Ly̲riker *der;* **~s, ~, Ly̲rikerin** *die;* **~, ~nen** lyric poet; lyricist

ly̲risch *Adj.* lyrical; lyric ‹*poetry*›

Lyze̲um *das;* **~s, Lyze̲en** girls' high school

Mm

m, M /ɛm/ *das;* **~, ~** m/M

m *Abk.* = **Meter** m

Mạch·art *die* style; (Schnitt) cut

mạchbar *Adj.* feasible

mạchen 1 *tr. V.* **(a)** make; **aus Plastik/Holz** *usw.* **gemacht** made of plastic/wood *etc.;* **sich** (*Dat.*) **etw. ~ lassen** have sth. made; **etw. aus jmdm. ~:** make sb. into sth.; **jmdn. zum Präsidenten** *usw.* **~:** make sb. president *etc.;* **jmdm./sich [einen] Kaffee ~:** make [some] coffee for sb./oneself **(b)** (verursachen) **jmdm. Arbeit ~:** make [extra] work for sb.; **das macht das Wetter** that's [because of] the weather **(c)** (ausführen) do ‹*job, repair, etc.*›; **einen Spaziergang ~:** go for a walk; **eine Reise ~:** go on a journey; **einen Besuch [bei jmdm.] ~:** pay [sb.] a visit **(d)** (tun) do; **was machst du da?** what are you doing?; **so etwas macht man nicht** that [just] isn't done **(e) was macht ...?** (wie ist es um ... bestellt?)

*old spelling - see note on page xiv

how is ...?; **was macht die Gesundheit/ Arbeit?** how are you keeping/how is the job [getting on]?
(f) (ergeben) (beim Rechnen) be; (bei Geldbeträgen) come to; **zwei mal zwei macht vier** two times two is four; **das macht 12 Euro** that is 12 euros; (Endsumme) that comes to 12 euros
(g) (schaden) **was macht das schon?** what does it matter?; **macht nichts!** (ugs.) it doesn't matter
(h) (teilnehmen an) **einen Kursus** *od.* **Lehrgang ~:** take a course
(i) mach's gut! (ugs.) look after yourself!; (auf Wiedersehen) so long!
2 *refl. V.* **(a) sich an etw.** (*Akk.*) **~:** get down to sth.
(b) (ugs.: sich entwickeln) do well
(c) mach dir nichts daraus! (ugs.) don't let it bother you
3 *itr. V.* **(a) mach schon!** (ugs.) get a move on! (coll.)
(b) das macht hungrig/durstig it makes you hungry/thirsty; **das macht dick** it's fattening

Machenschaften *Pl.* (abwertend) wheeling and dealing *sing.*

Macher *der;* **~s, ~, Macherin** *die;* **~, ~nen** (ugs.) doer; **der Typ des Machers** the dynamic type who just gets on with things

Macho /ˈmatʃ:o/ *der;* **~s, ~s** (abwertend) macho

Macht *die;* **~, Mächte** power; **an die ~ kommen** come to power

Macht-: ~bereich *der* sphere of influence; **~haber** *der;* **~~s, ~~, ~haberin** *die;* **~~, ~~nen** ruler

mächtig 1 *Adj.* **(a)** powerful
(b) (beeindruckend groß) mighty
2 *adv.* (ugs.) terribly (coll.)

macht-, Macht-: ~kampf *der* power struggle; **~los** *Adj.* powerless; **gegen etw. ~los sein** be powerless in the face of sth.; **~probe** *die* trial of strength

Mach·werk *das* (abwertend) shoddy effort

Macke *die;* **~, ~n (a)** (salopp: Tick) fad
(b) (ugs.: Defekt) defect

Mädchen *das;* **~s, ~ (a)** girl
(b) (Haus~) maid

mädchenhaft *Adj.* girlish

Mädchen·name *der* **(a)** girl's name
(b) (Name vor der Ehe) maiden name

Made *die;* **~, ~n** maggot

madig *Adj.* maggoty; **jmdn./etw. ~ machen** (ugs.) run sb./sth. down

Madonna *die;* **~, Madonnen** madonna

mag *1. u. 3. Pers. Sg. Präsens v.* MÖGEN

Magazin *das;* **~s, ~e (a)** (Lager) store; (für Waren) stockroom
(b) (für Patronen, Dias, Film usw.; Zeitschrift) magazine

Magazin·sendung *die* magazine programme

Magen *der;* **~s, Mägen** *od.* **~:** stomach

magen-, Magen-: ~bitter *der;* **~~s, ~~:** bitters *pl.;* **~geschwür** *das* stomach ulcer; **~krebs** *der* cancer of the stomach; **~schmerzen** *Pl.* stomach ache *sing.*

mager *Adj.* **(a)** thin
(b) (fettarm) low-fat; low in fat *pred.;* lean ‹*meat*›
(c) (fig.) poor ‹*soil, harvest*›; meagre ‹*profit, increase, success, report, etc.*›; thin ‹*programme*›

Mager-: ~milch *die* skim[med] milk; **~quark** *der* low-fat curd cheese; **~sucht** *die* (Med.) wasting disease; (Anorexie) anorexia

Magie *die;* **~:** magic

Magier /ˈma:gi̯ɐ/ *der;* **~s, ~, Magierin** *die;* **~, ~nen** (auch fig.) magician

magisch *Adj.* magic ‹*powers*›; (geheimnisvoll) magical

Magistrat *der;* **~[e]s, ~e** City Council

Magnat *der;* **~en, ~en** magnate

Magnet *der;* **~en** *od.* **~[e]s, ~e** magnet

Magnet·band *das; Pl.* **Magnet·bänder** magnetic tape

magnetisch 1 *Adj.* magnetic
2 *adv.* magnetically

magnetisieren *tr. V.* magnetize

Magnetismus *der;* **~:** magnetism

Magnet·nadel *die* [compass] needle

Mahagoni *das;* **~s** mahogany

Mäh·drescher *der* combine harvester

mähen 1 *tr. V.* mow; cut ‹*corn*›
2 *itr. V.* mow; (Getreide ~) reap

Mahl *das;* **~[e]s, Mähler** (geh.) meal; repast (formal)

mahlen *unr. tr., itr. V.* grind

Mahl·zeit meal

Mähne *die;* **~, ~n** mane

mahnen *tr. V.* urge; remind ‹*debtor*›

Mahn-: ~mal *das; Pl.* **~~e** *od.* **~mäler** memorial (erected as a warning to future generations); **~schreiben** *das* reminder

Mahnung *die;* **~, ~en (a)** exhortation; (Warnung) admonition
(b) ▶ MAHNSCHREIBEN

Mai *der;* **~[e]s** *od.* **~:** May

Mai-: ~baum *der* maypole; **~feiertag** *der* May Day *no def. art.;* **~glöckchen** *das* lily of the valley; **~käfer** *der* May bug

Mais *der;* **~es** maize; corn (esp. Amer.); (als Gericht) sweet corn

Mais·kolben *der* corn cob; (als Gericht) corn on the cob

Majestät *die;* **~, ~en (a)** (Titel) Majesty; **Eure ~:** Your Majesty
(b) (geh.) majesty

majestätisch 1 *Adj.* majestic
2 *adv.* majestically

Majonäse *die;* **~, ~n** mayonnaise

Major *der;* **~s, ~e** (Milit.) major

Majoran *der;* **~s, ~e** marjoram

makaber *Adj.* macabre

Makedonien /make'do:ni̯ən/ *(das);* **~s** Macedonia
Makel *der;* **~s, ~** (geh.) **(a)** (Schmach) stigma **(b)** (Fehler) blemish
makel·los 1 *Adj.* flawless; spotless ‹*white, cleanness*› 2 *adv.* immaculately; spotlessly ‹*clean*›
Make-up /me:k'|ap/ *das;* **~s, ~s** make-up
Makkaroni *Pl.* macaroni *sing.*
Makler *der;* **~s, ~, Maklerin** *die;* **~, ~nen (a)** (Häusermakler) estate agent (Brit.); realtor (Amer.) **(b)** (Börsenmakler) broker
Makrele *die;* **~, ~n** mackerel
Makro *der od. das;* **~s, ~s** (DV) macro
Makrone *die;* **~, ~n** macaroon
mal 1 *Adv.* times; (bei Flächen) by 2 *Partikel* **komm ~ her!** come here!
Mal[1] *das;* **~[e]s, ~e** time; **das erste/zweite ~, zum ersten/zweiten ~:** for the first/second time; **beim ersten/zweiten ~:** the first/second time; **das letzte, zum letzten ~:** for the last time; **letztes, beim letzten ~:** last time; **jedes ~:** every time; **mit einem ~[e]** all at once
Mal[2] *das;* **~[e]s, ~e** *od.* **Mäler** mark; (Muttermal) birthmark; (braun) mole
Malaie *der;* **~n, ~n, Malaiin** *die;* **~, ~nen** Malay
Malaria *die;* **~:** malaria
Malaysia *(das);* **~s** Malaysia
Mal·buch *das* colouring book
malen *tr., itr. V.* paint; decorate ‹*flat, room, walls*›
Maler *der;* **~s, ~:** painter
Malerei *die;* **~, ~en** painting
Malerin *der;* **~, ~nen** painter
malerisch 1 *Adj.* picturesque 2 *adv.* picturesquely
mal|nehmen *unr. tr., itr. V.* multiply **(mit** by)
malträtieren *tr. V.* maltreat; ill-treat
Malz·bier *das* malt beer
Mama *die;* **~, ~s** (fam.) mamma
Mami *die;* **~, ~s** (fam.) mummy (Brit. coll.); mommy (Amer. coll.)
Mammut *das;* **~s, ~e** *od.* **~s** mammoth
mampfen *tr., itr. V.* (salopp) munch; nosh (coll.)
man *Indefinitpron. im Nom.* one; you *2nd person;* (irgendjemand) somebody; (die Behörden; die Leute dort) they *pl.;* (die Menschen im Allgemeinen) people *pl;* **~ hat mir gesagt ...:** I was told ...
Management /'mɛnɪdʒ:mənt/ *das;* **~s, ~s** management
managen /'mɛnɪdʒ:n̩/ *tr. V.* **(a)** (ugs.) fix; organize **(b)** (betreuen) manage ‹*singer, artist, player*›

*alte Schreibung - vgl. Hinweis auf S. xiv

Manager /'mɛnɪdʒ:ɐ/ *der;* **~s, ~, Managerin** *die;* **~, ~nen** manager; (eines Fußballvereins) club secretary
manch *Indefinitpron.* **(a)** *attr.* many a; **in [so] ~er Beziehung** in many respects **(b)** *allein stehend* **~er** many a person/man; **~e** *Pl.* some; (viele) many; **[so] ~es** a number of things; (allerhand Verschiedenes) all kinds of things
mancherlei *indekl. Adj.* **(a)** *attr.* various; a number of **(b)** *allein stehend* various things
manch·mal *Adv.* sometimes
Mandant *der;* **~en, ~en, Mandantin** *die;* **~, ~nen** client
Mandarine *die;* **~, ~n** mandarin [orange]
Mandel *die;* **~, ~n (a)** almond **(b)** (Anat.) tonsil
Mandel·entzündung *die* tonsillitis *no indef. art.*
Manege /ma'ne:ʒə/ *die;* **~, ~n** (im Zirkus) ring; (in der Reitschule) arena
Mangel[1] *der;* **~s, Mängel (a)** (Fehlen) lack **(an** + *Dat.* of); (Knappheit) shortage, lack **(an** + *Dat.* of) **(b)** (Fehler) defect
Mangel[2] *die;* **~, ~n** [large] mangle
mangelhaft 1 *Adj.* faulty ‹*goods, German, English, etc.*›; (unzulänglich) inadequate ‹*knowledge, lighting*›; (Schulw.) **die Note „~"** the mark 'unsatisfactory'; (bei Prüfungen) the fail mark 2 *adv.* faultily; (unzulänglich) inadequately
mangeln[1] *itr. V.; unpers.* **es mangelt an etw.** *(Dat.)* (etw. fehlt) there is a lack of sth.; (etw. ist unzureichend vorhanden) there is a shortage of sth.; **jmdm./einer Sache mangelt es an etw.** *(Dat.)* sb./sth. lacks sth.
mangeln[2] *tr. V.* mangle
mangels *Präp. mit Gen.* in the absence of
Mango *die;* **~, ~s** mango
Mangold *der;* **~[e]s** [Swiss] chard
Manie *die;* **~, ~n** mania
Manier *die;* **~, ~en (a)** manner **(b)** *Pl.* (Umgangsformen) manners
manierlich 1 *Adj.* **(a)** (fam.) well-mannered; well-behaved ‹*child*› **(b)** (ugs.: einigermaßen gut) decent 2 *adv.* **(a)** (fam.) nicely **(b)** (ugs.: einigermaßen gut) **ganz/recht ~:** quite/really nicely
Manifest *das;* **~[e]s, ~e** manifesto
Maniküre *die;* **~:** manicure
maniküren *tr. V.* manicure
Manipulation *die;* **~, ~en** (geh.) manipulation
manipulieren *tr. V.* manipulate; rig ‹*election result etc.*›
Manko *das;* **~s, ~s** shortcoming; deficiency
Mann *der;* **~[e]s, Männer (a)** man **(b)** (Ehemann) husband
Männchen *das;* **~s, ~ (a)** little man

(b) (Tier~) male; ~ **machen** ‹*animal*› sit up and beg

Mannequin /'manəkɛ̃/ *das;* **~s, ~s** mannequin; [fashion] model

männer-, Männer-: ~beruf *der* all-male profession; (überwiegend von Männern ausgeübt) male-dominated profession; **~mordend** *Adj.* (ugs. scherzh.) man-eating (fig.); **~sache** *die:* **das ist ~sache** that's men's business; **~überschuss**, ***~überschuß** *der* surplus of men

mannig·fach *Adj.* multifarious

männlich 1 *Adj.* **(a)** male **(b)** ▶ MASKULIN 1; 2 *adv.* in a masculine way

Mannschaft *die;* **~, ~en** (Sport, auch fig.) team; (Schiffs-, Flugzeugbesatzung) crew; (Milit.) unit

Mannschafts-: ~führer *der*, **~führerin** *die* (Sport) team captain; **~kapitän** *der*, **~kapitänin** *die* (Sport) team captain; **~spiel** *das* (Sport) team game

Manöver *das;* **~s, ~ (a)** (Milit.) exercise; ~ *Pl.* manœuvres **(b)** (Bewegung; fig. abwertend: Trick) manœuvre

manövrieren *itr., tr. V.* manœuvre

Mansarde *die;* **~, ~n** attic; (Zimmer) attic room

Manschette *die;* **~, ~n** cuff

Manschetten·knopf *der* cuff link

Mantel *der;* **~s, Mäntel** coat

Manteltarif·vertrag *der* (Wirtsch.) framework collective agreement [on working conditions]

Manuskript *das;* **~[e]s, ~e (a)** manuscript; (Typoskript) typescript **(b)** (Notizen) notes *pl.*

Mappe *die;* **~, ~n (a)** folder **(b)** (Aktentasche) briefcase; (Schul~) schoolbag

Marathon·lauf /...tɔn.../ *der* marathon

Märchen *das;* **~s, ~:** fairy story; fairy tale; (ugs.: Lüge) [tall] story (coll.)

Märchen·buch *das* book of fairy stories

märchenhaft 1 *Adj.* magical 2 *adv.* magically; (ugs.) fantastically (coll.)

Margarine *die;* **~:** margarine

Margerite *die;* **~, ~n** ox-eye daisy

Maria *(die);* **~s** *od.* (Rel.) **Mariä** Mary

Marien·käfer *der* ladybird

Marihuana *das;* **~s** marijuana

Marinade *die;* **~, ~n** (Kochk.) marinade; (Salatsoße) [marinade] dressing

Marine *die;* **~, ~n** fleet; (Kriegs~) navy

marinieren *tr. V.* marinade; **marinierte Heringe** soused herrings

Marionette *die;* **~, ~n** puppet; marionette

Marionetten·theater *das* puppet theatre

Mark[1] *die;* **~, ~:** mark; **Deutsche ~:** Deutschmark

Mark[2] *das;* **~[e]s (a)** (Knochen~) marrow **(b)** (Frucht~) pulp

markant *Adj.* striking; prominent ‹*figure, nose, chin*›; clear-cut ‹*features, profile*›

Marke *die;* **~, ~n (a)** (Waren~) brand; (Fabrikat) make **(b)** (Brief~, Rabatt~, Beitrags~) stamp **(c)** (Essen~) meal ticket **(d)** (Erkennungs~) [identification] disc; (Dienst~) [police] identification badge; ≈ warrant card (Brit.) *or* (Amer.) ID card

Marken-: ~artikel *der* proprietary *or* (Brit.) branded article; **~zeichen** *das* trade mark

Marketing *das;* **~s** (Wirtsch.) marketing

markieren 1 *tr. V.* **(a)** mark **(b)** (ugs.: vortäuschen) sham ‹*illness, breakdown, etc.*› 2 *itr. V.* (ugs.: simulieren) put it on (coll.)

Markierung *die;* **~, ~en** marking

Markt *der;* **~[e]s, Märkte** market; (~platz) market place *or* square; **freitags ist ~:** Friday is market day

markt-, Markt-: ~anteil *der* share of the market; **~beherrschend** *Adj.* market-dominating *attrib.;* **~einführung** *die* launch; **~forschung** *die* market research *no def. art.;* **~frau** *die* market woman; **~führer** *der*, **~führerin** *die* market leader; **~halle** *die* covered market; **~lücke** *die* gap in the market; **~platz** *der* market place; **~stand** *der* market stall; **~wirtschaft** *die* market economy

Marmelade *die;* **~, ~n** jam; (Orangen~) marmalade

Marmor *der;* **~s** marble

Marokkaner *der;* **~s, ~, Marokkanerin** *die;* **~, ~nen** Moroccan

marokkanisch *Adj.* Moroccan

Marokko *(das);* **~s** Morocco

Marone *die;* **~, ~n** [sweet] chestnut

Mars *der;* **~:** Mars *no def. art.*

Marsch[1] *der;* **~[e]s, Märsche** march; (Wanderung) [long] walk

Marsch[2] *die;* **~, ~en** fertile marshland

Marsch·flug·körper *der* cruise missile

marschieren *itr. V.; mit sein* march; (wandern) walk

Marsch-: ~musik *die* march music; **~verpflegung** *die* (Milit.) marching rations *pl.;*

Mars-: ~mensch *der* Martian; **~sonde** *die* (Raumfahrt) Mars probe

Marter *die;* **~, ~n** (geh.) torture; (seelisch) torment

martern *tr. V.* (geh.) torture

Märtyrer *der;* **~s, ~, Märtyrerin** *die;* **~, ~nen** martyr

Martyrium *das;* **~s, Martyrien** martyrdom

Marxismus *der;* **~:** Marxism *no art.*

Marxist *der;* **~en, ~en, Marxistin** *die;* **~, ~nen** Marxist

marxistisch *Adj.* Marxist

März *der;* **~[es]** March

Marzipan *das;* **~s** marzipan
Masche *die;* **~, ~n** stitch; (Lauf~) run; ladder (Brit.); (beim Netz) mesh
Maschen·draht *der* wire netting
Maschine *die;* **~, ~n (a)** (auch ugs.: Motorrad) machine
(b) (ugs.: Automotor) engine
(c) (Flugzeug) [aero]plane
(d) (Schreib~) typewriter; **~ schreiben** type
maschine·geschrieben *Adj.* typewritten
maschinell [1] *Adj.* machine *attrib.;* by machine *postpos.;*
[2] *adv.* by machine; **~ hergestellt** machine-made
Maschinen-: ~gewehr *das* machine gun; **~pistole** *die* sub-machine gun; **~schlosser** *der,* **~schlosserin** *die* fitter
***maschine|schreiben** ▶ MASCHINE D
Masern *Pl.* measles *sing. or pl.*
Maserung *die;* **~, ~en** [wavy] grain
Maske *die;* **~, ~n** mask
Masken-: ~ball *der* masked ball; **~bildner** *der;* **~~s, ~~, ~bildnerin** *die;* **~~, ~~nen** make-up artist
Maskerade *die;* **~, ~n** [fancy-dress] costume
maskieren [1] *tr. V.* mask
[2] *refl. V.* put on a mask/masks
Maskottchen *das;* **~s, ~:** [lucky] mascot
maskulin /*auch:* '---/ [1] *Adj.* (auch Sprachw.) masculine
[2] *adv.* in a masculine way
Masochismus *der;* **~** (Psych.) masochism *no art.*
Masochist *der;* **~en, ~en, Masochistin** *die;* **~, ~nen** (Psych.) masochist
masochistisch (Psych.) [1] *Adj.* masochistic
[2] *adv.* masochistically; **~ veranlagt sein** have masochistic tendencies
maß *1. u. 3. Pers. Sg. Prät. v.* MESSEN
Maß[1] *das;* **~es, ~e (a)** measure (**für** of); (fig.) **das ~ ist voll** enough is enough
(b) (Größe) measurement
(c) (Grad) degree (**an** + *Dat.* of); **in großem/gewissem ~e** to a great/certain extent
(d) ~ halten exercise moderation
Maß[2] *die;* **~, ~[e]** (bayr., österr.) litre [of beer]
Massage /ma'sa:ʒə/ *die;* **~, ~n** massage
Massaker *das;* **~s, ~:** massacre
Maß-: ~anzug *der* made-to-measure suit; **~arbeit** *die* **(a)** custom-made item; (Kleidungsstück) made-to-measure item; **(b)** (genaue Arbeit) neat work
Masse *die;* **~, ~n (a)** mass
(b) (Gemisch) mixture
Maß·einheit *die* unit of measurement

*old spelling - see note on page xiv

Massen-: ~arbeitslosigkeit *die* mass unemployment; **~entlassungen** *Pl.* mass redundancies *pl.;* **~grab** *das* mass grave
massenhaft [1] *Adj.* in huge numbers *postpos.;*
[2] *adv.* on a huge scale
massen-, Massen-: ~karambolage *die* multiple crash; **~kommunikations·mittel** *das* medium of mass communication; mass medium; **~medium** *das* mass medium; **~mörder** *der,* **~mörderin** *die* mass murderer; **~produktion** *die* mass production; **~vernichtung** *die* mass extermination; **~vernichtungs·waffen** *Pl.* weapons of mass destruction; **~weise** *Adv.* in huge numbers
Masseur /ma'sø:ɐ̯/ *der;* **~s, ~e** masseur
Masseurin *die;* **~, ~nen, Masseuse** /ma'sø:zə/ *die;* **~, ~n** masseuse
maß·gebend, maß·geblich [1] *Adj.* authoritative ‹*book, expert, opinion*›; definitive ‹*text*›; influential ‹*person, circles, etc.*›; decisive ‹*factor, influence, etc.*›
[2] *adv.* ‹*influence*› to a considerable extent; (entscheidend) decisively
***maß|halten** ▶ MAß[1] D
massieren *tr. V.* massage
mäßig [1] *Adj.* moderate; (mittel~) mediocre
[2] *adv.* in moderation; moderately ‹*gifted, talented*›; (mittel~) indifferently
mäßigen *refl. V.* (geh.) **(a)** practise *or* exercise moderation
(b) (sich beherrschen) control *or* restrain oneself
Mäßigkeit *die;* **~:** moderation
Mäßigung *die;* **~:** moderation
massiv [1] *Adj.* **(a)** solid
(b) (heftig) massive ‹*demand*›; crude ‹*accusation, threat*›; strong ‹*attack, criticism, pressure*›
[2] *adv.* ‹*attack*› strongly; ‹*accuse, threaten*› crudely
maß-, Maß-: ~krug *der* (südd., österr.) litre beer mug; (aus Steingut) stein; **~los** [1] *Adj.* extreme; gross ‹*exaggeration, insult*›; excessive ‹*demand, claim*›; boundless ‹*ambition, greed, sorrow, joy*›; [2] *adv.* extremely; ‹*exaggerate*› grossly; **~nahme** *die;* **~~, ~~n** measure; **~regel** *die* regulation; (Maßnahme) measure; **~regeln** *tr. V.* (zurechtweisen) reprimand; (bestrafen) discipline; **~stab** *der* **(a)** standard; **(b)** (einer Karte, eines Modells usw.) scale; **~voll** [1] *Adj.* moderate; [2] *adv.* in moderation
Mast *der;* **~[e]s, ~en,** *auch:* **~e** (Schiffs~, Antennen~) mast; (Stange, Fahnen~) pole; (Hochspannungs~) pylon
masten *tr. V.* fatten
Masturbation *die;* **~, ~en** masturbation
masturbieren *itr., tr. V.* masturbate

Match /mɛtʃ/ *das od.* **der; ~[e]s, ~s** *od.* **~e** match

Material *das;* **~s, ~ien** material; (Bau~; Hilfsmittel) materials *pl.*

Materialismus *der;* **~:** materialism

Materialist *der;* **~en, ~en, Materialistin** *die;* **~, ~nen** materialist

materialistisch [1] *Adj.* materialistic [2] *adv.* materialistically

Materie *die;* **~, ~n (a)** matter **(b)** (geh.: Thema, Gegenstand) subject matter

materiell [1] *Adj.* (finanziell) financial [2] *adv.* materially; (finanziell) financially

Mathe *die;* **~** (ugs.) maths *sing.* (Brit. coll.); math (Amer. coll.)

Mathematik *die;* **~:** mathematics *sing., no art.*

mathematisch [1] *Adj.* mathematical [2] *adv.* mathematically

Matjes *der;* **~, ~:** matie [herring]

Matratze *die;* **~, ~n** mattress

Matrose *der;* **~n, ~n** sailor; seaman

Matsch *der;* **~[e]s** (ugs.) mud; (breiiger Schmutz) sludge; (Schnee~) slush

matschig *Adj.* (ugs.) **(a)** muddy; slushy ‹*snow*› **(b)** (weich) mushy; squashy ‹*fruit*›

matt [1] *Adj.* **(a)** weak; feeble ‹*applause, reaction*› **(b)** (glanzlos) matt; dull ‹*metal, mirror, etc.*› **(c)** (undurchsichtig) frosted ‹*glass*›; pearl ‹*lightbulb*› **(d)** subdued; (Schach) checkmated; **~!** checkmate! [2] *adv.* **(a)** (kraftlos) weakly **(b)** (mäßig) ‹*protest, contradict*› feebly

Matte *die;* **~, ~n** mat

Matt·scheibe *die* (ugs.) telly (Brit. coll.); box (coll.)

Matur *die;* **~** (schweiz.), **Matura** *die;* **~a** (österr., schweiz.) ▶ ABITUR

Mätzchen *das;* **~s, ~: ~ machen** (ugs.) fool about *or* around

Mauer *die;* **~, ~n** wall

mauern [1] *tr. V.* build [2] *itr. V.* lay bricks

Mauer-: ~segler *der* swift; **~werk** *das* **(a)** masonry; (aus Ziegeln) brickwork; **(b)** (Mauern) walls *pl.*

Maul *das;* **~[e]s, Mäuler** (von Tieren) mouth; (derb: Mund) gob (sl.)

Maul-: ~esel *der* mule; **~korb** *der* (auch fig.) muzzle; **~tier** *das* mule

Maul·wurf *der* mole

Maulwurfs-: ~haufen *der,* **~hügel** *der* molehill

Maurer *der;* **~s, ~, Maurerin** *die;* **~, ~nen** bricklayer

Maus *die;* **~, Mäuse** mouse

Mauschelei *die;* **~, ~en** (ugs. abwertend) shady wheeling and dealing *no indef. art.*

mauscheln *itr. V.* (ugs. abwertend) engage in shady wheeling and dealing

Mäuschen *das;* **~s, ~:** little mouse

mäuschen·still *Adj.* **~ sein** be as quiet as a mouse

Mause·falle *die* mousetrap

mausern *refl. V.* moult

Maus: ~klick *der;* **~~s, ~~s** (DV) mouse click; **~taste** *die* (DV) mouse button; **~zeiger** *der* (DV) mouse pointer

Maut *die;* **~, ~en** toll

maximal [1] *Adj.* maximum [2] *adv.* **~ zulässige Geschwindigkeit** maximum permitted speed

Maxime *die;* **~, ~n** maxim

maximieren *tr. V.* maximize

Maximum *das;* **~s, Maxima** maximum **(an** + *Dat.* of)

Maxi·single *die* maxi-single

Mayonnaise /majɔˈnɛːzə/ *die;* **~, ~n** mayonnaise

Mäzen *der;* **~s, ~e** (geh.) patron

Mäzenin *die;* **~, ~nen** patroness

MdB, M.d.B. *Abk.* = **Mitglied des Bundestages** Member of the Bundestag

m. E. *Abk.* = **meines Erachtens** in my opinion *or* view

Mechanik *die;* **~:** mechanics *sing., no art.*

Mechaniker *der;* **~s, ~, Mechanikerin** *die;* **~, ~nen** mechanic

mechanisch [1] *Adj.* mechanical; power *attrib.* ‹*loom, press*› [2] *adv.* mechanically

Mechanismus *der;* **~, Mechanismen** mechanism

meckern *itr. V.* **(a)** (auch fig.) bleat **(b)** (ugs.: nörgeln) grumble; moan

Mecklenburg-Vorpommern (*das*)*;* **~s** Mecklenburg-Western Pomerania

Medaille /meˈdaljə/ *die;* **~, ~n** medal

Medaillen·gewinner *der,* **Medaillen·gewinnerin** *die* medallist; medal winner

Medaillon /medalˈjõː/ *das;* **~s, ~s (a)** locket **(b)** (Kochk., bild. Kunst) medallion

medial *Adj.* (in den Medien) in the media *postpos.;* (von den Medien) by the media *postpos.;* **eine ~e Präsenz** a media presence; **ein ~es Spektakel** a media spectacle

Medien-: ~angebot *das* range of media; **~konzern** *der* media concern; **~landschaft** *die* media scene; **~politik** *die* media policy; **~präsenz** *die* media presence

Medikament *das;* **~[e]s, ~e** medicine; (Droge) drug

Meditation *die;* **~, ~en** meditation

meditieren *itr. V.* meditate **(über** + *Akk.* [up]on)

Medium *das;* **~s, Medien** medium

Medizin *die;* ~, **~en** medicine

Mediziner *der;* **~s, ~, Medizinerin** *die;* ~, **~nen** doctor; (Student[in]) medical student

medizinisch 1 *Adj.* medical; medicinal ‹*bath etc.*›; medicated ‹*toothpaste, soap, etc.*› 2 *adv.* medically

Meer *das;* **~[e]s, ~e** (auch fig.) sea; **am ~:** by the sea

Meer·enge *die* straits *pl.;* strait

Meeres-: ~boden *der* sea bed *or* bottom *or* floor; **~bucht** *die* bay; **~früchte** *Pl.* (Kochk.) seafood *sing.;* **~kunde** *die* oceanography *no art.;* **~spiegel** *der* sea level

Meer-: ~jungfrau *die* mermaid; **~katze** *die* guenon; **~rettich** *der* horseradish; **~schweinchen** *das;* **~~s, ~~:** guinea pig; **~wasser** *das* sea water

Meeting /'mi:tɪŋ/ *das;* **~s, ~s** meeting

mega-, Mega- mega-

Mega·byte *das* (DV) megabyte

Megaphon *das;* **~s, ~e** megaphone; loud hailer

Mehl *das;* **~[e]s** flour

mehlig *Adj.* **(a)** floury **(b)** mealy ‹*potato, apple, etc.*›

Mehl-: ~sack *der* flour sack; (Sack voll Mehl) sack of flour; **~tau** *der* mildew; **~wurm** *der* mealworm

mehr 1 *Indefinitpron.* more
2 *Adv.* **(a)** more
(b) nicht ~: not ... any more; no longer; **es war niemand ~ da** there was no one left; **das wird nie ~ vorkommen** it will never happen again; **da ist nichts ~ zu machen** there is nothing more to be done

mehr-, Mehr-: ~bändig *Adj.* in several volumes *postpos.;* **~bereichs·öl** *das* (Technik) multi-purpose oil; **~deutig** 1 *Adj.* ambiguous; 2 *adv.* ambiguously

mehren (geh.) *refl. V.* increase

mehrer... *Indefinitpron. u. unbest. Zahlwort*
(a) *attr.* several
(b) *allein stehend* **~e** several people; **~es** several things *pl.*

mehr·fach 1 *Adj.* multiple; (wiederholt) repeated
2 *adv.* several times; (wiederholt) repeatedly

Mehrheit *die;* **~, ~en** majority

Mehrheits-: ~beschluss, *~beschluß *der,* **~entscheidung** *die* majority decision

mehr-, Mehr-: ~jährig *Adj.* lasting several years *postpos.;* **~malig** *Adj.; nicht präd.* repeated; **~mals** *Adv.* several times; (wiederholt) repeatedly; **~parteien·system** *das* multi-party system; **~sprachig** *Adj.* multilingual; **~stimmig** (Musik) 1 *Adj.* for several voices *postpos.;* **ein ~stimmiges Lied** a part-song; 2 *adv.* **~stimmig singen** sing in harmony; **~teilig** *Adj.* in several parts *postpos.*

Mehrweg-: ~flasche *die* returnable *or* reusable bottle; **~verpackung** *die* reusable packaging

Mehr-: ~wert *der* (Wirtsch.) surplus value; **~wert·steuer** *die* (Wirtsch.) value added tax (Brit.); VAT (Brit.); sales tax (Amer.); **~zahl** *die* **(a)** (Sprachw.) plural; **(b)** (Mehrheit) majority

meiden *unr. tr. V.* (geh.) avoid

Meile *die;* **~, ~n** mile

mein *Possessivpron.* my; **~e Damen und Herren** ladies and gentlemen; **das Buch dort, ist das ~[e]s?** that book over there, is it mine?

Mein·eid *der* perjury *no indef. art.;* **einen ~ schwören** commit perjury

meinen 1 *itr. V.* think
2 *tr. V.* **(a)** think
(b) (sagen wollen, im Sinn haben) mean
(c) (beabsichtigen) mean; intend; **es gut mit jmdm. ~:** mean well by sb.
(d) (sagen) say

meiner *Gen. von* ICH (geh.) **gedenkt ~:** remember me; **erbarme dich ~:** have mercy upon me

meinerseits *Adv.* for my part; **ganz ~:** the pleasure is [all] mine

meinetwegen *Adv.* **(a)** because of me; (mir zuliebe) for my sake; (um mich) about me
(b) /*auch:* --'--/ (von mir aus) as far as I'm concerned; **~!** if you like

Meinung *die;* **~, ~en** opinion (**zu** on, **über** + *Akk.* about); **er ist der ~, dass ...** he is of the opinion *or* takes the view that ...; **meiner ~ nach** in my opinion; **ganz meine ~:** I agree entirely; **einer ~ sein** be of the same opinion

Meinungs-: ~forschung *die* opinion research; **~freiheit** *die* freedom to form and express one's own opinions; (Redefreiheit) freedom of speech; **~umfrage** *die* [public] opinion poll; **~verschiedenheit** *die* difference of opinion

Meise *die;* **~, ~n** tit[mouse]

Meißel *der;* **~s, ~:** chisel

meißeln *tr. V.* chisel; carve ‹*statue, sculpture*› with a chisel

meist *Adv.* mostly

meist... *Indefinitpron. u. unbest. Zahlw.* most; **die ~en Leute ...:** most people ...; **am ~en** most

meistens *Adv.* ▶ MEIST

Meister *der;* **~s, ~ (a)** master
(b) (Werk~, Polier) foreman
(c) (Sport) champion

Meister·brief *der* master craftsman's diploma *or* certificate

meisterhaft 1 *Adj.* masterly
2 *adv.* in a masterly manner

Meisterin *die;* **~, ~nen** ▶ MEISTER A,C

*alte Schreibung - vgl. Hinweis auf S. xiv

meistern *tr. V.* master
Meister·prüfung *die* examination for the/one's master craftsman's diploma *or* certificate
Meisterschaft *die;* ~, ~en **(a)** mastery **(b)** (Sport) championship
Meister-: **~stück** *das* masterpiece (**an** + *Dat.* of); **~titel** *der* (Sport) championship [title]; **~werk** *das* masterpiece (**an** + *Dat.* of)
Melancholie /melaŋko:'li:/ *die;* ~ melancholy
melancholisch [1] *Adj.* melancholy; melancholy, melancholic ‹*person, temperament*›
[2] *adv.* melancholically
melden [1] *tr. V.* report; (registrieren lassen) register ‹*birth, death, etc.*› (*Dat.* with)
[2] *refl. V.* **(a)** report
(b) (am Telefon) answer
(c) (ums Wort bitten) put one's hand up
(d) (von sich hören lassen) get in touch (**bei** with)
Meldung *die;* ~, ~en **(a)** report; (Nachricht) piece of news
(b) (Wort~) request to speak
meliert *Adj.* mottled; **[grau] ~es Haar** hair streaked with grey
melken *regelm.* (*auch unr.*) *tr. V.* milk
Melodie *die;* ~, ~n melody; (Weise) tune
melodisch [1] *Adj.* melodic
[2] *adv.* melodically
Melone *die;* ~, ~n **(a)** melon
(b) (ugs.: Hut) bowler [hat]
Membran *die;* ~, ~en **(a)** (Technik) diaphragm
(b) (Biol., Chemie) membrane
Memoiren /me'mo̯a:rən/ *Pl.* memoirs
Menge *die;* ~, ~n **(a)** quantity; amount
(b) (große) lot (coll.); **eine ~** (ugs.) lots [of it/them] (coll.)
(c) (Menschen~) crowd
(d) (Math.) set
Mengen-: **~lehre** *die* set theory *no art.;* **~rabatt** *der* bulk discount
Meniskus *der;* ~, **Menisken** (Anat., Optik) meniscus
Menopause *die;* ~, ~n (Physiol.) menopause
Mensa *die;* ~, ~s *od.* **Mensen** refectory, canteen (*of university, college*)
Mensch *der;* ~en, ~en **(a)** (Gattung) **der ~:** man; **die ~en** man *sing.;* human beings; mankind *sing.;*
(b) (Person) person; man/woman; **~en** people
menschen-, Menschen-: **~affe** *der* anthropoid [ape]; **~auflauf** *der* crowd [of people]; **~feind** *der,* **~feindin** *die* misanthropist; **~fresser** *der* (ugs.) cannibal; **~freund** *der,* **~freundin** *die* philanthropist; **~handel** *der* trade *or* traffic in human beings; **~kenner** *der,* **~kennerin** *die* judge of human nature; **~kenntnis** *die;* ability to judge human nature; **~leben** *das* life; **~leer** *Adj.* deserted; **~menge** *die* crowd [of people]; **~recht** *das* human right; **~rechtler** *der;* **~~s, ~~,** **~rechtlerin** *die;* **~~, ~~nen** human rights campaigner; **~schlag** *der* breed [of people]; **~seele** *die:* **keine ~seele** not a [living] soul
Menschens·kind: ~! (salopp) (erstaunt) good heavens; good grief; (vorwurfsvoll) for heaven's sake
menschen-, Menschen-: **~unwürdig** [1] *Adj.* ‹*accommodation*› unfit for human habitation; ‹*conditions*› unfit for human beings; ‹*behaviour*› unworthy of a human being; [2] *adv.* ‹*treat*› in a degrading and inhumane way; ‹*live, be housed*› in conditions unfit for human beings; **~verstand** *der* human intellect; **~würde** *die* human dignity *no art.*
Menschheit *die;* ~: mankind *no art.;* humanity *no art.;* human race
menschlich [1] *Adj.* **(a)** human
(b) (annehmbar) civilized
(c) (human) humane ‹*person, treatment, etc.*›
[2] *adv.* **(a) er ist mir ~ sympathisch** I like him as a person
(b) (human) humanely
Menschlichkeit *die;* ~: humanity *no art.*
Mensen ▸ MENSA
Menstruation *die;* ~, ~en (Physiol.) menstruation; (Periode) [menstrual] period
Mentalität *die;* ~, ~en mentality
Menü *das;* ~s, ~s (auch DV) menu
Menü·leiste *die* (DV) menu bar
merkbar [1] *Adj.* noticeable
[2] *adv.* noticeably
Merk·blatt leaflet
merken [1] *tr. V.* notice
[2] *refl. V.* **sich** (*Dat.*) **etw. ~:** remember sth.
merklich ▸ MERKBAR
Merkmal *das;* ~s, ~e feature
Merkur *der;* ~s Mercury
merkwürdig [1] *Adj.* strange; odd
[2] *adv.* strangely; oddly
messbar, ***meßbar** *Adj.* measurable
Messe[1] *die;* ~, ~n (Gottesdienst, Musik) mass
Messe[2] *die;* ~, ~n (Ausstellung) [trade] fair
messen [1] *unr. tr. V.* **(a)** *auch itr.* measure
(b) (beurteilen) judge (**nach** by)
[2] *unr. refl. V.* (geh.) compete (**mit** with)
Messer *das;* ~s, ~: knife
messer-, Messer-: **~scharf** [1] *Adj.* razor-sharp; (fig.) incisive ‹*logic*›; razor-sharp ‹*wit, intellect*›; [2] *adv.* (fig. ugs.) ‹*argue*› incisively; **~stecherei** *die;* **~~, ~~en** knife fight; **~stich** *der* knife thrust; (Wunde) knife wound
Mess·gerät, ***Meß·gerät** *das* measuring device; (Zähler) meter
Messias *der;* ~, ~se Messiah

Messing *das;* **~s** brass
Mess·instrument, *Meß·instrument *das* measuring instrument
Messung *die;* **~, ~en** measurement
Metall *das;* **~s, ~e** metal
metallic *indekl. Adj.* metallic [grey/blue/ *etc.*]
Metall·industrie *die* metal-processing and metal-working industries *pl.*
metallisch *Adj.* metallic; metal *attrib.*, metallic ‹*conductor*›
Metapher *die;* **~, ~n** metaphor
metaphorisch (Stilk.) 1 *Adj.* metaphorical 2 *adv.* metaphorically
Meta·physik *die;* **~:** metaphysics *sing., no art.*
Metastase *die;* **~, ~n** (Med.) metastasis
Meteor *der;* **~s, ~e** meteor
Meteorit *der;* **~en** *od.* **~s, ~e[n]** meteorite
Meteorologe *der;* **~n, ~n** meteorologist
Meteorologie *die;* **~:** meteorology *no art.*
Meteorologin *die;* **~, ~nen** meteorologist
meteorologisch 1 *Adj.* meteorological 2 *adv.* meteorologically
Meter *der od. das;* **~s, ~:** metre
meter-, Meter-: ~dick *Adj.* (sehr dick) metres thick *postpos.;* **~hoch** *Adj.* metres high *postpos.;* ‹*snow*› metres deep; **~maß** *das* tape measure; (Stab) [metre] rule
Methan *das;* **~s** methane
Methode *die;* **~, ~n** method
methodisch 1 *Adj.* methodological; (nach einer Methode vorgehend) methodical 2 *adv.* methodologically; (nach einer Methode) methodically
Metier /me'ti̯e:/ *das;* **~s, ~s** profession
Metrik *die;* **~, ~en** metrics
metrisch 1 *Adj.* **(a)** (Verslehre, Musik) metrical **(b)** (auf den Meter bezogen) metric 2 *adv.* metrically
Metropole *die;* **~, ~n** metropolis
Mett·wurst *die: soft smoked sausage made of minced pork and beef*
Metzger *der;* **~s, ~** (bes. westmd., südd., schweiz.) butcher
Metzgerei *die;* **~, ~en** (bes. westmd., südd., schweiz.) butcher's [shop]
Meute *die;* **~, ~n (a)** (Jägerspr.) pack **(b)** (ugs. abwertend) mob
Meuterei *die;* **~, ~en** mutiny
meutern *itr. V.* **(a)** mutiny; ‹*prisoners*› riot **(b)** (ugs.: Unwillen äußern) moan
Mexikaner *der;* **~s, ~, Mexikanerin** *die;* **~, ~** Mexican
mexikanisch *Adj.* Mexican
Mexiko *(das);* **~s** Mexico
MEZ *Abk.* = **mitteleuropäische Zeit** CET

*old spelling - see note on page xiv

mg *Abk.* = **Milligramm** mg
MG /ɛm'ge:/ *das;* **~s, ~s** *Abk.* = **Maschinengewehr**
Mi. *Abk.* = **Mittwoch** Wed.
miau *Interj.* miaow
miauen *itr. V.* miaow
mich 1 *Akk. von* ICH me 2 *Akk. des Reflexivpron. der 1.Pers. Sg.* myself
mick[e]rig *Adj.* (ugs.) miserable; measly (coll.); puny ‹*person*›
mied *1. u. 3. Pers. Sg. Prät. v.* MEIDEN
Mieder·waren *Pl.* corsetry *sing.*
Miene *die;* **~, ~n** expression
mies (ugs.) 1 *Adj.* lousy (coll.) 2 *adv.* lousily (coll.)
Mies-: ~macher *der,* **~macherin** *die* (ugs. abwertend) carping critic; (Spielverderber) killjoy; **~muschel** *die* [common] mussel
Miete *die;* **~, ~n** rent; (für ein Auto, Boot) hire charge; **zur ~ wohnen** live in rented accommodation
mieten *tr. V.* rent; (für kürzere Zeit) hire
Mieter *der;* **~s, ~, Mieterin** *die;* **~, ~nen** tenant
Miets·haus *das* block of rented flats (Brit.) *or* (Amer.) apartments
Miet-: ~erhöhung *die* rent increase; **~vertrag** *der* tenancy agreement; **~wagen** *der* hire car
Migräne *die;* **~, ~n** migraine
Migrant *der;* **~en, ~en, Migrantin** *die;* **~, ~nen** migrant
mikro-, Mikro- micro-
Mikrobe *die;* **~, ~n** microbe
mikro-, Mikro-: ~film *der* microfilm; **~phon** /--'-/ *das;* **~~s, ~~e** microphone; **~skop** /--'-/ *das;* **~~s, ~~e** microscope; **~skopisch** /--'--/ 1 *Adj.* microscopic; 2 *adv.* microscopically; **~welle** *die* (ugs.) microwave [oven]
Milbe *die;* **~, ~n** mite
Milch *die;* **~:** milk
Milch·flasche *die* milk bottle
milchig 1 *Adj.* milky 2 *adv.* **~ weiß** milky-white
Milch-: ~kaffee *der* coffee with plenty of milk; **~kännchen** *das;* **~~s, ~~:** milk jug; **~reis** *der* rice pudding; **~straße** *die* Milky Way; Galaxy; **~zahn** *der* milk tooth
mild, milde 1 *Adj.* mild; lenient ‹*judge, judgement*›; soft ‹*light*›; smooth ‹*brandy*› 2 *adv.* (gütig) leniently; (gelinde) mildly
Milde *die;* **~:** mildness; (Güte) leniency
mildern *tr. V.* moderate; mitigate ‹*punishment*›
Milderung *die;* **~:** ▶ MILDERN: moderation; mitigation
Milieu /mi'li̯ø:/ *das;* **~s, ~s** environment
militant *Adj.* militant

Militär¹ *das;* **~s** armed forces *pl.;* military; (Soldaten) soldiers *pl.*
Militär² *der;* **~s, ~s** [high-ranking military] officer
Militär-: ~dienst *der* military service; **~diktatur** *die* military dictatorship
militärisch *Adj.* military
militarisieren *tr. V.* militarize
Militarismus *der;* **~** (abwertend) militarism
Militarist *der;* **~en, ~en** (abwertend) militarist
Militär-: ~macht *die* military power; **~putsch** *der* military putsch
Military /'mılıtərı/ *die;* **~, ~s** (Reiten) three-day event
Miliz *die;* **~, ~en** militia; (Polizei) police
Mill. *Abk.* = **Million** m.
milli-, Milli- milli-
Milliarde *die;* **~, ~n** billion
Milli-: ~gramm *das* milligram; **~meter** *der od. das* millimetre; **~meter·papier** *das* [graph] paper ruled in millimetre squares
Million *die;* **~, ~en** million
Millionär *der;* **~s, ~e** millionaire
Millionen-: ~schaden *der* damage *no pl., no indef. art.* running into millions; **~stadt** *die* town with over a million inhabitants
millionst... *Ordinalz.* millionth
Milz *die;* **~:** spleen
Mimik *die;* **~:** gestures and facial expressions *pl.*
Mimose *die;* **~, ~n (a)** mimosa **(b)** (fig.) oversensitive person
mimosenhaft [1] *Adj.* oversensitive [2] *adv.* oversensitively
minder *Adv.* (geh.) less
minder... *Adj.* inferior ‹*goods, brand*›
minder·bemittelt *Adj.* without much money *postpos., not pred.;* **~ sein** not have much money; **geistig ~** (fig. salopp abwertend) not all that bright (coll.)
Minderheit *die;* **~, ~en** minority
minder·jährig *Adj.* ‹*child etc.*› who is/was a minor
Minder·jährige *der/die; adj. Dekl.* minor
mindern *tr. V.* (geh.) reduce
Minderung *die;* **~, ~en** reduction (*Gen.* in)
minder·wertig *Adj.* inferior
mindest... *Adj.* least; (geringst...) slightest; **das ist das Mindeste** *od.* **~e, was du tun kannst** it is the least you can do
mindestens *Adv.* at least
Mindest·haltbarkeits·datum *das* best-before date
Mine *die;* **~, ~n (a)** (Bergwerk, Sprengkörper) mine **(b)** (Bleistift~) lead; (Kugelschreiber~, Filzschreiber~) refill

Mineral *das;* **~s, ~e** *od.* **Mineralien** mineral
Mineralogie *die;* **~:** mineralogy *no art.*
Mineral-: ~öl *das* mineral oil; **~wasser** *das* mineral water
Mini *das;* **~s, ~s** (Mode) mini
Mini- mini-
Miniatur *die;* **~, ~en** miniature
minimal [1] *Adj.* minimal; marginal ‹*advantage, lead*›; very slight ‹*benefit, profit*› [2] *adv.* minimally
Minimum *das;* **~s, Minima** minimum (**an** + *Dat.* of)
minimieren *tr. V.* (bes. Math.) minimize
Minister *der;* **~s, ~, Ministerin** *die;* **~, ~nen** minister (**für** for); (eines britischen Hauptministeriums) Secretary of State (**für** for); (eines amerikanischen Hauptministeriums) Secretary (**für** of)
Ministerium *das;* **~s, Ministerien** Ministry; Department (Amer.)
Minister·präsident *der,* **Minister·präsidentin** *die* **(a)** (eines deutschen Bundeslandes) minister-president **(b)** (Premierminister[in]) Prime Minister
Minister·rat *der* Council of Ministers
Ministrant *der;* **~en, ~en, Ministrantin** *die;* **~, ~nen** (kath. Kirche) server
Minorität *die;* **~, ~en** ▶ MINDERHEIT
minus *Konj., Adv.* (bes. Math.) minus
Minus *das;* **~:** deficit
Minus·zeichen *das* minus sign
Minute *die;* **~, ~n** minute
minuten·lang [1] *Adj.* lasting [for] several minutes *postpos.;* [2] *adv.* for several minutes
Minuten·zeiger *der* minute hand
Mio. *Abk.* = **Million[en]** m.
mir [1] *Dat. von* ICH to me; (nach Präpositionen) me; **Freunde von ~:** friends of mine; **gehen wir zu ~:** let's go to my place; **von ~ aus** as far as I'm concerned [2] *Dat. des Reflexivpron. der 1. Pers. Sg.* myself
Mirabelle *die;* **~, ~n** mirabelle
Misch-: ~brot *das* bread made from wheat and rye flour; **~ehe** *die* mixed marriage
mischen [1] *tr. V.* mix [2] *refl. V.* **(a)** (sich ver~) mix (**mit** with); ‹*smell, scent*› blend (**mit** with) **(b)** (sich ein~) **sich in etw.** (*Akk.*) **~:** interfere in sth.
Misch·farbe *die* non-primary colour
Mischling *der;* **~s, ~e** half-caste
Mischmasch *der;* **~[e]s, ~e** (ugs., meist abwertend) hotchpotch; mishmash
Misch·pult *das* (Film, Rundf., Fems.) mixing desk *or* console
Mischung *die;* **~, ~en** mixture; (Tee~, Kaffee~, Tabak~) blend; (Pralinen~) assortment

m

Misch·wald *der* mixed [deciduous and coniferous] forest
miserabel (ugs.) [1] *Adj.* dreadful (coll.) [2] *adv.* dreadfully (coll.); **ihm geht es gesundheitlich ~:** he's in a bad way
Misere *die;* ~, **~n** (geh.) wretched *or* dreadful state; (Elend) misery; (Not) distress
miss, *miß *Imperativ Sg. v.* MESSEN
miss·achten, *miß·achten *tr. V.* **(a)** (ignorieren) disregard; ignore **(b)** (geringschätzen) be contemptuous of
miss·billigen, *miß·billigen *tr. V.* disapprove of
Miss·billigung, *Miß·billigung *die* disapproval
Miss·brauch, *Miß·brauch *der:* ▶ MISSBRAUCHEN: abuse; misuse
miss·brauchen, *miß·brauchen *tr. V.* abuse; misuse; abuse ‹*trust*›
missen *tr. V.* (geh.) **jmdn./etw. nicht ~ mögen** not want to be without sb./sth.
Miss·erfolg, *Miß·erfolg *der* failure
Misse·tat *die* (geh. veralt.) misdeed
miss·fallen, *miß·fallen *unr. itr. V.* **etw. missfällt jmdm.** sb. dislikes sth.
Missfallen, *Mißfallen *das;* **~s** displeasure; (Missbilligung) disapproval
Miss·geschick, *Miß·geschick *das* mishap
miss·glücken, *miß·glücken *itr. V.; mit sein* fail
miss·gönnen, *miß·gönnen *tr. V.* **jmdm. etw. ~:** begrudge sb. sth.
Miss·griff, *Miß·griff *der* error of judgement
miss·handeln, *miß·handeln *tr. V.* maltreat
Miss·handlung, *Miß·handlung *die* maltreatment
Mission *die;* ~, **~en** mission
Missionar *der;* **~s, ~e, Missionarin** *die;* ~, **~nen** missionary
Miss·kredit, *Miß·kredit *der:* **jmdn./etw. in ~ bringen** bring sb./sth. into discredit
misslang, *mißlang *1. u. 3. Pers. Sg. Prät. v.* MISSLINGEN
missliebig, *mißliebig *Adj.* unpopular
misslingen, *mißlingen *unr. itr. V.; mit sein* fail
Misslingen, *Mißlingen *das;* **~s** failure
misslungen, *mißlungen *2. Part. v.* MISSLINGEN
Miss·mut, *Miß·mut *der* ill humour *no indef. art.*
miß·mutig, *miss·mutig [1] *Adj.* bad-tempered; sullen ‹*face*› [2] *adv.* bad-temperedly
Miss·stand, *Miß·stand *der* deplorable state of affairs *no pl.*

*alte Schreibung - vgl. Hinweis auf S. xiv

misst, *mißt *2. u. 3. Pers. Sg. Präsens v.* MESSEN
miss·trauen, *miß·trauen *itr. V.* **jmdm./einer Sache ~:** mistrust *or* distrust sb./sth.
Misstrauen, *Miß·trauen *das;* **~s** mistrust, distrust (**gegen** of)
misstrauisch, *miß·trauisch [1] *Adj.* mistrustful; distrustful [2] *adv.* mistrustfully; distrustfully
miss·verständlich, *miß·verständlich [1] *Adj.* unclear; ‹*formulation, concept, etc.*› that could be misunderstood [2] *adv.* ‹*express oneself, describe*› in a way that could be misunderstood
Miss·verständnis, *Miß·verständnis *das* misunderstanding
miss·verstehen, *miß·verstehen *unr. tr. V.* **ich missverstehe, missverstanden, misszuverstehen** misunderstand
Miss·wirtschaft, *Miß·wirtschaft *die* mismanagement
Mist *der;* **~[e]s (a)** dung; (Dünger) manure; (mit Stroh usw. gemischt) muck **(b)** (Misthaufen) dung/manure/muck heap **(c)** (ugs. abwertend) (Unsinn) rubbish *no indef. art.;* (Minderwertiges) junk *no indef. art.*
Mistel *die;* ~, **~n** mistletoe
Mist·haufen *der* dung/manure/muck heap
mit [1] *Präp. mit Dat.* with; **ein Zimmer ~ Frühstück** a room with breakfast included; **~ 50 [km/h] fahren** drive at 50 [k.p.h]; **~ der Bahn/dem Auto fahren** go by train/car; **~ 20 [Jahren]** at [the age of] twenty [2] *adv.* **(a)** too; as well **(b) seine Arbeit war ~ am besten** (ugs.) his work was among the best
Mit·arbeit *die* collaboration (**bei/an** + *Dat.* on); (Mithilfe) assistance (**bei, in** + *Dat.* in); (Beteiligung) participation (**in** + *Dat.* in)
mit|arbeiten *itr. V.* collaborate (**bei/an** + *Dat.* on) (sich beteiligen) participate (**in** + *Dat.* in)
Mit·arbeiter *der,* **Mit·arbeiterin** *die* **(a)** collaborator; **freier ~:** freelance worker **(b)** (Angestellter) employee
mit|bekommen *unr. tr. V.* **(a) etw. ~:** be given sth. to take with one **(b)** (wahrnehmen) be aware of; (durch Hören, Sehen) hear/see
mit|bestimmen [1] *itr. V.* have a say [2] *tr. V.* have an influence on
Mit·bestimmung *die* participation (**bei** in); (der Arbeitnehmer) co-determination
mit|bringen *unr. tr. V.* **(a) etw. ~:** bring sth. with one; **jmdm./sich etw. ~:** bring sth. with one for sb./bring sth. back for oneself **(b)** (haben) have ‹*ability, gift, etc.*›
Mitbringsel *das;* **~s, ~:** [small] present; (Andenken) [small] souvenir

Mịt·bürger *der,* **Mịt·bürgerin** *die* fellow citizen; **ältere Mitbürger** (Amtsspr.) senior citizens

mit·einạnder *Adv.* **(a)** with each other *or* one another; ~ **sprechen** talk to each other *or* one another
(b) (gemeinsam) together

mịt|erleben *tr. V.* **(a)** witness ‹*events etc.*›
(b) (mitmachen) be alive during

mịt|fahren *unr. itr. V.; mit sein* **bei jmdm. [im Auto]** ~: go/travel with sb. [in his/her car]; (mitgenommen werden) get a lift with sb. [in his/her car]

mịt·fühlend [1] *Adj.* sympathetic
[2] *adv.* sympathetically

mịt|führen *tr. V.* **(a)** (Amtsspr.: bei sich tragen) **etw.** ~: carry sth. [with one]
(b) (transportieren) ‹*river, stream*› carry along

mịt|geben *unr. tr. V.* **jmdm. etw.** ~: give sb. sth. to take with him/her; (fig.) provide sb. with sth.

Mịt·gefühl *das* sympathy

mịt|gehen *unr. itr. V.; mit sein* **(a)** go too; **mit jmdm.** ~: go with sb.
(b) (sich mitreißen lassen) **begeistert** ~: respond enthusiastically

Mịt·gift *die;* ~, ~**en** (veralt.) dowry

Mịt·glied *das* member (*Gen.,* **in** + *Dat.* of)

Mịtglieder·versammlung *die* general meeting

Mịtglieds-: ~**ausweis** *der* membership card; ~**beitrag** *der* membership subscription

Mịtgliedschaft *die;* ~: membership (+ *Gen.,* **in** + *Dat.*) of

Mịtglied[s]·staat *der* member state *or* country

mịt|halten *unr. itr. V.* keep up (**bei** in, **mit** with)

mịt|helfen *unr. itr. V.* help (**bei, in** + *Dat.* with)

mit·hịlfe [1] *Präp. mit Gen.* with the help *or* aid of
[2] *Adv.* ~ **von** with the help *or* aid of

Mịt·hilfe *die* help; assistance

mịt|hören [1] *tr. V.* listen to; (zufällig) overhear ‹*conversation, argument, etc.*›; (abhören) listen in on
[2] *itr. V.* listen; (zufällig) overhear

mịt|kommen *unr. itr. V.; mit sein* **(a)** come too; **kommst du mit?** are you coming [with me/us]?
(b) (Schritt halten) keep up

Mịt·läufer *der,* **Mịt·läuferin** *die* (abwertend) [mere] supporter

Mịt·laut *der* consonant

Mịt·leid *das* pity, compassion (**mit** for); (Mitgefühl) sympathy (**mit** for)

Mịt·leidenschaft *die:* **jmdn./etw. in ~ ziehen** affect sb./sth.

mịt·leidig [1] *Adj.* compassionate; (mitfühlend) sympathetic
[2] *adv.* compassionately; (mitfühlend) sympathetically

mịt|machen [1] *tr. V.* **(a)** (teilnehmen an) go on ‹*trip*›; join in ‹*joke*›; follow ‹*fashion*›; fight in ‹*war*›; do ‹*course, seminar*›; **das mache ich nicht mit** (ugs.) I can't go along with it
(b) (ugs.: erleiden) **zwei Weltkriege/viele Bombenangriffe mitgemacht haben** have been through two world wars/many bomb attacks
[2] *itr. V.* **(a)** (sich beteiligen) join in
(b) (ugs.: funktionieren) **mein Herz/Kreislauf macht nicht mit** my heart/circulation can't take it

Mịt·mensch *der* fellow human being

mịt|nehmen *unr. tr. V.* **(a) jmdn.** ~: take sb. with one; **etw.** ~: take sth. with one; (verhüll.: stehlen) walk off with sth. (coll.); (kaufen) take sth.; **Essen/Getränke zum Mitnehmen** food/drinks to take away *or* (Amer.) to go
(b) (in Mitleidenschaft ziehen) **jmdn.** ~: take it out of sb.

mịt|reden *itr. V.* **(a)** join in the conversation
(b) (mitbestimmen) have a say

Mịt·reisende *der/die* fellow passenger

mịt|reißen *unr. tr. V.* **die Begeisterung/seine Rede hat alle Zuhörer mitgerissen** the audience was carried away with enthusiasm/by his speech

mit·sạmt *Präp. mit Dat.* together with

mịt|schneiden *unr. tr. V.* (Rundf., Ferns.) record [live]

Mịt·schuld *die* share of the blame *or* responsibility (**an** + *Dat.* for)

Mịt·schüler *der,* **Mịt·schülerin** *die* schoolfellow

mịt|spielen *itr. V.* **(a)** join in the game
(b) in einem Film ~: be in a film; **in einem Orchester/in** *od.* **bei einem Fußballverein** ~: play in an orchestra/for a football club

Mịt·spieler *der,* **Mịt·spielerin** *die* player; (in derselben Mannschaft) teammate

***mịttag** ▶ MITTAG

Mịttag *der;* ~**s**, ~**e** **(a)** midday *no art.;* **gegen** ~: around midday; **zu ~ essen** have lunch; **heute/Montag** ~: at midday today/on Monday
(b) (ugs.: Mittagspause) lunch hour

Mịttag·essen *das* lunch

mịttags *Adv.* at midday; **12 Uhr** ~: 12 noon

Mịttags-: ~**pause** *die* lunch hour; ~**ruhe** *die* period of quiet after lunch; ~**zeit** *die* **(a)** (Zeit gegen 12 Uhr) lunchtime *no art.;* **(b)** (Mittagspause) lunch hour

Mịtte *die;* ~, ~**n** middle; (eines Kreises, einer Kugel, Stadt) centre; ~ **des Monats/Jahres** in the middle of the month/year

mịt|teilen *tr. V.* **jmdm. etw.** ~: tell sb. sth.; (informieren) inform sb. of sth.

mitteilsam *Adj.* communicative; (gesprächig) talkative

Mit·teilung *die* communication; (Bekanntgabe) announcement

Mittel *das;* ~**s,** ~ **(a)** means; (Methode) way; method; (Werbe~, Propaganda~ usw.) device (*Gen.* for); **mit allen ~n versuchen, etw. zu tun** try by every means to do sth.
(b) (Arznei) **ein ~ gegen Husten** *usw.* a cure for coughs *etc.;*
(c) *Pl.* (Geldmittel) funds; [financial] resources; (Privatmittel) means

Mittel·alter *das* Middle Ages *pl.*

mittel·alterlich *Adj.* medieval

mittelbar 1 *Adj.* indirect
2 *adv.* indirectly

mittel-, Mittel-: ~**ding** *das* **ein ~ding sein** be something in between; ~**europa** (*das*) Central Europe; ~**finger** *der* middle finger; ~**gebirge** *das* low mountains *pl.;* ~**groß** *Adj.* medium-sized; ‹*person*› of medium height; ~**klasse·wagen** *der* medium-sized car; ~**linie** *die* centre line; (Fußball) half-way line; ~**los** *Adj.* without means *postpos.;* ~**mäßig** *Adj.* mediocre; ~**meer** *das* Mediterranean [Sea]; ~**punkt** *der* **(a)** (Geom.) centre; (einer Strecke) midpoint; **(b)** (Mensch/Sache im Zentrum) centre of attention; ~**scheitel** *der* centre parting; ~**schule** *die* ▶ REALSCHULE; ~**stand** *der* middle class; ~**strecken·rakete** *die* medium-range missile; ~**streifen** *der* central reservation; median strip (Amer.); ~**weg** *der* middle course; ~**welle** *die* (Physik, Rundf.) medium wave

mitten *Adv.* ~ **an/auf etw.** (*Akk./Dat.*) in the middle of sth.; ~ **durch die Stadt** right through the town

mitten-: ~**drin** *Adv.* [right] in the middle; ~**durch** *Adv.* [right] through the middle

Mitter·nacht *die* midnight *no art.*

Mitternachts·sonne *die* midnight sun

Mittler *der;* ~**s,** ~ mediator

mittler... *Adj.* middle; moderate ‹*speed*›; medium-sized ‹*company, town*›; medium ‹*quality, size*›; (durchschnittlich) average; **die ~e Reife** (Schulw.) *standard of achievement for school-leaving certificate at a Realschule or for entry to the sixth form in a Gymnasium*

Mittlerin *die;* ~, ~**nen** mediator

Mittler·rolle *die* mediating role

mittler·weile *Adv.* since then; (bis jetzt) by now; (unterdessen) in the meantime

Mittwoch *der;* ~**[e]s,** ~**e** Wednesday; *s. auch* DIENSTAG

mittwochs *Adv.* on Wednesday[s]

mit·unter *Adv.* from time to time

mit·wirken *itr. V.* **an etw.** (*Dat.*)**/bei etw.** ~: collaborate on/be involved in sth.; **in einem Orchester/Theaterstück** ~: play in an orchestra/act *or* appear in a play

Mitwirkende *der/die adj. Dekl.* (an einer Sendung) participant; (in einer Show) performer; (in einem Theaterstück) actor

Mit·wisser *der;* ~**s** ~, **Mit·wisserin** *die;* ~, ~**nen:** ~ **einer Sache** (*Gen.*) **sein** be an accessory to sth.

mixen *tr. V.* mix; **sich** (*Dat.*) **einen Drink** ~: fix oneself a drink

Mixer *der;* ~**s,** ~, **(a)** (Bar~) barman; bartender (Amer.)
(b) (Gerät) blender and liquidizer

Mixerin *die;* ~, ~**nen** barmaid

mm *Abk.* = **Millimeter** mm.

Mo. *Abk.* = **Montag** Mon.

Mob *der;* ~**s** (abwertend) mob

Möbel *das;* ~**s,** ~ **(a)** *Pl.* furniture *sing., no indef. art.;*
(b) piece of furniture

Möbel·wagen *der* furniture van; removal van

mobil *Adj.* **(a)** mobile; *s. auch* MOBILMACHEN;
(b) (ugs.) (lebendig) lively

Mobiliar *das;* ~**s** furnishings *pl.*

mobilisieren *tr. V.* **(a)** (Milit., fig.) mobilize
(b) (aktivieren) activate

mobil|machen *itr. V.* mobilize

Mobilmachung *die;* ~, ~**en** mobilization

Mobil·telefon *das* cellular phone

möblieren *tr. V.* furnish

mochte *1. u. 3. Pers. Sg. Prät. v.* MÖGEN

möchte *1. u. 3. Pers. Sg. Konjunktiv II v.* MÖGEN

Mode *die;* ~, ~**n** fashion

Mode·farbe *die* fashionable colour

Modell *das;* ~**s,** ~**e** (auch fig.) model; **jmdm.** ~ **sitzen** *od.* **stehen** sit for sb.

modellieren *tr. V.* model, mould ‹*figures, objects*›; mould ‹*clay, wax*›

Modell·kleid *das* model dress

Modem *der od. das;* ~**s,** ~**s** (DV) modem

Moden·schau *die* fashion show

Moder *der;* ~**s** mould; (~geruch) mustiness

Moderation *die;* ~, ~**en** (Rundf., Ferns.) presentation

Moderator *der;* ~**s,** ~**en, Moderatorin** *die;* ~, ~**nen** (Rundf., Ferns.) presenter

moderieren *tr. V.* (Rundf., Ferns.) present ‹*programme*›

modern[1] *itr. V.; auch mit sein* go mouldy

modern[2] 1 *Adj.* modern; (modisch) fashionable
2 *adv.* in a modern manner; (modisch) fashionably

modernisieren *tr. V.* modernize

Mode-: ~**schöpfer** *der* couturier; ~**schöpferin** *die* couturière; ~**wort** *das; Pl.* ~**wörter** vogue word; ~**zeitschrift** *die* fashion magazine

modifizieren *tr. V.* (geh.) modify

modisch 1 *Adj.* fashionable
2 *adv.* fashionably

*old spelling - see note on page xiv

Mofa *das;* **~s, ~s** [low-powered] moped
Mogelei *die;* **~, ~en** (ugs.) cheating *no pl.*
mogeln *itr. V.* cheat
Mogel·packung *die* (abwertend) deceptive packaging
mögen 1 *unr. Modalverb; 2.Part.* **mögen:** **(a)** (wollen) want to; **das hätte ich sehen ~:** I would have liked to see that
(b) (geh.: sollen) **das mag genügen** that should be enough
(c) (Vermutung, Möglichkeit) **sie mag/mochte vierzig sein** she must be/must have been [about] forty; **[das] mag sein** maybe
(d) *Konjunktiv II* (den Wunsch haben) **ich/sie möchte gern wissen ...:** I would/she would like to know ...
2 *unr. tr. V.* like; **sie mag keine Rosen** she does not like roses; **sie ~ sich** they're fond of one another; **möchten Sie ein Glas Wein?** would you like a glass of wine?; **ich möchte lieber Tee** I would prefer tea
3 *unr. itr. V.* **(a)** (es wollen) like to
(b) ich möchte nach Hause I want to go home; **er möchte zu Herrn A** he would like to see Mr A
möglich *Adj.* possible; **es war ihm nicht ~ [zu kommen]** he was unable [to come]; **alles Mögliche** (ugs.) all sorts of things; **[das ist doch] nicht ~!** impossible!; **sein Möglichstes tun** do one's utmost
möglicher·weise *Adv.* possibly
Möglichkeit *die;* **~, ~en (a)** possibility; (Methode) way; **es besteht die ~, dass ...:** there is a possibility that ...
(b) (Gelegenheit) opportunity; chance
möglichst *Adv.* **(a)** if [at all] possible
(b) ~ schnell as fast as possible
Mohammed (*der*) Muhammad
Mohammedaner *der;* **~s, ~, Mohammedanerin** *die;* **~, ~nen** Muslim; Muhammadan
mohammedanisch *Adj.* Muslim; Muhammadan
Mohn *der;* **~s** poppy; (Samen) poppy seed; (auf Brot, Kuchen) poppy seeds *pl.*
Mohn-: ~blume *die* poppy; **~brötchen** *das* poppy-seed roll; **~kuchen** *der* poppy-seed cake
Möhre *die;* **~, ~n** carrot
Mohren·kopf *der* chocolate marshmallow
Mohr·rübe *die* carrot
mokieren *refl. V.* (geh.) **sich über etw.** (*Akk.*) **~:** scoff at sth.; **sich über jmdn. ~:** mock sb.
Mokka *der;* **~s** strong black coffee
Molch *der;* **~[e]s, ~e** newt
Mole *die;* **~, ~n** [harbour] mole
Molekül *das;* **~s, ~e** molecule
molekular *Adj.* molecular
molk *1. u. 3. Pers. Sg. Prät. v.* MELKEN
Molkerei *die;* **~, ~en** dairy
Moll *das;* **~** (Musik) minor [key]
mollig 1 *Adj.* **(a)** (rundlich) plump
(b) (warm) snug
2 *adv.* snugly; **~ warm** warm and snug
Moment¹ *der;* **~[e]s, ~e** moment; **jeden ~** (ugs.) [at] any moment; **im ~:** at the moment
Moment² *das;* **~[e]s, ~e** factor, element (**für** in)
momentan 1 *Adj.* **(a)** present
(b) (vorübergehend) temporary; (flüchtig) momentary
2 *adv.* **(a)** at present
(b) (vorübergehend) temporarily
Monaco (*das*); **~s** Monaco
Monarch *der;* **~en, ~en** monarch
Monarchie *die;* **~, ~n** monarchy
Monarchin *die;* **~, ~nen** monarch
Monat *der;* **~s, ~e** month; **im ~ April** in the month of April
monatelang 1 *Adj.* lasting for months *postpos., not pred.;*
2 *adv.* for months [on end]
monatlich 1 *Adj.* monthly
2 *adv.* every month; (pro Monat) per month
Monats-: ~ende *das* end of the month; **~erste** *der; adj. Dekl.* first [day] of the month; **~hälfte** *die* half of the month; **~karte** *die* monthly season ticket; **~letzte** *der; adj. Dekl.* last day of the month
Mönch *der;* **~[e]s, ~e** monk
Mond *der;* **~[e]s, ~e** moon; **auf** *od.* **hinter dem ~ leben** (fig. ugs.) be a bit behind the times; **nach dem ~ gehen** (ugs.) ‹*clock, watch*› be hopelessly wrong
Mond-: ~fähre *die* (Raumf.) lunar module; **~finsternis** *die* eclipse of the moon; **~landung** *die* moon landing; **~licht** *das* moonlight; **~phase** *die* moon's phase
Mongole *der;* **~n, ~n (a)** Mongol
(b) (Bewohner der Mongolei) Mongolian
Mongolei *die;* **~:** Mongolia
Mongolin *die;* **~, ~nen** ▶ MONGOLE
Monitor *der;* **~s, ~en** monitor
mono-, Mono-: mono-
Mono·gramm *das;* **~s, ~e** monogram
Monographie *die;* **~, ~n** monograph
Monolog *der;* **~s, ~e** monologue
Monopol *das;* **~s, ~e** monopoly (**auf +** *Akk.*, **für** in, of)
monoton 1 *Adj.* monotonous
2 *adv.* monotonously
Monotonie *die;* **~, ~n** monotony
Monster *das;* **~s, ~:** monster; (hässlich) [hideous] brute
Monstren ▶ MONSTRUM
monströs *Adj.* monstrous
Monstrum *das;* **~s, Monstren (a)** monster
(b) (Sache) hulking great thing (coll.)
Monsun *der;* **~s, ~e** (Geogr.) monsoon
Mon·tag *der* Monday; *s. auch* DIENSTAG
Montage /mɔnˈtaːʒə/ *die;* **~, ~n (a)** ···

(Zusammenbau) assembly; (Einbau) installation; (Aufstellen) erection; (Anbringen) fitting (**an** + *Akk. od. Dat.* to); mounting (**auf** + *Akk. od. Dat.* on)
(b) (Film, bild. Kunst, Literaturw.) montage

montags *Adv.* on Monday[s]

montieren *tr. V.* **(a)** (zusammenbauen) assemble (**aus** from); erect ‹*building*›
(b) (anbringen) fit (**an** + *Akk. od. Dat.* to; **auf** + *Akk. od. Dat.* on); (einbauen) install (**in** + *Akk.* in); (befestigen) fix (**an** + *Akk. od. Dat.* to)

Monument *das;* **~[e]s, ~e** monument

monumental *Adj.* monumental

Moor *das;* **~[e]s, ~e** bog; (Bruch) marsh

Moos *das;* **~es, ~e** moss

Moped /'mo:pɛt/ *das;* **~s, ~s** moped

Mops *der;* **~es, Möpse** pug [dog]; (salopp: dicke Person) podge (coll.)

Moral *die;* **~ (a)** (Norm) morality
(b) (Sittlichkeit) morals *pl.;*
(c) (Selbstvertrauen) morale
(d) (Lehre) moral

moralisch 1 *Adj.* **(a)** moral
(b) (tugendhaft) virtuous
2 *adv.* **(a)** morally
(b) (tugendhaft) virtuously

moralisieren *itr. V.* (geh.) moralize

Moralist *der;* **~en, ~en, Moralistin** *die;* **~, ~nen** moralist

Moral·predigt *die* (abwertend) [moralizing] lecture; homily

Morast *der;* **~[e]s, ~e** *od.* **Moräste (a)** bog; swamp
(b) (Schlamm) mud

Mord *der;* **~[e]s, ~e** murder (**an** + *Dat.* of); (durch ein Attentat) assassination; **einen ~ begehen** commit murder

Mord-: ~anschlag *der* attempted murder (**auf** + *Akk.* of); (Attentat) assassination attempt (**auf** + *Akk.* on); **~drohung** *die* murder threat

morden *tr., itr. V.* murder

Mörder *der;* **~s, ~:** murderer (esp. Law); killer; (politischer) assassin

Mörderin *die;* **~, ~nen** murderer; murderess; (politische) assassin

mörderisch 1 *Adj.* murderous
2 *adv.* (ugs.) dreadfully (coll.)

Mord·fall *der* murder case

mords-, Mords- (ugs.) terrific (coll.)

mords·mäßig *Adj.* terrific (coll.); tremendous (coll.); (entsetzlich) terrible (coll.)

Mord-: ~verdacht *der* suspicion of murder; **~versuch** *der* attempted murder; (Attentat) assassination attempt; **~waffe** *die* murder weapon

morgen *Adv.* tomorrow; **~ in einer Woche** tomorrow week; a week tomorrow; **~ um diese Zeit** this time tomorrow; **bis ~!** until tomorrow!; see you tomorrow!

*alte Schreibung - vgl. Hinweis auf S. xiv

Morgen *der;* **~s, ~:** morning; **am ~:** in the morning; **am folgenden** *od.* **nächsten ~:** next morning; **früh am ~, am frühen ~:** early in the morning; **heute ~:** this morning; **guten ~!** good morning!

morgendlich *Adj.* morning

Morgen-: ~grauen *das* daybreak; **~mantel** *der* dressing gown; **~rot** *das* (geh.) rosy dawn

morgens *Adv.* in the morning; (jeden Morgen) every morning; **Dienstag** *od.* **dienstags ~:** on Tuesday morning[s]; **von ~ bis abends** from morning to evening

morgig *Adj.* tomorrow's

Morphium *das;* **~s** morphine

morphium·süchtig *Adj.* addicted to morphine *pred.*

morsch *Adj.* (auch fig.) rotten

Mörser *der;* **~s, ~** (Gefäß, Geschütz) mortar

Mörtel *der;* **~s** mortar

Mosaik *das;* **~s, ~en** *od.* **~e** mosaic

Mosambik *(das);* **~s** Mozambique

Moschee *die;* **~, ~n** mosque

Moschus *der;* **~:** musk

Mosel *die;* **~:** Moselle

Mosel·wein *der* Moselle [wine]

mosern *itr. V.* (ugs.) gripe (coll.) (**über** + *Akk.*)

Moskau *(das);* **~s** Moscow

Moskauer 1 *indekl. Adj.* Moscow *attrib.;*
2 *der;* **~s, ~:** Muscovite

Moskauerin *die;* **~, ~nen** Muscovite

Moskito *der;* **~s, ~s** mosquito

Moslem *der;* **~s, ~s** ▶ MUSLIM

Moslemin *die;* **~, ~nen** ▶ MUSLIMIN

moslemisch ▶ MUSLIMISCH

Most *der;* **~[e]s, ~e (a)** [cloudy fermented] fruit juice
(b) (landsch.: neuer Wein) new wine

Mostrich *der;* **~s** (nordostd.) mustard

Motel *das;* **~s, ~s** motel

Motiv *das;* **~s, ~e (a)** motive
(b) (fachspr.: Thema) motif; theme; (Kunst) subject

Motor *der;* **~s, ~en** engine; (Elektro~) motor

Motor·haube *die* (Kfz-W.) bonnet (Brit.); hood (Amer.)

motorisieren *tr. V.* motorize

Motor-: ~rad *das* motor cycle; **~rad·fahrer** *der,* **~rad·fahrerin** *die* motorcyclist; **~roller** *der* motor scooter; **~schaden** *der* engine trouble *no indef. art.*

Motte *die;* **~, ~n** moth

Motten·kugel *die* mothball

Motto *das;* **~s, ~s** motto; (Schlagwort) slogan

Möwe *die;* **~, ~n** gull

Mrd. *Abk.* = **Milliarde** bn.

Mücke *die;* **~, ~n** midge; (größer) mosquito

Mücken·stich *der* midge/mosquito bite

Mucks *der;* **~es, ~e** (ugs.) murmur [of protest]; **keinen ~ sagen** not utter a [single] word

müde [1] *Adj.* tired; (ermattet) weary; (schläfrig) sleepy; **jmdn./etw.** *od.* **jmds./einer Sache ~ sein** (geh.) be tired of sb./sth.
[2] *adv.* wearily; (schläfrig) sleepily

Müdigkeit *die;* **~:** tiredness

muffelig (ugs.) [1] *Adj.* grumpy
[2] *adv.* grumpily

muffig *Adj.* musty

Mühe *die;* **~, ~n** trouble; **sich** (*Dat.*) **mit jmdm./etw. ~ geben** take [great] pains over sb./sth.; **mit Müh und Not** with great difficulty

mühelos [1] *Adj.* effortless
[2] *adv.* effortlessly

mühe·voll *Adj.* laborious; painstaking ‹*work*›

Mühle *die;* **~, ~n (a)** mill; (Kaffee~) [coffee] grinder
(b) (Spiel) nine men's morris

Mühsal *die;* **~, ~e** (geh.) tribulation; (Strapaze) hardship

mühsam [1] *Adj.* laborious
[2] *adv.* laboriously

müh·selig (geh.) [1] *Adj.* laborious; arduous ‹*journey, life*›
[2] *adv.* with [great] difficulty

Mulde *die;* **~, ~n** hollow

Mull *der;* **~[e]s** (Stoff) mull; (Verband~) gauze

Müll *der;* **~s** refuse; rubbish; garbage (Amer.); trash (Amer.); (Industrie~) [industrial] waste

Müll-: ~abfuhr *die* refuse *or* (Amer.) garbage collection; **~ablade·platz** *der* [refuse] dump *or* (Brit.) tip

Mull·binde *die* gauze bandage

Müll·deponie *die* (Amtsspr.) refuse disposal site

Müller *der;* **~s, ~:** miller

Müll-: ~halde *die* refuse dump; **~kippe** *die* ▶ MÜLLABLADEPLATZ; **~mann** *der;* (ugs.) dustman (Brit.); garbage man (Amer.); **~sack** *der* refuse bag; **~schlucker** *der* rubbish *or* (Amer.) garbage chute; **~tonne** *die* dustbin (Brit.); garbage *or* trash can (Amer.); **~tüte** *die* bin bag; **~wagen** *der* dustcart (Brit.); garbage truck (Amer.)

mulmig *Adj.* (ugs.) uneasy

Multimedia·technik *die* (DV) multimedia technology

Multiplex *das;* **~es, ~e** multiplex

Multiplikation *die;* **~, ~en** (Math.) multiplication

multiplizieren *tr. V.* multiply (**mit** by)

Mumie /ˈmuːmi̯ə/ *die;* **~, ~n** mummy

Mumm *der;* **~s** (ugs.) (Mut) guts *pl.* (coll.); (Tatkraft) drive; zap (coll.); (Kraft) muscle power

Mumps *der od. die;* **~:** mumps *sing.*

München (*das*); **~s** Munich

Münch[e]ner [1] *indekl. Adj.* Munich *attrib*
[2] *der;* **~s, ~:** inhabitant/native of Munich

Münch[e]nerin *die;* **~, ~nen** ▶ MÜNCH[E]NER 2

Mund *der;* **~[e]s, Münder** mouth; **er küsste sie auf den ~:** he kissed her on the lips; **mit vollem ~ sprechen** speak with one's mouth full; **den ~ nicht aufmachen** (fig. ugs.) not say anything; **den** *od.* **seinen ~ halten** (ugs.) (zu sprechen aufhören) shut up (coll.); (nichts sagen) not say anything; (nichts verraten) keep quiet (**über** + *Akk.* about); **sie ist nicht auf den ~ gefallen** (fig. ugs.) she's never at a loss for words

Mund·art *die* dialect

münden *itr. V.; mit sein* **in etw.** (*Akk.*) **~:** ‹*river*› flow into sth.; ‹*corridor, street*› lead into sth.

mund-, Mund-: ~faul *Adj.* (ugs.) uncommunicative; **~gerecht** *Adj.* bite-sized; **~geruch** *der* bad breath *no indef. art.;* **~harmonika** *die* mouth organ

mündig *Adj.* of age *pred.;* **~ werden** come of age

mündlich [1] *Adj.* oral
[2] *adv.* orally

Mund·stück *das* mouthpiece; (bei Zigaretten) tip

mund·tot *Adj.* **jmdn. ~ machen** silence sb.

Mündung *die;* **~, ~en (a)** mouth; (größere Trichter~) estuary
(b) (bei Feuerwaffen) muzzle

Mund·wasser *das; Pl.* **~wässer** mouthwash

Mund-zu-Mund-Beatmung *die* mouth-to-mouth resuscitation

Munition *die;* **~:** ammunition

munkeln *tr., itr. V.* (ugs.) **man munkelt, dass ...:** there is a rumour that ...

Münster *das;* **~s, ~:** minster; (Dom) cathedral

munter [1] *Adj.* **(a)** cheerful; (lebhaft) lively ‹*eyes, game*›
(b) (wach) awake
[2] *adv.* cheerfully

Munterkeit *die;* **~:** cheerfulness

Münz·automat *der* slot machine

Münze *die;* **~, ~n** coin

Münz-: ~fernsprecher *der* payphone; pay station (Amer.); **~tankstelle** *die* coin-in-the-slot petrol (Brit.) *or* (Amer.) gas station; **~wechsler** *der* change machine

mürbe *Adj.* crumbly ‹*biscuit, cake, etc.*›; tender ‹*meat*›; soft ‹*fruit*›; **jmdn. ~ machen** (fig.) wear sb. down

Murmel *die;* **~, ~n** marble

murmeln *tr., itr. V.* mumble; mutter; (sehr leise) murmur

Murmel·tier *das* marmot

murren *itr. V.* grumble

mürrisch [1] *Adj.* grumpy

m

2 *adv.* grumpily

Mus *das od. der;* **~es, ~e** purée

Muschel *die;* **~, ~n (a)** mussel; (Schale) [mussel] shell
(b) (am Telefon) (Hör~) earpiece; (Sprech~) mouthpiece

Muse *die;* **~, ~n** muse

Museum *das;* **~s, Museen** museum

Musik *die;* **~, ~en** music

musikalisch 1 *Adj.* musical
2 *adv.* musically

Musikant *der;* **~en, ~en, Musikantin** *die;* **~, ~nen** musician

Musik·box *die* jukebox

Musiker *der;* **~s, ~, Musikerin** *die;* **~, ~nen** musician

Musik-: ~hochschule *die* college of music; **~instrument** *das* musical instrument; **~saal** *der* (in der Schule) music room; **~sender** *der* music station; **~stück** *das* piece of music; **ein ~stück Chopins/von Chopin** a piece by Chopin; **~stunde** *die* music lesson; **~szene** *die* music scene

musisch 1 *Adj.* artistic; ‹*education*› in the arts
2 *adv.* artistically

musizieren *itr. V.* play music; (bes. unter Laien) make music

Muskat *der;* **~[e]s, ~e** nutmeg

Muskat·nuss, *Muskat·nuß *die* nutmeg

Muskel *der;* **~s, ~n** muscle

Muskel-: ~kater *der* stiff muscles *pl.;* **~kraft** *die* muscle power; **~krampf** *der* cramp; **~pille** *die* (scherzh.) muscle-building pill; muscle builder **~protz** *der* (ugs.) muscleman; **~zerrung** *die* (Med.) pulled muscle; **sich** *(Dat.)* **eine ~zerrung zuziehen** pull a muscle

Muskulatur *die;* **~, ~en** musculature; muscular system

muskulös *Adj.* muscular

Müsli *das;* **~s, ~s** muesli

Muslim *der;* **~s, ~e** *od.* **~s** Muslim

Muslimin *die;* **~, ~nen** Muslim [woman]

muslimisch 1 *Adj.* Muslim
2 *adv.* on Muslim principles; **~ erzogen werden** be brought up in the Muslim faith

muss, *muß *1. u. 3.Pers. Sg. Präsens v.* MÜSSEN

Muss, *Muß *das;* **~:** necessity; must (coll.)

Muße *die;* **~:** leisure

müssen 1 *unr. Modalverb; 2.Part.* **müssen: (a)** have to; **er muss es tun** he must do it; he has to *or* (coll.) has got to do it; **das muss 1968 gewesen sein** it must have been in 1968; **er muss gleich hier sein** he will be here at any moment
(b) *Konjunktiv II* **es müsste doch möglich sein** it ought to be possible; **reich müsste man sein!** how nice it would be to be rich!
2 *unr. itr. V.* **ich muss nach Hause** I have to *or* must go home; **ich muss mal** (fam.) I need to spend a penny (Brit. coll.) *or* (Amer. coll.) go to the john

müßig 1 *Adj.* idle ‹*person*›; ‹*hours, weeks, life*› of leisure
2 *adv.* idly

Müßig-: ~gang *der* leisure; (Untätigkeit) idleness **~gänger** *der;* **~~s, ~~, ~gängerin** *die;* **~~, ~~nen** idler; **~gänger** *Pl.* people with time on their hands

musste, *mußte *1. u. 3. Pers. Sg. Prät. v.* MÜSSEN

Muster *das;* **~s, ~ (a)** (Vorlage) pattern
(b) (Vorbild) model (**an** + *Dat.* of)
(c) (Verzierung) pattern
(d) (Warenprobe) sample

muster-, Muster-: ~beispiel *das* perfect example; **~gültig** 1 *Adj.* exemplary; impeccable ‹*order*›; 2 *adv.* in an exemplary fashion; **~prozess, *~prozeß** *der* test case

mustern *tr. V.* **(a)** eye
(b) (Milit.: ärztlich untersuchen) **jmdn. ~:** give sb. his medical

Musterung *die;* **~, ~en (a)** scrutiny
(b) (Milit.: von Wehrpflichtigen) medical examination; medical

Mut *der;* **~[e]s** courage

mutig 1 *Adj.* brave
2 *adv.* bravely

mut·los *Adj.* dejected; (entmutigt) disheartened

Mut·losigkeit *die;* **~:** dejection

mutmaßen *tr., itr. V.* conjecture

mutmaßlich *Adj.* supposed; suspected ‹*murderer etc.*›

Mutmaßung *die;* **~, ~en** conjecture

Mut·probe *die* test of courage

Mutter¹ *die;* **~, Mütter** mother

Mutter² *die;* **~, ~n** nut

mütterlich 1 *Adj.* **(a)** maternal ‹*line, love, instincts, etc.*›
(b) (fürsorglich) motherly ‹*woman, care*›
2 *adv.* in a motherly way

mütterlicher·seits *Adv.* on the/his/her *etc.* mother's side

Mütterlichkeit *die;* **~:** motherliness; (mütterliche Gefühle) motherly feeling

Mutter-: ~liebe *die* motherly love *no art.;* **~mal** *das;* **~~e** birthmark

Mutterschaft *die;* **~:** motherhood

Mutterschafts·urlaub *der* maternity leave

mutter-, Mutter-: ~seelen·allein *Adj.* all alone; **~söhnchen** *das* mummy's *or* (Amer.) mama's boy; **~sprache** *die* mother tongue; **~tag** *der* Mother's Day *no def. art.*

*old spelling - see note on page xiv

Mutti *die;* ~, **~s** mummy (Brit. coll.); mum (Brit. coll.); mommy (Amer. coll.); mom (Amer. coll.)

mut·willig [1] *Adj.* wilful; wanton ‹*destruction*›
[2] *adv.* wilfully

Mütze *die;* ~, **~n** cap

MW *Abk.* (Rundf.) = **Mittelwelle** MW

Mw.-St., MwSt. *Abk.* **Mehrwertsteuer** VAT

mysteriös [1] *Adj.* mysterious
[2] *adv.* mysteriously

Mystik *die;* ~: mysticism

Mystery- /ˈmɪstəri/ mystery *attrib.*

Mythologie *die;* ~, **~n** mythology

mythologisch *Adj.* mythology

Mythos *der;* ~, **Mythen** myth

Nn

n, N /ɛn/ *das;* ~, ~: n/N

N *Abk.* = **Nord[en]** N

na *Interj.* (ugs.) well; **na so [et]was!** well I never!; **na und?** (wennschon) so what?; (beschwichtigend) **na, na, na!** now, now, come along; (triumphierend) **na also!** there you are!; (unsicher) **na, ich weiß nicht** hmm, I'm not sure; (ärgerlich) **na, was soll das denn?** now what's all this about?; (drohend) **na warte!** just [you] wait!

Nabe *die;* ~, **~n** hub

Nabel *der;* **~s,** ~: navel

Nabel-: ~bruch *der* (Med.) umbilical hernia; **~schnur** *die* umbilical cord

Naben·schaltung *die* hub gear

nach [1] *Präp. mit Dat.* **(a)** (räumlich) to; **der Zug ~ München** the train for Munich *or* the Munich train; **~ Hause gehen** go home; **~ Osten [zu]** eastwards; [towards the] east
(b) (zeitlich) after; **zehn [Minuten] ~ zwei** ten [minutes] past two
(c) (mit bestimmten Verben, bezeichnet das Ziel der Handlung) for
(d) (bezeichnet [räumliche und zeitliche] Reihenfolge) after; **~ Ihnen/dir!** after you
(e) (gemäß) according to; **~ meiner Ansicht** *od.* **Meinung, meiner Ansicht** *od.* **Meinung ~:** in my view *or* opinion; **~ der neusten Mode gekleidet** dressed in [accordance with] the latest fashion; **dem Gesetz ~:** in accordance with the law; by law; **~ etw. schmecken/riechen** taste/smell of sth.
[2] *Adv.* **(a)** (räumlich) **[alle] mir ~!** [everybody] follow me!
(b) (zeitlich) **~ und ~:** little by little; gradually; **~ wie vor** still

nach|ahmen *tr. V.* imitate

Nachahmung *die;* ~, **~en** imitation

Nachbar *der;* **~n, ~n** neighbour

Nachbar·haus *das* house next door

Nachbarin *die;* ~, **~nen** neighbour

Nachbar·land *das* neighbouring country

Nachbarschaft *die;* ~, **~en (a)** the whole neighbourhood
(b) (Beziehungen) **gute ~:** good neighbourliness
(c) (Gegend) neighbourhood; (Nähe) vicinity

Nach·beben *das* aftershock

nach|bestellen *tr. V.* **[noch] etw. ~:** order more of sth.; ‹*shop*› reorder sth.

Nach·bildung *die* **(a)** copying
(b) (Gegenstand) copy

nach|blicken *tr. V.* (geh.) **jmdm./einer Sache ~:** gaze after sb./sth.

nach|datieren *tr. V.* backdate

nach·dem *Konj.* **(a)** after
(b) ▶ JE[1] 3

nach|denken *unr. itr. V.* think; **denk mal [gut** *od.* **scharf] nach** have a [good] think

Nach·denken *das* thought

nachdenklich [1] *Adj.* thoughtful
[2] *adv.* thoughtfully

Nach·druck *der; Pl.* **~e (a) mit ~:** emphatically
(b) (Druckw.) reprint

nachdrücklich [1] *Adj.* emphatic
[2] *adv.* emphatically

Nachdrücklichkeit *die;* ~: emphatic nature

nach|dunkeln *itr. V.; mit sein* get darker

Nach·durst *der* morning-after thirst

nach|eifern *itr. V.* **jmdm. ~:** emulate sb.

nach·einander *Adv.* one after the other

nach|empfinden *unr. tr. V.* empathize with ‹*feeling*›; share ‹*delight, sorrow*›

Nach·erzählung *die* retelling [of a story]; (Schulw.) reproduction

Nachfahr *der;* **~en, ~en, Nachfahrin** *die;* ~, **~nen** (geh.) descendant

nach|fahren *unr. itr. V.; mit sein* follow [on]; **jmdm. ~:** follow sb.

Nach·folge *die* succession

Nachfolger *der;* **~s,** ~, **Nachfolgerin** *die;* ~, **~nen** successor

Nach·forschung *die* investigation
Nach·frage *die* demand (**nach** for)
nach|fragen *itr. V.* ask; inquire; **bei jmdm. ~**: ask sb.; **ob ich mal ~ soll?** should I ask about it *or* make inquiries?
nach|fühlen *tr. V.* empathize with; **das kann ich dir ~!** I know how you feel!
nach|füllen *tr. V.* top up; **Salz/Wein ~**: put [some] more salt/wine in
nach|geben *unr. itr. V.* give way
Nach·gebühr *die* excess postage
nach|gehen *unr. itr. V.; mit sein* **(a)** **jmdm./einer Sache ~**: follow sb./sth.; **einer Sache ~** (fig.) look into a matter; **einem Beruf ~**: practise a profession
(b) (nicht aus dem Kopf gehen) **jmdm. ~**: remain on sb.'s mind
(c) ‹*clock, watch*› be slow; **[um] eine Stunde ~**: be an hour slow
Nach·geschmack *der* aftertaste
nach·giebig *Adj.* indulgent
Nachgiebigkeit *die; ~*: indulgence
nach·haltig [1] *Adj.* **(a)** lasting
(b) (Ökologie) sustainable
[2] *adv.* **(a)** (auf längere Zeit) for a long time
(b) (Ökologie) sustainably
Nach·hause·weg *der* way home
nach|helfen *unr. itr. V.* help
nach·her /*auch:* '--/ *Adv.* afterwards; (später) later [on]; **bis ~!** see you later!
Nach·hilfe *die* coaching
Nachhilfe·unterricht *der* coaching
***nach·hinein, Nachhinein: im ~** (nachträglich) afterwards; later; (zurückblickend) with hindsight
nach|holen *tr. V.* (nachträglich erledigen) catch up on ‹*work, sleep*›; make up for ‹*working hours missed*›
nach|jagen *itr. V.; mit sein* **jmdm./einer Sache ~**: chase after sb./sth.
Nachkomme *der; ~n, ~n* descendant
nach|kommen *unr. itr. V.; mit sein* follow [later]; come [on] later
Nachkommenschaft *die; ~*: descendants *pl.*
Nachkömmling *der; ~s, ~e* much younger child (*than the rest*)
Nach·kriegs- post-war ‹*generation, period, etc.*›
Nach·lass, *Nach·laß *der;* **Nachlasses, Nachlasse** *od.* **Nachlässe (a)** estate
(b) (Kaufmannsspr.: Rabatt) discount
nach|lassen [1] *unr. itr. V.* let up; ‹*pain, stress, pressure*› ease; ‹*effect*› wear off; ‹*interest, enthusiasm, strength, courage*› wane; ‹*health, hearing, memory*› deteriorate; ‹*business*› drop off
[2] *unr. tr. V.* (Kaufmannsspr.) give a discount of
nach·lässig [1] *Adj.* careless
[2] *adv.* carelessly
Nach·lässigkeit *die; ~, ~en* carelessness
Nachlass·verwalter *der*, **Nachlass·verwalterin**, *die* (Rechtsw.) executor
nach|laufen *unr. itr. V.; mit sein* **jmdm./einer Sache ~**: run after sb./sth.
nach|lesen *unr. tr. V.* look up
nach|lösen [1] *tr. V.* **eine Fahrkarte ~**: buy a ticket [on the train, bus, etc.]
[2] *itr. V.* pay the excess [fare]
nach|machen *tr. V.* (auch tun) copy; (imitieren) imitate; (genauso herstellen) reproduce ‹*period furniture etc.*›; forge ‹*signature*›
***nach·mittag** ▶ NACHMITTAG
Nach·mittag *der* afternoon; **am ~**: in the afternoon; **am späten ~**: late in the afternoon; **heute ~**: this afternoon
nach·mittags *Adv.* in the afternoon; **dienstags** *od.* **Dienstag ~**: on Tuesday afternoons; **um vier Uhr ~**: at four in the afternoon; at 4 p.m.
Nachnahme *die; ~, ~n*: **per ~**: cash on delivery; COD
Nach·name *der* surname
Nach·porto *das* excess postage
nachprüfbar *Adj.* verifiable
nach|prüfen *tr., itr. V.* check
nach|rechnen *tr. V.* check ‹*figures*›
Nach·rede *die:* **üble ~**: malicious gossip; (Rechtsw.) defamation [of character]
nach|rennen *unr. itr. V.:* ▶ NACHLAUFEN
Nachricht *die; ~, ~en* **(a)** news *no pl.;* **das ist eine gute ~**: that is [a piece of] good news; **eine ~ hinterlassen** leave a message
(b) *Pl.* (Ferns., Rundf.) news *sing.;* **~en hören** listen to the news
Nachrichten-: ~sprecher *der*, **~sprecherin** *die* newsreader
nach|rücken *itr. V.; mit sein* move up
Nach·ruf *der* obituary (**auf** + *Akk.* of)
nach|rufen *unr. tr., itr. V.* **jmdm. [etw.] ~**: call [sth.] after sb.
nach|rüsten [1] *itr. V.* counter-arm
[2] *tr. V.* (Technik: zusätzlich ausstatten) **mit etw. ~** (+ *Akk.*) equip additionally with sth.; upgrade ‹*television, hi-fi, etc.*› with sth.
nach|sagen *tr. V.* **(a)** (wiederholen) repeat
(b) man sagt ihm nach, er sei ...: he is said to be ...; **jmdm. Schlechtes ~**: speak ill of sb.
Nach·saison *die* late season
nach|schicken *tr. V.* **(a)** (durch die Post o. Ä.) forward
(b) jmdm. jmdn. ~: send sb. after sb.
Nach·schlag *der* (ugs.: zusätzliche Portion) second helping; seconds *pl.*
nach|schlagen [1] *unr. tr. V.* look up
[2] *unr. itr. V.* **im Lexikon/Wörterbuch ~**: consult the encyclopaedia/dictionary
Nachschlage·werk *das* work of reference
Nach·schlüssel *der* duplicate key

*alte Schreibung - vgl. Hinweis auf S. xiv

nach|schmeißen *unr. tr. V.* (ugs.) **man kriegt sie nachgeschmissen** you get them for next to nothing

Nach·schub *der* (Milit.) **(a)** supply (**an** + *Dat.* of)
(b) (~material) supplies *pl.* (**an** + *Dat.* of)

nach|sehen 1 *unr. itr. V.* **(a) jmdm./einer Sache ~:** gaze after sb./sth.
(b) (kontrollieren) check
(c) (nachschlagen) have a look
2 *unr. tr. V.* **(a)** (nachlesen) look up
(b) (überprüfen) check [over]

Nach·sehen *das:* **das ~ haben** not get a look-in; (nichts abbekommen) be left with nothing

nach|senden *unr. od. regelm. tr. V.* forward

Nach·sicht *die* leniency

nachsichtig 1 *Adj.* lenient (**gegen, mit** towards)
2 *adv.* leniently

Nachsichtigkeit *die;* ~: leniency

Nach·silbe *die* (Sprachw.) suffix

nach|sitzen *unr. itr. V.* be in detention; **[eine Stunde] ~ müssen** have [an hour's] detention

Nach·spann *der;* **~[e]s, ~e** (Film, Ferns.) [final] credits *pl.*

Nach·speise *die* dessert; sweet

Nach·spiel *das:* **die Sache wird noch ein ~ haben** this affair will have repercussions; **ein gerichtliches ~ haben** result in court proceedings

nach|spionieren *itr. V.* **jmdm. ~:** spy on sb.

nach|sprechen *unr. tr. V.* **[jmdm.] etw. ~:** repeat sth. [after sb.]

nächst... *Sup. zu* NAH: *Adj.* next; (kürzest) shortest ‹*way*›; **am ~en Tag** the next day; **beim ~en Mal, das ~e Mal** the next time; **der ~e bitte!** next [one], please; **wer kommt als ~er dran?** whose turn is it next?

Nächste *der; adj. Dekl.* (geh.) neighbour

nach|stehen *unr. itr. V.* **jmdm. an etw.** (*Dat.*) **nicht ~:** be sb.'s match in sth.; **jmdm./einer Sache in nichts ~:** be in no way inferior to sb./sth.

nach·stehend 1 *Adj.* following
2 *adv.* below

Nächsten·liebe *die* charity [to one's neighbour]

nächstens *Adv.* **(a)** shortly
(b) (ugs.: wenn es so weitergeht) if it goes on like this

nächst-: ~liegend *Adj.* first, immediate ‹*problem*›; [most] obvious ‹*explanation etc.*›; **~möglich** *Adj.* earliest possible

nach|suchen *itr. V.* (geh.) **um etw. ~:** request sth.; (bes. schriftlich) apply for sth.

***nacht** ▶ NACHT

Nacht *die;* **~, Nächte** night; **gestern/morgen/Dienstag ~:** last night/tomorrow night/on Tuesday night; **heute ~:** tonight; **bei ~, in der ~:** at night[-time]; **über ~ bleiben** stay overnight; **gute ~!** good night!

nacht-, Nacht-: ~arbeit *die* night work *no art.;* **~blind** *Adj.* night-blind; **~blindheit** *die* night blindness; **~creme** *die* night cream; **~dienst** *der* night duty; **~dienst haben** be on night duty; ‹*chemist's shop*› be open late

Nach·teil *der* disadvantage

nachteilig 1 *Adj.* detrimental; harmful
2 *adv.* detrimentally; harmfully

Nacht-: ~essen *das* (bes. südd., schweiz.) ▶ ABENDESSEN; **~hemd** *das* nightshirt

Nachtigall *die;* **~, ~en** nightingale

nächtigen *itr. V.* (österr., sonst geh.) spend the night

Nach·tisch *der* dessert; sweet

nächtlich *Adj.* nocturnal; night ‹*sky*›; ‹*darkness, stillness*› of the night

Nacht·lokal *das* night spot (coll.)

nach|tragen *unr. tr. V.* (schriftlich ergänzen) insert; add

nach·tragend *Adj.* unforgiving; (rachsüchtig) vindictive

nachträglich 1 *Adj.* later; subsequent ‹*apology*›; (verspätet) belated ‹*greetings, apology*›
2 *adv.* afterwards; subsequently; (verspätet) belatedly

nach|trauern *itr. V.* **jmdm./einer Sache ~:** bemoan the passing of sb./sth.

Nacht·ruhe *die* night's sleep

nachts *Adv.* at night; **Montag** *od.* **montags ~:** on Monday nights; **um 3 Uhr ~:** at 3 o'clock in the morning

Nacht-: ~schicht *die* night shift; **~schwester** *die* night nurse; **~tisch** *der* bedside table; **~tisch·lampe** *die* bedside light; **~topf** *der* chamber pot; **~wächter** *der,* **~wächterin** *die* nightwatchman

Nach·untersuchung *die* follow-up examination; check-up

nach|vollziehen *unr. tr. V.* reconstruct; (begreifen) comprehend

nach|wachsen *unr. itr. V.; mit sein* **[wieder] ~:** grow again

Nach·wehen *Pl.* (Med.) afterpains; (fig. geh.) unpleasant after-effects

Nachweis *der;* **~es, ~e** proof *no indef. art.* (*Gen.,* **über** + *Akk.* of); (Zeugnis) certificate (**über** + *Akk.* of)

nachweisbar 1 *Adj.* demonstrable ‹*fact, truth, error, defect, guilt*›; detectable ‹*substance, chemical*›
2 *adv.* demonstrably

nach|weisen *unr. tr. V.* prove

nachweislich *Adv.* as can be proved

Nach·welt *die* posterity *no art.;* future generations *pl., no art.*

nach|winken *itr. V.* **jmdm./einer Sache ~:** wave after sb./sth.
Nach·wirkung *die* after-effect
Nach·wort *das; Pl.* **~e** afterword
Nach·wuchs *der* **(a)** (fam.: Kind[er]) offspring
(b) (junge Kräfte) new blood; (für eine Branche usw.) new recruits *pl.;* (in der Ausbildung) trainees *pl.*
nach|zahlen *tr., itr. V.* **(a)** pay later
(b) (zusätzlich zahlen) **25 Euro ~:** pay another 25 euros
nach|zählen *tr., itr. V.* [re]count
Nach·zahlung *die* additional payment
nach|ziehen *unr. itr. V.***(a)** (ugs.: ebenso handeln) do likewise; follow suit
(b) *mit sein* (nachträglich übersiedeln) **jmdm. ~:** [go to] join sb.
Nachzügler *der;* **~s, ~, Nachzüglerin** *die;* **~, ~nen** straggler; (spät Ankommende[r]) latecomer
Nackedei *der;* **~s, ~s** (fam. scherzh.) **[kleiner] ~:** naked little thing
Nacken *der;* **~s, ~:** back *or* nape of the neck; (Hals) neck
nackt *Adj.* naked; bare ‹*feet, legs, arms, skin, fists*›; (fig.) plain ‹*truth, fact*›; bare ‹*existence*›
Nackt·bade·strand *der* nudist beach
Nackte *der/die; adj. Dekl.* naked man/woman
Nackt·foto *das* nude photo
Nadel *die;* **~, ~n** needle; (Steck~, Hut~, Haar~) pin; **an der ~ hängen** (fig. ugs.) be on the needle (sl.)
Nadel·baum *der* conifer
Nadeldrucker *der* (DV) dot-matrix printer
nadeln *itr. V.* ‹*tree*› shed its needles
Nadel·wald *der* coniferous forest
Nagel *der;* **~s, Nägel** nail; **den ~ auf den Kopf treffen** (fig. ugs.) hit the nail on the head
Nagel-: ~bürste *die* nailbrush; **~feile** *die* nail file; **~lack** *der* nail varnish (Brit.); nail polish
nageln *tr. V.* nail (**an** + *Akk.* to, **auf** + *Akk.* on); (Med.) pin
nagel·neu *Adj.* (ugs.) brand-new
Nagel·schere *die* nail scissors *pl.*
nagen [1] *itr. V.* gnaw; **an etw.** (*Dat.*) **~:** gnaw [at] sth.
[2] *tr. V.* gnaw off; **ein Loch ins Holz ~:** gnaw a hole in the wood
Nage·tier *das* rodent
nah ▶ NAHE
Nah·aufnahme *die* (Fot.) close-up [photograph]
nahe /ˈnaːə,/ **näher** /ˈnɛːɐ,/ **nächst...** [1] *Adj.* **(a)** (räumlich) near *pred.;* close *pred.;* nearby *attrib.;*
(b) (zeitlich) imminent; near *pred.*
(c) (eng) close ‹*relationship etc.*›
[2] *adv.* **(a)** (räumlich) **~ an** (+ *Dat./Akk.*), **~ bei** close to; **~ gelegen** nearby; **von ~m** from close up; **jmdm. ~ gehen** affect sb. deeply; **eine Sache** (*Dat.*) **~ kommen** come close to sth.; ‹*amount*› approximate to sth.; **jmdm/sich [menschlich] ~ kommen** get to know sb./one another well; **jmdm/sich [menschlich] näher kommen** get on closer terms with sb.; **jmdm. ~ stehen** be on intimate terms with sb.; **jmdm. etw. ~ legen** (fig.) suggest sth. to sb.; **einen Verdacht/einen Gedanken** *usw.* **~ legen** give rise to a suspicion/thought *etc.*; **~ liegen** (fig.) ‹*thought*› suggest itself; ‹*suspicion, question*› arise
(b) (zeitlich) **~ an die achtzig** (ugs.) pushing eighty (coll.)
(c) (eng) closely
[3] *Präp. mit Dat.* (geh.) near; close to
Nähe *die;* **~:** closeness
nahe-: ~bei *Adv.* nearby; close by; **~|gehen** *usw.* ▶ NAHE 2A; **~liegend** *Adj.* obvious ‹*reason, solution*›
nahen *itr. V.; mit sein* (geh.) draw near; **sein/ihr** *usw.* **Ende nahte** the end was near
nähen [1] *itr. V.* sew; (Kleider machen) make clothes
[2] *tr. V.* **(a)** sew ‹*seam, hem*›; make ‹*dress etc.*›
(b) (Med.) stitch
näher [1] *Komp. zu* **nahe;**
[2] *Adj.* **(a)** (kürzer) shorter ‹*way, road*›
(b) (genauer) more precise ‹*information*›; closer ‹*investigation, inspection*›
[3] *adv.* **(a) bitte treten Sie ~!** please come in/nearer/this way
(b) (genauer) more closely; (im Einzelnen) in [more] detail
***näher|kommen** ▶ NAHE 2A
nähern *refl. V.* approach; **sich jmdm./einer Sache ~:** approach sb./sth.
nahe-: *~|stehen ▶ NAHE 2A; **~zu** *Adv.* almost; nearly; (mit Zahlenangabe) close on
Näh-: ~garn *das* [sewing] cotton; **~kasten** *der* sewing box
nahm *1. u. 3. Pers. Sg. Prät. v.* NEHMEN
Näh-: ~maschine *die* sewing machine; **~nadel** *die* sewing needle
nah·östlich *Adj.* Middle Eastern
Nähr·boden *der* culture medium; (fig.) breeding ground
nähren [1] *tr. V.* feed (**mit** on)
[2] *refl. V.* (geh.) **sich von etw. ~:** live on sth.; ‹*animal*› feed on sth.
nahrhaft *Adj.* nourishing
Nahrung *die;* **~:** food
Nahrungs·mittel *das* food [item]; **~** *Pl.* foodstuffs
Nähr·wert *der* nutritional value
Näh·seide *die* sewing silk
Naht *die;* **~, Nähte** seam
naht·los [1] *Adj.* seamless; (fig.) perfectly smooth ‹*transition*›

*old spelling - see note on page xiv

2 *adv.* **Studium und Beruf gehen nicht ~ ineinander über** there is not a perfectly smooth transition from study to work

Nah-: ~verkehr *der* local traffic; **~verkehrs·zug** *der* local train

Näh·zeug *das* sewing things *pl.*

naiv 1 *Adj.* naïve
2 *adv.* naïvely

Naivität *die;* ~: naïvety

Name *der;* **~ns, ~n** name

namens *Adv.* by the name of

Namens-: ~schild *das* **(a)** (an Türen usw.) nameplate; **(b)** (zum Anstecken) name badge; **~tag** *der* name day

namentlich 1 *Adj.* by name *postpos.;*
2 *adv.* by name
3 *Adv.* (besonders) particularly

namhaft *Adj.* **(a)** (berühmt) noted **(b)** (ansehnlich) noteworthy ‹*sum, difference*›; notable ‹*contribution, opportunity*›

nämlich *Adv.* **(a) er kann nicht kommen, er ist ~ krank** he cannot come, as he is ill **(b)** (und zwar) namely

nannte *1. u. 3. Pers. Sg. Prät. v.* NENNEN

nanu *Interj.* **~, was machst du denn hier?** hello, what are you doing here?; **~, Sie gehen schon?** what, you're going already?

Napf *der;* **~[e]s, Näpfe** bowl (esp. for animal's food)

Narbe *die;* **~, ~n** scar

narbig *Adj.* scarred

Narkose *die;* **~, ~n** (Med.) narcosis

narkotisieren *tr. V.* (Med.) anaesthetize ‹*patient*›; put ‹*patient*› under a general anaesthetic

Narr *der;* **~en, ~en** fool

Narren·freiheit *die* freedom to do as one pleases

Närrin *die;* **~, ~nen** fool

närrisch 1 *Adj.* crazy; carnival-crazy ‹*season*›
2 *adv.* crazily

Narzisse *die;* **~, ~n** narcissus

naschen 1 *itr. V.* (Süßes essen) eat sweet things; (heimlich essen) have a nibble
2 *tr. V.* eat ‹*sweets, chocolate, etc.*›; **er hat Milch genascht** he has been at the milk

Nascherei *die;* **~, ~en (a)** [continually] eating sweet things; **hör auf mit der ~!** don't keep eating sweet things all the time! **(b)** (Süßigkeit) **~en** sweets

naschhaft *Adj.* sweet-toothed; **~ sein** have a sweet tooth

Nase *die;* **~, ~n** nose; **die ~ voll haben** (ugs.) have had enough

Nasen-: ~bluten *das;* **~~s** bleeding from the nose; **~loch** *das* nostril; **~spitze** *die* tip of the/one's nose; **jmdm. etw. an der ~spitze ansehen** (fig. ugs.) tell sth. by sb.'s face; **~tropfen** *Pl.* nose drops; **~wurzel** *die* root of the nose

nase-: ~rümpfend 1 *Adj.* disapproving
2 *adv.* disdainfully; **~weis** 1 *Adj.* precocious; pert ‹*remark, reply*›; 2 *adv.* precociously

Nas·horn *das* rhinoceros

nass, *naß; **nasser** *od.* **nässer, nassest...** *od.* **nässest...**: *Adj.* wet; **sich/das Bett ~ machen** wet oneself/one's bed

Nässe *die;* ~: wetness

nass·kalt, *naß·kalt *Adj.* cold and wet

Nass·rasur, *Naß·rasur *die* wet shaving *no art.*

Nation *die;* **~, ~en** nation

national 1 *Adj.* national
2 *adv.* nationally

National-: ~elf *die* (Fußball) national side; **~hymne** *die* national anthem

Nationalisierung *die;* **~, ~en** nationalization

Nationalismus *der;* ~: nationalism *usu. no art.*

nationalistisch 1 *Adj.* nationalist; nationalistic
2 *adv.* nationalistically

Nationalität *die;* **~, ~en** nationality

national,- National-: ~mannschaft *die* national team; **~sozialismus** *der* National Socialism; **~sozialist** *der,* **~sozialistin** *die* National Socialist; **~sozialistisch** *Adj.* National Socialist; **~spieler** *der,* **~spielerin** *die* (Sport) national player; international; **~staat** *der* nation state; **~stolz** *der* national pride; **~versammlung** *die* National Assembly

NATO, Nato *die;* ~: NATO, Nato *no art.*

Natron *das;* **~s [doppeltkohlensaures] ~:** sodium bicarbonate; **[kohlensaures] ~:** sodium carbonate

Natter *die;* **~, ~n** colubrid

Natur *die;* **~, ~en** nature; **die freie ~:** [the] open countryside

Naturalien /natu'ra:li̯ən/ *Pl.* natural produce *sing.* (*used as payment*); **in ~** (*Dat.*) **bezahlen** pay in kind

Naturalismus *der;* ~: naturalism

naturalistisch 1 *Adj.* naturalistic
2 *adv.* naturalistically

Naturell *das;* **~s, ~e** temperament

natur-, Natur-: ~erscheinung *die* natural phenomenon; **~farben** *Adj.* natural-coloured; **~freund** *der,* **~freundin** *die* nature lover; **~gemäß** *Adv.* naturally; **~geschichte** *die* natural history; **~gesetz** *das* law of nature; **~getreu** 1 *Adj.* lifelike ‹*portrait, imitation*›; faithful ‹*reproduction*›; 2 *adv.* ‹*draw*› true to life; ‹*reproduce*› faithfully; **~heilkunde** *die* naturopathy *no art.;* **~katastrophe** *die* natural disaster

natürlich 1 *Adj.* natural
2 *adv.* ‹*laugh, behave*› naturally
3 *Adv.* **(a)** (selbstverständlich, wie erwartet) naturally; of course
(b) (zwar) of course

Natürlichkeit *die;* ~: naturalness

natur-, Natur-: ~park *der* ≈ national park; **~produkt** *das* natural product; **~schutz** *der* [nature] conservation; **unter ~schutz** (*Dat.*) **stehen** be protected by law; be a protected species/variety/area *etc.*; **~schutz·gebiet** *das* nature reserve; **~talent** *das* [great] natural talent *or* gift; (begabter Mensch) naturally talented *or* gifted person; **~verbunden** *Adj.* ‹*person*› in tune with nature; **~volk** *das* primitive people; **~wissenschaft** *die* natural science *no art.*; **~wissenschaftler** *der*, **~wissenschaftlerin** *die* [natural] scientist; **~wissenschaftlich** [1] *Adj.* scientific; [2] *adv.* scientifically; **~wunder** *das* miracle *or* wonder of nature

Navigation *die;* ~: navigation *no art.*

navigieren *tr., itr. V.* navigate

n. Chr. *Abk.* = **nach Christus** AD

Neandertaler *der;* **~s, ~**: Neanderthal man

Nebel *der;* **~s, ~**: fog; (weniger dicht) mist

nebelig ▶ NEBLIG

Nebel-: ~scheinwerfer *der* fog lamp; **~schluss·leuchte**, ***~schluß·leuchte** *die* rear fog lamp; **~schwaden** *Pl.* swathes of mist; **~wand** *die* wall of fog

neben [1] *Präp. mit Dat.* **(a)** (Lage) next to; beside
(b) (außer) apart from; aside from (Amer.)
(c) (verglichen mit) beside
[2] *Präp. mit Akk.* (Richtung) next to; beside

neben-, Neben-: ~an *Adv.* next door; **~bei** *Adv.* **(a)** ‹*work*› on the side; (zusätzlich) as well; **(b)** (beiläufig) ‹*remark, ask*› by the way; ‹*mention*› in passing; **~beruf** *der* second job; sideline; **~beruflich** [1] *Adj.* **eine ~berufliche Tätigkeit** a second job; [2] *adv.* on the side; **er arbeitet ~beruflich als Übersetzer** he translates as a sideline; **~beschäftigung** *die* second job; sideline; **~buhler** *der*, **~buhlerin** *die* rival

neben·einander *Adv.* **(a)** next to each other; ‹*be sitting, standing*› next to one another, side by side; (fig.: zusammen) ‹*live, exist*› side by side; **~ wohnen** live next door to each other; **~ legen** (+ *Akk.*) lay *or* place ‹*objects*› next to each other *or* side by side
(b) (gleichzeitig) together

***nebeneinander|legen** *usw.* ▶ NEBENEINANDER A

Neben-: ~erwerb *der* secondary occupation; **~fach** *das* subsidiary subject; minor (Amer.); **~fluss**, ***~fluß** *der* tributary; **~gebäude** *das* **(a)** annexe; outbuilding **(b)** (Nachbargebäude) neighbouring building; **~geräusch** *das* background noise; **~haus** *das* house next door

neben·her *Adv.* ▶ NEBENBEI

nebenher-: ~|fahren *unr. itr. V.; mit sein* drive/ride alongside; **~|gehen** *unr. itr. V.; mit sein* walk alongside

neben-, Neben-: ~höhle *die* (Anat.) paranasal sinus; **~kläger** *der*, **~klägerin** *die* (Rechtsw.) accessory prosecutor; **~kosten** *Pl.* **(a)** additional costs; **(b)** (bei Mieten) heating, lighting, and services; **~produkt** *das* by-product; **~rolle** *die* supporting role; **~sache** *die* minor matter; **~sachen** inessentials; **~sächlich** *Adj.* of minor importance *postpos.*; unimportant; minor ‹*detail*›; **~sächlichkeit** *die;* **~~, ~~en** (Unwichtiges) matter of minor importance; unimportant matter; **~satz** *der* (Sprachw.) subordinate clause; **~stelle** *die* extension; **~straße** *die* side street; **~tätigkeit** *die* second job; sideline; **~tisch** *der* next table; **~verdienst** *der* additional income; **~wirkung** *die* side effect; **~zimmer** *das* next room

neblig *Adj.* foggy; (weniger dicht) misty

Necessaire /nesɛˈsɛːɐ̯/ *das;* **~s, ~s** sponge bag (Brit.); toilet bag (Amer.)

necken *tr. V.* tease

Neckerei *die;* ~: teasing

nee (ugs.) no; nope (Amer. coll.)

Neffe *der;* **~n, ~n** nephew

negativ [1] *Adj.* negative
[2] *adv.* ‹*answer*› in the negative

Negativ *das;* **~s, ~e** (Fot.) negative

Neger *der;* **~s, ~**: Negro

Negerin *die;* **~, ~nen** Negress

nehmen *unr. tr. V.* take; **sich** (*Dat.*) **etw. ~**: take sth.; (sich bedienen) help oneself to sth.; **auf sich** (*Akk.*) **~**: take on ‹*responsibility, burden*›; **jmdm./einer Sache etw. ~**: deprive sb./sth. of sth.; **was nehmen Sie dafür?** how much do you charge for it?

Neid *der;* **~[e]s** envy; jealousy

neiden *tr. V.* (geh.) **jmdm. etw. ~**: envy sb. [for] sth.

Neid·hammel *der* (salopp abwertend) envious sod (sl.)

neidisch [1] *Adj.* envious
[2] *adv.* enviously

neigen [1] *tr. V.* tip; tilt; incline ‹*head, upper part of body*›
[2] *refl. V.:* ‹*person*› lean; ‹*ship*› heel over, list; ‹*scales*› tip
[3] *itr. V.* **(a) zu Erkältungen/Krankheiten ~**: be prone to colds/illnesses
(b) (tendieren) tend

Neigung *die;* **~, ~en** **(a)** (Vorliebe) inclination
(b) (Tendenz) tendency

nein *Interj.* no

Nein *das;* **~[s], ~[s]** no

Nein·stimme *die* no-vote

Nektar *der;* **~s, ~e** (Bot.) nectar

Nektarine *die;* **~, ~n** nectarine

*alte Schreibung - vgl. Hinweis auf S. xiv

Nelke *die;* **~, ~n (a)** pink; (Dianthus caryophyllus) carnation
(b) (Gewürz) clove

nennen [1] *unr. tr. V.* **(a)** call
(b) (angeben) give ‹*name, date of birth, address, reason, price, etc.*›
(c) (anführen) give ‹*example*›; (erwähnen) mention ‹*person, name*›
[2] *unr. refl. V.* ‹*person, thing*› be called

nennens·wert *Adj.* considerable ‹*influence, changes, delays, damage*›; **kaum ~e Veränderungen** changes scarcely worth mentioning

Nenner *der;* **~s, ~** (Math.) denominator

neo-, **Neo-** neo-

neo-: ~konservativ *Adj.* neo-conservative; neo-con (coll.), **~liberal** *Adj.* neo-liberal

Neon *das;* **~s** neon

Neon-: ~licht *das* neon light; **~röhre** *die* neon tube

Nepal (*das*); **~s** Nepal

Nepp *der;* **~s** (ugs. abwertend) daylight robbery *no art.*; rip-off (coll.)

neppen *tr. V.* (ugs. abwertend) rook; rip ‹*tourist, customer, etc.*› off (sl.)

Nepper *der;* **~s, ~**, **Nepperin** *die;* **~, ~nen** (ugs.) shark; rip-off merchant (coll.)

Nepp·lokal *das* (ugs.) clip joint (coll.)

Nerv *der;* **~s, ~en** nerve; **die ~en verlieren** lose control [of oneself]; **jmdm. auf die ~en gehen** *od.* **fallen** get on sb.'s nerves

nerven (salopp) [1] *tr. V.* **jmdn. ~:** get on sb.'s nerves
[2] *itr. V.* be wearing on the nerves

nerven-, Nerven-: ~aufreibend *Adj.* nerve-racking; **~bündel** *das* (ugs.) bundle of nerves (coll.); **~gift** *das* neurotoxin; **~heil·anstalt** *die* (veralt.) psychiatric hospital; **~krank** *Adj.* ‹*person*› suffering from a nervous disease; **~probe** *die* mental trial; **~säge** *die* (salopp) pain in the neck (coll.); **~zusammen·bruch** *der* nervous breakdown

nervig *Adj.* (auch fig.) sinewy

nervlich *Adj.* nervous ‹*strain*›

nervös [1] *Adj.* (auch Med.) nervous; jittery ‹*person*›
[2] *adv.* nervously

Nervosität *die;* **~** nervousness

nerv·tötend *Adj.* nerve-racking ‹*wait*›; soul-destroying ‹*activity, work*›

Nerz *der;* **~es, ~e** mink

Nerz·mantel *der* mink coat

Nessel *die;* **~, ~n** nettle

Nest *das;* **~[e]s, ~er (a)** nest
(b) (fam.: Bett) bed
(c) (ugs. abwertend: kleiner Ort) little place

nett [1] *Adj.* nice; (freundlich) kind
[2] *adv.* nicely; (freundlich) nicely; kindly

netter·weise *Adv.* kindly

netto *Adv.* ‹*weigh, earn, etc.*› net

Netto-: ~einkommen *das* net income; **~gehalt** *das* net salary; **~preis** *der* net price

Netz *das;* **~es, ~e (a)** net; (Einkaufs~) string bag; (Gepäck~) [luggage] rack
(b) (Spinnen~) web
(c) (Netzwerk) network; (für Strom, Wasser, Gas) mains *pl.*

Netz-: ~haut *die* (Anat.) retina; **~werk** *das* (auch Elektrot.) network

neu [1] *Adj.* new; **die ~este Mode** the latest fashion; **das ist mir ~:** that is news to me; **der/die Neue** the new man/woman/boy/girl
[2] *adv.* **(a) ~ tapeziert/gestrichen** repapered/repainted; **sich ~ einrichten** refurnish one's home
(b) (gerade erst) **diese Ware ist ~ eingetroffen** this item has just come in; **~ eröffnet** newly-opened; (wieder eröffnet) reopened

neu·artig *Adj.* new; **~e Lebensmittel** novel foods

Neu·artigkeit *die;* **~~:** novelty

neu-, Neu-: ~bau *der; Pl.* **~~ten** new house/building; **~bau·wohnung** *die* flat (Brit.) *or* (Amer.) apartment in a new block/house; **~beginn** *der* new beginning

neuerdings *Adv.* **er trägt ~ eine Brille** he has recently started wearing glasses

***neu·eröffnet** ▶ NEU 2B

Neu·eröffnung *die* **(a)** opening
(b) (Wiedereröffnung) reopening

Neuerung *die;* **~, ~en** innovation

neu·geboren *Adj.* newborn

Neu·gier, Neugierde *die;* **~:** curiosity; (Wissbegierde) inquisitiveness

neu·gierig [1] *Adj.* curious; inquisitive; inquisitive ‹*person*›; **ich bin ~, was er dazu sagt** I'm curious to know what he'll say about it
[2] *adv.* ‹*ask*› inquisitively; ‹*peer*› nosily (coll. derog.)

Neuheit *die;* **~, ~en (a)** novelty
(b) (Neues) new product/gadget/article *etc.*

Neuigkeit *die;* **~, ~en** piece of news; **~en** news *sing.*

Neu: ~jahr *das* New Year's Day; **~land** *das* (fig.) new ground

neulich *Adv.* recently; **~ morgens** the other morning

Neuling *der;* **~s, ~e** newcomer; (auf einem Gebiet) novice

Neu·mond *der* new moon

neun *Kardinalz.* nine

Neun *die;* **~, ~en** nine

neun-: ~hundert *Kardinalz.* nine hundred; **~jährig** *Adj.* (9 Jahre alt) nine-year-old *attrib.;* (9 Jahre dauernd) nine-year *attrib.;* **~mal** *Adv.* nine times

neunt... *Ordinalz.* ninth

neun·tausend *Kardinalz.* nine thousand

Neuntel *das* (schweiz. meist *der*); **~s, ~:** ninth

neuntens *Adv.* ninthly
neun·zehn *Kardinalz.* nineteen
neunzig *Kardinalz.* ninety
neunziger *indekl. Adj.* **die ~ Jahre** the nineties
neunzigst... *Ordinalz.* ninetieth
neuralgisch *Adj.* (Med.) neuralgic
neu·reich *Adj.* nouveau riche
Neurodermitis *die; ~,* **Neurodermitiden** (Med.) neurodermatitis
Neurologe *der; ~n, ~n* neurologist
Neurologie *die; ~:* neurology
Neurologin *die; ~, ~nen* neurologist
neurologisch *Adj.* neurological
Neurose *die; ~, ~n* (Med., Psych.) neurosis
Neurotiker *der; ~s, ~,* **Neurotikerin** *die; ~, ~nen* (Med., Psych., auch ugs.) neurotic
neurotisch *Adj.* (Med., Psych., auch ugs.) neurotic
Neu·see·land *(das); ~s* New Zealand
Neuseeländer *der; ~s, ~,* **Neuseeländerin** *die; ~, ~nen* New Zealander
neutral [1] *Adj.* neutral [2] *adv.* **sich ~ verhalten** remain neutral
Neutralität *die; ~, ~en* neutrality
Neutron *das; ~s, ~en* neutron
Neutrum *das; ~s,* **Neutra** (österr. nur so) *od.* **Neutren** (Sprachw.) neuter
neu-, Neu-: ~wert *der* value when new; **~wertig** *Adj.* as new; **~zeit** *die* modern age; **~zeitlich** *Adj.* modern
nicht *Adv.* not; **~!** [no,] don't!; **~ rostend** non-rusting ‹*blade*›; stainless ‹*steel*›; **~ [wahr]?** isn't it/he/she *etc.;* don't you/we/they *etc.;* **du magst das, ~ [wahr]?** you like that, don't you?; **was du ~ sagst!** you don't say!
nicht-, Nicht- non-
Nicht·angriffs·pakt *der* nonaggression pact
Nichte *die; ~, ~n* niece
nichtig *Adj.* **(a)** (geh.) vain ‹*things, pleasures, etc.*›; trivial ‹*reason*› **(b)** (Rechtsspr.) void
Nicht·raucher *der* non-smoker; **„~raucher“** 'no smoking'
***nicht·rostend** ▶ NICHT
nichts *Indefinitpron.* nothing; **ich möchte ~:** I don't want anything; **~ sagend** (fig.) empty; (ausdruckslos) expressionless ‹*face*›
nichts·desto·weniger *Adv.* nevertheless; none the less
nichts-, Nichts-: ~nutz *der; ~~es, ~~e* (veralt.) good-for-nothing; **~nutzig** *Adj.* (veralt.) good-for-nothing *attrib.;* worthless ‹*existence*›; ***~sagend** ▶ NICHTS; **~tun** *das* idleness *no art.*
Nicht·wähler *der,* **Nicht·wählerin** *die* non-voter; abstainer

*old spelling - see note on page xiv

Nickel *das; ~s* nickel
nicken *itr. V.* nod
nie *Adv.* never
nieder [1] *Adj.; nicht präd.* lower ‹*class, intelligence*›; minor ‹*official*›; lowly ‹*family, origins, birth*›; menial ‹*task*› [2] *Adv.* down
nieder-, Nieder-: ~gang *der* fall; decline; **~|gehen** *unr. itr. V.; mit sein* ‹*plane etc., rain, avalanche*› come down; **~geschlagen** *Adj.* dejected; **~geschlagenheit** *die; ~:* dejection; **~lage** *die* defeat
Nieder·lande *Pl.:* **die ~:** the Netherlands
Niederländer *der; ~s, ~:* Dutchman
Niederländerin *die; ~, ~nen* Dutchwoman
niederländisch *Adj.* Dutch; Netherlands *attrib.* ‹*government, embassy, etc.*›
nieder-, Nieder-: ~|lassen *unr. refl. V.* **(a)** set up in business; ‹*doctor, lawyer*› set up in practice; **(b)** (seinen Wohnsitz nehmen) settle; **~lassung** *die; ~~, ~~en* (Wirtsch.) branch; **~|legen** *tr. V.* **(a)** (geh.: hinlegen) lay *or* put down; lay ‹*wreath*›; **(b)** (fig.) resign [from] ‹*office*›; relinquish ‹*command*›
Nieder·sachsen *(das)* Lower Saxony
nieder-, Nieder-: ~schlag *der* precipitation; **~|schlagen** *unr. tr. V.* **(a) jmdn. ~schlagen** knock sb. down; **(b)** (beenden) suppress, put down ‹*revolt, uprising, etc.*›; **(c)** (senken) lower ‹*eyes, eyelids*›; **~schmetternd** *Adj.* shattering ‹*experience, news*›; devastating ‹*result, review*›; **~trächtig** [1] *Adj.* malicious ‹*person, slander, lie, etc.*›; (verachtenswert) despicable ‹*person*›; base ‹*misrepresentation, slander, lie*›; [2] *adv.* ‹*betray, lie, treat*› in a despicable way; **~trächtigkeit** *die; ~~, ~~en* **(a)** ▶ ~TRÄCHTIG 1: maliciousness; despicableness; baseness; **(b)** (gemeine Handlung) despicable act
Niederung *die; ~, ~en* low-lying area; (an Flussläufen, Küsten) flats *pl.;* (Tal) valley
niedlich [1] *Adj.* sweet; cute (Amer. coll.) [2] *adv.* sweetly
niedrig [1] *Adj.* low; lowly ‹*origins, birth*›; base ‹*instinct, desire, emotion*›; vile ‹*motive*› [2] *adv.* ‹*hang, fly*› low
Niedrig-: ~lohn·land *das* country with a low-wage country; **~wasser** *das* **(a)** (von Seen/Flüssen) **bei ~wasser** when the [level of the] lake/river is low; **(b)** (bei Ebbe) low tide; low water; **bei ~wasser** at low tide *or* low water
niemals *Adv.* never
niemand *Indefinitpron.* nobody; no one
Niemands·land *das* (auch fig.) no man's land
Niere *die; ~, ~n* kidney
Nieren-: ~entzündung *die* nephritis; **~stein** *der* kidney stone
nieseln *unpers. itr. V.* drizzle

Niesel·regen *der* drizzle
niesen *itr. V.* sneeze
Niete¹ *die;* ~, ~**n** **(a)** (Los) blank
(b) (ugs.: Mensch) dead loss (coll.) (**in** + *Dat.* at)
Niete² *die;* ~, ~**n** rivet
nieten *tr. V.* rivet
niet- und nagelfest: **[alles] was nicht ~ ist** (ugs.) [everything] that's not nailed *or* screwed down
Nikolaus /ˈnɪkolaʊs/ *der;* ~, ~**e** (ugs.) **Nikoläuse** **(a)** St Nicholas
(b) (Tag) St Nicholas' Day
Nikotin *das;* ~**s** nicotine
nikotin·arm *Adj.* low-nicotine *attrib.;* low in nicotine *pred.*
Nikotin·sucht *die* nicotine addiction
Nil *der;* ~**[s]** Nile
Nil·pferd *das* hippopotamus
nimm *Imperativ Sg. v.* NEHMEN
nippen *itr. V.* sip
nirgends, nirgend·wo *Adv.* nowhere
Nische *die;* ~, ~**n** niche; (Erweiterung eines Raumes) recess
nisten *itr. V.* nest
Nitrat *das;* ~**[e]s**, ~**e** nitrate
Niveau /niˈvoː/ *das;* ~**s**, ~**s** level; (Qualitäts~) standard
Nixe *die;* ~, ~**n** nixie; (mit Fischschwanz) mermaid
nobel *Adj.* **(a)** (geh.) noble; noble[-minded] ‹*person*›
(b) (oft spött.: luxuriös) elegant; posh (coll.)
Nobel·preis *der* Nobel prize
noch [1] *Adv.* **(a)** ([wie] bisher) still; **~ nicht** not yet; **sie sind immer ~ nicht da** they're still not here; **ich habe Großvater ~ gekannt** I'm old enough to have known grandfather; **er hat ~ Glück gehabt** he was lucky; **das geht ~**: that's [still] all right
(b) (als Rest einer Menge) **ich habe [nur] ~ zehn Euro** I've [only] ten euros left; **es sind ~ 10 km bis zur Grenze** it's another 10 km. to the border
(c) (bevor etw. anderes geschieht) just; **ich will ~ [schnell] duschen** I just want to have a [quick] shower
(d) (irgendwann einmal) some time; one day; **er wird ~ anrufen/kommen** he will still call/come
(e) (womöglich) if you're/he's *etc.* not careful; **du kommst ~ zu spät!** you'll be late if you're not careful
(f) (drückt eine geringe zeitliche Distanz aus) only; **gestern habe ich ihn ~ gesehen** I saw him only yesterday
(g) (nicht später als) **~ am selben Abend** the [very] same evening
(h) (außerdem, zusätzlich) **wer war ~ da?** who else was there?; **~ etwas Kaffee?** [would you like] some more coffee?; **Geld/Kleider** *usw.* **~ und ~** heaps and heaps of money/clothes *etc.* (coll.)
(i) **er ist ~ größer [als Karl]** he is even taller [than Karl]; **er will ~ mehr haben** he wants even more; **jeder ~ so dumme Mensch versteht das** anyone, however stupid, can understand that
(j) **wie heißt sie [doch] ~?** [now] what's her name again?
[2] *Partikel* **das ist ~ Qualität!** that's what I call quality; **der wird sich ~ wundern** (ugs.) he's in for a surprise; **er kann ~ nicht einmal lesen** he can't even read
[3] *Konj.* (und auch nicht) nor; **weder ... noch** neither ... nor
noch·mals *Adv.* again
Nominativ *der;* ~**s**, ~**e** (Sprachw.) nominative [case]
nominieren *tr. V.* nominate
Nominierung *die;* ~, ~**en** nomination
Nonne *die;* ~, ~**n** nun
Nord (bes. Seemannsspr., Met.) ▶ NORDEN
nord-, Nord-: ~**afrika** (*das*) North Africa; ~**amerika** (*das*) North America; ~**deutsch** *Adj.* North German
Norden *der;* ~**s** north; **der ~**: the North; **nach ~**: northwards
Nord·irland (*das*) Northern Ireland
nordisch *Adj.* Nordic
Nord·kap *das* North Cape
nördlich [1] *Adj.* **(a)** (im Norden gelegen) northern
(b) (nach, aus dem Norden) northerly
(c) (aus dem Norden kommend, für den Norden typisch) Northern
[2] *adv.* northwards; **~ von ...**: [to the] north of ...
[3] *Präp. mit Gen.* [to the] north of
Nord-: ~**licht** *das* northern lights *pl.;* aurora borealis; **ein ~licht/~lichter** the northern lights; ~**pol** *der* North Pole
Nordrhein-Westfalen (*das*); ~**s** North Rhine-Westphalia
Nord·see *die;* ~: North Sea
nord·wärts *Adv.* northwards
Nord·wind *der* northerly wind
Nörgelei *die;* ~ (abwertend) grumbling
nörgeln *itr. V.* (abwertend) moan, grumble (**an** + *Dat.* about)
Norm *die;* ~, ~**en** **(a)** norm
(b) (geforderte Arbeitsleistung) quota
(c) (Sport) qualifying standard
(d) (technische, industrielle ~) standard
normal [1] *Adj.* normal
[2] *adv.* normally
Normal·benzin *das* ≈ two-star petrol (Brit.); regular (Amer.)
normalerweise *Adv.* normally
normalisieren [1] *tr. V.* normalize
[2] *refl. V.* return to normal
Normalität *die;* ~: normality *no def. art.*
Normal·zustand *der* normal state
Normandie *die;* ~: Normandy
normen *tr. V.*, **normieren** *tr. V.* standardize

Norwegen *(das);* **~s** Norway
Norweger *der;* **~s, ~, Norwegerin** *die;* **~, ~nen** Norwegian
norwegisch *Adj.* Norwegian
Nostalgie *die;* **~:** nostalgia
Not *die;* **~, Nöte (a)** (Gefahr) **in ~ sein** be in desperate straits
(b) (Mangel, Armut) need; poverty [and hardship]; **~ leiden** suffer poverty [and hardship]; **in ~ geraten/sein** encounter hard times/be suffering want [and deprivation]
(c) (Verzweiflung) distress
(d) (Sorge, Mühe) trouble; **mit knapper ~:** by the skin of one's teeth
(e) (veralt.: Notwendigkeit) necessity; **zur ~:** if need be
Notar *der;* **~s, ~e** notary
Notariat *das;* **~[e]s, ~e (a)** (Amt) notaryship
(b) (Kanzlei) notary's office
not-, Not-: ~arzt *der* doctor on [emergency] call; **~aufnahme** *die* casualty department; casualty *no art.;* **~ausgang** *der* emergency exit; **~bremse** *die* emergency brake; **~dienst** *der* ▶ BEREITSCHAFTSDIENST; **~durft** *die;* **~** (geh.) **seine [große/kleine] ~durft verrichten** relieve oneself; **~dürftig** [1] *Adj.* makeshift ‹*shelter, repair*›; scanty ‹*cover, clothing*›;
[2] *adv.* scantily ‹*clothed*›
Note *die;* **~, ~n (a)** (Zeichen) note
(b) *Pl.* (Text) music *sing.;*
(c) (Schul~) mark
(d) (Eislauf, Turnen) score
Notebook /'noʊtbʊk/ *das;* **~s, ~s** (DV) notebook [computer]
not-, Not-: ~fall *der* **(a)** emergency; **(b) im ~fall** (nötigenfalls) if need be; **~falls** *Adv.* if need be; **~gedrungen** *Adv.* of necessity
notieren [1] *tr. V.* **[sich** *(Dat.)***] etw. ~:** make a note of sth.
[2] *itr. V.* (Börsenw., Wirtsch.) be quoted **(mit** at)
Notierung *die;* **~, ~en** (Börsenw., Wirtsch.) quotation; (Preis) quoted [price] **(für** of); (von Devisen) rate **(für** for)
nötig [1] *Adj.* necessary; **etw./jmdn. ~ haben** need sth./sb.
[2] *adv.* **er braucht ~ Hilfe** he is in urgent need of help
nötigen *tr. V.* compel; force; (Rechtsspr.) coerce
Nötigung *die;* **~, ~en** (bes. Rechtsspr.) intimidation; coercion
Notiz *die;* **~, ~en** note; (Zeitungs~) brief report; **von jmdm./etw. [keine] ~ nehmen** take [no] notice of sb./sth.
Notiz-: ~block *der; Pl.* **~blocks,** *schweiz.:* **~blöcke** notepad; **~buch** *das* notebook
not-, Not-: ~lage *die* serious difficulties *pl.;* **~landen** *itr. V.; mit sein;* **ich notlande, notgelandet, notzulanden** do an emergency landing; **~landung** *die* emergency landing; **~leidend** *Adj.* needy; **~lösung** *die* stopgap; **~lüge** *die* evasive lie; (aus Rücksichtnahme) white lie
notorisch [1] *Adj.* notorious
[2] *adv.* notoriously
Not-: ~ruf *der* **(a)** (Hilferuf) emergency call; (eines Schiffes) Mayday call; **(b)** (Nummer) emergency number; **~ruf·nummer** *die* emergency number; **~ruf·säule** *die* emergency telephone (mounted in a pillar); **~stand** *der* crisis; (Staatsrecht) state of emergency; **~unterkunft** *die* emergency accommodation *no pl., no indef. art.;* **~wehr** *die* self-defence
not·wendig *Adj.* necessary
Notwendigkeit *die;* **~, ~en** necessity
Not·zucht *die* (Rechtsw. veralt.) rape; **~ [an jmdm.] begehen** *od.* **verüben** commit rape [on sb.]
Novelle *die;* **~, ~n** (Literaturw.) novella
November *der;* **~[s], ~:** November
Novität *die;* **~, ~en** novelty; (neue Erfindung) innovation; (neue Schallplatte) new release; (neues Buch) new publication
Nr. *Abk.* = **Nummer** No
Nu *der:* **im Nu** in no time
Nuance /'nyã:sə/ *die;* **~, ~n** nuance; (Grad) shade
nüchtern [1] *Adj.* (nicht betrunken; realistisch) sober; (ungeschminkt) bare, plain ‹*fact*›; **der Patient muss ~ sein** the patient's stomach must be empty
[2] *adv.* soberly
Nüchternheit *die;* **~:** sobriety
nuckeln (ugs.) *itr. V.* suck **(an** + *Dat.* at)
Nudel *die;* **~, ~n** piece of spaghetti/vermicelli/tortellini *etc.;* (als Suppeneinlage) noodle; **~n** (Teigwaren) pasta *sing.;* (als Suppeneinlage) noodles
Nugat /'nu:gat/ *der; auch das;* **~s** nougat
nuklear [1] *Adj.* nuclear
[2] *adv.* **~ angetrieben** nuclear-powered
Nuklear-: ~medizin *die* nuclear medicine *no art.;* **~waffe** *die* nuclear weapon
null *Kardinalz.* nought; **~ Komma sechs** [nought] point six; **gegen ~ Uhr** around twelve midnight
Null *die;* **~, ~en (a)** nought; zero; **in ~ Komma nichts** (ugs.) in less than no time; **gleich ~ sein** (fig.) be practically zero; **auf ~ stehen** ‹*indicator, needle, etc.*› be at zero
(b) (ugs.: Versager) failure; dead loss (coll.)
Null-: ~punkt *der* zero; **~summen·spiel** *das* zero-sum game
***numerieren** *tr. V.* number
***Numerierung** *die;* **~, ~en** numbering
Numerus clausus *der;* **~:** *fixed number of students admissible to a university to study a particular subject;* numerus clausus
Nummer *die;* **~, ~n (a)** number; **ein Wagen**

*alte Schreibung - vgl. Hinweis auf S. xiv

mit [einer] Münchner ~: a car with a Munich registration; **ich bin unter der ~ 242679 zu erreichen** I can be reached on 242679
(b) (Ausgabe) issue
(c) (Größe) size

Nummern·schild *das* number plate; license plate (Amer.)

nummerieren *tr. V.* number

Nummerierung *die; ~, ~en* numbering

nun [1] *adv.* now
[2] *Partikel* now; **das hast du ~ davon!** it serves you right!; **kommst du ~ mit oder nicht?** now are you coming or not?; **~ gut** [well,] all right; **~, ~!** now, come on; **~ ja ...:** well, yes ...

nur [1] *adv.* **(a)** (nicht mehr als) only; just
(b) (ausschließlich) only; **nicht ~ ..., sondern auch ...:** not only ..., but also ...; **~ so zum Spaß** just for fun
[2] *Konj.* but; **ich kann dir das Buch leihen, ~ nicht heute** I can lend you the book, only not today
[3] *Partikel* **wenn er ~ hier wäre** if only he were here; **~ zu!** go ahead; **lass dich ~ nicht erwischen** just don't let me/them *etc.* catch you; **was sollen wir ~ tun?** what on earth are we going to do?; **so schnell er ~ konnte** just as fast as he could

Nürnberg *(das); ~s* Nuremberg

nuscheln *tr., itr. V.* (ugs.) mumble

Nuss, *Nuß *die; ~,* **Nüsse** nut

Nuss-, *Nuß-: ~baum, *der* walnut tree; **~knacker** *der* nutcrackers *pl.*; **~schale** *die* nutshell

Nüster *die; ~, ~n* nostril

Nut *die; ~, ~en* (Technik) groove

Nutte *die; ~, ~n* (derb) tart (sl.); hooker (Amer. sl.)

nutz-: ~bar *Adj.* usable; exploitable, utilizable ‹*mineral resources, invention*›; cultivatable ‹*land, soil*›; **~bringend**
[1] *Adj.* useful; (gewinnbringend) profitable
[2] *adv.* profitably

nutzen [1] *tr. V.* **(a)** use; exploit, utilize ‹*natural resources*›; cultivate ‹*land, soil*›; harness ‹*energy source*›; exploit ‹*advantage*›
(b) (be-, ausnutzen) use; make use of
[2] *itr. V.* ▶ NÜTZEN 1

Nutzen *der; ~s* **(a)** benefit; **[jmdm.] von ~ sein** be of use [to sb.]
(b) (Profit) profit

nützen [1] *itr. V.* be of use (*Dat.* to); **nichts ~:** be no use
[2] *tr. V.* ▶ NUTZEN 1

nützlich *Adj.* useful

Nützlichkeit *die; ~:* usefulness

nutzlos [1] *Adj.* useless; (vergeblich) vain *attrib.*; in vain *pred.*;
[2] *adv.* uselessly; (vergeblich) in vain

Nutz·losigkeit *die; ~:* uselessness; (Vergeblichkeit) futility

Nutznießer *der; ~s, ~,* **Nutznießerin** *die; ~, ~nen* beneficiary

Nutzung *die; ~, ~en* use; (des Landes, des Bodens) cultivation; (von Bodenschätzen) exploitation; utilization; (einer Energiequelle) harnessing

Nylon (Wz) /ˈnaiːlɔn/ *das; ~s* nylon

Nymphe *die; ~, ~n* (Myth., Zool.) nymph

Nymphomanin *die; ~, ~nen* (Psych.) nymphomaniac

Oo

o, O *das; ~, ~:* o/O

ö, Ö *das; ~, ~:* o/O umlaut

O *Abk.* = **Ost[en]** E

Oase *die; ~, ~n* (auch fig.) oasis

ob *Konj.* **(a)** whether
(b) und ob! of course!

OB *Abk.* = **Oberbürgermeister[in]**

Obacht *die; ~* (bes. südd.) caution; **~ auf jmdn./etw. geben** take care of sb./sth.; (aufmerksam sein) pay attention to sb./sth.

Obdach *das; ~[e]s* (geh.) shelter

obdach·los *Adj.* homeless

Obdachlose *der/die; adj. Dekl.* homeless person/man/woman; **die ~n** the homeless

Obdachlosen-: ~heim *das* hostel for the homeless; **~siedlung** *die* estate of houses for the homeless

Obdachlosigkeit *die; ~:* homelessness

Obduktion *die; ~, ~en* (Med., Rechtsw.) post mortem [examination]; autopsy

obduzieren *tr. V.* carry out *or* perform a/the postmortem [examination] *or* autopsy on

O-Beine *Pl.* bandy legs; bow legs

oben *Adv.* **(a) hier/dort ~:** up here/there; **weiter ~:** further up; **nach ~:** upwards; **von ~:** from above; **von ~ herab** (fig.) condescendingly
(b) (im Gebäude) upstairs; **nach ~:** upstairs
(c) (am oberen Ende, zum oberen Ende hin) at the top; **nach ~ [hin]** towards the top; **von ~:** from the top; **~ ohne** topless
(d) (an der Oberseite) on top
(e) (in einer Hierarchie, Rangfolge) at the top
(f) ([weiter] vorn im Text) above; **~ genannt** above-mentioned

*oben·genannt ▸ OBEN F
Ober *der;* ~**s**, ~: waiter; **Herr** ~! waiter!
ober... *Adj.* upper *attrib.*; top *attrib.*
Ober-: ~**arm** *der* upper arm; ~**bekleidung** *die* outer clothing; ~**bürgermeister** *der* mayor; ~**fläche** *die* surface; (Flächeninhalt) surface area
oberflächlich [1] *Adj.* superficial [2] *adv.* superficially
Ober·geschoss, *Ober·geschoß *das* upper storey; **im fünften** ~: on the fifth floor (Brit.) *or* (Amer.) the sixth floor
ober·halb [1] *Adv.* above; ~ **von** above [2] *Präp. mit Gen.* above
Ober-: ~**hand** *die* **die** ~**hand [über jmdn./etw.] haben** have the upper hand [over sb./sth.]; **die** ~**hand [über jmdn./etw.] gewinnen/bekommen** gain *or* get the upper hand [over sb./sth.]; ~**haupt** *das* head; (einer Verschwörung) leader; ~**hemd** *das* shirt; ~**kiefer** *der* upper jaw; ~**körper** *der* upper part of the body; ~**lippen·bart** *der* moustache; ~**schenkel** *der* thigh; ~**schicht** *die* (Soziol.) upper class; ~**schule** *die* secondary school; ~**seite** *die* top
oberst... ▸ OBER...
Ober-: ~**stufe** *die* (Schulw.) upper school; ~**teil** *das od. der* top [part]; (eines Bikinis, Anzugs, Kleids usw.) top [half]; ~**wasser** *das* headwater; (fig.) ~**wasser haben** feel in a strong position; ~**wasser bekommen/kriegen** have one's hand strengthened
ob·gleich *Konj.* ▸ OBWOHL
obig *Adj.* above
Objekt *das;* ~**s**, ~**e** object; (Kaufmannsspr.: Immobilie) property
objektiv [1] *Adj.* objective [2] *adv.* objectively
Objektiv *das;* ~**s**, ~**e** lens
Objektivität *die;* ~: objectivity
Obrigkeit *die;* ~, ~**en** authorities *pl.*
ob·schon *Konj.* (geh.) although
Obst *das;* ~**[e]s** fruit
Obst-: ~**baum** *der* fruit tree; ~**garten** *der* orchard; ~**kuchen** *der* fruit flan
Obstler *der;* ~**s**, ~ (bes. südd.) fruit brandy
Obst-: ~**saft** *der* fruit juice; ~**salat** *der* fruit salad; ~**wein** *der* fruit wine
obszön [1] *Adj.* obscene [2] *adv.* obscenely
Obszönität *die;* ~, ~**en** obscenity
ob·wohl *Konj.* although; though
Ochse /ˈɔksə/ *der;* ~**n**, ~**n** **(a)** ox; bullock **(b)** (salopp) numskull (coll.)
Ochsen·schwanz·suppe *die* oxtail soup
od. *Abk.* = **oder**
öde *Adj.* **(a)** deserted; desolate ‹*area, landscape*› **(b)** (unfruchtbar) barren **(c)** (langweilig) tedious; dreary ‹*life, time, existence*›
Öde *die;* ~ ▸ ÖDE A–C: desertedness; desolateness; barrenness; tediousness; dreariness
oder *Konj.* or; (in Fragen) **er ist doch hier,** ~? he is here, isn't he? (zweifelnd) he is here – or isn't he?
Öd·land *das* uncultivated land
Oeuvre /ˈøːvrə/ *das;* ~, ~**s** (geh.) œuvre
OEZ *Abk.* = **osteuropäische Zeit** EET
Ofen *der;* ~**s**, **Öfen** heater; (Kohle~) stove; (Back~) oven; (Brenn~, Trocken~) kiln
Ofen·rohr *das* [stove] flue
offen [1] *Adj.* **(a)** open; ~ **bleiben** stay open; **etw.** ~ **lassen** leave sth. open; ~ **stehen** be open; **ein** ~**es Hemd** a shirt with the collar unfastened; ~ **haben** *od.* **sein** be open; ~**es Licht** a naked light **(b)** (frei) vacant ‹*job, post*› **(c)** (ungewiss, ungeklärt) open ‹*question*›; uncertain ‹*result*›; ~ **bleiben** remain open; ‹*decision*› be left open **(d)** (noch nicht bezahlt) outstanding ‹*bill*› **(e)** (freimütig, aufrichtig) frank [and open] ‹*person*›; frank, candid ‹*look, opinion, reply*› [2] *adv.* openly; ~ **gesagt** frankly; to be frank
offen·bar [1] *Adj.* obvious [2] *adv.* obviously
Offenbarung *die;* ~, ~**en** revelation
***offen|bleiben** ▸ OFFEN 1A, C
Offen·heit *die;* ~ ▸ OFFEN E: frankness [and openness]; candour
offen-: ~**kundig** [1] *Adj.* obvious; [2] *adv.* obviously; *~**|lassen** ▸ OFFEN 1A; ~**sichtlich** [1] *Adj.* obvious; [2] *adv.* obviously
offensiv [1] *Adj.* **(a)** offensive **(b)** (Sport) attacking [2] *adv.* **(a)** offensively **(b)** (Sport) ~ **spielen** play an attacking game
Offensive *die;* ~, ~**n** (auch Sport) offensive
***offen|stehen** ▸ OFFEN 1A
öffentlich [1] *Adj.* public; state *attrib.*, [state-]maintained ‹*school*›; **der** ~**e Dienst** the civil service [2] *adv.* publicly; ‹*perform, appear*› in public
Öffentlichkeit *die;* ~: public
offiziell [1] *Adj.* official [2] *adv.* officially
Offizier *der;* ~**s**, ~**e**, **Offizierin** *die;* ~, ~**nen** officer
öffnen [1] *tr. V.* open; turn on ‹*tap*›; undo ‹*coat, blouse, button, zip*› [2] *itr. V.* **(a)** **[jmdm.]** ~: open the door [to sb.] **(b)** (geöffnet werden) ‹*shop, bank, etc.*› open [3] *refl. V.* open
Öffner *der;* ~**s**, ~: opener
Öffnung *die;* ~, ~**en** opening
Öffnungs·zeiten *Pl.* opening times

*old spelling - see note on page xiv

Offroader /ɔfrəʊdɐ/ *der;* **~s, ~**: offroader
oft *Adv.* **öfter, am öftesten** often; **wie oft soll ich dir noch sagen, dass ...?** how many [more] times do I have to tell you that ...?
öfter *Adv.* now and then
oftmals *Adv.* often; frequently
ohne [1] *Präp. mit Akk.* without; **~ mich!** [you can] count me out!; **~ weiteres** (leicht, einfach) easily; (ohne Einwand) readily [2] *Konj.* **~ zu zögern** without hesitation
ohne·hin *Adv.* anyway
Ohnmacht *die;* **~, ~en (a)** faint; **in ~ fallen** faint **(b)** (Machtlosigkeit) powerlessness; impotence
ohnmächtig [1] *Adj.* **(a)** unconscious; **~ werden** faint; **~ sein** have fainted **(b)** (machtlos) powerless; impotent [2] *adv.* impotently; **~ zusehen** watch helplessly
Ohr *das;* **~[e]s, ~en** ear; **gute/schlechte ~en haben** have good/poor hearing *sing.;* **jmdn. übers ~ hauen** (fig. ugs.) put one over on sb. (coll.)
Öhr *das,* **~[e]s, ~e** eye
ohren-, Ohren-: ~arzt, *der,* **~ärztin,** *die* otologist; ear specialist; **~betäubend** [1] *Adj.* ear-splitting; deafening; deafening ‹*applause*›; [2] *adv.* deafeningly; **~sausen** *das;* **~~s** ringing in the *or* one's ears; tinnitus (Med.); **~schmerz** *der* earache; **~schmerzen haben** have [an] earache *sing.*
ohr-, Ohr-: ~feige *die* box on the ears; **~feigen** *tr. V.* **jmdn. ~feigen** box sb.'s ears; **ich könnte mich ~feigen!** (ugs.) I could kick myself!; **~läppchen** *das* ear lobe; **~ring** *der* earring; **~wurm** *der* **(a)** earwig; **(b)** (ugs.: Melodie) catchy tune; **ein ~wurm sein** be really catchy
okay /o'ke/ (ugs.) *Interj., Adj., adv.* OK (coll.); okay (coll.)
öko-, Öko- eco-
Ökologie *die;* **~**: ecology
ökologisch [1] *Adj.* ecological [2] *adv.* ecologically
ökonomisch [1] *Adj.* **(a)** economic **(b)** (sparsam) economical [2] *adv.* economically
Öko-: ~produkt *das* ecoproduct; environmentally friendly *or* safe product; **~steuer** *die* eco-tax; **~system** *das* ecosystem; **~tourismus** *der* ecotourism
Oktober *der;* **~[s], ~**: October
ökumenisch *Adj.* (christl. Rel.) ecumenical
Öl *das;* **~[e]s, ~e** oil; **in Öl malen** paint in oils
ölen *tr. V.* oil
Öl-: ~embargo *das* oil embargo; **~farbe** *die* **(a)** oil-based paint; **(b)** (zum Malen) oil paint; **~gemälde** *das* oil painting
ölig *Adj.* oily
Olive *die;* **~, ~n** olive
Oliven-: ~baum *der* olive tree; **~öl** *das* olive oil
Öl-: ~ofen *der* oil heater; **~pest** *die* oil pollution *no indef. art.;* **~quelle** *die* oil well; **~sardine** *die* sardine in oil; **eine Dose ~sardinen** a tin of sardines; **~teppich** *der* oil slick; **~wechsel** *der* (bes. Kfz-W.) oil change
Olympiade *die;* **~, ~n** Olympic Games *pl.;* Olympics *pl.*
Olympia-: ~sieger *der,* **~siegerin** *die* Olympic champion; **~stadion** *das* Olympic stadium
olympisch *Adj.* Olympic; **die Olympischen Spiele** the Olympic Games; the Olympics
Oma *die;* **~, ~s** (fam.) granny (coll./child lang.)
Omelett /ɔm(ə)'lɛt/ *das;* **~[e]s, ~e** *od.* **~s** omelette
Omi *die;* **~, ~s** ▶ OMA
Omnibus *der;* **~ses, ~se** omnibus (formal); (Privat- und Reisebus auch) coach
Onanie *die;* **~**: onanism *no art.;* masturbation *no art.*
onanieren *itr. V.* masturbate
Onkel *der;* **~s, ~** *od.* (ugs.) **~s** uncle
online /'ɔnlaɪn/ [1] *Adj.* online; **~ gehen** go online [2] *Adv.* online
Online·shopping *das* online shopping
OP /o:'pe:/ *der;* **~[s], ~[s]** *Abk.* = **Operationssaal**
Opa *der;* **~s, ~s** (fam.) grandad (coll./child lang.)
Opal *der;* **~s, ~e** opal
OPEC /'o:pɛk/ *die;* **~**: *Abk.* OPEC
Oper *die;* **~, ~n** opera; (Opernhaus) Opera; opera house
Operation *die;* **~, ~en** operation
Operations·saal *der* operating theatre (Brit.) *or* room
operativ [1] *Adj.*(Med.) operative [2] *adv.* (Med.) by operative surgery; **etw. ~ entfernen** operate to remove sth.
Operette *die;* **~, ~n** operetta
operieren [1] *tr. V.* operate on ‹*patient*› [2] *itr. V.* operate
Opern·glas *das* opera glass[es *pl.*]
Opfer *das;* **~s, ~ (a)** sacrifice **(b)** (Geschädigter) victim
opfern *tr. V.* (auch fig.) sacrifice; offer up ‹*fruit, produce, etc.*›
Opi *der* **~s, ~s** ▶ OPA
Opium *das;* **~s** opium
opponieren *itr. V.* **gegen jmdn./etw. ~**: oppose sb./sth.
Opposition *die;* **~, ~en** opposition
oppositionell *Adj.* opposition *attrib.* ‹*group, movement, etc.*›; ‹*newspaper, writer, artist, etc.*› opposed to the government
Optik *die;* **~**: optics *sing., no art.*

Optiker *der;* **~s, ~, Optikerin** *die;* **~, ~nen** optician

optimal [1] *Adj.* optimal; optimum *attrib.;* [2] *adv.* **jmdn. ~ beraten** give sb. the best possible advice

optimieren *tr. V.* optimize

Optimierung *die;* **~, ~en** optimization

Optimismus *der;* **~:** optimism

Optimist *der;* **~en, ~en, Optimistin** *die;* **~, ~nen** optimist

optimistisch [1] *Adj.* optimistic [2] *adv.* optimistically

optisch [1] *Adj.* optical; visual ‹*impression*›; **eine ~e Täuschung** an optical illusion [2] *adv.* optically; visually ‹*impressive, effective*›

orange /o'rã:ʒ(ə)/ *indekl. Adj.* orange

Orange *die;* **~, ~n** orange

Orangen-: ~marmelade *die* orange marmalade; **~saft** *der* orange juice

Orchester /ɔr'kɛstɐ/ *das;* **~s, ~:** orchestra

Orden *der;* **~s, ~ (a)** order **(b)** (Ehrenzeichen) decoration

ordentlich [1] *Adj.* **(a)** [neat and] tidy; neat ‹*handwriting, clothes*› **(b)** (anständig) respectable; proper ‹*manners*› **(c)** (planmäßig) ordinary ‹*meeting*›; **~es Mitglied** full member **(d)** (ugs.: richtig) proper; real; **ein ~es Stück Kuchen** a nice big piece of cake **(e)** (ugs.: recht gut) decent ‹*wine, flat, marks, etc.*›; **ganz ~:** pretty good [2] *adv.* **(a)** tidily; neatly; ‹*write*› neatly **(b)** (anständig) properly **(c)** (ugs.: gehörig) **~ feiern** have a real good celebration (coll.) **(d)** (ugs.: recht gut) ‹*ski, speak, etc.*› really well

ordern *tr., itr. V.* (Kaufmannsspr.) order

Ordinal·zahl *die* ordinal [number]

ordinär [1] *Adj.* vulgar [2] *adv.* vulgarly

Ordinate *die;* **~, ~n** (Math.) ordinate

ordnen *tr. V.* arrange; **sein Leben/seine Finanzen ~:** straighten out one's life/put one's finances in order

Ordner *der;* **~s, ~** (Hefter) file

Ordnung *die;* **~, ~en** order; (geregelter Ablauf) routine; **~ halten** keep things tidy; **in ~ sein** (ugs.) be OK (coll.) *or* all right; **hier ist etw. nicht in ~:** there's something wrong here; **sie ist in ~** (ugs.) she's OK (coll.); **in ~!** (ugs.) OK! (coll.); all right!

ordnungs-, Ordnungs-: ~gemäß [1] *Adj.* ‹*conduct etc.*› in accordance with the regulations; [2] *adv.* in accordance with the regulations; **~halber** *Adv.* as a matter of form; **~widrig** (Rechtsw.) [1] *Adj.* ‹*actions, behaviour, etc.*› contravening the regulations; illegal ‹*parking*›; [2] *adv.* **~widrig parken** park illegally; **~widrigkeit** *die* (Rechtsw.) infringement of the regulations; **~zahl** *die* ordinal [number]

Organ *das;* **~s, ~e** organ; (ugs.: Stimme) voice

Organisation *die;* **~, ~en** organization

Organisator *der;* **~s, ~en, Organisatorin** *die;* **~, ~nen** organizer

organisatorisch *Adj.* organizational

organisch [1] *Adj.* organic [2] *adv.* organically

organisieren [1] *tr. V.* organize [2] *itr. V.* **gut ~ können** be a good organizer [3] *refl. V.* organize

Organismus *der;* **~, Organismen** organism

Organist *der;* **~en, ~en, Organistin** *die;* **~, ~nen** organist

Organ·spender *der,* **Organ·spenderin** *die* organ donor

Orgasmus *der;* **~, Orgasmen** orgasm

Orgel *die;* **~, ~n** organ

Orgie /'ɔrgi̯ə/ *die;* **~, ~n** (auch fig.) orgy

Orient /'o:ri̯ɛnt/ *der;* **~s** Middle East and south-western Asia (*including Afghanistan and Nepal*); **der Vordere ~:** the Middle East

orientalisch *Adj.* oriental

orientieren [1] *refl. V.* **(a)** get one's bearings **(b) sich über etw.** (*Akk.*) **~** (fig.) inform oneself about sth. **(c) sich an etw.** (*Dat.*) **~** (fig.) be oriented towards sth.; ‹*policy, advertising*› be geared towards sth. [2] *tr. V.* (unterrichten) inform (**über** + *Akk.* about)

Orientierung *die;* **~ (a) die ~ verlieren** lose one's bearings **(b)** (Unterrichtung) **zu Ihrer ~:** for your information

Orientierungs·sinn *der* sense of direction

original [1] *Adj.* original [2] *adv.* **~ italienischer Espresso** genuine Italian espresso coffee; **etw. ~ übertragen** broadcast sth. live

Original *das;* **~s, ~e** original

Original-: ~fassung *die* original version; **~gemälde** *das* original painting

Originalität *die;* **~:** originality

Original·ton *der; Pl.* **Original·töne** (Film, Ferns.) direct sound; original sound

originell [1] *Adj.* original [2] *adv.* with originality

Orkan *der;* **~[e]s, ~e** hurricane

Ornament *das;* **~[e]s, ~e** ornament

Ort[1] /ɔrt/ *der;* **~[e]s, ~e** place; (Dorf) village; (Stadt) town; **an ~ und Stelle** there and then

Ort[2]**: vor ~** (fig.) on the spot

orthodox *Adj.* orthodox

Orthographie *die;* **~, ~n** orthography

orthographisch [1] *Adj.* orthographic; **~e Fehler** spelling mistakes

*alte Schreibung - vgl. Hinweis auf S. xiv

2 *adv.* orthographically

Orthopäde *der;* **~n, ~n** orthopaedic specialist

orthopädisch 1 *Adj.* orthopaedic 2 *adv.* orthopaedically

örtlich 1 *Adj.* (auch Med.) local 2 *adv.* (auch Med.) locally; **~ betäubt werden** be given a local anaesthetic

Ortschaft *die;* **~, ~en** (Dorf) village; (Stadt) town

Orts-: ~gespräch *das* (Fernspr.) local call; **~name** *der* place name; **~netz·kennzahl** *die* (Fernspr.) dialling code; area code (Amer.)

Öse *die;* **~, ~n** eye

Ossi *der;* **~s, ~s** (salopp) East German

Ost (bes. Seemannsspr., Met.) ▶ OSTEN

ost-, Ost-: ~block *der* Eastern bloc; **~deutsch** *Adj.* Eastern German; (hist.: auf die DDR bezogen) East German; **~deutschland** *(das)* Eastern Germany; (hist.: DDR) East Germany

Osten *der;* **~s** east; **der ~**: the East; **der Ferne ~**: the Far East; **der Nahe ~**: the Middle East

Oster-: ~ei *das* Easter egg; **~glocke** *die* daffodil; **~hase** *der* Easter hare (*said to bring children their Easter Eggs*); **~montag** *der* Easter Monday *no def. art.*

Ostern *das;* **~, ~**: Easter; **Frohe** *od.* **Fröhliche ~**: Happy Easter!; **zu ~**: at Easter

Österreich *(das);* **~s** Austria

Österreicher *der;* **~s, Österreicherin** *die* **~, ~nen** Austrian

österreichisch *Adj.* Austrian

Oster·sonntag *der* Easter Sunday *no def. art.*

Ost·europa *(das)* Eastern Europe

Ostler *der;* **~s, ~, Ostlerin** *die;* **~, ~nen** (ugs.) East German

östlich 1 *Adj.* **(a)** (im Osten gelegen) eastern **(b)** (nach, aus dem Osten) easterly **(c)** (aus dem Osten kommend, für den Osten typisch; Politik) Eastern; ‹*influence, policies*› of the East 2 *adv.* eastwards; **~ von ...**: [to the] east of ... 3 *Präp. mit Gen.* [to the] east of

Ost·see *die;* **~**: Baltic [Sea]

ost·wärts *Adv.* eastwards

Ost·wind *der* easterly wind

Otter¹ *der;* **~s, ~** (Fisch~) otter

Otter² *die;* **~, ~n** (Viper) adder; viper

Otto·motor *der* Otto engine

out /aʊ:t/ *Adj.* **~ sein** (ugs.) be out

Outfit /'aʊ:tfɪt/ *das;* **~[s], ~s** outfit

Ouvertüre /uvɛr'ty:rə/ *die;* **~, ~n** (auch fig.) overture (*Gen.* to)

oval *Adj.* oval

Ovation *die;* **~, ~en** ovation; **jmdm. ~en darbringen** give sb. an ovation

Ozean *der;* **~s, ~e** ocean

Ozean·dampfer *der* ocean liner

Ozon *der od. das;* **~s** ozone

Ozon-: ~alarm *der* ozone alert; **~loch** *das* hole in the ozone layer; **~schicht** *die* ozone layer; **~zerstörung** *die* ozone destruction

Pp

p, P /pe/ *das;* **~, ~**: p/P

paar *indekl. Indefinitpron.* **ein ~ ...**: a few ...; (zwei od. drei) a couple of ...

Paar *das;* **~[e]s, ~e** pair; (Mann und Frau) couple; **ein ~ Würstchen** two sausages

paaren *refl. V.* ‹*animals*› mate; ‹*people*› copulate

Paar·lauf *der* pairs *pl.*

paar·mal *Adv.* **ein ~** a few times; (zwei- oder dreimal) a couple of times

Paarung *die;* **~, ~en** (Zool.) mating

paar·weise *Adv.* in pairs

Pacht *die;* **~, ~en** lease; **etw. in ~ nehmen** lease sth.; **etw. in ~ haben** have sth. on lease; **etw. in ~ geben** lease sth.

pachten *tr. V.* lease

Pächter *der;* **~s, ~, Pächterin** *die;* **~, ~nen** leaseholder; (eines Hofes) tenant

Pacht-: ~vertrag *der* lease; **~zins** *der; Pl.* **~~e** rent

Pack¹ *der;* **~[e]s, ~e** *od.* **Päcke (a)** pack **(b)** ▶ PACKEN

Pack² *das;* **~[e]s** (ugs. abwertend) rabble

Päckchen *das;* **~s, ~ (a)** package; (auch Postw.) small parcel; (Bündel) packet **(b)** ▶ PACKUNG A

packen 1 *tr. V.* **(a)** pack **(b)** (fassen) grab [hold of]; (fig.) **Furcht packte ihn/er wurde von Furcht gepackt** he was seized with fear 2 *itr. V.* (Koffer usw. ~) pack

Packen *der;* **~s, ~**: pile; (zusammengeschnürt) bundle; (von Geldscheinen) wad

packend 1 *Adj.* gripping
2 *adv.* grippingly

Pack·papier *das* [stout] wrapping paper

Packung *die;* ~, **~en** **(a)** packet; pack (esp. Amer.)
(b) (Med., Kosmetik) pack

Pädagoge *der;* **~n, ~n** (Erzieher, Lehrer) teacher; (Wissenschaftler) educationalist

Pädagogik *die;* ~: [theory and methodology of] education

Pädagogin *die;* ~, **~nen** ▶ PÄDAGOGE

pädagogisch 1 *Adj.* educational; **seine ~en Fähigkeiten** his teaching ability *sing.;*
2 *adv.* educationally ‹*sound, wrong*›

Paddel *das;* **~s,** ~: paddle

Paddel·boot *das* canoe

paddeln *itr. V.; mit sein* paddle; (als Sport) canoe

Päderast *der;* **~en, ~en** pederast

pädophil *Adj.* paedophile

Pädophile *der; adj. Dekl.* paedophile

paffen 1 *tr. V.* puff at ‹*pipe etc.*›
2 *itr. V.* puff away

Page /ˈpaːʒə/ *der;* **~n, ~n** bellboy

Paket *das;* **~[e]s, ~e** pile; (zusammengeschnürt) bundle; (Eingepacktes, Post~) parcel; (Packung) packet; pack (esp. Amer.)

Paket-: ~karte *die* parcel dispatch form; **~schalter** *der* parcels counter

Pakistan (*das*); **~s** Pakistan

Pakistaner *der;* **~s,** ~, **Pakistanerin** *die;* ~, **~nen, Pakistani** *der;* **~[s], ~[s]** Pakistani

pakistanisch *Adj.* Pakistani

Pakt *der;* **~[e]s, ~e** pact

paktieren *itr. V.* make *or* do a deal/deals

Palast *der;* **~[e]s, Paläste** palace

Palästina (*das*); **~s** Palestine

Palästinenser *der;* **~s,** ~, **Palästinenserin** *die;* ~, **~nen** Palestinian

palästinensisch *Adj.* Palestinian

Palaver /paˈlaːvɐ/ *das;* **~s,** ~ (ugs. abwertend) palaver

palavern *itr. V.* (ugs. abwertend) palaver

Palette *die;* ~, **~n** **(a)** palette
(b) (bes. Werbespr.: Vielfalt) diverse range; **die ganze ~:** the whole range
(c) (Technik, Wirtsch.: Untersatz) pallet

paletti *Adj.* **alles ~** (ugs.) everything's OK (coll.) *or* all right

Palme *die;* ~, **~n** palm [tree]

Pampelmuse *die;* ~, **~n** grapefruit

Panade *die;* ~, **~n** (Kochk.) breadcrumb coating

Panama (*das*); **~s** Panama

Panama·kanal *der;* **~s** Panama Canal

Panel /ˈpɛnl̩/ *das;* **~s, ~s** panel

Pan·flöte *die* pan pipes *pl.*

panieren *tr. V.* bread; coat ‹*sth.*› with breadcrumbs

Panier·mehl *das* breadcrumbs *pl.*

Panik *die;* ~, **~en** panic

Panik-: ~mache *die;* ~~ (abwertend) panicmongering; **~macher** *der,* **~macherin** *die* (abwertend) panicmonger

Panne *die;* ~, **~n** **(a)** breakdown; (Reifen~) puncture; flat [tyre]
(b) (Missgeschick) mishap

Pannen·dienst *der* breakdown service

Panorama *das;* **~s, Panoramen** panorama

Panter, *Panther *der;* **~s,** ~: panther

Pantoffel *der;* **~s, ~n** backless slipper

Pantomime *die;* ~, **~n** mime

Panzer *der;* **~s,** ~ **(a)** (Milit.) tank
(b) (Zool.) armour *no indef. art.;* (von Schildkröten, Krebsen) shell

Panzer·glas *das* bulletproof glass

panzern *tr. V.* armour[-plate]

Panzer·schrank *der* safe

Papa *der;* **~s, ~s** (ugs.) daddy (coll.)

Papagei *der;* **~en** *od.* **~s, ~e[n]** parrot

Paparazzo *der;* **~s, Paparazzi** paparazzo

Paperback /ˈpeɪpəbæk/ *das;* **~s, ~s** paperback

Papi *der;* **~s, ~s** (ugs.) daddy (coll.)

Papier *das;* **~s, ~e** **(a)** paper
(b) *Pl.* (Ausweis[e]) [identity] papers
(c) (Finanzw.: Wert~) security

Papier-: ~geld *das* paper money; **~korb** *der* waste-paper basket

Pappe *die;* ~, **~n** cardboard

Pappel *die;* ~, **~n** poplar

päppeln *tr. V.* feed up

Papp·karton *der* cardboard box

Paprika *der;* **~s, ~[s]** **(a)** pepper
(b) (Gewürz) paprika

Papst *der;* **~[e]s, Päpste, Päpstin** *die;* ~, **~nen** pope

päpstlich *Adj.* papal

Para *der;* **~s, ~s** para (coll.)

Parabel *die;* ~, **~n** **(a)** (bes. Literaturw.) parable
(b) (Math.) parabola

Parade *die;* ~, **~n** parade

Parade·beispiel *das* perfect example

Paradeiser *der;* **~s,** ~ (österr.) tomato

Paradies *das;* **~es, ~e** paradise

paradiesisch *Adj.* paradisical; (herrlich) heavenly

Paradigma *das;* **~s, Paradigmen** paradigm

paradox *Adj.* paradoxical

Para·gleiten *das;* **~s, Para·gliding** /ˈparaglaɪːdɪŋ/ *das;* **~s** paragliding

Paragraph *der;* **~en, ~en** section; (in Vertrag) clause

parallel 1 *Adj.* parallel
2 *adv.* **~ verlaufen** run parallel (**mit, zu** to)

*old spelling - see note on page xiv

Parallele *die;* ~, ~n parallel
Parallelogramm *das;* ~s, ~e parallelogram
Parallel·straße *die* street running parallel (*Gen.* to)
Para·nuss, ***Para·nuß** *die* Brazil nut
Parasit *der;* ~en, ~en (auch fig.) parasite
parat *Adj.* ready
Pardon /par'dõ/ *der od. das;* ~s pardon; ~! I beg your pardon
Parfum /par'fœ̃:/, **Parfüm** *das;* ~s, ~s perfume
Parfümerie *die;* ~, ~en perfumery
parfümieren *tr. V.* perfume
Pariser [1] *indekl. Adj.* Parisian; Paris *attrib.;*
[2] *der;* ~s, ~ **(a)** (Einwohner) Parisian
(b) (ugs.: Kondom) French letter (coll.)
Pariserin *die;* ~, ~nen Parisian
Parität *die;* ~, ~en parity
Park /park/ *der;* ~s, ~s park; (Schloss~ usw.) grounds *pl.*
Parka *der;* ~s, ~s parka
parken *tr., itr. V.* park; **„Parken verboten!"** 'No Parking'
Parkett *das;* ~[e]s, ~e **(a)** parquet floor
(b) (Theater) [front] stalls *pl.;* parquet (Amer.)
Parkett-: **~[fuß]boden** *der* parquet floor; **~handel** *der* (Börsenw.) floor trading
Park-: **~gebühr** *die* parking fee; **~haus** *das* multi-storey car park
parkieren *tr., itr. V.* (schweiz.) ▸ PARKEN
Park-: **~lücke** *die* parking space; **~platz** *der* car park; parking lot (Amer.); (für ein einzelnes Fahrzeug) parking space; **~scheibe** *die* parking disc; **~schein** *der* car park ticket; **~uhr** *die* parking meter; **~verbot** *das* ban on parking; **im ~verbot stehen** be parked illegally; **~verbots·schild** *das* no-parking sign
Parlament *das;* ~[e]s, ~e parliament
Parlamentarier *der;* ~s, ~, **Parlamentarierin** *die;* ~, ~nen member of parliament
parlamentarisch *Adj.* parliamentary
Parodie *die;* ~, ~n parody (**auf** + *Akk.* of)
Parole *die;* ~, ~n **(a)** (Wahlspruch) motto; (Schlagwort) slogan
(b) (bes. Milit.: Kennwort) password
Partei *die;* ~, ~en **(a)** (Politik, Rechtsw.) party
(b) (Gruppe, Mannschaft) side; **für jmdn. ~ ergreifen** *od.* **nehmen** side with sb.
Partei·gänger *der;* ~~s, ~~, **Partei·gängerin** *die;* ~~, ~~nen (oft abwertend) [loyal] party supporter
parteiisch [1] *Adj.* biased
[2] *adv.* in a biased manner
parteilich [1] *Adj.* (parteiisch) biased
[2] *adv.* in a biased manner
Parteilichkeit *die;* ~ (einseitige Parteinahme) bias; partiality
partei-, Partei-: **~los** *Adj.* (Politik) independent ‹*MP*›; **~lose** *der/die; adj. Dekl.* (Politik) independent; person not attached to a party; **~nahme** *die;* ~~, ~~n partisanship; taking sides *no art.;* **~politik** *die* party politics *sing.;* **~politisch** [1] *Adj.* party political;
[2] *adv.* from a party political point of view; **~tag** *der* party conference *or* (Amer.) convention
Parterre *das;* ~s, ~s ground floor; first floor (Amer.)
Partie *die;* ~, ~n **(a)** part
(b) (Spiel, Sport: Runde) game; (Golf) round
(c) eine gute ~ [für jmdn.] sein be a good match [for sb.]
Partisan *der;* ~s *od.* ~en, ~en, **Partisanin** *die,* ~, ~nen guerrilla; (gegen Besatzungstruppen im Krieg) partisan
Partitur *die;* ~, ~en (Musik) score
Partizip *das;* ~s, ~ien /-'ts:i:pi̯ən/ (Sprachw.) participle
Partner *der;* ~s, ~, **Partnerin** *die;* ~, ~nen partner
Partnerschaft *die;* ~, ~en partnership
partnerschaftlich [1] *Adj.* ‹*cooperation etc.*› on a partnership basis
[2] *adv.* in a spirit of partnership
Partner-: **~schule** *die* partner school; **~stadt** *die* twin town (Brit.); sister city *or* town (Amer.); **~vermittlung** *die* **(a)** matchmaking; **(b)** (Agentur) [introduction and] matchmaking agency; **~vermittlungs·büro** *das:* ▸ PARTNERVERMITTLUNG B
Party /'pa:ɐ̯ti/ *die;* ~, ~s party
Parzelle *die;* ~, ~n [small] plot [of land]
Pass, ***Paß** *der;* **Passes, Pässe (a)** (Reisepass) passport
(b) (Gebirgspass; Ballspiele) pass
passabel [1] *Adj.* reasonable; presentable ‹*appearance*›
[2] *adv.* reasonably well
Passage /pa'sa:ʒə/ *die;* ~, ~n **(a)** [shopping] arcade
(b) (Abschnitt) passage
Passagier /pasa'ʒi:ɐ̯/ *der;* ~s, ~e passenger; **blinder ~:** stowaway
Passagier-: **~dampfer** *der* passenger steamer; **~flugzeug** *das* passenger aircraft
Passagierin *die;* ~, ~nen passenger
Passagier·liste *die* passenger list
Pass·amt, ***Paß·amt** *das* passport office
Passant *der;* ~en, ~en, **Passantin** *die;* ~, ~nen passer-by
Pass·bild, ***Paß·bild** *das* passport photograph
Pässe ▸ PASS
passen *itr. V.* **(a)** (die richtige Größe/Form haben) fit
(b) (geeignet sein) be suitable (**auf** + *Akk.*, **zu** for); (harmonieren) ‹*colour etc.*› match; **zu etw./** ···>

jmdm. ~: go well with sth./be well suited to sb.; **zueinander** ~ ‹*things*› go well together; ‹*two people*› be suited to each other
(c) (genehm sein) **jmdm.** ~ ‹*time*› suit sb.
(d) (Kartenspiel) pass

passend *Adj.* **(a)** (geeignet) suitable ‹*dress, present, etc.*›; right ‹*words, expression, moment*›
(b) (harmonierend) matching ‹*shoes etc.*›

Pass·foto, *Paß·foto *das* ▶ PASSBILD

passierbar *Adj.* passable ‹*road*›; navigable ‹*river*›; negotiable ‹*path*›

passieren [1] *tr. V.* pass; **die Grenze** ~: cross the border
[2] *itr. V.; mit sein* happen

Passion *die;* ~, ~**en (a)** passion
(b) (christl. Rel.) Passion

passioniert *Adj.* passionate ‹*collector, card player, huntsman*›

passiv [1] *Adj.* passive
[2] *adv.* passively

Passiv *das;* ~**s**, ~**e** (Sprachw.) passive

Passivität *die;* ~: passivity

Passivraucher *der,* **Passivraucherin** *die* passive smoker

pass-, *paß, Pass-, *Paß-: ~**kontrolle** *die* passport check; ~**straße** *die* [mountain] pass road; ~**wort** *das; Pl.* ~**wörter** (DV) password; ~**wort·geschützt** (DV) [1] *Adj.* password-protected; [2] *adv.* with password protection; ~**zwang** *der* obligation to carry a passport

Paste *die;* ~, ~**n** paste

Pastell *das;* ~**[e]s**, ~**e (a)** (Farbton) pastel shade
(b) (Maltechnik) pastel *no art.*

Pastell-: ~**farbe** *die* pastel colour; ~**ton** *der* pastel shade

Pastete *die;* ~, ~**n (a)** (gefüllte) vol-au-vent
(b) (in einer Schüssel o. Ä. gegart) pâté; (in einer Hülle aus Teig gebacken) pie

pasteurisieren *tr. V.* pasteurize

Pastille *die;* ~, ~**n** pastille

Pastor *der;* ~**s**, ~**en**, **Pastorin** *die;* ~, ~**nen** pastor

Pate *der;* ~**n**, ~**n** godfather; (männlich od. weiblich) godparent

Paten-: ~**kind** *das* godchild; ~**onkel** *der* godfather; ~**stadt** *die* ▶ PARTNERSTADT

patent (ugs.) [1] *Adj.* **(a)** (tüchtig) capable
(b) (zweckmäßig) ingenious
[2] *adv.* ingeniously; neatly ‹*solved*›

Patent *das;* ~**[e]s**, ~**e (a)** (Schutz) patent; **etw. zum** *od.* **als** ~ **anmelden** apply for a patent for sth.
(b) (Erfindung) [patented] invention

Patent·amt *das* Patent Office

Paten·tante *die* godmother

patentieren *tr. V.* patent

Patent-: ~**lösung** *die* patent remedy (**für, zu** for); ~**rezept** *das* patent remedy (**gegen, für** for)

Pater *der;* ~**s**, ~ *od.* **Patres** (kath. Kirche) Father

pathetisch [1] *Adj.* emotional ‹*speech, manner*›; melodramatic ‹*gesture*›
[2] *adv.* emotionally; (dramatisch) [melo]dramatically

Pathos *das;* ~: emotionalism

Patience /pa'si̯ã:s/ *die;* ~, ~**n** [game of] patience; ~**n/eine** ~ **legen** play patience/a game of patience

Patient /pa'ts̯i̯ɛnt/ *der;* ~**en**, ~**en**, **Patientin** *die;* ~, ~**nen** patient

Patin *die;* ~, ~**nen** godmother

Patres ▶ PATER

Patriot *der;* ~**en**, ~**en**, **Patriotin** *die;* ~, ~**nen** patriot

patriotisch [1] *Adj.* patriotic
[2] *adv.* patriotically

Patriotismus *der;* ~: patriotism

Patrone *die;* ~, ~**n** cartridge

Patrouille /pa'trʊljə/ *die;* ~, ~**n** patrol

patrouillieren /patrʊl'ji:rən/ *itr. V.; auch mit sein* be on patrol

Patsche *die;* ~, ~**n** (ugs.) ▶ KLEMME

patschen *itr. V., mit sein* (ugs.) splash

patsch·nass, *patsch·naß *Adj.* (ugs.) sopping wet

patt *Adj.* (Schach) stalemated

Patt *das;* ~**s**, ~**s** (Schach; auch fig.) stalemate

Patt·situation *die* [position of] stalemate

Patzer *der;* ~**s**, ~ (ugs.) slip (coll.); boob (coll.)

patzig (ugs.) [1] *Adj.* snotty (coll.); (frech) cheeky
[2] *adv.* snottily (coll.); (frech) cheekily

Pauke *die;* ~, ~**n** kettledrum; **auf die** ~ **hauen** (ugs.) (feiern) paint the town red (coll.); (sich lautstark äußern) come right out with it

pauken (ugs.) [1] *tr. V.* swot up (Brit. sl.), bone up on (Amer. coll.) ‹*facts, figures, etc.*›; **Latein/Mathe** ~: swot up one's Latin/maths
[2] *itr. V.* swot (Brit. sl.); (fürs Examen) cram (coll.)

pausbäckig *Adj.* chubby-faced; chubby ‹*face*›

pauschal [1] *Adj.* **(a)** all-inclusive ‹*price, settlement*›
(b) (verallgemeinernd) sweeping ‹*judgement, criticism, statement*›; indiscriminate ‹*prejudice*›; wholesale ‹*discrimination*›
[2] *adv.* **(a)** ‹*cost*› all in all; ‹*pay*› in a lump sum
(b) (ohne zu differenzieren) wholesale

Pauschale *die;* ~, ~**n** flat-rate payment

Pauschal-: ~**preis** *der* flat rate; (Inklusivpreis) all-in price; ~**reise** *die* package holiday; (mit mehreren Reisezielen) package tour

Pause *die;* ~, ~**n** break; (Ruhe~) rest; (Theater) interval (Brit.); intermission (Amer.)

pausen *tr. V.* trace; (eine Lichtpause machen) Photostat (*Brit.* ®)

*alte Schreibung - vgl. Hinweis auf S. xiv

pausen-, Pausen-: ~brot *das* sandwich (*eaten during break*); **~hof** *der* school yard; **~los** [1] *Adj.* incessant ‹*noise, moaning, questioning*›; continous ‹*work, operation*›
[2] *adv.* incessantly; ‹*work*› non-stop
Pavian /'pa:vi̯a:n/ *der;* **~s, ~e** baboon
Pavillon /'pavɪljɔn/ *der;* **~s, ~s** pavilion
Pazifik *der;* **~s** Pacific
pazifisch *Adj.* Pacific ‹*area*›; **der Pazifische Ozean** the Pacific Ocean
Pazifismus *der;* **~:** pacifism *no art.*
Pazifist *der;* **~en, ~en, Pazifistin** *die;* **~, ~nen** pacifist
pazifistisch [1] *Adj.* pacifist
[2] *adv.* in a pacifist way
PC *der;* **~[s], ~[s]** (DV) PC
PDS *Abk.* = **Partei des Demokratischen Sozialismus** Party of Democratic Socialism
Peanuts /'pi:nʌts/ *Pl.* peanuts (coll.)
Pech *das;* **~[e]s, ~e (a)** pitch
(b) (Missgeschick) bad luck
pech·schwarz *Adj.* (ugs.) jet-black
Pedal *das;* **~s, ~e** pedal
Pedant *der;* **~en, ~en, Pedantin** *die;* **~, ~nen** pedant
pedantisch [1] *Adj.* pedantic
[2] *adv.* pedantically
Pediküre *die;* **~, ~n** pedicure
pediküren *tr. V.* pedicure
Pegel *der;* **~s, ~ (a)** water level indicator; (Tide~) tide gauge
(b) (Wasserstand) water level
peilen *tr. V.* take a bearing on ‹*transmitter, fixed point*›
Pein *die;* **~** (geh.) torment
peinigen *tr. V.* (geh.) torment; (foltern) torture
peinlich [1] *Adj.* **(a)** embarrassing; awkward ‹*question, position, pause*›; **es ist mir sehr ~:** I feel very bad (coll.) *or* embarrassed about it
(b) (äußerst genau) meticulous
[2] *adv.* **(a)** unpleasantly ‹*surprised*›
(b) (überaus [genau]) meticulously
Peinlichkeit *die;* **~, ~en (a)** embarrassment; **die ~ der Situation** the awkwardness of the situation
(b) (Genauigkeit) meticulousness
(c) (peinliche Situation) embarrassing situation
Peitsche *die;* **~, ~n** whip
peitschen *tr. V.* whip; (fig.) ‹*storm, waves, rain*› lash
Pelikan *der;* **~s, ~e** pelican
Pelle *die;* **~, ~n** (bes. nordd.) skin; (abgeschält) peel
pellen (bes. nordd.) *tr., refl. V.* peel
Pell·kartoffel *die* potato boiled in its skin
Pelz *der;* **~es, ~e (a)** fur; coat; (des toten Tieres) skin; pelt
(b) (Material) fur; (~mantel) fur coat
Pelz·mantel *der* fur coat
Pendel *das;* **~s, ~:** pendulum
pendeln *itr. V.* **(a)** swing [to and fro]; (mit weniger Bewegung) dangle
(b) *mit sein* ‹*bus, ferry, etc.*› operate a shuttle service; ‹*person*› commute
Pendler *der;* **~s, ~, Pendlerin** *die;* **~, ~nen** commuter
penetrant [1] *Adj.* **(a)** penetrating ‹*smell, taste*›; overpowering ‹*stink, perfume*›
(b) (aufdringlich) pushing, (coll.) pushy ‹*person*›; overbearing ‹*tone, manner*›; aggressive ‹*question*›
[2] *adv.* **(a)** overpoweringly
(b) (aufdringlich) overbearingly
penibel [1] *Adj.* over-meticulous ‹*person*›; (pedantisch) pedantic
[2] *adv.* painstakingly; over-meticulously ‹*dressed*›
Penis *der;* **~, ~se** penis
pennen *itr. V.* (salopp) **(a)** (schlafen) kip (coll.)
(b) (fig.: nicht aufpassen) be half asleep
(c) (koitieren) **mit jmdm. ~:** sleep with sb.
Penner *der;* **~s, ~, Pennerin** *die;* **~, ~nen** (salopp) tramp (Brit.); hobo (Amer.)
Pensen ▶ PENSUM
Pension /pã'zi̯o:n/ *die;* **~, ~en (a)** (Ruhestand) **in ~ gehen** retire; **in ~ sein** be retired
(b) (Ruhegehalt) [retirement] pension
(c) (Haus für [Ferien]gäste) guest house
(d) (Unterkunft u. Verpflegung) board
Pensionär /pãzi̯o'nɛ:ɐ̯/ *der;* **~s, ~e, Pensionärin** *die;* **~, ~nen** retired civil servant
pensionieren *tr. V.* pension off; retire; **sich [vorzeitig] ~ lassen** take [early] retirement; **ein pensionierter Schulmeister/Politiker** a retired schoolmaster/politician
Pensionierung *die;* **~, ~en** retirement
Pensions-: ~alter *das* retirement age; **~anspruch** *der* pension entitlement
Pensum *das;* **~s, Pensen** work quota
per *Präp. mit Akk.* **(a)** (mittels) by; **~ Adresse X** care of X; c/o X
(b) (Kaufmannsspr.: [bis] zum) by; (am) on
(c) (Kaufmannsspr.: pro) per
perfekt [1] *Adj.* **(a)** perfect ‹*crime, host*›; faultless ‹*English, French, etc.*›
(b) ~ sein (ugs.: abgeschlossen, fertig sein) be finalized
[2] *adv.* perfectly
Perfekt *das;* **~s** (Sprachw.) perfect
Perfektion *die;* **~:** perfection
perfektionieren *tr. V.* perfect
Perfektionismus *der;* **~:** perfectionism
Perfektionist *der;* **~en, ~en, Perfektionistin** *die;* **~, ~nen** perfectionist
perfektionistisch [1] *Adj.* perfectionist ‹*standards etc.*›
[2] *adv.* in a perfectionist manner

Pergament·papier *das* greaseproof paper
Periode *die;* ~, ~**n** period
Perle *die;* ~, ~**n** **(a)** (auch fig.) pearl **(b)** (aus Holz, Glas o. Ä.) bead
Perlmutt *das;* ~**s** mother-of-pearl
Perlon (Wz) *das;* ~**s** ≈ nylon
Perser *der;* ~**s**, ~ **(a)** Persian **(b)** ▶ PERSERTEPPICH
Perserin *die;* ~, ~**nen** Persian
Perser·teppich *der* Persian carpet
Persianer *der;* ~**s**, ~ (Mantel) Persian lamb coat
Persien (*das*); ~**s** Persia
persisch *Adj.* Persian
Person *die;* ~, ~**en** person; (in der Dichtung, im Film) character
Personal *das;* ~**s** (in einem Betrieb o. Ä.) staff; (im Haushalt) domestic staff *pl.*
Personal-: ~**abbau** *der* reduction in staff; (in mehreren Abteilungen/Betrieben) staff cuts *pl.;* ~**abteilung** *die* personnel department; ~**ausweis** *der* identity card; ~**büro** *das* personnel office; ~**chef** *der*, ~**chefin** *die* personnel manager
Personalien *Pl.* personal particulars
Personal-: ~**kosten** *Pl.* (Wirtsch., Verwaltung) staff costs; ~**mangel** *der* staff shortage; ~**pronomen** *das* (Sprachw.) personal pronoun; ~**rat** *der* **(a)** (Ausschuss) staff council (*for civil servants*); **(b)** (Mitglied) staff council representative; ~**rätin** *die:* ▶ ~RAT B
Personen-: ~**kraftwagen** *der* (bes. Amtsspr.) private car *or* (Amer.) automobile; ~**name** *der* personal name; ~**wagen** *der* (Auto) [private] car; automobile (Amer.); (im Unterschied zum Lastwagen) passenger car *or* (Amer.) automobile; ~**zug** *der* stopping train
Personifikation *die;* ~, ~**en** personification
personifizieren *tr. V.* personify
Personifizierung *die;* ~, ~**en** personification
persönlich [1] *Adj.* personal; ~ **werden** get personal [2] *adv.* personally; (auf Briefen) 'private [and confidential]'
Persönlichkeit *die;* ~, ~**en** **(a)** personality **(b)** (Mensch) person of character; **eine ~ sein** have a strong personality; ~**en des öffentlichen Lebens** public figures
Perspektive *die;* ~, ~**n** perspective; (Blickwinkel) angle; (Zukunftsaussicht) prospect
Peru (*das*); ~**s** Peru
Peruaner *der;* ~**s**, ~, **Peruanerin** *die;* ~, ~**nen** Peruvian
peruanisch *Adj.* Peruvian
Perücke *die;* ~, ~**n** wig
pervers *Adj.* perverted

*old spelling - see note on page xiv

Perversion *die;* ~, ~**en** perversion
Pessimismus *der;* ~: pessimism
Pessimist *der;* ~**en**, ~**en**, **Pessimistin** *die;* ~, ~**nen** pessimist
pessimistisch [1] *Adj.* pessimistic [2] *adv.* pessimistically
Pest *die;* ~: plague
Pestizid *das;* ~**s**, ~**e** pesticide
Petersilie /petɐ'zi:li̯ə/ *die;* ~: parsley
Petition *die;* ~, ~**en** (Amtsspr.) petition
Petroleum /pe'tro:leʊm/ *das;* ~**s** paraffin (Brit.); kerosene (Amer.)
Petrus (*der*); **Petri** (christl. Rel.: Apostel) St Peter
petzen (Schülerspr.) [1] *itr. V.* tell tales; sneak (Brit. school coll.) [2] *tr. V.* ~, **dass** ...: tell teacher/sb.'s parents that ...
Pf *Abk.* = **Pfennig**
Pfad *der;* ~[e]**s**, ~**e** path
Pfad-: ~**finder** *der* Scout; ~**finderin** *die;* ~, ~**nen** Guide (Brit.); girl scout (Amer.)
Pfaffe *der;* ~**n**, ~**n** (abwertend) cleric; Holy Joe (derog.)
Pfahl *der;* ~[e]**s**, **Pfähle** post; stake
Pfand *das;* ~[e]**s**, **Pfänder** **(a)** security; pledge (esp. fig.) **(b)** (für Flaschen usw.) deposit (**auf** + *Dat.* on)
pfänden *tr. V.* seize [under distress] (Law) ‹*goods, chattels*›; attach ‹*wages etc.*› (Law)
Pfand·flasche *die* returnable bottle (*on which a deposit is payable*)
Pfändung *die;* ~, ~**en** seizure; distraint (Law); (von Geldsummen, Vermögensrechten) attachment (Law)
Pfanne *die;* ~, ~**n** [frying] pan
Pfann·kuchen *der* **(a)** pancake **(b)** (Berliner) doughnut
Pfarrei *die;* ~, ~**en** **(a)** (Bezirk) parish **(b)** (Dienststelle) parish office **(c)** ▶ PFARRHAUS
Pfarrer *der;* ~**s**, ~ pastor; (anglikanisch) vicar; (von Freikirchen) minister
Pfarrerin *die;* ~, ~**nen** [woman] pastor; (in Freikirchen) [woman] minister
Pfarr·haus *das* vicarage; (katholisch) presbytery; (in Schottland) manse
Pfau *der;* ~[e]**s**, ~**en** peacock
Pfauen·auge *das* peacock butterfly
Pfd. *Abk.* = **Pfund** lb.
Pfeffer *der;* ~**s**, ~: pepper
Pfeffer-: ~**kuchen** *der* ≈ gingerbread; ~**minze** *die* peppermint [plant]; ~**minz·tee** *der* peppermint tea; ~**mühle** *die* pepper mill
pfeffern *tr. V.* season with pepper
Pfeffer·streuer *der;* ~**s**, ~: pepper pot
Pfeife *die;* ~, ~**n** pipe; (Triller~) whistle
pfeifen [1] *unr. itr. V.* whistle; ‹*bird*› sing;

(auf einer Trillerpfeife o. Ä.) ‹*policeman, referee, etc.*› blow one's whistle; **auf jmdn./etw. ~** (ugs.) not give a damn about sb./sth.
[2] *unr. tr. V.* whistle ‹*tune etc.*›; ‹*bird*› sing ‹*song*›; (auf einer Pfeife) pipe, play ‹*tune etc.*›

Pfeil *der;* **~[e]s, ~e** arrow

Pfeiler *der;* **~s, ~:** pillar; (Brücken~) pier

Pfennig *der;* **~s, ~e** pfennig; **es kostete damals 20 ~:** it cost 20 pfennig[s] at that time

pferchen *tr. V.* cram; pack

Pferd *das;* **~[e]s, ~e** horse; (Schachfigur) knight; **mit ihr kann man ~e stehlen** (ugs.) she's game for anything

Pferde-: ~rennen *das* horse race; (Sportart) horseracing; **~schwanz** *der* (Frisur) ponytail; **~stall** *der* stable

pfiff *1. u. 3. Pers. Sg. Prät. v.* PFEIFEN

Pfiff *der;* **~[e]s, ~e (a)** whistle
(b) (ugs.: besonderer Reiz) style

Pfifferling *der;* **~s, ~e** chanterelle; **keinen** *od.* **nicht einen ~ wert sein** (ugs.) be not worth a bean (coll.)

pfiffig [1] *Adj.* smart; bright ‹*idea*›; artful ‹*smile, expression*›
[2] *adv.* artfully

Pfingsten *das;* **~, ~:** Whitsun

Pfingst-: ~montag *der* Whit Monday *no def. art.*; **~sonntag** *der* Whit Sunday *no def. art.*

Pfirsich *der;* **~s, ~e** peach

Pflanze *die;* **~, ~n** plant

pflanzen *tr. V.* plant

Pflanzen·öl *das* vegetable oil

pflanzlich *Adj.* plant *attrib.* ‹*life, motif*›; vegetable ‹*dye, fat*›

Pflaster *das;* **~s, ~ (a)** (Straßen~) road surface; (auf dem Gehsteig) pavement; **ein teures/gefährliches ~** (ugs.) an expensive/dangerous place *or* spot to be
(b) (Wund~) sticking plaster

pflastern *tr.* (*auch itr.*) *V.* surface; (mit Kopfsteinpflaster, Steinplatten) pave

Pflaster·stein *der* paving stone; (Kopfstein) cobblestone

Pflaume *die;* **~, ~n** plum; **getrocknete ~n** [dried] prunes

Pflege *die;* **~:** care; (Maschinen~, Fahrzeug~) maintenance; (fig.: von Beziehungen, Kunst, Sprache) cultivation; **jmdn./etw. in ~** (*Akk.*) **nehmen** look after sb./sth.

pflege-, Pflege-: ~bedürftig *Adj.* needing care *or* attention *postpos.*; ‹*person*› in need of care; **~bedürftig sein** need looking after; need attention; **~eltern** *Pl.* foster-parents; **~fall** *der:* **ein ~fall sein** be in [permanent] need of nursing; **~heim** *das* nursing home (esp. Brit.); **~kind** *das* foster-child; **~leicht** *Adj.* easy-care *attrib.* ‹*textiles, flooring*›

pflegen [1] *tr. V.* look after; care for; take care of ‹*skin, teeth, floor*›; look after ‹*bicycle, car, machine*›; look after, tend ‹*garden, plants*›; cultivate ‹*relations, arts, interests*›; foster ‹*contacts, cooperation*›; pursue ‹*hobby*›
[2] *mod. V.* **etw. zu tun ~:** usually do sth.

Pflege·personal *das* nursing staff

Pfleger *der;* **~s, ~ (a)** (Krankenpfleger) [male] nurse
(b) (Tierpfleger) keeper

Pflegerin *die;* **~, ~nen (a)** (Krankenpflegerin) nurse
(b) (Tierpflegerin) keeper

Pflege·versicherung *die* (*long-term*) [nursing-]care insurance

Pflicht *die;* **~, ~en** duty

pflicht-, Pflicht-: ~bewusst, *~bewußt [1] *Adj.* conscientious; [2] *adv.* with a sense of duty; **~bewusstsein, *~bewußtsein** *das,* sense of duty; **~fach** *das* compulsory subject; **~gefühl** *das* sense of duty; **~übung** *die* (fig.) ritual exercise; **~verteidiger** *der,* **~verteidigerin** *die* (Rechtsw.) *defense counsel appointed by the court;* assigned counsel

Pflock *der;* **~[e]s, Pflöcke** peg

pflücken *tr. V.* pick

Pflug *der;* **~[e]s, Pflüge** plough

pflügen *tr., itr. V.* plough

Pforte *die;* **~, ~n** (Tor) gate; (Tür) door; (Eingang) entrance

Pförtner *der;* **~s, ~, Pförtnerin** *die;* **~, ~nen** porter; (eines Wohnblocks, Büros) doorkeeper; (am Tor) gatekeeper

Pförtner·loge *die* porter's lodge

Pfosten *der;* **~s, ~:** post

Pfote *die;* **~, ~n** paw

Pfropf *der;* **~[e]s, ~e** blockage

pfropfen *tr. V.* (ugs.) cram; stuff; **gepfropft voll** crammed [full]; packed

Pfropfen *der;* **~s, ~:** stopper; (Korken) cork; (für Fässer) bung

pfui *Interj.* ugh; **~ rufen** boo

Pfund *das;* **~[e]s, ~e** pound

Pfusch *der;* **~[e]s (a)** (ugs. abwertend) **das ist ~:** it's a botch-up
(b) (österr.: Schwarzarbeit) work done on the side (*and not declared for tax*); (nach Feierabend) moonlighting (coll.)

pfuschen *itr. V.* **(a)** (ugs. abwertend) botch it; do a botched-up job
(b) (österr.: schwarzarbeiten) do work on the side (*not declared for tax*); (nach Feierabend) moonlight (coll.)

Pfütze *die;* **~, ~n** puddle

Phänomen *das;* **~s, ~e** phenomenon

Phantasie *usw.:* ▶ FANTASIE *usw.*

Pharma-: ~berater *der,* **~beraterin** *die:* ▶ ~REFERENT; **~industrie** *die* pharmaceutical industry

Pharmakologie *die;* **~:** pharmacology *no art.*

Pharma·referent *der*, **Pharma·referentin** *die* pharmaceutical representative
pharmazeutisch *Adj.* pharmaceutical
Phase *die;* ~, ~**n** phase
Philosoph *der;* ~**en**, ~**en** philosopher
Philosophie *die;* ~, ~**n** philosophy
philosophieren *itr.* (*auch tr.*) *V.* philosophize
Philosophin *die;* ~, ~**nen** philosopher
philosophisch 1 *Adj.* philosophical; ‹*dictionary, principles*› of philosophy
2 *adv.* philosophically
Phosphat *das;* ~[**e**]**s**, ~**e** (Chemie) phosphate
Photo *das;* ~**s**, ~**s** ▶ FOTO
Phrase *die;* ~, ~**n** (abwertend) [empty] phrase; cliché
Physik *die;* ~: physics *sing., no art.*
physikalisch *Adj.* physics *attrib.* ‹*experiment, formula, research, institute*›; physical ‹*map, process*›
Physiker *der;* ~**s**, ~, **Physikerin** *die;* ~, ~**nen** physicist
physisch 1 *Adj.* physical
2 *adv.* physically
Pianist *der;* ~**en**, ~**en**, **Pianistin** *die;* ~, ~**nen** pianist
Pickel *der;* ~**s**, ~: pimple
picken 1 *itr. V.* peck (**nach** at; **an** + *Akk.*, **gegen** on, against)
2 *tr. V.* ‹*bird*› peck; (ugs.) ‹*person*› pick
Picknick *das;* ~**s**, ~**e** *od.* ~**s** picnic
piek·fein (ugs.) 1 *Adj.* posh (coll.)
2 *adv.* poshly (coll.)
piepe, piep·egal *Adj.* [**jmdm.**] ~ **sein** (ugs.) not matter at all [to sb.]; **es ist mir** ~ (ugs.) I don't give a damn
Piepen *Pl.* (salopp: Geld) dough *sing.* (coll.)
piep[s]en *itr. V.* (ugs.) squeak; ‹*small bird*› cheep; **bei dir piept's wohl!** (salopp) you must be off your rocker (coll.); **zum Piepen sein** (ugs.) be a hoot *or* a scream (coll.)
Pietät /pie'tɛ:t/ *die;* ~: respect; (Ehrfurcht) reverence
Pik *das;* ~[**s**], ~[**s**] (Kartenspiel) **(a)** (Farbe) spades *pl.;*
(b) (Karte) spade
pikant 1 *Adj.* **(a)** piquant
(b) (fig.: witzig) ironical
(c) (verhüll.: schlüpfrig) racy ‹*joke, story*›
2 *adv.* piquantly ‹*seasoned*›
pikiert 1 *Adj.* piqued
2 *adv.* ‹*reply, say*› in an aggrieved tone
Pilger *der;* ~**s**, ~, **Pilgerin** *die;* ~, ~**nen** pilgrim
pilgern *itr. V.* go on a pilgrimage
Pille *die;* ~, ~**n** pill
Pilot *der;* ~**en**, ~**en**, **Pilotin** *die;* ~, ~**nen** pilot

*alte Schreibung - vgl. Hinweis auf S. xiv

Pils *das;* ~, ~: Pils
Pilz *der;* ~**es**, ~**e** fungus; (Speise~, auch fig.) mushroom
Pinguin *der;* ~**s**, ~**e** penguin
Pinie /'pi:ni̯ə/ *die;* ~, ~**n** [stone *or* umbrella] pine
pinkeln *itr. V.* (salopp) pee (coll.)
Pinsel *der;* ~**s**, ~: brush; (Mal~) paintbrush
Pinzette *die;* ~, ~**n** tweezers *pl.*
Pionier *der;* ~**s**, ~**e** (Milit.) sapper; (fig.: Wegbereiter) pioneer
Pionierin *die;* ~, ~**nen** pioneer
Pionier·arbeit *die* pioneering work
Pipi *das;* ~**s** (Kinderspr.) ~ **machen** do wee-wees (sl.); ~ **müssen** have to do wee-wees *or* have a wee (sl.)
Pirat *der;* ~**en**, ~**en**, **Piratin** *die;* ~, ~**nen** pirate
pissen *itr. V.* (derb) piss (coarse)
Pistazie /pɪs'ta:tsi̯ə/ *die;* ~, ~**n** pistachio
Piste *die;* ~, ~**n** (Ski~) piste; (Renn~) course; (Flugw.) runway
Pistole *die;* ~, ~**n** pistol
Pizza *die;* ~, ~**s** *od.* **Pizzen** pizza
Pkw, PKW /'pe:ka:ve:/ *der;* ~[**s**], ~[**s**] [private] car; automobile (Amer.)
plädieren *itr. V.* (Rechtsw.) plead (**auf** + *Akk.* for); (fig.) argue
Plädoyer /plɛdo̯a'je:/ *das;* ~**s**, ~**s** (Rechtsw.) summing up (*for the defence/prosecution*); (fig.) plea
Plage *die;* ~, ~**n** **(a)** nuisance
(b) (ugs.: Mühe) bother; trouble
plagen 1 *tr. V.* **(a)** torment
(b) (ugs.: bedrängen) harass; (mit Bitten, Fragen) pester
2 *refl. V.* **(a)** (sich abmühen) slave away
(b) (leiden) **sich mit etw.** ~: be bothered by sth.
Plagiat *das;* ~[**e**]**s**, ~**e** plagiarism *no art.*
Plakat *das;* ~[**e**]**s**, ~**e** poster
Plakette *die;* ~, ~**n** badge
Plan *der;* ~[**e**]**s**, **Pläne** **(a)** plan
(b) (Karte) map; plan
Plane *die;* ~, ~**n** tarpaulin
planen *tr., itr. V.* plan
Planet *der;* ~**en**, ~**en** planet
planieren *tr. V.* level; grade
Planier·raupe *die* bulldozer
Planke *die;* ~, ~**n** plank
plan-: ~**los** 1 *Adj.* aimless; (ohne System) unsystematic; 2 *adv.* ▶ 1: aimlessly; unsystematically; ~**mäßig** 1 *Adj.* **(a)** scheduled ‹*service, steamer*›; ~**mäßige Ankunft/Abfahrt** scheduled time of arrival/departure; **(b)** (systematisch) systematic
2 *adv.* **(a)** (wie geplant) according to plan; (pünktlich) on schedule; **(b)** (systematisch) systematically
Plansch·becken *das* paddling pool
planschen *itr. V.* splash [about]

Plantage /plan'ta:ʒə/ *die;* ~, ~**n** plantation
Planung *die;* ~, ~**en** planning
Plan·wirtschaft *die* planned economy
Plastik¹ *die;* ~, ~**en** sculpture
Plastik² *das;* ~**s** (ugs.) plastic
Plastik·beutel *der,* **Plastik·tüte** *die* plastic bag
Platane *die;* ~, ~**n** plane tree
Platin *das;* ~**s** platinum
platschen *itr. V.* **(a)** splash
(b) *mit sein* (~d auftreffen) splash (**an** + *Akk.*, **gegen** against)
plätschern *itr. V.* **(a)** splash; ‹*rain*› patter; ‹*stream*› burble
(b) *mit sein* ‹*stream*› burble along
platt *Adj.* flat; **ein Platter** (ugs.) a flat (coll.); **etw.** ~ **machen** (salopp abwertend) close sth. down
Platt *das;* ~**[s]** [local] Low German dialect
Plättchen *das;* ~**s,** ~: small plate *or* disc
platt·deutsch *Adj.* Low German
Platte *die;* ~, ~**n** **(a)** (Stein~) slab; (Metall~) plate; sheet; (Span~, Hartfaser~ usw.) board; (Tisch~) [table] top; (Grab~) [memorial] slab
(b) (Koch~) hotplate
(c) (Schall~) [gramophone] record
(d) (Teller) plate; (zum Servieren, aus Metall) dish; **kalte** ~: selection of cold meats [and cheese]
Platten·spieler *der* record player
Platt·fuß *der* **(a)** flat foot
(b) (ugs.: Reifenpanne) flat (coll.)
Platz *der;* ~**es, Plätze** **(a)** square
(b) (Sport~) ground; (Spielfeld) field; (Tennis~, Volleyball~ usw.) court; (Golf~) course
(c) (Stelle, wo jmd., etw. hingehört) place; **nicht** *od.* **fehl am** ~**[e] sein** (fig.) be out of place
(d) (Sitz~) seat; (am Tisch, Steh~ usw.) place; ~ **nehmen** sit down
(e) (bes. Sport: Platzierung) place
(f) (Ort) place; **am** ~: in the town/village
(g) (Raum) space; room; ~ **machen** make room (*Dat.* for)
Platz·angst *die* (volkst.: Klaustrophobie) claustrophobia
Plätzchen *das;* ~**s,** ~ **(a)** little place
(b) (Keks) biscuit (Brit.); cookie (Amer.)
platzen *itr. V.; mit sein* **(a)** burst; (explodieren) explode
(b) (ugs.: scheitern) fall through; **der Wechsel/das Treffen ist geplatzt** the bill has bounced (coll.)/the meeting is off
(c) **in eine Versammlung** ~ (ugs.) burst into a meeting
Platz-: ~**karte** *die* reserved-seat ticket; ~**konzert** *das* open-air concert (*by a military or brass band*); ~**mangel** *der* lack of space; ~**not** *die* [acute] lack of space; ~**regen** *der* cloudburst; ~**wunde** *die* lacerated wound
Plauderei *die;* ~, ~**en** chat
plaudern *itr. V.* chat
plausibel *Adj.* plausible
Play·boy /'pleɪbɔɪ/ *der* playboy
Player /'pleɪɐ/ *der:* ~, ~: player
pleite (ugs.) ~ **sein** ‹*person*› be broke (coll.); ‹*company*› have gone bust (coll.); *s. auch* PLEITE A
Pleite *die;* ~, ~**n** (ugs.) **(a)** (Bankrott) bankruptcy *no def. art.;* ~ **gehen/machen** go bust (coll.)
(b) (Misserfolg) washout (coll.)
Pleite-: ~**geier** *der* (ugs.) spectre of bankruptcy; ~**wirtschaft** *die* (ugs.) bankrupt economy
Plissee *das;* ~**s,** ~**s** accordion pleats *pl.*
Plombe *die;* ~, ~**n** **(a)** (Siegel) [lead] seal
(b) (veralt.: Zahnfüllung) filling
plombieren *tr. V.* **(a)** (versiegeln) seal
(b) (veralt.) fill ‹*tooth*›
plötzlich [1] *Adj.* sudden
[2] *adv.* suddenly
Plötzlichkeit *die;* ~: suddenness
plump [1] *Adj.* **(a)** (dick) plump; (unförmig) ungainly ‹*shape*›; (rundlich) bulbous
(b) (schwerfällig) clumsy ‹*movements, style*›
(c) (fig.) (dreist) crude ‹*lie, deception, trick*›; (leicht durchschaubar) blatantly obvious; (unbeholfen) clumsy ‹*excuse, advances*›; crude ‹*joke, forgery*›
[2] *adv.* **(a)** (schwerfällig) clumsily
(b) (fig.) in a blatantly obvious manner
Plumpheit *die;* ~ **(a)** (Dicke) plumpness; (Unförmigkeit) ungainliness; (Rundlichkeit) bulbousness
(b) (Schwerfälligkeit) clumsiness
(c) (abwertend: Dreistigkeit) blatant nature
plumps *Interj.* bump; thud; (ins Wasser) splash; ~ **machen** go bump
Plumps *der;* ~**es,** ~**e** (ugs.) bump; thud; (ins Wasser) splash
plumpsen *itr. V.* fall with a bump; thud; (ins Wasser) splash
Plünderer *der;* ~**s,** ~, **Plünderin** *die;* ~, ~**nen** looter
plündern *itr., tr. V.* **(a)** loot; plunder ‹*town*›
(b) (scherzh.) raid ‹*larder, fridge, account*›
Plünderung *die;* ~, ~**en** looting; (einer Stadt) plundering; ~**en** cases of looting/plundering
Plural *der;* ~**s,** ~**e** plural
Pluralismus *der;* ~: pluralism
pluralistisch [1] *Adj.* pluralistic
[2] *adv.* pluralistically; along pluralistic lines
plus *Konj., Adv.* plus
Plus *das;* ~: surplus; (Vorteil) advantage
Plüsch *der;* ~**[e]s,** ~**e** plush
Plusquam·perfekt *das* pluperfect [tense]
PLZ *Abk.* = **Postleitzahl**
Po *der;* ~**s,** ~**s** (ugs.) bottom
Pöbel *der;* ~**s** rabble
pöbeln *itr. V.* make rude *or* coarse remarks

pochen *itr. V.* (klopfen) knock (**gegen/an** + *Akk.* at, on); (geh.: pulsieren) ‹*heart*› pound

Pocken *Pl.* smallpox *sing.*

Podest *das od. der;* **~[e]s, ~e** rostrum

Podium *das;* **~s, Podien** (Plattform) platform; (Bühne) stage; (trittartige Erhöhung) rostrum

Poesie *die;* **~**: poetry

Poet *der;* **~en, ~en** (veralt.) poet; bard (literary)

poetisch 1 *Adj.* poetic[al]
2 *adv.* poetically

Pogrom *das od. der;* **~s, ~e** pogrom

Pointe /'po̜ɛ̃:tə/ *die;* **~, ~n** (eines Witzes) punch line; (einer Geschichte) point; (eines Sketches) curtain line

pointiert /po̜ɛ̃'ti:ɐ̯t/ 1 *Adj.* pointed ‹*remark*›
2 *adv.* pointedly

Pokal *der;* **~s, ~e (a)** (Trinkgefäß) goblet **(b)** (Siegestrophäe, **~**wettbewerb) cup

Pökel·fleisch *das* salt meat

pökeln *tr. V.* salt

Poker *das od. der;* **~s** poker

Poker·gesicht *das* poker face

pokern *itr. V.* play poker

Pol *der;* **~s, ~e** pole

Polar·licht *das* aurora; polar lights *pl.*

Polaroid·kamera (Wz) *die* Polaroid camera ®

Pole *der;* **~n, ~n** Pole

polemisch 1 *Adj.* polemic[al]
2 *adv.* polemically

Polen *das;* **~s** Poland

Polente *die;* **~** (salopp) cops *pl.* (coll.)

Police /po'li:sə/ *die;* **~, ~n** (Versicherungsw.) policy

polieren *tr. V.* polish

Poli·klinik *die* outpatients' clinic

Polin *die;* **~n, ~nen** Pole

Polit·büro *das* politburo

Politik *die;* **~, ~en (a)** politics *sing., no art.* **(b)** (eine spezielle **~**) policy

Politiker *der;* **~s, ~, Politikerin** *die;* **~, ~nen** politician

politisch 1 *Adj.* political
2 *adv.* politically

politisieren 1 *itr. V.* talk politics
2 *tr. V.* make politically active

Politur *die;* **~, ~en** polish

Polizei *die;* **~, ~en** police *pl.*

Polizei-: ~auto *das* police car; **~beamte** *der* police officer; **~kontrolle** *die* police check

polizeilich 1 *Adj.* police; **~e Meldepflicht** obligation to register with the police
2 *adv.* by the police

Polizei-: ~präsidium *das* police headquarters *sing. or pl.;* **~revier** *das* police station; **~streife** *die* police patrol; **~stunde** *die* closing time; **~wache** *die* police station

Polizist *der;* **~en, ~en** policeman

Polizistin *die;* **~, ~nen** policewoman

Pollen *der;* **~s, ~** (Bot.) pollen

Poller *der;* **~s, ~**: bollard

polnisch *Adj.* Polish

Polster *das;* **~s, ~**: upholstery *no pl., no indef. art.*

Polster·möbel *Pl.* upholstered furniture *sing.*

polstern *tr. V.* upholster ‹*furniture*›

poltern *itr. V.* **(a)** crash about **(b)** *mit sein* **der Karren polterte über das Pflaster** the cart clattered over the cobblestones

Polyp *der;* **~en, ~en** (Zool., Med.) polyp

Pommern (*das*)*;* **~s** Pomerania

Pommes frites /pɔm'frit/ *Pl.* chips (Brit.); French fries (Amer.)

pompös 1 *Adj.* grandiose
2 *adv.* grandiosely

Pony[1] /'pɔni/ *das;* **~s, ~s** pony

Pony[2] *der;* **~s, ~s** (Frisur) fringe

Popel *der;* **~s, ~** (ugs.) bogy (sl.)

popelig (ugs. abwertend) 1 *Adj.* crummy (coll.); lousy (coll.); (durchschnittlich) second-rate
2 *adv.* crummily (sl.)

Popeline·mantel *der* poplin coat

popeln *itr. V.* (ugs.) **[in der Nase] ~**: pick one's nose

Pop-: ~musik *die* pop music; **~star** *der* pop star

populär 1 *Adj.* popular (**bei** with)
2 *adv.* popularly

popularisieren *tr. V.* popularize

Popularität *die;* **~**: popularity

Pore *die;* **~, ~n** pore

Porno *der;* **~s, ~s** (ugs.) porn[o] film/magazine *etc.*

Pornographie *die;* **~**: pornography

pornographisch 1 *Adj.* pornographic
2 *adv.* pornographically

Porree *der;* **~s** leek

Portal *das;* **~s, ~e** portal

Portemonnaie /pɔrtmɔ'ne:/ *das;* **~s, ~s** purse

Porti *Pl.* ▶ PORTO

Portier /pɔr'ti̯e:/ *der;* **~s, ~s,** *österr.:* /pɔr'ti:ɐ̯/ *der;* **~s, ~e** porter

Portion /pɔr'ts:i̯o:n/ *die;* **~, ~en (a)** (beim Essen) portion; helping **(b)** (ugs.: Anteil) amount

Porto *das;* **~s, ~s** *od.* **Porti** postage (**für** on, for)

Portugal (*das*)*;* **~s** Portugal

Portugiese *der;* **~n, ~n, Portugiesin** *die;* **~, ~nen** Portuguese

portugiesisch *Adj.* Portuguese

Portwein *der* port

*old spelling - see note on page xiv

Porzellan *das;* **~s** porcelain; china
Posaune *die;* **~, ~n** trombone
Position /pozi'tsi̯o:n/ *die;* **~, ~en** position
positiv [1] *Adj.* positive
[2] *adv.* positively
Positiv *das;* **~s, ~e** (Fot.) positive
Possessiv·pronomen *das* (Sprachw.) possessive pronoun
Post *die;* **~, ~en (a)** post (Brit.); mail; **etw. mit der** *od.* **per ~ schicken** send sth. by post *or* mail; **die ~ geht ab** (fig. ugs.) it's all happening; **ab 20 Uhr geht die ~ ab** (fig. ugs.) it'll all be happening from 8 o'clock; **auch beim Publikum geht die ~ ab** (fig. ugs.) the audience is having a ball too (coll.)
(b) (Postamt) post office
Post-: ~amt *das* post office; **~anweisung** *die* postal remittance form; **~auto** *das* mail van; **~bote** *der* (ugs.) postman (Brit.); mailman (Amer.); **~botin** *die* (ugs.) postwoman (Brit.); mailwoman (Amer.)
Posten *der;* **~s, ~ (a)** post
(b) (bes. Milit.: Wachmann) sentry
post-, Post-: ~fach *das* post office *or* PO box; (im Büro, Hotel usw.) pigeonhole; **~karte** *die* postcard; **~lagernd** *Adj., adv.* poste restante; general delivery (Amer.); **~leit·zahl** *die* postcode; Zip code (Amer.); **~stempel** *der* (Abdruck) postmark; **~wendend** *Adv.* by return [of post]
potent *Adj.* potent
Potenz *die;* **~, ~en (a)** potency
(b) (Math.) power
potenzieren *tr. V.* (Math.) **mit 5 ~:** raise to the power [of] 5
Pracht *die;* **~:** splendour
prächtig, pracht·voll [1] *Adj.* splendid
[2] *adv.* splendidly
prädestiniert *Adj.* predestined
Prädikat *das;* **~[e]s, ~e (a)** (Auszeichnung) rating
(b) (Sprachw.) predicate
Prag *(das);* **~s** Prague
prägen *tr. V.* **(a)** emboss
(b) mint ‹*coin*›
(c) (fig.: beeinflussen) shape
prägnant [1] *Adj.* concise; succinct
[2] *adv.* concisely; succinctly
Prägung *die;* **~, ~en** embossing; (von Münzen) minting
prahlen *itr. V.* boast, brag (**mit** about)
Prahler *der;* **~s, ~:** boaster; braggart
Prahlerei *die;* **~, ~en** (abwertend) boasting; bragging; **~en** boasts
Prahlerin *die;* **~, ~nen** boaster; braggart
Praktik *die;* **~, ~en** practice
Praktika ▶ PRAKTIKUM
praktikabel *Adj.* practicable; practical
Praktikant *der;* **~en, ~en, Praktikantin** *die;* **~, ~nen (a)** (in einem Betrieb) student trainee
(b) (an der Hochschule) physics/chemistry student (*doing a period of practical training*)
Praktikum *das;* **~s, Praktika** period of practical training
praktisch [1] *Adj.* practical; **~er Arzt** general practitioner
[2] *adv.* practically; (auf die Praxis bezogen; wirklich) in practice
praktizieren *tr. V.* practise
Praline *die;* **~, ~n** [filled] chocolate
prall *Adj.* **(a)** hard ‹*ball*›; bulging ‹*sack, wallet, bag*›; big strong *attrib.* ‹*thighs, muscles, calves*›; well-rounded ‹*breasts*›
(b) (intensiv) blazing ‹*sun*›
prallen *itr. V.; mit sein* crash (**gegen/auf/an** + *Akk.* into); collide (**gegen/auf/an** + *Akk.* with)
Prämie /'prɛ:mi̯ə/ *die;* **~, ~n (a)** (Leistungs~; Wirtschaft) bonus; (Belohnung) reward; (Spar~, Versicherungs~) premium
(b) (einer Lotterie) [extra] prize
prämieren *tr. V.* award a prize to ‹*person, film*›; give an award for ‹*best essay etc.*›
Pranger *der;* **~s, ~** (hist.) pillory
Pranke *die;* **~, ~n** paw
Präparat *das;* **~[e]s, ~e** preparation
präparieren [1] *tr. V.* prepare
[2] *refl. V.* (geh.: sich vorbereiten) prepare oneself
Präposition *die;* **~, ~en** (Sprachw.) preposition
Prärie *die;* **~, ~n** prairie
Präsens /'prɛ:zɛns/ *das;* **~** (Sprachw.) present [tense]
präsentieren *tr. V.* present
Präservativ *das;* **~s, ~e** condom
Präsident *der;* **~en, ~en, Präsidentin** *die;* **~, ~nen** president
Präsidium *das;* **~s, Präsidien (a)** committee
(b) (Vorsitz) chairmanship
(c) (Polizei~) police headquarters *sing. or pl.*
prasseln *itr. V.* pelt down; ‹*shots*› clatter; ‹*fire*› crackle
prassen *itr. V.* live extravagantly; (schlemmen) feast
Präteritum *das;* **~s** (Sprachw.) preterite [tense]
Prävention *die;* **~, ~en** prevention
Praxis *die;* **~, Praxen (a)** (im Unterschied zur Theorie) practice *no art.;* (Erfahrung) [practical] experience
(b) (eines Arztes, Anwalts usw.) practice; (Räume) (eines Arztes) surgery (Brit.); office (Amer.); (eines Anwalts usw.) office
präzise [1] *Adj.* precise
[2] *adv.* precisely
Präzision *die;* **~:** precision
predigen [1] *itr. V.* deliver a/the sermon
[2] *tr. V.* preach
Prediger *der;* **~s, ~, Predigerin** *die;* **~, ~nen** preacher

Predigt *die;* **~, ~en** sermon

Preis *der;* **~es, ~e: (a)** (Kaufpreis) price (**für** of)
(b) (Belohnung) prize

Preis-: ~anstieg *der* rise *or* increase in prices; **~aus·schreiben** *das* [prize] competition; **~bindung** *die* (Wirtsch.) price-fixing

Preisel·beere *die* cranberry

preisen *unr. tr. V.* (geh.) praise

preis-, Preis-: ~erhöhung *die* price increase *or* rise; **~geld** *das* prize money; **~günstig** 1 *Adj.* ‹*goods*› available at unusually low prices; ‹*purchases*› at favourable prices; inexpensive ‹*holiday*›; **das ~günstigste Angebot** the best bargain *or* value; **das ist [sehr] ~günstig** that is [very] good value; 2 *adv.* at a low price; **etw. ~günstig herstellen/verkaufen/bekommen** produce/sell/get sth. at a low price; **~kampf** *der* price war; **~liste** *die* price list; **~nachlass**, ***~nachlaß** *der* price reduction; **~richter** *der*, **~richterin** *die* judge; **~schild** *das* price tag; **~senkung** *die* price reduction *or* cut; **~steigerung** *die* rise *or* increase in prices; **~tafel** *die* price list; **~träger** *der*, **~trägerin** *die* prizewinner; **~verleihung** *die* presentation [of prizes/awards]; **~wert** 1 *Adj.* good value *pred.;* 2 *adv.* ‹*eat*› at a reasonable price; **dort kann man ~wert einkaufen** you get good value for money there

prellen *tr. V.* **(a)** (betrügen) cheat (**um** out of); **die Zeche ~:** avoid paying the bill
(b) (verletzen) bash; bruise

Prellung *die;* **~, ~en** bruise

Premiere /prə'mi̯e:rə/ *die;* **~, ~n** opening night

Presse *die;* **~, ~n (a)** press; (Zitronen~) squeezer
(b) (Zeitungen) press

Presse-: ~erklärung *die* press statement; **~freiheit** *die* freedom of the press; **~information** *die* press release; **~konferenz** *die* press conference; **~meldung** *die* press report

pressen *tr. V.* press

Presse·sprecher *der*, **~sprecherin** *die* spokesman; press officer

Press·luft-, ***Preß·luft-: ~bohrer** *der* pneumatic drill; **~hammer** *der* pneumatic hammer

Prestige /prɛs'ti:ʒə/ *das;* **~s** prestige

prickeln *itr. V.* tingle

pries *1. u. 3. Pers. Sg. Prät. v.* PREISEN

Priester *der;* **~s, ~:** priest

Priesterin *die;* **~, ~nen** priestess

prima (ugs.) 1 *indekl. Adj.* great (coll.)
2 *adv.* ‹*taste*› great (coll.); ‹*sleep*› fantastically well (coll.)

---

*alte Schreibung - vgl. Hinweis auf S. xiv

primär 1 *Adj.* primary
2 *adv.* primarily

Primel *die;* **~, ~n** primula; (Schlüsselblume) cowslip

primitiv 1 *Adj.* primitive; (einfach, schlicht) simple
2 *adv.* primitively; (einfach, schlicht) in a simple manner

Prim·zahl *die* (Math.) prime [number]

Prinz *der;* **~en, ~en** prince

Prinzessin *die;* **~, ~nen** princess

Prinzip *das;* **~s, ~ien** /-'tsi:pi̯ən/ principle; **aus ~:** on principle; **im ~:** in principle

prinzipiell 1 *Adj.* in principle *postpos., not pred.;* ‹*rejection*› on principle
2 *adv.* (im Prinzip) in principle; (aus Prinzip) on principle

Prion *das;* **~s, ~en** (Biol.) prion

Prise *die;* **~, ~n** pinch

privat 1 *Adj.* private; (persönlich) personal
2 *adv.* privately

Privat-: ~adresse *die* private *or* home address; **~angelegenheit** *die* private matter; **~besitz** *der* private property; **~eigentum** *das* private property

privatisieren *tr. V.* (Wirtsch.) privatize; transfer into private ownership

Privatisierung *die;* **~, ~en** (Wirtsch.) privatization; transfer into private ownership

Privat-: ~leben *das* private life; **~lehrer** *der*, **~lehrerin** *die* private tutor; **~patient** *der*, **~patientin** *die* private patient; **~schule** *die* private school; (Eliteschule in Großbritannien) public school; **~unterricht** *der* private tuition; **~vermögen** *das* private fortune; **~versicherung** *die* private insurance; **~weg** *der* private way; **~wirtschaftlich** *Adj.* private-sector *attrib.*

privilegiert *Adj.* privileged

pro *Präp. mit Akk.* per; **~ Stück** each; a piece

pro- pro-; **~westlich/~kommunistisch** pro-western/pro-communist

Probe *die;* **~, ~n (a)** test
(b) (Muster, Teststück) sample
(c) (Theater~, Orchester~) rehearsal

Probe-: ~fahrt *die* trial run; (vor dem Kauf, nach einer Reparatur) test drive; **~jahr** *das* probationary year

proben *tr., itr. V.* rehearse

probe·weise *Adv.* ‹*employ*› on a trial basis

Probe·zeit *die* probationary period

probieren 1 *tr. V.* **(a)** try; have a go at
(b) (kosten) taste; try
(c) (aus~) try out; (an~) try on ‹*clothes, shoes*›
2 *itr. V.* **(a)** (versuchen) try
(b) (kosten) have a taste

Problem *das;* **~s, ~e** problem

problematisch *Adj.* problematic[al]
problematisieren *tr. V.* **etw. ~:** expound the problems of sth.
problem·los 1 *Adj.* problem-free
2 *adv.* without any problems
Product-placement /'prɔdaktpleɪsmənt/ *das;* **~s, ~** product placement
Produkt *das;* **~[e]s, ~e** (auch Math., fig.) product
Produktion *die;* **~, ~en** production
produktiv 1 productive; prolific ‹*writer, artist, etc.*›
2 *adv.* ‹*work, cooperate*› productively
Produktivität *die;* **~:** productivity
Produzent *der;* **~en, ~en, Produzentin** *die;* **~, ~nen** producer
produzieren *tr. V.* produce
Prof. *Abk.* = **Professor** Prof.
professionell 1 *Adj.* professional
2 *adv.* professionally
Professor *der;* **~s, ~en, Professorin** *die;* **~, ~nen** professor
Professur *die;* **~, ~en** professorship, chair (**für** in)
Profi *der;* **~s, ~s** (ugs.) pro (coll.)
Profil *das;* **~s, ~e (a)** (Seitenansicht) profile; **im ~:** in profile
(b) (von Reifen, Schuhsohlen) tread
Profit *der;* **~[e]s, ~e** profit
profitieren *itr. V.* profit (**von, bei** by)
profund *Adj.* (geh.) profound; deep
Prognose *die;* **~, ~n** prognosis; (Wetter~, Wirtschafts~) forecast
prognostizieren *tr. V.* (geh.) forecast; predict
Programm *das;* **~s, ~e** programme; program (Amer., Computing); (Ferns.: Sender) channel
Programm-: ~fehler *der* (DV) program error; error in the/a program; **~heft** *das* programme; **~hinweis** *der* programme announcement
programmieren *tr. V.* **(a)** (DV) program **(b)** (auf etw. festlegen) programme
Programmierer *der;* **~s, ~, Programmiererin** *die;* **~, ~nen** (DV) programmer
Programm-: ~vorschau *die* (im Fernsehen) preview [of the week's/evening's *etc.* viewing]; (im Kino) trailers *pl.;* **~zeitschrift** *die* radio and television magazine
progressiv 1 *Adj.* progressive
2 *adv.* progressively
Projekt *das;* **~[e]s, ~e** project
Projekt·management *das* project management
Projektor /pro'jɛktɔr/ *der;* **~s, ~en** /-'to:rən/ projector
Projekt·tage *Pl.* (Schulw.) project[-work] days
projizieren /proji'tsi:rən/ *tr. V.* (Optik) project
proklamieren *tr. V.* proclaim
Prolet *der;* **~en, ~en** (abwertend) peasant
Proletariat *das;* **~[e]s** proletariat
Proletarier /prole'ta:ri̯ɐ/ *der;* **~s, ~:** proletarian
proletarisch *Adj.* proletarian
prollig *Adj.* (salopp) boorish
Promenade *die;* **~, ~n** promenade
Promille *das;* **~s, ~:** [part] per thousand; **er fährt nur ohne ~** (ugs.) he never drinks and drives; **er hatte 1,8 ~:** he had a blood alcohol level of 1.8 per thousand
Promille·grenze *die* (ugs.) legal [alcohol] limit
prominent *Adj.* prominent
Prominente *der/die; adj. Dekl.* prominent figure
Prominenz *die;* **~:** prominent figures *pl.*
Promotion /promo'tsi̯o:n/ *die;* **~** (Wirtsch.) promotion; **für etw. ~ machen** promote sth.
promovieren 1 *itr. V.* **(a)** (die Doktorwürde erlangen) gain *or* obtain a/one's doctorate **(b)** (eine Dissertation schreiben) do a doctorate (**über** + *Akk.* on)
2 *tr. V.* confer a doctorate *or* the degree of doctor on
prompt 1 *Adj.* prompt
2 *adv.* **(a)** promptly
(b) (ugs., meist iron.: wie erwartet) [and] sure enough
Promptheit *die;* **~:** promptness
Pronomen *das;* **~s, ~** *od.* **Pronomina** (Sprachw.) pronoun
Propaganda *die;* **~:** propaganda
propagieren *tr. V.* propagate
Propan·gas *das* propane
Propeller *der;* **~s, ~** propeller
Prophet *der;* **~en, ~en, Prophetin** *die;* **~, ~nen** prophet
prophezeien *tr. V.* prophesy (*Dat.* for); predict ‹*result, weather*›
Proportion *die;* **~, ~en** proportion
Prosa *die;* **~:** prose
Prosa·literatur *die* prose writing
prosit *Interj.* your [very good] health; **~ Neujahr!** happy New Year!
Prospekt *der od.* (bes. österr.) *das;* **~[e]s, ~e** (Werbeschrift) brochure; (Werbezettel) leaflet
prost *Interj.* (ugs.) cheers (Brit. coll.)
Prostituierte *die/der; adj. Dekl.* prostitute
Prostitution *die;* **~:** prostitution *no art.*
Protagonist *der;* **~en, ~en, Protagonistin** *die;* **~, ~nen** (geh.) protagonist
Protest *der;* **~[e]s, ~e** protest
Protestant *der;* **~en, ~en, Protestantin** *die;* **~, ~nen** Protestant
protestantisch *Adj.* Protestant

Protestantismus *der;* ~: Protestantism *no art.*

protestieren *itr. V.* protest, make a protest (**gegen** against, about)

Protest·kundgebung *die* protest rally

Prothese *die;* ~, **~n** artificial limb; prosthesis (Med.); (Zahn~) set of dentures; dentures *pl.*

Protokoll *das;* **~s, ~e (a)** (wörtlich mitgeschrieben) transcript; (Ergebnis~) minutes *pl.;* (bei Gericht) record; **etw. zu ~ geben** make a statement about sth.
(b) (diplomatisches Zeremoniell) protocol

protokollieren 1 *tr. V.* take down; take the minutes of ‹*meeting*›; minute ‹*remark*›
2 *itr. V.* take the minutes; (bei Gericht) keep the record

protzen *itr. V.* (ugs.) swank (coll.); show off; **mit etw. ~**: show sth. off

protzig (ugs. abwertend) 1 *Adj.* swanky (coll.); showy
2 *adv.* swankily (coll.)

Proviant *der;* **~s, ~e** provisions *pl.*

Provinz *die;* ~, **~en** province

provinziell 1 *Adj.* provincial
2 *adv.* provincially

Provision *die;* ~, **~en** (Kaufmannsspr.) commission

provisorisch 1 *Adj.* provisional; temporary
2 *adv.* temporarily

Pro·vitamin *das* provitamin

Provokation *die;* ~, **~en** provocation

provozieren *tr. V.* provoke

Prozedur *die;* ~, **~en** procedure

Prozent *das;* **~[e]s, ~e (a)** *nach Zahlenangaben Pl. ungebeugt* per cent *sing.;* **fünf ~**: five per cent
(b) *Pl.* (ugs.) (Gewinnanteil) share *sing.* of the profits; (Rabatt) discount *sing.;* **auf etw.** (*Akk.*) **~e bekommen** get a discount on sth.

-prozentig *adj.* -per-cent

Prozent-: ~punkt *der* percentage point; **~rechnung** *die* percentage calculation; **~satz** *der* percentage

prozentual 1 *Adj.* percentage
2 *adv.* **~ am Gewinn beteiligt sein** have a percentage share in the profits

Prozess, *Prozeß *der;* **Prozesses, Prozesse (a)** trial; (Fall) [court] case; **einen ~ gewinnen/verlieren** win/lose a case
(b) (Vorgang) process

prozessieren *itr. V.* go to court; **gegen jmdn. ~**: bring an action against sb.

Prozess·kosten, *Prozeß·kosten *Pl.* legal costs

Prozessor *der;* **~s, ~en** (DV) [central] processor

prüde (abwertend) 1 *Adj.* prudish
2 prudishly

*old spelling - see note on page xiv

Prüderie *die;* ~ (abwertend) prudery; prudishness

prüfen *tr. V.* **(a)** *auch itr.* examine ‹*pupil, student, etc.*›; **mündlich/schriftlich geprüft werden** have an oral/a written examination
(b) (untersuchen) examine (**auf** + *Akk.* for); check ‹*device, machine, calculation*› (**auf** + *Akk.* for); investigate ‹*complaint*›; (testen) test (**auf** + *Akk.* for)
(c) (kontrollieren) check; examine ‹*accounts, books*›
(d) (vor einer Entscheidung) check ‹*price*›; examine ‹*offer*›; consider ‹*application*›

Prüfer *der;* **~s, ~, Prüferin** *die;* **~, ~nen**
(a) inspector; (Buch~) auditor
(b) (im Examen) examiner

Prüfling *der;* **~s, ~e** examinee; [examination] candidate

Prüfung *die;* ~, **~en (a)** examination; exam (coll.); **eine ~ machen** *od.* **ablegen** take an examination
(b) ▶ PRÜFEN B–D: examination; check; investigation; test; consideration

Prügel *Pl.* (Schläge) beating *sing.;* (als Strafe für Kinder) hiding (coll.)

Prügelei *die;* ~, **~en** (ugs.) punch-up (coll.); fight

Prügel·knabe *der* whipping boy

prügeln 1 *tr.* (*auch itr.*) *V.* beat
2 *refl. V.* **sich ~**: fight; **sich mit jmdm. [um etw.] ~**: fight sb. [over *or* for sth.]

Prunk *der;* **~[e]s** splendour; magnificence

Prunk-: ~bau *der; Pl.* **~~ten** magnificent building; **~stück** *das* showpiece

PS /peːˈ|ɛs/ *das;* **~, ~**: *Abk.* = **Pferdestärke** h.p.

Psalm *der;* **~s, ~en** psalm

Psychiater *der;* **~s, ~, Psychiaterin** *die;* **~, ~nen** psychiatrist

Psychiatrie *die;* ~: psychiatry *no art.*

psychisch 1 *Adj.* psychological; mental ‹*process, illness*›
2 *adv.* psychologically; **~ gesund/krank sein** be mentally fit/ill

psycho-: Psycho- /psyːço-/: **~loge** *der;* **~~n, ~~n** psychologist; **~logie** *die;* **~~**: psychology; **~login** *die;* **~~, ~~nen** psychologist; **~logisch** 1 *Adj.* psychological; 2 *adv.* psychologically; **~path** *der;* **~~en, ~~en, ~pathin** *die;* **~~, ~~nen** psychopath

Psychose *die;* ~, **~n** psychosis

psychotisch *Adj.* psychotic

pubertär *Adj.* pubertal

Pubertät *die;* ~: puberty

pubertieren *itr. V.* reach puberty; **~d** pubescent

publik *Adj.* **~ sein/werden** be/become public knowledge

Publikum *das;* **~s (a)** (Zuschauer, Zuhörer) audience; (bei Sportveranstaltungen) crowd
(b) (Kreis von Interessierten) public; (eines Schriftstellers) readership

(c) (Besucher) clientele
Publikums-: ~erfolg *der* success with the public; **~liebling** *der* idol of the public; **~sport** *der* spectator sport
publizieren *tr.* (*auch itr.*) *V.* publish
Publizität *die;* **~:** publicity
Pudding *der;* **~s, ~e** *od.* **~s** *thick, usually flavoured, milk-based dessert;* ≈ blancmange
Pudel *der;* **~s, ~:** poodle
Puder *der;* **~s, ~:** powder
Puder·dose *die* powder compact
pudern *tr. V.* powder
Puder·zucker *der* icing sugar (Brit.); confectioners' sugar (Amer.)
Puff[1] *der;* **~[e]s, Püffe** (ugs.) **(a)** (Stoß) thump; (leichter/kräftiger Stoß mit dem Ellenbogen) nudge/dig
(b) (Knall) bang
Puff[2] *der od. das;* **~s, ~s** (salopp: Bordell) knocking shop (Brit. sl.); brothel
puffen (ugs.) *tr. V.:* ▶ PUFF[1] A: thump; nudge; dig
Puff·reis *der* puffed rice
Pulli *der;* **~s, ~s** (ugs.), **Pullover** *der;* **~s, ~:** pullover; sweater
Pullunder *der;* **~s, ~:** slipover
Puls *der;* **~es, ~e** pulse
Puls·ader *die* artery
Pult *das;* **~[e]s, ~e** desk; (Lese~) lectern
Pulver *das;* **~s, ~:** powder
pulverisieren *tr. V.* pulverize; powder
Pulver·kaffee *der* instant coffee
pumm[e]lig *Adj.* (ugs.) chubby
Pumpe *die;* **~, ~n** pump
pumpen *tr., itr. V.* **(a)** (auch fig.) pump
(b) (salopp) ▶ LEIHEN A, B
Pump-: ~spray *das* pump spray; **~zerstäuber** *der* pump-action atomizer
Punkt *der;* **~[e]s, ~e (a)** (Tupfen) dot; (größer) spot
(b) (Satzzeichen) full stop
(c) (I-Punkt) dot
(d) (Stelle) point; **ein schwacher/wunder ~** (fig.) a weak/sore point
(e) (Gegenstand, Thema, Abschnitt) point; (einer Tagesordnung) item
(f) (Bewertungs~) point; (bei einer Prüfung) mark
(g) ~ 12 Uhr at 12 o'clock on the dot
pünktlich [1] *Adj.* punctual
[2] *adv.* punctually; on time
Pünktlichkeit *die;* **~:** punctuality
Punsch *der;* **~[e]s, ~e** *od.* **Pünsche** punch
Pupille *die;* **~, ~n** pupil
Puppe *die;* **~, ~n (a)** doll[y]
(b) (Marionette) puppet; marionette
Puppen-: ~stube *die* doll's house; dollhouse (Amer.); **~wagen** *der* doll's pram
pur *Adj.* **(a)** (rein) pure
(b) (unvermischt) neat ‹*whisky etc.*›; straight
Püree *das;* **~s, ~s (a)** purée
(b) ▶ KARTOFFELBREI
pürieren *tr. V.* (Kochk.) purée ‹*potatoes, apples, etc.*›; (zerstampfen) mash
Purpur *der;* **~s** crimson
purzeln *itr. V.; mit sein* (fam.) tumble
pushen *tr. V.* **(a)** (Drogenjargon) push
(b) (Journalistenjargon) push
Puste *die;* **~** (salopp) puff; breath
Pustel *die;* **~, ~n** pimple; pustule (Med.)
pusten (ugs.) *tr., itr. V.* blow
Pute *die;* **~, ~n** turkey hen; (als Braten) turkey
Puter *der;* **~s, ~:** turkeycock; (als Braten) turkey
Putsch *der;* **~[e]s, ~e** putsch; coup [d'état]
putschen *itr. V.* organize a putsch *or* coup
Putsch·versuch *der* attempted putsch *or* coup
Putz *der;* **~es** plaster; (für Außenmauern) rendering
putzen *tr. V.* **(a)** (blank reiben) polish
(b) (säubern) clean; groom ‹*horse*›; **[sich** (*Dat.*)**] die Zähne/die Nase ~:** clean *or* brush one's teeth/blow one's nose
(c) *auch itr.* (sauber machen) clean ‹*room, shop, etc.*›; **~ gehen** work as a cleaner
(d) (vorbereiten) wash and prepare ‹*vegetables*›
Putz-: ~fimmel *der* (ugs. abwertend) mania for cleaning; **~frau** *die* cleaner
putzig *Adj.* (ugs.) (entzückend) sweet; cute (Amer.); (possierlich) funny; comical
Putz-: ~lappen *der* [cleaning] rag; cloth; **~leute** *Pl.* cleaners; **~mann** *der* cleaner; **~mittel** *das* cleaning agent; **~tuch** *das; Pl.* **~tücher** cloth; (Lappen) [cleaning] rag
puzzeln /ˈpʊzl̩n/ *itr. V.* do jigsaw puzzles/a jigsaw [puzzle]
Puzzle /ˈpʊzl̩/ *das;* **~s, ~s, Puzzlespiel** *das* jigsaw [puzzle]
Pyjama /pʏˈdʒaːma/ *der* (österr., schweiz. auch: *das*); **~s, ~s** pyjamas *pl.*
Pyramide *die;* **~, ~n** pyramid
pyramiden·förmig *Adj.* pyramidal; pyramid-shaped
Python *der;* **~s, ~s** *od.* **~en, Python·schlange** *die* python

Qq

q, Q /ku:/ *das;* ~, ~: q/Q

Quacksalber *der;* **~s, ~, Quacksalberin** *die;* **~, ~nen** (abwertend) quack [doctor]

Quader *der;* **~s, ~** *od.* (österr.:) **~n (a)** (Steinblock) ashlar block; [rectangular] block of stone
(b) (Geom.) rectangular parallelepiped; cuboid

Quadrat *das;* **~[e]s, ~e** square

quadratisch *Adj.* square

Quadrat-: ~meter *der od. das* square metre; **~wurzel** *die* (Math.) square root **(aus** of); **~zahl** *die* square number

quaken *itr. V.* ‹*duck*› quack; ‹*frog*› croak

Qual *die;* **~, ~en (a)** torment
(b) (Schmerzen) agony; **~en** pain *sing.;* agony *sing.;* (seelisch) torment *sing.*

quälen *tr. V.* **(a)** torment ‹*person, animal*›; be cruel to ‹*animal*›; (foltern) torture
(b) (plagen) ‹*cough etc.*› plague; (belästigen) pester

Quälerei *die;* **~, ~en (a)** torment; (Folter) torture; (Grausamkeit) cruelty
(b) (das Belästigen) pestering

Qualifikation *die;* **~, ~en (a)** (Ausbildung) qualifications *pl.*
(b) (Sport) qualification

qualifizieren *refl. V.* **(a)** gain qualifications
(b) (Sport) qualify

qualifiziert *Adj.* **(a)** ‹*work, post*› requiring particular qualifications
(b) (sachkundig) competent; skilled ‹*work*›

Qualität *die;* **~, ~en** quality

qualitativ **1** *Adj.* qualitative; ‹*difference, change*› in quality
2 *adv.* with regard to quality

Qualitäts·erzeugnis *das* quality product

Qualle *die;* **~, ~n** jellyfish

Qualm *der;* **~[e]s** [thick] smoke

qualmen *itr. V.* **(a)** give off clouds of [thick] smoke
(b) (ugs.: rauchen) puff away

qualmig *Adj.* (ugs.) thick with smoke *postpos.;* smoke-filled

qual·voll **1** *Adj.* agonizing
2 *adv.* agonizingly

Quantität *die;* **~, ~en** quantity

quantitativ **1** *Adj.* quantitative
2 *adv.* quantitatively

Quantum *das;* **~s, Quanten** quota **(an** + *Dat.* of); (Dosis) dose

*alte Schreibung - vgl. Hinweis auf S. xiv

Quarantäne /karan'tɛ:nə/ *die;* **~, ~n** quarantine

Quark *der;* **~s** quark

Quark·speise *die* quark dish

Quartal *das;* **~s, ~e** quarter [of the year]

Quartett *das;* **~[e]s, ~e (a)** quartet
(b) (Spiel) ≈ Happy Families; (Satz von vier Karten) set [of four]

Quartier *das;* **~s, ~e** accommodation *no indef. art.;* accommodations *pl.* (Amer.); place to stay; (Mil.) quarters *pl.*

Quarz *der;* **~es, ~e** quartz

Quarz·uhr *die* quartz clock; (Armbanduhr) quartz watch

quasi *Adv.* **[so] ~:** more or less; (so gut wie) as good as

quasseln (ugs.) **1** *itr. V.* chatter; rabbit on (Brit. sl.) **(von** about)
2 *tr. V.* spout, babble ‹*nonsense*›

Quaste *die;* **~, ~n** tassel

Quatsch *der;* **~[e]s** (ugs.) **(a)** (Äußerung) rubbish
(b) (Handlung) nonsense; (Unfug) messing about; **lass den ~:** stop that nonsense

quatschen (ugs.) **1** *itr. V.* **(a)** (dumm reden) rabbit on (Brit. coll.)
(b) (klatschen) gossip; **es wird so viel gequatscht** there is so much gossip
(c) (sich unterhalten) [have a] chat *or* (coll.) natter
2 *tr. V.* (äußern) spout ‹*nonsense, rubbish*›

Quatsch·kopf *der* (salopp) stupid chatterbox; (Schwätzer, Schwafler) windbag

Queck·silber *das* mercury

Quell·bewölkung *die* (Met.) cumulus clouds *pl.*

Quelle *die;* **~, ~n** spring; (eines Flusses; fig.) source

quellen *unr. itr. V.; mit sein* **(a)** ‹*liquid*› gush, stream; (aus der Erde) well up; ‹*smoke*› billow
(b) (sich ausdehnen) swell [up]

Quell·wasser *das; Pl.* **~** *od.* **Quell·wässer** spring water

quengeln *itr.* (*auch tr.*) *V.* (ugs.) **(a)** (weinen) ‹*baby*› whimper, (coll.) grizzle
(b) (drängen) nag
(c) (nörgeln) carp

quer *Adv.* sideways; (schräg) diagonally; (rechtwinklig) at right angles; **~ durch/über** (+ *Akk.*) straight through/across

Quer-: ~achse *die* transverse axis; **~denker** *der,* **~denkerin** *die* lateral thinker

Quere *die* **jmdm. in die ~ kommen** bump into sb. (coll.); (fig.: jmdn. behindern) get in sb.'s way (coll.)

quer-, Quer-: ~flöte *die* transverse flute; **~format** *das* landscape format; **~kopf** *der* (ugs.) awkward cuss (coll.); (komischer Kauz) oddball (coll.); **~köpfig** *Adj.* awkward; perverse; **~schläger** *der* deflected shot; ricochet; **~schnitt** *der* (*auch fig.*) cross section; **~schnitt[s]·gelähmt** *Adj.* (Med.) paraplegic; **~straße** *die* intersecting road; **~treiber** *der;* **~~s, ~~, ~treiberin** *die;* **~~, ~~nen** (ugs. abwertend) troublemaker

Querulant *der;* **~en, ~en, Querulantin** *die;* **~, ~nen** (abwertend) malcontent

quetschen *tr. V.* crush; **sich** (*Dat.*) **die Hand ~**: get one's hand caught

Quetschung *die;* **~, ~en** bruise; contusion (Med.)

quietschen *itr. V.* squeak; ‹*brakes, tyres*› squeal, screech; (ugs.) ‹*person*› squeal, shriek

Quirl *der;* **~[e]s, ~e** *long-handled blender with a star-shaped head*

quirlig *Adj.* lively; (flink) nimble

quitt *Adj.* (ugs.) quits

Quitte *die;* **~, ~n** quince

quittieren *tr. V.* **(a)** *auch itr.* acknowledge, confirm ‹*receipt, condition*›; give a receipt for ‹*sum, invoice*›
(b) etw. mit etw. ~: react *or* respond to sth. with sth.

Quittung *die;* **~, ~en (a)** receipt
(b) (fig.) come-uppance (coll.)

Quiz /kvɪs/ *das;* **~, ~**: quiz

quoll *1. u. 3. Pers. Sg. Prät. v.* QUELLEN

Quote *die;* **~, ~n** proportion

Quoten·regelung *die: requirement that women should be adequately represented*

Quotient *der;* **~en, ~en** (Math.) quotient **(aus** of)

Rr

r, R /ɛr/ *das;* **~, ~**: r/R

Rabatt *der;* **~[e]s, ~e** discount

Rabatte *die;* **~, ~n** border

Rabbi *der;* **~[s], ~nen** *od.* **~s (a)** (Titel) Rabbi
(b) (Person) rabbi

Rabbiner *der;* **~s, ~**: rabbi

Rabe *der;* **~n, ~n** raven

Rabenmutter *die*; *Pl.* **Rabenmütter** (abwertend) uncaring [brute of a] mother

rabiat 1 *Adj.* violent; brutal; ruthless ‹*methods*›
2 *adv.* (gewalttätig) violently; brutally

Rache *die;* **~**: revenge; **[an jmdm.] ~ nehmen** take revenge [on sb.]

Rache·akt *der* (geh.) act of revenge, reprisal (*Gen.* by, on the part of)

Rachen *der;* **~s, ~ (a)** (Schlund) pharynx (Anat.)
(b) (Maul) mouth; maw (literary); (fig.) jaws *pl.*

rächen 1 *tr. V.* avenge ‹*person, crime*›; take revenge for ‹*insult, crime*›
2 *refl. V.* **(a)** take one's revenge
(b) ‹*mistake etc.*› take its/their toll

Rachitis *die;* **~** (Med.) rickets *sing.*

Rach·sucht *die* (geh.) lust for revenge

rach·süchtig (geh.) 1 *Adj.* vengeful
2 *adv.* vengefully

Rad *das;* **~es, Räder (a)** wheel; **das fünfte ~ am Wagen sein** (fig. ugs.) be superfluous; **ein ~ abhaben** (fig. ugs.) have a screw loose (coll.)
(b) (Fahrrad) bicycle; bike (coll.); **~ fahren** cycle; ride a bicycle *or* (coll.) bike

Radar *der od. das;* **~s** radar

Radar-: ~falle *die* (ugs.) [radar] speed trap; **~kontrolle** *die* [radar] speed check; **~schirm** *der* radar screen

Rad·dampfer *der* paddle steamer

radeln *itr. V.; mit sein* (ugs., bes. südd.) cycle

Rädels·führer *der,* **Rädels·führerin** *die* (abwertend) ringleader

rad-, Rad-: ***~|fahren** ▶ RAD B; **~fahrer** *der,* **~fahrerin** *die* cyclist

Radien ▶ RADIUS

radieren *tr.* (*auch itr.*) *V.* erase

Radier·gummi *der* rubber [eraser]

Radierung *die;* **~, ~en** (Grafik) etching

Radieschen *das;* **~s, ~**: radish

radikal 1 *Adj.* radical; drastic ‹*measure, method, cure*›
2 *adv.* radically; (vollständig) totally

Radikalismus *der;* **~**: radicalism

Radikalität *die;* **~**: radicalness; radical nature

Radio *das* (südd., schweiz. auch: *der*); **~s, ~s** radio; **~ hören** listen to the radio

radio-, Radio-: ~aktiv /----'-/ 1 *Adj.* radioactive; 2 *adv.* radioactively; **~aktivität** /-----'-/ *die* radioactivity; **~sender** *der* radio station; **~wecker** *der* radio alarm clock

Radius *der;* **~, Radien** radius

Rad-: ~kappe *die* hubcap; **~lager** *das* wheel bearing

Radler *der;* **~s, ~: (a)** cyclist **(b)** (bes. südd.: Getränk) shandy

Radlerin *die;* **~, ~nen** cyclist

Rad-: ~rennbahn *die* cycle racing track; **~rennen** *das* cycle race; (Sport) cycle racing; **~sport** *der* cycling *no def. art.;* **~tour** *die* cycling tour; **~weg** *der* cycle path *or* track

raffen *tr. V.* **(a)** snatch; rake in (coll.) ‹*money*›; **etw. [an sich] ~:** seize sth.; (eilig) snatch sth.
(b) gather ‹*material, curtain*›

Raffinerie *die;* **~, ~n** refinery

Raffinesse *die;* **~, ~n (a)** (Schlauheit) guile; ingenuity
(b) (Finesse) refinement

raffiniert [1] *Adj.* **(a)** ingenious ‹*plan, design*›; (verfeinert) refined, subtle ‹*colour, scheme, effect*›; sophisticated ‹*dish, cut (of clothes)*›
(b) (gerissen) cunning ‹*person, trick*›
[2] *adv.* **(a)** ingeniously; (verfeinert) with great refinement/sophistication
(b) (gerissen) cunningly

Raffiniertheit *die;* **~ (a)** (Klugheit) ingenuity; (Verfeinerung) refinement; sophistication
(b) (Gerissenheit) cunning

Raft *das;* **~s, ~s** raft

raften *itr. V.* raft

Rafting *das;* **~s** rafting

Rage /ˈraːʒə/ *die;* **~** (ugs.) fury

ragen *itr. V.* **(a)** (vertikal) rise [up]; ‹*mountains*› tower up
(b) (horizontal) project, stick out (**in** + *Akk.* into; **über** + *Akk.* over)

r

Ragout /raˈguː/ *das;* **~s, ~s** ragout

Rahm *der;* **~[e]s** cream

rahmen *tr. V.* frame

Rahmen *der;* **~s, ~ (a)** frame; (Fahrgestell) chassis
(b) (fig.) framework

Rakete *die;* **~, ~n** rocket; (Lenkflugkörper) missile

rammen *tr. V.* ram

Rampe *die;* **~, ~n (a)** (Lade~) [loading] platform
(b) (schiefe Fläche) ramp

Rampen·licht *das:* **im ~ [der Öffentlichkeit] stehen** be in the limelight

Ramsch *der;* **~[e]s, ~e** (ugs.) **(a)** (Ware) trashy goods *pl.;*
(b) (Kram) junk

ran *Adv.* (ugs.) **(a)** ▶ HERAN;
(b) (fang[t] an) off you go; (fangen wir an) let's go
(c) (greif[t] an) go at him/them!

Rand *der;* **~[e]s, Ränder (a)** edge; (Einfassung) border; (Hut~) brim; (Brillen~, Gefäß~, Krater~) rim; (eines Abgrunds) brink; (auf einem Schriftstück) margin; (Weg~) verge; (Stadt~) outskirts *pl.;*
(b) (Schmutz~) mark; (rund) ring

*old spelling - see note on page xiv

randalieren *itr. V.* riot

Randalierer *der;* **~s, ~, Randaliererin** *die;* **~, ~nen** hooligan

rand-, Rand-: ~bemerkung *die* marginal note *or* comment; **~gruppe** *die* (Soziol.) fringe *or* marginal group; **~stein** *der* kerb; **~voll** *Adj.* ‹*glass etc.*› full to the brim

rang *1. u. 3. Pers. Sg. Prät. v.* RINGEN

Rang *der;* **~[e]s, Ränge (a)** rank; (in der Gesellschaft) status
(b) (im Theater) circle; **erster ~:** dress circle; **zweiter ~:** upper circle; **dritter ~:** gallery

rangieren /raŋˈʒiːrən/ *tr. V.* shunt ‹*trucks etc.*›; switch ‹*cars*› (Amer.)

Rang-: ~liste *die* ranking list; **Nummer eins der internationalen ~liste** number one in the world rankings; **~ordnung** *die* order of precedence; (Verhaltensf.) pecking order

Ranke *die;* **~, ~n** (Bot.) tendril

ranken *refl. V.* climb, grow (**an** + *Dat.* up, **über** + *Akk.* over)

Ranking /ˈræŋkɪŋ/ *das;* **~s** ranking

rann *1. u. 3. Pers. Sg. Prät. v.* RINNEN

rannte *1. u. 3. Pers. Sg. Prät. v.* RENNEN

Ranzen *der;* **~s, ~:** satchel

ranzig *Adj.* rancid

Rap /ræp/ *der;* **~[s], ~s** rap

Rappe *der;* **~n, ~n** black horse

rappen /ˈræpn̩/ *itr. V.* rap

Rappen *der;* **~s, ~:** [Swiss] centime

Rapper /ˈræpɐ/ *der;* **~s, ~, Rapperin** *die;* **~, ~nen** rapper

Raps *der;* **~es** (Bot.) rape

rar *Adj.* scarce; (selten) rare

Rarität *die;* **~, ~en** rarity

rasant (ugs.) [1] *Adj.* tremendously fast (coll.) ‹*car, horse, etc.*›
[2] *adv.* at terrific speed (coll.)

rasch [1] *Adj.* quick; speedy, swift ‹*end, action, decision, progress*›
[2] *adv.* quickly; ‹*decide, end, proceed*› swiftly, rapidly

rascheln *itr. V.* rustle; ‹*mouse etc.*› make a rustling noise

rasen *itr. V.* **(a)** *mit sein* (ugs.: eilen) dash *or* rush [along]; (fahren) tear *or* race along; (fig.) ‹*pulse*› race
(b) (toben) ‹*person*› rage

Rasen *der;* **~s, ~:** grass *no indef. art.;* (gepflegte Rasenfläche) lawn

rasend [1] *Adj.* **(a)** (sehr schnell) breakneck *attrib.* ‹*speed*›
(b) (tobend) raging
(c) (heftig) violent
[2] *adv.* (ugs.) incredibly (coll.)

Rasen·mäher *der;* **~s, ~**: lawn-mower
Raser *der;* **~s, ~** (ugs. abwertend) speed merchant (coll.); (rücksichtslos) road hog
Raserei *die;* **~, ~en** (ugs.) tearing along *no art.*
Raserin *die;* **~, ~nen** ▶ RASER
Rasier·apparat *der* [safety] razor; (elektrisch) electric shaver
rasieren *tr. V.* shave; **sich ~**: shave; **sich nass/trocken/elektrisch ~**: have a wet shave/have a dry shave/use an electric shaver
Rasierer *der;* **~s, ~** (ugs.) [electric] shaver
Rasier-: ~klinge *die* razor blade; **~messer** *das* cutthroat razor; **~pinsel** *der* shaving brush; **~schaum** *der* shaving foam; **~seife** *die* shaving soap; **~wasser** *das* aftershave; (vor der Rasur) pre-shave lotion
Räson /rɛˈzɔŋ/ *die* **zur ~ kommen** come to one's senses; **jmdn. zur ~ bringen** make sb. see reason
Rasse *die;* **~, ~n** **(a)** breed **(b)** (Menschen~) race
Rassel *die;* **~, ~n** rattle
rasseln *itr. V.* rattle
Rassen-: ~hass, *~haß *der* racial hatred *no art.;* **~krawall** *der* race riot; **~trennung** *die* racial segregation *no art.*
Rassismus *der;* **~**: racism; racialism
Rassist *der;* **~en, ~en, Rassistin** *die;* **~, ~nen** racist; racialist
rassistisch *Adj.* racist; racialist
Rast *die;* **~, ~en** rest; **~ machen** stop for a break
rasten *itr. V.* rest; take a rest *or* break
Raster *der;* **~s, ~** **(a)** (Druckw.) screen **(b)** (fig.) [conceptual] framework; set pattern
Rast-: ~haus *das* roadside café; (an der Autobahn) motorway restaurant; **~hof** *der* [motorway] motel [and service area]; **~platz** *der* **(a)** place to rest; **(b)** (an Autobahnen) parking place (*with benches and WCs*); picnic area; **~stätte** *die* service area
Rasur *die;* **~, ~en** shave
Rat *der;* **~[e]s, Räte** **(a)** advice; **ein ~**: a word of advice **(b)** (Gremium) council
rät *3. Pers. Sg. Präsens v.* RATEN
Rate *die,* **~, ~n** **(a)** (Teilbetrag) instalment; **etw. auf ~n kaufen** buy sth. by instalments *or* (Brit.) on hire purchase *or* (Amer.) on the installment plan **(b)** (Statistik) rate
raten **1** *unr. itr. V.* **(a) jmdm. ~**: advise sb. **(b)** (schätzen) guess
2 *tr. V.* **(a) jmdm. ~, etw. zu tun** advise sb. to do sth. **(b)** (erraten) guess
Raten·zahlung *die* payment by instalments
Rat·haus *das* town hall
Ratifizierung *die;* **~, ~en** ratification
Rätin *die;* **~, ~nen** councillor
Ration *die;* **~, ~en** ration
rational *Adj.* rational
rationalisieren *tr., itr. V.* rationalize
rationell **1** *Adj.* efficient; (wirtschaftlich) economic
2 *adv.* efficiently; (wirtschaftlich) economically
rationieren *tr. V.* ration
rat·los **1** *Adj.* baffled; helpless ‹*look*›
2 *adv.* helplessly
Rat·losigkeit *die;* **~**: helplessness
ratsam *Adj.* advisable
Ratschlag *der* [piece of] advice
Rätsel *das;* **~s, ~** **(a)** riddle, (Bilder~, Kreuzwort~ usw.) puzzle **(b)** (Geheimnis) mystery
rätselhaft **1** *Adj.* mysterious; (unergründlich) enigmatic
2 *adv.* mysteriously; (unergründlich) enigmatically
rätseln *itr. V.* puzzle, rack one's brains (**über** + *Akk.* over); **~, wer .../ob ...**: try to work out who .../whether ...
Ratte *die;* **~, ~n** (auch fig.) rat
rau **1** *Adj.* **(a)** (nicht glatt) rough **(b)** (nicht mild) harsh, raw ‹*climate, winter*›; raw ‹*wind*› **(c)** (kratzig) husky, hoarse ‹*voice*› **(d)** (entzündet) sore ‹*throat*› **(e)** (nicht feinfühlig) rough; harsh ‹*words, tone*›
2 *adv.* **(a)** (kratzig) ‹*speak etc.*› huskily, hoarsely **(b)** (nicht feinfühlig) roughly
Raub *der;* **~[e]s** **(a)** robbery **(b)** (Beute) stolen goods *pl.*
Raub·bau *der* overexploitation (**an** + *Dat.* of); **~ an etw.** (*Dat.*) **treiben** over-exploit sth.
rauben *tr. V.* steal; kidnap ‹*person*›; **jmdm. etw. ~**: rob sb. of sth.; (geh.: wegnehmen) deprive sb. of sth.
Räuber *der;* **~s, ~, Räuberin** *die;* **~, ~nen** robber
Raub-: ~fisch *der* predatory fish; **~kopie** *die* pirated copy; **~mord** *der* (Rechtsw.) murder (**an** + *Dat.* of) in the course of a robbery *or* with robbery as motive; **~tier** *das* predator; **~überfall** *der* robbery (**auf** + *Akk.* of); **~vogel** *der* bird of prey
Rauch *der;* **~[e]s** smoke
rauchen **1** *itr. V.* smoke
2 *tr.* (*auch itr.*) *V.* smoke ‹*cigarette, pipe, etc.*›; **„Rauchen verboten"** 'No smoking'
Raucher *der;* **~s, ~**: smoker
Raucher-: ~abteil *das* smoking compartment; smoker; **~husten** *der* smoker's cough
Raucherin *die;* **~, ~nen** smoker
räuchern *tr. V.* smoke ‹*meat, fish*›
rauch·frei *Adj.* smoke-free

···›

rauchig *Adj.* smoky; husky ‹*voice*›
Rauch-: **~melder** *der* smoke detector; **~schwaden** *der* cloud of smoke; **~verbot** *das* ban on smoking; **~wolke** *die* cloud of smoke
räudig *Adj.* mangy
rauf *Adv.* (ugs.) up; **~ mit euch!** up you go!; *s. auch* HERAUF; HINAUF
Rau·faser·tapete *die* woodchip wallpaper
raufen [1] *itr., refl. V.* fight [2] *tr. V.* **sich** (*Dat.*) **die Haare/den Bart ~:** tear one's hair/at one's beard
Rauferei *die;* **~, ~en** fight
***rauh** *usw.* ▶ RAU *usw.*
Raum *der;* **~[e]s, Räume (a)** (Wohn~, Nutz~) room
(b) (Gebiet) area; region
(c) (Platz) room; space
räumen *tr. V.* **(a)** clear [away]; clear ‹*snow*›
(b) (an einen Ort) clear; move
(c) (freimachen) clear ‹*street, building, warehouse, stocks, etc.*›
(d) (verlassen) vacate
Raum·fahrt *die;* **~:** space travel
räumlich [1] *Adj.* **(a)** spatial; **aus ~en Gründen** for reasons of space
(b) (dreidimensional) three-dimensional; stereoscopic ‹*vision*›
[2] *adv.* **(a)** spatially
(b) (dreidimensional) three-dimensionally
Räumlichkeit *die;* **~, ~en (a)** *Pl.* rooms
(b) (räumliche Wirkung) three-dimensionality
Raum-: **~schiff** *das* spaceship; **~sonde** *die* space probe
Räumung *die;* **~, ~en (a)** clearing
(b) (das Verlassen) vacation; vacating
(c) (wegen Gefahr) evacuation
(d) (eines Lagers) clearance
Räumungs·verkauf *der* (Kaufmannsspr.) clearance sale
raunen *tr., itr. V.* (geh.) whisper
Raupe *die;* **~, ~n** caterpillar
Rau·reif *der* hoar frost
raus *Adv.* (ugs.) out; **~ mit euch!** out you go!; *s. auch* HERAUS; HINAUS
Rausch *der;* **~[e]s, Räusche (a)** state of drunkenness
(b) (starkes Gefühl) transport; **der ~ der Geschwindigkeit** the exhilaration *or* thrill of speed
rauschen *itr. V.* ‹*water, wind, torrent*› rush; ‹*trees, leaves*› rustle; ‹*skirt, curtains, silk*› swish; ‹*waterfall, strong wind*› roar; ‹*rain*› pour down
Rausch·gift *das* drug; narcotic; **~ nehmen** take drugs; be on drugs
Rauschgift-: **~händler** *der,* **~händlerin** *die* drug trafficker; **~sucht** *die* drug addiction

*alte Schreibung - vgl. Hinweis auf S. xiv

raus|fliegen *unr. itr. V.; mit sein* (ugs.) be fired (coll.)
räuspern *refl. V.* clear one's throat
raus|schmeißen *unr. tr. V.* (ugs.) chuck (coll.) ‹*objects*› out *or* away; give ‹*employee*› the push (coll.) *or* sack (coll.); chuck (coll.) *or* throw ‹*customer, drunk, tenant*› out (**aus** of)
Raute *die;* **~, ~n** (Geom.) rhombus
Rave /reɪv/ *der;* **~s, ~s** rave
Raver /ˈreɪvɐ/ *der;* **~s, ~, Raverin** *die;* **~, ~nen** raver
Razzia *die;* **~, Razzien** raid
reagieren *itr. V.* react (**auf** + *Akk.* to)
Reaktion *die;* **~, ~en** reaction (**auf** + *Akk.* to)
reaktionär *Adj.* reactionary
Reaktionär *der;* **~s, ~e** reactionary
Reaktor *der;* **~s, ~en** /-ˈtoːrən/ reactor
real [1] *Adj.* real
[2] *adv.* actually
realisieren *tr. V.* (geh.) realize
Realismus *der;* **~:** realism
Realist *der;* **~en, ~en, Realistin** *die;* **~, ~nen** realist
realistisch [1] *Adj.* realistic
[2] *adv.* realistically
Realität *die;* **~, ~en** reality
Real·schule *die* ≈ secondary modern school (Brit. Hist.)
Rebe *die;* **~, ~n (a)** vine shoot
(b) (Weinstock) [grape] vine
Rebell *der;* **~en, ~en, Rebellin** *die;* **~, ~nen** rebel
rebellieren *itr. V.* rebel (**gegen** against)
Rebellion *die;* **~, ~en** rebellion
rebellisch *Adj.* rebellious
Reb-: **~huhn** *das* partridge; **~stock** *der* vine
rechen *tr. V.* (bes. südd.) rake
Rechen *der;* **~s, ~** (bes. südd.) rake
Rechen-: **~fehler** *der* arithmetical error; **~maschine** *die* calculator
Rechenschaft *die;* **~:** account; **jmdn. für etw. zur ~ ziehen** call *or* bring sb. to account for sth.
Rechenschafts·bericht *der* report
Recherche /reˈʃɛrʃə/ *die;* **~, ~n (a)** (geh.) investigation; enquiry
(b) (DV) search
recherchieren *itr., tr. V.* (geh.) investigate
rechnen [1] *tr. V.* **(a) eine Aufgabe ~:** work out a problem
(b) (veranschlagen) reckon; estimate; **gut/rund gerechnet** at a generous/rough estimate
(c) (berücksichtigen) take into account
(d) (einbeziehen) count
[2] *itr. V.* **(a)** do *or* make a calculation/calculations; **gut/schlecht ~ können** be good/bad at figures
(b) (zählen) reckon
(c) (ugs.: berechnen) calculate; estimate

(d) (wirtschaften) budget carefully
(e) **auf jmdn./etw.** *od.* **mit jmdm./etw. ~:** count on sb./sth.
(f) **mit etw. ~** (etw. einkalkulieren) reckon with sth.; (etw. erwarten) expect sth.

Rechnen *das;* **~s** arithmetic

Rechner *der;* **~s, ~:** calculator; (Computer) computer

rechnerisch *Adj.* arithmetical

Rechnung *die;* **~, ~en** **(a)** calculation **(b)** (schriftliche Kosten~) bill; invoice (Commerc.); **[jmdm.] etw. in ~ stellen** charge [sb.] for sth.

recht [1] *Adj.* **(a)** (geeignet, richtig) right **(b)** (gesetzmäßig, anständig) right; proper; **~ und billig** right and proper **(c)** (wunschgemäß) **jmdm. ~ sein** be all right with sb. **(d)** (wirklich, echt) real
[2] *adv.* **(a)** (geeignet) **du kommst gerade ~:** you are just in time **(b)** (richtig) correctly **(c)** (gesetzmäßig, anständig) properly **(d)** (wunschgemäß) **es jmdm. ~ machen** please sb. **(e)** (wirklich, echt) really **(f)** (ziemlich) quite; rather; *s. auch* RECHT D

Recht *das;* **~[e]s, ~e** **(a)** (Rechtsordnung) law **(b)** (Rechtsanspruch) right; **sein ~ fordern** *od.* **verlangen** demand one's rights **(c)** (Berechtigung) right (**auf** + *Akk.* to); **gleiches ~ für alle!** equal rights for all!; **im ~ sein** be in the right; **zu ~:** rightly **(d)** **~ haben** be right; **jmdm. ~ geben** admit that sb. is right

recht... *Adj.* **(a)** right; right[-hand] ‹*edge*› **(b)** (außen, sichtbar) right ‹*side*› **(c)** (in der Politik) right-wing

recht·fertigen *tr. V.* justify (**vor** + *Dat.* to)

Recht·fertigung *die* justification

rechtlich [1] *Adj.* legal
[2] *adv.* legally

Rechtlichkeit *die;* **~** *s.:* RECHTMÄSSIGKEIT

recht·los *Adj.* without rights *postpos.*

Rechtlosigkeit *die;* **~:** lack of rights

rechtmäßig [1] *Adj.* lawful; rightful; legitimate ‹*claim*›
[2] *adv.* lawfully; rightfully

Rechtmäßigkeit *die;* **~:** legality; (eines Anspruchs) legitimacy

rechts *Adv.* **(a)** on the right; **von ~:** from the right **(b)** (Politik) on the right wing

Rechts-: **~abbieger** *der,* **~abbiegerin** *die* (Verkehrsw.) motorist/cyclist/car *etc.* turning right; **~anwalt** *der,* **~anwältin** *die* lawyer; solicitor (Brit.); attorney (Amer.); (vor Gericht) barrister (Brit.); attorney[-at-law] (Amer.); advocate (Scot.); **~außen** /-'--/ *der;* **~, ~** (Ballspiele) right wing; outside right

recht-, Recht-: **~schaffen** [1] *Adj.* honest; [2] *adv.* honestly; **~schreib·fehler** *der* spelling mistake; **~schreibung** *die* orthography

rechts-, Rechts-: **~empfinden** *das* sense of [what is] right and wrong; **~extremist** *der,* **~extremistin** *die* (Politik) right-wing extremist; **~händer** *der;* **~~s, ~~, ~händerin** *die;* **~~, ~~nen** right-hander; **~kräftig** (Rechtsw.) [1] *Adj.* final [and absolute] ‹*decision, verdict, etc.*›; [2] *adv.* **jmdn. ~kräftig verurteilen** pass a final sentence on sb.; **~kurve** *die* right-hand bend

Recht·sprechung *die;* **~, ~en** administration of justice; (eines Gerichts) jurisdiction

rechts-, Rechts-: **~radikal** (Politik) [1] *Adj.* radical right-wing; [2] *adv.* **eine ~radikal orientierte Gruppe** a group with a radical right-wing orientation; **~radikale** *der/die* right-wing radical; **~radikalismus** *der* right-wing radicalism; **~staat** *der* [constitutional] state founded on the rule of law; **~staatlich** *Adj.* founded on the rule of law *postpos.*; **~verkehr** *der* driving *no art.* on the right; **~verletzung** *die* (Rechtsw.) infringement *or* violation of the law; **~widrig** [1] *Adj.* unlawful; [2] *adv.* unlawfully; **~widrigkeit** *die* **(a)** unlawfulness; **(b)** (Handlung) unlawful act

recht-: **~wink[e]lig** *Adj.* right-angled; **~zeitig** [1] *Adj.* timely; (pünktlich) punctual; [2] *adv.* in time; (pünktlich) on time

Reck *das;* **~[e]s, ~e** *od.* **~s** horizontal bar

recken [1] *tr. V.* stretch
[2] *refl. V.* stretch oneself

recyceln /ri'saiːkl̩n/ *tr. V.; 2. Part.* **recycelt** recycle

Recycling /ri'saiːklɪŋ/ *das;* **~s** recycling

Recycling·papier /ri'saiːklɪŋ-/ *das* recycled paper

Redakteur /redak'tøːɐ̯/ *der;* **~s, ~e, Redakteurin** *die;* **~, ~nen** editor

Redaktion *die;* **~, ~en** **(a)** (Redakteure) editorial staff **(b)** (Büro) editorial department *or* office/offices *pl.*

redaktionell [1] *Adj.* editorial
[2] *adv.* editorially

Rede *die;* **~, ~n** **(a)** (Ansprache) address; speech; **eine ~ halten** give *or* make a speech **(b)** (Vortrag) rhetoric **(c)** (Äußerung, Ansicht) **nicht der ~ wert sein** be not worth mentioning; **jmdn. zur ~ stellen** make someone explain himself/herself; **von jmdm./etw. ist die ~:** there is some talk about sb./sth.; **es ist die ~ davon, dass ...:** it is being said *or* people are saying that ...; **davon kann keine ~ sein** it's out of the question

reden [1] *tr. V.* talk; **Unsinn ~:** talk nonsense; **kein Wort ~:** not say *or* speak a word ⋯

[2] *itr. V.* **(a)** (sprechen) talk; speak; **viel/wenig ~:** talk a lot (coll.)/not talk much
(b) (sich äußern, eine Rede halten) speak; **gut ~ können** be a good speaker
(c) (sich unterhalten) talk; **mit jmdm./über jmdn. ~:** talk to/about sb.

Redens·art *die* **(a)** expression; (Sprichwort) saying
(b) *Pl.* (Phrase) empty *or* meaningless words

Rede·wendung *die* (Sprachw.) idiom

redlich [1] *Adj.* honest
[2] *adv.* honestly

Redlichkeit *die;* **~:** honesty

Redner *der;* **~s, ~, Rednerin** *die* **~, ~nen** **(a)** speaker
(b) (Rhetoriker) orator

red·selig *Adj.* talkative

reduzieren [1] *tr. V.* reduce (**auf** + *Akk.* to)
[2] *refl. V.* decrease; diminish

Reeder *der;* **~s, ~:** shipowner

Reederei *die;* **~, ~en** shipping firm

Reederin *die;* **~, ~nen** shipowner

reell [1] *Adj.* honest, straight ‹*person, deal, etc.*›; sound, solid ‹*business, firm, etc.*›; straight ‹*offer*›
[2] *adv.* honestly

Reet *das;* **~s** (nordd.) reeds *pl.*

Referat *das;* **~[e]s, ~e** **(a)** paper
(b) (kurzer schriftlicher Bericht) report

Referendar *der;* **~s, ~e, Referendarin** *die;* **~, ~nen** *candidate for a higher civil-service post who has passed the first state examination and is undergoing in-service training*

Referenz *die;* **~, ~en** (Person, Stelle) referee; **jmdn. als ~ angeben** give sb.'s name *or* give sb. as a reference

referieren *itr. V.* **über etw.** (*Akk.*) **~:** present a paper on sth.; (zusammenfassend) give a report on sth.

reflektieren *tr. V.* reflect

Reflex *der;* **~es, ~e** reflex

Reflexion *die;* **~, ~en** reflection

Reflexiv·pronomen *das* (Sprachw.) reflexive pronoun

Reform *die;* **~, ~en** reform

Reformation *die;* **~** (hist.) Reformation

Reformations·fest *das* Reformation Day

Reform·haus *das* health food shop

reformieren *tr. V.* reform

Refrain /rəˈfrɛ̃ː/ *der;* **~s, ~s** chorus

Regal *das;* **~s, ~e** [set *sing.* of] shelves *pl.*

rege [1] *Adj.* **(a)** (betriebsam) busy ‹*traffic*›; brisk ‹*demand, trade, business, etc.*›
(b) (lebhaft) lively; keen ‹*interest*›
[2] *adv.* **(a)** (betriebsam) actively
(b) (lebhaft) actively

Regel *die;* **~, ~n** **(a)** rule; **nach allen ~n der Kunst** (fig.) well and truly
(b) rule; custom; **die ~ sein** be the rule; **in der** *od.* **aller ~:** as a rule
(c) (Menstruation) period

regel·mäßig [1] *Adj.* regular
[2] *adv.* regularly

Regel·mäßigkeit *die* regularity

regeln [1] *tr. V.* **(a)** settle ‹*matter, question, etc.*›; put ‹*finances, affairs, etc.*› in order
(b) (einstellen, regulieren) regulate; (steuern) control
[2] *refl. V.* take care of itself

regelrecht [1] *Adj.* (ugs.: richtiggehend) proper (coll.); real; real ‹*shock*›; real, absolute ‹*scandal*›; complete, utter ‹*flop, disaster*›; **ich hatte ~e Angst** I was really afraid
[2] *adv.* (ugs.: richtiggehend) really

Regelung *die;* **~, ~en** **(a)** ▶ REGELN 1A, B: settlement; putting in order; regulation; control
(b) (Vorschrift) regulation

regen [1] *tr. V.* (geh.) move
[2] *refl. V.* **(a)** (sich bewegen) move
(b) (geh.) ‹*hope, doubt, desire, conscience*› stir

Regen *der;* **~s, ~** **(a)** rain; **vom** *od.* **aus dem ~ in die Traufe kommen** (fig.) jump out of the frying pan into the fire
(b) (fig.) shower

Regen-: ~bogen *der* rainbow; **~mantel** *der* raincoat; mackintosh; **~schirm** *der* umbrella; **~tag** *der* rainy day; **~wald** *der* (Geogr.) rainforest; **~wasser** *das* rainwater; **~wetter** *das* wet weather; **~wolke** *die* rain cloud; **~wurm** *der* earthworm; **~zeit** *die* rainy season

Regie /reˈʒiː/ *die;* **~** **(a)** (Theater, Film, Ferns., Rundf.) direction; **die ~ bei etw. haben** *od.* **führen** direct sth.
(b) (Leitung, Verwaltung) management

regieren [1] *itr. V.* rule (**über** + *Akk.* over); ‹*party, administration*› govern
[2] *tr. V.* rule; govern; ‹*monarch*› reign over

Regierung *die;* **~, ~en** **(a)** (Herrschaft) rule; (eines Monarchen) reign
(b) (Kabinett) government

Regierungs·sitz *der* seat of government

Regiment *das;* **~[e]s, ~e** *od.* **~er** **(a)** *Pl.* **~e** (Herrschaft) rule
(b) *Pl.* **~er** (Milit.) regiment

Region *die;* **~, ~en** region

regional [1] *Adj.* regional
[2] *adv.* regionally

Regisseur /reʒɪˈsøːɐ̯/ *der;* **~s, ~e, Regisseurin** *die;* **~, ~nen** director

Register *das;* **~s, ~** **(a)** index
(b) (amtliche Liste) register
(c) (Musik) (bei Instrumenten) register; (Orgel~) stop

registrieren *tr. V.* **(a)** register
(b) (bewusst wahrnehmen) note; register

Regler *der;* **~s, ~** (Technik) regulator; (Kybernetik) control

reg·los *Adj.* motionless

---

*old spelling - see note on page xiv

regnen 1 *itr., tr. V. (unpers.)* rain; **es regnet** it is raining
2 *itr. V.; mit sein* (fig.) rain down
regnerisch *Adj.* rainy
regulär *Adj.* **(a)** proper; normal ‹*working hours*›
(b) (normal, üblich) normal
regulieren *tr. V.* regulate
Regulierung *die; ~, ~en* regulation
Regung *die; ~, ~en* (geh.: Gefühl) stirring
regungs·los *Adj.* motionless
Reh *das; ~[e]s, ~e* roe deer
Rehabilitation *die; ~, ~en* rehabilitation
rehabilitieren *tr. V.* rehabilitate
Reh-: ~bock *der* roebuck; **~kitz** *das* fawn [of a/the roe deer]
Reibach *der; ~s* (ugs.) profits *pl.*; **einen [kräftigen] ~ machen** make a killing (coll.)
Reibe *die; ~, ~n,* **Reib·eisen** *das* grater
reiben 1 *unr. tr. V.* **(a)** rub
(b) (zerkleinern) grate
2 *unr. itr. V.* rub (**an** + *Dat.* on)
Reib·fläche *die* striking surface (*of matchbox*)
Reibung *die; ~, ~en* (Physik, fig.) friction
reibungs·los 1 *Adj.* smooth
2 *adv.* smoothly
reich 1 *Adj.* **(a)** (vermögend) rich
(b) (prächtig) costly ‹*goods, gifts*›; rich ‹*décor, finery*›
(c) (üppig) rich; abundant ‹*harvest*›; abundant ‹*mineral resources*›; **~ an etw.** (*Dat.*) **sein** be rich in sth.
(d) (vielfältig) rich ‹*collection, possibilities*›; wide, large ‹*selection, choice*›; wide ‹*knowledge, experience*›
2 *adv.* richly
Reich *das; ~[e]s, ~e* **(a)** empire; (König~) kingdom; realm; **das [Deutsche] ~** (hist.) the German Reich *or* Empire; **das Dritte ~** (hist.) the Third Reich
(b) (fig.) realm
reichen 1 *itr. V.* **(a)** (ausreichen) be enough; **das Geld reicht nicht** I/we *etc.* haven't got enough money; **jetzt reichts mir aber!** now I've had enough!; **danke, es reicht** that's enough, thank you
(b) (sich erstrecken) reach; ‹*forest, fields, etc.*› extend
2 *tr. V.* **(a)** pass; hand; **jmdm. die Hand ~:** hold out one's hand to sb.; **sich** (*Dat.*) **die Hand ~:** shake hands
(b) (servieren) serve ‹*food, drink*›
reich·haltig *Adj.* extensive; varied ‹*programme*›; substantial ‹*meal*›
Reich·haltigkeit *die; ~~:* extensiveness; (eines Programms) varied content; (einer Mahlzeit) substantialness
reichlich 1 *Adj.* large; ample ‹*space, time*›; good ‹*hour, year*›
2 *adv.* **(a)** amply
(b) (mehr als) over; more than
(c) (ugs.: ziemlich, sehr) a bit too ‹*cheeky, dear, late*›
Reichtum *der; ~s,* **Reichtümer (a)** wealth (**an** + *Dat.* of)
(b) *Pl.* (Vermögenswerte) riches
Reich·weite *die* reach; (eines Geschützes, Senders, Flugzeugs) range
reif *Adj.* **(a)** ripe ‹*fruit, grain, cheese*›; mature ‹*brandy, cheese*›; **~ für etw. sein** (ugs.) be ready for sth.
(b) (erwachsen, ausgewogen) mature
Reif[1] *der; ~[e]s* hoar frost
Reif[2] *der; ~[e]s, ~e* (geh.) ring; (Arm~) bracelet; (Diadem) circlet
Reife *die; ~* **(a)** ripeness; (von Menschen, Gedanken, Produkten) maturity
(b) (Reifung) ripening
(c) mittlere ~ (Schulw.) *school-leaving certificate usually taken after the fifth year of secondary school*
reifen 1 *itr. V.; mit sein* **(a)** ‹*fruit, cereal, cheese*› ripen
(b) (geh.: älter, reifer werden) mature (**zu** into)
(c) ‹*idea, plan, decision*› mature
2 *tr. V.* ripen ‹*fruit, cereal*›
Reifen *der; ~s, ~* **(a)** hoop
(b) (Gummi~) tyre
(c) ▶ REIF[2]
Reifen-: ~druck *der; Pl.* **~drücke** tyre pressure; **~panne** *die* puncture; **~wechsel** *der* tyre change
Reif·glätte *die* ice on the roads
reiflich 1 *Adj.* [very] careful
2 *adv.* [very] carefully
Reifung *die; ~:* ▶ REIFEN 1: ripening; maturing; maturation
Reigen *der; ~s, ~* **(a)** round dance
(b) (fig.) **den ~ eröffnen** start off
Reihe *die; ~, ~n* **(a)** row; **in Reih und Glied** (Milit.) in rank and file; **aus der ~ tanzen** (fig. ugs.) be different
(b) (Reihenfolge) series; **er/sie** *usw.* **ist an der ~:** it's his/her *etc.* turn; **der ~ nach, nach der ~:** in turn
(c) (größere Anzahl) number
reihen (geh.) *tr. V.* string; thread
Reihen-: ~folge *die* order; **~haus** *das* terraced house
Reiher *der; ~s, ~:* heron
Reim *der; ~[e]s, ~e* rhyme
reimen 1 *itr. V.* make up rhymes
2 *tr., refl. V.* rhyme (**auf** + *Akk.* with)
rein[1] *Adv.* (ugs.) **~ mit dir!** in you go/come!
rein[2] 1 *Adj.* **(a)** (unvermischt) pure
(b) (nichts anderes als) pure; sheer; plain, unvarnished ‹*truth*›
(c) (frisch, sauber) clean; fresh ‹*clothes, sheet of paper, etc.*›; pure, clean ‹*water, air*›; clear ‹*complexion*›; **etw. ins Reine schreiben** make a fair copy of sth.; **etw. ins Reine bringen** clear sth. up
2 *Adv.* purely; **~ gar nichts** (ugs.) absolutely nothing

r

Rein·fall *der* (ugs.) let-down
rein|fallen *unr. itr. V.; mit sein* (ugs.) ▶ HEREINFALLEN
Rein·gewinn *der* net profit
Reinheit *die;* ~ **(a)** purity **(b)** (Sauberkeit) cleanness; (des Wassers, der Luft) purity; (der Haut) clearness
reinigen *tr. V.* clean; purify ‹*effluents, air, water, etc.*›; **Kleider [chemisch] ~ lassen** have clothes [dry-]cleaned
Reinigung *die;* ~, ~**en (a)** ▶ REINIGEN: cleaning; purification; dry-cleaning **(b)** (Betrieb) [dry-]cleaner's
reinlich *Adj.* cleanly
Reinlichkeit *die;* ~: cleanliness
rein, Rein-: ~**rassig** *Adj.* thoroughbred ‹*animal*›; ~**|reiten** *tr. V.* (ugs.) **jmdn. ~reiten** drag sb. in (fig.); ~**schrift** *die* fair copy
rein|ziehen *unr. tr. V.* **(a)** ▶ HINEINZIEHEN; **(b) sich** (*Dat.*) **etw. ~ziehen** (salopp) take ‹*drug*›; watch ‹*film, show, video*›
Reis *der;* ~**es** rice
Reis·brei *der* rice pudding
Reise *die;* ~, ~**n** journey; (kürzere Fahrt, Geschäfts~) trip; (Ausflug) outing; trip; (Schiffs~) voyage; **eine ~ machen** go on a trip/an outing; **auf ~n sein** travel; (nicht zu Hause sein) be away; **glückliche** *od.* **gute ~!** have a good journey
reise-, Reise-: ~**andenken** *das* souvenir; ~**boom** *das* tourist boom; ~**büro** *das* travel agent's; travel agency; ~**bus** *der* coach; ~**freiheit** *die* freedom of travel; ~**führer** *der* **(a)** (Reiseleiter) courier; **(b)** (Buch) guidebook; ~**führerin** *die* courier; ~**gepäck** *das* luggage (Brit.); baggage (Amer.); (am Flughafen) baggage; ~**gesellschaft** *die* **(a)** (Reisegruppe) party of tourists; **(b)** (ugs.: Reiseveranstalter) tour operator; ~**kosten** *Pl.* travel expenses; ~**krank** *Adj.* travel-sick; ~**krankheit** *die* travel sickness *no pl.;* ~**leiter** *der,* ~**leiterin** *die* courier
reisen *itr. V.; mit sein* **(a)** travel **(b)** (abreisen) leave; set off
Reisende *der/die; adj. Dekl.* traveller; (Fahrgast) passenger
Reise-: ~**pass,** *~**paß** *der* passport; ~**planung** *die* travel planning; **die ~planung umstellen** change one's travel plans; ~**prospekt** *der* travel brochure; ~**route** *die* route; ~**scheck** *der* traveller's cheque; ~**tasche** *die* holdall; ~**verkehr** *der* holiday traffic; ~**wetterbericht** *der* holiday weather forecast; ~**ziel** *das* destination
Reisig *das;* ~**s** brushwood
Reiß·brett *das* drawing board
reißen 1 *unr. tr. V.* **(a)** tear; (in Stücke) tear up **(b)** (ziehen an) pull; (heftig) yank (coll.) **(c)** (werfen, ziehen) **jmdn. zu Boden/in die Tiefe ~:** knock sb. to the ground/drag sb. down into the depths **(d)** (töten) ‹*wolf, lion, etc.*› kill ‹*prey*› **(e) etw. an sich ~** (fig.) seize sth. 2 *unr. itr. V.* **(a)** *mit sein* ‹*paper, fabric*› tear, rip; ‹*rope, thread*› break, snap; ‹*film*› break; ‹*muscle*› tear **(b)** (ziehen) **an etw.** (*Dat.*) **~:** pull at sth. 3 *unr. refl. V.* (ugs.: sich bemühen um) **sie ~ sich um die Eintrittskarten** they are fighting each other to get tickets
reißend *Adj.* rapacious ‹*animal*›; raging ‹*torrent*›; ~**en Absatz finden** sell like hot cakes
reißerisch (abwertend) 1 *Adj.* sensational; lurid ‹*headline*›; garish, lurid ‹*colour*› 2 *adv.* sensationally
Reiß-: ~**leine** *die* (Flugw.) ripcord; ~**nagel** *der:* ▶ ~ZWECKE; ~**verschluss,** *~**verschluß** *der* zip [fastener]; ~**zwecke** *die* drawing pin (Brit.); thumbtack (Amer.)
reiten 1 *unr. itr. V.; meist mit sein* ride 2 *unr. tr. V.; auch mit sein* ride; **Schritt/Trab/Galopp ~:** ride at a walk/trot/gallop
Reiten *das;* ~**s** riding *no art.*
Reiter *der;* ~**s,** ~, **Reiterin** *die;* ~, ~**nen** rider
Reit-: ~**hose** *die* riding breeches *pl.;* ~**pferd** *das* saddle horse; ~**stiefel** *der* riding boot
Reiz *der;* ~**es,** ~**e (a)** (Physiol.) stimulus **(b)** (Anziehungskraft) attraction; appeal *no pl.;* (des Verbotenen, der Ferne usw.) lure **(c)** (Zauber) charm
reizbar *Adj.* irritable
Reizbarkeit *die;* ~: irritability
reizen 1 *tr. V.* **(a)** annoy; tease ‹*animal*›; (herausfordern, provozieren) provoke; *s. auch* GEREIZT **(b)** (Physiol.) irritate **(c)** (Interesse erregen bei) **jmdn. ~:** attract sb.; appeal to sb. **(d)** (Kartenspiele) bid 2 *itr. V.* (Kartenspiele) bid
reizend 1 *Adj.* charming; delightful, lovely ‹*child*› 2 *adv.* charmingly
reizlos *Adj.* unattractive; ‹*landscape, scenery*› lacking in charm
reizvoll *Adj.* **(a)** (hübsch) charming **(b)** (interessant) attractive
rekeln *refl. V.* (ugs.) stretch
Reklamation /reklama'ts̯io:n/ *die;* ~, ~**en** complaint (**wegen** about)
Reklame *die;* ~, ~**n (a)** advertising *no indef. art.;* **~ für jmdn./etw. machen** promote sb./advertise *or* promote sth. **(b)** (ugs.: Werbemittel) advert (Brit. coll.); ad (coll.); (im Fernsehen, Radio auch) commercial

*alte Schreibung - vgl. Hinweis auf S. xiv

Reklame-: ~schild *das* advertising sign; **~tafel** *die* advertising hoarding; (klein) advertising board

reklamieren [1] *itr. V.* complain [2] *tr. V.* **(a)** complain about (**bei** to, **wegen** on account of) **(b)** (beanspruchen) claim

rekonstruieren *tr. V.* reconstruct

Rekord *der;* **~[e]s, ~e** record

Rekord·halter *der,* **Rekord·halterin** *die,* **Rekord·inhaber** *der,* **Rekord·inhaberin** *die* record holder

Rekrut *der;* **~en, ~en** (Milit.) recruit

Rektor *der;* **~s, ~en (a)** (einer Schule) head[master] **(b)** (Universitäts~) Rector; ≈ Vice-Chancellor (Brit.); (einer Fachhochschule) principal

Rektorin *die;* **~, ~nen (a)** (einer Schule) head[mistress] **(b)** ▶ REKTOR B

Relation *die;* **~, ~en** relation

relativ [1] *Adj.* relative [2] *adv.* relatively

relativieren *tr. V.* relativize

Relativierung *die;* **~, ~en** relativization

Relativ-: ~pronomen *das* (Sprachw.) relative pronoun; **~satz** *der* (Sprachw.) relative clause

relaxed /ri'lɛkst/ *Adj.* (salopp) laid-back (coll.)

relevant /rele'vant/ *Adj.* relevant (**für** to)

Relevanz *die;* **~:** relevance (**für** to)

Relief *das;* **~s, ~s** *od.* **~e** relief

Religion *die;* **~, ~en** religion

religiös [1] *Adj.* religious [2] *adv.* in a religious manner

Religiosität *die;* **~:** religiousness

Relikt *das;* **~[e], ~e** relic

Reling *die;* **~, ~s** *od.* **~e** [deck] rail

Reliquie /re'li:kvi̯ə/ *die;* **~, ~n** relic

Remis *das;* **~** /rə'mi:(s)/, **~** /rə'mi:s/ (bes. Schach) draw

Ren *das;* **~s, ~s** *od.* **~e** reindeer

Renaissance /rənɛ'sã:s/ *die;* **~, ~n (a)** Renaissance **(b)** (Wiederaufleben) revival

Rendezvous /rãde'vu:/ *das;* **~** /...'vu:(s)/, **~** /'rãde'vu:s/ rendezvous

Renn·bahn *die* (Sport) racetrack; (für Pferde) racecourse

rennen *unr. itr. V.; mit sein* run; **an/gegen jmdn./etw. ~:** run *or* bang into sb./sth.

Rennen *das;* **~s, ~:** running; (Pferde~, Auto~) racing; (Wettbewerb) race

Renner *der;* **~s, ~** (ugs.: Verkaufserfolg) big seller

Renn-: ~fahrer *der,* **~fahrerin** *die* racing driver; **~pferd** *das* racehorse; **~rad** *das* racing cycle; **~wagen** *der* racing car

renommiert *Adj.* renowned

renovieren *tr. V.* renovate; redecorate ‹*room, flat*›

Renovierung *die;* **~, ~en** renovation; (eines Zimmers, einer Wohnung) redecoration

rentabel [1] *Adj.* profitable [2] *adv.* profitably

Rentabilität *die;* **~** (bes. Wirtsch.) profitability

Rente *die;* **~, ~n (a)** pension **(b)** (Kapitalertrag) annuity

Renten-: ~alter *das* pensionable age *no art.*; **~empfänger** *der,* **~empfängerin** *die* pensioner; **~versicherung** *die* pension scheme

Ren·tier *das* reindeer

rentieren *refl. V.* be profitable; ‹*equipment, machinery*› pay its way

Rentner *der;* **~s, ~, Rentnerin** *die;* **~, ~nen** pensioner

Reparatur *die;* **~, ~en** repair (**an** + *Dat.* to)

Reparatur·werkstatt *die* repair [work]shop; (für Autos) garage

reparieren *tr. V.* repair; mend

Repertoire /repɛ'to̯a:ɐ̯/ *das;* **~s, ~s** repertoire

Report *der;* **~[e]s, ~e, Reportage** /repɔr'ta:ʒə/ *die;* **~, ~n** report

Reporter *der;* **~s, ~, Reporterin** *die;* **~, ~nen** reporter

Repräsentant *der;* **~en, ~en, Repräsentantin** *die;* **~, ~nen** representative

repräsentativ *Adj.* representative

repräsentieren *tr. V.* represent

Repressalie /reprɛ'sa:li̯ə/ *die;* **~, ~n** repressive measure

Reproduktion *die* reproduction

reproduzieren *tr. V.* reproduce

Reptil *das;* **~s, ~ien** reptile

Republik *die;* **~, ~en** republic

republikanisch *Adj.* republican

Reservat *das;* **~[e]s, ~e (a)** reservation **(b)** (Naturschutzgebiet) reserve

Reserve *die;* **~, ~n** reserve

Reserve-: ~rad *das* spare wheel; **~reifen** *der* spare tyre

reservieren *tr. V.* reserve

reserviert [1] *Adj.* reserved [2] *adv.* in a reserved way

Reserviertheit *die;* **~:** reserve

Reservierung *die;* **~, ~en** reservation

Reservoir /rezɛr'vo̯a:ɐ̯/ *das;* **~s, ~e** (auch fig.) reservoir (**an** + *Dat.* of)

Residenz *die;* **~, ~en (a)** residence **(b)** (Hauptstadt) [royal] capital

Resignation *die;* **~, ~en** resignation

resignieren *itr. V.* give up

resigniert [1] *Adj.* resigned [2] *adv.* resignedly

resolut [1] *Adj.* resolute

··›

2 *adv.* resolutely
Resolution *die;* ~, ~**en** resolution
Resonanz *die;* ~, ~**en** resonance
resozialisieren *tr. V.* (bes. Rechtsspr.) reintegrate into society
Resozialisierung *die;* ~, ~**en** (bes. Rechtsspr.) reintegration into society
Respekt *der;* ~[e]**s** **(a)** (Achtung) respect (**vor** + *Dat.* for)
(b) (Furcht) **jmdm.** ~ **einflößen** intimidate sb.
respektabel 1 *Adj.* respectable
2 *adv.* respectably
respektieren *tr. V.* respect
respekt·los 1 *Adj.* disrespectful
2 *adv.* disrespectfully
Respekt·losigkeit *die;* ~: disrespectfulness
respekt·voll 1 *Adj.* respectful
2 *adv.* respectfully
Ressort /rɛˈsoːɐ̯/ *das;* ~**s**, ~**s** area of responsibility; (Abteilung) department
Ressource /rɛˈsʊrsə/ *die;* ~, ~**n** resource
Rest *der;* ~[e]**s**, ~**e** **(a)** rest; **ein** ~ **von** a little bit of
(b) (Endstück) remnant
(c) (Math.) remainder
Rest·alkohol *der* residual alcohol
Restaurant /rɛstoˈrãː/ *das;* ~**s**, ~**s** restaurant
restaurieren *tr. V.* restore
restlich *Adj.* remaining
rest·los 1 *Adj.* complete
2 *adv.* completely
Rest·müll *der* general waste; non-recyclable waste
Resultat *das;* ~[e]**s**, ~**e** result
resultieren *itr. V.* result
Retorte *die;* ~, ~**n** retort
Retorten·baby *das* (ugs.) test tube baby
Retrospektive *die;* ~, ~**n** **(a)** (Rückblick) retrospective view; **in der** ~: in retrospect
(b) (Ausstellung) retrospective
retten 1 *tr. V.* save; (vor Gefahr) save; rescue; (befreien) rescue; **jmdm. das Leben** ~: save sb.'s life
2 *refl. V.* (fliehen) escape (**aus** from)
Retter *der;* ~**s**, ~, **Retterin** *die;* ~, ~**nen** rescuer
Rettich *der;* ~**s**, ~**e** radish
Rettung *die* rescue; (vor Zerstörung) saving
rettungs-, Rettungs-: ~**aktion** *die* rescue operation; ~**boot** *das* lifeboat; ~**hubschrauber** *der* rescue helicopter; ~**los** 1 *Adj.* hopeless; inevitable ‹*disaster*›; 2 *adv.* hopelessly; ~**ring** *der* lifebelt
Reue *die;* ~: remorse (**über** + *Akk.* for); (Rel.) repentance
reuen *tr. V.* **etw. reut jmdn.** sb. regrets sth.

*old spelling - see note on page xiv

reu·mütig *Adj.* remorseful; repentant ‹*sinner*›
Reuse *die;* ~, ~**n** fish trap
Revanche /reˈvãːʃ(ə)/ *die;* ~, ~**n** revenge; (Sport) return match/fight/game
revanchieren *refl. V.* **(a)** get one's revenge, (coll.) get one's own back (**bei** on)
(b) **sich bei jmdm. für eine Einladung** ~ (ugs.) return sb.'s invitation
Revers /rəˈveːɐ̯/ *das od.* (österr.) *der;* ~ /rəˈvɛːɐ̯(s)/, ~ /rəˈvɛːɐ̯s/ lapel
reversibel /revɛrˈziːbl̩/ *Adj.* (Technik, Med.) reversible
revidieren /reviˈdiːrən/ *tr. V.* (abändern) revise; amend ‹*law, contract*›
Revier /reˈviːɐ/ *das;* ~**s**, ~**e** **(a)** (Aufgabenbereich) province
(b) (Zool.) territory
(c) (Polizei~) (Dienststelle) [police] station; (Bereich) district; (des einzelnen Polizisten) beat
Revision /reviˈzi̯oːn/ *die;* ~, ~**en** **(a)** revision; (Änderung) amendment
(b) (Rechtsw.) appeal [on a point/points of law]; ~ **einlegen, in die** ~ **gehen** lodge an appeal [on a point/points of law]
Revolte /reˈvɔltə/ *die;* ~, ~**n** revolt
revoltieren /revɔlˈtiːrən/ *itr. V.* revolt, rebel (**gegen** against); (fig.) ‹*stomach*› rebel
Revolution /revoluˈtsi̯oːn/ *die;* ~, ~**en** (auch fig.) revolution
revolutionär 1 *Adj.* revolutionary
2 *adv.* in a revolutionary way
Revolutionär *der;* ~**s**, ~**e**, **Revolutionärin** *die;* ~, ~**nen** revolutionary
Revolver /reˈvɔlvɐ/ *der;* ~**s**, ~: revolver
Rezept *das;* ~[e]**s**, ~**e** **(a)** (Med.) prescription
(b) (Anleitung) recipe
rezept·frei 1 *Adj.* ~**e Mittel** medicines obtainable without a prescription
2 *adv.* **etw.** ~ **verkaufen/erhalten** sell/obtain sth. without a prescription *or* over the counter
Rezeption *die;* ~, ~**en** reception *no art.*
rezept·pflichtig *Adj.* ‹*drug etc.*› obtainable only on prescription
Rezession *die;* ~, ~**en** (Wirtsch.) recession
R-Gespräch /ˈɛr-/ *das* (Fernspr.) reverse-charge call (Brit.); collect call (Amer.)
Rhabarber *der;* ~**s** rhubarb
Rhein *der;* ~[e]**s** Rhine
rheinisch *Adj.* Rhenish; ‹*speciality etc.*› of the Rhine region
Rhein·land *das;* ~[e]**s** Rhineland
Rheinland-Pfalz (*das*); ~: the Rhineland-Palatinate
Rhetorik *die;* ~, ~**en** rhetoric
Rheuma *das;* ~**s** (ugs.) rheumatism
rheumatisch (Med.) 1 *Adj.* rheumatic
2 *adv.* rheumatically

Rheumatismus *der;* ~, **Rheumatismen** (Med.) rheumatism

Rhinozeros *das;* ~[ses], ~se rhinoceros; rhino (coll.)

Rhododendron *der od. das;* ~s, **Rhododendren** rhododendron

rhythmisch 1 *Adj.* rhythmical; rhythmic 2 *adv.* rhythmically

Rhythmus *der;* ~, **Rhythmen** (auch fig.) rhythm

richten 1 *tr. V.* **(a)** direct ‹*gaze*› (**auf** + *Akk.* at, towards); turn ‹*eyes, gaze*› (**auf** + *Akk.* towards); point ‹*torch, telescope, gun*› (**auf** + *Akk.* at); aim ‹*gun, missile, telescope, searchlight*› (**auf** + *Akk.* on); (fig.) direct ‹*activity, attention*› (**auf** + *Akk.* towards); address ‹*letter, remarks, words*› (**an** + *Akk.* to); level ‹*criticism*› (**an** + *Akk.* at)
(b) (geraderichten) straighten
(c) (aburteilen) judge; (verurteilen) condemn; *s. auch* ZUGRUNDE A;
2 *refl. V.* **(a)** (sich hinwenden) **sich auf jmdn./etw.** ~ (auch fig.) be directed towards sb./sth.
(b) sich an jmdn./etw. ~ ‹*person*› turn on sb./sth.; ‹*appeal, explanation*› be directed at sb./sth.; **sich gegen jmdn./etw.** ~ ‹*person*› criticize sb./sth.; ‹*criticism, accusations, etc.*› be aimed *or* levelled at sb./sth.
(c) (sich orientieren) **sich nach jmdm./jmds. Wünschen** ~: fit in with sb./sb.'s wishes
(d) (abhängen) **sich nach jmdm./etw.** ~: depend on sb./sth.
3 *itr. V.* (urteilen) judge

Richter *der;* ~s, ~, **Richterin** *die;* ~, ~nen judge

Richt·geschwindigkeit *die* recommended maximum speed

richtig 1 *Adj.* **(a)** right; (zutreffend) right; correct; accurate ‹*prophecy, premonition*›; **etw.** ~ **stellen** correct sth.
(b) (ordentlich) proper
(c) (wirklich, echt) real
2 *adv.* **(a)** right; correctly
(b) (ordentlich) properly
(c) (richtiggehend) really

richtig·gehend 1 *Adj.* real; proper (coll.) 2 *adv.* really

Richtigkeit *die;* ~: correctness; **etw. hat seine** ~, **mit etw. hat es seine** ~: sth. is right; **das wird schon seine** ~ **haben** I'm sure it's all right *or* (coll.) OK

***richtig|stellen** ▶ RICHTIG 1A

Richt-: ~**linie** *die* guideline; ~**schnur** *die; Pl.* ~~**en** (fig.) guiding principle

Richtung *die;* ~, ~en **(a)** direction; **in** ~ **Ulm** in the direction of Ulm
(b) (fig.: Tendenz) movement; trend

richtung·weisend *Adj.* ‹*idea, resolution, paper, speech*› that points the way ahead

rieb *1. u. 3. Pers. Sg. Prät. v.* REIBEN

riechen 1 *unr. tr. V.* **(a)** smell
(b) (wittern) ‹*dog etc.*› pick up the scent of
2 *unr. itr. V.* **(a)** smell; **an jmdm./etw.** ~: smell sb./sth.
(b) (einen Geruch haben) smell (**nach** of)

rief *1. u. 3. Pers. Sg. Prät. v.* RUFEN

Riegel *der;* ~s, ~ **(a)** bolt
(b) ein ~ **Schokolade** a bar of chocolate

Riemen *der;* ~s, ~ **(a)** strap; (Treib~, Gürtel) belt; **sich am** ~ **reißen** (ugs.) pull oneself together; get a grip on oneself
(b) (Ruder) [long] oar

Riese *der;* ~n, ~n giant

rieseln *itr. V.; mit Richtungsangabe mit sein* trickle [down]; ‹*snow*› fall gently

Riesen- giant; enormous ‹*selection, profit, portion*›; tremendous (coll.) ‹*effort, rejoicing, success*›; terrific (coll.), terrible (coll.) ‹*stupidity, scandal, fuss*›

riesen-, Riesen-: ~**groß** *Adj.* enormous; huge; terrific (coll.) ‹*surprise*›; ~**schritt** *der* giant stride; ~**welle** *die* giant wave

riesig 1 *Adj.* enormous; huge; vast ‹*country*›; tremendous ‹*effort, progress*› 2 *adv.* (ugs.) tremendously (coll.)

Riesin *die;* ~, ~nen giantess

Riesling *der;* ~s, ~e Riesling

riet *1. u. 3. Pers. Sg. Prät. v.* RATEN

Riff *das;* ~[e]s, ~e reef

rigoros 1 *Adj.* rigorous 2 *adv.* rigorously

Rille *die;* ~, ~n groove

Rind *das;* ~[e]s, ~er **(a)** cow; (Stier) bull; ~er cattle *pl.;*
(b) (~fleisch) beef

Rinde *die;* ~, ~n **(a)** (Baum~) bark
(b) (Brot~) crust; (Käse~) rind

Rinder·braten *der* roast beef *no indef. art.;* (roh) roasting beef *no indef. art.*

Rinder·wahnsinn *der* mad cow disease

Rind-: ~**fleisch** *das* beef; ~**vieh** *das* **(a)** cattle *pl.;* **(b)** (ugs. abwertend) ass; [stupid] fool

Ring *der;* ~[e]s, ~e ring

Ringel·natter *die* ring snake

ringen 1 *unr. tr. V.* (Sport, fig.) wrestle; (fig.: kämpfen) struggle, fight (**um** for; **gegen, mit** with); **nach Luft** ~: struggle for breath
2 *unr. tr. V.* **die Hände** ~: wring one's hands

Ringen *das;* ~s (Sport) wrestling *no art.*

Ring-: ~**finger** *der* ring finger; ~**kampf** *der* **(a)** [stand-up] fight; **(b)** (Sport) wrestling bout

rings *Adv.* all around

rings·herum *Adv.* all around [it/them *etc.*]

Ring·straße *die* ring road

rings-: ~**um**, ~**umher** *Adv.* all around

Rinne *die;* ~, ~n channel; (Dach~, Rinnstein) gutter; (Abfluss) drainpipe

rinnen *unr. itr. V.; mit sein* run

Rinn·stein *der* gutter

Rippchen *das;* ~s, ~ (Kochk. südd.) rib [of pork]

Rippe *die;* ~, ~n rib

Rippen·bruch *der* (Med.) rib fracture
Risiko *das;* ~**s, Risiken** risk
Risiko-: ~**faktor** *der* risk factor; ~**gruppe** *die* risk group
riskant [1] *Adj.* risky
[2] *adv.* riskily
riskieren *tr. V.* risk
riss, *riß *1. u. 3. Pers. Sg. Prät. v.* REISSEN
Riss, *Riß *der;* **Risses, Risse** tear; (Spalt, Sprung) crack
rissig *Adj.* cracked; chapped ‹*lips*›
ritt *1. u. 3. Pers. Sg. Prät. v.* REITEN
Ritt *der;* ~**[e]s,** ~**e** ride
Ritter *der;* ~**s,** ~: knight
Ritter·sporn *der* delphinium
rittlings *Adv.* astride
Ritze *die;* ~, ~**n** crack; [narrow] gap
ritzen *tr. V.* scratch
Rivale *der;* ~**n,** ~**n, Rivalin** *die;* ~, ~**nen** rival
Rivalität *die;* ~, ~**en** rivalry *no indef. art.*
Roastbeef /'ro:stbi:f/ *das;* ~**s,** ~**s** roast [sirloin (Brit.) of] beef
Robbe *die;* ~, ~**n** seal
Robe *die;* ~, ~**n** robe; (schwarz) gown
Roboter *der;* ~**s,** ~: robot
robust *Adj.* robust
roch *1. u. 3. Pers. Sg. Prät. v.* RIECHEN
Rochade *die;* ~, ~**n** (Schach) castling
röcheln *itr. V.* give the death rattle
Rock[1] *der;* ~**[e]s, Röcke** skirt
Rock[2] *der;* ~**[s]** (Musik) rock [music]
Rock and Roll /'rɔk ɛnt 'rɔl/ *der;* ~**[s],** ~**[s]** rock and roll *no pl.*
Rock·band *die* rock band
rocken *itr. V.* rock
Rocker *der;* ~**s,** ~: rocker
rockig *Adj.* rock ‹*music*›; rock-like ‹*jazz etc.*›
Rock·musik *die* rock music
Rodel·bahn *die* toboggan run; (Sport) luge run
rodeln *itr. V.; mit sein* sledge; toboggan
roden *tr. V.* clear ‹*wood, land*›; (ausgraben) grub up ‹*tree*›
Rogen *der;* ~**s,** ~: roe
Roggen *der;* ~**s** rye
Roggen-: ~**brot** *das* rye bread; **ein** ~**brot** a loaf of rye bread; ~**brötchen** *das* rye-bread roll
roh [1] *Adj.* **(a)** raw ‹*food*›; unboiled ‹*milk*›; unfinished ‹*wood*›
(b) (ungenau) rough
(c) (brutal) brutish; brute *attrib.* ‹*force*›
[2] *adv.* **(a)** (ungenau) roughly
(b) (brutal) brutishly; (grausam) callously; (grob) coarsely
Roh-: ~**bau** *der* shell [of a/the building]; ~**kost** *die* raw fruit and vegetables *pl.;* ~**material** *das* raw material; ~**öl** *das* crude oil
Rohr *das;* ~**[e]s,** ~**e (a)** (Leitungs~) pipe; (als Bauteil) tube
(b) *o. Pl.* (Röhricht) reeds *pl.;*
(c) *o. Pl.* (Werkstoff) reed
Röhre *die;* ~, ~**n** tube; (Elektronen~) valve (Brit.); tube (Amer.)
Roh·stoff *der* raw material
Rokoko *das;* ~**[s]** rococo
***Rolladen** ▶ ROLLLADEN
Roll·bahn *die* (Flugw.) taxiway
Rolle *die;* ~, ~**n (a)** (Spule) reel
(b) (zylindrischer [Hohl]körper; Zusammengerolltes) roll
(c) (Walze) roller
(d) (Rad) [small] wheel; (an Möbeln usw.) castor; (für Gardine, Schiebetür usw.) runner
(e) (Turnen, Kunstflug) roll
(f) (Theater, Film usw., fig.) role; part; (Soziol.) role; **es spielt keine** ~: it is of no importance; (es macht nichts aus) it doesn't matter
rollen [1] *tr. V.* roll
[2] *itr. V. mit sein* ‹*ball, wheel, etc.*› roll; ‹*vehicle*› move; ‹*aircraft*› taxi
Roller *der;* ~**s,** ~: scooter
Roll-: ~**feld** *das* runway[s] and taxiway[s]; ~**kragen** *der* polo neck; ~**laden** *der* [roller] shutter; ~**mops** *der* rollmops; ~**schuh** *der* roller skate; ~**schuh laufen** roller-skate; ~**splitt** *der* loose chippings *pl.;* ~**stuhl** *der* wheelchair; ~**treppe** *die* escalator
Rom (*das*); ~**s** Rome
Roman *der;* ~**s,** ~**e** novel
Romantik *die;* ~: romanticism; **die** ~: Romanticism
romantisch [1] *Adj.* romantic
[2] *adv.* romantically
Romanze *die;* ~, ~**n** romance
Römer *der;* ~**s,** ~, **Römerin** *die;* ~, ~**nen** Roman
römisch-katholisch *Adj.* Roman Catholic
röntgen *tr. V.* X-ray
Röntgen-: ~**aufnahme** *die,* ~**bild** *das* X-ray [image/photograph *or* picture]; ~**strahlen** *Pl.* X-rays
rosa [1] *indekl. Adj.* pink
[2] *adv.* pink
Rosa *das;* ~**s,** ~ *od.* ~**s** pink
Rose *die;* ~, ~**n** rose
rosé *indekl. Adj.* pale pink
Rosé *der;* ~**s,** ~**s** rosé [wine]
Rosen-: ~**kohl** *der* [Brussels] sprouts *pl.;* ~**kranz** *der* (kath. Kirche) rosary; **einen** ~**kranz beten** say a rosary; ~**montag** *der* the day before Shrove Tuesday
rosig *Adj.* **(a)** rosy; pink ‹*piglet etc.*›
(b) (fig.) rosy; optimistic ‹*mood*›

*alte Schreibung - vgl. Hinweis auf S. xiv

Rosine *die;* ~, ~n raisin
Rosmarin *der;* ~s rosemary
Ross, *Roß *das;* **Rosses, Rosse** *od.* **Rösser** horse; steed (poet./joc.); **hoch zu** ~: on horseback; **auf dem** *od.* **seinem hohen** ~ **sitzen** (fig.) be on one's high horse
Ross-, *Roß-: ~**haar** *das* horsehair; ~**kastanie** *die* horse chestnut
Rost[1] *der;* ~[e]s, ~e **(a)** (Gitter) grating; (eines Ofens, einer Feuerstelle) grate; (Brat~) grill **(b)** (Bett~) base
Rost[2] *der;* ~[e]s rust
Rost-: ~**braten** *der* grilled steak; ~**bratwurst** *die* grilled sausage
rosten *itr. V.; auch mit sein* rust
rösten /'rœstn̩, 'rø:stn̩/ *tr. V.* roast; toast ‹*bread*›
rost·frei *Adj.* stainless ‹*steel*›
Rösti *die;* ~ (schweiz. Kochk.) thinly sliced fried potatoes *pl.*
rostig *Adj.* rusty
rot [1] *Adj.* red; ~ **werden** turn red; ‹*person*› blush; ‹*traffic light*› change to red
[2] *adv.* red
Rot *das;* ~s, ~ *od.* ~s red
Rot·barsch *der* rosefish
Röte *die;* ~: red[ness]
röten [1] *tr. V.* redden
[2] *refl. V.* go *or* turn red
rot·haarig *Adj.* red-haired
Rot·hirsch *der* red deer
rotieren *itr. V.* **(a)** rotate
(b) (ugs.: hektisch sein) get into a flap (coll.)
Rot-: ~**käppchen** *das;* ~~s Little Red Riding Hood; ~**kehlchen** *das;* ~~s, ~~: robin [redbreast]; ~**kohl** *der,* (bes. südd., österr.) ~**kraut** *das* red cabbage
rötlich *Adj.* reddish
Rot-: ~**licht** *das* red light; **bei** ~**licht** under a red light; ~**stift** *der* red pencil
Rötung *die;* ~, ~en reddening
Rot·wein *der* red wine
Rotz *der;* ~es (salopp) snot (sl.)
rotzen (derb) [1] *itr. V.* **(a)** blow one's nose loudly
(b) (Schleim in den Mund ziehen) sniff back one's snot (sl.)
(c) (ausspucken) gob (sl.)
[2] *tr. V.* spit
rotz·frech (salopp) [1] *Adj.* insolent; snotty (sl.)
[2] *adv.* insolently; snottily (sl.)
Rouge /ru:ʒ/ *das;* ~s, ~s rouge
Roulade /ru:la:də/ *die;* ~, ~n (Kochk.) [beef/veal/pork] olive
Route /'ru:tə/ *die;* ~, ~n route
Routine /ru'ti:nə/ *die;* ~ **(a)** (Erfahrung) experience; (Übung) practice
(b) (Gewohnheit) routine *no def. art.*
routiniert /ruti'ni:ɐ̯t/ [1] *Adj.* (gewandt) expert; skilled; (erfahren) experienced
[2] *adv.* expertly; skilfully
Rowdy /'raudi/ *der;* ~s, ~s (abwertend) hooligan
Rübe *die;* ~, ~n turnip; **Rote** ~: beetroot; **Gelbe** ~ (südd.) carrot
rüber *Adv.* (ugs.) over
Rubin *der;* ~s, ~e ruby
Rubrik *die;* ~, ~en column; (fig.: Kategorie) category
Ruck *der;* ~[e]s, ~e jerk
Rück·blick *der* look back (**auf** + *Akk.* at); retrospective view (**auf** + *Akk.* of)
rücken *itr., tr. V.* move
Rücken *der;* ~s, ~: back; (Buch~) spine
Rücken-: ~**deckung** *die* **(a)** (bes. Milit.) rear cover; **(b)** (fig.) backing; ~**lehne** *die* [chair/seat] back; ~**mark** *das* (Anat.) spinal cord; ~**schmerzen** *Pl.* backache *sing.;* ~**schwimmen** *das* backstroke; ~**wind** *der* tail wind
rück-, Rück-: ~|**erstatten** *tr. V.; nur im Inf. u. 2. Part.* repay; ~**erstattung** *die* repayment; ~**fahr·karte** *die,* ~**fahr·schein** *der* return [ticket]; ~**fahrt** *die* return journey; ~**fall** *der* (Med., auch fig.) relapse; ~**fällig** *Adj.* (Med., auch fig.) relapsed ‹*patient, alcoholic, etc.*›; ~**fällig werden** have a relapse; ‹*alcoholic etc.*› go back to one's old ways; ‹*criminal*› commit a second offence; ~**flug** *der* return flight; ~**frage** *die* query; ~**gabe** *die* return; ~**gang** *der* drop, fall (*Gen.* in); ~**gängig** *Adj.* ~**gängig machen** cancel ‹*agreement, decision, etc.*›; ~**grat** *das;* ~~[e]s, ~~e spine; (bes. fig.) backbone; ~**halt** *der* support; backing; ~**halt·los** [1] *Adj.* unreserved, unqualified ‹*support*›; [2] *adv.* unreservedly; ~**kehr** *die;* ~~: return; ~**kopp[e]lung** *die* (Elektrot.) feedback; ~**lage** *die* savings *pl.;* ~**läufig** *Adj.* decreasing ‹*number*›; declining ‹*economic growth etc.*›; falling ‹*rate, production, etc.*›; ~**licht** *das* rear *or* tail light
rücklings *Adv.* on one's back
Rück-: ~**nahme** *die;* ~~: taking back; ~**reise** *die* return journey; ~**ruf** *der* (Fernspr.) return call
Ruck·sack *der* rucksack; (Touren~) backpack
Rucksack·urlaub *der* backpacking holiday
rück-, Rück-: ~**schlag** *der* setback; ~**schritt** *der* retrograde step; ~**seite** *die* back; (einer Münze usw.) reverse; far side; ~**sicht** *die* consideration; ~**sicht auf jmdn. nehmen** show consideration for *or* towards sb.; ~**sicht·nahme** *die;* ~~: consideration; ~**sichts·los** [1] *Adj.* inconsiderate; thoughtless; (verantwortungslos) reckless ‹*driver*›; (schonungslos) ruthless; [2] *adv. s. Adj:* inconsiderately; recklessly; ruthlessly; ~**sichtslosigkeit** *die;* ~~, ~~en ▶ RÜCKSICHTSLOS: lack of consideration; recklessness; ruthlessness; ···›

~sichts·voll [1] *Adj.* considerate; [2] *adv.* considerately; **~sitz** *der* back seat; **~spiegel** *der* rear-view mirror; **~sprache** *die* consultation; **~stand** *der* **(a)** (Rest) residue; **(b)** (ausstehende Zahlung) arrears *pl.;* **(c)** (Zurückbleiben hinter dem gesetzten Ziel) backlog; (bes. Sport: hinter dem Gegner) deficit; [**mit etw.**] **im ~stand sein/in ~stand** (*Akk.*) **geraten** be/get behind [with sth.]; **~ständig** *Adj.* **(a)** backward; **(b)** (schon länger fällig) outstanding ‹*payment, amount*›; ‹*wages*› still owing; **~strahler** *der* reflector; **~tritt** *der* resignation (**von** from); (von einer Kandidatur, einem Vertrag usw.) withdrawal (**von** from)

rückwärts *Adv.* backwards

Rückwärts·gang *der* reverse [gear]

rück-, Rück-: ~weg *der* return journey; **~wirkend** [1] *Adj.* retrospective; backdated ‹*pay increase*›; [2] retrospectively; **~zahlung** *die* repayment; **~zug** *der* retreat

Rüde *der;* **~n, ~n** [male] dog

Rudel *das;* **~s, ~:** herd; (von Wölfen, Hunden) pack

Ruder *das;* **~s, ~ (a)** (Riemen) oar **(b)** (Steuer~) rudder

Ruder·boot *das* rowboat; rowing boat (Brit.)

Rudergänger *der;* **~~s, ~~, ~gast** *der* (Seemannsspr.) helmsman

rudern [1] *itr. V.; mit sein* row [2] *tr. V.* row

Ruder·regatta *die* rowing regatta

Ruf *der;* **~[e]s, ~e (a)** call; (Schrei) shout; cry; (Tierlaut) call **(b)** (fig.: Forderung) call (**nach** for) **(c)** (Telefonnummer) telephone [number] **(d)** (Leumund) reputation

rufen [1] *unr. itr. V.* call (**nach** for); (schreien) shout (**nach** for); ‹*animal*› call [2] *unr. tr. V.* **(a)** (ausrufen) call; (schreien) shout **(b)** (herbeirufen, anrufen) **jmdn. ~:** call sb.; **jmdn. zu Hilfe ~:** call to sb. to help

Ruf-: ~mord *der* character assassination; **~mord·kampagne** *die* smear campaign; **~name** *der* first name (*by which one is generally known*); **~nummer** *die* telephone number

Rüge *die;* **~, ~n** reprimand

rügen *tr. V.* reprimand ‹*person*› (**wegen** for); censure ‹*carelessness etc.*›

Ruhe *die;* **~ (a)** (Stille) silence; **~ [bitte]!** quiet *or* silence [please]! **(b)** (Ungestörtheit) peace; **jmdn. mit etw. in ~ lassen** stop bothering sb. with sth. **(c)** (Unbewegtheit) rest **(d)** (Erholung) rest *no def. art.;* **(e)** (Gelassenheit) calm[ness]; composure; **[die] ~ bewahren/die ~ verlieren** keep calm/lose one's composure; **in [aller] ~:** [really] calmly

ruhe·los [1] *Adj.* restless [2] *adv.* restlessly

ruhen *itr. V.* **(a)** (ausruhen) rest **(b)** (geh.: schlafen) sleep **(c)** (stillstehen) ‹*work, business*› have stopped; ‹*production, firm*› be at a standstill

Ruhe-: ~pause *die* break; **~stand** *der* retirement; **in den ~stand gehen/versetzt werden** go into retirement/be retired; **~störung** *die* disturbance; (Rechtsw.) disturbance of the peace; **~tag** *der* closing day; **„Dienstag ~tag"** 'closed on Tuesdays'

ruhig [1] *Adj.* **(a)** (still, leise) quiet **(b)** (friedlich, ungestört) peaceful ‹*times, life, valley, etc.*›; quiet ‹*talk, reflection, life*› **(c)** (unbewegt) calm ‹*sea, weather*›; still ‹*air*›; (fig.) peaceful ‹*melody*›; (gleichmäßig) steady ‹*breathing, hand, steps*›; smooth ‹*flight, crossing*› **(d)** (gelassen) calm ‹*voice etc.*›; quiet, calm ‹*person*› [2] *adv.* **(a)** (still, leise) quietly; **sich ~ verhalten** keep quiet **(b)** (friedlich, ohne Störungen) peacefully; (ohne Zwischenfälle) uneventfully; ‹*work, think*› in peace **(c)** (unbewegt) ‹*sit, lie, stand*› still; (gleichmäßig) ‹*burn, breathe*› steadily; ‹*run, fly*› smoothly **(d)** (gelassen) ‹*speak, watch, sit*› calmly [3] *Adv.* by all means

Ruhm *der;* **~[e]s** fame

rühmen [1] *tr. V.* praise [2] *refl. V.* boast (+ *Gen.* about)

ruhm·reich *Adj.* glorious ‹*victory, history*›; celebrated ‹*general, army, victory*›

Ruhr *die;* **~, ~en** dysentery *no art.*

Rühr·ei *das* scrambled egg[s *pl.*]

rühren [1] *tr. V.* **(a)** (umrühren) stir; (einrühren) stir ‹*egg, powder, etc.*› (**an, in** + *Akk.* into) **(b)** (bewegen) move ‹*limb, fingers, etc.*› **(c)** (fig.) move; touch [2] *itr. V.* **(a)** (umrühren) stir **(b)** (geh.: herrühren) **das rührt daher, dass ...:** that stems from the fact that ... [3] *refl. V.* **(a)** (sich bewegen) move **(b)** (Milit.) **rührt euch!** at ease!

rührend [1] *Adj.* touching [2] *adv.* touchingly

rühr·selig [1] *Adj.* **(a)** emotional ‹*person*› **(b)** (allzu gefühlvoll) over-sentimental; ‹*manner, mood, etc.*›; maudlin, (coll.) tear-jerking ‹*play, song, etc.*› [2] *adv.* (allzu gefühlvoll) in an over-sentimental manner

Rühr·seligkeit *die* sentimentality

Rührung *die;* **~:** emotion

Ruine *die;* **~, ~n** ruin

ruinieren *tr. V.* ruin

rülpsen *itr. V.* (ugs.) burp

rum *Adv.* (ugs.) ▶ HERUM

Rum *der;* **~s, ~s** rum

Rumäne *der;* **~n, ~n** Romanian

Rumänien *(das);* **~s** Romania

---

*old spelling - see note on page xiv

Rumänin *die;* ~, **~nen** Romanian
rumänisch *Adj.* Romanian
Rummel *der;* **~s** (ugs.) **(a)** commotion; (Aufhebens) fuss (**um** about)
(b) (Jahrmarkt) fair
Rummel·platz *der* (bes. nordd.) fairground
Rumpel·kammer *die* (ugs.) boxroom (Brit.); junk room
rumpeln *itr. V.* (ugs.) bump and bang about
Rumpf *der;* **~[e]s, Rümpfe (a)** trunk [of the body]
(b) (beim Schiff) hull
(c) (beim Flugzeug) fuselage
rümpfen *tr. V.* **die Nase [bei etw.] ~:** wrinkle one's nose [at sth.]; **über jmdn./etw. die Nase rümpfen** (fig.) look down one's nose at sb./turn up one's nose at sth.
Rumpsteak /'rʊmpste:k/ *das;* **~s, ~s** rump steak
rum|treiben *unr. refl. V.* (ugs.) ▶ HERUMTREIBEN
rund [1] *Adj.* **(a)** round
(b) (dicklich) plump ‹*arms etc.*›; chubby ‹*cheeks*›; fat ‹*stomach*›
(c) (ugs.: ganz) round ‹*dozen, number, etc.*›
[2] *Adv.* **(a)** (ugs.: etwa) about
(b) ~ um jmdn./etw. [all] around sb./sth.
Rund-: ~blick *der* panorama; view in all directions; **~brief** *der* circular [letter]
Runde *die;* ~, **~n (a)** (Sport: Strecke) lap
(b) (Sport: Durchgang usw.) round; **über die ~n kommen** (fig. ugs.) get by; manage
(c) (Personenkreis) circle; (Gesellschaft) company
(d) (Rundgang) round
(e) (Lage) round
rund-, Rund-: ~erneuern *tr. V.;* **ich runderneuere, runderneuert, rundzuerneuern** (Kfz-W.) remould; **~fahrt** *die* tour (**durch** of); **~funk** *der* **(a)** radio; **(b)** (Einrichtung, Gebäude) radio station
Rundfunk-: ~anstalt *die* broadcasting corporation; **~gebühren** *Pl.* radio licence fees; **~gerät** *das* radio set; **~sendung** *die* radio programme; **~sprecher** *der,* **~sprecherin** *die* radio announcer
rund-, Rund-: ~gang *der* round (**durch** of); **~herum** *Adv.* **(a)** (ringsum) all around; **(b)** (völlig) completely
rundlich *Adj.* **(a)** roundish
(b) (mollig) plump
Rund-: ~reise *die* [circular] tour (**durch** of); **~schreiben** *das:* ▶ ~BRIEF; **~weg** *der* circular path *or* walk
runter *Adv.* (ugs.) **~ [da]!** get off [there]; *s. auch* HERUNTER; HINUNTER
runter|scrollen *tr., auch itr. V.* (DV) scroll down
Runzel *die;* ~, **~n** wrinkle
runz[e]lig *Adj.* wrinkled
runzeln *tr. V.* **die Stirn/die Brauen ~:** wrinkle one's brow/knit one's brows; (ärgerlich) frown
rupfen *tr. V.* **(a)** pluck ‹*goose, hen, etc.*›
(b) (abreißen) pull up ‹*weeds, grass*›; pull off ‹*leaves etc.*›
ruppig *Adj.* (abwertend) gruff ‹*person, behaviour*›; sharp ‹*tone*›; **er war ~ zu ihr** he was short with her; he snapped at her
Rüsche *die;* ~, **~n** ruche; frill
Ruß *der;* **~es** soot
Russe *der;* **~n, ~n** Russian
Rüssel *der;* **~s, ~** (des Elefanten) trunk; (des Schweins) snout; (bei Insekten u. Ä.) proboscis
rußen *itr. V.* give off sooty smoke
Russin *die;* ~, **~nen** Russian
russisch [1] *Adj.* Russian
[2] *adv.* (auf ~) in Russian
Russisch *das;* **~[s]** Russian
Russ·land, *Ruß·land (*das*); **~s** Russia
rüsten *itr. V.* arm
rüstig *Adj.* sprightly; active
rustikal *Adj.* country-style ‹*food, inn, clothes, etc.*›; rustic ‹*furniture*›
Rüstung *die;* ~, **~en (a)** armament *no art.;* (Waffen) arms *pl.;* weapons *pl.*
(b) (hist.) suit of armour
Rüstungs-: ~industrie *die* armaments *or* arms industry; **~kontrolle** *die* arms control; **~stopp** *der* arms freeze; **~wettlauf** *der* arms race
Rute *die;* ~, **~n** switch; (Birken~, Angel~, Wünschel~) rod
Rutsch *der* **guten ~ [ins neue Jahr]!** (ugs.) happy New Year!
Rutsch·bahn *die* slide
Rutsche *die;* ~, **~n** chute
rutschen *itr. V.; mit sein* slide; ‹*clutch, carpet*› slip
rutschig *Adj.* slippery
rütteln *tr., itr. V.* shake

r

Ss

s, S /ɛs/ *das;* ~, ~ s/S
s *Abk.* = **Sekunde** sec.; s.
s. *Abk.* = **siehe**
S *Abk.* **(a)** = **Süden** S.
(b) (österr.) = **Schilling** Sch.
S. *Abk.* = **Seite** p.
Sa. *Abk.* = **Samstag** Sat.
Saal *der;* ~[e]s, **Säle** **(a)** hall; (Ballsaal) ballroom
(b) (Publikum) audience
Saar·land *das;* ~[e]s Saarland; Saar (esp. Hist.)
Saat *die;* ~, ~en **(a)** (das Gesäte) [young] crops *pl.*
(b) (das Säen) sowing
(c) (Samenkörner) seed[s *pl.*]
Säbel *der;* ~s, ~: sabre
Sabotage /zabo'ta:ʒə/ *die;* ~, ~n sabotage *no art.*
Sabotage·akt *der* act of sabotage
sabotieren *tr. V.* sabotage
Sach-: ~**bearbeiter** *der,* ~**bearbeiterin** *die* person responsible (**für** for); (Experte) specialist, expert (**für** on); ~**beschädigung** *die* (Rechtsw.) wilful damage to property; ~**buch** *das* [popular] non-fiction book; ~**bücher lesen** read non-fiction *sing.*
sach·dienlich *Adj.* useful
Sache *die;* ~, ~n **(a)** things
(b) (Angelegenheit) matter; business (esp. derog.); **zur** ~ **kommen** come to the point
(c) (Rechtssache) case
(d) (Anliegen) cause
sach-, Sach-: ~**gebiet** *das* subject [area]; field; ~**gemäß,** ~**gerecht** 1 *Adj.* proper; correct; 2 *adv.* properly; correctly; ~**kenntnis** *die* expertise; knowledge of the subject; ~**kundig** 1 *Adj.* with a knowledge of the subject *postpos., not pred.;* 2 *adv.* expertly
sachlich 1 *Adj.* **(a)** (objektiv) objective; (nüchtern) functional ‹*building, style, etc.*›; matter-of-fact ‹*letter etc.*›
(b) (sachbezogen) factual ‹*error*›
2 *adv.* **(a)** (objektiv) objectively; ‹*state*› as a matter of fact; (nüchtern) ‹*furnished*› in a functional style; ‹*written*› in a matter-of-fact way
(b) (sachbezogen) factually ‹*wrong*›
sächlich *Adj.* (Sprachw.) neuter
Sachlichkeit *die;* ~: objectivity; (Nüchternheit) functionalism

*alte Schreibung - vgl. Hinweis auf S. xiv

Sach-: ~**register** *das* [subject] index; ~**schaden** *der* damage [to property] *no indef. art.*
Sachse *der;* ~n, ~n Saxon
Sachsen (*das*); ~s Saxony
Sachsen-Anhalt (*das*); ~s Saxony-Anhalt
Sächsin *die;* ~, ~nen Saxon
sacht, sachte 1 *Adj.* **(a)** (behutsam) gentle
(b) (leise) quiet
2 *adv.* **(a)** gently
(b) (leise) quietly
Sach-: ~**verhalt** *der;* ~~[e]s, ~~e facts *pl.* [of the matter]; ~**verstand** *der* expertise; grasp of the subject; ~**verständige** *der/die; adj. Dekl.* expert
Sack *der;* ~[e]s, **Säcke** sack; (aus Papier, Kunststoff) bag
Sack-: ~**gasse** *die* cul-de-sac; ~**hüpfen** *das;* ~~s sack race
Sadismus *der;* ~: sadism *no art.*
Sadist *der;* ~en, ~en, **Sadistin** *die;* ~, ~nen sadist
sadistisch 1 *Adj.* sadistic
2 *adv.* sadistically
säen *tr.* (*auch itr.*) *V.* sow
Saft *der;* ~[e]s, **Säfte** **(a)** juice
(b) (in Pflanzen) sap
saftig *Adj.* **(a)** juicy; sappy ‹*stem*›; lush ‹*meadow, green*›
(b) (ugs.) hefty ‹*slap, blow*›; steep (coll.) ‹*prices, bill*›; crude ‹*joke, song, etc.*›; strongly-worded ‹*letter etc.*›
saft-, Saft-: ~**laden** *der* (salopp abwertend) lousy outfit (coll.); ~**los** *Adj.* **(a)** juiceless
(b) (fig.) feeble, anodyne ‹*language*›; ~- **und kraftlos** feeble; wishy-washy; (*adv.*) without any zest; ~**sack** *der* (derb abwertend) bastard (coll.)
Sage *die;* ~, ~n legend; (bes. nordische) saga
Säge *die;* ~, ~n saw
Säge-: ~**blatt** *das* saw blade; ~**mehl** sawdust
sagen 1 *tr. V.* **(a)** say; **was ich noch ~ wollte** [oh] by the way; **unter uns gesagt** between you and me
(b) (mitteilen) **jmdm. etw. ~:** say sth. to sb.; (zur Information) tell sb. sth.
(c) (nennen) **zu jmdm./etw. X ~:** call sb./sth. X
(d) (anordnen, befehlen) tell
2 *refl. V.* **sich** (*Dat.*) **etw. ~:** say sth. to oneself
sägen *tr., itr. V.* saw

Säge-: ~späne *Pl.* wood shavings; **~werk** *das* sawmill

sah *1. u. 3. Pers. Sg. Prät. v.* SEHEN

Sahne *die;* ~: cream

Saison /zɛ'zõ:/ *die;* ~, **~s** season

saisonal /zɛzo'na:l/ [1] *Adj.* seasonal [2] *adv.* ‹*fluctuate*› according to the season

Saite *die;* ~, **~n** string

Saiten·instrument *das* stringed instrument

Sakko *der od. das;* **~s, ~s** jacket

Sakrament *das;* **~[e]s, ~e** sacrament

Sakristei *die;* ~, **~en** sacristy

säkularisieren *tr. V.* secularize ‹*property, art, etc.*›; deconsecrate ‹*church*›

Salami *die;* ~, **~[s]** salami

Salami·taktik *die* step-by-step policy

Salat *der;* **~[e]s, ~e (a)** salad **(b)** **[grüner] ~**: lettuce; **ein Kopf ~**: a [head of] lettuce

Salat-: ~besteck *das* salad servers *pl.*; **~soße** *die* salad dressing

Salbe *die;* ~, **~n** ointment

Salbei *der od. die;* ~: sage

Saldo *der;* **~s, ~s** *od.* **Saldi** (Buchf., Finanzw.) balance

Säle ▸ SAAL

Salmiak *der od. das;* ~: sal ammoniac

Salmonelle *die;* ~, **~n** salmonella

Salon /za'lõ:/ *der;* **~s, ~s (a)** (Raum) drawing room **(b)** (Geschäft) [hair *etc.*] salon

salopp [1] *Adj.* casual ‹*clothes*›; informal ‹*behaviour*› [2] *adv.* ‹*dress*› casually

Salto *der;* **~s, ~s** *od.* **Salti** somersault

Salut *der;* **~[e]s, ~e** (Milit.) salute; **~ schießen** fire a salute

salutieren *itr. V.* (bes. Milit.) salute

Salut·schuss, *Salut·schuß *der* (Milit.) gun salute

Salve *die;* ~, **~n** (Milit.) salvo; (aus Gewehren) volley

Salz *das;* **~es, ~e** salt

salzen *tr. V.* salt

salzig *Adj.* salty

Salz-: ~kartoffel *die* boiled potato; **~säure** *die* (Chemie) hydrochloric acid; **~stange** *die* salt stick; **~streuer** *der;* **~~s, ~~**: salt sprinkler; salt shaker (Amer.); **~wasser** *das* **(a)** (zum Kochen) salted water; **(b)** (Meerwasser) salt water

Sambia (*das*); **~s** Zambia

Samen *der;* **~s, ~ (a)** (Samenkorn) seed **(b)** (Samenkörner) seed[s *pl.*] **(c)** (Sperma) sperm; semen

Samen-: ~bank *die; Pl.* **~~en** (Med., Tiermed.) sperm bank; **~erguss, *~erguß** *der* ejaculation; **~korn** *das* seed; **~spender** *der* (Med.) sperm donor

Sammel-: ~büchse *die* collecting box; **~mappe** *die* folder; file

sammeln [1] *tr. (auch itr.) V.* **(a)** collect; gather ‹*honey, firewood, fig.: experiences, impressions, etc.*›; gather, pick ‹*berries etc.*› **(b)** (zusammenkommen lassen) gather ‹*people*› [together]; assemble ‹*people*›; cause ‹*light rays*› to converge [2] *refl. V.* gather [together]

Sammler *der;* **~s, ~**: collector

Sammlung *die;* ~, **~en (a)** collection **(b)** **[innere] ~**: composure

Samstag *der;* **~[e]s, ~e** Saturday; *s. auch* DIENSTAG

samstags *Adv.* on Saturdays

samt [1] *Präp. mit Dat.* together with [2] *Adv.* **~ und sonders** one and all

Samt *der;* **~[e]s, ~e** velvet

samten *Adj.* velvet

Samt·handschuh *der* velvet glove; **jmdn. mit ~en anfassen** (fig.) handle sb. with kid gloves

samtig *Adj.* velvety

sämtlich *Indefinitpron. u. unbest. Zahlwort* all the

Sand *der;* **~[e]s** sand

Sandale *die;* ~, **~n** sandal

Sand-: ~bank *die; Pl.* **~bänke** sandbank; **~dorn** *der; Pl.* **~~e** (Bot.) hippopha; **[Echter] ~dorn** sea buckthorn **~düne** *die* sand dune

sandig *Adj.* sandy

sand-, Sand-: ~kasten *der* [child's] sandpit; sandbox (Amer.); **~kuchen** *der* Madeira cake; **~mann** *der,* **~männchen** *das* sandman; **~stein** *der* sandstone; **~strahlen** *tr. V.* (Technik) sandblast; **~strand** *der* sandy beach

sandte *1. u. 3. Pers. Sg. Prät. v.* SENDEN

sanft [1] *Adj.* gentle; (leise) soft; (friedlich) peaceful [2] *adv.* gently; (leise) softly; (friedlich) peacefully

Sänfte *die;* ~, **~n** litter; (geschlossen) sedan chair

Sanftheit *die;* ~: gentleness; (von Klängen, Licht, Farben) softness

Sanftmut *die;* ~: gentleness; **mit ~**: gently; (nachsichtig) leniently

sanftmütig [1] *Adj.* gentle; docile ‹*horse*› [2] *adv.* gently

Sanftmütigkeit *die;* ~: gentleness; (Fügsamkeit) docility

sang *1. u. 3. Pers. Sg. Prät. v.* SINGEN

Sänger *der;* **~s, ~, Sängerin** *die;* ~, **~nen** singer

sanieren [1] *tr. V.* **(a)** redevelop ‹*area*›; rehabilitate ‹*building*›; (renovieren) renovate [and improve] ‹*flat etc.*› **(b)** (Wirtsch.) restore ‹*firm*› to profitability ⋯

2 *refl. V.* ‹*company etc.*› restore itself to profitability; ‹*person*› get oneself out of the red
Sanierung *die;* ~, ~**en (a)** ▶ SANIEREN A: redevelopment; rehabilitation; renovation **(b)** ▶ SANIEREN B: restoration to profitability
sanitär *Adj.* sanitary
Sanitäter *der;* ~**s**, ~, **Sanitäterin** *die;* ~, ~**nen** first-aid worker; (im Krankenwagen) ambulance worker
sank *1. u. 3. Pers. Sg. Prät. v.* SINKEN
Sanktion *die;* ~, ~**en** sanction
sanktionieren *tr. V.* sanction
Sanktionierung *die;* ~, ~**en** sanctioning
sann *1. u. 3. Pers. Sg. Prät. v.* SINNEN
Saphir *der;* ~**s**, ~**e** sapphire
Sardelle *die;* ~, ~**n** anchovy
Sardine *die;* ~, ~**n** sardine
Sarg *der;* ~**[e]s, Särge** coffin
Sarkasmus *der;* ~: sarcasm
sarkastisch 1 *Adj.* sarcastic
2 *adv.* sarcastically
SARS, Sars /zars/ *das;* ~: SARS
saß *1. u. 3. Pers. Sg. Prät. v.* SITZEN
Satan *der* (bibl.) Satan *no def. art.*
Satellit *der;* ~**en**, ~**en** satellite
Satelliten-: ~**fernsehen** *das* satellite television; ~**navigation** *die* satellite navigation; ~**schüssel** *die* (ugs.) satellite dish; ~**technologie** *die* satellite technology
Satire *die;* ~, ~**n** satire
satirisch 1 *Adj.* satirical
2 *adv.* satirically; with a satirical touch
satt *Adj.* **(a)** full [up] *pred.;* well-fed; **sich ~ essen/trinken** eat/drink as much as one wants; eat/drink one's fill
(b) jmdn./etw. ~ haben (ugs.) be fed up with sb./sth. (coll.)
Sattel *der;* ~**s, Sättel** saddle
satteln 1 *tr. V.* saddle
2 *itr. V.* saddle the/one's horse
sättigen *itr. V.* be filling
Sattler *der;* ~**s**, ~, **Sattlerin** *die;* ~, ~**nen** saddler; (allgemein) leather worker
Satz *der;* ~**es, Sätze (a)** (sprachliche Einheit) sentence
(b) (Musik) movement
(c) (Tennis, Volleyball) set; (Tischtennis, Badminton) game
(d) (Sprung) leap; jump
(e) (Amtsspr.: Tarif) rate
(f) (Set) set
(g) (Bodensatz) sediment; (von Kaffee) grounds *pl.*
Satz·glied *das,* **Satz·teil** *der* (Sprachw.) component part [of a/the sentence]
Satzung *die;* ~, ~**en** articles of association *pl.;* statutes *pl.*
Satz·zeichen *das* punctuation mark

*old spelling - see note on page xiv

Sau *die;* ~, **Säue (a)** (weibliches Schwein) sow
(b) (bes. südd.: Schwein) pig
(c) die ~ rauslassen (fig. ugs.) let one's hair down
sau-, Sau- (salopp) bloody ... (Brit. sl.); damn ... (coll.)
sauber 1 *Adj.* **(a)** clean; **etw. ~ machen** clean sth.; **~ machen** (putzen) clean; do the cleaning
(b) (sorgfältig) neat
2 *adv.* **(a)** (sorgfältig) neatly
(b) (fehlerlos) **[sehr] ~:** [quite] perfectly
Sauberkeit *die;* ~: cleanness
säuberlich 1 *Adj.* neat
2 *adv.* neatly; **fein ~ geordnet/verpackt** *usw.* neatly arranged/packed *etc.*
***sauber|machen** ▶ SAUBER 1A
säubern *tr. V.* **(a)** clean
(b) (befreien) clear, rid (**von** of); purge ‹*party, government, etc.*› (**von** of)
Säuberung *die;* ~, ~**en (a)** cleaning
(b) (Entfernung) purging
(c) (Politik) purge; **ethnische ~** (verhüll.) ethnic cleansing
Säuberungs·aktion *die* (Politik) purge; clean-up operation
Sauce ▶ SOSSE
Saudi *der;* ~**s**, ~**s** Saudi
Saudi-Arabien (*das*) Saudi Arabia
sauer *Adj.* **(a)** sour; pickled ‹*herring, gherkin, etc.*›; acid[ic] ‹*wine, vinegar*›; **saurer Regen** acid rain
(b) (ugs.: verärgert) cross, annoyed (**auf** + *Akk.* with)
Sauer·braten *der: braised beef marinated in vinegar and herbs;* sauerbraten (Amer.)
Sauerei *die;* ~, ~**en** (salopp abwertend) **(a)** (Unflätigkeit) obscenity
(b) (Gemeinheit) bloody scandal (coll.)
Sauer-: ~**kirsche** *die* sour cherry; ~**kraut** *das* sauerkraut
säuerlich *Adj.* **[leicht] ~:** slightly sour; slightly sharp ‹*sauce*›
Sauer-: ~**stoff** *der* oxygen; ~**stoff·gerät** *das* oxygen apparatus; ~**stoff·mangel** *der* lack of oxygen; ~**teig** *der* leaven
saufen 1 *unr. itr. V.* (salopp: trinken) drink; swig (coll.); (Alkohol trinken) drink; booze (coll.)
2 *unr. tr. V.* (salopp: trinken) drink
Säufer *der;* ~**s**, ~ (salopp) boozer (coll.)
säuft *3. Pers. Sg. Präsens v.* SAUFEN
saugen 1 *tr. V.* **(a)** *auch unr.* suck
(b) *auch itr.* (staubsaugen) vacuum; hoover (coll.)
2 *regelm.* (*auch unr.*) *itr. V.* **an etw.** (*Dat.*) ~: suck [at] sth.
3 *unr.* (*auch regelm.*) *refl. V.* **sich voll etw. ~:** become soaked with sth.
säugen *tr. V.* suckle
Säuge·tier *das* (Zool.) mammal
Säugling *der;* ~**s**, ~**e** baby

Säuglings-: ~alter *das* infancy; babyhood; **~pflege** *die* baby care

Säule *die;* ~, ~n column; (nur als Stütze, auch fig.) pillar

Saum *der;* ~[e]s, **Säume** hem

säumen *tr. V.* hem; (fig. geh.) line

säumig (geh.) *Adj.* tardy

Sauna *die;* ~, ~s *od.* **Saunen** sauna

Säure *die;* ~, ~n **(a)** (von Früchten) sourness; (von Wein, Essig) acidity; (von Soßen) sharpness **(b)** (Chemie) acid

säure-: ~beständig *Adj.* acid-resistant; **~frei** *Adj.* acid-free

Saure·gurken·zeit, Saure-Gurken-Zeit *die* (ugs.) silly season (Brit.)

Saurier /'zauriɐ/ *der;* ~s, ~: large prehistoric reptile

Saus: **in ~ und Braus leben** live the high life

säuseln [1] *itr. V.* ‹*leaves, branches, etc.*› rustle; ‹*wind*› murmur
[2] *tr. V.* (iron.: sagen) whisper

sausen *itr. V.* **(a)** ‹*wind*› whistle; ‹*storm*› roar; ‹*head, ears*› buzz
(b) *mit sein* ‹*person*› rush; ‹*vehicle*› roar
(c) *mit sein* ‹*whip, bullet, etc.*› whistle

sau-, Sau-: ~stall *der* (fig. salopp abwertend) hole (coll.); dump (coll.); **~stark** *Adj.* (salopp) bloody brilliant (sl.); **~wetter** *das* (salopp abwertend) lousy weather (coll.); **~wohl** *Adj.* **sich ~wohl fühlen** (salopp) feel bloody (Brit. sl.) *or* (coll.) damn good *or* great

Savanne /za'vanə/ *die;* ~, ~n savannah

Saxophon *das;* ~s, ~e saxophone

SB- /ɛs'be:-/ self-service *attrib.*

S-Bahn /'ɛs-/ *die* city and suburban railway

Scanner /'skænɐ/ *der;* ~s, ~ (DV, Med., graf. Technik) scanner

Schabe *die;* ~, ~n cockroach

schaben *tr., itr. V.* scrape

Schaber *der;* ~s, ~: scraper

schäbig [1] *Adj.* **(a)** (abgenutzt) shabby
(b) (jämmerlich, gering) pathetic
(c) (gemein) shabby
[2] *adv.* **(a)** (abgenutzt) shabbily
(b) (jämmerlich) miserably
(c) (gemein) meanly

Schablone *die;* ~, ~n pattern

Schach *das;* ~s, ~s **(a)** (Spiel) chess
(b) (Stellung) check; **jmdn./etw. in ~ halten** (ugs. fig.) keep sb./sth. in check

Schach-: ~brett *das* chessboard; **~figur** *die* chess piece; **~spiel** *das* **(a)** (Spiel) chess; (das Spielen) chess-playing; **(b)** (Brett und Figuren) chess set

Schacht *der;* ~[e]s, **Schächte** shaft

Schachtel *die;* ~, ~n **(a)** box; **eine ~ Zigaretten** a packet *or* (Amer.) pack of cigarettes
(b) alte ~ (salopp abwertend) old bag (sl.)

schade *Adj.* **[ach, wie] ~!** [what a] pity *or* shame; **[es ist] ~ um jmdn./etw.** it's a pity *or* shame about sb./sth.; **für jmdn./für** *od.* **zu etw. zu ~ sein** be too good for sb./sth.

Schädel *der;* ~s, ~: skull; (Kopf) head

Schädel·basis·bruch *der* (Med.) basal skull fracture

Schädel·bruch *der* (Med.) skull fracture

schaden *itr. V.* **jmdm./einer Sache ~:** damage *or* harm sb./sth.

Schaden *der;* ~s, **Schäden** **(a)** damage *no pl., no indef. art.;* **ein kleiner/großer ~:** little/major damage
(b) (Nachteil) disadvantage

schaden-, Schaden-: ~ersatz *der* (Rechtsw.) damages *pl.;* **~freude** *die* malicious pleasure; **~froh** [1] *Adj.* gloating; **~froh sein** gloat; [2] *adv.* with malicious pleasure

schadhaft *Adj.* defective

Schadhaftigkeit *die;* ~: defectiveness

schädigen *tr. V.* damage ‹*health, reputation, interests*›; harm, hurt ‹*person*›; cause losses to ‹*firm, industry, etc.*›

Schädigung *die;* ~, ~en damage *no pl., no indef. art.* (*Gen.* to)

schädlich *Adj.* harmful

Schädling *der;* ~s, ~e pest

Schad·stoff *der* harmful chemical

schadstoff·arm *Adj.* (bes. Kfz-W.) low in harmful substances *postpos.;* clean-exhaust *attrib.* ‹*vehicle*›

Schaf *das;* ~[e]s, ~e **(a)** sheep
(b) (ugs.: Dummkopf) twit (Brit. coll.)

Schaf·bock *der* ram

Schäfchen *das;* ~s, ~: [little] sheep; (Lamm) lamb

Schäfchen·wolke *die* fleecy cloud

Schäfer *der;* ~s, ~: shepherd

Schäfer·hund *der* sheepdog; **[deutscher] ~:** Alsatian

Schäferin *die;* ~, ~nen shepherdess

Schaf·fell *das* sheepskin

schaffen [1] *unr. tr. V.* **(a)** create
(b) *auch regelm.* (herstellen) create ‹*conditions, jobs, situation, etc.*›; make ‹*room, space, fortune*›
[2] *tr. V.* **(a)** (bewältigen) manage; **es ~, etw. zu tun** manage to do sth.
(b) (ugs.: erschöpfen) wear out
(c) etw. aus etw./in etw. (*Akk.*) **~:** get sth. out of/into sth.
[3] *itr. V.* **(a)** (südd.: arbeiten) work
(b) sich (*Dat.*) **zu ~ machen** busy oneself; **jmdm. zu ~ machen** cause sb. trouble

Schaffner *der;* ~s ~ (im Bus) conductor; (im Zug) guard (Brit.); conductor (Amer.)

Schaffnerin *die;* ~, ~nen (im Bus) conductress (Brit.); (im Zug) guard (Brit.); conductress (Amer.)

Schaffung *die;* ~: creation

Schafott *das;* ~[e]s, ~e scaffold

Schafs·käse *der* sheep's milk cheese

Schaf·wolle *die* sheep's wool
Schakal *der;* **~s, ~e** jackal
schal *Adj.* stale ‹*drink, taste, smell, joke*›; empty ‹*words, feeling*›
Schal *der;* **~s, ~s** *od.* **~e** scarf
Schale *die;* **~, ~n** **(a)** (Obstschale) skin; (abgeschälte **~**) peel *no pl.;*
(b) (Nussschale, Eierschale) shell
(c) (Schüssel) bowl; (flacher) dish
(d) **sich in ~ werfen** *od.* **schmeißen** (ugs.) get dressed [up] to the nines
schälen [1] *tr. V.* peel ‹*fruit, vegetable*›; shell ‹*egg, nut, pea*›
[2] *refl. V.* peel
Schall *der;* **~[e]s, ~e** *od.* **Schälle** sound
Schall·dämpfer *der* **(a)** silencer
(b) (Musik) mute
schall·dicht *Adj.* soundproof
schallen *regelm.* (*auch unr.*) *itr. V.* ring out; **~des Gelächter** ringing laughter
Schall-: ~geschwindigkeit *die* speed *or* velocity of sound; **~mauer** *die* sound *or* sonic barrier; **~platte** *die* record
Schalotte *die;* **~, ~n** shallot
schalt *1. u. 3. Pers. Sg. Prät. v.* SCHELTEN
schalten [1] *tr. V.* switch
[2] *itr. V.* **(a)** (Schalter betätigen) switch, turn (**auf** + *Akk.* to)
(b) ‹*machine*› switch (**auf** + *Akk.* to)
(c) (im Auto) change [gear]
(d) **~ und walten** manage one's affairs
(e) (ugs.: begreifen) twig (coll.); catch on (coll.)
Schalter *der;* **~s, ~** **(a)** switch
(b) (Post-, Bankschalter usw.) counter
Schalter-: ~beamte *der,* **~beamtin** *die* counter clerk; (im Bahnhof) ticket clerk; **~halle** *die* hall; (im Bahnhof) booking hall (Brit.); ticket office
Schalt·jahr *das* leap year
Schaltung *die;* **~, ~en** (Elektrot.) circuit; wiring system
Scham *die;* **~:** shame
schämen *refl. V.* be ashamed (*Gen.,* **für, wegen** of)
Scham·gefühl *das* sense of shame
schamhaft [1] *Adj.* bashful
[2] *adv.* bashfully
scham·los [1] *Adj.* **(a)** (skrupellos, dreist) shameless
(b) (unanständig) indecent; shameless ‹*person*›
[2] *adv.* **(a)** (skrupellos, dreist) shamelessly
(b) (unanständig) indecently
Schampon *das;* **~s, ~s** ▶ SHAMPOO
schamponieren *tr. V.* shampoo
Schande *die;* **~:** disgrace
schändlich [1] *Adj.* disgraceful
[2] *adv.* disgracefully
Schändlichkeit *die;* **~:** disgracefulness
Schar *die;* **~, ~en** crowd; horde
scharen·weise *Adv.* in swarms *or* hordes

*alte Schreibung - vgl. Hinweis auf S. xiv

scharf; schärfer, schärfst... [1] *Adj.* **(a)** sharp
(b) (stark gewürzt, brennend, stechend) hot; strong ‹*drink, vinegar, etc.*›; caustic ‹*chemical*›; pungent ‹*smell*›
(c) (durchdringend) shrill; (hell) harsh; (kalt) biting ‹*cold, wind, etc.*›; sharp ‹*frost*›
(d) (deutlich wahrnehmend) keen
(e) (schnell) fast; hard ‹*ride, gallop, etc.*›
(f) (explosiv) live; (Ballspiele) powerful ‹*shot*›
(g) **das ~e S** (bes. österr.) the letter 'ß'
(h) **~ auf jmdn./etw. sein** (ugs.) really fancy sb. (coll.)/be really keen on sth.
[2] *adv.* **(a)** **~ würzen/abschmecken** season/flavour highly; **~ riechen** smell pungent
(b) (durchdringend) shrilly; (hell) harshly; (kalt) bitingly
(c) (deutlich wahrnehmend) ‹*listen, watch, etc.*› closely, intently; ‹*think, consider, etc.*› hard
(d) (deutlich hervortretend) sharply
(e) (schonungslos) ‹*attack, criticize, etc.*› sharply, strongly; ‹*watch, observe, etc.*› closely
(f) (schnell) fast; **~ bremsen** brake hard *or* sharply
Schärfe *die;* **~** **(a)** sharpness
(b) (von Geschmack) hotness; (von Chemikalien) causticity; (von Geruch) pungency
(c) (Intensität) shrillness; (des Frostes) sharpness
schärfen [1] *tr. V.* (auch fig.) sharpen
[2] *refl. V.* become sharper *or* keener
scharf-, Scharf-: ~kantig *Adj.* sharp-edged; **~macher** *der* (ugs.) rabble-rouser; **~macherei** *die;* **~~, ~~en** (ugs.) rabble-rousing; **~macherin** *die:* ▶ **~**MACHER; **~sichtig** *Adj.* sharp-sighted; perspicacious; **~sinn** *der* astuteness; **~sinnig** [1] *Adj.* astute; [2] *adv.* astutely
Scharlach *der;* **~s** (Med.) scarlet fever
Scharlatan *der;* **~s, ~e** (abwertend) charlatan
Scharnier *das;* **~s, ~e** hinge
scharren [1] *itr. V.* **(a)** scrape
(b) (wühlen) scratch
[2] *tr. V.* scrape, scratch out ‹*hole, hollow, etc.*›
Schaschlik *der od. das;* **~s, ~s** (Kochk.) shashlik
Schatten *der;* **~s, ~** **(a)** shadow
(b) (schattiger Bereich) shade
Schatten-: ~kabinett *das* (Politik) shadow cabinet; **~riss, *~riß** *der* silhouette; **~seite** *die* the shady side; **die ~seiten des Lebens kennen lernen** (fig.) get to know the dark side of life
schattig *Adj.* shady
Schatz *der;* **~es, Schätze** treasure *no indef. art.*
schätzen [1] *tr. V.* **(a)** estimate; **sich glücklich ~:** deem oneself lucky
(b) (ugs.: annehmen) reckon
(c) (würdigen, hoch achten) **jmdn. ~:** hold sb. in high esteem

[2] *itr. V.* guess

Schätzung *die;* ∼, **∼en** estimate

Schätz·wert *der* estimated value

Schau *die;* ∼, **∼en** **(a)** (Ausstellung) exhibition
(b) (Vorführung) show
(c) **zur ∼ stellen** (ausstellen) exhibit; display; (offen zeigen) display

Schauder *der;* **∼s, ∼:** shiver

schauderhaft [1] *Adj.* terrible
[2] *adv.* terribly

schaudern *itr. V.* **(a)** (vor Kälte) shiver
(b) (vor Angst) shudder

schauen (bes. südd., österr., schweiz.)
[1] *itr. V.* **(a)** look
(b) (sich kümmern um) **nach jmdm./etw. ∼:** take *or* have a look at sb./sth.
(c) (achten) **auf etw.** (*Akk.*) **∼:** set store by sth.
(d) (ugs.: sich bemühen) **schau, dass du ...:** see *or* mind that you ...
(e) (nachsehen) have a look
[2] *tr. V.* **Fernsehen ∼:** watch television

Schauer *der;* **∼s, ∼:** shower

Schauer·geschichte *die* horror story

schauerlich [1] *Adj.* **(a)** horrifying
(b) (ugs.: fürchterlich) terrible (coll.)
[2] (ugs.: fürchterlich) terribly (coll.)

Schaufel *die;* ∼, **∼n** shovel; (Kehr∼) dustpan

schaufeln *tr. V.* shovel; (graben) dig

Schau·fenster *das* shop window

Schaufenster-: ∼bummel *der:* **einen ∼bummel machen** go window shopping; **∼einbruch** *der* raid on a shop window

Schaukel *die;* ∼, **∼n** **(a)** swing
(b) (Wippe) see-saw

schaukeln [1] *itr. V.* **(a)** swing; (im Schaukelstuhl) rock
(b) (sich hin und her bewegen) sway [to and fro]; (sich auf und ab bewegen) ‹*ship, boat*› pitch and toss; ‹*vehicle*› bump [up and down]
[2] *tr. V.* rock

Schaukel-: ∼pferd *das* rocking horse; **∼stuhl** *der* rocking chair

Schau·lustige *der/die; adj. Dekl.* curious onlooker

Schaum *der;* **∼s, Schäume** **(a)** foam; (von Seife usw.) lather; (von Getränken, Suppen usw.) froth
(b) (Geifer) foam; froth

schäumen *itr. V.* foam; froth; ‹*soap etc.*› lather; ‹*beer, fizzy drink, etc.*› froth [up]

Schaum·gummi *der* foam rubber

schaumig *Adj.* frothy; **Butter und Zucker ∼ rühren** beat butter and sugar until fluffy

Schaum-: ∼schläger *der* (abwertend) boaster; **∼schlägerei** *die* (abwertend) boasting; **∼schlägerin** *die:* ▶ ∼SCHLÄGER; **∼stoff** *der* [plastic] foam; **∼wein** *der* sparkling wine

Schau·platz *der* scene

schaurig *Adj.* (furchtbar) dreadful; frightful; (unheimlich) eerie

Schau-: ∼spiel *das* **(a)** (Drama) drama *no art.;* **(b)** (ernstes Stück) play; **(c)** (geh.: Anblick) spectacle; **∼spieler** *der* actor; **∼spielerin** *die* actress; **∼steller** *der;* **∼∼s, ∼∼:** showman; **∼stellerin** *die;* **∼∼, ∼∼nen** showwoman

Scheck *der;* **∼s, ∼s** cheque

Scheck-: ∼heft *das* chequebook; **∼karte** *die* cheque card

scheel (ugs.) [1] *Adj.* disapproving; (neidisch) envious; jealous
[2] *adv.* disapprovingly; (neidisch) enviously; jealously

scheffeln *tr. V.* (ugs.) rake in (coll.)

Scheibe *die;* ∼, **∼n** **(a)** disc
(b) (abgeschnittene) slice
(c) (Glasscheibe) pane [of glass]; (Fensterscheibe) [window] pane

Scheiben-: ∼bremse *die* disc brake; **∼wasch·anlage** *die* (Kfz-W.) windscreen washer system *or* unit; **∼wischer** *der* windscreen wiper

Scheide *die;* ∼, **∼n** **(a)** sheath
(b) (Anat.) vagina

scheiden *unr. tr. V.* dissolve ‹*marriage*›; divorce ‹*married couple*›; **sich ∼ lassen** get divorced *or* get a divorce

Scheidung *die;* ∼, **∼en** divorce

Schein *der;* **∼[e]s, ∼e** **(a)** (Lichtschein) light
(b) (Anschein) appearances *pl., no art.;* (Täuschung) pretence; **etw. nur zum ∼ tun** [only] pretend to do sth.; make a show of doing sth.
(c) (Geldschein) note

scheinbar [1] *Adj.* apparent; seeming
[2] *adv.* seemingly

scheinen *unr. itr. V.* **(a)** shine
(b) (den Eindruck erwecken) seem; appear; **mir scheint, [dass] ...:** it seems *or* appears to me that ...

schein-, Schein-: ∼heilig [1] *Adj.* hypocritical; [2] *adv.* hypocritically; **∼heiligkeit** *die* hypocrisy; **∼tot** *Adj.* **(a)** (Med.) apparently *or* seemingly dead; **(b)** (salopp: sehr alt) with one foot in the grave *postpos.;* **∼werfer** *der* floodlight; (am Auto) headlight; **∼werfer·licht** *das* floodlight; (des Autos) headlights *pl.;* (im Theater, Museum usw.) spotlight [beam]

Scheiße *die;* ∼ (derb) shit (coarse); crap (coarse)

scheiß·egal *Adj.* (derb) **∼ sein** not matter a damn (sl.); **das ist mir ∼:** I don't give a damn (sl.) *or* (coarse) shit

scheißen *unr. itr. V.* (derb) [have *or* (Amer.) take a] shit (coarse); crap (coarse); have a crap (coarse)

Scheiß·kerl *der* (derb) bastard (coll.)

Scheitel *der;* **∼s, ∼:** parting

scheiteln *tr. V.* part ‹*hair*›

scheitern *itr. V.; mit sein* fail; ‹*talks, marriage*› break down; ‹*plan, project*› fail, fall through

Schelle *die;* **~, ~n** bell

schellen *itr. V.* (westd.) ▶ KLINGELN

Schell·fisch *der* haddock

Schelm *der;* **~[e]s, ~e** rascal; rogue

schelmisch 1 *Adj.* roguish
2 *adv.* roguishly

Schelte *die;* **~, ~n** (geh.) scolding

schelten (südd., geh.) 1 *unr. itr. V.* **auf** *od.* **über jmdn./etw. ~:** moan about sb./sth.
2 *unr. tr. V.* scold

Schema *das;* **~s, ~s** *od.* **~ta** *od.* **Schemen** pattern

schematisch 1 *Adj.* **(a)** diagrammatic
(b) (mechanisch) mechanical
2 *adv.* **(a)** in diagram form
(b) (mechanisch) mechanically

Schemel *der;* **~s, ~** **(a)** stool
(b) (südd.: Fußbank) footstool

Schenkel *der;* **~s, ~:** thigh

schenken *tr. V.* **(a)** give; **jmdm. etw. [zum Geburtstag] ~:** give sb. sth. *or* sth. to sb. [as a birthday present *or* for his/her birthday]
(b) (ugs.: erlassen) **jmdm./sich etw. ~:** spare sb./oneself sth.

scheppern *itr. V.* (ugs.) clank

Scherbe *die;* **~, ~n** fragment

Schere *die;* **~, ~n** **(a)** scissors *pl.;* **eine ~:** a pair of scissors
(b) (Zool.) claw

scheren¹ *unr. tr. V.* crop; (von Haar befreien) shear, clip ‹*sheep*›

scheren² *tr., refl. V.* **sich um jmdn./etw. nicht ~:** not care about sb./sth.

Scherereien *Pl.* (ugs.) trouble *no pl.*

Scherz *der;* **~es, ~e** joke

scherzen *itr. V.* joke

scherzhaft 1 *Adj.* jocular
2 *adv.* jocularly

scheu 1 *Adj.* shy; timid ‹*animal*›; (ehrfürchtig) awed
2 *adv.* shyly; (von Tieren) timidly

Scheu *die;* **~** **(a)** shyness; (Ehrfurcht) awe
(b) (von Tieren) timidity

scheuchen *tr. V.* shoo; drive

scheuen 1 *tr. V.* shrink from; shun ‹*people, light, company, etc.*›
2 *refl. V.* **sich vor etw.** (*Dat.*) **~:** be afraid of *or* shrink from sth.
3 *itr. V.* ‹*horse*› shy (**vor** + *Dat.* at)

scheuern 1 *tr., itr. V.* **(a)** (reinigen) scour; scrub
(b) (reiben) rub; chafe
2 *tr. V.* (reiben an) rub

Scheuer-: ~pulver *das* scouring powder; **~tuch** *das; Pl.* **~tücher** scouring cloth

Scheune *die;* **~, ~n** barn

Scheusal *das;* **~s, ~e** monster

scheußlich 1 *Adj.* **(a)** dreadful
(b) (ugs.: äußerst unangenehm) dreadful (coll.); ghastly (coll.) ‹*weather, taste, smell*›
2 *adv.* **(a)** dreadfully
(b) (ugs.: sehr) dreadfully (coll.)

Scheußlichkeit *die;* **~, ~en** **(a)** dreadfulness
(b) (etw. Scheußliches) dreadful thing

Schi *usw.* ▶ SKI *usw.*

Schicht *die;* **~, ~en** **(a)** (Lage) layer; (Geol.) stratum; (von Farbe) coat; (sehr dünn) film
(b) (Gesellschaftsschicht) stratum
(c) (Arbeitsschicht) shift; **~ arbeiten** work shifts; be on shift work

Schicht·arbeit *die* shift work

schichten *tr. V.* stack

schick 1 *Adj.* **(a)** stylish; chic ‹*clothes, fashions*›; smart ‹*woman, girl, man*›
(b) (ugs.: großartig, toll) great (coll.); fantastic (coll.)
2 *adv.* stylishly; smartly ‹*furnished, decorated*›

schicken 1 *tr. V.* send; **jmdm. etw. ~, etw. an jmdn. ~:** send sth. to sb.; send sb. sth.
2 *itr. V.* **nach jmdm. ~:** send for sb.
3 *refl. V.* (veralt.: sich ziemen) be proper *or* fitting

Schickeria *die;* **~** (ugs.) smart set

Schicksal *das;* **~s, ~e: [das] ~:** fate; destiny; (schweres Los) fate

Schicksals·schlag *der* stroke of fate

Schiebe·dach *das* sunroof

schieben 1 *unr. tr. V.* **(a)** push
(b) (stecken) put
(c) **etw. auf jmdn./etw. ~:** blame sb./sth. for sth.
2 *unr. refl. V.* **sich durch die Menge ~:** push one's way through the crowd
3 *unr. itr. V.* push; (heftig) shove

Schiebe·tür *die* sliding door

Schiebung *die;* **~, ~en** (ugs.) **(a)** shady deal
(b) (Begünstigung) pulling strings

schied *1. u. 3. Pers. Sg. Prät. v.* SCHEIDEN

Schieds·richter *der,* **Schieds·richterin** *die* referee; (Tennis, Hockey, Kricket) umpire

schief 1 *Adj.* **(a)** (schräg) leaning ‹*wall, fence, post*›; (nicht parallel) crooked; sloping ‹*surface*›; worn[-down] ‹*heels*›
(b) (fig.: verzerrt) distorted ‹*picture, presentation, view, impression*›; false ‹*comparison*›
2 *adv.* **(a)** (schräg) **das Bild hängt/der Teppich liegt ~:** the picture/carpet is crooked; **der Tisch steht ~:** the table isn't level
(b) (fig.: verzerrt) **etw. ~ darstellen** give a distorted account of sth.
(c) **~ gehen** *od.* **laufen** (ugs.) go wrong

Schiefer *der;* **~s** (Gestein) slate

***schief-: ~|gehen, ~|laufen** ▶ SCHIEF 2c

*old spelling - see note on page xiv

schielen *itr. V.* **(a)** squint; **auf dem rechten Auge ∼:** have a squint in one's right eye
(b) (ugs.: blicken) look out of the corner of one's eye

schien *1. u. 3. Pers. Sg. Prät. v.* SCHEINEN

Schien·bein *das* shinbone

Schiene *die;* **∼, ∼n (a)** rail
(b) (Gleitschiene) runner
(c) (Med.: Stütze) splint

schienen *tr. V.* **jmds. Arm/Bein ∼:** put sb.'s arm/leg in a splint/splints

schießen 1 *unr. itr. V.* **(a)** shoot; **auf jmdn./etw. ∼:** shoot/fire at sb./sth.
(b) *mit sein* (strömen) gush; (spritzen) spurt
(c) *mit sein* (schnell wachsen) shoot up
2 *unr. tr. V.* **(a)** shoot; fire ‹*bullet, missile, rocket*›
(b) (Fußball) score ‹*goal*›
(c) (ugs.: fotografieren) **einige Aufnahmen ∼:** take a few snaps

Schießerei *die;* **∼, ∼en (a)** shooting *no indef. art., no pl.;*
(b) (Schusswechsel) gun battle

Schiff *das;* **∼[e]s, ∼e (a)** ship; **mit dem ∼:** by ship *or* sea
(b) (Archit.) (Mittelschiff) nave; (Querschiff) transept; (Seitenschiff) aisle

***Schiffahrt** ▶ SCHIFFFAHRT

schiffbar *Adj.* navigable

Schiff-: ∼bau *der* shipbuilding *no art.;* **∼bruch** *der* (veralt.) shipwreck; **[mit etw.] ∼bruch erleiden** (fig.) fail [in sth.]; **∼brüchige** *der/die; adj. Dekl.* shipwrecked man/woman

Schiffer *der;* **∼s, ∼, Schifferin** *die;* **∼, ∼nen** boatman/boatwoman; (eines Lastkahns) bargee; (Kapitän[in]) skipper

Schiff·fahrt *die* shipping *no indef. art.*; (Schifffahrtskunde) navigation

Schiffs-: ∼arzt *der* ship's doctor; **∼brücke** *die* pontoon bridge; **∼junge** *der* ship's boy; **∼reise** *die* voyage; (Vergnügungsreise) cruise; **∼verkehr** *der* shipping traffic

Schikane *die;* **∼, ∼n (a)** harassment *no indef. art.*
(b) mit allen ∼n (ugs.) ‹*kitchen, house*› with all mod cons (Brit. coll.); ‹*car, bicycle, stereo*› with all the extras

schikanieren *tr. V.* harass

Schild[1] *der;* **∼[e]s, ∼e** shield

Schild[2] *das;* **∼[e]s, ∼er** sign; (Nummernschild) number plate; (Namensschild) nameplate; (auf Denkmälern, Gebäuden usw.) plaque; (Etikett) label

Schild·drüse *die* (Med.) thyroid [gland]

schildern *tr. V.* describe

Schild·kröte *die* tortoise; (Meeresschildkröte) turtle

Schilf *das;* **∼[e]s (a)** reed
(b) (Röhricht) reeds *pl.*

schillern *itr. V.* shimmer

Schilling *der;* **∼s, ∼e** schilling

schilt *3. Pers. Sg. Präsens v.* SCHELTEN

Schimmel *der;* **∼s, ∼ (a)** mould; (auf Leder, Papier) mildew
(b) (Pferd) white horse

schimmelig *Adj.* mouldy; mildewy ‹*paper, leather*›

schimmeln *itr. V.; auch mit sein* go mouldy; ‹*leather, paper*› get covered with mildew

Schimmel·pilz *der* mould

Schimmer *der;* **∼s** (Schein) gleam; (von Seide) shimmer; sheen; **keinen ∼ [von etw.] haben** (ugs.) not have the faintest idea [about sth.] (coll.)

schimmern *itr. V.* gleam; ‹*water, sea*› glisten, shimmer; ‹*metal*› glint, gleam; ‹*silk etc.*› shimmer

schimmlig ▶ SCHIMMELIG

Schimpanse *der;* **∼n, ∼n** chimpanzee

schimpfen 1 *itr. V.* **(a)** carry on (coll.) (**auf, über** + *Akk.* about); (meckern) grumble, moan (**auf, über** + *Akk.* at)
(b) mit jmdm. ∼: tell sb. off; scold sb.
2 *tr. V.* **jmdn. ∼:** tell sb. off

Schimpf·wort *das; Pl.* **Schimpf·wörter** (Beleidigung) insult; (derbes Wort) swear word

schinden *unr. tr. V.* maltreat; ill-treat; **Zeit ∼** (ugs.) play for time

Schinderei *die;* **∼, ∼en** (Strapaze, Qual) struggle; (Arbeit) toil

Schinken *der;* **∼s, ∼:** ham

Schinken·speck *der* bacon

Schippe *die;* **∼, ∼n** (Schaufel) shovel

Schirm *der;* **∼[e]s, ∼e** umbrella; brolly (Brit. coll.); (Sonnenschirm) sunshade

Schirm-: ∼herr *der* patron; **∼herrin** *die* patroness; **∼herrschaft** *die* patronage; **∼ständer** *der* umbrella stand

schiss, *schiß *1. u. 3. Pers. Sg. Prät. v.* SCHEISSEN

Schlacht *die;* **∼, ∼en** battle

schlachten *tr. (auch itr.) V.* slaughter; kill ‹*rabbit, chicken, etc.*›

Schlachter *der;* **∼s, ∼** (nordd.) butcher

Schlachterei *die;* **∼, ∼en** (nordd.) butcher's [shop]

Schlacht-: ∼feld *das* battlefield; **∼hof** *der* abattoir; **∼tier** *das* animal kept for meat; (kurz vor der Schlachtung) animal for slaughter

Schlachtung *die;* **∼, ∼en** slaughter[ing]

Schlacht·vieh *das* animals *pl.* kept for meat; (kurz vor der Schlachtung) animals *pl.* for slaughter

Schlacke *die;* **∼, ∼n** cinders *pl.;* (Hochofen∼) slag

Schlaf *der;* **∼[e]s** sleep; **einen leichten/festen/gesunden ∼ haben** be a light/heavy/good sleeper

Schlaf·anzug *der* pyjamas *pl.*

Schläfchen *das;* **∼s, ∼:** nap; snooze (coll.)

Schläfe *die;* **∼, ∼n** temple

schlafen *unr. itr. V.* **(a)** (auch fig.) sleep; **tief** *od.* **fest ∼**: be sound asleep; **lange ∼**: sleep for a long time; (am Morgen) sleep in; **∼ gehen** go to bed
(b) (ugs.: nicht aufpassen) be asleep

Schläfer *der;* **∼s, ∼, Schläferin** *die;* **∼, ∼nen** sleeper

schlaff [1] *Adj.* **(a)** slack; flabby ‹*stomach, muscles*›
(b) (schlapp, matt) limp ‹*body, hand, handshake*›; shaky ‹*knees*›
[2] *adv.* **(a)** slackly
(b) (schlapp, matt) limply

Schlaf-: ∼gelegenheit *die* place to sleep; **∼mittel** *das* sleep-inducing drug

schläfrig [1] *Adj.* sleepy
[2] *adv.* sleepily

Schläfrigkeit *die;* **∼**: sleepiness

Schlaf-: ∼saal *der* dormitory; **∼sack** sleeping bag

schläft *3. Pers. Sg. Präsens v.* SCHLAFEN

Schlaf-: ∼tablette *die* sleeping pill; **∼wagen** *der* sleeping car; sleeper; **∼zimmer** *das* bedroom

Schlag *der;* **∼[e]s, Schläge (a)** blow; (Faust∼) punch; (Klaps) slap; (Tennis, Golf) stroke; shot; **∼ auf ∼** (fig.) in quick succession
(b) (Aufprall) bang; (dumpf) thud; (Klopfen) knock
(c) (des Herzens, Pulses) beating; (eines Pendels) swinging
(d) (einzelne rhythmische Bewegung) beat; (eines Pendels) swing
(e) (Töne) (einer Uhr) striking; (einer Glocke) ringing
(f) (einzelner Ton) (Stundenschlag) stroke; (Glockenschlag) ring; **∼ acht Uhr** on the stroke of eight

schlag-, Schlag-: ∼ader *die* artery; **∼anfall** *der* stroke; **∼artig** [1] *Adj.* very sudden; [2] *adv.* quite suddenly; **∼baum** *der* barrier; **∼bohrer** *der,* **∼bohr·maschine** *die* percussion drill; hammer drill

schlagen [1] *unr. tr. V.* **(a)** hit; beat; strike; (mit der Faust) punch; hit; (mit der flachen Hand) slap
(b) (mit Richtungsangabe) hit ‹*ball*›; **einen Nagel in etw.** (*Akk.*) **∼**: knock a nail into sth.
(c) (rühren) beat ‹*mixture*›; whip ‹*cream*›; (mit einem Schneebesen) whisk
(d) (läuten) ‹*clock*› strike; ‹*bell*› ring
(e) (legen) throw
(f) (einwickeln) wrap (**in** + *Akk.* in)
(g) (besiegen, übertreffen) beat
[2] *unr. itr. V.* **(a) er schlug mit der Faust auf den Tisch** he beat the table with his fist
(b) mit den Flügeln ∼ ‹*bird*› beat or flap its wings
(c) *mit sein* (prallen) bang; **mit dem Kopf auf etw.** (*Akk.*)**/gegen etw. ∼**: bang one's head on/against sth.
(d) *mit sein* **jmdm. auf den Magen ∼**: affect sb.'s stomach
(e) (pulsieren) ‹*heart, pulse*› beat; (heftig) ‹*heart*› pound; ‹*pulse*› throb
(f) (läuten) ‹*clock*› strike; ‹*bell*› ring
[3] *unr. refl. V.* fight; **sich mit jmdm. ∼**: fight with sb.

Schlager *der;* **∼s, ∼ (a)** pop song
(b) (Erfolg) (Buch) best seller; (Ware) best-selling line; (Film, Stück, Lied) hit

Schläger *der;* **∼s, ∼ (a)** (Raufbold) tough; thug
(b) (Tennis, Federball, Squash) racket; (Tischtennis, Kricket) bat; ([Eis]hockey, Polo) stick; (Golf) club

Schlägerei *die;* **∼, ∼en** brawl; fight

Schlägerin *die;* **∼, ∼nen** ▶ SCHLÄGER A

Schlager·sänger *der,* **Schlager·sängerin** *die* pop singer

schlag-, Schlag-: ∼fertig *Adj.* quick-witted ‹*reply*›; ‹*person*› who is quick at repartee; **∼fertigkeit** *die* quickness at repartee; **∼licht** *das* (Kunst, Fot.) shaft of light; **ein ∼licht auf etw. werfen** highlight sth.; **∼loch** *das* pothole; **∼obers** *das;* **∼∼** (österr.), **∼rahm** *der* (bes. südd., österr., schweiz.), **∼sahne** *die* whipping cream; (geschlagen) whipped cream; **∼seite** *die* list; **[starke** *od.* **schwere] ∼seite haben/bekommen** be listing [heavily] *or* have a [heavy] list/ develop a [heavy] list; **∼stock** *der* cudgel; (für Polizei) truncheon; **∼wort** *das* **(a)** *Pl. meist* **∼∼e** (Parole) slogan; catchphrase; **(b)** *Pl.* **∼wörter** (Buchw.: Stichwort) headword; **∼zeile** *die* headline; **∼zeug** *das* drums *pl.*

schlaksig (ugs.) *Adj.* gangling; lanky

Schlamassel *der od. das;* **∼s** (ugs.) mess

Schlamm *der;* **∼[e]s, ∼e** *od.* **Schlämme (a)** mud
(b) (Schlick) sludge

schlammig *Adj.* **(a)** muddy
(b) (schlickig) sludgy; muddy

Schlamperei *die;* **∼, ∼en** (ugs. abwertend) sloppiness

schlampig (ugs. abwertend) [1] *Adj.* **(a)** (liederlich) slovenly
(b) (nachlässig) sloppy, slipshod ‹*work*›
[2] *adv.* **(a)** (liederlich) in a slovenly way
(b) (nachlässig) sloppily

schlang *1. u. 3. Pers. Sg. Prät. v.* SCHLINGEN

Schlange *die;* **∼, ∼n (a)** snake
(b) (Warteschlange) queue; line (Amer.); **∼ stehen** queue; stand in line (Amer.)
(c) (Autoschlange) tailback (Brit.); backup (Amer.)

schlängeln *refl. V.* ‹*snake*› wind [its way]; ‹*road*› wind, snake [its way]

Schlangen·linie *die* wavy line

schlank *Adj.* slim ‹*person*›; slim, slender ‹*build, figure*›

*alte Schreibung - vgl. Hinweis auf S. xiv

Schlankheit *die;* ~ ▶ SCHLANK: slimness; slenderness

Schlankheits·kur *die* slimming diet

schlapp *Adj.* **(a)** worn out; tired out; (wegen Schwüle) listless; (wegen Krankheit) run-down
(b) (ugs.: ohne Schwung) wet (coll.); feeble
(c) slack ‹*rope, cable*›; loose ‹*skin*›; flabby ‹*stomach, muscles*›

Schlappe *die;* ~, ~**n** setback

schlapp|machen *itr. V.* (ugs.) flag; (zusammenbrechen) flake out (coll.); (aufgeben) give up

Schlaraffen·land *das;* ~[e]s Cockaigne

schlau 1 *Adj.* **(a)** shrewd; astute; (gerissen) wily; crafty; cunning
(b) (ugs.: gescheit) clever, bright; smart; **aus jmdm. nicht ~ werden** (ugs.) not be able to make sb. out
2 *adv.* shrewdly; astutely; (gerissen) craftily; cunningly

Schlauch *der;* ~[e]s, **Schläuche (a)** hose
(b) (im Reifen) tube

Schlauch·boot *das* rubber dinghy; inflatable [dinghy]

schlauchen (ugs.) *tr., auch itr. V.* **jmdn. ~:** take it out of sb.

schlauch·los *Adj.* tubeless ‹*tyre*›

Schläue *die;* ~: shrewdness; astuteness; (Gerissenheit) wiliness; craftiness; cunning

Schlaufe *die;* ~, ~**n** loop

schlecht 1 *Adj.* **(a)** bad; poor, bad ‹*food, quality, style, harvest, health, circulation*›; poor ‹*salary, eater, appetite*›; poor-quality ‹*goods*›; bad, weak ‹*eyes*›; **um jmdn./mit etw. steht es ~:** sb./sth. is in a bad way; **jmdn. ~ machen** run sb. down; disparage sb.
(b) (böse) bad; wicked
(c) (ungenießbar) off; **das Fleisch ist ~ geworden** the meat has gone off
2 *adv.* **(a)** badly; **er sieht/hört ~:** his sight is poor/he has poor hearing; **über jmdn.** *od.* **von jmdm. ~ sprechen** speak ill of sb.; **~ bezahlt** badly *or* poorly paid
(b) (schwer) **heute geht es ~:** today is difficult
(c) ~ und recht, mehr ~ als recht after a fashion

schlecht-: ***~bezahlt** ▶ SCHLECHT 2A; ***~|gehen** ▶ GEHEN I; ***~gelaunt** ▶ GELAUNT

Schlechtigkeit *die;* ~: badness; wickedness

***schlecht|machen** ▶ SCHLECHT 1A

schlecken (bes. südd., österr.) *tr. V.* lap up

schleichen 1 *unr. itr. V.; mit sein* creep; (heimlich) creep; sneak; ‹*cat*› slink, creep; (langsam fahren) crawl along
2 *unr. refl. V.* creep; sneak; ‹*cat*› slink, creep

schleichend *Adj.* insidious ‹*disease*›; slow[-acting] ‹*poison*›; creeping ‹*inflation*›; gradual ‹*crisis*›

Schleich·werbung *die* surreptitious advertising

Schleier *der;* ~**s**, ~: veil

schleier·haft *Adj.* **jmdm. ~ sein/bleiben** be/remain a mystery to sb.

Schleife *die;* ~, ~**n (a)** bow; (Fliege) bow tie
(b) (starke Biegung) loop

schleifen[1] *unr. tr. V.* grind; cut ‹*diamond, glass*›; (mit Schleifpapier usw.) sand; (schärfen) sharpen

schleifen[2] 1 *tr. V.* **(a)** (auch fig.) drag
(b) (niederreißen) raze ‹*sth.*› [to the ground]
2 *itr. V.; auch mit sein* drag; **die Kupplung ~ lassen** (Kfz-W.) slip the clutch

Schleim *der;* ~[e]s, ~**e** mucus; (im Hals) phlegm; (von Schnecken) slime

schleimig *Adj.* (auch fig.) slimy; (Physiol., Zool.) mucous

schlemmen *itr. V.* have a feast

Schlemmer *der;* ~**s**, ~: gourmet

schlendern *itr. V.; mit sein* stroll

Schlenker *der;* ~**s**, ~ (ugs.) swerve; **einen ~ machen** swerve

schlenkern *tr., itr. V.* swing; **mit den Armen ~:** swing one's arms

Schleppe *die;* ~, ~**n** train

schleppen 1 *tr. V.* **(a)** (ziehen) tow ‹*vehicle, ship*›
(b) (tragen) carry; lug
(c) (ugs.: mitnehmen) drag
2 *refl. V.* drag *or* haul oneself

schleppend *Adj.* (nicht zügig) slow

Schlepper *der;* ~**s**, ~ **(a)** (Schiff) tug
(b) (Traktor) tractor

Schlepper·organisation *die: organization smuggling illegal immigrants and emigrants*

Schlepp-: **~lift** *der* T-bar [lift]; **~tau** *das* towline; **in jmds. ~tau** (fig.) in sb.'s wake

Schleswig-Holstein (*das*); ~**s** Schleswig-Holstein

Schleuder *die;* ~, ~**n** sling; (mit Gummiband) catapult (Brit.); slingshot (Amer.)

schleudern 1 *tr. V.* hurl
2 *itr. V.; mit sein* ‹*vehicle*› skid

schleunigst *Adv.* **(a)** (auf der Stelle) at once; immediately; straight away
(b) (eilends) hastily; with all haste

Schleuse *die;* ~, ~**n** lock

schlich *1. u. 3. Pers. Sg. Prät. v.* SCHLEICHEN

schlicht 1 *Adj.* **(a)** simple; plain ‹*pattern, furniture*›
(b) (unkompliziert) simple, unsophisticated ‹*person, view, etc.*›
2 *adv.* simply; simply, plainly ‹*dressed, furnished*›

schlichten 1 *tr. V.* settle ‹*argument etc.*›; settle ‹*industrial dispute etc.*› by mediation
2 *itr. V.* mediate

Schlichtheit *die;* ~ ▶ SCHLICHT A, B: simplicity; plainness; unsophisticatedness
Schlick *der;* **~[e]s, ~e** silt
schlief *1. u. 3. Pers. Sg. Prät. v.* SCHLAFEN
Schließe *die;* **~, ~n** clasp; (Schnalle) buckle
schließen [1] *unr. tr. V.* **(a)** close; shut; turn off ‹*tap*›; fasten ‹*belt, bracelet*›; do up ‹*button, zip*›; close ‹*street, route, border, electrical circuit*›; fill, close ‹*gap*›
(b) (außer Betrieb setzen) close [down] ‹*shop, school*›
(c) etw./jmdn./sich in etw. (*Akk.*) **~:** lock sth./sb./oneself in sth.
(d) (beenden) close ‹*meeting, proceedings, debate*›; end, conclude ‹*letter, speech, lecture*›
(e) (eingehen, vereinbaren) conclude ‹*treaty, pact, ceasefire, agreement*›; reach ‹*settlement, compromise*›; enter into ‹*contract*›
(f) (folgern) infer (**aus** from)
[2] *unr. itr. V.* **(a)** close, shut
(b) (enden) end; conclude
(c) [aus etw.] auf etw. (*Akk.*) **~:** infer sth. [from sth.]
[3] *unr. refl. V.* ‹*door, window*› close, shut; ‹*wound, circle*› close
Schließ·fach *das* locker; (bei der Post) PO box; (bei der Bank) safe-deposit box
schließlich *Adv.* **(a)** finally; in the end
(b) (immerhin, doch) after all
schliff *1. u. 3. Pers. Sg. Prät. v.* SCHLEIFEN
Schliff *der;* **~[e]s, ~e (a)** cutting; (von Messern, Sensen usw.) sharpening
(b) (Art, wie etw. geschliffen wird) cut; (von Messern, Scheren usw.) edge
(c) einem Brief/Text *usw.* **den letzten ~ geben** put the finishing touches *pl.* to a letter/text *etc.*
schlimm [1] *Adj.* **(a)** grave, serious ‹*error, mistake, accusation, offence*›; bad, serious ‹*error, mistake*›
(b) (übel) bad; nasty, bad ‹*experience*›; **[das ist alles] halb so ~:** it's not as bad as all that; **ist nicht ~!** [it] doesn't matter
[2] *adv.* **~ dran sein** be in a bad way; (in einer Notlage) be in dire straits
schlimmsten·falls *Adv.* if the worst comes to the worst
Schlinge *die;* **~, ~n (a)** loop; (für den Arm) sling; (zum Erhängen) noose
(b) (Fanggerät) snare
Schlingel *der;* **~s, ~:** rascal; rogue
schlingen [1] *unr. tr. V.* **etw. um etw. ~:** loop sth. round sth.
[2] *unr. refl. V.* **sich um etw. ~:** wind itself round sth.
[3] *unr. itr. V.* bolt one's food
schlingern *itr. V.; mit sein* ‹*ship, boat*› roll; ‹*train, vehicle*› lurch from side to side
Schlips *der;* **~es, ~e** tie
Schlitten *der;* **~s, ~:** sledge; sled; (Pferdeschlitten) sleigh; (Rodelschlitten) toboggan; **~ fahren** go tobogganing

*old spelling - see note on page xiv

schlittern *itr. V.* slide
Schlitt-: ~schuh *der* [ice] skate; **~schuh laufen** *od.* **fahren** [ice-]skate; **~schuh·laufen** *das* [ice] skating *no art.;* **~schuh·läufer** *der,* **~schuh·läuferin** *die* [ice] skater
Schlitz *der;* **~es, ~e (a)** slit; (am Briefkasten, Automaten) slot
(b) (Hosenschlitz) flies *pl.;* fly
schlitz-, Schlitz-: ~auge *das* slit eye; **~äugig** *Adj.* slit-eyed; **~ohr** *das* (ugs.) wily *or* crafty devil; **~ohrig** (ugs.) [1] *Adj.* wily; crafty; [2] *adv.* craftily
schloss, *schloß *1. u. 3. Pers. Sg. Prät. v.* SCHLIESSEN
Schloss, *Schloß *das;* **Schlosses, Schlösser (a)** lock; (Vorhänge~) padlock; **hinter ~ und Riegel** (ugs.) behind bars
(b) (Verschluss) clasp
(c) (Wohngebäude) castle; (Palast) palace; (Herrschaftshaus) mansion
Schlosser *der;* **~s, ~, Schlosserin** *die;* **~, ~nen** metalworker; (Maschinenschlosser) fitter; (für Schlösser) locksmith
Schlot *der;* **~[e]s, ~e** *od.* **Schlöte** chimney [stack]; (eines Schiffes) funnel
schlottern *itr. V.* **(a)** shake
(b) ‹*clothes*› hang loose
Schlucht *die;* **~, ~en** ravine
schluchzen *itr. V.* sob
Schluck *der;* **~[e]s, ~e** *od.* **Schlücke** swallow; mouthful; (großer ~) gulp; (kleiner ~) sip
Schluck·auf *der;* **~s** hiccups *pl.*
Schlückchen *das;* **~s, ~:** sip
schlucken [1] *tr. V.* swallow; **etw. hastig ~:** gulp sth. down
[2] *itr. V.* swallow
Schlucker *der;* **~s, ~: armer ~** (ugs.) poor devil *or* (Brit. coll.) blighter
schluderig ▶ SCHLUDRIG
schludern *itr. V.* (ugs.) work sloppily
schludrig (ugs.) [1] *Adj.* **(a)** slipshod ‹*work, examination*›; botched ‹*job*›; slapdash ‹*person, work*›
(b) (schlampig [aussehend]) scruffy
[2] *adv.* **(a)** in a slipshod *or* slapdash way
(b) (schlampig) scruffily
schlug *1. u. 3. Pers. Sg. Prät. v.* SCHLAGEN
Schlummer *der;* **~s** (geh.) slumber (poet./rhet.)
schlummern *itr. V.* (geh.) slumber (poet./rhet.)
Schlund *der;* **~[e]s, Schlünde** [back of the] throat; pharynx (Anat.)
schlüpfen *itr. V.; mit sein* slip; **[aus dem Ei] ~** ‹*chick*› hatch out
Schlüpfer *der;* **~s, ~** (für Damen) knickers *pl.* (Brit.); panties *pl.;* (für Herren) [under]pants *pl. or* trunks *pl.*
schlüpfrig *Adj.* **(a)** slippery
(b) (anstößig) lewd

Schlüpfrigkeit *die;* ~, ~**en (a)** (feuchte Glätte) slipperiness
(b) (Anstößigkeit) lewdness
schlurfen *itr. V.; mit sein* shuffle
schlürfen 1 *tr. V.* slurp [up] (coll.)
2 *itr. V.* slurp (coll.)
Schluss, *Schluß *der;* **Schlusses, Schlüsse (a)** end; (eines Vortrags o. Ä.) conclusion; (eines Buchs, Schauspiels usw.) ending; **am** *od.* **zum** ~: at the end; (schließlich) in the end
(b) (Folgerung) conclusion
Schlüssel *der;* ~**s**, ~: key
Schlüssel-: ~**bein** *das* collarbone; clavicle (Anat.); ~**blume** *die* cowslip; (Primel) primula; ~**bund** *der od. das* bunch of keys; ~**figur** *die* key figure; ~**loch** *das* keyhole; ~**stellung** *die* key position
schluss·folgern, *schlußfolgern *tr. V.* conclude (**aus** from)
Schluss·folgerung, *Schluß·folgerung *die* conclusion, inference (**aus** from); ~**en ziehen** draw conclusions
schlüssig 1 *Adj.* **(a)** conclusive ‹*proof, evidence*›; convincing, logical ‹*argument, conclusion*›
(b) sich (*Dat.*) ~ **werden** make up one's mind
2 *adv.* conclusively
Schlüssigkeit *die;* ~: conclusiveness
Schluss-, *Schluß-: ~**licht** *das* tail *or* rear light; ~**strich** *der* [bottom] line; ~**verkauf** *der* [end-of-season] sale[s *pl.*]
schmächtig *Adj.* slight
schmackhaft *Adj.* tasty
Schmähung *die;* ~, ~**en** diatribe; ~**en** abuse *sing.*; invective *sing.*
schmal; ~**er** *od.* **schmäler,** ~**st...** *od.* **schmälst...** *Adj.* narrow; slim, slender ‹*hips, hands, figure, etc.*›; thin ‹*lips, face, nose, etc.*›
schmälern *tr. V.* diminish; restrict ‹*rights*›
Schmalz[1] *das;* ~**es** dripping; (Schweineschmalz) lard
Schmalz[2] *der;* ~**es** (abwertend) schmaltz (coll.)
Schmalz·brot *das* slice of bread and dripping
schmalzig (abwertend) 1 *Adj.* schmaltzy (coll.)
2 *adv.* with slushy sentimentality
schmarotzen *itr. V.* (fig.) sponge; freeload (coll.)
Schmarren *der;* ~**s**, ~ (österr., auch südd.) *pancake broken up with a fork after frying*
schmatzen *itr. V.* smack one's lips; (geräuschvoll essen) eat noisily
Schmaus *der;* ~**es, Schmäuse** (veralt., scherzh.) [good] spread (coll.)
schmecken 1 *itr. V.* taste (**nach** of); **[gut]** ~: taste good; **schmeckt es [dir]?** are you enjoying it *or* your meal?
2 *tr. V.* taste; (kosten) sample
schmeicheln *itr. V.* **jmdm.** ~: flatter sb.
Schmeichler *der;* ~**s**, ~, **Schmeichlerin** *die;* ~, ~**nen** flatterer
schmeißen (ugs.) 1 *unr. tr. V.* chuck (coll.); sling (coll.); (schleudern) fling; hurl
2 *unr. refl. V.* throw oneself; (mit Wucht) hurl oneself
3 *unr. itr. V.* **mit etw. [nach jmdm.]** ~: chuck sth. [at sb.] (coll.)
Schmeiß·fliege *die* blowfly; (blaue) bluebottle
schmelzen 1 *unr. itr. V.; mit sein* melt; (fig.) ‹*doubts, apprehension, etc.*› dissolve, fade away
2 *unr. tr. V.* melt; smelt ‹*ore*›; render ‹*fat*›
Schmelz-: ~**käse** *der* processed cheese, ~**wasser** *das* melted snow and ice; meltwater (Geol.)
Schmerz *der;* ~**es**, ~**en (a)** (physisch) pain; (dumpf u. anhaltend) ache; **wo haben Sie** ~**en?** where does it hurt?; ~**en haben** be in pain
(b) (psychisch) pain; (Kummer) grief
schmerz·empfindlich *Adj.* sensitive to pain *pred.*
Schmerz·empfindlichkeit *die;* ~: sensitivity to pain
schmerzen 1 *tr. V.* **jmdn.** ~: hurt sb.; (jmdm. Kummer bereiten) grieve sb.; cause sb. sorrow
2 *itr. V.* hurt
schmerz·frei *Adj.* free of pain *pred.*; painless ‹*operation*›
Schmerz·grenze *die* (fig.) **jetzt/dann ist die** ~ **erreicht** this/that is the absolute limit
schmerzhaft *Adj.* painful
schmerzlich 1 *Adj.* painful; distressing
2 *adv.* painfully
schmerz-, Schmerz-: ~**lindernd** *Adj.* pain-relieving; ~**los** 1 *Adj.* painless;
2 *adv.* painlessly; ~**stillend** *Adj.* pain-killing; ~**tablette** *die* pain-killing tablet
Schmetterling *der;* ~**s**, ~**e** butterfly
schmettern 1 *tr. V.* **(a)** hurl (**an** + *Akk.* at, **gegen** against)
(b) (laut spielen, singen usw.) blare out ‹*march, music*›; ‹*person*› sing lustily ‹*song*›
(c) (Tennis usw.) smash ‹*ball*›
2 *itr. V.* ‹*trumpet, music, etc.*› blare out
Schmied *der;* ~**[e]s**, ~**e** blacksmith
Schmiede *die;* ~, ~**n** smithy; forge
schmieden *tr. V.* (auch fig.) forge
Schmiedin *die;* ~, ~**nen** ▶ SCHMIED
schmiegen 1 *refl. V.* snuggle, nestle (**in** + *Akk.* in); **sich an jmdn.** ~: snuggle [close] up to sb.
2 *tr. V.* press (**an** + *Akk.* against)
schmieren 1 *tr. V.* **(a)** lubricate
(b) (streichen) spread ‹*butter, jam, etc.*› (**auf** + *Akk.* on); **Brote** ~: spread slices of bread
2 *itr. V.* **(a)** ‹*oil, grease*› lubricate
(b) (ugs: unsauber schreiben) ‹*person*› scrawl, scribble; ‹*pen, ink*› smudge, make smudges

schmierig *Adj.* greasy
Schmier-: ~mittel *das* lubricant; **~seife** *die* soft soap
schmilzt *2. u. 3. Pers. Sg. Präsens v.* SCHMELZEN
Schminke *die;* ~, ~n make-up
schminken [1] *tr. V.* make up ‹*face, eyes*›
[2] *refl. V.* make oneself up
schmirgeln *tr. V.* rub down; (bes. mit Sandpapier) sand
Schmirgel·papier *das* emery paper; (Sandpapier) sandpaper
schmiss, *schmiß *1. u. 3. Pers. Sg. Prät. v.* SCHMEISSEN
Schmöker *der;* **~s, ~** (ugs.) lightweight adventure story/romance
schmökern (ugs.) [1] *itr. V.* bury oneself in a book
[2] *tr. V.* bury oneself in ‹*book*›
schmollen *itr. V.* sulk
Schmoll·mund *der* pouting mouth
schmolz *1. u. 3. Pers. Sg. Prät. v.* SCHMELZEN
Schmor·braten *der* braised beef
schmoren [1] *tr. V.* braise
[2] *itr. V.* **(a)** braise
(b) (ugs.: schwitzen) swelter
schmuck *Adj.* attractive
Schmuck *der;* **~[e]s (a)** jewelry; jewellery (esp. Brit.)
(b) ► SCHMUCKSTÜCK
(c) (Zierde) decoration
schmücken *tr. V.* decorate; embellish ‹*writings, speech*›
schmuck-, Schmuck-: ~kästchen *das,* **~kasten** *der* jewelry *or* (esp. Brit.) jewellery box; **~los** *Adj.* plain; bare ‹*room*›; **~losigkeit** *die;* **~~:** plainness; (eines Zimmers) bareness; **~stück** *das* piece of jewelry *or* (esp. Brit.) jewellery
schmuddelig *Adj.* (ugs.) grubby; mucky (coll.); (schmutzig u. unordentlich) messy; grotty (Brit. coll.)
Schmuggel *der;* **~s** smuggling *no art.*
schmuggeln *tr., itr. V.* smuggle (**in** + *Akk.* into; **aus** out of)
Schmuggler *der;* **~s, ~, Schmugglerin** *die;* **~, ~nen** smuggler
schmunzeln *itr. V.* smile to oneself
schmusen *itr. V.* (ugs.) cuddle; ‹*couple*› kiss and cuddle
Schmutz *der;* **~es** dirt; (Schlamm) mud
schmutzen *itr. V.* get dirty
schmutzig *Adj.* dirty
Schmutz·wasser *das* dirty water; (Abwasser) sewage
Schnabel *der;* **~s, Schnäbel (a)** beak
(b) (ugs.: Mund) gob (sl.)
Schnake *die;* **~, ~n (a)** daddy-long-legs
(b) (bes. südd.: Stechmücke) mosquito

*alte Schreibung - vgl. Hinweis auf S. xiv

Schnalle *die;* **~, ~n** buckle
schnallen *tr. V.* **(a)** (mit einer Schnalle festziehen) buckle ‹*shoe, belt*›; fasten ‹*strap*›
(b) (mit Riemen/Gurten befestigen) strap (**auf** + *Akk.* on to)
schnalzen *itr. V.* **[mit der Zunge/den Fingern] ~:** click one's tongue/snap one's fingers
Schnäppchen *das;* **~s, ~** (ugs.) snip (Brit. coll.); [real] bargain; **ein ~ machen** get a [real] bargain
schnappen [1] *itr. V.* **nach jmdm./etw. ~** ‹*animal*› snap at sb./sth.; **nach Luft ~:** gasp for breath
[2] *tr. V.* ‹*dog, bird, etc.*› snatch; **[sich** (*Dat.*)**] jmdn./etw. ~** (ugs.) ‹*person*› grab sb./sth.; (mit raschem Zugriff) snatch sb./sth
Schnapp·schuss, *Schnapp·schuß *der* snapshot
Schnaps *der;* **~es, Schnäpse (a)** spirit; (Klarer) schnapps
(b) (Spirituosen) spirits *pl.*
schnarchen *itr. V.* snore
schnattern *itr. V.* **(a)** ‹*goose etc.*› cackle, gaggle
(b) (ugs.: eifrig schwatzen) jabber [away]; chatter
schnauben *itr. V.* snort (**vor** with)
schnaufen *itr. V.* puff (**vor** with)
Schnauze *die;* **~, ~n (a)** (von Tieren) muzzle; (der Maus usw.) snout; (Maul) mouth
(b) (derb: Mund) gob (sl.); **[halt die] ~!** shut your trap! (sl.)
schnauzen *tr., itr. V.* (ugs.) bark; (ärgerlich) snap; snarl
Schnecke *die* snail; (Nacktschnecke) slug
Schnecken·haus *das* snail shell
Schnee *der;* **~s** snow
schnee-, Schnee-: ~ball *der* snowball; **~besen** *der* whisk; **~flocke** *die* snowflake; **~gestöber** *das* snow flurry; **~glöckchen** *das* snowdrop; **~kette** *die* snow chain; **~matsch** *der* slush; **~pflug** *der* snowplough; **~schmelze** *die;* **~~, ~~n** melting of the snow; thaw; **~sturm** *der* snowstorm; **~treiben** *das* driving snow; **~wehe** *die* snowdrift; **~weiß** *Adj.* snow-white; as white as snow *postpos.*
Schneewittchen *das;* **~s** Snow White
Schneid·brenner *der* (Technik) cutting torch; oxyacetylene cutter
Schneide *die;* **~, ~n** [cutting] edge
schneiden [1] *unr. itr. V.* cut (**in** + *Akk.* into)
[2] *unr. tr. V.* **(a)** cut; (in Scheiben) slice ‹*bread, sausage, etc.*›; (klein **~**) cut up, chop ‹*wood, vegetables*›; (stutzen) prune ‹*tree, bush*›; trim ‹*beard*›; cut, mow ‹*grass*›; **sich** (*Dat.*) **die Haare ~ lassen** have one's hair cut
(b) eine Kurve ~: cut a corner
Schneider *der;* **~s, ~:** tailor; (Damenschneider) dressmaker

Schneiderei *die;* ~, ~**en** tailor's shop; (Damenschneider) dressmaker's shop
Schneiderin *die;* ~, ~**nen** ▶ SCHNEIDER
schneidern *tr. V.* make; make, tailor ‹*suit*›
Schneide·zahn *der* incisor
schneien 1 *itr., tr. V.* (*unpers.*) snow; **es schneit** it is snowing
2 *itr. V.; mit sein* (fig.) rain down; fall like snow
Schneise *die;* ~, ~**n** (Wald~) aisle; (als Feuerschutz) firebreak
schnell 1 *Adj.* quick ‹*journey, decision, service, etc.*›; fast ‹*car, skis, road, track, etc.*›; quick, swift ‹*progress, movement, blow, action*›
2 *adv.* quickly, ‹*drive, move, etc.*› fast, quickly; ‹*spread*› quickly, rapidly; (bald) soon ‹*sold, past, etc.*›; **mach** ~! (ugs.) move it! (coll.)
schnellen *itr. V.; mit sein* shoot (**aus** + *Dat.* out of; **in** + *Akk.* into)
Schnelligkeit *die;* ~, ~**en** speed
Schnell-: ~**imbiss**, *~**imbiß** *der* snackbar; ~**koch·topf** *der* pressure cooker
schnellstens *Adv.* as quickly as possible
Schnell-: ~**straße** *die* expressway; ~**zug** *der* express [train]
Schnepfe *die;* ~, ~**n** snipe
schneuzen 1 *tr. V.* **sich/einem Kind die Nase** ~: blow one's/a child's nose
2 *refl. V.* blow one's nose
schnippeln (ugs.) 1 *itr. V.* snip [away] (**an** + *Dat.* at)
2 *tr. V.* shred ‹*vegetables*›; chop ‹*beans etc.*› [finely]
schnippen 1 *itr. V.* snap one's fingers (**nach** at)
2 *tr. V.* flick (**von** off, from)
schnippisch 1 *Adj.* pert ‹*reply, tone, etc.*›
2 *adv.* pertly
Schnipsel *der od. das;* ~**s**, ~: scrap; (aus Papier, Stoff) snippet; shred
schnipseln ▶ SCHNIPPELN
schnitt *1. u. 3. Pers. Sg. Prät. v.* SCHNEIDEN
Schnitt *der;* ~[**e**]**s**, ~**e** **(a)** cut
(b) (das Mähen) (von Gras) mowing; (von Getreide) harvest
Schnitt-: ~**blume** *die* cut flower; ~**bohne** *die* French bean
Schnittchen *das;* ~**s**, ~: canapé; [small] open sandwich
Schnitte *die;* ~, ~**n** slice; **eine** ~ [**Brot**] a slice of bread
Schnitt·fläche *die* cut surface
schnittig 1 *Adj.* stylish, smart ‹*suit, appearance, etc.*›; (sportlich) racy ‹*car, yacht, etc.*›
2 *adv.* stylishly; (sportlich) racily
Schnitt-: ~**lauch** *der* chives *pl.;* ~**menge** *die* (Math.) intersection; ~**punkt** *der* intersection; (Geom.) point of intersection; ~**stelle** *die* (DV) interface; ~**wunde** *die* cut; (lang u. tief) gash
Schnitzel *das;* ~**s**, ~ **(a)** (Fleisch) [veal/pork] escalope
(b) (von Papier) scrap; (von Holz) shaving
schnitzeln *tr. V.* chop up ‹*vegetables*› [into small pieces]; shred ‹*cabbage*›
schnitzen *tr., itr. V.* carve
schnodderig (ugs.) 1 *Adj.* brash
2 *adv.* brashly
schnöde (geh.) 1 *Adj.* **(a)** (verachtenswert) contemptible
(b) (gemein) contemptuous, scornful ‹*glance, reply, etc.*›
2 *adv.* (gemein) contemptuously; ‹*exploit, misuse*› flagrantly
Schnorchel *der;* ~**s**, ~: snorkel
Schnörkel *der;* ~**s**, ~: scroll; (der Handschrift, in der Rede) flourish
schnorren *tr., itr. V.* (ugs.) scrounge (coll.) (**bei, von** + *Dat.* off)
Schnorrer *der;* ~**s**, ~, **Schnorrerin** *die;* ~, ~**nen** (ugs.) scrounger (coll.)
Schnösel *der;* ~**s**, ~ (ugs. abwertend) young whippersnapper
schnüffeln *itr. V.* **(a)** sniff
(b) (ugs.: spionieren) snoop [about] (coll.)
(c) (Drogenjargon: Dämpfe ~) sniff [glue/paint *etc.*]
Schnüffler *der;* ~**s**, ~, **Schnüfflerin** *die;* ~, ~**nen** **(a)** (ugs.) Nosey Parker; (Spion) snooper (coll.)
(b) (Drogenjargon) [glue-, paint-, *etc.*]sniffer
Schnulze *die;* ~, ~**n** (ugs. abwertend) (Lied/Melodie) slushy song/tune; (Theaterstück, Film, Fernsehspiel) tear jerker (coll.); slushy play
schnupfen 1 *tr. V.* sniff; **Tabak** ~: take snuff
2 *itr. V.* take snuff
Schnupfen *der;* ~**s**, ~: [head] cold; [**den** *od.* **einen**] ~ **haben** have a [head] cold
Schnupf·tabak *der* snuff
schnuppe: **das/er ist mir** ~**/mir völlig** ~ (ugs.) I don't care/I couldn't care less about it/him (coll.)
schnuppern *itr. V.* sniff; **an etw.** (*Dat.*) ~: sniff sth.
Schnur *die;* ~, **Schnüre** **(a)** (Bindfaden) piece of string; (Kordel) piece of cord
(b) (ugs.: Kabel) flex (Brit.); lead; cord (Amer.)
schnüren *tr. V.* tie ‹*bundle, string, etc.*›; tie, lace up ‹*shoe, corset, etc.*›
schnur·los *Adj.* cordless
Schnurr·bart *der* moustache
schnurren *itr. V.* ‹*cat*› purr; ‹*machine*› hum
Schnür-: ~**schuh** *der* lace-up shoe; ~**senkel** *der;* ~~**s**, ~~ (bes. nordd.) [shoe]lace; (für Stiefel) bootlace
schnur·stracks *Adv.* (ugs.) straight
schob *1. u. 3. Pers. Prät. v.* SCHIESSEN

Schock *der;* **~[e]s, ~s** shock

schockieren *tr. V.* shock; **über etw.** (*Akk.*) **schockiert sein** be shocked at sth.

Schöffe *der;* **~n, ~n** lay judge (*acting together with another lay judge and a professional judge*)

Schöffen·gericht *das: court presided over by a professional judge and two lay judges*

Schöffin *die;* **~, ~nen** ▶ SCHÖFFE

Schokolade *die;* **~, ~n (a)** chocolate **(b)** (Getränk) [drinking] chocolate

Schokolade[n]-: ~eis *das* chocolate ice cream; **~guss, *~guß** *der* chocolate icing; **~pudding** *der* chocolate blancmange; **~torte** *die* chocolate cake *or* gateau

scholl *1. u. 3. Pers. Sg. Prät. v.* SCHALLEN

Scholle *die;* **~, ~n (a)** (Erdscholle) clod [of earth]
(b) (Eisscholle) [ice] floe
(c) (Fisch) plaice

schon [1] *Adv.* **(a)** (bereits) (oft nicht übersetzt) already; (in Fragen) yet; **wie lange bist du ~ hier?** how long have you been here?
(b) (fast gleichzeitig) there and then
(c) (jetzt) **~ [mal]** now; (inzwischen) meanwhile
(d) (selbst, sogar) even; (nur) only
(e) (ohne Ergänzung, ohne weiteren Zusatz) on its own; **[allein] ~ der Gedanke daran** the mere thought of it; **~ deshalb** for this reason alone
(f) (wohl) really; **Lust hätte ich ~, aber ...**: I'd certainly like to, but ...
[2] *Partikel* **(a)** (ugs. ungeduldig: endlich) **nun komm ~!** come on!; hurry up!
(b) (beruhigend: bestimmt) all right
(c) (durchaus) **das ist ~ möglich** that is quite possible
(d) (in Höflichkeitsformeln) **bitte ~, können Sie mir sagen, ...**: excuse me, could you tell me ...
(e) (iron.) **wie es so ~ heißt, wie man so ~ sagt** as they say
(f) (ugs.: beträchtlich) really; (vor einem Adjektiv) pretty; **ganz ~ arbeiten müssen** have to work jolly hard (Brit. coll.)
[3] *Partikel* (ugs.) **bleib ~ liegen!** lie there and be good

schön [1] *Adj.* **(a)** beautiful; handsome ‹*youth, man*›
(b) (angenehm) pleasant, nice ‹*day, holiday, dream, relaxation, etc.*›; fine ‹*weather*›; (nett) nice; **das war eine ~e Zeit** those were wonderful days
(c) (gut) good
(d) (in Höflichkeitsformeln) **~e Grüße** best wishes; **recht ~en Dank für ...**: thank you very much for ...
(e) ~! (ugs.: einverstanden) OK (coll.); all right
(f) (iron.: leer) **~e Worte** fine[-sounding] words; (schmeichlerisch) honeyed words
(g) (ugs.: beträchtlich) handsome, (coll.) tidy ‹*sum, fortune, profit*›; considerable ‹*quantity, distance*›; pretty good ‹*pension*›
(h) (iron.: unerfreulich) nice (coll. iron.); **das sind ja ~e Aussichten!** this is a fine lookout *sing.* (iron.)
(i) sich ~ machen smarten oneself up
[2] *adv.* **(a)** beautifully
(b) (angenehm, erfreulich) nicely; **~ warm/weich/langsam** nice and warm/soft/slow
(c) (gut) well

schonen [1] *tr. V.* treat ‹*clothes, books, furniture, etc.*› with care; (schützen) protect ‹*hands, furniture*›; (nicht strapazieren) spare ‹*voice, eyes, etc.*›; conserve ‹*strength*›
[2] *refl. V.* take things easy

Schönheit *die;* **~, ~en** beauty

Schönheits-: ~chirurgie *die* cosmetic surgery *no art.*; **~pflege** *die* beauty care *no art.*

Schon·kost *die* light food

***schön|machen** (ugs.) ▶ SCHÖN 1I

Schonung *die;* **~, ~en (a)** (Nachsicht) consideration; (nachsichtige Behandlung) considerate treatment; (nach Krankheit/Operation) [period of] rest; (von Gegenständen) careful treatment
(b) (Jungwald) [young] plantation

schonungs·los [1] *Adj.* unsparing, ruthless ‹*criticism etc.*›; blunt ‹*frankness*›
[2] *adv.* unsparingly; ‹*say*› without mincing one's words

Schonungslosigkeit *die;* **~**: ruthlessness; (Strenge) rigour

Schopf *der;* **~[e]s, Schöpfe** shock of hair

schöpfen *tr. V.* **(a)** scoop [up] ‹*water, liquid*›; (mit einer Kelle) ladle ‹*soup*›
(b) (geh.: einatmen) draw, take ‹*breath*›

Schöpfer *der;* **~s, ~**: creator; (Gott) Creator

Schöpferin *die;* **~, ~nen** creator

schöpferisch [1] *Adj.* creative
[2] *adv.* creatively

Schöpf-: ~kelle *die,* **~löffel** *der* ladle

Schöpfung *die;* **~, ~en** (geh.) creation; **die ~** (die Welt) Creation

Schoppen *der;* **~s, ~**: [quarter-litre/half-litre] glass of wine/beer

schor *1. u. 3. Pers. Sg. Prät. v.* SCHEREN

Schorf *der;* **~[e]s, ~e** scab

Schorle *die;* **~, ~n** wine with mineral water; ≈ spritzer

Schorn·stein *der* chimney; (Lokomotive, Schiff usw.) funnel

Schornstein·feger *der;* **~s, ~, Schornstein·fegerin** *die;* **~, ~nen** chimney sweep

schoss, *schoß *1. u. 3. Pers. Sg. Prät. v.* SCHIESSEN

Schoß *der;* **~es, Schöße** lap

Schote *die;* **~, ~n** pod

Schotte *der;* **~n, ~n** Scot; Scotsman; **die ~n** the Scots; the Scottish

*old spelling - see note on page xiv

Schotten·rock *der* tartan skirt; (Kilt) kilt

Schottin *die;* ~, **~nen** Scot; Scotswoman

schottisch *Adj.* Scottish; **~er Whisky** Scotch whisky

Schottland *(das);* **~s** Scotland

schräg [1] *Adj.* diagonal ‹*line, beam, cut, etc.*›; sloping ‹*surface, roof, wall, side, etc.*›; slanting, slanted ‹*writing, eyes, etc.*›; tilted ‹*position of the head etc., axis*›
[2] *adv.* at an angle; (diagonal) diagonally

Schräge *die;* ~, **~n** **(a)** (schräge Fläche) sloping surface
(b) (Neigung) slope

Schräg·strich *der* oblique stroke

schrak *1. u. 3. Pers. Sg. Prät. v.* SCHRECKEN

Schramme *die;* ~, **~n** scratch

schrammen *tr. V.* scratch

Schrank *der;* **~[e]s, Schränke** cupboard; closet (Amer.); (Glas~; kleiner Wand~) cabinet; (Kleiderschrank) wardrobe; (Bücher~) bookcase

Schränkchen *das;* **~s,** ~: cabinet

Schranke *die;* ~, **~n** **(a)** (auch fig.) barrier
(b) (fig.: Grenze) limit

Schraube *die;* ~, **~n** bolt; (Holz-, Blechschraube) screw

schrauben *tr. V.* **(a)** ▶ SCHRAUBE: bolt/screw (**an, auf** + *Akk.* on to)
(b) (drehen) screw ‹*nut, hook, lightbulb, etc.*› (**auf** + *Akk.* on to; **in** + *Akk.* into)

Schrauben-: ~schlüssel *der* spanner; **~zieher** *der;* **~s,** ~: screwdriver

Schraub·verschluss, *Schraub·verschluß *der* screw top

Schreber·garten *der* ≈ allotment (*cultivated primarily as a garden*)

Schreck *der;* **~[e]s, ~e** fright; scare; (Schock) shock; **jmdm. einen ~ einjagen** give sb. a fright

schrecken *regelm. (auch unr.) itr. V.* start [up]; **aus dem Schlaf ~:** awake with a start; start from one's sleep

Schrecken *der;* **~s,** ~: fright; scare; (Entsetzen) horror; (große Angst) terror; **jmdm. einen ~ einjagen** give sb. a fright

schreckhaft *Adj.* easily scared

Schreckhaftigkeit *die;* ~: easily scared nature; tendency to take fright

schrecklich [1] *Adj.* terrible
[2] *adv.* terribly

Schredder *der;* **~s,** ~: shredder

schreddern *tr. V.* shred

Schrei *der;* **~[e]s, ~e** cry; (lauter Ruf) shout; (durchdringend) yell; (gellend) scream; (kreischend) shriek

Schreib·block *der; Pl.* **~s** *od.* **Schreib·blöcke** writing pad

schreiben [1] *unr. itr. V.* write; (mit der Schreibmaschine) type; **an einem Roman** *usw.* **~:** be writing a novel *etc.;* **jmdm.** *od.* **an jmdn. ~:** write to sb.
[2] *unr. tr. V.* write; (mit der Schreibmaschine) type; **wie schreibt man dieses Wort?** how is this word spelt?
[3] *unr. refl. V.* be spelt

Schreiben *das;* **~s,** ~ **(a)** writing *no def. art.;*
(b) (Brief) letter

Schreiber *der;* **~s,** ~: writer; (Verfasser) author

Schreiberin *die;* ~, **~en** writer; (Verfasserin) authoress

Schreib-: ~marke *die* (DV) cursor; **~maschine** *die* typewriter; **~maschinen·papier** *das* typing paper; **~papier** *das* writing paper; **~schutz** *der* (DV) write protection; **~tisch** *der* desk

Schreibung *die;* ~, **~en** spelling

Schreib-: ~waren *Pl.* stationery *sing.;* **~waren·geschäft** *das* stationer's

schreien *unr. itr. V.* ‹*person*› cry [out]; (laut rufen/sprechen) shout; (durchdringend) yell; (gellend) scream; ‹*baby*› yell, bawl; **zum Schreien sein** (ugs.) be a scream (coll.)

Schrei·hals *der* (ugs.) **(a)** (Kind) bawler
(b) (abwertend: Randalierer) rowdy

Schreiner *der;* **~s,** ~, (bes. südd.) ▶ TISCHLER

Schreinerei *die;* ~, **~en** (bes. südd.) ▶ TISCHLEREI

Schreinerin *die;* ~, **~nen** (bes. südd.) ▶ TISCHLERIN

schreiten *unr. itr. V.; mit sein* (geh.) walk; (mit großen Schritten) stride

schrickst *2. Pers. Sg. Präsens v.* SCHRECKEN

schrickt *3. Pers. Sg. Präsens v.* SCHRECKEN

schrie *1. u. 3. Pers. Sg. Prät. v.* SCHREIEN

schrieb *1. u. 3. Pers. Sg. Prät. v.* SCHREIBEN

Schrieb *der;* **~[e]s, ~e** (ugs.) missive (coll.)

Schrift *die;* ~, **~en** **(a)** (System) script; (Alphabet) alphabet
(b) (Handschrift) [hand]writing
(c) (Werk) work

Schrift·art *die* (Druckw.) [type]face

schriftlich [1] *Adj.* written
[2] *adv.* in writing

Schrift-: ~steller *der;* **~~s, ~~, ~stellerin** *die;* **~~, ~~nen** writer; **~stück** *das* [official] document; **~wechsel** *der* correspondence; **~zeichen** *das* character; **~zug** *der* (Namenszug) lettering; (als Firmenzeichen) logo

schrill [1] *Adj.* shrill
[2] *adv.* shrilly

schrillen *itr. V.* shrill; sound shrilly

schritt *1. u. 3. Pers. Sg. Prät. v.* SCHREITEN

Schritt *der;* **~[e]s, ~e** **(a)** step; **einen ~ machen** *od.* **tun** take a step
(b) *Pl.* (Geräusch) footsteps
(c) (Entfernung) pace
(d) (Gleich~) **aus dem ~ kommen** get out of step

(e) (Gangart) walk; **seinen ~ verlangsamen/beschleunigen** slow/quicken one's pace; **[mit jmdm./etw.] ~ halten** (auch fig.) keep up *or* keep pace [with sb./sth.]
(f) (Schrittgeschwindigkeit) walking pace; **„~ fahren"** 'dead slow'
(g) (fig.: Maßnahme) step; measure

Schritt-: ~geschwindigkeit *die* walking pace; **~macher** *der,* **~macherin** *die* pacemaker

schroff 1 *Adj.* **(a)** precipitous ‹*rock etc.*›
(b) (plötzlich) sudden ‹*transition, change*›; (krass) stark ‹*contrast*›
(c) (barsch) curt ‹*refusal, manner*›; brusque ‹*manner, behaviour, tone*›
2 *adv.* **(a)** ‹*rise, drop*› sheer; ‹*fall away*› precipitously
(b) (plötzlich, unvermittelt) suddenly
(c) (barsch) curtly; ‹*interrupt*› abruptly; ‹*treat*› brusquely

schröpfen *tr. V.* (ugs.) fleece

Schrot *der od. das;* **~[e]s, ~e (a)** coarse meal; (aus Getreide) whole meal (Brit.); whole grain
(b) (Munition) shot

schroten *tr. V.* grind ‹*grain etc.*› [coarsely]; crush ‹*malt*› [coarsely]

Schrot-: ~flinte *die* shotgun; **~kugel** *die* pellet

Schrott *der;* **~[e]s, ~e (a)** scrap [metal]; **ein Auto zu ~ fahren** (ugs.) write a car off
(b) (salopp fig.) rubbish

schrott·reif *Adj.* ready for the scrap heap *postpos.*

schrubben *tr.* (*auch itr.*) *V.* scrub

Schrubber *der;* **~s, ~:** [long-handled] scrubbing brush

Schrulle *die;* **~, ~n** cranky idea; (Marotte) quirk

schrumpelig *Adj.* (ugs.) wrinkly

schrumpeln *itr. V.; mit sein* (ugs.) ‹*skin*› go wrinkled; ‹*apple etc.*› shrivel

schrumpfen *itr. V.; mit sein* shrink; ‹*metal, rock*› contract; ‹*apple etc.*› shrivel; ‹*skin*› go wrinkled; (abnehmen) decrease; ‹*supplies, capital, hopes*› dwindle

Schrumpf-: ~leber *die* cirrhotic liver; **~niere** *die* cirrhotic kidney

Schub *der;* **~[e]s, Schübe (a)** (Physik) thrust
(b) (Med.: Phase) phase; stage
(c) (Gruppe, Anzahl) batch

Schuber *der;* **~s, ~:** slip case

Schub-: ~fach *das* drawer; **~karre** *die,* **~karren** *der* wheelbarrow; **~lade** *die* drawer

Schubs *der;* **~es, ~e** (ugs.) shove

schubsen *tr.* (*auch itr.*) *V.* (ugs.) push; shove

schub·weise *Adv.* (Med.) in phases *or* stages

***alte Schreibung - vgl. Hinweis auf S. xiv**

schüchtern 1 *Adj.* **(a)** shy ‹*person, smile, etc.*›; shy, timid ‹*voice, knock, etc.*›
(b) (fig.: zaghaft) tentative, cautious ‹*attempt, beginnings, etc.*›
2 *adv.* shyly; ‹*knock, ask, etc.*› timidly

Schüchternheit *die;* **~:** shyness

Schuft *der;* **~[e]s, ~e** scoundrel

schuften (ugs.) *itr. V.* slave away

Schufterei *die;* **~** (ugs.) slaving away *no indef. art.;* slog

Schuh *der;* **~[e]s, ~e** shoe; (hoher ~, Stiefel) boot; **jmdm. etw. in die ~e schieben** (fig. ugs.) pin the blame for sth. on sb.

Schuh-: ~anzieher *der;* **~~s, ~~:** shoehorn; **~band** *das; Pl.* **~bänder** (bes. südd.) shoelace; **~creme** *die* shoe polish; **~größe** *die* shoe size; **welche ~größe hast du?** what size shoe[s] do you take?; **~löffel** *der* shoehorn; **~macher** *der,* **~macherin** *die* shoemaker; **~sohle** *die* sole [of a/one's shoe]

Schul-: ~abschluss, *~abschluß *der* school-leaving qualification; **~arbeit** *die* **(a)** ▶ ~AUFGABE; **(b)** (österr.: Klassenarbeit) [written] class test; **~aufgabe** *die* item of homework; **~aufgaben** homework *sing.;* **~beirat** *der* school advisory board; **~buch** *das* school book; **~bus** *der* school bus

schuld ▶ SCHULD B

Schuld *die;* **~, ~en (a)** guilt; **er ist sich** (*Dat.*) **keiner ~ bewusst** he is not conscious of having done any wrong
(b) (Verantwortlichkeit) blame; **es ist [nicht] seine ~:** it is [not] his fault; **[an etw.** (*Dat.*)**] ~ haben** *od.* **schuld sein** be to blame [for sth.]
(c) (Verpflichtung zur Rückzahlung) debt; **5 000 Euro ~en haben** have debts of 5,000 euros; owe 5,000 euros

schuld·bewusst, *schuld·bewußt
1 *Adj.* guilty ‹*look, face, etc.*›
2 *adv.* guiltily

schulden *tr. V.* owe; **was schulde ich Ihnen?** how much do I owe you?

Schuld·gefühl *das* feeling of guilt

schuldig *Adj.* **(a)** guilty; **der [an dem Unfall] ~e Autofahrer** the driver to blame [for the accident]
(b) jmdm. etw. ~ sein/bleiben owe sb. sth.
(c) (gebührend) due; proper

Schuldige *der/die; adj. Dekl.* guilty person; (im Strafprozess) guilty party

Schuldigkeit *die;* **~, ~en** duty; **meine [verdammte] Pflicht und ~:** my bounden duty; **seine ~ getan haben** (fig.) have served its/his purpose

Schul·direktor *der,* **Schul·direktorin** *die* head teacher; headmaster/headmistress

schuld-, Schuld-: ~los *Adj.* innocent (**an** + *Dat.* of); **~spruch** *der* verdict of guilty

Schule *die;* ~, ~n school; **zur** *od.* **in die ~ gehen, die ~ besuchen** go to school; **auf** *od.* **in der ~:** at school

schulen *tr. V.* train

Schüler *der;* ~s, ~: pupil; (Schuljunge) schoolboy

Schüler·austausch *der* school exchange

Schülerin *die;* ~, ~nen pupil; (Schulmädchen) schoolgirl

Schüler·mit·verwaltung *die* pupil participation *no art.* in school administration

schul-, Schul-: **~ferien** *Pl.* school holidays *or* (Amer.) vacation *sing.;* **~fernsehen** *das* educational television; television for schools; **~fest** *das* school open day; **~frei** *Adj.* ‹*day*› off school; **morgen ist/haben wir ~frei** there is/we have no school tomorrow; **~frei bekommen** be let off school; **~hof** *der* school yard; **~jahr** *das* **(a)** school year; **(b)** (Klasse) year; **~junge** *der* schoolboy; **~kind** *das* schoolchild; **~klasse** *die* [school] class; **~land·heim** *das* [school's] country hostel (*visited by school classes*); **~mädchen** *das* schoolgirl; **~ordnung** *die* school rules *pl.;* **~pflicht** *die* obligation to attend school; **die Einführung der [allgemeinen] ~pflicht** the introduction of compulsory school attendance [for all children]; **~pflichtig** *Adj.* required to attend school *postpos.;* **~pflichtig sein** have to attend school; **im ~pflichtigen Alter** of school age; **~ranzen** *der* [school] satchel; **~sportfest** *das* inter-school sports day; **~sprecher** *der* pupils' representative; ≈ head boy; **~sprecherin** *die* pupils' representative; ≈ head girl; **~tag** *der* school day; **~tasche** *die* schoolbag; (Ranzen) [school] satchel; **~uniform** *die* school uniform

Schulter *die;* ~, ~n shoulder; **jmdm. auf die ~ klopfen** pat sb. on the shoulder *or* (fig.) back

Schulter·blatt *das* (Anat.) shoulder blade

schultern *tr. V.* shoulder; **das Gewehr ~:** shoulder arms

Schul-: **~weg** *der* way to school; **~zeit** *die* schooldays *pl.*

Schummelei *die;* ~, ~en (ugs.) ▶ MOGELEI

schummeln *itr., tr., refl. V.* (ugs.) ▶ MOGELN

schummerig *Adj.* dim ‹*light etc.*›; dimly lit ‹*room etc.*›

Schummler *der;* ~s, ~, **Schummlerin** *die;* ~, ~nen (ugs.) cheat

Schund *der;* ~[e]s trash

Schuppe *die;* ~, ~n **(a)** scale **(b)** *Pl.* (auf dem Kopf) dandruff *sing.;* (auf der Haut) flaking skin *sing.*

schuppen **1** *tr. V.* scale ‹*fish*› **2** *refl. V.* ‹*skin*› flake; ‹*person*› have flaking skin

Schuppen *der;* ~s, ~ **(a)** shed **(b)** (ugs.: Lokal) joint (coll.)

schüren *tr. V.* **(a)** poke ‹*fire*› **(b)** (fig.) stir up ‹*hatred, envy, etc.*›

schürfen **1** *itr. V.* scrape **2** *tr. V.* **(a) sich** (*Dat.*) **das Knie** *usw.* **~:** graze one's knee *etc.;* **(b)** (Bergbau) mine ‹*ore etc.*› open-cast *or* (Amer.) opencut

Schürf·wunde *die* graze; abrasion

Schurke *der;* ~n, ~n, **Schurkin** *die;* ~, ~nen rogue

Schur·wolle *die* new wool

Schürze *die;* ~, ~n apron; (Latzschürze) pinafore

Schuss, *Schuß *der;* **Schusses, Schüsse** **(a)** shot (**auf** + *Akk.* at); **weit** *od.* **weitab vom ~** (fig. ugs.) well away from the action **(b)** (Menge Munition/Schießpulver) round; **drei ~ Munition** three rounds of ammunition **(c)** (Schusswunde) gunshot wound **(d)** (kleine Menge) dash **(e)** (Drogenjargon) shot; fix (sl.) **(f)** (Skisport) schuss; **~ fahren** schuss **(g)** (ugs.) **etw. in ~ bringen/halten** get sth. into/keep sth. in [good] shape

Schüssel *die;* ~, ~n bowl; (flacher) dish

schusselig (ugs.) **1** *Adj.* scatterbrained **2** *adv.* in a scatterbrained way

Schusseligkeit *die;* ~ (ugs.) scatterbrained way

Schuss-, *Schuß-: **~linie** *die* line of fire; **in die/jmds. ~linie geraten** *od.* **kommen** (auch fig.) come under fire/come under fire from sb.; **~verletzung** *die* gunshot wound; **~waffe** *die* weapon (*firing a projectile*); (Gewehr usw.) firearm; **~wechsel** *der* exchange of shots

Schuster *der;* ~s, ~, **Schusterin** *die;* ~, ~nen (ugs.) shoemaker; (jmd., der Schuhe repariert) shoe repairer

Schutt *der;* ~[e]s rubble; **„~ abladen verboten"** 'no tipping'; 'no dumping'

Schüttel·frost *der* [violent] shivering fit

schütteln **1** *tr. V.* **(a)** shake; **den Kopf [über etw.** (*Akk.*)**] ~:** shake one's head [over sth.]; **jmdm. die Hand ~:** shake sb.'s hand; shake sb. by the hand **(b)** (*unpers.*) **es schüttelte ihn [vor Kälte]** he was shaking [with *or* from cold] **2** *refl. V.* shake oneself/itself **3** *itr. V.* **mit dem Kopf ~:** shake one's head

schütten **1** *tr. V.* pour ‹*liquid, flour, etc.*›; (unabsichtlich) spill ‹*liquid, flour, etc.*›; tip ‹*rubbish, coal, etc.*› **2** *itr. V.* (*unpers.*) (ugs.: regnen) pour [down]

schütter *Adj.* sparse; thin

Schutt-: **~halde** *die* pile *or* heap of rubble; **~haufen** *der* pile of rubble; (Abfallhaufen) rubbish heap

Schutz *der;* ~es protection (**vor** + *Dat.*, **gegen** against); (Zuflucht) refuge; **~ suchend** seeking protection *postpos.*

schutz-, Schutz-: **~bedürftig** *Adj.* in

need of protection *postpos.*; **~behauptung** *die* (bes. Rechtsw.) attempt to justify one's behaviour; **~blech** *das* mudguard; **~brief** *der* (Kfz-W.) travel insurance; (Dokument) travel insurance certificate

Schụ̈tze *der;* **~n, ~n (a)** marksman **(b)** (Fußball usw.) scorer **(c)** (Milit.: einfacher Soldat) private **(d)** (Astrol.) Sagittarius

schụ̈tzen [1] *tr. V.* protect (**vor** + *Dat.* from, **gegen** against); safeguard ‹*interest, property, etc.*› (**vor** + *Dat.* from); **gesetzlich geschützt** registered [as a trade mark]
[2] *itr. V.* provide *or* give protection (**vor** + *Dat.* from, **gegen** against); (vor Wind, Regen) give shelter (**vor** + *Dat.* from)

Schụ̈tzen·fest *das: shooting competition with fair*

Schụtz·engel *der* guardian angel

Schụ̈tzen-: ~graben *der* trench; **~panzer** *der* armoured personnel carrier; **~verein** *der* rifle club

Schụtz-: ~helm *der* helmet; (bei Motorradfahrern usw.) crash helmet; (bei Bauarbeitern usw.) safety helmet; **~hütte** *die* **(a)** (Unterstand) shelter; **(b)** (Berghütte) mountain hut; **~impfung** *die* vaccination

Schụ̈tzin *die;* **~, ~nen (a)** markswoman **(b)** (Fußball usw.) scorer

Schụ̈tzling *der;* **~s, ~e** protégé; (Anvertrauter) charge

schụtz-, Schụtz-: ~los *Adj.* defenceless; **~mann** *der; Pl.* **~männer** *od.* **~leute** (ugs. veralt.) [police] constable; copper (Brit. coll.); **~patron** *der,* **~patronin** *die* patron saint; **~schicht** *die* protective layer (**aus** of); (flüssig aufgetragen) protective coating; *~**suchend** ▶ SCHUTZ; **~umschlag** *der* dust jacket

schwạbbelig *Adj.* flabby ‹*stomach, person, etc.*›; wobbly ‹*jelly etc.*›

schwạbbeln *itr. V.* (ugs.) wobble

Schwa̲be *der;* **~n, ~n** Swabian

Schwa̲ben (*das*); **~s** Swabia

Schwä̲bin *die;* **~, ~nen** Swabian

schwä̲bisch *Adj.* Swabian

schwạch; schwächer, schwạ̈chst... [1] *Adj.* **(a)** weak; weak, delicate ‹*child, woman*›; frail ‹*invalid, old person*›; low-powered ‹*engine, bulb, amplifier, etc.*›; weak, poor ‹*eyesight, memory, etc.*›; poor ‹*hearing*›; delicate ‹*health, constitution*›; **~ werden** grow weak; (fig.: schwanken) weaken; (fig.: nachgeben) give in
(b) (nicht gut) poor ‹*pupil, player, performance, result, etc.*›; weak ‹*argument, opponent, play, film, etc.*›
(c) (gering, niedrig) poor, low ‹*attendance etc.*›; slight ‹*effect, resistance, gradient, etc.*›; light ‹*wind, rain, current*›; faint ‹*voice, pressure, hope, smile, smell*›; weak, faint ‹*pulse*›; faint, dim ‹*light*›; pale ‹*colour*›
(d) (wenig konzentriert) weak ‹*solution, coffee, poison, etc.*›
(e) (Sprachw.) weak
[2] *adv.* **(a)** weakly
(b) (nicht gut) poorly
(c) (in geringem Maße) poorly ‹*attended, developed*›; slightly ‹*poisonous, sweetened, inclined*›; ‹*rain*› slightly; ‹*remember, glow, smile*› faintly
(d) (Sprachw.) **~ gebeugt** weak

Schwạ̈che *die;* **~, ~n** weakness; **eine ~ für jmdn./etw. haben** have a soft spot for sb./a weakness for sth.

Schwạ̈che·anfall *der* sudden feeling of faintness

schwạ̈chen *tr. V.* weaken

schwạ̈chlich *Adj.* weakly ‹*person*›; frail ‹*old person, constitution*›

Schwạ̈chling *der;* **~s, ~e** weakling

schwạch-, Schwạch-: ~punkt *der* weak point; **~sinn** *der* **(a)** (Med.) mental deficiency; **(b)** (ugs.) [idiotic (coll.)] rubbish; **~sinnig** [1] *Adj.* **(a)** (Med.) mentally deficient; **(b)** (ugs.) idiotic (coll.), nonsensical ‹*measure, policy, etc.*›; rubbishy ‹*film etc.*›; [2] *adv.* (ugs.) idiotically (coll.); stupidly

Schwạ̈chung *die;* **~, ~en** weakening

Schwa̲den *der;* **~s, ~:** [thick] cloud

schwa̲feln (ugs.) [1] *itr. V.* rabbit on (Brit. coll.), waffle (**von** about)
[2] *tr. V.* blether ‹*nonsense*›

Schwa̲ger *der;* **~s, Schwä̲ger** brother-in-law

Schwä̲gerin *die;* **~, ~nen** sister-in-law

Schwạlbe *die;* **~, ~n** swallow

Schwạll *der;* **~[e]s, ~e** torrent

schwạmm *1. u. 3. Pers. Sg. Prät. v.* SCHWIMMEN

Schwạmm *der;* **~[e]s, Schwạ̈mme (a)** sponge; **~ drüber!** (ugs.) [let's] forget it
(b) (südd., österr.: Pilz) mushroom

Schwạmmerl *das;* **~s, ~[n]** (bayr., österr.) mushroom

schwạmmig [1] *Adj.* **(a)** spongy
(b) (aufgedunsen) flabby, bloated ‹*face, body, etc.*›
(c) (abwertend: unpräzise) woolly ‹*concept, manner of expression, etc.*›
[2] *adv.* (unpräzise) vaguely

Schwạmmigkeit *die;* **~ (a)** sponginess
(b) (abwertend: Aufgedunsenheit) flabbiness; bloated appearence
(c) (abwertend: Vagheit) woolliness

Schwa̲n *der;* **~[e]s, Schwä̲ne** swan

schwạnd *1. u. 3. Pers. Sg. Prät. v.* SCHWINDEN

schwạng *1. u. 3. Pers. Sg. Prät. v.* SCHWINGEN

schwạnger *Adj.* pregnant (**von** by)

---

*old spelling - see note on page xiv

Schwangere *die; adj. Dekl.* expectant mother; pregnant woman

schwängern *tr. V.* make ‹*woman*› pregnant

Schwangerschaft *die;* ~, ~**en** pregnancy

Schwangerschafts-: ~**abbruch** *der* termination of pregnancy; abortion; ~**verhütung** *die* contraception; ~**vertretung** *die* **(a)** maternity[-leave] cover; **die** ~**vertretung für jmdn. machen** cover for sb. while she is on maternity leave; **(b)** (Person) person covering [a period of] maternity leave

Schwank *der;* ~[e]s, **Schwänke** comic tale; (auf der Bühne) farce

schwanken *itr. V.; mit Richtungsangabe mit sein* **(a)** sway; ‹*boat*› rock; (heftiger) roll; ‹*ground, floor*› shake
(b) (fig.: unbeständig sein) ‹*prices, temperature, etc.*› fluctuate; ‹*number, usage, etc.*› vary
(c) (fig.: unentschieden sein) waver; (zögern) hesitate

Schwankung *die;* ~, ~**en** variation; (der Kurse usw.) fluctuation

Schwanz *der;* ~**es, Schwänze** **(a)** tail
(b) (salopp: Penis) prick (coarse); cock (coarse)

Schwänzchen *das;* ~**s,** ~**(a)** [little] tail
(b) (fam.: Penis) willy (coll.)

schwänzeln *itr. V.* wag its tail/their tails

schwänzen *tr., itr. V.* (ugs.) skip, cut ‹*lesson etc.*›; **[die Schule]** ~: play truant *or* (Amer.) hookey

schwappen *itr. V.* slosh

Schwarm *der;* ~[e]s, **Schwärme** **(a)** swarm
(b) (fam.: Angebetete[r]) idol; heart-throb

schwärmen *itr. V.* **(a)** *mit Richtungsangabe mit sein* swarm
(b) (begeistert sein) **für jmdn./etw.** ~: be mad about *or* really keen on sb./sth.; **von etw.** ~: go into raptures about sth.

schwärmerisch [1] *Adj.* rapturous
[2] *adv.* rapturously

Schwarte *die;* ~, ~**n** **(a)** rind
(b) (ugs.: dickes Buch) tome

schwarz; schwärzer, schwärzest... [1] *Adj.*
(a) black; Black ‹*person*›; filthy[-black] ‹*hands, fingernails, etc.*›; **mir wurde Schwarz vor den Augen** everything went black **der** ~**e Erdteil** *od.* **Kontinent** the Dark Continent; **das Schwarze Meer** the Black Sea; **ins Schwarze treffen** (fig.) hit the nail on the head
(b) (illegal) illicit ‹*deal, exchange, etc.*›; **der** ~**e Markt** the black market
(c) ~ **sehen** look on the black side; be pessimistic (**für** about)
[2] *adv.* (illegal) illegally

Schwarz *das;* ~[es], ~: black

Schwarzbrot *das* black bread

Schwarze *der/die; adj. Dekl.* Black

schwärzen *tr. V.* blacken

schwarz-, Schwarz-: ~|**fahren** *unr. itr. V.; mit sein* dodge paying the fare; ~**fahrer** *der,* ~**fahrerin** *die* fare dodger; ~**haarig** *Adj.* black-haired; ~**handel** *der* black market (**mit** in); (Tätigkeit) black marketeering (**mit** in); ~**markt** *der* black market; ~|**sehen** *unr. itr. V.* watch television without a licence; *s. auch* SCHWARZ 1C; ~**seher** *der,* ~**seherin** *die* **(a)** (ugs.) pessimist; **(b)** (jmd, der schwarz fernsieht) [television] licence dodger

Schwärzung *die;* ~, ~**en** blackening

schwarz-, Schwarz-: ~**wald** *der;* ~[e]s Black Forest; ~**weiß** *Adj.* black and white; ~**weiß·film** *der* black and white film; ~**weiß·foto** *das* black and white photo; ~**wurzel** *die* black salsify

schwatzen, (bes. südd.) **schwätzen**
[1] *itr. V.* chat; (über belanglose Dinge) chatter; natter (coll.)
[2] *tr. V.* say; talk ‹*nonsense, rubbish*›

Schwätzer *der;* ~**s,** ~, **Schwätzerin** *die;* ~, ~**nen** chatterbox; (klatschhafter Mensch) gossip

schwatzhaft *Adj.* talkative; (klatschhaft) gossipy

Schwatzhaftigkeit *die;* ~: talkativeness; (Klatschsucht) gossipiness

Schwebe *die:* **in der** ~ **sein/bleiben** (fig.) be/remain in the balance

Schwebe-: ~**bahn** *die* cableway; ~**balken** *der* (Turnen) [balance] beam

schweben *itr. V.* **(a)** ‹*bird, balloon, etc.*› hover; ‹*cloud, balloon, mist*› hang; **in Gefahr** ~ (fig.) be in danger
(b) *mit sein* (durch die Luft) float

Schwede *der;* ~**n,** ~**n** Swede

Schweden (*das*); ~**s** Sweden

Schwedin *die;* ~, ~**nen** Swede

schwedisch *Adj.* Swedish

Schwefel *der;* ~**s** sulphur

Schwefel-: ~**dioxid,** ~**dioxyd** *das* (Chemie) sulphur dioxide; ~**säure** *die* (Chemie) sulphuric acid; ~**wasserstoff** *der* (Chemie) hydrogen sulphide

Schweif *der;* ~[e]s, ~**e** tail

schweifen *itr. V.; mit sein* (geh.; auch fig.) wander

Schweige·geld *das* hush money

schweigen *unr. itr. V.* remain *or* stay silent; say nothing; **ganz zu** ~ **von ...**: not to mention ...

Schweigen *das;* ~**s** silence

schweigsam *Adj.* silent; quiet

Schweigsamkeit *die;* ~: silence; quietness

Schwein *das;* ~[e]s, ~**e** **(a)** pig
(b) (Fleisch) pork
(c) (salopp: gemeiner Mensch) swine; (Schmutzfink) mucky devil (coll.); mucky pig (coll.)
(d) (salopp: Mensch) **ein armes** ~: a poor devil; **kein** ~ **war da** there wasn't a bloody (Brit. sl.) *or* (coll.) damn soul there

··›

(e) (ugs.: Glück) **[großes] ~ haben** have a [big] stroke of luck; (davonkommen) get away with it (coll.)

Schweine-: ~braten *der* roast pork *no indef. art.*; **~fleisch** *das* pork; **~kotelett** *das* (Kochk.) pork chop

Schweinerei *die*; **~, ~en** (ugs.) **(a)** (Schmutz) mess
(b) (Gemeinheit) mean *or* dirty trick

Schweine-: ~schnitzel *das* escalope of pork; **~stall** *der* (auch fig.) pigsty; pigpen (Amer.); **~steak** *das* pork steak;

schweinisch (ugs.) *Adj.* **(a)** (schmutzig) filthy
(b) (unanständig) dirty; smutty

Schweins·leder *das* pigskin

Schweiß *der*; **~es** sweat; **mir brach der ~ aus** I broke out in a sweat

Schweiß-: ~ausbruch *der* sweat; **~brenner** *der* welding torch; **~drüse** *die* (Anat.) sweat gland

schweißen *tr., itr. V.* weld

Schweißer *der*; **~s, ~**, **Schweißerin** *die*; **~, ~nen** welder

schweiß-, Schweiß-: ~fuß sweaty foot; **~gebadet** *Adj.* bathed in sweat *postpos.*; **~nass**, ***~naß** *Adj.* sweaty; damp with sweat *pred.*; **~perle** *die* bead of sweat

Schweiz *die*; **~**: Switzerland *no art.*

Schweizer *der*; **~s, ~**: Swiss

schweizer·deutsch *Adj.* Swiss German

Schweizerin *die*; **~, ~nen** Swiss

schweizerisch *Adj.* Swiss

schwelen (auch fig.) smoulder

schwelgen *itr. V.* feast

Schwelle *die*; **~, ~n** **(a)** threshold
(b) (Eisenbahnschwelle) sleeper (Brit.); [cross] tie (Amer.)

schwellen *unr. itr. V.; mit sein* swell; ‹*limb, face, cheek, etc.*› swell [up]

Schwellen·land *das: country at the stage of economic take-off*

Schwellung *die*; **~, ~en** (Med.) swelling

Schwemme *die*; **~, ~n** glut (**an** + *Dat.* of)

Schwemm·land *das* alluvial land

Schwengel *der*; **~s, ~** **(a)** (der Glocke) clapper
(b) (der Pumpe) handle

Schwenk *der*; **~s, ~s** **(a)** (Drehung) swing
(b) (Film, Ferns.) pan

schwenken [1] *tr. V.* **(a)** swing; wave ‹*flag, handkerchief*›
(b) (spülen) rinse
[2] *itr. V.; mit sein* ‹*marching column*› swing, wheel; ‹*camera*› pan; ‹*path, road, car*› swing

schwer [1] *Adj.* **(a)** heavy; **2 Kilo ~ sein** weigh two kilos
(b) (mühevoll) heavy ‹*work*›; hard, tough ‹*job*›; hard ‹*day*›; difficult ‹*birth*›; **es ~/nicht ~ haben** have it hard/easy; **sich mit** *od.* **bei etw. ~ tun** (ugs.) have trouble with sth.; **jmdm. fällt etw. ~**: sb. finds sth. difficult; **jmdm./sich etw. ~ machen** make sth. difficult for sb./oneself
(c) (schlimm) severe ‹*shock, disappointment, strain, storm*›; serious, grave ‹*wrong, injustice, error, illness, blow, reservation*›; serious ‹*accident, injury*›; heavy ‹*punishment, strain, loss, blow*›; **etw. ~ nehmen** take sth. seriously
[2] *adv.* **(a)** heavily ‹*built, laden, armed*›; **~ tragen** be carrying sth. heavy [with difficulty]
(b) ‹*work*› hard; ‹*breathe*› heavily; **~ hören** be hard of hearing
(c) (schwierig) with difficulty; **~ verdaulich** (auch fig.) hard to digest *pred.*
(d) (sehr) seriously ‹*injured, ill*›; greatly, deeply ‹*disappointed*›; ‹*punish*› severely, heavily; **~ verunglücken** have a serious accident

Schwer-: ~arbeiter *der* worker engaged in heavy physical work; **~behinderte** *der/die* severely handicapped person; (körperlich auch) severely disabled person; **die ~behinderten** the severely handicapped/disabled; **~beschädigte** *der/die; adj. Dekl.* severely disabled person

Schwere *die*; **~** **(a)** weight
(b) (Schwerkraft) gravity
(c) ▶ SCHWER 1C: severity; seriousness; gravity; heaviness

schwere·los *Adj.* weightless

Schwerelosigkeit *die*; **~**: weightlessness

schwer-, Schwer-: *~|fallen ▶ SCHWER 1B; **~fällig** [1] *Adj.* (auch fig.) ponderous; cumbersome ‹*bureaucracy, procedure*›; [2] *adv.* ponderously; **~fälligkeit** *die*: ▶ ~FÄLLIG: ponderousness; cumbersomeness; **~gewicht** *das* **(a)** (Sport) heavyweight; **(b)** (Schwerpunkt) main focus; **~hörig** *Adj.* hard of hearing *pred.*; **~hörigkeit** *die*; **~~**: hardness of hearing; **~industrie** *die* heavy industry; **~kraft** *die* gravity; ***~krank** ▶ SCHWER 2D

schwerlich *Adv.* hardly

schwer-, Schwer-: *~|machen ▶ SCHWER 1B; **~metall** *das* heavy metal; **~mütig** [1] *Adj.* melancholic; [2] *adv.* melancholically; ***~|nehmen** ▶ SCHWER 1C; **~punkt** *der* centre of gravity; (fig.) main focus; (Hauptgewicht) main stress

Schwert *das*; **~[e]s, ~er** sword

Schwert-: ~fisch *der* swordfish; **~lilie** *die* iris

schwer|tun ▶ SCHWER 1B

Schwert·wal *der* (Orka) killer whale

schwer-, Schwer-: ~verbrecher *der*, **~verbrecherin** *die* serious offender; ***~verdaulich** ▶ SCHWER 2C; ***~verletzt** ▶ SCHWER 2D; **~wiegend** *Adj.* serious; momentous ‹*decision*›

Schwester *die*; **~, ~n** **(a)** sister

*alte Schreibung - vgl. Hinweis auf S. xiv

(b) (Krankenschwester) nurse

schwesterlich 1 *Adj.* sisterly
2 *adv.* ~ **handeln** act in a sisterly way

schwieg *1. u. 3. Pers. Prät. v.* SCHWEIGEN

Schwieger-: **~eltern** *Pl.* parents-in-law; **~mutter** *die; Pl.* **~mütter** mother-in-law; **~sohn** *der* son-in-law; **~tochter** *die* daughter-in-law; **~vater** *der* father-in-law

Schwiele *die;* ~, **~n** callus; **~n an den Händen** horny hands

schwielig *Adj.* callused; **~e Hände** horny hands

schwierig *Adj.* difficult

Schwierigkeit *die;* ~, **~en** difficulty

Schwierigkeits·grad *der* degree of difficulty; (von Lehrmaterial usw.) level of difficulty

Schwimm-: **~bad** *das* swimming baths *pl.* (Brit.); swimming pool; **~becken** *das* swimming pool

schwimmen 1 *unr. itr. V.* **(a)** *meist mit sein* swim
(b) *meist mit sein* (treiben, nicht untergehen) float
(c) (ugs.: unsicher sein) be all at sea; **ins Schwimmen geraten** start to flounder
2 *unr. tr. V.; auch mit sein* swim

Schwimmen *das;* **~s:** swimming *no art.*

Schwimmer *der;* **~s,** ~ **(a)** swimmer
(b) (Technik) float

Schwimmerin *die;* ~, **~nen** swimmer

Schwimm-: **~flosse** *die* flipper; **~lehrer** *der,* **~lehrerin** *die* swimming instructor; **~weste** *die* life jacket

Schwindel *der;* **~s** **(a)** dizziness; giddiness
(b) (Betrug) swindle; (Lüge) lie

schwindel·frei *Adj.* ~ **sein** have a head for heights

schwindelig ▸ SCHWINDLIG

schwindeln *itr. V.* **(a)** *(unpers.)* **mich** *od.* **mir schwindelt** I feel dizzy *or* giddy
(b) (lügen) tell fibs

schwinden *unr. itr. V.; mit sein* fade; ‹*supplies, money*› run out; ‹*effect*› wear off; ‹*fear, mistrust*› lessen; ‹*powers, influence*› wane

Schwindler *der;* **~s,** ~, **Schwindlerin** *die;* ~, **~nen** (Lügner[in]) liar; (Betrüger[in]) swindler; (Hochstapler[in]) confidence trickster

schwindlig *Adj.* dizzy; giddy; **jmdm. wird es ~:** sb. gets dizzy *or* giddy

schwingen 1 *unr. itr. V.* **(a)** *mit sein* swing
(b) (vibrieren) vibrate
2 *unr. tr. V.* swing; wave ‹*flag, wand*›; brandish ‹*sword, axe, etc.*›
3 *unr. refl. V.* **sich aufs Pferd/Fahrrad ~:** leap on to one's horse/bicycle

Schwingung *die;* ~, **~en** **(a)** swinging; (Vibration) vibration
(b) (Physik) oscillation

Schwips *der;* **~es, ~e** (ugs.) **einen ~ haben** be tipsy

schwirren *itr. V. mit sein* ‹*arrow, bullet, etc.*› whiz; ‹*bird*› whir; ‹*insect*› buzz

schwitzen *itr. V.* (auch fig.) sweat

schwor *1. u. 3. Pers. Sg. Prät. v.* SCHWÖREN

schwören 1 *unr. tr., itr. V.* swear ‹*fidelity, friendship*›; swear, take ‹*oath*›
2 *unr. itr. V.* swear an/the oath

Schwuchtel *die;* ~, **~n** (salopp) queen (sl.)

schwul *Adj.* (ugs.) gay (coll.)

schwül *Adj.* sultry; close

Schwule *der; adj. Dekl.* (ugs.) gay (coll.); (abwertend) queer (sl.)

Schwüle *die;* ~: sultriness

schwülstig *Adj.* bombastic; pompous; over-ornate ‹*art, architecture*›

Schwund *der;* **~[e]s** decrease, drop (*Gen.* in); (an Interesse) waning; falling off

Schwung *der;* **~[e]s, Schwünge** **(a)** (Bewegung) swing
(b) (Linie) sweep
(c) (Geschwindigkeit) momentum; **~ holen** build *or* get up momentum
(d) (Antrieb) drive; energy
(e) (mitreißende Wirkung) sparkle

schwung·haft *Adj.* thriving; brisk, flourishing ‹*trade, business*›

schwung·voll 1 *Adj.* **(a)** lively
(b) (kraftvoll) vigorous; sweeping ‹*movement, gesture*›; bold ‹*handwriting, line, stroke*›
2 *adv.* spiritedly; (kraftvoll) with great vigour

Schwur *der;* **~[e]s, Schwüre** **(a)** (Gelöbnis) vow
(b) (Eid) oath

Schwur·gericht *das: court with a jury*

scrollen /'skrolən/ *itr., tr. V.* (DV) scroll

sechs *Kardinalz.* six

Sechs *die;* ~, **~en** six

sechs-, Sechs-: **~eck** *das* hexagon; **~eckig** *Adj.* hexagonal; **~fach** *Vervielfältigungsz.* sixfold; **~hundert** *Kardinalz.* six hundred; **~mal** *Adv.* six times

sechst... *Ordinalz.* sixth

sechs·tausend *Kardinalz.* six thousand

sechstel *Bruchz.* sixth

Sechstel *das,* (schweiz. meist *der*); **~s,** ~: sixth

sechstens *Adv.* sixthly

sechzehn *Kardinalz.* sixteen

sechzig *Kardinalz.* sixty

sechzigst... *Ordinalz.* sixtieth

SED *Abk.* (DDR) = **Sozialistische Einheitspartei Deutschlands** Socialist Unity Party of Germany (*state party of the former DDR*)

See¹ *der;* **~s, ~n** lake

See² *die;* ~: **die ~:** the sea; **an die ~ fahren** go to the seaside; **auf hoher ~:** on the high seas

see-, See-: **~bad** *das* seaside health ⇢

S

resort; **~fahrt** *die* seafaring *no art.;* sea travel *no art.;* **~gang** *der* **leichter/starker** *od.* **hoher** *od.* **schwerer ~gang** light/heavy *or* rough sea; **~hund** *der* [common] seal; (Pelz) seal[skin]; **~igel** *der* sea urchin; **~krank** *Adj.* seasick; **~krankheit** *die* seasickness; **~lachs** *der* pollack

Seele *die;* **~, ~n** soul; (Psyche) mind

Seelen·leben *das* (geh.) inner life

seelen·ruhig 1 *Adj.* calm; unruffled
2 *adv.* calmly

seelisch 1 *Adj.* psychological ‹*cause, damage, tension*›; mental ‹*equilibrium, breakdown, illness, health*›
2 *adv.* **~ bedingt sein** have psychological causes; **~ krank** mentally ill

Seel·sorge *die* pastoral care

Seelsorger *der;* **~s, ~, Seelsorgerin** *die;* **~, ~nen** pastoral worker; (Geistliche[r]) pastor

see-, See-: ~macht *die* sea power; **~mann** *der; Pl.* **~leute** seaman; sailor; **~meile** *die* nautical mile; **~not** *die* distress [at sea]; **in ~not geraten** get into difficulties *pl.;* **~pferd[chen]** *das* sea horse; **~räuber** *der,* **~räuberin** *die* pirate; **~reise** *die* voyage; (Kreuzfahrt) cruise; **~rose** *die* waterlily; **~stern** *der* starfish; **~tüchtig** *Adj.* seaworthy; **~zunge** *die* sole

Segel *das;* **~s, ~:** sail

Segel-: ~boot *das* sailing boat; **~flieger** *der,* **~fliegerin** *die* glider pilot; **~flugzeug** *das* glider

segeln *itr. V.; mit sein* sail

Segel-: ~schiff *das* sailing ship; **~tuch** *das; Pl.* **~~e** sailcloth

Segen *der;* **~s, ~:** blessing; (Gebet in der Messe) benediction

Segler *der;* **~s, ~:** yachtsman

Seglerin *die;* **~, ~nen** yachtswoman

segnen *tr. V.* bless

seh·behindert *Adj.* partially sighted; visually handicapped

sehen 1 *unr. itr. V.* **(a)** see; **schlecht/gut ~:** have bad/good eyesight; **mal ~, wir wollen** *od.* **werden ~** (ugs.) we'll see; **siehste!** (ugs.) there, you see!
(b) (hinsehen) look (**auf** + *Akk.* at); **sieh mal** *od.* **doch!** look!; **siehe da!** lo and behold!
2 *unr. tr. V.* **(a)** (auch fig.) see; **jmdn./etw. [nicht] zu ~ bekommen** [not] get to see sb./sth.; **ich habe ihn kommen [ge]~:** I saw him coming
(b) (ansehen) watch ‹*television programme*›

sehens·wert *Adj.* worth seeing *postpos.*

Sehens·würdigkeit *die;* **~, ~en** sight

Seher *der;* **~s, ~, Seherin** *die;* **~, ~nen** seer; prophet/prophetess

Seh-: ~fehler *der* sight defect; defect of vision; **~kraft** *die* sight

Sehne *die;* **~, ~n (a)** tendon
(b) (Bogen~) string

sehnen *refl. V.* **sich nach jmdm./etw. ~:** long *or* yearn for sb./sth.

sehnig *Adj.* **(a)** stringy ‹*meat*›
(b) (kräftig) sinewy ‹*figure, legs, etc.*›

sehnlichst 1 *Adj.* **das ist mein ~es Verlangen/mein ~er Wunsch** that's what I long for most/that's my dearest wish
2 *adv.* **etw. ~ herbeiwünschen** look forward longingly to sth.

Sehn·sucht *die* longing; **~ nach jmdm. haben** long to see sb.

sehn·süchtig *Adj.* longing *attrib.*, yearning *attrib.* ‹*desire, look, gaze, etc.*›

sehr *Adv.* **(a)** *mit Adj. u. Adv.* very; **~ viel** a great deal; **jmdn. ~ gern haben** like sb. a lot (coll.) *or* a great deal
(b) *mit Verben* very much; greatly; **danke ~!** thank you *or* thanks [very much]; **bitte ~, Ihr Steak!** here's your steak, sir/madam

Seh-: ~schärfe *die* visual acuity; **~test** *der* eye test; **~vermögen** *das* sight

sei *1. u. 3. Pers. Sg. Präsens Konjunktiv u. Imperativ Sg. v.* SEIN

seicht 1 *Adj.* (auch fig.) shallow
2 *adv.* (fig.) shallowly

Seichtheit *die;* **~** (auch fig.) shallowness

seid *2. Pers. Pl. Präsens u. Imperativ Pl. v.* SEIN

Seide *die;* **~, ~n** silk

Seidel *das;* **~s, ~:** beer mug

seiden *Adj.* silk

Seiden·papier *das* tissue paper

seidig 1 *Adj.* silky
2 *adv.* silkily

Seife *die;* **~, ~n** soap

Seifen-: ~blase *die* soap bubble; **~oper** *die* (ugs.) soap opera; **~schale** *die* soap dish; **~schaum** *der* lather

Seil *das;* **~s, ~e** rope; (Drahtseil) cable

Seil·bahn *die* cableway

seil|hüpfen *itr. V.; nur im Inf. u. 2. Part.; mit sein* ▶ SEILSPRINGEN

Seilschaft *die;* **~, ~en** (Bergsteigen) rope; (fig.) followers *pl.*

seil-, Seil-: ~|springen *unr. itr. V.; nur im Inf. u. 2. Part.; mit sein* skip; **~tänzer** *der,* **~tänzerin** *die* tightrope walker; **~winde** *die* cable winch

sein[1] 1 *unr. itr. V.* be; (existieren) be; exist; (sich ereignen) be; happen; **wie dem auch sei** be that as it may; **er ist Schwede/Lehrer** he is Swedish *or* a Swede/a teacher; **bist du es?** is that you?; **mir ist kalt/besser** I am *or* feel cold/better; **mir ist schlecht** I feel sick; **drei und vier ist** *od.* (ugs.) **sind sieben** three and four is *or* makes seven; **es ist drei Uhr/Mai/Winter** it is three o'clock/May/winter; **er ist aus Berlin** he is *or* comes from Berlin; **was darf es ~?** (im Geschäft) what can I get you?; **es war einmal ein Prinz** once upon a time there was a prince

---
*old spelling - see note on page xiv

2 *mod. V.* (in der Funktion von können/müssen + *Passiv*) **es ist niemand zu sehen** there's no one to be seen; **das war zu erwarten** that was to be expected; **die Schmerzen sind kaum zu ertragen** the pain is hardly bearable; **die Richtlinien sind strengstens zu beachten** the guidelines are to be strictly followed
3 *Hilfsverb* **(a)** (zur Perfektumschreibung) have; **er ist gestorben** he has died
(b) (zur Bildung des Zustandspassivs) be; **wir sind gerettet worden/wir waren gerettet** we were saved

sein² *Possessivpron.* (einer männlichen Person) his; (einer weiblichen Person) her; (einer Sache, eines Tiers) its; (nach man) one's; his (Amer.)

Sein *das;* **~s** (Philos.) being; (Dasein) existence; **~ und Schein** appearance and reality

seiner (geh.) *Gen. von* ER: **sich ~ erbarmen** have pity on him; **~ gedenken** remember him

seiner-: ~seits *Adv.* for his part; (von ihm) on his part; **~zeit** *Adv.* at that time

seines·gleichen *indekl. Pron.* his own kind

seinet·wegen *Adv.* ▶ MEINETWEGEN: because of him; for his sake; about him; as far as he is concerned

seismo-, Seismo-: ~graph *der;* **~~en, ~~en** seismograph; **~loge** *der;* **~~n, ~~n** seismologist; **~logie** *die;* **~~:** seismology *no art.;* **~login** *die;* **~~, ~~nen** seismologist; **~logisch** 1 *Adj.* seismological; 2 *adv.* seismologically

seit 1 *Präp. mit Dat.* (Zeitpunkt) since; (Zeitspanne) for; **ich bin ~ zwei Wochen hier** I've been here [for] two weeks
2 *Konj.* since; **~ du hier wohnst** since you have been living here

seit·dem 1 *Adv.* since then
2 *Konj.* ▶ SEIT 2

Seite *die;* **~, ~n (a)** side; **zur** *od.* **auf die ~ gehen** move aside *or* to one side; **~ an ~:** side by side; **jmdm. zur ~ stehen** stand by sb.; **von allen ~n** (auch fig.) from all sides; **nach allen ~n** in all directions; (fig.) on all sides
(b) (Buch-, Zeitungsseite) page

Seiten-: ~ansicht *die* side view; **~aufprall·schutz** *der* side impact protection; **~hieb** *der* (fig.) sideswipe (**auf** + *Akk.* at); **~ruder** *das* (Flugw.) rudder

seitens *Präp. mit Gen.* (Papierdt.) on the part of

Seiten-: ~sprung *der* infidelity; **~straße** *die* side street; **~wind** *der* side wind; crosswind; **~zahl** *die* **(a)** page number; **(b)** (Anzahl der Seiten) number of pages

seit·her *Adv.* since then

seitlich 1 *Adj.* at the side (postpos.)
2 *adv.* (an der Seite) at the side; (von der Seite) from the side; (nach der Seite) to the side

seit·wärts *Adv.* sideways

Sekretär *der;* **~s, ~e (a)** secretary
(b) (Schreibschrank) bureau (Brit.)

Sekretariat *das;* **~[e]s, ~e** [secretary's/ secretaries'] office

Sekretärin *die;* **~, ~nen** secretary

Sekt *der;* **~[e]s, ~e** high-quality sparkling wine; ≈ champagne

Sekte *die;* **~, ~n** sect

Sektor *der;* **~s, ~en (a)** (Fachgebiet) field; sphere; **industrieller/wirtschaftlicher ~:** industrial/economic sector
(b) (Geom.; Besatzungszone) sector

sekundär 1 *Adj.* secondary
2 *adv.* secondarily

Sekundar-: ~schule *die* (schweiz.) secondary school; **~stufe** *die* secondary stage (*of education*)

Sekunde *die;* **~, ~n (a)** (auch Math., Musik) second
(b) (ugs.: Augenblick) second; moment

Sekunden·zeiger *der* second hand

selb... *Demonstrativpron.* same;

selber *indekl. Demonstrativpron.* ▶ SELBST 1

selbst 1 *indekl. Demonstrativpron.* myself/ yourself/himself/herself/itself/ourselves/ yourselves/themselves; **von ~:** automatically; **~ gemacht** home-made
2 *Adv.* even

Selbst·achtung *die* self-respect; self-esteem

selb·ständig 1 *Adj.* independent; self-employed ‹*business man, tradesman, etc.*›; **sich ~ machen** set up on one's own
2 *adv.* independently; **~ denken** think for oneself

Selbständigkeit *die;* **~:** independence

selbst-, Selbst-: ~auslöser *der* (Fot.) delayed-action shutter release; **~bedienung** *die* self-service *no art.;* **~befriedigung** *die* masturbation *no art.;* **~beherrschung** *die* self-control *no art.;* **~bestätigung** *die* (Psych.) self-affirmation *no art.;* **~bewusst, *~bewußt** 1 *Adj.* self-confident; 2 *adv.* self-confidently; **~bewusstsein, *~bewußtsein** *das* self-confidence *no art.;* **~erkenntnis** *die* self-knowledge *no art.;* **~gefällig** 1 *Adj.* self-satisfied; smug; 2 *adv.* smugly; **~gefälligkeit** *die* self-satisfaction; smugness; ***~gemacht** ▶ SELBST 1; **~gespräch** *das* conversation with oneself; **~hilfe** *die* self-help *no art.;* **Hilfe zur ~hilfe leisten** help people to help themselves; **~hilfe·gruppe** *die* self-help group; **~los** 1 *Adj.* selfless; 2 *adv.* selflessly; unselfishly; **~mord** *der* suicide *no art.;* **~mörder** *der,* **~mörderin** *die* suicide; **~sicher** 1 *Adj.* self-confident; 2 *adv.* in a self-confident manner; **~ständig** *usw.:* ▶ SELBSTÄNDIG *usw.;* **~süchtig** 1 *Adj.* selfish; 2 *adv.* selfishly; **~tätig** 1 *Adj.* automatic; ···›

2 *adv.* automatically; **~verständlich** 1 *Adj.* natural; **etw. für ~verständlich halten** regard sth. as a matter of course; (für gegeben hinnehmen) take sth. for granted; 2 *adv.* naturally; of course; **~verständlichkeit** *die* matter of course; **etw. mit der größten ~verständlichkeit tun** do sth. as if it were the most natural thing in the world; **~vertrauen** *das* self-confidence; **~verwaltung** *die* self-government *no art.*; **~zweck** *der* end in itself

selektieren *tr. V.* select; pick out

Selektion *die; ~, ~en* selection

selektiv 1 *Adj.* selective 2 *adv.* selectively

selig 1 *Adj.* **(a)** (Rel.) blessed **(b)** (tot) late [lamented] **(c)** (glücklich) blissful ‹*idleness, slumber, etc.*›; blissfully happy ‹*person*› 2 *adv.* blissfully

Seligkeit *die; ~, ~en* bliss *no pl.*; [blissful] happiness *no pl.*

Sellerie *der; ~s, ~[s] od.* **die**; *~, ~*: celeriac; (Stangen~) celery

selten 1 *Adj.* rare; infrequent ‹*visit, visitor*› 2 *adv.* **(a)** rarely **(b)** (sehr) exceptionally; uncommonly

Seltenheit *die; ~, ~en* rarity

Seltenheits·wert *der; ~[es]* rarity value

Selters·wasser *das* seltzer [water]

seltsam 1 *Adj.* strange; odd 2 *adv.* strangely

Semester *das; ~s, ~*: semester

Semester·ferien *Pl.* [university] vacation *sing.*

Semi·finale *das* (Sport) semi-final

Semi·kolon *das; ~s, ~s* semicolon

Seminar *das; ~s, ~e* **(a)** seminar (**über** + *Akk.* on) **(b)** (Institut) department

Semit *der; ~en, ~en,* **Semitin** *die; ~, ~nen* Semite

semitisch *Adj.* Semitic

Semmel *die; ~, ~n* (bes. österr., bayr., ostmd.) [bread] roll

Semmel·knödel *der* (bayr., österr.) bread dumpling

Senat *der; ~[e]s, ~e* senate

Senator *der; ~s, ~en,* **Senatorin** *die; ~, ~nen* senator

senden[1] *unr.* (*auch regelm.*) *tr. V.* (geh.) send

senden[2] *regelm.* (*schweiz. unr.*) *tr., itr. V.* broadcast ‹*programme, play, etc.*›; transmit ‹*signals, Morse, etc.*›

Sender *der; ~s, ~*: [broadcasting] station; (Anlage) transmitter

Sende·reihe *die* series [of programmes]

Sender·such·lauf *der* (Rundf., Ferns.) [automatic] station search

Sende·schluss, *Sende·schluß *der* close down

Sende·zeit *die* (Rundf., Ferns.) broadcasting time; **die ~ um zehn Minuten überschreiten** overrun by ten minutes

Sendung *die; ~, ~en* **(a)** consignment **(b)** (Rundf., Ferns.) programme

Senf *der; ~[e]s, ~e* mustard

senil 1 *Adj.* (Med., auch abwertend) senile 2 *adv.* in a senile manner

senior *nach Personennamen* senior

Senior *der; ~s, ~en* **(a)** (Kaufmannsspr.) senior partner **(b)** (Sport) senior [player] **(c)** (Rentner) senior citizen

Senioren·heim *das* home for the elderly

Seniorin *die; ~, ~nen* ▶ SENIOR

Senke *die; ~, ~n* hollow

senken 1 *tr. V.* lower 2 *refl. V.* ‹*curtain, barrier, etc.*› fall, come down; ‹*ground, building, road*› subside, sink; ‹*water level*› fall, sink

senk-, Senk-: ~fuß *der* flat foot; **~recht** 1 *Adj.* vertical; **~recht zu etw.** perpendicular to sth.; 2 *adv.* vertically; **~rechte** *die; ~~, ~~n; auch adj. Dekl.* vertical; (Geom.: Gerade) perpendicular

Sensation *die; ~, ~en* sensation

sensationell 1 *Adj.* sensational 2 *adv.* sensationally

Sense *die; ~, ~n* scythe

sensibel 1 *Adj.* sensitive 2 *adv.* sensitively

sensibilisieren *tr. V.* (geh.) make ‹*person*› more sensitive (**für** to)

Sensibilität *die; ~*: sensitivity

sentimental 1 *Adj.* sentimental 2 *adv.* sentimentally

Sentimentalität *die; ~, ~en* sentimentality

separat 1 *Adj.* separate; self-contained ‹*flat etc.*› 2 *adv.* separately

September *der; ~[s], ~*: September

Serbe *der; ~n, ~n* Serb; Serbian

Serbien (*das*); *~s* Serbia

Serbin *die; ~, ~nen* ▶ SERBE

serbisch *Adj.* Serbian

Serenade *die; ~, ~n* serenade

Serie /ˈzeːri̯ə/ *die; ~, ~n* series

serien·mäßig 1 *Adj.* standard ‹*product, model, etc.*› 2 *adv.* **(a) ~ gefertigt** *od.* **gebaut** produced in series **(b)** (nicht als Sonderausstattung) ‹*fitted, supplied, etc.*› as standard

seriös *Adj.* respectable ‹*person, hotel, etc.*›; trustworthy ‹*firm, partner, etc.*›; serious ‹*offer, applicant, artist, etc.*›

*alte Schreibung - vgl. Hinweis auf S. xiv

Seriosität *die;* ~ (geh.) **(a)** (Solidität) respectability; (Vertrauenswürdigkeit) trustworthiness
(b) (Ernsthaftigkeit) seriousness

Serpentine *die;* ~, **~n** hairpin bend

Serum *das;* **~s, Seren** serum

Service¹ /zɛr'vi:s/ *das;* ~, ~: [dinner *etc.*] service

Service² /'zø:ɐ̯vɪs/ *der;* ~, **~s** /'zø:ɐ̯vɪsɪs/ (Bedienung, Kundendienst) service

servieren *tr. V.* serve

Serviererin *die;* ~, **~nen** waitress

Serviette /zɛr'vi̯ɛtə/ *die;* ~, **~n** napkin; serviette (Brit.)

Servo-: ~bremse *die* servo[-assisted] brake; **~lenkung** *die* power[-assisted] steering *no indef. art.*

Servus /'zɛrvʊs/ *Interj.* (bes. südd., österr.) (beim Abschied) goodbye; so long (coll.); (zur Begrüßung) hello

Sesam *der;* **~s** sesame seeds *pl.*

Sẹssel *der;* **~s,** ~ **(a)** armchair
(b) (österr.: Stuhl) chair

Sẹssel·lift *der* chairlift

sẹsshaft, *sẹßhaft *Adj.* settled; ~ **werden** settle down

Sẹsshaftigkeit, *Sẹßhaftigkeit *die;* ~: settled way of life

Sẹt *das od. der;* **~[s], ~s (a)** set, combination (**aus** of)
(b) (Deckchen) table- *or* place mat

sẹtzen [1] *refl. V.* **(a)** sit [down]; **setzen Sie sich** sit down; take a seat; **sich aufs Sofa** *usw.* ~: sit on the sofa *etc.;*
(b) ‹*coffee, froth, etc.*› settle; ‹*sediment*› sink to the bottom
[2] *tr. V.* **(a)** put
(b) (einpflanzen) plant ‹*tomatoes, potatoes, etc.*›
(c) (aufziehen) hoist ‹*flag etc.*›; set ‹*sails, navigation lights*›
(d) (Druckw.) set ‹*manuscript etc.*›
[3] *itr. V.* **(a)** *meist mit sein* (springen) leap; jump
(b) über einen Fluss ~ (mit einer Fähre o. Ä.) cross a river
(c) (beim Wetten) bet; **auf ein Pferd/auf Rot** ~: back a horse/put one's money on red

Sẹtzer *der;* **~s,** ~, **Sẹtzerin** *die;* ~, **~nen** (Druckw.) [type]setter

Sẹtzling *der;* **~s, ~e** seedling

Seuche *die;* ~, **~n** epidemic

Seuchen·gefahr *die* danger of an epidemic

seufzen *itr., tr. V.* sigh

Seufzer *der;* **~s,** ~: sigh

Sẹx *der;* **~[es]** sex *no art.*

Sexịsmus *der;* ~: sexism *no art.*

sexịstisch [1] *Adj.* sexist
[2] *adv.* ‹*behave, think, etc.*› in a sexist manner

Sexualität *die;* ~: sexuality *no art.*

Sexual-: ~kunde *die* (Schulw.) sex education *no art.;* **~leben** *das* sex life; **~partner** *der,* **~partnerin** *die* sexual partner; **~trieb** *der* sex[ual] drive *or* urge; **~verbrechen** *das* sex crime; **~verbrecher** *der* sex offender

sexuẹll [1] *Adj.* sexual
[2] *adv.* sexually

sezieren *tr. V.* dissect ‹*corpse*›

sfr., sFr. *Abk.* **Schweizer Franken**

Shampoo /ʃam'pu:/, **Shampoon** /ʃam'po:n/ *das;* **~s, ~s** shampoo

Shareholdervalue /'ʃeəhoʊldəvælju:/ *der;* **~s, ~s** shareholder value

Sherry /'ʃɛrɪ/ *der;* **~s, ~s** sherry

Show /ʃoʊ/ *die;* ~, **~s** show

siamesisch *Adj.* Siamese

Siam·katze *die* Siamese cat

Sibirien *(das);* **~s** Siberia

sịch *Reflexivpron. der 3. Pers. Sg. und Pl. Akk. und Dat.* **(a)** himself/herself/itself/themselves; (auf man bezogen) oneself; (auf das Anredepronomen Sie bezogen) yourself/yourselves; ~ **freuen/wundern/schämen/täuschen** be pleased/surprised/ashamed/mistaken; ~ **sorgen** worry
(b) (reziprok) one another, each other

Sịchel *die;* ~, **~n** sickle

sịcher [1] *Adj.* **(a)** safe ‹*road, procedure, etc.*›; secure ‹*job, investment, etc.*›
(b) reliable ‹*evidence, source*›; certain ‹*proof*›; reliable, sure ‹*judgment, taste, etc.*›
(c) (selbstbewusst) [self-]assured ‹*person, manner*›
(d) (gewiss) certain; sure
[2] *adv.* **(a)** safely
(b) (zuverlässig) reliably; ~ **[Auto] fahren** be a safe driver
(c) (selbstbewusst) [self-]confidently
[3] *Adv.* certainly

sịcher|gehen *unr. itr. V.; mit sein* play safe

Sịcherheit *die;* ~, **~en (a)** safety; (der Öffentlichkeit) security; **jmdn./etw. in** ~ **[vor etw.** (*Dat.*)**] bringen** save *or* rescue sb./sth. [from sth.]
(b) (Gewissheit) certainty
(c) (Wirtsch.: Bürgschaft) security

sịcherheits-, Sịcherheits-: ~abstand *der* (Verkehrsw.) safe distance between vehicles; **~gurt** *der* seat belt; **~halber** *Adv.* to be on the safe side; **~nadel** *die* safety pin; **~schloss, *~schloß** *das* safety lock

sịcherlich *Adv.* certainly

sịchern *tr. V.* **(a)** make ‹*door etc.*› secure; (garantieren) safeguard ‹*rights, peace*›; (schützen) protect ‹*rights etc.*›; **sich** (*Dat.*) **etw.** ~: secure sth.
(b) (DV) back up

sịcher|stellen *tr. V.* **(a)** impound ‹*goods, vehicle*›
(b) guarantee ‹*supply, freedom, etc.*›

S

Sicher·stellung *die* **(a)** ▶ SICHERSTELLEN A: impounding
(b) (Gewährleistung) guarantee

Sicherung *die;* ~, ~**en (a)** safeguarding; (das Schützen) protection
(b) (Elektrot.) fuse
(c) (techn. Vorrichtung) safety catch

Sicherungs·kopie *die* (DV) back-up [copy]

Sicht *die;* ~: view (**auf** + *Akk.*, **in** + *Akk.* of); **gute** *od.* **klare/schlechte** ~: good/poor visibility; **in** ~ **kommen** come into sight; **außer** ~ **sein** be out of sight

sichtbar [1] *Adj.* visible; (fig.) apparent ‹*reason*›
[2] *adv.* visibly

sichten *tr. V.* sight

sichtlich [1] *Adj.* obvious; evident
[2] *adv.* obviously; evidently; visibly ‹*impressed*›

Sichtung *die;* ~, ~**en** sighting

Sicht-: ~**verhältnisse** *Pl.* visibility *sing.;* ~**vermerk** *der* visa; ~**weite** *die* visibility *no art.;* **außer/in** ~**weite sein** be out of/in sight

sickern *itr. V.; mit sein* seep; (spärlich fließen) trickle

sie [1] *Personalpron.; 3. Pers. Sg. Nom. Fem.* she; (betont) her; (bei Dingen, Tieren) it; *s. auch* IHR[1], IHRER A
[2] *Personalpron.; 3. Pers. Pl. Nom.* they; (betont) them; *s. auch* IHNEN; IHRER B;
[3] *Akk. von* SIE 1: her; (bei Dingen, Tieren) it
[4] *Akk. von* SIE 2A: them

Sie *Personalpron.; 3. Pers. Pl. Nom. u. Akk; Anrede an eine od. mehrere Personen* you; *s. auch* IHNEN; IHRER

Sieb *das;* ~[e]**s**, ~**e** sieve; (für Tee) strainer

sieben[1] *tr. V.* **(a)** sieve ‹*flour etc.*›; riddle ‹*sand, gravel, etc.*›
(b) (auswählen) screen ‹*candidates*›

sieben[2] *Kardinalz.* seven

Sieben *die;* ~, ~**en** seven

sieben-, Sieben-: ~**fach** *Vervielfältigungsz.* sevenfold; ~**mal** *Adj.* seven times; ~**sachen** *Pl.* (ugs.) **meine/deine** *usw.* ~**sachen** my/your *etc.* belongings *or* (coll.) bits and pieces

siebt... *Ordinalz.* seventh

siebtel *Bruchz.* seventh

Siebtel *das,* (schweiz. meist *der*); ~**s**, ~: seventh

siebtens *Adv.* seventhly

sieb·zehn *Kardinalz.* seventeen

siebzig *Kardinalz.* seventy

siebzigst... *Ordinalz.* seventieth

siedeln *itr. V.* settle

sieden *unr. od. regelm. itr. V.* boil

Siede·punkt *der* (auch fig.) boiling point

Siedler *der;* ~**s**, ~: settler

Siedlung *die;* ~, ~**en (a)** (Wohngebiet) [housing] estate
(b) (Niederlassung) settlement

Sieg *der;* ~[e]**s**, ~**e** victory, (bes. Sport) win (**über** + *Akk.* over)

Siegel *das;* ~**s**, ~: seal; (von Behörden) stamp

siegen *itr. V.* win; **über jmdn.** ~: gain *or* win a victory over sb.; (bes. Sport) win against sb.; beat sb.

Sieger *der;* ~**s**, ~: winner; (Mannschaft) winners *pl.;* (einer Schlacht) victor

Sieger·ehrung *die* presentation ceremony; awards ceremony

Siegerin *die;* ~, ~**nen** winner

sieges·sicher *Adj., adv.* confident of victory

sieg·gewohnt *Adj.* ‹*army*› accustomed to victory; ‹*team*› used to winning

sieh, siehe *Imperativ Sg. v.* SEHEN

siehst *2. Pers. Sg. Präsens v.* SEHEN

sieht *3. Pers. Sg. Präsens v.* SEHEN

siezen *tr. V.* call ‹*sb.*› 'Sie' (*the polite form of address*)

Signal *das;* ~**s**, ~**e** signal

signalisieren *tr. V.* indicate ‹*danger, change, etc.*›

Signatur *die;* ~, ~**en (a)** initials *pl.;* (Kürzel) abbreviated signature; (des Künstlers) autograph
(b) (Unterschrift) signature
(c) (in einer Bibliothek) shelf mark

signieren *tr. V.* sign; autograph ‹*one's own work*›

Silbe *die;* ~, ~**n** syllable

Silber *das;* ~**s (a)** silver
(b) (silbernes Gerät) silver[ware]

Silber·medaille *die* silver medal

silbern [1] *Adj.* silver; silvery ‹*moonlight, shade, gleam, etc.*›
[2] *adv.* ‹*shine, shimmer, etc.*› with a silvery lustre

Silber·papier *das* silver paper

Silhouette /ziˈlu̯ɛtə/ *die;* ~, ~**n** silhouette

Silicium *das;* ~**s** silicon

Silikon *das;* ~**s**, ~**e** (Chemie) silicone

Silo *der od. das;* ~**s**, ~**s** silo

Silvester *der od. das;* ~**s**, ~: New Year's Eve

Silvester·nacht *die* night of New Year's Eve

Simbabwe (*das*); ~**s** Zimbabwe

Sim-Karte, SIM-Karte /ˈzɪm-/ *die* SIM card

simpel [1] *Adj.* **(a)** simple ‹*question, task*›
(b) (beschränkt) simple-minded ‹*person*›; simple ‹*mind*›
[2] *adv.* **(a)** simply
(b) (beschränkt) in a simple-minded manner

Simpel *der;* ~**s**, ~ (bes. südd. ugs.) simpleton; fool

Sims *der od. das;* ~**es**, ~**e** ledge; sill; (Kamin~) mantelpiece

---

*old spelling - see note on page xiv

simsen /ˈzɪmzn̩/ *itr. V.* (ugs.) send a text message/text messages
Simulant *der;* **~en, ~en Simulantin** *die;* **~, ~nen** malingerer
Simulation *die;* **~, ~en** simulation
simulieren [1] *tr. V.* feign, sham ‹*illness, emotion, etc.*›; simulate ‹*situation, condition*› [2] *itr. V.* feign illness
simultan [1] *Adj.* simultaneous [2] *adv.* simultaneously
sind *1. u. 3. Pers. Pl. Präsens v.* SEIN[1]
Sinfonie *die;* **~, ~n** symphony
Sinfonie·orchester *das* symphony orchestra
singen *unr. tr., itr. V.* sing
Single[1] /ˈzɪŋl̩/ *die;* **~, ~s** (Schallplatte) single
Single[2] *der;* **~s, ~s** single person; **~s** single people *no art.*
Single[3] *das;* **~s, ~s** (Badminton, Tennis) singles *sing. or pl.*
Singular *der;* **~s** singular
Sing·vogel *der* songbird
sinken *unr. itr. V.; mit sein* **(a)** ‹*ship, sun*› sink, go down; ‹*plane, balloon*› descend, go down
(b) (niedersinken) fall
(c) (niedriger werden) ‹*temperature, level*› fall, drop
(d) (an Wert verlieren; nachlassen; abnehmen) fall, go down
Sinn *der;* **~[e]s, ~e (a)** sense
(b) *Pl.* (geh.: Bewusstsein) senses; mind *sing.;* **nicht bei ~en sein** be out of one's senses
(c) (Gefühl, Verständnis) feeling
(d) (Bedeutung) meaning
(e) (Ziel u. Zweck) point
Sinn·bild *das* symbol
Sinnes-: ~organ *das* sense organ; sensory organ; **~täuschung** *die* trick of the senses
sinn·gemäß [1] *Adj.* **eine ~e Übersetzung** a translation which conveys the general sense
[2] *adv.* **etw. ~ übersetzen/wiedergeben** translate the general sense of sth./give the gist of sth.
sinnlich *Adj.* sensory ‹*impression, perception, stimulus*›; sensual ‹*love, mouth*›; sensuous ‹*pleasure, passion*›
Sinnlichkeit *die;* **~:** sensuality
sinn·los [1] *Adj.* **(a)** senseless
(b) (zwecklos) pointless
[2] *adv.* **(a)** senselessly
(b) (zwecklos) pointlessly
Sinnlosigkeit *die;* **~ (a)** senselessness
(b) (Zwecklosigkeit) pointlessness
sinn·voll [1] *Adj.* **(a)** (vernünftig) sensible
(b) (einen Sinn ergebend) meaningful
[2] *adv.* **(a)** (vernünftig) sensibly
(b) (einen Sinn ergebend) meaningfully
Sint·flut *die* Flood; Deluge
sintflut·artig [1] *Adj.* torrential
[2] *adv.* in torrents

Sinto *der;* **~, Sinti** Sinte
Sippe *die;* **~, ~n (a)** (Völkerk.) sib
(b) (ugs.: Verwandtschaft) clan
Sippschaft *die;* **~, ~en** (ugs.) ▶ SIPPE B
Sirene *die;* **~, ~n** siren
Sirup *der;* **~s, ~e** syrup
Sitte *die;* **~, ~n (a)** (Brauch) custom; tradition
(b) (moralische Norm) common decency
(c) *Pl.* (Benehmen) manners
sitten·widrig *Adj.* **(a)** (Rechtsw.) illegal ‹*methods, advertising, etc.*›
(b) (unmoralisch) immoral ‹*behaviour*›
sittlich [1] *Adj.* moral
[2] *adv.* morally
Sittlichkeit *die;* **~:** morality
Sittlichkeits-: ~verbrechen *das* sexual crime; **~verbrecher** *der,* **~verbrecherin** *die* sex offender
Situation *die;* **~, ~en** situation
situiert *Adj.* **gut/schlechter** (usw.) **~** well off/worse off *etc.*
Sitz *der;* **~es, ~e (a)** seat
(b) (Verwaltungssitz) headquarters *sing. or pl.;*
(c) (von Kleidungsstücken) fit
Sitz·bank *die; Pl.* **Sitzbänke** bench
sitzen *unr. itr. V.; südd., österr., schweiz. mit sein* **(a)** sit
(b) (sein) be
(c) ([gut] passen) fit
(d) ~ bleiben (nicht versetzt werden) stay down [a year]; (unverheiratet bleiben) be left on the shelf; **auf etw.** (*Dat.*) **~ bleiben** (für etw. keinen Käufer finden) be left *or* (coll.) stuck with sth.; **jmdn. ~ lassen** (ugs.) (nicht heiraten) jilt sb.; (im Stich lassen) leave sb. in the lurch; **etw. nicht auf sich** (*Dat.*) **~lassen** not take sth.
sitzen-: *~|bleiben ▶ SITZEN D; ***~|lassen** ▶ SITZEN D
Sitz·platz *der* seat
Sitzplatz·stadion *das* all-seater stadium
Sitzung *die;* **~, ~en** meeting; (eines Parlaments) sitting; session
Sitzungs·saal *der* conference hall
Skala *die;* **~, Skalen** scale
Skalp *der;* **~s, ~e** scalp
Skalpell *das;* **~s, ~e** scalpel
skalpieren *tr. V.* scalp
Skandal *der;* **~s, ~e** scandal
skandalös *Adj.* scandalous
Skandinavien (*das*)*;* **~s** Scandinavia
Skandinavier *der;* **~s, ~:** Scandinavian
skandinavisch *Adj.* Scandinavian
Skat *der;* **~[e]s, ~e** *od.* **~s** skat
Skateboard /ˈskeɪtbɔːd/ *das;* **~s, ~s** skateboard
Skateboarder /ˈskeɪtbɔːdɐ/ *der;* **~s, ~, Skateboarderin** *die;* **~, ~nen** skateboarder
Skelett *das;* **~[e]s, ~e** skeleton
Skepsis *die;* **~:** scepticism

skeptisch 1 *Adj.* sceptical
2 *adv.* sceptically

Ski /ʃi:/ *der;* **~s, ~er** *od.* **~**: ski; **~ laufen** *od.* **fahren** ski

Ski-: ~läufer *der,* **~läuferin** *die* skier; **~lehrer** *der,* **~lehrerin** *die* ski instructor; **~lift** *der* ski lift; **~springen** *das;* **~~s** ski jumping *no art.*

Skinhead /'skɪnhɛd/ *der;* **~s, ~s** skinhead

Skizze *die;* **~, ~n** sketch

Skizzen·block *der* sketch pad

skizzieren *tr. V.* sketch

Sklave *der;* **~n, ~n** slave

Sklaven·händler *der,* **Sklaven·händlerin** *die* slave trader

Sklaverei *die;* **~**: slavery *no art.*

Sklavin *die;* **~, ~nen** slave

sklavisch 1 *Adj.* slavish
2 *adv.* slavishly

Skonto *der od. das;* **~s, ~s** (Kaufmannsspr.) [cash] discount

Skorbut *der;* **~[e]s** scurvy *no art.*

Skorpion *der;* **~s, ~e** scorpion; (Astrol.) Scorpio

Skrupel *der;* **~s, ~**: scruple

skrupel·los 1 *Adj.* unscrupulous
2 *adv.* unscrupulously

Skrupellosigkeit *die;* **~**: unscrupulousness

Skulptur *die;* **~, ~en** sculpture

skurril 1 *Adj.* absurd; droll ‹*person*›
2 *adv.* absurdly

Skurrilität *die;* **~, ~en** absurdity

Slalom *der;* **~s, ~s** slalom

Slawe *der;* **~n, ~n, Slawin** *die;* **~, ~nen** Slav

slawisch *Adj.* Slav[ic]; Slavonic

Slip *der;* **~s, ~s** briefs *pl.*

Slogan /'slo:gn̩/ *der;* **~s, ~s** slogan

Slowake *der;* **~n, ~n** Slovak

Slowakei *die;* **~**: Slovakia *no art.*

Slowakin *die;* **~, ~nen** Slovak

Slowene *der;* **~n, ~n** Slovene; Slovenian

Slowenien /slo've:ni̯ən/ *(das);* **~s** Slovenia

Slowenin *die;* **~, ~nen** Slovene; Slovenian

Slum /slam/ *der;* **~s, ~s** slum

Smaragd *der;* **~[e]s, ~e** emerald

Smog *der;* **~[s], ~s** smog

Smoking *der;* **~s, ~s** dinner jacket *or* (Amer.) tuxedo and dark trousers

Snowboard /'snoʊbɔ:d/ *das;* **~s, ~s** snowboard

Snowboarder /'snoʊbɔ:dɐ/ *der;* **~s, ~, Snowboarderin** *die;* **~, ~nen** snowboarder

so 1 *Adv.* **(a)** (auf diese Weise; in, von dieser Art) like this/that; this/that way; **weiter so!** carry on in the same way!; **so gennant** so-called
(b) (dermaßen, überaus) so
(c) (genauso) as; **so wenig/viel wie** *od.* **als** as little/much as; **halb/doppelt so viel** half/ twice as much; **so weit wie möglich** as far as possible; **so weit** (im großen Ganzen) by and large; (bis jetzt) up to now; **so weit sein** (ugs.) be ready; **so gut ich konnte** as best I could
(d) (ugs.: solch) such; **so ein Idiot!** what an idiot!; **so einer/eine/eins** one like that
(e) *betont* (eine Zäsur ausdrückend) right; OK (coll.)
(f) (ugs.: schätzungsweise) about
2 *Partikel* **(a)** just; **ach, das hab' ich nur so gesagt** oh, I didn't mean anything by that
(b) (in Aufforderungssätzen verstärkend) **so komm doch** come on now

s. o. *Abk.* = **siehe oben**

So. *Abk.* = **Sonntag** Sun.

Soap /soʊp/ *die;* **~, ~s** soap [opera]

sobald *Konj.* as soon as

Socke *die;* **~, ~n** sock

Sockel *der;* **~s, ~ (a)** (einer Säule, Statue) plinth
(b) (unterer Teil eines Hauses, Schrankes) base

so·dass, *sodaß *Konj.* **(a)** (damit) so that
(b) (und deshalb) and so

Soda·wasser *das* soda; soda water

Sod·brennen *das;* **~s** heartburn

so·eben *Adv.* just

Sofa *das;* **~s, ~s** sofa; settee

so·fern *Konj.* provided [that]

soff *1. u. 3. Pers. Sg. Prät. v.* SAUFEN

so·fort *Adv.* immediately; at once

sofortig *Adj.* (unmittelbar) immediate

Sofort·maßnahme *die* immediate measure

Software /'sɔftvɛ:ɐ̯/ *die;* **~, ~s** (DV) software

sog *1. u. 3. Pers. Sg. Prät. v.* SAUGEN

Sog *der;* **~[e]s, ~e** suction; (bei Schiffen) wake; (bei Fahr-, Flugzeugen) slipstream; (von Wasser, auch fig.) current

so·gar *Adv.* even

***so·genannt** ▶ so 1A

so·gleich *Adv.* immediately; at once

Sohle *die;* **~, ~n (a)** (Schuh~) sole; (Einlege~) insole
(b) (Fuß~) sole [of the foot]

Sohn *der;* **~es, Söhne** son

Soja-: ~bohne *die* soy[a] bean; **~soße** *die* soy[a] sauce

so·lang[e] *Konj.* so *or* as long as

solar *Adj.* solar

Solar·energie *die* (Physik.) solar energy

Solarium *das;* **~s, Solarien** solarium

Solar-: ~kraftwerk *das:* ▶ SONNENKRAFTWERK; **~technik** *die* (Energietechnik) solar technology *no art.;* **~zelle** *die* (Physik, Elektrot.) solar cell

solch *Demonstrativpron.* **(a)** *attr.* such; **das macht ~en Spaß!** it's so much fun!
(b) *allein stehend* **~e wie die** people like that

---

*alte Schreibung - vgl. Hinweis auf S. xiv

Sold *der;* **~**[e]s, **~e** [military] pay

Soldat *der;* **~en, ~en** soldier

Soldaten·friedhof *der* military *or* war cemetery

Soldatin *die;* **~, ~nen** [female *or* woman] soldier

soldatisch 1 *Adj.* military ‹*discipline, expression, etc.*›; soldierly ‹*figure, virtue*› 2 *adv.* in a military manner

Söldner *der;* **~s, ~, Söldnerin** *die;* **~, ~nen** mercenary

solidarisch 1 *Adj.* **~es Verhalten zeigen** show one's solidarity 2 *adv.* **~ handeln/sich ~ verhalten** act in/show solidarity

solidarisieren *refl. V.* show [one's] solidarity

Solidarität *die;* **~:** solidarity

solide 1 *Adj.* **(a)** solid; sturdy ‹*shoes, material*›; [good-]quality ‹*goods*› **(b)** (gut fundiert) sound ‹*work, education, knowledge*›; solid ‹*firm*› **(c)** (anständig) respectable ‹*person, life, profession*› 2 *adv.* **(a)** solidly ‹*built*›; sturdily ‹*made*› **(b)** (gut fundiert) soundly ‹*educated, constructed*› **(c)** (anständig) ‹*live*› respectably, steadily

Solidität *die;* **~:** ▶ SOLIDE 1 A-C: solidness; sturdiness; soundness; respectability

Solist *der;* **~en, ~en, Solistin** *die;* **~, ~nen** soloist

Soll *das;* **~[s], ~[s] (a)** (Bankw.) debit **(b)** (Arbeits~) quota; **sein ~ erfüllen** *od.* **erreichen** achieve one's target

sollen 1 *unr. Modalverb; 2. Part.* **sollen: (a)** (bei Aufforderung, Anweisung, Auftrag) **was soll ich als Nächstes tun?** what should I do next?; **[sagen Sie ihm,] er soll hereinkommen** tell him to come in **(b)** (bei Wunsch, Absicht, Vorhaben) **das sollte ein Witz sein** that was meant to be a joke; **was soll denn das heißen?** what is that supposed to mean? **(c)** (bei Ratlosigkeit) **was soll ich nur machen?** what am I to do? **(d)** (Notwendigkeit ausdrückend) **man soll so etwas nicht unterschätzen** it shouldn't be taken so lightly **(e)** *häufig im Konjunktiv II* (Erwartung, Wünschenswertes ausdrückend) **du solltest dich schämen** you ought to be ashamed of yourself; **das hättest du besser nicht tun ~:** it would have been better if you hadn't done that **(f)** (jmdm. beschieden sein) **er sollte seine Heimat nicht wieder sehen** he was never to see his homeland again **(g)** *im Konjunktiv II* (eine Möglichkeit ausdrückend) **wenn du ihn sehen solltest, sage ihm bitte ...:** if you should see him, please tell him ... **(h)** *im Präsens* (sich für die Wahrheit nicht verbürgend) **das Restaurant soll sehr teuer sein** the restaurant is supposed *or* said to be very expensive **(i)** *im Konjunktiv II* (Zweifel ausdrückend) **sollte das sein Ernst sein?** is he really being serious? **(j)** (können) **mir soll es gleich sein** it's all the same to me 2 *tr., itr. V.* **was soll das?** what's the idea?; **was soll ich dort?** what would I do there?

Solo *das;* **~s, ~s** *od.* **Soli** solo

so·mit /*auch:* '--/ *Adv.* consequently; therefore

Sommer *der;* **~s, ~:** summer

Sommer·ferien *Pl.* summer holidays

sommerlich 1 *Adj.* summer; summery ‹*warmth, weather*›; summer's *attrib.* ‹*day, evening*› 2 *adv.* **es war ~ warm** it was as warm as summer

sommer-, Sommer-: ~reifen *der* standard tyre; **~schluss·verkauf,** ***~schluß·verkauf** *der* summer sale/sales; **~sprosse** *die* freckle; **~sprossig** *Adj.* freckled; **~zeit** *die* (Uhrzeit) summer time

Sonate *die;* **~, ~n** (Musik) sonata

Sonde *die;* **~, ~n** probe; (zur Ernährung) tube

Sonder-: ~angebot *das* special offer; **~ausgabe** *die* **(a)** special edition; **(b)** (Steuerw.: private Aufwendungen) tax-deductible expenditure; **(c)** (Extraausgabe) extra expense

sonderbar 1 *Adj.* strange; odd 2 *adv.* strangely; oddly

sonderbarer·weise *Adv.* strangely *or* oddly enough

Sonder-: ~fall *der* special case; **~genehmigung** *die* special permit

sonder·gleichen *Adv., nachgestellt* **eine Frechheit/Unverschämtheit ~:** the height of cheek/impudence

sonderlich *Adv.* particularly

Sonderling *der;* **~s, ~e** strange *or* odd person

Sonder-: ~marke *die* special issue [stamp]; **~müll** *der* hazardous waste

sondern¹ *tr. V.* (geh.) separate (**von** from)

sondern² *Konj.* but; **nicht nur ..., ~ [auch] ...:** not only ... but also ...

Sonder-: ~nummer *die* special edition *or* issue; **~preis** *der* special *or* reduced price; **~schule** *die* special school; **~schul·lehrer** *der,* **~schul·lehrerin** *die* teacher at a special school; **~wunsch** *der* special request *or* wish; **~zug** *der* special train

sondieren *tr. V.* sound out

Sonett *das;* **~[e]s, ~e** sonnet

Sonn·abend *der* (bes. nordd.) Saturday; *s. auch* DIENSTAG

sonn·abends *Adv.* on Saturday[s]

Sonne *die;* **~, ~n** sun; (Licht der ~) sun[light]

S

sonnen *refl. V.* sun oneself
sonnen-, Sonnen-: ~aufgang *der* sunrise; **~baden** *itr. V.* sunbathe; **~blume** *die* sunflower; **~brand** *der* sunburn *no indef. art.;* **~brille** *die* sunglasses *pl.;* **~energie** *die* solar energy; **~finsternis** *die* solar eclipse; **~hut** *der* sun hat; **~kollektor** *der* (Energietechnik) solar collector; **~kraftwerk** *das* solar power station; **~licht** *das* sunlight; **~milch** *die* suntan lotion; **~öl** *das* sun oil; **~schein** *der* sunshine; **~schirm** *der* sunshade; **~schutz·creme** *die* suntan lotion; **~stich** *der* sunstroke *no indef. art.;* **~strahl** *der* ray of sun[shine]; **~uhr** *die* sundial; **~untergang** *der* sunset
sonnig *Adj.* sunny
Sonn·tag *der* Sunday; *s. auch* DIENSTAG
sonn·täglich 1 *Adj.* Sunday *attrib.;* 2 *adv.* **~ gekleidet** dressed in one's Sunday best
sonntags *Adv.* on Sunday[s]
sonst *Adv.* **(a) der ~ so freundliche Mann ...**: the man, who is/was usually so friendly, ...; **alles war wie ~**: everything was [the same] as usual; **~ was** (ugs.) something else; (fragend, verneint) anything else; **~ wer** (ugs.) somebody else; (fragend, verneint) anybody else; **~ wo** (ugs.) somewhere else; (fragend, verneint) anywhere else; **~ noch was?** (ugs., auch iron.) anything else?; **wer/was/wie/wo [denn] ~?** who/what/how/where else?
(b) (andernfalls) otherwise; or
sonstig... *Adj.* other; further
***sonst·was** *usw.* ▶ SONST A
so·oft *Konj.* whenever
sophistisch 1 *Adj.* sophistic[al] 2 *adv.* sophistically
Sopran *der;* **~s, ~e** (Musik) soprano; (im Chor) sopranos *pl.*
Sopranistin *die;* **~, ~nen** soprano
Sorge *die;* **~, ~n** worry; **keine ~!** don't [you] worry!
sorgen 1 *refl. V.* worry (**um** about) 2 *itr. V.* **für jmdn./etw. ~**: take care of sb./sth.
sorgen-, Sorgen-: ~frei 1 *Adj.* carefree; 2 *adv.* **~frei leben** live in a carefree manner; **~kind** *das* (auch fig.) problem child; **~voll** 1 *Adj.* worried; 2 *adv.* worriedly
Sorg·falt *die;* **~**: care
sorg·fältig 1 *Adj.* careful 2 *adv.* carefully
sorg·los 1 *Adj.* **(a)** (ohne Sorgfalt) careless **(b)** (unbekümmert) carefree 2 *adv.* **~ mit etw. umgehen** treat sth. carelessly
Sorglosigkeit *die;* **~ (a)** (Mangel an Sorgfalt) carelessness **(b)** (Unbekümmertheit) carefreeness

*old spelling - see note on page xiv

sorgsam 1 *Adj.* careful 2 *adv.* carefully
Sorte *die;* **~, ~n (a)** sort; type; kind **(b)** *Pl.* (Devisen) foreign currency *sing.*
Sorten·kurs *der* (Bankw.) exchange rate
sortieren *tr. V.* sort [out] ‹*pictures, letters, washing, etc.*›; grade ‹*goods etc.*›
Sortiment *das;* **~[e]s, ~e** range (**an** + *Dat.* of)
so·sehr *Konj.* however much
Soße *die;* **~, ~n** sauce; (Bratensoße) gravy; sauce; (Salatsoße) dressing
sott *1. u. 3. Pers. Sg. Prät. v.* SIEDEN
Souffleur /zu'flø:ɐ̯/ *der;* **~s, ~e, Souffleuse** /zu'flø:zə/ *die;* **~, ~n** prompter
soufflieren /zu'fli:rən/ *tr. V.* prompt
Sound-: ~check /'saʊndtʃɛk/ *der;* **~~s, ~~s** sound check; **~karte** *die* (DV) sound card
Souvenir /suvə'ni:ɐ̯/ *das;* **~s, ~s** souvenir
souverän /zuvə'rɛ:n/ *Adj.* sovereign
Souveränität *die;* **~**: sovereignty
so·viel *Konj.* as *or* so far as; *s. auch* SO 1B
so·weit *Konj.* **(a)** as *or* so far as; *s. auch* SO 1B; **(b)** (in dem Maße, wie) [in] so far as; *s. auch* SO 1B
***so·wenig** ▶ SO 1B
so·wie *Konj.* **(a)** (und) as well as **(b)** (sobald) as soon as
so·wie·so *Adv.* anyway
sowjetisch *Adj.* Soviet
Sowjet·union *die* (1922–1991) Soviet Union
so·wohl *Konj.* **~ ... als** *od.* **wie [auch] ...**: both ... and ...; ... as well as ...
sozial 1 *Adj.* social 2 *adv.* socially
sozial-, Sozial-: ~abgaben *Pl.* social welfare contributions; **~arbeiter** *der,* **~arbeiterin** *die* social worker; **~demokrat** *der,* **~demokratin** *die* Social Democrat; **~demokratisch** *Adj.* social democratic; **~dienst** *der* community services department; **~hilfe** *die* social welfare; **~hilfe·empfänger** *der,* **~hilfe·empfängerin** *die* welfare recipient
Sozialismus *der;* **~**: socialism *no art.;*
Sozialist *der;* **~en, ~en, Sozialistin** *die;* **~, ~nen** socialist
sozialistisch 1 *Adj.* socialist 2 **~ regierte Länder** countries with socialist governments
Sozial-: ~kunde *die* social studies *sing., no art.;* **~politik** *die* social policy; **~produkt** *das* (Wirtsch.) national product; **~staat** *der* welfare state
Soziologe *der;* **~n, ~n** sociologist
Soziologie *die;* **~**: sociology
Soziologin *die;* **~, ~nen** sociologist
soziologisch 1 *Adj.* sociological

2 *adv.* sociologically

Sozius *der;* ~, ~se (a) *Pl. auch:* **Sozii** (Wirtsch.: Teilhaber) partner
(b) (beim Motorrad) pillion

so·zu·sagen *Adv.* as it were

Spachtel *der;* ~s, ~ *od. die;* ~, ~n putty knife; (zum Malen) palette knife

Spachtel·masse *die* filler

spachteln *tr. V.* (a) stop, fill ‹*hole, crack, etc.*›; smooth over ‹*wall, panel, surface, etc.*›
(b) (ugs.: essen) put away (coll.) ‹*food, meal*›

Spagat *der od. das;* ~[e]s, ~e splits *pl.;* [einen] ~ **machen** do the splits

Spaghetti *Pl.* spaghetti *sing.*

spähen *itr. V.* peer; (durch ein Loch, eine Ritze usw.) peep

Späher *der;* ~s, ~, **Späherin** *die;* ~, ~nen (Milit.) scout; (Posten) lookout; (Spitzel) informer

Spalier *das;* ~s, ~e (a) trellis
(b) (Ehren~) guard of honour; ~ **stehen** line the route; ‹*soldiers*› form a guard of honour

Spalt *der;* ~[e]s, ~e opening; (im Fels) fissure; crevice; (zwischen Vorhängen) chink; gap; (langer Riss) crack

Spalte *die;* ~, ~n (a) crack; (Felsspalte) crevice
(b) (Druckw.) column

spalten *unr. (auch regelm.) tr., refl. V.* split

Spaltung *die;* ~, ~en (auch fig.) splitting; (fig.: das Gespaltensein) split

Span *der;* ~[e]s, **Späne** (Hobelspan) shaving

Span·ferkel *das* suckling pig

Spange *die;* ~, ~n clasp; (Haarspange) hairslide (Brit.); barrette (Amer.); (Armspange) bracelet; bangle

Spaniel /'ʃpa:ni̯əl/ *der;* ~s, ~s spaniel

Spanien /'ʃpa:ni̯ən/ *(das);* ~s Spain

Spanier /'ʃpa:ni̯ɐ/ *der;* ~s, ~, **Spanierin** *die;* ~, ~nen Spaniard

spanisch *Adj.* Spanish

Span·korb *der* chip basket; chip

spann *1. u. 3. P. Sing. Prät. v.* SPINNEN

spannen 1 *tr. V.* (a) tighten ‹*violin string, violin bow, etc.*›; draw ‹*bow*›; tension ‹*spring, tennis net, drumhead, saw blade*›; stretch ‹*fabric, shoe, etc.*›; draw *or* pull ‹*line*› tight *or* taut; flex ‹*muscle*›; cock ‹*gun, camera shutter*›
(b) (befestigen) put up ‹*washing line*›; stretch ‹*net, wire, tarpaulin, etc.*› (**über** + *Akk.* over)
(c) (schirren) harness (**vor, an** + *Akk.* to)
2 *refl. V.* (a) become *or* go taut; ‹*muscles*› tense
(b) (geh.: sich wölben) **sich über etw.** (*Akk.*) ~: span sth.
3 *itr. V.* ‹*clothing*› be [too] tight; ‹*skin*› be taut

spannend 1 *Adj.* exciting; (stärker) thrilling
2 *adv.* excitingly; (stärker) thrillingly

Spannung *die;* ~, ~en (a) excitement; (Neugier) suspense
(b) (eines Romans, Films usw.) suspense
(c) (Zwistigkeit, Nervosität) tension
(d) (Elektrot.) voltage

Spannungs·gebiet *das* (Politik.) area of tension

Spann·weite *die* [wing]span

Span·platte *die* chipboard

Spar-: ~**buch** *das* savings book; ~**büchse** *die* money box

sparen 1 *tr. V.* save
2 *itr. V.* (a) save; **für** *od.* **auf etw.** (*Akk.*) ~: save up for sth.
(b) (sparsam wirtschaften) economize (**mit** on); **an etw.** (*Dat.*) ~: be sparing with sth.; (beim Einkauf) economize on sth.

Sparer *der;* ~s, ~, **Sparerin** *die;* ~, ~nen saver

Spargel *der;* ~s, ~, (schweiz. auch) *die;* ~, ~n asparagus *no pl., no indef. art.*

Spar-: ~**groschen** *der* (ugs.) nest egg; savings *pl.;* ~**kasse** *die* savings bank; ~**konto** *das* savings *or* deposit account

spärlich 1 *Adj.* sparse ‹*vegetation, beard, growth*›; thin ‹*hair, applause*›; scanty ‹*leftovers, knowledge, news, evidence, clothing*›; poor ‹*lighting*›
2 *adv.* sparsely, thinly ‹*populated, covered*›; poorly ‹*lit, attended*›; scantily ‹*dressed*›

sparsam 1 *Adj.* thrifty ‹*person*›; (wirtschaftlich) economical; **mit etw.** ~ **sein** be economical with sth.
2 *adv.* ~ **mit der Butter/dem Papier umgehen** use butter/paper sparingly; economize on butter/paper

Sparsamkeit *die;* ~: thrift[iness]; (Wirtschaftlichkeit) economicalness

Sparte *die;* ~, ~n (a) (Teilbereich) area; (eines Geschäfts) line [of business]
(b) (Rubrik) section

Sparten·kanal *der* special-interest channel

Spar-: ~**vertrag** *der* savings agreement; ~**zins** *der; Pl.* ~~en interest *no pl.* on a savings account

Spaß *der;* ~es, **Späße** (a) (Vergnügen) fun; ~ **an etw.** (*Dat.*) **haben** enjoy sth.; **[jmdm.]** ~ **machen** be fun [for sb.]; **viel** ~! have a good time!
(b) (Scherz) joke; (Streich) prank; **er macht nur** ~: he's only joking; ~ **beiseite!** joking aside; ~ **muss sein!** there's no harm in a joke; ~ **verstehen** be able to take a joke; **im** *od.* **zum** *od.* **aus** ~: as a joke; for fun

spaßen *itr. V.* (a) (Spaß machen) joke
(b) **er lässt nicht mit sich** ~: he won't stand for any nonsense; **mit ihm/damit ist nicht zu** ~: he/it is not to be trifled with

spaßes·halber *Adv.* for the fun of it; for fun

spaßig *Adj.* funny; comical; amusing

Spaß·macher *der,* **Spaß·macherin** *die* joker

spät [1] *Adj.* late; **wie ∼ ist es?** what time is it?
[2] *adv.* late; **∼ am Abend** late in the evening

Spaten *der;* **∼s, ∼:** spade

später [1] *Adj.* **(a)** later ‹*years, generations, etc.*›
(b) (zukünftig) future ‹*owner, wife, etc.*›
[2] *Adv.* later; **bis ∼!** see you later!

spätestens *Adv.* at the latest

Spatz *der;* **∼en, ∼en (a)** sparrow
(b) (fam.: Liebling) pet

Spätzle *Pl.* spaetzle; *kind of noodles*

spazieren *itr. V.; mit sein* stroll; **∼ gehen** go for a walk; **∼ fahren** go for a ride; **ein Kind [im Kinderwagen] ∼ fahren** take a baby for a walk [in a pram]

***spazieren|fahren** *usw.* ▶ SPAZIEREN

Spazier-: ∼gang *der* walk; **∼gänger** *der;* **∼∼s, ∼∼, ∼gängerin** *die;* **∼∼, ∼∼nen** person out for a walk

SPD ∼ *Abk.* = **Sozialdemokratische Partei Deutschlands** SPD

Specht *der;* **∼[e]s, ∼e** woodpecker

Speck *der;* **∼[e]s, ∼e (a)** bacon fat; (Schinkenspeck) bacon
(b) (ugs. scherzh.: Fettpolster) fat; flab (coll.)

speckig *Adj.* greasy

Spediteur /ʃpedi'tøːɐ̯/ *der;* **∼s, ∼e, Spediteurin** *die;* **∼, ∼nen** carrier; haulage contractor; (Möbelspediteur) furniture remover

Spedition *die;* **∼, ∼en** ▶ SPEDITIONSFIRMA

Speditions·firma *die* forwarding agency; (per Schiff) shipping agency; (Transportunternehmen) haulage firm; firm of hauliers; (per Schiff) firm of carriers; (Möbelspedition) removal firm

Speer *der;* **∼[e]s, ∼e (a)** spear
(b) (Sportgerät) javelin

Speichel *der;* **∼s** saliva

Speicher *der;* **∼s, ∼ (a)** storehouse; (Lagerhaus) warehouse
(b) (südd.: Dachboden) loft
(c) (Elektronik) memory

Speicher·kapazität *die* storage capacity; (DV) memory *or* storage capacity

speichern *tr. V.* store

speien (geh.) *unr. tr., itr. V.* spit

Speise *die;* **∼, ∼n (a)** (Gericht) dish
(b) (geh.: Nahrung) food

Speise-: ∼eis *das* ice cream; **∼fisch** *der* food fish; **∼gaststätte** *die* restaurant; **∼kammer** *die* larder; **∼karte** *die* menu; **∼lokal** *das* restaurant

speisen (geh.) [1] *itr. V.* eat; (dinieren) dine
[2] *tr. V.* eat; (dinieren) dine on

Speise-: ∼saal *der* dining hall; (im Hotel, in einer Villa usw.) dining room; **∼wagen** *der* restaurant car (Brit.); **∼zettel** *der* menu

*alte Schreibung - vgl. Hinweis auf S. xiv

Spektakel *der;* **∼s, ∼** (ugs.) (Lärm) row (coll.); rumpus (coll.)

spektakulär [1] *Adj.* spectacular
[2] *adv.* spectacularly

Spekulation *die;* **∼, ∼en** speculation

spekulieren *itr. V.* **(a)** (ugs.) **darauf ∼, etw. tun zu können** count on being able to do sth.
(b) (Wirtsch.) speculate (**mit** in)

Spelunke *die;* **∼, ∼n** (ugs. abwertend) dive (coll.)

Spelze *die;* **∼, ∼n** husk

Spende *die;* **∼, ∼n** donation; contribution

spenden *tr., itr. V.* **(a)** donate; give
(b) (fig. geh.) give ‹*light*›; afford, give ‹*shade*›; give off ‹*heat*›

Spenden·aktion *die* campaign for donations

Spender *der;* **∼s, ∼, Spenderin** *die;* **∼, ∼nen** donor; donator; (Organspender, Blutspender) donor

Spender·organ *das* donar organ

spendieren *tr. V.* (ugs.) get, buy ‹*drink, meal, etc.*›; stand ‹*round*›

Spengler *der;* **∼s, ∼, Spenglerin** *die;* **∼, ∼nen** (südd., österr., schweiz.) ▶ KLEMPNER

Sperling *der;* **∼s, ∼e** sparrow

Sperma *das;* **∼s, Spermen** sperm; semen

Sperma·bank *die; Pl.* **∼en** sperm bank

sperr-, Sperr-: ∼angel·weit *Adv.* (ugs.) **∼angel·weit offen** *od.* **geöffnet** wide open; **∼bezirk** *der* **(a)** restricted *or* prohibited area; **(b)** (für Prostituierte) *area in which prostitution is prohibited;* **(c)** (Gesundheitswesen) infected area

Sperre *die;* **∼, ∼n (a)** barrier; (Straßensperre) roadblock; (Milit.) obstacle
(b) (fig.) ban; (Handelssperre) embargo; (Import-, Exportsperre) blockade; (Nachrichten∼) [news] blackout

sperren [1] *tr. V.* **(a)** close; close off ‹*area*›; block ‹*entrance, access, etc.*›; lock ‹*mechanism etc.*›
(b) cut off ‹*water, gas, electricity, etc.*›
(c) (Bankw.) stop ‹*cheque, overdraft facility*›; freeze ‹*bank account*›
(d) (einsperren) **ein Tier/jmdn. in etw.** (*Akk.*) **∼:** shut an animal/sb. in sth.
(e) (Sport: von der Teilnahme ausschließen) ban
(f) (Druckw.: spationieren) print ‹*word, text*› with the letters spaced
[2] *refl. V.* **sich [gegen etw.] ∼:** balk [at sth.]

Sperr·holz *das* plywood

sperrig *Adj.* unwieldy

Sperr-: ∼müll *der* bulky refuse (*for which there is a separate collection service*); **∼sitz** *der* (im Kino) seat in the back stalls; (im Zirkus) front seat; (im Theater) seat in the front stalls; **∼stunde** *die* closing time

Sperrung *die;* **∼, ∼en** ▶ SPERREN A-C, E: closing; closing off; cutting off; stopping; freezing; banning

Spesen *Pl.* expenses; **auf ∼:** on expenses

Spezi *der;* **~s, ~[s]** (südd., österr., schweiz. ugs.) [bosom] pal (coll.); chum (coll.)

spezialisieren *refl. V.* specialize (**auf +** *Akk.* in)

Spezialist *der;* **~en, ~en, Spezialistin** *die;* **~, ~nen** specialist

Spezialität *die;* **~, ~en** speciality

speziell [1] *Adj.* special; specific ‹*question, problem, etc.*›
[2] *Adv.* especially; (eigens) specially

spezifisch [1] *Adj.* specific; characteristic ‹*smell, style*›
[2] *adv.* specifically

Sphäre *die;* **~, ~n** (auch fig.) sphere

spicken *tr. V.* lard

spie *1. u. 3. Pers. Sg. Prät. v.* SPEIEN

Spiegel *der;* **~s, ~ (a)** mirror
(b) (Wasserspiegel, fig.: Konzentration) level

spiegel-, Spiegel-: ~bild *das* reflection; **~blank** *Adj.* shining; **~ei** *das* fried egg; **~glatt** *Adj.* like glass *postpos.;* as smooth as glass *postpos.*

spiegeln [1] *itr. V.* **(a)** (glänzen) shine; gleam
(b) (als Spiegel wirken) reflect the light
[2] *tr. V.* reflect; mirror
[3] *refl. V.* be mirrored *or* reflected

Spiegel·reflex·kamera *die* reflex camera

Spiegelung *die;* **~, ~en (a)** (auch fig., Math.) reflection
(b) (Med.) speculum examination

spiegel·verkehrt [1] *Adj.* back-to-front ‹*lettering*›; **eine ~e Abbildung** a mirror image
[2] *adv.* **etw. ~ abbilden** reproduce sth. as a *or* in mirror image

Spiel *das;* **~[e]s, ~e (a)** play
(b) (Glücks, Gesellschaftsspiel) game; (Wettspiel) game; match; **auf dem ~ stehen** be at stake; **etw. aufs ~ setzen** put sth. at stake; risk sth.
(b) eine ~ mit Worten/Zahlen playing [around] with words/numbers

Spiel·bank *die; Pl.* **~en** casino

spielen [1] *itr. V.* **(a)** play; **auf der Gitarre ~:** play the guitar; **um Geld ~:** play for money
(b) (als Schauspieler) act; perform
(c) der Roman/Film spielt im 17. Jahrhundert/in Berlin the novel/film is set in the 17th century/in Berlin
(d) (fig.) **das Blau spielt ins Violette** the blue is tinged with purple
[2] *tr. V.* **(a)** play; **Cowboy ~:** play at being a cowboy; **Geige** *usw.* **~:** play the violin *etc.;*
(b) (aufführen, vorführen) put on ‹*play*›; show ‹*film*›; perform ‹*piece of music*›; play ‹*record*›; **den Beleidigten/Unschuldigen ~** (fig.) act offended/play the innocent

spielend *Adv.* easily

Spieler *der;* **~s, ~:** player; (Glücksspieler) gambler

Spielerei *die;* **~, ~en (a)** playing *no art.;* (im Glücksspiel) gambling *no art.;*

Spiel·ergebnis *das* match result

Spielerin *die;* **~, ~nen** ▶ SPIELER

spielerisch *Adj.* playful

Spiel-: ~feld *das* field; pitch (Brit.); (Tennis, Squash, Volleyball usw.) court; **~film** *der* feature film; **~kamerad** *der* playmate; **~karte** *die* playing card; **~leitung** *die* **(a)** (Sport) control of the match; **(b)** ▶ REGIE; **~plan** *der* programme; **~platz** *der* playground; **~raum** *der* room to move (fig.); scope; latitude; **~regel** *die* (auch fig.) rule of the game; **gegen die ~regeln verstoßen** (auch fig.) break the rules; **~sachen** *Pl.* toys; **~verderber** *der;* **~~s, ~~, ~verderberin** *die;* **~~, ~~nen** spoilsport; **~waren** *Pl.* toys; **~zeit** *die* **(a)** (Theater: Saison) season; **(b)** (Sport) playing time; **die normale ~zeit** normal time; **~zeug** *das* **(a)** toy; (fig.) toy; plaything; **(b)** (Gesamtheit) toys *pl.*

Spieß *der;* **~es, ~e (a)** (Waffe) spear; **den ~ umdrehen** *od.* **umkehren** (ugs.) turn the tables
(b) (Bratspieß) spit
(c) (Fleischspieß) kebab
(d) (Soldatenspr.) [company] sergeant major

Spieß·bürger *der,* **Spießbürgerin** *die* (abwertend) [petit] bourgeois

Spießer *der;* **~s, ~, Spießerin** *die;* **~, ~nen** (abwertend) [petit] bourgeois

spießig (abwertend) [1] *Adj.* [petit] bourgeois
[2] *adv.* ‹*think, behave, etc.*› in a [petit] bourgeois way

Spinat *der;* **~[e]s, ~e** spinach

Spind *der od. das;* **~[e]s, ~e** locker

Spindel *die;* **~, ~n** spindle

Spinne *die;* **~, ~n** spider

spinnen [1] *unr. tr. V.* spin (fig.); plot ‹*intrigue*›; think up ‹*idea*›; hatch ‹*plot*›
[2] *unr. itr. V.* **(a)** spin
(b) (ugs.: verrückt sein) be crazy *or* (coll.) nuts

Spinnen·netz *das* spider's web

Spinner *der;* **~s, ~ (a)** (Beruf) spinner
(b) (ugs. abwertend) nutcase (coll.); idiot

Spinnerei *die;* **~, ~en** spinning mill

Spinnerin *die;* **~, ~nen** ▶ SPINNER

Spinn-: ~rad *das* spinning wheel; **~webe** *die;* **~~, ~~n** cobweb

Spion *der;* **~s, ~e (a)** spy
(b) (Guckloch) spyhole

Spionage /ʃpio'naːʒə/ *die;* **~:** spying; espionage

spionieren *itr. V.* spy

Spionin *die;* **~, ~nen** spy

Spirale *die;* **~, ~n** spiral

Spiral·feder *die* coil spring

Spirituose *die;* **~, ~n** spirit *usu. in pl.*

Spiritus *der;* **~, ~se** spirit; ethyl alcohol

Spiritus·kocher *der* spirit stove

S

Spital *das;* **~s, Spitäler** (bes. österr., schweiz.) hospital

spitz 1 *Adj.* **(a)** pointed; sharp ‹*pencil, needle, stone, etc.*›; fine ‹*pen nib*›; (Geom.) acute ‹*angle*›
(b) (schrill) shrill ‹*cry etc.*›
(c) (boshaft) cutting ‹*remark etc.*›
2 *adv.* **(a) ~ zulaufen** taper to a point; **~ zulaufend** pointed
(b) (boshaft) cuttingly

Spitz *der;* **~es, ~e** spitz

spitz-, Spitz-: ~bart *der* goatee; **~bube** *der* (scherzh.: Schlingel) rascal; **~bübisch** 1 *Adj.* mischievous; 2 *adv.* mischievously

spitze *indekl. Adj.* (ugs.) ▶ KLASSE

Spitze *die;* **~, ~n (a)** point; (Pfeil~, Horn~ usw.) tip
(b) (oberes Ende) top; (eines Berges) summit
(c) (Zigarren-, Haar-, Zweigspitze) end; (Schuhspitze) toe; (Finger-, Nasenspitze) tip
(d) (vorderes Ende) front; **an der ~ liegen** (Sport) be in the lead *or* in front
(e) (führende Position) top
(f) (einer Firma, Organisation usw.) head; (einer Hierarchie) top; (leitende Gruppe) management
(g) (Höchstwert) maximum; peak
(h) **[absolute/einsame] ~ sein** (ugs.) be [absolutely] great (coll.)
(i) (fig.: Angriff) dig (**gegen** at)
(j) (Textilwesen) lace

Spitzel *der;* **~s, ~:** informer

spitzen *tr. V.* sharpen ‹*pencil*›; purse ‹*lips, mouth*›; prick up ‹*ears*›

Spitzen-: ~erzeugnis *das* top-quality product; **~kandidat** *der,* **~kandidatin** *die* leading *or* top candidate; **~klasse** *die* top class; **~qualität** *die* top quality; **~reiter** *der* **(a)** top rider; (fig.) leader; **(b)** (Mannschaft) top team; **(c)** (Ware) top *or* best seller; **~reiterin** *die:* ▶ ~REITER A; **~sportler** *der* top sportsman; **~sportlerin** *die* top sportswoman

Spitzer *der;* **~s, ~:** [pencil] sharpener

spitz-, Spitz-: ~findig *Adj.* hair-splitting; **~findigkeit** *die;* **~~, ~~en (a)** hair-splitting; **(b)** (etwas Spitzfindiges) nicety; **~hacke** *die* pick; **~|kriegen** *tr. V.* (ugs.) tumble to (coll.); **~maus** *die* shrew; **~name** *der* nickname

Spleen /ʃpli:n/ *der;* **~s, ~e** *od.* **~s** strange habit; eccentricity

Splitt *der;* **~[e]s, ~e** [stone] chippings *pl.;* (zum Streuen) grit

Splitter *der;* **~s, ~:** splinter; (Granat-, Bombensplitter) splinter

splitter·faser·nackt *Adj.* (ugs.) absolutely stark naked; completely starkers *pred.* (Brit. coll.)

splittern *itr. V.* **(a)** (Splitter bilden) splinter
(b) *mit sein* (in Splitter zerbrechen) ‹*glass, windscreen, etc.*› shatter

splitter·nackt *Adj.* (ugs.) stark naked; starkers *pred.* (Brit. coll.)

Splitter·partei *die* splinter party

SPÖ *Abk.* = **Sozialistische Partei Österreichs** Austrian Socialist Party

sponsern *tr. V.* sponsor

Sponsor *der;* **~s, ~en** sponsor

spontan 1 *Adj.* spontaneous
2 *adv.* spontaneously

Spontaneität /ʃpɔntanei'tɛ:t/ *die;* **~:** spontaneity

sporadisch 1 *Adj.* sporadic
2 *adv.* sporadically

Spore *die;* **~, ~n** spore

Sporn *der;* **~[e]s, Sporen** (des Reiters) spur; **einem Pferd die Sporen geben** spur a horse

Sport *der;* **~[e]s (a)** sport; (als Unterrichtsfach) sport; PE; **~ treiben** do sport
(b) (Hobby, Zeitvertreib) hobby; pastime

Sport-: ~art *die* [form of] sport; **~fest** *das* sports festival; (einer Schule) sports day; **~flugzeug** *das* sports plane; **~geist** *der* sportsmanship; **~halle** *die* sports hall; **~journalist** *der,* **~journalistin** *die* sports journalist; **~kleidung** *die* sportswear

Sportler *der;* **~s, ~:** sportsman

Sportlerin *die;* **~, ~nen** sportswoman

sportlich 1 *Adj.* **(a)** sporting *attrib.;*
(b) (fair) sportsmanlike; sporting
(c) (fig.: flott, rasant) sporty ‹*car, driving, etc.*›
(d) (zu sportlicher Leistung fähig) sporty, athletic ‹*person*›
(e) (jugendlich wirkend) sporty, smart but casual ‹*clothes*›; smart but practical ‹*hairstyle*›
2 *adv.* **(a)** as far as sport is concerned
(b) (fair) sportingly
(c) (fig.: flott, rasant) in a sporty manner

Sport-: ~platz *der* sports field; (einer Schule) playing field/fields *pl.;* **~schuh** *der* sports shoe; **~stadion** *das* [sports] stadium; **~teil** *der* sport[s] section; **~verein** *der* sports club; **~wagen** *der* **(a)** (Auto) sports car; **(b)** (Kinderwagen) pushchair (Brit.); stroller (Amer.); **~zentrum** *das* sports centre

Spot /spɔt/ *der;* **~s, ~s (a)** (Werbespot) commercial; advertisement; ad (coll.)
(b) (Leuchte) spotlight; spotlamp

Spott *der;* **~[e]s** mockery; (höhnischer) ridicule; derision

spott·billig *Adj., adv.* (ugs.) dirt cheap

spötteln *itr. V.* mock [gently]; poke *or* make [gentle] fun

spotten *itr. V.* **(a)** mock; poke *or* make fun; (höhnischer) ridicule; be derisive
(b) einer Sache (*Gen.*) **~:** be contemptuous of *or* scorn sth.

Spötter *der;* **~s, ~, Spötterin** *die;* **~, ~nen** mocker

spöttisch 1 *Adj.* mocking; (höhnischer) derisive
2 *adv.* mockingly

Spott·preis *der* (ugs.) ridiculously low price

sprach *1. u. 3. Pers. Sg. Prät. v.* SPRECHEN

Sprache *die;* ~, ~n **(a)** language; **in englischer ~:** in English
(b) (Sprechweise) way of speaking; speech; (Stil) style
(c) etw. zur ~ bringen bring sth. up; raise sth.; **heraus mit der ~!** come on, out with it!

Sprachen·schule *die* language school

Sprach-: ~fehler *der* speech impediment *or* defect; **~führer** *der* phrase book; **~grenze** *die* language boundary; **~kenntnisse** *Pl.* knowledge *sing.* of a language/languages; **~kurs** *der* language course; **~labor** *das* language laboratory *or* (coll.) lab

sprachlich **1** *Adj.* linguistic
2 *adv.* linguistically

sprach-, Sprach-: ~los *Adj.* (überrascht) speechless; **~problem** *das* language problem; **~rohr** *das* (Repräsentant) spokesman; (Propagandist) mouthpiece; **~schule** *die* language school; **~unterricht** *der* language teaching

sprang *1. u. 3. Pers. Sg. Prät. v.* SPRINGEN

Spray /ʃpreː/ *das od. der;* ~s, ~s spray

Spray·dose *die* aerosol [can]

sprayen *tr., itr. V.* spray

Sprech-: ~anlage *die* intercom (coll.); **~chor** *der* chorus

sprechen **1** *unr. itr. V.* speak (**über** + *Akk.* about; **von** about, of); (sich unterhalten, sich besprechen auch) talk (**über** + *Akk.*, **von** about); ‹*parrot etc.*› talk; **deutsch/flüsternd ~:** speak German/in a whisper; **für/gegen etw. ~:** speak in favour of/against sth.; **mit jmdm. ~:** speak *or* talk with *or* to sb.; **mit wem spreche ich?** who is speaking please?
2 *unr. tr. V.* **(a)** speak ‹*language, dialect*›; say ‹*word, sentence*›; **„Hier spricht man Deutsch"** 'German spoken'
(b) (rezitieren) say, recite ‹*poem, text*›; say ‹*prayer*›
(c) jmdn. ~: speak to sb.
(d) (aussprechen) pronounce ‹*name, word, etc.*›

Sprecher *der;* ~s, ~, **Sprecherin** *die;* ~, ~nen **(a)** spokesman/spokeswoman
(b) (Ansager[in]) announcer; (Nachrichtensprecher[in]) newscaster; newsreader
(c) (Kommentator[in], Erzähler[in]) narrator

Sprech-: ~funk·gerät *das* radio-telephone; (Walkie-talkie) walkie-talkie; **~stunde** *die* consultation hours *pl.;* (eines Arztes) surgery; **~stunden·hilfe** *die* (eines Arztes) receptionist; (eines Zahnarztes) assistant; **~zimmer** *das* consulting room

spreizen *tr. V.* spread ‹*fingers, toes, etc.*›; **die Beine ~:** spread one's legs apart; open one's legs

Spreiz·fuß *der* (Med.) spread foot

sprengen *tr. V.* **(a)** blow up; blast ‹*rock*›; **etw. in die Luft ~:** blow sth. up
(b) (gewaltsam öffnen, aufbrechen) force [open] ‹*door*›; force ‹*lock*›; burst, break ‹*bonds, chains*›; (fig.) break up ‹*meeting, demonstration*›
(c) (besprengen) water ‹*flower bed, lawn*›; sprinkle ‹*street, washing*› with water; (verspritzen) sprinkle; (mit dem Schlauch) spray

Spreng-: ~stoff *der* explosive; **~stoff·anschlag** *der* bomb attack

Sprenkel *der;* ~s, ~: spot; dot; speckle

sprenkeln *tr. V.* sprinkle spots of ‹*colour*›; sprinkle ‹*water*›

Spreu *die;* ~: chaff

sprich *Imperativ Sg. v.* SPRECHEN

sprichst *2. Pers. Sg. Präsens v.* SPRECHEN

spricht *3. Pers. Sg. Präsens v.* SPRECHEN

Sprich·wort *das; Pl.* **Sprichwörter** proverb

sprießen *unr. itr. V.; mit sein* ‹*leaf, bud*› shoot, sprout; ‹*seedlings*› come *or* spring up; ‹*beard*› sprout

Spring·brunnen *der* fountain

springen **1** *unr. itr. V.* **(a)** *mit sein* (auch Sport) jump; (mit Schwung) leap; spring; jump; ‹*frog, flea*› hop, jump; (sich in Sprüngen fortbewegen) bound
(b) *mit sein* (fig.) ‹*pointer, milometer, etc.*› jump (**auf** + *Akk.* to); ‹*traffic lights*› change (**auf** + *Akk.* to); ‹*spark*› leap; ‹*ball*› bounce
(c) *mit sein* ‹*string, glass, porcelain, etc.*› break; (Risse, Sprünge bekommen) crack
2 *unr. tr. V.; auch mit sein* (Sport) perform ‹*somersault, twist dive, etc.*›

Springer *der;* ~s, ~ **(a)** (Sport) jumper
(b) (Schachfigur) knight

Springerin *die;* ~, ~nen (Sport) jumper

spring·lebendig *Adj.* extremely lively; full of beans *pred.* (coll.)

Spring·reiten *das* showjumping *no art.*

Sprinkler *der;* ~s, ~: sprinkler

sprinten *itr. (auch tr.) V.; mit sein* sprint

Sprinter *der;* ~s, ~, **Sprinterin** *die;* ~, ~nen (Sport) sprinter

Sprit *der;* ~[e]s, ~e **(a)** (ugs.: Treibstoff) gas (Amer. coll.); juice (sl.); petrol (Brit.)
(b) (ugs.: Schnaps) shorts *pl.*

Spritze *die;* ~, ~n **(a)** syringe
(b) (Injektion) injection
(c) (der Feuerwehr) hose; (Löschfahrzeug) fire engine

spritzen **1** *tr. V.* **(a)** (versprühen) spray; (verspritzen) splash; (in Form eines Strahls) spray, squirt ‹*water, foam, etc.*›; pipe ‹*cream etc.*›
(b) (bespritzen, besprühen) water ‹*lawn, tennis court*›; water, spray ‹*street, yard*›; spray ‹*plants, crops, etc.*›; (mit Lack) spray ‹*car etc.*›; **jmdn. nass ~:** splash sb.; (mit Wasserpistole, Schlauch) spray sb.
(c) (injizieren) inject ‹*drug etc.*›; (ugs.: einer Injektion unterziehen) **jmdn./sich ~:** give sb. an injection/inject oneself

··›

2 *itr. V.; mit Richtungsangabe mit sein* ‹*hot fat*› spit; ‹*mud etc.*› spatter, splash; ‹*blood, water*› spurt

Spritzer *der;* **~s, ~** (kleiner Tropfen) splash; (von Farbe) splash; spot

spritzig 1 *Adj.* **(a)** sparkling ‹*wine*›; tangy ‹*fragrance, perfume*›
(b) lively ‹*show, music, article*›; sparkling ‹*performance*›; racy ‹*style*›; nippy (coll.); zippy ‹*car, engine*›; agile ‹*person*›
2 *adv.* sparklingly ‹*produced, performed, etc.*›; racily ‹*written*›

Spritz·tour *die* (ugs.) spin

spröd, spröde *Adj.* **(a)** brittle ‹*glass, plastic, etc.*›; dry ‹*hair, lips, etc.*›; (rissig) chapped ‹*lips, skin*›; (rauh) rough ‹*skin*›
(b) (fig.: abweisend) aloof ‹*person, manner, nature*›

Sprödheit, Sprödigkeit *die;* **~ (a)** ▶ SPRÖDE A: brittleness; dryness; roughness
(b) (fig.: abweisendes Wesen) aloofness

spross, *sproß *1. u. 3. Pers. Sg. Prät. v.* SPRIESSEN

Spross, *Sproß *der;* **Sprosses, Sprosse** (Bot.) shoot

Sprosse *die;* **~, ~n (a)** (auch fig.) rung
(b) (eines Fensters) glazing bar

Sprössling, *Sprößling *der;* **~s, ~e** (ugs. scherzh.) offspring; **seine ~e** his offspring *pl.*

Sprotte *die;* **~, ~n** sprat

Spruch *der;* **~[e]s, Sprüche** (Wahlspruch) motto; (Sinnspruch) maxim; (Ausspruch) saying; aphorism; (Zitat) quotation

spruch·reif *Adj.* **das ist noch nicht ~:** that's not definite, so people mustn't start talking about it yet

Sprudel *der;* **~s, ~ (a)** sparkling mineral water
(b) (österr.) fizzy drink

sprudeln *itr. V.; mit sein* bubble; ‹*lemonade, champagne, etc.*› fizz, effervesce

Sprudel·wasser *das* sparkling mineral water

Sprüh·dose *die* aerosol [can]

sprühen 1 *tr. V.* spray
2 *itr. V.; mit Richtungsangabe mit sein* ‹*sparks, spray*› fly; (fig.) ‹*eyes*› sparkle (**vor** + *Dat.* with); ‹*intellect, wit*› sparkle

Sprüh·regen *der* drizzle; fine rain

Sprung *der;* **~[e]s, Sprünge (a)** (auch Sport) jump; (schwungvoll) leap; (Satz) bound; (fig.) leap; **keine großen Sprünge machen können** (fig. ugs.) not be able to afford many luxuries; **auf dem ~[e] sein** (fig. ugs.) be in a rush
(b) (ugs.: kurze Entfernung) stone's throw
(c) (Riss) crack

Sprung·brett *das* (auch fig.) springboard

sprunghaft 1 *Adj.* **(a)** erratic ‹*person, character, manner*›; disjointed ‹*conversation, thoughts*›
(b) (unvermittelt) sudden
(c) (ruckartig) rapid ‹*change*›; sharp ‹*increase*›
2 *adv.* ▶ 1B–C: disjointedly; suddenly; rapidly; sharply

Sprunghaftigkeit *die;* **~:** ▶ SPRUNGHAFT 1A: erraticness; disjointedness

Sprung·tuch *das; Pl.* **Sprungtücher** safety blanket

Spucke *die;* **~:** spit

spucken 1 *itr. V.* spit; **in die Hände ~** (fig.: an die Arbeit gehen) go to work with a will
2 *tr. V.* spit; cough up ‹*blood, phlegm*›

Spuk *der;* **~[e]s, ~e** [ghostly *or* supernatural] manifestation

spuken *itr. V.; unpers.* **hier/in dem Haus spukt es** this place/the house is haunted

Spül·bürste *die* washing-up brush

Spule *die;* **~, ~n** spool; (für Tonband, Film) spool; reel

Spüle *die;* **~, ~n** sink unit; (Becken) sink

spulen *tr., itr. V.* spool; (am Tonbandgerät) wind

spülen 1 *tr. V.* **(a)** rinse; bathe ‹*wound*›
(b) (landsch.: abwaschen) wash up ‹*dishes, glasses, etc.*›; **Geschirr ~:** wash up
2 *itr. V.* **(a)** (beim WC) flush [the toilet]
(b) (den Mund ausspülen) rinse out [one's mouth]
(c) (landsch.) ▶ ABWASCHEN 2

Spül-: ~maschine *die* dishwasher; **~mittel** *das* washing-up liquid; **~tuch** *das; Pl.* **~tücher** dish cloth; **~wasser** *das* **(a)** rinse water; **(b)** (Abwaschwasser) dishwater

Spund *der;* **~[e]s, ~e/Spünde (a)** *Pl.* **Spünde** (Zapfen) bung
(b) *Pl.* **~e** (ugs.) **[junger** *od.* **grüner] ~** young greenhorn *or* tiro

Spur *die;* **~, ~en (a)** (Abdruck im Boden) track; (Folge von Abdrücken) tracks *pl.;* **eine heiße ~** (fig.) a hot trail; **jmdm./einer Sache auf der ~ sein** be on to the track *or* trail of sb./sth.
(b) (Anzeichen) trace; (eines Verbrechens) clue (*Gen.* to)
(c) (sehr kleine Menge; auch fig.) trace
(d) (Verkehrsw.: Fahrspur) lane; **die ~ wechseln** change lanes

spürbar 1 *Adj.* noticeable; distinct, perceptible ‹*improvement*›; evident ‹*relief, embarrassment*›
2 *adv.* noticeably; perceptibly; (sichtlich) clearly ‹*relieved, on edge*›

spüren *tr. V.* feel; (instinktiv) sense

spur·los 1 *Adj.* total, complete ‹*disappearance*›
2 *adv.* ‹*disappear*› completely *or* without trace

Spür·sinn *der* (feiner Instinkt) intuition

Spurt *der;* **~[e]s, ~s** *od.* **~e** spurt

spurten *itr. V.* **(a)** *mit Richtungsangabe mit sein* spurt
(b) *mit sein* (ugs.: schnell laufen) sprint

sputen *refl. V.* (veralt.) make haste

*alte Schreibung - vgl. Hinweis auf S. xiv

St. *Abk.* **(a)** = **Sankt** St.
(b) = **Stück**

Staat *der;* **~[e]s, ~en** state

staatlich 1 *Adj.* state *attrib.;* ‹*power, unity, etc.*› of the state; state-owned ‹*factory etc.*›
2 *adv.* by the state; **~ anerkannt/geprüft** state-approved/-certified

staats-, Staats-: ~angehörige *der/die* national; **~angehörigkeit** *die* nationality; **~anwalt** *der,* **~anwältin** *die* public prosecutor; **~bürger** *der,* **~bürgerin** *die* citizen; **er ist deutscher ~bürger** he is a German citizen *or* national; **~bürgerlich** *Adj.* civil ‹*rights*›; civic ‹*duties, loyalty*›; ‹*education, attitude*› as a citizen; **~bürgerschaft** *die* ▶ ~ANGEHÖRIGKEIT; **~gewalt** *die* authority of the state; (Exekutive) executive power; **~grenze** *die* state frontier *or* border; **~mann** *der; Pl.* **-männer** statesman; **~oberhaupt** *das* head of state; **~präsident** *der,* **~präsidentin** *die* [state] president; **~sicherheit** *die* **(a)** state security; **(b)** (DDR ugs.) ▶ ~SICHERHEITSDIENST; **~sicherheits·dienst** *der* (DDR) State Security Service

Stab *der;* **~[e]s, Stäbe (a)** rod; (länger) pole; (eines Käfigs, Gitters, Geländers) bar
(b) (Milit.) staff
(c) (Team) team

Stäbchen *das;* **~s, ~(a)** (kleiner Stab) little rod; [small] stick
(b) (Essstäbchen) chopstick

stabil 1 *Adj.* sturdy ‹*chair, cupboard*›; robust, sound ‹*health*›; stable ‹*prices, government, economy, etc.*›
2 *adv.* **~ gebaut** solidly built

stabilisieren 1 *tr. V.* stabilize
2 *refl. V.* **(a)** stabilize
(b) ‹*health, circulation, etc.*› become stronger

Stabilität *die;* **~ (a)** (einer Konstruktion) sturdiness; (von Gesundheit, Konstitution usw.) robustness; soundness
(b) (das Beständigsein) stability

Stab·lampe *die* torch (Brit.); flashlight (Amer.)

Stabs·arzt *der,* **Stabs·ärztin** *die* (Milit.) medical officer, MO (*with the rank of captain*)

stach *1. u. 3. Pers. Sg. Prät. v.* STECHEN

Stachel *der;* **~s, ~n (a)** spine; (Dorn) thorn
(b) (Giftstachel) sting
(c) (Spitze) spike; (an Stacheldraht) barb

Stachel-: ~beere *die* gooseberry; **~draht** *der* barbed wire

stachelig *Adj.* prickly

Stadion *das;* **~s, Stadien** stadium

Stadium *das;* **~s, Stadien** stage

Stadt *die;* **~, Städte (a)** town; (Großstadt) city; **die ~ Basel** the city of Basel; **in die ~ gehen** go into town; go downtown (Amer.)
(b) (Verwaltung) town council; (in der Großstadt) city council; city hall *no art.* (Amer.)

Stadt-: ~bahn *die* urban railway; **~bummel** *der* (ugs.) **einen ~bummel machen** take a stroll through the town/city centre

Städter *der;* **~s, ~, Städterin** *die;* **~, ~nen (a)** town-dweller; (Großstädter, -städterin) city-dweller
(b) (Stadtmensch) townie (coll.)

Städte·tour *die* city tour

Stadt-: ~führer *der* town/city guidebook; **~führung** *die* guided tour of the town/city; **~gespräch** *das.* **~gespräch sein** be the talk of the town

städtisch 1 *Adj.* **(a)** (kommunal) municipal
(b) (urban) urban ‹*life, way of life, etc.*›
2 *adv.* (kommunal) municipally

Stadt-: ~mauer *die* town/city wall; **~mitte** *die* town centre; (einer Großstadt) city centre; downtown area (Amer.); **~park** *der* municipal park; **~plan** *der* [town/city] street plan *or* map; **~rand** *der* outskirts *pl.* of the town/city; **am ~rand** on the outskirts of the town/city; **~rundfahrt** *die* sightseeing tour round a/the town/city; **~teil** *der* district; part [of a/the town]; **~tor** *das* town/city gate; **~viertel** *das* district

Staffel *die;* **~, ~n (a)** (Sport: Mannschaft) relay team
(b) (Sport: Staffellauf) relay race
(c) (Luftwaffe: Einheit) flight
(d) (Eskorte) escort formation

Staffelei *die;* **~, ~en** easel

staffeln *tr. V.* **(a)** (aufstellen, formieren) arrange in a stagger *or* in an echelon
(b) (einteilen, abstufen) grade ‹*salaries, fees, prices*›; stagger ‹*times, arrivals, starting places*›

stahl *1. u. 3. Pers. Sg. Prät. v.* STEHLEN

Stahl *der;* **~[e]s, Stähle** *od.* **~e** steel

Stahl-: ~beton *der* reinforced concrete; **~blech** *das* sheet steel

stählern *Adj.* steel

stak *1. u. 3. Pers. Sg. Prät. v.* STECKEN

Stall *der;* **~[e]s, Ställe** (Pferde-, Rennstall) stable; (Kuhstall) cowshed; (Hühnerstall) [chicken] coop; (Schweinestall) [pig]sty; (für Kaninchen, Kleintiere) hutch; (für Schafe) pen

Stallung *die;* **~, ~en** (Pferdestall) stable; (Kuhstall) cowshed; (Schweinestall) [pig]sty

Stamm *der;* **~[e]s, Stämme (a)** (Baumstamm) trunk
(b) (Volksstamm) tribe

Stamm-: ~aktie *die* (Wirtsch.) ordinary share; **~baum** *der* family tree; (eines Tieres) pedigree

stammeln *tr., itr. V.* stammer

S

stammen *itr. V.* come (**aus, von** from); (datieren) date (**aus, von** from)

Stamm-: **~gast** *der* (im Lokal/Hotel) regular customer/visitor; regular (coll.); **~tisch** *der* **(a)** (Tisch) regulars' table (coll.); **(b)** (Runde) group of regulars (coll.); **(c)** (Treffen) get-together with the regulars (coll.)

stampfen 1 *itr. V.* **(a)** (laut auftreten) stamp **(b)** *mit sein* (sich fortbewegen) tramp; (mit schweren Schritten) trudge
2 *tr. V.* **(a)** **mit den Füßen den Rhythmus ~:** tap the rhythm with one's feet
(b) (feststampfen) compress
(c) (zerkleinern) mash ‹*potatoes*›

stand *1. u. 3. Pers. Sg. Prät. v.* STEHEN

Stand *der;* **~[e]s, Stände (a)** (das Stehen) standing position; **[bei jmdm.** *od.* **gegen jmdn.] einen schweren ~ haben** (fig.) have a tough time [of it] [with sb.]
(b) (Standort) position
(c) (Verkaufsstand; Box für ein Pferd) stall; (Messestand, Informationsstand) stand; (Zeitungsstand) [newspaper] kiosk
(d) (erreichte Stufe; Zustand) state; **etw. auf den neu[e]sten ~ bringen** bring sth. up to date; **außer ~[e]** ▶ AUSSERSTANDE; **im ~[e]** ▶ IMSTANDE;
(e) (des Wassers, Flusses) level; (des Thermometers, Zählers, Barometers) reading; (der Kasse, Finanzen) state; (eines Himmelskörpers) position
(f) (Familienstand) status
(g) (Gesellschaftsschicht) class; (Berufsstand) trade; (Ärzte, Rechtsanwälte) [professional] group

Standard *der;* **~s, ~s** standard

standardisieren *tr. V.* standardize

Standardisierung *die;* **~, ~en** standardization

Ständchen *das;* **~s, ~:** serenade; **jmdm. ein ~ bringen** serenade sb.

Ständer *der;* **~s, ~:** stand; (Kleider~) coat stand; (Wäsche~) clothes horse

standes-, Standes-: **~amt** *das* registry office; **~amtlich** 1 *Adj.* registry office ‹*wedding, document*›; 2 *adv.* **~amtlich heiraten** get married in a registry office; **~beamte** *der,* **~beamtin** *die* registrar

stand-, Stand-: **~fest** *Adj.* steady; stable; strong ‹*stalk, stem*›; **~haft** 1 *Adj.* steadfast; 2 *adv.* steadfastly; **~haftigkeit** *die;* **~~:** steadfastness; **~|halten** *unr. itr. V.* stand firm; **einer Sache** (*Dat.*) **~halten** withstand sth.

ständig 1 *Adj.* constant ‹*noise, worry, pressure, etc.*›; permanent ‹*residence, correspondent, staff, member, etc.*›; standing ‹*committee*›; regular ‹*income*›
2 *adv.* constantly

Stand-: **~licht** *das* (Kfz-W.) sidelights *pl.;* **~ort** *der* **(a)** position; (eines Betriebes usw.) location; site; **(b)** (Milit.: Garnison) garrison; base; **~punkt** *der* (fig.) point of view; viewpoint; **auf dem ~punkt stehen, dass ...:** take the view that ...; **~spur** *die* (Verkehrsw.) hard shoulder; **~uhr** *die* grandfather clock

Stange *die;* **~, ~n** pole; (aus Metall) bar; (dünner) rod; (Kleiderstange) rail; (Vogelstange) perch; **ein Anzug von der ~** (ugs.) an off-the-peg-suit

Stängel *der;* **~s, ~:** stem; stalk

Stangen-: **~brot** *das* French bread; **~spargel** *der* asparagus spears *pl.*

stank *1. u. 3. Pers. Sg. Prät. v.* STINKEN

Stapel *der;* **~s, ~:** pile; **ein ~ Holz** a pile *or* stack of wood

stapeln 1 *tr. V.* pile up; stack
2 *refl. V.* pile up

stapfen *itr. V.; mit sein* tramp

Star[1] *der;* **~[e]s, ~e** *od.* (schweiz.) **~en** (Vogel) starling

Star[2] *der;* **~s, ~s** (berühmte Persönlichkeit) star

Star[3] *der;* **~[e]s** (Med.) **grauer ~:** cataract; **grüner ~:** glaucoma

starb *1. u. 3. Pers. Sg. Prät. v.* STERBEN

stark; **stärker, stärkst...** 1 *Adj.* **(a)** strong; potent ‹*drink, medicine, etc.*›; powerful ‹*engine, lens, voice, etc.*›; (ausgezeichnet) excellent; *s. auch* STÜCK C;
(b) (dick) thick; stout ‹*rope, string*›; (verhüll.: korpulent) well-built (euphem.)
(c) (zahlenmäßig groß, umfangreich) sizeable, large; big ‹*demand*›; **eine 100 Mann ~e Truppe** a 100-strong unit
(d) (heftig, intensiv) heavy; severe ‹*frost, pain*›; strong ‹*impression, current, resistance, dislike*›; grave ‹*doubt, reservations*›; great ‹*exaggeration, interest*›; loud ‹*applause*›
(e) (Jugendspr.: großartig) great (coll.); fantastic (coll.)
2 *adv.* **(a)** (sehr, überaus, intensiv) (mit Adj.) very; heavily ‹*indebted, stressed*›; greatly ‹*increased, reduced, enlarged*›; strongly ‹*emphasized, characterized*›; badly ‹*damaged, worn, affected*›; (mit Verb) heavily; ‹*exaggerate, impress*› greatly; ‹*enlarge, reduce, increase*› considerably; ‹*support, oppose, suspect*› strongly; ‹*remind*› very much; **~ erkältet sein** have a heavy *or* bad cold
(b) (Jugendspr.: großartig) fantastically (coll.)

Stark·bier *das* strong beer

Stärke *die;* **~, ~n (a)** strength; (eines Motors) power; (einer Glühbirne) wattage
(b) (Dicke) thickness; (Technik) gauge
(c) (zahlenmäßige Größe) strength
(d) (besondere Fähigkeit, Vorteil) strength; **jmds. ~/nicht jmds. ~ sein** be sb.'s forte/not be sb.'s strong point
(e) (Intensität) strength; (von Sturm, Schmerzen, Abneigung) intensity; (von Frost) severity; (von Lärm, Verkehr) volume
(f) (organischer Stoff) starch

stärken 1 *tr. V.* **(a)** strengthen; boost ‹*power, prestige*›; ‹*drink, food, etc.*› fortify ‹*person*›
(b) (steif machen) starch ‹*washing etc.*›

*old spelling - see note on page xiv

2 *refl. V.* refresh oneself
Stärkung *die;* ~, **~en (a)** strengthening **(b)** (Erfrischung) refreshment
starr 1 *Adj.* **(a)** rigid; (steif) stiff (**vor** + *Dat.* with); fixed ‹*expression, smile, stare*› **(b)** (nicht abwandelbar) inflexible, rigid ‹*law, rule, principle*› **(c)** (unnachgiebig) inflexible ‹*person, attitude, etc.*›
2 *adv.* rigidly; (steif) stiffly
starren *itr. V.* **(a)** stare (**in** + *Akk.* into, **auf, an, gegen** + *Akk.* at); **jmdm. ins Gesicht ~:** stare sb. in the face **(b) vor/von Schmutz ~:** be filthy
starr-, Starr-: ~sinn *der* pigheadedness; **~sinnig** *Adj.* pigheaded; **~sinnigkeit** *die* pigheadedness
Start *der;* **~[e]s, ~s** start; (eines Flugzeugs) take-off; (einer Rakete) launch
Start·bahn *die* [take-off] runway
start·bereit *Adj.* ready to start *postpos.;* ‹*aircraft*› ready for take-off
starten 1 *itr. V.; mit sein* **(a)** start; ‹*aircraft*› take off; ‹*rocket*› blast off, be launched **(b)** (den Motor anlassen) start the engine
2 *tr. V.* start; launch ‹*rocket, satellite, attack*›; start [up] ‹*engine, machine, car*›
Stasi *die;* ~: *Abk.* (DDR ugs.) **Staatssicherheit**
Stasi·akte *die* Stasi file
Station *die;* ~, **~en (a)** station **(b)** (Haltestelle) stop **(c)** (Zwischenhalt, Aufenthalt) stopover; **~ machen** stop over *or* off **(d)** (im Krankenhaus) ward
stationär 1 *Adj.* (Med.) ‹*treatment*› in hospital, as an inpatient
2 *adv.* (Med.) in hospital; **jmdn. ~ behandeln** treat sb. as an inpatient
stationieren *tr. V.* station ‹*troops*›; deploy ‹*weapons, bombers, etc.*›
Stationierung *die;* ~, **~en** stationing; (von Waffen, Raketen usw.) deployment
Stations-: ~arzt *der,* **~ärztin** *die* ward doctor; **~schwester** *die* ward sister; **~taste** *die* (Rundf.) preset [tuning] button; preset
statisch *Adj.* static
Statistik *die;* ~: statistics *sing., no art.*
statistisch 1 *Adj.* statistical
2 *adv.* statistically
statt 1 *Präp. mit Gen.* instead of; *s. auch* STATTDESSEN;
2 *Konj.* ▶ ANSTATT
statt·dessen *Adv.* instead [of this]
statt|finden *unr. itr. V.* take place; ‹*process, development*› occur
statthaft *Adj.* permissible
stattlich 1 *Adj.* **(a)** well-built; imposing ‹*figure, stature, building, etc.*›; fine ‹*farm, estate*›; impressive ‹*trousseau, collection*› **(b)** (beträchtlich) considerable
2 *adv.* impressively
Statue *die;* ~, **~n** statue
Statur *die;* ~, **~en** build
Status *der;* ~, ~ /ˈʃtaːtuːs/ status
Status quo *der;* ~ (geh.) status quo
Statut *das;* **~[e]s, ~en** statute
Stau *der;* **~[e]s, ~s** *od.* **~e (a)** build-up **(b)** (von Fahrzeugen) tailback (Brit.); backup (Amer.)
Staub *der;* **~[e]s** dust; **~ wischen** dust; **~ saugen** vacuum; *or* (Brit. coll.) hoover; **sich aus dem ~[e] machen** (fig. ugs.) make oneself scarce (coll.)
stauben *itr. V.* cause dust
staubig *Adj.* dusty
staub-, Staub-: ~saugen *itr., tr. V.* **ich staubsauge, staubgesaugt, staubzusaugen** vacuum; (Brit. coll.) hoover; **~sauger** *der* vacuum cleaner; Hoover (*Brit.* ®); **~tuch** *das; Pl.* **~tücher** duster
Stau·damm *der* dam
Staude *die;* ~, **~n** (Bot.) herbaceous perennial
stauen 1 *tr. V.* dam [up] ‹*stream, river*›; staunch ‹*blood*›
2 *refl. V.* ‹*water, blood, etc.*› accumulate, build up; ‹*people*› form a crowd; ‹*traffic*› form a tailback/tailbacks (Brit.) *or* (Amer.) backup/backups
staunen *itr. V.* be amazed *or* astonished (**über** + *Akk.* at); (beeindruckt sein) marvel (**über** + *Akk.* at); **~d** with *or* in amazement
Staunen *das;* **~s** amazement (**über** + *Akk.* at); (Bewunderung) wonderment
Stau-: ~see *der* reservoir; **~stufe** *die* barrage
Stauung *die;* ~, **~en (a)** (eines Bachs, Flusses) damming; (des Blutes, Wassers) stemming the flow; (das Sichstauen) build-up **(b)** (Verkehrsstau) tailback (Brit.); backup (Amer.); jam
Std. *Abk.* = **Stunde** hr.
Steak /steːk/ *das;* **~s, ~s** steak
stechen 1 *unr. itr. V.* **(a)** prick; ‹*wasp, bee*› sting; ‹*mosquito*› bite **(b)** (hineinstechen) **mit etw. in etw.** (*Akk.*) **~:** stick *or* jab sth. into sth.
2 *unr. tr. V.* (mit dem Messer, Schwert) stab; (mit der Nadel, mit einem Dorn usw.) prick; ‹*bee, wasp*› sting; ‹*mosquito*› bite; **sich in den Finger ~:** prick one's finger
stechend *Adj.* penetrating, pungent ‹*smell*›; penetrating ‹*glance, eyes*›
Stech-: ~mücke *die* mosquito; gnat; **~uhr** *die* time clock
Steck-: ~brief *der* description [of a/the wanted person]; (Plakat) 'wanted' poster; **~dose** *die* socket; power point
stecken 1 *tr. V.* **(a)** put **(b)** (mit Nadeln) pin ‹*hem, lining, etc.*›; pin [on] ‹*badge*›; pin up ‹*hair*›
2 *itr. V.* be; **~ bleiben** get stuck; **den Schlüssel [im Schloss] ~ lassen** leave the ···>

key in the lock; **wo steckt meine Brille?** (ugs.) where have my glasses got to *or* gone?; **hinter etw.** (*Dat.*) ~ (fig. ugs.) be behind sth.

stecken-, Stecken-: *~|bleiben ▶ STECKEN 2; ***~|lassen** ▶ STECKEN 2; **~pferd** *das* **(a)** (Spielzeug) hobby horse; **(b)** (Liebhaberei) hobby

Stecker *der;* **~s, ~**: plug

Steck·nadel *die* pin

Steg *der;* **~[e]s, ~e** (Brücke) [narrow] bridge; (Laufbrett) gangplank; (Boots~) landing stage

Steg·reif *der:* **aus dem ~**: impromptu

Steh·auf·männchen *das* tumbling figure; tumbler

stehen *unr. itr. V.; südd., österr., schweiz. mit sein* **(a)** stand
(b) (sich befinden) be; ‹*upright object, building*› stand
(c) (einen bestimmten Stand haben) **auf etw.** (*Dat.*) ~ ‹*needle, hand*› point to sth.; **das Barometer steht tief/auf Regen** the barometer is reading low/indicating rain; **das Spiel/es steht 1:1** (Sport) the score is one all; **die Sache steht gut/schlecht** things are going well/badly
(d) (einen bestimmten Kurs, Wert haben) ‹*currency*› stand (**bei** at); **wie steht das Pfund?** what is the rate for the pound?
(e) (nicht in Bewegung sein) be stationary; ‹*machine etc.*› be at a standstill; **meine Uhr steht** my watch has stopped; **~ bleiben** (anhalten) stop; ‹*traffic*› come to a standstill; (stehen gelassen werden) stay; be left; (zurückgelassen werden) be left behind; (der Zerstörung entgehen) ‹*building*› be left standing; **etw. ~ lassen** (nicht entfernen) leave sth.; (vergessen) leave sth. [behind]
(f) (geschrieben, gedruckt sein) be; **in der Zeitung steht, dass ...**: it says in the paper that ...
(g) (Sprachw.: gebraucht werden) ‹*subjunctive etc.*› occur; be found
(h) **jmdm. [gut] ~** ‹*dress etc.*› suit sb. [well]
(i) **auf etw.** (*Akk.*) ~ (ugs., bes. Jugendspr.: mögen) be into sth. (coll.); **sie steht total auf ihn** she's nuts about him

***stehen|bleiben**, ***stehen|lassen** ▶ STEHEN E

Steh·lampe *die* standard lamp (Brit.); floor lamp (Amer.)

stehlen *unr. tr., itr. V.* steal; *s. auch* GESTOHLEN 2

Steh·platz *der* (im Theater usw.) standing place; (im Bus) space to stand

Steiermark *die;* **~**: Styria *no art.*

steif [1] *Adj.* **(a)** stiff; (ugs.: erigiert) erect ‹*penis*›
(b) (Seemannsspr.: stark) stiff ‹*wind, breeze*›
(c) (förmlich) stiff; formal
[2] *adv.* stiffly

Steifheit *die;* **(a)** ~ stiffness
(b) (Förmlichkeit) formality; stiffness

steigen [1] *unr. itr. V.; mit sein* **(a)** climb; ‹*mist, smoke, sun*› rise; ‹*balloon*› climb, rise; **auf die Leiter ~**: get on to the ladder; **in den/aus dem Bus/Zug ~**: board *or* get on/get off *or* out of the bus/train
(b) (ansteigen, zunehmen) rise; ‹*price, cost, salary, output*› increase, rise; ‹*debts, tension*› increase, mount; ‹*chances*› improve
[2] *unr. tr. V.; mit sein* climb ‹*stairs, steps*›

Steiger *der;* **~s, ~** (Bergbau) overman

steigern [1] *tr. V.* **(a)** increase ‹*speed, value, sales, consumption, etc.*› (**auf** + *Akk.* to); step up ‹*demands, production, etc.*›; raise ‹*standards, requirements*›; (verstärken) intensify ‹*fear, tension*›; heighten ‹*effect*›
(b) (Sprachw.) compare ‹*adjective*›
[2] *refl. V.* ‹*confusion, speed, profit, etc.*› increase; ‹*pain, excitement, tension, etc.*› become more intense; ‹*costs*› escalate; ‹*effect*› be heightened

Steigerung *die;* **~, ~en** **(a)** increase (*Gen.* in); (Verstärkung) intensification; (einer Wirkung) heightening; (Verbesserung) improvement (*Gen.* in); (bes. Sport: Leistungssteigerung) improvement [in performance]
(b) (Sprachw.) comparison

Steigung *die;* **~, ~en** gradient

steil [1] *Adj.* steep; meteoric ‹*career*›; rapid ‹*rise*›
[2] *adv.* steeply

Steil-: ~hang *der* steep escarpment; **~küste** *die* (Geogr.) cliffs *pl.*

Stein *der;* **~[e]s, ~e** stone; (Fels) rock; (Baustein) [stone]block; **mir fällt ein ~ vom Herzen** that's a weight off my mind

Stein-: ~bock *der* **(a)** ibex; **(b)** (Astrol.) Capricorn; the Goat; **~bruch** *der* quarry

steinern *Adj.* stone

Stein·gut *das* earthenware

stein·hart *Adj.* rock-hard

steinig *Adj.* stony

steinigen *tr. V.* stone ‹*person*›

Stein-: ~kohle *die* [hard] coal; **~metz** *der;* **~~en, ~~en**, **~metzin** *die;* **~~, ~~nen** stonemason; **~obst** *das* stone fruit; **~pilz** *der* cep; **~schlag** *der* rock fall; **„Achtung ~schlag"** 'beware falling rocks'; **~zeit** *die* Stone Age; (fig.) stone age

Steiß·bein *das* (Anat.) coccyx

Stelle *die;* **~, ~n** **(a)** place; **an jmds. ~ treten** take sb.'s place; **ich an deiner ~ ...**: ... if I were you; **an achter ~ liegen** be in eighth place; **die erste ~ hinter** *od.* **nach dem Komma** (Math.) the first decimal place; **an ~** (+ *Gen.*) instead of; **auf der ~**: immediately
(b) (begrenzter Bereich) patch; (am Körper) spot
(c) (Passage) passage; (Punkt im Ablauf einer Rede usw.) point
(d) (Arbeitsstelle) job; post; **eine freie ~**: a vacancy
(e) (Dienststelle) office; (Behörde) authority

stellen [1] *tr. V.* **(a)** put; (mit Sorgfalt) place; (aufrecht hin~) stand
(b) (ein~) set ‹*points, clock, scales*›; **den**

*alte Schreibung - vgl. Hinweis auf S. xiv

Wecker auf 6 Uhr ~: set the alarm for 6 o'clock; **die Heizung höher/niedriger ~**: turn the heating up/down
(c) (bereitstellen) provide
(d) jmdn. besser ~: ‹*firm*› improve sb.'s pay; **gut/schlecht/besser gestellt** comfortably/badly/better off
(e) *verblasst* put ‹*question*›; set ‹*task, topic, condition*›; make ‹*application, demand, request*›; **jmdm. eine Frage ~**: ask sb. a question
[2] *refl. V.* **(a)** place oneself; **sich auf die Zehenspitzen ~**: stand on tiptoe
(b) sich schlafend/taub/tot *usw.* **~**: feign sleep/deafness/death *etc.*; pretend to be asleep/deaf/dead *etc.*

stellen-, Stellen-: ~angebot *das* offer of a job; (Inserat) job advertisement; **„~angebote"** 'situations vacant'; **~anzeige** *die* job advertisement; **~gesuch** *das* 'situation wanted' advertisement; **~markt** *der* job market; **~profil** *das* job profile; **~suche** *die* job-hunting *no art.*; search for a job; **~weise** *Adv.* in places; **~wert** *der* **(a)** (Math.) place value; **(b)** (fig.: Bedeutung) standing; status

Stellung *die;* **~, ~en** position; **zu etw. ~ nehmen** express one's opinion on sth.

Stellungnahme *die;* **~, ~n** opinion; (kurze Äußerung) statement

stell-, Stell-: ~vertretend [1] *Adj.* acting; (von Amts wegen) deputy ‹*minister, director, etc.*›; [2] *adv.* as a deputy; **~vertreter** *der,* **~vertreterin** *die* deputy

Stelze *die;* **~, ~n** stilt

stelzen *itr. V.; mit sein* strut; stalk

stemmen [1] *tr. V.* **(a)** (hochstemmen) lift [above one's head]
(b) (drücken) brace ‹*feet, knees*› **(gegen** against)
[2] *refl. V.* **sich gegen etw. ~**: brace oneself against sth.

Stempel *der;* **~s, ~**: stamp; (Poststempel) postmark

stempeln *tr. V.* stamp ‹*passport, form*›; postmark ‹*letter*›; cancel ‹*postage stamp*›

***Stengel** ▶ STÄNGEL

steno-, Steno-: ~gramm *das* shorthand text; **~graph** *der;* **~~en, ~~en** stenographer; **~graphie** *die;* **~~, ~~n** stenography *no art.*; shorthand *no art.*; **~graphieren** *itr. V.* do shorthand; **~graphin** *die;* **~~, ~~nen** stenographer; **~typistin** *die;* **~~, ~~nen** shorthand typist

Stepp·decke *die* quilt

Steppe *die;* **~, ~n** steppe

steppen¹ *tr. (auch itr.) V.* backstitch

steppen² *itr. V.* (tanzen) tap dance

Steppke *der;* **~s, ~s** (ugs., bes. berlin.) lad; nipper (coll.)

sterben *unr. itr. V.; mit sein* die; **im Sterben liegen** lie dying

sterbens·krank *Adj.* mortally ill

sterblich *Adj.* mortal

Sterbliche *der/die; adj. Dekl.* mortal; **ein gewöhnlicher ~r** an ordinary mortal *or* person

Sterblichkeit *die;* **~**: mortality

stereo *Adv.* in stereo

Stereo *das;* **~s** stereo

Stereo-: ~anlage *die* stereo [system]; **~aufnahme** *die* stereo recording

steril *Adj.* sterile

Sterling /'stɛːlɪŋ/: **Pfund ~**: pound/pounds sterling

Stern *der;* **~[e]s, ~e** star

Sternchen *das;* **~s, ~** (Druckw.) asterisk

Stern·schnuppe *die;* **~, ~n** shooting star

Stethoskop *das;* **~s, ~e** (Med.) stethoscope

Steuer¹ *das;* **~s, ~**: [steering] wheel; (von Schiffen) helm

Steuer² *die;* **~, ~n** tax

steuer-, Steuer-: ~belastung *die* tax burden; **~berater** *der,* **~beraterin** *die* tax consultant *or* adviser; **~bord** *das od.* (österr.) *der* (Seew., Flugw.) starboard; **~erhöhung** *die* tax increase; **~erklärung** *die* tax return; **~ermäßigung** *die* tax relief; **~frau** *die* (Rudersport) cox; **~frei** *Adj.* tax-free

steuerlich [1] *Adj.* tax ‹*advantages, benefits, etc.*›
[2] *adv.* **~ absetzbar** tax-deductible

Steuer·mann *der; Pl.* **~leute** *od.* **~männer** (Rudersport) cox

steuern [1] *tr. V.* (fahren) steer; (fliegen) pilot, fly ‹*aircraft*›; fly ‹*course*›
[2] *itr. V.* **(a)** be at the wheel; (auf dem Schiff) be at the helm
(b) *mit sein* (Kurs nehmen, ugs.: sich hinbewegen; auch fig.) head

Steuer-: ~oase *die* (ugs.) tax haven; **~senkung** *die* (Steuerw.) tax cut; reduction in taxation

Steuerung *die;* **~, ~en (a)** (System) controls *pl.*;
(b) ▶ STEUERN 1: steering; piloting; flying

Steward /'stjuːɐt/ *der;* **~s, ~s** steward

Stewardess, *Stewardeß /'stjuːɐdɛs/ *die;* **~, Stewardessen** stewardess

stich *Imper. Sg. v.* STECHEN

Stich *der;* **~[e]s, ~e (a)** (mit einer Waffe) stab
(b) (mit einem Dorn, einer Nadel) prick; (von Wespe, Biene usw.) sting; (Mückenstich usw.) bite
(c) (Stichwunde) stab wound
(d) (beim Nähen) stitch
(e) (Schmerz) stabbing *or* shooting pain
(f) (Kartenspiel) trick

(g) **jmdn./etw. im ~ lassen** leave sb. in the lurch/abandon sth.

Stichelei *die; ~,* **~en** (ugs. abwertend) **(a)** (Bemerkung) dig; gibe
(b) hör auf mit deiner ~: stop getting at me/him *etc.* (coll.)

sticheln *itr. V.* make snide remarks (coll.) (**gegen** about)

stich-, Stich-: ~flamme *die* tongue of flame; **~haltig** *Adj.* sound ‹*argument, reason*›; valid ‹*assertion, reply*›; conclusive ‹*evidence*›; **~haltigkeit** *die;* **~~:** ▶ ~HALTIG: soundness; validity; conclusiveness

Stichling *der;* **~s, ~e** stickleback

Stich·probe *die* [random] sample; (bei Kontrollen) spot check

stichst *2. Pers. Sg. Präsens v.* STECHEN

sticht *3. Pers. Sg. Präsens v.* STECHEN

Stich-: ~tag *der* set date; deadline; **~wunde** *die* stab wound

sticken 1 *itr. V.* do embroidery
2 *tr. V.* embroider

Stickerei *die; ~,* **~en** embroidery *no pl.;* (gestickte Arbeit) piece of embroidery

Stick·garn *das* embroidery thread

stickig *Adj.* stuffy; stale ‹*air*›

Stick-: ~oxid, ~oxyd *das* nitrogen oxide; **~oxid·emission, ~oxyd·emission** *die* nitrogen oxide emission; **~stoff** *der* nitrogen; **~stoff·oxid, ~stoff·oxyd** *das* nitrogen oxide

Stief- step ‹*brother, child, mother, etc.*›

Stiefel *der;* **~s, ~** boot

stief-, Stief-: ~mutter *die; Pl.* **~mütter** stepmother; **~mütterchen** *das;* **~~s, ~~** (Bot.) pansy; **~mütterlich** 1 *Adj.* poor, shabby ‹*treatment*›; 2 *adv.* **~mütterlich behandeln** treat ‹*person*› poorly *or* shabbily; neglect ‹*pet, flowers, doll, problem*›; **~vater** *der* stepfather

stieg *1. u. 3. Pers. Sg. Prät. v.* STEIGEN

Stieglitz *der;* **~es, ~e** goldfinch

stiehl *Imp. Sg. v.* STEHLEN

stiehlst *2. Pers. Sg. Präsens v.* STEHLEN

stiehlt *3. Pers. Sg. Präsens v.* STEHLEN

Stiel *der;* **~[e]s, ~e** (Griff) handle; (Besenstiel) [broom]stick; (für Süßigkeiten) stick; (bei Gläsern) stem; (bei Blumen) stem; (an Obst usw.) stalk

Stier *der;* **~[e]s, ~e** bull; (Astrol.) Taurus; the Bull

stieren *itr. V.* stare [vacantly] (**auf** + *Akk.* at)

Stier·kampf *der* bullfight

stieß *1. u. 3. Pers. Sg. Prät. v.* STOßEN

Stift *der;* **~[e]s, ~e (a)** (aus Metall) pin; (aus Holz) peg
(b) (Bleistift) pencil; (Malstift) crayon; (Schreibstift) pen

*old spelling - see note on page xiv

stiften *tr. V.* **(a)** found, establish ‹*monastery, hospital, etc.*›; endow ‹*prize, scholarship*›; (als Spende) donate, give (**für** to)
(b) (herbeiführen) cause, create ‹*unrest, confusion, strife, etc.*›; bring about ‹*peace, order, etc.*›; arrange ‹*marriage*›

Stifter *der;* **~s, ~, Stifterin** *die;* **~, ~nen** founder; (Spender) donor

Stiftung *die;* **~, ~en** (Rechtsspr.) foundation; endowment

Stift·zahn *der* (Zahnmed.) post crown

stigmatisieren *tr. V.* stigmatize

Stil *der;* **~[e]s, ~e** style

Stil·bruch *der* inconsistency of style

stilistisch 1 *Adj.* stylistic
2 *adv.* stylistically

still 1 *Adj.* quiet; (ohne Geräusche) silent; still; (reglos) still; (wortlos) silent; (heimlich) secret; **der Stille Ozean** the Pacific [Ocean]
2 *adv.* quietly; (geräuschlos) silently; (wortlos) in silence

Stille *die;* **~:** quiet; (Geräuschlosigkeit) silence; stillness

***stillegen** ▶ STILLLEGEN

stillen 1 *tr. V.* **(a) ein Kind ~:** breastfeed a baby
(b) (befriedigen) satisfy; quench ‹*thirst*›
(c) (eindämmen) stop ‹*bleeding, tears, pain*›
2 *itr. V.* breastfeed

still-, Still-: ~|halten *unr. itr. V.* keep *or* stay still; **~|legen** *tr. V.* close *or* shut down; close ‹*railway line*›; **~schweigen** *das* silence; **~schweigen bewahren** maintain silence; keep silent; **~schweigend** 1 *Adj.* silent; (ohne Abmachung) tacit ‹*assumption, agreement*›; 2 *adv.* in silence; (ohne Abmachung) tacitly; **~|sitzen** *unr. itr. V.* sit still; **~stand** *der* standstill; **~|stehen** *unr. itr. V.* **(a)** ‹*factory, machine*› stand idle; ‹*traffic*› be at a standstill; ‹*heart etc.*› stop; **(b)** (Milit.) stand to attention

Stimm·bruch *der:* **er ist im ~:** his voice is breaking

Stimme *die;* **~, ~n (a)** voice
(b) (bei Wahlen) vote

stimmen 1 *itr. V.* **(a)** be right *or* correct; **stimmt es, dass ...?** is it true that ...?
(b) (seine Stimme geben) vote; **mit Ja ~:** vote yes *or* in favour
2 *tr. V.* **(a)** (in eine Stimmung versetzen) make
(b) (Musik) tune ‹*instrument*›

Stimm-: ~enthaltung *die* abstention; **~gabel** *die* (Musik) tuning fork

stimmig *Adj.* harmonious; **die Argumentation ist [in sich** (*Dat.*)**] ~:** the argument is consistent

Stimm-: ~lage *die* **(a)** voice; **(b)** (Musik) voice; register; **~recht** *das* right to vote

Stimmung *die;* **~, ~en (a)** mood
(b) (Atmosphäre) atmosphere

stimmungs·voll 1 *Adj.* atmospheric
2 *adv.* ‹*describe, light*› atmospherically; ‹*sing, recite*› with great feeling

Stimm·zettel *der* ballot paper
stimulieren *tr. V.* stimulate
Stink·bombe *die* stink bomb
stinken *unr. itr. V.* stink **(nach** of)
stink·faul *Adj.* (salopp abwertend) bone idle (coll.)
stinkig *Adj.* (salopp abwertend) stinking; smelly
stink-: ~normal (salopp) [1] *Adj.* dead (coll.) *or* boringly ordinary; [2] *adv.* in a dead ordinary way (coll.); **~reich** *Adj.* (salopp) stinking rich (coll.)
Stipendium *das;* **~s, Stipendien** (als Auszeichnung) scholarship; (als finanzielle Unterstützung) grant
stirb *Imp. Sg. v.* STERBEN
stirbst *2. Pers. Sg. Präsens v.* STERBEN
stirbt *3. Pers. Sg. Präsens v.* STERBEN
Stirn *die;* **~, ~en** forehead; brow
Stirn-: ~höhle *die* (Anat.) frontal sinus; **~runzeln** *das;* **~~s** frown; **~seite** *die* front [side]
stöbern *itr. V.* (ugs.) rummage
stochern *itr. V.* poke
Stock[1] *der;* **~[e]s, Stöcke (a)** stick; (Zeigestock) pointer; stick; (Taktstock) baton; (Skistock) pole; stick
(b) (Pflanze) (Rosenstock) [rose] bush; (Rebstock) vine
Stock[2] *der;* **~[e]s, ~** (Etage) floor; storey; **in welchem ~?** on which floor?
stock·dunkel *Adj.* (ugs.) pitch-dark
stocken *itr. V.* **(a)** ‹*traffic*› be held up; ‹*conversation, production*› stop; ‹*business*› slacken; ‹*journey*› be interrupted
(b) (innehalten) falter
stock·finster *Adj.* (ugs.) pitch-dark
Stöckel·schuhe *Pl.* high heels
-stöckig -storey *attr.;* -storeyed
stock·nüchtern *Adj.* (ugs.) stone-cold sober
Stockung *die;* **~, ~en** hold-up (*Gen.* in)
Stockwerk *das* floor; storey
Stoff *der;* **~[e]s, ~e (a)** material; fabric
(b) (Materie) substance
(c) (Philos.) matter
(d) (Thema) subject [matter]; (Gesprächsthema) topic
(e) (salopp: Rauschgift) stuff (sl.); dope (sl.)
stofflich *Adj.* material
Stofflichkeit *die;* **~:** materiality
Stoff·wechsel *der* metabolism
stöhnen *itr. V.* moan; (vor Schmerz) groan
Stola *die;* **~, Stolen** shawl; (Pelzstola) stole
Stollen *der;* **~s, ~ (a)** (Kuchen) Stollen
(b) (Bergbau) gallery
(c) (bei Sportschuhen) stud
stolpern *itr. V.; mit sein* stumble; trip
stolz [1] *Adj.* proud **(auf +** *Akk.* of); **eine ~e Summe** (ugs.) a tidy sum
[2] *adv.* proudly
Stolz *der;* **~es** pride **(auf +** *Akk.* in)
stolzieren *itr. V.; mit sein* strut
stop /stɔp/ *Interj.* stop; (Verkehrsw.) halt
stopfen *tr. V.* **(a)** darn
(b) (hineintun) stuff
(c) (füllen) stuff ‹*cushion, quilt, etc.*›; fill ‹*pipe*›; plug, stop [up] ‹*hole, leak*›
Stopf-: ~garn *das* darning cotton; **~nadel** *die* darning needle
Stopp *der;* **~s, ~s** stop; (Einstellung) freeze (*Gen.* on)
Stoppel *die;* **~, ~n** stubble *no pl.*
stoppelig *Adj.* stubbly
stoppen *tr., itr. V.* stop
Stopp-: ~licht *das* stop light; **~schild** *das* stop sign; **~uhr** *die* stopwatch
Stöpsel *der;* **~s, ~:** plug
Stör *der;* **~s, ~e** sturgeon
Storch *der;* **~[e]s, Störche** stork
stören [1] *tr. V.* **(a)** disturb; disrupt ‹*court proceedings, lecture, church service, etc.*›; interfere with ‹*transmitter, reception*›
(b) (missfallen) bother
[2] *itr. V.* **(a)** disturb
(b) (Unruhe stiften) make *or* cause trouble
[3] *refl. V.* **sich an jmdm./etw. ~:** take exception to sb./sth.
Störenfried *der;* **~[e]s, ~e** troublemaker
Stör·fall *der* (Technik) fault
störrisch [1] *Adj.* stubborn
[2] *adv.* stubbornly
Störung *die;* **~, ~en (a)** disturbance; (einer Gerichtsverhandlung, Vorlesung, eines Gottesdienstes usw.) disruption; **bitte entschuldigen Sie die ~, aber ...:** I'm sorry to bother you, but ...
(b) eine technische ~: a technical fault
Stoß *der;* **~es, Stöße (a)** (mit der Faust) punch; (mit dem Fuß) kick; (mit dem Kopf, den Hörnern) butt; (mit dem Ellbogen) dig
(b) (mit einer Waffe) (Stich) thrust; (Schlag) blow
(c) (beim Schwimmen, Rudern) stroke
(d) (Stapel) pile; stack
stoßen [1] *unr. tr. V.* **(a)** *auch itr.* (mit der Faust) punch; (mit dem Fuß) kick; (mit dem Kopf, den Hörnern) butt; (mit dem Ellbogen) dig
(b) (hineintreiben) plunge, thrust ‹*dagger, knife*›; push ‹*stick, pole*›
(c) (schleudern) push; **die Kugel ~:** put the shot
[2] *unr. itr. V.* **(a)** *mit sein* (auftreffen) bump **(gegen** into); **mit dem Kopf gegen etw. ~:** bump one's head on sth.
(b) *mit sein* (fig.) **auf etw.** (*Akk.*) **~** (etw. entdecken) come upon sth.; **auf Ablehnung ~** (abgelehnt werden) meet with disapproval
(c) (grenzen) **an etw.** (*Akk.*) **~** ‹*room, property, etc.*› be [right] next to sth.
[3] *unr. refl. V.* bump *or* knock oneself; **sich an etw.** (*Dat.*) **~** (fig.) object to sth.
Stoß-: ~seufzer *der* heartfelt groan; **~stange** *die* bumper
stößt *3. Pers. Sg. Präsens v.* STOSSEN
stoß-, Stoß-: ~weise *Adv.* **(a)** ⋯

spasmodically; **(b)** (in Stapeln) by the pile; in piles; **~zahn** *der* tusk; **~zeit** *die* peak time; (Hauptverkehrszeit) rush hour

Stotterer *der;* **~s, ~, Stotterin** *die;* **~, ~nen** stutterer

stottern 1 *itr. V.* stutter
2 *tr. V.* stutter [out]

Str. *Abk.* **Straße** St./Rd.

stracks *Adv.* **(a)** (direkt) straight
(b) (sofort) straight away

straf·bar *Adj.* punishable

Strafe *die;* **~, ~n** punishment; (Rechtsspr.) penalty; (Freiheitsstrafe) sentence; (Geldstrafe) fine

strafen *tr. V.* punish

straff 1 *Adj.* **(a)** tight, taut ‹*rope, lines, etc.*›; firm ‹*breasts, skin*›
(b) (energisch) tight ‹*organization, planning, etc.*›; strict ‹*discipline, leadership, etc.*›
2 *adv.* **(a) [zu] ~ sitzen** ‹*clothes*› be [too] tight
(b) (energisch) tightly, strictly

straf·fällig *Adj.* **~ werden** commit a criminal offence

straffen *tr. V.* **(a)** tighten; firm ‹*skin*›
(b) (fig.) tighten up ‹*text, procedure, organization, etc.*›

straf-, Straf-: ~frei *Adj.* **~frei ausgehen** go unpunished; **~freiheit** *die* exemption from punishment; **~gefangene** *der/die* prisoner; **~gericht** *das* (fig.) judgement; **ein ~gericht des Himmels** divine judgement; **~gesetz·buch** *das* penal code

sträflich 1 *Adj.* criminal
2 *adv.* criminally

Sträfling *der;* **~s, ~e** prisoner

straf-, Straf-: ~los *Adj.* unpunished; **~rechtlich** 1 *Adj.* criminal *attrib.* ‹*case, investigation, responsibility*›; 2 *adv.* under criminal law; **etw. ~rechtlich verfolgen** prosecute sth.; **~tat** *die* criminal offence; **~täter** *der,* **~täterin** *die* offender; **~verfahren** *das* criminal proceedings *pl.;* **~vollzug** *der* (System) penal system; **~zettel** *der* (ugs.) [parking, speeding, *etc.*] ticket

Strahl *der;* **~[e]s, ~en** (auch Phys., Math., fig.) ray; (von Scheinwerfern, Taschenlampen) beam; (von Flüssigkeit) jet

Strahle·mann *der* (ugs.) man/boy with the smiling face

strahlen *itr. V.* **(a)** shine; **bei ~dem Wetter/Sonnenschein** in glorious sunny weather/in glorious sunshine; **~d weiß** sparkling white
(b) (glänzen) sparkle
(c) (lächeln) beam (**vor** + *Dat.* with)

Strahler *der;* **~s, ~ (a)** radiator
(b) (Heizstrahler) radiant heater

Strahlung *die;* **~, ~en** radiation

Strähne *die;* **~, ~n** strand; **eine graue ~:** a grey streak

*alte Schreibung - vgl. Hinweis auf S. xiv

strähnig 1 *Adj.* straggly ‹*hair*›
2 *adv.* in strands

stramm 1 *Adj.* **(a)** (straff) tight, taut ‹*rope, line, etc.*›; tight ‹*clothes*›
(b) (kräftig) strapping ‹*girl, boy*›; sturdy ‹*legs, body*›
(c) (gerade) upright, erect ‹*posture, etc.*›
2 *adv.* **(a)** (straff) tightly
(b) (kräftig) sturdily ‹*built*›

strampeln *itr. V.* ‹*baby*› kick [his/her feet]

Strand *der;* **~[e]s, Strände** beach; **am ~:** on the beach

Strand-: ~bad *das* bathing beach (*on river, lake*); **~burg** *die* sand den (*built as a windbreak*)

stranden *itr. V.; mit sein* ‹*ship*› run aground

Strand-: ~korb *der* basket chair; **~urlaub** *der* beach holiday; beach vacation (Amer.)

Strang *der;* **~[e]s, Stränge** rope

Strapaze *die;* **~, ~n** strain *no pl.*

strapazieren *tr. V.* be a strain on ‹*person, nerves*›

strapazier·fähig *Adj.* hard-wearing ‹*clothes, shoes*›; durable ‹*material*›

Straße *die;* **~, ~n** (in Ortschaften) street; road; (außerhalb) road

Straßen-: ~bahn *die* tram (Brit.); streetcar (Amer.); **~bahn·haltestelle** *die* tram stop (Brit.); **~bau·arbeiten** *Pl.* roadworks; **~café** *das* pavement café; street café; **~ecke** *die* street corner; **~feger** *der,* **~fegerin** *die;* **~~, ~~nen** (bes. nordd.) road sweeper; **~graben** *der* ditch [at the side of the road]; **~karte** *die* road map; **~kehrer** *der;* **~~s, ~~, ~kehrerin** *die;* **~~, ~~nen** (bes. südd.) road sweeper; **~kriminalität** *die* street crime; **~musikant** *der,* **~musikantin** *die* street musician; busker; **~raub** *der* street robbery; (gewalttätig) mugging; **~räuber** *der,* **~räuberin** *die* street robber; (gewalttätig) mugger; **~schild** *das* street name sign; **~sperre** *die* roadblock; **~verkehr** *der* traffic

Strategie *die;* **~, ~n** strategy

strategisch 1 *Adj.* strategic
2 *adv.* strategically

Strato·sphäre *die* stratosphere

sträuben 1 *tr. V.* ruffle [up] ‹*feathers*›; bristle ‹*fur, hair*›
2 *refl. V.* **(a)** ‹*hair, fur*› bristle, stand on end; ‹*feathers*› become ruffled
(b) (sich widersetzen) resist

Strauch *der;* **~[e]s, Sträucher** shrub

straucheln *itr. V.; mit sein* (geh.) stumble

Strauß[1] *der;* **~es, Sträuße** bunch of flowers; bouquet [of flowers]

Strauß[2] *der;* **~es, ~e** (Vogel) ostrich

Sträußchen *das;* **~s, ~:** posy

streben *itr. V.* **(a)** *mit sein* make one's way briskly

(b) (trachten) strive (**nach** for)

Streber *der;* **~s; ~** (abwertend) pushy person (coll.); (in der Schule) swot (Brit. coll.); grind (Amer. coll.)

strebsam *Adj.* ambitious and industrious

Strecke *die;* **~, ~n** distance; (Abschnitt, Route) route; (Eisenbahn~) line

strecken 1 *tr. V.* (gerade machen) stretch ‹*arms, legs*›; (dehnen) stretch [out] ‹*arms, legs, etc.*›; **den Kopf aus dem Fenster ~:** stick one's head out of the window (coll.) 2 *refl. V.* stretch out

strecken·weise *Adv.* in places; (fig.: zeitweise) at times

Streich *der;* **~[e]s, ~e** trick; prank; **jmdm. einen ~ spielen** play a trick on sb.

streicheln *tr. V.* stroke

streichen 1 *unr. tr. V.* **(a)** stroke
(b) (anstreichen) paint; **„frisch gestrichen"** 'wet paint'
(c) (auftragen) spread ‹*butter, jam, ointment, etc.*›; (bestreichen) **ein Brötchen mit Butter/mit Honig ~:** butter a roll/spread honey on a roll
(d) (tilgen) delete; cancel ‹*train, flight*›
2 *unr. itr. V.* **(a)** stroke; **jmdm. über den Kopf ~:** stroke sb.'s head
(b) (anstreichen) paint

Streicher *der;* **~s, ~, Streicherin** *die;* **~, ~nen** (Musik) string player; **die Streicher:** the strings

Streich-: ~holz *das* match; **~instrument** *das* string[ed] instrument; **~käse** *der* cheese spread; **~wurst** *die* [soft] sausage for spreading; ≈ meat spread

Streife *die;* **~, ~n (a)** (Personen) patrol
(b) (Streifengang) patrol

streifen 1 *tr. V.* **(a)** (leicht berühren) touch; ‹*shot*› graze
(b) (kurz behandeln) touch [up]on ‹*problem, subject, etc.*›
(c) den Ring vom Finger ~: slip the ring off one's finger; **die Ärmel nach oben ~:** pull/push up one's sleeves
2 *itr. V. mit sein* roam

Streifen *der;* **~s, ~ (a)** stripe
(b) (Stück, Abschnitt) strip

Streifen·wagen *der* patrol car

streifig *Adj.* streaky

Streif·licht *das* streak of light; **ein ~licht auf etw.** (*Akk.*) **werfen** (fig.) highlight sth.

Streik *der;* **~[e]s, ~s** strike; **in den ~ treten** come out *or* go on strike

Streik·brecher *der,* **Streik·brecherin** *die;* **~, ~nen** strike-breaker; blackleg (derog.)

streiken *itr. V.* **(a)** strike; be on strike; (in den Streik treten) come out *or* go on strike; strike
(b) (ugs.: nicht mitmachen) go on strike
(c) (ugs.: nicht funktionieren) pack up (coll.)

Streikende *der/die; adj. Dekl.* striker

Streik·posten *der* picket

Streit *der;* **~[e]s, ~e** (Zank) quarrel; (Auseinandersetzung) dispute; argument

streiten *unr. itr., refl. V.* quarrel; argue; (sich zanken) quarrel

Streiterei *die;* **~, ~en** arguing *no pl., no indef. art.;* (Gezänk) quarrelling *no pl.*

Streitigkeit *die;* **~, ~en** *meist Pl.* **(a)** quarrel; argument
(b) (Streitfall) dispute

Streit·kräfte *Pl.* armed forces

streng 1 *Adj.* **(a)** strict; severe ‹*punishment*›; stringent, strict ‹*rule, regulation, etc.*›; stringent ‹*measure*›; rigorous ‹*examination, check, test, etc.*›; stern ‹*reprimand, look*›; absolute ‹*discretion*›; complete ‹*rest*›
(b) (schmucklos, herb) austere, severe ‹*cut, collar, style, etc.*›; severe ‹*face, features, hairstyle, etc.*›
(c) (durchdringend) pungent, sharp ‹*taste, smell*›
(d) (rau) severe ‹*winter*›; sharp, severe ‹*frost*›
2 *adv.* ‹*mark, judge, etc.*› strictly, severely; ‹*punish*› severely; ‹*look, reprimand*› sternly; ‹*smell*› strongly

Strenge *die;* **~ (a)** ▶ STRENG A: strictness; severity; stringency; rigour; sternness
(b) (von [Gesichts]zügen) severity
(c) (von Geruch, Geschmack) pungency; sharpness
(d) ▶ STRENG D: severity; sharpness

strengstens *Adv.* [most] strictly

Stress, ***Streß** *der;* **Stresses** stress

stressen (ugs.) 1 *tr. V.* **jmdn. ~:** put sb. under stress; **vollkommen gestresst sein** be under an enormous amount of stress; **die gestressten Großstädter** the stressed city-dwellers
2 *itr. V.* be stressful

Streu *die;* **~, ~en** straw

streuen *tr. V.* **(a)** spread ‹*manure, sand, grit*›; sprinkle ‹*salt, herbs, etc.*›; strew, scatter ‹*flowers*›
(b) *auch itr.* **die Straßen [mit Sand/Salz] ~:** grit/salt the roads

streunen *itr. V.; meist mit sein* wander *or* roam about *or* around; **~de Katzen/Hunde** stray cats/dogs

Streusel·kuchen *der* streusel cake

strich *1. u. 3. Pers. Sg. Prät. v.* STREICHEN

Strich *der;* **~[e]s, ~e** (Linie) line; (Gedankenstrich) dash; (Schrägstrich) diagonal; (Binde-, Trennungsstrich) hyphen; **auf den ~ gehen** (salopp) walk the streets

stricheln *tr. V.* **(a)** sketch in [with short lines]
(b) (schraffieren) hatch

Strich-: ~junge *der* (salopp) [young] male prostitute; **~mädchen** *das* (salopp) streetwalker; hooker (Amer. sl.); **~punkt** *der* semicolon

Strick *der;* **~[e]s, ~e** cord; (Seil) rope; **jmdm. aus etw. einen ~ drehen** (fig.) use sth. against sb.

S

stricken *tr., itr. V.* knit
Strick-: **~jacke** *die* cardigan; **~nadel** *die* knitting needle; **~zeug** *das* knitting
striegeln *tr. V.* groom ‹*horse*›
strikt [1] *Adj.* strict
[2] *adv.* strictly
Strip *der;* **~s, ~s** strip[tease]
Strippe *die;* **~, ~n** (ugs.) string; **an der ~ hängen** (fig.) be on the phone (coll.); (dauernd) hog the phone (coll.)
Stripper *der;* **~s, ~, Stripperin** *die;* **~, ~nen** (ugs.) stripper
Striptease /ˈʃtrɪptiːs/ *der od. das;* **~:** striptease
stritt *1. u. 3. Pers. Sg. Prät. v.* STREITEN
strittig *Adj.* contentious ‹*point, problem*›; disputed ‹*territory*›; ‹*question*› in dispute, at issue
Stroh *das;* **~[e]s** straw
Stroh-: **~blume** *die* **(a)** (Immortelle) immortelle; **(b)** (Korbblütler) strawflower; **~halm** *der* straw; **~witwe** *die* (ugs. scherzh.) grass widow; **~witwer** *der* (ugs. scherzh.) grass widower
Strolch *der;* **~[e]s, ~e** (fam. scherzh.: Junge) rascal
Strom *der;* **~[e]s, Ströme** river; (fig.) stream; (Strömung; Elektrizität) current; (**~**versorgung) electricity; **unter ~ stehen** be live
strom-: **~abwärts** *Adv.* downstream; **~auf[wärts]** *Adv.* upstream
strömen *itr. V.; mit sein* stream
Strömung *die;* **~, ~en** current; (Met.) airstream; (fig.) trend
Strophe *die;* **~, ~n** verse; (einer Ode) strophe
strotzen *itr. V.* **von** *od.* **vor etw.** (*Dat.*) **~:** be full of sth.; **von** *od.* **vor Gesundheit ~:** be bursting with health
strubbelig *Adj.* tousled
Strudel *der;* **~s, ~ (a)** whirlpool
(b) (bes. südd., österr.: Gebäck) strudel
Struktur *die;* **~, ~en** structure
strukturieren *tr. V.* structure; **neu ~:** restructure
Strumpf *der;* **~[e]s, Strümpfe** stocking; (Socke, Knie**~**) sock
Strumpf-: **~band** *das* garter; (Straps) suspender (Brit.); garter (Amer.); **~hose** *die* tights *pl.* (Brit.); pantyhose (esp. Amer.)
Strunk *der;* **~[e]s, Strünke** stem; stalk; (Baumstrunk) stump
struppig *Adj.* shaggy; tangled, tousled ‹*hair*›
Stube *die;* **~, ~n (a)** (veralt.: Wohnraum) [living] room; parlour (dated)
(b) (Milit.) [barrack] room
Stuben·fliege *die* [common] housefly
Stück *das;* **~[e]s, ~e (a)** piece; (kleines) bit; (Teil, Abschnitt) part; **ein ~ Kuchen** a piece *or* slice of cake; **ein ~ Zucker/Seife** a lump of sugar/a piece *or* bar of soap; **im** *od.* **am ~:** unsliced ‹*sausage, cheese, etc.*›
(b) (Einzelstück) item; (Exemplar) specimen; **ich nehme 5 ~:** I'll take five [of them]; **30 Cent das ~:** thirty cents each; **~ für ~:** piece by piece; (eins nach dem andern) one by one; **das ist [ja] ein starkes ~** (ugs.) that's a bit much; **ein faules/freches ~** (salopp) a lazy/cheeky thing *or* devil
(c) (Bühnenstück) play; (Musikstück) piece
Stückchen *das;* **~s, ~:** [little] piece; bit
stückeln *tr. V.* put together ‹*sleeve, curtain*› with patches
Student *der;* **~en, ~en (a)** student
(b) (österr.: Schüler) [secondary-school] pupil
Studenten·wohnheim *das* student hostel; hall of residence
Studentin *die;* **~, ~nen** ▶ STUDENT
Studie /ˈʃtuːdi̯ə/ *die;* **~, ~n** study
Studien-: **~aufenthalt** *der* study visit (**in** + *Dat.* to); **~dauer** *die* length of study; **eine neunsemestrige ~dauer** nine semesters of study; **~freund** *der,* **~freundin** *die* university/college friend; **~gebühr** *die* tuition fee; **~platz** *der* university/college place; **~reise** *die* study trip
studieren *tr., itr. V.* study
Studierende *der/die; adj. Dekl.* student
Studio *das;* **~s, ~s** studio
Studium *das;* **~s, Studien** study; (Studiengang) course of study
Stufe *die;* **~, ~n (a)** step; (einer Treppe) stair; **„Vorsicht, ~!"** 'mind the step'
(b) (Raketenstufe, Geol., fig.: Stadium) stage; (Niveau) level; (Grad) degree; (Rang) grade
Stuhl *der;* **~[e]s, Stühle** chair
Stuhl-: **~gang** *der* bowel movement[s]; (Kot) stool; **~lehne** *die* (Rückenlehne) chair back; (Armlehne) chair arm
stülpen *tr. V.* **etw. auf** *od.* **über etw.** (*Akk.*) **~:** pull/put sth. on to *or* over sth.
stumm *Adj.* dumb ‹*person*›; (schweigsam) silent; (wortlos) wordless; mute ‹*glance, gesture*›
Stumme *der/die; adj. Dekl.* mute; **die ~n** the dumb
Stummel *der;* **~s, ~:** stump; (Bleistiftstummel) stub; (Zigaretten-/Zigarrenstummel) [cigarette/cigar] butt
Stumm·film *der* silent film
Stümper *der;* **~s, ~:** botcher; bungler
stümperhaft [1] *Adj.* incompetent; botched ‹*job*›; (laienhaft) amateurish ‹*attempt, drawing*›
[2] *adv.* incompetently; (laienhaft) amateurishly
Stümperin *die;* **~, ~nen** botcher; bungler
stümpern *itr. V.* work incompetently; (pfuschen) bungle
stumpf *Adj.* **(a)** blunt ‹*pin, needle, knife, etc.*›

*old spelling - see note on page xiv

(b) (glanzlos, matt) dull ‹*paint, hair, metal, colour, etc.*›

Stumpf *der;* **~[e]s, Stümpfe** stump

Stumpf·sinn *der* **(a)** apathy
(b) (Monotonie) monotony; tedium

stumpf·sinnig 1 *Adj.* **(a)** apathetic; vacant ‹*look*›
(b) (monoton) tedious; soul-destroying ‹*job, work*›
2 *adv.* **(a)** apathetically; ‹*stare*› vacantly
(b) (monoton) tediously

Stunde *die;* **~, ~n** hour; (Unterrichts~) lesson; **eine ~ Aufenthalt/Pause** an hour's stop/break; a stop/break of an hour

stünde *1. u. 3. Pers. Sg. Konjunktiv II v.* STEHEN

stunden *tr. V.* **jmdm. einen Betrag** *usw.* **~:** allow sb. to defer payment of a sum *etc.*

stunden-, Stunden-: ~kilometer *der* kilometre per hour; k.p.h.; **~lang** 1 *Adj.* lasting hours *postpos.;* 2 *adv.* for hours; **~lohn** *der* hourly wage; **~plan** *der* timetable; **~zeiger** *der* hour hand

-stündig *adj.* -hour

stündlich *Adj., adv.* hourly

-stündlich *adj.* -hourly; **zwei~/halb~:** two-hourly/half-hourly; *adv.* every two hours/ half an hour

Stundung *die;* **~, ~en** deferment of payment

Stups *der;* **~es, ~e** (ugs.) push; shove; (leicht) nudge

stupsen *tr. V.* (ugs.) push; shove; (leicht) nudge

Stups·nase *die* snub nose

stur (ugs.) 1 *Adj.* **(a)** obstinate; dogged ‹*insistence*›; (phlegmatisch) dour
(b) (unbeirrbar) dogged; persistent
(c) (stumpfsinnig) tedious
2 *adv.* **(a)** obstinately
(b) (unbeirrbar) doggedly
(c) (stumpfsinnig) tediously; ‹*learn, copy*› mechanically

stürbe *1. u. 3. Pers. Sg. Konjunktiv II v.* STERBEN

Sturheit *die;* **~** (ugs.) **(a)** obstinacy; pigheadedness; (phlegmatisches Wesen) dourness
(b) (Stumpfsinnigkeit) deadly monotony

Sturm *der;* **~[e]s, Stürme (a)** storm; (heftiger Wind) gale
(b) (Milit.) assault (**auf** + *Akk.* on); **~ klingeln** ring the [door]bell like mad

stürmen 1 *itr. V.* **(a)** *unpers.* **es stürmt [heftig]** it's blowing a gale
(b) *mit sein* (rennen) rush; (verärgert) storm
2 *tr. V.* (Milit.) storm ‹*town, position, etc.*›; (fig.) besiege ‹*booking office, shop, etc.*›

Stürmer *der;* **~s, ~** (Sport) striker; forward

stürmisch 1 *Adj.* **(a)** stormy; (fig.) tempestuous, turbulent
(b) (ungestüm) tumultuous ‹*applause, welcome, reception*›; wild ‹*enthusiasm*›; passionate ‹*lover, embrace, temperament*›; vehement ‹*protest*›
2 *adv.* ‹*protest*› vehemently; ‹*embrace*› impetuously, passionately; ‹*demand*› clamorously; ‹*applaud*› wildly

Sturz *der;* **-es, Stürze (a)** fall; (Unfall) accident
(b) (fig.: von Preis, Temperatur usw.) [sharp] fall, drop (*Gen.* in)
(c) (Verlust des Amtes, der Macht) fall; (Absetzung) overthrow; (Amtsenthebung) removal from office

Sturz·bach *der* [mountain] torrent; (fig.: von Fragen usw.) torrent

sturz·besoffen *Adj* (ugs.) paralytic [drunk] (coll.)

stürzen 1 *itr. V.; mit sein* **(a)** fall; (fig.) ‹*temperature, exchange rate, etc.*› drop [sharply]; ‹*prices*› tumble; ‹*government*› fall, collapse
(b) (laufen) rush; dash
(c) (fließen) stream; pour
2 *refl. V.* **sich auf jmdn./etw. ~** (auch fig.) pounce on sb./sth.; **sich in etw.** (*Akk.*) **~:** throw oneself into sth.
3 *tr. V.* **(a)** throw; (mit Wucht) hurl
(b) (umdrehen) upturn ‹*mould*›; turn out ‹*pudding, cake, etc.*›
(c) (des Amtes entheben) oust ‹*person*› [from office]; (gewaltsam) overthrow ‹*leader, government*›

Sturz-: ~flug *der* (Flugw.) [nose]dive; **im ~flug** in a [nose]dive; **~helm** *der* crash helmet

Stuss, *Stuß *der;* **Stusses** (ugs. abwertend) rubbish; twaddle (coll.)

Stute *die;* **~, ~n** mare

Stütze *die;* **~, ~n** (auch fig.) support

stutzen¹ *itr. V.* stop short

stutzen² *tr. V.* trim; dock ‹*tail*›; clip ‹*ear, hedge, wing*›; prune ‹*tree, bush*›

stützen 1 *tr. V.* support; (mit Pfosten o. Ä.) prop up; (aufstützen) rest ‹*head, hands, arms, etc.*›
2 *refl. V.* **sich auf jmdn./etw. ~:** lean *or* support oneself on sb./sth.

stutzig *Adj.* **~ werden** begin to wonder; **jmdn. ~ machen** make sb. wonder

Styropor Ⓦⓩ *das;* **~s** polystyrene [foam]

s. u. *Abk.* = **siehe unten** see below

Subjekt *das;* **~[e]s, ~e (a)** subject
(b) (abwertend: Mensch) creature

subjektiv 1 *Adj.* subjective
2 *adv.* subjectively

Subjektivität *die;* **~:** subjectivity

***substantiell** ▶ SUBSTANZIELL

Substantiv *das;* **~s, ~e** (Sprachw.) noun

Substanz *die;* **~, ~en (a)** (auch fig.) substance
(b) (Grundbestand) **die ~:** the reserves *pl.*

substanziell 1 *Adj.* substantial
2 *adv.* substantially

S

subtil 1 *Adj.* subtle
2 *adv.* subtly
Subtilität *die;* ~, ~**en** subtlety
sub·tropisch *Adj.* subtropical
Subvention *die;* ~, ~**en** (Wirtsch.) subsidy
Suche *die;* ~, ~**n** search (**nach** for); **auf der** ~ **[nach jmdm./etw.] sein** be looking/ (intensiver) searching [for sb./sth.]
suchen 1 *tr. V.* **(a)** look for; (intensiver) search for; **„Leerzimmer gesucht"** 'unfurnished room wanted'
(b) (bedacht sein auf, sich wünschen) seek ‹*protection, advice, company, warmth, etc.*›; look for ‹*adventure*›
2 *itr. V.* search; **nach jmdm./etw.** ~: look/ search for sb./sth.
Sucherei *die;* ~, ~**en** (ugs., oft abwertend) [endless] searching *no pl.*
Sucht *die;* ~, **Süchte** *od.* ~**en** **(a)** addiction (**nach** to); **[bei jmdm.] zur** ~ **werden** (auch fig.) become addictive [in sb.'s case]
(b) *Pl.* **Süchte** (übermäßiges Verlangen) craving (**nach** for)
süchtig *Adj.* **(a)** addicted
(b) (fig.) **nach etw.** ~ **sein** be obsessed with sth.
Sucht·kranke *die/der* addict
Süd (bes. Seemannsspr., Met.) ▶ SÜDEN
Süd-: ~**afrika** (*das*) South Africa; ~**amerika** (*das*) South America
Sudan (*das*); ~**s** *od. der;* ~**s** Sudan
Süden *der;* ~**s** south; **der** ~: the South;
Süd·frucht *die* tropical [or sub-tropical] fruit
Südländer *der;* ~**s**, ~, **Südländerin** *die;* ~, ~**nen** Southern European
südländisch *Adj.* Southern [European]; Latin ‹*temperament*›; ~ **aussehen** have Latin looks
südlich 1 *Adj.* **(a)** southern
(b) (nach, von Süden) southerly
(c) (aus dem Süden) Southern
2 *adv.* southwards
3 *Präp. mit Gen.* [to the] south of
süd-, Süd-: ~**licht** *das* southern lights *pl.;* (einzelne Erscheinung) display of the southern lights; ~**pol** *der* South Pole; ~**see** *die;* ~~: **die** ~**see:** the South Seas *pl.;* ~**see·insel** *die* South Sea island; ~**tirol** (*das*) South Tyrol; ~**wärts** *Adv.* southwards; ~**wind** *der* south *or* southerly wind
Sues·kanal *der;* ~**s** Suez Canal
Sühne *die;* ~, ~**n** (geh.) atonement; expiation
sühnen *tr., itr. V.* **[für] etw.** ~: atone for *or* pay the penalty for sth.
Sultanine *die;* ~, ~**n** sultana
Sülze *die;* ~, ~**n** **(a)** diced meat/fish in aspic; (vom Schweinskopf) brawn
(b) (Aspik) aspic

*alte Schreibung - vgl. Hinweis auf S. xiv

sülzen *tr., itr. V.* (salopp) ▶ QUATSCHEN 1A, 2
Summe *die;* ~, ~**n** sum
summen 1 *itr. V.* hum; (lauter, heller) buzz
2 *tr. V.* hum ‹*tune, song, etc.*›
summieren *refl. V.* add up (**auf** + *Akk.* to)
Sumpf *der;* ~**[e]s, Sümpfe** marsh; (bes. in den Tropen) swamp
sumpfig *Adj.* marshy
Sund *der;* ~**[e]s**, ~**e** (Geogr.) sound
Sünde *die;* ~, ~**n** sin; (fig.) misdeed; transgression
Sünden·bock *der* (ugs.) scapegoat
Sünder *der;* ~**s**, ~, **Sünderin** *die;* ~, ~**nen** sinner
sündigen *itr. V.* sin
Super *das;* ~**s**, ~: four star (Brit.); premium (Amer.)
super- ultra- ‹*long, high, fast, modern, masculine, etc.*›
Super- super‹*hero, car, group, etc.*›; terrific (coll.), tremendous (coll.) ‹*success, offer, chance, idea, etc.*›
Super·benzin *das* four-star petrol (Brit.); premium (Amer.)
Superlativ *der;* ~**s**, ~**e** (Sprachw.) superlative
Super-: ~**macht** *die* super power; ~**markt** *der* supermarket
Suppe *die;* ~; ~**n** soup
Suppen·löffel *der* soup spoon
Surf·brett /'sə:f-/ *das* surfboard
surfen /'sə:fn̩/ *itr. V.* surf
Surfer /'sə:fɐ/ *der;* ~**s**, ~, **Surferin** *die;* ~, ~**nen** surfer
surren *itr. V.* **(a)** (summen) hum; ‹*camera, fan*› whirr
(b) *mit sein* (schwirren) whirr
suspekt 1 *Adj.* suspicious; **jmdm.** ~ **sein** arouse sb.'s suspicions
2 *adv.* suspiciously
süß 1 *Adj.* sweet
2 *adv.* sweetly
süßen *tr. V.* sweeten
Süßigkeit *die;* ~, ~**en** sweet (Brit.); candy (Amer.); ~**en** sweets (Brit.); candy *sing.* (Amer.); (als Ware) confectionery *sing.*
süßlich 1 *Adj.* **(a)** [slightly] sweet; on the sweet side *pred.;*
(b) (sentimental) mawkish
2 *adv.* ‹*write, paint*› mawkishly
süß-, Süß-: ~**most** *der* unfermented fruit juice; ~**-sauer** 1 *Adj.* sweet-and-sour; (fig.) wry ‹*smile, face*›; 2 *adv.* **(a)** **etw.** ~**-sauer zubereiten** give sth. a sweet-and-sour flavour; **(b)** (fig.) ‹*smile*› wryly; ~**speise** *die* sweet; dessert; ~**stoff** *der* sweetener; ~**wasser** *das* fresh water
Symbol *das;* ~**s**, ~**e** symbol
symbolisch 1 *Adj.* symbolic
2 *adv.* symbolically
Sympathie *die;* ~, ~**n** sympathy (**für** with)

sympathisch [1] *Adj.* congenial, likeable ‹*person, manner*›; appealing ‹*voice, appearance, material*›
[2] *adv.* in an appealing way; (angenehm) agreeably
Symphonie *usw.* ▶ SINFONIE *usw.*
Symptom *das;* ~s, ~e (Med., geh.) symptom (*Gen.*, **für, von** of)
symptomatisch (Med., geh.) *Adj.* symptomatic (**für** of)
Synagoge *die;* ~, ~n synagogue
synchron [1] *Adj.* **(a)** synchronous
(b) (Sprachw.) synchronic
[2] *adv.* **(a)** synchronously
(b) (Sprachw.) synchronically
Synchronisation *die;* ~, ~en ▶ SYNCHRONISIERUNG
synchronisieren *tr. V.* **(a)** (Film) dub ‹*film*›
(b) (Technik, fig.) synchronize ‹*watches, operations, etc.*›; **synchronisiertes Getriebe** synchromesh [gearbox]
Synchronisierung *die;* ~, ~en **(a)** (Film) dubbing
(b) (Technik, fig.) synchronization
Synthese *die;* ~, ~n synthesis (*Gen.*, **von, aus** of)
Synthesizer /'sɪntəsaiːzɐ/ *der;* ~s, ~ (Musik) synthesizer
synthetisch [1] *Adj.* synthetic
[2] *adv.* synthetically
Syrer *der;* ~s, ~, **Syrerin** *die;* ~, ~nen Syrian
Syrien /'zyːriən/ (*das*); ~s Syria
syrisch *Adj.* Syrian
System *das;* ~s, ~e system
systematisch [1] *Adj.* systematic
[2] *adv.* systematically
System·fehler *der* fault in the system
Szenario *das;* ~s, ~s scenario
Szene /'stsːeːnə/ *die;* ~, ~n (auch fig.) scene
Szenen·wechsel *der* (Theater) scene change

Tt

t, T /teː/ *das;* ~, ~: t/T
t *Abk.* = **Tonne** t
Tab. *Abk.* = **Tabelle**
Tabak *der;* ~s, ~e tobacco
Tabaks·pfeife *die* [tobacco] pipe
tabellarisch *Adj.* tabular; **ein ~er Lebenslauf** a curriculum vitae in tabular form
Tabelle *die;* ~, ~n table
Tabellen·kalkulation *die* (DV) performing calculations using a spreadsheet; (Program) spreadsheet program
Tabernakel *das od.* **der;** ~s, ~: tabernacle
Tablett *das;* ~[e]s, ~s *od.* ~e tray
Tablette *die;* ~, ~n tablet
tabletten·süchtig *Adj.* addicted to pills *postpos.*
tabu *Adj.* taboo
Tabu *das;* ~s, ~s taboo
tabuisieren *tr. V.* **etw.** ~: taboo sth.; make sth. taboo
Ta·cheles [**mit jmdm.**] ~ **reden** (ugs.) do some straight talking [to sb.]
Tacho *der;* ~s, ~s (ugs.) speedo (coll.)
Tacho-: ~**meter** *der od. das* speedometer; ~**stand** *der* (ugs.: Kilometerstand) mileometer *or* odometer reading
Tadel *der;* ~s, ~ **(a)** censure
(b) (im Klassenbuch) black mark
tadel·los [1] *Adj.* impeccable; immaculate ‹*hair, clothing, suit, etc.*›; perfect ‹*condition, teeth, pronunciation, German, etc.*›
[2] *adv.* ‹*dress*› impeccably; ‹*fit, speak, etc.*› perfectly; ‹*live, behave, etc.*› irreproachably
tadeln *tr. V.* **jmdn.** [**für** *od.* **wegen etw.**] ~: rebuke sb. [for sth.]
Tafel *die;* ~, ~n **(a)** (Schiefertafel) slate; (Wandtafel) blackboard
(b) (plattenförmiges Stück) slab; **eine ~ Schokolade** a bar of chocolate
(c) (Gedenktafel) plaque
(d) (geh.: festlicher Tisch) table
Täfelchen *das;* ~s, ~: ▶ TAFEL B: [small] slab; [small] bar
tafeln *itr. V.* (geh.) feast
täfeln *tr. V.* panel
Tafel-: ~**spitz** *der* (österr.) boiled fillet of beef; ~**wasser** *das* [bottled] mineral water; ~**wein** *der* table wine
taff *Adj.* (ugs.) tough
Taft *der;* ~[e]s, ~e taffeta
Tag *der;* ~[e]s, ~e day; **am ~[e]** during the day[time]; **guten ~!** hello; (bei Vorstellung) how do you do?; **an diesem ~:** on this day; **dreimal am ~:** three times a day; **am folgenden ~:** the next day; **eines ~es** one day; some day
tag·aus *Adv.* ~, **tagein** day in, day out; day after day
Tage·buch *das* diary

tag·ein *Adv.* ▶ TAGAUS

tage·lang [1] *Adj.* lasting for days *postpos.;* **nach ~em Regen** after days of rain
[2] *adv.* for days [on end]

tagen *itr. V.* meet; **das Gericht/Parlament tagt** the court/parliament is in session

tages-, Tages-: ~aktuell *Adj.* **die ~aktuellen Nachrichten** the [current] news of the day; **die ~aktuellen Kurse** the rates of exchange current on the day; **~anbruch** *der* daybreak; dawn; **~ausflug** *der* day's outing; **~karte** *die* **(a)** (Gastron.) menu of the day; **(b)** (Fahr-, Eintrittskarte) day ticket; **~kasse** *die* **(a)** box office (*open during the day*); **(b)** (Tageseinnahme) day's takings *pl.;* **~licht** *das* daylight; **~licht·projektor** *der* overhead projector; **~zeit** *die* time of day; **~zeitung** *die* daily newspaper; daily

-tägig (a) (... Tage alt) **ein sechstägiges Küken** a six-day-old chick
(b) (... Tage dauernd) **nach dreitägiger Vorbereitung** after three days' preparation

täglich [1] *Adj.* daily
[2] *adv.* every day; **zweimal ~:** twice a day; **~ drei Tabletten einnehmen** take three tablets daily

tags *Adv.* **(a)** by day; in the daytime
(b) ~ zuvor/davor the day before; **~ darauf** the next *or* following day; the day after

tags·über *Adv.* during the day

tag·täglich (intensivierend) [1] *Adj.* day-to-day; daily
[2] *adv.* every single day

Tagung *die;* **~, ~en** conference

Taifun *der;* **~s, ~e** typhoon

Taille /'taljə/ *die;* **~, ~n** waist

Taiwan (*das*)*;* **~s** Taiwan

Takt *der;* **~[e]s, ~e (a)** (Musik) time; (Einheit) bar; measure (Amer.); **aus dem ~ kommen** lose the beat
(b) (rhythmischer Bewegungsablauf) rhythm
(c) (Feingefühl) tact

Takt·gefühl *das* sense of tact

taktieren *itr. V.* proceed tactically; **vorsichtig/klug ~:** use caution/clever tactics

Taktik *die;* **~, ~en: [eine] ~:** tactics *pl.*

taktisch [1] *Adj.* tactical
[2] *adv.* tactically

taktlos [1] *Adj.* tactless
[2] *adv.* tactlessly

Taktlosigkeit *die;* **~, ~en (a)** (taktlose Art) tactlessness
(b) (taktlose Handlung) piece of tactlessness

taktvoll [1] *Adj.* tactful
[2] *adv.* tactfully

Tal *das;* **~[e]s, Täler** valley

Talent *das;* **~[e]s, ~e** talent **(zu, für** for); (Mensch) talented person

talentiert *Adj.* talented

***old spelling - see note on page xiv**

Talg *der;* **~[e]s, ~e** suet; (zur Herstellung von Seife, Kerzen usw.) tallow

Talisman *der;* **~s, ~e** talisman

Tampon *der;* **~s, ~s** tampon

Tamtam *das;* **~s** (ugs. abwertend) **[großes] ~:** [a big] fuss

Tang *der;* **~[e]s, ~e** seaweed

Tangente *die;* **~, ~n** (Math.) tangent

Tank *der;* **~s, ~s** tank

tanken *tr., itr. V.* fill up; **Öl ~:** fill up with oil

Tanker *der;* **~s, ~:** tanker

Tank-: ~säule *die* petrol pump (Brit.); gasoline pump (Amer.); **~stelle** *die* petrol station (Brit.); gas station (Amer.); **~wagen** *der* tanker; **~wart** *der;* **~~s, ~~e, ~wartin** *die;* **~~, ~~nen** petrol pump attendant (Brit.); gas station attendant (Amer.)

Tanne *die;* **~, ~n** fir [tree]

Tannen-: ~baum *der* (ugs.) fir tree; (Weihnachtsbaum) Christmas tree; **~grün** *das* fir sprigs *pl.;* **~zapfen** *der* fir cone; **~zweig** *der* fir branch

Tansania (*das*)*;* **~s** Tanzania

Tante *die;* **~, ~n (a)** aunt
(b) (Kinderspr.: Frau) lady
(c) (ugs.: Frau) woman

Tanz *der;* **~es, Tänze** dance

Tanz-: ~abend *der* evening dance; **~bar** *die* night spot (coll.) with dancing; **~café** *das* coffee house with dancing

tanzen *itr., tr. V.* dance

Tänzer *der;* **~s, ~, Tänzerin** *die;* **~, ~nen** dancer; (Balletttänzer[in]) ballet dancer

Tanz-: ~fläche *die* dance floor; **~lokal** *das* café/restaurant with dancing; **~orchester** *das* dance band; **~stunde** *die* **(a)** (~kurs) dancing class; **(b)** (einzelne Stunde) dancing lesson

Tapete *die;* **~, ~n** wallpaper

Tapeten·wechsel *der* (ugs.) change of scene

tapezieren *tr. V.* [wall]paper

tapfer [1] *Adj.* brave
[2] *adv.* bravely

Tapferkeit *die;* **~:** courage; bravery

tappen *itr. V.* **(a)** *mit sein* patter
(b) (tastend greifen) grope **(nach** for)

Taps *der;* **~es, ~e** (ugs. abwertend) clumsy oaf

Tarif *der;* **~s, ~e** charge; (Post-, Wassertarif) rate; (Verkehrstarif) fares *pl.;* (Zolltarif) tariff; (Lohntarif) [wage] rate; (Gehaltstarif) [salary] scale

tarnen [1] *tr., itr. V.* camouflage
[2] *refl. V.* camouflage oneself

Tasche *die;* **~, ~n** bag; (in Kleidung, Rucksack usw.) pocket; **jmdm. auf der ~ liegen** (fig. ugs.) live off sb.

Taschen-: ~buch *das* paperback; **~dieb** *der,* **~diebin** *die* pickpocket; **~geld** *das* pocket money; **~lampe** *die* [pocket] torch (Brit.) *or* (Amer.) flashlight;

~messer *das* penknife; **~rechner** *der* pocket calculator; **~tuch** *das; Pl.* **~tücher** handkerchief; **~uhr** *die* pocket watch

Tasse *die;* **~, ~n** cup

Tastatur *die;* **~, ~en** keyboard

Taste *die;* **~, ~n (a)** (eines Musikinstruments, einer Schreibmaschine) key
(b) (Pedal) pedal [key]
(c) (am Telefon, Radio, Fernsehgerät, Taschenrechner usw.) button

tasten 1 *itr. V.* (fühlend suchen) grope, feel (**nach** for)
2 *refl. V.* (sich tastend bewegen) grope *or* feel one's way

Tasten-: ~feld *das* (Elektrot.) keypad; **~telefon** *das* push-button telephone

tat *1. u. 3. Pers. Sg. Prät. v.* TUN

Tat *die;* **~, ~en** act; (das Tun) action; **eine gute ~:** a good deed; **in der ~** (verstärkend) actually; (zustimmend) indeed

Tatar *das;* **~[s]** steak tartare

Tat·bestand *der* **(a)** facts *pl.* [of the matter *or* case]
(b) (Rechtsw.) elements *pl.* of an offence

Täter *der;* **~s, ~, Täterin** *die;* **~, ~nen** culprit

tätig *Adj.* **(a) ~ sein** work
(b) (rührig, aktiv) active

tätigen *tr. V.* (Kaufmannsspr., Papierdt.) transact ‹*business, deal, etc.*›

Tätigkeit *die;* **~, ~en** activity; (Arbeit) job

tat-, Tat-: ~kraft *die* energy; drive; **~kräftig** 1 *Adj.* energetic ‹*person*›;
2 *adv.* energetically

tätlich 1 *Adj.* physical ‹*clash, attack, resistance, etc.*›; **gegen jmdn. ~ werden** become violent towards sb.
2 *adv.* physically; **jmdn. ~ angreifen** attack sb. physically; assault sb.

Tat·ort *der* scene of a/the crime

tätowieren *tr. V.* tattoo

Tätowierung *die;* **~, ~en** tattoo

Tat·sache *die* fact

tatsächlich 1 *Adj.* actual; real
2 *adv.* actually; really

tätscheln *tr. V.* pat

Tattoo /tɛˈtuː/ *das;* **~s, ~s** tattoo

tat·verdächtig *Adj.* suspected

Tat·waffe *die* weapon [used in the crime]

Tatze *die;* **~, ~n** paw

Tat·zeit *die* time of the crime

Tau[1] *der;* **~[e]s** dew

Tau[2] *das;* **~[e]s, ~e** (Seil) rope

taub *Adj.* **(a)** deaf
(b) (wie abgestorben) numb
(c) empty ‹*nut*›

Taube[1] *die;* **~, ~n** pigeon; (Turteltaube; auch Politik fig.) dove

Taube[2] *der/die; adj. Dekl.* deaf person; deaf man/woman; **die ~n** the deaf

Taubheit *die;* **~:** deafness

taub·stumm *Adj.* deaf and dumb

Taub·stumme *der/die; adj. Dekl.* deaf mute

tauchen 1 *itr. V.* **(a)** *auch mit sein* dive (**nach** for)
(b) *mit sein* (eintauchen) dive; (auftauchen) rise; emerge
2 *tr. V.* **(a)** (eintauchen) dip
(b) (untertauchen) duck

Taucher *der;* **~s, ~:** diver; (mit Flossen und Atemgerät) skin diver

Taucher-: ~anzug *der* diving suit; **~brille** *die* diving goggles *pl.*

Taucherin *die;* **~, ~nen** ▶ TAUCHER

Tauch·sieder *der;* **~s, ~:** portable immersion heater

tauen 1 *itr. V.* **(a)** *unpers.* **es taut** it's thawing
(b) *mit sein* (schmelzen) melt
2 *tr. V.* melt; thaw

Taufe *die;* **~, ~n** (christl. Rel.) **(a)** (Sakrament) baptism
(b) (Zeremonie) christening; baptism

taufen *tr. V.* **(a)** baptize
(b) (einen Namen geben) christen

taugen *itr. V.* **nichts/nicht viel/etwas ~:** be no/not much/some good *or* use

tauglich *Adj.* **[nicht] ~:** [un]suitable; (für Militärdienst) fit [for service]

Taumel *der;* **~s (a)** [feeling of] dizziness
(b) (Rausch) frenzy; fever

taumelig *Adj.* dizzy; giddy

taumeln *itr. V.* **(a)** *auch mit sein* (wanken) reel, sway (**vor** + *Dat.* with)
(b) *mit sein* (taumelnd gehen) stagger

Tausch *der;* **~[e]s, ~e** exchange; **ein guter/schlechter ~:** a good/bad deal

tauschen 1 *tr. V.* exchange (**gegen** for); **sie tauschten die Plätze** they changed places
2 *itr. V.* **mit jmdm. ~** (fig.) change places with sb.

täuschen 1 *tr. V.* deceive; **wenn mich nicht alles täuscht** unless I'm completely mistaken
2 *itr. V.* be deceptive
3 *refl. V.* be mistaken (**in** + *Dat.* about)

täuschend 1 *Adj.* remarkable, striking ‹*similarity, imitation*›
2 *adv.* remarkably

Täuschung *die;* **~, ~en** deception; (Selbst~) delusion

tausend *Kardinalz.* **(a)** a *or* one thousand
(b) (ugs.: sehr viele) thousands of; **~ Dank/Küsse** a thousand thanks/kisses

Tausend *das;* **~s, ~e** thousand

tausend·ein[s] *Kardinalz.* a *or* one thousand and one

Tausender *der;* **~s, ~** (ugs.) (Tausendmarkschein usw.) thousand-mark/-dollar *etc.* note; (Betrag) thousand marks/dollars *etc.*

t

tausenderlei *indekl. Adj.* (ugs.) a thousand and one different ‹*answers, kinds, etc.*›
tausend·mal *Adv.* a thousand times
tausendst... *Ordinalz.* thousandth; *s. auch* ACHT...
tausendstel *Bruchz.* thousandth
Tausendstel *das* (schweiz. meist *der*); **~s, ~**: thousandth
Tau-: ~wasser *das* meltwater; **~wetter** *das* thaw; **~ziehen** *das;* **~~s** (auch fig.) tug-of-war
Taxe *die;* **~, ~n (a)** (Taxi) taxi
(b) (Gebühr) charge
Taxi *das;* **~s, ~s** taxi
taxieren *tr. V.* estimate
Taxi-: ~fahrer *der,* **~fahrerin** *die* taxi driver; **~stand** *der* taxi rank (Brit.); taxi stand
Tb /te:ˈbe:/, **Tbc** /te:be:ˈts:e:/ *die;* **~**: *Abk.* = **Tuberkulose** TB
Team /ti:m/ *das;* **~s, ~s** team
Team·arbeit *die* teamwork
Technik *die;* **~, ~en (a)** technology; (Studienfach) engineering *no art.;*
(b) (technische Ausrüstung) equipment
(c) (Arbeitsweise, Verfahren) technique
Techniker *der;* **~s, ~, Technikerin** *die;* **~, ~nen** technical expert
technisch **1** *Adj.* technical; technological ‹*progress, age*›
2 *adv.* technically; technologically ‹*advanced*›
Techno /ˈtɛkno/ *das od. der;* **~s** techno
Technologie *die;* **~, ~n** technology
technologisch **1** *Adj.* technological
2 *adv.* technologically
Techno·party *die* techno party
Tee *der;* **~s, ~s** tea
TEE /te:|e:ˈ|e:/ *der;* **~[s], ~[s]** *Abk.* = **Trans-Europ-Express** TEE
Tee-: ~beutel *der* tea bag; **~kanne** *die* teapot; **~löffel** *der* teaspoon
Teenie /ˈti:ni/ *der;* **~s, ~s** (ugs.) young teenager
Tee-: sieb *das* tea strainer; **~tasse** *die* teacup
Teich *der;* **~[e]s, ~e** pond
Teig *der;* **~[e]s, ~e** dough; (Kuchen-, Biskuitteig) pastry; (Pfannkuchen-, Waffelteig) batter
Teig·waren *Pl.* pasta *sing.*
Teil (a) *der;* **~[e]s, ~e** part; **fünfter ~**: fifth
(b) *der od. das;* **~[e]s, ~e** (Anteil; Beitrag) share
(c) *der;* **~[e]s, ~e** (beteiligte Person[en]; Rechtsw.: Partei) party
(d) *das;* **~[e]s, ~e** (Einzelteil) part
teil·bar *Adj.* divisible (**durch** by)
Teilbarkeit *die;* **~**: divisibility
Teilchen *das;* **~s, ~ (a)** (kleines Stück) [small] part
(b) (Partikel) particle

teilen **1** *tr. V.* **(a)** divide (**durch** by)
(b) (aufteilen) share (**unter** + *Dat.* among)
2 *refl. V.* **sich** (*Dat.*) **etw. [mit jmdm.] ~**: share sth. [with sb.]
Teiler *der;* **~s, ~** (Math.) factor
teil|haben *unr. itr. V.* share (**an** + *Dat.* in)
Teilhaber *der;* **~s, ~, Teilhaberin** *die;* **~, ~nen** partner
Teil·kasko·versicherung *die: insurance giving limited cover*
Teilnahme *die;* **~, ~n (a)** participation (**an** + *Dat.* in); **~ an einem Kurs** attendance at a course
(b) (Interesse) interest (**an** + *Dat.* in)
(c) (geh.: Mitgefühl) sympathy
teilnahms·los *Adj.* indifferent
Teilnahmslosigkeit *die;* **~**: indifference
teilnahms·voll **1** *Adj.* compassionate
2 *adv.* compassionately
teil|nehmen *unr. itr. V.* **[an etw.** (*Dat.*)**] ~**: take part [in sth.]; **[an einem Lehrgang] ~**: attend [a course]
Teilnehmer *der;* **~s, ~, Teilnehmerin** *die;* **~, ~nen (a)** participant (*Gen.*, **an** + *Dat.* in); (bei Wettbewerb auch) competitor, contestant (**an** + *Dat.* in)
(b) (Fernspr.) subscriber
teils *Adv.* partly
Teilung *die;* **~, ~en** division
teil·weise **1** *Adv.* partly
2 *adj.* partial
Teilzeit-: ~arbeit *die* part-time work *no indef. art.;* **~beschäftigt** *Adj.* ‹*person*› in part-time work; **~beschäftigt sein** work part-time; **~beschäftigte** *der/die; adj. Dekl.* part-time employee; **~job** *der* part-time job
Teint /tɛ̃:/ *der;* **~s, ~s** complexion
Telefon /ˈte:lefo:n, *auch* teleˈfo:n/ *das;* **~s, ~e** telephone; phone; **ans ~ gehen** answer the [tele]phone
Telefon-: ~anruf *der* [tele]phone call; **~anschluss, *~anschluß** *der* telephone; line; **~apparat** *der* telephone
Telefonat *das;* **~[e]s, ~e** telephone call
Telefon-: ~buch *das* [tele]phone book *or* directory; **~gespräch** *das* telephone conversation
telefonieren *itr. V.* make a [tele]phone call; **mit jmdm. ~**: talk to sb. [on the telephone]
telefonisch **1** *Adj.* telephone *attrib.*
2 *adv.* by telephone
Telefonist *der;* **~en, ~en, Telefonistin** *die;* **~, ~nen** telephonist; (in einer Firma) switchboard operator
Telefon-: ~karte *die* phonecard; **~nummer** *die* [tele]phone number; **~rechnung** *die* [tele]phone bill; **~verzeichnis** *das* [tele]phone list; **~zelle** *die* [tele]phone booth *or* (Brit.) box; call box (Brit.); **~zentrale** *die* telephone exchange

*alte Schreibung - vgl. Hinweis auf S. xiv

Telegraf *der;* **~en, ~en** telegraph
Telegrafie *die;* ~: telegraphy *no art.*
telegrafieren *itr., tr. V.* telegraph
telegrafisch [1] *Adj.* telegraphic [2] *adv.* by telegraph *or* telegram
Telegramm *das* telegram
Tele·objektiv *das* (Fot.) telephoto lens
Tele·text *der* teletext *no art.*
Teller *der;* **~s,** ~: plate
Tempel *der;* **~s,** ~: temple
Temperament *das;* **~[e]s, ~e (a)** (Wesensart) temperament **(b)** (Schwung) **eine Frau mit ~:** a woman with spirit
temperament·voll *Adj.* spirited ‹*person, speech, dance, etc.*›
Temperatur *die;* **~, ~en** temperature
Temperatur-: ~anstieg *der* rise in temperature; **~rückgang** *der* drop *or* fall in temperature
Tempo *das;* **~s, ~s** *od.* **Tempi (a)** *Pl.* **~s** speed **(b)** (Musik) tempo; time
Tempo·limit *das* (Verkehrsw.) speed limit
Tempus *das;* **~, Tempora** (Sprachw.) tense
Tendenz *die;* **~, ~en** trend
tendieren *itr. V.* tend (**zu** towards)
Teneriffa (*das*)*;* **~s** Tenerife
Tennis *das;* ~: tennis *no art.*
Tennis-: ~ball *der* tennis ball; **~platz** *der* tennis court; **~schläger** *der* tennis racket; **~schuh** *der* tennis shoe; **~schule** *die* tennis school; **~spieler** *der,* **~spielerin** *die* tennis player
Tenor *der;* **~s, Tenöre,** (österr. auch:) **~e** (Musik) tenor; (im Chor) tenors *pl.*
Teppich *der;* **~s, ~e** carpet; (kleiner) rug
Teppich·boden *der* fitted carpet
Termin *der;* **~s, ~e** date; (Anmeldung) appointment; (Verabredung) engagement; (Rechtsw.) hearing
Terminal /'tø:ɐ̯minəl/ *das;* **~s, ~s** terminal
Termin-: ~geschäft *das* (Börsenw.) forward transaction *or* operation; **~kalender** *der* appointments book
Terminus *der;* **~, Termini** term
Terpentin *das,* (österr. meist:) *der;* **~s (a)** (Harz) turpentine **(b)** (ugs.: Terpentinöl) turps *sing.* (coll.)
Terrain /tɛ'rɛ̃:/ *das;* **~s, ~s** terrain
Terrasse *die;* **~, ~n** terrace
Terrier /'tɛri̯ɐ/ *der;* **~s,** ~: terrier
Terrine *die;* **~, ~n** tureen
Territorium *das;* **~s, Territorien** territory
Terror *der;* **~s** terrorism *no art.*
Terror-: ~angriff *der* terrorist attack; **~anschlag** *der* terrorist attack; **~gruppe** *die* terrorist group
terrorisieren *tr. V.* **(a)** terrorize **(b)** (ugs.: belästigen) pester
Terrorismus *der;* ~: terrorism *no art.*
Terrorist *der;* **~en, ~en, Terroristin** *die;* **~, ~nen** terrorist
Terror-: ~verdächtige *der/die* terrorist suspect; **~zelle** *die* terrorist cell
Test *der;* **~[e]s, ~s** *od.* **~e** test
Testament *das;* **~[e]s, ~e (a)** will **(b)** (christl. Rel.) Testament
Test·bogen *der* test paper
testen *tr. V.* test (**auf** + *Akk.* for)
teuer [1] *Adj.* expensive; dear *usu. pred.;* **wie ~ war das?** how much did that cost? [2] *adv.* expensively; dearly; **etw. ~ kaufen/verkaufen** pay a great deal for sth./sell sth. at a high price
Teuerung *die;* **~, ~en** rise in prices
Teuerungs·rate *die* rate of price increases
Teufel *der;* **~s,** ~: devil
Teufels·zeug *das* (ugs.) terrible stuff (coll.)
teuflisch [1] *Adj.* **(a)** devilish, fiendish ‹*plan, trick, etc.*›; diabolical ‹*laughter, pleasure, etc.*› **(b)** (ugs.: groß, intensiv) terrible (coll.); dreadful (coll.) [2] *adv.* **(a)** diabolically **(b)** (ugs.) terribly (coll.)
Text *der;* **~[e]s, ~e** text; (Wortlaut) wording; (eines Theaterstücks) script; (einer Oper) libretto; (eines Liedes, Chansons usw.) words *pl.;* (eines Schlagers) words *pl.;* lyrics *pl.;* (zu einer Abbildung) caption
texten *tr. V.* write ‹*song, advertisement, etc.*›
Textilien *Pl.* **(a)** textiles **(b)** (Fertigwaren) textile goods
Textil·industrie *die* textile industry
Text·verarbeitung *die* text processing; word processing
Thailand (*das*)*;* **~s** Thailand
Theater *das;* **~s, ~ (a)** theatre; **ins ~ gehen** go to the theatre; **im ~:** at the theatre; **~ spielen** act; (fig.) play-act; pretend **(b)** (fig. ugs.) fuss
Theater-: ~abonnement *das* theatre subscription [ticket]; **~stück** *das* [stage] play
Theke *die;* **~, ~n (a)** (Schanktisch) bar **(b)** (Ladentisch) counter
Thema *das;* **~s, Themen** subject; topic; (einer Abhandlung) subject; theme; (Leitgedanke) theme
Themse *die;* ~: Thames
Theologe *der;* **~n, ~n** theologian
Theologie *die;* **~, ~n** theology *no art.*
Theologin *die;* **~, ~:** theologian
theologisch [1] *Adj.* theological [2] *adv.* theologically
theoretisch [1] *Adj.* theoretical [2] *adv.* theoretically
Theorie *die;* **~, ~n** theory

Therapeut *der;* **~en, ~en, Therapeutin** *die;* **~, ~nen** therapeutist

therapeutisch 1 *Adj.* therapeutic
2 *adv.* therapeutically

Therapie *die;* **~, ~n** therapy (**gegen** for)

therapieren *tr. V.* treat

Thermo·meter *das* (*österr. u. schweiz. der od. das*) thermometer

Thermos·flasche (Wz) *die* Thermos flask ®; vacuum flask

Thermostat *der;* **~[e]s** *od.* **~en, ~e** *od.* **~en** thermostat

These *die;* **~, ~n** thesis

Thron *der;* **~[e]s, ~e** throne

Thun·fisch *der* tuna

Thüringen (*das*)*;* **~s** Thuringia

Thymian *der;* **~s, ~e** thyme

Tick *der;* **~[e]s, ~s (a)** (ugs.: Schrulle) quirk; thing (coll.)
(b) (ugs.: Nuance) tiny bit; shade

ticken *itr. V.* tick; **du tickst wohl nicht richtig** (salopp) you must be off your rocker (coll.)

Ticket *das;* **~s, ~s** ticket

tief 1 *Adj.* (auch fig.) deep; (niedrig) low; low ‹*neckline, bow*›; deep; intense ‹*pain, suffering*›
2 *adv.* deep; (niedrig) low; (intensiv) deeply; ‹*stoop, bow*› low; ‹*breathe, inhale*› deeply

Tief *das;* **~s, ~s** (Met.) low

tief·blau *Adj.* deep blue

Tief·druck *der* (Met.) low pressure

Tiefe *die;* **~, ~n** depth; **in die ~ stürzen** plunge into the depths

tief-, Tief-: ~garage *die* underground car park; **~greifend** 1 *Adj.* profound; profound, deep ‹*crisis*›; far-reaching ‹*improvement*›; 2 *adv.* profoundly; **~gründig** *Adj.* profound; **~|kühlen** *tr. V.* [deep-]freeze

Tief·kühl-: ~fach *das* freezer [compartment]; **~kost** *die* frozen food

tief-, Tief-: ~punkt *der* low [point]; **~schlag** *der* (Boxen) low punch; punch below the belt (lit. or fig.); **~see** *die* (Geogr.) deep sea; **~sinnig** 1 *Adj.* profound; 2 *adv.* profoundly

Tiefst·temperatur *die* minimum *or* lowest temperature

Tiegel *der;* **~s, ~** (zum Kochen) pan; (Schmelztiegel) crucible; (Behälter) pot

Tier *das;* **~[e]s, ~e** animal

Tier-: ~arzt *der,* **~ärztin** *die* veterinary surgeon; vet; **~garten** *der* zoo; zoological garden; **~heim** *das* animal home

tierisch 1 *Adj.* **(a)** animal *attrib.;* savage ‹*cruelty, crime*›
(b) (ugs.: unerträglich groß) terrible (coll.); **~er Ernst** deadly seriousness
2 *adv.* **(a)** ‹*roar*› like an animal; savagely ‹*cruel*›
(b) (ugs.: unerträglich) terribly (coll.)

tier-, Tier-: ~kreis *der* (Astron., Astrol.) zodiac; **~kreis·zeichen** *das* (Astron., Astrol.) sign of the zodiac; **~lieb** *Adj.* animal-loving *attrib.;* fond of animals *postpos.;* **~park** *der* zoo; **~pfleger** *der,* **~pflegerin** *die* animal keeper; **~quälerei** /---'-/ *die* cruelty to animals; **~rechtler** *der;* **~~s, ~~, ~rechtlerin** *die;* **~~, ~~nen** animal rights campaigner; **~reich** *das* animal kingdom

Tiger *der;* **~s, ~:** tiger

tilgen *tr. V.* **(a)** (geh.) delete ‹*word, letter, error*›; erase ‹*record, endorsement*›; (fig.) wipe out ‹*shame, guilt, traces*›
(b) (Wirtsch., Bankw.) repay; pay off

Tilgung *die;* **~, ~en (a)** (geh.) ▶ TILGEN A: deletion; erasure; wiping out
(b) (Wirtsch., Bankw.) repayment

Tilsiter *der;* **~s, ~:** Tilsit [cheese]

Tinte *die;* **~, ~n** ink; **in der ~ sitzen** (ugs.) be in the soup (coll.)

Tinten-: ~fisch *der* cuttlefish; (Krake) octopus; **~strahl·drucker** *der* (DV) ink-jet printer

***Tip, Tipp** *der;* **~s, ~s (a)** (ugs.) tip
(b) (bei Toto, Lotto usw.) [row of] numbers

tippen 1 *itr. V.* **(a) an/gegen etw.** (*Akk.*) **~:** tap sth.
(b) (ugs.: Maschine schreiben) type
(c) (wetten) do the pools/lottery *etc.;* **im Lotto ~:** do the lottery
2 *tr. V.* **(a)** tap
(b) (ugs.: mit der Maschine schreiben) type
(c) (setzen auf) choose; **sechs Richtige ~:** make six correct selections

Tipp-: ~fehler *der* typing error *or* mistake; **~gemeinschaft** *die* pools/lottery *etc.* syndicate

tipp·topp (ugs.) 1 *Adj.* (tadellos) immaculate; (erstklassig) tip-top
2 *adv.* immaculately

Tirol (*das*)*;* **~s** [the] Tyrol

Tiroler *der;* **~s, ~, Tirolerin** *die;* **~, ~nen** Tyrolese; Tyrolean

Tisch *der;* **~[e]s, ~e** table; **reinen ~ machen** (ugs.) sort things out

Tisch-: ~dame *die* dinner partner; **~decke** *die* tablecloth; **~gebet** *das* grace *no pl.*; **~herr** *der* dinner partner; **~lampe** *die* table lamp

Tischler *der;* **~s, ~:** joiner; (bes. Kunst~) cabinetmaker

Tischlerei *die;* **~, ~en** ▶ TISCHLER: **(a)** (Werkstatt) joiner's/cabinetmaker's [workshop]
(b) (Handwerk) joinery/cabinetmaking

Tischlerin *die;* **~, ~nen** ▶ TISCHLER

Tisch-: ~nachbar *der* person next to one [at table]; **~platte** *die* table top; **~tennis** *das* table tennis; **~tuch** *das; Pl.* **~tücher**

*old spelling - see note on page xiv

tablecloth; **~wäsche** *die* table linen; **~wein** *der* table wine; **~zeit** *die* lunchtime

Titel *der;* **~s, ~ (a)** title
(b) (ugs.: Musikstück, Song usw.) number

Titel-: ~bild *das* cover picture; **~blatt** *das* title page; **~rolle** *die* title role; **~seite** *die* **(a)** (einer Zeitung, Zeitschrift) [front] cover; **(b)** (eines Buchs) title page

Titte *die;* **~, ~n** (derb) tit (coarse)

titulieren *tr. V.* call

tja /tja(:)/ *Interj.* [yes] well; (Resignation ausdrückend) oh, well

Toast /to:st/ *der;* **~[e]s, ~e** *od.* **~s** toast

Toast·brot *das* [sliced white] bread for toasting

toasten *tr. V.* toast

Toaster *der;* **~s, ~:** toaster

toben *itr. V.* **(a)** go wild (**vor** + *Dat.* with); (fig.) ‹*storm, sea, battle*› rage
(b) (tollen) romp *or* charge about
(c) *mit sein* (laufen) charge

Tochter *die;* **~, Töchter (a)** daughter
(b) (Wirtsch.) subsidiary

Tochter·gesellschaft *die* (Wirtsch.) subsidiary [company]

Tod *der;* **~[e]s, ~e** death; **eines natürlichen/ gewaltsamen ~es sterben** die a natural/ violent death; **jmdn. zum ~e verurteilen** sentence sb. to death

tod·ernst [1] *Adj.* deadly serious
[2] *adv.* deadly seriously

Todes-: ~anzeige *die* **(a)** (in einer Zeitung) death notice; **(b)** (Karte) *card announcing a person's death;* **~fall** *der* death; (in der Familie) bereavement; **~nachricht** *die* news of his/her/their *etc.* death; **~opfer** *das* death; fatality; **~strafe** *die* death penalty; **~ursache** *die* cause of death; **~urteil** *das* death sentence; **~verachtung** *die* [utter] fearlessness in the face of death; **etw. mit ~verachtung essen/trinken** (ugs.) force sth. down [without showing one's distaste]

Tod·feind *der,* **Tod·feindin** *die* deadly enemy

tod·krank *Adj.* critically ill

tödlich [1] *Adj.* **(a)** fatal ‹*accident, illness, outcome, etc.*›; lethal, deadly ‹*poison, bite, shot, trap, etc.*›; lethal ‹*dose*›
(b) (sehr groß, ausgeprägt) deadly ‹*hatred, seriousness, certainty, boredom*›
[2] *adv.* **(a)** fatally
(b) (sehr) terribly (coll.)

tod-, Tod-: ~müde *Adj.* dead tired; **~schick** (ugs.) [1] *Adj.* dead smart (coll.); [2] *adv.* dead smartly (coll.); **~sicher** (ugs.) [1] *Adj.* sure-fire (coll.); [2] *adv.* for certain *or* sure; **~sünde** *die* (auch fig.) deadly *or* mortal sin; **~unglücklich** *Adj.* (ugs.) extremely *or* desperately unhappy

Toilette /toa'lɛtə/ *die;* **~, ~n** toilet

Toiletten·papier *das* toilet paper

toi, toi, toi /'tɔy: 'tɔy: 'tɔy:/ *Interj.* good luck!; (unberufen!) touch wood!

Tokio *(das);* **~s** Tokyo

tolerant [1] *Adj.* tolerant (**gegen** of)
[2] *adv.* tolerantly

Toleranz *die;* **~:** tolerance

tolerierbar *Adj.* tolerable

tolerieren *tr. V.* tolerate

toll [1] *Adj.* **(a)** (ugs.) (großartig) great (coll.); fantastic (coll.); (erstaunlich) amazing; (heftig, groß) enormous ‹*respect*›; terrific (coll.) ‹*noise, storm*›
(b) (wild) wild
[2] *adv.* **(a)** (ugs.: großartig) terrifically well (coll.)
(b) (ugs.: heftig) ‹*rain, snow*› like billy-o (coll.)
(c) (wild) **bei dem Fest ging es ~ zu** it was a wild party

Tolle *die;* **~, ~n** quiff

tollen *itr. V.* **(a)** romp about
(b) *mit sein* romp

toll-, Toll-: ~kühn [1] *Adj.* daredevil *attrib.;* daring; [2] *adv.* daringly; **~wut** *die* rabies *sing.;* **~wütig** *Adj.* rabid

Tollpatsch *der;* **~[e]s, ~e** (ugs.) clumsy *or* awkward creature

tollpatschig (ugs.) [1] *Adj.* clumsy; awkward
[2] *adv.* clumsily; awkwardly

***Tolpatsch** *usw.* ▶ TOLLPATSCH *usw.*

Tölpel *der;* **~s, ~:** fool

tölpelhaft [1] *Adj.* foolish
[2] *adv.* foolishly

Tomate *die;* **~, ~n** tomato

Tomaten·mark *das* tomato purée

Tombola *die;* **~, ~s** raffle

Ton[1] *der;* **~[e]s, ~e** clay

Ton[2] *der;* **~[e]s, Töne (a)** (auch Physik, Musik; beim Telefon) tone; (Klang) note
(b) (Film, Ferns. usw., Tonwiedergabe) sound
(c) (ugs.: Äußerung) word
(d) (Farb~) shade
(e) (Akzent) stress

ton-, Ton-: ~angebend *Adj.* predominant; **~art** *die* **(a)** (Musik) key; **(b)** (fig.) tone; **~band** *das; Pl.* **~bänder** tape; **~band·gerät** *das* tape recorder; **~effekt** *der* sound effect

tönen [1] *itr. V.* (geh.) sound; ‹*bell*› sound, ring; (schallen, widerhallen) resound
[2] *tr. V.* (färben) tint

Ton-: ~fall *der* tone; (Intonation) intonation; **~höhe** *die* pitch; **~leiter** *die* (Musik) scale

Tonne *die;* **~, ~n (a)** (Behälter) drum; (Mülltonne) bin; (Regentonne) water butt
(b) (Gewicht) tonne

tonnen·weise *Adv., adj.* by the ton

Ton·qualität *die* sound quality

Tönung *die;* **~, ~en** tint; shade

Tool /tu:l/ *das;* **~s, ~s** (DV) tool

Topf *der;* **~es, Töpfe (a)** pot; (Braten~, Schmor~) casserole; (Stielkasserolle) saucepan ⋯

(b) (zur Aufbewahrung) pot
(c) (Krug) jug
(d) (Nachttopf) chamber pot; (für Kinder) potty (Brit. coll.)
(e) (Blumentopf) [flower]pot

Topf·blume *die* [flowering] pot plant
Töpfchen *das;* ~s, ~: potty (Brit. coll.)
Töpfer *der;* ~s, ~ potter
Töpferei *die;* ~, ~en (a) (Handwerk) pottery *no art.;*
(b) (Werkstatt) pottery; potter's workshop
(c) (Erzeugnis) piece of pottery; ~en pottery *sing.*
Töpferin *die;* ~, ~nen ▶ TÖPFER
Topf-: ~**lappen** *der* oven cloth; ~**pflanze** *die* pot plant
Tor[1] *das;* ~[e]s, ~e (a) gate; (einer Garage, Scheune) door; (fig.) gateway
(b) (Ballspiele) goal
(c) (Ski) gate
Tor[2] *der;* ~en, ~en (geh.: Narr) fool
Torf *der;* ~[e]s, ~e peat
Torheit *die;* ~, ~en (geh.) (a) foolishness
(b) (Handlung) foolish act
Tor·hüter *der,* **Tor·hüterin** *die* (Ballspiele) goalkeeper
töricht (geh.) 1 *Adj.* foolish
2 *adv.* foolishly
torkeln *itr. V.; mit sein* stagger
Tor·mann *der; Pl.* **Tormänner** *od.* **Torleute** (Ballspiele) goalkeeper
Tornister /tɔrˈnɪstɐ/ *der;* ~s, ~: knapsack; (Schulranzen) satchel
torpedieren *tr. V.* (Milit., fig.) torpedo
Torpedo *der;* ~s, ~s torpedo
Törtchen *das;* ~s, ~: tartlet
Torte *die;* ~, ~n (Creme-, Sahnetorte) gateau; (Obsttorte) [fruit] flan
Torten-: ~**boden** *der* flan case; (ohne Rand) flan base; ~**guss,** *~**guß** *der* glaze; ~**heber** *der;* ~~s, ~~: cake slice
Tortur *die;* ~, ~en (a) ordeal
(b) (veralt.: Folter) torture
Tor-: ~**wart** *der;* ~~[e]s, ~~e, ~**wartin** *die;* ~~, ~~nen (Ballspiele) goalkeeper; ~**weg** *der* gateway
tosen *itr. V.* roar; ‹*storm*› rage
tot *Adj.* dead; ~ **umfallen** drop dead; **sich ~ stellen** pretend to be dead; play dead; ~ **geboren** stillborn
total 1 *Adj.* total
2 *adv.* totally
Total·ausverkauf *der* clearance sale
totalitär (Politik) 1 *Adj.* totalitarian
2 *adv.* in a totalitarian way; ‹*organized, run*› along totalitarian lines
Total·schaden *der* (Versicherungsw.) **an beiden Fahrzeugen entstand ~:** both vehicles were a write-off
tot|ärgern *refl. V.* (ugs.) get livid (coll.)

*alte Schreibung - vgl. Hinweis auf S. xiv

Tote *der/die; adj. Dekl.* dead person; **die ~n** the dead
töten *tr., itr. V.* kill; deaden ‹*nerve etc.*›
toten-, Toten-: ~**blass,** *~**blaß,** ~**bleich** *Adj.* deathly pale; ~**gräber** *der;* ~~s, ~~, ~**gräberin** *die;* ~~, ~~nen gravedigger; ~**kopf** *der* (a) skull; (b) (als Symbol) death's head; (mit gekreuzten Knochen) skull and crossbones; ~**schädel** *der* skull; ~**sonntag** *der* (ev. Kirche) *Sunday before Advent on which the dead are commemorated;* ~**still** *Adj.* deathly quiet; ~**stille** *die* deathly silence; ~**wache** *die* vigil by the body
tot-, Tot-: ~**|fahren** *unr. tr. V.* [run over and] kill; *~**geboren** ▶ TOT; ~**geburt** *die* still birth; ~**|lachen** *refl. V.* (ugs.) kill oneself laughing; **zum Totlachen sein** be killing (coll.)
Toto *das od. der;* ~s, ~s (a) (Pferdetoto) tote (coll.); **im ~:** on the tote
(b) (Fußballtoto) [football] pools *pl.;* **[im] ~ spielen** do the pools
Toto·schein *der:* ▶ TOTO: pools coupon/ (coll.) tote ticket
tot-, Tot-: ~**|schießen** *unr. tr. V.* (ugs.) **jmdn. ~schießen** shoot sb. dead; ~**schlag** *der* (Rechtsw.) manslaughter *no indef. art.;* ~**|schlagen** *unr. tr. V.* beat to death; *~**|stellen** ▶ TOT; ~**|treten** *unr. tr. V.* trample ‹*person*› to death; step on and kill ‹*insect*›
Tötung *die;* ~, ~en killing; **fahrlässige ~** (Rechtsspr.) manslaughter by culpable negligence
Touch /tatʃ:/ *der;* ~s, ~s (ugs.) touch
tough /taf/ *Adj.* (ugs.) tough
Toupet /tuˈpe:/ *das;* ~s, ~s toupee
toupieren /tuˈpi:rən/ *tr. V.* backcomb
Tour /tu:ɐ̯/ *die;* ~, ~en tour (**durch** of); (kürzere Fahrt, Ausflug) trip; (mit dem Auto) drive; (mit dem Fahrrad) ride; (feste Strecke) route; **in einer ~** (ugs.) the whole time
touren /ˈtu:rən/ *itr. V.; mit sein* tour
Tourismus /tuˈrɪsmʊs/ *der;* ~: tourism
Tourismus·branche *die* tourism industry; tourist industry;
Tourist *der;* ~en, ~en tourist
Touristen-: ~**klasse** *die* tourist class; ~**paradies** *das* tourist paradise; ~**zentrum** *das* tourist centre
Touristin *die;* ~, ~nen tourist
Tournee /tʊrˈne:/ *die;* ~, ~s *od.* ~n tour; **auf ~ sein/gehen** be/go on tour
Trab *der;* ~[e]s trot; **im ~:** at a trot; **im ~ reiten** trot
traben *itr. V.; mit sein* (auch ugs.: laufen) trot
Tracht *die;* ~, ~en (a) (Volkstracht) national costume; (Berufstracht) uniform
(b) **eine ~ Prügel** a thrashing; (als Strafe) a hiding
trachten *itr. V.* (geh.) strive (**nach** for, after)
Tradition *die;* ~, ~en tradition

traditionell [1] *Adj.* traditional
[2] *adv.* traditionally

traf *1. u. 3. Pers. Sg. Prät. v.* TREFFEN

träfe *1. u. 3. Pers. Sg. Konjunktiv II v.* TREFFEN

Trafik *die;* ~, **~en** (österr.) tobacconist's [shop]

Trag·bahre *die* stretcher

tragbar *Adj.* **(a)** portable
(b) wearable ‹*clothes*›
(c) (finanziell) supportable ‹*cost, debt, etc.*›
(d) (erträglich) bearable; tolerable

träge [1] *Adj.* sluggish
[2] *adv.* sluggishly

Trage *die;* ~, **~n** **(a)** (Bahre) stretcher
(b) (Traggestell) pannier

tragen [1] *unr. tr. V.* **(a)** carry
(b) (bringen) take
(c) (ertragen) bear ‹*fate, destiny*›; bear, endure ‹*suffering*›
(d) (halten) hold; **einen/den linken Arm in der Schlinge ~:** have one's arm/one's left arm in a sling
(e) (von unten stützen) support
(f) (belastbar sein durch) be able to carry *or* take ‹*weight*›
(g) (übernehmen, aufkommen für) bear, carry ‹*costs etc.*›; take ‹*blame, responsibility, consequences*›
(h) (am Körper) wear ‹*clothes, wig, glasses, jewellery, etc.*›
(i) have ‹*false teeth, beard, etc.*›
(j) (hervorbringen) ‹*tree*› bear ‹*fruit*›; ‹*field*› produce ‹*crops*›
[2] *unr. itr. V.* **(a)** carry
(b) (am Körper) **man trägt [wieder] kurz/lang** short/long skirts are in fashion [again]
(c) der Baum trägt gut the tree produces a good crop

tragend *Adj.* (Stabilität gebend) load-bearing; supporting ‹*wall, column, function, etc.*›

Träger *der;* **~s,** ~ **(a)** porter
(b) (Austräger) paper boy/girl; delivery boy/girl
(c) (Bauw.) girder; [supporting] beam
(d) (an Kleidung) strap; (Hosenträger) braces *pl.;*
(e) (Inhaber) (eines Amts) holder; (eines Namens, Titels) bearer; (eines Preises) winner

Trägerin *die;* ~, **~nen** ▶ TRÄGER A, B, E

Trage·tasche *die* carrier bag

Trag-: ~fähigkeit *die* load-bearing capacity; **~fläche** *die* wing; **~flügel·boot** *das* hydrofoil

Trägheit *die;* ~, **~en** sluggishness

Tragik *die;* **~:** tragedy

tragi·komisch [1] *Adj.* tragicomic
[2] *adv.* tragicomically

tragisch [1] *Adj.* tragic; **das ist nicht [so] ~** (ugs.) it's not the end of the world (coll.)
[2] *adv.* tragically

Tragödie /tra'gø:di̯ə/ *die;* ~, **~n** tragedy

Trag·weite *die* consequences *pl.*

Trainer /'trɛ:nɐ/ *der;* **~s,** ~, **Trainerin** *die;* ~, **~nen** coach; trainer; (einer Fußballmannschaft) manager

trainieren [1] *tr. V.* **(a)** train; coach ‹*swimmer, tennis player*›; manage ‹*football team*›; exercise ‹*muscles etc.*›
(b) (üben, einüben) practise ‹*exercise, jump, etc.*›; **Fußball ~:** do football training
[2] *itr. V.* train

Training /'trɛ:nɪŋ/ *das;* **~s, ~s** training *no indef. art.*

Trainings-: ~anzug *der* track suit; **~hose** *die* track-suit bottoms *pl.* **~lager** *das* training camp

Trakt *der;* **~[e]s, ~e** section; (Flügel) wing

Traktor *der;* **~s, ~en** tractor

trällern *itr., tr. V.* warble

trampeln [1] *itr. V.* **(a) [mit den Füßen] ~:** stamp one's feet
(b) *mit sein* (treten) trample **(auf** + *Akk.* on)
[2] *tr. V.* trample

Trampel·pfad *der* [beaten] path

trampen /'trɛmpn̩/ *itr. V. mit sein* hitch-hike

Tramper *der;* **~s,** ~, **Tramperin** *die;* ~, **~nen** hitch-hiker

Trampolin *das;* **~s, ~e** trampoline

Tramway /'tramve/ *die;* ~, **~s** (österr.) tram (Brit.); streetcar (Amer.)

Tran *der;* **~[e]s** train-oil

Trance /'trã:s(ə)/ *die;* ~, **~n** trance; **in ~:** in a trance

tranchieren /trã'ʃi:rən/ *tr. V.* carve

Träne *die;* ~, **~n** tear; **~n lachen** laugh till one cries

tränen *itr. V.* ‹*eyes*› water

tranig *Adj.* (ugs. abwertend: langsam) sluggish; slow

trank *1. u. 3. Pers. Sg. Prät. v.* TRINKEN

Tränke *die;* ~, **~n** watering place

tränken *tr. V.* **(a)** water
(b) (sich voll saugen lassen) soak

Transfer *der;* **~s, ~s** (bes. Wirtsch., Sport) transfer

Transfer·summe *die* transfer fee

Trans·formator *der;* **~s, ~en** transformer

Transistor *der;* **~s, ~en** transistor

Transit /tran'zi:t, *auch:* 'tranzɪt/ *das;* **~s, ~s** transit visa

transitiv (Sprachw.) [1] *Adj.* transitive
[2] *adv.* transitively

Transit·verkehr *der* transit traffic

transparent *Adj.* transparent; (Licht durchlassend) translucent

Transparent *das;* **~[e]s, ~e** (Spruchband) banner; (Bild) transparency

Transparenz *die;* ~ transparency

Transport *der;* **~[e]s, ~e (a)** transportation ⇢

(b) (beförderte Lebewesen od. Sachen) (mit dem Zug) trainload; (mit mehreren Fahrzeugen) convoy; (Fracht) consignment

transportabel *Adj.* transportable; (tragbar) portable

Transporteur /...'tø:ɐ̯/ *der;* **~s, ~e, Transporteurin** *die;* **~, ~nen** carrier

transport·fähig *Adj.* moveable

transportieren *tr. V.* transport ‹*goods, people*›; move ‹*patient*›

Transport·kosten *Pl.* carriage *sing.;* transport costs

Transvestit *der;* **~en, ~en** transvestite

Trapez *das;* **~es, ~e (a)** (Geom.) trapezium (Brit.); trapezoid (Amer.)
(b) (im Zirkus) trapeze

trappeln *itr. V.; mit sein* patter [along]; ‹*feet*› patter; ‹*hoofs*› go clip-clop

Trara *das;* **~s** (ugs.) razzmatazz (coll.)

Trasse *die;* **~, ~n** (Verkehrsweg) [marked-out] route *or* line

trat *1. u. 3. Pers. Sg. Prät. v.* TRETEN

Tratsch *der;* **~[e]s** (ugs.) gossip; tittle-tattle

tratschen *itr. V.* (ugs.) gossip; (schwatzen) chatter

Traube *die;* **~, ~n (a)** bunch; (von Johannisbeeren usw.) cluster
(b) (Weinbeere~) grape
(c) (Menschenmenge) bunch; cluster

trauen [1] *itr. V.* **jmdm./einer Sache ~:** trust sb./sth.
[2] *refl. V.* dare
[3] *tr. V.* (verheiraten) ‹*vicar, registrar, etc.*› marry

Trauer *die;* **~ (a)** grief (**über** + *Akk.* over); (um einen Toten) mourning (**um** + *Akk.* for)
(b) (Trauerzeit) [period of] mourning
(c) ~ tragen be in mourning

Trauer-: ~fall *der* bereavement; **~feier** *die* memorial ceremony; (beim Begräbnis) funeral ceremony; **~karte** *die* [pre-printed] card of condolence; **~kleidung** *die* mourning clothes *pl.*

trauern *itr. V.* mourn; **um jmdn. ~:** mourn for sb.

Trauer-: ~spiel *das* tragedy; (fig. ugs.) deplorable business; **~weide** *die* weeping willow

träufeln *tr. V.* [let] trickle (**in** + *Akk.* into); drip ‹*ear drops etc.*›

Traum *der;* **~[e]s, Träume** /'trɔy:mə/ dream

Trauma *das;* **~s, Traumen** *od.* **~ta** (Psych., Med.) trauma

traumatisch (Psych., Med.) [1] *Adj.* traumatic
[2] *adv.* traumatically

träumen [1] *itr. V.* dream (**von** of, about); (unaufmerksam sein) [day]dream
[2] *tr. V.* dream

*old spelling - see note on page xiv

Träumer *der;* **~s, ~, Träumerin** *die;* **~, ~nen** dreamer

träumerisch [1] *Adj.* dreamy
[2] *adv.* dreamily

traumhaft (ugs.) [1] *Adj.* marvellous; fabulous (coll.)
[2] *adv.* fabulously (coll.)

Traum·urlaub *der* dream holiday

traurig [1] *Adj.* **(a)** sad; unhappy ‹*childhood, youth*›; painful ‹*duty*›
(b) (kümmerlich) sorry ‹*state etc.*›; miserable ‹*result*›
[2] *adv.* sadly

Traurigkeit *die;* **~:** sadness; sorrow

Trau-: ~ring *der* wedding ring; **~schein** *der* marriage certificate

Trauung *die;* **~, ~en** wedding [ceremony]

Trau·zeuge *der,* **Trau·zeugin** *die* witness (*at wedding ceremony*)

Trecker *der;* **~s, ~:** tractor

Treff *der;* **~s, ~s** (ugs.) rendezvous; (Ort) meeting place

treffen [1] *unr. tr. V.* **(a)** hit; ‹*punch, blow, object*› strike; **ihn trifft keine Schuld** he is in no way to blame
(b) (erschüttern) affect [deeply]; (verletzen) hurt
(c) (begegnen) meet
(d) (vorfinden) come upon, find ‹*anomalies etc.*›; **es gut/schlecht ~:** be *or* strike lucky/ be unlucky
(e) (als Funktionsverb) make ‹*arrangements, choice, preparations, decision, etc.*›
[2] *unr. itr. V.* **(a)** ‹*person, shot, etc.*› hit the target; **nicht ~:** miss [the target]
(b) *mit sein* **auf etw.** (*Akk.*) **~:** come upon sth.; **auf Widerstand/Ablehnung/ Schwierigkeiten ~:** meet with resistance/ rejection/difficulties
[3] *unr. refl. V.* **(a) sich mit jmdm. ~:** meet sb.
(b) *unpers.* **es trifft sich gut/schlecht** it is convenient/inconvenient

Treffen *das;* **~s, ~:** meeting

treffend [1] *Adj.* apt
[2] *adv.* aptly

Treffer *der;* **~s, ~ (a)** (Milit., Boxen, Fechten usw.) hit; (Schlag) blow; (Ballspiele) goal
(b) (Gewinn) win; (Los) winner

trefflich (geh.) [1] *Adj.* excellent; splendid ‹*person*›
[2] *adv.* excellently; splendidly

treff-, Treff-: ~punkt *der* meeting place; **~sicher** [1] *Adj.* accurate ‹*language, mode of expression*›; unerring ‹*judgement*›; [2] *adv.* accurately; **~sicherheit** *die* accuracy

Treib·eis *das* drift-ice

treiben [1] *unr. tr. V.* **(a)** drive
(b) (sich beschäftigen mit) go in for ‹*farming, cattle breeding, etc.*›; study ‹*French etc.*›; carry on, pursue ‹*studies, trade, craft*›; **viel Sport ~:** do a lot of sport; **es wüst/übel/toll ~** (ugs.) lead a dissolute/bad life/live it up

2 *unr. itr. V. meist, mit Richtungsangabe nur, mit sein* drift

Treiben *das;* ~s **(a)** (Durcheinander) bustle **(b)** (Tun) activities *pl.*; doings *pl.*

Treib-: ~**gas** *das* propellant; ~**haus** *das* hothouse; ~**haus·effekt** *der* greenhouse effect; ~**haus·gas** *das* greenhouse gas; ~**stoff** *der* fuel

trekken /'trɛkn̩/ *itr. V.; mit sein* trek

Trekking *das;* ~s trekking

Trenchcoat /'trɛntʃkoʊt/ *der;* ~s, ~s trench coat

Trend *der;* ~s, ~s trend (**zu** + *Dat.* towards); (Mode) vogue

trendig *Adj.* (ugs.) modern and fashionable

trennen 1 *tr. V.* **(a)** separate (**von** from); sever ‹*head, arm*›
(b) (auftrennen) unpick ‹*dress, seam*›
(c) (teilen) divide ‹*word, parts of a room etc., fig.: people*›
2 *refl. V.* **(a)** (voneinander weggehen) part [company]
(b) (eine Partnerschaft auflösen) ‹*couple, partners*› split up
(c) sich von etw. ~: part with sth.

Trennung *die;* ~, ~en (von Menschen) separation (**von** from); (von Gegenständen) parting; (von Wörtern) division

trepp-: ~**ab** *Adv.* down the stairs; ~**auf** *Adv.* up the stairs

Treppe *die;* ~, ~n staircase; [flight *sing.* of] stairs *pl.*; (im Freien, auf der Bühne) [flight *sing.* of] steps *pl.*

Treppen-: ~**absatz** *der* half-landing; ~**geländer** *das* banisters *pl.*; ~**haus** *das* stairwell; ~**stufe** *die* stair; (im Freien) step

Tresen *der;* ~s, ~ (bes. nordd.) bar; (Ladentisch) counter

Tresor *der;* ~s, ~e safe

Tret·boot *das* pedalo

treten 1 *unr. itr. V.* **(a)** *mit sein* step (**in** + *Akk.* into, **auf** + *Akk.* on to)
(b) (seinen Fuß setzen) **auf etw.** (*Akk.*) ~ tread on sth.
(c) (ausschlagen) kick
2 *unr. tr. V.* **(a)** (Tritt versetzen) kick ‹*person, ball, etc.*›
(b) (trampeln) trample ‹*path*›
(c) (mit dem Fuß niederdrücken) step on ‹*brake, pedal*›; operate ‹*bellows, clutch*›

treu 1 *Adj.* faithful; loyal; faithful ‹*husband, wife*›; loyal ‹*ally, subject*›; **jmdm. ~ sein** be true to sb.; **sich selbst** (*Dat.*)/**seinem Glauben ~ bleiben** be true to oneself/one's faith
2 *adv.* faithfully; loyally

Treue *die;* ~ **(a)** loyalty; (von [Ehe]partnern) fidelity
(b) (*Genauigkeit*) accuracy

treu-, Treu-: ~**hand[anstalt]** *die* (Wirtschaft) German privatization agency; ~**herzig** 1 *Adj.* ingenuous; (naiv) naïve; (unschuldig) innocent; 2 *adv.* ingenuously; (naiv) naïvely; (unschuldig) innocently; ~**herzigkeit** *die;* ~~: ingenuousness; (Naivität) naivety; (Unschuld) innocence; ~**los** *Adj.* disloyal, faithless ‹*friend, person*›; unfaithful ‹*husband, wife, lover*›

Tribunal *das;* ~s, ~e tribunal

Tribüne *die;* ~, ~n [grand]stand

Tribut *der;* ~[e]s, ~e (fig.) due; **einer Sache** (*Dat.*) **~ zollen** pay the price for sth.

Trichter *der;* ~s, ~ funnel

Trick *der;* ~s, ~s trick; (fig.: List) ploy

Trick·film *der* animated cartoon [film]

trieb *1. u. 3. Pers. Sg. Prät. v.* TREIBEN

Trieb *der;* ~[e]s, ~e **(a)** (innerer Antrieb) impulse; (Drang) urge; (Verlangen) [compulsive] desire
(b) (Spross) shoot

trieb-, Trieb-: ~**feder** *die* mainspring; (fig.) driving *or* motivating force; ~**haft** 1 *Adj.* compulsive; carnal ‹*sensuality*›; 2 *adv.* compulsively; ~**täter** *der*, ~**täterin** *die*, ~**verbrecher** *der*, ~**verbrecherin** *die: offender committing a crime in gratifying a compulsive desire;* (Sexualtäter) sexual offender; ~**wagen** *der* (Eisenb.) railcar; ~**werk** *das* engine

triefen *unr. od. regelm. itr. V.* **(a)** *mit sein* (fließen) (in Tropfen) drip; (in kleinen Rinnsalen) trickle
(b) (nass sein) be dripping wet; ‹*nose*› run

triff *Imperativ Sg. v.* TREFFEN

trifft *3. Pers. Sg. Präsens v.* TREFFEN

triftig *Adj.* good ‹*reason, excuse*›; valid, convincing ‹*motive, argument*›

Trikot[1] /tri'ko:/ *der od. das;* ~s, ~s (Stoff) cotton jersey

Trikot[2] /tri'ko:/ *das;* ~s, ~ (ärmellos) singlet; (eines Tänzers) leotard; (eines Fußballspielers) shirt

Triller *der;* ~s, ~: trill

trillern 1 *itr. V.* trill
2 *tr. V.* warble ‹*song*›

Triller·pfeife *die* police/referee's whistle

Trillion *die;* ~, ~en quintillion

Trimm-dich-Pfad *der* keep-fit trail

trimmen *tr. V.* (durch Sport) get ‹*person*› into shape

trinken 1 *unr. itr. V.* drink; **auf jmdn./etw. ~**: drink to sb./sth.
2 *unr. tr. V.* drink; **einen Kaffee/ein Bier ~**: have a coffee/beer

Trinker *der;* ~s, ~: alcoholic

Trinkerei *die;* ~, ~en drinking *no art.*

Trinkerin *die;* ~, ~nen alcoholic

Trink-: ~**geld** *das* tip; ~**halle** *die* **(a)** (in einem Heilbad) pump room; **(b)** (Kiosk) refreshment kiosk; (größer) refreshment stall; ~**wasser** *das* drinking water; **„kein ~wasser"** 'not for drinking'

Trio *das;* ~s, ~s (Musik, fig.) trio

Trip *der;* ~s, ~s **(a)** (ugs.: Ausflug) trip; jaunt **(b)** (Drogenjargon: Rausch) trip (coll.)

⋯

(c) (Drogenjargon: Dosis) fix (sl.)

trippeln *itr. V.; mit sein* trip; ‹*child*› patter

trist *Adj.* dreary; dismal

tritt *Imperativ Sg. u. 3. Pers. Sg. Präsens v.* TRETEN

Tritt *der;* **~[e]s, ~e** (Schritt; Trittbrett) step; (Fußtritt) kick

Tritt-: ~brett *das* step; **~brett·fahrer** *der,* **~brett·fahrerin** *die* (fig. abwertend) ≈ free rider (Amer.); *person who profits from another's work*

Triumph *der;* **~[e]s, ~e** triumph

triumphieren *itr. V.* **(a)** exult **(b)** (siegen) be triumphant; triumph (lit. or fig.) (**über** + *Akk.* over)

trivial **1** *Adj.* **(a)** (platt) banal; trite; (unbedeutend) trivial **(b)** (alltäglich) humdrum ‹*life, career*› **2** *adv.* (platt) banally; ‹*say etc.*› tritely

trocken **1** *Adj.* (auch fig.) dry **2** *adv.* drily

Trocken·haube *die* [hood-type] hairdrier

Trockenheit *die;* **~, ~en (a)** dryness **(b)** (Dürreperiode) drought

trocken-, Trocken-: ~|legen *tr. V.* **(a) ein Baby ~legen** change a baby's nappies (Brit.) *or* (Amer.) diapers; **(b)** (entwässern) drain ‹*marsh, pond, etc.*›; **~milch** *die* dried milk; **~|reiben** *unr. tr. V.* rub ‹*hair, child, etc.*› dry; wipe ‹*crockery, window, etc.*› dry

trocknen **1** *itr. V.; meist mit sein* dry **2** *tr. V.* dry

Troddel *die;* **~, ~n** tassel

Trödel *der;* **~s** (ugs.) junk; (für den Flohmarkt) jumble

trödeln *itr. V.* **(a)** (ugs.) dawdle (**mit** over) **(b)** *mit sein* (ugs.: schlendern) saunter

Trödler *der;* **~s, ~, Trödlerin** *die;* **~, ~nen** (ugs.) junk dealer

troff *1. u. 3. Pers. Sg. Prät. v.* TRIEFEN

trog *1. u. 3. Pers. Sg. Prät. v.* TRÜGEN

Trog *der;* **~[e]s, Tröge** trough

trollen (ugs.) *refl. V.* push off (coll.)

Trommel *die;* **~, ~n** drum

Trommel·bremse *die* drum brake

trommeln *itr. V.* **(a)** beat the drum; (als Beruf, Hobby usw.) play the drums **(b)** ([auf etw.] schlagen, auftreffen) drum (**auf** + *Akk.* on, **an** + *Akk.* against)

Trommel·wirbel *der* drum roll

Trommler *der;* **~s, ~** drummer

Trompete *die;* **~, ~n** trumpet

trompeten **1** *itr. V.* play the trumpet; (fig.) ‹*elephant*› trumpet **2** *tr. V.* play ‹*piece*› on the trumpet

Trompeter *der;* **~s, ~, Trompeterin** *die;* **~, ~nen** trumpeter

Tropen *Pl.* tropics

Tropen- tropical

Tropen·helm *der* sun helmet

Tropf *der;* **~[e]s, ~e** (Med.) drip

Tröpfchen *das;* **~s, ~:** droplet; (kleine Menge) drop

tröpfeln **1** *itr. V.* **(a)** *mit sein* drip (**auf** + *Akk.* on to, **aus, von** from) **(b)** *unpers.* (ugs.: leicht regnen) **es tröpfelt** it's spitting [with rain] **2** *tr. V.* let ‹*sth.*› drip (**in** + *Akk.* into, **auf** + *Akk.* on to)

tropfen **1** *itr. V.; mit Richtungsangabe mit sein* drip; ‹*tears*› fall; *unpers.* **es tropft [vom Dach** *usw.*] water is dripping from the roof *etc.;* **2** *tr. V.* let ‹*sth.*› drip (**in** + *Akk.* into, **auf** + *Akk.* on to)

Tropfen *der;* **~s, ~** drop; **ein guter/edler ~:** a good/fine vintage

Tropf·stein·höhle *die* limestone cave with stalactites and/or stalagmites

Trophäe *die;* **~, ~n** (hist., Jagd, Sport) trophy

tropisch *Adj.* tropical

Tross, *Troß *der;* **Trosses, Trosse** **(a)** (Milit.) baggage train **(b)** (Gefolge) retinue; (fig.: Zug) procession [of hangers-on]

Trost *der;* **~[e]s** consolation; (bes. geistlich) comfort; **nicht [ganz** *od.* **recht] bei ~ sein** (ugs.) be out of one's mind

trösten **1** *tr. V.* comfort, console (**mit** with) **2** *refl. V.* console oneself

tröstlich *Adj.* comforting

trost·los *Adj.* **(a)** hopeless; (verzweifelt) in despair *postpos.;* **(b)** (deprimierend, öde) miserable; dreary; hopeless ‹*situation*›

Trostlosigkeit *die;* **~ (a)** (einer Person, der Lage usw.) hopelessness; (Verzweiflung) despair **(b)** (Öde) dreariness

Trost·preis *der* consolation prize

Tröstung *die;* **~, ~en** comfort *no indef. art.*

Trott *der;* **~[e]s, ~e** trot; (fig.) routine

Trottel *der;* **~s, ~** (ugs.) fool

trottelig (ugs.) **1** *Adj.* doddery **2** *adv.* in a feeble-minded way

trotten *itr. V.; mit sein* trot [along]

trotz *Präp. mit Gen., seltener mit Dat.* in spite of; despite

Trotz *der;* **~es** defiance

trotz·dem /*auch:* '-'-/ *Adv.* nevertheless

trotzen *itr. V.* **(a)** (geh.: widerstehen) **jmdm./einer Sache ~** (auch fig.) defy sb./sth. **(b)** (trotzig sein) be contrary

trotzig **1** *Adj.* defiant; (widerspenstig) contrary; difficult ‹*child*› **2** *adv.* defiantly

trüb[e] **1** *Adj.* **(a)** (nicht klar) murky ‹*stream, water*›; cloudy ‹*liquid, wine, juice*›; (schlammig) muddy ‹*puddle*›; (schmutzig) dirty ‹*glass, window pane*›; dull ‹*eyes*›

---

*alte Schreibung - vgl. Hinweis auf S. xiv

(b) (nicht hell) dim ‹*light*›; dull, dismal ‹*day, weather*›; grey, overcast ‹*sky*›
2 *adv.* ‹*shine, light*› dimly

Trubel *der;* **~s** [hustle and] bustle; **sie stürzten sich in den dicksten ~:** they plunged into the thick of the hurly-burly

trüben **1** *tr. V.* **(a)** make ‹*liquid*› cloudy; cloud ‹*liquid*›
(b) (beeinträchtigen) dampen ‹*mood*›; mar ‹*relationship*›; cloud ‹*judgement*›
2 *refl. V.* ‹*liquid*› become cloudy; ‹*eyes*› become dull; ‹*sky*› darken

Trübsal *die;* **~, ~e** (geh.) **(a)** (Leiden) affliction
(b) (Kummer) grief; **~ blasen** (ugs.) mope (**wegen** over, about)

trüb-, Trüb-: ~selig **1** *Adj.* **(a)** (öde) dreary, depressing ‹*place, area, colour*›; **(b)** (traurig) gloomy; **2** *adv.* (traurig) gloomily; **~seligkeit** *die:* **(a)** (Ödheit) dreariness; **(b)** (Traurigkeit) gloom; **~sinn** *der* melancholy; **~sinnig** **1** *Adj.* melancholy; **2** *adv.* gloomily

Trübung *die;* **~, ~en** **(a)** clouding; (des Auges) dimming
(b) (Beeinträchtigung) deterioration; (der Stimmung) dampening

trudeln *itr. V. mit sein* roll

Trüffel *die;* **~, ~n** truffle

trug *1. u. 3. Pers. Prät. v.* TRAGEN

trüge *1. u. 3. Pers. Sg. Konjunktiv II v.* TRAGEN

trügen **1** *unr. tr. V.* deceive
2 *unr. itr. V.* be deceptive; ‹*feeling, deception*› be a delusion

trügerisch **1** *Adj.* deceptive; false ‹*hope, sign, etc.*›; treacherous ‹*ice*›
2 *adv.* deceptively

Truhe *die;* **~, ~n** chest

Trümmer *Pl.* (eines Gebäudes) rubble *sing.;* (Ruinen) ruins; (eines Flugzeugs usw.) wreckage *sing.;* (kleinere Teile) debris *sing.*

Trümmer·haufen *der* pile *or* heap of rubble

Trumpf *der;* **~[e]s, Trümpfe** (auch fig.) trump [card]; (Farbe) trumps *pl.;* **~ sein** (fig.: Mode sein) be the in thing

trumpfen *itr. V.* play a trump

Trunk *der;* **~[e]s, Trünke** (geh.) (Getränk) drink; beverage (formal)

Trunkenheit *die;* **~:** drunkenness; **~ am Steuer** drink-driving

Trunk·sucht *die* alcoholism *no art.*

trunk·süchtig *Adj.* alcoholic; **~ sein** be an alcoholic

Trupp *der;* **~s, ~s** troop; (von Arbeitern, Gefangenen) gang; (von Soldaten, Polizisten) squad

Truppe *die;* **~, ~n** **(a)** (Einheit der Streitkräfte) unit
(b) *Pl.* (Soldaten) troops
(c) (Streitkräfte) [armed] forces *pl.;* (Heer) army
(d) (Gruppe von Schauspielern, Artisten) troupe; (von Sportlern) squad

Trut·hahn *der* turkey [cock]

tschau *Interj.* (ugs.) ciao (coll.)

Tscheche *der;* **~n, ~n** Czech

Tschechien *(das);* **~s** Czech Republic

Tschechin *die;* **~, ~nen** Czech

tschechisch *Adj.* Czech

Tschechoslowakei *die;* **~** (hist.) Czechoslovakia *no art.*

tschechoslowakisch *Adj.* (hist.) Czechoslovak[ian]

tschüs *Interj.* (ugs.) bye (coll.)

Tsd. *Abk.* = **Tausend**

T-Shirt /'ti:ʃə:t/ *das;* **~s, ~s** T-shirt

Tube *die;* **~, ~n** tube

Tuberkulose *die;* **~, ~n** (Med.) tuberculosis *no art.*

Tuch *das;* **~[e]s, Tücher** *od.* **~e** **(a)** *Pl.* **Tücher** cloth; (Kopf-, Halstuch) scarf
(b) *Pl.* **~e** (Gewebe) cloth

Tuch·fühlung *die* (scherzh.) physical contact

tüchtig **1** *Adj.* **(a)** efficient; (fähig) capable, competent (**in** + *Dat.* at)
(b) (ugs.: beträchtlich) sizeable ‹*piece, portion*›; big ‹*gulp*›; hearty ‹*eater, appetite*›
2 *adv.* **(a)** efficiently; (fähig) competently
(b) (ugs.: sehr) really ‹*cold, warm*›; ‹*snow, rain*› good and proper (coll.); ‹*eat*› heartily

Tüchtigkeit *die;* **~:** efficiency; (Fähigkeit) ability; competence; (Fleiß) industry

Tücke *die;* **~, ~n** **(a)** (Hinterhältigkeit) deceit[fulness]; (List) guile
(b) ([verborgene] Gefahr/Schwierigkeit) [hidden] danger/difficulty

tuckern *itr. V.; mit Richtungsangabe mit sein* chug

tückisch **1** *Adj.* **(a)** (hinterhältig) wily; (betrügerisch) deceitful
(b) (gefährlich) treacherous ‹*bend, slope, spot, etc.*›
2 *adv.* craftily

tüfteln *itr. V.* (ugs.) fiddle (**an** + *Dat.* with); do finicky work (**an** + *Dat.* on); (geistig) rack one's brains (**an** + *Dat.* over)

Tugend *die;* **~, ~en** virtue

tugendhaft **1** *Adj.* virtuous
2 *adv.* virtuously

Tüll *der;* **~s, ~e** tulle

Tülle *die;* **~, ~n** (bes. nordd.) spout

Tulpe *die;* **~, ~n** tulip

tummeln *refl. V.* romp [about]

Tummel·platz *der* (auch fig.) playground

Tumor *der;* **~s, ~en** (Med.) tumour

Tümpel *der;* **~s, ~:** pond

Tumult *der;* **~[e]s, ~e** tumult; commotion; (Protest) uproar

tun **1** *unr. tr. V.* **(a)** do; **so etwas tut man nicht** that is just not done; **[etwas] mit etw./jmdm. zu ~ haben** be concerned with sth./have dealings with sb.
(b) *als Funktionsverb* make ‹*remark, catch, etc.*›; take ‹*step, jump*›; do ‹*deed*› ···

(c) (bewirken) work, perform ‹*miracle*›
(d) (antun) **jmdm. etw. ~:** do sth. to sb.
(e) **es ~** (ugs.: genügen) be good enough
(f) (ugs.: irgendwohin bringen) put
2 *unr. itr. V.* **(a)** (ugs.: funktionieren) work
(b) freundlich/geheimnisvoll ~: pretend to be *or* (coll.) act friendly/act mysteriously
3 *unr. refl. V.; unpers.* **es hat sich einiges getan** quite a bit has happened

Tünche *die; ~, ~n* distemper; wash; **[weiße] ~:** whitewash

tünchen *tr.* (*auch itr.*) *V.* distemper; **weiß ~:** whitewash

Tunell *das; ~s, ~s* (südd., österr., schweiz.) ▶ TUNNEL

tunen /'tju:nən/ *tr. V.* (Kfz-W.) tune

Tuner /'tju:nɐ/ *der; ~s, ~* **(a)** (Elektronik) tuner
(b) (Kfz-W.) tuner; tuning expert

Tunesien /tu'ne:zi̯ən/ (*das*)*; ~s* Tunisia

tunesisch *Adj.* Tunisian

Tunke *die; ~, ~n* (bes. ostmd.) sauce; (Bratensoße) gravy

tunken *tr. V.* (bes. ostmd.) dip

tunlichst *Adv.* (geh.) **(a)** (möglichst) as far as possible
(b) (unbedingt) at all costs

Tunnel *der; ~s, ~ od. ~s* tunnel

tupfen *tr. V.* **(a)** dab
(b) (mit Tupfen versehen) dot

Tupfen *der; ~s, ~:* dot; (größer) spot

Tupfer *der; ~s, ~* (Med.) swab

Tür *die; ~, ~en* door; (Garten~) gate; **an die ~ gehen** (öffnen) [go and] answer the door; **vor die ~ gehen** go outside

Turban *der; ~s, ~e* turban

Turbine *die; ~, ~n* turbine

turbulent 1 *Adj.* (auch fachspr.) turbulent
2 *adv.* (auch fachspr.) turbulently

Turbulenz *die; ~, ~en* (auch Physik, Astron., Met.) turbulence *no pl.*

Tür·griff *der* door handle

Türke *der; ~n, ~n* Turk

Türkei *die; ~:* Turkey *no art.*

türken *tr. V.* (ugs.) fake ‹*scene, letter, document, etc.*›; make up ‹*story, report*›

Türkin *die; ~, ~nen* Turk

türkis *indekl. Adj.* turquoise

Türkis *der; ~es, ~e* turquoise

türkisch *Adj.* Turkish

Tür·klinke *die* door handle

Turm *der; ~[e]s, Türme* **(a)** tower; (spitzer Kirchturm) spire; steeple
(b) (Schach) rook
(c) (Sprungturm) diving platform

Türmchen *das; ~s, ~:* turret

türmen[1] 1 *tr. V.* (stapeln) stack up; (häufen) pile up
2 *refl. V.* be piled up; ‹*clouds*› gather

türmen[2] *itr. V.; mit sein* (salopp) scarper (Brit. coll.)

Turm·falke *der* kestrel

turnen 1 *itr. V.* do gymnastics; (Schulw.) do gym
2 *tr. V.* do, perform ‹*exercise, routine*›

Turnen *das; ~s* gymnastics *sing., no art.;* (Schulw.) gym *no art.;* PE *no art.*

Turner *der; ~s, ~,* **Turnerin** *die; ~, ~nen* gymnast

Turn-: ~halle *die* gymnasium; **~hemd** *das* [gym] singlet; **~hose** *die* gym shorts *pl.*

Turnier *das; ~s, ~e* (auch hist.) tournament; (Reitturnier) show; (Tanzturnier) competition

Turn·schuh *der* gym shoe

Turnus *der; ~, ~se* regular cycle

Turn·verein *der* gymnastics club

Tür-: ~öffner *der* door-opener; **~rahmen** *der* doorframe

turteln *itr. V.* (scherzh.: zärtlich sein) bill and coo

Tusch *der; ~[e]s, ~e* fanfare

Tusche *die; ~, ~n* Indian (Brit.) *or* (Amer.) India ink

Tuschelei *die; ~, ~en* **(a)** (das Tuscheln) whispering
(b) (Äußerung) whisper

tuscheln *itr., tr. V.* whisper

Tussi *die; ~, ~s* (salopp) female (derog.)

Tüte *die; ~, ~n* bag

tuten *itr. V.* hoot; ‹*siren, [fog]horn*› sound

Tutor *der; ~s, ~en,* **Tutorin** *die; ~, ~nen* (Päd.) tutor

Tycoon /tai'ku:n/ *der; ~s, ~s* tycoon

Typ *der; ~s, ~en* **(a)** type
(b) *Gen. auch* **~en** (ugs.: Mann) bloke (Brit. coll.)

Type *die; ~, ~n* (Druck-, Schreibmaschinentype) type

Typhus *der; ~:* typhoid [fever]

typisch 1 *Adj.* typical (**für** of)
2 *adv.* typically

Typographie *die; ~, ~n* (Druckw.) typography

typographisch (Druckw.) 1 *Adj.* typographical
2 *adv.* typographically

Tyrann *der; ~en, ~en* (auch fig.) tyrant

Tyrannei *die; ~, ~en* (auch fig.) tyranny

Tyrannin *die; ~, ~nen* ▶ TYRANN

tyrannisch 1 *Adj.* tyrannical
2 *adv.* tyrannically

tyrannisieren *tr. V.* tyrannize

*old spelling - see note on page xiv

t

U u

u, U /u:/ *das;* **~, ~**: u/U

u. *Abk.* = **und**

ü, Ü /y:/ *das;* **~, ~**: u umlaut

U-Bahn *die* underground (Brit.); subway (Amer.); (bes. in London) tube

U-Bahnhof *der*; **U-Bahn-Station** *die* underground station (Brit.); subway station (Amer.); (bes. in London) tube station

übel *Adj.* **(a)** foul, nasty ‹*smell, weather*›; bad, nasty ‹*headache, cold, taste*›; nasty ‹*consequences, situation*›; sorry ‹*state, affair*›; foul, (coll.) filthy ‹*mood*›; **nicht ~** (ugs.) not bad at all
(b) (unwohl) **jmdm. ist/wird ~**: sb. feels sick
(c) (verwerflich) bad; wicked; nasty, dirty ‹*trick*›
(d) jmdm. etw. ~ nehmen hold sth. against sb.; **etw. ~ nehmen** take offence at sth.

Übel *das;* **~s, ~**: evil

Übelkeit *die;* **~, ~en** nausea

***übel|nehmen** ▶ ÜBEL D

Übel·täter *der*, **Übel·täterin** *die* wrongdoer

üben *tr. V.* **(a)** (*auch itr.*) practise; rehearse ‹*scene, play*›; practise on ‹*musical instrument*›
(b) (trainieren, schulen) exercise ‹*fingers*›; train ‹*memory*›

über [1] *Präp. mit Dat.* **(a)** (Lage, Standort) over; above; (in einer Rangfolge) above; **~ jmdm. wohnen** live above sb.; **zehn Grad ~ Null** ten degrees above zero; **sie trug eine Jacke ~ dem Kleid** she wore a jacket over her dress
(b) (während) during; **~ dem Lesen/der Arbeit einschlafen** fall asleep over one's book/magazine *etc.*/over one's work
[2] *Präp. mit Akk.* **(a)** (Richtung) over; (quer hinüber) across; **~ Ulm nach Stuttgart** via Ulm to Stuttgart
(b) (während) over; (für die Dauer von) for
(c) (betreffend) about; **~ etw. reden/schreiben** talk/write about sth.; **ein Scheck/eine Rechnung ~ 100 Euro** a cheque/bill for 100 euros
(d) Kinder ~ 10 Jahre children over ten [years of age]
[3] *Adv.* **(a)** (mehr als) over
(b) ~ und ~: all over

über·all /*od.* --'-/ *Adv.* **(a)** everywhere
(b) (bei jeder Gelegenheit) always

überall-: ~her *Adv.* from all over the place; **~hin** *Adv.* everywhere

Über·angebot *das* surplus (**an** + *Dat.* of); (Schwemme) glut (**an** + *Dat.* of)

über·anstrengen *tr. V.;* **ich überanstrenge, überanstrengt, zu überanstrengen** overtax ‹*person, energy*›; strain ‹*eyes, nerves, heart*›; **sich ~**: overexert oneself

über·arbeiten [1] *tr. V.* rework; revise ‹*text, edition*›
[2] *refl. V.* overwork

über·aus *Adv.* (geh.) extremely

über·backen *unr. tr. V.* **etw. mit Käse** *usw.* **~**: top sth. with cheese *etc.* and brown it lightly [under the grill/in a hot oven]

Über·bein *das* (Med.) ganglion

überbelichten *tr. V.;* **ich überbelichte, überbelichtet, überzubelichten** (Fot.) overexpose

über·bieten *unr. tr. V.* **(a)** outbid (**um** by)
(b) (übertreffen) surpass; outdo ‹*rival*›; break ‹*record*› (**um** by); exceed ‹*target*› (**um** by)

Über·blick *der* **(a)** view; **einen guten ~ über etw.** (*Akk.*) **haben** have a good view over sth.
(b) (Abriss) survey
(c) (Einblick) overall view

über·blicken *tr. V.* ▶ ÜBERSEHEN A, B

über·bringen *unr. tr. V.* deliver; convey ‹*greetings, congratulations*›

über·brücken *tr. V.* bridge ‹*gap, gulf*›; reconcile ‹*difference*›

Überbrückung *die;* **~, ~en** (fig.) bridging; (von Gegensätzen) reconciliation

über·buchen *tr. V.* overbook

überdacht *Adj.* covered ‹*terrace, station platform, etc.*›

über·dauern *tr. V.* survive ‹*war, separation, hardship*›

über·dehnen *tr. V.* overstretch; strain ‹*muscle*›

über·dies *Adv.* moreover

Über·dosis *die* overdose

Über·druck *der; Pl.* **Überdrücke** excess pressure

Überdruss, ***Überdruß** *der;* **Überdrusses** surfeit (**an** + *Dat.* of)

überdrüssig *Adj.* **jmds./einer Sache ~ sein/werden** be/grow tired of sb./sth.

über·eignen *tr. V.* **jmdm. etw. ~**: transfer sth. *or* make sth. over to sb.

Über·eignung *die* transfer (**an** + *Akk.* to)

über·eilen *tr. V.* rush; **übereilt** overhasty

über·einander *Adv.* **(a)** one on top of the other; **Holzscheite** *usw.*: **~ legen** lay pieces of wood *etc.* one on top of the other; **Arme/Beine ~ schlagen** fold one's arms/cross one's legs
(b) ‹*talk etc.*› about each other

U

***übereinander|legen** *usw.* ▶ ÜBEREINANDER A

überein|kommen *unr. itr. V.; mit sein* agree; come to an agreement

Überein·kommen *das;* **~s, ~, Übereinkunft** *die;* **~, Übereinkünfte** agreement

überein|stimmen *itr. V.* **(a)** (einer Meinung sein) agree (**in** + *Dat.* on) **(b)** (sich gleichen) ‹*colours, styles*› match; ‹*figures, statements, reports, results*› tally, agree; ‹*views, opinions*› coincide

Überein·stimmung *die* agreement (**in** + *Dat.* on; *Gen.* between)

über·empfindlich [1] *Adj.* oversensitive (**gegen** to); (Med.) hypersensitive (**gegen** to) [2] *adv.* oversensitively; (Med.) hypersensitively

Über·empfindlichkeit *die* oversensitivity (**gegen** to); (Med.) hypersensitivity (**gegen** to)

über|fahren¹ [1] *unr. tr. V.* **jmdn. ~:** ferry *or* take sb. over [2] *unr. itr. V.; mit sein* cross over

über·fahren² *unr. tr. V.* **(a)** run over **(b)** (hinwegfahren über) cross; go over ‹*crossroads*›

Über·fahrt *die* crossing (**über** + *Akk.* of)

Über·fall *der* attack (**auf** + *Akk.* on); (aus dem Hinterhalt) ambush (**auf** + *Akk.* on); (mit vorgehaltener Waffe) hold-up; (auf eine Bank o. Ä.) raid (**auf** + *Akk.* on)

über·fallen *unr. tr. V.* **(a)** attack; raid ‹*bank, enemy position, village, etc.*›; (hinterrücks) ambush; (mit vorgehaltener Waffe) hold up **(b)** (überkommen) ‹*tiredness, homesickness, fear*› come over

über·fällig *Adj.* overdue

über·fischen *tr. V.* overfish

über·fliegen *unr. tr. V.* **(a)** fly over; overfly (formal) **(b)** (flüchtig lesen) skim [through]

über·flügeln *tr. V.* outshine; outstrip

Über·fluss, *Über·fluß *der* abundance (**an** + *Dat.* of); (Wohlstand) affluence

über·flüssig *Adj.* superfluous; unnecessary ‹*purchase, words, work*›

über·fluten *tr. V.* (auch fig.) flood

Über|flutung *die;* **~, ~en** (auch fig.) flooding

über·fordern *tr. V.* **jmdn. [mit etw.] ~:** overtax sb. [with sth.]; ask *or* demand too much of sb. [with sth.]

über·fragen *tr. V.* **da bin ich überfragt** I don't know the answer to that

über·fremden *tr. V.* **überfremdet werden/sein** ‹*country*› be dominated [by foreign influences]

*****alte Schreibung - vgl. Hinweis auf S. xiv

Über·fremdung *die;* **~, ~en** domination [by foreign influences]

über·frieren *unr. itr. V.; mit sein* freeze over; **~de Nässe** black ice

über|führen¹ *tr. V.* transfer

über·führen² *tr. V.* **(a)** ▶ ÜBERFÜHREN¹; **(b) jmdn. [eines Verbrechens] ~:** convict sb. [of a crime]

Über·führung *die* **(a)** transfer **(b)** (eines Verdächtigen) conviction **(c)** (Brücke) bridge; (Hochstraße) overpass; (für Fußgänger) [foot]bridge

über·füllt *Adj.* crammed full (**von** with); (mit Menschen) overcrowded (**von** with); oversubscribed ‹*course*›

Über·gabe *die* **(a)** handing over (**an** + *Akk.* to); (von Macht) handing over **(b)** (Auslieferung an den Gegner) surrender (**an** + *Akk.* to)

Über·gang *der* **(a)** crossing **(b)** (Stelle zum Überqueren) crossing; (Bahnübergang) level crossing (Brit.); grade crossing (Amer.); (Grenzübergang) crossing point **(c)** (Wechsel, Überleitung) transition (**zu, auf** + *Akk.* to)

über·geben [1] *unr. tr. V.* **(a)** hand over; pass ‹*baton*› **(b)** (übereignen) transfer, make over (*Dat.* to) **(c)** (ausliefern) surrender (*Dat.*, **an** + *Akk.* to) **(d) eine Straße dem Verkehr ~:** open a road to traffic [2] *unr. refl. V.* (sich erbrechen) vomit

über|gehen¹ *unr. itr. V.; mit sein* **(a)** pass **(b) zu etw. ~:** go over to sth. **(c) in etw.** (*Akk.*) **~** (zu etw. werden) turn into sth.

über·gehen² *unr. tr. V.* **(a)** (nicht beachten) ignore **(b)** (auslassen, überspringen) skip [over] **(c)** (nicht berücksichtigen) pass over

über·geordnet *Adj.* higher ‹*court, authority, position*›; greater ‹*significance*›; superordinate ‹*concept*›

Über·gewicht *das* **(a)** excess weight **(b)** (fig.) predominance

über·gewichtig *Adj.* overweight

über·glücklich *Adj.* blissfully happy; (hocherfreut) overjoyed

über|greifen *unr. itr. V.* **auf etw.** (*Akk.*) **~:** spread to sth.

Über·griff *der* (unrechtmäßiger Eingriff) encroachment (**auf** + *Akk.* on); infringement (**auf** + *Akk.* of); (Angriff) attack (**auf** + *Akk.* on)

Über·größe *die* outsize

überhand: **~ nehmen** get out of hand; ‹*attacks, muggings, etc.*› increase alarmingly

über|hängen *tr. V.* **sich** (*Dat.*) **eine Jacke ~:** put a jacket round one's shoulders; **sich** (*Dat.*) **das Gewehr/die Tasche ~:** hang the rifle/bag over one's shoulder

über·häufen *tr. V.* **jmdn. mit etw. ~:** heap *or* shower sth. on sb.

überhaupt *Adv.* **(a)** in general **(b)** ~ **nicht** not at all; ~ **keine Zeit haben** have no time at all; ~ **nichts** nothing at all

überheblich [1] *Adj.* arrogant; supercilious ‹*grin*› [2] *adv.* arrogantly; ‹*grin*› superciliously

Überheblichkeit *die;* ~: arrogance

über·holen [1] *tr. V.* **(a)** overtake (esp. Brit.); pass (esp. Amer.) **(b)** (übertreffen) outstrip **(c)** (wieder instand setzen) overhaul [2] *itr. V.* overtake (esp. Brit.); pass (esp. Amer.)

Überholspur *die* overtaking lane (esp. Brit.); pass lane (esp. Amer.)

überholt *Adj.* (veraltet) outdated

Überholung *die;* ~, ~**en** overhaul

Überhol·verbot *das* ban on overtaking

über·hören *tr. V.* not hear

über·irdisch [1] *Adj.* celestial; heavenly; (übernatürlich) supernatural [2] *adv.* celestially; (übernatürlich) supernaturally

über|kochen *itr. V.; mit sein* (auch fig. ugs.) boil over

über·kommen *unr. tr. V.* **Mitleid/Ekel/Furcht überkam mich** I was overcome by pity/revulsion/fear

über·laden *unr. tr. V.* (auch fig.) overload

über·lassen *unr. tr. V.* **(a) jmdm. etw.** ~: let sb. have sth. **(b) sich** (*Dat.*) **selbst** ~ **sein** be left to one's own devices **(c) etw. jmdm.** ~ (etw. jmdn. entscheiden/tun lassen) leave sth. to sb.

über·lasten *tr. V.* overload; overtax ‹*person*›; (mit Arbeit) overwork ‹*person*›

Über·lauf *der* overflow

über|laufen[1] *unr. itr. V.; mit sein* **(a)** overflow **(b)** (auf die gegnerische Seite überwechseln) defect; ‹*partisan*› go over to the other side

über·laufen[2] *unr. tr. V.* seize; **ein Frösteln/Schauer überlief mich, es überlief mich [eis]kalt** a cold shiver ran down my spine

überlaufen[3] *Adj.* overcrowded

Über·läufer *der,* **Über·läuferin** *die* (auch fig.) defector

über·leben *tr. V.* survive

Über·lebende *der/die; adj. Dekl.* survivor

über|legen[1] *tr. V.* **jmdm. etw.** ~: put sth. over sb.

über·legen[2] [1] *tr. V.* consider; think about; **es sich anders** ~: change one's mind [2] *itr. V.* think

überlegen[3] [1] *Adj.* **(a)** superior; clear, convincing ‹*win, victory*›; **jmdm.** ~ **sein** be superior to sb. (**an** + *Dat.* in) **(b)** (herablassend) supercilious [2] *adv.* **(a)** in a superior manner; ‹*play*› much the better: ‹*win, argue*› convincingly **(b)** (herablassend) superciliously

Überlegenheit *die;* ~: superiority

überlegt [1] *Adj.* carefully considered [2] *adv.* in a carefully considered way

Überlegung *die;* ~, ~**en** **(a)** thought **(b)** (Gedanke) idea; ~**en** (Gedankengang) thoughts

über·liefern *tr. V.* hand down

Über·lieferung *die* tradition

überlisten *tr. V.* outwit

überm *Präp.* + *Art.* = **über dem**

Über·macht *die* superior strength; (zahlenmäßig) superior numbers *pl.*

über·mannen *tr. V.* overcome

Über·maß *das* excessive amount, excess (**an** + *Dat.* of)

über·mäßig [1] *Adj* excessive [2] *adv.* excessively

über·menschlich *Adj.* superhuman

über·mitteln *tr. V.* send; (als Mittler weitergeben) pass on, convey ‹*greetings, regards, etc.*›

über·morgen *Adv.* the day after tomorrow

über·müden *tr. V.* overtire; **übermüdet** overtired; exhausted

Übermüdung *die;* ~: overtiredness; exhaustion

Über·mut *der* high spirits *pl.*

übermütig [1] *Adj.* high-spirited [2] *adv.* high-spiritedly

über·nächst... *Adj.* **im** ~**en Jahr,** ~**es Jahr** the year after next; **am** ~**en Tag** two days later

über·nachten *itr. V.* stay overnight

übernächtigt *Adj.* ‹*person*› tired *or* worn out [through lack of sleep]; tired ‹*face, look, etc.*›

Übernachtung *die;* ~, ~**en** overnight stay; ~ **und Frühstück** bed and breakfast

Übernahme *die;* ~ (von Waren, einer Sendung) taking delivery *no art.;* (einer Idee usw.) adoption, taking over *no indef. art.;* (der Macht, einer Praxis usw.) take over

über·natürlich *Adj.* supernatural

über·nehmen [1] *unr. tr. V.* **(a)** take delivery of ‹*goods, consignment*›; take over ‹*power, practice, business, etc.*›; take on ‹*job, position, etc.*›; undertake to pay ‹*costs*› **(b)** (sich zu Eigen machen) adopt ‹*ideas, methods, subject, etc.*› (**von** from); borrow ‹*word, phrase*› (**von** from) [2] *unr. refl. V.* overdo things *or* it; **sich mit etw.** ~: take on too much with sth.

Über·produktion *die* (Wirtsch., Med.) overproduction

über·prüfen *tr. V.* check (**auf** + *Akk.* for); review ‹*issue, situation, results*›

Über·prüfung *die* **(a)** checking *no indef. art.* (**auf** + *Akk.* for) **(b)** (Kontrolle) check; (einer Lage, Frage usw.) review

über·queren *tr. V.* cross

über·ragen *tr. V.* **(a) jmdn./etw. ~:** tower above sb./sth.
(b) (übertreffen) **jmdn. an etw.** (*Dat.*) **~:** be head and shoulders above sb. in sth.

überragend [1] *Adj.* outstanding
[2] *adv.* outstandingly

über·raschen *tr. V.* surprise

Überraschung *die;* **~, ~en** surprise

über·reden *tr. V.* persuade

Überredung *die;* **~:** persuasion

über·regional [1] *Adj.* national ‹*newspaper, radio station*›
[2] *adv.* nationally

über·reichen *tr. V.* **[jmdm.] etw. ~:** present sth. [to sb.]

Überreichung *die;* **~:** presentation

über·reif *Adj.* over-ripe

über·rumpeln *tr. V.* **jmdn. ~:** take sb. by surprise

über·runden *tr. V.* **(a)** (Sport) lap
(b) (übertreffen) outstrip

übers *Präp. + Art.* = **über das**

über·sättigen *tr. V.* supersaturate ‹*solution*›; glut ‹*market*›; satiate ‹*public*›

Überschall-: ~flugzeug *das* supersonic aircraft; **~geschwindigkeit** *die* supersonic speed

über·schatten *tr. V.* overshadow; cast its/their shadow over; (fig.) cast a shadow over

über·schätzen *tr. V.* overestimate; overrate ‹*artist, talent, etc.*›

Über·schätzung *die* ▶ ÜBERSCHÄTZEN: overestimation; overrating

überschaubar *Adj.* **eine ~e Menge/Zahl** a manageable quantity/number

über·schauen *tr. V.* ▶ ÜBERSEHEN A, B

Über·schlag *der* **(a)** rough calculation *or* estimate
(b) (Turnen) handspring
(c) ▶ LOOPING

über|schlagen¹ [1] *unr. tr. V.* **die Beine ~:** cross one's legs
[2] *unr. itr. V.; mit sein* ‹*wave*› break

über·schlagen² [1] *unr. tr. V.* **(a)** skip ‹*chapter, page, etc.*›
(b) (ungefähr berechnen) calculate *or* estimate roughly
[2] *unr. refl. V.* go head over heels; ‹*car*› turn over

über|schnappen *itr. V.; mit sein* (ugs.) go crazy

über·schneiden *unr. refl. V.* cross, intersect; (fig.) overlap

über·schreiben *unr. tr. V.* **(a)** entitle; head ‹*chapter, section*›
(b) etw. jmdm. *od.* **auf jmdn. ~:** transfer sth. to sb.

über·schreiten *unr. itr. V.* cross; (fig.) exceed

*old spelling - see note on page xiv

Über·schrift *die* heading; (in einer Zeitung) headline; (Titel) title

Über·schuss, ***Über·schuß** *der* surplus (**an** + *Dat.* of)

überschüssig *Adj.* surplus

über·schütten *tr. V.* cover

Überschwang *der;* **~[e]s** exuberance

über·schwänglich [1] *Adj.* effusive ‹*words etc.*›; wild ‹*joy, enthusiasm*›
[2] *adv.* effusively

über·schwemmen *tr. V.* (auch fig.) flood

Überschwemmung *die;* **~, ~en** flood; (das Überschwemmen) flooding *no pl.*

***über·schwenglich** ▶ ÜBERSCHWÄNGLICH

Über·see: aus *od.* **von ~:** from overseas; **in/nach ~:** overseas

über·sehen *unr. tr. V.* **(a)** look out over
(b) (abschätzen) assess ‹*damage, situation, consequences, etc.*›
(c) (nicht sehen) overlook; miss; miss ‹*turning, signpost*›
(d) (ignorieren) ignore

über·senden *unr.* (*auch regelm.*) *tr. V.* send

über|setzen¹ [1] *tr. V.* ferry over
[2] *itr. V.; auch mit sein* cross [over]

über·setzen² *tr., itr. V.* (auch fig.) translate

Über·setzer *der,* **Übersetzerin** *die;* **~, ~nen** translator

Übersetzung *die;* **~, ~en** translation

Über·sicht *die* **(a)** overall view, overview (**über** + *Akk.* of)
(b) (Darstellung) survey; (Tabelle) summary

über·sichtlich [1] *Adj.* clear; ‹*crossroads*› which allows a clear view
[2] *adv.* clearly

Übersichtlichkeit *die;* **~:** clarity; (einer Kreuzung) clear layout

über|siedeln¹, über·siedeln² *itr. V.; mit sein* move (**nach** to)

Über·siedler *der,* **Über·siedlerin** *die* migrant

überspannt *Adj.* exaggerated ‹*ideas, behaviour, gestures*›; extreme ‹*views*›; inflated ‹*demands, expectations*›

über·spielen *tr. V.* **(a)** (hinweggehen über) cover up; smooth over ‹*difficult situation*›
(b) (aufnehmen) **[auf ein Tonband] ~:** transfer ‹*record*› to tape; put ‹*record*› on tape

über·spitzen *tr. V.* **etw. ~:** push *or* carry sth. too far

über·springen *unr. tr. V.* **(a)** jump ‹*obstacle*›
(b) (auslassen) miss out

über|stehen¹ *unr. itr. V.; südd., österr., schweiz. mit sein* jut out

über·stehen² *unr. tr. V.* come through ‹*danger, war, operation*›; get over ‹*illness*›

über·steigen *unr. tr. V.* **(a)** climb over
(b) (fig.) exceed

über·stimmen *tr. V.* outvote

über|streifen *tr. V.* **[sich (*Dat.*)] etw. ~:** slip sth. on
über|stülpen *tr. V.* pull on ‹*hat etc.*›
Über·stunde *die:* **~n machen** do overtime
über·stürzen 1 *tr. V.* rush
2 *refl. V.* rush; (rasch aufeinander folgen) ‹*events, news, etc.*› come thick and fast
überstürzt 1 *Adj.* hurried ‹*escape, departure*›; overhasty ‹*decision*›
2 *adv.* ‹*decide, act*› overhastily; ‹*depart*› hurriedly
über·tölpeln *tr. V.* dupe; con (coll.)
über·tönen *tr. V.* drown out
Übertrag *der;* **~[e]s, Überträge** (bes. Buchf.) carry-over
über·tragbar *Adj.* transferable (**auf** + *Akk.* to); (auf etw. anderes anwendbar) applicable (**auf** + *Akk.* to); (übersetzbar) translatable; (ansteckend) infectious ‹*disease*›
über·tragen *unr. tr. V.* **(a)** transfer (**auf** + *Akk.* to); transmit ‹*power, torque, etc.*› (**auf** + *Akk.* to); communicate ‹*disease, illness*› (**auf** + *Akk.* to); carry over ‹*subtotal*›; (auf etw. anderes anwenden) apply (**auf** + *Akk.* to); (übersetzen) translate
(b) (senden) broadcast ‹*concert, event, match, etc.*›; (im Fernsehen) televise
(c) (geben) **jmdm. Aufgaben/Pflichten** *usw.* **~:** hand over tasks/duties *etc.* to sb.; (anvertrauen) entrust sb. with tasks/duties *etc.*
Übertragung *die;* **~, ~en (a)**
▶ ÜBERTRAGEN A: transference; transmission; communication; carrying over; application; translation
(b) (das Senden) broadcasting; (Sendung) broadcast; (im Fernsehen) televising/television broadcast
über·treffen *unr. tr. V.* **(a)** surpass, outdo (**an** + *Dat.* in); break ‹*record*›
(b) (übersteigen) exceed
über·treiben *unr. tr. V.* **(a)** *auch itr.* exaggerate
(b) (zu weit treiben) overdo
Übertreibung *die;* **~, ~en** exaggeration
über|treten¹ *unr. itr. V.; mit sein* change sides; **zum Katholizismus/Islam ~:** convert to Catholicism/Islam
über·treten² *unr. tr. V.* contravene ‹*law*›; violate ‹*regulation, prohibition*›
Übertretung *die;* **~, ~en (a)**
▶ ÜBERTRETEN²: contravention; violation
(b) (Vergehen) misdemeanour
übertrieben *Adj.* 1 exaggerated; (übermäßig) excessive ‹*care, thrift, etc.*›
2 *adv.* excessively
Über·tritt *der* change of allegiance, switch (**zu** to); (Rel.) conversion (**zu** to)
über·trumpfen *tr. V.* outdo
über·tünchen *tr. V.* cover with whitewash; (fig.) cover up
über·vorteilen *tr. V.* cheat
über·wachen *tr. V.* keep under surveillance ‹*suspect, agent, area, etc.*›; supervise ‹*factory, workers, process*›; control ‹*traffic*›; monitor ‹*progress, production process, experiment, patient*›
Überwachung *die;* **~, ~en**
▶ ÜBERWACHEN: surveillance; supervision; controlling; monitoring
über·wältigen *tr. V.* **(a)** overpower
(b) (fig.) ‹*sleep, emotion, fear, etc.*› overcome; ‹*sight, impressions, beauty, etc.*› overwhelm
überwältigend 1 *Adj.* overwhelming ‹*sight, impression, victory, majority, etc.*›; overpowering ‹*smell*›; stunning ‹*beauty*›
2 *adv.* stunningly ‹*beautiful*›
über·weisen *unr. tr. V.* **(a)** transfer ‹*money*› (**an, auf** + *Akk.* to)
(b) refer ‹*patient*› (**an** + *Akk.* to)
Über·weisung *die* **(a)** transfer (**an, auf** + *Akk.* to)
(b) (Summe) remittance
(c) (eines Patienten) referral (**an** + *Akk.* to)
überwiegend 1 */auch --'--/ Adj.* overwhelming
2 *adv.* mainly
über·winden 1 *unr. tr. V.* overcome; get past ‹*stage*›
2 *unr. refl. V.* overcome one's reluctance; **sich [dazu] ~, etw. zu tun** bring oneself to do sth.
Über·windung *die* **(a)** ▶ ÜBERWINDEN 1: overcoming; getting past
(b) (das Sichüberwinden) **es war eine große ~ für ihn** it cost him a great effort
über·wuchern *tr. V.* overgrow
Über·zahl *die* majority
überzählig *Adj.* surplus
über·zeugen 1 *tr. V.* convince
2 *itr. V.* be convincing
überzeugend 1 *Adj.* convincing
2 *adv.* convincingly
überzeugt *Adj.* convinced
Über·zeugung *die* (feste Meinung) conviction
über|ziehen¹ *unr. tr. V.* pull on
über·ziehen² *unr. tr. V.* **(a) etw. mit etw. ~:** cover sth. with sth.
(b) overdraw ‹*account*› (**um** by)
Überziehungs·kredit *der* (Finanzw.) overdraft facility
überzüchtet *Adj.* overbred; over-sophisticated ‹*engines, systems*›
Überzug *der* **(a)** (Beschichtung) coating
(b) (Bezug) cover
üblich *Adj.* usual; (normal) normal; (gebräuchlich) customary
üblicher·weise *Adv.* usually
U-Boot *das* submarine; sub (coll.)
übrig *Adj.* remaining *attrib.;* (ander...) other; **alle ~en Gäste ...:** all the other guests ...; **im Übrigen** besides; **es ist etwas ~:** there is some left; **~ bleiben** be left; ‹*food, drink*› be left over; **~ lassen** (+ *Akk.*) leave; leave ‹*food, drink*› over

***übrig|bleiben** ▶ ÜBRIG
übrigens *Adv.* by the way
***übrig|lassen** ▶ ÜBRIG
Übung *die;* ~, ~**en** **(a)** exercise
(b) (das Üben, Geübtsein) practice
UdSSR *Abk. die;* ~ (1922–1991) = **Union der Sozialistischen Sowjetrepubliken** USSR
Ufer *das;* ~**s**, ~: bank; (des Meers) shore
UG *Abk.* = **Untergeschoss**
Uganda *(das);* ~**s** Uganda
Uhr *die;* ~, ~**en** **(a)** clock; (Armband-, Taschenuhr) watch; (Wasser-, Gasuhr) meter; (an Messinstrumenten) dial; gauge; **auf die** *od.* **nach der** ~ **sehen** look at the time; **rund um die** ~ (ugs.) round the clock
(b) **acht** ~: eight o'clock; **wie viel** ~ **ist es?** what's the time?; what time is it?
Uhr-: ~**armband** *das* watch strap; ~**kette** *die* watch chain; ~**macher** *der,* ~**macherin** *die* watchmaker/clockmaker; ~**werk** *das* clock/watch mechanism; ~**zeiger** *der* clock/watch hand; ~**zeiger·sinn** *der:* **im/entgegen dem** ~**zeigersinn** clockwise/anticlockwise; ~**zeit** *die* time; **jmdn. nach der** ~**zeit fragen** ask sb. the time
Uhu *der;* ~**s**, ~**s** eagle owl
Ukraine *die;* ~: Ukraine
Ukrainer *der;* ~**s**, ~, **Ukrainerin** *die;* ~, ~**nen** Ukrainian
UKW *Abk.* = **Ultrakurzwelle** VHF
UKW-Sender *der* VHF station; ≈ FM station
Ulk *der;* ~**s**, ~**e** lark (coll.); (Streich) trick; [practical] joke
ulkig (ugs.) 1 *Adj.* funny
2 *adv.* in a funny way
Ulme *die;* ~, ~**n** elm
Ultimatum *das;* ~**s**, **Ultimaten** ultimatum
Ultra·kurz·welle *die* ultra-short wave; (Rundf.: Wellenbereich) very high frequency; VHF
Ultra·schall *der* (Physik, Med.) ultrasound
Ultraschall·untersuchung *die* (Med.) ultrasound examination
ultra·violett *Adj.* ultraviolet
um 1 *Präp. mit Akk.* **(a)** (räumlich) [a]round; **um die Ecke** round the corner
(b) (zeitlich) (genau) at; (etwa) around [about]
(c) **Tag um Tag/Stunde um Stunde** day after day/hour after hour
(d) (bei Maß- u. Mengenangaben) by
2 *Adv.* around; about; **um [die] 10 Euro/50 Personen [herum]** around *or* about 10 euros/50 people
3 *Konj.* **(a)** (final) **um ... zu** [in order] to
(b) (konsekutiv) **er ist groß genug/ist noch zu klein, um ... zu ...:** he is big enough/is still too young to ...

*alte Schreibung - vgl. Hinweis auf S. xiv

um|ändern *tr. V.* change; revise ‹*text, novel*›; alter ‹*garment*›
um·armen *tr. V.* embrace; (an sich drücken) hug
Umarmung *die;* ~, ~**en** embrace; hug
Um·bau *der;* ~**[e]s**, ~**ten** ▶ UMBAUEN: rebuilding; alteration; conversion; (fig.) reorganization
um|bauen *tr., auch itr. V.* rebuild; (leicht ändern) alter; (zu etw. anderem) convert (**zu** into); (fig.) reorganize ‹*system, administration, etc.*›
um|benennen *unr. tr. V.* change the name of; rename
um|biegen 1 *unr. tr. V.* bend
2 *unr. itr. V.; mit sein* turn
um|binden *unr. tr. V.* put on
um|blättern 1 *tr. V.* turn [over]
2 *itr. V.* turn the page/pages
um|blicken *refl. V.* **(a)** look around
(b) (zurückblicken) [turn to] look back (**nach** at)
um|bringen *unr. tr. V.* kill
Um·bruch *der* **(a)** radical change; (Umwälzung) upheaval
(b) (Druckw.) make-up; (Ergebnis) page proofs *pl.*
um|buchen 1 *tr. V.* change (**auf** + *Akk.* to)
2 *itr. V.* change one's booking (**auf** + *Akk.* to)
Um·buchung *die* change of booking
um|datieren *tr. V.* change the date of; redate ‹*contract, letter, etc.*›
um|denken *unr. itr. V.* revise one's thinking; rethink; **ein Prozess des Umdenkens** a process of rethinking
um|drehen 1 *tr. V.* turn round; turn over ‹*coin, hand, etc.*›; turn ‹*key*›
2 *refl. V.* turn round; (den Kopf wenden) turn one's head
3 *itr. V.; auch mit sein* (ugs.: umkehren) turn back; (ugs.: wenden) turn round
Um·drehung *die* turn; (eines Motors usw.) revolution; rev (coll.)
um·einander *Adv.* **sich** ~ **kümmern/sorgen** take care of/worry about each other *or* one another
um|fahren¹ *unr. tr. V.* knock down
um·fahren² *unr. tr. V.* go round; make a detour ‹*obstruction etc.*›; (im Auto) drive round; (im Schiff) sail round; (auf einer Umgehungsstraße) bypass ‹*town, village, etc.*›
um|fallen *unr. itr. V.; mit sein* **(a)** fall over
(b) (zusammenbrechen) collapse; **tot** ~: fall down dead
Um·fang *der* **(a)** circumference; (eines Quadrats usw.) perimeter; (eines Baums, Menschen usw.) girth
(b) (Größe) size
(c) (Ausmaß) extent
umfang·reich *Adj.* extensive; substantial ‹*book*›
um·fassen *tr. V.* **(a)** grasp; (umarmen) embrace

(b) (enthalten) contain; (einschließen) include; span, cover ‹*period*›

umfassend [1] *Adj.* full ‹*reply, information, survey, confession*›; extensive, wide ‹*knowledge, powers*›
[2] *adv.* ‹*inform*› fully

Um·feld *das* (Psych., Soziol.) milieu

um|formen *tr. V.* reshape; revise ‹*poem, novel*›; transform ‹*person*›

Um·frage *die* survey; (Politik) opinion poll

um|füllen *tr. V.* **etw. in etw.** (*Akk.*) **~:** transfer sth. into sth.

um|funktionieren *tr. V.* change the function of; **etw. zu etw. ~:** turn sth. into sth.

Um·gang *der* **(a)** (gesellschaftlicher Verkehr) contact
(b) (das Umgehen) **den ~ mit Pferden lernen** learn how to handle horses

umgänglich *Adj.* affable; (gesellig) sociable

Umgangs-: ~form *die* **gute/schlechte/keine ~formen haben** have good/bad/no manners; **~sprache** *die* colloquial language

um·garnen *tr. V.* beguile

um·geben *unr. tr. V.* **(a)** surround; ‹*hedge, fence, wall, etc.*› enclose
(b) etw. mit etw. ~: surround sth. with sth.; (einfrieden) enclose sth. with sth.

Umgebung *die; ~, ~en* surroundings *pl.;* (Nachbarschaft) neighbourhood; (eines Ortes) surrounding area

um|gehen¹ *unr. itr. V.; mit sein* **(a)** (im Umlauf sein) ‹*list, rumour, etc.*› go round, circulate; ‹*illness, infection*› go round
(b) (spuken) **hier geht ein Gespenst um** this place is haunted
(c) (behandeln) **mit jmdm. freundlich/liebevoll** *usw.* **~:** treat sb. kindly/lovingly *etc.;* **er kann mit Geld nicht ~:** he can't handle money

um·gehen² *unr. tr. V.* **(a)** go round; make a detour round; (auf einer Umgehungsstraße) bypass ‹*town etc.*›
(b) (vermeiden) avoid; evade ‹*question, issue*›
(c) (nicht befolgen) circumvent ‹*law, restriction, etc.*›; evade ‹*obligation, duty*›

umgehend [1] *Adj.* immediate
[2] *adv.* immediately

Umgehung *die; ~, ~en* **(a) durch ~ der Innenstadt** by bypassing *or* avoiding the town centre
(b) ▶ UMGEHEN² c: circumvention; evasion

Umgehungs·straße *die* bypass

umgekehrt [1] *Adj.* inverse ‹*ratio, proportion*›; reverse ‹*order*›; opposite ‹*sign*›
[2] *adv.* inversely ‹*proportional*›; **vom Englischen ins Deutsche und ~ übersetzen** translate from English into German and vice versa

um|gestalten *tr. V.* reshape; remodel; redesign ‹*square, park, room, etc.*›

um|graben *unr. tr. V.* dig over

Um·hang *der* cape

um|hängen *tr. V.* **(a) etw. ~:** hang sth. somewhere else
(b) jmdm./sich einen Mantel/eine Decke ~: drape a coat/blanket round sb.'s/one's shoulders

um|hauen *unr. tr. V.* fell; (fig.) knock down

um·her *Adv.* around

umher- ▶ HERUM-

um|hören *refl. V.* keep one's ears open; (direkt fragen) ask around

um·jubeln *tr. V.* cheer

um|kehren [1] *itr. V.; mit sein* turn back
[2] *tr. V.* turn upside down; turn over ‹*sheet of paper*›; (nach links drehen) turn ‹*garment etc.*› inside out; (nach rechts drehen) turn ‹*garment etc.*› right side out

um|kippen [1] *itr. V.; mit sein* **(a)** fall over; ‹*boat*› capsize, turn over; ‹*vehicle*› overturn
(b) (ugs.: ohnmächtig werden) keel over
(c) (Ökologie) ‹*river, lake*› reach the stage of biological collapse
[2] *tr. V.* tip over; knock over ‹*lamp, vase, glass, cup*›; capsize ‹*boat*›; turn ‹*boat*› over; overturn ‹*vehicle*›

um|klappen *tr. V.* fold down

Umkleide·kabine *die* changing cubicle

um|knicken *itr. V.; mit sein* **(a)** [**mit dem Fuß**] **~:** go over on one's ankle
(b) bend; ‹*branch*› bend and snap

um|kommen *unr. itr. V.; mit sein* die; (bei einem Unglück, durch Gewalt) get killed; die; ‹*food*› go off

Um·kreis *der* surrounding area; **im ~ von 5 km** within a radius of 5 km.

um·kreisen *tr. V.* circle; ‹*spacecraft, satellite*› orbit; ‹*planet*› revolve [a]round

Um·lauf *der* **(a)** (von Planeten) revolution
(b) (Zirkulation) circulation; **in** *od.* **im ~ sein** be circulating; ‹*coin, banknote*› be in circulation; **in ~ bringen** circulate; bring ‹*coin, banknote*› into circulation

Umlauf·bahn *die* (Astron., Raumf.) orbit

Um·laut *der* (Sprachw.) umlaut

um|legen *tr. V.* **(a)** (um einen Körperteil) put on
(b) (verlegen) transfer ‹*patient, telephone call*›
(c) (salopp: ermorden) **jmdn. ~:** bump sb. off (coll.)

um|leiten divert

Um·leitung *die* diversion

umliegend *Adj.* surrounding ‹*area*›; (nahe) nearby ‹*building*›

um|modeln *tr. V.* (ugs.) change ‹*house, flat*› round; refashion, alter ‹*jacket etc.*›

um·nachtet *Adj.* (geh.) deranged

Umnachtung *die; ~, ~en* (geh.) derangement

um|pflanzen *tr. V.* transplant

um|pflügen *tr. V.* plough up

um|räumen [1] *tr. V.* rearrange
[2] *itr. V.* rearrange things

um|rechnen *tr. V.* convert (**in** + *Akk.* into)
Um·rechnung *die* conversion (**in** + *Akk.* into)
Umrechnungs·kurs *der* exchange rate
um|reißen[1] *unr. tr. V.* pull ‹*mast, tree*› down; knock ‹*person*› down; ‹*wind*› tear ‹*tent etc.*› down
um·reißen[2] *unr. tr. V.* outline; summarize ‹*subject, problem, situation*›
um|rennen *unr. tr. V.* [run into and] knock down
um·ringen *tr. V.* surround
Um·riss, *Um·riß *der* (auch fig.) outline
um|rühren *tr.* (*auch itr.*) *V.* stir
um|rüsten *tr. V.* (Technik) convert (**auf** + *Akk.* to, **zu** into)
ums /ʊms/ *Präp.* + *Art.* **(a)** = **um das;**
(b) **~ Leben kommen** lose one's life
um|satteln *itr. V.* (ugs.) change jobs; ‹*student*› change courses
Um·satz *der* turnover; (Verkauf) sales *pl.* (**an** + *Dat.* of); **~ machen** (ugs.) make money
um|säumen *tr. V.* hem
um|schalten 1 *tr. V.* (auch fig.) switch [over] (**auf** + *Akk.* to); move ‹*lever*›
2 *itr. V.* switch *or* change over (**auf** + *Akk.* to)
Um·schlag *der* **(a)** cover
(b) (Briefumschlag) envelope
(c) (Schutzumschlag) jacket; (einer Broschüre, eines Heftes) cover
(d) (Med.: Wickel) compress; (warm) poultice
um|schlagen 1 *unr. tr. V.* **(a)** turn up ‹*sleeve, collar, trousers*›; turn over ‹*page*›
(b) (umladen, verladen) turn round, trans-ship ‹*goods*›
2 *unr. itr. V.; mit sein* change (**in** + *Akk.* into); ‹*wind*› veer [round]
um|schreiben[1] *unr. tr. V.* rewrite
um·schreiben[2] *unr. tr. V.* **(a)** (in Worte fassen) describe; (definieren) define ‹*meaning, sb.'s task, etc.*›; (paraphrasieren) paraphrase ‹*word, expression*›
(b) (Sprachw.) construct (**mit** with)
Um·schreibung *die* description; (Definition) definition; (Verhüllung) circumlocution (*Gen.* for)
Um·schrift *die* (Sprachw.) transcription
um|schulen 1 *tr. V.* (beruflich) retrain
2 *itr. V.* retrain (**auf** + *Akk.* as)
Umschulung *die;* **~:** retraining (**auf** + *Akk.* as)
um|schütten *tr. V.* **(a)** pour [into another container]; decant ‹*liquid*›
(b) (verschütten) spill
Um·schweif *der* circumlocution; **ohne ~e** without beating about the bush
Um·schwung *der* complete change; (in der Politik usw.) U-turn

*old spelling - see note on page xiv

um|sehen *unr. refl. V.* **(a)** look; **sich im Zimmer ~:** look [a]round the room
(b) (zurücksehen) look round *or* back
umseitig *Adj., adv.* overleaf
um|setzen *tr. V.* **(a)** move; (auf anderen Posten usw.) move, transfer (**in** + *Akk.* to); (umpflanzen) transplant; (in anderen Topf) repot
(b) (verwirklichen) implement ‹*plan*›; translate ‹*plan, intention, etc.*› into action *or* reality; realize ‹*ideas*›
(c) (Wirtsch.) turn over, have a turnover of ‹*x euros etc.*›; sell ‹*shares, goods*›
Um·sicht *die* circumspection
um·sichtig 1 *Adj.* circumspect
2 *adv.* circumspectly
um|siedeln 1 *tr. V.* resettle
2 *itr. V.; mit sein* move (**in** + *Akk.*, **nach** to)
um·so *Konj.* **je ... ~:** the ..., the; **~ besser/schlimmer!** all the better/worse!
um·sonst *Adv.* **(a)** (unentgeltlich) free; for nothing
(b) (vergebens) in vain
Um·stand *der* **(a)** (Gegebenheit) circumstance; (Tatsache) fact; **unter Umständen** possibly
(b) (Aufwand) business; **macht keine [großen] Umstände** please don't go to any bother
umstände·halber *Adv.* owing to circumstances; **„~ zu verkaufen"** 'forced to sell'
umständlich 1 *Adj.* involved, elaborate ‹*procedure, method, description, explanation, etc.*›; elaborate, laborious ‹*preparation, check, etc.*›; awkward, difficult ‹*journey, job*›; (weitschweifig) long-winded; (Umstände machend) awkward ‹*person*›
2 *adv.* in an involved *or* roundabout way; (weitschweifig) at great length
Umstands·kleid *das* maternity dress
umstehend *Adj.* standing round *postpos.*
um|steigen *unr. itr. V.* change (**in** + *Akk.* [on] to)
um|stellen[1] 1 *tr. V.* **(a)** rearrange, change round ‹*furniture, books, etc.*›; reorder ‹*words etc.*›; transpose ‹*two words*›
(b) (anders einstellen) reset ‹*lever, switch, points, clock*›
(c) (ändern) change *or* switch over (**auf** + *Akk.* to)
2 *refl. V.* adjust (**auf** + *Akk.* to)
um·stellen[2] *tr. V.* surround
um|stimmen *tr. V.* win ‹*person*› round
um|stoßen *unr. tr. V.* **(a)** knock over
(b) (rückgängig machen) change ‹*plan, decision*›; (zunichte machen) upset, wreck ‹*plan, theory*›
umstritten *Adj.* disputed; controversial ‹*book, author, policy, etc.*›
Um·sturz *der* coup
um|stürzen 1 *tr. V.* overturn; (fig.) topple, overthrow ‹*political system, government*›
2 *itr. V.* overturn; ‹*wall, building, chimney*› fall down
umstürzlerisch *Adj.* subversive

Umsturz·versuch *der* attempted coup
Um·tausch *der* exchange
um|tauschen *tr. V.* exchange ‹*goods, article*› (**gegen** for); change ‹*dollars, pounds, etc.*› (**in** + *Akk.* into)
um|topfen *tr. V.* repot ‹*plant*›
Um·trunk *der* communal drink
um|tun *unr. refl. V.* (ugs.) look [a]round; **sich nach etw.** ~: be on the lookout for sth.
Umwälzung *die;* ~, ~**en** (fig.) revolution
um|wandeln *tr. V.* convert ‹*substance, building, etc.*› (**in** + *Akk.* into); (ändern) change; alter
Um·weg *der* detour
Um·welt *die* **(a)** environment
(b) (Menschen) people *pl.* around sb.
umwelt-, Umwelt-: ~**bedingt** *Adj.* caused by the *or* one's environment *postpos.;* ~**belastung** *die* environmental pollution *no indef. art.;* ~**bewusst,** *~**bewußt** *Adj.* environmentally conscious *or* aware; ~**feindlich** [1] *Adj.* inimical to the environment *postpos.;* ecologically undesirable; [2] *adv.* in an ecologically undesirable way; ‹*drive, behave*› without regard for the environment; ~**freundlich** [1] *Adj.* environmentally friendly; [2] *adv.* in an environmentally friendly way; ~**katastrophe** *die* environmental disaster; ~**schädlich** [1] *Adj.* harmful to the environment *postpos.;* ecologically harmful; [2] *adv.* in an ecologically harmful way; ~**schutz** *der* environmental protection *no art.;* ~**schützer** *der;* ~~**s**, ~~, ~**schützerin** *die;* ~~, ~, ~**nen** environmentalist; conservationist; ~**verschmutzung** *die* pollution [of the environment]
um|wenden *regelm.* (*auch unr.*) *tr. V.* **(a)** turn over ‹*page, joint, etc.*›
(b) turn round ‹*vehicle, horse*›
um·werben *unr. tr. V.* court; woo; **viel umworben** much-courted
um|werfen *unr. tr. V.* **(a)** knock over; knock ‹*person*› down *or* over; (fig. ugs.: aus der Fassung bringen) bowl ‹*person*› over; stun ‹*person*›
(b) (fig. ugs.: umstoßen) knock ‹*plan*› on the head (coll.)
umwerfend (ugs.) [1] *Adj.* fantastic (coll.); stunning (coll.)
[2] *adv.* fantastically [well] (coll.); brilliantly
um·wickeln *tr. V.* wrap; bind; (mit einem Verband) bandage
Umzäunung *die;* ~, ~**en** fence, fencing (*Gen.* round)
um|ziehen [1] *unr. itr. V.; mit sein* move (**an** + *Akk.*, **in** + *Akk.*, **nach** to)
[2] *unr. tr. V.* **jmdn.** ~: change sb. *or* get sb. changed; **sich** ~: change *or* get changed
um·zingeln *tr. V.* surround; encircle
Umzingelung *die;* ~: encirclement
Um·zug *der* **(a)** move; (von Möbeln) removal
(b) (Festzug) procession
UN *Pl.* UN *sing.*
unabänderlich [1] *Adj.* unalterable; irrevocable ‹*decision*›
[2] *adv.* irrevocably
unabhängig [1] *Adj.* independent (**von** of); (unbeeinflusst) unaffected (**von** by)
[2] *adv.* independently (**von** of); ~ **davon, ob .../was .../wo ...** *usw.* irrespective *or* regardless of whether .../what .../where ... *etc*
Unabhängigkeit *die;* ~: independence
unabkömmlich *Adj.* indispensable; **sie ist im Moment** ~: she is otherwise engaged
unablässig [1] *Adj.* incessant
[2] *adv.* incessantly
unabsichtlich [1] *Adj.* unintentional
[2] *adv.* unintentionally
unabwendbar *Adj.* inevitable
unachtsam [1] *Adj.* **(a)** inattentive
(b) (nicht sorgfältig) careless
[2] *adv.* (ohne Sorgfalt) carelessly
Unachtsamkeit *die;* ~ **(a)** inattentiveness
(b) (mangelnde Sorgfalt) carelessness
unangebracht *Adj.* inappropriate
unangefochten *Adj.* unchallenged; (Rechtsw.) uncontested ‹*verdict, will, etc.*›
unangenehm [1] *Adj.* unpleasant (*Dat.* for); (peinlich) embarrassing ‹*question, situation*›
[2] *adv.* unpleasantly
unannehmbar *Adj.* unacceptable
Unannehmlichkeit *die;* ~, ~**en** trouble
unansehnlich *Adj.* unprepossessing; plain ‹*girl*›
unanständig [1] *Adj.* improper; (anstößig) indecent; dirty ‹*joke*›; rude ‹*word, song*›
[2] *adv.* improperly
Unanständigkeit *die;* ~, ~**en** impropriety; indecency; (Obszönität) obscenity
unappetitlich [1] *Adj.* unappetizing; (fig.) unsavoury ‹*joke*›; disgusting ‹*washbasin, nails, etc.*›
[2] *adv.* unappetizingly
Unart *die;* ~, ~**en** bad habit
unartig *Adj.* naughty
unästhetisch *Adj.* unpleasant ‹*sight etc.*›; ugly ‹*building etc.*›
unauffällig [1] *Adj.* inconspicuous; unobtrusive ‹*scar, defect, skill, behaviour, surveillance, etc.*›; discreet ‹*signal, elegance*›
[2] *adv.* inconspicuously; unobtrusively
unauffindbar *Adj.* untraceable; ~ **sein** *od.* **bleiben** be nowhere to be found
unaufgefordert *Adv.* without being asked
unaufhaltsam [1] *Adj.* inexorable
[2] *adv.* inexorably
unaufmerksam *Adj.* inattentive (**gegenüber** to); careless ‹*driver*›
unaufrichtig *Adj.* insincere

U

Unaufrichtigkeit *die;* ~, ~**en** insincerity
unausbleiblich *Adj.* inevitable
unausgegoren *Adj.* (abwertend) immature
unausstehlich *Adj.* unbearable ‹*person, noise, smell, etc.*›; insufferable ‹*person*›; intolerable ‹*noise, smell*›.
unausweichlich *Adj.* unavoidable; inevitable
unbändig [1] *Adj.* **(a)** boisterous **(b)** (überaus groß/stark) unbridled [2] *adv.* **(a)** wildly **(b)** (sehr, äußerst) unrestrainedly; tremendously (coll.)
unbarmherzig *Adj.* merciless
unbeabsichtigt [1] *Adj.* unintentional [2] *adv.* unintentionally
unbeachtet *Adj.* unnoticed
unbedacht [1] *Adj.* rash; thoughtless [2] *adv.* rashly; thoughtlessly
unbedenklich *adv.* without second thoughts
unbedeutend [1] *Adj.* insignificant; minor ‹*artist, poet*›; slight, minor ‹*improvement, change, error*› [2] *adv.* slightly
unbedingt [1] *Adj.* absolute [2] *adv.* absolutely [3] *Adv.* (auf jeden Fall) whatever happens
unbefangen *Adj.* **(a)** (ungehemmt) uninhibited **(b)** (unvoreingenommen) impartial
Unbefangenheit *die:* ▶ UNBEFANGEN A, B: uninhibitedness; impartiality
unbefriedigend *Adj.* unsatisfactory
unbefristet [1] *Adj.* for an indefinite period *postpos.;* indefinite ‹*strike*›; unlimited ‹*visa*› [2] *adv.* for an indefinite period
unbefugt [1] *Adj.* unauthorized [2] *adv.* without authorization
unbegreiflich *Adj.* incomprehensible (*Dat.*, **für** to); incredible ‹*love, goodness, stupidity, carelessness, etc.*›
unbegrenzt [1] *Adj.* unlimited [2] *adv.* ‹*stay, keep, etc.*› indefinitely
Unbehagen *das;* ~**s** uneasiness, disquiet; (Sorge) concern (**an** + *Dat.* about)
unbehaglich [1] *Adj.* uneasy ‹*feeling, atmosphere*›; uncomfortable ‹*thought, room*› [2] *adv.* uneasily
unbeherrscht *Adj.* uncontrolled; **er ist** ~: he has no self-control
Unbeherrschtheit *die;* ~: lack of self-control
unbeholfen [1] *Adj.* clumsy [2] *adv.* clumsily
unbekannt *Adj.* **(a)** unknown; (nicht vertraut) unfamiliar; unidentified ‹*caller, donor*›; **„Empfänger** ~**"** 'not known at this address' **(b)** (nicht vielen bekannt) little known; obscure ‹*poet, painter, etc.*›
Unbekannte[1] *der/die; adj. Dekl.* unknown *or* unidentified man/woman; (Fremde[r]) stranger
Unbekannte[2] *die; adj. Dekl.* (Math.; auch fig.) unknown
unbekleidet *Adj.* without any clothes on *postpos.;* bare ‹*torso etc.*›; naked ‹*corpse*›
unbekümmert [1] *Adj.* carefree; (ohne Bedenken, lässig) casual [2] *adv.* **(a)** in a carefree way **(b)** (ohne Bedenken) without caring *or* worrying
unbeleuchtet *Adj.* unlit ‹*street, corridor, etc.*›; ‹*vehicle*› without [any] lights
unbeliebt *Adj.* unpopular (**bei** with)
unbemannt *Adj.* unmanned
unbemerkt *Adj., adv.* unnoticed
unbenutzt *Adj.* unused
unbequem [1] *Adj.* **(a)** uncomfortable **(b)** (lästig) awkward, embarrassing ‹*question, opinion*›; troublesome ‹*politician etc.*›; unpleasant ‹*criticism, truth, etc.*› [2] *adv.* uncomfortably
unberechenbar [1] *Adj.* unpredictable [2] *adv.* unpredictably
unberechtigt *Adj.* **(a)** (ungerechtfertigt) unjustified **(b)** (unbefugt) unauthorized
unberührt *Adj.* untouched; **sie ist noch** ~: she is still a virgin
unbescheiden *Adj.* presumptuous
unbeschrankt *Adj.* ‹*crossing*› without gates, with no gates
unbeschreiblich [1] *Adj.* indescribable; unimaginable ‹*fear, beauty*›; ‹*fear, beauty*› beyond description [2] *adv.* indescribably ‹*beautiful*›; unbelievably ‹*busy*›
unbesorgt *Adj.* unconcerned; **seien Sie** ~: don't [you] worry
unbeständig *Adj.* changeable ‹*weather*›; fickle ‹*lover etc.*›
unbestimmt [1] *Adj.* **(a)** indefinite; indeterminate ‹*age, number*›; (ungewiss) uncertain **(b)** (ungenau) vague **(c)** (Sprachw.) indefinite ‹*article, pronoun*› [2] *adv.* (ungenau) vaguely
unbestreitbar *Adj.* indisputable; unquestionable
unbestritten [1] *Adj.* undisputed; ~ **ist, dass ...** it is undisputed that ...; there is no disputing that ... [2] *adv.* indisputably
unbewacht *Adj.* unsupervised; unattended ‹*car park*›
unbewaffnet *Adj.* unarmed
unbeweglich *Adj.* motionless; still ‹*air, water*›; fixed ‹*gaze, expression*›

*alte Schreibung - vgl. Hinweis auf S. xiv

unbewegt *Adj.* motionless; fixed ‹*expression*›
unbewohnbar *Adj.* uninhabitable
unbewohnt *Adj.* uninhabited ‹*area*›; unoccupied ‹*house, flat*›
unbewusst, *unbewußt *Adj.* unconscious
unbrauchbar *Adj.* unusable; (untauglich) useless ‹*method, person*›
und *Konj.* and; (folglich) [and] so; **ich ~ tanzen?** what, me dance?; **sei so gut ~ mach das Fenster zu** be so good as to shut the window
Undank *der;* **~[e]s:** ingratitude
undankbar *Adj.* ungrateful ‹*person, behaviour*›
undenkbar *Adj.* unthinkable; inconceivable
undeutlich [1] *Adj.* unclear; indistinct; (ungenau) vague ‹*idea, memory, etc.*›
[2] *adv.* indistinctly; (ungenau) vaguely
undicht *Adj.* leaky; leaking; **~e Fenster** windows which do not fit tightly
Unding *das* **ein ~ sein** be preposterous *or* ridiculous
undurchführbar *Adj.* impracticable
undurchlässig *Adj.* impermeable; (wasserdicht) watertight; waterproof; (luftdicht) airtight
uneben *Adj.* uneven
Unebenheit *die;* **~, ~en (a)** unevenness **(b)** (unebene Stelle) lumpy *or* uneven patch
unehelich *Adj.* illegitimate ‹*child*›; unmarried ‹*mother*›
unehrlich [1] *Adj.* dishonest
[2] *adv.* dishonestly; by dishonest means
uneigennützig *Adj.* unselfish
Uneigennützigkeit *die;* **~:** unselfishness
uneinig *Adj.* ‹*party*› divided by disagreement; **[sich** (*Dat.*)**] ~ sein** disagree
Uneinigkeit *die;* **~:** disagreement (**in** + *Dat.* on)
uneins *Adj.* **~ sein** be divided (**in** + *Dat.* on); ‹*persons*› be at variance *or* at cross purposes (**in** + *Dat.* over)
unempfindlich *Adj.* **(a)** insensitive (**gegen** to)
(b) (immun) immune (**gegen** to, against)
(c) (strapazierfähig) hard-wearing
unendlich [1] *Adj.* infinite; boundless; (zeitlich) endless; (Math.) infinite
[2] *adv.* infinitely ‹*lovable, sad*›; immeasurably ‹*happy*›; ‹*happy*› beyond measure
unentbehrlich *Adj.* indispensable (*Dat.*, **für** to)
unentgeltlich /*od.* '----/ [1] *Adj.* free
[2] *adv.* free of charge; ‹*work*› for nothing
unentschieden [1] *Adj.* unsettled; undecided ‹*question*›; (Sport, Schach) drawn
[2] *adv.* **~ spielen** draw
Unentschieden *das;* **~s, ~** (Sport, Schach) draw
unentwegt /*od.* --'-/ [1] *Adj.* **(a)** (beharrlich) persistent ‹*fighter, champion, efforts*›
(b) (unaufhörlich) constant; incessant
[2] *adv.* **(a)** (beharrlich) persistently
(b) (unaufhörlich) constantly; incessantly
unerbittlich [1] *Adj.* (auch fig.) inexorable; unsparing ‹*critic*›; relentless ‹*battle, struggle*›; implacable ‹*hate, enemy*›
[2] *adv.* (auch fig.) inexorably
unerfahren *Adj.* inexperienced
unerfreulich [1] *Adj.* unpleasant; bad ‹*news*›
[2] *adv.* unpleasantly
unerheblich *Adj.* insignificant
unerhört [1] *Adj.* (empörend) outrageous
[2] *adv.* outrageously
unerlaubt [1] *Adj.* unauthorized
[2] *adv.* without authorization
unerledigt *Adj.* not dealt with *postpos.*
unermüdlich [1] *Adj.* tireless, untiring (**bei, in** + *Dat.* in)
[2] *adv.* tirelessly
unerreichbar *Adj.* inaccessible; (fig.) unattainable
unerreicht *Adj.* unequalled
unersättlich *Adj.* insatiable
unerschöpflich *Adj.* inexhaustible
unersetzlich *Adj.* irreplaceable
unerträglich /*od.* '----/ *Adj.* unbearable; intolerable ‹*situation, conditions, etc.*›
unerwartet [1] *Adj.* unexpected; **es kam für alle ~:** it came as a surprise to everybody
[2] *adv.* unexpectedly
unerwünscht *Adj.* unwanted; unwelcome ‹*interruption, visit, visitor*›; undesirable ‹*side effects*›
unethisch [1] *Adj.* unethical
[2] *adv.* unethically
unfähig *Adj.* **(a) ~ sein, etw. zu tun** (ständig) be incapable of doing sth.; (momentan) be unable to do sth.
(b) (inkompetent) incompetent
Unfähigkeit *die* **(a)** inability
(b) (Inkompetenz) incompetence
unfair [1] *Adj.* unfair (**gegen** to)
[2] *adv.* unfairly
Un·fall *der;* **~[e]s, Unfälle** accident
Unfall-: ~arzt *der,* **~ärztin** *die* casualty doctor; **~flucht** *die* (Rechtsspr.) **~flucht begehen** fail to stop after [being involved in] an accident; **~opfer** *das* accident victim; **~stelle** *die* scene of an/the accident; **~versicherung** *die* accident insurance
unfehlbar *Adj.* infallible
Unfehlbarkeit *die;* **~:** infallibility
unförmig *Adj.* shapeless; huge ‹*legs, hands, body*›; bulky, ungainly ‹*shape, shoes*›
unfrei *Adj.* not free *pred.;* subject, dependent ‹*people*›; ‹*life*› of bondage

unfreiwillig 1 *Adj.* involuntary; (erzwungen) enforced ‹*stay*›; (nicht beabsichtigt) unintended ‹*publicity, joke, humour*›
2 *adv.* involuntarily; without wanting to; (unbeabsichtigt) unintentionally

unfreundlich 1 *Adj.* unfriendly (**zu, gegen** to); unkind ‹*words, remark*›
2 *adv.* in an unfriendly way

Unfreundlichkeit *die;* ~: unfriendliness

unfrisiert *Adj.* ungroomed ‹*hair*›

unfruchtbar *Adj.* infertile; (fig.) unproductive

Unfruchtbarkeit *die;* ~: infertility; (fig.) unproductiveness

Unfug *der;* ~[e]s **(a)** [piece of] mischief; **grober** ~: public nuisance
(b) (Unsinn) nonsense

Ungar *der;* ~n, ~n, **Ungarin** *die;* ~, ~nen Hungarian

ungarisch *Adj.* Hungarian

Ungarn *(das);* ~s Hungary

ungeachtet *Präp. mit Gen.* (geh.) notwithstanding; despite

ungebildet *Adj.* uneducated

ungeboren *Adj.* unborn

ungebräuchlich *Adj.* uncommon; rare; rarely used ‹*method, process*›

ungebrochen *Adj.* (fig.) unbroken ‹*will, person*›; undiminished ‹*strength, courage*›

ungedeckt *Adj.* uncovered ‹*cheque*›

Ungeduld *die;* ~: impatience

ungeduldig 1 *Adj.* impatient
2 *adv.* impatiently

ungeeignet *Adj.* unsuitable; (für eine Aufgabe) unsuited (**für, zu** to, for)

ungefähr 1 *Adj.* approximate; rough ‹*idea, outline*›
2 *adv.* approximately; roughly

ungefährlich *Adj.* safe; harmless ‹*animal, person, illness, etc.*›

ungeheizt *Adj.* unheated

ungeheuer 1 *Adj.* enormous; tremendous ‹*strength, energy, effort, enthusiasm, fear, success, pressure, etc.*›; vast, immense ‹*fortune, knowledge*›; (schrecklich) terrible (coll.), terrific (coll.) ‹*pain, rage*›
2 *adv.* tremendously; terribly (coll.) ‹*difficult, clever*›

Ungeheuer *das;* ~s, ~ (auch fig.) monster

ungeheuerlich *Adj.* monstrous; outrageous

Ungeheuerlichkeit *die;* ~, ~en **(a)** monstrous nature; outrageousness
(b) (Vorgang) monstrous *or* outrageous thing

ungehindert *Adj.* unimpeded

ungehörig 1 *Adj.* improper; (frech) impertinent
2 *adv.* improperly; (frech) impertinently

ungehorsam *Adj.* disobedient (**gegenüber** to)

*old spelling - see note on page xiv

Ungehorsam *der;* ~s disobedience (**gegenüber** to)

ungekürzt *Adj.* unabridged ‹*edition, book*›; uncut ‹*film, speech*›

ungelegen 1 *Adj.* **das kommt mir sehr ~/ nicht ~:** that is very inconvenient *or* awkward/quite convenient for me
2 *adv.* inconveniently

ungelernt *Adj.* unskilled

ungemütlich 1 *Adj.* uninviting, cheerless ‹*room, flat*›; uncomfortable, unfriendly ‹*atmosphere*›
2 *adv.* uncomfortably ‹*furnished*›

ungenau 1 *Adj.* inaccurate; imprecise, inexact ‹*definition, formulation, etc.*›; (undeutlich) vague ‹*memory, idea, impression*›
2 *adv.* inaccurately; ‹*define*› imprecisely, inexactly; ‹*remember*› vaguely

ungeniert /'ʊnʒeniːɐ̯t/ 1 *Adj.* free and easy; uninhibited
2 *adv.* openly; ‹*yawn*› unconcernedly; ‹*undress etc.*› without any embarrassment

ungenießbar *Adj.* (nicht essbar) inedible; (nicht trinkbar) undrinkable; (fig. ugs.) unbearable

ungenügend 1 *Adj.* inadequate; **die Note „~"/ein Ungenügend** (Schulw.) the/an 'unsatisfactory' [mark]
2 *adv.* inadequately

ungepflegt *Adj.* neglected ‹*garden, park, car, etc.*›; unkempt ‹*person, appearance, hair*›; uncared-for ‹*hands*›

ungerade *Adj.* odd ‹*number*›

ungerecht 1 *Adj.* unjust, unfair (**gegen, zu, gegenüber** to)
2 *adv.* unjustly; unfairly

Ungerechtigkeit *die;* ~, ~en injustice

ungern *Adv.* reluctantly; **etw. ~ tun** not like *or* dislike doing sth.

ungerührt *Adj.* unmoved

ungeschält *Adj.* unpeeled ‹*fruit*›

ungeschehen *Adj.* **etw. ~ machen** undo sth.

Ungeschicklichkeit *die;* ~, ~en
(a) clumsiness
(b) (etwas Ungeschicktes) piece of clumsiness

ungeschickt 1 *Adj.* clumsy; awkward
2 *adv.* clumsily; awkwardly

ungesetzlich 1 *Adj.* unlawful; illegal
2 *adv.* unlawfully; illegally

ungestempelt *Adj.* uncancelled ‹*stamp*›

ungestört *Adj.* undisturbed; uninterrupted ‹*development*›

ungesund *Adj.* (auch fig.) unhealthy

Ungetüm *das;* ~s, ~e monster

ungewiss, *ungewiß *Adj.* uncertain; **über etw.** *(Akk.)* **im Ungewissen sein** be uncertain *or* unsure about sth.

Ungewissheit, *Ungewißheit *die;* ~, ~en uncertainty

ungewöhnlich 1 *Adj.* **(a)** unusual

(b) (sehr groß) exceptional ‹*strength, beauty, ability, etc.*›; outstanding ‹*achievement, success*›
2 *adv.* (a) ‹*behave*› abnormally, strangely
(b) (enorm) exceptionally

ungewohnt 1 *Adj.* unaccustomed; (nicht vertraut) unfamiliar ‹*method, work, surroundings, etc.*›
2 *adv.* unusually

ungewollt 1 *Adj.* unwanted; (unbeabsichtigt) unintentional; inadvertent
2 *adv.* unintenionally; inadvertently

Ungeziefer *das;* **~s** vermin *pl.*

ungezogen 1 *Adj.* naughty; badly behaved; bad ‹*behaviour*›; (frech) cheeky
2 *adv.* naughtily; ‹*behave*› badly

ungezwungen *Adj.* natural, unaffected ‹*person, behaviour, cheerfulness*›; (nicht förmlich) informal, free and easy ‹*tone, conversation, etc.*›

ungläubig 1 *Adj.* (a) disbelieving
(b) (Rel.) unbelieving
2 *adv.* in disbelief

unglaublich 1 *Adj.* incredible
2 *adv.* (ugs.: äußerst) incredibly (coll.)

unglaubwürdig *Adj.* implausible; untrustworthy, unreliable ‹*witness etc.*›

ungleich 1 *Adj.* unequal; odd, unmatching ‹*socks, gloves, etc.*›; (unähnlich) dissimilar
2 *adv.* (a) unequally
(b) (ungleichmäßig) unevenly

ungleichmäßig 1 *Adj.* uneven
2 *adv.* unevenly

Unglück *das;* **~[e]s, ~e** (a) (Unfall) accident; (Flugzeugunglück, Zugunglück) crash; accident
(b) (Not) misfortune; (Leid) suffering
(c) (Pech) bad luck; **~ haben** be unlucky; **das bringt ~:** that's unlucky
(d) (Schicksalsschlag) misfortune

unglücklich 1 *Adj.* (a) unhappy
(b) (nicht vom Glück begünstigt) unfortunate ‹*person*›; (bedauernswert, arm) hapless ‹*person, animal*›
(c) (ungünstig, ungeschickt) unfortunate ‹*moment, combination, meeting, etc.*›; unhappy ‹*end, choice, solution*›
2 *adv.* (a) unhappily
(b) (ungünstig) unfortunately; (ungeschickt) unhappily, clumsily ‹*translated, expressed*›

unglücklicher·weise *Adv.* unfortunately

Unglücks·fall *der* accident

Ungnade *die* **[bei jmdm.] in ~** (*Akk.*) **fallen/in ~** (*Dat.*) **sein** fall/be out of favour [with sb.]

ungnädig *Adj.* bad-tempered; grumpy

ungültig *Adj.* invalid; void (esp. Law); spoilt ‹*vote, ballot paper*›; disallowed ‹*goal*›

Ungunst *die* **zu jmds. ~en** to sb.'s disadvantage

ungünstig 1 *Adj.* (a) unfavourable; unfortunate, bad ‹*shape, layout*›
(b) (unpassend) inconvenient ‹*time*›; (ungeeignet) inappropriate, inconvenient ‹*time, place*›
2 *adv.* (a) unfavourably; badly ‹*designed, laid out*›
(b) (unpassend) inconveniently

ungut *Adj.* **nichts für ~!** no offence [meant]! (coll.)

unhandlich *Adj.* unwieldy

Unheil *das;* **~s** disaster

unheilbar 1 *Adj.* incurable
2 *adv.* incurably

unheil·voll *Adj.* disastrous; (verhängnisvoll) fateful

unheimlich 1 *Adj.* (a) eerie
(b) (ugs.) (schrecklich) terrible (coll.) ‹*hunger, headache, etc.*› terrific (coll.) ‹*fun etc.*›
2 *adv.* (a) eerily
(b) (ugs.: äußerst) terribly (coll.); incredibly (coll.) ‹*quick, long*›

unhöflich 1 *Adj.* impolite
2 *adv.* impolitely

Unhöflichkeit *die;* **~, ~en** impoliteness

unhygienisch 1 *Adj.* unhygienic
2 *adv.* unhygienically

Uni *die;* **~, ~s** (ugs.) university

Uniform *die;* **~, ~en** uniform

uninteressant *Adj.* uninteresting; (nicht von Belang) of no interest *postpos.;* unimportant

Union *die;* **~, ~en** union

Universität *die;* **~, ~en** university

Universum *das;* **~s** universe

unkenntlich *Adj.* unrecognizable ‹*person, face*›; indecipherable ‹*writing, stamp*›

Unkenntnis *die;* **~:** ignorance

unklar *Adj.* unclear; **sich** (*Dat.*) **über etw.** (*Akk.*) **im Unklaren sein** be unclear *or* unsure about sth.

unkonventionell 1 *Adj.* unconventional
2 *adv.* unconventionally

Unkosten *Pl.* (a) [extra] expense *sing.;* expenses
(b) (ugs.: Ausgaben) costs; expenditure *sing.*

Unkosten·beitrag *der* contribution towards expenses

Unkraut *das;* **~[e]s, Unkräuter** weeds *pl.*

unkultiviert *Adj.* uncultivated

unlauter *Adj.* (geh.) dishonest; **~er Wettbewerb** (Rechtsspr.) unfair competition

unleserlich 1 *Adj.* illegible
2 *adv.* illegibly

unmäßig 1 *Adj.* immoderate; excessive
2 *adv.* excessively; ‹*eat, drink*› to excess

Unmenge *die* mass; enormous number/ amount

Unmensch *der;* **~en, ~en** brute

unmenschlich 1 *Adj.* (a) inhuman; brutal; appalling ‹*conditions*›
(b) (entsetzlich) appalling ··›

2 *adv.* **(a)** in an inhuman way
(b) (entsetzlich) appallingly (coll.)

unmissverständlich, *unmißverständlich 1 *Adj.* **(a)** (eindeutig) unambiguous
(b) (offen, direkt) blunt ‹*answer, refusal*›; unequivocal ‹*language*›
2 *adv.* **(a)** (eindeutig) unambiguously
(b) (offen, direkt) bluntly; unequivocally

unmittelbar 1 *Adj.* immediate; direct ‹*contact, connection, influence, etc.*›
2 *adv.* immediately; directly

unmöbliert *Adj.* unfurnished

unmodern 1 *Adj.* old-fashioned; (nicht modisch) unfashionable
2 *adv.* in an old-fashioned way; (nicht modisch) unfashionably

unmöglich 1 *Adj.* impossible; (ugs.: seltsam) incredible
2 *adv.* (ugs.) ‹*behave*› impossibly; ‹*dress*› ridiculously
3 *Adv.* (ugs.) **ich/es** *usw.* **kann ~ …**: I/it *etc.* can't possibly …

unmoralisch 1 *Adj.* immoral
2 *adv.* immorally

unmündig *Adj.* under-age

Unmut *der;* **~[e]s** (geh.) displeasure; annoyance

unnachsichtig 1 *Adj.* merciless; unmerciful
2 *adv.* mercilessly; ‹*punish*› unmercifully

unnahbar *Adj.* unapproachable

unnatürlich 1 *Adj.* unnatural; forced ‹*laugh*›
2 *adv.* unnaturally; ‹*laugh*› in a forced way; ‹*speak*› affectedly

unnötig 1 *Adj.* unnecessary
2 *adv.* unnecessarily

unnütz *Adj.* useless

UNO *die;* **~**: UN

unordentlich 1 *Adj.* **(a)** untidy
(b) (ungeregelt) disorderly ‹*life*›
2 *adv.* untidily; ‹*tie, treat, etc.*› carelessly

Unordnung *die;* **~**: disorder; mess

unparteiisch 1 *Adj.* impartial
2 *adv.* impartially

unpassend 1 *Adj.* inappropriate; unsuitable ‹*dress etc.*›
2 *adv.* inappropriately; unsuitably ‹*dressed etc.*›

unpersönlich 1 *Adj.* impersonal; distant, aloof ‹*person*›
2 *adv.* impersonally; ‹*answer, write*› in impersonal terms

unpraktisch 1 *Adj.* unpractical
2 *adv.* in an unpractical way

unproblematisch *Adj.* unproblematic

unproduktiv *Adj.* unproductive

unpünktlich 1 *Adj.* unpunctual ‹*person*›; late, unpunctual ‹*payment*›
2 *adv.* late

*alte Schreibung - vgl. Hinweis auf S. xiv

Unpünktlichkeit *die;* **~**: lack of punctuality

Unrecht *das;* **~[e]s** wrong; **zu ~**: wrongly; **~ haben** be wrong; **jmdm. ~ tun** do sb. an injustice

unrechtmäßig 1 *Adj.* unlawful
2 *adv.* unlawfully

unredlich (geh.) 1 *Adj.* dishonest
2 *adv.* dishonestly

Unredlichkeit *die;* **~, ~en (a)** dishonesty
(b) (Handlung) dishonest act

unregelmäßig 1 *Adj.* irregular
2 *adv.* irregularly

Unregelmäßigkeit *die;* **~, ~en** irregularity

unreif *Adj.* **(a)** unripe
(b) (nicht erwachsen) immature

unrentabel *Adj.* unprofitable

Unruhe *die;* **~, ~n** (auch fig.) unrest; (Lärm) noise; (Unrast) restlessness; (Besorgnis) anxiety

unruhig 1 *Adj.* **(a)** restless; (besorgt) anxious; unsettled, troubled ‹*time*›
(b) (laut) noisy
(c) (ungleichmäßig) uneven ‹*breathing, pulse, etc.*›; fitful ‹*sleep*›; disturbed ‹*night*›
2 *adv.* **(a)** restlessly; (besorgt) anxiously
(b) (ungleichmäßig) unevenly; ‹*sleep*› fitfully

uns 1 **(a)** *Akk. von* WIR us
(b) *Dat. von* WIR; **gib es ~**: give it to us; **bei ~**: at our home *or* (coll.) place
2 *Reflexivpron. der 1. Pers. Pl.* **(a)** *refl.* ourselves
(b) *reziprok* one another

unsachlich 1 *Adj.* unobjective
2 *adv.* without objectivity

unsauber 1 *Adj.* **(a)** dirty
(b) (nachlässig) untidy; sloppy
2 *adv.* (nachlässig) untidily

unschädlich *Adj.* harmless

unscharf *Adj.* blurred ‹*photo, picture*›

unscheinbar *Adj.* inconspicuous

unschlagbar *Adj.* unbeatable

Unschuld *die;* **~**: innocence; (Jungfräulichkeit) virginity

unschuldig 1 *Adj.* innocent
2 *adv.* innocently

unselbständig, unselbstständig *Adj.* dependent [on other people]

unser[1] *Possessivpron. der 1. Pers. Pl.* our; **das ist ~s** that is ours

unser[2] *Gen. von* WIR (geh.) of us; **in ~ aller/beider Interesse** in the interest of all/both of us

unser·einer, unsereins *Indefinitpron.* (ugs.) the likes of us *pl.;* our sort (coll.)

unserer·seits *Adv.* for our part; (von uns) on our part

unser[e]s·gleichen *indekl. Indefinitpron.* people *pl.* like us

unsert·wegen *Adv.:* ▶ MEINETWEGEN: because of us; for our sake; about us; as far as we are concerned

unsicher 1 *Adj.* uncertain; (nicht selbstsicher) insecure
2 *adv.* ‹*walk, stand, etc.*› unsteadily; (nicht selbstsicher) ‹*smile, look*› diffidently

Unsicherheit *die;* ~: uncertainty; (fehlende Selbstsicherheit) insecurity

unsichtbar *Adj.* invisible (**für** to)

Unsinn *der;* ~[e]s nonsense; ~ **machen** mess *or* fool about

unsinnig *Adj.* nonsensical ‹*statement, talk, etc.*›; absurd, ridiculous ‹*demand etc.*›

Unsitte *die;* ~, ~**n** bad habit

unsittlich 1 *Adj.* indecent
2 *adv.* indecently

unsr... ▶ UNSER[1]

unsterblich *Adj.* immortal

Unsterblichkeit *die;* ~: immortality

unstreitig 1 *Adj.* indisputable
2 *adv.* indisputably

unsympathisch *Adj.* uncongenial, disagreeable ‹*person*›; unpleasant ‹*characteristic, nature, voice*›

Untat *die;* ~, ~**en** misdeed; evil deed

untätig *Adj.* idle; ~ **herumsitzen/zusehen** sit around doing nothing/stand idly by

untauglich *Adj.* unsuitable; (für Militärdienst) unfit [for service] *postpos.*

unten *Adv.* **(a)** down; **hier/da** ~: down here/there; **von** ~: from below
(b) (in Gebäuden) downstairs; **nach** ~: downstairs
(c) (am unteren Ende, zum unteren Ende hin) at the bottom; ~ **[links] auf der Seite/im Schrank** at the bottom [left] of the page/cupboard
(d) (an der Unterseite) underneath
(e) (im Text) below; ~ **genannt** undermentioned (Brit.); mentioned below *postpos.*

***unten·genannt** ▶ UNTEN E

unter 1 *Präp. mit Dat.* (Lage, Standort) under; (zwischen) among[st]; **Mengen** ~ **100 Stück** quantities of less than 100; ~ **Angst/Tränen** in *or* out of fear/in tears
2 *Präp. mit Akk.* under; (zwischen) among[st]; ~ **Null sinken** drop below zero
3 *Adv.* less than; ~ **30 [Jahre alt] sein** be under 30 [years of age]

unter... *Adj.* lower; bottom; (ganz unten) bottom; (in der Rangfolge o. Ä.) lower

Unter·arm *der* forearm

unterbelichten *tr. V.;* **ich unterbelichte, unterbelichtet, unterzubelichten** (Fot.) underexpose

Unter·bewusstsein, *Unter·bewußtsein *das* subconscious

unter·bleiben *unr. itr. V.; mit sein* **etw. unterbleibt** sth. does not occur *or* happen

unter·brechen *unr. tr. V.* interrupt; break ‹*journey, silence*›

Unter·brechung *die* ▶ UNTERBRECHEN: interruption; break (*Gen.* in)

unter|bringen *unr. tr. V.* **(a)** put
(b) (beherbergen) put up

Unterbringung *die;* ~, ~**en** accommodation *no indef. art.*

unter|buttern *tr. V.* (ugs.) push aside (fig.)

***unter·der·hand** ▶ HAND

unter·dessen ▶ INZWISCHEN

unter·drücken *tr. V.* suppress; hold back ‹*comment, question, answer, criticism, etc.*›; oppress ‹*minority etc.*›

Unterdrückung *die;* ~, ~**en (a)** (das Unterdrücken) suppression
(b) (das Unterdrücktwerden, -sein) oppression

unter·einander *Adv.* **(a)** (räumlich) one below the other
(b) (miteinander) among[st] ourselves/themselves *etc.*

unter·ernährt *Adj.* undernourished

Unter·ernährung *die* malnutrition

Unter·führung *die* underpass; (für Fußgänger) subway (Brit.); [pedestrian] underpass (Amer.)

unter-, Unter-: ~**gang** *der* **(a)** (Sonnenuntergang, Monduntergang usw.) setting; **(b)** (von Schiffen) sinking; **(c)** (das Zugrundegehen) decline; ~**|gehen** *unr. itr. V.; mit sein* **(a)** ‹*sun, star, etc.*› set; ‹*ship*› sink, go down; ‹*person*› drown, go under; **(b)** (zugrunde gehen) come to an end; ~**geordnet** *Adj.* secondary ‹*role, importance, etc.*›; subordinate ‹*position, post, etc.*›; ~**geschoss**, *~**geschoß** *das* basement; ~**gewicht** *das* underweight; ~**grund** *der* (bes. Politik) underground; ~**grund·bahn** *die* underground [railway] (Brit.); subway (Amer.); ~**|haken** *tr. V.* (ugs.) **jmdn.** ~**haken** take sb.'s arm; ~**halb** 1 *Adv.* below; ~**halb von** below; 2 *Präp. mit Gen.* below; ~**halt** *der* **(a)** living; **(b)** (Zahlung) maintenance; **(c)** (Instandhaltung[skosten]) upkeep

unter-, Unter-: ~**halten** 1 *unr. tr. V.* **(a)** support; **(b)** (instand halten) maintain ‹*building*›; **(c)** (betreiben) run, keep ‹*car, hotel*›; **(d)** (pflegen) maintain, keep up ‹*contact, correspondence*›; **(e)** entertain ‹*guest, audience*›; 2 *unr. refl. V.* **(a)** talk; converse; **(b)** (sich vergnügen) enjoy oneself; ~**haltsam** *Adj.* entertaining; ~**haltung** *die* **(a)** (Versorgung) support; **(b)** (Instandhaltung) maintenance; **(c)** (Gespräch) conversation; **(d)** (Zeitvertreib) entertainment

unter-, Unter-: ~**händler** *der,* ~**händlerin** *die* (bes. Politik) negotiator; ~**hemd** *das* vest (Brit.); undershirt (Amer.); ~**holz** *das* underwood; undergrowth; ~**hose** *die* (für Männer) briefs *pl.;* [under]pants *pl.;* (für Frauen) panties *pl.*; knickers *pl.* (Brit.); ~**irdisch** 1 *Adj.* underground; 2 *adv.* underground; ~**|jubeln** *tr. V.* (ugs.) **jmdm. etw.** ~**jubeln** palm sth. off on sb.; ~**kiefer** *der* lower ⋯

jaw; ~|**kommen** *unr. itr. V.; mit sein* find accommodation; ~**kühlt** *Adj.* ~**kühlt sein** be suffering from hypothermia *or* exposure

Unterkunft *die;* ~, **Unterkünfte** accommodation *no indef. art.;* lodging *no indef. art.;* ~ **und Frühstück** bed and breakfast; ~ **und Verpflegung** board and lodging

Unter·lage *die* **(a)** (Schreibunterlage) pad; (für eine Schreibmaschine usw.) mat **(b)** *Pl.* documents; papers

unter-, Unter-: ~**lassen** *unr. tr. V.* refrain from [doing]; ~**lassung** *die;* ~~, ~~**en** omission; failure; ~**lassungs·sünde** *die* (ugs.) sin of omission; ~**laufen** *unr. itr. V.; mit sein* occur; **jmdm. ist ein Fehler/Irrtum** ~**laufen** sb. made a mistake; ~**legen** *Adj.* inferior; **jmdm.** ~**legen sein** be inferior to sb. (**an** + *Dat.* in); ~**leib** *der* lower abdomen

unter·liegen *unr. itr. V.* **(a)** *mit sein* (besiegt werden) lose; be beaten *or* defeated **(b)** (unterworfen sein) be subject to

Unter·lippe *die* lower lip

unterm *Präp. + Art.* = **unter dem**

unter·malen *tr. V.* accompany

Unter·malung *die;* ~, ~**en** accompaniment (*Gen.* to)

unter·mauern *tr. V.* (mit Argumenten, Fakten absichern) back up

Unter-: ~**miete** *die* subtenancy; sublease; ~**mieter** *der,* ~**mieterin** *die* subtenant; lodger

untern (ugs.) *Präp. + Art.* = **unter den**

unter-, Unter-: ~**nehmen** *unr. tr. V.* **(a)** (durchführen) undertake; make; take ‹*steps*›; **(b)** **etwas** ~**nehmen** do something; ~**nehmen** *das;* ~~**s**, ~~ **(a)** (Vorhaben) enterprise; **(b)** (Firma) concern; ~**nehmer** *der;* ~~**s**, ~~, ~**nehmerin** *die;* ~~, ~~**nen** employer

unternehmerisch [1] *Adj.* entrepreneurial [2] *adv.* ‹*think*› in an entrepreneurial *or* businesslike way

unter·nehmungs·lustig *Adj.* active; **sie ist sehr** ~ she is always out doing things

Unter·offizier *der* **(a)** non-commissioned officer **(b)** (Dienstgrad) corporal

unter|ordnen [1] *tr. V.* subordinate [2] *refl. V.* accept a subordinate role

Unterredung *die;* ~, ~**en** discussion

Unterricht *der;* ~[e]**s**, ~**e** instruction; (Schulunterricht) teaching; (Schulstunden) classes *pl.*

unterrichten [1] *tr. V.* **(a)** teach **(b)** (informieren) inform (**über** + *Akk.* of, about) [2] *itr. V.* (Unterricht geben) teach [3] *refl. V.* (sich informieren) inform oneself (**über** + *Akk.* about)

Unterrichts·stunde *die* lesson; period

*old spelling - see note on page xiv

Unter·rock *der* [half] slip

unter|rühren *tr. V.* stir in

unters *Präp. + Art.* = **unter das**

unter·sagen *tr. V.* forbid; prohibit

Unter·satz *der* ▶ UNTERSETZER

unter-, Unter-: ~**schätzen** *tr. V.* underestimate ‹*amount, effect, etc.*›; underrate ‹*talent, ability, etc.*›; ~**scheiden** [1] *unr. tr. V.* distinguish; [2] *unr. refl. V.* differ (**durch** in, **von** from); ~**scheidung** *die* (Vorgang) differentiation; (Resultat) distinction

Unter-: ~**schenkel** *der* shank; lower leg; ~**schicht** *die* (Soziol.) lower class

Unter·schied *der;* ~[e]**s**, ~**e** difference

unterschiedlich [1] *Adj.* different; (uneinheitlich) variable; varying [2] *adv.* **[sehr/ganz]** ~: in [very/quite] different ways

unterschieds·los [1] *Adj.* uniform; equal ‹*treatment*› [2] *adv.* ‹*treat*› equally; (ohne Benachteiligung) without discrimination

unter·schlagen *unr. tr. V.* embezzle ‹*money, funds, etc.*›; (unterdrücken) intercept ‹*letter*›; withhold ‹*fact, news, information, etc.*›

Unter·schlupf *der;* ~[e]**s**, ~**e** shelter; (Versteck) hiding place; hideout

unter|schlüpfen *itr. V.; mit sein* (ugs.) hide out

unter·schreiben *unr. itr., tr. V.* sign

Unter-: ~**schrift** *die* signature; (Bild~) caption; ~**see·boot** *das* submarine; ~**setzer** *der* mat; (für Gläser) coaster

untersetzt *Adj.* stocky

Unter·stand *der* (Schutzbunker) dugout; (Unterschlupf) shelter

unter|stehen [1] *unr. itr. V.* **jmdm.** ~: be subordinate *or* answerable to sb. [2] *unr. refl. V.* dare

unter|stellen[1] [1] *tr. V.* (zur Aufbewahrung) keep; store ‹*furniture*› [2] *refl. V.* take shelter

unter·stellen[2] *tr. V.* **(a)** **jmdm. eine Abteilung** ~: put sb. in charge of a department; **die Behörde ist dem Ministerium unterstellt** the office is under the ministry **(b)** (unterschieben) **jmdm. böse Absichten** *usw.* ~: insinuate that sb.'s intentions *etc.* are bad

Unter·stellung *die* (falsche Behauptung) insinuation

unter·streichen *unr. tr. V.* **(a)** underline **(b)** (hervorheben) emphasize

Unter·streichung *die;* ~, ~**en** **(a)** underlining **(b)** (das Betonen) emphasizing

unter·stützen *tr. V.* support

Unter·stützung *die;* ~, ~**en** **(a)** support **(b)** (finanzielle Hilfe) allowance; (für Arbeitslose) [unemployment] benefit *no art.*

unter·suchen *tr. V.* examine; (überprüfen)

test (**auf** + *Akk.* for); (aufzuklären suchen) investigate; (durchsuchen) search (**auf** + *Akk.*, **nach** for)

Untersuchung *die;* ~, ~en (a) ▶ UNTERSUCHEN: examination; test; investigation; search (b) (wissenschaftliche Arbeit) study

Untersuchungs·haft *die* imprisonment *or* detention while awaiting trial

Unter·tasse *die* saucer

unter|tauchen [1] *itr. V.; mit sein* **(a)** (im Wasser) dive [under] **(b)** (verschwinden) disappear [2] *tr. V.* duck

Unter·teil *das od. der* bottom part

unter·teilen *tr. V.* divide; (gliedern) subdivide

Unter·titel *der* subtitle

unter·treiben *unr. itr. V.* play things down

Untertreibung *die;* ~, ~en understatement

unter·vermieten *tr., itr. V.* sublet

unter·wandern *tr. V.* infiltrate

Unter·wanderung *die* infiltration *no indef. art.*

Unter·wäsche *die* underwear

unterwegs *Adv.* on the way; (nicht zu Hause) out [and about]

unter·weisen *unr. tr. V.* (geh.) instruct

Unter·welt *die;* ~: underworld

unter·werfen [1] *unr. tr. V.* **(a)** subjugate ‹*people, country*› **(b)** (unterziehen) subject (*Dat.* to) [2] *unr. refl. V.* **sich [jmdm./einer Sache] ~:** submit [to sb./sth.]

Unterwerfung *die;* ~, ~en **(a)** (das Unterwerfen) subjugation (**unter** + *Akk.* to) **(b)** (das Sichunterwerfen) submission (**unter** + *Akk.* to)

unterwürfig [1] *Adj.* obsequious [2] *adv.* obsequiously

unter·zeichnen *tr. V.* sign

unter·ziehen [1] *unr. tr. V.* **etw. einer Untersuchung/Überprüfung** (*Dat.*) **~:** examine/check sth. [2] *unr. refl. V.* **sich einer Operation** (*Dat.*) **~:** undergo *or* have an operation

untragbar *Adj.* unbearable

untreu *Adj.* disloyal; (in der Ehe, Liebe) unfaithful

Untreue *die;* ~: disloyalty; (in der Ehe, Liebe) unfaithfulness

untröstlich *Adj.* inconsolable

Untugend *die;* ~, ~en bad habit

unüberlegt [1] *Adj.* rash [2] *adv.* rashly

unübersehbar [1] *Adj.* **(a)** (offenkundig) conspicuous **(b)** (sehr groß) enormous [2] *adv.* (sehr) extremely

unübersichtlich [1] *Adj.* unclear; confusing ‹*arrangement*›; blind ‹*bend*›; broken ‹*country etc.*› [2] *adv.* unclearly; confusingly ‹*arranged*›

unübertrefflich [1] *Adj.* superb [2] *adv.* superbly

unübertroffen *Adj.* unsurpassed

unumgänglich *Adj.* [absolutely] necessary

Unumgänglichkeit *die;* ~: absolute necessity

unumwunden [1] *Adj.* frank [2] *adv.* frankly; openly

ununterbrochen [1] *Adj.* incessant [2] *adv.* incessantly

unveränderlich *Adj.* unchangeable

unverantwortlich [1] *Adj.* irresponsible [2] *adv.* irresponsibly

unverbesserlich *Adj.* incorrigible

unverbindlich [1] *Adj.* **(a)** not binding *pred.;* without obligation *postpos;* **(b)** (reserviert) non-committal ‹*answer, words*›; impersonal ‹*attitude*› [2] *adv.* ‹*send, reserve*› without obligation

unverbleit *Adj.* unleaded

unverblümt [1] *Adj.* blunt [2] *adv.* bluntly

unverbraucht *Adj.* untouched; unspent ‹*energy*›; fresh ‹*air*›

unverdaut *Adj.* undigested

unverdorben *Adj.* unspoilt

unverdrossen *Adj.* undeterred; (unverzagt) undaunted

unvereinbar *Adj.* incompatible (**mit** with)

Unvereinbarkeit *die;* ~: incompatibility (**mit** with)

unverfänglich *Adj.* harmless

unverfroren *Adj.* insolent; impudent

unvergänglich *Adj.* immortal ‹*fame*›; unchanging ‹*beauty*›; abiding ‹*recollection*›

unvergesslich, *unvergeßlich *Adj.* unforgettable

unvergleichlich [1] *Adj.* incomparable [2] *adv.* incomparably

unverheiratet *Adj.* unmarried

unverhofft [1] *Adj.* unexpected [2] *adv.* unexpectedly

unverhohlen [1] *Adj.* unconcealed [2] *adv.* openly

unverkäuflich *Adj.* **diese Vase ist ~:** this vase is not for sale/(nicht absetzbar) unsaleable

unvermeidlich *Adj.* unavoidable; (sich als Folge ergebend) inevitable

Unvermögen *das;* ~s lack of ability

unvermutet [1] *Adj.* unexpected [2] *adv.* unexpectedly

unvernünftig *Adj.* stupid; foolish

unverrichtet *Adj.* **~er Dinge** without having achieved anything

U

unverschämt [1] *Adj.* **(a)** impertinent ‹*person, manner, words, etc.*›; barefaced ‹*lie*› **(b)** (ugs.: sehr groß) outrageous ‹*price, luck, etc.*›
[2] *adv.* impertinently; ‹*lie*› barefacedly; blatantly
Unverschämtheit *die;* ~, ~**en** impertinence
unversehens *Adv.* suddenly
unversehrt *Adj.* unscathed; (unbeschädigt) undamaged
unverständlich *Adj.* incomprehensible
Unverständnis *das;* ~**ses** lack of understanding
unverträglich *Adj.* **(a)** quarrelsome **(b)** incompatible ‹*blood groups, medicines, transplant tissue*›
unverwechselbar *Adj.* unmistakable; distinctive
unverwüstlich *Adj.* indestructible
unverzeihlich *Adj.* unforgivable
unverzüglich [1] *Adj.* prompt
[2] *adv.* promptly
unvollkommen [1] *Adj.* **(a)** imperfect **(b)** (unvollständig) incomplete
[2] *adv.* **(a)** imperfectly
(b) (unvollständig) incompletely
Unvollkommenheit *die;* ~: **(a)** imperfectness
(b) (Unvollständigkeit) incompleteness
unvollständig *Adj.* incomplete
Unvollständigkeit *die;* ~: incompleteness
unvorhergesehen *Adj.* unforeseen; unexpected ‹*visit*›
unvorhersehbar *Adj.* unforeseeable
unvorsichtig [1] *Adj.* careless; (unüberlegt) rash
[2] *adv.* carelessly; (unüberlegt) rashly
Unvorsichtigkeit *die;* ~ ▶ UNVORSICHTIG 1: carelessness; rashness
unvorstellbar [1] *Adj.* inconceivable
[2] *adv.* unimaginably
unvorteilhaft *Adj.* **(a)** unattractive ‹*figure, appearance*›
(b) (ohne Vorteil) unfavourable, poor ‹*purchase, exchange*›; unprofitable ‹*business*›
unwahr *Adj.* untrue
Unwahrheit *die;* ~, ~**en** **(a)** untruthfulness
(b) (Äußerung) untruth
unwahrscheinlich [1] *Adj.* **(a)** improbable; unlikely
(b) (ugs.: sehr viel) incredible (coll.)
[2] *adv.* (ugs.: sehr) incredibly (coll.)
Unwahrscheinlichkeit *die;* ~: improbability
unwegsam *Adj.* [almost] impassable
unweiblich *Adj.* unfeminine
unweigerlich [1] *Adj.* inevitable
[2] *adv.* inevitably
Unwesen *das:* **sein ~ treiben** (abwertend) be up to one's mischief *or* one's tricks
Unwetter *das;* ~**s**, ~: [thunder]storm
unwichtig *Adj.* unimportant
Unwichtigkeit *die;* ~, ~**en** **(a)** unimportance
(b) (etw. Unwichtiges) unimportant thing
unwiderruflich [1] *Adj.* irrevocable
[2] *adv.* irrevocably
unwiderstehlich *Adj.* irresistible
unwiederbringlich (geh.) [1] *Adj.* irretrievable
[2] *adv.* irretrievably
Unwille[n] *der;* **Unwillens** displeasure
unwillig [1] *Adj.* indignant; (widerwillig) unwilling
[2] *adv.* indignantly; (widerwillig) unwillingly
unwillkürlich [1] *Adj.* **(a)** spontaneous ‹*cry, sigh*›; instinctive ‹*reaction, movement, etc.*›
(b) (Physiol.) involuntary ‹*movement etc.*›
[2] *adv.* **(a)** ‹*shout etc.*› spontaneously; ‹*react, move, etc.*› instinctively
(b) (Physiol.) ‹*move etc.*› involuntarily
unwirklich (geh.) *Adj.* unreal
Unwirklichkeit *die;* ~, ~**en** unreality
unwirksam *Adj.* ineffective
Unwirksamkeit *die;* ~: ineffectiveness
unwirsch [1] *Adj.* surly; ill-natured
[2] *adv.* ill-naturedly
unwirtschaftlich [1] *Adj.* uneconomic ‹*procedure etc.*›; (nicht sparsam) uneconomical ‹*driving etc.*›
[2] *adv.* ‹*work, drive, etc.*› uneconomically
Unwissenheit *die;* ~: ignorance
unwissentlich [1] *Adj.* unconscious
[2] *adv.* unknowingly; unwittingly
unwohl *Adv.* unwell; **mir ist ~:** I don't feel well
Unwohlsein *das;* ~**s** indisposition
unwürdig *Adj.* **(a)** undignified ‹*person, behaviour*›; degrading ‹*treatment*›
(b) (unangemessen) unworthy
unzählig *Adj.* innumerable; countless
Unze *die;* ~, ~**n** ounce
unzeitgemäß *Adj.* anachronistic
unzerbrechlich *Adj.* unbreakable
unzertrennlich *Adj.* inseparable
Unzucht *die:* ~ **treiben** fornicate; **gewerbsmäßige ~:** prostitution
unzüchtig [1] *Adj.* obscene ‹*letter, gesture*›
[2] *adv.* ‹*touch, approach, etc.*› indecently; ‹*speak*› obscenely
unzufrieden *Adj.* dissatisfied; (stärker) unhappy
Unzufriedenheit *die;* ~: dissatisfaction; (stärker) unhappiness
unzugänglich *Adj.* inaccessible ‹*area, building, etc.*›; unapproachable ‹*character, person, etc.*›

*alte Schreibung - vgl. Hinweis auf S. xiv

unzulänglich (geh.) 1 *Adj.* insufficient 2 *adv.* insufficiently

unzumutbar *Adj.* unreasonable

unzurechnungsfähig *Adj.* not responsible for one's actions *pred.;* (geistesgestört) of unsound mind *postpos.*

unzustellbar *Adj.* (Postw.) „~": 'not known [at this address]'

unzutreffend *Adj.* inappropriate; (falsch) incorrect

unzuverlässig *Adj.* unreliable

Unzuverlässigkeit *die;* ~: unreliability

unzweckmäßig 1 *Adj.* unsuitable; (unpraktisch) impractical 2 *adv.* unsuitably; (unpraktisch) impractically

Update /'apdeit/ *das;* **~s, ~s** (DV) update

üppig 1 *Adj.* lush ‹*vegetation*›; thick ‹*hair, beard*›; full ‹*bosom, lips*›; voluptuous ‹*figure, woman*›; (fig.) sumptuous, opulent ‹*meal*› 2 *adv.* luxuriantly; (fig.) sumptuously

Ur·abstimmung *die* [*esp.* strike] ballot

Ural *der;* **~[s]** Urals *pl.;* Ural Mountains *pl.*

ur·alt *Adj.* very old; ancient

Uran *das;* **~s** uranium

Ur·aufführung *die* première; first night *or* performance; (eines Films) première; first showing

urbar *Adj.* **ein Stück Land ~ machen** cultivate a piece of land

Ur·einwohner *der,* **Ur·einwohnerin** *die* native inhabitant

Ur·enkel *der* great-grandson

Urgroß-: ~eltern *Pl.* great-grandparents; **~mutter** *die; Pl.* **~mütter** great-grandmother; **~vater** *der* great-grandfather

Ur·heber *der;* **~s, ~**: originator; initiator; (bes. Rechtsspr.: Verfasser, Autor) author

Urheber·recht *das* copyright

urig *Adj.* natural ‹*person*›; real ‹*beer*›; cosy ‹*pub*›

Urin *der;* **~s, ~e** (Med.) urine

urinieren *itr. V.* urinate

Ur·knall *der* big bang

Ur·kunde *die;* **~, ~n** document; (Bescheinigung, Siegerurkunde, Diplom usw.) certificate

Urlaub *der;* **~[e]s, ~e** holiday[s] (Brit.); vacation (esp. Amer.); (bes. Milit.) leave

urlaubs-, Urlaubs-: ~geld *das* holiday pay *or* money; (gespartes Geld) holiday money; **~ort** *der* holiday resort; **~reif** *Adj.* **~reif sein** (ugs.) be ready for a holiday; **~reise** *die* holiday [trip]; **~zeit** *die* holiday period *or* season

Urne *die;* **~, ~n** urn; (Wahlurne) [ballot] box

Ur·oma *die* (fam.) great-granny (coll./child lang.)

Ur·opa *der* (fam.) great-grandpa (coll./child lang.)

Ur·sache *die* cause

Ur·sprung *der* origin

ur·sprünglich 1 *Adj.* **(a)** original ‹*plan, price, form, material, etc.*› **(b)** (natürlich) natural 2 *adv.* **(a)** originally **(b)** (natürlich) naturally

Urteil *das;* **~s, ~e** judgement; (Strafe) sentence; (Gerichtsurteil) verdict

urteilen *itr. V.* form an opinion; judge; **über etw./jmdn. ~**: judge sth./sb.

urteils-, Urteils-: ~fähig *Adj.* competent *or* able to judge *postpos.;* **~fähigkeit** *die* competence *or* ability to judge; **~vermögen** *das* competence to judge

Ur·wald *der* primeval forest; (tropisch) jungle

ur·wüchsig *Adj.* natural ‹*landscape, power*›; earthy ‹*language, humour*›

Urwüchsigkeit *die;* **~** ▶ URWÜCHSIG: naturalness; earthiness

USA *Pl.* USA

User /'ju:zɐ/ *der;* **~s, ~, Userin** *die;* **~, ~nen** (bes. DV, Drogenjargon) user

usw. *Abk.* = **und so weiter** etc.

Utensil *das;* **~s, ~ien** /...i̯ən/ piece of equipment; **~ien** equipment *sing.*

Utopie *die;* **~, ~n** utopian dream

utopisch *Adj.* utopian

UV *Abk.* = **Ultraviolett** UV

Vv

v, V /vau:/ *das;* ~, ~: v/V
v. *Abk.* = **von**
vage /'va:ga/ [1] *Adj.* vague
[2] *adv.* vaguely
Vagina /va'gi:na/ *die;* ~, **Vaginen** (Anat.) vagina
vaginal *Adj.* (Anat.) vaginal
vakant /va'kant/ *Adj.* vacant
Vakuum *das;* ~s, **Vakuen** vacuum
vakuum·verpackt *Adj.* vacuum-packed
Valentins·tag /'va:lɛnti:ns-/ *der* [St] Valentine's Day
Van /væn/ *der;* ~s, ~s (Kfz.-W.) multi-purpose vehicle; MPV
Vandale /van'da:la/ *usw.* ▶ WANDALE
Vanille /va'nɪljə/ *die;* ~: vanilla
Vanille-: ~**eis** *das* vanilla ice cream; ~**pudding** *der* vanilla pudding; ~**zucker** *der* vanilla sugar
variabel /va'ri̯a:bl̩/ [1] *Adj.* variable
[2] *adv.* variably
Variante /va'ri̯antə/ *die;* ~, ~n (geh.) variant; variation
variieren *tr., itr. V.* vary
Vase /'va:zə/ *die;* ~, ~n vase
Vaseline /vaze'li:nə/ *die;* ~: Vaseline ®
Vater *der;* ~s, **Väter** father; **Gott** ~: God the Father
Vater·land *das* fatherland
väterlich [1] *Adj.* **(a)** paternal ‹*line, love, instincts, etc.*›
(b) (fürsorglich) fatherly
[2] *adv.* in a fatherly way
väterlicherseits *Adv.* on the/his/her *etc.* father's side
Vaterschaft *die;* ~, ~en fatherhood
Vater-: ~**tag** *der* Father's Day *no def. art.*; ~**unser** *das;* ~~s, ~~: Lord's Prayer
Vati *der;* ~s, ~s (fam.) dad[dy] (coll.)
Vatikan /vati'ka:n/ *der;* ~s Vatican
v. Chr. *Abk.* = **vor Christus** BC
Vegetarier /vege'ta:ri̯ɐ/ *der;* ~s, ~, **Vegetarierin** *die;* ~, ~nen vegetarian
vegetarisch [1] *Adj.* vegetarian
[2] *adv.* **er isst** *od.* **lebt** ~: he is a vegetarian
Vegetation *die;* ~, ~en vegetation *no indef. art.*
vegetieren *itr. V.* vegetate
Veilchen *das;* ~s, ~: violet
Vene /'ve:nə/ *die;* ~, ~n vein
Venedig /ve'ne:dɪç/ *(das);* ~s Venice

*old spelling - see note on page xiv

Venezolaner /venets:o'la:nɐ/ *der;* ~s, ~, **Venezolanerin** *die;* ~, ~nen Venezuelan
venezolanisch *Adj.* Venezuelan
Venezuela *(das);* ~s Venezuela
Ventil /vɛn'ti:l/ *das;* ~s, ~e valve
Ventilator /vɛnti'la:tɔr/ *der;* ~s, ~en ventilator
Venus /'ve:nʊs/ *die;* ~: Venus *no def. art.*
verabreden [1] *tr. V.* arrange
[2] *refl. V.* **sich im Park/zum Tennis/für den folgenden Abend** ~: arrange to meet in the park/for tennis/next evening
Verabredung *die;* ~, ~en **(a)** arrangement
(b) (verabredete Zusammenkunft) appointment; **eine** ~ **absagen** call off a meeting
verabscheuen *tr. V.* detest; loathe
verabschieden [1] *tr. V.* **(a)** say goodbye to
(b) (aus dem Dienst) retire ‹*general, civil servant, etc.*›
[2] *refl. V.* **sich [von jmdm.]** ~: say goodbye [to sb.]
Verabschiedung *die;* ~, ~en **(a)** leave-taking
(b) (aus dem Dienst) retirement
verachten *tr. V.* despise
verächtlich [1] *Adj.* **(a)** contemptuous
(b) (verachtenswürdig) contemptible
[2] *adv.* contemptuously
Verächtlichkeit *die;* ~: contempt; contemptuousness
Verachtung *die;* ~: contempt
verallgemeinern *tr., itr. V.* generalize
Verallgemeinerung *die;* ~, ~en generalization
veralten *itr. V.; mit sein* become obsolete
Veranda /ve'randa/ *die;* ~, **Veranden** veranda; porch
veränderlich *Adj.* changeable
verändern *tr., refl. V.* change
Veränderung *die;* ~, ~en change (*Gen.* in)
verängstigen *tr. V.* frighten; scare
verankern *tr. V.* fix ‹*tent, mast, pole, etc.*›; (mit einem Anker) anchor
veranlagen *tr. V.* (Steuerw.) assess (**mit** at)
veranlagt *Adj.* **künstlerisch/praktisch** ~ **sein** have an artistic bent/be practically minded
Veranlagung *die;* ~, ~en [pre]disposition
veranlassen *tr. V.* cause; induce; ~, **dass** ... see to it that ...

Veranlassung *die;* **~, ~en** reason
veranschaulichen *tr. V.* illustrate
veranschlagen *tr. V.* estimate (**mit** at)
veranstalten *tr. V.* organize; hold, give ‹*party*›; hold ‹*auction*›; do ‹*survey*›
Veranstalter *der;* **~s, ~, Veranstalterin** *die;* **~, ~nen** organizer
Veranstaltung *die;* **~, ~en (a)** (das Veranstalten) organizing; organization
(b) (etw., was veranstaltet wird) event
verantworten 1 *tr. V.* **etw. ~:** take responsibility for sth.
2 *refl. V.* **sich für etw. ~:** answer for sth.; **sich vor jmdm. ~:** answer to sb
verantwortlich *Adj.* responsible
Verantwortung *die;* **~, ~en** responsibility (**für** for)
verantwortungs-: ~bewusst, *~bewußt *Adj.* responsible; **~los** *Adj.* irresponsible; **~voll** *Adj.* responsible
verarbeiten *tr. V.* use; **etw. zu etw. ~:** make sth. into sth.; (geistig bewältigen) assimilate ‹*film, experience, impressions*›
Verarbeitung *die;* **~, ~en (a)** (das Verarbeiten) use
(b) (Art der Fertigung) finish; **Schuhe in erstklassiger ~:** shoes with a first-class finish
verärgern *tr. V.* annoy
verarzten *tr. V.* (ugs.) patch up (coll.) ‹*person*›; fix (coll.) ‹*wound etc.*›
verausgaben *refl. V.* wear oneself out; **sie hat sich total verausgabt** (finanziell) she has completely spent out
veräußern *tr. V.* dispose of ‹*property*›
Verb /vɛrp/ *das;* **~s, ~en** verb
verbal /vɛr'ba:l/ *Adj.* 1 (auch Sprachw.) verbal
2 *adv.* verbally
Verband *der* **(a)** (Binde) bandage; dressing
(b) (Vereinigung) association
verbandeln *tr. V.* link closely
Verband[s]-: ~kasten *der* first-aid box; **~material** *das* dressing materials *pl.*
Verband·zeug *das* first-aid things *pl.*
Verbannung *die;* **~, ~en** banishment
verbeamten *tr. V.* make ‹*person*› a civil servant
verbergen *unr. tr. V.* hide; conceal
verbessern 1 *tr. V.* **(a)** improve
(b) (korrigieren) correct
2 *refl. V.* **(a)** improve
(b) ([beruflich] aufsteigen) better oneself
Verbesserung *die* **(a)** improvement
(b) (Korrektur) correction
Verbesserungs·vorschlag *der* suggestion for improvement
verbeugen *refl. V.* bow (**vor** + *Dat.* to)
Verbeugung *die;* **~, ~en** bow
verbeulen *tr. V.* dent
verbieten *unr. tr. V.* **(a)** forbid; **jmdm. etw. ~:** forbid sb. sth.; **„Betreten des Rasens/Rauchen verboten"** 'keep off the grass'/'no smoking'
(b) (für unzulässig erklären) ban
verbinden 1 *unr. tr. V.* **(a)** (bandagieren) bandage; dress
(b) (zubinden) bind; **jmdm. die Augen ~:** blindfold sb.
(c) (zusammenfügen) join
(d) (in Beziehung bringen) connect (**durch** by); link ‹*towns, lakes, etc.*› (**durch** by)
(e) (verknüpfen) combine ‹*abilities, qualities, etc.*›
(f) *auch itr.* (telefonisch) **jmdn. [mit jmdm.] ~:** put sb. through [to sb.]
2 *unr. refl. V.* **(a)** (auch Chemie) combine (**mit** with)
(b) (sich zusammentun) join [together]; join forces
verbindlich 1 *Adj.* **(a)** friendly
(b) (bindend) obligatory; compulsory; binding ‹*agreement, decision, etc.*›
2 *adv.* **(a)** (freundlich) in a friendly manner
(b) ~ zusagen definitely agree; **jmdm. etw. ~ zusagen** make sb. a firm offer of sth
Verbindung *die;* **~, ~en (a)** (das Verknüpfen) linking
(b) (Zusammenhalt) join; connection
(c) (verknüpfende Strecke) link
(d) (durch Telefon, Funk, Verkehrsmittel) connection (**nach** to)
(e) (Kombination) combination; **in ~ mit etw.** in conjunction with sth.
(f) (Kontakt) contact; **sich mit jmdm. in ~ setzen** get in touch *or* contact with sb.
(g) (Zusammenhang) connection
verbissen 1 *Adj.* dogged; doggedly determined
2 *adv.* doggedly
verbitten *unr. refl. V.* **sich** (*Dat.*) **etw. ~:** refuse to tolerate sth.
verbittern *tr. V.* embitter
Verbitterung *die;* **~, ~en** bitterness; embitterment
verblassen *itr. V.; mit sein* (auch fig. geh.) fade
Verbleib *der;* **~[e]s** (geh.) whereabouts *pl.*
verbleiben *unr. itr. V.; mit sein* remain; **wie seid ihr verblieben?** what did you arrange?
verbleien *tr. V.* (Technik) lead ‹*petrol*›
Verblendung *die;* **~, ~en** blindness
verblüffen *tr.* (*auch itr.*) *V.* amaze
verblüffend 1 *Adj.* amazing
2 *adv.* amazingly
Verblüffung *die;* **~, ~en** amazement
verblühen *itr. V.; mit sein* (auch fig.) fade
verbluten *itr.* (*auch refl.*) *V.; mit sein* bleed to death
verbohrt *Adj.* pigheaded
verborgen *Adj.* (abgelegen) secluded; (nicht sichtbar) hidden
Verbot *das;* **~[e]s, ~e** ban (*Gen.*, **von** on)

V

Verbots·schild *das; Pl.* **~er** sign (prohibiting sth.); (Verkehrsw.) prohibitive sign
Verbrauch *der;* **~[e]s** consumption (**von, an** + *Dat.* of)
verbrauchen *tr. V.* use; consume ‹*food, drink*›; use up ‹*provisions*›; spend ‹*money*›; consume, use ‹*fuel*›; (fig.) use up ‹*strength, energy*›
Verbraucher *der;* **~s, ~, Verbraucherin** *die;* **~, ~nen** consumer
Verbraucher·schutz *der* consumer protection
Verbrechen *das;* **~s, ~:** crime (**an** + *Dat.*, **gegen** against)
Verbrechens-: ~rate *die* crime rate; **~verhütung** *die* crime prevention
Verbrecher *der;* **~s, ~, Verbrecherin** *die;* **~, ~nen** criminal
verbrecherisch *Adj.* criminal
verbreiten 1 *tr. V.* spread; radiate ‹*optimism, calm, etc.*›
2 *refl. V.* spread
Verbreitung *die;* **~, ~en (a)** ▶ VERBREITEN 1: spreading; radiation
(b) (Ausbreitung) spread
verbrennen 1 *unr. itr. V.; mit sein* burn
2 *tr. V.* burn; cremate ‹*dead person*›; **sich** (*Dat.*) **den Mund ~** (fig.) say too much
Verbrennung *die;* **~, ~en (a)** ▶ VERBRENNEN 2: burning; cremation
(b) (Wunde) burn
Verbrennungs·anlage *die* incineration plant; incinerator
verbringen *unr. tr. V.* spend
verbummeln *tr. V.* (ugs.) **(a)** waste ‹*time*›
(b) (vergessen) forget [all] about; clean forget; (verlieren) lose
verbünden *refl. V.* form an alliance
Verbündete *der/die; adj. Dekl.* ally
verbüßen *tr. V.* serve ‹*sentence*›
Verdacht *der;* **~[e]s, ~e** *od.* **Verdächte** suspicion; **wen hast du in ~?** who do you suspect?
verdächtig 1 *Adj.* suspicious
2 *adv.* suspiciously

Verdächtige *der/die; adj. Dekl.* suspect
verdächtigen *tr. V.* suspect
Verdächtigung *die;* **~, ~en** suspicion
verdammen *tr. V.* condemn; (Rel.) damn
verdampfen 1 *itr. V.; mit sein* evaporate
2 *tr. V.* evaporate
verdanken *tr. V.* **jmdm./einer Sache etw. ~:** owe sth. to sb./sth.
verdarb *1. u. 3. Pers. Sg. Prät. v.* VERDERBEN
verdattert (ugs.) *Adj.* flabbergasted; (verwirrt) dazed; stunned
verdauen 1 *tr. V.* (auch fig.) digest
2 *itr. V.* digest [one's food]
verdaulich *Adj.* digestible

Verdauung *die;* **~:** digestion
Verdeck *das;* **~[e]s, ~e** top; hood (Brit.); (bei Kinderwagen) hood
verdecken *tr. V.* hide; cover
verderben 1 *unr. itr. V.; mit sein* go bad *or* off; spoil
2 *unr. tr. V.* spoil; (stärker) ruin; spoil ‹*appetite, enjoyment, fun, etc.*›
3 *unr. refl. V.* **sich** (*Dat.*) **den Magen/die Augen ~:** give oneself an upset stomach/ruin one's eyesight
Verderben *das;* **~s** ruin
verderblich *Adj.* perishable ‹*food*›; pernicious ‹*influence, effect, etc.*›
verdeutlichen *tr. V.* **etw. ~:** make sth. clear; (erklären) explain sth.
verdichten *refl. V.* ‹*fog, smoke*› thicken, become thicker; (fig.) ‹*suspicion, rumour*› grow; ‹*feeling*› intensify
verdienen 1 *tr. V.* **(a)** earn
(b) (wert sein) deserve
2 *itr. V.* **beide Eheleute ~:** husband and wife are both earning
Verdiener *der;* **~s, ~, Verdienerin** *die;* **~, ~nen** wage earner
Verdienst[1] *der;* **~[e]s, ~e** income
Verdienst[2] *das;* **~[e]s, ~e** merit
verdienst·voll 1 *Adj.* commendable; ‹*person*› of outstanding merit
2 *adv.* commendably
verdient 1 *Adj.* **(a)** ‹*person*› of outstanding merit; **sich um etw. ~ machen** render outstanding services to sth.
(b) (gerecht, zustehend) well-deserved
2 *adv.* deservedly
verdientermaßen *Adv.* deservedly
verdoppeln 1 *tr. V.* double; (fig.) double, redouble ‹*efforts etc.*›
2 *refl. V.* double
verdorben *2. Part. v.* VERDERBEN
verdorren *itr. V.; mit sein* wither [and die]; ‹*meadow*› scorch
verdrängen *tr. V.* **(a)** drive out ‹*inhabitants*›; (fig.: ersetzen) displace
(b) (Psych.) repress; (bewusst) suppress
verdrehen *tr. V.* **(a)** twist ‹*joint*›; roll ‹*eyes*›
(b) (ugs. abwertend: entstellen) twist ‹*words, facts, etc.*›
verdrießen *unr. tr. V.* (geh.) irritate; annoy
verdrießlich 1 *Adj.* morose
2 *adv.* morosely
verdross, *verdroß *1. u. 3. Pers. Sg. Prät. v.* VERDRIESSEN
verdrossen 1 *Adj.* (missmutig) morose; (missmutig und lustlos) sullen
2 *adv.* (missmutig) morosely; (missmutig und lustlos) sullenly
Verdruss, *Verdruß *der;* **Verdrusses, Verdrusse** annoyance
verdunkeln *tr. V.* darken; (vollständig) black out ‹*room, house, etc.*›

*alte Schreibung - vgl. Hinweis auf S. xiv

Verdunk[e]lung *die;* ~, ~**en** darkening; (vollständig) blackout
verdünnen *tr. V.* dilute
verdunsten *itr. V.; mit sein* evaporate
verdünnen *tr. V.* dilute
verdunsten *itr. V.; mit sein* evaporate
Verdunstung *die;* ~: evaporation
verdursten *itr. V.; mit sein* die of thirst
verdutzt *Adj.* taken aback *pred.;* nonplussed; (verwirrt) baffled
Verdutztheit *die;* ~: bafflement
verehren *tr. V.* **(a)** venerate **(b)** (geh.: bewundern) admire; (ehrerbietig lieben) worship
Verehrer *der;* ~**s**, ~, **Verehrerin** *die;* ~, ~**en** admirer
Verehrung *die;* ~ **(a)** veneration **(b)** (Bewunderung) admiration
vereidigen *tr. V.* swear in
Vereidigung *die;* ~, ~**en** swearing in
Verein *der;* ~**s**, ~**e** organization; (der Kunstfreunde usw.) association; society; (Sportverein) club
vereinbar *Adj.* compatible
vereinbaren *tr. V.* agree; arrange ‹*meeting etc.*›
Vereinbarung *die;* ~, ~**en** **(a)** agreeing; (eines Termins usw.) arranging **(b)** (Abmachung) agreement
vereinfachen *tr. V.* simplify
Vereinfachung *die;* ~, ~**en** simplification
vereinheitlichen *tr. V.* standardize
Vereinheitlichung *die;* ~, ~**en** standardization
vereinigen *tr., refl. V.* unite; (in der Wirtschaft) merge
vereinigt *Adj.* united
Vereinigung *die;* ~, ~**en** **(a)** organization **(b)** (das Vereinigen) uniting; (von Unternehmen) merging
vereinsamen *itr. V.; mit sein* become [increasingly] lonely *or* isolated
Vereinsamung *die;* ~: loneliness; isolation
vereinzelt 1 *Adj.* occasional 2 *adv.* (zeitlich) occasionally; (örtlich) here and there
Vereinzelung *die;* ~, ~**en** isolation
vereisen *itr. V.; mit sein* freeze *or* ice over; ‹*wing*› ice up; ‹*lock*› freeze up
vereiteln *tr. V.* thwart
Vereitelung *die;* ~: thwarting
vereitern *itr. V.; mit sein* go septic
verenden *itr. V.; mit sein* perish; die
verengen *refl. V.* narrow; ‹*pupils*› contract
vererben *tr. V.* leave, bequeath ‹*property*› (*Dat.*, **an** + *Akk.* to)
Vererbung *die;* ~, ~**en** heredity *no art.*
verewigen 1 *tr. V.* immortalize 2 *refl. V.* (ugs.: Spuren hinterlassen) leave one's mark
verfahren 1 *unr. refl. V.* lose one's way 2 *unr. itr. V.; mit sein* proceed
Verfahren *das;* ~**s**, ~ **(a)** procedure; (Technik) process; (Methode) method **(b)** (Rechtsw.) proceedings *pl.*
Verfall *der;* ~[e]**s** **(a)** decay; (fig.: der Preise, einer Währung) collapse **(b)** (Auflösung) decline
verfallen *unr. itr. V.; mit sein* **(a)** (baufällig werden) fall into disrepair **(b)** (körperlich) ‹*strength*› decline **(c)** (untergehen) ‹*empire*› decline; ‹*morals, morale*› deteriorate **(d)** (ungültig werden) expire
Verfalls·datum *das* use-by date; (ugs.: Mindesthaltbarkeitsdatum) best-before date
verfälschen *tr. V.* distort, misrepresent ‹*statement, message*›; falsify, misrepresent ‹*facts, history, truth*›; falsify ‹*painting, banknote*›; adulterate ‹*wine, milk, etc.*›
Verfälschung *die* ▶ VERFÄLSCHEN: distortion; misrepresentation; falsification; adulteration
verfassen *tr. V.* write; draw up ‹*resolution*›
Verfasser *der;* ~**s**, ~, **Verfasserin** *die;* ~, ~**nen** writer; (eines Buchs, Artikels usw.) author; writer
Verfassung *die;* ~, ~**en** **(a)** (Politik) constitution **(b)** (Zustand) state [of health/mind]; **in guter/schlechter ~ sein** be in good/poor shape
verfassungs·gemäß 1 *Adj.* constitutional; in accordance with the constitution *postpos.;* 2 *adv.* constitutionally; in accordance with the constitution
verfaulen *itr. V.; mit sein* rot
verfehlen *tr. V.* miss
Verfehlung *die;* ~, ~**en** misdemeanour; (Rel.: Sünde) transgression
verfeinden *refl. V.* **sich ~ mit** make an enemy of
verfeinern *tr. V.* improve; refine ‹*method, procedure*›
Verfeinerung *die;* ~, ~**en** ▶ VERFEINERN: improvement; refinement
verfertigen *tr. V.* produce
verfilmen *tr. V.* film; make a film of
Verfilmung *die;* ~, ~**en** **(a)** (das Verfilmen) filming **(b)** (Film) film [version]
verfinstern 1 *tr. V.* obscure ‹*sun etc.*› 2 *refl. V.* (auch fig.) darken
Verfinsterung *die;* ~, ~**en** darkening
verflixt (ugs.) 1 *Adj.* **(a)** (ärgerlich) awkward, unpleasant ‹*situation, business, etc.*› **(b)** (verdammt) blasted (Brit.); blessed; confounded; ~ **[noch mal]!** [damn and] blast! (Brit. coll.)

(c) (sehr groß) **er hat ~es Glück gehabt** he was damned lucky (coll.)
2 *adv.* (sehr) damned (coll.)

verflossen *Adj.* (ugs.) former

verfluchen *tr. V.* curse

verflucht **1** *Adj.* (salopp) damned (coll.); bloody (Brit. sl.); **~ [noch mal]!** damn [it]! (coll.)
2 *adv.* (sehr) damned (coll.)

verfolgen *tr. V.* pursue; hunt, track ‹*animal*›; **etw. [strafrechtlich] ~:** prosecute sth.

Verfolgte *der/die; adj. Dekl.* victim of persecution

Verfolgung *die; ~, ~en* **(a)** pursuit; (eines Ziels, Plans usw.) pursuance
(b) **[strafrechtliche] ~:** prosecution

Verfolgungs-: ~jagd *die* pursuit; chase; **~wahn** *der* (Psych.) persecution mania

verfressen *Adj.* (salopp) greedy

verfügen **1** *tr. V.* (anordnen) order; (dekretieren) decree
2 *itr. V.* **über etw.** (*Akk.*) **[frei] ~ können** be free to decide what to do with sth.; **über etw.** (*Akk.*) **~** (etw. haben) have sth. at one's disposal

Verfügung *die; ~, ~en* **(a)** (Anordnung) order; (Dekret) decree
(b) (Disposition) **etw. zur ~ haben** have sth. at one's disposal; **jmdm. etw. zur ~ stellen** put sth. at sb.'s disposal

verführen *tr. V.* **(a)** (verleiten) tempt
(b) (sexuell) seduce

Verführer *der; ~s, ~:* seducer

Verführerin *der; ~, ~nen* seductress

verführerisch **1** *Adj.* **(a)** (verlockend) tempting
(b) (aufreizend) seductive
2 *adv.* **(a)** (verlockend) temptingly
(b) (aufreizend) seductively

Verführung *die; ~, ~en* **(a)** temptation
(b) (sexuell) seduction

vergangen *Adj.* **(a)** (vorüber, vorbei) bygone, former ‹*times, years, etc.*›
(b) (letzt...) last ‹*year, week, etc.*›

Vergangenheit *die; ~* **(a)** past
(b) (Grammatik: Präteritum) past tense

vergänglich *Adj.* transient; transitory; ephemeral

Vergänglichkeit *die; ~:* transience

Vergaser *der; ~s, ~:* carburettor

vergaß *1. u. 3. Pers. Sg. Prät. v.* VERGESSEN

Vergasung *die; ~, ~en* **(a)** (von Kohle) gasification
(b) (Tötung) gassing
(c) **bis zur ~** (ugs.) ad nauseam

vergeben *unr. tr. V.* **(a)** *auch itr.* (geh.: verzeihen) forgive; **jmdm. etw. ~:** forgive sb. [for] sth.
(b) throw away ‹*chance, goal, etc.*›
(c) (geben) place ‹*order*› **(an** + *Akk.* with); award ‹*grant, prize*› **(an** + *Akk.* to)

vergebens **1** *Adv.* in vain; vainly
2 *adj.* **es war ~:** it was of *or* to no avail

vergeblich **1** *Adj.* futile; vain, futile ‹*attempt, efforts*›
2 *adv.* in vain

Vergebung *die; ~:* (geh.) forgiveness

vergegenwärtigen /*od.* ---'---/ *refl. V.* **sich** (*Dat.*) **etw. ~:** imagine sth.; (erinnern) recall sth.

vergehen *unr. itr. V.; mit sein* ‹*time*› pass [by], go by; ‹*pain*› wear off, pass; ‹*pleasure*› fade

Vergehen *das; ~s, ~:* crime; (Rechtsspr.) offence

vergeigen *tr. V.* (ugs.) botch up ‹*test, performance, etc.*›; lose ‹*game, match*›

vergelten *unr. tr. V.* repay

vergessen *unr. tr.* (*auch itr.*) *V.* forget

Vergessenheit *die; ~:* oblivion

vergesslich, *vergeßlich *Adj.* forgetful

vergeuden *tr. V.* waste

Vergeudung *die; ~, ~en* waste

vergewaltigen *tr. V.* rape

Vergewaltigung *die; ~, ~en* rape

vergewissern *refl. V.* make sure (*Gen.* of)

vergießen *unr. tr. V.* spill; **Tränen ~:** shed tears

vergiften *tr. V.* (auch fig.) poison

Vergiftung *die; ~, ~en* poisoning

vergiss, *vergiß *Imper. Sg. v.* VERGESSEN

Vergiss·mein·nicht, *Vergiß·mein·nicht *das; ~[e]s, ~[e]* forget-me-not

vergisst, *vergißt *2. u. 3. Pers. Sg. Präs. v.* VERGESSEN

Vergleich *der; ~[e]s, ~e* **(a)** comparison; **im ~ zu** *od.* **mit etw.** in comparison with sth.; compared with *or* to sth.
(b) (Rechtsw.) settlement

vergleichbar *Adj.* comparable

vergleichen *unr. tr. V.* compare

Vergleichs·form *die* (Sprachw.) comparative/superlative form

verglühen *itr. V.; mit sein* ‹*log, wick, fire, etc.*› smoulder and go out; ‹*satellite, rocket, wire, etc.*› burn out

vergnügen *refl. V.* enjoy oneself; have a good time

Vergnügen *das; ~s, ~:* pleasure; (Spaß) fun; **viel ~!** (auch iron.) have fun!

vergnüglich *Adj.* amusing; entertaining

vergnügt **1** *Adj.* cheerful
2 *adv.* cheerfully

Vergnügungs·viertel *das* pleasure district

vergolden *tr. V.* gold-plate ‹*jewellery etc.*›; (mit Blattgold) gild

vergraben *unr. tr. V.* bury

vergrämt *Adj.* careworn

---
*old spelling - see note on page xiv

vergraulen *tr. V.* (ugs.) put off
vergreifen *unr. refl. V.* **sich an jmdm. ~:** assault sb.
vergriffen *Adj.* out of print *pred.*
vergrößern [1] *tr. V.* **(a)** (erweitern) extend ‹*room, area, building, etc.*›
(b) (vermehren) increase
(c) (größer reproduzieren) enlarge ‹*photograph etc.*›
[2] *refl. V.* **(a)** (größer werden) ‹*firm, business, etc.*› expand
(b) (zunehmen) increase
[3] *itr. V.* ‹*lens etc.*› magnify
Vergrößerung *die; ~, ~en* **(a)** ▶ VERGRÖSSERN 1, 2: extension; increase; enlargement; expansion
(b) (Foto) enlargement
Vergrößerungs·glas *das* magnifying glass
Vergünstigung *die; ~, ~en* privilege
vergüten *tr. V.* **(a)** (erstatten) **jmdm. etw. ~:** reimburse sb. for sth.
(b) (bes. Papierdt.: bezahlen) remunerate, pay for ‹*work, services*›
Vergütung *die; ~, ~en* **(a)** (Rückerstattung) reimbursement
(b) (Geldsumme) remuneration
verhaften *tr. V.* arrest; **Sie sind verhaftet** you are under arrest
Verhaftung *die; ~, ~en* arrest
verhalten *unr. refl. V.* **(a)** behave; (reagieren) react
(b) (beschaffen sein) be
Verhalten *das; ~s* behaviour
Verhaltens·weise *die* behaviour
Verhältnis *das; ~ses, ~se* **(a) ein ~ von drei zu eins** a ratio of three to one
(b) (persönliche Beziehung) relationship (**zu** with); **mit jmdm. ein ~ haben** (ugs.) have an affair with sb.
(c) *Pl.* (Umstände) conditions
verhältnis·mäßig *Adv.* relatively; comparatively
Verhältnis·wort *das; Pl.* **~wörter** (Sprachw.) preposition
verhandeln [1] *itr. V.* **(a)** negotiate (**über** + *Akk.* about)
(b) (strafrechtlich) try a case; (zivilrechtlich) hear a case
[2] *tr. V.* **(a) etw. ~:** negotiate over sth.
(b) (strafrechtlich) try ‹*case*›; (zivilrechtlich) hear ‹*case*›
Verhandlung *die; ~, ~en* **(a) ~en** negotiations
(b) (strafrechtlich) trial; (zivilrechtlich) hearing; **die ~ gegen X** the trial of X
verhängen *tr. V.* impose ‹*fine, punishment*› (**über** + *Akk.* on); declare ‹*state of emergency, state of siege*›; (Sport) award, give ‹*penalty etc.*›
Verhängnis *das; ~ses, ~se* undoing
verhängnis·voll *Adj.* disastrous
verharmlosen *tr. V.* play down
Verharmlosung *die; ~, ~en* playing down
verhärmt *Adj.* careworn
verharren *itr. V.* (geh.) remain
verhärten [1] *tr. V.* harden; make ‹*person*› hard
[2] *refl. V.* ‹*tissue*› become hardened
verhasst, *verhaßt *Adj.* hated; detested
verhätscheln *tr. V.* (ugs.) pamper
verhauen (ugs.) *unr. tr. V.* beat up; (als Strafe) beat
verheben *unr. refl. V.* do oneself an injury [while lifting sth.]
verheeren *tr. V.* devastate; lay waste [to]
verheerend *Adj.* **(a)** devastating
(b) (ugs.: scheußlich) ghastly (coll.)
verhehlen *tr. V.* (geh.) conceal (*Dat.* from)
verheilen *itr. V.; mit sein* ‹*wound*› heal [up]
verheimlichen *tr. V.* **[jmdm.] etw. ~:** keep sth. secret [from sb.]
Verheimlichung *die; ~, ~en* concealment
verheiraten *refl. V.* get married; **sich mit jmdm. ~:** marry sb.; get married to sb.
Verheiratete *der/die; adj. Dekl.* married person; married man/woman
Verheiratung *die; ~, ~en* marriage
verheizen *tr. V.* **(a)** burn; use as fuel
(b) (abwertend: rücksichtslos einsetzen) burn out ‹*athlete, skier, etc.*›; use ‹*troops*› as cannon fodder
verhelfen *unr. itr. V.* **jmdm./einer Sache zu etw. ~:** help sb./sth. to get/achieve sth.
verherrlichen *tr. V.* glorify
Verherrlichung *die; ~, ~en* glorification
verheult *Adj.* (ugs.) ‹*eyes*› red from crying; ‹*face*› puffy *or* swollen from crying
verhexen *tr. V.* (auch fig.) bewitch
verhindern *tr. V.* prevent
Verhinderung *die; ~, ~en* prevention
verhöhnen *tr. V.* mock
Verhöhnung *die; ~, ~en* mockery
Verhör *das; ~[e]s, ~e* interrogation; questioning; (bei Gericht) examination
verhören [1] *tr. V.* interrogate; question; (bei Gericht) examine
[2] *refl. V.* mishear
verhüllen *tr. V.* cover; (fig.) disguise
verhüllend *Adj.* (Literaturw.) euphemistic
Verhüllung *die; ~, ~en* covering; (fig.) disguising
verhungern *itr. V.; mit sein* die of starvation; starve [to death]
verhunzen *tr. V.* (ugs. abwertend) ruin; mess up; ruin ‹*landscape, townscape, etc.*›
verhüten *tr. V.* prevent
Verhütung *die; ~, ~en* prevention; (Empfängnisverhütung) contraception
Verhütungs·mittel *das* contraceptive

verirren *refl. V.* **(a)** get lost; lose one's way; ‹*animal*› stray
(b) (irgendwohin gelangen) stray (**in, an** + *Akk.* into)

verjagen *tr. V.* chase away

verjüngen 1 *tr. V.* rejuvenate
2 *refl. V.* (schmaler werden) taper; become narrower; narrow

verkalken *itr. V.; mit sein* **(a)** ‹*tissue*› calcify; ‹*arteries*› become hardened
(b) (ugs.: senil werden) become senile

Verkauf *der;* **~[e]s, Verkäufe** sale

verkaufen *tr. V.* (auch fig.) sell (*Dat.*, **an** + *Akk.* to); **„zu ~"** 'for sale'

Verkäufer *der;* **~s, ~ Verkäuferin** *die;* **~, ~nen (a)** seller; vendor (formal)
(b) (Berufsbez.) sales *or* shop assistant; (im Außendienst) salesman/saleswoman

verkäuflich *Adj.* (zum Verkauf geeignet) saleable; (zum Verkauf bestimmt) for sale *postpos.*

verkaufs·offen *Adj.* **der ~e Samstag** Saturday on which the shops are open all day

Verkaufs·preis *der* retail price

Verkehr *der;* **~s (a)** traffic
(b) (Kontakt) contact; communication
(c) (Geschlechtsverkehr) intercourse

verkehren *itr. V.* **(a)** *auch mit sein* (fahren) run; ‹*aircraft*› fly
(b) (in Kontakt stehen) **mit jmdm. ~:** associate with sb.
(c) (zu Gast sein) **bei jmdm. ~:** visit sb. regularly

verkehrs-, Verkehrs-: ~ampel *die* traffic lights *pl.;* **~amt** *das* tourist information office; **~aufkommen** *das* volume of traffic; **~hindernis** *das* obstruction to traffic; **~knotenpunkt** *der* [traffic] junction; **~kontrolle** *die* traffic check; **~meldung** *die* traffic announcement *or* flash; **~mittel** *das* means of transport; **die öffentlichen ~mittel** public transport *sing.;* **~polizist** *der* traffic policeman; **~polizistin** *die* traffic policewoman; **~schild** *das; Pl.* **~~er** traffic sign; road sign; **~sicher** *Adj.* roadworthy; **~teilnehmer** *der,* **~teilnehmerin** *die* road user; **~unfall** *der* road accident; **~weg** *der* traffic route; **~zeichen** *das* traffic sign; road sign

verkehrt 1 *Adj.* wrong
2 *adv.* wrongly; **alles ~ machen** do everything wrong

verkennen *unr. tr. V.* fail to recognize; misjudge ‹*situation*›

verklagen *tr. V.* sue; take to court; **eine Firma auf Schadenersatz ~:** sue a company for damages

verkleben 1 *itr. V.; mit sein* stick together
2 *tr. V.* (zukleben) seal up ‹*hole*›; (festkleben) stick [down] ‹*floor covering etc.*›

*alte Schreibung - vgl. Hinweis auf S. xiv

verkleiden *tr. V.* disguise; (kostümieren) dress up; **sich ~:** disguise oneself/dress [oneself] up

Verkleidung *die;* **~, ~en (a)** disguising; (das Kostümieren) dressing up
(b) (Kleidung) disguise; (bei einer Party) fancy dress

verkleinern 1 *tr. V.* **(a)** make smaller
(b) (verringern) reduce ‹*size, number, etc.*›
(c) (kleiner reproduzieren) reduce ‹*photograph etc.*›
2 *refl. V.* become smaller; ‹*number*› decrease

Verkleinerungs·form *die* (Sprachw.) diminutive form

verknallen *refl. V.* (ugs.: sich verlieben) fall head over heels in love (**in** + *Akk.* with); **in jmdn. verknallt sein** be crazy about sb. (coll.)

verknittern *tr. V.* crumple

verknoten *tr. V.* tie; knot

verknüpfen *tr. V.* **(a)** (knoten) tie; knot
(b) (in Beziehung setzen) link

verkochen *itr. V.; mit sein* **(a)** boil away
(b) (breiig werden, zerfallen) boil down to a pulp

verkohlen *itr. V.* char

verkommen¹ *unr. itr. V.; mit sein* go to the dogs; (moralisch, sittlich) go to the bad

verkommen² *Adj.* depraved

verköstigen *tr. V.* feed; provide with meals

verkraften *tr. V.* cope with

verkrampfen *refl. V.* ‹*muscle*› become cramped; ‹*person*› tense up

Verkrampfung *die;* **~, ~en** tenseness; tension

verkriechen *unr. refl. V.* ‹*animal*› creep [away]; ‹*person*› hide [oneself away]

verkrümeln *refl. V.* (ugs.: sich entfernen) slip off *or* away

verkrümmt *Adj.* bent ‹*person*›; crooked ‹*finger*›; curved ‹*spine*›

Verkrümmung *die;* **~, ~en** crookedness

verkrüppeln *tr. V.* cripple

verkümmern *itr. V.; mit sein* ‹*person, animal*› go into a decline; ‹*plant etc.*› become stunted; ‹*talent, emotional life, etc.*› wither away

verkünden *tr. V.* announce; pronounce ‹*judgement*›; promulgate ‹*law, decree*›

verkündigen *tr. V.* (geh.) announce; proclaim

Verkündigung *die;* **~, ~en** announcement; proclamation

Verkündung *die;* **~, ~en** announcement; (von Urteilen) pronouncement; (von Gesetzen, Verordnungen) promulgation

verkürzen *tr. V.* **(a)** (verringern) reduce; (abkürzen) shorten
(b) (abbrechen) cut short ‹*stay, life*›; put an end to, end ‹*suffering*›

verladen *unr. tr. V.* load

V

Verlag *der;* **~[e]s, ~e** publishing house *or* firm; publisher's

verlagern *tr. V.* shift; (an einen anderen Ort) move; (fig.) transfer; shift ‹*emphasis*›

Verlagerung *die* moving; **eine ~ des Schwergewichts** (fig.) a shift in emphasis

verlanden *itr. V.; mit sein* silt up

Verlandung *die;* **~, ~en** silting up

verlangen *tr. V.* demand; (nötig haben) ‹*task etc.*› require, call for ‹*patience, knowledge, experience, skill, etc.*›; (berechnen) charge; (sehen/sprechen wollen) ask for; **du wirst am Telefon verlangt** you're wanted on the phone (coll.)

Verlangen *das;* **~s, ~** **(a)** desire (**nach** for)
(b) auf ~: on request

verlängern *tr. V.* extend; lengthen, make longer ‹*skirt, sleeve, etc.*›; renew ‹*passport, driving licence, etc.*›

Verlängerung *die;* **~, ~en** ▶ VERLÄNGERN: extension; lengthening; renewal

Verlängerungs·schnur *die* extension lead *or* (Amer.) cord

verlangsamen *tr. V.* **das Tempo/seine Schritte ~:** reduce speed/slacken one's pace; slow down

verlassen¹ **1** *unr. refl. V.* rely, depend (**auf** + *Akk.* on)
2 *unr. tr. V.* **(a)** leave
(b) (sich trennen von) desert; abandon; forsake; leave, desert ‹*wife, family, etc.*›

verlassen² *Adj.* deserted ‹*street etc.*›; empty ‹*house*›; (öd) desolate ‹*region etc.*›

verlässlich, *verläßlich **1** *Adj.* reliable
2 *adv.* reliably

Verlauf *der;* **~[e]s, Verläufe** course

verlaufen **1** *unr. itr. V.; mit sein* **(a)** (sich erstrecken) run
(b) (ablaufen) ‹*test, rehearsal, etc.*› go; ‹*party etc.*› go off
2 *unr. refl. V.* get lost; lose one's way

Verlaufs·form *die* (Sprachw.) progressive *or* continuous form

verlautbaren *tr. V.* announce [officially]

Verlautbarung *die;* **~, ~en** announcement

verlauten *itr. V.; mit sein* be reported; **wie verlautet** according to reports

verleben *tr. V.* spend

verlebt *Adj.* dissipated

verlegen¹ *tr. V.* **(a)** mislay
(b) (verschieben) postpone (**auf** + *Akk.* until); (vor~) bring forward (**auf** + *Akk.* to); **einen Termin ~:** alter an appointment
(c) (verlagern) move; transfer ‹*patient*›
(d) (legen) lay ‹*cable, pipe, carpet, etc.*›

verlegen² **1** *Adj.* embarrassed
2 *adv.* in embarrassment

Verlegenheit *die;* **~, ~en** **(a)** (Befangenheit) embarrassment; **jmdn. in ~ bringen** embarrass sb.
(b) (Unannehmlichkeit) embarrassing situation

Verleger *der;* **~s, ~,** **Verlegerin** *die;* **~, ~nen** publisher

Verleih *der;* **~[e]s, ~e** **(a)** hiring out; (von Autos) renting *or* hiring out
(b) (Unternehmen) hire firm; (Filmverleih) distribution company; (Videoverleih) video library; (Autoverleih) rental *or* hire firm

verleihen *unr. tr. V.* **(a)** hire out; rent *or* hire out ‹*car*›; (umsonst) lend [out]
(b) (überreichen) award; confer ‹*award, honour*›

Verleihung *die;* **~, ~en** **(a)** ▶ VERLEIHEN A: hiring out; renting out; lending [out]
(b) ▶ VERLEIHEN B: awarding; conferring; (Zeremonie) award; conferment

verleiten *tr. V.* **jmdn. dazu ~, etw. zu tun** lead *or* induce sb. to do sth.

verlernen *tr. V.* forget

verlesen **1** *unr. tr. V.* read out
2 *unr. refl. V.* (falsch lesen) make a mistake/mistakes in reading

verletzen *tr. V.* **(a)** injure; (durch Schuss, Stich) wound
(b) (kränken) hurt ‹*person, feelings*›
(c) (verstoßen gegen) violate; infringe ‹*regulation*›; break ‹*agreement, law*›

verletzlich *Adj.* vulnerable

Verletzlichkeit *die;* **~:** vulnerability

Verletzte *der/die; adj. Dekl.* casualty; (durch Schuss, Stich) wounded person

Verletzung *die;* **~, ~en** **(a)** (Wunde) injury
(b) (Kränkung) hurting
(c) ▶ VERLETZEN C: violation; infringement; breaking

verleugnen *tr. V.* deny; disown ‹*friend, relation*›

Verleugnung *die;* **~, ~en** denial; (eines Freundes, Verwandten) disownment

verleumden *tr. V.* slander; (schriftlich) libel

verleumderisch *Adj.* slanderous; (in Schriftform) libellous

Verleumdung *die;* **~, ~en** slander; (in Schriftform) libel

verlieben *refl. V.* fall in love (**in** + *Akk.* with)

Verliebte *der/die; adj. Dekl.* lover

verlieren *unr. tr., itr. V.* lose

Verlierer *der;* **~s, ~,** **Verliererin** *die;* **~, ~nen** loser

verloben *refl. V.* get engaged; **verlobt sein** be engaged

Verlobte *der/die; adj. Dekl.* fiancé/fiancée

verlockend *Adj.* tempting

Verlockung *die;* **~, ~en** temptation

verlogen *Adj.* lying, mendacious ‹*person*›; false ‹*morality etc.*›

verlor *1. u. 3. Pers. Sg. Prät. v.* VERLIEREN

verloren **1** *2. Part. v.* VERLIEREN 

[2] *Adj.* lost; wasted ‹*effort*›; ~ **gehen** get lost

***verloren|gehen** ▶ VERLOREN 2

verlosen *tr. V.* raffle

Verlosung *die;* ~, **~en** raffle; draw

verlottern *itr. V.; mit sein* ‹*person*› go to seed

Verlust *der;* **~[e]s, ~e** loss (**an** + *Dat.* of)

vermachen *tr. V.* **jmdm. etw. ~:** leave *or* bequeath sth. to sb.; (fig.: schenken, überlassen) give sth. to sb.

vermählen *refl. V.* (geh.) **sich [jmdm.** *od.* **mit jmdm.] ~:** marry *or* wed [sb.]

Vermählung *die;* ~, **~en** (geh.) **(a)** marriage
(b) (Fest) wedding ceremony

vermarkten *tr. V.* market ‹*goods etc.*›

Vermarktung *die;* ~, **~en** marketing

vermehren [1] *tr. V.* increase (**um** by)
[2] *refl. V.* **(a)** increase
(b) (sich fortpflanzen) reproduce

Vermehrung *die;* ~, **~en (a)** increase (*Gen.* in)
(b) (Fortpflanzung) reproduction

vermeiden *unr. tr. V.* avoid

Vermeidung *die;* ~, **~en** avoidance

vermeintlich *Adj.* supposed

vermengen *tr. V.* mix (**miteinander** together)

Vermerk *der;* **~[e]s, ~e** note; (amtlich) remark

vermerken *tr. V.* make a note of; note [down]; (in Akten, Wachbuch usw.) record

vermessen[1] *unr. tr. V.* measure; survey ‹*land, site*›

vermessen[2] *Adj.* (geh.) presumptuous

vermieten *tr.* (*auch itr.*) *V.* rent [out], let [out] (**an** + *Akk.* to); hire [out] ‹*boat, car, etc.*›; **„Zimmer zu ~"** 'room to let'

Vermieter *der;* **~s,** ~: landlord

Vermieterin *die;* ~, **~nen** landlady

Vermietung *die;* ~, **~en** ▶ VERMIETEN: renting [out]; letting [out]; hiring [out]

vermindern [1] *tr. V.* reduce; decrease; reduce, lessen ‹*danger, stress*›; lower ‹*resistance*›; reduce ‹*debt*›
[2] *refl. V.* decrease; ‹*resistance*› diminish

Verminderung *die* ▶ VERMINDERN 1: reduction; decreasing; lessening; lowering; **eine ~ der Einnahmen** a decrease in revenues

verminen *tr. V.* mine

vermischen [1] *tr. V.* mix (**miteinander** together); blend ‹*teas, tobaccos, etc.*›
[2] *refl. V.* mix; (fig.) mingle; ‹*races, animals*› interbreed

Vermischung *die;* ~ ▶ VERMISCHEN: mixing; blending; (fig.) mingling

vermissen *tr. V.* **(a)** miss
(b) (nicht haben) **ich vermisse meinen Ausweis** my identity card is missing

*old spelling - see note on page xiv

Vermisste, *Vermißte *der/die; adj. Dekl.* missing person

vermitteln [1] *itr. V.* mediate, act as [a] mediator (**in** + *Dat.* in)
[2] *tr. V.* **(a)** (herbeiführen) arrange; negotiate ‹*transaction, ceasefire, compromise*›
(b) (besorgen) **jmdm. eine Stelle ~:** find sb. a job
(c) (weitergeben) impart ‹*knowledge, insight, values, etc.*›; communicate ‹*message, information, etc.*›; convey ‹*feeling*›; pass on ‹*experience*›

Vermittler *der;* **~s,** ~, **Vermittlerin** *die;* ~, **~nen (a)** (Mittler) mediator
(b) ▶ VERMITTELN 2C: imparter; communicator; conveyer
(c) (von Berufs wegen) agent

Vermittlung *die;* ~, **~en (a)** (Schlichtung) mediation
(b) ▶ VERMITTELN 2A: arrangement; negotiation
(c) ▶ VERMITTELN 2C: imparting; communicating; conveying
(d) (Telefonzentrale) exchange; (in einer Firma) switchboard

vermöbeln *tr. V.* (ugs.) beat up; (als Strafe) thrash

vermögen (geh.) *unr. tr. V.* **etw. zu tun ~:** be able to do sth.; be capable of doing sth.

Vermögen *das;* **~s,** ~ **(a)** (geh.: Fähigkeit) ability
(b) (Besitz) fortune; **er hat ~:** he has money

vermögend *Adj.* wealthy; well-off

Vermögen[s]·steuer *die* wealth tax

vermummen *tr. V.* wrap up [warmly]; (verbergen) disguise

vermurksen *tr. V.* (ugs.) mess up; muck up (Brit. sl.)

vermuten *tr. V.* suspect; **das ist zu ~:** that is what one would suppose *or* expect; we may assume that;

vermutlich [1] *Adj.* probable
[2] *Adv.* presumably; (wahrscheinlich) probably

Vermutung *die;* ~, **~en** supposition

vernachlässigen *tr. V.* neglect; (unberücksichtigt lassen) ignore; disregard

Vernachlässigung *die;* ~, **~en** neglect

vernarben *itr. V.; mit sein* [form a] scar; heal (lit. or fig.)

vernehmbar *Adj.* (geh.) audible

vernehmen *unr. tr. V.* **(a)** (geh.: hören, erfahren) hear
(b) (verhören) question

vernehmlich [1] *Adj.* [clearly] audible
[2] *adv.* audibly

Vernehmung *die;* ~, **~en** questioning

verneigen *refl. V.* (geh.) bow (**vor** + *Dat.* to, (literary) before)

verneinen *tr.* (*auch itr.*) *V.* **(a)** say 'no' to ‹*question*›; answer ‹*question*› in the negative
(b) (Sprachw.) negate

Verneinung *die;* ~, **~en** (Sprachw.) negation

vernetzen *tr. V.* (Chemie, Technik) interlink
vernichten *tr. V.* destroy; exterminate ‹*pests, vermin*›
vernichtend 1 *Adj.* crushing ‹*defeat*›; shattering ‹*blow*›; (fig.) devastating ‹*criticism*›; devastating, withering ‹*glance*› 2 *adv.* **den Feind ~ schlagen** inflict a crushing defeat on the enemy
Vernichtung *die; ~, ~en* destruction; (von Schädlingen) extermination
Vernichtungs-: ~lager *das* extermination camp; **~waffe** *die* weapon of annihilation
Vernunft *die; ~:* reason
vernünftig 1 *Adj.* **(a)** sensible
(b) (ugs.: ordentlich, richtig) decent
2 *adv.* **(a)** sensibly
(b) (ugs.: ordentlich, richtig) ‹*talk, eat*› properly; ‹*dress*› sensibly
veröffentlichen *tr. V.* publish
Veröffentlichung *die; ~, ~en* publication
verordnen *tr. V.* **[jmdm. etw.] ~:** prescribe [sth. for sb.]
Verordnung *die; ~, ~en* prescribing
verpachten *tr. V.* lease
verpacken *tr. V.* pack; wrap up ‹*present, parcel*›
Verpackung *die* **(a)** packing
(b) (Umhüllung) packaging *no pl.;* wrapping
verpassen *tr. V.* miss
verpennen (salopp) 1 *itr. V.* oversleep
2 *tr. V.* **(a)** (vergessen) forget
(b) (verschlafen) sleep through ‹*morning etc.*›
verpesten *tr. V.* (abwertend) pollute
Verpestung (abwertend) *die; ~, ~en* pollution
verpflanzen *tr. V.* (auch Med.) transplant; graft ‹*skin*›
Verpflanzung *die; ~, ~en* (Med.) transplant[ing]; (von Haut) graft
verpflegen *tr. V.* cater for; feed
Verpflegung *die; ~, ~en* **(a)** catering *no indef. art.* (*Gen.* for)
(b) (Nahrung) food; **Unterkunft und ~:** board and lodging
verpflichten 1 *tr. V.* **(a)** oblige; commit; (festlegen, binden) bind
(b) (einstellen, engagieren) engage ‹*manager, actor, etc.*›
2 *refl. V.* undertake; promise; **sich vertraglich ~:** sign a contract
Verpflichtung *die; ~, ~en* **(a)** obligation; commitment
(b) (Engagement) engaging; engagement
verpfuschen *tr. V.* (ugs.) make a mess of; muck up (Brit. sl.)
verpissen *refl. V.* (salopp) piss off (Brit. sl.); beat it (coll.)
verpönt *Adj.* scorned; (tabu) taboo
verprügeln *tr. V.* beat up; (zur Strafe) thrash
Verputz *der; ~es* plaster; (auf Außenwänden) rendering
verputzen *tr. V.* plaster; render ‹*outside wall*›
verquer *Adj.* (absonderlich) weird, outlandish ‹*idea*›
verquirlen *tr. V.* mix [with a whisk]; whisk
verquollen *Adj.* swollen
verrammeln *tr. V.* barricade
Verrat *der; ~[e]s* betrayal (**an** + *Dat.* of)
verraten *unr. tr. V.* **(a)** betray (**an** + *Akk.* to)
(b) (ugs.: mitteilen) **jmdm. den Grund** *usw.* **~:** tell sb. the reason *etc.;*
(c) (erkennen lassen) show, betray ‹*feelings, surprise, fear, etc.*›; show ‹*influence, talent*›
Verräter *der; ~s, ~:* traitor
Verräterin *die; ~, ~nen* traitress
verräterisch *Adj.* treacherous ‹*plan, purpose, act, etc.*›
verraucht *Adj.* smoke-filled; smoky
verrechnen 1 *tr. V.* include ‹*amount etc.*›; (gutschreiben) credit ‹*cheque etc.*› to another account
2 *refl. V.* miscalculate
Verrechnungs·scheck *der* crossed cheque
verregnen *itr. V.; mit sein* be spoilt *or* ruined by rain
verreiben *unr. tr. V.* rub in
verreisen *itr. V.; mit sein* go away
verrenken *tr. V.* dislocate
Verrenkung *die; ~, ~en* dislocation
verrichten *tr. V.* perform
verriegeln *tr. V.* bolt
verringern 1 *tr. V.* reduce
2 *refl. V.* decrease
Verringerung *die; ~:* reduction; decrease (*Gen.*, **von** in)
Verriss, *Verriß *der* (ugs.) damning review *or* criticism (**über** + *Akk.* of)
verrosten *itr. V.; mit sein* rust; **verrostet** rusty
verrückt (ugs.) 1 *Adj.* **(a)** mad; **~ werden** go mad *or* insane
(b) (überspannt, ausgefallen) crazy ‹*idea, fashion, prank, day, etc.*›
2 *adv.* crazily; ‹*behave*› crazily *or* like a madman; ‹*dress etc.*› in a mad *or* crazy way
Verrückte *der/die; adj. Dekl.* (ugs.) madman/madwoman; lunatic
verrufen *Adj.* disreputable
verrühren *tr. V.* stir together; mix
verrutschen *itr. V.* slip
Vers *der; ~es, ~e* verse
versagen *itr. V.* fail; ‹*machine, engine*› stop [working]; **menschliches Versagen** human error
Versager *der; ~s, ~,* **Versagerin** *die; ~, ~nen* failure

versalzen *unr. tr. V.* put too much salt in/on; (fig. ugs.) spoil

versammeln *tr., refl. V.* assemble

Versammlung *die;* ~, **~en (a)** meeting **(b)** (Gremium) assembly

Versand *der;* **~[e]s (a)** dispatch **(b)** (ugs.: Versandhaus) mail order firm

Versand-: ~handel *der* mail order business; **~haus** *das* mail order firm

versauen *tr. V.* (salopp) **(a)** (verschmutzen) mess up; make mucky (coll.) **(b)** (verderben) foul up (coll.)

versäumen *tr. V.* **(a)** (verpassen) miss; lose ‹*time, sleep*› **(b)** (vernachlässigen, unterlassen) neglect ‹*duty, task*›

verschaffen *tr. V.* **jmdm. etw. ~:** provide sb. with sth.; get sb. sth.; **sich** (*Dat.*) **etw. ~:** get hold of sth.; obtain sth.

verschämt 1 *Adj.* bashful 2 *adv.* bashfully

verschandeln *tr. V.* (ugs.) spoil; ruin

verschenken *tr. V.* give away

verscheuchen *tr. V.* chase away

verscheuern *tr. V.* (ugs.) flog (Brit. sl.) (*Dat.*, **an** + *Akk.* to)

verschicken *tr. V.* ▶ VERSENDEN

verschieben 1 *unr. tr. V.* **(a)** shift; move **(b)** (aufschieben) put off, postpone (**auf** + *Akk.* till) 2 *unr. refl. V.* be postponed (**um** for); ‹*start*› be put back *or* delayed (**um** by)

Verschiebung *die;* ~, **~en** postponement

verschieden 1 *Adj.* **(a)** different (**von** from) **(b)** (vielfältig) various; **die ~sten ...:** all sorts of ...; **die ~en ...:** the various ... **(c) Verschiedenes** various things *pl.;* 2 *adv.* differently

verschieden·artig 1 *Adj.* different in kind *pred.;* (mehr als zwei) diverse 2 *adv.* diversely

Verschiedenheit *die;* ~, **~en** difference; (unter mehreren) diversity

verschiedentlich *Adv.* on various occasions

verschimmeln *itr. V.; mit sein* go mouldy; **verschimmelt** mouldy

verschlafen[1] 1 *unr. itr.* (*auch refl.*) *V.* oversleep 2 *unr. tr. V.* **(a)** (schlafend verbringen) sleep through ‹*morning, journey, etc.*› **(b)** (versäumen) not wake up in time for ‹*appointment*›; not wake up in time to catch ‹*train, bus*› **(c)** (ugs.: vergessen) forget about ‹*appointment etc.*›

verschlafen[2] *Adj.* half asleep; (fig.) sleepy ‹*town*›

Verschlag *der;* **~[e]s, Verschläge** shed

verschlagen[1] *unr. tr. V.* **die Seite ~:** lose one's place *or* page; **jmdm. die Sprache ~:** leave sb. speechless

verschlagen[2] 1 *Adj.* sly; shifty 2 *adv.* slyly; shiftily

verschlechtern 1 *tr. V.* make worse 2 *refl. V.* get worse; deteriorate

Verschlechterung *die;* ~, **~en** worsening, deterioration (*Gen.* in)

Verschleiß *der;* **~es, ~e (a)** wear *no indef. art.;* **(b)** (Verbrauch) consumption (**an** + *Dat.* of)

verschleißen 1 *unr. itr. V.; mit sein* wear out 2 *unr. tr. V.* wear out; (fig.) run down, ruin ‹*one's nerves, one's health*›; use up ‹*energy, ability, etc.*›

verschleppen *tr. V.* **(a)** carry off; take away ‹*person*› **(b)** (weiterverbreiten) carry, spread ‹*disease, bacteria, mud, etc.*› **(c)** (verzögern) delay; (in die Länge ziehen) draw out; let ‹*illness*› drag on [and get worse]

verschleudern *tr. V.* **(a)** sell dirt cheap (coll.); (mit Verlust) sell at a loss **(b)** (verschwenden) squander

verschließbar *Adj.* closable; lockable ‹*suitcase, drawer, etc.*›; **[luftdicht] ~:** sealable ‹*container etc.*›

verschließen *unr. tr. V.* **(a)** close; stop, (mit einem Korken) cork ‹*bottle*› **(b)** (abschließen) lock; lock up ‹*house etc.*› **(c)** (wegschließen) lock away (**in** + *Dat. od. Akk.* in)

verschlimmern 1 *tr. V.* make worse 2 *refl. V.* get worse; ‹*position, conditions*› deteriorate, worsen

Verschlimmerung *die;* ~, **~en** worsening

verschlingen *unr. tr. V.* **(a)** [inter]twine ‹*threads etc.*› (**zu** into) **(b)** (essen, fressen) devour ‹*food*›; (fig.) devour ‹*novel, money, etc.*›

verschlissen *2. Part. v.* VERSCHLEISSEN 2

verschlossen *Adj.* (wortkarg) taciturn; (zurückhaltend) reserved

Verschlossenheit *die;* ~**:** taciturnity; (Zurückhaltung) reserve

verschlucken 1 *tr. V.* swallow 2 *refl. V.* choke

Verschluss, *Verschluß *der* (am BH, an Schmuck usw.) fastener; fastening; (an Taschen, Schmuck) clasp; (an Schuhen, Gürteln) buckle; (am Schrank, Fenster, Koffer usw.) catch; (an Flaschen) top; (Stöpsel) stopper

verschmähen *tr. V.* (geh.) spurn

verschmerzen *tr. V.* get over

verschmieren *tr. V.* smear ‹*window etc.*›; (beim Schreiben) mess up ‹*paper*›; scrawl all over ‹*page*›; smudge ‹*ink*›

verschmitzt 1 *Adj.* mischievous 2 *adv.* mischievously

---

*alte Schreibung - vgl. Hinweis auf S. xiv

verschmụtzen 1 *itr. V.; mit sein* get dirty; ‹*river etc.*› become polluted
2 *tr. V.* dirty; soil; pollute ‹*air, water, etc.*›
Verschmụtzung *die;* ~, ~**en** (der Umwelt) pollution; (von Stoffen, Teppichen usw.) soiling
verschnaufen *itr.* (*auch refl.*) *V.* have *or* take a breather
verschneit *Adj.* snow-covered *attrib.;* covered with snow *postpos.*
verschnọ̈rkelt *Adj.* ornate
verschnüren *tr. V.* tie up
verschọllen *Adj.* missing
verschonen *tr. V.* spare; **jmdn. mit etw. ~:** spare sb. sth.
verschönern *tr. V.* brighten up
verschrạ̈nken *tr. V.* fold ‹*arms*›; cross ‹*legs*›; clasp ‹*hands*›
verschrẹcken *tr. V.* frighten *or* scare [off *or* away]
verschreiben 1 *unr. tr. V.* (Med.: verordnen) prescribe
2 *unr. refl. V.* **(a)** make a slip of the pen
(b) sich einer Sache (*Dat.*) **~:** devote oneself to sth.
verschreibungs·pflichtig *Adj.* available only on prescription *postpos.*
verschrie[e]n *Adj.* notorious (**wegen** for)
verschroben *Adj.* eccentric, cranky ‹*person*›; cranky, weird ‹*ideas*›
verschrọtten *tr. V.* scrap
Verschrọttung *die;* ~, ~**en** scrapping
verschụlden 1 *tr. V.* be to blame for ‹*accident, death, etc.*›
2 *refl. V.* get into debt
Verschụlden *das;* ~**s** guilt; **durch eigenes ~:** through one's own fault
verschụldet *Adj.* in debt *postpos.* (**bei** to); **hoch ~:** deeply in debt
verschụ̈tt: **~ gehen** (ugs.) do a vanishing trick *or* disappearing act (coll.)
verschụ̈tten *tr. V.* **(a)** spill
(b) (begraben) bury ‹*person*› [alive]
***verschụ̈tt|gehen** ▸ VERSCHÜTT
verschwägert *Adj.* related by marriage *postpos.*
verschweigen *unr. tr. V.* conceal (*Dat.* from)
verschwẹnden *tr. V.* waste (**an** + *Akk.* on)
Verschwẹnder *der;* ~**s**, ~, **Verschwẹnderin** *die;* ~, ~**nen** (von Geld) spendthrift; (von Dingen) wasteful person
verschwẹnderisch 1 *Adj.* wasteful ‹*person*›; ‹*life*› of extravagance
2 *adv.* wastefully
Verschwẹndung *die;* ~, ~**en** wastefulness; extravagance
verschwiegen *Adj.* discreet; (still, einsam) secluded
Verschwiegenheit *die;* ~**:** secrecy; (Diskretion) discretion
verschwịmmen *unr. itr. V.; mit sein* blur
verschwịnden *unr. itr. V.; mit sein* disappear; vanish; **verschwinde [hier]!** off with you!; go away!; hop it! (coll.); **ich muss mal ~** (ugs. verhüll.) I have to pay a visit (coll.) *or* (Brit. coll.) spend a penny
verschwịndend 1 *Adj.* tiny
2 *adv.* **~ klein** tiny; minute; **~ wenig** a tiny amount
verschwọmmen 1 *Adj.* blurred ‹*photograph, vision*›; blurred, hazy ‹*outline*›; vague, woolly ‹*idea, concept, formulation, etc.*›
2 *adv.* vaguely; ‹*remember*› hazily
versehen 1 *unr. tr. V.* **(a)** (ausstatten) provide; equip ‹*car, factory, machine, etc.*›
(b) (ausüben, besorgen) perform ‹*duty etc.*›
2 *unr. refl. V.* make a slip; slip up
Versehen *das;* ~**s**, ~**:** oversight; slip; **aus ~:** by mistake; inadvertently
versehentlich 1 *Adv.* by mistake; inadvertently
2 *adj.* inadvertent
Versehrte *der/die; adj. Dekl.* disabled person; **die ~n** the disabled
versẹnden *unr.* (*auch regelm.*) *tr. V.* send ‹*letter, parcel*›; send out ‹*invitations*›; dispatch ‹*goods*›
versẹtzen 1 *tr. V.* **(a)** move; transfer, move ‹*employee*›; (in die nächsthöhere Klasse) move ‹*pupil*› up, (Amer.) promote ‹*pupil*› (**in** + *Akk.* to); (umpflanzen) transplant, move ‹*plant*›; (fig.) transport (**in** + *Akk.* to)
(b) (nicht geradlinig anordnen) stagger
(c) (verpfänden) pawn
(d) (verkaufen) sell
(e) (ugs.: vergeblich warten lassen) stand ‹*person*› up (coll.)
(f) (vermischen) mix
(g) (erwidern) retort
(h) etw. in Bewegung/Tätigkeit ~: set sth. in motion/operation; **jmdn. in die Lage ~, etw. zu tun** put sb. in a position to do sth.; **jmdm. einen Stoß/Fußtritt/Schlag** *usw.* **~:** give sb. a push/kick/deal sb. a blow *etc.;*
2 *refl. V.* **sich in jmds. Lage** (*Akk.*) **~:** put oneself in sb.'s position *or* place
Versẹtzung *die;* ~, ~**en** (eines Schülers) moving up, (Amer.) promotion (**in** + *Akk.* to); (eines Angestellten) transfer
verseuchen *tr. V.* (auch fig.) contaminate; **radioaktiv ~:** contaminate with radioactivity
Verseuchung (auch fig.) *die;* ~, ~**en** contamination
Versịcherer *der;* ~**s**, ~, **Versịcherin** *die;* ~, ~**nen** insurer
versịchern *tr. V.* **(a)** assert ‹*sth.*›
(b) (vertraglich schützen) insure (**bei** with)
Versịcherte *der/die; adj. Dekl.* insured [person]
Versịcherung *die* **(a)** (Beteuerung) assurance
(b) (Schutz durch Vertrag) insurance; (Vertrag) insurance [policy] (**über** + *Akk.* for); (Gesellschaft) insurance [company]

Versicherungs-: ~beitrag *der* insurance premium; **~betrug** *der* insurance fraud; **~gesellschaft** *die* insurance company; **~nehmer** *der;* **~~s, ~~, ~nehmerin** *die;* **~~, ~~nen** policy holder; **~police** *die* insurance policy

versickern *itr. V.; mit sein ‹river etc.›* drain *or* seep away

versiegeln *tr. V.* seal

versiegen *itr. V.; mit sein* (geh.) dry up; run dry

versinken *unr. itr. V.; mit sein* sink; **im Schlamm ~:** sink into the mud

verslumen /...'slamən/ *itr. V.; mit sein* turn into a slum; **ein verslumter Stadtteil** a slum district

versoffen *Adj.* (salopp abwertend) boozy (coll.)

versöhnen [1] *refl. V.* **sich [miteinander] ~:** become reconciled; **sich mit jmdm. ~:** make it up with sb.
[2] *tr. V.* reconcile

Versöhnung *die;* **~, ~en** reconciliation

versonnen [1] *Adj.* dreamy
[2] *adv.* dreamily

versorgen *tr. V.* **(a)** supply
(b) (unterhalten, ernähren) provide for *‹children, family›*
(c) (sorgen für) look after; **jmdn. ärztlich ~:** give sb. medical care; (kurzzeitig) give sb. medical attention

Versorger *der;* **~s, ~, Versorgerin** *die;* **~, ~nen** breadwinner

Versorgung *die;* **~, ~en (a)** supply[ing]
(b) (Unterhaltung, Ernährung) support[ing]
(c) (Bedienung, Pflege) care; **ärztliche ~:** medical care *or* treatment; (kurzzeitig) medical attention

Verspannung *die* (Med.: der Muskulatur) tension

verspäten *refl. V.* be late

verspätet *Adj.* late *‹arrival etc.›*; belated *‹greetings, thanks›*; **~ eintreffen** arrive late

Verspätung *die;* **~, ~en** lateness; (verspätetes Eintreffen) late arrival; **[fünf Minuten] ~ haben** be [five minutes] late

versperren *tr. V.* block; obstruct *‹view›*

verspielen *tr. V.* gamble away; (fig.) squander, throw away *‹opportunity, chance›*; forfeit *‹right, credibility, etc›*

verspielt [1] *Adj.* (auch fig.) playful; fanciful, fantastic *‹form, design, etc.›*
[2] *adv.* playfully (lit. or fig.); *‹dress, designed›* fancifully, fantastically

verspotten *tr. V.* mock; ridicule

Verspottung *die;* **~, ~en** mocking; ridiculing

versprechen [1] *unr. tr. V.* promise; **sich** *(Dat.)* **etw. von etw./jmdm. ~:** hope for sth. *or* to get sth. from sth./sb.
[2] *unr. refl. V.* make a slip/slips of the tongue

Versprechen *das;* **~s, ~, Versprechung** *die;* **~, ~en** promise

versprühen *tr. V.* spray

verspüren *tr. V.* feel

verstaatlichen *tr. V.* nationalize

Verstaatlichung *die;* **~, ~en** nationalization

Verstand *der;* **~[e]s** (Fähigkeit zu denken) reason *no art.;* (Fähigkeit, Begriffe zu bilden) mind; (Vernunft) [common] sense *no art.;* **hast du denn den ~ verloren?** (ugs.) have you taken leave of your senses?

verständig [1] *Adj.* sensible
[2] *adv.* sensibly

verständigen [1] *tr. V.* notify, inform **(von, über** + *Akk.* of)
[2] *refl. V.* **(a)** make oneself understood; **sich mit jmdm. ~:** communicate with sb.
(b) (sich einigen) **sich [mit jmdm.] über/auf etw.** *(Akk.)* **~:** come to an understanding [with sb.] about *or.* on sth

Verständigkeit *die;* **~:** understanding; intelligence

Verständigung *die;* **~, ~en (a)** notification
(b) (das Sichverständlichmachen) communication *no art.;*
(c) (Einigung) understanding

Verständigungs·schwierigkeit *die* difficulty of communication

verständlich [1] *Adj.* **(a)** comprehensible; (deutlich) clear *‹pronunciation, presentation, etc.›*; **sich ~ machen** make oneself understood; **jmdm. etw. ~ machen** make sth. clear to sb.
(b) (begreiflich, verzeihlich) understandable
[2] *adv.* comprehensibly; (deutlich) *‹speak, express oneself, present›* clearly

verständlicher·weise *Adv.* understandably

Verständlichkeit *die;* **~:** comprehensibility; clarity

Verständnis *das;* **~ses, ~se** understanding; **ich habe volles ~ dafür, dass ...:** I fully understand that ...; **für die Unannehmlichkeiten bitten wir um [Ihr] ~:** we apologize for the inconvenience caused

verständnis-: ~los [1] *Adj.* uncomprehending; [2] *adv.* uncomprehendingly; **~voll** [1] *Adj.* understanding; [2] *adv.* understandingly

verstärken [1] *tr. V.* **(a)** strengthen
(b) (zahlenmäßig) reinforce *‹troops etc.›* **(um** by); enlarge *‹orchestra, choir›* **(um** by)
(c) (intensiver machen) intensify, increase *‹effort, contrast›*; strengthen, increase *‹impression, suspicion›*; (größer machen) increase *‹pressure, voltage, effect, etc.›*; (lauter machen) amplify *‹signal, sound, guitar, etc.›*
[2] *refl. V.* increase

Verstärker *der;* **~s, ~:** amplifier

Verstärkung *die;* **~, ~en (a)** strengthening

*old spelling - see note on page xiv

(b) (zahlenmäßig) reinforcement (esp. Mil.)
(c) (Zunahme) increase (*Gen.* in); (der Lautstärke) amplification
(d) (zusätzliche Person[en]) reinforcements *pl.*

verstauben *itr. V.; mit sein* get dusty; gather dust (lit. or fig.)

verstaubt *Adj.* (fig. abwertend) old-fashioned; outmoded

verstauchen *tr. V.* sprain; **sich** (*Dat.*) **den Fuß/die Hand ~:** sprain one's ankle/wrist

Verstauchung *die;* **~, ~en** sprain

verstauen *tr. V.* pack (**in** + *Dat. od. Akk.* in[to]); (bes. im Boot/Auto) stow (**in** + *Dat. od. Akk.* in)

Versteck *das;* **~[e]s, ~e** hiding place: **~ spielen** play hide-and-seek

verstecken **1** *tr. V.* hide (**vor** + *Dat.* from)
2 *refl. V.* **sich [vor jmdm./etw.] ~:** hide [from sb./sth.]

versteckt *Adj.* hidden; (heimlich) secret ‹*malice, activity, etc.*›; disguised ‹*foul*›

verstehen **1** *unr. tr. V.* understand; **wie soll ich das ~?** how am I to interpret that?; **jmdn./etw. falsch ~:** misunderstand sb./sth.
2 *unr. refl. V.* **sich mit jmdm. ~:** get on with sb.; **das versteht sich [von selbst]** that goes without saying

versteigern *tr. V.* auction; **etw. ~ lassen** put sth. up for auction

Versteigerung *die;* **~, ~en** auction

versteinern *itr. V.; mit sein* ‹*plant, animal*› fossilize, become fossilized; ‹*wood etc.*› petrify, become petrified

Versteinerung *die;* **~, ~en (a)** (das Versteinern) fossilization; (von Holz) petrification
(b) (Fossil) fossil

verstellbar *Adj.* adjustable

verstellen **1** *tr. V.* **(a)** (falsch platzieren) misplace
(b) (anders einstellen) adjust ‹*seat etc.*›; alter [the adjustment of] ‹*mirror etc.*›; reset ‹*alarm clock, points, etc.*›
(c) (versperren) block, obstruct
(d) (zur Täuschung verändern) disguise ‹*voice, handwriting*›
2 *refl. V.* pretend

Verstellung *die;* **~, ~en** pretence; (der Stimme, Schrift) disguising

versteuern *tr. V.* pay tax on

verstimmen *tr. V.* put ‹*person*› in a bad mood; (verärgern) annoy

verstimmt *Adj.* **(a)** (Musik) out of tune *pred.;*
(b) (verärgert) put out, peeved, disgruntled (**über** + *Akk.* by, about); **ein ~er Magen** an upset stomach

Verstimmung *die;* **~, ~en** bad mood

verstockt *Adj.* obdurate; stubborn

Verstocktheit *die;* **~:** obduracy; stubbornness

verstohlen **1** *Adj.* furtive
2 *adv.* furtively

verstopfen **1** *tr. V.* block; **verstopft sein** ‹*pipe, drain, jet, nose, etc.*› be blocked [up] (**durch, von** with)
2 *itr. V.; mit sein* become blocked

Verstopfung *die;* **~, ~en** (Med.) constipation

verstorben *Adj.* late (*deceased*)

Verstorbene *der/die; adj. Dekl.* (geh.) deceased

verstören *tr. V.* distress

verstört *Adj.* distraught

Verstoß *der;* **~es, Verstöße** violation (**gegen** of)

verstoßen **1** *unr. tr. V.* disown
2 *unr. itr. V.* **gegen etw. ~:** infringe sth

verstreichen **1** *unr. tr. V.* apply, put on ‹*paint*›; spread ‹*butter etc.*›
2 *unr. itr. V.; mit sein* (geh.) ‹*time*› pass [by]

verstreuen *tr. V.* scatter; put down ‹*bird food, salt*›; (versehentlich) spill

verstricken **1** *tr. V.* **jmdn. in etw.** (*Akk.*) **~:** involve sb. in sth.; draw sb. into sth.
2 *refl. V.* **sich in etw.** (*Akk.*) **~:** become entangled *or* caught up in sth

verstümmeln *tr. V.* mutilate; (fig.) garble ‹*report*›; chop, mutilate ‹*text*›

verstummen *itr. V.; mit sein* (geh.) fall silent; ‹*music, noise, conversation*› cease

Versuch *der;* **~[e]s, ~e** attempt; (Experiment) experiment (**an** + *Dat.* on); (Probe) test

versuchen *tr. V.* **(a)** try; attempt
(b) (probieren) try ‹*cake etc.*›

versündigen *refl. V.* **sich an jmdm./etw. ~:** sin against sb./sth.

versüßen *tr. V.* **jmdm./sich etw. ~** (fig.) make sth. more pleasant for sb./oneself

vertauschen *tr. V.* exchange; switch; reverse ‹*roles, poles*›; **etw. mit** *od.* **gegen etw. ~:** exchange sth. for sth.

verteidigen *tr. V.* defend

Verteidiger *der;* **~s, ~, Verteidigerin** *die;* **~, ~nen** (auch Sport) defender; (Rechtsw.) defence counsel

Verteidigung *die,* **~, ~en** defence

Verteidigungs·minister *der,* **Verteidigungs·ministerin** *die* minister of defence

verteilen *tr. V.* distribute, hand out ‹*leaflets, prizes, etc.*› (**an** + *Akk.* to, **unter** + *Akk.* among); share [out], distribute ‹*money, food*› (**an** + *Akk.* to, **unter** + *Akk.* among); allocate ‹*work*›; distribute ‹*weight etc.*› (**auf** + *Akk.* over); spread ‹*cost*› (**auf** + *Akk.* among); distribute, spread ‹*butter, seed, dirt, etc.*›

Verteilung *die;* **~, ~en** distribution; (der Rollen, der Arbeit) allocation

verteuern **1** *tr. V.* make ‹*goods*› more expensive
2 *refl. V.* become more expensive

verteufeln *tr. V.* condemn; denigrate

Verteufelung *die;* ~, **~en** condemnation; denigration

vertiefen 1 *tr. V.* (auch fig.) deepen (**um** by) 2 *refl. V.* **sich ~ in** (+ *Akk.*) bury oneself in ‹*book, work, etc.*›; **in etw.** (*Akk.*) **vertieft sein** be engrossed in sth

Vertiefung *die;* ~, **~en** (Mulde) depression; hollow

vertikal 1 *Adj.* vertical
2 *adv.* vertically

Vertikale *die;* ~, **~n** ▶ SENKRECHTE

vertilgen *tr. V.* **(a)** (vernichten) exterminate ‹*vermin*›; kill off ‹*weeds*›
(b) (ugs.: verzehren) devour, (joc.) demolish ‹*food*›

vertonen *tr. V.* set ‹*text, poem*› to music

Vertonung *die;* ~, **~en** setting

Vertrag *der;* **~[e]s, Verträge** contract; (zwischen Staaten) treaty

vertragen 1 *unr. tr. V.* endure; tolerate (esp. Med.); (aushalten, leiden können) stand; bear; **ich vertrage keinen Kaffee** coffee disagrees with me
2 *unr. refl. V.* **sich mit jmdm. ~**: get on *or* along with sb.; (passen) **sich mit etw. ~**: go with sth

vertraglich 1 *Adj.* contractual
2 *adv.* contractually; by contract

verträglich *Adj.* **(a)** digestible ‹*food*›
(b) (umgänglich) goodnatured; easy to get on with *pred.*

vertrauen *itr. V.* **jmdm./einer Sache ~**: trust sb./sth.; **auf etw.** (*Akk.*) **~**: [put one's] trust in sth.

Vertrauen *das;* **~s** trust; confidence; **jmdn. ins ~ ziehen** take sb. into one's confidence

vertrauen·erweckend *Adj.* inspiring

vertrauens-, Vertrauens-: ~bruch *der* breach of trust; **~lehrer** *der,* **~lehrerin** *die* (Schulw.) liaison teacher (liaising between staff and pupils); **~person** *die* person in a position of trust; **~sache** *die* matter *or* question of trust; **~selig** *Adj.* all too trusting; **~voll** 1 *Adj.* trusting ‹*relationship*›; ‹*collaboration, cooperation*› based on trust; (zuversichtlich) confident;
2 *adv.* trustingly; (zuversichtlich) confidently; **~würdig** *Adj.* trustworthy

vertraulich 1 *Adj.* **(a)** confidential
(b) (freundschaftlich, intim) familiar ‹*manner, tone, etc.*›; intimate ‹*conversation*›
2 *adv.* **(a)** confidentially
(b) (freundschaftlich, intim) in a familiar way

Vertraulichkeit *die;* ~, **~en (a)** confidentiality
(b) (vertrauliche Information) confidence
(c) (distanzloses Verhalten) familiarity; (Intimität) intimacy

vertraut *Adj.* **(a)** close ‹*friend etc.*›; intimate ‹*circle, conversation, etc.*›
(b) (bekannt) familiar; **jmdn./sich mit etw. ~ machen** familiarize sb./oneself with sth.

Vertraute *der/die; adj. Dekl.* close friend

vertreiben *unr. tr. V.* **(a)** drive out (**aus** of); drive away ‹*animal, smoke, clouds*› (**aus** from); fight off ‹*tiredness, troubles*›
(b) (verkaufen) sell

vertreten 1 *unr. tr. V.* **(a)** stand in *or* deputize for ‹*colleague etc.*›; ‹*teacher*› cover for ‹*colleague*›
(b) (eintreten für, repräsentieren) represent ‹*person, firm, interests, constituency, country, etc.*›; (Rechtsw.) act for ‹*person, prosecution, etc.*›; **~ sein** be represented
(c) (einstehen für, verfechten) support ‹*point of view, principle*›; hold ‹*opinion*›; advocate ‹*thesis etc.*›
2 *unr. refl. V.* **sich** (*Dat.*) **die Füße** *od.* **Beine ~** (ugs.) stretch one's legs

Vertreter *der;* **~s, ~, Vertreterin** *die;* ~, **~nen (a)** (Stellvertreter[in]) deputy; stand-in
(b) (Repräsentant[in]) representative; (Handelsvertreter[in]) sales representative; commercial traveller
(c) (Verfechter[in], Anhänger[in]) supporter; advocate

Vertretung *die;* ~, **~en** deputy; (Delegierte[r]) representative; (Delegation) delegation (Handelsvertretung) [sales] agency; **eine diplomatische ~**: a diplomatic mission

Vertriebene *der/die; adj. Dekl.* expellee [from his/her homeland]

vertrocknen *itr. V.; mit sein* dry up

vertrödeln *tr. V.* (ugs. abwertend) dawdle away, waste ‹*time*›

vertrösten *tr. V.* put ‹*person*› off (**auf** + *Akk.* until)

vertun 1 *unr. tr. V.* waste
2 *unr. refl. V.* (ugs.) make a slip

vertuschen *tr. V.* hush up ‹*scandal etc.*›; keep ‹*truth etc.*› secret

Vertuschung *die;* ~, **~en** hushing up; **eine ~**: a hush-up *or* cover-up

verübeln *tr. V.* **jmdm. eine Äußerung** *usw.* **~**: take sb.'s remark *etc.* amiss

verüben *tr. V.* commit ‹*crime etc.*›

verunglücken *itr. V.; mit sein* have an accident; ‹*car etc.*› be involved in an accident; **mit dem Auto/Flugzeug ~**: be in a car/an air accident *or* crash

Verunglückte *der/die; adj. Dekl.* accident victim; casualty

verunreinigen *tr. V.* pollute; contaminate ‹*water, milk, flour, oil*›

verunsichern *tr. V.* **jmdn. ~**: make sb. feel unsure *or* uncertain

verunstalten *tr. V.* disfigure

Verunstaltung *die;* ~, **~en** disfigurement

veruntreuen *tr. V.* embezzle

Veruntreuung *die;* ~, **~en** embezzlement

verunzieren *tr. V.* spoil the look of

verursachen *tr. V.* cause

*alte Schreibung - vgl. Hinweis auf S. xiv

verurteilen *tr. V.* pass sentence on; sentence; (fig.) condemn ‹*behaviour, action*›; **jmdn. zum Tode ~:** sentence *or* condemn sb. to death
Verurteilte *der/die; adj. Dekl.* convicted man/woman
Verurteilung *die; ~, ~en* sentencing; (fig.) condemnation
vervollkommnen *tr. V.* perfect
vervollständigen *tr. V.* complete
verwachsen *Adj.* deformed
verwählen *refl. V.* misdial
verwahren 1 *tr. V.* keep [safe]
2 *refl. V.* protest
verwahrlosen *itr. V.; mit sein* get in a bad state; ‹*house, building*› fall into disrepair; ‹*garden, hedge*› become overgrown; ‹*person*› let oneself go; **verwahrlost** neglected; overgrown ‹*hedge, garden*›; dilapidated ‹*house, building*›; unkempt ‹*person, appearance, etc.*›; (in der Kleidung) ragged ‹*person*›
Verwahrlosung *die; ~:* (eines Gebäudes) dilapidation; (einer Person) advancing decrepitude
verwaisen *itr. V.* be orphaned
verwalten *tr. V.* **(a)** administer ‹*estate, property*›; run ‹*house*›; hold ‹*money*› in trust
(b) (leiten) run, manage ‹*hostel, kindergarten, etc.*›; (regieren) administer ‹*area, colony, etc.*›; govern ‹*country*›
Verwalter *der; ~s, ~,* **Verwalterin** *die; ~, ~nen* administrator; (eines Amts usw.) manager; (eines Nachlasses) trustee
Verwaltung *die; ~, ~en* **(a)** administration; (eines Landes) government; (eines Amtes) tenure; (einer Aufgabe) performance
(b) (Organ) administration
verwandeln 1 *tr. V.* convert (**in** + *Akk.*, **zu** into); (völlig verändern) transform (**in** + *Akk.*, **zu** into)
2 *refl. V.* **sich in etw.** (*Akk.*) *od.* **zu etw. ~:** turn *or* change into sth.; (bei chemischen Vorgängen usw.) be converted into sth
Verwandlung *die; ~, ~en* conversion (**in** + *Akk.*, **zu** into); (völlige Veränderung, das Sichverwandeln) transformation (**in** + *Akk.*, **zu** into)
verwandt[1] *2. Part. v.* VERWENDEN
verwandt[2] *Adj.* related (**mit** to); (fig.) similar ‹*views, ideas, forms*›
Verwandte *der/die; adj. Dekl.* relative; relation
Verwandtschaft *die; ~, ~en* **(a)** relationship (**mit** to); (fig.) affinity
(b) (Verwandte) relatives *pl.*; relations *pl.*; **die ganze ~:** all one's relatives
verwandtschaftlich *Adj.* family ‹*ties, relationships, etc.*›
verwarnen *tr. V.* warn, caution (**wegen** for)
Verwarnung *die; ~, ~en* warning; caution
verwechseln *tr. V.* **(a)** [**miteinander**] **~:** confuse ‹*two things/people*›; **etw. mit etw./jmdn. mit jmdm. ~:** mistake sth. for sth./sb. for sb.; confuse sth. with sth./sb. with sb.
(b) (vertauschen) mix up
Verwechslung *die; ~, ~en* **(a)** [case of] confusion
(b) (Vertauschung) mixing up; **eine ~:** a mix-up
verwegen 1 *Adj.* daring; (auch fig.) audacious
2 *adv.* (auch fig.) audaciously
Verwegenheit *die; ~:* daring; (auch fig.) audacity
verwehren *tr. V.* **jmdm. etw. ~:** refuse *or* deny sb. sth.
Verwehung *die; ~, ~en* [snow]drift
verweigern *tr. V.* refuse
Verweigerung *die; ~, ~en* refusal
Verweis *der; ~es, ~e* **(a)** reference (**auf** + *Akk.* to); (Querverweis) cross reference
(b) (Tadel) reprimand
verweisen *unr. tr. V.* **(a) jmdn./einen Fall** *usw.* **an jmdn./etw. ~** (auch Rechtsspr.) refer sb./a case *etc.* to sb./sth.
(b) (wegschicken) **jmdn. von der Schule/aus dem Saal ~:** expel sb. from the school/send sb. out of the room; **einen Spieler vom Platz ~:** send a player off [the field]
(c) *auch itr.* (hinweisen) **[jmdn.] auf etw.** (*Akk.*) **~:** refer [sb.] to sth.
verwelken *itr. V.; mit sein* wilt
verwendbar *Adj.* usable
Verwendbarkeit *die; ~:* usability
verwenden *unr. od. regelm. tr. V.* **(a)** use (**zu, für** for)
(b) (aufwenden) spend ‹*time*› (**auf** + *Akk.* on)
Verwendung *die; ~, ~en* use
verwerfen *unr. tr. V.* reject; dismiss ‹*thought*›
verwerflich (geh.) 1 *Adj.* reprehensible
2 *adv.* reprehensibly
verwertbar *Adj.* utilizable; usable
verwerten *tr. V.* utilize, use (**zu** for); make use of ‹*suggestion, experience, knowledge, etc.*›
verwesen *itr. V.; mit sein* decompose
Verwesung *die; ~:* decomposition
verwickeln 1 *refl. V.* get tangled up *or* entangled; **sich in etw.** (*Akk. od. Dat.*) **~:** get caught [up] in sth.
2 *tr. V.* involve
Verwicklung *die; ~, ~en* complication
verwildern *itr. V.* ‹*garden*› become overgrown; ‹*domestic animal*› return to the wild
verwirklichen 1 *tr. V.* realize ‹*dream*›; realize, put into practice ‹*plan, proposal, idea, etc.*›; carry out ‹*project, intention*›
2 **(a)** *refl. V.* ‹*hope, dream*› be realized

(b) (sich voll entfalten) **sich [selbst] ~**: realize one's [full] potential; fulfil oneself
Verwirklichung *die; ~, ~en* realization; (eines Wunsches, einer Hoffnung) fulfilment
verwirren *tr. (auch itr.) V.* confuse; **verwirrt** confused; **~d** bewildering
Verwirrung *die; ~, ~en* confusion
verwischen *tr. V.* smudge ‹*signature, writing, etc.*›; smear ‹*paint*›; (fig.) cover up ‹*tracks*›
verwittern *itr. V.; mit sein* weather
Verwitterung *die; ~, ~en* weathering
verwitwet *Adj.* widowed
verwöhnen *tr. V.* spoil
verwöhnt *Adj.* spoilt; (anspruchsvoll) discriminating; ‹*taste, palate*› of a gourmet
verworren *Adj.* confused, muddled ‹*ideas, situation, etc.*›
verwunden *tr. V.* wound; injure
Verwundete *der/die; adj. Dekl.* casualty; **die ~n** the wounded
Verwundung *die; ~, ~en* wound
verwünschen *tr. V.* curse
verwüsten *tr. V.* devastate
Verwüstung *die; ~, ~en* devastation
verzagen *itr. V.; mit sein od. haben* despair; lose heart; **verzagt sein** be despondent
Verzagtheit *die; ~*: despondency; despair
verzählen *refl. V.* miscount
verzanken *refl. V.* (ugs.) **sich [mit jmdm. wegen etw.] ~**: fall out [with sb. over sth.]
verzaubern *tr. V.* cast a spell on; bewitch; (fig.) enchant; **jmdn. in etw.** *(Akk.)* **~**: transform sb. into sth.
Verzehr *der; ~[e]s* consumption
verzehren *tr. V.* consume
Verzeichnis *das; ~ses, ~se* list; (Register) index
verzeihen *unr. tr., itr. V.* forgive; (entschuldigen) excuse ‹*behaviour, remark, etc.*›; **~ Sie [bitte], können Sie mir sagen ...?** excuse me, could you tell me ...?
Verzeihung *die; ~*: forgiveness; **~!** sorry!; **jmdn. um ~ bitten** apologize to sb.
verzerren *tr. V.* **(a)** contort ‹*face etc.*› **(zu** into)
(b) (akustisch, optisch) distort ‹*sound, image*›; **etw. verzerrt darstellen** (fig.) present a distorted account *or* picture of sth.
Verzicht *der; ~[e]s, ~e* **(a)** renunciation **(auf** + *Akk.* of)
(b) (auf Reichtum, ein Amt usw.) relinquishment **(auf** + *Akk.* of)
verzichten *itr. V.* do without; **~ auf** (+ *Akk.*) do without; (sich enthalten) refrain from; (aufgeben) give up ‹*share, smoking, job, etc.*›; renounce ‹*inheritance*›; relinquish ‹*right, privilege*›; (opfern) sacrifice ‹*holiday, salary*›
verziehen[1] *2. Part. v.* VERZEIHEN
verziehen[2] **1** *unr. tr. V.* **(a)** screw up ‹*face, mouth, etc.*›
(b) (schlecht erziehen) spoil
2 *unr. refl. V.* **(a)** (aus der Form geraten) go out of shape; ‹*wood*› warp
(b) (wegziehen) ‹*clouds, storm*› move away, pass over: ‹*fog, mist*› disperse
(c) (ugs.: weggehen) take oneself off
3 *unr. itr. V.; mit sein* move [away]; **„Empfänger [unbekannt] verzogen"** 'no longer at this address'
verzieren *tr. V.* decorate
Verzierung *die; ~, ~en* decoration
verzögern **1** *tr. V.* **(a)** delay **(um** by)
(b) (verlangsamen) slow down
2 *refl. V.* be delayed **(um** by)
Verzögerung *die; ~, ~en* delay *(Gen.* in); (Verlangsamung) slowing down
verzollen *tr. V.* pay duty on
Verzug *der; ~[e]s* delay; **im ~ sein/in ~ kommen** be/fall behind
verzweifeln *itr. V.; mit sein* despair; **über etw./jmdn. ~**: despair at sth./of sb.
verzweifelt **1** *Adj.* despairing ‹*person*›; desperate ‹*situation, attempt, effort, struggle, etc*›; **~ sein** be in despair
2 *adv.* desperately
Verzweiflung *die; ~*: despair
verzweigen *refl. V.* branch [out]
Veteran /vete'ra:n/ *der; ~en, ~en,* **Veteranin** *die; ~, ~nen* (auch fig.) veteran
Vetter *der; ~s, ~n* cousin
vgl. *Abk.* = **vergleiche** cf.
v. H. *Abk.* = **vom Hundert** per cent
via /'vi:a/ *Präp.* via
Viadukt /via'dʊkt/ *das od. der; ~[e]s, ~e* viaduct
Viagra (Wz) /'vi̯agra/ *das; ~s* Viagra ®
vibrieren /vi'bri:rən/ *itr. V.* vibrate
Video *das; ~s, ~s* (ugs.) video
video-, Video- /'vi:deo-/: video
Video-: ~clip *der; ~~s, ~~s* video; **~gerät** *das* video machine; **~kassette** *die* video cassette; **~recorder, ~rekorder** *der* video recorder; **~text** *der* videotex[t]
Videothek *die; ~, ~en* video library
Vieh *das; ~[e]s* **(a)** (Nutztiere) livestock *sing. or pl.;*
(b) (Rinder) cattle *pl.*
Vieh·zucht *die* [live]stock/cattle breeding *no art.*
viel **1** *Indefinitpron. u. unbest. Zahlw.* **(a)** *Sg.* a great deal of; a lot of (coll.); **wie/nicht/zu ~**: how/not/too much; **~[es]** (vielerlei) much; **der ~e Regen** all the rain; **um ~es jünger** a great deal younger
(b) *Pl.* many; **gleich ~[e]** the same number of; **die ~en Menschen** all the people
2 *Adv.* **(a)** (oft, lange) a great deal; a lot (coll.)
(b) (wesentlich) much; a great deal; a lot (coll.); **~ zu klein** much too small

*old spelling - see note on page xiv

vielerlei *indekl. Adj.* **(a)** *attr.* many different; all kinds *or* sorts of **(b)** *allein stehend* all kinds of things

viel-, Viel-: ~fach [1] *Adj.* **(a)** multiple; **die ~fache Menge** many times the amount; **(b)** (vielfältig) many kinds of; [2] *adv.* many times; **~falt** *die; ~~:* diversity; **~fältig** [1] *Adj.* many and diverse; [2] *adv.* in many different ways

vielleicht *Adv.* perhaps; maybe

viel-: ~mals *Adv.* **ich bitte ~mals um Entschuldigung** I'm very sorry; **danke ~mals** thank you very much; **~mehr** /*od.* -'-/ *Konj. u. Adv.* rather; **~sagend** [1] *Adj.* meaningful; [2] *adv.* meaningfully; **~seitig** *Adj.* versatile ‹*person*›; **~versprechend** [1] *Adj.* [very] promising; [2] *adv.* [very] promisingly

vier *Kardinalz.* four

Vier *die; ~, ~en* four; **eine ~ schreiben/bekommen** (Schulw.) ≈ get a D

vier-, Vier-: (*s. auch* ACHT-, ACHT-); **~beiner** *der; ~~s, ~~* (ugs.) four-legged friend; **~beinig** *Adj.* four-legged; **~eck** *das* quadrilateral; (Rechteck) rectangle; (Quadrat) square; **~eckig** *Adj.* quadrilateral; (rechteckig) rectangular; **~fach** *Vervielfältigungsz.* fourfold; quadruple; **~fache** *das; adj. Dekl.* **um das ~fache:** fourfold; by four times the amount; **~hundert** *Kardinalz.* four hundred

Vierling *der; ~s, ~e* quadruplet

vier-, Vier-: ~mal *Adv.* four times; **~spurig** *Adj.* four-lane ‹*road, motorway*›; **~spurig sein** have four lanes; **~stellig** *Adj.* four-figure *attrib.*; **~sterne·hotel** /-'----/ *das* four-star hotel

viert... *Ordinalz.* fourth

vier·tausend *Kardinalz.* four thousand;

viertel /'fɪrtl̩/ *Bruchz.* quarter; **ein ~ Pfund** a quarter of a pound; **drei ~ Liter** three quarters of a litre

Viertel /'fɪrtl̩/ *das* (schweiz. meist *der*); *~s, ~* **(a)** quarter; **~ vor/nach eins** [a] quarter to/past one; **drei ~:** three-quarters **(b)** (Stadtteil) quarter; district

viertel-, Viertel-: ~finale *das* (Sport) quarter-final; **~jahr** *das* three months *pl.*; **~jährlich** [1] *Adj.* quarterly; [2] *adv.* quarterly; **~liter** *der* quarter of a litre; **~note** *die* (Musik) crotchet (Brit.); quarter note (Amer.); **~pfund** *das* quarter [of a] pound; **~stunde** *die* quarter of an hour; **~stündig** *Adj.* quarter-of-an-hour; **~stündlich** *Adj., adv* every quarter of an hour

viertens *Adv.* fourthly

viertürig *Adj.* four-door *attrib.*; **~ sein** have four doors

Vierwaldstätter See, (schweiz.:) **Vierwaldstättersee** *der* Lake Lucerne

vier- /'fɪr-:/ ~zehn *Kardinalz.* fourteen; **für vierzehn Tage** for a fortnight; **~zehn·tägig** *Adj.* two-week; **~zehn·täglich** [1] *Adj.* fortnightly; [2] *adv.* fortnightly

vierzig /'fɪrtsɪç/ *Kardinalz.* forty; *s. auch* ACHTZIG

vierzigst... *Ordinalz.* fortieth; *s. auch* ACHT...

Vikar /vi'kaːɐ̯/ *der; ~s, ~e,* **Vikarin** *die; ~, ~nen* **(a)** (kath. Kirche) locum tenens **(b)** (ev. Kirche) ≈ [trainee] curate

Villa /'vɪla/ *die; ~,* **Villen** villa

Villen·viertel *das* exclusive residential district

violett /vi̯o'lɛt/ purple; violet

Violett *das; ~s, ~e od. ugs. ~s* purple; violet; (im Spektrum) violet

Violine /vi̯o'liːnə/ *die; ~, ~n* (Musik) violin

Viper /'viːpɐ/ *die; ~, ~n* viper; adder

Viren ▶ VIRUS

Viren·schutz *der* (DV, Med.) virus protection

virtuell /vɪr'tu̯ɛl/ [1] *Adj.* **(a)** potential **(b)** (DV, Optik) virtual ‹*memory, image;*› **~e Wirklichkeit** virtual reality [2] *adv.* virtually

virtuos /vɪr'tu̯oːs/ [1] *Adj.* virtuoso ‹*performance etc.*› [2] *adv.* in a virtuoso manner

Virtuose *der; ~n, ~n,* **Virtuosin** *die; ~, ~nen* virtuoso

Virtuosität *die; ~:* virtuosity

Virus /'viːrʊs/ *das; ~,* **Viren** virus

Visa ▶ VISUM

Visage /vi'zaːʒə/ *die; ~, ~n* (salopp abwertend) mug (coll.); (Miene) expression

Visen ▶ VISUM

Visier /vi'ziːɐ̯/ *das; ~s, ~e* (am Helm) visor; (an der Waffe) backsight

Vision /vi'zi̯oːn/ *die; ~, ~en* vision

Visite /vi'ziːtə/ *die; ~, ~n* round; **~ machen** do one's round

Visiten·karte *die* visiting card

Visum /'viːzʊm/ *das; ~s,* **Visa** *od.* **Visen** visa

vital *Adj.* vital

Vitalität *die; ~:* vitality

Vitamin /vita'miːn/ *das; ~s, ~e* vitamin

vitamin-, Vitamin-: ~arm *Adj.* low in vitamins *postpos.*; **~mangel** *der* vitamin deficiency; **~reich** *Adj.* rich in vitamins *postpos.*

Vitrine /vi'triːnə/ *die; ~, ~n* display case; (Möbel) display cabinet

Vize- vice-

Vogel *der; ~s,* **Vögel** bird; **einen ~ haben** (salopp) be off one's rocker (coll.)

Vogel-: ~grippe *die* bird flu; **~käfig** *der* birdcage; **~nest** *das* bird's nest; **~perspektive** *die* bird's-eye view; **~scheuche** *die; ~~, ~~n* scarecrow

Vokabel /vo'kaːbl̩/ *die; ~, ~n* word; **~n** vocabulary *sing.*

Vokal /vo'ka:l/ *der;* **~s, ~e** (Sprachw.) vowel

Vọlk *das;* **~[e]s, Vọlker** people

vọlks-, Vọlks-: ~abstimmung *die* plebiscite; **~eigen** *Adj.* (DDR) publicly *or* nationally owned; **~entscheid** *der* (Politik) referendum; **~fest** *das* public festival; (Jahrmarkt) fair; **~hochschule** *die* adult education centre; **~kammer** *die* (DDR) Volkskammer; People's Chamber; **~kunde** *die* folklore; **~lied** *das* folk song; **~musik** *die* folk music; **~polizei** *die* (DDR) People's Police; **~republik** *die* People's Republic; **~stamm** *der* tribe; **~tanz** *der* folk dance; **~tracht** *die* traditional costume; (eines Landes) national costume; **~trauer·tag** *der* (Bundesrepublik Deutschland) national remembrance day

vọlkstümlich 1 *Adj.* popular
2 *adv.* **~ schreiben** write in terms readily comprehensible to the layman

vọlks-, Vọlks-: ~verhetzung *die;* **~~:** incitement of the people; **~vertreter** *der,* **~vertreterin** *die* representative of the people; **~wirt** *der,* **~wirtin** *die* economist; **~wirtschaft** *die* national economy; (Fach) economics *sing., no art.*; **~wirtschaftlich** 1 *Adj.* economic; 2 *adv.* economically; **~zählung** *die* [national] census; **~zorn** *der* public anger

vọll 1 *Adj.* full; ample ‹*bosom*›; (salopp: betrunken) plastered (sl.); **~ von** *od.* **mit etw. sein** be full of sth.; **~ laufen** fill up; **etw. ~ laufen lassen** fill sth. [up]; **etw. ~ füllen** fill sth. up; **etw. ~ gießen** fill sth. [up]; **etw. ~ tanken** fill sth. up; **bitte ~ tanken** fill it up, please; **etw. ~ machen** fill sth. up; **[sich]** (*Dat.*)**] die Hosen/Windeln ~ machen** (ugs.) mess one's pants/nappy; **jmdn. nicht für ~ nehmen** not take sb. seriously
2 *adv.* fully; **~ und ganz** completely

***vọllabern▶** VOLLABERN

voll·auf /*od.* '--/ *Adv.* completely

***vọllaufen ▶** VOLL 1

vọll-, Vọll-: ~automatisch 1 *Adj.* fully automatic; 2 *adv.* fully automatically; **~bad** *das* bath; **~bart** *der* full beard; **~bringen** /-'--/ *unr. tr. V.* (geh.) accomplish

Vọlle·gefühl *das* feeling of fullness

voll·ẹnden *tr. V.* complete

vollẹndet 1 *Adj.* accomplished ‹*performance*›; perfect ‹*gentleman, host, manners, reproduction*›
2 *adv.* ‹*play*› in an accomplished manner

vọllends *Adv.* completely

Voll·ẹndung *die* completion

vọller *indekl. Adj.* full of; **~ Flecken** covered with stains

Volley·ball /'vɔlibal/ *der* volleyball

vọll-, Vọll-: ~führen /-'--/ *tr. V.* perform; ***~|füllen ▶** VOLL 1; **~gas** *das* **~gas geben** put one's foot down; **mit ~gas** at full throttle; ***~|gießen ▶** VOLL 1

vọ̈llig 1 *Adj.* complete; total
2 *adv.* completely; totally; **du hast ~ Recht** you are absolutely right

vọll-, Vọll-: ~jährig *Adj.* of age *pred.;* **~jährig werden** come of age; **~jährigkeit** *die;* **~:** majority *no art.;* **~kasko·versicherung** *die* fully comprehensive insurance

voll·kommen 1 *Adj.* **(a)** /-'-- *od.* '---/ (vollendet) perfect
(b) /'---/ (vollständig) complete; total
2 /'---/ *adv.* completely; totally

vọll-, Vọll-: ~korn·brot *das* wholemeal (Brit.) *or* (Amer.) wholewheat bread; **~|labern** *tr. V.* (ugs.) **jmdn. ~labern** rabbit on at sb. (coll.); ***~|laufen ▶** VOLL 1; ***~|machen ▶** VOLL 1; **~macht** *die;* **~~, ~~en (a)** authority; **(b)** (Urkunde) power of attorney; **~milch** *die* full-cream milk; **~milch·schokolade** *die* full-cream milk chocolate; **~mond** *der* full moon; **~pension** *die* full board *no art.;* **~ständig** 1 *Adj.* complete; full ‹*text, address, etc.*›; 2 *adv.* completely; ‹*list*› in full; **~ständigkeit** *die;* **~:** completeness; **~strecken** /-'--/ *tr. V.* enforce ‹*penalty, fine, law*›; carry out ‹*sentence*› **(an** + *Dat.* on); ***~|tanken ▶** VOLL 1; **~treffer** *der* direct hit; **ein ~treffer sein** (fig.) hit the bull's eye; **~versammlung** *die* general meeting; (der UNO) General Assembly; **~zählig** *Adj.* complete; **~zeit·beschäftigt** *Adj.* emloyed full-time *postpos.*; **~zeit·beschäfligte** *der/die* full-time employee

voll·ziehen *unr. tr. V.* carry out **(an** + *Dat.* on); execute, carry out ‹*order*›; perform ‹*sacrifice, ceremony, sexual intercourse*›

Voll·zug *der:* **▶** VOLLZIEHEN: carrying out; execution; performance

Volt /vɔlt/ *das;* **~** *od.* **~[e]s, ~:** (Physik, Elektrot.) volt

Volumen /vo'lu:mən/ *das;* **~s, ~:** volume

vọm *Präp.* + *Art.* **(a) = von dem;**
(b) (räumlich) from the; **links/rechts ~ Eingang** to the left/right of the entrance; **~ Stuhl aufspringen** jump up out of one's chair
(c) (zeitlich) **~ Morgen bis zum Abend** from morning till night; **~ ersten Januar an** [as] from the first of January
(d) (zur Angabe der Ursache) **das kommt ~ Rauchen/Alkohol** that comes from smoking/drinking alcohol; **jmdn. ~ Sehen kennen** know sb. by sight

vọn *Präp. mit Dat.* **(a)** (räumlich) from; **nördlich/südlich ~ Mannheim** to the north/south of Mannheim; **rechts/links ~ mir** on my right/left; **~ hier an** *od.* (ugs.) **ab** from here on[ward]; **~ Mannheim aus** from Mannheim
(b) (zeitlich) from; **~ jetzt an** *od.* (ugs.) **ab** from now on; **~ heute/morgen an** [as] from today/tomorrow; starting today/tomorrow; **in der**

*alte Schreibung - vgl. Hinweis auf S. xiv

Nacht ~ Freitag auf *od.* **zu Samstag** during Friday night; **das Brot ist ~ gestern** it's yesterday's bread
(c) (anstelle eines Genitivs) of; **acht ~ hundert/zehn** eight out of a hundred/ten
(d) (zur Angabe des Urhebers, der Ursache, beim Passiv) by; **der Roman ist ~ Fontane** the novel is by Fontane; **müde ~ der Arbeit sein** be tired from work[ing]; **sie hat ein Kind ~ ihm** she has a child by him
(e) (zur Angabe von Eigenschaften) of; **eine Fahrt ~ drei Stunden** a three-hour drive

von·einander *Adv.* from each other *or* one another

vonstatten *Adv.* **~ gehen** proceed

vor 1 *Präp. mit Dat.* **(a)** (räumlich) in front of; (weiter vorn) ahead of, in front of; (nicht ganz so weit wie) before; (außerhalb) outside; **kurz ~ der Abzweigung** just before the turn-off; **~ der Stadt** outside the town; **etw. ~ sich haben** (fig.) have sth. before one; **das liegt noch ~ mir** (fig.) I still have that to come *or* have that ahead of me
(b) (zeitlich) before; **es ist fünf [Minuten] ~ sieben** it is five [minutes] to seven
(c) (bei Reihenfolge, Rangordnung) before; **knapp ~ jmdm. siegen** win just ahead *or* in front of sb.
(d) (aufgrund von) with; **~ Freude strahlen** beam with joy; **~ Hunger/Durst umkommen** (ugs.) die of hunger/thirst
(e) ~ fünf Minuten/10 Jahren/Wochen *usw.* five minutes/ten years/weeks ago; **heute ~ einer Woche** a week ago today
2 *Präp. mit Akk.* in front of; **~ sich hin** to oneself

Vor·abend *der* evening before; (fig.) eve

Vor·ahnung *die* premonition; presentiment; **dunkle/schlimme ~en** dark forebodings

vor·an *Adv.* forward[s] ahead; first

voran-: ~|gehen *unr. itr. V.; mit sein* **(a)** go first; **(b)** (Fortschritte machen) make progress; **~|kommen** *unr. itr. V.; mit sein* **(a)** make headway; **(b)** (Fortschritte machen) make progress; **~|treiben** *unr. tr. V.* push ahead

Vor·arbeiter *der* foreman

Vor·arbeiterin *die* forewoman

vor·aus 1 /-'-/ *Präp. mit Dat., nachgestellt* in front; **jmdm./seiner Zeit ~ sein** (fig.) be ahead of sb./one's time
2 *Adv.* **im Voraus** /'--/ in advance

voraus-, Voraus-: ~|gehen *unr. itr. V.; mit sein* **(a)** go [on] ahead; **(b)** (zeitlich) **einem Ereignis ~gehen** precede an event; **~sage** *die* ▶ VORHERSAGE; **~|sagen** *tr. V.* predict; **~|sehen** *unr. tr. V.* foresee; **~|setzen** *tr. V.* **(a)** (als gegeben ansehen) assume; **~gesetzt, [dass] ...:** provided [that] ...; **(b)** (erfordern) require ‹*skill, experience, etc.*›; presuppose ‹*good organization, planning, etc.*›; **~setzung** *die;* **~~, ~~en (a)** (Annahme) assumption; (Prämisse) premiss; **(b)** (Vorbedingung) prerequisite; **unter der ~setzung, dass ...:** on condition *or* on the precondition that ...; **~sichtlich** 1 *Adj.* anticipated; 2 *adv.* probably

Vor·bau *der; Pl.* **~ten** porch

Vorbehalt *der;* **~[e]s, ~e** reservation; **unter dem ~, dass ...:** with the reservation that ...

vor|behalten *unr. tr. V.* **sich** (*Dat.*) **etw. ~:** reserve oneself sth.; **„Änderungen ~"** 'subject to alterations'

vorbehalt·los 1 *Adj.* unreserved; unconditional
2 *adv.* unreservedly; without reservation[s]

vor·bei *Adv.* **(a)** (räumlich) past; by; **an etw.** (*Dat.*) **~:** past sth.
(b) (zeitlich) past; over; (beendet) finished, over; **es ist acht Uhr ~** (ugs.) it is past *or* gone eight o'clock

vorbei-: ~|fahren *unr. itr. V.; mit sein* **(a)** drive/ride past; pass; **an jmdm. ~fahren** drive/ride past *or* pass sb.; **(b)** (ugs.: einen kurzen Besuch machen) **[bei jmdm./der Post] ~fahren** drop in (coll.) [at sb.'s/at the post office]; **~|gehen** *unr. itr. V.; mit sein* **(a)** pass; go past; **an jmdm./etw. ~gehen** pass *or* go past sb./sth.; **der Schuss ist ~gegangen** the shot missed; **(b)** (ugs.: einen kurzen Besuch machen) **[bei jmdm./der Post] ~gehen** drop in (coll.) [at sb.'s/at the post office]; **(c)** (vergehen) pass; **~|kommen** *unr. itr. V.; mit sein* pass; **an etw.** (*Dat.*) **~kommen** pass sth.; **~|reden** *itr. V.* **an etw.** (*Dat.*) **~reden** talk round sth. without getting to the point; **aneinander ~reden** talk at cross purposes; **~|schießen** *unr. itr. V.* miss

vor·belastet *Adj.* handicapped (**durch** by); **erblich ~ sein** have an inherited defect

vor|bereiten *tr. V.* prepare; **jmdn./sich auf** *od.* **für etw. ~:** prepare sb./oneself for sth.

Vor·bereitung *die;* **~, ~en** preparation; **~en [für etw.] treffen** make preparations for sth.

vor|bestellen *tr. V.* order in advance

Vor·bestellung *die* advance order

vor·bestraft *Adj.* with a previous conviction/previous convictions *postpos., not pred.*

vor|beugen 1 *tr. V.* bend ‹*head, upper body*› forward; **sich ~:** lean forward
2 *itr. V.* **einer Sache** (*Dat.*) *od.* **gegen etw. ~:** prevent sth.

Vor·beugung *die* prevention (**gegen** of); **zur ~:** as a preventive

Vor·bild *das* model; **jmdm. ein gutes ~ sein** be a good example to sb.

vor·bildlich 1 *Adj.* exemplary
2 *adv.* in an exemplary way

vor|bringen *unr. tr. V.* say; **eine Forderung/ein Anliegen ~:** make a demand/express a desire; **Argumente ~:** present arguments

vor·christlich *Adj.* pre-Christian

vor|datieren *tr. V.* postdate
vorder... *Adj.* front; **der Vordere Orient** the Middle East
Vorder-: ~grund *der* foreground; **im ~grund stehen** (fig.) be prominent *or* to the fore; **~mann** *der; Pl.* **~männer** person in front; **jmdn. auf ~mann bringen** (ugs.) lick sb. into shape
vor|drängen *refl. V.* push [one's way] forward *or* to the front; (fig.) push oneself forward
vor|dringen *unr. itr. V.; mit sein* push forward; advance
vor·dringlich 1 *Adj.* **(a)** priority *attrib.* ‹*treatment*›
(b) (dringlich) urgent
2 *adv.* **(a)** as a matter of priority
(b) (dringlich) as a matter of urgency
Vor·druck *der; Pl.* **~e** form
vor·eilig 1 *Adj.* rash
2 *adv.* rashly
vor·einander *Adv.* **(a)** one in front of the other
(b) (einer dem anderen gegenüber) opposite each other; face to face
(c) Angst ~ haben be afraid of each other
vor·eingenommen *Adj.* prejudiced; biased; **für/gegen jmdn. ~ sein** be prejudiced in sb.'s favour/against sb.
Vor·eingenommenheit *die;* **~, ~en** prejudice; bias
vorenthalten *unr. tr. V.;* **ich enthalte vor** (*od. seltener:* **vorenthalte), vorenthalten, vorzuenthalten: jmdm. etw. ~:** withhold sth. from sb.
vor·erst /*od.* -'-/ *Adv.* for the present
Vorfahr *der;* **~en, ~en** forefather
vor|fahren *unr. itr. V.; mit sein* **(a)** (ankommen) drive/ride up
(b) (weiter nach vorn fahren) ‹*person*› drive *or* move forward; ‹*car*› move forward
(c) (vorausfahren) drive *or* go on ahead
Vor·fahrt *die* right of way; **„~ beachten/gewähren"** 'give way'
Vorfahrt[s]-: ~schild *das; Pl.* **~~er** right-of-way sign; **~straße** *die* main road
Vor·fall *der* incident; occurrence
vor|fallen *unr. itr. V.; mit sein* **(a)** (sich ereignen) happen; occur
(b) (nach vorn fallen) fall forward
Vor·film *der* supporting film
vor|finden *unr. tr. V.* find
Vor·freude *die* anticipation
vor|führen *tr. V.* show ‹*film, slides, etc.*›; present ‹*circus act, programme*›; perform ‹*play, trick, routine*›; (demonstrieren) demonstrate; **jmdn. dem Richter ~:** bring sb. before the judge
Vor·führung *die* show; (eines Theaterstücks) performance

*old spelling - see note on page xiv

Vor·gang *der* occurrence; (Amtsspr.) file
Vorgänger *der;* **~s, ~, Vorgängerin** *die;* **~, ~nen** predecessor
Vor·garten *der* front garden
vor|geben *unr. tr. V.* pretend
Vor·gebirge *das* promontory
vor·gefasst, *vor·gefaßt *Adj.* preconceived
vor|gehen *unr. itr. V.; mit sein* **(a)** (ugs.: nach vorn gehen) go forward
(b) (vorausgehen) go on ahead; **jmdn. ~ lassen** let sb. go first
(c) ‹*clock*› be fast
(d) (einschreiten) **gegen jmdn./etw. ~:** take action against sb./sth.
(e) (verfahren) proceed
(f) (sich abspielen) happen; go on
(g) (Vorrang haben) have priority; come first
Vor·geschmack *der* foretaste
Vor·gesetzte *der/die; adj. Dekl.* superior
vor·gestern *Adv.* the day before yesterday
vor|greifen *unr. itr. V.* **jmdm. ~:** anticipate sb.; jump in ahead of sb.
vor|haben *unr. tr. V.* intend; (geplant haben) plan
Vor·haben *das;* **~s, ~:** plan; (Projekt) project
Vor·halle *die* entrance hall; (eines Theaters, Hotels) foyer
vor|halten *unr. tr. V.* **(a)** hold up; **mit vorgehaltener Schusswaffe** at gunpoint
(b) (zum Vorwurf machen) **jmdm. etw. ~:** reproach sb. for sth.
Vor·haltungen *Pl.* **jmdm. [wegen etw.] ~ machen** reproach sb. [for sth.]
vorhanden *Adj.* existing; (verfügbar) available; **~ sein** exist *or* be in existence/be available
Vor·hang *der* (auch Theater) curtain
Vorhänge·schloss, *Vorhänge·schloß *das* padlock
Vor·haut *die* foreskin
vor·her /*od.* -'-/ beforehand; (davor) before
vorher|gehen *unr. itr. V.; mit sein* **in den ~den Wochen** in the preceding weeks
Vor·herrschaft *die* supremacy
vor|herrschen *itr. V.* predominate
vorher-, Vorher-: ~sage *die* prediction; (des Wetters) forecast; **~|sagen** *tr. V.* predict; forecast ‹*weather*›; **~|sehen** *unr. tr. V.* ▶ VORAUSSEHEN
vor·hin /*od.* -'-/ *Adv.* a short time *or* while ago
vorig... *Adj.* last
Vor·jahr *das* previous year
vor·jährig *Adj.* of the previous year
Vor·kämpfer *der,* **Vor·kämpferin** *die* pioneer
Vorkehrungen *Pl.* precautions
Vor·kenntnis *die* background knowledge

vor|kommen *unr. itr. V.; mit sein* **(a)** (sich ereignen) happen
(b) (vorhanden sein) occur
(c) (erscheinen) seem; **das Lied kommt mir bekannt vor** I seem to know the song

Vorkommnis *das;* **~ses, ~se** incident; occurrence

vor|laden *unr. tr. V.* summon

Vor·ladung *die* summons

Vor·lage *die* **(a)** ▶ VORLEGEN: presentation; showing; production; submission; tabling
(b) (Entwurf) draft
(c) (Muster) pattern; (Modell) model

Vor·lauf *der* (eines Bandgeräts) fast forward

Vor·läufer *der,* **Vor·läuferin** *die* precursor; forerunner

vor·läufig [1] *Adj.* temporary; provisional; interim ‹*order, agreement*›
[2] *adv.* for the time being

vor·laut [1] *Adj.* forward
[2] *adv.* forwardly

vor|legen *tr. V.* present; show, produce ‹*certificate, identity card, etc.*›; show ‹*sample*›; submit ‹*evidence*›; table ‹*parliamentary bill*›

vor|lesen *unr. tr., itr. V.* read aloud *or* out; read ‹*story, poem, etc.*› aloud; **jmdm. [etw.] ~:** read [sth.] to sb.

Vor·lesung *die* lecture; (Vorlesungsreihe) series *or* course of lectures

vor·letzt... *Adj.* last but one; penultimate ‹*page, episode, etc.*›

vorlieb: **mit jmdm./etw. ~ nehmen** put up with sb./sth.; (sich begnügen) make do with sb./sth.

Vor·liebe *die* preference

***vorlieb|nehmen** ▶ VORLIEB

vor|liegen *unr. itr. V.* **jmdm. ~:** be with sb.; **die Ergebnisse liegen uns noch nicht vor** we do not have the results yet; **im ~den Fall** in the present case

vor|lügen *unr. tr. V.* (ugs.) **jmdm. etwas ~:** lie to sb.

vorm *Präp. + Art.* **(a)** = **vor dem;**
(b) (räumlich) in front of the
(c) (zeitlich, bei Reihenfolge) before the

vor|machen *tr. V.* (ugs.) **jmdm. etw. ~:** show sb. sth.; (vortäuschen) kid (coll.) *or* fool sb.

vormalig *Adj.* former

vormals *Adv.* formerly

Vor·marsch *der* (auch fig.) advance

vor|merken *tr. V.* make a note of; **ich habe Sie für den Kurs vorgemerkt** I've put you down for the course

***vor·mittag** ▶ VORMITTAG

Vor·mittag *der* morning; **heute/morgen/gestern ~:** this/tomorrow/yesterday morning

vor·mittags *Adv.* in the morning

Vor·mund *der; Pl.* **~e** *od.* **Vormünder** guardian

Vor·name *der* first *or* Christian name

vorn[e] *Adv.* at the front; **nach ~:** to the front; **von ~:** from the front; **noch einmal von ~ anfangen** start afresh; **von ~ bis hinten** (ugs.) from beginning to end

vornehm [1] *Adj.* (nobel; adelig) noble; (kultiviert) distinguished; (elegant) exclusive ‹*district, hotel, restaurant, resort*›; elegant ‹*villa, clothes*›
[2] *adv.* nobly; (elegant) elegantly

vor|nehmen *unr. refl. V.* **sich** (*Dat.*) **etw. ~:** plan sth.; **sich** (*Dat.*) **~, mit dem Rauchen aufzuhören** resolve to give up smoking

vorn-: ~herein: von ~herein from the outset; **~über** *Adv.* forwards

Vor·ort *der* suburb

vor|programmieren *tr. V.* (auch fig.) pre-programme

Vor·rang *der* **(a)** priority (**vor** + *Dat.* over)
(b) (bes. österr.: Vorfahrt) right of way

Vor·rat *der* supply, stock (**an** + *Dat.* of)

vorrätig *Adj.* in stock *postpos.*

Vor·raum *der* anteroom

vor|rechnen *tr. V.* **jmdm. etw. ~:** work sth. out *or* calculate sth. for sb.; **jmdm. seine Fehler ~** (fig.) enumerate sb.'s mistakes

Vor·recht *das* privilege

Vor·redner *der,* **Vor·rednerin** *die* previous speaker; **mein Vorredner:** the previous speaker

Vor·richtung *die* device

vor|rücken [1] *tr. V.* move forward; advance ‹*chess piece*›
[2] *itr. V.; mit sein* move forward; **auf den 5. Platz ~:** move up to fifth place

Vor·ruhestand *der* early retirement

vors *Präp. + Art.* = **vor das**

vor|sagen *tr. V.* **(a)** *auch itr.* **jmdm. [die Antwort] ~:** tell sb. the answer; (flüsternd) whisper the answer to sb.
(b) (aufsagen) recite

Vor·saison *die* start of the season; early [part of the] season

Vor·satz *der* intention

vorsätzlich [1] *Adj.* intentional; wilful ‹*murder, arson, etc.*›
[2] *adv.* intentionally

Vor·schau *die* preview

Vor·schein *der:* **zum ~ kommen** appear; (entdeckt werden) come to light

vor|schieben *unr. tr. V.* **(a)** push ‹*bolt*› across
(b) (nach vorn schieben) push forward

vor|schießen *unr. tr. V.* **jmdm. Geld ~:** advance sb. money

Vorschlag *der* suggestion; proposal

vor|schlagen *unr. tr. V.* **[jmdm.] etw. ~:** suggest *or* propose sth. [to sb.]

vor·schreiben *unr. tr. V.* stipulate, set ‹*conditions*›; lay down ‹*rules*›; prescribe ‹*dose*›

V

Vor·schrift *die* instruction; order; (gesetzliche od. amtliche Bestimmung) regulation

vorschrifts·mäßig [1] *Adj.* correct; proper
[2] *adv.* correctly; properly

Vor·schub *der* **jmdm./einer Sache ~ leisten** encourage sb./encourage *or* promote *or* foster sth.

Vorschul·alter *das* preschool age

Vor·schuss, *Vor·schuß *der* advance

vor|schwärmen *itr. V.* **jmdm. von jmdm./etw. ~:** rave about sb./sth. to sb. (coll.)

vor|schweben *itr. V.* **jmdm. schwebt etw. vor** sb. has sth. in mind

vor|sehen [1] *unr. tr. V.* **(a)** plan; **etw. für/als etw. ~:** intend sth. for/as sth.
(b) ‹*law, plan, contract, etc.*› provide for
[2] *unr. refl. V.* **sich [vor jmdm./etw.] ~:** be careful [of sb./sth.]

vor|setzen *tr. V.* **jmdm. etw. ~:** serve sb. sth.; (fig.) serve *or* dish sb. up sth.

Vor·sicht *die* care; (bei Risiko, Gefahr) caution; care; **zur ~:** as a precaution; **~!** be careful!; **„~, Stufe!"** 'mind the step!'

vorsichtig [1] *Adj.* careful; (bei Risiko, Gefahr) cautious; **sei ~!** be careful!; take care!
[2] *adv.* carefully; with care

vorsichts·halber *Adv.* as a precaution; to be on the safe side

Vorsichts·maßnahme *die* precautionary measure; precaution

Vor·silbe *die* [monosyllabic] prefix

vor|singen *unr. tr. V.* **[jmdm.] etw. ~:** sing sth. [to sb.]

Vor·sitz *der* chairmanship

Vorsitzende *der/die; adj. Dekl.* chair[person]; (bes. Mann) chairman; (Frau auch) chairwoman

Vor·sorge *die* precautions *pl.;* (für den Todesfall, Krankheit, Alter) provisions *pl.*

vor|sorgen *itr. V.* **für etw. ~:** make provisions for sth.; provide for sth.

Vorsorge·untersuchung *die* (Med.) medical check-up

vorsorglich *adv.* as a precaution

Vor·spann *der* (Film, Ferns.) opening credits *pl.*

Vor·speise *die* starter; hors d'œuvre

Vor·spiel *das* (Theater) prologue; (Musik) prelude

vor|spielen *tr. V.* **(a)** play ‹*piece of music*› (*Dat.* to, for); act out, perform ‹*scene*› (*Dat.* for, in front of)
(b) (vorspiegeln) **jmdm. etw. ~:** feign sth. to sb.

vor|sprechen [1] *unr. tr. V.* **(a)** (zum Nachsprechen) **jmdm. etw. ~:** pronounce *or* say sth. first for sb.
(b) (zur Prüfung) recite
[2] *unr. itr. V.* audition

Vor·sprung *der* lead (**vor** + *Dat.* over)

*alte Schreibung - vgl. Hinweis auf S. xiv

Vor·stadt *die* suburb

Vor·stand *der* (einer Firma) board [of directors]; (eines Vereins, einer Gesellschaft) executive committee; (einer Partei) executive

vor|stehen *unr. itr. V.* **(a)** project; jut out; ‹*teeth, chin*› stick out; **~de Zähne** buck teeth; projecting teeth
(b) (geh.: leiten) **einer Institution ~:** be the head of an institution

vorstell·bar *Adj.* conceivable; imaginable; **es ist durchaus/[nur] schwer ~, dass ...:** it is quite/scarcely conceivable that ...

vor|stellen [1] *tr. V.* **jmdn./sich jmdm. ~:** introduce sb./oneself to sb.; (bei Bewerbung) **sich ~:** come/go for [an] interview; **die Uhr [um eine Stunde] ~:** put the clock forward [one hour]
[2] *refl. V.* **sich** (*Dat.*) **etw. ~:** imagine sth.

Vor·stellung *die* **(a)** (Begriff) idea
(b) (Fantasie) imagination
(c) (Aufführung) performance; (im Kino) showing

Vorstellungs·gespräch *das* interview

Vor·stoß *der* advance

vor|stoßen *unr. itr. V.; mit sein* advance; push forward

Vor·strafe *die* previous conviction

vor|strecken *tr. V.* stretch ‹*arm, hand*› out; advance ‹*money, sum*›

Vor·tag *der* day before

vor|täuschen *tr. V.* feign; simulate ‹*reality etc.*›; fake ‹*crime*›

Vor·teil /*od.* 'fɔrtai̯l/ *der* advantage

vorteilhaft [1] *Adj.* advantageous
[2] *adv.* advantageously

Vortrag *der;* **~[e]s, Vorträge** talk; (wissenschaftlich) lecture; **einen ~ halten** give a talk/lecture

vor|tragen *unr. tr. V.* **(a)** sing ‹*song*›; perform, play ‹*piece of music*›; recite ‹*poem*›
(b) (darlegen) present ‹*case, matter, request, demands*›; lodge, make ‹*complaint*›; express ‹*wish, desire*›

vor·trefflich [1] *Adj.* excellent
[2] *adv.* excellently

Vortrefflichkeit *die;* **~:** excellence

vorüber *Adv.* over; (räumlich) past

vorüber|gehen *unr. itr. V.; mit sein* **(a)** go *or* walk past; pass by; **an jmdm./etw. ~:** go past sb./sth.; pass sb./sth.; (achtlos) pass sb./sth. by
(b) (vergehen) pass; ‹*pain*› go

vorübergehend [1] *Adj.* temporary; passing ‹*interest, infatuation*›; brief ‹*illness, stay*›
[2] *adv.* temporarily; (für kurze Zeit) for a short time; briefly

Vor·urteil *das* bias; (voreilige Schlussfolgerung) prejudice

Vor·vergangenheit *die* (Sprachw.) pluperfect

Vor·verkauf *der* advance sale of tickets

vor|verlegen *tr. V.* (zeitlich) bring forward (**auf** + *Akk.* to; **um** by)

Vor·wahl *die,* **Vorwähl·nummer** *die* (Fernspr.) dialling code

Vorwand *der;* **~[e]s, Vorwände** pretext; (Ausrede) excuse

vor|warnen *tr. V.* **jmdn. ~:** give sb. advance warning; warn sb. [in advance]; **vorgewarnt sein** be forewarned

Vor·warnung *die* [advance] warning

vor·wärts *Adv.* forwards; (weiter) onwards; **~ kommen** make progress; (im Beruf, Leben) get on; get ahead

***vorwärts|kommen** ▶ VORWÄRTS

vor·weg *Adv.* beforehand

vorweg|nehmen *unr. tr. V.* anticipate

vor|weisen *unr. tr. V.* produce

vor|werfen *unr. tr. V.* **jmdm. etw. ~:** reproach sb. with sth.; (beschuldigen) accuse sb. of sth.

vor·wiegend *Adv.* mainly

vor·witzig *Adj.* bumptious; pert ‹*child*›

Vor·wort *das; Pl.* **~e** foreword

Vor·wurf *der* reproach; (Beschuldigung) accusation

vorwurfs·voll 1 *Adj.* reproachful
2 *adv.* reproachfully

Vor·zeichen *das* **(a)** (Omen) omen
(b) (Math.) [algebraic] sign

vor|zeigen *tr. V.* produce; show

Vor·zeit *die* prehistory

vorzeitig 1 *Adj.* premature; early ‹*retirement*›
2 *adv.* prematurely

vor|ziehen *unr. tr. V.* prefer

Vor·zimmer *das* outer office

Vor·zug *der* **(a)** preference (**gegenüber** over)
(b) (gute Eigenschaft) good quality; merit

vorzüglich 1 *Adj.* excellent; first-rate
2 *adv.* excellently

vulgär /vʊl'gɛːɐ̯/ 1 *Adj.* vulgar
2 *adv.* in a vulgar way

Vulgarität /vʊlgari'tɛːt/ *die;* **~, ~en** vulgarity

Vulkan /vʊl'kaːn/ *der;* **~s, ~e** volcano

vulkanisch *Adj.* volcanic

vulkanisieren *tr. V.* vulcanize

v. u. Z. *Abk.* = **vor unserer Zeit[rechnung]** BC

Ww

w, W /veː/ *das;* **~s, ~:** w/W

W *Abk.* **(a)** = **West, Westen** W.
(b) = **Watt** W.

Waage *die;* **~, ~n (a)** [pair *sing.* of] scales *pl.*
(b) (Astrol.) **[die] ~:** Libra; **er ist [eine] ~:** he is a Libra *or* Libran

waage·recht 1 *Adj.* horizontal
2 *adv.* horizontally

Waage·rechte *die;* **~, ~n;** *also adj. Dekl.* horizontal

Waag·schale *die* scale pan

Wabe *die;* **~, ~n** honeycomb

wach 1 *Adj.* awake
2 *adv.* alertly; attentively

Wache *die;* **~, ~n (a)** (Milit.) guard *or* sentry duty; (Seew.) watch [duty]
(b) (Wächter, Milit.) guard; (Seew.) watch
(c) (Polizei~) police station

wachen *itr. V.* (geh.) be awake; **bei jmdm. ~:** stay up at sb.'s bedside; sit up with sb.

Wachheit *die;* **~:** alertness

Wach·hund *der* guard dog

Wacholder *der;* **~s, ~:** juniper

Wach·posten *der* (Milit.) guard

Wachs *das;* **~es, ~e** wax

wachsam *Adj.* watchful; vigilant

Wachsamkeit *die;* **~:** vigilance

wachsen[1] *unr. itr. V.; mit sein* grow

wachsen[2] *tr. V.* wax

Wachs-: ~figur *die* waxwork; **~figuren·kabinett** *das* waxworks *sing. or pl.;* waxworks museum

wächst *2. u. 3. Pers. Sg. Präsens v.* WACHSEN

Wachs·tuch *das Pl.* **Wachstücher** (Tischtuch) oilcloth tablecloth

Wachstum *das;* **~s** growth

Wachtel *die;* **~, ~n** quail

Wächter *der;* **~s, ~:** guard; (Nacht-, Turmwächter) watchman; (Parkwächter) [park-]keeper

Wächterin *die;* **~, ~nen** ▶ WÄCHTER

Wach[t]·turm *der* watchtower

wackelig *Adj.* **(a)** wobbly ‹*chair, table, etc.*›; loose ‹*tooth*›
(b) (ugs.: kraftlos, schwach) frail

Wackel·kontakt *der* (Elektrot.) loose connection

wackeln *itr. V.* wobble; ‹*tooth etc.*› be loose; ‹*house, window, etc.*› shake; **mit dem Kopf/den Ohren ~:** waggle one's head/ears

wacker (veralt.) 1 *Adj.* upright

[2] *adv.* valiantly; **sich ~ halten** put up a good show

Wade *die;* **~, ~n** (Anat.) calf

Waden·krampf *der* cramp in one's calf

Waffe *die;* **~, ~n** weapon

Waffel *die;* **~, ~n** waffle; (dünne Waffel, Eiswaffel) wafer; (Eistüte) cone

Waffen-: ~gewalt *die* **mit ~gewalt** by force of arms; **~handel** *der* arms trade; **~händler** *der,* **~händlerin** *die* arms dealer; **~schein** *der* firearms licence; **~stillstand** *der* armistice

Wage·mut *der* daring

wage·mutig *Adj.* daring

wagen [1] *tr. V.* risk; **[es] ~, etw. zu tun** dare to do sth.
[2] *refl. V.* **sich irgendwohin/nicht irgendwohin ~:** venture somewhere/not dare to go somewhere

Wagen *der;* **~s, ~:** (PKW) car; (Pferdewagen) cart; (Eisenb.: Personenwagen) coach; (Eisenb.: Güterwagen) truck; (Straßenbahnwagen) car; (Kinder-, Puppenwagen) pram (Brit.); baby carriage (Amer.); (Sportwagen) pushchair (Brit.); stroller (Amer.)

Wagen·heber *der* jack

Waggon /va'gɔŋ, *südd., österr.:* va'go:n/ *der;* **~s, ~s,** *südd., österr.:* **~s, ~e** wagon; truck (Brit.); car (Amer.)

waghalsig [1] *Adj.* daring; (leichtsinnig) reckless
[2] *adv.* daringly; ‹*speculate*› riskily; (leichtsinnig) recklessly

Wagnis *das;* **~ses, ~se** daring exploit *or* feat; (Risiko) risk

Wahl *die;* **~, ~en (a)** choice; **eine/seine ~ treffen** make a/one's choice
(b) (in ein Gremium, Amt usw.) election; **geheime ~:** secret ballot

wahl·berechtigt *Adj.* eligible *or* entitled to vote *postpos.*

Wahl·beteiligung *die* turn-out

wählen [1] *tr. V.* **(a)** choose; (aus~) select
(b) (Fernspr.) dial ‹*number*›
(c) (durch Stimmabgabe) elect
(d) (stimmen für) vote for ‹*party, candidate*›
[2] *itr. V.* **(a)** choose
(b) (Fernspr.) dial
(c) (stimmen) vote

Wähler *der;* **~s, ~:** voter

Wahl·ergebnis *das* election result

Wählerin *die;* **~, ~nen** voter

wählerisch *Adj.* choosy; particular (**in +** *Dat.* about)

Wählerschaft *die;* **~, ~en** electorate; **die ~ der SPD** the SPD's voters *pl.;* those who vote for the SPD

wahl-, Wahl-: ~fach *das* (Schulw.) optional subject; **~gang** *der* ballot; **~geheimnis** *das* secrecy of the ballot; **~geschenk** *das* pre-election bonus; **~kabine** *die* polling booth; **~kampf** *der* election campaign; **~kreis** *der* constituency; **~lokal** *das* polling station; **~los** [1] *Adj.* indiscriminate; [2] *adv.* indiscriminately; **~niederlage** *die* election defeat; **~recht** *das* right to vote

Wähl·scheibe *die* (Fernspr.) dial

Wahl-: ~sieg *der* election victory; **~spruch** *der* motto; **~system** *das* electoral system; **~urne** *die* ballot box

Wahn *der;* **~[e]s** mania; delusion

Wahn·sinn *der* **(a)** insanity; madness
(b) (ugs.: Unvernunft) madness; lunacy

wahnsinnig [1] *Adj.* **(a)** (geistesgestört) insane; mad
(b) (ugs.: ganz unvernünftig) mad; crazy
(c) (ugs.: groß, heftig, intensiv) terrific (coll.) ‹*effort, speed, etc.*›; terrible (coll.) ‹*fright, job, pain*›
[2] *adv.* (ugs.) incredibly (coll.); terribly (coll.)

wahr *Adj.* **(a)** true; **nicht ~?** *translation depends on preceding verb form:* **du hast Hunger, nicht ~?** you're hungry, aren't you?; **nicht ~, er weiß es doch?** he does know, doesn't he?
(b) (wirklich) real ‹*reason, motive, feelings, joy, etc.*›; actual ‹*culprit*›; (echt) true, real ‹*friend, friendship, love, art*›

wahren *tr. V.* (geh.) preserve ‹*balance, equality, neutrality, etc.*›; maintain ‹*authority, right*›; (verteidigen) defend

währen *itr. V.* (geh.) last

während [1] *Konj.* **(a)** (zeitlich) while
(b) (adversativ) whereas
[2] *Präp. mit Gen.* during; (über einen Zeitraum von) for

wahr|haben *unr. tr. V.* **etw. nicht ~ wollen** not want to admit sth.

wahrhaft (geh.) [1] *Adj.* true
[2] *adv.* truly

wahrhaftig [1] *Adj.* (geh.) truthful ‹*person*›
[2] *adv.* really; genuinely

Wahrheit *die;* **~, ~en** truth

wahrheits·getreu [1] *Adj.* truthful; faithful ‹*account*›
[2] *adv.* truthfully; ‹*portray*› faithfully

wahr|nehmen *unr. tr. V.* **(a)** (mit den Sinnen erfassen) perceive; (spüren) feel; detect ‹*sound, smell*›; (bemerken) notice; (erkennen, ausmachen) make out
(b) (nutzen) take advantage of ‹*opportunity*›; exploit ‹*advantage*›; exercise ‹*right*›
(c) (vertreten) look after ‹*sb.'s interests, affairs*›
(d) (erfüllen, ausführen) carry out, perform ‹*function, task, duty*›; fulfil ‹*responsibility*›

Wahrnehmung *die;* **~, ~en (a)** perception; (eines Sachverhalts) awareness; (eines Geruchs, eines Tons) detection
(b) (Nutzung) (eines Rechts) exercise; (einer Gelegenheit, eines Vorteils) exploitation
(c) (Vertretung) representation
(d) (einer Funktion, Aufgabe, Pflicht) performance; execution; (einer Verantwortung) fulfilment

*old spelling - see note on page xiv

wahr·sagen *2. Part.* **gewahrsagt** [1] *itr. V.* tell fortunes
[2] *tr. V.* predict, foretell ‹*future*›
Wahrsager *der;* **~s, ~, Wahrsagerin** *die;* **~, ~nen** fortune-teller
wahrscheinlich [1] *Adj.* probable; likely
[2] *adv.* probably
Wahrscheinlichkeit *die;* **~, ~en** probability; likelihood
Währung *die;* **~, ~en** currency
Währungs-: ~reform *die* currency reform; **~union** *die* currency union; **~-, Wirtschafts- und Sozialunion** social, economic, and currency union
Wahr·zeichen *das* symbol; (einer Stadt, einer Landschaft) [most famous] landmark
Waise *die;* **~, ~n** orphan
Waisen·haus *das* orphanage
Wal *der;* **~[e]s, ~e** whale
Wald *der;* **~[e]s, Wälder** wood; (größer) forest
Wald·brand *der* forest fire
Wäldchen *das;* **~s, ~:** copse
Wald-: ~meister *der* (Bot.) woodruff; **~sterben** *das;* **~~s** death of the forest [as a result of pollution]
Wal·fang *der* whaling *no def. art.;* **auf ~ gehen/sein** go/be whaling
Waliser *der;* **~s, ~:** Welshman
Waliserin *die;* **~, ~nen** Welshwoman
walisisch *Adj.* Welsh
Walkman (Wz) /'wɔkmən/ *der;* **~s, Walkmen** /'wɔkmən/ Walkman ®; personal stereo
Wall *der;* **~[e]s, Wälle** earthwork; embankment; rampart (esp. Mil.)
Wall-: ~fahrer *der* pilgrim; **~fahrt** *die* pilgrimage; **~fahrts·ort** *der* place of pilgrimage
Wal·nuss, *Wal·nuß *die* walnut
Wal·ross, *Wal·roß *das; Pl.* **-rosse** walrus
walten *itr. V.* (geh.) ‹*good sense, good spirit*› prevail; ‹*peace, silence, harmony, etc.*› reign
Walze *die;* **~, ~n** roller; (Straßen~) [road] roller; (Schreib~) platen
walzen *tr. V.* roll ‹*field, road, steel, etc.*›
wälzen [1] *tr. V.* roll; heave ‹*heavy object*›; (fig.) shove ‹*blame, responsibility*› (**auf** + *Akk.* on); **etw. in Mehl** *usw.* **~** (Kochk.) toss sth. in flour *etc.;* **Probleme ~** (fig. ugs.) mull over problems
[2] *refl. V.* roll; (auf der Stelle) roll about *or* around; (im Krampf, vor Schmerzen) writhe around
Walzer *der;* **~s, ~:** waltz
wand *1. u. 3. Pers. Sg. Prät. v.* WINDEN
Wand *die;* **~, Wände** wall; (Trennwand) partition; (bewegliche Trennwand) screen; (eines Behälters, Schiffs) side
Wandale *der;* **~n, ~n, Wandalin** *die;* **~, ~nen** vandal
Wandalismus *der;* **~:** vandalism
Wandel *der;* **~s** change
wandeln *refl., tr. V.* change (**in** + *Akk.* into)
Wanderer *der;* **~s, ~, Wanderin** *die;* **~, ~nen** rambler; hiker
Wander·karte *die* rambler's [path] map
wandern *itr. V.; mit sein* **(a)** hike; ramble
(b) (ugs.: gehen; fig.) wander (lit. or fig.)
(c) (ziehen, reisen) travel; (ziellos) roam; ‹*exhibition, circus, theatre*› tour, travel; ‹*animal, people, tribe*› migrate
Wander·tag *der* day's hike (*for a class or school*)
Wanderung *die;* **~, ~en (a)** hike; walking tour; **eine ~ machen** go on a hike *or* a walking tour
(b) (Zool., Soziol.) migration
Wander-: ~urlaub *der* walking holiday; **~weg** *der* footpath (*constructed for ramblers*)
Wand-: ~gemälde *das* mural; **~lampe** *die* wall light
Wandlung *die;* **~, ~en** change; (grundlegend) transformation
Wand-: ~malerei *die* (Bild) mural; **~schrank** *der* wall cupboard *or* (Amer.) closet
wandte *1. u. 3. Pers. Prät. v.* WENDEN
Wange *die;* **~, ~n** (geh.) cheek
Wankelmut *der* (geh.) vacillation
wankel·mütig *Adj.* (geh.) vacillating
wanken *itr. V.* **(a)** sway; ‹*person*› totter; (unter einer Last) stagger
(b) *mit sein* (unsicher gehen) stagger; totter
wann *Adv.* when; **seit ~ wohnst du dort?** how long have you been living there?
Wanne *die;* **~, ~n** bath[tub]
Wanze *die;* **~, ~n** bug (coll.)
Wappen *das;* **~s, ~:** coat of arms
wappnen *refl. V.* (geh.) forearm oneself
war *1. u. 3. Pers. Sg. Prät. v.* SEIN
warb *1. u. 3. Pers. Sg. Prät. v.* WERBEN
ward (geh.) *1. u. 3. Pers. Sg. Prät. v.* WERDEN
Ware *die;* **~, ~n (a) ~[n]** goods *pl.;*
(b) (Artikel) article; commodity (Econ., fig.); (Erzeugnis) product
Waren-: ~angebot *das* supply [of goods]; (Sortiment) range of goods; **~haus** *das* department store; **~korb** *der* (Statistik) basket of goods; **~lager** *das* (einer Fabrik o. Ä.) stores *pl.;* (eines Geschäftes) stockroom; (größer) warehouse; **~muster** *das,* **~probe** *die* sample; **~zeichen** *das* trade mark
warf *1. u. 3. Pers. Sg. Prät. v.* WERFEN
warm; wärmer, wärmst ... [1] *Adj.* (auch fig.) warm; hot ‹*meal, food, bath, spring*›; keen, lively ‹*interest*› **das Essen ~ machen** heat up the food; „~" (auf Wasserhahn) 'hot'
[2] *adv.* warmly; **~ essen/duschen** have a hot meal/shower
Wärme *die;* **~:** warmth; (Hitze; auch Physik) heat

W

wärmen [1] *tr. V.* warm; (aufwärmen) warm up ‹*food, drink*›
[2] *itr. V.* be warm; (warm halten) keep one warm

Wärme·pumpe *die* (Technik) heat pump

Warm·front *die* (Met.) warm front

warm|halten *unr. tr. V.* (ugs.) **sich** (*Dat.*) **jmdn.** ~: keep on the right side of sb.

Warm·wasser-: ~bereiter *der;* **~s, ~:** water heater; **~heizung** *die* hot-water heating

Warn-: ~blinkanlage *die* (Kfz-W.) hazard warning lights *pl.;* **~dreieck** *das* (Kfz-W.) hazard warning triangle

warnen *tr.* (*auch itr.*) *V.* warn (**vor** + *Dat.* of, about); **jmdn. [davor] ~, etw. zu tun** warn sb. against doing sth.

Warn-: ~schild *das; Pl.* **~~er** warning sign; **~schuss, *~schuß** *der* warning shot; **~signal** *das* warning signal; **~streik** *der* token strike

Warnung *die;* **~, ~en** warning (**vor** + *Dat.* of, about)

Warschau (*das*)*;* **~s** Warsaw

Warte-: ~halle *die* waiting room; (Flugw.) departure lounge; **~liste** *die* waiting list

warten [1] *itr. V.* wait (**auf** + *Akk.* for)
[2] *tr. V.* service ‹*car etc.*›

Wärter *der;* **~s, ~, Wärterin** *die;* **~, ~nen** attendant; (Tier-, Zoo-, Leuchtturmwärter[in]) keeper; (Krankenwärter[in]) orderly; (Gefängniswärter[in]) warder

Warte-: ~saal *der* waiting room; **~zimmer** *das* waiting room

Wartung *die;* **~, ~en** service; (das Warten) servicing; (Instandhaltung) maintenance

warum *Adv.* why

Warze *die;* **~, ~n** wart; (Brust~) nipple

was [1] *Interrogativpron. Nom. u. Akk. u.* (*nach Präp.*) *Dat. Neutr.;* **~ kostet das?** what *or* how much does that cost?; **ach ~!** (ugs.) oh, come on!; **~ für ein …/~ für …:** what sort *or* kind of …
[2] *Relativpron. Nom. u. Akk. u.* (*nach Präp.*) *Dat. Neutr.;* **[das,] ~:** what; **alles, ~ …:** everything *or* all that …; **vieles/nichts/etwas, ~ …:** much/nothing/something that …; **~ mich betrifft, [so] …:** as far as I'm concerned, …
[3] *Indefinitpron. Nom. u. Akk. u.* (*nach Präp.*) *Dat. Neutr.* (ugs.) ▶ ETWAS;
[4] *Adv.* (ugs.) (warum, wozu) why; what … for

Wasch-: ~anlage *die* car wash; **~automat** *der* washing machine; **~becken** *das* washbasin

Wäsche *die;* **~, ~n (a)** (zu waschende Textilien) washing; (für die Wäscherei) laundry
(b) (Unterwäsche) underwear
(c) (das Waschen) washing *no pl.;* (einmalig) wash; **in der ~ sein** be in the wash

*alte Schreibung - vgl. Hinweis auf S. xiv

wasch·echt *Adj.* **(a)** colour-fast ‹*textile, clothes*›; fast ‹*colour*›
(b) (fig.) genuine

Wäsche-: ~klammer *die* clothes peg (Brit.); clothespin (Amer.); **~korb** *der* laundry basket; **~leine** *die* clothes line

waschen [1] *unr. tr. V.* wash; **sich ~:** wash [oneself]; have a wash; **Wäsche ~:** do the/some washing
[2] *unr. itr. V.* do the washing

Wäscherei *die;* **~, ~en** laundry

Wäsche-: ~schleuder *die* spin drier; **~trockner** *der* **(a)** (Maschine) tumble drier; **(b)** (Gestell) clothes airer

wasch-, Wasch-: ~gelegenheit *die* washing facilities *pl.;* **~küche** *die* laundry room; **~lappen** *der* [face] flannel; washcloth (Amer.); **~maschine** *die* washing machine; **~maschinen·fest** *Adj.* machine washable; **~mittel** *das* detergent; **~pulver** *das* washing powder; **~raum** *der* washing room; **~schüssel** *die* washing bowl; **~straße** *die* [automatic] car wash

wäscht *3. Pers. Sg. Präsens v.* WASCHEN

Wasch·wasser *das* washing water

Wasser *das;* **~s, ~/Wässer (a)** water
(b) *Pl.* **Wässer** (Mineral-, Tafelwasser) mineral water; (Heilwasser) water
(c) (Gewässer) **ein fließendes/stehendes ~:** a moving/stagnant stretch of water
(d) ~ lassen pass water

wasser-, Wasser-: ~bad *das* (Kochk.) bain-marie; **~ball** *der* **(a)** beachball; **(b)** (Spiel) water polo; **~dampf** *der* steam; **~dicht** *Adj.* waterproof ‹*clothing, watch, etc.*›; watertight ‹*container, seal, etc.*›; **~fall** *der* waterfall; **~farbe** *die* watercolour; **~hahn** *der* water tap; faucet (Amer.)

wässerig ▶ WÄSSRIG

Wasser-: ~kessel *der* kettle; **~leitung** *die* water pipe; (Hauptleitung) water main; **~mann** *der* (Astrol.) **[der] ~mann** Aquarius; **er/sie ist [ein] ~~:** he/she is an Aquarian

wassern *itr. V.; mit sein* land [on the water]

wässern *tr. V.* soak; (Fot.) wash ‹*negative, print*›

wasser-, Wasser-: ~pflanze *die* aquatic plant; **~qualität** *die* water quality; **~rohr** *das* water pipe; **~scheu** *Adj.* scared of water; **~schlauch** *der* [water] hose; **~schutz·polizei** *die* river/lake police; **~ski**[1] *der* waterski; **~ski fahren** waterski; **~ski**[2] *das;* **~~s** waterskiing *no art.;* **~spiegel** *der* **(a)** (Oberfläche) surface [of the water]; **(b)** (Niveau) water level; **~sport** *der* water sport *no art.;* **~spülung** *die* flush

Wasser·stoff *der* hydrogen

Wasser·stoff-: ~bombe *die* hydrogen

bomb; ~per·oxid, ~per·oxyd, ~super·oxid, ~super·oxyd *das* (Chemie) hydrogen peroxide

Wasser-: ~strahl *der* jet of water; **~straße** *die* waterway; **~temperatur** *die* water temperature; **~tiefe** *die* depth of the water; **~tropfen** *der* drop of water; **~turm** *der* water tower; **~werfer** *der* water cannon; **~werk** *das* waterworks *sing.*; **~zeichen** *das* watermark

wässrig, *wäßrig *Adj.* watery

waten *itr. V.; mit sein* wade

Waterloo *das;* **~s, ~s** Waterloo *no art.*; **sein ~ erleben** meet one's Waterloo

watscheln *itr. V.; mit sein* waddle

Watt[1] *das;* **~[e]s, ~en** mudflats *pl.*

Watt[2] *das;* **~s, ~** (Technik, Physik) watt

Watte *die;* **~, ~n** cotton wool

Watte·bausch *der* wad of cotton wool

Watten·meer *das* tidal shallows *pl.*

wattiert *Adj.* quilted; padded ‹*shoulder etc., envelope*›

WC *das;* **~[s], ~[s]** toilet; WC

weben *tr., itr. V.* weave

Weber *der;* **~s, ~, Weberin** *die;* **~, ~nen** weaver

Website /web'saɪt/ *die;* **~, ~s** (DV) Web site

Web·stuhl *der* loom

Wechsel *der;* **~s, ~ (a)** (das Auswechseln) change; (Geldwechsel) exchange
(b) (Aufeinanderfolge) alternation; **im ~:** alternately; (bei mehr als zwei) in rotation
(c) (das Überwechseln) move; (Sport) transfer
(d) (Bankw.) bill of exchange (**über** + *Akk.* for)

wechsel-, Wechsel-: ~geld *das* change; **~haft** *Adj.* changeable; **~jahre** *Pl.* change of life *sing.*; menopause *sing.*; **~kurs** *der* exchange rate

wechseln 1 *tr. V.* **(a)** change; **das Hemd ~:** change one's shirt; **die Wohnung ~:** move home
(b) ([aus]tauschen) exchange ‹*letters, glances, etc.*›
(c) (umwechseln) change ‹*money, note, etc.*› (**in** + *Akk.* into)
2 *itr. V.* change

wechsel-, Wechsel-: ~seitig 1 *Adj.* mutual; 2 *adv.* mutually; **~strom** *der* (Elektrot.) alternating current; **~stube** *die* bureau de change; **~wähler** *der,* **~wählerin** *die* (Politik) floating voter; **~wirkung** *die* interaction

wecken *tr. V.* **jmdn. [aus dem Schlaf] ~:** wake sb. [up]; (fig.: hervorrufen) arouse ‹*interest, curiosity, anger*›

Wecker *der;* **~s, ~:** alarm clock

wedeln *itr. V.* ‹*tail*› wag; **[mit dem Schwanz] ~** ‹*dog*› wag its tail

weder *Konj.* **~ A noch B** neither A nor B

weg *Adv.* away; (verschwunden, weggegangen) gone; **er ist schon seit einer Stunde ~:** he left an hour ago; **weit ~:** far away; a long way away

Weg *der;* **~[e]s,~e (a)** (Fußweg) path; (Feldweg) track
(b) (Zugang) way; (Passage, Durchgang) passage; **sich** (*Dat.*) **einen ~ durch etw. bahnen** clear a path *or* way through sth.
(c) (Route, Verbindung) way; route
(d) (Strecke, Entfernung) distance; (Gang) walk; (Reise) journey; **auf dem kürzesten ~:** by the shortest route; **auf halbem ~[e]** (auch fig.) half-way; **sich auf den ~ machen** set off; **etw. in die ~e leiten** get sth. under way
(e) (ugs.: Besorgung) errand
(f) (Methode) way; (Mittel) means

weg-: ~|bleiben *unr. itr. V.; mit sein* (nicht kommen) stay away; (nicht nach Hause kommen) stay out; **~|bringen** *unr. tr. V.* take away; (zur Reparatur, Wartung usw.) take in

Wegelagerei *die;* **~:** highway robbery

Wegelagerer *der;* **~s, ~:** highwayman

Wegelagerin *die;* **~, ~nen** highwaywoman

wegen *Präp. mit Gen.* **(a)** because of; **~ Umbau[s] geschlossen** closed for alterations
(b) (um ... willen) for the sake of; **~ der Kinder**/(ugs.) **dir** for the children's/your sake
(c) (bezüglich) about; regarding

weg-: ~|fahren 1 *unr. itr. V.; mit sein* **(a)** leave; (im Auto) drive off; (losfahren) set off; **(b)** (irgendwohin fahren) go away; 2 *unr. tr. V.* drive away; (mit dem Handwagen usw.) take away; **~|fallen** *unr. itr. V.; mit sein* be discontinued; (nicht mehr zutreffen) no longer apply; **~|fliegen** *unr. itr. V.; mit sein* fly away; (weggeblasen werden) fly off; **~|gehen** *unr. itr. V.* **(a)** leave; (ugs.: ausgehen) go out; (ugs.: wegziehen) move away; **(b)** (verschwinden) ‹*spot, fog, etc.*› go away; **(c)** (sich entfernen lassen) ‹*stain*› come out; **~|jagen** *tr. V.* chase away; **~|kommen** *unr. itr. V.; mit sein* **(a)** get away; **(b)** (abhanden kommen) go missing; **(c) gut/schlecht** *usw.* **[bei etw.] ~kommen** (ugs.) come off well/badly *etc.* [in sth.]; **~|kriegen** *tr. V.* get rid of ‹*cold, pain, etc.*›; get out, get rid of ‹*stain*›; **~|lassen** *unr. tr. V.* **(a) jmdn. ~lassen** let sb. go; (ausgehen lassen) let sb. go out; **(b)** (auslassen) leave out; omit; **~|laufen** *unr. itr. V.; mit sein* run away (**von, vor** + *Dat.* from); **~|legen** *tr. V.* put aside; (an seinen Platz legen) put away; **~|nehmen** *unr. tr. V.* **(a)** take away; move ‹*head, arm*›; **(b) jmdm. etw. ~nehmen** take sth. away from sb.; **~|schicken** *tr. V.* **(a)** send off ‹*letter, parcel*›; **(b)** send ‹*person*› away; **~|schmeißen** *unr. tr. V.* (ugs.) chuck away (coll.); **~|schnappen** *tr. V.* (ugs.) **jmdm. etw. ~schnappen/vor der Nase ~schnappen** snatch sth. away from sb./from under sb.'s nose; **~|schütten** *tr. V.* pour away; **~|sehen** *unr. itr. V.* look away; **~|stellen** *tr. V.* put away; (beiseite stellen) ⋯

put aside; ~|**stoßen** *unr. tr. V.* push *or* shove away; ~|**tragen** *unr. tr. V.* carry away

Weg·weiser *der;* ~**s**, ~: signpost

weg-: ~|**werfen** *unr. tr. V.* (auch fig.) throw away; ~**werfend** *Adj.* dismissive ‹*gesture, remark*›; ~|**wischen** *tr. V.* wipe away; ~**zappen** (ugs.) [1] *tr. V.* **etw. ~zappen** switch sth. off [by changing channels]; [2] *itr. V.* switch to another channel; ~**ziehen** [1] *unr. tr. V.* pull away; draw back curtain; pull off blanket; [2] *unr. itr. V.; mit sein* **(a)** (umziehen) move away; **(b)** (wandern) ‹*animals, nomads, etc.*› leave [on their migration]

weh (ugs.) *Adj.* sore; *s. auch* WEHTUN

Wehe *die;* ~, ~**n**: ~**n haben** have contractions; **in den ~n liegen** be in labour

wehen *itr. V.* **(a)** (blasen) blow **(b)** (flattern) flutter

weh-, Weh-: ~**leidig** (abwertend) [1] *Adj.* (überempfindlich) soft; (weinerlich) whining *attrib.;* [2] *adv.* self-pityingly; (weinerlich) whiningly; ~**mut** *die;* ~ (geh.) wistful nostalgia; ~**mütig** *Adj.* wistfully nostalgic

Wehr[1] *die;* ~, ~**en: sich [gegen jmdn./etw.] zur ~ setzen** make a stand [against sb./sth.]; resist [sb./sth.]

Wehr[2] *das;* ~**[e]s**, ~**e** weir

Wehrdienst *der* military service *no art.;* **seinen ~ ableisten** do one's military service

Wehr·dienst-: ~**verweigerer** *der;* ~**s**, ~: conscientious objector; ~**verweigerung** *die* conscientious objection

wehren *refl. V.* defend oneself

wehr-, Wehr-: ~**los** *Adj.* defenceless; ~**losigkeit** *die;* ~~: defencelessness; ~**pflicht** *die* military service; **die allgemeine ~pflicht** compulsory military service; ~**pflichtig** *Adj.* liable for military service *postpos.;* ~**sold** *der* military pay; ~**übung** *die* reserve duty [re]training exercise

weh|tun *unr. itr. V.* (ugs.) hurt; **mir tut der Magen/Kopf/Rücken weh** my stomach/head/ back is aching *or* hurts; **jmdm./sich ~**: hurt sb./oneself

Weib *das;* ~**[e]s**, ~**er** (veralt., ugs.) woman; female (derog.)

Weibchen *das;* ~**s**, ~: female

Weiber·held *der* (ugs.) ladykiller

weiblich [1] *Adj.* **(a)** female **(b)** (für die Frau typisch; Sprachw.) feminine [2] *adv.* femininely

Weiblichkeit *die;* ~: femininity

Weibs·bild *das* **(a)** (ugs.) woman **(b)** (salopp abwertend) female

weich [1] *Adj.* (auch fig.) soft; **ein ~es** *od.* **~ gekochtes Ei** a soft-boiled egg [2] *adv.* softly

*old spelling - see note on page xiv

Weiche[1] *die;* ~, ~**n** (Flanke) flank

Weiche[2] *die;* ~, ~**n** points *pl.* (Brit.); switch (Amer.)

weichen *unr. itr. V.; mit sein* move; **vor jmdm./einer Sache ~**: give way to sb./sth.

***weich·gekocht** ▶ WEICH 1

weichlich [1] *Adj.* soft; (ohne innere Festigkeit) weak [2] *adv.* softly

Weich·macher *der* (Chemie, Technik) plasticizer

Weide[1] *die;* ~, ~**n** willow

Weide[2] *die;* ~, ~**n** pasture

weiden *itr., tr. V.* graze

Weiden·kätzchen *das* willow catkin

weigern *refl. V.* refuse

Weigerung *die;* ~, ~**en** refusal

Weih·bischof *der* (kath. Kirche) suffragan bishop

Weihe *die;* ~, ~**n** (Rel.) consecration; (kath. Kirche: Priester-, Bischofsweihe) ordination

weihen *tr. V.* **(a)** (Rel.) consecrate; (zueignen) dedicate (*Dat.* to) **(b)** (kath. Kirche: ordinieren) ordain

Weiher *der;* ~**s**, ~: [small] pond

Weihnachten *das;* ~, ~: Christmas; **frohe** *od.* **fröhliche** *od.* **gesegnete ~!** Merry *or* Happy Christmas!

weihnachtlich *Adj.* Christmassy

Weihnachts-: ~**baum** *der* Christmas tree; ~**feiertag** *der:* **der erste/zweite ~feiertag** Christmas Day/Boxing Day; ~**fest** *das* Christmas; ~**geld** *das* Christmas bonus; ~**geschenk** *das* Christmas present *or* gift; ~**lied** *das* Christmas carol; ~**mann** *der; Pl.* ~**männer** Father Christmas; Santa Claus; ~**markt** *der* Christmas fair; ~**tag** *der:* ▶ ~FEIERTAG; ~**zeit** *die* Christmas time

Weih-: ~**rauch** *der* incense; ~**wasser** *das* (kath. Kirche) holy water

weil *Konj.* because

Weile *die;* ~: while

weilen *itr. V.* (geh.) stay; (sein) be

Wein *der;* ~**[e]s**, ~**e** wine

Wein-: ~**berg** *der* vineyard; ~**berg·schnecke** *die* [edible] snail; ~**brand** *der* brandy

weinen *itr. V.* cry (**über** + *Akk.* over, about); (aus Trauer, Kummer) cry, weep (**um** for)

weinerlich [1] *Adj.* tearful; weepy [2] *adv.* tearfully

wein-, Wein-: ~**essig** *der* wine vinegar; ~**flasche** wine bottle; ~**glas** *das* wineglass; ~**handlung** *die* wine merchant's; ~**karte** *die* wine list; ~**krampf** *der* crying fit; fit of crying; ~**lokal** *das* wine bar; ~**probe** *die* wine-tasting [session]; ~**rebe** *die* grapevine; ~**rot** *Adj.* wine-red; ~**schaum·creme**

die (Kochk.) zabaglione; **~stock** *der; Pl.* **~stöcke** [grape]vine; **~stube** *die* wine bar; **~traube** *die* grape

weise 1 *Adj.* wise
2 *adv.* wisely

Weise *die;* **~, ~n** **(a)** (Art, Verfahren) way
(b) (Melodie) tune; melody

weisen 1 *unr. tr. V.* (geh.: zeigen) show; **jmdn. aus dem Zimmer ~:** send sb. out of the room
2 *unr. itr. V.* (irgendwohin zeigen) point

Weisheit *die;* **~, ~en** **(a)** wisdom
(b) (Erkenntnis) wise insight; (Spruch) wise saying

Weisheits·zahn *der* wisdom tooth

weis|machen *tr. V.* (ugs.) **das kannst du mir nicht ~!** you can't expect me to swallow that!

weiß[1] *1. u. 3. Pers. Sg. Präsens v.* WISSEN

weiß[2] *Adj.* white

Weiß *das;* **~[e]s, ~:** white

weis·sagen *tr. V.* prophesy

Weissagung *die;* **~, ~en** prophecy

Weiß-: ~bier *das* wheat beer; white beer; **~brot** *das* white bread; **~dorn** *der;* **~~s, ~~e** hawthorn

Weiße *der/die; adj. Dekl.* white; white man/woman

weißen *tr. V.* paint white; (tünchen) whitewash

weiß-, Weiß-: ~gold *das* white gold; **~haarig** *Adj.* white-haired; **~haarig sein** have white hair; **~herbst** *der* ≈ rosé wine; **~kohl** *der,* (bes. südd., österr.) **~kraut** *das* white cabbage

weißlich *Adj.* whitish

Weiß·macher *der* whitener

weißt *2. Pers. Sg. Präsens v.* WISSEN

Weiß-: ~wein *der* white wine; **~wurst** *die* veal sausage

Weisung *die;* **~, ~en** (geh., sonst Amtsspr.) instruction; (Direktive) directive

Weisungs·befugnis *die* authority to issue instructions/directives

weit 1 *Adj.* wide; long ‹*way*›; **jmdm. zu ~ sein** ‹*clothes*› be too loose on sb.
2 *adv.* **(a)** (räumlich ausgedehnt) **~ geöffnet** wide open; **~ und breit war niemand zu sehen** there was no one to be seen anywhere; **~ verbreitet** widespread; common; common ‹*plant, animal*›; **~ gereist** widely travelled
(b) (lang) far; **~er** further; farther; **am ~esten** [the] furthest *or* farthest; **~ [entfernt** *od.* **weg] wohnen** live a long way away *or* off; live far away; **~ reichend** long-range; (fig.) far-reaching ‹*importance, consequences*›; sweeping ‹*changes, powers*›; extensive ‹*relations, influence*›; **von ~em** from a distance; **das geht zu ~** (fig.) that is going too far
(c) (zeitlich entfernt) **~ nach Mitternacht** well past midnight
(d) (in der Entwicklung) far

Weit·blick *der* far-sightedness

Weite *die;* **~, ~n** **(a)** (räumliche Ausdehnung) expanse
(b) (bes. Sport: Entfernung) distance
(c) (eines Kleidungsstückes) width

weiten 1 *tr. V.* widen
2 *refl. V.* widen; ‹*pupil*› dilate

weiter *Adv.* **(a)** ▶ WEIT 2;
(b) **und so ~:** and so on
(c) (weithin, anschließend) then
(d) (außerdem, sonst) **~ nichts** nothing more *or* else

weiter... *Adj.* further; **bis auf ~es** for the time being; *s. auch* OHNE

weiter-, Weiter-: ~|bilden *tr. V.:* ▶ FORTBILDEN; **~bildung** *die:* ▶ FORTBILDUNG; **~|bringen** *unr. tr. V.* **die Diskussion brachte uns nicht ~:** the discussion did not get us any further [forward]; **~|erzählen** *tr. V.* **(a)** continue telling; *itr.* **erzähl weiter!** do carry *or* go on; **(b)** (~sagen) pass on; **~|fahren** *unr. itr. V.; mit sein* continue [on one's way]; (weiterreisen) travel on; **~|führen** *tr., itr. V.* continue; **~|geben** *unr. tr. V.* pass on; **~|gehen** *unr. itr. V.; mit sein* go on; **bitte ~gehen!** please move along *or* keep moving!; **~hin** *Adv.* **(a)** (immer noch) still; **(b)** (künftig) in future; **(c)** (außerdem) in addition; **~|kommen** *unr. itr. V.; mit sein* **(a)** get further; **(b)** (Fortschritte machen) make progress; **im Beruf ~kommen** get on in one's career; **~|machen** (ugs.) *itr. V.* carry on; go on; **~|reichen** *tr. V.* pass on; **~|sagen** *tr. V.* pass on; **~|sehen** *unr. itr. V.* see

Weiterungen *Pl.* complications; difficulties

weiter-, Weiter-: ~verarbeiten *tr. V.* process; **~verarbeitung** *die* processing

weit-, Weit-: ~gehend 1 *Adj.* extensive, wide, sweeping ‹*powers*›; far-reaching ‹*support, concessions, etc.*›; wide ‹*support, agreement, etc.*›; general ‹*renunciation*›; 2 *adv.* to a large *or* great extent; ***~gereist** ▶ WEIT 2A; **~hin** *Adv.* for miles around; **~läufig** 1 *Adj.* **(a)** (ausgedehnt) extensive; (geräumig) spacious; **(b)** (entfernt) distant; 2 *adv.* **(a)** (ausgedehnt) spaciously; **(b)** (entfernt) distantly; **~räumig** 1 *Adj.* spacious ‹*room, area, etc.*›; wide ‹*gap, space*›; 2 *adv.* spaciously; ***~reichend** ▶ WEIT 2B; **~sichtig** *Adj.* long-sighted; **~sichtigkeit** *die;* **~~:** long-sightedness; **~sprung** *der* (Sport) long jump (Brit.); broad jump (Amer.); ***~verbreitet** ▶ WEIT 2A; **~winkel·objektiv** *das* wide-angle lens

Weizen *der;* **~s** wheat

Weizen·bier *das:* ▶ WEISSBIER

welch 1 *Interrogativpron.* (bei Wahl aus einer ⋯

W

unbegrenzten Menge) what; (bei Wahl aus einer begrenzten Menge) (*adj.*) which; (*subst.*) which one
[2] *Relativpron.* (bei Menschen) who; (bei Sachen) which
[3] *Indefinitpron.* some; (in Fragen) any

welk *Adj.* withered ‹*skin, hands, etc.*›; wilted ‹*leaves, flower*›; limp ‹*lettuce*›

welken *itr. V.; mit sein* ‹*plant, flower*› wilt

Well·blech *das* corrugated iron

Welle *die;* ~, ~**n** **(a)** (auch fig.) wave; (Rundf.: Wellenlänge) wavelength
(b) (Technik) shaft

wellen-, Wellen-: ~**bad** *das* artificial wave pool; ~**bereich** *der* (Rundf.) waveband; ~**brecher** *der* breakwater; ~**gang** *der* swell; **bei starkem ~gang** in heavy seas; ~**länge** *die* wavelength; ~**sittich** *der* budgerigar

Well·fleisch *das* boiled belly pork

wellig *Adj.* wavy ‹*hair*›; undulating ‹*scenery, hills, etc.*›; uneven ‹*surface, track, etc.*›

Well·pappe *die* corrugated cardboard

Wels *der;* ~**es**, ~**e** catfish

Welt *die;* ~, ~**en** **(a)** world; **auf der ~:** in the world; **die Alte/Neue ~:** the Old/New World; **die Dritte/Vierte ~** the Third/Fourth World; **auf die** *od.* **zur ~ kommen** be born; **alle ~** (fig. ugs.) the whole world; everybody
(b) (Weltall) universe

welt-, Welt-: ~**all** *das* universe; ~**anschauung** *die* world view; ~**ausstellung** *die* world fair; ~**berühmt** *Adj.* world-famous; ~**bevölkerung** *die* world population; population of the world

Welten·bummler *der;* ~**s**, ~, **Welten·bummlerin** *die;* ~, ~**nen** globetrotter

welt-, Welt-: ~**erfolg** *der* worldwide success; ~**fremd** [1] *Adj.* unworldly; [2] *adv.* unrealistically; ~**frieden** *der* world peace; ~**karte** *die* map of the world; ~**klima** *das* world climate; ~**krieg** *der* world war; **der Erste/Zweite ~krieg** the First/Second World War

weltlich *Adj.* **(a)** worldly
(b) (nicht geistlich) secular

welt-, Welt-: ~**literatur** *die* world literature *no art.;* ~**macht** *die* world power; ~**markt** *der* (Wirtsch.) world market; ~**meister** *der,* ~**meisterin** *die* world champion; ~**meisterschaft** *die* world championship; ~**politik** *die* world politics *pl.;* ~**rangliste** *die* world ranking list; world rankings *pl.;* ~**raum** *der* space *no art.;* ~**reise** *die* world tour; ~**rekord** *der* world record; ~**religion** *die* world religion; ~**sicherheits·rat** *der* (Pol.) [United Nations] Security Council; ~**sprache** *die* world language; ~**stadt** *die* cosmopolitan city; ~**weit** [1] *Adj.* worldwide; [2] *adv.* throughout the world; ~**wirtschaft** *die* world economy; ~**wunder** *das:* **die sieben ~wunder** the Seven Wonders of the World

wem *Dat. von* WER [1] *Interrogativpron.* to whom; who … to; **mit/von/zu ~:** with/from/ to whom; who … with/from/to
[2] *Relativpron.* the person to whom …; the person who … to
[3] *Indefinitpron.* (ugs.: jemandem) to somebody *or* someone; (fragend od. verneint) to anybody *or* anyone

wen *Akk. von* WER [1] *Interrogativpron.* whom; who (coll.); **an/für ~:** to/for whom …; who … to/for
[2] *Relativpron.* the person whom
[3] *Indefinitpron.* (ugs.: jemanden) somebody; someone; (fragend od. verneint) anybody; anyone

Wende *die;* ~, ~**n** change (**zu** for)

Wende·kreis *der* **(a)** (Geogr.) tropic
(b) (Kfz-W.) turning circle

Wendel·treppe *die* spiral staircase

wenden[1] [1] *tr., auch itr. V.* (auf die andere Seite) turn [over]; (in die entgegengesetzte Richtung) turn [round]; **bitte ~!** please turn over
[2] *itr. V.* turn [round]
[3] *refl. V.* **sich zum Besseren/Schlechteren ~:** take a turn for the better/worse

wenden[2] [1] *unr.* (*auch regelm.*) *tr. V.* turn
[2] *unr.* (*auch regelm.*) *refl. V.* **(a)** ‹*person*› turn
(b) (sich richten) **sich an jmdn. [um Rat] ~:** turn to sb. [for advice]

Wende-: ~**platz** *der* turning area; ~**punkt** *der* turning point

wendig [1] *Adj.* **(a)** agile; manœuvrable ‹*vehicle, boat, etc.*›
(b) (gewandt) astute
[2] *adv.* **(a)** (beweglich) agilely
(b) (gewandt) astutely

Wendigkeit *die;* ~ **(a)** agility; (eines Flugzeugs) manœuvrability
(b) (Gewandtheit) astuteness

Wendung *die;* ~, ~**en** **(a)** (Änderung der Richtung) turn
(b) (Veränderung) change

wenig [1] *Indefinitpron. u. unbest. Zahlw.* **(a)** *Sing.* little; **das ist ~:** that isn't much; **zu ~ Zeit/Geld haben** not have enough time/ money; **ein Exemplar/50 Euro zu ~:** one copy too few/50 euros too little
(b) *Pl.* a few; **mit ~en Worten** in a few words
[2] *Adv.* little; **~ mehr** not much more

weniger [1] *Komp. von* WENIG; *Indefinitpron. u. unbest. Zahlw.* (+ *Sg.*) less; (+ *Pl.*) fewer; **immer ~:** less and less
[2] *Komp. von* WENIG; *Adv.* less; **das ist ~ angenehm/erfreulich/schön** that is not very pleasant/pleasing/nice; *s. auch* MEHR 1;
[3] *Konj.* less; **fünf ~ drei** five, take away three

*alte Schreibung - vgl. Hinweis auf S. xiv

wenigst... 1 *Sup. von* WENIG 1; least; **am ~en** least
2 *Sup. von* WENIG 2: **am ~en** the least

wenigstens *Adv.* at least

wenn *Konj.* **(a)** (konditional) if; **außer ~:** unless; **~ es nicht anders geht** if there's no other way
(b) (temporal) when; **jedes Mal** *od.* **immer, ~:** whenever
(c) (konzessiv) **wenn ... auch** even though
(d) (in Wunschsätzen) if only

wenn·gleich *Konj.* (geh.) even though; although

wer *Nom. Mask. u. Fem.; s. auch (Gen.)* WESSEN; *(Dat.)* WEM; *(Akk.)* WEN
1 *Interrogativpron.* who; **~ von ...:** which of ...
2 *Relativpron.* the person who; (jeder, der) anyone *or* anybody who
3 *Indefinitpron.* (ugs.: jemand) someone; (in Fragen, Konditionalsätzen) anyone; anybody

Werbe-: ~abteilung *die* advertising *or* publicity department; **~agentur** *die* advertising agency; **~aktion** *die* advertising campaign; **~block** *der; pl.* **~blöcke** commercial break; **~fernsehen** *das* television commercials *pl.;* **~funk** *der* radio commercials *pl.;* **~geschenk** *das* [promotional] free gift

werben 1 *unr. itr. V.* advertise; **für etw. ~:** advertise sth.
2 *unr. tr. V.* attract ‹*readers, customers, etc.*›; recruit ‹*soldiers, members, etc.*›

Werbe-: ~pause *die* commercial break; **~spot** *der* commercial; advertisement; ad (coll.); **~spruch** *der* advertising slogan

Werbung *die;* **~:** advertising; **für etw. ~ machen** advertise sth.

Werde·gang *der* career

werden 1 *unr. itr. V.; mit sein* become; get; **älter ~:** get *or* grow old[er]; **wahnsinnig** *od.* **verrückt ~:** go mad; **das muss anders ~:** things have to change; **wach ~:** wake up; **rot ~:** go *or* turn red; **Arzt/Professor ~:** become a doctor/professor; **zu etw. ~:** become sth.; **es wird [höchste] Zeit** it is [high] time; **es wird 10 Uhr** it is nearly 10 o'clock; **es wird Herbst** autumn is coming; **sind die Fotos [etwas] geworden?** (ugs.) have the photos turned out [well]?
2 *Hilfsverb; 2. Part.* **worden (a)** (zur Bildung des Futurs) **wir ~ uns um ihn kümmern** we will take care of him; **es wird gleich regnen** it is going to rain any minute; **es wird um die 80 Euro kosten** (ich vermute, es kostet um die 80 Euro) it will cost around 80 euros
(b) (zur Bildung des Passivs) **du wirst gerufen** you are being called; **er wurde gebeten** he was asked

werfen 1 *unr. tr. V.* throw; drop ‹*bombs*›
2 *unr. itr. V.* **(a)** throw; **mit etw. ~:** throw sth.
(b) (Junge kriegen) give birth; ‹*dog, cat*› litter
3 *unr. refl. V.* throw oneself; **sich vor einen Zug ~:** throw oneself under a train

Werft *die;* **~, ~en** shipyard

Werk *das;* **~[e]s, ~e (a)** work
(b) (Betrieb, Fabrik) factory; works *sing. or pl.;* **ab ~:** ex works

Werk·bank *die; Pl.* **Werkbänke** workbench

werken *itr. V.* work

Werken *das;* **~s** (Schulw.) handicraft

Werk[s]-: ~angehörige *der/die* factory *or* works employee; **~arzt** *der*, **~ärztin** *die* factory *or* works doctor

werk-, Werk-: ~statt *die;* **~statt, ~stätten** workshop; (Kfz-W.) garage; **~stoff** *der* material; **~tag** *der* working day; workday; **~tags** *Adv.* on weekdays; **~tätig** *Adj.* working; **~tätige** *der/die; adj. Dekl.* worker; **~zeug** *das* (auch fig.) tool; (Gesamtheit von Werkzeugen) tools *pl.*

Werkzeug-: ~kasten *der* toolbox; **~macher** *der*, **~macherin** *die* tool maker

Wermut *der;* **~[e]s, ~s (a)** (Pflanze) wormwood
(b) (Wein) vermouth

wert *Adj.* (geh.) esteemed; (als Anrede) my dear ...; **etw./nichts ~ sein** be worth sth./be worthless

Wert *der;* **~[e]s, ~e** value; **im ~[e] von ...:** worth ...; **~ auf etw.** *(Akk.)* **legen** set great store by *or* on sth.

wert·beständig *Adj.* of lasting value *postpos.*

werten *tr., itr. V.* judge; assess

wert-, Wert-: ~gegenstand *der* valuable object; **~gegenstände** valuables; **~los** *Adj.* worthless; valueless; **~papier** *das* (Wirtsch.) security; **~sache** *die* valuable item; **~sachen** valuables; **~sendung** *die* (Postw.) registered item; **~stoff** *der* recyclable material

Wertung *die;* **~, ~en** judgement

Wert·urteil *das* value judgement

wert·voll *Adj.* valuable; (moralisch) estimable

Wesen *das;* **~s** nature

wesentlich 1 *Adj.* fundamental (**für** to); **im W~en** essentially
2 *adv.* (erheblich) considerably; much

wes·halb *Adv.* ▶ WARUM

Wespe *die;* **~, ~n** wasp

Wespen·nest *das* wasp's nest; **in ein ~stechen** (fig. ugs.) stir up a hornets' nest

wessen *Interrogativpron.* **(a)** *Gen. von* WER whose
(b) *Gen. von* WAS: **~ wird er beschuldigt?** what is he accused of?

Wessi *der;* **~s, ~s** (salopp) West German

West (bes. Seemannsspr., Met.) ▶ WESTEN

west·deutsch *Adj.* Western German; (hist.: auf die alte BRD bezogen) West German

West·deutschland *(das)* Western Germany; (hist.: alte BRD) West Germany
Weste *die;* ~, ~**n** waistcoat (Brit.); vest (Amer.)
Westen *der;* ~**s** west; **der** ~: the West
Western *der;* ~[**s**], ~: western
West·europa *(das)* Western Europe
Westfalen *(das);* ~**s** Westphalia
westfälisch *Adj.* Westphalian
West·indien *(das)* the West Indies *pl.*
westlich [1] *Adj.* **(a)** western **(b)** (nach Westen) westerly **(c)** (aus dem Westen) Western [2] *adv.* westwards [3] *Präp. mit Gen.* [to the] west of
west·wärts *Adv.* [to the] west
West·wind *der* west[erly] wind
wes·wegen *Adv.* ▶ WARUM
Wett·bewerb *der;* ~[**e**]**s**, ~**e** **(a)** competition **(b)** (Wirtsch.) competition *no indef. art.*
Wette *die;* ~, ~**n** bet; **eine** ~ [**mit jmdm.**] **abschließen** make a bet [with sb.]; **mit jmdm. um die** ~ **laufen** race sb.
wett·eifern *itr. V.; 2. Part.* **gewetteifert: mit jmdm.** [**um etw.**] ~: compete with sb. [for sth.]
wetten *itr. V.* bet; **mit jmdm.** ~: have a bet with sb.; **mit jmdm. um etw.** ~: bet sb. sth.
Wetter *das;* ~**s** weather
wetter-, Wetter-: ~**aussichten** *Pl.* weather outlook *sing.;* ~**bedingungen** *Pl.* weather conditions; ~**bericht** *der* weather report; (Vorhersage) weather forecast; ~**dienst** *der* weather *or* meteorological service; ~**fühlig** *Adj.* sensitive to [changes in] the weather *postpos.;* ~**fühligkeit** *die;* ~~: sensitivity to [changes in] the weather; ~**karte** *die* weather chart; weather map; ~**lage** *die* weather situation; ~**satellit** *der* weather satellite; ~**vorhersage** *die* weather forecast; ~**warte** *die* weather station
wett-, Wett-: ~**kampf** *der* competition; ~**lauf** *der* race; ~|**machen** *tr. V.* make up for (**durch** with); ~**rennen** *das* race; ~**rüsten** *das;* ~~**s** arms race; ~**streit** *der* contest
wetzen *tr. V.* sharpen; whet
WEZ *Abk.* = **Westeuropäische Zeit** GMT
Whirlpool /'wə:lpu:l/ *der;* ~**s**, ~**s** whirlpool [bath]
Whiskey /'vɪski/ *der;* ~**s** ~**s** whiskey
Whisky /'vɪski/ *der;* ~**s**, ~**s** whisky
wich *1. u. 3. Pers. Sg. Prät. v.* WEICHEN
wichtig *Adj.* important
Wichtigkeit *die;* ~: importance
Wicke *die;* ~, ~**n** vetch; (im Garten) sweet pea

*old spelling - see note on page xiv

Wickel *der;* ~**s**, ~: compress
wickeln *tr. V.* wind; (einwickeln) wrap (**in** + *Akk.* in); (auswickeln) unwrap (**aus** + *Dat.* from); (abwickeln) unwind (**von** from); **ein Kind** ~: change a baby's nappy
Widder *der;* ~**s**, ~: **(a)** ram **(b)** (Astrol.) Aries
wider *Präp. mit Akk.* (geh.) against
wider-: ~**fahren** *unr. itr. V.; mit sein* (geh.) **etw.** ~**fährt jmdm.** sth. happens to sb.; ~**legen** *tr. V.* **etw.** ~**legen** refute sth.; **jmdn.** ~**legen** prove sb. wrong
widerlich [1] *Adj.* revolting; repulsive ‹*person, behaviour, etc.*›; awful ‹*headache*› [2] *adv.* revoltingly; ‹*behave*› in a repugnant *or* repulsive manner; awfully ‹*cold, sweet, etc.*›
Widerlichkeit *die;* ~, ~**en** (abwertend) **(a)** repulsiveness **(b)** (Äußerung/Handlung) revolting remark/ action
wider-, Wider-: ~**rede** *die:* **keine** ~**rede!** don't argue!; ~**ruf** *der* retraction; [**bis**] **auf** ~**ruf** until revoked; ~**rufen** /--'--/ *unr. tr., auch itr. V.* retract ‹*statement, claim, confession, etc.*›; ~**setzen** /--'--/ *refl. V.* **sich jmdm./einer Sache** ~**setzen** oppose sb./sth.; ~**spenstig** [1] *Adj.* unruly; stubborn ‹*horse, mule, etc.*›; [2] *adv.* wilfully; ~|**spiegeln,** ~**spiegeln** /--'--/ [1] *tr. V.* mirror; (fig.) reflect; [2] *refl. V.* be mirrored; (fig.) be reflected; ~**sprechen** /--'--/ *unr. itr. V.* contradict; ~**spruch** *der* **(a)** (Widerrede, Protest) opposition; protest; **(b)** (etw. Unvereinbares) contradiction; **in** ~**spruch zu** *od.* **mit etw. stehen** contradict sth.; be contradictory to sth.; ~**sprüchlich** *Adj.* contradictory ‹*news, statements, etc.*›; inconsistent ‹*behaviour, attitude, etc.*›
Wider·stand *der* **(a)** resistance (**gegen** to) **(b)** (Hindernis) opposition
widerstands-, Widerstands-: ~**fähig** *Adj.* robust; resistant ‹*material etc.*›; hardy ‹*animal, plant*›; ~**fähigkeit** *die* robustness; (von Material usw.) resistance; (von Tier, Pflanze) hardiness; ~**los** *Adj., adv.* without resistance *postpos.*
wider-, Wider-: ~**stehen** /--'--/ *unr. itr. V.* **(a)** (nicht nachgeben) [**jmdm./einer Sache**] ~**stehen** resist [sb./sth.]; **(b)** (standhalten) **jmdm./einer Sache** ~**stehen** withstand sb./ sth.; ~**streben** /--'--/ *itr. V.* **etw.** ~**strebt jmdm.** sb. dislikes *or* detests sth.; ~**wärtig** [1] *Adj.* revolting, repugnant ‹*smell, taste, etc.*›; offensive ‹*person, behaviour, etc.*›; [2] *adv.* ‹*behave etc.*› in an offensive manner; ~**wille** *der* aversion (**gegen** to); ~**willig** [1] *Adj.* reluctant; unwilling; [2] *adv.* reluctantly; unwillingly
widmen [1] *tr. V.* **(a)** dedicate **(b)** (verwenden für/auf) devote [2] *refl. V.* **sich jmdm./einer Sache** ~: attend to sb./sth.; (ausschließlich) devote oneself to sb./sth.

Widmung *die;* ~, **~en** dedication (**an** + *Akk.* to)
widrig *Adj.* unfavourable; adverse
Widrigkeit *die;* ~, **~en** adversity
wie [1] *Interrogativadv.* how; **~ viel/viele** how much/many; **~ [bitte]?** [I beg your] pardon?; **~ spät ist es?** what time is it?
[2] *Relativadv.* **~ er es tut** the way *or* manner in which he does it
[3] *Konj.* **(a)** *Vergleichspartikel* as; **[so] … ~ …**: as … as …; **ich fühlte mich ~ …**: I felt as if I were …; **„N" ~ „Nordpol"** N for November
(b) (zum Beispiel) like; such as
(c) (und, sowie) as well as; both
wieder *Adv.* again; **alles ist ~ beim Alten** everything is back as it was before; **ich bin gleich ~ da** I'll be right back (coll.); **etw. ~ finden** find sth. again; **etw. ~ gutmachen** make sth. good; put sth. right; **den Schaden ~ gutmachen** pay for the damage; **jmdn. ~ wählen** re-elect sb.; **jmdn. ~ beleben** revive *or* resuscitate sb.; **jmdn./etw. ~ erkennen** recognize sb./sth.
wieder-, Wieder-: ~aufbau /--'--/ *der* reconstruction; rebuilding; **der wirtschaftliche ~aufbau** economic recovery; **~|bekommen** *unr. tr. V.* get back; ***~|beleben** ▶ WIEDER; **~belebungs·versuch** *der* attempt at resuscitation; **~eingliederung** *die* reintegration (**in** + *Akk.* in); ***~|erkennen** ▶ WIEDER; ***~|finden** ▶ WIEDER; **~gabe** *die* (Bericht) report; (Übersetzung) rendering; (Reproduktion) reproduction; **~|geben** *unr. tr. V.* **(a)** (zurückgeben) give back; **(b)** (berichten) report; (wiederholen) repeat; **~geburt** *die* (christl. Rel., fig. geh.) rebirth
***wieder·gut|machen** ▶ WIEDER
wieder|haben *unr. tr. V.* (auch fig.) have back
wieder-: ~her|stellen *tr. V.* **(a)** re-establish ‹*contact, peace*›; **(b)** (reparieren) restore ‹*building*›; **~holen** [1] *tr. V.* repeat; (repetieren) revise ‹*lesson, vocabulary, etc.*›;
[2] *refl. V.* **(a)** (wieder dasselbe sagen) repeat oneself; **(b)** (erneut geschehen) happen again; **(c)** (wiederkehren) be repeated; recur
wieder|holen *tr. V.* fetch *or* get back
wiederholt [1] *Adj.* repeated
[2] *adv.* repeatedly
Wiederholung *die;* ~, **~en** repetition; (eines Fußballspiels usw.) replay; (einer Sendung) repeat; (einer Aufführung) repeat performance; (von Lernstoff) revision
Wiederholungs·täter *der*, **Wiederholungs·täterin** *die* habitual offender
Wieder·hören *das:* **[auf** *od.* **Auf] ~!** goodbye! (*at end of telephone call*)
wieder-, Wieder-: ~kehr *die;* ~~ (geh.) return; **~|kehren** *itr. V.; mit sein* (geh.) return; **~|kommen** *unr. itr. V.; mit sein* **(a)** (zurückkommen) return; come back; **(b)** (noch einmal kommen) come back *or* again; **(c)** (sich noch einmal ereignen) ‹*opportunity, past*› come again; **~|kriegen** *tr. V.* (ugs.) get back; **~schauen** *das:* **[auf] ~schauen!** (südd., österr.) goodbye!; **~|sehen** *unr. tr. V.* see again; **~sehen** *das;* **~s**, ~: reunion; **[auf] ~sehen!** goodbye!; **~um** *Adv.* **(a)** (erneut) again; **(b)** (andererseits) on the other hand; **~verwendung** *die* reuse; **~verwertung** *die* recycling; **~wahl** *die* re-election; ***~|wählen** *tr. V.* WIEDER
Wiege *die;* ~, **~n** (auch fig.) cradle
wiegen¹ *unr. itr., tr. V.* weigh
wiegen² *tr. V.* rock; shake ‹*head*›
Wiegen·lied *das* lullaby; cradle song
wiehern *itr. V.* whinny; (lauter) neigh
Wien (*das*); **~s** Vienna
Wiener¹ *der;* **~s**, ~: Viennese
Wiener² *Adj.* Viennese; *s. auch* WÜRSTCHEN
Wienerin *die;* ~, **~nen** Viennese
wienerisch *Adj.* Viennese
wies *1. u. 3. Pers. Sg. Prät. v.* WEISEN
Wiese *die;* ~, **~n** meadow; (Rasen) lawn
wie·so *Interrogativadv.* why
***wie·viel** /*od.* '--/ ▶ VIEL, WIE, UHR B
wie·viel·mal /*od.* -'--/ *Interrogativadv.* how many times
wievielt… /*od.* '--/ *Interrogativadj.* **der ~e Band?** which number volume?; **der Wievielte ist heute?** what is the date today?
wie·weit *Interrogativadv.* to what extent; how far
wild [1] *Adj.* (auch fig.) wild; (wütend) furious ‹*cursing, shouting, etc.*›; **~es Parken** illegal parking; **~er Streik** wildcat strike; **~ auf etw./jmdn. sein** (ugs.) be mad *or* crazy about sth./sb. (coll.); **~ werden** get furious; **jmdn. ~ machen** infuriate sb.
[2] *adv.* **(a)** wildly; **wie ~** (ugs.) like mad (coll.)
(b) (ordnungswidrig) illegally
Wild *das;* **~[e]s** **(a)** (Tiere, Fleisch) game
(b) (einzelnes Tier) [wild] animal
Wild·bret /-brɛt/ *das;* **~s** (geh.) game
Wilde *der/die; adj. Dekl.* savage
Wilderei *die;* ~, **~en** poaching *no pl., no art.*
Wilderer *der;* **~s**, ~, **Wilderin** *die;* ~, **~nen** poacher
wild·fremd *Adj.* completely strange
Wild·gans *die* wild goose
Wildheit *die;* ~: wildness
Wild-: ~katze *die* wild cat; **~leder** *das* suede
Wildnis *die;* ~, **~se** wilderness
Wild-: ~pferd *das* wild horse; **~schwein** *das* wild boar; **~wasser** *das Pl.* ~~: mountain torrent; **~wechsel** *der* game crossing; **~west·film** *der* western
will *1. u. 3. Pers. Sg. Präsens v.* WOLLEN
Wille *der;* **~ns** will; (Wunsch) wish

W

willen *Präp. mit Gen.* **um jmds./einer Sache ~**: for sb.'s/sth.'s sake
Willen *der;* **~s** ▶ WILLE
willen·los [1] *Adj.* will-less
[2] *adv.* will-lessly
willens *Adj.* **~ sein, etw. zu tun** (geh.) be willing to do sth.
willens-, Willens-: ~schwach *Adj.* weak-willed; **~schwäche** *die* weakness of will; **~stark** *Adj.* strong-willed; **~stärke** *die* strength of will
willentlich [1] *Adj.* deliberate
[2] *adv.* deliberately; on purpose
willig [1] *Adj.* willing
[2] *adv.* willingly
will·kommen *Adj.* welcome; **jmdn. ~ heißen** welcome sb.
Will·kür *die;* **~**: arbitrary use of power; (Handlung o. Ä.) arbitrariness
willkürlich [1] *Adj.* arbitrary; (vom Willen gesteuert) voluntary ‹*muscle, movement, etc.*›
[2] *adv.* arbitrarily; (vom Willen gesteuert) voluntarily
wimmeln *itr. V.* **von Fischen/Fehlern ~**: be teeming with fish/mistakes
wimmern *itr. V.* whimper
Wimpel *der;* **~s, ~**: pennant
Wimper *die;* **~, ~n** [eye]lash
Wimpern·tusche *die* mascara
Wind *der;* **~[e]s, ~e** wind
Wind·beutel *der* cream puff
Winde *die;* **~, ~n** winch
Windel *die;* **~, ~n** nappy (Brit.); diaper (Amer.)
Windel·höschen *das* nappy pants *pl.*
winden [1] *unr. tr. V.* (geh.) make ‹*wreath, garland*›; **etw. um etw. ~**: wind sth. around sth.
[2] *unr. refl. V.* ‹*plant, tendrils*› wind (**um** around); ‹*snake*› coil [itself], wind itself (**um** around); **sich vor Schmerzen ~**: writhe in pain
Windes·eile *die:* **in ~**: in next to no time
Wind-: ~hose *die* (Met.) whirlwind; **~hund** *der* greyhound
windig *Adj.* windy
Wind-: ~kanal *der* (Technik) wind tunnel; **~mühle** *die* windmill; **~pocken** *Pl.* chickenpox *sing.;* **~schatten** *der* lee; **~schutz·scheibe** *die* windscreen (Brit.); windshield (Amer.); **~stärke** *die:* **~stärke 7/9** *usw.* wind force 7/9 *etc.;* **~still** *Adj.* windless; still; **~stoß** *der* gust of wind; **~surfer** *der,* **~surferin** *die* windsurfer; **~surfing** *das;* **~~s** windsurfing *no art.*
Windung *die;* **~, ~en (a)** bend
(b) (spiralförmiger Verlauf) spiral; (einer Spule usw.) winding
Wink *der;* **~[e]s, ~e** sign; (Hinweis) hint; (Ratschlag) tip; hint

*alte Schreibung - vgl. Hinweis auf S. xiv

Winkel *der;* **~s, ~ (a)** (Math.) angle; **toter ~**: blind spot
(b) (Ecke; auch fig.) corner
winkelig *Adj.* twisty ‹*streets*›
winken [1] *itr. V.* **(a)** wave; **mit etw. ~**: wave sth.
(b) (auffordern heranzukommen) **jmdm. ~**: beckon sb. over; **einem Taxi ~**: hail a taxi
[2] *tr. V.* beckon; **jmdn. zu sich ~**: beckon sb. over [to one]
winklig *Adj.* ▶ WINKELIG
winseln *itr. V.* ‹*dog*› whimper
Winter *der;* **~s, ~**: winter
Winter-: ~anfang *der* beginning of winter; **~garten** *der* conservatory
winterlich [1] *Adj.* wintry; winter *attrib.* ‹*clothing, break*›
[2] *adv.* **~ kalt** cold and wintry
Winter-: ~reifen *der* winter tyre; **~schlussverkauf,** ***~schlußverkauf** *der* winter sale[s *pl.*]; **~sport** *der* winter sports *pl.;* **~urlaub** *der* winter holiday; **~zeit** *die* wintertime
Winzer *der;* **~s, ~, Winzerin** *die;* **~, ~nen** winegrower
winzig [1] *Adj.* tiny
[2] *adv.* **~ klein** tiny; minute
Winzigkeit *die;* **~, ~en (a)** tininess; minuteness
(b) (Kleinigkeit) tiny thing; triviality
Wipfel *der;* **~s, ~**: treetop
Wippe *die;* **~, ~n** see-saw
wippen *itr. V.* bob up and down; (hin und her) bob about; (auf einer Wippe) see-saw
wir *Personalpron.; 1. Pers. Pl. Nom.* we; *s. auch (Gen.)* UNSER; *(Dat.)* UNS; *(Akk.)* UNS
wirb *Imperativ Sg. v.* WERBEN
Wirbel *der;* **~s, ~ (a)** (kreisende Bewegung) (im Wasser) whirlpool; (in der Luft) whirlwind; (kleiner) eddy; (von Rauch, beim Tanz) whirl
(b) (Trubel) hurly-burly
(c) (Aufsehen) fuss
(d) (Anat.) vertebra
wirbeln [1] *itr. V. mit sein* whirl; ‹*water, snowflakes*› swirl
[2] *tr. V.* swirl ‹*leaves, dust*›; whirl ‹*dancer*›
Wirbel-: ~säule *die* spinal column; **~sturm** *der* cyclone
wirbt *3. Pers. Sg. Präsens v.* WERBEN
wird *3. Pers. Sg. Präsens v.* WERDEN
wirf *Imperativ Sg. v.* WERFEN
wirft *3. Pers. Sg. Präsens v.* WERFEN
wirken *itr. V.* **(a)** (eine Wirkung haben) have an effect; **gegen etw. ~**: be effective against sth.
(b) (erscheinen) seem; appear
wirklich [1] *Adj.* real
[2] *Adv.* really
Wirklichkeit *die;* **~, ~en** reality; **in ~**: in reality
wirksam [1] *Adj.* effective
[2] *adv.* effectively
Wirksamkeit *die;* **~**: effectiveness

Wirk·stoff *der* active agent

Wirkung *die;* **~, ~en** effect (**auf** + *Akk.* on); **mit ~ vom 1. Juli** (Amtsspr.) with effect from 1 July

wirkungs-, Wirkungs-: ~grad *der* (Technik) efficiency; **~los** [1] *Adj.* ineffective; [2] *adv.* ineffectively; **~losigkeit** *die;* **~~:** ineffectiveness; **~voll** [1] *Adj.* effective; [2] *adv.* effectively

wirr *Adj.* (unordentlich) tousled ‹*hair, beard*›; tangled ‹*ropes, roots*›; (unklar, verwirrt) confused

Wirren *Pl.* turmoil *sing.*

Wirrwarr *der;* **~s** chaos; (von Stimmen) clamour

Wirsing *der;* **~s, Wirsing·kohl** *der* savoy [cabbage]

Wirt *der;* **~[e]s, ~e** landlord

Wirtin *die;* **~, ~nen** landlady

Wirtschaft *die;* **~, ~en (a)** economy; (Geschäftsleben) commerce and industry
(b) (Gaststätte) public house; pub (Brit. coll.); bar (Amer.)
(c) (Haushalt) household
(d) (ugs. abwertend: Unordnung) mess; shambles *sing.*

wirtschaften *itr. V.* **mit dem Geld gut ~:** manage one's money well; **mit Verlust/Gewinn ~:** run at a loss/profit

wirtschaftlich [1] *Adj.* **(a)** economic
(b) (finanziell) financial
(c) (sparsam, rentabel) economical
[2] *adv.; s. Adj.:* economically; financially

Wirtschaftlichkeit *die;* **~:** economic viability

Wirtschafts-: ~hilfe *die* economic aid *no indef. art.;* **~krieg** *der* economic war; (Kriegsführung) economic warfare; **~kriminalität** *die* economic crime *no art.;* **~krise** *die* economic crisis; **~lehre** *die* economics *sing.;* **~minister** *der,* **~ministerin** *die* minister for economic affairs; **~politik** *die* economic policy; **~union** *die* economic union; *s. auch* WÄHRUNGSUNION; **~wunder** *das* (ugs.) economic miracle

Wirts-: ~haus *das* pub (Brit. coll.); **~leute** *Pl.* landlord and landlady

Wisch *der;* **~[e]s, ~e** (salopp) piece *or* bit of paper

wischen *itr., tr. V.* wipe; **Staub ~:** do the dusting; dust

wispern *itr., tr. V.* whisper

wiss-, *wiß-, Wiss, *Wiß-: ~begier, ~begierde *die* thirst for knowledge; **~begierig** *Adj.* eager for knowledge; ‹*child*› eager to learn

wissen [1] *unr. tr. V.* know; **von jmdm./etw. nichts [mehr] ~ wollen** want to have nothing [more] to do with sb./sth.
[2] *unr. itr. V.* **von etw./um etw. ~:** know about sth.

Wissen *das;* **~s** knowledge; **meines/unseres ~s** to my/our knowledge

Wissenschaft *die;* **~, ~en** science

Wissenschaftler *der;* **~s ~, Wissenschaftlerin** *die;* **~, ~nen** academic; (Naturwissenschaft) scientist

wissenschaftlich [1] *Adj.* scholarly; (naturwissenschaftlich) scientific
[2] *adv.* in a scholarly manner; (naturwissenschaftlich) scientifically

wissens·wert *Adj.* **~ sein** be worth knowing

wissentlich [1] *Adj.* deliberate
[2] *adv.* knowingly; deliberately

wittern [1] *itr. V.* sniff the air
[2] *tr. V.* get wind of; (fig.: ahnen) sense

Witterung *die;* **~, ~en (a)** (Wetter) weather *no indef. art;*
(b) (Jägerspr.) (Geruchssinn) sense of smell; (Geruch) scent

Witwe *die;* **~, ~n** widow; **~ werden** be widowed

Witwen·rente *die* widow's pension

Witwer *der;* **~s, ~:** widower; **~ werden** be widowed

Witz *der;* **~es, ~e** joke

Witz-: ~blatt *das* humorous magazine; **~bold** *der;* **~~es, ~~e** joker

Witzelei *die;* **~, ~en (a)** teasing
(b) (witzelnde Bemerkung) joke

witzeln *itr. V.* joke (**über** + *Akk.* about)

Witz·figur *die* **(a)** (in Witzen) joke character
(b) (ugs. abwertend) figure of fun

witzig [1] *Adj.* funny
[2] *adv.* amusingly

witz·los *Adj.* **(a)** dull
(b) (ugs.: sinnlos) pointless

wo [1] *Adv.* where
[2] *Konj.* **(a)** (da, weil) seeing that
(b) (obwohl) although; when

wo·anders *Adv.* somewhere else

wo·bei *Adv.* **(a)** (interrogativ) **~ hast du sie ertappt?** what did you catch her doing?
(b) (relativisch) **er gab sechs Schüsse ab, ~ einer der Täter getötet wurde** he fired six shots – one of the criminals was killed

Woche *die;* **~, ~n** week; **in dieser/der nächsten/der letzten ~:** this/next/last week; **heute in/vor einer ~:** a week today/a week ago today

wochen-, Wochen-: ~bett *das:* **im ~bett liegen** be lying in; **~ende** *das* weekend; **~lang** [1] *Adj.* lasting weeks *postpos;* [2] *adv.* for weeks [on end]; **~stunde** *die* (Schulw.) period per week; **~tag** *der* weekday (*including Saturday*); **~tags** *Adv.* on weekdays [and Saturdays]

wöchentlich *Adj., adv.* weekly

Wochen·zeitung *die* weekly newspaper

-wöchig (a) (... Wochen alt) ... -week-old
(b) (... Wochen dauernd) ... week's/weeks'; ...-week

W

Wöchnerin *die;* ~, ~**nen** woman who has just given birth

Wodka *der;* ~**s,** ~**s** vodka

wo·durch *Adv.* **(a)** (interrogativ) how **(b)** (relativisch) as a result of which

wo·für *Adv.* **(a)** (interrogativ) for what **(b)** (relativisch) for which

wog *1. u. 3. Pers. Sg. Prät. v.* WIEGEN

Woge *die;* ~, ~**n** wave

wo·gegen [1] *Adv.* **(a)** (interrogativ) against what; what ... against **(b)** (relativisch) against which; which ... against [2] *Konj.* whereas

wogen *itr. V.* (geh.) ‹*sea*› surge; (fig.) ‹*corn*› wave

wo·her *Adv.* **(a)** (interrogativ) where ... from; ~ **weißt du das?** how do you know that? **(b)** (relativisch) where ... from

wo·hin *Adv.* **(a)** (interrogativ) where [... to] **(b)** (relativisch) where

wo·hingegen *Konj.* whereas

wohl [1] *Adv.* **(a)** well; **jmdm. ist nicht** ~, **jmd. fühlt sich nicht** ~: sb. does not feel well **(b)** (behaglich) at ease; happy; **leb** ~**!/leben Sie** ~**!** farewell! **(c)** (durchaus) well **(d)** (ungefähr) about **(e) etw. tut jmdm.** ~: sth. does sb. good [2] *Partikel* probably; ~ **kaum** hardly

Wohl *das;* ~**[e]s** welfare; **auf jmds.** ~ **trinken** drink sb.'s health; **zum** ~**!** cheers!

wohl-, Wohl-: ~**auf** /-'-/ *Adj.* (geh.) ~**auf sein** be well; ~**befinden** *das* well-being; ~**behagen** *das* sense of well-being; ~**behalten** *Adj.* safe and well ‹*person*›; undamaged ‹*thing*›; ~**fahrts·staat** *der* welfare state; ~**gefallen** *das;* ~~**s** pleasure; ~**gemerkt** *Adv.* please note; ~**habend** *Adj.* prosperous; ~**habenheit** *die;* ~~: prosperity

wohlig [1] *Adj.* pleasant; agreeable [2] *adv.* ‹*sigh, purr, etc.*› with pleasure

wohl-, Wohl-: ~**klang** *der* (geh.) melodious sound; ~**schmeckend** *Adj.* (geh.) delicious; ~**stand** *der* prosperity; ~**stands·gesellschaft** *die* affluent society; ~**tat** *die* **(a)** (gute Tat) good deed; (Gefallen) favour; **(b)** (*Genuss*) blissful relief; ~**tätig** *Adj.* charitable; ~**tuend** *Adj.* agreeable; *~|**tun** ▶ WOHL 1 E; ~**verdient** *Adj.* well-earned; ~**weislich** *Adv.* deliberately; ~**wollen** *das;* ~~**s** goodwill; ~**wollend** [1] *Adj.* benevolent; favourable ‹*judgement, opinion*›; [2] *adv.* benevolently; ‹*judge, consider*› favourably

Wohn-: ~**anhänger** *der* caravan; trailer (Amer.); ~**block** *der; Pl.* ~~**s,** *od.* ~**blöcke** residential block

wohnen *itr. V.* live; (kurzfristig) stay

wohn-, Wohn-: ~**gemeinschaft** *die* group sharing a flat (Brit.) *or* (Amer.) apartment/house; ~**haft** *Adj.* resident (**in** + *Dat.* in); ~**heim** *das* (für Alte, Behinderte) home; (für Obdachlose, Lehrlinge) hostel; (für Studenten) hall of residence

wohnlich *Adj.* homely

Wohn-: ~**mobil** *das;* ~~**s,** ~~**e** motor home; ~**ort** *der* place of residence; ~**siedlung** *die* residential estate; (mit gleichartigen Häusern) housing estate; ~**sitz** *der* place of residence; **ohne festen** ~**sitz** of no fixed abode

Wohnung *die;* ~, ~**en** **(a)** flat (Brit.); apartment (Amer.) **(b)** (Unterkunft) lodging

Wohnungs-: ~**not** *die* housing crisis; serious housing shortage; ~**schlüssel** *der* key to the flat (Brit.) *or* (Amer.) apartment; ~**suche** *die* search for a flat (Brit.) *or* (Amer.) apartment; **auf** ~**suche sein** be flat-hunting; ~**tür** *die* door of the flat (Brit.) *or* (Amer.) apartment; ~**verlust** *der* loss of one's home

Wohn-: ~**verhältnisse** *Pl.* living conditions; ~**wagen** *der* caravan; trailer (Amer.); ~**zimmer** *das* living room

wölben [1] *tr. V.* curve; vault, arch ‹*roof, ceiling*› [2] *refl. V.* curve; ‹*bridge, ceiling*› arch

Wölbung *die;* ~, ~**en** curve; (einer Decke) arch; vault

Wolf *der;* ~**[e]s, Wölfe** wolf

Wolke *die;* ~, ~**n** cloud

wolken-, Wolken-: ~**bruch** *der* cloudburst; ~**bruch·artig** *Adj.* torrential; ~**decke** *die* [unbroken] cloud *no indef. art.;* **die** ~**decke riss auf** the clouds broke; ~**kratzer** *der* skyscraper; ~**los** *Adj.* cloudless

wolkig *Adj.* cloudy

Wolle *die;* ~, ~**n** wool

wollen[1] *Adj.* woollen

wollen[2] [1] *unr. Modalverb; 2. Part. wollen:* **etw. tun** ~ (den Wunsch haben, etw. zu tun) want to do sth.; (die Absicht haben, etw. zu tun) be going to do sth.; **die Wunde will nicht heilen** the wound [just] won't heal [2] *unr. itr. V.* **du musst nur** ~, **dann ...** you only have to want to enough, then ... **ganz wie du willst** just as you like; **ich will nach Hause** (ugs.) I want to go home; **zu wem** ~ **Sie?** whom do you want to see? [3] *unr. tr. V.* want; **das habe ich nicht gewollt** I never meant that to happen

wo·mit *Adv.* **(a)** (interrogativ) ~ **schreibst du?** what do you write with? **(b)** (relativisch) ~ **du schreibst** which *or* that you write with; (more formal) with which you write

wo·möglich *Adv.* possibly

wo·nach *Adv.* **(a)** (interrogativ) after what; what ... after; ~ **suchst du?** what are you looking for?

*old spelling - see note on page xiv

(b) (relativisch) after which; which ... after

Wonne *die;* **~, ~n** (geh.) bliss *no pl.;* ecstasy; (etw., was Freude macht) joy

wonnig *Adj.* sweet

woran *Adv.* **(a)** (interrogativ) **~ denkst du?** what are you thinking of?
(b) (relativisch) **nichts, ~ man sich anlehnen könnte** nothing one could lean against

worauf (a) (interrogativ) **~ wartest du?** what are you waiting for?
(b) (relativisch) **etwas, ~ man sich verlassen kann** something one can rely on
(c) (relativisch: woraufhin) whereupon

woraus *Adv.* **(a)** (interrogativ) **~ schließt du das?** what do you infer that from?
(b) (relativisch) **es gab nichts, ~ wir den Wein hätten trinken können** there was nothing for us to drink the wine out of

worden *2. Part. v.* WERDEN 2

worin *Adv.* **(a)** (interrogativ) in what; what ... in
(b) (relativisch) in which; which ... in

Workaholic /wə:kəˈhɔlɪk/ *der;* **~s, ~s:** workaholic

Wort *das;* **~[e]s, Wörter/~e (a)** *Pl.* **Wörter,** (auch:) **~e** word; **~ für ~:** word for word; **1 000 € (in ~en: tausend)** 1,000 € (in words: one thousand)
(b) *Pl.* **~e** (Äußerung) word; **mir fehlen die ~e** I'm lost for words; **Dr. Meyer hat das ~:** it's Dr Meyer's turn to speak
(c) *Pl.* **~e** (Spruch) saying; (Zitat) quotation
(d) *Pl.* **~e** (geh.: Text) words *pl.;* **in ~ und Bild** in words and pictures
(e) *Pl.* **~e** (Versprechen) word; **[sein] ~ halten** keep one's word

Wort·bruch *der* breaking one's word *no art.*

wort·brüchig *Adj.* **~ werden** break one's word

Wörter·buch *das* dictionary

wort-, Wort-: ~getreu *Adj.* word-for-word; **~karg** [1] *Adj.* taciturn ‹*person*›; [2] *adv.* taciturnly; **~kargheit** *die* taciturnity; **~laut** *der* wording; **im [vollen] ~laut** verbatim

wörtlich [1] *Adj.* **(a)** word-for-word
(b) (der eigentlichen Bedeutung entsprechend) literal
[2] *adv.: s. Adj.:* word for word; literally

wort-, Wort-: ~los [1] *Adj.* silent; wordless; [2] *adv.* without saying a word; **~meldung** *die:* **gibt es noch ~meldungen?** does anyone else wish to speak?; **~spiel** *das* play on words; pun; **~wechsel** *der* exchange of words; **~wörtlich** *Adj.* word-for-word

worüber *Adv.* **(a)** (interrogativ) over what ...; what ... over
(b) (relativisch) over which; which ... over

worum *Adv.* **(a)** (interrogativ) around what; what ... around
(b) (relativisch) around which; which ... around

worunter *Adv.* **(a)** (interrogativ) under what; what ... under
(b) (relativisch) under which; which ... under

wo·von *Adv.* **(a)** (interrogativ) from where; where ... from
(b) (relativisch) from which; which ... from

wo·vor *Adv.* **(a)** (interrogativ) in front of what; what ... in front of
(b) (relativisch) in front of which; which ... in front of

wo·zu *Adv.* **(a)** (interrogativ) to what; what ... to; (wofür) what ... for
(b) (relativisch) **~ du dich auch entschließt** whatever you decide on

Wrack *das;* **~[e]s, ~s** *od.* **~e** wreck

wrang *1. und 3. Pers. Sg. Prät. v.* WRINGEN

wringen *unr. tr. V.* (bes. nordd.) wring

Wucher *der;* **~s** profiteering; (beim Verleihen von Geld) usury

wuchern *itr. V.* **(a)** *auch mit sein* ‹*plants, weeds, etc.*› proliferate, run wild
(b) (Wucher treiben) **[mit etw.] ~:** profiteer [on sth.]; (beim Verleihen von Geld) lend [sth.] at extortionate interest rates

Wucherung *die;* **~, ~en** growth

wuchs *1. u. 3. Pers. Sg. Prät. v.* WACHSEN

Wuchs *der;* **~es** (Gestalt) stature

Wucht *die;* **~:** force; (von Schlägen) power; weight

wuchtig [1] *Adj.* **(a)** (voller Wucht) powerful; mighty
(b) (schwer, massig) massive
[2] *adv.* powerfully

wühlen [1] *itr. V.* **(a)** dig; (mit der Schnauze, dem Schnabel) root (**nach** for); ‹*mole*› tunnel, burrow
(b) (ugs.: suchen) rummage [around] (**nach** for)
[2] *tr. V.* burrow; tunnel out ‹*burrow*›

wulstig *Adj.* bulging

wund *Adj.* sore; **sich ~ liegen** get bed sores

Wunde *die;* **~, ~n** wound

wunder, Wunder[1] (ugs.): **er denkt, er sei ~ wer** he thinks he's really something; **sie bildet sich ~ was darauf ein** she's terribly pleased with herself about it (coll.)

Wunder[2] *das;* **~s, ~ (a)** miracle; **~ wirken** (fig. ugs.) work wonders; **ein/kein ~ sein** (ugs.) be a/no wonder
(b) (etw. Erstaunliches) wonder

wunderbar [1] *Adj.* **(a)** miraculous
(b) (sehr schön, herrlich) wonderful; marvellous
[2] *adv.* **(a)** (sehr schön, herrlich) wonderfully; marvellously
(b) (ugs.: sehr) wonderfully

Wunder-: ~kerze *die* sparkler; **~kind** *das* child prodigy

wunderlich [1] *Adj.* strange; odd
[2] *adv.* strangely; oddly

W

wundern [1] *tr. V.* surprise; **mich wundert** *od.* **es wundert mich, dass ...:** I'm surprised that ...
[2] *refl. V.* **sich über jmdn./etw. ~:** be surprised at sb./sth

wunder-: ~schön [1] *Adj.* simply beautiful; (herrlich) simply wonderful; [2] *adv.* quite beautifully; **~voll** [1] *Adj.* wonderful; [2] *adv.* wonderfully

***wund|liegen** ▶ WUND

Wund·starr·krampf *der* (Med.) tetanus

Wunsch *der;* **~[e]s, Wünsche** wish (**nach** to have); (Sehnen) desire (**nach** for); **haben Sie [sonst] noch einen ~?** will there be anything else?; **auf jmds. ~:** at sb.'s wish; **mit den besten/herzlichsten Wünschen** with best/warmest wishes

wünschbar *Adj.* (bes. schweiz.) desirable

Wünschel-: ~rute *die* divining rod; **~ruten·gänger** *der;* **~~s, ~~, ~ruten·gängerin** *die;* **~~, ~~nen** diviner

wünschen *tr. V.* **(a) sich** (*Dat.*) **etw. ~:** want sth.; (im Stillen) wish for sth.
(b) (in formelhaften Wünschen) wish; **jmdm. alles Gute/frohe Ostern ~:** wish sb. all the best/a happy Easter
(c) *auch itr. V.* (begehren) want; **was ~ Sie?, Sie ~?** (im Lokal) what would you like?; (in einem Geschäft) can I help you?

Wunsch-: ~kind *das* wanted child; **~konzert** *das* request concert; (im Rundfunk) request programme; **~zettel** *der* (zum Geburtstag *usw.*) list of presents one would like

wurde *1. u. 3. Pers. Sg. Prät. v.* WERDEN

würde *1. u. 3. Pers. Sg. Konjunktiv II v.* WERDEN

Würde *die;* **~:** dignity

würde·los [1] *Adj.* undignified; (schimpflich) disgraceful
[2] *adv.* in an undignified way; (schimpflich) disgracefully

Würdelosigkeit *die;* **~** ▶ WÜRDELOS: lack of dignity; disgracefulness

Würden·träger *der,* **Würden·trägerin** *die* dignitary

würde·voll [1] *Adj.* dignified
[2] *adv.* with dignity

würdig [1] *Adj.* **(a)** dignified
(b) (wert) worthy
[2] *adv.* **(a)** with dignity
(b) (angemessen) worthily

würdigen *tr. V.* **(a)** (anerkennen, beachten) recognize; (schätzen) appreciate; (lobend hervorheben) acknowledge
(b) (für wert halten) **jmdn. keines Blickes/keiner Antwort ~:** not deign to look at/answer sb.

Wurf *der;* **~[e]s, Würfe (a)** throw; (beim Kegeln) bowl
(b) *o. Pl.* (das Werfen) throwing/pitching/bowling
(c) (Zool.) litter

Würfel *der;* **~s, ~:** cube; (Spielwürfel) dice; die (formal)

Würfel·becher *der* dice cup

würfeln [1] *itr. V.* throw the dice; **um etw. ~:** play dice for sth.
[2] *tr. V.* **(a)** throw
(b) (in Würfel schneiden) dice

Würfel-: ~spiel *das* dice; (Brettspiel) dice game; **~zucker** *der* cube sugar

Wurf·geschoss, *Wurf·geschoß *das* missile

würgen [1] *tr. V.* strangle; throttle
[2] *itr. V.* (Brechreiz haben) retch

Wurm *der;* **~[e]s, Würmer** worm; (Made) maggot

wurmig *Adj.,* **wurm·stichig** *Adj.* worm-eaten; (madig) maggoty

Wurst *die;* **~, Würste** sausage; **es geht um die ~** (fig. ugs.) the crunch has come; **jmdm. ist jmd./etw. ~** (ugs.) sb. doesn't care about sb./sth.

Wurst·bude *die* ▶ WÜRSTCHENBUDE

Würstchen *das;* **~s, ~ (a)** [small] sausage; **Frankfurter/Wiener ~:** frankfurter/wienerwurst
(b) (fig. ugs.) nobody; (hilfloser Mensch) poor soul

Würstchen·bude *die* sausage stand

Wurstelei *die;* **~, ~en** (ugs. abwertend) pottering about *no pl.*

wursteln *itr. V.* (ugs.) potter

Wurst·salat *der: piquant salad with pieces of sausage, onion rings, boiled eggs and/or cheese*

Würze *die;* **~, ~n** spice; seasoning

Wurzel *die;* **~, ~n** (auch fig.) root

wurzeln *itr. V.* take root

würzen *tr. V.* season

würzig *Adj.* tasty; full-flavoured ‹*beer, wine*›; aromatic ‹*fragrance*›; tangy ‹*air*›

Würzigkeit *die;* **~** ▶ WÜRZIG 1: tastiness; full flavour; aromatic fragrance; tanginess

wusch *1. u. 3. Pers. Sg. Prät. v.* WASCHEN

wusste, *wußte *1. und 3. Pers. Sg. Prät. v.* WISSEN

wüsste, *wüßte *1. und 3. Pers. Sg. Konjunktiv II v.* WISSEN

wüst [1] *Adj.* **(a)** (öde) desolate
(b) (unordentlich) chaotic
(c) (ungezügelt) wild; (unanständig) rude
[2] *adv.* **(a)** (unordentlich) chaotically
(b) (ungezügelt) wildly

Wust *der;* **~[e]s** (abwertend) jumble; (fig.) welter; **ein ~ von Daten/Vorschriften** a mass of data/regulations

Wüste *die;* **~, ~n** desert

Wut *die;* **~:** rage; fury

*alte Schreibung - vgl. Hinweis auf S. xiv

wüten *itr. V.* (auch fig.) rage; (zerstören) wreak havoc

wütend [1] *Adj.* furious; angry ‹*voice, mob*› [2] *adv.* furiously; in a fury

x[1], X /ɪks/ *das;* ~, ~: x/X

x[2] *unbest. Zahlwort* (ugs.) umpteen (coll.)

x-Achse *die* (Math.) x-axis

X-Beine *Pl.* knock knees

x-beinig *Adj.* knock-kneed

x-beliebig *Adj.* (ugs.) **[irgend]ein ~er/[irgend]eine ~e/[irgend]ein ~es** any old (coll. attrib.); **jeder ~e Ort** any old place (coll.)

X-Chromosom *das* (Biol.) X-chromosome

x-fach [1] *Vervielfältigungsz.* **die ~e Menge** (Math.) x times the amount; (ugs.) umpteen times the amount (coll.) [2] *adv.* (ugs.) ~ **erprobt sein** ‹*tested etc.*› umpteen times (coll.)

x-mal *Adv.* (ugs.) umpteen times (coll.)

x-t... *Ordinalz.* (ugs.) umpteenth (coll.)

Xylophon *das;* **~s, ~e** xylophone

Yy

y, Y /'ʏpsilɔn/ *das;* ~, ~: y/Y

y-Achse *die* (Math.) y-axis

Yacht ▶ JACHT

Y-Chromosom *das* (Biol.) Y-chromosome

Yoga ▶ JOGA

Ypsilon *das;* **~[s], ~s** y, Y; (im griechischen Alphabet) upsilon

Zz

z, Z /tsɛt/ *das;* ~, ~: z/Z

Zack: **auf ~ sein** (ugs.: tüchtig sein) be on the ball (coll.) *or* one's toes; **jmdn. auf ~ bringen** (ugs.) knock sb. into shape (coll.)

Zacke *die;* ~, **~n** point; peak; (einer Säge, eines Kamms) tooth; (einer Gabel, Harke) prong

Zacken *der;* **~s**: ▶ ZACKE

zackig [1] *Adj.* **(a)** (gezackt) jagged; (mit kleinen, regelmäßigen Zacken) serrated **(b)** (schneidig) dashing; smart; rousing ‹*music*›; brisk ‹*orders, tempo*›; lively ‹*organization*› [2] *adv.* **(a)** (gezackt) jaggedly **(b)** (schneidig) smartly; ‹*play music*› rousingly

zaghaft [1] *Adj.* timid; (zögernd) hesitant [2] *adv.* timidly; (zögernd) hesitantly

Zaghaftigkeit *die;* ~: timidity; (Zögern) hesitancy

zäh [1] *Adj.* **(a)** tough; heavy ‹*dough, soil*›; (dickflüssig) glutinous; viscous ‹*oil*› **(b)** (widerstandsfähig) tough ‹*person*› **(c)** (beharrlich) tenacious; tough ‹*negotiations*›; dogged ‹*resistance*› [2] *adv.* (beharrlich) tenaciously; ‹*resist*› doggedly

Zähheit *die;* ~: **(a)** (Festigkeit) toughness; (des Teigs, Bodens) heaviness; (Dickflüssigkeit) glutinousness; (von Öl) viscosity **(b)** (Widerstandsfähigkeit) toughness **(c)** (Beharrlichkeit) tenacity; (des Widerstands) doggedness

Zähigkeit *die;* ~ **(a)** (Widerstandsfähigkeit) toughness **(b)** (Beharrlichkeit) tenacity; **mit ~**: tenaciously

Zahl *die;* ~, **~en** number; (Ziffer) numeral; (Zahlenangabe, Geldmenge) figure; **in den roten/schwarzen ~en** in the red/black

zahlbar *Adj.* (Kaufmannsspr.) payable

zahlen [1] *tr. V.* pay (**an** + *Akk.* to) ···>

X

[2] *itr. V.* pay; **[ich möchte] bitte ~** (im Lokal) [can I have] the bill, please!

zählen [1] *itr. V.* **(a)** count; **zu einer Gruppe** *usw.* **~**: be one of *or* belong to a group *etc.*; **(b) auf jmdn./etw. ~**: count on sb./sth
[2] *tr. V.* count; **jmdn. zu seinen Freunden ~**: count sb. among one's friends

zahl-, Zahl-: ~karte *die* (Postw.) paying-in slip; **~los** *Adj.* countless; **~reich** *Adj.* numerous

Zahlung *die;* **~, ~en** payment

Zählung *die;* **~, ~en** counting; **eine ~**: a count

zahlungs-, Zahlungs-: ~bilanz *die* (Wirtsch.) balance of payments; **~fähig** *Adj.* solvent; **~fähigkeit** *die* solvency; **~mittel** *das* means of payment; **~unfähig** *Adj.* insolvent; **~unfähigkeit** *die* insolvency

Zahl·wort *das; Pl.* **Zahl·wörter** (Sprachw.) numeral

zahm [1] *Adj.* tame
[2] *adv.* tamely

zähmen *tr. V.* (auch fig.) tame

Zahn *der;* **~[e]s, Zähne** tooth; (Reißzahn) fang; (an einer Briefmarke usw.) serration

Zahn-: ~arzt *der,* **~ärztin** *die* dentist; (mit chirurgischer Ausbildung) dental surgeon; **~bürste** *die* toothbrush

zahnen *itr. V.* ‹*baby*› be teething

zahn-, Zahn-: ~ersatz *der* denture; **~fleisch** *das* gum; (als Ganzes) gums *pl.;* **~fleisch·bluten** *das;* **~~s** bleeding gums *pl.;* **~los** *Adj.* toothless; **~lücke** *die* gap in one's teeth; **~pasta** *die;* **~~, ~pasten** toothpaste; **~pflege** *die* dental care; **~prothese** *die* dentures *pl.;* [set *sing.* of] false teeth *pl.;* **~rad** *das* gearwheel; (für Ketten) sprocket; **~schmerzen** *Pl.* toothache *sing.;* **~seide** *die* dental floss; **~spange** *die* [tooth] brace; **~stein** *der* tartar; **~stocher** *der;* **~~s, ~~**: toothpick; **~weh** *das* (ugs.) toothache

Zange *die;* **~, ~n (a)** (Werkzeug) pliers *pl.;* (Eiswürfel-, Zuckerzange) tongs *pl.;* (Geburtszange) forceps *pl.;* (Kneifzange) pincers *pl.;* **eine ~**: a pair of pliers/tongs/forceps/pincers
(b) (bei Tieren) pincer

Zank *der;* **~[e]s** squabble; row

zanken *refl.* (*auch itr.*) *V.* squabble, bicker (**um** *od.* **über** + *Akk.* over)

zänkisch *Adj.* quarrelsome

Zäpfchen *das;* **~s, ~**: suppository

zapfen *tr. V.* tap, draw ‹*beer, wine*›

Zapfen *der;* **~s, ~ (a)** (Bot.) cone
(b) (Stöpsel) bung

Zapf·säule *die* petrol pump (Brit.); gasoline pump (Amer.)

zappeln *itr. V.* wriggle; ‹*child*› fidget

zappen /'zɛpn̩/ *itr. V.* (ugs.) zap (coll.)

Zar *der;* **~en, ~en** (hist.) Tsar

***old spelling - see note on page xiv**

Zarin *die;* **~, ~nen** (hist.) Tsarina

zart [1] *Adj.* (auch fig.) delicate; soft ‹*skin*›; tender ‹*bud, shoot; meat, vegetables*›; fine ‹*biscuits*›; gentle ‹*kiss, touch*›; soft ‹*pastel colours*›
[2] *adv.* (empfindlich) delicately; ‹*kiss, touch*› gently

Zartheit *die;* **~**: delicacy; (der Haut) softness; (von Fleisch, Gemüse) tenderness; (eines Kusses, einer Berührung) gentleness

zärtlich [1] *Adj.* tender
[2] *adv.* tenderly

Zärtlichkeit *die;* **~, ~en (a)** (Zuneigung) tenderness; affection
(b) (Liebkosung) caress

Zauber *der;* **~s, ~ (a)** (auch fig.) magic; (Bann) [magic] spell
(b) (ugs. abwertend: Aufheben) fuss

Zauberei *die;* **~, ~en (a)** (das Zaubern) magic
(b) (Zaubertrick) magic trick

Zauberer *der;* **~s, ~**: magician

zauber·haft [1] *Adj.* enchanting
[2] *adv.* enchantingly

Zauberin *die;* **~, ~nen (a)** sorceress
(b) (Zauberkünstlerin) conjurer

Zauber·künstler *der,* **Zauberkünstlerin** *die* conjurer; magician

zaubern [1] *itr. V.* **(a)** do magic
(b) (Zaubertricks ausführen) do conjuring tricks
[2] *tr. V.* (auch fig.) conjure

zaudern *itr. V.* (geh.) delay

Zaum *der;* **~[e]s, Zäume** bridle

zäumen *tr. V.* bridle

Zaum·zeug *das* bridle

Zaun *der;* **~[e]s, Zäune** fence

Zaun·könig *der* wren

z. B. *Abk.* = **zum Beispiel** e.g.

ZDF *das;* **~**: *Abk.* = **Zweites Deutsches Fernsehen** Second German Television Channel

Zebra *das;* **~s, ~s** zebra

Zebra·streifen *der* zebra crossing (Brit.); pedestrian crossing

Zeche *die;* **~, ~n (a)** (Rechnung) bill (Brit.); check (Amer.)
(b) (Bergwerk) pit; mine

zechen *itr. V.* (veralt., scherzh.) tipple

Zecke *die;* **~, ~n** (Zool.) tick

Zeder *die;* **~, ~n** cedar

Zedern·holz *das* cedarwood

Zeh *der;* **~s, ~en, Zehe** *die;* **~, ~n (a)** toe
(b) (Knoblauchzehe) clove

Zehen·spitze *die:* **auf ~n** on tiptoe

zehn *Kardinalz.* ten

Zehn *die;* **~, ~en** ten

Zehner *der;* **~s, ~ (a)** (ugs.: Geldschein, Münze) ten
(b) (ugs.: Autobus) number ten
(c) (Math.) ten

zehn·fach *Vervielfältigungsz.* tenfold
Zehnfache *das; adj. Dekl.* **das ~:** ten times as much
zehn-, Zehn-: ~kampf *der* (Sport) decathlon; **~mal** *Adv.* ten times; **~mark·schein** *der* ten-mark note; **~pfennig·[brief]marke** *die* ten-pfennig stamp; **~pfennig·stück** *das* ten-pfennig piece
zehnt... *Ordinalz.* tenth;
zehn·tausend *Kardinalz.* ten thousand
zehntel *Bruchz.* tenth
Zehntel *das* (schweiz. meist *der*); **~s, ~:** tenth
zehntens *Adv.* tenthly
zehren *itr. V.* **von etw. ~:** live on *or* off sth.
Zeichen *das;* **~s, ~:** sign; (Markierung) mark; (Chemie, Math., auf Landkarten usw.) symbol; (Schrift~) character; **jmdm. ein ~ geben** signal to sb.
Zeichen-: ~setzung *die;* **~~:** punctuation; **~sprache** *die* sign language
zeichnen [1] *tr. V.* draw; (fig.) portray ‹*character*›
[2] *itr. V.* draw
Zeichner *der;* **~s, ~, Zeichnerin** *die;* **~, ~nen** graphic artist; (Technik) draughtsman/-woman
Zeichnung *die;* **~, ~en** drawing
zeichnungs·berechtigt *Adj.* with signatory powers *postpos.;* **~ sein** have signatory powers
Zeige·finger *der* index finger; forefinger
zeigen [1] *itr. V.* point
[2] *tr. V.* show
[3] *refl. V.* **(a)** (sich sehen lassen) appear
(b) (sich erweisen) prove to be; **es wird sich ~, ...:** time will tell ...
Zeiger *der;* **~s, ~:** pointer; (Uhrzeiger) hand
Zeile *die;* **~, ~n** line; (Reihe) row
zeit *Präp. mit Gen.* **~ meines** *usw.*/**unseres** *usw.* **Lebens** all my *etc.* life/our *etc.* lives
Zeit *die;* **~, ~en (a)** time *no art.;* **mit der ~:** with *or* in time; (allmählich) gradually; **eine ~ lang** for a while
(b) (Zeitpunkt) time; **alles zu seiner ~:** all in good time; ***zur ~:** at the moment
(c) (Zeit-, Lebensabschnitt) time; period; (Geschichtsabschnitt) age; period
(d) (Sprachw.) tense
zeit-, Zeit-: ~alter *das* age; era; **~arbeit** *die* (Wirtsch.) temporary work; work as a temp (coll.); **~druck** *der* pressure of time; **unter ~druck** under pressure; **unter ~druck stehen** be pressed for time; **~geist** *der* spirit of the age; **~gemäß** *Adj.* (modern) up-to-date; (aktuell) topical ‹*theme*›; contemporary ‹*views*›; **~genosse** *der,* **~genossin** *die* contemporary; **~genössisch** *Adj.* contemporary; **~geschehen** *das:* **das [aktuelle] ~geschehen** current events *pl.;* **~geschichte** *die* contemporary history
zeitig *Adj., adv.* early
zeit-, Zeit-: ~karte *die* (Verkehrsw.) season ticket; ***~lang** ▶ ZEIT A; **~lebens** *Adv.* all my/his/her *etc.* life
zeitlich [1] *Adj.* ‹*length, interval*› in time; chronological ‹*order, sequence*›
[2] *adv.* with regard to time
zeit-, Zeit-: ~los [1] *Adj.* timeless; classic ‹*fashion, shape*›; [2] *adv.* timelessly; **~lupe** *die* slow motion; **~mangel** *der* lack of time; **~punkt** *der* moment; **~raubend** *Adj.* time-consuming; **~raum** *der* period; **~schrift** *die* magazine; (bes. wissenschaftlich) journal; periodical; **~spanne** *die* period
Zeitung *die;* **~, ~en** [news]paper
Zeitungs-: ~ausschnitt *der* newspaper cutting; **~bericht** *der* newspaper report; **~notiz** *die* newspaper item
zeit-, Zeit-: ~unterschied *der* time difference; **~verschwendung** *die* waste of time; **~vertreib** *der;* **~~[e]s, ~~e** pastime; **zum ~vertreib** to pass the time; **~weilig** [1] *Adj.* temporary; [2] *adv.* temporarily; **~weise** *Adv.* (gelegentlich) occasionally; (von Zeit zu Zeit) from time to time; **~wort** *das; Pl.* **~wörter** (Sprachw.) verb; **~zünder** *der* time fuse
Zelle *die;* **~, ~n** cell
Zelluloid /tsɛlu'lɔy:t/ *das;* **~[e]s** celluloid
Zelt *das;* **~[e]s, ~e** tent; (Festzelt) marquee; (Zirkuszelt) big top
zelten *itr. V.* camp
Zelt-: ~lager *das* camp; **~plane** *die* tarpaulin
Zement *der;* **~[e]s, ~e** cement
Zensur *die;* **~, ~en (a)** (Schulw.: Note) mark; grade (Amer.)
(b) (Kontrolle) censorship
(c) (Behörde) censors *pl.*
Zenti-: ~meter *der, auch: das* centimetre; **~meter·maß** *das* [centimetre] measuring tape
Zentner *der;* **~s, ~ (a)** metric hundredweight
(b) (österr., schweiz.) ▶ DOPPELZENTNER
zentral [1] *Adj.* central
[2] *adv.* centrally
Zentral·bank *die; Pl.* **~en** (Finanzw.) central bank
Zentrale *die;* **~, ~n (a)** (zentrale Stelle) head *or* central office; (der Polizei, einer Partei) headquarters *sing. or pl.;* (Funkzentrale) control centre
(b) (Telefonzentrale) [telephone] exchange; (eines Hotels, einer Firma o. Ä.) switchboard
Zentral-: ~figur *die* central figure; **~heizung** *die* central heating; **~speicher** *der* (DV) main memory
Zentren ▶ ZENTRUM
Zentrifugal·kraft *die* (Physik) centrifugal force

Zentrifuge *die;* ~, ~**n** centrifuge
Zentrum *das;* ~**s, Zentren** centre; **im** ~: at the centre; (im Stadtzentrum) in the town/city centre
Zeppelin *der;* ~**s,** ~**e** Zeppelin
Zepter *das, auch: der;* ~**s,** ~: sceptre
zerbeißen *unr. tr. V.* bite in two
zerbersten *unr. itr. V.; mit sein* burst apart
zerbrechen [1] *unr. itr. V.; mit sein* break [into pieces]; smash [to pieces]; ‹*glass*› shatter; (fig.) ‹*marriage, relationship*› break up
[2] *unr. tr. V.* break; smash, shatter ‹*dishes, glass*›
zerbrechlich *Adj.* fragile; (fig.) frail
Zerbrechlichkeit *die;* ~: fragility; (fig.) frailty
zerbröckeln [1] *itr. V.; mit sein* crumble away
[2] *tr. V.* break into small pieces
zerdrücken *tr. V.* mash
Zeremonie *die;* ~, ~**n** ceremony; (fig.) ritual
Zeremoniell *das;* ~**s,** ~**e** ceremonial
zerfallen *unr. itr. V.; mit sein* (auch fig.) disintegrate (**in** + *Akk.*, **zu** into); ‹*building*› fall into ruin, decay; ‹*corpse*› decompose, decay
zerfetzen *tr. V.* rip *or* tear to pieces; (fig.) tear apart ‹*body, limb*›
zerfleischen *tr. V.* tear ‹*person, animal*› limb from limb
zerfressen *unr. tr. V.* **(a)** eat away; ‹*moth etc.*› eat holes in
(b) (zersetzen) corrode ‹*metal*›; eat away ‹*bone*›
zergehen *unr. itr. V.; mit sein* melt; (in Wasser, im Mund) ‹*tablet etc.*› dissolve
zerhacken *tr. V.* chop up (**zu** into)
zerhauen *unr. tr. V.* chop up
zerkleinern *tr. V.* chop up; (zermahlen) crush ‹*rock etc.*›
zerknautschen *tr. V.* (ugs.) crumple
zerknirscht [1] *Adj.* remorseful
[2] *adv.* remorsefully
zerknittern *tr. V.* crease; crumple
zerknüllen *tr. V.* crumple up [into a ball]
zerkratzen *tr. V.* scratch
zerkrümeln *tr. V.* crumble up
zerlegen *tr. V.* **(a)** dismantle; take to pieces
(b) (zerschneiden) cut up ‹*animal, meat*›; carve ‹*joint*›
zerlumpt *Adj.* ragged ‹*clothes, person*›
zerplatzen *itr. V.; mit sein* burst
Zerr·bild *das* distorted image
zerreiben *unr. tr. V.* crush
zerreißen [1] *unr. tr. V.* **(a)** tear up; (in kleine Stücke) tear to pieces; break ‹*thread*›
(b) (beschädigen) tear ‹*stocking, trousers, etc.*› (**an** + *Dat.* on)
[2] *unr. itr. V.; mit sein* ‹*thread, string, rope*› break; ‹*paper, cloth, etc.*› tear
Zerreiß·probe *die* acid test
zerren [1] *tr. V.* **(a)** drag
(b) sich (*Dat.*) **einen Muskel/eine Sehne** ~: pull a muscle/tendon
[2] *itr. V.* **an etw.** (*Dat.*) ~: tug *or* pull at sth
Zerrung *die;* ~, ~**en** pulled muscle/tendon
zerrütten *tr. V.* ruin; shatter ‹*nerves*›
zerschellen *itr. V.; mit sein* be dashed *or* smashed to pieces
zerschlagen [1] *unr. tr. V.* smash ‹*plate, windscreen, etc.*›; smash up ‹*furniture*›; (fig.) smash ‹*spy ring etc.*›
[2] *unr. refl. V.* ‹*plan, deal*› fall through
zerschmettern *tr. V.* smash; shatter ‹*glass, leg, bone*›
zerschneiden *unr. tr. V.* cut; (in Stücke) cut up; (in zwei Teile) cut in two
zersetzen *tr. V.* corrode ‹*metal*›; decompose ‹*organism*›
zersplittern *itr. V.; mit sein* ‹*wood, bone*› splinter; ‹*glass*› shatter
zerspringen *unr. itr. V.; mit sein* shatter; (Sprünge bekommen) crack
zerstäuben *tr. V.* spray
zerstören *tr. V.* destroy; ‹*hooligan*› smash up, vandalize; (fig.) ruin ‹*health, life*›
Zerstörung *die;* ~, ~**en** ▶ ZERSTÖREN: destruction; smashing up; vandalization; (fig.) ruin[ation]
Zerstörungs·wut *die* destructive frenzy
zerstreuen [1] *tr. V.* scatter; disperse ‹*crowd*›; **jmdn./sich** ~ (ablenken) take sb.'s/one's mind off things
[2] *refl. V.* disperse; (schneller) scatter
zerstreut [1] *Adj.* distracted; (vergesslich) absent-minded
[2] *adv.* absentmindedly
Zerstreuung *die;* ~, ~**en** (Ablenkung) diversion
zerstückeln *tr. V.* break ‹*sth.*› up into small pieces; (zerschneiden) cut *or* chop ‹*sth.*› up into small pieces; dismember ‹*corpse*›
zerteilen *tr. V.* divide into pieces; (zerschneiden) cut into pieces; cut up
Zertifikat *das;* ~**[e]s,** ~**e** certificate
zertrampeln *tr. V.* trample all over ‹*flower bed etc.*›; trample ‹*child etc.*› underfoot
zertreten *unr. tr. V.* stamp on; stamp out ‹*cigarette, match*›
zertrümmern *tr. V.* smash; smash, shatter ‹*glass*›; smash up ‹*furniture*›; wreck ‹*car, boat*›; reduce ‹*building*› to ruins
Zerwürfnis *das;* ~**ses,** ~**se** (geh.) quarrel; dispute; (Bruch) rift
zerzausen *tr. V.* ruffle; **zerzaust aussehen** look dishevelled
zetern *itr. V.* scold [shrilly]; (sich beklagen) moan (**über** + *Akk.* about)

*alte Schreibung - vgl. Hinweis auf S. xiv

Zettel *der;* **~s, ~**: slip *or* piece of paper; (mit einigen Zeilen) note; (Bekanntmachung) notice; (Formular) form; (Kassenzettel) receipt; (Handzettel) leaflet

Zeug *das;* **~[e]s, ~e (a)** (ugs.) stuff; **dummes ~**: nonsense; rubbish **(b)** (Kleidung) things *pl.*

Zeuge *der;* **~n, ~n** witness

zeugen *tr. V.* procreate; ‹*man*› father ‹*child*›

Zeugen·aussage *die* testimony

Zeugin *die;* **~, ~nen** witness

Zeugnis *das;* **~ses, ~se (a)** (Schulw.) report **(b)** (Arbeitszeugnis) reference; testimonial **(c)** (Gutachten) certificate

Zeugung *die;* **~, ~en** procreation; (eines Kindes) fathering

zeugungs·fähig *Adj.* fertile

z. Hd. *Abk.* = **zu Händen** attn.

Zicke *die;* **~, ~n (a)** ▸ ZIEGE; **(b)** *Pl.* (ugs.: Dummheiten) stupid tricks; monkey business *sing.* (coll.); **~n machen** mess about; (Schwierigkeiten machen) make trouble

Zickzack *der;* **~[e]s, ~e** zigzag

Ziege *die;* **~, ~n** goat; (Schimpfwort: Frau) cow (sl. derog.)

Ziegel *der;* **~s, ~** brick; (Dachziegel) tile

Ziegelei *die;* **~, ~en** brickworks *sing.*

Ziegel·stein *der* brick

Ziegen-: ~bock *der* he- *or* billy goat; **~käse** *der* goat's cheese

ziehen [1] *unr. tr. V.* **(a)** pull; (sanfter) draw; (zerren) tug; (schleppen) drag; **etw. nach sich ~** (fig.) result in sth.; entail sth. **(b)** (herausziehen) extract ‹*tooth*›; take out, remove ‹*stitches*›; draw ‹*cord, sword, pistol*›; **den Hut ~**: raise one's hat; **die [Quadrat]wurzel ~** (Math.) extract the square root **(c)** (dehnen) stretch ‹*elastic etc.*›; stretch out ‹*sheets etc.*› **(d)** (Gesichtspartien bewegen) make ‹*face, grimace*› **(e)** (bei Brettspielen) move ‹*chessman etc.*› **(f)** (zeichnen) draw ‹*line etc.*› **(g)** (anlegen) dig ‹*trench*›; build ‹*wall*›; erect ‹*fence*›; put up ‹*washing line*›; run, lay ‹*cable, wires*›; draw ‹*frontier*› **(h)** (aufziehen) grow ‹*plants, flowers*›; breed ‹*animals*›

[2] *unr. itr. V.* **(a)** (reißen) pull; **an etw.** (*Dat.*) **~**: pull on sth. **(b)** (funktionieren) ‹*stove, pipe, chimney*› draw **(c)** *mit sein* (umziehen) move (**nach, in** + *Akk.* to) **(d)** *mit sein* (gehen) go; (marschieren) march; (umherstreifen) roam; (weggehen) go away; leave; ‹*fog, clouds*› drift **(e)** (saugen) draw; **an einer Zigarette/Pfeife ~**: draw on a cigarette/pipe **(f)** ‹*tea, coffee*› draw **(g)** (Kochk.) simmer **(h)** *unpers.* **es zieht** there's a draught

[3] *unr. refl. V.* ‹*road*› run, stretch; ‹*frontier*› run

Zieh·harmonika *die* piano accordion

Ziehung *die;* **~, ~en** draw

Ziel *das;* **~[e]s, ~e (a)** destination **(b)** (Sport) finish; (Ziellinie) finishing line; (Pferderennen) finishing post **(c)** (Zielscheibe; auch Milit.) target **(d)** (Zweck) aim; goal; **sein ~ erreichen** achieve one's objective *or* aim

ziel·bewusst, ***ziel·bewußt** [1] *Adj.* determined [2] *adv.* determinedly

zielen *itr. V.* aim (**auf** + *Akk.*, at); (fig.) **auf jmdn./etw. ~** ‹*reproach, efforts, etc.*› be aimed at sb./sth.

ziel-, Ziel-: ~gruppe *die* target group; **~los** [1] *Adj.* aimless; [2] *adv.* aimlessly; **~losigkeit** *die;* **~~**: aimlessness; **~scheibe** *die* (auch fig.) target (*Gen.* for); **~strebig** [1] *Adj.* **(a)** purposeful; **(b)** (energisch) single-minded ‹*person*›; [2] *adv.* **(a)** purposefully; **(b)** (energisch) single-mindedly; **~strebigkeit** *die;* **~~** ▸ ~STREBIG: **(a)** purposefulness; **(b)** single-mindedness; **~wahl** *die* (Fernspr.) one-touch dialling

ziemlich [1] *Adj.* (ugs.) fair, sizeable ‹*quantity, number*› [2] *adv.* **(a)** quite; fairly **(b)** (ugs.: fast) pretty well

Zierde *die;* **~, ~n** (auch fig.) ornament

zieren *refl. V.* be coy

zierlich [1] *Adj.* dainty; petite, dainty ‹*woman, figure*› [2] *adv.* daintily

Zierlichkeit *die;* **~**: daintiness; (einer Frau, Gestalt) petiteness; daintiness

Zier·pflanze *die* ornamental plant

Ziffer *die;* **~, ~n** numeral; (in einer mehrstelligen Zahl) digit; figure

Ziffer·blatt *das* dial; face

zig *unbest. Zahlwort* (ugs.) umpteen (coll.)

Zigarette *die;* **~, ~n** cigarette

Zigaretten·werbung *die* cigarette advertising

Zigarillo *der od. das;* **~s, ~s** cigarillo; small cigar

Zigarre *die;* **~, ~n** cigar

Zigeuner *der;* **~s, ~**, **Zigeunerin** *die;* **~, ~nen** gypsy

zig·mal *Adv.* (ugs.) umpteen times (coll.)

zig·tausend *unbest. Zahlwort* (ugs.) umpteen thousand (coll.)

Zimmer *das;* **~s, ~**: room

Zimmer·mädchen *das* chambermaid

zimmern *tr. V.* make ‹*shelves etc.*›

Zimmer-: ~suche *die* room-hunt; **~vermittlung** *die* accommodation office

zimperlich [1] *Adj.* timid; (leicht angeekelt) squeamish; (prüde) prissy [2] *adv.: s. Adj.:* timidly; squeamishly; prissily

Zimperlichkeit *die;* ~, ~**en** (abwertend) timidity; (Neigung zum Ekel) squeamishness; (Prüderie) prissiness
Zimt *der;* ~[**e**]**s**, ~**e** cinnamon
Zink *das;* ~[**e**]**s** zinc
Zinke *die;* ~, ~**n** prong; (eines Kamms) tooth
Zinn *das;* ~[**e**]**s** tin; (Gegenstände) pewter[ware]
Zins *der;* ~**es**, ~**en** interest
Zinses·zins *der* compound interest
zins·los [1] *Adj.* interest-free
[2] *adv.* free of interest
Zins·satz *der* interest rate
Zipfel *der;* ~**s**, ~ (einer Decke, eines Tisch-, Handtuchs usw.) corner; (Wurstzipfel, eines Halstuchs) [tail] end
Zipfel·mütze *die* [long-]pointed cap
zirka *Adv.* about; approximately
Zirkulation *die,* ~, ~**en** circulation
zirkulieren *itr. V.; auch mit sein* circulate
Zirkus *der;* ~, ~**se** **(a)** circus
(b) (ugs.) (Trubel) hustle and bustle; (Krach) to-do
zirpen *itr. V.* chirp
zischeln *tr. V.* whisper angrily
zischen *itr. V.* **(a)** hiss; ‹*hot fat*› sizzle
(b) *mit sein* hiss
Zitat *das;* ~[**e**]**s**, ~**e** quotation (**aus** from)
zitieren *tr., itr. V.* **(a)** quote; (Rechtsspr.) cite
(b) (rufen) summon
Zitronat *das;* ~[**e**]**s** candied lemon peel
Zitrone *die;* ~, ~**n** lemon
Zitronen-: ~**limonade** *die* lemonade; ~**presse** *die* lemon squeezer; ~**saft** *der* lemon juice
Zitrus·frucht *die* citrus fruit
zittern *itr. V.* tremble (**vor** + *Dat.* with); (vor Kälte) shiver; (beben) ‹*walls, windows*› shake; **vor jmdm./etw.** ~: be terrified of sb./sth.
Zitter·partie *die* nail-biting affair
zittrig *Adj.* shaky; doddery ‹*old man*›
Zitze *die;* ~, ~**n** teat
zivil [1] *Adj.* **(a)** civilian; non-military ‹*purposes*›; civil ‹*aviation, marriage, law, defence*›
(b) (annehmbar) decent
[2] *adv.* (annehmbar) decently
Zivil *das;* ~**s** civilian clothes *pl.*
Zivil·bevölkerung *die* civilian population
Zivilisation /tsːiviliza'tsːi̯oːn/ *die;* ~, ~**en** civilization
zivilisieren *tr. V.* civilize
zivilisiert [1] *Adj.* civilized
[2] *adv.* in a civilized way
Zivilist *der;* ~**en**, ~**en**, **Zivilistin** *die;* ~, ~**nen** civilian
Zivil·kleidung *die* civilian clothes *pl.*
Zofe *die;* ~, ~**n** (hist.) lady's maid
zoffen *refl. V.* (ugs.) quarrel (**mit** with)

*old spelling - see note on page xiv

zog *1. u. 3. Pers. Sg. Prät. v.* ZIEHEN
zögerlich [1] *Adj.* hesitant; tentative
[2] *adv.* hesitantly; tentatively
zögern *itr. V.* hesitate; **ohne zu** ~: without hesitation
Zoll *der;* ~[**e**]**s**, **Zölle** **(a)** [customs] duty
(b) (Behörde) customs *pl.*
zoll-, Zoll-: ~**amt** *das* customs house *or* office; ~**beamte** *der,* ~**beamtin** *die* customs officer; ~**erklärung** *die* customs declaration; ~**frei** [1] *Adj.* duty-free; free of duty *pred.;* [2] *adv.* free of duty; ~**kontrolle** *die* customs examination *or* check; ~**stock** *der* folding rule
Zone *die;* ~, ~**n** zone
Zoo *der;* ~**s**, ~**s** zoo
Zoologe *der;* ~**n**, ~**n** zoologist
Zoologie *die;* ~: zoology *no art.*
Zoologin *die;* ~, ~**nen** zoologist
zoologisch *Adj.* zoological; ~**er Garten** zoological gardens *pl.*
Zoom *das;* ~**s**, ~**s** (Film, Fot.) zoom
Zoom·objektiv *das* (Film, Fot.) zoom lens
Zopf *der;* ~[**e**]**s**, **Zöpfe** plait; (am Hinterkopf) pigtail
Zorn *der;* ~[**e**]**s** anger; (stärker) wrath; fury
zornig [1] *Adj.* furious
[2] *adv.* furiously
Zote *die;* ~, ~**n** dirty joke
zotig [1] *Adj.* smutty; dirty ‹*joke*›
[2] *adv.* smuttily
zottig *Adj.* shaggy
zu [1] *Präp. mit Dat.* **(a)** (Richtung) to; **zu ... hin** towards ...
(b) (zusammen mit) with; **zu dem Käse gab es Wein** there was wine with the cheese
(c) (Lage) at; **zu beiden Seiten** on both sides
(d) (zeitlich) at; **zu Weihnachten** at Christmas
(e) (Art u. Weise) **zu meiner Zufriedenheit/ Überraschung** to my satisfaction/surprise; (bei Mengenangaben) **zu Dutzenden/zweien** by the dozen/in twos
(f) (ein Zahlenverhältnis ausdrückend) **ein Verhältnis von 3 zu 1** a ratio of 3 to 1
(g) (einen Preis zuordnend) at; for
(h) (Zweck) for
(i) (Ziel, Ergebnis) into; **zu etw. werden** turn into sth.
(j) (über) about; on; **sich zu etw. äußern** comment on sth.
(k) (gegenüber) **freundlich/hässlich zu jmdm. sein** be friendly/nasty to sb.; *s. auch* ZUM; ZUR;
[2] *Adv.* **(a)** (allzu) too; **zu sehr/viel** too much; **zu wenig** too little
(b) *nachgestellt* (Richtung) towards
[3] *Konj.* **(a)** *mit Infinitiv* to; **was gibts da zu lachen?** what is there to laugh about?
(b) *mit 1. Part.* **die zu erledigende Post** the letters *pl.* to be dealt with
Zubehör *das;* ~[**e**]**s**, ~**e** *od. schweiz.* ~**den** accessories *pl.;* (eines Staubsaugers, Mixers usw.) attachments *pl.;* (Ausstattung) equipment

zu|bereiten *tr. V.* prepare ‹*meal etc.*›; make up ‹*medicine, ointment*›; (kochen) cook ‹*fish, meat, etc.*›

zu|billigen *tr. V.* **jmdm. etw. ~:** grant *or* allow sb. sth.

zu|binden *unr. tr. V.* tie [up]

zu|blinzeln *itr. V.* **jmdm. ~:** wink at sb.

zu|bringen *unr. tr. V.* spend

Zu·bringer *der;* **~s, ~ (a)** (Straße) access road
(b) (Verkehrsmittel) shuttle

Zucht *die;* **~, ~en (a)** breeding; (von Pflanzen) cultivation; **ein Pferd aus deutscher ~:** a German-bred horse
(b) (geh.: Disziplin) discipline

züchten *tr. V.* (auch fig.) breed; cultivate ‹*plants*›; culture ‹*bacteria, pearls*›

Züchter *der;* **~s, ~, Züchterin** *die;* **~, ~nen** breeder; (von Pflanzen) grower [of new varieties]

züchtigen *tr. V.* (geh.) beat; thrash; (fig.: bestrafen) castigate

Züchtigung *die;* **~, ~en** (geh.) beating; thrashing; (fig.: Bestrafung) castigation

Züchtung *die;* **~, ~en (a)** breeding; (von Pflanzen) cultivation
(b) (Zuchtergebnis) strain

zucken *itr. V.; mit Richtungsangabe mit sein* twitch; ‹*body, arm, leg, etc.*› jerk; (vor Schreck) start; ‹*flames*› flicker; **mit den Achseln/Schultern ~:** shrug one's shoulders

zücken *tr. V.* draw ‹*sword, dagger, knife*›

Zucker *der;* **~s, ~ (a)** sugar
(b) (ugs.: Diabetes) diabetes; **~ haben** be a diabetic

zucker-, Zucker-: ~dose *die* sugar bowl; **~hut** *der* sugar loaf; **~krank** *Adj.* diabetic

zuckern *tr. V.* sugar

Zucker·wasser *das* sugar water

Zuckung *die;* **~, ~en** twitch

zu|decken *tr. V.* cover up; cover [over] ‹*well, ditch*›; **jmdn./sich ~:** tuck sb./oneself up

zu|drehen *tr. V.* **(a)** (abdrehen) turn off
(b) (zuwenden) **jmdm. den Rücken ~:** turn one's back on sb.

zu·dringlich [1] *Adj.* pushy (coll.), pushing ‹*person, manner*›; (sexuell) importunate ‹*person, manner*›; prying ‹*glance*›
[2] *adv.* importunately

Zu·dringlichkeit *die;* **~, ~en (a)** pushiness (coll.); (in sexueller Hinsicht) importunate manner
(b) (Handlung) **~en** insistent advances *or* attentions

zu|drücken *tr. V.* press shut; push ‹*door*› shut; **jmdm. die Kehle ~:** choke *or* throttle sb.

zu·einander *Adv.* to one another

zu·erst *Adv.* **(a)** first
(b) (anfangs) at first; to start with
(c) (erstmals) first

Zu·fahrt *die* **(a)** access [for vehicles]
(b) (Straße, Weg) access road; (zum Haus) driveway

Zufahrts·straße *die* access road

Zu·fall *der* chance; (zufälliges Zusammentreffen von Ereignissen) coincidence; **durch ~:** by chance

zu|fallen *unr. itr. V.; mit sein* **(a)** ‹*door etc.*› slam shut; ‹*eyes*› close
(b) (zukommen) **jmdm. ~** ‹*task*› fall to sb.; ‹*prize, inheritance*› go to sb.

zu·fällig [1] *Adj.* accidental; chance *attrib.* ‹*meeting, acquaintance*›; random ‹*selection*›
[2] *adv.* by chance; **wissen Sie ~, wie spät es ist?** (ugs.) do you by any chance know the time?

Zufalls·treffer *der* fluke

zu|fassen *itr. V.* make a snatch *or* grab

zu|faxen *tr.V.* **jmdm. etw. ~:** fax sth. to sb.; fax sb. sth.

zu|fliegen *unr. itr. V.; mit sein* (ugs.) ‹*door, window, etc.*› slam shut

Zu·flucht *die* refuge (**vor** + *Dat.* from); (vor Unwetter o. Ä.) shelter (**vor** + *Dat.* from)

Zufluchts·ort *der* place of refuge; sanctuary

Zu·fluss, *Zu·fluß *der* **(a)** (das Zufließen) inflow; supply; (fig.) influx
(b) (Gewässer) feeder stream/river

zu|flüstern *tr. V.* **jmdm. etw. ~:** whisper sth. to sb.

zu·folge *Präp. mit Dat.; nachgestellt* according to

zu·frieden [1] *Adj.* contented; (befriedigt) satisfied; **mit etw. ~ sein** be satisfied with sth.; **sich ~ geben** be satisfied; **jmdn. ~ stellen** satisfy sb.
[2] *adv.* contentedly

***zufrieden|geben** ▶ ZUFRIEDEN 1

Zufriedenheit *die;* **~:** contentment; (Befriedigung) satisfaction

***zufrieden|stellen** ▶ ZUFRIEDEN 1

zufriedenstellend [1] *Adj.* satisfactory
[2] *adv.* satisfactorily

zu|frieren *unr. itr. V.; mit sein* freeze over

zu|fügen *tr. V.* **jmdm. etw. ~:** inflict sth. on sb.; **jmdm. Schaden/[ein] Unrecht ~:** do sb. harm/an injustice

Zufuhr *die;* **~:** supply; (Material) supplies *pl.*

zu|führen [1] *itr. V.* **auf etw.** (*Akk.*) **~:** lead towards sth.
[2] *tr. V.* **(a)** (zuleiten) **einer Sache** (*Dat.*) **etw. ~:** supply sth. to sth.
(b) (bringen) **einer Partei Mitglieder ~:** bring new members to a party

Zug *der;* **~[e]s, Züge (a)** (Bahn) train
(b) (Kolonne) column; (Umzug) procession; (Demonstrationszug) march
(c) (das Ziehen) pull; traction (Phys.)
(d) (Vorrichtung) pull
(e) (Wanderung) migration
(f) (beim Brettspiel) move ···>

(g) (Schluck) swig (coll.); mouthful; (großer Schluck) gulp; **das Glas auf einen** *od.* **in einem ~ leeren** empty the glass at one go
(h) (beim Rauchen) pull; drag (coll.)
(i) (Atemzug) breath
(j) (Zugluft; beim Ofen) draught
(k) (Gesichtszug) feature; (Wesenszug) characteristic; trait

Zu·gabe *die* **(a)** (Geschenk) [free] gift
(b) (im Konzert, Theater) encore

Zu·gang *der* **(a)** (Weg, auch fig.) access; (Eingang) entrance
(b) (das Hinzukommen) (von Personen) intake; (von Patienten) admission
(c) (Zuwachs) increase (**von** in)

zu·gange: **~ sein** (ugs.) be busy *or* occupied

zugänglich *Adj.* **(a)** accessible; (geöffnet) open
(b) (zur Verfügung stehend) available (*Dat.*, **für** to); (verständlich) accessible (*Dat.*, **für** to)
(c) (aufgeschlossen) approachable ‹*person*›

zu|geben *unr. tr. V.* admit; admit to ‹*deed, crime*›

zu·gegen *Adj.* **~ sein** be present

zu|gehen *unr. itr. V.; mit sein* **(a) auf jmdn./etw. ~:** approach sb./sth.
(b) jmdm. ~ (zugeschickt werden) be sent to sb.
(c) (ugs.: sich schließen) close; shut; **die Tür geht nicht zu** the door will not shut

zu·gehörig *Adj.* belonging to it/them *postpos., not pred.*

Zugehörigkeit *die;* **~:** belonging (**zu** to)

Zügel *der;* **~s, ~:** rein

zügel·los (fig.) [1] *Adj.* unrestrained; unbridled ‹*rage, passion*›
[2] *adv.* without restraint

Zügellosigkeit *die;* **~, ~en** lack of restraint; (Unzüchtigkeit) licentiousness

zügeln *tr. V.* rein [in] ‹*horse*›; (fig.) curb, restrain ‹*desire etc.*›

zu|gesellen *refl. V.* **sich jmdm./einer Sache ~:** join sb./sth.

Zu·geständnis *das* concession

zu|gestehen *unr. tr. V.* admit; concede

zu·getan *Adj.* **jmdm. [herzlich] ~ sein** (geh.) be [very] attached to sb.

zugig *Adj.* draughty, (im Freien) windy

zügig [1] *Adj.* speedy; rapid
[2] *adv.* speedily; rapidly

Zügigkeit *die;* **~:** speediness; rapidity

zu·gleich *Adv.* at the same time

Zug-: ~luft *die* draught; **~maschine** *die* tractor; (von Sattelzug) tractor [unit]

zu|greifen *unr. itr. V.* **(a)** take hold
(b) (sich bedienen) help oneself
(c) (fleißig arbeiten) **[hart** *od.* **kräftig] ~:** [really] knuckle down to it

Zu·griff *der* (Zugang) access (**auf** + *Akk.* to)

zu·grunde *Adv.* **(a) ~ gehen** (sterben) die (**an** + *Dat.* of); (zerstört werden) be destroyed (**an** + *Dat.* by); **~ richten** destroy; (finanziell) ruin ‹*company, person*›
(b) etw. einer Sache (*Dat.*) **~ legen** base sth. on sth.; **etw. liegt einer Sache ~:** sth. is based on sth.

zu|gucken *itr. V.* (ugs.) ▶ ZUSEHEN

zu·gunsten [1] *Präp. mit Gen.* in favour of
[2] *Adv.* **~ von** in favour of

zu·gute *Adv.* **jmdm. seine Unerfahrenheit** *usw.* **~ halten** (geh.) make allowances for sb.'s inexperience *etc.;* **sich** (*Dat.*) **etwas/viel auf etw.** (*Akk.*) **~ tun** *od.* **halten** (geh.) be proud/very proud of sth.; **jmdm./einer Sache ~ kommen** stand sb./sth. in good stead

zu|haben *unr. itr. V.* (ugs.) ‹*shop, office*› be shut *or* closed

zu|halten *unr. tr. V.* hold closed; (nicht öffnen) keep closed

zu|hängen *tr. V.* cover ‹*window, cage*›

zu|hauen (ugs.) [1] *unr. itr. V.* bang *or* slam ‹*door, window*› shut
[2] *unr. itr. V.* hit *or* strike out

Zu·hause *das;* **~s** home

Zuhilfenahme *die;* **~:** utilization; **ohne/unter ~ einer Sache** (*Gen.*)**/von etw.** without/with the aid of sth.

zu|hören *itr. V.* **jmdm./einer Sache ~:** listen to sb./sth.

Zu·hörer *der,* **Zu·hörerin** *die* listener

zu|kleben *tr. V.* seal ‹*letter, envelope*›

zu|knallen (ugs.) [1] *tr. V.* slam
[2] *itr. V.; mit sein* slam

zu|knöpfen *tr. V.* button up

zu|kommen *itr. V.; mit sein* **auf jmdn. ~:** approach sb.

Zukunft *die;* **~:** future

Zukunfts·technologie *die* technology of the future

Zu·lage *die* extra pay *no indef. art.;* additional allowance *no indef. art.*

zu|lassen *unr. tr. V.* **(a)** allow; permit
(b) (teilnehmen lassen) admit
(c) (mit einer Lizenz usw. versehen) **jmdn. als Arzt ~:** register sb. as a doctor
(d) (Kfz-W.) register ‹*vehicle*›
(e) (geschlossen lassen) leave closed *or* shut

zu·lässig *Adj.* permissible; admissible ‹*appeal*›

Zulassung *die;* **~, ~en** registration

Zu·lauf *der* **[viel] ~ haben** ‹*shop, restaurant, etc.*› enjoy a large clientele; ‹*doctor, lawyer*› have a large practice

zu|laufen *unr. itr. V.; mit sein* **(a) auf jmdn./etw. ~** (auch fig.) run towards sb./sth.
(b) jmdm. ~ ‹*cat, dog, etc.*› adopt sb. as a new owner

zu|legen *refl. V.* **sich** (*Dat.*) **etw. ~:** get oneself sth.

zu·letzt *Adv.* **(a)** last [of all]
(b) (als Letzter/Letzte/Letztes) last
(c) (fig.: am wenigsten) least of all
(d) (schließlich, am Ende) in the end; **bis ~:** [right up] to *or* until the end

*alte Schreibung - vgl. Hinweis auf S. xiv

zu·liebe *Adv.* **jmdm./einer Sache ~:** for sb.'s sake/for the sake of sth.
Zulieferer *der;* **~s, ~, Zulieferin** *die;* **~, ~nen** supplier
zum *Präp. + Art.* **(a)** = **zu dem;**
(b) (räumlich: Richtung) to the
(c) (räumlich: Lage) **etw. ~ Fenster hinauswerfen** throw sth. out of the window
(d) (Hinzufügung) **Milch ~ Tee nehmen** take milk with [one's] tea
(e) (zeitlich) at the; **spätestens ~ 15. April** by 15 April at the latest
(f) (Zweck) **~ Spaß/Vergnügen** for fun/ pleasure
(g) (Folge) **~ Ärger seines Vaters** to the annoyance of his father
zu|machen *tr. V.* close; fasten, do up ‹*dress*›; seal ‹*envelope, letter*›; turn off ‹*tap*›; put the top on ‹*bottle*›; (stilllegen) close *or* shut down ‹*factory, mine, etc.*›
zu·mal 1 *Adv.* especially; particularly
2 *Konj.* especially *or* particularly since
zumindest *Adv.* at least
zu|müllen *tr. V.* (ugs.) **etw. ~:** bury sth. under rubbish; **mit etw. zugemüllt werden** be buried under sth.; **von etw. zugemüllt werden** (fig.) be buried under sth.
zu·mute *Adj.* **jmdm. ist unbehaglich** *usw.* **~:** sb. feels uncomfortable *etc.*; **mir war nicht danach ~:** I didn't feel like it
zu|muten *tr. V.* **jmdm. etw. ~** (abverlangen) expect *or* ask sth. of sb.; (antun) expect sb. to put up with sth.
Zumutung *die;* **~, ~en** unreasonable demand; **eine ~ sein** be unreasonable
zu·nächst *Adv.* **(a)** (als erstes) first; (anfangs) at first
(b) (im Moment, vorläufig) for the moment
Zunahme *die;* **~, ~n** increase (*Gen.*, **an** + *Dat.* in)
Zu·name *der* surname; last name
zünden 1 *tr. V.* ignite ‹*gas, fuel, etc.*›; detonate ‹*bomb, explosive device, etc.*›; let off ‹*fireworks*›; fire ‹*rocket*›
2 *itr. V.* ‹*rocket, engine*› fire; ‹*lighter, match*› light; ‹*gas, fuel, explosive*› ignite
Zünd-: ~holz *das* (bes. südd., österr.) match; **~schlüssel** *der* (Kfz-W.) ignition key
Zündung *die;* **~, ~en (a)** ▶ ZÜNDEN 1: ignition; detonation; letting off; firing
(b) (Kfz-W.: Anlage) ignition
zu|nehmen *unr. itr. V.* **(a)** increase (**an** + *Dat.* in); ‹*moon*› wax
(b) (schwerer werden) put on *or* gain weight
Zu·neigung *die* affection
Zunge *die;* **~, ~n** tongue; **[jmdm.] die ~ herausstrecken** put one's tongue out [at sb.]
zu·nichte *Adj.* **etw. ~ machen** ruin sth.
zu·oberst *Adv.* [right] on [the] top
zu·pass, *zu·paß: jmdm. ~ kommen come [to sb.] at just the right moment
zupfen 1 *itr. V.* **an etw.** (*Dat.*) **~:** pluck *or* pull at sth.
2 *tr. V.* **(a) etw. aus/von** *usw.* **etw. ~:** pull sth. out of/from *etc.* sth.
(b) (auszupfen) pull out; pluck ‹*eyebrows*›
(c) pluck ‹*string, guitar, tune*›
(d) jmdn. am Ärmel ~: pull *or* tug [at] sb.'s sleeve
zur *Präp. + Art.* **(a)** = **zu der;**
(b) (räumlich, fig.: Richtung) to the; **~ Schule/ Arbeit gehen** go to school/work
(c) (räumlich: Lage) **~ Tür hereinkommen** come [in] through the door
(d) (Zusammengehörigkeit, Hinzufügung) with the
(e) (zeitlich) at the; **~ Stunde** at the moment; at present **~ Zeit** ▶ ZURZEIT
(f) (Zweck) **~ Entschuldigung** by way of [an] excuse
(g) (Folge) **~ vollen Zufriedenheit ihres Chefs** to the complete satisfaction of her boss
zurechnungs·fähig *Adj.* sound of mind *pred.*
zurecht-: ~|finden *unr. refl. V.* find one's way [around]; **~|kommen** *unr. itr. V.; mit sein* get on (**mit** with); **~|legen** *tr. V.* lay out [ready]; **jmdm. etw. ~legen** lay sth. out ready for sb.; **~|machen** *tr. V.* (ugs.) **(a)** (vorbereiten) get ready; **(b)** (herrichten) do up; **(c) jmdn./sich ~machen** get sb. ready/get [oneself] ready; (schminken) make sb. up/put on one's make-up; **~|weisen** *unr. tr. V.* rebuke; reprimand ‹*pupil, subordinate, etc.*›
zu|reden *itr. V.* **jmdm. ~:** persuade sb.; (ermutigen) encourage sb.
Zürich (*das*); **~s** Zurich
zu·rück *Adv.* back; (weiter hinten) behind; **einen Schritt ~:** a step backwards; **~!** get *or* go back!
zurück-, Zurück-: ~|behalten *unr. tr. V.* **(a)** keep [back]; retain; **(b)** be left with ‹*scar, heart defect, etc.*›; **~|bekommen** *unr. tr. V.* get back; **Sie bekommen 10 Euro ~:** you get 10 euros change; **~|bleiben** *unr. itr. V.; mit sein* **(a)** remain; **(b)** (nicht mithalten) lag behind; (fig.) fall behind; **(c)** (bleiben) remain; **~|blicken** *itr. V.* look back; **~|erstatten** *tr. V.* refund; **jmdm. etw. ~erstatten** refund sth. to sb.; **~|fahren** *unr. itr. V.; mit sein* **(a)** go back; return; **(b)** (nach hinten fahren) go back[wards]; **~|fallen** *unr. itr. V.; mit sein* **(a)** (in Rückstand geraten) fall behind; **(b)** (auf einen niedrigeren Rang) drop (**auf** + *Akk.* to); **(c) an jmdn. ~fallen** ‹*property*› revert to sb.; **(d) auf jmdn. ~fallen** ‹*actions, behaviour*› reflect [up]on sb.; **~|fliegen** *unr. itr. V.; mit sein* fly back; **~|führen** *tr. V.* **etw. auf etw.** (*Akk.*) **~führen** attribute sth. to sth.; **~|geben** *unr. tr. V.* give back; return; take back ‹*defective goods*›; **~|gehen** *unr. itr. V.; mit sein* **(a)** go back; return; **(b)** (nach hinten) go back; **(c)** (verschwinden) disappear; ‹*swelling, inflammation*› go down; ‹*pain*› subside; **(d)** (sich verringern) decrease; ‹*fever*› abate; ‹*flood*› subside; ‹*business*› fall off; **(e)** (zurückgeschickt werden) be returned *or* sent back; **~|greifen** *unr. itr. V.* **auf jmdn./etw.** ···›

~**zurückgreifen** fall back on sb./sth.; ~|**halten** 1 *unr. tr. V.* **(a)** **jmdn. ~halten** hold sb. back; (von etw. abhalten) stop sb.; **(b)** (am Vordringen hindern) keep back ‹*crowd, mob, etc.*›; **(c)** (behalten) withhold ‹*news, letter, etc.*›; **(d)** (nicht austreten lassen) hold back ‹*tears etc.*›; 2 *unr. refl. V.* restrain *or* control oneself; **sich in einer Diskussion ~halten** keep in the background in a discussion; ~**haltend** 1 *Adj.* **(a)** reserved; **(b)** (kühl, reserviert) cool, restrained ‹*reception, response*›; **(c)** (Wirtsch.: schwach) slack ‹*demand*›; 2 *adv.* ‹*behave*› with reserve *or* restraint; (kühl, reserviert) coolly; ~**haltung** *die* reserve; (Kühle, Reserviertheit) coolness; (Wirtsch.) caution; ~|**kehren** *itr. V.; mit sein* return; come back; ~|**kommen** *unr. itr. V.; mit sein* come back; return; (zurückgelangen) get back; ~**kommen auf** (+ *Akk.*) come back to ‹*subject, question, point, etc.*›; ~|**kriegen** *tr. V.* (ugs.) ▶ ~BEKOMMEN; ~|**lassen** *unr. tr. V.* leave; ~|**legen** *tr. V.* **(a)** put back; **(b)** (reservieren) put aside, keep (*Dat.*, **für** for); **(c)** (sparen) put away; **(d)** (hinter sich bringen) cover ‹*distance*›; ~|**lehnen** *refl. V.* lean back; ~|**nehmen** *unr. tr. V.* (auch fig. widerrufen) take back; ~|**rufen** *unr. tr. V.* **(a)** call back; recall ‹*ambassador*›; **(b)** *auch itr.* (telefonisch) call *or* (Brit.) ring back; ~|**schauen** *itr. V.* (bes. südd., österr., schweiz.) ▶ ~BLICKEN; ~|**schicken** *tr. V.* send back; ~|**schlagen** 1 *unr. tr. V.* **(a)** (nach hinten schlagen) fold back ‹*cover, hood, etc.*›; turn down ‹*collar*›; **(b)** (durch einen Schlag zurückbefördern) hit back; (mit dem Fuß) kick back; **(c)** (zum Rückzug zwingen, abwehren) beat off, repulse ‹*enemy, attack*›; 2 *unr. itr. V.* **(a)** hit back; ‹*enemy*› strike back, retaliate; **(b)** *mit sein* ‹*pendulum*› swing back; ~|**schrecken** *regelm.*, (veralt.) *unr., itr. V., mit sein* **vor etw.** (*Dat.*) ~**schrecken** (fig.) shrink from sth.; **er schreckt vor nichts ~:** he will stop at nothing; ~|**senden** *unr. od. regelm. tr. V.* (geh.) ▶ ~SCHICKEN; ~|**treten** *unr. itr. V.; mit sein* step back; (von einem Amt) resign; step down; ‹*government*› resign; (von einem Vertrag usw.) withdraw (**von** from); back out (**von** of); (fig.: in den Hintergrund treten) become less important; ~|**weisen** *unr. tr. V.* reject ‹*proposal, question, demand, application, etc.*›; turn down, refuse ‹*offer, request, help, etc.*›; turn away ‹*petitioner, unwelcome guest*›; repudiate ‹*accusation, claim, etc.*›; ~|**werfen** *unr. tr. V.* throw back; reflect ‹*light, sound*›; repulse ‹*enemy*›; (fig.: in einer Entwicklung) set back; ~|**zahlen** *tr. V.* pay back; ~|**ziehen** 1 *unr. tr. V.* **(a)** pull back; draw back ‹*bolt, curtains, one's hand, etc.*›; **(b)** (abziehen, zurückbeordern) withdraw ‹*troops*›; recall ‹*ambassador*›; **(c)** (rückgängig machen) withdraw; cancel ‹*order, instruction*›; 2 *unr. refl. V.* withdraw

Zu·ruf *der* shout

zu|rufen *unr. tr. V.* **jmdm. etw. ~:** shout sth. to sb.

zur·zeit *Adv.* at the moment

Zu·sage *die* **(a)** (auf eine Einladung hin) acceptance; (auf eine Stellenbewerbung hin) offer **(b)** (Versprechen) promise; undertaking

zu|sagen 1 *itr. V.* **(a)** accept **(b)** **jmdm. ~** (gefallen) appeal to sb. 2 *tr. V.* promise

zusammen *Adv.* together; **~ sein** (zusammenleben) be *or* live together

zusammen-, Zusammen-: ~**arbeit** *die* cooperation *no indef. art.;* ~|**arbeiten** *itr. V.* cooperate; ~|**binden** *unr. tr. V.* tie together; ~|**brechen** *unr. itr. V.; mit sein* collapse; (fig.) ‹*order, communications, system, telephone network*› break down; ‹*traffic*› come to a standstill; ~**bruch** *der* collapse; (fig., auch psychisch, nervlich) breakdown; ~|**drücken** *tr. V.* press together; ~|**fahren** *unr. itr. V.; mit sein* (zusammenzucken) start; jump; ~|**fallen** *unr. itr. V.; mit sein* **(a)** collapse; **(b)** **[zeitlich] ~fallen** coincide; ~|**fassen** *tr. V.* summarize; ~**fassung** *die* summary; ~|**fegen** *tr. V.* (bes. nordd.) sweep together; ~|**fließen** *unr. itr. V.; mit sein* ‹*rivers, streams*› flow into each other; ~**fluss,** *~**fluß** *der* confluence; ~|**fügen** *tr. V.* fit together; ~|**führen** *tr. V.* bring together; ~|**gehören** *itr. V.* belong together; ~**gehörig** *Adj.* [closely] related *or* connected ‹*subjects, problems, etc.*›; matching *attrib.* ‹*pieces of tea service, cutlery, etc.*›; ~**gehörigkeit** *die;* **~~: ein starkes Gefühl der ~gehörigkeit** a strong sense of belonging together; ~**gehörigkeits·gefühl** *das* sense *or* feeling of belonging together; ~**hang** *der* connection; (einer Geschichte, Rede) coherence; (Kontext) context; ~|**hängen** *unr. itr. V.* **(a)** be joined [together]; **(b)** **mit etw. ~hängen** (fig.) be related to sth.; (durch etw. [mit] verursacht sein) be the result of sth.; ~|**kehren** *tr. V.* (bes. südd.) sweep together; ~**klappbar** *Adj.* folding; ~|**klappen** *tr. V.* fold up; ~|**kommen** *unr. itr. V.; mit sein* **(a)** meet; **mit jmdm. ~kommen** meet sb.; **(b)** (zueinanderkommen; auch fig.) get together; (gleichzeitig auftreten) occur *or* happen together; ~**kunft** *die;* **~~, ~künfte** meeting; ~|**laufen** *unr. itr. V.; mit sein* **(a)** ‹*people, crowd*› gather, congregate; **(b)** ‹*rivers, streams*› flow into each other, join up; ~|**leben** *itr. V.* live together; ~**leben** *das* living together *no art.;* ~|**legen** 1 *tr. V.* **(a)** put *or* gather together; **(b)** (zusammenfalten) fold [up]; **(c)** (miteinander verbinden) amalgamate, merge ‹*classes, departments, etc.*›; combine ‹*events*›; **(d)** put ‹*patients, guests, etc.*› together [in the same room]; 2 *itr. V.* club together; ~|**nehmen** 1 *unr. tr. V.* summon up ‹*courage, strength, understanding*›; 2 *unr. refl. V.* get *or* take a grip on oneself; **nimm dich ~!** pull yourself

*old spelling - see note on page xiv

Z

together!; ~|**passen** *itr. V.* go together; ‹*persons*› be suited to each other; ~**prall** *der;* ~~[e]s, ~~e collision; ~|**prallen** *itr. V.; mit sein* collide (mit with); ~|**schlagen** *unr. tr. V.* (verprügeln) beat up; *~|**sein** ▶ ZUSAMMEN; ~|**setzen** 1 *tr. V.* put together; 2 *refl. V.* (a) **sich aus etw. ~setzen** be made up *or* composed of sth.; (b) (sich zueinander setzen) sit together; (zu einem Gespräch) get together; ~**setzung** *die;* ~~, ~~en (a) putting together; (b) (Aufbau) composition; „~**setzung:** ..." (als Aufschrift auf Medikamentenpackung) 'ingredients: ...'; (c) (Sprachw.) compound; ~**spiel** *das* (a) (von Musikern) ensemble playing; (von Darstellern) ensemble acting; (einer Mannschaft) teamwork; (b) (fig.) interplay; ~|**stehen** *unr. itr. V.* stand together; ~|**stellen** *tr. V.* put together; draw up ‹*list*›; ~**stoß** *der* collision; (fig.) clash (mit with); ~|**stoßen** *unr. itr. V.; mit sein* collide (mit with); ~|**treffen** *unr. itr. V.; mit sein* (a) meet; **mit jmdm. ~treffen** meet sb.; (b) (zeitlich) coincide; ~|**wachsen** *unr. itr. V.; mit sein* grow together; join [up]; ‹*bones*› knit together; (fig.) ‹*towns*› merge into one; ~|**zählen** *tr. V.* add up; ~|**ziehen** *unr. itr. V.; mit sein* move in together; **mit jmdm. ~ziehen** move in with sb.; ~|**zucken** *itr. V.; mit sein* start; jump

Zu·satz *der* addition; (Zugesetztes, Additiv) additive

zusätzlich 1 *Adj.* additional
2 *adv.* in addition

zu|schauen *itr. V.* (südd., österr., schweiz.) ▶ ZUSEHEN

Zu·schauer *der,* **Zu·schauerin** *die;* ~, ~nen spectator; (im Theater, Kino) member of the audience; (an einer Unfallstelle) onlooker; (Fernsehzuschauer) viewer; **die Zuschauer** (im Theater, Kino) the audience *sing.*

Zuschauer·zahl *die* (bes. Ferns.) audience [numbers]; (Sport) attendance

zu|schicken *tr. V.* send; **jmdm. etw. ~:** send sth. to sb.

zu|schieben *unr. tr. V.* (a) push ‹*drawer, door*› shut
(b) (fig.) **jmdm. die Schuld ~:** lay the blame on sb.

Zu·schlag *der* (a) additional *or* extra charge; (für Nacht-, Feiertagsarbeit usw.) additional *or* extra payment
(b) (Eisenb.) supplement

zu|schlagen 1 *unr. tr. V.* bang *or* slam ‹*door, window, etc.*› shut; close ‹*book*›; (heftig) slam ‹*book*› shut
2 *unr. itr. V.* (a) *mit sein* ‹*door, trap*› slam *or* bang shut
(b) (einen Schlag/Schläge führen) throw a blow/blows; (losschlagen) hit *or* strike out; (fig.) ‹*army, police, murderer*› strike

zu|schließen 1 *unr. tr. V.* lock
2 *unr. itr. V.* lock up

zu|schnüren *tr. V.* tie up

zu|schrauben *tr. V.* screw the lid *or* top on ‹*jar, flask*›; screw ‹*lid, top*› on

Zu·schrift *die* letter; (auf eine Anzeige) reply

Zu·schuss, ***Zu·schuß** *der* contribution (zu towards)

zu|sehen *unr. itr. V.* (a) watch; **jmdm. [beim Arbeiten** *usw.*] **~:** watch sb. [working *etc.*]
(b) (dafür sorgen) make sure; see to it

zu|senden *unr. od. regelm. tr. V.* ▶ ZUSCHICKEN

Zu·sendung *die* sending

zu|spitzen *refl. V.* become aggravated

zu|sprechen 1 *unr. tr. V.* (a) **er sprach ihr Trost/Mut zu** his words gave her comfort/courage
(b) **jmdm. ein Erbe** *usw.* **~:** award sb. an inheritance *etc.;*
2 *unr. itr. V.* **jmdm. ermutigend/tröstend ~:** speak encouragingly/comfortingly to sb.

Zu·stand *der* (a) condition; (bes. abwertend) state
(b) (Stand der Dinge) state of affairs

zu·stande *Adv.* **etw. ~ bringen** [manage to] bring about sth.; **~ kommen** come into being; (geschehen) take place

zu·ständig *Adj.* appropriate relevant ‹*authority, office, etc.*›; **[für etw.] ~ sein** (verantwortlich) be responsible [for sth.]

Zuständigkeit *die;* ~, ~en (Verantwortlichkeit) responsibility; (Kompetenz) competence

zu|stehen *unr. itr. V.* **etw. steht jmdm. zu** sb. is entitled to sth.

zu|steigen *unr. itr. V.; mit sein* get on; **ist noch jemand zugestiegen?** (im Bus) ≈ any more fares, please?; (im Zug) ≈ tickets, please!

zu|stellen *tr. V.* deliver ‹*letter, parcel, etc.*›

zu|stimmen *itr. V.* agree; **jmdm. [in einem Punkt] ~:** agree with sb. [on a point]; **einer Sache** (*Dat.*) **~:** agree to sth.

Zu·stimmung *die* (Billigung) approval (zu of); (Einverständnis) agreement (zu to, with)

zu|stoßen *unr. itr. V.; mit sein* **jmdm. ~:** happen to sb.

Zu·tat *die* ingredient

zu·teil *Adv.* **jmdm./einer Sache ~ werden** (geh.) be granted to sb./sth.

zu|teilen *tr. V.* **jmdm. jmdn./etw. ~:** allot *or* assign sb./sth. to sb.; **jmdm. seine Portion ~:** mete out his/her share to sb.

zu|tragen *unr. refl. V.* (geh.) occur

zuträglich *Adj.* healthy ‹*climate*›; **jmdm./einer Sache ~ sein** be good for sb./sth.; be beneficial to sb./sth.

zu|trauen *tr. V.* **jmdm. etw. ~:** believe sb. [is] capable of [doing] sth.; **sich** (*Dat.*) **etw. ~:** think one can do sth.

Zutrauen *das;* ~s confidence, trust (zu in)

zutraulich 1 *Adj.* trusting
2 *adv.* trustingly

Zutraulichkeit *die; ~:* trust[fulness]

zu|treffen *unr. itr. V.* **(a)** be correct **(b) auf** *od.* **für jmdn./etw. ~:** apply to sb./sth.

zutreffend 1 *Adj.* **(a)** correct; (treffend) accurate **(b)** (geltend) applicable; relevant 2 *adv.* correctly

zu|trinken *unr. itr. V.* **jmdm. ~:** raise one's glass and drink to sb.

Zu·tritt *der* entry; admittance; **„kein ~", „~ verboten"** 'no entry'; 'no admittance'; **~ [zu etw.] haben** have access [to sth.]

Zu·tun *das;* **~s: ohne jmds. ~:** without sb.'s being involved

zu·unterst *Adv.* right at the bottom

zuverlässig 1 *Adj.* reliable; (verlässlich) dependable ‹*person*› 2 *adv.* reliably

Zuverlässigkeit *die; ~:* reliability; (Verlässlichkeit) dependability

Zuversicht *die; ~:* confidence

zuversichtlich 1 *Adj.* confident 2 *adv.* confidently

***zuviel** ▶ ZU 2A

zu·vor *Adv.* before

zuvor|kommen *unr. itr. V.; mit sein* **(a) jmdm. ~:** beat sb. to it **(b) einer Sache** (*Dat.*) **~:** anticipate sth.

zuvorkommend 1 *Adj.* obliging; (höflich) courteous 2 *adv.* obligingly; (höflich) courteously

Zuvorkommenheit *die; ~:* courteousness; courtesy

Zuwachs *der;* **~es, Zuwächse** increase (*Gen.*, **an** + *Dat.* in)

Zuwachs·rate *die* (bes. Wirtsch.) growth rate

Zu·wanderer *der,* **Zu·wanderin** *die* immigrant

Zu·wanderung *die* immigration

zu·weilen *Adv.* (geh.) now and again

zu|weisen *unr. tr. V.* **jmdm. etw. ~:** allocate *or* allot sb. sth.

zu|wenden *unr. od. regelm. refl. V.* **sich jmdm./einer Sache ~** (auch fig.) turn to sb./sth.

***zu·wenig** ▶ ZU 2A

zuwider *Adj.* **jmdm. ~ sein** be repugnant to sb.

zu|winken *itr. V.* **jmdm./einander ~:** wave to sb./one another

zu|zahlen *tr. V.* pay ‹*five euros etc.*› extra

zu|ziehen 1 *unr. tr. V.* pull ‹*door*› shut; draw ‹*curtain*›; do up ‹*zip*› 2 *unr. refl. V.* **sich** (*Dat.*) **eine Krankheit ~:** catch an illness 3 *unr. itr. V.; mit sein* move into the area

Zu·zug *der* influx

zuzüglich *Präp. mit Gen.* plus

zwang *1. u. 3. Pers. Sg. Prät. v.* ZWINGEN

*alte Schreibung - vgl. Hinweis auf S. xiv

Zwang *der;* **~[e]s, Zwänge (a)** compulsion **(b)** (unwiderstehlicher Drang) irresistible urge

zwängen 1 *tr. V.* squeeze 2 *refl. V.* squeeze [oneself]

zwanghaft *Adj.* obsessive

zwanglos 1 *Adj.* **(a)** informal; casual ‹*behaviour*› **(b)** (unregelmäßig) haphazard ‹*arrangement*› 2 *adv.* **(a)** informally **(b)** (unregelmäßig) haphazardly ‹*arranged*›

Zwanglosigkeit *die; ~:* **(a)** informality **(b)** (Unregelmäßigkeit) haphazard *or* casual manner

Zwangs·lage *die* predicament

zwangs·läufig 1 *Adj.* inevitable 2 *adv.* inevitably

zwanzig *Kardinalz.* twenty; *s. auch* ACHTZIG

zwanziger *indekl. Adj.* **die ~ Jahre** the twenties

Zwanzig·mark·schein *der* twenty-mark note

zwanzigst... *Ordinalz.* twentieth

zwar *Adv.* **(a)** admittedly **(b) und ~:** to be precise

Zweck *der;* **~[e]s, ~e** purpose; (Sinn) point; **es hat keinen ~:** it's pointless; **es hat keinen ~, das zu tun** there is no point in doing that

zweck-, Zweck-: ~entfremden *tr. V.* use for another purpose; **~los** *Adj.* pointless; **~losigkeit** *die; ~~:* pointlessness; **~mäßig** 1 *Adj.* appropriate; expedient ‹*behaviour, action*›; functional ‹*building, fittings, furniture*›; 2 *adv.* appropriately ‹*arranged, clothed*›; ‹*act*› expediently; ‹*equip, furnish*› functionally; **~mäßigkeit** *die* appropriateness; (einer Handlung) expediency; (eines Gebäudes) functionalism

zwecks *Präp. mit Gen.* (Papierdt.) for the purpose of

zwei *Kardinalz.* two; *s. auch* ACHT[1]

Zwei *die;* **~, ~en (a)** (Zahl) two **(b)** (Schulnote) B

zwei-, Zwei-: ~bettzimmer *das* twin-bedded room; **~deutig** 1 *Adj.* ambiguous; (fig.: schlüpfrig) suggestive ‹*remark, joke*›; 2 *adv.* ambiguously; (fig.) suggestively; **~deutigkeit** *die; ~~, ~~en* ambiguity; (fig.) suggestiveness; **~dimensional** 1 *Adj.* two-dimensional; 2 *adv.* two-dimensionally; **~ein·halb** *Bruchz.* two and a half

zweierlei *indekl. Adj.* **(a)** *attr.* two sorts *or* kinds of; two different ‹*sizes, kinds, etc.*›; odd ‹*socks, gloves*› **(b)** *allein stehend* two [different] things

zwei·fach *Vervielfältigungsz.* double; (zweimal) twice

Zwei·fache *das; adj. Dekl.* **das ~:** twice as much

Zweifel *der;* **~s, ~:** doubt (**an** + *Dat.* about); **etw. in ~ ziehen** question sth.

zweifelhaft *Adj.* **(a)** doubtful

(b) (fragwürdig) dubious; (suspekt) suspicious

zweifel·los *Adv.* undoubtedly

zweifeln *itr. V.* doubt; **an jmdm./etw. ~:** doubt sb./sth.; have doubts about sb./sth.

zweifels-, Zweifels-: ~fall *der* case of doubt; doubtful *or* problematic case; **im ~fall[e]** in case of doubt; if in doubt; **~ohne** *Adv.* undoubtedly; without doubt

Zweig *der;* **~[e]s, ~e** [small] branch; (meist ohne Blätter) twig

zwei-, Zwei-: ~hundert *Kardinalz.* two hundred; **~mal** *Adv.* twice; **~mark·stück** *das* two-mark piece; **~pfennig·stück** *das* two-pfennig piece; **~reiher** *der* double-breasted suit/coat/jacket; **~schneidig** *Adj.* double-edged; **~sprachig** [1] *Adj.* bilingual; ‹*sign*› in two languages; [2] *adv.* bilingually; ‹*written*› in two languages; ‹*published*› in a bilingual edition; **~spurig** *Adj.* **(a)** two-lane ‹*road*›; **(b)** two-track ‹*vehicle*›; **(c)** two- *or* twin-track ‹*recording*›; **~stellig** *Adj.* two-figure *attrib.* ‹*number, sum*›; **~stöckig** *Adj.* two-storey *attrib.;* **~stöckig sein** have two storeys

zweit... *Ordinalz.* second; **jeder Zweite** every other one; *s. auch* ERST...

zwei·tägig *Adj.* (2 Tage alt) two-day-old *attrib.;* (2 Tage dauernd) two-day *attrib.*

zweit·ältest... *Adj.* second oldest

zwei·tausend *Kardinalz.* two thousand

zweit·best... *Adj.* second best

***zweite·mal** ▶ MAL[1]

***zweiten·mal** ▶ MAL[1]

zweitens *Adv.* secondly; in the second place

Zweite[r]-Klasse-Abteil *das* second-class compartment

zweit·rangig *Adj.* of secondary importance *postpos.;* (zweitklassig) second-rate

Zweit·stimme *die* second vote

zwei·türig *Adj.* two-door ‹*car*›

Zweit-: ~wagen *der* second car; **~wohnung** *die* second home

Zwei·zimmer·wohnung *die* two-room flat (Brit.) *or* (Amer.) apartment

Zwerch·fell *das* (Anat.) diaphragm

Zwerg *der;* **~[e]s, ~e** dwarf; (Gartenzwerg) gnome

Zwetsche *die;* **~, ~n** damson plum

Zwieback *der;* **~[e]s, ~e** *od.* **Zwiebäcke** rusk; (unzählbar) rusks *pl.*

Zwiebel *die;* **~, ~n** onion; (Blumenzwiebel) bulb

zwie-, Zwie-: ~gespräch *das* (geh.) dialogue; **~spalt** *der;* **~~[e]s, ~~e** *od.* **~spälte** [inner] conflict; **~spältig** *Adj.* conflicting ‹*mood, feelings*›; discordant ‹*impression*›; (widersprüchlich) contradictory ‹*nature, attitude, person, etc.*›

Zwilling *der;* **~s, ~e (a)** twin **(b)** *Pl.* (Astrol.) Gemini; the Twins; **er/sie ist [ein] ~:** he/she is a Gemini

Zwillings-: ~bruder *der* twin brother; **~paar** *das* pair of twins; **~schwester** *die* twin sister

zwingen *unr. tr. V.* force; **jmdn. [dazu] ~, etw. zu tun** force *or* compel sb. to do sth.

zwingend *Adj.* compelling ‹*reason, logic*›; conclusive ‹*proof, argument*›; imperative ‹*necessity*›

zwinkern *itr. V.* **[mit den Augen] ~:** blink; (als Zeichen) wink

Zwirn *der;* **~[e]s, ~e** [strong] thread *or* yarn

zwischen *Präp. mit Dat./Akk.* between; (mitten unter) among[st]

zwischen-, Zwischen-: ~durch /-'-/ *Adv.* (zeitlich) between times; (zwischen zwei Zeitpunkten) in between; (von Zeit zu Zeit) from time to time; **~fall** *der* incident; **~|landen** *itr. V.; mit sein* **in X ~landen** land in X on the way; **~mahlzeit** *die* snack [between meals]; **~menschlich** [1] *Adj.* interpersonal ‹*relations*›; ‹*contacts*› between people; [2] *adv.* on a personal level; **~raum** *der* space; gap; (Lücke) gap; **~ruf** *der* interruption; **viele ~rufe** a great deal of heckling *sing.;* **~wand** *die* dividing wall; partition; **~zeit** *die* interim

Zwist *der;* **~[e]s, ~e** (geh.) strife *no indef. art.;* (Fehde) feud; dispute

Zwistigkeit *die;* **~, ~en** (geh.) dispute

zwitschern *itr. (auch tr.) V.* chirp

Zwitter *der;* **~s, ~** (Biol.) hermaphrodite

zwo *Kardinalz.* (ugs.; bes. zur Verdeutlichung) two

zwölf *Kardinalz.* twelve; **~ Uhr mittags/nachts** [twelve o'clock] midday/midnight; *s. auch* ACHT[1]

zwölft... *Ordinalz.* twelfth; *s. auch* ACHT...

zwölftel *Bruchz.* twelfth; *s. auch* ACHTEL

Zwölftel *das* (schweiz. meist *der*); **~s, ~:** twelfth

zwot... *Ordinalz.* (ugs.; bes. zur Verdeutlichung) second

zwotens *Adv.* (ugs.; bes. zur Verdeutlichung) secondly

Zylinder /tsi'lɪndɐ/ *der;* **~s, ~ (a)** cylinder; **(b)** (Hut) top hat

zylindrisch [1] *Adj.* cylindrical [2] *adv.* cylindrically

Zyniker *der;* **~s, ~, Zynikerin** *die;* **~, ~nen** cynic

zynisch [1] *Adj.* cynical [2] *adv.* cynically

Zynismus *der;* **~:** cynicism

Zypern *(das);* **~s** Cyprus

Zyprer *der;* **~s, ~, Zyprerin** *die;* **~, ~nen** Cypriot

Zypresse *die;* **~, ~n** cypress

Zypriot *der;* **~en, ~en, Zypriotin** *die;* **~, ~nen** Cypriot

zypriotisch, zyprisch *Adj.* Cypriot

Zyste *die;* **~, ~n** (Med.) cyst

Contents

Traditions, festivals, and holidays in German-speaking countries

1 January Neujahr (New Year's Day) is always a public holiday and tends to be a quiet day when people are recovering from the Silvester celebrations.

6 January Heilige Drei Könige Epiphany or Twelfth Night is a public holiday in Austria and some parts of southern Germany. In some areas, children dress up as the Three Kings and go from house to house to bless homes for the coming year and collect money for charity.

2 February Mariä Lichtmess Candlemas is celebrated in the Catholic Church but is not a public holiday.

1 April Erster April April Fool's Day is the time to make an April fool of your family and friends (*jdn. in den April schicken*) or to play an April fool trick (*Aprilscherz*).

1 May Erster Mai May Day is a public holiday in Germany, Austria, and Switzerland. It is celebrated by trade unions as Labour Day, often with rallies and demonstrations. Many people go on a family outing; in rural areas maypoles are put up in the villages.

3 October Tag der deutschen Einheit Germany's national holiday, the Day of German Unity, commemorates German reunification on 3 October 1990.

26 October Nationalfeiertag Austria's national holiday.

31 October Reformationstag Reformation Day is a public holiday in some mainly Protestant parts of Germany and commemorates the Reformation.

1 November Allerheiligen All Saints' Day is a public holiday in Catholic parts of Germany and Austria.

2 November Allerseelen All Souls' Day is the day when Catholics remember their dead by visiting the cemeteries to pray and place wreaths, flowers, and candles on the graves. This is often done on 1 November as Allerseelen is not a public holiday.

11 November Martinstag (St Martin's Day) is not a public holiday, but in Catholic areas the charitable saint is commemorated with processions where children carry lanterns and sing songs. Traditional food includes the *Martinsgans* (roast goose) and *Martinsbrezel* (a soft pretzel).

6 December Nikolaustag On the eve of St Nicholas' Day, children put out their boots in the hope of finding presents and fruit, nuts, and sweets in the morning. St Nicholas is always depicted as looking much like Santa Claus or Father Christmas.

25 December Weihnachten (Christmas) is a family event in Germany, and preparations begin with the *Adventskranz*, an Advent wreath with four candles. On each Sunday of Advent one more candle is lit. Christmas decorations are generally very traditional, with fir branches, candles and wooden Christmas figurines, which can be bought at the *Weihnachtsmarkt* (Christmas market). Typical Christmas baking includes *Stollen* or *Christstollen* (a rich fruit bread), *Lebkuchen* (spicy honey biscuits), and lots of biscuits in the shape of stars, bells, etc. The decorated Christmas tree should only be seen by the children on Heiligabend (Christmas Eve), when presents are given out. The erster Weihnachtstag (Christmas Day) is a public holiday in Germany, Austria, and Switzerland. It tends to be a quiet day for family gatherings, often with a traditional lunch of goose or carp.

The zweiter Weihnachtstag (Boxing Day) is also a public holiday; in Austria and Switzerland it is called Stephanstag (St Stephen's Day).

31 December Silvester New Year's Eve is not a bank holiday, but firms and shops tend to close early. Many people celebrate with a party, or a meal with friends, toasting in the new year at midnight with Sekt (German sparkling wine), and watching fireworks.

Movable feasts

Rosenmontag The day before Shrove Tuesday is not an official holiday but many people, especially in the Rhineland, get the day off to take part in the *Karneval* celebrations, including masked balls, fancy-dress parties, and parades. Almost every town has its own carnival prince and princess. The street parades in Düsseldorf, Cologne, Mainz, and other cities are attended by thousands of revellers wearing fancy dress and shown live on television.

Faschingsdienstag Shrove Tuesday is the final day of *Fasching* (Carnival) in southern Germany, with processions and fancy-dress parties similar to Rosenmontag in the northwest. In the far south, ancient customs to drive out the winter with bells and drums survive.

Aschermittwoch Ash Wednesday marks the end of the carnival season and the beginning of Lent. It is celebrated in the Catholic Church but it is not a pubic holiday.

Karfreitag Good Friday is a public holiday and generally quiet. Catholics traditionally eat fish on this day.

Ostern Easter traditions include hiding Easter eggs (often dyed hardboiled eggs, or the chocolate variety) in the garden for the children, supposedly left by the *Osterhase* (Easter bunny). Ostermontag (Easter Monday) is also a public holiday.

Weißer Sonntag (Sunday after Easter) In the Catholic Church, first communion is traditionally taken on this Sunday.

Muttertag (second Sunday in May). On Mother's Day, children of all ages give their mothers small gifts, cards, or flowers.

Christi Himmelfahrt (40 days after Easter). Ascension Day is a public holiday in Germany, Austria, and Switzerland. This is also Father's Day, when fathers traditionally go out on day trips or pub crawls.

Pfingsten (Whitsun – seventh Sunday after Easter). As Pfingstmontag (Whit Monday) is a public holiday in Germany, Austria, and Switzerland, Whitsun is a popular time to have a long weekend away.

Fronleichnam (second Thursday after Whitsun). Corpus Christi is a public holiday in Austria and in parts of Germany and Switzerland. In Catholic areas, processions and open-air masses are held.

Erntedankfest Harvest festival is not a legal holiday in Germany, but is celebrated with church services on the first Sunday in October in many rural areas. In Switzerland there is a harvest thanksgiving holiday in mid-September.

Buß- und Bettag (third Wednesday in November). This day of 'repentance and prayer' is a public holiday only in some parts of Germany.

Volkstrauertag (second Sunday before the beginning of Advent). In Germany, this is a national day of mourning to commemorate the dead of both world wars, and the victims of the Nazis.

Totensonntag (last Sunday before the beginning of Advent). Protestants remember their dead on this day.

Advent The four weeks leading up to Christmas, beginning with the **1. Adventssonntag** (first Sunday in Advent), still have a special significance in Germany, even for people who are not religious.

A–Z of life and culture in German-speaking countries

Abendbrot, Abendessen For most Germans, MITTAGESSEN is still the main meal of the day. *Abendbrot* or *Abendessen* normally consists of bread, cheese, meats, perhaps a salad, and a hot drink. It is eaten by the whole family at about 6 or 7 p.m. *Abendessen* can also refer to a cooked meal, especially for people who are out at work all day.

Abitur The *Abitur*, or *Matura* in Austria, is the final exam taken by pupils at a GYMNASIUM, usually when they are aged about 19. The result is based on continuous assessment during the last two years before the *Abitur*, plus examinations in four subjects. On passing the *Abitur*, a *Zeugnis der allgemeinen Hochschulreife* is issued. This certificate is the obligatory qualification for university entrance.

Adventskranz A garland made of fir springs, traditionally decorated with ribbons and four candles. The wreath is either suspended from the ceiling or put on a table. One candle is lit on the first Sunday in Advent, two on the next, and so on until the fourth Sunday.

Allerheiligen ▸ TRADITIONS, FESTIVALS, AND HOLIDAYS

Allerseelen ▸ TRADITIONS, FESTIVALS, AND HOLIDAYS

Amerikahaus In Germany and Austria, Amerikahäuser are US information centres. They have reference libraries and offer language courses and lectures.

Ampelkoalition A term describing any coalition between the SPD (the party colour is red), the FDP (yellow), and the Green Party (*see* BÜNDNIS 90). This type of coalition has become increasingly common in local government over the last ten years, with some LÄNDER ruled in this way.

Amtsgericht *Amtsgerichte* (local or district courts) are the lowest level of ordinary courts in Germany. They work in a two-tier system with the *Landgerichte* (regional courts) and deal with minor cases. There are four levels of ordinary courts hearing both civil and criminal cases: beside the *Amtsgericht* and *Landgericht* there are the *Oberlandesgericht* (higher regional court) and the *Bundesgerichtshof* (federal supreme court). Most legal proceedings at the local court are handled by magistrates. The regional courts handle more serious cases and deal with local court appeals; a panel of lay judges sits with a professional judge in a regional court.

Arbeitsagentur The local employment office to be found in every German town (formerly called *Arbeitsamt*). It provides career guidance, helps the unemployed find new jobs, and processes all claims for ARBEITSLOSENGELD I and related benefits. Unemployed people have to report to the *Arbeitsagentur* once every three months to prove that they are still looking for work.

Arbeitsgericht Industrial tribunals are held at administrative courts (local, higher, and federal), which handle all proceedings under administrative law. They deal with disputes between employers and employees, between employers and trade unions, and matters connected with the *Betriebsverfassungsgesetz* (industrial relations law).

Arbeitslosengeld I, or earnings-related unemployment benefit, is paid to all unemployed people who are looking for a new job and have already made a minimum contribution to the ARBEITSLOSENVERSICHERUNG. The benefit is a proportion of the person's previous pay, and is higher for people supporting children. It is generally paid for up to one year. People unemployed for longer than twelve months, or those who are not entitled to *Arbeitslosengeld I*, can apply for the so-called *Arbeitslosengeld II* (unemployment benefit II), which has replaced *Arbeitslosenhilfe* and is a reduced-rate benefit.

Arbeitsamt ▶ ARBEITSAGENTUR

Arbeitslosenversicherung This is the compulsory state-run insurance against unemployment. All employees have to pay into this scheme, and in return are entitled to ARBEITSLOSENGELD I and related benefits. Employees and employers each pay half of the contributions. This area has been subject to wide-ranging reforms in recent years.

Archiv der Jugendkulturen Since 1998 the Archive of Youth Culture in Berlin has been collecting and cataloguing books, magazines, CDs, and other materials of special interest to young people. The Archive is open to the public and publishes a magazine called *Journal der Jugendkulturen* (Journal of Youth Culture).

ARD – Arbeitsgemeinschaft der öffentlich-rechtlichen Rundfunkanstalten der Bundesrepublik Deutschland An umbrella organization for the regional broadcasting stations of the various German LÄNDER, financed by licence fees plus a certain amount of advertising. The ARD broadcasts das ERSTE.

Aschermittwoch ▶ TRADITIONS, FESTIVALS, AND HOLIDAYS

AStA — Allgemeiner Studentenausschuss A students' union which consists of twelve student boards elected by a student parliament that is voted in annually. AStA deals with all student issues, including financial, cultural, and social concerns, offering advice and support.

Ausbildungsplatz Over 500,000 firms in all branches of the economy, including the independent professions and the public sector, provide trainee posts for AZUBIS. Young people can only apply for these in state-recognized occupations for which vocational training is required. Large firms have their own training workshops, but smaller firms train their apprentices on the job.

Autobahn Germany's motorway network is very extensive and not subject to a general speed limit, other than a recommended limit of about 80 mph (130 km/h). But increasingly speed limits are in force on long stretches of the *Autobahn*. Many motorways have only two lanes. To ease congestion, lorries are not allowed to use the *Autobahn* on Sundays. German motorways are free for passenger traffic. Lorries over twelve tonnes pay a toll known as *Autobahngebühren*. On Austrian and Swiss motorways, all vehicles must display a VIGNETTE.

Azubi Trainees and apprentices are known as *Azubis* or *Auszubildende*. They are trained within the German dual system (*das duale Ausbildungssystem*), which combines practical on-the-job training in recognized occupations with theoretical instruction at a BERUFSSCHULE. During the training period, *Azubis* receive a small wage from their employer. In order to gain professional qualifications, *Azubis* take an examination at the end of their two- or three-year apprenticeship; this is conducted by a board of examiners such as the chamber of industry and commerce, the chamber of crafts, or representatives of employers and vocational schoolteachers.

Bachfest This ten-day music festival is held annually in honour of the great German composer Johann Sebastian Bach (1685–1750), and takes place in Leipzig, where Bach spent many years of his life. The Bachfest is one of more than a hundred important music festivals in Germany.

BAföG – Bundesausbildungsförderungsgesetz Federal education and training assistance, which about a quarter of German students receive from the state. Whether they are entitled to a *BAföG* grant or loan, and how much they get, depends on the students' and their parents' financial circumstances. Half of this assistance is awarded in the form of a grant, and the rest as an interest-free loan which usually has to be repaid within five years of the end of the maximum entitlement period. The payments are made by the STUDENTENWERKE (student welfare services).

BahnCard A rail pass for frequent rail travellers within Germany. *Bahncard 25*/*Bahncard 50*/*Bahncard 100* entitle the holder to 25 per cent, 50 per cent, or 100 per cent discount respectively. There are a number of other passes and saver tickets offering reductions throughout Germany, Austria, Switzerland, and neighbouring countries.

Bauhaus A school of architecture and the applied arts founded in 1919 in Weimar and later housed at Dessau. Under the leadership of Walter Gropius (1883–1969) and Ludwig Mies van der Rohe (1886–1969), it became the centre of modern design in the 1920s and played a key role in establishing a relationship between architecture, technology, and functionality. The Bauhaus was closed down by the Nazis in 1933.

Bausparen German building societies expect people to have saved up a sizeable sum towards the purchase of a house before they will give them a mortgage. For this reason, many Germans have a *Bausparvertrag* (a tax-efficient savings contract for an agreed sum) with a building society, even if they are not planning to buy their EIGENHEIM for some time.

Bayern Bayern, or Bavaria, the largest and most southerly of Germany's LÄNDER, is known for its beautiful scenery (the Alps and their foothills, as well as forests, rivers, and lakes, picturesque towns and villages), its excellent BIER (beer) and food, and its lively cosmopolitan capital, München (Munich). The Bavarians are said to be warm and hospitable, but also fiercely independent and very conservative.

Bayreuth The Franconian city of Bayreuth in Bavaria is a magnet for opera fans. The German composer Richard Wagner (1813–83) lived there from 1872. Since 1876 the Richard Wagner Festival has been staged annually in the Festspielhaus, the festival theatre built between 1872 and 1876 with funding by the Bavarian King Ludwig II, one of Wagner's greatest admirers.

Beamte This term, meaning 'official', covers civil servants and other local government officers, but also teachers and lecturers. *Beamte* are legally obliged to support the democratic system in Germany and are not allowed to go on strike. In return, they enjoy many privileges, such as total job security, private health insurance, and exemption from social security contributions.

Berlin After WIEDERVEREINIGUNG, Berlin took over from Bonn as the capital of Germany, though the German government did not start moving there until 1998. This vibrant city lies on the River Spree. It has about 3.5 million inhabitants and is a major cultural and commercial centre.

Berlinale This is the short name for the Internationale Filmfestspiele Berlin, an annual film festival that was first held in 1951. A *Goldener Bär* (Golden Bear) statuette is awarded for the best film, and a *Gläserner Bär* (Glass Bear) for the best children's film. The bear is Berlin's symbol.

Berliner Theatertreffen Founded in 1964, the Berlin Theatre Encounter presents the best German-language plays. Some dramatic productions are broadcast on 3SAT, which also presents one of the Theatertreffen prizes, awarded for innovative drama.

Berufsfachschule A full-time vocational college that offers preparation courses for a period of one to three years. Only pupils with a *Haupt-* or *Realschulabschluss* (school-leaving certificates) can attend a *Berufsfachschule.* The courses count as part of an apprenticeship, or can even replace it. *See also* SCHULE.

Berufsschule A college for young people who are doing a LEHRE. They attend *Berufsschule* one or two days a week (or sometimes in blocks of several weeks) to continue their general education and receive formal training in their chosen type of job.

Besenwirtschaft An inn set up temporarily by a local winegrower for a few weeks after the new wine has been made. A blown-up pig's bladder hung outside the door indicates that the new vintage may be sampled here. This is mainly found in southern Germany and is similar to the Austrian HEURIGE. *See also* STRAUßWIRTSCHAFT.

Betriebsrat The staff in any German company with at least five employees are entitled to have a *Betriebsrat.* This is a committee elected by the workers to represent their interests, as opposed to those of management. It allows workers to participate in decisions on pay and other benefits, redundancies, and even some business matters.

Bier Germany and Austria rank among the world's top beer producers and consumers, with a vast range of beer varieties (Bock, Alt, Dunkel, Export, Hell, Kölsch, Lager, Malzbier, Pils, Märzen, Weizenbier or Weißbier, and Berliner Weiße) to choose from. Germans brew more than 5,000 varieties, and each beer tastes different depending on the ratio of ingredients, brewing temperature and technique, alcoholic content, ageing time, and colour. Although there are now some big brewing conglomerates, the local brews from small independent breweries (there are about 1,300 in Germany) are still the best and most popular. German beer is brewed according to the *Reinheitsgebot* (beer purity regulation) of 1516, which stipulates that no ingredients other than hops, malted barley, yeast, and water can be used. Dortmund and Munich are among the top beer-producing cities in the world. Drinking beer is a vital part of everyday life for many people; they regularly meet up at their STAMMTISCH in a *Kneipe* (pub) or BIERGARTEN.

Biergarten A rustic open-air pub, or beer garden, which is traditional in Bavaria and Austria but can now also be found throughout Germany. It is usually set up for the summer in the yard of a pub or restaurant and serves beer and simple meals. In Munich beer gardens, the drink comes in a litre-sized glass, called a *Maß.* The standard everyday pale beer most people order is a *Helles*, a dark beer is a *Dunkles*, and a wheat beer is a *Weißbier*.

Bild Zeitung Germany's largest-selling daily newspaper, *Bild* is a typical tabloid with huge headlines, lots of photos, scandal stories, gossip, and nude models. It is known for its right-wing views. *Bild* sells about 4.5 million copies every day, almost eight times more than any other newspaper in Germany. Its Sunday edition is called *Bild am Sonntag*.

Bioladen A health-food shop which sells only organically grown products.

Biotonne ▶ RECYCLING

BKJ ▶ DBJR

Blauer Brief A letter sent by a school to inform parents that their son or daughter is in danger of having to repeat the year, a concept colloquially known as SITZEN BLEIBEN.

Blauer Engel The Blue Angel label on goods for sale shows consumers that the product is environmentally friendly.

Bodensee This is the German name for Lake Constance, Germany's biggest lake, bordered by Germany, Switzerland, and Austria. The River Rhine flows through it. This popular recreation area enjoys a particularly mild climate, especially on the three islands, Lindau, Mainau, and Reichenau.

Bonn Bonn was the capital of the Federal Republic of Germany (*see* BUNDESREPUBLIK DEUTSCHLAND) from 1949 until Berlin was made the capital of reunified Germany in 1991. It is still home to a number of government institutions. This relatively small city of about 300,000 inhabitants enjoys a picturesque location on the River Rhine.

Brandenburger Tor Once a symbol of divided Berlin, the Brandenburg Gate triumphal arch has become a symbol of reunited Germany. It was designed in the neoclassical style by Karl Gotthard Langhans (1732–1808) and opened in 1791 as an entrance to the boulevard Unter den Linden. Topped by the goddess of peace, the monument was part of the closed border between East and West Berlin from 1961 to 1989.

Brothers Grimm ▶ KINDER- UND HAUSMÄRCHEN

Bund This term refers to the federal state as the top level of government, as opposed to the individual LÄNDER which make up the BUNDESREPUBLIK. *Bund* and *Länder* have different responsibilities, with the *Bund* in charge of foreign policy, defence, transport, health, employment, etc.

Bundesbank Properly called the Deutsche Bundesbank, Germany's central bank is an autonomous non-governmental institution located in Frankfurt am Main. With the introduction of the EURO in 1999, some of the bank's functions passed to the European Central Bank (also in Frankfurt).

Bundesheer The Bundesheer is the Austrian federal army, which ensures the country's neutrality. All 18-year-old Austrian males must serve for a compulsory six months, plus two further months reserve duty at later dates. Conscientious objectors do public service. No foreign military bases are allowed on Austrian territory. *See also* WEHRDIENST, ZIVILDIENST.

Bundeskanzler The chancellor is the head of government in Germany and Austria. The German chancellor is normally elected for four years by the ministers in the BUNDESTAG after being proposed by the BUNDESPRÄSIDENT. The *Bundeskanzler* chooses the ministers and decides on government policies.

Bundesländer ▶ LÄNDER

Bundesliga The German national soccer league is split into two divisions of eighteen teams: *Bundesliga* and *2nd Bundesliga*. League games attract hundreds of thousands of spectators every week during the regular season.

Bundesminister The Federal Government consists of the BUNDESKANZLER and the *Bundesministerin* (federal ministers). The chancellor appoints ministers and determines their number and responsibilities in the Cabinet. Ministers run their ministries independently but within the framework of the guidelines of the chancellor's policy.

Bundespräsident The president is the head of state in Germany and Austria. The German president is elected for five years by the members of the BUNDESTAG and delegates from the LÄNDER. The *Bundespräsident* acts mainly as a figurehead, representing Germany abroad, and does not get involved in party politics, although he often takes a moral lead in major issues and can exercise personal authority through his neutral mediating function. The *Bundespräsident* can only be re-elected once.

Bundesrat This is the upper house of the German parliamentary system. The Bundesrat members are appointed by the LÄNDER governments and represent them. The Bundesrat has to approve laws affecting the *Länder*, and also any changes to the GRUNDGESETZ. The opposition parties can sometimes hold a majority in the Bundesrat, which allows them to influence German legislation.

Bundesrepublik Deutschland, or Bundesrepublik for short, is the official name of the German state (the Federal Republic of Germany, or FRG). Before reunification, the shortened form was used to distinguish the West German state from the East German (*see* GDR), but it is now commonly used to refer to the reunified state. Established on 23 May 1949, the republic became fully independent from British, French, and US control in May 1955. In October 1990 the Federal Republic merged with the GDR to form a single, unified Germany. *See also* WIEDERVEREINIGUNG.

Bundestag The lower house of the German parliament, which is elected every four years by the German people. The Bundestag is responsible for federal legislation, the federal budget, and electing the BUNDESKANZLER. Half of the ministers are elected directly and half by proportional representation, in a system in which each voter has two votes. *See also* NATIONALRAT.

Bundesverfassungsgericht As the supreme court in Germany, the federal constitutional court in Karlsruhe is the guardian of the GRUNDGESETZ and the final arbiter in any German legal appeal. It passes judgement on constitutional complaints and has the power to order a party's dissolution if it is unconstitutional and may pose a threat to democracy. The Federal Government has to accept the judges' ruling, however controversial the case may be. The Bundesverfassungsgericht consists of two panels, each with eight judges, who are elected for a single twelve-year term. Half of the panel is elected by the BUNDESTAG and half by the BUNDESRAT.

Bundeswappen The federal coat of arms is the eagle. This heraldic bird – emblem of the Roman emperors – was adopted by Charlemagne and became the coat of arms of the German Empire when it was founded in 1871. The Weimar Republic adopted it in its present form in 1919, and since 1950 it has been used by the BUNDESREPUBLIK DEUTSCHLAND.

Bundeswehr This is the name for the Federal Armed Forces, which come under the control of the defence minister. The Bundeswehr consists of professional soldiers and conscripts serving their WEHRDIENST. Until 1994, the GRUNDGESETZ did not allow German forces to be deployed abroad, but they now take part in certain operations, notably UN peacekeeping missions.

Bündnis 90/Die Grünen This party came into being in 1993 as a result of the merger of the West German Green party and civil-rights movements of the former East Germany (GDR). It is an important force in the German parliament, committed to environmental and social issues.

Burschenschaft A students' duelling society, like a fraternity, which was founded in Jena in 1815 to strengthen patriotic feeling. The tradition was abolished in 1935, but a decade later male students formed a new fraternity, the Deutsche Burschenschaft. Most of these generally right-wing social organizations for students are now called studentische Verbindungen (*Verbindung* means 'link' or 'connection'). There are now also Verbindungen for women.

CDU – Christlich-Demokratische Union One of the main German political parties, it was founded in 1945 and is committed to Christian and conservative values. Led by Angela Merkel, the CDU and its sister party, the CSU, were well ahead in opinion polls at the start of the 2005 election campaign. However, results announced after the 18 September ballot showed the CDU/CSU had gained only four more seats than its rivals, the SPD, headed by former chancellor Gerhard Schröder. Extended negotiations between the SPD and CDU/CSU resulted in an agreement to form a Grand Coalition between the parties, with Merkel as BUNDESKANZLER.

Christkind Traditionally, it is *das* Christkind (the Christ child) who brings Christmas presents to children on Christmas Eve. The concept of *der* Weihnachtsmann (Father Christmas or Santa Claus) is relatively new in Germany.

Christopher Street Day Gay Pride festivals and parades in Germany and Switzerland are called Christopher Street Days (or CSDs), after the New York street in which the gay protests known as the Stonewall Rebellion took place in 1969. Pride parades are held in most German cities, and the most famous are in Berlin and Cologne. In Austria, the parade is called the Regenbogenparade (Rainbow Parade).

CSU – Christlich-Soziale Union The Bavarian sister party of the CDU was founded in 1946 and has enjoyed an absolute majority in Bavaria for over 30 years. It now forms part of the governing Grand Coalition in Germany.

DAAD – Deutscher Akademischer Austauschdienst The German Academic Exchange Service is a joint organization of universities and other institutions of higher education for the promotion of academic exchange. The DAAD is the central source of information on study and research opportunities in Germany and abroad. It awards scholarships to students and academics and acts as a national agency for grants from the European Union.

DBJR – Deutscher Bundesjugendring The German Federal Youth Association, based in Berlin, is made up of twenty-four national youth organizations and sixteen regional youth councils. The Bundesjugendring aims to represent young people in their everyday lives. The Bundesvereinigung Kulturelle Jugendbildung (BKJ), a separate Federation of Youth Cultural Associations based in Remscheid, specializes in cultural activities that are followed by more than 12 million young people.

Deutsche Bibliothek The German Library in Frankfurt am Main is the central archive of all German-language writing, and the national bibliographical information centre of the BUNDESREPUBLIK. The first national library bringing together all German-language literature under one roof was set up in Leipzig in 1912. The division of Germany after the Second World War resulted in a new national library, established in 1947 in Frankfurt. After reunification in 1990, the German library in Leipzig was merged with the Frankfurt library.

Deutsche Post The previously state-run German postal system has undergone wide-ranging reforms in recent years, which will effectively remove the Deutsche Post monopoly by 2007. The number of post offices has been reduced, but small post-office agencies can now be found in shops, newsagents, and petrol stations. German letter boxes are yellow. Postal charges are relatively high, but the service is very reliable.

Deutsche Telekom The previously state-run German telecommunications service has undergone extensive reforms and gradual privatization and is now a public limited company. Since 1998, when the market was opened up to competition, Deutsche Telekom has ceased to have a monopoly.

Deutsche Welle Aimed at listeners abroad, this radio station is financed and controlled by the German government and broadcasts programmes on German politics, business, arts, and culture.

Deutscher Kulturrat The German Arts Council was founded in 1982 as a non-governmental commission representing cultural associations and institutions. The Arts Council comprises eight independent organizations, among them the Sociocultural Council (SOZIOKULTUR). The function of the Kulturrat is to coordinate, advise, and inform on matters concerning cultural affairs, make recommendations on cultural policy, and further international cultural relations.

Deutscher Sportbund – DSB Around 27 million people are members of a sports club in Germany, while another 12 million take part in sport. The German Sports Federation (DSB) has 16 regional sports federations and many individual sports associations. There are more than 2.5 million volunteer coaches and officials working for the Sports Federation. The DSB also promotes programmes such as *Trimm dich* (Get fit), a programme aimed at physical fitness, and *Sport für alle* (Sport for all), a programme encouraging people to run, swim, cycle, ski, and hike. About 750,000 people a year pass DSB tests and qualify for a gold, silver, or bronze sports medal.

Deutschlandlied This has been the German national anthem since 1922, when it was chosen by the first president of the Weimar Republic. The song entitled *Lied der Deutschen* (Song of the Germans) was written by Hoffmann von Fallersleben in 1841 and set to a melody composed by Joseph Haydn (1732–1809). Only the third stanza of the song is now used as the national anthem.

Diplomprüfung Final (degree) examination at a university or equivalent higher education institution in a technical or scientific subject, especially in engineering, business administration, design, agriculture, and social work. On passing the exam, a degree or diploma is awarded.

Duales System This waste-disposal and recycling system was introduced in Germany in 1993 and is operated by the private company DSD. All packaging materials marked with the GRÜNER PUNKT symbol are collected separately, and sorted into plastics, glass, paper, and metal for recycling. All other waste is still collected by the local refuse collection service. *See also* RECYCLING.

Eigenheim Germany and Switzerland have the lowest levels of home ownership in Europe, while Austria has among the highest. In Germany, many people happily live in rented flats or houses, but most dream of buying or building their *Eigenheim* (own home) one day, and save up towards it through the system of BAUSPAREN. First-time buyers are usually middle-aged and expect to stay in their home for the rest of their lives.

Einwohnermeldeamt (residents' registration office) Anybody who moves to Germany or relocates within Germany is legally obliged to register their address with the *Einwohnermeldeamt* within a week.

Eisschießen, Eisstockschießen Ice-stick shooting or Bavarian curling is a popular sport in Bavaria and Austria. There are two kinds of *Eisschießen*: in one, the aim is to slide the ice stick, a heavy metal plate with a handle, as far as possible across the ice; in the other, players slide a metal-plated wooden ice stick as close as possible to the *Daube*, a wooden tee.

Elternzeit A German mother or father who looks after a child at home is entitled to up to three years' extended maternity or paternity leave. At the end of this *Elternzeit* – formerly called *Erziehungsurlaub* (parental leave) – they are entitled to return to their old job. Around 95 per cent of German mothers take time out of work for at least one year after the birth.

Entwerter In many German cities, *Entwerter* (ticket-cancelling machines) are located on U-Bahn and S-Bahn platforms, or on trains, trams, or buses. When travelling on public transport in Germany, it is important to remember to cancel (*entwerten*) the ticket in one of the machines. Even if just bought from the driver, your ticket is not valid without this stamp.

Erntedankfest ▶ TRADITIONS, FESTIVALS, AND HOLIDAYS

Erste, Das Also called Erstes Programm, this is the first German public TV channel, broadcast by ARD. Programming includes news, information, films, and entertainment. There is a limited amount of advertising, which is concentrated in blocks at certain times of day and not after 8 p.m.

Erziehungsgeld A state benefit paid for up to two years to any mother or father who stays at home after the birth of a child to look after it. In 98 per cent of cases, it is still the mother who claims *Erziehungsgeld*. In addition to this, parents receive *Kindergeld* (child benefit) for each child.

Erziehungsurlaub ▶ **ELTERNZEIT**

Euro The *Euro* was introduced as a *gemeinsame Währung* (common currency) in twelve states of the European Union in 2002. It replaced the *Mark* in Germany and the *Schilling* in Austria. Switzerland is not a member of the EU and retained the *Franken*.

Eurocheque The *Eurocheque* is the standard cheque issued by banks in Germany. It is backed up by the *Eurochequekarte*, which can also be used at cash machines and for payments in shops. Although plastic cards have become more popular in Germany, many people (and shops and restaurants) still prefer cash.

Fachhochschule This type of college provides shorter, more vocational and practical courses than those available at a HOCHSCHULE. A third of new students now enrol at a *Fachhochschule* to take the DIPLOMPRÜFUNG.

Fachhochschulreife ▶ **FACHOBERSCHULE**

Fachoberschule This vocationally orientated college takes students with an intermediate school certificate and leads to the *Fachhochschulreife*, a certificate qualifying students for the FACHHOCHSCHULE. Courses last for two to three years and cover theoretical instruction as well as on-the-job training.

Fasching, Fastnachtszeit This is the carnival season, which begins in November and ends on Aschermittwoch for Lent. Depending on the region it is called *Karneval*, *Fastnacht*, *Fasnet*, or *Fasching*, and is celebrated in Germany, Austria, and Switzerland. Every town and village has its own carnival customs. Whether it is the Kölner Karneval or the Münchner Fasching, celebrations reach a climax in the last week, especially on Rosenmontag and Faschingsdienstag. On Ash Wednesday everything returns to normal. *See also* ASCHERMITTWOCH, FASCHINGSDIENSTAG, ROSENMONTAG in TRADITIONS, FESTIVALS, AND HOLIDAYS.

Faschingsdienstag ▶ **TRADITIONS, FESTIVALS, AND HOLIDAYS**

FDP – Freie Demokratische Partei The German Liberal party, founded in 1948. This relatively small party has held the balance of power in coalitions in the past, even though it tends to gain only 5 to 10 per cent of the vote at general elections (9.9 per cent in 2005). It supports a free-market economy and the freedom of the individual.

Flohmarkt There is a *Flohmarkt* (flea market) on Sundays in most big cities. Stalls are set up along a main street, in a park or central square, to sell knick-knacks, second-hand clothes, furniture, and other bargains.

Focus A relatively new weekly news and current affairs magazine published in Munich. It was set up in 1993 and is aimed at a centre-right, professional readership. *Focus* has become a serious competitor of DER SPIEGEL, with shorter, easier-to-read articles, and a more modern presentation.

Formel 1 Formula 1 motor racing enjoys a large following in Germany, particularly since local hero Michael Schumacher has won the drivers' world championship seven times between 1994 and 2004. The German Grand Prix, which has been won three times by Michael and once by his brother Ralf, takes place each year at Hockenheim near Mannheim. The European Grand Prix has been held at the Nürburgring in Rheinland-Pfalz since 1999.

FPÖ – Freiheitliche Partei Österreichs The Austrian Freedom Party, also known as Die Freiheitlichen, was founded in 1955. It is right wing and is the third largest party. It advocates a minimum monthly wage and stricter asylum policies.

Frankfurter Allgemeine Zeitung (FAZ) One of Germany's most serious and widely respected daily newspapers. It tends to have a centre-left to liberal outlook.

Frankfurter Buchmesse The annual Book Fair was first held in Frankfurt in 1964. Since then it has become the most important publishing trade fair in the world. Held every October, it includes the award of the Friedenspreis des deutschen Buchhandels (Peace Prize of the German Book Trade). Leipzig also stages an important annual book fair.

Die Freiheitlichen ▶ FPÖ

FRG – Federal Republic of Germany ▶ BUNDESREPUBLIK DEUTSCHLAND

Frühstück Breakfast in Germany typically consists of strong coffee, slices of bread or fresh rolls with butter, jam, honey, sliced cheese and meat, and maybe a boiled egg. For working people and schoolchildren, who have little time for breakfast first thing in the morning, a *zweites Frühstück* is common at around 10 a.m.

Fünfprozentklausel The 5 per cent clause, introduced in 1953, stipulates that only parties gaining at least 5 per cent of the valid second votes, or at least three constituency seats, can be represented in parliament.

Fußballweltmeisterschaft The Football World Cup takes place in Germany in 2006, with matches spread across twelve cities, including the opening match in Munich and the final in Berlin. The German team won the *Weltmeisterschaft* (World Cup) in 1954, 1974, and 1990, and has been runner-up four times. Women's football is also strong in Germany; the German team won the Women's World Cup in 2003.

Gastarbeiter The term used for workers from foreign countries, mainly Turkey, former Yugoslavia, and Italy, many of whom came to Germany in the 1960s and 1970s. Despite the time that they have lived in Germany, and the fact that their children have grown up there, the issue of integration is still widely discussed.

GDR – German Democratic Republic The communist state, established in the Soviet-occupied zone of Germany after the Second World War. Also known as East Germany, or the Deutsche Demokratische Republik (DDR), it lasted from 1949 to 1990. *See also* BUNDESREPUBLIK DEUTSCHLAND, MAUER, WIEDERVEREINIGUNG.

Gemeinde The lowest level of local government, run by a local council chaired by the *Bürgermeister* (mayor). *Gemeinden* have their own budget, with income from local taxes. They pass local legislation and administer local affairs.

Gesamthochschule A type of university established in some LÄNDER following reforms in the 1960s and combining HOCHSCHULE and FACHHOCHSCHULE under one roof, thereby offering greater flexibility and a wider choice of subjects to the student.

Gesamtschule A comprehensive secondary school introduced in the 1970s and designed to replace the traditional division into GYMNASIUM, REALSCHULE, and HAUPTSCHULE. Pupils are taught different subjects at their own level and may take any of the school-leaving exams, including the ABITUR.

Glascontainer ▶ RECYCLING

Goethe-Institut An organization promoting German language and culture abroad. It is based in Munich and runs about 140 institutes in over seventy countries, offering German language classes, cultural events such as exhibitions, films, and seminars, and a library, which is open to the public, of German books and magazines and other documentation.

Goldener Bär ▶ BERLINALE

Grundgesetz The written German constitution which came into force in May 1949. It lays down the basic rights of German citizens, the relationship between BUND and LÄNDER, and the legal framework of the German state.

Grundschule The primary school which all German children attend for four years from the age of six (some children do not start until they are seven). Lessons are intense but pupils only attend school for about four hours a day. At the end of the *Grundschule*, teachers and parents decide together which type of secondary school – HAUPTSCHULE, REALSCHULE, GESAMTSCHULE, or GYMNASIUM – the child should attend.

Grünen, Die ▶ **BÜNDNIS 90**

Grüner Punkt A symbol used to mark packaging materials that can be recycled. Any packaging carrying this logo is collected separately under the DUALES SYSTEM recycling scheme. Manufacturers have to buy a licence from the recycling company DSD (Duales System Deutschland) to entitle them to use this symbol.

Gruppe 47 This German literary group was founded (in 1947, hence its name) by the writer Hans Werner Richter (1908–93), who organized regular meetings to encourage young German-language authors in the postwar era. The group's two most famous representatives both won Nobel Prizes in Literature: Heinrich Böll in 1972, for his 'renewal of German literature', and Günter Grass, in 1999, for portraying 'the forgotten face of history'.

Gymnasium The secondary school which prepares pupils for the ABITUR. The GYMNASIUM is attended after the GRUNDSCHULE by the most academically inclined pupils. They spend nine years at this school, and during the last three years they have some choice as to which subjects they study. *See also* SCHULE.

Hansestadt Hansestädte (Hanseatic cities), such as Bremen and Hamburg, were once part of an association of trading cities along the North Sea and Baltic coasts. The Hanse (Hanseatic League or Hansa) was formed in the 13th century to protect the economic interests of its members. Meetings were held at Lübeck, where members developed a system of commercial laws. The Hanse remained a powerful force until the late sixteenth century, after which it declined.

Hauptschule The secondary school which prepares pupils for the *Hauptschulabschluss* (school-leaving certificate). The *Hauptschule* aims to give less academically inclined pupils a sound educational grounding. Pupils stay at the *Hauptschule* for five or six years after the GRUNDSCHULE. *See also* LEHRE, SCHULE.

Hausordnung These 'house rules' are what a tenant has to adhere to in order to maintain a harmonious relationship with neighbours. They might cover the maintenance of common areas and the appearance of the house or apartment block; for example, forbidding a tenant from hanging washing from a front window. But usually the *Hausordnung*, whether written or unwritten, refer to restrictions on noise, possibly even including running a late-night bath. *See also* RUHEZEIT.

Heiligabend ▶ **TRADITIONS, FESTIVALS, AND HOLIDAYS**

Heilige Drei Könige ▶ **TRADITIONS, FESTIVALS, AND HOLIDAYS**

Heurige This is an Austrian term for both a new wine and an inn with new wine on tap, especially an inn with its own vineyard in the environs of

Vienna. On warm, late summer evenings Viennese wine devotees sit on wooden benches and sample the new wine of the year. A garland of pine twigs outside the gates of the *Heurige* shows that the barrel has been breached. *See also* BESENWIRTSCHAFT and STRAUẞWIRTSCHAFT.

Hochdeutsch There are many regional variations and dialects in Germany, Austria, and Switzerland (64 per cent of Swiss people speak Schwyzerdütsch). Hochdeutsch is the standard German that can be understood by all German speakers. It is probably the only way for a Bavarian, Austrian, or Swiss to communicate with a North German. Newspapers and other publications are generally printed in Hochdeutsch, which is regarded as 'proper' German.

Hochschule German *Hochschulen* (universities and colleges) have up to now generally not charged fees, but at least some LÄNDER will in the near future introduce them. Anybody who has passed the ABITUR is entitled to go to university (except for some subjects which have a restriction on numbers, or NUMERUS CLAUSUS). They tend to be very large and impersonal institutions. Students may receive a BAFÖG grant and often take more than the minimum eight semesters (four years) to complete their course.

Hochzeit Church weddings are not legally recognized in Germany, Austria, or Switzerland, and all couples must be married in a civil ceremony. The civil ceremony is held in a *Standesamt* (registry office, called a *Zivilstandsamt* in Switzerland). The civil marriage tends to be a private family affair; if the couple also has a church ceremony afterwards, that is usually a more public event. Various traditions are associated with weddings: often a car procession takes place (where the wedding party and guests drive around honking their horns, and well-wishers honk back), or children strew flowers in front of the couple for good luck. The bachelor party or stag night is known as *Junggesellenabschied*, and there is often also an informal party held before the wedding known as POLTERABEND. Since 2001, same-sex couples have been able to register a civil union called a *Lebenspartnerschaft*.

ICE – Intercityexpresszug This high-speed train runs at one- or two-hour intervals on a number of main routes in Germany, offering shorter journey times and better facilities than ordinary trains.

IM – inoffizieller Mitarbeiter This term refers to 'unofficial collaborators' of the STASI. These informers were often ordinary people in the former GDR who had been recruited or pressurized by the Stasi to spy on neighbours, family, and friends. However, some were prominent figures in the West.

Jüdisches Museum The new Jewish Museum in Berlin opened in 1999, a stunning, angular silver building designed by the American architect Daniel Libeskind. It stands in dramatic contrast to its Baroque neighbour, a former appeal court built in 1734–35. The collection covers two millennia of German Jewish history, and includes a Holocaust Tower memorial.

Kaffee This refers not only to coffee as a drink but also to the small meal taken at about four in the afternoon, consisting of coffee and cakes or biscuits. It is often a social occasion, as it is common to invite family or friends for *Kaffee und Kuchen* (rather than for tea or dinner), especially on birthdays and other family occasions.

Kanton The name for the individual autonomous states that make up Switzerland. There are 26 *Kantone*, each with its own government and constitution.

Karneval ▶ FASCHING, FASTNACHTSZEIT

Kfz-Kennzeichen This is the number plate on German motor vehicles, which have to be licensed by the *Zulassungsstelle* (vehicle registration office) for the owner's registered place of residence. The first letter, or first two or three letters, on the *Kfz-Kennzeichen* indicate where the car comes from.

KI.KA – Kinderkanal This publicly funded children's TV channel was set up in 1997 by ARD and ZDF. Based in Erfurt, the channel broadcasts German children's favourites, as well as classic programmes from around the world.

Kindergarten Every German pre-school child has the right to attend *Kindergarten* (nursery or play school) between the ages of three and six. *Kindergarten* concentrates on play, crafts, singing, etc., and aims to foster the child's social and emotional development. There is no formal teaching at all, this being reserved for the GRUNDSCHULE.

Kindertagesstätte Often called *Kita* for short, these day nurseries are intended for the children of working parents and usually cater for babies to 6-year-olds, though some *Kitas* also offer after-school care for older children.

Kinder- und Hausmärchen Jakob Grimm (1785–1863) and his brother Wilhelm (1786–1859) collected fairy tales for their book of *Kinder- und Hausmärchen* (Household and Nursery Tales). In 1852 they started compiling a comprehensive German dictionary, but the work was so vast that it was only completed in 1961, a century after their deaths.

Kirchensteuer Any taxpayer who is a member of one of the established churches in Germany (mainly Catholic and Protestant) has to pay *Kirchensteuer* (church tax). It is calculated as a proportion of income tax and is collected at source by the tax office, which then passes on the money to the relevant church.

Kita ▶ KINDERTAGESSTÄTTE

Knecht Ruprecht ▶ KRAMPUS

Krampus – Knecht Ruprecht The legendary figure known as Krampus in Austria and Bavaria, and Knecht Ruprecht in other regions, is St Nicholas's helper. While St Nicholas carries presents, Krampus is a scary – sometimes horned – figure, who carries a sack in which he is supposed to place disobedient children. Other traditions have him carrying a birch and a sack full of coal for the naughty ones. He visits on St Nicholas' Day (6 December). He is also believed to help the CHRISTKIND carry Christmas presents. *See also* TRADITIONS, FESTIVALS, AND HOLIDAYS.

Krankenkasse There are many different health insurance organizations in Germany. Contributions are high, due to the high standard (and cost) of health care in Germany. Members of the *Krankenkassen* are given plastic cards entitling them to treatment by the doctor of their choice.

Kriminalpolizei – Kripo The criminal investigation department deals with serious offences, including murder, terrorism, and organized crime.

Kulturstadt Weimar This thousand-year-old city has played an important role in Germany's cultural history. The composer Johann Sebastian Bach (1685–1750) and the artist Lucas Cranach (1472–1553) lived and worked here. Other important writers and poets such as Johann Wolfgang von Goethe (1749–1832), Johann Gottfried von Herder (1744–1803) and Christoph Martin Wieland (1733–1813) – who translated Shakespeare's plays – made the city their home. Friedrich von Schiller (1759–1805) wrote many of his plays in Weimar, while the composer Franz Liszt (1811–86) composed and gave concerts here. In 1919 the Bauhaus was founded in Weimar; in the same year, the constitution of the first German republic – the Weimar Republic – was drafted in the city.

Kur A health cure in a spa town lasting about three to six weeks and usually involving a special diet, exercise programmes, physiotherapy, massage, etc. These are intended for people with minor complaints or recovering from illness. *Kuren* are paid for by the KRANKENKASSEN, with the patient making a contribution. The *Kur* is not taken as frequently as it once was.

Kuratorium Junger Deutscher Film Young creative directors are given financial support by the LÄNDER. The Young German Film Board awards prizes for first films (sometimes also second films) of artistic value. The Filmförderungsanstalt – FFA (German Film Board) – provides financial assistance for film productions and cinemas.

Ladenschlusszeit Strict regulations governing *Ladenschlusszeit* (shop closing times) in Germany were relaxed in 1996. Shops are allowed to stay open until 8 p.m. on weekdays and 4 p.m. on Saturdays, and bakeries may open for three hours on Sundays. However, actual opening times vary, depending on the location and size of the shop.

Länder Germany is a federal republic consisting of sixteen member states called *Länder* or *Bundesländer*. Five so-called *neue Bundesländer* were added after reunification in 1990. Each *Land* has a degree of autonomy and is responsible for educational and cultural affairs, the police, the environment, and local government. Austria is a federal state consisting of nine *Länder*. The Swiss equivalent of a German or Austrian *Land* is a KANTON.

Landtag The parliament of a *Land*. It is elected every four to five years using a similar mixed system of voting as for the BUNDESTAG elections.

Lebenspartnerschaft ▶ HOCHZEIT

Lehre This type of apprenticeship is still the normal way to learn a trade or train for a practical career in Germany. A *Hauptschulabschluss* is the minimum requirement, although many young people with a *Realschulabschluss* or ABITUR opt to train in this way. A *Lehre* takes about two to three years and involves practical training by a MEISTER(IN) backed up by lessons at a BERUFSSCHULE, with an exam at the end.

Linkspartei, Die (Left Party) Formerly known as the PDS, this ultra left-wing party formed in 1990 from the old East German SED, the Communist party which ruled in the former GDR. In the 2005 federal elections, the Left Party joined forces with the newly formed Arbeit & soziale Gerechtigkeit – Die Wahlalternative, or WASG (the Labour and Social Justice Party) and won an 8.7 per cent share of the vote.

Loveparade A techno music and dance festival which takes place in Berlin every summer, with hundreds of thousands of mainly young people attending. Originally a celebration of youth culture, it has become a major tourist attraction.

Markt Weekly markets are still held in most German cities and towns, usually laid out very attractively in the picturesque market squares. Fresh fruit and vegetables, flowers, eggs, cheese and other dairy products, bread, meat, and fish are available directly from the producer. Many Germans still buy most of their provisions '*auf dem Markt*'.

Matura ▶ ABITUR

Mauer *Die Mauer*, or the Berlin Wall, a 42-km (26-mile) structure of concrete blocks, was put up almost overnight in 1961. It was designed to halt the exodus of inhabitants from the Communist-controlled East of the city to the West. Over the following twenty-eight years, numerous people were killed trying to escape East Berlin. On 9 November 1989, an announcement by the East German Government that border checkpoints in the city had been abandoned resulted in a flood of people crossing to the West, the gradual dismantling of the wall, and eventually the WIEDERVEREINIGUNG. Parts of the Berlin Wall were sold to museums and private collectors. A few small sections remain as a memorial and tourist attraction.

Meister(in) A master craftsman or craftswoman who has completed rigorous training in his/her trade or vocation and has passed a final exam after several years' experience in a job. A *Meister(in)* is allowed to set up in business and train young people who are doing their LEHRE.

Meldepflicht An 'obligation to register' that applies to all German residents, regardless of nationality. Residents must inform the EINWOHNERMELDEAMT every time they change their address. The applicant is issued with an *Abmeldebestätigung* (notification of intention to leave) and must then register the new address. The system means that every resident can quickly be traced.

Mitfahrzentrale An agency that puts drivers and passengers in contact with each other (including via the Internet) to save petrol costs and reduce pollution. The Mitfahrzentrale charges a small fee, complies with particular requests (non-smoking, female drivers, etc.), and is popular throughout Germany for long-distance travel.

Mittagessen This is a cooked meal eaten in the middle of the day and is the main meal of the day for most Germans. Schoolchildren come home from school in time for *Mittagessen*, and most large companies have canteens where hot meals are served at lunchtime. On a Sunday, *Mittagessen* might consist of a starter such as clear broth, followed by a roast with gravy, boiled potatoes and vegetables, and a dessert.

Museumsinsel The Museum Island on the River Spree in Berlin is home to the renowned Pergamon Museum of Antiquities, attracting more than 850,000 visitors a year, as well as to the Altes Museum and Neues Museum. The island was designated a World Heritage Site by UNESCO in 1999.

Namenstag This day is celebrated by many Germans, especially Catholics, in the same way as a birthday. It is the day dedicated to the saint whose name the person carries, so someone called Martin, for example, would celebrate their *Namenstag* on Martinstag (11 November). *See also* TRADITIONS, FESTIVALS, AND HOLIDAYS.

Nationalrat In Austria the Nationalrat is the Federal Assembly's lower house, whose 183 members are elected for four years under a system of proportional representation. The BUNDESKANZLER commands the majority in the Nationalrat. The BUNDESRAT, the 64-member upper house, is elected by provincial assemblies. In Switzerland, the National Council is made up of 200 representatives, and together with the STÄNDERAT forms the Federal Assembly.

Neue Kronen Zeitung An Austrian tabloid that is published in Vienna and is read by around half the population. It is regarded as right wing, as is the *Kurier*, Austria's other tabloid.

Neue Zürcher Zeitung A Swiss quality daily which is held in high esteem at home and abroad.

Numerus clausus The *Numerus clausus* system is used to limit the number of students studying certain oversubscribed subjects such as medicine at German universities. It means that only those students who have achieved a minimum average mark in their ABITUR are admitted.

Oktoberfest Germany's most famous beer festival (the Munich October Festival) actually starts each year in September. Over 5 million litres of beer are drunk over a period of sixteen days. The Oktoberfest goes back to the year 1810, when the Bavarian crown prince (later King Ludwig I) married Therese of Saxony-Hildburghausen. A horse race was organized in honour of the couple on the Theresienwiese (Therese's Meadow, named after the bride), and almost the entire population of Munich joined in the celebrations. The party was such a success that it became an annual event. Today the *Wies'n* (meadow), as the locals call the Oktoberfest, looks more like a giant fairground, with huge marquees in which the big breweries set up beer halls for visitors to drink many a *Maß* (a litre of beer), eat *Weißwurst* (veal sausage), *Schweinshaxe* (pork knuckles) and giant *Brezen* (pretzels) while listening and singing along to Bavarian music.

Orientierungsstufe A two-year orientation stage following GRUNDSCHULE, during which pupils can find out if they are more suited to a HAUPTSCHULE, GESAMTSCHULE, GYMNASIUM, or REALSCHULE. Students can transfer to a different school during this phase.

Ossi A colloquial and sometimes derogatory term for someone from the former East Germany (GDR), as opposed to a WESSI (someone from the former West Germany).

Ostern ▶ TRADITIONS, FESTIVALS, AND HOLIDAYS

ÖVP – Österreichische Volkspartei The conservative People's Party is Austria's centrist party. It was founded in 1945 and is the second largest party.

Papiertonne ▶ RECYCLING

Parkscheibe In Germany, some areas only allow limited parking time; here you have to display a *Parkscheibe* (parking disc) on your windscreen, with the hands of its clock set to your arrival time. These blue cardboard or plastic discs are available at newsagents and department stores.

Passionsspiel The famous Passion Play is held every ten years in the small Bavarian mountain village of Oberammergau. It has its origin in a vow sworn by the villagers in 1633 that they would perform the passion of Jesus if God delivered them from the plague.

PDS – Partei des Demokratischen Sozialismus ▶ LINKSPARTIE

Personalausweis The standard German identity card, with the holder's photograph and particulars, should in theory be carried at all times. If you are stopped by the police without any ID, you might be taken to a police station and kept there for up to six hours. The *Personalausweis* acts as a passport for Germans and Austrians travelling within the EU.

Pflegeversicherung Compulsory nursing-care insurance which all employees have to pay into as part of their SOZIALABGABEN. It was introduced in Germany in 1995 and pays for the long-term nursing care of the elderly and the severely disabled. Employers and employees make equal contributions to the scheme.

Pinakothek der Moderne This gallery of modern art, design, graphics, and architecture opened in Munich in 2002. Its collections concentrate on 20th- and 21st-century art, complementing the nearby Neue Pinakothek (exhibiting 19th-century art) and Alte Pinakothek (14th–18th century art).

Polterabend In Germany the *Polterabend* usually takes place a few days before the wedding and takes the form of a large party for the family and friends of both bride and groom. Traditionally, the guests smash some crockery, as this is supposed to bring good luck to the couple. *See also* HOCHZEIT.

Popmusik At the beginning of the 1980s, the *Neue Deutsche Welle* (New German Wave) of popular music brought German pop groups to the fore. Today all the different pop genres are represented by German groups, and in 2005 the German hip-hop band *Die Fantastischen Vier* won an ECHO music award. Some chart-topping German pop groups such as No Angels and Bro'Sis were discovered via the Popstars REALITY-TV show.

Post ▶ DEUTSCHE POST

Prater Vienna's largest and most popular amusement park. In 1766 Joseph II, the son of Empress Maria Theresa, decreed that Der Prater should be open to everyone. Earlier it had been forbidden to enter forests and meadows reserved for imperial hunts. The Prater has old-fashioned swings, skittle alleys, and merry-go-rounds, including the oldest carousel in Europe. A *Riesenrad* (big wheel) with a diameter of 67 m (200 ft) was put up for the World Exhibition of 1897 and is a famous Viennese landmark.

Premiere Germany's main pay-TV channel, introduced in 1991, can be received via satellite or cable. Premiere subscribers can watch feature films, sports events, documentaries, and so on, uninterrupted by advertising.

Pro 7 Germany's third largest private television channel, Pro 7 is financed entirely by advertising. It offers documentaries, films, and news programmes.

profil An Austrian news and current affairs magazine, with a circulation of over 100,000. It has a reputation for hard-hitting journalism.

Reality-TV *Reality-Shows* are as popular in the German-speaking world as elsewhere. They include *Big Brother* (shown on RTL II in Germany and TV3 in Switzerland) and a mobile version called *Taxi Orange*, shown on ORF, the public broadcaster in Austria, in which contestants have to run a taxi company in Vienna and live off the profits. So-called *Casting-Shows* such as Popstars have produced chart-topping pop groups. *See also* POPMUSIK.

Realschule The secondary school that prepares pupils for the *Realschulabschluss* (school-leaving certificate). It is in between HAUPTSCHULE and GYMNASIUM, catering for less academic students who will probably train for a practical career. Pupils stay at the *Realschule* for six years after the GRUNDSCHULE. *See also* LEHRE, SCHULE.

Rechtschreibreform After much controversy, a reform aiming to simplify the rules governing German spelling was implemented in 1998. The old spellings were officially acceptable for a transitional period until 2005, and further modifications to the reform were agreed during that period. The new spellings are still controversial and are only binding for schools and public authorities. Some newspapers have retained or returned to the old spellings, so it remains to be seen whether the changes will gain general acceptance.

Recycling All *Hausmüll* (domestic waste) in Germany is collected in at least three bins, and waste materials are recycled and reused. The *Biotonne* is for biodegradable kitchen waste (vegetable and fruit peel, meat, cheese, nutshells, tea leaves, and coffee filters, etc.). The *Wertstofftonne* can be used for plastic containers, metal objects, cans, aluminium, textiles, etc., and anything with a GRÜNER PUNKT. A separate *Papiertonne* is used for paper and cardboard, although most wrapping is discarded at source or reused – German supermarkets don't hand out a free supply of plastic bags. The *Restmüll* is for sweepings and general household rubbish. Bottles and glass are taken to the *Glascontainer* (bottle bank). A deposit on drinks bottles encourages returning empties to the shop. There are also collection points for fridges, freezers, and bulky items. *See also* DUALES SYSTEM.

Regenbogenparade ▶ CHRISTOPHER STREET DAY

Reichstag This historic building in the centre of Berlin became the seat of the BUNDESTAG in 1999. The refurbishment of the REICHSTAG included the addition of a glass cupola, with a walkway open to visitors, which provides a spectacular viewing platform and further enhances the Berlin skyline.

Religion In Germany, the Christian community is divided almost equally between Roman Catholics (26.6 million people) and Protestants (mostly Lutheran, 26.3 million). In April 2005, a German, Cardinal Joseph Ratzinger, was appointed head of the Roman Catholic Church as Papst Benedikt XVI (Pope Benedict XVI). There are also more than 3 million Muslims, mostly from Turkey and former Yugoslavia, living in Germany. Eighty-eight per cent of Austrians are Catholic, while in Switzerland there are slightly more Catholics than Protestants, with Muslims – again mainly from Turkey and former Yugoslavia – making up just over 4 per cent of the population. *See also* KIRCHENSTEUER.

Rentenversicherung This is the compulsory state pension insurance in Germany. All employees have to pay into it as part of their SOZIALABGABEN, with employers and the state also making a contribution. The amount of the German state pension depends on the contributions made by the individual, with allowances for years spent as a student or carer.

Restmüll ▶ RECYCLING

Rosenmontag ▶ TRADITIONS, FESTIVALS, AND HOLIDAYS

RTL – Radio Télévision Luxembourg Germany's largest privately owned television channel is the market leader in commercial television. It broadcasts films, sport, news, and entertainment, and regularly achieves top viewing figures.

Ruhezeit This is the accepted 'quiet time', usually between one and three o'clock in the afternoon, late evening, and on Sundays. *Ruhezeit* prohibits loud music and any noisy work, including drilling and vacuuming. But many young Germans no longer adhere to the letter of the *Ruhezeit*. *See also* HAUSORDNUNG.

Salzburger Festspiele Since 1920, this annual festival has been held in Salzburg, the home of Wolfgang Amadeus Mozart (1756–91), as a tribute to the great composer.

SAT 1 Germany's second largest privately owned television channel broadcasts films, news, sport, and entertainment. It was the first commercial channel in the country.

3SAT This satellite TV channel is run jointly by ARD, ZDF, and Swiss and

Austrian TV. It offers programmes that are not broadcast by other TV stations, and almost half of 3SAT's output is devoted to cultural reports.

S-Bahn ▶ U-BAHN

Schnellimbiss Usually a *Schnellimbiss* is just a stand, selling different kinds of *Würstchen* (sausages), rissoles, *Döner* (doner kebab) or *Leberkäse* (meat loaf), depending on which region you are in. You can eat there or take the snack away. *Currywurst* – sausages served with ketchup (or a tomato-based sauce) mixed with curry powder – is a *Schnellimbiss* favourite.

Schrebergarten A *Schrebergarten* is an enclosed mini-garden in a large common garden, usually just outside an urban area. As most German city-dwellers live in blocks of flats, many rent a *Schrebergarten* to provide them with a place where they can grow fruit and flowers and relax. The gardens are named after the Leipzig physician D. G. M. Schreber (1808–61), who had the idea of creating playgrounds for children and small gardens for adults, set within a common plot. By law, the size of each mini-garden is limited to no more than 400 sq. m (4,306 sq. ft). Most *Schrebergärten* have a shed or summer house at one end that often looks like a fairy-tale cottage, and tidy flower beds. The gardeners are members of an association (*Schrebergartenverein*) which represents their interests.

Schule German children have to attend school from the ages of 6 to 18. Full-time schooling is compulsory for nine or ten years, until pupils are at least 15. All children go to a GRUNDSCHULE for four years (six in Berlin) and move on to a HAUPTSCHULE, REALSCHULE, GYMNASIUM, or GESAMTSCHULE, depending on their ability. From the age of 15, some pupils attend a BERUFSSCHULE, a part-time vocational school. Some students stay at school until they are over 20, due to the system of SITZEN BLEIBEN.

Schultüte The first day at school (*der 1. Schultag*) is a big event for a German child, involving a ceremony at school and sometimes at church. The child is given a *Schultüte*, a large cardboard cone containing pens, small gifts, and sweets, to mark this special occasion.

Schützenfest An annual festival celebrated in most towns, involving a shooting competition, parade, and fair. The winners of the shooting competition are crowned *Schützenkönig* and *Schützenkönigin* (shooting king and queen) for the year.

Schutzpolizei (Schupo) Colloquially referred to as the Schupo, the Schutzpolizei is the general police force dealing with public security, order, and traffic offences. Most people know the Schupo only as traffic police.

Schwarzwald The Black Forest, a mountainous area in Baden-Württemberg in southwestern Germany, is a popular holiday destination for Germans and foreign tourists alike. The name refers to the large coniferous forests in the region. *See also* WALDSTERBEN.

Schweizerische Eidgenossenschaft The Swiss Confederation is the official name for Switzerland. The confederation was established in 1291 when farmers from the mountain cantons of Uri, Schwyz, and Unterwalden swore that they would jointly defend their traditional rights against the House of Habsburg. The unified federal state as it is today, with twenty-six self-governing cantons, was formed in 1848. *See also* KANTON.

Seniorenbüro There are 170 *Seniorenbüros* (senior citizens' offices) spread throughout Germany. They were set up in the early 1990s to organize events, publicize sources of help and advice, and help older people take part in volunteer work. They are government funded.

siezen/duzen German has two forms for 'you', the formal *Sie* and the familiar *du*. *Du* is used when speaking to a friend, a child, or a family member. Young people always address each other as *du*. If someone says, *wir duzen uns* (we call each other *du*), it means that they are friends. When speaking to a person you do not know very well, the polite form *Sie* is used. Even though there has been a tendency for less formality in recent years, it is still best to say *Sie*, especially in work situations and when you would normally address someone in English as Mrs or Mr.

sitzen bleiben If German pupils fail more than one subject in their end-of-year school report, they have to repeat the year. This is colloquially referred to as *sitzen bleiben*. Some students might even have to repeat two years, not sitting their ABITUR until they are 20.

Skat A popular card game for three players playing with thirty-two German cards. Keen players even join a *Skat* club.

Solidaritätszuschlag A tax surcharge introduced to help pay for the cost of German reunification and rebuilding the economy in former East Germany (GDR). It is payable by every German taxpayer and firm.

Sozialabgaben This term refers to the contributions every German taxpayer has to make towards the four main state insurance schemes: pension, health, nursing care, and unemployment. This amounts to over 40 per cent of gross income, with employee and employer paying half each.

Soziokultur The sociocultural movement has its origins in the alternative cultural scene which developed in the 1970s in Germany. Groups of artists and performers developed new, independent centres such as theatres, art schools, and women's cultural groups.

SPD — Sozialdemokratische Partei Deutschlands One of the main German political parties. Reformed after the war in 1945, it is a workers' party supporting social-democratic values. In the 2005 federal elections, the SPD gained only 1 per cent fewer votes than the CDU/CSU; after protracted negotiations, the three parties agreed to form a Grand Coalition, headed by the CDU leader, Angela Merkel.

Der Spiegel One of Germany's best-selling weekly news and current affairs magazines, *Der Spiegel* was founded in 1947 and is published in Hamburg. It has a liberal outlook and has become synonymous with investigative journalism in Germany, as it has brought to light a number of major scandals in German business and politics over the years.

SPÖ — Sozialistische Partei Österreichs The Austrian Social-Democratic Party was founded in 1888 as the Sozialdemokratische Arbeiterpartei Österreichs (Social Democratic Workers' Party of Austria). It was reformed in 1945 and is the largest political party in Austria.

Stadtumbau Ost This government programme was set up to regenerate inner-city housing and improve the urban environment between the years 2002 and 2009 in the eastern part of Germany (the former GDR).

Stammtisch A large table reserved for regulars in most German pubs. The word is also used to refer to the group of people who meet around the table for a drink and lively discussion.

Der Standard An Austrian daily printed on pink paper and considered to be liberal in its views.

Ständerat The Ständerat (Council of States) is the upper chamber in Switzerland. It is composed of forty-six representatives from the various cantons. *See also* KANTON.

Stasi, Staatssicherheitsdienst *Stasi* is the shortened nickname of the State Security Service, the much-despised secret police and their agents in the former GDR. With the help of an extensive network of informers, the *Stasi* built up personal files on a third of the East German population. It was disbanded a year before the WIEDERVEREINIGUNG. Since then there have been many charges relating to political crimes committed by *Stasi* agents, as well as enquiries into the number of former GDR citizens who cooperated with the *Stasi*. *See also* IM.

Straußwirtschaft An inn set up temporarily by a local winegrower for a few weeks after the new wine has been made. A bunch of flowers and vine leaves above the door shows that the new vintage is ready for tasting. *See also* BESENWIRTSCHAFT and HEURIGE.

Studentenwerke The *Studentenwerke* (student welfare services) are responsible for the economic, social, cultural, and health care of students at higher educational institutions.

Süddeutsche Zeitung This respected daily national newspaper was founded in 1945 and is published in Munich. It has a liberal outlook and is read mainly in southern Germany.

Tempolimit Speed limits are either compulsory – 50 km/h (30 mph) in towns, 100 km/h (60 mph) on other roads – or recommended when driving in bad weather conditions, on dangerous stretches, and in urban areas. On the *Autobahn* the *Richtgeschwindigkeit* (recommended maximum speed) is 130 km/h (80 mph). In residential areas the limit can be as low as 30 km/h (20 mph); the 30-Zone was introduced to protect children and pedestrians.

Trabant A make of car produced in the former GDR. A Trabant, or Trabi, with its two-stroke engine and plastic body, was a prized possession, and people had to wait for years to get one. After reunification, the Trabant came to symbolize the GDR era and has achieved cult status in Germany.

U-Bahn Most large cities have a *U-Bahn* (*Untergrundbahn*) (underground railway network) that connects with an *S-Bahn* (*Schnellbahn* or *Stadtbahn*) (city and suburban railway). The same ticket can normally be used for both services.

Umweltschutz (Environmental protection) Most Germans feel a strong sense of responsibility for the environment, especially after seeing so many forests dying (WALDSTERBEN). The *Bundesumweltministerium* is the government ministry responsible for all environmental matters. Its policy is based on the 'polluter must pay' principle, by which manufacturers are obliged to collect, sort, and recycle their waste; on the cooperation principle, by which every individual is responsible for the environment; and on the prevention principle, which encourages manufacturers to develop environmentally friendly products. Other focal points are a more efficient use of energy, a clean air and water programme, less road traffic, and cleaner fuels, nature conservation, and soil protection. *See also* DUALES SYSTEM, GRÜNER PUNKT, RECYCLING.

Verein There are over 300,000 officially registered *Vereine* (clubs or associations) with their own constitution and by-laws. Millions of Germans belong to a club; nearly one in four is a member of a sports club, and there are around 15 million hiking-club members. Stamp collectors, marksmen, dog breeders, music fans – in fact those who follow any kind of activity or hobby – are soon organized into a *Verein*. Membership fees are usually low, and everybody is encouraged to socialize at club level.

Vignette In order to be able to use Austrian and Swiss motorways, all vehicles must display a sticker on the windscreen called a *Vignette*. These stickers are usually valid for one year, but foreign tourists in Austria can buy stickers for a period of ten days or two months. The sticker can be bought at all Austrian border crossings and petrol stations.

Volkshochschule (VHS) A local adult education centre that can be found in every German town. The *VHS* offers low-cost day and evening classes in a wide range of subjects, including crafts, languages, music, and exercise.

Waldsterben *Waldsterben* (the death of forests) is due mainly to pollution from factories and cars. By 1996 over half of Germany's trees were damaged. The threat to forests has strengthened support for Germany's ecological political movement, BÜNDNIS 90/DIE GRÜNEN.

WASG ▶ LINKSPARTEI

Wehrdienst Compulsory military service for young men in Germany (nine months), Switzerland (three months), and Austria (six months). Young Germans are generally called up when they are 18 or 19, although there are certain exemptions. Conscientious objectors may apply to do ZIVILDIENST instead.

Weihnachten ▶ TRADITIONS, FESTIVALS, AND HOLIDAYS

Weihnachtsmarkt During the weeks of Advent, Christmas markets take place in most German towns, selling Christmas decorations, handmade toys and crib figures, traditional Christmas biscuits, and mulled wine to sustain the shoppers.

Wein Germany, Switzerland, and Austria are wine-producing countries, best known for their white wines. Germany's main wine regions are Franconia, the Rhineland-Palatinate, the Moselle area, and Baden-Württemberg. Rhine wine (or hock) is sold in tall brown bottles and wine from the Moselle in green bottles; Franconian Bocksbeutel comes in wide, bulbous bottles. There are two categories of German wine, the cheap *Tafelwein* (table wine) and the superior *Qualitätswein* (quality wine). The best wines are designated *Qualitätswein mit Prädikat*. Sekt is a champagne-like sparkling wine. In August and September there are festivals in German wine towns and villages. Austria grows red and white wines, mainly in the Burgenland, in Styria, and around the Neusiedler See where the HEURIGE is celebrated. More than a third of the total area of grape cultivation in Austria is devoted to Grüner Veltliner, a full-bodied, fruity white wine. Wines from Switzerland are mostly drunk locally and are produced in the Thurgau region. The Swiss reputation rests with their spirits, such as Kirsch, Pflümli, Mirabelle, and Enzian. *See also* BESENWIRTSCHAFT and STRAUẞWIRTSCHAFT.

Weinstube A cosy wine bar which offers a wide choice of wines and usually also serves a few dishes that are considered to go well with wine. A *Weinstube* can be more upmarket than an ordinary pub, or else fairly rustic, especially in wine-growing areas.

Die Welt A national daily newspaper published in Hamburg. It has a large business section and is considered right-wing in its views.

Wende This word can refer to any major political or social change or turning point, but it is used especially to refer to the collapse of Communism in 1989, symbolized by the fall of die MAUER (the Berlin Wall), which eventually led to the WIEDERVEREINIGUNG in 1990.

Wertstofftonne ▶ RECYCLING

Wessi A colloquial and sometimes derogatory term for someone from West Germany, as opposed to an OSSI. The expression *Besserwessi*, a pun on *Besserwisser* (know-all), is sometimes used to describe overly confident West Germans.

Westdeutsche Allgemeine Zeitung (WAZ) Germany's highest-circulation serious national paper. It is published in Essen, and caters mainly for the densely populated Ruhr area.

Wiedervereinigung The German word for the reunification of Germany, which officially took place on 3 October 1990, when the former GDR was incorporated into the BUNDESREPUBLIK. The huge financial and social costs of reunification are still being felt throughout Germany. *See also* SOLIDARITÄTSZUSCHLAG.

Wirtschaftswunder, or German economic miracle, which resulted from the country's rapid reconstruction after the Second World War. The economy boomed in the decades after 1950.

Die Woche A relatively new weekly newspaper, which was founded in 1993 and is published in Hamburg. It is less comprehensive and easier to read than DIE ZEIT, but is also an important opinion leader with a liberal outlook offering background information, analyses, and reports.

ZDF – Zweites Deutsches Fernsehen The second German public TV channel, founded in 1961. It broadcasts the Zweites Programm with entertainment, news, information, and a limited amount of advertising.

Die Zeit Germany's 'heaviest' weekly newspaper, published in Hamburg, is considered essential reading for academics and intellectuals. Former BUNDESKANZLER Helmut Schmidt is a joint editor. The paper offers in-depth analysis of current issues in politics, society, culture, and the arts.

Zeugnis der allgemeinen Hochschulreife ▶ ABITUR

Zivildienst Community service, which recognized conscientious objectors in Germany, Austria, and Switzerland can choose to carry out instead of WEHRDIENST. It lasts longer than WEHRDIENST and usually involves caring for children, the elderly, the disabled, or the sick.

Letter-writing / Briefeschreiben

Holiday postcard

- *Beginnings (informal)*: 'Lieber' *here because it's a man; if it's a woman, use e.g.* Liebe Elke.

  To two people, repeat 'Liebe(r)': Lieber Hans, liebe Elke.

  To a family: Liebe Schmidts, Liebe Familie Schmidt, *or just* Liebe Leute.

- *Address*: *Note that the title* (Herrn, Frau, Fräulein) *stands on the line above the name. Herr always has an n on the end in addresses.*

  The house number comes after the street name.

  The postcode comes before the place, and if you're writing from outside the country put a D- for Germany, A- for Austria or CH- for Switzerland in front of it.

Heidelberg, den 6.8. 2000

Lieber Hans!

Einen schönen Gruß aus Alt-Heidelberg! Wir sind erst zwei Tage hier, aber schon sehr angetan von der Stadt und Umgebung, trotz der vielen Touristen. Allerdings ist es ziemlich schwül. Wir waren gestern abend in einem Konzert im Schlosshof, eine wunderbare Stimmung! Und dann die herrliche Aussicht auf Altstadt und Neckar von der Terrasse. Morgen machen wir eine Bootsfahrt, dann geht's am Donnerstag wieder nach Hause. Hoffentlich ist deine Mutter inzwischen wieder gesund.

Bis bald

Max und Sophie

Herrn
Hans Matthäus
Brucknerstr. 26
91052 Erlangen

- *Endings (informal)*: Herzlich *or* Herzlichst, Herzliche Grüße; *more affectionately:* Alles Liebe; Bis bald = *See you soon* .

Postkarte aus dem Urlaub

- *Anrede: sehr einfach auf Postkarten, immer 'Dear' und der Vorname, der im englischen Sprachraum viel häufiger verwendet wird. Die Anrede kann auch entfallen.*

- *Meist keine Ortsangabe, wenn der Ort aus dem Inhalt oder dem Bild auf der Postkarte klar hervorgeht.*
  Datum – in den USA verwendet man die Reihenfolge Monat, Tag, Jahr, wenn ein Datum mit Ziffern angegeben ist – 8.6.2000

- *Adresse: Der Titel (*Mr, Mrs, Miss, Ms*) steht direkt vor dem Namen auf der gleichen Zeile.*

  Das Haus hat oft einen Namen anstelle einer (oder zusätzlich zur) Hausnummer, die übrigens vor dem Straßennamen steht.

  *Es folgen (in GB) Ortschaft, meist auch Grafschaft, dann Postleitzahl (*postcode*), alles jeweils auf einer eigenen Zeile; in den USA Ortschaft und Postleitzahl (*zipcode*), mit dem auf zwei Buchstaben abgekürzten Namen des Staates davor:*

  John Splaine Jr.
  1067 Blackwall Avenue
  Studio City
  CA 91604
  USA

6.8.2000

Dear John,

Greetings from old Heidelberg! Got here ① a couple of days ago, but already in love with the place (in spite of all the tourists). It's pretty sultry though. Last night we went to a concert in the castle courtyard, very atmospheric. And a terrific view of the river and the old town from the terrace. Tomorrow we're taking a boat trip, and then on Thursday we head for home. Hope ① your mother's fully recovered by now.

See you soon,

Mark and Juliet

Mr J. Roberts
The Willows
49 North Terrace
Kings Barton
Nottinghamshire
NG8 4LQ
England

- *Schlussformel:*
  All the best, Best wishes, *oder einfach* Yours; *auch* Love (from)*, wenn man den Addressaten näher steht.*

① *Telegrammstil: die Angabe der Person entfällt auf Postkarten oft.*

Christmas and New Year wishes

On a card:

Frohe Weihnachten und viel Glück im neuen Jahr

A bit more formal: Ein gesegnetes Weihnachtsfest und die besten Wünsche zum neuen Jahr

A bit less formal: Fröhliche Weihnachten und einen guten Rutsch ins neue Jahr

In a letter:

- *On most personal letters German speakers don't put their address at the top, but just the name of the place and the date*

Würzburg, den 20.12.2000

Liebe Karin, lieber Ferdinand,

euch und euren Kindern wünschen wir von Herzen frohe Weihnachten und ein glückliches neues Jahr. Wir hoffen, es geht euch allen gut, und dass wir uns bald mal wieder sehen werden. Es kommt uns so vor, als hätten wir uns eine Ewigkeit nicht gesehen.

Das vergangene Jahr war für uns sehr ereignisreich. Thomas hatte im Sommer einen Unfall mit dem Fahrrad, und brach sich den Arm und das Schlüsselbein. Sabine hat das Abitur gerade noch bestanden und ist jetzt an der Uni in Erlangen, studiert Sport. Der arme Michael ist im Oktober arbeitslos geworden und sucht immer noch nach einer Stelle.

Ihr müsst unbedingt vorbeikommen, wenn ihr das nächste Mal in der Gegend seid. Ruft doch einfach ein paar Tage vorher an, damit wir etwas ausmachen können.

Mit herzlichen Grüßen

Eure Gabi und Michael

Weihnachts- und Neujahrsgrüße

Auf einer Karte:

[Best wishes for a] Happy ① Christmas and a Prosperous New Year

All best wishes for Christmas and the New Year

Wishing you every happiness this Christmas[tide] and in the New Year

① *Oder etwas altmodisch:* Merry

In einem Brief:

44 Louis Gardens
London NW6 4GM

December 20th 2000

Dear Peter and Claire,

First of all, a very happy Christmas and all the best for the New Year to you and the children.① We hope you're all well② and that we'll see you again soon. It seems ages since we last met up.

We've had a very eventful year. Last summer Gavin came off his bike and broke his arm and collarbone. Kathy scraped through her A levels and is now at Sussex doing European Studies. Poor Tony was made redundant in October and is still looking for a job.

Do come and see us next time you are over this way. Just give us a ring a couple of days before so we can fix something.

All best wishes

Tony and Ann

① *Oder (vor allem, wenn die Kinder älter sind):* to you and the family.
② *Informeller:* flourishing.

Invitation (informal)

Hamm, den 22.4.2000

Liebe Jennie,

wäre es möglich, dass du ① in den Sommerferien zu uns kommst? Katrin und Gottfried würden sich riesig freuen (ich und mein Mann natürlich auch). Wir planen eine Reise zum Bodensee Ende Juli/Anfang August, du ① könntest gerne mitfahren. Es ist wirklich sehr schön dort unten. Wir werden wahrscheinlich zelten – hoffentlich hast du ① nichts dagegen!

Schreib bald, ob das für dich ① in Frage kommt.

Herzliche Grüße

Monika Pfortner

■ *Beginning: if you put a comma after the name on the first line (which is usual), the letter proper should start with a small letter.*

① du, dich, dein etc.: although many people still write these with a capital in letters, this is not necessary. But the formal Sie, Ihnen, Ihr must always have a capital.

Invitation (formal)

Invitations to parties are usually by word of mouth, while for weddings, announcements rather than invitations are usually sent out:

Irene Brinkmann — Stefan Hopf

Wir heiraten am Samstag, den 20. April 2000, um 14 Uhr in der Pfarrkirche Landsberg.

Goethestraße 12 — Ulrichsweg 4

Landsberg — Altötting

Einladung (informell)

- *Die Absenderadresse befindet sich oben auf dem Brief selbst, entweder rechts oder in der Mitte, darunter das Datum.*
- *Das Datum im Englischen hat viele Formen:* May 10, 10 May, May 10th, 10th May *sind alle möglich und gleichermaßen richtig. In den USA verwendet man die Reihenfolge Monat, Tag, Jahr, wenn das Datum in Ziffern angegeben wird:* 05/10/2000

35 Winchester
Drive
Stoke Gifford
Bristol
BS34 8PD

April 22nd 2000

Dear Klaus,

Is there any chance of your coming to stay with us in the summer holidays? Roy and Debbie would be delighted if you could (as well as David and me, of course). We hope to go to North Wales at the end of July/beginning of August, and you'd be very welcome to come too. It's really beautiful up there. We'll probably take tents – I hope that's OK by you.

Let me know as soon as possible if you can manage it.

All best wishes

Rachel Hemmings

Einladung (förmlich)

Zu einer Hochzeit mit anschließendem Empfang

Mr and Mrs Peter Thompson
request the pleasure of your company
at the marriage of their daughter
Hannah Louise
to
Steven David Warner

at St. Mary's Church, Little Bourton
on Saturday 25th July 2000 at 2 p.m.
and afterwards at the
Golden Cross Hotel, Billing

R.S.V.P. *23 Santers Lane*
Little Bourton
Northampton
NN6 1AZ

Accepting an invitation

Edinburgh, den 2.5.2000

Liebe Frau Pfortner,

recht herzlichen Dank für Ihre liebe Einladung. Da ich noch keine festen Pläne für die Sommerferien habe, möchte ich sie sehr gerne annehmen. Allerdings darf ich nicht mehr als vier bis fünf Tage weg sein, da es meiner Mutter nicht sehr gut geht. Sie ① müssen mir sagen, was ich mitbringen soll (außer Edinburgh Rock!). Ist es sehr warm am Bodensee? Kann man im See schwimmen?

Natürlich habe ich nichts gegen Zelten. Auch hier in Schottland bei Wind und Regen macht es mir Spaß!

Ich freue mich auf ein baldiges Wiedersehen.

Herzliche Grüße

Jennie Stewart

① *Since this is a letter from a younger person writing to the mother of a friend, she uses the formal* Sie *form and possessive* Ihr *(always with capitals), and writes to her as* "Frau Pfortner". *On the other hand it was quite natural for* Frau Pfortner *to use the* du *form to her.*

Antwort auf eine Einladung (informell)

Mozartstraße 5
32756 Detmold
Germany

2 May 2000

Dear Mrs Hemmings,

Many thanks for your letter and kind invitation. Since I don't have anything fixed yet for the summer holidays, I'd be delighted to come. However I mustn't be away for more than four or five days since my mother hasn't been very well.

You must let me know what I should bring. How warm is it in North Wales? Can one swim in the sea? Camping is fine as far as I'm concerned, we take our tent everywhere.

Looking forward to seeing you again soon,

Yours

Klaus

Antwort auf eine Einladung (förmlich)

Greenacres
Westway
Balsall Common
West Midlands
CV7 8RR

Annahme:

Richard Willis has great pleasure in accepting Mr and Mrs Peter Thompson's kind invitation to the marriage of their daughter Hannah Louise to Steven Warner at St. Mary's Church, Little Bourton, on Saturday 25th July.

- *Man wiederholt die Details von der Einladung, etwas vereinfacht.*

Absage:

Richard Willis regrets that he is unable to accept Mr and Mrs Peter Thompson's kind invitation ... , due to a prior engagement.

- *Im Falle einer Absage ist es oft höflicher, einen Brief zu schreiben, vor allem wenn man die Brauteltern gut kennt.*

Replying to a job advertisement

David Baker
67 Whiteley Avenue
St George
Bristol
BS5 6TW

Softwarehaus WSO GmbH
Personalabteilung
Kanalstr. 75
D-75757 Pforzheim

Bristol, den 26.2.2000

Ihre Stellenanzeige im Tagblatt vom 23.2.2000

Sehr geehrte Damen und Herren, ①

ich interessiere mich für die von Ihnen im Tagblatt vom 23. September ausgeschriebene Stelle eines Computergrafikers und würde mich freuen, wenn Sie mir nähere Informationen zuschicken könnten. ②

Derzeit bin ich bei der Firma Wondersoft Ltd in Bristol tätig, aber mein Vertrag läuft schon Ende des Monats aus, ③ und ich möchte gerne in Deutschland arbeiten. Wie Sie meinem Lebenslauf entnehmen können, verfüge ich über ausgezeichnete Sprachkenntnisse sowie die geforderten Qualifikationen und einschlägige Berufserfahrung.

Zu einem Vorstellungsgespräch stehe ich jederzeit ab dem 6. Oktober zur Verfügung. Sie können mich ab diesem Datum unter der folgenden Adresse in Deutschland erreichen:

bei Gerber
Rudolfstr. 22
81925 München
Tel. (089) 460 99 507

Ich freue mich darauf, von Ihnen zu hören. ④

Mit freundlichen Grüßen

David Baker

Anlage: Lebenslauf

① *Correct if the letter is addressed to the personnel department, but if it is addressed to the personnel manager (*An den Personalleiter, ...*) the letter begins:* Sehr geehrter Herr XY *or* Sehr geehrte Frau XY.

② *Or if you have enough details and want to apply for the job right away:* und möchte mich um diese Stellung bewerben.

③ *Or if you are unemployed:* Derzeit bin ich arbeitslos, ...

④ *Or:* Ihre Antwort erwarte ich mit Interesse.

Bewerbung auf eine Stellenanzeige hin

Humboldtweg 16
60247 Frankfurt a. M.
Germany
Tel. (069) 724 689

13th February 2000

The Personnel Manager ①
Patterson Software plc
Milton Estate
Bath BA6 8YZ

Dear Sir or Madam,②

I am interested in the post of programmer advertised in the Guardian of 12th February and would be grateful if you could send me further particulars. ③

I am currently working for the Sempo Corporation in Frankfurt, but my contract finishes at the end of the month, and I would like ④ to come and work in the UK. As you can see from my CV (enclosed), I have an excellent command of English and also the required qualifications and experience.

I will be available for interview any time after 6th October, from which date I can be contacted at the following address in the UK:

c/o Lewis
51 Dexter Road
London N7 6BW
Tel. 0207 607 5512

I look forward to hearing from you.⑤

Yours sincerely

Rita Steinmüller

Encl.

① *Den Brief so addressieren, wenn in der Anzeige kein Name vorkommt; aber wenn es z.B. heißt* "Reply to Angela Summers", *dann* "Ms Angela Summers, ..."
② *Wenn der Name bekannt ist, dann* "Dear Ms Summers", "Dear Mr Wright" *etc.*
③ *Oder falls Sie schon genügend Informationen haben und sich bewerben wollen:* "and would like to apply for this position".
④ *Oder falls Sie arbeitslos sind:* "I am currently unemployed and would like ..."
⑤ *Oder:* "Thanking you in anticipation".

Curriculum Vitae (CV) or (*Amer.*) Résumé

Lebenslauf

David Baker
67 Whiteley Avenue
St George
Bristol
BS5 6TW
Großbritannien

Tel. +43 (0)117 945 3421

geboren am 30.06.1970 in London, ledig ①

Ausbildung

1986 O Levels in 7 Fächern (ungefähr = mittlere Reife), John Radcliffe School, Croydon

1988 A Levels in Mathematik, Höherer Mathematik, Informatik, Deutsch (ungefähr = Abitur), Croydon Sixth Form College

1989 Teilzeitarbeit in München, Abendkurse an der VHS

1990-94 University of Aston, Birmingham, B.Sc in Informatik

Berufstätigkeit

08/94 - 08/97 Traineeausbildung, anschließend Sotwareentwickler bei IBM

seit 09/97 Programmierer bei Wondersoft plc, Bristol

Entwicklung von Programmen für die Industrie; Schwerpunkt: Grafiksoftware

Besondere Kenntnisse

Fremdsprachen: Deutsch (fließend), Französisch (gut)

① *Or:* Verheiratet (mit einem Kind/zwei Kindern etc.); Geschieden (mit einem Kind/zwei Kindern etc.)

Lebenslauf

CURRICULUM VITAE ①

Name:	Rita Steinmüller
Address:	Humboldtweg 16 60247 Frankfurt a. M. Germany
Telephone:	+44 (0)69 724 689
Nationality:	German
Date of Birth:	11/3/1973
Marital status:	Single ②

Education:

1991-1995	Degree Course in Information Technology at Stuttgart University
1984-1991	Theodor-Heuss-Gymnasium, Eichborn Abitur examination (approx. A Level) in Mathematics, Physics, Economics and English

Employment:

1996-present	Program development engineer with Sempo-Informatik, Frankfurt, specializing in computer graphics
1995-1996	Trainee programmer with Oregon Germany, Rüsselsheim

Further skills:

Languages:	German (mother tongue), English (fluent spoken and written), French (good)
Interests:	Travel (many trips to the UK), chess, tennis

① *Oder (Amer.):* RÉSUMÉ
② *Oder:* Married (with one/two/three etc. children), Divorced (with one/two/three etc. children)

Booking a hotel room

Hotel Goldener Pflug
Ortsstraße 7
69235 Steinbach

Tobias Schwarz
Gartenstr. 19
76530 Baden-Baden

16. Juli 2000

Sehr geehrte Damen und Herren,

Ich wurde durch die Broschüre "Hotels und Pensionen im Naturpark Odenwald (Ausgabe 2000)" auf ihr Hotel aufmerksam.

Ich möchte für mich und meine Frau für die Zeit vom 2. bis 11. August (neun Nächte) ein ruhiges Doppelzimmer mit Dusche reservieren, sowie ein Einzelzimmer für unseren Sohn.

Falls Sie für diese Zeit etwas Passendes haben, informieren Sie mich doch bitte über den Preis und darüber, ob Sie eine Anzahlung wünschen.

Mit freundlichen Grüßen

Tobias Schwarz

Booking a campsite

Camilla Stumpf
Saalgasse 10
60311 Frankfurt

Camping am See
Frau Bettina Sattler
Auweg 6-10
87654 Waldenkirchen

■ *For a business letter to a particular person, use* "Sehr geehrte(r)" *and the name. (If this letter were to a man, it would start* "Sehr geehrter Herr Sattler").

Frankfurt, den 16.04.2000

Sehr geehrte Frau Sattler,

Ihr Campingplatz wurde mir von Herrn Stephan Seidel empfohlen, der schon mehrmals bei Ihnen war. ① *Ich würde nun gerne vom 18. bis 25. Juli mit zwei Freunden eine Woche bei Ihnen verbringen. Könnten Sie uns bitte einen Zeltplatz* ② *möglichst in unmittelbarer Nähe des Sees* ③ *reservieren?*

Würden Sie mir freundlicherweise mitteilen, ob Sie meine Reservierung annehemen können und ob Sie eine Anzahlung wünschen?

Außerdem wäre ich Ihnen dankbar für eine kurze Wegbeschreibung von der Autobahn.

Mit vielem Dank im Voraus und freundlichen Grüßen

Camilla Stumpf

① *Or if you have found the campsite in a guide, say e.g.:* "Ich habe Ihre Anschrift dem ACDA-Campingführer 2000 entnommen".
② *Or if you have a caravan:* "einen Stellplatz für einen Wohnwagen".
③ *Alternatives*: "in schattiger/geschützter Lage".

Hotelzimmerreservierung

The Manager
Torbay Hotel
Dawlish
Devon
EX37 2LR

35 Prince Edward Road
Oxford OX7 3AA

Tel. 01865 322435
23rd April 2000

Dear Sir or Madam,

I saw your hotel listed in the Inns of Devon guide for last year, and wish to reserve a double (or twin-bedded) room with shower ① in a quiet position from August 2nd - 11th (nine nights), also a single room for our son.

If you have anything suitable for this period please let me know the price and whether you require a deposit.

Yours sincerely

Charles Fairhurst

① *Alternativen:* "with bath", "with ensuite".

Campingplatzreservierung

22 Daniel Avenue
Caldwood
Leeds LS8 7RR
Tel. 01132 998767

25th April 2000

Mr Joseph Vale
Lakeside Park
Rydal
Cumbria
LA22 9RZ

Dear Mr Vale

Your campsite was recommended to me by James Dallas, who knows it from several visits.① I and two friends would like to come for a week from July 18th to 25th Could you please reserve us a site for one tent, ② preferably close to the shore.③

Please confirm the booking and let me know if you require a deposit. Would you also be good enough to send me instructions on how to reach you from the motorway.

Yours sincerely

Frances Good

① *Oder falls Sie den Campingplatz einem Führer entnommen haben, etwa:* "I found your site in the Tourist Board's list/ the Good Camper's Guide" *etc.*
② *Oder falls Sie einen Wohnwagen haben:* "a caravan site".
③ *Andere Möglichkeiten:* "in a shady/sheltered spot".

Cancelling a reservation

Herrn
Hans Knauer
Gasthaus Sonnenblick
Hauptstr. 6
D-94066 Bad Füssing
Germany

Aberdeen, den 2.6.2000

Sehr geehrter Herr Knauer,

leider muss ich meine/unsere Reservierung für die Woche vom 7. bis 13. August ① rückgängig machen. Wegen unvorhergesehener Umstände ② muss ich/müssen wir auf meinen/unseren Urlaub verzichten.

Es tut mir aufrichtig Leid, dass ich so spät abbestellen muss, und hoffe, dass Sie deswegen keine Unannehmlichkeiten haben.

Mit freundlichen Grüßen

Robert McDonald

① *Or:* "für die Zeit vom 7. bis 20. August" *etc.*
② *Or more precisely:* "Durch den überraschenden Tod meines Vaters/die Krankheit meines Mannes" *etc.*

Stornierung einer Reservierung

Mrs J. Warrington
Downlands
Steyning
West Sussex
BN44 6LZ

Wernerstr. 17
49835 Wietmarschen
Germany

July 20th 2000

Dear Mrs Warrington,

Unfortunately I have to cancel my/our reservation for the week of August 7th. ① Due to unforeseen circumstances ② I/we have had to abandon my/our holiday plans.

I very much regret having to cancel [at such a late stage] and hope it does not cause you undue inconvenience.

Yours sincerely

Elke Nordrup

① *Oder:* "for the period from August 7th to 14th".
② *Oder genauer:* "Owing to my father's sudden death/my husband's illness" *etc*

Sending an e-mail

The illustration shows a typical interface for sending e-mail.

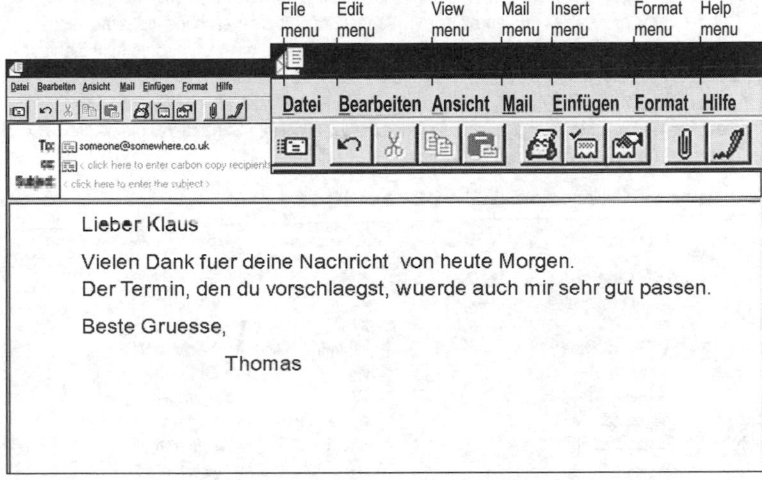

Das Verschicken von E-Mails

Die Abbildung zeigt eine typische Oberfläche zum Verschicken von E-Mails.

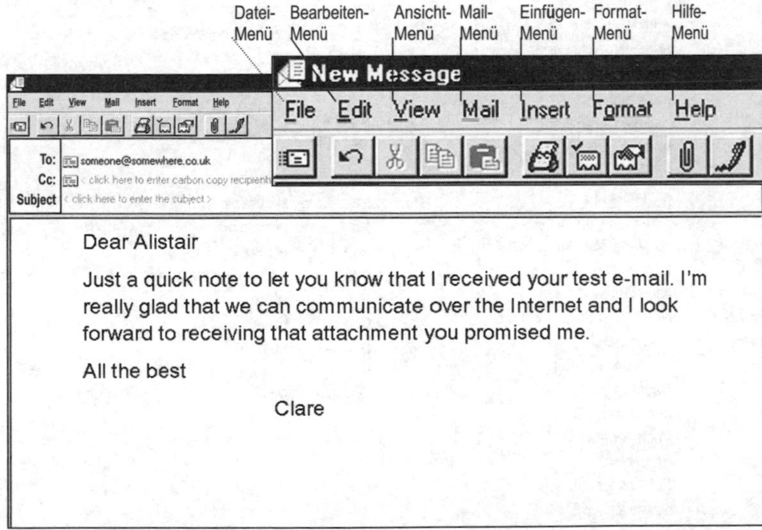

SMS (electronic text-messaging)

The basic principles governing German SMS abbreviations are similar to those governing English SMS. Certain words or syllables are represented by letters or numbers that sound the same. Most punctuation is usually omitted, umlauts are rarely used, and there are no strict rules about upper and lower case. For example 'viele Grüße' can be 'vlg'. Sentences are shortened by leaving out certain letters – 'bist du noch wach?' might read 'bidunowa'. Often just the initial letter of a word is used, as in 'ff' for 'Fortsetzung folgt'. Many English abbreviations have made it into German text messages. For example '4u' (for you) is often used for 'für dich'.

Glossary of German SMS abbreviations

Abbreviation	*Meaning*
8ung	Achtung
ads	alles deine Schuld
akla?	alles klar?
aws	auf Wiedersehen
bb	bis bald
bda	bis dann
bidunowa?	bist du noch wach?
braduhi?	brauchst du Hilfe?
bs	bis später
dad	denke an dich
d	der
div	danke im Voraus
dubido	du bist doof
ff	Fortsetzung folgt
g	grinsen
g&k	Gruß und Kuss
gn8	gute Nacht
gngn	geht nicht, gibts nicht
hahu	habe Hunger
hdl	habe dich lieb
hdos	halt die Ohren steif
hegl	herzlichen Glückwunsch
ild	ich liebe dich
jon	jetzt oder nie
katze?	kannst du tanzen?
ko5mispä	komme 5 Minuten später
l8er	later = später
lg	liebe Grüße
lidumino	liebst du mich noch?
mamima	mail mir mal
mumidire	muss mit dir reden
n8	Nacht
nfd	nur für dich
pg	Pech gehabt
rumian	ruf mich an
sfh	Schluss für heute
siw	soweit ich weiß

Abbreviation	*Meaning*
sms	schreib mir schnell
sz	schreib zurück
tabu	tausend Bussis
vegimini	vergiss mich nicht
vlg	viele Grüße
vv	viel Vergnügen
wamaduheu?	was machst du heute?
waudi	warte auf dich
we	Wochenende
zdom?	zu dir oder zu mir?

Emoticons	
:-)	lächeln, glücklich
:-))	sehr glücklich
:-|	Stirnrunzeln
:-e	enttäuscht
:-(	unglücklich, traurig
:-((	sehr unglücklich
:->	sarkastisch
%-)	verwirrt
:~(or **:'-(**	weinen
;-)	zwinkern
|-o	müde
:-	skeptisch
:-D	lachen
:-<>	erstaunt
:-p	rausgestreckte Zunge
:-O	schreien
O:-)	Engel
:-* or **:-x**	Kuss
:-o	Schock
@}-,-'–	Rose

SMS (elektronische Textmitteilungen über das Handy)

SMS ist die englische Abkürzung für "Short Message Service", was sich als "Kurznachrichtendienst" übersetzen lässt. Im Englischen gibt es zahllose Abkürzungen, die es erlauben, viele Informationen mit wenigen Zeichen und Zahlen zu übermitteln. Zum Beispiel: 2L8 = 'too late'. Für die meisten Nachrichten tippt man nur die Anfangsbuchstaben jedes Wortes ein, zum Beispiel: ttyl = 'talk to you later' oder fyi = 'for your information'.

Verzeichnis von englischen SMS-Abkürzungen

Abkürzung	*Bedeutung*
adn	any day now
afaik	as far as I know
atb	all the best
b	be
b4	before
b4n	bye for now
bbl	be back late(r)
bcnu	be seeing you
bfn	bye for now
brb	be right back
btw	by the way
bwd	backward
c	see
cu	see you
cul8r	see you later
f2f	face to face
f2t	free to talk
fwd	forward
fwiw	for what it's worth
fyi	for your information
gal	get a life
gr8	great
h8	hate
hand	have a nice day
hak	hugs and kisses
hth	hope this helps
ic	I see
iluvu	I love you
imho	in my humble opinion
imo	in my opinion
iow	in other words
jic	just in case
jk	just kidding
kit	keep in touch
kwim	know what I mean?
l8	late
l8r	later
lol	lots of luck/ laughing out loud
mob	mobile
msg	message
myob	mind your own business
ne	any
ne1	anyone
no1	no one
oic	oh, I see
otoh	on the other hand
pcm	please call me
pls	please
ppl	people
r	are
rofl	rolling on the floor, laughing
ru	are you
ruok	are you OK?
sit	stay in touch
som1	someone
spk	speak
thkq	thank you
ttyl	talk to you later
tx	thanks
u	you
ur	you are
w/	with
wan2	want to
wan2 tlk	want to talk?
werv u bin	where have you been?
wknd	weekend
wot	what
wu	what's up?
x	kiss
xlnt	excellent
xoxoxo	hugs and kisses
yr	your
2	to, too
2day	today
2l8	too late
2moro	tomorrow
2nite	tonight
3sum	threesome
4	for

<table>
<tr><th colspan="2">Emoticons</th></tr>
<tr><td>:-)</td><td>smiling, happy face</td></tr>
<tr><td>:-))</td><td>very happy face</td></tr>
<tr><td>:-|</td><td>frowning</td></tr>
<tr><td>:-e</td><td>disappointed</td></tr>
<tr><td>:-(</td><td>unhappy, sad face</td></tr>
<tr><td>:-((</td><td>very unhappy face</td></tr>
<tr><td>:-></td><td>sarcastic</td></tr>
<tr><td>%-)</td><td>confused</td></tr>
<tr><td>:~(or :'-(</td><td>crying</td></tr>
<tr><td>;-)</td><td>winking happy face</td></tr>
<tr><td>|-o</td><td>tired, asleep</td></tr>
<tr><td>:-\</td><td>sceptical</td></tr>
<tr><td>:-D</td><td>big smile, laughing face</td></tr>
<tr><td>:-<></td><td>amazed</td></tr>
<tr><td>X=</td><td>fingers crossed</td></tr>
<tr><td>:-p</td><td>tongue sticking out</td></tr>
<tr><td>:-O</td><td>shouting</td></tr>
<tr><td>O:-)</td><td>angel</td></tr>
<tr><td>:-* or :-x</td><td>big kiss!</td></tr>
<tr><td>:-o</td><td>shocked face</td></tr>
<tr><td>@}-,-'—</td><td>a rose</td></tr>
</table>

Aa

A, a[1] /eɪ/ *n.* A, a, *das;* **A road** Straße 1. Ordnung; ≈ Bundesstraße, *die*

a[2] /ə, *stressed* eɪ/ *indef. art.* ein/eine/ein; **he is a gardener/a Frenchman** er ist Gärtner/Franzose; **she did not say a word** sie sagte kein Wort

AA *abbr.* (Brit.) = **Automobile Association** *britischer Automobilklub*

aback /ə'bæk/ *adv.* **be taken ~**: erstaunt sein

abacus /'æbəkəs/ *n., pl.* **~es** *or* **abaci** /'æbəsaɪ/ Abakus, *der*

abandon /ə'bændən/ *v.t.* verlassen ‹*Ort, Person*›; aufgeben ‹*Prinzip*›; **~ed** verlassen, ausgesetzt ‹*Kind, Tier*›

abase /ə'beɪs/ *v.t.* erniedrigen

abashed /ə'bæʃt/ *adj.* beschämt

abate /ə'beɪt/ *v.i.* nachlassen

abattoir /'æbətwɑ:(r)/ *n.* Schlachthof, *der*

abbey /'æbɪ/ *n.* Abtei, *die*

abbot /'æbət/ *n.* Abt, *der*

abbreviate /ə'bri:vɪeɪt/ *v.t.* abkürzen

ab'breviated dialling *n.* (Teleph.) Kurzwahl, *die*

abbreviation /əbri:vɪ'eɪʃn/ *n.* Abkürzung, *die*

abdicate /'æbdɪkeɪt/ *v.t.* abdanken

abdication /æbdɪ'keɪʃn/ *n.* Abdankung, *die*

abdomen /'æbdəmən/ *n.* Bauch, *der*

abdominal /æb'dɒmɪnl/ *adj.* Bauch-

abduct /əb'dʌkt/ *v.t.* entführen

abduction /əb'dʌkʃn/ *n.* Entführung, *die*

aberration /æbə'reɪʃn/ *n.* Abweichung, *die*

abet /ə'bet/ *v.t.,* **-tt-** helfen (+ *Dat.*); **aid and ~**: Beihilfe leisten (+ *Dat.*)

abhor /əb'hɔ:(r)/ *v.t.,* **-rr-** verabscheuen

abhorrent /əb'hɒrənt/ *adj.* abscheulich

abide /ə'baɪd/ [1] *v.i.* **~ by** befolgen ‹*Gesetz, Vorschrift*›; [ein]halten ‹*Versprechen*›
[2] *v.t.* ertragen; **I can't ~ dogs** ich kann Hunde nicht ausstehen

ability /ə'bɪlɪtɪ/ *n.* **(a)** (capacity) Fähigkeit, *die;* **have the ~ to do sth.** etw. können
(b) (cleverness) Intelligenz, *die*
(c) (talent) Begabung, *die*

abject /'æbdʒekt/ *adj.* elend; bitter ‹*Armut*›; demütig ‹*Entschuldigung*›

ablaze /ə'bleɪz/ *adj.* **be ~**: in Flammen stehen

able /'eɪbl/ *adj.* **(a) be ~ to do sth.** etw. tun können
(b) (competent) fähig

able-bodied /'eɪblbɒdɪd/ *adj.* kräftig; tauglich ‹*Soldat, Matrose*›

ably /'eɪblɪ/ *adv.* geschickt; gekonnt

abnormal /æb'nɔ:ml/ *adj.* abnorm; a[b]normal ‹*Interesse, Verhalten*›

abnormality /æbnɔ:'mælɪtɪ/ *n.* Abnormität, *die*

aboard /ə'bɔ:d/ [1] *adv.* an Bord
[2] *prep.* an Bord (+ *Gen.*); **~ the bus** imC **~ ship** an Bord

abode /ə'bəʊd/ *n.* **of no fixed ~**: ohne festen Wohnsitz

abolish /ə'bɒlɪʃ/ *v.t.* abschaffen

abolition /æbə'lɪʃn/ *n.* Abschaffung, *die*

abominable /ə'bɒmɪnəbl/ *adj.* abscheulich; scheußlich

aborigine /æbə'rɪdʒɪnɪ/ *n.* Ureinwohner, *der*

abort /ə'bɔ:t/ *v.t.* abtreiben ‹*Baby*›

abortion /ə'bɔ:ʃn/ *n.* Abtreibung, *die;* 1776991/ann>**back-street ~**: illegale Abtreibung (durch Engelmacherin)

a'bortion pill *n.* Abtreibungspille, *die*

abortive /ə'bɔ:tɪv/ *adj.* misslungen ‹*Plan*›; fehlgeschlagen ‹*Versuch*›

abound /ə'baʊnd/ *v.i.* **~ in sth.** an etw. (*Dat.*) reich sein

about /ə'baʊt/ [1] *adv.* **(a)** (all around) rings[her]um; (here and there) überall; **all ~**: ringsumher
(b) (near) **be ~**: da sein; hier sein
(c) be ~ to do sth. gerade etw. tun wollen
(d) be out and ~: aktiv sein
(e) (approximately) ungefähr
[2] *prep.* **(a)** (all round) um [... herum]
(b) (concerning) über (+ *Akk.*); **know ~ sth.** von etw. wissen; **a question ~ sth.** eine Frage zu etw.; **what was it ~?** worum ging es?

above /ə'bʌv/ [1] *adv.* **(a)** (position) oben; (higher up) darüber
(b) (direction) nach oben
[2] *prep.* (position) über (+ *Dat.*); (direction, more than) über (+ *Akk.*); **~ all** vor allem

above 'board *pred. adj.* einwandfrei; korrekt

a'bove-mentioned *adj.* oben erwähnt *od.* genannt

abrasion /ə'breɪʒn/ *n.* (graze) Hautabschürfung, *die*

abrasive /ə'breɪsɪv/ [1] *adj.* **(a)** scheuernd; Scheuer-
(b) (fig.: harsh) aggressiv
[2] *n.* Scheuermittel, *das*

abreast /ə'brest/ *adv.* **(a)** nebeneinander

a

(b) (fig.) **keep ~ of sth.** sich über etw. (*Akk.*) auf dem Laufenden halten

abroad /ə'brɔ:d/ *adv.* im Ausland; (direction) ins Ausland

abrupt /ə'brʌpt/ *adj.*, **a'bruptly** *adv.* **(a)** (sudden[ly]) abrupt; plötzlich
(b) (brusque[ly]) schroff

ABS *abbr.* = **anti-lock brake** *or* **braking system** ABS

abscess /'æbsɪs/ *n.* Abszess, *der*

abscond /əb'skɒnd/ *v.t.* sich entfernen

absence /'æbsəns/ *n.* Abwesenheit, *die;* **the ~ of sth.** der Mangel an etw. (*Dat.*)

absent /'æbsənt/ *adj.* abwesend; **be ~ from school/work** in der Schule/am Arbeitsplatz fehlen

absentee /æbsən'ti:/ *n.* Fehlende, *der/die;* Abwesende, *der/die;* **~ballot** (Amer.) Briefwahl, *die;* **~ landlord** nicht auf seinem Gut lebender Gutsherr

absenteeism /æbsən'ti:ɪzm/ *n.* [häufiges] Fernbleiben; (without good reason) Krankfeiern, *das* (ugs.)

absent-minded /æbsənt'maɪndɪd/ *adj.* geistesabwesend; (habitually) zerstreut

absolute /'æbsəlu:t/ *adj.* absolut; ausgemacht ‹*Lüge, Skandal*›; **~ majority** absolute Mehrheit

abso'lutely *adv.* absolut; völlig ‹*verrückt*›; **you're ~ right!** du hast völlig Recht; **~ not!** auf keinen Fall!

absolve /əb'zɒlv/ *v.t.* **~ from** entbinden von ‹*Pflichten*›; lossprechen von ‹*Schuld*›

absorb /əb'sɔ:b/ *v.t.* **(a)** aufsaugen ‹*Flüssigkeit*›
(b) abfangen ‹*Schlag, Stoß*›

absorbency /əb'sɔ:bənsɪ/ *n.* Saugfähigkeit, *die*

absorbent /əb'sɔ:bənt/ *adj.* saugfähig

ab'sorbing *adj.* faszinierend

abstain /əb'steɪn/ *v.i.* **~ from sth.** sich einer Sache (*Gen.*) enthalten; **~ [from voting]** sich der Stimme enthalten

abstemious /əb'sti:mɪəs/ *adj.* enthaltsam

abstention /əb'stenʃn/ *n.* (from voting) Stimmenthaltung, *die*

abstinence /'æbstɪnəns/ *n.* Abstinenz, *die*

abstinent /'æbstɪnənt/ *adj.* abstinent

abstract /'æbstrækt/ **1** *adj.* abstrakt
2 *n.* Zusammenfassung, *die*

absurd /əb'sɜ:d/ *adj.* absurd; (ridiculous) lächerlich

absurdity /əb'sɜ:dɪtɪ/ *n.* Absurdität, *die*

ab'surdly *adv.* lächerlich

abundance /ə'bʌndəns/ *n.* **[an] ~ of sth.** eine Fülle von etw.

abundant /ə'bʌndənt/ *adj.* reich (**in** an + *Dat.*)

abuse **1** /ə'bju:z/ *v.t.* beschimpfen
2 /ə'bju:s/ *n.* Beschimpfungen *Pl.*

abusive /ə'bju:sɪv/ *adj.* beleidigend; **become ~:** ausfallend werden

abysmal /ə'bɪzml/ *adj.* (coll.: bad) katastrophal (ugs.)

abyss /ə'bɪs/ *n.* Abgrund, *der*

AC *abbr.* = **alternating current** Ws

academic /ækə'demɪk/ *adj.* akademisch

academy /ə'kædəmɪ/ *n.* Akademie, *die*

accede /æk'si:d/ *v.i.* **(a)** zustimmen (**to** *Dat.*)
(b) ~ [to the throne] den Thron besteigen

accelerate /ək'seləreɪt/ **1** *v.t.* beschleunigen
2 *v.i.* sich beschleunigen; ‹*Auto, Fahrer:*› beschleunigen

acceleration /əkselə'reɪʃn/ *n.* Beschleunigung, *die*

accelerator /ək'seləreɪtə(r)/ *n.* **~ [pedal]** Gas[pedal], *das*

accent /'æksənt/ *n.* Akzent, *der*

accentuate /ək'sentjʊeɪt/ *v.t.* betonen

accept /ək'sept/ *v.t.* **(a)** annehmen; entgegennehmen ‹*Dank, Spende*›; übernehmen ‹*Verantwortung*›
(b) (acknowledge) akzeptieren

acceptable /ək'septəbl/ *adj.* akzeptabel; annehmbar ‹*Preis, Gehalt*›

acceptance /ək'septəns/ *n.* **(a)** Annahme, *die*
(b) (acknowledgement) Anerkennung, *die*

access /'ækses/ *n.* **(a)** (admission) **gain ~:** Einlass finden
(b) (opportunity to use or approach) Zugang, *der* (**to** zu)

accessible /ək'sesɪbl/ *adj.* **(a)** (reachable) erreichbar
(b) (available, understandable) zugänglich (**to** für)

accession /ək'seʃn/ *n.* Amtsantritt, *der;* **~ [to the throne]** Thronbesteigung, *die*

accessory /ək'sesərɪ/ *n.* **(a) accessories** *pl.* Zubehör, *das*
(b) (dress article) Accessoire, *das*

'access road *n.* Zufahrtsstraße, *die*

accident /'æksɪdənt/ *n.* **(a)** Unfall, *der*
(b) (chance) Zufall, *der;* **by ~:** zufällig
(c) (mistake) Versehen, *das;* **by ~:** versehentlich

accidental /æksɪ'dentl/ *adj.* (chance) zufällig; (unintended) unbeabsichtigt

acci'dentally *adv.* (by chance) zufällig; (by mistake) versehentlich

'accident-prone *adj.* **~ person** Unfäller, *der* (Psych.); **he's such an ~ boy** mit dem Jungen ist aber auch immer irgendwas (ugs.)

acclaim /ə'kleɪm/ *v.t.* feiern

acclimatisation, acclimatise ▶ ACCLIMATIZ-

acclimatization /əklaɪmətaɪ'zeɪʃn/ *n.* (lit. or fig.) Akklimatisation, *die*

acclimatize /ə'klaɪmətaɪz/ *v.t.* **get** *or* **become ~d** sich akklimatisieren

accolade /'ækəleɪd/ *n.* **~[s]** (praise) Lob, *das*

accommodate /ə'kɒmədeɪt/ *v.t.* **(a)** unterbringen; (hold) Platz bieten (+ *Dat.*) **(b)** (oblige) gefällig sein (+ *Dat.*)
accommodating /ə'kɒmədeɪtɪŋ/ *adj.* zuvorkommend
accommodation /əkɒmə'deɪʃn/ *n.* Unterkunft, *die*
accommo'dation address *n.* Gefälligkeitsadresse, *die*
accompaniment /ə'kʌmpənɪmənt/ *n.* Begleitung, *die*
accompanist /ə'kʌmpənɪst/ *n.* Begleiter, *der*/Begleiterin, *die*
accompany /ə'kʌmpənɪ/ *v.t.* begleiten
accomplice /ə'kʌmplɪs/ *n.* Komplize, *der*/ Komplizin, *die*
accomplish /ə'kʌmplɪʃ/ *v.t.* vollbringen ‹*Tat*›; erfüllen ‹*Aufgabe*›
accomplished /ə'kʌmplɪʃt/ *adj.* fähig; **he is an ~ speaker/dancer** er ist ein erfahrener Redner/vollendeter Tänzer
ac'complishment *n.* **(a)** (completion) Vollendung, *die*
(b) (achievement) Leistung, *die;* (skill) Fähigkeit, *die*
accord /ə'kɔ:d/ **1** *n.* Übereinstimmung, *die;* **of one's own ~**: aus eigenem Antrieb; **with one ~**: geschlossen
2 *v.t.* **~ sb. sth.** jmdm. etw. gewähren
accordance /ə'kɔ:dəns/ *n.* **in ~ with** in Übereinstimmung mit
ac'cording *adv.* **~ to** nach; **~ to him** nach seiner Aussage
ac'cordingly *adv.* (as appropriate) entsprechend; (therefore) folglich
accordion /ə'kɔ:dɪən/ *n.* Akkordeon, *das*
accost /ə'kɒst/ *v.t.* ansprechen
account /ə'kaʊnt/ *n.* **(a)** (Finance) Rechnung, *die;* (at bank, shop) Konto, *das*
(b) (consideration) **take ~ of sth., take sth. into ~**: etw. berücksichtigen; **take no ~ of sth./sb.** etw./jmdn. unberücksichtigt lassen; **don't change your plans on my ~**: ändert nicht meinetwegen eure Pläne; **on ~ of** wegen; **on no ~**: auf [gar] keinen Fall
(c) (report) Bericht, *der*
(d) call sb. to ~: jmdn. zur Rechenschaft ziehen
▪ **ac'count for** *v.t.* Rechenschaft ablegen über; (explain) erklären
accountable /ə'kaʊntəbl/ *adj.* verantwortlich
accountancy /ə'kaʊntənsɪ/ *n.* Buchhaltung, *die*
accountant /ə'kaʊntənt/ *n.* [Bilanz]buchhalter, *der*/-halterin, *die*
account: ~ holder *n.* Kontoinhaber, *der*/-inhaberin, *die;* **~ number** *n.* Kontonummer, *die*
accredited /ə'kredɪtɪd/ *adj.* anerkannt ‹*Schule, Anstalt, Buch, Regierung*›; akkreditiert ‹*Botschafter, Diplomat*›; zugelassen ‹*Journalist*›

accrue /ə'kru:/ *v.i.* ‹*Zinsen:*› auflaufen; **~ to sb.** ‹*Reichtümer, Einnahmen:*› jmdm. zufließen
accumulate /ə'kju:mjʊleɪt/ **1** *v.t.* sammeln
2 *v.i.* ‹*Menge, Staub:*› sich ansammeln; ‹*Geld:*› sich anhäufen
accumulation /əkju:mjʊ'leɪʃn/ *n.* [An]sammeln, *das;* (being accumulated) Anhäufung, *die*
accuracy /'ækjʊrəsɪ/ *n.* Genauigkeit, *die*
accurate /'ækjʊrət/ *adj.*, **'accurately** *adv.* genau; (correct[ly]) richtig
accusation /ækju:'zeɪʃn/ *n.* Anschuldigung, *die;* (Law) Anklage, *die*
accusative /ə'kju:zətɪv/ *adj. & n.* **~ [case]** Akkusativ, *der*
accuse /ə'kju:z/ *v.t.* beschuldigen; (Law) anklagen (**of** wegen + *Gen.*)
accustom /ə'kʌstəm/ *v.t.* gewöhnen (**to** an + *Akk.*); **grow/be ~ed to sth.** sich an etw. (*Akk.*) gewöhnen/an etw. (*Akk.*) gewöhnt sein
accustomed /ə'kʌstəmd/ *attrib. adj.* gewohnt; üblich
ace /eɪs/ **1** *n.* As, *das*
2 *adj.* (coll.) klasse (ugs.); spitze (ugs.)
ache /eɪk/ **1** *v.i.* schmerzen; wehtun
2 *n.* Schmerz, *der*
achieve /ə'tʃi:v/ *v.t.* zustande bringen; erreichen ‹*Ziel, Standard*›
a'chievement *n.* **(a)** ▶ ACHIEVE: Zustandebringen, *das;* Erreichen, *das*
(b) (thing accomplished) Leistung, *die*
acid /'æsɪd/ **1** *adj.* sauer
2 *n.* Säure, *die*
'acid house *n* Acidhouse, *das;* **~ music/party** Acidhousemusik, *die*/Acidhouseparty, *die*
'acid: ~'rain *n.* saurer Regen; **~ test** *n.* (fig.) Feuerprobe, *die*
acidic /ə'sɪdɪk/ *adj.* säuerlich
acidity /ə'sɪdɪtɪ/ *n.* Säure, *die*
acknowledge /ək'nɒlɪdʒ/ *v.t.* **(a)** zugeben ‹*Tatsache, Fehler, Schuld*›
(b) sich erkenntlich zeigen für ‹*Dienste, Bemühungen*›; erwidern ‹*Gruß*›
(c) bestätigen ‹*Empfang, Bewerbung*›; **~ a letter** den Empfang eines Briefes bestätigen
acknowledg[e]ment /ək'nɒlɪdʒmənt/ *n.* **(a)** (admission) Eingeständnis, *das*
(b) (thanks) Dank, *der* (**of** für)
(c) (of letter) Bestätigung [des Empfangs]
acne /'æknɪ/ *n.* Akne, *die*
acorn /'eɪkɔ:n/ *n.* Eichel, *die*
acoustic /ə'ku:stɪk/ *adj.* akustisch
a'coustics *n. pl.* Akustik, *die*
acquaint /ə'kweɪnt/ *v.t.* **be ~ed with sb.** mit jmdm. bekannt sein
acquaintance /ə'kweɪntəns/ *n.* **(a)** **~ with sb.** Bekanntschaft mit jmdm.; **make sb.'s ~**: jmds. Bekanntschaft machen

a

(b) (person) Bekannte, *der/die*

acquiesce /ækwɪ'es/ *v.i.* einwilligen (**in** in + *Akk.*)

acquire /ə'kwaɪə(r)/ *v.t.* sich (*Dat.*) anschaffen ‹*Gegenstände*›; erwerben ‹*Besitz, Kenntnisse*›

acquisition /ækwɪ'zɪʃn/ *n.* Erwerb, *der;* (thing) Anschaffung, *die*

acquisitive /ə'kwɪzɪtɪv/ *adj.* raffsüchtig

acquit /ə'kwɪt/ *v.t.*, **-tt-** freisprechen

acquittal /ə'kwɪtl/ *n.* Freispruch, *der*

acre /'eɪkə(r)/ *n.* Acre, *der*

acrid /'ækrɪd/ *adj.* beißend ‹*Geruch, Rauch*›; bitter ‹*Geschmack*›

acrimonious /ækrɪ'məʊniəs/ *adj.* bitter; erbittert ‹*Streit*›

acrobat /'ækrəbæt/ *n.* Akrobat, *der*/Akrobatin, *die*

acrobatic /ækrə'bætɪk/ *adj.* akrobatisch

acrobatics /ækrə'bætɪks/ *n.* Akrobatik, *die*

acronym /'ækrənɪm/ *n.* Akronym, *das*

across /ə'krɒs/ **1** *adv.* (from one side to the other) darüber; (from here to there) hinüber; **be 9 miles ~**: 9 Meilen breit sein
2 *prep.* über (+ *Akk.*); (on the other side of) auf der anderen Seite (+ *Gen.*)

a'cross-the-board *adj.* pauschal; **an ~ pay rise** eine pauschale *od.* generelle Lohnerhöhung

acrylic /ə'krɪlɪk/ **1** *adj.* aus Acryl *nachgestellt;* Acryl-; **~ paint/fibre** Acrylfarbe, *die*/-faser, *die*
2 *n.* Acryl, *das*

act /ækt/ **1** *n.* **(a)** (deed) Tat, *die*
(b) (Theatre) Akt, *der*
(c) (pretence) Theater, *das;* **put on an ~**: Theater spielen
(d) (Law) Gesetz, *das*
2 *v.t.* spielen ‹*Stück*›
3 *v.i.* **(a)** (perform actions) handeln
(b) (behave) sich verhalten; **~ as** fungieren als
(c) (perform play) spielen
(d) (have effect) **~ on sth.** auf etw. (*Akk.*) wirken

'acting **1** *n.* (Theatre etc.) die Schauspielerei
2 *adj.* (temporary) stellvertretend

action /'ækʃn/ *n.* **(a)** (doing sth.) Handeln, *das;* **take ~**: Schritte *od.* etwas unternehmen; **put a plan into ~**: einen Plan in die Tat umsetzen; **put sth. out of ~**: etw. außer Betrieb setzen
(b) (act) Tat, *die*
(c) (legal process) [Gerichts]verfahren, *das*
(d) **die in ~**: im Kampf fallen

action: ~ committee, ~ group *ns.* [Eltern-/Bürger- *usw.*]initiative, *die;* **~-packed** *adj.* spannend ‹*Buch, Roman*›; **an ~-packed film** ein Film mit viel Aktion; **~'replay** *n.* Wiederholung [in Zeitlupe]

activate /'æktɪveɪt/ *v.t.* **(a)** in Gang setzen
(b) (Chem., Phys.) aktivieren

active /'æktɪv/ *adj.*, **'actively** *adv.* aktiv

activist /'æktɪvɪst/ *n.* Aktivist, *der*/Aktivistin, *die*

activity /æk'tɪvɪtɪ/ *n.* Aktivität, *die;* **outdoor activities** Betätigung an der frischen Luft; **~ holiday** Aktivurlaub, *der*

actor /'æktə(r)/ *n.* Schauspieler, *der*

actress /'æktrɪs/ *n.* Schauspielerin, *die*

actual /'æktʃʊəl/ *adj.* eigentlich; wirklich ‹*Name*›

'actually *adv.* (in fact) eigentlich; (by the way) übrigens; (believe it or not) sogar

acumen /'ækjʊmen/ Scharfsinn, *der;* **business ~**: Geschäftssinn, *der*

acupressure /'ækju:preʃə(r)/ *n.* (Med.) Akupressur, *die*

acupuncture /'ækjʊpʌnktʃə(r)/ *n.* Akupunktur, *die*

acute /ə'kju:t/ *adj.* **(a)** spitz ‹*Winkel*›
(b) (critical; Med.) akut

ad /æd/ *n.* (coll.) Annonce, *die*

AD *abbr.* = **Anno Domini** n.Chr.

adamant /'ædəmənt/ *adj.* unnachgiebig; **be ~ that ...**: darauf bestehen, dass ...

adapt /ə'dæpt/ *v.t.* **(a)** anpassen (**to** *Dat.*); **~ oneself to sth.** sich an etw. (*Akk.*) gewöhnen
(b) bearbeiten ‹*Text, Theaterstück*›

adaptable /ə'dæptəbl/ *adj.* anpassungsfähig

adaptation /ædəp'teɪʃn/ *n.* **(a)** Anpassung, *die*
(b) (version) Adap[ta]tion, *die;* (of story, text) Bearbeitung, *die*

adapter, adaptor /ə'dæptə(r)/ *n.* Adapter, *der*

add /æd/ **1** *v.t.* hinzufügen (**to** *Dat.*); **~ two and two** zwei und zwei zusammenzählen
2 *v.i.* **~ to** vergrößern ‹*Schwierigkeiten, Einkommen*›

■ **add 'up** **1** *v.i.* **~ up to sth.** (fig.) auf etw. (*Akk.*) hinauslaufen
2 *v.t.* zusammenzählen

adder /'ædə(r)/ *n.* Viper, *die*

addict **1** /ə'dɪkt/ *v.t.* **be ~ed** süchtig sein (**to** nach); **be ~ed to alcohol/smoking/drugs** alkohol-/nikotin-/drogensüchtig sein
2 /'ædɪkt/ *n.* Süchtige, *der/die*

addiction /ə'dɪkʃn/ *n.* Sucht, *die* (**to** nach)

addictive /ə'dɪktɪv/ *adj.* **be ~**: süchtig machen

addition /ə'dɪʃn/ *n.* **(a)** Hinzufügen, *das;* (adding up) Addieren, *das;* (process) Addition, *die;* **in ~**: außerdem; **in ~ to** zusätzlich zu
(b) (thing added) Ergänzung, *die* (**to** zu)

additional /ə'dɪʃənl/ *adj.* zusätzlich

additionally /ə'dɪʃənəlɪ/ *adv.* außerdem

additive /'ædɪtɪv/ *n.* Zusatz, *der*

'add-on **1** *n.* (accessory) Zubehörteil, *das;* (for electrical appliance) Zusatzgerät, *das;* (addition) Zusatz, *der*

2 *adj.* ~ **accessory** Zubehörteil, *das*; (for electrical appliance) Zusatzgerät, *das*

address /ə'dres/ 1 *v.t.* **(a)** (mark with ~) adressieren (**to** an + *Akk.*) **(b)** (speak to) anreden; sprechen zu ‹*Zuhörern*› 2 *n.* **(a)** (on letter) Adresse, *die* **(b)** (speech) Ansprache, *die*

ad'dress book *n.* Adressenbüchlein, *das*

addressee /ædre'si:/ *n.* Adressat, *der*/ Adressatin, *die*

ad'dress label *n.* Adressenaufkleber, *der*

adept /'ædept, ə'dept/ *adj.* geschickt (**in, at** in + *Dat.*)

adequate /'ædıkwət/ *adj.* **(a)** angemessen (**to** *Dat.*); (suitable) passend **(b)** (sufficient) ausreichend

'adequately *adv.* **(a)** (sufficiently) ausreichend **(b)** (suitably) angemessen ‹*gekleidet, qualifiziert usw.*›

adhere /əd'hıə(r)/ *v.i.* haften, (by glue) kleben (**to** an + *Dat.*)

adhesion /əd'hi:ʒn/ *n.* Haften, *das*

adhesive /əd'hi:sıv/ 1 *adj.* gummiert ‹*Briefmarke*›; Klebe‹*band*›; ~ **plaster** Heftpflaster, *das* 2 *n.* Klebstoff, *der*

adjacent /ə'dʒeısənt/ *adj.* angrenzend; ~ **to** neben (*position:* + *Dat.; direction:* + *Akk.*)

adjective /'ædʒıktıv/ *n.* Adjektiv, *das*

adjoin /ə'dʒɔın/ *v.t.* grenzen an (+ *Akk.*)

adjourn /ə'dʒɜ:n/ 1 *v.t.* (break off) unterbrechen; (put off) aufschieben 2 *v.i.* sich vertagen; ~ **for lunch/half an hour** eine Mittagspause/halbstündige Pause einlegen

a'djournment *n.* (of court) Vertagung, *die;* (of meeting) Unterbrechung, *die*

adjudicate /ə'dʒu:dıkeıt/ *v.i.* (in court, tribunal) das Urteil fällen; (in contest) entscheiden

adjust /ə'dʒʌst/ 1 *v.t.* einstellen; ~ **sth. [to sth.]** etw. [an etw. (*Akk.*)] anpassen 2 *v.i.* ‹*Person:*› sich anpassen (**to** an + *Akk.*)

adjustable /ə'dʒʌstəbl/ *adj.* einstellbar; verstellbar ‹*Gerät*›

a'djustment *n.* Einstellung, *die;* (to situation etc.) Anpassung, *die*

ad-lib /æd'lıb/ 1 *adj.* improvisiert 2 *v.i.,* **-bb-** improvisieren

admin /'ædmın/ *n.* (coll.) Verwaltung, *die;* **an ~ problem** ein Verwaltungsproblem

administer /æd'mınıstə(r)/ **(a)** (manage) verwalten **(b)** leisten ‹*Hilfe*›; verabreichen ‹*Medikamente*›

administration /ədmını'streıʃn/ *n.* Verwaltung, *die*

administrative /əd'mınıstrətıv/ *adj.* Verwaltungs-; **an ~ job** ein Verwaltungsposten

administrator /əd'mınıstreıtə(r)/ *n.* Administrator, *der;* Verwalter, *der*

admirable /'ædmərəbl/ *adj.* bewundernswert

admiral /'ædmərəl/ *n.* Admiral, *der*

admiration /ædmə'reıʃn/ *n.* Bewunderung, *die* (**of, for** für)

admire /əd'maıə(r)/ *v.t.* bewundern

admirer /əd'maıərə(r)/ *n.* Bewunderer, *der*/ Bewunderin, *die*

admiring /əd'maıərıŋ/ *adj.* bewundernd

admission /əd'mıʃn/ *n.* **(a)** (entry) Zutritt, *der* **(b)** (charge) Eintritt, *der* **(c)** (confession) Eingeständnis, *das*

admission: ~ charge, ~ fee *ns* Eintrittspreis, *der;* ~ **money** *n.* Eintrittsgeld, *das;* ~**price** *n.* Eintrittspreis, *der;* ~ **ticket** *n.* Eintrittskarte, *die*

admit /əd'mıt/ *v.t.,* **-tt-**: **(a)** (let in) hinein-/ hereinlassen **(b)** (acknowledge) zugeben

admittance /əd'mıtəns/ *n.* Zutritt, *der*

admittedly /əd'mıtıdlı/ *adv.* zugegeben[ermaßen]

admonish /əd'mɒnıʃ/ *v.t.* ermahnen

ado /ə'du:/ *n.* **without more ~**: ohne weiteres Aufheben

adolescence /ædə'lesns/ *n.* die Zeit des Erwachsenenwerdens

adolescent /ædə'lesnt/ 1 *n.* Heranwachsende, *der/die* 2 *adj.* heranwachsend

adopt /ə'dɒpt/ *v.t.* **(a)** adoptieren **(b)** (take over) annehmen ‹*Glaube, Kultur*› **(c)** (take up) übernehmen ‹*Methode*›; einnehmen ‹*Standpunkt, Haltung*›

adoption /ə'dɒpʃn/ *n.* **(a)** Adoption, *die* **(b)** (taking over) Annahme, *die* **(c)** (taking up) Übernahme, *die;* (of point of view) Einnahme, *die*

adorable /ə'dɔ:rəbl/ *adj.* bezaubernd

adoration /ædə'reıʃn/ *n.* Verehrung, *die*

adore /ə'dɔ:(r)/ *v.t.* verehren

adorn /ə'dɔ:n/ *v.t.* schmücken

a'dornment *n.* Verzierung, *die;* ~**s** Schmuck, *der*

adrenalin /ə'drenəlın/ *n.* Adrenalin, *das*

Adriatic /eıdrı'ætık/ *pr. n.* ~ **[Sea]** Adriatisches Meer

adrift /ə'drıft/ *adj.* **be ~**: treiben

adroit /ə'drɔıt/ *adj.* geschickt

ADSL *abbr.* (Teleph.) = **asymmetric digital subscriber line** ADSL

adulation /ædjʊ'leıʃn/ *n.* Vergötterung, *die*

adult /'ædʌlt, ə'dʌlt/ 1 *adj.* erwachsen; **an ~ film/book** *etc.* ein Film/Buch *usw.* [nur] für Erwachsene 2 *n.* Erwachsene, *der/die;* ~ **education** Erwachsenenbildung, *die*

a

adulterate /ə'dʌltəreɪt/ *v.t.* verunreinigen
adultery /ə'dʌltərɪ/ *n.* Ehebruch, *der*
advance /əd'vɑːns/ **1** *v.t.* **(a)** (also Mil.) vorrücken lassen
(b) (put forward) vorbringen ‹*Plan, Meinung*›
(c) (further) fördern
(d) (pay before due date) vorschießen; ‹*Bank:*› leihen
2 *v.i.* **(a)** (also Mil.) vorrücken; ‹*Prozession:*› sich vorwärts bewegen
(b) (fig.: make progress) vorankommen
3 *n.* **(a)** Vorrücken, *das;* (fig.: progress) Fortschritt, *der*
(b) *usu. in pl.* (personal approach) Annäherungsversuch, *der*
(c) (on salary) Vorschuss, *der*
(d) in ~: im Voraus
ad'vance booking *n.* (for a film, play) [vorherige] Kartenreservierung; (of a table in a restaurant) [vorherige] Tischreservierung
advanced /əd'vɑːnst/ *adj.* fortgeschritten
advance: ~ 'notice *n.* **a week's ~ notice** Benachrichtigung eine Woche [im] Voraus; **give sb. ~ notice of sth.** jmdn. im Voraus von etw. in Kenntnis setzen; **~ 'payment** *n.* Vorauszahlung, *die*
advantage /əd'vɑːntɪdʒ/ *n.* Vorteil, *der;* **take ~ of sb.** jmdn. ausnutzen; **be to one's ~:** für jmdn. von Vorteil sein; **turn sth. to [one's] ~:** etw. ausnutzen
advantageous /ædvən'teɪdʒəs/ *adj.* vorteilhaft
advent /'ædvent/ *n.* Beginn, *der;* **A~:** Advent, *der*
adventure /əd'ventʃə(r)/ *n.* Abenteuer, *das*
adventure: ~ holiday *n* Abenteuerurlaub, *der*; **~ playground** *n.* (Brit.) Abenteuerspielplatz, *der*
adventurous /əd'ventʃərəs/ *adj.* abenteuerlustig
adverb /'ædvɜːb/ *n.* Adverb, *das*
adversary /'ædvəsərɪ/ *n.* (enemy) Widersacher, *der*/Widersacherin, *die;* (opponent) Kontrahent, *der*/Kontrahentin, *die*
adverse /'ædvɜːs/ *adj.* **(a)** (unfavourable) ungünstig
(b) (contrary) widrig ‹*Wind, Umstände*›
adversity /əd'vɜːsɪtɪ/ *n.* **(a)** *no pl.* Not, *die*
(b) *usu. in pl.* Widrigkeit, *die*
advert /'ædvɜːt/ (Brit. coll.) ▶ ADVERTISEMENT
advertise /'ædvətaɪz/ **1** *v.t.* werben für; (by small ad) inserieren; ausschreiben ‹*Stelle*›
2 *v.i.* werben; (in newspaper) inserieren; annoncieren
advertisement /əd'vɜːtɪsmənt/ *n.* Anzeige, *die;* **TV ~:** Fernsehspot, *der;* **classified ~:** Kleinanzeige, *die*
advertiser /'ædvətaɪzə(r)/ *n.* (in newspaper) Inserent, *der*/Inserentin, *die;* (on radio, TV) Auftraggeber/Auftraggeberin [der Werbesendung]
advertising /'ædvətaɪzɪŋ/ *n.* Werbung, *die; attrib.* Werbe-; **~ agency/campaign/industry** Werbeagentur, *die*/-kampagne, *die*/-branche, *die*
advice /əd'vaɪs/ *n.* Rat, *der;* **take sb.'s ~:** jmds. Rat (*Dat.*) folgen
advisable /əd'vaɪzəbl/ *adj.* ratsam
advise /əd'vaɪz/ *v.t.* beraten; **~ sth.** zu etw. raten; (inform) unterrichten (**of** über + *Akk.*); **~ sb. to do sth.** jmdm. raten, etw. zu tun
adviser, advisor /əd'vaɪzə(r)/ *n.* Berater, *der*/Beraterin, *die*
advisory /əd'vaɪzərɪ/ *adj.* beratend
advocate **1** /'ædvəkət/ *n.* (of a cause) Befürworter, *der*/Befürworterin, *die;* (Law) [Rechts]anwalt, *der*/-anwältin, *die*
2 /'ædvəkeɪt/ *v.t.* befürworten
advt. *abbr.* = **advertisement**
aerial /'eərɪəl/ **1** *adj.* Luft-; **~ bombardment** Bombardierung [aus der Luft]; **~ photograph/photography** Luftaufnahme, *die*/Luftaufnahmen *Pl.*
2 *n.* Antenne, *die*
aero- /eərəʊ/ *in comb.* Aero-
aerobic /eə'rəʊbɪk/ *adj.* (Biol.) aerob
ae'robics *n.* Aerobic, *das*
aerody'namic *adj.* aerodynamisch
aeronautics /eərə'nɔːtɪks/ *n.* Aeronautik, *die*
aeroplane /'eərəpleɪn/ *n.* (Brit.) Flugzeug, *das*
aerosol /'eərəsɒl/ *n.* (spray) Spray, *der od. das;* (container) **~ [spray]** Spraydose, *die*
'aerospace *n., no art.* Erdatmosphäre und Weltraum; (technology) Luft- und Raumfahrt, *die*
aesthetic /iːs'θetɪk/ *adj.* ästhetisch
afar /ə'fɑː/ *adv.* **from ~:** aus der Ferne
affable /'æfəbl/ *adj.* freundlich
affair /ə'feə(r)/ *n.* **(a)** (concern) Angelegenheit, *die*
(b) *in pl.* (business) Geschäfte *Pl.*
(c) (love **~**) Affäre, *die;* **have an ~ with sb.** eine Affäre *od.* ein Verhältnis mit jmdm. haben
affect /ə'fekt/ *v.t.* **(a)** sich auswirken auf (+ *Akk.*)
(b) (emotionally) betroffen machen
affectation /æfek'teɪʃn/ *n.* (studied display) Verstellung, *die;* (artificiality) Affektiertheit, *die*
affected /ə'fektɪd/ *adj.* affektiert; gekünstelt ‹*Sprache, Stil*›
affection /ə'fekʃn/ *n.* Zuneigung, *die*
affectionate /ə'fekʃənət/ *adj.* anhänglich; liebevoll ‹*Umarmung*›
af'fectionately *adv.* liebevoll
affiliate /ə'fɪlɪeɪt/ *v.t.* **be ~d to sth.** an etw. (*Akk.*) angegliedert sein
affinity /ə'fɪnɪtɪ/ *n.* **(a)** (relationship) Verwandtschaft, *die* (**to** mit)
(b) (liking) Neigung, *die* (**for** zu); **feel an ~ to** *or* **for sb./sth.** sich zu jmdm./etw. hingezogen fühlen

affirm /ə'fɜ:m/ *v.t.* (assert) bekräftigen ‹*Absicht*›; beteuern ‹*Unschuld*›; (state as a fact) bestätigen

affirmation /æfə'meɪʃn/ *n.* (of intention) Bekräftigung, *die;* (of fact) Bestätigung, *die*

affirmative /ə'fɜ:mətɪv/ 1 *adj.* affirmativ; bejahend ‹*Antwort*›
2 *n.* **answer in the ~:** bejahend antworten

affirmative 'action *n.* (Amer.) positive Diskriminierung (fachspr.); Bevorzugung, *die*

afflict /ə'flɪkt/ *v.t.* (physically) plagen; (mentally) quälen; peinigen; **be ~ed with sth.** von etw. befallen sein

affliction /ə'flɪkʃn/ *n.* Leiden, *das*

affluence /'æflʊəns/ *n.* Reichtum, *der*

affluent /'æflʊənt/ *adj.* reich; **the ~ society** die Überflussgesellschaft

afford /ə'fɔ:d/ *v.t.* **(a)** sich (*Dat.*) leisten
(b) (provide) bieten; gewähren ‹*Schutz*›

affordable /ə'fɔ:dəbl/ *adj.* erschwinglich

affray /ə'freɪ/ *n.* Schlägerei, *die*

affront /ə'frʌnt/ 1 *v.t.* beleidigen
2 *n.* Beleidigung, *die*

afield /ə'fi:ld/ *adv.* **far ~** (direction) weit hinaus; (place) weit draußen

afloat /ə'fləʊt/ *pred. adj.* **(a)** (floating) über Wasser; flott ‹*Schiff*›
(b) (at sea) auf See; **be ~:** auf dem Meer treiben

afoot /ə'fʊt/ *pred. adj.* im Gange

aforementioned /ə'fɔ:menʃnd/, **aforesaid** /ə'fɔ:sed/ *adjs.* oben erwähnt *od.* genannt

afraid /ə'freɪd/ *adj.* **be ~ [of sb./sth.]** [vor jmdm./etw.] Angst haben; **be ~ to do sth.** Angst davor haben, etw. zu tun; **I'm ~ so/not** ich fürchte ja/nein

afresh /ə'freʃ/ *adv.* von neuem

Africa /'æfrɪkə/ *pr. n.* Afrika (*das*)

African /'æfrɪkən/ 1 *adj.* afrikanisch; **sb. is ~:** jmd. ist Afrikaner/Afrikanerin
2 *n.* Afrikaner, *der*/Afrikanerin, *die*

Afro-Carib'bean 1 *adj.* afrokaribisch
2 *n.* Mensch afrokaribischer Herkunft *od.* Abstammung

after /'ɑ:ftə(r)/ 1 *adv.* **(a)** (later) danach
(b) (behind) hinterher
2 *prep.* **(a)** (in time) nach; **two days ~:** zwei Tage danach
(b) (behind) hinter (+ *Dat.*)
(c) ask ~ sb./sth. nach jmdm./etw. fragen
(d) ~ all schließlich
3 *conj.* nachdem

after: ~care *n.* (Med.) Nachbehandlung, *die* **~-effect** *n.* Nachwirkung, *die*

aftermath /'ɑ:ftəmæθ, 'ɑ:ftəmɑ:θ/ *n.* Nachwirkungen *Pl.*

after: ~'noon *n.* Nachmittag, *der;* **this/tomorrow ~noon** heute/morgen Nachmittag; **in the ~noon** am Nachmittag; (regularly) nachmittags; **~-sales service** *n.* Kundendienst, *der;* **~shave** *n.* Aftershave, *das;* **~taste** *n.* Nachgeschmack, *der;* **~thought** *n.* nachträglicher Einfall

afterwards /'ɑ:ftəwədz/ *adv.* danach

again /ə'gen, ə'geɪn/ *adv.* wieder; (one more time) noch einmal; **~ and ~, time and [time] ~:** immer wieder; **back ~:** wieder zurück

against /ə'genst, ə'geɪnst/ *prep.* gegen

age /eɪdʒ/ 1 *n.* **(a)** Alter, *das;* **what ~ are you?** wie alt bist du?; **at the ~ of** im Alter von; **come of ~:** volljährig werden; **be under ~:** zu jung sein
(b) (great period) Zeitalter, *das;* **~s** (coll.: a long time) eine Ewigkeit
2 *v.t.* altern lassen
3 *v.i.* altern

'age bracket *n.* Altersstufe, *die*

aged *adj.* **(a)** /eɪdʒd/ **be ~ five** fünf Jahre alt sein; **a boy ~ five** ein fünfjähriger Junge
(b) /'eɪdʒɪd/ (elderly) bejahrt

'age group *n.* Altersgruppe, *die*

ageism /'eɪdʒɪzm/ *n.* Diskriminierung aufgrund des Alters

ageist /'eɪdʒɪst/ *adj.* das Alter diskriminierend

ageless /'eɪdʒlɪs/ *adj.* nicht alternd ‹*Person*›; (eternal) zeitlos

'age limit *n.* Altersgrenze, *die*

agency /'eɪdʒənsɪ/ *n.* (business establishment) Geschäftsstelle, *die;* (news/advertising ~) Agentur, *die*

agenda /ə'dʒendə/ *n.* Tagesordnung, *die*

agent /'eɪdʒənt/ *n.* Vertreter, *der*/Vertreterin, *die;* (spy) Agent, *der*/Agentin, *die*

age: ~-old *adj.* uralt; **~ range** *n.* Altersstufe, *die*

aggravate /'ægrəveɪt/ *v.t.* **(a)** (make worse) verschlimmern
(b) (annoy) aufregen; ärgern

aggravating /'ægrəveɪtɪŋ/ *adj.* ärgerlich

aggravation /ægrə'veɪʃn/ *n.* **(a)** Verschlimmerung, *die*
(b) (annoyance) Ärger, *der*

aggregate /'ægrɪgət/ 1 *n.* Gesamtmenge, *die*
2 *adj.* gesamt

aggression /ə'greʃn/ *n.* Aggression, *die*

aggressive /ə'gresɪv/ *adj.*, **ag'gressively** *adv.* aggressiv

ag'gressiveness *n.* Aggressivität, *die*

aggressor /ə'gresə(r)/ *n.* Aggressor, *der*

aggrieved /ə'gri:vd/ *v.t.* (resentful) verärgert; (offended) gekränkt

aggro /'ægrəʊ/ *n.* (Brit. sl.) Zoff, *der* (ugs.); Krawall, *der;* **they are looking for ~:** sie suchen Streit

aghast /ə'gɑ:st/ *pred. adj.* bestürzt (**über** + *Akk.*)

agile /'ædʒaɪl/ *adj.* beweglich; flink ‹*Bewegung*›

agility /ə'dʒɪlɪtɪ/ *n.* Beweglichkeit, *die;* (of movement) Flinkheit, *die*

a

agitate /'ædʒɪteɪt/ 1 *v.t.* **(a)** (shake) schütteln
(b) (disturb) erregen
2 *v.i.* agitieren

agitation /ædʒɪ'teɪʃn/ *n.* **(a)** (shaking) Schütteln, *das*
(b) (emotional) Erregung, *die*

agitator /'ædʒɪteɪtə(r)/ *n.* Agitator, *der*

AGM *abbr.* = **Annual General Meeting** JHV

agnostic /æg'nɒstɪk/ *n.* Agnostiker, *der*/Agnostikerin, *die*

ago /ə'gəʊ/ *adv.* **ten years ~:** vor zehn Jahren; **[not] long ~:** vor [nicht] langer Zeit

agog /ə'gɒg/ *pred. adj.* gespannt

agonize /'ægənaɪz/ *v.i.* **~ over sth.** sich (*Dat.*) den Kopf über etw. (*Akk.*) zermartern

agony /'ægənɪ/ *n.* Todesqualen *Pl.*

'agony aunt *n.* (coll.) Briefkastentante, *die* (ugs. scherzh.)

agoraphobia /ægərə'fəʊbɪə/ *n.* (Psych.) Agoraphobie, *die;* Platzangst, *die*

agoraphobic /ægərə'fəʊbɪk/ *adj.* (Psych.) an Agoraphobie *od.* Platzangst leidend; **be ~:** an Agoraphobie *od.* Platzangst leiden

agree /ə'gri:/ 1 *v.i.* **(a)** (consent) einverstanden sein (**to, with** mit)
(b) (hold similar opinion) einer Meinung sein; **they ~d [with me]** sie waren derselben Meinung [wie ich]
(c) (reach similar opinion) **~ on sth.** sich über etw. (*Akk.*) einigen
(d) (harmonize) übereinstimmen
(e) ~ with sb. (suit) jmdm. bekommen
2 *v.t.* vereinbaren

agreeable /ə'gri:əbl/ *adj.* **(a)** (pleasing) angenehm
(b) be ~ [to sth.] [mit etw.] einverstanden sein

agreeably /ə'gri:əblɪ/ *adv.* angenehm

agreed /ə'gri:d/ *adj.* einig; vereinbart ‹*Summe, Zeit*›

a'greement *n.* Übereinstimmung, *die;* **be in ~ [about sth.]** sich (*Dat.*) [über etw. (*Akk.*)] einig sein

agricultural /ægrɪ'kʌltʃərl/ *adj.* landwirtschaftlich

agriculture /'ægrɪkʌltʃə(r)/ *n.* Landwirtschaft, *die*

aground /ə'graʊnd/ *adj.* **go** *or* **run ~:** auf Grund laufen

aha /ɑ:'hɑ:/ *int.* aha

ahead /ə'hed/ *adv.* voraus; **~ of** vor (+ *Dat.*); **be ~ of the others** (fig.) den anderen voraus sein

AI *abbr.* = **artificial intelligence** KI

aid /eɪd/ 1 *v.t.* **(a) ~ sb. [to do sth.]** jmdm. helfen[, etw. zu tun]; **~ed by** unterstützt von
(b) (promote) fördern
2 *n.* **(a)** (help) Hilfe, *die;* **with the ~ of sth./sb.** mit Hilfe einer Sache (*Gen.*)/mit jmds. Hilfe; **in ~ of sb./sth.** zugunsten von jmdm./etw.
(b) (source of help) Hilfsmittel, *das* (**to** für)

'aid agency *n.* Hilfsorganisation, *die;* Hilfswerk, *das*

aide /eɪd/ *n.* Berater, *der*/Beraterin, *die*

Aids /eɪdz/ *n.* Aids (*das*); **~ test** Aidstest, *der*

'Aids-related *adj.* **~ disease/illness** durch Aids hervorgerufene Krankheit

'aid worker *n.* Helfer, *der*/Helferin, *die;* **~s** Hilfskräfte *Pl.;* Hilfspersonal, *das*

ailment /'eɪlmənt/ *n.* Gebrechen, *das*

aim /eɪm/ 1 *v.t.* ausrichten ‹*Schusswaffe, Rakete*›; **~ sth. at sb./sth.** etw. auf jmdn./etw. richten
2 *v.i.* **(a)** zielen (**at** auf + *Akk.*)
(b) ~ to do sth. beabsichtigen, etw. zu tun; **~ at** *or* **for sth.** (fig.) etwas anstreben
3 *n.* Ziel, *das;* **take ~ [at sth./sb.]** [auf etw./jmdn.] zielen

'aimless *adj.*, **'aimlessly** *adv.* ziellos

air /eə(r)/ 1 *n.* **(a)** Luft, *die;* **be/go on the ~:** senden; ‹*Programm:*› gesendet werden; **by ~:** mit dem Flugzeug; (by ~ mail) mit Luftpost
(b) (facial expression) Miene, *die*
(c) put on ~s sich aufspielen
2 *v.t.* (ventilate) lüften; (make public) [öffentlich] darlegen

air: ~ bag *n.* (Motor Veh.) Airbag *der;* **side ~ bag** Seitenairbag, *der;* **~base** *n.* Luftwaffenstützpunkt, *der;* **~bed** *n.* Luftmatratze, *die;* **~borne** *adj.* **be ~borne** sich in der Luft befinden; **~ brake** *n.* Druckluftbremse, *die;* (flap) Luftbremse, *die;* **~brush** *n.* Spritzpistole, *die;* **~ bubble** *n.* Luftblase, *die;* **~ bus** *n.* Airbus, *der;* **~-conditioned** *adj.* klimatisiert; **~ conditioner** *n.* Klimaanlage, *die;* **~ conditioning** *n.* Klimaanlage, *die;* **~-cooled** *adj.* luftgekühlt; **~craft** *n., pl. same* Flugzeug, *das;* **~craft carrier** *n.* Flugzeugträger, *der;* **~ crew** *n.* Besatzung, *die;* Flugpersonal, *das;* **~ cushion** *n.* Luftkissen, *das;* **~ fare** *n.* Flugpreis, *der;* **~field** *n.* Flugplatz, *der;* **~ force** *n.* Luftwaffe, *die;* **~ freshener** *n.* Lufterfrischer, *der;* Luftverbesserer, *der;* **~gun** *n.* Luftgewehr, *das;* **~ hostess** *n.* Stewardess, *die*

airing /'eərɪŋ/ *n.* Auslüften, *das;* **these clothes need a good ~:** diese Kleider müssen gründlich gelüftet werden

airless /'eəlɪs/ *adj.* stickig ‹*Zimmer, Büro*›; windstill ‹*Nacht*›

air: ~ letter *n.* Aerogramm, *das;* **~lift** *n.* Luftbrücke, *die* (**of** für); **~line** *n.* Fluggesellschaft, *die;* Fluglinie, *die;* **~line pilot** [für eine Fluggesellschaft fliegender] Pilot; **~ liner** *n.* Verkehrsflugzeug, *das;* **~ mail** *n.* Luftpost, *die;* **by ~ mail** mit Luftpost; **~man** /'eəmən/ *n., pl.* **~men** /-mən/ Flieger, *der;* **~ mile** *n.* Flugmeile, *die;* **~plane** *n.* (Amer.) Flugzeug, *das;* **~ play** *n.* (Radio) *das Spielen einer Platte im Radio;*

the record receives *or* **gets no/a great deal of ~play** die Platte wird [überhaupt] nicht/ wird sehr häufig im Radio gespielt; **~ pocket** *n.* (Aeronaut.) Luftloch, *das;* **~ pollution** *n.* Luftverschmutzung, *die;* **~port** *n.* Flughafen, *der;* **~port tax** Flughafengebühr, *die;* **~ pressure** *n.* Luftdruck, *der;* **~ raid** *n.* Luftangriff, *der;* **~-raid shelter** *n.* Luftschutzraum, *der;* **~ rifle** *n.* Luftgewehr, *das;* **~-sea 'rescue** *n.* Seenotrettungseinsatz aus der Luft; **~ship** *n.* Luftschiff, *das;* **~ show** *n.* Flugschau, *die;* **~sick** *adj.* luftkrank; **~stream** *n.* (Meteorol.) Luftströmung, *die;* **~strike** *n.* Luftanschlag, *der;* **~ terminal** *n.* [Air-]Terminal, *der od. das;* **~tight** *adj.* luftdicht; **~time** *n.* Sendezeit, *die;* **~ traffic** *n.* Flugverkehr, *der;* **~-traffic control** *n.* Flugsicherung, *die;* **~-traffic controller** *n.* Fluglotse, *der;* **~ travel** *n.* Fliegen, *das;* **~waves** *n. pl.* Äther, *der*

'airy *adj.* luftig ‹*Büro, Zimmer*›

aisle /aɪl/ *n.* Gang, *der;* (of church) Seitenschiff, *das*

ajar /ə'dʒɑː(r)/ *adj.* **be ~:** einen Spaltbreit offen stehen

a.k.a. *abbr.* = **also known as** al.

akin /ə'kɪn/ *adj.* **be ~ to sth.** einer Sache (*Dat.*) ähnlich sein

alarm /ə'lɑːm/ [1] *n.* **(a)** Alarm, *der;* **give** *or* **raise the ~:** Alarm schlagen
(b) (fear) Angst, *die*
[2] *v.t.* aufschrecken

alarm: ~ call *n.* Weck[an]ruf, *der;* **~ 'clock** *n.* Wecker, *der*

alas /ə'læs/ *int.* ach

Albania /æl'beɪnɪə/ *pr. n.* Albanien (*das*)

Albanian /æl'beɪnɪən/ [1] *adj.* albanisch; **sb. is ~:** jmd. ist Albaner/Albanerin
[2] *n.* **(a)** (person) Albaner, *der*/Albanerin, *die*
(b) (language) Albanisch, *das; see also* ENGLISH 2 A

albatross /'ælbətrɒs/ *n.* Albatros, *der*

album /'ælbəm/ *n.* Album, *das*

alcohol /'ælkəhɒl/ *n.* Alkohol, *der*

'alcohol-free *adj.* alkoholfrei

alcoholic /ælkə'hɒlɪk/ [1] *adj.* alkoholisch
[2] *n.* Alkoholiker, *der*/Alkoholikerin, *die*

Alcoholics A'nonymous *n.* die Anonymen Alkoholiker

alcoholism /'ælkəhɒlɪzm/ *n.* Alkoholismus, *der*

alcopop /'ælkəʊpɒp/ *n.* Alcopop, *der od. das*

alcove /'ælkəʊv/ *n.* Alkoven, *der*

ale /eɪl/ *n.* Ale, *das*

alert /ə'lɜːt/ [1] *adj.* wachsam
[2] *n.* Alarmbereitschaft, *die;* **on the ~:** auf der Hut
[3] *v.t.* alarmieren; **~ sb. [to sth.]** jmdn. [vor etw. (*Dat.*)] warnen

'A level *n.* (Brit. Sch.) ≈ Abitur, *das*

algebra /'ældʒɪbrə/ *n.* Algebra, *die*

Algeria /æl'dʒɪərɪə/ *pr. n.* Algerien (*das*)

Algerian /æl'dʒɪərɪən/ [1] *adj.* algerisch; **sb. is ~:** jmd. ist Algerier/Algerierin
[2] *n.* Algerier, *der*/Algerierin, *die*

alias /'eɪlɪəs/ [1] *adv.* alias
[2] *n.* **(a)** angenommener Name;
(b) (Comp.) Alias, *das*

alibi /'ælɪbaɪ/ *n.* Alibi, *das*

alien /'eɪlɪən/ [1] *adj.* **(a)** (strange) fremd
(b) (foreign) ausländisch
[2] *n.* **(a)** (from another world) Außerirdische, *der/die*
(b) (Admin.: foreigner) Ausländer, *der*/Ausländerin, *die*

alienate /'eɪlɪəneɪt/ *v.t.* befremden

alienation /eɪlɪə'neɪʃn/ *n.* Entfremdung, *die*

alight¹ /ə'laɪt/ *v.i.* **(a)** aussteigen (**from** aus)
(b) ‹*Vogel:*› sich niedersetzen

alight² *adj.* **be/catch ~:** brennen; **set sth. ~:** etw. in Brand setzen

align /ə'laɪn/ *v.t.* **(a)** (place in a line) ausrichten
(b) (bring into line) in eine Linie bringen

a'lignment *n.* Ausrichtung, *die;* **out of ~:** nicht richtig ausgerichtet

alike /ə'laɪk/ *pred. adj.* ähnlich; (indistinguishable) gleich

alimony /'ælɪmənɪ/ *n.* Unterhaltszahlung, *die*

alive /ə'laɪv/ *pred. adj.* **(a)** lebendig
(b) (aware) **be ~ to sth.** sich (*Dat.*) einer Sache (*Gen.*) bewusst sein
(c) (swarming) **be ~ with** wimmeln von

alkali /'ælkəlaɪ/ *n., pl.* **~s** *or* **~es** Alkali, *das*

alkaline /'ælkəlaɪn/ *adj.* alkalisch

all /ɔːl/ [1] *attrib. adj.* **(a)** (entire extent or quantity of) ganz; **~ day** den ganzen Tag; **~ my money** mein ganzes Geld
(b) (entire number of) alle; **~ the books** alle Bücher; **~ my books** all[e] meine Bücher; **~ the others** alle anderen
(c) (any whatever) jeglicher/jegliche/jegliches
(d) (greatest possible) **in ~ innocence** in aller Unschuld
[2] *n.* **(a)** (~ persons) alle; **~ of us** wir alle; **the happiest of ~:** der/die Glücklichste unter *od.* von allen
(b) (every bit) **~ of it** alles; **~ of the money** das ganze Geld
(c) ~ of (coll.: as much as) **be ~ of seven feet tall** gut sieben Fuß groß sein
(d) (~ things) alles; **~ I need is the money** ich brauche nur das Geld; **that is ~:** das ist alles; **the most beautiful of ~:** der/die/das Schönste von allen; **most of ~:** am meisten; **it was ~ but impossible** es war fast unmöglich; **it's ~ the same to me** es ist mir ganz egal; **can I help you at ~?** kann ich Ihnen irgendwie behilflich sein?; **she has no talent at ~:** sie hat überhaupt kein Talent; ⋯

a

nothing at ~: gar nichts; **not at ~ happy/well** überhaupt nicht glücklich/gesund; **not at ~!** überhaupt nicht!; (acknowledging thanks) gern geschehen!; **if at ~**: wenn überhaupt; **in ~**: insgesamt; **~ in ~**: alles in allem
(e) (Sport) **two [goals] ~**: zwei zu zwei; (Tennis) **thirty ~**: dreißig beide
[3] *adv.* ganz; **~ but** fast; **~ the better/worse [for that]** um so besser/schlimmer; **~ at once** (suddenly) plötzlich; **be ~ 'in** (exhausted) total erledigt sein (ugs.); **sth. is ~ right** etw. ist in Ordnung; (tolerable) etw. ist ganz gut; **I'm ~ right** mir geht es ganz gut; **yes, ~ right** ja, gut; **it's ~ right by me** das ist mir recht

allay /ə'leɪ/ *v.t.* zerstreuen ‹*Besorgnis, Befürchtungen*›

all: ~-'clear *n.* Entwarnung, *die;* **~-day** *adj.* ganztägig ‹*Ausflug, Versammlung*›

allegation /ælɪ'geɪʃn/ *n.* Behauptung, *die;* **make ~s against sb.** Beschuldigungen gegen jmdn. erheben

allege /ə'ledʒ/ *v.t.* behaupten

alleged /ə'ledʒd/ *adj.*, **allegedly** /ə'ledʒɪdlɪ/ *adv.* angeblich

allegiance /ə'li:dʒəns/ *n.* Loyalität, *die* (**to** gegenüber)

allegorical /ælɪ'gɒrɪkl/ *adj.* allegorisch

allegory /'ælɪgərɪ/ *n.* Allegorie, *die*

allergic /ə'lɜ:dʒɪk/ *adj.* allergisch (**to** gegen)

allergy /'ælədʒɪ/ *n.* Allergie, *die*

alleviate /ə'li:vɪeɪt/ *v.t.* abschwächen

alley /'ælɪ/ *n.* [schmale] Gasse

alliance /ə'laɪəns/ *n.* Bündnis, *das;* (league) Allianz, *die*

allied /'ælaɪd/ *adj.* **be ~ to** *or* **with sb./sth.** mit jmdm./etw. verbündet sein

alligator /'ælɪgeɪtə(r)/ *n.* Alligator, *der*

all: ~-in *adj.* Pauschal-; **~-night** *adj.* die ganze Nacht dauernd ‹*Sitzung*›; nachts durchgehend geöffnet ‹*Gaststätte*›

allocate /'æləkeɪt/ *v.t.* zuweisen, zuteilen (**to** *Dat.*)

allocation /ælə'keɪʃn/ *n.* Zuweisung, *die;* (ration) Zuteilung, *die*

allot /ə'lɒt/ *v.t.*, **-tt-**: **~ sth. to sb.** jmdm. etw. zuteilen

al'lotment *n.* (Brit.: plot of land) ≈ Schrebergarten, *der*

all: ~-out *attrib. adj.* mit allen [verfügbaren] Mitteln *nachgestellt;* **~-over** *attrib. adj.* **~-over tan** nahtlose Bräune

allow /ə'laʊ/ [1] *v.t.* erlauben; zulassen; **~ sb. to do sth.** jmdm. erlauben, etw. zu tun; **be ~ed to do sth.** etw. tun dürfen
[2] *v.i.* **~ for sth.** etw. berücksichtigen

allowance /ə'laʊəns/ *n.* **(a)** Zuteilung, *die;* (for special expenses) Zuschuss, *der*
(b) make ~s for sth./sb. etw./jmdn. berücksichtigen

alloy /'ælɔɪ/ *n.* Legierung, *die*

all: ~-purpose *adj.* Universal-; Allzweck-; **~-risks** *attrib. adj.* **an ~-risks insurance** eine alle gängigen Risiken abdeckende Versicherung; **~-round** *adj.* Allround-; **~-'rounder** *n.* Allroundtalent, *das;* **~-seater** *adj.* voll bestuhlt ‹*Stadion*›; **~-time** *adj.* **~-time record** absoluter Rekord

allude /ə'lu:d/ *v.i.* **~ to** sich beziehen auf (+ *Akk.*); (indirectly) anspielen auf (+ *Akk.*)

allusion /ə'lu:ʒn/ *n.* Hinweis, *der;* (indirect) Anspielung, *die*

ally /'ælaɪ/ *n.* Verbündete, *der/die;* **the Allies** die Alliierten

almighty /ɔ:l'maɪtɪ/ *adj.* allmächtig; **the A~**: der Allmächtige

almond /'ɑ:mənd/ *n.* Mandel, *die*

almost /'ɔ:lməʊst/ *adv.* fast; beinahe

alms /ɑ:mz/ *n.* Almosen, *das*

alone /ə'ləʊn/ [1] *pred. adj.* allein; alleine (ugs.)
[2] *adv.* allein

along /ə'lɒŋ/ [1] *prep.* entlang (*position:* + Dat.; direction: + Akk.)
[2] *adv.* weiter; **I'll be ~ shortly** ich komme gleich; **all ~**: die ganze Zeit [über]

along'side [1] *adv.* daneben
[2] *prep.* neben (*position:* + *Dat.; direction:* + Akk.)

aloof /ə'lu:f/ [1] *adv.* abseits; **hold ~ from sb.** sich von jmdm. fern halten
[2] *adj.* distanziert

aloud /ə'laʊd/ *adv.* laut; **read [sth.] ~**: [etw.] vorlesen

alphabet /'ælfəbet/ *n.* Alphabet, *das*

alphabetical /ælfə'betɪkl/ *adj.*, **alpha'betically** *adv.* alphabetisch

alpine /'ælpaɪn/ *adj.* alpin

Alps /ælps/ *pr. n. pl.* **the ~**: die Alpen

already /ɔ:l'redɪ/ *adv.* schon

Alsation /æl'seɪʃn/ *n.* [deutscher] Schäferhund

also /'ɔ:lsəʊ/ *adv.* auch; (moreover) außerdem

altar /'ɔ:ltə(r), 'ɒltə(r)/ *n.* Altar, *der*

alter /'ɔ:ltə(r), 'ɒltə(r)/ [1] *v.t.* ändern
[2] *v.i.* sich verändern

alteration /ɔ:ltə'reɪʃn, ɒltə'reɪʃn/ *n.* Änderung, *die*

alternate [1] /ɔ:l'tɜ:nət/ *adj.* sich abwechselnd
[2] /'ɔ:ltəneɪt/ *v.t.* abwechseln lassen
[3] /'ɔ:ltəneɪt/ *v.i.* sich abwechseln

al'ternately *adv.* abwechselnd

'alternating current *n.* (Electr.) Wechselstrom, *der*

alternative /ɔ:l'tɜ:nətɪv/ [1] *adj.* alternativ; Alternativ-; **~ energy** alternative Energie; **~ fuel** Alternativkraftstoff, *der* (*für Verbrennungsmotoren*); **~ medicine** Alternativmedizin, *die*
[2] *n.* **(a)** (choice) Alternative, *die*
(b) (possibility) Möglichkeit, *die*

al'ternatively *adv.* oder aber; **or ~**: oder aber auch

although /ɔːlˈðəʊ/ *conj.* obwohl
altimeter /ˈæltɪmiːtə(r)/ *n.* Höhenmesser, *der*
altitude /ˈæltɪtjuːd/ *n.* Höhe, *die*
altogether /ɔːltəˈgeðə(r)/ *adv.* völlig; (on the whole) im Großen und Ganzen; (in total) insgesamt; **not ~ [true/convincing]** nicht ganz [wahr/überzeugend]
altruist /ˈæltrʊɪst/ *n.* Altruist, *der*/Altruistin, *die* (geh.)
altruistic /æltrʊˈɪstɪk/ *adj.* altruistisch
aluminium /æljʊˈmɪnɪəm/ (Brit.), **aluminum** /əˈluːmɪnəm/ (Amer.) *ns.* Aluminium, *das*
always /ˈɔːlweɪz/ *adv.* immer; (repeatedly) ständig
Alzheimer's disease /ˈæltshaɪmez dɪziːz/ *n.* Alzheimerkrankheit, *die*
am ▶ BE
AM *abbr.* = **amplitude modulation** AM
a.m. /eɪˈem/ *adv.* vormittags; [at] **one/four ~**: [um] ein/vier Uhr früh
amalgamate /əˈmælgəmeɪt/ [1] *v.t.* vereinigen
[2] *v.i.* sich vereinigen; ‹*Firmen:*› fusionieren
amalgamation /əmælgəˈmeɪʃn/ *n.* Vereinigung, *die;* (of firms) Fusion, *die*
amass /əˈmæs/ *v.t.* anhäufen
amateur /ˈæmətə(r)/ *n.* Amateur, *der; attrib.* Amateur-; Laien-
'amateurish *adj.* laienhaft; amateurhaft
amaze /əˈmeɪz/ *v.t.* verblüffen; verwundern
a'mazement *n.* Verblüffung, *die;* Verwunderung, *die*
amazing /əˈmeɪzɪŋ/ *adj.* (remarkable) erstaunlich; (astonishing) verblüffend
Amazon /ˈæməzən/ *pr. n.* **the ~**: der Amazonas
ambassador /æmˈbæsədə(r)/ *n.* Botschafter, *der*/Botschafterin, *die*
amber /ˈæmbə(r)/ [1] *n.* **(a)** Bernstein, *der* **(b)** (traffic light) Gelb, *das*
[2] *adj.* Bernstein-; (colour) bernsteinfarben; gelb ‹*Verkehrslicht*›
ambiguity /æmbɪˈgjuːɪtɪ/ *n.* Zweideutigkeit, *die*
ambiguous /æmˈbɪgjʊəs/ *adj.* zweideutig
ambition /æmˈbɪʃn/ *n.* Ehrgeiz, *der;* (aspiration) Ambition, *die*
ambitious /æmˈbɪʃəs/ *adj.* ehrgeizig
ambivalent /æmˈbɪvələnt/ *adj.* ambivalent
amble /ˈæmbl/ *v.i.* schlendern
ambulance /ˈæmbjʊləns/ *n.* Krankenwagen, *der;* Ambulanz, *die*
ambulance: ~ chaser *n.* (Amer.) *Anwalt oder sein Agent, der Unfallopfer dazu überredet, auf Schadenersatz zu klagen;* **~ driver** *n.* Fahrer/Fahrerin eines/des Krankenwagens; **~ man** *n.* Sanitäter, *der;* **~ service** *n.* Rettungsdienst, *der*
ambush /ˈæmbʊʃ/ [1] *n.* Hinterhalt, *der;* **lie in ~**: im Hinterhalt liegen
[2] *v.t.* [aus dem Hinterhalt] überfallen
amen /ɑːˈmen, eɪˈmen/ [1] *int.* amen
[2] *n.* Amen, *das*
amenable /əˈmiːnəbl/ *adj.* zugänglich, aufgeschlossen (**to** *Dat.*)
amend /əˈmend/ *v.t.* berichtigen; abändern ‹*Gesetzentwurf, Antrag*›
a'mendment *n.* (to motion) Abänderungsantrag, *der;* (to bill) Änderungsantrag, *der*
amends /əˈmendz/ *n. pl.* **make ~ [to sb.]** es [bei jmdm.] wieder gutmachen; **make ~ for sth.** etw. wieder gutmachen
amenity /əˈmiːnɪtɪ/ *n., usu. in pl.* **amenities** (of town) kulturelle und Freizeiteinrichtungen
America /əˈmerɪkə/ *pr. n.* Amerika (*das*)
American /əˈmerɪkən/ [1] *adj.* amerikanisch; **sb. is ~**: jmd. ist Amerikaner/Amerikanerin; **~ English** amerikanisches Englisch
[2] *n.* (person) Amerikaner, *der*/Amerikanerin, *die*
American: ~ 'football *n.* Football, *der;* **~ 'Indian** *n.* Indianer, *der*/Indianerin, *die*
Americanism /əˈmerɪkənɪzm/ *n.* (Ling.) Amerikanismus, *der*
Americanization /əmerɪkənaɪˈzeɪʃn/ *n.* Amerikanisierung, *die*
Americanize /əˈmerɪkənaɪz/ *v.t.* amerikanisieren
amiable /ˈeɪmɪəbl/ *adj.* umgänglich
amicable /ˈæmɪkəbl/ *adj.* freundschaftlich; gütlich ‹*Einigung*›
amicably /ˈæmɪkəblɪ/ *adv.* in [aller] Freundschaft
amid[st] /əˈmɪd(st)/ *prep.* inmitten; (fig.: during) bei
amiss /əˈmɪs/ [1] *pred. adj.* verkehrt; **is anything ~?** stimmt irgendetwas nicht?
[2] *adv.* **take sth. ~**: etw. übel nehmen
ammonia /əˈməʊnɪə/ *n.* Ammoniak, *das*
ammunition /æmjʊˈnɪʃn/ *n.* Munition, *die*
amnesia /æmˈniːzɪə/ Amnesie, *die*
amnesty /ˈæmnɪstɪ/ *n.* Amnestie, *die*
amniocentesis /æmnɪəʊsenˈtiːsɪs/ *n.* (Med.) Fruchtwasserentnahme, *die*
amok /əˈmɒk/ *adv.* **run ~**: Amok laufen
among[st] /əˈmʌŋ(st)/ *prep.* unter (+ *Dat.*); **~ other things** unter anderem; **they often quarrel ~ themselves** sie streiten oft miteinander
amoral /eɪˈmɒrl/ *adj.* amoralisch
amorous /ˈæmərəs/ *adj.* verliebt; amourös ‹*Abenteuer, Beziehung*›
amorphous /əˈmɔːfəs/ *adj.* formlos; amorph ‹*Masse*›

a

amount /ə'maʊnt/ [1] *v.i.* ~ **to sth.** sich auf etw. (*Akk.*) belaufen; (fig.) etw. bedeuten
[2] *n.* **(a)** (total) Betrag, *der;* Summe, *die*
(b) (quantity) Menge, *die*

amp /æmp/ *n.* Ampere, *das*

amphetamine /æm'fetəmɪn/ *n.* (Med.) Amphetamin, *das*

amphibian /æm'fɪbɪən/ [1] *adj.* amphibisch
[2] *n.* Amphibie, *die*

amphibious /æm'fɪbɪəs/ *adj.* amphibisch

amphitheatre /'æmfɪθɪətə(r)/ *n.* Amphitheater, *das*

ample /'æmpl/ *adj.* **(a)** (spacious) weitläufig ‹*Garten, Räume*›; reichhaltig ‹*Mahl*›
(b) (enough) ~ **room/food** reichlich Platz/zu essen

amplifier /'æmplɪfaɪə(r)/ *n.* Verstärker, *der*

amplify /'æmplɪfaɪ/ *v.t.* verstärken; (enlarge on) weiter ausführen

amputate /'æmpjʊteɪt/ *v.t.* amputieren

amputation /æmpjʊ'teɪʃn/ *n.* Amputation, *die*

amuse /ə'mju:z/ *v.t.* **(a)** (interest) unterhalten; ~ **oneself by doing sth.** sich (*Dat.*) die Zeit damit vertreiben, etw. zu tun
(b) (make laugh or smile) amüsieren

a'musement *n.* Belustigung, *die;* ~ **arcade** Spielhalle, *die*

amusing /ə'mju:zɪŋ/ *adj.* amüsant

an /ən, *stressed* æn/ *indef. art. see also* A²: ein/eine/ein

anaemia /ə'ni:mɪə/ *n.* Blutarmut, *die;* Anämie, *die*

anaemic /ə'ni:mɪk/ *adj.* blutarm; anämisch

anaesthetic /ænɪs'θetɪk/ *n.* Anästhetikum, *das;* **general** ~: Narkosemittel, *das;* **local** ~: Lokalanästhetikum, *das*

anaesthetist /ə'ni:sθətɪst/ *n.* Anästhesist, *der*/Anästhesistin, *die;* Narkose[fach]arzt, *der*/-ärztin, *die*

anagram /'ænəgræm/ *n.* Anagramm, *das*

analgesia /ænæl'dʒi:zɪə/ *n.* (Med.) Analgesie, *die*

analgesic /ænæl'dʒi:sɪk/ (Med.) [1] *adj.* analgetisch
[2] *n.* Analgetikum, *das*

analog (Amer.) ▶ ANALOGUE

analogue /'ænəlɒg/ *n.* Entsprechung, *die;* Analogon, *das* (geh.); ~ **computer** Analogrechner, *der;* ~ **watch** Analoguhr, *die*

analogy /ə'næləd3ɪ/ *n.* Analogie, *die*

analyse /'ænəlaɪz/ *v.t.* analysieren

analysis /ə'nælɪsɪs/ *n., pl.* **analyses** /ə'nælɪsi:z/ Analyse, *die*

analyst /'ænəlɪst/ *n.* **(a)** (Psych.) Analytiker, *der*/Analytikerin, *die*
(b) (Econ., Polit., etc.) Experte, *der*/Expertin, *die*

analytic /ænə'lɪtɪk/, **analytical** /ænə'lɪtɪkl/ *adj.* analytisch

analyze (Amer.) ▶ ANALYSE

anarchic /ə'nɑ:kɪk/, **anarchical** /ə'nɑ:kɪkl/ *adj.* anarchisch; (anarchistic) anarchistisch

anarchist /'ænəkɪst/ *n.* Anarchist, *der*/Anarchistin, *die*

anarchy /'ænəkɪ/ *n.* Anarchie, *die*

anatomical /ænə'tɒmɪkl/ *adj.* anatomisch

anatomy /ə'nætəmɪ/ *n.* Anatomie, *die*

ANC *abbr.* = **African National Congress** ANK

ancestor /'ænsestə(r)/ *n.* Vorfahr, *der*

ancestry /'ænsestrɪ/ *n.* Abstammung, *die*

anchor /'æŋkə(r)/ [1] *n.* Anker, *der*
[2] *v.t.* verankern
[3] *v.i.* ankern

anchorage /'æŋkərɪdʒ/ *n.* Ankerplatz, *der*

anchorman/'ægkəmæn/ *n.* (Telev., Radio) Moderator, *der*

anchovy /'æntʃəvɪ/ *n.* Sardelle, *die*

ancient /'eɪnʃənt/ *adj.* alt; historisch ‹*Gebäude usw.*›; (of antiquity) antik

and /ənd, *stressed* ænd/ *conj.* und; **for weeks ~ weeks** wochenlang; **better ~ better** immer besser

androgynous /æn'drɒdʒɪnəs/ *adj.* (Biol.) zwittrig

anecdote /'ænɪkdəʊt/ *n.* Anekdote, *die*

anemia, anemic (Amer.) ▶ ANAEM-

anesthetic *etc.* (Amer.) ▶ ANAESTHETIC *etc.*

angel /'eɪndʒl/ *n.* Engel, *der*

angelic /æn'dʒelɪk/ *adj.* engelhaft

anger /'æŋgə(r)/ [1] *n.* Zorn, *der* (**at** über + Akk.); (fury) Wut, *die* (**at** über + *Akk.*)
[2] *v.t.* verärgern; (infuriate) wütend machen

angina [pectoris] /æn'dʒaɪnə ('pektərɪs)/ *n.* (Med.) Angina pectoris, *die*

angle¹ /'æŋgl/ *n.* **(a)** (Geom.) Winkel, *der;* **at an ~ of 60°** im Winkel von 60°; **at an ~:** schief
(b) (fig.) Gesichtspunkt, *der*

angle² *v.i.* angeln; (fig.) ~ **for sth.** sich um etw. bemühen

angle: ~ **brackets** *n. pl.* spitze Klammern; ~ **grinder** *n.* Winkelschleifer, *der;* (with cutting disc) Flex, *die;* ~**-parking** *n.* Schrägparken, *das*

angler /'æŋglə(r)/ *n.* Angler, *der*/Anglerin, *die*

Anglican /'æŋglɪkən/ [1] *adj.* anglikanisch
[2] *n.* Anglikaner, *der*/Anglikanerin, *die*

Anglo- /æŋgləʊ/ *in comb.* anglo-/Anglo-

Anglo-Saxon /-'sæksn/ [1] *n.* Angelsachse, *der*/Angelsächsin, *die;* (language) Angelsächsisch, *das*
[2] *adj.* angelsächsisch

angora [wool] /æŋ'gɔ:rə/ *n.* Angorawolle, *die;* Mohair, *der*

angrily /'æŋgrɪlɪ/ *adv.* verärgert; (stronger) zornig

angry /'æŋgrɪ/ *adj.* böse; verärgert ‹*Person, Stimme, Geste*›; (stronger) zornig; wütend; **be**

~ **at** *or* **about sth.** wegen etw. böse sein; **be ~ with** *or* **at sb.** mit jmdm. *od.* auf jmdn. böse sein; **get ~**: böse werden

anguish /'æŋgwɪʃ/ *n.* Qualen *Pl.*

angular /'æŋgjʊlə(r)/ *adj.* eckig ‹*Gebäude, Struktur*›; kantig ‹*Gesicht*›

animal /'ænɪməl/ [1] *n.* Tier, *das* [2] *adj.* tierisch

animal: A~ Libe'ration Front *n.* Tierbefreiungsfront, *die;* **~ lover** *n.* Tierfreund, *der*/-freundin, *die;* **~ pro'tectionist** *n.* Tierschützer, *der*/-schützerin, *die;* **~ 'rights** *n. pl.* Tierrechte *Pl.;* **~ rights supporter** Tierrechtler, *der*/ Tierrechtlerin, *die*

animate [1] /'ænɪmeɪt/ *v.t.* beleben [2] /'ænɪmət/ *adj.* beseelt ‹*Leben, Körper*›; belebt ‹*Objekt, Welt*›

animated /'ænɪmeɪtɪd/ *adj.* lebhaft ‹*Diskussion, Gebärde*›; **~ cartoon** Zeichentrickfilm, *der*

animation /ænɪ'meɪʃn/ *n.* **(a)** Lebhaftigkeit, *die* **(b)** (Cinemat.) Animation, *die*

animosity /ænɪ'mɒsɪtɪ/ *n.* Feindseligkeit, *die*

aniseed /'ænɪsi:d/ *n.* Anis[samen], *der*

ankle /'æŋkl/ *n.* Fußgelenk, *das*

ankle: ~-deep *adj.* knöcheltief; **~ sock** *n.* Socke, *die;* (esp. for children) Söckchen, *das*

annex [1] /ə'neks/ *v.t.* annektieren ‹*Land, Territorium*› [2] /'æneks/ *n.* Anbau, *der*

annexation /ænɪk'seɪʃn/ *n.* Annexion, *die;* Annektierung, *die*

annexe ▸ ANNEX 2

annihilate /ə'naɪɪleɪt/ *v.t.* vernichten

annihilation /ənaɪɪ'leɪʃn/ *n.* Vernichtung, *die*

anniversary /ænɪ'vɜ:sərɪ/ *n.* Jahrestag, *der;* **wedding ~**: Hochzeitstag, *der*

annotate /'ænəteɪt/ *v.t.* kommentieren

announce /ə'naʊns/ *v.t.* bekannt geben; ansagen ‹*Programm*›; (over Tannoy etc.) durchsagen; (in newspaper) anzeigen ‹*Heirat usw.*›

an'nouncement *n.* Bekanntgabe, *die;* (over Tannoy etc.) Durchsage, *die;* (in newspaper) Anzeige, *die*

an'nouncer *n.* Ansager, *der*/Ansagerin, *die*

annoy /ə'nɔɪ/ *v.t.* **(a)** ärgern **(b)** (harass) schikanieren

annoyance /ə'nɔɪəns/ *n.* Verärgerung, *die;* (nuisance) Plage, *die*

annoyed /ə'nɔɪd/ *adj.* **be ~ [at** *or* **with sb./sth.]** ärgerlich [auf *od.* über jmdn./über etw.] sein; **he got very ~**: er hat sich darüber sehr geärgert

an'noying *adj.* ärgerlich; lästig ‹*Gewohnheit, Person*›

annual /'ænjʊəl/ [1] *adj.* **(a)** (reckoned by the year) Jahres-; **~ income/subscription/rent/turnover/production/leave/salary** Jahreseinkommen, *das*/-abonnement, *das*/-miete, *die*/-umsatz, *der*/-produktion, *die*/-urlaub, *der*/-gehalt, *das;* **~ rainfall** jährliche Regenmenge **(b)** (recurring yearly) [all]jährlich ‹*Ereignis, Feier*›; Jahres‹*bericht, -hauptversammlung*› [2] *n.* **(a)** Jahrbuch, *das;* (of comic etc.) Jahresalbum, *das* **(b)** (plant) einjährige Pflanze

'annually *adv.* jährlich

annul /ə'nʌl/ *v.t.*, **-ll-** annullieren; auflösen ‹*Vertrag*›

anodyne /'ænadaɪn/ *adj.* (fig.) wohltuend; (soothing) einlullend

anon. /ə'nɒn/ *abbr.* = **anonymous [author]** anon.

anonymity /ænə'nɪmɪtɪ/ *n.* Anonymität, *die*

anonymous /ə'nɒnɪməs/ *adj.* anonym

anorak /'ænəræk/ *n.* Anorak, *der*

anorexia /ænə'reksɪə/ *n.* Anorexie, *die* (Med.); Magersucht, *die*

anorexic /ænə'reksɪk/ *adj.* anorektisch (fachspr.); magersüchtig; **be ~**: an Anorexie (Med.) *od.* Magersucht leiden

another /ə'nʌðə(r)/ [1] *pron.* **(a)** (an additional one) noch einer/eine/eins; ein weiterer/eine weitere/ein weiteres **(b)** (counterpart) wieder einer/eine/eins **(c)** (a different one) ein anderer/eine andere/ein anderes [2] *adj.* **(a)** (additional) noch ein/eine; ein weiterer/eine weitere/ein weiteres; **after ~ six weeks** nach weiteren sechs Wochen **(b)** (different) ein anderer/eine andere/ein anderes

answer /'ɑ:nsə(r)/ [1] *n.* **(a)** (reply) Antwort, *die* (**to** auf + *Akk.*) **(b)** (to problem) Lösung, *die* (**to** *Gen.*); (to calculation) Ergebnis, *das* [2] *v.t.* **(a)** beantworten ‹*Brief, Frage*›; antworten auf (+ *Akk.*) ‹*Frage, Hilferuf, Einladung, Inserat*›; eingehen auf (+ *Akk.*) ‹*Angebot, Vorschlag*›; sich stellen zu ‹*Beschuldigung*›; erhören ‹*Gebet*›; erfüllen ‹*Bitte, Wunsch*›; **~ sb.** jmdm. antworten **(b) ~ the door/bell** an die Tür gehen [3] *v.i.* **(a)** (reply) antworten; **~ to sth.** sich zu etw. äußern **(b)** (be responsible) **~ for sth.** für etw. die Verantwortung übernehmen **(c) ~ to a description** einer Beschreibung (*Dat.*) entsprechen

answerable /'ɑ:nsərəbl/ *adj.* verantwortlich (**for** für; **to** *Dat.*)

answering: ~machine *n.* Anrufbeantworter, *der;* **~ service** *n* Fernsprechauftragsdienst, *der*

'answerphone (Brit.) ▸ ANSWERING MACHINE

ant /ænt/ *n.* Ameise, *die*

a

antagonism /æn'tæɡənɪzm/ *n.* Feindseligkeit, *die* **(towards, against** gegenüber)

antagonist /æn'tæɡənɪst/ *n.* Gegner, *der*/Gegnerin, *die*

antagonistic /æntæɡə'nɪstɪk/ *adj.* feindlich

antagonize /æn'tæɡənaɪz/ *v.t.* **~ sb.** sich (*Dat.*) jmdn. zum Feind machen

antarctic /ænt'ɑːktɪk/ **1** *adj.* antarktisch **2** *n.* **the A~:** die Antarktis

antelope /'æntɪləʊp/ *n.* Antilope, *die*

antenatal /æntɪ'neɪtl/ *adj.* (concerning pregnancy) Schwangerschafts-; Schwangeren-; **~ care** Schwangerenfürsorge, *die;* **~ clinic** Klinik für werdende Mütter

antenna /æn'tenə/ *n.* **(a)** *pl.* **~e** /æn'teniː/ (Zool.) Fühler, *der*
(b) *pl.* **~s** (tech., Amer.: aerial) Antenne, *die*

anthem /'ænθəm/ *n.* Chorgesang, *der*

anthology /æn'θɒlədʒɪ/ *n.* Anthologie, *die*

anthropologist /ænθrə'pɒlədʒɪst/ *n.* Anthropologe, *der*/Anthropologin, *die*

anthropology /ænθrə'pɒlədʒɪ/ *n.* Anthropologie, *die*

anti /'æntɪ/ **1** *prep.* gegen **2** *adj.* ablehnend

anti- /æntɪ/ *pref.* anti-/Anti-

anti: ~-a'bortion *attrib. adj.* **~-abortion protester** Abtreibungsgegner, *der*/-gegnerin, *die;* **~-abortion protest/law** Protest/Gesetz gegen Abtreibung; **~-abortion demonstration/movement** Antiabtreibungsdemonstration, *die*/-bewegung, *die;* **~-abortionist** /æntɪə'bɔːʃənɪst/ *n.* Abtreibungsgegner, *der*/-gegnerin, *die;* **~-'aircraft** *adj.* (Mil.) Flugabwehr-; **~-aircraft gun** Flak, *die*

antibiotic /æntɪbaɪ'ɒtɪk/ *n.* Antibiotikum, *das*

'antibody *n.* Antikörper, *der*

antic /'æntɪk/ *n.* (trick) Mätzchen, *das* (ugs.); (of clown) Possen, *der*

anticipate /æn'tɪsɪpeɪt/ *v.t.* **(a)** (expect) erwarten; (foresee) voraussehen; **~ trouble** mit Ärger rechnen
(b) (consider before due time) vorwegnehmen

anticipation /æntɪsɪ'peɪʃn/ *n.* Erwartung, *die*

anti'climax *n.* Abstieg, *der*

anti'clockwise *adv., adj.* gegen den Uhrzeigersinn

anti'cyclone *n.* Hochdruckgebiet, *das*

antidepressant /æntɪdɪ'presənt/ *n.* Antidepressivum, *das*

antidote /'æntɪdəʊt/ *n.* Gegenmittel, *das* **(for, against, to** gegen)

'antifreeze *n.* Frostschutzmittel, *das*

antiglobalization /æntɪɡləʊbəlaɪ'zeɪʃn/ *n.* Antiglobalisierung, *die*

'anti-hero *n.* Antiheld, *der*

antihistamine /æntɪ'hɪstəmɪn/ *n.* (Med.) Antihistamin[ikum], *das*

'anti-lock *adj.* Antiblockier-; **~ brake** *or* **braking system** Antiblockiersystem, *das*

anti'nuclear *adj.* Anti-Atom[kraft]-

antipathy /æn'tɪpəθɪ/ *n.* Antipathie, *die;* Abneigung, *die*

anti-person'nel *adj.* gegen Menschen gerichtet; **~ mine** Schützenmine, *die*

antiperspirant /æntɪ'pɜːspɪrənt/ **1** *adj.* schweißhemmend; **~ spray** Deodorantspray, *der od. das*
2 *n.* Antitranspirant, *das*

antiquated /'æntɪkweɪtɪd/ *adj.* antiquiert; veraltet

antique /æn'tiːk/ **1** *adj.* antik
2 *n.* Antiquität, *die;* **~ shop** Antiquitätenladen, *der*

antiquity /æn'tɪkwɪtɪ/ *n.* Altertum, *das;* Antike, *die*

anti-Semitic /æntɪsɪ'mɪtɪk/ *adj.* antisemitisch; judenfeindlich

anti-Semitism /æntɪ'semɪtɪzm/ *n.* Antisemitismus, *der;* Judenhass, *der*

anti'septic **1** *adj.* antiseptisch
2 *n.* Antiseptikum, *das*

anti'social *adj.* asozial

anti-'theft *attrib. adj.* Antidiebstahl-

antithesis /æn'tɪθəsɪs/ *n., pl.* **antitheses** /æn'tɪθəsiːz/ Gegenstück, *das* **(of, to** zu)

anti: ~'toxin *n.* (Med.) Antitoxin, *das;* **~'virus** *attrib. adj.* (Comp.) Antivirus-; **~virus software** Antivirensoftware, *die*

antivivisectionist /æntɪvɪvɪ'sekʃənɪst/ *n.* Vivisektionsgegner, *der*/-gegnerin, *die*

antler /'æntlə(r)/ *n.* Geweihsprosse, *die;* **[pair of] ~s** Geweih, *das*

anvil /'ænvɪl/ *n.* Amboss, *der*

anxiety /æŋ'zaɪətɪ/ *n.* Angst, *die;* (concern about future) Sorge, *die* **(about** wegen)

anxious /'æŋkʃəs/ *adj.* **(a)** (troubled) besorgt **(about** um)
(b) (eager) sehnlich; **be ~ for sth.** sich nach etw. sehnen

'anxiously *adv.* **(a)** besorgt
(b) (eagerly) sehnsüchtig

any /'enɪ/ **1** *adj.* **(a)** (some) [irgend]ein/[irgend]eine; **not ~:** kein/keine; **have you ~ wool/wine?** haben Sie Wolle/Wein?
(b) (one) ein/eine
(c) (all, every) jeder/jede/jedes; **[at] ~ time** jederzeit
(d) (whichever) jeder/jede/jedes [beliebige]; **choose ~ [one] book/~ books you like** suchen Sie sich (*Dat.*) irgendein Buch/irgendwelche Bücher aus
2 *pron.* **(a)** (some) *in condit., interrog., or neg. sentence* (replacing sing. n.) einer/eine/ein[e]s; (replacing collect. n.) welcher/welche/welches; (replacing pl. n.) welche; **not ~:** keiner/keine/kein[e]s/*Pl.* keine
(b) (no matter which) irgendeiner/irgendeine/irgendein[e]s/irgendwelche *Pl.*

3 *adv.* **do you feel ~ better today?** fühlen Sie sich heute [etwas] besser?; **if it gets ~ colder** wenn es noch kälter wird; **I can't wait ~ longer** ich kann nicht [mehr] länger warten

'anybody *n. & pron.* **(a)** (whoever) jeder **(b)** (somebody) [irgend]jemand; *after neg.* niemand

'anyhow *adv.* **(a)** ▶ ANYWAY **(b)** (haphazardly) irgendwie

'anyone ▶ ANYBODY

'anything 1 *n. & pron.* **(a)** (whatever thing) was [immer]; alles, was **(b)** (something) irgendetwas; *after neg.* nichts **(c)** (a thing of any kind) alles 2 *adv.* **not ~ like as … as** keineswegs so … wie

'anyway *adv.* **(a)** (in any case, besides) sowieso **(b)** (at any rate) jedenfalls

'anywhere *adv.* **(a)** (in any place) (wherever) überall, wo; wo [immer]; (somewhere) irgendwo; **not ~ near as … as** (coll.) nicht annähernd so … wie **(b)** (to any place) (wherever) wohin [auch immer]; (somewhere) irgendwohin

aorta /eɪ'ɔːtə/ *n.* (Anat.) Aorta, *die*

apart /ə'pɑːt/ *adv.* **(a)** (separately) getrennt; **~ from …:** außer … **(b)** (into pieces) auseinander

apartheid /ə'pɑːteɪt/ *n.* Apartheid, *die*

apartment /ə'pɑːtmənt/ *n.* **(a)** (room) Apartment, *das* **(b)** (Amer.: flat) Wohnung, *die*

apathetic /æpə'θetɪk/ *adj.* apathisch (**about** gegenüber)

apathy /'æpəθɪ/ *n.* Apathie, *die* (**about** gegenüber)

ape /eɪp/ 1 *n.* [Menschen]affe, *der* 2 *v.t.* nachahmen

aperitif /əperɪ'tiːf/ *n.* Aperitif, *der*

aperture /'æpətʃə(r)/ *n.* Öffnung, *die*

apex /'eɪpeks/ *n.* Spitze, *die*

aphid /'eɪfɪd/ *n.* Blattlaus, *die*

aphrodisiac /æfrə'dɪzɪæk/ *n.* Aphrodisiakum, *das*

apiece /ə'piːs/ *adv.* je; **they cost a penny ~:** sie kosten einen Penny das Stück

apolitical /eɪpə'lɪtɪkl/ *adj.* apolitisch; unpolitisch

apologetic /əpɒlə'dʒetɪk/ *adj.* entschuldigend; **be ~:** sich entschuldigen

apologize /ə'pɒlədʒaɪz/ *v.i.* sich entschuldigen (**to** bei)

apology /ə'pɒlədʒɪ/ *n.* Entschuldigung, *die;* **make an ~:** sich entschuldigen (**to** bei)

apoplectic /æpə'plektɪk/ *adj.* apoplektisch; **~ fit** Schlaganfall, *der*

apoplexy /'æpəpleksɪ/ *n.* Apoplexie, *die* (fachspr.); Schlaganfall, *der*

apostle /ə'pɒsl/ *n.* Apostel, *der*

apostrophe /ə'pɒstrəfɪ/ *n.* Apostroph, *der;* Auslassungszeichen, *das*

appal (*Amer.:* **appall**) /ə'pɔːl/ *v.t.,* **-ll-** entsetzen

ap'palling *adj.* entsetzlich

apparatus /æpə'reɪtəs/ *n.* (equipment) Gerät, *das;* (gymnastic ~) Geräte *Pl.;* (machinery, lit. or fig.) Apparat, *der;* **a piece of ~:** ein Gerät

apparel /ə'pærəl/ *n.* Kleidung, *die;* Gewänder *Pl.* (geh.)

apparent /ə'pærənt/ *adj.* **(a)** (clear) offensichtlich; offenbar ‹*Bedeutung, Wahrheit*› **(b)** (seeming) scheinbar

ap'parently *adv.* **(a)** (clearly) offensichtlich **(b)** (seemingly) scheinbar

apparition /æpə'rɪʃn/ *n.* [Geister]erscheinung, *die*

appeal /ə'piːl/ 1 *v.i.* **(a)** (Law etc.) Einspruch einlegen **(b)** (make earnest request) **~ to sb. for sth./to do sth.** jmdn. um etw. ersuchen/jmdn. ersuchen, etw. zu tun **(c)** (address oneself) **~ to sb./sth.** an jmdn./etw. appellieren **(d)** (be attractive) **~ to sb.** jmdm. zusagen 2 *n.* **(a)** (Law etc.) Einspruch, *der* (**to** bei); (to higher court) Berufung, *die* (**to** bei) **(b)** (request) Appell, *der;* **an ~ to sb. for sth.** eine Bitte an jmdn. um etw. **(c)** (attraction) Reiz, *der*

ap'pealing *adj.* **(a)** (imploring) flehend **(b)** (attractive) ansprechend; verlockend ‹*Idee*›

appear /ə'pɪə(r)/ *v.i.* **(a)** (become visible, arrive) erscheinen; ‹*Licht, Mond:*› auftauchen; (present oneself) auftreten **(b)** (occur) vorkommen **(c)** (seem) **~ [to be] …:** scheinen … [zu sein]

appearance /ə'pɪərəns/ *n.* **(a)** (becoming visible) Auftauchen, *das;* (arrival) Erscheinen, *das;* (of performer etc.) Auftritt, *der* **(b)** (look) Äußere, *das;* **to all ~s** allem Anschein nach **(c)** (semblance) Anschein, *der* **(d)** (occurrence) Vorkommen, *das*

appease /ə'piːz/ *v.t.* besänftigen; (Polit.) beschwichtigen

append /ə'pend/ *v.t.* anhängen (**to** an + *Akk.*); (add) anfügen (+ *Dat.*)

appendage /ə'pendɪdʒ/ *n.* Anhängsel, *das;* (addition) Anhang, *der*

appendicitis /əpendɪ'saɪtɪs/ *n.* Blinddarmentzündung, *die*

appendix /ə'pendɪks/ *n., pl.* **appendices** /ə'pendɪsiːz/ *or* **~es** **(a)** Anhang, *der* (**to** zu) **(b)** (Anat.) Blinddarm, *der*

appetite /'æpɪtaɪt/ *n.* **(a)** Appetit, *der* (**for** auf + *Akk.*) **(b)** (fig.) Verlangen, *das* (**for** nach)

appetizer /'æpɪtaɪzə(r)/ *n.* Appetitanreger, *der*

appetizing /'æpɪtaɪzɪŋ/ *adj.* appetitlich

a

applaud /ə'plɔ:d/ [1] *v.i.* applaudieren; [Beifall] klatschen
[2] *v.t.* applaudieren (+ *Dat.*)

applause /ə'plɔ:z/ *n.* Beifall, *der;* Applaus, *der*

apple /'æpl/ *n.* Apfel, *der*

apple: ~ 'pie gedeckte Apfeltorte; **~ 'sauce** *n.* Apfelmus, *das*

applet /'æplɪt/ *n.* (Comp.) Applet, *das*

'apple tree *n.* Apfelbaum, *der*

appliance /ə'plaɪəns/ *n.* Gerät, *das*

applicable /ə'plɪkəbl/ *adj.* **(a)** anwendbar (**to** auf + *Akk.*)
(b) (appropriate) geeignet; zutreffend ‹*Fragebogenteil*›

applicant /'æplɪkənt/ *n.* Bewerber, *der*/Bewerberin, *die* (**for** um); (claimant) Antragsteller, *der*/-stellerin, *die*

application /æplɪ'keɪʃn/ *n.* **(a)** (request) Bewerbung, *die* (**for** um); (for passport, licence, etc.) Antrag, *der* (**for** auf + *Akk.*); **~ form** Antragsformular, *das*
(b) (putting) Auftragen, *das* (**to** auf + *Akk.*)
(c) (use) Anwendung, *die*
(d) (Comp.) Applikation, *die*

applicator /'æplɪkeɪtə(r)/ *n.* Applikator, *der*

apply /ə'plaɪ/ [1] *v.t.* **(a)** auftragen ‹*Creme, Farbe*› (**to** auf + *Akk.*)
(b) (make use of) anwenden
[2] *v.i.* **(a)** (have relevance) zutreffen (**to** auf + *Akk.*)
(b) ~ [to sb.] for sth. [jmdn.] um etw. bitten; (for passport etc.) [bei jmdm.] etw. beantragen; (for job) sich [bei jmdm.] um etw. bewerben

appoint /ə'pɔɪnt/ *v.t.* **(a)** (fix) bestimmen; festlegen ‹*Zeitpunkt, Ort*›
(b) (to job) einstellen; (to office) ernennen

appointee /əpɔɪn'ti:/ *n.* Ernannte, *der/die;* Berufene, *der/die*

ap'pointment *n.* **(a)** (to job) Einstellung, *die;* (to office) Ernennung, *die* (**as** zum/zur)
(b) (job) Stelle, *die*
(c) (arrangement) Termin, *der;* **make an ~ with sb.** sich (*Dat.*) von jmdm. einen Termin geben lassen; **by ~:** nach Anmeldung

appraisal /ə'preɪzl/ *n.* (evaluation) Bewertung, *die*

appraise /ə'preɪz/ *v.t.* (evaluate) bewerten

appreciable /ə'pri:ʃəbl/ *adj.* **(a)** (perceptible) nennenswert ‹*Unterschied, Einfluss*›; spürbar ‹*Veränderung, Wirkung*›; merklich ‹*Verringerung, Anstieg*›
(b) (considerable) beträchtlich

appreciably /ə'pri:ʃəblɪ/ *adv.* **(a)** (perceptibly) spürbar ‹*verändern*›; merklich ‹*sich unterscheiden*›
(b) (considerably) beträchtlich

appreciate /ə'pri:ʃɪeɪt/ [1] *v.t.* **(a)** ([correctly] estimate) [richtig] einschätzen; (understand) verstehen; (be aware of) sich (*Dat.*) bewusst sein (+ *Gen.*)
(b) (be grateful for) schätzen; (enjoy) genießen
[2] *v.i.* im Wert steigen

appreciation /əpri:ʃɪ'eɪʃn/ *n.* **(a)** ([correct] estimation) [richtige] Einschätzung; (understanding) Verständnis, *das* (**of** für); (awareness) Bewusstsein, *das*
(b) (gratefulness) Dankbarkeit, *die;* (enjoyment) Gefallen, *das* (**of** an + *Dat.*)

appreciative /ə'pri:ʃətɪv/ *adj.* (grateful) dankbar (**of** für); (approving) anerkennend

apprehend /æprɪ'hend/ *v.t.* **(a)** (arrest) festnehmen
(b) (understand) erfassen

apprehension /æprɪ'henʃn/ *n.* Besorgnis, *die*

apprehensive /æprɪ'hensɪv/ *adj.* besorgt

apprentice /ə'prentɪs/ *n.* Lehrling, *der* (**to** bei)

ap'prenticeship *n.* (training) Lehre, *die;* (learning period) Lehrzeit, *die*

approach /ə'prəʊtʃ/ [1] *v.i.* sich nähern; (in time) nahen
[2] *v.t.* **(a)** (come near to) sich nähern (+ *Dat.*)
(b) (approximate to) nahe kommen (+ *Dat.*)
(c) (appeal to) sich wenden an (+ *Akk.*)
[3] *n.* **(a)** [Heran]nahen, *das*
(b) (approximation) Annäherung, *die* (**to** an + *Akk.*)
(c) (appeal) Herantreten, *das* (**to** an + *Akk.*)
(d) (access) Zugang, *der;* (road) Zufahrtsstraße, *die*

approachable /ə'prəʊtʃəbl/ *adj.* **(a)** (friendly) umgänglich
(b) (accessible) zugänglich

ap'proach road *n.* Zufahrtsstraße, *die*

appropriate [1] /ə'prəʊprɪət/ *adj.* geeignet (**to, for** für)
[2] /ə'prəʊprɪeɪt/ *v.t.* sich (*Dat.*) aneignen

appropriately /ə'prəʊprɪətlɪ/ *adv.* gebührend; passend ‹*gekleidet, genannt*›

approval /ə'pru:vl/ *n.* **(a)** (sanctioning) Genehmigung, *die;* (of proposal) Billigung, *die;* (agreement) Zustimmung, *die*
(b) on ~ (Commerc.) zur Probe

approve /ə'pru:v/ [1] *v.t.* **(a)** (sanction) genehmigen ‹*Plan, Projekt*›; billigen ‹*Vorschlag*›
(b) (find good) gutheißen
[2] *v.i.* **~ of** billigen; zustimmen (+ *Dat.*) ‹*Plan*›

approving /ə'pru:vɪŋ/ *adj.* zustimmend ‹*Worte*›; anerkennend ‹*Blicke*›

approx. /ə'prɒks/ *abbr.* = **approximately** ca.

approximate /ə'prɒksɪmət/ *adj.* ungefähr *attr.*

ap'proximately *adv.* ungefähr

approximation /əprɒksɪ'meɪʃn/ *n.* **(a)** Annäherung, *die* (**to** an + *Dat.*)
(b) (estimate) Annäherungswert, *der*

APR *abbr.* = **annualized percentage rate** Jahreszinssatz, *der*

Apr. *abbr.* = **April** Apr.

après-ski /æpreɪ'ski:/ *n.* Après-Ski, *der; attrib.* Après-Ski-
apricot /'eɪprɪkɒt/ *n.* Aprikose, *die*
April /'eɪprəl/ *n.* April, *der;* **~ fool** April[s]narr, *der; see also* AUGUST
apron /'eɪprən/ *n.* Schürze, *die*
apt /æpt/ *adj.* **(a)** (suitable) passend; treffend ‹*Bemerkung*›
(b) be ~ to do sth. dazu neigen, etw. zu tun
aptitude /'æptɪtju:d/ *n.* Begabung, *die*
'aptly *adv.* passend
aqualung /'ækwəlʌŋ/ *n.* Tauchgerät, *das*
aquaplane /'ækwəpleɪn/ *v.i.* ‹*Reifen:*› aufschwimmen; ‹*Fahrzeug:*› [durch Aquaplaning] ins Rutschen geraten
aquarium /ə'kweərɪəm/ *n., pl.* **~s** *or* **aquaria** /ə'kweərɪə/ Aquarium, *das*
Aquarius /ə'kweərɪəs/ *n.* (Astrol., Astron.) der Wassermann
aquatic /ə'kwætɪk/ *adj.* aquatisch; Wasser-; **~ plant** Wasserpflanze, *die*
aqueduct /'ækwɪdʌkt/ *n.* Aquädukt, *der od. das*
aqueous /'eɪkwɪəs, 'ækwɪəs/ *adj.* wässerig; wässrig
Arab /'ærəb/ **1** *adj.* arabisch
2 *n.* Araber, *der*/Araberin, *die*
Arabian /ə'reɪbɪən/ **1** *adj.* arabisch
2 *n.* Araber, *der*/Araberin, *die*
Arabic /'ærəbɪk/ **1** *adj.* arabisch
2 *n.* Arabisch, *das; see also* ENGLISH 2A
arable /'ærəbl/ *adj.* bebaubar, landwirtschaftlich nutzbar ‹*Land*›; **~ land** (cultivated) Ackerland, *das*
arbitrary /'ɑ:bɪtrərɪ/ *adj.* willkürlich
arbitrate /'ɑ:bɪtreɪt/ **1** *v.t.* schlichten ‹*Streit*›
2 *v.i.* **~ [upon sth.]** [in einer Sache] vermitteln
arbitration /ɑ:bɪ'treɪʃn/ *n.* Vermittlung, *die;* (in industry) Schlichtung, *die*
arbitrator /'ɑ:bɪtreɪtə(r)/ *n.* Vermittler, *der;* (in industry) Schlichter, *der*
arboretum /ɑ:bə'ri:təm/ *n., pl.* **arboreta** /ɑ:bə'ri:tə/ *or* (Amer.) **~s** Arboretum, *das;* Baumgarten, *der*
arbour /'ɑ:bə(r)/ *n.* (Brit.) Laube, *die*
arc /ɑ:k/ *n.* [Kreis]bogen, *der;* **~ lamp, ~ light** Lichtbogenlampe, *die;* **~ welding** Lichtbogen-, Elektroschweißung, *die*
arcade /ɑ:'keɪd/ *n.* Arkade, *die*
arch /ɑ:tʃ/ **1** *n.* Bogen, *der;* (of foot) Wölbung, *die*
2 *v.t.* beugen ‹*Rücken*›; **~ its back** ‹*Katze:*› einen Buckel machen
arch- *pref.* Erz-
archaeological /ɑ:kɪə'lɒdʒɪkl/ *adj.* archäologisch
archaeologist /ɑ:kɪ'ɒlədʒɪst/ *n.* Archäologe, *der*/Archäologin, *die*
archaeology /ɑ:kɪ'ɒlədʒɪ/ *n.* Archäologie, *die*
archaic /ɑ:'keɪɪk/ *adj.* veraltet
arch'bishop *n.* Erzbischof, *der*
arch-'enemy *n.* Erzfeind, *der*/Erzfeindin, *die*
archeology *etc.* (*Amer.*) ▶ ARCHAEOLOGY *etc.*
archer /'ɑ:tʃə(r)/ *n.* Bogenschütze, *der*
archery /'ɑ:tʃərɪ/ *n.* Bogenschießen, *das*
archetype /'ɑ:kɪtaɪp/ *n.* (original) Urfassung, *die;* (typical specimen) Prototyp, *der*
architect /'ɑ:kɪtekt/ *n.* Architekt, *der*/Architektin, *die*
architectural /ɑ:kɪ'tektʃərl/ *adj.* architektonisch
architecture /'ɑ:kɪtektʃə(r)/ *n.* Architektur, *die*
archive /'ɑ:kaɪv/ **1** *n.* Archiv, *das;* **~s** Archiv, *das*
2 *v.t.* archivieren
arctic /'ɑ:ktɪk/ **1** *adj.* arktisch; **A~ Circle** nördlicher Polarkreis; **A~ Ocean** Nordpolarmeer, *das*
2 *n.* **the A~**: die Arktis
ardent /'ɑ:dənt/ *adj.* leidenschaftlich; brennend ‹*Wunsch*›; (eager) begeistert
ardor (Amer.), **ardour** (Brit.) /'ɑ:də(r)/ *n.* Leidenschaft, *die*
arduous /'ɑ:djʊəs/ *adj.* anstrengend
are ▶ BE
area /'eərɪə/ *n.* **(a)** (surface measure) Fläche, *die;* Flächeninhalt, *der*
(b) (region) Gelände, *das;* (of wood, marsh, desert) Gebiet, *das;* (of city, country) Gegend, *die;* **parking/picnic ~**: Park-/Picknickplatz, *der*
(c) (subject field) Gebiet, *das*
'area code *n.* (Amer. Teleph.) Gebietsvorwahl[nummer], *die*
arena /ə'ri:nə/ *n.* Arena, *die;* **the political ~**: die politische Arena
aren't /ɑ:nt/ (coll.) = **are not;** ▶ BE
Argentina /ɑ:dʒən'ti:nə/ *pr. n.* Argentinien (*das*)
Argentinian /ɑ:dʒən'tɪnɪən/ **1** *adj.* argentinisch; **sb. is ~**: jmd. ist Argentinier/Argentinierin
2 *n.* Argentinier, *der*/Argentinierin, *die*
arguable /'ɑ:gjʊəbl/ *adj.* (questionable) fragwürdig
arguably /'ɑ:gjʊəblɪ/ *adv.* möglicherweise
argue /'ɑ:gju:/ **1** *v.t.* **(a)** (maintain) **~ that ...**: die Ansicht vertreten, dass ...
(b) (with reasoning) darlegen ‹*Grund, Standpunkt*›
2 *v.i.* **~ with sb.** sich mit jmdm. streiten; **~ for/against sth.** für/gegen etw. eintreten; **~ about sth.** sich über/um etw. (*Akk.*) streiten
argument /'ɑ:gjʊmənt/ *n.* **(a)** (reason) Begründung, *die;* **~s for/against sth.** Argumente für/gegen etw.
(b) (reasoning process) Argumentieren, *das* ⇢

(c) (disagreement, quarrel) Auseinandersetzung, *die*

argumentative /ɑ:gjʊ'mentətɪv/ *adj.* widerspruchsfreudig

arid /'ærɪd/ *adj.* trocken

Aries /'eəri:z/ *n.* (Astrol; Astron.) der Widder

arise /ə'raɪz/ *v.i.*, **arose** /ə'rəʊz/, **arisen** /ə'rɪzn/ **(a)** (originate) entstehen
(b) (present itself) auftreten; ‹*Gelegenheit:*› sich bieten
(c) (result) **~ from** *or* **out of sth.** von etw. herrühren

aristocracy /ærɪ'stɒkrəsɪ/ *n.* Aristokratie, *die*

aristocrat /'ærɪstəkræt/ *n.* Aristokrat, *der*/ Aristokratin, *die*

aristocratic /ærɪstə'krætɪk/ *adj.* aristokratisch

arithmetic /ə'rɪθmətɪk/ *n.* Arithmetik, *die*

arm¹ /ɑ:m/ *n.* Arm, *der*

arm² [1] *n.* **(a)** *usu. in pl.* (weapon) Waffe, *die;* **up in ~s** (fig.) in Harnisch (**about** wegen)
(b) *in pl.* (heraldic device) Wappen, *das*
[2] *v.t.* bewaffnen

armada /ɑ:'mɑ:də/ *n.* Armada, *die*

arm: ~band *n.* Armbinde, *die;* **~chair** *n.* Sessel, *der;* **~chair politician/strategist** politischer Amateur/Amateurstratege, *der;* **~chair critic** Hobby- *od.* Amateurkritiker, *der;* **~chair travel** Reisen *Pl.* in der Fantasie

armed /ɑ:md/ *adj.* bewaffnet; **~ forces** Streitkräfte *Pl.*

armistice /'ɑ:mɪstɪs/ *n.* Waffenstillstand, *der*

armor (Amer.), **armour** (Brit.) /'ɑ:mə(r)/ *n.*
(a) (Hist.) Rüstung, *die*
(b) (steel plates) Panzerung, *die*

arm: ~pit *n.* Achselhöhle, *die;* **~rest** *n.* Armlehne, *die*

arms: ~ control *n.* Rüstungskontrolle, *die; attrib.* Rüstungskontroll-; **~ race** *n.* Rüstungswettlauf, *der;* **~ trade** *n.* Waffenhandel, *der*

army /'ɑ:mɪ/ *n.* Heer, *das;* **join the ~:** zum Militär gehen

aroma /ə'rəʊmə/ *n.* Duft, *der*

aromatherapy /ərəʊmə'θerəpɪ/ *n.* Aromatherapie, *die*

aromatic /ærə'mætɪk/ *adj.* aromatisch

arose ▶ ARISE

around /ə'raʊnd/ [1] *adv.* **(a)** (on every side) **[all] ~:** überall
(b) (round) herum
(c) (in various places) **ask/look ~:** herumfragen/sich umsehen
[2] *prep.* **(a)** um [... herum]
(b) (approximately) **~ 3 o'clock** gegen 3 Uhr; **sth. [costing] ~ £2** etw. für ungefähr 2 Pfund

arouse /ə'raʊz/ *v.t.* **(a)** (awake) [auf]wecken
(b) (excite) erregen; erwecken ‹*Interesse, Begeisterung*›; **~ suspicion** Verdacht erregen

arrange /ə'reɪndʒ/ [1] *v.t.* **(a)** (order) anordnen
(b) (settle, agree) ausmachen, vereinbaren ‹*Termin*›; planen ‹*Urlaub*›; **they ~d to meet the following day** sie verabredeten sich für den nächsten Tag
[2] *v.i.* (plan) sorgen (**for** für)

ar'rangement *n.* **(a)** (ordering, order) Anordnung, *die*
(b) (settling, agreement) Vereinbarung, *die*
(c) *in pl.* (plans) Vorkehrungen *Pl.*; **make ~s** Vorkehrungen treffen

arrears /ə'rɪəz/ *n. pl.* Schulden *Pl.;* **be in ~ with sth.** mit etw. im Rückstand sein; **be paid in ~:** rückwirkend bezahlt werden

arrest /ə'rest/ [1] *v.t.* **(a)** verhaften, (temporarily) festnehmen ‹*Person*›
(b) (stop) aufhalten
[2] *n.* Verhaftung, *die;* **under ~:** festgenommen

arrival /ə'raɪvl/ *n.* Ankunft, *die;* **new ~s** Neuankömmlinge

arrive /ə'raɪv/ *v.i.* **(a)** ankommen; **~ at a conclusion/an agreement** zu einem Schluss/ einer Einigung kommen
(b) ‹*Stunde, Tag, Augenblick:*› kommen

arrogance /'ærəgəns/ *n.* Arroganz, *die*

arrogant /'ærəgənt/ *adj.* arrogant

arrow /'ærəʊ/ *n.* Pfeil, *der*

arse /ɑ:s/ *n.* (coarse) Arsch, *der* (derb)

■ **arse a'bout, arse a'round** *v. i.* (Brit. coarse) herumalbern (ugs.); herumblödeln (ugs.)

'arsehole *n.* (coarse) Arschloch, *das* (derb)

arsenal /'ɑ:sənl/ *n.* Waffenlager, *das*

arsenic /'ɑ:sənɪk/ *n.* **(a)** Arsenik, *das*
(b) (element) Arsen, *das*

arson /'ɑ:sn/ *n.* Brandstiftung, *die;* **~ attack** Brandanschlag, *der*

arsonist /'ɑ:sənɪst/ *n.* Brandstifter, *der*/ Brandstifterin, *die*

art /ɑ:t/ *n.* **(a)** Kunst, *die;* **works of ~:** Kunstwerke *Pl.;* **~ college** *or* **school** Kunsthochschule, *die;* **~s and crafts** Kunsthandwerk, *das*
(b) *in pl.* (branch of study) Geisteswissenschaften *Pl.*

artery /'ɑ:tərɪ/ *n.* (Anat.) Schlagader, *die;* Arterie, *die* (bes. fachspr.)

artful /'ɑ:tfl/ *adj.* schlau

'art gallery *n.* Kunstgalerie, *die*

arthritic /ɑ:'θrɪtɪk/ *adj.* arthritisch

arthritis /ɑ:'θraɪtɪs/ *n.* Arthritis, *die* (fachspr.); Gelenkentzündung, *die*

artichoke /'ɑ:tɪtʃəʊk/ *n.* **[globe] ~:** Artischocke, *die*

article /'ɑ:tɪkl/ *n.* **(a)** (in magazine, newspaper; Ling.) Artikel, *der*
(b) **an ~ of furniture/clothing** ein Möbel-/ Kleidungsstück; **an ~ of value** ein Wertgegenstand

articulate /ɑːˈtɪkjʊlət/ *adj.* redegewandt; **be ~/not very ~:** sich gut/nicht sehr gut ausdrücken [können]

articulated /ɑːˈtɪkjʊleɪtɪd/ *adj.* **~ 'lorry** Sattelzug, *der*

artificial /ɑːtɪˈfɪʃl/ *adj.* **(a)** künstlich; Kunst-; (not real) unecht; **~ limb** Prothese, *die* **(b)** (affected) gekünstelt

artificial: ~ insemi'nation *n.* künstliche Befruchtung; (of animal) künstliche Besamung; **~ in'telligence** *n.* künstliche Intelligenz; **~ 'language** *n.* Kunstsprache, *die;* **~ respi'ration** *n.* künstliche Beatmung

artillery /ɑːˈtɪlərɪ/ *n.* Artillerie, *die*

artisan /ˈɑːtɪzn, ɑːtɪˈzæn/ *n.* [Kunst]handwerker, *der*

artist /ˈɑːtɪst/ *n.* Künstler, *der*/Künstlerin, *die*

artiste /ɑːˈtiːst/ *n.* Artist, *der*/Artistin, *die*

artistic /ɑːˈtɪstɪk/ *adj.* **(a)** (of art) Kunst-; künstlerisch **(b)** (naturally skilled in art) künstlerisch veranlagt

'artless *adj.* arglos

art nouveau /ɑː nuːˈvəʊ/ *n.* Jugendstil, *der*

'art room *n.* Zeichensaal, *der*

'arts centre *n.* Kunstzentrum, *das*

'art work *n.* Bildmaterial, *das*

as /əz, *stressed* æz/ **1** *adv., conj.* **(a) he is as tall as I am** er ist so groß wie ich; **as quickly as you can/as possible** so schnell du kannst/wie möglich **(b)** (though) **small as he was** obwohl er klein war **(c)** (however much) **try as he might/would, he could not concentrate** sosehr er sich auch bemühte, er konnte sich nicht konzentrieren **(d)** *expr. manner* wie; **as you may already have heard, ...:** wie Sie vielleicht schon gehört haben, ...; **as it were** sozusagen **(e)** *expr. time* als; während; **as we climbed the stairs** als wir die Treppe hinaufgingen; **as we were talking** während wir uns unterhielten **(f)** *expr. reason* da **2** *prep.* **(a)** (in the function of) als; **as an artist** als Künstler; **speaking as a mother ...:** als Mutter ... **(b)** (like) wie **(c) the same as ...:** der-/die-/dasselbe wie ...; **such as** wie zum Beispiel **3 as for ...:** was ... angeht *od.* betrifft; **as [it] is** wie die Dinge liegen; **the place is untidy enough as it is** es ist hier [so] schon unordentlich genug; **as of ...** (Amer.) von ... an; **as to** hinsichtlich (+ *Gen.*); **as yet** bis jetzt; noch

a.s.a.p. *abbr.* = **as soon as possible**

asbestos /æzˈbestɒs/ *n.* Asbest, *der*

asbestosis /æzbesˈtəʊsɪs/ *n.* (Med.) Asbestose, *die*

ASBO /ˈæzbəʊ/ *abbr.* (Brit.) = **antisocial behaviour order** Verfügung gegen antisoziales Verhalten

ascend /əˈsend/ **1** *v.i.* **(a)** (go up) hinaufsteigen; (climb up) hinaufklettern; (by vehicle) hinauffahren **(b)** (rise) aufsteigen; ‹*Hubschrauber:*› höhersteigen **(c)** (slope upwards) ‹*Hügel, Straße:*› ansteigen **2** *v.t.* **(a)** (go up) hinaufsteigen ‹*Treppe, Leiter, Berg*› **(b) ~ the throne** den Thron besteigen

Ascension Day /əˈsenʃn/ *n.* Himmelfahrtstag, *der*

ascent /əˈsent/ *n.* Aufstieg, *der*

ascertain /æsəˈteɪn/ *v.t.* feststellen; ermitteln ‹*Fakten, Daten*›

ascribe /əˈskraɪb/ *v.t.* zuschreiben (**to** *Dat.*)

ash¹ /æʃ/ *n.* (tree) Esche, *die*

ash² *n.* (from fire etc.) Asche, *die*

ashamed /əˈʃeɪmd/ *adj.* beschämt; **be ~:** sich schämen (**of** wegen)

ash: ~ bin *n.* Mülleimer, *der;* **~ blonde** **1** *adj.* aschblond; **2** *n.* Aschblonde, *der/die;* **~can** (Amer.) ▶ ~ BIN

ashen /ˈæʃn/ *adj.* aschfahl ‹*Gesicht*›

ashore /əˈʃɔː(r)/ *adv.* an Land

'ashtray *n.* Aschenbecher, *der*

Ash 'Wednesday *n.* Aschermittwoch, *der*

Asia /ˈeɪʃə/ *pr. n.* Asien (*das*)

Asian /ˈeɪʃən/ **1** *adj.* asiatisch **2** *n.* Asiat, *der*/Asiatin, *die*

aside /əˈsaɪd/ *adv.* beiseite; zur Seite

ask /ɑːsk/ **1** *v.t.* **(a)** fragen; **~ sb. [sth.]** jmdn. [nach etw.] fragen **(b)** (seek to obtain) **~ sth.** um etw. bitten; **how much are you ~ing for that car?** wie viel verlangen Sie für das Auto?; **~ sb. to do sth.** jmdn. [darum] bitten, etw. zu tun **(c)** (invite) einladen **2** *v.i.* **~ after sb./sth.** nach jmdm./etw. fragen; **~ for sth./sb.** etw./jmdn. verlangen

askance /əˈskæns, əˈskɑːns/ *adv.* **look ~ at sb.** jmdn. befremdet ansehen

askew /əˈskjuː/ *adv., pred. adj.* schief

asleep /əˈsliːp/ *pred. adj.* schlafend; **be/lie ~:** schlafen; **fall ~:** einschlafen

asparagus /əˈspærəgəs/ *n.* Spargel, *der*

aspect /ˈæspekt/ *n.* Aspekt, *der*

aspersion /əˈspɜːʃn/ *n.* **cast ~s on sb./sth.** jmdn./etw in den Schmutz ziehen

asphalt /ˈæsfælt/ *n.* Asphalt, *der*

asphyxiate /æsˈfɪksɪeɪt/ *v.t. & i.* ersticken

aspiration /æspəˈreɪʃn/ *n.* Streben, *das*

aspire /əˈspaɪə(r)/ *v.i.* **~ to** *or* **after sth.** nach etw. streben

aspirin /ˈæspərɪn/ *n.* Aspirin (Wz), *das;* Kopfschmerztablette, *die*

ass¹ /æs/ *n.* Esel, *der*

ass² (Amer.) ▶ ARSE

a

assailant /ə'seɪlənt/ *n.* Angreifer, *der*/Angreiferin, *die*
assassin /ə'sæsɪn/ *n.* Mörder, *der*/Mörderin, *die*
assassinate /ə'sæsɪneɪt/ *v.t.* ermorden; **be ~d** einem Attentat zum Opfer fallen
assassination /əsæsɪ'neɪʃn/ *n.* Mord, *der* (**of** an + *Dat.*); **~ attempt** Attentat, *das* (**on** auf + *Akk.*)
assault /ə'sɔ:lt/ **1** *n.* Angriff, *der;* (fig.) Anschlag, *der*
2 *v.t.* angreifen
assemble /ə'sembl/ **1** *v.t.* **(a)** zusammentragen; zusammenrufen ‹*Menschen*›
(b) (fit together) zusammenbauen
2 *v.i.* sich versammeln
assembly /ə'semblɪ/ *n.* **(a)** (meeting) Versammlung, *die;* (in school) Morgenandacht, *die*
(b) (fitting together) Zusammenbau, *der*
as'sembly line *n.* Fließband, *das*
assent /ə'sent/ **1** *v.i.* zustimmen (**to** *Dat.*)
2 *n.* Zustimmung, *die*
assert /ə'sɜ:t/ *v.t.* **(a)** geltend machen; **~ oneself** sich durchsetzen
(b) (declare) behaupten; beteuern ‹*Unschuld*›
assertion /ə'sɜ:ʃn/ *n.* **(a)** Geltendmachen, *das*
(b) (declaration) Behauptung, *die*
assertive /ə'sɜ:tɪv/ *adj.* energisch ‹*Person*›; bestimmt ‹*Ton, Verhalten*›
assertiveness /ə'sɜ:tɪvnɪs/ *n.* Bestimmtheit, *die*
assess /ə'ses/ *v.t.* einschätzen; festsetzen ‹*Steuer*› (**at** auf + *Akk.*)
as'sessment *n.* **(a)** Einschätzung, *die*
(b) (tax to be paid) Steuerbescheid, *der*
asset /'æset/ *n.* **(a)** Vermögenswert, *der*
(b) (useful quality) Vorzug, *der* (**to** für); (person) Stütze, *die;* (thing) Hilfe, *die*
'asset-stripping *n.: Ankauf unrentabler Unternehmen, von denen einzelne Teile Gewinn bringend weiterverkauft werden*
assiduous /ə'sɪdjʊəs/ *adj.* **(a)** (diligent) eifrig
(b) (conscientious) gewissenhaft
assign /ə'saɪn/ *v.t.* **(a)** (allot) zuweisen (**to** *Dat.*)
(b) (appoint) zuteilen; **~ sb. to do sth.** jmdn. damit betrauen, etw. zu tun
as'signment *n.* **(a)** (allotment) Zuweisung, *die;* (appointment) Zuteilung, *die*
(b) (task) Aufgabe, *die*
assimilate /ə'sɪmɪleɪt/ *v.t.* angleichen (**to, with** an + *Akk.*)
assimilation /əsɪmɪ'leɪʃn/ *n.* Angleichung, *die* (**to, with** an + *Akk.*)
assist /ə'sɪst/ **1** *v.t.* helfen (+ *Dat.*)
2 *v.i.* helfen; **~ with sth./in doing sth.** bei etw. helfen/helfen, etw. zu tun
assistance /ə'sɪstəns/ *n.* Hilfe, *die*
assistant /ə'sɪstənt/ *n.* (helper) Helfer, *der*/Helferin, *die;* (subordinate) Mitarbeiter, *der*/Mitarbeiterin, *die;* (of professor, artist) Assistent, *der*/Assistentin, *die;* (in shop) Verkäufer, *der*/Verkäuferin, *die;* **~ manager** stellvertretender Geschäftsführer
associate **1** /ə'səʊʃɪət, ə'səʊsɪət/ *n.* (partner) Partner, *der*/Partnerin, *die;* (colleague) Kollege, *der*/Kollegin, *die*
2 /ə'səʊʃɪeɪt, ə'səʊsɪeɪt/ *v.t.* in Verbindung bringen; **be ~d** in Verbindung stehen
3 /ə'səʊʃɪeɪt, ə'səʊsɪeɪt/ *v.i.* **~ with sb.** mit jmdm. Umgang haben
association /əsəʊsɪ'eɪʃn/ *n.* **(a)** (organization) Vereinigung, *die*
(b) (mental connection) Assoziation, *die*
(c) (connection) Verbindung, *die*
assorted /ə'sɔ:tɪd/ *adj.* gemischt
assortment /ə'sɔ:tmənt/ *n.* Sortiment, *das;* **a good ~ of hats [to choose from]** eine gute Auswahl an Hüten
Asst. *abbr.* = **Assistant** Ass.
assume /ə'sju:m/ *v.t.* **(a)** voraussetzen; **assuming that ...:** vorausgesetzt, dass ...
(b) (undertake) übernehmen ‹*Amt, Pflichten*›
(c) (take on) annehmen ‹*Namen, Rolle*›
assumption /ə'sʌmpʃn/ *n.* Annahme, *die;* **going on the ~ that ...:** vorausgesetzt, dass ...; **the A~** (Relig.) Mariä Himmelfahrt
assurance /ə'ʃʊərəns/ *n.* **(a)** Zusicherung, *die*
(b) (self-confidence) Selbstsicherheit, *die*
assure /ə'ʃʊə(r)/ *v.t.* **(a)** versichern (+ *Dat.*)
(b) (convince) **~ sb./oneself** jmdn./sich überzeugen
(c) (make certain or safe) gewährleisten
assured /ə'ʃʊəd/ *adj.* gewährleistet ‹*Erfolg*›; **be ~ of sth.** sich (*Dat.*) einer Sache (*Gen.*) sicher sein
asterisk /'æstərɪsk/ *n.* Sternchen, *das*
astern /ə'stɜ:n/ *adv.* (Naut., Aeronaut.) achtern; (towards the rear) achteraus
asteroid /'æstərɔɪd/ *n.* Asteroid, *der*
asthma /'æsmə/ *n.* Asthma, *das*
asthmatic /æs'mætɪk/ **1** *adj.* asthmatisch
2 *n.* Asthmatiker, *der*/Asthmatikerin, *die*
astonish /ə'stɒnɪʃ/ *v.t.* erstaunen
a'stonishing *adj.* erstaunlich
a'stonishment *n.* Erstaunen, *das*
astound /ə'staʊnd/ *v.t.* verblüffen
a'stounding *adj.* erstaunlich
astray /ə'streɪ/ *adv.* **sth. goes ~** (is mislaid) etw. wird verlegt; (is lost) etw. geht verloren; **go/lead ~** (fig.) in die Irre gehen/führen
astride /ə'straɪd/ **1** *adv.* rittlings ‹*sitzen*›
2 *prep.* rittlings auf (+ *Dat.*)
astringent /ə'strɪndʒənt/ **1** *adj.* scharf
2 *n.* Adstringens, *das*
astrologer /ə'strɒlədʒə(r)/ *n.* Astrologe, *der*/Astrologin, *die*
astrological /æstrə'lɒdʒɪkl/ *adj.* astrologisch
astrology /ə'strɒlədʒɪ/ *n.* Astrologie, *die*

a

astronaut /'æstrənɔ:t/ *n.* Astronaut, *der*/ Astronautin, *die*
astronautics /æstrə'nɔ:tɪks/ *n.* Astronautik, *die;* Raumfahrt, *die*
astronomer /ə'strɒnəmə(r)/ *n.* Astronom, *der*/Astronomin, *die*
astronomical /æstrə'nɒmɪkl/ *adj.* astronomisch
astronomy /ə'strɒnəmɪ/ *n.* Astronomie, *die*
astrophysics /æstrəʊ'fɪzɪks/ *n.* Astrophysik, *die*
astute /ə'stju:t/ *adj.* scharfsinnig
asylee /æsaɪ'lɪ:/ *n.* Asylant, *der*/Asylantin, *die*
asylum /ə'saɪləm/ *n.* **(a)** (Polit.) Asyl, *das;* **grant sb. ~:** jmdm. Asyl gewähren; **~ seeker** Asylsuchende, *der/die*
(b) ▶ LUNATIC ASYLUM
asymmetric /æsɪ'metrɪk, eɪsɪ'metrɪk/ *adj.* asymmetrisch; unsymmetrisch
at /ət, *stressed* æt/ *prep.* **(a)** *expr. place* an (+ *Dat.*); **at the station** am Bahnhof; **at the baker's/butcher's/grocer's** beim Bäcker/ Fleischer/Kaufmann; **at the chemist's** in der Apotheke/Drogerie; **at the supermarket** im Supermarkt; **at the party** auf der Party; **at the office/hotel** im Büro/Hotel; **at Dover** in Dover
(b) *expr. time* **at Christmas** [zu *od.* an] Weihnachten; **at six o'clock** um sechs Uhr; **at midnight** um Mitternacht; **at midday** am Mittag; **at [the age of] 40** mit 40; im Alter von 40; **at this/the moment** in diesem/im Augenblick *od.* Moment
(c) *expr. price* **at £2.50 [each]** zu *od.* für [je] 2,50 Pfund
(d) *expr. speed* **at 30 m.p.h.** *etc.* mit dreißig Meilen pro Stunde *usw.*
(e) at that (at that point) dabei; (at that provocation) daraufhin; (moreover) noch dazu
ate ▶ EAT
atheism /'eɪθɪɪzm/ *n.* Atheismus, *der*
atheist /'eɪθɪɪst/ *n.* Atheist, *der*/Atheistin, *die*
Athens /'æθɪnz/ *pr. n.* Athen *(das)*
athlete /'æθli:t/ *n.* Athlet, *der*/Athletin, *die;* (runner, jumper) Leichtathlet, *der*/-athletin, *die*
athletic /æθ'letɪk/ *adj.* sportlich
ath'letics *n.* Leichtathletik, *die*
Atlantic /ət'læntɪk/ **1** *adj.* atlantisch; **~ Ocean** Atlantischer Ozean
2 *pr. n.* Atlantik, *der*
atlas /'ætləs/ *n.* Atlas, *der*
ATM *abbr.* = **automated teller machine**
atmosphere /'ætməsfɪə(r)/ *n.* Atmosphäre, *die*
atmospheric /ætməs'ferɪk/ *adj.* **(a)** atmosphärisch
(b) (fig.: evocative) stimmungsvoll
atom /'ætəm/ *n.* Atom, *das*
'atom bomb *n.* Atombombe, *die*
atomic /ə'tɒmɪk/ *adj.* Atom-
atomizer /'ætəmaɪzə(r)/ *n.* Zerstäuber, *der*
atone /ə'təʊn/ *v.i.* es wieder gutmachen; **~ for sth.** etw. wieder gutmachen
a'tonement *n.* Buße, *die*
atrocious /ə'trəʊʃəs/ *adj.* grauenhaft; scheußlich ‹*Wetter, Benehmen*›
atrocity /ə'trɒsɪtɪ/ *n.* **(a)** (wickedness) Grauenhaftigkeit, *die*
(b) (deed) Gräueltat, *die*
'at sign *n.* At-Zeichen, *das;* Klammeraffe, *der* (ugs.)
attach /ə'tætʃ/ *v.t.* **(a)** (fasten) befestigen (**to** an + *Dat.*); **please find ~ed a copy of the letter** beigeheftet ist eine Kopie des Briefes
(b) (fig.) **~ importance to sth.** einer Sache (*Dat.*) Gewicht beimessen
attaché /ə'tæʃeɪ/ *n.* Attaché, *der*
at'taché case *n.* Diplomatenkoffer, *der*
attached /ə'tætʃt/ *adj.* (emotionally) **be ~ to sb./sth.** an jmdm./etw. hängen
at'tachment *n.* **(a)** (act or means of fastening) Befestigung, *die*
(b) (affection) Anhänglichkeit, *die* (**to** an + *Akk.*)
(c) (accessory) Zusatzgerät, *das*
(d) (Comp.) Attachment, *das;* Anlage, *die*
attack /ə'tæk/ **1** *v.t.* **(a)** angreifen; (ambush, raid) überfallen; (fig.: criticize) attackieren
(b) (affect) ‹*Krankheit:*› befallen
2 *v.i.* angreifen
3 *n.* Angriff, *der;* (ambush) Überfall, *der;* (fig.: criticism) Attacke, *die;* (of illness) Anfall, *der*
at'tacker *n.* Angreifer, *der*/Angreiferin, *die*
attacking /ə'tækɪŋ/ *adj.* offensiv ‹*Spielweise, Spieler*›; angreifend ‹*Truppen*›
attain /ə'teɪn/ *v.t.* erreichen
attainable /ə'teɪnəbl/ *adj.* erreichbar ‹*Ziel*›; realisierbar ‹*Hoffnung, Ziel*›
at'tainment *n.* Verwirklichung, *die*
attempt /ə'tempt/ **1** *v.t.* versuchen
2 *n.* Versuch, *der*
attend /ə'tend/ **1** *v.i.* **(a)** (give care and thought) aufpassen; (apply oneself) **~ to sth.** (deal with sth.) sich um etw. kümmern
(b) (be present) anwesend sein (**at** bei)
2 *v.t.* (be present at) teilnehmen an (+ *Dat.*); (go regularly to) besuchen
attendance /ə'tendəns/ *n.* Anwesenheit, *die;* (number of people) Teilnehmerzahl, *die*
attendant /ə'tendənt/ *n.* **(a) [lavatory] ~:** Toilettenmann, *der*/-frau, *die;* **[cloakroom] ~:** Garderobenmann, *der*/-frau, *die;* **museum ~:** Museumswärter, *der*/-wärterin, *die*
(b) (member of entourage) Begleiter, *der*/ Begleiterin, *die*
attention /ə'tenʃn/ **1** *n.* **(a)** Aufmerksamkeit, *die;* **attract [sb.'s] ~:** [jmdn.] auf sich (*Akk.*) aufmerksam machen; **pay ~ to sb./sth.** jmdn./etw. beachten; **pay** ···›

a

~! gib Acht!; pass auf!; **hold sb.'s ~:** jmds. Interesse wach halten; **~ Miss Jones** (on letter) zu Händen [von] Miss Jones
(b) (Mil.) **stand to ~:** stillstehen
2 *int.* **(a)** Achtung
(b) (Mil.) stillgestanden

attentive /ə'tentɪv/ *adj.* aufmerksam

attic /'ætɪk/ *n.* (room) Dachboden, *der;* (habitable) Dachkammer, *die*

attire /ə'taɪə(r)/ *n.* Kleidung, *die*

attitude /'ætɪtju:d/ *n.* **(a)** Haltung, *die*
(b) (mental ~) Einstellung, *die*

attn. *abbr.* = **for the attention of** z. H[d].

attorney /ə'tɜ:nɪ/ *n.* **(a)** Bevollmächtigte, *der/die;* **power of ~:** Vollmacht, *die*
(b) (Amer.: lawyer) [Rechts]anwalt, *der*/-anwältin, *die*

attract /ə'trækt/ *v.t.* **(a)** (draw) anziehen; auf sich (*Akk.*) ziehen ‹*Interesse, Blick, Kritik*›
(b) (arouse pleasure in) anziehend wirken auf (+ *Akk.*)
(c) (arouse interest in) reizen (**about** an + *Dat.*)

attraction /ə'trækʃn/ *n.* **(a)** Anziehung, *die;* (force, lit. or fig.) Anziehung[skraft], *die*
(b) (fig.: thing that attracts) Attraktion, *die;* (charm) Verlockung, *die;* Reiz, *der*

attractive /ə'træktɪv/ *adj.* **(a)** anziehend
(b) (fig.) attraktiv; reizvoll ‹*Vorschlag, Möglichkeit, Idee*›

attribute 1 /'ætrɪbju:t/ *n.* Eigenschaft, *die*
2 /ə'trɪbju:t/ *v.t.* zuschreiben (**to** *Dat.*)

attributive /ə'trɪbjʊtɪv/ *adj.* (Ling.) attributiv

atypical /eɪ'tɪpɪkl/ *adj.* atypisch; untypisch

aubergine /'əʊbəʒi:n/ *n.* Aubergine, *die*

auburn /'ɔ:bən/ *adj.* rötlich braun

auction /'ɔ:kʃn/ 1 *n.* Versteigerung, *die*
2 *v.t.* versteigern

auctioneer /ɔ:kʃə'nɪə(r)/ *n.* Auktionator, *der*/Auktionatorin, *die*

audacious /ɔ:'deɪʃəs/ *adj.* **(a)** (daring) kühn; verwegen
(b) (impudent) dreist

audacity /ɔ:'dæsɪtɪ/ *n.* **(a)** (daringness) Kühnheit, *die;* Verwegenheit, *die*
(b) (impudence) Dreistigkeit, *die*

audible /'ɔ:dɪbl/ *adj.* hörbar

audience /'ɔ:dɪəns/ *n.* **(a)** Publikum, *das*
(b) (formal interview) Audienz, *die* (**with** bei)

audio /'ɔ:dɪəʊ/ *adj.* Ton-; **~ frequency** Tonfrequenz, *die;* **~ equipment** Audioanlage, *die*

audio: ~book *n.* Hörbuch, *das;* **~ cassette** *n.* Audiokassette, *die;* Tonkassette, *die;* **~ typist** *n.* Phonotypist, *der*/-typistin, *die;* **~visual** *adj.* audiovisuell

audit /'ɔ:dɪt/ 1 *n.* **~ [of the accounts]** Rechnungsprüfung, *die*
2 *v.t.* prüfen

audition /ɔ:'dɪʃn/ 1 *n.* (singing) Vorsingen, *das;* (dancing) Vortanzen, *das;* (acting) Vorsprechen, *das*
2 *v.i.* (sing) vorsingen; (dance) vortanzen; (act) vorsprechen
3 *v.t.* vorsingen/vortanzen/vorsprechen lassen

auditor /'ɔ:dɪtə(r)/ *n.* Buchprüfer, *der*/-prüferin, *die*

auditorium /ɔ:dɪ'tɔ:rɪəm/ *n.* Zuschauerraum, *der*

Aug. *abbr.* = **August** Aug.

augment /ɔ:g'ment/ *v.t.* verbessern ‹*Einkommen*›; aufstocken ‹*Fonds*›

augur /'ɔ:gə(r)/ 1 *v.t.* bedeuten; versprechen ‹*Erfolg*›
2 *v.i.* **~ well/ill for sth./sb.** ein gutes/schlechtes Zeichen für etw./jmdn. sein

August /'ɔ:gəst/ *n.* August, *der;* **in ~:** im August; **last/next ~:** letzten/nächsten August; **the first of/on the first of ~:** der erste/am ersten August

aunt /ɑ:nt/ *n.* Tante, *die*

auntie, aunty /'ɑ:ntɪ/ *n.* (coll.) Täntchen, *das;* (with name) Tante, *die*

au pair /əʊ 'peə(r)/ *n.* Aupairmädchen, *das*

aura /'ɔ:rə/ *n.* Aura, *die*

auspices /'ɔ:spɪsɪs/ *n. pl.* **under the ~ of sb./sth.** unter jmds./einer Sache Schirmherrschaft

auspicious /ɔ:'spɪʃəs/ *adj.* günstig; viel versprechend ‹*Anfang*›

Aussie /'ɒzɪ/ (coll.) 1 *adj.* australisch
2 *n.* Australier, *der*/Australierin, *die*

austere /ɒ'stɪə(r)/ *adj.* **(a)** (strict, stern) streng
(b) (severely simple) karg

austerity /ɒ'sterɪtɪ/ *n.* **(a)** (strictness) Strenge, *die*
(b) (severe simplicity) Kargheit, *die*
(c) (lack of luxuries) wirtschaftliche Einschränkung

Australia /ɒ'streɪlɪə/ *pr. n.* Australien (*das*)

Australian /ɒ'streɪlɪən/ 1 *adj.* australisch; **sb. is ~:** jmd. ist Australier/Australierin
2 *n.* Australier, *der*/Australierin, *die*

Austria /'ɒstrɪə/ *pr. n.* Österreich (*das*)

Austrian /'ɒstrɪən/ 1 *adj.* österreichisch; **sb. is ~** jmd. ist Österreicher/Österreicherin
2 *n.* Österreicher, *der*/Österreicherin, *die*

authentic /ɔ:'θentɪk/ *adj.* authentisch

authenticate /ɔ:'θentɪkeɪt/ *v.t.* authentifizieren; **~ sth.** die Echtheit einer Sache (*Gen.*) bestätigen

authentication /ɔ:θentɪ'keɪʃn/ *n.* Bestätigung der Echtheit; (of information, report) Bestätigung, *die*

authenticity /ɔ:θen'tɪsɪtɪ/ *n.* Authentizität, *die*

author /'ɔ:θə(r)/ *n.* Autor, *der*/Autorin, *die;* (profession) Schriftsteller, *der*/Schriftstellerin, *die*

authoritarian /ɔ:θɒrɪ'teərɪən/ 1 *adj.* autoritär
2 *n.* autoritäre Person

authoritative /ɔːˈθɒrɪtətɪv/ *adj.* maßgebend; zuverlässig ‹*Bericht, Information*›
authority /ɔːˈθɒrɪtɪ/ *n.* **(a)** Autorität, *die;* **in ~:** verantwortlich
(b) the authorities die Behörde[n]
authorization /ɔːθəraɪˈzeɪʃn/ *n.* Genehmigung, *die*
authorize /ˈɔːθəraɪz/ *v.t.* **(a)** ermächtigen; bevollmächtigen
(b) (sanction) genehmigen
auto /ˈɔːtəʊ/ *n., pl.* **~s** (Amer. coll.) Auto, *das*
auto- /ɔːtəʊ/ *in comb.* auto-/Auto-
autobioˈgraphical *adj.* autobiographisch
autobiˈography *n.* Autobiographie, *die*
autocrat /ˈɔːtəkræt/ *n.* Autokrat, *der*/ Autokratin, *die*
autocratic /ɔːtəˈkrætɪk/ *adj.* autokratisch
ˈautocross *n.* Autocross, *das*
Autocue ® /ˈɔːtəʊkjuː/ *n.* Teleprompter (Wz), *der*
ˈautofocus *n.* (Photog.) Autofokus, *der*
autograph /ˈɔːtəgrɑːf/ **1** *n.* Autogramm, *das*
2 *v.t.* signieren
auto-imˈmune *adj.* (Med.) autoimmun; **~ response** Autoimmunantwort, *die*
automat /ˈɔːtəmæt/ *n.* (Amer.) **(a)** (slot machine) [Münz]automat, *der*
(b) (cafeteria) Automatenrestaurant, *das*
automate /ˈɔːtəmeɪt/ *v.t.* automatisieren
automated ˈteller machine *n.* Geldautomat, *der*
automatic /ɔːtəˈmætɪk/ **1** *adj.* automatisch; **~ gear system, ~ transmission** Automatikgetriebe, *das*
2 *n.* (weapon) automatische Waffe; (vehicle) Fahrzeug mit Automatikgetriebe
automatically /ɔːtəˈmætɪkəlɪ/ *adv.* automatisch
automation /ɔːtəˈmeɪʃn/ *n.* Automation, *die*
automaton /ɔːˈtɒmətən/ *n., pl.* **~s** *or* automata /ɔːˈtɒmətə/ Automat, *der*
automobile /ˈɔːtəməbiːl/ *n.* (Amer.) Auto, *das*
autonomous /ɔːˈtɒnəməs/ *adj.* autonom
autonomy /ɔːˈtɒnəmɪ/ *n.* Autonomie, *die*
ˈautopilot *n.* Autopilot, *der;* **[fly] on ~:** mit Autopilot [fliegen]
autopsy /ˈɔːtɒpsɪ/ *n.* Autopsie, *die*
auto: ~save (Comp.) **1** *n.* automatisches Speichern; **2** *v.t.* automatisch speichern; **~-suggestion** *n.* Autosuggestion, *die;* **~timer** *n.* [automatische] Schaltuhr
autumn /ˈɔːtəm/ *n.* Herbst, *der;* **in [the] ~:** im Herbst
autumnal /ɔːˈtʌmnl/ *adj.* herbstlich
auxiliary /ɔːgˈzɪljərɪ/ **1** *adj.* Hilfs-
2 *n.* **(a)** Hilfskraft, *die*
(b) (Ling.) Hilfsverb, *das*

avail /əˈveɪl/ **1** *n.* **be of no ~:** nichts nützen; **to no ~:** vergebens
2 *v. refl.* **~ oneself of sth.** von etw. Gebrauch machen
available /əˈveɪləbl/ *adj.* **(a)** (at one's disposal) verfügbar
(b) (obtainable) erhältlich; lieferbar ‹*Waren*›
avalanche /ˈævəlɑːnʃ/ *n.* Lawine, *die*
avarice /ˈævərɪs/ *n.* Geldgier, *die;* Habsucht, *die*
avaricious /ævəˈrɪʃəs/ *adj.* geldgierig; habsüchtig
avenge /əˈvendʒ/ *v.t.* rächen
avenue /ˈævənjuː/ *n.* Allee, *die;* (fig.) Weg, *der* (to zu)
average /ˈævərɪdʒ/ **1** *n.* Durchschnitt, *der;* **on ~:** im Durchschnitt; durchschnittlich
2 *adj.* durchschnittlich
3 *v.t.* **(a)** (find the ~ of) den Durchschnitt ermitteln von
(b) (amount on ~ to) durchschnittlich betragen
4 *v.i.* **~ out at** im Durchschnitt betragen
averse /əˈvɜːs/ *adj.* **be ~ to sth.** einer Sache (*Dat.*) abgeneigt sein
aversion /əˈvɜːʃn/ *n.* Abneigung, *die* (to gegen)
avert /əˈvɜːt/ *v.t.* abwenden; verhüten ‹*Unfall*›
aviary /ˈeɪvɪərɪ/ *n.* Vogelhaus, *das*
aviation /eɪvɪˈeɪʃn/ *n.* Luftfahrt, *die*
avid /ˈævɪd/ *adj.* (enthusiastic) begeistert; **be ~ for sth.** (eager, greedy) begierig auf etw. (*Akk.*) sein
avocado /ævəˈkɑːdəʊ/ *n., pl.* **~s: ~ [pear]** Avocado[birne], *die*
avoid /əˈvɔɪd/ *v.t.* **(a)** meiden ‹*Ort*›; **~ a cyclist** einem Radfahrer ausweichen; **~ the boss when he's in a temper** geh dem Chef aus dem Weg, wenn er schlechte Laune hat
(b) (refrain from, escape) vermeiden
avoidable /əˈvɔɪdəbl/ *adj.* vermeidbar
avoidance /əˈvɔɪdəns/ *n.* Vermeidung, *die*
await /əˈweɪt/ *v.t.* erwarten
awake /əˈweɪk/ **1** *v.i.,* **awoke** /əˈwəʊk/, **awoken** /əˈwəʊkn/ erwachen
2 *v.t.,* **awoke, awoken** wecken
3 *pred. adj.* wach; **wide ~:** hellwach
awaken /əˈweɪkn/ *v.t. & i.* (esp. fig.) ▶ AWAKE 1, 2
award /əˈwɔːd/ **1** *v.t.* verleihen ‹*Preis, Auszeichnung*›; zusprechen ‹*Sorgerecht, Entschädigung*›; gewähren ‹*Zahlung, Gehaltserhöhung*›
2 *n.* (prize) Auszeichnung, *die*
aˈward-winning *adj.* preisgekrönt
aware /əˈweə(r)/ *adj.* **be ~ of sth.** sich (*Dat.*) einer Sache (*Gen.*) bewusst sein; **be ~ that ...:** sich (*Dat.*) [dessen] bewusst sein, dass ...
aˈwareness *n.* Bewusstsein, *das*

awash /əˈwɒʃ/ *adj.* **be ~** (flooded) unter Wasser stehen

away /əˈweɪ/ [1] *adv.* **(a)** (at a distance) entfernt; **play ~** (Sport) auswärts spielen
(b) (to a distance) weg; fort
(c) (absent) nicht da
[2] *adj.* (Sport) auswärts *präd.;* Auswärts-; **~ match** Auswärtsspiel, *das;* **~ team** Gastmannschaft, *die*

awe /ɔː/ *n.* Ehrfurcht, *die* (**of** vor + *Dat.*)

ˈawe-inspiring *adj.* Ehrfurcht gebietend; beeindruckend

awesome /ˈɔːsəm/ *adj.* überwältigend; eindrucksvoll ‹*Schweigen*›; übergroß ‹*Verantwortung*›

awe: ~stricken, ~struck *adj.* [von Ehrfurcht] ergriffen; ehrfurchtsvoll ‹*Ausdruck, Staunen*›

awful /ˈɔːfl/ *adj.*, **ˈawfully** *adv.* furchtbar

awkward /ˈɔːkwəd/ *adj.* **(a)** (difficult to use) ungünstig; **be ~ to use** unhandlich sein
(b) (clumsy) unbeholfen
(c) (embarrassing) peinlich
(d) (difficult) schwierig; ungünstig ‹*Zeitpunkt*›

awning /ˈɔːnɪŋ/ *n.* (on house) Markise, *die;* (of tent) Vordach, *das*

awoke, awoken ▶ AWAKE

awry /əˈraɪ/ *adv.* schief; **go ~** (fig.) schief gehen (ugs.); ‹*Plan:*› fehlschlagen

axe (*Amer.:* **ax**) /æks/ *n.* Axt, *die;* Beil, *das*

axis /ˈæksɪs/ *n., pl.* **axes** /ˈæksiːz/ Achse, *die*

axle /ˈæksl/ *n.* Achse, *die*

Bb

B, b /biː/ *n.* B, b, *das;* **B road** Straße 2. Ordnung; ≈ Landstraße, *die*

BA *abbr.* = **Bachelor of Arts**

babble /ˈbæbl/ *v.i.* **(a)** (talk incoherently) stammeln
(b) (talk foolishly) [dumm] schwatzen
(c) ‹*Bach:*› plätschern

baboon /bəˈbuːn/ *n.* Pavian, *der*

baby /ˈbeɪbɪ/ *n.* **(a)** Baby, *das;* **have a ~/be going to have a ~:** ein Kind bekommen; **throw out** *or* **away the ~ with the bathwater** (fig.) das Kind mit dem Bade ausschütten
(b) (childish person) **be a ~:** sich wie ein kleines Kind benehmen

baby: ~ boom *n.* Babyboom, *der;* **~-bouncer** *n.: federnd aufgehängter Sitz für Kleinkinder, in dem sie durch Wippen ihre Beine kräftigen sollen;* **~ buggy, ~ carriage** *ns.* (Amer.) Kinderwagen, *der;* **~ clothes** *n. pl.* Babykleidung, *die;* **~ food** *n.* Babynahrung, *die*

ˈbabyish *adj.* kindlich ‹*Aussehen*›; kindisch ‹*Benehmen, Person*›

baby: ~-minder *n.* Tagesmutter, *die;* **~sit** *v.i., forms as* SIT 1: babysitten (ugs.); auf das Kind/die Kinder aufpassen; **~sitter** *n.* Babysitter, *der*/Babysitterin, *die;* **~sitting** *n.* Babysitting, *das;* **~-snatcher** *n.* Kindesentführer, *der* /-entführerin, *die;* **~-talk** *n.* Babysprache, *die;* **~ walker** *n.* Laufstuhl, *der;* **~ wipe** *n.* feuchtes Baby[pflege]tuch

bachelor /ˈbætʃələ(r)/ *n.* **(a)** Junggeselle, *der*
(b) (Univ.) **B~ of Arts/Science** Bakkalaureus der philosophischen Fakultät/der Naturwissenschaften

back /bæk/ [1] *n.* **(a)** (of person, animal) Rücken, *der;* (of house, cheque) Rückseite, *die;* (of vehicle) Heck, *das;* (inside car) Rücksitz, *der;* **stand ~ to ~:** Rücken an Rücken stehen; **~ to front** verkehrt rum; **turn one's ~ on sb.** jmdm. den Rücken zuwenden; (fig.) jmdn. im Stich lassen; **turn one's ~ on sth.** (fig.) sich um etw. nicht kümmern; **get** *or* **put sb.'s ~ up** (fig.) jmdn. wütend machen; **be glad to see the ~ of sb./sth.** (fig.) froh sein, jmdn./etw. nicht mehr sehen zu müssen; **have one's ~ to the wall** (fig.) mit dem Rücken zur Wand stehen; **put one's ~ into sth.** (fig.) sich für etw. mit allen Kräften einsetzen; **with the ~ of one's hand** mit dem Handrücken; **at the ~ [of the book]** hinten [im Buch]
(b) (Sport: player) Verteidiger, *der*
[2] *adj.* hinter...
[3] *adv.* zurück; **two miles ~:** vor zwei Meilen; **~ and forth** hin und her; **there and ~:** hin und zurück; **a week/month ~:** vor einer Woche/vor einem Monat
[4] *v.t.* **(a)** (assist) unterstützen
(b) (bet on) wetten *od.* setzen auf (+ *Akk.*)
(c) zurücksetzen [mit] ‹*Fahrzeug*›
[5] *v.i.* zurücksetzen; **~ into/out of sth.** rückwärts in etw. (*Akk.*)/aus etw. fahren; **~ on to sth.** hinten an etw. (*Akk.*) grenzen

▪ **back ˈdown** *v.i.* nachgeben

▪ **back ˈout** *v.i.* rückwärts herausfahren; **~ out of sth.** (fig.) von etw. zurücktreten

▪ **back ˈup** *v.t.* **(a)** unterstützen; untermauern ‹*Anspruch, These*›

(b) (Comp.) sichern ‹*Daten, Dokumente*›; **~ up a file on to a floppy disk** von einer Datei eine Sicherungskopie auf Diskette machen

back: ~ache *n.* Rückenschmerzen *Pl.;* **~-bencher** /bæk'bentʃə(r)/ *n.* (Brit. Parl.) [einfacher] Abgeordneter/[einfache] Abgeordnete; **~bone** *n.* Rückgrat, *das;* **~chat** *n.* (coll.) [freche] Widerrede; **~date** *v.t.* zurückdatieren (**to** auf + *Akk.*); **~ 'door** *n.* Hintertür, *die*

'backer *n.* Geldgeber, *der*

back: ~'fire *v.i.* knallen; (fig.) fehlschlagen; **it ~fired on me/him** *etc.* der Schuss ging nach hinten los (ugs.); **~gammon** /'bækgæmən/ *n.* (game) Backgammon, *das;* ≈ Tricktrack, *das;* ≈ Puff, *das;* **~ground** *n.* Hintergrund, *der;* (social status) Herkunft, *die;* **~hand** (Tennis etc.) [1] *adj.* Rückhand-; [2] *n.* Rückhand, *die;* **~'handed** *adj.* **(a)** (Tennis etc.) Rückhand-; **(b)** (fig.) indirekt; zweifelhaft ‹*Kompliment*›; **~'hander** *n.* (coll.: bribe) Schmiergeld, *das*

'backing *n.* (support) Unterstützung, *die*

back: ~ issue ▶ ~ NUMBER; **~lash** *n.* (fig.) Gegenreaktion, *die;* **~log** *n.* Rückstand, *der;* **~ number** *n.* (of periodical, magazine) alte Nummer; **~pack** [1] *n.* Rucksack, *der;* [2] *v.i.* mit dem Rucksack [ver]reisen; **~packer** *n.* Rucksackreisende, *der/die;* Rucksacktourist, *der*/-touristin, *die;* (hiker) Wanderer, *der*/ Wanderin, *die* mit Rucksack; **~packing** *n.* das [Ver]reisen mit dem Rucksack; (hiking) das Wandern mit dem Rucksack; *attrib.* ‹*Reise usw.*› mit dem Rucksack; **~ pay** *n.* ausstehender Lohn/ausstehendes Gehalt; **he was reinstated with ~ pay** er wurde wieder eingestellt und erhielt eine Lohn-/ Gehaltsnachzahlung; **she was awarded £7,850 in ~ pay** sie erhielt eine Nachzahlung von 7 850 Pfund; **~-'pedal** *v.i.* **(a)** die Pedale rückwärts treten; **(b)** (fig.) einen Rückzieher machen (ugs.); **~scratching** *n.* (fig. coll.) **[mutual] ~scratching** Klüngelei, *die* (abwertend); **~ 'seat** *n.* Rücksitz, *der;* **~side** *n.* Hinterteil, *das* (ugs.); **~space** *v.i.* die Rücktaste betätigen; **~'stage** *adv.* **go ~stage** hinter die Bühne gehen; **~ street** *n.* kleine Seitenstraße; **~stroke** *n.* Rückenschwimmen, *das;* **~track** *v.i.* wieder zurückgehen; (fig.) eine Kehrtwendung machen; **~-up** *n.* (support) Unterstützung, *die;* **~-up [copy]** (Comp.) Sicherungskopie, *die*

backward /'bækwəd/ [1] *adj.* **(a)** rückwärts gerichtet; Rückwärts-
(b) (reluctant, shy) zurückhaltend
(c) (underdeveloped) rückständig ‹*Land, Region*›
[2] *adv.* ▶ BACKWARDS

backwards /'bækwədz/ *adv.* **(a)** nach hinten; **the child fell [over] ~ into the water** das Kind fiel rückwärts ins Wasser; **bend** *or* **lean over ~ to do sth.** (fig. coll.) sich zerreißen, um etw. zu tun (ugs.)
(b) (oppositely to normal direction) rückwärts; **~ and forwards** hin und her

back: ~water *n.* (fig.) Kaff, *das* (ugs.); **~ 'yard** *n.* Hinterhof, *der*

bacon /'beɪkn/ *n.* [Frühstücks]speck, *der*

bacterial /bæk'tɪərɪəl/ *adj.* bakteriell

bacterium /bæk'tɪərɪəm/ *n., pl.* **bacteria** /bæk'tɪərɪə/ Bakterie, *die*

bad /bæd/ *adj.,* **worse** /wɜːs/, **worst** /wɜːst/
(a) schlecht; (rotten) schlecht, verdorben ‹*Fleisch, Fisch, Essen*›; faul ‹*Ei, Apfel*›; **not ~** (coll.) nicht schlecht; nicht übel
(b) (naughty) ungezogen, böse ‹*Kind, Hund*›
(c) (offensive) **[use] ~ language** Kraftausdrücke [benutzen]
(d) (regretful) **feel ~ about sth.** etw. bedauern; **I feel ~ about him** ich habe seinetwegen ein schlechtes Gewissen
(e) (serious) schlimm ‹*Sturz, Krise*›; schwer ‹*Fehler, Krankheit, Unfall*›
(f) (Commerc.) **a ~ debt** eine uneinbringliche Schuld

bade ▶ BID 1B

badge /bædʒ/ *n.* Abzeichen, *das*

badger /'bædʒə(r)/ *n.* Dachs, *der*

'badly *adv.,* **worse** /wɜːs/, **worst** /wɜːst/ **(a)** schlecht
(b) schwer ‹*verletzt, beschädigt*›
(c) (urgently) dringend

bad-mannered /bæd'mænəd/ *adj.* **be ~:** schlechte Manieren haben

badminton /'bædmɪntən/ *n.* Federball, *der;* (als Sport) Badminton, *das*

bad-tempered /bæd'tempəd/ *adj.* griesgrämig

baffle /'bæfl/ *v.t.* **~ sb.** jmdm. unverständlich sein

baffling /'bæflɪŋ/ *adj.* rätselhaft

bag /bæg/ [1] *n.* Tasche, *die;* (sack) Sack, *der;* (hand~) Handtasche, *die;* (plastic ~) Beutel, *der;* (small paper ~) Tüte, *die;* **~s of** (coll.: large amount) jede Menge
[2] *v.t.,* **-gg-: (a)** in Säcke/Beutel/Tüten füllen
(b) (claim possession of) sich (*Dat.*) schnappen (ugs.)

baggage /'bægɪdʒ/ *n.* Gepäck, *das*

baggage: ~ allowance *n.* Freigepäck, *das;* **be over/within one's ~ allowance** Übergepäck/kein Übergepäck haben; **~ handler** *n.* Gepäckverlader, *der*/ -verladerin, *die;* **~ handling** *n.* Gepäckverladung, *die;* **~ reclaim** *n.* Gepäckausgabe, *die*

baggy /'bægɪ/ *adj.* weit [geschnitten] ‹*Kleid, Hose*›; (through long use) ausgebeult ‹*Hose*›

'bagpipe[s] *n.* [*pl.*] Dudelsack, *der*

baguette /bæ'get/ *n.* Baguette, *die;* [französisches] Stangenweißbrot

b

Bahamas /bəˈhɑːməz/ *pr. n. pl.* **the ~:** die Bahamas *Pl.*

bail¹ /beɪl/ 1 *n.* Kaution, *die;* **be [out] on ~:** gegen Kaution auf freiem Fuß sein
2 *v.t.* **~ sb. out** jmdn. gegen Kaution freibekommen; (fig.) jmdm. aus der Klemme helfen (ugs.)

bail² *v.t.* (scoop) **~ [out]** ausschöpfen
■ **ˈbail out** *v.i.* ‹*Pilot:*› abspringen

bailiff /ˈbeɪlɪf/ *n.* ≈ Gerichtsvollzieher, *der*

bait /beɪt/ 1 *v.t.* mit einem Köder versehen
2 *n.* Köder, *der*

bake /beɪk/ *v.t. & i.* backen; **~d beans** gebackene Bohnen [in Tomatensoße]; **~d potato** [in der Schale] gebackene Kartoffel

ˈbaker *n.* Bäcker, *der*

bakery /ˈbeɪkərɪ/ *n.* Bäckerei, *die*

baking: ~ powder *n.* Backpulver, *das;* **~ sheet** *n.* Backblech, *das;* **~ soda** *n.* Natron, *das;* **~ tin** *n.* Backform, *die;* **~ tray** *n.* Kuchenblech, *das*

balance /ˈbæləns/ 1 *n.* **(a)** (instrument) Waage, *die*
(b) (fig.) **be** *or* **hang in the ~:** in der Schwebe sein
(c) (steady position) Gleichgewicht, *das;* **keep/lose one's ~:** das Gleichgewicht halten/verlieren; (fig.) sein Gleichgewicht bewahren/verlieren; **strike a ~ between** (fig.) den Mittelweg finden zwischen (+ *Dat.*)
(d) (Bookk.: difference) Bilanz, *die;* (state of bank account) Kontostand, *der;* **on ~** (fig.) alles in allem; **~ sheet** Bilanz, *die*
(e) (Econ.) **~ of payments** Zahlungsbilanz, *die;* **~ of trade** Handelsbilanz, *die*
(f) (remainder) Rest, *der*
2 *v.t.* **(a)** (weigh up) abwägen
(b) (bring into or keep in ~) balancieren; auswuchten ‹*Rad*›
(c) (equal, neutralize) ausgleichen; **~ each other, be ~d** sich (*Dat.*) die Waage halten

ˈbalanced *adj.* ausgewogen; ausgeglichen ‹*Person, Team, Gemüt*›

balcony /ˈbælkənɪ/ *n.* Balkon, *der*

bald /bɔːld/ *adj.* kahl ‹*Kopf*›; kahlköpfig, glatzköpfig ‹*Person*›; **be/go ~:** eine Glatze haben/bekommen

bald: ~head *n.* kahlköpfiger *od.* glatzköpfiger Mensch; Kahlkopf, *der* (ugs.); Glatzkopf, *der* (ugs.); **~-ˈheaded** *adj.* glatzköpfig; kahlköpfig

ˈbalding *adj.* mit beginnender Glatze *nachgestellt;* **be ~:** kahl werden

ˈbaldness *n.* Kahlheit, *die*

bale /beɪl/ *n.* Ballen, *der*

balk /bɔːlk/ 1 *v.t.* **they were ~ed in their plan** ihr Plan wurde blockiert
2 *v.i.* sich sträuben (**at** gegen)

Balkan /ˈbɔːlkn/ 1 *adj.* Balkan-
2 *n. pl.* **the ~s** der Balkan

ball¹ /bɔːl/ *n.* **(a)** Ball, *der;* (Billiards etc., Croquet) Kugel, *die;* **be on the ~** (coll.: be alert) auf Zack sein (ugs.)
(b) (of wool, string, fluff, etc.) Knäuel, *das*

ball² *n.* (dance) Ball, *der*

ballad /ˈbæləd/ *n.* Ballade, *die*

ballast /ˈbæləst/ *n.* Ballast, *der*

ball: ~ ˈbearing *n.* Kugellager, *das;* **~boy** *n.* Balljunge, *der;* **~cock** *n.* Schwimmer[regel]ventil, *das*

ballerina /bæləˈriːnə/ *n.* Ballerina, *die*

ballet /ˈbæleɪ/ *n.* Ballett, *das;* **~ dancer** Balletttänzer, *der*/-tänzerin, *die*

ˈball game *n.* **(a)** Ballspiel, *das*
(b) (Amer.) Baseballspiel, *das;* **a whole new ~** (fig. coll.) eine ganz neue Geschichte (ugs.); **a different ~** (fig. coll.) eine andere Sache

ballistic /bəˈlɪstɪk/ *adj.* ballistisch; **go ~** (fig. coll.) ausrasten (salopp)

balloon /bəˈluːn/ *n.* **(a)** Ballon, *der;* **hot-air ~:** Heißluftballon, *der*
(b) (toy) Luftballon, *der*

ballot /ˈbælət/ *n.* Abstimmung, *die;* **[secret] ~:** geheime Wahl

ballot: ~ box *n.* Wahlurne, *die;* **~ paper** *n.* Stimmzettel, *der*

ball: ~park *n.* (Amer.) Baseballfeld, *das;* **your estimate is not in the right ~park** (fig.) mit deiner Schätzung liegst du völlig falsch (ugs.); **~ pen, ~point ˈpen** *ns.* Kugelschreiber, *der;* **~room** *n.* Tanzsaal, *der*

balls-up /ˈbɔːlzʌp/ *n.* (coarse) Scheiß, *der* (salopp abwertend); **make a ~ of sth.** bei etw. Scheiße bauen (derb)

balm /bɑːm/ *n.* Balsam, *der*

balmy /ˈbɑːmɪ/ *adj.* (mild) mild

balsa /ˈbɔːlsə, ˈbɒlsə/ *n.* **~ [wood]** Balsaholz, *das*

Baltic /ˈbɔːltɪk/ 1 *pr. n.* Ostsee, *die*
2 *adj.* **~ Sea** Ostsee, *die*

balustrade /bæləˈstreɪd/ *n.* Balustrade, *die*

bamboo /bæmˈbuː/ *n.* Bambus, *der*

ban /bæn/ 1 *v.t.*, **-nn-** verbieten; **~ sb. from doing sth.** jmdm. verbieten, etw. zu tun
2 *n.* Verbot, *das*

banal /bəˈnɑːl/ *adj.* banal

banality /bəˈnælɪtɪ/ *n.* Banalität, *die*

banana /bəˈnɑːnə/ *n.* Banane, *die*

baˈnana skin *n.* Bananenschale, *die*

band /bænd/ 1 *n.* **(a)** Band, *das;* **a ~ of light/colour** ein Streifen Licht/Farbe
(b) (range of values) Bandbreite, *die*
(c) (organized group) Gruppe, *die;* (of robbers, outlaws, etc.) Bande, *die*
(d) (Mus.) [Musik]kapelle, *die;* (pop group, jazz ~) Band, *die*
2 *v.i.* **~ together [with sb.]** sich [mit jmdm.] zusammenschließen

bandage /ˈbændɪdʒ/ 1 *n.* Verband, *der;* (as support) Bandage, *die*
2 *v.t.* verbinden; bandagieren ‹[*verstauchtes*] *Gelenk usw.*›

b. & b. /biː ən ˈbiː/ *abbr.* = **bed & breakfast**

bandit /'bændɪt/ *n.* Bandit, *der*
band: ~**stand** *n.* Musiktribüne, *die;* ~**wagon** *n.* **climb** *or* **jump on [to] the ~wagon** (fig.) auf den fahrenden Zug aufspringen (fig.)
bandy[1] /'bændɪ/ *v.t.* **they were ~ing words/insults** sie stritten sich/beschimpften sich gegenseitig
bandy[2] *adj.* krumm; **he is ~-legged** er hat O-Beine (ugs.)
bang /bæŋ/ [1] *v.t.* knallen (ugs.); schlagen; zuknallen (ugs.) ‹*Tür, Fenster, Deckel*›; ~ **one's head on sth.** mit dem Kopf an etw. (*Akk.*) knallen (ugs.)
[2] *v.i.* (strike) ~ **[against sth.]** [gegen etw.] knallen (ugs.); ~ **shut** ‹*Tür:*› zuknallen (ugs.)
[3] *n.* **(a)** (blow) Schlag, *der*
(b) (noise) Knall, *der*
[4] *adv.* **go ~** ‹*Gewehr, Feuerwerkskörper:*› krachen
'**banger** *n.* (coll.) **(a)** (sausage) Würstchen, *das*
(b) (firework) Kracher, *der* (ugs.)
(c) (car) Klapperkiste, *die* (ugs.)
bangle /'bæŋgl/ *n.* Armreif, *der*
banish /'bænɪʃ/ *v.t.* verbannen (**from** aus)
banister /'bænɪstə(r)/ *n.* [Treppen]geländer, *das*
banjo /'bændʒəʊ/ *n., pl.* ~**s** *or* ~**es** Banjo, *das*
bank[1] /bæŋk/ *n.* **(a)** (slope) Böschung, *die*
(b) (of river) Ufer, *das*
bank[2] [1] *n.* (Finance) Bank, *die*
[2] *v.i.* ~ **at/with ...:** ein Konto haben bei ...; ~ **on sth.** (fig.) auf etw. (*Akk.*) zählen
[3] *v.t.* zur Bank bringen
bank: ~ **account** *n.* Bankkonto, *das;* ~ **balance** *n.* Kontostand, *der;* ~ **book** *n.* Sparbuch, *das;* ~ **card** *n.* Scheckkarte, *die;* ~ **charges** *n. pl.* Kontoführungskosten *Pl.*; ~ **clerk** *n.* Bankangestellte, *der/die;* ~ **draft** *n.* Bankakzept, *das*
'**banker** *n.* Bankier, *der*
banker's: ~ **card** ▸ BANK CARD; ~ **draft** ▸ BANK DRAFT; ~ '**order** *n.* Bankanweisung, *die*
bank 'holiday *n.* (Brit.) Feiertag, *der*
'**banking** *n.* Bankwesen, *das*
bank: ~ **loan** *n.* Bankdarlehen, *das;* **take out a ~ loan** bei einer Bank einen Kredit *od.* ein Darlehen aufnehmen; ~ **manager** *n.* Zweigstellenleiter/-leiterin [einer/der Bank]; ~**note** *n.* Banknote, *die*
bankrupt /'bæŋkrʌpt/ [1] *n.* Bankrotteur, *der*
[2] *adj.* **go ~:** Bankrott machen
[3] *v.t.* Bankrott machen
bankruptcy /'bæŋkrʌptsɪ/ *n.* Konkurs, *der;* Bankrott, *der*
'**bank statement** *n.* Kontoauszug, *der*
banner /'bænə(r)/ *n.* Banner, *das;* (on two poles) Spruchband, *das*
banns /bænz/ *n. pl.* Aufgebot, *das*
banquet /'bæŋkwɪt/ *n.* Bankett, *das*
bap /bæp/ *n.* ≈ Brötchen, *das*
baptism /'bæptɪzm/ *n.* Taufe, *die*
Baptist /'bæptɪst/ *n.* Baptist, *der*/Baptistin, *die*
baptize /bæp'taɪz/ *v.t.* taufen
bar /bɑː(r)/ [1] *n.* **(a)** Stange, *die;* (shorter, thinner also) Stab, *der;* (of cage, prison) Gitterstab, *der;* **a ~ of soap** ein Stück Seife; **a ~ of chocolate** eine Tafel Schokolade
(b) (for refreshment) Bar, *die;* (counter) Theke, *die*
[2] *v.t.*, **-rr-: (a)** (fasten) verriegeln
(b) ~ **sb.'s way** jmdm. den Weg versperren
(c) (prohibit, hinder) verbieten; ~ **sb. from doing sth.** jmdn. daran hindern, etw. zu tun
[3] *prep.* abgesehen von; ~ **none** ohne Einschränkung
barb /bɑːb/ *n.* Widerhaken, *der*
barbarian /bɑː'beərɪən/ *n.* Barbar, *der*
barbaric /bɑː'bærɪk/ *adj.* barbarisch
barbarity /bɑː'bærɪtɪ/ *n.* Grausamkeit, *die*
barbecue /'bɑːbɪkjuː/ [1] *n.* **(a)** (party) Grillparty, *die*
(b) (food) Grillgericht, *das;* ~ **sauce** Grillsoße, *die;* Barbecuesoße, *die*
[2] *v.t.* grillen
barbed wire /bɑːbd 'waɪə(r)/ *n.* Stacheldraht, *der*
barber /'bɑːbə(r)/ *n.* [Herren]friseur, *der;* ~**'s shop** (Brit.) Friseursalon, *der*
barbiturate /bɑː'bɪtjʊrət/ *n.* (Chem.) Barbiturat, *das*
bar: ~ **chart** *n.* Stabdiagramm, *das;* ~ **code** *n.* Strichcode, *der*
bare /beə(r)/ [1] *adj.* nackt; (leafless, unfurnished) kahl; (empty) leer; äußerst ‹*Notwendige*›; **do sth. with one's ~ hands** etw. mit den bloßen Händen tun
[2] *v.t.* entblößen ‹*Kopf, Arm, Bein*›; blecken ‹*Zähne*›
bare: ~**faced** /'beəfeɪst/ *adj.* (fig.) unverhüllt; ~**foot** [1] *adj.* barfüßig; [2] *adv.* barfuß
barely /'beəlɪ/ *adv.* kaum; knapp ‹*vermeiden, entkommen*›
bargain /'bɑːgɪn/ [1] *n.* **(a)** (agreement) Abmachung, *die;* **into the ~:** darüber hinaus
(b) (thing offered cheap) günstiges Angebot; (thing acquired cheaply) guter Kauf
[2] *v.i.* **(a)** (discuss) handeln
(b) ~ **for** *or* **on sth.** (expect sth.) mit etw. rechnen
bargain: ~ '**basement** *n.* Untergeschoss mit Sonderangeboten; ~ **hunter** *n.* Schnäppchenjäger, *der*/-jägerin, *die;* ~ **price** *n.* Sonderpreis, *der*
barge /bɑːdʒ/ [1] *n.* Kahn, *der*
[2] *v.i.* ~ **into sb.** jmdn. anrempeln; ~ **in** (intrude) hineinplatzen/hereinplatzen (ugs.)
baritone /'bærɪtəʊn/ [1] *n.* Bariton, *der*
[2] *adj.* Bariton-

bark¹ /bɑ:k/ *n.* (of tree) Rinde, *die*
bark² 1 *n.* (of dog) Bellen, *das*
2 *v.i.* bellen; **be ~ing up the wrong tree** auf dem Holzweg sein
barley /'bɑ:lɪ/ *n.* Gerste, *die*
bar: ~maid *n.* (Brit.) Bardame, *die;* **~man** /'bɑ:mən/ *n., pl.* **~men** /'bɑ:mən/ Barmann, *der*
barmy /'bɑ:mɪ/ *adj.* (coll.: crazy) bescheuert (salopp)
barn /bɑ:n/ *n.* (Brit.: for grain etc.) Scheune, *die;* (Amer.: for animals) Stall, *der*
barnacle /'bɑ:nəkl/ *n.* Rankenfüßer, *der*
barn: ~ dance *n.* ≈ Schottische, *der;* **~storming** /'bɑ:nstɔ:mɪŋ/ *adj.* mitreißend
barometer /bə'rɒmɪtə(r)/ *n.* Barometer, *das*
baron /'bærn/ *n.* Baron, *der;* Freiherr, *der*
baroness /'bærənɪs/ *n.* Baronin, *die;* Freifrau, *die*
baroque /bə'rɒk/ 1 *n.* Barock, *das*
2 *adj.* barock
barracks /'bærəks/ *n. pl.* Kaserne, *die*
barrage /'bærɑ:ʒ/ *n.* (Mil.) Sperrfeuer, *das;* **a ~ of questions** ein Bombardement von Fragen
barrel /'bærl/ *n.* **(a)** Fass, *das*
(b) (of gun) Lauf, *der*
barren /'bærn/ *adj.* unfruchtbar
barricade /bærɪ'keɪd/ 1 *n.* Barrikade, *die*
2 *v.t.* verbarrikadieren
barrier /'bærɪə(r)/ *n.* Barriere, *die;* (at level crossing etc.) Schranke, *die*
barring /'bɑ:rɪŋ/ *prep.* außer im Falle (+ *Gen.*)
barrister /'bærɪstə(r)/ *n.* (Brit.) **~[-at-law]** Barrister, *der;* ≈ [Rechts]anwalt/-anwältin vor höheren Gerichten
barrow /'bærəʊ/ *n.* **(a)** Karre, *die;* Karren, *der*
(b) ▶ WHEELBARROW
barter /'bɑ:tə(r)/ 1 *v.t.* [ein]tauschen; **~ sth. for sth. [else]** etw. für *od.* gegen etw. [anderes] [ein]tauschen
2 *v.i.* Tauschhandel treiben
3 *n.* Tauschhandel, *der*
base /beɪs/ 1 *n.* **(a)** (of lamp, mountain) Fuß, *der;* (of cupboard, statue) Sockel, *der;* (fig.: support) Basis, *die*
(b) (Mil.) Basis, *die;* Stützpunkt, *der*
2 *v.t.* **(a) be ~d on sth.** sich auf etw. (*Akk.*) gründen; **~ sth. on sth.** etw. auf etw. (*Dat.*) aufbauen
(b) *in pass.* **be ~d in Paris** (permanently) in Paris sitzen; (temporarily) in Paris sein
base: ~ball *n.* Baseball, *der;* **~line** *n.* Grundlinie, *die*
basement /'beɪsmənt/ *n.* Untergeschoss, *das;* **a ~ flat** eine Kellerwohnung
'base rate *n.* (Finance) Eckzins, *der*
bash /bæʃ/ *v.t.* [heftig] schlagen
bashful /'bæʃfl/ *adj.* schüchtern
basic /'beɪsɪk/ *adj.* grundlegend; Grund⟨*prinzip, -bestandteil, -lohn, -gehalt usw.*⟩; Haupt⟨*problem, -grund, -sache*⟩; **be ~ to sth.** wesentlich für etw. sein
basically /'beɪsɪkəlɪ/ *adv.* im Grunde; grundsätzlich ⟨*übereinstimmen*⟩; (mainly) hauptsächlich
basil /'bæzɪl/ *n.* Basilikum, *das*
basin /'beɪsn/ *n.* **(a)** Becken, *das;* (wash~) Waschbecken, *das;* (bowl) Schüssel, *die*
(b) (of river) Becken, *das*
basis /'beɪsɪs/ *n., pl.* **bases** /'beɪsi:z/ Basis, *die;* Grundlage, *die*
bask /bɑ:sk/ *v.i.* sich [wohlig] wärmen
basket /'bɑ:skɪt/ *n.* Korb, *der*
'basketball *n.* Basketball, *der*
Basle /bɑ:l/ *pr. n.* Basel (*das*)
bass /beɪs/ 1 *n.* **(a)** Bass, *der*
(b) (coll.) (double ~) [Kontra]bass, *der;* (~ guitar) Bass, *der*
2 *adj.* Bass-
bass gui'tar *n.* Bassgitarre, *die*
bassoon /bə'su:n/ *n.* Fagott, *das*
'bass player *n.* Bassist, *der*/Bassistin, *die*
bastard /'bɑ:stəd/ 1 *adj.* unehelich
2 *n.* **(a)** uneheliches Kind
(b) (sl.: disliked person) Schweinehund, *der* (derb)
baste /'beɪst/ *v.t.* [mit Fett] begießen
bastion /'bæstɪən/ *n.* Bastei, *die*
bat¹ /bæt/ *n.* (Zool.) Fledermaus, *die*
bat² 1 *n.* (Sport) Schlagholz, *das;* (for table tennis) Schläger, *der;* **do sth. off one's own ~** (fig.) etw. auf eigene Faust tun
2 *v.t.,* **-tt-** schlagen
bat³ *v.t.* **not ~ an eyelid** nicht mit der Wimper zucken
batch /bætʃ/ *n.* **(a)** (of loaves) Schub, *der*
(b) (of people) Gruppe, *die;* (of books, papers) Stapel, *der*
batch: ~ file *n.* (Comp.) Stapeldatei, *die;* **~ 'processing** *n.* (Comp.) Schub-, Stapelverarbeitung, *die*
bated /'beɪtɪd/ *v.t.* **with ~ breath** mit angehaltenem Atem
bath /bɑ:θ/ 1 *n., pl.* **~s** /bɑ:ðz/ **(a)** Bad, *das;* **have** *or* **take a ~:** ein Bad nehmen
(b) (tub) Badewanne, *die;* **room with ~:** Zimmer mit Bad
(c) *usu. in pl.* (building) Bad, *das*
2 *v.t. & i.* baden
'bath cubes *n. pl.* Badesalz, *das*
bathe /beɪð/ *v.t. & i.* baden
bather /'beɪðə(r)/ *n.* Badende, *der*/*die*
bathing /'beɪðɪŋ/ *n.* Baden, *das*
bathing: ~ beach *n.* Badestrand, *der;* **~ costume, ~ suit** *ns.* Badeanzug, *der;* **~ trunks** *n. pl.* Badehose, *die*
bath: ~ mat *n.* Badematte, *die;* **~robe** *n.* Bademantel, *der;* **~room** *n.* Badezimmer,

das; ~ **salts** *n. pl.* Badesalz, *das;* ~ **towel** *n.* Badetuch, *das;* ~**tub** ▶ BATH 1B; ~**water** *n.* Badewasser, *das*

baton /ˈbætn/ *n.* **(a)** (truncheon) Schlagstock, *der*
(b) (Mus.) Taktstock, *der*

batsman /ˈbætsmən/ *n., pl.* **batsmen** /ˈbætsmən/ Schlagmann, *der*

battalion /bəˈtæljən/ *n.* Bataillon, *das*

batter¹ /ˈbætə(r)/ *v.t.* (strike) einschlagen auf (+ *Akk.*)

batter² *n.* (Cookery) [Back]teig, *der*

battery /ˈbætərɪ/ *n.* Batterie, *die*

battery: ~ **charger** *n.* Batterieladegerät, *das;* ~ **'chicken** *n.* Batteriehuhn, *das;* ~ **'farming** *n.* Batteriehaltung, *die;* ~ **'hen** *n.* Batteriehuhn, *das;* ~**-operated** *adj.* batteriebetrieben

battle /ˈbætl/ **1** *n.* Schlacht, *die;* (fig.) Kampf, *der*
2 *v.i.* kämpfen

battle: ~**axe** *n.* (coll.: woman) Schreckschraube, *die* (ugs.); ~**field,** ~**ground** *ns.* Schlachtfeld, *das*

battlements /ˈbætlmənts/ *n. pl.* Zinnen *Pl.*

'battleship *n.* Schlachtschiff, *das*

batty /ˈbætɪ/ *adj.* (coll.) bekloppt (salopp)

bauble /ˈbɔːbl/ *n.* Flitter, *der*

baulk ▶ BALK

Bavaria /bəˈveərɪə/ *pr. n.* Bayern (*das*)

Bavarian /bəˈveərɪən/ **1** *adj.* bay[e]risch; **sb. is** ~: jmd. ist Bayer/Bayerin
2 *n.* Bayer, *der*/Bayerin, *die*

bawdy /ˈbɔːdɪ/ *adj.* zweideutig; (stronger) obszön

bay¹ /beɪ/ *n.* (of sea) Bucht, *die*

bay² *n.* **(a)** (space in room) Erker, *der*
(b) [parking] ~: Stellplatz, *der*

bay³ *n.* **hold** *or* **keep sb./sth. at** ~: sich (*Dat.*) jmdn./etw. vom Leib halten

'bayleaf *n.* Lorbeerblatt, *das*

bayonet /ˈbeɪənɪt/ *n.* Bajonett, *das*

bayonet: ~ **fitting** *n.* Bajonettfassung, *die;* ~ **plug** *n.* Stecker mit Bajonettverschluss *od.* -fassung; ~ **socket** *n.* Steckdose mit Bajonettfassung

bay 'window *n.* Erkerfenster, *das*

bazaar /bəˈzɑː(r)/ *n.* Basar, *der*

BBC *abbr.* = **British Broadcasting Corporation** BBC, *die*

BC *abbr.* = **before Christ** v.Chr.

be /biː/ *v., pres. t.* **I am** /əm, *stressed* æm/, **he is** /ɪz/, **we are** /ə(r), *stressed* ɑː(r)/; *p.t.* **I was** /wəz, *stressed* wɒz/, **we were** /wə(r), *stressed* wɜː(r)/; *pres.p.* **being** /ˈbiːɪŋ/; *p.p.* **been** /bɪn, *stressed* biːn/ **1** *copula* **(a)** sein; **she is a mother/an Italian/a teacher** sie ist Mutter/Italienerin/Lehrerin; **be sensible!** sei vernünftig!; **be ill/unwell** krank sein/sich nicht wohl fühlen; **I am well** es geht mir gut; **I am hot** mir ist heiß; **I am freezing** mich friert es; **how are you/is she?** wie gehts (ugs.)/geht es ihr?; **it is the 5th today** heute haben wir den Fünften; **who's that?** wer ist das?; **if I were you** an deiner Stelle; **it's hers** es ist ihrs
(b) (cost) kosten; **how much are the eggs?** was kosten die Eier?; **two times three is six, two threes are six** zweimal drei ist *od.* sind sechs
(c) (constitute) bilden
2 *v.i.* **(a)** (exist) [vorhanden] sein; **there is/are ...:** es gibt ...; **for the time being** vorläufig; **be that as it may** wie dem auch sei
(b) (remain) bleiben; **I shan't be a moment** ich komme sofort; **let it be** lass es sein; **let him/her be** lass ihn/sie in Ruhe
(c) (happen) stattfinden; sein
(d) (go, come) **be off with you!** geh/geht!; **I'm off home** ich gehe jetzt nach Hause; **she's from Australia** sie stammt *od.* ist aus Australien
(e) (go or come on visit) sein; **have you [ever] been to London?** bist du schon einmal in London gewesen?; **has anyone been?** ist jemand da gewesen?
3 *v. aux.* **(a)** *forming passive* werden; **the child was found** das Kind wurde gefunden; **German is spoken here** hier wird Deutsch gesprochen
(b) *forming continuous tenses, active* **he is reading** er liest [gerade]; **I am leaving tomorrow** ich reise morgen [ab]; **the train was departing when I got there** der Zug fuhr gerade ab, als ich ankam
(c) *forming continuous tenses, passive* **the house is/was being built** das Haus wird/wurde [gerade] gebaut
(d) *expr. arrangement, obligation* **be to** sollen; **I am to go/to inform you** ich soll gehen/Sie unterrichten
(e) *expr. destiny* **they were never to meet again** sie sollten sich nie wieder treffen
(f) *expr. condition* **if I were to tell you that ...:** wenn ich dir sagen würde, dass ...
4 **bride-/husband-to-be** zukünftige Braut/zukünftiger Ehemann

beach /biːtʃ/ *n.* Strand, *der;* **on the** ~: am Strand; ~ **hat/holiday/shoe** Strandhut/-urlaub/-schuh, *der*

beach: ~**ball** *n.* Wasserball, *der;* ~**wear** *n.* Strandkleidung, *die*

beacon /ˈbiːkn/ *n.* Leuchtfeuer, *das;* (Naut.) Leuchtbake, *die*

bead /biːd/ *n.* Perle, *die;* ~**s** Perlen *Pl.;* Perlenkette, *die;* ~**s of dew/sweat** Tau-/Schweißtropfen

beady /ˈbiːdɪ/ *adj.* ~ **eyes** Knopfaugen *Pl.*

beak /biːk/ *n.* Schnabel, *der*

beaker /ˈbiːkə(r)/ *n.* Becher, *der*

beam /biːm/ **1** *n.* **(a)** (timber etc.) Balken, *der*
(b) (ray etc.) [Licht]strahl, *der*
2 *v.i.* **(a)** (shine) strahlen; glänzen

⋯

(b) (smile) strahlen; **~ at sb.** jmdn. anstrahlen

bean /bi:n/ *n.* Bohne, *die;* **full of ~s** (fig. coll.) putzmunter (ugs.)

bean: ~bag *n.* **(a)** *mit Bohnen gefülltes Säckchen zum Spielen;* **(b)** (cushion) Knautschsessel, *der;* **~ curd** *n.* Soja[bohnen]quark, *der;* **~pole** *n.* (lit. or fig.) Bohnenstange, *die;* **~sprout** *n.* Sojabohnenkeim, *der*

bear¹ /beə(r)/ *n.* Bär, *der*

bear² 1 *v.t.,* **bore** /bɔ:(r)/, **borne** /bɔ:n/ **(a)** tragen; aufweisen ‹*Spuren, Ähnlichkeit*›; tragen, führen ‹*Namen, Titel*›; **~ some/little relation to sth.** einen gewissen/wenig Bezug zu etw. haben
(b) (endure, tolerate) ertragen ‹*Schmerz, Kummer*›; *with neg.* ertragen, aushalten ‹*Schmerz*›; ausstehen ‹*Geruch, Lärm*›
(c) (be fit for) vertragen; **it will not ~ scrutiny** es hält einer Überprüfung nicht stand; **it does not ~ thinking about** daran darf man gar nicht denken
(d) (give birth to) gebären ‹*Kind, Junges*›
2 *v.i.,* **bore, borne: ~ left** ‹*Person:*› sich links halten; **the path ~s to the left** der Weg führt nach links

■ **bear 'out** *v.t.* (fig.) bestätigen ‹*Bericht, Erklärung*›; **~ sb. out** jmdm. Recht geben

■ **'bear with** *v.t.* Nachsicht haben mit

bearable /'beərəbl/ *adj.* erträglich

beard /bɪəd/ *n.* Bart, *der*

'bearded *adj.* bärtig. **be ~:** einen Bart haben

'bearer *n.* (carrier) Träger, *der*/Trägerin, *die;* (of message, cheque) Überbringer, *der*/Überbringerin, *die*

'bear hug *n.* kräftige Umarmung

'bearing *n.* **(a)** (behaviour) Verhalten, *das*
(b) (relation) Bezug, *der;* **have some/no ~ on sth.** relevant/irrelevant für etw. sein
(c) (Mech. Engin.) Lager, *das*
(d) (compass ~) Position, *die;* **take a compass ~:** den Kompasskurs feststellen; **get one's ~s** sich orientieren; (fig.) sich zurechtfinden

beast /bi:st/ *n.* Tier, *das;* (fig.: brutal person) Bestie, *die*

'beastly *adj., adv.* (coll.) scheußlich

beat /bi:t/ 1 *v.t.,* **beat, beaten** /'bi:tn/ schlagen; klopfen ‹*Teppich*›; (surpass) brechen ‹*Rekord*›; **hard to ~:** schwer zu schlagen; **it ~s me how/why ...:** es ist mir ein Rätsel wie/warum ...; **~ time** den Takt schlagen; **~ it!** (coll.) hau ab! (ugs.); *see also* BEATEN 2
2 *v.i.,* **beat, beaten** schlagen (**on** auf + *Akk.*); ‹*Regen, Hagel:*› prasseln (**against** gegen)
3 *n.* **(a)** (stroke, throbbing) Schlagen, *das;* (*Mus.*) (*rhythm*) Takt, *der;* (single ~) Schlag, *der*
(b) (of policeman) Runde, *die*

■ **beat 'off** *v.t.* abwehren ‹*Angriff*›

■ **beat 'up** *v.t.* zusammenschlagen ‹*Person*›

beaten /'bi:tn/ 1 ▶ BEAT 1, 2
2 *adj.* **(a) off the ~ track** weit abgelegen
(b) gehämmert ‹*Silber, Gold*›

'beating *n.* **(a)** (punishment) **a ~:** Schläge *Pl.;* Prügel *Pl.*
(b) (defeat) Niederlage, *die*
(c) take some/a lot of ~: nicht leicht zu übertreffen sein

'beat-up *adj.* (coll.) ramponiert (ugs.)

beautician /bju:'tɪʃn/ *n.* Kosmetiker, *der*/Kosmetikerin, *die*

beautiful /'bju:tɪfl/ *adj.* schön; wunderschön ‹*Augen, Aussicht, Morgen*›

beautify /'bju:tɪfaɪ/ *v.t.* verschönern

beauty /'bju:tɪ/ *n.* Schönheit, *die;* (beautiful feature) Schöne, *das;* **the ~ of it** das Schöne daran

beauty: ~ competition, ~ contest *ns.* Schönheitswettbewerb, *der;* **~ parlour** ▶ ~ SALON; **~ queen** *n.* Schönheitskönigin, *die;* **~ salon** *n.* Kosmetiksalon, *der;* **~ spot** *n.* Schönheitsfleck, *der;* (place) schönes Fleckchen [Erde]; **~ treatment** *n.* Schönheitsbehandlung, *die*

beaver /'bi:və(r)/ *n.* Biber, *der*

became ▶ BECOME

because /bɪ'kɒz/ 1 *conj.* weil
2 *adv.* **~ of** wegen (+ *Gen.*)

beckon /'bekn/ *v.t. & i.* winken (**to sb.** jmdm.); (fig.) locken

become /bɪ'kʌm/ 1 *copula,* **became** /bɪ'keɪm/, **become** werden; **~ a politician** Politiker werden; **~ a nuisance/rule** zu einer Plage/zur Regel werden
2 *v.i.,* **became, become** werden; **what has ~ of him?** was ist aus ihm geworden?
3 *v.t.,* **became, become** (suit) **~ sb.** jmdm. stehen

becoming /bɪ'kʌmɪŋ/ *adj.* **(a)** (fitting) schicklich (geh.)
(b) (flattering) vorteilhaft ‹*Hut, Kleid, Frisur*›

bed /bed/ *n.* **(a)** Bett, *das;* (without bedstead) Lager, *das;* **in ~:** im Bett; **~ and breakfast** Zimmer mit Frühstück; **get out of/into ~:** aufstehen/ins Bett gehen; **go to ~:** ins Bett gehen; **put sb. to ~:** jmdn. ins Bett bringen; **make the ~:** das Bett machen
(b) (flat base) Unterlage, *die;* (of machine) Bett, *das*
(c) (in garden) Beet, *das*
(d) (of sea, lake) Grund, *der;* (of river) Bett, *das*

'bedclothes *n. pl.* Bettzeug, *das*

bedding /'bedɪŋ/ *n.* Matratze und Bettzeug

'bedding plant *n.* Freilandpflanze, *die*

bedlam /'bedləm/ *n., no indef. art.* Tumult, *der*

bed: ~linen *n.* Bettwäsche, *die;* **~pan** *n.* Bettpfanne, *die*

bedraggled /bɪ'drægld/ *adj.* (soaked) durchnässt; (with mud) verdreckt

bed: ~ridden *adj.* bettlägerig; **~room** *n.* Schlafzimmer, *das;* **~ set'tee** *n.* Bettcouch, *die;* **~side** *n.* Seite des Bettes, *die;* **~side table/lamp** Nachttisch, *der*/Nachttischlampe, *die;* **~sit, ~'sitter** *ns.* (coll.)

Wohnschlafzimmer, *das;* **~spread** *n.* Tagesdecke, *die;* **~stead** *n.* Bettgestell, *das;* **~time** *n.* Schlafenszeit, *die;* **at ~time** vor dem Zubettgehen; **a ~time story** eine Gutenachtgeschichte; **~-wetting** *n.* Bettnässen, *das*

bee /bi:/ *n.* Biene, *die*

beech /bi:tʃ/ *n.* Buche, *die*

beef /bi:f/ 1 *n.* **(a)** Rindfleisch, *das* **(b)** (coll.: muscles) Muskeln *Pl.*
2 *v.t.* **~ up** stärken

beef: ~burger *n.* Beefburger, *der;* **~cake** *n.* (Amer. coll.) Muskeln *Pl.;* Bizeps, *der* (ugs.)

bee: ~hive *n.* Bienenstock, *der;* **~-keeper** *n.* Imker, *der*/Imkerin, *die;* **~-keeping** *n.* Imkerei, *die;* **~line** *n.* **make a ~line for oth./sb.** schnurstracks auf etw./jmdn. zustürzen

been ▶ BE

beep /bi:p/ 1 *n.* Piepton, *der;* (of car horn) Tuten, *das*
2 *v.i.* piepen; ‹*Signalhorn:*› hupen
3 *v.t.* (esp. Amer.) ▶ BLEEP 3

beeper /ˈbi:pə(r)/ *n.* Piepser, *der*

beer /bɪə(r)/ *n.* Bier, *das*

beer: ~ barrel *n.* Bierfass, *das;* **~ belly** *n.* (coll.) Bierbauch, *der* (ugs.); **~ bottle** *n.* Bierflasche, *die;* **~ can** *n.* Bierdose, *die;* **~ cellar** *n.* Bierkeller, *der;* **~ drinker** *n.* Biertrinker, *der;* **~ garden** *n.* Biergarten, *der;* **~ glass** *n.* Bierglas, *das;* **~ mat** *n.* Bierdeckel, *der;* Bieruntersetzer, *der;* **~ mug** *n.* Bierkrug, *der*

beet /bi:t/ *n.* Rübe, *die*

beetle /ˈbi:tl/ *n.* Käfer, *der*

ˈbeetroot *n.* rote Beete *od.* Rübe

before /bɪˈfɔ:(r)/ 1 *adv.* **(a)** (of time) vorher; (already) schon; **the day ~**: am Tag zuvor; **never ~**: noch nie
(b) (ahead in position) vor[aus]
2 *prep.* (of time; position) vor (+ *Dat.*); (direction) vor (+ *Akk.*); **the day ~ yesterday** vorgestern; **~ now/then** früher/vorher; **~ Christ** vor Christus; **~ leaving, he phoned** bevor er wegging, rief er an
3 *conj.* bevor

beˈforehand *adv.* vorher; (in anticipation) im Voraus

befriend /bɪˈfrend/ *v.t.* **(a)** (act as a friend to) sich anfreunden mit
(b) (help) sich annehmen (+ *Gen.*)

beg /beg/ 1 *v.t.*, **-gg-**: **(a)** betteln um
(b) (ask earnestly for) **~ sth.** um etw. bitten
2 *v.i.*, **-gg-** betteln (**for** um)

began ▶ BEGIN

beggar /ˈbegə(r)/ *n.* **(a)** Bettler, *der*/Bettlerin, *die*
(b) (coll.) **poor ~**: armer Teufel

begin /bɪˈgɪn/ 1 *v.t.*, **-nn-, began** /bɪˈgæn/, **begun** /bɪˈgʌn/ **~ sth.** [mit] etw. beginnen; **~ doing** *or* **to do sth.** anfangen *od.* beginnen, etw. zu tun
2 *v.i.*, **-nn-, began, begun** anfangen; **~ [up]on sth.** etw. anfangen

beˈginner *n.* Anfänger, *der*/Anfängerin, *die*

beˈginning *n.* Anfang, *der;* **at** *or* **in the ~**: am Anfang; **at the ~ of February/the month** Anfang Februar/des Monats; **from the ~**: von Anfang an

begrudge /bɪˈgrʌdʒ/ *v.t.* **~ sb. sth.** jmdm. etw. missgönnen; **~ doing sth.** etw. ungern tun

begun ▶ BEGIN

behalf /bɪˈhɑ:f/ *n.* **on** *or* (Amer.) **in ~ of sb./sth.** für jmdn./etw.; (more formally) im Namen von jmdm./etw.

behave /bɪˈheɪv/ 1 *v.i.* sich verhalten; sich benehmen; **well-/ill-** *or* **badly ~d** brav/ungezogen
2 *v. refl.* **~ oneself** sich benehmen

behaviour /bɪˈheɪvjə(r)/ *n.* Verhalten, *das*

behead /bɪˈhed/ *v.t.* enthaupten

behind /bɪˈhaɪnd/ 1 *adv.* hinten; (further back) **be miles ~**: kilometerweit zurückliegen; **stay ~**: dableiben; **leave sb./sth. ~**: jmdn./etw. zurücklassen; **fall ~**: zurückbleiben; (fig.) in Rückstand geraten; **be/get ~ with one's payments/rent** mit seinen Zahlungen/der Miete im Rückstand sein/in Rückstand geraten
2 *prep.* **(a)** hinter (+ *Dat.*); **one ~ the other** hintereinander
(b) (towards rear of) hinter (+ *Akk.*)

beige /beɪʒ/ 1 *n.* Beige, *das*
2 *adj.* beige

being /ˈbi:ɪŋ/ *n.* **(a)** (existence) Dasein, *das;* **in ~**: bestehend; **come into ~**: entstehen
(b) (person etc.) Wesen, *das*

belated /bɪˈleɪtɪd/ *adj.*, **beˈlatedly** *adv.* verspätet

belch /beltʃ/ 1 *v.i.* heftig aufstoßen; rülpsen (ugs.)
2 *n.* Rülpser, *der* (ugs.)

beleaguer /bɪˈli:gə(r)/ *v.t.* (lit. or fig.) belagern

belfry /ˈbelfrɪ/ *n.* Glockenturm, *der*

Belgian /ˈbeldʒən/ 1 *adj.* belgisch; **sb. is ~**: jmd. ist Belgier/Belgierin
2 *n.* Belgier, *der*/Belgierin, *die*

Belgium /ˈbeldʒəm/ *pr. n.* Belgien (*das*)

belie /bɪˈlaɪ/ *v.t.*, **belying** /bɪˈlaɪɪŋ/ hinwegtäuschen über ‹*Tatsachen, wahren Zustand*›; nicht erfüllen ‹*Versprechen*›; nicht entsprechen ‹*Vorstellung* (*Dat.*)›

belief /bɪˈli:f/ *n.* **(a)** Glaube, *der* (**in** an + *Akk.*); **in the ~ that ...**: in der Überzeugung, dass ...
(b) (Relig.) Glaube[n], *der*

believable /bɪˈli:vəbl/ *adj.* glaubhaft

believe /bɪˈli:v/ 1 *v.i.* glauben (**in** an + *Dat.*); (have faith) glauben (**in** an + *Akk.*) ‹*Gott, Himmel usw.*›; **I ~ so/not** ich glaube schon/nicht ···›

2 *v.t.* glauben; **~ sb.** jmdm. glauben; **I don't ~ you** das glaube ich dir nicht; **make ~ that ...:** so tun, als ob ...

believer /bɪ'li:və(r)/ *n.* **(a)** Gläubige, *der/die* **(b) be a great** *or* **firm ~ in sth.** viel von etw. halten

Belisha beacon /bəli:ʃə 'bi:kn/ *n.* (Brit.) *gelbes Blinklicht an Zebrastreifen*

belittle /bɪ'lɪtl/ *v.t.* herabsetzen

bell /bel/ *n.* Glocke, *die;* (door~) Klingel, *die*

belligerent /bɪ'lɪdʒərənt/ *adj.* Krieg führend ‹*Nation*›; streitlustig ‹*Person*›

bellow /'beləʊ/ 1 *v.i.* brüllen
2 *v.t.* **~ [out]** brüllen ‹*Befehl*›

bellows /'beləʊz/ *n. pl.* Blasebalg, *der*

bell: ~-ringer *n.* Glöckner, *der;* **~-ringing** *n.* Glockenläuten, *das*

belly /'belɪ/ *n.* Bauch, *der*

belly: ~ache *n.* Bauchschmerzen *Pl.;* **~ button** *n.* (coll.) Bauchnabel, *der;* **~ dance** *n.* Bauchtanz, *der*

belong /bɪ'lɒŋ/ *v.i.* **~ to sb./sth.** jmdm./zu etw. gehören; **~ to a club** einem Verein angehören; **where does this ~?** wo gehört das hin?

be'longings *n. pl.* Habe, *die;* Sachen *Pl.;* **personal ~:** persönlicher Besitz; persönliches Eigentum

beloved /bɪ'lʌvɪd/ 1 *adj.* geliebt
2 *n.* Geliebte, *der/die*

below /bɪ'ləʊ/ 1 *adv.* **(a)** (position) unten; (lower down) darunter; **from ~:** von unten [herauf]
(b) (direction) nach unten; hinunter
2 *prep.* unter (*position:* + *Dat.; direction:* + *Akk.*)

belt /belt/ *n.* Gürtel, *der;* (for tools, weapons, ammunition) Gurt, *der;* (of trees) Streifen, *der*

■ **belt along** *v.i.* (coll.) rasen (ugs.)

■ **belt 'up** *v.i.* (Brit. coll.) die Klappe halten (salopp)

bemused /bɪ'mju:zd/ *adj.* verwirrt

bench /bentʃ/ *n.* Bank, *die;* (work table) Werkbank, *die*

bench: ~mark *n.* Höhenmarke, *die;* (fig.) Maßstab, *der;* Fixpunkt, *der;* **~marking** *n.* Benchmarking, *das* (fachspr.); Leistungsvergleich, *der;*

bend /bend/ 1 *n.* Beuge, *die;* (in road) Kurve, *die*
2 *v.t.,* **bent** /bent/ biegen; beugen ‹*Arm, Knie*›; anwinkeln ‹*Bein*›
3 *v.i.,* **bent** sich biegen; (bow) sich bücken

■ **bend 'down** *v.i.* sich bücken

■ **bend 'over** *v.i.* sich nach vorn beugen

beneath /bɪ'ni:θ/ *prep.* **(a)** (unworthy of) **~ sb., ~ sb.'s dignity** unter jmds. Würde (*Dat.*)
(b) (arch./literary: under) unter (+ *Dat.*)

benefactor /'benɪfæktə(r)/ *n.* Wohltäter, *der;* (patron) Gönner, *der*

beneficial /benɪ'fɪʃl/ *adj.* nützlich; vorteilhaft ‹*Einfluss*›

benefit /'benɪfɪt/ 1 *n.* **(a)** Vorteil, *der;* **be of ~ to sb./sth.** jmdm./einer Sache von Nutzen sein; **have the ~ of** den Vorteil (+ *Gen.*) haben; **with the ~ of** mit Hilfe (+ *Gen.*); **for sb.'s ~:** in jmds. Interesse (*Dat.*)
(b) (allowance) Beihilfe, *die;* **unemployment ~:** Arbeitslosenunterstützung, *die*
2 *v.t.* nützen (+ *Dat.*)
3 *v.i.* **~ by/from sth.** von etw. profitieren

benevolent /bɪ'nevələnt/ *adj.* **(a)** gütig **(b)** wohltätig ‹*Institution, Verein*›

benign /bɪ'naɪn/ *adj.* gütig; (Med.) gutartig

bent /bent/ 1 ▶ BEND 2, 3
2 *n.* (liking) Neigung, *die* (**for** zu)
3 **(a)** *adj.* krumm
(b) (Brit. sl.: corrupt) link (salopp)

bequeath /bɪ'kwi:ð/ *v.t.* **~ sth. to sb.** jmdm. etw. hinterlassen

bequest /bɪ'kwest/ *n.* Legat, *das* (**to** an + *Akk.*)

bereaved /bɪ'ri:vd/ *n.* **the ~:** der/die Hinterbliebene/die Hinterbliebenen

bereavement /bɪ'ri:vmənt/ *n.* Trauerfall, *der*

beret /'bereɪ/ *n.* Baskenmütze, *die*

Berlin /bɜ:'lɪn/ *pr. n.* Berlin (*das*)

Berne /bɜ:n/ *pr. n.* Bern (*das*)

berry /'berɪ/ *n.* Beere, *die*

berserk /bə'sɜ:k/ *adj.* rasend; **go ~:** durchdrehen (ugs.)

berth /bɜ:θ/ *n.* (for ship) Liegeplatz, *der;* (sleeping place) (in ship) Koje, *die;* (in train) Schlafwagenbett, *das*

beside /bɪ'saɪd/ *prep.* **(a)** neben (+ *Dat.*); **~ the sea/lake** am Meer/See
(b) be ~ the point nichts damit zu tun haben
(c) ~ oneself außer sich

besides /bɪ'saɪdz/ 1 *adv.* außerdem
2 *prep.* außer

besiege /bɪ'si:dʒ/ *v.t.* belagern

besotted /bɪ'sɒtɪd/ *adj.* **be ~ by** *or* **with sb.** in jmdn. vernarrt sein

bespectacled /bɪ'spektəkld/ *adj.* bebrillt

best /best/ 1 *adj.* best...; **the ~ part of an hour** fast eine ganze Stunde
2 *adv.* am besten
3 *n.* **the ~:** der/die/das Beste; **do one's ~:** sein Bestes tun; **make the ~ of it** das Beste daraus machen; **at ~:** bestenfalls

best: ~-before date *n.* Mindesthaltbarkeitsdatum, *das;* **~ 'friend** *n.* bester Freund/beste Freundin; **be ~ friends with sb.** sehr gut mit jmdm. befreundet sein; **~ 'man** *n.* Trauzeuge, *der* (*des Bräutigams*); **~ 'seller** *n.* Bestseller, *der;* (author) Bestsellerautor, *der;* **~-selling** *attrib. adj.* meistverkauft ‹*Schallplatte*›; **~-selling book/novel** Bestseller, *der;* **a ~-selling author/novelist** ein Bestsellerautor

bet /bet/ 1 *v.t. & i.,* **-tt-, ~** *or* **~ted** wetten; **I ~ him £10** ich habe mit ihm um 10 Pfund gewettet; **~ on sth.** auf etw. (*Akk.*) setzen

2 *n.* Wette, *die;* (fig. coll.) Tipp, *der*

beta-blocker /'bi:təblɒkə(r)/ *n.* (Med.) Beta[rezeptoren]blocker, *der*

betray /bɪ'treɪ/ *v.t.* verraten (**to** an + *Akk.*)

betrayal /bɪ'treɪəl/ *n.* Verrat, *der*

better /'betə(r)/ 1 *adj.* besser; **~ and ~**: immer besser; **be much ~** (recovered) sich viel besser fühlen; **get ~** (recover) besser werden; **the ~ part of sth.** der größte Teil einer Sache (*Gen.*)
2 *adv.* besser; **~ 'off** (financially) [finanziell] besser gestellt; **be ~ off than sb.** besser als jmd. dran sein (ugs.); **be ~ off without sb./sth.** ohne jmdn./etw. besser dran sein; **I'd ~ be off now** ich gehe jetzt besser
3 *n.* **get the ~ of sb./sth.** jmdn./etw. unterkriegen (ugs.); **a change for the ~**: eine vorteilhafte Veränderung
4 *v.t.* übertreffen

better-'quality *attrib. adj.* qualitativ besser

'betting shop *n.* Wettbüro, *das*

between /bɪ'twi:n/ 1 *prep.* **(a)** **[in] ~**: zwischen (*position:* + *Dat.; direction:* + *Akk.*)
(b) (amongst) unter (+ *Dat.*); **~ ourselves, ~ you and me** unter uns (*Dat.*) gesagt
(c) **~ them/us** (by joint action of) gemeinsam; **~ us we had 40p** wir hatten zusammen 40 Pence
2 *adv.* **[in] ~**: dazwischen; (in time) zwischendurch

beverage /'bevərɪdʒ/ *n.* Getränk, *das*

beware /bɪ'weə(r)/ *v.t. & i.; only in imper. and inf.* **~ [of] sb./sth.** sich vor jmdm./etw. in Acht nehmen; **~ of doing sth.** sich davor hüten, etw. zu tun; **'~ of the dog'** „Vorsicht, bissiger Hund!"

bewilder /bɪ'wɪldə(r)/ *v.t.* verwirren

be'wildering *adj.* verwirrend

be'wilderment *n.* Verwirrung, *die*

bewitch /bɪ'wɪtʃ/ *v.t.* verzaubern; (fig.) bezaubern

beyond /bɪ'jɒnd/ 1 *adv.* **(a)** (in space) jenseits; (on other side of wall, mountain range, etc.) dahinter
(b) (in time) darüber hinaus
(c) (in addition) außerdem
2 *prep.* **(a)** (at far side of) jenseits (+ *Gen.*)
(b) (later than) nach
(c) (out of reach or comprehension or range) über ... (+ *Akk.*) hinaus

bias /'baɪəs/ 1 *n.* Voreingenommenheit, *die*
2 *v.t.*, **-s-** *or* **-ss-** beeinflussen; **be ~ed in favour of/against sth./sb.** für etw./jmdn. eingestellt sein/gegen etw./jmdn. voreingenommen sein

bib /bɪb/ *n.* Lätzchen, *das*

Bible /'baɪbl/ *n.* Bibel, *die*

biblical /'bɪblɪkl/ *adj.* biblisch

bibliography /bɪblɪ'ɒgrəfɪ/ *n.* Bibliographie, *die*

biceps /'baɪseps/ *n.* Bizeps, *der*

bicker /'bɪkə(r)/ *v.i.* sich zanken

bicycle /'baɪsɪkl/ 1 *n.* Fahrrad, *das; attrib.* Fahrrad-
2 *v.i.* Rad fahren

bicycle: ~ clip *n.* Hosenklammer, *die;* **~ courier** *n.* Fahrradkurier, *der*/-kurierin, *die;* **~ lane** *n.* (reserved for cyclists) Radfahrstreifen, *der;* (with priority for cyclists) Schutzstreifen, *der* [für Radfahrer]; **~ path** *n.* [Fahr]radweg, *der*

bid /bɪd/ 1 *v.t.* **(a)** **-dd-, bid** (at auction) bieten
(b) **-dd-, bade** /bæd, beɪd/ *or* **bid, bidden** /'bɪdn/ *or* **bid: ~ sb. welcome/goodbye** jmdn. willkommen heißen/sich von jmdm. verabschieden
2 *v.i.*, **-dd-, bid** **(a)** werben (**for** um)
(b) (at auction) bieten
3 *n.* **(a)** (at auction) Gebot, *das*
(b) (attempt) Versuch, *der*

bidden ▶ BID 1B

'bidder *n.* Bieter, *der*/Bieterin, *die*

bide /'baɪd/ *v.t.* **~ one's time** den richtigen Augenblick abwarten

biennial /baɪ'enɪəl/ *n.* (Bot.) zweijährige Pflanze; Bienne, *die* (fachspr.)

bifocal /baɪ'fəʊkl/ 1 *adj.* Bifokal-
2 *n. in pl.* Bifokalgläser *Pl.*

big /bɪg/ *adj.* groß

bigamist /'bɪgəmɪst/ *n.* Bigamist, *der*/Bigamistin, *die*

bigamy /'bɪgəmɪ/ *n.* Bigamie, *die*

big: ~head *n.* (coll.) Fatzke, *der* (ugs. abwertend); **~-'headed** *adj.* (coll.) eingebildet

bigot /'bɪgət/ *n.* bornierter Mensch; (Relig.) bigotter Mensch

bigoted /'bɪgətɪd/ *adj.* borniert

big: ~ 'toe *n.* große Zehe; **~ 'top** *n.* Zirkuszelt, *das;* **~ 'wheel** *n.* (at fair) Riesenrad, *das*

bike /baɪk/ (coll.) 1 *n.* (bicycle) Rad, *das;* (motor cycle) Maschine, *die*
2 *v.i.* Rad fahren/[mit dem] Motorrad fahren

bike: ~ courier, ~ messenger *ns.* (on motorbike) Motorradkurier, *der*/-kurierin, *die;* (on bicycle) Fahrradkurier, *der*/-kurierin, *die;* **~ path** (esp. Amer.) ▶ BICYCLE PATH

bikini /bɪ'ki:nɪ/ *n.* Bikini, *der*

bilingual /baɪ'lɪŋgwəl/ *adj.* zweisprachig

bilious /'bɪljəs/ *adj.* (Med.) Gallen-; **~ attack** Gallenanfall, *der*

bill[1] /bɪl/ *n.* (of bird) Schnabel, *der*

bill[2] *n.* **(a)** (Parl.) Gesetzentwurf, *der*
(b) (note of charges) Rechnung, *die;* **could we have the ~ please?** wir möchten zahlen
(c) (poster) **'[stick] no ~s'** „[Plakate] ankleben verboten"

'billboard *n.* Reklametafel, *die*

billet /'bɪlɪt/ 1 *n.* Quartier, *das*
2 *v.t.* einquartieren (**with, on** bei)

'billfold *n.* (Amer.) Brieftasche, *die*

'billiard ball *n.* Billardkugel, *die*
billiards /'bɪljədz/ *n.* Billard[spiel], *das*
billion /'bɪljən/ *n.* (thousand million) Milliarde, *die*
billionaire /bɪljə'neə(r)/ *n.* Milliardär, *der*
bimbo /'bɪmbəʊ/ *n.* (coll. derog.) Puppe, *die* (salopp)
bin /bɪn/ *n.* Behälter, *der;* (for bread) Brotkasten, *der;* (for rubbish) Mülleimer, *der*
binary /'baɪnərɪ/ *adj.* binär
'bin bag *n.* Müllbeutel, *der*
bind /baɪnd/ *v.t.*, **bound** /baʊnd/ **(a)** fesseln ‹*Person, Tier*›; (bandage) wickeln ‹*Glied, Baum*›; verbinden ‹*Wunde*› **(with** mit)
(b) binden ‹*Buch*›
(c) be bound up with sth. (fig.) eng mit etw. verbunden sein
(d) be bound to do sth. (required) verpflichtet sein, etw. zu tun; (certain) etw. ganz bestimmt tun; **it is bound to rain** es wird bestimmt regnen
'binder *n.* (for papers) Hefter, *der;* (for magazines) Mappe, *die*
'binding 1 *adj.* bindend ‹*Vertrag, Abkommen*› **(on** für)
2 *n.* (of book) Einband, *der*
bingo /'bɪŋgəʊ/ *n.* Bingo, *das*
'bin liner *n.* Müllbeutel, *der*
binoculars /bɪ'nɒkjʊləz/ *n. pl.* **[pair of]** ~: Fernglas, *das*
bio'chemistry *n.* Biochemie, *die*
biodegradable /baɪəʊdɪ'greɪdəbl/ *adj.* biologisch abbaubar
biode'grade *v.i.* sich biologisch abbauen
brodi'versity *n.* biologische Vielfalt
biographer /baɪ'ɒgrəfə(r)/ *n.* Biograph, *der*/Biographin, *die*
biographical /baɪə'græfɪkl/ *adj.* biographisch
biography /baɪ'ɒgrəfɪ/ *n.* Biographie, *die*
'biohazard *n.* Biogefahr, *die*
biological /baɪə'lɒdʒɪkl/ *adj.* biologisch
biological: ~ 'clock *n.* biologische Uhr; **~ 'warfare** *n.* biologische Kriegführung; Bakterienkrieg, *der;* **~ 'waste** *n.* Bio-Abfall, *der*; Biomüll, *der*
biologist /baɪ'ɒlədʒɪst/ *n.* Biologe, *der*/ Biologin, *die*
biology /baɪ'ɒlədʒɪ/ *n.* Biologie, *die*
biopsy /'baɪɒpsɪ/ *n.* Biopsie, *die*
'biorhythm *n.* Biorhythmus, *der*
'biosphere *n.* Biosphäre, *die*
biotech'nology *n.* Biotechnologie, *die*
bio'terrorism *n.* Bioterrorismus, *der*
birch /bɜːtʃ/ *n.* Birke, *die*
bird /bɜːd/ *n.* Vogel, *der*
bird: ~ bath *n.* Vogelbad, *das;* **~ cage** *n.* Vogelkäfig, *der;* **~ flu** *n.* Vogelgrippe, *die;* **~'s-eye 'view** *n.* Vogelperspektive, *die;* **~'s nest** *n.* Vogelnest, *das;* **~ table** *n.* Futterstelle für Vögel; **~watcher** *n.* Vogelbeobachter, *der*/-beobachterin, *die;* **~-watching** *n.* das Beobachten von Vögeln
Biro ® /'baɪrəʊ/ *n., pl.* **~s** Kugelschreiber, *der;* Kuli, *der* (ugs.)
birth /bɜːθ/ *n.* **(a)** Geburt, *die;* **give ~** ‹*Frau:*› entbinden; ‹*Tier:*› jungen; werfen; **give ~ to a child** ein Kind zur Welt bringen **(b)** (of movement, fashion, etc.) Aufkommen, *das*
birth: ~ certificate *n.* Geburtsurkunde, *die;* **~ control** *n.* Geburtenkontrolle, *die;* **~day** *n.* Geburtstag, *der; attrib.* Geburtstags; **~mark** *n.* Muttermal, *das;* **~place** *n.* Geburtsort, *der;* **~ rate** *n.* Geburtenrate, *die*
biscuit /'bɪskɪt/ *n.* (Brit.) Keks, *der*
bisect /baɪ'sekt/ *v.t.* halbieren
bisexual /baɪ'seksjʊəl/ 1 *adj.* bisexuell
2 *n.* Bisexuelle, *der/die*
bishop /'bɪʃəp/ *n.* **(a)** (Eccl.) Bischof, *der*
(b) (Chess) Läufer, *der*
bit¹ /bɪt/ *n.* **(a)** (for horse) Gebiss, *das*
(b) (of drill) [Bohr]einsatz, *der*
bit² *n.* (piece) Stück, *das;* **not a** *or* **one ~** (not at all) überhaupt nicht; **a ~ tired/too early** ein bisschen müde/zu früh; **be a ~ of a coward/ bully** ein ziemlicher Feigling sein/den starken Mann markieren (ugs.)
bit³ *n.* (Comp.) Bit, *das*
bit⁴ ▶ BITE 1, 2
bitch /bɪtʃ/ *n.* **(a)** (dog) Hündin, *die*
(b) (sl. derog.: woman) Miststück, *das* (derb)
bitchy /'bɪtʃɪ/ *adj.* (coll.) gemein; gehässig
bite /baɪt/ 1 *v.t.*, **bit** /bɪt/, **bitten** /'bɪtn/ beißen; ‹*Moskito usw.:*› stechen
2 *v.i.*, **bit, bitten** beißen/stechen; (take bait) anbeißen
3 *n.* Biss, *der;* (piece) Bissen, *der;* (wound) Bisswunde, *die;* (by mosquito etc.) Stich, *der*
■ **bite 'off** *v.t.* abbeißen
'bite-size *adj.* mundgerecht
biting /'baɪtɪŋ/ *adj.* beißend
bitten ▶ BITE 1, 2
bitter /'bɪtə(r)/ *adj.* bitter
'bitterly *adv.* bitterlich ‹*weinen, sich beschweren*›; **~ cold** bitterkalt
'bitterness *n.* Bitterkeit, *die*
bizarre /bɪ'zɑː(r)/ *adj.* bizarr
black /blæk/ 1 *adj.* **(a)** schwarz; **~ and blue** (fig.) grün und blau; **in ~ and white** (fig.) schwarz auf weiß; **~ and white film** Schwarzweißfilm, *der;* **in the ~** (in credit) in den schwarzen Zahlen
(b) B~ (dark-skinned) schwarz
2 *n.* **(a)** Schwarz, *das*
(b) B~ (person) Schwarze, *der/die*
3 *v.t.* bestreiken ‹*Betrieb*›; boykottieren ‹*Arbeit*›
■ **black 'out** 1 *v.t.* verdunkeln
2 *v.i.* das Bewusstsein verlieren

black: ~berry /'blækbərɪ/ *n.* Brombeere, *die;* **~bird** *n.* Amsel, *die;* **~board** *n.* [Wand]tafel, *die;* **~ 'box** *n.* (flight recorder) Flugschreiber, *der;* **~'currant** *n.* schwarze Johannisbeere

blacken /'blækn/ *v.t.* schwärzen; verfinstern ‹*Himmel*›

black: ~ 'eye *n.* blaues Auge; **B~ 'Forest** *pr. n.* Schwarzwald, *der;* **~ 'hole** *n.* (Astron.) schwarzes Loch; **~ 'ice** *n.* Glatteis, *das;* **~leg** *n.* (Brit.) Streikbrecher, *der*/-brecherin, *die;* **~ list** *n.* schwarze Liste; **~list** *v.t.* auf die schwarze Liste setzen; **~mail** [1] *v.t.* erpressen; [2] *n.* Erpressung, *die;* **~ market** *n.* schwarzer Markt

'blackness *n.* Schwärze, *die;* (darkness) Finsternis, *die*

black: ~out *n.* **(a)** Verdunkelung, *die;* (Theatre, Radio) Blackout, *der;* **(b)** (Med.) **have a ~out** das Bewusstsein verlieren; **~ 'pudding** *n.* Blutwurst, *die;* **B~ 'Sea** *pr. n.* Schwarze Meer, *das;* **~smith** *n.* Schmied, *der;* **~ spot** *n.* Gefahrenstelle, *die*

bladder /'blædə(r)/ *n.* Blase, *die*

blade /bleɪd/ *n.* **(a)** (of sword, knife, razor, etc.) Klinge, *die;* (of saw, oar, propeller) Blatt, *das* **(b)** (of grass) Spreite, *die*

Blairite /'bleəraɪt/ [1] *adj.* blairsch; Blairsch
[2] *n.* Blair-Anhänger, *der*/-Anhängerin, *die*

blame /bleɪm/ [1] *v.t.* **~ sb. [for sth.]** jmdm. die Schuld [an etw. (*Dat.*)] geben; **be to ~ [for sth.]** an etw. (*Dat.*) schuld sein; **~ sth. [for sth.]** etw. [für etw.] verantwortlich machen
[2] *n.* Schuld, *die*

'blameless *adj.* untadelig

blancmange /blə'mɒnʒ/ *n.* Flammeri, *der*

bland /blænd/ *adj.* mild; (suave) verbindlich

blank /blæŋk/ [1] *adj.* **(a)** leer; kahl ‹*Wand, Fläche*›
(b) (empty) frei
[2] *n.* **(a)** (space) Lücke, *die*
(b) (cartridge) Platzpatrone, *die*
(c) draw a ~: kein Glück haben

blank 'cheque *n.* Blankoscheck, *der;* (fig.) Blankovollmacht, *die*

blanket /'blæŋkɪt/ *n.* Decke, *die;* **wet '~** (fig.) Trauerkloß, *der* (ugs.)

blare /'bleə(r)/ [1] *v.i.* ‹*Lautsprecher:*› plärren; ‹*Trompete:*› schmettern
[2] *v.t.* **~ [out]** [hinaus]plärren ‹*Worte*›; [hinaus]schmettern ‹*Melodie*›

blasé /'blɑ:zeɪ/ *adj.* blasiert

blasphemous /'blæsfəməs/ *adj.* lästerlich

blasphemy /'blæsfəmɪ/ *n.* Blasphemie, *die*

blast /blɑ:st/ [1] *n.* **(a) a ~ [of wind]** ein Windstoß
(b) (of horn) Tuten, *das*
[2] *v.t.* (blow up) sprengen
[3] *int.* verdammt

■ **blast 'off** *v.i.* abheben

blasted /'blɑ:stɪd/ *adj.* (damned) verdammt (salopp)

'blast-off *n.* Abheben, *das*

blatant /'bleɪtənt/ *adj.* **(a)** (flagrant) eklatant **(b)** (unashamed) unverhohlen; unverfroren ‹*Lüge*›

'blatantly *adv.* ▶ BLATANT: eklatant; unverhohlen

blaze /bleɪz/ [1] *n.* Feuer, *das*
[2] *v.i.* brennen; lodern (geh.)

blazer /'bleɪzə(r)/ *n.* Blazer, *der*

bleach /bli:tʃ/ [1] *v.t.* bleichen
[2] *n.* Bleichmittel, *das*

bleak /'bli:k/ *adj.* **(a)** öde ‹*Landschaft usw.*› **(b)** (unpromising) düster

bleat /bli:t/ *v.i.* ‹*Schaf:*› blöken; ‹*Ziege:*› meckern

bled ▶ BLEED

bleed /bli:d/ *v.i.*, **bled** /bled/ bluten

bleep /bli:p/ [1] *n.* Piepen, *das*
[2] *v.i.* ‹*Geigerzähler, Funksignal:*› piepen
[3] *v.t.* **~ sb.** jmdn. über seinen Kleinempfänger *od.* (ugs.) Piepser rufen

bleeper /'bli:pə(r)/ *n.* Kleinempfänger, *der;* Piepser, *der* (*ugs.*)

blemish /'blemɪʃ/ *n.* Fleck, *der*

blend /blend/ [1] *v.t.* mischen
[2] *v.i.* sich mischen lassen
[3] *n.* Mischung, *die*

'blender *n.* Mixer, *der*

bless /bles/ *v.t.* segnen; **~ you!** (after sb. sneezes) Gesundheit!

blessed /'blesɪd/ *adj.* **(a)** (revered) heilig **(b)** (cursed) verdammt (salopp)

'blessing *n.* Segen, *der*

blew ▶ BLOW[1]

blight /blaɪt/ *n.* (fig.) Fluch, *der*

blind /blaɪnd/ [1] *adj.* blind; **~ in one eye** auf einem Auge blind
[2] *adv.* blindlings
[3] *n.* **(a)** Jalousie, *die;* (made of cloth) Rouleau, *das;* (of shop) Markise, *die*
(b) *pl.* **the n~:** die Blinden *Pl.*
[4] *v.t.* blenden

blind: ~ 'alley *n.* (lit. or fig.) Sackgasse, *die;* **~ 'corner** *n.* unübersichtliche Ecke; **~ 'date** *n.* Verabredung mit einem/einer Unbekannten; **~fold** [1] *v.t.* die Augen verbinden (+ *Dat.*); [2] *adj.* mit verbundenen Augen *nachgestellt*

'blinding *adj.* blendend; **a ~ headache** rasende Kopfschmerzen *Pl.*

'blindly *adv.* [wie] blind; (fig.) blindlings

'blindness *n.* Blindheit, *die*

'blind spot *n.* (Motor Veh.) toter Winkel; (fig.: weak spot) schwacher Punkt;

blink /blɪŋk/ *v.i.* **(a)** blinzeln **(b)** (shine intermittently) blinken

'blinkers *n. pl.* Scheuklappen *Pl.*

bliss /blɪs/ *n.* [Glück]seligkeit, *die*

blissful /'blɪsfl/ *adj.* [glück]selig

blister /'blɪstə(r)/ [1] *n.* Blase, *die* ⋯

2 v.i. ‹Haut:› Blasen bekommen; ‹Anstrich:› Blasen werfen

'blister pack *n.* Klarsichtpackung, *die*

blizzard /'blɪzəd/ *n.* Schneesturm, *der*

bloated /'bləʊtɪd/ *adj.* (having overeaten) aufgedunsen; **I feel ~:** ich bin voll (ugs.)

blob /blɒb/ *n.* (drop) Tropfen, *der;* (small mass) Klacks, *der* (ugs.)

block /blɒk/ 1 *n.* **(a)** Klotz, *der;* (for chopping on) Hackklotz, *der;* (of concrete or stone, building stone) Block, *der*
(b) (building) [Häuser]block, *der;* **~ of flats/offices** Wohnblock, *der*/Bürohaus, *das*
2 *v.t.* versperren ‹*Tür, Straße, Durchgang, Sicht*›; verstopfen ‹*Pfeife, Abfluss*›; verhindern ‹*Fortschritt*›

■ **block 'out** *v.t.* ausschließen ‹*Licht, Lärm*›

■ **block 'up** *v.t.* verstopfen; versperren ‹*Eingang*›

blockade /blɒ'keɪd/ 1 *n.* Blockade, *die*
2 *v.t.* blockieren

blockage /'blɒkɪdʒ/ *n.* Block, *der;* (of pipe, gutter) Verstopfung, *die*

block: ~ 'booking *n.* Gruppenbuchung, *die;* **~buster** *n.* **(a)** (bomb) [große] Fliegerbombe; **(b)** (fig.) Knüller, *der* (ugs.); **~ 'capital** *n.* Blockbuchstabe, *der;* **~head** *n.* Dummkopf, *der;* **~ 'letters** *n. pl.* Blockschrift, *die*

blog /blɒg/ (Comp.) 1 *n.* Blog, *das* (Jargon)
2 *v.i.* ein Weblog unterhalten

blogger /'blɒgə(r)/ *n.* (author of a weblog) Weblogautor, *der*/-autorin, *die*

bloke /bləʊk/ *n.* (Brit. coll.) Typ, *der* (ugs.)

blonde /blɒnd/ 1 *adj.* blond
2 *n.* Blondine, *die*

blood /blʌd/ *n.* Blut, *das*

blood: ~ bank *n.* Blutbank, *die;* **~bath** *n.* Blutbad, *das;* **~ cell** *n.* Blutkörperchen, *das;* **~ clot** *n.* Blutgerinnsel, *das;* **~ donor** *n.* Blutspender, *der*/-spenderin, *die;* **~ group** *n.* Blutgruppe, *die;* **~hound** *n.* Bluthund, *der;* **~ plasma** *n.* Blutplasma, *das;* **~ poisoning** *n.* Blutvergiftung, *die;* **~ pressure** *n.* Blutdruck, *der;* **~ sample** *n.* Blutprobe, *die;* **~shed** *n.* Blutvergießen, *das;* **~shot** *adj.* blutunterlaufen; **~ sports** *n. pl.* Hetzjagd, *die;* **~stain** *n.* Blutfleck, *der;* **~stained** *adj.* blutbefleckt; **~stream** *n.* Blutstrom, *der;* **~ sugar** *n.* Blutzucker, *der;* **~ test** *n.* Blutprobe, *die;* **~thirsty** *adj.* blutrünstig; **~ transfusion** *n.* Bluttransfusion, *die;* **~ vessel** *n.* Blutgefäß, *das*

'bloody 1 *adj.* **(a)** blutig; (running with blood) blutend
(b) (sl.: damned) verdammt (salopp)
2 *adv.* (sl.: damned) verdammt (salopp)

bloom /blu:m/ 1 *n.* Blüte, *die;* **be in ~:** in Blüte stehen
2 *v.i.* blühen

blossom /'blɒsəm/ 1 *n.* (flower) Blüte, *die;* (mass) Blütenmeer, *das* (geh.)
2 *v.i.* blühen; ‹*Mensch:*› aufblühen

blot /blɒt/ 1 *n.* (of ink) Tintenklecks, *der;* (stain) Fleck, *der*
2 *v.t.,* **-tt-** ablöschen ‹*Tinte, Papier*›

■ **blot 'out** *v.t.* (fig.) auslöschen

'blotting paper *n.* Löschpapier, *das*

blouse /blaʊz/ *n.* Bluse, *die*

blow¹ /bləʊ/ 1 *v.i.,* **blew** /blu:/, **blown** /bləʊn/ ‹*Wind:*› wehen; ‹*Sturm:*› blasen
2 *v.t.,* **blew, blown: (a)** blasen; ‹*Wind:*› wehen; machen ‹*Seifenblase*›; **~ sb. a kiss** jmdm. eine Kusshand zuwerfen
(b) ~ one's nose sich (*Dat.*) die Nase putzen
(c) ~ sth. to pieces etw. in die Luft sprengen

■ **blow 'out** 1 *v.t.* ausblasen
2 *v.i.* ausgeblasen werden

■ **blow 'over** 1 *v.i.* umgeblasen werden; ‹*Streit, Sturm:*› sich legen
2 *v.t.* umblasen

■ **blow 'up** 1 *v.t.* **(a)** (shatter) [in die Luft] sprengen
(b) aufblasen ‹*Ballon*›; aufpumpen ‹*Reifen*›
(c) (coll.: exaggerate) hochspielen
2 *v.i.* (explode) explodieren

blow² *n.* **(a)** Schlag, *der;* (with axe) Hieb, *der;* **come to ~s** handgreiflich werden
(b) (disaster) [schwerer] Schlag

blow: ~dry *v.t.* fönen; **~lamp, ~torch** *n.* Lötlampe, *die*

blown ▸ BLOW¹

blubber /'blʌbə(r)/ *n.* Walspeck, *der*

blue /blu:/ 1 *adj.* blau
2 *n.* **(a)** Blau, *das*
(b) have the ~s deprimiert sein
(c) (Mus.) **the ~s** der Blues
(d) out of the ~: aus heiterem Himmel

blue: ~bell *n.* Glockenblume, *die;* **~bottle** *n.* Schmeißfliege, *die;* **~ 'cheese** *n.* Blauschimmelkäse, *der;* Edelpilzkäse, *der;* **~-collar** *adj.* **~-collar worker** Arbeiter, *der*/Arbeiterin, *die;* **~-eyed** *adj.* blauäugig; **be ~-eyed** blaue Augen haben; **~ 'moon** *n.* **once in a ~ moon** alle Jubeljahre (ugs.); **~print** *n.* (fig.) Entwurf, *der;* **~ tit** *n.* (Ornith.) Blaumeise, *die;* **~ 'whale** *n.* Blauwal, *der*

bluff /blʌf/ 1 *n.* Bluff, *der* (ugs.); **call sb.'s ~:** es darauf ankommen lassen (ugs.)
2 *v.i. & t.* bluffen (ugs.)

blunder /'blʌndə(r)/ 1 *n.* [schwerer] Fehler
2 *v.i.* **(a)** (make mistake) einen [schweren] Fehler machen
(b) (move blindly) tappen

blunt /blʌnt/ 1 *adj.* **(a)** stumpf
(b) (outspoken) direkt; glatt (ugs.) ‹*Ablehnung*›
2 *v.t.* **~ [the edge of]** stumpf machen

'bluntly *adv.* direkt; glatt ‹*ablehnen*›

blur /blɜ:(r)/ *v.t.,* **-rr-:** verwischen; **his vision was ~red** er sah alles verschwommen

blurt /blɜːt/ *v.t.* ~ **out** herausplatzen mit (ugs.)
blush /blʌʃ/ [1] *v.i.* rot werden
[2] *n.* Rotwerden, *das*
bluster /ˈblʌstə(r)/ *v.i.* sich aufplustern (ugs.)
blustery /ˈblʌstərɪ/ *adj.* stürmisch
BO *abbr.* (coll.) = **body odour** Körpergeruch, *der*
boar /bɔː(r)/ *n.* [**wild**] ~: Keiler, *der*
board /bɔːd/ [1] *n.* **(a)** Brett, *das;* (black~) Tafel, *die;* (notice~) schwarzes Brett; **above** ~ (fig.) einwandfrei; korrekt
(b) (Commerc.) ~ [**of directors**] Vorstand, *der;* (supervisory ~) Aufsichtsrat, *der*
(c) (Naut., Aeronaut.) **on** ~: an Bord
(d) ~ **and lodging** Unterkunft und Verpflegung; **full** ~: Vollpension, *die*
[2] *v.t.* ~ **the ship/plane** an Bord des Schiffes/Flugzeuges gehen; ~ **the train/bus** in den Zug/Bus einsteigen
▪ **board 'up** *v.t.* mit Brettern vernageln
'boarder *n.* (Sch.) Internatsschüler, *der*/-schülerin, *die*
'board game *n.* Brettspiel, *das*
boarding: ~ **house** *n.* Pension, *die;* ~ **pass** *n.* Bordkarte, *die;* ~ **school** *n.* Internat, *das*
board: ~ **meeting** *n.* Vorstandssitzung, *die;* ~**room** *n.* Sitzungssaal, *der*
boast /bəʊst/ *v.i.* prahlen
boastful /ˈbəʊstfl/ *adj.* prahlerisch
boat /bəʊt/ *n.* Boot, *das*
boat: ~**house** *n.* Bootshaus, *das;* ~ **trip** *n.* Bootsfahrt, *die*
bob[1] /bɒb/ *v.i.*, **-bb-:** ~ [**up and down**] sich auf und nieder bewegen
bob[2] *n.* (~sled) Bob, *der*
bob: ~**sled,** ~**sleigh** *ns.* Bobschlitten, *der*
bodice /ˈbɒdɪs/ *n.* Mieder, *das;* (part of dress) Oberteil, *das*
bodily /ˈbɒdɪlɪ/ *adj.* körperlich; ~ **needs** leibliche Bedürfnisse
body /ˈbɒdɪ/ *n.* **(a)** Körper, *der*
(b) (corpse) Leiche, *die*
(c) (group) Gruppe, *die;* (with particular function) Organ, *das*
body: ~ **bag** *n.* Leichensack, *der;* ~**building** [1] *n.* Bodybuilding, *das;* [2] *adj.* ~**building food** Aufbaukost, *die;* ~ **clock** ▶ BIOLOGICAL CLOCK; ~**guard** *n.* (single) Leibwächter, *der;* (group) Leibwache, *die;* ~ **language** *n.* Körpersprache, *die;* ~ **odour** *n.* Körpergeruch, *der;* ~ **part** *n.* Körperteil, *der;* ~ **piercing** *n.* Piercing, *das;* ~ **weight** *n.* Körpergewicht, *das;* ~**work** *n.* Karosserie, *die*
bog /bɒg/ [1] *n.* Moor, *das;* (marsh, swamp) Sumpf, *der*
[2] *v.t.*, **-gg-: be/get** ~**ged down** (fig.) sich verzettelt haben/sich verzetteln
boggle /ˈbɒgl/ *v.i.* (coll.) **the mind** ~**s** da kann man nur [noch] staunen
bogus /ˈbəʊgəs/ *adj.* falsch
boil[1] /bɔɪl/ [1] *v.i. & t.* kochen
[2] *n.* **come to/go off the** ~: zu kochen anfangen/aufhören; **bring to the** ~: zum Kochen bringen
▪ **boil 'down** *v.i.* ~ **down to sth.** (fig.) auf etw. hinauslaufen
▪ **boil 'over** *v.i.* überkochen
boil[2] *n.* (Med.) Furunkel, *der*
'boiler *n.* Kessel, *der*
boiler: ~**room** *n.* Kesselraum, *der;* ~ **suit** *n.* Overall, *der*
'boiling point *n.* Siedepunkt, *der*
boisterous /ˈbɔɪstərəs/ *adj.* ausgelassen
bold /bəʊld/ *adj.* **(a)** (courageous) mutig; (daring) kühn
(b) auffallend ‹*Farbe, Muster*›
'boldly *adv.* (courageously) mutig; (daringly) kühn
Bolivia /bəˈlɪvɪə/ *pr. n.* Bolivien (*das*)
bollard /ˈbɒlɑːd/ *n.* (Brit.) Poller, *der*
bollocks /ˈbɒləks/ (coarse) [1] *n. pl.* Eier (derb)
[2] *int.* Scheiße
bolster /ˈbəʊlstə(r)/ [1] *n.* (pillow) Nackenrolle, *die*
[2] *v.t.* (fig.) stärken
bolt /bəʊlt/ [1] *n.* **(a)** (on door or window) Riegel, *der;* (on gun) Kammerverschluss, *der*
(b) (metal pin) Schraube, *die;* (without thread) Bolzen, *der*
[2] *v.i.* davonlaufen; ‹*Pferd:*› durchgehen; ‹*Fuchs, Kaninchen:*› flüchten
[3] *v.t.* **(a)** verriegeln ‹*Tür, Fenster*›
(b) (fasten with ~s) verschrauben/mit Bolzen verbinden
(c) ~ [**down**] hinunterschlingen ‹*Essen*›
[4] *adv.* ~ **upright** kerzengerade
bomb /bɒm/ [1] *n.* Bombe, *die;* ~ **attack** Bombenanschlag, *der*
[2] *v.t.* bombardieren
bombard /bɒmˈbɑːd/ *v.t.* beschießen
bom'bardment *n.* Beschuss, *der*
bombastic /bɒmˈbæstɪk/ *adj.* bombastisch
bomb: ~ **blast** *n.* (blast wave) Druckwelle, *die*; (explosion) Bombenexplosion, *die;* ~ **disposal** *n.* Räumung von Bomben; ~ **disposal squad** Bombenräumkommando, *das*
bomber /ˈbɒmə(r)/ *n.* (Air Force) Bomber, *der* (ugs.)
bombing /ˈbɒmɪŋ/ *n.* Bombardierung, *die*
bomb: ~ **scare** *n.* Bombendrohung, *die;* ~**shell** *n.* Bombe, *die;* (fig.) Sensation, *die*
bond /bɒnd/ *n.* **(a)** Band, *das; in pl.* (shackles) Fesseln *Pl.*
(b) (adhesion) Verbindung, *die*
(c) (Commerc.) Anleihe, *die*
bone /bəʊn/ [1] *n.* Knochen, *der;* (of fish) Gräte, *die*

b

2 *v.t.* den/die Knochen herauslösen aus; entgräten ‹*Fisch*›

bone: ~ **'china** *n.* Knochenporzellan, *das;* ~ **'dry** *adj.* knochentrocken (ugs.); ~ **'idle** *adj.* stinkfaul (salopp); ~ **marrow** *n.* (Anat.) Knochenmark, *das;* **~meal** *n.* Knochenmehl, *das*

bonfire /'bɒnfaɪə(r)/ *n.* Freudenfeuer, *das;* (for rubbish) Feuer, *das;* **B~ Night** (Brit.) [Abend des] Guy Fawkes Day (*mit Feuerwerk*)

bonnet /'bɒnɪt/ *n.* **(a)** (woman's) Haube, *die;* (child's) Häubchen, *das*
(b) (Brit. Motor Veh.) Motorhaube, *die*

bonus /'bəʊnəs/ *n.* zusätzliche Leistung; (to shareholders) Bonus, *der;* **Christmas ~:** Weihnachtsgratifikation, *die*

bony /'bəʊnɪ/ *adj.* **(a)** Knochen-; (like bone) knochenartig
(b) (skinny) knochendürr (ugs.); spindeldürr

boo /bu:/ 1 *int.* (to surprise sb.) huh; (expr. disapproval, contempt) buh
2 *n.* Buh, *das* (ugs.)
3 *v.t.* ausbuhen (ugs.)
4 *v.i.* buhen (ugs.)

boob /bu:b/ (Brit. coll.) *n.* **(a)** (mistake) Fehler, *der;* Schnitzer, *der* (ugs.)
(b) (breast) Titte, *die* (derb)

booby /'bu:bɪ/ *n.* Trottel, *der* (ugs.)

booby: ~ **prize** *n: Preis für den schlechtesten Teilnehmer an einem Wettbewerb;* ~ **trap** *n.* **(a)** *Falle, mit der man jmdm. einen Streich spielen will;* **(b)** (Mil.) versteckte Sprengladung

book /bʊk/ 1 *n.* Buch, *das;* (for accounts) Rechnungsbuch, *das;* (for exercises) [Schreib]heft, *das*
2 *v.t.* buchen ‹*Reise, Flug, Platz* [*im Flugzeug*]›; [vor]bestellen ‹*Eintrittskarte, Tisch, Zimmer, Platz* [*im Theater*]›
3 *v.i.* buchen

■ **book 'in** 1 *v.i.* sich eintragen
2 *v.t.* eintragen

■ **book 'up** *v.i. & t.* buchen; **be ~ed up** ‹*Hotel usw.:*› ausgebucht sein

book: **~case** *n.* Bücherschrank, *der;* ~ **club** *n.* Buchklub, *der;* Buchgemeinschaft, *die;* **~ends** *n. pl.* Buchstützen *Pl.*

bookie /'bʊkɪ/ *n.* (coll.) Buchmacher, *der*

'booking office *n.* [Fahrkarten]schalter, *der*

book: **~keeper** *n.* Buchhalter, *der*/ -halterin, *die;* **~keeping** *n.* Buchführung, *die;* Buchhaltung, *die*

booklet /'bʊklɪt/ *n.* Broschüre, *die*

book: **~maker** *n.* (in betting) Buchmacher, *der;* **~mark** *n.* 1 (also Comp.) Lesezeichen, *das;* 2 *v.t.* (Comp.) mit einem Lesezeichen versehen; **~seller** *n.* Buchhändler, *der*/ -händlerin, *die;* **~shelf** *n.* Bücherbord, *das;* **~shop** *n.* Buchhandlung, *die;* **~stall** *n.* Bücherstand, *der;* **~store** *n.* (Amer.) Buchhandlung, *die;* ~ **token** *n.* Büchergutschein, *der;* **~worm** *n.* Bücherwurm, *der*

boom¹ /bu:m/ *n.* **(a)** (for camera or microphone) Ausleger, *der*
(b) (Naut.) Baum, *der*

boom² 1 *v.i.* **(a)** dröhnen
(b) ‹*Geschäft, Verkauf, Gebiet:*› sich sprunghaft entwickeln
2 *n.* **(a)** Dröhnen, *das*
(b) (in business or economy) Boom, *der*

boomerang /'bu:məræŋ/ *n.* Bumerang, *der*

boon /bu:n/ *n.* Segen, *der* (**to** für)

boor /bʊər/ *n.* Rüpel, *der*

boorish /'bʊərɪʃ/ *adj.* rüpelhaft

boost /bu:st/ 1 *v.t.* ankurbeln ‹*Wirtschaft*›; in die Höhe treiben ‹*Preis, Wert*›; stärken ‹*Selbstvertrauen, Moral*›
2 *n.* Auftrieb, *der*

boot /bu:t/ 1 *n.* **(a)** Stiefel, *der;* **give sb. the ~** (fig. coll.) jmdn. rausschmeißen (ugs.)
(b) (Brit.: of car) Kofferraum, *der*
2 *v.t.* **(a)** (coll.: kick) kicken (ugs.)
(b) (Comp.) ~ **[up]** booten

bootable /'bu:təbl/ *adj.* (Comp.) bootbar ‹*System*›; ~ **disk** Bootdiskette, *die*

'boot disk *n.* (Comp.) Bootdiskette, *die*

booth /bu:ð/ *n.* **(a)** Bude, *die*
(b) (telephone ~) Zelle, *die*

'bootleg *adj.* (illegally sold/distilled) schwarz verkauft/gebrannt

booze /bu:z/ (coll.) 1 *v.i.* saufen (derb)
2 *n.* Alkohol, *der*

'booze-up *n.* (coll.) Besäufnis, *das* (salopp); **have a ~:** saufen gehen (salopp) (ugs.)

border /'bɔ:də(r)/ 1 *n.* **(a)** Rand, *der;* (of tablecloth, handkerchief) Bordüre, *die*
(b) (of country) Grenze, *die*
(c) (flower bed) Rabatte, *die*
2 *attrib. adj.* Grenz‹*stadt, -streit*›
3 *v.t.* **(a)** (adjoin) [an]grenzen an (+ *Akk.*)
(b) (put a ~ to, act as ~ to) umranden; einfassen
4 *v.i.* ~ **on (a)** ▶ 3A
(b) (resemble) grenzen an (+ *Akk.*)

border: ~ **crossing** *n.* Grenzübergang, *der;* **~line** 1 *n.* Grenzlinie, *die;* 2 *adj.* **be ~line** auf der Grenze liegen; **a ~line case/ candidate** ein Grenzfall

bore¹ /bɔ:(r)/ 1 *v.t.* bohren
2 *n.* (of firearm) Kaliber, *das*

bore² 1 *n.* **(a)** **it's a real ~:** es ist wirklich ärgerlich; **what a ~!** wie ärgerlich!
(b) (person) Langweiler, *der* (ugs.)
2 *v.t.* langweilen; **be ~d** sich langweilen

bore³ ▶ BEAR²

boredom /'bɔ:dəm/ *n.* Langeweile, *die*

'borehole *n.* Bohrloch, *das*

boring /'bɔ:rɪŋ/ *adj.* langweilig

born /bɔ:n/ 1 **be ~:** geboren werden
2 *adj.* geboren; **be a ~ orator** der geborene Redner sein

borne ▶ BEAR²

borough /'bʌrə/ *n.* (town) Stadt, *die;* (village) Gemeinde, *die*

borrow /'bɒrəʊ/ *v.t.* leihen (**from** von, bei); (from library) entleihen

'borrower *n.* (from bank) Kreditnehmer, *der;* (from library) Entleiher, *der*

Bosnia /'bɔznɪə/ *n.* Bosnien (*das*)

Bosnian /'bɔznɪən/ [1] *adj.* bosnisch; **sb. is ~**: jmd. ist Bosnier/Bosnierin
[2] *n.* Bosnier, *der*/Bosnierin, *die*

bosom /'bʊzəm/ *n.* Brust, *die*

boss /bɒs/ (coll.) [1] *n.* Boss, *der* (ugs.); Chef, *der*
[2] *v.t.* **~ [about** *or* **around]** herumkommandieren (ugs.)

'bossy *adj.* (coll.) herrisch

botanical /bə'tænɪkl/ *adj.* botanisch

botanist /'bɒtənɪst/ *n.* Botaniker, *der*/ Botanikerin, *die*

botany /'bɒtənɪ/ *n.* Botanik, *die*

botch /bɒtʃ/ [1] *v.t.* pfuschen bei (ugs.)
[2] *v.i.* pfuschen (ugs.)

■ **botch 'up** *v.t.* (bungle) verpfuschen (ugs.)

both /bəʊθ/ [1] *adj.* beide; **~ [the] brothers** beide Brüder
[2] *pron.* beide; **~ [of them] are dead** beide sind tot; **~ of you/them are ...**: ihr seid/sie sind beide ...
[3] *adv.* **~ A and B** sowohl A als [auch] B; **he and I were ~ there** er und ich waren beide da

bother /'bɒðə(r)/ [1] *v.t.* **(a) I can't be ~ed** ich habe keine Lust
(b) (annoy) lästig sein (+ *Dat.*); ‹*Lärm, Licht:*› stören; ‹*Schmerz, Zahn:*› zu schaffen machen (+ *Dat.*); **I'm sorry to ~ you, but ...**: es tut mir Leid, wenn ich Sie störe, aber ...
(c) (worry) Sorgen machen (+ *Dat.*); ‹*Problem, Frage:*› beschäftigen
[2] *v.i.* **don't ~ to do it** Sie brauchen es nicht zu tun; **you needn't/shouldn't have ~ed** das wäre nicht nötig gewesen; **don't ~!** nicht nötig!
[3] *n.* **(a)** (trouble) Ärger, *der*
(b) (effort) Mühe, *die*
[4] *int.* (coll.) wie ärgerlich!

bottle /'bɒtl/ [1] *n.* Flasche, *die;* **a ~ of beer** eine Flasche Bier
[2] *v.t.* **(a)** (put into **~s**) in Flaschen [ab]füllen
(b) ~d beer Flaschenbier, *das*
(c) (preserve in jars) einmachen

■ **bottle 'up** *v.t.* **(a)** (conceal) in sich (*Dat.*) aufstauen
(b) (trap) einschließen

bottle: ~ bank *n.* Altglasbehälter, *der;* **~neck** *n.* (fig.) Flaschenhals, *der* (ugs.); **~-opener** *n.* Flaschenöffner, *der;* **~ top** *n.* Flaschenverschluss, *der*

bottom /'bɒtəm/ [1] *n.* **(a)** unteres Ende; (of cup, glass, box) Boden, *der;* (of valley, well, shaft) Sohle, *die;* (of hill, cliff, stairs) Fuß, *der*
(b) (buttocks) Hinterteil, *das* (ugs.)
(c) (of sea, lake) Grund, *der*
(e) (farthest point) **at the ~ of the garden/street** hinten im Garten/am Ende der Straße
(e) (underside) Unterseite, *die*
(f) (fig.) **start at the ~**: ganz unten anfangen; **be ~ of the class** der/die Letzte in der Klasse sein
[2] *adj.* **(a)** (lowest) unterst...; (lower) unter...
(b) (fig.: last) letzt...

'bottomless *adj.* bodenlos; unendlich tief ‹*Meer, Ozean*›

'botulism /'bɒtju:lɪzm/ *n.* (Med.) Botulismus, *der*

bough /baʊ/ *n.* Ast, *der*

bought ▶ BUY 1

boulder /'bəʊldə(r)/ *n.* Felsbrocken, *der*

boulevard /'bu:ləvɑ:d/ *n.* Boulevard, *der*

bounce /baʊns/ [1] *v.i.* **(a)** springen
(b) (coll.) ‹*Scheck:*› platzen (ugs.)
[2] *v.t.* aufspringen lassen ‹*Ball*›
[3] *n.* Aufprall, *der*

'bouncer *n.* (coll.) Rausschmeißer, *der* (ugs.)

bouncing /'baʊnsɪŋ/ *adj.* stramm ‹*Baby*›

bouncy /'baʊnsɪ/ *adj.* gut springend ‹*Ball*›; (fig.: lively) munter

bound¹ /baʊnd/ [1] *n., usu. in pl.* (limit) Grenze, *die;* **within the ~s of possibility** im Bereich des Möglichen; **sth. is out of ~s [to sb.]** der Zutritt zu etw. ist [für jmdn.] verboten
[2] *v.t.* **be ~ed by sth.** durch etw. begrenzt werden

bound² [1] *v.i.* hüpfen
[2] *n.* Satz, *der*

bound³ *pred. adj.* **be ~ for home/Frankfurt** auf dem Heimweg/nach Frankfurt unterwegs sein; **homeward ~**: auf dem Weg nach Hause

bound⁴ ▶ BIND

boundary /'baʊndərɪ/ *n.* Grenze, *die*

'boundless *adj.* grenzenlos

bounty /'baʊntɪ/ *n.* Kopfgeld, *das*

bouquet /bʊ'keɪ/ *n.* [Blumen]strauß, *der*

bourgeois /'bʊəʒwɑ:/ [1] *n., pl. same* Bürger, *der*/Bürgerin, *die*
[2] *adj.* bürgerlich

bout /baʊt/ *n.* **(a)** (contest) Wettkampf, *der*
(b) (fit) Anfall, *der*

boutique /bu:'ti:k/ *n.* Boutique, *die*

bow¹ /bəʊ/ **(a)** (curve, weapon, Mus.) Bogen, *der*
(b) (knot, ribbon) Schleife, *die*

bow² /baʊ/ [1] *v.i.* **(a) ~ [to sb.]** sich [vor jmdm.] verbeugen
(b) (submit) sich beugen (**to** *Dat.*)
[2] *n.* Verbeugung, *die*

bow³ /baʊ/ *n.* (Naut.) Bug, *der*

bowel /'baʊəl/ *n.* (Anat.) **~s** *pl.*, (Med.) **~**: Darm, *der*

bowl¹ /bəʊl/ *n.* (basin) Schüssel, *die;* (shallower) Schale, *die;* (of spoon) Schöpfteil, *der;* (of pipe) Kopf, *der*

bowl² [1] *n.* **(a)** (ball) Kugel, *die*

(b) *in pl.* (game) Bowls, *das*
[2] *v.i.* **(a)** (play ~s) Bowls spielen
(b) (Cricket) werfen

bow-legged /ˈbəʊlegɪd/ o-beinig (ugs.)

bowler¹ /ˈbəʊlə(r)/ *n.* (Cricket) Werfer, *der*

bowler² *n.* ~ [hat] Bowler, *der*

ˈbowling *n.* [tenpin] ~: Bowling, *das;* **go ~:** bowlen gehen

bowling: ~ alley *n.* Bowlingbahn, *die;* **~ green** *n.: Rasenfläche für Bowls*

bow /bəʊ/**: ~string** *n.* Bogensehne, *die;* **~ ˈtie** *n.* Fliege, *die;* **~ window** *n.* Erkerfenster, *das*

box¹ /bɒks/ *n.* **(a)** Kasten, *der;* (bigger) Kiste, *die;* (of cardboard) Schachtel, *die*
(b) the ~ (coll.: television) der Kasten (ugs. abwertend); die Flimmerkiste (scherzh.)

box² [1] *n.* **he gave him a ~ on the ear[s]** er gab ihm eine Ohrfeige
[2] *v.t.* **(a) he ~ed his ears** *or* **~ed him round the ears** er ohrfeigte ihn
(b) (Sport) **~ sb.** gegen jmdn. boxen
[3] *v.i.* (Sport) boxen

■ **box ˈin** *v.t.* (enclose tightly) einklemmen

ˈboxer *n.* Boxer, *der*

ˈboxer shorts *n. pl.* Boxershorts *Pl.*

ˈboxing *n.* Boxen, *das*

boxing: B~ Day *n.* zweiter Weihnachtsfeiertag; **~ glove** *n.* Boxhandschuh, *der;* **~ match** *n.* Boxkampf, *der;* **~ ring** *n.* Boxring, *der*

box: ~ junction *n.* (Brit.) *gelb markierter Kreuzungsbereich, in den man bei Stau nicht einfahren darf;* **~ number** *n.* (at newspaper office) Chiffre, *die;* (at post office) Postfach, *das;* **~ office** *n.* Kasse, *die;* **be a ~ office success** ein Kassenerfolg sein; **~room** *n.* (Brit.) Abstellraum, *der*

boy /bɔɪ/ *n.* Junge, *der*

ˈboy band *n.* Boyband, *die*

boycott /ˈbɔɪkɒt/ [1] *v.t.* boykottieren
[2] *n.* Boykott, *der*

ˈboyfriend *n.* Freund, *der*

ˈboyish *adj.* jungenhaft

boy ˈscout ▶ SCOUT 1A

bra /brɑː/ *n.* BH, *der* (ugs.)

brace /breɪs/ [1] *n.* **(a)** (connecting piece) Klammer, *die;* (strut) Strebe, *die;* (Dent.) [Zahn]spange, *die*
(b) *in pl.* (trouser straps) Hosenträger *Pl.*
[2] *v. refl.* **~ oneself for sth.** sich auf etw. (*Akk.*) vorbereiten

bracelet /ˈbreɪslɪt/ *n.* Armband, *das*

bracing /ˈbreɪsɪŋ/ *adj.* belebend

bracken /ˈbrækn/ *n.* [Adler]farn, *der*

bracket /ˈbrækɪt/ [1] *n.* **(a)** (support) Konsole, *die*
(b) (mark) Klammer, *die*
[2] *v.t.* einklammern

brag /bræg/ *v.i. & t.*, **-gg-** prahlen (**about** mit)

braid /breɪd/ [1] *n.* **(a)** (plait) Flechte, *die* (geh.); Zopf, *der*
(b) (woven band) Borte, *die;* (on uniform) Litze, *die*
[2] *v.t.* flechten

Braille /breɪl/ *n.* Blindenschrift, *die*

brain /breɪn/ *n.* Gehirn, *das*

brain: ~child *n.* (coll.) Geistesprodukt, *das;* **~-dead** *adj.* **(a)** (Med.) hirntot; **(b)** (coll. derog.) hirnlos ‹*Person*›; **~less** *adj.* hirnlos; **~storm** *n.* **(a)** Anfall geistiger Umnachtung; **(b)** (Amer. coll.) ▶ ~WAVE; **~storming** *n.* Brainstorming, *das;* **~ tumour** *n.* Gehirntumor, *der;* **~wash** *v.t.* einer Gehirnwäsche unterziehen; **~wave** *n.* (coll.: inspiration) genialer Einfall

ˈbrainy *adj.* intelligent

brake /breɪk/ [1] *n.* Bremse, *die*
[2] *v.t. & i.* bremsen

brake: ~ block *n.* Bremsklotz, *der;* **~ cable** *n.* Bremszug, *der;* Bremsseil, *das;* **~ fluid** *n.* Bremsflüssigkeit, *die;* **~ light** *n.* Bremslicht, *das;* **~ pad** *n.* Bremsbelag, *der;* **~ shoe** *n.* Bremsbacke, *die*

ˈbraking distance *n.* Bremsweg, *der*

bramble /ˈbræmbl/ *n.* Dornenstrauch, *der*

bran /bræn/ *n.* Kleie, *die*

branch /brɑːntʃ/ [1] *n.* **(a)** (bough) Ast, *der;* (twig) Zweig, *der*
(b) (of artery, antlers) Ast, *der*
(c) (office) Zweigstelle, *die;* (shop) Filiale, *die*
[2] *v.i.* sich verzweigen

■ **branch ˈoff** *v.i.* abzweigen

■ **branch ˈout** *v.i.* (fig.) **~ out into sth.** sich auch mit etw. befassen

branch: ~ line *n.* (Railw.) Nebenstrecke, *die;* **~ manager** *n.* Filialleiter, *der*/-leiterin, *die;* **~ office** *n.* Zweigstelle, *die*

brand /brænd/ *n.* **(a)** (trade mark) Markenzeichen, *das;* (goods of particular make) Marke, *die*
(b) (mark) Brandmal, *das*

ˈbrand image *n.* Markenimage, *das*

brandish /ˈbrændɪʃ/ *v.t.* schwenken; schwingen ‹*Waffe*›

brand: ~ leader *n.* (product) marktführendes Produkt; (brand) führende Marke; **~ name** *n.* Markenname, *der;* **~-ˈnew** *adj.* nagelneu (ugs.)

brandy /ˈbrændɪ/ *n.* Weinbrand, *der;* Kognak, *der*

brash /bræʃ/ *adj.* dreist

brass /brɑːs/ *n.* Messing, *das; attrib.* Messing-; **the ~** (Mus.) das Blech; **~ player** (Mus.) Blechbläser, *der;* **get down to ~ tacks** zur Sache kommen

brass ˈband *n.* Blaskapelle, *die*

brassière /ˈbræzjə(r)/ *n.* Büstenhalter, *der*

brat /bræt/ *n.* Balg, *das od. der* (ugs.)

bravado /brəˈvɑːdəʊ/ *n.* **do sth. out of ~:** so waghalsig sein, etw. zu tun

brave /breɪv/ [1] *adj.* tapfer
[2] *n.* [indianischer] Krieger

3 *v.t.* trotzen (+ *Dat.*)

'bravely *adv.* tapfer

bravery /'breɪvərɪ/ *n.* Tapferkeit, *die*

bravo /brɑː'vəʊ/ *int.* bravo

brawl /brɔːl/ 1 *v.i.* sich schlagen
2 *n.* Schlägerei, *die*

brawny /'brɔːnɪ/ *adj.* muskulös

bray /breɪ/ 1 Iah, *das*
2 *v.i.* ‹*Esel*:› iahen

brazen /'breɪzn/ 1 *adj.* dreist; (shameless) schamlos
2 *v.t.* ~ [out] trotzen (+ *Dat.*); **~ it out** (deny guilt) es abstreiten; (not admit guilt) es nicht zugeben

brazier /'breɪzɪə(r)/ *n.* Kohlenbecken, *das*

Brazil /brə'zɪl/ *pr. n.* Brasilien (*das*)

Bra'zil nut *n.* Paranuss, *die*

breach /briːtʃ/ 1 *n.* **(a)** (violation) Verstoß, *der* (of gegen); **~ of faith/duty** Vertrauensbruch, *der*/Pflichtverletzung, *die*
(b) (of relations) Bruch, *der*
(c) (gap) Bresche, *die*; (fig.) Riss, *der*
2 *v.t.* durchbrechen

bread /bred/ *n.* Brot, *das*; **a piece of ~ and butter** ein Butterbrot

bread: ~ bin *n.* Brotkasten, *der*; **~board** *n.* [Brot]brett, *das*; **~crumb** *n.* Brotkrume, *die*; **~crumbs** (coating) Paniermehl, *das*; **~ knife** *n.* Brotmesser, *das*; **~line** *n.* **be** *or* **live on/below the ~line** gerade noch/nicht einmal mehr das Notwendigste zum Leben haben; **~ 'roll** *n.* Brötchen, *das*

breadth /bredθ/ *n.* Breite, *die*

'breadwinner *n.* Ernährer, *der*/Ernährerin, *die*

break /breɪk/ 1 *v.t.*, **broke** /brəʊk/, **broken** /'brəʊkn/ **(a)** brechen; (so as to damage) zerbrechen; kaputtmachen (ugs.); zerreißen ‹*Seil*›; (fig.: interrupt) unterbrechen; brechen ‹*Bann, Zauber, Schweigen*›; **the TV/my watch is broken** der Fernseher/meine Uhr ist kaputt (ugs.); **~ the habit** es sich (*Dat.*) abgewöhnen
(b) (fracture) sich (*Dat.*) brechen ‹*Arm, Bein usw.*›
(c) brechen ‹*Vertrag, Versprechen*›; verstoßen gegen ‹*Regel, Gesetz*›
(d) (surpass) brechen ‹*Rekord*›
(e) (cushion) auffangen ‹*Schlag, jmds. Fall*›
2 *v.i.*, **broke, broken (a)** kaputtgehen (ugs.); ‹*Faden, Seil*:› [zer]reißen; ‹*Glas, Tasse, Teller*:› zerbrechen; ‹*Eis*:› brechen; **~ in two/in pieces** durchbrechen/zerbrechen
(b) ~ into einbrechen in (+ *Akk.*) ‹*Haus*›; aufbrechen ‹*Auto, Safe*›; **~ into laughter/tears** in Gelächter/Tränen ausbrechen; **~ into a trot/run** zu traben/laufen anfangen
(c) (escape) **~ out of prison** aus dem Gefängnis ausbrechen; **~ free** *or* **loose** sich losreißen
(d) ‹*Welle*:› sich brechen (**on/against** an + *Dat.*)
(e) ‹*Tag*:› anbrechen; ‹*Sturm*:› losbrechen
(f) **sb's voice is ~ing** jmd. kommt in den Stimmbruch
3 *n.* **(a)** Bruch, *der*; (of rope) Reißen, *das*; **a ~ with sb./sth.** ein Bruch mit jmdm./etw.
(b) (gap) Lücke, *die*; (broken place) Sprung, *der*
(c) (dash) **they made a sudden ~**: sie stürmten plötzlich davon
(d) (interruption) Unterbrechung, *die*; (pause, holiday) Pause, *die*; **take** *or* **have a ~**: Pause machen
(e) (coll.: chance) Chance, *die*

■ **break 'down** 1 *v.i.* zusammenbrechen; ‹*Verhandlungen*:› scheitern; ‹*Auto*:› eine Panne haben
2 *v.t.* **(a)** aufbrechen ‹*Tür*›; brechen ‹*Widerstand*›; niederreißen ‹*Barriere, Schranke*›
(b) (analyse) aufgliedern

■ **break 'in** 1 *v.i.* (into building etc.) einbrechen
2 *v.t.* **(a)** zureiten ‹*Pferd*›
(b) einlaufen ‹*Schuhe*›
(c) **~ the door in** die Tür aufbrechen

■ **'break into** ▶ ~ 2B

■ **break 'off** 1 *v.t.* abbrechen; abreißen ‹*Faden*›; auflösen ‹*Verlobung*›
2 *v.i.* **(a)** abbrechen
(b) (cease) aufhören

■ **break 'out** *v.i.* ausbrechen; **~ out in spots/a rash** Pickel/einen Ausschlag bekommen

■ **break 'up** 1 *v.t.* **(a)** (**~** into pieces) zerkleinern; ausschlachten ‹*Auto*›; aufbrechen ‹*Erde*›
(b) (disband) auflösen
2 *v.i.* **(a)** (**~** into pieces, lit. or fig.) zerbrechen
(b) (disband) sich auflösen; ‹*Schule*:› schließen; ‹*Schüler, Lehrer*:› in die Ferien gehen
(c) **~ up [with sb.]** sich [von jmdm.] trennen

breakable /'breɪkəbl/ 1 *adj.* zerbrechlich
2 *n.* **~s** zerbrechliche Dinge

breakage /'breɪkɪdʒ/ *n.* Zerbrechen, *das*; **~s must be paid for** zerbrochene Ware muss bezahlt werden

'breakdown *n.* **(a)** (of vehicle) Panne, *die*; (in machine) Störung, *die*; **~ truck/van** Abschleppwagen, *der*
(b) (Med.) Zusammenbruch, *der*
(c) (analysis) Aufschlüsselung, *die*

'breaker *n.* **(a)** (wave) Brecher, *der*
(b) **~'s [yard]** Autoverwertung, *die*

breakfast /'brekfəst/ 1 *n.* Frühstück, *das*; **for ~**: zum Frühstück
2 *v.i.* frühstücken

breakfast: ~ cereal *n.* ≈ Frühstücksflocken *Pl.*; **~ 'television** *n.* Frühstücksfernsehen, *das*

'break-in *n.* Einbruch, *der*

'breaking *n.* **~ and entering** (Law) Einbruch, *der*; **be at ~ point** (mentally) die Grenze der Belastbarkeit erreicht haben

break: ~neck *adj.* halsbrecherisch; ···

~through *n.* Durchbruch, *der;* **~-up** *n.* Auflösung, *die;* (of relationship) Bruch, *der;* **~water** *n.* Wellenbrecher, *der*

breast /brest/ *n.* Brust, *die*

breast: ~bone *n.* Brustbein, *das;* **~ cancer** *n.* Brustkrebs, *der;* **~feed** *v.t. & i.* stillen; **~stroke** *n.* Brustschwimmen, *das*

breath /breθ/ *n.* **(a)** Atem, *der;* **get one's ~ back** wieder zu Atem kommen; **hold one's ~**: den Atem anhalten; **be out of ~**: außer Atem sein; **say sth. under one's ~**: etw. vor sich (*Akk.*) hin murmeln
(b) (one respiration) Atemzug, *der*

Breathalyser (Brit.), **Breathalyzer** ® /ˈbreθəlaɪzə(r)/ *n.* Alcotest-Röhrchen Ⓦⓩ, *das;* **~ test** Alcotest Ⓦⓩ, *der*

breathe /bri:ð/ 1 *v.i.* atmen; **~ in** einatmen; **~ out** ausatmen
2 *v.t.* **(a) ~ [in/out]** ein-/ausatmen
(b) (utter) hauchen

ˈbreather /ˈbri:ðə(r)/ *n.* Verschnaufpause, *die*

ˈbreathing space *n.* Zeit zum Luftholen; (fig.) Atempause, *die*

ˈbreathless *adj.* atemlos (**with** vor + *Dat.*)

breath: ~taking *adj.* atemberaubend; **~ test** *n.* Alcotest Ⓦⓩ, *der*

bred ▶ BREED 1, 2

breeches /ˈbrɪtʃɪz/ *n. pl.* **[pair of] ~**: [Knie]bundhose, *die;* **[riding]~**: Reithose, *die*

breed /bri:d/ 1 *v.t.,* **bred** /bred/ **(a)** (cause) erzeugen
(b) züchten ‹*Tiere, Pflanzen*›
2 *v.i.,* **bred** sich vermehren
3 *n.* (of animals) Rasse, *die*

ˈbreeding *n.* **[good] ~**: gute Erziehung

ˈbreeding ground *n.* (lit. or fig.) Brutstätte, *die*

breeze /bri:z/ *n.* Brise, *die*

ˈbreeze block *n.* (Building) ≈ Leichtstein, *der*

breezy /ˈbri:zɪ/ *adj.* windig

brevity /ˈbrevɪtɪ/ *n.* Kürze, *die*

brew /bru:/ 1 *v.t.* brauen ‹*Bier*›; **~ [up]** kochen ‹*Kaffee, Tee usw.*›
2 *v.i.* **(a)** ‹*Bier:*› gären; ‹*Kaffee, Tee:*› ziehen
(b) ‹*Unwetter:*› sich zusammenbrauen
3 *n.* (brewed beer/tea) Bier, *das*/Tee, *der*

ˈbrewer *n.* Brauer, *der;* (firm) Brauerei, *die*

brewery /ˈbru:ərɪ/ *n.* Brauerei, *die*

bribe /braɪb/ 1 *n.* Bestechung, *die*
2 *v.t.* bestechen; **~ sb. to do/into doing sth.** jmdn. bestechen, damit er etw. tut

bribery /ˈbraɪbərɪ/ *n.* Bestechung, *die*

brick /brɪk/ 1 *n.* Ziegelstein, *der;* (toy) Bauklötzchen, *das*
2 *adj.* Ziegelstein-

brick: ~layer *n.* Maurer, *der;* **~laying** *n.* Mauern, *das;* **~ ˈwall** *n.* Backsteinmauer, *die;* **bang one's head against a ~ wall** (fig.) mit dem Kopf gegen die Wand rennen (fig.)

bridal /ˈbraɪdl/ *adj.* Braut-

bride /braɪd/ *n.* Braut, *die*

ˈbridegroom *n.* Bräutigam, *der*

bridesmaid /ˈbraɪdzmeɪd/ *n.* Brautjungfer, *die*

bridge[1] /brɪdʒ/ 1 *n.* **(a)** Brücke, *die*
(b) (Naut.) [Kommando]brücke, *die*
(c) (of nose) Nasenbein, *das*
(d) (of spectacles) Steg, *der*
2 *v.t.* eine Brücke bauen über (+ *Akk.*)

bridge[2] *n.* (Cards) Bridge, *das*

ˈbridging loan *n.* (Commerc.) Überbrückungskredit, *der*

bridle /ˈbraɪdl/ *n.* Zaum, *der*

ˈbridle path *n.* Reitweg, *der*

brief[1] /bri:f/ *adj.* **(a)** kurz; gering ‹*Verspätung*›
(b) (concise) knapp; **in ~, to be ~**: kurz gesagt

brief[2] 1 *n.* (instructions) Instruktionen *Pl.;* (Law: case) Mandat, *das*
2 *v.t.* Instruktionen geben (+ *Dat.*); (inform) unterrichten

ˈbriefcase *n.* Aktentasche, *die*

ˈbriefing *n.* Briefing, *das;* (of reporters) Unterrichtung, *die*

ˈbriefly *adv.* **(a)** kurz
(b) (concisely) knapp; kurz

briefs /bri:fs/ *n. pl.* **[pair of] ~**: Slip, *der*

brigade /brɪˈgeɪd/ *n.* (Mil.) Brigade, *die*

brigadier /brɪgəˈdɪə(r)/ *n.* Brigadegeneral, *der*

bright /braɪt/ *adj.* **(a)** hell; grell ‹*Scheinwerfer[licht], Sonnenlicht*›; strahlend ‹*Sonnenschein, Augen, Tag*›; leuchtend ‹*Farbe, Blume*›; **~ intervals/periods** Aufheiterungen *Pl.*
(b) (cheerful) fröhlich
(c) (clever) intelligent

brighten /ˈbraɪtn/ 1 *v.t.* **~ [up]** aufhellen
2 *v.i.* **the weather** *or* **it is ~ing [up]** es klärt sich auf

ˈbrightly *adv.* **(a)** hell
(b) (cheerfully) fröhlich

ˈbrightness *n.* ▶ BRIGHT: **(a)** Helligkeit, *die;* Grelle, *die;* Strahlen, *das;* Leuchtkraft, *die*
(b) Fröhlichkeit, *die*
(c) Intelligenz, *die*

brilliance /ˈbrɪlɪəns/ *n.* ▶ BRILLIANT: **(a)** Helligkeit, *die;* Leuchten, *das*
(b) Genialität, *die;* Glanz, *der*

brilliant /ˈbrɪljənt/ *adj.* **(a)** hell ‹*Licht*›; leuchtend ‹*Farbe*›
(b) genial ‹*Mensch, Gedanke, Leistung*›; glänzend ‹*Verstand, Aufführung, Idee*›

brim /brɪm/ 1 *n.* Rand, *der;* (of hat) [Hut]krempe, *die*
2 *v.i.,* **-mm-: be ~ming with sth.** randvoll mit etw. sein

brim-ˈfull *pred. adj.* randvoll (**with** mit)

brine /braɪn/ *n.* Salzwasser, *das*

bring /brɪŋ/ *v.t.*, **brought** /brɔ:t/ **(a)** bringen; (as a present or favour) mitbringen; **~ sth. with one** etw. mitbringen
(b) ~ sb. to do sth. jmdn. dazu bringen, etw. zu tun; **I could not ~ myself to do it** ich konnte es nicht über mich bringen, es zu tun
■ **bring a'bout** *v.t.* verursachen
■ **bring 'back** *v.t.* **(a)** (return) zurückbringen; (from a journey) mitbringen
(b) (recall) in Erinnerung bringen
(c) (restore, reintroduce) wieder einführen
■ **bring 'down** *v.t.* **(a)** herunterbringen
(b) (kill, wound) zur Strecke bringen
(c) senken ‹*Preise, Inflationsrate, Fieber*›
■ **bring 'forward** *v.t.* **(a)** nach vorne bringen
(b) vorverlegen ‹*Termin*› (**to** auf + *Akk.*)
■ **bring 'in** *v.t.* hereinbringen; einbringen ‹*Gesetzesvorlage, Verdienst, Summe*›
■ **bring 'off** *v.t.* (conduct successfully) zustande bringen
■ **bring 'on** *v.t.* **(a)** (cause) verursachen
(b) (Sport) einsetzen
■ **bring 'out** *v.t.* **(a)** herausbringen
(b) hervorheben ‹*Unterschied*›
(c) einführen ‹*Produkt*›; herausbringen ‹*Buch, Zeitschrift*›
■ **bring 'up** *v.t.* **(a)** heraufbringen
(b) (educate) erziehen; (rear) aufziehen
(c) zur Sprache bringen ‹*Angelegenheit, Thema, Problem*›

brink /brɪŋk/ *n.* Rand, *der;* **be on the ~ of doing sth.** nahe daran sein, etw. zu tun

brisk /brɪsk/ *adj.* flott ‹*Gang*›; forsch ‹*Person, Art*›; frisch ‹*Wind*›; (fig.) rege ‹*Handel, Nachfrage*›; lebhaft ‹*Geschäft*›

'briskly *adv.* flott

bristle /'brɪsl/ [1] *n.* Borste, *die*
[2] *v.i.* **(a) ~ [up]** ‹*Haare:*› sich sträuben
(b) ~ with (fig.) starren vor (+ *Dat.*)

bristly /'brɪslɪ/ *adj.* borstig

Brit /brit/ *n.* (coll.) Brite, *der*/Britin, *die;* Engländer, *der*/Engländerin, *die* (ugs.)

Britain /'brɪtn/ *pr. n.* Großbritannien (*das*)

British /'brɪtɪʃ/ [1] *adj.* britisch; **he/she is ~**: er ist Brite/sie ist Britin
[2] *n. pl.* **the ~**: die Briten

British 'Isles *pr. n. pl.* Britische Inseln

Briton /'brɪtn/ *n.* Brite, *der*/Britin, *die*

Brittany /'brɪtənɪ/ *pr. n.* Bretagne, *die*

brittle /'brɪtl/ *adj.* spröde ‹*Material*›

broach /brəʊtʃ/ *v.t.* anschneiden ‹*Thema*›

broad /brɔ:d/ *adj.* **(a)** breit; (extensive) weit ‹*Ebene, Land*›; ausgedehnt ‹*Fläche*›
(b) (explicit) klar ‹*Hinweis*›; breit ‹*Lächeln*›
(c) (main) grob; (generalized) allgemein
(d) stark ‹*Akzent*›

'broadband *n.* (Comp.) Breitband, *das; attrib.* Breitband-

broad 'bean *n.* Saubohne, *die*

broadcast /'brɔ:dkɑ:st/ [1] *n.* Sendung, *die;* (live) Übertragung, *die*
[2] *v.t.*, **broadcast** senden; übertragen ‹*Livesendung*›
[3] *v.i.*, **broadcast** senden

'broadcaster *n.* (Radio, Telev.) *jmd., der durch häufige Auftritte im Rundfunk und Fernsehen, besonders als Interviewpartner, Diskussionsteilnehmer od. Kommentator, bekannt ist*

'broadcasting *n.* Senden, *das;* (live) Übertragen, *das;* **work in ~**: beim Funk arbeiten

broaden /'brɔ:dn/ [1] *v.t.* **(a)** verbreitern
(b) ausweiten ‹*Diskussion*›
[2] *v.i.* sich verbreitern; (fig.) sich erweitern

'broadly *adv.* **(a)** deutlich ‹*hinweisen*›; breit ‹*grinsen, lächeln*›
(b) (in general) allgemein ‹*beschreiben*›; **~ speaking** allgemein gesagt

broad: ~-'minded *adj.* tolerant; **~sheet** *n.* **(a)** (Printing) Einblattdruck, *der;* **(b)** (pamphlet) Flugblatt, *das;* **~-'shouldered** *adj.* breitschultrig; **~side** *n.* Breitseite, *die*

brocade /brə'keɪd/ *n.* Brokat, *der*

broccoli /'brɒkəlɪ/ *n.* Brokkoli, *der*

brochure /'brəʊʃə(r)/ *n.* Broschüre, *die;* Prospekt, *der*

broil /'brɔɪl/ *v.t.* (esp. Amer.) grillen

broke /brəʊk/ [1] ▶ BREAK 1, 2
[2] *pred. adj.* (coll.) pleite (ugs.)

broken /'brəʊkn/ [1] ▶ BREAK 1, 2
[2] *adj.* **(a)** zerbrochen; gebrochen ‹*Bein, Hals*›; verletzt ‹*Haut*›; abgebrochen ‹*Zahn*›; gerissen ‹*Seil*›; kaputt (ugs.) ‹*Uhr, Fernsehen, Fenster*›; **~ glass** Glasscherben *Pl.*
(b) (imperfect) gebrochen; **in ~ English** in gebrochenem Englisch
(c) (fig.) ruiniert ‹*Ehe*›; gebrochen ‹*Mensch, Herz*›

broken: ~-down *adj.* baufällig ‹*Gebäude*›; kaputt (ugs.) ‹*Wagen*›; **~-'hearted** *adj.* untröstlich

broker /'brəʊkə(r)/ *n.* Makler, *der*

brolly /'brɒlɪ/ *n.* (Brit. coll.) [Regen]schirm, *der*

bronchitis /brɒŋ'kaɪtɪs/ *n.* Bronchitis, *die*

bronze /brɒnz/ [1] *n.* Bronze, *die*
[2] *attrib. adj.* Bronze-; (coloured like ~) bronzefarben

brooch /brəʊtʃ/ *n.* Brosche, *die*

brood /bru:d/ [1] *n.* Brut, *die*
[2] *v.i.* [vor sich (*Akk.*) hin] brüten

brook /brʊk/ *n.* Bach, *der*

broom /bru:m/ *n.* **(a)** Besen, *der*
(b) (Bot.) Ginster, *der*

broom: ~ cupboard *n.* Besenschrank, *der;* **~stick** *n.* Besenstiel, *der*

broth /brɒθ/ *n.* Brühe, *die*

brothel /'brɒθl/ *n.* Bordell, *das*

brother /'brʌðə(r)/ *n.* Bruder, *der;* **my ~s and sisters** meine Geschwister ···›

b

'brotherhood *n.* (organization) Bruderschaft, *die*

'brother-in-law *n., pl.* **brothers-in-law** Schwager, *der*

brought ▶ BRING

brow /braʊ/ *n.* **(a)** (eye~) Braue, *die* **(b)** (forehead) Stirn, *die* **(c)** (of hill) Kuppe, *die*

'browbeat *v.t., forms as* BEAT 1 einschüchtern

brown /braʊn/ 1 *adj.* braun 2 *n.* Braun, *das*

brown: ~ 'bread *n.* ≈ Mischbrot, *das;* **~-eyed** *adj.* braunäugig; **be ~-eyed** braune Augen haben

Brownie /'braʊnɪ/ *n.* Wichtel, *die*

brown: ~ 'paper *n.* Packpapier, *das;* **~ 'rice** *n.* Naturreis, *der*

browse /braʊz/ *v.i.* 1 **(a)** weiden **(b)** (in shop) sich umsehen; (read) blättern (**through** in + *Dat.*) **(c)** (Comp.) suchen; **~ through sth.** etw. durchsuchen 2 **(a)** abgrasen ‹*Weide*›; abfressen ‹*Blätter*› **(b)** (Comp.) **~ sth** in etw. (*Dat.*) suchen

browser /'braʊzə(r)/ *n.* (Comp.) Browser, *der*

bruise /bru:z/ 1 *n.* **(a)** (Med.) blauer Fleck **(b)** (on fruit) Druckstelle, *die* 2 *v.t.* quetschen ‹*Obst, Pflanzen*›; **~ oneself/one's leg** sich stoßen/sich am Bein stoßen

brunch /brʌntʃ/ *n.* (coll.) Brunch, *der;* ausgedehntes, spätes Frühstück

brunette /bru:'net/ 1 *n.* Brünette, *die* 2 *adj.* brünett

brunt /brʌnt/ *n.* **bear the ~ of the attack/financial cuts** von dem Angriff/von den Einsparungen am meisten betroffen sein

brush /brʌʃ/ 1 *n.* **(a)** Bürste, *die;* (for sweeping) Besen, *der;* (with short handle) Handfeger, *der;* (for painting or writing) Pinsel, *der* **(b)** (skirmish) Zusammenstoß, *der* **(c)** (light touch) flüchtige Berührung 2 *v.t.* **(a)** kehren; fegen; abbürsten ‹*Kleidung*›; **~ one's teeth/hair** sich (*Dat.*) die Zähne putzen/die Haare bürsten **(b)** (touch in passing) streifen 3 *v.i.* **~ past sb./sth.** jmdn./etw. streifen

■ **brush 'up** *v.t. & i.* **~ up [on]** auffrischen ‹*Kenntnisse usw.*›

brusque /brʌsk/ *adj.*, **'brusquely** *adv.* schroff

Brussels /'brʌslz/ *pr. n.* Brüssel (*das*)

Brussels 'sprouts *n. pl.* Rosenkohl, *der*

brutal /'bru:tl/ *adj.* brutal

brutality /bru:'tælɪtɪ/ *n.* Brutalität, *die*

brutally /'bru:təlɪ/ *adv.* brutal

brute /bru:t/ 1 *n.* **(a)** (animal) Bestie, *die* **(b)** (person) Rohling, *der* 2 *attrib. adj.* **by ~ force** mit roher Gewalt

B.Sc. *abbr.* = **Bachelor of Science**

BSE *abbr.* = **bovine spongiform encephalopathy** BSE

BST *abbr.* = **British Summer Time** Britische Sommerzeit

bubble /'bʌbl/ 1 *n.* Blase, *die;* (small) Perle, *die* 2 *v.i.* ‹*Wasser, Schlamm, Lava:*› Blasen bilden

bubble: ~ bath *n.* Schaumbad, *das;* **~ pack** *n.* Klarsichtpackung, *die;* **~-wrapped** *adj.* in Luftpolsterfolie verpackt

buck¹ /bʌk/ *n.* (deer, chamois) Bock, *der;* (rabbit, hare) Rammler, *der*

buck² *n.* **pass the ~ to sb.** jmdm. die Verantwortung aufhalsen

buck³ (coll.) 1 *v.i.* **~ 'up (a)** (make haste) sich ranhalten (ugs.) **(b)** (cheer up) **~ up!** Kopf hoch! 2 *v.t.* **~ one's ideas up** (coll.) sich zusammenreißen

buck⁴ *n.* (Amer. coll.) Dollar, *der*

bucket /'bʌkɪt/ *n.* Eimer, *der*

bucketful /'bʌkɪtfʊl/ *n.* Eimer [voll]

bucket: ~ seat *n.* Schalensitz, *der;* **~ shop** *n.* [nicht ganz seriöses] Maklerbüro; (for air tickets) Reisebüro (*das vor allem Billigflüge vermittelt*)

buckle /'bʌkl/ 1 *n.* Schnalle, *die* 2 *v.t.* **(a)** zuschnallen; **~ sth. on/up** etw. anschnallen/festschnallen **(b)** verbiegen ‹*Stoßstange, Rad*› 3 *v.i.* ‹*Rad, Metallplatte:*› [sich] verbiegen

bud /bʌd/ 1 *n.* Knospe, *die;* **come into ~/be in ~:** Knospen treiben 2 *v.i.*, **-dd-** Knospen treiben

Buddha /'bʊdə/ *n.* Buddha, *der*

Buddhism /'bʊdɪzm/ *n.* Buddhismus, *der*

Buddhist /'bʊdɪst/ 1 *n.* Buddhist, *der*/Buddhistin, *die* 2 *adj.* buddhistisch

budge /bʌdʒ/ 1 *v.i.* sich rühren; ‹*Gegenstand:*› sich bewegen 2 *v.t.* bewegen

budgerigar /'bʌdʒərɪgɑ:(r)/ *n.* Wellensittich, *der*

budget /'bʌdʒɪt/ 1 *n.* Etat, *der;* Haushalt[splan], *der* 2 *v.i.* **~ for sth.** etw. [im Etat] einplanen

'budget account *n.* Konto für laufende Zahlungen

budgie /'bʌdʒɪ/ *n.* (coll.) Wellensittich, *der*

buff /bʌf/ 1 *adj.* gelbbraun 2 *n.* (coll.: enthusiast) Fan, *der* (ugs.)

buffalo /'bʌfələʊ/ *n., pl.* **~es** *or same* Büffel, *der*

buffer /'bʌfə(r)/ *n.* Prellbock, *der;* (on vehicle; also fig.) Puffer, *der*

buffet /'bʊfeɪ/ *n.* Büfett, *das*

'buffet car *n.* Büfettwagen, *der*

bug /bʌg/ *n.* (also coll.: microphone) Wanze, *die*

bugger /'bʌgə(r)/ (coarse) [1] *n.* (as insult) Scheißkerl, *der* (derb)
[2] *v.t.* (damn) ~ **you/him** du kannst/der kann mich mal (derb); ~ **it!** ach du Scheiße! (derb)
■ ~ **'off** *v.i.* abhauen (ugs.)

buggy /'bʌgɪ/ *n.* (pushchair) Sportwagen, *der*

bugle /'bju:gl/ *n.* Bügelhorn, *das*

build /bɪld/ [1] *v.t.*, **built** /bɪlt/ bauen; (fig.) aufbauen ‹*System, Gesellschaft, Zukunft*›
[2] *v.i.*, **built** bauen
[3] *n.* Körperbau, *der*
■ **build 'in** *v.t.* einbauen
■ **build 'on** *v.t.* aufbauen auf (+ *Dat.*); bebauen ‹*Gebiet*›
■ **build 'up** [1] *v.t.* aufhäufen ‹*Reserven, Mittel*›; kräftigen ‹*Personen, Körper*›; steigern ‹*Produktion, Kapazität*›; stärken ‹[*Selbst*]*vertrauen*›; aufbauen ‹*Firma, Geschäft*›
[2] *v.i.* ‹*Spannung, Druck:*› zunehmen; ‹*Schlange, Rückstau:*› sich bilden; ‹*Verkehr:*› sich verdichten

'builder *n.* Bauunternehmer, *der*

'building *n.* **(a)** Bau, *der*
(b) (structure) Gebäude, *das*

building: ~ **site** *n.* Baustelle, *die;* ~ **society** *n.* (Brit.) Bausparkasse, *die*

built ▶ BUILD 1, 2

built: ~**-in** *adj.* **(a)** eingebaut; Einbau‹*schrank, küche usw.*›; **(b)** (fig.: instinctive) angeboren; ~**-up** *adj.* bebaut; ~**-up area** Wohngebiet, *das;* (Motor Veh.) geschlossene Ortschaft

bulb /bʌlb/ *n.* **(a)** (Bot., Hort.) Zwiebel, *die*
(b) (of lamp) [Glüh]birne, *die*

Bulgaria /bʌl'geərɪə/ *pr. n.* Bulgarien (*das*)

Bulgarian /bʌl'geərɪən/ [1] *adj.* bulgarisch; **sb. is** ~: jmd. ist Bulgare/Bulgarin
[2] *n.* **(a)** (person) Bulgare, *der*/Bulgarin, *die*
(b) (language) Bulgarisch, *das; see also* ENGLISH 2A

bulge /bʌldʒ/ [1] *n.* Ausbeulung, *die;* ausgebeulte Stelle
[2] *v.i.* sich wölben

bulimia (nervosa) /bʊ'li:mɪə (nɜ:'vəʊsə)/ *n.* Bulimie, *die;* Bulimia nervosa, *die* (fachspr.)

bulimic /bʊ'lɪmɪk/ [1] *n.* Bulimiker, *der*/Bulimikerin, *die*
[2] *adj.* bulimisch

bulk /bʌlk/ *n.* **(a)** (large quantity) **in** ~: in großen Mengen
(b) (large shape) massige Gestalt
(c) (size) Größe, *die*
(d) (greater part) der größte Teil; (of population, votes) Mehrheit, *die*

bulk 'buying *n.* Großeinkauf, *der*

'bulky *adj.* sperrig ‹*Gegenstand*›; massig ‹*Gestalt, Körper*›

bull /bʊl/ *n.* Bulle, *der;* (esp. for bullfight) Stier, *der*

bull: ~ **bar** *n.* Rammschutz, *der;* Rammbügel, *der;* ~**dog** *n.* Bulldogge, *die*

bulldozer /'bʊldəʊzə(r)/ *n.* Planierraupe, *die*

bullet /'bʊlɪt/ *n.* Kugel, *die*

'bullet hole *n.* Einschuss, *der;* Einschussloch, *das*

bulletin /'bʊlɪtɪn/ *n.* Bulletin, *das*

'bulletin board *n.* (Comp.) schwarzes Brett

'bulletproof *adj.* kugelsicher

bull: ~**fight** *n.* Stierkampf, *der;* ~**fighter** *n.* Stierkämpfer, *der;* ~**fighting** *n.* Stierkämpfe *Pl.*

bullion /'bʊljən/ *n.* **gold** ~: Goldbarren *Pl.*

'bull neck *n.* Stiernacken, *der*

bullock /'bʊlək/ *n.* Ochse, *der*

bull: ~**ring** *n.* Stierkampfarena, *die;* ~**seye** *n.* (of target) Schwarze, *das;* ~**shit** (coarse) *n.* Scheiße, *die* (salopp abwertend)

bully /'bʊlɪ/ [1] *n.* (schoolboy etc.) ≈ Rabauke, *der;* (boss) Tyrann, *der*
[2] *v.t.* schikanieren; (frighten) einschüchtern

bullying /'bʊlɪɪŋ/ *n.* Schikanieren, *das*

bum¹ /bʌm/ *n.* (Brit. coll.) Hintern, *der* (ugs.)

bum² *n.* (Amer. coll.: tramp) Penner, *der* (salopp)

bumble-bee /'bʌmblbi:/ *n.* Hummel, *die*

bumf /bʌmf/ *n.* (Brit. coll. derog.: papers) Papierkram, *der* (ugs.)

bump /bʌmp/ [1] *n.* **(a)** (sound) Bums, *der;* (impact) Stoß, *der*
(b) (swelling) Beule, *die*
(c) (hump) Buckel, *der* (ugs.)
[2] *adv.* bums
[3] *v.t.* anstoßen
■ **'bump into** *v.t.* **(a)** stoßen an (+ *Akk.*)
(b) (meet by chance) zufällig [wieder]treffen

'bumper [1] *n.* Stoßstange, *die;* ~**-to-**~ Stoßstange an Stoßstange
[2] *attrib. adj.* Rekord‹*ernte, -jahr*›

'bumpy *adj.* holp[e]rig ‹*Straße, Fahrt, Fahrzeug*›; uneben ‹*Fläche*›; unruhig ‹*Flug*›

bun /bʌn/ *n.* süßes Brötchen; (currant ~) Korinthenbrötchen, *das*

bunch /bʌntʃ/ *n.* **(a)** (of flowers) Strauß, *der;* (of grapes, bananas) Traube, *die;* (of parsley, radishes) Bund, *das;* ~ **of flowers/grapes** Blumenstrauß, *der*/Traube, *die;* **a** ~ **of keys** ein Schlüsselbund
(b) (lot) Anzahl, *die;* **the best** *or* **pick of the** ~: der/die/das Beste [von allen]
(c) (of people) Haufen, *der* (ugs.)

bundle /'bʌndl/ *n.* Bündel, *das;* (of papers) Packen, *der*

bung /bʌŋ/ [1] *n.* Spund, *der*
[2] *v.t.* (coll.) schmeißen (ugs.)
■ **bung 'up** *v.i.* **be/get** ~**ed up** verstopft sein/verstopfen

bungalow /'bʌŋgələʊ/ *n.* Bungalow, *der*

'bungee jumping /'bʌndʒɪ/ *n.* Bungeespringen, *das*

bungle /'bʌŋgl/ *v.t.* stümpern bei

bunk /bʌŋk/ *n.* (in ship, lorry) Koje, *die;* (in sleeping car) Bett, *das;* (~ bed) Etagenbett, *das*

b

bunker /'bʌŋkə(r)/ *n.* Bunker, *der*

bunny /'bʌnɪ/ *n.* Häschen, *das*

buoy /bɔɪ/ *n.* Boje, *die*

buoyancy /'bɔɪənsɪ/ *n.* Auftrieb, *der*

buoyant /'bɔɪənt/ *adj.* **(a)** schwimmend; **be ~**: schwimmen
(b) (fig.) rege, lebhaft ‹*Markt*›; heiter, munter ‹*Person*›; **in ~ spirits** in Hochstimmung

burden /'bɜ:dn/ **1** *n.* Last, *die;* **become a ~** (fig.) zur Last werden
2 *v.t.* belasten (**with** mit)

bureau /'bjʊərəʊ, bjʊə'rəʊ/ *n.* **(a)** (Brit.: writing desk) Sekretär, *der*
(b) (office) Büro, *das*

bureaucracy /bjʊə'rɒkrəsɪ/ *n.* Bürokratie, *die*

bureaucrat /'bjʊərəkræt/ *n.* Bürokrat, *der*/Bürokratin, *die*

bureaucratic /bjʊərə'krætɪk/ *adj.* bürokratisch

burger /'bɜ:gə(r)/ *n.* (coll.) Hamburger, *der*

'burger bar *n.* (coll.) Hamburgerlokal, *das*

burglar /'bɜ:glə(r)/ *n.* Einbrecher, *der*

burglar: ~ alarm *n.* Alarmanlage, *die;* **~-proof** *adj.* einbruch[s]sicher

burglary /'bɜ:glərɪ/ *n.* Einbruch, *der*

burgle /'bɜ:gl/ *v.t.* einbrechen in (+ *Akk.*); **the shop/he was ~d** in dem Laden/bei ihm wurde eingebrochen

burial /'berɪəl/ *n.* Begräbnis, *das*

burly /'bɜ:lɪ/ *adj.* stämmig

Burma /'bɜ:mə/ *pr. n.* Birma (*das*)

Burmese /bɜ:'mi:z/ **1** *adj.* birmanisch; **sb. is ~**: jmd. ist Birmane/Birmanin
2 *n., pl. same* **(a)** (person) Birmane, *der*/ Birmanin, *die*
(b) (language) Birmanisch, *das; see also* ENGLISH 2A

burn /bɜ:n/ **1** *n.* (on the skin) Verbrennung, *die;* (on material) Brandfleck, *der*
2 *v.t.*, **~t** /bɜ:nt/ *or* **~ed** **(a)** verbrennen; **~ oneself/one's hand** sich verbrennen/sich (*Dat.*) die Hand verbrennen; **~ a hole in sth.** ein Loch in etw. (*Akk.*) brennen
(b) als Brennstoff verwenden ‹*Gas, Öl usw.*›; heizen mit ‹*Kohle, Holz, Torf*›
(c) (spoil) anbrennen lassen ‹*Fleisch, Kuchen*›; **be ~t** angebrannt sein
(d) (Comp.) brennen ‹*CD, CD-ROM*›
3 *v.i.*, **~t** *or* **~ed** brennen; **~ to death** verbrennen; **she ~s easily** sie bekommt leicht einen Sonnenbrand

■ **burn 'down** *v.t. & i.* niederbrennen

'burned-out *adj.* (lit. or fig.) ausgebrannt

'burner *n.* Brenner, *der*

'burning *adj.* glühend ‹*Leidenschaft, Hass, Wunsch*›; brennend ‹*Wunsch, Frage*›

'burn-out *n.* Burn-out, *das* (Med.); totale Erschöpfung *od.* Entkräftung; **risk ~**: Gefahr laufen, sich zu übernehmen

burnt ▶ BURN 2, 3

'burnt-out ▶ BURNED-OUT

burp /bɜ:p/ (coll.) **1** *n.* Rülpser, *der* (ugs.)
2 *v.i.* rülpsen (ugs.)

burrow /'bʌrəʊ/ **1** *n.* Bau, *der*
2 *v.i.* [sich (*Dat.*)] einen Gang graben

burst /bɜ:st/ **1** *n.* **(a)** (split) Bruch, *der*
(b) (of firing) Salve, *die*
(c) (fig.) **a ~ of applause/cheering** ein Beifallsausbruch/Beifallsrufe *Pl.*
2 *v.t.*, **burst** zum Platzen bringen; platzen lassen ‹*Luftballon*›; **~ pipe** Rohrbruch, *der*
3 *v.i.*, **burst** **(a)** platzen; ‹*Bombe:*› explodieren; ‹*Damm:*› brechen; ‹*Flussufer:*› überschwemmt werden; ‹*Furunkel, Geschwür:*› aufgehen
(b) be ~ing with sth. zum Bersten voll sein mit etw.; **be ~ing with pride/impatience/ excitement** vor Stolz/Ungeduld platzen/vor Aufregung außer sich sein

■ **'burst into** *v.t.* **(a)** eindringen in
(b) ~ into tears/laughter in Tränen/ Gelächter ausbrechen; **~ into flames** in Brand geraten

■ **burst 'out** *v.i.* **(a)** herausstürzen
(b) (exclaim) losplatzen
(c) ~ out laughing/crying in Lachen/Tränen ausbrechen

bury /'berɪ/ *v.t.* **(a)** begraben
(b) (hide) vergraben; **~ one's face in one's hands** das Gesicht in den Händen vergraben
(c) ~ one's teeth in sth. seine Zähne in etw. (*Akk.*) graben

bus /bʌs/ *n.* Bus, *der*

bus: ~ company *n.* ≈ Verkehrsbetrieb, *der;* **~ conductor** *n.* Busschaffner, *der*/ -schaffnerin, *die;* **~ depot** ▶ **~** GARAGE; **~ driver** *n.* Busfahrer, *der*/-fahrerin, *die;* **~ fare** *n.* [Bus]fahrpreis, *der;* **~ garage** *n.* Busdepot, *das*

bush /bʊʃ/ *n.* **(a)** Busch, *der*
(b) (shrubs) Gebüsch, *das*

'bushy *adj.* buschig

busily /'bɪzɪlɪ/ *adj.* eifrig

business /'bɪznɪs/ *n.* **(a)** (trading operation) Geschäft, *das;* (company, firm) Betrieb, *der;* (large) Unternehmen, *das;* **how's ~ with you?** (lit. or fig.) was machen die Geschäfte [bei Ihnen]?; **~ is ~** (fig.) Geschäft ist Geschäft; **go out of ~**: Pleite gehen (ugs.); **go into ~**: Geschäftsmann/-frau werden
(b) (buying and selling) Geschäfte *Pl.*
(c) (task, province) Aufgabe, *die;* **mind your own ~!** kümmere dich um deine [eigenen] Angelegenheiten!
(d) (difficult matter) Problem, *das*

business: ~ address *n.* Geschäftsadresse, *die;* **~ card** *n.* Geschäftskarte, *die;* **~ class** **1** *n., no pl.* Businessklasse, *die; attrib.* Businessklasse-;
2 *adv.* **fly/travel ~ class** in der Businessklasse fliegen/reisen;
~ correspondence *n.* Geschäftskorrespondenz, *die;* **~ hours** *n. pl.* Geschäftszeit, *die;* (in office) Dienstzeit, *die;* **~ letter** *n.* Geschäftsbrief, *der;* **~-like**

adj. geschäftsmäßig ‹*Art*›; geschäftstüchtig ‹*Person*›; ~ **lunch** *n.* Arbeitsessen, *das;* ~**man** *n.* Geschäftsmann, *der;* ~ **park** *n.* Gewerbepark, *der;* ~ **plan** *n.* Geschäftsplan, *der;* ~ **premises** *n. pl.* Geschäftsräume *Pl.*; ~ **school** *n.* kaufmännische Fachschule; ~ **studies** *n. pl.* Wirtschaftslehre, *die;* ~ **trip** *n.* Geschäftsreise, *die;* **on a ~ trip** auf Geschäftsreise; ~**woman** *n.* Geschäftsfrau, *die*

busker /'bʌskə(r)/ *n.* Straßenmusikant, *der*

bus: ~ **lane** *n.* (Brit.) Busspur, *die;* ~ **ride** *n.* Busfahrt, *die;* **B. is only an hour's ~ ride away** B. ist nur eine Busstunde entfernt; ~ **route** *n.* Buslinie, *die;* ~ **service** *n.* Omnibusverkehr, *der;* (specific service) Busverbindung, *die;* ~ **shelter** *n.* Wartehäuschen, *das;* ~ **station** *n.* Omnibusbahnhof, *der;* ~ **stop** *n.* Bushaltestelle, *die*

bust¹ /bʌst/ *n.* **(a)** (sculpture) Büste, *die* **(b)** ~ **[measurement]** Oberweite, *die*

bust² (coll.) **1** *adj.* kaputt (ugs.) **2** *v.t.*, ~**ed** *or* **bust** (break) kaputtmachen (ugs.); ~ **sth. open** etw. aufbrechen **3** *v.i.*, ~**ed** *or* **bust** kaputtgehen (ugs.)

bus: ~ **terminal** *n.* Busbahnhof, *der;* ~ **ticket** *n.* Busfahrkarte, *die;* Busfahrschein, *der*

bustle /'bʌsl/ **1** *v.i.* ~ **about** geschäftig hin und her eilen **2** *n.* Betrieb, *der*

bustling /'bʌslɪŋ/ *adj.* belebt ‹*Straße, Stadt, Markt usw.*›; rege ‹*Tätigkeit*›

busy /'bɪzɪ/ **1** *adj.* **(a)** beschäftigt (**at, with** mit); arbeitsreich ‹*Leben*›; ziemlich hektisch ‹*Zeit*›; **I'm ~ now** ich habe jetzt zu tun; **he was ~ packing** er war mit Packen beschäftigt **(b)** (Amer. Teleph.) besetzt **2** *v. refl.* ~ **oneself** sich beschäftigen (**with** mit)

'busybody *n.* G[e]schaftlhuber, *der*

but **1** /bət, *stressed* bʌt/ *conj.* aber; *correcting after a negative* sondern; **not that book ~ this one** nicht das Buch, sondern dieses **2** /bət/ *prep.* außer (+ *Dat.*); **the next/last ~ one** der/die/das übernächste/vorletzte

butcher /'bʊtʃə(r)/ **1** *n.* Fleischer, *der*/Fleischerin, *die* **2** *v.t.* (murder) niedermetzeln

butler /'bʌtlə(r)/ *n.* Butler, *der*

butt¹ /bʌt/ *n.* **(a)** (of rifle) Kolben, *der* **(b)** (of cigarette, cigar) Stummel, *der*

butt² *n.* (object of teasing or ridicule) Zielscheibe, *die*

butt³ **1** *n.* (push) (by person) [Kopf]stoß, *der;* (by animal) Stoß [mit den Hörnern] **2** *v.t. & i.* mit dem Kopf/den Hörnern stoßen

■ **butt 'in** *v.i.* dazwischenreden

butter /'bʌtə(r)/ **1** *n.* Butter, *die* **2** *v.t.* buttern

butter: ~ **bean** *n.* Mondbohne, *die;* ~**cup** *n.* Butterblume, *die;* ~ **dish** *n.* Butterdose, *die;* ~**fingers** *n. sing.* Tollpatsch, *der* (*beim Fangen usw.*); ~**fly** *n.* **(a)** Schmetterling, *der;* **(b)** ~**fly [stroke]** Delphinstil, *der;* ~ **mountain** *n.* Butterberg, *der*

buttock /'bʌtək/ *n.* Hinterbacke, *die;* Gesäßhälfte, *die;* ~**s** Gesäß, *das*

button /'bʌtn/ **1** *n.* Knopf, *der* **2** *v.t.* ~ **[up]** zuknöpfen

'buttonhole **1** *n.* **(a)** Knopfloch, *das* **(b)** (flower) Knopflochblume, *die* **2** *v.t.* zu fassen kriegen (ugs.)

buttress /'bʌtrɪs/ *n.* (Archit.) Mauerstütze, *die*

buxom /'bʌksəm/ *adj.* drall

buy /baɪ/ **1** *v.t.*, **bought** /bɔːt/ kaufen; ~ **sb./oneself sth.** jmdm./sich etw. kaufen **2** *n.* [Ein]kauf, *der;* **be a good ~**: preiswert sein

■ **buy 'up** *v.t.* aufkaufen

'buyer *n.* **(a)** Käufer, *der*/Käuferin, *die* **(b)** (Commerc.) Einkäufer, *der*/Einkäuferin, *die*

'buying power /'baɪɪŋ/ *n.* Kaufkraft, *die*

'buyout *n.* Aufkauf, *der*; Management-Buy-Out, *das* (Wirtsch.)

buzz /bʌz/ **1** *n.* Summen, *das* **2** *v.i.* summen

■ **buzz 'off** *v.i.* (coll.) abhauen (salopp)

'buzzer *n.* Summer, *der*

by /baɪ/ **1** *prep.* **(a)** (near, beside) an (+ *Dat.*); bei; (next to) neben; ~ **the window/river** am Fenster/Fluss **(b)** (to position beside) zu **(c)** (about, in the possession of) bei **(d)** **[all] by herself/himself** *etc.* [ganz] allein[e] **(e)** (along) entlang; (via) über (+ *Akk.*) **(f)** (passing) vorbei an (+ *Dat.*) **(g)** (during) bei; **by day/night** bei Tag/Nacht **(h)** (through the agency of) von; **written by ...**: geschrieben von ... **(i)** (through the means of) durch; **by bus/ship** *etc.* mit dem Bus/Schiff *usw.;* **by air/sea** mit dem Flugzeug/Schiff **(j)** (not later than) bis; **by now/this time** inzwischen **(k)** (indicating unit) pro; **by the minute/hour** pro Minute/Stunde; **day by day/month by month** Tag für Tag/Monat für Monat; **10 ft. by 20 ft.** 10 [Fuß] mal 20 Fuß **(l)** (indicating amount) **one by one** einzeln; **two by two/three by three** zu zweit/dritt **(m)** (indicating factor) durch; **8 divided by 2 is 4** 8 geteilt durch 2 ist 4 **(n)** (indicating extent) um; **wider by a foot** um einen Fuß breiter **(o)** (according to) nach **2** *adv.* **(a)** (past) vorbei **(b)** (near) **close/near by** in der Nähe **(c)** **by and large** im Großen und Ganzen

C

bye[-bye] /'baɪ(baɪ)/ *int.* (coll.) tschüs (ugs.)
bye-law ▶ BY-LAW
'by-election *n.* Nachwahl, *die*
bygone /'baɪgɒn/ *adj.* vergangen
'by-law *n.* (esp. Brit.) Verordnung, *die*
'bypass [1] *n.* **(a)** Umgehungsstraße, *die* **(b)** (Med.) Bypass, *der;* **~ surgery** (Med.) eine Bypassoperation/Bypassoperationen *Pl.* [2] *v.t.* **(a) the road ~es the town** die Straße führt um die Stadt herum **(b)** (fig.) übergehen
'by-product *n.* Nebenprodukt, *das*
'byroad *n.* Nebenstraße, *die*
bystander /'baɪstændə(r)/ *n.* Zuschauer, *der*/Zuschauerin, *die*
byte /'baɪt/ *n.* (Comp.) Byte, *das*
'byway *n.* Seitenweg, *der*
'byword *n.* Inbegriff, *der* (**for** *Gen.*)

Cc

C, c /si:/ *n.* C, c, *das*
C. *abbr.* **(a)** = **Celsius** C **(b)** = **Centigrade** C
cab /kæb/ *n.* **(a)** (taxi) Taxi, *das* **(b)** (of lorry, truck) Fahrerhaus, *das;* (of train) Führerstand, *der*
cabaret /'kæbəreɪ/ *n.* Varietee, *das;* (satirical) Kabarett, *das*
cabbage /'kæbɪdʒ/ *n.* Kohl, *der;* **red/white ~**: Rot-/Weißkohl, *der*
'cab driver *n.* Taxifahrer, *der*/-fahrerin, *die*
cabin /'kæbɪn/ *n.* (in ship) (for passengers) Kabine, *die;* (for crew) Kajüte, *die;* (in aircraft) Kabine, *die*
cabinet /'kæbɪnɪt/ *n.* **(a)** Schrank, *der;* (in bathroom, for medicines) Schränkchen, *das;* **[display] ~**: Vitrine, *die* **(b) the C~** (Polit.) das Kabinett; **C~ Minister** Minister, *der*
cable /'keɪbl/ [1] *n.* **(a)** (rope) Kabel, *das;* (of ~ car etc.) Seil, *das* **(b)** (Electr., Teleph.) Kabel, *das* **(c)** (message) Kabel, *das* [2] *v.t.* kabeln ‹*Mitteilung, Nachricht*›
cable: ~ car *n.* Drahtseilbahn, *die;* **~ 'television, ~ T'V** *ns.* Kabelfernsehen, *das*
'cab rank *n.* (Brit.) Taxistand, *der;* Droschken[halte]platz, *der* (Amtsspr.)
cache /kæʃ/ *n.* geheimes [Waffen-/Proviant-]lager
cackle /'kækl/ [1] *n.* **(a)** (of hen) Gackern, *das* **(b)** (laughter) [meckerndes] Gelächter [2] *v.i.* **(a)** ‹*Henne:*› gackern **(b)** (laugh) meckernd lachen
cactus /'kæktəs/ *n., pl.* **cacti** /'kæktaɪ/ *or* **~es** Kaktus, *der*
CAD *abbr.* = **computer-aided design** CAD
caddie /'kædɪ/ *n.* (Golf) Caddie, *der*
caddy /'kædɪ/ *n.* Dose, *die*
cadet /kə'det/ *n.* Offiziersschüler, *der;* **naval/police ~**: Marinekadett/Anwärter für den Polizeidienst
cadge /kædʒ/ *v.t.* [sich (*Dat.*)] erbetteln
café, cafe /'kæfeɪ/ *n.* Lokal, *das;* (tea room) Café, *das*
cafeteria /kæfɪ'tɪərɪə/ *n.* Cafeteria, *die*
cafetière /kæfə'tjeə/ *n.* Kaffeebereiter, *der*
caffeinated /'kæfɪneɪtɪd/ *adj.* koffeinhaltig
caffeine /'kæfi:n/ *n.* Koffein, *das*
cage /keɪdʒ/ [1] *n.* **(a)** Käfig, *der* **(b)** (of lift) Fahrkabine, *die* [2] *v.t.* einsperren
cagey /'keɪdʒɪ/ *adj.* (coll.) zugeknöpft (ugs.); **be ~ about sth.** mit etw. hinterm Berg halten (ugs.)
Cairo /'kaɪərəʊ/ *pr. n.* Kairo (*das*)
cajole /kə'dʒəʊl/ *v.t.* **~ sb. into sth./doing sth.** jmdm. etw. einreden/jmdm. einreden, etw. zu tun
cake /keɪk/ [1] *n.* Kuchen, *der;* **a ~ of soap** ein Riegel *od.* Stück Seife [2] *v.t.* verkrusten; **~d with dirt/blood** schmutz-/blutverkrustet
cal. *abbr.* = **calorie[s]** cal.
calamity /kə'læmɪtɪ/ *n.* Unheil, *das*
calcium /'kælsɪəm/ *n.* Kalzium, *das*
calculate /'kælkjʊleɪt/ [1] *v.t.* **(a)** berechnen; (by estimating) ausrechnen **(b) be ~d to do sth.** darauf abzielen, etw. zu tun [2] *v.i.* **~ on doing sth.** damit rechnen, etw. zu tun
'calculated *adj.* kalkuliert ‹*Risiko*›; vorsätzlich ‹*Handlung*›
calculation /kælkjʊ'leɪʃn/ *n.* **(a)** (result) Rechnung, *die;* **he is out in his ~s** er hat sich verrechnet **(b)** (calculating) Berechnung, *die*
calculator /'kælkjʊleɪtə(r)/ *n.* Rechner, *der*

calculus /ˈkælkjʊləs/ *n.* **differential/integral ~:** Differenzial-/Integralrechnung, *die*

calendar /ˈkælɪndə(r)/ *n.* Kalender, *der; attrib.* Kalender-

calf¹ /kɑːf/ *n., pl.* **calves** Kalb, *das*

calf² *n., pl.* **calves** (Anat.) Wade, *die*

calibre (*Brit.; Amer.:* **caliber**) /ˈkælɪbə(r)/ *n.* Kaliber, *das*

calico /ˈkælɪkəʊ/ *n.* Kattun, *der*

California /kælɪˈfɔːnɪə/ *pr. n.* Kalifornien (*das*)

caliper ▶ CALLIPER

call /kɔːl/ 1 *v.i.* **(a)** rufen; **~ to sb.** jmdm. etwas zurufen; **~ [out] for help** um Hilfe rufen
(b) (pay brief visit) [kurz] besuchen (**at** *Akk.*); **~ on sb.** jmdn. besuchen; **~ round** vorbeikommen (ugs.); **~ at a port/station** einen Hafen anlaufen/an einem Bahnhof halten
(c) (Teleph.) **who is ~ing, please?** wer spricht da, bitte?; **thank you for ~ing** vielen Dank für Ihren Anruf!
2 *v.t.* **(a)** rufen; aufrufen ‹*Namen, Nummer*›
(b) (cry to, summon) rufen; (to a duty, to do sth.) aufrufen
(c) (by radio/telephone) rufen/anrufen; (initially) Kontakt aufnehmen mit
(d) (rouse) wecken
(e) einberufen ‹*Konferenz*›; ausrufen ‹*Streik*›
(f) (name) nennen; **he is ~ed Bob** er heißt Bob; **what is it ~ed in English?** wie heißt das auf Englisch?
3 *n.* **(a)** Ruf, *der;* **a ~ for help** ein Hilferuf; **be on ~:** Bereitschaftsdienst haben
(b) (visit) Besuch, *der;* **make** *or* **pay a ~ on sb., make** *or* **pay sb. a ~:** jmdn. besuchen
(c) (telephone ~) Anruf, *der;* **give sb. a ~:** jmdn. anrufen; **make a ~:** telefonieren
(d) (invitation, summons) Aufruf, *der*
(e) (need, occasion) Anlass, *der*

■ **call ˈback** 1 *v.t.* zurückrufen
2 *v.i.* zurückrufen; (come back) zurückkommen

■ **ˈcall for** *v.t.* **(a)** (send for, order) bestellen
(b) (collect) abholen
(c) (require, demand) erfordern; **this ~s for a celebration** das muss gefeiert werden

■ **call ˈin** 1 *v.i.* vorbeikommen (ugs.) (**on** bei)
2 *v.t.* zu Rate ziehen ‹*Fachmann usw.*›

■ **call ˈoff** *v.t.* absagen ‹*Treffen, Verabredung*›; rückgängig machen ‹*Geschäft*›; lösen ‹*Verlobung*›; (end) abbrechen ‹*Streik*›

■ **ˈcall on** *v.t.* **(a)** ▶ ~ 1B
(b) ▶ ~ [UP]ON

■ **call ˈout** 1 *v.t.* alarmieren ‹*Truppen*›; zum Streik aufrufen ‹*Arbeitnehmer*›
2 *v.i.* ▶ ~ 1A

■ **call ˈup** *v.t.* **(a)** (by telephone) anrufen
(b) (Mil.) einberufen

■ **ˈcall [up]on** *v.t.* **~ upon sb.'s generosity** an jmds. Großzügigkeit (*Akk.*) appellieren; **~ [up]on sb. to do sth.** jmdn. auffordern, etw. zu tun

ˈcall box *n.* Telefonzelle, *die*

ˈcaller *n.* (visitor) Besucher, *der*/Besucherin, *die;* (on telephone) Anrufer, *der*/Anruferin, *die*

ˈcall girl *n.* Callgirl, *das*

ˈcalling *n.* Beruf, *der*

calliper /ˈkælɪpə(r)/ *n.* **(a)** **[a pair of] ~s** Tasterzirkel, *der*
(b) (Med.) Beinschiene, *die*

callous /ˈkæləs/ *adj.* gefühllos; herzlos ‹*Handlung, Verhalten*›

ˈcall-up *n.* (Mil.) Einberufung, *die*

calm /kɑːm/ 1 *n.* (stillness) Stille, *die;* (serenity) Ruhe, *die*
2 *adj.* ruhig
3 *v.t.* **~ sb. [down]** jmdn. beruhigen
4 *v.i.* **~ [down]** sich beruhigen

ˈcalmly *adv.* ruhig; gelassen

ˈcalmness *n.* Ruhe, *die;* (of water) Stille, *die*

Calor gas ® /ˈkælə gæs/ *n.* Butangas, *das*

calorie /ˈkælərɪ/ *n.* Kalorie, *die*

calorific /kæləˈrɪfɪk/ *adj.* **~ value** Heizwert, *der*

calves *pl. of* CALF¹, ²

CAM *abbr.* = **computer-aided manufacturing** CAM

camber /ˈkæmbə(r)/ *n.* Wölbung, *die*

camcorder /ˈkæmkɔːdə(r)/ *n.* Camcorder, *der;* Kamerarecorder, *der*

came ▶ COME

camel /ˈkæml/ *n.* Kamel, *das*

camera /ˈkæmərə/ *n.* Kamera, *die*

camera: ~ case *n.* Kameratasche, *die;* **~ crew** *n.* Kamerateam, *das;* **~man** *n.* Kameramann, *der;* **~work** *n., no indef. art.* Kameraführung, *die*

camomile /ˈkæməmaɪl/ *n.* Kamille, *die;* **~ tea** Kamillentee, *der*

camouflage /ˈkæməflɑːʒ/ 1 *n.* Tarnung, *die*
2 *v.t.* tarnen

camp /kæmp/ 1 *n.* Lager, *das*
2 *v.i.* **~ [out]** campen; (in tent) zelten; **go ~ing** Campen/Zelten fahren/gehen

campaign /kæmˈpeɪn/ 1 *n.* **(a)** (Mil.) Feldzug, *der*
(b) (organized action) Kampagne, *die;* **publicity ~:** Werbekampagne, *die*
2 *v.i.* **~ for/against sth.** sich für etw. einsetzen/gegen etw. etwas unternehmen; **be ~ing** ‹*Politiker:*› im Wahlkampf stehen

ˈcamp bed *n.* Campingliege, *die*

ˈcamper *n.* (person) Camper, *der*/Camperin, *die*

ˈcampfire *n.* Lagerfeuer, *das*

ˈcamping *n.* Camping, *das;* (in tent) Zelten, *das*

camping: ~ ground ▶ ~ SITE;

~ holiday *n.* Campingurlaub, *der;* **~ site** *n.* Campingplatz, *der;* **~ stove** *n.* Campingkocher, *der*

'campsite *n.* Campingplatz, *der*

campus /'kæmpəs/ *n.* Campus, *der*

can¹ /kæn/ **1** *n.* **(a)** (milk ~, watering ~) Kanne, *die;* (for oil, petrol) Kanister, *der;* (Amer.: for refuse) Eimer, *der*
(b) (for preserving) [Konserven]dose, *die;* **a ~ of tomatoes/beer** eine Dose Tomaten/Bier
2 *v.t.,* **-nn-** konservieren

can² /kən, *stressed* kæn/ *v. aux., only in pres.* **can,** *neg.* **cannot** /'kænət/, (coll.) **can't** /kɑ:nt/, *past* **could** /kʊd/, *neg.* (coll.) **couldn't** /'kʊdnt/ können; (have right, be permitted) dürfen; können; **I can't do that** das kann ich nicht; (it would be wrong) das kann ich nicht tun; **you can't smoke here** hier dürfen Sie nicht rauchen; **could you ring me tomorrow?** könnten Sie mich morgen anrufen?; **I could have killed him** ich hätte ihn umbringen können; **[that] could be [so]** das könnte *od.* kann sein

Canada /'kænədə/ *pr. n.* Kanada *(das)*

Canadian /kə'neɪdɪən/ **1** *adj.* kanadisch; **sb. is ~:** jmd. ist Kanadier/Kanadierin
2 *n.* Kanadier, *der*/Kanadierin, *die*

canal /kə'næl/ *n.* Kanal, *der*

canary /kə'neərɪ/ *n.* Kanarienvogel, *der*

Ca'nary Islands *pr. n. pl.* Kanarische Inseln *Pl.*

cancel /'kænsl/ **1** *v.t.,* (Brit.) **-ll- (a)** absagen ‹*Besuch, Urlaub, Reise, Sportveranstaltung*›; ausfallen lassen ‹*Veranstaltung, Vorlesung, Zug, Bus*›; fallen lassen ‹*Pläne*›; rückgängig machen ‹*Einladung, Vertrag*›; zurücknehmen ‹*Befehl*›; stornieren ‹*Bestellung, Auftrag*›; kündigen ‹*Abonnement*›; abbestellen ‹*Zeitung*›
(b) (Comp.) abbrechen
2 *v.i.,* (Brit.) **-ll-: (a) ~ [out]** sich [gegenseitig] aufheben
(b) (Comp.) abbrechen

cancellation /kænsə'leɪʃn/ *n.* ▶ CANCEL 1A: Absage, *die;* Ausfall, *der;* Fallenlassen, *das;* Rückgängigmachen, *das;* Zurücknahme, *die;* Stornierung, *die;* Kündigung, *die;* Abbestellung, *die*

cancer /'kænsə(r)/ *n.* **(a)** (Med.) Krebs, *der;* **~ of the liver** Leberkrebs, *der*
(b) C~ (Astrol., Astron.) der Krebs

candelabra /kændɪ'lɑ:brə/ *n.* Leuchter, *der*

candid /'kændɪd/ *adj.* offen; ehrlich ‹*Ansicht, Bericht*›

candidate /'kændɪdət, 'kændɪdeɪt/ *n.* Kandidat, *der*/Kandidatin, *die*

candle /'kændl/ *n.* Kerze, *die*

candle: ~light *n.* Kerzenlicht, *das;* **~stick** *n.* Kerzenhalter, *der;* (elaborate) Leuchter, *der;* **~wick** *n.* (material) Frottierplüsch, *der*

candour (*Brit., Amer.:* **candor**) /'kændə(r)/ *n.* ▶ CANDID: Offenheit, *die;* Ehrlichkeit, *die*

candy /'kændɪ/ *n.* (Amer.) (sweets) Süßigkeiten *Pl.;* (sweet) Bonbon, *das od. der*

'candyfloss /'kændɪflɒs/ *n.* Zuckerwatte, *die*

cane /keɪn/ **1** *n.* **(a)** (stem) Rohr, *das;* (of raspberry, blackberry) Spross, *der*
(b) (material) Rohr, *das*
(c) (stick) [Rohr]stock, *der*
2 *v.t.* [mit dem Stock] schlagen

'cane sugar *n.* Rohrzucker, *der*

canine /'keɪnaɪn/ *adj.* **(a)** (of dog[s]) Hunde-
(b) ~ tooth Eckzahn, *der*

canister /'kænɪstə(r)/ *n.* Büchse, *die;* (for petrol, oil, etc.) Kanister, *der*

cannabis /'kænəbɪs/ *n.* (hashish) Haschisch, *das;* (marijuana) Marihuana, *das*

canned /kænd/ *adj.* Dosen-; in Dosen *nachgestellt;* **~ meat/fruit** Fleisch-/Obstkonserven *Pl.;* **~ beer** Dosenbier; **~ food** [Lebensmittel]konserven *Pl.;* **~ music** Musikkonserve, *die*

cannibal /'kænɪbl/ *n.* Kannibale, *der*/Kannibalin, *die*

cannibalism /'kænɪbəlɪzm/ *n.* Kannibalismus, *der*

cannon /'kænən/ **1** *n.* Kanone, *die*
2 *v.i.* (Brit.) **~ into sb./sth.** mit etw./jmdm. zusammenprallen

'cannon ball *n.* Kanonenkugel, *die*

cannot ▶ CAN²

canny /'kænɪ/ *adj.* (shrewd) schlau

canoe /kə'nu:/ *n.* Paddelboot, *das;* (Indian ~, Sport) Kanu, *das*

canoeing /kə'nu:ɪŋ/ *n.* Paddeln, *das;* (Sport) Kanufahren, *das;* Kanusport, *der*

canoeist /kə'nu:ɪst/ *n.* Paddelbootfahrer, *der*/-fahrerin, *die*

canon /'kænən/ *n.* **(a)** (general law, criterion) Grundregel, *die*
(b) (Eccl.: person) Kanoniker, *der*

canonize /'kænənaɪz/ *v.t.* kanonisieren ‹*Heiligen*›; heilig sprechen ‹*Märtyrer*›

'can-opener *n.* Dosenöffner, *der*

canopy /'kænəpɪ/ *n.* Baldachin, *der;* (over entrance) Vordach, *das*

can't /kɑ:nt/ (coll.) = CANNOT; ▶ CAN²

cantankerous /kæn'tæŋkərəs/ *adj.* streitsüchtig

canteen /kæn'ti:n/ *n.* Kantine, *die*

canter /'kæntə(r)/ **1** *n.* Handgalopp, *der*
2 *v.i.* leicht galoppieren

canvas /'kænvəs/ *n.* Leinwand, *die*

canvass /'kænvəs/ **1** *v.t.* Wahlwerbung treiben in ‹*einem Wahlkreis, Gebiet*›; Wahlwerbung treiben bei ‹*Wählern, Bürgern*›
2 *v.i.* werben (**on behalf of** für); **~ for votes** um Stimmen werben

'canvasser *n.* (for votes) Wahlhelfer, *der*/

-helferin, *die*
canyon /'kænjən/ *n.* Cañon, *der*
cap /kæp/ [1] *n.* **(a)** Mütze, *die;* (nurse's, servant's) Haube, *die;* (with peak) Schirmmütze, *die;* (skull~) Kappe, *die*
(b) (of bottle, jar) [Verschluss]kappe, *die;* (petrol ~, radiator ~) Deckel, *der*
[2] *v.t.*, **-pp-**: **(a)** verschließen ‹*Flasche*›; zudecken ‹*Bohrloch*›; mit einer Schutzkappe versehen ‹*Zahn*›
(b) (fig.) überbieten; **to ~ it all** obendrein
CAP *abbr.* = **Common Agricultural Policy** gemeinsame Agrarpolitik
capability /keɪpə'bɪlɪtɪ/ *n.* Fähigkeit, *die*
capable /'keɪpəbl/ *adj.* **(a) be ~ of sth.** ‹*Person:*› zu etw. imstande sein
(b) (gifted, able) fähig
capacity /kə'pæsɪtɪ/ *n.* **(a)** Fassungsvermögen, *das;* **the machine is working to ~**: die Maschine ist voll ausgelastet; **a seating ~ of 300** 300 Sitzplätze
(b) (measure) Rauminhalt, *der;* Volumen, *das;* **measure of ~**: Hohlmaß, *das*
(c) (position) Eigenschaft, *die;* **in his ~ as ...**: in seiner Eigenschaft als ...
cape¹ /keɪp/ *n.* (garment) Umhang, *der;* Cape, *das*
cape² *n.* (Geog.) Kap, *das;* **the C~ [of Good Hope]** das Kap der Guten Hoffnung; **C~ Town** Kapstadt (*das*)
caper /'keɪpə(r)/ *v.i.* **~ [about]** [herum]tollen
capful /'kæpfʊl/ *n.* **one ~**: der Inhalt einer Verschlusskappe
capillary /kə'pɪlərɪ/ *n.* Kapillare, *die* (fachspr.)
capital /'kæpɪtl/ [1] *attrib. adj.* **(a)** Todes‹*strafe, -urteil*›; Kapital‹*verbrechen*›
(b) groß, Groß‹*buchstabe*›
(c) (principal) Haupt‹*stadt*›
[2] *n.* **(a)** (letter) Großbuchstabe, *der*
(b) (city, town) Hauptstadt, *die*
(c) (stock, wealth) Kapital, *das*
capitalism /'kæpɪtəlɪzm/ *n.* Kapitalismus, *der*
capitalist /'kæpɪtəlɪst/ [1] *n.* Kapitalist, *der*/Kapitalistin, *die*
[2] *adj.* kapitalistisch
capitalize /'kæpɪtəlaɪz/ [1] *v.t.* großschreiben ‹*Buchstaben, Wort*›
[2] *v.i.* **~ on sth.** aus etw. Kapital schlagen (ugs.)
capital 'punishment *n.* Todesstrafe, *die*
capitulate /kə'pɪtjʊleɪt/ *v.i.* kapitulieren
capitulation /kəpɪtjʊ'leɪʃn/ *n.* Kapitulation, *die*
cappuccino /kɑːpʊ'tʃiːnəʊ/ *n., pl.* **~s** Cappuccino, *der*
capricious /kə'prɪʃəs/ *adj.* launisch
Capricorn /'kæprɪkɔːn/ *n.* (Astrol., Astron.) der Steinbock
capsize /kæp'saɪz/ [1] *v.t.* zum Kentern bringen
[2] *v.i.* kentern
capsule /'kæpsjuːl/ *n.* Kapsel, *die*
Capt. *abbr.* = **Captain** Kapt.; Hptm.
captain /'kæptɪn/ [1] *n.* Kapitän, *der;* (Army) Hauptmann, *der*
[2] *v.t.* **~ a team** Kapitän einer Mannschaft sein
caption /'kæpʃn/ *n.* (heading) Überschrift, *die;* (under photograph, drawing) Bildunterschrift, *die;* (Cinemat., Telev.) Untertitel, *der*
captivate /'kæptɪveɪt/ *v.t.* fesseln
captivating /'kæptɪveɪtɪŋ/ *adj.* bezaubernd; einnehmend ‹*Lächeln*›
captive /'kæptɪv/ [1] *adj.* gefangen; **be taken ~**: gefangen genommen werden; **~ audience** unfreiwilliges Publikum
[2] *n.* Gefangener, *der*/Gefangene, *die*
captivity /kæp'tɪvɪtɪ/ *n.* Gefangenschaft, *die;* **be held in ~**: gefangen gehalten werden
captor /'kæptə(r)/ *n.* **his ~**: der, der/die, die ihn gefangen nahm
capture /'kæptʃə(r)/ [1] *n.* **(a)** (of thief etc.) Festnahme, *die;* (of town) Einnahme, *die*
(b) (thing, person) Fang, *der*
[2] *v.t.* festnehmen ‹*Person*›; [ein]fangen ‹*Tier*›; einnehmen ‹*Stadt*›; gefangen nehmen ‹*Fantasie*›
car /kɑː(r)/ *n.* Auto, *das;* Wagen, *der;* **by ~**: mit dem Auto
carafe /kə'ræf/ *n.* Karaffe, *die*
caramel /'kærəmel/ *n.* Karamell, *der;* (toffee) Karamellbonbon, *das*
carat /'kærət/ *n.* Karat, *das;* **a 22-~ gold ring** ein 22-karätiger Goldring
caravan /'kærəvæn/ *n.* (Brit.) Wohnwagen, *der*
'caravan site *n.* Campingplatz für Wohnwagen
carbohydrate /kɑːbəʊ'haɪdreɪt/ *n.* Kohlenhydrat, *das*
'car bomb *n.* Autobombe, *die*
carbon /'kɑːbən/ *n.* Kohlenstoff, *der*
carbon: ~ 'copy *n.* Durchschlag, *der;* **~ dioxide** /- daɪ'ɒksaɪd/ *n.* Kohlendyoxid, *das;* **~ mo'noxide** /-mə'nɒksaɪd/ *n.* (Chem.) Kohlenmonoxyd, *das;* **~ paper** *n.* Kohlepapier, *das*
car 'boot sale *n.: Trödelmarkt, bei dem die Händler ihre Waren aus dem Kofferraum ihrer Autos heraus verkaufen*
carburettor (*Amer.:* **carburetor**) /kɑːbə'retə(r)/ *n.* Vergaser, *der*
carcass (*Brit. also:* **carcase**) /'kɑːkəs/ *n.* Kadaver, *der*
'car crash *n.* Autounfall, *der*
card /kɑːd/ *n.* Karte, *die;* **play ~s** Karten spielen
card: ~board *n.* Pappe, *die;* **~board 'box** *n.* [Papp]karton, *der;* (smaller) [Papp]schachtel, *die;* **~ game** *n.* Kartenspiel, *das;* **~holder** *n.* Karteninhaber, *der*/-inhaberin, *die*

C

cardiac /'kɑːdɪæk/ *adj.* (of heart) Herz-
cardiac ar'rest *n.* Herzstillstand, *der*
cardigan /'kɑːdɪgən/ *n.* Strickjacke, *die*
cardinal /'kɑːdɪnl/ 1 *adj.* grundlegend ‹*Frage, Doktrin, Pflicht*›; Kardinal‹*fehler, -problem*›; Haupt‹*punkt, -merkmal*›
2 *n.* (Eccl.) Kardinal, *der*
cardinal: ~ 'number *n.* Kardinalzahl, *die;* **~ 'sin** *n.* Todsünde, *die*
'cardphone *n.* Kartentelefon, *das*
care /keə(r)/ 1 *n.* **(a)** (anxiety) Sorge, *die*
(b) (pains) Sorgfalt, *die*
(c) (caution) Vorsicht, *die;* **take ~:** aufpassen
(d) medical ~: ärztliche Betreuung
(e) (charge) Obhut, *die* (geh.); **put sb. in ~/take sb. into ~:** jmdn. in Pflege geben/nehmen; **~ of** (on letter) bei; **take ~ of sb./sth.** (ensure safety of) auf jmdn./etw. aufpassen; (attend to) sich um jmdn./etw. kümmern
2 *v.i.* **~ for sb./sth.** (look after) sich um jmdn./etw. kümmern; (like) jmdn./etw. mögen; **~ to do sth.** etw. tun mögen; **I don't ~ [whether/how/what** *etc.*] es ist mir gleich[, ob/wie/was *usw.*]
career /kə'rɪə(r)/ 1 *n.* Beruf, *der*
2 *v.i.* rasen; ‹*Pferd, Reiter:*› galoppieren
career: ~ break *n.* Karriereknick, *der;* **~s adviser** *n.* Berufsberater, *der*/-beraterin, *die;* **~s [advisory] service** *n.* Berufsberatung, *die;* **~ woman** *n.* Karrierefrau, *die*
'carefree *adj.* sorgenfrei
careful /'keəfl/ *adj.* (thorough) sorgfältig; (cautious) vorsichtig; **[be] ~!** Vorsicht!; **be ~ of sb./sth.** (be cautious of) sich vor jmdm./etw. in Acht nehmen; **be ~ with sb./sth.** vorsichtig mit jmdm./etw. umgehen
'carefully *adv.* (thoroughly) sorgfältig; (attentively) aufmerksam; (cautiously) vorsichtig
careless /'keəlɪs/ *adj.* **(a)** (inattentive) unaufmerksam; (thoughtless) gedankenlos; leichtsinnig ‹*Fahrer*›; nachlässig ‹*Arbeiter, Arbeit*›; gedankenlos ‹*Bemerkung, Handlung*›; unachtsam ‹*Fahren*›
(b) (nonchalant) ungezwungen
'carelessly *adv.* (without care) nachlässig; (thoughtlessly) gedankenlos
'carelessness *n.* (lack of care) Nachlässigkeit, *die;* (thoughtlessness) Gedankenlosigkeit, *die*
carer /'keərə(r)/ *n.* (for sick person) Pfleger, *der*/Pflegerin, *die*
caress /kə'res/ 1 *n.* Liebkosung, *die*
2 *v.t.* liebkosen
'caretaker *n.* Hausmeister, *der*/-meisterin, *die*
'car ferry *n.* Autofähre, *die*
cargo /'kɑːgəʊ/ *n.* Fracht, *die*
'cargo boat, 'cargo ship *ns.* Frachter, *der*
'car hire *n.* Autovermietung, *die*
Caribbean /kærɪ'biːən/ 1 *n.* **the ~:** die Karibik
2 *adj.* karibisch
caricature /'kærɪkətjʊə(r)/ 1 *n.* Karikatur, *die*
2 *v.t.* karikieren
caring /'keərɪŋ/ *adj.* sozial ‹*Gesellschaft*›; fürsorglich ‹*Person*›
carnage /'kɑːnɪdʒ/ *n.* Gemetzel, *das*
carnal /'kɑːnl/ *adj.* sinnlich
carnation /kɑː'neɪʃn/ *n.* [Garten]nelke, *die*
carnet /'kɑːneɪ/ *n.* (of motorist) Triptyk, *das;* **[camping] ~:** Ausweis für Camper
carnival /'kɑːnɪvl/ *n.* Volksfest, *das*
carnivorous /kɑː'nɪvərəs/ *adj.* Fleisch fressend
carol /'kærl/ *n.* **[Christmas] ~:** Weihnachtslied, *das*
'car owner *n.* Autobesitzer, *der*/-besitzerin, *die*
carp /kɑːp/ *n., pl. same* Karpfen, *der*
car: ~ park *n.* Parkplatz, *der;* (building) Parkhaus, *das;* **~ parking** *n.* Parken, *das;* **~ parking facilities are available** Parkplätze [sind] vorhanden
carpenter /'kɑːpɪntə(r)/ *n.* Zimmermann, *der;* (for furniture) Tischler, *der*/Tischlerin, *die*
carpentry /'kɑːpɪntrɪ/ *n.* Zimmerhandwerk, *das;* (in furniture) Tischlerhandwerk, *das*
carpet /'kɑːpɪt/ *n.* Teppich, *der*
carpet: ~ slipper *n.* Hausschuh, *der;* **~ sweeper** *n.* Teppichkehrer, *der*
car: ~ phone *n.* Autotelefon, *das;* **~port** *n.* Einstellplatz, *der;* **~ radio** *n.* Autoradio, *das;* **~ rental** ▶ CAR HIRE
carriage /'kærɪdʒ/ *n.* **(a)** (horse-drawn) Kutsche, *die*
(b) (Railw.) Wagen, *der*
'carriageway *n.* Fahrbahn, *die*
'car ride *n.* Autofahrt, *die*
carrier /'kærɪə(r)/ *n.* **(a)** (bearer) Träger, *der*
(b) (firm) Transportunternehmen, *das*
carrier: ~ bag *n.* Tragetasche, *die;* **~ pigeon** *n.* Brieftaube, *die*
carrot /'kærət/ *n.* Möhre, *die*
carry /'kærɪ/ *v.t.* **(a)** tragen; (emphasizing destination) bringen
(b) (possess) besitzen ‹*Autorität, Gewicht*›
▪ **carry a'way** *v.t.* forttragen; **be** *or* **get carried away** sich hinreißen lassen
▪ **carry 'on** 1 *v.t.* fortführen; **~ on [doing sth.]** weiterhin etw. tun
2 *v.i.* weitermachen
▪ **carry 'out** *v.t.* durchführen; ausführen ‹*Anweisung, Auftrag*›; vornehmen ‹*Verbesserungen*›
carry: ~cot *n.* Babytragetasche, *die;* **~-out** *n.* **~-out [meal]** Essen *od.* Mahlzeit zum Mitnehmen; **get a ~-out** sich (*Dat.*) in einem Restaurant was zu essen holen
'carsick *adj.* **children are often ~:** Kindern wird beim Autofahren oft schlecht
cart /kɑːt/ 1 *n.* Wagen, *der*

2 *v.t.* (coll.) schleppen

'car thief *n.* Autodieb, *der*/-diebin, *die*

cartilage /'kɑ:tɪlɪdʒ/ *n.* Knorpel, *der*

carton /'kɑ:tn/ *n.* [Papp]karton, *der;* (of drink) Tüte, *die;* (of cream, yoghurt) Becher, *der*

cartoon /kɑ:'tu:n/ *n.* humoristische Zeichnung; (satirical) Karikatur, *die;* (film) Zeichentrickfilm, *der*

cartridge /'kɑ:trɪdʒ/ *n.* **(a)** (for gun) Patrone, *die*
(b) (of film; cassette) Kassette, *die*

'cartwheel *n.* (Gymnastics) Rad, *das;* **turn** *or* **do ~s** Rad schlagen

carve /kɑ:v/ 1 *v.t.* **(a)** tranchieren ‹*Fleisch, Braten, Hähnchen*›
(b) (from wood) schnitzen; (from stone) meißeln
2 *v.i.* **~ in wood/stone** in Holz schnitzen/in Stein meißeln

carving /'kɑ:vɪŋ/ *n.* (in or from wood) Schnitzerei, *die;* (in or from stone) Skulptur, *die*

'carving knife *n.* Tranchiermesser, *das*

'car wash *n.* Waschanlage, *die*

cascade /kæs'keɪd/ *n.* Kaskade, *die*

case[1] /keɪs/ *n.* **(a)** (instance, matter, set of arguments) Fall, *der;* **it is [not] the ~ that ...:** es trifft [nicht] zu, dass ...; **in ~ ...:** falls ...; **[just] in ~:** für alle Fälle; **in ~ of emergency** im Notfall; **in any ~:** jedenfalls; **in that ~:** in diesem Fall; **in any ~** (regardless of anything else) jedenfalls; **I don't need it in any ~:** ich brauche es sowieso nicht
(b) (Med., Police, Soc. Serv., etc.) Fall, *der*
(c) (Law) Fall, *der;* (action) Verfahren, *das*
(d) (Ling.) Fall, *der;* Kasus, *der* (fachspr.)

case[2] *n.* **(a)** Koffer, *der;* (brief~) [Akten]tasche, *die*
(b) (for spectacles, cigarettes) Etui, *das*
(c) (crate) Kiste, *die*
(d) **[display] ~:** Schaukasten, *der*

cash /kæʃ/ 1 *n.* Bargeld, *das;* **pay [in] ~, pay ~ down** bar zahlen
2 *v.t.* einlösen ‹*Scheck*›

cash: ~ account *n.* Kassekonto, *das;* **~ and 'carry** *n.* cash and carry; (store) Cash-and-carry-Laden, *der;* **~back** *n., no art.: Barauszahlung eines Differenzbetrages bei Kauf mit Geldkarte;* **~card** *n.* Geldautomatenkarte, *die;* **~ desk** *n.* (Brit.) Kasse, *die;* **~ discount** *n.* Skonto, *der od. das;* Barzahlungsrabatt, *der;* **~ dispenser** *n.* Geldautomat, *der*

cashew nut /'kæʃu:/ *n.* Cashewnuss, *die*

'cash flow *n.* Cashflow, *der*

cashier /kæ'ʃɪə(r)/ *n.* Kassierer, *der*/ Kassiererin, *die*

'cashless *adj.* bargeldlos; **the ~ society** die bargeldlose Gesellschaft

cashmere /'kæʃmɪə(r)/ *n.* Kaschmir, *der;* **~ wool/sweater** Kaschmirwolle, *die*/ Kaschmirpullover, *der*

cash: ~ payment *n.* Barzahlung, *die;* **make ~ payment** bar bezahlen; **~point** *n.* Geldautomat, *der;* **~ register** *n.* [Registrier]kasse, *die*

casino /kə'si:nəʊ/ *n.* Kasino, *das*

cask /kɑ:sk/ *n.* Fass, *das*

casket /'kɑ:skɪt/ *n.* **(a)** Kästchen, *das*
(b) (Amer.: coffin) Sarg, *der*

casserole /'kæsərəʊl/ *n.* Schmortopf, *der*

cassette /kə'set, kæ'set/ *n.* Kassette, *die*

cassette: ~ deck *n.* Kassettendeck, *das;* **~ player** *n.* Kassettengerät, *das;* **~ recorder** *n.* Kassettenrekorder, *der*

cast /kɑ:st/ 1 *v.t.,* **cast** **(a)** werfen
(b) (shape, form) gießen
(c) abgeben ‹*Stimme*›
2 *n.* **(a)** (Med.) Gipsverband, *der*
(b) (actors) Besetzung, *die*

■ **cast a'side** *v.t.* beiseite schieben ‹*Vorschlag*›; vergessen ‹*Sorgen*›; fallen lassen ‹*Hemmungen*›

■ **cast 'off** *v.i. & t.* (Naut.) losmachen

castanets /kæstə'nets/ *n. pl.* Kastagnetten *Pl.*

'castaway *n.* Schiffbrüchige, *der*/*die*

caste /kɑ:st/ *n.* Kaste, *die*

cast 'iron *n.* Gusseisen, *das*

castle /'kɑ:sl/ *n.* Burg, *die;* (mansion) Schloss, *das*

'cast-offs *n. pl.* abgelegte Sachen *Pl.*

castor /'kɑ:stə(r)/ *n.* (wheel) Rolle, *die*

castor: ~ 'oil *n.* Rizinusöl, *das;* **~ sugar** *n.* Raffinade, *die*

castrate /kæ'streɪt/ *v.t.* kastrieren

castration /kæ'streɪʃn/ *n.* Kastration, *die*

casual /'kæʒjʊəl/ *adj.* ungezwungen; leger ‹*Kleidung*›; beiläufig ‹*Bemerkung*›; flüchtig ‹*Bekannter, Bekanntschaft, Blick*›; unbekümmert ‹*Haltung, Einstellung*›

casual 'labour *n.* Gelegenheitsarbeit, *die*

'casually *adv.* ungezwungen; beiläufig ‹*bemerken*›; flüchtig ‹*anschauen*›; leger ‹*sich kleiden*›

casualty /'kæʒjʊəltɪ/ *n.* **(a)** (injured person) Verletzte, *der*/*die;* (in battle) Verwundete, *der*/ *die;* (dead person) Tote, *der*/*die*
(b) (hospital department) Unfallstation, *die*

'casualty ward *n.* Unfallstation, *die*

cat /kæt/ *n.* Katze, *die*

catalogue (*Amer.:* **catalog**) /'kætəlɒg/ 1 *n.* Katalog, *der*
2 *v.t.* katalogisieren

catalyst /'kætəlɪst/ *n.* Katalysator, *der*

catalytic /kætə'lɪtɪk/ *adj.* **~ converter** Katalysator, *der*

catamaran /kætəmə'ræn/ *n.* Katamaran, *der*

catapult /'kætəpʌlt/ 1 *n.* Katapult, *das*
2 *v.t.* katapultieren

cataract /'kætərækt/ *n.* **(a)** Katarakt, *der*
(b) (Med.) grauer Star

catarrh /kə'tɑ:(r)/ *n.* Katarrh, *der*

C

catastrophe /kəˈtæstrəfɪ/ *n.* Katastrophe, *die*
catastrophic /kætəˈstrɒfɪk/ *adj.* katastrophal
catch /kætʃ/ 1 *v.t.*, **caught** /kɔ:t/ **(a)** fangen; **~ hold of sb./sth.** jmdn./etw. festhalten; (to stop oneself falling) sich an jmdm./etw. festhalten; **get sth. caught** *or* **~ sth. on/in sth.** mit etw. an/in etw. (*Dat.*) hängen bleiben; **~ one's finger in the door** sich (*Dat.*) den Finger in der Tür einklemmen
(b) (travel by) nehmen; (be in time for) [noch] erreichen
(c) (surprise) **~ sb. doing sth.** jmdn. [dabei] erwischen, wie er etw. tut (ugs.)
(d) (become infected with) sich (*Dat.*) zuziehen; **~ sth. from sb.** sich bei jmdm. mit etw. anstecken; **~ a cold** sich erkälten; **~ it** (fig. coll.) etwas kriegen (ugs.)
(e) **~ sb.'s attention/interest** jmds. Aufmerksamkeit erregen/jmds. Interesse wecken
2 *v.i.*, **caught (a)** (begin to burn) [anfangen zu] brennen
(b) (become hooked up) hängenbleiben; ‹*Haar, Faden:*› sich verfangen
3 *n.* **(a)** (of ball) **make a ~:** fangen
(b) (amount caught, lit. or fig.) Fang, *der*
(c) (difficulty) Haken, *der* (**in** an + *Dat.*)
(d) (of door) Schnapper, *der*
■ **catch 'on** *v.i.* (coll.) **(a)** (become popular) [gut] ankommen (ugs.)
(b) (understand) kapieren (ugs.)
■ **catch 'up** 1 *v.t.* **~ sb. up, ~ up with sb.** jmdn. einholen
2 *v.i.* **~ up** gleichziehen; **~ up on sth.** etw. nachholen
'catching *adj.* ansteckend
'catchphrase *n.* Slogan, *der*
'catchy *adj.* eingängig
'cat door *n.* Katzentür, *die*
categorical /kætɪˈgɒrɪkl/ *adj.* kategorisch
categorize (categorise) /ˈkætɪgəraɪz/ *v.t.* kategorisieren
category /ˈkætɪgərɪ/ *n.* Kategorie, *die*
cater /ˈkeɪtə(r)/ *v.i.* **~ for sb./sth.** für jmdn./etw. [die] Speisen und Getränke liefern; (fig.) auf jmdn./etw. eingestellt sein
'caterer *n.* Lieferant von Speisen und Getränken
'catering *n.* **(a)** (trade) Gastronomie, *die*
(b) (service) Lieferung von Speisen und Getränken
caterpillar /ˈkætəpɪlə(r)/ *n.* Raupe, *die*
'cat flap ▶ CAT DOOR
cathedral /kəˈθi:drl/ *n.* Dom, *der*
Catherine wheel /ˈkæθrɪn wi:l/ *n.* Feuerrad, *das*
Catholic /ˈkæθəlɪk/ 1 *adj.* katholisch
2 *n.* Katholik, *der*/Katholikin, *die*
Catholicism /kəˈθɒlɪsɪzm/ *n.* Katholizismus, *der*
catkin /ˈkætkɪn/ *n.* (Bot.) Kätzchen, *das*
'Cat's-eye ® *n.* (Brit.: on road) Bodenrückstrahler, *der*
cattle /ˈkætl/ *n. pl.* Rinder *Pl.*
'cattle market *n.* Viehmarkt, *der;* (fig.) Fleischbeschau, *die* (ugs. scherzh.)
'catwalk *n.* Laufsteg, *der*
caught ▶ CATCH 1, 2
cauldron /ˈkɔ:ldrən/ *n.* Kessel, *der*
cauliflower /ˈkɒlɪflaʊə(r)/ *n.* Blumenkohl, *der*
cause /kɔ:z/ 1 *n.* **(a)** Ursache, *die* (**of** für *od. Gen.*); (person) Verursacher, *der*/ Verursacherin, *die;* **be the ~ of sth.** etw. verursachen
(b) (reason) Grund, *der;* **~ for sth.** Grund zu etw.
(c) (object of support) Sache, *die;* **[in] a good ~:** [für] eine gute Sache
2 *v.t.* verursachen; erregen ‹*Aufsehen, Ärgernis*›; hervorrufen ‹*Unruhe, Verwirrung*›; **~ sb. worry/pain** jmdm. Sorge/ Schmerzen bereiten; **~ sb. to do sth.** jmdn. veranlassen, etw. zu tun
causeway /ˈkɔ:zweɪ/ *n.* Damm, *der*
caustic /ˈkɔ:stɪk/ *adj.* ätzend; (fig.) bissig; beißend ‹*Spott*›
caution /ˈkɔ:ʃn/ 1 *n.* **(a)** Vorsicht, *die*
(b) (warning) Warnung, *die*
2 *v.t.* (warn) warnen; (warn and reprove) verwarnen (**for** wegen)
cautious /ˈkɔ:ʃəs/ *adj.*, **'cautiously** *adv.* vorsichtig
cavalry /ˈkævəlrɪ/ *n.* Kavallerie, *die*
cave /keɪv/ *n.* Höhle, *die*
■ **cave 'in** *v.i.* einbrechen
'caveman *n.* Höhlenbewohner, der
cavern /ˈkævən/ *n.* Höhle, *die*
cavernous /ˈkævənəs/ *adj.* höhlenartig
caviar[e] /ˈkævɪɑ:(r)/ *n.* Kaviar, *der*
cavity /ˈkævɪtɪ/ *n.* Hohlraum, *der;* (in tooth) Loch, *das*
'cavity wall *n.* Hohlmauer, *die*
cc /si:ˈsi:/ *abbr.* = **cubic centimetre(s)** cm^3
CCTV *abbr.* = **closed-circuit television** CCTV
CD *abbr.* = **compact disc** CD, *die*; **CD burner, CD writer** CD-Brenner; **CD player** CD-Spieler, *der*
CD-ROM /si:di:ˈrɒm/ *n.* CD-ROM, *die;* **~ drive** CD-ROM-Laufwerk, *das*
cease /si:s/ 1 *v.i.* aufhören
2 *v.t.* **(a)** (stop) aufhören
(b) (end) aufhören mit; einstellen ‹*Bemühungen*›
'ceasefire *n.* Waffenruhe, *die*
cedar /ˈsi:də(r)/ *n.* Zeder, *die*
Ceefax ® /ˈsi:fæks/ *n.* (Brit.) *Bildschirmtextdienst der BBC*
ceiling /ˈsi:lɪŋ/ *n.* **(a)** Decke, *die*
(b) (upper limit) Maximum, *das*

celebrate /'selɪbreɪt/ *v.t. & i.* feiern
'celebrated *adj.* berühmt
celebration /selɪ'breɪʃn/ *n.* Feier, *die*
celebrity /sɪ'lebrɪtɪ/ *n.* Berühmtheit, *die*
celery /'selərɪ/ *n.* Sellerie, *der od. die*
celibate /'selɪbət/ *adj.* zölibatär (Rel.); ehelos
cell /sel/ *n.* Zelle, *die*
cellar /'selə(r)/ *n.* Keller, *der*
cellist /'tʃelɪst/ *n.* Cellist, *der*/Cellistin, *die*
cello /'tʃeləʊ/ *n., pl.* **~s** Cello, *das*
Cellophane ® /'seləfeɪn/ *n.* Cellophan Ⓦⓩ, *das*
'cellphone, cellular 'phone /'seljʊlə(r)/ *ns.* Mobiltelefon, *das*
cellulite /'seljʊlaɪt/ *n., no indef. art.: überschüssige Fettdepots an Oberschenkeln und Hüften*
Celsius /'selsɪəs/ *adj.* Celsius
cement /sɪ'ment/ [1] *n.* Zement, *der*
[2] *v.t.* zementieren; (stick together) zusammenkleben
ce'ment mixer *n.* Betonmischmaschine, *die*
cemetery /'semɪtərɪ/ *n.* Friedhof, *der*
censor /'sensə(r)/ [1] *n.* Zensor, *der*
[2] *v.t.* zensieren
'censorship *n.* Zensur, *die*
censure /'senʃə(r)/ *v.t.* tadeln
census /'sensəs/ *n.* Volkszählung, *die*
cent /sent/ *n.* Cent, *der*
centenary /sen'ti:nərɪ/ *adj. & n.* **~ [celebrations]** Hundertjahrfeier, *die*
center (Amer.) ▶ CENTRE
centigrade /'sentɪgreɪd/ ▶ CELSIUS
centimetre (*Brit.; Amer.:* **centimeter**) /'sentɪmi:tə(r)/ *n.* Zentimeter, *der*
centipede /'sentɪpi:d/ *n.* Tausendfüßler, *der*
central /'sentrl/ *adj.* zentral
Central: ~ A'merica *pr. n.* Mittelamerika (*das*); **~ 'Europe** *pr. n.* Mitteleuropa (*das*); **~ Euro'pean** *adj.* mitteleuropäisch; **c~ 'heating** *n.* Zentralheizung, *die*
centralize /'sentrəlaɪz/ *v.t.* zentralisieren
central: ~ 'locking *n.* (Motor Veh.) Zentralverriegelung, *die;* **~ 'nervous system** *n.* Zentralnervensystem, *das;* **~ 'processing unit** *n.* (Comp.) Zentraleinheit, *die;* **~ reservation** *n.* (Brit.) Mittelstreifen, *der*
centre /'sentə(r)/ (Brit.) [1] *n.* **(a)** Mitte, *die;* (of circle) Mittelpunkt, *der*
(b) (of area, city) Zentrum, *das*
[2] *adj.* mittler...
[3] *v.i.* **~ on sth.** sich auf etw. (*Akk.*) konzentrieren; **~ [a]round sth.** sich um etw. drehen
[4] *v.t.* **(a)** in der Mitte anbringen
(b) (concentrate) **be ~d [a]round sth.** etw. zum Mittelpunkt haben; **~ sth. on sth.** etw. auf etw. (*Akk.*) konzentrieren
centre 'forward *n.* Mittelstürmer, *der*
centrifugal /sentrɪ'fju:gl/ *adj.* **~ force** Zentrifugalkraft, *die;* Fliehkraft, *die*
century /'sentʃərɪ/ *n.* (hundred-year period from a year ..00) Jahrhundert, *das;* (hundred years) hundert Jahre
ceramic /sɪ'ræmɪk/ *adj.* keramisch
cereal /'sɪərɪəl/ *n.* Getreide, *das;* (breakfast dish) Getreideflocken *Pl.*
cerebral /'serɪbrl/ *adj.* (intellectual) intellektuell
ceremonial /serɪ'məʊnɪəl/ [1] *adj.* feierlich; (prescribed for ceremony) zeremoniell
[2] *n.* Zeremoniell, *das*
ceremony /'serɪmənɪ/ *n.* Feier, *die;* (formal act) Zeremonie, *die*
certain /'sɜ:tn, 'sɜ:tɪn/ *adj.* **(a)** (settled, definite) bestimmt
(b) be ~ to do sth. etw. bestimmt tun
(c) (confident, sure to happen) sicher
(d) (indisputable) unbestreitbar
(e) a ~ Mr Smith ein gewisser Herr Smith; **to a ~ extent** in gewisser Weise
'certainly *adv.* **(a)** (admittedly) sicher[lich]; (definitely) bestimmt
(b) (in answer) [aber] sicher; **[most] ~ 'not!** auf [gar] keinen Fall!
certainty /'sɜ:tntɪ, 'sɜ:tɪntɪ/ *n.* **(a) be a ~:** sicher sein
(b) (absolute conviction) Gewissheit, *die*
certificate /sə'tɪfɪkət/ *n.* Urkunde, *die;* (of action performed) Schein, *der*
certify /'sɜ:tɪfaɪ/ *v.t.* bescheinigen; bestätigen; **this is to ~ that ...:** hiermit wird bescheinigt *od.* bestätigt, dass ...
cf. *abbr.* = **compare** vgl.
CFC *abbr.* = **chlorofluorocarbon** FCKW, *das;* **~-free** FCKW-frei
chafe /tʃeɪf/ *v.t.* wund scheuern
chaff /tʃɑ:f/ *n.* Spreu, *die*
chaffinch /'tʃæfɪntʃ/ *n.* Buchfink, *der*
chagrin /'ʃægrɪn/ *n.* Kummer, *der*
chain /tʃeɪn/ [1] *n.* Kette, *die;* **~ of shops/hotels** Laden-/Hotelkette, *die*
[2] *v.t.* [an]ketten (**to** an + *Akk.*)
chain: ~ re'action *n.* Kettenreaktion, *die;* **~saw** *n.* Kettensäge, *die;* **~-smoke** *v.t. & i.* Kette rauchen (ugs.); **~-smoker** *n.* Kettenraucher, *der*/-raucherin, *die;* **~ store** *n.* Kettenladen, *der*
chair /tʃeə(r)/ [1] *n.* **(a)** Stuhl, *der;* (arm~, easy ~) Sessel, *der*
(b) (professorship) Lehrstuhl, *der*
(c) (at meeting) Vorsitz, *der;* (~person) Vorsitzende, *der*/*die*
[2] *v.t.* den Vorsitz haben bei
chair: ~ back *n.* Rückenlehne, *die;* **~lift** *n.* Sessellift, *der;* **~man** /'tʃeəmən/ *n., pl.*

~men /ˈtʃeəmən/ Vorsitzende, *der/die;* **~person** *n.* Vorsitzende, *der/die;* **~woman** *n.* Vorsitzende, *die*

chalet /ˈʃæleɪ/ *n.* Chalet, *das*

chalk /tʃɔːk/ 1 *n.* Kreide, *die*
2 *v.t.* mit Kreide schreiben/malen *usw*

challenge /ˈtʃælɪndʒ/ 1 *n.* Herausforderung, *die*
2 *v.t.* **(a)** (to contest etc.) herausfordern
(b) (fig.) auffordern; (question) infrage stellen

challenged /ˈtʃælɪndʒd/ *adj.* (euphem. or joc.) behindert; **mentally ~**: geistig behindert

ˈchallenger *n.* Herausforderer, *der*/ Herausforderin, *die*

challenging /ˈtʃælɪndʒɪŋ/ *adj.* herausfordernd; fesselnd ‹*Problem*›; anspruchsvoll ‹*Arbeit*›

chamber /ˈtʃeɪmbə(r)/ *n.* Kammer, *die*

chamber: ~maid *n.* Zimmermädchen, *das;* **~ music** *n.* Kammermusik, *die;* **C~ of ˈCommerce** *n.* Industrie- und Handelskammer, *die;* **~ pot** *n.* Nachttopf, *der*

chameleon /kəˈmiːljən/ *n.* Chamäleon, *das*

chamois /ˈʃæmwɑː/ *n.* **(a)** Gämse, *die*
(b) /ˈʃæmɪ/ **~ [leather]** Chamois[leder], *das*

champagne /ʃæmˈpeɪn/ *n.* Sekt, *der;* (from Champagne) Champagner, *der*

chamˈpagne glass *n.* Sektglas, *das*

champion /ˈtʃæmpɪən/ 1 *n.* **(a)** (defender) Verfechter, *der*/Verfechterin, *die*
(b) (Sport) Meister, *der*/Meisterin, *die*
2 *v.t.* verfechten ‹*Sache*›; sich einsetzen für ‹*Person*›

ˈchampionship *n.* Meisterschaft, *die*

chance /tʃɑːns/ 1 *n.* **(a)** (fortune, trick of fate) Zufall, *der; attrib.* zufällig; **~ encounter** Zufallsbegegnung, *die;* **game of ~**: Glücksspiel, *das;* **by ~**: zufällig; **take a ~**: es riskieren; **the ~s are that ...**: es ist wahrscheinlich, dass ...; **by [any] ~, by some ~ or other** zufällig
(b) (opportunity, possibility) Chance, *die;* **get a/the ~ to do sth.** eine/die Gelegenheit haben, etw. zu tun
2 *v.t.* riskieren

chancellor /ˈtʃɑːnsələ(r)/ *n.* Kanzler, *der;* **C~ of the Exchequer** (Brit.) Schatzkanzler, *der*

chandelier /ʃændəˈlɪə(r)/ *n.* Kronleuchter, *der*

change /tʃeɪndʒ/ 1 *n.* **(a)** Veränderung, *die;* Änderung, *die;* (of job, surroundings, government, etc.) Wechsel, *der*
(b) (for the sake of variety) Abwechslung, *die;* **for a ~**: zur Abwechslung
(c) (money) Wechselgeld, *das;* **[loose** *or* **small] ~**: Kleingeld, *das;* **[here is] £5 ~**: 5 Pfund zurück; **keep the ~**: [es] stimmt so
2 *v.t.* **(a)** (switch) wechseln; auswechseln ‹*Glühbirne, Batterie*›; **~ one's clothes** sich umziehen; **~ one's address/name** seine Anschrift/seinen Namen ändern; **~ trains/buses** umsteigen
(b) (transform) verwandeln **(into** in + *Akk.*); (alter) ändern
(c) (exchange) eintauschen **(for** für); wechseln ‹*Geld*›
3 *v.i.* **(a)** (alter) sich ändern; ‹*Person, Land:*› sich verändern
(b) (into something else) sich verwandeln
(c) (put on other clothes) sich umziehen
(d) (~trains, buses, etc.) umsteigen

■ **change ˈover** *v.i.* **~ over from sth. to sth.** von etw. zu etw. übergehen

changeable /ˈtʃeɪndʒəbl/ *adj.* veränderlich

ˈchange[-giving] machine *n.* Geldwechsler, *der*

ˈchangeover *n.* Wechsel, *der;* **~ from sth. to sth.** Umstellung von etw. auf etw. (*Akk.*)

ˈchanging room *n.* (Brit.) Umkleideraum, *der*

channel /ˈtʃænl/ 1 *n.* (also Telev., Radio) Kanal, *der;* **the C~** (Brit.) der [Ärmel]kanal
2 *v.t.* (fig.) lenken

Channel: c~-hop *v.i.* (coll.) **(a)** (Telev.) zappen (ugs.); **(b)** (cross the English Channel) kurz mal über den Kanal fahren; **~ Islands** *pr. n. pl.* Kanalinseln *Pl.;* **~ ˈTunnel** *n.* [Ärmel]kanaltunnel, *der*

chant /tʃɑːnt/ 1 *v.t.* skandieren; (Eccl.) singen
2 *v.i.* Sprechchöre anstimmen; (Eccl.) singen
3 *n.* Sprechchor, *der;* (Eccl.) Gesang, *der*

chaos /ˈkeɪɒs/ *n.* Chaos, *das*

chaotic /keɪˈɒtɪk/ *adj.* chaotisch

chap¹ /tʃæp/ *n.* (Brit. coll.) Bursche, *der;* Kerl, *der*

chap² *v.t.*, **-pp-** aufplatzen lassen

chapel /ˈtʃæpl/ *n.* Kapelle, *die*

chaperon /ˈʃæpərəʊn/ 1 *n.* Anstandsdame, *die*
2 *v.t.* beaufsichtigen

chaplain /ˈtʃæplɪn/ *n.* Kaplan, *der*

chapter /ˈtʃæptə(r)/ *n.* Kapitel, *das*

char /tʃɑː(r)/ *v.t. & i.*, **-rr-** verkohlen

character /ˈkærɪktə(r)/ *n.* **(a)** Charakter, *der*
(b) (in novel etc.) Figur, *die*
(c) (coll.: extraordinary person) Original, *das*
(d) (symbol) Zeichen, *das*

characteristic /kærɪktəˈrɪstɪk/ 1 *adj.* charakteristisch **(of** für)
2 *n.* charakteristisches Merkmal

characterize /ˈkærɪktəraɪz/ *v.t.* charakterisieren

ˈcharacterless *adj.* nichts sagend

charade /ʃəˈrɑːd/ *n.* Scharade, *die;* (fig.) Farce, *die*

charcoal /ˈtʃɑːkəʊl/ *n.* Holzkohle, *die*

charge /tʃɑːdʒ/ 1 *n.* **(a)** (price) Preis, *der;* (for services) Gebühr, *die*
(b) be in ~ of sth. für etw. die Verantwortung haben; **take ~**: die Verantwortung übernehmen
(c) (Law: accusation) Anklage, *die*

(d) (attack) Angriff, *der*
(e) (of explosives, electricity) Ladung, *die*
[2] *v.t.* (a) ~ sb. sth., ~ sth. to sb. jmdm. etw. berechnen
(b) (Law: accuse) anklagen (with wegen)
(c) (Electr.) [auf]laden ‹*Batterie*›
(d) (rush at) angreifen
[3] *v.i.* (a) (attack) angreifen
(b) (coll.: hurry) sausen
charge: ~ account *n.* (Amer.) Kreditkonto, *das;* ~ **card** *n.* Kreditkarte, *die*
charisma /kə'rɪzmə/ *n.* Charisma, *das*
charitable /'tʃærɪtəbl/ *adj.* (a) wohltätig (b) (lenient) großzügig
charity /'tʃærɪtɪ/ *n.* (a) Wohltätigkeit, *die* (b) (organization) wohltätige Organisation
charity: ~ concert *n.* Benefizkonzert, *das;* ~ **match** *n.* Benefizspiel, *das;* ~ **performance** *n.* Benefizvorstellung, *die;* Wohltätigkeitsvorstellung, *die;* ~ **shop** *n.: Secondhandladen, dessen Erlöse einem wohltätigen Zweck dienen*
charlady /'tʃɑːleɪdɪ/ *n.* (Brit.) Putzfrau, *die*
charlatan /'ʃɑːlətən/ *n.* Scharlatan, *der*
charm /tʃɑːm/ [1] *n.* (a) (act) Zauber, *der*
(b) (talisman) Talisman, *der*
(c) (attractiveness) Reiz, *der;* (of person) Charme, *der*
[2] *v.t.* bezaubern
'charming *adj.* bezaubernd
chart /tʃɑːt/ [1] *n.* (a) (map) Karte, *die*
(b) (graph etc.) Schaubild, *das*
(c) the ~s die Hitliste
[2] *v.t.* (fig.: describe) schildern
charter /'tʃɑːtə(r)/ [1] *n.* (a) Charta, *die*
(b) on ~ gechartert
[2] *v.t.* chartern ‹*Schiff, Flugzeug*›
chartered: ~ ac'countant *n.* (Brit.) Wirtschaftsprüfer, *der*/-prüferin, *die;* ~ **'aircraft** *n.* Charterflugzeug, *das;* Chartermaschine, *die*
charter: ~ flight *n.* Charterflug, *der;* ~ **plane** ▶ CHARTERED AIRCRAFT
charwoman /'tʃɑːwʊmən/ *n.* Putzfrau, *die*
chase /tʃeɪs/ [1] *n.* Verfolgungsjagd, *die*
[2] *v.t.* (pursue) jagen; ~ sth. (fig.) einer Sache (*Dat.*) nachjagen
[3] *v.i.* ~ after sb./sth. hinter jmdm./etw. herjagen
▪ **chase 'up** *v.t.* (coll.) ausfindig machen
chasm /'kæzm/ *n.* Kluft, *die*
chassis /'ʃæsɪ/ *n., pl. same* /'ʃæsɪz/ Chassis, *das;* Fahrgestell, *das*
chaste /tʃeɪst/ *adj.* keusch
chastening /'tʃeɪsənɪŋ/ *adj.* ernüchternd
chastise /tʃæ'staɪz/ *v.t.* züchtigen
chastity /'tʃæstɪtɪ/ *n.* Keuschheit, *die*
chat /tʃæt/ [1] *n.* Schwätzchen, *das*
[2] *v.i.,* -tt-: (a) plaudern; ~ with *or* to sb. about sth. mit jmdm. von etw. plaudern
(b) (Comp.) chatten
▪ **chat 'up** *v.t.* (Brit. coll.) anmachen (ugs.)
chat: ~ line *n.* Chatline, *die;* ~ **room** *n.* (Comp.) Chat-Room, *der;* ~ **show** *n.* Talkshow, *die*
chattels /'tʃætəlz/ *n. pl.* bewegliche Habe (geh.)
chatter /'tʃætə(r)/ [1] *v.i.* (a) schwatzen
(b) ‹*Zähne:*› klappern
[2] *n.* Schwatzen, *das*
'chatterbox *n.* Quasselstrippe, *die* (ugs.)
chatty /'tʃætɪ/ *adj.* gesprächig
chauffeur /'ʃəʊfə(r)/ [1] *n.* Fahrer, *der;* Chauffeur, *der*
[2] *v.t.* fahren
chauvinist /'ʃəʊvɪnɪst/ *n.* Chauvinist, *der*/Chauvinistin, *die*
chauvinistic /ʃəʊvɪ'nɪstɪk/ *adj.* chauvinistisch
cheap /tʃiːp/ *adj., adv.* billig
cheapen /'tʃiːpn/ *v.t.* (fig.) herabsetzen
'cheaply *adv.* billig
cheat /tʃiːt/ [1] *n.* Schwindler, *der*/Schwindlerin, *die*
[2] *v.t. & i.* betrügen
check[1] /tʃek/ [1] *n.* (a) Kontrolle, *die;* make/keep a ~ on kontrollieren
(b) (Amer.: bill) Rechnung, *die*
[2] *v.t.* (a) (restrain) unter Kontrolle halten
(b) (examine) nachprüfen; kontrollieren ‹*Fahrkarte*›
(c) (stop) aufhalten
[3] *v.i.* ~ on sth. etw. überprüfen; ~ with sb. bei jmdm. nachfragen
▪ **check 'in** *v.t. & i.* (at airport) einchecken
▪ **check 'out** [1] *v.t.* überprüfen
[2] *v.i.* abreisen
▪ **check 'up** *v.i.* ~ up [on] überprüfen
check[2] *n.* (pattern) Karo, *das*
checkers /'tʃekəz/ (Amer.) ▶ DRAUGHTS
check: ~-in *n.* Abfertigung, *die;* ~**list** *n.* Checkliste, *die;* ~**mate** [1] *n.* [Schach]matt, *das;* [2] *int.* [schach]matt; ~**out [desk]** *n.* Kasse, *die;* ~**point** *n.* Kontrollpunkt, *der;* ~**-up** *n.* (Med.) Untersuchung, *die*
cheek /tʃiːk/ *n.* (a) Backe, *die;* Wange, *die* (geh.)
(b) (impertinence) Frechheit, *die*
'cheekbone *n.* Backenknochen, *der*
'cheekily *adv.,* **'cheeky** *adj.* frech
cheep /tʃiːp/ [1] *v.i.* piep[s]en
[2] *n.* Piep[s]en, *das*
cheer /tʃɪə(r)/ [1] *n.* (a) (applause) Beifallsruf, *der*
(b) *in pl.* (Brit. coll.: as a toast) prost!
(c) (Brit. coll.: thank you) danke
[2] *v.t.* (a) (applaud) ~ sth./sb. etw. bejubeln/jmdm. zujubeln
(b) (gladden) aufmuntern
[3] *v.i.* jubeln
▪ **cheer 'on** *v.t.* anfeuern ‹*Sportler*›
▪ **cheer 'up** [1] *v.t.* aufheitern
[2] *v.i.* bessere Laune bekommen; ~ up! Kopf hoch!

cheerful /'tʃɪəfl/ *adj.* (in good spirits) fröhlich; (bright, pleasant) heiter
'cheerfully *adv.* vergnügt
'cheering [1] *adj.* fröhlich stimmend [2] *n.* Jubeln, *das*
cheerio /tʃɪərɪ'əʊ/ *int.* (Brit. coll.) tschüs (ugs.)
'cheery *adj.* fröhlich
cheese /tʃi:z/ *n.* Käse, *der*
cheese: ~board *n.* Käseplatte, *die;* **~cake** *n.* Käsetorte, *die*
cheetah /'tʃi:tə/ *n.* Gepard, *der*
chef /ʃef/ *n.* Küchenchef, *der;* (as profession) Koch, *der*
chemical /'kemɪkl/ [1] *adj.* chemisch [2] *n.* Chemikalie, *die*
chemical 'warfare *n.* chemische Krieg[s]führung
chemist /'kemɪst/ *n.* **(a)** (scientist) Chemiker, *der*/Chemikerin, *die*
(b) (Brit.: pharmacist) Drogist, *der*/Drogistin, *die;* **~'s [shop]** Drogerie, *die*
chemistry /'kemɪstrɪ/ *n.* Chemie, *die*
chemotherapy /ki:mə'θerəpɪ/ *n.* Chemotherapie, *die*
cheque /tʃek/ *n.* Scheck, *der;* **pay by ~:** mit [einem] Scheck bezahlen
cheque: ~book *n.* Scheckbuch, *das;* **~book 'journalism** *n.* Scheckbuchjournalismus, *der;* **~ card** *n.* Scheckkarte, *die*
cherish /'tʃerɪʃ/ *v.t.* hegen ‹*Hoffnung, Gefühl*›; in Ehren halten ‹*[Erinnerungs]gegenstand*›
cherry /'tʃerɪ/ *n.* Kirsche, *die*
chess /tʃes/ *n., no art.* das Schach[spiel]
chess: ~board *n.* Schachbrett, *das;* **~man** *n.* Schachfigur, *die;* **~ player** *n.* Schachspieler, *der*/-spielerin, *die*
chest /tʃest/ *n.* **(a)** Kiste, *die*
(b) (Anat.) Brust, *die;* **get sth. off one's ~** (fig. coll.) sich (*Dat.*) etw. von der Seele reden
(c) ~ [measurement] Brustumfang, *der*
chestnut /'tʃesnʌt/ [1] *n.* **(a)** Kastanie, *die*
(b) (colour) Kastanienbraun, *das*
[2] *adj.* (colour) **~[-brown]** kastanienbraun
'chestnut tree *n.* Kastanie, *die*
chest of 'drawers *n.* Kommode, *die*
chew /tʃu:/ *v.t. & i.* kauen
'chewing gum *n.* Kaugummi, *der od. das*
chic /ʃɪ:k/ *adj.* schick; elegant
chick /tʃɪk/ *n.* **(a)** Küken, *das*
(b) (sl.: young woman) Biene, *die* (ugs.)
chicken /'tʃɪkɪn/ [1] *n.* **(a)** Huhn, *das;* (grilled, roasted) Hähnchen, *das*
(b) (coll.: coward) Angsthase, *der*
[2] *adj.* (coll.) feig[e]
[3] *v.i.* **~ out** (coll.) kneifen
chicken: ~pox /-pɒks/ *n.* Windpocken *Pl.;* **~ 'soup** *n.* Hühnersuppe, *die;* **~ wire** *n.* Maschendraht, *der*
'chickpea *n.* Kichererbse, *die*
chicory /'tʃɪkərɪ/ *n.* (plant) Chicorée, *der od. die;* (for coffee) Zichorie, *die*
chief /tʃi:f/ [1] *n.* **(a)** Oberhaupt, *das;* (of tribe) Häuptling, *der*
(b) (of department) Leiter, *der;* **~ of police** Polizeipräsident, *der*
[2] *adj., usu. attrib.* **(a)** Haupt-
(b) (leading) führend
'chiefly *adv.* hauptsächlich
chieftain /'tʃi:ftən/ *n.* Stammesführer, *der*
chilblain /'tʃɪlbleɪn/ *n.* Frostbeule, *die*
child /tʃaɪld/ *n., pl.* **~ren** /'tʃɪldrən/ Kind, *das*
child: ~ abuse *n.* Kindesmisshandlung, *die;* **~bearing** [1] *n.* Schwangerschaften *Pl.;* [2] *adj.* **~bearing age** Gebäralter, *das;* **of ~bearing age** im gebärfähigen Alter; **~birth** *n.* Geburt, *die;* **~care** *n.* Kinderbetreuung *die*
'childhood *n.* Kindheit, *die*
childish /'tʃaɪldɪʃ/ *adj.,* **'childishly** *adv.* kindisch
'childishness *n.* (behaviour) kindisches Benehmen
child: ~less *adj.* kinderlos; **~like** *adj.* kindlich; **~minder** /-maɪndə(r)/ *n.* (Brit.) Tagesmutter, *die;* **~proof** *adj.* kindersicher; **~proof door lock** (in car) Kindersicherung, *die*
children *pl. of* CHILD
'child's play *n.* (fig.) ein Kinderspiel
Chile /'tʃɪlɪ/ *pr. n.* Chile (*das*)
chill /tʃɪl/ [1] *n.* Kühle, *die;* (illness) Erkältung, *die*
[2] *v.t.* kühlen
■ **chill out** *v.i.* (coll.) (relax) sich entspannen; (calm down) sich abregen (ugs.)
chilli /'tʃɪlɪ/ *n., pl.* **~es** Chili, *der*
chilling /'tʃɪlɪŋ/ *adj.* (fig.) ernüchternd
'chilly *adj.* kühl; **I am rather ~:** mir ist ziemlich kühl
chime /tʃaɪm/ [1] *n.* Geläute, *das*
[2] *v.i.* läuten; ‹*Turmuhr:*› schlagen
chimney /'tʃɪmnɪ/ *n.* Schornstein, *der*
chimney: ~ breast *n.* Kaminmantel, *der;* **~ pot** *n.* ≈ Schornsteinkopf, *der;* **~ sweep** *n.* Schornsteinfeger, *der*
chimpanzee /tʃɪmpən'zi:/ *n.* Schimpanse, *der*
chin /tʃɪn/ *n.* Kinn, *das*
china *n.* Porzellan, *das;* (crockery) Geschirr, *das*
China /'tʃaɪnə/ *pr. n.* China (*das*)
Chinese /tʃaɪ'ni:z/ [1] *adj.* chinesisch; **sb. is ~:** jmd. ist Chinese/Chinesin
[2] *n.* **(a)** *pl. same* (person) Chinese, *der*/Chinesin, *die*
(b) (language) Chinesisch, *das; see also* ENGLISH 2A
chink *n.* (gap) Spalt, *der*
chip /tʃɪp/ [1] *n.* **(a)** Splitter, *der*
(b) *in pl.* (Brit.: potato ~s) Pommes frites *Pl.*

(c) (Gambling, Comp.) Chip, *der*
2 *v.t.*, **-pp-** anschlagen
■ **chip 'in** (coll.) 1 *v.i.* **(a)** (interrupt) sich einmischen
(b) (contribute money) etwas beisteuern
2 *v.t.* (contribute) beisteuern
'chipboard *n.* Spanplatte, *die*
chipmunk /'tʃɪpmʌŋk/ *n.* Chipmunk, *das*
chippy /'tʃɪpɪ/ *n.* (Brit. coll.) Pommes-frites-Bude, *die;* Frittenbude, *die* (ugs.)
'chip shop (Brit.) ▶ CHIPPY
chiropodist /kɪ'rɒpədɪst/ *n.* Fußpfleger, *der*/-pflegerin, *die*
chiropody /kɪ'rɒpədɪ/ *n.* Fußpflege, *die*
chirp /tʃɜːp/ 1 *v.i.* zwitschern; ‹*Grille:*› zirpen
2 *n.* Zwitschern, *das;* Zirpen, *das*
chisel /'tʃɪzl/ 1 *n.* Meißel, *der;* (for wood) Stemmeisen, *das*
2 *v.t.*, (Brit.) **-ll-** meißeln; (in wood) hauen
chit /tʃɪt/ *n.* Notiz, *die*
chit-chat /'tʃɪttʃæt/ *n.* Plauderei, *die*
chivalrous /'ʃɪvlrəs/ *adj.* ritterlich
chivalry /'ʃɪvlrɪ/ *n.* Ritterlichkeit, *die*
chives /tʃaɪvz/ *n.* Schnittlauch, *der*
chloride /'klɔːraɪd/ *n.* Chlorid, *das*
chlorine /'klɔːriːn/ *n.* Chlor, *das*
chlorofluorocarbon /klɔːrəʊflʊərəʊ'kɑːbən/ *n.* Chlorfluorkohlenstoff, *der*
chock /tʃɒk/ *n.* Bremsklotz, *der*
'chock-a-block *pred adj.* voll gepfropft
chocolate /'tʃɒklət/ *n.* Schokolade, *die*
chocolate 'biscuit *n.* Schokoladenkeks, *der*
choice /tʃɔɪs/ 1 *n.* **(a)** Wahl, *die;* **from ~:** freiwillig
(b) (variety) Auswahl, *die*
2 *adj.* ausgewählt
choir /kwaɪə(r)/ *n.* Chor, *der*
'choirboy *n.* Chorknabe, *der*
choke /tʃəʊk/ 1 *v.t.* **(a)** ersticken
(b) (block up) verstopfen
2 *v.i.* (temporarily) keine Luft [mehr] bekommen; (permanently) ersticken (**on** an + *Dat.*)
3 *n.* (Motor Veh.) Choke, *der*
cholera /'kɒlərə/ *n.* Cholera, *die*
cholesterol /kə'lestərɒl/ *n.* Cholesterin, *das*
choose /tʃuːz/ 1 *v.t.*, **chose** /tʃəʊz/, **chosen** /'tʃəʊzn/ **(a)** wählen
(b) (decide) **~/~ not to do sth.** sich dafür/dagegen entscheiden, etw. zu tun
2 *v.i.*, **chose, chosen** wählen (**between** zwischen); **~ from sth.** aus etw./(from several) unter etw. (*Dat.*) [aus]wählen
choos[e]y /'tʃuːzɪ/ *adj.* wählerisch
chop /tʃɒp/ 1 *n.* **(a)** Hieb, *der*
(b) (of meat) Kotelett, *das*
(c) get the ~ (coll.: be dismissed) rausgeworfen werden (ugs.)
2 *v.t.*, **-pp-** hacken ‹*Holz*›; klein schneiden ‹*Fleisch, Gemüse*›
'chopper *n.* (axe) Beil, *das;* (cleaver) Hackbeil, *das*
'chopping board *n.* Hackbrett, *das*
'choppy *adj.* bewegt
'chopstick *n.* [Ess]stäbchen, *das*
choral /'kɔːrl/ *adj.* Chor-
chord /kɔːd/ *n.* (Mus.) Akkord, *der*
chore /tʃɔː(r)/ *n.* [lästige] Routinearbeit
choreographer /kɒrɪ'ɒgrəfə(r)/ *n.* Choreograph, *der*/Choreographin, *die*
choreography /kɒrɪ'ɒgrəfɪ/ *n.* Choreographie, *die*
chortle /'tʃɔːtl/ 1 *v.i.* vor Lachen glucksen
2 *n.* Glucksen, *das*
chorus /'kɔːrəs/ *n.* **(a)** Chor, *der*
(b) (of song) Refrain, *der;* (in jazz) Chorus, *der*
chose, chosen ▶ CHOOSE
chow /tʃaʊ/ *n.* (Amer. sl.: food) Futter, *das* (salopp)
Christ /kraɪst/ *n.* Christus (*der*)
christen /'krɪsn/ *v.t.* taufen
'christening *n.* Taufe, *die*
Christian /'krɪstjən/ 1 *adj.* christlich
2 *n.* Christ, *der*/Christin, *die*
Christianity /krɪstɪ'ænɪtɪ/ *n.* das Christentum
'Christian name *n.* Vorname, *der*
Christmas /'krɪsməs/ *n.* Weihnachten, *das od. Pl.;* **merry** *or* **happy ~**: frohe *od.* fröhliche Weihnachten; **at ~**: [zu] Weihnachten
Christmas: ~ cake *n.* Weihnachtskuchen, *der;* **~ card** *n.* Weihnachtskarte, *die;* **~ 'carol** *n.* Weihnachtslied, *das;* **~ 'Day** *n.* erster Weihnachtsfeiertag; **~ 'Eve** *n.* Heiligabend, *der;* **~ present** *n.* Weihnachtsgeschenk, *das;* **~ tree** *n.* Weihnachtsbaum, *der*
chrome /krəʊm/**, chromium** /'krəʊmɪəm/ *ns.* Chrom, *das*
'chromium-plated *adj.* verchromt
chromosome /'krəʊməsəʊm/ *n.* Chromosom, *das*
chronic /'krɒnɪk/ *adj.* chronisch; **~ fatigue syndrome** chronisches Müdigkeitssyndrom
chronically /'krɒnɪkəlɪ/ *adv.* chronisch
chronicle /'krɒnɪkl/ *n.* Chronik, *die*
chronological /krɒnə'lɒdʒɪkl/ *adj.* chronologisch
chrysalis /'krɪsəlɪs/ *n., pl.* **~es** Puppe, *die*
chrysanthemum /krɪ'sænθɪməm/ *n.* Chrysantheme, *die*
chubby /'tʃʌbɪ/ *adj.* pummelig
chuck /tʃʌk/ *v.t.* (coll.) schmeißen (ugs.)
■ **chuck 'away, chuck 'out** *v.t.* (coll.) wegschmeißen (ugs.)
chuckle /'tʃʌkl/ 1 *v.i.* leise [vor sich hin] lachen (**at** über + *Akk.*)
2 *n.* leises, glucksendes Lachen

C

chug /tʃʌg/ *v.i.*, **-gg-** tuckern
chum /tʃʌm/ *n.* (coll.) Kumpel, *der* (salopp)
chunk /tʃʌŋk/ *n.* dickes Stück
'chunky *adj.* **(a)** (small and sturdy) stämmig **(b)** dick ‹*Pullover*›
Chunnel /'tʃʌnl/ *n.* (Brit. coll.) [Ärmel]kanaltunnel, *der*
church /tʃɜ:tʃ/ *n.* Kirche, *die;* **go to ~:** in die Kirche gehen; **the C~ of England** die Kirche von England
'churchyard *n.* Friedhof, *der* (*bei einer Kirche*); Kirchhof, *der* (veralt.)
churlish /'tʃɜ:lɪʃ/ *adj.* (ill-bred) ungehobelt; (surly) griesgrämig
churn /tʃɜ:n/ *n.* (Brit.) Butterfass, *das*
churn 'out *v.t.* massenweise produzieren (ugs.)
chute /ʃu:t/ *n.* Schütte, *die;* (for persons) Rutsche, *die*
chutney /'tʃʌtnɪ/ *n.* Chutney, *das*
CIA *abbr.* (Amer.) = **Central Intelligence Agency** CIA, *der od. die*
cicada /sɪ'kɑ:də/ *n.* Zikade, die
CID *abbr.* (Brit.) = **Criminal Investigation Department** C.I.D.; **the ~:** die Kripo
cider /'saɪdə(r)/ *n.* ≈ Apfelwein, *der*
cigar /sɪ'gɑ:(r)/ *n.* Zigarre, *die*
cigarette /sɪgə'ret/ *n.* Zigarette, *die*
cigarette: ~ end *n.* Zigarettenstummel, *der;* **~ lighter** *n.* Feuerzeug, *das;* **~ packet** *n.* Zigarettenschachtel, *die;* **~ paper** *n.* Zigarettenpapier, *das*
cinders /'sɪndəz/ *n. pl.* Asche, *die*
cine /'sɪnɪ/**: ~ camera** *n.* Filmkamera, *die;* **~ film** *n.* Schmalfilm, *der*
cinema /'sɪnɪmə/ *n.* Kino, *das;* **go to the ~:** ins Kino gehen
cinema: ~ complex *n.* Kinocenter, *das;* **~-goer** *n.* (Brit.) Kinogänger, *der*/-gängerin, *die*
cinematography /sɪnɪmə'tɒgrəfɪ/ *n.* Kinematographie, *die*
cinnamon /'sɪnəmən/ *n.* Zimt, *der*
cipher /'saɪfə(r)/ *n.* Geheimschrift, *die;* **in ~:** chiffriert
circle /'sɜ:kl/ **1** *n.* Kreis, *der* **2** *v.i.* kreisen **3** *v.t.* umkreisen
circuit /'sɜ:kɪt/ *n.* **(a)** (Electr.) Schaltung, *die* **(b)** (Motor racing) Rundkurs, *der*
circular /'sɜ:kjʊlə(r)/ **1** *adj.* (round) kreisförmig **2** *n.* (letter, notice) Rundbrief, *der;* Rundschreiben, *das;* (advertisement) Werbeprospekt, *der*
circular: ~ 'letter ▶ CIRCULAR 2; **~ 'saw** *n.* Kreissäge, *die*
circulate /'sɜ:kjʊleɪt/ **1** *v.i.* zirkulieren; ‹*Personen, Wein usw.:*› herumgehen (ugs.) **2** *v.t.* in Umlauf setzen; herumgehen lassen ‹*Buch, Bericht*› (**around** in + *Dat.*)
circulation /sɜ:kjʊ'leɪʃn/ *n.* **(a)** (Physiol.) Kreislauf, *der;* **poor ~:** Kreislaufstörungen *Pl.* **(b)** (copies sold) verkaufte Auflage
circulatory /sɜ:kjʊ'leɪtərɪ, 'sɜ:kjʊleɪtərɪ/ *adj.* (Physiol., Bot.) Kreislauf-; **~ system** Kreislauf, *der*
circumcise /'sɜ:kəmsaɪz/ *v.t.* beschneiden
circumcision /sɜ:kəm'sɪʒn/ *n.* Beschneidung, *die*
circumference /sə'kʌmfərəns/ *n.* Umfang, *der*
circumstances /'sɜ:kəmstənsɪz/ *n. pl.* Umstände *Pl.*; **in** *or* **under the ~:** unter diesen Umständen; **under no ~:** unter keinen Umständen
circus /'sɜ:kəs/ *n.* Zirkus, *der*
CIS *abbr.* = **Commonwealth of Independent States** GUS
cissy /'sɪsɪ/ ▶ SISSY
cistern /'sɪstən/ *n.* Wasserkasten, *der;* (in roof) Wasserbehälter, *der*
citation /saɪ'teɪʃn/ *n.* Zitat, *das*
cite /saɪt/ *v.t.* (quote) zitieren; anführen ‹*Beispiel*›
citizen /'sɪtɪzən/ *n.* **(a)** (of town, city) Bürger, *der*/Bürgerin, *die* **(b)** (of state) [Staats]bürger, *der*/-bürgerin, *die*
'citizenship *n.* Staatsbürgerschaft, *die*
citrus /'sɪtrəs/ *n.* **~ [fruit]** Zitrusfrucht, *die*
city /'sɪtɪ/ *n.* [Groß]stadt, *die*
city 'centre *n.* Stadtzentrum, *das*
civic /'sɪvɪk/ *adj.* [staats]bürgerlich; **~ centre** Verwaltungszentrum der Stadt
civil /'sɪvl/ *adj.* **(a)** (not military) zivil **(b)** (polite, obliging) höflich **(c)** (Law) Zivil-
civil: ~ engi'neer *n.* Bauingenieur, *der*/-ingenieurin, *die;* **~ engi'neering** *n.* Hoch- und Tiefbau, *der*
civilian /sɪ'vɪljən/ **1** *n.* Zivilist, *der* **2** *adj.* Zivil-
civility /sɪ'vɪlɪtɪ/ *n.* Höflichkeit, *die*
civilization /sɪvɪlaɪ'zeɪʃn/ *n.* Zivilisation, *die*
civilized /'sɪvɪlaɪzd/ *adj.* zivilisiert
civil: ~ 'law *n.* Zivilrecht, *das;* **~ 'rights** *n. pl.* Bürgerrechte *Pl.*; **~ 'servant** *n.* ≈ Staatsbeamte, *der*/-beamtin, *die;* **C~ 'Service** *n.* öffentlicher Dienst; **~ 'war** *n.* Bürgerkrieg, *der*
CJD *abbr.* = **Creutzfeldt-Jakob disease**
clad /klæd/ *adj.* (arch./literary) gekleidet (**in** in + *Akk.*)
claim /kleɪm/ **1** *v.t.* **(a)** beanspruchen ‹*Thron, Gebiete*›; fordern ‹*Lohnerhöhung, Schadensersatz*›; beantragen ‹*Sozialhilfe usw.*› **(b)** (assert) behaupten **2** *v.i.* (Insurance) Ansprüche geltend machen

3 *n.* Anspruch, *der* (**to** auf + *Akk.*); **lay ~ to sth.** auf etw. (*Akk.*) Anspruch erheben

claimant /ˈkleɪmənt/ *n.* Antragsteller, *der*/-stellerin, *die*

ˈclaim form *n.* **(a)** (Insurance) Antragsformular, *das*
(b) (for expenses) Spesenabrechnungsformular, *das*

clairvoyant /kleəˈvɔɪənt/ 1 *n.* Hellseher, *der*/Hellseherin, *die*
2 *adj.* hellseherisch

clam /klæm/ 1 *n.* Klaffmuschel, *die*
2 *v.i.*, **-mm-: ~ up** (coll.) den Mund nicht [mehr] aufmachen

clamber /ˈklæmbə(r)/ *v.i.* klettern

clammy /ˈklæmɪ/ *adj.* feucht; kalt und schweißig ‹*Haut*›; klamm ‹*Kleidung*›

clamour (*Brit.; Amer.:* **clamor**) /ˈklæmə(r)/ 1 *n.* (noise, shouting) Lärm, *der;* lautes Geschrei
2 *v.i.* **~ for sth.** nach etw. schreien

clamp /klæmp/ 1 *n.* Klammer, *die;* (for holding) Schraubzwinge, *die*
2 *v.t.* klemmen; einspannen ‹*Werkstück*›
3 *v.i.* (fig.) **~ down on sb./sth.** gegen jmdn./etw. rigoros vorgehen

clan /klæn/ *n.* Sippe, *die;* (of Scottish Highlanders) Clan, *der*

clandestine /klænˈdestɪn/ *adj.* heimlich

clang /klæŋ/ 1 *n.* (of bell) Läuten, *das;* (of hammer) Klingen, *das*
2 *v.i.* ‹*Glocke:*› läuten; ‹*Hammer:*› klingen

clap /klæp/ 1 *n.* **(a)** Klatschen, *das*
(b) ~ of thunder Donnerschlag, *der*
2 *v.i.*, **-pp-** klatschen
3 *v.t.*, **-pp-: ~ one's hands** in die Hände klatschen; **~ sth.** etw. beklatschen; **~ sb.** jmdm. Beifall klatschen

ˈclapping *n.* Applaus, *der*

claret /ˈklærət/ 1 *n.* roter Bordeauxwein
2 *adj.* weinrot

clarification /klærɪfɪˈkeɪʃn/ *n.* Klarstellung, *die*

clarify /ˈklærɪfaɪ/ *v.t.* klären ‹*Situation usw.*›; (by explanation) klarstellen; erläutern ‹*Bedeutung, Aussage*›

clarinet /klærɪˈnet/ *n.* Klarinette, *die*

clarity /ˈklærɪtɪ/ *n.* Klarheit, *die*

clash /klæʃ/ 1 *v.i.* **(a)** scheppern (ugs.)
(b) (meet in conflict) zusammenstoßen
(c) (disagree) sich streiten
(d) ‹*Interesse, Ereignis:*› kollidieren; ‹*Farbe:*› sich beißen (ugs.) (**with** mit)
2 *v.t.* gegeneinander schlagen
3 *n.* **(a)** (of cymbals) Dröhnen, *das*
(b) (meeting in conflict) Zusammenstoß, *der*
(c) (disagreement) Auseinandersetzung, *die*
(d) (of personalities, colours) Unverträglichkeit, *die;* (of events) Überschneiden, *das*

clasp /klɑːsp/ 1 *n.* Verschluss, *der*
2 *v.t.* umklammern

class /klɑːs/ 1 *n.* Klasse, *die;* (in society) Gesellschaftsschicht, *die;* (Sch.: lesson) Stunde, *die*
2 *v.t.* einstufen (**as** als)

ˈclass-conscious *adj.* klassenbewusst

classic /ˈklæsɪk/ 1 *adj.* klassisch
2 *n.* Klassiker, *der;* **~s** Altphilologie, *die*

classical /ˈklæsɪkl/ *adj.* klassisch

classifiable /ˈklæsɪfaɪəbl/ *adj.* klassifizierbar

classification /klæsɪfɪˈkeɪʃn/ *n.* Klassifikation, *die*

classified /ˈklæsɪfaɪd/ *adj.* **(a)** (secret) geheim
(b) ~ advertisement Kleinanzeige, *die*

classify /ˈklæsɪfaɪ/ *v.t.* klassifizieren

ˈclassless *adj.* klassenlos ‹*Gesellschaft*›

class: ~mate *n.* Klassenkamerad, *der*/-kameradin, *die;* **~room** *n.* Klassenzimmer, *das;* **~room assistant** Unterrichtsassistent, *der*/-assistentin, *die;* **~ trip** *n.* Klassenfahrt, *die;* Klassenausflug, *der*

ˈclassy *adj.* (coll.) klasse

clatter /ˈklætə(r)/ 1 *n.* Klappern, *das*
2 *v.i.* **(a)** klappern
(b) (move or fall with a ~) poltern

clause /klɔːz/ *n.* **(a)** Klausel, *die*
(b) (Ling.) Teilsatz, *der;* [**subordinate**] **~:** Nebensatz, *der*

claustrophobia /klɒstrəˈfəʊbɪə/ *n.* Klaustrophobie, *die*

claustrophobic /klɒstrəˈfəʊbɪk/ *adj.* beengend ‹*Ort*›

claw /klɔː/ 1 *n.* Kralle, *die;* (of crab etc.) Schere, *die*
2 *v.t.* kratzen

clay /kleɪ/ *n.* Lehm, *der;* (for pottery) Ton, *der*

clean /kliːn/ 1 *adj.* sauber; frisch ‹*Wäsche, Hemd*›
2 *adv.* glatt
3 *v.t.* sauber machen; putzen ‹*Zimmer, Schuh*›; reinigen ‹*Teppich, Kleidung, Wunde*›; **~ one's teeth** sich (*Dat.*) die Zähne putzen
4 *n.* **give sth. a ~:** etw. putzen

■ **clean ˈout** *v.t.* **(a)** sauber machen
(b) (coll.) **~ sb. out** (take all sb.'s money) jmdn. [total] schröpfen (ugs.)

■ **clean ˈup** 1 *v.t.* **(a)** aufräumen
(b) (fig.) säubern
2 *v.i.* aufräumen

ˈclean-cut *adj.* klar [umrissen]; **his ~ features** seine klar geschnittenen Gesichtszüge

ˈcleaner *n.* **(a)** Raumpfleger, *der*/-pflegerin, *die;* (woman also) Putzfrau, *die*
(b) *usu. in pl.* (dry-~) Reinigung, *die;* **take sth. to the ~'s** etw. in die Reinigung bringen

cleanliness /ˈklenlɪnɪs/ *n.* Reinlichkeit, *die*

ˈclean-living *adj.* von untadeligem Lebenswandel *nachgestellt*

C

C

cleanse /klenz/ *v.t.* [gründlich] reinigen
'cleanser *n.* Reinigungsmittel, *das*
'clean-shaven *adj.* glatt rasiert
'cleansing cream *n.* Reinigungscreme, *die*
clear /klɪə(r)/ **1** *adj.* **(a)** klar; scharf ‹*Bild*›; **make oneself ~:** sich deutlich [genug] ausdrücken; **make it ~ [to sb.] that …:** [jmdm.] klar und deutlich sagen, dass …
(b) (complete) **three ~ days** volle drei Tage
(c) (unobstructed) frei; **keep sth. ~** (not block) etw. freihalten
2 *adv.* **keep ~ of sth./sb.** etw./jmdn. meiden; **please stand** *or* **keep ~ of the door** bitte von der Tür zurücktreten
3 *v.t.* **(a)** räumen ‹*Straße*›; abräumen ‹*Schreibtisch*›; freimachen ‹*Abfluss, Kanal*›; **~ a space for sb./sth.** für jmdn./etw. Platz machen
(b) (empty) räumen; leeren ‹*Briefkasten*›
(c) (remove) wegräumen; beheben ‹*Verstopfung*›
(d) (show to be innocent) freisprechen
(e) (get permission for) **~ sth. with sb.** etw. von jmdm. genehmigen lassen
4 *v.i.* **(a)** ‹*Wetter, Himmel:*› sich aufheitern
(b) (disperse) sich verziehen
5 *n.* **we're in the ~** (free of suspicion) auf uns fällt kein Verdacht; (free of trouble) wir haben es geschafft
■ **clear 'off** *v.i.* abhauen (salopp)
■ **clear 'out** **1** *v.t.* ausräumen
2 *v.i.* (coll.) verschwinden
■ **clear 'up** **1** *v.t.* **(a)** wegräumen ‹*Abfall*›; aufräumen ‹*Platz, Sachen*›
(b) (explain) klären
2 *v.i.* **(a)** aufräumen
(b) ‹*Wetter:*› sich aufhellen
clearance /'klɪərəns/ *n.* **(a)** (of obstruction) Beseitigung, *die*
(b) (clear space) Spielraum, *der*
'clearance sale *n.* Räumungsverkauf, *der*
'clear cut *adj.* klar umrissen; klar ‹*Abgrenzung, Ergebnis*›
'clearing *n.* Lichtung, *die*
'clearing bank *n.* Clearingbank, *die*
'clearly *adv.* **(a)** (distinctly) klar; deutlich ‹*sprechen*›
(b) (manifestly, unambiguously) eindeutig; klar ‹*denken*›
'clearway *n.* (Brit.) Straße mit Halteverbot
cleavage /'kli:vɪdʒ/ *n.* (between breasts) Dekolleté, *das*
cleaver /'kli:və(r)/ *n.* Hackbeil, *das*
clef /klef/ *n.* Notenschlüssel, *der*
cleft /kleft/ *n.* Spalte, *die*
clematis /'klemətɪs, klə'meɪtɪs/ *n.* Klematis, *die*
clementine /'kleməntiːn, 'keməntaɪn/ *n.* Klementine, *die*
clench /klentʃ/ *v.t.* zusammenpressen; **~ one's fist** *or* **fingers** die Faust ballen; **~ one's teeth** die Zähne zusammenbeißen
clergy /'klɜ:dʒɪ/ *n. pl.* Geistlichkeit, *die;* Klerus, *der*
clergyman /'klɜ:dʒɪmən/ *n., pl.* **~men** /'klɜ:dʒɪmən/ Geistliche, *der*
clerical /'klerɪkl/ *adj.* Büro‹*arbeit, -personal*›; **~ error** Schreibfehler, *der*
clerk /klɑ:k/ *n.* (in bank) Bankangestellte, *der/die;* (in office) Büroangestellte, *der/die*
clever /'klevə(r)/ *adj.* **(a)** klug
(b) (skilful) geschickt
(c) (ingenious) geistreich ‹*Idee, Argument*›
(d) (smart, cunning) clever
'cleverly *adv.* **(a)** klug
(b) (skilfully) geschickt
cliché /'kli:ʃeɪ/ *n.* Klischee, *das*
click /klɪk/ **1** *n.* Klicken, *das*
2 *v.i.* klicken
3 *v.t.* (Comp.) drücken ‹*Maustaste*›
■ **click on** *v.t.* (Comp.) anklicken
client /'klaɪənt/ *n.* **(a)** Klient, *der*/Klientin, *die*
(b) (customer) Kunde, *der*/Kundin, *die*
clientele /kli:ɒn'tel/ *n.* (of shop) Kundschaft, *die*
cliff /klɪf/ *n.* Kliff, *das*
'cliffhanger *n.* Thriller, *der*
climate /'klaɪmət/ *n.* Klima, *das*
'climate change *n.* Klimawandel, *der*
climatic /klaɪ'mætɪk/ *adj.* klimatisch
climax /'klaɪmæks/ *n.* Höhepunkt, *der*
climb /klaɪm/ **1** *v.t.* hinaufsteigen; klettern auf ‹*Baum*›; ‹*Auto:*› hinaufkommen ‹*Hügel*›
2 *v.i.* **(a)** klettern (**up** auf + *Akk.*)
(b) ‹*Flugzeug, Sonne:*› aufsteigen
3 *n.* Aufstieg, *der*
■ **climb 'down** *v.i.* **(a)** hinunterklettern
(b) (fig.) nachgeben
'climbdown *n.* Rückzieher, *der* (ugs.)
climber /'klaɪmə(r)/ *n.* Bergsteiger, *der*
'climbing frame *n.* Klettergerüst, *das*
clinch /klɪntʃ/ **1** *v.t.* zum Abschluss bringen; perfekt machen (ugs.) ‹*Geschäft*›
2 *n.* (Boxing) Clinch, *der*
cling /klɪŋ/ *v.i.,* **clung** /klʌŋ/ sich klammern (**to** an + *Akk.*)
'cling film *n.* Klarsichtfolie, *die*
clinic /'klɪnɪk/ *n.* Klinik, *die*
clinical /'klɪnɪkl/ *adj.* **(a)** (Med.) klinisch
(b) (dispassionate) nüchtern
clink /klɪŋk/ **1** *n.* (of glasses) Klirren, *das;* (of coins) Klimpern, *das*
2 *v.i.* ‹*Flaschen:*› klirren; ‹*Münzen:*› klimpern
3 *v.t.* klirren mit ‹*Glas*›
clip[1] /klɪp/ **1** *n.* Klammer, *die;* (for paper) Büroklammer, *die*
2 *v.t.,* **-pp-** klammern (**[on] to** an + *Akk.*)
clip[2] *v.t.,* **-pp-** (cut) schneiden ‹*Fingernägel, Haar, Hecke*›; stutzen ‹*Flügel*›
clip: ~board *n.* **(a)** Klemmbrett, *das;* **(b)** (Comp.) Zwischenablage, *die;* **~ frame** *n.* [rahmenloser] Bilderhalter

clipping /ˈklɪpɪŋ/ *n.* **(a)** (piece clipped off) Schnipsel, *der od. das*
(b) (newspaper cutting) Ausschnitt, *der*

clique /kliːk/ *n.* Clique, *die*

clitoris /ˈklɪtərɪs/ *n.* Kitzler, *der;* Klitoris, *die* (fachspr.)

cloak /kləʊk/ **1** *n.* Umhang, *der*
2 *v.t.* [ein]hüllen

ˈcloakroom *n.* Garderobe, *die;* (Brit. euphem.: lavatory) Toilette, *die*

clock /klɒk/ **1** *n.* **(a)** Uhr, *die;* **[work] against the ~**: gegen die Zeit [arbeiten]; **round the ~**: rund um die Uhr
(b) (coll.) (speedometer) Tacho, *der* (ugs.); (milometer) ≈ Kilometerzähler, *der*
2 *v.t.* **~ [up]** zu verzeichnen haben ‹*Erfolg*›; erreichen ‹*Geschwindigkeit*›

■ **clock ˈin, clock ˈon** *v.i.* [bei Arbeitsantritt] stechen

■ **clock ˈoff, clock ˈout** *v.i.* [bei Arbeitsschluss] stechen

clock ˈradio *n.* Radiowecker, *das*

ˈclockwise *adv., adj.* im Uhrzeigersinn

ˈclockwork *n.* Uhrwerk, *das;* **a ~ car** ein Aufziehauto; **as regular as ~** (fig.) absolut regelmäßig

clod /klɒd/ *n.* (of earth) Scholle, *die*

clog /klɒg/ **1** *n.* Clog, *der;* (traditional) Holzschuh, *der*
2 *v.t.*, **-gg-**: **~ [up]** verstopfen

cloister /ˈklɔɪstə(r)/ *n.* Kreuzgang, *der*

clone /kləʊn/ **1** *n.* Klon, *der*
2 *v.t.* klonen

close **1** /kləʊs/ *adj.* **(a)** (in space) dicht; nahe; **be ~ to sth.** nahe bei *od.* an etw. (*Dat.*) sein; **at ~ quarters** aus der Nähe betrachtet
(b) (in time) nahe (**to** an + *Dat.*)
(c) eng ‹*Freund, Zusammenarbeit*›; nahe ‹*Verwandte, Bekanntschaft*›
(d) eingehend ‹*Untersuchung, Prüfung usw.*›
(e) hart ‹*Wett[kampf], Spiel*›; knapp ‹*Ergebnis*›; **that was a ~ call** *or* **shave**! (coll.) das war knapp!
2 /kləʊs/ *adv.* nah[e]; **~ by** in der Nähe; **~ to sb./sth.** nahe bei jmdm./etw.
3 /kləʊz/ *v.t.* **(a)** (shut) schließen; zuziehen ‹*Vorhang*›; schließen ‹*Laden, Fabrik*›; sperren ‹*Straße*›
(b) (conclude) schließen ‹*Diskussion, Versammlung*›
4 /kləʊz/ *v.i.* **(a)** (shut) sich schließen
(b) ‹*Laden, Fabrik:*› schließen, (ugs.) zumachen
5 /kləʊz/ *n.* Ende, *das;* Schluss, *der;* **come** *or* **draw to a ~**: zu Ende gehen; **bring** *or* **draw sth. to a ~**: etw. zu Ende bringen

■ **close ˈdown** /kləʊz/ **1** *v.t.* schließen; stilllegen ‹*Werk*›
2 *v.i.* geschlossen werden; ‹*Werk:*› stillgelegt werden

■ **close ˈin** *v.i.* ‹*Nacht, Dunkelheit:*› hereinbrechen; ‹*Tage:*› kürzer werden; **~ in on** umzingeln

■ **close ˈoff** *v.t.* [ab]sperren

close-cropped /ˈkləʊskrɒpt/ *adj.* kurz geschoren

closed /kləʊzd/ *adj.* geschlossen; **we're ~**: wir haben geschlossen

ˈclosed-circuit *adj.* **~ television** interne Fernsehanlage; (for supervision) Videoüberwachungsanlage, *die*

close-down /ˈkləʊzdaʊn/ *n.* (Radio, Telev.) Sendeschluss, *der*

closed ˈshop *n.* Closed Shop, *der*

ˈclose-knit /kləʊsˈnɪt/ *adj.* fest zusammengewachsen

closely /ˈkləʊslɪ/ *adv.* **(a)** dicht
(b) (intimately) eng
(c) genau ‹*befragen, prüfen*›; streng ‹*bewachen*›

ˈclose-range /ˈkləʊsreɪndʒ/ *adj.* ‹*Sicht, Betrachtung*› aus nächster Nähe

closet /ˈklɒzɪt/ *n.* (Amer.: cupboard) Schrank, *der*

close-up /ˈkləʊsʌp/ *n.* **~ [picture/shot]** Nahaufnahme, *die*

closing /ˈkləʊzɪŋ/**: ~ date** *n.* (for competition) Einsendeschluss, *der;* (to take part) Meldefrist, *die;* **~ time** *n.* (of pub) Polizeistunde, *die*

closure /ˈkləʊʒə(r)/ *n.* Schließung, *die;* (of road) Sperrung, *die*

clot /klɒt/ **1** *n.* **(a)** (blood) Gerinnsel, *das*
(b) (Brit. coll.: stupid person) Trottel, *der*
2 *v.i.*, **-tt-** ‹*Blut:*› gerinnen

cloth /klɒθ/ *n., pl.* **~s** /klɒθs/ **(a)** Stoff, *der;* Tuch, *das*
(b) (dish~) Spültuch, *das;* (table~) [Tisch]decke, *die*

clothe /kləʊð/ *v.t.* kleiden

clothes /kləʊðz/ *n. pl.* Kleider *Pl.;* **put one's ~ on** sich anziehen; **take one's ~ off** sich ausziehen

clothes: ~ brush *n.* Kleiderbürste, *die;* **~ hanger** *n.* Kleiderbügel, *der;* **~ horse** *n.* Wäscheständer, *der;* **~ line** *n.* Wäscheleine, *die;* **~ peg** (Brit.), **~pin** (Amer.) *ns.* Wäscheklammer, *die*

clothing /ˈkləʊðɪŋ/ *n.* Kleidung, *die*

clotted cream /klɒtɪd ˈkriːm/ *n. sehr fetter Rahm*

cloud /klaʊd/ *n.* **(a)** Wolke, *die;* **every ~ has a silver lining** (prov.) es hat alles sein Gutes
(b) ~ of dust/smoke Staub-/Rauchwolke, *die*

■ **cloud ˈover** *v.i.* sich bewölken

ˈcloudburst *n.* Wolkenbruch, *der*

ˈcloudless *adj.* wolkenlos

ˈcloudy *adj.* bewölkt ‹*Himmel*›; trübe ‹*Wetter, Flüssigkeit, Glas*›

clout /klaʊt/ (coll.) **1** *n.* Schlag, *der*
2 *v.t.* hauen (ugs.)

clove[1] /kləʊv/ *n.* **~ [of garlic]** [Knoblauch]zehe, *die*

clove[2] *n.* (spice) [Gewürz]nelke, *die*

clover /ˈkləʊvə(r)/ *n.* Klee, *der*

'cloverleaf *n.* Kleeblatt, *das*

clown /klaʊn/ [1] *n.* Clown, *der*
[2] *v.i.* ~ **[about** *or* **around]** den Clown spielen

cloying /'klɔɪɪŋ/ *adj.* süßlich

club /klʌb/ [1] *n.* **(a)** (weapon) Keule, *die;* (golf ~) Schläger, *der*
(b) (association) Klub, *der;* Verein, *der*
(c) (Cards) Kreuz, *das;* **~s are trumps** Kreuz ist Trumpf; **the ace/seven of ~s** das Kreuzas/die Kreuzsieben
[2] *v.t.,* **-bb-** (beat) prügeln; (with ~) knüppeln
[3] *v.i.,* **-bb-: ~ together** (to buy something) zusammenlegen

club 'sandwich *n.* (Amer.) Club-Sandwich, *das;* Doppeldecker, *der* (ugs.)

cluck /klʌk/ [1] *n.* Gackern, *das*
[2] *v.i.* gackern

clue /klu:/ *n.* Anhaltspunkt, *der;* (in criminal investigation) Spur, *die;* **not have a ~:** keine Ahnung haben

'clueless *adj.* (coll.) unbedarft (ugs.)

clump /klʌmp/ *n.* Gruppe, *die;* (of grass) Büschel, *das*

clumsily /'klʌmzɪlɪ/ *adv.* ▶ CLUMSY: schwerfällig; unbeholfen; plump

clumsiness /'klʌmzɪnɪs/ *n.* ▶ CLUMSY: Schwerfälligkeit, *die;* Plumpheit, *die*

clumsy /'klʌmzɪ/ *adj.* schwerfällig, unbeholfen ‹*Person, Bewegung*›; plump ‹*Form, Figur, Nachahmung*›

clung ▶ CLING

cluster /'klʌstə(r)/ [1] *n.* (of grapes, berries) Traube, *die;* (of fruit, flowers) Büschel, *das;* (of stars, huts) Haufen, *der*
[2] *v.i.* ~ **[a]round sb./sth.** sich um jmdn./etw. scharen *od.* drängen

clutch /klʌtʃ/ [1] *v.t.* umklammern
[2] *v.i.* ~ **at sth.** nach etw. greifen; (fig.) sich an etw. (*Akk.*) klammern
[3] *n.* **(a)** *in pl.* (fig.: control) Klauen *Pl.*
(b) (Motor Veh.) Kupplung, *die*

clutter /'klʌtə(r)/ [1] *n.* Durcheinander, *das*
[2] *v.t.* ~ **[up] the table/room** überall auf dem Tisch/im Zimmer herumliegen

cm. *abbr.* = **centimetre[s]** cm

c/o *abbr.* = **care of** bei; c/o

Co. *abbr.* **(a)** = **company** Co.
(b) = **county**

coach /kəʊtʃ/ [1] *n.* **(a)** (horse-drawn) Kutsche, *die*
(b) (Railw.) Wagen, *der*
(c) (bus) [Reise]bus, *der;* **by ~:** mit dem Bus
(d) (Sport) Trainer, *der*/Trainerin, *die*
[2] *v.t.* trainieren

coaching /'kəʊtʃɪŋ/ *n.* **(a)** (teaching) Privatunterricht, *der*
(b) (Sport) Training, *das*

coach: ~ party *n.* Reisegesellschaft, *die;* **~ station** *n.* Busbahnhof, *der;* **~ tour** *n.* Rundreise [im Omnibus]

coagulate /kəʊ'ægjʊleɪt/ [1] *v.t.* gerinnen lassen
[2] *v.i.* gerinnen

coal /kəʊl/ *n.* Kohle, *die*

coal: ~field *n.* Kohlenrevier, *das;* **~ fire** *n.* Kohlenfeuer, *das;* **~-fired** *adj.* mit Kohle beheizt; kohlebeheizt

coalition /kəʊə'lɪʃn/ *n.* (Polit.) Koalition, *die*

coal: ~ mine *n.* [Kohlen]bergwerk, *das;* **~ miner** *n.* [im Kohlenbergbau tätiger] Grubenarbeiter; **~ mining** *n.* Kohlenbergbau, *der*

coarse /kɔ:s/ *adj.* **(a)** (in texture) grob
(b) (unrefined, obscene) derb

coast /kəʊst/ [1] *n.* Küste, *die*
[2] *v.i.* im Freilauf fahren

coastal /'kəʊstl/ *adj.* Küsten-

'coaster *n.* **(a)** (mat) Untersetzer, *der*
(b) (ship) Küstenmotorschiff, *das*

coast: ~guard *n.* Küstenwache, -wacht, *die;* **~line** *n.* Küste, *die*

coat /kəʊt/ [1] *n.* **(a)** Mantel, *der*
(b) (layer) Schicht, *die;* (of paint) Anstrich, *der*
(c) (animal's hair, fur, etc.) Fell, *das*
[2] *v.t.* überziehen; (with paint) streichen

'coat hanger *n.* Kleiderbügel, *der*

'coating *n.* Schicht, *die*

coat of 'arms *n.* Wappen, *das*

coax /kəʊks/ *v.t.* überreden

cobble /'kɒbl/ *n.* Kopfstein, *der*

cobbler /'kɒblə(r)/ *n.* Schuster, *der*

'cobblestone ▶ COBBLE

cobra /'kɒbrə/ *n.* Kobra, *die*

cobweb /'kɒbweb/ *n.* Spinnengewebe, *das;* Spinnennetz, *das*

cocaine /kə'keɪn/ *n.* Kokain, *das*

cock /kɒk/ [1] *n.* Hahn, *der*
[2] *v.t.* spitzen ‹*Ohren*›; ~ **a/the gun** den Hahn spannen

cock-a-hoop /kɒkə'hu:p/ *adj.* überschwänglich

cockatoo /kɒkə'tu:/ *n.* Kakadu, *der*

'cockcrow *n.* **at ~:** beim ersten Hahnenschrei

cockerel /'kɒkərəl/ *n.* junger Hahn

cock-eyed /'kɒkaɪd/ *adj.* **(a)** (crooked) schief
(b) (absurd) verrückt

cockle /'kɒkl/ *n.* Herzmuschel, *die*

cockney /'kɒknɪ/ [1] *adj.* Cockney-
[2] *n.* Cockney, *der*

'cockpit *n.* Cockpit, *das*

cockroach /'kɒkrəʊtʃ/ *n.* [Küchen-, Haus-]schabe, *die*

cocktail /'kɒkteɪl/ *n.* Cocktail, *der*

cocktail: ~ cabinet *n.* Hausbar, *die;* **~ party** *n.* Cocktailparty, *die*

cocoa /'kəʊkəʊ/ *n.* Kakao, *der*

coconut /'kəʊkənʌt/ *n.* Kokosnuss, *die*

cocoon /kə'ku:n/ *n.* (Zool.) Kokon, *der*

cod /kɒd/ *n., pl. same* Kabeljau, *der*

COD *abbr.* = **cash on delivery,** (Amer.) = **collect on delivery** p. Nachn.

code /kəʊd/ [1] *n.* **(a)** (statutes etc.) Gesetzbuch, *das;* **~s of behaviour** Verhaltensnormen
(b) (system of signals) Code, *der;* **be in ~:** verschlüsselt sein
[2] *v.t.* chiffrieren; verschlüsseln

code: ~ name *n.* Deckname, *der;* **~ word** *n.* Kennwort, *das*

cod-liver 'oil *n.* Lebertran, *der*

co-driver /'kəʊdraɪvə(r)/ *n.* Beifahrer, *der*/-fahrerin, *die*

coed /'kəʊed/ (esp. Amer. coll.) [1] *n.* Studentin, *die*
[2] *adj.* **~ school** gemischte Schule

coeducational /kəʊedjʊ'keɪʃənl/ *adj.* koedukativ; Koedukations-

coerce /kəʊ'ɜːs/ *v.t.* zwingen; **~ sb. into sth.** jmdn. zu etw. zwingen

coercion /kəʊ'ɜːʃn/ *n.* Zwang, *der*

coexist /kəʊɪg'zɪst/ *v.i.* koexistieren

coexistence /kəʊɪg'zɪstəns/ *n.* Koexistenz, *die*

C. of E. /siːəv'iː/ *abbr.* = **Church of England**

coffee /'kɒfɪ/ *n.* Kaffee, *der;* **three black/white ~s** drei [Tassen] Kaffee ohne/mit Milch

coffee: ~ bar *n.* Café, *das;* **~ bean** *n.* Kaffeebohne, *die;* **~ break** *n.* Kaffeepause, *die;* **~ cup** *n.* Kaffeetasse, *die;* **~ machine, ~ maker** *ns.* Kaffeeautomat, *der;* **~ pot** *n.* Kaffeekanne, *die;* **~ shop** *n.* Kaffeestube, *die;* **~ table** *n.* Couchtisch, *der*

coffin /'kɒfɪn/ *n.* Sarg, *der*

cog /kɒg/ *n.* (Mech.) Zahn, *der*

cogent /'kəʊdʒənt/ *adj.* überzeugend ‹*Argument*›; zwingend ‹*Grund*›

cognac /'kɒnjæk/ *n.* Cognac, *der* (Wz)

cog: ~ railway *n.* Zahnradbahn, *die;* **~wheel** *n.* Zahnrad, *das*

cohabit /kəʊ'hæbɪt/ *v.i.* zusammenleben; in eheähnlicher Gemeinschaft leben (Rechtsspr.)

cohere /kəʊ'hɪə(r)/ *v.i.* zusammenhalten

coherent /kəʊ'hɪərənt/ *adj.* zusammenhängend

coherently /kəʊ'hɪərəntlɪ/ *adv.* zusammenhängend; im Zusammenhang

coil /kɔɪl/ [1] *v.t.* aufwickeln; (twist) aufdrehen
[2] *v.i.* **~ round sth.** etw. umschlingen
[3] *n.* **(a)** **~s of rope/wire** aufgerollte Seile *Pl.*/aufgerollter Draht
(b) (single turn) Windung, *die*
(c) (Electr.) Spule, *die*

'coil spring *n.* Spiralfeder, *die*

coin /kɔɪn/ [1] *n.* Münze, *die*
[2] *v.t.* prägen ‹*Wort, Redewendung*›

coincide /kəʊɪn'saɪd/ *v.i.* **(a)** (in time) zusammenfallen
(b) (agree) übereinstimmen (**with** mit)

coincidence /kəʊ'ɪnsɪdəns/ *n.* Zufall, *der*

coincidental /kəʊɪnsɪ'dentl/ *adj.* zufällig

coincidentally /kəʊɪnsɪ'dentəlɪ/ *adv.* gleichzeitig; (by coincidence) zufälligerweise

'coin-operated *adj.* Münz-

coke /kəʊk/ *n.* Koks, *der*

Col. *abbr.* = **Colonel** Obst.

colander /'kʌləndə(r)/ *n.* Sieb, *das*

cold /kəʊld/ [1] *adj.* **(a)** kalt; **I am/feel ~:** mir ist kalt
(b) (fig.) [betont] kühl ‹*Person, Aufnahme, Begrüßung*›
[2] *adv.* kalt
[3] *n.* **(a)** Kälte, *die*
(b) (illness) Erkältung, *die;* **~ [in the head]** Schnupfen, *der;* **have a ~:** eine Erkältung/[einen] Schnupfen haben

cold-blooded /'kəʊldblʌdɪd/ *adj.* **(a)** wechselwarm ‹*Tier*›
(b) kaltblütig ‹*Person, Mord*›

'coldly *adv.* [betont] kühl

cold: ~-'shoulder *v.t.* schneiden (fig.); **~ 'storage** *n.* Kühllagerung, *die;* **~ 'war** *n.* kalter Krieg

coleslaw /'kəʊlslɔː/ *n.* Krautsalat, *der*

collaborate /kə'læbəreɪt/ *v.i.* **(a)** zusammenarbeiten; **~ [with sb.] on sth.** zusammen [mit jmdm.] an etw. (*Dat.*) arbeiten
(b) (with enemy) kollaborieren

collaboration /kəlæbə'reɪʃn/ *n.* Zusammenarbeit, *die;* (with enemy) Kollaboration, *die*

collaborator /kə'læbəreɪtə(r)/ *n.* Mitarbeiter, *der*/-arbeiterin, *die;* (with enemy) Kollaborateur, *der*/Kollaborateurin, *die*

collage /'kɒlɑːʒ/ *n.* Collage, *die*

collapse /kə'læps/ [1] *n.* **(a)** (of person) Zusammenbruch, *der*
(b) (of structure) Einsturz, *der*
(c) (of negotiations) Scheitern, *das;* (of company) Zusammenbruch, *der*
[2] *v.i.* **(a)** ‹*Person:*› zusammenbrechen
(b) ‹*Stuhl:*› zusammenbrechen; ‹*Gebäude:*› einstürzen
(c) ‹*Verhandlungen:*› scheitern; ‹*Unternehmen:*› zusammenbrechen
(d) (fold down) ‹*Regenschirm, Fahrrad, Tisch:*› sich zusammenklappen lassen

collapsible /kə'læpsɪbl/ *adj.* Klapp‹*stuhl, -tisch, -fahrrad*›

collar /'kɒlə(r)/ [1] *n.* **(a)** Kragen, *der*
(b) (for dog) [Hunde]halsband, *das*
[2] *v.t.* schnappen (ugs.)

'collarbone *n.* Schlüsselbein, *das*

colleague /'kɒliːg/ *n.* Kollege, *der*/Kollegin, *die*

collect /kə'lekt/ [1] *v.i.* sich versammeln; ‹*Staub, Müll usw.:*› sich ansammeln
[2] *v.t.* sammeln; aufsammeln ‹*Müll, leere Flaschen usw.*›; (fetch) abholen ‹*Menschen, Dinge*›; **~ one's wits/thoughts** seine Gedanken sammeln

C

col'lected *adj.* **(a)** (gathered) gesammelt **(b)** (calm) gesammelt; gelassen

collection /kə'lekʃn/ *n.* **(a)** (collecting) Sammeln, *das;* (of goods, persons) Abholen, *das* **(b)** (amount of money collected) Sammlung, *die;* (in church) Kollekte, *die* **(c)** (from postbox) Leerung, *die* **(d)** (of stamps etc.) Sammlung, *die*

collective /kə'lektɪv/ *adj.* kollektiv *nicht präd*

collective 'bargaining *n.* Tarifverhandlungen *Pl.*

collector /kə'lektə(r)/ *n.* **(a)** (of stamps etc.) Sammler, *der*/Sammlerin, *die* **(b)** (of taxes) Einnehmer, *der*/Einnehmerin, *die*

col'lector's item, col'lector's piece *ns.* Sammlerstück, *das*

college /'kɒlɪdʒ/ *n.* **(a)** (esp. Brit. Univ.) College, *das* **(b)** (place of further education) Fach[hoch]schule, *die;* **go to ~** (esp. Amer.) studieren

collide /kə'laɪd/ *v.i.* zusammenstoßen (**with** mit)

collie /'kɒlɪ/ *n.* Collie, *der*

colliery /'kɒljərɪ/ *n.* Kohlengrube, *die*

collision /kə'lɪʒn/ *n.* Zusammenstoß, *der;* **on a ~ course** (lit. or fig.) auf Kollisionskurs

colloquial /kə'ləʊkwɪəl/ *adj.* umgangssprachlich

collusion /kə'lu:ʒn/ *n.* geheime Absprache

cologne ▶ EAU-DE-COLOGNE

Cologne /kə'ləʊn/ 1 *pr. n.* Köln (*das*) 2 *attrib. adj.* Kölner

Colombia /kə'lɒmbɪə/ *pr. n.* Kolumbien (*das*)

colon¹ /'kəʊlən/ *n.* Doppelpunkt, *der*

colon² /'kəʊlən, 'kəʊlɒn/ *n.* (Anat.) Grimmdarm, *der*

colonel /kɜ:nl/ *n.* Oberst, *der*

colonial /kə'ləʊnɪəl/ *adj.* Kolonial-; kolonial

colonize /'kɒlənaɪz/ *v.t.* kolonisieren

colony /'kɒlənɪ/ *n.* Kolonie, *die*

color *etc.* (*Amer.*) ▶ COLOUR *etc.*

colossal /kə'lɒsl/ *adj.* ungeheuer; gewaltig ‹*Bauwerk*›

colour /'kʌlə(r)/ (Brit.) 1 *n.* Farbe, *die;* **what ~ is it?** welche Farbe hat es?; **change ~**: die Farbe ändern; **he is off ~**: ihm ist nicht gut 2 *v.t.* **(a)** (give ~ to) Farbe geben (+ *Dat.*) **(b)** (paint) malen **(c)** (stain, dye) färben 3 *v.i.* ~ **[up]** erröten

'colour-blind *adj.* farbenblind

coloured /'kʌləd/ (Brit.) 1 *adj.* **(a)** farbig **(b)** (of non-white descent) farbig; **~ people** Farbige *Pl.* 2 *n.* Farbige, *der/die*

colour: ~-fast *adj.* farbecht; **~ film** *n.* Farbfilm, *der*

colourful /'kʌləfl/ *adj.* (Brit.) bunt; anschaulich ‹*Sprache, Stil, Bericht*›

'colouring *n.* (Brit.) **(a)** (colours) Farben *Pl.* **(b)** ~ **[matter]** (in food etc.) Farbstoff, *der*

'colourless *adj.* (Brit.) farblos

colour: ~ photograph *n.* Farbaufnahme, *die;* **~ printer** *n.* Farbdrucker, *der;* **~ scheme** *n.* Farb[en]zusammenstellung, *die;* **~ supplement** *n.* Farbbeilage, *die;* **~ television** *n.* Farbfernsehen, *das;* (set) Farbfernsehgerät, *das;* **~ transparency** *n.* Farbdia, *das*

colt /kəʊlt/ *n.* [Hengst]fohlen, *das*

column /'kɒləm/ *n.* **(a)** Säule, *die* **(b)** (of page) Spalte, *die;* **sports ~**: Sportteil, *der*

columnist /'kɒləmɪst/ *n.* Kolumnist, *der*/Kolumnistin, *die*

coma /'kəʊmə/ *n.* Koma, *das;* **in a ~**: im Koma

comb /kəʊm/ 1 *n.* Kamm, *der* 2 *v.t.* **(a)** kämmen; **~ sb.'s/one's hair** jmdm./sich die Haare kämmen **(b)** (search) durchkämmen

combat /'kɒmbæt/ 1 *n.* Kampf, *der* 2 *v.t.* bekämpfen

combatant /'kɒmbətənt/ *n.* Kombattant, *der*

combination /kɒmbɪ'neɪʃn/ *n.* Kombination, *die;* **in ~**: zusammen

combi'nation lock *n.* Kombinationsschloss, *das*

combine 1 /kəm'baɪn/ *v.t.* zusammenfügen (**into** zu); verbinden ‹*Substanzen*› 2 *v.i.* (join together) ‹*Stoffe:*› sich verbinden 3 /'kɒmbaɪn/ *n.* ~ **[harvester]** Mähdrescher, *der*

combustible /kəm'bʌstɪbl/ *adj.* brennbar

combustion /kəm'bʌstʃn/ *n.* Verbrennung, *die*

come /kʌm/ *v.i.*, **came** /keɪm/, **come** /kʌm/ kommen; **~ here!** komm [mal] her!; **[I'm] coming!** [ich] komme schon!; **the train came into the station** der Zug fuhr in den Bahnhof ein; **Christmas is coming** bald ist Weihnachten; **the handle has ~ loose** der Griff ist lose; **nothing came of it** es ist nichts daraus geworden

■ **come a'bout** *v.i.* passieren

■ **come across** 1 /--'-/ *v.i.* (be understood) verstanden werden 2 /'---/ *v.t.* begegnen (+ *Dat.*)

■ **come a'long** *v.i.* (coll.) **(a)** (hurry up) **~ along!** komm/kommt! **(b)** (make progress) **~ along nicely** gute Fortschritte machen **(c)** (to place) mitkommen (**with** mit)

■ **come 'back** *v.i.* zurückkommen

■ **come by** 1 /'--/ *v.t.* (obtain) bekommen 2 /-'-/ *v.i.* vorbeikommen

■ **come 'down** *v.i.* **(a)** (fall) ‹*Schnee, Regen, Preis:*› fallen **(b)** (~ lower) herunterkommen **(c)** (land) [not]landen; (crash) abstürzen

C

▪ **come 'in** *v.i.* (enter) hereinkommen; **~ in!** herein!

▪ **'come into** *v.t.* **(a)** (enter) hereinkommen in (+ *Akk.*)
(b) (inherit) erben

▪ **come off** **1** /-'-/ *v.i.* **(a)** ‹*Griff, Knopf:*› abgehen; (be removable) sich abnehmen lassen
(b) (succeed) ‹*Pläne, Versuche:*› Erfolg haben
(c) (take place) stattfinden
2 /'--/ *v.t.* **~ off a horse/bike** vom Pferd/Fahrrad fallen; **~ 'off it!** (coll.) nun mach mal halblang! (ugs.)

▪ **come on** **1** /-'-/ *v.i.* **(a)** (continue coming, follow) kommen; **~ on!** komm, komm/kommt, kommt!; (encouraging) na, komm!
(b) (make progress) **~ on very well** gute Fortschritte machen
2 /'--/ *v.t.* ▶ ~ UPON

▪ **come 'out** *v.i.* **(a)** herauskommen
(b) (fig.) ‹*Sonne, Wahrheit, Buch:*› herauskommen
(c) **~ out with** herausrücken mit (ugs.)

▪ **come 'over** **1** *v.i.* herüberkommen
2 *v.t.* kommen über (+ *Akk.*)

▪ **come 'round** *v.i.* **(a)** (visit) vorbeischauen
(b) (recover) wieder zu sich kommen

▪ **come 'through** **1** *v.i.* durchkommen
2 *v.t.* (survive) überleben

▪ **come to** **1** /'--/ *v.t.* (amount to) ‹*Rechnung, Kosten:*› sich belaufen auf (+ *Akk.*), machen
2 /-'-/ *v.i.* wieder zu sich kommen

▪ **'come under** *v.t.* **(a)** (be classed as or among) kommen unter (+ *Akk.*)
(b) (be subject to) kommen unter (+ *Akk.*)

▪ **come 'up** *v.i.* **(a)** (~ higher) hochkommen
(b) **~ up to sb.** (approach for talk) auf jmdn. zukommen
(c) (present itself) sich ergeben
(d) **~ up to** (reach) reichen bis an (+ *Akk.*); entsprechen (+ *Dat.*) ‹*Erwartungen*›
(e) **~ up against sth.** (fig.) auf etw. (*Akk.*) stoßen
(f) **~ up with** vorbringen ‹*Vorschlag*›; wissen ‹*Lösung, Antwort*›

▪ **'come upon** *v.t.* (meet by chance) begegnen (+ *Dat.*)

'comeback *n.* (to profession etc.) Come-back, *das*

comedian /kə'mi:dɪən/ *n.* Komiker, *der*

comedienne /kəmi:dɪ'en/ *n.* Komikerin, *die*

'comedown *n.* Abstieg, *der*

comedy /'kɒmɪdɪ/ **(a)** *n.* Lustspiel, *das;* Komödie, *die*
(b) (humour) Witz, *der;* Witzigkeit, *die*

comer /'kʌmə(r)/ *n.* **the competition is open to all ~s** an dem Wettbewerb kann sich jeder beteiligen; **the first ~:** derjenige, der zuerst kommt

comet /'kɒmɪt/ *n.* Komet, *der*

comeuppance /kʌm'ʌpəns/ *n.* **get one's ~:** die Quittung kriegen (fig.)

comfort /'kʌmfət/ **1** *n.* **(a)** (consolation) Trost, *der*
(b) (physical well-being) Behaglichkeit, *die*
(c) *in pl.* Komfort, *der*
2 *v.t.* trösten

comfortable /'kʌmfətəbl/ *adj.* **(a)** bequem ‹*Bett, Schuhe*›; komfortabel ‹*Haus, Zimmer*›; **a ~ victory** ein leichter Sieg
(b) (at ease) **be/feel ~:** sich wohl fühlen

comfortably /'kʌmfətəblɪ/ *adv.* bequem; leicht ‹*gewinnen*›

comforting /'kʌmfətɪŋ/ *adj.* beruhigend ‹*Gedanke*›; tröstend ‹*Worte*›; wohlig ‹*Wärme*›

'comfort station *n.* (Amer.) öffentliche Toilette

comfy /'kʌmfɪ/ *adj.* (coll.) bequem; gemütlich ‹*Haus, Zimmer*›

comic /'kɒmɪk/ **1** *adj.* komisch
2 *n.* **(a)** (comedian) Komiker, *der*/Komikerin, *die*
(b) (periodical) Comicheft, *das*

comical /'kɒmɪkl/ *adj.* komisch

coming /'kʌmɪŋ/ **1** *adj.* **in the ~ week** kommende Woche
2 *n.* **~s and goings** das Kommen und Gehen

comma /'kɒmə/ *n.* Komma, *das*

command /kə'mɑ:nd/ **1** *v.t.* **(a)** (order) befehlen (**sb.** jmdm.)
(b) (be in ~ of) befehligen ‹*Schiff, Armee*›
(c) verfügen über (+ *Akk.*) ‹*Gelder, Wortschatz*›
2 *n.* **(a)** Kommando, *das;* (in writing) Befehl, *der;* **have/take ~ of** das Kommando über (+ *Akk.*) ... haben/übernehmen
(b) (mastery, possession) Beherrschung, *die*

commandeer /kɒmən'dɪə(r)/ *v.t.* requirieren

com'mander *n.* Führer, *der*

com'manding *adj.* **(a)** gebieterisch ‹*Erscheinung, Stimme*›; imposant ‹*Gestalt*›
(b) beherrschend ‹*Ausblick, Lage*›

commanding 'officer *n.* Befehlshaber, *der*/Befehlshaberin, *die*

com'mandment *n.* Gebot, *das*

commemorate /kə'meməreɪt/ *v.t.* gedenken (+ *Gen.*)

commemoration /kəmemə'reɪʃn/ *n.* Gedenken, *das;* **in ~ of** zum Gedenken an (+ *Akk.*)

commemorative /kə'memərətɪv/ *adj.* Gedenk-; **~ of** zum Gedenken an (+ *Akk.*)

commence /kə'mens/ *v.t. & i.* beginnen

com'mencement *n.* Beginn, *der*

commend /kə'mend/ *v.t.* (praise) loben

commendable /kə'mendəbl/ *adj.* lobenswert; löblich

commendation /kɒmen'deɪʃn/ *n.* (praise) Lob, *das;* (official) Belobigung, *die;* (award) Auszeichnung, *die*

comment /'kɒment/ **1** *n.* Bemerkung, *die* (**on** über + *Akk.*); (note) Anmerkung, *die* (**on** über + *Akk.*); **no ~!** (coll.) kein Kommentar! ⇢

C

[2] *v.i.* ~ **on sth.** über etw. (*Akk.*) Bemerkungen machen; **he ~ed that ...:** er bemerkte, dass ...

commentary /'kɒməntərɪ/ *n.* **(a)** Kommentar, *der* (**on** zu)
(b) (Radio, Telev.) **[live** *or* **running]** ~: Livereportage, *die*

commentate /'kɒmənteɪt/ *v.i.* ~ **on sth.** etw. kommentieren

commentator /'kɒmənteɪtə(r)/ *n.* Kommentator, *der*/Kommentatorin, *die;* (Sport) Reporter, *der*/Reporterin, *die*

commerce /'kɒmɜːs/ *n.* Handel, *der*

commercial /kə'mɜːʃl/ [1] *adj.* Handels-; kaufmännisch ‹*Ausbildung*›
[2] *n.* Werbespot, *der*

commercial: ~ **'bank** *n.* private Geschäftsbank; ~ **'break** *n.* Werbepause, *die*

commercialism /kə'mɜːʃəlɪzm/ *n.* Kommerzialismus, *der*

commercialize /kə'mɜːʃəlaɪz/ *v.t.* kommerzialisieren

commercial: ~ **'radio** *n.* Werbefunk, *der;* ~ **'television** *n.* Werbefernsehen, *das;* ~ **'traveller** *n.* Handelsvertreter, *der*/-vertreterin, *die;* ~ **'vehicle** *n.* Nutzfahrzeug, *das*

commiserate /kə'mɪzəreɪt/ *v.i.* ~ **with sb.** jmdm. sein Mitgefühl aussprechen (**on** zu)

commission /kə'mɪʃn/ [1] *n.* **(a)** (official body) Kommission, *die*
(b) (instruction, piece of work) Auftrag, *der*
(c) (Mil.) Ernennungsurkunde, *die*
(d) (pay of agent) Provision, *die*
(e) in/out of ~ ‹*Auto, Maschine*› in/außer Betrieb
[2] *v.t.* beauftragen ‹*Künstler*›; in Auftrag geben ‹*Gemälde usw.*›

commissionaire /kəmɪʃə'neə(r)/ *n.* (esp. Brit.) Portier, *der*

commissioner /kə'mɪʃənə(r)/ *n.* (of police) Präsident, *der*

commit /kə'mɪt/ *v.t.*, **-tt-: (a)** begehen ‹*Verbrechen, Fehler, Ehebruch*›
(b) (pledge, bind) ~ **oneself/sb. to doing sth.** sich/jmdn. verpflichten, etw. zu tun
(c) (entrust) anvertrauen (**to** *Dat.*)
(d) ~ **sb. for trial** jmdm. dem Gericht überstellen

com'mitment *n.* Verpflichtung (**to** gegenüber)

com'mitted *adj.* engagiert

committee /kə'mɪtɪ/ *n.* Ausschuss, *der*

commodity /kə'mɒdɪtɪ/ *n.* **(a) household** ~: Haushaltsartikel, *der*
(b) (St. Exch.) [vertretbare] Ware; (raw material) Rohstoff, *der*

common /'kɒmən/ [1] *adj.* **(a)** (belonging to all) gemeinsam
(b) (public) öffentlich
(c) (usual) gewöhnlich; (frequent) häufig; allgemein verbreitet ‹*Sitte, Redensart*›
(d) (vulgar) ordinär
[2] *n.* **(a)** (land) Gemeindeland, *das*
(b) have sth./nothing/a lot in ~ **[with sb.]** etw./nichts/viel [mit jmdm.] gemein[sam] haben

common 'cold *n.* Erkältung, *die*

'commoner *n.* Bürgerliche *der*/*die*

common: ~ **'ground** *n.* gemeinsame Basis; ~ **'knowledge** *n.* **it's [a matter of]** ~ **knowledge that ...** es ist allgemein bekannt, dass ...; ~**-law** *adj.* **she's his** ~**-law wife** sie lebt mit ihm in eheähnlicher Gemeinschaft

'commonly *adv.* im Allgemeinen

common: C~ 'Market *n.* gemeinsamer Markt; ~**place** [1] *n.* Gemeinplatz, *der;* [2] *adj.* alltäglich; ~ **room** *n.* (Brit.) Gemeinschaftsraum, *der;* (for lecturers) Dozentenzimmer, *das*

Commons /'kɒmənz/ *n. pl.* **the [House of]** ~: das Unterhaus

common: ~ **'sense** *n.* gesunder Menschenverstand; ~**-sense** *adj.* vernünftig; gesund ‹*Ansicht, Standpunkt*›; ~**wealth** *n.* **the [British] C~wealth** das Commonwealth

commotion /kə'məʊʃn/ *n.* Tumult, *der*

communal /'kɒmjʊnl/ *adj.* **(a)** (of or for the community) gemeindlich
(b) (for common use) gemeinsam

commune /'kɒmjuːn/ *n.* Kommune, *die*

communicate /kə'mjuːnɪkeɪt/ [1] *v.t.* übertragen ‹*Krankheit*›; übermitteln ‹*Informationen*›; vermitteln ‹*Gefühle, Ideen*›
[2] *v.i.* ~ **with sb.** mit jmdm. kommunizieren

communication /kəmjuːnɪ'keɪʃn/ *n.* **(a)** (of information) Übermittlung, *die*
(b) (message) Mitteilung, *die* (**to** an + *Akk.*)

communication: ~ **cord** *n.* Notbremse, *die;* ~**s satellite** *n.* Nachrichtensatellit, *der*

communicative /kə'mjuːnɪkətɪv/ *adj.* gesprächig

Communion /kə'mjuːnɪən/ *n.* **[Holy]** ~ (Protestant Ch.) das [heilige] Abendmahl; (RC Ch.) die [heilige] Kommunion

communiqué /kə'mjuːnɪkeɪ/ *n.* Kommuniqué, *das*

communism /'kɒmjʊnɪzm/ *n.* Kommunismus, *der;* **C~**: der Kommunismus

Communist, communist /'kɒmjʊnɪst/ [1] *n.* Kommunist, *der*/Kommunistin, *die*
[2] *adj.* kommunistisch

community /kə'mjuːnɪtɪ/ *n.* **(a)** (organized body) Gemeinwesen, *das;* **the Jewish** ~: die jüdische Gemeinde
(b) *no pl.* (public) Öffentlichkeit, *die*

community: ~ **'care** *n.* ≈ ambulante Betreuung; ~ **centre** *n.* Gemeindezentrum, *das;* ~ **'charge** *n.* (Brit.) Gemeindesteuer, *die;* ~ **'service** *n.*:

[*freiwilliger od. als Strafe auferlegter*] *sozialer Dienst;* ~ **spirit** *n.* Gemeinschaftsgeist, *der*

commute /kə'mju:t/ [1] *v.t.* umwandeln ‹*Strafe*› (to in + *Akk.*)
[2] *v.i.* pendeln

commuter /kə'mju:tə(r)/ *n.* Pendler, *der*/ Pendlerin, *die*

com'muter: ~ **belt** *n.* großstädtischer Einzugsbereich; ~ **train** *n.* Pendlerzug, *der*

compact¹ /kəm'pækt/ *adj.* kompakt

compact² /'kɒmpækt/ *n.* Puderdose [mit Puder(stein)]

compact 'disc *n.* Compactdisc, *die;* ~ **player** CD-Spieler, *der*

companion /kəm'pænjən/ *n.* Begleiter, *der*/Begleiterin, *die*

com'panionship *n.* Gesellschaft, *die*

company /'kʌmpənɪ/ *n.* **(a)** (persons assembled, companionship) Gesellschaft, *die;* **expect** ~: Besuch *od.* Gäste erwarten; **keep sb.** ~: jmdm. Gesellschaft leisten
(b) (firm) Gesellschaft, *die;* ~ **car** Firmenwagen, *der;* ~ **policy** Unternehmenspolitik, *die;* Firmenpolitik, *die*
(c) (of actors) Truppe, *die;* Ensemble, *das*
(d) (Mil.) Kompanie, *die*

comparable /'kɒmpərəbl/ *adj.* vergleichbar (**to, with** mit)

comparably /'kɒmpərəblɪ/ *adv.* in vergleichbarer Weise; vergleichbar

comparative /kəm'pærətɪv/ [1] *adj.* **(a)** (relative) relativ; **in** ~ **comfort** relativ komfortabel
(b) (Ling.) komparativ (fachspr.); **a** ~ **adjective/adverb** ein Adjektiv/Adverb im Komparativ
[2] *n.* (Ling.) Komparativ, *der*

com'paratively *adv.* verhältnismäßig

compare /kəm'peə(r)/ [1] *v.t.* vergleichen (**to, with** mit); ~**d with** *or* **to sb./sth.** verglichen mit *od.* im Vergleich zu jmdm./ etw.
[2] *v.i.* sich vergleichen lassen

comparison /kəm'pærɪsn/ *n.* Vergleich, *der;* **in** *or* **by** ~ [**with sb./sth.**] im Vergleich [zu jmdm./etw.]

compartment /kəm'pɑ:tmənt/ *n.* (in drawer, desk, etc.) Fach, *das;* (of railway carriage) Abteil, *das*

compass /'kʌmpəs/ *n.* **(a)** *in pl.* [**a pair of**] ~**es** ein Zirkel
(b) (for navigating) Kompass, *der*

compassion /kəm'pæʃn/ *n.* Mitgefühl, *das* (**for** mit)

compassionate /kəm'pæʃənət/ *adj.* mitfühlend; **on** ~ **grounds** aus persönlichen Gründen; (for family reasons) aus familiären Gründen

compatibility /kəmpætɪ'bɪlɪtɪ/ *n.* Vereinbarkeit, *die;* (of people) Zueinanderpassen, *das;* (Comp.) Kompatibilität, *die*

compatible /kəm'pætɪbl/ *adj.* vereinbar; zueinander passend ‹*Personen*›; (Comp.) kompatibel

compel /kəm'pel/ *v.t.,* **-ll-** zwingen

compelling /kəm'pelɪŋ/ *adj.* bezwingend

compendium /kəm'pendɪəm/ *n.* Kompendium, *das*

compensate /'kɒmpenseɪt/ [1] *v.i.* ~ **for sth.** etw. ersetzen
[2] *v.t.* ~ **sb. for sth.** jmdn. für etw. entschädigen

compensation /kɒmpen'seɪʃn/ *n.* Ersatz, *der;* (for damages, injuries, etc.) Schaden[s]ersatz, *der*

compère /'kɒmpeə(r)/ *n.* (Brit.) Conférencier, *der*

compete /kəm'pi:t/ *v.i.* konkurrieren (**for** um); (Sport) kämpfen

competence /'kɒmpɪtəns/ *n.* Fähigkeiten *Pl.*

competent /'kɒmpɪtənt/ *adj.* fähig; **not** ~ **to do sth.** nicht kompetent, etw. zu tun

'competently *adv.* kompetent

competition /kɒmpɪ'tɪʃn/ *n.* **(a)** (contest) Wettbewerb, *der;* (in magazine etc.) Preisausschreiben, *das*
(b) (those competing) Konkurrenz, *die*

competitive /kəm'petɪtɪv/ *adj.* wettbewerbsfähig ‹*Preis, Unternehmen*›; ~ **sports** Leistungssport, *der*

competitor /kəm'petɪtə(r)/ *n.* Konkurrent, *der*/Konkurrentin, *die;* (in contest, race) Teilnehmer, *der*/-nehmerin, *die*

compile /kəm'paɪl/ *v.t.* zusammenstellen

complacency /kəm'pleɪsənsɪ/ *n.* Selbstzufriedenheit, *die*

complacent /kəm'pleɪsənt/ *adj.* selbstzufrieden

complain /kəm'pleɪn/ *v.i.* sich beklagen (**about, at** über + *Akk.;* **to** bei); ~ **of sth.** über etw. (*Akk.*) klagen

complaint /kəm'pleɪnt/ *n.* **(a)** Beschwerde, *die*
(b) (ailment) Leiden, *das*

complement [1] /'kɒmplɪmənt/ *n.* **(a)** (what completes) Vervollständigung, *die*
(b) (full number) **a** [**full**] ~: die volle Zahl; (of people) die volle Stärke
[2] /'kɒmplɪment/ *v.t.* ergänzen

complementary /kɒmplɪ'mentərɪ/ *adj.* **(a)** (completing) ergänzend
(b) (completing each other) einander ergänzend

complementary 'medicine *n.* Komplementärmedizin, *die*

complete /kəm'pli:t/ [1] *adj.* **(a)** vollständig; (in number) vollzählig
(b) (finished) fertig
(c) (absolute) völlig ‹*Idiot*›; absolut ‹*Katastrophe*›; total, (ugs.) blutig ‹*Anfänger*›
[2] *v.t.* **(a)** (finish) beenden; fertig stellen ‹*Gebäude, Arbeit*›
(b) ausfüllen ‹*Formular*›

com'pletely *adv.* völlig; absolut ‹*erfolgreich*›

completion /kəm'pli:ʃn/ *n.* Beendigung, *die;* (of building, work) Fertigstellung, *die*

complex /'kɒmpleks/ **1** *adj.* kompliziert **2** *n.* Komplex, *der*

complexion /kəm'plekʃn/ *n.* Gesichtsfarbe, *die;* (fig.) Gesicht, *das*

-complexioned /kəm'plekʃnd/ *adj. in comb.* **sallow-/fair-~:** mit gelblichem Teint/ mit hellem Teint

complexity /kəm'pleksɪtɪ/ *n.* Kompliziertheit, *die*

complicate /'kɒmplɪkeɪt/ *v.t.* komplizieren.

'complicated *adj.* kompliziert

complication /kɒmplɪ'keɪʃn/ *n.* Komplikation, *die*

complicity /kəm'plɪsɪtɪ/ *n.* Mittäterschaft, *die* (in bei)

compliment **1** /'kɒmplɪmənt/ *n.* Kompliment, *das; in pl.* (formal greetings) Grüße *Pl.;* **pay sb. a ~:** jmdn. ein Kompliment machen
2 /'kɒmplɪment/ *v.t.* **~ sb. on sth.** jmdm. Komplimente wegen etw. machen

complimentary /kɒmplɪ'mentərɪ/ *adj.* **(a)** schmeichelhaft
(b) (free) Frei-

comply /kəm'plaɪ/ *v.i.* **~ with sth.** sich nach etw. richten; **he refused to ~:** er wollte sich nicht danach richten

component /kəm'pəʊnənt/ **1** *n.* Bestandteil, *der*
2 *adj.* **a ~ part** ein Bestandteil

compose /kəm'pəʊz/ *v.t.* **(a)** bilden; **be ~d of** sich zusammensetzen aus
(b) verfassen ‹*Rede, Gedicht*›; abfassen ‹*Brief*›
(c) (Mus.) komponieren

com'posed *adj.* (calm) gefasst

com'poser *n.* Komponist, *der*/ Komponistin, *die*

composition /kɒmpə'zɪʃn/ *n.* **(a)** (constitution) (of soil etc.) Zusammensetzung, *die;* (of picture) Aufbau, *der*
(b) (essay) Aufsatz, *der;* (Mus.) Komposition, *die*

compost /'kɒmpɒst/ *n.* Kompost, *der*

compostable /'kɒmpɒstəbl/ *adj.* kompostierbar

'compost heap *n.* Komposthaufen, *der*

composure /kəm'pəʊʒə(r)/ *n.* Gleichmut, *der*

compound[1] **1** /'kɒmpaʊnd/ *adj.* **(a)** zusammengesetzt
(b) (Med.) **~ fracture** komplizierter Bruch
2 /'kɒmpaʊnd/ *n.* **(a)** (mixture) Mischung, *die*
(b) (Ling.) Kompositum, *das*
(c) (Chem.) Verbindung, *die*
3 /'kəm'paʊnd/ *v.t.* verschlimmern ‹*Schwierigkeiten, Verletzung usw.*›

compound[2] /'kɒmpaʊnd/ *n.* umzäuntes Gelände

compound 'interest *n.* Zinseszinsen *Pl.*

comprehend /kɒmprɪ'hend/ *v.t.* verstehen

comprehensible /kɒmprɪ'hensɪbl/ *adj.* verständlich

comprehension /kɒmprɪ'henʃn/ *n.* Verständnis, *das*

comprehensive /kɒmprɪ'hensɪv/ **1** *adj.* **(a)** umfassend
(b) **~ school** Gesamtschule, *die*
(c) (Insurance) Vollkasko-
2 *n.* Gesamtschule, *die*

compress **1** /kəm'pres/ *v.t.* **(a)** (squeeze) zusammenpressen (**into** zu)
(b) komprimieren ‹*Luft, Gas, Bericht*›
(c) (Comp.) komprimieren
2 /'kɒmpres/ *n.* Kompresse, *die*

compression /kəm'preʃn/ *n.* Kompression, *die*

compressor /kəm'presə(r)/ *n.* Kompressor, *der*

comprise /kəm'praɪz/ *v.t.* (include) umfassen; (consist of) bestehen aus

compromise /'kɒmprəmaɪz/ **1** *n.* Kompromiss, *der*
2 *v.i.* Kompromisse/einen Kompromiss schließen
3 *v.t.* kompromittieren

compromising /'kɒmprəmaɪzɪŋ/ *adj.* kompromittierend

compulsion /kəm'pʌlʃn/ *n.* Zwang, *der;* **be under no ~ to do sth.** keineswegs etw. tun müssen

compulsive /kəm'pʌlsɪv/ *adj.* **(a)** zwanghaft; **he is a ~ gambler** er ist dem Spiel verfallen
(b) **this book is ~ reading** von diesem Buch kann man sich nicht losreißen

compulsory /kəm'pʌlsərɪ/ *adj.* obligatorisch

compunction /kəm'pʌŋkʃn/ *n.* Schuldgefühle

computer /kəm'pju:tə(r)/ *n.* Computer, *der*

computer: ~-aided *adj.* computergestützt; **~ ani'mation** *n.* Computeranimation, *die;* **~-assisted** *adj.* computergestützt; **~ 'dating** *n.* Partnervermittlung per Computer; **~ dating agency/service** Computer-Partnervermittlung[sagentur], *die;* **~ game** *n.* Computerspiel, *das;* **~ 'graphics** *n. pl.* Computergraphik, *die*

computerisation, computerise ▶ COMPUTERIZ-

computerization /kəmpju:təraɪ'zeɪʃn/ *n.* Computerisierung, *die*

computerize /kəm'pju:təraɪz/ *v.t.* computerisieren

computer: ~-'literate *adj.* mit Computern vertraut; **~-'operated** *adj.* computergesteuert; rechnergesteuert; **~ program** *n.* Programm, *das;*

~ programmer *n.* Programmierer, *der*/Programmiererin, *die;* **~ programming** *n.* Programmieren, *das;* **~ room** *n.* Computerraum, *der;* **~ 'science** *n.* Computerwissenschaft, *die;* **~ terminal** *n.* Terminal, *das;* **~ 'typesetting** *n.* Computersatz, *der;* **~ virus** *n.* [Computer]virus, *das od. der*

computing /kəm'pju:tɪŋ/ *n.* EDV, *die;* elektronische Datenverarbeitung; **~ skills** Computerkenntnisse *Pl.*

comrade /'kɒmreɪd, 'kɒmrɪd/ *n.* Kamerad, *der*/Kameradin, *die*

'comradeship *n.* Kameradschaft, *die*

con /kɒn/ (coll.) [1] *n.* Schwindel, *der* [2] *v.t.*, **-nn-** reinlegen (ugs.); **~ sb. into sth.** jmdm. etw. aufschwatzen (ugs.)

concave /'kɒnkeɪv/ *adj.* konkav

conceal /kən'si:l/ *v.t.* verbergen (**from** vor + *Dat.*)

con'cealment *n.* Verbergen, *das*

concede /kən'si:d/ *v.t.* zugeben

conceit /kən'si:t/ *n.* Einbildung, *die*

con'ceited *adj.* eingebildet

conceivable /kən'si:vəbl/ *adj.* vorstellbar; **it is scarcely ~ that ...:** man kann sich (*Dat.*) kaum vorstellen, dass ...

conceivably /kən'sɪ:vəblɪ/ *adj.* möglicherweise; **he cannot ~ have done it** er kann es unmöglich getan haben

conceive /kən'si:v/ [1] *v.t.* **(a)** empfangen ‹*Kind*›
(b) (form in mind) sich (*Dat.*) vorstellen; haben ‹*Idee, Plan*›
[2] *v.i.* **(a)** (become pregnant) empfangen
(b) ~ of sth. sich (*Dat.*) etw. vorstellen

concentrate /'kɒnsəntreɪt/ [1] *v.t.* konzentrieren
[2] *v.i.* sich konzentrieren (**on** auf + *Akk.*)

'concentrated *adj.* konzentriert

concentration /kɒnsən'treɪʃn/ *n.* Konzentration, *die*

concen'tration camp *n.* Konzentrationslager, *das;* KZ, *das*

concentric /kən'sentrɪk/ *adj.* konzentrisch

concept /'kɒnsept/ *n.* Begriff, *der;* (idea) Vorstellung, *die*

conception /kən'sepʃn/ **(a)** Vorstellung, *die* (**of** von)
(b) (of child) Empfängnis, *die*

conceptual /kən'septjʊəl/ *adj.* begrifflich

conceptualize /kən'septjʊəlaɪz/ *v.t.* begrifflich fassen

concern /kən'sɜ:n/ [1] *v.t.* **(a)** (affect) betreffen; **so far as ... is ~ed** was ... betrifft; **'to whom it may ~'** ≈ „Bestätigung“; (on certificate, testimonial) ≈ „Zeugnis“
(b) (interest) **~ oneself with** *or* **about sth.** sich mit etw. befassen
(c) (trouble) beunruhigen
[2] *n.* **(a)** (anxiety) Besorgnis, *die;* (interest) Interesse, *das*
(b) (matter) Angelegenheit, *die*
(c) (firm) Unternehmen, *das*

con'cerned /kən'sɜ:nd/ *adj.* **(a)** (involved) betroffen; (interested) interessiert; **as** *or* **so far as I'm ~:** was mich betrifft
(b) (troubled) besorgt

con'cerning *prep.* bezüglich

concert /'kɒnsət/ *n.* Konzert, *das*

concerted /kən'sɜ:tɪd/ *adj.* vereint

concert: ~-goer *n.* Konzertbesucher, *der*/-besucherin, *die;* **~ hall** *n.* Konzertsaal, *der*

concertina /kɒnsə'ti:nə/ *n.* Konzertina, *die*

concerto /kən'tʃeətəʊ/ *n.* Konzert, *das*

concession /kən'seʃn/ *n.* Konzession, *die*

concessionary /kən'seʃənərɪ/ *adj.* Konzessions-; **~ rate/fare** ermäßigter Tarif

conciliatory /kən'sɪljətərɪ/ *adj.* versöhnlich

concise /kən'saɪs/ *adj.* kurz und prägnant; knapp, konzis ‹*Stil*›

conclude /kən'klu:d/ [1] *v.t.* **(a)** (end) beschließen
(b) (infer) schließen (**from** aus)
(c) (reach decision) beschließen
[2] *v.i.* (end) schließen

concluding /kən'klu:dɪŋ/ *adj.* abschließend

conclusion /kən'klu:ʒn/ *n.* **(a)** (end) Abschluss, *der;* **in ~:** zum Abschluss
(b) (result) Ausgang, *der*
(c) (inference) Schluss, *der;* **draw** *or* **reach a ~:** zu einem Schluss kommen

conclusive /kən'klu:sɪv/ *adj.*, **con'clusively** *adv.* schlüssig

concoct /kən'kɒkt/ *v.t.* zubereiten; zusammenbrauen ‹*Trank*›

concoction /kən'kɒkʃn/ *n.* Gebräu, *das*

concourse /'kɒnkɔ:s/ *n.* Halle, *die;* **station ~:** Bahnhofshalle, *die*

concrete /'kɒnkri:t/ [1] *adj.* konkret
[2] *n.* Beton, *der; attrib.* Beton-; aus Beton *präd*

concrete/'kɒnkri:t/**: ~ mixer** *n.* Betonmischer, *der;* Betonmischmaschine, *die;* **~ 'poetry** *n.* konkrete Poesie

concur /kən'kɜ:(r)/ *v.i.*, **-rr-: ~ [with sb.] [in sth.]** [jmdm.] [in etw. (*Dat.*)] zustimmen

concurrent /kən'kʌrənt/ *adj.*, **con'currently** *adv.* gleichzeitig

concussion /kən'kʌʃn/ *n.* Gehirnerschütterung, *die*

condemn /kən'dem/ *v.t.* **(a)** (censure) verdammen
(b) (Law: sentence) verurteilen (**to** zu)
(c) für unbewohnbar erklären ‹*Gebäude*›

condemnation /kɒndem'neɪʃn/ *n.* Verdammung, *die*

condensation /kɒnden'seɪʃn/ *n.* **(a)** (condensing) Kondensation, *die*
(b) (water) Kondenswasser, *das*

C

condense /kən'dens/ [1] *v.t.* **(a)** komprimieren; **~d milk** Kondensmilch, *die*
(b) (Phys., Chem.) kondensieren
[2] *v.i.* kondensieren

condescend /kɒndɪ'send/ *v.i.* **~ to do sth.** sich dazu herablassen, etw. zu tun

conde'scending *adj.* herablassend

condescension /kɒndɪ'senʃn/ *n.* (derog.: patronizing manner) Herablassung, *die*

condiment /'kɒndɪmənt/ *n.* Gewürz, *das*

condition /kən'dɪʃn/ *n.* **(a)** (stipulation) [Vor]bedingung, *die;* **on [the] ~ that ...:** unter der Voraussetzung, dass ...
(b) *in pl.* (circumstances) Umstände *Pl.;* **weather/living ~s** Witterungs-/Wohnverhältnisse; **working ~s** Arbeitsbedingungen
(c) (of athlete etc.) Form, *die;* (of thing) Zustand, *der;* (of patient) Verfassung, *die*
(d) (Med.) Leiden, *das*

conditional /kən'dɪʃənl/ *adj.* **(a)** bedingt; **be ~ [up]on sth.** von etw. abhängen
(b) (Ling.) Konditional-

con'ditioner *n.* Frisiermittel, *das*

condolence /kən'dəʊləns/ *n.* Anteilnahme, die; **letter of ~:** Beileidsbrief, *der*

condom /'kɒndɒm/ *n.* Kondom, *das od. der*

condominium /'kɒndə'mɪnɪəm/ *n.* (Amer.) Appartementhaus [mit Eigentumswohnungen]

condone /kən'dəʊn/ *v.t.* hinwegsehen über (+ *Akk.*); (approve) billigen

conducive /kən'dju:sɪv/ *adj.* **be ~ to sth.** einer Sache (*Dat.*) förderlich sein

conduct [1] /'kɒndʌkt/ *n.* **(a)** (behaviour) Verhalten, *das*
(b) (way of ~ing) Führung, *die*
[2] /kən'dʌkt/ *v.t.* **(a)** führen
(b) (Mus.) dirigieren
(c) (Phys.) leiten
(d) **~ed tour** Führung, *die*

conduction /kən'dʌkʃn/ *n.* (Phys.) Leitung, *die*

conductor /kən'dʌktə(r)/ *n.* **(a)** (Mus.) Dirigent, *der*/Dirigentin, *die*
(b) (of bus, tram) Schaffner, *der*

conductress /kən'dʌktrɪs/ *n.* Schaffnerin, *die*

conduit /'kɒndjʊɪt/ *n.* **(a)** Leitung, *die;* Kanal, *der* (auch fig.)
(b) (Electr.) Isolierrohr, *das*

cone /kəʊn/ *n.* **(a)** Kegel, *der;* (traffic ~) Leitkegel, *der*
(b) (Bot.) Zapfen, *der*
(c) **ice-cream ~:** Eistüte, *die*

confectioner /kən'fekʃənə(r)/ *n.* **~'s [shop]** Süßwarengeschäft, *das*

con'fectionery *n.* Süßwaren *Pl.*

confederate /kən'fedərət/ *adj.* verbündet

confederation /kənfedə'reɪʃn/ *n.* [Staaten]bund, *der*

confer /kən'fɜ:(r)/ [1] *v.t.,* **-rr-: ~ sth. [up]on sb.** jmdm. etw. verleihen
[2] *v.i.,* **-rr-: ~ with sb.** sich mit jmdm. beraten

conference /'kɒnfərəns/ *n.* **(a)** Konferenz, *die*
(b) **be in ~:** in einer Besprechung sein

conference: ~ room *n.* Konferenzraum, *der;* **~ table** *n.* Konferenztisch, *der*

confess /kən'fes/ [1] *v.t.* **(a)** gestehen
(b) (Eccl.) beichten
[2] *v.i.* **(a)** **~ to sth.** etw. gestehen
(b) (Eccl.) beichten **(to sb.** jmdm.)

confession /kən'feʃn/ *n.* **(a)** Geständnis, *das*
(b) (Eccl.: of sins etc.) Beichte, *die*

confetti /kən'fetɪ/ *n.* Konfetti, *das*

confidant /'kɒnfɪdænt, kɒnfɪ'dænt/ *n.* Vertraute, *der*

confidante /'kɒnfɪdænt, kɒnfɪ'dænt/ *n.* Vertraute, *die*

confide /kən'faɪd/ [1] *v.i.* **~ in sb.** sich jmdm. anvertrauen
[2] *v.t.* **~ sth. to sb.** jmdm. etw. anvertrauen

confidence /'kɒnfɪdəns/ *n.* **(a)** (firm trust) Vertrauen, *das;* **have ~ in sb./sth.** Vertrauen zu jmdm./etw. haben; **have [absolute] ~ that ...:** [absolut] sicher sein, dass ...
(b) (assured expectation) Gewissheit, *die*
(c) (self-reliance) Selbstvertrauen, *das*
(d) **in ~:** im Vertrauen; **this is in [strict] ~:** das ist [streng] vertraulich

'confidence trick *n.* (Brit.) Trickbetrug, *der*

confident /'kɒnfɪdənt/ *adj.* zuversichtlich (**about** in Bezug auf + *Akk.*)

confidential /kɒnfɪ'denʃl/ *adj.* vertraulich

confidentiality /kɒnfɪdenʃɪ'ælɪtɪ/ *n.* Vertraulichkeit, *die*

confi'dentially *adv.* vertraulich

'confidently *adv.* zuversichtlich

configure /kən'fɪgə(r)/ *v.t.* (esp. Comp.) konfigurieren

confine /kən'faɪn/ *v.t.* **(a)** einsperren; **be ~d to bed/the house** ans Bett/Haus gefesselt sein
(b) (fig.) **~ oneself to doing sth.** sich darauf beschränken, etw. zu tun

con'fined *adj.* begrenzt

con'finement *n.* (imprisonment) Einsperrung, *die*

confines /'kɒnfaɪnz/ *n. pl.* Grenzen

confirm /kən'fɜ:m/ *v.t.* bestätigen

confirmation /kɒnfə'meɪʃn/ *n.* **(a)** Bestätigung, *die*
(b) (Protestant Ch.) Konfirmation, *die;* (RC Ch.) Firmung, *die*

con'firmed *adj.* eingefleischt ‹*Junggeselle*›; überzeugt ‹*Vegetarier*›

confiscate /'kɒnfɪskeɪt/ *v.t.* beschlagnahmen

confiscation /kɒnfɪsˈkeɪʃn/ *n.* Beschlagnahme, *die*

conflict 1 /ˈkɒnflɪkt/ *n.* **(a)** (fight) Kampf, *der*
(b) (clashing) Konflikt, *der*
2 /kənˈflɪkt/ *v.i.* (be incompatible) sich (*Dat.*) widersprechen; ~ **with sth.** einer Sache (*Dat.*) widersprechen

conˈflicting *adj.* widersprüchlich

conform /kənˈfɔːm/ *v.i.* **(a)** entsprechen (**to** *Dat.*)
(b) (comply) sich einfügen; ~ **to** *or* **with sth./with sb.** sich nach etw./jmdm. richten

conformist /kənˈfɔːmɪst/ *n.* Konformist, *der*/Konformistin, *die*

conformity /kənˈfɔːmɪtɪ/ *n.* Übereinstimmung, *die* (**with, to** mit)

confound /kənˈfaʊnd/ *v.t.* **(a)** (defeat) vereiteln
(b) (confuse) verwirren

conˈfounded *adj.* (coll. derog.) verdammt

confront /kənˈfrʌnt/ *v.t.* **(a)** gegenüberstellen; ~ **sb. with sth./sb.** jmdn. mit etw./[mit] jmdm. konfrontieren
(b) (stand facing) gegenüberstehen (+ *Dat.*)

confrontation /kɒnfrənˈteɪʃn/ *n.* Konfrontation, *die*

confuse /kənˈfjuːz/ *v.t.* **(a)** (disorder) durcheinander bringen
(b) (mix up mentally) verwechseln
(c) (perplex) verwirren

conˈfused *adj.* konfus; wirr ‹*Gedanken, Gerüchte*›; verworren ‹*Lage, Situation*›

confusing /kənˈfjuːzɪŋ/ *adj.* verwirrend

confusion /kənˈfjuːʒn/ *n.* **(a)** Verwirrung, *die;* (mixing up) Verwechslung, *die*
(b) (embarrassment) Verlegenheit, *die*

congeal /kənˈdʒiːl/ *v.i.* gerinnen

congenial /kənˈdʒiːnɪəl/ *adj.* (agreeable) angenehm

congenital /kənˈdʒenɪtl/ *adj.* angeboren; kongenital (fachspr.)

conger /ˈkɒŋgə(r)/ *n.* ~ **[eel]** Seeaal, *der*

congested /kənˈdʒestɪd/ *adj.* verstopft ‹*Straße, Nase*›

congestion /kənˈdʒestʃn/ *n.* (of traffic) Stauung, *die;* **nasal** ~: verstopfte Nase

conglomerate /kənˈglɒmərət/ *n.* (Commerc.) Großkonzern, *der*

conglomeration /kənglɒməˈreɪʃn/ *n.* Anhäufung, *die*

congratulate /kənˈgrætjʊleɪt/ *v.t.* gratulieren (+ *Dat.*); ~ **sb./oneself on sth.** jmdm./sich zu etw. gratulieren

congratulations /kəngrætjʊˈleɪʃnz/
1 *int.* ~! herzlichen Glückwunsch! (**on** zu); (on passing exam etc.) ich gratuliere!
2 *n. pl.* Glückwünsche *Pl.*

congregate /ˈkɒŋgrɪgeɪt/ *v.i.* sich versammeln

congregation /kɒŋgrɪˈgeɪʃn/ *n.* (Eccl.) Gemeinde, *die*

congress /ˈkɒŋgres/ *n.* Kongress, *der;* **C~** (Amer.) der Kongress

congressional /kənˈgreʃənl/ *adj.* Kongress-

conical /ˈkɒnɪkl/ *adj.* kegelförmig

conifer /ˈkɒnɪfə(r)/ *n.* Nadelbaum, *der*

coniferous /kəˈnɪfərəs/ *adj.* Nadel-; ~ **tree** Nadelbaum, *der;* Konifere, *die*

conjecture /kənˈdʒektʃə(r)/ 1 *n.* Vermutung, *die*
2 *v.t.* vermuten
3 *v.i.* Vermutungen anstellen

conjugate /ˈkɒndʒʊgeɪt/ *v.t.* (Ling.) konjugieren

conjugation /kɒndʒʊˈgeɪʃn/ *n.* (Ling.) Konjugation, *die*

conjunction /kənˈdʒʌŋkʃn/ *n.* **(a)** Verbindung, *die;* **in** ~ **with** in Verbindung mit
(b) (Ling.) Konjunktion, *die*

conjure /ˈkʌndʒə(r)/ *v.i.* zaubern; **conjuring trick** Zaubertrick, *der*

■ **conjure ˈup** *v.t.* heraufbeschwören

conjurer, conjuror /ˈkʌndʒərə(r)/ *n.* Zauberkünstler, *der*/-künstlerin, *die*

connect /kəˈnekt/ 1 *v.t.* verbinden (**to, with** mit)
2 *v.i.* ~ **with sth.** mit etw. zusammenhängen

conˈnected *adj.* zusammenhängend

connection, (Brit. also) **connexion** /kəˈnekʃn/ *n.* **(a)** (act, state) Verbindung, *die*
(b) (fig.: of ideas) Zusammenhang, *der;* **in** ~ **with** im Zusammenhang mit
(c) (train, bus, etc.) Anschluss, *der*

connoisseur /kɒnəˈsɜː(r)/ *n.* Kenner, *der*

connotation /kɒnəˈteɪʃn/ *n.* Assoziation, *die*

conquer /ˈkɒŋkə(r)/ *v.t.* besiegen; erobern ‹*Land*›

conqueror /ˈkɒŋkərə(r)/ *n.* (of a country) Eroberer, *der*

conquest /ˈkɒŋkwest/ *n.* Eroberung, *die*

conscience /ˈkɒnʃəns/ *n.* Gewissen, *das;* **have a clear/guilty** ~: ein gutes/schlechtes Gewissen haben

ˈconscience-stricken, ˈconscience-struck *adjs.* schuldbewusst

conscientious /kɒnʃɪˈenʃəs/ *adj.* pflichtbewusst; (meticulous) gewissenhaft; ~ **objector** Wehrdienstverweigerer [aus Gewissensgründen]

consciˈentiously *adv.* pflichtbewusst; (meticulously) gewissenhaft

conscious /ˈkɒnʃəs/ *adj.* **(a) he is not** ~ **of it** es ist ihm nicht bewusst
(b) *pred.* (awake) bei Bewusstsein *präd.*
(c) (realized by doer) bewusst ‹*Versuch, Bemühung*›

ˈconsciously *adv.* bewusst

ˈconsciousness *n.* Bewusstsein, *das*

conscript [1] /kən'skrɪpt/ *v.t.* einberufen [2] /'kɒnskrɪpt/ *n.* Einberufene, *der/die*

conscription /kən'skrɪpʃn/ *n.* Wehrpflicht, *die*

consecrate /'kɒnsɪkreɪt/ *v.t.* weihen

consecutive /kən'sekjʊtɪv/ *adj.* aufeinander folgend ‹*Monate, Jahre*›; fortlaufend ‹*Zahlen*›

con'secutively *adj.* hintereinander

consensus /kən'sensəs/ *n.* Einigkeit, *die*

consent /kən'sent/ [1] *v.i.* zustimmen [2] *n.* (agreement) Zustimmung, *die* (**to** zu); **by common** *or* **general** ~: nach allgemeiner Auffassung; **age of** ~: Ehemündigkeitsalter, *das*

consequence /'kɒnsɪkwəns/ *n.* **(a)** (result) Folge, *die;* **in** ~: folglich; **as a** ~: infolgedessen **(b)** (importance) Bedeutung, *die*

consequent /'kɒnsɪkwənt/ *adj.* daraus folgend

'consequently *adv.* infolgedessen

conservation /kɒnsə'veɪʃn/ *n.* Erhaltung, *die;* **wildlife** ~: Schutz wild lebender Tierarten

conser'vation area *n.* (Brit.) (rural) Landschaftsschutzgebiet, *das;* (urban) unter Denkmalschutz stehendes Gebiet

conservationist /kɒnsə'veɪʃənɪst/ *n.* Naturschützer, *der*/-schützerin, *die*

conservative /kən'sɜ:vətɪv/ [1] *adj.* **(a)** konservativ **(b)** vorsichtig ‹*Schätzung*› **(c) C~** (Brit. Polit.) konservativ; **the C~ Party** die Konservative Partei [2] *n.* **C~** (Brit. Polit.) Konservative, *der/die*

con'servatively *adv.* vorsichtig ‹*geschätzt*›

conservatory /kən'sɜ:vətərɪ/ *n.* Wintergarten, *der*

conserve /kən'sɜ:v/ *v.t.* erhalten; schonen ‹*Kräfte*›

consider /kən'sɪdə(r)/ *v.t.* **(a)** (think about) ~ **sth.** an etw. (*Akk.*) denken; **he's ~ing emigrating** er denkt daran, auszuwandern **(b)** (reflect on) sich (*Dat.*) überlegen **(c)** (regard as) halten für; **all things ~ed** alles in allem

considerable /kən'sɪdərəbl/ *adj.*, **con'siderably** *adv.* erheblich

considerate /kən'sɪdərət/ *adj.* rücksichtsvoll; (thoughtfully kind) entgegenkommend

considerately /kən'sɪdərətlɪ/ *adv.* rücksichtsvoll; (obligingly) entgegenkommend

consideration /kənsɪdə'reɪʃn/ *n.* **(a)** Überlegung, *die;* **take sth. into** ~: etw. berücksichtigen; **the matter is under** ~: die Angelegenheit wird geprüft **(b)** (thoughtfulness) Rücksichtnahme, *die*

considered /kən'sɪdəd/ *adj.* **(a)** ~ **opinion** feste *od.* ernsthafte Überzeugung **(b) be highly** ~ **[by others]** [bei anderen] in hohem Ansehen stehen

con'sidering *prep.* ~ **sth.** wenn man etw. bedenkt; ~ **[that]** ...: wenn man bedenkt, dass ...

consign /kən'saɪn/ *v.t.* anvertrauen (**to** *Dat.*)

con'signment *n.* (Commerc.) Sendung, *die;* (large) Ladung, *die*

consist /kən'sɪst/ *v.i.* ~ **of** bestehen aus

consistency /kən'sɪstənsɪ/ *n.* **(a)** (density) Konsistenz, *die* **(b)** (being consistent) Konsequenz, *die*

consistent /kən'sɪstənt/ *adj.* **(a)** (compatible) [miteinander] vereinbar **(b)** (uniform) gleich bleibend ‹*Qualität*› **(c)** (unchanging) konsequent

consolation /kɒnsə'leɪʃn/ *n.* Trost, *der*

conso'lation prize *n.* Trostpreis, *der*

console /kən'səʊl/ *v.t.* trösten

consolidate /kən'sɒlɪdeɪt/ *v.t.* festigen

consolidation /kənsɒlɪ'deɪʃn/ *n.* Festigung, *die*

consoling /kən'səʊlɪŋ/ *adj.* tröstlich

consonant /'kɒnsənənt/ *n.* Konsonant, *der*

consort /kən'sɔ:t/ *v.i.* verkehren (**with** mit)

consortium /kən'sɔ:tɪəm/ *n., pl.* **consortia** /kən'sɔ:tɪə/ Konsortium, *das*

conspicuous /kən'spɪkjʊəs/ *adj.* **(a)** (visible) unübersehbar **(b)** (obvious) auffallend

con'spicuously *adv.* **(a)** (visibly) unübersehbar **(b)** (obviously) auffallend

conspiracy /kən'spɪrəsɪ/ *n.* (conspiring) Verschwörung, *die;* (plot) Komplott, *das*

conspire /kən'spaɪə(r)/ *v.i.* sich verschwören

constable /'kʌnstəbl, 'kɒnstəbl/ *n.* (Brit.) Polizist, *der*/Polizistin, *die*

constabulary /kən'stæbjʊlərɪ/ *n.* Polizei, *die*

constant /'kɒnstənt/ *adj.* **(a)** (unceasing) ständig **(b)** (unchanging) gleich bleibend

'constantly *adv.* **(a)** (unceasingly) ständig **(b)** (unchangingly) konstant

constellation /kɒnstə'leɪʃn/ *n.* Sternbild, *das*

consternation /kɒnstə'neɪʃn/ *n.* Bestürzung, *die*

constipated /'kɒnstɪpeɪtɪd/ *adj.* **be** ~: an Verstopfung leiden

constipation /kɒnstɪ'peɪʃn/ *n.* Verstopfung, *die*

constituency /kən'stɪtjʊənsɪ/ *n.* Wahlkreis, *der*

constituent /kən'stɪtjʊənt/ *n.* **(a)** (part) Bestandteil, *der* **(b)** (Polit.) Wähler, *der*/Wählerin, *die*

constitute /'kɒnstɪtju:t/ *v.t.* **(a)** (form, be) sein; ~ **a threat to** eine Gefahr sein für

(b) (make up) bilden
constitution /kɒnstɪ'tjuːʃn/ *n.* **(a)** (of person) Konstitution, *die*
(b) (of state) Verfassung, *die*
constitutional /kɒnstɪ'tjuːʃənl/ *adj.* (of constitution) der Verfassung *nachgestellt;* (in harmony with constitution) verfassungsmäßig
constrain /kən'streɪn/ *v.t.* zwingen
constraint /kən'streɪnt/ *n.* (limitation) Einschränkung, *die*
constrict /kən'strɪkt/ *v.t.* verengen
constriction /kən'strɪkʃn/ *n.* Verengung, *die*
construct /kən'strʌkt/ *v.t.* bauen; (fig.) erstellen ‹*Plan*›
construction /kən'strʌkʃn/ *n.* **(a)** (conctructing) Bau, *der;* **be under ~:** im Bau sein
(b) (thing constructed) Bauwerk, *das*
constructive /kən'strʌktɪv/ *adj.* konstruktiv
consul /'kɒnsl/ *n.* Konsul, *der*
consulate /'kɒnsjʊlət/ *n.* Konsulat, *das*
consult /kən'sʌlt/ *v.t.* konsultieren ‹*Arzt, Fachmann*›; **~ a book** in einem Buch nachsehen
consultant /kən'sʌltənt/ *n.* Berater, *der*/ Beraterin, *die;* (Med.) Chefarzt, *der*/-ärztin, *die*
consultation /kɒnsəl'teɪʃn/ *n.* Beratung, *die*
con'sulting room *n.* Sprechzimmer, *das*
consume /kən'sjuːm/ *v.t.* verbrauchen; (eat, drink) konsumieren
con'sumer *n.* Verbraucher, *der*/ Verbraucherin, *die*
con'sumer goods *n. pl.* Konsumgüter *Pl.*
consumerism /kən'sjuːmərɪzm/ *n.*, *no art.* Konsumerismus, *der*
consumer: ~ pro'tection *n.* Verbraucherschutz, *der;* **~ research** *n.* Verbrauchsforschung, *die;* Konsumforschung, *die*
consumption /kən'sʌmpʃn/ *n.* Verbrauch, *der* (**of** an + *Dat.*); (eating or drinking) Verzehr, *der* (**of** von)
cont. *abbr.* = **continued** Forts.
contact [1] /'kɒntækt/ *n.* Berührung, *die;* (fig.) Kontakt, *der;* **be in ~ with sth.** etw. berühren; **be in ~ with sb.** (fig.) mit jmdm. Kontakt haben
[2] /'kɒntækt, kən'tækt/ *v.t.* sich in Verbindung setzen mit
'contact lens *n.* Kontaktlinse, *die*
contagious /kən'teɪdʒəs/ *adj.* ansteckend
contain /kən'teɪn/ *v.t.* **(a)** (hold, include) enthalten
(b) (prevent from spreading) aufhalten
con'tainer *n.* Behälter, *der;* (cargo ~) Container, *der;* **cardboard/wooden ~:** Pappkarton, *der*/Holzkiste, *die*
contaminate /kən'tæmɪneɪt/ *v.t.* verunreinigen; (with radioactivity) verseuchen
contamination /kəntæmɪ'neɪʃn/ *n.* Verunreinigung, *die;* (with radioactivity) Verseuchung, *die*
contemplate /'kɒntəmpleɪt/ *v.t.* **(a)** betrachten; (mentally) nachdenken über (+ *Akk.*)
(b) (expect) rechnen mit; (consider) **~ sth./ doing sth.** an etw. (*Akk.*) denken/daran denken, etw. zu tun
contemplation /kɒntəm'pleɪʃn/ *n.* Betrachtung, *die;* (mental) Nachdenken, *das* (**of** über + *Akk.*)
contemporary /kən'tempərərɪ/ [1] *adj.* zeitgenössisch
[2] *n.* Zeitgenosse, *der*/-genossin, *die*
contempt /kən'tempt/ *n.* Verachtung, *die* (**of, for** für)
contemptible /kən'temptɪbl/ *adj.* verachtenswert
contemptuous /kən'temptjʊəs/ *adj.* verächtlich
contend /kən'tend/ *v.i.* **be able/have to ~ with** fertig werden können/müssen mit
con'tender *n.* Bewerber, *der*/Bewerberin, *die*
content¹ /'kɒntent/ *n.* **(a)** *in pl.* Inhalt, *der;* **[table of] ~s** Inhaltsverzeichnis, *das*
(b) (amount contained) Gehalt, *der* (**of** an + *Dat.*)
content² /kən'tent/ [1] *pred. adj.* zufrieden
[2] *v.t.* zufrieden stellen; **~ oneself with sth./ sb.** sich mit etw./jmdm. zufrieden geben
con'tented *adj.*, **con'tentedly** *adv.* zufrieden
contention /kən'tenʃn/ *n.* **(a)** Streit, *der*
(b) (point asserted) Behauptung, *die*
contentious /kən'tenʃəs/ *adj.* strittig ‹*Punkt, Thema*›
con'tentment *n.* Zufriedenheit, *die*
contest [1] /'kɒntest/ *n.* Wettbewerb, *der*
[2] /kən'test/ *v.t.* **(a)** bestreiten; infrage stellen ‹*Behauptung*›
(b) (Brit.: compete for) kandidieren für
contestant /kən'testənt/ *n.* (competitor) Teilnehmer, *der*/Teilnehmerin, *die*
context /'kɒntekst/ *n.* Kontext, *der;* **in/out of ~:** im/ohne Kontext; **in this ~:** in diesem Zusammenhang
contextual /kən'tekstjʊəl/ *adj.* kontextuell
contextualize /kən'tekstjʊəlaɪz/ *v.t.* (place in context) in einen Kontext einordnen
continent /'kɒntɪnənt/ *n.* Kontinent, *der;* **the C~:** das europäische Festland
continental /kɒntɪ'nentl/ *adj.* **(a)** kontinental
(b) C~ (mainland European) kontinental[europäisch]
continental: ~ 'breakfast *n.* kontinentales Frühstück; **~ 'quilt** *n.* (Brit.) [Stepp]federbett, *das*

con'tingency plan /kən'tɪndʒənsɪ/ *n.* Alternativplan, *der*

contingent /kən'tɪndʒənt/ *n.* Kontingent, *das*

continual /kən'tɪnjʊəl/ *adj.*, **con'tinually** *adv.* (frequent[ly]) ständig; (without stopping) unaufhörlich

continuation /kəntɪnjʊ'eɪʃn/ *n.* Fortsetzung, *die*

continue /kən'tɪnju:/ 1 *v.t.* fortsetzen; **'~d on page 2'** „Fortsetzung auf Seite 2"; **~ doing** *or* **to do sth.** etw. weiter tun; **it ~d to rain** es regnete weiter
2 *v.i.* (persist) ‹*Wetter, Zustand, Krise usw.:*› andauern; (persist in doing sth.) nicht aufhören; **~ with sth.** mit etw. fortfahren

continuity /kɒntɪ'nju:ɪtɪ/ *n.* Kontinuität, *die*

continuous /kən'tɪnjʊəs/ *adj.* **(a)** ununterbrochen; anhaltend ‹*Regen, Sonnenschein*›; ständig ‹*Kritik, Streit*›; durchgezogen ‹*Linie*›
(b) (Ling.) **~ [form]** Verlaufsform, *die*

con'tinuously *adv.* ununterbrochen; ständig ‹*sich ändern*›

contort /kən'tɔ:t/ *v.t.* verdrehen

contortion /kən'tɔ:ʃn/ *n.* Verdrehung, *die*

contour /'kɒntʊə(r)/ *n.* Kontur, *die;* **~ map** Höhenlinienkarte, *die*

contraband /'kɒntrəbænd/ *n.* Schmuggelware, *die*

contraception /kɒntrə'sepʃn/ *n.* Empfängnisverhütung, *die*

contraceptive /kɒntrə'septɪv/ 1 *adj.* empfängnisverhütend
2 *n.* Verhütungsmittel, *das*

contract 1 /'kɒntrækt/ *n.* Vertrag, *der;* **~ of employment** Arbeitsvertrag, *der;* **be under ~ to do sth.** vertraglich verpflichtet sein, etw. zu tun
2 /kən'trækt/ *v.t.* (Med.) sich (*Dat.*) zuziehen
3 /kən'trækt/ *v.i.* **(a) ~ to do sth.** sich vertraglich verpflichten, etw. zu tun
(b) (become smaller, be drawn together) sich zusammenziehen

contraction /kən'trækʃn/ *n.* Kontraktion, *die*

'contract killer *n.* Auftragskiller, *der*/-killerin, *die*

contractor /kən'træktə(r)/ *n.* Auftragnehmer, *der*/-nehmerin, *die*

contradict /kɒntrə'dɪkt/ *v.t.* widersprechen (+ *Dat.*)

contradiction /kɒntrə'dɪkʃn/ *n.* Widerspruch, *der;* **in ~ to sb./sth.** im Widerspruch zu jmdm./etw.

contradictory /kɒntrə'dɪktərɪ/ *adj.* widersprüchlich

contraflow /'kɒntrəfləʊ/ *n.* **~ system** Gegenverkehr auf einem Fahrstreifen

contralto /kən'træltəʊ/ *n., pl.* **~s** Alt, *der*

contraption /kən'træpʃn/ *n.* (coll.) [komisches] Gerät

contrary /'kɒntrərɪ/ 1 *adj.* **(a)** entgegengesetzt; **be ~ to sth.** im Gegensatz zu etw. stehen
(b) /kən'treərɪ/ (perverse) widerspenstig
2 *n.* **the ~**: das Gegenteil; **on the ~**: im Gegenteil
3 *adv.* **~ to sth.** entgegen einer Sache

contrast 1 /kən'trɑ:st/ *v.t.* gegenüberstellen
2 /'kɒntrɑ:st/ *n.* Kontrast, *der* **(with** zu**)**; **in ~, ...**: im Gegensatz dazu, ...; **[be] in ~ with sth.** im Gegensatz zu etw. [stehen]

con'trasting *adj.* gegensätzlich

contravene /kɒntrə'vi:n/ *v.t.* verstoßen gegen

contravention /kɒntrə'venʃn/ *n.* Verstoß, *der* **(of** gegen**)**

contribute /kən'trɪbju:t/ 1 *v.t.* **~ sth. [to** *or* **towards sth.]** etw. [zu etw.] beitragen
2 *v.i.* **~ to charity** für karitative Zwecke spenden; **~ to the success of sth.** zum Erfolg einer Sache (*Gen.*) beitragen

contribution /kɒntrɪ'bju:ʃn/ *n.* Beitrag, *der;* (for charity) Spende, *die* **(to** für**)**; **make a ~**: einen Beitrag leisten; (to charity) etwas spenden

contributor /kən'trɪbjʊtə(r)/ *n.* (to encyclopaedia etc.) Mitarbeiter, *der*/Mitarbeiterin, *die*

'con trick (Brit. coll.) ▶ CONFIDENCE TRICK

contrite /'kɒntraɪt/ *adj.* zerknirscht

contrive /kən'traɪv/ *v.t.* **~ to do sth.** es fertig bringen, etw. zu tun

contrived /kən'traɪvd/ *adj.* künstlich

control /kən'trəʊl/ 1 *n.* **(a)** Kontrolle, *die* **(of** über + *Akk.*); **keep ~ of sth.** etw. unter Kontrolle halten; **be in ~ [of sth.]** die Kontrolle [über etw. (*Akk.*)] haben; **[go** *or* **get] out of ~**: außer Kontrolle [geraten]; **[get sth.] under ~**: [etw.] unter Kontrolle [bringen]
(b) (device) Regler, *der;* **~s** Schalttafel, *die*
2 *v.t.*, **-ll-** kontrollieren; lenken ‹*Auto*›; zügeln ‹*Zorn*›; regeln ‹*Verkehr*›

control: ~ centre *n.* Kontrollzentrum, *das;* **~ con'trol desk** *n.* Schaltpult, *das*

con'troller *n.* (director) Leiter, *der*/Leiterin, *die*

control: ~ panel *n.* Schalttafel, *die;* **~ room** *n.* Kontrollraum, *der;* **~ tower** *n.* Kontrollturm, *der*

controversial /kɒntrə'vɜ:ʃl/ *adj.* umstritten

controversy /'kɒntrəvɜ:sɪ, kən'trɒvəsɪ/ *n.* Auseinandersetzung, *die*

conurbation /kɒnɜ:'beɪʃn/ *n.* Konurbation, *die* (Soziol.); ≈ Stadtregion, *die*

convalesce /kɒnvə'les/ *v.i.* genesen

convalescence /kɒnvə'lesəns/ *n.* Genesung, *die*

convection /kən'vekʃn/ *n.* (Phys., Meteorol.) Konvektion, *die*

convector /kən'vektə(r)/ *n.* Konvektor, *der*

convene /kən'vi:n/ 1 *v.t.* einberufen
2 *v.i.* zusammenkommen

convenience /kən'vi:nɪəns/ *n.* **(a)** **for sb.'s ~** zu jmds. Bequemlichkeit; **at your ~:** wann es Ihnen passt
(b) (toilet) **[public] ~:** [öffentliche] Toilette

con'venience food *n.* Fertignahrung, *die*

convenient /kən'vi:nɪənt/ *adj.* günstig; (useful) praktisch; **would it be ~ to** *or* **for you?** würde es Ihnen passen?

con'veniently *adv.* **(a)** günstig ‹*gelegen, angebracht*›
(b) (opportunely) angenehmerweise

convent /'kɒnvənt/ *n.* Kloster, *das*

convention /kən'venʃn/ *n.* **(a)** Brauch, *der*
(b) (assembly) Konferenz, *die*
(c) (agreement) Konvention, *die*

conventional /kən'venʃənl/ *adj.* konventionell

converge /kən'vɜ:dʒ/ *v.i.* **~ [on each other]** aufeinander zulaufen

conversant /kən'vɜ:sənt/ *pred. adj.* vertraut **(with** mit)

conversation /kɒnvə'seɪʃn/ *n.* Unterhaltung, *die;* **have a ~:** ein Gespräch führen

conversational /kɒnvə'seɪʃənl/ *adj.* **~ English** gesprochenes Englisch

converse¹ /kən'vɜ:s/ *v.i.* (formal) **~ [with sb.] [about** *or* **on sth.]** sich [mit jmdm.] [über etw. (*Akk.*)] unterhalten

converse² /'kɒnvɜ:s/ 1 *adj.* entgegengesetzt; umgekehrt ‹*Fall, Situation*›
2 *n.* Gegenteil, *das*

conversely /kən'vɜ:slɪ/ *adj.* umgekehrt

conversion /kən'vɜ:ʃn/ *n.* **(a)** Umwandlung, *die* **(into** in + *Akk.*)
(b) (adaptation) Umbau, *der*
(c) (of person) Bekehrung, *die* **(to** zu)

con'version table *n.* Umrechnungstabelle, *die*

convert 1 /kən'vɜ:t/ *v.t.* umwandeln **(into** in + *Akk.*); (Comp.) konvertieren ‹*Daten*›; **~ sb. [to sth.]** jmdn. [zu etw.] bekehren
2 /kən'vɜ:t/ *v.i.* **~ into sth.** sich in etw. (*Akk.*) umwandeln lassen
3 /'kɒnvɜ:t/ *n.* Konvertit, *der*/Konvertitin, *die*

convertible /kən'vɜ:tɪbl/ 1 *adj.* **be ~ into sth.** sich in etw. (*Akk.*) umwandeln lassen
2 *n.* Kabrio[lett], *das*

convex /'kɒnveks/ *adj.* konvex

convey /kən'veɪ/ *v.t.* **(a)** befördern
(b) (impart) vermitteln

conveyance /kən'veɪəns/ *n.* **(a)** (transportation) Beförderung, *die*
(b) (formal: vehicle) Beförderungsmittel, *das*

con'veyancing *n.* (Law) **~ [of property]** [Eigentums]übertragung, *die*

conveyor /kən'veɪə(r)/ *n.* **~ [belt]** Förderband, *das*

convict 1 /'kɒnvɪkt/ *n.* Strafgefangene, *der/die*
2 /kən'vɪkt/ *v.t.* verurteilen

conviction /kən'vɪkʃn/ *n.* **(a)** (Law) Verurteilung, *die* **(for** wegen)
(b) (belief) Überzeugung, *die*

convince /kən'vɪns/ *v.t.* überzeugen; **~ sb. that ...:** jmdn. davon überzeugen, dass ...; **be ~d that ...:** davon überzeugt sein, dass ...

convincing /kən'vɪnsɪŋ/ *adj.*, **con'vincingly** *adv.* überzeugend

convivial /kən'vɪvɪəl/ *adj.* fröhlich

convoluted /'kɒnvəlu:tɪd/ *adj.* (complex) kompliziert

convoy /'kɒnvɔɪ/ *n.* Konvoi, *der;* **in ~:** im Konvoi

convulse /kən'vʌls/ *v.t.* **be ~d with** sich krümmen vor (+ *Dat.*)

convulsions /kən'vʌlʃnz/ *n. pl.* Krämpfe *Pl.*

convulsive /kən'vʌlsɪv/ *adj.*, **con'vulsively** *adv.* konvulsivisch

coo /ku:/ *v.i.* gurren

cook /kʊk/ 1 *n.* Koch, *der*/Köchin, *die*
2 *v.t.* kochen ‹*Mahlzeit*›; (fry, roast) braten; (boil) kochen
3 *v.i.* kochen

■ **cook 'up** *v.t.* erfinden ‹*Geschichte*›

'cookbook *n.* (Amer.) Kochbuch, *das*

'cooker *n.* (Brit.) Herd, *der*

cookery /'kʊkərɪ/ *n.* Kochen, *das*

'cookery book *n.* (Brit.) Kochbuch, *das*

cookie /'kʊkɪ/ *n.* **(a)** (Amer.) Keks, *der*
(b) (Comp.) Cookie, *der*

'cooking *n.* Kochen, *das*

cooking: ~ apple *n.* Kochapfel, *der;* **~ utensil** *n.* Küchengerät, *das*

cool /ku:l/ 1 *adj.* **(a)** kühl; **store in a ~ place** kühl aufbewahren
(b) (unemotional, unfriendly) kühl; (calm) ruhig
2 *n.* Kühle, *die*
3 *v.i.* abkühlen
4 *v.t.* kühlen; (from high temperature) abkühlen

■ **cool 'down, cool 'off** *v.i. & t.* abkühlen

cool: ~ box *n.* Kühlbox, *die;* **~-headed** *adj.* kühl; nüchtern

coolly /'ku:llɪ/ *adv.* (calmly) ruhig; (unemotionally) kühl

coop /ku:p/ 1 *n.* (for poultry) Hühnerstall, *der*
2 *v.t.* **~ up** einpferchen

cooperate /kəʊ'ɒpəreɪt/ *v.i.* mitarbeiten **(in** bei); (with each other) zusammenarbeiten **(in** bei)

cooperation /kəʊɒpə'reɪʃn/ *n.* Zusammenarbeit, *die*

cooperative /kəʊ'ɒpərətɪv/ 1 *adj.* kooperativ; (helpful) hilfsbereit
2 *n.* Genossenschaft, *die*

coordinate /kəʊ'ɔ:dɪneɪt/ *v.t.* koordinieren

coordination /kəʊɔːdɪˈneɪʃn/ *n.* Koordination, *die*

co-owner /kəʊˈəʊnə(r)/ *n.* Miteigentümer, *der*/-eigentümerin, *die;* (of business) Mitinhaber, *der*/-inhaberin, *die*

cop /kɒp/ *n.* (coll.: police officer) Bulle, *der* (salopp)

cope /kəʊp/ *v.i.* ~ **with sb./sth.** mit jmdm./etw. fertig werden

Copenhagen /kəʊpnˈheɪgn/ *pr. n.* Kopenhagen (*das*)

copier /ˈkɒpɪə(r)/ *n.* (machine) Kopiergerät, *das*

co-pilot /ˈkəʊpaɪlət/ *n.* Kopilot, *der*/Kopilotin, *die*

copious /ˈkəʊpɪəs/ *adj.* reichhaltig

ˈcop-out *n.* (coll.) Drückebergerei, *die* (ugs. abwertend); **that's a ~:** das ist Drückebergerei (ugs. abwertend)

copper¹ /ˈkɒpə(r)/ *n.* Kupfer, *das*

copper² (Brit. coll.) ▶ COP

coppice /ˈkɒpɪs/, **copse** /kɒps/ *ns.* Wäldchen, *das*

ˈcop shop *n.* (Brit. coll.) Wache, *die;* Revier, *das*

copula /ˈkɒpjʊlə/ *n.* (Ling.) Kopula, *die*

copulate /ˈkɒpjʊleɪt/ *v.i.* kopulieren

copy /ˈkɒpɪ/ **1** *n.* **(a)** (reproduction) Kopie, *die*
(b) (specimen) Exemplar, *das*
2 *v.t. & i.* kopieren; (transcribe) abschreiben

copy: ~cat *n.* (coll.) **you're such a ~cat!** du musst immer alles nachmachen!; **~ editor** *n.* Redakteur, *der*/Redakteurin, *die* (der/die nur nach schriftlichen Vorlagen arbeitet); **~ protection** *n.* (Comp.) Kopierschutz, *der;* **~right** *n.* Urheberrecht, *das* **~writer** *n.* [Werbe]texter, *der*/-texterin, *die*

coral /ˈkɒrl/ *n.* Koralle, *die*

cord /kɔːd/ *n.* **(a)** Kordel, *die;* (strong string) Schnur, *die*
(b) (cloth) Cord, *der*
(c) *in pl.* (trousers) **[pair of] ~s** Cordhose, *die*

cordial /ˈkɔːdɪəl/ **1** *adj.* herzlich
2 *n.* (drink) Sirup, *der*

cordiality /kɔːdɪˈælɪtɪ/ *n.* Herzlichkeit, *die*

ˈcordially *adv.* herzlich

ˈcordless phone /ˈkɔːrdlɪs/ *n.* Schnurlostelefon, *das*

cordon /ˈkɔːdn/ **1** *n.* Kordon, *der*
2 *v.t.* **~ [off]** absperren

corduroy /ˈkɔːdərɔɪ, ˈkɔːdjʊrɔɪ/ *n.* Cordsamt, *der*

core /kɔː(r)/ **1** *n.* (of fruit) Kerngehäuse, *das*
2 *v.t.* entkernen

co-respondent /kəʊrɪˈspɒndənt/ *n.* Mitbeklagte, *der/die* (*im Scheidungsprozess*)

cork /kɔːk/ **1** *n.* **(a)** (bark) Kork, *der*
(b) (bottle stopper) Korken, *der*
2 *v.t.* zukorken

cork: ~screw *n.* Korkenzieher, *der;* **~ ˈtile** *n.* Korkplatte, *die*

cormorant /ˈkɔːmərənt/ *n.* Kormoran, *der*

corn¹ /kɔːn/ *n.* Getreide, *das*

corn² *n.* (on foot) Hühnerauge, *das*

cornea /ˈkɔːnɪə/ *n.* (Anat.) Hornhaut, *die;* Cornea, *die* (fachspr.)

corned beef /kɔːnd ˈbiːf/ *n.* Cornedbeef, *das*

corner /ˈkɔːnə(r)/ **1** *n.* **(a)** Ecke, *die;* (curve) Kurve, *die;* **on the ~:** an der Ecke/in der Kurve
(b) (of mouth, eye) Winkel, *der*
2 *v.t.* (fig.) in die Enge treiben
3 *v.i.* die Kurve nehmen

corner: ~ kick *n.* (Footb.) Eckball, *der;* **~ shop** *n.* Tante-Emma-Laden, *der* (ugs.); **~stone** *n.* (fig.) Eckpfeiler, *der*

cornet /ˈkɔːnɪt/ *n.* **(a)** (Brit.: for ice cream) [Eis]tüte, *die*
(b) (Mus.) Kornett, *das*

corn: ~flakes *n. pl.* Cornflakes *Pl.;* **~flour** (Brit.) *n.* Maismehl, *das;* **~flower** *n.* Kornblume, *die;* **~ starch** (Amer.) *n.* Maismehl, *das*

ˈcorny *adj.* (coll.: trite) abgedroschen

coronary /ˈkɒrənərɪ/ **1** *adj.* (Anat.) koronar
2 *n.* (Med.) ▶ CORONARY THROMBOSIS

coronary: ~ ˈartery *n.* Herzkranzarterie, *die;* Koronararterie, *die* (fachspr.); **~ thromˈbosis** *n.* Koronarthrombose, *die*

coronation /kɒrəˈneɪʃn/ *n.* Krönung, *die*

coroner /ˈkɒrənə(r)/ *n.* Coroner, *der; Beamter, der gewaltsame od. unnatürliche Todesfälle untersucht*

coronet /ˈkɒrənet/ *n.* Krone, *die*

corporal¹ /ˈkɔːpərl/ *adj.* körperlich

corporal² *n.* ≈ Hauptgefreite, *der*

corporate /ˈkɔːpərət/ *adj.* körperschaftlich

corporation /kɔːpəˈreɪʃn/ *n.* Stadtverwaltung, *die*

corpoˈration tax *n.* Körperschaftssteuer, *die*

corps /kɔː(r)/ *n., pl. same* /kɔːz/ Korps, *das*

corpse /kɔːps/ *n.* Leiche, *die*

corpulent /ˈkɔːpjʊlənt/ *adj.* korpulent

Corpus Christi /kɔːpəs ˈkrɪstɪ/ *n.* (Eccl.) Fronleichnam (*der*)

corpuscle /ˈkɔːpəsl/ *n.* **[blood] ~** Blutkörperchen, *das*

corral /kəˈrɑːl/ (Amer.) **1** *n.* Pferch, *der*
2 *v.t.*, **-ll-** einpferchen

correct /kəˈrekt/ **1** *v.t.* korrigieren
2 *adj.* korrekt; **that is ~:** das stimmt

correction /kəˈrekʃn/ *n.* Korrektur, *die*

corˈrectly *adv.* korrekt

correspond /kɒrɪˈspɒnd/ *v.i.* **(a) ~ [to each other]** einander entsprechen; **~ to sth.** einer Sache (*Dat.*) entsprechen
(b) (communicate) **~ with sb.** mit jmdm. korrespondieren

correspondence /kɒrɪˈspɒndəns/ *n.* **(a)** Übereinstimmung, *die* **(with, to** mit)
(b) (communication) Briefwechsel, *der*

corre'spondence course *n.* Fernkurs, *der*

correspondent /kɒrɪ'spɒndənt/ *n.* (reporter) Korrespondent, *der*/ Korrespondentin, *die*

corre'sponding *adj.* entsprechend (**to** *Dat.*)

corre'spondingly *adv.* entsprechend

corridor /'kɒrɪdɔ:(r)/ *n.* **(a)** Flur, *der* **(b)** (Railw.) [Seiten]gang, *der*

corroborate /kə'rɒbəreɪt/ *v.t.* bestätigen

corroboration /kərɒbə'reɪʃn/ *n.* Bestätigung, *die*

corrode /kə'rəʊd/ **1** *v.t.* zerfressen **2** *v.i.* zerfressen werden

corrosion /kə'rəʊʒn/ *n.* Korrosion, *die*

corrugated /'kɒrəgeɪtɪd/ *adj.* **~ cardboard** Wellpappe, *die;* **~ iron** Wellblech, *das*

corrupt /kə'rʌpt/ **1** *adj.* (depraved) verdorben (geh.); (influenced by bribery) korrupt **2** *v.t.* (deprave) korrumpieren; (bribe) bestechen

corruption /kə'rʌpʃn/ *n.* (moral deterioration) Verdorbenheit, *die* (geh.); (corrupt practices) Korruption, *die*

corset /'kɔ:sɪt/ *n.* Korsett, *das*

Corsica /'kɔ:sɪkə/ *pr. n.* Korsika (*das*)

cortège /kɔ:'teɪʒ/ *n.* Trauerzug, *der*

cortisone /'kɔ:tɪzəʊn/ *n.* Kortison, *das;* Cortison, *das* (fachspr.)

cosh /kɒʃ/ (Brit. coll.) **1** *n.* Totschläger, *der* **2** *v.t.* niederknüppeln

cosmetic /kɒz'metɪk/ **1** *adj.* kosmetisch **2** *n.* Kosmetikum, *das*

cosmic /'kɒzmɪk/ *adj.* kosmisch

cosmonaut /'kɒzmənɔ:t/ *n.* Kosmonaut, *der*/Kosmonautin, *die*

cosmopolitan /kɒzmə'pɒlɪtən/ *adj.* kosmopolitisch

cosmos /'kɒzmɒs/ *n.* Kosmos, *der*

cosset /'kɒsɪt/ *v.t.* [ver]hätscheln

cost /kɒst/ **1** *n.* **(a)** Kosten *Pl.* **(b)** (fig.) Preis, *der;* **at all ~s, at any ~:** um jeden Preis **2** *v.t.* **(a)** *p.t., p.p.* **cost** (lit. or fig.) kosten; **how much does it ~?** was kostet es? **(b)** *p.t., p.p.* **costed** (Commerc.: fix price of) **~ sth.** den Preis für etw. kalkulieren

co-star /'kəʊstɑ:(r)/ (Cinemat., Theatre) **1** *n.* **be a/the ~:** eine der Hauptrollen/die zweite Hauptrolle spielen **2** *v.i.,* **-rr-** eine der Hauptrollen spielen **3** *v.t.,* **-rr-: the film ~red Robert Redford** der Film zeigte Robert Redford in einer der Hauptrollen

cost: ~ cutting *n.* Kostensenkung, *die;* **~-cutting** *adj.* Spar-; **~-effective** *adj.* rentabel

'costly *adj.* teuer

cost: ~ of 'living *n.* Lebenshaltungskosten *Pl.;* **~-of-living index** Lebenshaltungsindex, *der;* **~ price** *n.* Selbstkostenpreis, *der*

costume /'kɒstju:m/ *n.* Kleidermode, *die;* (theatrical ~) Kostüm, *das*

costume 'jewellery *n.* Modeschmuck, *der*

cosy /'kəʊzɪ/ *adj.* gemütlich

cot /kɒt/ *n.* Kinderbett, *das*

'cot death *n.* (Brit.) plötzlicher Kindstod; Cot-death, *der* (Med.)

cottage /'kɒtɪdʒ/ *n.* Cottage, *das*

cottage: ~ 'cheese *n.* Hüttenkäse, *der;* **~ 'hospital** *n.: kleines [Land]krankenhaus ohne ständige ärztliche Betreuung;* **~ industry** *n.* Heimarbeit, *die;* **~ 'pie** *n.: mit Kartoffelbrei überbackenes Hackfleisch*

cotton /'kɒtən/ **1** *n.* Baumwolle, *die;* (thread) Baumwollgarn, *das* **2** *attrib. adj.* Baumwoll- **3** *v.i.* **~ 'on** (coll.) kapieren (ugs.)

cotton: ~ reel *n.* [Näh]garnrolle, *die;* **~ 'wool** *n.* Watte, *die*

couch /kaʊtʃ/ *n.* Couch, *die*

couchette /ku:'ʃet/ *n.* (Railw.) Liegewagenplatz, *der*

couch po'tato *n.* (coll.) Couchpotato[e], *der*

cough /kɒf/ **1** *n.* Husten, *der* **2** *v.i.* husten

cough: ~ medicine *n.* Hustenmittel, *das;* **~ mixture** *n.* Hustensaft, *der*

could ▶ CAN²

couldn't /'kʊdnt/ (coll.) = **could not;** ▶ CAN²

council /'kaʊnsl/ *n.* Rat, *der;* **local ~:** Gemeinderat, *der;* **city/town ~:** Stadtrat, *der;* **C~ of Ministers** Ministerrat, *der*

council: ~ estate *n.* Wohnviertel mit Sozialwohnungen; **~ flat** *n.* Sozialwohnung, *die;* **~ house** *n.* Haus des sozialen Wohnungsbaus; **~ housing** *n.* sozialer Wohnungsbau

councillor /'kaʊnsələ(r)/ *n.* Ratsmitglied, *das*

'council tax *n.* (Brit.) Gemeindesteuer, *die*

counsel /'kaʊnsl/ **1** *n.* **(a)** Rat[schlag], *der* **(b)** *pl. same* (Law) Rechtsanwalt, *der*/ -anwältin, *die* **2** *v.t.,* (Brit.) **-ll-** beraten

counselling (*Amer.:* **counseling**) /'kaʊnsəlɪŋ/ *n.* Beratung, *die;* **marriage ~:** Eheberatung, *die*

counsellor, (*Amer.* **counselor**) /'kaʊnsələ(r)/ *n.* Berater, *der*/Beraterin, *die*

count¹ /kaʊnt/ **1** *n.* Zählen, *das;* **keep ~ [of sth.]** [etw.] zählen; **lose ~:** sich verzählen **2** *v.t.* **(a)** zählen **(b)** (include) mitzählen; **not ~ing** abgesehen von **(c)** (consider) halten für; **~ oneself lucky** sich glücklich schätzen können ⇢

[3] *v.i.* **(a)** zählen; ~ **[up] to ten** bis zehn zählen
(b) (be included) zählen
■ **'count on** *v.t.* ~ **on sb./sth.** sich auf jmdn./etw. verlassen
■ **count 'up** *v.t.* zusammenzählen
count² *n.* (nobleman) Graf, *der*
'countdown *n.* Count-down, *der od. das*
countenance /'kaʊntɪnəns/ [1] *n.* (literary: face) Antlitz, *das*
[2] *v.t.* (formal: approve) gutheißen
counter¹ /'kaʊntə(r)/ *n.* **(a)** (in shop) Ladentisch, *der;* (in cafeteria) Büfett, *das;* (in bank) Schalter, *der*
(b) (for games) Spielmarke, *die*
counter² [1] *adj.* Gegen-
[2] *v.t.* **(a)** (oppose) begegnen (+ *Dat.*)
(b) (act against) kontern
[3] *adv.* **go ~ to** zuwiderlaufen (+ *Dat.*)
counter: ~'act *v.t.* entgegenwirken (+ *Dat.*); **~-attack** *n.* Gegenangriff, *der;* **~balance** *v.t.* (fig.) ausgleichen; **~-'espionage** *n.* Spionageabwehr, *die*
counterfeit /'kaʊntəfɪt/ [1] *adj.* gefälscht; ~ **money** Falschgeld, *das*
[2] *v.t.* fälschen
'counterfeiter *n.* Fälscher, *der*/Fälscherin, *die*
counterfoil /'kaʊntəfɔɪl/ *n.* Kontrollabschnitt, *der*
counter: ~part *n.* Gegenstück, *das* (**of** zu); **~pro'ductive** *adj.* **sth. is ~productive** etw. bewirkt das Gegenteil des Gewünschten; **~sign** *v.t.* gegenzeichnen; **~weight** *n.* Gegengewicht, *das*
countess /'kaʊntɪs/ *n.* Gräfin, *die*
'countless *adj.* zahllos
countrified /'kʌntrɪfaɪd/ *adj.* ländlich
country /'kʌntrɪ/ *n.* **(a)** Land, *das;* **sb's [home]** ~: jmds. Heimat
(b) (~side) Landschaft, *die;* **in the** ~: auf dem Land; ~ **road/air** Landstraße, *die*/Landluft, *die*
country 'dancing *n.* Kontertanz, *der*
countryfied ▶ COUNTRIFIED
country: ~man /'kʌntrɪmən/, *n. pl.* **~men** /'kʌntrɪmən/ Landsmann, *der;* **~side** *n.* **(a)** (rural areas) Land, *das;* **(b)** (rural scenery) Landschaft, *die*
county /'kaʊntɪ/ *n.* (Brit.) Grafschaft, *die*
coup /ku:/ *n.* **(a)** Coup, *der*
(b) ▶ COUP D'ÉTAT
coup d'état /ku: deɪ'ta:/ *n.* Staatsstreich, *der*
coupé /'ku:peɪ/ *n.* Coupé, *das*
couple /kʌpl/ [1] *n.* **(a)** (pair) Paar, *das;* (married) [Ehe]paar, *das*
(b) a ~ [of] (a few) ein paar; (two) zwei
[2] *v.t.* koppeln
coupon /'ku:pɒn/ *n.* **(a)** (for rations) Marke, *die*
(b) (in advertisement) Coupon, *der*
courage /'kʌrɪdʒ/ *n.* Mut, *der*
courageous /kə'reɪdʒəs/ *adj.*, **cou'rageously** *adv.* mutig
courgette /kʊə'ʒet/ *n.* (Brit.) Zucchino, *der*
courier /'kʊrɪə(r)/ *n.* **(a)** (Tourism) Reiseleiter, *der*/-leiterin, *die*
(b) (messenger) Kurier, *der*
'courier company *n.* Kurierdienst, *der*
course /kɔ:s/ *n.* **(a)** (of ship, plane) Kurs, *der;* ~ **[of action]** Vorgehensweise, *die*
(b) of ~: natürlich
(c) in due ~: zu gegebener Zeit; **in the ~ of the day/his life** im Lauf[e] des Tages/seines Lebens
(d) (of meal) Gang, *der*
(e) (Sport) Kurs, *der;* **[golf]~**: [Golf]platz, *der*
(f) (Educ.) Kurs[us], *der;* **go to** *or* **attend/do a ~ in sth.** einen Kurs in etw. (*Dat.*) besuchen/machen
(g) (Med.) **a ~ of treatment** eine Kur
court /kɔ:t/ [1] *n.* **(a)** Hof, *der*
(b) (Tennis, Squash) Platz, *der*
(c) (Law) Gericht, *das*
[2] *v.t.* ~ **sb.** jmdn. umwerben
courteous /'kɜ:tɪəs/ *adj.* höflich
courtesy /'kɜ:təsɪ/ *n.* Höflichkeit, *die*
'courtesy light *n.* (Motor Veh.) Innenbeleuchtung, *die*
court: ~ house *n.* (Law) Gerichtsgebäude, *das;* **~ 'martial** *n., pl.* **~s martial** (Mil.) Kriegsgericht, *das;* **~room** *n.* (Law) Gerichtssaal, *der*
courtship /'kɔ:tʃɪp/ *n.* Werben, *das*
court: ~ shoe *n.* Pumps, *der;* **~yard** *n.* Hof, *der*
cousin /'kʌzn/ *n.* **[first]** ~: Cousin, *der*/Cousine, *die*
couturier /ku:'tjʊərjeɪ/ *n.* Couturier, *der;* Modeschöpfer, *der*
cove /kəʊv/ *n.* (Geog.) [kleine] Bucht
covenant /'kʌvənənt/ *n.* formelle Übereinkunft
cover /'kʌvə(r)/ [1] *n.* **(a)** (piece of cloth) Decke, *die;* (of cushion, bed) Bezug, *der;* (lid) Deckel, *der;* (of hole, engine, typewriter, etc.) Abdeckung, *die*
(b) (of book) Einband, *der;* (of magazine) Umschlag, *der*
(c) [send sth.] under separate ~: [etw.] mit getrennter Post [schicken]
(d) take ~ [from sth.] Schutz [vor etw. (*Dat.*)] suchen; **under ~** (from rain) überdacht
[2] *v.t.* **(a)** bedecken; beziehen ‹*Sessel, Kissen*›; zudecken ‹*Pfanne*›; **the roses are ~ed with greenfly** die Rosen sind voller Blattläuse
(b) (include) abdecken
(c) (Journ.) berichten über (+ *Akk.*)
(d) decken ‹*Kosten*›
■ **cover 'up** [1] *v.t.* zudecken; (fig.) vertuschen
[2] *v.i.* ~ **up for sb.** jmdn. decken
coverage /'kʌvərɪdʒ/ *n.* (Journ.) Berichterstattung, *die*

'cover charge *n.* [Preis für das] Gedeck
'covering *n.* Decke, *die;* (of chair, bed) Bezug, *der*
'covering letter *n.* Begleitbrief, *der*
'cover story *n.* (Journ.) Titelgeschichte, *die*
covert /'kʌvət/ *adj.* versteckt
cover: **~-up** *n.* Verschleierung, *die;* **~ version** *n.* Coverversion, *die*
covet /'kʌvɪt/ *v.t.* begehren (geh.)
covetous /'kʌvɪtəs/ *adj.* begehrlich (geh.)
cow /kaʊ/ *n.* Kuh, *die*
coward /'kaʊəd/ *n.* Feigling, *der*
cowardice /'kaʊədɪs/ *n.* Feigheit, *die*
'cowardly *adj.* feig[e]
'cowboy *n.* Cowboy, *der*
cower /'kaʊə(r)/ *v.i.* sich ducken
cowherd *n.* Kuhhirte, *der*
'co-worker *n.* Kollege, *der*/Kollegin, *die*
cow: **~ parsley** *n.* (Bot.) Wiesenkerbel, *der;* **~pat** *n.* Kuhfladen, *der;* **~shed** *n.* Kuhstall, *der;* **~slip** *n.* Schlüsselblume, *die*
coy /kɔɪ/ *adj.* gespielt schüchtern
cozy (Amer.) ▶ COSY
CPU *abbr.* (Comp.) = **central processing unit** ZE
crab /kræb/ *n.* Krabbe, *die*
'crab apple *n.* Holzapfel, *der*
crack /kræk/ **1** *n.* **(a)** (noise) Krachen, *das*
(b) (in china etc.) Sprung, *der;* (in rock) Spalte, *die;* (chink) Spalt, *der*
(c) (coll.: try) **have a ~ at sth./doing sth.** versuchen, etw. zu tun
(d) (sl.: drug) **~ [cocaine]** Crack, *das*
2 *attrib. adj.* (coll.) erstklassig
3 *v.t.* **(a)** knacken ‹*Nuss, Problem, Kode*›
(b) (make a ~ in) anschlagen ‹*Porzellan usw.*›
(c) **~ a joke** einen Witz machen
(d) **~ a whip** mit einer Peitsche knallen
4 *v.i.* ‹*Porzellan usw.:*› einen Sprung/ Sprünge bekommen
■ **crack 'down** *v.i.* (coll.) **~ down [on sb./sth.]** [gegen jmdn./etw.] [hart] vorgehen
■ **crack 'up** *v.i.* (coll.) ‹*Person:*› zusammenbrechen
'crack-down *n.* (coll.) **there will be a ~:** man wird hart durchgreifen; **have/order a ~ on sb./sth.** drastische Maßnahmen gegen jmdn./etw. ergreifen/anordnen
cracked /krækt/ *adj.* gesprungen ‹*Porzellan usw.*›; rissig ‹*Verputz*›
cracker /'krækə(r)/ *n.* **(a)** **[Christmas] ~** ≈ Knallbonbon, *der od. das*
(b) (biscuit) Cracker, *der*
'crackers *pred. adj.* (Brit. coll.) übergeschnappt (ugs.)
crackle /'krækl/ **1** *v.i.* knistern; ‹*Feuer:*› prasseln
2 *n.* Knistern, *das*
cradle /'kreɪdl/ **1** *n.* Wiege, *die*
2 *v.t.* wiegen
cradle:~ -snatch *v.i.* (coll.) **Your boyfriend/girlfriend is much younger than you. You're ~-snatching** Dein Freund/deine Freundin ist viel jünger als du. Du vergreifst dich ja an kleinen Kindern (ugs. scherzh.); **~ -snatcher** *n.* (fig. coll.) *jmd., der mit einer sehr viel jüngeren Person eine Liebesbeziehung eingeht*
craft /krɑːft/ *n.* **(a)** (trade) Handwerk, *das;* (art) Kunsthandwerk, *das*
(b) *pl. same* (boat) Boot, *das*
craftily /'krɑːftɪlɪ/ *adv.* listig
craftsman /'krɑːftsmən/ *n., pl.* **craftsmen** /'krɑːftsmən/ Handwerker, *der*
craftsmanship /'krɑːftsmənʃɪp/ *n.* (skilled workmanship) handwerkliches Können
crafty /'krɑːftɪ/ *adj.* listig
crag /kræg/ *n.* Felsspitze, *die*
'craggy *adj.* **(a)** felsig
(b) zerfurcht ‹*Gesicht*›
cram /kræm/ **1** *v.t.,* **-mm-** (overfill) voll stopfen (ugs.); (force) stopfen
2 *v.i.,* **-mm-** (for exam) büffeln (ugs.)
cramp /kræmp/ **1** *n.* (Med.) Krampf, *der*
2 *v.t.* einengen
cramped /kræmpt/ *adj.* eng ‹*Raum*›; gedrängt ‹*Handschrift*›
cranberry /'krænbərɪ/ *n.* Preiselbeere, *die*
crane /kreɪn/ **1** *n.* Kran, *der*
2 *v.t.* **~ one's neck** den Hals recken
crane: **~ driver** *n.* Kranführer, *der*/ -führerin, *die;* **~ fly** *n.* Schnake, *die*
crank¹ /kræŋk/ *n.* (Mech. Engin.) [Hand]kurbel, *die*
crank² *n.* Irre, *der*/*die* (salopp)
crank: **~ arm** *n.* (of bicycle) Tretkurbel, *die;* **~shaft** *n.* (Mech. Engin.) Kurbelwelle, *die*
'cranky *adj.* (eccentric) schrullig
cranny /'krænɪ/ *n.* Ritze, *die*
crap /kræp/ *n.* (coarse) **(a)** (faeces) Scheiße, *die* (derb); **have a ~:** scheißen (derb)
(b) (nonsense) Scheiß, *der* (salopp)
crash /kræʃ/ **1** *n.* **(a)** (noise) Krachen, *das*
(b) (collision) Zusammenstoß, *der;* **have a ~:** einen Unfall haben
2 *v.i.* **(a)** (make a noise, go noisily) krachen
(b) (have a collision) einen Unfall haben; ‹*Flugzeug, Flieger:*› abstürzen; **~ into sth.** gegen etw. krachen
(c) (Finance etc., Computing) zusammenbrechen
3 *v.t.* **(a)** (smash) schmettern
(b) (cause to have collision) einen Unfall haben mit
crash: **~ barrier** *n.* Leitplanke, *die;* **~ course** *n.* Intensivkurs, *der;* **~ diet** *n.* radikale Diät; ≈ Nulldiät, *die;* **~ helmet** *n.* Sturzhelm, *der;* **~-land** **1** *v.t.* **~-land a plane** mit einem Flugzeug bruchlanden; **2** *v.i.* bruchlanden; **~-landing** *n.* Bruchlandung, *die*
crass /kræs/ *adj.* haarsträubend ‹*Dummheit, Unwissenheit*›; (grossly stupid) strohdumm
crate /kreɪt/ *n.* Kiste, *die*
crater /'kreɪtə(r)/ *n.* Krater, *der*

cravat /krəˈvæt/ *n.* Krawatte, *die*

crave /kreɪv/ *v.t.* **(a)** (beg) erbitten
(b) (long for) sich sehnen nach

ˈ**craving** *n.* Verlangen, *das* (**for** nach)

crawl /krɔːl/ **1** *v.i.* **(a)** kriechen; ‹*Baby, Insekt:*› krabbeln
(b) (coll.) **~ to sb.** vor jmdm. kriechen
2 *n.* **(a)** **go at a ~:** im Schneckentempo fahren
(b) (swimming stroke) Kraulen, *das*

ˈ**crawler lane** *n.* Kriechspur, *die*

crayfish /ˈkreɪfɪʃ/ *n., pl. same* Flusskrebs, *der*

crayon /ˈkreɪən/ *n.* **[coloured] ~:** Buntstift, *der;* (wax) Wachsmalstift, *der*

craze /kreɪz/ *n.* Begeisterung, *die*

crazy /ˈkreɪzɪ/ *adj.* verrückt; **be ~ about sb./sth.** (coll.) nach jmdm./etw. verrückt sein (ugs.)

creak /kriːk/ **1** *n.* Knarren, *das*
2 *v.i.* knarren

cream /kriːm/ **1** *n.* **(a)** Sahne, *die*
(b) (dessert, cosmetic) Creme, *die*
2 *adj.* **~[-coloured]** creme[farben]

cream: ~ cake *n.* Cremetorte, *die;* (small) Cremetörtchen, *das;* (with whipped ~) Sahnetorte, *die*/Sahnetörtchen, *das;* **~ ˈcheese** *n.* ≈ Frischkäse, *der;* **~ ˈcracker** *n.* ≈ Cracker, *der;* **~ ˈtea** *n.* Tee mit Marmeladetörtchen und Sahne

ˈ**creamy** *adj.* (with cream) sahnig; (like cream) cremig

crease /kriːs/ **1** *n.* (pressed) Bügelfalte, *die;* (accidental) Falte, *die*
2 *v.t.* (press) eine Falte bügeln in (+ *Akk.*); (accidentally) zerknittern
3 *v.i.* Falten bekommen; knittern

ˈ**crease-resistant** *adj.* knitterfrei

create /kriːˈeɪt/ *v.t.* schaffen; verursachen ‹*Verwirrung*›; machen ‹*Eindruck*›

creation /kriːˈeɪʃn/ *n.* Schaffung, *die;* (of the world) Schöpfung, *die* (geh.)

creative /kriːˈeɪtɪv/ *adj.* kreativ

creator /kriːˈeɪtə(r)/ *n.* Schöpfer, *der*/Schöpferin, *die*

creature /ˈkriːtʃə(r)/ *n.* Geschöpf, *das*

crèche /kreʃ/ *n.* [Kinder]krippe, *die*

credentials /krɪˈdenʃlz/ *n. pl.* Zeugnis, *das*

credibility /kredɪˈbɪlɪtɪ/ *n.* Glaubwürdigkeit, *die*

credible /ˈkredɪbl/ *adj.* glaubwürdig

credit /ˈkredɪt/ **1** *n.* **(a)** (honour) Ehre, *die;* **take the ~ for sth.** die Anerkennung für etw. einstecken
(b) (Commerc.) Kredit, *der*
(c) **~s, ~ titles** (at beginning of film) Vorspann, *der;* (at end) Nachspann, *der*
2 *v.t.* **(a)** glauben
(b) (Finance) gutschreiben

creditable /ˈkredɪtəbl/ *adj.* anerkennenswert

creditably /ˈkredɪtəblɪ/ *adv.* achtbar

credit: ~ account *n.* Kreditkonto, *das;* **~ card** *n.* Kreditkarte, *die;* **~ facilities** *n. pl.* [Kredit]fazilität, *die* (fachspr.); **~ limit** *n.* Kreditlinie, *die*

creditor /ˈkredɪtə(r)/ *n.* Gläubiger, *der*/Gläubigerin, *die*

credit: ~ rating *n.* [Einschätzung der] Kreditwürdigkeit; **have a good/bad ~ rating** als kreditwürdig/kreditunwürdig eingeschätzt werden; **~worthy** *adj.* kreditwürdig

creed /kriːd/ *n.* Glaubensbekenntnis, *das*

creek /kriːk/ *n.* **(a)** (Brit.: of coast) [kleine] Bucht
(b) (of river) [kurzer] Flussarm

creep /kriːp/ **1** *v.i.,* **crept** [krept] kriechen; (move timidly, slowly, stealthily) schleichen
2 *n.* **(a)** (coll.: person) Fiesling, *der* (salopp)
(b) (coll.) **give sb. the ~s** jmdn. nicht [ganz] geheuer sein

ˈ**creeper** *n.* Kletterpflanze, *die*

ˈ**creepy** *adj.* unheimlich

cremate /krɪˈmeɪt/ *v.t.* einäschern

cremation /krɪˈmeɪʃn/ *n.* Einäscherung, *die*

crematorium /kreməˈtɔːrɪəm/ *n.* Krematorium, *das*

creosote /ˈkriːəsəʊt/ *n.* Kreosot, *das*

crept ▶ CREEP 1

crescendo /krɪˈʃendəʊ/ *n., pl.* **~s** (Mus.) Crescendo, *das;* (fig.) Zunahme, *die*

crescent /ˈkresənt/ *n.* Mondsichel, *die*

cress /kres/ *n.* Kresse, *die*

crest /krest/ *n.* Kamm, *der*

ˈ**crestfallen** *adj.* niedergeschlagen

Crete /kriːt/ *pr. n.* Kreta (*das*)

cretin /ˈkretɪn/ *n.* (coll.) Trottel, *der*

Creutzfeldt-Jakob disease /ˈkrɔɪtsfeltˈjækɒb/ *n.* Creutzfeldt-Jakob-Krankheit, *die*

crevasse /krɪˈvæs/ *n.* Gletscherspalte, *die*

crevice /ˈkrevɪs/ *n.* Spalt, *der*

crew /kruː/ *n.* Besatzung, *die*

crew: ~cut *n.* Bürstenschnitt, *der;* **~ neck** *n.* enger, runder Halsausschnitt; **a ~-neck pullover** ein Pullover mit engem, rundem Halsausschnitt

crib /krɪb/ **1** *n.* Krippe, *die*
2 *v.t.,* **-bb-** (coll.) abkupfern (salopp)

crick /krɪk/ *n.* **a ~ [in one's neck/back]** ein steifer Hals/Rücken

cricket[1] /ˈkrɪkɪt/ *n.* Kricket, *das*

cricket[2] *n.* (Zool.) Grille, *die*

cricket: ~ ball *n.* Kricketball, *der;* **~ bat** Schlagholz, *das*

ˈ**cricketer** *n.* Kricketspieler, *der*/-spielerin, *die*

ˈ**cricket match** *n.* Kricketspiel, *das*

cried ▶ CRY

crime /kraɪm/ *n.* **(a)** Verbrechen, *das*

(b) *collect.* **a wave of ~:** eine Welle von Straftaten; **~ doesn't pay** Verbrechen lohnen sich nicht

crime: ~ prevention *n.* Verbrechensverhütung, *die;* **C~ Prevention Officer** *Polizeibeamter, dessen/-beamtin, deren Aufgabe aktive, vorbeugende Verbrechensbekämpfung ist;* **~ rate** *n.* Kriminalitätsrate, *die;* **~ wave** *n.* Welle von Straftaten; **~ writer** *n.* Kriminalschriftsteller, *der*/-schriftstellerin, *die*

criminal /'krɪmɪnl/ **1** *adj.* kriminell; strafbar; **~ act** *or* **deed/offence** Straftat, *die*
2 *n.* Kriminelle, *der/die*

criminal: ~ charge *n.* Anklage, *die;* **face ~ charges [for sth.]** sich [wegen etw.] vor Gericht zu verantworten haben; **there are ~ charges against him** er steht unter Anklage; **~ 'court** *n.* Strafgericht, *das;* **~ 'law** *n.* Strafrecht, *das;* **~ 'lawyer** *n.* Anwalt/Anwältin für Strafsachen; **~ 'record** *n.* Strafregister, *das;* **have a ~ record** vorbestraft sein

crimson /'krɪmzn/ **1** *adj.* purpurrot
2 *n.* Purpurrot, *das*

cringe /krɪndʒ/ *v.i.* zusammenzucken

crinkle /'krɪŋkl/ **1** *n.* Knitterfalte, *die*
2 *v.t.* zerknittern
3 *v.i.* knittern

cripple /'krɪpl/ **1** *n.* Krüppel, *der*
2 *v.t.* zum Krüppel machen; (fig.) lähmen

crippled /'krɪpld/ *adj.* verkrüppelt

crippling /'krɪplɪŋ/ *adj.* zur Verkrüppelung führend ‹*Krankheit, Verletzung*›; (fig.) erdrückend ‹*Preise, Inflationsrate, Steuern, Mieten*›; lähmend ‹*Streik, Schmerzen*›

crisis /'kraɪsɪs/ *n., pl.* **crises** /'kraɪsi:z/ Krise, *die*

crisis: ~ area *n.* Krisengebiet, *das;* **~ 'management** *n.* Krisenmanagement, *das*

crisp /krɪsp/ **1** *adj.* knusprig
2 *n.* **(a)** *usu. in pl.* (Brit.: potato **~**) [Kartoffel]chip, *der*
(b) be burned to a ~: verbrannt sein

'crispbread *n.* Knäckebrot, *das*

'crispy *adj.* knusprig

criss-cross /'krɪskrɒs/ **1** *adj.* **~ pattern** Muster aus gekreuzten Linien
2 *adv.* kreuz und quer
3 *v.t.* wiederholt schneiden

criterion /kraɪ'tɪərɪən/ *n., pl.* **criteria** /kraɪ'tɪərɪə/ Kriterium, *das*

critic /'krɪtɪk/ *n.* Kritiker, *der*/Kritikerin, *die*

critical /'krɪtɪkl/ *adj.* kritisch; **be ~ of sb./sth.** jmdn./etw. kritisieren

critically /'krɪtɪkəlɪ/ *adv.* kritisch; **~ ill** ernstlich krank

critical 'mass *n.* (Phys.) kritische Masse

criticism /'krɪtɪsɪzm/ *n.* Kritik, *die* **(of** an + *Dat.*)

criticize /'krɪtɪsaɪz/ *v.t.* kritisieren **(for** wegen)

critique /krɪ'ti:k/ *n.* Kritik, *die*

croak /krəʊk/ **1** *n.* (of frog) Quaken, *das;* (of person) Krächzen, *das*
2 *v.i.* ‹*Frosch:*› quaken; ‹*Person:*› krächzen
3 *v.t.* krächzen

Croat /'krəʊæt/ *n.* **(a)** (person) Kroate, *der*/Kroatin, *die*
(b) (language) Kroatisch, *das*

Croatia /krəʊ'eɪʃə/ *pr. n.* Kroatien **(***das***)**

Croatian /krəʊ'eɪʃən/ **1** *adj.* kroatisch; **sb. is ~:** jmd. ist Kroate/Kroatin
2 *n.* ▶ CROAT

crochet /'krəʊʃeɪ/ **1** *n.* Häkelarbeit, *die;* **~ hook** Häkelhaken, *der*
2 *v.t.* häkeln

crock /krɒk/ *n.* (coll.) **[old] ~** (person) altes Wrack, *das* (fig.); (vehicle) [alte] Klapperkiste (ugs.)

crockery /'krɒkərɪ/ *n.* Geschirr, *das*

crocodile /'krɒkədaɪl/ *n.* Krokodil, *das*

crocus /'krəʊkəs/ *n.* Krokus, *der*

croft /krɒft/ *n.* **(a)** [kleines] Stück Acker-/Weideland
(b) (smallholding) [kleines] Pachtgut

'crofter *n.* (Brit.) Pächter, *der*/Pächterin, *die*

croissant /'krwɑ:sɑ̃/ *n.* Hörnchen, *das*

crony /'krəʊnɪ/ *n.* Kumpel, *der* (ugs.)

crook /krʊk/ *n.* **(a)** (coll.: rogue) Gauner, *der*
(b) (shepherd's) Hirtenstab, *der*

crooked /'krʊkɪd/ *adj.* krumm; (fig.: dishonest) betrügerisch

crop /krɒp/ **1** *n.* [Feld]frucht, *die;* (season's yield) Ernte, *die*
2 *v.t.* stutzen ‹*Haare usw.*›

■ **crop 'up** *v.i.* auftauchen

'crop dusting *n.* Schädlingsbekämpfung aus der Luft

'cropper *n.* (coll.) **come a ~:** einen Sturz bauen (ugs.)

crop: ~-spraying *n.* Schädlingsbekämpfung (*mit Sprühmitteln*); **~ top** *n.* bauch- *od.* nabelfreies Top

croquet /'krəʊkeɪ/ *n.* Krocket[spiel], *das*

croquette /krə'ket/ *n.* Krokette, *die*

cross /krɒs/ **1** *n.* **(a)** Kreuz, *das*
(b) (mixture) Mischung, *die* **(between** aus)
2 *v.t.* **(a)** [über]kreuzen; **~ one's arms/legs** die Arme verschränken/die Beine übereinander schlagen; **keep one's fingers ~ed [for sb.]** (fig.) [jmdm.] die *od.* den Daumen drücken
(b) (go across) kreuzen; überqueren ‹*Straße, Gebirge*›; durchqueren ‹*Land, Zimmer*›; **~ sb.'s mind** (fig.) jmdm. einfallen; **'~ now'** „Gehen"
(c) (Brit.) **a ~ed cheque** ein Verrechnungsscheck
(d) ~ oneself sich bekreuzigen
3 *v.i.* aneinander vorbeigehen; **~ [in the post]** ‹*Briefe:*› sich kreuzen

4 *adj.* verärgert; **sb. will be ~:** jmd. wird ärgerlich *od.* böse werden; **be ~ with sb.** böse auf jmdn. sein

■ **cross 'out** *v.t.* ausstreichen

■ **cross 'over** *v.t.* überqueren; *abs.* hinübergehen

cross: ~bar *n.* **(a)** [Fahrrad]stange, *die;* **(b)** (Sport) Querlatte, *die;* **~bones** *n. pl.* gekreuzte Knochen *Pl.* (*unter Totenkopf*); **~bow** /'krɒsbəʊ/ *n.* Armbrust, *die;* **~-breed** 1 *n.* Hybride, *die;* (animal) Bastard, *der;* 2 *v.t.* kreuzen; **~-Channel** *adj.* **~-Channel traffic/ferry** Verkehr/Fähre über den Kanal; **~-check** 1 *n.* Gegenprobe, *die;* 2 *v.t.* [nochmals] nachprüfen; nachkontrollieren; **~-country** 1 *adj.* Querfeldein-; 2 *adv.* querfeldein; **~-cultural** *adj.* interkulturell; **~-dressing** *n.* Crossdressing, *das;* **~-examination** *n.* Kreuzverhör, *das;* **~-examine** *v.t.* ins Kreuzverhör nehmen; **~-eyed** /'krɒsaɪd/ *adj.* [nach innen] schielend; **be ~-eyed** schielen; **~-'fertilize** *v.t.* fremdbestäuben; kreuzbefruchten; (fig.) sich gegenseitig befruchten; **~fire** *n.* Kreuzfeuer, *das;* **get caught in the ~fire** (fig.) ins Kreuzfeuer geraten

'crossing *n.* **(a)** (act) Überquerung, *die* **(b)** (pedestrian ~) Überweg, *der*

cross-legged /'krɒslegd/ *adv.* mit gekreuzten Beinen; (with feet across thighs) im Schneidersitz

'crossly *adv.* verärgert

cross: ~ 'purposes *n. pl.* **talk at ~ purposes** aneinander vorbeireden; **~-'question** *v.t.* ins Kreuzverhör nehmen; **~-refer** *v.i.* einen Querverweis machen (**to** auf + *Akk.*); **~ reference** *n.* Querverweis, *der;* **~roads** *n. sing.* Kreuzung, *die;* (fig.) Wendepunkt, *der;* **~ section** *n.* Querschnitt, *der;* **~word** *n.* **~word [puzzle]** Kreuzworträtsel, *das*

crotch /krɒtʃ/ *n.* (of trousers, body) Schritt, *der*

crotchet /'krɒtʃɪt/ *n.* (Brit. Mus.) Viertelnote, *die*

crouch /kraʊtʃ/ *v.i.* [sich zusammen]kauern

croupier /'kru:pɪə(r), 'kru:pɪeɪ/ *n.* Croupier, *der*

crow /krəʊ/ *n.* Krähe, *die;* **as the ~ flies** Luftlinie

'crowbar *n.* Brechstange, *die*

crowd /kraʊd/ 1 *n.* [Menschen]menge, *die* 2 *v.t.* füllen 3 *v.i.* sich sammeln

'crowded *adj.* überfüllt

'crowd-puller *n.* (coll.) Publikumsmagnet, *der*

crown /kraʊn/ 1 *n.* Krone, *die* 2 *v.t.* **(a)** krönen **(b)** überkronen ‹*Zahn*›

crown 'jewels *n. pl.* Kronjuwelen *Pl.*

'crow's-foot *n., usu. in pl.* Krähenfuß, *der*

crucial /'kru:ʃl/ *adj.* entscheidend (**to** für)

crucially /'kru:ʃəlɪ/ *adv.* entscheidend; **be ~ important** von entscheidender Wichtigkeit sein

crucifix /'kru:sɪfɪks/ *n.* Kruzifix, *das*

crucifixion /kru:sɪ'fɪkʃn/ *n.* Kreuzigung, *die*

crucify /'kru:sɪfaɪ/ *v.t.* kreuzigen

crude /kru:d/ *adj.* **(a)** roh; **~ oil** Rohöl, *das* **(b)** (fig.) grob ‹*Entwurf, Worte*›

cruel /'kru:əl/ *adj.* grausam

cruelty /'kru:əltɪ/ *n.* Grausamkeit, *die*

cruet /'kru:ɪt/ *n.* **(a)** Essig-/Ölfläschchen, *das* **(b)** ▶ CRUET STAND

'cruet stand *n.* Menage, *die*

cruise /kru:z/ 1 *v.i.* (at random) ‹*Fahrzeug, Fahrer:*› herumfahren 2 *n.* Kreuzfahrt, *die*

'cruise missile *n.* Marschflugkörper, *der*

'cruiser *n.* Kreuzer, *der*

crumb /krʌm/ *n.* Krümel, *der*

crumble /'krʌmbl/ 1 *v.t.* zerkrümeln ‹*Keks, Kuchen*› 2 *v.i.* ‹*Mauer:*› zusammenfallen

crumbly /'krʌmblɪ/ *adj.* krümelig ‹*Keks, Kuchen*›; bröckelig ‹*Gestein*›

crumpet /'krʌmpɪt/ *n. weiches Hefeküchlein zum Toasten*

crumple /'krʌmpl/ 1 *v.t.* **(a)** (crush) zerdrücken **(b)** (wrinkle) zerknittern 2 *v.i.* knittern

'crumple zone *n.* (Motor Veh.) Knautschzone, *die*

crunch /krʌntʃ/ 1 *v.t.* [geräuschvoll] knabbern ‹*Keks*› 2 *v.i.* ‹*Schnee, Kies:*› knirschen 3 *n.* Knirschen, *das;* **when it comes to the ~:** wenn es hart auf hart geht

'crunchy *adj.* knusprig

crusade /kru:'seɪd/ 1 *n.* (Hist.; also fig.) Kreuzzug, *der* 2 *v.i.* (fig.) zu Felde gehen

cru'sader *n.* (Hist.) Kreuzfahrer, *der*

crush /krʌʃ/ 1 *v.t.* **(a)** quetschen **(b)** (powder) zerstampfen **(c)** (fig.) niederschlagen 2 *n.* **(a)** (crowd) Gedränge, *das* **(b)** (coll.) **have/get a ~ on sb.** in jmdn. verknallt sein/sich in jmdn. verknallen (ugs.)

crush: ~ bar *n.* Bar, *die* (*im Foyer eines Theaters*); **~-barrier** *n.* Absperrgitter, *das*

crushing /'krʌʃɪŋ/ *adj.* niederschmetternd ‹*Antwort*›; vernichtend ‹*Niederlage, Schlag*›

crust /krʌst/ *n.* Kruste, *die*

'crusty *adj.* knusprig

crutch /krʌtʃ/ *n.* Krücke, *die;* **go about on ~es** an Krücken gehen

crux /krʌks/ *n.* **the ~ of the matter** der springende Punkt bei der Sache

cry /kraɪ/ **1** *n.* (of grief) Schrei, *der;* (of words) Schreien, *das;* **a far ~ from …** (fig.) etwas ganz anderes als …
2 *v.i.* **(a)** rufen; (loudly) schreien
(b) (weep) weinen (**over** wegen)
▪ **cry 'off** *v.i.* absagen
▪ **cry 'out** *v.i.* aufschreien
'crying *adj.* **it's a ~ shame** es ist eine wahre Schande
crypt /krɪpt/ *n.* Krypta, *die*
cryptic /'krɪptɪk/ *adj.* geheimnisvoll
crystal /'krɪstl/ **1** *n.* **(a)** Kristall, *der*
(b) (glass) Bleikristall, *das*
2 *adj.* (made of ~ glass) kristallen; Kristalle‹*schale, -vase*›
crystal: ~ clear *adj.* kristallklar; ; (fig.) glasklar; **~ 'glass** *n.* Bleikristall, *das;* Kristallglas, *das*
crystallize /'krɪstəlaɪz/ *v.i.* kristallisieren; (fig.) feste Form annehmen
cub /kʌb/ *n.* **(a)** Junge, *das;* (of wolf, fox, dog) Welpe, *der*
(b) Cub ▶ CUB SCOUT
Cuba /'kju:bə/ *pr. n.* Kuba *(das)*
cubby[hole] /'kʌbɪ(həʊl)/ *n.* Kämmerchen, *das*
cube /kju:b/ *n.* Würfel, *der*
'cube sugar *n.* Würfelzucker, *der*
cubic /'kju:bɪk/ *adj.* **(a)** würfelförmig
(b) Kubik‹*meter usw.*›
cubicle /'kju:bɪkl/ *n.* Kabine, *die*
cubism /'kju:bɪzm/ *n.* (Art) Kubismus, *der*
cubist /'kju:bɪst/ *n.* (Art) Kubist, *der*/ Kubistin, *die*
'Cub Scout *n.* Wölfling, *der*
cuckoo /'kʊku:/ *n.* Kuckuck, *der*
'cuckoo clock *n.* Kuckucksuhr, *die*
cucumber /'kju:kʌmbə(r)/ *n.* [Salat]gurke, *die*
cuddle /'kʌdl/ **1** *n.* enge Umarmung
2 *v.t.* schmusen mit; hätscheln ‹*kleines Kind*›
3 *v.i.* schmusen
cuddly /'kʌdlɪ/ *adj.* zum Schmusen *nachgestellt*
cuddly 'toy *n.* Plüschtier, *das*
cudgel /'kʌdʒl/ *n.* Knüppel, *der*
cue¹ /kju:/ *n.* (Billiards etc.) Queue, *das*
cue² *n.* (Theatre) Stichwort, *das*
cuff¹ /kʌf/ *n.* **(a)** Manschette, *die;* **off the ~** (fig.) aus dem Stegreif
(b) (Amer.: trouser turn-up) [Hosen]aufschlag, *der*
cuff² **1** *v.t.* **~ sb.** jmdm. einen Klaps geben
2 *n.* Klaps, *der*
'cuff link *n.* Manschettenknopf, *der*
cuisine /kwɪ'zi:n/ *n.* Küche, *die*
cul-de-sac /'kʌldəsæk/ *n.* Sackgasse, *die*
culinary /'kʌlɪnərɪ/ *adj.* kulinarisch
culminate /'kʌlmɪneɪt/ *v.i.* gipfeln; **~ in sth.** in etw. (*Dat.*) seinen Höchststand erreichen
culmination /kʌlmɪ'neɪʃn/ *n.* Höhepunkt, *der*
culottes /kju:'lɒts/ *n. pl.* Hosenrock, *der*
culpable /'kʌlpəbl/ *adj.* schuldig ‹*Person*›; strafbar ‹*Handlung*›
culprit /'kʌlprɪt/ *n.* Täter, *der*/Täterin, *die*
cult /kʌlt/ *n.* Kult, *der*
cultivate /'kʌltɪveɪt/ *v.t.* kultivieren (auch fig.); bestellen ‹*Acker, Land*›; anbauen ‹*Pflanzen*›
cultivated /'kʌltɪveɪtɪd/ *adj.* kultiviert ‹*Manieren, Sprache, Geschmack*›; kultiviert, gebildet ‹*Person*›
cultivation /kʌltɪ'veɪʃn/ *n.* ▶ CULTIVATE: Kultivierung, *die;* Bestellen *das;* Anbau, *der*
culture /'kʌltʃə(r)/ *n.* Kultur, *die*
'cultured *adj.* kultiviert
'culture shock *n.* Kulturschock, *der*
cumbersome /'kʌmbəsəm/ *adj.* hinderlich ‹*Kleider*›; sperrig ‹*Pakete*›; schwerfällig ‹*Arbeitsweise*›
cunning /'kʌnɪŋ/ **1** *n.* Schläue, *die*
2 *adj.* schlau
cup /kʌp/ *n.* **(a)** Tasse, *die*
(b) (prize, competition) Pokal, *der*
(c) (~ful) Tasse, *die;* **a ~ of coffee/tea** eine Tasse Kaffee/Tee
cupboard /'kʌbəd/ *n.* Schrank, *der*
'Cup Final *n.* Pokalendspiel, *das*
cupful /'kʌpfl/ *n.* Tasse, *die;* **a ~ of water** eine Tasse Wasser
'cup tie *n.* Pokalspiel, *das*
curable /'kjʊərəbl/ *adj.* heilbar
curate /'kjʊərət/ *n.* Kurat, *der*
curator /kjʊə'reɪtə(r)/ *n.* (of museum) Direktor, *der*/Direktorin, *die*
curb /kɜ:b/ *v.t.* zügeln
'curd cheese *n.* ≈ Quark, *der*
curdle /'kɜ:dl/ *v.i.* gerinnen
cure /kjʊə(r)/ **1** *n.* [Heil]mittel, *das* (**for** gegen); (fig.) Mittel, *das*
2 *v.t.* **(a)** heilen
(b) [ein]pökeln ‹*Fleisch*›
'cure-all *n.* Allheilmittel, *das*
curfew /'kɜ:fju:/ *n.* Ausgangssperre, *die*
curiosity /kjʊərɪ'ɒsɪtɪ/ *n.* **(a)** Neugier[de], *die*
(b) (object) Wunderding, *das*
curious /'kjʊərɪəs/ *adj.* **(a)** (inquisitive) neugierig
(b) (strange, odd) seltsam
curl /kɜ:l/ **1** *n.* Locke, *die*
2 *v.t.* locken
3 *v.i.* **(a)** sich locken
(b) ‹*Straße, Fluss:*› sich winden
'curler *n.* Lockenwickler, *der*
'curly *adj.* lockig

'curly-haired *adj.* lockenköpfig; mit lockigem Haar
currant /'kʌrənt/ *n.* Korinthe, *die*
currency /'kʌrənsɪ/ *n.* (money) Währung, *die;* **foreign currencies** Devisen *Pl.*
current /'kʌrənt/ 1 *adj.* **(a)** verbreitet ‹*Meinung*›; gebräuchlich ‹*Wort*›
(b) laufend ‹*Jahr, Monat*›
(c) (the present) aktuell ‹*Ereignis, Mode*›; Tages‹*politik, -preis*›; **~ affairs** Tagespolitik, *die*
2 *n.* **(a)** (of water, air) Strömung, *die*
(b) (Electr.) Strom, *der*
'current account *n.* Girokonto, *das*
'currently *adv.* zur Zeit
curriculum /kə'rɪkjʊləm/ *n.* Lehrplan, *der*
curriculum vitae /- 'vi:taɪ/ *n.* Lebenslauf, *der*
curry¹ /'kʌrɪ/ *n.* Curry[gericht], *das*
curry² *v.t.* **~ favour [with sb.]** sich [bei jmdm.] einschmeicheln
curse /kɜ:s/ 1 *n.* Fluch, *der*
2 *v.t.* verfluchen
3 *v.i.* fluchen
cursor /'kɜ:sə(r)/ *n.* Läufer, *der;* (on screen) Cursor, *der;* Schreibmarke, *die*
cursory /'kɜ:sərɪ/ *adj.* flüchtig
curt /kɜ:t/ *adj.* kurz angebunden; kurz und schroff ‹*Brief*›
curtail /kɜ:'teɪl/ *v.t.* kürzen; abkürzen ‹*Urlaub*›; beschneiden ‹*Macht*›
curtain /'kɜ:tən/ *n.* Vorhang, *der;* **draw** *or* **pull the ~s** (open) die Vorhänge aufziehen; (close) die Vorhänge zuziehen
curtain: ~ call *n.* Vorhang, *der;* **~ hook** *n.* Gardinenhaken, *der;* **~ rod** *n.* Gardinenstange, *die*
curtsy /'kɜ:tsɪ/ 1 *n.* Knicks, *der*
2 *v.i.* einen Knicks machen (**to** vor + *Dat.*)
curvaceous /kɜ:'veɪʃəs/ *adj.* kurvenreich (ugs.); **a ~ figure** eine üppige Figur
curve /kɜ:v/ 1 *v.t.* krümmen
2 *v.i.* ‹*Straße, Fluss:*› eine Biegung machen
3 *n.* Kurve, *die*
cushion /'kʊʃn/ 1 *n.* Kissen, *das*
2 *v.t.* dämpfen ‹*Aufprall, Stoß*›
cushy /'kʊʃɪ/ *adj.* (coll.) bequem
custard /'kʌstəd/ *n.* ≈ Vanillesoße, *die*
'custard powder *n.* Vanillesoßenpulver, *das*
custodian /kʌs'təʊdɪən/ *n.* (of museum) Wächter, *der*/Wächterin, *die;* (of valuables) Hüter, *der*/Hüterin, *die*
custody /'kʌstədɪ/ *n.* **(a)** (care) Obhut, *die*
(b) (imprisonment) **[be] in ~:** in Haft [sein]; **take sb. into ~:** jmdn. verhaften *od.* festnehmen
custom /'kʌstəm/ *n.* **(a)** Brauch, *der*
(b) *in pl.* (duty on imports) Zoll, *der*
customary /'kʌstəmərɪ/ *adj.* üblich
'custom-built *adj.* spezial[an]gefertigt
customer /'kʌstəmə(r)/ *n.* Kunde, *der*/Kundin, *die*
customize (customise) /'kʌstəmaɪz/ *v.t.* speziell anfertigen; (alter) umbauen
'custom-made *adj.* spezial[an]gefertigt; maßgeschneidert ‹*Kleidung*›
customs: ~ duty *n.* Zoll, *der;* **~ inspection** *n.* Zollkontrolle, *die;* **~ officer** *n.* Zollbeamter, *der*/-beamtin, *die*
cut /kʌt/ 1 *v.t.*, **-tt-, cut (a)** schneiden; durchschneiden ‹*Seil*›; **~ one's leg** sich (*Dat. od. Akk.*) ins Bein schneiden
(b) abschneiden ‹*Scheibe*›; schneiden ‹*Hecke*›; mähen ‹*Getreide, Gras*›; **~ one's nails** sich (*Dat.*) die Nägel schneiden
(c) (reduce) senken ‹*Preise*›; kürzen ‹*Lohn*›; abbauen ‹*Arbeitsplätze*›
(d) ~ sth. short (interrupt) etw. abbrechen
(e) (Comp.) **~ and paste** ausschneiden und einfügen
2 *v.i.*, **-tt-, cut (a)** ‹*Messer:*› schneiden
(b) ~ through *or* **across the field/park** [quer] über das Feld/durch den Park gehen
3 *n.* **(a)** (act of cutting) Schnitt, *der*
(b) (stroke, blow) (with knife) Schnitt, *der;* (with sword, whip) Hieb, *der*
(c) (reduction) Kürzung, *die;* (in prices) Senkung, *die;* (in services) Verringerung, *die*
(d) (of meat) Stück, *das*
■ **cut a'way** *v.t.* abschneiden
■ **cut 'back** *v.t.* **(a)** (reduce) einschränken
(b) (prune) stutzen
■ **cut 'down** 1 *v.t.* **(a)** fällen ‹*Baum*›
(b) (reduce) einschränken
2 *v.i.* **~ down on sth.** etw. einschränken
■ **cut 'off** *v.t.* abschneiden; unterbrechen ‹*Telefongespräch, Sprecher*›
■ **cut 'out** 1 *v.t.* **(a)** ausschneiden (**of** aus)
(b) be ~ out for geeignet sein zu
2 *v.i.* ‹*Motor:*› aussetzen
■ **cut 'up** *v.t.* zerschneiden
cut: ~back *n.* (reduction) Kürzung, *die;* **~ 'glass** *n.* Kristall[glas], *das;* **~-glass** *adj.* Kristall-
cutlery /'kʌtlərɪ/ *n.* Besteck, *das*
cutlet /'kʌtlɪt/ *n.* Kotelett, *das*
cut: ~-off *n.* **~-off point** Trennungslinie, *die;* **~-out** *n.* (figure) Ausschneidefigur, *die;* **~-price** *adj.* herabgesetzt; **~-price offer** Billigangebot, *das*
'cutting 1 *adj.* beißend ‹*Bemerkung, Antwort*›
2 *n.* (from newspaper) Ausschnitt, *der*
'cutting edge *n.* **be at the ~ of technology** auf dem Gebiet der Technologie führend sein; die Speerspitze der Technologie sein; **be at the ~ of fashion** auf dem Gebiet der Mode führend sein
c. v. *abbr.* = **curriculum vitae**
cyber: ~cafe /'saɪbəkæfeɪ/ *n.* Internet-Café *das;* **~sex** /'saɪbəseks/ *n., no art.* Cybersex, *der;* **~space** /'saɪbəspeɪs/ *n., no art.* Cyberspace, *der*

cycle /'saɪkl/ [1] *n.* **(a)** (recurrent period) Zyklus, *der*
(b) (bicycle) Rad, *das*
[2] *v.i.* Rad fahren

cycle: ~ lane *n.* Fahrradspur, *die;* **~ race** *n.* Radrennen, *das;* **~ track** *n.* Rad[fahr]weg, *der;* (for racing) Radrennbahn, *die*

cycling /'saɪklɪŋ/ *n.* (activity) Radfahren, *das;* (sport) Radsport, *der;* **~ shorts** Radlerhose, *die*

cyclist /'saɪklɪst/ *n.* Radfahrer, *der*/-fahrerin, *die*

cyclone /'saɪkləʊn/ *n.* (violent hurricane) Zyklon, *der*

cylinder /'sɪlɪndə(r)/ *n.* Zylinder, *der*

cylindrical /sɪ'lɪndrɪkl/ *adj.* zylindrisch

cymbal /'sɪmbl/ *n.* Beckenteller, *der;* **~s** Becken *Pl.*

cynic /'sɪnɪk/ *n.* Zyniker, *der*

cynical /'sɪnɪkl/ *adj.* zynisch; bissig ‹*Bemerkung, Worte*›

cynicism /'sɪnɪsɪzm/ *n.* Zynismus, *der*

Cyprus /'saɪprəs/ *pr. n.* Zypern (*das*)

czar ▶ TSAR

Czech /tʃek/ [1] *adj.* tschechisch; **sb. is ~:** jmd. ist Tscheche/Tschechin
[2] *n.* **(a)** (language) Tschechisch, *das*
(b) (person) Tscheche, *der*/Tschechin, *die*

Czechoslovakia /tʃekəʊslə'vækɪə/ *pr. n.* (Hist.) die Tschechoslowakei

Czechoslovakian /tʃekəʊslə'vækɪən/ (Hist.) [1] *adj.* tschechoslowakisch
[2] *n.* Tschechoslowake, *der*/Tschechoslowakin, *die*

Czech Re'public *pr. n.* Tschechische Republik; Tschechien (*das*)

Dd

D, d /di:/ *n.* D, d, *das*

dab /dæb/ [1] *n.* Tupfer, *der*
[2] *v.t.*, **-bb-** abtupfen; **~ sth. on** *or* **against sth.** etw. auf etw. (*Akk.*) tupfen

dabble /'dæbl/ *v.i.* **~ in sth.** sich in etw. (*Dat.*) versuchen

dachshund /'dækshʊnd/ *n.* Dackel, *der*

dad /dæd/ *n.* (coll.) Vater, *der*

daddy /'dædɪ/ *n.* (coll.) Vati, *der* (fam.)

daddy-'long-legs *n.* Schnake, *die*

daffodil /'dæfədɪl/ *n.* Osterglocke, *die*

daft /dɑ:ft/ *adj.* doof (ugs.)

dagger /'dægə(r)/ *n.* Dolch, *der*

daily /'deɪlɪ/ [1] *adj.* täglich; **~ [news]paper** Tageszeitung, *die*
[2] *adv.* täglich
[3] *n.* Tageszeitung, *die*

dainty /'deɪntɪ/ *adj.* zierlich; anmutig ‹*Bewegung, Person*›; zart ‹*Gesichtszüge*›

dairy /'deərɪ/ *n.* **(a)** Molkerei, *die*
(b) (shop) Milchladen, *der*

dairy: ~ cattle *n.* Milchvieh, *das;* **~ farm** *n.* Milchbetrieb, *der;* **~ farmer** *n.* Milchbauer, *der;* **~ produce** *n.*, **~ products** *n. pl.* Molkereiprodukte

dais /'deɪɪs/ *n.* Podium, *das*

daisy /'deɪzɪ/ *n.* Gänseblümchen, *das*

'daisy chain *n.* Kranz aus Gänseblümchen

dam /dæm/ [1] *n.* [Stau]damm, *der*
[2] *v.t.*, **-mm-: (a) ~ [up] sth.** etw. abblocken
(b) aufstauen ‹*Fluss*›

damage /'dæmɪdʒ/ [1] *n.* Schaden, *der*
[2] *v.t.* beschädigen

damaging /'dæmɪdʒɪŋ/ *adj.* schädlich **(to** für)

damn /dæm/ [1] *v.t.* verdammen
[2] *adj., adv., int.* (coll.) verdammt (ugs.)
[3] *n.* **he doesn't give** *or* **care a ~:** ihm ist es völlig wurscht (ugs.)

damp /dæmp/ [1] *adj.* feucht
[2] *v.t.* ▶ DAMPEN
[3] *n.* Feuchtigkeit, *die*

dampen /'dæmpn/ *v.t.* befeuchten; (fig.) dämpfen ‹*Begeisterung, Eifer*›

'dampness *n.* Feuchtigkeit, *die*

'damp-proof *adj.* feuchtigkeitsbeständig; **~ course** Sperrschicht, *die* (*gegen aufsteigende Bodenfeuchtigkeit*)

dance /dɑ:ns/ [1] *v.i. & t.* tanzen
[2] *n.* **(a)** Tanz, *der*
(b) (party) Tanzveranstaltung, *die;* (private) Tanzparty, *die*

dance: ~ floor *n.* Tanzfläche, *die;* **~ hall** *n.* Tanzsaal, *der*

'dancer *n.* Tänzer, *der*/Tänzerin, *die*

'dance step *n.* Tanzschritt, *der*

dandelion /'dændɪlaɪən/ *n.* Löwenzahn, *der*

dandruff /'dændrʌf/ *n.* [Kopf]schuppen *Pl.*

Dane /deɪn/ *n.* Däne, *der*/Dänin, *die*

danger /'deɪndʒə(r)/ *n.* Gefahr, *die;* **in/out of ~:** in/außer Gefahr; **be in ~ of doing sth.** ‹*Person:*› Gefahr laufen, etw. zu tun

danger: ~ area *n.* Gefahrenzone, *die;* **~ list** *n.* **be on/off the ~ list** in/außer Lebensgefahr sein
dangerous /ˈdeɪndʒərəs/ *adj.*, **ˈdangerously** *adv.* gefährlich
danger: ~ signal *n.* Warnzeichen, *das;* **~ zone** *n.* Gefahrenzone, *die*
dangle /ˈdæŋgl/ 1 *v.i.* baumeln (**from** an + *Dat.*)
2 *v.t.* baumeln lassen
Danish /ˈdeɪnɪʃ/ 1 *adj.* dänisch; **sb. is ~:** jmd. ist Däne/Dänin
2 *n.* Dänisch, *das; see also* ENGLISH 2A
dank /dæŋk/ *adj.* feucht
Danube /ˈdænjuːb/ *pr. n.* Donau, *die*
dare /deə(r)/ 1 *v.t.* **(a)** [es] wagen; **~ to do sth.** [es] wagen, etw. zu tun
(b) (challenge) **~ sb. to do sth.** jmdn. aufstacheln, etw. zu tun; **I ~ you!** trau dich!
2 *n.* Mutprobe, *die*
daring /ˈdeərɪŋ/ *adj.* (bold) kühn; waghalsig ‹*Kunststück, Tat*›; (fearless) wagemutig
dark /dɑːk/ 1 *adj.* dunkel; (dark-haired) dunkelhaarig; **~-blue/-brown** dunkelblau/ -braun; **~ glasses** dunkle Brille
2 *n.* **(a)** Dunkel, *das;* **in the ~:** im Dunkeln; **keep sb. in the ~** (fig.) jmdn. im Dunkeln lassen
(b) *no art.* (nightfall) Einbruch der Dunkelheit
darken /ˈdɑːkn/ *v.t.* verdunkeln
dark: ~-haired *adj.* dunkelhaarig; **~ ˈhorse** *n.* **be a ~ horse** ein stilles Wasser sein
ˈdarkness *n.* Dunkelheit, *die*
ˈdarkroom *n.* Dunkelkammer, *die*
darling /ˈdɑːlɪŋ/ *n.* Liebling, *der*
darn /dɑːn/ *v.t.* stopfen
dart /dɑːt/ 1 *n.* **(a)** (missile) Pfeil, *der*
(b) (Sport) Wurfpfeil, *der;* **~s** *sing.* (game) Darts, *das*
2 *v.i.* sausen
ˈdartboard *n.* Dartsscheibe, *die*
dash /dæʃ/ 1 *v.i.* sausen
2 *v.t.* (fling) schleudern
3 *n.* **(a) make a ~:** rasen (ugs.) (**for** zu)
(b) (horizontal stroke) Gedankenstrich, *der*
(c) (small amount) Schuss, *der*
ˈdashboard *n.* Armaturenbrett, *das*
data /ˈdeɪtə, ˈdɑːtə/ *n.* Daten *Pl.*
data: ~base *n.* Datenbank, *die;* **~ capture** *n.* (Comp.) Datenerfassung, *die;* **~ file** *n.* (Comp.) Datei, *die;* **~ highway** *n.* (Comp.) Datenautobahn, *die;* **~ proˈtection** *n.* (Comp.) Datenschutz, *der;* **~ retrieval** *n.* (Comp.) Retrieval, *das;* Datenabruf, *der;* **~ security** *n.* (Comp.) Datensicherung, *die;* **~ storage** *n.* (Comp.) Datenspeicherung, *die;* (capacity) Speicherkapazität, *die*
date¹ /deɪt/ *n.* (Bot.) Dattel, *die*
date² 1 *n.* **(a)** Datum, *das;* (on coin etc.) Jahreszahl, *die;* **~ of birth** Geburtsdatum, *das;* **be out of ~:** altmodisch sein; **to ~:** bis heute
(b) (coll.: appointment) Verabredung, *die;* **have/make a ~ with sb.** mit jmdm. verabredet sein/sich mit jmdm. verabreden
2 *v.t.* **(a)** datieren
(b) (coll.: make seem old) alt machen
3 *v.i.* **~ back to/~ from** stammen aus
dated /ˈdeɪtɪd/ *adj.* altmodisch
date: ~ line *n.* Datumsgrenze, *die;* **~ rape** *n.: Vergewaltigung der eigenen Freundin oder Vergewaltigung einer Frau während einer Verabredung mit ihr;* **~ stamp** *n.* Datumsstempel, *der;* **~-stamp** *v.t.* abstempeln; mit einem Datumsstempel versehen
ˈdating agency /ˈdeɪtɪŋ/ *n.* Partnervermittlung, *die*
dative /ˈdeɪtɪv/ *adj. & n.* **~ [case]** Dativ, *der*
daub /dɔːb/ *v.t.* (smear) beschmieren; (put crudely) schmieren
daughter /ˈdɔːtə(r)/ *n.* Tochter, *die*
ˈdaughter-in-law *n., pl.* **daughters-in-law** Schwiegertochter, *die*
daunt /dɔːnt/ *v.t.* entmutigen
dawdle /ˈdɔːdl/ *v.i.* bummeln (ugs.)
dawn /dɔːn/ 1 *v.i.* dämmern; **sth. ~s [up]on sb.** etw. dämmert jmdm
2 *n.* [Morgen]dämmerung, *die;* **at ~:** im Morgengrauen
dawn ˈchorus *n.* morgendlicher Gesang der Vögel
day /deɪ/ *n.* Tag, *der;* **all ~ [long]** den ganzen Tag [lang]; **for two ~s** zwei Tage [lang]; **the ~ before yesterday/after tomorrow** vorgestern/übermorgen; **~ after ~:** Tag für Tag; **~ in ~ out** tagaus, tagein; **in the ~s when ...:** zu der Zeit, als ...; **these ~s** heutzutage; **in those ~s** damals
day: ~bed *n.* Liegesofa, *das;* **~break** *n.* Tagesanbruch, *der;* **~ care** *n.* Ganztagsbetreuung, *die;* **~dream** 1 *n.* Tagtraum, *der;* 2 *v.i.* träumen; **~dreamer** *n.* Tagträumer, *der*/-träumerin, *die;* **~light** *n.* Tageslicht, *das;* **in broad ~light** am helllichten Tag[e]; **~ release** *n.* (Brit.) [tageweise] Freistellung zur Fortbildung; **~ reˈturn** *n.* Tagesrückfahrkarte, *die;* **~time** *n.* Tag, *der;* **~-to-~** *adj.* [tag]täglich; **~ trip** *n.* Tagesausflug, *der;* **~ tripper** *n.* Tagesausflügler, *der*/ -ausflüglerin, *die*
daze /ˈdeɪz/ *v.t.* benommen machen
dazed /ˈdeɪzd/ *adj.* benommen
dazzle /ˈdæzl/ *v.t.* blenden
DC *abbr.* = **direct current** GS
dead /ded/ 1 *adj.* **(a)** tot
(b) plötzlich ‹*Halt*›; genau ‹*Mitte*›
(c) (numb) taub
2 *adv.* völlig; **~ straight** schnurgerade; **~ easy/slow** kinderleicht/ganz langsam; **~ on time** auf die Minute; **~ tired** todmüde
3 *n. pl.* **the ~:** die Toten *Pl.*
deaden /ˈdedn/ *v.t.* dämpfen; betäuben ‹*Schmerz*›

dead: ~ **'end** *n.* Sackgasse, *die;* ~ **'heat** *n.* totes Rennen; **~line** *n.* [letzter] Termin; **~lock** *n.* völliger Stillstand; ~ **'loss** *n.* (coll.) (worthless thing) totaler Reinfall (ugs.); (person) hoffnungsloser Fall (ugs.)

deadly /'dedlɪ/ *adj.* tödlich; (fig. coll.: boring) todlangweilig

dead: **~pan** *adj.* unbewegt; **he looked ~pan** *or* **had a ~pan expression** er verzog keine Miene; **D~ 'Sea** *pr. n.* Totes Meer; ~ **'wood** *n.* (fig.) **be just ~ wood** völlig überflüssig sein

deaf /def/ *adj.* 1 taub; ~ **and dumb** taubstumm
2 *n. pl.* **the ~**: die Gehörlosen *Pl.*

'deaf aid *n.* Hörgerät, *das*

deafen /'defn/ *v.t.* ~ **sb.** bei jmdm. zur Taubheit führen; **I was ~ed by the noise** (fig.) ich war von dem Lärm wie betäubt

'deafening *adj.* ohrenbetäubend

'deafness *n.* Taubheit, *die*

deal[1] /di:l/ 1 *v.t.*, **dealt** /delt/ **(a)** (Cards) austeilen
(b) ~ **sb. a blow** jmdm. einen Schlag versetzen
2 *v.i.*, **dealt (a)** (do business) ~ **in sth.** mit etw. handeln
(b) ~ **with sth.** (occupy oneself) sich mit etw. befassen; (manage) mit etw. fertig werden; (be about) von etw. handeln; ~ **with sb.** mit jmdm. fertig werden
3 *n.* (coll.: arrangement) Geschäft, *das;* **it's a ~!** abgemacht!; **big ~!** (iron.) na, und?

■ **deal 'out** *v.t.* verteilen

deal[2] *n.* **a great** *or* **good ~**: viel; (often) ziemlich viel; **a great** *or* **good ~ of** viel

'dealer *n.* **(a)** Händler, *der*
(b) (Cards) Geber, *der;* **he's the ~**: er gibt

'dealings *n. pl.* **have ~ with sb.** mit jmdm. zu tun haben

dealt ▶ DEAL[1] 1, 2

dean /di:n/ *n.* (Eccl.) Dechant, *der*

dear /dɪə(r)/ 1 *adj.* **(a)** lieb; **sb./sth. is ~ to sb.['s heart]** jmd. liebt jmdn./etw.; (beginning letter) **D~ Sir/Madam** Sehr geehrter Herr/Sehr geehrte Dame; **D~ Mr Jones/Mrs Jones** Sehr geehrter Herr Jones/Sehr geehrte Frau Jones; **D~ Malcolm/Emily** Lieber Malcolm/Liebe Emily
(b) (expensive) teuer
2 *int.* ~, **~!**, ~ **me!**, **oh ~!** [ach] du liebe *od.* meine Güte!

'dearly *adv.* **(a)** von ganzem Herzen
(b) (at high price) teuer

dearth /dɜ:θ/ *n.* Mangel, *der* (**of** an + *Dat.*)

death /deθ/ *n.* **(a)** Tod, *der;* **... to ~**: zu Tode ...; **bleed to ~**: verbluten
(b) (instance) Todesfall, *der*

death: **~bed** *n.* Totenbett, *das;* **on one's ~bed** auf dem Sterbebett; ~ **certificate** *n.* (from doctor) Totenschein, *der*

deathly /'deθlɪ/ 1 *adj.* tödlich
2 *adv.* tödlich; ~ **still/quiet** totenstill

death: ~ **penalty** *n.* Todesstrafe, *die;* ~ **sentence** *n.* Todesurteil, *das;* ~ **trap** *n.* lebensgefährliche Sache; ~ **threat** *n.* Morddrohung, *die*

debatable /dɪ'beɪtəbl/ *adj.* (questionable) fraglich

debate /dɪ'beɪt/ *n.* Debatte, *die*

debilitating /dɪ'bɪlɪteɪtɪŋ/ *adj.* anstrengend ‹*Klima*›; schwächend ‹*Krankheit*›

debit /'debɪt/ 1 *n.* Soll, *das*
2 *v.t.* belasten ‹*Konto*›

debris /'debri:/ *n.* Trümmer *Pl.*

debt /det/ *n.* Schuld, *die;* **be in ~**: Schulden haben; **get into ~**: in Schulden geraten

debtor /'detə(r)/ *n.* Schuldner, *der*/Schuldnerin, *die*

debug /di:'bʌg/ *v.t.*, **-gg-** (coll.: remove defects from) von Fehlern befreien

début (*Amer.*: **debut**) /'deɪbu:, 'deɪbju:/ *n.* Debüt, *das*

Dec. *abbr.* = **December** Dez.

decade /'dekeɪd/ *n.* Jahrzehnt, *das*

decadent /'dekədənt/ *adj.* dekadent

decaf, decaff /'di:kæf/ *n.* (coll.) *or* ® koffeinfreier Kaffee

decaffeinated /di:'kæfɪneɪtɪd/ *adj.* entkoffeiniert

decanter /dɪ'kæntə(r)/ *n.* Karaffe, *die*

decay /dɪ'keɪ/ 1 *v.i.* verrotten; ‹*Gebäude:*› zerfallen; ‹*Zahn:*› faul werden
2 *n.* Verrotten, *das;* (of building) Zerfall, *der;* (of tooth) Fäule, *die*

deceased /dɪ'si:st/ 1 *adj.* verstorben
2 *n.* Verstorbene, *der/die*

deceit /dɪ'si:t/ *n.* Täuschung, *die*

deceitful /dɪ'si:tfl/ *adj.* falsch ‹*Person, Art*›; hinterlistig ‹*Trick*›

deceive /dɪ'si:v/ *v.t.* täuschen; (be unfaithful to) betrügen

December /dɪ'sembə(r)/ *n.* Dezember, *der; see also* AUGUST

decency /'di:sənsɪ/ *n.* Anstand, *der*

decent /'di:sənt/ *adj.* anständig

decentralization /di:sentrəlaɪ'zeɪʃn/ *n.* Dezentralisierung, *die*

decentralize /di:'sentrəlaɪz/ *v.t.* dezentralisieren

deception /dɪ'sepʃn/ *n.* Betrug, *der;* (being deceived) Täuschung, *die*

deceptive /dɪ'septɪv/ *adj.* trügerisch

decibel /'desɪbel/ *n.* Dezibel, *das*

decide /dɪ'saɪd/ 1 *v.t.* **(a)** (settle, judge) entscheiden über (+ *Akk.*)
(b) (resolve) ~ **that ...**: beschließen, dass ...; ~ **to do sth.** sich entschließen, etw. zu tun
2 *v.i.* sich entscheiden (**in favour of** zugunsten von, **against** gegen)

de'cided *adj.*, **de'cidedly** *adv.* entschieden

deciduous /dɪ'sɪdjʊəs/ *adj.* ~ **tree** ≈ Laubbaum, *der*

decimal /'desɪml/ [1] *n.* Dezimalbruch, *der* [2] *adj.* Dezimal-
decimal: ~ 'currency *n.* Dezimalwährung, *die;* **~ 'fraction** *n.* Dezimalbruch, *der;* **~ 'point** *n.* Komma, *das*
decimate /'desɪmeɪt/ *v.t.* dezimieren
decipher /dɪ'saɪfə(r)/ *v.t.* entziffern
decision /dɪ'sɪʒn/ *n.* Entscheidung, *die*
decisive /dɪ'saɪsɪv/ *adj.* entscheidend
deck /dek/ *n.* **(a)** Deck, *das;* **on ~:** an Deck; **below ~[s]** unter Deck
(b) (Amer.: pack) **a ~ of cards** ein Spiel Karten
'deckchair *n.* Liegestuhl, *der*
declaration /deklə'reɪʃn/ *n.* Erklärung, *die*
declare /dɪ'kleə(r)/ *v.t.* erklären; kundtun (geh.) ‹*Wunsch, Absicht*›; **~ sth./sb. [to be] sth.** etw./jmdn. für etw. erklären
declension /dɪ'klenʃn/ *n.* Deklination, *die*
decline /dɪ'klaɪn/ [1] *v.i.* nachlassen; ‹*Anzahl:*› sinken
[2] *v.t.* **(a)** ablehnen
(b) (Ling.) deklinieren
[3] *n.* ▶ 1: Nachlassen, *das*/Sinken, *das* **(in** *Gen.*); **be on the ~:** nachlassen/sinken
decode /di:'kəʊd/ *v.t.* entziffern
decommission /di:kə'mɪʃən/ *v.t.* stilllegen; außer Dienst stellen ‹*Schiff*›
decompose /di:kəm'pəʊz/ *v.i.* sich zersetzen
décor /'deɪkɔ:(r)/ *n.* Ausstattung, *die*
decorate /'dekəreɪt/ *v.t.* **(a)** schmücken ‹*Raum, Straße, Baum*›; verzieren ‹*Kuchen, Kleid*›; (paint) streichen; (wallpaper) tapezieren
(b) (award medal etc. to) auszeichnen
decoration /dekə'reɪʃn/ *n.* **(a)** Schmücken, *das;* (with paint) Streichen, *das;* (with wallpaper) Tapezieren, *das;* (of cake, dress) Verzieren, *das*
(b) (adornment) Schmuck, *der*
(c) (medal etc.) Auszeichnung, *die*
decorative /'dekərətɪv/ *adj.* dekorativ
decorator /'dekəreɪtə(r)/ *n.* Maler, *der;* (paperhanger) Tapezierer, *der*
decorous /'dekərəs/ *adj.*, **'decorously** *adv.* schicklich (geh.)
decorum /dɪ'kɔ:rəm/ *n.* Schicklichkeit, *die* (geh.)
decoy /'dɪ:kɔɪ/ *n.* Lockvogel, *der*
decrease [1] /dɪ'kri:s/ *v.i.* abnehmen; ‹*Stärke:*› nachlassen
[2] /dɪ'kri:s/ *v.t.* [ver]mindern ‹*Wert, Lärm*›; schmälern ‹*Popularität, Macht*›
[3] /'di:kri:s/ *n.* Rückgang, *der;* (in weight) Abnahme, *die;* (in strength) Nachlassen, *das;* (in value, noise) Minderung, *die*
decree /dɪ'kri:/ [1] *n.* Dekret, *das;* Erlass, *der*
[2] *v.t.* verfügen
decrepit /dɪ'krepɪt/ *adj.* altersschwach; (dilapidated) heruntergekommen
decriminalize /di:'krɪmɪnəlaɪz/ *v.t.* entkriminalisieren
dedicate /'dedɪkeɪt/ *v.t.* **~ sth. to sb.** jmdm. etw. widmen
'dedicated *adj.* **(a)** (devoted) **be ~ to sth./sb.** nur für etw./jmdn. leben
(b) (to vocation) hingebungsvoll; **a ~ teacher** ein Lehrer mit Leib und Seele
dedication /dedɪ'keɪʃn/ *n.* **(a)** Widmung, *die* **(to** *Dat.*)
(b) (devotion) Hingabe, *die*
deduce /dɪ'dju:s/ *v.t.* **~ sth. [from sth.]** etw. [aus etw.] schließen
deduct /dɪ'dʌkt/ *v.t.* **~ sth. [from sth.]** etw. [von etw.] abziehen
deduction /dɪ'dʌkʃn/ *n.* **(a)** (deducting) Abzug, *der*
(b) (deducing, thing deduced) Ableitung, *die*
(c) (amount) Abzüge *Pl.*
deed /di:d/ *n.* **(a)** Tat, *die*
(b) (Law) Urkunde, *die*
deejay /di:'dʒeɪ/ *n.* (coll.) Diskjockey, *der*
deem /di:m/ *v.t.* erachten für
deep /di:p/ [1] *adj.* (lit. or fig.) tief; tiefgründig ‹*Bemerkung*›; **water ten feet ~:** drei Meter tiefes Wasser; **take a ~ breath** tief Atem holen; **be ~ in thought** in Gedanken versunken sein
[2] *adv.* tief
'deepen [1] *v.t.* vertiefen
[2] *v.i.* sich vertiefen
deep: ~-'freeze *v.t.* tiefgefrieren; **~-fried** *adj.* frittiert
'deeply *adv.* (lit. or fig.) tief; äußerst ‹*interessiert, dankbar*›
deep-'rooted *adj.* tief ‹*Abneigung*›; tief verwurzelt ‹*Tradition*›
deer /dɪə(r)/ *n., pl. same* Hirsch, *der;* (roe ~) Reh, *das*
de-escalate /di:'eskəleɪt/ *v.t.* deeskalieren
deface /dɪ'feɪs/ *v.t.* verunstalten
defamation /defə'meɪʃn/ *n.* Diffamierung, *die*
defamatory /dɪ'fæmətərɪ/ *adj.* diffamierend
default /dɪ'fɔ:lt, dɪ'fɒlt/ [1] *n.* **(a) lose/go by ~:** durch Abwesenheit verlieren/nicht zur Geltung kommen; **win by ~:** durch Nichterscheinen des Gegners gewinnen
(b) (Comp.) Voreinstellung, *die*
[2] *v.i.* **~ on one's payments/debts** seinen Zahlungsverpflichtungen nicht nachkommen
defeat /dɪ'fi:t/ [1] *v.t.* besiegen
[2] *n.* (being ~ed) Niederlage, *die;* (~ing) Sieg, *der* **(of** über + *Akk.*)
de'featist *adj.* defätistisch
defect [1] /'di:fekt/ *n.* **(a)** (lack) Mangel, *der*
(b) (shortcoming) Fehler, *der*
[2] /dɪ'fekt/ *v.i.* überlaufen **(to** zu)
defection /dɪ'fekʃn/ *n.* Flucht, *die*

defective /dɪˈfektɪv/ *adj.* defekt ‹*Maschine*›; fehlerhaft ‹*Material, Arbeiten, Methode*›
defector /dɪˈfektə(r)/ *n.* Überläufer, *der*/-läuferin, *die*
defence /dɪˈfens/ *n.* (Brit.) Verteidigung, *die;* (means of ~) Schutz, *der*
deˈfenceless *adj.* wehrlos
deˈfence mechanism *n.* (Physiol., Psych.) Abwehrmechanismus, *der*
defend /dɪˈfend/ *v.t.* verteidigen
defendant /dɪˈfendənt/ *n.* (Law) (accused) Angeklagte, *der/die;* (sued) Beklagte, *der/die*
deˈfender *n.* Verteidiger, *der*
defense *etc.* (*Amer.*) ▶ DEFENCE *etc.*
defensive /dɪˈfensɪv/ [1] *adj.* defensiv
[2] *n.* **be on the ~:** in der Defensive sein
defer¹ /dɪˈfɜː(r)/ *v.t.*, **-rr-** aufschieben
defer² *v.i.*, **-rr-: ~ [to sb.]** sich [jmdm.] beugen
deference /ˈdefərəns/ *n.* Respekt, *der;* **in ~ to sb./sth.** aus Achtung vor jmdm./etw.
deferential /defəˈrenʃl/ *adj.* respektvoll
defiance /dɪˈfaɪəns/ *n.* Trotz, *der;* **in ~ of sb./sth.** jmdm./einer Sache zum Trotz
defiant /dɪˈfaɪənt/ *adj.*, **deˈfiantly** *adv.* trotzig
deficiency /dɪˈfɪʃənsɪ/ *n.* Mangel, *der*
deficient /dɪˈfɪʃənt/ *adj.* unzulänglich; **sb./sth. is ~ in sth.** jmdm./einer Sache mangelt es an etw. (*Dat.*)
deficit /ˈdefɪsɪt/ *n.* Defizit, *das* (**of** an + *Dat.*)
defile /dɪˈfaɪl/ *v.t.* verpesten ‹*Luft*›; beflecken ‹*Reinheit, Unschuld*›
define /dɪˈfaɪn/ *v.t.* definieren
definite /ˈdefɪnɪt/ *adj.* bestimmt; eindeutig ‹*Antwort, Entscheidung, Beschluss, Verbesserung*›; klar umrissen ‹*Ziel, Plan*›; klar ‹*Vorstellung*›; genau ‹*Zeitpunkt*›
ˈdefinitely [1] *adv.* bestimmt; eindeutig ‹*festlegen, größer sein, verbessert*›; endgültig ‹*entscheiden*›
[2] *int.* (coll.) na, klar (ugs.)
definition /defɪˈnɪʃn/ *n.* Definition, *die;* (Telev., Phot.) Schärfe, *die*
definitive /dɪˈfɪnɪtɪv/ *adj.* endgültig ‹*Beschluss, Antwort, Urteil*›; (authoritative) maßgeblich
deflate /dɪˈfleɪt/ *v.t.* die Luft ablassen aus; (fig.) ernüchtern
deflation /dɪˈfleɪʃn/ *n.* (Econ.) Deflation, *die*
deflect /dɪˈflekt/ *v.t.* brechen ‹*Licht*›; **~ sb./sth. [from sb./sth.]** jmdn./etw. [von jmdm./einer Sache] ablenken
deforestation /diːfɒrɪˈsteɪʃn/ *n.* Entwaldung, *die;* Abholzung, *die*
deform /dɪˈfɔːm/ *v.t.* deformieren
deformed /dɪˈfɔːmd/ *adj.* entstellt ‹*Gesicht*›; verunstaltet ‹*Person, Körperteil*›
deformity /dɪˈfɔːmɪtɪ/ *n.* (malformation) Verunstaltung, *die*
defraud /dɪˈfrɔːd/ *v.t.* **~ sb. [of sth.]** jmdn. [um etw.] betrügen
defray /dɪˈfreɪ/ *v.t.* bestreiten
defrost /diːˈfrɒst/ *v.t.* auftauen ‹*Speisen*›; abtauen ‹*Kühlschrank*›
deft /deft/ *adj.*, **ˈdeftly** *adv.* sicher und geschickt
defunct /dɪˈfʌŋkt/ *adj.* defekt ‹*Maschine*›; veraltet ‹*Gesetz*›
defuse /dɪˈfjuːz/ *v.t.* entschärfen
defy /dɪˈfaɪ/ *v.t.* **(a)** (resist openly) **~ sb.** jmdm. trotzen
(b) (refuse to obey) **~ sb./sth.** sich jmdm./einer Sache widersetzen
degenerate /dɪˈdʒenəreɪt/ *v.i.* **~ [into sth.]** [zu etw.] verkommen
degradation /degrəˈdeɪʃn/ *n.* Erniedrigung, *die*
degrade /dɪˈgreɪd/ *v.t.* erniedrigen
degrading /dɪˈgreɪdɪŋ/ *adj.* entwürdigend; erniedrigend
degree /dɪˈgriː/ *n.* **(a)** Grad, *der;* **20 ~s** 20 Grad
(b) (academic rank) [akademischer] Grad
deˈgree course *n.* Studium, *das*
dehydrate /diːˈhaɪdreɪt/ *v.t.* austrocknen ‹*Körper*›; **~d** dehydratisiert (fachspr.)
dehydration /diːhaɪˈdreɪʃn/ *n.* Dehydration, *die* (fachspr.); Austrocknung, *die*
de-ice /diːˈaɪs/ *v.t.* enteisen
deign /deɪn/ *v.t.* **~ to do sth.** sich [dazu] herablassen, etw. zu tun
deity /ˈdiːɪtɪ/ *n.* Gottheit, *die*
dejected /dɪˈdʒektɪd/ *adj.* niedergeschlagen
dejection /dɪˈdʒekʃn/ *n.* Niedergeschlagenheit, *die*
delay /dɪˈleɪ/ [1] *v.t.* (make late) aufhalten; verzögern ‹*Ankunft, Abfahrt*›; **the train has been ~ed** der Zug hat Verspätung
[2] *v.i.* warten
[3] *n.* **(a)** Verzögerung, *die* (**to** bei)
(b) (Transport) Verspätung, *die*
delectable /dɪˈlektəbl/ *adj.* köstlich
delegate [1] /ˈdelɪgət/ *n.* Delegierte, *der/die*
[2] /ˈdelɪgeɪt/ *v.t.* delegieren (**to** an + *Akk.*)
delegation /delɪˈgeɪʃn/ *n.* Delegation, *die*
delete /dɪˈliːt/ *v.t.* streichen (**from** in + *Dat.*); (Comp.) löschen
deˈlete key *n.* (Comp.) Löschtaste, *die*
deletion /dɪˈliːʃn/ *n.* Streichung, *die;* (Comp.) Löschung, *die*
deli /ˈdelɪ/ (coll.) ▶ DELICATESSEN
deliberate /dɪˈlɪbərət/ *adj.* **(a)** (intentional) absichtlich; bewusst ‹*Lüge, Irreführung*›
(b) (fully considered) wohl überlegt
deˈliberately *adv.* absichtlich
deliberation /dɪlɪbəˈreɪʃn/ *n.* Überlegung, *die;* (discussion) Beratung, *die*
delicacy /ˈdelɪkəsɪ/ *n.* **(a)** (tactfulness and care) Feingefühl, *das*

(b) (food) Delikatesse, *die*
delicate /'delɪkət/ *adj.* zart; (requiring careful handling) empfindlich; delikat ‹*Frage, Angelegenheit*›
delicatessen /delɪkə'tesən/ *n.* Feinkostgeschäft, *das*
delicious /dɪ'lɪʃəs/ *adj.* köstlich
delight /dɪ'laɪt/ **1** *v.t.* erfreuen
2 *v.i.* **sb. ~s in doing sth.** es macht jmdm. Freude, etw. zu tun
3 *n.* Freude, *die* (**at** über + *Akk.*; **in** an + *Dat.*)
de'lighted *adj.* **be ~** ‹*Person:*› hocherfreut sein; **be ~ by** *or* **with sth.** sich über etw. (*Akk.*) freuen
delightful /dɪ'laɪtfl/ *adj.* wunderbar; köstlich ‹*Geschmack*›; reizend ‹*Person, Landschaft*›
de'lightfully *adv.* wunderbar
delinquent /dɪ'lɪŋkwənt/ **1** *n.* Randalierer, *der*
2 *adj.* kriminell
delirious /dɪ'lɪrɪəs/ *adj.* **be ~**: im Delirium sein; **be ~ [with sth.]** (fig.) außer sich [vor etw. (*Dat.*)] sein
delirium /dɪ'lɪrɪəm/ *n.* Delirium, *das*
deliver /dɪ'lɪvə(r)/ *v.t.* **(a)** bringen; liefern ‹*Ware*›; zustellen ‹*Post, Telegramm*›; überbringen ‹*Botschaft*›
(b) halten ‹*Rede*›
delivery /dɪ'lɪvərɪ/ *n.* Lieferung, *die;* (of letters, parcels) Zustellung, *die*
delivery: ~ date *n.* Liefertermin, *der;* **~ note** *n.* Lieferschein, *der;* **~ service** *n.* Zustelldienst, *der;* **~ van** *n.* Lieferwagen, *der*
delta /'deltə/ *n.* Delta, *das*
delude /dɪ'lju:d/ *v.t.* täuschen
deluge /'delju:dʒ/ **1** *n.* sintflutartiger Regen
2 *v.t.* überschwemmen
delusion /dɪ'lju:ʒn/ *n.* Illusion, *die*
de luxe /də'lʌks/ *adj.* Luxus-
demand /dɪ'mɑ:nd/ **1** *n.* Forderung, *die* (**for** nach); (for commodity) Nachfrage, *die;* **sth./sb. is in ~**: etw. ist gefragt/jmd. ist begehrt
2 *v.t.* verlangen (**of, from** von); fordern ‹*Recht*›
de'manding *adj.* anspruchsvoll
demean /dɪ'mi:n/ *v. refl.* (lower one's dignity) **~ oneself [to do sth.]** sich [dazu] erniedrigen[, etw. zu tun]; **~ oneself by sth./doing sth.** sich durch etw. erniedrigen/sich dadurch erniedrigen, dass man etw. tut
demeaning /dɪ'mi:nɪŋ/ *adj.* erniedrigend
demeanour (*Brit.; Amer.:* **demeanor**) /dɪ'mi:nə(r)/ *n.* Benehmen, *das*
demented /dɪ'mentɪd/ *adj.* wahnsinnig
dementia /dɪ'menʃə/ *n.* (Med.) Demenz, *die*
demerara /demə'reərə/ *n.* **~ [sugar]** brauner Zucker; Farin, *der*
demise /dɪ'maɪz/ *n.* (death) Ableben, *das* (geh.); (of firm, party, etc.) Untergang, *der*
demo /'deməʊ/ *n., pl.* **~s** (coll.) Demo, *die* (ugs.)
de'mobilize *v.t.* demobilisieren ‹*Armee*›; aus dem Kriegsdienst entlassen ‹*Soldat*›
democracy /dɪ'mɒkrəsɪ/ *n.* Demokratie, *die*
Democrat /'deməkræt/ *n.* (Amer. Polit.) Demokrat, *der*/Demokratin, *die*
democratic /demə'krætɪk/ *adj.*, **democratically** /demə'krætɪkəlɪ/ *adv.* demokratisch
demolish /dɪ'mɒlɪʃ/ *v.t.* abreißen
demolition /demə'lɪʃn/ *n.* Abriss, *der;* **~ work** Abbrucharbeit, *die*
demon /'di:mən/ *n.* Dämon, *der*
demonstrably /'demənstrəblɪ, dɪ'mɒnstrəblɪ/ *adv.* nachweislich
demonstrate /'demənstreɪt/ **1** *v.t.* zeigen; (be proof of) zeigen; beweisen
2 *v.i.* demonstrieren
demonstration /demən'streɪʃn/ *n.* (also Pol. etc.) Demonstration, *die;* (proof) Beweis, *der*
demonstrative /də'mɒnstrətɪv/ *adj.* **(a)** offen ‹*Person*›
(b) (Ling.) Demonstrativ-
demonstrator /'demənstreɪtə(r)/ *n.* (Pol. etc.) Demonstrant, *der*/Demonstrantin, *die*
demoralize /dɪ'mɒrəlaɪz/ *v.t.* demoralisieren
demote /di:'məʊt/ *v.t.* degradieren (**to** zu)
demotion /di:'məʊʃn/ *n.* Degradierung, *die* (**to** zu)
demur /dɪ'mɜ:(r)/ *v.i.*, **-rr-** Einwände erheben
demure /dɪ'mjʊə(r)/ *adj.* betont zurückhaltend
den /den/ *n.* Höhle, *die*
denial /dɪ'naɪəl/ *n.* (refusal) Verweigerung, *die;* (of request) Ablehnung, *die;* **be in ~**: die Augen vor der Wahrheit schließen
denier /'denjə(r)/ *n.* Denier, *das*; **20 ~ stockings** 20-den-Strümpfe
denim /'denɪm/ *n.* Denim (Wz), *der;* Jeansstoff, *der;* **~ jacket** Jeansjacke, *die;* **~s** Bluejeans *Pl.*
Denmark /'denmɑ:k/ *pr. n.* Dänemark (*das*)
denomination /dɪnɒmɪ'neɪʃn/ *n.* (Relig.) Konfession, *die*
denote /dɪ'nəʊt/ *v.t.* bezeichnen
dénouement, denouement /deɪ'nu:mɑ̃/ *n.* Ausgang, *der*
denounce /dɪ'naʊns/ *v.t.* denunzieren; (accuse publicly) beschuldigen
dense /dens/ *adj.* **(a)** dicht; massiv ‹*Körper*›
(b) (stupid) dumm
'densely *adv.* dicht; **~ packed** dicht gedrängt
density /'densɪtɪ/ *n.* Dichte, *die*
dent /dent/ **1** *n.* Beule, *die*

2 *v.t.* einbeulen

dental /'dentl/ *adj.* Zahn-; ~ **care** Zahnpflege, *die;* ~ **treatment** zahnärztliche Behandlung

dental: ~ **floss** /'dentl flɒs/ *n.* Zahnseide, *die;* ~ **practitioner,** ~ **surgeon** *ns.* Zahnarzt, *der*/-ärztin, *die*

dentist /'dentɪst/ *n.* Zahnarzt, *der*/-ärztin, *die*

dentistry /'dentɪstrɪ/ *n.* Zahnheilkunde, *die*

denture /'dentʃə(r)/ *n.* ~**[s]** Zahnprothese, *die*

denunciation /dɪnʌnsɪ'eɪʃn/ *n.* Denunziation, *die;* (public accusation) Beschuldigung, *die*

deny /dɪ'naɪ/ *v.t.* (declare untrue) bestreiten; (refuse) ~ **sb. sth.** jmdm. etw. verweigern; ~ **sb.'s request** jmdm. seine Bitte abschlagen

deodorant /di:'əʊdərənt/ **1** *adj.* deodorierend

2 *n.* Deodorant, *das*

depart /dɪ'pɑ:t/ *v.i.* **(a)** (go away) weggehen

(b) (set out, leave) abfahren; (on one's journey) abreisen

(c) (fig.: deviate) abweichen (**from** von)

department /dɪ'pɑ:tmənt/ *n.* Abteilung, *die;* (government ~) Ministerium, *das;* (of university) Seminar, *das*

de'partment store *n.* Kaufhaus, *das*

departure /dɪ'pɑ:tʃə(r)/ *n.* **(a)** Abreise, *die;* (of train, bus, ship) Abfahrt, *die;* (of aircraft) Abflug, *der*

(b) (deviation) ~ **from sth.** Abweichen von etw.

departure: ~ **gate** *n.* Flugsteig, *der;* ~ **lounge** *n.* Abflughalle, *die;* ~ **time** *n.* (of train, bus) Abfahrtzeit, *die;* (of aircraft) Abflugzeit, *die*

depend /dɪ'pend/ *v.i.* **(a)** ~ **[up]on** abhängen von; **it/that** ~**s** es kommt drauf an

(b) (rely, trust) ~ **[up]on** sich verlassen auf (+ *Akk.*); (have to rely on) angewiesen sein auf (+ *Akk.*)

dependable /dɪ'pendəbl/ *adj.* zuverlässig

dependant /dɪ'pendənt/ *n.* Abhängige, *der/die*

dependence /dɪ'pendəns/ *n.* Abhängigkeit, *die*

dependent /dɪ'pendənt/ **1** *n.* ▶ DEPENDANT

2 *adj.* abhängig

depict /dɪ'pɪkt/ *v.t.* darstellen

deplete /dɪ'pli:t/ *v.t.* erheblich verringern

deplorable /dɪ'plɔ:rəbl/ *adj.* beklagenswert

deplore /dɪ'plɔ:(r)/ *v.t.* **(a)** (disapprove of) verurteilen

(b) (regret) beklagen

deploy /dɪ'plɔɪ/ *v.t.* einsetzen

deport /dɪ'pɔ:t/ *v.t.* ausweisen

deportation /di:pɔ:'teɪʃn/ *n.* Ausweisung, *die*

depose /dɪ'pəʊz/ *v.t.* absetzen

deposit /dɪ'pɒzɪt/ **1** *n.* **(a)** (in bank) Depot, *das;* (credit) Guthaben, *das;* (Brit.: at interest) Sparguthaben, *das*

(b) (first instalment) Anzahlung, *die;* **put down a** ~ **on sth.** eine Anzahlung für etw. leisten

(c) (on bottle) Pfand, *das*

2 *v.t.* **(a)** (lay down) ablegen; abstellen ‹*etw. Senkrechtes*›

(b) (in bank) deponieren

de'posit account *n.* (Brit.) Sparkonto, *das*

depot /'depəʊ/ *n.* Depot, *das*

depraved /dɪ'preɪvd/ *adj.* verdorben

depravity /dɪ'prævɪtɪ/ *n.* Verdorbenheit, *die*

depreciate /dɪ'pri:ʃɪeɪt/ *v.i.* an Wert verlieren

depreciation /dɪpri:ʃɪ'eɪʃn/ *n.* Wertverlust, *der*

depress /dɪ'pres/ *v.t.* **(a)** (deject) deprimieren

(b) (push down) herunterdrücken

depressed /dɪ'prest/ *adj.* deprimiert

de'pressing *adj.*, **de'pressingly** *adv.* deprimierend

depression /dɪ'preʃn/ *n.* **(a)** Depression, *die*

(b) (sunk place) Vertiefung, *die*

(c) (Meteorol.) Tief[druckgebiet], *das*

(d) (Econ.) Wirtschaftskrise, *die*

deprivation /deprɪ'veɪʃn/ *n.* Entbehrung, *die*

deprive /dɪ'praɪv/ *v.t.* ~ **sb. of sth.** jmdm. etw. nehmen; (prevent from having) jmdm. etw. vorenthalten

deprived /dɪ'praɪvd/ *adj.* benachteiligt ‹*Kind, Familie usw.*›

depth /depθ/ *n.* Tiefe, *die;* **in** ~: gründlich; **in the** ~**s of winter** im tiefsten Winter

'depth charge *n.* Wasserbombe, *die*

deputation /depjʊ'teɪʃn/ *n.* Abordnung, *die*

deputize /'depjʊtaɪz/ *v.i.* ~ **for sb.** jmdn. vertreten

deputy /'depjʊtɪ/ *n.* [Stell]vertreter, *der*/-vertreterin, *die; attrib.* stellvertretend

derail /dɪ'reɪl/ *v.t.* **be** ~**ed** entgleisen

de'railment *n.* Entgleisung, *die*

deranged /dɪ'reɪndʒd/ *adj.* **[mentally]** ~: geistesgestört

deregulate /di:'regjʊleɪt/ *v.t.* deregulieren (fachspr.); dem freien Wettbewerb überlassen

deregulation /di:regjʊ'leɪʃn/ *n.* Deregulation, *die* (fachspr.); Deregulierung, *die* (fachspr.)

derelict /'derɪlɪkt/ **1** *adj.* verlassen und verfallen

2 *n.* Ausgestoßene, *der/die*

deride /dɪ'raɪd/ *v.t.* sich lustig machen über (+ *Akk.*)
derision /dɪ'rɪʒn/ *n.* Spott, *der*
derisive /dɪ'raɪsɪv/ *adj.* (ironical) spöttisch; (scoffing) verächtlich
derisory /dɪ'raɪzərɪ/ *adj.* (ridiculously inadequate) lächerlich
derivation /derɪ'veɪʃn/ *n.* Ableitung, *die*
derivative /dɪ'rɪvətɪv/ [1] *adj.* abgeleitet; (lacking originality) nachahmend
[2] *n.* Ableitung, *die*
derive /dɪ'raɪv/ [1] *v.t.* **~ sth. from sth.** etw. aus etw. gewinnen; **~ pleasure from sth.** Freude an etw. (*Dat.*) haben
[2] *v.i.* **~ from** beruhen auf (+ *Dat.*)
derogatory /dɪ'rɒgətərɪ/ *adj.* abfällig
derrick /'derɪk/ *n.* [Derrick]kran, *der*
derv /dɜ:v/ *n.* Diesel[kraftstoff], *der*
descale /di:'skeɪl/ *v.t.* entkalken
descend /dɪ'send/ [1] *v.i.* **(a)** (go down) hinuntergehen/-steigen/-klettern/-fahren; (come down) herunterkommen; ‹*Fallschirm, Flugzeug:*› niedergehen
(b) (slope downwards) abfallen
(c) ~ on sb. jmdn. überfallen
[2] *v.t.* (go/come down) hinunter-/heruntergehen/-steigen/-klettern/-fahren
descendant /dɪ'sendənt/ *n.* Nachkomme, *der*
de'scended *adj.* **be ~ from sb.** von jmdm. abstammen
descent /dɪ'sent/ *n.* **(a)** Abstieg, *der;* (of parachute, plane) Niedergehen, *das*
(b) (lineage) Herkunft, *die;* **be of Russian ~:** russischer Abstammung sein
describe /dɪ'skraɪb/ *v.t.* beschreiben
description /dɪ'skrɪpʃn/ *n.* **(a)** Beschreibung, *die*
(b) (sort, class) Art, *die*
descriptive /dɪ'skrɪptɪv/ *adj.* beschreibend; (vivid) anschaulich; **a purely ~ report** ein reiner Tatsachenbericht
desecrate /'desɪkreɪt/ *v.t.* entweihen
desert[1] /'dezət/ *n.* Wüste, *die*
desert[2] /dɪ'zɜ:t/ [1] *v.t.* verlassen
[2] *v.i.* ‹*Soldat:*› desertieren
de'serted *adj.* verlassen
de'serter *n.* Deserteur, *der*
desertion /dɪ'zɜ:ʃn/ *n.* Desertion, *die*
desert 'island /dezət 'aɪlənd/ *n.* einsame Insel
deserts /dɪ'zɜ:ts/ *n. pl.* **get one's [just] ~:** das bekommen, was man verdient hat
deserve /dɪ'zɜ:v/ *v.t.* verdienen
deserving /dɪ'zɜ:vɪŋ/ *adj.* verdienstvoll; **a ~ cause** ein guter Zweck
design /dɪ'zaɪn/ [1] *n.* Entwurf, *der;* (pattern) Muster, *das;* (established form of machine, engine, etc.) Bauweise, *die;* (general idea, construction) Konstruktion, *die*
[2] *v.t.* entwerfen; **be ~ed to do sth.** etw. tun sollen
designate /'dezɪgneɪt/ *v.t.* **(a)** bezeichnen
(b) (appoint) designieren (geh.)
designation /dezɪg'neɪʃn/ *n.* Bezeichnung, *die*
'designer *n.* Designer, *der*/Designerin, *die;* (of machines) Konstrukteur, *der*/Konstrukteurin, *die; attrib.* Modell‹*-kleidung, -jeans*›
desirability /dɪzaɪərə'bɪlɪtɪ/ *n.* Wunschbarkeit, *die*
desirable /dɪ'zaɪərəbl/ *adj.* wünschenswert
desire /dɪ'zaɪə(r)/ [1] *n.* Wunsch, *der* (**for** nach); (longing) Sehnsucht, *die* (**for** nach)
[2] *v.t.* sich (*Dat.*) wünschen; (long for) sich sehnen nach
desist /dɪ'zɪst/ *v.i.* (literary) einhalten (geh.); **~ from sth.** von etw. ablassen (geh.)
desk /desk/ *n.* **(a)** Schreibtisch, *der;* (in school) Tisch, *der*
(b) (cash ~) Kasse, *die;* (reception ~) Rezeption, *die*
desk: ~-bound *adj.* an den Schreibtisch gefesselt (fig.); **~ calendar, ~ diary** *ns.* Tischkalender, *der;* **~ editor** *n.* Manuskriptbearbeiter, *der*/-bearbeiterin, *die;* Lektor, *der*/Lektorin, *die;* **~ lamp** *n.* Schreibtischlampe, *die;* **~top** *adj.* **~top publishing** Desktoppublishing, *das;* **~top computer** Tischcomputer, *der*
desolate /'desələt/ *adj.* trostlos
desolation /desə'leɪʃn/ *n.* Trostlosigkeit, *die*
despair /dɪ'speə(r)/ [1] *n.* Verzweiflung, *die;* **be the ~ of sb.** jmdn. zur Verzweiflung bringen
[2] *v.i.* verzweifeln
desperate /'despərət/ *adj.* verzweifelt; extrem ‹*Maßnahmen*›; **be ~ for sth.** etw. dringend brauchen
desperation /despə'reɪʃn/ *n.* Verzweiflung, *die*
despicable /dɪ'spɪkəbl/ *adj.* verabscheuungswürdig
despise /dɪ'spaɪz/ *v.t.* verachten
despite /dɪ'spaɪt/ *prep.* trotz
despondent /dɪ'spɒndənt/ *adj.* bedrückt
despot /'despɒt/ *n.* Despot, *der*
dessert /dɪ'zɜ:t/ *n.* Nachtisch, *der*
dessert: ~spoon *n.* Esslöffel, *der;* **~spoonful** *n.* Esslöffel, *der;* **~ wine** *n.* Dessertwein, *der*
destabilize /di'steɪbɪlaɪz/ *v.t.* (Polit.) destabilisieren
destination /destɪ'neɪʃn/ *n.* Reiseziel, *das;* (of goods) Bestimmungsort, *der;* (of train, bus) Zielort, *der*
destine /'destɪn/ *v.t.* bestimmen; **be ~d to do sth.** dazu bestimmt sein, etw. zu tun
destiny /'destɪnɪ/ *n.* Schicksal, *das*
destitute /'destɪtju:t/ *adj.* mittellos
destroy /dɪ'strɔɪ/ *v.t.* zerstören
de'stroyer *n.* (also Naut.) Zerstörer, *der*

destruction /dɪ'strʌkʃn/ *n.* Zerstörung, *die*

destructive /dɪ'strʌktɪv/ *adj.* zerstörerisch; verheerend ‹*Sturm, Feuer*›

desultory /'desəltərɪ/ *adj.* sprunghaft; zwanglos, ungezwungen ‹*Gespräch*›

detach /dɪ'tætʃ/ *v.t.* entfernen; abnehmen ‹*wieder zu Befestigendes*›; herausnehmen ‹*innen Befindliches*›

detachable /dɪ'tætʃəbl/ *adj.* abnehmbar

detached /dɪ'tætʃt/ *adj.* **(a)** (impartial) unvoreingenommen; (unemotional) unbeteiligt **(b)** **a ~ house** ein Einzelhaus

de'tachment *n.* **(a)** ▶ DETACH: Entfernen, *das;* Abnehmen, *das;* Herausnehmen, *das* **(b)** (Mil.) Abteilung, *die*

detail /'di:teɪl/ [1] *n.* Einzelheit, *die;* Detail, *das;* **in ~:** Punkt für Punkt; **go into ~[s]** ins Detail gehen
[2] *v.t.* **(a)** einzeln ausführen
(b) (Mil.) abkommandieren

detailed /'di:teɪld/ *adj.* detailliert; eingehend ‹*Studie*›

detain /dɪ'teɪn/ *v.t.* **(a)** festhalten; (take into confinement) verhaften
(b) (delay) aufhalten

detainee /di:teɪ'ni:/ *n.* Verhaftete, *der/die*

detect /dɪ'tekt/ *v.t.* entdecken; wahrnehmen ‹*Bewegung*›; aufdecken ‹*Irrtum, Verbrechen*›

detection /dɪ'tekʃn/ *n.* Entdeckung, *die;* (of error, crime) Aufdeckung, *die*

detective /dɪ'tektɪv/ *n.* Detektiv, *der;* **private ~:** Privatdetektiv, *der;* **~ work** Ermittlungsarbeit, *die;* **~ story** Detektivgeschichte, *die*

detector /dɪ'tektə(r)/ *n.* Detektor, *der*

detention /dɪ'tenʃn/ *n.* **(a)** Festnahme, *die;* (confinement) Haft, *die*
(b) (Sch.) Nachsitzen, *das*

de'tention centre *n.* (Brit.) Jugendstrafanstalt, *die*

deter /dɪ'tɜ:(r)/ *v.t.*, **-rr-** abschrecken

detergent /dɪ'tɜ:dʒənt/ *n.* Waschmittel, *das*

deteriorate /dɪ'tɪərɪəreɪt/ *v.i.* sich verschlechtern; ‹*Haus:*› verfallen

deterioration /dɪtɪərɪə'reɪʃn/ *n.* ▶ DETERIORATE: Verschlechterung, *die;* Verfall, *der*

determination /dɪtɜ:mɪ'neɪʃn/ *n.* Entschlossenheit, *die*

determine /dɪ'tɜ:mɪn/ *v.t.* **(a)** (decide) beschließen
(b) (be a decisive factor for) bestimmen
(c) (ascertain) feststellen

determined /dɪ'tɜ:mɪnd/ *adj.* **(a)** **be ~ to do sth.** etw. unbedingt tun wollen
(b) (resolute) entschlossen

deterrent /dɪ'terənt/ *n.* Abschreckungsmittel, *das* (**to** für)

detest /dɪ'test/ *v.t.* verabscheuen

detestable /dɪ'testəbl/ *adj.* verabscheuenswert

detonate /'detəneɪt/ [1] *v.t.* zünden
[2] *v.i.* detonieren

detonation /detə'neɪʃn/ *n.* Detonation, *die*

detonator /'detəneɪtə(r)/ *n.* Sprengkapsel, *die*

detour /'di:tʊə(r)/ *n.* Umweg, *der;* (diversion) Umleitung, *die*

detoxify /di:'tɒksɪfaɪ/ *v.t.* entgiften; unschädlich machen ‹*Gift usw.*›

detract /dɪ'trækt/ *v.i.* **~ from sth.** etw. beeinträchtigen

detriment /'detrɪmənt/ *n.* **to the ~ of sth.** zum Nachteil einer Sache (*Gen.*)

detrimental /detrɪ'mentl/ *adj.* schädlich; **be ~ to sth.** einer Sache (*Dat.*) schaden

deuce /dju:s/ *n.* (Tennis) Einstand, *der*

devaluation /di:vælju:'eɪʃn/ *n.* Abwertung, *die*

devalue /di:'vælju:/ *v.t.* abwerten

devastate /'devəsteɪt/ *v.t.* verwüsten; (fig.) niederschmettern

devastating /'devəsteɪtɪŋ/ *adj.* verheerend; (fig.) niederschmetternd

devastation /devə'steɪʃn/ *n.* Verwüstung, *die*

develop /dɪ'veləp/ [1] *v.t.* entwickeln; erschließen ‹*natürliche Ressourcen*›; bekommen ‹*Krankheit, Fieber, Lust*›; **~ a taste for sth.** Geschmack an etw. (*Akk.*) finden
[2] *v.i.* sich entwickeln (**from** aus; **into** zu)

de'veloper *n.* **(a)** (Photog.) Entwickler, *der* **(b)** (of land) Bauunternehmer, *der*

developing: ~ country *n.* Entwicklungsland, *das;* **~ world** *n.* Entwicklungsländer *Pl.*

de'velopment *n.* Entwicklung, *die* (**from** aus; **into** zu); (of natural resources etc.) Erschließung, *die*

de'velopment area *n.* (Brit.) Entwicklungsgebiet, *das*

deviant /'di:vɪənt/ *adj.* abweichend

deviate /'di:vɪeɪt/ *v.i.* abweichen

deviation /di:vɪ'eɪʃn/ *n.* Abweichung, *die*

device /dɪ'vaɪs/ *n.* Gerät, *das;* (as part of sth.) Vorrichtung, *die;* **leave sb. to his own ~s** jmdn. sich (*Dat.*) selbst überlassen

devil /'devl/ *n.* Teufel, *der;* **the D~:** der Teufel

'devilish *adj.* teuflisch

devious /'di:vɪəs/ *adj.* **(a)** (winding) verschlungen; **~ route** Umweg, *der*
(b) (unscrupulous, insincere) hinterhältig

devise /dɪ'vaɪz/ *v.t.* entwerfen; schmieden ‹*Pläne*›

devoid /dɪ'vɔɪd/ *adj.* **~ of sth.** (lacking) ohne etw.; (free from) frei von etw.

devolution /di:və'lu:ʃn/ *n.* (Polit.) Dezentralisierung, *die*

devote /dɪ'vəʊt/ *v.t.* widmen (**to** *Dat.*)

d

de'voted *adj.* treu; aufrichtig ‹*Freundschaft, Liebe, Verehrung*›; **be ~ to sb.** jmdn. innig lieben

devotion /dɪ'vəʊʃn/ *n.* **~ to sb./sth.** Hingabe an jmdn./etw.

devour /dɪ'vaʊə(r)/ *v.t.* verschlingen

devout /dɪ'vaʊt/ *adj.* fromm

dew /dju:/ *n.* Tau, *der*

'dewdrop *n.* Tautropfen, *der*

dexterity /dek'sterɪtɪ/ *n.* Geschicklichkeit, *die*

dextrous /'dekstrəs/ *adj.* geschickt

diabetes /daɪə'bi:ti:z/ *n.* Zuckerkrankheit, *die*

diabetic /daɪə'betɪk/ [1] *adj.* zuckerkrank ‹*Person*›
[2] *n.* Diabetiker, *der*/Diabetikerin, *die*

diabolical /daɪə'bɒlɪkl/ *adj.* teuflisch

diagnose /daɪəg'nəʊz/ *v.t.* diagnostizieren; feststellen ‹*Fehler*›

diagnosis /daɪəg'nəʊsɪs/ *n., pl.* **diagnoses** /daɪəg'nəʊsi:z/ Diagnose, *die;* **make a ~:** eine Diagnose stellen

diagonal /daɪ'ægənl/ [1] *adj.* diagonal
[2] *n.* Diagonale, *die*

di'agonally *adv.* diagonal

diagram /'daɪəgræm/ *n.* Diagramm, *das*

dial /'daɪəl/ [1] *n.* (of clock or watch) Zifferblatt, *das;* (of gauge, meter, etc.) Skala, *die;* (Teleph.) Wählscheibe, *die*
[2] *v.t. & i.,* (Brit.) **-ll-** (Teleph.) wählen; **~ direct** selbst wählen; (dial extension) durchwählen

dialect /'daɪəlekt/ *n.* Dialekt, *der*

dialling, (Amer.) **dialing: ~ code** *n.* Vorwahl, *die;* **~ tone** Wählton, *der*

dialogue /'daɪəlɒg/ *n.* Dialog, *der*

'dialogue box *n.* (Comp.) Dialogbox, *die;* Dialogfenster, *das*

'dial tone *n.* (Amer.) Wählton, *der*

dialysis /daɪ'ælɪsɪs/ *n.* [Hämo]dialyse, *die* (fachspr.); Blutwäsche, *die;* **~ machine** Dialyseapparat, *der*

diameter /daɪ'æmɪtə(r)/ *n.* Durchmesser, *der*

diametrical /daɪə'metrɪkl/ *adj.,* **dia'metrically** *adv.* diametral

diamond /'daɪəmənd/ *n.* **(a)** Diamant, *der*
(b) (figure) Raute, *die*
(c) (Cards) Karo, *das; see also* CLUB 1C

diaper /'daɪəpə(r)/ *n.* (Amer.) Windel, *die*

diaphragm /'daɪəfræm/ *n.* Diaphragma, *das* (Fachspr.); (*Anat. also*) Zwerchfell, *das;* (*Photog. also*) Blende, *die*

diarrhoea (*Amer.:* **diarrhea**) /daɪə'ri:ə/ *n.* Durchfall, *der*

diary /'daɪərɪ/ *n.* **(a)** Tagebuch, *das*
(b) (for appointments) Terminkalender, *der*

dice /daɪs/ [1] *n.* Würfel, *der*
[2] *v.t.* (Cooking) würfeln

dicey /'daɪsɪ/ *adj.* (coll.) riskant

Dictaphone ® /'dɪktəfəʊn/ *n.* Diktaphon, *das* (fachspr.); Diktiergerät, *das*

dictate /dɪk'teɪt/ *v.t. & i.* diktieren; (prescribe) vorschreiben; **~ to** Vorschriften machen (+ *Dat.*)

dic'tating machine *n.* Diktiergerät, *das*

dictation /dɪk'teɪʃn/ *n.* Diktat, *das*

dictator /dɪk'teɪtə(r)/ *n.* Diktator, *der*

dictatorial /dɪktə'tɔ:rɪəl/ *adj.* diktatorisch

dic'tatorship *n.* Diktatur, *die*

dictionary /'dɪkʃənərɪ/ *n.* Wörterbuch, *das*

did ▶ DO

diddle /'dɪdl/ *v.t.* (coll.) übers Ohr hauen (ugs.)

didn't /'dɪdnt/ (coll.) = **did not;** ▶ DO

die /daɪ/ *v.i.,* **dying** /'daɪɪŋ/ sterben **(of, from** an + *Dat.*); ‹*Tier, Pflanze:*› eingehen; **be dying to do sth.** darauf brennen, etw. zu tun; **be dying for sth.** etw. unbedingt brauchen

■ **die 'down** *v.i.* ‹*Sturm, Wind, Protest:*› sich legen; ‹*Flammen:*› kleiner werden; ‹*Feuer:*› herunterbrennen; ‹*Lärm:*› leiser werden

■ **die 'out** *v.i.* aussterben

'diehard *n.* Ewiggestrige, *der/die*

diesel /'di:zl/ *n.* **~ [engine]** Diesel[motor], *der;* **~ [fuel]** Diesel[kraftstoff], *der*

diet /'daɪət/ [1] *n.* Diät, *die;* **be/go on a ~:** eine Schlankheitskur machen
[2] *v.i.* eine Schlankheitskur machen

'diet sheet *n.* Diätplan, *der*

differ /'dɪfə(r)/ *v.i.* (be different) sich unterscheiden

difference /'dɪfərəns/ *n.* **(a)** Unterschied, *der;* **make no ~ [to sb.]** [jmdm.] nichts ausmachen; **it makes a ~:** es ist ein *od.* (ugs.) macht einen Unterschied
(b) (disagreement) Meinungsverschiedenheit, *die*

different /'dɪfərənt/ *adj.* verschieden; (*pred. also*) anders; (*attrib. also*) ander...; **be ~ from** *or* (esp. Brit.) **to** *or* (Amer.) **than ...:** anders sein als ...

differentiate /dɪfə'renʃɪeɪt/ *v.t. & i.* unterscheiden (**between** zwischen + *Dat.*)

'differently *adv.* anders (**from,** *esp. Brit.* **to** als)

difficult /'dɪfɪkəlt/ *adj.* schwierig

'difficulty *n.* Schwierigkeit, *die;* **with [great] ~:** [sehr] mühsam; **get into difficulties** in Schwierigkeiten kommen

diffident /'dɪfɪdənt/ *adj.* zaghaft; (modest) zurückhaltend

diffuse [1] /dɪ'fju:z/ *v.t.* verbreiten
[2] *v.i.* sich ausbreiten (**through** in + *Dat.*)
[3] /dɪ'fju:s/ *adj.* diffus

dig /dɪg/ [1] *v.i.,* **-gg-, dug** /dʌg/ graben (**for** nach)
[2] *v.t.,* **-gg-, dug** graben; umgraben ‹*Erde, Garten*›

■ **dig 'out** *v.t.* ausgraben

■ **dig 'up** *v.t.* ausgraben; umgraben ‹*Garten*›; aufreißen ‹*Straße*›

digest /dɪ'dʒest, daɪ'dʒest/ *v.t.* verdauen

digestion /dɪ'dʒestʃn, daɪ'dʒestʃn/ *n.* Verdauung, *die*

'digger *n.* Bagger, *der*

digit /'dɪdʒɪt/ *n.* Ziffer, *die*

digital /'dɪdʒɪtl/ *adj.* Digital-; ~ **audio tape** Digitaltonband, *das;* ~ **camera** Digitalkamera, *die;* ~ **television** Digitalfernsehen, *das;* ~ **video disc** DVD, *die;* Digital Video Disc, *die*

dignified /'dɪgnɪfaɪd/ *adj.* würdig; (stately) würdevoll

dignify /'dɪgnɪfaɪ/ *v.t.* Würde verleihen (+ *Dat.*)

dignitary /'dɪgnɪtərɪ/ *n.* Würdenträger, *der*; **dignitaries** (prominent people) Honoratioren *Pl.*

dignity /'dɪgnɪtɪ/ *n.* Würde, *die*

digress /daɪ'gres/ *v.i.* abschweifen

digression /daɪ'greʃn/ *n.* Abschweifung, *die*

dike /daɪk/ *n.* Deich, *der*

dilapidated /dɪ'læpɪdeɪtɪd/ *adj.* verfallen ‹*Gebäude*›; verwahrlost ‹*Erscheinung*›

dilate /daɪ'leɪt/ [1] *v.i.* sich weiten [2] *v.t.* ausdehnen

dilemma /dɪ'lemə, daɪ'lemə/ *n.* Dilemma, *das*

diligence /'dɪlɪdʒəns/ *n.* Fleiß, *der*

diligent /'dɪlɪdʒənt/ *adj.*, **'diligently** *adv.* fleißig

dilute [1] /daɪ'lju:t, 'daɪlju:t/ *adj.* verdünnt [2] /daɪ'lju:t/ *v.t.* verdünnen

dim /dɪm/ [1] *adj.* **(a)** schwach ‹*Licht, Flackern*›; dunkel ‹*Zimmer*›; verschwommen ‹*Gestalt*›
(b) (vague) verschwommen
(c) (coll.: stupid) beschränkt
[2] *v.i.* schwächer werden

dime /daɪm/ *n.* (Amer. coll.) Zehncentstück, *das*

dimension /dɪ'menʃn, daɪ'menʃn/ *n.* Dimension, *die;* ~**s** (measurements) Abmessungen; Maße

diminish /dɪ'mɪnɪʃ/ [1] *v.i.* nachlassen; ‹*Vorräte, Einfluss:*› abnehmen; ‹*Wert, Ansehen:*› geringer werden
[2] *v.t.* verringern; schmälern ‹*Ansehen, Ruf*›

dimple /'dɪmpl/ *n.* Grübchen, *das*

dim: ~wit *n.* (coll.) Dummkopf, *der* (ugs.); **~-witted** /'dɪmwɪtɪd/ *adj.* (coll.) dusselig (salopp)

din /dɪn/ *n.* Lärm, *der*

dine /daɪn/ *v.i.* [zu Mittag/zu Abend] essen

'diner *n.* Gast, *der*

dinghy /'dɪŋgɪ, 'dɪŋɪ/ *n.* Ding[h]i, *das;* (inflatable) Schlauchboot, *das*

dingy /'dɪndʒɪ/ *adj.* schmuddelig

dining /'daɪnɪŋ/**:** ~ **area** *n.* ≈ Essecke, *die;* ~ **car** *n.* Speisewagen, *der;* ~ **room** *n.* Esszimmer, *das;* (in hotel etc.) Speisesaal, *der;* ~ **table** *n.* Esstisch, *der*

dinner /'dɪnə(r)/ *n.* (at midday) Mittagessen, *das;* (in the evening) Abendessen, *das;* (formal) Diner, *das*

dinner: ~ **jacket** *n.* (Brit.) Dinnerjacket, *das;* ~ **party** *n.* Abendeinladung, *das* (*mit Essen*); (more formal) Abendgesellschaft, *die;* ~ **plate** *n.* flacher Teller; Essteller, *der;* ~ **table** *n.* Esstisch, *der;* ~ **time** *n.* Essenszeit, *die;* **at** ~ **time** zur Essenszeit; (12-2 p.m.) mittags

dinosaur /'daɪnəsɔ:(r)/ *n.* Dinosaurier, *der*

dint /dɪnt/ *n.* **by** ~ **of** durch; **by** ~ **of doing sth.** indem jmd. etw. tut

dip /dɪp/ [1] *v.t.*, **-pp-: (a)** [ein]tauchen (in in + *Akk.*)
(b) ~ **one's headlights** abblenden
[2] *v.i.* sinken; (incline) abfallen
[3] *n.* **(a)** (in road) Senke, *die*
(b) (bathe) [kurzes] Bad

diphtheria /dɪf'θɪərɪə/ *n.* Diphtherie, *die*

diphthong /'dɪfθɒŋ/ *n.* Diphthong, *der*

diploma /dɪ'pləʊmə/ *n.* Diplom, *das*

diplomacy /dɪ'pləʊməsɪ/ *n.* Diplomatie, *die*

diplomat /'dɪpləmæt/ *n.* Diplomat, *der*/ Diplomatin, *die*

diplomatic /dɪplə'mætɪk/ *adj.*, **diplo'matically** *adv.* diplomatisch

diplo'matic service *n.* diplomatischer Dienst

'dipstick *n.* [Öl-/Benzin]messstab, *der*

dire /'daɪə(r)/ *adj.* furchtbar

direct /dɪ'rekt, daɪ'rekt/ [1] *v.t.* **(a)** (turn) richten (**to[wards]** auf + *Akk.*); ~ **sb. to a place** jmdn. den Weg zu einem Ort weisen
(b) (control) leiten; regeln ‹*Verkehr*›
(c) (order) anweisen
(d) (Theatre, Cinemat., etc.) Regie führen bei
[2] *adj.* direkt; durchgehend ‹*Zug*›; unmittelbar ‹*Ursache, Auswirkung, Erfahrung, Verantwortung*›; genau ‹*Gegenteil*›; direkt ‹*Widerspruch*›; diametral ‹*Gegensatz*›; ~ **speech** direkte Rede
[3] *adv.* direkt

direct: ~ **'current** *n.* (Electr.) Gleichstrom, *der;* ~ **'debit** *n.* (Brit.) Lastschriftverfahren, *das;* ~ **'dialling** *n.* Durchwahl, *die;* **we will soon have** ~ **dialling** wir werden bald ein Durchwahlsystem haben; ~ **'flight** *n.* Direktflug, *der;* ~ **'hit** *n.* Volltreffer, *der*

direction /dɪ'rekʃn, daɪ'rekʃn/ *n.* **(a)** Richtung, *die;* **in the** ~ **of London** in Richtung London
(b) (guidance) Führung, *die;* (Theatre, Cinemat., etc.) Regie, *die;* Spielleitung, *die*
(c) *usu. in pl.* (order) Anordnung, *die;* **~s [for use]** Gebrauchsanweisung, *die*

di'rectly *adv.* **(a)** direkt; unmittelbar ‹*folgen, verantwortlich sein*› ···›

(b) (exactly) genau
(c) (at once) umgehend
(d) (shortly) gleich

di'rect object *n.* direktes Objekt

director /daɪ'rektə(r), dɪ'rektə(r)/ *n.* **(a)** (Commerc.) Direktor, *der*/Direktorin, *die;* **board of ~s** Aufsichtsrat, *der*
(b) (Theatre, Cinemat., etc.) Regisseur, *der*/Regisseurin, *die*

directory /daɪ'rektərɪ, dɪ'rektərɪ/ *n.* (telephone ~) Telefonbuch, *das;* (of tradesmen etc.) Branchenverzeichnis, *das;* (Comp.) Verzeichnis, *das;* **~ enquiries** (Brit.), **~ information** (Amer.) [Fernsprech]auskunft, *die*

dirt /dɜːt/ *n.* Schmutz, *der;* **~ cheap** (coll.) spottbillig

'dirty [1] *adj.* schmutzig; **get sth. ~:** etw. schmutzig machen
[2] *v.t.* schmutzig machen

disa'bility *n.* Behinderung, *die*

disa'bility allowance *n.* Erwerbsunfähigkeitsentschädigung, *die*

disabled /dɪs'eɪbld/ *adj.* behindert

disad'vantage *n.* Nachteil, *der;* **at a ~:** im Nachteil

disad'vantaged *adj.* benachteiligt

disa'gree *v.i.* anderer Meinung sein; **~ with sb./sth.** mit jmdm./etw. nicht übereinstimmen; **~ [with sb.] about** *or* **over sth.** sich [mit jmdm.] über etw. (*Akk.*) nicht einig sein

disa'greeable *adj.* unangenehm

disa'greement *n.* **(a)** (difference of opinion) Uneinigkeit, *die;* **be in ~ with sb./sth.** mit jmdm./etw. nicht übereinstimmen
(b) (quarrel) Meinungsverschiedenheit, *die*
(c) (discrepancy) Diskrepanz, *die*

disal'low *v.t.* verbieten; (Sport) nicht geben ‹*Tor*›

disap'pear *v.i.* verschwinden; ‹*Brauch, Tierart:*› aussterben

disap'pearance *n.* Verschwinden, *das*

disap'point *v.t.* enttäuschen

disap'pointed *adj.* enttäuscht

disap'pointing *adj.* enttäuschend

disap'pointment *n.* Enttäuschung, *die*

disap'proval *n.* Missbilligung, *die*

disap'prove *v.i.* dagegen sein; **~ of sb./sth.** jmdn. ablehnen/etw. missbilligen

dis'arm *v.t.* entwaffnen

disarmament /dɪs'ɑːməmənt/ *n.* Abrüstung, *die*

disarray /dɪsə'reɪ/ *n.* Unordnung, *die;* **in ~:** in Unordnung

disaster /dɪ'zɑːstə(r)/ *n.* Katastrophe, *die;* **~ area** Katastrophengebiet, *das;* **~ fund** Nothilfefonds, *der*

disastrous /dɪ'zɑːstrəs/ *adj.* katastrophal; verhängnisvoll ‹*Irrtum, Entscheidung, Politik*›

dis'band [1] *v.t.* auflösen
[2] *v.i.* sich auflösen

disbe'lief *n.* Unglaube, *der;* **in ~:** ungläubig

disbe'lieve *v.t.* **~ sb./sth.** jmdm./etw. nicht glauben

disc /dɪsk/ *n.* **(a)** Scheibe, *die;* (record) Platte, *die*
(b) (Comp.) ▶ DISK A

discard /dɪs'kɑːd/ *v.t.* wegwerfen; fallenlassen ‹*Vorschlag, Idee*›

'disc brake *n.* Scheibenbremse, *die*

discern /dɪ'sɜːn/ *v.t.* wahrnehmen

discernible /dɪ'sɜːnɪbl/ *adj.* erkennbar

di'scerning *adj.* kritisch

discharge [1] /dɪs'tʃɑːdʒ/ *v.t.* **(a)** entlassen (**from** aus); freisprechen ‹*Angeklagte*›
(b) ablassen ‹*Flüssigkeit, Gas*›
[2] /'dɪstʃɑːdʒ/ *n.* **(a)** Entlassung, *die* (**from** aus); (of defendant) Freispruch, *der*
(b) (emission) Ausfluss, *der*

disciple /dɪ'saɪpl/ *n.* **(a)** (Relig.) Jünger, *der*
(b) (follower) Anhänger, *der*/Anhängerin, *die*

disciplinary /dɪsɪ'plɪnərɪ/ *adj.* disziplinarisch; **~ action** Disziplinarmaßnahmen *Pl.*

discipline /'dɪsɪplɪn/ [1] *n.* Disziplin, *die*
[2] *v.t.* disziplinieren; (punish) bestrafen

disciplined /'dɪsɪplɪnd/ *adj.* diszipliniert

'disc jockey *n.* Diskjockey, *der*

dis'claim *v.t.* abstreiten

dis'claimer *n.* Gegenerklärung, *die;* (Law) Verzichterklärung, *die*

disclose /dɪs'kləʊz/ *v.t.* enthüllen; bekannt geben ‹*Information, Nachricht*›

dis'closure *n.* Enthüllung, *die;* (of information, news) Bekanntgabe, *die*

disco /'dɪskəʊ/ *n., pl.* **~s** (coll.) Disko, *die*

'disco dancing *n.* Diskotanz, *der*

dis'colour (*Brit.; Amer.:* **discolor**) *v.t.* verfärben

dis'comfort *n.* **(a)** *no pl.* (slight pain) Beschwerden *Pl.*
(b) (hardship) Unannehmlichkeit, *die*

'disco music *n.* Diskomusik, *die*

disconcert /dɪskɒn'sɜːt/ *v.t.* irritieren

discon'nect *v.t.* abtrennen; abstellen ‹*Telefon*›

disconsolate /dɪs'kɒnsələt/ *adj.* **(a)** (unhappy) unglücklich
(b) (inconsolable) untröstlich

discon'tent *n.* Unzufriedenheit, *die*

discon'tented *adj.* unzufrieden

discon'tinue *v.t.* einstellen

discord /'dɪskɔːd/ *n.* **(a)** Zwietracht, *die*
(b) (Mus.) Dissonanz, *die*

discordant /dɪs'kɔːdənt/ *adj.* **(a)** (conflicting) gegensätzlich
(b) **a ~ note** ein Misston

discothèque /'dɪskətek/ *n.* Diskothek, *die*

discount [1] /'dɪskaʊnt/ *n.* (Commerc.) Rabatt, *der* (**on** auf + *Akk.*)

2 /dɪ'skaʊnt/ *v.t.* (disbelieve) unberücksichtigt lassen

discourage /dɪ'skʌrɪdʒ/ *v.t.* **(a)** entmutigen
(b) (advise against) abraten

di'scouragement *n.* **(a)** Entmutigung, *die*
(b) (depression) Mutlosigkeit, *die*

discouraging /dɪ'skʌrɪdʒɪŋ/ *adj.* entmutigend

dis'courteous *adj.* unhöflich

dis'courtesy *n.* Unhöflichkeit, *die*

discover /dɪ'skʌvə(r)/ *v.t.* entdecken; (by search) herausfinden

di'scovery *n.* Entdeckung, *die*

dis'credit 1 *n.* Misskredit, *der;* **bring ~ on sb./sth., bring sb./sth. into ~:** jmdn./etw. in Misskredit bringen
2 *v.t.* in Misskredit bringen

discreet /dɪ'skri:t/ *adj.*, **di'screetly** *adv.* diskret

discrepancy /dɪ'skrepənsɪ/ *n.* Diskrepanz, *die*

discrepant /dɪ'skrepənt/ *adj.* [voneinander] abweichend

discretion /dɪ'skreʃn/ *n.* (prudence) Umsicht, *die*

discriminate /dɪ'skrɪmɪneɪt/ *v.i.* **(a)** unterscheiden
(b) ~ against/in favour of sb. jmdn. diskriminieren/bevorzugen

discrimination /dɪskrɪmɪ'neɪʃn/ *n.* **(a)** Unterscheidung, *die*
(b) Diskriminierung, *die* (**against** *Gen.*); **~ in favour of** Bevorzugung (+ *Gen.*)

discus /'dɪskəs/ *n.* Diskus, *der*

discuss /dɪ'skʌs/ *v.t.* besprechen; (debate) diskutieren über (+ *Akk.*)

discussion /dɪ'skʌʃn/ *n.* Gespräch, *das;* (debate) Diskussion, *die*

disdain /dɪs'deɪn/ 1 *n.* Verachtung, *die*
2 *v.t.* verachten; **~ to do sth.** zu stolz sein, etw. zu tun

disdainful /dɪs'deɪnfl/ *adj.* verächtlich

disease /dɪ'zi:z/ *n.* Krankheit, *die*

diseased /dɪ'zi:zd/ *adj.* krank

disem'bark *v.i.* von Bord gehen

disen'chant *v.t.* ernüchtern; **he became ~ed with her/it** sie/es hat ihn desillusioniert

disen'gage *v.t.* lösen (**from** aus, von); **~ the clutch** auskuppeln

disen'tangle *v.t.* entwirren; (extricate) befreien (**from** aus)

dis'figure *v.t.* entstellen

disgrace /dɪs'greɪs/ 1 *n.* Schande, *die* (**to** für)
2 *v.t.* Schande machen (+ *Dat.*); **~ oneself** sich blamieren

di'sgraceful /dɪs'greɪsfl/ *adj.* skandalös; **it's ~:** es ist ein Skandal

disgruntled /dɪs'grʌntld/ *adj.* verstimmt

disguise /dɪs'gaɪz/ 1 *v.t.* verkleiden ‹*Person*›; verstellen ‹*Stimme*›; tarnen ‹*Gegenstand*›
2 *n.* Verkleidung, *die*

disgust /dɪs'gʌst/ 1 *n.* (nausea) Ekel, *der* (**at** vor + *Dat.*); (revulsion) Abscheu, *der* (**at** vor + *Dat.*); (indignation) Empörung, *die* (**at** über + *Akk.*)
2 *v.t.* anwidern; (fill with nausea) ekeln; (fill with indignation) empören

dis'gusted *adj.* angewidert; (nauseated) angeekelt; (indignant) empört

dis'gusting *adj.* widerlich

dish /dɪʃ/ *n.* **(a)** Schale, *die;* (deeper) Schüssel, *die;* **~es** (crockery) Geschirr, *das;* **wash** *or* (coll.) **do the ~es** Geschirr spülen
(b) (type of food) Gericht, *das*

■ **dish 'out** *v.t.* **(a)** austeilen ‹*Essen*›
(b) (coll.: distribute) verteilen

■ **dish 'up** *v.t.* auftragen

'dishcloth *n.* Spültuch, *das*

dis'hearten *v.t.* entmutigen

dishevelled (*Amer.:* **disheveled**) /dɪ'ʃevld/ *adj.* zerzaust ‹*Haar*›; ungepflegt ‹*Erscheinung*›

dis'honest *adj.*, **dis'honestly** *adv.* unehrlich

dis'honesty *n.* Unehrlichkeit, *die*

dis'honour 1 *n.* Unehre, *die*
2 *v.t.* beleidigen

dishonourable /dɪs'ɒnərəbl/ *adj.* unehrenhaft

dish: ~ rack *n.* Abtropfgestell, *das;* (in dishwasher) Geschirrwagen, *der;* **~washer** *n.* Geschirrspülmaschine, *die*

disil'lusion 1 *v.t.* ernüchtern
2 *n.* Desillusion, *die* (**with** über + *Akk.*)

disil'lusionment *n.* Desillusionierung, *die*

disincentive /dɪsɪn'sentɪv/ *n.* Hemmnis, *das;* **act as** *or* **be a ~ to sb. to do sth.** jmdn. davon abhalten, etw. zu tun

disin'fect *v.t.* desinfizieren

disinfectant /dɪsɪn'fektənt/ 1 *adj.* desinfizierend
2 *n.* Desinfektionsmittel, *das*

disinformation /dɪsɪnfə'meɪʃn/ *n.* Desinformation, *die*

disingenuous /dɪsɪn'dʒenjʊəs/ *adj.* unaufrichtig

dis'integrate *v.i.* zerfallen

disinte'gration *n.* Zerfall, *der*

dis'interested *adj.* **(a)** (impartial) unvoreingenommen
(b) (coll.: uninterested) desinteressiert

disjointed /dɪs'dʒɔɪntɪd/ *adj.* unzusammenhängend

disk *n.* **(a)** (Comp.) **[floppy] ~:** Floppydisk, *die;* Diskette, *die;* **[hard] ~** (exchangeable) [harte] Magnetplatte; (fixed) Festplatte, *die*
(b) ▶ DISC A

'disk drive *n.* (Comp.) Diskettenlaufwerk, *das*
diskette /dɪ'sket/ *n.* Diskette, *die*
dis'like 1 *v.t.* nicht mögen; ~ **doing sth.** etw. ungern tun
2 *n.* Abneigung, *die* (**of, for** gegen); **take a ~ to sb./sth.** eine Abneigung gegen jmdn./etw. empfinden
dislocate /'dɪsləkeɪt/ *v.t.* ausrenken; auskugeln ‹*Schulter, Hüfte*›
dis'lodge *v.t.* entfernen (**from** aus)
dis'loyal *adj.* illoyal (**to** gegenüber)
dis'loyalty *n.* Illoyalität, *die* (**to** gegenüber)
dismal /'dɪzməl/ *adj.* trist
dismantle /dɪs'mæntl/ *v.t.* demontieren; abbauen ‹*Schuppen, Gerüst*›
dismay /dɪs'meɪ/ 1 *v.t.* bestürzen
2 *n.* Bestürzung, *die* (**at** über + *Akk.*)
dismiss /dɪs'mɪs/ *v.t.* entlassen; (reject) ablehnen
dismissal /dɪs'mɪsl/ *n.* Entlassung, *die*
dismissive /dɪs'mɪsɪv/ *adj.* abweisend; (disdainful) abschätzig
dis'mount *v.i.* absteigen
diso'bedience *n.* Ungehorsam, *der*
diso'bedient *adj.* ungehorsam
diso'bey *v.t.* nicht gehorchen (+ *Dat.*); nicht befolgen ‹*Befehl*›
dis'order *n.* **(a)** Durcheinander, *das*
(b) (Med.) Störung, *die*
dis'orderly *adj.* (untidy) unordentlich; ~ **conduct** ungebührliches Benehmen
dis'organized *adj.* chaotisch
dis'orientated, dis'oriented *adjs.* desorientiert
dis'own *v.t.* verleugnen
disparage /dɪ'spærɪdʒ/ *v.t.* herabsetzen
disparaging /dɪ'spærɪdʒɪŋ/ *adj.* abschätzig
disparity /dɪ'spærɪtɪ/ *n.* Ungleichheit, *die*
dispatch /dɪ'spætʃ/ 1 *v.t.* **(a)** schicken
(b) (kill) töten
2 *n.* Bericht, *der*
di'spatch note *n.* Versandanzeige, *die*
dispel /dɪ'spel/ *v.t.*, **-ll-** vertreiben; zerstreuen ‹*Besorgnis, Befürchtung*›
dispensable /dɪ'spensəbl/ *adj.* entbehrlich
dispensary /dɪ'spensərɪ/ *n.* Apotheke, *die*
dispense /dɪ'spens/ *v.i.* ~ **with** verzichten auf (+ *Akk.*)
dispensing 'chemist *n.* Apotheker, *der*/Apothekerin, *die*
dispersal /dɪ'spɜ:sl/ *n.* Zerstreuung, *die*
disperse /dɪ'spɜ:s/ 1 *v.t.* zerstreuen
2 *v.i.* sich zerstreuen
dispirited /dɪ'spɪrɪtɪd/ *adj.* entmutigt
dis'place *v.t.* verschieben; (supplant) ersetzen
displaced 'person *n.* Vertriebene, *der*/*die*
display /dɪ'spleɪ/ 1 *v.t.* **(a)** zeigen; ausstellen ‹*Waren*›
(b) (Comp.) anzeigen
2 *n.* **(a)** Ausstellung, *die;* (of goods) Auslage, *die;* (ostentatious show) Zurschaustellung, *die*
(b) (Comp. etc.) Display, *das;* Anzeige, *die*
dis'please *v.t.* ~ **sb.** jmds. Missfallen erregen
dis'pleasure *n.* Missfallen, *das*
disposable /dɪ'spəʊzəbl/ *adj.* Wegwerf-
disposal /dɪ'spəʊzl/ *n.* Beseitigung, *die;* **have sth./sb. at one's ~:** etw./jmdn. zur Verfügung haben; **be at sb.'s ~:** jmdm. zur Verfügung stehen
dispose /dɪ'spəʊz/ *v.t.* ~ **sb. to sth.** jmdn. zu etw. veranlassen; ~ **sb. to do sth.** jmdn. dazu veranlassen, etw. zu tun
■ **di'spose of** *v.t.* beseitigen; (settle) erledigen
disposed /dɪ'spəʊzd/ *adj.* **be ~ to do sth.** dazu neigen, etw. zu tun; **be well ~ towards sb./sth.** jmdm. wohl gesinnt sein/einer Sache (*Dat.*) positiv gegenüberstehen
disposition /dɪspə'zɪʃn/ *n.* Veranlagung, *die;* (nature) Art, *die*
dis'prove *v.t.* widerlegen
disputable /dɪ'spju:təbl, 'dɪspjʊtəbl/ *adj.* strittig
dispute /dɪ'spju:t/ 1 *n.* Streit, *der* (**over** um)
2 *v.t.* **(a)** (discuss) sich streiten über (+ *Akk.*)
(b) (oppose) bestreiten
disqualifi'cation *n.* Ausschluss, *der;* (Sport) Disqualifikation, *die*
dis'qualify *v.t.* ausschließen (**from** von); (Sport) disqualifizieren
disre'gard 1 *v.t.* ignorieren
2 *n.* Missachtung, *die* (**of, for** *Gen.*); (of wishes, feelings) Gleichgültigkeit, *die* (**for, of** gegenüber)
dis'reputable *adj.* verrufen
disrepute /dɪsrɪ'pju:t/ *n.* Verruf, *der;* **bring sb./sth. into ~:** jmdn./etw. in Verruf bringen
disre'spect *n.* Missachtung, *die;* **show ~ for sb./sth.** keine Achtung vor jmdm./etw. haben
disre'spectful *adj.* respektlos
disrupt /dɪs'rʌpt/ *v.t.* stören
disruption /dɪs'rʌpʃn/ *n.* Störung, *die*
disruptive /dɪs'rʌptɪv/ *adj.* störend
dissatis'faction *n.* Unzufriedenheit, *die*
dis'satisfied *adj.* unzufrieden
dissect /dɪ'sekt/ *v.t.* sezieren
disseminate /dɪ'semɪneɪt/ *v.t.* verbreiten
dissent /dɪ'sent/ 1 *v.i.* **(a)** (refuse to assent) nicht zustimmen; ~ **from sth.** mit etw. nicht übereinstimmen
(b) (disagree) ~ **from sth.** von etw. abweichen
2 *n.* Ablehnung, *die;* (from majority) Abweichung, *die*
dissertation /dɪsə'teɪʃn/ *n.* Dissertation, *die*
dis'service *n.* **do sb. a ~:** jmdm. einen schlechten Dienst erweisen

dissident /'dɪsɪdənt/ *n.* Dissident, *der*/ Dissidentin, *die*
dis'similar *adj.* unähnlich (**to** *Dat.*)
dissociate /dɪ'səʊʃɪeɪt/ *v.t.* trennen; **~ oneself** sich distanzieren (**from** von)
dissolve /dɪ'zɒlv/ **1** *v.t.* auflösen **2** *v.i.* sich auflösen
dissuade /dɪ'sweɪd/ *v.t.* abbringen (**from** von)
distance /'dɪstəns/ *n.* **(a)** Entfernung, *die* (**from** zu)
(b) (way to cover) Strecke, *die;* **from a ~:** von weitem; **in/into the ~:** in der/die Ferne
'distance learning *n.* Fernstudium, *das*
distant /'dɪstənt/ *adj.* **(a)** fern; entfernt ‹*Ähnlichkeit, Verwandtschaft, Verwandte*›
(b) (reserved) distanziert
dis'taste *n.* Abneigung, *die* (**for** gegen)
dis'tasteful *adj.* unangenehm
distend /dɪ'stend/ *v.t.* erweitern
distil, (Amer.) **distill** /dɪ'stɪl/ *v.t.* destillieren; brennen ‹*Branntwein*›
distillation /dɪstɪ'leɪʃn/ *n.* Destillation, *die*
distillery /dɪ'stɪlərɪ/ *n.* Brennerei, *die*
distinct /dɪ'stɪŋkt/ *adj.* deutlich; (different) verschieden
distinction /dɪ'stɪŋkʃn/ *n.* Unterschied, *der*
distinctive /dɪ'stɪŋktɪv/ *adj.* unverwechselbar
dis'tinctly *adv.* deutlich
distinguish /dɪ'stɪŋgwɪʃ/ **1** *v.t.* **(a)** (make out) erkennen
(b) (differentiate) unterscheiden
(c) (characterize) kennzeichnen
(d) ~ oneself [by sth.] sich [durch etw.] hervortun
2 *v.i.* unterscheiden; **~ between** auseinander halten
distinguished /dɪ'stɪŋgwɪʃt/ *adj.* angesehen; glänzend ‹*Laufbahn*›; vornehm ‹*Aussehen*›
distort /dɪ'stɔ:t/ *v.t.* verzerren; (fig.) verdrehen
distortion /dɪ'stɔ:ʃn/ *n.* Verzerrung, *die;* (fig.) Verdrehung, *die*
distract /dɪ'strækt/ *v.t.* ablenken; **~ sb.['s attention from sth.]** jmdn. [von etw.] ablenken
di'stracted *adj.* von Sinnen *nachgestellt;* (mentally far away) abwesend
distraction /dɪ'strækʃn/ *n.* **(a)** (diversion) Ablenkung, *die;* (interruption) Störung, *die*
(b) drive sb. to ~: jmdn. zum Wahnsinn treiben
distraught /dɪ'strɔ:t/ *adj.* aufgelöst (**with** vor + *Dat.*); verstört ‹*Blick*›
distress /dɪ'stres/ **1** *n.* **(a)** Kummer, *der* (**at** über + *Akk.*)
(b) (pain) Qualen *Pl.*
(c) an aircraft/ship in ~: ein Flugzeug in Not/ein Schiff in Seenot
2 *v.t.* nahe gehen (+ *Dat.*)
di'stressing *adj.* erschütternd
di'stress signal *n.* Notsignal, *das*
distribute /dɪ'strɪbju:t/ *v.t.* verteilen (**to** an + *Akk.;* **among** unter + *Akk.*); (Commerc.) vertreiben
distribution /dɪstrɪ'bju:ʃn/ *n.* Verteilung, *die;* (Commerc.) Vertrieb, *der*
distributor /dɪ'strɪbjʊtə(r)/ *n.* Verteiler, *der*/Verteilerin, *die;* (Commerc.) Vertreiber, *der*
district /'dɪstrɪkt/ *n.* Gegend, *die;* (Admin.) Bezirk, *der*
district: ~ at'torney *n.* (Amer. Law) [Bezirks]staatsanwalt, *der*/-anwältin, *die;* **~ 'nurse** *n.* (Brit.) Gemeindeschwester, *die*
dis'trust /dɪs'trʌst/ **1** *n.* Misstrauen, *das* (**of** gegen)
2 *v.t.* misstrauen (+ *Dat.*)
dis'trustful *adj.* misstrauisch
disturb /dɪ'stɜ:b/ *v.t.* **(a)** stören; **'do not ~!'** „bitte nicht stören!"
(b) (worry) beunruhigen
disturbance /dɪ'stɜ:bəns/ *n.* Störung, *die;* **political ~s** politische Unruhen
disturbed /dɪ'stɜ:bd/ *adj.* besorgt; **[mentally] ~:** geistig gestört
disturbing /dɪs'tɜ:bɪŋ/ *adj.* bestürzend
disuse /dɪs'ju:s/ *n.* **fall into ~:** außer Gebrauch kommen
disused /dɪs'ju:zd/ *adj.* stillgelegt; leer stehend ‹*Gebäude*›
ditch /dɪtʃ/ **1** *n.* Graben, *der*
2 *v.t.* (coll.) sausen lassen ‹*Plan*›; sitzen lassen ‹*Familie, Freund*›
dither /'dɪðə(r)/ *v.i.* schwanken
ditto /'dɪtəʊ/ *n., pl.* **~s** ebenso; ditto; **~ marks** Unterführungszeichen, *das*
divan /dɪ'væn/ *n.* [Polster]liege, *die*
dive /daɪv/ **1** *v.i.,* **dived** *or* (Amer.) **dove** /dəʊv/ **(a)** einen Kopfsprung machen; (when already in water) tauchen
(b) ‹*Vogel, Flugzeug usw.:*› einen Sturzflug machen
2 *n.* **(a)** Kopfsprung, *der;* (of bird, aircraft, etc.) Sturzflug, *der*
(b) (coll.: place) Spelunke, *die*
'diver *n.* **(a)** (Sport) Kunstspringer, *der*/ -springerin, *die*
(b) (as profession) Taucher, *der*/Taucherin, *die*
diverge /daɪ'vɜ:dʒ/ *v.i.* auseinander gehen
divergent /daɪ'vɜ:dʒənt/ *adj.* auseinander gehend
diverse /daɪ'vɜ:s/ *adj.* verschieden
diversify /daɪ'vɜ:sɪfaɪ, dɪ'vɜ:sɪfaɪ/ *v.i.* ‹*Firma:*› sich auf neue Produktions-/ Produktbereiche umstellen
diversion /daɪ'vɜ:ʃn/ *n.* **(a)** Ablenkung, *die;* **create a ~:** ein Ablenkungsmanöver durchführen
(b) (Brit.: alternative route) Umleitung, *die*
diversity /daɪ'vɜ:sɪtɪ/ *n.* Vielfalt, *die*

divert /daɪ'vɜːt/ *v.t.* umleiten ‹*Verkehr, Fluss*›; ablenken ‹*Aufmerksamkeit*›

divide /dɪ'vaɪd/ [1] *v.t.* **(a)** teilen; **~ sth. in two** etw. [in zwei Teile] zerteilen
(b) (distribute) aufteilen (**among/between** unter + *Akk. od. Dat.*)
(c) (Math.) dividieren (fachspr.), teilen (**by** durch)
[2] *v.i.* sich teilen; **~ [from sth.]** von etw. abzweigen

■ **divide 'out** *v.t.* aufteilen (**among/between** unter + *Akk. od. Dat.*); (distribute) verteilen an (+ *Akk.*)

■ **divide 'up** *v.t.* aufteilen

dividend /'dɪvɪdend/ *n.* Dividende, *die*

dividers /dɪ'vaɪdəz/ *n. pl.* Stechzirkel, *der*

divine /dɪ'vaɪn/ *adj.* göttlich

diving /'daɪvɪŋ/ *n.* Kunstspringen, *das*

diving: ~ board *n.* Sprungbrett, *das;* **~ suit** *n.* Taucheranzug, *der*

divinity /dɪ'vɪnɪtɪ/ *n.* **(a)** Göttlichkeit, *die*
(b) (god) Gottheit, *die*

divisible /dɪ'vɪzɪbl/ *adj.* teilbar (**by** durch)

division /dɪ'vɪʒn/ *n.* **(a)** Teilung, *die*
(b) (Math.) Dividieren, *das;* **do ~**: dividieren; **long ~**: ausführliche Division (*mit Aufschreiben der Zwischenprodukte*); **short ~**: verkürzte Division (*ohne Aufschreiben der Zwischenprodukte*)
(c) (section, part) Abteilung, *die*
(d) (group) Gruppe, *die*
(e) (Mil. etc.) Division, *die*
(f) (Footb. etc.) Liga, *die;* Spielklasse, *die;* (in British football) Division, *die*

divorce /dɪ'vɔːs/ [1] *n.* [Ehe]scheidung, *die*
[2] *v.t.* **~ one's husband/wife** sich von seinem Mann/seiner Frau scheiden lassen

divorcee /dɪvɔː'siː/ *n.* Geschiedene, *der/die;* **be a ~**: geschieden sein

divorced /dɪ'vɔːst/ *adj.* geschieden; **get ~**: sich scheiden lassen

divulge /daɪ'vʌldʒ/ *v.t.* preisgeben

DIY *abbr.* = **do-it-yourself**

dizzy /'dɪzɪ/ *adj.* schwind[e]lig; **I feel ~**: mir ist schwindlig

DJ /diː'dʒeɪ/ *abbr.* = **disc jockey** Diskjockey, *der*

DNA *abbr.* = **deoxyribonucleic acid** DNS

do /də, *stressed* duː/ [1] *v.t., neg.* (coll.) **don't** /dəʊnt/, *pres.t.* **he does** /dʌz/, *neg.* (coll.) **doesn't** /'dʌznt/, *p.t.* **did** /dɪd/, *neg.* (coll.) **didn't** /'dɪdnt/, *pres.p.* **doing** /'duːɪŋ/, *p.p.* **done** /dʌn/ **(a)** machen ‹*Hausaufgaben, Hausarbeit, Examen, Übersetzung, Kopie, Bett, Handstand*›; erfüllen ‹*Pflicht*›; verrichten ‹*Arbeit*›; vorführen ‹*Trick, Nummer, Tanz*›; durchführen ‹*Test*›; schaffen ‹*Pensum*›; (clean) putzen; (arrange) [zurecht]machen ‹*Haare*›; schminken ‹*Lippen, Augen, Gesicht*›; machen (ugs.) ‹*Nägel*›; (cut) schneiden ‹*Nägel*›; (paint) machen (ugs.) ‹*Zimmer*›; streichen ‹*Haus, Möbel*›; (repair) in Ordnung bringen; **do the shopping/washing-up/cleaning** einkaufen [gehen]/abwaschen/sauber machen; **what can I do for you?** (in shop) was darfs sein?; **do sth. about sth./sb.** etw. gegen etw./jmdn. unternehmen
(b) (cook) braten; **well done** durch[gebraten]
(c) (solve) lösen ‹*Problem, Rätsel*›; machen ‹*Puzzle, Kreuzworträtsel*›
(d) (coll.: swindle) reinlegen (ugs.); **do sb. out of sth.** jmdn. um etw. bringen
(e) (satisfy) zusagen (+ *Dat.*)
[2] *v.i., forms as* 1: **(a)** (act) tun; **do as they do** mach es wie sie
(b) (fare) **how are you doing?** wie gehts dir?
(c) (get on) vorankommen; (in exams) abschneiden; **do well/badly at school** gut/schlecht in der Schule sein
(d) how do you do? (formal) guten Tag/Morgen/Abend!
(e) (serve purpose) es tun; (suffice) [aus]reichen; (be suitable) gehen; **that won't do** das geht nicht; **that will do!** jetzt aber genug!
[3] *v. substitute, forms as* 1: **you mustn't act as he does** du darfst nicht so wie er handeln; **You went to Paris, didn't you? – Yes, I did** Du warst doch in Paris, nicht wahr? – Ja[, stimmt]; **come in, do!** komm doch herein!
[4] *v. aux. forms as* 1: **I do love Greece** Griechenland gefällt mir wirklich gut; **little did he know that ...**: er hatte keine Ahnung, dass ...; **do you know him?** kennst du ihn?; **what does he want?** was will er?; **I don't** *or* **do not wish to take part** ich möchte nicht teilnehmen; **don't be so noisy!** seid [doch] nicht so laut!
[5] *n.* /duː/, *pl.* **do's** *or* **dos** /duːz/ (Brit. coll.) Feier, *die;* Fete, *die* (ugs.)

■ **do a'way with** *v.t.* abschaffen

■ **'do for** *v.t.* (coll.) **do for sb.** jmdn. fertig machen (ugs.); **be done for** erledigt sein

■ **do 'in** *v.t.* (sl.) kaltmachen (salopp)

■ **do 'up** *v.t.* **(a)** (fasten) zumachen; binden ‹*Schnürsenkel, Fliege*›
(b) (wrap) einpacken

■ **'do with** *v.t.* **I could do with ...**: ich brauche ...

■ **'do without** *v.t.* **do without sth.** auf etw. (*Akk.*) verzichten

docile /'dəʊsaɪl/ *adj.* sanft; (submissive) unterwürfig

dock¹ /dɒk/ [1] *n.* **(a)** Dock, *das*
(b) *usu. in pl.* (area) Hafen, *der*
[2] *v.t.* [ein]docken
[3] *v.i.* anlegen

dock² *n.* (in lawcourt) Anklagebank, *die;* **stand/be in the ~**: ≈ auf der Anklagebank sitzen

'docker *n.* Hafenarbeiter, *der*

dock: ~land *n.* das Hafenviertel; **~yard** *n.* Schiffswerft, *die*

doctor /'dɒktə(r)/ [1] *n.* **(a)** Arzt, *der*/Ärztin, *die; as address* Herr/Frau Doktor
(b) (holder of degree) Doktor, *der*

2 *v.t.* (coll.) verfälschen
doctorate /'dɒktərət/ *n.* Doktorwürde, *die*
doctrine /'dɒktrɪn/ *n.* Lehre, *die*
document /'dɒkjʊmənt/ *n.* **(a)** Dokument, *das;* Urkunde, *die*
(b) (Comp.) Dokument, *das*
documentary /dɒkjʊ'mentərɪ/ 1 *adj.* dokumentarisch
2 *n.* (film) Dokumentarfilm, *der*
documentation /dɒkjʊmen'teɪʃn/ *n.* (material) beweiskräftige Dokumente *Pl.*
dodge /dɒdʒ/ 1 *v.i.* ausweichen
2 *v.t.* ausweichen (+ *Dat.*) ‹*Schlag, Hindernis usw.*›; entkommen (+ *Dat.*) ‹*Polizei, Verfolger*›
3 *n.* (trick) Trick, *der*
dodgems /'dɒdʒəmz/ *n. pl.* [Auto]skooterbahn, *die;* **have a ride/go on the ~**: Autoskooter fahren
dodgy /'dɒdʒɪ/ *adj.* (Brit. coll.) (unreliable) unsicher; (risky) gewagt
doe /dəʊ/ *n.* (deer) Damtier, *das;* (rabbit) [Kaninchen]weibchen, *das*
does /dʌz/ ▶ DO
doesn't /'dʌznt/ (coll.) = **does not;** ▶ DO
dog /dɒg/ 1 *n.* Hund, *der*
2 *v.t.*, **-gg-** verfolgen; (fig.) heimsuchen
dog: ~ biscuit *n.* Hundekuchen, *der;* **~ collar** *n.* [Hunde]halsband, *das;* (joc.: clerical collar) Kollar, *das;* **~-eared** *adj.* **a ~-eared book** ein Buch mit Eselsohren; **~-end** *n.* (coll.) Kippe, *die* (ugs.)
dogged /'dɒgɪd/ *adj.* hartnäckig ‹*Weigerung, Verurteilung*›; zäh ‹*Durchhaltevermögen, Ausdauer*›
'dog licence *n.* Hundesteuerbescheinigung, *die*
dogma /'dɒgmə/ *n.* Dogma, *das*
dogmatic /dɒg'mætɪk/ *adj.* dogmatisch
do-gooder /du:'gʊdə(r)/ *n.* Wohltäter, *der* (iron.)
dog: ~sbody *n.* (Brit. coll.) Mädchen für alles; **~'s life** *n.* **a ~'s life** ein Hundeleben; **give** *or* **lead sb. a ~'s life** jmdn. schäbig behandeln; **~-'tired** *adj.* hundemüde
doing /'du:ɪŋ/ *n.* Tun, *das*
do-it-yourself /du:ɪtjə'self/ 1 *adj.* Do-it-yourself-
2 *n.* Heimwerken, *das*
doldrums /'dɒldrəmz/ *n. pl.* **in the ~** (in low spirits) niedergeschlagen; (Econ.) in einer Flaute
dole /dəʊl/ 1 *n.* (coll.) **the ~**: Stempelgeld, *das* (ugs.); **be/go on the ~**: stempeln gehen (ugs.)
2 *v.t.* **~ out** [in kleinen Mengen] verteilen
doll /dɒl/ *n.* Puppe, *die*
dollar /'dɒlə(r)/ *n.* Dollar, *der*
dollar: ~ 'bill *n.* Dollarnote, *die;* Dollarschein, *der;* **~ sign** *n.* Dollarzeichen, *das*
dollop /'dɒləp/ *n.* (coll.) Klacks, *der* (ugs.)
'doll's house *n.* Puppenhaus, *das*
dolphin /'dɒlfɪn/ *n.* Delphin, *der*
domain /də'meɪn/ *n.* **(a)** Gebiet, *das*
(b) (Comp.) Domäne, *die;* Domain, *die;* **~ name** Domänenname, *der*
dome /dəʊm/ *n.* Kuppel, *die*
domestic /də'mestɪk/ *adj.* **(a)** (household) häuslich; (family) familiär ‹*Angelegenheit, Reibereien*›
(b) (Econ.) inländisch; Binnen-
(c) ~ animal/cat Haustier, *das*/-katze, *die*
domesticated /də'mestɪkeɪtɪd/ *adj.* gezähmt ‹*Tier*›; (fig.) häuslich
domesticity /dəʊmes'tɪsɪtɪ, dɒmes'tɪsɪtɪ/ *n.* (being domestic) Häuslichkeit, *die*
domestic 'science *n.* Hauswirtschaftslehre, *die*
dominant /'dɒmɪnənt/ *adj.* vorherrschend
dominate /'dɒmɪneɪt/ *v.t.* beherrschen
domination /dɒmɪ'neɪʃn/ *n.* [Vor]herrschaft, *die* (**over** über + *Akk.*)
domineering /dɒmɪ'nɪərɪŋ/ *adj.* herrisch
domino /'dɒmɪnəʊ/ *n.* Domino[stein], *der;* **~es** *sing.* (game) Domino[spiel], *das;* **play ~es** Domino spielen
'domino effect *n.* Dominoeffekt, *der*
don¹ /dɒn/ *v.t.* (Liter.) anlegen (geh.)
don² *n.* (Univ.) Dozent, *der*
donate /dəʊ'neɪt/ *v.t.* spenden; (on large scale) stiften
donation /də'neɪʃn/ *n.* Spende, *die* (**to** für); (large-scale) Stiftung, *die*
done /dʌn/ ▶ DO
donkey /'dɒŋkɪ/ *n.* Esel, *der*
donor /'dəʊnə(r)/ *n.* Spender, *der*/Spenderin, *die*
don't /dəʊnt/ (coll.) = **do not;** ▶ DO
doodle /'du:dl/ *v.i.* [herum]kritzeln
doom /du:m/ 1 *n.* Verhängnis, *das*
2 *v.t.* verurteilen; **be ~ed** verloren sein; **be ~ed to fail** *or* **failure** zum Scheitern verurteilt sein
door /dɔ:(r)/ *n.* Tür, *die;* (of castle, barn) Tor, *das;* **out of ~s** im Freien; **go out of ~s** nach draußen gehen
door: ~bell *n.* Türklingel, *die;* **~frame** *n.* Türrahmen, *der;* **~ handle** *n.* Türklinke, *die;* **~keeper** *n.* Pförtner, *der;* Portier, *der;* **~knob** *n.* Türknopf, -knauf, *der;* **~man** *n.* Portier, *der;* **~mat** *n.* Fußmatte, *die;* **~step** *n.* Türstufe, *die;* **on one's/the ~step** (fig.) vor jmds. Tür; **~way** *n.* Eingang, *der*
dope /dəʊp/ 1 *n.* **(a)** (sl.: narcotic) Stoff, *der* (salopp)
(b) (coll.: fool) Dussel, *der*
2 *v.t.* dopen ‹*Pferd, Athleten*›
dormant /'dɔ:mənt/ *adj.* ruhend ‹*Tier, Pflanze*›; untätig ‹*Vulkan*›
dormitory /'dɔ:mɪtərɪ/ *n.* Schlafsaal, *der*
dormouse /'dɔ:maʊs/ *n., pl.* **dormice** /'dɔ:maɪs/ Haselmaus, *die*

d

DOS /dɒs/ *abbr.* (Comp.) = **disk operating system** DOS
dosage /'dəʊsɪdʒ/ *n.* (size of dose) Dosis, *die*
dose /dəʊs/ 1 *n.* Dosis, *die*
2 *v.t.* ~ **sb. with sth.** jmdm. etw. geben
dot /dɒt/ *n.* Punkt, *der;* **on the ~**: auf den Punkt genau
dot.com /'dɒtkɒm/ 1 *adj.* Dot-com-
2 *n.* Dot-com-Firma, *die*
dote /dəʊt/ *v.i.* ~ **on sb./sth.** jmdn./etw. abgöttisch lieben
'dot matrix *n.* (Comp.) Punktmatrix, *die;* ~ **printer** Nadeldrucker, *der*
dotted /'dɒtɪd/ *adj.* gepunktet
dotty /'dɒtɪ/ *adj.* (coll.) (silly) dümmlich; (feeble-minded) vertrottelt (ugs.); (absurd) blödsinnig (ugs.)
double /'dʌbl/ 1 *adj.* doppelt; ~ **bed/room** Doppelbett, *das*/-zimmer, *das;* **be ~ the height/width/length** doppelt so hoch/breit/lang sein
2 *adv.* doppelt
3 *n.* **(a)** Doppelte, *das*
(b) (twice as much) doppelt so viel; (twice as many) doppelt so viele
(c) (person) Doppelgänger, *der*/-gängerin, *die*
(d) *in pl.* (Tennis etc.) Doppel, *das*
(e) at the ~ (Mil.) im Laufschritt; (fig.) ganz schnell
4 *v.t.* verdoppeln
5 *v.i.* sich verdoppeln
■ **double 'back** *v.i.* kehrtmachen (ugs.).
■ **double 'up** *v.i.* sich krümmen (**with** vor + *Dat.*)
double: ~ 'agent *n.* Doppelagent, *der*/-agentin, *die;* **~-barrelled** (*Amer.:* **~-barreled**) /'dʌblbærəld/ *adj.* doppelläufig; **~-barrelled surname** (Brit.) Doppelname, *der;* **~ 'bass** *n.* Kontrabass, *der;* **~ 'bill** *n.* Doppelprogramm, *das;* **~-breasted** /dʌbl'brestɪd/ *adj.* zwei- *od.* doppelreihig; **~-breasted jacket** Zweireiher, *der;* **~-'check** *v.t.* (verify twice) zweimal kontrollieren; (verify in two ways) zweifach überprüfen; **~ 'chin** *n.* Doppelkinn, *das;* **~-click** (Comp.) 1 *v.i.* doppelklicken;
2 *v.t.* **~click sth.** auf etw. (*Dat.*) doppelklicken; **~ 'cream** *n.* Sahne mit hohem Fettgehalt; **~-'cross** *v.t.* ein Doppelspiel treiben mit; **~-decker** /dʌbl'dekə(r)/ *n.* Doppeldeckerbus, *der*
double entendre /du:bl ɑ̃'tɑ̃dr/ *n.* Zweideutigkeit, *die*
double: ~-'glazed *adj.* Doppel‹*fenster*›; **~ 'glazing** *n.* Doppelverglasung, *die;* **~-'jointed** *adj.* sehr gelenkig; **~ lesson** *n.* Doppelstunde, *die;* **~-'lock** *v.t.* zweimal abschließen; **~ 'meaning** ▶ DOUBLE ENTENDRE; **~-page 'spread** *n.* **the advertisement was a ~-page spread** die Anzeige war doppelseitig; **~-'parking** *n.* Parken in der zweiten Reihe; **~ 'room** *n.* Doppelzimmer, *das;* **~ 'standard** *n.* (rule) Doppelmoral, *die;* **apply** *or* **operate a ~ standard** *or* **~ standards** mit zweierlei Maß messen; **~ 'vision** *n.* Doppeltsehen, *das;* **~ yellow 'lines** *n. pl.: am Fahrbahnrand verlaufende gelbe Doppellinie, die ein Halteverbot signalisiert*
doubly /'dʌblɪ/ *adv.* doppelt
doubt /daʊt/ 1 *n.* Zweifel, *der* (**about, as to,** of an + *Dat.*); **~[s] [about** *or* **as to sth./as to whether ...]** (as to future) Ungewissheit, (as to fact) Unsicherheit [über etw. (*Akk.*)/darüber, ob ...]; **there's no ~ that ...**: es besteht kein Zweifel daran, dass ...; **~[s]** (hesitations) Bedenken *Pl.* (**about** gegen); **no ~** (certainly) gewiss; (probably) sicherlich
2 *v.i.* zweifeln
3 *v.t.* zweifeln an (+ *Dat.*); **I don't ~ that** *or* **it** ich bezweifle das nicht; **I ~ whether** *or* **if** *or* **that ...**: ich bezweifle, dass ...
doubtful /'daʊtfl/ *adj.* skeptisch ‹*Wesen*›; ungläubig ‹*Blick*›
doubtless /'daʊtlɪs/ *adv.* **(a)** (certainly) gewiss
(b) (probably) sicherlich
dough /dəʊ/ *n.* **(a)** Teig, *der*
(b) (coll.: money) Knete, *die* (salopp)
'doughnut *n.* [Berliner] Pfannkuchen, *der*
douse /daʊs/ *v.t.* übergießen; (extinguish) ausmachen
dove¹ /dʌv/ *n.* Taube, *die*
dove² /dəʊv/ ▶ DIVE 1
dovecot, dovecote /'dʌvkɒt/ *n.* Taubenschlag, *der;* **flutter the ~cots** (fig.) für einige Aufregung sorgen
dowdy /'daʊdɪ/ *adj.* unansehnlich; (shabby) schäbig
down¹ /daʊn/ *n.* (feathers) Daunen *Pl.*
down² 1 *adv.* **(a)** (to lower place) herunter/hinunter; (in lift) abwärts
(b) (in lower place, downstairs) unten; **~ there/here** da/hier unten; **the next floor ~**: ein Stockwerk tiefer; **be ~ with an illness** eine Krankheit haben; **be three points/games ~**: mit drei Punkten/Spielen zurückliegen
2 *prep.* herunter/hinunter; **lower ~ the river** weiter unten am Fluss; **walk ~ the hill/road** den Berg/die Straße heruntergehen; **fall ~ the stairs/steps** die Treppe/Stufen herunterstürzen; **fall ~ a hole/ditch** in ein Loch/ einen Graben fallen; **go ~ the pub** in die Kneipe gehen; **live just ~ the road** ein Stück weiter unten in der Straße wohnen; **be ~ the pub/town** in der Kneipe/Stadt sein; **I've got coffee [all] ~ my skirt** mein ganzer Rock ist voll Kaffee
3 *v.t.* (coll.) schlucken (ugs.) ‹*Getränk*›; **~ tools** die Arbeit niederlegen
down: ~-and-'out *n.* Stadtstreicher, *der*/-streicherin, *die;* **~cast** *adj.* niedergeschlagen; **~fall** *n.* Untergang, *der;* **~-'hearted** *adj.* niedergeschlagen; **~'hill** *adv.* bergab; **~'load** *v.t.* (Comp.) herunterladen; **~market** *adj.* weniger anspruchsvoll; **~ payment** *n.* Anzahlung, *die;* **~pour** *n.* Regenguss, *der;* **~right** *adj.*

ausgemacht; glatt ‹*Lüge*›; **~size** 1 *v.t.* verschlanken; 2 *v.i.* abspecken; **~stairs** 1 /-'-/ *adv.* die Treppe hinunter‹*gehen, -fallen, -kommen*›; unten ‹*wohnen, sein*›; 2 /'--/ *adj.* im Erdgeschoss *nachgestellt;* **~'stream** *adv.* flussabwärts; **~-to-'earth** *adj.* sachlich; **~town** *adv.* im/(direction) ins Stadtzentrum; **~trodden** *adj.* unterdrückt; **~turn** *n.* (Econ., Commerc.) Abschwung, *der;* **~ 'under** *adv.* (coll.) in/(to) nach Australien/Neuseeland

downward /'daʊnwəd/ 1 *adj.* nach unten gerichtet
2 *adv.* abwärts ‹*sich bewegen*›; nach unten ‹*sehen, gehen*›

downwards /'daʊnwədz/ ▶ DOWNWARD 2

dowry /'daʊrɪ/ *n.* Aussteuer, *die*

doz. *abbr.* = **dozen** Dtzd.

doze /dəʊz/ 1 *v.i.* dösen (ugs.)
2 *n.* Nickerchen, *das* (ugs.)

▪ **doze 'off** *v.i.* eindösen (ugs.)

dozen /'dʌzn/ *n.* **(a)** Dutzend, *das;* **half a ~:** sechs
(b) *in pl.* (coll.: many) Dutzende *Pl.*

Dr *abbr.* = **doctor** Dr.

drab /dræb/ *adj.* langweilig; trostlos ‹*Landschaft*›; eintönig ‹*Leben*›

draft /drɑːft/ 1 *n.* **(a)** (of speech) Konzept, *das;* (of treaty, bill) Entwurf, *der*
(b) (Amer.) ▶ DRAUGHT
2 *v.t.* entwerfen

drafty (Amer.) ▶ DRAUGHTY

drag /dræg/ 1 *v.t.*, **-gg-** schleppen; (Comp.) ziehen; **~ and drop** ziehen und ablegen
2 *v.i.*, **-gg-** schleifen; (fig.: pass slowly) sich [hin]schleppen
3 *n.* **(a)** (coll.) **in ~:** in Frauenkleidung
(b) (coll.: at cigarette) Zug, *der*

▪ **drag 'down** *v.t.* nach unten ziehen; **~ sb. down to one's own level** (fig.) jmdn. auf sein Niveau herabziehen

▪ **drag 'on** *v.i.* sich [da]hinschleppen

dragon /'drægn/ *n.* Drache, *der*

'dragonfly *n.* Libelle, *die*

drain /dreɪn/ 1 *n.* Abflussrohr, *das;* (underground) Kanalisationsrohr, *das;* (grating at roadside) Gully, *der;* **go down the ~** (fig. coll.) für die Katz sein (ugs.)
2 *v.t.* **(a)** trockenlegen ‹*Teich*›; entwässern ‹*Land*›; ableiten ‹*Wasser*›
(b) (Cookery) abgießen ‹*Wasser, Gemüse*›
(c) austrinken ‹*Glas*›
3 *v.i.* ‹*Flüssigkeit:*› ablaufen; ‹*Geschirr, Gemüse:*› abtropfen

drainage /'dreɪnɪdʒ/ *n.* Kanalisation, *die*

'draining board (*Brit.; Amer.:* **'drainboard**) *n.* Abtropfbrett, *das*

'drainpipe *n.* Regen[abfall]rohr, *das*

drake /dreɪk/ *n.* Enterich, *der*

drama /'drɑːmə/ *n.* Drama, *das*

dramatic /drə'mætɪk/ *adj.* dramatisch

dramatist /'dræmətɪst/ *n.* Dramatiker, *der*/Dramatikerin, *die*

dramatize /'dræmətaɪz/ *v.t.* dramatisieren

drank ▶ DRINK 2

drape /dreɪp/ 1 *v.t.* drapieren
2 *n.* (Amer.: curtain) Vorhang, *der*

'draper *n.* (Brit.) Textilkaufmann, *der;* **~'s [shop]** Textilgeschäft, *das*

drastic /'dræstɪk/ *adj.* drastisch

draught /drɑːft/ *n.* [Luft]zug, *der;* **there's a ~:** es zieht

draught: ~ 'beer *n.* Fassbier, *das;* **~ board** *n.* (Brit.) Damebrett, *das;* **~ excluder** *n.* Abdichtvorrichtung, *die;* Zugluft-Verhinderer, *der;* **~proof** *adj.* winddicht

draughts /drɑːfts/ *n.* (Brit.) Damespiel, *das*

'draughtsman /-mən/ *n., pl.* **draughtsmen** /-mən/ Zeichner, *der*/Zeichnerin, *die*

'draughty *adj.* zugig

draw /drɔː/ 1 *v.t.*, **drew** /druː/, **drawn** /drɔːn/ **(a)** (pull) ziehen; **~ the curtains/blinds** (close) die Vorhänge zuziehen/die Jalousien herunterlassen; **~ sth. towards one** etw. zu sich heranziehen
(b) (attract) anlocken; **be ~n to sb.** von jmdm. angezogen werden
(c) (take out) herausziehen; schöpfen ‹*Wasser*›; **~ money from the bank** Geld bei der Bank holen/abheben
(d) beziehen ‹*Gehalt, Rente, Arbeitslosenunterstützung*›
(e) ziehen ‹*Strich*›; zeichnen ‹*geometrische Figur, Bild*›
(f) ziehen ‹*Parallele, Vergleich*›; herausstellen ‹*Unterschied*›
2 *v.i.* **(a) drew, drawn: ~ to an end** zu Ende gehen
(b) (Sport) **they drew [three-all]** sie spielten [3 : 3] unentschieden
3 *n.* **(a)** (raffle) Tombola, *die*
(b) (of lottery) Ziehung, *die*
(c) ([result of] drawn game) Unentschieden, *das;* **end in a ~:** mit einem Unentschieden enden

▪ **draw 'back** 1 *v.t.* zurückziehen
2 *v.i.* zurückweichen

▪ **draw 'in** *v.i.* einfahren; ‹*Tage:*› kürzer werden

▪ **draw 'out** *v.i.* abfahren; ‹*Tage:*› länger werden

▪ **draw 'up** 1 *v.t.* **(a)** aufsetzen ‹*Vertrag*›; aufstellen ‹*Liste*›
(b) (pull closer) heranziehen
2 *v.i.* [an]halten

draw: ~back *n.* Nachteil, *der;* **~bridge** *n.* Zugbrücke, *die*

drawer /drɔː(r), 'drɔːə(r)/ *n.* Schublade, *die*

'drawing *n.* (sketch) Zeichnung, *die*

drawing: ~ board *n.* Zeichenbrett, *das;* **~ pin** *n.* (Brit.) Reißzwecke, *die;* **~ room** *n.* Salon, *der*

drawl /drɔːl/ 1 *v.i.* gedehnt sprechen
2 *n.* gedehntes Sprechen

drawn ▶ DRAW 1, 2

dread /dred/ [1] *v.t.* sich sehr fürchten vor (+ *Dat.*); **the ~ed day/moment** der gefürchtete Tag/Augenblick
[2] *n.* Angst, *die*

dreadful /'dredfl/ *adj.* schrecklich; (coll.: very bad) fürchterlich; **I feel ~** (unwell) ich fühle mich scheußlich (ugs.)

'dreadfully *adv.* schrecklich; (coll.: very badly) fürchterlich

dream /dri:m/ [1] *n.* Traum, *der; attrib.* traumhaft; Traum‹*haus, -auto, -urlaub*›; **have a ~ about sb./sth.** von jmdm./etw. träumen
[2] *v.i. & t.* **dreamt** /dremt/ *or* **dreamed** träumen

'dreamer *n.* (in sleep) Träumende, *der/die;* (day~) Träumer, *der*/Träumerin, *die*

dreary /'drɪərɪ/ *adj.* trostlos

dredge /dredʒ/ *v.t.* ausbaggern

'dredger *n.* Bagger, *der*

dregs /dregz/ *n. pl.* [Boden]satz, *der*

drench /drentʃ/ *v.t.* durchnässen

dress /dres/ [1] *n.* Kleid, *das;* (clothing) Kleidung, *die*
[2] *v.t.* **(a)** anziehen; **be well ~ed** gut gekleidet sein; **get ~ed** sich anziehen
(b) verbinden ‹*Wunde*›
[3] *v.i.* sich anziehen

■ **dress 'up** *v.i.* sich fein machen

dress: ~ circle *n.* (Theatre) erster Rang; **~ designer** *n.* Modeschöpfer, *der*/-schöpferin, *die*

'dresser *n.* **(a)** Anrichte, *die*
(b) (Amer.) ▶ DRESSING TABLE

'dressing *n.* **(a)** *no pl.* Anziehen, *das*
(b) (Cookery) Dressing, *das*
(c) (Med.) Verband, *der*

dressing: ~ gown *n.* Bademantel, *der;* **~ room** *n.* (Sport) Umkleideraum, *der;* (for actor) Garderobe, *die;* **~ table** *n.* Frisierkommode, *die*

dress: ~maker *n.* Damenschneider, *der*/-schneiderin, *die;* **~making** *n.* Damenschneiderei, *die;* **~ rehearsal** *n.* Generalprobe, *die*

drew ▶ DRAW 1, 2

dribble /'drɪbl/ *v.i.* **(a)** (slobber) sabbern
(b) (Sport) dribbeln

dried /draɪd/ *adj.* getrocknet; **~ fruit[s]** Dörrobst, *das;* **~ milk** Trockenmilch, *die*

drier /'draɪə(r)/ *n.* (for hair) Trockenhaube, *die;* (hand-held) Föhn, *der;* (for laundry) [Wäsche]trockner, *der*

drift /drɪft/ [1] *n.* **(a)** (of snow or sand) Verwehung, *die*
(b) (gist) **get** *or* **catch the ~ of sth.** etw im Wesentlichen verstehen
[2] *v.i.* **(a)** treiben; ‹*Wolke:*› ziehen
(b) ‹*Sand, Schnee:*› zusammengeweht werden

'driftwood *n.* Treibholz, *das*

drill /drɪl/ [1] *n.* **(a)** (tool) Bohrer, *der*
(b) (Mil.: training) Drill, *der*
[2] *v.t. & i.* bohren (**for** nach)

'drill bit *n.* Bohrer, *der*

drink /drɪŋk/ [1] *n.* Getränk, *das;* (alcoholic) Glas, *das;* (not with food) Drink, *der;* **have a ~:** [etwas] trinken; (alcoholic) ein Glas trinken
[2] *v.t. & i.* **drank** /dræŋk/, **drunk** /drʌŋk/ trinken

drinkable /'drɪŋkəbl/ *adj.* trinkbar

'drink-driving *n.* Fahren unter Alkoholeinfluss; Alkohol am Steuer; **~ offence** Alkoholdelikt, *das*

drinker /'drɪŋkə(r)/ *n.* Trinker, *der*/Trinkerin, *die*

drinking /'drɪŋkɪŋ/**: ~ fountain** *n.* Trinkbrunnen, *der;* **~ water** *n.* Trinkwasser, *das*

drip /drɪp/ [1] *n.* **(a)** Tropfen, *das*
(b) (coll.: feeble person) Schlappschwanz, *der* (salopp)
[2] *v.i.*, **-pp-** tropfen; **be ~ping with water/moisture** triefend nass sein

'drip-dry *adj.* bügelfrei

'dripping *n.* (Cookery) Schmalz, *das*

drive /draɪv/ [1] *n.* **(a)** Fahrt, *die*
(b) (private road) Zufahrt, *die;* (entrance) (to small building) Einfahrt, *die;* (to large building) Auffahrt, *die*
(c) (energy) Tatkraft, *die*
(d) (Psych.) Trieb, *der*
(e) (Motor Veh.) **left-hand/right-hand ~:** Links-/Rechtssteuerung, *die*
[2] *v.t.*, **drove** /drəʊv/, **driven** /'drɪvn/ **(a)** fahren
(b) treiben ‹*Tier*›
(c) (compel to move) vertreiben (**out of, from** aus)
(d) (fig.) **~ sb. to sth.** jmdn. zu etw. treiben; **~ sb. to do sth.** *or* **into doing sth.** jmdn. dazu treiben, etw. zu tun
(e) (power) antreiben
[3] *v.i.*, **drove, driven (a)** fahren; **can you ~?** kannst du Auto fahren?
(b) (go by car) mit dem [eigenen] Auto fahren

■ **'drive at** *v.t.* (fig.) hinauswollen auf (+ *Akk.*); **what are you driving at?** worauf wollen Sie hinaus?

■ **drive a'way** [1] *v.i.* wegfahren
[2] *v.t.* **(a)** wegfahren
(b) (chase away) vertreiben

■ **drive 'off** ▶ DRIVE AWAY

■ **drive 'on** *v.i.* weiterfahren

■ **drive 'up** *v.i.* vorfahren (**to** vor + *Dat.*)

'drive-in *adj.* Drive-in-; **~ cinema** *or* (Amer.) movie [theater] Autokino, *das*

drivel /'drɪvl/ *n.* Gefasel, *das* (ugs.); **talk ~:** faseln (ugs.)

driven ▶ DRIVE 2, 3

driver /'draɪvə(r)/ *n.* **(a)** Fahrer, *der*/Fahrerin, *die;* (of locomotive) Führer, *der*/Führerin, *die;* **~'s license** (Amer.) Führerschein, *der*
(b) (Comp.) Treiber, *der*

driving /'draɪvɪŋ/ [1] *n.* Fahren, *das*
[2] *adj.* peitschend ‹*Regen*›

driving: ~ force *n.* treibende Kraft;

Triebfeder, *die;* **the ~ force behind sth.** die treibende Kraft hinter etw.; ~ **gloves** *n. pl.* Autohandschuhe *Pl.*; ~ **instructor** *n.* Fahrlehrer, *der*/-lehrerin, *die;* ~ **lesson** *n.* Fahrstunde, *die;* ~ **licence** *n.* Führerschein, *der;* ~ **mirror** *n.* Rückspiegel, *der;* ~ **school** *n.* Fahrschule, *die;* ~ **test** *n.* Fahrprüfung, *die*

drizzle /ˈdrɪzl/ 1 *n.* Nieseln, *das* 2 *v.i.* **it's drizzling** es nieselt

drone /drəʊn/ 1 *v.i.* **(a)** ‹*Biene:*› summen; ‹*Maschine:*› brummen **(b)** ‹*Rezitator:*› leiern 2 *n.* ▶ 1: Summen, *das;* Brummen, *das;* Geleier, *das*

drool /druːl/ *v.i.* ~ **over** eine kindische Freude haben an (+ *Dat.*)

droop /druːp/ *v.i.* herunterhängen, ‹*Blume:*› den Kopf hängen lassen

drop /drɒp/ 1 *n.* **(a)** Tropfen, *der;* **in ~s** tropfenweise **(b)** (decrease) Rückgang, *der* 2 *v.i.*, **-pp-**: **(a)** (fall) (accidentally) [herunter]fallen; (deliberately) sich [hinunter]fallen lassen **(b)** (in amount etc.) sinken; ‹*Preis, Wert:*› sinken, fallen; ‹*Wind:*› sich legen; ‹*Stimme:*› sich senken 3 *v.t.*, **-pp-**: **(a)** fallen lassen; abwerfen ‹*Bomben, Nachschub*› **(b)** (discontinue, abandon) fallen lassen; ~ **out of university/the course** das Studium abbrechen *od.* aufgeben **(c)** (omit) auslassen

▪ **drop 'by, drop 'in** *v.i.* vorbeikommen

▪ **drop 'off** 1 *v.i.* **(a)** (fall off) abfallen **(b)** (fall asleep) einnicken 2 *v.t.* absetzen ‹*Fahrgast*›

▪ **drop 'out** *v.i.* **(a)** herausfallen (**of** aus) **(b)** (withdraw) aussteigen (ugs.) (**of** aus); (beforehand) seine Teilnahme absagen

drop: ~-down menu *n.* (Comp.) Dropdownmenü, *das;* ~ **handlebars** *n. pl.* Rennlenker, *der;* ~ **kick** *n.* (Football) Dropkick, *der*

droplet /ˈdrɒplɪt/ *n.* Tröpfchen, *das*

dropout /ˈdrɒpaʊt/ *n.* Aussteiger, *der*/Aussteigerin, *die*

dropper /ˈdrɒpə(r)/ *n.* (esp. Med.) Tropfer, *der*

drop shot *n.* (Tennis etc.) Stoppball, *der*

drought /draʊt/ *n.* Dürre, *die*

drove ▶ DRIVE 2, 3

drown /draʊn/ 1 *v.i.* ertrinken 2 *v.t.* ertränken; **be ~ed** ertrinken

drowse /draʊz/ *v.i.* [vor sich hin]dösen

drowsy /ˈdraʊzɪ/ *adj.* schläfrig; (on just waking) verschlafen

drudgery /ˈdrʌdʒərɪ/ *n.* Schufterei, *die*

drug /drʌg/ 1 *n.* **(a)** (Med.) [Arznei]mittel, *das* **(b)** (narcotic) Droge, *die;* **be on ~s** Rauschgift nehmen 2 *v.t.*, **-gg-** betäuben ‹*Person*›; ~ **sb.'s food/drink** jmds. Essen/Getränk (*Dat.*) ein Betäubungsmittel beimischen

drug: ~ abuse *n.* Drogenmissbrauch, *der;* ~ **abuser** *n.* Drogenmissbrauch Treibender/Treibende; ~ **addict** *n.* Drogensüchtige, *der/die;* ~ **addiction** *n.* Drogensucht, *die;* ~ **dealer** *n.* Drogenhändler, *der*/-händlerin, *die;* Dealer, *der*/Dealerin, *die* (Drogenjargon); ~ **peddler** ▶ DRUG DEALER; **~-related** *adj.* Drogen‹*-tote, -kriminalität, -delikt, probleme*›; ~ **scene** *n.* Drogenszene, *die;* **~store** *n.* (Amer.) Drugstore, *der;* **~-taking** *n.* Drogeneinnahme, *die;* ~ **trafficking** *n.* Drogenhandel, *der;* ~ **test** *n.* Dopingkontrolle, *die;* Dopingtest, *der;* **~user** *n.* Drogenkonsument, *der*/-konsumentin, *die*

drum /drʌm/ 1 *n.* **(a)** Trommel, *die* **(b)** *in pl.* (in jazz or pop) Schlagzeug, *das* **(c)** (container) Fass, *das* 2 *v.i.* trommeln

▪ **drum 'up** *v.i.* auftreiben

'drum beat *n.* Trommelschlag, *der*

'drummer *n.* Schlagzeuger, *der*

'drumstick *n.* **(a)** Trommelschlägel, *der* **(b)** (Cookery) Keule, *die*

drunk /drʌŋk/ 1 *adj.* **be ~**: betrunken sein; **get ~**: betrunken werden (**on** von); (intentionally) sich betrinken (**on** mit) 2 *n.* Betrunkene, *der/die*

drunkard /ˈdrʌŋkəd/ *n.* Trinker, *der*/Trinkerin, *die*

drunken /ˈdrʌŋkn/ *attrib. adj.* betrunken; (habitually) ständig betrunken; ~ **driving** Trunkenheit am Steuer

'drunkenness *n.* Betrunkenheit, *die;* (habitual) Trunksucht, *die*

dry /draɪ/ 1 *adj.* trocken; trocken, (very ~) herb ‹*Wein*›; ausgetrocknet ‹*Flussbett*›; **get** *or* **become ~**: trocknen 2 *v.t.* **(a)** trocknen ‹*Haare, Wäsche*›; abtrocknen ‹*Geschirr, Baby*›; ~ **oneself** sich abtrocknen; ~ **one's eyes** *or* **tears/hands** sich (*Dat.*) die Tränen abwischen/die Hände abtrocknen **(b)** (preserve) trocknen; dörren ‹*Obst, Fleisch*› 3 *v.i.* trocknen

▪ **dry 'out** *v.t. & i.* trocknen

▪ **dry 'up** 1 *v.t.* abtrocknen 2 *v.i.* **(a)** (~ the dishes) abtrocknen **(b)** ‹*Brunnen, Quelle:*› versiegen; ‹*Fluss, Teich:*› austrocknen

dry: ~-'clean *v.t.* chemisch reinigen; **~-'cleaner's** *n.* chemische Reinigung; **~-'cleaning** *n.* chemische Reinigung

'dryer ▶ DRIER

dry: ~-eyed *adj.* ohne Rührung; ~ **'ice** *n.* Trockeneis, *das*

drying-'up *n.* Abtrocknen, *das;* **do the ~** abtrocknen; *attrib.* ~ **cloth** Geschirrtuch, *das*

'dryness *n.* Trockenheit, *die*
dry 'rot *n.* Trockenfäule, *die*
dual /'dju:əl/ *adj.* doppelt
dual: ~ 'carriageway *n.* (Brit.) Straße mit Mittelstreifen; **~ con'trol** *n.* (Aeronaut.) Doppelsteuerung, *die;* (Motor Veh.) doppelte Bedienungselemente *Pl.;* **~-'purpose** *adj.* zweifach verwendbar

d

dub /dʌb/ *v.t.*, **-bb-** (Cinemat.) synchronisieren
dubious /'dju:bɪəs/ *adj.* (doubting) unschlüssig; (suspicious) zweifelhaft
duchess /'dʌtʃɪs/ *n.* Herzogin, *die*
duck /dʌk/ 1 *n.* Ente, *die*
2 *v.i.* sich [schnell] ducken
3 *v.t.* **~ one's head** den Kopf einziehen
duckling /'dʌklɪŋ/ *n.* Entenküken, *das*
'duck pond *n.* Ententeich, *der*
duct /dʌkt/ *n.* Rohr, *das;* (for air) Ventil, *das*
dud /dʌd/ 1 *n.* (useless thing) Niete, die (ugs.); (counterfeit) Fälschung, *die*
2 *adj.* mies (ugs.); schlecht; (fake) gefälscht; geplatzt ‹*Scheck*›
dude /dju:d, du:d/ *n.* (esp. Amer. coll.) Typ, *der* (ugs.)
due /dju:/ 1 *adj.* **(a)** (owed) geschuldet; zustehend ‹*Eigentum, Recht usw.*›; **there's sth. ~ to me, I've got sth. ~:** mir steht etw. zu
(b) (immediately payable) fällig
(c) (that it is proper to give or use) gebührend; angemessen ‹*Belohnung*›; **be ~ to sb.** jmdm. gebühren; **with all ~ respect** bei allem gebotenen Respekt
(d) (attributable) **the mistake was ~ to negligence** der Fehler war durch Nachlässigkeit verursacht; **it's ~ to her that we missed the train** ihretwegen verpassten wir den Zug
(e) (scheduled, expected); **be ~ to do sth.** etw. tun sollen; **be ~ [to arrive]** ankommen sollen
(f) (likely to get, deserving) **be ~ for sth.** etw. verdienen
2 *adv.* **(a) ~ north** genau nach Norden
(b) ~ to aufgrund (+ *Gen.*); auf Grund (+ *Gen.*)
3 *n.* **(a) give sb. his ~:** jmdm. Gerechtigkeit widerfahren lassen
(b) ~s (fees) Gebühren *Pl.*
duel /'dju:əl/ *n.* Duell, *das*
duet /dju:'et/ *n.* (for voices) Duett, *das;* (instrumental) Duo, *das*
duffle /'dʌfl/**: ~ bag** *n.* Matchbeutel, *der;* **~ coat** *n.* Dufflecoat, *der*
dug ▶ DIG
duke /dju:k/ *n.* Herzog, *der*
dull /dʌl/ 1 *adj.* **(a)** (stupid) beschränkt; (slow to understand) begriffsstutzig
(b) (boring) langweilig
(c) (gloomy) trübe ‹*Wetter, Tag*›
2 *v.t.* abstumpfen ‹*Geist, Sinne, Verstand*›
duly /'dju:lɪ/ *adv.* ordnungsgemäß
dumb /dʌm/ *adj.* **(a)** stumm
(b) (coll.: stupid) doof (ugs.)

■ **dumb down** *v.t. & i.* (coll.) verflachen
dumbfounded /dʌm'faʊndɪd/ *adj.* sprachlos
dummy /'dʌmɪ/ *n.* **(a)** (of tailor) Schneiderpuppe, *die;* (in shop) Schaufensterpuppe, *die;* (of ventriloquist) Puppe, *die;* (stupid person) Dummkopf, *der* (ugs.); **like a stuffed ~:** wie ein Ölgötze (ugs.)
(b) (imitation) Attrappe, *die*
(c) (esp. Brit.: for baby) Schnuller, *der*
dump /dʌmp/ 1 *n.* **(a)** (place) Müllkippe, *die;* (heap) Müllhaufen, *der;* (permanent) Müllhalde, *die*
(b) (Mil.) Depot, *das*
(c) (coll.: town) Kaff, *das* (ugs.)
2 *v.t.* (dispose of) werfen; (deposit) abladen ‹*Sand, Müll usw.*›; (leave) lassen; (place) abstellen
'dumping ground *n.* Müllkippe, *die;* (fig.) Abstellplatz, *der*
dumpling /'dʌmplɪŋ/ *n.* Kloß, *der*
dumps /dʌmps/ *n. pl.* **be** *or* **feel down in the ~:** ganz down sein (ugs.)
'dump truck *n.* Kipper, *der*
dunce /dʌns/ *n.* Null, *die* (ugs.)
dune /dju:n/ *n.* Düne, *die*
dung /dʌŋ/ *n.* Dung, *der*
dungarees /dʌŋgə'ri:z/ *n. pl.* Latzhose, *die*
dungeon /'dʌndʒən/ *n.* Kerker, *der*
dunk /dʌŋk/ *v.t.* tunken
dupe /dju:p/ 1 *v.t.* übertölpeln
2 *n.* Dumme, *der/die*
duplex /'dju:pleks/ *adj.* (esp. Amer.) (two-storey) zweistöckig ‹*Wohnung*›; (two-family) Zweifamilien‹*haus*›
duplicate 1 /'dju:plɪkət/ *adj.* **(a)** (identical) Zweit-
(b) (twofold) doppelt
2 *n.* Kopie, *die;* (second copy of letter/document/key) Duplikat, *das;* **in ~:** in doppelter Ausfertigung
3 /'dju:plɪkeɪt/ *v.t.* **(a)** (make a copy of, make in ~) **~ sth.** eine zweite Anfertigung von etw. machen
(b) (on machine) vervielfältigen
(c) (do twice) noch einmal tun
duplicity /dju:'plɪsɪtɪ/ *n.* Falschheit, *die*
durability /djʊərə'bɪlɪtɪ/ *n.* (of friendship, peace, etc.) Dauerhaftigkeit, *die;* (of garment, material) Haltbarkeit, die
durable /'djʊərəbl/ *adj.* haltbar; dauerhaft ‹*Friede, Freundschaft usw.*›
duration /djʊə'reɪʃn/ *n.* Dauer, *die*
duress /djʊə'res/ *n.* Zwang, *der*
during /'djʊərɪŋ/ *prep.* während; (at a point in) in (+ *Dat.*)
dusk /dʌsk/ *n.* Einbruch der Dunkelheit
dust /dʌst/ 1 *n.* Staub, *der*
2 *v.t.* abstauben ‹*Möbel*›; **~ a room/ house** in einem Zimmer/Haus Staub wischen
3 *v.i.* Staub wischen

dust: **~bin** *n.* (Brit.) Mülltonne, *die;* **~cart** *n.* (Brit.) Müllwagen, *der;* **~ cloth** *n.* Schonbezug, *der;* (duster) Staubtuch, *das*

'duster *n.* Staubtuch, *das*

dust: **~ jacket** *n.* Schutzumschlag, *der;* **~man** /-mən/ *n., pl.* **~men** /-mən/ (Brit.) Müllmann, *der;* **~pan** *n.* Kehrschaufel, *die*

'dusty *adj.* staubig; verstaubt ‹*Bücher, Möbel*›

Dutch /dʌtʃ/ [1] *adj.* holländisch; **sb. is ~:** jmd. ist Holländer/Holländerin
[2] *n.* **(a)** (language) Holländisch, *das; see also* ENGLISH 2A
(b) the **~** *pl.* die Holländer *Pl.*

Dutch: **~ 'courage** *n.* angetrunkener Mut; **~ 'elm disease** *n.* Ulmensterben, *das;* **~man** /-mən/ *n., pl.* **~men** /-mən/ Holländer, *der;* **~woman** *n.* Holländerin, *die*

dutiful /'dju:tɪfl/ *adj.*, **'dutifully** *adv.* pflichtbewusst

duty /'dju:tɪ/ *n.* **(a)** Pflicht, *die;* (task) Aufgabe, *die;* **be on ~:** Dienst haben; **off ~:** nicht im Dienst; **be off ~:** keinen Dienst haben; ‹*ab ... Uhr*› dienstfrei sein
(b) (tax) Zoll, *der;* **pay ~ on sth.** Zoll für etw. bezahlen

'duty-free *adj., adv.* zollfrei

duvet /'du:veɪ/ *n.* Federbett, *das;* **~ cover** Bettbezug, *der*

DVD *abbr.* = **digital video disc** DVD

dwarf /dwɔ:f/ *n., pl.* **~s** *or* **dwarves** /'dwɔ:vz/ Zwerg, *der*/Zwergin, *die*

dwell /dwel/ *v.i.*, **dwelt** /dwelt/ (literary) wohnen
■ **'dwell [up]on** *v.t.* (in discussion) sich ausführlich befassen mit; (in thought) in Gedanken verweilen bei

'dwelling *n.* Wohnung, *die*

dwelt ▶ DWELL

dwindle /'dwɪndl/ *v.i.* **~ [away]** abnehmen; ‹*Unterstützung, Interesse:*› nachlassen; ‹*Vorräte:*› schrumpfen

dye /daɪ/ [1] *n.* Färbemittel, *das*
[2] *v.t.*, **~ing** /'daɪɪŋ/ färben

dying /'daɪɪŋ/ *adj.* sterbend; absterbend ‹*Baum*›

dyke ▶ DIKE

dynamic /daɪ'næmɪk/ *adj.* dynamisch

dynamism /'daɪnəmɪzm/ *n.* Dynamik, *die*

dynamite /'daɪnəmaɪt/ *n.* Dynamit, *das*

dynamo /'daɪnəməʊ/ *n.* Dynamo, *der;* (in car) Lichtmaschine, *die*

dynasty /'dɪnəstɪ/ *n.* Dynastie, *die*

dysentry /'dɪsəntrɪ/ *n.* Ruhr, *die*

Ee

E, e /i:/ *n.* E, e, *das*

E. *abbr.* **(a)** = **east** O
(b) = **eastern** ö

each /i:tʃ/ [1] *adj.* jeder/jede/jedes; **they cost** *or* **are a pound ~:** sie kosten ein Pfund pro Stück
[2] *pron.* **(a)** jeder/jede/jedes
(b) ~ other sich

eager /'i:gə(r)/ *adj.* eifrig; **be ~ to do sth.** etw. unbedingt tun wollen

'eagerly *adv.* eifrig; gespannt ‹*warten*›

eagle /'i:gl/ *n.* Adler, *der*

eagle-'eyed *adj.* adleräugig

ear[1] /ɪə(r)/ *n.* Ohr, *das;* **up to one's ~s in work/debt** bis zum Hals in Arbeit/Schulden; **be[come] all ~s** [plötzlich] ganz Ohr sein; **play by ~** (Mus.) nach dem Gehör spielen

ear[2] *n.* (Bot.) Ähre, *die*

ear: **~ache** *n.* Ohrenschmerzen *Pl.;* **~ clip** *n.* Ohr[en]klipp, *der;* **~ drops** *n. pl.* **(a)** (Med.) Ohrentropfen *Pl.;* **(b)** (earrings) Ohrgehänge, *das;* **~drum** *n.* Trommelfell, *das*

earl /ɜ:l/ *n.* Graf, *der*

'ear lobe *n.* Ohrläppchen, *das*

early /'ɜ:lɪ/ [1] *adj.* früh
[2] *adv.* früh; **I am a bit ~:** ich bin etwas zu früh gekommen; **~ next week** Anfang der nächsten Woche; **~ in June** Anfang Juni; **from ~ in the morning till late at night** von früh [morgens] bis spät [nachts]; **~ on** schon früh

early: **~ 'closing** *n.* **it is ~ closing** die Geschäfte haben nachmittags geschlossen; **~-'closing day** *n.: Tag, an dem die Geschäfte nachmittags geschlossen haben*

ear: **~mark** *v.t.* vorsehen; **~muffs** *n. pl.* Ohrenschützer *Pl.*

earn /ɜ:n/ *v.t.* verdienen; (bring in as income or interest) einbringen

earnest /'ɜ:nɪst/ [1] *adj.* ernsthaft
[2] *n.* **in ~:** mit vollem Ernst

earnings /'ɜ:nɪŋz/ *n. pl.* Verdienst, *der;* (of business etc.) Ertrag, *der*

ear: **~phones** *n. pl.* Kopfhörer, *der;* **~piece** *n.* Hörmuschel, *die;* **~-piercing** [1] *adj.* durch Mark und Bein gehend ‹*Lärm*›; [2] *n.* Durchstechen der Ohrläppchen; **~plug** *n.* Ohropax, *das* (Wz);

~ring *n.* Ohrring, *der;* **~shot** *n.* **out of/within ~shot** außer/in Hörweite; **~-splitting** *adj.* ohrenbetäubend

earth /ɜːθ/ 1 *n.* (also Brit. Electr.) Erde, *die;* **how/what** *etc.* **on ~ ...?** wie/was *usw.* in aller Welt ...?
2 *v.t.* (Brit. Electr.) erden

earthenware /ˈɜːθnweə(r)/ 1 *n.* Tonwaren *Pl.*
2 *adj.* Ton-

earthly /ˈɜːθlɪ/ *adj.* irdisch; **no ~ use** *etc.* (coll.) nicht der geringste Nutzen *usw.*

earth: ~quake *n.* Erdbeben, *das;* **~ sciences** *n. pl.* Geowissenschaften *Pl.;* **~worm** *n.* Regenwurm, *der*

ˈearthy *adj.* **(a)** erdig
(b) (coarse) derb

ˈearwax *n.* Ohrenschmalz, *das*

earwig /ˈɪəwɪɡ/ *n.* Ohrwurm, *der*

ease /iːz/ 1 *n.* **(a) set sb. at ~:** jmdn. beruhigen; **at [one's] ~:** entspannt; **be** *or* **feel at [one's] ~:** sich wohl fühlen; **[stand] at ~!** (Mil.) rührt euch!
(b) with ~ (without difficulty) mit Leichtigkeit
2 *v.t.* lindern ‹*Schmerz, Kummer*›; entspannen ‹*Lage*›; verringern ‹*Belastung, Druck, Spannung*›
3 *v.i.* nachlassen

easel /ˈiːzl/ *n.* Staffelei, *die*

easily /ˈizɪlɪ/ *adv.* leicht

east /iːst/ 1 *n.* **(a)** Osten, *der;* **in/to[wards]/from the ~:** im/nach/von Osten; **to the ~ of** östlich von
(b) *usu.* **E~** (Geog., Polit.) Osten, *der*
2 *adj.* östlich; Ost‹*küste, -wind, -grenze*›
3 *adv.* nach Osten; **~ of** östlich von

ˈEast Berˈlin *pr. n.* (Hist.) Ostberlin, *das*

ˈeastbound *adj.* ‹*Zug, Verkehr usw.*› in Richtung Osten

Easter /ˈiːstə(r)/ *n.* Ostern, *das od. Pl.*

ˈEaster egg *n.* Osterei, *das*

easterly /ˈiːstəlɪ/ *adj.* östlich; ‹*Wind*› aus östlichen Richtungen

Easter ˈMonday *n.* Ostermontag, *der*

eastern /ˈiːstən/ *adj.* östlich; Ost‹*grenze, -hälfte, -seite*›; **~ Germany** Ostdeutschland (*das*)

Eastern: ~ ˈEurope *pr. n.* Osteuropa, (*das*); **~ Euroˈpean** 1 *adj.* osteuropäisch; 2 *n.* Osteuropäer, *der*/Osteuropäerin, *die*

Easter ˈSunday *n.* Ostersonntag, *der*

East: ~ ˈGerman (Hist.) 1 *adj.* ostdeutsch; **he/she is ~ German** er ist Ostdeutscher/sie ist Ostdeutsche; 2 *n.* Ostdeutsche, *der/die;* **~ ˈGermany** *pr. n.* (Hist.) Ostdeutschland (*das*); **~ ˈTimor** /ˈtiːmɔː(r)/ *pr. n.* Osttimor (*das*)

eastward(s) /iːstwəd(z)/ *adv.* ostwärts

easy /ˈiːzɪ/ 1 *adj.* **(a)** leicht; **on ~ terms** auf Raten ‹*kaufen*›
(b) sorglos ‹*Leben, Zeit*›
2 *adv.* leicht; **easier said than done** leichter gesagt als getan; **take it ~!** (calm down!) beruhige dich!

easy: ~-care *attrib. adj.* pflegeleicht; **~ chair** *n.* Sessel, *der;* **~-ˈgoing** *adj.* gelassen; (lax) nachlässig; **~ ˈmoney** *n.* leicht verdientes Geld

eat /iːt/ *v.t. & i.,* **ate** /et, eɪt/, **eaten** /ˈiːtn/ essen; ‹*Tier:*› fressen
■ **eat aˈway** *v.t.* ‹*Rost, Säure:*› zerfressen
■ **eat ˈout** *v.i.* essen gehen
■ **eat ˈup** *v.t.* aufessen; ‹*Tier:*› auffressen

ˈeat-by date *n.* Verfallsdatum, *das*

eaten ▶ EAT

eating: ~ apple *n.* Essapfel, *der;* **~ disorder** *n.* Essstörung, *die* (*meist Pl.*); **~ place** *n.* Essgelegenheit, *die*

eau-de-Cologne /əʊdəkəˈləʊn/ *n.* Kölnischwasser, *das*

eaves /iːvz/ *n. pl.* Dachgesims, *das*

ˈeavesdrop *v.i.* lauschen; **~ on** belauschen

ˈeavesdropper *n.* Lauscher, *der*/Lauscherin, *die*

ˈe-banking *n.* E-Banking, *das*

ebb /eb/ 1 *n.* Ebbe, *die;* **be at a low ~** (fig.) ‹*Person, Stimmung, Moral:*› auf dem Nullpunkt sein
2 *v.i.* zurückgehen; **~ away** (fig.) dahinschwinden

ˈebb tide *n.* Ebbe, *die*

ebony /ˈebənɪ/ *n.* Ebenholz, *das*

EC *abbr.* = **European Community** EG

eccentric /ikˈsentrɪk/ 1 *adj.* exzentrisch
2 *n.* Exzentriker, *der*/Exzentrikerin, *die*

eccentricity /eksenˈtrɪsɪtɪ/ *n.* Exzentrizität, *die*

ecclesiastical /ɪkliːzɪˈæstɪkl/ *adj.* kirchlich; geistlich ‹*Musik*›

ECG *abbr.* = **electrocardiogram** EKG

echo /ˈekəʊ/ 1 *n.* Echo, *das*
2 *v.t.* zurückwerfen; (fig.: repeat) wiederholen

éclair /eɪˈkleə(r)/ *n.* Eclair, *das*

eclipse /ɪˈklɪps/ *n.* (Astron.) Finsternis, *die;* **~ of the sun** Sonnenfinsternis, *die*

ˈeco-friendly *adj.* umweltfreundlich

ecological /iːkəˈlɒdʒɪkl/ *adj.* ökologisch

ecoˈlogically *adv.* ökologisch; **~ aware/sound/harmful** umweltbewusst/-gerecht/-schädlich

ecologist /iːˈkɒlədʒɪst/ *n.* Ökologe, *der*/Ökologin, *die*

ecology /iːˈkɒlədʒɪ/ *n.* Ökologie, *die*

e-commerce /iːˈkɒmɜːs/ *n.* (Comp.) elektronischer Handel; E-Commerce, *der*

economic /iːkəˈnɒmɪk/ *adj.* **(a)** Wirtschafts‹*politik, -abkommen, -system, -krise, -wunder*›; wirtschaftlich ‹*Entwicklung, Zusammenbruch*›; **~ refugee** Wirtschaftsflüchtling, *der*
(b) (giving adequate return) wirtschaftlich

economical /iːkəˈnɒmɪkl/ *adj.* wirtschaftlich; sparsam ‹*Person*›; **be ~ with sth.** mit etw. haushalten

eco'nomically *adv.* wirtschaftlich; (not wastefully) sparsam

economics /iːkəˈnɒmɪks/ *n.* Wirtschaftswissenschaft, *die* (*meist Pl.*)

economist /ɪˈkɒnəmɪst/ *n.* Wirtschaftswissenschaftler, *der*/ -wissenschaftlerin, *die*

economize /ɪˈkɒnəmaɪz/ *v.i.* sparen; **~ on sth.** etw. sparen

economy /ɪˈkɒnəmɪ/ *n.* **(a)** (frugality) Sparsamkeit, *die*
(b) (instance) Einsparung, *die;* **make economies** zu Sparmaßnahmen greifen
(c) (of country etc.) Wirtschaft, *die*

economy: ~ class *n.* Touristenklasse, *die;* Economyklasse, *die;* **~-class syndrome** Economyclasssyndrom, *das;* **~ size** *n.* Haushaltspackung, *die*

'ecosystem *n.* Ökosystem, *das*

ecstasy /ˈekstəsɪ/ *n.* **(a)** Ekstase, *die*
(b) E~ (drug) Ecstasy, *das*

ecstatic /ɪkˈstætɪk/ *adj.* ekstatisch

eddy /ˈedɪ/ *n.* Strudel, *der*

edge /edʒ/ **1** *n.* **(a)** (of knife, razor, weapon) Schneide, *die;* **on ~** (fig.) nervös *od.* gereizt (**about** wegen)
(b) (of solid, bed, table) Kante, *die;* (of sheet of paper, road, forest, cliff) Rand, *der*
2 *v.i.* sich schieben

edgy /ˈedʒɪ/ *adj.* nervös

edible /ˈedɪbl/ *adj.* essbar

edict /ˈiːdɪkt/ *n.* Erlass, *der*

edit /ˈedɪt/ *v.t.* herausgeben ‹*Zeitung*›; redigieren ‹*Buch, Artikel, Manuskript*›

edition /ɪˈdɪʃn/ *n.* Ausgabe, *die*

editor /ˈedɪtə(r)/ *n.* Redakteur, *der*/ Redakteurin, *die;* (of particular work) Bearbeiter, *der*/Bearbeiterin, *die;* (of newspaper) Herausgeber, *der*/Herausgeberin, *die*

editorial /edɪˈtɔːrɪəl/ **1** *n.* Leitartikel, *der*
2 *adj.* redaktionell

EDP *abbr.* = **electronic data processing** EDV

educate /ˈedjʊkeɪt/ *v.t.* **(a)** (bring up) erziehen; (train mind and character of) bilden
(b) (provide schooling for) **he was ~d at ...:** er hat seine Ausbildung in ... erhalten

educated /ˈedjʊkeɪtɪd/ *adj.* gebildet

education /edjʊˈkeɪʃn/ *n.* Erziehung, *die;* (system) Erziehungswesen, *das*

educational /edjʊˈkeɪʃənl/ *adj.* pädagogisch; Lehr‹*film, -spiele, -anstalt*›; Erziehungs‹*methoden, -arbeit*›

edu'cation system *n.* Bildungssystem, *das*

EEC *abbr.* = **European Economic Community** EWG

eel /iːl/ *n.* Aal, *der*

eerie /ˈɪːrɪ/ *adj.* unheimlich

eff /ef/ *v.i.* (sl.) **~ and blind** fluchen

effect /ɪˈfekt/ *n.* **(a)** Wirkung, *die* (**on** auf + *Akk.*); **the ~s of sth. on sth.** die Auswirkungen einer Sache (*Gen.*) auf etw. (*Akk.*); **take ~:** die erwünschte Wirkung erzielen; **in ~:** in Wirklichkeit
(b) come into ~: gültig werden; ‹*Gesetz:*› in Kraft treten; **put into ~:** in Kraft setzen ‹*Gesetz*›; verwirklichen ‹*Plan*›; **with ~ from 2 November/Monday** mit Wirkung vom 2. November/von Montag
(c) personal ~s persönliches Eigentum; Privateigentum, *das;* **household ~s** Hausrat, *der*

effective /ɪˈfektɪv/ *adj.* **(a)** wirksam ‹*Mittel, Maßnahmen*›; **be ~** ‹*Arzneimittel:*› wirken
(b) (in operation) gültig; **~ from/as of** mit Wirkung vom

ef'fectively *adv.* (in fact) effektiv; (with effect) wirkungsvoll

effectual /ɪˈfektjʊəl/ *adj.* wirksam

effeminate /ɪˈfemɪnət/ *adj.* unmännlich

effervescent /efəˈvesənt/ *adj.* sprudelnd; (fig.) übersprudelnd

effete /eˈfiːt/ *adj.* verweichlicht

efficiency /ɪˈfɪʃənsɪ/ *n.* (of person) Fähigkeit, *die;* Tüchtigkeit, *die;* (of machine, factory, engine) Leistungsfähigkeit, *die;* (of organization, method) gutes Funktionieren

efficient /ɪˈfɪʃənt/ *adj.* fähig ‹*Person*›; tüchtig ‹*Arbeiter, Sekretärin*›; leistungsfähig ‹*Maschine, Motor, Fabrik*›; gut funktionierend ‹*Methode, Organisation*›

ef'ficiently *adj.* gut

effigy /ˈefɪdʒɪ/ *n.* Bildnis, *das*

effing /ˈefɪŋ/ *adj.* (sl.) Scheiß- (salopp)

effluent /ˈeflʊənt/ Abwässer *Pl.*

effort /ˈefət/ *n.* **(a)** Anstrengung, *die;* Mühe, *die;* **make an/every ~** (physically) sich anstrengen; (mentally) sich bemühen
(b) (attempt) Versuch, *der*

'effortless *adj.* mühelos

effrontery /ɪˈfrʌntərɪ/ *n.* Dreistigkeit, *die;* **have the ~ to do sth.** die Stirn besitzen, etw. zu tun

effusive /ɪˈfjuːsɪv/ *adj.* überschwänglich; exaltiert (geh.) ‹*Person*›

EFL *abbr.* = **English as a foreign language**

e.g. /iːˈdʒiː/ *abbr.* = **for example** z.B.

egg /eg/ *n.* Ei, *das*

■ **egg 'on** *v.t.* anstacheln

egg: ~cup *n.* Eierbecher, *der;* **~plant** *n.* Aubergine, *die;* (fruit also) Eierfrucht, *die;* (plant also) Eierpflanze, *die;* **~shell** *n.* Eierschale, *die;* **~ timer** *n.* Eieruhr, *die;* **~ white** *n.* Eiweiß, *das;* **~ yolk** *n.* Eigelb, *das*

ego /ˈegəʊ, ˈiːgəʊ/ *n., pl.* **~s (a)** (Psych.) Ego, *das*
(b) (self-esteem) Selbstbewusstsein, *das*

egotism /ˈegətɪzm/ *n.* **(a)** Egotismus, *der* (fachspr.); Ichbezogenheit, *die*

(b) (self-conceit) Egotismus, *der;* Selbstgefälligkeit, *die*

egotist /'egətɪst/ *n.* Egotist, *der*/Egotistin, *die* (fachspr.); (self-centred person) Egozentriker, *der*/Egozentrikerin, *die*

egotistic /egə'tɪstɪk/, **egotistical** /egə'tɪstɪkl/ *adj.* **(a)** ichbezogen ‹*Rede, Gespräch*›
(b) selbstsüchtig, selbstgefällig ‹*Person*›

Egypt /'i:dʒɪpt/ *pr. n.* Ägypten (*das*)

Egyptian /ɪ'dʒɪpʃn/ [1] *adj.* ägyptisch; **sb. is ~**: jmd. ist Ägypter/Ägypterin
[2] *n.* (person) Ägypter, *der*/Ägypterin, *die*

eiderdown /'aɪdədaʊn/ *n.* Federbett, *das*

eight /eɪt/ [1] *adj.* acht; **at ~**: um acht; **half past ~**: halb neun; **~ thirty** acht Uhr dreißig; **~ ten/fifty** zehn nach acht/vor neun; (esp. in timetable) acht Uhr zehn/fünfzig; **~-year-old boy** achtjähriger Junge; **an ~-year-old** ein Achtjähriger/eine Achtjährige; **at [the age of] ~, aged ~**: mit acht Jahren; **~ times** achtmal
[2] *n.* Acht, *die;* **the first/last ~**: die ersten/letzten acht; **there were ~ of us present** wir waren [zu] acht

eighteen /eɪ'ti:n/ [1] *adj.* achtzehn
[2] *n.* Achtzehn, *die. See also* EIGHT

eighteenth /eɪ'ti:nθ/ [1] *adj.* achtzehnt...
[2] *n.* (fraction) Achtzehntel, *das. See also* EIGHTH

eighth /eɪtθ/ [1] *adj.* acht...; **be/come ~**: Achter sein/als Achter ankommen; **~largest** achtgrößt...
[2] *n.* (in sequence, rank) Achte, *der/die/das;* (fraction) Achtel, *das;* **the ~ of May** der achte Mai

eightieth /'eɪtɪɪθ/ *adj.* achtzigst...

eighty /'eɪtɪ/ [1] *adj.* achtzig
[2] *n.* Achtzig, *die;* **the eighties** (years) die Achtzigerjahre; **be in one's eighties** in den Achtzigern sein. *See also* EIGHT

Eire /'eərə/ *pr. n.* Irland, *das;* Eire, *das*

either /'aɪðə(r), 'i:ðə(r)/ [1] *adj.* **(a)** (each) **at ~ end of the table** an beiden Enden des Tisches
(b) (one or other) [irgend]ein ... [von beiden]; **take ~ one** nimm einen/eine/eins von [den] beiden
[2] *pron.* **(a)** (each) beide *Pl.;* **I can't cope with ~**: ich kann mit keinem von beiden fertig werden
(b) (one or other) einer/eine/ein[e]s [von beiden]
[3] *adv.* auch [nicht]; **'I don't like that ~**: ich mag es auch nicht
[4] *conj.* **~ ... or ...**: entweder ... oder ...; (after negation) weder ... noch ...

ejaculate /ɪ'dʒækjʊleɪt/ [1] *v.t.* (utter suddenly) ausstoßen
[2] *v.i.* (eject semen) ejakulieren

eject /'ɪdʒekt/ [1] *v.t.* **(a)** (from hall, meeting) hinauswerfen (**from** aus)
(b) ‹*Gerät:*› auswerfen, ‹*Person:*› herausholen ‹*Kassette*›
[2] *v.i.* sich hinauskatapultieren

ejector seat /ɪ'dʒektə si:t/ *n.* Schleudersitz, *der*

eke out /i:k 'aʊt/ *v.t.* strecken; **~ out a living** sich (*Dat.*) seinen Lebensunterhalt notdürftig verdienen

elaborate [1] /ɪ'læbərət/ *adj.* kompliziert; kunstvoll [gearbeitet] ‹*Arrangement, Verzierung*›
[2] /ɪ'læbəreɪt/ *v.i.* mehr ins Detail gehen; **~ on** näher ausführen

elapse /ɪ'læps/ *v.i.* ‹*Zeit:*› vergehen

elastic /ɪ'læstɪk/ [1] *adj.* elastisch
[2] *n.* (~ band) Gummiband, *das*

elastic 'band *n.* Gummiband, *das*

elated /ɪ'leɪtɪd/ *adj.* freudig erregt; **be** *or* **feel ~**: in Hochstimmung sein

elation /ɪ'leɪʃn/ *n.* freudige Erregung

elbow /'elbəʊ/ [1] *n.* Ell[en]bogen, *der*
[2] *v.t.* **~ sb. aside** jmdn. mit dem Ellenbogen zur Seite stoßen

elbow: ~ grease *n.* (joc.) Muskelkraft, *die;* **~ room** *n.* Ell[en]bogenfreiheit, *die*

elder[1] /'eldə(r)/ [1] *attrib. adj.* älter...
[2] *n.* **(a)** (senior) Ältere, *der/die*
(b) (village ~, church ~) Älteste, *der/die*

elder[2] *n.* (Bot.) Holunder, *der*

'elderberry *n.* Holunderbeere, *die*

elderly /'eldəlɪ/ [1] *adj.* älter
[2] *n. pl.* **the ~**: ältere Menschen

eldest /'eldɪst/ *adj.* ältest...

elect /ɪ'lekt/ [1] *adj. postpos.* gewählt; **the President ~**: der designierte Präsident
[2] *v.t.* wählen; **~ sb. chairman** jmdn. zum Vorsitzenden wählen

election /ɪ'lekʃn/ *n.* Wahl, *die;* **general ~**: allgemeine Wahlen *Pl.*; **~ results** Wahlergebnisse *Pl.*

e'lection campaign *n.* Wahlkampagne, *die*

electioneer /ɪlekʃə'nɪə(r)/ *v.i.* **be/go ~ing** Wahlkampf machen

elector /ɪ'lektə(r)/ *n.* Wähler, *der*/Wählerin, *die*

electoral /ɪ'lektərl/ *adj.* Wahl-

electoral 'college *n.* Wahlmännergremium, *das;* Wahlausschuss, *der*

electorate /ɪ'lektərət/ *n.* Wähler *Pl.*

electric /ɪ'lektrɪk/ *adj.* elektrisch; Elektro‹*kabel, -motor, -herd, -kessel*›; Strom‹*versorgung*›; (fig.) spannungsgeladen ‹*Atmosphäre*›

electrical /ɪ'lektrɪkl/ *adj.* elektrisch; Elektro‹*abteilung, -handel, -geräte*›

electric: ~ 'blanket *n.* Heizdecke, *die;* **~ 'chair** *n.* elektrischer Stuhl; **~ cooker** *n.* Elektroherd, *der;* **~ 'fire** *n.* [elektrischer] Heizofen; **~ gui'tar** *n.* elektrische Gitarre; E-Gitarre, *die*

electrician /ɪlek'trɪʃn/ *n.* Elektriker, *der*/Elektrikerin, *die*

electricity /ɪlek'trɪsɪtɪ/ *n.* Elektrizität, *die*
electricity: ~ bill *n.* Stromrechnung, *die;* **~ man** *n.* (fitter) Elektroinstallateur, *der;* (meter reader, collector) Stromableser, *der;* **~ meter** *n.* Stromzähler, *der*
electric 'shock *n.* Stromschlag, *der*
electrify /ɪ'lektrɪfaɪ/ *v.t.* elektrifizieren; (fig.) elektrisieren
electro'cardiogram *n.* Elektrokardiogramm, *das*
electrocute /ɪ'lektrəkju:t/ *v.t.* durch Stromschlag töten
electrode /ɪ'lektrəʊd/ *n.* Elektrode, *die*
electro'magnet *n.* Elektromagnet, *der*
electromag'netic *adj.* elektromagnetisch
electron /ɪ'lektrɒn/ *n.* Elektron, *das*
electronic /ɪlek'trɒnɪk/ *adj.* elektronisch
electronic: ~ 'cash *n.* elektronisches Geld; **~ 'mail** *n.* elektronische Post; **~ 'publishing** *n.* elektronisches Publizieren
electronics /ɪlek'trɒnɪks/ *n.* Elektronik, *die*
electronic: ~ 'shopping basket *n.* elektronischer Warenkorb; **~'storefront** *n.* elektronisches Schaufenster
electron 'microscope *n.* Elektronenmikroskop, *das*
elegance /'elɪgəns/ *n.* Eleganz, *die*
elegant /'elɪgənt/ *adj.* elegant
elegy /'elɪdʒɪ/ *n.* Elegie, *die*
element /'elɪmənt/ *n.* **(a)** Element, *das* **(b)** (Electr.) Heizelement, *das* **(c) ~s** (rudiments) Grundlagen *Pl.*
elementary /elɪ'mentərɪ/ *adj.* elementar; grundlegend ‹*Fakten, Wissen*›; Grundschul‹*bildung*›; Grund‹*kurs, -ausbildung, -kenntnisse*›
elementary: ~ 'particle *n.* (Phys.) Elementarteilchen, *das;* **~ school** *n.* Grundschule, *die*
elephant /'elɪfənt/ *n.* Elefant, *der;* **white ~** (fig.) nutzloser Besitz; **be a white ~** ‹*Gebäude, Einkaufszentrum usw.:*› reine Geldverschwendung sein
elevate /'elɪveɪt/ *v.t.* [empor]heben
elevation /elɪ'veɪʃn/ *n.* **(a)** (height) Höhe, *die* **(b)** (Archit.) Aufriss, *der*
elevator /'elɪveɪtə(r)/ *n.* (Amer.) Aufzug, *der;* Fahrstuhl, *der*
eleven /ɪ'levn/ **1** *adj.* elf **2** *n.* (also Sport) Elf, *die. See also* EIGHT
elevenses /ɪ'levnzɪz/ *n. sing. or pl.* (Brit. coll.) ≈ zweites Frühstück [gegen elf Uhr]
eleventh /ɪ'levnθ/ **1** *adj.* elft...; **at the ~ hour** in letzter Minute **2** *n.* (fraction) Elftel, *das. See also* EIGHTH
elf /elf/ *n., pl.* **elves** /elvz/ Elf, *der*/ Elfe, *die*
elicit /ɪ'lɪsɪt/ *v.t.* entlocken (**from** *Dat.*); gewinnen ‹*Unterstützung*›
eligible /'elɪdʒɪbl/ *adj.* **be ~ for sth.** (fit) für etw. geeignet sein; (entitled) zu etw. berechtigt sein
eliminate /ɪ'lɪmɪneɪt/ *v.t.* **(a)** (remove) beseitigen; ausschließen ‹*Möglichkeit*› **(b)** (exclude) ausschließen; **be ~d** (Sport) ausscheiden
elimination /ɪlɪmɪ'neɪʃn/ *n.* **(a)** (removal) Beseitigung, *die;* **process of ~:** Ausleseverfahren, *das* **(b)** (exclusion) Ausschluss, *der;* (Sport) Ausscheiden, *das*
élite /eɪ'li:t/ *n.* Elite, *die*
élitist /eɪ'li:tɪst/*adj.* elitär; Elite‹*denken*›
elk /elk/ *n., pl.* **~s** *or same* **(a)** (deer) Elch, *der* **(b)** (moose) Riesenelch, *der*
ellipse /ɪ'lɪps/ *n.* Ellipse, *die*
elliptical /ɪ'lɪptɪkl/ *adj.* elliptisch
elm /elm/ *n.* Ulme, *die*
elongated /'i:lɒŋgeɪtɪd/ *adj.* lang gestreckt
elope /ɪ'ləʊp/ *v.i.* durchbrennen (ugs.)
eloquence /'eləkwəns/ *n.* Beredtheit, *die*
eloquent /'eləkwənt/ *adj.* beredt ‹*Person*›; gewandt ‹*Stil, Redner*›
else /els/ *adv.* **(a)** (besides) sonst [noch]; **somebody/something ~:** [noch] jemand anders/noch etwas; **everybody/everything ~:** alle anderen/alles andere; **who/what/when/how ~?** wer/was/wann/wie sonst noch?; **why ~?** warum sonst? **(b)** (instead) ander...; **sb. ~'s hat** der Hut von jmd. anders; **anybody/anything ~?** [irgend]jemand anders/[irgend]etwas anderes?; **somebody/something ~:** jemand anders/etwas anderes; **everybody/everything ~:** alle anderen/alles andere **(c)** (otherwise) sonst; **or ~:** oder aber; **do it or ~ ...!** tun Sie es, sonst ...!
'elsewhere *adv.* woanders
elude /ɪ'lju:d/ *v.t.* (avoid) ausweichen (+ *Dat.*); (escape from) entkommen (+ *Dat.*)
elusive /ɪ'lju:sɪv/ *adj.* schwer zu erreichen ‹*Person*›; schwer zu fassen ‹*Straftäter*›; schwer definierbar ‹*Begriff, Sinn*›
elves *pl. of* ELF
emaciated /ɪ'meɪsɪeɪtɪd/ *adj.* abgezehrt
e-mail /'i:meɪl/ **1** *n.* E-Mail, *die;* **~ address** E-Mail-Adresse, *die;* **~ message** E-Mail, *die* **2** *v.t.* per E-Mail übermitteln ‹*Ergebnisse, Datei usw.*›; **~ sb.** jmdm. eine E-Mail schicken
emancipated /ɪ'mænsɪpeɪtɪd/ *adj.* emanzipiert: **become ~:** sich emanzipieren
emancipation /ɪmænsɪ'peɪʃn/ *n.* Emanzipation, *die*
embalm /ɪm'bɑ:m/ *v.t.* einbalsamieren
embankment /ɪm'bæŋkmənt/ *n.* Damm, *der*
embargo /em'bɑ:gəʊ/ *n., pl.* **~es** Embargo, *das;* **put** *or* **lay an ~ on sth.** etw. mit einem Embargo belegen

embark /ɪm'bɑːk/ *v.i.* **(a)** sich einschiffen (**for** nach)
(b) ~ **[up]on sth.** etw. in Angriff nehmen

embarkation /embɑː'keɪʃn/ *n.* Einschiffung, *die*

embarrass /ɪm'bærəs/ *v.t.* in Verlegenheit bringen

embarrassed /ɪm'bærəst/ *adj.* verlegen; **feel ~**: verlegen sein

em'barrassing *adj.* peinlich

em'barrassment *n.* Verlegenheit, *die*

embassy /'embəsɪ/ *n.* Botschaft, *die*

embed /ɪm'bed/ *v.t.*, **-dd-**: **(a)** (fix) einlassen; **~ sth. in cement/concrete** etw. einzementieren/einbetonieren; **~ded in the mud** im Schlamm versunken; **~ded journalist** eingebetteter Journalist; **~ded sentence** (Ling.) eingeschobener Satz

embellish /em'belɪʃ/ *v.t.* beschönigen ‹*Wahrheit*›; ausschmücken ‹*Geschichte, Bericht*›

embers /'embəz/ *n. pl.* Glut, *die*

embezzle /ɪ'mbezl/ *v.t.* unterschlagen

embitter /ɪm'bɪtə(r)/ *v.t.* verbittern

emblem /'embləm/ *n.* Emblem, *das*

embody /ɪm'bɒdɪ/ *v.t.* verkörpern

embrace /ɪm'breɪs/ [1] *v.t.* umarmen; (fig.: accept, adopt) annehmen
[2] *v.i.* sich umarmen
[3] *n.* Umarmung, *die*

embroider /ɪm'brɔɪdə(r)/ *v.t.* sticken ‹*Muster*›; besticken ‹*Tuch, Kleid*›; (fig.) ausschmücken

embroidery /ɪm'brɔɪdərɪ/ *n.* Stickerei, *die*

embroil /ɪm'brɔɪl/ *v.t.* **become/be ~ed in sth.** in etw. (*Akk.*) verwickelt werden/sein

embryo /'embrɪəʊ/ *n.* Embryo, *der;* **~ research** Embryonenforschung, *die*

embryonic /embrɪ'ɒnɪk/ *adj.* (Biol., fig.) Embryonal‹*entwicklung, -struktur, -zustand, -stadium*›; unausgereift ‹*Vorstellung*›

emerald /'emərəld/ [1] *n.* Smaragd, *der*
[2] *adj.* smaragdgrün; **the E~ Isle** die Grüne Insel

emerald 'green *n.* Smaragdgrün, *das*

emerge /ɪ'mɜːdʒ/ *v.i.* auftauchen (**from** aus, **from behind** hinter + *Dat.*); ‹*Wahrheit:*› an den Tag kommen; **it ~s that ...**: es stellt sich heraus, dass ...

emergency /ɪ'mɜːdʒənsɪ/ [1] *n.* Notfall, *der;* **in an** *or* **in case of ~**: im Notfall; **declare a state of ~**: den Ausnahmezustand ausrufen
[2] *adj.* Not-

emergency: ~ exit *n.* Notausgang, *der;* **~ services** *n. pl.* Hilfsdienste *Pl.*

'emery paper *n.* Schmirgelpapier, *das*

emigrant /'emɪgrənt/ *n.* Auswanderer, *der*/ Auswanderin, *die*

emigrate /'emɪgreɪt/ *v.i.* auswandern (**to** nach, **from** aus)

emigration /emɪ'greɪʃn/ *n.* Auswanderung, *die* (**to** nach, **from** aus)

eminence /'emɪnəns/ *n.* hohes Ansehen

eminent /'emɪnənt/ *adj.* bedeutend; herausragend

emission /ɪ'mɪʃn/ *n.* Emission, *die* (fachspr.); (process also) Abgabe, *die*

emit /ɪ'mɪt/ *v.t.*, **-tt-** abgeben, emittieren (fachspr.) ‹*Wärme, Strahlung usw.*›; ausstoßen ‹*Rauch*›

emoticon /ɪ'mɒtɪkɒn/ *n.* (Comp.) Emoticon, *das*

emotion /ɪ'məʊʃn/ *n.* Gefühl, *das*

emotional /ɪ'məʊʃənl/ *adj.* emotional; Gemüts‹*zustand, -störung*›; gefühlvoll ‹*Stimme*›

e'motionally *adv.* emotional; gefühlvoll ‹*sprechen*›; **~ disturbed** seelisch gestört

emotive /ɪ'məʊtɪv/ *adj.* emotional

empathize /'empəθaɪz/ *v.i.* **~ with sb.** sich in jmdn. hineinversetzen; **~ with sth.** etw. nachempfinden

empathy /'empəθɪ/ *n.* Empathie, *die* (Psych.); Einfühlung, *die*

emperor /'empərə(r)/ *n.* Kaiser, *der*

emphasis /'emfəsɪs/ *n., pl.* **emphases** /'emfəsiːz/ Betonung, *die;* **lay** *or* **place** *or* **put ~ on sth.** etw. betonen

emphasize /'emfəsaɪz/ *v.t.* betonen

emphatic /ɪm'fætɪk/ *adj.* nachdrücklich; demonstrativ ‹*Ablehnung*›; **be ~ that ...**: darauf bestehen, dass ...

em'phatically *adv.* nachdrücklich

empire /'empaɪə(r)/ *n.* Reich, *das*

empirical /ɪm'pɪrɪkl/ *adj.* empirisch

employ /ɪm'plɔɪ/ *v.t.* **(a)** (take on) einstellen; (have working for one) beschäftigen; **be ~ed by a company** bei einer Firma arbeiten
(b) (use) einsetzen (**for, in, on** für); anwenden ‹*Methode, List*› (**for, in, on** bei)

employee (*Amer.:* **employe**) /emplɔɪ'iː, em'plɔɪiː/ *n.* Angestellte, *der/die*

employer /ɪm'plɔɪə(r)/ *n.* Arbeitgeber, *der*/ -geberin, *die*

employment /ɪm'plɔɪmənt/ *n.* **(a)** (work) Arbeit, *die*
(b) (regular trade or profession) Beschäftigung, *die*

employment: ~ agency *n.* Stellenvermittlung, *die;* **~ office** *n.* (Brit.) Arbeitsamt, *das*

empower /ɪm'paʊə(r)/ *v.t.* (authorize) ermächtigen; (enable) befähigen

empress /'emprɪs/ *n.* Kaiserin, *die*

emptiness /'emptɪnɪs/ *n.* Leere, *die*

empty /'emptɪ/ [1] *adj.* leer; frei ‹*Sitz, Parkplatz*›
[2] *v.t.* leeren; (pour) schütten (**over** über + *Akk.*)
[3] *v.i.* sich leeren

'empty-handed *adj.* mit leeren Händen

EMS *abbr.* = **European Monetary System** EWS
emu /'iːmjuː/ *n.* (Ornith.) Emu, *der*
EMU *abbr.* = **Economic and Monetary Union** WWU
emulate /'emjʊleɪt/ *v.t.* nacheifern (+ *Dat.*)
emulsion /ɪ'mʌlʃn/ *n.* **(a)** Emulsion, *die*
(b) ▶ EMULSION PAINT
e'mulsion paint *n.* Dispersionsfarbe, *die*
enable /ɪ'neɪbl/ *v.t.* **~ sb. to do sth.** es jmdm. ermöglichen, etw. zu tun
enamel /ɪ'næml/ **1** *n.* Email, *das*
2 *v.t.*, (Brit.) **-ll-** emaillieren
enchant /ɪn'tʃɑːnt/ *v.t.* verzaubern; (delight) entzücken
en'chanted *adj.* verzaubert
en'chanting *adj.* entzückend
en'chantment *n.* Verzauberung, *die;* (fig.) Zauber, *der*
encircle /ɪn'sɜːkl/ *v.t.* umgeben
encl. *abbr.* = **enclosed, enclosure[s]** Anl.
enclave /'enkleɪv/ *n.* Enklave, *die*
enclose /ɪn'kləʊz/ *v.t.* **(a)** (surround) umgeben; (shut up or in) einschließen
(b) (with letter) beilegen (**with, in** *Dat.*); **please find ~d** anbei erhalten Sie
enclosure /ɪn'kləʊʒə(r)/ *n.* **(a)** (in zoo) Gehege, *das*
(b) (with letter) Anlage, *die*
encode /ɪn'kəʊd/ *v.t.* verschlüsseln; chiffrieren
encore /'ɒŋkɔː(r)/ **1** *int.* Zugabe!
2 *n.* Zugabe, *die*
encounter /ɪn'kaʊntə(r)/ **1** *v.t.* (as adversary) treffen auf (+ *Akk.*); (by chance) begegnen (+ *Dat.*); stoßen auf (+ *Akk.*) ‹*Problem, Widerstand usw.*›
2 *n.* (chance meeting) Begegnung, *die*
encourage /ɪn'kʌrɪdʒ/ *v.t.* ermutigen; (promote) fördern
encouragement *n.* Ermutigung, *die* (**from** durch)
encroach /ɪn'krəʊtʃ/ *v.i.* **~ on** eindringen in (+ *Akk.*); in Anspruch nehmen ‹*Zeit*›
encrypt /en'krɪpt/ *v.t.* (Comp.) verschlüsseln ‹*Daten etc.*›
encumber /ɪn'kʌmbə(r)/ *v.t.* belasten
encumbrance /ɪn'kʌmbrəns/ *n.* Belastung, *die*
encyclopaedia /ɪnsaɪklə'piːdɪə/ *n.* Lexikon, *das;* Enzyklopädie, *die*
encyclopaedic /ɪnsaɪklə'piːdɪk/ *adj.* enzyklopädisch
end /end/ **1** *n.* **(a)** Ende, *das;* (of nose, hair, finger) Spitze, *die;* **from ~ to ~**: von einem Ende zum anderen; **at the ~ of 1987/March** Ende 1987/März; **in the ~**: schließlich; **come to an ~**: ein Ende nehmen; **be at an ~**: zu Ende sein
(b) (of box, packet, etc.) Schmalseite, *die;* (top/bottom surface) Ober-/Unterseite, *die;* **on ~**: hochkant; **make ~s meet** (fig.) zurechtkommen; **no ~ of** (coll.) unendlich viel/viele
(c) (remnant) Rest, *der;* (of cigarette) Stummel, *der*
(d) (purpose, object) Ziel, *das;* **~ in itself** Selbstzweck, *der*
2 *v.t.* beenden
3 *v.i.* enden
■ **end 'up** *v.i.* enden; **~ up in** (coll.) landen in (+ *Dat.*); **~ up [as] a teacher** (coll.) schließlich Lehrer werden
endanger /ɪn'deɪndʒə(r)/ *v.t.* gefährden
endear /ɪn'dɪə(r)/ *v.t.* **~ sb./sth./oneself to sb.** jmdn./etw./sich bei jmdm. beliebt machen
en'dearing *adj.* reizend; gewinnend ‹*Lächeln, Art*›
endeavour (*Brit.; Amer.:* **endeavor**) /ɪn'devə(r)/ **1** *v.i.* **~ to do sth.** sich bemühen, etw. zu tun
2 *n.* Bemühung, *die;* (attempt) Versuch, *der*
'ending *n.* Schluss, *der;* (of word) Endung, *die*
endive /'endaɪv/ *n.* Endivie, *die*
'endless *adj.* endlos
'endlessly *adv.* unaufhörlich ‹*streiten, schwatzen*›
endorse /ɪn'dɔːs/ *v.t.* **(a)** indossieren ‹*Scheck*›
(b) beipflichten (+ *Dat.*) ‹*Meinung*›; billigen ‹*Entscheidung, Handlung*›; unterstützen ‹*Vorschlag*›
(c) (Brit. Law) einen Strafvermerk machen auf (+ *Akk. od. Dat.*)
en'dorsement *n.* **(a)** (of cheque) Indossament, *das*
(b) (support) Billigung, *die;* (of proposal) Unterstützung, *die*
(c) (Brit. Law) Strafvermerk, *der*
endow /ɪn'daʊ/ *v.t.* [über Stiftungen/ eine Stiftung] finanzieren; stiften ‹*Preis, Lehrstuhl*›; **be ~ed with charm/a talent for music** Charme/musikalisches Talent besitzen
en'dowment mortgage *n.* ≈ Tilgungslebensversicherung, *die;*
end: ~ 'product *n.* Endprodukt, *das;* **~ re'sult** *n.* Ergebnis, *das;* (consequence) Folge, *die*
endurable /ɪn'djʊərəbl/ *adj.* erträglich
endurance /ɪn'djʊərəns/ *n.* Ausdauer, *die*
en'durance test *n.* Belastungsprobe, *die*
endure /ɪn'djʊə(r)/ *v.t.* ertragen
enema /'enəmə/ *n.* Einlauf, *der*
enemy /'enəmɪ/ **1** *n.* Feind, *der* (**of, to** *Gen.*)
2 *adj.* feindlich
energetic /enə'dʒetɪk/ *adj.* energiegeladen; (active) tatkräftig
energy /'enədʒɪ/ *n.* Energie, *die*
energy: ~ consumption *n.* Energieverbrauch, *der;* **~ crisis** *n.* ⇢

Energiekrise, *die;* ~ **resources** *n. pl.* Energieressourcen *Pl.;* **~-saving** *adj.* Energie sparend; **~-saving lamp** Energiesparlampe, *die*

enforce /ɪn'fɔ:s/ *v.t.* durchsetzen; sorgen für ‹*Disziplin*›; **~d** erzwungen ‹*Schweigen*›; unfreiwillig ‹*Untätigkeit*›

ENG *abbr.* = **electronic news-gathering** elektronische Berichterstattung; EB

engage /ɪn'geɪdʒ/ **1** *v.t.* **(a)** (hire) einstellen ‹*Arbeiter*›; engagieren ‹*Sänger*›
(b) wecken ‹*Interesse*›; auf sich (*Akk.*) ziehen ‹*Aufmerksamkeit*›
(c) ~ **the clutch/first gear** einkuppeln/den ersten Gang einlegen
2 *v.i.* ~ **in sth.** sich an etw. (*Dat.*) beteiligen; ~ **in politics** sich politisch engagieren

engaged /ɪn'geɪdʒd/ *adj.* **(a) be ~ [to be married] [to sb.]** [mit jmdm.] verlobt sein; **get ~ [to be married] [to sb.]** sich [mit jmdm.] verloben
(b) be ~ in sth./in doing sth. mit etw. beschäftigt sein/damit beschäftigt sein, etw. zu tun; **be otherwise ~:** etwas anderes vorhaben
(c) besetzt ‹*Toilette, [Telefon]anschluss, Nummer*›; ~ **signal** *or* **tone** (Brit.) Besetztzeichen, *das*

en'gagement *n.* **(a)** (to be married) Verlobung, *die* (**to** mit)
(b) (appointment) Verabredung, *die*

en'gagement ring *n.* Verlobungsring, *der*

engaging /ɪn'geɪdʒɪŋ/ *adj.* bezaubernd; einnehmend ‹*Persönlichkeit, Art*›

engine /'endʒɪn/ *n.* **(a)** Motor, *der;* (rocket/jet ~) Triebwerk, *das*
(b) (locomotive) Lok[omotive], *die*

'engine driver *n.* Lok[omotiv]führer, *der*

engineer /endʒɪ'nɪə(r)/ **1** *n.* **(a)** Ingenieur, *der*/Ingenieurin, *die;* (service ~, installation ~) Techniker, *der*/Technikerin, *die*
(b) (Amer.: engine driver) Lok[omotiv]führer, *der*
2 *v.t.* arrangieren

engi'neering *n.* Technik, *die*

England /'ɪŋglənd/ *pr. n.* England (*das*)

English /'ɪŋglɪʃ/ **1** *adj.* englisch; **he/she is ~:** er ist Engländer/sie ist Engländerin
2 *n.* **(a)** Englisch, *das;* **say sth. in ~:** etw. auf Englisch sagen; **I cannot** *or* **do not speak ~:** ich spreche kein Englisch; **translate into/from [the] ~:** ins Englische/aus dem Englischen übersetzen
(b) *pl.* **the ~:** die Engländer *Pl.*

English: ~ **'breakfast** *n.* englisches Frühstück; ~ **'Channel** *pr. n.* **the ~ Channel** der [Ärmel]kanal; **~man** /-mən/ *n., pl.* **~men** /-mən/ Engländer, *der;* **~woman** *n.* Engländerin, *die*

engrave /ɪn'greɪv/ *v.t.* gravieren; eingravieren ‹*Namen, Figur usw.*›

engraving /ɪn'greɪvɪŋ/ *n.* Stich, *der;* (from wood) Holzschnitt, *der*

engross /ɪn'grəʊs/ *v.t.* fesseln; **be ~ed in sth.** in etw. (*Akk.*) vertieft sein; **become** *or* **get ~ed in sth.** sich in etw. (*Akk.*) vertiefen

engrossing /ɪn'grəʊsɪŋ/ *adj.* fesselnd

engulf /ɪn'gʌlf/ *v.t.* verschlingen

enhance /ɪn'hɑ:ns/ *v.t.* erhöhen ‹*Wert, Aussichten, Schönheit*›; verstärken ‹*Wirkung*›; heben ‹*Aussehen*›

enigma /ɪ'nɪgmə/ *n.* Rätsel, *das*

enigmatic /enɪg'mætɪk/ *adj.* rätselhaft

enjoy /ɪn'dʒɔɪ/ **1** *v.t.* **(a) I ~ed the book/work** das Buch/die Arbeit hat mir gefallen; **he ~s reading/travelling** er liest/reist gern
(b) genießen ‹*Rechte, Privilegien, Vorteile*›
2 *v. refl.* sich amüsieren

enjoyable /ɪn'dʒɔɪəbl/ *adj.* schön; angenehm ‹*Empfindung, Arbeit*›; unterhaltsam ‹*Buch, Film, Stück*›

en'joyment *n.* Vergnügen, *das* (**of** an + *Dat.*)

enlarge /ɪn'lɑ:dʒ/ **1** *v.t.* vergrößern; verbreitern ‹*Straße, Durchgang*›
2 *v.i.* ~ **[up]on sth.** etw. weiter ausführen

en'largement *n.* Vergrößerung, *die;* (making wider) Verbreiterung, *die*

enlighten /ɪn'laɪtn/ *v.t.* aufklären (**on, as to** über + *Akk.*).

en'lightenment *n.* Aufklärung, *die*

enlist /ɪn'lɪst/ **1** *v.t.* (obtain) gewinnen
2 *v.i.* ~ **[for the army/navy]** in die Armee/Marine eintreten; ~ **[as a soldier]** Soldat werden

enliven /ɪn'laɪvn/ *v.t.* beleben

enmity /'enmɪtɪ/ *n.* Feindschaft, *die*

enormous /ɪ'nɔ:məs/ *adj.* enorm; riesig, gewaltig ‹*Figur, Tier, Menge*›

e'normously *adv.* enorm

enough /ɪ'nʌf/ **1** *adj.* genug; **there's ~ room** es ist Platz genug
2 *n.* genug; **be ~ to do sth.** genügen, etw. zu tun; **have had ~ [of sb./sth.]** genug [von jmdm./etw.] haben; **I've had ~!** jetzt reicht's mir aber!
3 *adv.* genug; **oddly/funnily ~:** merkwürdigerweise/(ugs.) komischerweise

enquire /ɪn'kwaɪə(r)/ **1** *v.i.* sich erkundigen (**about, after** nach, **of** bei); ~ **into** untersuchen
2 *v.t.* sich erkundigen nach ‹*Weg, Namen*›

enquiring /ɪn'kwaɪərɪŋ/ *adj.* fragend; forschend ‹*Geist*›

enquiry /ɪn'kwaɪərɪ/ *n.* **(a)** (question) Erkundigung, *die* (**into** über + *Akk.*); **make enquiries** Erkundigungen einziehen; ~ **desk,** ~ **office** Auskunft, *die*
(b) (investigation) Untersuchung, *die*

enrage /ɪn'reɪdʒ/ *v.t.* wütend machen; **be ~d by sth.** über etw. (*Akk.*) wütend werden

enrich /ɪn'rɪtʃ/ *v.t.* reich machen; (fig.) bereichern

enrol (*Amer.*: **enroll**) /ɪn'rəʊl/ [1] *v.i.*, **-ll-** sich einschreiben; ~ **for a course** sich zu einem Kurs anmelden
[2] *v.t.* einschreiben

en'rolment (*Amer.*: **en'rollment**) *n.* Einschreibung, *die*

en route /ɑ̃ 'ru:t/ *adv.* unterwegs; ~ **to Scotland/for Edinburgh** auf dem Weg nach Schottland/Edinburgh

ensign /'ensaɪn, 'ensn/ *n.* Hoheitszeichen, *das*

enslave /ɪn'sleɪv/ *v.t.* versklaven

ensue /ɪn'sju:/ *v.i.* folgen (**from** aus); **the discussion which ~d** die anschließende Diskussion

ensure /ɪn'ʃʊə(r)/ *v.t.* ~ **that ...** (see to it that) gewährleisten, dass ...; ~ **sth.** etw. gewährleisten

entail /ɪn'teɪl/ *v.t.* mit sich bringen; **sth. ~s doing sth.** etw. bedeutet, dass man etw. tun muss

entangle /ɪn'tæŋgl/ *v.t.* sich verfangen lassen; **get** *or* **become ~d in** *or* **with sth.** sich in etw. (*Dat.*) verfangen

enter /'entə(r)/ [1] *v.i.* **(a)** hineingehen; ‹*Fahrzeug*:› hineinfahren; (come in) hereinkommen; (into room) eintreten
(b) (register as competitor) sich zur Teilnahme anmelden (**for** an + *Dat.*)
[2] *v.t.* **(a)** [hinein]gehen in (+ *Akk.*); ‹*Fahrzeug*:› [hinein]fahren in (+ *Akk.*); betreten ‹*Gebäude, Zimmer*›; einlaufen in (+ *Akk.*) ‹*Hafen*›; einreisen in (+ *Akk.*) ‹*Land*›; (come into) [herein]kommen in (+ *Akk.*)
(b) teilnehmen an (+ *Dat.*) ‹*Rennen, Wettbewerb*›
(c) (in book etc.) eintragen (**in** in + *Akk.*)
(d) (Comp.) eingeben ‹*Daten usw.*›; **press ~:** 'Enter' drücken
■ **'enter into** *v.t.* aufnehmen ‹*Verhandlungen*›; eingehen ‹*Verpflichtung*›; schließen ‹*Vertrag*›
■ **'enter [up]on** *v.t.* beginnen

'enter key *n.* (Comp.) Entertaste, *die*, Eingabetaste, *die*

enterprise /'entəpraɪz/ *n.* **(a)** (undertaking) Unternehmen, *das;* **free/private ~:** freies/privates Unternehmertum
(b) (enterprising spirit) Unternehmungsgeist, *der*

enterprising /'entəpraɪzɪŋ/ *adj.* unternehmungslustig

entertain /entə'teɪn/ *v.t.* **(a)** (amuse) unterhalten
(b) (receive as guest) bewirten
(c) haben ‹*Vorstellung*›; hegen (geh.) ‹*Gefühl, Verdacht, Zweifel*›; (consider) in Erwägung ziehen

enter'tainer *n.* Unterhalter, *der*/Unterhalterin, *die*

enter'taining *adj.* unterhaltsam

enter'tainment *n.* **(a)** (amusement) Unterhaltung, *die*
(b) (performance, show) Veranstaltung, *die*

enthral (*Amer.*: **enthrall**) /ɪn'θrɔ:l/ *v.t.*, **-ll-** gefangen nehmen (fig.)

enthuse /ɪn'θju:z/ [1] *v.i.* in Begeisterung ausbrechen (**about** über + *Akk.*)
[2] *v.t.* begeistern

enthusiasm /ɪn'θju:zɪæzm/ *n.* Begeisterung, *die*

enthusiast /ɪn'θju:zɪæst/ *n.* Enthusiast, *der;* (for sports) Fan, *der;* **a great DIY ~:** ein begeisterter Heimwerker

enthusiastic /ɪnθju:zɪ'æstɪk/ *adj.* begeistert; **not be very ~ about doing sth.** keine große Lust haben, etw. zu tun

entice /ɪn'taɪs/ *v.t.* locken (**into** in + *Akk.*); ~ **sb. into doing** *or* **to do sth.** jmdn. dazu verleiten, etw. zu tun

entire /ɪn'taɪə(r)/ *adj.* **(a)** (whole) ganz
(b) (intact) vollständig

en'tirely *adv.* **(a)** (wholly) völlig
(b) (solely) ganz ‹*für sich behalten*›; voll ‹*verantwortlich sein*›; **it's up to you ~:** es liegt ganz bei dir

entirety /ɪn'taɪərətɪ/ *n.* **in its ~:** in seiner/ihrer Gesamtheit

entitle /ɪn'taɪtl/ *v.t.* berechtigen (**to** zu); ~ **sb. to do sth.** jmdm. das Recht geben, etw. zu tun; **be ~d to [claim] sth.** Anspruch auf etw. (*Akk.*) haben; **be ~d to do sth.** das Recht haben, etw. zu tun

entomologist /entə'mɒlədʒɪst/ *n.* Entomologe, *der*/Entomologin, *die*

entomology /entə'mɒlədʒɪ/ *n.* Entomologie, *die;* Insektenkunde, *die*

entourage /ɒntʊ'rɑ:ʒ/ *n.* Gefolge, *das*

entrails /'entreɪlz/ *n. pl.* Eingeweide *Pl.*

entrance¹ /ɪn'trɑ:ns/ *v.t.* hinreißen

entrance² /'entrəns/ *n.* (way in) Eingang, *der* (**to** *Gen. od.* zu); (for vehicles) Einfahrt, *die*

entrance /'entrəns/**:** ~ **examination** *n.* Aufnahmeprüfung, *die;* ~ **fee** *n.* Eintrittsgeld, *das;* ~ **hall** *n.* Eingangshalle, *die;* ~ **ticket** *n.* Eintrittskarte, *die*

entrant /'entrənt/ *n.* (for competition, race, etc.) Teilnehmer, *der*/Teilnehmerin, *die* (**for** *Gen.*, an + *Dat.*)

entreat /ɪn'tri:t/ *v.t.* anflehen

en'treaty *n.* flehentliche Bitte

entrepreneur /ɒntrəprə'nɜ:(r)/ *n.* Unternehmer, *der*/Unternehmerin, *die*

entrepreneurial /ɒntrəprə'nɜ:rɪəl/ *adj.* unternehmerisch

entrust /ɪn'trʌst/ *v.t.* ~ **sb. with sth.** jmdm. etw. anvertrauen; ~ **sb./sth. to sb./sth.** jmdn./etw. jmdm./einer Sache anvertrauen; ~ **a task to sb.** jmdn. mit einer Aufgabe betrauen

entry /'entrɪ/ *n.* **(a)** Eintritt, *der* (**into** in + *Akk.*); (into country) Einreise, *die;* **'no ~'** (for people) „Zutritt verboten"; (for vehicles) „Einfahrt verboten"
(b) (way in) Eingang, *der;* (for vehicle) Einfahrt, *die*

(c) (registration, item) Eintragung, *die* **(in, into** in + *Akk. od. Dat.*); (in dictionary, encyclopaedia) Eintrag, *der*

entry: ~ fee *n.* Eintrittsgeld, *das;* **~ form** *n.* Anmeldeformular, *das;* **~ visa** *n.* Einreisevisum, *das*

envelop /ɪn'veləp/ *v.t.* [ein]hüllen **(in** in + *Akk.*); **be ~ed in flames** ganz von Flammen umgeben sein

envelope /'envələʊp, 'ɒnvələʊp/ *n.* [Brief]umschlag, *der*

enviable /'envɪəbl/ *adj.* beneidenswert

envious /'envɪəs/ *adj.* neidisch **(of** auf + *Akk.*)

environment /ɪn'vaɪərənmənt/ *n.* Umwelt, *die;* (surrounding objects, region) Umgebung, *die*

environmental /ɪnvaɪərən'mentl/ *adj.* Umwelt‹*verschmutzung, -schutz, -katastrophe*›; **for ~ reasons** aus Gründen des Umweltschutzes; **~ group** Umweltschutzorganisation, *die;* **~ protection** Umweltschutz, *der*

environmental 'health *n.* Umwelthygiene, *die;* **~ health officer** Umwelthygienebeauftragte, *der/die;* **~ health department** Umwelthygieneamt, *das*

environ'mentalist *n.* Umweltschützer, *der*/-schützerin, *die*

environ'mentally *adv.* **~ friendly** umweltfreundlich; **~ sensitive** ökologisch sensibel; **~ sound** umweltverträglich; umweltgerecht

envisage /ɪn'vɪzɪdʒ/, **envision** /ɪn'vɪʒn/ *v.t.* sich (*Dat.*) vorstellen

envoy /'envɔɪ/ *n.* Gesandte, *der*/Gesandtin, *die*

envy /'envɪ/ **1** *n.* Neid, *der;* **you'll be the ~ of all your friends** alle deine Freunde werden dich beneiden
2 *v.t.* beneiden; **~ sb. sth.** jmdn. um etw. beneiden

enzyme /'enzaɪm/ *n.* Enzym, *das*

ephemeral /ɪ'femərl/ *adj.* kurzlebig

epic /'epɪk/ **1** *adj.* episch
2 *n.* Epos, *das*

epidemic /epɪ'demɪk/ **1** *adj.* epidemisch
2 *n.* Epidemie, *die*

epilepsy /'epɪlepsɪ/ *n.* Epilepsie, *die*

epileptic /epɪ'leptɪk/ **1** *adj.* epileptisch; **~ fit** epileptischer Anfall
2 *n.* Epileptiker, *der*/Epileptikerin, *die*

Epiphany /ɪ'pɪfənɪ/ *n.* **[Feast of the] ~:** Epiphanias, *das;* Dreikönigsfest, *das;* **at ~:** am Dreikönigstag

episode /'epɪsəʊd/ *n.* **(a)** Episode, *die*
(b) (of serial) Folge, *die*

epistle /ɪ'pɪsl/ *n.* Epistel, *die*

epitaph /'epɪtɑːf/ *n.* Grab[in]schrift, *die*

epithet /'epɪθet/ *n.* Beiname, *der;* (as term of abuse) Schimpfname, *der*

epitome /ɪ'pɪtəmɪ/ *n.* Inbegriff, *der*

epitomize /ɪ'pɪtəmaɪz/ *v.t.* **~ sth.** der Inbegriff einer Sache (*Gen.*) sein

epoch /'iːpɒk/ *n.* Epoche, *die*

'epoch-making *adj.* Epoche machend

equal /'iːkwl/ **1** *adj.* **(a)** gleich; **~ in** *or* **of ~ height/size/importance** *etc.* gleich hoch/groß/wichtig *usw.*
(b) be ~ to sth./sb. (strong, clever, etc. enough) einer Sache/jmdm. gewachsen sein
2 *n.* Gleichgestellte, *der/die;* **have no ~:** nicht seines-/ihresgleichen haben
3 *v.t.*, (Brit.) **-ll-: ~ sb.** es jmdm. gleichtun; **three times four ~s twelve** drei mal vier ist [gleich] zwölf

equality /ɪ'kwɒlɪtɪ/ *n.* Gleichheit, *die;* (equal rights) Gleichberechtigung, *die;* **~ between the sexes** Gleichheit von Mann und Frau

equalize /'iːkwəlaɪz/ *v.i.* (Sport) den Ausgleich[streffer] erzielen

'equalizer *n.* (Sport) Ausgleich[streffer], *der*

'equally *adv.* gleich; (just as) ebenso; in gleiche Teile ‹*aufteilen*›; gleichmäßig ‹*verteilen*›

Equal Oppor'tunities Commission *n.* (Brit.) *Ausschuss für Chancengleichheit;* ≈ Gleichstellungsausschuss, *der*

equal oppor'tunity *n.* Chancengleichheit, *die*

'equals sign *n.* (Math.) Gleichheitszeichen, *das*

equanimity /ekwə'nɪmɪtɪ/ *n.* Gelassenheit, *die*

equate /ɪ'kweɪt/ *v.t.* gleichsetzen **(with** mit)

equation /ɪ'kweɪʒn/ *n.* (Math.) Gleichung, *die*

equator /ɪ'kweɪtə(r)/ *n.* Äquator, *der*

equilibrium /iːkwɪ'lɪbrɪəm/ *n., pl.* **equilibria** /iːkwɪ'lɪbrɪə/ *or* **~s** Gleichgewicht, *das*

equinox /'ekwɪnɒks/ *n.* Tagundnachtgleiche, *die*

equip /ɪ'kwɪp/ *v.t.*, **-pp-** ausrüsten ‹*Fahrzeug, Armee*›; ausstatten ‹*Küche*›; **fully ~ped** komplett ausgerüstet/ausgestattet; **~ sb./oneself [with sth.]** jmdn./sich [mit etw.] ausrüsten

e'quipment *n.* Ausrüstung, *die;* (of kitchen, laboratory) Ausstattung, *die;* (needed for activity) Geräte *Pl.*

equity /'ekwɪtɪ/ *n.* **(a)** (fairness) Gerechtigkeit, *die;* **with ~:** gerecht
(b) *in pl.* (stocks and shares without fixed interest) [Stamm]aktien *Pl.*
(c) (value of shares) Eigenkapital, *das*
(d) (net value of mortgaged property) *Wert eines Besitzes nach Abzug der Belastungen*

'equity market *n.* (Commerc.) Aktienmarkt, *der*

equivalent /ɪ'kwɪvələnt/ **1** *adj.* gleichwertig; **be ~ to sth.** einer Sache (*Dat.*) entsprechen
2 *n.* **(a)** (thing, person) Pendant, *das;* Gegenstück, *das* **(of** zu)

(b) be the ~ of sth. (have same result) einer Sache (*Dat.*) entsprechen
equivocal /ɪ'kwɪvəkl/ *adj.* zweideutig
er /ɜ:(r)/ *int.* äh
era /'ɪərə/ *n.* Ära, *die*
eradicate /ɪ'rædɪkeɪt/ *v.t.* ausrotten
erase /ɪ'reɪz/ *v.t.* auslöschen; (with rubber, knife) ausradieren; (from tape, also Comp.) löschen
e'raser *n.* [**pencil**] ~: Radiergummi, *der*
erect /ɪ'rekt/ 1 *adj.* aufrecht
2 *v.t.* errichten; aufstellen ‹*Standbild, Mast, Verkehrsschild, Gerüst, Zelt*›
erection /ɪ'rekʃn/ *n.* **(a)** ▶ ERECT 2: Errichtung, *die;* Aufstellen, *das*
(b) (Physiol.) Erektion, *die*
ergonomic /ɜ:gə'nɒmɪk/ *adj.*, **ergo'nomically** *adv.* ergonomisch
ermine /'ɜ:mɪn/ *n.* Hermelin, *der*
erode /ɪ'rəʊd/ *v.t.* **(a)** ‹*Säure, Rost:*› angreifen; ‹*Wasser:*› auswaschen; ‹*Wind:*› verwittern lassen
(b) (fig.) unterminieren
erosion /ɪ'rəʊʒn/ *n.* **(a)** ▶ ERODE A: Angreifen, *das;* Auswaschung, *die;* Verwitterung, *die*
(b) (fig.) Unterminierung, *die*
erotic /ɪ'rɒtɪk/ *adj.* erotisch
err /ɜ:(r)/ *v.i.* sich irren
errand /'erənd/ *n.* Botengang, *der;* (shopping) Besorgung, *die;* **go on** *or* **run an** ~: einen Botengang/eine Besorgung machen
'errand boy *n.* Laufbursche, *der*
erratic /ɪ'rætɪk/ *adj.* unregelmäßig; sprunghaft ‹*Wesen, Person, Art*›; launenhaft ‹*Verhalten*›
erroneous /ɪ'rəʊnɪəs/ *adj.* falsch; irrig ‹*Schlussfolgerung, Annahme*›
error /'erə(r)/ *n.* (mistake) Fehler, *der;* (wrong opinion) Irrtum, *der;* **in** ~: irrtümlich[erweise]
'error message *n.* (Comp.) Fehlermeldung, *die*
erudite /'eru:daɪt/ *adj.* gelehrt
erupt /ɪ'rʌpt/ *v.i.* ausbrechen
eruption /ɪ'rʌpʃn/ *n.* Ausbruch, *der*
escalate /'eskəleɪt/ *v.i.* 1 sich ausweiten (**into** zu); ‹*Preise, Kosten:*› [ständig] steigen
2 *v.t.* ausweiten (**into** zu)
escalator /'eskəleɪtə(r)/ *n.* Rolltreppe, *die*
escapade /eskə'peɪd/ *n.* Eskapade, *die* (geh.)
escape /ɪ'skeɪp/ 1 *n.* Flucht, *die* (**from** aus); **have a narrow** ~: gerade noch einmal davonkommen
2 *v.i.* **(a)** fliehen (**from** aus); (successfully) entkommen (**from** *Dat.*)
(b) ‹*Gas:*› ausströmen; ‹*Flüssigkeit:*› auslaufen
3 *v.t.* **(a)** entkommen (+ *Dat.*) ‹*Verfolger, Feind*›; entgehen (+ *Dat.*) ‹*Bestrafung, Gefangennahme, Tod*›; verschont bleiben von ‹*Zerstörung, Auswirkungen*›
(b) (not be remembered by) entfallen sein (+ *Dat.*)
escape: ~ artist ▶ ESCAPOLOGIST; **~ attempt, ~ bid** *ns.* Fluchtversuch, *der;* (from prison) Ausbruchsversuch, *der;* **~ hatch** *n.* Notausstieg, *der;* (fig.) Rettungsanker, *der;* **~ key** *n.* (Comp.) Escapetaste, *die;* **~ road** *n.* Auslaufstrecke, *die;* **~ route** *n.* Fluchtweg, *der*
escapism /ɪ'skeɪpɪzm/ *n.* Realitätsflucht, *die*
escapologist /eskə'pɒlədʒɪst/ *n.* (Brit.) Entfesselungskünstler, *der*/-künstlerin, *die*
escarpment /ɪ'skɑ:pmənt/ *n.* (Geog.) Steilhang, *der*
escort 1 /'eskɔ:t/ *n.* **(a)** Begleitung, *die;* (Mil.) Eskorte, *die*
(b) (hired companion) Begleiter, *der*/ Begleiterin, *die*
2 /ɪ'skɔ:t/ *v.t.* begleiten; (lead) führen; (Mil.) eskortieren
Eskimo /'eskɪməʊ/ 1 *adj.* Eskimo-
2 *n., pl.* **~s** *or same* Eskimo, *der*/ Eskimofrau, *die;* **the ~[s]** die Eskimos
esoteric /esəʊ'terɪk/ *adj.* esoterisch
especial /ɪ'speʃl/ *attrib. adj.* [ganz] besonder...
especially /ɪ'speʃəlɪ/ *adv.* besonders
espionage /'espɪənɑ:ʒ/ *n.* Spionage, *die*
esplanade /esplə'neɪd, esplə'nɑ:d/ *n.* Esplanade, *die* (geh.)
espouse /ɪ'spaʊz/ *v.t.* eintreten für
espresso /e'spresəʊ/ *n., pl.* **~s** (coffee) Espresso, *der*
e'spresso bar *n.* Espressobar, *die*
Esq. /ɪ'skwaɪə(r)/ *abbr.* = **Esquire** ≈ Hr.; (on letter) ≈ Hrn.; **Jim Smith, ~:** Hr./Hrn. Jim Smith
essay /'eseɪ/ *n.* Essay, *der;* Aufsatz, *der* (bes. Schulw.)
essence /'esəns/ *n.* **(a)** Wesen, *das;* (gist) Wesentliche, *das;* **in ~:** im Wesentlichen
(b) (Cookery) Essenz, *die*
essential /ɪ'senʃl/ 1 *adj.* **(a)** (fundamental) wesentlich
(b) (indispensable) unentbehrlich; lebensnotwendig ‹*Versorgungseinrichtungen, Güter*›; unabdingbar ‹*Qualifikation, Voraussetzung*›; **it is ~ that ...:** es ist unbedingt notwendig, dass ...
2 *n. pl.* **the ~s** (fundamentals) das Wesentliche; (items) das Notwendigste
es'sentially *adv.* im Grunde
establish /ɪ'stæblɪʃ/ *v.t.* **(a)** schaffen ‹*Einrichtung, Präzedenzfall*›; gründen ‹*Organisation, Institut*›; errichten ‹*Geschäft, System*›
(b) (secure acceptance for) etablieren; **become ~ed** sich einbürgern
(c) (prove) beweisen

(d) (discover) feststellen
established /ɪ'stæblɪʃt/ *adj.* bestehend ‹*Ordnung*›; etabliert ‹*Schriftsteller*›; (accepted) üblich; fest ‹*Brauch*›; feststehend ‹*Tatsache*›; **become ~**: sich durchsetzen
e'stablishment *n.* **(a)** (setting up, foundation) Gründung, *die*
(b) **[business] ~**: Unternehmen, *das*
estate /ɪ'steɪt/ *n.* **(a)** (landed property) Gut, *das*
(b) (Brit.: housing ~) [Wohn]siedlung, *die*
(c) (of deceased person) Erbmasse, *die*
estate: ~ agent *n.* (Brit.) Grundstücksmakler, *der*/-maklerin, *die;* **~ car** *n.* (Brit.) Kombiwagen, *der;* **~ duty** (Brit.)**, e'state tax** (Amer.) *ns.* Erbschaftssteuer, *die*
esteem /ɪ'sti:m/ [1] *n.* Wertschätzung, *die* (geh.) (**for** *Gen.*, für)
[2] *v.t.* schätzen; **highly ~ed** hoch geschätzt
estimate [1] /'estɪmət/ *n.* **(a)** Schätzung, *die;* **at a rough ~**: grob geschätzt
(b) (Commerc.) Kostenvoranschlag, *der*
[2] /'estɪmeɪt/ *v.t.* schätzen (**at** auf + *Akk.*)
estimation /estɪ'meɪʃn/ *n.* Schätzung, *die;* **in sb.'s ~**: nach jmds. Schätzung
Estonia /e'stəʊnɪə/ *pr. n.* Estland (*das*)
Estonian /e'stəʊnɪən/ [1] *adj.* estländisch; estnisch; **sb. is ~**: jmd. ist Este/Estin
[2] *n.* **(a)** (language) Estnisch, *das;* Estländisch, *das; see also* ENGLISH 2A
(b) (person) Este, *der*/Estin, *die;* Estländer, *der*/Estländerin, *die*
estuary /'estjʊərɪ/ *n.* [Trichter]mündung, *die*
ETA *abbr.* = **estimated time of arrival** voraussichtliche Ankunftszeit
etc. *abbr.* = **et cetera** usw.
etch /etʃ/ *v.t.* ätzen (**on** auf + *Akk.*); (on metal also) ‹*bes. Künstler:*› radieren; (fig.) einprägen (**in, on** *Dat.*)
'etching *n.* (Art) Radierung, *die*
eternal /ɪ'tɜ:nl/ *adj.*, **e'ternally** *adv.* ewig
eternity /ɪ'tɜ:nɪtɪ/ *n.* Ewigkeit, *die*
ether /'i:θə(r)/ *n.* Äther, *der*
ethereal /ɪ'θɪərɪəl/ *adj.* ätherisch
ethical /'eθɪkl/ *adj.* ethisch
ethics /'eθɪks/ *n.* **(a)** Moral, *die;* (moral philosophy) Ethik, *die*
(b) *usu. constr. as pl.* (moral code) Ethik, *die* (geh.)
Ethiopia /i:θɪ'əʊpɪə/ *pr. n.* Äthiopien (*das*)
Ethiopian /i:θɪ'əʊpɪən/ [1] *adj.* äthiopisch; **sb. is ~**: jmd. ist Äthiopier/Äthiopierin
[2] *n.* Äthiopier, *der*/Äthiopierin, *die*
ethnic /'eθnɪk/ *adj.* ethnisch; **~ minority** ethnische Minderheit
ethnic 'cleansing *n.* ethnische Säuberung
ethnology /eθ'nɒlədʒɪ/ *n.* Ethnologie, *die*
ethos /'i:θɒs/ *n.* (guiding beliefs) Gesinnung, *die;* (fundamental values) Ethos, *das* (geh.)
etiquette /'etɪket/ *n.* Etikette, *die*
etymology /etɪ'mɒlədʒɪ/ *n.* Etymologie, *die*
EU *abbr.* = **European Union** EU
eulogy /'ju:lədʒɪ/ *n.* Lobrede, *die*
euphemism /'ju:fəmɪzm/ *n.* Euphemismus, *der*
euphemistic /ju:fə'mɪstɪk/ *adj.* verhüllend
euphoria /ju:'fɔ:rɪə/ *n.* Euphorie, *die* (geh.)
euro /'jʊərəʊ/ *n.* Euro, *der*
Euro: ~cheque *n.* Euroscheck, *der;* **~land** *n.* Euroland, *das;* **~-MP** *n.* Europaabgeordnete, *der*/*die*
Europe /'jʊərəp/ *pr. n.* Europa (*das*)
European /jʊərə'pi:ən/ [1] *adj.* europäisch; **sb. is ~**: jmd. ist Europäer/Europäerin; **~ [Economic] Community** Europäische [Wirtschafts]gemeinschaft
[2] *n.* Europäer, *der*/Europäerin, *die*
European: ~ Central 'Bank *n.* Europäische Zentralbank; **~ Com'mission** *n.* Europäische Kommission; **~ 'Council** *n.* Europäischer Rat; **~ Court of 'Justice** *n.* Europäischer Gerichtshof; **~ 'Cup** *n.* (Footb.) Europacup, *der;* Europapokal, *der;* **~ 'currency unit** *n.* Europäische Währungseinheit; **~ 'Monetary System** *n.* Europäisches Währungssystem; **~ Monetary 'Union** *n.* Europäische Währungsunion; **~ 'Parliament** *n.* Europäisches Parlament; **~ 'Union** *n.* Europäische Union
Euro-: ~-rebel *n.* (esp. Brit.) [innerparteilicher] Europagegner/ [innerparteiliche] Europagegnerin; **~sceptic** *n.* Euroskeptiker, *der*/ -skeptikerin, *die;* **~star** ® *n.* Eurostar, *der;* **go by ~star** mit dem Eurostar fahren; **~zone** *n.* Eurozone, *die*
euthanasia /ju:θə'neɪzɪə/ *n.* Euthanasie, *die*
evacuate /ɪ'vækjʊeɪt/ *v.t.* evakuieren (**from** aus)
evacuation /ɪvækjʊ'eɪʃn/ *n.* Evakuierung, *die* (**from** aus)
evade /ɪ'veɪd/ *v.t.* ausweichen (+ *Dat.*) ‹*Angriff, Angreifer, Schlag, Problem, Frage*›; sich entziehen (+ *Dat.*) ‹*Verhaftung, Verantwortung*›; entkommen (+ *Dat.*) ‹*Verfolger, Verfolgung*›; hinterziehen ‹*Steuern*›; **~ doing sth.** vermeiden, etw. zu tun
evaluate /ɪ'væljʊeɪt/ *v.t.* einschätzen; bewerten ‹*Daten*›
evangelical /i:væn'dʒelɪkl/ *adj.* missionarisch (fig.); (Protestant) evangelikal
evangelist /ɪ'vændʒəlɪst/ *n.* Evangelist, *der*
evaporate /ɪ'væpəreɪt/ [1] *v.i.* verdunsten
[2] *v.t.* verdunsten lassen
evaporated 'milk *n.* Kondensmilch, *die*

evaporation /ɪvæpəˈreɪʃn/ *n.* Verdunstung, *die*

evasion /ɪˈveɪʒn/ *n.* Umgehung, *die;* (of responsibility, question) Ausweichen, *das* (**of** vor + *Dat.*); **tax ~:** Steuerhinterziehung, *die*

evasive /ɪˈveɪsɪv/ *adj.* **(a) be/become ~:** ausweichen
(b) ausweichend ‹*Antwort*›

eve /iːv/ *n.* Vorabend, *der* (**of** *Gen.*); (day) Vortag, *der* (**of** *Gen.*)

even /ˈiːvn/ **1** *adj.* **(a)** eben ‹*Boden, Fläche*›; gleich hoch ‹*Stapel, Stuhl-, Tischbein*›; **be of ~ height/length** gleich hoch/lang sein
(b) gerade ‹*Zahl, Seite, Hausnummer*›
(c) be *or* **get ~ with sb.** (quits) es jmdm. heimzahlen; **break ~:** die Kosten decken
2 *adv.* sogar; selbst; sogar noch ‹*weniger, schlimmer usw.*›; **~ if** selbst wenn; **~ so** [aber] trotzdem; **not** *or* **never ~ …:** [noch] nicht einmal …
■ **even ˈup** *v.t.* ausgleichen

evening /ˈiːvnɪŋ/ *n.* Abend, *der;* **this/tomorrow ~:** heute/morgen Abend; **in the ~:** am Abend; (regularly) abends

evening: ~ class *n.* Abendkurs, *der;* **~ dress** *n.* Abendkleidung, *die;* **~ ˈmeal** *n.* Abendessen, *das;* **~ ˈpaper** *n.* Abendzeitung, *die*

ˈevenly *adv.* gleichmäßig

ˈeven-numbered *adj.* gerade

event /ɪˈvent/ *n.* **(a) in the ~ of his dying** *or* **death** im Falle seines Todes; **in the ~:** letzten Endes; **in the ~ of rain** bei Regenwetter
(b) (occurrence) Ereignis, *das*
(c) (planned public or social occasion) Veranstaltung, *die*

eˈventful *adj.* ereignisreich

eventual /ɪˈventjʊəl/ *adj.* **predict sb.'s ~ downfall** vorhersagen, dass jmd. schließlich zu Fall kommen wird; **the career of Napoleon and his ~ defeat** der Aufstieg Napoleons und schließlich seine Niederlage

eventuality /ɪventjʊˈælɪtɪ/ *n.* Eventualität, *die*

eˈventually *adv.* schließlich

ever /ˈevə(r)/ *adv.* **(a)** (always) immer; **for ~:** für immer; ewig ‹*lieben, da sein, leben*›; **~ since** [**then**] seit [dieser Zeit]
(b) (at any time) je[mals]; **hardly ~:** so gut wie nie; **as ~:** wie gewöhnlich
(c) *in comb. with compar. adj. or adv.* noch; **~-increasing** ständig zunehmend
(d) what ~ does he want? was will er nur?; **why ~ not?** warum denn nicht?

ˈever: ~green **1** *adj.* immergrün;
2 *n.* immergrüne Pflanze; **~lasting** *adj.* **(a)** (eternal) immer während; ewig ‹*Leben*›; unvergänglich ‹*Ruhm, Ehre*›; **(b)** (incessant) endlos

every /ˈevrɪ/ *adj.* **(a)** jeder/jede/jedes; **~ one** jeder/jede/jedes [einzelne]; **your ~ wish** all[e] deine Wünsche; **she comes ~ day** sie kommt jeden Tag; **~ three/few days** alle drei/paar Tage; **~ other** (**~** second, almost **~**) jeder/jede/jedes zweite
(b) (the greatest possible) all ‹*Respekt, Aussicht*›

every: ~body *n. & pron.* jeder; **~body else** alle anderen; **~day** *attrib. adj.* alltäglich; Alltags‹*kleidung, -sprache*›; **in ~day life** im Alltag; **~one** ▶ **~BODY**; **~place** (Amer.) ▶ **~WHERE**; **~thing** *n. & pron.* alles; **~where** *adv.* überall; **~where you go/look** wohin man auch geht/sieht

evict /ɪˈvɪkt/ *v.t.* **~ sb.** [**from his home**] jmdn. zur Räumung [seiner Wohnung] zwingen

eviction /ɪˈvɪkʃn/ *n.* Zwangsräumung, *die;* **the ~ of the tenant** die zwangsweise Vertreibung des Mieters

evidence /ˈevɪdəns/ *n.* **(a)** Beweis, *der;* (indication) Anzeichen, *das;* **be ~ of sth.** etw. beweisen
(b) (Law) Beweismaterial, *das;* **give ~:** aussagen

evident /ˈevɪdənt/ *adj.* offensichtlich; **be ~ to sb.** jmdm. klar sein; **it soon became ~ that …:** es stellte sich bald heraus, dass …

ˈevidently *adv.* offensichtlich

evil /ˈiːvl, ˈiːvɪl/ **1** *adj.* böse; schlecht ‹*Charakter, Einfluss, System*›
2 *n.* **(a)** Böse, *das*
(b) (bad thing) Übel, *das*

evocative /ɪˈvɒkətɪv/ *adj.* **be ~ of sth.** etw. heraufbeschwören

evoke /ɪˈvəʊk/ *v.t.* heraufbeschwören; hervorrufen ‹*Bewunderung, Überraschung*›; erregen ‹*Interesse*›

evolution /iːvəˈluːʃn/ *n.* Entwicklung, *die;* (Biol.) Evolution, *die*

evolve /ɪˈvɒlv/ **1** *v.i.* sich entwickeln (**from** aus, **into** zu)
2 *v.t.* entwickeln

ewe /juː/ *n.* Mutterschaf, *das*

ex¹ /eks/ *n.* (coll.) Verflossene, *der/die* (ugs.)

ex² *prep.* (Commerc.) **ex works/store** ‹*Güter*› ab Werk/Lager

ex- *pref.* Ex-‹*Freundin, Präsident, Champion*›; Alt‹[*bundes*]*kanzler*›

exacerbate /ekˈsæsəbeɪt/ *v.t.* verschärfen ‹*Lage*›; verschlechtern ‹*Zustand*›

exact /ɪgˈzækt/ **1** *adj.* genau
2 *v.t.* fordern; erheben ‹*Gebühr*›

exacting /ɪgˈzæktɪŋ/ *n.* anspruchsvoll; hoch ‹*Anforderung*›

exactitude /ɪgˈzæktɪtjuːd/ Genauigkeit, *die*

exactly /ɪgˈzæktlɪ/ *adv.* genau; **not ~** (coll. iron.) nicht gerade

exactness /ɪgˈzæktnɪs/ *n.* Genauigkeit, *die*

exaggerate /ɪgˈzædʒəreɪt/ *v.t.* übertreiben

exaggeration /ɪgzædʒəˈreɪʃn/ *n.* Übertreibung, *die*

exam /ɪgˈzæm/ (coll.) ▶ EXAMINATION B

examination /ɪgzæmɪ'neɪʃn/ *n.* **(a)** (inspection; Med.) Untersuchung, *die*
(b) (Sch. etc.) Prüfung, *die;* (final ~ at university) Examen, *das*
exami'nation paper *n.* **(a)** ~[s] schriftliche Prüfungsaufgaben *Pl.*
(b) (with candidate's answers) ≈ Klausurarbeit, *die*
examine /ɪg'zæmɪn/ *v.t.* **(a)** (inspect; Med.) untersuchen (**for** auf + *Akk.*); prüfen ‹*Dokument, Gewissen*›; kontrollieren ‹*Ausweis, Gepäck*›
(b) (Sch. etc.) prüfen (**in** in + *Dat.*)
(c) (Law) verhören
examiner /ɪg'zæmɪnə(r)/ *n.* Prüfer, *der*/Prüferin, *die*
example /ɪg'zɑ:mpl/ *n.* Beispiel, *das;* **for ~:** zum Beispiel; **make an ~ of sb.** ein Exempel an jmdm. statuieren
exasperate /ɪg'zæspəreɪt/ *v.t.* (irritate) verärgern; (infuriate) zur Verzweiflung bringen
exasperation /ɪg'zæspəreɪʃn/ *n.* ▶ EXASPERATE: Ärger, *der*/Verzweiflung, *die* (**with** über + *Akk.*); **in ~:** verärgert/verzweifelt
excavate /'ekskəveɪt/ *v.t.* **(a)** ausschachten; (with machine) ausbaggern
(b) (Archaeol.) ausgraben
excavation /ekskə'veɪʃn/ *n.* **(a)** Ausschachtung, *die;* (with machine) Ausbaggerung, *die*
(b) (Archaeol.) Ausgrabung, *die*
excavator /'ekskəveɪtə(r)/ *n.* Bagger, *der*
exceed /ɪk'si:d/ *v.t.* **(a)** (be greater than) übertreffen (**in** an + *Dat.*); ‹*Kosten, Summe, Anzahl:*› übersteigen (**by** um)
(b) (go beyond) überschreiten; hinausgehen über (+ *Akk.*) ‹*Auftrag, Befehl*›
ex'ceedingly *adv.* äußerst; ausgesprochen ‹*hässlich, dumm*›
excel /ɪk'sel/ **1** *v.t.*, **-ll-** übertreffen; **~ oneself** (lit. or iron.) sich selbst übertreffen
2 *v.i.*, **-ll-** sich hervortun (**at, in** in + *Dat.*)
excellence /'eksələns/ *n.* hervorragende Qualität
excellent /'eksələnt/ *adj.* hervorragend
except /ɪk'sept/ **1** *prep.* **~ [for]** außer (+ *Dat.*); **~ for** (in all respects other than) abgesehen von
2 *v.t.* ausnehmen (**from** bei); **~ed** ausgenommen
ex'cepting *prep.* außer (+ *Dat.*)
exception /ɪk'sepʃn/ *n.* Ausnahme, *die;* **take ~ to** Anstoß nehmen an (+ *Dat.*)
exceptional /ɪk'sepʃənl/ *adj.* außergewöhnlich
ex'ceptionally *adv.* **(a)** (as an exception) ausnahmsweise
(b) (remarkably) ungewöhnlich
excerpt /'eksɜ:pt/ *n.* Auszug, *der* (**from** aus)
excess /ɪk'ses/ *n.* **(a)** Übermaß, *das* (**of** an + *Dat.*); **eat/drink to ~:** übermäßig essen/trinken
(b) *esp. in pl.* (over-indulgence) Exzess, *der*
(c) be in ~ of sth. etw. übersteigen
(d) (surplus) Überschuss, *der*
excess /'ekses/**: ~ 'baggage** *n.* Mehrgepäck, *das;* **~ 'fare** *n.* Mehrpreis, *der;* **pay the ~ fare** nachlösen
excessive /ɪk'sesɪv/ *adj.* übermäßig; übertrieben ‹*Forderung, Lob, Ansprüche*›; unmäßig ‹*Esser, Trinker*›
ex'cessively *adv.* übertrieben; unmäßig ‹*essen, trinken*›
excess: ~ 'luggage ▶ ~ BAGGAGE; **~ 'postage** *n.* Nachgebühr, *die*
exchange /ɪks'tʃeɪndʒ/ **1** *v.t.* **(a)** tauschen ‹*Plätze, Ringe, Küsse*›; umtauschen ‹*Geld*›; wechseln ‹*Blicke, Worte*›; **~ insults** sich beleidigen
(b) (give in place of another) eintauschen (**for** für, gegen); umtauschen ‹*[gekaufte] Ware*› (**for** gegen)
2 *n.* **(a)** Tausch, *der;* **in ~:** dafür; **in ~ for sth.** für etw.
(b) (Educ.) Austausch, *der;* **an ~ student** ein Austauschstudent/eine Austauschstudentin
(c) (of money) Umtausch, *der;* **~ rate, rate of ~:** Wechselkurs, *der*
(d) (Teleph.) Fernmeldeamt, *das*
exchequer /ɪks'tʃekə(r)/ *n.* (Brit.) Schatzamt, *das*
excise /'eksaɪz/ *n.* Verbrauchsteuer, *die;* **Customs and E~** (Brit.) *Amt für Zölle und Verbrauchsteuer*
excitable /ek'saɪtəbl/ *adj.* leicht erregbar
excite /ɪk'saɪt/ *v.t.* **(a)** (thrill) begeistern
(b) (agitate) aufregen
ex'cited *adj.* aufgeregt (**at** über + *Akk.*); **get ~:** sich aufregen
ex'citement *n.* Aufregung, *die;* (enthusiasm) Begeisterung, *die*
exciting /ɪk'saɪtɪŋ/ *adj.* aufregend; (full of suspense) spannend
exclaim /ɪk'skleɪm/ **1** *v.t.* ausrufen
2 *v.i.* aufschreien
exclamation /eksklə'meɪʃn/ *n.* Ausruf, *der*
excla'mation mark, (Amer.) **excla'mation point** *ns.* Ausrufezeichen, *das*
exclude /ɪk'sklu:d/ *v.t.* ausschließen
excluding /ɪk'sklu:dɪŋ/ *prep.* **~ drinks/VAT** Getränke ausgenommen/ohne Mehrwertsteuer
exclusion /ɪk'sklu:ʒn/ *n.* Ausschluss, *der*
exclusive /ɪk'sklu:sɪv/ *adj.* **(a)** alleinig ‹*Besitzer, Kontrolle*›; Allein‹*eigentum*›; (Journ.) Exklusiv‹*bericht, -interview*›
(b) (select) exklusiv
(c) ~ of ohne
ex'clusively *adv.* ausschließlich
excommunicate /ekskə'mju:nɪkeɪt/ *v.t.* exkommunizieren
excrement /'ekskrɪmənt/ *n.* Kot, *der* (geh.)
excrete /ɪk'skri:t/ *v.t.* ausscheiden

excruciating /ɪk'skru:'ʃɪeɪtɪŋ/ *adj.* unerträglich
excursion /ɪk'skɜ:ʃn/ *n.* Ausflug, *der*
excusable /ɪk'skju:zəbl/ *adj.* entschuldbar; verzeihlich
excuse 1 /ɪk'skju:z/ *v.t.* **(a)** entschuldigen; **~ oneself** sich entschuldigen; **~ me** Entschuldigung **(b)** (release, exempt) befreien (**from** von) 2 /ɪk'skju:s/ *n.* Entschuldigung, *die*
ex-di'rectory *adj.* (Brit. Teleph.) Geheim‹*nummer, -anschluss*›; **be ~:** nicht im Telefonbuch stehen
execute /'eksɪkju:t/ *v.t.* **(a)** hinrichten **(b)** (put into effect) ausführen
execution /eksɪ'kju:ʃn/ *n.* **(a)** Hinrichtung, *die* **(b)** (putting into effect) Ausführung, *die*
exe'cutioner *n.* Scharfrichter, *der*
executive /ɪg'zekjʊtɪv/ 1 *n.* leitender Angestellter/leitende Angestellte 2 *adj.* leitend ‹*Stellung, Funktion*›
executive: ~ 'stress *n.* Managerstress, *der;* **~ 'toy** *n.* Managerspielzeug, *das*
executor /ɪg'zekjʊtə(r)/ *n.* (Law) Testamentsvollstrecker, *der*
exemplary /ɪg'zemplərɪ/ *adj.* **(a)** (model) vorbildlich **(b)** (deterrent) exemplarisch
exemplify /ɪg'zemplɪfaɪ/ *v.t.* veranschaulichen
exempt /ɪg'zempt/ 1 *adj.* **[be] ~ [from sth.]** [von etw.] befreit [sein] 2 *v.t.* befreien
exemption /ɪg'zempʃn/ *n.* Befreiung, *die*
exercise /'eksəsaɪz/ 1 *n.* **(a)** Übung, *die* **(b)** *no pl.* (physical exertion) Bewegung, *die;* **take ~:** sich (*Dat.*) Bewegung schaffen 2 *v.t.* ausüben ‹*Recht, Macht, Einfluss*›; walten lassen ‹*Vorsicht*› 3 *v.i.* sich (*Dat.*) Bewegung schaffen
exercise: ~ bicycle, (coll.) **~ bike** *ns.* Heimtrainer, *der;* **~ book** *n.* [Schul]heft, *das*
exert /ɪg'zɜ:t/ 1 *v.t.* aufbieten ‹*Kraft*›; ausüben ‹*Einfluss, Druck*› 2 *v. refl.* sich anstrengen
exertion /ɪg'zɜ:ʃn/ *n.* **(a)** (of strength, force) Aufwendung, *die;* (of influence, pressure) Ausübung, *die* **(b)** (effort) Anstrengung, *die*
exhale /eks'heɪl/ *v.t. & i.* ausatmen
exhaust /ɪg'zɔ:st/ 1 *v.t.* erschöpfen; erschöpfend behandeln ‹*Thema*› 2 *n.* (Motor Veh.) Auspuff, *der;* (gases) Auspuffgase *Pl.;* **~ emissions** Auspuffabgase *Pl.;* **~ emissions test** Abgasuntersuchung, *die*
ex'hausted *adj.* erschöpft
ex'hausting *adj.* anstrengend
exhaustion /ɪg'zɔ:stʃn/ *n.* Erschöpfung, *die*
exhaustive /ɪg'zɔ:stɪv/ *adj.* umfassend
ex'haust pipe *n.* Auspuffrohr, *das*
exhibit /ɪg'zɪbɪt/ 1 *v.t.* ausstellen; zeigen ‹*Mut, Symptome, Angst usw.*› 2 *n.* Ausstellungsstück, *das*
exhibition /eksɪ'bɪʃn/ *n.* Ausstellung, *die;* **make an ~ of oneself** sich unmöglich aufführen
exhibitionism /eksɪ'bɪʃənɪzm/ *n.* Exhibitionismus, *der*
exhibitionist /eksɪ'bɪʃənɪst/ *n.* Exhibitionist, *der*/Exhibitionistin, *die*
exhibitor /ɪg'zɪbɪtə(r)/ *n.* Aussteller, *der*/Ausstellerin, *die*
exhilarated /ɪg'zɪləreɪtɪd/ *adj.* belebt
exhilarating /ɪg'zɪləreɪtɪŋ/ *adj.* belebend
exhilaration /ɪgzɪlə'reɪʃn/ *n.* **[feeling of] ~:** Hochgefühl, *das*
exhort /ɪg'zɔ:t/ *v.t.* ermahnen
exile /'eksaɪl/ 1 *n.* **(a)** Exil, *das;* **in/into ~:** im/ins Exil **(b)** (person) Verbannte, *der/die* 2 *v.t.* verbannen
exist /ɪg'zɪst/ *v.i.* existieren; ‹*Zweifel, Gefahr, Problem, Einrichtung:*› bestehen; **~ on sth.** von etw. leben
existence /ɪg'zɪstəns/ *n.* Existenz, *die;* (mode of living) Dasein, *das;* **be in/come into ~:** existieren/entstehen
exit /'eksɪt/ *n.* (way out) Ausgang, *der* (**from** aus); (for vehicle) Ausfahrt, *die*
exit: ~ permit *n.* Ausreiseerlaubnis, *die;* **~ poll** *n.: Befragung der ein Wahllokal verlassenden Wähler;* **~ visa** *n.* Ausreisevisum, *das*
exonerate /ɪg'zɒnəreɪt/ *v.t.* entlasten
exorbitant /ɪg'zɔ:bɪtənt/ *adj.* [maßlos] überhöht
exorcize /'eksɔ:saɪz/ *v.t.* austreiben
exotic /ɪg'zɒtɪk/ *adj.* exotisch
expand /ɪk'spænd/ 1 *v.i.* **(a)** sich ausdehnen; (Commerc.) expandieren **(b) ~ on** weiter ausführen 2 *v.t.* ausdehnen; (Commerc.) erweitern
expanse /ɪk'spæns/ *n.* [weite] Fläche
expansion /ɪk'spænʃn/ *n.* Ausdehnung, *die;* (Commerc.) Expansion, *die*
expect /ɪk'spekt/ *v.t.* **(a)** erwarten; **~ to do sth.** damit rechnen, etw. zu tun; **~ sb. to do sth.** damit rechnen, dass jmd. etw. tut; (require) von jmdm. erwarten, dass er etw. tut **(b)** (coll.: think, suppose) glauben; **I ~ so** ich glaube schon
expectancy /ɪk'spektənsɪ/ *n.* Erwartung, *die*
expectant /ɪk'spektənt/ *adj.* erwartungsvoll; **~ mother** werdende Mutter
ex'pectantly *adv.* erwartungsvoll; gespannt ‹*warten*›
expectation /ekspek'teɪʃn/ *n.* Erwartung, *die*
expedient /ɪk'spi:dɪənt/ 1 *adj.* angebracht

2 *n.* Mittel, *das*

expedition /ekspɪ'dɪʃn/ *n.* Expedition, *die*

expel /ɪk'spel/ *v.t.*, **-ll-** ausweisen (**from** aus); **~ sb. from school** jmdn. von der Schule verweisen

expend /ɪk'spend/ *v.t.* **(a)** aufwenden ([**up**]**on** für)
(b) (use up) aufbrauchen ([**up**]**on** für)

expendable /ɪk'spendəbl/ *adj.* entbehrlich; **be ~**: geopfert werden können

expenditure /ɪk'spendɪtʃə(r)/ *n.* **(a)** (amount spent) Ausgaben *Pl.* (**on** für)
(b) (spending) Ausgabe, *die*

expense /ɪk'spens/ *n.* **(a)** Kosten *Pl.*; **at sb.'s ~**: auf jmds. Kosten (*Akk.*); **at one's own ~**: auf eigene Kosten
(b) *usu. in pl.* (Commerc. etc.: amount spent [and repaid]) Spesen *Pl.*
(c) (fig.) [**be**] **at the ~ of sth.** auf Kosten von etw. [gehen]

ex'pense account *n.* Spesenabrechnung, *die;* **put sth. on one's ~**: etw. als Spesen abrechnen

expensive /ɪk'spensɪv/ *adj.*, **ex'pensively** *adv.* teuer

experience /ɪk'spɪərɪəns/ 1 *n.* Erfahrung, *die;* (incident) Erlebnis, *das*
2 *v.t.* erleben; haben ‹*Schwierigkeiten*›; verspüren ‹*Kälte, Schmerz, Gefühl*›

ex'perienced *adj.* erfahren

experiment 1 /ɪk'sperɪmənt/ *n.* **(a)** Experiment, *das*, Versuch, *der* (**on** an + *Dat.*)
(b) (fig.) Experiment, *das*
2 /ɪk'sperɪment/ *v.i.* Versuche anstellen (**on** an + *Dat.*)

experimental /ɪksperɪ'mentl/ *adj.* experimentell; Experimentier‹*theater, -kino*›

expert /'ekspɜːt/ 1 *adj.* ausgezeichnet; **be ~ in** *or* **at sth.** Fachmann *od.* Experte für etw. sein; **be ~ in** *or* **at doing sth.** etw. ausgezeichnet können
2 *n.* Fachmann, *der;* Experte, *der*/Expertin, *die;* **be an ~ in** *or* **at/on sth.** Fachmann *od.* Experte in etw. (*Dat.*)/für etw. sein

expertise /ekspɜː'tiːz/ *n.* Fachkenntnisse *Pl.*; (skill) Können, *das*

expert: ~ system *n.* (Comp.) Expertensystem, *das;* **~ 'witness** *n.* sachverständiger Zeuge

expire /ɪk'spaɪə(r)/ *v.i.* ablaufen

expiry /ɪk'spaɪərɪ/ *n.* Ablauf, *der*

explain /ɪk'spleɪn/ 1 *v.t., also abs.* erklären
2 *v. refl., often abs.* **please ~** [**yourself**] bitte erklären Sie mir das

■ **explain a'way** *v.t.* eine [plausible] Erklärung finden für

explanation /eksplə'neɪʃn/ *n.* Erklärung, *die;* **need ~**: einer Erklärung bedürfen

explanatory /ɪk'splænətərɪ/ *adj.* erklärend; erläuternd ‹*Bemerkung*›

explicable /ɪk'splɪkəbl/ *adj.* erklärbar

explicit /ɪk'splɪsɪt/ *adj.* klar; ausdrücklich ‹*Zustimmung, Erwähnung*›

ex'plicitly *adv.* ausdrücklich; deutlich ‹*beschreiben, ausdrücken*›

explode /ɪk'spləʊd/ 1 *v.i.* explodieren
2 *v.t.* zur Explosion bringen

exploit 1 /'eksplɔɪt/ *n.* Heldentat, *die*
2 /ɪk'splɔɪt/ *v.t.* ausbeuten ‹*Arbeiter usw.*›; ausnutzen ‹*Gutmütigkeit, Freund, Unwissenheit*›

exploitation /eksplɔɪ'teɪʃn/ *n.* ▶ EXPLOIT 2: Ausbeutung, *die;* Ausnutzung, *die*

exploration /eksplə'reɪʃn/ *n.* Erforschung, *die;* (fig.) Untersuchung, *die*

exploratory /ɪk'splɒrətərɪ/ *adj.* Forschungs-

explore /ɪk'splɔː(r)/ *v.t.* erforschen; (fig.) untersuchen

ex'plorer *n.* Entdeckungsreisende, *der/die*

explosion /ɪk'spləʊʒn/ *n.* Explosion, *die*

explosive /ɪk'spləʊsɪv/ 1 *adj.* explosiv
2 *n.* Sprengstoff, *der*

export 1 /ɪk'spɔːt, 'ekspɔːt/ *v.t.* exportieren; ausführen
2 /'ekspɔːt/ *n.* Export, *der*

export /'ekspɔːt/**: ~ drive** *n.* Exportkampagne, *die;* **~ duty** *n.* Exportzoll, *der*

ex'porter *n.* Exporteur, *der*

export /'ekspɔːt/**: ~ licence** *n.* Ausfuhrlizenz, *die;* **~ market** *n.* Exportmarkt, *der;* **~ permit** *n.* Exporterlaubnis, *die;* Ausfuhrerlaubnis, *die*

expose /ɪk'spəʊz/ *v.t.* **(a)** (uncover) freilegen; entblößen ‹*Haut, Körper*›
(b) offenbaren ‹*Schwäche*›; aufdecken ‹*Missstände, Verbrechen*›; entlarven ‹*Täter, Spion*›
(c) (subject) **~ to sth.** einer Sache (*Dat.*) aussetzen
(d) (Photog.) belichten

exposed /ɪk'spəʊzd/ *adj.* (unprotected) ungeschützt; **~ position** exponierte Stellung

exposure /ɪk'spəʊʒə(r)/ *n.* **(a)** (to cold etc.) **die of/suffer from ~**: an Unterkühlung (*Dat.*) sterben/leiden
(b) (Photog.) (exposing time) Belichtung, *die;* (picture) Aufnahme, *die*

ex'posure meter *n.* Belichtungsmesser, *der*

expound /ɪk'spaʊnd/ *v.t.* darlegen

express /ɪk'spres/ 1 *v.t.* ausdrücken; äußern ‹*Meinung, Wunsch, Dank, Bedauern*›; **~ oneself** sich ausdrücken
2 *attrib. adj.* **(a)** Eil‹*brief, -bote usw.*›; Schnell‹*paket, -sendung*›
(b) ausdrücklich ‹*Wunsch, Absicht*›
3 *adv.* als Eilsache ‹*senden*›
4 *n.* (train) Schnellzug, *der*

express de'livery *n.* Eilzustellung, *die*

expression /ɪk'spreʃn/ *n.* Ausdruck, *der*

expressive /ɪk'spresɪv/ *adj.* ausdrucksvoll

express: ~ 'letter *n.* Eilbrief, *der;* **~ 'lift** *n.* Schnellaufzug, *der*

ex'pressly *adv.* ausdrücklich

express: ~ 'train *n.* D-Zug, *der;* **~way** *n.* (Amer.) Schnellstraße, *die*

expulsion /ɪk'spʌlʃn/ *n.* Ausweisung, *die* **(from** aus); (from school) Verweisung, *die* **(from** von)

exquisite /'ekskwɪzɪt, ɪk'skwɪzɪt/ *adj.* erlesen

ex'quisitely *adv.* vorzüglich; kunstvoll ‹*verziert, geschnitzt*›

extend /ɪk'stend/ [1] *v.t.* verlängern; ausstrecken ‹*Arm, Bein, Hand*›; ausziehen ‹*Leiter, Teleskop*›; verlängern lassen ‹*Leihbuch, Visum*›; ausdehnen ‹*Einfluss, Macht*›; vergrößern ‹*Haus, Geschäft, Fabrik*›; gewähren ‹*[Gast]freundschaft, Hilfe, Kredit*› **(to** *Dat.*); **~ the time limit** den Termin hinausschieben

[2] *v.i.* sich erstrecken; **the season ~s from November to March** die Saison geht von November bis März

extended 'family *n.* Großfamilie, *die*

extension /ɪk'stenʃn/ *n.* **(a)** Verlängerung, *die*

(b) (part of house) Anbau, *der*

(c) (telephone) Nebenanschluss, *der;* (number) Apparat, *der*

extension: ~ cord (Amer.) ▶ ~ LEAD; **~ ladder** *n.* Ausziehleiter, *die;* **~ lead** *n.* (Brit.) Verlängerungsschnur, *die*

extensive /ɪk'stensɪv/ *adj.* ausgedehnt; umfangreich ‹*Reparatur, Wissen, Nachforschungen*›; beträchtlich ‹*Schäden*›; weit reichend ‹*Änderungen*›

ex'tensively *adv.* beträchtlich ‹*ändern, beschädigen*›; ausführlich ‹*berichten, schreiben*›

extent /ɪk'stent/ *n.* Ausdehnung, *die;* (scope) Umfang, *der;* (of damage) Ausmaß, *das;* **to what ~?** inwieweit?

exterior /ɪk'stɪərɪə(r)/ [1] *adj.* äußer...; Außen‹*fläche, -wand*›

[2] *n.* Äußere, *das;* (of house) Außenwände *Pl.*

exterminate /ɪk'stɜ:mɪneɪt/ *v.t.* ausrotten ‹*Nation, Volk*›; vertilgen ‹*Ungeziefer*›; liquidieren ‹*Person*›

extermination /ɪkstɜ:mɪ'neɪʃn/ *n.* Ausrottung, *die;* (of pests) Vertilgung, *die*

extermi'nation camp *n.* Vernichtungslager, *das*

external /ɪk'stɜ:nl/ *adj.* äußer...; Außen‹*fläche, -abmessungen*›; **purely ~:** rein äußerlich; **for ~ use only** nur äußerlich anzuwenden

extinct /ɪk'stɪŋkt/ *adj.* erloschen ‹*Vulkan*›; ausgestorben ‹*Art, Rasse, Gattung*›

extinction /ɪk'stɪŋkʃn/ *n.* Aussterben, *das*

extinguish /ɪk'stɪŋgwɪʃ/ *v.t.* löschen

ex'tinguisher *n.* Feuerlöscher, *der*

extol /ɪk'stɒl/ *v.t.*, **-ll-** rühmen; preisen

extort /ɪk'stɔ:t/ *v.t.* erpressen **(out of** von)

extortion /ɪk'stɔ:ʃn/ *n.* Erpressung, *die*

extortionate /ɪk'stɔ:ʃənət/ *adj.* Wucher‹*preis, -zinsen usw.*›; maßlos überzogen ‹*Forderung*›

extra /'ekstrə/ [1] *adj.* zusätzlich; Mehr‹*arbeit, -kosten, -ausgaben*›; Sonder‹*bus, -zug*›

[2] *adv.* **(a)** (more than usually) besonders; extra ‹*lang, stark, fein*›

(b) (additionally) extra; **packing and postage ~:** zuzüglich Verpackung und Porto

[3] *n.* **(a)** (added to services, salary, etc.) zusätzliche Leistung; (on car etc.) Extra, *das*

(b) (in play, film, etc.) Statist, *der*/Statistin, *die*

extract [1] /'ekstrækt/ *n.* **(a)** Extrakt, *der* (fachspr. auch: *das*)

(b) (from book, music, etc.) Auszug, *der*

[2] /ɪk'strækt/ *v.t.* ziehen ‹*Zahn*›; herausziehen ‹*Dorn, Splitter usw.*›

extraction /ɪk'strækʃn/ *n.* (of tooth) Extraktion, *die;* (of thorn, splinter, etc.) Herausziehen, *das*

ex'tractor fan *n.* Entlüfter, *der*

extra-curricular /ekstrəkə'rɪkjʊlə(r)/ *adj.* extracurricular (fachspr.); ‹*Aktivität*› außerhalb des Lehrplans

extradite /'ekstrədaɪt/ *v.t.* ausliefern

extradition /ekstrə'dɪʃn/ *n.* Auslieferung, *die*

extra'marital *adj.* außerehelich

extraordinary /ɪk'strɔ:dɪnərɪ/ *adj.* außergewöhnlich; merkwürdig ‹*Benehmen*›; **how ~!** wie seltsam!

extravagance /ɪk'strævəgəns/ *n.* **(a)** Extravaganz, *die*

(b) (extravagant thing) Luxus, *der*

extravagant /ɪk'strævəgənt/ *adj.* verschwenderisch; aufwendig ‹*Lebensstil*›

extreme /ɪk'stri:m/ [1] *adj.* **(a)** äußerst... ‹*Spitze, Rand, Ende*›; extrem ‹*Gegensätze, Hitze, Kälte*›; höchst... ‹*Gefahr*›; äußerst... ‹*Notfall, Höflichkeit, Bescheidenheit*›; stärkst... ‹*Schmerzen*›; größt... ‹*Wichtigkeit*›; **at the ~ edge/left** ganz am Rand/ganz links

(b) (not moderate) extrem; drastisch ‹*Maßnahme*›

[2] *n.* Extrem, *das;* **go to ~s** vor nichts zurückschrecken; **go from one ~ to the other** von einem Extrem ins andere fallen

ex'tremely *adv.* äußerst

extreme 'sport *n.* Extremsportart, *die*

extremist /ɪk'stri:mɪst/ *n.* Extremist, *der*/Extremistin, *die; attrib.* extremistisch

extremity /ɪk'stremɪtɪ/ *n.* äußerstes Ende

extricate /'ekstrɪkeɪt/ *v.t.* **~ sth. from sth.** etw. aus etw. herausziehen; **~ oneself/sb. from sth.** sich/jmdn. aus etw. befreien

extrovert /'ekstrəvɜ:t/ [1] *n.* extravertierter Mensch; **be an ~:** extravertiert sein

[2] *adj.* extravertiert

exuberant /ɪg'zju:bərənt/ *adj.* **be ~:** sich überschwänglich freuen

exude /ɪg'zju:d/ *v.t.* absondern; (fig.) ausstrahlen

exult /ɪg'zʌlt/ *v.i.* jubeln (**in, at, over** über + *Akk.*)

eye /aɪ/ 1 *n.* **(a)** Auge, *das;* **keep an ~ on sb./sth.** auf jmdn./etw. aufpassen; **see ~ to ~**: einer Meinung sein; **with one's ~s shut** (fig.) blind; (easily) im Schlaf; **be up to one's ~s in work/debt** bis über beide Ohren in Arbeit/Schulden stecken (ugs.)
(b) (of needle) Öhr, *das;* (metal loop) Öse, *die*
2 *v.t.*, beäugen; **~ sb. up and down** jmdn. von oben bis unten mustern

eye: ~ball *n.* Augapfel, *der;* **~brow** *n.* Augenbraue, *die;* **~-catching** *adj.* ins Auge springend *od.* fallend ‹*Inserat, Plakat, Buchhülle usw.*›; **be [very] ~-catching** ein [wirkungsvoller] Blickfang sein; **~ drops** *n. pl.* (Med.) Augentropfen *Pl.;* **~ hospital** *n.* Augenklinik, *die;* **~lash** *n.* Augenwimper, *die;* **~ level** *n.* Augenhöhe, *die;* **~-level** *attrib.* in Augenhöhe *nachgestellt;* **at ~ level** in Augenhöhe; **~lid** *n.* Augenlid, *das;* **~ make-up** *n.* Augen-Make-up, *das;* **~shadow** *n.* Lidschatten, *der;* **~sight** *n.* Sehkraft, *die;* **have good ~sight** gute Augen haben; **his ~sight is poor** er hat schlechte Augen; **~sore** *n.* Schandfleck, *der;* **~wash** *n.* **(a)** (Med.: lotion) Augenwasser, *das;* **(b)** (coll.) (nonsense) Gewäsch, *das* (ugs.); (concealment) Augen[aus]wischerei, *die* (ugs.); **~witness** *n.* Augenzeuge, *der*/-zeugin, *die*

Ff

F, f /ef/ *n.* F, f, *das*

fable /'feɪbl/ *n.* Fabel, *die;* (myth, lie) Märchen, *das*

fabric /'fæbrɪk/ *n.* Gewebe, *das*

fabricate /'fæbrɪkeɪt/ *v.t.* (invent) erfinden

fabrication /fæbrɪkeɪʃn/ *n.* Erfindung, *die*

'fabric softener /'sɒfənə(r)/ *n.* Weichspülmittel, *das;* Weichspüler, *der*

fabulous /'fæbjʊləs/ *adj.* **(a)** sagenhaft
(b) (coll.: marvellous) fabelhaft (ugs.)

façade /fə'sɑ:d/ *n.* (lit. or fig.) Fassade, *die;* **that's just a ~** (fig.) das ist alles nur Fassade

face /feɪs/ 1 *n.* **(a)** Gesicht, *das;* **lie ~ down[ward]** ‹*Person/Buch:*› auf dem Bauch/Gesicht liegen; **make** *or* **pull a ~/~s** Grimassen schneiden; **on the ~ of it** dem Anschein nach; **in the ~ of sth.** trotz etw. (*Gen.*)
(b) (of mountain, cliff) Wand, *die;* (of clock, watch) Zifferblatt, *das;* (of dice) Seite, *die;* (of coin, playing card) Vorderseite, *die*
2 *v.t.* **(a)** sich wenden zu; **[stand] facing one another** sich (*Dat.*) gegenüber[stehen]
(b) (fig.) ins Auge sehen (+ *Dat.*) ‹*Tod, Vorstellung*›; stehen vor (+ *Dat.*) ‹*Ruin, Entscheidung*›; **~ the facts** den Tatsachen ins Gesicht sehen; **be ~d with sth.** sich einer Sache (*Dat.*) gegenübersehen
(c) (coll.: bear) verkraften
3 *v.i.* (in train etc.) **~ backwards/forwards** ‹*Person:*› entgegen der/in Fahrtrichtung sitzen

■ **face 'up to** *v.t.* ins Auge sehen (+ *Dat.*); sich abfinden mit ‹*Möglichkeit*›

face: ~ cream *n.* Gesichtscreme, *die;* **~ flannel** *n.* (Brit.) Waschlappen, *der;* **~less** /'feɪslɪs/ *adj.* (anonymous) anonym (fig.); **~lift** *n.* **(a)** Facelifting, *das;* **have** *or* **get a ~lift** sich liften lassen; **(b)** (fig.) Verschönerung, *die;* **~ pack** *n.* [Gesichts]maske, *die;* **~-saving** *adj.* zur Wahrung des Gesichts *nachgestellt*

facet /'fæsɪt/ *n.* Facette, *die;* (fig.) Aspekt, *der*

facetious /fə'si:ʃəs/ *adj.* [gewollt] witzig

face: ~-to-~ *adj.* persönlich ‹*Gespräch, Treffen*›; **~ value** *n.* Nennwert, *der;* **accept sth. at [its] ~ value** (fig.) etw. für bare Münze nehmen

facial /'feɪʃl/ *adj.* Gesichts-

facile /'fæsaɪl/ *adj.* nichts sagend

facilities /fə'sɪlɪtɪz/ *n. pl.* Einrichtungen *Pl.*; **cooking/washing ~**: Koch-/Waschgelegenheit, *die;* **sports ~**: Sportanlagen *Pl.*; **shopping ~**: Einkaufsmöglichkeiten *Pl.*

facsimile /fæk'sɪmɪlɪ/ *n.* **(a)** Faksimile, *das* **(b)** ▶ FAX 1

fact /fækt/ *n.* Tatsache, *die;* **~s and figures** Fakten und Zahlen; **the ~ remains that ...**: Tatsache bleibt: ...; **the true ~s of the case** *or* **matter** der wahre Sachverhalt; **know for a ~ that ...**: genau wissen, dass ...; **in ~**: tatsächlich

faction /'fækʃn/ *n.* Splittergruppe, *die*

factor /'fæktə(r)/ *n.* Faktor, *der*

factory /'fæktərɪ/ *n.* Fabrik, *die*

factory: ~ 'farm *n.* [voll]automatisierter landwirtschaftlicher Betrieb; **~ 'farming** *n.* [fabrikmäßige] Massentierhaltung; **the ~ farming of salmon** die massenweise Lachsproduktion; **~ worker** *n.* Fabrikarbeiter, *der*/-arbeiterin, *die*

'fact sheet *n.* Infoblatt, *das*

factual /'fæktjʊəl/ *adj.* sachlich

faculty /ˈfækəltɪ/ *n.* **(a)** Fähigkeit, *die;* **mental ~:** geistige Kraft
(b) (Univ.) Fakultät, *die*

fad /fæd/ *n.* Marotte, *die*

fade /feɪd/ *v.i.* **(a)** ‹*Blätter, Blumen:*› [ver]welken
(b) ~ **[in colour]** [ver]bleichen; **the light ~d** es dunkelte
(c) ‹*Laut:*› verklingen
(d) (fig.) verblassen; ‹*Schönheit:*› verblühen; ‹*Hoffnung:*› schwinden
(e) (blend) übergehen (**into** in + *Akk.*).

▪ **fade aˈway** *v.i.* schwinden; ‹*Laut:*› verklingen (**into** in + *Dat.*)

faded /ˈfeɪdɪd/ *adj.* welk ‹*Blume, Blatt, Laub*›; verblichen ‹*Stoff, Farbe*›

faeces /ˈfi:si:z/ *n. pl.* Fäkalien *Pl.*

fag /fæg/ *n.* **(a)** (Brit. coll.) Schinderei, *die* (ugs.)
(b) (coll.: cigarette) Stäbchen, *das* (ugs.)

fail /feɪl/ **1** *v.i.* **(a)** scheitern; (in examination) nicht bestehen, (ugs.) durchfallen (**in** in + *Dat.*)
(b) (become weaker) ‹*Augenlicht, Gehör, Stärke:*› nachlassen
(c) (break down, stop) ‹*Versorgung:*› zusammenbrechen; ‹*Motor:*› aussetzen; ‹*Batterie, Pumpe:*› ausfallen; ‹*Bremse:*› versagen
2 *v.t.* **(a)** ~ **to do sth.** (not succeed in doing) etw. nicht tun [können]; ~ **to achieve one's purpose/aim** seine Absicht/sein Ziel verfehlen
(b) (be unsuccessful in) nicht bestehen, (ugs.) durchfallen in (+ *Dat.*) ‹*Prüfung*›
(c) (reject) durchfallen lassen (ugs.) ‹*Prüfling*›
(d) ~ **to do sth.** (not do) etw. nicht tun; (neglect to do) [es] versäumen, etw. zu tun; **not ~ to do sth.** etw. tun
(e) words ~ me mir fehlen die Worte; **his courage ~ed him** ihn verließ der Mut
3 *n.* **without ~:** auf jeden Fall

ˈfailing **1** *n.* Schwäche, *die*
2 *prep.* ~ **that** andernfalls

failure /ˈfeɪljə(r)/ *n.* **(a)** (omission, neglect) Versäumnis, *das*
(b) (lack of success) Scheitern, *das;* **end in ~:** scheitern
(c) (person or thing) Versager, *der;* **our plan/attempt was a ~:** unser Plan/Versuch war fehlgeschlagen

faint /feɪnt/ **1** *adj.* **(a)** matt ‹*Licht, Farbe, Stimme, Lächeln*›; schwach ‹*Geruch, Duft*›; leise ‹*Flüstern, Geräusch, Stimme*›; entfernt ‹*Ähnlichkeit*›; undeutlich ‹*Umriss, Linie, Spur, Fotokopie*›
(b) (giddy, weak) matt; **she felt ~:** ihr war schwindelig
2 *v.i.* ohnmächtig werden (**from** vor + *Dat.*)
3 *n.* Ohnmacht, *die*

faint-ˈhearted *adj.* hasenherzig; zaghaft ‹*Versuch*›

ˈfaintly *adv.* schwach; entfernt ‹*sich ähneln*›

fair¹ /feə(r)/ *n.* (fun~) Jahrmarkt, *der;* (exhibition) Messe, *die;* **book/trade ~:** Buch-/Handelsmesse, *die*

fair² *adj.* **(a)** (just) gerecht; begründet ‹*Beschwerde, Annahme*›; fair ‹*Spiel, Kampf, Prozess, Preis, Beurteilung, Handel*›; ~ **play** Fairness, *die*
(b) (not bad, pretty good) ganz gut ‹*Bilanz, Anzahl, Chance*›; ziemlich ‹*Maß, Geschwindigkeit*›
(c) (blond) blond ‹*Haar, Person*›; (light) hell ‹*Haut*›; (~-skinned) hellhäutig ‹*Person*›
(d) schön ‹*Wetter, Tag*›

fair: ~ground *n.* Festplatz, *der;* **~-haired** *adj.* blond; **~-haired boy** (Amer. fig.) Liebling, *der;* Favorit, *der*

ˈfairly *adv.* **(a)** fair ‹*kämpfen, spielen*›; gerecht ‹*bestrafen, beurteilen, behandeln*›
(b) (rather) ziemlich

ˈfair-minded *adj.* unvoreingenommen

ˈfairness *n.* Gerechtigkeit, *die;* **in all ~ [to sb.]** um fair [gegen jmdn.] zu sein

fairy /ˈfeərɪ/ *n.* Fee, *die*

fairy: ~ ˈgodmother *n.* gute Fee; **~ story, ~ tale** *ns.* Märchen, *das*

faith /feɪθ/ *n.* **(a)** (reliance, trust) Vertrauen, *das* (**in** zu); **have ~ in oneself** Selbstvertrauen haben; **in good ~:** in gutem Glauben
(b) (religious belief) Glaube, *der*

faithful /ˈfeɪθfl/ *adj.* **(a)** treu (**to** *Dat.*)
(b) (conscientious) pflichtbewusst; [ge]treu ‹*Diener*›
(c) (accurate) [wahrheits]getreu; originalgetreu ‹*Wiedergabe, Kopie*›

ˈfaithfully *adv.* **(a)** treu ‹*dienen*›; pflichtbewusst ‹*überbringen, zustellen*›; hoch und heilig ‹*versprechen*›
(b) (accurately) wahrheitsgetreu ‹*erzählen*›; originalgetreu ‹*wiedergeben*›; genau ‹*befolgen*›
(c) yours ~: hochachtungsvoll

faith: ~ healer *n.* Gesundbeter, *der*/-beterin, *die;* **~ healing** *n.* Gesundbeten, *das*

fake /feɪk/ **1** *adj.* unecht; gefälscht ‹*Dokument, Banknote, Münze*›
2 *n.* **(a)** Imitation, *die;* (painting) Fälschung, *die*
(b) (person) Schwindler, *der*/Schwindlerin, *die*
3 *v.t.* fälschen ‹*Unterschrift*›; vortäuschen ‹*Krankheit, Unfall*›

falcon /ˈfɔ:lkn/ *n.* Falke, *der*

fall /fɔ:l/ **1** *n.* **(a)** Fallen, *das;* (of person) Sturz, *der;* ~ **of snow/rain** Schnee-/Regenfall, *der;* **have a ~:** stürzen
(b) (collapse, defeat) Fall, *der;* (of dynasty, empire) Untergang, *der*
(c) (decrease) Rückgang, *der*
(d) (Amer.: autumn) Herbst, *der*
2 *v.i.*, **fell** /fel/, **fallen** /ˈfɔ:ln/ **(a)** fallen; ‹*Baum:*› umstürzen; ‹*Pferd:*› stürzen; ~ **off sth., ~ down from sth.** von etw. ··›

[herunter]fallen; ~ **down [into] sth.** in etw. (*Akk.*) [hinein]fallen; ~ **to the ground** auf den Boden fallen; ~ **down the stairs** *or* **downstairs** die Treppe herunter-/hinunterfallen
(b) ‹*Nacht, Dunkelheit:*› hereinbrechen; ‹*Abend:*› anbrechen
(c) ‹*Blätter:*› [ab]fallen
(d) (sink) sinken; ‹*Barometer:*› fallen; ‹*Absatz, Verkauf:*› zurückgehen; ~ **by 10 per cent/from 10[°C] to 0[°C]** um 10%/von 10[°C] auf 0[°C] sinken
(e) (be killed) ‹*Soldat:*› fallen
(f) (collapse) einstürzen; ~ **to pieces,** ~ **apart** auseinander fallen
(g) (occur) fallen (**on** auf + *Akk.*)
■ **fall 'back** *v.i.* zurückweichen
■ **fall 'back on** *v.t.* zurückgreifen auf (+ *Akk.*)
■ **fall 'down** *v.i.* **(a)** ▶ FALL 2A
(b) ‹*Brücke, Gebäude:*› einstürzen
■ **'fall for** *v.t.* (coll.) ~ **for sb.** sich in jmdn. verknallen (ugs.); ~ **for sth.** auf etw. (*Akk.*) hereinfallen (ugs.)
■ **fall 'in** *v.i.* **(a)** hineinfallen
(b) (Mil.) antreten; ~ **in!** angetreten!
(c) ‹*Gebäude, Wand usw.:*› einstürzen
■ **fall 'off** *v.i.* **(a)** herunterfallen
(b) (diminish) nachlassen
■ **fall 'out** *v.i.* **(a)** herausfallen; ‹*Haare, Federn*› ausfallen
(b) (quarrel) ~ **out [with sb.]** sich [mit jmdm.] streiten
■ **fall 'over** *v.i.* umfallen; ‹*Person:*› [hin]fallen
■ **fall 'through** *v.i.* (fig.) ins Wasser fallen (ugs.)

fallacy /'fæləsɪ/ *n.* Irrtum, *der*

fallen ▶ FALL 2

fallible /'fælɪbl/ *adj.* nicht unfehlbar; fehlbar ‹*Person*›

'fallout *n.* radioaktiver Niederschlag

fallow /'fæləʊ/ *adj.* brachliegend; ~ **ground/land** Brache, *die*/Brachland, *das;* **lie** ~: brachliegen

false /fɔ:ls, fɒls/ *adj.* falsch; gefälscht ‹*Urkunde, Dokument*›; künstlich ‹*Wimpern*›; **under a** ~ **name** unter falschem Namen

false 'alarm *n.* blinder Alarm

'falsely *adv.* falsch; fälschlich[erweise] ‹*annehmen, glauben, behaupten, beschuldigen*›

false: ~ **'move** ▶ FALSE STEP; ~ **pre'tences** *n. pl.* Vorspiegelung falscher Tatsachen; ~ **'start** *n.* Fehlstart, *der;* ~ **'step** *n.* (lit. or fig.) falscher Schritt; **make a** ~ **step** einen falschen Schritt tun; ~ **'teeth** *n. pl.* [künstliches] Gebiss

falsify /'fɔ:lsɪfaɪ/ *v.t.* (alter) fälschen; (misrepresent) verfälschen ‹*Tatsachen, Wahrheit*›

falter /'fɔ:ltə(r)/ *v.i.* stocken

fame /feɪm/ *n.* Ruhm, *der*

familiar /fə'mɪljə(r)/ *adj.* **(a)** vertraut; bekannt ‹*Gesicht, Name, Lied*›; **he looks** ~: er kommt mir bekannt vor
(b) (informal) ungezwungen ‹*Sprache, Art*›

familiarity /fəmɪlɪ'ærɪtɪ/ *n.* Vertrautheit, *die*

familiarize /fə'mɪljəraɪz/ *v.t.* vertraut machen (**with** mit)

family /'fæməlɪ/ *n.* Familie, *die*

family: ~ **'doctor** *n.* Hausarzt, *der;* ~ **name** *n.* Familienname, *der;* ~ **'planning** *n.* Familienplanung, *die;* ~ **'tree** *n.* Stammbaum, *der*

famine /'fæmɪn/ *n.* Hungersnot, *die*

famished /'fæmɪʃt/ *adj.* ausgehungert; **I'm absolutely** ~ (coll.) ich sterbe vor Hunger (ugs.)

famous /'feɪməs/ *adj.* berühmt

fan¹ /fæn/ [1] *n.* Fächer, *der;* (apparatus) Ventilator, *der*
[2] *v.t.*, **-nn-** fächeln ‹*Gesicht*›; anfachen ‹*Feuer*›; ~ **oneself/sb.** sich/jmdm. Luft zufächeln
■ **fan 'out** *v.i.* fächern; ‹*Soldaten:*› ausfächern

fan² *n.* (devotee) Fan, *der*

fanatic /fə'nætɪk/ *n.* Fanatiker, *der*/Fanatikerin, *die*

fanatical /fə'nætɪkl/ *adj.* fanatisch

fanaticism /fə'nætɪsɪzm/ *n.* Fanatismus, *der*

'fan belt *n.* Keilriemen, *der*

fanciful /'fænsɪfl/ *adj.* überspannt ‹*Vorstellung, Gedanke*›; fantastisch ‹*Gemälde, Design*›

'fan club *n.* Fanklub, *der*

fancy /'fænsɪ/ [1] *n.* **(a)** (taste, inclination) **he has taken a** ~ **to a new car/her** ein neues Auto/sie hat es ihm angetan; **take** *or* **catch sb.'s** ~: jmdm. gefallen
(b) (whim) Laune, *die;* **tickle sb.'s** ~: jmdn. reizen
[2] *attrib. adj.* kunstvoll ‹*Arbeit, Muster*›; fein[st...] ‹*Kuchen, Spitzen*›
[3] *v.t.* **(a)** (imagine) sich (*Dat.*) einbilden; ~ **that!** (coll.) sieh mal einer an!
(b) (suppose) glauben
(c) (wish to have) mögen; **what do you** ~ **for dinner?** was hättest du gern zum Abendessen?; **do you think she fancies him?** glaubst du, sie mag ihn?

fancy 'dress *n.* [Masken]kostüm, *das;* **in** ~: kostümiert; **fancy-dress party** Kostümfest, *das;* **fancy-dress ball** Maskenball, *der*

fanfare /'fænfeə(r)/ *n.* Fanfare, *die*

fang /fæŋ/ *n.* Reißzahn, *der;* (of snake) Giftzahn, *der*

fan: ~ **heater** *n.* Heizlüfter, *der;* ~**light** *n.* Oberlicht, *das;* ~ **mail** *n.* Fanpost, *die;* ~ **oven** *n.* Heißluftofen, *der*

fantastic /fæn'tæstɪk/ *adj.* **(a)** (grotesque, quaint) bizarr
(b) (coll.: excellent) fantastisch (ugs.)

fantasy /'fæntəzɪ/ *n.* Fantasie, *die;* (mental image) Fantasiegebilde, *das*

FAQ /fæk/ *abbr.* (Comp.) FAQ

far /fɑː(r)/ 1 *adv.* weit; ~ **above/below** hoch über/tief unter (+ *Dat.*); hoch oben/tief unten; **as ~ as Munich/the church** bis [nach] München/bis zur Kirche; ~ **and wide** weit und breit; **from ~ and wide** von fern und nah; ~ **too** viel zu; ~ **longer/better** weit[aus] länger/besser; **as ~ as I remember/know** soweit ich mich erinnere/weiß; **go so ~ as to do sth.** so weit gehen und etw. tun; **so ~** (until now) bisher; **so ~ so good** so weit, so gut; **by ~**: bei weitem; ~ **from easy/good** alles andere als leicht/gut
2 *adj.* **(a)** (remote) weit entfernt; (in time) fern; **in the ~ distance** in weiter Ferne
(b) (more remote) weiter entfernt; **the ~ bank of the river/side of the road** das andere Flussufer/die andere Straßenseite; **the ~ door/wall** *etc.* die hintere Tür/Wand *usw.*

farce /fɑːs/ *n.* Farce, *die*

farcical /'fɑːsɪkl/ *adj.* (absurd) farcenhaft

fare /feə(r)/ *n.* **(a)** (price) Fahrpreis, *der;* (money) Fahrgeld, *das;* **what** *or* **how much is the ~?** was kostet die Fahrt?
(b) (food) Kost, *die*

Far: ~ 'East *n.* **the ~ East** der Ferne Osten; ~ **'Eastern** *adj.* fernöstlich; des Fernen Ostens *nachgestellt*

farewell /feə'wel/ 1 *int.* leb[e] wohl (veralt.)
2 *n. attrib.* ~ **speech/gift** Abschiedsrede, *die*/-geschenk, *das*

far-'fetched *adj.* weit hergeholt

farm /fɑːm/ 1 *n.* [Bauern]hof, *der;* (larger) Gut, *das;* ~ **animals** Nutzvieh, *das*
2 *v.t.* bebauen ‹*Land*›
3 *v.i.* Landwirtschaft treiben

'farmer *n.* Landwirt, *der*/-wirtin, *die*

farm: ~hand *n.* Landarbeiter, *der*/-arbeiterin, *die;* **~house** *n.* Bauernhaus, *das;* (larger) Gutshaus, *das*

'farming *n.* Landwirtschaft, *die*

farm: ~land *n.* Acker- und Weideland, *das;* **~worker** *n.* Landarbeiter, *der*/-arbeiterin, *die;* **~yard** *n.* Hof, *der*

far: ~-'reaching *adj.* weit reichend; **~sighted** *adj.* **(a)** (fig.) weit blickend; **(b)** (Amer.: long-sighted) weitsichtig

fart /fɑːt/ (coarse) 1 *v.i.* furzen (derb)
2 *n.* Furz, *der* (derb)

farther /'fɑːðə(r)/ ▶ FURTHER 1A, 2

farthest /'fɑːðɪst/ ▶ FURTHEST

fascinate /'fæsɪneɪt/ *v.t.* fesseln; bezaubern

fascinated /'fæsɪneɪtɪd/ *adj.* fasziniert

fascinating /'fæsɪneɪtɪŋ/ *adj.* faszinierend (geh.); bezaubernd; hochinteressant ‹*Thema, Faktum, Meinung*›; spannend, fesselnd ‹*Buch*›

fascination /fæsɪ'neɪʃn/ *n.* Zauber, *der;* **have a ~ for sb.** einen besonderen Reiz auf jmdn. ausüben

fascism /'fæʃɪzm/ *n.* Faschismus, *der*

fascist /'fæʃɪst/ 1 *n.* Faschist, *der*/Faschistin, *die*
2 *adj.* faschistisch

fashion /'fæʃn/ 1 *n.* **(a)** Mode, *die*
(b) (manner) Art [und Weise]; **talk/behave in a peculiar ~**: merkwürdig sprechen/sich merkwürdig verhalten
2 *v.t.* formen **(out of, from** aus; **[in]to** zu)

fashionable /'fæʃənəbl/ *adj.* modisch; vornehm ‹*Hotel, Restaurant*›; Mode‹*farbe, -autor*›

fashionably /'fæʃənəblɪ/ *adv.* modisch

fashion: ~-conscious *adj.* modebewusst; ~ **designer** *n.* Modeschöpfer, *der*/-schöpferin, *die;* ~ **parade,** ~ **show** *ns.* Mode[n]schau, *die*

fast¹ /fɑːst/ 1 *v.i.* fasten
2 *n.* Fasten, *das*

fast² 1 *adj.* **(a)** (fixed, attached) fest; **make [the boat] ~**: das Boot festmachen; **hard and ~**: fest; bindend ‹*Regel*›; klar ‹*Entscheidung*›
(b) (rapid) schnell; ~ **train** Schnellzug, *der;* D-Zug, *der*
(c) be [ten minutes] ~ ‹*Uhr:*› [zehn Minuten] vorgehen
2 *adv.* **(a) be ~ asleep** fest schlafen; (when one should be awake) fest eingeschlafen sein
(b) (quickly) schnell

'fastback *n.* (back of car) Fließheck, *das;* Fastback, *das;* (car) Wagen mit Fließheck; Fastback, *das*

fasten /'fɑːsn/ *v.t.* befestigen **(on, to** an + *Dat.*); zumachen ‹*Kleid, Spange, Jacke*›; [ab]schließen ‹*Tür*›; anstecken ‹*Brosche*› **(to** an + *Akk.*); ~ **one's seat belt** sich anschnallen

'fastener, 'fastening *ns.* Verschluss, *der*

fast: ~ 'food *n.: im Schnellrestaurant angebotenes Essen;* Fastfood, *das; attrib.* **~-food restaurant** Schnellrestaurant, *das;* ~ **'forward** *n.* schneller Vorlauf; (playback) Zeitrafferwiedergabe, *die;* **~-forward** 1 *attrib. adj.* Vorspul‹*taste, -funktion*›;
2 *v.t. & i.* vorspulen

fastidious /fæ'stɪdɪəs/ *adj.* wählerisch; (hard to please) heikel

fast: ~ lane *n.* Überholspur, *die;* **life in the ~ lane** (fig.) Leben auf vollen Touren (ugs.); ~ **track** *n.* Überholspur, *die;* **a career on the ~ track** eine Blitzkarriere; **be on the ~ track** eine Blitzkarriere machen; **~-track** 1 *v.t.* beschleunigen ‹*Projekt*›;
2 *attrib. adj.* Schnell-

fat /fæt/ 1 *adj.* dick; rund ‹*Wangen, Gesicht*›
2 *n.* Fett, *das;* **animal/vegetable ~**: tierisches/pflanzliches Fett

fatal /'feɪtl/ *adj.* **(a)** (disastrous) verheerend (to für); **it would be ~:** das wäre das Ende **(b)** (deadly) tödlich ‹*Unfall, Verletzung*›

fatality /fə'tælɪtɪ/ *n.* Todesopfer, *das*

'fatally *adv.* tödlich; **be ~ ill** todkrank sein

fate /feɪt/ *n.* Schicksal, *das*

fat-free *adj.* fettfrei

'fathead *n.* Dummkopf, *der* (ugs.)

father /'fɑːðə(r)/ *n.* Vater, *der*

father: F~ 'Christmas *n.* der Weihnachtsmann; **~ figure** *n.* Vaterfigur, *die*

fatherhood /'fɑːðəhʊd/ *n.* Vaterschaft, *die*

'father-in-law *n., pl.* **~s-in-law** Schwiegervater, *der*

'fatherly *adj.* väterlich

'Father's Day *n.* Vatertag, *der*

fathom /'fæðəm/ [1] *n.* (Naut.) Faden, *der* [2] *v.t.* (comprehend) verstehen; **~ sb./sth. out** jmdn./etw. ergründen

fatigue /fə'tiːg/ [1] *n.* Ermüdung, *die* [2] *v.t.* ermüden

'fatness *n.* Dicke, *die*

fatten /'fætn/ *v.t.* herausfüttern ‹*Person*›; mästen ‹*Tier*›

'fattening *adj.* **be ~:** dick machen

fatty /'fætɪ/ *adj.* fett ‹*Fleisch, Soße*›; fetthaltig ‹*Speise, Nahrungsmittel*›

faucet /'fɔːsɪt/ *n.* (Amer.) Wasserhahn, *der*

fault /fɔːlt, fɒlt/ *n.* **(a)** Fehler, *der* **(b)** (responsibility) Schuld, *die;* **it's your ~:** du bist schuld; **it isn't my ~:** ich habe keine Schuld; **be at ~:** im Unrecht sein **(c)** (in machinery; also Electr.) Defekt, *der*

'faultless *adj.* einwandfrei

'faulty *adj.* fehlerhaft; defekt ‹*Gerät, usw.*›

fauna /'fɔːnə/ *n., pl.* **~e** /'fɔːnɪ/ *or* **~s** Fauna, *die*

favor *etc.* (*Amer.*) ▶ FAVOUR *etc.*

favour /'feɪvə(r)/ [1] *n.* **(a)** Gunst, *die* **(b)** (kindness) Gefallen, *der;* **ask sb. a ~, ask a ~ of sb.** jmdn. um einen Gefallen bitten; **do sb. a ~, do a ~ for sb.** jmdm. einen Gefallen tun; **as a ~:** aus Gefälligkeit **(c) be in ~ of sth.** für etw. sein [2] *v.t.* bevorzugen

favourable /'feɪvərəbl/ *adj.* (Brit.) **(a)** günstig ‹*Eindruck, Licht*›; gewogen ‹*Haltung, Einstellung*›; freundlich ‹*Erwähnung*›; positiv ‹*Bericht*[*erstattung*], *Bemerkung*› **(b)** (helpful) günstig (**to** für) ‹*Wetter, Wind, Umstand*›

favourably /'feɪvərəblɪ/ *adv.* (Brit.) wohlwollend; **be ~ disposed towards sb./sth.** jmdm./einer Sache positiv gegenüberstehen

favourite /'feɪvərɪt/ (Brit.) [1] *adj.* Lieblings- [2] *n.* **(a)** Liebling, *der;* (food/country etc.) Lieblingsessen, *das*/-land, *das usw.;* **this/he is my ~:** das/ihn mag ich am liebsten **(b)** (Sport) Favorit, *der*/Favoritin, *die*

favouritism /'feɪvərɪtɪzm/ *n.* (Brit.) Begünstigung, *die;* (when selecting sb. for a post etc.) Günstlingswirtschaft, *die*

fawn /fɔːn/ [1] *n.* **(a)** (colour) Rehbraun, *das* **(b)** (young deer) [Dam]kitz, *das* [2] *adj.* rehfarben

fax /fæks/ [1] *n.* [Tele]fax, *das* [2] *v.t.* faxen

fax: ~ machine *n.* Faxgerät, *das;* **~ modem** *n.* (Comp.) Faxmodem, *das;* **~ number** *n.* Faxnummer, *die*

FBI *abbr.* (Amer.) = **Federal Bureau of Investigation** FBI, *das*

fear /fɪə(r)/ [1] *n.* Angst, *die* (**of** vor + *Dat.*); (instance) Befürchtung, *die;* **~ of death** *or* **dying/heights** Todes-/Höhenangst, *die;* **~ of doing sth.** Angst davor, etw. zu tun; **in ~:** angstvoll; **no ~!** (coll.) keine Bange! (ugs.) [2] *v.t.* **(a) ~ sb./sth.** vor jmdm./etw. Angst haben; **~ to do** *or* **doing sth.** Angst haben, etw. zu tun **(b)** (be worried about) befürchten; **~ [that ...]** fürchten[, dass ...]

fearful /'fɪəfl/ *adj.* **(a)** (terrible) furchtbar **(b)** (frightened) ängstlich; **be ~ of sth./sb.** vor etw./jmdm. Angst haben

'fearless *adj.*, **'fearlessly** *adv.* furchtlos

feasibility /fiːzɪ'bɪlɪtɪ/ *n.* Durchführbarkeit, *die*

feasible /'fiˈzɪbl/ *adj.* durchführbar

feast /fiːst/ [1] *n.* **(a)** (Relig.) Fest, *das* **(b)** (banquet) Festessen, *das* [2] *v.i.* schlemmen; **~ on sth.** sich an etw. (*Dat.*) gütlich tun

feat /fiːt/ *n.* Meisterleistung, *die*

feather /'feðə(r)/ *n.* Feder, *die*

feather: ~ 'bed *n.* mit Federn gefüllte Matratze; **~ 'duster** *n.* Flederwisch, *der;* **~weight** *n.* (Boxing) Federgewicht, *das*

feature /'fiːtʃə(r)/ [1] *n.* **(a)** *usu. in pl.* (of face) Gesichtszug, *der* **(b)** (characteristic) [charakteristisches] Merkmal; **be a ~ of sth.** charakteristisch für etw. sein **(c)** (Journ.) Feature, *das* **(d)** (Cinemat.) **~ [film]** Hauptfilm, *der* [2] *v.t.* vorrangig vorstellen; (in film) in der Hauptrolle zeigen [3] *v.i.* vorkommen; **~ in** (be important) eine bedeutende Rolle haben bei

Feb. *abbr.* = **February** Febr.

February /'febrʊərɪ/ *n.* Februar, *der*

feces (Amer.) ▶ FAECES

fed /fed/ [1] ▶ FEED 1, 2 [2] *pred. adj.* (coll.) **be/get ~ up with sb./sth.** jmdn./etw. satt haben/kriegen (ugs.); **I'm ~ up** ich hab die Nase voll (ugs.)

federal /'fedərl/ *adj.* Bundes-; föderativ ‹*System*›

federation /fedə'reɪʃn/ *n.* Föderation, *die*

fee /fiː/ *n.* Gebühr, *die;* (of doctor, lawyer, etc.) Honorar, *das*

feeble /'fi:bl/ *adj.* schwach; wenig überzeugend ‹*Entschuldigung*›; zaghaft ‹*Versuch*›; lahm (ugs.) ‹*Witz*›

feed /fi:d/ **1** *v.t.*, **fed** /fed/ **(a)** füttern; **~ sb./an animal with sth.** jmdm. etw. zu essen/einem Tier [etw.] zu fressen geben **(b)** (provide food for) ernähren (**on, with** mit) **2** *v.i.*, **fed** ‹*Tier:*› fressen (**from** aus); ‹*Person:*› essen (**off** von); **~ on sth.** ‹*Tier:*› etw. fressen **3** *n.* **(a)** (for baby) Mahlzeit, *die* **(b)** (fodder) Futter, *das*

'feedback *n.* Reaktion, *die*

feel /fi:l/ **1** *v.t.*, **felt** /felt/ **(a)** (explore by touch) befühlen **(b)** (perceive by touch) fühlen; (become aware of) bemerken; (have sensation of) spüren **(c)** (experience) empfinden; verspüren ‹*Drang*›; **~ the cold/heat** unter der Kälte/Hitze leiden; **~ [that] ...**: das Gefühl haben, dass ...; (think) glauben, dass ... **2** *v.i.*, **felt**: **(a) ~ [about] in sth. [for sth.]** in etw. (*Dat.*) [nach etw.] [herum]suchen **(b)** (be conscious that one is) sich ... fühlen; **~ angry/sure/disappointed** böse/sicher/enttäuscht sein; **~ like sth./doing sth.** auf etw. (*Akk.*) Lust haben/Lust haben, etw. zu tun **(c)** (be consciously perceived as) sich ... anfühlen

■ **'feel for** *v.t.* **~ for sb.** mit jmdm. Mitleid haben

'feeler *n.* Fühler, *der*

'feeling *n.* **(a)** Gefühl, *das;* (sense of touch) **[sense of] ~**: Tastsinn, *der;* **hurt sb.'s ~s** jmdn. verletzen **(b)** (opinion) Ansicht, *die*

feet *pl. of* FOOT

feign /fein/ *v.t.* vortäuschen; **~ to do sth.** vorgeben, etw. zu tun

feline /'fi:laın/ *adj.* (of cat[s]) Katzen-; (catlike) katzenartig; katzenhaft

fell[1] ▸ FALL 2

fell[2] /fel/ *v.t.* fällen ‹*Baum*›

fell[3] *adj.* **in one ~ swoop** auf einen Schlag

fellow /'feləʊ/ **1** *n.* **(a)** (comrade) Kamerad, *der* **(b)** (Brit. Univ.) Fellow, *der* **(c)** (of academy or society) Mitglied, *das* **(d)** (coll.: man, boy) Kerl, *der* (ugs.) **2** *attrib. adj.* Mit-; **~ man** *or* **human being** Mitmensch, *der*

fellowship /'feləʊʃıp/ *n.* (companionship) Gesellschaft, *die*

felt[1] /felt/ *n.* Filz, *der*

felt[2] ▸ FEEL

felt[-tipped] 'pen *n.* Filzstift, *der*

female /'fi:meıl/ **1** *adj.* weiblich; Frauen‹*stimme, -chor, -verein*› **2** *n.* Frau, *die;* (foetus, child) Mädchen, *das;* (animal) Weibchen, *das*

feminine /'femının/ *adj.* weiblich; Frauen‹*angelegenheit, -leiden*›; (womanly) feminin

femininity /femı'nınıtı/ *n.* Weiblichkeit, *die*

feminism /'femınızm/ *n.* Feminismus, *der*

feminist /'femınıst/ **1** *adj.* feministisch; Feministen‹*bewegung, -gruppe*› **2** *n.* Feministin, *die*/Feminist, *der*

fence /fens/ **1** *n.* Zaun, *der* **2** *v.i.* (Sport) fechten **3** *v.t.* **~ [in]** einzäunen

'fencer *n.* Fechter, *der*/Fechterin, *die*

fencing /'fensıŋ/ *n.* (Sport) Fechten, *das*

fend /fend/ *v.i.* **~ for oneself** für sich selbst sorgen; (in hostile surroundings) sich allein durchschlagen

■ **fend 'off** *v.t.* abwehren

fender /'fendə(r)/ *n.* **(a)** (for fire) Kaminschutz, *der* **(b)** (Amer.) (car bumper) Stoßstange, *die;* (car mudguard) Kotflügel, *der*

ferment /fə'ment/ **1** *v.i.* gären **2** *v.t.* zur Gärung bringen

fermentation /fɜ:men'teıʃn/ *n.* Gärung, *die*

fern /fɜ:n/ *n.* Farnkraut, *das*

ferocious /fə'rəʊʃəs/ *adj.* wild

ferocity /fə'rɒsıtı/ *n.* Wildheit, *die*

ferret /'ferıt/ *n.* Frettchen, *das*

ferrous /'ferəs/ *adj.* (containing iron) eisenhaltig; Eisen-

ferry /'ferı/ **1** *n.* Fähre, *die;* (service) Fährverbindung, *die* **2** *v.t.* (in boat) **~ [across** *or* **over]** übersetzen

'ferry service *n.* **(a)** Fährverbindung, *die* **(b)** (business) Fährbetrieb, *der*

fertile /'fɜ:taıl/ *adj.* (fruitful) fruchtbar; (capable of developing) befruchtet

fertility /fɜ:'tılıtı/ *n.* Fruchtbarkeit, *die*

fer'tility drug *n.* Hormonpräparat, *das* (*zur Steigerung der Fruchtbarkeit*)

fertilization /fɜ:tılaı'zeıʃn/ *n.* **(a)** (Biol.) Befruchtung, *die* **(b)** (Agric.) Düngung, *die*

fertilize /'fɜ:tılaız/ *v.t.* befruchten

'fertilizer *n.* Dünger, *der*

fervent /'fɜ:vənt/ *adj.* leidenschaftlich; inbrünstig ‹*Gebet, Wunsch, Hoffnung*›

fervour (*Brit.; Amer.:* **fervor**) /'fɜ:və(r)/ *n.* Leidenschaftlichkeit, *die*

fester /'festə(r)/ *v.i.* eitern

festival /'festıvl/ *n.* **(a)** (feast day) Fest, *das* **(b)** (of music etc.) Festival, *das*

festive /'festıv/ *adj.* festlich; fröhlich; **the ~ season** die Weihnachtszeit

festivity /fe'stıvıtı/ *n.* **(a)** (gaiety) Feststimmung, *die* **(b)** (celebration) Feier, *die;* **festivities** Feierlichkeiten *Pl.*

festoon /fe'stu:n/ **1** *n.* Girlande, *die* **2** *v.t.* schmücken (**with** mit)

fetch /fetʃ/ *v.t.* **(a)** holen; (collect) abholen (**from** von); **~ sb. sth., ~ sth. for sb.** jmdm. etw. holen
(b) (be sold for) erzielen ‹*Preis*›

'fetching *adj.* einnehmend

fête /feɪt/ *n.* [Wohltätigkeits]basar, *der*

fetish /'fetɪʃ/ *n.* Fetisch, *der*

fetishism /'fetɪʃɪzm/ *n.* Fetischismus, *der*

fetishist /'fetɪʃɪst/ *n.* Fetischist, *der*/ Fetischistin, *die*

fetter /'fetə(r)/ *v.t.* fesseln

fetus (Amer.) ▶ FOETUS

feud /fju:d/ *n.* Fehde, *die*

feudal /'fju:dl/ *adj.* Feudal-; feudalistisch; **~ system** Feudalsystem, *das*

fever /'fi:və(r)/ *n.* **(a)** (high temperature) Fieber, *das;* **have a [high] ~:** [hohes] Fieber haben
(b) (disease) Fieberkrankheit, *die*

'feverish *adj.* **(a)** (Med.) fiebrig; **be ~:** Fieber haben
(b) (excited) fiebrig

'fever pitch *n.* Siedepunkt, *der* (fig.); **reach ~:** auf dem Siedepunkt angelangt sein; **at ~:** auf dem Siedepunkt

few /fju:/ **1** *adj.* **(a)** (not many) wenige; *abs.* nur wenige; **with very ~ exceptions** mit ganz wenigen Ausnahmen; **his ~ belongings** seine paar Habseligkeiten; **a ~ ...:** wenige ...
(b) (some) wenige; **a ~ ...:** ein paar ...; **a ~ more ...:** noch ein paar ...
2 *n.* **(a)** (not many) wenige; **a ~:** wenige; **just a ~ of you/her friends** nur ein paar von euch/ihrer Freunde
(b) (some) **with a ~ of our friends** mit einigen unserer Freunde; **quite a ~:** ziemlich viele

fiancé /fɪ'ɑ̃seɪ/ *n.* Verlobte, *der*

fiancée /fɪ'ɑ̃seɪ/ *n.* Verlobte, *die*

fiasco /fɪ'æskəʊ/ *n., pl.* **~s** Fiasko, *das*

fib /fɪb/ **1** *n.* Flunkerei, *die* (ugs.); **tell ~s** flunkern (ugs.)
2 *v.i.,* **-bb-** flunkern (ugs.)

fibre (*Brit.; Amer.:* **fiber**) /'faɪbə(r)/ *n.* **(a)** Faser, *die*
(b) (material) [Faser]gewebe, *das*

fibre: ~glass *n.* (plastic) glasfaserverstärkter Kunststoff; **~ optic 'cable** *n.* Glasfaserkabel, *das;* **~ 'optics** *n.* Faseroptik, *die*

fibrous /'faɪbrəs/ *adj.* faserig ‹*Aufbau, Beschaffenheit, Eigenschaft*›; Faser‹*gewebe, -holz, -stoff*›

fiche /fi:ʃ/ *n., pl. same or* **~s** Mikrofiche, *das od. der*

fickle /'fɪkl/ *adj.* unberechenbar

fiction /'fɪkʃn/ *n.* erzählende Literatur; **a ~/~s** eine Erfindung

fictional /'fɪkʃənl/ *adj.* erfunden ‹*Geschichte*›; fiktiv ‹*Figur*›

'fiction writer *n.* Belletrist, *der*/ Belletristin, *die*

fictitious /fɪk'tɪʃəs/ *adj.* fingiert; falsch ‹*Name, Identität*›

fiddle /'fɪdl/ **1** *n.* **(a)** (Mus.) (coll./derog.) Fiedel, *die;* (violin for traditional music) Geige, *die;* **[as] fit as a ~:** kerngesund
(b) (coll.: swindle) Gaunerei, *die*
2 *v.t.* (coll.) frisieren (ugs.) ‹*Bücher, Rechnungen*›
3 *v.i.* herumspielen (**with** mit)

fiddler /'fɪdlə(r)/ *n.* Geiger, *der*/Geigerin, *die*

fiddly /'fɪdlɪ/ *adj.* (coll.) knifflig

fidelity /fɪ'delɪtɪ/ *n.* Treue, *die* (**to** zu)

fidget /'fɪdʒɪt/ **1** *v.i.* **~ [about]** herumrutschen
2 *n.* (person) Zappelphilipp, *der* (ugs.)

'fidgety *adj.* unruhig; zappelig ‹*Kind*›

field /fi:ld/ *n.* **(a)** Feld, *das*
(b) (for game) Platz, *der;* [Spiel]feld, *das*
(c) (subject area) [Fach]gebiet, *das;* **in the ~ of medicine** auf dem Gebiet der Medizin; **that is outside my ~:** das fällt nicht in mein Fach

field: ~ day *n.* **have a ~ day** seinen großen Tag haben; **~ events** *n. pl.* technische Disziplinen *Pl.* **~ glasses** *n. pl.* Feldstecher, *der;* **F~ 'Marshal** *n.* (Brit. Mil.) Feldmarschall, *der;* **~ mouse** *n.* Brandmaus, *die;* **~ trip** *n.* Exkursion, *die*

fiend /fi:nd/ *n.* **(a)** (wicked person) Scheusal, *das*
(b) (evil spirit) böser Geist

'fiendish *adj.* **(a)** teuflisch
(b) (very awkward) höllisch

fierce /'fɪəs/ *adj.* wild; erbittert ‹*Widerstand, Kampf*›; scharf ‹*Kritik*›

'fiercely *adv.* heftig ‹*angreifen, Widerstand leisten*›; wütend ‹*brüllen*›; aufs heftigste ‹*kritisieren, bekämpfen*›

fiery /'faɪərɪ/ *adj.* glühend; (looking like fire) feurig; (blazing red) feuerrot

fifteen /fɪf'ti:n/ **1** *adj.* fünfzehn
2 *n.* Fünfzehn, *die. See also* EIGHT

fifteenth /fɪf'ti:nθ/ **1** *adj.* fünfzehnt...
2 *n.* (fraction) Fünfzehntel, *das. See also* EIGHTH

fifth /fɪfθ/ **1** *adj.* fünft...
2 *n.* (in sequence, rank) Fünfte, *der/die/das;* (fraction) Fünftel, *das. See also* EIGHTH

fiftieth /'fɪftɪɪθ/ *adj.* fünfzigst...

fifty /'fɪftɪ/ **1** *adj.* fünfzig
2 *n.* Fünfzig, *die. See also* EIGHT; EIGHTY 2

fig /fɪg/ *n.* Feige, *die*

fig. *abbr.* = **figure** Abb.

fight /faɪt/ **1** *v.i.,* **fought** /fɔ:t/ **(a)** kämpfen; (with fists) sich schlagen
(b) (squabble) [sich] streiten (**about** wegen)
2 *v.t.,* **fought: (a) ~ sb./sth.** gegen jmdn./ etw. kämpfen; (using fists) **~ sb.** sich mit jmdm. schlagen
(b) (seek to overcome) bekämpfen; (resist) **~ sb./sth.** gegen jmdn./etw. ankämpfen
(c) ~ a battle einen Kampf austragen
(d) kandidieren bei ‹*Wahl*›
3 *n.* Kampf, *der* (**for** um)

■ **'fight against** *v.t.* kämpfen gegen; ankämpfen gegen ‹*Wellen, Wind*›

■ **fight 'back** 1 *v.i.* zurückschlagen
2 *v.t.* (suppress) zurückhalten
■ **fight 'off** *v.t.* abwehren
■ **'fight with** *v.t.* **(a)** kämpfen mit
(b) (squabble with) [sich] streiten mit
'fighter *n.* Kämpfer, *der*/Kämpferin, *die;* (aircraft) Kampfflugzeug, *das*
'fighting *n.* Kämpfe *Pl.*
fighting 'chance *n.* **have a ~ of succeeding/of doing sth.** Aussicht auf Erfolg haben/gute Chancen haben, etw. zu tun
'fig leaf *n.* (lit. or fig.) Feigenblatt, *das*
figment /'fɪgmənt/ *n.* **a ~ of one's** *or* **the imagination** pure Einbildung
'fig tree *n.* Feigenbaum, *der*
figurative /'fɪgərətɪv/ *adj.* übertragen
figure /'fɪgə(r)/ 1 *n* **(a)** (shape) Form, *die*
(b) (carving, sculpture, one's bodily shape) Figur, *die*
(c) (illustration) Abbildung, *die*
(d) (person as seen) Gestalt, *die;* (literary ~) Figur, *die*
(e) (numerical symbol) Ziffer, *die;* (number) Zahl, *die;* (amount of money) Betrag, *der*
(f) ~ of speech Redewendung, *die*
2 *v.i.* **(a)** vorkommen
(b) that ~s (coll.) das kann gut sein
■ **figure 'out** *v.t.* **(a)** (by arithmetic) ausrechnen
(b) (understand) verstehen
figure: ~head *n.* (lit. or fig.) Galionsfigur, *die;* **~ skating** *n.* Eiskunstlauf, *der*
filament /'fɪləmənt/ *n.* **(a)** Faden, *der*
(b) (Electr.) Glühfaden, *der*
filch /'fɪltʃ/ *v.t.* stibitzen (ugs.)
file¹ /faɪl/ 1 *n.* Feile, *die*
2 *v.t.* feilen ‹*Fingernägel*›; mit der Feile bearbeiten ‹*Holz, Eisen*›
file² 1 *n.* **(a)** (holder) Ordner, *der;* (box) Kassette, *die*
(b) (papers) Ablage, *die;* (cards) Kartei, *die*
2 *v.t.* **(a)** [in die Kartei] einordnen/[in die Akten] aufnehmen
(b) einreichen ‹*Antrag*›
file³ 1 *n.* (Mil. etc.) Reihe, *die;* **[in] single** *or* **Indian ~:** [im] Gänsemarsch
2 *v.i.* **~ [in/out]** in einer Reihe [hinein-/hinaus]gehen
file: ~ copy *n.* Belegexemplar, *das;* (of letter) Kopie für die Akten; **~ extension** *n.* (Comp.) Dateierweiterung, *die;* **~ name** *n.* (Comp.) Dateiname, *der*
filigree /'fɪlɪgri:/ *n.* Filigran, *das*
'filing cabinet *n.* Aktenschrank, *der*
filings /'faɪlɪŋz/ *n. pl.* Späne *Pl.*
fill /fɪl/ 1 *v.t.* **(a)** füllen; besetzen ‹*Sitzplätze*›; (fig.) ausfüllen ‹*Gedanken, Zeit*›; (pervade) erfüllen; **~ed with** voller ‹*Reue, Bewunderung, Neid usw.*›
(b) (appoint sb. to) besetzen ‹*Posten*›
2 *v.i.* **~ [with sth.]** sich [mit etw.] füllen
3 *n.* **eat/drink one's ~:** sich satt essen/trinken

■ **fill 'in** 1 *v.t.* **(a)** füllen; zuschütten ‹*Erdloch*›
(b) (complete) ausfüllen
(c) ~ sb. in [on sth.] (coll.) jmdn. [über etw. (*Akk.*)] ins Bild setzen
2 *v.i.* **~ in for sb.** für jmdn. einspringen
■ **fill 'out** *v.t.* ausfüllen
■ **fill 'up** *v.t.* **(a)** füllen (**with** mit)
(b) (put petrol into) **~ up the tank** tanken; **~ her up!** (coll.) voll [tanken]!
fillet /'fɪlɪt/ 1 *n.* Filet, *das*
2 *v.t.* entgräten ‹*Fisch*›
'filling *n.* **(a)** (for teeth) Füllung, *die*
(b) (for pancakes etc.) Füllung, *die;* (for sandwiches etc.) Belag, *der;* (for spreading) Aufstrich, *der*
'filling station *n.* Tankstelle, *die*
filly /'fɪlɪ/ *n.* junge Stute
film /fɪlm/ 1 *n.* **(a)** Film, *der*
(b) (thin layer) Schicht, *die*
2 *v.t.* filmen; drehen ‹*Kinofilm, Szene*›
film: ~ crew *n.* Kamerateam, *das;* **~ director** *n.* Filmregisseur, *der*/-regisseurin, *die;* **~ industry** *n.* Filmindustrie, *die;* **~ music** *n.* Filmmusik, *die;* **~ poster** *n.* Filmplakat, *das;* **~ projector** *n.* Projektor, *der;* **~ script** *n.* Drehbuch, *das;* **~ set** *n.* Dekoration, *die;* **~ star** *n.* Filmstar, *der;* **~strip** *n.* Filmstreifen, *der;* **~ studio** *n.* Filmstudio, *das*
filter /'fɪltə(r)/ 1 *n.* Filter, *der*
2 *v.t.* filtern
■ **filter 'through** *v.t.* durchsickern
filter: ~ ciga'rette *n.* Filterzigarette, *die;* **~ coffee** *n.* Filterkaffee, *der;* **~ lane** *n.* Abbiegespur, *die;* **~-tip** *n.* **(a)** Filter, *der;* **(b) ~-tip [cigarette]** Filterzigarette, *die*
filth /fɪlθ/ *n.* Dreck, *der*
'filthy *adj.* dreckig (ugs.); schmutzig
fin /fɪn/ *n.* Flosse, *die*
final /'faɪnl/ 1 *adj.* letzt...; End‹*spiel, -stadium, -stufe, -ergebnis*›; endgültig ‹*Entscheidung*›
2 *n.* **(a)** (Sport etc.) Finale, *das*
(b) ~s *pl.* (university examination) Examen, *das*
finale /fɪ'nɑ:lɪ/ *n.* Finale, *das*
finalist /'faɪnəlɪst/ *n.* Teilnehmer/Teilnehmerin in der Endausscheidung; (Sport) Finalist, *der*/Finalistin, *die*
finality /faɪ'nælɪtɪ/ *n.* Endgültigkeit, *die;* (of tone of voice) Entschiedenheit, *die*
finalize /'faɪnəlaɪz/ *v.t.* [endgültig] beschließen; (complete) zum Abschluss bringen
finally /'faɪnəlɪ/ *adv.* **(a)** (in the end) schließlich; (expressing impatience etc.) endlich
(b) (in conclusion) abschließend
(c) (conclusively) entschieden ‹*sagen*›
finance /faɪ'næns, 'faɪnæns/ 1 *n.* **(a)** *in pl.* (resources) Finanzen *Pl.*
(b) (management of money) Geldwesen, *das*
(c) (support) Geldmittel *Pl.*

f

2 *v.t.* finanzieren

'finance company *n.* Finanzierungsgesellschaft, *die*

financial /faɪ'nænʃl/ *adj.* finanziell; Finanz‹*mittel, -experte, -lage*›; **~ year** Geschäftsjahr, *das*

fi'nancially *adv.* finanziell

financier /faɪ'nænsɪə(r)/ *n.* Finanzexperte, *der*/-expertin, *die*

finch /fɪntʃ/ *n.* Fink[envogel], *der*

find /faɪnd/ 1 *v.t.*, **found** /faʊnd/ finden; (come across unexpectedly) entdecken; auftreiben ‹*Geld, Gegenstand*›; aufbringen ‹*Kraft, Energie*›; **want to ~:** suchen; **~ that ...:** herausfinden, dass ...; **~ sth. necessary** etw. für nötig erachten; **~ sth./sb. to be ...:** herausfinden, dass etw./jmd. ... ist/war; **you will ~ [that] ...:** Sie werden sehen, dass ...
2 *n.* Fund, *der*

■ **find 'out** *v.t.* herausfinden

'finder *n.* Finder, *der*/Finderin, *die*

'findings *n. pl.* Ergebnisse *Pl.*

fine¹ /faɪn/ 1 *n.* Geldstrafe, *die*
2 *v.t.* mit einer Geldstrafe belegen

fine² *adj.* **(a)** hochwertig ‹*Qualität, Lebensmittel*›; fein ‹*Gewebe, Spitze*›; edel ‹*Holz, Wein*›
(b) (delicate) fein; zart ‹*Porzellan*›; (thin) hauchdünn; **cut** *or* **run it ~:** knapp kalkulieren
(c) (in small particles) [hauch]fein ‹*Sand, Staub*›; **~ rain** Nieselregen, *der*
(d) (sharp) scharf ‹*Spitze, Klinge*›; spitz ‹*Nadel, Schreibfeder*›
(e) (excellent) ausgezeichnet ‹*Sänger, Schauspieler*›
(f) (satisfactory) schön; **that's ~ by** *or* **with me** ja, ist mir recht
(g) (in good health or state) gut; **feel ~:** sich wohl fühlen
(h) schön ‹*Wetter*›

fine 'arts *n. pl.* schöne Künste *Pl.*

finery /'faɪnərɪ/ *n.* Pracht, *die;* (garments etc.) Staat, *der*

finger /'fɪŋgə(r)/ 1 *n.* Finger, *der*
2 *v.t.* berühren; (meddle with) befingern

finger: ~mark *n.* Fingerabdruck, *der;* **~nail** *n.* Fingernagel, *der;* **~print** *n.* Fingerabdruck, *der;* **~tip** *n.* Fingerspitze, *die;* **have sth. at one's ~tips** (fig.) etw. im kleinen Finger haben (ugs.)

finish /'fɪnɪʃ/ 1 *v.t.* **(a)** beenden ‹*Unterhaltung*›; erledigen ‹*Arbeit*›; abschließen ‹*Kurs, Ausbildung*›; **have ~ed sth.** etw. fertig haben; **~ writing/reading sth.** etw. zu Ende schreiben/lesen
(b) aufessen ‹*Mahlzeit*›; auslesen ‹*Buch, Zeitung*›; austrinken ‹*Flasche, Glas*›
2 *v.i.* **(a)** aufhören; **have you ~ed?** sind Sie fertig?; **when does the concert ~?** wann ist das Konzert aus?; **have you ~ed with the sugar?** brauchen Sie den Zucher noch?; **~ with one's boyfriend/girlfriend** mit seinem Freund/seiner Freundin Schluss machen
(b) (in race) das Ziel erreichen
3 *n.* **(a)** Ende, *das*
(b) (~ing line) Ziel, *das*

■ **finish 'off** *v.t.* abschließen

finishing: ~ post *n.* Zielpfosten, *der;* **~ 'touch** *n.* **as a ~ touch to sth.** zur Vollendung *od.* Vervollkommnung einer Sache; **put the ~ touches to sth.** einer Sache (*Dat.*) den letzten Schliff geben

finite /'faɪnaɪt/ *adj.* begrenzt

Finland /'fɪnlənd/ *pr. n.* Finnland (*das*)

Finn /fɪn/ *n.* Finne, *der*/Finnin, *die*

Finnish /'fɪnɪʃ/ 1 *adj.* finnisch; **sb. is ~:** jmd. ist Finne/Finnin
2 *n.* Finnisch, *das; see also* ENGLISH 2A

fiord /fɪ'ɔ:d/ *n.* Fjord, *der*

fir /fɜ:(r)/ *n.* Tanne, *die*

fire /'faɪə(r)/ 1 *n.* **(a)** Feuer, *das;* **be on ~:** brennen; **catch ~:** Feuer fangen; ‹*Wald, Gebäude:*› in Brand geraten; **set ~ to sth.** etw. anzünden
(b) (in grate) [offenes] Feuer; (electric or gas ~) Heizofen, *der;* **light the ~:** den Ofen anstecken; (in grate) das [Kamin]feuer anmachen
(c) (destructive burning) Brand, *der*
(d) (of guns) **come/be under ~:** unter Beschuss geraten/beschossen werden
2 *v.t.* **(a)** abschießen ‹*Gewehr*›; abfeuern ‹*Kanone*›; abgeben ‹*Schuss*›; **~ one's gun/pistol/rifle at sb.** auf jmdn. schießen; **two shots were ~d** es fielen zwei Schüsse; **~ questions at sb.** jmdn. mit Fragen bombardieren
(b) (coll.: dismiss) feuern (ugs.)
3 *v.i.* feuern; **~ at/on** schießen auf (+ *Akk.*); **~!** Feuer!

fire: ~ alarm *n.* Feuermelder, *der;* **~arm** *n.* Schusswaffe, *die;* **~bomb** *n.* Brandsatz, *der;* (aerial bomb) Brandbombe, *die;* **~ brigade** (Brit.), **~ department** (Amer.) *ns.* Feuerwehr, *die;* **~ drill** *n.* Probe[feuer]alarm, *der;* **~ engine** *n.* Löschfahrzeug, *das;* **~ escape** *n.* (staircase) Feuertreppe, *die;* **~ exit** *n.* Notausgang, *der;* **~ extinguisher** *n.* Feuerlöscher, *der;* **~fighter** *n.* Feuerwehrmann, *der*/-frau, *die;* **~fighting** *n.* Feuerbekämpfung, *die;* Brandbekämpfung, *die;* **~ hazard** *n.* Brandrisiko, *das;* **~lighter** *n.* (Brit.) Feueranzünder, *der;* **~man** /'faɪəmən/ *n., pl.* **~men** /-mən/ Feuerwehrmann, *der;* **~place** *n.* Kamin, *der;* **~ precautions** *n. pl.* Feuerschutz, *der;* **~proof** 1 *adj.* feuerfest; 2 *v.t.* feuerfest machen; **~-resistant** *adj.* feuerbeständig; **~ risk** ▸ **~** HAZARD; **~side** *n.* **at** *or* **by the ~side** am Kamin; **~ station** *n.* Feuerwache, *die;* **~ tongs** *n. pl.* Feuerzange, *die;* **a pair of ~ tongs** eine Feuerzange; **~wood** *n.* Brennholz, *das;* **~work** *n.* Feuerwerkskörper, *der;* **~works** (display) Feuerwerk, *das*

firm¹ /fɜ:m/ *n.* Firma, *die*

firm² *adj.* **(a)** fest; stabil ‹*Konstruktion, Stuhl*›
(b) (resolute, strict) bestimmt

'firmly *adv.* **(a)** fest
(b) (resolutely, strictly) bestimmt

first /fɜːst/ **1** *adj.* erst...; **he was ~ to arrive** er kam als Erster an
2 *adv.* **(a)** (before anyone else) zuerst; als Erster/Erste ‹*sprechen, ankommen*›; (before anything else) an erster Stelle ‹*stehen, kommen*›; **~ come ~ served** wer zuerst kommt, mahlt zuerst (Spr.)
(b) (beforehand) vorher
(c) (for the ~ time) zum ersten Mal
(d) ~ of all zuerst; (in importance) vor allem
3 *n.* **(a) the ~** (in sequence, rank) der/die/das Erste; *pl.* die Ersten
(b) at ~: zuerst; **from the ~:** von Anfang an

first: ~ 'aid *n.* erste Hilfe; **~-aid box/kit** Verbandkasten, *der*/Erste-Hilfe-Ausrüstung, *die;* **~-class** **1** /'--/ *adj.* **(a)** erster Klasse *nachgestellt;* Erste[r]-Klasse-‹*Fahrkarte, Abteil, Post, Brief usw.*›; **(b)** (excellent) erstklassig; **2** /-'-/ *adv.* erster Klasse ‹*reisen*›

'firstly *adv.* zunächst [einmal]; (followed by 'secondly') erstens

first: ~ name *n.* Vorname, *der;* **~ 'night** *n.* (Theatre) Premiere, *die;* **~ of'fender** *n.* Ersttäter, *der*/-täterin, *die;* **~-rate** *adj.* erstklassig; **~ school** *n.* (Brit.) ≈ Grundschule, *die*

'fir tree *n.* Tanne, *die*

fish /fɪʃ/ **1** *n.* Fisch, *der*
2 *v.i.* fischen; (with rod) angeln; **go ~ing** fischen/angeln gehen

■ **fish 'out** *v.t.* (coll.) herausfischen (ugs.)

fish: ~ bone *n.* [Fisch]gräte, *die;* **~ cake** *n.* Fischfrikadelle, *die*

fisherman /'fɪʃəmən/ *n., pl.* **fishermen** /'fɪʃəmən/ Fischer, *der;* (angler) Angler, *der*

fish: ~eye lens *n.* Fischaugenobjektiv, *das;* **~ farm** *n.* Fischzucht[anlage], *die;* **~ farming** *n.* Fischzucht, *die;* **~ 'finger** *n.* Fischstäbchen, *das;* **~ hook** *n.* Angelhaken, *der*

'fishing *n.* Fischen, *das;* (with rod) Angeln, *das*

fishing: ~ boat *n.* Fischerboot, *das;* **~ industry** *n.* Fischerei[industrie], *die;* **~ net** *n.* Fischernetz, *das;* **~ rod** *n.* Angelrute, *die* **~ tackle** *n.* Angelgeräte *Pl.;* **~ vessel** *n.* Fischereifahrzeug, *das;* **~ village** *n.* Fischerdorf, *das*

fish: ~ kettle *n.* Fischkessel, *der;* **~monger** /'fɪʃmʌŋgə(r)/ *n.* (Brit.) Fischhändler, *der*/-händlerin, *die;* **~ pond** *n.* Fischteich, *der;* **~ shop** *n.* Fischgeschäft, *das;* **~ slice** *n.* Wender, *der;* **~ tank** *n.* Fischkasten, *der;* Fischbehälter, *der*

'fishy *adj.* **(a)** fischartig; Fisch‹*geschmack, -geruch*›
(b) (coll.: suspicious) verdächtig

fist /fɪst/ *n.* Faust, *die*

fit¹ /fɪt/ *n.* Anfall, *der;* (fig.) [plötzliche] Anwandlung; **be in ~s of laughter** sich vor Lachen biegen; **in a ~ of ...:** in einem Anfall von ...

fit² **1** *adj.* **(a)** (suitable) geeignet; **~ to eat** essbar
(b) (worthy) würdig; wert
(c) (proper) richtig; **see** *or* **think ~ [to do sth.]** es für richtig halten[, etw. zu tun]
(d) (healthy) fit (ugs.); **keep ~:** sich fit halten
2 *n.* Passform, *die;* **it is a good/bad ~:** es sitzt *od.* passt gut/nicht gut
3 *v.t.*, **-tt-: (a)** ‹*Kleider:*› passen (+ *Dat.*); ‹*Deckel, Bezug:*› passen auf (+ *Akk.*)
(b) (put into place) anbringen (**to** an + *Dat. od. Akk.*); einbauen ‹*Motor, Ersatzteil*›
4 *v.i.*, **-tt-** passen

■ **fit 'in** **1** *v.t.* unterbringen
2 *v.i.* **(a)** ‹*Person:*› sich anpassen (**with** an + *Akk.*)
(b) (be in accordance with) **~ in with sth.** mit etw. übereinstimmen

fitful /'fɪtfl/ *adj.* unbeständig; unruhig ‹*Schlaf*›; launisch ‹*Brise*›

'fitment *n.* Einrichtung, *die*

'fitness *n.* **(a)** (physical) Fitness, *die*
(b) (suitability) Eignung, *die*

'fitness studio *n.* Fitnessstudio, *das*

'fitted *adj.* **(a)** (suited) geeignet (**for** für, zu)
(b) (shaped) tailliert ‹*Kleider*›; Einbau‹*küche, schrank*›; **~ carpet** Teppichboden, *der*

'fitter *n.* Monteur, *der;* (of pipes) Installateur, *der;* (of machines) Maschinenschlosser, *der*

'fitting **1** *adj.* (appropriate) passend; (becoming) schicklich (geh.) ‹*Benehmen*›
2 *n.* **(a)** *usu. in pl.* (fixture) Anschluss, *der;* **~s** (furniture) Ausstattung, *die*
(b) (Brit.: size) Größe, *die*

'fitting-room *n.* Anprobe, *die*

five /faɪv/ **1** *adj.* fünf
2 *n.* Fünf, *die. See also* EIGHT

fiver /'faɪvə(r)/ *n.* (Brit. coll.) Fünfpfundschein, *der*

five: ~-star *adj.* Fünf-Sterne-‹*Hotel, General*›; (fig.) ausgezeichnet; **~-'year plan** *n.* Fünfjahresplan, *der*

fix /fɪks/ **1** *v.t.* **(a)** befestigen
(b) festsetzen ‹*Termin, Preis, Grenze*›; (agree on) ausmachen
(c) (repair) reparieren
(d) (arrange) arrangieren
2 *n.* (coll.: predicament) Klemme, *die* (ugs.); **be in a ~:** in der Klemme sitzen

■ **fix 'up** *v.t.* **(a)** (arrange) arrangieren; festsetzen ‹*Termin, Treffpunkt*›
(b) (provide) versorgen; **~ sb. up with sth.** jmdm. etw. verschaffen

fixed: ~ price Festpreis, *der;* **~-rate** *attrib. adj.* Festzins-; mit festem Zins *nachgestellt*

fixture /'fɪkstʃə(r)/ *n.* **(a)** (furnishing) eingebautes Teil
(b) (Sport) Veranstaltung, *die*

fizz /fɪz/ *v.i.* [zischend] sprudeln
fizzle /'fɪzl/ *v.i.* zischen
■ **fizzle 'out** *v.i.* ‹*Kampagne:*› im Sande verlaufen
fizzy /'fɪzɪ/ *adj.* sprudelnd; **~ lemonade** Brause[limonade], *die*
flabbergast /'flæbəgɑ:st/ *v.t.* umhauen (ugs.)
flabby /'flæbɪ/ *adj.* schlaff
flag¹ /flæg/ *n.* Fahne, *die;* (national ~, on ship) Flagge, *die*
flag² *v.i.*, **-gg-** ‹*Person:*› abbauen; ‹*Kraft, Begeisterung usw.:*› nachlassen
flagon /'flægn/ *n.* Kanne, *die*
'flagpole *n.* Flaggenmast, *der*
flagrant /'fleɪgrənt/ *adj.* eklatant; flagrant ‹*Verstoß*›
'flagstone *n.* Steinplatte, *die*
flair /fleə(r)/ *n.* Gespür, *das;* (special ability) Talent, *das*
flak /flæk/ *n.* Flakfeuer, *das* (Milit.); (gun) Flak, *die* (Milit.); **get a lot of ~ for sth.** (fig.) wegen etw. [schwer] unter Beschuss geraten
flake /fleɪk/ [1] *n.* Flocke, *die;* (of dry skin) Schuppe, *die*
[2] *v.i.* abblättern
'flak jacket *n.* kugelsichere Weste
flaky /'fleɪkɪ/ *adj.* blättrig ‹*Kruste*›; **~ pastry** Blätterteig, *der*
flamboyant /flæm'bɔɪənt/ *adj.* extravagant
flame /fleɪm/ *n.* Flamme, *die;* **be in ~s** in Flammen stehen
'flameproof nicht entflammbar; flammfest
flan /flæn/ *n.* **[fruit] ~:** [Obst]torte, *die*
flank /flæŋk/ *n.* Seite, *die;* (of animal; also Mil.) Flanke, *die*
flannel /'flænl/ *n.* **(a)** (fabric) Flanell, *der*
(b) (Brit.: for washing) Waschlappen, *der*
flap /flæp/ [1] *v.t.*, **-pp-: ~ its wings** mit den Flügeln schlagen
[2] *v.i.*, **-pp-** ‹*Flügel:*› schlagen; ‹*Segel, Fahne, Vorhang:*› flattern
[3] *n.* **(a)** Klappe, *die;* (envelope seal, of shoe) Lasche, *die*
(b) (fig. coll.) **in a ~:** furchtbar aufgeregt
flare /fleə(r)/ [1] *v.i.* flackern; (fig.) ausbrechen; **tempers ~d** die Gemüter erhitzten sich
[2] *n.* Leuchtsignal, *das*
■ **flare 'up** *v.i.* **(a)** aufflackern
(b) (break out) [wieder] ausbrechen
flash /flæʃ/ [1] *n.* Aufleuchten, *das;* (as signal) Lichtsignal, *das;* **~ of lightning** Blitz, *der;* **in a ~:** (quickly) im Nu
[2] *v.t.* **(a)** aufleuchten lassen; **~ one's headlights** die Lichthupe betätigen; **~ sb. a smile/glance** jmdm. ein Lächeln/einen Blick zuwerfen
(b) (display briefly) kurz zeigen
[3] *v.i.* aufleuchten; **~ by** *or* **past** ‹*Zeit, Ferien:*› wie im Fluge vergehen
flash: ~back *n.* Rückblende, *die* (**to** auf + *Akk.*); **~ bulb** *n.* Blitzbirnchen, *das;* **~ cube** *n.* Blitzwürfel, *der;* **~ flood** *n.* Überschwemmung, *die* (durch heftige Regenfälle); **~gun** *n.* Blitzgerät, *das;* **~light** *n.* **(a)** (for signals) Blinklicht, *das;* **(b)** (Amer.: torch) Taschenlampe, *die;* **~point** *n.* Flammpunkt, *der;* (fig.) Siedepunkt, *der*
'flashy *adj.* auffällig
flask /flɑ:sk/ *n.* **(a)** ▶ THERMOS
(b) (for wine, oil) [bauchige] Flasche
(c) (Chem.) Kolben, *der*
flat¹ /flæt/ *n.* (Brit.) Wohnung, *die*
flat² [1] *adj.* **(a)** flach; eben ‹*Fläche*›; platt ‹*Nase, Reifen*›
(b) (downright) glatt (ugs.) ‹*Absage, Weigerung, Widerspruch*›
(c) (Mus.) [um einen Halbton] erniedrigt ‹*Note*›
(d) schal, abgestanden ‹*Bier, Sekt*›
(e) leer ‹*Batterie*›
[2] *adv.* (Mus.) zu tief
flat: ~-chested /flæt'tʃestɪd/ *adj.* flachbrüstig; flachbusig; **~ 'feet** *n. pl.* Plattfüße *Pl.*; **~'fish** *n.* Plattfisch, *der;* **~-'footed** *adj.* plattfüßig; **~-heeled** *adj.* ‹*Schuh*› mit flachem Absatz; flach ‹*Schuh*›
'flatly *adv.* rundweg
flat: ~ mate *n.* (Brit.) Mitbewohner, *der/* Mitbewohnerin, *die;* **they were ~ mates** sie haben zusammen gewohnt; **~ 'out** *adv.* (at top speed) **he ran/worked ~ out** er rannte/ arbeitete, so schnell er konnte; **~-pack** *adj.* ‹*Möbel*› zum Selbstbauen; **~ rate** *n.* Einheitstarif, *der;* **~ screen** *n.* (Comp.) Flachbildschirm, *der;* **~ 'spin** *n.* (Aeronaut.) Flachtrudeln, *das;* **go into a ~ spin** (fig. coll.) durchdrehen (ugs.)
flatten /'flætn/ [1] *v.t.* flach drücken ‹*Schachtel*›; dem Erdboden gleichmachen ‹*Stadt, Gebäude*›
[2] *v. refl.* **~ oneself against sth.** sich flach gegen etw. drücken
flatter /'flætə(r)/ *v.t.* schmeicheln (+ *Dat.*)
'flattering *adj.* schmeichelhaft
'flattery *n.* Schmeichelei, *die*
flat 'tyre *n.* Reifenpanne, *die*
flatulence /'flætjʊləns/ *n.* Blähungen *Pl.;* Flatulenz, *die* (Med.)
flaunt /flɔ:nt/ *v.t.* zur Schau stellen
flavor *etc.* (*Amer.*) ▶ FLAVOUR *etc.*
flavour /'fleɪvə(r)/ (Brit.) [1] *n.* **(a)** Geschmack, *der*
(b) (fig.) Anflug, *der*
[2] *v.t.* abschmecken
'flavouring *n.* (Brit.) Aroma, *das*
'flavourless *adj.* (Brit.) fade
flavoursome /'fleɪvəsəm/ *adj.* (Brit.) schmackhaft
flaw /flɔ:/ *n.* Fehler, *der;* (imperfection) Makel, *der;* (in workmanship or goods) Mangel, *der*
flax /flæks/ *n.* Flachs, *der*
flea /fli:/ *n.* Floh, *der*

flea: ~ **bite** *n.* Flohbiss, *der;* ~ **market** *n.* (coll.) Flohmarkt, *der*

fled ▶ FLEE

flee /fliː/ [1] *v.i.*, **fled** /fled/ fliehen; ~ **from sth./sb.** aus etw./vor jmdm. flüchten [2] *v.t.*, **fled** fliehen aus

fleece /fliːs/ [1] *n.* [Schaf]fell, *das* [2] *v.t.* (fig.) ausplündern

fleecy /ˈfliːsɪ/ *adj.* flauschig

fleet /fliːt/ *n.* Flotte, *die*

fleeting /ˈfliːtɪŋ/ *adj.* flüchtig

flesh /fleʃ/ *n.* Fleisch, *das;* (of fruit, plant) [Frucht]fleisch, *das*

flesh: ~**-coloured** *adj.* fleischfarben; ~ **wound** *n.* Fleischwunde, *die*

ˈfleshy *adj.* fett; fleischig ‹*Hände*›

flew ▶ FLY² 1, 2

flex¹ /fleks/ *n.* (Brit. Electr.) Kabel, *das*

flex² *v.t.* beugen ‹*Arm, Knie*›; ~ **one's muscles** seine Muskeln spielen lassen

flexible /ˈfleksɪbl/ *adj.* **(a)** biegsam; elastisch
(b) (fig.) flexibel; ~ **working hours** *or* **time** gleitende Arbeitszeit

flexitime /ˈfleksɪtaɪm/ (Brit.), **flextime** /ˈflekstaɪm/ (Amer.) *ns.* Gleitzeit, *die;* **be on** *or* **work** ~: gleitende Arbeitszeit haben

flick /flɪk/ *v.t.* schnippen; anknipsen ‹*Schalter*›; verspritzen ‹*Tinte*›
■ **ˈflick through** *v.t.* durchblättern

flicker /ˈflɪkə(r)/ [1] *v.i.* flackern; ‹*Fernsehapparat:*› flimmern
[2] *n.* Flackern, *das;* (of TV) Flimmern, *das*

ˈflick knife *n.* (Brit.) Schnappmesser, *das*

flight¹ /flaɪt/ *n.* **(a)** Flug, *der*
(b) ~ **[of stairs** *or* **steps]** Treppe, *die*

flight² *n.* (fleeing) Flucht, *die;* **take** ~: die Flucht ergreifen; **put to** ~: in die Flucht schlagen

flight: ~ **attendant** *n.* Flugbegleiter, *der*/-begleiterin, *die;* ~ **control** *n.* ≈ Flugsicherung, *die;* ~ **controller** *n.* (Aeronaut.) Fluglotse, *der;* ~ **deck** *n.* **(a)** (of aircraft carrier) Flugdeck, *das;* **(b)** (of aircraft) Cockpit, *das;* ~ **number** *n.* Flugnummer, *die;* ~ **path** *n.* (Aeronaut.) Flugweg, *der;* (Astronaut.) Flugbahn, *die;* ~ **recorder** *n.* Flugschreiber, *der*

flimsy /ˈflɪmzɪ/ *adj.* **(a)** dünn; nicht sehr haltbar ‹*Verpackung*›
(b) (fig.) fadenscheinig ‹*Entschuldigung, Argument*›

flinch /flɪntʃ/ *v.i.* zurückschrecken (**from** vor + *Dat.*); (wince) zusammenzucken

fling /flɪŋ/ [1] *n.* **have a** *or* **one's** ~: sich ausleben
[2] *v.t.*, **flung** /flʌŋ/ werfen; ~ **oneself into sth.** (fig.) sich in etw. (*Akk.*) stürzen

flint /flɪnt/ *n.* Feuerstein, *der*

flip /flɪp/ *v.t.*, **-pp-** schnipsen; ~ **[over]** (turn over) umdrehen
■ **ˈflip through** *v.t.* durchblättern

flippant /ˈflɪpənt/ *adj.* leichtfertig

flipper /ˈflɪpə(r)/ *n.* Flosse, *die*

ˈflip side *n.* B-Seite, *die*

flirt /flɜːt/ *v.i.* flirten

flirtation /flɜːˈteɪʃn/ *n.* Flirt, *der*

flirtatious /flɜːˈteɪʃəs/ *adj.* kokett ‹*Blick, Art*›

flit /flɪt/ *v.i.* huschen

float /fləʊt/ [1] *v.i.* treiben; (in air) schweben
[2] *n.* (for carnival) Festwagen, *der*
[3] *v.t.* (set afloat) flottmachen; (fig.) lancieren ‹*Plan, Idee*›

floating: ~ **ˈdock** *n.* Schwimmdock, *das;* ~ **ˈvoter** *n.* Wechselwähler, *der*/-wählerin, *die*

flock /flɒk/ [1] *n.* **(a)** Herde, *die;* (of birds) Schwarm, *der*
(b) (of people) Schar, *die*
[2] *v.i.* strömen; ~ **round sb.** sich um jmdn. scharen

flog /flɒg/ *v.t.*, **-gg-**: **(a)** auspeitschen
(b) (Brit. coll.: sell) verscheuern (salopp)

flood /flʌd/ [1] *n.* Überschwemmung, *die;* **the F**~ (Bibl.) die Sintflut
[2] *v.i.* ‹*Fluss:*› über die Ufer treten; (fig.) strömen
[3] *v.t.* überschwemmen

flood: ~ **damage** *n.* Hochwasserschaden, *der;* **the area suffered extensive** ~ **damage** in dem Gebiet gab es beträchtliche Hochwasserschäden; ~**gate** *n.* (Hydraulic Engin.) Schütze, *die;* **open the** ~**gates to sth.** (fig.) einer Sache (*Dat.*) Tür und Tor öffnen; ~**light** [1] *n.* Scheinwerfer, *der.* [2] *v.t.*, **floodlit** /ˈflʌdlɪt/ anstrahlen; ~ **tide** *n.* Flut, *die;* ~ **warning** *n.* Hochwasserwarnung, *die;* ~ **water** *n.* Hochwasser, *das*

floor /flɔː(r)/ [1] *n.* **(a)** Boden, *der*
(b) (storey) Stockwerk, *das;* **first** ~ (Amer.) Erdgeschoss, *das;* **first** ~ (Brit.), **second** ~ (Amer.) erster Stock; **ground** ~: Erdgeschoss, *das;* Parterre, *das*
[2] *v.t.* **(a)** (confound) überfordern
(b) (knock down) zu Boden schlagen

floor: ~**board** *n.* Dielenbrett, *das;* ~**cloth** *n.* (Brit.) Scheuertuch, *das;* ~ **polish** *n.* Bohnerwachs, *das;* ~ **show** *n.* ≈ Unterhaltungsprogramm, *das*

flop /flɒp/ [1] *v.i.*, **-pp-**: **(a)** plumpsen
(b) (coll.: fail) fehlschlagen; ‹*Theaterstück, Show:*› durchfallen
[2] *n.* (coll.: failure) Reinfall, *der* (ugs.)

floppy /ˈflɒpɪ/ *adj.* weich und biegsam

floppy disk n. (Comp.) Floppy Disk, *die;* Diskette, *die*

flora /ˈflɔːrə/ *n.* Flora, *die*

floral /ˈflɔːrl, ˈflɒrl/ *adj.* geblümt ‹*Kleid, Stoff*›; Blumen‹*muster*›

Florence /ˈflɒrəns/ *pr. n.* Florenz (*das*)

florid /ˈflɒrɪd/ *adj.* blumig ‹*Stil, Redeweise*›; gerötet ‹*Teint*›

florist /ˈflɒrɪst/ *n.* Florist, *der*/Floristin, *die*

flotsam /ˈflɒtsəm/ *n.* ~ **[and jetsam]** Treibgut, *das*
flounder /ˈflaʊndə(r)/ *v.i.* taumeln
flour /ˈflaʊə(r)/ *n.* Mehl, *das*
flourish /ˈflʌrɪʃ/ 1 *v.i.* gedeihen; ‹*Geschäft:*› florieren, gut gehen
2 *v.t.* schwingen
3 *n.* **do sth. with a ~:** etw. schwungvoll tun
flout /flaʊt/ *v.t.* missachten
flow /fləʊ/ 1 *v.i.* fließen; ‹*Körner, Sand:*› rinnen, rieseln; ‹*Gas:*› strömen
2 *n.* **(a)** Fließen, *das;* **~ of water/people** Wasser-/Menschenstrom, *der;* **~ of information** Informationsfluss, *der*
(b) (of tide, river) Flut, *die*
ˈflow chart *n.* Flussdiagramm, *das*
flower /ˈflaʊə(r)/ 1 *n.* (blossom) Blüte, *die;* (plant) Blume, *die;* **come into ~:** zu blühen beginnen
2 *v.i.* blühen
ˈflower bed *n.* Blumenbeet, *das*
flowering /ˈflaʊərɪŋ/ *adj.* **~ cherry/shrub** Zierkirsche, *die*/Blütenstrauch, *der*
ˈflowerpot *n.* Blumentopf, *der*
ˈflowery *adj.* geblümt ‹*Stoff, Muster*›; (fig.) blumig ‹*Sprache*›
ˈflowing *adj.* fließend; wallend ‹*Haar*›
flown ▶ FLY² 1, 2
flu /fluː/ *n.* (coll.) Grippe, *die*
fluctuate /ˈflʌktjʊeɪt/ *v.i.* schwanken
fluctuation /flʌktjʊˈeɪʃn/ *n.* Schwankung, *die*
fluency /ˈfluːənsɪ/ *n.* Gewandtheit, *die;* (spoken) Redegewandtheit, *die*
fluent /ˈfluːənt/ *adj.* gewandt ‹*Stil, Redeweise, Redner, Schreiber*›; **be ~ in Russian, speak ~ Russian** fließend Russisch sprechen
fluff /flʌf/ *n.* Flusen *Pl.*; Fusseln *Pl.*
fluffy /ˈflʌfɪ/ *adj.* [flaum]weich ‹*Kissen, Küken*›; flauschig ‹*Spielzeug, Decke*›
fluid /ˈfluːɪd/ 1 *n.* Flüssigkeit, *die*
2 *adj.* flüssig
fluke /fluːk/ *n.* (piece of luck) Glücksfall, *der*
flung ▶ FLING 2
fluorescent /fluːəˈresənt/ *adj.* fluoreszierend
fluorescent ˈlight *n.* Leuchtstofflampe, *die*
fluoride /ˈfluːəraɪd/ *n.* Fluorid, *das;* **~ toothpaste** fluorhaltige Zahnpasta
flurry /ˈflʌrɪ/ *n.* **(a)** Aufregung, *die*
(b) (of rain/snow) [Regen-/Schnee]schauer, *der*
flush¹ /flʌʃ/ 1 *v.i.* rot werden
2 *v.t.* ausspülen ‹*Becken*›; **~ the toilet** *or* **lavatory** spülen
3 *n.* Rotwerden, *das*
flush² *adj.* (level) bündig; **be ~ with sth.** mit etw. bündig abschließen
flush ˈtoilet *n.* Toilette mit Wasserspülung
fluster /ˈflʌstə(r)/ *v.t.* aus der Fassung bringen
flustered /ˈflʌstəd/ *adj.* nervös
flute /fluːt/ *n.* Flöte, *die*
flutter /ˈflʌtə(r)/ 1 *v.i.* flattern
2 *v.t.* flattern mit ‹*Flügel*›
flux /flʌks/ *n.* **in a state of ~:** im Fluss
fly¹ /flaɪ/ *n.* Fliege, *die*
fly² 1 *v.i.*, **flew** /fluː/, **flown** /fləʊn/ **(a)** fliegen; **~ away** *or* **off** wegfliegen
(b) (fig.) **~ [by** *or* **past]** wie im Fluge vergehen
(c) ‹*Fahne:*› gehisst sein
2 *v.t.*, **flew, flown** fliegen ‹*Flugzeug, Fracht, Einsatz usw.*›; fliegen über (+ *Akk.*) ‹*Strecke*›
3 *n. in sing. or pl.* (on trousers) Hosenschlitz, *der*
■ **fly ˈin** *v.i.* [mit dem Flugzeug] eintreffen **(from** aus)
■ **fly ˈout** *v.i.* abfliegen **(of** von)
ˈfly-fishing *n.* Fliegenfischerei, *die*
flying /ˈflaɪɪŋ/**: ~ ˈdoctor** *n.:* *Arzt, der seine Krankenbesuche mit dem Flugzeug macht;* **~ ˈsaucer** *n.* fliegende Untertasse; **~ ˈstart** *n.* (Sport) fliegender Start; **~ ˈvisit** *n.* Stippvisite, *die* (ugs.)
fly: ~leaf *n.* Vorsatzblatt, *das;* **~over** *n.* (Brit.) [Straßen]überführung, *die;* **~ spray** *n.* Insektenspray, *der od. das;* **~ swatter** *n.* Fliegenklappe, *die;* Fliegenklatsche, *die*
foal /fəʊl/ *n.* Fohlen, *das*
foam /fəʊm/ 1 *n.* Schaum, *der*
2 *v.i.* schäumen
foam: ~-backed *adj.* schaumstoffverstärkt; **~ ˈmattress** *n.* Schaumgummimatratze, *die;* **~ ˈrubber** *n.* Schaumgummi, *der*
fob /fɒb/ *v.t.*, **-bb-: ~ sb. off with sth.** jmdn. mit etw. abspeisen (ugs.)
ˈfocal point *n.* Brennpunkt, *der* (auch fig.)
focus /ˈfəʊkəs/ 1 *n., pl.* **~es** *or* **foci** /ˈfəʊsaɪ/ Brennpunkt, *der;* **out of/in ~:** unscharf/scharf eingestellt; unscharf/scharf ‹*Foto, Film usw.*›; (fig.) **be the ~ of attention** im Brennpunkt des Interesses stehen
2 *v.t.*, **-s-** *or* **-ss-** einstellen **(on** auf + *Akk.*); bündeln ‹*Licht, Strahlen*›
3 *v.i.*, **-s-** *or* **-ss-** (fig.) sich konzentrieren **(on** auf + *Akk.*)
ˈfocus group *n.* Fokusgruppe, *die*
fodder /ˈfɒdə(r)/ *n.* [Vieh]futter, *das*
foe /fəʊ/ *n.* (poet./rhet.) Feind, *der*
foetus /ˈfiːtəs/ *n.* Fötus, *der*
fog /fɒg/ *n.* Nebel, *der*
ˈfoglight *n.* Nebelscheinwerfer, *der*
foggy /ˈfɒgɪ/ *adj.* neblig
fogy /ˈfəʊgɪ/ *n.* **[old] ~:** [alter] Opa (salopp)/[alte] Oma (salopp)
foible /ˈfɔɪbl/ *n.* Eigenheit, *die*
foil¹ /fɔɪl/ *n.* Folie, *die*
foil² *v.t.* vereiteln
foist /fɔɪst/ *v.t.* **~ [off] on to sb.** jmdm. andrehen (ugs.); auf jmdn. abwälzen ‹*Probleme, Verantwortung*›

fold /fəʊld/ [1] *v.t.* [zusammen]falten; **~ one's arms** die Arme verschränken
[2] *v.i.* **(a)** (become ~ed) sich zusammenfalten
(b) (be able to be ~ed) sich falten lassen
(c) (go bankrupt) Konkurs machen
[3] *n.* Falte, *die;* (line made by ~ing) Kniff, *der*

■ **fold 'up** *v.t.* zusammenfalten ‹*Laken*›; zusammenklappen ‹*Stuhl*›

'folder *n.* **(a)** Mappe, *die*
(b) (Comp.) Ordner, *der*

foliage /'fəʊlɪɪdʒ/ *n.* Blätter *Pl.;* (of tree also) Laub, *das*

folk /fəʊk/ *n.* **(a)** Volk, *das*
(b) *in pl.* **~[s]** (people) Leute *Pl.*

folk: ~ dance *n.* Volkstanz, *der;* **~ hero** *n.* Volksheld, *der;* **~lore** /-lɔ:(r)/ *n.* Folklore, *die;* **~ music** *n.* Volksmusik, *die;* **~ singer** *n.* Sänger/Sängerin von Volksliedern; (modern) Folksänger, *der*/-sängerin, *die;* **~ song** Volkslied, *das;* (modern) Folksong, *der*

follow /'fɒləʊ/ [1] *v.t.* **(a)** folgen (+ *Dat.*)
(b) entlanggehen/-fahren ‹*Straße usw.*›
(c) (come after) folgen auf (+ *Akk.*)
(d) (result from) die Folge sein von
(e) (treat or take as guide) sich orientieren an (+ *Dat.*)
(f) folgen (+ *Dat.*) ‹*Prinzip, Instinkt, Trend*›; verfolgen ‹*Politik*›; befolgen ‹*Regel, Vorschrift, Rat, Warnung*›; sich halten an (+ *Akk.*) ‹*Konventionen, Diät*›
(g) (grasp meaning of) folgen (+ *Dat.*); **do you ~ me?** verstehst du, was ich meine?
[2] *v.i.* **(a)** (go, come) **~ after sb./sth.** jmdm./einer Sache folgen
(b) (come next in order or time) folgen; **as ~s** wie folgt
(c) ~ from sth. (result) die Folge von etw. sein; (be deducible) aus etw. folgen

■ **follow 'on** *v.i.* (continue) **~ on from sth.** die Fortsetzung von etw. sein

■ **follow 'up** *v.t.* **(a)** ausbauen ‹*Erfolg, Sieg*›
(b) nachgehen (+ *Dat.*) ‹*Hinweis*›

'follower *n.* Anhänger, *der*/Anhängerin, *die*

'following [1] *adj.* folgend; **the ~:** Folgendes
[2] *prep.* nach
[3] *n.* Anhängerschaft, *die*

folly /'fɒlɪ/ *n.* Torheit, *die* (geh.)

fond /fɒnd/ *adj.* liebevoll; lieb ‹*Erinnerung*›; **be ~ of sb.** jmdn. mögen; **be ~ of doing sth.** etw. gern tun

fondle /'fɒndl/ *v.t.* streicheln

'fondness *n.* Liebe, *die;* **~ for sth.** Vorliebe für etw.

font¹ /fɒnt/ *n.* Taufstein, *der*

font² *n.* (Comp., Printing) Schrift, *die;* Font, *der* (fachspr.); **~ size** Schriftgröße, *die;* Fontgröße, *die*

food /fu:d/ *n.* **(a)** Nahrung, *die;* (for animals) Futter, *das*
(b) (as commodity) Lebensmittel *Pl.*
(c) (in solid form) Essen, *das*
(d) (particular kind) Nahrungsmittel, *das;* Kost, *die*

food: ~ chain *n.* Nahrungskette, *die;* **~ poisoning** *n.* Lebensmittelvergiftung, *die;* **~ processor** *n.* Küchenmaschine, *die;* **~ shop, ~ store** *ns.* Lebensmittelgeschäft, *das;* **~stuff** *n.* Nahrungsmittel, *das;* **perishable ~stuffs** leicht verderbliche Lebensmittel

fool /fu:l/ [1] *n.* Dummkopf, *der* (ugs.)
[2] *v.t.* **~ sb. into doing sth.** jmdn. [durch Tricks] dazu bringen, etw. zu tun

■ **fool a'bout, fool a'round** *v.i.* Unsinn machen

foolhardy /'fu:lhɑ:dɪ/ *adj.* tollkühn

'foolish *adj.* töricht; verrückt (ugs.) ‹*Idee, Vorschlag*›

'foolproof *adj.* (infallible) absolut sicher

foot /fʊt/ [1] *n., pl.* **feet** /fi:t/ **(a)** Fuß, *der;* **on ~:** zu Fuß; **put one's ~ in it** (fig. coll.) ins Fettnäpfchen treten (ugs.)
(b) (far end) unteres Ende; (of bed) Fußende, *das*
(c) (measure) Fuß, *der* (30,48 cm)
[2] *v.t.* **~ the bill** die Rechnung bezahlen

football /'fʊtbɔ:l/ *n.* (game, ball) Fußball, *der*

'football boot *n.* Fußballschuh, *der*

'footballer *n.* Fußballspieler, *der*/-spielerin, *die*

football: ~ pitch *n.* Fußballplatz, *der;* **~ pools** *n. pl.* **the ~ pools** das Fußballtoto

foot: ~ brake *n.* Fußbremse, *die;* **~ bridge** *n.* Fußgängerbrücke, *die;* **~hold** *n.* Halt, *der*

'footing *n.* **(a)** (fig.) **be on an equal ~ [with sb.]** [jmdm.] gleichgestellt sein
(b) (foothold) Halt, *der*

foot: ~note *n.* Fußnote, *die;* **~ passenger** *n.* Fußpassagier, *der;* **~path** *n.* Fußweg, *der;* **~print** *n.* Fußabdruck, *der;* **~rest** *n.* Fußstütze, *die;* (on bicycle or motorcycle) Fußraste, *die;* **~step** *n.* Schritt, *der;* **follow in sb.'s ~steps** (fig.) in jmds. Fußstapfen (*Akk.*) treten; **~stool** *n.* Fußbank, *die;* Fußschemel, *der;* **~wear** *n.* Schuhe *Pl.;* **~work** *n.* (Sport, Dancing) Beinarbeit, *die*

for /fə(r), *stressed* fɔ:(r)/ [1] *prep.* **(a)** für; **what is it ~?** wofür ist das?; **reason ~ living** Grund zu leben; **a request ~ help** eine Bitte um Hilfe; **study ~ a university degree** auf einen Hochschulabschluss hin studieren; **take sb. ~ a walk** mit jmdm. einen Spaziergang machen; **be '~ doing sth.** (in favour) dafür sein, etw. zu tun; **cheque/bill ~ £5** Scheck/Rechnung über 5 Pfund; **what have you got ~ a cold?** was haben Sie gegen Erkältungen da?
(b) (on account of, as penalty of) wegen; **were it not ~ you/ your help** ohne dich/deine Hilfe; **~ fear of** aus Angst vor (+ *Dat.*)
(c) (in spite of) **~ all ...:** trotz ...; **~ all that, ...:** trotzdem ...

⋯

(d) ~ **all I know/care ...**: möglicherweise/was mich betrifft, ...; ~ **one thing, ...**: zunächst einmal ...
(e) (during) **stay ~ a week** eine Woche bleiben; **we've/we haven't been here ~ three years** wir sind seit drei Jahren hier/nicht mehr hier gewesen
(f) **walk ~ 20 miles** 20 Meilen gehen
[2] *conj.* denn

forage /'fɒrɪdʒ/ [1] *n.* Futter, *das*
[2] *v.i.* ~ **for sth.** auf der Suche nach etw. sein

forbad, forbade ▸ FORBID

forbid /fə'bɪd/ *v.t.*, **-dd-, forbad** /fə'bæd/ *or* **forbade** /fə'bæd, fə'beɪd/, **forbidden** /fə'bɪdn/ ~ **sb. to do sth.** jmdm. verbieten, etw. zu tun; ~ **[sb.] sth.** [jmdm.] etw. verbieten; **it is ~den [to do sth.]** es ist verboten[, etw. zu tun]

forbidden ▸ FORBID

for'bidding *adj.* Furcht einflößend

force /fɔːs/ [1] *n.* **(a)** (strength, power) Stärke, *die;* (of explosion, storm) Wucht, *die;* (Phys.; physical strength) Kraft, *die;* **in ~**: mit einem großen Aufgebot
(b) (validity) Kraft, *die;* **in ~**: in Kraft; **come into ~** ‹*Gesetz usw.*:› in Kraft treten
(c) (violence) Gewalt, *die;* **by ~**: gewaltsam
(d) (group) (of workers) Kolonne, *die;* Trupp, *der;* (Mil.) Armee, *die;* **the ~** (Police) die Polizei; **the ~s** die Armee; **be in the ~s** beim Militär sein
[2] *v.t.* **(a)** zwingen; ~ **sth. [up]on sb.** jmdm. etw. aufzwingen
(b) ~ **[open]** aufbrechen; ~ **one's way in** sich (*Dat.*) mit Gewalt Zutritt verschaffen

forced /fɔːst/ *adj.* **(a)** (contrived, unnatural) gezwungen
(b) (compelled by force) erzwungen; Zwangs‹*arbeit*›

forced 'landing *n.* Notlandung, *die*

'force-feed *v.t.* zwangsernähren

forceful /'fɔːsfl/ *adj.* stark ‹*Persönlichkeit, Charakter*›; energisch ‹*Person, Art*›; eindrucksvoll ‹*Sprache*›

forceps /'fɔːseps/ *n., pl. same* **[pair of] ~**: Zange, *die*

forcible /'fɔːsɪbl/ *adj.*, **forcibly** /'fɔːsɪblɪ/ *adv.* gewaltsam

ford /fɔːd/ [1] *n.* Furt, *die*
[2] *v.t.* durchqueren; (wade through) durchwaten

fore /fɔː(r)/ [1] *adj., esp. in comb.* vorder...; Vorder‹*teil, -front usw.*›
[2] *n.* **to the ~**: im Vordergrund

'forearm *n.* Unterarm, *der*

foreboding /fɔː'bəʊdɪŋ/ *n.* Vorahnung, *die*

'forecast [1] *v.t.*, **forecast** *or* **forecasted** vorhersagen
[2] *n.* Voraussage, *die*

'forecaster *n.* Meteorologe, *der*/Meteorologin, *die*

'forecourt *n.* Vorhof, *der*

'forefather *n., usu. in pl.* Vorfahr, *der*

'forefinger *n.* Zeigefinger, *der*

'forefront *n.* **[be] in the ~ of** in vorderster Linie (+ *Gen.*) [stehen]

'foregone *adj.* **be a ~ conclusion** von vornherein feststehen; (be certain) so gut wie sicher sein

'foreground *n.* Vordergrund, *der*

forehead /'fɒrɪd, 'fɔːhed/ *n.* Stirn, *die*

foreign /'fɒrɪn/ *adj.* **(a)** (from abroad) ausländisch; Fremd‹*kapital, -sprache*›; **he is ~**: er ist Ausländer
(b) (abroad) fremd; Außen‹*politik, -handel*›; **from a ~ country** aus einem anderen Land; aus dem Ausland; **~ countries** Ausland, *das*
(c) (from outside) fremd; **~ body/substance** Fremdkörper, *der*

foreign corre'spondent *n.* (Journ.) Auslandskorrespondent, *der*/-korrespondentin, *die*

'foreigner *n.* Ausländer, *der*/Ausländerin, *die*

foreign: ~ ex'change *n.* Devisen *Pl.;* **~ 'language** *n.* Fremdsprache, *die;* **~-language assistant** Fremdsprachenassistent, *der*/-assistentin, *die;* **~-language newspaper/broadcast** fremdsprachige Zeitung/Rundfunksendung; **~-language teaching** Fremdsprachenunterricht, *der;* **F~ 'Minister** *n.* Außenminister, *der*/-ministerin, *die;* **F~ 'Ministry** *n.* Außenministerium, *das;* **F~ Office** *n.* (Brit. Hist./coll.) Außenministerium, *das;* **~ policy** *n.* Außenpolitik, *die;* **F~ 'Secretary** *n.* (Brit.) Außenminister, *der*/-ministerin, *die;* **~ trade** *n.* Außenhandel, *der*

foreman /'fɔːmən/ *n., pl.* **foremen** /'fɔːmən/ Vorarbeiter, *der*

foremost /'fɔːməʊst, 'fɔːməst/ [1] *adj.* **(a)** vorderst...
(b) (fig.) führend
[2] *adv.* **first and ~**: zunächst einmal

'forename *n.* Vorname, *der*

forensic /fə'rensɪk/ *adj.* **~ medicine** Gerichtsmedizin, *die;* **~ science** Kriminaltechnik, *die*

'foreplay *n.* Vorspiel, *das*

'forerunner *n.* Vorläufer, *der*/Vorläuferin, *die*

foresaw ▸ FORESEE

foresee /fɔː'siː/ *v.t., forms as* SEE voraussehen

foreseeable /fɔː'siːəbl/ *adj.* vorhersehbar; **in the ~ future** in nächster Zukunft

foreseen ▸ FORESEE

'foresight *n.* Weitblick, *der*

'foreskin *n.* (Anat.) Vorhaut, *die*

forest /'fɒrɪst/ *n.* Wald, *der;* (commercially exploited) Forst, *der*

fore'stall *v.t.* zuvorkommen (+ *Dat.*)

forested /'fɒrɪstɪd/ *adj.* bewaldet

forestry /'fɒrɪstrɪ/ *n.* Forstwirtschaft, *die*
'foretaste *n.* Vorgeschmack, *der*
fore'tell *v.t.*, **fore'told** voraussagen
'forethought *n.* (prior deliberation) [vorherige] Überlegung; (care for the future) Vorausdenken, *das*
forever /fə'revə(r)/ *adv.* (constantly) ständig
fore'warn *v.t.* vorwarnen
fore'warning *n.* Vorwarnung, *die*
'foreword *n.* Vorwort, *das*
forfeit /'fɔ:fɪt/ 1 *v.t.* verlieren; verwirken (geh.) ‹*Recht, jmds. Gunst*›
2 *n.* Strafe, *die;* (games) Pfand, *das*
forgave ▶ FORGIVE
forge¹ /fɔ:dʒ/ 1 *n.* **(a)** (workshop) Schmiede, *die*
(b) (blacksmith's hearth) Esse, *die*
2 *v.t.* **(a)** schmieden **(into** zu)
(b) (fig.) schmieden ‹*Plan*›; schließen ‹*Vereinbarung, Freundschaft*›
(c) (counterfeit) fälschen
forge² *v.i.* **~ ahead** [das Tempo] beschleunigen; (fig.) Fortschritte machen
'forger *n.* Fälscher, *der*/Fälscherin, *die*
forgery /'fɔ:dʒərɪ/ *n.* Fälschung, *die*
forget /fə'get/ 1 *v.t.*, **-tt-, forgot** /fə'gɒt/, **forgotten** /fə'gɒtn/ vergessen; (~ learned ability) verlernen
2 *v.i.*, **-tt-, forgot, forgotten** es vergessen; **~ about sth.** etw. vergessen; **~ about it!** (coll.) schon gut!
forgettable /fə'getəbl/ *adj.* **easily ~:** leicht zu vergessen
forgetful /fə'getfl/ *adj.* vergesslich
for'getfulness *n.* Vergesslichkeit, *die*
for'get-me-not *n.* (Bot.) Vergissmeinnicht, *das*
forgive /fə'gɪv/ *v.t.*, **forgave** /fə'geɪv/, **forgiven** /fə'gɪvn/ verzeihen; vergeben ‹*Sünden*›; **~ sb. [sth.** *or* **for sth.]** jmdm. [etw.] verzeihen
for'giveness *n.* Verzeihung, *die;* (of sins) Vergebung, *die*
for'giving /fə'gɪvɪŋ/ *adj.* versöhnlich
forgo /fɔ:'gəʊ/ *v.t.*, *forms as* GO: verzichten auf (+ *Akk.*)
forgone ▶ FORGO
forgot, forgotten ▶ FORGET
fork /fɔ:k/ 1 *n.* **(a)** Gabel, *die;* **knives and ~s** Besteck, *das*
(b) (in road) Gabelung, *die;* (one branch) Abzweigung, *die*
2 *v.i.* (divide) sich gabeln; (turn) abbiegen; **~ left** links abbiegen
■ **fork 'out** *v.i.* (coll.) blechen (ugs.)
forked 'lightning *n.*, *no indef. art.* Linienblitz, *der*
'forklift truck *n.* Gabelstapler, *der*
forlorn /fə'lɔ:n/ *adj.* **(a)** (desperate) verzweifelt
(b) (forsaken) verlassen

form /fɔ:m/ 1 *n.* **(a)** (shape, type, style) Form, *die;* **take ~:** Gestalt annehmen
(b) (printed sheet) Formular, *das*
(c) (Brit. Sch.) Klasse, *die*
(d) (bench) Bank, *die*
(e) (Sport: physical condition) Form, *die;* (fig.) **true to ~:** wie üblich
2 *v.t.* **(a)** bilden
(b) (shape) formen, gestalten **(into** zu)
(c) sich (*Dat.*) bilden ‹*Meinung, Urteil*›; gewinnen ‹*Eindruck*›; fassen ‹*Plan*›; entwickeln ‹*Vorliebe, Gewohnheit*›; schließen ‹*Freundschaft*›
(d) (set up) bilden ‹*Regierung*›; gründen ‹*Bund, Firma, Partei*›
3 *v.i.* sich bilden; ‹*Idee:*› Gestalt annehmen
formal /'fɔ:ml/ *adj.* formell; förmlich ‹*Person, Art, Einladung, Begrüßung*›; (official) offiziell; **a ~ 'yes'/'no'** eine bindende Zusage/endgültige Absage
formality /fɔ:'mælɪtɪ/ *n.* **(a)** (requirement) Formalität, *die*
(b) (being formal) Förmlichkeit, *die*
formalize /'fɔ:məlaɪz/ *v.t.* **(a)** (specify and systematize) formalisieren
(b) (make official) formell bekräftigen
format /'fɔ:mæt/ *n.* 1 (also Comp.) Format, *das*
2 *v.t.*, **-tt-** (Comp.) formatieren
formation /fɔ:'meɪʃn/ *n.* **(a)** ▶ FORM 2A, D: Bildung, *die;* Gründung, *die*
(b) (Mil., Aeronaut.) Formation, *die*
formative /'fɔ:mətɪv/ *adj.* formend, prägend ‹*Einfluss*›; **the ~ years of life** die entscheidenden Lebensjahre
former /'fɔ:mə(r)/ *attrib. adj.* ehemalig; **in ~ times** früher; **the ~:** der/die/das Erstere; *pl.* die Ersteren
'formerly *adv.* früher
formidable /'fɔ:mɪdəbl/ *adj.* gewaltig; gefährlich ‹*Herausforderung, Gegner*›
formula /'fɔ:mjʊlə/ *n.* Formel, *die*
formulate /'fɔ:mjʊleɪt/ *v.t.* formulieren; (devise) entwickeln
formulation /fɔ:mjʊ'leɪʃn/ *n.* Formulierung, *die*
forsake /fə'seɪk/ *v.t.*, **forsook** /fə'sʊk/, **~n** /fə'seɪkn/ **(a)** (give up) verzichten auf (+ *Akk.*)
(b) (desert) verlassen
for'saken *adj.* verlassen
forsook ▶ FORSAKE
fort /fɔ:t/ *n.* (Mil.) Fort, *das*
forte /'fɔ:teɪ/ *n.* Stärke, *die*
forth /fɔ:θ/ *adv.* **and so ~:** und so weiter; *see also* BACK 3
forthcoming /'---, -'--/ *adj.* **(a)** (approaching) bevorstehend; in Kürze erscheinend ‹*Buch usw.*›
(b) *pred.* **be ~** ‹*Geld, Antwort:*› kommen; ‹*Hilfe:*› geleistet werden; **not be ~:** ausbleiben
(c) (responsive) mitteilsam ‹*Person*›

'forthright *adj.* direkt
forth'with *adv.* unverzüglich
fortieth /'fɔ:tɪɪθ/ *adj.* vierzigst...
fortify /'fɔ:tɪfaɪ/ *v.t.* **(a)** (Mil.) befestigen
(b) (strengthen) stärken
fortitude /'fɔ:tɪtju:d/ *n.* innere Stärke
fortnight /'fɔ:tnaɪt/ *n.* vierzehn Tage *Pl.*
fortnightly /'fɔ:tnaɪtlɪ/ **1** *adj.* vierzehntäglich; zweiwöchentlich
2 *adv.* alle vierzehn Tage; alle zwei Wochen
fortress /'fɔ:trɪs/ *n.* Festung, *die*
fortuitous /fɔ:'tju:ɪtəs/ *adj.*, **for'tuitously** *adv.* zufällig
fortunate /'fɔ:tʃənət/ *adj.* glücklich
'fortunately *adv.* glücklicherweise
fortune /'fɔ:tʃən, 'fɔ:tʃu:n/ *n.* **(a)** (wealth) Vermögen, *das*
(b) (luck) Schicksal, *das;* **bad/good ~:** Pech/Glück, *das*
'fortune teller *n.* Wahrsager, *der*/Wahrsagerin, *die*
forty /'fɔ:tɪ/ **1** *adj.* vierzig; **have ~ 'winks** ein Nickerchen machen (ugs.)
2 *n.* Vierzig, *die. See also* EIGHT; EIGHTY 2
forum /'fɔ:rəm/ *n.* Forum, *das*
forward /'fɔ:wəd/ **1** *adv.* **(a)** (in direction faced) vorwärts
(b) (to the front) nach vorn; vor‹*laufen, -rücken, -schieben*›
(c) (closer) heran; **he came ~ to greet me** er kam auf mich zu, um mich zu begrüßen
(d) come ~ ‹*Zeuge, Helfer:*› sich melden
2 *adj.* **(a)** (directed ahead) vorwärts gerichtet
(b) (at or to the front) Vorder-; vorder...
3 *n.* (Sport) Stürmer, *der*/Stürmerin, *die*
4 *v.t.* (send on) nachschicken ‹*Post*› **(to** an + *Akk.*)
forwarding ad'dress /'fɔ:wədɪŋ/ *n.* Nachsendeanschrift, *die*
forward: ~-looking *adj.* vorausschauend; **~ 'planning** *n.* Vorausplanung, *die*
forwards /'fɔ:wədz/ ▶ FORWARD 1A, B
forwent ▶ FORGO
fossil /'fɒsɪl/ *n.* Fossil, *das;* **~ fuel** fossiler Brennstoff
foster /'fɒstə(r)/ **1** *v.t.* **(a)** fördern; pflegen ‹*Freundschaft*›
(b) in Pflege haben ‹*Kind*›
2 *adj.* **~-:** Pflege‹*kind, -eltern, -sohn usw.*›
fought ▶ FIGHT 1, 2
foul /faʊl/ **1** *adj.* **(a)** abscheulich ‹*Geruch, Geschmack*›
(b) (polluted) verschmutzt ‹*Wasser, Luft*›; (putrid) faulig ‹*Wasser*›; stickig ‹*Luft*›
(c) (coll.: awful) scheußlich (ugs.); anstößig ‹*Sprache*›
2 *n.* (Sport) Foul, *das*
3 *v.t.* **(a)** beschmutzen; verpesten ‹*Luft*›
(b) (Sport) foulen
foul: ~-mouthed /'faʊlmaʊðd/ *adj.* unanständig; unflätig; **~-smelling** *adj.* übel riechend

found¹ /faʊnd/ *v.t.* **(a)** (establish) gründen; stiften ‹*Krankenhaus, Kloster*›; begründen ‹*Wissenschaft, Religion*›
(b) (fig.: base) begründen; **be ~ed [up]on sth.** [sich] auf etw. (*Akk.*) gründen
found² ▶ FIND 1
foundation /faʊn'deɪʃn/ *n.* **(a)** Gründung, *die;* (of hospital, monastery) Stiftung, *die*
(b) *usu. in pl.* **~[s]** (lit. or fig.) Fundament, *das;* **be without ~** (fig.) unbegründet sein
foundation: ~ course *n.* (Univ. etc.) Grundkurs, *der;* **~ cream** *n.* Grundierungscreme, *die;* **~ stone** *n.* (lit. or fig.) Grundstein, *der*
'founder¹ *n.* Gründer, *der*/Gründerin, *die;* (of hospital) Stifter, *der*/Stifterin, *die*
founder² *v.i.* **(a)** ‹*Schiff:*› sinken
(b) (fig.: fail) sich zerschlagen
foundry /'faʊndrɪ/ *n.* Gießerei, *die*
fountain /'faʊntɪn/ *n.* Fontäne, *die;* (structure) Springbrunnen, *der;* (fig.) Quelle, *die*
'fountain pen *n.* Füllfederhalter, *der*
four /fɔ:(r)/ **1** *adj.* vier
2 *n.* Vier, *die;* **on all ~s** auf allen vieren (ugs.). *See also* EIGHT
four: ~-by-~ **1** *adj.* Allrad-; **2** *n.* Allradler, *der;* Allradfahrzeug, *das;* **~-door** *attrib. adj.* viertürig ‹*Auto*›; **~fold** /'fɔ:fəʊld/ *adj., adv.* vierfach; **a ~fold increase** ein Anstieg auf das Vierfache; **~-legged** /'fɔ:legɪd, 'fɔ:legd/ *adj.* vierbeinig; **~-letter 'word** *n.* vulgärer Ausdruck; (expressing anger) ≈ Kraftausdruck, *der;* **~-poster** *n.* Himmelbett, *das;* **~some** /'fɔ:səm/ *n.* Quartett, *das;* **go in** *or* **as a ~some** zu viert gehen; **~-star** *n.* **~-star [petrol]** Super[benzin], *das*
fourteen /fɔ:'ti:n/ **1** *adj.* vierzehn
2 *n.* Vierzehn, *die. See also* EIGHT
fourteenth /fɔ:'ti:nθ/ **1** *adj.* vierzehnt...
2 *n.* (fraction) Vierzehntel, *das. See also* EIGHTH
fourth /fɔ:θ/ **1** *adj.* viert...
2 *n.* (in sequence, rank) Vierte, *der/die/das;* (fraction) Viertel, *das. See also* EIGHTH
'fourthly *adv.* viertens
four-wheel 'drive *n.* (Motor Veh.) Vier- *od.* Allradantrieb, *der*
fowl /faʊl/ *n.* Haushuhn, *das;* (collectively) Geflügel, *das*
fox /fɒks/ **1** *n.* Fuchs, *der*
2 *v.t.* verwirren
'fox-hunting *n.* Fuchsjagd, *die*
foyer /'fɔɪeɪ/ *n.* Foyer, *das*
fraction /'frækʃn/ *n.* **(a)** (Math.) Bruch, *der*
(b) (small part) Bruchteil, *der*
fracture /'fræktʃə(r)/ **1** *n.* Bruch, *der*
2 *v.t.* brechen
fragile /'frædʒaɪl/ *adj.* zerbrechlich
fragility /frə'dʒɪlɪtɪ/ *n.* Zerbrechlichkeit, *die*
fragment /'frægmənt/ *n.* Bruchstück, *das*

fragmentary /ˈfrægməntərɪ/ *adj.* bruchstückhaft

fragrance /ˈfreɪgrəns/ *n.* Duft, *der*

fragrant /ˈfreɪgrənt/ *adj.* duftend

frail /freɪl/ *adj.* zerbrechlich; gebrechlich ‹*Greis, Greisin*›

frame /freɪm/ [1] *n.* **(a)** (of vehicle) Rahmen, *der;* (of bed) Gestell, *das*
(b) (border) Rahmen, *der;* **[spectacle] ~s** [Brillen]gestell, *das*
[2] *v.t.* **(a)** rahmen
(b) formulieren ‹*Frage, Antwort*›
(c) (coll.: incriminate) **~ sb.** jmdm. etwas anhängen (ugs.)

frame: ~-up *n.* (coll.) abgekartetes Spiel (ugs.); **~work** *n.* Gerüst, *das*

franc /fræŋk/ *n.* Franc, *der;* (Swiss) Franken, *der*

France /frɑːns/ *pr. n.* Frankreich (*das*)

franchise /ˈfræntʃaɪz/ *n.* **(a)** Stimmrecht, *das*
(b) (Commerc.) Lizenz, *die*

frank¹ *adj.* offen; freimütig ‹*Geständnis, Äußerung*›; **be ~ with sb.** zu jmdm. offen sein

frank² *v.t.* (Post) frankieren

frankfurter /ˈfræŋkfɜːtə(r)/ (*Amer.:* **frankfurt** /ˈfræŋkfɜːt/) *n.* Frankfurter [Würstchen]

ˈfrankly *adv.* offen; (honestly) offen gesagt

frantic /ˈfræntɪk/ *adj.* **(a)** verzweifelt ‹*Hilferufe, Gestikulieren*›; **be ~ with fear/rage** *etc.* außer sich (*Dat.*) sein vor Angst/Wut *usw.*
(b) hektisch ‹*Aktivität, Suche*›

frantically /ˈfræntɪkəlɪ/, **ˈfranticly** *adv.* verzweifelt

fraternal /frəˈtɜːnl/ *adj.* brüderlich

fraternize /ˈfrætənaɪz/ *v.i.* **~ [with sb.]** sich verbrüdern [mit jmdm.]

fraud /frɔːd/ *n.* **(a)** *no pl.* Betrug, *der*
(b) (trick) Schwindel, *der*
(c) (person) Betrüger, *der*/Betrügerin, *die*

fraudulent /ˈfrɔːdjʊlənt/ *adj.* betrügerisch

fraught /frɔːt/ *adj.* **be ~ with danger** voller Gefahren sein

fray¹ /freɪ/ *n.* [Kampf]getümmel, *das;* **enter** *or* **join the ~:** sich in den Kampf stürzen

fray² *v.i.* [sich] durchscheuern; ‹*Hosenbein, Teppich, Seilende:*› ausfransen; **our nerves/tempers began to ~** (fig.) wir verloren langsam die Nerven/unsere Gemüter erhitzten sich

freak /friːk/ *n.* **(a)** Missgeburt, *die; attrib.* ungewöhnlich ‹*Wetter, Ereignis*›
(b) (coll.: fanatic) Freak, *der*

freakish /ˈfriːkɪʃ/ *adj.* (capricious) launisch; verrückt (ugs.); (abnormal) absonderlich

freaky /ˈfriːkɪ/ *adj.* **(a)** ▶ FREAKISH
(b) (coll.: bizarre) irre (salopp); verrückt (ugs.)

freckle /ˈfrekl/ *n.* Sommersprosse, *die*

ˈfreckled *adj.* sommersprossig

free /friː/ [1] *adj.*, **freer** /ˈfriːə(r)/, **freest** /ˈfriːɪst/ **(a)** frei; **get ~:** freikommen; **set ~:** freilassen; **~ of charge/cost** gebührenfrei/kostenlos; **sb. is ~ to do sth.** es steht jmdm. frei, etw. zu tun; **~ time** Freizeit, *die;* **he's ~ in the mornings** er hat morgens Zeit
(b) (without payment) kostenlos; frei ‹*Unterkunft, Verpflegung*›; Frei‹*karte, -exemplar*›; Gratis‹*probe*›; **'admission ~'** „Eintritt frei"; **for ~** (coll.) umsonst
[2] *adv.* gratis; umsonst
[3] *v.t.* (set at liberty) freilassen; (disentangle) befreien (**of, from** von); **~ sb./oneself from** jmdn./sich befreien aus ‹*Gefängnis, Sklaverei*›

free ˈagent *n.* **be a ~:** sein eigener Herr sein

freedom /ˈfriːdəm/ *n.* Freiheit, *die;* **~ of the press** Pressefreiheit, *die;* **~ of action/speech/movement** Handlungs-/Rede-/Bewegungsfreiheit, *die;* **~ of information** Auskunftsrecht, *das*

ˈfreedom fighter *n.* Freiheitskämpfer, *der*/-kämpferin, *die*

free: ~ ˈenterprise *n.* freies Unternehmertum; **~ ˈfall** *n.* freier Fall; **~-fall parachuting** Fallschirmspringen mit freiem Fall; **F~fone** ® /ˈfriːfəʊn/ *n.* ≈ Service 130; **phone us on F~fone 0800 343 027** rufen Sie uns unter 0800 343 027 zum Nulltarif an; **~ ˈgift** *n.* Gratisgabe, *die;* **~hold** [1] *n.* Besitzrecht, *das;* [2] *adj.* Eigentums-; **~holder** *n.* Grundeigentümer, *der;* **~ house** *n.* (Brit.) *brauereiunabhängiges Wirtshaus;* **~ ˈkick** *n.* (Footb.) Freistoß, *der;* **~lance** [1] *n.* freier Mitarbeiter/freie Mitarbeiterin; [2] *adj.* freiberuflich; **~lancer** /ˈfriːlɑːnsə(r)/ ▶ ~LANCE 1

ˈfreely *adv.* (willingly) großzügig; freimütig ‹*eingestehen*›; (without restriction) frei; (frankly) offen

free: ~ ˈmarket *n.* (Econ.) freier Markt; **F~mason** *n.* Freimaurer, *der;* **F~phone** ▶ FREEFONE; **~-range** *adj.* frei laufend ‹*Huhn*›; **~-range eggs** Eier von frei laufenden Hühnern; **~ speech** *n.* Redefreiheit; **~-standing** *adj.* frei stehend; **~ware** /ˈfriːweə(r)/ *n., no indef. art.* (Comp.) Freeware, *die;* kostenlose Software; **~way** *n.* (Amer.) Autobahn, *die;* **~-wheel** *v.i.* im Freilauf fahren; **~ ˈworld** *n.* freie Welt

freeze /friːz/ [1] *v.i.*, **froze** /frəʊz/, **frozen** /ˈfrəʊzn/ **(a)** frieren; (become covered with ice) zufrieren; ‹*Straße:*› vereisen; ‹*Flüssigkeit:*› gefrieren; ‹*Rohr, Schloss:*› einfrieren
(b) (become rigid) steif frieren
[2] *v.t.*, **froze, frozen (a)** (preserve) tiefkühlen
(b) einfrieren ‹*Kredit, Löhne, Preise usw.*›

ˈfreeze-dry *v.t.* gefriertrocknen

ˈfreezer *n.* Tiefkühltruhe, *die;* **[upright] ~:** Tiefkühlschrank, *der;* **~ compartment** Tiefkühlfach, *das*

freezing /'fri:zɪŋ/ 1 *adj.* (lit. or fig.) frostig; **it's ~:** es ist eiskalt
2 *n.* **above/below ~:** über/unter dem/den Gefrierpunkt

freezing: ~ 'fog *n.* gefrierender Nebel; **~ point** *n.* Gefrierpunkt, *der*

freight /freɪt/ *n.* Fracht, *die*

'freighter *n.* Frachter, *der*

'freight train *n.* Güterzug, *der*

French /frentʃ/ 1 *adj.* französisch; **he/she is ~:** er ist Franzose/sie ist Französin
2 *n.* **(a)** (language) Französisch, *das; see also* ENGLISH 2A
(b) the ~ *pl.* die Franzosen *Pl.*

French: ~ 'bean *n.* (Brit.) Gartenbohne, *die;* **~ 'bread** *n.* französisches [Stangen]weißbrot; **~ 'dressing** *n.* Vinaigrette, *die;* **~ 'fries** *n. pl.* Pommes frites *Pl.;* **~ 'kiss** *n.* französischer Kuss (ugs.); Zungenkuss, *der;* **~man** /'frentʃmən/ *n., pl.* **~men** /'frentʃmən/ Franzose, *der;* **~ 'polish** *n.* Schellackpolitur, *die;* **~ 'window** *n.* französisches Fenster; **~woman** *n.* Französin, *die*

frenzied /'frenzɪd/ *adj.* rasend

frenzy /'frenzɪ/ *n.* Wahnsinn, *der;* (fury) Raserei, *die*

frequency /'fri:kwənsɪ/ *n.* **(a)** Häufigkeit, *die*
(b) (Phys.) Frequenz, *die*

frequent 1 /'fri:kwənt/ *adj.* **(a)** häufig; **become less ~:** seltener werden
(b) (habitual) eifrig
2 /fri:'kwent/ *v.t.* häufig besuchen ‹*Café, Klub, usw.*›

frequently /'fri:kwəntlɪ/ *adv.* häufig

fresco /'freskəʊ/ *n. pl.* **~es** *or* **~s** Fresko, *das*

fresh /freʃ/ *adj.* frisch; neu ‹*Beweise, Anstrich, Mut, Energie*›; **~ supplies** Nachschub, *der* (**of** an + *Dat.*); **make a ~ start** noch einmal von vorne anfangen; (fig.) neu beginnen

freshen /'freʃn/ *v.i.* auffrischen
■ **freshen 'up** *v.i.* sich auffrischen

'freshly *adv.* frisch

'freshness *n.* Frische, *die*

fresh 'water *n.* Süßwasser, *das*

fret /fret/ *v.i.*, **-tt-** sich (*Dat.*) Sorgen machen

fretful /'fretfl/ *adj.* verdrießlich; quengelig (ugs.)

'fretsaw *n.* Laubsäge, *die*

Fri. *abbr.* = **Friday** Fr.

friar /'fraɪə(r)/ *n.* Ordensbruder, *der*

friction /'frɪkʃn/ *n.* Reibung, *die*

Friday /'fraɪdeɪ, 'fraɪdɪ/ *n.* Freitag, *der;* **on ~:** [am] Freitag; **on a ~, on ~s** freitags; **~ 13 August** Freitag, der 13. August; (at top of letter etc.) Freitag, den 13. August; **next/last ~:** [am] nächsten/letzten Freitag; **Good ~:** Karfreitag, *der*

fridge /frɪdʒ/ *n.* (Brit. coll.) Kühlschrank, *der*

fried ▶ FRY[1]

friend /frend/ *n.* Freund, *der*/Freundin, *die;* **be ~s with sb.** mit jmdm. befreundet sein; **make ~s [with sb.]** [mit jmdm.] Freundschaft schließen

friendliness /'frendlɪnɪs/ *n.* Freundlichkeit, *die*

'friendly 1 *adj.* freundlich (**to** zu); freundschaftlich ‹*Rat, Beziehungen, Wettkampf*›
2 *n.* (Sport) Freundschaftsspiel, *das*

'friendship *n.* Freundschaft, *die*

fries /fraɪz/ *n. pl.* (Amer.) Pommes frites *Pl.*

frigate /'frɪgət/ *n.* (Naut.) Fregatte, *die*

fright /fraɪt/ *n.* Schreck, *der;* **take ~:** erschrecken

frighten /'fraɪtn/ *v.t.* ‹*Explosion, Schuss:*› erschrecken; ‹*Gedanke, Drohung:*› Angst machen (+ *Dat.*); **be ~ed at** *or* **by sth.** vor etw. (*Dat.*) erschrecken

'frightful *adj.*, **'frightfully** *adv.* furchtbar

frigid /'frɪdʒɪd/ *adj.* frostig; (sexually) frigid[e]

frill /frɪl/ *n.* **(a)** Rüsche, *die*
(b) *in pl.* (embellishments) Beiwerk, *das*

'frilly *adj.* mit Rüschen besetzt; Rüschen‹*kleid, -bluse*›

fringe /frɪndʒ/ *n.* **(a)** Fransenkante, *die* (**on** an + *Dat.*)
(b) (hair) [Pony]fransen *Pl.* (ugs.)
(c) (edge) Rand, *der*

frisk /frɪsk/ 1 *v.i.* **~ [about]** [herum]springen
2 *v.t.* (coll.) filzen (ugs.)

'frisky *adj.* munter

fritter[1] /'frɪtə(r)/ *n.* **apple** *etc.* **~s** Apfelstücke *usw.* in Pfannkuchenteig

fritter[2] *v.t.* **~ away** vergeuden

frivolity /frɪ'vɒlɪtɪ/ *n.* Oberflächlichkeit, *die*

frivolous /'frɪvələs/ *adj.* **(a)** frivol
(b) (trifling) belanglos

frizzy /'frɪzɪ/ *adj.* kraus

fro /frəʊ/ *adv.* ▶ TO 2

frock /frɒk/ *n.* Kleid, *das*

frog /frɒg/ *n.* Frosch, *der*

frog: ~man /'frɒgmən/ *n., pl.* **~men** /'frɒgmən/ Froschmann, *der;* **~spawn** *n.* Froschlaich, *der*

frolic /'frɒlɪk/ *v.i.*, **-ck-: ~ [about** *or* **around]** [herum]springen

from /frəm, *stressed* frɒm/ *prep.* von; (~ within; expr. origin) aus; **~ Paris** aus Paris; **~ Paris to Munich** von Paris nach München; **be a mile ~ sth.** eine Meile von etw. entfernt sein; **where do you come ~?, where are you ~?** woher kommen Sie?; **painted ~ life** nach dem Leben gemalt; **weak ~ hunger** schwach vor Hunger; **~ the year 1972** seit 1972; **~ [the age of] 18** ab 18 Jahre; **~ 4 to 6 eggs** 4 bis 6 Eier

front /frʌnt/ 1 *n.* **(a)** Vorderseite, *die;* (of house) Vorderfront, *die;* **in** *or* **at the ~ [of**

sth.] vorn [in etw. *position: Dat., movement: Akk.*]; **to the ~**: nach vorn; **in ~**: vorn[e]; **be in ~ of sth./sb.** vor etw./jmdm. sein
(b) (Mil.) Front, *die*
(c) (at seaside) Strandpromenade, *die*
(d) (Metereol.) Front, *die*
(e) (bluff) Fassade, *die*
2 *adj.* vorder...; Vorder‹*rad, -zimmer, -zahn*›; **~ garden** Vorgarten, *der;* **~ row** erste Reihe

frontal /ˈfrʌntl/ *adj.* Frontal-

front ˈdoor *n.* (of flat) Wohnungstür, *die;* (of house) Haustür, *die*

frontier /ˈfrʌntɪə(r)/ *n.* Grenze, *die*

front: ~ ˈpage *n.* Titelseite, *die;* **~-wheel drive** **1** *n.* Vorderradantrieb, *der;* Frontantrieb, *der;* **2** *adj.* **a ~-wheel drive vehicle** ein Fahrzeug mit Vorderrad- od. Frontantrieb

frost /frɒst/ **1** *n.* Frost, *der;* **ten degrees of ~** (Brit.) zehn Grad minus
2 *v.t.* **~ed glass** Mattglas, *das*

ˈfrostbite *n.* Erfrierung, *die*

ˈfrosting *n.* (esp. Amer.) Glasur, *die*

ˈfrosty *adj.* frostig

froth /frɒθ/ **1** *n.* Schaum, *der*
2 *v.i.* schäumen

ˈfrothy *adj.* schaumig

frown /fraʊn/ **1** *v.i.* die Stirn runzeln ([**up**]**on** über + *Akk.*)
2 *n.* Stirnrunzeln, *das*

froze ▶ FREEZE

frozen /ˈfrəʊzn/ **1** ▶ FREEZE
2 *adj.* **(a)** zugefroren ‹*Fluss, See*›; eingefroren ‹*Wasserleitung*›; **I'm ~** (fig.) mir ist eiskalt
(b) (to preserve) tiefgekühlt; **~ food** Tiefkühlkost, *die*

frugal /ˈfru:gl/ *adj.* genügsam ‹*Lebensweise, Mensch*›; frugal ‹*Mahl*›

fruit /fru:t/ *n.* Frucht, *die; collect.* Obst, *das*

ˈfruit cake *n.* englischer Teekuchen

fruitful /ˈfru:tfl/ *adj.* fruchtbar

ˈfruit juice *n.* Obstsaft, *der*

ˈfruitless *adj.* nutzlos ‹*Versuch, Gespräch*›; fruchtlos ‹*Verhandlung, Suche*›

fruit: ~ machine *n.* (Brit.) Spielautomat, *der;* **~ ˈsalad** *n.* Obstsalat, *der*

ˈfruity *adj.* fruchtig ‹*Geschmack, Wein*›

frustrate /frʌˈstreɪt/ *v.t.* vereiteln ‹*Plan, Versuch*›; zunichte machen ‹*Hoffnung, Bemühungen*›

ˈfrustrated *adj.* frustriert

frustration /frʌˈstreɪʃn/ *n.* Frustration, *die*

fry¹ /fraɪ/ *v.t. & i.*, **fried** /fraɪd/ braten; **fried egg** Spiegelei, *das*

fry² *n.* (fishes) Brut, *die;* **small ~** (fig.) unbedeutende Leute

ˈfrying pan *n.* Bratpfanne, *die*

ft. *abbr.* = **feet, foot** ft.

fuchsia /ˈfju:ʃə/ *n.* (Bot.) Fuchsie, *die*

fuck /fʌk/ (coarse) **1** *v.t. & i.* ficken (vulg.); **[oh,] ~!, [oh,] ~ it!** [au,] Scheiße! (derb.)
2 *n.* Fick, *der* (vulg.)

fuddy-duddy /ˈfʌdɪdʌdɪ/ (coll.) **1** *adj.* verkalkt (ugs.)
2 *n.* Fossil, *das* (fig.)

fudge /fʌdʒ/ *n.* Karamellbonbon, *der od. das*

fuel /ˈfju:əl/ *n.* Brennstoff, *der;* (for vehicle) Kraftstoff, *der;* (for ship, aircraft) Treibstoff, *der*

fuel: ~ consumption *n.* (of vehicle) Kraftstoffverbrauch, *der;* **~ gauge** *n.* Kraftstoffanzeiger *der;* **~ injection** *n.* Benzineinspritzung, *die*

fugitive /ˈfju:dʒɪtɪv/ *n.* Flüchtige, *der/die*

fugue /fju:g/ *n.* (Mus.) Fuge, *die*

fulfil (*Amer.:* **fulfill**) /fʊlˈfɪl/ *v.t.*, **-ll-** erfüllen; halten ‹*Versprechen;*› **~ oneself** sich selbst verwirklichen

fulˈfilment (*Amer.:* **fulˈfillment**) *n.* Erfüllung, *die*

full /fʊl/ **1** *adj.* **(a)** voll; satt ‹*Person*›; **~ of** voller; **be ~ up** voll [besetzt] sein; ‹*Behälter:*› randvoll sein; ‹*Flug:*› völlig ausgebucht sein; **I'm ~ [up]** (coll.) ich bin voll [bis obenhin] (ugs.); **be ~ of oneself** sehr von sich eingenommen sein
(b) ausführlich ‹*Bericht, Beschreibung*›; erfüllt ‹*Leben*›; ganz ‹*Stunde, Jahr, Monat, Seite*›; voll ‹*Name, Bezahlung, Verständnis*›; **~ details** alle Einzelheiten; **at ~ speed** mit Höchstgeschwindigkeit
(c) voll ‹*Gesicht*›; füllig ‹*Figur*›; weit ‹*Rock*›
2 *n.* **in ~**: vollständig
3 *adv.* (exactly) genau

full: ~-blown *adj.* ausgewachsen ‹*Skandal*›; ausgereift ‹*Theorie, Plan, Gedanke*›; **~-blown AIDS** Vollbild-Aids, *das;* **~-bodied** *adj.* vollmundig, (fachspr.) körperreich ‹*Wein*›; **~-cream** *adj.* **~-cream milk/cheese** Vollmilch, *die*/ Vollfettkäse, *der;* **~ -length** *adj.* lang ‹*Kleid*›; **~ ˈmoon** *n.* Vollmond, *der;* **~-scale** *adj.* **(a)** in Originalgröße; **(b)** groß angelegt ‹*Untersuchung, Suchaktion*›; **~ ˈstop** *n.* Punkt, *der;* **~-time** *adj.* ganztägig; Ganztags‹*arbeit*›; **~-ˈtimer** *n.* Ganztagsbeschäftigte, *der/die*

fully /ˈfʊlɪ/ *adv.* voll [und ganz]; reich ‹*belohnt*›; ausführlich ‹*erklären*›

fulsome /ˈfʊlsəm/ *adj.* übertrieben

fumble /ˈfʌmbl/ *v.i.* **~ at** *or* **with** [herum]fingern an (+ *Dat.*); **~ in one's pockets for sth.** in seinen Taschen nach etw. kramen (ugs.)

fume /fju:m/ **1** *n. in pl.* **~s** Dämpfe *Pl.*; (from car exhaust) Abgase *Pl.*
2 *v.i.* vor Wut schäumen

fumigate /ˈfju:mɪgeɪt/ *v.t.* ausräuchern

fun /fʌn/ *n.* Spaß, *der;* **have ~!** viel Spaß!; **make ~ of sb.** sich über jmdn. lustig machen; **for ~, for the ~ of it** zum Spaß

function /'fʌŋkʃn/ [1] *n.* Aufgabe, *die;* Funktion, *die;* (formal event) Veranstaltung, *die* [2] *v.i.* ‹*Maschine, System:*› funktionieren; **~ as** fungieren als; (serve as) dienen als

functional /'fʌŋkʃənl/ *adj.* **(a)** (useful) funktionell
(b) (working) funktionsfähig

'function key *n.* (Comp.) Funktionstaste, *die*

fund /fʌnd/ [1] *n.* **(a)** (money) Fonds, *der*
(b) (fig.: stock) Fundus, *der* (**of** von, an + *Dat.*)
[2] *v.t.* finanzieren

fundamental /fʌndə'mentl/ *adj.* grundlegend (**to** für); elementar ‹*Bedürfnisse*›

fundamentalism /fʌndə'mentəlɪzm/ *n.* Fundamentalismus, *der*

fundamentalist /fʌndə'mentəlɪst/ *n.* Fundamentalist, *der*/Fundamentalistin, *die*

funda'mentally *adv.* grundlegend; von Grund auf ‹*verschieden, ehrlich*›

fund: ~-raiser /'fʌndreɪzə(r)/ *n.* **(a)** (person) Geldbeschaffer, *der*/-beschafferin, *die;* **(b)** (event) Benefizveranstaltung, *die;* **~-raising** /'fʌndreɪzɪŋ/ *n.* Geldbeschaffung, *die; attrib.* zur Geldbeschaffung *nachgestellt*

funeral /'fju:nərl/ *n.* Beerdigung, *die.* **~ director** Bestattungsunternehmer, *der;* **~ service** Trauerfeier, *die*

'funfair *n.* (Brit.) Jahrmarkt, *der*

fungus /'fʌŋgəs/ *n., pl.* **fungi** /'fʌŋgaɪ, 'fʌndʒaɪ/ *or* **~es** Pilz, *der*

funicular /fju:'nɪkjʊlə(r)/ *adj.* & *n.* **~ [railway]** [Stand]seilbahn, *die*

'fun-loving *adj.* lebenslustig

funnel /'fʌnl/ *n.* Trichter, *der;* (of ship etc.) Schornstein, *der*

funnily /'fʌnɪlɪ/ *adv.* komisch; **~ enough** komischerweise

funny /'fʌnɪ/ *adj.* **(a)** komisch; lustig; witzig ‹*Mensch, Einfall*›
(b) (strange) komisch

'funny bone *n.* Musikantenknochen, *der*

fur /fɜ:(r)/ *n.* **(a)** Fell, *das;* (garment) Pelz, *der;* **~ coat** Pelzmantel, *der*
(b) (in kettle) Kesselstein, *der*

furious /'fjʊərɪəs/ *adj.* wütend; heftig ‹*Streit*›; wild ‹*Tanz, Tempo, Kampf*›; **be ~ with sb.** wütend auf jmdn. sein

'furiously *adv.* wütend; wild ‹*kämpfen*›: wie wild (ugs.) ‹*arbeiten*›

furl /fɜ:l/ *v.t.* einrollen ‹*Segel, Flagge*›

furnace /'fɜ:nɪs/ *n.* Ofen, *der*

furnish /'fɜ:nɪʃ/ *v.t.* **(a)** möblieren
(b) (supply) liefern; **~ sb. with sth.** jmdm. etw. liefern

'furnishings *n. pl.* Einrichtungsgegenstände *Pl.*

furniture /'fɜ:nɪtʃə(r)/ *n.* Möbel *Pl.;* **piece of ~:** Möbel[stück], *das*

furniture: ~ polish *n.* Möbelpolitur, *die;* **~ van** *n.* Möbelwagen, *der*

furrow /'fʌrəʊ/ *n.* Furche, *die*

furry /'fɜ:rɪ/ *adj.* haarig; **~ animal** (toy) Plüschtier, *das*

further /'fɜ:ðə(r)/ [1] *adj.* **(a)** (in space) weiter entfernt
(b) (additional) weiter...
[2] *adv.* weiter
[3] *v.t.* fördern

further edu'cation *n.* Weiterbildung, *die;* (for adults also) Erwachsenenbildung, *die*

further'more *adv.* außerdem

'furthermost *adj.* äußerst...

furthest /'fɜ:ðɪst/ [1] *adj.* am weitesten entfernt
[2] *adv.* am weitesten ‹*springen, laufen*›; am weitesten entfernt ‹*sein, wohnen*›

furtive /'fɜ:tɪv/ *adj.*, **furtively** *adv.* verstohlen

fury /'fjʊərɪ/ *n.* Wut, *die;* (of sea, battle) Wüten, *das*

fuse¹ /fju:z/ [1] *v.t.* (blend) verschmelzen (**into** zu)
[2] *v.i.* **~ together** miteinander verschmelzen

fuse² *n.* **[time] ~:** [Zeit]zünder, *der;* (cord) Zündschnur, *die*

fuse³ (Electr.) [1] *n.* Sicherung, *die*
[2] *v.i.* **the lights have ~d** die Sicherung ist durchgebrannt

'fuse box *n.* Sicherungskasten, *der*

fuselage /'fju:zəlɑ:ʒ/ *n.* [Flugzeug]rumpf, *der*

fusion /'fju:ʒn/ *n.* **(a)** Verschmelzung, *die*
(b) (Phys.) Fusion, *die*

fuss /fʌs/ [1] *n.* Theater, *das* (ugs.); **make a ~ [about sth.]** einen Wirbel [um etw.] machen
[2] *v.i.* Wirbel machen; (get agitated) sich [unnötig] aufregen

'fussy *adj.* (fastidious) eigen; penibel; **I'm not ~** (I don't mind) ich bin nicht wählerisch

futile /'fju:taɪl/ *adj.* vergeblich ‹*Versuch, Bemühung*›; zum Scheitern verurteilt ‹*Plan*›

futility /fju:'tɪlɪtɪ/ *n.* (of attempt, effort) Vergeblichkeit, *die;* (of plan) Zwecklosigkeit, *die*

futon /'fu:tɒn/ *n.* Futon, *der*

future /'fju:tʃə(r)/ [1] *adj.* [zu]künftig; **at some ~ date** zu einem späteren Zeitpunkt
[2] *n.* **(a)** Zukunft, *die;* **in ~:** in Zukunft; künftig
(b) (Ling.) Futur, *das;* Zukunft, *die*
(c) *in pl.* (Commerc.) Terminware, *die;* (contracts) Lieferungsverträge *Pl.*

futuristic /fju:tʃə'rɪstɪk/ *adj.* futuristisch

fuze /fju:z/ ▶ FUSE²

fuzzy /'fʌzɪ/ *adj.* **(a)** (frizzy) kraus
(b) (blurred) verschwommen

Gg

G, g /dʒiː/ *n.* G, g, *das*
gab /gæb/ *n.* (coll.) **have the gift of the ~:** reden können
gabble /'gæbl/ *v.i.* brabbeln (ugs.)
gable /'geɪbl/ *n.* Giebel, *der*
gad /gæd/ *v.i.*, **-dd-** (coll.) **~ about** herumziehen (ugs.)
gadget /'gædʒɪt/ *n.* Gerät, *das*
gadgetry /'gædʒɪtrɪ/ *n.* [hoch technisierte] Ausstattung
Gaelic /'geɪlɪk, 'gælɪk/ **1** *adj.* gälisch **2** *n.* Gälisch, *das*
gaffe /gæf/ *n.* Fauxpas, *der*
gag /gæg/ **1** *n.* **(a)** Knebel, *der* **(b)** (joke) Gag, *der* **2** *v.t.*, **-gg-** knebeln
gaiety /'geɪətɪ/ *n.* Fröhlichkeit, *die*
gaily /'geɪlɪ/ *adv.* fröhlich; in leuchtenden Farben ‹*bemalt, geschmückt*›
gain /geɪn/ **1** *n.* **(a)** Gewinn, *der* **(b)** (increase) Zunahme, *die* (**in** an + *Dat.*) **2** *v.t.* **(a)** gewinnen; finden ‹*Zugang, Zutritt*›; erwerben ‹*Wissen, Ruf*›; erlangen ‹*Freiheit*›; erzielen ‹*Vorteil, Punkte*›; verdienen ‹*Lebensunterhalt, Geldsumme*›; **~ weight/five pounds [in weight]** zunehmen/fünf Pfund zunehmen; **~ speed** schneller werden **(b)** ‹*Uhr:*› vorgehen um **3** *v.i.* **(a) ~ by sth.** von etw. profitieren **(b)** ‹*Uhr:*› vorgehen
gainful /'geɪnfl/ *adj.* **~ employment** Erwerbstätigkeit, *die*
gainfully /'geɪnfəlɪ/ *adv.* **~ employed** erwerbstätig
gait /geɪt/ *n.* Gang, *der*
gala /'gɑːlə, 'geɪlə/ *n.* Festveranstaltung, *die*; *attrib.* Gala‹*abend, -vorstellung*›; **swimming ~:** Schwimmfest, *das*
galaxy /'gæləksɪ/ *n.* Galaxie, *die*
gale /geɪl/ *n.* Sturm, *der*
gall /gɔːl/ *n.* Unverschämtheit, *die*
gallant /'gælənt/ *adj.* (brave) tapfer; (chivalrous) ritterlich
gallantry /'gæləntrɪ/ *n.* (bravery) Tapferkeit, *die*
'gall bladder *n.* Gallenblase, *die*
gallery /'gælərɪ/ *n.* **(a)** Galerie, *die* **(b)** (Theatre) dritter Rang
galley /'gælɪ/ *n.* **(a)** (ship's kitchen) Kombüse, *die* **(b)** (Hist.) Galeere, *die*
gallivant /'gælɪvænt/ *v.i.* (coll.) herumziehen (ugs.)
gallon /'gælən/ *n.* Gallone, *die*
gallop /'gæləp/ **1** *n.* Galopp, *der* **2** *v.i.* ‹*Pferd, Reiter:*› galoppieren
gallows /'gæləʊz/ *n. sing.* Galgen, *der*
Gallup poll ® /'gæləp pəʊl/ *n.* Meinungsumfrage, *die*
galore /gə'lɔː(r)/ *adv.* im Überfluss; in Hülle und Fülle
galvanize /'gælvənaɪz/ *v.t.* wachrütteln; **~ sb. into action** jmdn. veranlassen, sofort aktiv zu werden
gambit /'gæmbɪt/ *n.* Gambit, *das*
gamble /'gæmbl/ *v.i.* **(a)** [um Geld] spielen; **~ at cards/on horses** um Geld Karten spielen/auf Pferde wetten **(b)** (fig.) spekulieren; **~ on sth.** sich auf etw. (*Akk.*) verlassen
gambler /'gæmblə(r)/ *n.* Glücksspieler, *der*
gambling /'gæmblɪŋ/ *n.* Spiel[en], *das;* Glücksspiel, *das;* (on horses, dogs) Wetten, *das*
game¹ /geɪm/ *n.* **(a)** Spiel, *das;* (of [table] tennis, chess, cards, cricket) Partie, *die* **(b)** (fig.: scheme) Vorhaben, *das* **(c)** *in pl.* (athletic contests) Spiele *Pl.*; (in school) (sports) Sport, *der;* (athletics) Leichtathletik, *die* **(d)** (Hunting, Cookery) Wild, *das*
game² *adj.* mutig; **be ~ to do sth.** bereit sein, etw. zu tun
'gamekeeper *n.* Wildheger, *der*
gamma rays /'gæmə/ *n. pl.* (Phys.) Gammastrahlen *Pl.*
gammon /'gæmən/ *n.* Räucherschinken, *der*
gamut /'gæmət/ *n.* Skala, *die*
gander /'gændə(r)/ *n.* Gänserich, *der*
gang /gæŋ/ **1** *n.* Bande, *die;* (of workmen, prisoners) Trupp, *der* **2** *v.i.* **~ up against** *or* **on** (coll.) sich verbünden gegen
gangling /'gæŋglɪŋ/ schlaksig (ugs.)
gangster /'gæŋstə(r)/ *n.* Gangster, *der*
'gang warfare *n.* Bandenkrieg, *der*
'gangway *n.* Gangway, *die;* (Brit.: between seats) Gang, *der*
gaol /dʒeɪl/ ▶ JAIL
gap /gæp/ *n.* **(a)** Lücke, *die* **(b)** (in time) Pause, *die* **(c)** (divergence) Kluft, *die*
gape /geɪp/ *v.i.* **(a)** den Mund aufsperren; ‹*Loch, Abgrund, Wunde:*› klaffen **(b)** (stare) Mund und Nase aufsperren (ugs.); **~ at sb./sth.** jmdn./etw. mit offenem Mund anstarren

garage /ˈgærɪdʒ/ *n.* Garage, *die;* (selling petrol) Tankstelle, *die;* (for repairing cars) [Kfz-]Werkstatt, *die*

garb /gɑːb/ *n.* Tracht, *die*

garbage /ˈgɑːbɪdʒ/ *n.* **(a)** Abfall, *der;* Müll, *der*
(b) (coll.: nonsense) Quatsch, *der* (salopp)

garbage: ~ can *n.* (Amer.) Mülltonne, *die;* **~ disˈposal unit, ~ disposer** *ns.* Abfallvernichter, *der;* Müllwolf, *der*

garble /ˈgɑːbl/ *v.t.* verstümmeln

garden /ˈgɑːdn/ *n.* Garten, *der*

garden: ~ centre *n.* Gartencenter, *das;* **~ ˈcity** *n.* Gartenstadt, *die*

gardener /ˈgɑːdnə(r)/ *n.* Gärtner, *der*/ Gärtnerin, *die*

gardening /ˈgɑːdnɪŋ/ *n.* Gartenarbeit, *die*

garden: ~ ˈshed *n.* Geräteschuppen, *der* **~ ˈwaste** *n.* Gartenabfälle *Pl.;* Gartenabfall, *der*

gargle /ˈgɑːgl/ *v.i.* gurgeln

gargoyle /ˈgɑːgɔɪl/ *n.* (Archit.) Wasserspeier, *der*

garish /ˈgeərɪʃ/ *adj.* grell ‹*Farbe, Licht*›; knallbunt ‹*Kleidung*›

garland /ˈgɑːlənd/ *n.* Girlande, *die*

garlic /ˈgɑːlɪk/ *n.* Knoblauch, *der*

garment /ˈgɑːmənt/ *n.* Kleidungsstück, *das;* **~s** *pl.* (clothes) Kleidung, *die;* Kleider *Pl.*

garnish /ˈgɑːnɪʃ/ [1] *v.t.* garnieren
[2] *n.* Garnierung, *die*

garret /ˈgærət/ *n.* Dachkammer, *die*

garrison /ˈgærɪsn/ *n.* Garnison, *die*

garter /ˈgɑːtə(r)/ *n.* Strumpfband, *das*

gas /gæs/ [1] *n.* **(a)** *pl.* **~es** /ˈgæsɪz/ Gas, *das*
(b) (Amer. coll.: petrol) Benzin, *das*
[2] *v.t.,* **-ss-** mit Gas vergiften

gas: ~ chamber *n.* Gaskammer, *die;* **~ ˈcooker** *n.* (Brit.) Gasherd, *der;* **~ cylinder** *n.* Gasflasche, *die;* **~ ˈfire** *n.* Gasofen, *der*

gash /gæʃ/ [1] *n.* Schnittwunde, *die*
[2] *v.t.* aufritzen ‹*Haut*›; **~ one's finger** sich (*Dat. od. Akk.*) in den Finger schneiden

gas: ~ heater *n.* Gasofen, *der;* **~ mask** *n.* Gasmaske, *die;* **~ meter** *n.* Gaszähler, *der*

gasoline (**gasolene**) /ˈgæsəliːn/ *n.* (Amer.) Benzin, *das*

gasometer /gæˈsɒmɪtə(r)/ *n.* Gasometer, *der*

gasp /gɑːsp/ [1] *v.i.* nach Luft schnappen (**with** vor); **he was ~ing for air** er rang nach Luft
[2] *v.t.* **~ out** hervorstoßen
[3] *n.* Keuchen, *das*

ˈgas station *n.* (Amer.) Tankstelle, *die*

gastric: ~ ˈflu (coll.)**, ~ influˈenza** *ns.* Darmgrippe, *die;* **~ ˈulcer** *n.* Magengeschwür, *das*

gastro-enteritis /gæstrəʊentəˈraɪtɪs/ *n.* Gastroenteritis, *die* (fachspr.); Magen-Darm-Katarrh, *der*

gastronomy /gæˈstrɒnəmɪ/ *n.* Gastronomie, *die*

ˈgasworks *n. sing.* Gaswerk, *das*

gate /geɪt/ *n.* Tor, *das;* (barrier) Sperre, *die;* (to field etc.) Gatter, *das;* (of level crossing) [Bahn]schranke, *die;* (in airport) Flugsteig, *der*

gateau /ˈgætəʊ/ *n., pl.* **~s** *or* **~x** /ˈgætəʊz/ Torte, *die*

gate: ~crasher /ˈgeɪtkræʃə(r)/ *n.* ungeladener Gast; **~way** *n.* Tor, *das*

gather /ˈgæðə(r)/ [1] *v.t.* **(a)** sammeln; zusammentragen ‹*Informationen*›; pflücken ‹*Obst, Blumen*›
(b) (infer, deduce) schließen (**from** aus)
(c) **~ speed/force** schneller/stärker werden
[2] *v.i.* sich versammeln; ‹*Wolken:*› sich zusammenziehen

ˈgathering *n.* Versammlung, *die*

GATT /gæt/ *abbr.* = **General Agreement on Tariffs and Trade** GATT, *das*

gauche /gəʊʃ/ *adj.* linkisch

gaudy /ˈgɔːdɪ/ *adj.* protzig; grell ‹*Farben*›

gauge /geɪdʒ/ *n.* [1] **(a)** (measure) Maß, *das*
(b) (instrument) Messgerät, *das*
[2] *v.t.* messen; (fig.) beurteilen

gaunt /gɔːnt/ *adj.* hager

gauntlet /ˈgɔːntlɪt/ *n.* Stulpenhandschuh, *der*

gauze /gɔːz/ *n.* Gaze, *die*

gave ▶ GIVE 1, 2

gay /geɪ/ [1] *adj.* **(a)** fröhlich; (brightly coloured) farbenfroh
(b) (coll.: homosexual) schwul (ugs.); Schwulen‹*lokal*›
[2] *n.* (coll.) Schwule, *der* (ugs.)

gay ˈrights *n. pl.* Schwulenrechte *Pl.*

gaze /geɪz/ *v.i.* blicken; (fixedly) starren; **~ at sb./sth.** jmdn./etw. anstarren

GB *abbr.* = **Great Britain** GB

GCSE *abbr.* (Brit.) = **General Certificate of Secondary Education**

gear /gɪə(r)/ [1] *n.* **(a)** (Motor Veh.) Gang, *der;* **top/bottom ~** (Brit.) der höchste/erste Gang; **change** *or* **shift ~**: schalten; **put the car into ~**: einen Gang einlegen; **out of ~**: im Leerlauf
(b) (coll.: clothes) Aufmachung, *die*
(c) (equipment) Gerät, *das;* Ausrüstung, *die*
[2] *v.t.* ausrichten (**to** auf + *Akk.*)

gear: ~box *n.* Getriebekasten, *der;* **~ lever,** (Amer.) **~ shift** *ns.* Schalthebel, *der*

geese *pl. of* GOOSE

geezer /ˈgiːzə(r)/ (coll.: old man) Opa, *der* (ugs.)

gel /dʒel/ *n.* Gel, *das*

gelatin /ˈdʒelətɪn/, (Brit.) **gelatine** /ˈdʒelətiːn/ *n.* Gelatine, *die*
gelignite /ˈdʒelɪgnaɪt/ *n.* Gelatinedynamit, *das*
gem /dʒem/ *n.* Edelstein, *der*
Gemini /ˈdʒemɪnaɪ, ˈdʒemɪnɪ/ *n.* (Astrol., Astron.) Zwillinge *Pl.*
ˈgemstone *n.* Edelstein, *der*
gender /ˈdʒendə(r)/ *n.* (Ling.) [grammatisches] Geschlecht
gene /dʒiːn/ *n.* (Biol.) Gen, *das*
general /ˈdʒenrl/ 1 *adj.* allgemein; weit verbreitet ‹*Ansicht*›; (true of [nearly] all cases) allgemein gültig; ungefähr ‹*Vorstellung, Beschreibung usw.*›; **the ~ public** weite Kreise der Bevölkerung; **in ~ use** allgemein verbreitet; **as a ~ rule, in ~**: im Allgemeinen
2 *n.* (Mil.) General, *der*
general: ~ eˈlection ▶ ELECTION; **~ ˈhospital** *n.* Allgemeinkrankenhaus, *das*
generalization /dʒenrəlaɪˈzeɪʃn/ *n.* Verallgemeinerung, *die*
generalize /ˈdʒenrəlaɪz/ 1 *v.t.* verallgemeinern
2 *v.i.* **~ about sth.** etw. verallgemeinern
general ˈknowledge *n.* Allgemeinwissen, *das*
generally /ˈdʒenrəlɪ/ *adv.* **(a)** allgemein; **~ available** überall erhältlich; **~ speaking** im Allgemeinen
(b) (usually) im Allgemeinen
general: ~ ˈmanager *n.* [leitender] Direktor/[leitende] Direktorin; **~ ˈmeeting** *n.* Generalversammlung, *die;* Hauptversammlung, *die;* **~ National Voˈcational Qualification** *n.* (Brit.) *staatliches Berufsausbildungsprogramm;* **~ pracˈtitioner** *n.* (Med.) Arzt/Ärztin für Allgemeinmedizin
generate /ˈdʒenəreɪt/ *v.t.* erzeugen (**from** aus); (result in) führen zu
generation /dʒenəˈreɪʃn/ *n.* **(a)** Generation, *die*
(b) (production) Erzeugung, *die*
generator /ˈdʒenəreɪtə(r)/ *n.* Generator, *der*
generosity /dʒenəˈrɒsɪtɪ/ *n.* Großzügigkeit, *die*
generous /ˈdʒenərəs/ *adj.* großzügig; reichlich ‹*Vorrat, Portion*›
ˈgenerously *adv.* großzügig
genetic /dʒɪˈnetɪk/ *adj.* genetisch
genetically /dʒɪˈnetɪkəlɪ/ *adv.* genetisch; **~ modified** gentechnisch verändert; **~ engineered** gentechnisch verändert ‹*Organismen, Pflanzen, Tiere, Nahrungsmittel*›; genetisch hergestellt ‹*Medikament, Enzym*›
genetic engiˈneering *n.* Gentechnologie, *die*
genetics /dʒɪˈnetɪks/ *n.* Genetik, *die*
Geneva /dʒɪˈniːvə/ 1 *pr. n.* Genf (*das*)
2 *attrib. adj.* Genfer
genial /ˈdʒiːnɪəl/ *adj.* freundlich
genitals /ˈdʒenɪtlz/ *n. pl.* Geschlechtsorgane *Pl.*
genitive /ˈdʒenɪtɪv/ *adj.* & *n.* **~ [case]** Genitiv, *der*
genius /ˈdʒiːnɪəs/ *n.* **(a)** (person) Genie, *das*
(b) (ability) Talent, *das*
genome /ˈdʒiːnəʊm/ *n.* (Biol.) Genom, *das*
genre /ˈʒɑ̃rə/ *n.* Genre, *das*
gent /dʒent/ *n.* **(a)** (coll./joc.) Gent, *der* (iron.)
(b) the G~s (Brit. coll.) die Herrentoilette
genteel /dʒenˈtiːl/ *adj.* vornehm
gentle /ˈdʒentl/ *adj.*, **~r** /ˈdʒentlə(r)/, **~st** /ˈdʒentlɪst/ sanft; liebenswürdig ‹*Person, Verhalten*›; leicht, schwach ‹*Brise*›; leise ‹*Geräusch*›; gemächlich ‹*Spaziergang, Tempo*›; mäßig ‹*Hitze*›
gentleman /ˈdʒentlmən/ *n., pl.* **gentlemen** /ˈdʒentlmən/ Herr, *der;* (well-mannered) Gentleman, *der;* **Ladies and Gentlemen!** meine Damen und Herren!; **'Gentlemen'** (sign) „Herren"
ˈgentleness *n.* Sanftheit, *die;* (of nature) Sanftmütigkeit, *die*
gently /ˈdʒentlɪ/ *adv.* (tenderly) zart; zärtlich; (mildly) sanft; (carefully) behutsam; (quietly, softly) leise
genuine /ˈdʒenjʊɪn/ *adj.* **(a)** (real) echt
(b) (true) aufrichtig; wahr ‹*Grund, Not*›
ˈgenuinely *adv.* wirklich
genus /ˈdʒiːnəs, ˈdʒenəs/ *n., pl.* **genera** /ˈdʒenərə/ (Biol.) Gattung, *die*
geographical /dʒiːəˈgræfɪkl/ *adj.* geographisch
geography /dʒɪˈɒgrəfɪ/ *n.* Geographie, *die;* Erdkunde, *die* (Schulw.)
geological /dʒiːəˈlɒdʒɪkl/ *adj.* geologisch
geologist /dʒɪˈɒlədʒɪst/ *n.* Geologe, *der*/ Geologin, *die*
geology /dʒɪˈɒlədʒɪ/ *n.* Geologie, *die*
geometric /dʒiːəˈmetrɪk/, **geometrical** /dʒiːəˈmetrɪkl/ *adj.* geometrisch
geometry /dʒɪˈɒmɪtrɪ/ *n.* Geometrie, *die*
geranium /dʒəˈreɪnɪəm/ *n.* Geranie, *die;* Pelargonie, *die*
geriatric /dʒerɪˈætrɪk/ *adj.* geriatrisch
germ /dʒɜːm/ *n.* Keim, *der*
German /ˈdʒɜːmən/ 1 *adj.* deutsch; **he/she is ~**: er ist Deutscher/sie ist Deutsche
2 *n.* **(a)** (person) Deutsche, *der/die*
(b) (language) Deutsch, *das; see also* ENGLISH 2A
German Democratic Reˈpublic *pr. n.* (Hist.) Deutsche Demokratische Republik
Germanic /dʒɜːˈmænɪk/ *adj.* germanisch
German ˈmeasles *n.* Röteln *Pl.*
Germany /ˈdʒɜːmənɪ/ *pr. n.* Deutschland (*das*); **Federal Republic of ~**: Bundesrepublik Deutschland, *die*
germinate /ˈdʒɜːmɪneɪt/ *v.i.* keimen

germ 'warfare *n.* Bakterienkrieg, *der*

gesticulate /dʒe'stɪkjʊleɪt/ *v.i.* gestikulieren

gesticulation /dʒestɪkjʊ'leɪʃn/ *n.* Gesten *Pl.*

gesture /'dʒestʃə(r)/ *n.* Geste, *die*

get /get/ 1 *v.t.*, **-tt-, got** /gɒt/, **got** *or* (Amer.) gotten /'gɒtn/ **(a)** (obtain, receive) bekommen; kriegen (ugs.); sich (*Dat.*) besorgen ‹*Visum, Genehmigung*›; sich (*Dat.*) beschaffen ‹*Geld*›; (find) finden ‹*Zeit*›; (fetch) holen; (buy) kaufen; **where did you ~ that?** wo hast du das her?; **~ sb. a job/taxi, ~ a job/taxi for sb.** jmdm. einen Job verschaffen/ein Taxi besorgen; **~ oneself sth.** sich (*Dat.*) etw. zulegen
(b) ~ the bus *etc.* (be in time for, catch) den Bus *usw.* erreichen *od.* (ugs.) kriegen; (travel by) den Bus *usw.* nehmen
(c) (prepare) machen (ugs.), zubereiten ‹*Essen*›
(d) (win) bekommen; finden ‹*Anerkennung*›; erzielen ‹*Tor, Punkt, Treffer*›; gewinnen ‹*Spiel, Preis, Belohnung*›; **~ permission** die Erlaubnis erhalten
(e) finden ‹*Schlaf, Ruhe*›; bekommen ‹*Einfall, Vorstellung, Gefühl, Kopfschmerzen, Grippe*›; gewinnen ‹*Eindruck*›
(f) have got (coll.: have) haben; **have got a cold** eine Erkältung haben; **have got to do sth.** etw. tun müssen
(g) (succeed in placing, bringing, etc.) bringen; kriegen (ugs.); **~ a message to sb.** jmdm. eine Nachricht zukommen lassen; **~ things going** *or* **started** die Dinge in Gang bringen
(h) ~ everything packed/prepared alles [ein]packen/vorbereiten; **~ sth. ready/done** etw. fertig machen; **~ one's feet wet** nasse Füße kriegen; **~ one's hands dirty** sich (*Dat.*) die Hände schmutzig machen; **~ one's hair cut** sich (Dat.) die Haare schneiden lassen; **~ sb. to do sth.** (induce) jmdn. dazu bringen, etw. zu tun
(i) ~ sb. [on the telephone] jmdn. [telefonisch] erreichen
(j) (coll.) (understand) kapieren (ugs.); (hear) mitkriegen (ugs.)
2 *v.i.*, **-tt-, got, got** *or* (Amer.) **gotten (a)** (succeed in coming or going) kommen; **~ to London before dark** London vor Einbruch der Dunkelheit erreichen
(b) (come to be) **~ working** sich an die Arbeit machen; **~ going** *or* **started** (leave) losgehen; (become lively or operative) in Schwung kommen; **~ going on** *or* **with sth.** mit etw. anfangen
(c) ~ to know sb. jmdn. kennen lernen
(d) (become) werden; **~ ready/washed** sich fertig machen/waschen; **~ frightened/hungry** Angst/Hunger kriegen

■ **get a'bout** *v.i.* **(a)** (travel) herumkommen **(b)** ‹*Gerücht:*› sich verbreiten

■ **'get at** *v.t.* **(a)** herankommen an (+ *Akk.*) **(b)** (find out) [he]rausfinden ‹*Wahrheit usw.*›; **what are you ~ting at?** worauf wollen Sie hinaus?
(c) (coll.: attack, taunt) anmachen (salopp)

■ **get a'way** *v.i.* **(a)** (leave) wegkommen **(b)** (escape) entkommen

■ **get 'back** 1 *v.i.* zurückkommen; **~ back home** nach Hause kommen
2 *v.t.* (recover) zurückbekommen; **~ one's own back** (coll.) sich rächen

■ **get 'by** *v.i.* **(a)** vorbeikommen **(b)** (coll.: manage) über die Runden kommen (ugs.)

■ **get 'down** 1 *v.i.* hinunter-/heruntersteigen; **~ down to sth.** (start) sich an etw. (*Akk.*) machen
2 *v.t.* **(a) ~ sb./sth. down** jmdn./etw. hinunter-/herunterbringen
(b) (coll.: depress) fertig machen (ugs.)

■ **get 'in** 1 *v.i.* (into bus etc.) einsteigen; (arrive) ankommen
2 *v.t.* (fetch) reinholen

■ **get 'off** 1 *v.i.* **(a)** (alight) aussteigen; (dismount) absteigen
(b) (leave) [weg]gehen
(c) (escape punishment) davonkommen
2 *v.t.* **(a)** (remove) ausziehen ‹*Kleidung usw.*›; entfernen ‹*Fleck usw.*›; abbekommen ‹*Deckel usw.*›
(b) (alight from) aussteigen aus; absteigen von ‹*Fahrrad*›
(c) ~ off the subject vom Thema abkommen

■ **get 'on** *v.i.* **(a)** (mount) aufsteigen; (enter vehicle) einsteigen
(b) (make progress) vorankommen; **he's ~ting on well** es geht ihm gut
(c) (manage) zurechtkommen

■ **get 'on with** *v.t.* **(a)** weitermachen mit **(b) ~ on [well] with sb.** mit jmdm. [gut] auskommen

■ **get 'out** 1 *v.i.* **(a)** rausgehen/rausfahren (**of** aus)
(b) (alight) aussteigen
(c) (escape) ausbrechen (**of** aus); (fig.) herauskommen; **~ out of** (avoid) herumkommen um (ugs.)
2 *v.t.* **(a)** (cause to leave) rausbringen
(b) (withdraw) abheben ‹*Geld*› (**of** von)

■ **get 'over** *v.t.* **(a)** (cross) gehen über (+ *Akk.*); (climb) klettern über (+ *Akk.*)
(b) (recover from) überwinden; hinwegkommen über (+ *Akk.*).

■ **get 'round** *v.i.* **~ round to doing sth.** dazu kommen, etw. zu tun

■ **get 'through** *v.i.* durchkommen

■ **get 'up** *v.i.* aufstehen

■ **get 'up to** *v.t.* **~ up to mischief** etwas anstellen

get: ~away *n.* Flucht, *die; attrib.* Flucht‹*plan, -wagen*›; **make one's ~away** entkommen; **~-together** *n.* (coll.) gemütliches Beisammensein; **~-up** *n.* (coll.) Aufmachung, *die*

geyser /'gi:zə(r)/ *n.* **(a)** (spring) Geysir, *der* **(b)** (Brit.) Durchlauferhitzer, *der*

ghastly /'gɑ:stlɪ/ *adj.* grauenvoll; entsetzlich ‹*Verletzungen*›; schrecklich ‹*Fehler*›

gherkin /'gɜ:kɪn/ *n.* Essiggurke, *die*

ghetto /ˈgetəʊ/ *n., pl.* **~s** Getto, *das*
ghetto blaster /ˈgetəʊblɑːstə(r)/ *n.* (coll.) [großer, tragbarer] Radiorekorder
ghost /gəʊst/ *n.* Geist, *der;* Gespenst, *das*
ˈghostly *adj.* gespenstisch
ghost: ~ story *n.* Gespenstergeschichte, *die;* **~ writer** *n.* Ghostwriter, *der*
giant /ˈdʒaɪənt/ **1** *n.* Riese, *der*
2 *attrib. adj.* riesig
gibberish /ˈdʒɪbərɪʃ/ *n.* Kauderwelsch, *das*
gibe /dʒaɪb/ *n.* Stichelei, *die*
giblets /ˈdʒɪblɪts/ *n. pl.* [Geflügel]klein, *das*
giddiness /ˈgɪdɪnɪs/ *n.* Schwindel, *der*
giddy /ˈgɪdɪ/ *adj.* schwind[e]lig
gift /gɪft/ *n.* **(a)** Geschenk, *das;* **make sb. a ~ of sth., make a ~ of sth. to sb.** jmdm. etw. schenken; **a ~ box/pack** eine Geschenkpackung
(b) (talent) Begabung, *die;* **have a ~ for languages/ mathematics** sprachbegabt/ mathematisch begabt sein
ˈgifted *adj.* begabt (**in, at** für)
gift: ~ shop *n.* Geschenkboutique, *die;* Geschenkladen, *der;* **~ token, ~ voucher** *ns.* Geschenkgutschein, *der;* **~-wrap** *v.t.* als Geschenk einpacken; in Geschenkpapier einpacken
gigantic /dʒaɪˈgæntɪk/ *adj.* gigantisch; riesig; enorm ‹*Verbesserung, Appetit*›
giggle /ˈgɪgl/ **1** *n.* Kichern, *das*
2 *v.i.* kichern
gild /gɪld/ *v.t.* vergolden
gill /gɪl/ *n.* Kieme, *die*
gilt /gɪlt/ **1** *n.* Goldauflage, *die;* (paint) Goldfarbe, *die*
2 *adj.* vergoldet
gimmick /ˈgɪmɪk/ *n.* (coll.) Gag, *der*
gin /dʒɪn/ *n.* Gin, *der*
ginger /ˈdʒɪndʒə(r)/ *n.* **(a)** Ingwer, *der*
(b) (colour) Rötlichgelb, *das*
ginger: ~ ˈbeer *n.* Ingwerbier, *das;* **~bread** *n.* Pfefferkuchen, *der*
gingerly /ˈdʒɪndʒəlɪ/ *adv.* vorsichtig
gipsy ▸ GYPSY
giraffe /dʒɪˈrɑːf/ *n.* Giraffe, *die*
girder /ˈgɜːdə(r)/ *n.* Träger, *der*
girl /gɜːl/ *n.* Mädchen, *das;* (teenager) junges Mädchen
girl: ~ band *n.* Girlgroup, *die;* **~friend** *n.* Freundin, *die*
ˈgirlish *adj.* mädchenhaft
ˈgirl power *n.* (coll.) Girlpower, *die*
giro /ˈdʒaɪərəʊ/ *n.* **(a)** Giro, *das; attrib.* Giro-; **bank ~:** Giroverkehr, *der*
(b) (cheque) Scheck, *der*
girth /gɜːθ/ *n.* **(a)** Umfang, *der*
(b) (for horse) Bauchgurt, *der*
gismo /ˈgɪzməʊ/ *n.* (coll.) Ding, *das* (ugs.)
gist /dʒɪst/ *n.* Wesentliche, *das;* (of tale, question, etc.) Kern, *der*

give /gɪv/ **1** *v.t.,* **gave** /geɪv/, **given** /ˈgɪvn/
(a) geben (**to** *Dat.*)
(b) (as gift) schenken; **~ sb. sth., ~ sth. to sb.** jmdm. etw. schenken; **~ and take** (fig.) Kompromisse eingehen
(c) (assign) aufgeben ‹*Hausaufgaben usw.*›; (grant, award, offer, allow to have) geben; verleihen ‹*Preis, Titel usw.*›; lassen ‹*Wahl, Zeit*›; verleihen ‹*Gewicht, Nachdruck*›; bereiten, machen ‹*Freude, Mühe, Kummer*›; bieten ‹*Schutz*›; leisten ‹*Hilfe*›; gewähren ‹*Unterstützung*›; **be ~n sth.** etw. bekommen; **~n that** (because) da; (if) wenn; **~ sb. hope** jmdm. Hoffnung machen
(d) (tell) angeben ‹*Namen, Anschrift, Alter, Grund*›; nennen ‹*Einzelheiten*›; geben ‹*Rat, Befehl, Anweisung, Antwort*›; fällen ‹*Urteil, Entscheidung*›; sagen ‹*Meinung*›; bekannt geben ‹*Nachricht*›; **~ him my best wishes** richte ihm meine besten Wünsche aus
(e) (perform, sing, etc.) geben ‹*Vorstellung, Konzert*›; halten ‹*Vortrag, Seminar*›
(f) (produce) geben ‹*Licht, Milch*›; ergeben ‹*Zahlen, Resultat*›
(g) (make, show) geben ‹*Zeichen, Stoß, Tritt*›; machen ‹*Satz, Ruck*›; ausstoßen ‹*Schrei, Seufzer, Pfiff*›; **~ sb. a [friendly] look** jmdm. einen [freundlichen] Blick zuwerfen
(h) (inflict) versetzen ‹*Schlag, Stoß*›; **sth. ~s me a headache** von etw. bekomme ich Kopfschmerzen
(i) geben ‹*Party, Essen usw.*›
2 *v.i.,* **gave, given** (yield) nachgeben; ‹*Knie:*› weich werden; ‹*Bett:*› federn
3 *n.* Nachgiebigkeit, *die;* (elasticity) Elastizität, *die*
▪ **give aˈway** *v.t.* **(a)** verschenken
(b) (in marriage) dem Bräutigam zuführen
(c) (betray) verraten
▪ **give ˈback** *v.t.* zurückgeben
▪ **give in** **1** /ˈ--/ *v.t.* abgeben
2 /-ˈ-/ *v.i.* nachgeben (**to** *Dat.*)
▪ **give ˈoff** *v.t.* ausströmen ‹*Geruch*›; aussenden ‹*Strahlen*›
▪ **give ˈup** **1** *v.i.* aufgeben
2 *v.t.* aufgeben; widmen ‹*Zeit*›; **~ sth. up** (abandon habit) sich (*Dat.*) etw. abgewöhnen; **~ oneself up** sich stellen
▪ **give ˈway** *v.i.* **(a)** (yield) nachgeben
(b) (in traffic) **~ way [to traffic from the right]** [dem Rechtsverkehr] die Vorfahrt lassen; **'G~ Way'** „Vorfahrt beachten"
(c) (collapse) einstürzen
given ▸ GIVE 1, 2
ˈgiven name *n.* (Amer.) Vorname, *der*
give-ˈway sign *n.* (Brit.) Vorfahrtsschild, *das*
gizmo ▸ GISMO
glacier /ˈglæsɪə(r)/ *n.* Gletscher, *der*
glad /glæd/ *adj.* froh; **be ~ of sth.** über etw. (*Akk.*) froh sein; für etw. dankbar sein
gladden /ˈglædn/ *v.t.* erfreuen
glade /gleɪd/ *n.* Lichtung, *die*
ˈgladly *adv.* gern

glamor (Amer.) ▶ GLAMOUR

glamorous /ˈglæmərəs/ *adj.* glanzvoll; glamourös ‹*Filmstar*›

glamour /ˈglæmə(r)/ *n.* Glanz, *der;* (of person) Ausstrahlung, *die*

glance /glɑːns/ 1 *n.* Blick, *der*
2 *v.i.* blicken; **~ at sb./sth.** jmdn./etw. anblicken; **~ at one's watch** auf seine Uhr blicken; **~ at the newspaper** *etc.* einen Blick in die Zeitung *usw.* werfen; **~ round [the room]** sich [im Zimmer] umsehen

gland /glænd/ *n.* Drüse, *die*

glandular /ˈglændjʊlə(r)/ *adj.* Drüsen-

glare /gleə(r)/ 1 *n.* **(a)** grelles Licht
(b) (hostile look) feindseliger Blick; **with a ~:** feindselig
2 *v.i.* (glower) [finster] starren; **~ at sb./sth.** jmdn./etw. anstarren

glaring /ˈgleərɪŋ/ *adj.* grell; (fig.: conspicuous) schreiend; grob ‹*Fehler*›; krass ‹*Gegensatz*›

glass /glɑːs/ *n.* **(a)** (substance) Glas, *das;* **pieces of/broken ~:** Glasscherben *Pl.;* (smaller) Glassplitter *Pl.*
(b) (drinking ~) Glas, *das;* **a ~ of milk** ein Glas Milch
(c) (pane) [Glas]scheibe, *die*
(d) *in pl.* (spectacles) **[a pair of] ~es** eine Brille

glass 'ceiling *n.* (fig.) unsichtbare Barriere

'glassy *adj.* gläsern

glaze /gleɪz/ 1 *n.* Glasur, *die*
2 *v.t.* **(a)** glasieren
(b) (fit with glass) verglasen

glazed /gleɪzd/ *adj.* glasig ‹*Blick*›

glazier /ˈgleɪzɪə(r)/ *n.* Glaser, *der*

gleam /gliːm/ 1 *n.* Schein, *der;* (fainter) Schimmer, *der;* **~ of hope** Hoffnungsschimmer, *der*
2 *v.i.* ‹*Licht:*› scheinen; ‹*Fußboden, Stiefel:*› glänzen; ‹*Zähne:*› blitzen; ‹*Augen:*› leuchten

'gleaming *adj.* glänzend

glean /gliːn/ *v.t.* zusammentragen ‹*Informationen usw.*›; **~ sth. from sth.** einer Sache (*Dat.*) etw. entnehmen

glee /gliː/ *n.* Freude, *die;* (gloating joy) Schadenfreude, *die*

gleeful /ˈgliːfl/ *adj.* freudig; (gloating) schadenfroh

glen /glen/ *n.* [schmales] Tal

glib /glɪb/ *adj.* aalglatt ‹*Person*›; leicht dahingesagt ‹*Antwort*›

glide /glaɪd/ *v.i.* gleiten; (through the air) schweben

'glider *n.* Segelflugzeug, *das*

glimmer /ˈglɪmə(r)/ 1 *n.* Schimmer, *der* (of von); (of fire) Glimmen, *das*
2 *v.i.* glimmen

glimpse /glɪmps/ 1 *n.* [kurzer] Blick; **catch** *or* **have** *or* **get a ~ of sb./sth.** jmdn./etw. [kurz] zu sehen bekommen
2 *v.t.* flüchtig sehen

glint /glɪnt/ 1 *n.* Schimmer, *der*
2 *v.i.* blinken; glitzern

glisten /ˈglɪsn/ *v.i.* glitzern

glitter /ˈglɪtə(r)/ 1 *v.i.* glitzern; ‹*Juwelen, Sterne:*› funkeln
2 *n.* Glitzern, *das;* (of diamonds) Funkeln, *das*

glitz /glɪts/ *n.* Glanz, *der*

glitzy /ˈglɪtsɪ/ *adj.* glanzvoll

gloat /gləʊt/ *v.i.* **~ over sth.** sich hämisch über etw. (*Akk.*) freuen

global /ˈgləʊbl/ *adj.* weltweit; **G~ Positioning System** GPS[-Navigationssystem] *das*; **~ warming** globaler Temperaturanstieg; **the ~ village** das Weltdorf

globalization /gləʊbəlaɪˈzeɪʃn/ *n.* Globalisierung, *die*

globalize /ˈgləʊbəlaɪz/ *v.t.* globalisieren

globe /gləʊb/ *n.* **(a)** (*sphere*) Kugel, *die*
(b) (with map) Globus, *der*
(c) (world) **the ~:** der Globus; der Erdball

'globetrotter *n.* Globetrotter, *der;* Weltenbummler, *der*

gloom /gluːm/ *n.* **(a)** (darkness) Dunkel, *das* (geh.)
(b) (despondency) düstere Stimmung

'gloomy *adj.* **(a)** (*dark*) düster; finster
(b) (depressing) düster; (depressed) trübsinnig

glorify /ˈglɔːrɪfaɪ/ *v.t.* verherrlichen; **a glorified messenger boy** ein besserer Botenjunge

glorious /ˈglɔːrɪəs/ *adj.* **(a)** (illustrious) ruhmreich ‹*Held, Sieg*›
(b) (delightful) wunderschön; herrlich

glory /ˈglɔːrɪ/ 1 *n.* **(a)** (splendour) Schönheit, *die;* (majesty) Herrlichkeit, *die*
(b) (fame) Ruhm, *der*
2 *v.i.* **~ in sth.** (be proud of) sich einer Sache (*Gen.*) rühmen

gloss /glɒs/ *n.* Glanz, *der;* **~ paint** Lackfarbe, *die*

■ **'gloss over** *v.t.* bemänteln; beschönigen ‹*Fehler*›

glossary /ˈglɒsərɪ/ *n.* Glossar, *das*

'glossy 1 *adj.* glänzend; (fig.) glanzvoll
2 *n.* (coll.) (magazine) auf [Hoch]glanzpapier gedruckte Zeitschrift

glove /glʌv/ *n.* Handschuh, *der*

glove: ~ box *n.* **(a)** ▶ **~** COMPARTMENT; **(b)** (for toxic material etc.) Handschuhkasten, *der;* **~ compartment** *n.* Handschuhfach, *das;* **~ puppet** *n.* Handpuppe, *die*

glow /gləʊ/ *v.i.* **(a)** glühen; ‹*Lampe, Leuchtfarbe:*› schimmern, leuchten
(b) (fig.) (with warmth or pride) ‹*Gesicht, Wangen:*› glühen (**with** vor + *Dat.*); (with health or vigour) strotzen (**with** vor + *Dat.*)

glower /ˈglaʊə(r)/ *v.i.* finster dreinblicken; **~ at sb.** jmdn. finster anstarren

'glowing *adj.* glühend; begeistert ‹*Bericht*›

'glow-worm *n.* Glühwürmchen, *das*

glucose /ˈgluːkəʊz/ *n.* Glucose, *die*

glue /gluː/ 1 *n.* Klebstoff, *der*

2 *v.t.* kleben; ~ **sth. to sth.** etw. an etw. (*Dat.*) an- *od.* festkleben

'glue-sniffing *n.* Schnüffeln, *das* (ugs.); Sniefen, *das* (ugs.)

glum /glʌm/ *adj.* verdrießlich

glut /glʌt/ *n.* Überangebot, *das* (**of** an, von + *Dat.*)

glutton /'glʌtən/ *n.* Vielfraß, *der* (ugs.); **a ~ for punishment** (iron.) ein Masochist (fig.)

gluttony /'glʌtənɪ/ *n.* Gefräßigkeit, *die*

glycerine /'glɪsəri:n/ (*Amer.*: **glycerin** /'glɪsərɪn/) *n.* Glyzerin, *das*

GM *abbr.* = **genetically modified**; **GM crops/food** gentechnisch veränderte Feldfrüchte *Pl.*/Nahrungsmittel *Pl.*

gm. *abbr.* = **gram[s]** g

GMO *abbr.* = **genetically modified organism** GVO

GMT *abbr.* = **Greenwich Mean Time** GMT; WEZ

gnarled /nɑ:ld/ *adj.* knorrig; knotig ‹*Hand*›

gnash /næʃ/ *v.t.* ~ **one's teeth** mit den Zähnen knirschen

gnat /næt/ *n.* [Stech]mücke, *die*

gnaw /nɔ:/ **1** *v.i.* ~ **[away] at sth.** an etw. (*Dat.*) nagen
2 *v.t.* nagen an (+ *Dat.*); abnagen ‹*Knochen*›

gnome /nəʊm/ *n.* Gnom, *der*

GNVQ *abbr.* = **General National Vocational Qualification**

go /gəʊ/ **1** *v.i., pres.* **he goes** /gəʊz/, *p.t.* **went** /went/, *pres. p.* **going** /'gəʊɪŋ/, *p.p.* **gone** /gɒn/ **(a)** gehen; ‹*Fahrzeug:*› fahren; ‹*Flugzeug:*› fliegen; ‹*Vierfüßer:*› laufen; (on horseback etc.) reiten; (in lift) fahren; (on outward journey) weg-, abfahren; (travel regularly) ‹*Verkehrsmittel:*› verkehren (**from … to** zwischen + *Dat.* … und); **go by bicycle/car/bus/train** *or* **rail/boat** *or* **sea** *or* **ship** mit dem [Fahr]rad/Auto/Bus/Zug/Schiff fahren; **go by plane** *or* **air** fliegen; **go on foot** zu Fuß gehen; laufen (ugs.); **go on a journey** verreisen; **have far to go** es weit haben; **go to the toilet/cinema/a museum** auf die Toilette/ins Kino/ins Museum gehen; **go to the doctor['s]** *etc.* zum Arzt *usw.* gehen; **go bathing** baden gehen; **go cycling** Rad fahren; **go to see sb.** jmdn. aufsuchen; **go and see whether …:** nachsehen [gehen], ob …; **I'll go!** ich geh schon!; (answer phone) ich geh ran *od.* nehme ab; (answer door) ich mache auf
(b) (start) losgehen; (in vehicle) losfahren
(c) (pass, circulate) gehen; **a shiver went up** *or* **down my spine** ein Schauer lief mir über den Rücken; **go to** (be given to) ‹*Preis, Gelder, Job:*› gehen an (+ *Akk.*); ‹*Titel, Besitz:*› übergehen auf (+ *Akk.*); **go towards** (be of benefit to) zugute kommen (+ *Dat.*)
(d) (act, function effectively) gehen; ‹*Mechanismus, Maschine:*› laufen; **keep going** (in movement) weitergehen/-fahren; (in activity) weitermachen; (not fail) sich aufrecht halten; **keep sth. going** etw. in Gang halten; **make sth. go, get/set sth. going** etw. in Gang bringen
(e) go to work zur Arbeit gehen; **go to school** in die Schule gehen; **go to a comprehensive school** auf eine Gesamtschule gehen
(f) (depart) gehen; ‹*Bus, Zug:*› [ab]fahren; ‹*Post:*› rausgehen (ugs.)
(g) (cease to function) kaputtgehen; ‹*Sicherung:*› durchbrennen; (break) brechen; ‹*Seil usw.:*› reißen
(h) (disappear) weggehen; ‹*Mantel, Hut, Fleck:*› verschwinden; ‹*Geruch, Rauch:*› sich verziehen; ‹*Geld, Zeit:*› draufgehen (ugs.) (**in, on** für)
(i) to go (still remaining) **have sth. [still] to go** [noch] etw. übrig haben, **one week** *etc.* **to go to …:** noch eine Woche *usw.* bis …; **there's hours to go** es dauert noch Stunden
(j) (be sold) weggehen (ugs.); verkauft werden; **going! going! gone!** zum Ersten! zum Zweiten! zum Dritten!; **go to sb.** an jmdn. gehen
(k) (run) ‹*Grenze, Straße usw.:*› verlaufen, gehen; (lead) gehen; führen; (extend) reichen; **as** *or* **so far as he/it goes** so weit
(l) (turn out, progress) ‹*Projekt, Interview, Abend:*› verlaufen; **how did your holiday go?** wie war Ihr Urlaub?; **things have been going well/badly** in der letzten Zeit läuft alles gut/schief
(m) (be, have form or nature) sein; ‹*Sprichwort, Gedicht, Titel:*› lauten; **that's the way it goes** so ist es nun mal; **go hungry** hungern; **go without food/water** es ohne Essen/Wasser aushalten
(n) (become) werden; **the tyre has gone flat** der Reifen ist platt
(o) (have usual place) kommen; (belong) gehören; **where does the box go?** wo kommt *od.* gehört die Kiste hin?
(p) (fit) passen; **go in[to] sth.** in etw. (*Akk.*) gehen *od.* [hinein]passen; **go through sth.** durch etw. [hindurch]gehen
(q) (match) passen (**with** zu)
(r) ‹*Turmuhr, Gong:*› schlagen; ‹*Glocke:*› läuten
(s) (coll.: be acceptable or permitted) erlaubt sein; **it/that goes without saying** es/das ist doch selbstverständlich. *See also* GOING 2
2 *n., pl.* **goes** /gəʊz/ (coll.) **(a)** (attempt, try) Versuch, *der;* (chance) Gelegenheit, *die;* **have a go** es versuchen; **let me have a go/can I have a go?** lass mich [auch ein]mal/kann ich [auch ein]mal? (ugs.); **it's 'my go** ich bin an der Reihe *od.* dran; **at one go** auf einmal; **at the first go** auf Anhieb
(b) (vigorous activity) **it's all go** es ist alles eine einzige Hetzerei (ugs.); **be on the go** auf Trab sein (ugs.)
(c) (success) **make a go of sth.** mit etw. Erfolg haben

▪ **go a'head** *v.i.* **(a)** (in advance) vorausgehen (**of** *Dat.*)

(b) (proceed) weitermachen; (make progress) ‹*Arbeit:*› fortschreiten, vorangehen
▪ **go a'long with** *v.t.* **go along with sth.** (agree to) sich einer Sache (*Dat.*) anschließen
▪ **go a'way** *v.i.* weggehen; (on holiday or business) verreisen
▪ **go 'back** *v.i.* zurückgehen/-fahren; (restart) ‹*Schule, Fabrik:*› wieder anfangen; (fig.) zurückgehen; **go back to the beginning** noch mal von vorne anfangen
▪ **go by** 1 /'--/ *v.t.* **go by sth.** sich nach etw. richten; (adhere to) sich an etw. (*Akk.*) halten
2 /-'-/ *v.i.* ‹*Zeit:*› vergehen
▪ **go 'down** *v.i.* hinuntergehen/-fahren; ‹*Sonne:*› untergehen; ‹*Schiff:*› untergehen; (fall to ground) ‹*Flugzeug usw.:*› abstürzen.
▪ **'go for** *v.t.* **go for sb./sth.** (go to fetch) jmdn./etw. holen; (apply to) für jmdn./etw. gelten; (like) jmdn./etw. gut finden
▪ **go 'in** *v.i.* hineingehen; reingehen (ugs.)
▪ **go 'off** 1 *v.i.* **(a) go off with sb./sth.** sich mit jmdm./etw. auf- und davonmachen (ugs.)
(b) ‹*Alarm, Schusswaffe:*› losgehen; ‹*Wecker:*› klingeln; ‹*Bombe:*› hochgehen
(c) (turn bad) schlecht werden
(d) ‹*Strom:*› ausfallen
2 *v.t.* (begin to dislike) **go off sth.** von etw. abkommen
▪ **go 'on** *v.i.* **(a)** weitergehen/-fahren
(b) (continue) weitermachen
(c) (happen) passieren
▪ **go 'out** *v.i.* ausgehen; **go out to work/for a meal** arbeiten/essen gehen; **go out with sb.** (date sb.) mit jmdm. gehen (ugs.)
▪ **go over** 1 /-'--/ *v.i.* hinübergehen
2 /'---, -'--/ *v.t.* (re-examine) durchgehen
▪ **go 'round** *v.i.* **(a)** (call) **go round and** *or* **to see sb.** bei jmdm. vorbeigehen (ugs.)
(b) (look round) sich umschauen
(c) (suffice) reichen; langen (ugs.)
(d) (spin) sich drehen
▪ **go through** 1 /-'-/ *v.i.* ‹*Ernennung:*› durchkommen; ‹*Antrag:*› durchgehen
2 /'--/ **(a)** (rehearse) durchgehen
(b) (examine) durchsehen
(c) (endure) durchmachen
▪ **go 'through with** *v.t.* zu Ende führen
▪ **go 'under** *v.i.* untergehen; (fig.: fail) eingehen
▪ **go 'up** *v.i.* **(a)** hinaufgehen/-fahren; ‹*Ballon:*› aufsteigen; (Theatre) ‹*Vorhang:*› aufgehen; ‹*Lichter:*› angehen
(b) (increase) ‹*Zahl:*› wachsen; ‹*Preis, Wert, Niveau:*› steigen; (in price) ‹*Ware:*› teurer werden
▪ **go without** 1 /'---/ *v.t.* verzichten auf (+ *Akk.*)
2 /--'-/ *v.i.* verzichten

goad /gəʊd/ *v.t.* ~ **sb. into sth./doing sth.** jmdn. zu etw. anstacheln/dazu anstacheln, etw. zu tun

'go-ahead 1 *adj.* unternehmungslustig; (progressive) fortschrittlich
2 *n.* **give sb./sth. the ~:** jmdm./einer Sache grünes Licht geben

goal /gəʊl/ *n.* **(a)** (aim) Ziel, *das*
(b) (Footb., Hockey) Tor, *das;* **score/kick a ~:** einen Treffer erzielen
goalie /'gəʊlɪ/ *n.* (coll.) Tormann, *der*
goal: ~keeper *n.* Torwart, *der;* **~post** *n.* Torpfosten, *der;* **move the ~posts** (fig. coll.) sich nicht an die Spielregeln halten
goat /gəʊt/ *n.* Ziege, *die*
gobble /'gɒbl/ 1 *v.t.* ~ [**down** *or* **up**] hinunterschlingen
2 *v.i.* schlingen
'go-between *n.* Vermittler, *der*/Vermittlerin, *die*
goblet /'gɒblɪt/ *n.* Kelchglas, *das*
goblin /'gɒblɪn/ *n.* Kobold, *der*
god /gɒd/ *n.* **(a)** Gott, *der*
(b) God (Theol.) Gott
god: ~child *n.* Patenkind, *das;* **~-daughter** *n.* Patentochter, *die*
goddess /'gɒdɪs/ *n.* Göttin, *die*
god: ~father *n.* Pate, *der;* **G~-forsaken** *adj.* gottverlassen; **~mother** *n.* Patentante, *die;* **~send** *n.* Gottesgabe, *die;* **be a ~send to sb.** für jmdn. ein Geschenk des Himmels sein; **~son** *n.* Patensohn, *der*
'go-getter *n.* Draufgänger, *der*
'goggle-box *n.* (Brit. coll.) Glotze, *die* (salopp); Glotzkiste, *die* (salopp)
goggles /'gɒglz/ *n. pl.* Schutzbrille, *die*
going /'gəʊɪŋ/ 1 *n.* (progress) Vorankommen, *das;* **while the ~ is good** solange es noch geht
2 *adj.* **(a)** (available) erhältlich; **there is sth. ~:** es gibt etw.
(b) be ~ to do sth. etw. tun [werden/wollen]; **I was ~ to say** ich wollte sagen; **it's ~ to snow** es wird schneien; **a ~ concern** eine gesunde Firma
(c) (current) [derzeit/damals/dann] geltend; **the ~ rate of exchange** der augenblickliche Wechselkurs
(d) a ~ concern eine gesunde Firma
goings-'on *n. pl.* Ereignisse *Pl.*
gold /gəʊld/ 1 *n.* Gold, *das*
2 *attrib. adj.* golden; Gold‹*münze, -kette usw.*›
'gold-digger *n.* Goldgräber, *der;* **she's a ~-digger** (fig. coll.) sie ist nur auf das Geld der Männer aus
golden /'gəʊldn/ *adj.* golden
golden 'wedding *n.* goldene Hochzeit
gold: ~fish *n.* Goldfisch, *der;* **~fish bowl** *n.* Goldfischglas, *das;* **like being in a ~fish bowl** (fig.) wie auf dem Präsentierteller; **~ 'medal** *n.* Goldmedaille, *die;* **~ 'medallist** *n.* Goldmedaillengewinner, *der*/-gewinnerin, *die;* **~ mine** *n.* Goldmine, *die;* (fig.) Goldgrube, *die;* **~-'plated** *adj.* vergoldet; **~smith** *n.* Goldschmied, *der*/-schmiedin, *die*
golf /gɒlf/ *n.* Golf, das

golf: ~ **ball** *n.* Golfball, *der;* ~ **club** *n.* **(a)** (implement) Golfschläger, *der;* **(b)** (association) Golfklub, *der;* **~course** *n.* Golfplatz, *der*

'golfer *n.* Golfer, *der*/Golferin, *die*

golf links *n.* Golfplatz, *der*

gondola /'gɒndələ/ *n.* Gondel, *die*

gondolier /gɒndə'lɪə(r)/ *n.* Gondoliere, *der*

gone /gɒn/ [1] ▶ GO 1
[2] *pred. adj.* **(a)** (away) weg; **it's time you were ~:** es ist *od.* wird Zeit, dass du gehst
(b) (of time: after) nach; **it's ~ ten o'clock** es ist zehn Uhr vorbei

gong /gɒŋ/ *n.* Gong, *der*

good /gʊd/ [1] *adj.*, **better** /'betə(r)/, **best** /best/ **(a)** gut; günstig ‹*Gelegenheit, Angebot*›; ausreichend ‹*Vorrat*›; ausgiebig ‹*Mahl*›; **as ~ as** so gut wie; **his ~ eye/leg** sein gesundes Auge/Bein; **in ~ time** frühzeitig; **all in ~ time** alles zu seiner Zeit; **be ~ at sth.** in etw. (*Dat.*) gut sein; **too ~ to be true** zu schön, um wahr zu sein; **apples are ~ for you** Äpfel sind gesund; **be too much of a ~ thing** zu viel des Guten sein; **~ times** eine schöne Zeit; **feel ~:** sich wohl fühlen; **take a ~ look round** sich gründlich umsehen; **give sb. a ~ beating/scolding** jmdn. tüchtig verprügeln/ausschimpfen; **~ afternoon/day** guten Tag!; **~ evening/morning** guten Abend/Morgen!; **~ night** gute Nacht!
(b) (enjoyable) schön ‹*Leben, Urlaub, Wochenende*›; **the ~ life** das angenehme[, sorglose] Leben; **have a ~ time!** viel Spaß!; **have a ~ journey!** gute Reise!
(c) (well-behaved) gut; brav; **be ~!, be a ~ girl/boy!** sei brav *od.* lieb!; **[as] ~ as gold** ganz artig *od.* brav
(d) (virtuous) rechtschaffen; (kind) nett; gut ‹*Absicht, Wünsche, Benehmen, Tat*›; **be ~ to sb.** gut zu jmdm. sein; **would you be so ~ as to** *or* **~ enough to do that?** wären Sie so freundlich *od.* nett, das zu tun?; **that/it is ~ of you** das/es ist nett *od.* lieb von dir
(e) (commendable) gut; **~ for 'you** *etc.* (coll.) bravo!
(f) (attractive) schön; gut ‹*Figur*›; **look ~:** gut aussehen
(g) (considerable) [recht] ansehnlich ‹*Menschenmenge*›; ganz schön, ziemlich (ugs.) ‹*Entfernung, Strecke*›; gut ‹*Preis, Erlös*›
(h) make ~ (succeed) erfolgreich sein; (compensate for) wieder gutmachen; (indemnify) ersetzen
[2] *n.* **(a)** (use) Nutzen, *der;* **be some ~ to sb./sth.** jmdm./einer Sache nützen; **be no ~ to sb./sth.** für jmdn./etw. nicht zu gebrauchen sein; **it is no/not much ~ doing sth.** es hat keinen/kaum einen Sinn, etw. zu tun; **what's the ~ of …?, what ~ is …?** was nützt …?
(b) (benefit) **for your/his** *etc.* **own ~:** zu deinem/seinem *usw.* Besten; **do no/little ~:** nichts/wenig helfen *od.* nützen; **do sb./sth. ~:** jmdm./einer Sache nützen; ‹*Ruhe, Erholung:*› jmdm./einer Sache gut tun; ‹*Arznei:*› jmdm./einer Sache helfen
(c) (goodness) Gute, *das;* **be up to no ~:** nichts Gutes im Sinn haben
(d) for ~ (finally) ein für alle Mal; (permanently) für immer
(e) *in pl.* (wares etc.) Waren *Pl.*; (belongings) Habe, *die;* (Brit. Railw.) Fracht, *die; attrib.* Güter‹*wagen, -zug*›

good: **~'bye** (*Amer.:* **~'by**) *int.* auf Wiedersehen!; (on telephone) auf Wiederhören!; **~-for-nothing** [1] *adj.* nichtsnutzig; [2] *n.* Taugenichts, *der;* **~-'looking** *adj.* gut aussehend

'goodness [1] *n.* Güte, *die*
[2] *int.* **[my] ~!** meine Güte! (ugs.)

good: **~s train** *n.* (Brit.) Güterzug, *der;* **~-'tempered** *adj.* ausgeglichen; verträglich ‹*Person*›; **~'will** *n.* guter Wille; *attrib.* Goodwill‹*botschaft, -reise usw.*›

'goody *n.* (coll.: hero) Gute, *der/die*

gooey /'gu:ɪ/ *adj.*, **gooier** /'gu:ɪə(r)/, **gooiest** /'gu:ɪɪst/ (coll.) klebrig

goose /gu:s/ *n.*, *pl.* **geese** /gi:s/ Gans, *die*

gooseberry /'gʊzbərɪ/ *n.* Stachelbeere, *die*

goose bumps (Amer.), **goose pimples** *ns. pl.* **have ~:** eine Gänsehaut haben

gore[1] /gɔ:(r)/ *v.t.* [mit den Hörnern] aufspießen *od.* durchbohren

gore[2] *n.* Blut, *das*

gorge /gɔ:dʒ/ [1] *n.* Schlucht, *die*
[2] *v.i. & refl.* **~ [oneself]** sich voll stopfen (ugs.) **(on** mit)

gorgeous /'gɔ:dʒəs/ *adj.* prächtig; hinreißend ‹*Frau, Mann, Lächeln*›

gorilla /gə'rɪlə/ *n.* Gorilla, *der*

gormless /'gɔ:mlɪs/ *adj.* (Brit. coll.) dämlich (ugs.)

gorse /gɔ:s/ *n.* Stechginster, *der*

gory /'gɔ:rɪ/ *adj.* (fig.) blutrünstig

gosh /gɒʃ/ *int.* (coll.) Gott!

'go-slow *n.* (Brit.) Bummelstreik, *der*

gospel /'gɒspl/ *n.* Evangelium, *das*

'gospel singer *n.* Gospelsänger, *der*/-sängerin, *die*

gossamer /'gɒsəmə(r)/ *n.* Altweibersommer, *der; attrib.* hauchdünn

gossip /'gɒsɪp/ [1] *n.* **(a)** (talk) Klatsch, *der* (ugs.)
(b) (person) Klatschbase, *die* (ugs.)
[2] *v.i.* klatschen (ugs.)

gossip: **~ column** *n.* Klatschspalte, *die* (ugs.); **~ columnist** *n.* Klatschspaltenkolumnist, *der*/-kolumnistin, *die*

got ▶ GET

Gothic /'gɒθɪk/ *adj.* gotisch

gotten ▶ GET

gouge /gaʊdʒ/ *v.t.* aushöhlen

goulash /'gu:læʃ/ *n.* Gulasch, *das od. der*

gourmet /'gʊəmeɪ/ *n.* Gourmet, *der*
govern /'gʌvn/ 1 *v.t.* **(a)** regieren ‹*Land, Volk*›; verwalten ‹*Provinz*›
(b) (dictate) bestimmen
2 *v.i.* regieren
governess /'gʌvənɪs/ *n.* Gouvernante, *die* (veraltet); Hauslehrerin, *die*
government /'gʌvnmənt/ *n.* Regierung, *die; attrib.* Regierungs-
government: ~ department *n.* Regierungsstelle, *die;* **~-funded** *adj.* staatlich finanziert; **~ official** *n.* Regierungsbeamte, *der*/-beamtin, *die*
governor /'gʌvənə(r)/ *n.* **(a)** (of province etc.) Gouverneur, *der*
(b) (of institution) Direktor, *der*/Direktorin, *die;* **[board of] ~s** Vorstand, *der*
(c) (coll.: employer) Boss, *der* (ugs.)
gown /gaʊn/ *n.* **(a)** [elegantes] Kleid
(b) (official or uniform robe) Talar, *der*
GP *abbr.* = **general practitioner**
GPS *abbr.* = **Global Positioning System**
grab /græb/ 1 *v.t.*, **-bb-** greifen nach; (seize) packen; **~ the chance** die Gelegenheit ergreifen; **~ hold of sb./sth.** sich (*Dat.*) jmdn./etw. schnappen (ugs.)
2 *v.i.*, **-bb-: ~ at sth.** nach etw. greifen
3 *n.* **make a ~ at** *or* **for sb./sth.** nach jmdm./etw. greifen
grace /greɪs/ *n.* **(a)** (charm) Anmut, *die* (geh.)
(b) (decency) **have the ~ to do sth.** so anständig sein und etw. tun
(c) (delay) Frist, *die;* **give sb. a day's ~:** jmdm. einen Tag Aufschub gewähren
(d) (prayers) **say ~:** das Tischgebet sprechen
graceful /'greɪsfl/ *adj.* elegant; graziös ‹*Bewegung, Eleganz*›
gracious /'greɪʃəs/ 1 *adj.* **(a)** liebenswürdig
(b) (merciful) gnädig
2 *int.* **good ~!** [ach] du meine Güte!
grade /greɪd/ 1 *n.* **(a)** Rang, *der;* (Mil.) Dienstgrad, *der*
(b) (position) Stufe, *die*
(c) (Amer. Sch.: class) Klasse, *die*
(d) (Sch., Univ.: mark) Note, *die;* Zensur, *die*
2 *v.t.* **(a)** einstufen ‹*Schüler*›; [nach Größe/ Qualität] sortieren ‹*Eier, Kartoffeln*›
(b) (mark) benoten
gradient /'greɪdɪənt/ *n.* (ascent) Steigung, *die;* (descent) Gefälle, *das*
gradual /'grædʒʊəl/ *adj.*, **'gradually** *adv.* allmählich
graduate 1 /'grædʒʊət/ *n.* Graduierte, *der/die;* (who has left university) Akademiker, *der*/Akademikerin, *die;* **university ~:** Hochschulabsolvent, *der*/-absolventin, *die*
2 /'grædʒʊeɪt/ *v.i.* einen akademischen Grad/Titel erwerben; (Amer. Sch.) die [Schul]abschlussprüfung bestehen (**from** an + *Dat.*)
graduation /grædʒʊ'eɪʃn/ *n.* **(a)** (Univ.) Graduierung, *die*
(b) (Amer. Sch.) Entlassung, *die*
graffiti /grə'fi:ti:/ *n. sing. or pl.* Graffiti *Pl.;* **~ artist** Graffitikünstler, *der*/-künstlerin, *die*
graft /grɑ:ft/ 1 *n.* **(a)** (Bot.) Edelreis, *das*
(b) (Med.) (operation) Transplantation, *die;* (thing ~ed) Transplantat, *das*
(c) (Brit. coll.: work) Plackerei, *die* (ugs.)
2 *v.t.* **(a)** (Bot.) pfropfen
(b) (Med.) transplantieren
3 *v.i.* (Brit. coll.) schuften (ugs.)
grain /greɪn/ *n.* **(a)** Korn, *das; collect.* Getreide, *das*
(b) (particle) Korn, *das*
(c) (in wood) Maserung, *die;* (in paper) Faser, *die;* (in leather) Narbung, *die;* **go against the ~ [for sb.]** (fig.) jmdm. gegen den Strich gehen (ugs.)
'grainy *adj.* körnig; gemasert ‹*Holz*›; genarbt ‹*Leder*›
gram /græm/ *n.* Gramm, *das*
grammar /'græmə(r)/ *n.* Grammatik, *die*
grammar: ~ book *n.* Grammatik, *die;* **~ school** *n.* (Brit.) ≈ Gymnasium, *das*
grammatical /grə'mætɪkl/ *adj.* **(a)** grammat[ikal]isch richtig *od.* korrekt
(b) (of grammar) grammatisch
grammatically /grə'mætɪkəlɪ/ *adv.* grammati[kal]isch ‹*richtig, falsch*›
gramme ▸ GRAM
gramophone /'græməfəʊn/ *n.* (dated) Plattenspieler, *der*
gran /græn/ *n.* (coll./child lang.) Oma, *die* (Kinderspr./ugs.)
granary /'grænərɪ/ *n.* Getreidesilo, *der od. das;* Kornspeicher, *der*
'granary bread *n.* Ganzkornbrot, *das*
grand /grænd/ *adj.* **(a)** (most or very important) groß; **~ finale** großes Finale
(b) (splendid) grandios
(c) (coll.: excellent) großartig
grandad /'grændæd/ *n.* (coll./child lang.); Opa, *der* (Kinderspr./ugs.)
grand: ~child *n.* Enkel, *der*/Enkelin, *die;* Enkelkind, *das;* **~dad[dy]** /'grændæd(i)/ ▸ GRANDAD; **~daughter** *n.* Enkelin, *die*
grandeur /'grændʒə(r), 'grændjə(r)/ *n.* Erhabenheit, *die*
'grandfather *n.* Großvater, *der;* **~ clock** Standuhr, *die*
grandiose /'grændɪəʊs/ *adj.* grandios; (pompous) bombastisch
grand: ~ma *n.* (coll./child lang.) Oma, *die* (Kinderspr./ugs.); **~mother** *n.* Großmutter, *die;* **~pa** *n.* (coll./child lang.) Opa, *der* (Kinderspr./ugs.); **~parent** *n.* (male) Großvater, *der;* (female) Großmutter, *die;* **~parents** Großeltern *Pl.;* **~ pi'ano** *n.* [Konzert]flügel, *der;* **~son** *n.* Enkel, *der;* **~stand** *n.* [Haupt]tribüne, *die*
granite /'grænɪt/ *n.* Granit, *der*
granny /'grænɪ/ *n.* (coll./child lang.) Oma, *die* (Kinderspr./ugs.)
'granny flat *n.* Einliegerwohnung, *die*

grant /grɑːnt/ 1 *v.t.* **(a)** erfüllen ‹*Wunsch*›; stattgeben (+ *Dat.*) ‹*Gesuch*›
(b) (concede, give) gewähren; geben ‹*Zeit*›; bewilligen ‹*Geldmittel*›; zugestehen ‹*Recht*›; erteilen ‹*Erlaubnis*›
(c) (in argument) zugeben; **take sb./sth. for ~ed** sich (*Dat.*) jmds. sicher sein/etw. für selbstverständlich halten
2 *n.* Zuschuss, *der;* (financial aid [to student]) [Studien]beihilfe, *die;* (scholarship) Stipendium, *das*

granulated sugar /grænjʊleɪtɪd 'ʃʊgə(r)/ *n.* Kristallzucker, *der*

granule /'grænjuːl/ *n.* Körnchen, *das*

grape /greɪp/ *n.* Weintraube, *die;* **a bunch of ~s** eine Traube

grape: ~fruit *n., pl. same* Grapefruit, *die;* **~ juice** *n.* Traubensaft, *der;* **~vine** *n.* (fig.) **the ~vine** die Flüsterpropaganda; **I heard on the ~vine that ...:** es wird geflüstert, dass ...

graph /grɑːf/ *n.* grafische Darstellung; **~ paper** Diagrammpapier, *das*

graphic /'græfɪk/ *adj.* **(a)** grafisch
(b) (vivid) plastisch; anschaulich

graphically /'græfɪkəlɪ/ *adv.* **(a)** (vividly) plastisch
(b) (using graphics) grafisch

graphic 'arts *n. pl.* Grafik, *die*

graphics /'græfɪks/ *n.* (use of diagrams) grafische Darstellung; **computer ~:** Computergraphik, *die*

grapple /'græpl/ *v.i.* handgemein werden; **~ with** (fig.) sich auseinander setzen mit

grasp /grɑːsp/ 1 *v.i.* **~ at** ergreifen; sich stürzen auf (+ *Akk.*) ‹*Angebot*›
2 *v.t.* **(a)** (seize) ergreifen
(b) (hold firmly) festhalten
(c) (understand) verstehen; erfassen ‹*Bedeutung*›
3 *n.* **(a)** (firm hold) Griff, *der*
(b) (mental ~) **have a good ~ of sth.** etw. gut beherrschen

'grasping *adj.* habgierig

grass /grɑːs/ *n.* **(a)** Gras, *das*
(b) (lawn) Rasen, *der*
(c) (Brit. sl.: police informer) Spitzel, *der*

grass: ~hopper *n.* Grashüpfer, *der;* **~-root[s]** *attrib. adj.* (Polit.) Basis-; **~ seed** *n.* Grassamen, *der;* (collect.) Grassamen *Pl.*

grassy /'grɑːsɪ/ *adj.* mit Gras bewachsen

grate¹ /greɪt/ *n.* Rost, *der;* (recess) Kamin, *der*

grate² *v.t.* **(a)** reiben; (less finely) raspeln
(b) (grind) **~ one's teeth** mit den Zähnen knirschen

grateful /'greɪtfl/ *adj.* dankbar (**to** *Dat.*)

'gratefully *adv.* dankbar

'grater *n.* Reibe, *die;* Raspel, *die*

gratify /'grætɪfaɪ/ *v.t.* freuen; **be gratified by** *or* **with** *or* **at sth.** über etw. (*Akk.*) erfreut sein

'gratifying *adj.* erfreulich

grating /'greɪtɪŋ/ *n.* Gitter, *das*

gratitude /'grætɪtjuːd/ *n.* Dankbarkeit, *die* (**to** gegenüber)

gratuitous /grə'tjuːɪtəs/ *adj.* (motiveless) grundlos

gratuity /grə'tjuːɪtɪ/ *n.* Trinkgeld, *das*

grave¹ /greɪv/ *n.* Grab, *das*

grave² *adj.* **(a)** (important, solemn) ernst
(b) (serious) schwer ‹*Fehler, Irrtum*›; ernst ‹*Situation, Lage*›; groß ‹*Gefahr*›; schlimm ‹*Nachricht*›

'gravedigger *n.* Totengräber, *der*

gravel /'grævl/ *n.* Kies, *der*

grave: ~stone *n.* Grabstein, *der;* **~yard** *n.* Friedhof, *der*

gravity /'grævɪtɪ/ *n.* **(a)** (of mistake, offence) Schwere, *die;* (of situation) Ernst, *der*
(b) (Phys., Astron.) Gravitation, *die;* Schwerkraft, *die*

gravy /'greɪvɪ/ *n.* **(a)** (juices) Bratensaft, *der*
(b) (dressing) [Braten]soße, *die*

gravy: ~ boat *n.* Sauciere, *die;* Soßenschüssel, *die;* **~ train** *n.* **ride/board the ~ train** (coll.) leichtes Geld machen (ugs.)

gray *etc.* (*Amer.*) ▶ GREY *etc.*

graze¹ /greɪz/ *v.i.* grasen; weiden

graze² 1 *n.* Schürfwunde, *die*
2 *v.t.* **(a)** (touch lightly) streifen
(b) (scrape) abschürfen ‹*Haut*›; zerkratzen ‹*Oberfläche*›

grease /griːs/ 1 *n.* Fett, *das;* (lubricant) Schmierfett, *das*
2 *v.t.* einfetten; (lubricate) schmieren

'greaseproof *adj.* fettdicht; **~ paper** Pergament- *od.* Butterbrotpapier, *das*

greasy /'griːsɪ/ *adj.* fettig; fett ‹*Essen*›; (lubricated) geschmiert; (dirty with lubricant) schmierig

great /greɪt/ *adj.* **(a)** groß; **a ~ many** sehr viele; sehr gut ‹*Freund*›; (impressive; coll.: splendid) großartig; **be a ~ one for sth.** etw. sehr gern tun
(b) Groß‹*onkel, -tante, -neffe, -nichte*›; Ur‹*großmutter, -großvater, -enkel, -enkelin*›

great: G~ 'Bear *n.* (Astron.) Großer Bär; **G~ 'Britain** *pr. n.* Großbritannien (*das*)

'greatly *adv.* sehr; höchst ‹*verärgert*›; stark ‹*beeinflusst*›; bedeutend ‹*verbessert*›

'greatness *n.* Größe, *die*

Great 'War *n.* Erster Weltkrieg

Greece /griːs/ *pr. n.* Griechenland (*das*)

greed /griːd/ *n.* Gier, *die* (**for** nach); (gluttony) Gefräßigkeit, *die*

'greedy *adj.* gierig; (gluttonous) gefräßig

Greek /griːk/ 1 *adj.* griechisch; **sb. is ~:** jmd. ist Grieche/Griechin
2 *n.* **(a)** (person) Grieche, *der*/Griechin, *die*
(b) (language) Griechisch, *das; see also* ENGLISH 2A

green /griːn/ 1 *adj.* **(a)** grün
(b) (environmentally safe) ökologisch ··>

(c) (gullible) naiv; (inexperienced) grün **(d)** (Polit.) **G~**: grün; **the G~s** die Grünen
2 *n.* **(a)** (colour) Grün, *das*
(b) (piece of land) Grünfläche, *die;* **village ~**: Dorfanger, *der*
(c) *in pl.* (~ vegetables) Grüngemüse, *das*

green: ~ belt *n.* Grüngürtel, *der;* **~ 'card** *n.* (Motor Veh.) grüne Karte

greenery /'gri:nərɪ/ *n.* Grün, *das*

green: ~fly *n.* (Brit.) grüne Blattlaus; **~gage** /'gri:ngeɪdʒ/ *n.* Reineclaude, *die;* **~grocer** *n.* (Brit.) Obst- und Gemüsehändler, *der*/-händlerin, *die*

'greenhouse *n.* Gewächshaus, *das*

greenhouse: ~ effect *n.* Treibhauseffekt, *der;* **~ gas** *n.* Treibhausgas, *das*

green: ~ light *n.* **(a)** grünes Licht; (as signal) Grün, *das;* **(b)** (fig.) **give sb./get the ~**: jmdm. grünes Licht geben/grünes Licht erhalten; **G~ Party** *n.* (Polit.) die Grünen *Pl.*

greet /gri:t/ *v.t.* begrüßen; (in passing) grüßen; (receive) empfangen

'greeting *n.* Begrüßung, *die;* (in passing) Gruß, *der;* (words) Grußformel, *die*

'greetings card *n.* Grußkarte, *die;* (for birthday) Glückwunschkarte, *die*

gregarious /grɪ'geərɪəs/ *adj.* gesellig

grenade /grɪ'neɪd/ *n.* Granate, *die*

grew ▶ GROW

grey /greɪ/ **1** *adj.* grau
2 *n.* Grau, *das*

grey: ~-haired *adj.* grauhaarig; **~hound** *n.* Windhund, *der;* **~hound racing** *n.* Windhundrennen, *das*

greyish /'greɪɪʃ/ *adj.* gräulich

grid /grɪd/ *n.* **(a)** (grating) Rost, *der*
(b) (of lines) Gitter[netz], *das*
(c) (for supply) Versorgungsnetz, *das*

grid: ~lock *n.* Verkehrsinfarkt, *der;* (fig.) völliger Stillstand; **~locked** /'grɪdlɒkt/ *adj.* total verstopft ‹*Straße, Stadt*›; (fig.) festgefahren

grief /gri:f/ *n.* Kummer, *der* (**over, at** über + *Akk.*, um); (at loss of sb.) Trauer, *die* (**for** um); **come to ~** (fail) scheitern

'grief-stricken *adj.* untröstlich (**at** über + *Akk.*)

grievance /'gri:vəns/ *n.* (complaint) Beschwerde, *die;* (grudge) Groll, *der*

grieve /gri:v/ **1** *v.t.* betrüben; bekümmern
2 *v.i.* trauern (**for** um)

grievous /'gri:vəs/ *adj.* schwer ‹*Verwundung, Krankheit;*› **~ bodily harm** (Law) schwere Körperverletzung

grill[1] /grɪl/ **1** *v.t.* (cook) grillen; (fig.: question) in die Mangel nehmen (ugs.)
2 *n.* **(a) mixed ~**: gemischte Grillplatte
(b) (on cooker) Grill, *der*

grille (**grill[2]**) *n.* **(a)** Gitter, *das*
(b) (Motor Veh.) [Kühler]grill, *der*

grim /grɪm/ *adj.* (stern) streng; grimmig ‹*Lächeln, Schweigen*›; (unrelenting) erbittert ‹*Widerstand, Kampf*›; (ghastly) grauenvoll ‹*Aufgabe, Nachricht*›; trostlos ‹*Aussichten*›

grimace /grɪ'meɪs/ **1** *n.* Grimasse, *die*
2 *v.i.* Grimassen schneiden; **~ with pain** vor Schmerz das Gesicht verziehen

grime /graɪm/ *n.* Schmutz, *der*

grimy /'graɪmɪ/ *adj.* schmutzig

grin /grɪn/ **1** *n.* Grinsen, *das*
2 *v.i.*, **-nn-** grinsen; **~ at sb.** jmdn. angrinsen

grind /graɪnd/ **1** *v.t.*, **ground** /graʊnd/ **(a) ~ [up]** zermahlen; mahlen ‹*Kaffee, Pfeffer, Getreide*›
(b) (sharpen) schleifen ‹*Schere, Messer*›; schärfen ‹*Klinge*›
(c) (rub harshly) zerquetschen; **~ one's teeth** mit den Zähnen knirschen
2 *v.i.*, **ground: ~ to a halt** ‹*Fahrzeug:*› quietschend zum Stehen kommen; (fig.) ‹*Verkehr:*› zum Erliegen kommen
3 *n.* (coll.) Plackerei, *die* (ugs.)

'grinder *n.* Schleifmaschine, *die;* (coffee ~ etc.) Mühle, *die*

'grindstone *n.* Schleifstein, *der*

grip /grɪp/ **1** *n.* **(a)** (firm hold) Halt, *der;* (fig.: power) Umklammerung, *die;* **have a ~ on sth.** etw. festhalten; (fig.) etwas im Griff haben; **loosen one's ~**: loslassen; **lose one's ~** (fig.) nachlassen
(b) (strength or way of ~ping) Griff, *der*
2 *v.t.*, **-pp-** [fest] halten; ‹*Reifen:*› greifen; (fig.) fesseln ‹*Publikum, Aufmerksamkeit*›
3 *v.i.*, **-pp-** ‹*Räder, Bremsen usw.:*› greifen

gripe /graɪp/ *v.i.* (coll.) meckern (ugs.) (**about** über + *Akk.*)

gripping /'grɪpɪŋ/ *adj.* (fig.) packend

grisly /'grɪzlɪ/ *adj.* grausig

gristle /'grɪsl/ *n.* Knorpel, *der*

grit /grɪt/ **1** *n.* **(a)** Sand, *der*
(b) (coll.: courage) Schneid, *der* (ugs.)
2 *v.t.*, **-tt-: (a)** streuen ‹*Straßen*›
(b) ~ one's teeth die Zähne zusammenbeißen (ugs.)

grizzly /'grɪzlɪ/ *n.* **~ [bear]** Grislybär, *der*

groan /grəʊn/ **1** *n.* Stöhnen, *das;* (of thing) Ächzen, *das*
2 *v.i.* [auf]stöhnen (**at** bei); ‹*Tisch, Planken:*› ächzen
3 *v.t.* stöhnen

grocer /'grəʊsə(r)/ *n.* Lebensmittelhändler, *der*/-händlerin, *die*

grocery /'grəʊsərɪ/ *n.* **(a)** *in pl.* (goods) Lebensmittel *Pl.*
(b) ~ [store] Lebensmittelgeschäft, *das*

groggy /'grɒgɪ/ *adj.* groggy *präd.* (ugs.)

groin /grɔɪn/ *n.* Leistengegend, *die*

groom /gru:m, grʊm/ **1** *n.* **(a)** (stable boy) Stallbursche, *der*
(b) (bride~) Bräutigam, *der*
2 *v.t.* striegeln ‹*Pferd*›; (fig.) vorbereiten (**for** auf + *Akk.*)

groove /gruːv/ *n.* Rille, *die*

grope /grəʊp/ *v.i.* tasten (**for** nach)

gross[1] /grəʊs/ *adj.* **(a)** (flagrant) grob ‹*Fahrlässigkeit, Fehler*›
(b) (obese) fett
(c) (total) Brutto-

gross[2] *n., pl. same* Gros, *das*

'**grossly** *adj.* (flagrantly) äußerst; grob ‹*übertreiben*›

grotesque /grəʊ'tesk/ *adj.* grotesk

grotto /'grɒtəʊ/ *n., pl.* **~es** *or* **~s** Grotte, *die*

grotty /'grɒtɪ/ *adj.* (Brit. coll.) mies (ugs.)

ground[1] /graʊnd/ [1] *n.* **(a)** Boden, *der;* **get off the ~** (coll.) konkrete Gestalt annehmen
(b) [**sports**] **~**: Sportplatz, *der*
(c) *in pl.* (attached to house) Anlage, *die*
(d) (reason) Grund, *der;* **on the ~[s] of** auf Grund (+ *Gen.*); **on the ~[s] that ...**: unter Berufung auf die Tatsache, dass ...
(e) *in pl.* (sediment) Satz, *der*
[2] *v.t.* (Aeronaut.) am Boden festhalten

ground[2] [1] ▶ GRIND 1, 2
[2] *adj.* gemahlen ‹*Kaffee, Getreide*›

ground: ~ control *n.* (Aeronaut.: personnel, equipment, etc.;) Flugsicherungskontrolldienst, *der;* **~ 'floor** ▶ FLOOR 1B; **~ forces** *n. pl.* Bodentruppen *Pl.;* **~ frost** *n.* Bodenfrost, *der*

'**grounding** *n.* Grundkenntnisse *Pl.*

'**groundless** *adj.* unbegründet

ground: ~sheet *n.* Bodenplane, *die;* **~sman** /'graʊndzmən/ *n., pl.* **-smen** /'graʊndzmən/ (Sport) Platzwart, *der;* **~work** *n.* Vorarbeiten *Pl.;* **~ 'zero** *n.* [Boden]nullpunkt, *der*

group /gruːp/ [1] *n.* Gruppe, *die*
[2] *v.t.* gruppieren

group: ~ practice *n.* Gemeinschaftspraxis, *die;* **~ therapy** *n.* Gruppentherapie, *die*

grouse[1] /graʊs/ *n., pl. same* Raufußhuhn, *das;* [**red**] **~** (Brit.) Schottisches Moorschneehuhn

grouse[2] *v.i.* (coll.) meckern (ugs.)

grove /grəʊv/ *n.* Wäldchen, *das*

grovel /'grɒvl/ *v.i.,* (Brit.) **-ll-** (fig.) katzbuckeln

grow /grəʊ/ [1] *v.i.,* **grew** /gruː/, **grown** /grəʊn/ **(a)** wachsen; **~ out of** *or* **from sth.** sich aus etw. entwickeln; (from sth. abstract) von etw. herrühren; **~ in** gewinnen an (+ *Dat.*) ‹*Größe, Bedeutung*›
(b) (become) werden; **~ apart** (fig.) sich auseinander leben; **~ to love/hate sb./sth.** jmdn./etw. lieben lernen/hassen lernen; **~ to like sb./sth.** nach und nach Gefallen an jmdm./etw. finden
[2] *v.t.,* **grew, grown** ziehen; (on a large scale) anpflanzen; züchten ‹*Blumen*›

■ **grow 'up** *v.i.* **(a)** aufwachsen; (become adult) erwachsen werden
(b) ‹*Legende:*› entstehen

growl /graʊl/ [1] *n.* Knurren, *das;* (of bear) Brummen, *das*
[2] *v.i.* knurren; ‹*Bär:*› [böse] brummen

grown /grəʊn/ [1] ▶ GROW
[2] *adj.* erwachsen

'**grown-up** [1] *n.* Erwachsene, *der/die*
[2] *adj.* erwachsen

growth /grəʊθ/ *n.* **(a)** Wachstum, *das* (**of, in** *Gen.*); (increase) Zunahme, *die* (**of, in** *Gen.*)
(b) (Med.) Gewächs, *das*

growth: ~ area *n.* Wachstumsbereich, *der;* **~ industry** *n.* Wachstumsindustrie, *die;* **~ rate** *n.* Wachstumsrate, *die*

grub /grʌb/ *n.* **(a)** Larve, *die;* (maggot) Made, *die*
(b) (coll.: food) Fressen, *das* (salopp)

grubby /'grʌbɪ/ *adj.* schmudd[e]lig (ugs.)

grudge /grʌdʒ/ [1] *v.t.* **~ sb. sth.** jmdm. etw. missgönnen; **~ doing sth.** etw. ungern tun
[2] *n.* Groll, *der;* **bear sb. a. ~** *or* **a ~ against sb.** jmdm. gegenüber nachtragend sein

grudging /'grʌdʒɪŋ/ *adj.* widerwillig; widerwillig gewährt ‹*Zuschuss*›

'**grudgingly** *adv.* widerwillig

gruelling (*Amer.*: **grueling**) /'gruːəlɪŋ/ *adj.* aufreibend; strapaziös ‹*Reise*›

gruesome /'gruːsəm/ *adj.* grausig

gruff /grʌf/ *adj.* barsch; rau ‹*Stimme*›

grumble /'grʌmbl/ *v.i.* murren; **~ about** *or* **over sth.** sich über etw. (*Akk.*) beklagen

grumpily /'grʌmpɪlɪ/ *adv.* unleidlich

grumpy /'grʌmpɪ/ *adj.* unleidlich

grunge /grʌndʒ/ *n.* Grunge, *der*

grunt /grʌnt/ [1] *n.* Grunzen, *das*
[2] *v.i.* grunzen

guarantee /gærən'tiː/ [1] *v.t.* **(a)** garantieren für; [eine] Garantie geben auf (+ *Akk.*); **the clock is ~d for a year** die Uhr hat ein Jahr Garantie
(b) (promise) garantieren (ugs.); (ensure) bürgen für ‹*Qualität*›
[2] *n.* **(a)** (Commerc. etc.) Garantie, *die;* (document) Garantieschein, *der*
(b) (promise) Garantie, *die* (ugs.); **give sb. a ~ that ...**: jmdm. garantieren, dass ...

guarantor /'gærəntə(r), gærən'tɔː(r)/ *n.* Bürge, *der*/Bürgin, *die*

guaranty /'gærəntɪ/ *n.* (basis of security) Garantie, *die;* Gewähr, *die*

guard /gɑːd/ [1] *n.* **(a)** (guardsman) Wachtposten, *der;* (group of soldiers) Wache, *die;* **be on ~**: Wache haben; **be on [one's] ~** (lit. or fig.) sich hüten
(b) (Brit. Railw.) [Zug]schaffner, *der*/-schaffnerin, *die*
(c) (Amer.: prison warder) [Gefängnis]wärter, *der*/-wärterin, *die*
[2] *v.t.* bewachen; hüten ‹*Geheimnis*›; schützen ‹*Leben*›; beschützen ‹*Prominenten*› ⋯

■ **'guard against** *v.t.* sich hüten vor (+ *Dat.*); vorbeugen (+ *Dat.*) ‹*Krankheit, Irrtum*›
guard: ~ dog *n.* Wachhund, *der;* **~ duty** *n.* Wachdienst, *der*
'guarded *adj.* zurückhaltend
guardian /'gɑːdɪən/ *n.* **(a)** Hüter, *der;* Wächter, *der*
(b) (Law) Vormund, *der*
guardian 'angel *n.* Schutzengel, *der*
guerrilla /gə'rɪlə/ *n.* Guerillakämpfer, *der*/-kämpferin, *die; attrib.* Guerilla-
guess /ges/ **1** *v.t.* **(a)** (estimate) schätzen; (surmise) raten; (surmise correctly) erraten; raten ‹*Rätsel*›; **~ what!** (coll.) stell dir vor!
(b) (esp. Amer.: suppose) **I ~:** ich glaube
2 *v.i.* (estimate) schätzen; (make assumption) vermuten; (surmise correctly) es erraten; **~ at sth.** etw. schätzen; **keep sb. ~ing** (coll.) jmdn. im Unklaren lassen
3 *n.* Schätzung, *die;* **make** *or* **have a ~:** schätzen
'guesswork *n.* **be ~:** eine Vermutung sein
guesstimate /'gestɪmət/ *n.* (coll.) grobe Schätzung
guest /gest/ *n.* Gast, *der*
guest: ~ house *n.* Pension, *die;* **~ list** *n.* Gästeliste, *die*; **~ room** *n.* Gästezimmer, *das;* **~ worker** *n.* Gastarbeiter, *der*/-arbeiterin, *die*
guffaw /gʌ'fɔː/ **1** *n.* brüllendes Gelächter
2 *v.i.* brüllend lachen
guidance /'gaɪdəns/ *n.* **(a)** (leadership) Führung, *die;* (by teacher etc.) [An]leitung, *die*
(b) (advice) Rat, *der*
guide /gaɪd/ **1** *n.* **(a)** Führer, *der*/Führerin, *die;* (Tourism) [Fremden]führer, *der*/-führerin, *die*
(b) (indicator) **be a [good] ~ to sth.** ein [guter] Anhaltspunkt für etw. sein; **be no ~ to sth.** keine Rückschlüsse auf etw. (*Akk.*) zulassen
(c) (Brit.) **[Girl] G~:** Pfadfinderin, *die*
(d) (handbook) Handbuch, *das*
(e) (for tourists) [Reise]führer, *der*
2 *v.t.* führen; (fig.) bestimmen ‹*Handeln, Urteil*›; **be ~d by sth./sb.** sich von etw./jmdm. leiten lassen
'guidebook *n.* [Reise]führer, *der*
guided 'missile *n.* Lenkflugkörper, *der*
'guide dog *n.* Blinden[führ]hund, *der*
guided 'tour *n.* Führung, *die* (**of** durch)
'guideline *n.* Richtlinie, *die*
guild /gɪld/ *n.* **(a)** Verein, *der*
(b) (Hist.) Gilde, *die;* Zunft, *die*
guile /gaɪl/ *n.* Hinterlist, *die*
guillotine /'gɪlətiːn/ *n.* Guillotine, *die*
guilt /gɪlt/ *n.* **(a)** Schuld, *die* (**of, for** an + *Dat.*)
(b) (guilty feeling) Schuldgefühle *Pl.*
'guiltless *adj.* unschuldig (**of** an + *Dat.*)
'guilty *adj.* **(a)** schuldig; **be ~ of murder** des Mordes schuldig sein; **find sb. ~/not ~ [of sth.]** jmdn. [an etw. (*Dat.*)] schuldig sprechen/[von etw.] freisprechen; **feel ~** ein schlechtes Gewissen haben
(b) schuldbewusst ‹*Miene, Blick, Verhalten*›; schlecht ‹*Gewissen*›
guinea: ~fowl, ~ hen *ns.* Perlhuhn, *das;* **~ pig** *n.* **(a)** (animal) Meerschweinchen, *das;*
(b) (fig.: subject of experiment) (person) Versuchsperson, *die;* Versuchskaninchen, *das* (ugs. abwertend); (thing) Versuchsobjekt, *das;* **act as ~ pig** Versuchskaninchen spielen
guise /gaɪz/ *n.* Gestalt, *die;* **in the ~ of** in Gestalt (+ *Gen.*)
guitar /gɪ'tɑː(r)/ *n.* Gitarre, *die*
guitarist /gɪ'tɑːrɪst/ *n.* Gitarrist, *der*/Gitarristin, *die*
gulf /gʌlf/ *n.* **(a)** (Geog.) Golf, *der*
(b) (wide gap) Kluft, *die*
gull /gʌl/ *n.* Möwe, *die*
gullet /'gʌlɪt/ *n.* **(a)** Speiseröhre, *die*
(b) (throat) Kehle, *die*
gullible /'gʌlɪbl/ *adj.* leichtgläubig
gully /'gʌlɪ/ *n.* (artificial channel) Abzugsrinne, *die;* (drain) Gully, *der*
gulp /gʌlp/ **1** *v.t.* hinunterschlingen; hinuntergießen ‹*Getränk*›
2 *n.* **(a)** Schlucken, *das*
(b) (large mouthful of drink) kräftiger Schluck
■ **gulp 'down** *v.t.* hinunterschlingen; hinuntergießen ‹*Getränk*›
gum¹ /gʌm/ *n.* (Anat.) **~[s]** Zahnfleisch, *das*
gum² **1** *n.* **(a)** Gummi, *das;* (glue) Klebstoff, *der*
(b) (Amer.) ▶ CHEWING GUM
2 *v.t.*, **-mm-: (a)** (smear with ~) mit Klebstoff bestreichen; gummieren ‹*Briefmarken, Etiketten usw.*›
(b) (fasten with ~) kleben
'gumboot *n.* Gummistiefel, *der*
gumption /'gʌmpʃn/ *n.* (coll.) Grips, *der*
gun /gʌn/ *n.* Schusswaffe, *die;* (rifle) Gewehr, *das;* (pistol) Pistole, *die;* (revolver) Revolver, *der*
■ **gun 'down** *v.t.* niederschießen
gun: ~fight *n.* (Amer. coll.) Schießerei, *die;* **~fire** *n.* Geschützfeuer, *das;* **~ laws** *pl.* Waffengesetze *Pl.*; **~man** /'gʌnmən/ *n., pl.* **~men** /'gʌnmən/ bewaffneter Mann; **~powder** *n.* Schießpulver, *das;* **~shot** *n.* Schuss, *der;* **~shot wound** Schusswunde, *die;* **~smith** *n.* Büchsenmacher, *der*
gurgle /'gɜːgl/ **1** *n.* Gluckern, *das;* (of brook) Plätschern, *das*
2 *v.i.* gluckern; ‹*Bach:*› plätschern; ‹*Baby:*› lallen; (with delight) glucksen
guru /'gʊruː/ *n.* Guru, *der*
gush /gʌʃ/ **1** *n.* Schwall, *der*
2 *v.i.* **(a)** strömen; **~ out** herausströmen
(b) (fig.: enthuse) schwärmen
'gushing *adj.* **(a)** reißend ‹*Strom*›
(b) (effusive) exaltiert
gust /gʌst/ *n.* **~ [of wind]** Bö[e], *die*
gusto /'gʌstəʊ/ *n.* Genuss, *der;* (vitality) Schwung, *der*

'gusty *adj.* böig
gut /gʌt/ [1] *n.* **(a)** (material) Darm, *der*
(b) *in pl.* (bowels) Eingeweide *Pl.*; Gedärme *Pl.*
(c) *in pl.* (coll.: courage) Schneid, *der* (ugs.)
[2] *v.t.*, **-tt-**: **(a)** (remove **~s** of) ausnehmen
(b) (remove fittings from) ausräumen; **the house was ~ted [by fire]** das Haus brannte aus
[3] *attrib. adj.* **~ feeling** instinktives Gefühl; **have a ~ feeling that ...** es im Gefühl *od.* (salopp) Urin haben, dass ...
gutter /'gʌtə(r)/ *n.* (below edge of roof) Dachrinne, *die*; (at side of street) Rinnstein, *der*; Gosse, *die*
'guttering *n.* (on roof) Dachrinnen *Pl.*
gutter 'press *n.* Sensationspresse, *die*
guttural /'gʌtərl/ *adj.* guttural; kehlig
guy /gaɪ/ *n.* **(a)** (coll.: man) Typ, *der* (ugs.)
(b) *in pl.* (Amer.: everyone) **[listen,] you ~s!** [hört mal,] Kinder! (ugs.)
'guy rope *n.* Zelt[spann]leine, *die*
guzzle /'gʌzl/ [1] *v.t.* (eat) hinunterschlingen; (drink) hinuntergießen
[2] *v.i.* schlingen
gym /dʒɪm/ *n.* (coll.) **(a)** (gymnasium) Turnhalle, *die*
(b) (gymnastics) Turnen, *das*
gymnasium *n.* /dʒɪm'neɪzɪəm/ *n., pl.* **~s** *or* **gymnasia** /dʒɪm'neɪzɪə/ Turnhalle, *die*
gymnast /'dʒɪmnæst/ *n.* Turner, *der*/ Turnerin, *die*
gymnastic /dʒɪm'næstɪk/ *adj.* turnerisch ‹*Können*›; **~ equipment** Turngeräte *Pl.*
gymnastics /dʒɪm'næstɪks/ *n.* Gymnastik, *die*; (esp. with apparatus) Turnen, *das*
'gymslip *n.* Trägerrock, *der*
gynaecologist /gaɪnɪ'kɒlədʒɪst/ *n.* Frauenarzt, *der*/-ärztin, *die*
gynaecology /gaɪnɪ'kɒlədʒɪ/ *n.* Gynäkologie, *die*
gypsy, Gypsy /'dʒɪpsɪ/ *n.* Zigeuner, *der*/ Zigeunerin, *die*
gyrate /dʒaɪə'reɪt/ *v.i.* sich drehen

Hh

H¹, h /eɪtʃ/ *n.* H, h, *das*
haberdashery /'hæbədæʃərɪ/ *n.* (goods) Kurzwaren *Pl.*; (Amer.: menswear) Herrenmoden *Pl.*
habit /'hæbɪt/ *n.* **(a)** Gewohnheit, *die*; **good/bad ~**: gute/schlechte [An]gewohnheit; **get** *or* **fall into a** *or* **the ~ of doing sth.** [es] sich (*Dat.*) angewöhnen, etw. zu tun
(b) (coll.: addiction) Süchtigkeit, *die*
habitable /'hæbɪtəbl/ *adj.* bewohnbar
habitat /'hæbɪtæt/ *n.* Habitat, *das*
habitation /hæbɪ'teɪʃn/ *n.* **fit/unfit for human ~**: bewohnbar/unbewohnbar
habitual /hə'bɪtjʊəl/ *adj.* **(a)** gewohnt
(b) (given to habit) gewohnheitsmäßig; Gewohnheits‹*trinker*›
ha'bitually *adv.* (regularly) regelmäßig
hack¹ /hæk/ *v.t.* **(a)** hacken ‹*Holz*›; **~ sth. to bits** *or* **pieces** etw. in Stücke hacken
(b) (Comp.) eindringen in (+ *Akk.*) ‹*Computersystem*›; **~ into sth.** in etw. (*Akk.*) eindringen
▪ **hack 'off** *v.t.* abhacken
▪ **hack 'out** *v.t.* heraushauen (**from** aus)
hack² *n.* (derog.: writer) Schreiberling, *der*
hacker /'hækə(r)/ *n.* (Comp.) Hacker, *der*
hackneyed /'hæknɪd/ *adj.* abgegriffen; abgedroschen (ugs.)
'hacksaw *n.* [Metall]bügelsäge, *die*
had ▶ HAVE
haddock /'hædək/ *n., pl. same* Schellfisch, *der*
hadn't /'hædnt/ (coll.) = **had not;** ▶ HAVE
haemoglobin /hi:mə'gləʊbɪn/ *n.* Hämoglobin, *das*
haemophilia /hi:mə'fɪlɪə/ *n.* Hämophilie, *die* (fachspr.); Bluterkrankheit, *die*
haemophiliac /hi:mə'fɪlɪæk/ *n.* Bluter, *der*/Bluterin, *die*
haemorrhage /'hemərɪdʒ/ *n.* Blutung, *die*
haemorrhoid /'hemərɔɪd/ *n.* Hämorrhoide, *die*
hag /hæg/ *n.* [alte] Hexe
haggard /'hægəd/ *adj.* ausgezehrt; (with worry) abgehärmt
haggle /'hægl/ *v.i.* sich zanken (**over, about** wegen); (over price) feilschen (**over, about** um)
Hague /heɪg/ *pr. n.* **The ~**: Den Haag (*das*)
hail¹ /heɪl/ [1] *n.* Hagel, *der*
[2] *v.i.* **it ~s** *or* **is ~ing** es hagelt; **~ down** (fig.) niederprasseln (**on** auf + *Akk.*)
hail² *v.t.* **(a)** (call out to) anrufen; (signal to) anhalten ‹*Taxi*›
(b) (acclaim) zujubeln (+ *Dat.*); bejubeln (**as** als)
'hailstone *n.* Hagelkorn, *das*
hair /heə(r)/ *n.* **(a)** (one strand) Haar, *das*

(b) *collect.* Haar, *das;* Haare *Pl.; attrib.* Haar-; **have** *or* **get one's ~ done** sich (*Dat.*) das Haar *od.* die Haare machen lassen (ugs.)

hair: ~brush *n.* Haarbürste, *die;* **~ conditioner** *n.* Pflegespülung, *die;* **~ cream** *n.* Haarcreme, *die;* Pomade, *die;* **~ curler** *n.* Lockenwickler, *der;* **~cut** *n.* **(a)** (act) Haareschneiden, *das;* **go for/need a ~cut** zum Friseur gehen/müssen; **get/have a ~cut** sich (*Dat.*) die Haare schneiden lassen; **(b)** (style) Haarschnitt, *der;* **~do** *n.* (style) Frisur, *die;* **~dresser** *n.* Friseur, *der*/Friseurin, *die;* **go to the ~dresser's** zum Friseur gehen; **~ dye** *n.* Haarfärbemittel, *das;* **~grip** *n.* (Brit.) Haarklammer, *die;* **~line** *n.* **(a)** (edge of hair) Haaransatz, *der;* **his ~line is receding, he has a receding ~line** er bekommt eine Stirnglatze; **(b)** (crack) Haarriss; **~line fracture** (Med.) Fissur, *die;* **~pin** *n.* Haarnadel, *die;* **~pin 'bend** *n.* Haarnadelkurve, *die;* **~-raising** /'heəreɪzɪŋ/ *adj.* haarsträubend; **~spray** *n.* Haarspray, *das;* **~style** *n.* Frisur, *die*

'hairy *adj.* **(a)** behaart; flauschig ‹*Pullover, Teppich*›
(b) (coll.: difficult) haarig

hale /heɪl/ *adj.* **~ and hearty** gesund und munter

half /hɑːf/ [1] *n., pl.* **halves** /hɑːvz/ **(a)** Hälfte, *die;* **~ [of sth.]** die Hälfte [von etw.]; **~ of Europe** halb Europa; **one and a ~ hours, one hour and a ~:** anderthalb *od.* eineinhalb Stunden; **divide sth. in ~** *or* **into halves** etw. halbieren; **she is three and a ~:** sie ist dreieinhalb
(b) (Footb. etc.: period) Halbzeit, *die*
[2] *adj.* halb; **~ the house/books/time** die Hälfte des Hauses/der Bücher/der Zeit; **~ an hour** eine halbe Stunde
[3] *adv.* **(a)** zur Hälfte; halb ‹*schließen, aufessen, fertig, voll, geöffnet*›; (almost) fast ‹*ersticken, tot sein*›; **~ as much/many** halb so viel/viele; **only ~ hear what ...:** nur zum Teil hören, was ...
(b) ~ past *or* (coll.) **~** one/two/three *etc.* halb zwei/drei/vier *usw.*; **~ past twelve** halb eins

half: ~-'board *n.* Halbpension, *die;* **~-caste** *n.* Mischling, *der;* **~-'hearted** *adj.* halbherzig; **~-'hour** *n.* halbe Stunde; **~ 'mast** *n.* **be [flown] at ~ mast** auf Halbmast stehen; **~ 'moon** *n.* Halbmond, *der;* **~ note** *n.* (Amer. Mus.) halbe Note; **~-'price** [1] *n.* halber Preis; [2] *adj.* zum halben Preis *nachgestellt;* [3] *adv.* zum halben Preis; **~-'term** *n.* (Brit.) (holiday) **~-term [holiday/break]** Ferien in der Mitte des Trimesters; **~-'time** *n.* (Sport) Halbzeit, *die;* **~'way** [1] *adj.* **~way point** Mitte, *die;* [2] *adv.* die Hälfte des Weges ‹*begleiten, fahren*›; **~wit** *n.* Schwachkopf, *der;* (scatterbrain) Schussel, *der*

halibut /'hælɪbət/ *n., pl. same* Heilbutt, *der*

hall /hɔːl/ *n.* **(a)** Saal, *der;* (building) Halle, *die;* **school/church ~:** Aula, *die*/Gemeindehaus, *das*
(b) (entrance ~) Flur, *der*
(c) (Univ.) **~ [of residence]** Studentenwohnheim, *das*

'hallmark *n.* [Feingehalts]stempel, *der;* (fig.) Kennzeichen, *das*

hallo /hə'ləʊ/ *int.* **(a)** (to call attention) hallo
(b) (Brit.) ▶ HELLO

Hallowe'en /hæləʊ'iːn/ *n.* Halloween, *das; Abend vor Allerheiligen*

hallucination /həluːsɪ'neɪʃn/ *n.* Halluzination, *die*

hallucinogen /hə'luːsɪnədʒen/ *n.* (Med.) Halluzinogen, *das*

hallucinogenic /həluːsɪnə'dʒenɪk/ *adj.* (Med.) halluzinogen

'hallway *n.* Flur, *der*

halo /'heɪləʊ/ *n., pl.* **~es** Heiligenschein, *der*

halt /hɒlt, hɔːlt/ [1] *n.* **(a)** Pause, *die;* (interruption) Unterbrechung, *die;* **call a ~ to sth.** mit etw. Schluss machen
(b) (Brit. Railw.) Haltepunkt, *der*
[2] *v.i.* **(a)** stehen bleiben; ‹*Fahrer:*› anhalten; (for a rest) eine Pause machen; (esp. Mil.) Halt machen; **~, who goes there?** (Mil.) halt, wer da?
(b) (end) eingestellt werden
[3] *v.t.* anhalten; einstellen ‹*Projekt*›

'halting *adj.* schleppend; zögernd ‹*Antwort*›

halve /hɑːv/ *v.t.* halbieren

halves *pl. of* HALF

ham /hæm/ *n.* Schinken, *der*

hamburger /'hæmbɜːgə(r)/ *n.* Hacksteak, *das;* (in roll) Hamburger, *der*

hamlet /'hæmlɪt/ *n.* Weiler, *der*

hammer /'hæmə(r)/ [1] *n.* Hammer, *der*
[2] *v.t.* hämmern
[3] *v.i.* hämmern (**at** an + *Dat.*)

■ **hammer 'out** *v.t.* ausklopfen ‹*Delle, Beule*›; (fig.: devise) ausarbeiten

hammock /'hæmək/ *n.* Hängematte, *die*

hamper¹ /'hæmpə(r)/ *n.* [Deckel]korb, *der*

hamper² *v.t.* behindern

hamster /'hæmstə(r)/ *n.* Hamster, *der*

'hamstring [1] *n.* (Anat.) Kniesehne, *die*
[2] *vt.* (fig.) lähmen

hand /hænd/ [1] *n.* **(a)** Hand, *die;* **by ~** (manually) mit der *od.* von Hand; **give** *or* **lend [sb.] a ~ [with** *or* **in sth.]** [jmdm.] [bei etw.] helfen
(b) (share) **have a ~ in sth.** bei etw. seine Hände im Spiel haben
(c) (worker) Arbeiter, *der;* (Naut.: seaman) Matrose, *der*
(d) (of clock or watch) Zeiger, *der*
(e) at ~: in der Nähe; **on the one ~ ..., [but] on the other [~] ...:** einerseits ..., andererseits ...
(f) (Cards) Karte, *die*
[2] *v.t.* geben; ‹*Überbringer:*› übergeben ‹*Sendung, Lieferung*›

■ **hand 'in** *v.t.* abgeben (**to, at** bei); einreichen ‹*Petition*›

■ **hand 'out** *v.t.* austeilen

■ **hand 'over** *v.t.* übergeben (to *Dat.*)

hand: ~bag *n.* Handtasche, *die;* **~ baggage** *n.* Handgepäck, *das;* **~book** *n.* Handbuch, *das;* **~brake** *n.* Handbremse, *die;* **~cuff** 1 *n., usu. in pl.* Handschelle, *die;* 2 *v.t.* **~cuff sb.** jmdm. Handschellen anlegen

handful /'hændfʊl/ *n.* Handvoll, *die;* **be a ~:** (fig. coll.) einen ständig auf Trab halten (ugs.)

hand: ~ grenade *n.* Handgranate, *die;* **~gun** *n.* Faustfeuerwaffe, *die;* **~-held** *adj.* **~-held camera** Handkamera, *die*

handicap /'hændɪkæp/ 1 *n.* **(a)** (Sport, also fig.) Handikap, *das*
(b) (physical) Behinderung, *die*
2 *v.t.*, **-pp-** benachteiligen

handicapped /'hændɪkæpt/ *adj.* [**mentally/physically**] **~:** [geistig/körperlich] behindert

handicraft /'hændɪkrɑːft/ *n.* [Kunst]handwerk, *das;* (needlework, knitting, etc.) Handarbeit, *die*

handiwork /'hændɪwɜːk/ *n.* handwerkliche Arbeit; **it's all his own ~:** das hat er selbst gemacht

handkerchief /'hæŋkətʃɪf/ *n., pl.* **~s** *or* **handkerchieves** /'hæŋkətʃiːvz/ Taschentuch, *das*

handle /'hændl/ 1 *n.* Griff, *der;* (of door) Klinke, *die;* (of axe, brush, comb, broom, saucepan) Stiel, *der;* (of cup, jug) Henkel, *der*
2 *v.t.* **(a)** (touch, feel) anfassen
(b) (control) handhaben ‹*Fahrzeug, Flugzeug*›
(c) (deal/cope with) umgehen/fertig werden mit

'handlebars *n. pl.* Lenkstange, *die*

'handling charge /'hændlɪŋ/ *n.* (Commerc.) Bearbeitungsgebühr, *die*

hand: ~ lotion *n.* Handlotion, *die;* **~ luggage** *n.* Handgepäck, *das;* **~made** *adj.* handgearbeitet; **~over** *n.* Übergabe, *die;* **~-painted** *adj.* handbemalt; **~picked** *adj.* sorgfältig ausgewählt; **~s-free** *adj.* Freisprech‹*einrichtung, -betrieb*›; **~s-free kit** Freisprechanlage, *die;* Freisprecheinrichtung, *die;* **~shake** *n.* Händedruck, *der*

handsome /'hænsəm/ *adj.* gut aussehend

hand: ~s-'on *adj.* praktisch; **~stand** *n.* Handstand, *der;* **~ towel** *n.* [Hände]handtuch, *das;* **~writing** *n.* [Hand]schrift, *die;* **~written** *adj.* handgeschrieben; handschriftlich

handy /'hændɪ/ *adj.* greifbar; **keep/have sth. ~:** etw. greifbar haben

'handyman *n.* Handwerker, *der;* [**home**] **~:** Heimwerker, *der*

hang /hæŋ/ 1 *v.t.* **(a)** *p.t., p.p.* **hung** /hʌŋ/ hängen; aufhängen ‹*Bild, Gardinen*›; ankleben ‹*Tapete*›
(b) *p.t., p.p.* **hanged** (execute) hängen (**for** wegen); **~ oneself** sich erhängen
2 *v.i.*, **hung (a)** hängen; ‹*Kleid usw.:*› fallen
(b) (be executed) hängen
3 *n.* **get the ~ of sth.** (coll.) mit etw. klarkommen (ugs.)

■ **hang a'bout, hang a'round** *v.i.* **(a)** (loiter) herumlungern (salopp)
(b) (coll.: wait) warten

■ **hang 'on** *v.i.* **(a)** sich festhalten (**to** an + *Dat.*)
(b) (coll.: wait) warten
(c) ~ on to (coll.: keep) behalten

■ **hang 'out** 1 *v.t.* aufhängen ‹*Wäsche*›
2 *v.i.* **(a)** heraushängen
(b) (coll.) (live) wohnen; (be often present) sich herumtreiben (ugs.)

■ **hang 'up** *v.t.* 1 aufhängen
2 *v.i.* (Teleph.) auflegen

hangar /'hæŋə(r)/ *n.* Hangar, *der*

'hanger *n.* Bügel, *der*

hang: ~-glider *n.* Hängegleiter, *der;* Drachen, *der;* **~-glider pilot** Drachenflieger, *der*/-fliegerin, *die;* **~-gliding** *n.* Drachenfliegen, *das*

'hanging 1 *n.* (execution) Hinrichtung, *die* [durch den Strang]
2 *adj.* **~ basket** Hängekorb, *der*

hang: ~man /hæŋmən/ *n., pl.* **~men** /hæŋmən/ Henker, *der;* **~over** *n.* Kater, *der* (ugs.); **~-up** *n.* (coll.) Macke, *die* (ugs.)

hanker /'hæŋkə(r)/ *v.i.* **~ after** ein heftiges Verlangen haben nach

hanky /'hæŋkɪ/ *n.* (coll.) Taschentuch, *das*

haphazard /hæp'hæzəd/ *adj.*, **hap'hazardly** *adv.* willkürlich

happen /'hæpn/ *v.i.* geschehen; ‹*Vorhergesagtes:*› eintreffen; **~ to sb.** jmdm. passieren; **~ to do sth./be sb.** zufällig etw. tun/jmd. sein; **as it ~s** *or* **it so ~s I have ...:** zufällig habe ich ...

'happening *n.* Ereignis, *das*

happily /'hæpɪlɪ/ *adv.* **(a)** glücklich ‹*lächeln*›; vergnügt ‹*spielen, lachen*›
(b) (gladly) mit Vergnügen

happiness /'hæpɪnɪs/ *n.* ▶ HAPPY A: Glück, *das;* Heiterkeit, *die;* Zufriedenheit, *die*

happy /'hæpɪ/ *adj.* **(a)** (joyful) glücklich; heiter ‹*Bild, Veranlagung*›; erfreulich ‹*Erinnerung, Szene*›; froh ‹*Ereignis*›; (contented) zufrieden
(b) be ~ to do sth. (glad) etw. gern tun

happy: ~ 'ending *n.* Happyend, *das;* **~-go-'lucky** *adj.* sorglos

harass /'hærəs/ *v.t.* schikanieren

harassed /'hærəst/ *adj.* geplagt (**with** von); gequält ‹*Blick, Ausdruck*›

'harassment *n.* Schikanierung, *die;* **sexual ~:** [sexuelle] Belästigung

harbour (*Brit.; Amer.:* **harbor**) /'hɑːbə(r)/
1 *n.* Hafen, *der;* **in ~:** im Hafen
2 *v.t.* Unterschlupf gewähren (+ *Dat.*) ‹*Verbrecher, Flüchtling*›; hegen (geh.) ‹*Groll, Verdacht*›

hard /hɑːd/ 1 *adj.* **(a)** hart; fest ‹*Gelee*›; stark ‹*Regen*›; streng ‹*Frost, Winter*›; gesichert ‹*Beweis, Daten*›

(b) (difficult) schwer; **this is ~ to believe** das ist kaum zu glauben; **do sth. the ~ way** es sich (*Dat.*) bei etw. unnötig schwer machen
(c) (strenuous) hart
(d) (vigorous) kräftig ‹*Schlag, Stoß, Tritt*›
(e) (harsh) hart
2 *adv.* **(a)** (strenuously) hart ‹*arbeiten, trainieren*›; fleißig ‹*studieren, üben*›; genau ‹*überlegen*›; gut ‹*aufpassen, zuhören*›; **try ~:** sich sehr bemühen
(b) (vigorously) heftig; fest ‹*schlagen, drücken, klopfen*›
(c) (severely) hart; **be ~ up** knapp bei Kasse sein (ugs.); **feel ~ done by** sich schlecht behandelt fühlen

hard: ~back *n.* gebundene Ausgabe; **~board** *n.* Hartfaserplatte, *die;* **~-boiled** *adj.* **(a)** hart gekocht ‹*Ei*›; **(b)** (tough) hartgesotten; **~ 'cash** *n.* **in ~ cash** in bar ‹*bezahlen*›; **~ copy** *n.* (Comp.) Hardcopy, *die;* **~-core** *attrib. adj.* hart ‹*Pornographie*›; **~ court** *n.* (Tennis) Hartplatz, *der;* **~ 'currency** *n.* harte Währung; **~ 'disk** ▶ DISK A; **~ drug** *n.* harte Droge; **~-earned** *adj.* schwer verdient

harden /'hɑ:dn/ 1 *v.t.* härten; (fig.) abhärten (**to** gegen)
2 *v.i.* hart werden; (become confirmed) sich verhärten

hardened /'hɑ:dnd/ *adj.* abgehärtet (**to** gegen); hartgesotten ‹*Verbrecher*›

hard: ~ 'hat *n.* Schutzhelm, *der;* **~-headed** *adj.* nüchtern; **~-hearted** *adj.* hartherzig (**towards** gegenüber); **~-'hitting** *adj.* (fig.) aggressiv ‹*Rede, Politik, Kritik*›; **~ 'labour** *n.* Zwangsarbeit, *die*

hardly /'hɑ:dlɪ/ *adv.* kaum; **~ anyone** *or* **anybody/anything** fast niemand/nichts; **~ ever** so gut wie nie; **~ at all** fast überhaupt nicht

'hardness *n.* Härte, *die*

hard: ~ porn (coll.)**, ~ pornography** *ns.* harte Pornographie; harte Pornos *Pl.* (ugs.); **~ 'pressed** *adj.* hart bedrängt; **be ~ pressed** große Schwierigkeiten haben; **~ sell** *n.* aggressive Verkaufsmethoden *Pl.*

'hardship *n.* **(a)** Not, *die;* Elend, *das*
(b) (instance) Notlage, *die*

hard: ~ 'shoulder *n.* (Brit.) Standspur, *die;* **~ware** *n.* **(a)** (goods) Eisenwaren *Pl.; attrib.* Eisenwaren‹*geschäft*›; **(b)** (Comp.) Hardware, *die;* **~-wearing** *adj.* strapazierfähig; **~-working** *adj.* fleißig; **~wood** *n.* Hartholz, *das*

hardy /'hɑ:dɪ/ *adj.* abgehärtet; zäh ‹*Rasse*›; winterhart ‹*Pflanze*›

hare /heə(r)/ *n.* Hase, *der*

harem /'hɑ:ri:m, hɑ:'ri:m/ *n.* Harem, *der*

hark /hɑ:k/ *v.i.* **[just] ~ at him** hör ihn dir/hört ihn euch nur an!; **~ back to** zurückkommen auf (+ *Akk.*)

harm /hɑ:m/ 1 *n.* Schaden, *der;* **do sb. ~, do ~ to sb.** jmdm. schaden
2 *v.t.* etwas [zuleide] tun (+ *Dat.*); schaden (+ *Dat.*) ‹*Beziehungen, Land, Ruf*›

harmful /'hɑ:mfl/ *adj.* schädlich (**to** für)

'harmless *adj.* harmlos

harmonica /hɑ:'mɒnɪkə/ *n.* Mundharmonika, *die*

harmonious /hɑ:'məʊnɪəs/ *adj.* harmonisch

harmonize /'hɑ:mənaɪz/ 1 *v.t.* aufeinander abstimmen
2 *v.i.* harmonieren (**with** mit)

harmony /'hɑ:mənɪ/ *n.* Harmonie, *die;* **be in ~:** harmonieren

harness /'hɑ:nɪs/ 1 *n.* Geschirr, *das*
2 *v.t.* anschirren; (fig.) nutzen

harp /hɑ:p/ 1 *n.* Harfe, *die*
2 *v.i.* **~ on [about] sth.** immer wieder von etw. reden; (critically) auf etw. (*Dat.*) herumreiten (salopp)

harpoon /hɑ:'pu:n/ *n.* Harpune, *die*

harpsichord /'hɑ:psɪkɔ:d/ *n.* Cembalo, *das*

harrowing /'hærəʊɪŋ/ *adj.* entsetzlich; grauenhaft ‹*Anblick, Geschichte*›

harsh /hɑ:ʃ/ *adj.* **(a)** rau ‹*Gewebe, Klima*›; schrill ‹*Ton, Stimme*›; grell ‹*Licht*›; hart ‹*Bedingungen, Leben*›
(b) (excessively severe) [sehr] hart; [äußerst] streng ‹*Disziplin*›; rücksichtslos ‹*Tyrann, Herrscher, Politik*›

'harshly *adv.* [sehr] hart

harvest /'hɑ:vɪst/ 1 *n.* Ernte, *die*
2 *v.t.* ernten

harvest 'festival *n.* Erntedankfest, *das*

has ▶ HAVE

has-been /'hæzbi:n/ *n.* (coll.) **be a ~:** seine besten Jahre hinter sich haben

hash /hæʃ/ *n.* **(a)** (Cookery) Haschee, *das*
(b) make a ~ of sth. (coll.) etw. verpfuschen (ugs.)

'hash browns *n. pl.: Bratkartoffeln mit Zwiebeln;* ≈ Rösti mit Zwiebeln

hashish /'hæʃɪʃ/ *n.* Haschisch, *das*

hasn't /'hæznt/ = **has not;** ▶ HAVE

hassle /'hæsl/ (coll.) 1 *n.* Ärger, *der*
2 *v.t.* schikanieren

haste /heɪst/ *n.* Eile, *die;* (rush) Hast, *die;* **make ~:** sich beeilen

hasten /'heɪsn/ 1 *v.t.* beschleunigen
2 *v.i.* eilen

hastily /'heɪstɪlɪ/ *adv.* (hurriedly) eilig; (rashly) übereilt

hasty /'heɪstɪ/ *adj.* eilig; flüchtig ‹*Skizze, Blick*›; (rash) übereilt

hat /hæt/ *n.* Hut, *der*

hatch¹ /hætʃ/ *n.* Luke, *die;* (serving ~) Durchreiche, *die*

hatch² 1 *v.t.* ausbrüten
2 *v.i.* [aus]schlüpfen

■ **hatch 'out** 1 *v.i.* ausschlüpfen
2 *v.t.* ausbrüten

'hatchback *n.* (car) Schräghecklimousine, *die*
hatchet /ˈhætʃɪt/ *n.* Beil, *das;* **bury the ~** (fig.) das Kriegsbeil begraben
hate /heɪt/ [1] *n.* Hass, *der*
[2] *v.t.* hassen; **I ~ to say this** (coll.) ich sage das nicht gern
hateful /ˈheɪtfl/ *adj.* abscheulich
'hate mail *n.* hasserfüllte Briefe *Pl.*
'hatpin *n.* Hutnadel, *die*
hatred /ˈheɪtrɪd/ *n.* Hass, *der*
hat: ~stand *n.* Hutständer, *der;* **~ trick** *n.* Hattrick, *der*
haughty /ˈhɔːtɪ/ *adj.* hochmütig
haul /hɔːl/ [1] *v.i. & t.* ziehen
[2] *n.* **(a)** Ziehen, *das*
(b) (catch) Fang, *der;* (fig.) Beute, *die*
haulage /ˈhɔːlɪdʒ/ *n.* Transport, *der*
haunch /hɔːntʃ/ *n.* **sit on one's/its ~es** auf seinem Hinterteil sitzen
haunt /hɔːnt/ *v.t.* **~ a house/castle** in einem Haus/Schloss spuken; **a ~ed house** ein Haus, in dem es spukt
'haunting *adj.* sehnsüchtig
have [1] /hæv/ *v.t., pres.* **he has** /hæz/, *p.t. & p.p.* **had** /hæd/ haben; (obtain) bekommen; (take) nehmen; bekommen ‹*Kind*›; **~ breakfast/dinner/lunch** frühstücken/zu Abend/zu Mittag essen; **~ a cup of tea** eine Tasse Tee trinken; **~ sb. to stay** jmdn. zu Besuch haben; **you've had it now** (coll.) jetzt ist es aus (ugs.); **~ a game of football** Fußball spielen
[2] /həv, əv, *stressed* hæv/ *v. aux.*, **he has** /həz, əz, *stressed* hæz/, **had** /həd, əd, *stressed* hæd/ **I ~/I had read** ich habe/hatte gelesen; **I ~/I had gone** ich bin/war gegangen; **if I had known ...:** wenn ich gewusst hätte ...; **~ sth. made** etw. machen lassen; **~ to** müssen
■ **have 'on** *v.t.* **(a)** (wear) tragen
(b) (Brit. coll.: deceive) **~ sb. on** jmdn. auf den Arm nehmen (ugs.)
■ **have 'out** *v.t.* **(a) ~ a tooth/one's tonsils out** sich (*Dat.*) einen Zahn ziehen lassen/sich (*Dat.*) die Mandeln herausnehmen lassen
(b) ~ it out with sb. mit jmdm. offen sprechen
haven /ˈheɪvn/ *n.* geschützte Anlegestelle, *die;* (fig.) Zufluchtsort, *der*
haven't /ˈhævnt/ = **have not;** ▶ HAVE
haversack /ˈhævəsæk/ *n.* Brotbeutel, *der*
havoc /ˈhævək/ *n.* **(a)** (devastation) Verwüstungen *Pl.*; **cause** *or* **wreak ~:** Verwüstungen anrichten
(b) (confusion) Chaos; **play ~ with sth.** etw. völlig durcheinander bringen
hawk[1] /hɔːk/ *n.* Falke, *der*
hawk[2] *v.t.* hausieren mit
'hawker *n.* Hausierer, *der*/Hausiererin, *die*
hawthorn /ˈhɔːθɔːn/ *n.* (Bot.) (white) Weißdorn, *der;* (red) Rotdorn, *der*
hay /heɪ/ *n.* Heu, *das*
hay: ~ fever *n.* Heuschnupfen, *der;* **~making** *n.* Heuernte, *die;* **~stack** *n.* Heuschober, *der* (südd.); Heudieme, *die* (nordd.); **~wire** *adj.* (coll.) **go ~wire** ‹*Instrument:*› verrückt spielen (ugs.)
hazard /ˈhæzəd/ [1] *n.* Gefahr, *die*
[2] *v.t.* **~ a guess** es mit Raten probieren
'hazard lights *n. pl.* Warnblinkanlage, *die*
hazardous /ˈhæzədəs/ *adj.* gefährlich; **~ waste** Sondermüll, *der*
hazard 'warning lights ▶ HAZARD LIGHTS
haze /heɪz/ *n.* Dunst[schleier], *der*
hazel /ˈheɪzl/ *adj.* haselnussbraun
hazelnut /ˈheɪzlnʌt/ *n.* Haselnuss, *die*
hazy /ˈheɪzɪ/ *adj.* dunstig; (fig.) vage
HDTV *abbr.* – **high-definition television** HDTV
he /hɪ, *stressed* hiː/ *pron.* er
head /hed/ [1] *n.* **(a)** Kopf, *der;* **~ first** mit dem Kopf voran; **~ over heels** kopfüber; **keep/lose one's ~:** einen klaren Kopf behalten/den Kopf verlieren; **in one's ~:** im Kopf; **enter sb.'s ~:** jmdm. in den Sinn kommen; **use your ~:** gebrauch deinen Verstand; **a** *or* **per ~:** pro Kopf
(b) *in pl.* (on coin) **~s** Kopf; **~s or tails?** Kopf oder Zahl?
(c) (leader) Leiter, *der*/Leiterin, *die*
(d) (on beer) Blume, *die*
[2] *attrib. adj.* **~ waiter** Oberkellner, *der;* **~ office** Hauptverwaltung, *die;* **~ boy/girl** ≈ Schulsprecher, *der*/-sprecherin, *die* (*vom Lehrkörper eingesetzt*)
[3] *v.t.* **(a)** (stand at top of) anführen ‹*Liste*›; (lead) leiten; führen ‹*Bewegung*›
(b) (Football) köpfen
[4] *v.i.* steuern; **~ for London** ‹*Flugzeug, Schiff:*› Kurs auf London nehmen; ‹*Auto:*› in Richtung London fahren; **you're ~ing for trouble** du wirst Ärger bekommen
head: ~ache *n.* Kopfschmerzen *Pl.;* **~band** *n.* Stirnband, *das;* **~board** *n.* Kopfende, *das;* **~ count** *n.* Kopfzahl, *die*
'header *n.* (Footb.) Kopfball, *der*
'headgear *n.* Kopfbedeckung, *die*
'heading *n.* Überschrift, *die*
head: ~lamp *n.* Scheinwerfer, *der;* **~land** *n.* Landspitze, *die;* **~light** *n.* Scheinwerfer, *der;* **~line** *n.* Schlagzeile, *die;* **be ~line news, make [the] ~lines, hit the ~lines** Schlagzeilen machen; **~long** *adv.* kopfüber; **~'master** *n.* Schulleiter, *der;* **~'mistress** *n.* Schulleiterin, *die;* **~ 'office** *n.* Hauptsitz, *der;* **~-on** [1] /'--/ *adj.* frontal; Frontal‹*zusammenstoß*›; [2] /-'-/ *adv.* frontal; **~phones** *n. pl.* Kopfhörer, *der;* **~'quarters** *n. sing. or pl.* Hauptquartier, *das;* **~rest** *n.* Kopfstütze, *die;* **~room** *n.* [lichte] Höhe, *die;* **~scarf** *n.* Kopftuch, *das;* **~set** *n.* Kopfhörer, *der;* **~stone** *n.* **(a)** (gravestone) Grabstein, *der;* **(b)** (of building) Grundstein, *der;* (fig.) Grundpfeiler, *der;* **~strong** *adj.*

eigensinnig; ~ **'teacher** ▶ ~MASTER; ~MISTRESS; ~**way** *n.* **make ~way** Fortschritte machen; ~ **wind** *n.* Gegenwind, *der*

heady /'hedɪ/ *adj.* berauschend

heal /hi:l/ **1** *v.t.* heilen **2** *v.i.* ~ **[up]** [ver]heilen

healer /'hi:lə(r)/ *n.* (person) Heilkundige, *der/die*

health /helθ/ *n.* Gesundheit, *die;* **in good/very good ~:** bei guter/bester Gesundheit; **good** *or* **your ~!** auf deine Gesundheit!

health: ~ care *n.* Gesundheitsfürsorge, *die;* ~ **care worker** im Gesundheitswesen Beschäftigte, *der/die;* **inadequate ~ care** unzureichende medizinische Versorgung; ~ **centre** *n.* Poliklinik, *die;* ~ **certificate** *n.* Gesundheitszeugnis, *das;* ~ **check** *n.* Gesundheitsuntersuchung, *die;* ~ **farm** *n.* Gesundheitsfarm, *die* (ugs.); ~ **food** *n.* Reformhauskost, *die;* ~ **food shop** Reformhaus, *das;* ~ **hazard** *n.* Gesundheitsrisiko, *das*

healthily /'helθɪlɪ/ *adv.* gesund

health: ~ insurance *n.* Krankenversicherung, *die;* ~ **resort** *n.* Kurort, *der;* ~ **service** *n.* Gesundheitsdienst, *der;* ~ **visitor** *n.* Krankenschwester/-pfleger im Sozialdienst; ~ **warning** *n.* Warnhinweis, *der; Hinweis auf die Gesundheitsgefährdung*

healthy /'helθɪ/ *adj.* gesund

heap /hi:p/ **1** *n.* Haufen, *der;* ~**s of** (coll.) jede Menge (ugs.) **2** *v.t.* aufhäufen

hear /hɪə(r)/ **1** *v.t.,* **heard** /hɜ:d/ **(a)** hören **(b)** (understand) verstehen **2** *v.i.,* **heard: ~ about sb./sth.** von jmdm./etw. [etwas] hören; **he wouldn't ~ of it** er wollte nichts davon hören **3** *int.* **H~! H~!** bravo!; richtig!

■ **hear 'out** *v.t.* ausreden lassen

heard ▶ HEAR 1, 2

'hearing *n.* Gehör, *das;* **be hard of ~:** schwerhörig sein

'hearing aid *n.* Hörgerät, *das*

hearsay /'hɪəseɪ/ *n.* Gerücht, *das;* **it's only ~:** es ist nur ein Gerücht

hearse /hɜ:s/ *n.* Leichenwagen, *der*

heart /hɑ:t/ *n.* (also Cards) Herz, *das;* **by ~:** auswendig; **at ~:** im Grunde seines/ihres Herzens; **take/lose ~:** Mut schöpfen/verlieren; **my ~ sank** mein Mut sank; **the ~ of the matter** der wahre Kern der Sache; *see also* CLUB 1c

heart: ~ache *n.* [seelische] Qual; ~ **attack** *n.* Herzanfall, *der;* (fatal) Herzschlag, *der;* ~**beat** *n.* Herzschlag, *der;* ~**breaking** *adj.* herzzerreißend; ~**broken** *adj.* **she was ~broken** ihr Herz war gebrochen; ~**burn** *n.* Sodbrennen, *das;* ~ **disease** *n.* Herzkrankheiten *Pl.*

hearten /'hɑ:tn/ *v.t.* ermutigen

'heartening *adj.* ermutigend

heart: ~ failure *n.* Herzversagen, *das;* ~**felt** *adj.* tief empfunden ‹*Beileid*›; aufrichtig ‹*Dankbarkeit*›

hearth /hɑ:θ/ *n.: Platz vor dem Kamin*

'hearthrug *n.* Kaminvorleger, *der*

heartily /'hɑ:tɪlɪ/ *adv.* von Herzen; **eat ~:** tüchtig essen

'heartless *adj.* herzlos

heart: ~ rate *n.* Herzfrequenz, *die;* ~**-shaped** *adj.* herzförmig; ~**-throb** *n.* Idol, *das;* ~ **transplant** *n.* Herztransplantation, *die* (fachspr.); ~**-warming** *adj.* herzerfreuend

hearty /'hɑ:tɪ/ *adj.* herzlich; ungeteilt ‹*Zustimmung*›; herzhaft ‹*Mahlzeit*›

heat /hi:t/ **1** *n.* **(a)** (hotness) Hitze, *die* **(b)** (Phys.) Wärme, *die* **(c)** (Sport) Vorlauf, *der* **2** *v.t.* heizen

■ **heat 'up** *v.t.* heiß machen

'heated *adj.* (angry) hitzig

'heater *n.* Ofen, *der;* (for water) Boiler, *der*

heath /hi:θ/ *n.* Heide, *die*

heathen /'hi:ðn/ **1** *adj.* heidnisch **2** *n.* Heide, *der*/Heidin, *die*

heather /'heðə(r)/ *n.* Heidekraut, *das*

'heating *n.* Heizung, *die*

heat: ~proof *adj.* feuerfest; ~ **rash** *n.* Hitzebläschen *Pl.;* ~**-resistant** *adj.* hitzebeständig; ~**stroke** *n.* Hitzschlag, *der;* ~ **treatment** *n.* (Med.) Wärmebehandlung, *die;* ~**wave** *n.* Hitzewelle, *die*

heave /hi:v/ **1** *v.t.* **(a)** heben **(b)** (coll.: throw) schmeißen (ugs.) **(c)** ~ **a sigh** aufseufzen **2** *v.i.* (pull) ziehen **3** *n.* Zug, *der*

heaven /'hevn/ *n.* Himmel, *der;* **in ~:** im Himmel; **for H~'s sake!** um Gottes willen!

'heavenly *adj.* himmlisch

heavily /'hevɪlɪ/ *adj.* schwer; (to a great extent) stark; schwer ‹*bewaffnet*›; tief ‹*schlafen*›; dicht ‹*bevölkert*›; **smoke/drink ~:** ein starker Raucher/Trinker sein; **it rained/snowed ~:** es regnete/schneite stark

heavy /'hevɪ/ *adj.* schwer; unmäßig ‹*Trinken, Rauchen*›; **a ~ smoker/drinker** ein starker Raucher/Trinker; **be a ~ sleeper** sehr fest schlafen

heavy: ~-duty *adj.* strapazierfähig ‹*Kleidung, Material*›; schwer ‹*Werkzeug, Maschine*›; ~ **'goods vehicle** *n.* (Brit.) Schwerlastwagen, *der;* ~**-'handed** *adj.* (clumsy) ungeschickt ‹*Person*›; ~ **'industry** *n.* Schwerindustrie, *die;* ~ **'metal** *n.* **(a)** Schwermetall, *das;* **(b)** (Mus.) Heavy metal, *das;* ~**weight** *n.* Schwergewicht, *das*

Hebrew /'hi:bru:/ **1** *adj.* hebräisch **2** *n.* (language) Hebräisch, *das*

heckle /'hekl/ *v.t.* durch Zwischenrufe unterbrechen

heckler /'heklə(r)/ *n.* Zwischenrufer, *der*/ Zwischenruferin, *die*
hectic /'hektɪk/ *adj.* hektisch
he'd /hɪd, *stressed* hi:d/ **(a)** = **he had;** **(b)** = **he would**
hedge /hedʒ/ [1] *n.* Hecke, *die*
[2] *v.t.* **~ one's bets** (fig.) nicht alles auf eine Karte setzen
[3] *v.i.* sich nicht festlegen
'hedge clippers *n. pl.* Heckenschere, *die*
hedgehog /'hedʒhɒg/ *n.* Igel, *der*
'hedgerow *n.* Hecke, *die* [als Feldbegrenzung]
hedonism /'hi:dənɪzm/ *n.* Hedonismus, *der*
hedonist /'hi:dənɪst/ *n.* Hedonist, *der*/ Hedonistin, *die*
heed /hi:d/ [1] *v.t.* beachten; beherzigen ‹*Rat, Lektion*›; **~ the danger/risk** sich (*Dat.*) der Gefahr/des Risikos bewusst sein
[2] *n.* **give** *or* **pay ~ to, take ~ of** Beachtung schenken (+ *Dat.*)
'heedless *adj.* unachtsam; **be ~ of sth.** auf etw. (*Akk.*) nicht achten
heel /hi:l/ *n.* Ferse, *die;* (of shoe) Absatz, *der;* **Achilles' ~** (fig.) Achillesferse, *die;* **down at ~** (fig.) heruntergekommen; **take to one's ~s** Fersengeld geben (ugs.)
hefty /'heftɪ/ *adj.* kräftig; (heavy) schwer
height /haɪt/ *n.* **(a)** Höhe, *die;* (of person, animal, building) Größe, *die*
(b) (fig.: highest point) Höhepunkt, *der*
heighten /'haɪtn/ *v.t.* aufstocken; (fig.) verstärken
heir /eə(r)/ *n.* Erbe, *der*/Erbin, *die*
heiress /'eərɪs/ *n.* Erbin, *die*
heirloom /'eəlu:m/ *n.* Erbstück, *das*
held ▶ HOLD[2] 1, 2
helicopter /'helɪkɒptə(r)/ *n.* Hubschrauber, *der*
heliport /'helɪpɔ:t/ *n.* Heliport, *der*
helium /'hi:lɪəm/ *n.* Helium, *das*
hell /hel/ *n.* **(a)** Hölle, *die*
(b) (coll.) **[oh] ~!** verdammter Mist! (ugs.); **what the ~!** ach, zum Teufel! (ugs.); **run like ~:** wie der Teufel rennen (ugs.)
he'll /hɪl, *stressed* hi:l/ = **he will**
hello /hə'ləʊ, he'ləʊ/ *int.* (greeting) hallo; (surprise) holla
hell's 'angel *n.* Rocker, *der*
helm /helm/ *n.* (Naut.) Ruder, *das*
helmet /'helmɪt/ *n.* Helm, *der*
help /help/ [1] *v.t.* **(a) ~ sb. [to do sth.]** jmdm. helfen[, etw. zu tun]; **can I ~ you?** (in shop) was möchten Sie bitte?
(b) (serve) **~ oneself** sich bedienen; **~ oneself to sth.** sich (*Dat.*) etw. nehmen; (coll.: steal) etw. mitgehen lassen (ugs.)
(c) (avoid) **if I/you can ~ it** wenn es irgend zu vermeiden ist; (remedy) **I can't ~ it** ich kann nichts dafür (ugs.); **it can't be ~ed** es lässt sich nicht ändern
(d) (refrain from) **I can't ~ thinking** *or* **can't ~ but think that ...:** ich kann mir nicht helfen, ich glaube, ...; **I can't ~ laughing** ich muss einfach lachen
[2] *n.* Hilfe, *die;* **with the ~ of ...:** mit Hilfe ... (+ *Gen.*); **be of [some]/no/much ~ to sb.** jmdm. eine gewisse/keine/eine große Hilfe sein
■ **help 'out** [1] *v.i.* aushelfen
[2] *v.t.* **~ sb. out** jmdm. helfen
'help desk *n.* Help Desk, *das* (fachspr.); *Auskunftsstelle für Computerbenutzer*
'helper *n.* Helfer, *der*/Helferin, *die*
helpful /'helpfl/ *adj.* (willing) hilfsbereit; (useful) hilfreich; nützlich
'helping [1] *adj.* **lend [sb.] a ~ hand [with sth.]** (fig.) [jmdm.] [bei etw.] helfen
[2] *n.* Portion, *die*
'helpless *adj.*, **'helplessly** *adv.* hilflos
'helpline *n.* Hotline, *die*
helter-skelter /heltə'skeltə(r)/ *n.* [spiralförmige] Rutschbahn
hem /hem/ [1] *n.* Saum, *der*
[2] *v.t.*, **-mm-** säumen
■ **hem 'in** *v.t.* einschließen; **feel ~med in** sich eingeengt fühlen
hemisphere /'hemɪsfɪə(r)/ *n.* Halbkugel, *die*
'hemline *n.* Saum, *der*
hemo- (*Amer.*) ▶ HAEMO-
hemp /hemp/ *n.* Hanf, *der*
hen /hen/ *n.* Huhn, *das;* Henne, *die*
hence /hens/ *adv.* (therefore) daher
hence'forth *adv.* von nun an
henchman /'hentʃmən/ *n., pl.* **henchmen** /'hentʃmən/ Handlanger, *der*
hen: ~ party *n.* (coll.) [Damen]kränzchen, *das;* **~pecked** /'henpekt/ *adj.* **a ~ husband** ein Pantoffelheld, *der* (ugs.)
hepatitis /hepə'taɪtɪs/ *n.* (Med.) Leberentzündung, *die*
her[1] /hə(r), *stressed* hɜ:(r)/ *pron.* sie; *as indirect object* ihr; **it was ~:** sie wars
her[2] *poss. pron. attr.* ihr
herald /'herəld/ [1] *n.* Herold, *der*
[2] *v.t.* ankündigen
heraldic /he'rældɪk/ *adj.* heraldisch
heraldry /'herəldrɪ/ *n.* Heraldik, *die*
herb /hɜ:b/ *n.* Kraut, *das*
herbaceous /hɜ:'beɪʃəs/ *adj.* krautartig; **~ border** Staudenrabatte, *die*
herbal /'hɜ:bl/ *attrib. adj.* Kräuter-
herbivore /'hɜ:bɪvɔ:(r)/ *n.* Pflanzenfresser, *der*
'herb tea *n.* Kräuteraufguss, *der*
herd /hɜ:d/ [1] *n.* Herde, *die;* (of wild animals) Rudel, *das*
[2] *v.t.* **(a)** treiben; **~ people together** Menschen zusammenpferchen
(b) (tend) hüten
here /hɪə(r)/ [1] *adv.* **(a)** (in or at this place) hier; **down/in/up ~:** hier unten/drin/oben; **~ you are** (coll.: giving sth.) hier

(b) (to this place) hierher; **in[to] ~**: hierherein; **come/bring ~**: hierher kommen/bringen
[2] *int.* (attracting attention) he
here'by *adv.* (formal) hiermit
hereditary /hɪ'redɪtərɪ/ *adj.* **(a)** erblich ‹*Titel, Amt*›
(b) (Biol.) angeboren
heresy /'herɪsɪ/ *n.* Ketzerei, *die*
heretic /'herɪtɪk/ *n.* Ketzer, *der*/Ketzerin, *die*
heretical /hɪ'retɪkl/ *adj.* ketzerisch
here'with *adv.* in der Anlage
heritage /'herɪtɪdʒ/ *n.* Erbe, *das*
hermetic /hɜ:'metɪk/ *adj.* luftdicht
hermetically /hɜ:'metɪkəlɪ/ *adv.* hermetisch
hermit /'hɜ:mɪt/ *n.* Einsiedler, *der*/ Einsiedlerin, *die*
hernia /'hɜ:nɪə/ *n.* Bruch, *der*
hero /'hɪərəʊ/ *n., pl.* **~es** Held, *der*
heroic /hɪ'rəʊɪk/ *adj.* heldenhaft
heroin /'herəʊɪn/ *n.* Heroin, *das*
heroine /'herəʊɪn/ *n.* Heldin, *die*
heroism /'herəʊɪzm/ *n.* Heldentum, *das*
heron /'hern/ *n.* Reiher, *der*
herpes /'hɜ:pi:z/ *n.* (Med.) Herpes, *der*
herring /'herɪŋ/ *n.* Hering, *der*
hers /hɜ:z/ *poss. pron. pred.* ihrer/ihre/ihres; **the book is ~**: das Buch gehört ihr
her'self *pron.* **(a)** *emphat.* selbst; **[all] by ~**: [ganz] allein[e]
(b) *refl.* sich; allein[e] ‹*tun, wählen*›; **younger than/as heavy as ~**: jünger als/so schwer wie sie selbst
he's /hɪz, *stressed* hi:z/ **(a)** = **he is**;
(b) = **he has**
hesitant /'hezɪtənt/ *adj.* zögernd ‹*Reaktion*›; stockend ‹*Rede*›
hesitate /'hezɪteɪt/ *v.i.* zögern; (falter) ins Stocken geraten; **~ to do sth.** Bedenken haben, etw. zu tun
hesitation /hezɪ'teɪʃn/ *n.* **(a)** (indecision) Unentschlossenheit, *die;* **without ~**: ohne zu zögern
(b) (instance of faltering) Unsicherheit, *die*
(c) (reluctance) Bedenken *Pl.*
hetero /'hetərəʊ/ *n.* (coll.) *n.* Hetero *der/die*
heterosexual /hetərəʊ'seksjʊəl/ [1] *adj.* heterosexuell
[2] *n.* Heterosexuelle, *der/die*
het up /het 'ʌp/ *adj.* aufgeregt
hew /hju:/ *v.t., p.p.* **hewn** /hju:n/ *or* **hewed** /hju:d/ hacken ‹*Holz*›; losschlagen ‹*Kohle, Gestein*›
hewn ▶ HEW
hexagon /'heksəgən/ *n.* Sechseck, *das*
hey /heɪ/ *int.* he; **~ presto!** simsalabim!
heyday /'heɪdeɪ/ *n.* Blütezeit, *die*
HGV *abbr.* (Brit.) = **heavy goods vehicle**
hi /haɪ/ *int.* hallo (ugs.)
hiatus /haɪ'eɪtəs/ *n.* Unterbrechung, *die*
hibernate /'haɪbəneɪt/ *v.i.* Winterschlaf halten
hibernation /haɪbə'neɪʃn/ *n.* Winterschlaf, *der*
hiccup /'hɪkʌp/ [1] *n.* **(a)** Schluckauf, *der;* **have/get [the] ~s** den Schluckauf haben/ bekommen
(b) (fig.: stoppage) Störung, *die*
[2] *v.i.* schlucksen (ugs.)
hid ▶ HIDE[1]
hidden ▶ HIDE[1]
hide[1] /haɪd/ [1] *v.t.,* **hid** /hɪd/, **hidden** /'hɪdn/ **(a)** verstecken ‹*Gegenstand, Person usw.*› (**from** vor + *Dat.*); verbergen ‹*Gefühle, Sinn usw.*› (**from** vor + *Dat.*); verheimlichen ‹*Tatsache, Absicht usw.*› (**from** *Dat.*)
(b) (obscure) verdecken
[2] *v.i.,* **hid, hidden** sich verstecken (**from** vor + *Dat.*)
hide[2] *n.* Haut, *die;* (of furry animal) Fell, *das;* (dressed) Leder, *das*
hide-and-'seek *n.* Versteckspiel, *das;* **play ~**: Verstecken spielen
hideous /'hɪdɪəs/ *adj.* scheußlich
'hideout *n.* Versteck, *das*
hiding[1] /'haɪdɪŋ/ *n.* **go into ~**: sich verstecken; (to avoid police, public attention) untertauchen; **be in ~**: sich versteckt halten; (to avoid police, public attention) untergetaucht sein
hiding[2] *n.* (coll.: beating) Tracht Prügel; **give sb. a [good] ~**: jmdm. eine [ordentliche] Tracht Prügel verpassen (ugs.)
'hiding place *n.* Versteck, *das*
hierarchic /haɪə'rɑ:kɪk/, **hierarchical** /haɪə'rɑ:kɪkl/ *adj.* hierarchisch
hierarchy /'haɪərɑ:kɪ/ *n.* Hierarchie, *die*
hi-fi /'haɪfaɪ/ (coll.) [1] *adj.* Hi-Fi-
[2] *n.* Hi-Fi-Anlage, *die*
high /haɪ/ [1] *adj.* **(a)** hoch; groß ‹*Höhe*›; stark ‹*Wind*›
(b) (coll.: on a drug) high (ugs.)
(c) it's ~ time you left es ist höchste Zeit, dass du gehst
[2] *adv.* hoch; **search** *or* **look ~ and low** überall suchen
[3] *n.* **(a)** (**~est** level/figure) Höchststand, *der*
(b) (Meteorol.) Hoch, *das*
(c) (coll.: drug-induced euphoria) Rausch[zustand], *der;* **give sb. a ~** ‹*Droge:*› jmdn. high machen (ugs.)
high: ~brow [1] *n.* Intellektuelle, *der/die;* [2] *adj.* intellektuell ‹*Person, Gerede usw.*›; hochgestochen (abwertend) ‹*Person, Musik, Literatur usw.*›; **~ chair** *n.* Hochstuhl, *der;* **~-definition 'television** *n.* hoch auflösendes Fernsehen
higher edu'cation *n.* Hochschulbildung, *die*
high: ~ fi'nance *n.* Hochfinanz, *die;* **~-'flier, ~-'flyer** *n.* (successful person) Senkrechtstarter, *der;* (person with great

potential) Hochbegabte, *der/die;* **~ 'frequency** *n.* Hochfrequenz, *die;* **~-'handed** *adj.* selbstherrlich; **~-heeled** /haɪ'hi:ld/ *adj.* ‹*Schuhe*› mit hohen Absätzen; **~-income** *adj.* einkommensstark; **~ jump** *n.* Hochsprung, *der;* **~land** /'haɪlənd/ *n.* Hochland, *das;* **~light** [1] *n.* **(a)** Höhepunkt, *der;* **(b)** (bright area) Licht, *das;* [2] *v.t.,* **~lighted** ein Schlaglicht werfen auf (+ *Akk.*) ‹*Probleme usw.*›

'highly *adv.* sehr; hoch ‹*angesehen, bezahlt*›; hoch‹*interessant, -gebildet*›; leicht ‹*entzündlich*›; stark ‹*gewürzt*›; **think ~ of sb./sth.** eine hohe Meinung von jmdm./etw. haben; **speak ~ of sb./sth.** jmdn./etw. sehr loben

highly-strung /'haɪlɪstrʌŋ/ *adj* übererregbar

Highness /'haɪnɪs/ *n.* **His/her** *etc.* **~:** Seine/Ihre *usw.* Hoheit

high: ~-pitched /'haɪpɪtʃt/ *adj.* hoch ‹*Ton, Stimme*›; **~-powered** /'haɪpaʊəd/ *adj.* (forceful) dynamisch ‹*Geschäftsmann*›; **~ 'pressure** *n.* **(a)** (Meteorol.) Hochdruck, *der;* **(b)** (Mech. Engin.) Überdruck, *der;* **~-rise** *adj.* **~-rise building** Hochhaus, *das;* **~-rise block of flats/office block** Wohn-/Bürohochhaus, *das;* **~-risk** *attrib. adj.* risikoreich; Risiko‹*gruppe, -sportart*›; **a ~-risk investment** eine Geldanlage mit hohem Risiko; **~ school** *n.* ≈ Oberschule, *die;* **~ 'seas** *n. pl.* **the ~ seas** die hohe See; **~ season** *n.* Hochsaison, *die;* **~-speed** *adj.* **~-speed train** Hochgeschwindigkeitszug, *der;* **~ street** *n.* Hauptstraße, *die;* **~ 'tech** (coll.) ▶ ~ TECHNOLOGY; **~-tech** *adj.* (coll.) Hightech-; **~ tech'nology** *n.* Spitzentechnologie, *die;* Hochtechnologie, *die;* **~-'voltage** *adj.* Hochspannungs-; **~way** *n.* öffentliche Straße

hijack /'haɪdʒæk/ *v.t.* entführen

'hijacker *n.* Entführer, *der;* (of aircraft) Hijacker, *der*

hike /haɪk/ *n.* Wanderung, *die*

'hiker *n.* Wanderer, *der*/Wanderin, *die*

hilarious /hɪ'leərɪəs/ *adj.* urkomisch

hill /hɪl/ *n.* Hügel, *der;* (higher) Berg, *der;* (slope) Hang, *der*

hill: ~billy /'hɪlbɪlɪ/ *n.* (Amer.) Hinterwäldler, *der*/Hinterwäldlerin, *die;* **~side** *n.* Hang, *der;* **~top** *n.* [Berg]gipfel, *der*

'hilly *adj.* hüg[e]lig

hilt /hɪlt/ *n.* Griff, *der;* **[up] to the ~** (fig.) voll und ganz

him /ɪm, *stressed* hɪm/ *pron.* ihn; *as indirect object* ihm; **it was ~:** er war's

Himalayas /hɪmə'leɪəz/ *pr. n. pl.* Himalaya, *der*

him'self *pron.* **(a)** *emphat.* selbst **(b)** *refl.* sich. *See also* HERSELF

hind /haɪnd/ *adj.* hinter...; **~ legs** Hinterbeine *Pl.*

hinder /'hɪndə(r)/ *v.t.* (impede) behindern; (delay) verzögern ‹*Vollendung einer Arbeit, Vorgang*›; aufhalten ‹*Person*›; **~ sb. from doing sth.** jmdn. daran hindern, etw. zu tun

'hindquarters *n. pl.* Hinterteil, *das*

hindrance /'hɪndrəns/ *n.* Hindernis, *das* **(to** für)

'hindsight *n.* **with [the benefit of] ~:** im Nachhinein

Hindu /'hɪndu:, hɪn'du:/ [1] *n.* Hindu, *der* [2] *adj.* hinduistisch; Hindu‹*gott, -tempel*›

Hinduism /'hɪndu:ɪzm/ *n.* Hinduismus, *der*

hinge /hɪndʒ/ [1] *n.* Scharnier, *das* [2] *v.t.* mit Scharnieren versehen [3] *v.i.* (depend) abhängen (**[up]on** von)

hint /hɪnt/ [1] *n.* **(a)** (suggestion) Wink, *der* **(b)** (slight trace) Spur, *die* (**of** von); **the ~/no ~ of a smile** der Anflug/nicht die Spur eines Lächelns **(c)** (information) Tipp, *der* (**on** für) [2] *v.i.* **~ at** andeuten

hip /hɪp/ *n.* Hüfte, *die*

hip: ~ bone *n.* Hüftbein, *das;* **~ flask** *n.* Taschenflasche, *die;* **~ joint** *n.* Hüftgelenk, *das*

hippie /'hɪpɪ/ *n.* (coll.) Hippie, *der*

hippopotamus /hɪpə'pɒtəməs/ *n.* Nilpferd, *das*

hippy ▶ HIPPIE

hire /haɪə(r)/ [1] *n.* Mieten, *das;* **be on ~ [to sb.]** [an jmdn.] vermietet sein; **for ~:** zu vermieten [2] *v.t.* **(a)** (employ) anwerben; engagieren ‹*Anwalt, Berater usw.*› **(b)** (obtain use of) mieten; **~ sth. from sb.** etw. bei jmdm. mieten **(c)** (grant use of) **~ [out]** vermieten; **~ sth. [out] to sb.** etw. jmdm. *od.* an jmdn. vermieten

hire: ~ car *n.* Mietwagen, *der;* **~ 'purchase** *n.* (Brit.) Ratenkauf, *der; attrib.* Raten-; **pay for/buy sth. on ~ purchase** etw. in Raten bezahlen/auf Raten kaufen

his /ɪz, *stressed* hɪz/ *poss. pron.* **(a)** *attrib.* sein **(b)** *pred.* seiner/seine/sein[e]s; *see also* HERS

hiss /hɪs/ [1] *n.* Zischen, *das* [2] *v.i.* zischen

historian /hɪ'stɔ:rɪən/ *n.* Historiker, *der*/Historikerin, *die*

historic /hɪ'stɒrɪk/ *adj.* historisch

historical /hɪ'stɒrɪkl/ *adj.* historisch; geschichtlich ‹*Belege, Hintergrund*›

history /'hɪstərɪ/ *n.* Geschichte, *die*

hit /hɪt/ [1] *v.t.,* **-tt-, hit** schlagen; (with missile) treffen; ‹*Geschoss, Ball usw.*:› treffen; ‹*Fahrzeug*:› prallen gegen; ‹*Schiff*:› laufen gegen; **~ one's head on sth.** mit dem Kopf gegen etw. stoßen; **~ it off with sb.** gut mit jmdm. auskommen [2] *v.i.,* **-tt-, hit** schlagen

···>

3 *n.* **(a)** (blow) Schlag, *der;* (shot or bomb striking target) Treffer, *der*
(b) (success) Erfolg, *der;* (in entertainment) Schlager, *der;* Hit, *der* (ugs.)
■ **hit 'back** *v.t. & i.* zurückschlagen
■ **'hit [up]on** *v.t.* kommen auf (+ *Akk.*) ‹*Idee*›; finden ‹*richtige Antwort, Methode*›

hit-and-'run *adj.* unfallflüchtig ‹*Fahrer*›; ~ **accident** Unfall mit Fahrerflucht

hitch /hɪtʃ/ 1 *v.t.* **(a)** binden ‹*Seil*› **(round** um + *Akk.*); [an]koppeln ‹*Anhänger usw.*› **(to** an + *Akk.*); spannen ‹*Zugtier usw.*› **(to** vor + *Akk.*)
(b) ~ **a lift** *or* **ride** (coll.) per Anhalter fahren
2 *n.* (problem) Problem, *das*
■ **hitch 'up** *v.t.* hochheben ‹*Rock*›

'hitch-hike *v.i.* per Anhalter fahren

'hitch-hiker *n.* Anhalter, *der*/Anhalterin, *die*

hit: ~ **man** *n.* (Amer.) Killer, *der* (salopp); ~**-or-'miss** *adj.* (coll.: random) unsicher, unzuverlässig ‹*Methode*›; ~ **parade** *n.* Hitparade, *die;* ~ **'record** *n.* Hit, *der* (ugs.)

HIV *abbr.* = **human immunodeficiency virus** HIV; ~**-positive/-negative** HIV-positiv/-negativ

hive /haɪv/ *n.* [Bienen]stock, *der*

HMS *abbr.* (Brit.) = **Her/His Majesty's Ship** H.M.S.

hoard /hɔːd/ 1 *n.* Vorrat, *der*
2 *v.t.* ~ **[up]** horten; hamstern ‹*Lebensmittel*›

hoarding /'hɔːdɪŋ/ *n.* (fence) Bauzaun, *der;* (Brit.: for advertisements) Reklamewand, *die*

hoar frost /'hɔːfrɒst/ *n.* [Rau]reif, *der*

hoarse /hɔːs/ *adj.* heiser

hoax /həʊks/ 1 *v.t.* anführen (ugs.); foppen
2 *n.* (deception) Schwindel, *der;* (practical joke) Streich, *der;* (false alarm) blinder Alarm

hob /hɒb/ *n.* [Koch]platte, *die*

hobble /'hɒbl/ *v.i.* ~ **[about]** [herum]humpeln

hobby /'hɒbɪ/ *n.* Hobby, *das*

'hobby horse *n.* Steckenpferd, *das*

hobnailed /'hɒbneɪld/ *adj.* Nagel‹*schuh, -stiefel*›

hobo /'həʊbəʊ/ *n., pl.* **-es** (Amer.) Landstreicher, *der*/-streicherin, *die*

hockey /'hɒkɪ/ *n.* Hockey, *das*

'hockey stick *n.* Hockeyschläger, *der*

hoe /həʊ/ 1 *n.* Hacke, *die*
2 *v.t. & i.* hacken

hog /hɒg/ 1 *n.* [Mast]schwein
2 *v.t.,* **-gg-** (coll.) mit Beschlag belegen

hoist /hɔɪst/ 1 *v.t.* hochziehen, hissen ‹*Flagge usw.*›; hieven ‹*Last*›; setzen ‹*Segel*›
2 *n.* [Lasten]aufzug, *der*

hold¹ /həʊld/ *n.* (of ship) Laderaum, *der;* (of aircraft) Frachtraum, *der*

hold² 1 *v.t.,* **held** /held/ **(a)** halten; (carry) tragen; (keep fast) festhalten; ~ **the door open for sb.** jmdm. die Tür aufhalten; ~ **sth. in place** etw. halten
(b) (contain) enthalten; (be able to contain) fassen ‹*Liter, Personen usw.*›
(c) (possess) besitzen; haben
(d) (keep possession of) halten ‹*Stützpunkt, Stadt, Stellung*›; ~ **the line** (Teleph.) am Apparat bleiben; ~ **one's own** sich behaupten
(e) (cause to take place) stattfinden lassen; abhalten ‹*Veranstaltung, Konferenz, Gottesdienst, Sitzung*›; veranstalten ‹*Festival, Auktion*›; austragen ‹*Meisterschaften*›; führen ‹*Unterhaltung, Gespräch*›; durchführen ‹*Untersuchung*›; halten ‹*Vortrag, Rede*›
(f) (think, believe) ~ **a view** *or* **an opinion** eine Ansicht haben **(on** über + *Akk.*); ~ **that ...:** der Ansicht sein, dass ...; ~ **oneself responsible for sth.** sich für etw. verantwortlich fühlen; ~ **sth. against sb.** jmdm. etw. vorwerfen
2 *v.i.,* **held** halten; ‹*Wetter:*› sich halten
3 *n.* **(a)** (grasp) Griff, *der;* **grab** *or* **seize** ~ **of sth.** etw. ergreifen; **get** *or* **lay** *or* **take** ~ **of sth.** etw. fassen *od.* packen; **keep** ~ **of sth.** etw. festhalten; **get** ~ **of sth.** (fig.) etw. auftreiben; **get** ~ **of sb.** (fig.) jmdn. erreichen
(b) (influence) Einfluss, *der* **(on, over** auf + *Akk.*)
(c) (Sport) Griff, *der*
■ **hold 'back** 1 *v.t.* zurückhalten
2 *v.i.* zögern
■ **hold 'on** 1 *v.t.* [fest]halten
2 *v.i.* **(a)** sich festhalten; ~ **on to** sich festhalten an (+ *Dat.*); (keep) behalten
(b) (coll.: wait) warten
■ **hold 'out** 1 *v.t.* ausstrecken ‹*Hand, Arm usw.*›; hinhalten ‹*Tasse, Teller*›
2 *v.i.* (resist) sich halten
■ **hold 'up** *v.t.* **(a)** (raise) hochhalten; heben ‹*Hand, Kopf*›
(b) (delay) aufhalten
(c) (rob) überfallen
■ **'hold with** *v.t.* **not** ~ **with sth.** etw. ablehnen

'holdall *n.* Reisetasche, *die*

'holder *n.* **(a)** (of post, title) Inhaber, *der*/Inhaberin, *die*
(b) ‹*Zigaretten*›spitze, *die;* ‹*Papier-, Zahnputzglas*›halter, *der*

'hold-up *n.* **(a)** (robbery) [Raub]überfall, *der*
(b) (delay) Verzögerung, *die*

hole /həʊl/ *n.* Loch, *das;* (of fox, badger, rabbit) Bau, *der;* **pick** ~**s in** (fig.) zerpflücken (ugs.)

holiday /'hɒlɪdeɪ/ *n.* **(a)** [arbeits]freier Tag; (public ~) Feiertag, *der*
(b) *in sing. or pl.* (Brit.: vacation) Urlaub, *der;* (Sch.) [Schul]ferien *Pl.*

holiday: ~ **home** *n.* Feriendomizil, *das;* ~ **job** *n.* Ferienjob, *der;* ~**maker** *n.* Urlauber, *der*/Urlauberin, *die;* ~ **resort** *n.* Ferienort, *der;* ~ **season** *n.* Urlaubszeit, *die*

Holland /'hɒlənd/ *pr. n.* Holland (*das*)

hollow /'hɒləʊ/ [1] *adj.* hohl; eingefallen ‹*Wangen, Schläfen*›; (fig.) leer ‹*Versprechen*›
[2] *n.* [Boden]senke, *die*
[3] *v.t.* ~ **out** aushöhlen

holly /'hɒlɪ/ *n.* Stechpalme, *die*

holocaust /'hɒləkɔ:st/ *n.* (destruction) Massenvernichtung, *die;* **the H~**: der Holocaust

hologram /'hɒləgræm/ *n.* Hologramm, *der*

holster /'həʊlstə(r)/ *n.* [Pistolen]halfter, *die od. das*

holy /'həʊlɪ/ *adj.* heilig

Holy: H~ 'Bible *n.* Heilige Schrift; ~ **'Ghost** ▶ ~ SPIRIT; ~ **Land** *n.* **the ~ Land** das Heilige Land; ~ **'Spirit** *n.* Heiliger Geist

homage /'hɒmɪdʒ/ *n.* Huldigung, *die* (**to** an + *Akk.*); **pay** *or* **do ~ to sb./sth.** jmdm./einer Sache huldigen

home /həʊm/ [1] *n.* **(a)** Heim, *das;* (flat) Wohnung, *die;* (house) Haus, *das;* (household) [Eltern]haus, *das;* (native country) Heimat, *die;* **at ~**: zu Hause; **be/feel at ~** (fig.) sich wohl fühlen; **make yourself at ~**: fühl dich wie zu Hause
(b) (institution) Heim, *das*
[2] *adj.* **(a)** Haus-
(b) (Sport) Heim-; ~ **match** Heimspiel, *das*
[3] *adv.* nach Hause

home: ~ address *n.* Privatanschrift, *die;* ~ **'banking** *n.* Homebanking, *das;* **~-based** /'həʊmbeɪst/ *adj.* zu Hause arbeitend; **be ~-based** zu Hause arbeiten; seinen Arbeitsplatz zu Hause haben; **~coming** *n.* Heimkehr, *die;* ~ **com'puter** *n.* Heimcomputer, *der;* ~ **'ground** *n.* **on ~ ground** auf heimischem Boden; (fig.) zu Hause (ugs.); **~-grown** *adj.* selbst gezogen; **~land** *n.* Heimat, *die;* **~land security** (esp. Amer.) Heimatschutz, *der*

'homeless [1] *adj.* obdachlos
[2] *n. pl.* **the ~**: die Obdachlosen *Pl.*

'homelessness *n.* Obdachlosigkeit, *die*

homely /'həʊmlɪ/ *adj.* wohnlich ‹*Zimmer usw.*›; behaglich ‹*Atmosphäre*›

home: ~-made *adj.* selbst gemacht; selbst gebacken ‹*Brot*›; hausgemacht ‹*Lebensmittel*›; **H~ Office** *n.* (Brit.) Innenministerium, *das*

homeopathic *etc.* (*Amer.*) ▶ HOMOEO-

home: ~owner *n.* Eigenheimbesitzer, *der*/-besitzerin, *die;* ~ **page** *n.* (Comp.) Homepage, *die;* **H~ 'Secretary** *n.* (Brit.) Innenminister, *der;* ~ **'shopping** *n.* Teleshopping, *das;* **~sick** *adj.* heimwehkrank; **become/be ~sick** Heimweh bekommen/haben; **~sickness** *n.* Heimweh, *das;* ~ **'town** *n.* Heimatstadt, *die;* **~work** *n.* Hausaufgaben *Pl.;* **piece of ~work** Hausaufgabe, *die*

homicide /'hɒmɪsaɪd/ *n.* Tötung, *die;* (manslaughter) Totschlag, *der*

homoeopathic /həʊmɪə'pæθɪk, hɒmɪə'pæθɪk/ *adj.* homöopathisch

homoeopathy /həʊmɪ'ɒpəθɪ, hɒmɪ'ɒpəθɪ/ *n.* Homöopathie, *die*

homosexual /həʊməʊ'seksjʊəl/ [1] *adj.* homosexuell
[2] *n.* Homosexuelle, *der/die*

homosexu'ality *n.* Homosexualität, *die*

hone /həʊn/ *v.t.* wetzen

honest /'ɒnɪst/ *adj.* ehrlich

'honestly *adv.* ehrlich; redlich ‹*handeln*›; **~!** ehrlich!; (annoyed) also wirklich!

honesty /'ɒnɪstɪ/ *n.* Ehrlichkeit, *die*

honey /'hʌnɪ/ *n.* Honig, *der*

honey: ~ bee *n.* Honigbiene, *die;* **~comb** *n.* Honigwabe, *die;* **~moon** *n.* Flitterwochen *Pl.;* (journey) Hochzeitsreise, *die;* **~suckle** *n.* Geißblatt, *das*

honk /hɒŋk/ [1] *v.i.* ‹*Fahrzeug, Fahrer:*› hupen
[2] *n.* Hupen, *das*

honor, honorable (Amer.) ▶ HONOUR, HONOURABLE

honorary /'ɒnərərɪ/ *adj.* Ehren‹*mitglied, -präsident, -doktor, -bürger*›

honour /'ɒnə(r)/ (Brit.) [1] *n.* **(a)** Ehre, *die*
(b) (distinction) Auszeichnung, *die*
[2] *v.t.* ehren; (Commerc.) honorieren

honourable /'ɒnərəbl/ *adj.* (Brit.) ehrenwert (geh.)

'honours degree *n.* Examen mit Auszeichnung

hood /hʊd/ *n.* **(a)** Kapuze, *die*
(b) (Amer. Motor Veh.) Motorhaube, *die*
(c) (of pram) Verdeck, *das*

hoodlum /'hu:dləm/ *n.* Rowdy, *der*

hoodwink /'hʊdwɪŋk/ *v.t.* hinters Licht führen

hoof /hu:f/ *n., pl.* **~s** *or* **hooves** /hu:vz/ Huf, *der*

hook /hʊk/ [1] *n.* Haken, *der;* **by ~ or by crook** mit allen Mitteln
[2] *v.t.* **(a)** (grasp) mit Haken/mit einem Haken greifen
(b) (fasten) mit Haken/mit einem Haken befestigen (**to** an + *Dat.*)
(c) be ~ed [on sth.] (addicted) [von etw.] abhängig sein; (harmlessly) auf etw. (*Akk.*) stehen (ugs.)

■ **hook 'up** *v.t.* festhaken (**to** an + *Akk.*)

hooligan /'hu:lɪgən/ *n.* Rowdy, *der*

hooliganism /'hu:lɪgənɪzm/ *n.* Rowdytum, *das*

hoop /hu:p/ *n.* Reifen, *der*

hooray /hʊ'reɪ/ *int.* hurra

hoot /hu:t/ [1] *v.i.* **(a)** (call out) johlen
(b) ‹*Eule:*› schreien
(c) ‹*Fahrzeug, Fahrer:*› hupen
[2] *n.* **(a)** (shout) **~s of derision** verächtliches Gejohle
(b) (of owl) Schrei, *der*

⋯

'hooter *n.* (Brit.: siren) Sirene, *die*

hoover /'hu:və(r)/ (Brit.) **1** *n.* **(a) H~** ® [Hoover]staubsauger, *der*
(b) (made by any company) Staubsauger, *der*
2 *v.t.* staubsaugen

hooves *pl. of* HOOF

hop¹ /hɒp/ *n.* **(a)** (plant) Hopfen, *der*
(b) *in pl.* (Brewing) Hopfen, *der*

hop² **1** *v.i.*, **-pp-**: **(a)** hüpfen; ‹*Hase:*› hoppeln
(b) (fig. coll.) **~ out of bed** aus dem Bett springen; **~ into the car/on [to] the bus/train** sich ins Auto/in den Bus/Zug schwingen (ugs.)
2 *v.t.*, **-pp-** (Brit. coll.) **~ it** sich verziehen (ugs.)
3 *n.* **(a)** Hüpfer, *der*
(b) (Brit. coll.) **catch sb. on the ~:** jmdn. überraschen

hope /həʊp/ **1** *n.* Hoffnung, *die;* **sb.'s ~[s] of sth.** jmds. Hoffnung auf etw. (*Akk.*); **raise sb.'s ~s** jmdm. Hoffnung machen
2 *v.i. & t.* hoffen (**for** auf + *Akk.*); **I ~ so/not** hoffentlich/hoffentlich nicht; **~ for the best** das Beste hoffen

hopeful /'həʊpfl/ *adj.* **(a)** zuversichtlich; **be ~ of sth./of doing sth.** auf etw. (*Akk.*) hoffen/ voller Hoffnung sein, etw. zu tun
(b) (promising) viel versprechend

'hopefully *adv.* **(a)** (expectantly) voller Hoffnung
(b) (coll.: it is hoped that) hoffentlich

'hopeless *adj.*, **'hopelessly** *adv.* **(a)** hoffnungslos
(b) (inadequate) miserabel

'hopelessness *n.* Hoffnungslosigkeit, *die*

hopscotch /'hɒpskɒtʃ/ *n.* Himmel-und-Hölle-Spiel, *das*

horde /hɔ:d/ *n.* Horde, *die*

horizon /hə'raɪzn/ *n.* Horizont, *der;* **on the ~:** am Horizont; (fig.) **broaden one's/sb.'s ~s** seinen/jmds. Horizont erweitern

horizontal /hɒrɪ'zɒntl/ *adj.* horizontal; waagerecht

hori'zontally *adv.* horizontal; (flat) waagerecht

hormone /'hɔ:məʊn/ *n.* Hormon, *das*

hormone re'placement therapy *n.* Hormonsubstitutionstherapie, *die*

horn /hɔ:n/ *n.* Horn, *das;* (of vehicle) Hupe, *die*

hornet /'hɔ:nɪt/ *n.* Hornisse, *die*

'horny *adj.* (hard) hornig

horoscope /'hɒrəskəʊp/ *n.* Horoskop, *das*

horrendous /hə'rendəs/ *adj.* (coll.) schrecklich (ugs.)

horrible /'hɒrɪbl/ *adj.* grauenhaft; grausig ‹*Monster*›; grauenvoll ‹*Verbrechen, Albtraum*›

horrid /'hɒrɪd/ *adj.* scheußlich

horrific /hə'rɪfɪk/ *adj.* schrecklich

horrify /'hɒrɪfaɪ/ *v.t.* mit Schrecken erfüllen; **be horrified** (shocked, scandalized) entsetzt sein (**at, by** über + *Akk.*)

'horrifying *adj.* grauenhaft

horror /'hɒrə(r)/ **1** *n.* Entsetzen, *das* (**at** über + *Akk.*); (repugnance) Grausen, *das;* (horrifying thing) Gräuel, *der*
2 *attrib. adj.* Horror-; **~ film/story** Horrorfilm, *der*/-geschichte, *die*

'horror-stricken, 'horror-struck *adjs.* von Entsetzen gepackt

hors d'œuvre /ɔ:'dɜ:vr/ *n.* Horsd'œuvre, *das;* ≈ Vorspeise, *die*

horse /hɔ:s/ *n.* Pferd, *das*

horse: ~back *n.* **on ~back** zu Pferd; **~ 'chestnut** *n.* Rosskastanie, *die;* **~fly** *n.* Pferdebremse, *die;* **~man** /'hɔ:smən/ *n., pl.* **~men** /'hɔ:smən/ ([skilled] rider) [guter] Reiter; **~play** *n.* Balgerei, *die;* **~power** *n., pl. same* (Mech.) Pferdestärke, *die;* **~racing** *n.* Pferderennsport, *der;* **~radish** *n.* Meerrettich, *der;* **~shoe** *n.* Hufeisen, *das*

horticulture /'hɔ:tɪkʌltʃə(r)/ *n.* Gartenbau, *der*

hose /həʊz/**, 'hosepipe** *ns.* Schlauch, *der*

hospice /'hɒspɪs/ *n.* (Brit.: for the terminally ill) Sterbehospiz, *das*

hospitable /hɒ'spɪtəbl/ *adj.* gastfreundlich ‹*Person, Wesensart*›; **be ~ to sb.** jmdn. gastfreundlich aufnehmen

hospital /'hɒspɪtl/ *n.* Krankenhaus, *das;* **in ~** (Brit.), **in the ~** (Amer.) im Krankenhaus

'hospital bed *n.* Krankenhausbett, *das*

hospitality /hɒspɪ'tælɪtɪ/ *n.* Gastfreundschaft, *die*

'hospital nurse *n.* ≈ Krankenschwester, *die*

host¹ /həʊst/ *n.* (large number) Menge, *die;* **a ~ of people/children** eine Menge Leute/eine Schar von Kindern

host² *n.* Gastgeber, *der*/-geberin, *die*

hostage /'hɒstɪdʒ/ *n.* Geisel, *die*

'host country *n.* Gastland, *das*

hostel /'hɒstl/ *n.* (Brit.) Wohnheim, *das*

hostess /'həʊstɪs/ *n.* Gastgeberin, *die;* (in nightclub) Animierdame, *die*

hostile /'hɒstaɪl/ *adj.* **(a)** feindlich
(b) (unfriendly) feindselig (**to[wards]** gegenüber); **be ~ to sth.** etw. ablehnen

hostility /hɒ'stɪlɪtɪ/ *n.* Feindseligkeit, *die*

hot /hɒt/ *adj.* **(a)** heiß; warm ‹*Mahlzeit, Essen*›; **I am/feel ~:** mir ist heiß
(b) (pungent) scharf ‹*Gewürz, Senf usw.*›; scharf gewürzt ‹*Essen*›
(c) (recent) noch warm ‹*Nachrichten*›
(d) (coll.: illegally obtained) heiß ‹*Ware, Geld*›

hot: ~ 'air *n.* (coll.) leeres Gerede (ugs.); **~bed** *n.* (Hort.) Mistbeet, *das;* (fig.: of vice, corruption) Brutstätte, *die* (**of** für)

hotchpotch /'hɒtʃpɒtʃ/ *n.* Mischmasch, *der* (ugs.) (**of** aus)

hot: ~-desking *n.: Mehrfachnutzung von Arbeitsplätzen;* **~ dog** *n.* (coll.) Hotdog, *der od. das*

hotel /həʊ'tel/ *n.* Hotel, *das*

hotelier /hə'telɪə(r)/ *n.* Hotelier, *der*

ho'tel room *n.* Hotelzimmer, *das*

hot: ~head *n.* Hitzkopf, *der;* **~house** *n.* Treibhaus, *das;* **~ line** *n.* Hotline, *die;* (Polit.) heißer Draht

'hotly *adv.* heftig

hot: ~plate *n.* Kochplatte, *die;* (to keep food ~) Warmhalteplatte, *die;* **~ seat** *n.* (coll.) **be in the ~ seat** den Kopf hinhalten müssen (ugs.); **~-tempered** *adj.* heißblütig; **~-'water bottle** *n.* Wärmflasche, *die*

hound /haʊnd/ [1] *n.* Jagdhund, *der* [2] *v.t.* verfolgen

hour /'aʊə(r)/ *n.* **(a)** Stunde, *die;* **half an ~:** eine halbe Stunde; **an ~ and a half** anderthalb Stunden; **be paid by the ~:** stundenweise bezahlt werden; **the 24-~ clock** die Vierundzwanzigstundenuhr **(b)** (time o'clock) Zeit, *die;* **the small ~s [of the morning]** die frühen Morgenstunden; **0100/0200/1700/1800 ~s** (on 24-~ clock) 1.00/2.00/17.00/18.00 Uhr

'hourly *adj., adv.* stündlich; **be paid ~:** stundenweise bezahlt werden

house [1] /haʊs/ *n., pl.* **~s** /'haʊzɪz/ Haus, *das;* **to/at my ~:** zu mir [nach Hause]/bei mir [zu Hause] [2] /haʊz/ *v.t.* **(a)** ein Heim geben (+ *Dat.*) **(b)** (keep, store) unterbringen

house/haʊs/**: ~ arrest** *n.* Hausarrest, *der;* **~boat** *n.* Hausboot, *das;* **~-bound** *adj.* ans Haus gefesselt

household /'haʊshəʊld/ *n.* Haushalt, *der; attrib.* Haushalts-

'householder *n.* Wohnungsinhaber, *der/* -inhaberin, *die*

household 'name *n.* geläufiger Name; **be a ~:** ein Begriff sein

house /haʊs/**: ~ husband** *n.* Hausmann, *der;* **~keeper** *n.* Haushälterin, *die;* **~keeping** *n.* Hauswirtschaft, *die;* **~ plant** *n.* Zimmerpflanze, *die;* **~-proud** *adj.* **he/she is ~-proud** Ordnung und Sauberkeit [im Haushalt] gehen ihm/ihr über alles; **~-sit** *v.i.* das Haus hüten; **~-sitter** *n.* Housesitter, *der* (ugs.); *Person, die für jemanden das Haus hütet;* **~-trained** *adj.* (Brit.) stubenrein ‹*Hund, Katze*›; **~-warming** *n.* **~-warming [party]** Einzugsfeier, *die;* **~wife** *n.* Hausfrau, *die;* **~work** *n.* Hausarbeit, *die*

housing /'haʊzɪŋ/ *n.* (dwellings) Wohnungen *Pl.*; (provision of dwellings) Wohnungsbeschaffung, *die*

housing: ~ association *n.* (Brit.) Gesellschaft für sozialen Wohnungsbau; **~ benefit** *n.* (Brit.) Wohngeld, *das;* **~ estate** *n.* (Brit.) Wohnsiedlung, *die;* **~ shortage** *n.* Wohnraummangel, *der*

hovel /'hɒvl/ *n.* [armselige] Hütte

hover /'hɒvə(r)/ *v.i.* **(a)** schweben **(b)** (linger) sich herumdrücken (ugs.)

'hovercraft *n., pl. same* Hovercraft, *das;* Luftkissenfahrzeug, *das*

'hover mower *n.* Luftkissenmäher, *der*

how /haʊ/ *adv.* wie; **learn ~ to ride a bike/swim** Rad fahren/schwimmen lernen; **~ 'are you?** wie geht es dir?; (greeting) guten Morgen/Tag/Abend!; **~ do you 'do?** (formal) guten Morgen/Tag/Abend!; **~ much?** wieviel?; **~ many?** wie viel?; wie viele?

however /haʊ'evə(r)/ *adv.* **(a)** wie ... auch **(b)** (nevertheless) jedoch; aber

howl /haʊl/ [1] *n.* (of animal) Heulen, *das;* (of distress) Schrei, *der;* **~s of laughter** brüllendes Gelächter [2] *v.i.* ‹*Tier, Wind:*› heulen; (with distress) schreien [3] *v.t.* [hinaus]schreien

howler /'haʊlə(r)/ *n.* (coll.: blunder) Schnitzer, *der* (ugs.)

HP *abbr.* (Brit.) = **hire purchase**

HQ *abbr.* = **headquarters** HQ

HTML *abbr.* (Comp.) = **hypertext markup language** HTML

hub /hʌb/ *n.* [Rad]nabe, *die;* (fig.) Mittelpunkt, *der*

hubbub /'hʌbʌb/ *n.* Lärm, *der;* **a ~ of voices** ein Stimmengewirr

hub: ~cap *n.* Radkappe, *die;* **~ dynamo** *n.* Nabendynamo, *der;* **~ gear** *n.* Nabenschaltung, *die*

huddle /'hʌdl/ *v.i.* sich drängen; **~ together** sich zusammendrängen

■ **huddle 'up** *v.i.* (nestle up) sich zusammenkauern; (crowd together) sich [zusammen]drängen

hue[1] /hju:/ *n.* Farbton, *der*

hue[2] *n.* **~ and cry** lautes Geschrei; (protest) Gezeter, *das*

huff /hʌf/ [1] *v.i.* **~ and puff** schnaufen und keuchen [2] *n.* **in a ~:** beleidigt

hug /hʌg/ [1] *n.* Umarmung, *die;* **give sb. a ~:** jmdn. umarmen [2] *v.t.,* **-gg-** umarmen

huge /hju:dʒ/ *adj.* riesig; gewaltig ‹*Unterschied, Verbesserung, Interesse*›

hulking /'hʌlkɪŋ/ *adj.* (coll.) **~ great** klobig

hull /hʌl/ *n.* (Naut.) Schiffskörper, *der*

hum /hʌm/ [1] *v.i.,* **-mm-: (a)** summen; ‹*Maschine:*› brummen **(b) ~ and haw** (coll.) herumdrucksen (ugs.) [2] *v.t.,* **-mm-** summen [3] *n.* **(a)** Summen, *das;* (of machinery) Brummen, *das* **(b)** (of voices, conversation) Gemurmel, *das;* (of traffic) Brausen, *das*

human /'hju:mən/ [1] *adj.* menschlich; **the ~ race** die menschliche Rasse [2] *n.* Mensch, *der*

human 'being *n.* Mensch, *der*

humane /hju:'meɪn/ *adj.* human

humanitarian /hju:mænɪ'teərɪən/ *adj.* humanitär

humanity /hju:'mænɪtɪ/ *n.* **(a)** (mankind) Menschheit, *die;* (people collectively) Menschen *Pl.*
(b) (being humane) Humanität, *die*

human 'rights *n. pl.* Menschenrechte *Pl.;* **~ activist** Menschenrechtsaktivist, *der*/-aktivistin, *die;* **~ group** Menschenrechtsorganisation, *die*

humble /'hʌmbl/ [1] *adj.* **(a)** demütig
(b) (modest) bescheiden
(c) (low-ranking) einfach; niedrig ‹*Status, Rang*›
[2] *v.t.* **(a)** demütigen; **~ oneself** sich demütigen *od.* erniedrigen
(b) (defeat decisively) [vernichtend] schlagen

humbly /'hʌmblɪ/ *adv.* demütig

humdrum /'hʌmdrʌm/ *adj.* alltäglich; eintönig ‹*Leben*›

humid /'hju:mɪd/ *adj.* feucht

humidifier /hju:'mɪdɪfaɪə(r)/ *n.* Luftbefeuchter, *der*

humidify /hju:'mɪdɪfaɪ/ *v.t.* befeuchten

humidity /hju:'mɪdɪtɪ/ *n.* Feuchtigkeit, *die*

humiliate /hju:'mɪlɪeɪt/ *v.t.* demütigen

humiliation /hju:mɪlɪ'eɪʃn/ *n.* Demütigung, *die*

humility /hju:'mɪlɪtɪ/ *n.* Demut, *die*

humor (Amer.) ▶ HUMOUR

humorous /'hju:mərəs/ *adj.* lustig, komisch ‹*Geschichte, Name, Situation*›; witzig ‹*Bemerkung*›

humour /'hju:mə(r)/ (Brit.) [1] *n.* **(a)** Humor, *der;* **sense of ~:** Sinn für Humor; **have no sense of ~:** keinen Humor haben
(b) (mood) Laune, *die*
[2] *v.t.* **~ sb.** jmdm. seinen Willen lassen

hump /hʌmp/ [1] *n.* **(a)** (of person) Buckel, *der;* (of animal) Höcker, *der*
(b) (mound) Hügel, *der*
[2] *v.t.* (Brit. coll.: carry) schleppen

humpback 'bridge *n.* gewölbte Brücke

hunch¹ /hʌntʃ/ *v.t.* **~ [up]** hochziehen

hunch² *n.* (feeling) Gefühl, *das*

'hunchback *n.* (back) Buckel, *der;* (person) Bucklige, *der/die;* **be a ~:** einen Buckel haben

hundred /'hʌndrəd/ [1] *adj.* hundert; **a** *or* **one ~:** [ein]hundert; **two/several ~:** zweihundert/mehrere hundert; **a** *or* **one ~ and one** [ein]hundert[und]eins
[2] *n.* **(a)** (number) hundert; **a** *or* **one/two ~:** [ein]hundert/zweihundert
(b) (written figure; group) Hundert, *das*
(c) (indefinite amount) **~s** Hunderte. *See also* EIGHT

hundredth /'hʌndrədθ/ [1] *adj.* hundertst...; **a ~ part** ein Hundertstel
[2] *n.* (fraction) Hundertstel, *das;* (in sequence, rank) Hundertste, *der/die/das*

'hundredweight *n., pl. same* (Brit.) 50,8 kg; ≈ Zentner, *der*

hung ▶ HANG 1, 2

Hungarian /hʌŋ'geərɪən/ [1] *adj.* ungarisch; **sb. is ~:** jmd. ist Ungar/Ungarin
[2] *n.* **(a)** (person) Ungar, *der*/Ungarin, *die*
(b) (language) Ungarisch, *das; see also* ENGLISH 2A

Hungary /'hʌŋgərɪ/ *pr. n.* Ungarn (*das*)

hunger /'hʌŋgə(r)/ [1] *n.* Hunger, *der*
[2] *v.i.* **~ after** *or* **for sb./sth.** [heftiges] Verlangen nach jmdm./etw. haben

'hunger strike *n.* Hungerstreik, *der;* **go on ~:** in den Hungerstreik treten

hung 'over *adj.* (coll.) verkatert (ugs.)

hungry /'hʌŋgrɪ/ *adj.* hungrig; **be ~:** Hunger haben; **go ~:** hungern

hunk /hʌŋk/ *n.* [großes] Stück

hunt /hʌnt/ [1] *n.* Jagd, *die;* (search) Suche, *die*
[2] *v.t.* jagen; (search for) Jagd machen auf (+ *Akk.*) ‹*Mörder usw.*›
[3] *v.i.* jagen; **go ~ing** auf die Jagd gehen; **~ after** *or* **for** Jagd machen auf (+ *Akk.*); (seek) suchen

'hunter *n.* Jäger, *der*

'hunting *n.* die Jagd (**of** auf + *Akk.*); (searching) Suche, *die* (**for** nach)

hurdle /'hɜ:dl/ *n.* Hürde, *die*

hurl /hɜ:l/ *v.t.* werfen; (violently) schleudern; **~ insults at sb.** jmdm. Beleidigungen ins Gesicht schleudern

hurly-burly /'hɜ:lɪbɜ:lɪ/ *n.* Tumult, *der;* **the ~ of city life** der Großstadtrummel (ugs.)

hurrah /hʊ'rɑ:/, **hurray** /hʊ'reɪ/ *int.* hurra

hurricane /'hʌrɪkən/ *n.* (tropical cyclone) Hurrikan, *der;* (storm, lit. or fig.) Orkan, *der*

hurried /'hʌrɪd/ *adj.* eilig; überstürzt ‹*Abreise*›; in Eile ausgeführt ‹*Arbeit*›

hurry /'hʌrɪ/ [1] *n.* Eile, *die;* **in a ~:** eilig; **be in a ~:** es eilig haben; **there's no ~:** es eilt nicht
[2] *v.t.* antreiben ‹*Person*›; hinunterschlingen ‹*Essen*›; **~ one's work** seine Arbeit in zu großer Eile erledigen
[3] *v.i.* sich beeilen; (to or from place) eilen

■ **hurry 'up** [1] *v.i.* sich beeilen
[2] *v.t.* antreiben

hurt /hɜ:t/ [1] *v.t.,* **hurt (a)** wehtun (+ *Dat.*); (injure) verletzen; **~ oneself** sich (*Dat.*) weh tun; (injure oneself) sich verletzen; **~ one's arm/back** sich (*Dat.*) am Arm/Rücken wehtun; (injure) sich (*Dat.*) den Arm/am Rücken verletzen
(b) (damage, be detrimental to) schaden (+ *Dat.*)
(c) (upset) verletzen ‹*Person, Stolz*›
[2] *v.i.,* **hurt (a)** wehtun
(b) (cause damage, be detrimental) schaden
[3] *adj.* gekränkt ‹*Tonfall, Miene*›
[4] *n.* (emotional pain) Schmerz, *der*

hurtful /'hɜ:tfl/ *adj.* verletzend

hurtle /'hɜ:tl/ *v.i.* rasen (ugs.)

husband /'hʌzbənd/ *n.* Ehemann, *der;* **my/your/her ~:** mein/dein/ihr Mann; **~ and wife** Mann und Frau

hush /hʌʃ/ [1] *n.* (silence) Schweigen, *das;* (stillness) Stille, *die*
[2] *v.t.* (silence) zum Schweigen bringen; (still) beruhigen
[3] *v.i.* still sein; **~!** still!

▪ **hush 'up** *v.t.* vertuschen
husk /hʌsk/ *n.* Spelze, *die*
husky¹ /'hʌskɪ/ *adj.* heiser
husky² *n.* Eskimohund, *der*
hustle /'hʌsl/ [1] *v.t.* drängen (**into** zu) [2] *n.* ~ **and bustle** geschäftiges Treiben
hut /hʌt/ *n.* Hütte, *die*
hutch /hʌtʃ/ *n.* Stall, *der*
hyacinth /'haɪəsɪnθ/ *n.* Hyazinthe, *die*
hybrid /'haɪbrɪd/ [1] *n.* Hybride, *die od. der* (**between** aus); (fig.: mixture) Mischung, *die* [2] *adj.* hybrid ‹*Züchtung*›
'hybrid bike *n.* Crossrad, *das*
hydrangea /haɪ'dreɪndʒə/ *n.* Hortensie, *die*
hydrant /'haɪdrənt/ *n.* Hydrant, *der*
hydraulic /haɪ'drɔːlɪk/ *adj.* hydraulisch
hydrochloric acid /haɪdrəklɔːrɪk 'æsɪd/ *n.* Salzsäure, *die*
hydroelectric /haɪdrəʊɪ'lektrɪk/ *adj.* hydroelektrisch; ~ **power station** Wasserkraftwerk, *das*
hydrofoil /'haɪdrəfɔɪl/ *n.* Tragflächenboot, *das*
hydrogen /'haɪdrədʒən/ *n.* Wasserstoff, *der;* ~ **bomb** Wasserstoffbombe, *die*
hyena /haɪ'iːnə/ *n.* Hyäne, *die*
hygiene /'haɪdʒiːn/ *n.* Hygiene, *die*
hygienic /haɪ'dʒiːnɪk/ *adj.* hygienisch
hymn /hɪm/ *n.* Hymne, *die;* (sung in service) Kirchenlied, *das*
'hymn book *n.* Gesangbuch, *das*
hyper /'haɪpə(r)/ *adj.* (coll.) aufgedreht (ugs.)
hyperactive /haɪpə'ræktɪv/ *adj.* überaktiv
hyperbole /haɪ'pɜːbəlɪ/ *n.* Hyperbel, *die*
hyper: ~link *n.* (Comp.) Hyperlink, *der;* **~market** *n.* (Brit.) Verbrauchermarkt, *der;* **~text** *n.* (Comp.) Hypertext, *der;* **~'ventilate** *v.i.* hyperventilieren
hyphen /'haɪfn/ [1] *n.* Bindestrich, *der* [2] *v.t.* mit Bindestrich schreiben
hyphenate /'haɪfəneɪt/ ▶ HYPHEN 2
hyphenation /haɪfə'neɪʃn/ *n.* Kopplung, *die*
hypnosis /hɪp'nəʊsɪs/ *n., pl.* **hypnoses** /hɪp'nəʊsiːz/ Hypnose, *die;* (act, process) Hypnotisierung, *die;* **under ~**: in Hypnose (*Dat.*)
hypnotic /hɪp'nɒtɪk/ *adj.* hypnotisch
hypnotism /'hɪpnətɪzm/ *n.* Hypnotik, *die;* (act) Hypnotisieren, *das*
hypnotist /'hɪpnətɪst/ *n.* Hypnotiseur, *der*/Hypnotiseurin, *die*
hypnotize /'hɪpnətaɪz/ *v.t.* hypnotisieren
hypochondria /haɪpə'kɒndrɪə/ *n.* Hypochondrie, *die*
hypochondriac /haɪpə'kɒndrɪæk/ *n.* Hypochonder, *der*
hypocrisy /hɪ'pɒkrɪsɪ/ *n.* Heuchelei, *die*
hypocrite /'hɪpəkrɪt/ *n.* Heuchler, *der*/Heuchlerin, *die*
hypocritical /hɪpə'krɪtɪkl/ *adj.* heuchlerisch
hypodermic /haɪpə'dɜːmɪk/ *adj.* & *n.* ~ **[syringe]** Injektionsspritze, *die*
hypotenuse /haɪ'pɒtənjuːz/ *n.* Hypotenuse, *die*
hypothermia /haɪpə'θɜːmɪə/ *n.* (Med.) Hypothermie, *die* (fachspr.); Unterkühlung, *die*
hypothesis /haɪ'pɒθɪsɪs/ *n., pl.* **hypotheses** /haɪ'pɒθɪsiːz/ Hypothese, *die*
hypothetical /haɪpə'θetɪkl/ *adj.* hypothetisch
hysterectomy /hɪstə'rektəmɪ/ *n.* (Med.) Hysterektomie, *die* (fachspr.)
hysteria /hɪ'stɪərɪə/ *n.* Hysterie, *die*
hysterical /hɪ'sterɪkl/ *adj.* hysterisch
hysterics /hɪ'sterɪks/ *n. pl.* (laughter) hysterischer Lachanfall; (crying) hysterischer Weinkrampf; **have ~**: hysterisch lachen/weinen

Ii

I¹, i /aɪ/ *n.* I, i, *das*
I² *pron.* ich
ice /aɪs/ [1] *n.* **(a)** Eis, *das;* **feel/be like ~** (be very cold) eiskalt sein
(b) (~ cream) [Speise]eis, *das;* **an ~/two ~s** ein/zwei Eis
[2] *v.t.* glasieren ‹*Kuchen*›
▪ **ice 'over, ice 'up** *v.i.* ‹*Gewässer:*› zufrieren
'ice age *n.* Eiszeit, *die*
iceberg /'aɪsbɜːg/ *n.* Eisberg, *der*
ice: ~box *n.* (Amer.) Kühlschrank, *der;* **~ bucket** *n.* Eisbehälter, *der;* **~-cold** *adj.* eiskalt; **~ 'cream** *n.* Eis, *das;* Eiscreme, *die;* **one ~ cream/two/too many ~ creams** ein/zwei/zu viel Eis; **~ 'cream parlour** *n.* Eisdiele, *die;* **~ cube** *n.* Eiswürfel, *die;* **~ hockey** *n.* Eishockey, *das*

Iceland /'aɪslənd/ *pr. n.* Island (*das*)
Icelandic /aɪs'lændɪk/ 1 *adj.* isländisch 2 *n.* Isländisch, *das; see also* ENGLISH 2A
ice: ~ **'lolly** *n.* Eis am Stiel; ~ **rink** *n.* Eisbahn, *die;* ~ **skate** *n.* Schlittschuh, *der;* ~**-skate** *v.i.* Schlittschuh laufen; ~ **skating** *n.* Schlittschuhlaufen, *das*
icicle /'aɪsɪkl/ *n.* Eiszapfen, *der*
icing /'aɪsɪŋ/ *n.* Zuckerguss, *der*
'icing sugar *n.* (Brit.) Puderzucker, *der*
icon /'aɪkɒn/ *n.* **(a)** Ikone, *die* **(b)** (Comp.) Icon, *das*
icy /'aɪsɪ/ *adj.* **(a)** vereist ‹*Berge, Landschaft, Straße*›; eisreich ‹*Region, Land*›; **in ~ conditions** bei Eis **(b)** (very cold) eiskalt; eisig; (fig.) frostig
I'd /aɪd/ **(a)** = **I had; (b)** = **I would**
idea /aɪ'dɪə/ *n.* Idee, *die;* Gedanke, *der;* (mental picture) Vorstellung, *die;* (vague notion) Ahnung, *die;* **have you any ~ [of] how ...?** weißt du ungefähr, wie ...?; **have no ~ [of] where ...:** keine Ahnung haben, wo ...; **not have the slightest** *or* **faintest ~:** nicht die leiseste Ahnung haben
ideal /aɪ'dɪəl/ 1 *adj.* ideal; vollendet ‹*Ehemann, Gastgeber*›; vollkommen ‹*Welt*› 2 *n.* Ideal, *das*
idealism /aɪ'dɪəlɪzm/ *n.* Idealismus, *der*
idealist /aɪ'dɪəlɪst/ *n.* Idealist, *der*/ Idealistin, *die*
idealistic /aɪdɪə'lɪstɪk/ *adj.* idealistisch
idealize /aɪ'dɪəlaɪz/ *v.t.* idealisieren
ideally /aɪ'dɪəlɪ/ *adv.* ideal; **~, ...:** idealerweise *od.* im Idealfall ...
identical /aɪ'dentɪkl/ *adj.* identisch; **be ~:** sich (*Dat.*) völlig gleichen; **~ twins** eineiige Zwillinge
identification /aɪdentɪfɪ'keɪʃn/ *n.* Identifizierung, *die;* (of plants, animals) Bestimmung, *die*
identifi'cation parade *n.* (Brit.) Gegenüberstellung [zur Identifizierung], *die*
identify /aɪ'dentɪfaɪ/ 1 *v.t.* identifizieren; bestimmen ‹*Pflanze, Tier*› 2 *v.i.* **~ with sb.** sich mit jmdm. identifizieren
Identikit ® /aɪ'dentɪkɪt/ *n.* Phantombild, *das*
identity /aɪ'dentɪtɪ/ *n.* Identität, *die;* **proof of ~:** Identitätsnachweis, *der;* **[case of] mistaken ~:** [Personen]verwechslung, *die*
identity: ~ **card** *n.* [Personal]ausweis, *der;* ~ **crisis** *n.* Identitätskrise, *die;* ~ **parade** ▶ IDENTIFICATION PARADE; ~ **theft** *n.* Identitätsdiebstahl, *der*
ideological /aɪdɪə'lɒdʒɪkl/ *adj.* ideologisch
ideology /aɪdɪ'ɒlədʒɪ/ *n.* Ideologie, *die*
idiocy /'ɪdɪəsɪ/ *n.* Idiotie, *die*
idiom /'ɪdɪəm/ *n.* [Rede]wendung, *die*
idiomatic /ɪdɪə'mætɪk/ *adj.* idiomatisch
idiosyncrasy /ɪdɪə'sɪŋkrəsɪ/ *n.* Eigentümlichkeit, *die*
idiosyncratic /ɪdɪəsɪŋ'krætɪk/ *adj.* eigenwillig
idiot /'ɪdɪət/ *n.* Idiot, *der* (ugs.)
idiotic /ɪdɪ'ɒtɪk/ *adj.* idiotisch (ugs.)
idle /'aɪdl/ 1 *adj.* **(a)** (lazy) faul **(b)** (not in use) außer Betrieb *nachgestellt;* **be ~** ‹*Maschinen, Fabrik:*› stillstehen **(c)** bloß ‹*Neugier, Spekulation*›; leer ‹*Geschwätz*› 2 *v.i.* ‹*Motor:*› leer laufen
■ **idle a'way** *v.t.* vertun
'idleness *n.* Faulheit, *die*
idol /'aɪdl/ *n.* Idol, *das*
idolize /'aɪdəlaɪz/ *v.t.* vergöttern
idyllic /ɪ'dɪlɪk/ *adj.* idyllisch
i.e. /aɪ'i:/ *abbr.* = **that is** d.h.; i.e.
if /ɪf/ *conj.* **(a)** wenn; **if anyone should ask ...:** falls jemand fragt, ...; **if I knew what to do ...:** wenn ich wüsste, was ich tun soll ...; **if I were you** an deiner Stelle; **if so/not** wenn ja/ nein *od.* nicht; **if then/that/at all** wenn überhaupt; **as if** als ob; **if I only knew, if only I knew!** wenn ich das nur wüsste!; **if it isn't Ronnie!** das ist doch Ronnie! **(b)** (whenever) [immer] wenn **(c)** (whether) ob **(d)** (though) auch *od.* selbst wenn **(e)** (despite being) wenn auch
iffy /'ɪfɪ/ *adj.* (coll.) ungewiss; zweifelhaft
igloo /'ɪglu:/ *n.* Iglu, *der od. das*
ignite /ɪg'naɪt/ 1 *v.t.* anzünden 2 *v.i.* sich entzünden
ignition /ɪg'nɪʃn/ *n.* **(a)** (igniting) Zünden, *das* **(b)** (Motor Veh.) Zündung, *die;* **~ key** Zündschlüssel, *der*
ignorance /'ɪgnərəns/ *n.* Unwissenheit, *die;* **keep sb. in ~ of sth.** jmdn. in Unkenntnis über etw. (*Akk.*) lassen
ignorant /'ɪgnərənt/ *adj.* unwissend; **be ~ of sth.** (uninformed) über etw. (*Akk.*) nicht informiert sein
ignore /ɪg'nɔ:(r)/ *v.t.* ignorieren; nicht befolgen ‹*Befehl, Rat*›; übergehen ‹*Frage, Bemerkung*›
ill /ɪl/ 1 *adj.*, **worse** /wɜ:s/, **worst** /wɜ:st/ krank; **fall ~:** krank werden 2 *adv.* **be ~ at ease** sich nicht wohl fühlen 3 *n.* Übel, *das*
I'll /aɪl/ **(a)** = **I shall (b)** = **I will**
'ill-advised *adj.* unklug
illegal /ɪ'li:gl/ *adj.*, **il'legally** *adv.* illegal
il'legal immigrant *n.* illegaler Einwanderer/illegale Einwanderin
illegality /ɪlɪ'gælɪtɪ/ *n.* Ungesetzlichkeit, *die*
illegible /ɪ'ledʒɪbl/ *adj.* unleserlich
illegitimate /ɪlɪ'dʒɪtɪmət/ *adj.* unehelich ‹*Kind*›

ill 'health *n.* schwache Gesundheit
illicit /ɪ'lɪsɪt/ *adj.* unerlaubt ‹*Beziehung, [Geschlechts]verkehr*›; Schwarz‹*handel, -verkauf, -arbeit*›
'ill-informed *adj.* schlecht informiert
illiteracy /ɪ'lɪtərəsɪ/ *n.* Analphabetentum, *das*
illiterate /ɪ'lɪtərət/ *adj.* des Lesens und Schreibens unkundig; analphabetisch ‹*Bevölkerung*›
illness /'ɪlnɪs/ *n.* Krankheit, *die*
illogical /ɪ'lɒdʒɪkl/ *adj.* unlogisch
ill-'treat *v.t.* misshandeln
ill-'treatment *n.* Misshandlung, *die*
illuminate /ɪ'lu:mɪneɪt/ *v.t.* beleuchten
illuminating /ɪ'lu:mɪneɪtɪŋ/ *adj.* aufschlussreich
illumination /ɪlu:mɪ'neɪʃn/ *n.* Beleuchtung, *die*
illusion /ɪ'lu:ʒn/ *n.* Illusion, *die;* **be under the ~ that ...:** sich (*Dat.*) einbilden, dass ...
illusory /ɪ'lu:sərɪ/ *adj.* illusorisch
illustrate /'ɪləstreɪt/ *v.t.* **(a)** (serve as example of) veranschaulichen
(b) illustrieren ‹*Buch, Erklärung*›
illustration /ɪlə'streɪʃn/ *n.* **(a)** (example) Beispiel, *das* (**of** für)
(b) (picture) Abbildung, *die*
illustrious /ɪ'lʌstrɪəs/ *adj.* berühmt ‹*Person*›
ill 'will *n.* Böswilligkeit, *die*
I'm /aɪm/ = **I am**
image /'ɪmɪdʒ/ *n.* **(a)** Bildnis, *das* (geh.)
(b) (Optics) Bild, *das*
(c) **[public] ~:** Image, *das*
'image-conscious *adj.* imagebewusst
imaginable /ɪ'mædʒɪnəbl/ *adj.* **the best solution ~:** die denkbar beste Lösung
imaginary /ɪ'mædʒɪnərɪ/ *adj.* imaginär (geh.); eingebildet ‹*Krankheit*›
imagination /ɪmædʒɪ'neɪʃn/ *n.* **(a)** Fantasie, *die*
(b) (fancy) Einbildung, *die*
imaginative /ɪ'mædʒɪnətɪv/ *adj.* fantasievoll; (showing imagination) einfallsreich
imagine /ɪ'mædʒɪn/ *v.t.* **(a)** sich (*Dat.*) vorstellen
(b) (suppose) glauben
(c) (get the impression) **~ that ...:** sich (*Dat.*) einbilden[, dass ...]
imbalance /ɪm'bæləns/ *n.* Unausgeglichenheit, *die*
imbecile /'ɪmbɪsi:l/ *n.* Idiot, *der* (ugs.)
IMF *abbr.* = **International Monetary Fund** IWF, *der*
imitate /'ɪmɪteɪt/ *v.t.* nachahmen
imitation /ɪmɪ'teɪʃn/ *n.* **(a)** Nachahmung, *die*
(b) (counterfeit) Imitation, *die*
immaculate /ɪ'mækjʊlət/ *adj.* (spotless) makellos; (faultless) tadellos
immaterial /ɪmə'tɪərɪəl/ *adj.* unerheblich
immature /ɪmə'tjʊə(r)/ *adj.* unreif; noch nicht voll entwickelt ‹*Lebewesen*›
immaturity /ɪmə'tjʊərɪtɪ/ *n.* Unreife, *die*
immediate /ɪ'mi:djət/ *adj.* **(a)** unmittelbar; (nearest) nächst... ‹*Nachbar[schaft], Umgebung, Zukunft*›; engst... ‹*Familie*›
(b) (occurring at once) prompt; unverzüglich ‹*Handeln, Maßnahmen*›; umgehend ‹*Antwort*›
im'mediately **1** *adv.* **(a)** unmittelbar
(b) (without delay) sofort
2 *conj.* sobald
immemorial /ɪmɪ'mɔ:rɪəl/ *adj.* **from time ~:** seit undenklichen Zeiten
immense /ɪ'mens/ *adj.* **(a)** ungeheuer
(b) (coll.: great) enorm
im'mensely *adv.* **(a)** ungeheuer
(b) (coll.: very much) unheimlich (ugs.)
immerse /ɪ'mɜ:s/ *v.t.* [ein]tauchen; **be ~d in thought/one's work** in Gedanken versunken/in seine Arbeit vertieft sein
immersion /ɪ'mɜ:ʃn/ *n.* Eintauchen, *das*
im'mersion heater *n.* Heißwasserbereiter, *der*
immigrant /'ɪmɪgrənt/ **1** *n.* Einwanderer, *der*/Einwanderin, *die*
2 *adj.* Einwanderer-; **~ workers** ausländische Arbeitnehmer *Pl.*
immigration /ɪmɪ'greɪʃn/ *n.* Einwanderung *die* (**into** nach, **from** aus); *attrib.* Einwanderungs‹*kontrolle, -gesetz*›; **~ officer** Beamter/Beamtin der Einwanderungsbehörde; **~ authorities** Einwanderungsbehörden *Pl.;* **go through ~:** durch die Passkontrolle gehen
imminent /'ɪmɪnənt/ *adj.* unmittelbar bevorstehend; drohend ‹*Gefahr*›; **be ~:** unmittelbar bevorstehen/drohen
immobile /ɪ'məʊbaɪl/ *adj.* (immovable) unbeweglich
immobilize /ɪ'məʊbɪlaɪz/ *v.t.* verankern; (fig.) lähmen
immobilizer /ɪ'məʊbɪlaɪzə(r)/ *n.* (Motor Veh.) Wegfahrsperre, *die*
immodest /ɪ'mɒdɪst/ *adj.* unbescheiden; (improper) unanständig
immoral /ɪ'mɒrəl/ *adj.* unmoralisch; (in sexual matters) sittenlos
immorality /ɪmə'rælɪtɪ/ *n.* Unmoral, *die;* (in sexual matters) Sittenlosigkeit, *die*
immortal /ɪ'mɔ:tl/ *adj.* unsterblich
immortality /ɪmɔ:'tælɪtɪ/ *n.* Unsterblichkeit, *die*
immortalize /ɪ'mɔ:təlaɪz/ *v.t.* unsterblich machen
immovable /ɪ'mu:vəbl/ *adj.* unbeweglich; **be ~:** sich nicht bewegen lassen
immune /ɪ'mju:n/ *adj.* **(a)** (exempt) sicher (**from** vor + *Dat.*)
(b) (not susceptible) unempfindlich (**to** gegen) ···›

(c) (Med.) immun (**to** gegen); **~ system** Immunsystem, *das;* **~ therapy** *n.* Immuntherapie, *die*

immunity /ɪ'mju:nɪtɪ/ *n.* **(a) diplomatic ~:** diplomatische Immunität
(b) (Med.) Immunität, *die*

immunization /ɪmjʊnaɪ'zeɪʃn/ *n.* Immunisierung, *die*

immunize /'ɪmjʊnaɪz/ *v.t.* immunisieren

immunodeficiency /ɪ'mju:nəʊdɪfɪʃənsɪ/ *n.* Immunschwäche, *die*

immunology /ɪmjʊ'nɒlədʒɪ/ *n.* Immunologie, *die*

immunotherapy /ɪmju:nəʊ'θerəpɪ/ *n.* Immuntherapie, *die*

immutable /ɪ'mju:təbl/ *adj.* unveränderlich

imp /ɪmp/ *n.* **(a)** Kobold, *der*
(b) (fig.: child) Racker, *der* (fam.)

impact /'ɪmpækt/ *n.* **(a)** Aufprall, *der* (**on, against** auf + *Akk.*); (collision) Zusammenprall, *der*
(b) (fig.) Wirkung, *die*

impair /ɪm'peə(r)/ *v.t.* beeinträchtigen; schaden (+ *Dat.*) ‹*Gesundheit*›

impale /ɪm'peɪl/ *v.t.* aufspießen

impart /ɪm'pɑ:t/ *v.t.* **(a)** (give) [ab]geben (**to** an + *Akk.*)
(b) (communicate) kundtun (geh.) (**to** *Dat.*); vermitteln ‹*Kenntnisse*› (**to** *Dat.*)

impartial /ɪm'pɑ:ʃl/ *adj.* unparteiisch; gerecht ‹*Entscheidung, Urteil*›

impassable /ɪm'pɑ:səbl/ *adj.* unpassierbar (**to** für); (to vehicles) unbefahrbar (**to** für)

impasse /'æmpɑ:s/ *n.* Sackgasse, *die*

impassive /ɪm'pæsɪv/ *adj.* ausdruckslos

impatience /ɪm'peɪʃəns/ *n.* Ungeduld, *die* (**at** über + *Akk.*)

impatient /ɪm'peɪʃənt/ *adj.* ungeduldig; **~ at sth./with sb.** ungeduldig über etw. (*Akk.*)/mit jmdm.

im'patiently *adv.* ungeduldig

impeccable /ɪm'pekəbl/ *adj.* makellos; tadellos ‹*Manieren*›

impeccably /ɪm'pekəblɪ/ *adv.* tadellos; makellos ‹*rein*›

impede /ɪm'pi:d/ *v.t.* behindern

impediment /ɪm'pedɪmənt/ *n.* **(a)** Hindernis, *das* (**to** für)
(b) (speech defect) Sprachfehler, *der*

impel /ɪm'pel/ *v.t.*, **-ll-** treiben; **feel ~led to do sth.** sich genötigt *od.* gezwungen fühlen, etw. zu tun

impending /ɪm'pendɪŋ/ *adj.* bevorstehend

impenetrable /ɪm'penɪtrəbl/ *adj.* undurchdringlich (**by, to** für)

imperative /ɪm'perətɪv/ **1** *adj.* dringend erforderlich
2 *n.* (Ling.) Imperativ, *der*

imperceptible /ɪmpə'septɪbl/ *adj.* nicht wahrnehmbar; (very slight or gradual) unmerklich

imperfect /ɪm'pɜ:fɪkt/ **1** *adj.* **(a)** (incomplete) unvollständig
(b) (faulty) mangelhaft
2 *n.* (Ling.) Imperfekt, *das*

imperfection /ɪmpə'fekʃn/ *n.* **(a)** (incompleteness) Unvollständigkeit, *die*
(b) (fault) Mangel, *der*

im'perfectly *adv.* **(a)** (incompletely) unvollständig
(b) (faultily) fehlerhaft

imperial /ɪm'pɪərɪəl/ *adj.* kaiserlich

imperialism /ɪm'pɪərɪəlɪzm/ *n.* Imperialismus, *der*

imperious /ɪm'pɪərɪəs/ *adj.* herrisch

impermeable /ɪm'pɜ:mɪəbl/ *adj.* undurchlässig

impersonal /ɪm'pɜ:sənl/ *adj.* unpersönlich

impersonate /ɪm'pɜ:səneɪt/ *v.t.* sich ausgeben als; (to entertain) imitieren; nachahmen

impertinence /ɪm'pɜ:tɪnəns/ *n.* Unverschämtheit, *die*

impertinent /ɪm'pɜ:tɪnənt/ *adj.* unverschämt

imperturbable /ɪmpə'tɜ:bəbl/ *adj.* gelassen; **be completely ~:** durch nichts zu erschüttern sein

impervious /ɪm'pɜ:vɪəs/ *adj.* undurchlässig; **be ~ to sth.** (fig.) unempfänglich für etw. sein

impetuous /ɪm'petjʊəs/ *adj.* unüberlegt; impulsiv ‹*Person*›

impetus /'ɪmpɪtəs/ *n.* **(a)** Kraft, *die*
(b) (fig.) Motivation, *die*

impinge /ɪm'pɪndʒ/ *v.i.* **~ on sth.** auf etw. (*Akk.*) Einfluss nehmen

'impish *adj.* lausbübisch

implacable /ɪm'plækəbl/ *adj.* unversöhnlich; erbittert ‹*Gegner*›

implausible /ɪm'plɔ:zɪbl/ *adj.* unglaubwürdig

implement **1** /'ɪmplɪmənt/ *n.* Gerät, *das*
2 /'ɪmplɪment/ *v.t.* [in die Tat] umsetzen ‹*Politik, Plan usw.*›

implicate /'ɪmplɪkeɪt/ *v.t.* belasten; **be ~d in a scandal** in einen Skandal verwickelt sein

implication /ɪmplɪ'keɪʃn/ *n.* Implikation, *die;* **by ~:** implizit

implicit /ɪm'plɪsɪt/ *adj.* **(a)** (implied) implizit (geh.); unausgesprochen ‹*Drohung, Zweifel*›
(b) (resting on authority) unbedingt; blind ‹*Vertrauen*›

implicitly /ɪm'plɪsɪtlɪ/ *adv.* **(a)** (by implication) implizit (geh.)
(b) (unquestioningly) blind ‹*vertrauen, gehorchen usw.*›

implode /ɪm'pləʊd/*v.i.* implodieren

implore /ɪm'plɔ:(r)/ *v.t.* anflehen (**for** um)

imply /ɪm'plaɪ/ *v.t.* **(a)** implizieren (geh.); (say indirectly) hindeuten auf (+ *Akk.*)
(b) (insinuate) unterstellen

impolite /ɪmpəˈlaɪt/ *adj.* unhöflich

import 1 /ɪmˈpɔːt/ *v.t.* importieren, einführen ‹*Waren*› (**from** aus, **into** nach)
2 /ˈɪmpɔːt/ *n.* **(a)** (process) Import, *der*
(b) (article) Importgut, *das*

importance /ɪmˈpɔːtəns/ *n.* Wichtigkeit, *die* (**to** für); (significance) Bedeutung, *die;* **be of ~**: wichtig sein; **full of one's own ~**: von seiner eigenen Wichtigkeit überzeugt

important /ɪmˈpɔːtənt/ *adj.* wichtig (**to** für); (significant) bedeutend

ˈimport duty *n.* Einfuhrzoll, *der*

imˈporter *n.* Importeur, *der*

impose /ɪmˈpəʊz/ *v.t.* auferlegen (geh.) ‹*Bürde, Verpflichtung*› (**[up]on** *Dat.*); erheben ‹*Steuer*› (**on** auf + *Akk.*); verhängen ‹*Kriegsrecht*›; anordnen ‹*Rationierung*›

■ **imˈpose on** *v.t.* ausnutzen ‹*Gutmütigkeit, Toleranz usw.*›; **~ on sb.** sich jmdm. aufdrängen

imposing /ɪmˈpəʊzɪŋ/ *adj.* imposant

imposition /ɪmpəˈzɪʃn/ *n.* **(a)** Auferlegung, *die;* (of tax) Erhebung, *die*
(b) (unreasonable demand) Zumutung, *die*

impossibility /ɪmpɒsɪˈbɪlɪtɪ/ *n.* Unmöglichkeit, *die*

impossible /ɪmˈpɒsɪbl/ *adj.*, **impossibly** /ɪmˈpɒsɪblɪ/ *adv.* unmöglich

impostor /ɪmˈpɒstə(r)/ *n.* Hochstapler, *der*/-staplerin, *die;* (swindler) Betrüger, *der*/ Betrügerin, *die*

impotence /ˈɪmpətəns/ *n.* **(a)** (powerlessness) Machtlosigkeit, *die*
(b) (lack of sexual power) Impotenz, *die*

impotent /ˈɪmpətənt/ *adj.* **(a)** (powerless) machtlos
(b) (lacking in sexual power; in popular use: sterile) impotent

impound /ɪmˈpaʊnd/ *v.t.* beschlagnahmen

impoverished /ɪmˈpɒvərɪʃt/ *adj.* **be/ become ~**: verarmt sein/verarmen

impracticable /ɪmˈpræktɪkəbl/ *adj.* undurchführbar

impractical /ɪmˈpræktɪkl/ *adj.* **(a)** (unpractical) unpraktisch
(b) ▶ IMPRACTICABLE

imprecise /ɪmprɪˈsaɪs/ *adj.* ungenau

impregnable /ɪmˈpregnəbl/ *adj.* uneinnehmbar ‹*Festung, Bollwerk*›; (fig.) unanfechtbar ‹*Ruf, Stellung*›

impregnate /ˈɪmpregneɪt/ *v.t.* imprägnieren

impress /ɪmˈpres/ *v.t.* beeindrucken; *abs.* Eindruck machen; **be ~ed by** *or* **with sth.** von etw. beeindruckt sein

■ **imˈpress [up]on** *v.t.* einschärfen (+ *Dat.*); **~ sth. [up]on sb.'s memory** jmdm. etw. einschärfen

impression /ɪmˈpreʃn/ *n.* **(a)** Eindruck, *der;* **form an ~ of sb.** sich (*Dat.*) ein Bild von jmdm. machen
(b) (impersonation) **do an ~ of sb.** jmdn. imitieren; **do ~s** andere Leute imitieren

impressionable *adj.* beeinflussbar

impressionist /ɪmˈpreʃənɪst/ *n.* Impressionist, *der*/Impressionistin, *die*

impressive /ɪmˈpresɪv/ *adj.* beeindruckend; imponierend

imprint 1 /ˈɪmprɪnt/ *n.* Abdruck, *der;* (fig.) Stempel, *der*
2 /ɪmˈprɪnt/ *v.t.* aufdrucken; (fig.) einprägen (**on** *Dat.*)

imprison /ɪmˈprɪzn/ *v.t.* in Haft nehmen; **be ~ed** sich in Haft befinden

imˈprisonment *n.* Haft, *die;* **a long term of ~**: eine lange Haftstrafe

improbable /ɪmˈprɒbəbl/ *adj.* unwahrscheinlich

impromptu /ɪmˈprɒmptjuː/ 1 *adj.* improvisiert; **an ~ speech** eine Stegreifrede
2 *adv.* aus dem Stegreif

improper /ɪmˈprɒpə(r)/ *adj.* **(a)** (wrong) unrichtig
(b) (unseemly) unpassend; (indecent) unanständig

imˈproperly *adv.* ▶ IMPROPER: unrichtig; unpassend; unanständig

improvable /ɪmˈpruːvəbl/ *adj.* verbesserungsfähig

improve /ɪmˈpruːv/ 1 *v.i.* besser werden; ‹*Person, Wetter:*› sich bessern
2 *v.t.* verbessern
3 *v. refl.* **~ oneself** sich weiterbilden

■ **imˈprove [up]on** *v.t.* überbieten ‹*Rekord, Angebot*›; verbessern ‹*Leistung*›

improvement /ɪmˈpruːvmənt/ *n.* Verbesserung, *die* (**on, over** gegenüber); **make ~s to sth.** Verbesserungen an etw. (*Dat.*) vornehmen

improvisation /ɪmprəvaɪˈzeɪʃn/ *n.* Improvisieren, *das*

improvise /ˈɪmprəvaɪz/ *v.t.* improvisieren

imprudent /ɪmˈpruːdənt/ *adj.* unklug; (showing rashness) unbesonnen

impudence /ˈɪmpjʊdəns/ *n.* Unverschämtheit, *die;* (brazenness) Dreistigkeit, *die*

impudent /ˈɪmpjʊdənt/ *adj.*, **ˈimpudently** *adv.* unverschämt; (brazen[ly]) dreist

impulse /ˈɪmpʌls/ *n.* Impuls, *der;* **on [an] ~**: impulsiv

ˈimpulse buying *n.* Spontankäufe *Pl.*

impulsive /ɪmˈpʌlsɪv/ *adj.* impulsiv

impunity /ɪmˈpjuːnɪtɪ/ *v.t.* **with ~**: ungestraft

impure /ɪmˈpjʊə(r)/ *adj.* unrein

impurity /ɪmˈpjʊərɪtɪ/ *n.* Unreinheit, *die;* (foreign body) Fremdstoff, *der*

impute /ɪmˈpjuːt/ *v.t.* zuschreiben (**to** *Dat.*)

in /ɪn/ 1 *prep.* (position; also fig.) in (+ *Dat.*); (into) in (+ *Akk.*); **in this heat** bei dieser Hitze; **two feet in diameter** mit einem Durchmesser von zwei Fuß; **there are three feet in a yard** ein Yard hat drei Fuß; **draw in** ···

crayon/ink mit Kreide/Tinte zeichnen; **pay in pounds/dollars** in Pfund/Dollars bezahlen; **in fog/rain** *etc.* bei Nebel/Regen *usw.*; **in the 20th century** im 20. Jahrhundert; **4 o'clock in the morning/afternoon** 4 Uhr morgens/abends; **in 1990** [im Jahre] 1990; **in three minutes/years** in drei Minuten/Jahren; **in doing this, he ...:** indem er das tut/tat, ... er ...; **in that ...:** insofern als...
2 *adv.* **(a)** (inside) hinein‹*gehen usw.*›; herein‹*kommen usw.*›
(b) (at home, work, etc.) **be in** da sein
(c) have it in for sb. es auf jmdn. abgesehen haben (ugs.); **sb. is in for sth.** (about to undergo) jmdm. steht etw. bevor
3 *adj.* (coll.: in fashion) in (ugs.)
4 *n.* **know the ins and outs of sth.** sich in einer Sache genau auskennen

in. *abbr.* = **inch[es]**

ina'bility *n.* Unfähigkeit, *die*

inaccessible /ɪnək'sesɪbl/ *adj.* unzugänglich

in'accuracy *n.* **(a)** (incorrectness) Unrichtigkeit, *die*
(b) (imprecision) Ungenauigkeit, *die*

in'accurate *adj.* **(a)** (incorrect) unrichtig
(b) (imprecise) ungenau

in'active *adj.* untätig

inac'tivity *n.* Untätigkeit, *die*

inadequacy /ɪn'ædɪkwəsɪ/ *n.* **(a)** Unzulänglichkeit, *die*
(b) (incompetence) mangelnde Eignung

in'adequate *adj.* unzulänglich; (incompetent) ungeeignet; **feel ~:** sich überfordert fühlen

inadvertent /ɪnəd'vɜ:tənt/ *adj.*, **inad'vertently** *adv.* versehentlich

inad'visable *adj.* nicht ratsam

inane /ɪ'neɪn/ *adj.* dümmlich

in'animate *adj.* unbelebt

inap'plicable *adj.* nicht zutreffend

inap'propriate *adj.* unpassend

in'apt *adj.* unpassend

inar'ticulate *adj.* **(a) she's rather/very ~:** sie kann sich ziemlich schlecht/sehr schlecht ausdrücken
(b) (indistinct) unverständlich

inat'tentive *adj.* unaufmerksam (**to** gegenüber)

in'audible *adj.* unhörbar

inau'spicious *adj.* (ominous) unheilvoll; (unlucky) unglücklich

'inborn *adj.* angeboren (**in** *Dat.*)

'in-box *n.* (Comp.) Inbox, *die;* Posteingang, *der*

in'bred *adj.* **they are/have become ~:** bei ihnen herrscht Inzucht

in'breeding *n.* Inzucht, *die*

'inbuilt *adj.* jmdm./einer Sache eigen

Inc. *abbr.* (Amer.) = **Incorporated** e. G.

incalculable /ɪn'kælkjʊləbl/ *adj.* (very great) unermesslich

in'capable *adj.* **(a) be ~ of doing sth.** außerstande sein, etw. zu tun; **be ~ of sth.** zu etw. unfähig sein
(b) be ~ of nicht zulassen ‹*Beweis, Messung usw.*›

incapacitate /ɪnkə'pæsɪteɪt/ *v.t.* unfähig machen

incarcerate /ɪn'kɑ:səreɪt/ *v.t.* einkerkern (geh.)

incarceration /ɪnkɑ:sə'reɪʃn/ *n.* Einkerkerung, *die* (geh.)

incendiary /ɪn'sendɪərɪ/ *adj. & n.* **~ device** Brandsatz, *der;* **~ [bomb]** Brandbombe, *die*

incense¹ /'ɪnsens/ *n.* Weihrauch, *der*

incense² /ɪn'sens/ *v.t.* erzürnen

incentive /ɪn'sentɪv/ *n.* Anreiz, *der*

incessant /ɪn'sesənt/ *adj.*, **in'cessantly** *adv.* unablässig

incest /'ɪnsest/ *n.* Inzest, *der*

incestuous /ɪn'sestjʊəs/ *adj.* inzestuös

inch /ɪntʃ/ 1 *n.* Inch, *der;* Zoll, *der* (veralt.)
2 *v.t. & i.* **~ [one's way] forward** sich Zoll für Zoll vorwärts bewegen

incident /'ɪnsɪdənt/ *n.* **(a)** (notable event) Vorfall, *der*
(b) (clash) Zwischenfall, *der*

incidental /ɪnsɪ'dentl/ *adj.* beiläufig ‹*Bemerkung*›; Neben‹*ausgaben, -einnahmen*›

incidentally /ɪnsɪ'dentəlɪ/ *adv.* nebenbei [bemerkt]

inci'dental music *n.* Begleitmusik, *die*

incinerate /ɪn'sɪnəreɪt/ *v.t.* verbrennen

incinerator /ɪn'sɪnəreɪtə(r)/ *n.* Verbrennungsofen, *der*

incision /ɪn'sɪʒn/ *n.* Einschnitt, *der*

incisive /ɪn'saɪsɪv/ *adj.* schneidend ‹*Ton*›; scharf ‹*Verstand*›; scharfsinnig ‹*Kritik, Frage, Bemerkung, Argument*›

incite /ɪn'saɪt/ *v.t.* anstiften; aufstacheln ‹*Massen, Volk*›

in'citement *n.* Anstiftung, *die*/ Aufstachelung, *die*

incl. *abbr.* = **including** inkl.

inclination /ɪnklɪ'neɪʃn/ *n.* Neigung, *die*

incline 1 /ɪn'klaɪn/ *v.t.* **(a)** (bend) neigen
(b) (dispose) veranlassen
2 *v.i.* (be disposed) neigen (**to[wards]** zu)
3 /'ɪnklaɪn/ *n.* Steigung, *die*

inclined /ɪn'klaɪnd/ *adj.* geneigt; **they are ~ to be slow** sie neigen zur Langsamkeit; **if you feel [so] ~:** wenn Sie Lust [dazu] haben

include /ɪn'klu:d/ *v.t.* einschließen; (contain) enthalten; **~d in the price** im Preis inbegriffen

including /ɪn'klu:dɪŋ/ *prep.* einschließlich (+ *Gen.*); **~ VAT** inklusive Mehrwertsteuer

inclusion /ɪn'klu:ʒn/ *n.* Aufnahme, *die*

inclusive /ɪn'klu:sɪv/ *adj.* einschließlich; **be ~ of sth.** etw. einschließen; **from 2 to 6 January ~:** vom 2. bis einschließlich 6. Januar; **cost £50 ~:** 50 Pfund kosten, alles inbegriffen

incognito /ɪnkɒɡ'ni:təʊ/ *adj., adv.* inkognito
inco'herent *adj.* zusammenhanglos
income /'ɪnkəm/ *n.* Einkommen, *das*
income: ~ bracket, ~ group *ns.* Einkommensklasse, *die;* **~ sup'port** *n.* (Brit.) zusätzliche Hilfe zum Lebensunterhalt; **~ tax** *n.* Einkommensteuer, *die;* (on wages, salary) Lohnsteuer, *die*
'incoming *adj.* ankommend; landend ‹*Flugzeug*›; einfahrend ‹*Zug*›; eingehend ‹*Telefongespräch, Auftrag*›
incomings /'ɪnkʌmɪŋz/ *n. pl.* (revenue, income) Einnahmen *Pl.*
in'comparable *adj.* unvergleichlich
incom'patible *adj.* unvereinbar; **be ~** ‹*Menschen:*› nicht zueinander passen
in'competence /ɪn'kɒmpɪtəns/ *n.* Unfähigkeit, *die;* Unvermögen, *das*
in'competent *adj.* unfähig
incom'plete *adj.* unvollständig
incompre'hensible *adj.* unbegreiflich; unverständlich ‹*Rede, Argument*›
incon'ceivable *adj.* unvorstellbar
incon'clusive *adj.* ergebnislos; nicht schlüssig ‹*Beweis, Argument*›
incongruous /ɪn'kɒŋɡrʊəs/ *adj.* unpassend
inconsequential /ɪnkɒnsɪ'kwenʃl/ *adj.* belanglos
incon'siderate *adj.* rücksichtslos
incon'sistency *n.* ▶ INCONSISTENT: Widersprüchlichkeit, *die;* Inkonsequenz, *die;* Unbeständigkeit, *die*
incon'sistent *adj.* widersprüchlich; (illogical) inkonsequent; (irregular) unbeständig
inconsolable /ɪnkən'səʊləbl/ *adj.* untröstlich
incon'spicuous *adj.* unauffällig
incontinence /ɪn'kɒntɪnəns/ *n.* (Med.) Inkontinenz, *die*
incontinent /ɪn'kɒntɪnənt/ *adj.* (Med.) inkontinent; **be ~:** an Inkontinenz leiden
incontrovertible /ɪnkɒntrə'vɜ:təbl/ *adj.* unbestreitbar; unwiderlegbar ‹*Beweis*›
incon'venience [1] *n.* Unannehmlichkeiten *Pl.* **(to** für); **put sb. to a lot of ~:** jmdm. große Unannehmlichkeiten bereiten
[2] *v.t.* Unannehmlichkeiten bereiten (+ *Dat.*); (disturb) stören
incon'venient *adj.* unbequem; ungünstig ‹*Lage, Standort*›; **come at an ~ time** zu ungelegener Zeit kommen; **be ~ for sb.** jmdm. nicht passen
incorporate /ɪn'kɔ:pəreɪt/ *v.t.* aufnehmen **(in[to], with** in + *Akk.*)
incorporated /ɪn'kɔ:pəreɪtɪd/ *adj.* eingetragen ‹*[Handels]gesellschaft*›
incor'rect *adj.* **(a)** unrichtig; **be ~:** nicht stimmen; **it is ~ to say that ...:** es stimmt nicht, dass ...
(b) (improper) inkorrekt
incor'rectly *adv.* **(a)** unrichtigerweise; falsch ‹*beantworten, aussprechen*›
(b) (improperly) inkorrekt
incorrigible /ɪn'kɒrɪdʒɪbl/ *adj.* unverbesserlich
increase [1] /ɪn'kri:s/ *v.i.* zunehmen; ‹*Lärm:*› größer werden; ‹*Preise, Nachfrage:*› steigen; **~ in weight/size/price** schwerer/größer/teurer werden
[2] *v.t.* **(a)** (make greater) erhöhen
(b) (intensify) verstärken
[3] /'ɪnkri:s/ *n.* Zunahme, *die* **(in** *Gen.*); **be on the ~:** ständig zunehmen
increasing /ɪn'kri:sɪŋ/ *adj.* steigend; **an ~ number of people** mehr und mehr Menschen
in'creasingly *adv.* in zunehmendem Maße; **become ~ apparent** immer deutlicher werden
in'credible *adj.* (also coll.: remarkable) unglaublich
in'credibly *adv.* (also coll.: remarkably) unglaublich
incredulity /ɪnkrɪ'dju:lɪtɪ/ *n.* Ungläubigkeit, *die*
incredulous /ɪn'kredjʊləs/ *adj.* ungläubig
increment /'ɪnkrɪmənt/ *n.* Erhöhung, *die;* (amount of growth) Zuwachs, *der*
incriminate /ɪn'krɪmɪneɪt/ *v.t.* belasten
incubate /'ɪŋkjʊbeɪt/ *v.t.* bebrüten; (to hatching) ausbrüten
incubation /ɪŋkjʊ'beɪʃn/ *n.* Bebrütung, *die*
incubator /'ɪŋkjʊbeɪtə(r)/ *n.* Inkubator, *der;* (for babies also) Brutkasten, *der*
incur /ɪn'kɜ:(r)/ *v.t.*, **-rr-** sich (*Dat.*) zuziehen ‹*Unwillen, Ärger*›; **~ debts/expenses/risks** Schulden machen/Ausgaben haben/Risiken eingehen
in'curable *adj.* unheilbar
incurably /ɪn'kjʊərəblɪ/ *adv.* unheilbar ‹*krank*›
incursion /ɪn'kɜ:ʃn/ *n.* Eindringen, *das;* (by sudden attack) Einfall, *der*
indebted /ɪn'detɪd/ *pred. adj.* **be [much] ~ to sb. for sth.** jmdm. für etw. [sehr] zu Dank verpflichtet sein
in'decency *n.* Unanständigkeit, *die*
in'decent *adj.*, **in'decently** *adv.* unanständig
indecipherable /ɪndɪ'saɪfərəbl/ *adj.* unentzifferbar
inde'cision *n.* Unentschlossenheit, *die*
inde'cisive *adj.* **(a)** ergebnislos ‹*Streit, Diskussion*›; nichtssagend ‹*Ergebnis*›
(b) (hesitating) unentschlossen
indeed /ɪn'di:d/ *adv.* **(a)** in der Tat; **thank you very much ~:** haben Sie vielen herzlichen Dank; **~ it is** in der Tat
(b) (in fact) ja sogar; **~, he can ...:** ja, er kann sogar ...
(c) (admittedly) zugegebenermaßen

indefatigable /ɪndɪˈfætɪgəbl/ *adj.* unermüdlich

indefensible /ɪndɪˈfensɪbl/ *adj.* (intolerable) unverzeihlich

inˈdefinite *adj.* **(a)** (vague) unbestimmt **(b)** (unlimited) unbegrenzt

inˈdefinitely *adv.* **(a)** (vaguely) unbestimmt **(b)** (unlimitedly) unbegrenzt; auf unbestimmte Zeit ‹*verschieben*›

indelible /ɪnˈdelɪbl/ *adj.* unauslöschlich; **~ ink** Wäschetinte, *die*

indelibly /ɪnˈdelɪblɪ/ *adv.* unauslöschlich

indemnify /ɪnˈdemnɪfaɪ/ *v.t.* absichern (**against** gegen); (compensate) entschädigen

indemnity /ɪnˈdemnɪtɪ/ *n.* Absicherung, *die;* (compensation) Entschädigung, *die*

indentation /ɪndenˈteɪʃn/ *n.* **(a)** (indenting, notch) Einkerbung, *die* **(b)** (recess) Einschnitt, *der*

indeˈpendence *n.* Unabhängigkeit, *die*

indeˈpendent *adj.*, **indeˈpendently** *adv.* unabhängig (**of** von)

indescribable /ɪndɪˈskraɪbəbl/ *adj.* unbeschreiblich

indestructible /ɪndɪˈstrʌktɪbl/ *adj.* unzerstörbar

indeterminable /ɪndɪˈtɜːmɪnəbl/ *adj.* unbestimmbar

indeterminate /ɪndɪˈtɜːmɪnət/ *adj.* unbestimmt; unklar ‹*Konzept*›

index /ˈɪndeks/ [1] *n.* Register, *das* [2] *v.t.* mit einem Register versehen

index: ~card *n.* Karteikarte, *die;* **~ finger** *n.* Zeigefinger, *der;* **~ gears** *pl.* Indexschaltung, *die;* **~-linked** *adj.* (Econ.) indexiert; dynamisch ‹*Rente*›; **~ number** *n.* Indexzahl, *die*

India /ˈɪndɪə/ *n.* Indien (*das*)

Indian /ˈɪndɪən/ [1] *adj.* **(a)** indisch; **sb. is ~**: jmd. ist Inder/Inderin **(b) [American] ~**: indianisch [2] *n.* **(a)** Inder, *der*/Inderin, *die* **(b) [American] ~**: Indianer, *der*/Indianerin, *die*

Indian: ~ ˈOcean *pr. n.* Indischer Ozean; **~ ˈsummer** *n.* Altweibersommer, *der*

indicate /ˈɪndɪkeɪt/ [1] *v.t.* **(a)** (be a sign of) erkennen lassen **(b)** (state briefly) andeuten **(c)** (mark, point out) anzeigen **(d)** (suggest, make evident) zum Ausdruck bringen (**to** gegenüber) [2] *v.i.* (Motor Veh.) blinken

indication /ɪndɪˈkeɪʃn/ *n.* [An]zeichen, *das* (**of** *Gen.*, für)

indicative /ɪnˈdɪkətɪv/ [1] *adj.* **(a) be ~ of sth.** auf etw. (*Akk.*) schließen lassen **(b)** (Ling.) indikativisch [2] *n.* (Ling.) Indikativ, *der*

indicator /ˈɪndɪkeɪtə(r)/ *n.* (on vehicle) Blinker, *der*

indict /ɪnˈdaɪt/ *v.t.* anklagen (**for, on a charge of** *Gen.*)

indie /ˈɪndɪ/ (coll.) [1] *adj.* Indie-‹*Gruppe, Szene, Charts etc.*› [2] *n.* (record company) Indie-Label, *das;* (band) Indie-Band, *die*

inˈdifference *n.* Gleichgültigkeit, *die* (**to[wards]** gegenüber)

inˈdifferent *adj.* **(a)** gleichgültig **(b)** (not good) mittelmäßig

indigenous /ɪnˈdɪdʒɪnəs/ *adj.* einheimisch; eingeboren ‹*Bevölkerung*›

indigestible /ɪndɪˈdʒestɪbl/ *adj.* (lit. or fig.) unverdaulich

indiˈgestion *n.* Magenverstimmung, *die;* (chronic) Verdauungsstörungen *Pl.*

indignant /ɪnˈdɪgnənt/ *adj.* entrüstet (**at, over, about** über + *Akk.*); indigniert ‹*Blick, Geste*›

inˈdignantly *adv.* entrüstet; indigniert

indignation /ɪndɪgˈneɪʃn/ *n.* Entrüstung, *die* (**about, at, against, over** über + *Akk.*)

inˈdignity *n.* Demütigung, *die*

indigo /ˈɪndɪgəʊ/ [1] *adj.* **~ [blue]** indigoblau [2] *n.* **~ [blue]** Indigoblau, *das*

indiˈrect *adj.* indirekt; **~ speech** indirekte Rede

indiˈrectly *adv.* indirekt

indirect ˈobject *n.* indirektes Objekt; (in German) Dativobjekt, *das*

indiscipline /ɪnˈdɪsɪplɪn/ *n., no indef. art.* Disziplinlosigkeit, *die*

indiˈscreet *adj.* indiskret

indiˈscretion *n.* Indiskretion, *die*

indiscriminate /ɪndɪˈskrɪmɪnət/ *adj.* (lacking judgement) unkritisch; (random, unrestrained) wahllos

indiˈspensable *adj.* unentbehrlich (**to** für); unabdingbar ‹*Voraussetzung*›

indisposed /ɪndɪˈspəʊzd/ *adj.* (unwell) unpässlich; indisponiert ‹*Sänger, Schauspieler*›

indisputable /ɪndɪˈspjuːtəbl/ *adj.*, **indisputably** /ɪndɪˈspjuːtəblɪ/ *adv.* unbestreitbar

indiˈstinct *adj.*, **indiˈstinctly** *adv.* undeutlich

indiˈstinguishable *adj.* nicht unterscheidbar

individual /ɪndɪˈvɪdjʊəl/ [1] *adj.* **(a)** einzeln **(b)** (distinctive, characteristic) individuell [2] *n.* Einzelne, *der/die*

individualist /ɪndɪˈvɪdjʊəlɪst/ *n.* Individualist, *der*/Individualistin, *die*

individualistic /ɪndɪvɪdjʊəˈlɪstɪk/ *adj.* individualistisch

individuality /ɪndɪvɪdjʊˈælɪtɪ/ *n.* (character) eigene Persönlichkeit

indiˈvidually *adv.* einzeln

indiˈvisible *adj.* unteilbar

indoctrinate /ɪnˈdɒktrɪneɪt/ *v.t.* indoktrinieren

indoctrination /ɪndɒktrɪˈneɪʃn/ *n.* Indoktrination, *die*

indolence /ˈɪndələns/ *n.* Trägheit, *die*
indolent /ˈɪndələnt/ *adj.* träge
indomitable /ɪnˈdɒmɪtəbl/ *adj.* unbeugsam
Indonesia /ɪndəˈni:zɪə/ *pr. n.* Indonesien (*das*)
ˈindoor *adj.* ~ **swimming pool/sports** Hallenbad, *das*/-sport, *der;* ~ **plants** Zimmerpflanzen; ~ **games** Spiele im Haus; (Sport) Hallenspiele
indoors /ɪnˈdɔ:z/ *adv.* drinnen; im Haus; **go/come** ~: nach drinnen gehen/kommen
indubitable /ɪnˈdju:bɪtəbl/ *adj.* unzweifelhaft
indubitably /ɪnˈdju:bɪtəblɪ/ *adv.* zweifellos; zweifelsohne
induce /ɪnˈdju:s/ *v.t.* ~ **sb. to do sth.** jmdn. dazu bringen, etw. zu tun
inˈducement *n.* (incentive) Anreiz, *der*
induction /ɪnˈdʌkʃn/ *n.* Amtseinführung, *die;* ~ **course** Einführungskurs[us], *der*
indulge /ɪnˈdʌldʒ/ **1** *v.t.* **(a)** nachgeben (+ *Dat.*) ‹*Wunsch, Verlangen, Verlockung*›; frönen (geh.) (+ *Dat.*) ‹*Leidenschaft*› **(b)** (please) verwöhnen **2** *v.i.* ~ **in** frönen (geh.) (+ *Dat.*) ‹*Leidenschaft*›
indulgence /ɪnˈdʌldʒəns/ *n.* **(a)** Nachsicht, *die;* (humouring) Nachgiebigkeit, *die* (**with** gegenüber) **(b)** (thing indulged in) Luxus, *der*
indulgent /ɪnˈdʌldʒənt/ *adj.* nachsichtig (**with, to[wards]** gegenüber)
industrial /ɪnˈdʌstrɪəl/ *adj.* industriell; Arbeits‹*unfall, -medizin, -psychologie*›
industrial: ~ **ˈaction** *n.* Arbeitskampfmaßnahmen *Pl.*; **take** ~ **action** in den Ausstand treten; ~ **area** *n.* Industriegebiet, *das;* ~ **diˈsease** *n.* Berufskrankheit, *die;* ~ **dispute** *n.* Arbeitskonflikt, *der;* ~ **ˈespionage** *n.* Industriespionage, *die;* ~ **estate** *n.* Industriegebiet, *das* ~ **ˈinjury** *n.* Arbeitsverletzung, *die*
industrialist /ɪnˈdʌstrɪəlɪst/ *n.* Industrielle, *der/die*
industrialization /ɪndʌstrɪəlaɪˈzeɪʃn/ *n.* Industrialisierung, *die*
industrialize /ɪnˈdʌstrɪəlaɪz/ *v.t.* industrialisieren
industrial: ~ **park** *n.* Industriegebiet, *das;* ~ **plant** *n.* Industrieanlage, *die;* ~ **reˈlations** *n. pl.* Industrialrelations *Pl.;* ~ **town** *n.* Industriestadt, *die;* ~ **tribunal** *n.* Arbeitsgericht, *das;* ~ **ˈwaste** *n.* Industriemüll, *der*
industrious /ɪnˈdʌstrɪəs/ *adj.* fleißig; (busy) emsig
industry /ˈɪndəstrɪ/ *n.* **(a)** Industrie, *die* **(b)** ▶ INDUSTRIOUS: Fleiß, *der;* Emsigkeit, *die*
inebriated /ɪˈni:brɪeɪtɪd/ *adj.* betrunken
inebriation /ini:brɪˈeɪʃn/ *n.* Betrunkenheit, *die;* betrunkener Zustand

inˈedible *adj.* ungenießbar
inefˈfective *adj.* unwirksam; fruchtlos ‹*Anstrengung, Versuch*›
ineffectual /ɪnɪˈfektjʊəl/ *adj.* unwirksam; fruchtlos ‹*Versuch, Bemühung*›; ineffizient ‹*Methode, Person*›
inefˈficiency *n.* Leistungsschwäche, *die;* (of organization, method) schlechtes Funktionieren
inefˈficient *adj.* leistungsschwach; schlecht funktionierend ‹*Organisation, Methode*›
inˈelegant *adj.* unelegant
inˈeligible *adj.* ungeeignet; **be** ~ **for** nicht infrage kommen für ‹*Beförderung, Position*›; nicht berechtigt sein zu ‹*Leistungen des Staats usw.*›
inept /ɪˈnept/ *adj.* unbeholfen
ineptitude /ɪˈneptɪtju:d/ *n.* Unbeholfenheit, *die*
ineˈquality *n.* Ungleichheit, *die*
inert /ɪˈnɜ:t/ *adj.* **(a)** reglos; (sluggish) träge **(b)** (Chem.) inert; ~ **gas** Edelgas, *das*
inertia /ɪˈnɜ:ʃə/ *n.* Trägheit, *die*
inertia reel ˈseat belt *n.* Automatikgurt, *der*
inescapable /ɪnɪˈskeɪpəbl/ *adj.* unausweichlich
inesˈsential *adj.* unwesentlich; (dispensable) entbehrlich
inestimable /ɪnˈestɪməbl/ *adj.* unschätzbar
inevitable /ɪnˈevɪtəbl/ *adj.* unvermeidlich; unabwendbar ‹*Ereignis, Krieg, Schicksal*›; zwangsläufig ‹*Ergebnis, Folge*›
inevitably /ɪnˈevɪtəblɪ/ *adv.* zwangsläufig
ineˈxact *adj.* ungenau
inexˈcusable *adj.* unverzeihlich
inexhaustible /ɪnɪgˈzɔ:stɪbl/ *adj.* unerschöpflich; unverwüstlich ‹*Person*›
inexorable /ɪnˈeksərəbl/ *adj.* unerbittlich
inexˈpensive *adj.* preisgünstig
inexˈperience *n.* Unerfahrenheit, *die*
inexˈperienced *adj.* unerfahren; ~ **in sth.** wenig vertraut mit etw.
inexpert /ɪnˈekspɜ:t/ *adj.* unerfahren
inexˈplicable *adj.* unerklärlich
inexpressive /ɪnɪkˈspresɪv/ *adj.* ausdruckslos ‹*Gesicht, Augen*›; trocken ‹*Ausdrucksweise, Sprache*›
inextricably /ɪnˈekstrɪkəblɪ/ *adv.* **become** ~ **entangled** sich vollkommen verheddern (ugs.); **[be]** ~ **linked** untrennbar verbunden [sein]
infallibility /ɪnfælɪˈbɪlɪtɪ/ *n.* Unfehlbarkeit, *die*
inˈfallible *adj.* unfehlbar
infamous /ˈɪnfəməs/ *adj.* berüchtigt
infancy /ˈɪnfənsɪ/ *n.* frühe Kindheit; **be in its** ~ (fig.) noch in den Anfängen stecken
infant /ˈɪnfənt/ *n.* kleines Kind

infantile /ˈɪnfəntaɪl/ *adj.* kindlich; (childish) kindisch

infant morˈtality *n.* Säuglingssterblichkeit, *die*

infantry /ˈɪnfəntrɪ/ *n.* Infanterie, *die*

ˈinfant school *n.* (Brit.) ≈ Vorschule, *die*

infatuated /ɪnˈfætjʊeɪtɪd/ *adj.* **be ~ with sb.** in jmdn. vernarrt sein

infect /ɪnˈfekt/ *v.t.* anstecken; infizieren; **the wound became ~ed** die Wunde entzündete sich

infection /ɪnˈfekʃn/ *n.* Infektion, *die;* **throat/ear/eye ~:** Hals-/Ohren-/Augenentzündung, *die*

infectious /ɪnˈfekʃəs/ *adj.* ansteckend; **be ~** ‹*Person:*› eine ansteckende Krankheit haben

infer /ɪnˈfɜː(r)/ *v.t.,* **-rr-** schließen (**from** aus); ziehen ‹*Schlussfolgerung*›

inference /ˈɪnfərəns/ *n.* [Schluss]folgerung, *die*

inferior /ɪnˈfɪərɪə(r)/ **1** *adj.* (of lower quality) minderwertig ‹*Ware*›; minder... ‹*Qualität*›; unterlegen ‹*Gegner*›; **~ to sth.** schlechter als etw.; **feel ~:** Minderwertigkeitsgefühle haben **2** *n.* Untergebene, *der/die*

inferiority /ɪnfɪərɪˈɒrɪtɪ/ *n.* Minderwertigkeit, *die;* (of opponent) Unterlegenheit, *die*

inferiˈority complex *n.* Minderwertigkeitskomplex, *der*

infernal /ɪnˈfɜːnl/ *adj.* **(a)** (of hell) höllisch **(b)** (coll.) verdammt (salopp)

inferno /ɪnˈfɜːnəʊ/ *n.* Inferno, *das*

inˈfertile *adj.* unfruchtbar

inferˈtility *n.* Unfruchtbarkeit, *die*

infest /ɪnˈfest/ *v.t.* ‹*Ungeziefer:*› befallen; ‹*Unkraut:*› überwuchern; **~ed with** befallen/überwuchert von

infestation /ɪnfesˈteɪʃn/ *n.* **~ of rats/insects** Ratten-/Insektenplage, *die*

infidelity /ɪnfɪˈdelɪtɪ/ *n.* Untreue, *die* (**to** gegenüber)

ˈinfighting *n.* (in organization) interne Machtkämpfe *Pl.*

infiltrate /ˈɪnfɪltreɪt/ *v.t.* **(a)** infiltrieren; unterwandern ‹*Partei, Organisation*› **(b)** einschleusen ‹*Agenten*›

infinite /ˈɪnfɪnɪt/ *adj.* **(a)** (endless) unendlich **(b)** (very great) ungeheuer

infinitesimal /ɪnfɪnɪˈtesɪml/ *adj.* **(a)** (Math.) infinitesimal **(b)** (very small) äußerst gering; winzig ‹*Menge*›

infinitive /ɪnˈfɪnɪtɪv/ *n.* Infinitiv, *der*

infinity /ɪnˈfɪnɪtɪ/ *n.* Unendlichkeit, *die*

infirm /ɪnˈfɜːm/ *adj.* gebrechlich

infirmary /ɪnˈfɜːmərɪ/ *n.* (hospital) Krankenhaus, *das*

infirmity /ɪnˈfɜːmɪtɪ/ *n.* Gebrechlichkeit, *die;* (malady) Gebrechen, *das*

inflamed /ɪnˈfleɪmd/ *adj.* (Med.) **be/become ~:** entzündet sein/sich entzünden

inflammable /ɪnˈflæməbl/ *adj.* feuergefährlich

inflammation /ɪnfləˈmeɪʃn/ *n.* (Med.) Entzündung, *die*

inflammatory /ɪnˈflæmətərɪ/ *adj.* aufrührerisch; **an ~ speech** eine Hetzrede

inflatable /ɪnˈfleɪtəbl/ *adj.* aufblasbar; **~ dinghy** Schlauchboot, *das*

inflate /ɪnˈfleɪt/ *v.t.* aufblasen; (with pump) aufpumpen

inflated /ɪnˈfleɪtɪd/ *adj.* (lit or fig.) aufgeblasen

inflation /ɪnˈfleɪʃn/ *n.* (Econ.) Inflation, *die*

inˈflexible *adj.* **(a)** (stiff) unbiegsam **(b)** (obstinate) [geistig] unbeweglich

inflict /ɪnˈflɪkt/ *v.t.* zufügen ‹*Leid, Schmerzen*›, beibringen ‹*Wunde*›, versetzen ‹*Schlag*› (**on** *Dat.*)

infliction /ɪnˈflɪkʃn/ *n.* ▸ INFLICT: Zufügen, *das;* Beibringen, *das;* Versetzen, *das*

ˈin-flight *adj.* Bord‹*verpflegung, -programm*›

influence /ˈɪnflʊəns/ **1** *n.* Einfluss, *der;* **be a good/bad ~ [on sb.]** einen guten/schlechten Einfluss [auf jmdn.] ausüben **2** *v.t.* beeinflussen

influential /ɪnflʊˈenʃl/ *adj.* einflussreich

influenza /ɪnflʊˈenzə/ *n.* Grippe, *die*

influx /ˈɪnflʌks/ *n.* Zustrom, *der*

info /ˈɪnfəʊ/ *n.* (coll.) Infos *Pl.* (ugs.)

inform /ɪnˈfɔːm/ **1** *n.* informieren (**of, about** über + *Akk.*); **keep sb. ~ed** jmdn. auf dem Laufenden halten **2** *v.i.* **~ against** *or* **on sb.** jmdn. denunzieren (**to** bei)

inˈformal *adj.* **(a)** zwanglos **(b)** (unofficial) informell

inforˈmality *n.* Zwanglosigkeit, *die*

informant /ɪnˈfɔːmənt/ *n.* Informant, *der*/Informantin, *die*

information /ɪnfəˈmeɪʃn/ *n.* Informationen *Pl.;* **give ~ on sth.** Auskunft über etw. (*Akk.*) erteilen; **piece** *or* **bit of ~:** Information, *die*

information: ~ bureau, ~ centre *ns.* Auskunftsbüro, *das;* **~ desk** *n.* Informationsschalter, *der;* **~ explosion** *n.* Informationsflut, *die;* **~ highway** *n.* (Comp.) Datenautobahn, *die;* **~ office** ▸ **~** BUREAU; **~ pack** *n.* Informationspaket, *das;* (folder etc.) Informationsmappe, *die;* **~ retrieval** *n.* (Comp.) Retrieval, *das;* **~ science** *n.* Informatik, *die;* **~ superhighway** *n.* (Comp.) Datenautobahn, *die;* Datensuperhighway, *der;* **~ system** *n.* Informationssystem, *das;* **~ technology** *n.* Informationstechnologie, *die*

informative /ɪnˈfɔːmətɪv/ *adj.* informativ; **not very ~:** nicht sehr aufschlussreich ‹*Dokument, Schriftstück*›

informed /ɪnˈfɔːmd/ *adj.* informiert

in'former *n.* Denunziant, *der*/ Denunziantin, *die*
infra-red /ɪnfrəˈred/ *adj.* infrarot
infrastructure /ˈɪnfrəstrʌktʃə(r)/ *n.* Infrastruktur, *die*
infrequency /ɪnˈfri:kwənsɪ/ *n.* Seltenheit, *die*
in'frequent *adj.*, **in'frequently** *adv.* selten
infringe /ɪnˈfrɪndʒ/ *v.t. & i.* **~ [on]** verstoßen gegen
in'fringement *n.* Verstoß, *der* (**of** gegen)
infuriate /ɪnˈfjʊərɪeɪt/ *v.t.* wütend machen; **be ~d** wütend sein (**by** über + *Akk.*)
infuriating /ɪnˈfjʊərɪeɪtɪŋ/ *adj.* ärgerlich
ingenious /ɪnˈdʒi:nɪəs/ *adj.* einfallsreich; genial ‹*Methode, Idee*›; raffiniert ‹*Spielzeug, Maschine*›
ingenuity /ɪndʒɪˈnju:ɪtɪ/ *n.* Genialität, *die*
ingot /ˈɪŋgət/ *n.* Ingot, *der*
ingratiate /ɪnˈgreɪʃɪeɪt/ *v. refl.* **~ oneself with sb.** sich bei jmdm. einschmeicheln
in'gratitude *n.* Undankbarkeit, *die* (**to[wards]** gegenüber)
ingredient /ɪnˈgri:dɪənt/ *n.* Zutat, *die*
ingrowing /ˈɪngrəʊɪŋ/ *adj.* eingewachsen ‹*Zehennagel usw.*›
inhabit /ɪnˈhæbɪt/ *v.t.* bewohnen
inhabitable /ɪnˈhæbɪtəbl/ *adj.* bewohnbar
inhabitant /ɪnˈhæbɪtənt/ *n.* Bewohner, *der*/Bewohnerin, *die*
inhale /ɪnˈheɪl/ *v.t. & i.* einatmen; inhalieren (ugs.) ‹*Zigarettenrauch usw.*›
inherent /ɪnˈhɪərənt, ɪnˈherənt/ *adj. adj.* (belonging by nature) innewohnend (geh.); natürlich ‹*Anmut, Eleganz*›
inherit /ɪnˈherɪt/ *v.t.* erben
inheritance /ɪnˈherɪtəns/ *n.* Erbe, *das;* (inheriting) Erbschaft, *die*
in'heritance tax *n.* Erbschaftssteuer, *die*
inhibit /ɪnˈhɪbɪt/ *v.t.* hemmen
in'hibited *adj.* gehemmt
inhibition /ɪnhɪˈbɪʃn/ *n.* Hemmung, *die*
inho'spitable *adj.* ungastlich ‹*Person, Verhalten*›; unwirtlich ‹*Gegend, Klima*›
'in-house *adj.* hausintern
in'human *adj.* unmenschlich
inhumane /ɪnhju:ˈmeɪn/ *adj.* unmenschlich
initial /ɪˈnɪʃl/ **1** *adj.* anfänglich; Anfangs‹*stadium, -schwierigkeiten*›
2 *n. esp. in pl.* Initiale, *die*
3 *v.t.*, (Brit.) **-ll-** abzeichnen ‹*Scheck, Quittung*›; paraphieren ‹*Vertrag, Abkommen usw.*›
initial 'letter *n.* Anfangsbuchstabe, *der*
i'nitially *adv.* anfangs; am Anfang
initiate /ɪˈnɪʃɪeɪt/ *v.t.* **(a)** (introduce) einführen (**into** in + *Akk.*); (into knowledge, mystery) einweihen (**into** in + *Akk.*)
(b) (begin) einleiten
initiation /ɪnɪʃɪˈeɪʃn/ *n.* **(a)** (introduction) Einführung, *die*
(b) (into knowledge, mystery) Einweihung, *die*
initiative /ɪˈnɪʃətɪv/ *n.* Initiative, *die;* **lack ~**: keine Initiative haben
inject /ɪnˈdʒekt/ *v.t.* [ein]spritzen; injizieren (Med.)
injection /ɪnˈdʒekʃn/ *n.* Spritze, *die;* Injektion, *die*
injure /ˈɪndʒə(r)/ *v.t.* **(a)** verletzen; **his leg was ~d** er wurde/(state) war am Bein verletzt
(b) (impair) schaden (+ *Dat.*)
injured /ˈɪndʒəd/ *adj.* verletzt; verwundet ‹*Soldat*›
injury /ˈɪndʒərɪ/ *n.* Verletzung, *die* (**to** *Gen.*)
'injury time *n.* (Brit. Footb.) Nachspielzeit, *die;* **be into/play ~**: nachspielen
in'justice *n.* Ungerechtigkeit, *die*
ink /ɪŋk/ *n.* Tinte, *die*
'ink-jet printer *n.* Tintenstrahldrucker, *der*
inkling /ˈɪŋklɪŋ/ *n.* Ahnung, *die;* **have an ~ of sth.** etw. ahnen
'ink pad *n.* Stempelkissen, *das*
inland /ˈɪnlənd, ˈɪnlænd/ *adj.* Binnen-; binnenländisch
Inland 'Revenue *n.* (Brit.) ≈ Finanzamt, *das*
'in-laws *n. pl.* (coll.) Schwiegereltern *Pl.*
inlet /ˈɪnlət/ *n.* [schmale] Bucht
'inmate *n.* Insasse, *der*/Insassin, *die*
inn /ɪn/ *n.* (hotel) Gasthof, *der;* (pub) Wirtshaus, *das*
innate /ɪˈneɪt/ *adj.* angeboren
inner /ˈɪnə(r)/ *adj.* inner...; Innen‹*hof, -tür, -fläche, -seite usw.*›; **~ tube** Schlauch, *der*
inner 'city *n.* Innenstadt, *die;* **~ areas** Innenbezirke
innermost /ˈɪnəməʊst/ *adj.* innerst...
'innkeeper *n.* [Gast]wirt, *der*/-wirtin, *die*
innocence /ˈɪnəsəns/ *n.* **(a)** Unschuld, *die*
(b) (naïvity) Naivität, *die*
innocent /ˈɪnəsənt/ *adj.* **(a)** unschuldig (**of** an + *Dat.*)
(b) (naïve) naiv
innocuous /ɪˈnɒkjʊəs/ *adj.* harmlos
innovation /ɪnəˈveɪʃn/ *n.* Innovation, *die;* (thing, change) Neuerung, *die*
innovative /ˈɪnəvətɪv/ *adj.* innovativ
innuendo /ɪnju:ˈendəʊ/ *n., pl.* **~es** *or* **~s** versteckte Andeutung
innumerable /ɪˈnju:mərəbl/ *adj.* unzählig
innumeracy /ɪˈnju:mərəsɪ/ *n.* Nicht-Rechnen-Können, *das*
innumerate /ɪˈnju:mərət/ *adj.* **be ~**: nicht rechnen können
inoculate /ɪˈnɒkjʊleɪt/ *v.t.* impfen
inoculation /ɪnɒkjʊˈleɪʃn/ *n.* Impfung, *die*
inof'fensive *adj.* harmlos

inoperable /ɪn'ɒpərəbl/ *adj.* (Surg.) inoperabel (fachspr.)
inoperative /ɪn'ɒpərətɪv/ *adj.* ungültig
in'opportune *adj.* unpassend; unangebracht ‹*Bemerkung*›
inordinate /ɪ'nɔ:dɪnət/ *adj.* unmäßig; ungeheuer ‹*Menge*›
inor'ganic *adj.* anorganisch
'inpatient *n.* stationär behandelter Patient/behandelte Patientin
'input *n.* Input, *der od. das*
inquest /'ɪŋkwest/ *n.* gerichtliche Untersuchung der Todesursache
inquire, inquiry ▶ ENQUIR-
inquisitive /ɪn'kwɪzɪtɪv/ *adj.* neugierig
'inroad *n.* Eingriff, *der* (**on, into** in + *Akk.*); **make ~s into sb.'s savings** jmds. Ersparnisse angreifen
in'sane *adj.* geisteskrank
in'sanitary *adj.* unhygienisch
in'sanity *n.* Geisteskrankheit, *die*
insatiable /ɪn'seɪʃəbl/ *adj.* unersättlich; unstillbar ‹*Verlangen*›
inscribe /ɪn'skraɪb/ *v.t.* schreiben; (on stone, rock) einmeißeln; mit einer Inschrift versehen ‹*Denkmal, Grabstein*›
inscription /ɪn'skrɪpʃn/ *n.* Inschrift, *die;* (on coin) Aufschrift, *die*
inscrutable /ɪn'skru:təbl/ *adj.* unergründlich; undurchdringlich ‹*Miene*›
insect /'ɪnsekt/ *n.* Insekt, *das*
insect: ~ bite *n.* Insektenstich, *der;* **~-borne** *adj.* durch Insekten übertragen ‹*Krankheit*›
insecticide /ɪn'sektɪsaɪd/ *n.* Insektizid, *das*
'insect repellent *n.* Insektenschutzmittel, *das*
inse'cure *adj.* unsicher
inse'curity *n.* Unsicherheit, *die*
insemination /ɪnsemɪ'neɪʃn/ *n.* (of woman) Befruchtung, *die* (of animal) Besamung, *die*
in'sensitive *adj.* **(a)** gefühllos ‹*Person, Art*›; (unappreciative) unempfänglich (**to** für) **(b)** (physically) unempfindlich (**to** gegen)
in'separable *adj.* untrennbar; (fig.) unzertrennlich
insert /ɪn'sɜ:t/ *v.t.* **(a)** einlegen ‹*Film*›; einwerfen ‹*Münze*›; hineinstecken ‹*Schlüssel*›; einstechen ‹*Nadel*› **(b)** (Comp.) einfügen; **~ key** Einfügetaste, *die*
insertion /ɪn'sɜ:ʃn/ *n.* ▶ INSERT: Einlegen, *das;* Einwerfen, *das;* Hineinstecken, *das;* Einstechen, *das;* Einfügen, *das*
'inset *n.* (small map) Nebenkarte, *die;* (small photograph, diagram) Nebenbild, *das*
inside 1 /-'-, '--/ *n.* **(a)** (internal side) Innenseite, *die;* **on the ~**: innen; **to/from the ~**: nach/von innen **(b)** (inner part) Innere, *das*
2 /'--/ *adj.* inner...; Innen‹*wand, -einrichtung, -ansicht*›; (fig.) intern
3 /-'-/ *adv.* (on or in the ~) innen; (to the ~) nach innen hinein/herein; (indoors) drinnen; **come ~**: hereinkommen; **take a look ~**: hineinsehen; **go ~**: [ins Haus] hineingehen; **turn a jacket ~ out** eine Jacke nach links wenden; **know sth. ~ out** etw. in- und auswendig kennen
4 /-'-/ *prep.* (position) in (+ *Dat.*); (direction) in (+ *Akk.*) hinein
inside-'leg *adj.* **~ measurement** Schrittlänge, *die*
insidious /ɪn'sɪdɪəs/ *adj.* heimtückisch
'insight *n.* (discernment) Verständnis, *das;* **gain an ~ into sth.** Einblick in etw. (*Akk.*) gewinnen
insig'nificant *adj.* unbedeutend; geringfügig ‹*Summe*›
insin'cere *adj.* unaufrichtig
insin'cerity *n.* Unaufrichtigkeit, *die*
insinuate /ɪn'sɪnjʊeɪt/ *v.t.* andeuten (**to sb.** jmdm. gegenüber)
insinuation /ɪnsɪnjʊ'eɪʃn/ *n.* Anspielung, *die* (**about** auf + *Akk.*)
insipid /ɪn'sɪpɪd/ *adj.* fade
insist /ɪn'sɪst/ *v.i.* bestehen (**[up]on** auf + *Dat.*); **~ on doing sth./on sb.'s doing sth.** darauf bestehen, etw. zu tun/dass jmd. etw. tut; **if you ~**: wenn du darauf bestehst
insistence /ɪn'sɪstəns/ *n.* Bestehen, *das* (**on** auf + *Dat.*)
insistent /ɪn'sɪstənt/ *adj.* **be ~ that ...**: darauf bestehen, dass ...
insolence /'ɪnsələns/ *n.* Unverschämtheit, *die;* Frechheit, *die*
insolent /'ɪnsələnt/ *adj.*, **'insolently** *adv.* unverschämt; frech
in'soluble *adj.* **(a)** (esp. Chem.) unlöslich **(b)** (not solvable) unlösbar
insolvency /ɪn'sɒlvənsɪ/ *n.* Zahlungsunfähigkeit, *die*
in'solvent *adj.* zahlungsunfähig
insomnia /ɪn'sɒmnɪə/ *n.* Schlaflosigkeit, *die*
insomniac /ɪn'sɒmnɪæk/ *n.* **be an ~**: an Schlaflosigkeit leiden
inspect /ɪn'spekt/ *v.t.* prüfend betrachten; (examine officially) überprüfen; kontrollieren ‹*Räumlichkeiten*›
inspection /ɪn'spekʃn/ *n.* Überprüfung, *die;* (of premises) Kontrolle, *die;* Inspektion, *die;* **on [closer] ~**: bei näherer Betrachtung
inspector /ɪn'spektə(r)/ *n.* **(a)** (on bus, train, etc.) Kontrolleur, *der*/Kontrolleurin, *die* **(b)** (Brit.) ≈ Polizeiinspektor, *der*
inspiration /ɪnspə'reɪʃn/ *n.* Inspiration, *die* (geh.)
inspire /ɪn'spaɪə(r)/ *v.t.* **(a)** inspirieren (geh.) ‹*Person*› **(b)** (instil) einflößen (**in** *Dat.*)
inspiring /ɪn'spaɪərɪŋ/ *adj.* inspirierend (geh.)
insta'bility *n.* Instabilität, *die;* (of person) Labilität, *die*

install /ɪn'stɔ:l/ *v.t.* installieren; einbauen ‹*Badezimmer*›; anschließen ‹*Telefon, Herd*›; **~ oneself** sich installieren

installation /ɪnstə'leɪʃn/ *n.* **(a)** Installation, *die;* (of bathroom) Einbau, *der;* (of telephone, cooker) Anschluss, *der*
(b) (apparatus etc. installed) Anlage, *die*

instalment (*Amer.:* **installment**) /ɪn'stɔ:lmənt/ *n.* **(a)** (part payment) Rate, *die;* **pay by** *or* **in ~s** in Raten zahlen
(b) (of serial, novel) Fortsetzung, *die;* (Radio, Telev.) Folge, *die*

instance /'ɪnstəns/ *n.* (example) Beispiel, *das* (**of** für); **for ~:** zum Beispiel; **in many ~s** (cases) in vielen Fällen; **in the first ~:** zunächst einmal

instant /'ɪnstənt/ **1** *adj.* unmittelbar; sofortig ‹*Wirkung, Linderung, Ergebnis*›; **~ coffee/tea** Pulverkaffee/Instanttee, *der;* **~ potatoes** fertiger Kartoffelbrei
2 *n.* Augenblick, *der;* **at that very ~:** genau in dem Augenblick; **come here this ~:** komm sofort her; **in an ~:** augenblicklich

instantaneous /ɪnstən'teɪnɪəs/ *adj.* unmittelbar; **his reaction was ~:** er reagierte sofort

'instantly *adv.* sofort

instead /ɪn'sted/ *adv.* stattdessen; **~ of doing sth.** [an]statt etw. zu tun; **~ of sth.** anstelle einer Sache (*Gen.*); **I will go ~ of you** ich gehe an deiner Stelle

'instep *n.* (of foot) Spann, *der;* Fußrücken, *der;* (of shoe) Blatt, *das*

instigate /'ɪnstɪgeɪt/ *v.t.* anstiften (**to** zu); initiieren (geh.) ‹*Reformen, Projekt usw.*›

instigation /ɪnstɪ'geɪʃn/ *n.* Anstiftung, *die;* (of reforms, project, etc.) Initiierung, *die;* **at sb.'s ~:** auf jmds. Betreiben (*Akk.*)

instil (*Amer.:* **instill**) /ɪn'stɪl/ *v.t.*, **-ll-** einflößen (**in** *Dat.*); beibringen ‹*gutes Benehmen, Wissen*› (**in** *Dat.*)

instinct /'ɪnstɪŋkt/ *n.* Instinkt, *der*

instinctive /ɪn'stɪŋktɪv/ *adj.*, **in'stinctively** *adv.* instinktiv

institute /'ɪnstɪtju:t/ **1** *n.* Institut, *das*
2 *v.t.* einführen; einleiten ‹*Suche, Verfahren*›; anstrengen ‹*Prozess*›

institution /ɪnstɪ'tju:ʃn/ *n.* Institution, *die;* (home) Heim, *das;* Anstalt, *die*

instruct /ɪn'strʌkt/ *v.t.* **(a)** (teach) unterrichten ‹*Klasse, Fach*›
(b) (direct, command) anweisen

instruction /ɪn'strʌkʃn/ *n.* **(a)** (teaching) Unterricht, *der*
(b) *esp. in pl.* (direction, order) Anweisung, *die;* **~ manual/~s for use** Gebrauchsanleitung, *die*

instructive /ɪn'strʌktɪv/ *adj.* aufschlussreich; lehrreich ‹*Erfahrung, Buch*›

instructor /ɪn'strʌktə(r)/ *n.* Lehrer, *der*/Lehrerin, *die;* (Mil.) Ausbilder, *der*

instrument /'ɪnstrʊmənt/ *n.* Instrument, *das*

instrumental /ɪnstrə'mentl/ *adj.* **(a)** (Mus.) Instrumental-
(b) (helpful) dienlich (**to** *Dat.*); **he was ~ in finding me a job** er hat mir zu einer Stelle verholfen

instrumentalist /ɪnstrʊ'mentəlɪst/ *n.* Instrumentalist, *der*/Instrumentalistin, *die*

insubordinate /ɪnsə'bɔ:dɪnət/ *adj.* aufsässig

insubordination /ɪnsəbɔ:dɪ'neɪʃn/ *n.* Aufsässigkeit, *die*

insubstantial /ɪnsəb'stænʃl/ *adj.* wenig substanziell (geh.)

insufferable /ɪn'sʌfərəbl/ *adj.* (unbearably arrogant) unausstehlich

insuf'ficient *adj.* nicht genügend; unzulänglich ‹*Beweise*›; unzureichend ‹*Versorgung, Beleuchtung*›

insuf'ficiently *adv.* ungenügend

insular /'ɪnsjʊlə(r)/ *adj.* **(a)** Insel-; insular (fachspr.)
(b) (fig.: narrow-minded) provinziell (abwertend)

insulate /'ɪnsjʊleɪt/ *v.t.* isolieren (**against, from** gegen); **insulating tape** Isolierband, *das*

insulation /ɪnsjʊ'leɪʃn/ *n.* Isolierung, *die*

insulin /'ɪnsjʊlɪn/ *n.* Insulin, *das*

insult **1** /'ɪnsʌlt/ *n.* Beleidigung, *die* (**to** *Gen.*)
2 /ɪn'sʌlt/ *v.t.* beleidigen

insulting /ɪn'sʌltɪŋ/ *adj.* beleidigend

insuperable /ɪn'su:pərəbl/ *adj.* unüberwindlich

insupportable /ɪnsə'pɔ:təbl/ *adj.* (unendurable) unerträglich

insurance /ɪn'ʃʊərəns/ *n.* Versicherung, *die;* (fig.) Sicherheit, *die;* **take out ~ against/on sth.** eine Versicherung gegen etw. abschließen/etw. versichern lassen; **travel ~:** Reisegepäck- und -unfallversicherung, *die*

insurance: ~ agent *n.* Versicherungsvertreter, *der*/-vertreterin, *die;* **~ broker** *n.* Versicherungsmakler, *der*/-maklerin, *die*; **~ claim** *n.* Versicherungsanspruch, *der;* **~ company** *n.* Versicherungsgesellschaft, *die;* **~ stamp** *n.* (Brit.) Versicherungsmarke, *die*

insure /ɪn'ʃʊə(r)/ *v.t.* versichern ‹*Person*›; versichern lassen ‹*Gepäck, Gemälde usw.*›; **~ [oneself] against sth.** [sich] gegen etw. versichern

insurer /ɪn'ʃʊərə(r)/ *n.* Versicherer, *der*

insurmountable /ɪnsə'maʊntəbl/ *adj.* unüberwindlich

intact /ɪn'tækt/ *adj.* **(a)** (entire) unbeschädigt; intakt ‹*Uhr, Maschine usw.*›
(b) (unimpaired) unversehrt

'intake *n.* **(a)** (action) Aufnahme, *die*
(b) (persons, things) Neuzugänge *Pl.*; (amount) aufgenommene Menge

in'tangible *adj.* nicht greifbar; (mentally) unbestimmbar

integral /'ɪntɪgrl/ *adj.* **(a)** wesentlich ‹*Bestandteil*›
(b) (whole) vollständig

integrate /'ɪntɪgreɪt/ *v.t.* integrieren **(into** in + *Akk.*)

integration /ɪntɪ'greɪʃn/ *n.* Integration, *die* **(into** in + *Akk.*)

integrity /ɪn'tegrɪtɪ/ *n.* Redlichkeit, *die*

intellect /'ɪntəlekt/ *n.* Verstand, *der;* Intellekt, *der*

intellectual /ɪntə'lektjʊəl/ [1] *adj.* intellektuell; geistig anspruchsvoll ‹*Person, Publikum*›
[2] *n.* Intellektuelle, *der/die*

intelligence /ɪn'telɪdʒəns/ *n.* **(a)** Intelligenz, *die*
(b) (information) Informationen *Pl.*
(c) military ~ (organization) militärischer Geheimdienst

intelligence: ~ quotient *n.* Intelligenzquotient, *der;* **~ test** *n.* Intelligenztest, *der*

intelligent /ɪn'telɪdʒənt/ *adj.* intelligent

intelligible /ɪn'telɪdʒɪbl/ *adj.* verständlich **(to** für)

intend /ɪn'tend/ *v.t.* beabsichtigen; **it was ~ed as a joke** das sollte ein Witz sein

in'tended *adj.* beabsichtigt ‹*Wirkung*›; **be ~ for sb./sth.** für jmdn./etw. gedacht sein

intense /ɪn'tens/ *adj.* **(a)** intensiv; groß ‹*Hitze, Belastung, Interesse*›; stark ‹*Schmerzen*›
(b) (earnest) ernst

in'tensely *adv.* äußerst; intensiv ‹*studieren, fühlen*›

intensify /ɪn'tensɪfaɪ/ [1] *v.t.* intensivieren
[2] *v.i.* zunehmen

intensity /ɪn'tensɪtɪ/ *n.* ▶ INTENSE A: Intensität, *die;* Größe, *die;* Stärke, *die*

intensive /ɪn'tensɪv/ *adj.* intensiv; Intensiv‹*kurs*›; **be in ~ care** auf der Intensivstation sein

in'tensively *adv.* intensiv

intent /ɪn'tent/ [1] *n.* Absicht, *die;* **to all ~s and purposes** im Grunde
[2] *adj.* **be ~ on achieving sth.** etw. unbedingt erreichen wollen

intention /ɪn'tenʃn/ *n.* Absicht, *die*

intentional /ɪn'tenʃənl/ *adj.*, **in'tentionally** *adv.* absichtlich

in'tently *adv.* aufmerksam

interact /ɪntər'ækt/ *v.i.* interagieren

interaction /ɪntər'ækʃn/ *n.* Interaktion, *die*

interactive /ɪntər'æktɪv/ *adj.* (Sociol., Psych., Comp.) interaktiv; **~ television** interaktives Fernsehen

intercede /ɪntə'si:d/ *v.i.* sich einsetzen **(with** bei; **for, on behalf of** für)

intercept /ɪntə'sept/ *v.t.* abfangen

interchange [1] /'ɪntətʃeɪndʒ/ *n.* **(a)** Austausch, *der*
(b) (road junction) [Autobahn]kreuz, *das*
[2] /ɪntə'tʃeɪndʒ/ *v.t.* austauschen

interchangeable /ɪntə'tʃeɪndʒəbl/ *adj.* austauschbar

inter-city /ɪntə'sɪtɪ/ *adj.* Intercity-; **~ train** Intercity[-Zug], *der*

intercom /'ɪntəkɒm/ *n.* (coll.) Gegensprechanlage, *die*

interconnect /ɪntəkə'nekt/ [1] *v.t.* miteinander verbinden
[2] *v.i.* miteinander in Zusammenhang stehen

intercontinental /ɪntəkɒntɪ'nentl/ *adj.* interkontinental

intercourse /'ɪntəkɔ:s/ *n.* (sexual) [Geschlechts]verkehr, *der*

interest /'ɪntrəst/ [1] *n.* **(a)** Interesse, *das;* **take** *or* **have an ~ in sb./sth.** sich für jmdn./etw. interessieren; **[just] for** *or* **out of ~:** [nur] interessehalber; **with ~:** interessiert; **act in one's own/sb.'s ~[s]** im eigenen/in jmds. Interesse handeln; **be of ~:** interessant sein **(to** für)
(b) (Finance) Zinsen *Pl.*
[2] *v.t.* interessieren; **be ~ed** sich interessieren **(in** für)

interest-'free *adj., adv.* unverzinslich ‹*Schuldverschreibung*›; zinsfrei ‹*Darlehen*›

'interesting *adj.* interessant

'interest rate *n.* Zinssatz, *der;* Zinsfuß, *der*

interface /'ɪntəfeɪs/ *n.* (Comp.) Schnittstelle, *die*

interfere /ɪntə'fɪə(r)/ *v.i.* sich einmischen **(in** in + *Akk.*); **~ with sth.** sich (*Dat.*) an etw. (*Dat.*) zu schaffen machen

interference /ɪntə'fɪərəns/ *n.* **(a)** (interfering) Einmischung, *die*
(b) (Radio, Telev.) Störung, *die*

interim /'ɪntərɪm/ [1] *n.* **in the ~:** in der Zwischenzeit
[2] *adj.* vorläufig

interior /ɪn'tɪərɪə(r)/ [1] *adj.* inner...; Innen‹*fläche, -wand*›
[2] *n.* Innere, *das*

interior: ~ deco'ration *n.* Raumgestaltung, *die;* **~ 'decorator** *n.* Raumgestalter, *der*/-gestalterin, *die;* **~ de'sign** *n.* Innenarchitektur, *die;* **~ de'signer** *n.* Innenarchitekt, *der*/-architektin, *die*

interject /ɪntə'dʒekt/ *v.t.* einwerfen

interjection /ɪntə'dʒekʃn/ *n.* Ausruf, *der*

interloper /'ɪntələʊpə(r)/ *n.* Eindringling, *der*

interlude /'ɪntəlu:d/ *n.* Pause, *die;* (music) Zwischenspiel, *das*

intermediary /ɪntə'mi:dɪərɪ/ *n.* Vermittler, *der*/Vermittlerin, *die*

intermediate /ɪntə'mi:djət/ *adj.* Zwischen-

interminable /ɪn'tɜ:mɪnəbl/ *adj.* endlos

intermingle /ɪntə'mɪŋgl/ *v.i.* sich vermischen

intermission /ɪntə'mɪʃn/ *n.* Pause, *die*

intermittent /ɪntə'mɪtənt/ *adj.* in Abständen auftretend

inter'mittently *adv.* in Abständen

intern /ɪn'tɜ:n/ *v.t.* gefangen halten

internal /ɪn'tɜ:nl/ *adj.* inner...; Innen‹*fläche, -abmessungen*›

internally /ɪn'tɜ:nəlɪ/ *adv.* innerlich

international /ɪntə'næʃənl/ [1] *adj.* international
[2] *n.* **(a)** (Sport) (contest) Länderspiel, *das*
(b) (participant) Nationalspieler, *der*/ -spielerin, *die*

international: ~ **call** *n.* Auslandsgespräch, *das;* ~ **'law** *n.* Völkerrecht, *das*

inter'nationally *adv.* international

International 'Monetary Fund *n.* Internationaler Währungsfonds

internee /ɪntɜ:'ni:/ *n.* Internierte, *der/die*

Internet /'ɪntənet/ *n.* **the** ~ das Internet; **on the** ~: im Internet

Internet: ~ **access** *n.* Internetzugang, *der;* ~ **cafe** *n.* Internetcafé, *das;* ~ **'Service Provider** *n.* Internetprovider, *der;* ~ **site** *n.* Internetseite, *die*

in'ternment *n.* Internierung, *die*

interplay /'ɪntəpleɪ/ *n.* Zusammenspiel, *das*

interpret /ɪn'tɜ:prɪt/ [1] *v.t.* **(a)** interpretieren; deuten ‹*Traum, Zeichen*›
(b) (between languages) dolmetschen
[2] *v.i.* dolmetschen

interpretation /ɪntɜ:prɪ'teɪʃn/ *n.* Interpretation, *die;* (of dream, symptoms) Deutung, *die*

in'terpreter *n.* Dolmetscher, *der*/ Dolmetscherin, *die*

interrogate /ɪn'terəgeɪt/ *v.t.* verhören; ausfragen ‹*Freund, Kind usw.*›

interrogation /ɪnterə'geɪʃn/ *n.* Verhör, *das*

interrogative /ɪntə'rɒgətɪv/ *adj.* (Ling.) Interrogativ-

interrogator /ɪn'terəgeɪtə(r)/ *n.* Vernehmer, *der*

interrupt /ɪntə'rʌpt/ [1] *v.t.* unterbrechen; **don't** ~ **me when I'm busy** stör mich nicht, wenn ich zu tun habe
[2] *v.i.* unterbrechen; stören

interruption /ɪntə'rʌpʃn/ *n.* Unterbrechung, *die;* Störung, *die*

intersect /ɪntə'sekt/ *v.i.* **(a)** ‹*Straßen:*› sich kreuzen
(b) (Geom.) sich schneiden

intersection /ɪntə'sekʃn/ *n.* **(a)** (road junction) Kreuzung, *die*
(b) (Geom.) Schnittpunkt, *der*

intersperse /ɪntə'spɜ:s/ *v.t.* **be** ~**d with** durchsetzt sein mit

interval /'ɪntəvl/ *n.* **(a)** [Zeit]abstand, *der;* **at** ~**s** in Abständen
(b) (break; also Brit. Theatre etc.) Pause, *die;* **sunny** ~**s** Aufheiterungen *Pl.*

intervene /ɪntə'vi:n/ *v.i.* **(a)** [vermittelnd] eingreifen (**in** in + *Akk.*)
(b) the intervening years die dazwischenliegenden Jahre

intervention /ɪntə'venʃn/ *n.* Eingreifen, *das;* Intervention, *die* (bes. Politik)

interview /'ɪntəvju:/ [1] *n.* **(a)** (for job) Vorstellungsgespräch, *das*
(b) (Journ., Radio, Telev.) Interview, *das*
[2] *v.t.* ein Vorstellungsgespräch führen mit; interviewen ‹*Politiker, Filmstar usw.*›

'interviewer *n.* Interviewer, *der*/ Interviewerin, *die*

intestine /ɪn'testɪn/ *n.* Darm, *der*

intimacy /'ɪntɪməsɪ/ *n.* **(a)** Vertrautheit, *die*
(b) (sexual) Intimität, *die*

intimate [1] /'ɪntɪmət/ *adj.* **(a)** eng ‹*Freund, Verhältnis*›; genau, (geh.) intim ‹*Kenntnis*›
(b) (sexually) intim
[2] /'ɪntɪmeɪt/ *v.t.* (imply) andeuten

intimately /'ɪntɪmətlɪ/ *adv.* genau[estens] ‹*kennen*›; eng ‹*verbinden*›

intimidate /ɪn'tɪmɪdeɪt/ *v.t.* einschüchtern

intimidation /ɪntɪmɪ'deɪʃn/ *n.* Einschüchterung, *die*

into /*before vowel* 'ɪntʊ, *before consonant* 'ɪntə/ *prep.* in (+ *Akk.*); (against) gegen; **I went out** ~ **the street** ich ging auf die Straße hinaus; **translate sth.** ~ **English** etw. ins Englische übersetzen

in'tolerable *adj.* unerträglich

in'tolerance *n.* Intoleranz, *die*

in'tolerant *adj.* intolerant (**of** gegenüber)

intonation /ɪntə'neɪʃn/ *n.* Intonation, *die*

intoxicant /ɪn'tɒksɪkənt/ *n.* Rauschmittel, *das*

intoxicate /ɪn'tɒksɪkeɪt/ *v.t.* betrunken machen

intoxication /ɪntɒksɪ'keɪʃn/ *n.* Rausch, *der*

intractable /ɪn'træktəbl/ *adj.* hartnäckig ‹*Problem*›

intransigent /ɪn'trænsɪdʒənt/ *adj.* unnachgiebig

in'transitive *adj.* (Ling.) intransitiv

intra-uterine /ɪntrə'ju:təraɪn/ *adj.* (Med.) intrauterin; ~ **[contraceptive] device** Intrauterinpessar, *das*

intravenous /ɪntrə'vi:nəs/ *adj.* (Med.) intravenös

'in-tray *n.* Eingangskorb, *der*

intrepid /ɪn'trepɪd/ *adj.* unerschrocken

intricacy /'ɪntrɪkəsɪ/ *n.* Kompliziertheit, *die*

intricate /'ɪntrɪkət/ *adj.* kompliziert

intrigue /ɪn'tri:g/ *v.t.* faszinieren

intriguing /ɪn'tri:gɪŋ/ *adj.* faszinierend
intrinsic /ɪn'trɪnsɪk/ *adj.* innewohnend; inner...; ~ **value** innerer Wert
intrinsically /ɪn'trɪnsɪkəlɪ/ *adv.* im Wesentlichen
intro /'ɪntrəʊ/ *n., pl.* ~**s** (coll.) (presentation) Vorstellung, *die;* (*Mus.*) Einleitung, *die*
introduce /ɪntrə'dju:s/ *v.t.* einführen; ~ **oneself/sb. [to sb.]** sich/jmdn. [jmdm.] vorstellen
introduction /ɪntrə'dʌkʃn/ *n.* Einführen, *das;* Einführung, *die;* (to person) Vorstellung, *die;* (to book) Einleitung, *die*
intro'duction agency *n.* Partnervermittlung[sagentur], *die*
introductory /ɪntrə'dʌktərɪ/ *adj.* einleitend; Einführungs‹*kurs, -vortrag*›
introspective /ɪntrə'spektɪv/ *adj.* in sich (*Akk.*) gerichtet
introvert /'ɪntrəvɜ:t/ **1** *n.* Introvertierte, *der/die;* **be an** ~: introvertiert sein **2** *adj.* introvertiert
introverted /'ɪntrəvɜ:tɪd/ *adj.* introvertiert
intrude /ɪn'tru:d/ *v.i.* stören
in'truder *n.* Eindringling, *der*
in'truder alarm *n.* Einbruchmeldeanlage, *die*
intrusion /ɪn'tru:ʒn/ *n.* Störung, *die*
intrusive /ɪn'tru:sɪv/ *adj.* aufdringlich
intuition /ɪntju:'ɪʃn/ *n.* Intuition, *die*
intuitive /ɪn'tju:ɪtɪv/ *adj.,* **in'tuitively** *adv.* intuitiv
inundate /'ɪnəndeɪt/ *v.t.* überschwemmen
inure /ɪ'njʊə(r)/ *v.t.* gewöhnen (**to** an + *Akk.*)
invade /ɪn'veɪd/ *v.t.* einfallen in (+ *Akk.*)
in'vader *n.* Angreifer, *der*
invalid[1] /'ɪnvəlɪd/ (Brit.) **1** *n.* Kranke, *der/die;* (disabled) Körperbehinderte, *der/die* **2** *adj.* körperbehindert
invalid[2] /ɪn'vælɪd/ *adj.* nicht schlüssig ‹*Argument, Theorie*›; ungültig ‹*Fahrkarte, Garantie, Vertrag*›
invalidate /ɪn'vælɪdeɪt/ *v.t.* aufheben; widerlegen ‹*Theorie, These*›
in'valuable *adj.* unersetzlich ‹*Person*›; unschätzbar ‹*Dienst, Hilfe*›; außerordentlich wichtig ‹*Rolle*›
in'variable *adj.* unveränderlich
invariably /ɪn'veərɪəblɪ/ *adv.* immer; ausnahmslos ‹*falsch, richtig*›
invasion /ɪn'veɪʒn/ *n.* Invasion, *die*
invective /ɪn'vektɪv/ *n.* Beschimpfungen *Pl.*
invent /ɪn'vent/ *v.t.* erfinden
invention /ɪn'venʃn/ *n.* Erfindung, *die*
inventive /ɪn'ventɪv/ *adj.* **(a)** schöpferisch ‹*Person, Begabung*› **(b)** (original) originell
inventor /ɪn'ventə(r)/ *n.* Erfinder, *der/* Erfinderin, *die*
inventory /'ɪnvəntərɪ/ *n.* Bestandsliste, *die;* **make** *or* **take an** ~ **of sth.** von etw. ein Inventar aufstellen
inverse /'ɪnvɜ:s/ *adj.* umgekehrt
invert /ɪn'vɜ:t/ *v.t.* umstülpen
in'vertebrate *n.* wirbelloses Tier
inverted 'commas *n. pl.* (Brit.) Anführungszeichen *Pl.*
invest /ɪn'vest/ *v.t.* **(a)** (Finance) anlegen (**in** in + *Dat.*); investieren (**in** in + *Dat. od. Akk.*) **(b)** (fig.) investieren; ~ **sb. with sth.** jmdm. etw. übertragen; ~ **sth. with sth.** einer Sache (*Dat.*) etw. verleihen
investigate /ɪn'vestɪgeɪt/ *v.t.* untersuchen
investigation /ɪnvestɪ'geɪʃn/ *n.* Untersuchung, *die*
investigative /ɪn'vestɪgətɪv/ *adj.* detektivisch; ~ **journalism** Enthüllungsjournalismus, *der*
investigator /ɪn'vestɪgeɪtə(r)/ *n.* **[private]** ~: [Privat]detektiv, *der/*-detektivin, *die*
in'vestment *n.* Investition, *die;* (money invested) angelegtes Geld; **be a good** ~ (fig.) sich bezahlt machen
investor /ɪn'vestə(r)/ *n.* [Kapital]anleger, *der/*-anlegerin, *die*
inveterate /ɪn'vetərət/ *adj.* eingefleischt ‹*Trinker, Raucher*›; unverbesserlich ‹*Lügner*›
invigilate /ɪn'vɪdʒɪleɪt/ *v.i.* (Brit.: in examination) Aufsicht führen
invigilator /ɪn'vɪdʒɪleɪtə(r)/ *n.* (Brit.) Aufsichtsperson, *die*
invigorate /ɪn'vɪgəreɪt/ *v.t.* stärken; (physically) kräftigen
invigorating /ɪn'vɪgəreɪtɪŋ/ *adj.* kräftigend ‹*Getränk, Klima*›
invincible /ɪn'vɪnsɪbl/ *adj.* unbesiegbar
in'visible *adj.* unsichtbar
invitation /ɪnvɪ'teɪʃn/ *n.* Einladung, *die;* **at sb.'s** ~: auf jmds. Einladung (*Akk.*)
invite /ɪn'vaɪt/ *v.t.* **(a)** (request to come) einladen **(b)** (request to do sth.) auffordern **(c)** (bring on) herausfordern ‹*Kritik, Verhängnis*›
inviting /ɪn'vaɪtɪŋ/ *adj.* einladend; verlockend ‹*Gedanke, Vorstellung*›
in-vitro fertili'zation /ɪn'vi:trəʊ fɜ:tɪlaɪ'zeɪʃn/ *n.* künstliche Befruchtung [im Reagenzglas]; In-vitro-Fertilisation, *die* (fachspr.)
invoice /'ɪnvɔɪs/ **1** *n.* (bill) Rechnung, *die* **2** *v.t.* ~ **sb.** jmdm. eine Rechnung schicken; ~ **sb. for sth.** jmdm. etw. in Rechnung stellen
invoke /ɪn'vəʊk/ *v.t.* anrufen
in'voluntarily *adv.,* **in'voluntary** *adj.* unwillkürlich
involve /ɪn'vɒlv/ *v.t.* **(a)** (implicate) verwickeln

(b) **become** *or* **get ~d in a fight** in eine Schlägerei verwickelt werden; **get ~d with sb.** sich mit jmdm. einlassen
(c) (entail) mit sich bringen

involved /ɪn'vɒlvd/ *adj.* verwickelt; (complicated) kompliziert

invulnerable /ɪn'vʌlnərəbl/ *adj.* unverwundbar; (fig.) unantastbar

inward /'ɪnwəd/ [1] *adj.* inner...
[2] *adv.* einwärts ‹*gerichtet, gebogen*›; **open ~**: nach innen öffnen

'inwardly *adv.* im Inneren; innerlich

inwards /'ɪnwədz/ ▶ INWARD 2

iodine /'aɪədi:n/ *n.* Jod, *das*

ion /'aɪən/ *n.* Ion, *das*

iota /aɪ'əʊtə/ *n.* **not one** *or* **an ~**: nicht ein Jota (geh.)

IOU /aɪəʊ'ju:/ *n.* Schuldschein, *der*

IQ *abbr.* = **intelligence quotient** IQ, *der;* **IQ-test** IQ-Test, *der*

IRA *abbr.* = **Irish Republican Army** IRA, *die*

Iran /ɪ'rɑ:n/ *pr. n.* Iran, *der od.* (*das*)

Iraq /ɪ'rɑ:k/ *pr. n.* Irak, *der od.* (*das*)

Iraq 'War *n.* Irakkrieg, *der*

irate /aɪ'reɪt/ *adj.* wütend

Ireland /'aɪələnd/ *pr. n.* Irland (*das*)

iris /'aɪərɪs/ *n.* (Bot., Anat.) Iris, *die*

Irish /'aɪərɪʃ/ [1] *adj.* irisch; **sb. is ~**: jmd. ist Ire/Irin
[2] *n.* **(a)** (language) Irisch, *das; see also* ENGLISH 2A
(b) *constr. as pl.* **the ~**: die Iren *Pl.*

Irish: ~man /'aɪərɪʃmən/ *n., pl.* **~men** /'aɪərɪʃmən/ Ire, *der;* **~ Re'public** *pr. n.* Irische Republik; **~ 'Sea** *pr. n.* Irische See; **~woman** *n.* Irin, *die*

irk /ɜ:k/ *v.t.* ärgern

irksome /'ɜ:ksəm/ *adj.* lästig

iron /'aɪən/ [1] *n.* **(a)** (metal) Eisen, *das*
(b) (for smoothing) Bügeleisen, *das*
[2] *attrib. adj.* eisern; Eisen‹*platte usw.*›
[3] *v.t. & i.* bügeln

▪ **iron 'out** *v.t.* herausbügeln; (fig.) aus dem Weg räumen

Iron 'Curtain *n.* (Hist.) Eiserner Vorhang

ironic /aɪ'rɒnɪk/, **ironical** /aɪ'rɒnɪkl/ *adj.* ironisch

ironing /'aɪənɪŋ/ *n.* Bügeln, *das;* (items) Bügelwäsche, *die;* **do the ~**: bügeln

'ironing board *n.* Bügelbrett, *das*

ironmonger /'aɪənmʌŋgə(r)/ *n.* (Brit.) Eisenwarenhändler, *der*/-händlerin, *die*

irony /'aɪrənɪ/ *n.* Ironie, *die;* **the ~ was that ...**: die Ironie lag darin, dass ...

irradiate /ɪ'reɪdɪeɪt/ *v.t.* bestrahlen

irrational /ɪ'ræʃənl/ *adj.* irrational

irreconcilable /ɪ'rekənsaɪləbl/ *adj.* (incompatible) unvereinbar

irrefutable /ɪrɪ'fju:təbl/ *adj.* unwiderlegbar

irregular /ɪ'regjʊlə(r)/ *adj.* unregelmäßig; unkorrekt ‹*Verhalten, Handlung usw.*›

irregularity /ɪregjʊ'lærɪtɪ/ *n.* ▶ IRREGULAR: Unregelmäßigkeit, *die;* Unkorrektheit, *die*

irrelevance /ɪ'relɪvəns/, **irrelevancy** /ɪ'relɪvənsɪ/ *ns.* Belanglosigkeit, *die;* Irrelevanz, *die* (geh.)

irrelevant /ɪ'relɪvənt/ *adj.* belanglos; irrelevant (geh.)

irreparable /ɪ'repərəbl/ *adj.* nicht wieder gutzumachend *nicht präd.;* irreparabel (geh., Med.)

irreplaceable /ɪrɪ'pleɪsəbl/ *adj.* unersetzlich

irrepressible /ɪrɪ'presɪbl/ *adj.* nicht zu unterdrückend *nicht präd.;* **she is ~**: sie ist nicht unterzukriegen (ugs.)

irresistible /ɪrɪ'zɪstɪbl/ *adj.* unwiderstehlich; bestechend ‹*Argument*›

irresolute /ɪ'rezəlu:t/ *adj.* unentschlossen

irrespective /ɪrɪ'spektɪv/ *adj.* **~ of** ungeachtet (+ *Gen.*)

irresponsible /ɪrɪ'spɒnsɪbl/ *adj.* verantwortungslos ‹*Person*›; unverantwortlich ‹*Benehmen*›

irretrievable /ɪrɪ'tri:vəbl/ *adj.* nicht mehr wiederzubekommen *nicht attr.*

irreverence /ɪ'revərəns/ *n.* Respektlosigkeit, *die*

irreverent /ɪ'revərənt/ *adj.* respektlos

irreversible /ɪrɪ'vɜ:sɪbl/, **irrevocable** /ɪ'revəkəbl/ *adjs.* unwiderruflich

irrigate /'ɪrɪgeɪt/ *v.t.* bewässern

irrigation /ɪrɪ'geɪʃn/ *n.* Bewässerung, *die*

irritable /'ɪrɪtəbl/ *adj.* (quick to anger) reizbar; (temporarily) gereizt

irritant /'ɪrɪtənt/ *n.* Reizstoff, *der*

irritate /'ɪrɪteɪt/ *v.t.* **(a)** ärgern; **get ~d** ärgerlich werden; **be ~d by sth.** sich über etw. (*Akk.*) ärgern
(b) (Med.) reizen

irritating /'ɪrɪteɪtɪŋ/ *adj.* lästig

irritation /ɪrɪ'teɪʃn/ *n.* **(a)** Ärger, *der*
(b) (Med.) Reizung, *die*

is ▶ BE

Islam /'ɪzlɑ:m/ *n.* Islam, *der*

Islamist /'ɪzlæmɪst/ [1] *n.* Islamist, *der*/Islamistin *die*
[2] *adj.* islamistisch

island /'aɪlənd/ *n.* Insel, *die*

'islander *n.* Inselbewohner, *der*/-bewohnerin, *die*

island: ~-hop *v.i.* **go ~-hopping** eine Inselhoppingtour machen; **~-hopping** *n.* Inselhopping, *das*

isle /aɪl/ *n.* Insel, *die*

isn't /'ɪznt/ (coll.) = **is not;** ▶ BE

isolate /'aɪsəleɪt/ *v.t.* isolieren

isolated /'aɪsəleɪtɪd/ *adj.* **(a)** (single) einzeln; **~ cases/instances** Einzelfälle
(b) (remote) abgelegen

isolation /aɪsə'leɪʃn/ *n.* **(a)** (act) Isolierung, *die*
(b) (state) Isolation, *die*

ISP *abbr.* = **Internet service provider** ISP

Israel /'ɪzreɪl/ *pr. n.* Israel *(das)*

Israeli /ɪz'reɪlɪ/ 1 *adj.* israelisch; **sb. is ~:** jmd. ist Israeli
2 *n.* Israeli, *der/die*

issue /'ɪʃu:, 'ɪsju:/ 1 *n.* **(a)** (point in question) Frage, *die;* **make an ~ of sth.** etw. aufbauschen; **evade** *or* **dodge the ~:** ausweichen
(b) (of magazine etc.) Ausgabe, *die*
(c) (result, outcome) Ergebnis, *das*
2 *v.t.* **(a)** (give out) ausgeben; ausstellen ‹*Pass*›; erteilen ‹*Lizenz, Befehl*›; **~ sb. with sth.** etw. an jmdn. austeilen
(b) (publish) herausgeben ‹*Publikation*›

it /ɪt/ *pron.* **(a)** es; **I can't cope with it any more** ich halte das nicht mehr länger aus; **what is it?** was ist los?
(b) (the thing, animal, young child previously mentioned) er/sie/es; *as direct obj.* ihn/sie/es; *as indirect obj.* ihm/ihr/ihm
(c) (the person in question) **who is it?** wer ist da?; **it was the children** es waren die Kinder; **is it you, Dad?** bist du es, Vater?

IT *abbr.* = **information technology** IT

Italian /ɪ'tæljən/ 1 *adj.* italienisch; **sb. is ~:** jmd. ist Italiener/Italienerin
2 *n.* **(a)** (person) Italiener, *der*/Italienerin, *die*
(b) (language) Italienisch, *das; see also* ENGLISH 2A

italic /ɪ'tælɪk/ 1 *adj.* kursiv
2 *n. in pl.* Kursivschrift, *die;* **in ~s** kursiv

Italy /'ɪtəlɪ/ *pr. n.* Italien *(das)*

itch /ɪtʃ/ 1 *n.* Juckreiz, *der;* **I have an ~:** es juckt mich
2 *v.i.* **(a)** einen Juckreiz haben; **it ~es** es juckt
(b) ~ *or* **be ~ing to do sth.** darauf brennen, etw. zu tun

'itchy *adj.* kratzig; **be ~** ‹*Körperteil:*› jucken

it'd /'ɪtəd/ (coll.) **(a)** = **it had**
(b) = **it would**

item /'aɪtəm/ *n.* **(a)** Ding, *das;* Sache, *die;* (in shop, catalogue) Artikel, *der;* (on radio, TV) Nummer, *die;* **~ of clothing** Kleidungsstück, *das*
(b) ~ [of news] Nachricht, *die*

itemize /'aɪtəmaɪz/ *v.t.* einzeln aufführen

itinerary /aɪ'tɪnərərɪ/ *n.* Reiseroute, *die*

it'll /ɪtl/ (coll.) = **it will**

its /ɪts/ *poss. pron. attrib.* sein/ihr/sein

it's /ɪts/ **(a)** = **it is**
(b) = **it has**

itself /ɪt'self/ *pron.* **(a)** *emphat.* selbst
(b) *refl.* sich

IUD *abbr.* = **intrauterine device** IUP

I've /aɪv/ = **I have**

IVF *abbr.* = **in-vitro fertilization** IVF

ivory /'aɪvərɪ/ *n.* Elfenbein, *das; attrib.* elfenbeinern; Elfenbein-

ivy /'aɪvɪ/ *n.* Efeu, *der*

Jj

J, j /dʒeɪ/ *n.* J, j, *das*

jab /dʒæb/ 1 *v.t.,* **-bb-** stoßen
2 *n.* **(a)** Stoß, *der;* (with needle) Stich, *der*
(b) (Brit. coll.: injection) Spritze, *die*

jabber /'dʒæbə(r)/ *v.i.* plappern (ugs.)

jack /dʒæk/ *n.* **(a)** (for car) Wagenheber, *der*
(b) (Cards) Bube, *der*

jackal /'dʒækl/ *n.* Schakal, *der*

jackdaw /'dʒækdɔ:/ *n.* Dohle, *die*

jacket /'dʒækɪt/ *n.* **(a)** Jacke, *die;* (of suit) Jackett, *das;* **sports ~:** Sakko, *der*
(b) (of book) Schutzumschlag, *der*
(c) ~ potatoes in der Schale gebackene Kartoffeln

jack: ~-knife *v.i.* **the lorry ~-knifed** der Anhänger des Lastwagens stellte sich quer; **~pot** *n.* Jackpot, *der;* **hit the ~pot** (fig.) das große Los ziehen

jacuzzi (Amer.: ®) /dʒə'ku:zɪ/ *n.* ≈ Whirlpool, *der*

jaded /'dʒeɪdɪd/ *adj.* abgespannt

jagged /'dʒægɪd/ *adj.* gezackt

jaguar /'dʒægjʊə(r)/ *n.* Jaguar, *der*

jail /dʒeɪl/ 1 *n.* Gefängnis, *das*
2 *v.t.* ins Gefängnis bringen

jail: ~bird Knastbruder, *der* (ugs.); **~break** *n.* Gefängnisausbruch, *der*

jailer, jailor /'dʒeɪlə(r)/ *n.* Gefängniswärter, *der*/-wärterin, *die*

jam¹ /dʒæm/ 1 *v.t.,* **-mm-: (a)** (between two surfaces) einklemmen
(b) (make immovable) blockieren; (fig.) lähmen
2 *v.i.,* **-mm-: (a)** (become wedged) sich verklemmen
(b) ‹*Maschine:*› klemmen
3 *n.* **(a)** (crush, stoppage) Blockierung, *die*

(b) (coll.: dilemma) **be in a ~:** in der Klemme stecken (ugs.)

■ **jam 'on** *v.t.* **~ the brakes [full] on** [voll] auf die Bremse steigen (ugs.)

jam² *n.* Marmelade, *die*

Jamaica /dʒə'meɪkə/ *pr. n.* Jamaika (*das*)

jamb /dʒæm/ *n.* (of doorway, window) Pfosten, *der*

'jam-packed *adj.* (coll.) knallvoll (ugs.), proppenvoll (ugs.) (**with** von)

Jan. *abbr.* = **January** Jan.

jangle /'dʒæŋgl/ **1** *v.i.* klimpern; ‹*Klingel*:› bimmeln
2 *v.t.* rasseln mit

janitor /'dʒænɪtə(r)/ *n.* Hausmeister, *der*

January /'dʒænjʊərɪ/ *n.* Januar, *der; see also* AUGUST

Japan /dʒə'pæn/ *n.* Japan (*das*)

Japanese /dʒæpə'ni:z/ **1** *adj.* japanisch; **sb. is ~** jmd. ist Japaner/Japanerin
2 *n., pl. same* **(a)** (person) Japaner, *der*/Japanerin, *die*
(b) (language) Japanisch, *das; see also* ENGLISH 2A

jar¹ /dʒɑ:(r)/ **1** *v.i.*, **-rr-** quietschen; (fig.) **~ on sb./sb.'s nerves** jmdm. auf die Nerven gehen
2 *v.t.*, **-rr-** erschüttern

jar² *n.* Topf, *der;* (glass **~**) Glas, *das*

jargon /'dʒɑ:gən/ *n.* Jargon, *der*

jasmin[e] /'dʒæsmɪn/ *n.* Jasmin, *der*

jaundice /'dʒɔ:ndɪs/ *n.* (Med.) Gelbsucht, *die*

jaundiced /'dʒɔ:ndɪst/ *adj.* (fig.) verbittert

jaunt /dʒɔ:nt/ *n.* Ausflug, *der*

jaunty /'dʒɔ:ntɪ/ *adj.* unbeschwert; keck ‹*Hut*›; **he wore his hat at a ~ angle** er hatte sich (*Dat.*) den Hut keck aufs Ohr gesetzt

javelin /'dʒævlɪn/ *n.* **(a)** Speer, *der*
(b) (Sport: event) Speerwerfen, *das*

jaw /dʒɔ:/ Kiefer, *der*

'jawbone *n.* Kieferknochen, *der*

jay /dʒeɪ/ *n.* Eichelhäher, *der*

'jay-walk *v.i.* als Fußgänger im Straßenverkehr unachtsam sein

jazz /dʒæz/ **1** *n.* Jazz, *der; attrib.* Jazz-
2 *v.t.* **~ up** aufpeppen (ugs.)

jazz: ~ band *n.* Jazzband, *die;* **~ dance** *n.* Jazztanz, *der;* **~ 'rock** *n.* Jazzrock, *der*

jazzy /'dʒæzɪ/ *adj.* poppig; **a ~ sports car** ein aufgemotzter Sportwagen (ugs.)

jealous /'dʒeləs/ *adj.* eifersüchtig (**of** auf + *Akk.*)

'jealousy *n.* Eifersucht, *die*

jeans /dʒi:nz/ *n. pl.* Jeans *Pl.*

Jeep ® /dʒi:p/ *n.* Jeep (Wz), *der*

jeer /dʒɪə(r)/ *v.i.* höhnen (geh.); **~ at sb.** jmdn. verhöhnen

jelly /'dʒelɪ/ *n.* Gelee, *das;* (dessert) Götterspeise, *die*

'jellyfish *n.* Qualle, *die*

jeopardize /'dʒepədaɪz/ *v.t.* gefährden

jeopardy /'dʒepədɪ/ *n.* **in ~:** in Gefahr; gefährdet

jerk /dʒɜ:k/ **1** *n.* Ruck, *der*
2 *v.t.* reißen an (+ *Dat.*)
3 *v.i.* zucken

jersey /'dʒɜ:zɪ/ *n.* Pullover, *der;* (Sport) Trikot, *das*

jest /dʒest/ **1** *n.* Scherz, *der;* **in ~:** im Scherz
2 *v.i.* scherzen

Jesus /'dʒi:zəs/ *pr. n.* Jesus (*der*)

jet /dʒet/ *n.* **(a)** (stream) Strahl, *der*
(b) (nozzle) Düse, *die*
(c) (aircraft) Düsenflugzeug, *das;* Jet, *der*

jet: ~-black *adj.* pechschwarz; **~ engine** *n.* Düsentriebwerk, *das;* **~foil** *n.* [Jetfoil-]Tragflügelboot, *das;* **~ lag** *n.* Jetlag, *der;* **~-lagged** *adj.* **sb. is ~-lagged** jmdm. macht der Jetlag zu schaffen; **~ plane** *n.* Düsenflugzeug, *das;* **~-propelled** *adj.* düsengetrieben; **~ pro'pulsion** *n.* Düsen- *od.* Strahlantrieb, *der*

jetsam /'dʒetsəm/ *n.* ▶ FLOTSAM

jet: ~ set *n.* Jet-set, *der;* **~ ski** *n.* Jetski, *der*

jettison /'dʒetɪsən/ *v.t.* über Bord werfen; (discard) wegwerfen

jetty /'dʒetɪ/ *n.* Landungsbrücke, *die*

Jew /dʒu:/ *n.* Jude, *der*/Jüdin, *die*

jewel /'dʒu:əl/ *n.* Juwel, *das od. der*

'jewel box, 'jewel case *ns.* Schmuckkasten, *der*

jeweller (*Amer.:* **jeweler**) /'dʒu:ələ(r)/ *n.* Juwelier, *der*

jewellery (Brit.), **jewelry** /'dʒu:əlrɪ/ *n.* Schmuck, *der*

Jewish /'dʒu:ɪʃ/ *adj.* jüdisch; **he/she is ~:** er ist Jude/sie ist Jüdin

jib /dʒɪb/ *v.i.*, **-bb-** sich sträuben (**at** gegen)

jibe ▶ GIBE

jiffy /'dʒɪfɪ/ *n.* (coll.) **in a ~:** sofort

'Jiffy bag ® *n.* gefütterte Versandtasche

jig /dʒɪg/ *n.* Jig, *die*

'jigsaw *n.* **(a)** Dekupiersäge, *die;* (electric) Stichsäge, *die*
(b) ~ [puzzle] Puzzle, *das*

jilt /dʒɪlt/ *v.t.* sitzenlassen (ugs.)

jingle /'dʒɪŋgl/ **1** *n.* (Commerc.) Werbespruch, *der;* Jingle, *der* (Werbespr.)
2 *v.i.* klimpern; ‹*Glöckchen*:› bimmeln
3 *v.t.* klimpern mit ‹*Münzen, Schlüsseln*›

jinx /dʒɪŋks/ (coll.) **1** *n.* Fluch, *der*
2 *v.t.* verhexen

jitters /'dʒɪtəz/ *n. pl.* (coll.) großes Zittern

jittery /'dʒɪtərɪ/ *adj.* (coll.) (nervous) nervös; (frightened) verängstigt

job /dʒɒb/ *n.* **(a)** (piece of work) Arbeit, *die;* **I have a ~ for you** ich habe eine Aufgabe für dich
(b) (employment) Stelle, *die;* Job, *der* (ugs.)

job: ~ advert *n.* Stellenanzeige, *die;* **~centre** *n.* (Brit.) Arbeitsvermittlungsstelle, *die;* **~ creation scheme** *n.* Beschäftigungsprogramm, *das;* Arbeitsbeschaffungsprogramm, *das;* **~ description** *n.* Arbeitsplatzbeschreibung, *die;* **~ evaluation** *n.* Arbeitsbewertung, *die;* **~-hunt** *v.i.* **go/be ~-hunting** auf Arbeits- *od.* Stellensuche gehen/sein; **~-hunter** *n.* Stellen- *od.* Arbeitssuchende, *der/die;* **~-hunting** *n.* Arbeitssuche, *die;* Stellensuche, *die*

'jobless *adj.* arbeitslos

job: ~ market *n.* Arbeitsmarkt, *der;* Stellenmarkt, *der;* **~ offer** *n.* Stellenangebot, *das;* **~ satisfaction** *n.* Arbeitszufriedenheit, *die;* **~ security** *n.* Arbeitsplatzsicherheit, *die;* **~-share** [1] *n.* geteilter Arbeitsplatz; [2] *v.i.* sich (*Dat.*) einen Arbeitsplatz teilen (**with** mit); **~-sharing** *n.* Jobsharing, *das*

jockey /'dʒɒkɪ/ *n.* Jockei, *der*

jockey shorts *n. pl.* (Amer.) Unterhose, *die;* Unterhosen *Pl.*

jocular /'dʒɒkjʊlə(r)/ *adj.* lustig

jodhpurs /'dʒɒdpəz/ *n. pl.* Reithose, *die*

jog /dʒɒg/ [1] *v.t.*, **-gg-**: **(a)** (shake) rütteln
(b) (nudge) [an]stoßen
(c) ~ sb.'s memory jmds. Gedächtnis (*Dat.*) auf die Sprünge helfen
[2] *v.i.*, **-gg-**: **(a)** (up and down) auf und ab hüpfen
(b) (trot) ‹*Pferd:*› [dahin]trotten
(c) (Sport) joggen
[3] *n.* **go for a ~**: joggen gehen

jogger /'dʒɒgə(r)/ *n.* Jogger, *der*/Joggerin, *die*

'jogging *n.* Jogging, *das*

'jogtrot *n.* (lit. or fig.) Trott, *der*

john /dʒɒn/ *n.* (Amer. sl.: lavatory) Lokus, *der* (salopp)

join /dʒɔɪn/ [1] *v.t.* **(a)** (connect) verbinden (**to** mit)
(b) (come into company of) sich gesellen zu
(c) eintreten in (+ *Akk.*) ‹*Armee, Firma, Verein, Partei*›
[2] *v.i.* ‹*Straßen:*› zusammenlaufen

▪ **join in** [1] /-'-/ *v.i.* mitmachen (**with** bei)
[2] /'--/ *v.t.* mitmachen bei

▪ **join 'up** [1] *v.i.* (Mil.) einrücken
[2] *v.t.* miteinander verbinden

'joiner *n.* Tischler, *der*/Tischlerin, *die*

joinery /'dʒɔɪnərɪ/ *n., no art.* (craft) Tischlerei, *die;* Tischlerhandwerk, *das*

joint /dʒɔɪnt/ [1] *n.* **(a)** (Building) Fuge, *die*
(b) (Anat.) Gelenk, *das*
(c) a ~ [of meat] ein Stück Fleisch; (for roasting) ein Braten
(d) (coll.: place) Laden, *der*
(e) (sl.: marijuana cigarette) Joint, *der*
[2] *adj.* **(a)** (of two or more) gemeinsam
(b) Mit‹*autor, -erbe, -besitzer*›

'jointly *adv.* gemeinsam

joint 'venture *n.* (Commerc.) Jointventure, *das*

joist /dʒɔɪst/ *n.* (Building) Deckenbalken, *der;* (steel) [Decken]träger, *der*

joke /dʒəʊk/ [1] *n.* Witz, *der;* Scherz, *der*
[2] *v.i.* scherzen, Witze machen (**about** über + *Akk.*); **joking apart** Scherz beiseite!

'joker *n.* **(a)** Spaßvogel, *der*
(b) (Cards) Joker, *der*

jollity /'dʒɒlɪtɪ/ *n.* Fröhlichkeit, *die;* (merrymaking) Festlichkeit, *die*

jolly /'dʒɒlɪ/ [1] *adj.* fröhlich
[2] *adv.* (Brit. coll.) ganz schön (ugs.); **~ good!** ausgezeichnet!

jolt /dʒəʊlt/ [1] *v.t.* ‹*Fahrzeug:*› durchrütteln
[2] *v.i.* ‹*Fahrzeug:*› holpern
[3] *n.* **(a)** (jerk) Stoß, *der;* Ruck, *der*
(b) (fig.: shock) Schock, *der*

Jordan /'dʒɔ:dn/ *pr. n.* Jordanien (*das*)

jostle /'dʒɒsl/ [1] *v.i.* **~ [against each other]** aneinander stoßen
[2] *v.t.* stoßen

jot /dʒɒt/ *n.* **[not] a ~**: [k]ein bisschen

▪ **jot 'down** *v.t.* [rasch] aufschreiben

jotter /'dʒɒtə(r)/ *n.* Notizblock, *der*

journal /'dʒɜ:nl/ *n.* Zeitschrift, *die*

journalism /'dʒɜ:nəlɪzm/ *n.* Journalismus, *der*

journalist /'dʒɜ:nəlɪst/ *n.* Journalist, *der*/Journalistin, *die*

journey /'dʒɜ:nɪ/ *n.* **(a)** Reise, *die*
(b) (of vehicle) Fahrt, *die*

jovial /'dʒəʊvɪəl/ *adj.* herzlich ‹*Gruß*›; fröhlich ‹*Person*›

jowl /dʒaʊl/ *n.* (jaw) Unterkiefer, *der;* (lower part of face) Kinnbacken *Pl.;* (double chin) Doppelkinn, *das*

joy /dʒɔɪ/ *n.* Freude, *die*

joyful /'dʒɔɪfl/ *adj.* froh [gestimmt] ‹*Person*›; freudig ‹*Blick, Ereignis, Gesang*›

joy: ~ride *n.* (coll.) Spritztour, *die* [im gestohlenen Auto]; **~stick** *n.* **(a)** (Aeronaut.) Knüppel, *der;* **(b)** (on computer etc.) Hebel, *der;* Joystick, *der*

JP *abbr.* = **Justice of the Peace**

jubilant /'dʒu:bɪlənt/ *adj.* jubelnd; **be ~** ‹*Person:*› frohlocken

jubilation /dʒu:bɪ'leɪʃn/ *n.* Jubel, *der*

jubilee /'dʒu:bɪli:/ *n.* Jubiläum, *das*

Judaism /'dʒu:deɪɪzm/ *n., no art.* Judentum, *das;* Judaismus, *der*

judge /dʒʌdʒ/ [1] *n.* **(a)** Richter, *der*/Richterin, *die*
(b) (in contest) Preisrichter, *der*/-richterin, *die*
(c) (fig.: critic) Kenner, *der*/Kennerin, *die*
[2] *v.t.* **(a)** (sentence) richten (geh.)
(b) (form opinion about) [be]urteilen

'judg[e]ment *n.* **(a)** Urteil, *das*
(b) (critical faculty) Urteilsvermögen, *das*

judicial /dʒu:'dɪʃl/ *adj.* gerichtlich

judiciary /dʒu:'dɪʃərɪ/ *n.* Richterschaft, *die*

judicious /dʒu:'dɪʃəs/ *adj.* klar blickend

judo /'dʒu:dəʊ/ *n.* Judo, *das*
jug /dʒʌg/ *n.* Krug, *der;* (with lid, water ~) Kanne, *die*
juggernaut /'dʒʌgənɔ:t/ *n.* (Brit.: lorry) schwerer Brummer (ugs.)
juggle /'dʒʌgl/ *v.i.* jonglieren
juggler /'dʒʌglə(r)/ *n.* Jongleur, *der*/Jongleurin, *die*
juice /dʒu:s/ *n.* Saft, *der*
juicy /'dʒu:sɪ/ *adj.* saftig
jukebox /'dʒu:kbɒks/ *n.* Jukebox, *die;* Musikbox, *die*
Jul. *abbr.* = **July** Jul.
July /dʒʊ'laɪ/ *n.* Juli, *der; see also* AUGUST
jumble /'dʒʌmbl/ [1] *v.t.* ~ **up** durcheinander bringen
[2] *n.* Durcheinander, *das*
'jumble sale *n.* (Brit.) Trödelmarkt, *der*
jumbo jet /dʒʌmbəʊ 'dʒet/ *n.* Jumbojet, *der*
jump /dʒʌmp/ [1] *n.* **(a)** Sprung, *der*
(b) (in prices) sprunghafter Anstieg
[2] *v.i.* **(a)** springen; ~ **for joy** einen Freudensprung machen
(b) ~ **to conclusions** voreilige Schlüsse ziehen
[3] *v.t.* **(a)** überspringen
(b) ~ **the queue** (Brit.) sich vordrängeln
■ **jump a'bout, jump a'round** *v.i.* herumspringen (ugs.)
■ **'jump at** *v.t.* (fig.) sofort zugreifen bei ‹*Angebot, Gelegenheit*›
jumped-up /'dʒʌmptʌp/ *adj.* (coll.) emporgekommen
'jumper *n.* Pullover, *der*
jump: ~ jet *n.* Senkrechtstarter, *der;* ~ **leads** *n. pl.* (Brit. Motor Veh.) Starthilfekabel *Pl.* ; **~-start** [1] *v.t.* Starthilfe geben (+ *Dat.*) ‹*Auto*›; (fig.) [wieder] in Gang bringen; [wieder] ankurbeln ‹*Wirtschaft, Industrie*›; [2] *n.* Start durch Starthilfe; (fig.) neuer Impuls *od.* Auftrieb; **~suit** *n.* Overall, *der*
jumpy /'dʒʌmpɪ/ *adj.* nervös
Jun. *abbr.* = **June** Jun.
junction /'dʒʌŋkʃn/ *n.* **(a)** (of railway lines, roads) ≈ Einmündung, *die*
(b) (crossroads) Kreuzung, *die*
'junction box *n.* (Electr.) Verteilerkasten, *der*
juncture /'dʒʌŋktʃə(r)/ *n.* **at this ~:** zu diesem Zeitpunkt
June /dʒu:n/ *n.* Juni, *der; see also* AUGUST
jungle /'dʒʌŋgl/ *n.* Dschungel, *der*
junior /'dʒu:nɪə(r)/ *adj.* **(a)** (in age) jünger; ~ **team** (Sport) Juniorenmannschaft, *die*
(b) (in rank) rangniedriger ‹*Person*›; niedriger ‹*Rang*›
junior: ~ 'partner *n.* Juniorpartner, *der*/-partnerin, *die;* ~ **school** *n.* (Brit.) Grundschule, *die*
junk /dʒʌŋk/ *n.* Trödel, *der* (ugs.); (trash) Ramsch, *der* (ugs.)
junk 'e-mail *n.* Junkmail, *die*
'junk food *n.* minderwertige Kost
junkie /'dʒʌŋkɪ/ *n.* (sl.) Junkie, *der* (Drogenjargon)
junk: ~ mail *n.* Postwurfsendungen *Pl.;* Reklame, *die;* (e-mail) Junkmail, *die;* ~ **shop** *n.* Trödelladen, *der* (ugs.)
Jupiter /'dʒu:pɪtə(r)/ *pr. n.* (Astron.) Jupiter, *der*
jurisdiction /dʒʊərɪs'dɪkʃn/ *n.* Gerichtsbarkeit, *die*
juror /'dʒʊərə(r)/ *n.* Geschworene, *der*/*die*
jury /'dʒʊərɪ/ *n.* **(a)** (in court) **the ~:** die Geschworenen *Pl.*
(b) (in competition) Jury, *die*
just /dʒʌst/ [1] *adj.* (morally right) gerecht
[2] *adv.* **(a)** (exactly) genau; ~ **then/enough** gerade da/genug; ~ **as** (exactly as) genauso wie; (when) gerade, als; ~ **as you like** *or* **please** ganz wie Sie wünschen/du magst; ~ **as good** *etc.* genauso gut *usw.*
(b) (barely) gerade [eben]; (with little time to spare) gerade noch; (no more than) nur; ~ **under £10** nicht ganz zehn Pfund
(c) (at this moment) gerade; **not ~ now** im Moment nicht
(d) (coll.) (simply) einfach; (only) nur; *esp. with imper.* mal [eben]; ~ **look at that!** guck dir das mal an!; ~ **a moment** einen Moment mal; ~ **in case** für alle Fälle
justice /'dʒʌstɪs/ *n.* **(a)** Gerechtigkeit, *die*
(b) (magistrate) Schiedsrichter, *der*/-richterin, *die;* **J~ of the Peace** Friedensrichter, *der*/-richterin, *die*
justifiable /dʒʌstɪ'faɪəbl/ *adj.* berechtigt
justifiably /dʒʌstɪ'faɪəblɪ/ *adv.* zu Recht
justification /dʒʌstɪfɪ'keɪʃn/ *n.* Rechtfertigung, *die*
justify /'dʒʌstɪfaɪ/ *v.t.* rechtfertigen; **be justified in doing sth.** etw. zu Recht tun
jut /dʒʌt/ *v.i.*, **-tt-:** ~ **[out]** [her]vorragen; herausragen
juvenile /'dʒu:vənaɪl/ [1] *adj.* **(a)** jugendlich
(b) (immature) kindisch
[2] *n.* Jugendliche, *der*/*die*
juvenile delinquency /dɪ'lɪŋkwənsɪ/ *n.* Jugendkriminalität, *die*
juvenile delinquent /dɪ'lɪŋkwənt/ *n.* jugendlicher Straftäter/jugendliche Straftäterin
juxtapose /dʒʌkstə'pəʊz/ *v.t.* nebeneinander stellen (**with, to** und)
juxtaposition /dʒʌkstəpə'zɪʃn/ *n.* Nebeneinanderstellung, *die*

Kk

K, k /keɪ/ *n.* K, k, *das*

kale /keɪl/ *n.* Grünkohl, *der;* Krauskohl, *der*

kaleidoscope /kəˈlaɪdəskəʊp/ *n.* Kaleidoskop, *das*

kangaroo /kæŋgəˈruː/ *n.* Känguru, *das*

karaoke /kærɪˈəʊkɪ/ *n., no indef. art.* Karaoke, *das; attrib.* Karaoke-

karate /kəˈrɑːtɪ/ *n.* Karate, *das*

kebab /kɪˈbæb/ *n.* Kebab, *der*

keel /kiːl/ *n.* [1] (Naut.) Kiel, *der*
[2] *v.i.* ~ **over** umstürzen; ‹*Schiff:*› kentern; ‹*Person:*› umkippen

keen /kiːn/ *adj.* **(a)** (sharp) scharf
(b) (cold) schneidend ‹*Wind, Kälte*›
(c) (eager) begeistert ‹*Fußballfan, Sportler*›; lebhaft ‹*Interesse*›; **be ~ to do sth.** darauf erpicht sein, etw. zu tun; **be ~ on doing sth.** etw. gern[e] tun
(d) (sensitive) scharf ‹*Augen*›; fein ‹*Sinne*›

ˈkeenly *adv.* **(a)** (sharply) scharf
(b) (eagerly) eifrig; brennend ‹*interessiert sein*›
(c) (acutely) **be ~ aware of sth.** sich (*Dat.*) einer Sache (*Gen.*) voll bewusst sein

keep /kiːp/ [1] *v.t.,* **kept** /kept/ **(a)** halten ‹*Versprechen, Schwur, Sabbat, Fasten*›; einhalten ‹*Verabredung, Vereinbarung*›; begehen, feiern ‹*Fest*›
(b) (have charge of) aufbewahren
(c) (retain) behalten; (not lose or destroy) aufheben ‹*Quittung, Rechnung*›
(d) halten ‹*Bienen, Hund usw*›
(e) führen ‹*Tagebuch, Geschäft, Ware*›
(f) (support) versorgen ‹*Familie*›
(g) (detain) festhalten; **~ sb. waiting** jmdn. warten lassen; **what kept you?** wo bleibst du denn?
(h) (reserve) aufheben
[2] *v.i.,* **kept (a)** (remain) bleiben; **are you ~ing well?** gehts dir gut?
(b) ~ [to the] left/right sich links/rechts halten; **~ doing sth.** (repeatedly) etw. immer wieder tun; **~ talking/working** *etc.* **until ...:** weiterreden/-arbeiten *usw.,* bis ...
(c) (remain good) ‹*Lebensmittel:*› sich halten
[3] *n.* **(a)** (maintenance) Unterhalt, *der*
(b) for ~s (coll.) auf Dauer
(c) (Hist.: tower) Bergfried, *der*

■ **keep ˈback** [1] *v.i.* zurückbleiben
[2] *v.t.* **(a)** (restrain) zurückhalten ‹*Menschenmenge, Tränen*›
(b) (withhold) verschweigen ‹*Informationen, Tatsachen*› **(from** *Dat.*)

■ **keep ˈdown** [1] *v.i.* unten bleiben
[2] *v.t.* **(a)** niedrig halten ‹*Steuern, Preise usw.*›; **~ one's weight down** nicht zunehmen
(b) keep your voice down! rede nicht so laut!

■ **keep ˈoff** [1] *v.i.* ‹*Person:*› wegbleiben
[2] *v.t.* fern halten; **'~ off the grass'** „Betreten des Rasens verboten“

■ **keep ˈon** *v.i.* weitermachen (**with** *Akk.*); **~ on doing sth.** etw. [immer] weiter tun; (repeatedly) etw. immer wieder tun

■ **keep ˈout** [1] *v.i.* **'~out** „Zutritt verboten“
[2] *v.t.* nicht hereinlassen

■ **keep ˈup** [1] *v.i.* **~ up with sb./sth.** mit jmdm./etw. Schritt halten
[2] *v.t.* aufrechterhalten ‹*Freundschaft, jmds. Moral*›; **~ one's strength up** sich bei Kräften halten; **~ it up!** weiter so!

keep-ˈfit *n.* Fitnesstraining, *das*

keep-ˈfit class *n.* Fitnessgruppe, *die;* **go to ~es** zu Fitnessübungen gehen

ˈkeeping *n.* **be in ~ with sth.** einer Sache (*Dat.*) entsprechen

ˈkeepsake *n.* Andenken, *das*

keg /keg/ *n.* [kleines] Fass

kelp /kelp/ *n.* [See]tang, *der*

kennel /ˈkenl/ *n.* Hundehütte, *die*

Kenya /ˈkenjə/ *pr. n.* Kenia (*das*)

kept ▶ KEEP 1, 2

kerb /kɜːb/ *n.* (Brit.) Bordstein, *der*

kerb: ~-crawling *n.* (Brit.) (*langsames*) *Fahren auf dem Autostrich zur Kontaktaufnahme mit einer Prostituierten;* **~stone** *n.* (Brit.) Bordstein, *der*

kernel /ˈkɜːnl/ *n.* Kern, *der*

kerosene, kerosine /ˈkerəsiːn/ *n.* (Amer., Austral., NZ/as tech. term) Paraffin[öl], *das;* (for jet engines) Kerosin, *das*

kestrel /ˈkestrəl/ *n.* Turmfalke, *der*

ketchup /ˈketʃʌp/ *n.* Ketschup, *der od. das*

kettle /ˈketl/ *n.* [Wasser]kessel, *der*

key /kiː/ [1] *n.* **(a)** Schlüssel, *der*
(b) (on piano, typewriter, computer, etc.) Taste, *die*
(c) (Mus.) Tonart, *die*
[2] *v.t.* (Comp.) eintasten

key: ~board *n.* (of piano etc.) Klaviatur, *die;* (of typewriter, computer, etc.) Tastatur, *die;* **~board operator** Taster, *der*/Tasterin, *die;* **~boarder** *n.* Taster, *der*/Tasterin, *die;* **~boarding** *n.* Tasten, *das;* **~boarding error** Tastfehler, *der;* **~ card** *n.* Schlüsselkarte, *die;* **~hole** *n.* Schlüsselloch, *das;* **~hole surgery** *n.* Schlüssellochchirurgie, *die;* Knopflochchirurgie, *die*

ˈkeying ▶ KEYBOARDING

key: ~ring *n.* Schlüsselring, *der;* **~stone** *n.* (Archit.) Schlussstein, *der;* (fig.) Grundpfeiler, *der;* **~stroke** *n.* Anschlag, *der*

kg. *abbr.* = **kilogram[s]** kg

khaki /'kɑːkɪ/ [1] *adj.* khakifarben [2] *n.* (cloth) Khaki, *der*

kick /kɪk/ [1] *n.* **(a)** [Fuß]tritt, *der;* (Footb.) Schuss, *der;* **give sb. a ~**: jmdm. einen Tritt geben
(b) (coll.: thrill) **do sth. for ~s** etw. zum Spaß tun; **he gets a ~ out of it** er hat Spaß daran
[2] *v.i.* treten; ‹*Pferd:*› ausschlagen
[3] *v.t.* einen Tritt geben (+ *Dat.*) ‹*Person, Hund*›; treten gegen ‹*Gegenstand*›; kicken (ugs.), schießen ‹*Ball*›

■ **kick a'bout, kick a'round** *v.t.* [in der Gegend] herumkicken (ugs.)

■ **kick 'off** *v.i.* (Footb.) anstoßen

■ **kick 'up** *v.t.* (coll.) **~ up a fuss/row** Krach schlagen/anfangen (ugs.)

kick: ~-off *n.* (Footb.) Anstoß, *der;* **~-start** [1] *n.* **(a)** Kickstarter, *der;* **(b)** (fig.) [neuer] Auftrieb; [2] *v.t.* **(a)** [mit dem Kickstarter] starten; **(b)** (fig.) ankurbeln ‹*Industrie, Wirtschaft*›; vorantreiben, forcieren ‹*Friedensprozess, Entwicklung*›

kid /kɪd/ [1] *n.* **(a)** (young goat) Kitz, *das*
(b) (coll.: child) Kind, *das*
[2] *v.t.*, **-dd-** (coll.) auf den Arm nehmen (ugs.); **~ oneself** sich (*Dat.*) was vormachen

kiddie /'kɪdɪ/ *n.* (coll.) Kindchen, *das*

kid-'glove *adj.* sanft

kidnap /'kɪdnæp/ *v.t.*, (Brit.) **-pp-** entführen

'kidnapper *n.* Entführer, *der*/Entführerin, *die*

kidney /'kɪdnɪ/ *n.* Niere, *die*

kidney: ~ bean *n.* Gartenbohne, *die;* (scarlet runner bean) Feuerbohne, *die;* **red ~ bean** Kidneybohne, *die;* **~ machine** *n.* künstliche Niere; **~-shaped** *adj.* nierenförmig

kill /kɪl/ *v.t.* **(a)** töten; (deliberately) umbringen; **be ~ed in action** im Kampf fallen; **be ~ed in a car crash** bei einem Autounfall ums Leben kommen
(b) ~ time die Zeit totschlagen

'killer *n.* Mörder, *der*/Mörderin, *die*

'killer whale *n.* Mörderwal, *der*

'killing *n.* **(a)** Töten, *das*
(b) make a ~ (coll.: great profit) einen [Mords]reibach machen (ugs.)

'killjoy *n.* Spielverderber, *der*/-verderberin, *die*

kiln /kɪln/ *n.* Brennofen, *der*

kilo /'kiːləʊ/ *n.*, *pl.* **~s** Kilo, *das*

kilogram, kilogramme /'kɪləgræm/ *n.* Kilogramm, *das*

kilometre (*Brit.; Amer.:* **kilometer**) /'kɪləmiːtə(r) (Brit.), kɪ'lɒmɪtə(r)/ *n.* Kilometer, *der*

kilowatt *n.* /'kɪləwɒt/ Kilowatt, *das*

kilt /kɪlt/ *n.* Kilt, *der*

kimono /kɪ'məʊnəʊ/ *n.*, *pl.* **~s** Kimono, *der*

kin /kɪn/ *n.* (relatives) Verwandte *Pl.;* (relative) Verwandte, *der/die*

kind¹ /kaɪnd/ *n.* **(a)** (class, sort) Art, *die;* **several ~s of apples** mehrere Sorten Äpfel; **all ~s of things/excuses** alles Mögliche/alle möglichen Ausreden; **no ... of any ~**: keinerlei ...; **what ~ is it?** was für einer/eine/eins ist es?; **what ~ of [a] tree is this?** was für ein Baum ist das?
(b) (implying vagueness) **a ~ of ...**: [so] eine Art ...; **~ of cute** (coll.) irgendwie niedlich (ugs.)

kind² *adj.* liebenswürdig; (showing friendliness) freundlich; **be ~ to animals** gut zu Tieren sein; **how ~!** wie nett [von ihm/Ihnen *usw.*]!

kindergarten /'kɪndəgɑːtn/ *n.* Kindergarten, *der*

kind-hearted /kaɪnd'hɑːtɪd/ *adj.* gutherzig

kindle /'kɪndl/ (fig.) wecken

kindly /'kaɪndlɪ/ [1] *adv.* **(a)** freundlich; nett
(b) *in polite request etc.* freundlicherweise; **thank you ~**: herzlichen Dank
[2] *adj.* freundlich; nett; (kind-hearted) gütig

'kindness *n.* **(a)** *no pl.* (kind nature) Freundlichkeit, *die*
(b) do sb. a ~ (kind act) jmdm. eine Gefälligkeit erweisen

kindred /'kɪndrɪd/ *adj.* verwandt; **~ 'spirit** Gleichgesinnte, *der/die*

king /kɪŋ/ *n.* König, *der*

kingdom /'kɪŋdəm/ *n.* Königreich, *das*

'kingfisher *n.* Eisvogel, *der*

'king-size[d] *adj.* extragroß; King-size- ‹*Zigaretten*›

kink /kɪŋk/ *n.* (in pipe, wire, etc.) Knick, *der;* (in hair, wool) Welle, *die*

'kinky *adj.* (coll.) spleenig; (sexually) abartig

kinsman /'kɪnzmən/ *n.*, *pl.* **kinsmen** /'kɪnzmən/ Verwandte, *der*

kinswoman /'kɪnzwʊmn/ *n.* Verwandte, *die*

kiosk /'kiːɒsk/ *n.* **(a)** Kiosk, *der*
(b) (telephone booth) [Telefon]zelle, *die*

kip /kɪp/ *n.* (Brit. coll.: sleep) **have a/get some ~**: eine Runde pennen (salopp)

kipper /'kɪpə(r)/ *n.* Kipper, *der*

kiss /kɪs/ [1] *n.* Kuss, *der*
[2] *v.t.* küssen; **~ sb. good night/goodbye** jmdm. einen Gutenacht-/Abschiedskuss geben
[3] *v.i.* **they ~ed** sie küssten sich

kit /kɪt/ *n.* **(a)** (Brit.: set of items) Set, *das*
(b) (Brit.: clothing etc.) **sports ~**: Sportzeug, *das;* **riding/skiing ~**: Reit-/Skiausrüstung, *die*

'kitbag *n.* Tornister, *der*

kitchen /'kɪtʃɪn/ *n.* Küche, *die; attrib.* Küchen-

kitchen: ~ paper *n.* Küchenkrepp, *der;* **~ roll** *n.* Küchenrolle, *die;* (kitchen paper) Küchenkrepp, *der;* **~ 'sink** *n.* [Küchen]ausguss, *der;* **~ unit** *n.* ···>

Küchenelement, *das;* ~ **units** Küchenmöbel *Pl.*; ~ **utensil** *n.* Küchengerät, *das;* ~**ware** *n.* Küchengeräte *Pl.*

kite /kaɪt/ *n.* Drachen, *der*

kith /kɪθ/ *n.* ~ **and kin** Freunde und Verwandte

kitten /'kɪtn/ *n.* Kätzchen, *das*

kitty /'kɪtɪ/ *n.* (money) Kasse, *die*

kleptomania /kleptə'meɪnɪə/ *n.* Kleptomanie, *die*

kleptomaniac /kleptə'meɪnɪæk/ *n.* Kleptomane, *der*/Kleptomanin, *die*

km. *abbr.* = **kilometre[s]** km

knack /næk/ *n.* Talent, *das;* **get the** ~ **[of doing sth.]** den Bogen rauskriegen [, wie man etw. macht] (ugs.); **have lost the** ~: es nicht mehr zustande bringen

knapsack /'næpsæk/ *n.* Rucksack, *der;* (Mil.) Tornister, *der*

knead /ni:d/ *v.t.* kneten

knee /ni:/ *n.* Knie, *das*

knee: ~**cap** *n.* Kniescheibe, *die;* ~**-deep** *adj.* knietief; ~**-high** *adj.* kniehoch; ~**-jerk reaction** *n.* (fig.) automatische Reaktion; ~ **joint** *n.* Kniegelenk, *das*

kneel /ni:l/ *v.i.*, **knelt** /nelt/ *or* (esp. Amer.) **kneeled** knien; ~ **down** niederknien

'knee-length *adj.* knielang

knelt ▶ KNEEL

knew ▶ KNOW

knickers /'nikəz/ *n. pl.* (Brit.) [Damen]schlüpfer, *der*

knife /naɪf/ [1] *n., pl.* **knives** /naɪvz/ Messer, *das*
[2] *v.t.* (stab) einstechen auf (+ *Akk.*); (kill) erstechen

'knife-edge *n.* Schneide, *die;* **be [balanced] on a** ~ (fig.) auf des Messers Schneide stehen

knight /naɪt/ *n.* **(a)** (Hist.) Ritter, *der*
(b) (Chess) Springer, *der*

'knighthood *n.* Ritterwürde, *die*

knit /nɪt/ *v.t.*, **-tt-** stricken; ~ **one's brow** die Stirn runzeln

'knitting *n.* Stricken, *das;* (work being knitted) Strickarbeit, *die*

'knitting needle *n.* Stricknadel, *die*

'knitwear *n.* Strickwaren *Pl.*

knives *pl. of* KNIFE 1

knob /nɒb/ *n.* **(a)** (on door, walking stick, etc.) Knauf, *der*
(b) (control on radio etc.) Knopf, *der*
(c) (of butter) Klümpchen, *das*

knock /nɒk/ [1] *v.t.* **(a)** (strike) (lightly) klopfen an (+ *Akk.*); (forcefully) schlagen gegen *od.* an (+ *Akk.*); ~ **a hole in sth.** ein Loch in etw. (*Akk.*) schlagen
(b) (coll.: criticize) herziehen über (+ *Akk.*) (ugs.)
[2] *v.i.* klopfen (**at** an + *Akk.*)
[3] *n.* Klopfen, *das*

■ **knock 'down** *v.t.* **(a)** (in car) umfahren
(b) (demolish) abreißen

■ **knock 'off** [1] *v.t.* **(a)** ~ **off work** (coll.: leave) Feierabend machen
(b) (deduct) ~ **five pounds off the price** es fünf Pfund billiger machen
(c) (coll.: do quickly) aus dem Ärmel schütteln (ugs.)
(d) (coll.: steal) klauen (salopp)
[2] *v.i.* (coll.) Feierabend machen

■ **knock 'out** *v.t.* **(a)** (make unconscious) bewusstlos umfallen lassen
(b) (Boxing) k.o. schlagen
(c) (coll.: exhaust) kaputtmachen (ugs.)

■ **knock 'over** *v.t.* umstoßen; ‹*Fahrer, Fahrzeug:*› umfahren ‹*Person*›

'knock-down *adj.* ~ **prices** Schleuderpreise

'knocker *n.* [Tür]klopfer, *der*

knock: ~**-kneed** /'nɒkni:d/ *adj.* x-beinig ‹*Person*›; ~**out** *n.* (Boxing) K.-o.-Schlag, *der*

knot /nɒt/ [1] *n.* Knoten, *der*
[2] *v.t.*, **-tt-** knoten ‹*Seil, Faden usw.*›

'knotty *adj.* (fig.: puzzling) verwickelt

know /nəʊ/ *v.t.*, **knew** /nju:/, **known** /nəʊn/
(a) (recognize) erkennen (**by** an + *Dat.*, **for** als + *Akk.*)
(b) (be able to distinguish) ~ **sth. from sth.** etw. von etw. unterscheiden können
(c) (be aware of) wissen
(d) (have understanding of) können ‹*ABC, Einmaleins, Deutsch usw.*›; ~ **how to mend fuses** wissen, wie man Sicherungen repariert; ~ **how to drive a car** Auto fahren können
(e) kennen ‹*Person*›

'know-all *n.* Neunmalkluge, *der/die*

'know-how *n.* praktisches Wissen; (technical expertise) Know-how, *das*

'knowing *adj.* **(a)** wissend ‹*Blick, Lächeln*›
(b) (cunning) verschlagen

'knowingly *adv.* **(a)** (intentionally) wissentlich
(b) viel sagend ‹*lächeln, anblicken*›

knowledge /'nɒlɪdʒ/ *n.* **(a)** (familiarity) Kenntnisse *Pl.* (**of** in + *Dat.*)
(b) (awareness) Wissen, *das;* **have no** ~ **of sth.** nichts von etw. wissen; keine Kenntnis von etw. haben (geh.)
(c) **[a]** ~ **of languages/French** Sprach-/Französischkenntnisse *Pl.*

knowledgeable /'nɒlɪdʒəbl/ *adj.* **be** ~ **about** *or* **on sth.** viel über etw. (*Akk.*) wissen

known /nəʊn/ [1] ▶ KNOW
[2] *adj.* bekannt

knuckle /'nʌkl/ *n.* [Finger]knöchel, *der*

Koran /kɔ:'rɑ:n, kə'rɑ:n/ *n.* Koran, *der*

Korea /kə'rɪə/ *pr. n.* Korea (*das*)

Korean /kə'ri:ən/ [1] *adj.* koreanisch; **sb. is** ~: jmd. ist Koreaner/Koreanerin
[2] *n.* **(a)** (person) Koreaner, *der*/Koreanerin, *die*
(b) (language) Koreanisch, *das; see also* ENGLISH 2A

kosher /'kəʊʃə(r)/ *adj.* koscher

Kosovan /'kɒsəvən/ [1] *adj.* **~ town/immigrant** Stadt im Kosovo/Einwanderer aus dem Kosovo; **~ Albanian** Kosovoalbaner, *der*/-albanerin, *die;* **he/she is ~:** er ist Kosovarer/sie ist Kosovarin
[2] *n.* (person) Kosovare, *der*/Kosovarin, *die*

Kosovo /'kɒsəvə/ *pr. n.* Kosovo, *der od. das od.* (*das*)

kudos /'kju:dɒs/ *n.* Prestige, *das*

Kurd /kɜ:d/ *n.* Kurde, *der*/Kurdin, *die*

Kurdish /'kɜ:dɪʃ/ [1] *adj.* kurdisch; **sb. is ~:** jmd. ist Kurde/Kurdin
[2] *n.* (language) Kurdisch, *das*

Kurdistan /kɜ:dɪ'stɑ:n/ *pr. n.* Kurdistan (*das*)

Kuwait /kʊ'weɪt/ *pr. n.* Kuwait (*das*)

Kuwaiti /kʊ'weɪtɪ/ [1] *adj.* kuwaitisch; **sb. is ~:** jmd. ist Kuwaiti
[2] *n.* Kuwaiti, *der*/*die*

kW *abbr.* = **kilowatt[s]** kW

Ll

L, l /el/ *n.* L, l, *das*

l. *abbr.* = **litre[s]** l

£ *abbr.* = **pound[s]** £; **cost £5** 5 £ *od.* Pfund kosten

lab /læb/ *n.* (coll.) Labor, *das*

label /'leɪbl/ [1] *n.* Schildchen, *das;* (on bottles, in clothes) Etikett, *das;* (tied/stuck to an object) Anhänger/Aufkleber, *der*
[2] *v.t.,* (Brit.) **-ll-: (a)** etikettieren; auszeichnen ‹*Waren*›; (write on) beschriften
(b) (fig.) **~ sb./sth. [as] sth.** jmdn./etw. als etw. etikettieren

labor (Amer.) ▶ LABOUR

laboratory /lə'bɒrətərɪ/ *n.* Labor[atorium], *das*

labored, laborer (Amer.) ▶ LABOUR-

laborious /lə'bɔ:rɪəs/ *adj.* mühsam

la'boriously *adv.* mühevoll

labour /'leɪbə(r)/ (Brit.) [1] *n.* **(a)** Arbeit, *die*
(b) (workers) Arbeiterschaft, *die;* **immigrant ~:** ausländische Arbeitskräfte *Pl.*
(c) L~, the L~ Party (Polit.) die Labour Party
(d) (childbirth) Wehen *Pl.;* **be in ~:** in den Wehen liegen
[2] *v.i.* hart arbeiten (**at, on** an + *Dat.*)
[3] *v.t.* **~ the point** sich lange darüber verbreiten

laboured /'leɪbəd/ *adj.* (Brit.) mühsam; schwerfällig ‹*Stil*›; **his breathing was ~:** er atmete schwer

'labourer *n.* (Brit.) Arbeiter, *der*/Arbeiterin, *die*

labour: ~ pains *n. pl.* Wehenschmerzen *Pl.*; **~-saving** *adj.* arbeit[s]sparend

laburnum /lə'bɜ:nəm/ *n.* (Bot.) Goldregen, *der*

labyrinth /'læbərɪnθ/ *n.* Labyrinth, *das*

lace /leɪs/ [1] *n.* **(a)** (for shoe) Schnürsenkel, *der*
(b) (fabric) Spitze, *die; attrib.* Spitzen-
[2] *v.t.* **~ [up]** [zu]schnüren

lacerate /'læsəreɪt/ *v.t.* aufreißen

'lace-up [1] *attrib. adj.* Schnür-
[2] *n.* Schnürschuh/-stiefel, *der*

lack /læk/ [1] *n.* Mangel, *der* (**of** an + *Dat.*)
[2] *v.t.* **sb./sth. ~s sth.** jmdm./einer Sache fehlt es an etw. (*Dat.*)

lackey /'lækɪ/ *n.* Lakai, *der*

'lacking *adj.* **be ~:** fehlen

laconic /lə'kɒnɪk/ *adj.* lakonisch

lacquer /'lækə(r)/ *n.* Lack, *der*

lacrosse /lə'krɒs/ *n.* Lacrosse, *das*

lacy /'leɪsɪ/ *adj.* Spitzen-

lad /læd/ *n.* Junge, *der*

ladder /'lædə(r)/ [1] *n.* **(a)** Leiter, *die*
(b) (Brit.: in tights etc.) Laufmasche, *die*
[2] *v.i.* (Brit.) Laufmaschen/eine Laufmasche bekommen
[3] *v.t.* (Brit.) Laufmaschen/eine Laufmasche machen in (+ *Akk.*)

laden /'leɪdn/ beladen (**with** mit)

ladle /'leɪdl/ *n.* Schöpfkelle, *die*

lady /'leɪdɪ/ *n.* **(a)** Dame, *die;* **~-in-waiting** (Brit.) Hofdame, *die*
(b) 'Ladies' (WC) „Damen"
(c) (as form of address) **Ladies** meine Damen
(d) (Brit.) (as title) **L~:** Lady

lady: ~bird, (Amer.) **~bug** *ns.* Marienkäfer, *der;* **~like** *adj.* damenhaft

lag¹ /læg/ *v.i.,* **-gg-: ~ [behind]** zurückbleiben; (fig.) im Rückstand sein

lag² *v.t.,* **-gg-** (insulate) isolieren

lager /'lɑ:gə(r)/ *n.* Lagerbier, *das*

'lager lout *n.* Bier trinkender Rüpel

'lagging *n.* Isolierung, *die*

lagoon /lə'gu:n/ *n.* Lagune, *die*

laid ▶ LAY²

'laid-back *adj.* (coll.) gelassen

lain ▶ LIE²

lair /leər/ *n.* (of wild animal) Unterschlupf, *der;* (of pirates, bandits) Schlupfwinkel, *der*

lake /leɪk/ *n.* See, *der*

Lake Constance /leɪk 'kɒnstəns/ *pr. n.* der Bodensee

lama /'lɑːmə/ *n.* Lama, *der*
lamb /læm/ *n.* **(a)** Lamm, *das* **(b)** (meat) Lamm[fleisch], *das*
lamb 'chop *n.* Lammkotelett, *das*
lambswool /'læmzwʊl/ *n.* Lambswool, *die*
lame /leɪm/ *adj.*, **'lamely** *adv.* lahm
lament /lə'ment/ 1 *n.* Klage, *die* **(for** um) 2 *v.t.* ~ **that ...:** beklagen, dass ... 3 *v.i.* klagen (geh.); ~ **over sth.** etw. beklagen (geh.)
lamentable /'læməntəbl/ *adj.* beklagenswert
laminated /'læmɪmeɪtɪd/ *adj.* lamelliert; ~ **glass** Verbundglas, *das*
lamp /læmp/ *n.* Lampe, *die;* (in street) [Straßen]laterne, *die*
lamp: ~ **post** *n.* Laternenpfahl, *der;* ~**shade** *n.* Lampenschirm, *der*
lance /lɑːns/ 1 *n.* Lanze, *die* 2 *v.t.* (Med.) mit der Lanzette öffnen
lance 'corporal *n.* Obergefreite, *der*
land /lænd/ 1 *n.* Land, *das;* **have** *or* **own** ~**:** Grundbesitz haben 2 *v.t.* **(a)** (set ashore) [an]landen **(b)** (Aeronaut.) landen **(c)** ~ **oneself in trouble** sich in Schwierigkeiten bringen; ~ **sb. with sth.,** ~ **sth. on sb.** jmdm. etw. aufhalsen (ugs.) 3 *v.i.* **(a)** ‹*Boot usw.:*› anlegen, landen; ‹*Passagier:*› aussteigen (**from** aus); **we** ~**ed at Dieppe** wir gingen in Dieppe an Land **(b)** (Aeronaut.) landen **(c)** ~ **on one's feet** (fig.) [wieder] auf die Füße fallen
'landed *adj.* ~ **gentry/aristocracy** Landadel, *der*
'landing *n.* **(a)** (of ship, aircraft) Landung, *die* **(b)** (on stairs) Treppenabsatz, *der;* (passage) Treppenflur, *der*
landing: ~ **card** *n.* Landekarte, *die;* ~ **stage** *n.* Landesteg, *der*
land: ~**lady** *n.* **(a)** (of rented property) Vermieterin, *die;* **(b)** (of public house) [Gast]wirtin, *die;* ~**locked** *adj.* vom Land eingeschlossen ‹*Bucht, Hafen*›; ‹*Staat*› ohne Zugang zum Meer; ~**lord** *n.* **(a)** (of rented property) Vermieter, *der;* **(b)** (of public house) [Gast]wirt, *der;* ~**mark** *n.* **(a)** Orientierungspunkt, *der;* **(b)** (fig.) Markstein, *der;* ~ **mass** *n.* Landmasse, *die;* ~**mine** *n.* Landmine, *die;* ~**owner** *n.* Grundbesitzer, *der*/-besitzerin, *die;* ~**scape** /'lændskeɪp/ *n.* Landschaft, *die;* ~**scape architect** *n.* Landschaftsarchitekt, *der*/-architektin, *die;* ~**scape gardener** *n.* Landschaftsgärtner, *der*/-gärtnerin, *die;* ~**scape gardening** *n.* Landschaftsgärtnerei, *die;* ~**slide** *n.* Erdrutsch, *der;* **a** ~**slide [victory]** (Polit.) ein Erdrutsch[wahl]sieg
lane /leɪn/ *n.* **(a)** (in the country) Landsträßchen, *das;* Weg, *der* **(b)** (in town) Gasse, *die* **(c)** (part of road) [Fahr]spur, *die;* **'get in** ~**'** „bitte einordnen" **(d)** (Sport) Bahn, *die*
language /'læŋgwɪdʒ/ *n.* Sprache, *die;* (style) Ausdrucksweise, *die*
language: ~ **course** *n.* Sprachkurs[us], *der;* ~ **school** *n.* Sprachenschule; *die;* ~ **teacher** *n.* Sprachlehrer, *der*/-lehrerin, *die*
languid /'læŋgwɪd/ *adj.* träge
languish /'læŋgwɪʃ/ *v.i.* **(a)** (lose vitality) ermatten (geh.) **(b)** ~ **under sth.** unter etw. (*Dat.*) schmachten (geh.)
lank /læŋk/ *adj.* **(a)** hager **(b)** glatt herabhängend ‹*Haar*›
lanky /'læŋkɪ/ *adj.* schlaksig (ugs.)
lantern /'læntən/ *n.* Laterne, *die*
lap¹ /læp/ *n.* (part of body) Schoß, *der*
lap² *n.* (Sport) Runde, *die*
lap³ 1 *v.i.*, **-pp-** schlecken 2 *v.t.*, **-pp-:** ~ **[up]** [auf]schlecken
■ **lap 'up** *v.t.* (fig.) schlucken
'lap belt *n.* Beckengurt, *der*
lapel /lə'pel/ *n.* Revers, *das*
Lapland /'læplænd/ *pr. n.* Lappland (*das*)
lapse /læps/ 1 *n.* **(a)** (interval) **a/the** ~ **of ...:** eine/die Zeitspanne von ... **(b)** (mistake) Fehler, *der;* ~ **of memory** Gedächtnislücke, *die* 2 *v.i.* **(a)** ‹*Vertrag, usw.:*› ungültig werden **(b)** ~ **into** verfallen in (+ *Akk.*)
'laptop 1 *adj.* tragbar, Laptop‹*gerät, -PC*› 2 *n.* Laptop, *der;* tragbarer PC
larceny /'lɑːsənɪ/ *n.* Diebstahl, *der*
lard /lɑːd/ *n.* Schweineschmalz, *das*
larder /'lɑːdə(r)/ *n.* Speisekammer, *die*
large /lɑːdʒ/ 1 *adj.* groß 2 *n.* **at** ~ (not in prison etc.) auf freiem Fuß 3 *adv.* ▶ BY 2D
'largely *adv.* weitgehend
larger-than-'life *attrib. adj.* überlebensgroß
large: ~**-scale** *attrib. adj.* groß angelegt; groß ‹*Erfolg, Misserfolg*›; ‹*Katastrophe*› großen Ausmaßes; ‹*Modell*› in großem Maßstab; ~**-scale manufacture** Massenproduktion, *die;* ~**-size[d]** *adj.* groß
lark¹ /lɑːk/ *n.* (Ornith.) Lerche, *die*
lark² (coll.) 1 *n.* Jux, *der* (ugs.) 2 *v.i.* ~ **[about** *or* **around]** herumalbern (ugs.)
larva /'lɑːvə/ *n., pl.* ~**e** /'lɑːviː/ Larve, *die*
laryngitis /lærɪn'dʒaɪtɪs/ *n.* Kehlkopfentzündung, *die*
larynx /'lærɪŋks/ *n.* Kehlkopf, *der*
lascivious /lə'sɪvɪəs/ *adj.* lüstern (geh.)
laser /'leɪzə(r)/ *n.* Laser, *der*
laser: ~ **beam** *n.* Laserstrahl, *der;* ~**disc** *n.* Laserplatte, *die;* ~ **printer** *n.* Laserdrucker, *der*

lash /læʃ/ 1 *n.* **(a)** (stroke) [Peitschen]hieb, *der*
(b) (on eyelid) Wimper, *die*
2 *v.i.* ‹*Welle, Regen:*› peitschen (**against** gegen, **on** auf + *Akk.*)
3 *v.t.* **(a)** (fasten) festbinden (**to** an + *Dat.*)
(b) (as punishment) auspeitschen
■ **lash 'down** 1 *v.t.* festbinden
2 *v.i.* ‹*Regen:*› niederprasseln
■ **lash 'out** *v.i.* **(a)** (hit out) um sich schlagen; ~ **out at sb.** nach jmdm. schlagen
(b) ~ **out on sth.** (coll.: spend freely) sich (*Dat.*) etw. leisten

lashings /'læʃɪŋz/ *n. pl.* ~ **of sth.** Unmengen von etw.

lass /læs/ *n.* Mädchen, *das*

lasso /lə'su:/ Lasso, *das*

last¹ /lɑ:st/ 1 *adj.* letzt...; **be ~ to arrive** als Letzter/Letzte ankommen; ~ **night** gestern Nacht/Abend
2 *adv.* **(a)** [ganz] zuletzt; als Letzter/Letzte ‹*sprechen, ankommen*›
(b) (on ~ previous occasion) das letzte Mal; zuletzt
3 *n.* **(a)** (person or thing) **the ~**: der/die/das Letztere; *pl.* die Letzteren
(b) at [long] ~: endlich

last² *v.i.* **(a)** (continue) dauern; ‹*Wetter, Ärger:*› anhalten
(b) (suffice) reichen

'last-ditch *adj.* ~ **attempt** letzter verzweifelter Versuch

'lasting *adj.* bleibend; dauerhaft ‹*Beziehung*›; nachhaltig ‹*Eindruck, Wirkung*›

'lastly *adv.* schließlich

last: ~-minute *attrib. adj.* in letzter Minute vorgebracht ‹*Plan, Aufruf, Ergänzung, Gesuch, Bewerbung*›; ~ **name** *n.* Zuname, *der;* Nachname, *der*

latch /lætʃ/ *n.* Riegel, *der;* **on the ~**: nur eingeklinkt
■ **latch 'on to** *v.t.* (coll.:) kapieren (ugs.)

late /leɪt/ 1 *adj.* **(a)** spät; **am I ~?** komme ich zu spät?; **be ~ for the train** den Zug verpassen; **the train is [an hour] ~**: der Zug hat [eine Stunde] Verspätung; ~ **shift** Spätschicht, *die;* ~ **summer** Spätsommer, *der*
(b) (dead) verstorben
(c) (former) ehemalig. *See also* LATER 1; LATEST
2 *adv.* **(a)** (after proper time) verspätet
(b) (at/till a ~ hour) spät; **be up ~**: bis spät in die Nacht aufbleiben; **work ~ at the office** [abends] lange im Büro arbeiten; **[a bit] ~ in the day** (fig. coll.) reichlich spät
3 *n.* **of ~**: in letzter Zeit

latecomer /'leɪtkʌmə(r)/ *n.* Zuspätkommende, *der/die*

'lately *adv.* in letzter Zeit

'lateness *n.* **(a)** (delay) Verspätung, *die*
(b) the ~ of the performance der späte Beginn der Vorstellung

'late-night *attrib. adj.* Spät‹*programm, -vorstellung*›

latent /'leɪtənt/ *adj.* latent

later /'leɪtə(r)/ 1 *adv.* ~ **[on]** später
2 *adj.* später; (more recent) neuer

lateral /'lætərl/ *adj.* seitlich (**to** von); ~ **thinking** Querdenken, *das*

latest /'leɪtɪst/ *adj.* **(a)** (modern) neu[e]st...
(b) (most recent) letzt...
(c) at [the] ~/the very ~: spätestens/allerspätestens

lathe /leɪð/ *n.* Drehbank, *die*

lather /'lɑ:ðə(r)/ 1 *n.* [Seifen]schaum, *der*
2 *v.t.* einschäumen

Latin /'lætɪn/ 1 *adj.* lateinisch
2 *n.* Latein, *das; see also* ENGLISH 2A

Latin A'merica *pr. n.* Lateinamerika (*das*)

Latin-A'merican *adj.* lateinamerikanisch

latitude /'lætɪtju:d/ *n.* **(a)** (freedom) Freiheit, *die*
(b) (Geog.) Breite, *die*

latrine /lə'tri:n/ *n.* Latrine, *die*

latter /'lætə(r)/ *attrib. adj.* letzter...; **the ~**: der/die/das Letztere; *pl.* die Letzteren

'latterly *adv.* in letzter Zeit

lattice /'lætɪs/ *n.* Gitter, *das*

laudable /'lɔ:dəbl/ *adj.* lobenswert

laugh /lɑ:f/ 1 *n.* Lachen, *das;* (continuous) Gelächter, *das*
2 *v.i.* lachen; ~ **out loud** laut auflachen; ~ **at sb./sth.** über jmdn./etw. lachen; (jeer) jmdn. auslachen/etw. verlachen
■ **laugh 'off** *v.t.* mit einem Lachen abtun

laughable /'lɑ:fəbl/ *adj.* lachhaft; lächerlich

'laughing *n.* **be no ~ matter** nicht zum Lachen sein

laughing: ~ gas *n.* Lachgas, *das;* ~ **stock** *n.* **make sb. a ~ stock, make a ~ stock of sb.** jmdn. zum Gespött machen

laughter /'lɑ:ftə(r)/ *n.* Lachen, *das;* (continuous) Gelächter, *das*

'laughter lines *n. pl.* Lachfältchen *Pl.*

launch /lɔ:ntʃ/ *v.t.* **(a)** zu Wasser lassen ‹*Boot*›; vom Stapel lassen ‹*neues Schiff*›; abschießen ‹*Harpune, Torpedo*›; schleudern ‹*Speer*›
(b) (fig.) auf den Markt bringen ‹*Produkt*›; vorstellen ‹*Buch, Schallplatte, Sänger*›; ~ **an attack** einen Angriff durchführen
■ **launch 'out** *v.i.* (fig.) ~ **out into films/a new career/on one's own** sich beim Film versuchen/beruflich etwas ganz Neues anfangen/sich selbstständig machen

'launching pad, launch pad *ns.* [Raketen]abschussrampe, *die*

launder /'lɔ:ndə(r)/ *v.t.* waschen und bügeln

launderette /lɔ:ndə'ret/, **laundrette** /lɔ:n'dret/, (Amer.) **laundromat** /'lɔ:ndrəmæt/ *ns.* Waschsalon, *der*

laundry /ˈlɔːndrɪ/ *n.* **(a)** (place) Wäscherei, *die*
(b) (clothes etc.) Wäsche, *die*

ˈlaundry basket *n.* Wäschekorb, *der*

lava /ˈlɑːvə/ *n.* Lava, *die*

lavatory /ˈlævətərɪ/ *n.* Toilette, *die*

lavender /ˈlævɪndə(r)/ *n.* Lavendel, *der*

lavish /ˈlævɪʃ/ **1** *adj.* großzügig
2 *v.t.* **~ sth. on sb.** jmdn. mit etw. überhäufen

law /lɔː/ *n.* **(a)** Gesetz, *das;* **break the ~:** gegen das Gesetz verstoßen; **take the ~ into one's own hands** sich (*Dat.*) selbst Recht verschaffen; **~ and order** Ruhe und Ordnung
(b) (of game) Regel, *die*
(c) (as subject) Jura *o. Art.*

law: ~-abiding /ˈlɔːəbaɪdɪŋ/ *adj.* gesetzestreu; **~court** *n.* Gerichtsgebäude, *das;* (room) Gerichtssaal, *der;* **~ firm** *n.* (Amer.) Anwaltskanzlei, *die*

lawful /ˈlɔːfl/ *adj.* rechtmäßig ‹*Besitzer, Erbe*›; legal, gesetzmäßig ‹*Vorgehen, Maßnahme*›

ˈlawless *adj.* gesetzlos

lawn /lɔːn/ *n.* Rasen, *der*

lawn: ~mower *n.* Rasenmäher, *der;* **~ sprinkler** *n.* Rasensprenger, *der;* **~ tennis** *n.* Rasentennis, *das*

ˈlaw suit *n.* Prozess, *der*

lawyer /ˈlɔːjə(r)/ *n.* Rechtsanwalt, *der*/ Rechtsanwältin, *die*

lax /læks/ *adj.* lax; **be ~ about hygiene/paying the rent** *etc.* es mit der Hygiene/der Zahlung der Miete *usw.* nicht so genau nehmen

laxative /ˈlæksətɪv/ *n.* Abführmittel, *das*

laxity /ˈlæksɪtɪ/, **ˈlaxness** *ns.* Laxheit, *die*

lay¹ /leɪ/ *adj.* Laien-

lay² *v.t.*, **laid** /leɪd/ **(a)** legen ‹*Teppichboden, Rohr, Kabel*›
(b) (impose) auferlegen ‹*Verantwortung, Verpflichtung*› (**on** *Dat.*); verhängen ‹*Strafe*› (**on** über + *Akk.*)
(c) **~ the table** den Tisch decken
(d) (Biol.) legen ‹*Ei*›

▪ **lay aˈside** *v.t.* beiseite legen

▪ **lay ˈby** *v.t.* beiseite legen

▪ **lay ˈdown** *v.t.* **(a)** hinlegen
(b) festlegen ‹*Regeln, Bedingungen*›

▪ **lay ˈoff** **1** *v.t.* (from work) vorübergehend entlassen
2 *v.i.* (coll.: stop) aufhören

▪ **lay ˈout** *v.t.* **(a)** (spread out) ausbreiten
(b) anlegen ‹*Garten*›

▪ **lay ˈup** *v.t.* **(a)** (store) lagern
(b) **I was laid up in bed for a week** ich musste eine Woche das Bett hüten

lay³ ▶ LIE²

lay: ~about *n.* (Brit.) Gammler, *der* (ugs.); **~-by** *n., pl.* **~-bys** (Brit.) Parkbucht, *die;* Haltebucht, *die*

layer /ˈleɪə(r)/ *n.* Schicht, *die*

layette /leɪˈet/ *n.* **[baby's] ~:** Babyausstattung, *die*

lay: ~man /ˈleɪmən/ *n., pl.* **~men** /ˈleɪmən/ Laie, *der;* **~out** *n.* (of garden, park) Anlage, *die;* (of book, advertisement, etc.) Layout, *das*

laze /leɪz/ *v.i.* faulenzen; **~ around** *or* **about** herumfaulenzen (ugs.)

lazily /ˈleɪzɪlɪ/ *adv.* faul

laziness /ˈleɪzɪnɪs/ *n.* Faulheit, *die*

lazy /ˈleɪzɪ/ *adj.* faul

ˈlazybones *n. sing.* Faulpelz, *der*

lb. *abbr.* = **pound[s]** ≈ Pfd.

LCD *abbr.* = **liquid crystal display** LCD

lead¹ /led/ **1** *n.* **(a)** (metal) Blei, *das*
(b) (in pencil) [Bleistift]mine, *die*
2 *attrib. adj.* Blei-
3 *v.t.* **(a)** in Blei fassen ‹*Fenster*›; **~ed** bleigefasst
(b) **~ed petrol** bleihaltiges Benzin

lead² /liːd/ **1** *v.t.*, **led** /led/ **(a)** führen; **~ sb. to do sth.** (fig.) jmdn. dazu bringen, etw. zu tun
(b) (fig.: influence) **~ sb. to do sth.** jmdn. veranlassen, etw. zu tun; **be easily led** sich leicht beeinflussen lassen; **he led me to believe that ...:** er machte mich glauben, dass ...
(c) (be first in) anführen
(d) (direct) anführen ‹*Bewegung, Abordnung*›; leiten ‹*Diskussion, Orchester*›
2 *v.i.*, **led** **(a)** ‹*Straße usw., Tür:*› führen
(b) (be first) führen; (go in front) vorangehen
3 *n.* **(a)** (precedent) Beispiel, *das;* (clue) Anhaltspunkt, *der;* **follow sb.'s ~:** jmds. Beispiel (*Dat.*) folgen
(b) (first place) Führung, *die;* **be in the ~:** in Führung liegen
(c) (distance ahead) Vorsprung, *der*
(d) (leash) Leine, *die;* **on a ~:** an der Leine
(e) (Electr.) Kabel, *das*
(f) (Theatre) Hauptrolle, *die*

▪ **lead aˈway** *v.t.* abführen ‹*Gefangenen, Verbrecher*›

▪ **lead ˈoff** **1** *v.t.* abführen
2 *v.i.* beginnen

▪ **lead ˈon** **1** *v.t.* **~ sb. on** (entice) jmdn. reizen; (deceive) jmdn. auf den Leim führen
2 *v.i.* **~ on to the next topic** *etc.* zum nächsten Thema *usw.* führen

▪ **lead ˈup to** *v.t.* schließlich führen zu

ˈleader *n.* **(a)** Führer, *der*/Führerin, *die;* (of political party) Vorsitzende, *der*/*die;* (of expedition) Leiter, *der*/Leiterin, *die*
(b) (Brit. Journ.) Leitartikel, *der*

ˈleadership *n.* Führung, *die*

ˈleader writer *n.* Leitartikelschreiber, *der*/-schreiberin, *die;* Leitartikler, *der*/ -artiklerin, *die* (Pressejargon)

lead-free /ˈledfriː/ *adj.* bleifrei

leading /ˈliːdɪŋ/ *adj.* führend

leading: ~ ˈlady *n.* Hauptdarstellerin, *die;* **~ ˈman** *n.* Hauptdarsteller, *der;*

~ 'question *n.* Suggestivfrage, *die;* **~ role** *n.* Hauptrolle, *die;* (fig.) führende Rolle

lead: ~ 'pencil /led 'pensl/ *n.* Bleistift, *der;* **~ poisoning** /'led pɔɪzənɪŋ/ *n.* Bleivergiftung, *die;* **~ singer** /li:d 'sɪŋə(r)/ *n.* Leadsänger *der*/-sängerin, *die;* **~ story** /'li:d stɔ:rɪ/ *n.* (Journ.) Titelgeschichte, *die;* **~ time** /'li:d taɪm/ *n.* (Econ.) Entwicklungszeit, *die*

leaf /li:f/ *n., pl.* **leaves** /li:vz/ Blatt, *das;* (of table) Platte *die*

■ **leaf 'through** *v.t.* durchblättern

leaflet /'li:flɪt/ *n.* [Hand]zettel, *der;* (advertising) Reklamezettel, *der;* (political) Flugblatt, *das*

'leafy *adj.* belaubt

league /li:g/ *n.* **(a)** (agreement) Bündnis, *das;* **be in ~ with sb.** mit jmdm. im Bunde sein
(b) (Sport) Liga, *die*

league: ~ 'football *n.* Ligafußball, *der;* **~ match** *n.* Ligaspiel, *das;* **~ table** *n.* Tabelle, *die* (Sport); **be at the top/bottom of the ~ table** an der Tabellenspitze/am Tabellenende sein (fig.); an der Spitze rangieren/das Schlusslicht bilden (ugs.) (**of** unter + *Dat.*)

leak /li:k/ **1** *n.* **(a)** (hole) Leck, *das;* (in roof, tent; also fig.) undichte Stelle
(b) (escaping gas) durch ein Leck austretendes Gas
2 *v.i.* **(a)** (escape) austreten (**from** aus)
(b) ‹*Fass, Tank, Schiff:*› lecken; ‹*Rohr, Leitung, Dach:*› undicht sein; ‹*Gefäß, Füller:*› auslaufen
(c) (fig.) **~ [out]** durchsickern
3 *v.t.* **~ sth. to sb.** jmdm. etw. zuspielen

leakage /'li:kɪdʒ/ *n.* Auslaufen, *das;* (of fluid, gas) Ausströmen, *das*

'leaky *adj.* undicht; leck ‹*Boot*›

lean¹ /li:n/ **1** *adj.* mager
2 *n.* (meat) Magere, *das*

lean² **1** *v.i.*, **leaned** /li:nd, lent/ *or* (Brit.) **leant** /lent/ **(a)** sich beugen; **~ against the door** sich gegen die Tür lehnen; **~ down/forward** sich herab-/vorbeugen; **~ back** sich zurücklehnen
(b) (support oneself) **~ against/on sth.** sich gegen/an etw (*Akk.*) lehnen
(c) (be supported) lehnen (**against** an + *Dat.*)
(d) (fig.) **~ [up]on sb.** (rely) auf jmdn. bauen; **~ to[wards] sth.** (tend) zu etw. neigen
2 *v.t.*, **leaned** *or* (Brit.) **leant** lehnen (**against** gegen *od.* an + *Akk.*)

■ **lean 'over** *v.i.* sich hinüberbeugen

'leaning *n.* Neigung, *die*

leant ▸ LEAN²

leap /li:p/ **1** *v.i.*, **leaped** /li:pt, lept/ *or* **leapt** /lept/ **(a)** springen; ‹*Herz:*› hüpfen
(b) (fig.) **~ at the chance** die Gelegenheit beim Schopf packen
2 *v.t.*, **leaped** *or* **leapt** überspringen
3 *n.* Sprung, *der;* **with** *or* **in one ~:** mit einem Satz; **by ~s and bounds** (fig.) mit Riesenschritten

'leapfrog **1** *n.* Bockspringen, *das*
2 *v.i.*, **-gg-** Bockspringen machen
3 *v.t.* **(a) ~frog sb.** einen Bocksprung über jmdn. machen
(b) (fig.) übertreffen ‹*Konkurrenz, Kollegen usw.*›

leapt ▸ LEAP 1, 2

'leap year *n.* Schaltjahr, *das*

learn /lɜ:n/ **1** *v.t.*, **learned** /lɜ:nd, lɜ:nt/ *or* **learnt** /lɜ:nt/ **(a)** lernen; **~ to swim** schwimmen lernen
(b) (find out) erfahren
2 *v.i.*, **learned** *or* **learnt** **(a)** lernen; **~ about sth.** etwas über etw. (*Akk.*) lernen
(b) (get to know) erfahren (**of** von)

learned /'lɜ:nɪd/ *adj.* gelehrt

'learner *n.* (beginner) Anfänger, *der*/Anfängerin, *die;* **~ [driver]** Fahrschüler, *der*/-schülerin, *die*

'learning *n.* (of person) Gelehrsamkeit, *die*

learning: ~ curve *n.* Lernkurve, *die;* **~ difficulties** *n. pl.* Lernschwierigkeiten *Pl.*; **~ disability** *n.* Lernbehinderung, *die*

learnt ▸ LEARN

lease /li:s/ **1** *n.* (of land, business premises) Pachtvertrag, *der;* (of house, flat, office) Mietvertrag, *der*
2 *v.t.* **(a)** (grant ~ on) verpachten ‹*Grundstück, Geschäft, Rechte*›; vermieten ‹*Haus, Wohnung, Büro*›
(b) (take ~ on) pachten ‹*Grundstück, Geschäft*›; mieten ‹*Haus, Wohnung, Büro*›

'leasehold *n.* ▸ LEASE 2: **have the ~ of** *or* **on sth.** etw. gepachtet/gemietet haben

leash /li:ʃ/ *n.* Leine, *die*

least /li:st/ **1** *adj.* (smallest) kleinst...; (in quantity) wenigst...; (in status) geringst...
2 *n.* Geringste, *das;* **the ~ I can do** das Mindeste, was ich tun kann; **at ~:** mindestens; (anyway) wenigstens; **at the [very] ~:** [aller]mindestens; **not [in] the ~:** nicht im Geringsten
3 *adv.* am wenigsten

leather /'leðə(r)/ **1** *n.* Leder, *das*
2 *adj.* ledern; Leder‹*jacke, -mantel*›

'leather goods *n. pl.* Lederwaren *Pl.*

'leathery *adj.* ledern

leave¹ /li:v/ *n.* **(a)** (permission) Erlaubnis, *die*
(b) (from duty or work) Urlaub, *der;* **~ [of absence]** Urlaub, *der*
(c) take one's ~ sich verabschieden

leave² *v.t.*, **left** /left/ **(a)** (make or let remain) hinterlassen; **~ sb. to do sth.** es jmdm. überlassen, etw. zu tun; (in will) **~ sb. sth., ~ sth. to sb.** jmdm. etw. hinterlassen
(b) (refrain from doing, using, etc.) stehen lassen ‹*Abwasch, Essen*›

···>

(c) (in given state) lassen; **~ sb. alone** (allow to be alone) jmdn. allein lassen; (stop bothering) jmdn. in Ruhe lassen
(d) (refer, entrust) **~ sth. to sb./sth.** etw. jmdm./einer Sache überlassen
(e) (go away from, quit, desert) verlassen; **~ home at 6 a.m.** um 6 Uhr früh von zu Hause weggehen/-fahren; **~ Bonn at 6 p.m.** (by car, in train) um 18 Uhr von Bonn abfahren; (by plane) um 18 Uhr in Bonn abfliegen; *abs.* **the train ~s at 8.30 a.m.** der Zug fährt *od.* geht um 8.30 Uhr; **~ on the 8 a.m. train/flight** mit dem Achtuhrzug fahren/der Achtuhrmaschine fliegen

■ **leave a'side** *v.t.* beiseite lassen
■ **leave be'hind** *v.t.* zurücklassen; (by mistake) vergessen; liegen lassen
■ **leave 'off** *v.t.* (stop) aufhören mit; *abs.* aufhören
■ **leave 'out** *v.t.* auslassen
■ **leave 'over** *v.t.* **be left over** übrig [geblieben] sein

leaves *pl. of* LEAF

Lebanon /'lebənən/ *pr. n.* **[the] ~:** [der] Libanon

lecherous /'letʃərəs/ *adj.* lüstern (geh.)

lecture /'lektʃə(r)/ [1] **(a)** *n.* Vortrag, *der;* (Univ.) Vorlesung, *die*
(b) (reprimand) Strafpredigt, *die* (ugs.)
[2] *v.i.* **~ [to sb.] [on sth.]** [vor jmdm.] einen Vortrag/(Univ.) eine Vorlesung [über etw. (*Akk.*)] halten
[3] *v.t.* (scold) **~ sb.** jmdm. eine Strafpredigt halten

'lecture hall *n.* Hörsaal, *der*

'lecturer *n.* Vortragende, *der/die;* **senior ~:** Dozent, *der*/Dozentin, *die*

'lecture room *n.* Vortragsraum, *der;* (Univ.) Vorlesungsraum, *der*

lectureship /'lektʃəʃɪp/ *n.* Dozentur, *die*

lecture: ~ theatre *n.* Hörsaal, *der;* **~ tour** *n.* Vortragsreise, *die*

led ▶ LEAD² 1, 2

LED *abbr.* = **light-emitting diode** LED

ledge /ledʒ/ *n.* Sims, *der od. das;* (of rock) Vorsprung, *der*

ledger /'ledʒə(r)/ *n.* Hauptbuch, *das*

lee /li:/ *n.* **(a)** (shelter) Schutz, *der*
(b) ~ [side] (Naut.) Leeseite, *die*

leech /li:tʃ/ *n.* [Blut]egel, *der*

leek /li:k/ *n.* Stange Porree *od.* Lauch; **~s** Porree, *der;* Lauch, *der*

leek 'soup *n.* Lauch[creme]suppe, *die*

leer /lɪə(r)/ [1] *n.* anzüglicher Blick
[2] *v.i.* **~ at sb.** jmdm. einen anzüglichen/spöttischen [Seiten]blick zuwerfen

leeward /'li:wəd/ [1] *adj.* **to/on the ~ side of the ship** nach/in Lee
[2] *n.* Leeseite, *die;* **to ~:** leewärts

'leeway *n.* **(a)** (Naut.) Leeweg, *der;* Abdrift, *die*
(b) (fig.) Spielraum, *der*

left¹ ▶ LEAVE²

left² /left/ [1] *adj.* **(a)** link...; **on the ~ side** auf der linken Seite; links
(b) L~ (Polit.) link...
[2] *adv.* nach links
[3] *n.* **(a)** (~-hand side) linke Seite; **on** *or* **to the ~ [of sb./sth.]** links [von jmdm./etw.]
(b) (Polit.) **the L~:** die Linke

left: ~-hand *adj.* link...; **~-'handed** [1] *adj.* linkshändig; ‹*Werkzeug*› für Linkshänder; **be ~-handed** Linkshänder/Linkshänderin sein; [2] *adv.* linkshändig; **~ 'luggage [office]** *n.* (Brit. Railw.) Gepäckaufbewahrung, *die;* **~overs** *n. pl.* Reste *Pl.* **~ 'wing** *n.* linker Flügel; **~-wing** *adj.* (Polit.) linksgerichtet; Links‹*extremist, -intellektueller*›; **~-'winger** *n.* **(a)** (Sport) Linksaußen, *der;* **(b)** (Polit.) Angehöriger/Angehörige des linken Flügels

leg /leg/ *n.* **(a)** Bein, *das;* **pull sb.'s ~** (fig.) jmdn. auf den Arm nehmen (ugs.); **stretch one's ~s** sich (*Dat.*) die Beine vertreten
(b) ~ of lamb Lammkeule, *die*
(c) (of journey) Etappe, *die*

legacy /'legəsɪ/ *n.* Vermächtnis, *das* (Rechtsspr.); Erbschaft, *die*

legal /'li:gl/ *adj.* **(a)** (concerning the law) juristisch; Rechts‹*beratung, -streit, -experte, -schutz*›; gesetzlich ‹*Vertreter*›; rechtlich ‹*Gründe, Stellung*›; Gerichts‹*kosten*›
(b) (required by law) gesetzlich ‹*Verpflichtung*›; gesetzlich verankert ‹*Recht*›
(c) (lawful) legal; rechtsgültig ‹*Vertrag, Testament*›

legal: ~ 'action *n.* Gerichtsverfahren, *das;* Prozess, *der;* **take ~ action against sb.** gerichtlich gegen jmdn. vorgehen; **~ 'aid** *n.* ≈ Prozesskostenhilfe, *die*

legality /lɪ'gælɪtɪ/ *n.* Legalität, *die*

legalization /li:gəlaɪ'zeɪʃn/ *n.* Legalisierung, *die*

legalize /'li:gəlaɪz/ *v.t.* legalisieren

legend /'ledʒənd/ *n.* Sage, *die;* (unfounded belief) Legende, *die*

legendary /'ledʒəndərɪ/ *adj.* legendär

leggings /'legɪŋz/ *n. pl.* Ledergamaschen *Pl.* (veralt.); (of baby) Strampelhose, *die*

legibility /ledʒɪ'bɪlɪtɪ/ *n.* Leserlichkeit, *die*

legible /'ledʒɪbl/ *adj.* leserlich; **easily/scarcely ~:** leicht/kaum lesbar

legion /'li:dʒn/ *n.* Legion, *die*

legion'naires' disease *n.* (Med.) Legionärskrankheit, *die*

legislate /'ledʒɪsleɪt/ *v.i.* Gesetze verabschieden

legislation /ledʒɪs'leɪʃn/ *n.* **(a)** (laws) Gesetze *Pl.*
(b) (legislating) Gesetzgebung, *die*

legislative /'ledʒɪslətɪv/ *adj.* gesetzgebend

legislator /'ledʒɪsleɪtə(r)/ *n.* Gesetzgeber, *der*

legislature /'ledʒɪsleɪtʃə(r)/ *n.* Legislative, *die*

legitimacy /lɪ'dʒɪtɪməsɪ/ *n.* **(a)** Rechtmäßigkeit, *die;* Legitimität, *die*
(b) (of child) Ehelichkeit, *die*

legitimate /lɪ'dʒɪtɪmət/ *adj.* **(a)** (lawful) legitim; rechtmäßig ‹*Besitzer, Regierung*›
(b) (valid) berechtigt
(c) ehelich ‹*Kind*›

legitimatize (legitimatise) /lɪ'dʒɪtɪmətaɪz/, **legitimize (legitimise)** /lɪ'dʒɪtɪmaɪz/ *v.t.* legitimieren

leisure /'leʒə(r)/ *n.* Freizeit, *die; attrib.* Freizeit-

'leisurely *adj.* gemächlich

'leisurewear *n., no indef. art.* Freizeitkleidung, *die*

lemon /'lemən/ *n.* Zitrone, *die*

lemonade /lemə'neɪd/ *n.* [Zitronen]limonade, *die*

lend /lend/ *v.t.,* **lent** /lent/ leihen; **~ sth. to sb.** jmdm. etw. leihen

'lender *n.* Verleiher, *der*/Verleiherin, *die*

length /leŋθ, leŋkθ/ *n.* **(a)** (also of time) Länge, *die;* **be six feet in ~**: sechs Fuß lang sein; **a short ~ of time** kurze Zeit
(b) at ~ (for a long time) lange; (eventually) schließlich; **at [great] ~** (in great detail) lang und breit; **at some ~**: ziemlich ausführlich
(c) go to any/great ~s alles nur/alles Erdenkliche tun
(d) (piece of material) Länge, *die;* Stück, *das*

lengthen /'leŋθən/ 1 *v.i.* länger werden
2 *v.t.* verlängern; länger machen ‹*Kleid*›

lengthways /'leŋθweɪz/ *adv.* der Länge nach; längs

'lengthy *adj.* überlang

lenient /'li:nɪənt/ *adj.* nachsichtig

lens /lenz/ *n.* Linse, *die;* (of spectacles) Glas, *das*

lens cap *n.* Objektivdeckel, *der*

lent ▶ LEND

Lent /lent/ *n.* Fastenzeit, *die*

lentil /'lentl/ *n.* Linse, *die*

Leo /'li:əʊ/ *n., pl.* **~s** (Astrol., Astron.) der Löwe

leopard /'lepəd/ *n.* Leopard, *der*

leotard /'li:ətɑ:d/ *n.* Turnanzug, *der*

leper /'lepə(r)/ *n.* Leprakranke, *der/die*

leprosy /'leprəsɪ/ *n.* Lepra, *die*

lesbian /'lezbɪən/ 1 *n.* Lesbierin, *die*
2 *adj.* lesbisch

less /les/ 1 *adj.* weniger; **of ~ value/importance** weniger wertvoll/wichtig
2 *adv.* weniger; **~ and ~**: immer weniger; **~ and ~ [often]** immer seltener
3 *n.* weniger
4 *prep.* (deducting) **ten ~ three** zehn weniger drei

lessen /'lesn/ 1 *v.t.* verringern
2 *v.i.* sich verringern

lesser /'lesə(r)/ *attrib. adj.* geringer...

lessee /le'si:/ *n.* Pächter, *der*/Pächterin, *die;* Mieter, *der*/Mieterin, *die*

lesson /'lesn/ *n.* **(a)** (class) [Unterrichts]stunde, *die*
(b) (example, warning) Lehre, *die*
(c) (Eccl.) Lesung, *die*

let /let/ 1 *v.t.,* **-tt-, let (a)** (allow to) lassen; **~ sb. do sth.** jmdn. etw. tun lassen; **~ alone** (far less) geschweige denn
(b) (cause to) **~ sb. know** jmdn. wissen lassen
(c) (Brit.: rent out) vermieten
2 *v. aux.,* **-tt-, let** lassen; **Let's go to the cinema. – Yes, ~'s/No, ~'s not** Komm/Kommt, wir gehen ins Kino. – Ja, gut/Nein, lieber nicht; **~ them come in** sie sollen hereinkommen

■ **let 'down** *v.t.* **(a)** (lower) herunter-/hinunterlassen
(b) (Dressm.) auslassen
(c) (disappoint, fail) im Stich lassen

■ **let 'in** *v.t.* **(a)** (admit) herein-/hineinlassen
(b) ~ oneself in for sth. sich auf etw. (*Akk.*) einlassen
(c) ~ sb. in on a secret/plan *etc.* jmdn. in ein Geheimnis/einen Plan *usw.* einweihen

■ **'let into** *v.t.* **(a)** (admit into) lassen in (+ *Akk.*)
(b) (fig.: acquaint with) **~ sb. into a secret** jmdn. in ein Geheimnis einweihen

■ **let 'off** *v.t.* **(a)** (excuse) laufen lassen (ugs.); **~ sb. off sth.** jmdm. etw. erlassen
(b) (allow to alight) aussteigen lassen
(c) abbrennen ‹*Feuerwerk*›

■ **let 'on** (coll.) 1 *v.i.* **don't ~ on!** nichts verraten!
2 *v.t.* **sb. ~ on to me that ...**: man hat mir gesteckt, dass ... (ugs.)

■ **let 'out** *v.t.* **(a) ~ sb./an animal out** jmdn./ein Tier heraus-/hinaus lassen
(b) ausstoßen ‹*Schrei*›; **~ out a groan** aufstöhnen
(c) verraten ‹*Geheimnis*›
(d) (Dressm.) auslassen
(e) (Brit.: rent out) vermieten

■ **let 'through** *v.t.* durchlassen

■ **let 'up** *v.i.* (coll.) nachlassen

'let-down *n.* Enttäuschung, *die*

lethal /'li:θl/ *adj.* tödlich

lethargic /lɪ'θɑ:dʒɪk/ *adj.* träge; (apathetic) lethargisch

lethargy /'leθədʒɪ/ *n.* Trägheit, *die;* (apathy) Lethargie, *die*

letter /'letə(r)/ *n.* **(a)** Brief, *der* (**to** an + *Akk.*)
(b) (of alphabet) Buchstabe, *der*

letter: ~ bomb *n.* Briefbombe, *die;* **~ box** *n.* Briefkasten, *der;* **~head, ~-heading** *ns.* Briefkopf, *der*

'lettering *n.* Typographie, *die*

letter: ~ pad *n.* Briefblock, *der;* **~s page** *n.* Leserbriefseite, *die*

lettuce /'letɪs/ *n.* [Kopf]salat, *der*

leukaemia, (Amer.) **leukemia** /lu:'ki:mɪə/ *n.* Leukämie, *die*

level /'levl/ [1] *n.* **(a)** Höhe, *die;* (storey) Etage, *die*
(b) (fig.: steady state) Niveau, *das;* **be on a ~ [with sb./sth.]** auf dem gleichen Niveau sein [wie jmd./etw.]
(c) (of computer game) Level, *der*
[2] *adj.* **(a)** waagerecht; eben ‹*Boden, Land*›
(b) (on a ~) **be ~ [with sth./sb.]** auf gleicher Höhe [mit etw./jmdm.] sein
(c) (fig.) **keep a ~ head** einen kühlen Kopf bewahren; **do one's ~ best** (coll.) sein Möglichstes tun
[3] *v.t.,* (Brit.) **-ll-: (a)** (make ~) ebnen
(b) (aim) richten ‹*Blick, Gewehr*› (**at** auf + *Akk.*); (fig.) richten ‹*Kritik usw.*› (**at** gegen)

level: ~ 'crossing *n.* (Brit. Railw.) [schienengleicher] Bahnübergang; **~-'headed** *adj.* besonnen

lever /'li:və(r)/ [1] *n.* Hebel, *der*
[2] *v.t.* **~ sth. open** etw. aufhebeln

leverage /'li:vərɪdʒ/ *n.* Hebelwirkung, *die*

levity /'levɪtɪ/ *n.* (frivolity) Unernst, *der*

levy /'levɪ/ [1] *n.* (tax) Steuer, *die*
[2] *v.t.* erheben

lewd /lju:d/ *adj.* geil; anzüglich ‹*Geste*›; schlüpfrig ‹*Witz*›

lexicon /'leksɪkən/ *n.* **(a)** (dictionary) Wörterbuch, *das;* Lexikon, *das* (veralt.)
(b) (vocabulary) Wortschatz, *der*

liability /laɪə'bɪlɪtɪ/ *n.* **(a)** Haftung, *die*
(b) (handicap) Belastung, *die* (**to** für)

liable /'laɪəbl/ *pred. adj.* **(a)** (legally bound) **be ~ for sth.** für etw. haftbar sein *od.* haften
(b) (prone) **be ~ to sth.** ‹*Person:*› zu etw. neigen; **be ~ to do sth.** ‹*Sache:*› leicht etw. tun; ‹*Person:*› dazu neigen, etw. zu tun

liaise /lɪ'eɪz/ *v.i.* eine Verbindung herstellen; **~ on a project** bei einem Projekt zusammenarbeiten

liaison /lɪ'eɪzɒn/ *n.* (cooperation) Zusammenarbeit, *die*

liar /'laɪə(r)/ *n.* Lügner, *der*/Lügnerin, *die*

libel /'laɪbl/ [1] *n.* Verleumdung, *die*
[2] *v.t.,* (Brit.) **-ll-** verleumden

libellous (*Amer.:* **libelous**) /'laɪbələs/ *adj.* verleumderisch

liberal /'lɪbərl/ [1] *adj.* **(a)** großzügig
(b) (Polit.) liberal; **the L~ Democrats** (Brit.) die Liberaldemokraten
[2] *n.* **L~** (Polit.) Liberale, *der/die*

liberate /'lɪbəreɪt/ *v.t.* befreien (**from** aus); **a ~d woman** eine emanzipierte Frau

liberation /lɪbə'reɪʃn/ *n.* Befreiung, *die; see also* WOMEN'S LIBERATION

liberator /'lɪbəreɪtə(r)/ *n.* Befreier, *der*/ Befreierin, *die*

liberty /'lɪbətɪ/ *n.* Freiheit, *die;* **take the ~ of doing sth.** sich (*Dat.*) die Freiheit nehmen, etw. zu tun; **take liberties with sb.** sich (*Dat.*) Freiheiten gegen jmdn. herausnehmen (ugs.)

Libra /'li:brə/ *n.* (Astrol., Astron.) die Waage

librarian /laɪ'breərɪən/ *n.* Bibliothekar, *der*/ Bibliothekarin, *die*

library /'laɪbrərɪ/ *n.* Bibliothek, *die;* **public ~**: öffentliche Bücherei

library: ~ book *n.* Buch aus der Bibliothek; **~ ticket** *n.* Lesekarte, *die*

Libya /'lɪbɪə/ *pr. n.* Libyen (*das*)

lice *pl. of* LOUSE

licence /'laɪsəns/ [1] *n.* [behördliche] Genehmigung; Lizenz, *die;* **[driving] ~**: Führerschein, *der*
[2] *v.t.* ▶ LICENSE 1

'licence fee *n.* Lizenzgebühr, *die*

license /'laɪsəns/ [1] *v.t.* ermächtigen; **the restaurant is ~d to sell drinks** das Restaurant hat eine Schankerlaubnis *od.* -konzession; **~d** ‹*Händler, Makler, Buchmacher*› mit [einer] Lizenz; **licensing laws** Schankgesetze; **~d premises** Gaststätte mit Schankerlaubnis; **get a car ~d** ≈ die Kfz-Steuer für ein Auto bezahlen
[2] *n.* (Amer.) ▶ LICENCE 1

'license plate *n.* (Amer.) Nummernschild, *das*

licentious /laɪ'senʃəs/ *adj.* zügellos ‹*Person*›; unzüchtig ‹*Benehmen*›

lichen /'laɪkn, 'lɪtʃn/ *n.* Flechte, *die*

lick /lɪk/ [1] *v.t.* **(a)** lecken
(b) (coll.: beat) verdreschen (ugs.)
[2] *n.* Lecken, *das*

■ **lick 'off** *v.t.* ablecken

lid /lɪd/ *n.* **(a)** Deckel, *der*
(b) (eyelid) Lid, *das*

lido /'li:dəʊ/ *n., pl.* **~s** Freibad, *das*

lie¹ /laɪ/ [1] *n.* Lüge, *die;* **tell ~s/a ~**: lügen
[2] *v.i.,* **lying** /'laɪɪŋ/ lügen; **~ to sb.** jmdn. be- *od.* anlügen

lie² *v.i.,* **lying** /'laɪɪŋ/, **lay** /leɪ/, **lain** /leɪn/ **(a)** liegen; (assume horizontal position) sich legen
(b) ~ idle ‹*Maschine, Fabrik:*› stillstehen

■ **lie a'bout, lie a'round** *v.i.* herumliegen (ugs.).

■ **lie 'back** *v.i.* sich zurücklegen; (sitting) sich zurücklehnen

■ **lie 'down** *v.i.* sich hinlegen

lie detector /'laɪdɪ'tektə(r)/ *n.* Lügendetektor, *der*

'lie-in *n.* (coll.) **have a ~**: [sich] ausschlafen

lieu /lju:/ *n.* **in ~ of sth.** anstelle einer Sache (*Gen.*); **get holiday in ~**: stattdessen Urlaub bekommen

lieutenant /lef'tenənt/ *n.* (Army) Oberleutnant, *der*

life /laɪf/ *n., pl.* **lives** /laɪvz/ Leben, *das;* **for ~**: lebenslänglich ‹*inhaftiert*›; **true to ~**: wahrheitsgetreu; **get a ~** (coll.) was aus seinem Leben machen

life: ~-and-death *adj.* ‹*Kampf*› auf Leben und Tod; (fig.) überaus wichtig ‹*Frage, Brief*›; **~ assurance** *n.* (Brit.) Lebensversicherung, *die;* **~belt** *n.* Rettungsring, *der;* **~boat** *n.* Rettungsboot, *das;* **~buoy** *n.* Rettungsring, *der;* **~ cycle**

n. Lebenszyklus, *der;* ~ **expectancy** *n.* Lebenserwartung, *die;* ~**guard** *n.* Rettungsschwimmer, *der*/-schwimmerin, *die;* ~ **insurance** *n.* Lebensversicherung, *die;* ~ **jacket** *n.* Schwimmweste, *die;* ~**less** *adj.* leblos; (fig.) farblos; ~**like** *adj.* lebensecht; ~**line** *n.* Rettungsleine, *die;* (fig.) Rettungsanker, *der;* ~**long** *adj.* lebenslang

lifer /'laɪfə(r)/ *n.* (coll.) Lebenslängliche, *der*/*die* (ugs.)

life: ~**-saving** *n.* Rettungsschwimmen, *das; attrib.* Rettungs-; ~ **sciences** *n. pl.* Biowissenschaften *Pl.;* ~ **sentence** *n.* lebenslängliche Freiheitsstrafe; ~**-size,** ~**-sized** *adj.* lebensgroß; in Lebensgröße *nachgestellt;* ~**span** *n.* Lebenserwartung, *die;* (Biol.) Lebensdauer, *die;* ~**style** *n.* Lebensstil, *der;* ~**time** *n.* Lebenszeit, *die;* **during my** ~**time** während meines Lebens; **once in a** ~**time** einmal im Leben; ~ **vest** *n.* Schwimmweste, *die*

lift /lɪft/ [1] *v.t.* heben; (fig.) erheben ‹*Gemüt, Geist*›
[2] *n.* **(a)** (in vehicle) **get a** ~: mitgenommen werden; **give sb. a** ~: jmdn. mitnehmen
(b) (Brit.: elevator) Aufzug, *der*
[3] *v.i.* ‹*Nebel:*› sich auflösen

■ **'lift off** *v.t. & i.* abheben

■ **lift 'up** *v.t.* hochheben; heben ‹*Kopf*›

'lift-off *n.* Abheben, *das*

ligament /'lɪgəmənt/ *n.* Band, *das*

light[1] /laɪt/ [1] *n.* **(a)** Licht, *das;* ~ **of day** Tageslicht, *das*
(b) (lamp) Licht, *das;* (fitting) Lampe, *die*
(c) (signal to traffic) Ampel, *die*; **as far as the** ~**s** bis zur Ampel
(d) (to ignite) **have you got a** ~**?** haben Sie Feuer? **set** ~ **to sth.** etw. anzünden
(e) bring sth. to ~: etw. ans [Tages]licht bringen; **throw** *or* **shed** ~ **[up]on sth.** Licht in etw. (*Akk.*) bringen
(f) (aspect) **in that** ~: aus dieser Sicht; **seen in this** ~: so gesehen; **in the** ~ **of** angesichts (+ *Gen.*); **show sb. in a bad** ~: ein schlechtes Licht auf jmdn. werfen
[2] *adj.* hell; ~**-blue**/**-brown** *etc.* hellblau/-braun *usw.*
[3] *v.t.,* **lit** /lɪt/ *or* **lighted (a)** (ignite) anzünden
(b) (illuminate) erhellen

■ **light 'up** [1] *v.i.* **(a)** (become lit) erleuchtet werden
(b) (become bright) aufleuchten (**with** vor)
[2] *v.t.* **(a)** (illuminate) erleuchten
(b) anzünden ‹*Zigarette*›

light[2] [1] *adj.* leicht; (mild) mild ‹*Strafe*›
[2] *adv.* **travel** ~: mit wenig *od.* leichtem Gepäck reisen

light: ~ **'aircraft** *n.* Leichtflugzeug, *das;* ~**bulb** *n.* Glühbirne, *die*

'lighted *adj.* brennend ‹*Kerze, Zigarette*›; angezündet ‹*Streichholz*›

light-emitting 'diode /'daɪəʊd/ *n.* Leuchtdiode, *die*

lighten[1] /'laɪtn/ *v.t.* (make less heavy, difficult) leichter machen

lighten[2] [1] *v.t.* (make brighter) aufhellen; heller machen ‹*Raum*›
[2] *v.i.* sich aufhellen

'lighter *n.* Feuerzeug, *das*

light: ~**-'headed** *adj.* leicht benommen; ~**-'hearted** *adj.* **(a)** (humorous) unbeschwert; **(b)** (optimistic) unbekümmert; ~**house** *n.* Leuchtturm, *der;* ~ **'industry** *n.* Leichtindustrie, *die*

'lighting *n.* Beleuchtung, *die*

'lightly *adv.* **(a)** leicht
(b) (without serious consideration) leichtfertig
(c) (cheerfully) leichthin; **not treat sth.** ~: etw. nicht auf die leichte Schulter nehmen
(d) get off ~: glimpflich davonkommen

'light meter *n.* Lichtmesser, *der;* (exposure meter) Belichtungsmesser, *der*

'lightness[1] *n.* (of weight; also fig.) Leichtigkeit, *die*

lightness[2] *n.* (of colour) Helligkeit, *die*

lightning /'laɪtnɪŋ/ *n.* Blitz, *der;* **flash of** ~: Blitz, *der*

lightning: ~ **conductor** *n.* Blitzableiter, *der;* ~ **strike** *n.* Blitzschlag, *der*

light: ~**weight** [1] *adj.* leicht. [2] *n.* Leichtgewicht, *das;* ~ **year** *n.* Lichtjahr, *das*

like[1] /laɪk/ [1] *adj.* **(a)** (resembling) wie; **your dress is** ~ **mine** dein Kleid ist so ähnlich wie meins; **in a case** ~ **that** in so einem Fall; **what is sb./sth.** ~**?** wie ist jmd./etw.?
(b) (characteristic of) typisch für ‹*dich, ihn usw.*›
(c) (similar) ähnlich
[2] *prep.* (in the manner of) wie; **[just]** ~ **that** [einfach] so
[3] *n.* **(a)** (equal) **his/her** ~: seines-/ihresgleichen
(b) (similar things) **the** ~: so etwas; **and the** ~: und dergleichen

like[2] [1] *v.t.* (be fond of, wish for) mögen; ~ **vegetables** Gemüse mögen; gern Gemüse essen; ~ **doing sth.** etw. gern tun; **would you** ~ **a drink?** möchtest du etwas trinken?; **would you** ~ **me to do it?** möchtest du, dass ich es tue?; **how do you** ~ **it?** wie gefällt es dir?; **if you** ~ *expr. assent* wenn du willst
[2] *n., in pl.* ~**s and dislikes** Vorlieben und Abneigungen

likeable /'laɪkəbl/ *adj.* nett; sympathisch

likelihood /'laɪklɪhʊd/ *n.* Wahrscheinlichkeit, *die*

likely /'laɪklɪ/ [1] *adj.* wahrscheinlich; **there are** ~ **to be [traffic] hold-ups** man muss mit [Verkehrs]staus rechnen; **they are [not]** ~ **to come** sie werden wahrscheinlich [nicht] kommen; **is it** ~ **to rain tomorrow?** wird es morgen wohl regnen?; **this is not** ~ **to happen** es ist unwahrscheinlich, dass das geschieht

···

[2] *adv.* wahrscheinlich; **as ~ as not** höchstwahrscheinlich; **not ~!** (coll.) auf keinen Fall!

'like-minded *adj.* gleich gesinnt

liken /'laɪkn/ *v.t.* **~ sth./sb. to sth./sb.** etw./jmdn. mit etw./jmdm. vergleichen

'likeness *n.* Ähnlichkeit, *die* (**to** mit)

likewise /'laɪkwaɪz/ *adv.* ebenso

liking /'laɪkɪŋ/ *n.* Vorliebe, *die;* **take a ~ to sb./sth.** an jmdm./etw. Gefallen finden; **sth. is [not] to sb.'s ~:** etw. ist [nicht] nach jmds. Geschmack

lilac /'laɪlək/ [1] *n.* **(a)** (Bot.) Flieder, *der*
(b) (colour) Zartlila, *das*
[2] *adj.* zartlila; fliederfarben

Lilo ® /'laɪləʊ/ *n.* Luftmatratze, *die*

lily /'lɪlɪ/ *n.* Lilie, *die*

limb /lɪm/ *n.* **(a)** (Anat.) Glied, *das*
(b) be out on a ~ (fig.) exponiert sein

limber up /lɪmbər 'ʌp/ *v.i.* (loosen up) die Muskeln lockern

lime¹ /laɪm/ *n.* **[quick]~:** [ungelöschter] Kalk

lime² *n.* (fruit) Limone, *die*

lime³ ▶ LIME TREE

'limelight *n.* **be in the ~:** im Rampenlicht [der Öffentlichkeit] stehen

limerick /'lɪmərɪk/ *n.* Limerick, *der*

lime: ~stone *n.* Kalkstein, *der;* **~ tree** *n.* Linde, *die*

limit /'lɪmɪt/ [1] *n.* **(a)** Grenze, *die;* **set** *or* **put a ~ on sth.** etw. begrenzen; **be over the ~** ‹*Autofahrer:*› zu viele Promille haben; **lower/upper ~:** Untergrenze/Höchstgrenze, *die;* **without ~:** unbegrenzt; **within ~s** innerhalb gewisser Grenzen
(b) (coll.) **this is the ~!** das ist [doch] die Höhe!; **he/she is the [very] ~:** er/sie ist [einfach] unmöglich
[2] *v.t.* begrenzen (**to** auf + *Akk.*); einschränken ‹*Freiheit*›

limitation /lɪmɪ'teɪʃn/ *n.* Beschränkung, *die*

'limited *adj.* **(a)** (restricted) begrenzt
(b) (intellectually narrow) beschränkt

'limitless *adj.* grenzenlos

limousine /'lɪmʊzi:n/ *n.* Limousine, *die*

limp¹ /lɪmp/ [1] *v.i.* hinken
[2] *n.* Hinken, *das*

limp² *adj.* schlaff

'limply *adv.* schlaff; (weakly) schwach

limpet /'lɪmpɪt/ *n.* (Zool.) Napfschnecke, *die*

limpid /'lɪmpɪd/ *adj.* klar

linctus /'lɪŋktəs/ *n.* Hustensaft, *der*

line¹ /laɪn/ [1] *n.* **(a)** (string, cord, rope, etc.) Leine, *die*
(b) (telephone cable) Leitung, *die*
(c) (long mark; also Math., Phys.) Linie, *die*
(d) (row, series) Reihe, *die;* (Amer.: queue) Schlange, *die;* **bring sb. into ~:** dafür sorgen, dass jmd. nicht aus der Reihe tanzt (ugs.)
(e) (row of words on a page) Zeile, *die*
(f) (wrinkle) Falte, *die*
(g) (direction, course) Richtung, *die;* **on the ~s of** nach Art (+ *Gen.*); **be on the right/wrong ~s** in die richtige/falsche Richtung gehen; **along** *or* **on the same ~s** in der gleichen Richtung
(h) (Railw.) Bahnlinie, *die;* (track) Gleis, *das*
(i) (field of activity) Branche, *die*
(j) (Commerc.: product) Artikel, *der;* Linie, *die* (fachspr.)
[2] *v.t.* **(a)** linieren ‹*Papier*›; **a ~d face** ein faltiges Gesicht
(b) säumen (geh.) ‹*Straße, Strecke*›

■ **line 'up** [1] *v.t.* antreten lassen ‹*Gefangene, Soldaten usw.*›; [in einer Reihe] aufstellen ‹*Gegenstände*›
[2] *v.i.* ‹*Gefangene, Soldaten:*› antreten; (queue up) sich anstellen

line² *v.t.* füttern ‹*Kleidungsstück*›; ausschlagen ‹*Schublade usw.*›

lineage /'lɪnɪɪdʒ/ *n.* Abstammung, *die*

linear /'lɪnɪə(r)/ *adj.* linear

line: ~ dance [1] *n.* Linedance, *der;* [2] *v.i.* Linedance tanzen; **~ dancing** *n.* Linedance-Tanzen, *das;* **~ manager** *n.* [unmittelbarer] Vorgesetzter; Linienmanager, *der*

linen /'lɪnɪn/ [1] *n.* **(a)** Leinen, *das*
(b) (shirts, sheets, etc.) Wäsche, *die*
[2] *adj.* Leinen‹*faden, -bluse*›; Lein‹*tuch*›

linen: ~ basket *n.* (Brit.) Wäschekorb, *der;* **~ cupboard** *n.* Wäscheschrank, *der*

'line printer *n.* (Comp.) Zeilendrucker, *der*

liner /'laɪnə(r)/ Linienschiff, *das*

'line-up *n.* Aufstellung, *die*

linger /'lɪŋgə(r)/ *v.i.* verweilen (geh.); bleiben

lingerie /'læ̃ʒərɪ/ *n.* **[women's] ~:** Damenunterwäsche, *die*

lingo /'lɪŋgəʊ/ *n.* (coll.) Sprache, *die*

linguist /'lɪŋgwɪst/ *n.* Sprachkundige, *der/die*

linguistic /lɪŋ'gwɪstɪk/ *adj.* (of ~s) linguistisch; (of language) sprachlich

linguistics /lɪŋ'gwɪstɪks/ *n.* Linguistik, *die*

lining /'laɪnɪŋ/ *n.* (of clothes) Futter, *das;* (of objects, machines, etc.) Auskleidung, *die*

'lining paper *n.* Schrankpapier, *das*

link /lɪŋk/ [1] *n.* **(a)** (of chain) Glied, *das*
(b) (connection) Verbindung, *die*
[2] *v.t.* verbinden; **~ arms** sich unterhaken

■ **link 'up** *v.t.* miteinander verbinden

links /lɪŋks/ *n.* **[golf] ~:** Golfplatz, *der*

lino /'laɪnəʊ/ *n., pl.* **~s** Linoleum, *das*

linoleum /lɪ'nəʊlɪəm/ *n.* Linoleum, *das*

linseed /'lɪnsi:d/ *n.* Leinsamen, *der*

linseed 'oil *n.* Leinöl, *das*

lint /lɪnt/ *n.* Mull, *der*

lintel /'lɪntl/ *n.* (Archit.) Sturz, *der*

lion /'laɪən/ *n.* Löwe, *der*

lioness /'laɪənɪs/ *n.* Löwin, *die*

lip /lɪp/ *n.* **(a)** Lippe, *die;* **lower/upper ~:** Unter-/Oberlippe, *die*

(b) (of cup) [Gieß]rand, *der;* (of jug) Schnabel, *der*

liposuction /'laɪpəʊsʌkʃn, 'lɪpəʊsʌkʃn/ *n.* Fettabsaugung, *die*; Liposuktion, *die*

lip: ~-read *v.i.* von den Lippen lesen; **~-reading** *n.* Lippenlesen, *das;* **~ service** *n.* **pay ~ service to sth.** ein Lippenbekenntnis zu etw. ablegen; **~stick** *n.* Lippenstift, *der*

liquefy /'lɪkwɪfaɪ/ **1** *v.t.* verflüssigen **2** *v.i.* sich verflüssigen

liqueur /lɪ'kjʊə(r)/ *n.* Likör, *der*

liquid /'lɪkwɪd/ **1** *adj.* flüssig **2** *n.* Flüssigkeit, *die*

liquidate /'lɪkwɪdeɪt/ *v.t.* (Commerc.) liquidieren

liquidation /lɪkwɪ'deɪʃn/ *n.* (Commerc.) Liquidation, *die*

liquid crystal dis'play *n.* Flüssigkristallanzeige, *die*

liquidize /'lɪkwɪdaɪz/ *v.t.* auflösen; (Cookery) [im Mixer] pürieren

'liquidizer *n.* Mixer, *der*

liquid 'measure *n.* Flüssigkeitsmaß, *das*

liquor /'lɪkə(r)/ *n.* (drink) Alkohol, *der*

liquorice /'lɪkərɪs/ *n.* Lakritze, *die*

Lisbon /'lɪzbən/ *pr. n.* Lissabon (*das*)

lisp /lɪsp/ **1** *v.i. & t.* lispeln **2** *n.* Lispeln, *das*

list¹ /lɪst/ **1** *n.* Liste, *die* **2** *v.t.* aufführen; auflisten; (verbally) aufzählen

list² *v.i.* (Naut.) Schlagseite haben

listed 'building *n.* (Brit.) Gebäude unter Denkmalsschutz

listen /'lɪsn/ *v.i.* zuhören; **~ to music/the radio** Musik/Radio hören; **they ~ed to his words** sie hörten ihm zu

listener /'lɪsnə(r)/ *n.* Zuhörer, *der*/ Zuhörerin, *die;* (to radio) Hörer, *der*/Hörerin, *die*

listless /'lɪstlɪs/ *adj.* lustlos

'list price *n.* Katalogpreis, *der*

lit ▶ LIGHT¹ 3

litany /'lɪtənɪ/ *n.* Litanei, *die*

lite, Lite ® /laɪt/ **1** *adj.* kalorienreduziert ‹*Bier, Käse etc.*› **2** *n.* Leichtbier, *das*

liter (Amer.) ▶ LITRE

literacy /'lɪtərəsɪ/ *n.* Lese- und Schreibfertigkeit, *die*

literal /'lɪtərl/ *adj.* **(a)** wörtlich **(b)** (not exaggerated) buchstäblich

literally /'lɪtərəlɪ/ *adv.* **(a)** wörtlich **(b)** (actually) buchstäblich **(c)** (coll.: with some exaggeration) geradezu

literary /'lɪtərərɪ/ *adj.* literarisch

literary 'agent *n.* Literaturagent, *der*/ -agentin, *die*

literate /'lɪtərət/ *adj.* des Lesens und Schreibens kundig; (educated) gebildet

literature /'lɪtrətʃə(r)/ *n.* Literatur, *die*

lithe /laɪð/ *adj.* geschmeidig

litigation /lɪtɪ'geɪʃn/ *n.* Rechtsstreit, *der*

litre /'li:tə(r)/ *n.* (Brit.) Liter, *der od. das*

litter /'lɪtə(r)/ **1** *n.* **(a)** (rubbish) Abfall, *der* **(b)** (of animals) Wurf, *der* **2** *v.t.* verstreuen

litter: ~ basket *n.* Abfallkorb, *der;* **~ bin** *n.* Abfalleimer, *der;* **~bug, ~ lout** *ns.* Schmutzfink, *der* (ugs.)

little /'lɪtl/ **1** *adj.*, **~r** /'lɪtlə(r)/, **~st** /'lɪtlɪst/ (*Note: it is more common to use the compar. and superl. forms* **smaller, smallest**) **(a)** klein; **a ~ way** ein kurzes Stück; **after a ~ while** nach kurzer Zeit **(b)** (not much) wenig; **there is very ~ tea left** es ist kaum noch Tee da; **a ~ ...** (a small quantity of) etwas ...; ein bisschen ... **2** *n.* wenig; **a ~** (a small quantity) etwas; (somewhat) ein wenig; **~ by ~**: nach und nach

little: ~ 'finger *n.* kleiner Finger; **~-known** *adj.* wenig bekannt

liturgy /'lɪtədʒɪ/ *n.* Liturgie, *die*

live¹ /laɪv/ **1** *adj.* **(a)** *attrib.* (alive) lebend **(b)** (Radio, Telev.) **~ performance** Liveaufführung, *die;* **~ broadcast** Livesendung, *die* **(c)** (Electr.) Strom führend **2** *adv.* (Radio, Telev.) live ‹*übertragen usw.*›

live² /lɪv/ **1** *v.i.* **(a)** leben **(b)** (make permanent home) wohnen; leben **2** *v.t.* leben

■ **live 'down** *v.t.* Gras wachsen lassen über (+ *Akk.*); **he will never be able to ~ it down** das wird ihm ewig anhängen

■ **live on** **1** /'--/ *v.t.* leben von **2** /-'-/ *v.i.* weiterleben

■ **live 'up to** *v.t.* gerecht werden (+ *Dat.*)

live-in /'lɪvɪn/ *attrib. adj.* im Haus wohnend ‹*Personal*›

livelihood /'laɪvlɪhʊd/ *n.* Lebensunterhalt, *der*

liveliness /'laɪvlɪnɪs/ *n.* Lebhaftigkeit, *die*

lively /'laɪvlɪ/ *adj.* lebhaft; lebendig ‹*Schilderung*›; rege ‹*Handel*›

liven up /laɪvn 'ʌp/ **1** *v.t.* Leben bringen in (+ *Akk.*) **2** *v.i.* ‹*Person:*› aufleben

liver /'lɪvə(r)/ *n.* Leber, *die*

livery /'lɪvərɪ/ *n.* Livree, *die*

lives *pl. of* LIFE

live /laɪv/**: ~stock** *n. pl.* Vieh, *das;* **~ 'wire** *n.* (fig.) Energiebündel, *das* (ugs.)

livid /'lɪvɪd/ *adj.* (Brit. coll.) fuchtig (ugs.)

living /'lɪvɪŋ/ **1** *n.* **(a)** Leben, *das* **(b)** **make a ~**: seinen Lebensunterhalt verdienen **(c)** *pl.* **the ~**: die Lebenden *Pl.* **2** *adj.* lebend; **within ~ memory** seit Menschengedenken

living: ~ room *n.* Wohnzimmer, *das;* **~ 'will** *n.* Patientenverfügung, *die*

lizard /'lɪzəd/ *n.* Eidechse, *die*
llama /'lɑːmə/ *n.* Lama, *das*
load /ləʊd/ [1] *n.* (burden, weight; also fig.) Last, *die;* (amount carried) Ladung, *die*
[2] *v.t.* **(a)** (put ~ on) beladen; (put as load) **~ sb. with work** (fig.) jmdm. Arbeit auftragen
(b) laden ‹*Gewehr*›; **~ a camera** einen Film [in einen Fotoapparat] einlegen
▪ **load 'up** *v.i.* laden (**with** *Akk.*)
'loaded *adj.* **a ~ question** eine suggestive Frage; **be ~** (coll.: rich) [schwer] Kohle haben (salopp)
'loading bay *n.* Ladeplatz, *der*
loaf[1] /ləʊf/ *n., pl.* **loaves** /ləʊvz/ Brot, *das;* [Brot]laib, *der;* **a ~ of bread** ein Laib Brot
loaf[2] *v.i.* **~ round town/the house** in der Stadt/zu Hause herumlungern (ugs.)
loan /ləʊn/ [1] *n.* **(a)** (thing lent) Leihgabe, *die;* **be out on ~**: ausgeliehen sein; **have sth. on ~ [from sb.]** etw. [von jmdm.] geliehen haben
(b) (money lent) Darlehen, *das*
[2] *v.t.* **~ sth. to sb.** jmdm. etw. leihen
loan shark *n.* (coll.) Kredithai, *der* (ugs.)
loath /ləʊθ/ *pred. adj.* **be ~ to do sth.** etw. ungern tun
loathe /ləʊð/ *v.t.* verabscheuen
loathing /'ləʊðɪŋ/ *n.* Abscheu, *der* (**of, for** vor + *Dat.*)
loathsome /'ləʊðsəm/ *adj.* abscheulich; widerlich
loaves *pl. of* LOAF[1]
lobby /'lɒbɪ/ *n.* **(a)** (pressure group) Lobby, *die*
(b) (of hotel) Eingangshalle, *die;* (of theatre) Foyer, *das*
lobe /ləʊb/ *n.* (ear~) Ohrläppchen, *das*
lobster /'lɒbstə(r)/ *n.* Hummer, *der*
'lobster pot *n.* Hummerkorb, *der*
local /'ləʊkl/ [1] *adj.* lokal (bes. Zeitungsw.); Kommunal‹*wahl, -abgaben*›; (of this area) hiesig; (of that area) dortig; ortsansässig ‹*Firma, Familie*›; ‹*Wein, Produkt, Spezialität*› [aus] der Gegend; **she's a ~ girl** sie ist von hier/dort
[2] *n.* **(a)** (person) Einheimische, *der/die*
(b) (Brit. coll.: pub) [Stamm]kneipe, *die*
local: ~ anaes'thetic *n.* Lokalanästhetikum, *das;* **~ au'thority** *n.* (Brit.) Kommunalverwaltung, *die;* **~ call** *n.* (Teleph.) Ortsgespräch, *das;* **~ 'government** *n.* Kommunalverwaltung, *die*
locality /ləʊ'kælɪtɪ/ *n.* Ort, *der*
localization /ləʊkəlaɪ'zeɪʃn/ *n.* (Comp.) Lokalisierung, *die*
'locally *adv.* im/am Ort
locate /ləʊ'keɪt/ *v.t.* **(a)** **be ~d** liegen
(b) (determine position of) ausfindig machen
location /ləʊ'keɪʃn/ *n.* **(a)** Lage, *die*
(b) (Cinemat.) Drehort, *der;* **be on ~**: bei Außenaufnahmen sein
loch /lɒx, lɒk/ *n.* (Scot.) See, *der*
lock[1] /lɒk/ *n.* (of hair) [Haar]strähne, *die*
lock[2] [1] *n.* **(a)** (of door etc.) Schloss, *das*
(b) (on canal etc.) Schleuse, *die*
[2] *v.t.* zuschließen
▪ **lock a'way** *v.t.* einschließen; einsperren ‹*Person*›
▪ **lock 'in** *v.t.* einschließen; (deliberately) einsperren
▪ **lock 'out** *v.t.* aussperren (**of** aus); **~ oneself out** sich aussperren
▪ **lock 'up** [1] *v.i.* abschließen
[2] *v.t.* **(a)** abschließen ‹*Haus, Tür*›
(b) (imprison) einsperren
locker /'lɒkə(r)/ *n.* Schließfach, *das*
locket /'lɒkɪt/ *n.* Medaillon, *das*
lock: ~jaw *n.* (Med.) Kieferklemme, *die;* **~out** *n.* Aussperrung, *die;* **~smith** *n.* Schlosser, *der*
locomotive /ləʊkə'məʊtɪv/ *n.* Lokomotive, *die*
locust /'ləʊkəst/ *n.* Heuschrecke, *die*
lodge /lɒdʒ/ [1] *n.* **(a)** (cottage) Pförtner-/Gärtnerhaus, *das*
(b) (porter's room) [Pförtner]loge, *die*
[2] *v.t.* **(a)** einlegen ‹*Beschwerde, Protest usw.*›
(b) einreichen ‹*Klage*›
[3] *v.i.* [zur Miete] wohnen
'lodger *n.* Untermieter, *der*/Untermieterin, *die*
lodging /'lɒdʒɪŋ/ *n.* [möbliertes] Zimmer
loft /lɒft/ *n.* (attic) [Dach]boden, *der*
lofty /'lɒftɪ/ *adj.* **(a)** (exalted) hoch
(b) (haughty) hochmütig
log /lɒg/ *n.* **(a)** (timber) [geschlagener] Baumstamm; (as firewood) [Holz]scheit, *das*
(b) **~[book]** (Naut.) Logbuch, *das*
▪ **log 'in** ▸ LOG ON
▪ **log 'off** *v.i.* (Comp.) sich abmelden
▪ **log 'on** *v.i.* (Comp.) sich anmelden
▪ **log 'out** ▸ LOG OFF
log: ~ 'cabin *n.* Blockhütte, *die;* **~ 'fire** *n.* Holzfeuer, *das*
loggerheads /'lɒgəhedz/ *n. pl.* **be at ~ with sb.** mit jmdm. im Clinch liegen
logic /'lɒdʒɪk/ *n.* Logik, *die*
logical /'lɒdʒɪkl/ *adj.* logisch; **she has a ~ mind** sie denkt logisch
logically /'lɒdʒɪkəlɪ/ *adv.* logisch
logistics /lə'dʒɪstɪks/ *n. pl.* Logistik, *die*
logo /'ləʊgəʊ/ *n., pl.* **~s** Signet, *das*
loin /lɔɪn/ *n.* Lende, *die*
'loincloth *n.* Lendenschurz, *der*
loiter /'lɔɪtə(r)/ *v.i.* trödeln; (linger suspiciously) herumlungern
loll /lɒl/ *v.i.* sich lümmeln (ugs.)
lollipop /'lɒlɪpɒp/ *n.* Lutscher, *der*
London /'lʌndən/ [1] *pr. n.* London (*das*)
[2] *attrib. adj.* Londoner
'Londoner *n.* Londoner, *der*/Londonerin, *die*
lone /ləʊn/ *attrib. adj.* einsam

loneliness /'ləʊnlɪnɪs/ *n.* Einsamkeit, *die*

lonely /'ləʊnlɪ/ *adj.* einsam

lone 'parent *n.* allein erziehender Elternteil; **she/he is a ~**: sie/er ist allein erziehend

loner /'ləʊnə(r)/ *n.* Einzelgänger, *der*/ -gängerin, *die*

lonesome /'ləʊnsəm/ *adj.* einsam

long¹ /lɒŋ/ 1 *adj.*, **~er** /'lɒŋgə(r)/, **~est** /'lɒŋgɪst/ **(a)** lang; weit ‹*Reise, Weg*›
(b) (elongated) länglich; schmal
(c) in the '~ run auf die Dauer
2 *n.* (~ interval) **take ~**: lange dauern; **for ~**: lange; (since ~ ago) seit langem; **before ~**: bald
3 *adv.*, **~er, ~est (a)** lang[e]; **as** *or* **so ~ as** solange; **you should have finished ~ before now** du hättest schon längst fertig sein sollen; **much ~er** viel länger
(b) as *or* **so ~ as** (provided that) solange; wenn

long² *v.i.* **~ for sb./sth.** sich nach jmdm./ etw. sehnen; **~ to do sth.** sich danach sehnen, etw. zu tun

long-distance 1 /'---/ *adj.* Fern‹*gespräch, -verkehr usw.*›; Langstrecken‹*läufer, -flug usw.*›
2 /-'--/ *adv.* **phone ~**: ein Ferngespräch führen

longevity /lɒn'dʒevɪtɪ/ *n.* Langlebigkeit, *die*

long: ~-haired *adj.* langhaarig; Langhaar‹*dackel, -katze*›; **~hand** *n.* Langschrift, *die;* **~-haul** *adj.* Fern‹*verkehr, -lastwagen*›; Langstrecken‹*[flug]verkehr*›

'longing 1 *n.* Sehnsucht, *die*
2 *adj.* sehnsüchtig

'longingly *adv.* sehnsüchtig

longitude /'lɒŋgɪtju:d/ *n.* (Geog.) Länge, *die*

long: ~ jump *n.* (Brit. Sport) Weitsprung, *der;* **~-lasting** *adj.* langandauernd; dauerhaft ‹*Beziehung, Freundschaft*›; **~-legged** *adj.* langbeinig; **~ 'lens** *n.* Fernobjektiv, *das;* **~-life** *adj.* haltbar [gemacht]; **~-life battery** Batterie mit langer Lebensdauer; **~-life milk** H-Milch, *die;* **~-lived** /'lɒŋlɪvd/ *adj.* langlebig; **~-playing 'record** *n.* Langspielplatte, *die;* **~-range** *adj.* **(a)** Langstrecken‹*flugzeug, -rakete usw.*›; **(b)** (relating to time) langfristig; **~-sighted** /lɒŋ'saɪtɪd/ *adj.* weitsichtig; (fig.) weitblickend; **~-sleeved** /'lɒŋsli:vd/ *adj.* langärmelig; **~-standing** *attrib. adj.* seit langem bestehend; alt ‹*Schulden, Streit*›; **~-suffering** *adj.* schwer geprüft; **~-term** *adj.* langfristig; **~ wave** *n.* (Radio) Langwelle, *die;* **~-winded** /lɒŋ'wɪndɪd/ *adj.* langatmig

loo /lu:/ *n.* (Brit. coll.) Klo, *das* (ugs.)

look /lʊk/ 1 *v.i.* **(a)** sehen; gucken (ugs.)
(b) (search) nachsehen
(c) (face) zugewandt sein (**to[wards]** *Dat.*)
(d) (appear) aussehen; **~ well/ill** gut/schlecht aussehen
2 *n.* **(a)** Blick, *der;* **have** *or* **take a ~ at sb./ sth.** sich (*Dat.*) jmdn./etw. ansehen
(b) (appearance) Aussehen, *das;* **good ~s** gutes Aussehen

■ **look 'after** *v.t.* (care for) sorgen für

■ **look a'head** *v.i.* (fig.) an die Zukunft denken

■ **'look at** *v.t.* **(a)** (regard) ansehen
(b) (consider) betrachten

■ **look 'back** *v.i.* **(a)** sich umsehen
(b) ~ back on *or* **to sth.** an etw. (*Akk.*) zurückdenken

■ **look 'down [up]on** *v.t.* **(a)** herunter-/ hinuntersehen auf (+ *Akk.*)
(b) (fig.: despise) herabsehen auf (+ *Akk.*)

■ **'look for** *v.t.* **(a)** (seek) suchen nach
(b) (expect) erwarten

■ **look 'out** *v.i.* **(a)** hinaus-/heraussehen (**of** aus)
(b) (take care) aufpassen
(c) ~ out on sth. ‹*Zimmer, Wohnung usw.*:› zu etw. hin liegen

■ **look 'out for** *v.t.* (be prepared for) achten auf (+ *Akk.*); (keep watching for) Ausschau halten nach ‹*Arbeit, Gelegenheit, Sammelobjekt usw.*›

■ **look 'over** *v.t.* **(a)** sehen über (+ *Akk.*)
(b) (survey) sich (*Dat.*) ansehen ‹*Haus*›

■ **look 'round** *v.i.* sich umsehen

■ **'look through** *v.t.* **(a) ~ through sth.** durch etw. [hindurch] sehen
(b) (inspect) durchsehen ‹*Papiere*›

■ **'look to** *v.t.* (rely on) **~ to sb./sth. for sth.** etw. von jmdm./etw. erwarten

■ **look 'up** 1 *v.i.* **(a)** aufblicken
(b) (improve) besser werden
2 *v.t.* nachschlagen ‹*Wort*›; heraussuchen ‹*Telefonnummer, Zugverbindung usw.*›

■ **look 'up to** *v.t.* **~ up to sb.** zu jmdm. aufsehen

'look-alike *n.* Doppelgänger, *der*/-gängerin, *die*

looker-'on *n.* Zuschauer, *der*/Zuschauerin, *die*

'looking glass *n.* Spiegel, *der*

'lookout *n., pl.* **~s (a)** (observation post) Ausguck, *der*
(b) (person) Wache, *die*
(c) (Brit. fig.) **that's a bad ~**: das sind schlechte Aussichten; **that's his ~**: das ist sein Problem
(d) keep a ~ [for sb./sth.] [nach jmdm./etw] Ausschau halten

loom¹ /lu:m/ *n.* (Weaving) Webstuhl, *der*

loom² *v.i.* auftauchen

loop /lu:p/ 1 *n.* **(a)** Schleife, *die*
(b) (cord) Schlaufe, *die*
2 *v.t.* zu einer Schlaufe formen

'loophole *n.* (fig.) Lücke, *die*

loopy /'lu:pɪ/ *adj.* (coll.) verrückt (ugs.)

loose /lu:s/ *adj.* **(a)** (not firm) locker ‹*Zahn, Schraube, Knopf*›

(b) (not fixed) lose ‹*Knopf, Buchseite, Brett, Stein*›; offen ‹*Haar*›
(c) be at a ~ end (fig.) nichts zu tun haben
(d) (inexact) ungenau

loose: ~-fitting *adj.* bequem geschnitten; **~-leaf** *adj.* Loseblatt-; **~-leaf file** Ringbuch, *das;* **~-limbed** *adj.* gelenkig

'loosely *adv.* locker; lose ‹*zusammenhängen*›; frei ‹*übersetzen*›

loosen /'lu:sn/ *v.t.* lockern

■ **loosen 'up** *v.i.* sich auflockern; (relax) auftauen

'looseness *n.* Lockerheit, *die*

loot /lu:t/ **1** *v.t.* plündern
2 *n.* Beute, *die*

'looter *n.* Plünderer, *der*

lop /lɒp/ *v.t.* **~ sth. [off** *or* **away]** etw. abbauen *od.* abhacken

lopsided /lɒp'saɪdɪd/ *adj.* schief

loquacious /lə'kweɪʃəs/ *adj.* redselig

lord /lɔ:d/ **1** *n.* **(a)** (master) Herr, *der*
(b) L~ (Relig.) Herr, *der*
(c) (Brit.: as title) Lord, *der;* **the House of L~s** (Brit.) das Oberhaus
2 *int.* (coll.) Gott; **oh/good L~!** du lieber Himmel!

'lordship *n.* Lordschaft, *die*

lore /lɔ:(r)/ *n.* Überlieferung, *die*

lorry /'lɒrɪ/ *n.* (Brit.) Lastwagen, *der;* Lkw, *der*

'lorry driver *n.* (Brit.) Lastwagenfahrer, *der;* Lkw-Fahrer, *der*

lose /lu:z/ **1** *v.t.,* **lost** /lɒst/ **(a)** verlieren; **~ one's way** sich verlaufen/verfahren
(b) ‹*Uhr:*› nachgehen
(c) (waste) vertun ‹*Zeit*›; (miss) versäumen ‹*Gelegenheit*›
(d) ~ weight abnehmen
2 *v.i.,* **lost (a)** (in match, contest) verlieren
(b) ‹*Uhr:*› nachgehen

'loser *n.* Verlierer, *der*/Verliererin, *die*

loss /lɒs/ *n.* **(a)** Verlust, *der* (**of** *Gen.*); **sell at a ~:** mit Verlust verkaufen
(b) be at a ~: nicht [mehr] weiterwissen; **be at a ~ for words** um Worte verlegen sein; **be at a ~ what to do** nicht wissen, was zu tun ist

loss: ~ adjuster *n.* (Finance) Schaden[s]regulierer, *der*/-reguliererin, *die;* **~-making** *adj.* mit Verlust arbeitend

lost /lɒst/ **1** ▶ LOSE
2 *adj.* **(a)** verloren; **get ~** ‹*Person:*› sich verlaufen/verfahren; **get ~!** (coll.) verdufte! (salopp); **~ cause** aussichtslose Sache
(b) (wasted) vertan ‹*Zeit*›; (missed) versäumt ‹*Gelegenheit*›

lot /lɒt/ *n.* **(a)** (destiny) Los, *das*
(b) (set of persons) Haufen, *der;* **the ~:** [sie] alle
(c) (set of things) Menge, *die;* **the ~:** alle/alles
(d) (coll.: large quantity) **~s** *or* **a ~ of money** *etc.* viel *od.* eine Menge Geld *usw.;* **sing** *etc.* **a ~:** viel singen *usw.;* **like sth. a ~:** etw. sehr mögen; **have ~s to do** viel zu tun haben
(e) (for choosing) Los, *das;* **draw/cast/throw ~s [for sth.]** um etw. losen

lotion /'ləʊʃn/ *n.* Lotion, *die*

lottery /'lɒtərɪ/ *n.* Lotterie, *die*

'lottery number *n.* Lottozahl, *die*

loud /laʊd/ **1** *adj.* **(a)** laut; lautstark ‹*Protest, Kritik*›
(b) (flashy, conspicuous) aufdringlich; grell ‹*Farbe*›
2 *adv.* laut; **laugh out ~:** laut auflachen; **say sth. out ~:** etw. aussprechen

loud'hailer *n.* Megaphon, *das*

'loudly *adv.* laut

loud: ~mouth *n.* Großmaul, *das;* **~-mouthed** /'laʊdmaʊðd/ *adj.* großmäulig (ugs.)

'loudness *n.* Lautstärke, *die*

loud'speaker *n.* Lautsprecher, *der*

lounge /laʊndʒ/ **1** *v.i.* **~ [about** *or* **around]** [faul] herumliegen/-sitzen/-stehen
2 *n.* **(a)** (in hotel) [Hotel]halle, *die;* (at airport) Wartehalle, *die*
(b) (sitting room) Wohnzimmer, *das*

lounger /'laʊndʒə(r)/ *n.* (sunbed) Liege, *die*

'lounge suit *n.* (Brit.) Straßenanzug, *der*

louse /laʊs/ *n., pl.* **lice** /laɪs/ Laus, *die*

lousy /'laʊzɪ/ *adj.* (coll.) **(a)** (disgusting) ekelhaft
(b) (very poor) lausig (ugs.); **feel ~:** sich mies (ugs.) fühlen

lout /laʊt/ *n.* Rüpel, *der;* Flegel, *der*

loutish /'laʊtɪʃ/ *adj.* rüpelhaft; flegelhaft

louver, louvre /'lu:və(r)/ *n.* **~ window** Jalousiefenster, *das;* **~ door** Jalousietür, *die*

lovable /'lʌvəbl/ *adj.* liebenswert

love /lʌv/ **1** *n.* **(a)** Liebe, *die* (**of, for** zu); **in ~ [with]** verliebt [in (+ *Akk.*)]; **fall in ~ [with]** sich verlieben [in (+ *Akk.*)]; **for ~:** aus Liebe; **~ from Beth** (in letter) herzliche Grüße von Beth; **send one's ~ to sb.** jmdn. grüßen lassen
(b) (sweetheart) Geliebte, *der/die;* **[my] ~** (coll.: form of address) [mein] Liebling *od.* Schatz
(c) (Tennis) **fifteen/thirty ~:** fünfzehn/dreißig null
2 *v.t.* **(a)** lieben; **our/their ~d ones** unsere/ihre Lieben
(b) (like) **I'd ~ a cigarette** ich hätte sehr gerne eine Zigarette; **~ to do** *or* **~ doing sth.** etw. gern tun

love: ~ affair *n.* Liebesverhältnis, *das;* **~ letter** *n.* Liebesbrief, *der;* **~ life** *n.* Liebesleben, *das*

loveliness /'lʌvlɪnɪs/ *n.* Schönheit, *die*

lovely /'lʌvlɪ/ *adj.* [wunder]schön; herrlich ‹*Tag, Essen*›

lover /'lʌvə(r)/ *n.* **(a)** Liebhaber, *der;* Geliebte, *der;* (woman) Geliebte, *die;* **be ~s** ein Liebespaar sein
(b) (person who likes sth.) Freund, *der*/Freundin, *die*

love: ~sick *adj.* an Liebeskummer

leidend; liebeskrank (geh.); ~ **song** *n.* Liebeslied, *das;* ~ **story** *n.* Liebesgeschichte, *die*

loving /ˈlʌvɪŋ/ *adj.* **(a)** (affectionate) liebend **(b)** (expressing love) liebevoll

ˈlovingly *adv.* liebevoll

low /ləʊ/ **1** *adj.* **(a)** niedrig; tief ausgeschnitten ‹*Kleid*›; tief ‹*Ausschnitt*›; tief liegend ‹*Grund*›
(b) (of humble rank) nieder...; niedrig
(c) (inferior) niedrig; gering ‹*Intelligenz, Bildung*›
(d) (in pitch) tief; (in loudness) leise
2 *adv.* **(a)** (to a ~ position) tief
(b) (not loudly) leise
(c) lie ~ (hide) untertauchen

low: ~-alcohol *adj.* alkoholarm ‹*Getränk*›; **~brow** *adj.* schlicht ‹*Person*›; [geistig] anspruchslos ‹*Buch, Programm*›; **~-budget** *adj.* Lowbudget-, Billig‹*film, -produktion usw.*›; **~-calorie** *adj.* kalorienarm ‹*Kost, Getränk*›; **~-cost** *adj.* preiswert; **~-cut** *adj.* [tief] ausgeschnitten ‹*Kleid*›; **~-cut neck** tiefer Ausschnitt; **~-cut shoes** Halbschuhe

lower¹ /ˈləʊə(r)/ *v.t.* **(a)** herab-/hinablassen **(b)** senken ‹*Blick*›; auslassen ‹*Saum*›; senken ‹*Preis, Miete, Zins usw.*›; ~ **one's voice** leiser sprechen

lower² **1** *compar. adj.* unter...; Unter‹*grenze, -arm, -lippe usw.*›
2 *compar. adv.* tiefer

lower ˈcase **1** *n.* Kleinbuchstaben *Pl.;*
2 *adj.* klein ‹*Buchstabe*›

low: ~-fat *adj.* fettarm; **~-flying** *adj.* tief fliegend; **~-flying aircraft** Tiefflieger, *der;* ~ **ˈfrequency** *n.* Niederfrequenz, *die;* **~-grade** *adj.* minderwertig; **~-income** *adj.* einkommenschwach; **~-income families** Familien mit niedrigem Einkommen; **~-key** *adj.* zurückhaltend; unaufdringlich ‹*Beleuchtung, Unterhaltung*›; unauffällig ‹*Einsatz*›; **~land** /ˈləʊlənd/ *n.* Tiefland, *das*

lowly /ˈləʊlɪ/ *adj.* (modest) bescheiden

low: ~-lying *adj.* tief liegend; **~-nicotine** *adj.* nikotinarm; **~-paid** *adj.* niedrig bezahlt; **~-paid families** Familien mit geringem Einkommen; ~ **point** *n.* Tiefpunkt, *der;* ~ **pressure** *n.* (Meteorol.) Tiefdruck, *der;* **~-priced** *adj.* preisgünstig; ~ **season** *n.* Nebensaison, *die;* **~-tech** *adj.* Lowtech‹*-system, -ausrüstung etc.*›; **~-voltage** *adj.* Niederspannungs-; **~-wage** *attrib. adj.* schlecht bezahlt; Niedriglohn‹*land*›

loyal /ˈlɔɪəl/ *adj.* treu

loyalty /ˈlɔɪəltɪ/ *n.* Treue, *die*

ˈloyalty card *n.* Treuekarte, *die* (*für Kunden*)

lozenge /ˈlɒzɪndʒ/ *n.* Pastille, *die*

LP *abbr.* = **long-playing record** LP, *die*

ˈL-plate *n.* (Brit.) 'L'-Schild, *das;* ≈ „Fahrschule"-Schild, *das*

Ltd. *abbr.* = **Limited** GmbH

lubricant /ˈlu:brɪkənt/ *n.* Schmiermittel, *das*

lubricate /ˈlu:brɪkeɪt/ *v.t.* schmieren

lubrication /lu:brɪˈkeɪʃn/ *n.* Schmierung, *die; attrib.* Schmier‹*system, -vorrichtung*›

lucid /ˈlu:sɪd/ *adj.* klar

lucidity /lu:ˈsɪdɪtɪ/ *n.* Klarheit, *die*

luck /lʌk/ *n.* Glück, *das;* **good** ~: Glück, *das;* **bad** *or* **hard** ~: Pech, *das;* **good** ~! viel Glück!; **be in/out of** ~: Glück/kein Glück haben; **no such** ~: schön wärs

luckily /ˈlʌkɪlɪ/ *adv.* glücklicherweise

lucky /ˈlʌkɪ/ *adj.* **(a)** glücklich; **be** ~: Glück haben
(b) (bringing good luck) Glücks‹*zahl, -tag usw.*›; ~ **charm** Glücksbringer, *der*

lucrative /ˈlu:krətɪv/ *adj.* einträglich; lukrativ

ludicrous /ˈlu:dɪkrəs/ *adj.* lächerlich; lachhaft ‹*Angebot, Ausrede*›

lug /lʌg/ *v.t.,* **-gg-** (drag) schleppen

luggage /ˈlʌgɪdʒ/ *n.* Gepäck, *das*

luggage: ~ **locker** *n.* [Gepäck]schließfach, *das;* ~ **rack** *n.* Gepäckablage, *die*

lugubrious /lu:ˈgu:brɪəs/ *adj.* (mournful) kummervoll; (dismal) düster

lukewarm /ˈlu:kwɔ:m/ *adj.* lauwarm

lull /lʌl/ **1** *v.t.* **(a)** (soothe) lullen
(b) (fig.) einlullen; ~ **sb. into a false sense of security** jmdn. in einer trügerischen Sicherheit wiegen
2 *n.* Pause, *die*

lullaby /ˈlʌləbaɪ/ *n.* Schlaflied, *das*

lumbago /lʌmˈbeɪgəʊ/ *n., pl.* **~s** (Med.) Hexenschuss, *der*

lumber /ˈlʌmbə(r)/ **1** *n.* **(a)** (furniture) Gerümpel, *das*
(b) (useless material) Kram, *der* (ugs.)
(c) (Amer.: timber) [Bau]holz, *das*
2 *v.t.* ~ **sb. with sth./sb.** jmdm. etw./jmdn. aufhalsen (ugs.)

ˈlumbering *adj.* schwerfällig

lumberjack /ˈlʌmbədʒæk/ *n.* (Amer.) Holzfäller, *der*

luminous /ˈlu:mɪnəs/ *adj.* [hell] leuchtend; Leucht‹*anzeige, -zeiger usw.*›

lump /lʌmp/ **1** *n.* **(a)** Klumpen, *der;* (of sugar, butter, etc.) Stück, *das;* (of wood) Klotz, *der;* (of dough) Kloß, *der;* (of bread) Brocken, *der*
(b) (swelling) Beule, *die*
2 *v.t.* ~ **sth. with sth.** etw. und etw. zusammentun

lump: ~ **ˈpayment** *n.* einmalige Zahlung [einer größeren Summe]; ~ **ˈsum** *n.* Pauschalsumme, *die*

ˈlumpy *adj.* klumpig ‹*Brei*›; ‹*Kissen, Matratze*› mit klumpiger Füllung

lunacy /ˈlu:nəsɪ/ *n.* Wahnsinn, *der*

lunar /ˈlu:nə(r)/ *adj.* Mond-

lunatic /'lu:nətɪk/ [1] *adj.* wahnsinnig [2] *n.* Wahnsinnige, *der/die;* Irre, *der/die*

lunch /lʌntʃ/ [1] *n.* Mittagessen, *das;* **have** *or* **eat [one's] ~:** zu Mittag essen [2] *v.i.* zu Mittag essen

lunch: ~ box *n.* Lunchbox, *die;* **~ break** ▶ ~ HOUR

luncheon: ~ meat *n.* Frühstücksfleisch, *das;* **~ voucher** *n.* (Brit.) Essenmarke, *die*

lunch: ~ hour *n.* Mittagspause, *die;* **~time** *n.* Mittagszeit, *die;* **at ~time** mittags

lung /lʌŋ/ *n.* (right or left) Lungenflügel, *der;* **~s** Lunge, *die*

'lung cancer *n.* Lungenkrebs, *der*

lunge /lʌndʒ/ [1] *n.* Sprung nach vorn [2] *v.i.* **~ at sb. with a knife** jmdn. mit einem Messer angreifen

lurch¹ /lɜ:tʃ/ *n.* **leave sb. in the ~:** jmdn. im Stich lassen

lurch² [1] *n.* Rucken, *das* [2] *v.i.* rucken; ‹*Betrunkener:*› torkeln

lure /ljʊə(r), lʊə(r)/ [1] *v.t.* locken [2] *n.* Lockmittel, *das*

lurid /'ljʊərɪd, 'lʊərɪd/ *adj.* **(a)** (in colour) grell **(b)** (sensational) reißerisch

lurk /lɜ:k/ *v.i.* lauern

lurker /lɜ:kə(r)/ *n.* (Comp. sl.) Lurker, *der*/Lurkerin, *die*

luscious /'lʌʃəs/ *adj.* köstlich [süß]; saftig [süß] ‹*Obst*›

lush /lʌʃ/ *adj.* saftig ‹*Wiese*›; grün ‹*Tal*›; üppig ‹*Vegetation*›

lust /lʌst/ [1] *n.* **(a)** (sexual) Sinnenlust, *die* **(b)** (strong desire) Gier, *die* (**for** nach) [2] *v.i.* **~ after** [lustvoll] begehren (geh.)

lustful /'lʌstfl/ *adj.* lüstern (geh.)

lustily /'lʌstɪlɪ/ *adv.* kräftig; aus voller Kehle ‹*rufen, singen*›

lustre /'lʌstə(r)/ *n.* (Brit.) **(a)** Schimmer, *der* **(b)** (fig.: splendour) Glanz, *der*

lusty /'lʌstɪ/ *adj.* kräftig

Luxembourg, Luxemburg /'lʌksəmbɜ:g/ *pr. n.* Luxemburg (*das*)

luxuriant /lʌg'zjʊərɪənt/ *adj.* üppig

luxuriate /lʌg'zjʊərɪeɪt/ *v.i.* **~ in** sich aalen in (+ *Dat.*)

luxurious /lʌg'zjʊərɪəs/ *adj.* luxuriös

luxury /'lʌkʃərɪ/ *n.* **(a)** Luxus, *der; attrib.* Luxus- **(b)** (article) Luxusgegenstand, *der;* **luxuries** Luxus, *der*

LW *abbr.* (Radio) = **long wave** LW

lying /'laɪɪŋ/ *adj.* verlogen ‹*Person*›. *See also* LIE¹ 2

lymph gland *n.* Lymphknoten, *der*

lynch /lɪntʃ/ *v.t.* lynchen

lynx /lɪŋks/ *n.* Luchs, *der*

lyre /'laɪə(r)/ *n.* Lyra, *die*

lyric /'lɪrɪk/ [1] *adj.* lyrisch; **~ poetry** Lyrik, *die* [2] *n. in pl.* (of song) Text, *der*

lyrical /'lɪrɪkl/ *adj.* **(a)** lyrisch **(b)** (coll.: enthusiastic) gefühlvoll

Mm

M, m /em/ *n.* M, m, *das*

m. *abbr.* **(a)** = **masculine** m. **(b)** = **metre[s]** m **(c)** = **million[s]** Mill. **(d)** = **minute[s]** Min.

MA *abbr.* = **Master of Arts** M.A.

mac /mæk/ *n.* (Brit. coll.) Regenmantel, *der*

macaroni /mækə'rəʊnɪ/ *n.* Makkaroni *Pl.*

Macedonia /mæsɪ'dəʊnɪə/ *pr. n.* Makedonien (*das*)

machine /mə'ʃi:n/ *n.* Maschine, *die*

machine: ~ gun *n.* Maschinengewehr, *das;* **~-made** *adj.* maschinell hergestellt; **~ operator** *n.* [Maschinen]bediener, *der*/-bedienerin, *die;* **~-readable** *adj.* (Comp.) maschinenlesbar

machinery /mə'ʃi:nərɪ/ *n.* **(a)** (machines) Maschinen *Pl.* **(b)** (mechanism) Mechanismus, *der*

machine: ~ tool *n.* Werkzeugmaschine, *die;* **~-wash** *v.t.* in der Waschmaschine waschen; **~-washable** *adj.* waschmaschinenfest

machinist /mə'ʃi:nɪst/ *n.* Maschinist, *der*/Maschinistin, *die;* **[sewing] ~:** [Maschinen]näherin, *die*/-näher, *der*

machismo /mə'tʃɪzməʊ, mə'kɪzməʊ/ *n.* Machismo, *der;* Männlichkeitswahn, *der*

macho /'mætʃəʊ/ *adj.* Macho-; **he is ~:** er ist ein Macho

mackerel /'mækərl/ *n., pl. same or* **~s** Makrele, *die*

mackintosh /'mækɪntɒʃ/ *n.* Regenmantel, *der*

macro /'mækrəʊ/ *n.* (Comp.) Makro, *das*

macrobiotic /mækrəʊbaɪ'ɒtɪk/ *adj.* makrobiotisch

mad /mæd/ *adj.* **(a)** (insane) geisteskrank **(b)** (frenzied) wahnsinnig; **drive sb. mad** jmdn. um den Verstand bringen

(c) (foolish) verrückt (ugs.)
(d) (very enthusiastic) **be ~ about** *or* **on sb./sth.** auf jmdn./etw. wild sein (ugs.)
(e) (coll.: annoyed) ~ [**with** *or* **at sb.**] sauer [auf jmdn.] (ugs.)
(f) (with rabies) toll[wütig]; [**run** etc.] **like ~** (coll.) wie wild [laufen *usw.*]

madam /ˈmædəm/ *n.* gnädige Frau; **Dear M~** (in letter) Sehr geehrte Dame

mad ˈcow disease *n.* (coll.) Rinderwahnsinn, *der*

madden /ˈmædn/ *v.t.* (irritate) [ver]ärgern

maddening /ˈmædənɪŋ/ *adj.* (irritating) [äußerst] ärgerlich

made ▶ MAKE 1

made-to-ˈmeasure *attrib. adj.* Maß-

ˈmadly *adv.* (coll.) wahnsinnig (ugs.)

madman /ˈmædmən/ *n., pl.* **madmen** /ˈmædmən/ *n.* Wahnsinnige, *der*

ˈmadness *n.* Wahnsinn, *der*

magazine /mægəˈziːn/ *n.* **(a)** Zeitschrift, *die*
(b) (of firearm) Magazin, *das*

maggot /ˈmægət/ *n.* Made, *die*

magic /ˈmædʒɪk/ 1 *n.* **(a)** Magie, *die;* **work like ~:** wie ein Wunder wirken
(b) (conjuring) Zauberei, *die*
2 *adj.* **(a)** magisch; Zauber‹*trank, -baum*›
(b) (fig.) wunderbar

magical /ˈmædʒɪkl/ *adj.* zauberhaft

magician /məˈdʒɪʃn/ *n.* Magier, *der*/ Magierin, *die;* (conjurer) Zauberer, *der*/ Zauberin, *die*

magic ˈwand *n.* Zauberstab, *der*

magistrate /ˈmædʒɪstreɪt/ *n.* Friedensrichter, *der*/-richterin, *die*

magnanimity /mægnəˈnɪmɪtɪ/ *n.* Großmut, *die*

magnanimous /mægˈnænɪməs/ *adj.* großmütig (**towards** gegen)

magnate /ˈmægneɪt/ *n.* Magnat, *der*/ Magnatin, *die*

magnesium /mægˈniːzɪəm/ *n.* Magnesium, *das*

magnet /ˈmægnɪt/ *n.* Magnet, *der*

magnetic /mægˈnetɪk/ *adj.* magnetisch

magnetic: ~ ˈnorth magnetisch Nord, *das;* **~ ˈtape** *n.* Magnetband, *das*

magnetism /ˈmægnɪtɪzm/ *n.* **(a)** (force, lit. or fig.) Magnetismus, *der*
(b) (fig.: charm) Anziehungskraft, *die*

magnetize /ˈmægnɪtaɪz/ *v.t.* magnetisieren

magnification /mægnɪfɪˈkeɪʃn/ *n.* Vergrößerung, *die*

magnificence /mægˈnɪfɪsəns/ *n.* Pracht, *die;* (beauty) Herrlichkeit, *die;* (lavishness) Üppigkeit, *die*

magnificent /mægˈnɪfɪsənt/ *adj.* **(a)** prächtig; herrlich ‹*Garten, Kunstwerk, Wetter*›; (lavish) üppig ‹*Mahl*›
(b) (coll.: excellent) fabelhaft (ugs.)

magnifier /ˈmægnɪfaɪə(r)/ *n.* (Optics) Lupe, *die*

magnify /ˈmægnɪfaɪ/ *v.t.* **(a)** vergrößern
(b) (exaggerate) aufbauschen

ˈmagnifying glass *n.* Lupe, *die*

magnitude /ˈmægnɪtjuːd/ *n.* **(a)** (size) Größe, *die*
(b) (importance) Wichtigkeit, *die*

magnolia /mægˈnəʊlɪə/ *n.* Magnolie, *die*

magnum /ˈmægnəm/ *n.* (bottle) Magnum, *die*

magpie /ˈmægpaɪ/ *n.* Elster, *die*

mahogany /məˈhɒgənɪ/ *n.* Mahagoni[holz], *das; attrib.* Mahagoni-

maid /meɪd/ *n.* Dienstmädchen, *das*

maiden /ˈmeɪdn/ 1 *n.* Jungfrau, *die*
2 *adj.* **(a)** (unmarried) unverheiratet
(b) (first) **~ voyage/speech** Jungfernfahrt/ -rede, *die*

ˈmaiden name *n.* Mädchenname, *der*

mail /meɪl/ 1 *n.* ▶ POST² 1
2 *v.t.* abschicken

mail: ~bag *n.* Postsack, *der;* **~box** *n.* (Amer.) Briefkasten, *der;* **~ing address** *n.* Postanschrift, *die;* **~ing list** *n.* Adressenliste, *die;* **~man** *n.* (Amer.) Briefträger, *der;* **~ order** *n.* Bestellung per Post; **~ order catalogue** *n.* Versandhauskatalog, *der;* **~ order firm** *n.* Versandhaus, *das;* **~ room** *n.* Poststelle, *die*

maim /meɪm/ *v.t.* verstümmeln

main /meɪn/ 1 *n.* **(a)** (channel, pipe) Hauptleitung, *die;* **~s** (Electr.) Stromnetz, *das*
(b) in the ~: im Großen und Ganzen
2 *attrib. adj.* Haupt-; **the ~ thing is that ...:** die Hauptsache ist, dass ...

main: ~ beam *n.* (Motor Veh.) **on ~ beam** aufgeblendet; **~ course** *n.* Hauptgang, *der;* Hauptgericht, *das;* **~frame** *n.* (Comp.) Großrechner, *der;* **~land** /ˈmeɪnlənd/ *n.* Festland, *das;* **~ ˈline** *n.* (Railw.) Hauptstrecke, *die;* **~-line station/train** Fernbahnhof/-zug, *der*

ˈmainly *adv.* hauptsächlich

main: ~ ˈroad *n.* Hauptstraße, *die;* **~stay** *n.* [wichtigste] Stütze; **~ street** /*Brit.* -ˈ-, *Amer.* ˈ--/ *n.* Hauptstraße, *die*

maintain /meɪnˈteɪn/ *v.t.* **(a)** (keep up) aufrechterhalten
(b) (provide for) **~ sb.** für jmds. Unterhalt aufkommen
(c) (preserve) instand halten; warten ‹*Maschine*›
(d) ~ that ...: behaupten, dass ...

maintenance /ˈmeɪntənəns/ *n.* **(a)** (keeping up) Aufrechterhaltung, *die*
(b) (preservation) Instandhaltung, *die;* (of machinery) Wartung, *die*
(c) (Law: money paid to support sb.) Unterhalt, *der*

maintenance-ˈfree *adj.* wartungsfrei

maison[n]ette /meɪzə'net/ *n.* [zweistöckige] Wohnung
maize /meɪz/ *n.* Mais, *der*
majestic /mə'dʒestɪk/ *adj.*, **majestically** /mə'dʒestɪkəlɪ/ *adv.* majestätisch
majesty /'mædʒɪstɪ/ *n.* Majestät, *die* (geh.); **Your/Her** *etc.* **M~**: Eure/Seine *usw.* Majestät
major /'meɪdʒə(r)/ [1] *adj.* **(a)** *attrib.* (greater) größer...
(b) *attrib.* (important) bedeutend...; (serious) schwer; **~ road** Hauptverkehrsstraße, *die*
(c) (Mus.) Dur-; **C ~**: C-Dur
[2] *n.* (Mil.) Major, *der*
[3] *v.i.* (Amer. Univ.) **~ in sth.** etw. als Hauptfach haben
Majorca /mə'jɔːkə/ *pr. n.* Mallorca (*das*)
majority /mə'dʒɒrɪtɪ/ *n.* Mehrheit, *die;* **be in the ~**: in der Mehrzahl sein
majority 'rule *n.* Mehrheitsregierung, *die*
make /meɪk/ [1] *v.t.*, **made** /meɪd/ **(a)** machen (**of** aus); bauen ‹*Straße, Flugzeug*›; anlegen ‹*Teich, Weg usw.*›; zimmern ‹*Tisch, Regal*›; basteln ‹*Spielzeug, Vogelhäuschen usw.*›; nähen ‹*Kleider*›; (manufacture) herstellen; (prepare) zubereiten ‹*Mahlzeit*›; machen, kochen ‹*Kaffee, Tee*›; backen ‹*Brot, Kuchen*›
(b) (establish, enact) treffen ‹*Unterscheidung, Übereinkommen*›; ziehen ‹*Vergleich*›; erlassen ‹*Gesetz*›; aufstellen ‹*Regeln, Behauptung*›; stellen ‹*Forderung*›; geben ‹*Bericht*›; vornehmen ‹*Zahlung*›; erheben ‹*Protest, Beschwerde*›
(c) (cause to be or become) **~ happy/known** *etc.* glücklich/bekannt *usw.* machen; **~ sb. captain** jmdn. zum Kapitän machen
(d) **~ sb. do sth.** (cause) jmdn. dazu bringen, etw. zu tun; (compel) jmdn. zwingen, etw. zu tun; **be made to do sth.** etw. tun müssen
(e) (earn) machen ‹*Profit, Verlust*›; verdienen ‹*Lebensunterhalt*›
(f) **what do you ~ of him?** was hältst du von ihm?
(g) (arrive at) erreichen; **make it** (succeed in arriving) es schaffen
(h) **~ 'do** vorlieb nehmen; **~ 'do with/without sth.** mit/ohne etw. auskommen
[2] *n.* (brand) Marke, *die*
▪ **'make for** *v.t.* zusteuern auf (+ *Akk.*)
▪ **make 'off** *v.i.* sich davonmachen
▪ **make 'off with** *v.t.* **~ off with sb./sth.** sich mit jmdm./etw. auf und davon machen
▪ **make 'out** [1] *v.t.* **(a)** (write) ausstellen; **~ out a cheque to sb.** einen Scheck auf jmdn. ausstellen
(b) (claim) behaupten
(c) (manage to see or hear) ausmachen; (manage to read) entziffern
(d) (pretend) vorgeben
[2] *v.i.* (coll.) zurechtkommen (**at** bei)
▪ **make 'over** *v.t.* überschreiben (**to** auf + *Akk.*)
▪ **make 'up** [1] *v.t.* **(a)** (assemble) zusammenstellen
(b) (invent) erfinden
(c) (constitute) bilden; **be made up of ...**: bestehen aus ...
(d) (apply cosmetics to) schminken; **~ up one's face** sich schminken
[2] *v.i.* (be reconciled) sich wieder vertragen
▪ **make 'up for** *v.t.* wieder gutmachen; **~ up for lost time** Versäumtes nachholen
make: ~-believe [1] *n.* **it's only ~-believe** das ist bloß Fantasie; [2] *adj.* nicht echt; **~-or-'break** *attrib. adj.* alles entscheidend; **~over** *n.* (of a person's appearance) [grundlegende] Verwandlung; (of a building) Umbau, *der*
'maker *n.* (manufacturer) Hersteller, *der*
make: ~shift *adj.* behelfsmäßig; **~-up** *n.* Make-up, *das;* **~-up bag** Kosmetiktasche, *die*
making /'meɪkɪŋ/ *n.* **in the ~**: im Entstehen; **have the ~s of a leader** das Zeug zum Führer haben (ugs.)
maladjusted /mælə'dʒʌstɪd/ *adj.* verhaltensgestört
malady /'mælədɪ/ *n.* Leiden, *das*
malaise /mə'leɪz/ *n.* Unbehagen, *das*
malaria /mə'leərɪə/ *n.* Malaria, *die*
Malaysia /mə'leɪzɪə/ *pr. n.* Malaysia (*das*)
male /meɪl/ [1] *adj.* männlich; Männer‹*stimme, -chor, -verein*›; **~ doctor/nurse** Arzt, *der*/Krankenpfleger, *der*
[2] *n.* (person) Mann, *der;* (animal) Männchen, *das*
'male-dominated *adj.* von Männern dominiert
malevolence /mə'levələns/ *n.* Boshaftigkeit, *die*
malevolent /mə'levələnt/ *adj.* boshaft
malfunction /mæl'fʌŋkʃn/ [1] *n.* Störung, *die;* (Med.) Funktionsstörung, *die*
[2] *v.i.* nicht richtig funktionieren
malice /'mælɪs/ *n.* Bosheit, *die*
malicious /mə'lɪʃəs/ *adj.* böse
malign /mə'laɪn/ *v.t.* verleumden
malignant /mə'lɪgnənt/ *adj.* bösartig
malinger /mə'lɪŋgə(r)/ *v.i.* simulieren
ma'lingerer *n.* Simulant, *der*/Simulantin, *die*
malleable /'mælɪəbl/ *adj.* formbar
mallet /'mælɪt/ *n.* Holzhammer, *der*
malnourished /mæl'nʌrɪʃt/ *adj.* unterernährt
malnutrition /mælnjuː'trɪʃn/ *n.* Unterernährung, *die*
malpractice /mæl'præktɪs/ *n.* (Law, Med.) Kunstfehler, *der*
malt /mɔːlt/ *n.* Malz, *das*
Malta /'mɔːltə/ *pr. n.* Malta (*das*)
maltreat /mæl'triːt/ *v.t.* misshandeln
mal'treatment *n.* Misshandlung, *die*
malt 'whisky *n.* Malzwhisky, *der*
mammal /'mæml/ *n.* Säugetier, *das*
mammoth /'mæməθ/ [1] *n.* Mammut, *das*

2 *adj.* Mammut-; gigantisch ‹*Vorhaben*›

man /mæn/ **1** *n.* **(a)** *pl.* **men** [men] Mann, *der*
(b) (human race) der Mensch
2 *v.t.*, **-nn-** bemannen ‹*Schiff*›; besetzen ‹*Büro, Stelle usw.*›; bedienen ‹*Telefon, Geschütz*›

manacle /ˈmænəkl/ **1** *n., usu. in pl.* [Hand]fessel, *die*
2 *v.t.* Handfesseln anlegen (+ *Dat.*)

manage /ˈmænɪdʒ/ **1** *v.t.* **(a)** leiten ‹*Geschäft*›
(b) (Sport) betreuen ‹*Mannschaft*›
(c) (cope with) schaffen
(d) ~ **to do sth.** es fertig bringen, etw. zu tun; **he ~d to do it** es gelang ihm, es zu tun
2 *v.i.* zurechtkommen; ~ **without sth.** ohne etw. auskommen; **I can ~:** es geht

manageable /ˈmænɪdʒəbl/ *adj.* leicht frisierbar ‹*Haar*›; fügsam ‹*Person, Tier*›; überschaubar ‹*Größe, Menge*›

ˈmanagement *n.* **(a)** (of a business) Leitung, *die*
(b) (managers) **the ~:** die Geschäftsleitung

management: ~ consultancy *n.* Unternehmensberatung, *die;* **~ consultant** *n.* Unternehmensberater, *der*/-beraterin, *die*

ˈmanager *n.* (of shop or bank) Filialleiter, *der*/-leiterin, *die;* (of football team) [Chef]trainer, *der*/-trainerin, *die;* (of restaurant, shop, hotel) Geschäftsführer, *der*/-führerin, *die*

manageress /mænɪdʒəˈres/ *n.* Geschäftsführerin, *die*

managerial /mænəˈdʒɪərɪəl/ *adj.* führend, leitend ‹*Stellung*›; ~ **skills** Führungsqualitäten

managing /ˈmænɪdʒɪŋ/ *adj.* ~ **director** Geschäftsführer, *der*/-führerin, *die*

mandarin¹ /ˈmændərɪn/ *n.* ~ **[orange]** Mandarine, *die*

mandarin² *n.* (bureaucrat) Bürokrat, *der*/Bürokratin, *die*

mandarine /ˈmændəri:n/ ▸ MANDARIN¹

mandate /ˈmændeɪt/ *n.* Mandat, *das*

mandatory /ˈmændətərɪ/ *adj.* obligatorisch

mandolin[e] /mændəˈlɪn/ *n.* Mandoline, *die*

mane /meɪn/ *n.* Mähne, *die*

maneuver[able] (Amer.) ▸ MANŒUVR-

manful /ˈmænfl/ *adj.*, **manfully** /ˈmænfəlɪ/ *adv.* mannhaft

manger /ˈmeɪndʒə(r)/ *n.* Krippe, *die*

mangetout /mɑ̃ʒˈtu:/ *n.* Zuckererbse, *die*

mangle /ˈmæŋgl/ *v.t.* verstümmeln ‹*Person*›; demolieren ‹*Sache*›

mango /ˈmæŋgəʊ/ *n., pl.* **~es** *or* **~s** (fruit) Mango[frucht], *die*

mangy /ˈmeɪndʒɪ/ *adj.* **(a)** (Vet. Med.) räudig
(b) (shabby) schäbig

man: ~handle *v.t.* **(a)** von Hand bewegen ‹*Gegenstand*›; **(b)** grob behandeln ‹*Person*›; **~hole** *n.* Mannloch, *das*

ˈmanhood *n.* Mannesalter, *das*

man: ~-hour *n.* Arbeitsstunde, *die;* **~hunt** *n.* Verbrecherjagd, *die*

mania /ˈmeɪnɪə/ *n.* Manie, *die*

maniacal /məˈnaɪəkl/ *adj.* wahnsinnig

manicure /ˈmænɪkjʊə(r)/ **1** *n.* Maniküre, *die*
2 *v.t.* maniküren

manifest /ˈmænɪfest/ **1** *adj.* offenkundig
2 *v.t.* (reveal) offenbaren

ˈmanifestly *adv.* offenkundig

manifesto /mænɪˈfestəʊ/ *n., pl.* **~s** Manifest, *das*

manifold /ˈmænɪfəʊld/ *adj.* (literary) mannigfaltig (geh.)

manipulate /məˈnɪpjʊleɪt/ *v.t.* **(a)** manipulieren
(b) (handle) handhaben

manipulation /mənɪpjʊˈleɪʃn/ *n.* **(a)** Manipulation, *die*
(b) (handling) Handhabung, *die*

manipulative /məˈnɪpjʊlətɪv/ *adj.* manipulativ

mankind /mænˈkaɪnd/ *n.* Menschheit, *die*

manly /ˈmænlɪ/ *adj.* männlich

ˈman-made *adj.* künstlich; (synthetic) Kunst‹*faser, -stoff*›

manned /mænd/ *adj.* bemannt

manner /ˈmænə(r)/ *n.* **(a)** Art, *die;* Weise, *die;* **in this ~:** auf diese Art und Weise
(b) (general behaviour) Art, *die*
(c) *in pl.* Manieren *Pl.*

mannerism /ˈmænərɪzm/ *n.* Eigenart, *die*

manœuvrable /məˈnu:vrəbl/ *adj.* (Brit.) manövrierfähig

manœuvre /məˈnu:və(r)/ (Brit.) **1** *n.* Manöver, *das*
2 *v.t. & i.* manövrieren

manor /ˈmænə(r)/ *n.* **(a)** (land) [Land]gut, *das*
(b) ▸ MANOR HOUSE

ˈmanor house *n.* Herrenhaus, *das*

ˈmanpower *n.* Arbeitskräfte *Pl.*

mansion /ˈmænʃn/ *n.* Herrenhaus, *das*

manslaughter /ˈmænslɔ:tə(r)/ *n.* Totschlag, *der*

mantel: ~piece /ˈmæntlpi:s/ *n.* **(a)** (above fireplace) Kaminsims, *der od. das;* **(b)** (around fireplace) Kamineinfassung, *die;* **~shelf** ▸ ~PIECE A

mantle /ˈmæntl/ *n.* Umhang, *der*

manual /ˈmænjʊəl/ **1** *adj.* **(a)** manuell; ~ **work** Handarbeit; ~ **worker** Handarbeiter, *der*/-arbeiterin, *die*
(b) (not automatic) handbetrieben; ‹*Bedienung, Schaltung*› von Hand
2 *n.* Handbuch, *das*

manually /ˈmænjʊəlɪ/ *adv.* manuell; **a ∼ operated machine** eine handbetriebene Maschine
manufacture /mænjʊˈfæktʃə(r)/ **1** *n.* Herstellung, *die*
2 *v.t.* herstellen
manuˈfacturer *n.* Hersteller, *der*
manure /məˈnjʊə(r)/ **1** *n.* Dung, *der*
2 *v.t.* düngen
manuscript /ˈmænjʊskrɪpt/ *n.* Manuskript, *das*
many /ˈmenɪ/ **1** *adj.* viele; **how ∼ people/books?** wie viele *od.* wie viel Leute/Bücher?
2 *n.* viele [Leute]; **∼ of us** viele von uns; **a good/great ∼**: eine Menge
map /mæp/ **1** *n.* [Land]karte, *die;* (street plan) Stadtplan, *der*
2 *v.t.,* **-pp-** kartographieren
▪ **map ˈout** *v.t.* im Einzelnen festlegen
maple /ˈmeɪpl/ *n.* Ahorn, *der*
ˈmap-reading *n.* Kartenlesen, *das*
mar /mɑː(r)/ *v.t.* verderben
marathon /ˈmærəθən/ *n.* **(a)** Marathon[lauf], *der*
(b) (fig.) Marathon, *das*
marauder /məˈrɔːdə(r)/ *n.* Plünderer, *der*
marble /ˈmɑːbl/ *n.* **(a)** (stone) Marmor, *der*
(b) (toy) Murmel, *die;* **[game of] ∼s** Murmelspiel, *das*
march **1** *n.* Marsch, *der;* **[protest] ∼**: Protestmarsch, *der*
2 *v.i.* marschieren
▪ **march ˈoff** **1** *v.i.* losmarschieren
2 *v.t.* abführen
▪ **march ˈpast** *v.i.* vorbeimarschieren
March /mɑːtʃ/ *n.* März, *der; see also* AUGUST
ˈmarcher *n.* **[protest] ∼**: Demonstrant, *der*/Demonstrantin, *die*
mare /meə(r)/ *n.* Stute, *die*
margarine /mɑːdʒəˈriːn/**,** (coll.) **marge** /mɑːdʒ/ *ns.* Margarine, *die*
margin /ˈmɑːdʒɪn/ *n.* **(a)** (of page) Rand, *der*
(b) (extra amount) Spielraum, *der;* **[profit] ∼**: [Gewinn]spanne, *die;* **by a narrow ∼**: knapp
marginal /ˈmɑːdʒɪnl/ *adj.,* **ˈmarginally** *adv.* unwesentlich
marigold /ˈmærɪgəʊld/ *n.* Ringelblume, *die*
marijuana /mærɪjʊˈɑːnə/ *n.* Marihuana, *das*
marina /məˈriːnə/ *n.* Jachthafen, *der*
marinade /mærɪˈneɪd/ **1** *n.* Marinade, *die*
2 ▸ MARINATE
marinate /ˈmærɪneɪt/ *v.t.* marinieren
marine /məˈriːn/ **1** *adj.* Meeres-; See‹*versicherung, -recht usw.*›; Schiffs‹*ausrüstung, -turbine usw.*›
2 *n.* (person) Marineinfanterist, *der*
mariner /ˈmærɪnə(r)/ *n.* Seemann, *der*
marionette /mærɪəˈnet/ *n.* Marionette, *die*
marital /ˈmærɪtl/ *adj.* ehelich; **∼ status** Familienstand, *der*
maritime /ˈmærɪtaɪm/ *adj.* See-

mark¹ /mɑːk/ **1** *n.* **(a)** (trace) Spur, *die;* (stain etc.) Fleck, *der;* (scratch) Kratzer, *der*
(b) (sign) Zeichen, *das*
(c) (Sch.) Note, *die*
(d) (target) Ziel, *das*
2 *v.t.* **(a)** (dirty) schmutzig machen; (scratch) zerkratzen
(b) (put distinguishing ∼ on) kennzeichnen, markieren (**with** mit)
(c) (Sch.) (correct) korrigieren; (grade) benoten
(d) **∼ time** auf der Stelle treten
▪ **mark ˈoff** *v.t.* abgrenzen (**from** von, gegen)
▪ **mark ˈout** *v.t.* markieren
mark² *n.* (monetary unit) Mark, *die*
marked /mɑːkt/ *adj.,* **markedly** /ˈmɑːkɪdlɪ/ *adv.* deutlich
ˈmarker *n.* Markierung, *die*
ˈmarker pen *n.* Markierstift, *der*
market /ˈmɑːkɪt/ **1** *n.* Markt, *der*
2 *v.t.* vermarkten
market: ∼ day *n.* Markttag, *der;* **∼ eˈconomy** *n.* Marktwirtschaft, *die;* **∼ ˈforces** *n. pl.* Kräfte des freien Marktes; **∼ ˈgardening** *n.* (Brit.) Gemüseanbau, *der*
ˈmarketing *n.* Marketing, *das*
market: ∼ ˈleader *n.* (company, brand) Marktführer, *der;* (product) meistverkauftes Produkt; **the company is the ∼ leader in its field** die Firma ist marktführend auf ihrem Gebiet; **∼ place** *n.* Marktplatz, *der;* (fig.) Markt, *der;* **∼ ˈprice** *n.* Marktpreis, *der;* **∼ ˈresearch** *n.* Marktforschung, *die;* **∼ share** *n.* Marktanteil, *der;* **∼ town** *n.* Marktort, *der;* **∼ ˈvalue** *n.* Marktwert, *der*
ˈmarking *n.* **(a)** Markierung, *die*
(b) (on animal) Zeichnung, *die*
marksman /ˈmɑːksmən/ *n., pl.* **marksmen** /ˈmɑːksmən/ Scharfschütze, *der*
marmalade /ˈmɑːməleɪd/ *n.* **[orange] ∼**: Orangenmarmelade, *die*
maroon¹ /məˈruːn/ **1** *adj.* kastanienbraun
2 *n.* Kastanienbraun, *das*
maroon² *v.t.* **(a)** (Naut.: put ashore) aussetzen
(b) ‹*Flut, Hochwasser:*› von der Außenwelt abschneiden
marquee /mɑːˈkiː/ *n.* Festzelt, *das*
marquess, marquis /ˈmɑːkwɪs/ *n.* Marquis, *der*
marquetry /ˈmɑːkɪtrɪ/ *n.* Marketerie, *die*
marriage /ˈmærɪdʒ/ *n.* **(a)** Ehe, *die* (**to** mit)
(b) (wedding) Hochzeit, *die*
marriage: ∼ broker *n.* Heiratsvermittler, *der*/-vermittlerin, *die;* **∼ bureau** *n.* Eheanbahnungs- *od.* Ehevermittlungsinstitut, *das;* **∼ certificate** *n.* Trauschein, *der;* (record of civil marriage also) Heiratsurkunde, *die;* **∼ ˈguidance** *n.* Eheberatung, *die;* **∼ licence** *n.* Heirats- *od.* Eheerlaubnis, *die*
married /ˈmærɪd/ *adj.* **(a)** verheiratet; **∼ couple** Ehepaar, *das*
(b) (marital) Ehe‹*leben, -name*›

marrow /'mærəʊ/ *n.* **(a)** [**vegetable**] **~**: Speisekürbis, *der*
(b) (Anat.) [Knochen]mark, *das*
marry /'mærɪ/ 1 *v.t.* **(a)** heiraten
(b) (join) trauen; **they were** *or* **got/have got married** sie haben geheiratet
2 *v.i.* heiraten
Mars /mɑ:z/ *pr. n.* (Astron.) Mars, *der*
marsh /mɑ:ʃ/ *n.* Sumpf, *der*
marshal /'mɑ:ʃl/ 1 *n.* **(a)** (officer in army) Marschall, *der*
(b) (Sport) Ordner, *der*
2 *v.t.*, (Brit.) **-ll-** aufstellen ‹*Truppen*›; ordnen ‹*Fakten*›
'marshalling yard *n.* Rangierbahnhof, *der*
marshmallow /mɑ:ʃ'mæləʊ/ *n.* (sweet) ≈ Mohrenkopf, *der*
'marshy *adj.* sumpfig
marsupial /mɑ:'sju:pɪəl/ *n.* Beuteltier, *das*
martial /'mɑ:ʃl/ *adj.* kriegerisch
martial 'law *n.* Kriegsrecht, *das*
martyr /'mɑ:tə(r)/ 1 *n.* Märtyrer, *der*/ Märtyrerin, *die*
2 *v.t.* **be ~ed** den Märtyrertod sterben
marvel /'mɑ:vl/ 1 *n.* Wunder, *das*
2 *v.i.*, (Brit.) **-ll-** (literary) **~ at sth.** über etw (*Akk.*) staunen
marvellous /'mɑ:vələs/ *adj.*, **'marvellously** *adv.* wunderbar
marvelous[ly] (Amer.) ▶ MARVELLOUS[LY]
Marxism /'mɑ:ksɪzm/ *n.* Marxismus, *der*
Marxist /'mɑ:ksɪst/ 1 *n.* Marxist, *der*/ Marxistin, *die*
2 *adj.* marxistisch
marzipan /'mɑ:zɪpæn/ *n.* Marzipan, *das*
mascara /mæ'skɑ:rə/ *n.* Mascara, *das*
mascot /'mæskɒt/ *n.* Maskottchen, *das*
masculine /'mæskjʊlɪn/ *adj.* männlich
masculinity /mæskju'lɪnɪtɪ/ *n.* Männlichkeit, *die*
mash /mæʃ/ 1 *n.* **(a)** Brei, *der*
(b) (Brit. coll.: **~**ed potatoes) Kartoffelbrei, *der*
2 *v.t.* zerdrücken; **~ed potatoes** Kartoffelbrei, *der*
mask /mɑ:sk/ 1 *n.* Maske, *die*
2 *v.t.* maskieren
'masking tape *n.* Abklebeband, *das*
masochism /'mæsəkɪzm/ *n.* Masochismus, *der*
masochist /'mæsəkɪst/ *n.* Masochist, *der*/ Masochistin, *die*
masochistic /mæsə'kɪstɪk/ *adj.* masochistisch
mason /'meɪsn/ *n.* **(a)** Steinmetz, *der*
(b) M~ (Free**~**) [Frei]maurer, *der*
Masonic /mə'sɒnɪk/ *adj.* [frei]maurerisch; **~ lodge** [Frei]maurerloge, *die*
masonry /'meɪsnrɪ/ *n.* Mauerwerk, *das*
masquerade /mæskə'reɪd, mɑ:skə'reɪd/ 1 *n.* Maskerade, *die*
2 *v.i.* **~ as sb./sth.** sich als jmd./etw. ausgeben
mass¹ /mæs/ *n.* (Eccl.) Messe, *die*
mass² 1 *n.* **(a)** Masse, *die*
(b) a ~ of ...: eine Unmenge von ...
(c) *attrib.* (for many people) Massen-
2 *v.t.* anhäufen
3 *v.i.* sich ansammeln; ‹*Truppen:*› sich massieren
massacre /'mæsəkə(r)/ 1 *n.* Massaker, *das*
2 *v.t.* massakrieren
massage /'mæsɑ:ʒ/ 1 *n.* Massage, *die*
2 *v.t.* massieren
mass communi'cations *n. pl.* Massenkommunikation, *die*
masseur /mæ'sɜ:(r)/ *n.* Masseur, *der*
masseuse /mæ'sɜ:z/ *n. fem.* Masseurin, *die*
mass hy'steria *n.* Massenhysterie, *die*
massive /'mæsɪv/ *adj.* massiv; gewaltig ‹*Aufgabe*›; enorm ‹*Schulden*›
mass: ~ market *attrib. adj.* für den Massenmarkt *nachgestellt;* **~ 'media** *n. pl.* Massenmedien *Pl.;* **~ 'murderer** *n.* Massenmörder, *der*/-mörderin, *die;* **~-pro'duced** *adj.* serienmäßig produziert; **~ pro'duction** *n.* Massenproduktion, *die*
mast /mɑ:st/ *n.* Mast, *der*
mastectomy /mæ'stektəmɪ/ *n.* (Med.) Mastektomie, *die*
master /'mɑ:stə(r)/ 1 *n.* **(a)** Herr, *der*
(b) (of dog) Herrchen, *das;* (of ship) Kapitän, *der*
(c) (Sch.: teacher) Lehrer, *der*
(d) (expert, great artist) Meister, *der* (**at** in + *Dat.*)
(e) M~ of Arts/Science Magister Artium/ rerum naturalium
2 *adj.* Haupt-
3 *v.t.* (learn) erlernen; **have ~ed a language** eine Sprache beherrschen
masterful /'mɑ:stəfl/ *adj.* (masterly) meisterhaft
'master key *n.* Hauptschlüssel, *der*
masterly /'mɑ:stəlɪ/ *adj.* meisterhaft
master: ~mind 1 *n.* führender Kopf;
2 *v.t.* **~mind the plot** der Kopf des Komplotts sein; **~piece** *n.* (work of art) Meisterwerk, *das;* **~ stroke** *n.* Geniestreich, *der;* **be a ~ stroke** genial sein; **~ switch** *n.* Hauptschalter, *der*
mastery /'mɑ:stərɪ/ *n.* **(a)** (skill) Meisterschaft, *die*
(b) (knowledge) Beherrschung, *die* (**of** *Gen.*)
masturbate /'mæstəbeɪt/ *v.i.* & *t.* masturbieren
masturbation /mæstə'beɪʃn/ *n.* Masturbation, *die*
mat /mæt/ *n.* **(a)** Matte, *die*
(b) (to protect table etc.) Untersetzer, *der*
matador /'mætədɔ:(r)/ *n.* Matador, *der*

match¹ /mætʃ/ 1 *n.* **(a) be no ~ for sb.** sich mit jmdm. nicht messen können; **meet one's ~**: seinen Meister finden
(b) be a [good *etc.*] ~ for sth. [gut *usw.*] zu etw. passen
(c) (Sport) Spiel, *das;* (Boxing) Kampf, *der*
2 *v.t.* **(a)** (equal) **~ sb. at chess** es mit jmdm. im Schach aufnehmen [können]
(b) (harmonize with) passen zu; **a handbag and ~ing shoes** eine Handtasche und [dazu] passende Schuhe; **~ each other** zueinander passen
3 *v.i.* zusammenpassen

match² *n.* (~stick) Streichholz, *das*

'matchbox *n.* Streichholzschachtel, *die*

'matchless *adj.* unvergleichlich

match: ~maker *n.* Ehestifter, *der*/Ehestifterin, *die;* **~stick** *n.* Streichholz, *das*

mate¹ /meɪt/ 1 *n.* **(a)** Kumpel, *der* (ugs.); **look** *or* **listen, ~, ...**: jetzt hör [mir] mal gut zu, Freundchen, ...
(b) (Naut.) ≈ Kapitänleutnant, *der*
(c) (workman's assistant) Gehilfe, *der*
(d) (Zool.) (male) Männchen, *das;* (female) Weibchen, *das*
2 *v.i.* sich paaren
3 *v.t.* paaren ‹*Tiere*›

mate² (Chess) ▶ CHECKMATE

material /məˈtɪərɪəl/ 1 *adj.* **(a)** materiell
(b) (relevant) wesentlich
2 *n.* **(a) ~[s]** Material, *das;* **building/writing ~s** Bau-/Schreibmaterial, *das*
(b) (cloth) Stoff, *der*

materialism /məˈtɪərɪəlɪzm/ *n.* Materialismus, *der*

materialistic /mətɪərɪəˈlɪstɪk/ *adj.* materialistisch

materialize /məˈtɪərɪəlaɪz/ *v.i.* ‹*Plan, Idee:*› sich verwirklichen; ‹*Treffen:*› zustande kommen

maternal /məˈtɜːnl/ *adj.* mütterlich; Mutter‹*instinkt*›

maternity /məˈtɜːnɪtɪ/ *n.* Mutterschaft, *die*

maternity: ~ benefit *n.* Mutterschaftsgeld, *das;* **~ dress** *n.* Umstandskleid, *das;* **~ hospital** *n.* Entbindungsheim, *das;* **~ leave** *n.* Mutterschaftsurlaub, *der;* **~ nurse** *n.* Hebamme, *die;* **~ pay** *n.* Mutterschaftsgeld, *das;* **~ unit, ~ ward** *ns.* Entbindungsstation, *die;* **~ wear** *n.* Umstandskleidung, *die*

matey /ˈmeɪtɪ/ *adj.*, **matier** /ˈmeɪtɪə(r)/, **matiest** /ˈmeɪtɪɪst/ (Brit. coll.) kameradschaftlich

math /mæθ/ (Amer. coll.) ▶ MATHS

mathematical /mæθɪˈmætɪkl/ *adj.*, **mathematically** /mæθɪˈmætɪkəlɪ/ *adv.* mathematisch

mathematician /mæθɪməˈtɪʃn/ *n.* Mathematiker, *der*/Mathematikerin, *die*

mathematics /mæθɪˈmætɪks/ *n.* Mathematik, *die*

maths /mæθs/ *n.* (Brit. coll.) Mathe, *die* (Schülerspr.)

matinée /ˈmætɪneɪ/ *n.* Nachmittagsvorstellung, *die*

matriarchal /meɪtrɪˈɑːkl/ *adj.* matriarchalisch

matriarchy /ˈmeɪtrɪɑːkɪ/ *n.* Matriarchat, *das*

matrices *pl. of* MATRIX

matriculate /məˈtrɪkjʊleɪt/ 1 *v.t.* immatrikulieren (**in** an + *Dat.*)
2 *v.i.* sich immatrikulieren

matriculation /mətrɪkjʊˈleɪʃn/ *n.* Immatrikulation, *die*

matrimonial /mætrɪˈməʊnɪəl/ *adj.* Ehe-

matrimony /ˈmætrɪmənɪ/ *n.* Ehestand, *der*

matrix /ˈmeɪtrɪks/ *n., pl.* **matrices** /ˈmeɪtrɪsiːz/ *or* **~es** Matrix, *die*

matron /ˈmeɪtrən/ *n.* (in school) ≈ Hausmutter, *die;* (in hospital) Oberschwester, *die*

matt /mæt/ *adj.* matt

'matted *adj.* verfilzt

matter /ˈmætə(r)/ 1 *n.* **(a)** (affair) Angelegenheit, *die;* **~s** die Dinge; **money ~s** Geldangelegenheiten
(b) it's a ~ of taste das ist Geschmackssache; **[only] a ~ of time** [nur noch] eine Frage der Zeit
(c) what's the ~? was ist [los]?
(d) (physical material) Materie, *die*
2 *v.i.* etwas ausmachen; **what does it ~?** was macht das schon?; **[it] doesn't ~**: [das] macht nichts (ugs.)

'matter-of-fact *adj.* sachlich

mattress /ˈmætrɪs/ *n.* Matratze, *die*

mature /məˈtjʊə(r)/ 1 *adj.* reif; ausgereift ‹*Stil, Käse, Portwein, Sherry*›
2 *v.t.* reifen lassen
3 *v.i.* reifen

maturity /məˈtjʊərɪtɪ/ *n.* Reife, *die*

Maundy Thursday /mɔːndɪ ˈθɜːzdɪ/ *n.* Gründonnerstag, *der*

mausoleum /mɔːsəˈliːəm/ *n.* Mausoleum, *das*

mauve /məʊv/ *adj.* mauve

mawkish /ˈmɔːkɪʃ/ *adj.* rührselig

max. *abbr.* = **maximum** (*adj.*) max., (*n.*) Max.

maxim /ˈmæksɪm/ *n.* Maxime, *die*

maximum /ˈmæksɪməm/ 1 *n., pl.* **maxima** /ˈmæksɪmə/ Maximum, *das*
2 *adj.* maximal; Maximal-; **~ speed/temperature** Höchstgeschwindigkeit, *die*/-temperatur, *die*

'maximum-security *attrib. adj.* Hochsicherheits‹[*gefängnis*]*trakt*›

may *v. aux., only in pres.* **may**, *neg.* (coll.) **mayn't** /meɪnt/, *past* **might** /maɪt/, *neg.* (coll.) **mightn't** /ˈmaɪtnt/ **(a)** (expr. possibility) können; **it ~ be true** das kann stimmen; **I ~ be wrong** vielleicht irre ich mich; **it ~ not be possible**

das wird vielleicht nicht möglich sein; **he ~ have missed his train** vielleicht hat er seinen Zug verpasst; **it ~** *or* **might rain** es könnte regnen; **we ~** *or* **might as well go** wir könnten eigentlich ebenso gut [auch] gehen
(b) (expr. permission) dürfen
(c) (expr. wish) mögen; **~ the best man win!** auf dass der Beste gewinnt!

May /meɪ/ *n.* Mai, *der; see also* AUGUST

maybe /'meɪbi:, 'meɪbɪ/ *adv.* vielleicht

'May Day *n.* der Erste Mai; **the ~ holiday** der Maifeiertag

'mayfly *n.* Eintagsfliege, *die*

mayhem /'meɪhem/ *n.* Chaos, *das*

mayn't /meɪnt/ (coll.) = **may not;** ▶ MAY

mayonnaise /meɪə'neɪz/ *n.* Mayonnaise, *die*

mayor /meə(r)/ *n.* Bürgermeister, *der*

mayoress /'meərɪs/ *n.* (woman mayor) Bürgermeisterin, *die;* (mayor's wife) [Ehe]frau des Bürgermeisters

maze /meɪz/ *n.* Labyrinth, *das*

MBA *abbr.* = **Master of Business Administration** *Diplom in Betriebswirtschaft*

me /mɪ, *stressed* mi:/ *pron.* mich; *as indirect object* mir; **who, me?** wer, ich?; **not me** ich nicht; **it's me** ich bins

ME *abbr.* (Med.) = **myalgic encephalomyelitis**

meadow /'medəʊ/ *n.* Wiese, *die*

meagre /'mi:gə(r)/ *adj.* dürftig

meal /mi:l/ *n.* Mahlzeit, *die;* **go out for a ~:** essen gehen; **enjoy your ~:** guten Appetit!; **~s on wheels** (Brit.) Essen auf Rädern

meal: ~ ticket *n.* Essenmarke, *die;* (fig. coll.) melkende Kuh (ugs.); **~time** *n.* Essenszeit, *die;* **~ voucher** *n.* Essenmarke, *die*

mean¹ /mi:n/ *n.* **(a)** Mittelweg, *der*
(b) (Math.) Mittelwert, *der*

mean² *adj.* **(a)** (miserly) geizig
(b) (unkind) gemein
(c) (shabby) schäbig

mean³ *v.t.*, **meant** /ment/ **(a)** (intend) beabsichtigen; **~ to do sth.** etw. tun wollen
(b) (design, destine) **be ~t to do sth.** etw. tun sollen
(c) (intend to convey) meinen; **I [really] ~ it** ich meine das ernst; **what do you ~ by that?** was hast du damit gemeint?
(d) (signify) bedeuten

meander /mɪ'ændə(r)/ *v.i.* **(a)** ‹*Fluss:*› sich winden
(b) ‹*Person:*› schlendern

'meaning *n.* Bedeutung, *die;* (of text etc., life) Sinn, *der*

meaningful /'mi:nɪŋfl/ *adj.* bedeutungsvoll ‹*Blick, Ergebnis*›; sinnvoll ‹*Aufgabe, Gespräch*›

'meaningless *adj.* ‹*Wort, Gespräch:*› ohne Sinn; sinnlos ‹*Aktivität*›

means /mi:nz/ *n.* **(a)** Möglichkeit, *die;* [Art und] Weise; **by this ~:** hierdurch; **~ of transport** Transportmittel, *das*
(b) *pl.* (resources) Mittel *Pl.;* **live within/beyond one's ~:** seinen Verhältnissen entsprechend/über seine Verhältnisse leben
(c) by all ~! selbstverständlich!; **by no [manner of] ~:** ganz und gar nicht; **by ~ of** durch; mit [Hilfe von]

'means test *n.* Überprüfung der Bedürftigkeit

meant ▶ MEAN³

mean: ~time [1] *n.* **in the ~time** inzwischen; [2] *adv* inzwischen; **~while** *adv.* inzwischen

measles /'mi:zlz/ *n.* Masern *Pl.*

measly /'mi:zlɪ/ *adj.* (coll.) pop[e]lig (ugs.)

measurable /'meʒərəbl/ *adj.* messbar

measure /'meʒə(r)/ [1] *n.* **(a)** Maß, *das;* **for good ~:** sicherheitshalber; (as an extra) zusätzlich; **made to ~:** maßgeschneidert
(b) (degree) **in some/large ~:** in gewisser Hinsicht/ in hohem Maße
(c) (for measuring) Maß, *das*
(d) (step) Maßnahme, *die;* **take ~s** Maßnahmen treffen
[2] *v.t.* messen ‹*Größe, Menge usw.*›; ausmessen ‹*Raum*›
[3] *v.i.* messen

■ **measure 'up to** *v.t.* entsprechen (+ *Dat.*)

'measured /'meʒəd/ *adj.* gemessen ‹*Schritt, Worte*›

'measurement *n.* **(a)** Messung, *die*
(b) (dimension) Maß, *das*

'measuring tape *n.* Bandmaß, *das*

meat /mi:t/ *n.* Fleisch, *das*

'meaty *adj.* **(a)** fleischig
(b) (fig.) gehaltvoll

mechanic /mɪ'kænɪk/ *n.* Mechaniker, *der*/ Mechanikerin, *die*

mechanical /mɪ'kænɪkl/ *adj.* mechanisch

mechanical engi'neering *n.* Maschinenbau, *der*

me'chanically *adv.* mechanisch

mechanical 'pencil *n.* (Amer.) Drehbleistift, *der*

me'chanics *n.* **(a)** Mechanik, *die*
(b) *pl.* (mechanism) Mechanismus, *der*

mechanism /'mekənɪzm/ *n.* Mechanismus, *der*

mechanize /'mekənaɪz/ *v.t.* mechanisieren

medal /'medl/ *n.* Medaille, *die;* (decoration) Orden, *der*

medallion /mɪ'dæljən/ *n.* [große] Medaille

medallist /'medəlɪst/ *n.* Medaillengewinner, *der*/-gewinnerin, *die*

meddle /'medl/ *v.i.* **~ with sth.** sich (*Dat.*) an etw. (*Dat.*) zu schaffen machen; **~ in sth.** sich in etw. (*Akk.*) einmischen

media /'mi:dɪə/ ▶ MASS MEDIA; MEDIUM 1

mediaeval ▶ MEDIEVAL

'media studies *n. sing.* Medienwissenschaft, *die;* (school subject) Medienkunde, *die*

mediate /'miːdɪeɪt/ *v.i.* vermitteln

mediator /'miːdɪeɪtə(r)/ *n.* Vermittler, *der*/ Vermittlerin, *die*

medical /'medɪkl/ *adj.* medizinisch; ärztlich ‹*Behandlung, Untersuchung*›

medical: ~ certificate *n.* Attest, *das;* **~ exami'nation** *n.* ärztliche Untersuchung; **~ 'history** *n.* (of person) Krankengeschichte, *die;* **~ insurance** *n.* Krankenversicherung, *die;* **have ~ insurance** krankenversichert sein; **~ prac'titioner** *n.* praktischer Arzt/praktische Ärztin; **~ report** *n.* medizinisches Gutachten; **~ school** *n.* medizinische Hochschule; **~ student** *n.* Medizinstudent, *der*/ -studentin *die*

medicament /mɪ'dɪkəmənt, 'medɪkəmənt/ *n.* Medikament, *das*

Medicare /'medɪkeə(r)/ *n.* (Amer.) [*bundes*]*staatliches Krankenversicherungssystem für Personen über 65 Jahre*

medicated /'medɪkeɪtɪd/ *adj.* medizinisch

medication /medɪ'keɪʃn/ *n.* (medicine) Medikament, *das*

medicinal /mɪ'dɪsɪnl/ *adj.* medizinisch

medicine /'medsən, 'medɪsɪn/ *n.* **(a)** (science) Medizin, *die*
(b) (preparation) Medikament, *das*

'medicine chest *n.* Medikamentenschränkchen, *das;* (in home) Hausapotheke, *die*

medieval /medɪ'iːvl/ *adj.* mittelalterlich

mediocre /miːdɪ'əʊkə(r)/ *adj.* mittelmäßig

mediocrity /miːdɪ'ɒkrɪtɪ/ *n.* Mittelmäßigkeit, *die*

meditate /'medɪteɪt/ *v.i.* nachdenken, (esp. Relig.) meditieren (**[up]on** über + *Akk.*)

meditation /medɪ'teɪʃn/ *n.* **(a)** (act) Nachdenken, *das*
(b) (Relig.) Meditation, *die*

Mediterranean /medɪtə'reɪnɪən/ *pr. n.* **the ~**: das Mittelmeer

medium /'miːdɪəm/ **1** *n., pl.* **media** /'miːdɪə/ *or* **~s (a)** (substance) Medium, *das*
(b) (means) Mittel, *das;* **by** *or* **through the ~ of** durch
(c) *pl.* **~s** (Spiritualism) Medium, *das*
(d) *in pl.* **media** (mass media) Medien *Pl.*
2 *adj.* mittler ...; medium *nur präd.* ‹*Steak*›

medium: ~-range *adj.* Mittelstrecken‹*flugzeug, -rakete*›; **~-size[d]** *adj.* mittelgroß

medley /'medlɪ/ *n.* **(a)** buntes Gemisch
(b) (Mus.) Potpourri, *das*

meek /miːk/ *adj.* **(a)** (humble) sanftmütig
(b) (submissive) zu nachgiebig

meet /miːt/ **1** *v.t.,* **met** /met/ **(a)** treffen; (collect) abholen
(b) (make the acquaintance of) kennen lernen; **pleased to ~ you** [sehr] angenehm
(c) (experience) stoßen auf (+ *Akk.*) ‹*Widerstand, Problem*›
(d) (satisfy) entsprechen (+ *Dat.*) ‹*Wunsch, Bedürfnis, Kritik*›; einhalten ‹*Termin, Zeitplan*›
(e) (pay) decken ‹*Kosten*›; bezahlen ‹*Rechnung*›
2 *v.i.,* **met (a)** (by chance) sich (*Dat.*) begegnen; (by arrangement) sich treffen; **we've met before** wir kennen uns bereits
(b) ‹*Komitee, Ausschuss usw.*:› tagen

▪ **meet 'up** *v.i.* sich treffen; **~ up with sb.** (coll.) sich treffen

▪ **'meet with** *v.t.* **(a)** begegnen (+ *Dat.*)
(b) (experience) haben ‹*Erfolg, Unfall*›; stoßen auf (+ *Akk.*) ‹*Widerstand*›

'meeting *n.* **(a)** Begegnung, *die;* (by arrangement) Treffen, *das*
(b) (assembly) Versammlung, *die;* (of committee etc.) Sitzung, *die*

'meeting place *n.* Treffpunkt, *der*

mega /'megə/ (coll.) **1** *adj.* **(a)** (enormous) Mega- (Jugendspr.)
(b) (excellent) geil (Jugendspr.)
2 *adv.* äußerst; **be ~ rich** super- *od.* (Jugendspr.) megareich sein

'megabyte *n.* (Comp.) Megabyte, *das*

megalomania /megələ'meɪnɪə/ *n.* Größenwahn, *der*

megaphone /'megəfəʊn/ *n.* Megaphon, *das*

melancholic /melən'kɒlɪk/ *adj.* melancholisch

melancholy /'melənkəlɪ/ **1** *n.* Melancholie, *die*
2 *adj.* melancholisch

mellow /'meləʊ/ **1** *adj.* **(a)** (softened by age or experience) abgeklärt
(b) (ripe, well-matured) reif
2 *v.i.* reifen

melodic /mɪ'lɒdɪk/, **melodious** /mɪ'ləʊdɪəs/ *adjs.*, **me'lodiously** *adv.* melodisch

melodrama /'melədrɑːmə/ *n.* Melodrama, *das*

melodramatic /melədrə'mætɪk/ *adj.* melodramatisch

melody /'melədɪ/ *n.* Melodie, *die*

melon /'melən/ *n.* Melone, *die*

melt /melt/ **1** *v.i.* schmelzen
2 *v.t.* schmelzen; zerlassen ‹*Butter*›

▪ **melt a'way** *v.i.* [weg]schmelzen

▪ **melt 'down** **1** *v.i.* schmelzen
2 *v.t.* einschmelzen

melting: ~ point *n.* Schmelzpunkt, *der;* **~ pot** *n.* (fig.) Schmelztiegel, *der*

member /'membə(r)/ *n.* **(a)** Mitglied, *das;* **be a ~**: Mitglied sein; **~ of a/the family** Familienangehörige, *der/die*
(b) M~ [of Parliament] (Brit.) Abgeordnete [des Unterhauses], *der/die*

'membership *n.* **(a)** Mitgliedschaft, *die* (**of** in + *Dat.*)
(b) (number of members) Mitgliederzahl, *die*
(c) (members) Mitglieder *Pl.*

'member state *n.* Mitglied[s]staat, *der*

membrane /'membreɪn/ *n.* (Biol.) Membran, *die*

memento /mɪ'mentəʊ/ *n., pl.* **~es** *or* **~s** Andenken, *das* (**of** an + *Akk.*)

memo /'meməʊ/ *n., pl.* **~s** (coll.) ▶ MEMORANDUM

memoirs /'memwɑːz/ *n. pl.* Memoiren *Pl.*

memorable /'memərəbl/ *adj.* denkwürdig ‹*Ereignis, Tag*›; unvergesslich ‹*Film, Buch, Aufführung*›

memorandum /memə'rændəm/ *n., pl.* **memoranda** /memə'rændə/ *or* **~s** Mitteilung, *die*

memorial /mɪ'mɔːrɪəl/ **1** *adj.* Gedenk-
2 *n.* Denkmal, *das* (**to** für)

memorize /'meməraɪz/ *v.t.* sich (*Dat.*) merken *od.* einprägen; (learn by heart) auswendig lernen

memory /'memərɪ/ *n.* **(a)** Gedächtnis, *das*
(b) (thing remembered, act of remembering) Erinnerung, *die* (**of** an + *Akk.*); **from ~:** aus dem Gedächtnis; **in ~ of** zur Erinnerung an (+ *Akk.*)
(c) (Comp.) Speicher, *der*

memory: ~ bank *n.* Speicherbank, *die;* **~ stick** *n.* (Comp.) Memorystick, *der;* Speicherstab, *der*

men *pl. of* MAN

menace /'menəs/ **1** *v.t.* bedrohen
2 *n.* Plage, *die*

menacing /'menəsɪŋ/ *adj.* drohend

mend /mend/ **1** *v.t.* reparieren; ausbessern ‹*Kleidung*›; kleben ‹*Glas, Porzellan*›
2 *v.i.* ‹*Knochen, Bein usw.:*› heilen
3 *n.* **be on the ~:** auf dem Wege der Besserung sein

'menfolk *n. pl.* Männer *Pl.*

menial /'miːnɪəl/ *adj.* niedrig; untergeordnet ‹*Aufgabe*›

meningitis /menɪn'dʒaɪtɪs/ *n.* Hirnhautentzündung, *die*

menopause /'menəpɔːz/ *n.* Wechseljahre *Pl.*

menstruate /'menstrʊeɪt/ *v.i.* menstruieren

menstruation /menstrʊ'eɪʃn/ *n.* Menstruation, *die*

menswear /'menzweə(r)/ *n.* Herrenbekleidung, *die*

mental /'mentl/ *adj.* **(a)** (of the mind) geistig; Geistes‹*zustand, -störung*›
(b) (Brit. coll.: mad) verrückt (salopp)

mental: ~ a'rithmetic *n.* Kopfrechnen, *das;* **~ 'health** *n.* seelische Gesundheit; **~ hospital** *n.* Nervenklinik, *die* (ugs.); **~ 'illness** *n.* Geisteskrankheit, *die*

mentality /men'tælɪtɪ/ *n.* Mentalität, *die*

'mentally *adv.* geistig

mention /'menʃn/ **1** *n.* Erwähnung, *die*
2 *v.t.* erwähnen (**to** gegenüber); **don't ~ it** keine Ursache

menu /'menjuː/ *n.* **(a)** [Speise]karte, *die*
(b) (Comp., Telev.) Menü, *das*

'menu bar *n.* (Comp.) Menüleiste, *die*

mercenary /'mɜːsɪnərɪ/ **1** *adj.* gewinnsüchtig
2 *n.* Söldner, *der*

merchandise /'mɜːtʃəndaɪz/ *n.* [Handels]ware, *die*

merchant /'mɜːtʃənt/ *n.* Kaufmann, *der*

merchant: ~ 'bank *n.* Handelsbank, *die;* **~ 'navy** *n.* (Brit.) Handelsmarine, *die*

merciful /'mɜːsɪfl/ *adj.* gnädig

mercifully /'mɜːsɪfəlɪ/ *adv.* (fortunately) glücklicherweise

merciless /'mɜːsɪlɪs/ *adj.*, **'mercilessly** *adv.* gnadenlos

mercury /'mɜːkjʊrɪ/ **1** *n.* Quecksilber, *das*
2 *pr. n.* **M~** (Astron.) Merkur, *der*

mercy /'mɜːsɪ/ *n.* Erbarmen, *das* (**on** mit); **show sb. [no] ~:** mit jmdm. [kein] Erbarmen haben; **be at the ~ of sb./sth.** jmdm./einer Sache [auf Gedeih und Verderb] ausgeliefert sein

mere /mɪə(r)/ *adj.*, **'merely** *adv.* bloß

merge /mɜːdʒ/ **1** *v.t.* **(a)** (combine) zusammenschließen
(b) (blend gradually) verschmelzen (**with** mit)
2 *v.i.* **(a)** (combine) fusionieren (**with** mit)
(b) ‹*Straße:*› zusammenlaufen (**with** mit)

merger /'mɜːdʒə(r)/ *n.* Fusion, *die*

meringue /mə'ræŋ/ *n.* Meringe, *die;* Baiser, *das*

merit /'merɪt/ **1** *n.* **(a)** (worth) Verdienst, *das*
(b) (good feature) Vorzug, *der*
2 *v.t.* verdienen

mermaid /'mɜːmeɪd/ *n.* Nixe, *die*

merrily /'merɪlɪ/ *adv.* munter

merriment /'merɪmənt/ *n.* Fröhlichkeit, *die*

merry /'merɪ/ *adj.* fröhlich; **~ Christmas!** frohe *od.* fröhliche Weihnachten!

'merry-go-round *n.* Karussell, *das*

'merrymaking *n.* Feiern, *das*

mesh /meʃ/ *n.* **(a)** Masche, *die*
(b) (netting; also fig.: network) Geflecht, *das;* **wire ~:** Maschendraht, *der*

mesmerize /'mezməraɪz/ *v.t.* faszinieren

mess /mes/ *n.* **(a)** (dirty/untidy state) **[be] a ~** *or* **in a ~:** schmutzig/unaufgeräumt [sein]; **what a ~!** was für ein Dreck (ugs.)/ Durcheinander!
(b) (bad state) **be [in] a ~:** sich in einem schlimmen Zustand befinden; ‹*Person:*› schlimm dran sein; **get into a ~:** in Schwierigkeiten geraten; **make a ~ of** verpfuschen (ugs.) ‹*Arbeit, Leben*›
(c) (Mil.) Kasino, *das*

■ **mess a'bout, mess a'round** [1] *v.i.* (potter) herumwerken; (fool about) herumalbern
[2] *v.t.* ~ **sb. about** *or* **around** mit jmdm. nach Belieben umspringen
■ **mess 'up** *v.t.* **(a)** (make dirty) schmutzig machen; (make untidy) in Unordnung bringen **(b)** (bungle) ~ **it/things up** Mist bauen (ugs.)
message /'mesɪdʒ/ *n.* Nachricht, *die;* **give sb. a** ~: jmdm. etwas ausrichten
messenger /'mesɪndʒə(r)/ *n.* Bote, *der*/Botin, *die*
Messiah /mɪ'saɪə/ *n.* Messias, *der*
Messrs /'mesəz/ *n. pl.* **(a)** (in name of firm) ≈ Fa.
(b) *pl. of* MR; (in list of names) ~ **A and B** die Herren A und B
'**messy** *adj.* (dirty) schmutzig; (untidy) unordentlich
met ▶ MEET
metabolism /mɪ'tæbəlɪzm/ *n.* Stoffwechsel, *der*
metal /'metl/ [1] *n.* Metall, *das*
[2] *adj.* Metall-
'**metal detector** *n.* Metallsuchgerät, *das*
metallic /mɪ'tælɪk/ *adj.* metallisch; **have a** ~ **taste** nach Metall schmecken
metallurgy /mɪ'tælədʒɪ/ *n.* Metallurgie, *die*
'**metalwork** *n.* (products) Metallarbeiten *Pl.*
metamorphosis /metə'mɔ:fəsɪs/ *n., pl.* **metamorphoses** /metə'mɔ:fəsi:z/ Metamorphose, *die*
metaphor /'metəfə(r)/ *n.* Metapher, *die*
metaphorical /metə'fɒrɪkl/ *adj.*, **metaphorically** /metə'fɒrɪkəlɪ/ *adv.* metaphorisch
meteor /'mi:tɪə(r)/ *n.* Meteor, *der*
meteoric /mi:tɪ'ɒrɪk/ *adj.* (fig.) kometenhaft
meteorological /mi:tɪərə'lɒdʒɪkl/ *adj.* meteorologisch ‹*Instrument*›; Wetter‹*ballon, -bericht*›
meteorologist /mi:tɪə'rɒlədʒɪst/ *n.* Meteorologe, *der*/Meteorologin, *die*
meteorology /mi:tɪə'rɒlədʒɪ/ *n.* Meteorologie, *die*
meter¹ /'mi:tə(r)/ *n.* **(a)** Zähler, *der;* (for coins) Münzzähler, *der*
(b) (parking ~) Parkuhr, *die*
meter² (Amer.) ▶ METRE¹, ²
methane /'mi:θeɪn/ *n.* Methan, *das*
method /'meθəd/ *n.* Methode, *die*
methodical /mɪ'θɒdɪkl/ *adj.*, **me'thodically** *adv.* systematisch
Methodist /'meθədɪst/ *n.* Methodist, *der*/Methodistin, *die*
meths /meθs/ *n.* (Brit. coll.) [Brenn]spiritus, *der*
methylated spirit[s] /meθɪleɪtɪd 'spɪrɪt(s)/ *n.* [*pl.*] Brennspiritus, *der*
meticulous /mɪ'tɪkjʊləs/ *adj.*, **me'ticulously** *adv.* (scrupulous[ly]) sorgfältig; (overscrupulous[ly]) übergenau

metre¹ /'mi:tə/ *n.* (Brit.: poetic rhythm) Metrum, *das*
metre² *n.* (Brit.: unit) Meter, *der od. das*
metric /'metrɪk/ *adj.* metrisch; ~ **system** metrisches System
metrication /metrɪ'keɪʃn/ *n.* Umstellung auf das metrische System
metro /'metrəʊ/ *n., pl.* ~**s** U-Bahn, *die;* **the Paris M**~ die [Pariser] Metro
metronome /'metrənəʊm/ *n.* Metronom, *das*
metropolis /mɪ'trɒpəlɪs/ *n.* Metropole, *die*
metropolitan /metrə'pɒlɪtən/ *adj.* ~ **New York** der Großraum New York; ~ **London** Großlondon (*das*)
Mexican /'meksɪkən/ [1] *adj.* mexikanisch; **sb. is** ~: jmd. ist Mexikaner/Mexikanerin
[2] *n.* Mexikaner, *der*/Mexikanerin, *die*
Mexico /'meksɪkəʊ/ *pr. n.* Mexiko (*das*)
miaow /mɪ'aʊ/ [1] *v.i.* miauen
[2] *n.* Miauen, *das*
mice *pl. of* MOUSE
microbe /'maɪkrəʊb/ *n.* Mikrobe, *die*
micro /'maɪkrəʊ/: ~**chip** *n.* Mikrochip, *der;* ~**computer** *n.* Mikrocomputer, *der;* ~**dot** *n.* Mikrat, *das;* ~**fibre** *n.* Mikrofaser, *die;* ~**fiche** *n.* Mikrofiche, *das od. der;* ~**film** [1] *n.* Mikrofilm, *der;* [2] *v.t.* auf Mikrofilm aufnehmen; ~**light ['aircraft]** *n.* Ultraleichtflugzeug, *das*
microphone /'maɪkrəfəʊn/ *n.* Mikrofon, *das*
microprocessor /maɪkrəʊ'prəʊsesə(r)/ *n.* Mikroprozessor, *der*
microscope /'maɪkrəskəʊp/ *n.* Mikroskop, *das*
microscopic /maɪkrə'skɒpɪk/ *adj.* mikroskopisch; (fig.: very small) winzig
'**microwave** *n.* Mikrowelle, *die;* ~ **[oven]** Mikrowellenherd, *der*
mid- /mɪd/ *in comb.* **in** ~**-air** in der Luft; **in** ~**-sentence** mitten im Satz; ~**-July** Mitte Juli; **the** ~**-60s** die Mitte der Sechzigerjahre; **a man in his** ~**-fifties** ein Mittfünfziger; **be in one's** ~**-thirties** Mitte dreißig sein
midday /'mɪddeɪ, mɪd'deɪ/ *n.* **(a)** (noon) zwölf Uhr
(b) (middle of day) Mittag, *der; attrib.* Mittags-
middle /'mɪdl/ [1] *attrib. adj.* mittler...
[2] *n.* **(a)** Mitte, *die;* **in the** ~ **of the forest/night** mitten im Wald/in der Nacht
(b) (waist) Taille, *die*
middle: ~ **'age** *n.* mittleres [Lebens]alter; ~**-aged** /'mɪdleɪdʒd/ *adj.* mittleren Alters *nachgestellt;* **M**~ **'Ages** *n. pl.* **the M**~ **Ages** das Mittelalter; ~ **'class** *n.* Mittelstand, *der;* ~**-class** *adj.* bürgerlich; **M**~ **'East** *pr. n.* **the M**~ **East** der Nahe [und Mittlere] Osten; **M**~ **'Eastern** *adj.* nahöstlich; ~**man** *n.* (Commerc.) Zwischenhändler, *der*/-händlerin, *die;* (fig.) Vermittler, *der*/

Vermittlerin, *die;* ~ '**management** *n.* mittleres Management; ~ **name** *n.* zweiter Vorname
middling /'mɪdlɪŋ/ *adj.* mittelmäßig
'**midfield** *n.* (Footb.) Mittelfeld, *das*
midge /mɪdʒ/ *n.* Stechmücke, *die*
midget /'mɪdʒɪt/ [1] *n.* Liliputaner, *der*/ Liliputanerin, *die*
[2] *adj.* winzig
Midlands /'mɪdləndz/ *n. pl.* **the** ~ (Brit.) Mittelengland (*das*)
midlife crisis /mɪdlaɪf 'kraɪsɪs/ *n.* Midlifecrisis, *die*
'**midnight** *n.* Mitternacht, *die*
'**midpoint** *n.* Mitte, *die*
midriff /'mɪdrɪf/ *n.* Bauch, *der*
midst /mɪdst/ *n.* **in the** ~ **of sth.** mitten in einer Sache; **in our/their/your** ~: in unserer/ ihrer/eurer Mitte
midsummer /'---, -'--/ *n.* die [Zeit der] Sommersonnenwende
midway /'--, -'-/ *adv.* auf halbem Weg[e] ‹*sich treffen, sich befinden*›
midweek /'mɪdwi:k, mɪd'wi:k/ *n.* **in** ~: in der Wochenmitte
'**midwife** *n., pl.* '**midwives** Hebamme, *die*
midwifery /'mɪdwɪfrɪ, mɪd'wɪfərɪ/ *n., no art.* Geburtshilfe, *die*
mid'winter *n.* die [Zeit der] Wintersonnenwende
might[1] ▶ MAY
might[2] /maɪt/ *n.* **(a)** (force) Gewalt, *die*
(b) (power) Macht, *die*
mightn't /'maɪtnt/ (coll.) = **might not;** ▶ MAY
mighty /'maɪtɪ/ [1] *adj.* mächtig
[2] *adv.* (coll.) verdammt (ugs.)
migraine /'mi:greɪn/ *n.* Migräne, *die*
migrant /'maɪgrənt/ *n.* **(a)** Auswanderer, *der*/Auswanderin, *die*
(b) (bird) Zugvogel, *der*
migrate /maɪ'greɪt/ *v.i.* **(a)** (to a town) abwandern; (to another country) auswandern
(b) ‹*Vogel:*› fortziehen
migration /maɪ'greɪʃn/ *n.* **(a)** (to a town) Abwandern, *das;* (to another country) Auswandern, *das*
(b) (of birds) Zug, *der*
migratory /maɪ'greɪtərɪ/ *adj.* ~ **bird/fish** Zugvogel, *der*/Wanderfisch, *der*
mike /maɪk/ *n.* (coll.) Mikro, *das*
Milan /mɪ'læn/ *pr. n.* Mailand (*das*)
mild /maɪld/ *adj.* mild; sanft ‹*Person*›
mildew /'mɪldju:/ *n.* **(a)** Schimmel, *der*
(b) (on plant) Mehltau, *der*
'**mildly** *adv.* **(a)** (gently) mild[e]
(b) (slightly) ein bisschen
(c) to put it ~: gelinde gesagt
mile /maɪl/ *n.* **(a)** Meile, *die*
(b) (fig. coll.) ~**s better/too big** tausendmal besser/viel zu groß; **be** ~**s ahead of sb.** jmdm. weit voraus sein
mileage /'maɪlɪdʒ/ *n.* [Anzahl der] Meilen *Pl.;* **a low** ~: ein niedriger Meilenstand
'**milestone** *n.* Meilenstein, *der*
militant /'mɪlɪtənt/ [1] *adj.* militant
[2] *n.* Militante, *der*/*die*
military /'mɪlɪtərɪ/ [1] *adj.* militärisch; Militär‹*regierung, -akademie, -uniform, -parade*›; ~ **service** Militärdienst, *der*
[2] *n.* **the** ~: das Militär
militate /'mɪlɪteɪt/ *v.i.* ~ **against/in favour of sth.** [deutlich] gegen/für etw. sprechen
militia /mɪ'lɪʃə/ *n.* Miliz, *die*
milk /mɪlk/ [1] *n.* Milch, *die*
[2] *v.t.* melken
milk: ~ **bottle** *n.* Milchflasche, *die;* ~ '**chocolate** *n.* Milchschokolade, *die;* ~ **float** *n.* (Brit.) Milchwagen, *der*
milking /'mɪlkɪŋ/ *n.* Melken, *das*
milk: ~ **jug** *n.* Milchkännchen, *das;* ~**man** /'mɪlkmən/ *n., pl.* ~**men** /'mɪlkmən/ Milchmann, *der;* ~ **shake** *n.* Milchshake, *der;* ~ **tooth** *n.* Milchzahn, der
'**milky** *adj.* milchig
Milky 'Way *n.* Milchstraße, *die*
mill /mɪl/ [1] *n.* **(a)** Mühle, *die*
(b) (factory) Fabrik, *die*
[2] *v.t.* **(a)** mahlen ‹*Getreide*›
(b) fräsen ‹*Metallgegenstand*›
mill a'bout (Brit.), **mill a'round** *v.i.* durcheinander laufen
millennium /mɪ'lenɪəm/ *n., pl.* ~**s** *or* **millennia** /mɪ'lenɪə/ Jahrtausend, *das;* Millennium, *das*
mil'lennium bug *n.* (Comp.) Jahrtausendvirus, *der od. das*
'**miller** *n.* Müller, *der*
millet /'mɪlɪt/ *n.* Hirse, *die*
milligram /'mɪlɪgræm/ *n.* Milligramm, *das*
millilitre (*Brit.; Amer.:* **milliliter**) /'mɪlɪli:tə(r)/ *n.* Milliliter, *der od. das*
millimetre (*Brit.; Amer.:* **millimeter**) /'mɪlɪmi:tə(r)/ *n.* Millimeter, *der*
milliner /'mɪlɪnə(r)/ *n.* Modist, *der*/ Modistin, *die*
'**millinery** *n.* Hutmacherei, *die*
million /'mɪljən/ [1] *adj.* **a** *or* **one/two** ~: eine Million/zwei Millionen; **half a** ~: eine halbe Million
[2] *n.* **(a)** Million, *die*
(b) (indefinite amount) ~**s of people** eine Unmenge Leute
millionaire /mɪljə'neə(r)/ *n.* Millionär, *der*/Millionärin, *die*
millionth /'mɪljənθ/ [1] *adj.* millionst...
[2] *n.* (fraction) Millionstel, *das*
'**millstone** *n.* Mühlstein, *der*
mime /maɪm/ [1] *n.* **(a)** (performance) Pantomime, *die*
(b) (art) Pantomimik, *die*
[2] *v.i.* pantomimisch agieren
[3] *v.t.* pantomimisch darstellen
mimic /'mɪmɪk/ [1] *n.* Imitator, *der* ···

2 *v.t.*, **-ck-** nachahmen

min. *abbr.* **(a)** = **minute[s]** Min. **(b)** = **minimum** (*adj.*) mind., (*n.*) Min.

mince /mɪns/ **1** *n.* Hackfleisch, *das* **2** *v.t.* durch den [Fleisch]wolf drehen ‹*Fleisch*›

'mincemeat *n.* **(a)** Hackfleisch, *das* **(b)** (sweet) *süße Pastetenfüllung aus Obst, Rosinen, Gewürzen, Nierenfett usw.*

mince 'pie *n. mit „mincemeat" B gefüllte Pastete*

'mincer *n.* Fleischwolf, *der*

mind /maɪnd/ **1** *n.* **(a)** Geist, *der* **(b)** (remembrance) **bear** *or* **keep sth. in ~:** an etw. (*Akk.*) denken; **have [got] sb./sth. in ~:** an jmdn./etw. denken **(c)** (opinion) **give sb. a piece of one's ~:** jmdm. gründlich die Meinung sagen; **to my ~:** meiner Meinung *od.* Ansicht nach; **change one's ~:** seine Meinung ändern; **I have a good ~ to do that** ich hätte große Lust, das zu tun; **make up one's ~, make one's ~ up** sich entscheiden **(d)** ([normal] mental powers) Verstand, *der;* **be out of one's ~:** den Verstand verloren haben **(e) frame of ~:** [seelische] Verfassung **2** *v.t.* **(a) I can't afford a bicycle, never ~ a car** ich kann mir kein Fahrrad leisten, geschweige denn ein Auto; **we've got some decorations up, - not many, ~ you** wir haben etwas dekoriert, allerdings nicht viel **(b)** *usu. neg. or interrog.* (object to) **would you ~ opening the door?** würdest du bitte die Tür öffnen?; **I wouldn't ~ a walk** ich hätte nichts gegen einen Spaziergang **(c)** (take care) **~ you don't go too near the cliff edge!** pass auf, dass du nicht zu nah an den Felsenrand gehst!; **~ how you go!** pass auf! **(d)** (have charge of) aufpassen auf (+ *Akk.*) **3** *v.i.* **(a) ~!** Vorsicht!; Achtung! **(b)** (care, object) **do you ~ if I smoke?** stört es Sie, wenn ich rauche? **(c) never ~** (it's not important) macht nichts

■ **mind 'out** *v.i.* aufpassen (**for** auf + *Akk.*); **~ out!** Vorsicht!

mind: ~-bending, (coll.) **~-blowing** *adjs.* bewusstseinsverändernd; **~-boggling** /'maɪndbɒglɪŋ/ *adj.* (coll.) wahnsinnig (ugs.)

'minded *adj.* **mechanically ~:** technisch veranlagt; **not politically ~:** unpolitisch

minder /'maɪndə(r)/ *n.* **(a)** (for child) **we need a ~ for the child** wir brauchen jemanden, der auf das Kind aufpasst *od.* das Kind betreut **(b)** (sl.: protector of criminal) Gorilla, *der* (salopp)

mindful /'maɪndfl/ *adj.* **be ~ of sth.** etw. berücksichtigen

'mindless *adj.* geistlos ‹*Person*›; sinnlos ‹*Gewalt*›

mine¹ /maɪn/ *n.* **(a)** Bergwerk, *das* **(b)** (explosive) Mine, *die*

mine² *poss. pron. pred.* meiner/meine/mein[e]s; *see also* HERS

mine: ~-detector *n.* Minensuchgerät, *das;* **~field** *n.* Minenfeld, *das*

'miner *n.* Bergmann, *der*

mineral /'mɪnərl/ **1** *adj.* mineralisch; Mineral‹*salz, -quelle*› **2** *n.* **(a)** Mineral, *das* **(b)** (Brit.: soft drink) Erfrischungsgetränk, *das*

'mineral water *n.* Mineralwasser, *das*

minesweeper /'maɪnswi:pə(r)/ *n.* Minensuchboot, *das*

mingle /'mɪŋgl/ **1** *v.t.* [ver]mischen **2** *v.i.* sich [ver]mischen (**with** mit)

mini /'mɪnɪ/ *n.* (coll.) **(a)** (car) **M~** ® Mini, *der* **(b)** (skirt) Mini, *der* (ugs.)

mini- /'mɪnɪ/ *in comb.* Mini-; Klein‹*bus, -wagen, -taxi*›

miniature /'mɪnɪtʃə(r)/ **1** *n.* (picture) Miniatur, *die* **2** *adj.* Miniatur-

mini: ~bus *n.* Kleinbus, *der;* **~cab** *n.* Minicar, *das*

minim /'mɪnɪm/ *n.* (Brit. Mus.) halbe Note

minimal /'mɪnɪml/ *adj.* minimal

minimize /'mɪnɪmaɪz/ *v.t.* **(a)** (reduce) auf ein Mindestmaß reduzieren **(b)** (understate) bagatellisieren

minimum /'mɪnɪməm/ **1** *n., pl.* **minima** /'mɪnɪmə/ Minimum, *das* (**of** an + *Dat.*) **2** *attrib. adj.* Mindest-

minimum: ~ 'lending rate *n.* *Mindestausleihsatz [der Bank von England];* ≈ Mindestdiskontsatz, *der;* **~ 'wage** *n.* Mindestlohn, *der*

mining /'maɪnɪŋ/ *n.* Bergbau, *der; attrib.* Bergbau-

mining: ~ industry *n.* Bergbau, *der;* **~ town** *n.* Bergbaustadt, *die*

minion /'mɪnjən/ *n.* Lakai, *der*

mini: ~ roundabout *n.* (Brit.) *sehr kleiner, oft nur aufs Pflaster aufgezeichneter Kreisverkehr;* **~skirt** *n.* Minirock, *der*

minister /'mɪnɪstə(r)/ **1** *n.* **(a)** (Polit.) Minister, *der*/Ministerin, *die* **(b)** (Eccl.) Geistliche, *der/die;* Pfarrer, *der*/Pfarrerin, *die* **2** *v.i.* **~ to sb.** sich um jmdn. kümmern

ministerial /mɪnɪ'stɪərɪəl/ *adj.* (Polit.) Minister-; ministeriell

ministry /'mɪnɪstrɪ/ *n.* **(a)** (Polit.) Ministerium, *das* **(b)** (Eccl.) geistliches Amt

mink /mɪŋk/ *n.* Nerz, *der*

minnow /'mɪnəʊ/ *n.* Elritze, *die*

minor /'maɪnə(r)/ **1** *adj.* **(a)** (lesser) kleiner... **(b)** (unimportant) weniger bedeutend; (not serious) leicht; **~ road** kleine Straße **(c)** (Mus.) Moll-; **A ~:** a-Moll **2** *n.* Minderjährige, *der/die*

minority /maɪ'nɒrɪtɪ, mɪ'nɒrɪtɪ/ *n.* Minderheit, *die;* **in the ~:** in der Minderheit

minstrel /'mɪnstrl/ *n.* fahrender Sänger

mint¹ /mɪnt/ [1] *n.* (place) Münzanstalt, *die*
[2] *adj.* funkelnagelneu (ugs.); **in ~ condition** in tadellosem Zustand
[3] *v.t.* prägen

mint² *n.* **(a)** (plant) Minze, *die*
(b) (peppermint) Pfefferminz, *das; attrib.* Pfefferminz-

mint 'sauce *n.* Minzsoße, *die*

minuet /mɪnjʊ'et/ *n.* Menuett, *das*

minus /'maɪnəs/ *prep.* minus; weniger; (without) abzüglich (+ *Gen.*)

minuscule /'mɪnəskju:l/ *adj.* winzig

minute¹ /'mɪnɪt/ *n.* **(a)** Minute, *die;* (moment) Moment, *der*
(b) **~s** (of meeting) Protokoll, *das;* **take the ~s of a meeting** bei einer Sitzung [das] Protokoll führen

minute² /maɪ'nju:t/ *adj.* (tiny) winzig

minute hand /'mɪnɪthænd/ *n.* Minutenzeiger, *der;* großer Zeiger

minutiae /maɪ'nju:ʃɪi:, mɪ'nju:ʃɪi:/ *n. pl.* Details *Pl.*

miracle /'mɪrəkl/ *n.* Wunder, *das*

miraculous /mɪ'rækjʊləs/ *adj.* wunderbar

mirage /'mɪrɑ:ʒ/ *n.* Fata Morgana, *die*

mire /maɪə(r)/ *n.* Morast, *der*

mirror /'mɪrə(r)/ [1] *n.* Spiegel, *der*
[2] *v.t.* [wider]spiegeln

mirror 'image *n.* Spiegelbild, *das*

misadventure /mɪsəd'ventʃə(r)/ *n.* Missgeschick, *das*

misanthropist /mɪ'zænθrəpɪst/ *ns.* Misanthrop, *der* (geh.); Menschenfeind, *der*

misanthropy /mɪ'zænθrəpɪ/ *n.* Menschenfeindlichkeit, *die*

misapprehension /mɪsæprɪ'henʃn/ *n.* Missverständnis, *das;* **be under a ~:** einem Irrtum unterliegen

misbehave /mɪsbɪ'heɪv/ *v.i. & refl.* sich schlecht benehmen

misbehaviour (*Amer.:* **misbehavior**) /mɪsbɪ'heɪvjə(r)/ *n.* schlechtes Benehmen

miscalculate /mɪs'kælkjʊleɪt/ [1] *v.t.* falsch berechnen; (misjudge) falsch einschätzen
[2] *v.i.* sich verrechnen

miscalculation /mɪskælkjʊ'leɪʃn/ *n.* Rechenfehler, *der;* (misjudgement) Fehleinschätzung, *die*

miscarriage /mɪs'kærɪdʒ/ *n.* **(a)** Fehlgeburt, *die*
(b) **~ of justice** Justizirrtum, *der*

miscarry /mɪs'kærɪ/ *v.i.* **(a)** (Med.) eine Fehlgeburt haben
(b) ‹*Plan, Vorhaben usw.:*› fehlschlagen

miscellaneous /mɪsə'leɪnɪəs/ *adj.* **(a)** [kunter]bunt
(b) *with pl. n.* verschieden

miscellany /mɪ'selənɪ/ *n.* [bunte] Sammlung; [buntes] Gemisch

mischief /'mɪstʃɪf/ *n.* **(a)** Unfug, *der;* **get up to ~:** etwas anstellen
(b) (harm) Schaden, *der*

mischievous /'mɪstʃɪvəs/ *adj.* spitzbübisch; schelmisch

misconception /mɪskən'sepʃn/ *n.* falsche Vorstellung (**about** von); **be [labouring] under a ~ about sth.** sich (*Dat.*) eine falsche Vorstellung von etw. machen

misconduct /mɪs'kɒndʌkt/ *n.* unkorrektes Verhalten

misconstrue /mɪskən'stru:/ *v.t.* missverstehen

miscount /mɪs'kaʊnt/ [1] *v.i.* sich vorzählen
[2] *v.t.* falsch zählen

misdeed /mɪs'di:d/ *n.* Missetat, *die* (veralt., scherzh.)

misdemeanour (*Amer.:* **misdemeanor**) /mɪsdɪ'mi:ne(r)/ *n.* Missetat, *die* (veralt., scherzh.)

misdirect /mɪsdɪ'rekt, mɪsdaɪ'rekt/ *v.t.* falsch adressieren ‹*Brief*›; in die falsche Richtung schicken ‹*Person*›

miser /'maɪzə(r)/ *n.* Geizhals, *der*

miserable /'mɪzərəbl/ *adj.* **(a)** unglücklich; **feel ~:** sich elend fühlen
(b) trist ‹*Wetter, Urlaub*›

miserably /'mɪzərəblɪ/ *adv.* unglücklich; jämmerlich ‹*versagen*›; **~ poor** bettelarm

miserly /'maɪzəlɪ/ *adj.* geizig

misery /'mɪzərɪ/ *n.* **(a)** Elend, *das*
(b) (coll.: discontented person) **~ [guts]** Miesepeter, *der* (ugs.)

misfire /mɪs'faɪə(r)/ *v.i.* **(a)** ‹*Motor:*› Fehlzündungen haben
(b) ‹*Plan, Versuch:*› fehlschlagen; ‹*Streich, Witz:*› danebengehen

misfit /'mɪsfɪt/ *n.* Außenseiter, *der*/ Außenseiterin, *die*

misfortune /mɪs'fɔ:tʃu:n/ *n.* Missgeschick, *das*

misgiving /mɪs'gɪvɪŋ/ *n.* **~[s]** Bedenken *Pl.*

misguided /mɪs'gaɪdɪd/ *adj.* töricht

mishandle /mɪs'hændl/ *v.t.* falsch behandeln

mishap /'mɪshæp/ *n.* Missgeschick, *das*

mishear /mɪs'hɪə(r)/ [1] *v.i.,* **misheard** /mɪs'hɜ:d/ sich verhören
[2] *v.t.,* **misheard** falsch verstehen

mishit [1] /'mɪshɪt/ *n.* Fehlschlag, *der*
[2] /mɪs'hɪt/ *v.t.,* **-tt-, mishit** verschlagen

mishmash /'mɪʃmæʃ/ *n.* Mischmasch, *der* (ugs.) (**of** aus)

misinform /mɪsɪn'fɔ:m/ *v.t.* falsch informieren

misinterpret /mɪsɪn'tɜ:prɪt/ *v.t.* (make wrong inference from) falsch deuten; missdeuten ⋯

misinterpretation /mɪsɪntɜ:prɪ'teɪʃn/ *n.* **be open to ~:** leicht missdeutet werden können

misjudge /mɪs'dʒʌdʒ/ *v.t.* falsch einschätzen; falsch beurteilen ‹*Person*›

misjudgement, misjudgment /mɪs'dʒʌdʒmənt/ *n.* Fehleinschätzung, *die;* (of person) falsche Beurteilung

mislay /mɪs'leɪ/ *v.t.,* **mislaid** /mɪs'leɪd/ verlegen

mislead /mɪs'li:d/ *v.t.,* **misled** /mɪs'led/ irreführen

mis'leading *adj.* irreführend

mismanage /mɪs'mænɪdʒ/ *v.t.* schlecht abwickeln ‹*Geschäft, Projekt*›

mismanagement /mɪs'mænɪdʒmənt/ *n.* schlechte Abwicklung

misnomer /mɪs'nəʊmə(r)/ *n.* unzutreffende Bezeichnung

misogynist /mɪ'sɒdʒɪnɪst/ *n.* Frauenhasser, *der*

misplace /mɪs'pleɪs/ *v.t.* an den falschen Platz stellen/legen/setzen *usw.*

misprint [1] /'mɪsprɪnt/ *n.* Druckfehler, *der* [2] /mɪs'prɪnt/ *v.t.* verdrucken

mispronounce /mɪsprə'naʊns/ *v.t.* falsch aussprechen

misquote /mɪs'kwəʊt/ *v.t.* falsch zitieren; **he was ~d as saying that ...:** man unterstellte ihm, gesagt zu haben, dass ...

misread /mɪs'ri:d/ *v.t.,* **misread** /mɪs'red/ falsch lesen

misrepresent /mɪsreprɪ'zent/ *v.t.* falsch darstellen

misrepresentation /mɪsreprɪzen'teɪʃn/ *n.* falsche Darstellung

miss [1] *n.* Fehlschlag, *der;* (shot) Fehlschuss, *der;* (throw) Fehlwurf, *der*
[2] *v.t.* **(a)** (fail to hit) verfehlen
(b) (let slip) verpassen; **~ an opportunity** sich (*Dat.*) eine Gelegenheit entgehen lassen
(c) (fail to catch) verpassen ‹*Zug*›
(d) (fail to take part in) versäumen; **~ school** in der Schule fehlen
(e) (fail to see) übersehen; (fail to hear) nicht mitbekommen
(f) (feel the absence of) vermissen; **she ~es him** er fehlt ihr
[3] *v.i.* (not hit sth.) danebentreffen

■ **miss 'out** [1] *v.t.* weglassen
[2] *v.i.* **~ out on sth.** (coll.) sich (*Dat.*) etw. entgehen lassen

Miss /mɪs/ *n.* **~ Brown** (unmarried woman) Frau Brown; Fräulein Brown (veralt.); (girl) Fräulein Brown

misshapen /mɪs'ʃeɪpn/ *adj.* missgebildet

missile /'mɪsaɪl/ *n.* **(a)** (thrown) [Wurf]geschoss, *das*
(b) (Mil.) Rakete, *die*

'missile base, 'missile site *ns.* Raketenbasis, *die*

'missing *adj.* fehlend; **be ~:** fehlen; ‹*Person:*› (Mil. etc.) vermisst werden; (not present) fehlen; **~ person** Vermisste, *der/die*

mission /'mɪʃn/ *n.* **(a)** Mission, *die*
(b) (planned operation) Einsatz, *der*

missionary /'mɪʃənərɪ/ *n.* Missionar, *der/* Missionarin, *die*

'mission statement *n.* Unternehmensleitbild, *das*

misspell /mɪs'spel/ *v.t., forms as* SPELL[1] falsch schreiben

mist /mɪst/ *n.* (fog) Nebel, *der;* (haze) Dunst, *der;* (on windscreen etc.) Beschlag, *der*

■ **mist 'up** *v.i.* [sich] beschlagen

mistake /mɪ'steɪk/ [1] *n.* Fehler, *der;* **by ~:** versehentlich
[2] *v.t., forms as* TAKE 1: **(a)** falsch verstehen
(b) ~ x for y x mit y verwechseln

mistaken /mɪ'steɪkn/ *adj.* **be ~:** sich täuschen; **a case of ~ identity** eine Verwechslung

mi'stakenly *adv.* irrtümlicherweise

mistletoe /'mɪsltəʊ/ *n.* Mistel, *die*

mistook ▶ MISTAKE 2

mistranslate /mɪstræns'leɪt/ *v.t.* falsch übersetzen

mistreat /mɪs'tri:t/ *v.t.* schlecht behandeln; (violently) misshandeln

mistreatment /mɪs'tri:tmənt/ *n.* schlechte Behandlung; (violent) Misshandlung, *die*

mistress /'mɪstrɪs/ *n.* **(a)** (Brit. Sch.: teacher) Lehrerin, *die*
(b) (lover) Geliebte, *die*

mistrust /mɪs'trʌst/ [1] *v.t.* misstrauen (+ *Dat.*)
[2] *n.* Misstrauen, *das* (**of** gegenüber + *Dat.*)

mistrustful /mɪs'trʌstfl/ *adj.* misstrauisch (**of** gegenüber)

'misty *adj.* dunstig

misunderstand /mɪsʌndə'stænd/ *v.t., forms as* UNDERSTAND: missverstehen

misunder'standing *n.* Missverständnis, *das*

misuse [1] /mɪs'ju:z/ *v.t.* missbrauchen
[2] /mɪs'ju:s/ *n.* Missbrauch, *der*

mite /maɪt/ *n.* **(a)** (Zool.) Milbe, *die*
(b) (small child) Würmchen, *das* (fam.); **poor little ~:** armes Kleines

miter (Amer.) ▶ MITRE

mitigate /'mɪtɪgeɪt/ *v.t.* **(a)** (reduce) lindern
(b) (make less severe) mildern; **mitigating circumstances** mildernde Umstände

mitre /'maɪtə(r)/ *n.* (Brit. Eccl.) Mitra, *die*

mitten /'mɪtn/ *n.* Fausthandschuh, *der*

mix /mɪks/ [1] *v.t.* [ver]mischen; verrühren ‹*Zutaten*›
[2] *v.i.* **(a)** (become ~ed) sich vermischen
(b) (be sociable, participate) Umgang mit anderen [Menschen] haben; **~ with** Umgang haben mit; **~ well** kontaktfreudig sein
[3] *n.* (coll.) Mischung, *die;* **[cake] ~:** Backmischung, *die*

■ **mix 'up** *v.t.* **(a)** vermischen **(b)** (muddle) durcheinander bringen; (confuse) verwechseln **(c) be/get ~ed up in sth.** in etw. (*Akk.*) verwickelt sein/werden

mixed /mɪkst/ *adj.* **(a)** gemischt **(b)** (diverse) unterschiedlich

mixed: ~ 'bag *n.* bunte Mischung; **~ 'blessing** *n.* **be a ~ blessing** nicht nur Vorteile haben; **~ 'grill** *n.* Mixedgrill, *der* (Gastr.); gemischte Grillplatte; **~ 'marriage** *n.* Mischehe, *die;* **~ 'up** *adj.* (fig. coll.) verwirrt, konfus ‹*Person*›; **be/feel very ~ up** völlig durcheinander sein

'mixer *n.* (for food) Küchenmaschine, *die*; **hand ~:** Handrührgerät, *das*

mixture /'mɪkstʃə(r)/ *n.* **(a)** Mischung, *die* (**of** aus) **(b)** (Med.) Mixtur, *die*

'mix-up *n.* Durcheinander, *das;* (misunderstanding) Missverständnis, *das*

mm. *abbr.* = **millimetre[s]** mm

moan /məʊn/ [1] *n.* **(a)** Stöhnen, *das* **(b) have a ~** (complain) jammern [2] *v.i.* **(a)** stöhnen (**with** vor + *Dat.*) **(b)** (complain) jammern (**about** über + *Akk.*) [3] *v.t.* stöhnen

moat /məʊt/ *n.* **[castle] ~:** Burggraben, *der*

mob /mɒb/ [1] *n.* **(a)** (rabble) Mob, *der* **(b)** (coll.: group) **Peter and his ~:** Peter und seine ganze Blase (salopp) [2] *v.t.,* **-bb-** belagern (ugs.) ‹*Star*›

mobile /'məʊbaɪl/ [1] *adj.* beweglich; (on wheels) fahrbar; **upwardly ~:** sozial aufsteigend [2] *n.* Mobile, *das;* (**~** phone) Handy, *das*

mobile: ~ 'home *n.* transportable Wohneinheit; **~ 'phone** *n.* Mobiltelefon, *das*

mobility /mə'bɪlɪtɪ/ *n.* Beweglichkeit, *die*

mobilization /məʊbɪlaɪ'zeɪʃn/ *n.* Mobilisierung, *die*

mobilize /'məʊbɪlaɪz/ *v.t.* mobilisieren

moccasin /'mɒkəsɪn/ *n.* Mokassin, *der*

mocha /'mɒkə/ *n.* Mokka, *der*

mock /mɒk/ [1] *v.t.* sich lustig machen über (+ *Akk.*) [2] *v.i.* sich lustig machen (**at** über + *Akk.*) [3] *adj.* Schein‹*kampf, -angriff, -ehe*›

mockery /'mɒkərɪ/ *n.* Spott, *der;* **make a ~ of sth.** etw. zur Farce machen

'mock-up *n.* Modell [in Originalgröße]

mode /məʊd/ *n.* **(a)** Art [und Weise], *die* **(b)** (fashion) Mode, *die*

model /'mɒdl/ [1] *n.* **(a)** Modell, *das* **(b)** (example to be imitated) Vorbild, *das* **(c)** (Art) Modell, *das;* (Fashion) Mannequin, *das;* (male) Dressman, *der* [2] *adj.* **(a)** (exemplary) Muster- **(b)** (miniature) Modell- [3] *v.t.,* (Brit.) **-ll-: (a)** modellieren; **~ sth. after** *or* **[up]on sth.** etw. einer Sache (*Dat.*) nachbilden **(b)** (Fashion) vorführen [4] *v.i.* (Fashion) als Mannequin/Dressman arbeiten; (Art) Modell stehen/sitzen

modem /'məʊdem/ *n.* Modem, *der*

moderate [1] /'mɒdərət/ *adj.* **(a)** gemäßigt ‹*Ansichten*›; maßvoll ‹*Trinker, Forderungen*› **(b)** mittler... ‹*Größe, Menge, Wert*›; (reasonable) angemessen ‹*Preis, Summe*› [2] /'mɒdərət/ *n.* Gemäßigte, *der/die* [3] /'mɒdəreɪt/ *v.t.* mäßigen [4] *v.i.* nachlassen

moderately /'mɒdərətlɪ/ *adv.* einigermaßen; mäßig ‹*begeistert, groß, begabt*›

moderation /mɒdə'reɪʃn/ *n.* Mäßigkeit, *die;* **in ~:** mit Maßen

modern /'mɒdn/ *adj.* modern; heutig ‹*Zeit[alter], Welt, Mensch*›; **~ art/music** moderne Kunst/Musik; **~ history** neuere Geschichte; **~ languages** neuere Sprachen

modernize /'mɒdənaɪz/ *v.t.* modernisieren

modest /'mɒdɪst/ *adj.* bescheiden; einfach ‹*Haus, Kleidung*›

'modestly *adv.* bescheiden

'modesty *n.* Bescheidenheit, *die*

modification /mɒdɪfɪ'keɪʃn/ *n.* [Ab]änderung, *die*

modify /'mɒdɪfaɪ/ *v.t.* [ab]ändern

modulate /'mɒdjʊleɪt/ *v.t. & i.* modulieren

modulation /mɒdjʊ'leɪʃn/ *n.* Modulation, *die*

module /'mɒdju:l/ *n.* **(a)** Bauelement, *das* **(b)** (Astronaut.) **command ~:** Kommandoeinheit, *die* **(c)** (Educ.) Unterrichtseinheit, *die*

mohair /'məʊheə(r)/ *n.* Mohair, *der*

moist /mɔɪst/ *adj.* feucht (**with** von)

moisten /'mɔɪsn/ *v.t.* anfeuchten

moisture /'mɔɪstʃə(r)/ *n.* Feuchtigkeit, *die*

moisturize /'mɔɪstjʊraɪz, 'mɔɪstʃəraɪz/ *v.t.* befeuchten; **~ the skin** der Haut (*Dat.*) Feuchtigkeit zuführen; ‹*Creme:*› der Haut (*Dat.*) Feuchtigkeit verleihen

moisturizer /'mɔɪstʃəraɪzə(r)/, **moisturizing cream** /'mɔɪstʃəraɪzɪŋ kri:m/ *ns.* Feuchtigkeitscreme, *die*

molar /'məʊlə(r)/ *n.* Backenzahn, *der*

molasses /mə'læsɪz/ *n.* Melasse, *die*

mold (Amer.) ▶ MOULD[1, 2]

molder, molding, moldy (Amer.) ▶ MOULD-

mole[1] /məʊl/ *n.* (on skin) Leberfleck, *der*

mole[2] *n.* (animal) Maulwurf, *der*

molecular /mə'lekjʊlə(r)/ *adj.* molekular

molecule /'mɒlɪkju:l/ *n.* Molekül, *das*

'molehill *n.* Maulwurfshügel, *der*

molest /mə'lest/ *v.t.* belästigen

mollify /'mɒlɪfaɪ/ *v.t.* besänftigen

mollusc, (Amer.) **mollusk** /'mɒləsk/ *n.* Weichtier, *das*

mollycoddle /'mɒlɪkɒdl/ *v.t.* [ver]hätscheln
molt (Amer.) ▶ MOULT
molten /'məʊltn/ *adj.* geschmolzen
mom /mɒm/ (Amer. coll.) ▶ MUM[2]
moment /'məʊmənt/ *n.* Augenblick, *der;* **at any ~,** (coll.) **any ~:** jeden Augenblick; **one** *or* **just a** *or* **wait a ~!** einen Augenblick!; **in a ~** (very soon) sofort; **at the ~:** im Augenblick; **the ~ of truth** die Stunde der Wahrheit
momentarily /'məʊməntərɪlɪ/ *adv.* einen Augenblick lang
momentary /'məʊməntərɪ/ *adj.* kurz
momentous /mə'mentəs/ *adj.* (important) bedeutsam; (of consequence) folgenschwer
momentum /mə'mentəm/ *n.* Schwung, *der*
Mon. *abbr.* = **Monday** Mo.
monarch /'mɒnək/ *n.* Monarch, *der*/Monarchin, *die*
'monarchy *n.* Monarchie, *die*
monastery /'mɒnəstrɪ/ *n.* Kloster, *das*
monastic /mə'næstɪk/ *adj.* mönchisch
Monday /'mʌndeɪ, 'mʌndɪ/ *n.* Montag, *der; see also* FRIDAY
monetary /'mʌnɪtərɪ/ *adj.* **(a)** (of currency) monetär; Währungs‹*politik, -system*›; **~ union** Währungsunion, *die*
(b) (of money) finanziell
money /'mʌnɪ/ *n.* Geld, *das;* **make ~** ‹*Person:*› [viel] Geld verdienen; ‹*Geschäft:*› etwas einbringen; **for 'my ~:** wenn man mich fragt
money: ~ bag *n.* Geldsack, *der;* **~ belt** *n.* Geldgürtel, *der;* **~ box** *n.* Sparbüchse, *die;* **~making** *adj.* Gewinn bringend; **~ order** *n.* Postanweisung, *die*
Mongolia /mɒŋ'gəʊlɪə/ *pr. n.* Mongolei, *die*
Mongolian /mɒŋ'gəʊlɪən/ [1] *adj.* mongolisch; **sb. is ~:** jmd. ist Mongole/Mongolin
[2] *n.* (person) Mongole, *der*/Mongolin, *die*
mongrel /'mʌŋgrəl/ *n.* **~ [dog]** Promenadenmischung, *die*
monitor /'mɒnɪtə(r)/ [1] *n.* **(a)** (Sch.) Aufsichtsschüler, *der*/-schülerin, *die*
(b) (Med., Telev., Comp.) Monitor, *der*
[2] *v.t.* beobachten ‹*Wetter, Flugzeug*›; abhören ‹*Sendung, Telefongespräch*›
monk /mʌŋk/ *n.* Mönch, *der*
monkey /'mʌŋkɪ/ *n.* Affe, *der*
monkey: ~ business *n.* (coll.: mischief) Schabernack, *der;* **~ nut** *n.* Erdnuss, *die;* **~ wrench** *n.* Universalschraubenschlüssel, *der*
mono /'mɒnəʊ/ *adj.* Mono‹*platte*[*nspieler*], *-wiedergabe*›
monochrome /'mɒnəkrəʊm/ *adj.* monochrom (fachspr.); einfarbig; Schwarzweiß- (Ferns.)
monocle /'mɒnəkl/ *n.* Monokel, *das*
monogamous /mə'nɒgəməs/ *adj.* monogam
monogamy /mə'nɒgəmɪ/ *n.* Monogamie, *die;* Einehe, *die*
monogram /'mɒnəgræm/ *n.* Monogramm, *das*
monogrammed /'mɒnəgræmd/ *adj.* monogrammiert; ‹*Taschentuch usw.:*› mit Monogramm
monologue (*Amer.:* **monolog**) /'mɒnəlɒg/ *n.* Monolog, *der*
monopolize /mə'nɒpəlaɪz/ *v.t.* (Econ.) monopolisieren; (fig.) mit Beschlag belegen; **~ the conversation** den/die anderen nicht zu Wort kommen lassen
monopoly /mə'nɒpəlɪ/ *n.* **(a)** (Econ.) Monopol, *das* (**of** auf + *Akk.*)
(b) (exclusive possession) alleiniger Besitz
monotone /'mɒnətəʊn/ *n.* gleich bleibender Ton
monotonous /mə'nɒtənəs/ *adj.*, **mo'notonously** *adv.* eintönig
monotony /mə'nɒtənɪ/ *n.* Eintönigkeit, *die*
monsoon /mɒn'suːn/ *n.* Monsun, *der*
monster /'mɒnstə(r)/ *n.* **(a)** (creature) Ungeheuer, *das;* (huge thing) Ungetüm, *das*
(b) (inhuman person) Unmensch, *der*
monstrosity /mɒn'strɒsɪtɪ/ *n.* **(a)** (outrageous thing) Ungeheuerlichkeit, *die*
(b) (hideous building etc.) Ungetüm, *das*
monstrous /'mɒnstrəs/ *adj.* **(a)** (huge) riesig
(b) (outrageous) ungeheuerlich
(c) (atrocious) scheußlich
month /mʌnθ/ *n.* Monat, *der;* **for a ~/~s** einen Monat [lang]/monatelang
'monthly [1] *adj.* monatlich; Monats‹*einkommen, -gehalt*›
[2] *adv.* einmal im Monat
[3] *n.* Monatsschrift, *die*
monument /'mɒnjʊmənt/ *n.* Denkmal, *das*
monumental /mɒnjʊ'mentl/ *adj.* **(a)** (massive) monumental
(b) gewaltig ‹*Misserfolg, Irrtum*›
moo /muː/ [1] *n.* Muhen, *das*
[2] *v.i.* muhen
mooch /muːtʃ/ *v.i.* (coll.) **~ about** *or* **around/along** herumschleichen (ugs.)/zockeln (ugs.)
mood /muːd/ *n.* **(a)** Stimmung, *die;* **be in a good/bad ~:** [bei] guter/schlechter Laune sein; **I'm not in the ~:** ich hab keine Lust dazu
(b) (bad ~) Verstimmung, *die*
'moody *adj.* **(a)** (sullen) missmutig
(b) (subject to moods) launenhaft
moon /muːn/ *n.* Mond, *der*
moon: ~beam *n.* Mondstrahl, *der;* **~light** [1] *n.* Mondlicht, *das;* Mondschein, *der;* [2] *v.i.* (coll.) nebenberuflich abends arbeiten; **~lit** *adj.* mondbeschienen (geh.)
moor[1] /mʊə(r), mɔː(r)/ *n.* (Geog.) [Hoch]moor, *das*
moor[2] *v.t. & i.* festmachen; vertäuen
'moorhen *n.* [Grünfüßiges] Teichhuhn

'mooring *n.* **~[s]** Anlegestelle, *die*

'mooring post *n.* Pfahl, *der;* ≈ Duckdalben, *der*

moorland /'mʊələnd, 'mɔ:lənd/ *n.* Moorland, *das*

moose /mu:s/ *n., pl. same* Amerikanischer Elch

moot /mu:t/ **1** *adj.* umstritten; offen ‹*Frage*›; strittig ‹*Punkt*›
2 *v.t.* erörtern ‹*Frage, Punkt*›

mop /mɒp/ **1** *n.* **(a)** Mopp, *der*
(b) **~ [of hair]** Wuschelkopf, *der*
2 *v.t.*, **-pp-** moppen ‹*Fußboden*›; (wipe) abwischen ‹*Träne, Schweiß, Stirn*›

■ **mop 'up** *v.t.* aufwischen

mope /məʊp/ *v.i.* Trübsal blasen

moped /'məʊped/ *n.* Moped, *das*

moral /'mɒrl/ **1** *adj.* **(a)** moralisch; sittlich ‹*Wert*›; Moral‹*begriff, -prinzip*›
(b) (virtuous) moralisch ‹*Leben, Person*›
2 *n.* **(a)** Moral, *die*
(b) *in pl.* (habits) Moral, *die*

morale /mə'rɑ:l/ Moral, *die;* **low/high ~:** schlechte/gute Moral

mo'rale-booster *n.* **be a** *or* **act as a ~ for sb.** jds. Moral heben *od.* stärken

morality /mə'rælɪtɪ/ *n.* Moral, *die*

moral sup'port *n.* moralische Unterstützung

morbid /'mɔ:bɪd/ *adj.* krankhaft; morbid (geh.) ‹*Faszination, Neigung*›

more /mɔ:(r)/ **1** *adj.* mehr; **any** *or* **some ~** (apples, books, etc.) noch welche; **any** *or* **some ~** (tea, paper, etc.) noch etwas; **any** *or* **some ~ apples/tea** noch Äpfel/Tee; **I haven't any ~ [apples/tea]** ich habe keine [Äpfel]/keinen [Tee] mehr; **~ and ~:** immer mehr
2 *n.* mehr; **~ and ~:** immer mehr; **six or ~:** mindestens sechs
3 *adv.* **(a)** mehr; **~ interesting** interessanter
(b) (nearer, rather) eher
(c) (again) wieder; **no ~, not any ~:** nicht mehr; **once ~:** noch einmal
(d) **~ and ~:** immer mehr; **~ and ~ absurd** immer absurder
(e) **~ or less** (fairly) mehr oder weniger; (approximately) annähernd

moreish /'mɔ:rɪʃ/ *adj.* (coll.) lecker

more'over *adv.* und außerdem

morgue /mɔ:g/ ▸ MORTUARY

morning /'mɔ:nɪŋ/ *n.* Morgen, *der;* (not afternoon) Vormittag, *der; attrib.* morgendlich; Morgen-; **this ~:** heute Morgen; **tomorrow ~,** (coll.) **in the ~:** morgen früh; **[early] in the ~:** am [frühen] Morgen; (regularly) [früh]morgens

morning: ~ 'after *n.* **~-'after [feeling]** (coll.: hangover) Katzenjammer, *der;* **~-'after pill** *n.* Pille [für den Morgen] danach; **~ 'star** *n.* Morgenstern, *der*

Moroccan /mə'rɒkən/ **1** *adj.* marokkanisch; **sb. is ~:** jmd. ist Marokkaner/Marokkanerin
2 *n.* Marokkaner, *der*/Marokkanerin, *die*

Morocco /mə'rɒkəʊ/ *pr. n.* Marokko (*das*)

moron /'mɔ:rɒn/ *n.* (coll.) Schwachkopf, *der* (ugs.)

morose /mə'rəʊs/ *adj.* verdrießlich

morphine /'mɔ:fi:n/ *n.* Morphin, *das*

Morse [code] /mɔ:s ('kəʊd)/ *n.* Morsealphabet, *das*

morsel /'mɔ:sl/ *n.* (of food) Bissen, *der*

mortal /'mɔ:tl/ **1** *adj.* **(a)** sterblich
(b) (fatal) tödlich (**to** für)
2 *n.* Sterbliche, *der/die*

mortality /mɔ:'tælɪtɪ/ *n.* **(a)** Sterblichkeit, *die*
(b) **~ [rate]** Sterblichkeitsrate, *die*

'mortally *adv.* tödlich

mortar /'mɔ:tə(r)/ *n.* **(a)** Mörtel, *der*
(b) (vessel) Mörser, *der*
(c) (weapon) Minenwerfer, *der;* Mörser, *der*

mortgage /'mɔ:gɪdʒ/ **1** *n.* Hypothek, *die*
2 *v.t.* mit einer Hypothek belasten

mortuary /'mɔ:tjʊərɪ/ *n.* (building) Leichenschauhaus, *das;* (room) Leichenkammer, *die*

mosaic /məʊ'zeɪɪk/ *n.* Mosaik, *das*

Moscow /'mɒskəʊ/ *pr. n.* Moskau (*das*)

Moselle /məʊ'zel/ *pr. n.* Mosel, *die*

Moslem /'mɒzləm/ ▸ MUSLIM

mosque /mɒsk/ *n.* Moschee, *die*

mosquito /mɒs'ki:təʊ/ *n., pl.* **~es** Stechmücke, *die;* (in tropics) Moskito, *der*

mos'quito net *n.* Moskitonetz, *das*

moss /mɒs/ *n.* Moos, *das*

'mossy *adj.* moosig

most /məʊst/ **1** *adj.* (in number, majority of) die meisten; (in amount) meist...; **make the ~ mistakes/the ~ noise** die meisten Fehler/den größten Lärm machen; **for the ~ part** größtenteils
2 *n.* **(a)** (greatest amount) **the ~ it will cost is £10** es wird höchstens zehn Pfund kosten; **pay the ~:** am meisten bezahlen
(b) (greater part) **~ of the girls** die meisten Mädchen; **~ of his friends** die meisten seiner Freunde; **~ of the poem** der größte Teil des Gedichts; **~ of the time** die meiste Zeit
(c) (on ~ occasions) meistens
3 *adv.* **(a)** am meisten; **the ~ interesting book** das interessanteste Buch; **~ often** am häufigsten
(b) (exceedingly) äußerst

'mostly *adv.* (most of the time) meistens; (mainly) größtenteils

MOT ▸ MOT TEST

motel /məʊ'tel/ *n.* Motel, *das*

moth /mɒθ/ *n.* Nachtfalter, *der;* (in clothes) Motte, *die*

moth: ~ball *n.* Mottenkugel, *die;* **~-eaten** *adj.* von Motten zerfressen
mother /'mʌðə(r)/ [1] *n.* Mutter, *die* [2] *v.t.* (over-protect) bemuttern
'motherboard *n.* (Comp.) Mutterplatine, *die*
'motherhood *n.* Mutterschaft, *die*
Mothering Sunday /'mʌðərɪŋ sʌndɪ/ (Brit. Eccl.) ▶ MOTHER'S DAY
mother: ~-in-law *n., pl.* **~s-in-law** Schwiegermutter, *die;* **~land** *n.* Vaterland, *das*
motherly /'mʌðəlɪ/ *adj.* mütterlich; **~ love** Mutterliebe, *die*
mother: ~-of-'pearl *n.* Perlmutt, *das;* **M~'s Day** *n.* Muttertag, *der;* **~ 'tongue** *n.* Muttersprache, *die*
moth: ~ hole *n.* Mottenloch, *das;* **~proof** *adj.* mottenfest
motif /məʊ'ti:f/ *n.* Motiv, *das*
motion /'məʊʃn/ [1] *n.* **(a)** Bewegung, *die* **(b)** (proposal) Antrag, *der* [2] *v.t. & i.* **~ [to] sb. to do sth.** jmdm. bedeuten (geh.), etw. zu tun
'motionless *adj.* bewegungslos
motivate /'məʊtɪveɪt/ *v.t.* motivieren
motivation /məʊtɪ'veɪʃn/ *n.* Motivation, *die*
motive /'məʊtɪv/ *n.* Beweggrund, *der;* **the ~ for the crime** das Tatmotiv
motley /'mɒtlɪ/ *adj.* bunt gemischt
motor /'məʊtə(r)/ [1] *n.* **(a)** Motor, *der* **(b)** (Brit.: **~** car) Auto, *das* [2] *adj.* Motor‹*mäher, -jacht usw.*› [3] *v.i.* (Brit.) [mit dem Auto] fahren
motor: ~bike *n.* (coll.) Motorrad, *das;* **~ boat** *n.* Motorboot, *das*
motorcade /'məʊtəkeɪd/ *n.* Fahrzeug- *od.* Wagenkolonne, *die*
motor: ~ car *n.* (Brit.) Kraftfahrzeug, *das;* **~ cycle** *n.* Motorrad, *das;* **~cyclist** *n.* Motorradfahrer, *der*/-fahrerin, *die*
'motoring *n.* (Brit.) Autofahren, *das*
'motorist *n.* Autofahrer, *der*/-fahrerin, *die*
motorize /'məʊtəraɪz/ *v.t.* motorisieren
motor: ~ racing *n.* Autorennsport, *der;* **~ show** *n.* Auto[mobil]ausstellung, *die;* **~ vehicle** *n.* Kraftfahrzeug, *das;* **~way** *n.* (Brit.) Autobahn, *die*
MO'T test *n.* (Brit.) ≈ TÜV, *der*
mottled /'mɒtld/ *adj.* gesprenkelt
motto /'mɒtəʊ/ *n., pl.* **~es** Motto, *das*
mould¹ /məʊld/ [1] *n.* (hollow container) Form, *die* [2] *v.t.* formen (**out of, from** aus)
mould² *n.* (Bot.) Schimmel, *der*
moulder /'məʊldə(r)/ *v.i.* **~ [away]** [ver]modern
'moulding *n.* **(a)** Formteil, *das* (**of, in** aus); (Archit.) Zierleiste, *die* **(b)** (wooden) Leiste, *die*
'mouldy *adj.* schimmlig; **go ~**: schimmeln
moult /məʊlt/ *v.i.* ‹*Vogel:*› sich mausern; ‹*Hund, Katze:*› sich haaren
mound /maʊnd/ *n.* **(a)** (of earth) Hügel, *der* **(b)** (heap) Haufen, *der*
mount /maʊnt/ [1] *n.* **(a)** **M~ Vesuvius/Everest** der Vesuv/der Mount Everest **(b)** (animal) Reittier, *das;* (horse) Pferd, *das* **(c)** (of picture, photograph) Passepartout, *das* **(d)** (for gem) Fassung, *die* [2] *v.t.* **(a)** hinaufsteigen ‹*Treppe*›; steigen auf (+ *Akk.*) ‹*Plattform, Reittier, Fahrzeug*› **(b)** aufziehen ‹*Bild*›; einfassen ‹*Edelstein usw.*› **(c)** inszenieren ‹*Stück, Oper*›; organisieren ‹*Ausstellung*›; durchführen ‹*Angriff, Operation*› [3] *v.i.* **~ [up]** (increase) steigen (**to** auf + *Akk.*)
mountain /'maʊntɪn/ *n.* Berg, *der;* **in the ~s** im Gebirge
mountain: ~ bike *n.* Mountainbike, *das;* **~ chain** *n.* Gebirgszug, *der*
mountaineer /maʊntɪ'nɪə(r)/ *n.* Bergsteiger, *der*/Bergsteigerin, *die*
mountai'neering *n.* Bergsteigen, *das*
mountainous /'maʊntɪnəs/ *adj.* **(a)** gebirgig **(b)** (huge) riesig
mountain: ~ 'range *n.* Gebirgszug, *der;* **~side** *n.* [Berg][ab]hang, *der;* **~ top** *n.* Berggipfel, *der*
mourn /mɔ:n/ [1] *v.i.* trauern; **~ for** *or* **over** trauern um ‹*Toten*› [2] *v.t.* betrauern
'mourner *n.* Trauernde, *der/die*
mournful /'mɔ:nfl/ *adj.* klagend ‹*Stimme, Ton, Schrei*›; trauervoll (geh.) ‹*Person*›
'mourning *n.* Trauer, *die;* **be in/go into ~**: Trauer tragen/anlegen
mouse /maʊs/ *n., pl.* **mice** /maɪs/ Maus, *die*
mouse: ~ button *n.* (Comp.) Maustaste, *die;* **~ click** *n.* (Comp.) Mausklick, *der;* **~ mat** *n.* (Comp.) Mauspad, *das;* **~ pointer** *n.* (Comp.) Mauszeiger, *der;* **~trap** *n.* Mausefalle, *die*
mousse /mu:s/ *n.* Mousse, *die*
moustache /mə'stɑ:ʃ/ *n.* Schnurrbart, *der*
mousy /'maʊsɪ/ *adj.* **(a)** mattbraun ‹*Haar*› **(b)** (timid) scheu
mouth [1] /maʊθ/ *n.* **(a)** (of person) Mund, *der;* (of animal) Maul, *das;* **with one's ~ open/full** mit offenem/vollem Mund **(b)** (harbour entrance) [Hafen]einfahrt, *die;* (of tunnel, cave) Eingang, *der;* (of river) Mündung, *die* [2] /maʊð/ *v.t.* mit Lippenbewegungen sagen
mouthful /'maʊθfʊl/ *n.* Mundvoll, *der*
mouth: ~ organ *n.* Mundharmonika, *die;* **~piece** *n.* **(a)** Mundstück, *das;* **(b)** (fig.) Sprachrohr, *das*
movable /'mu:vəbl/ *adj.* beweglich
move /mu:v/ [1] *n.* **(a)** (change of home) Umzug, *der*

(b) (action taken) Schritt, *der;* (Footb. etc.) Spielzug, *der*
(c) (turn in game) Zug, *der;* **make a ~:** ziehen; **it's your ~:** du bist am Zug
(d) be on the ~ ‹*Person:*› unterwegs sein
(e) make a ~ (do sth.) etwas tun; (coll.: leave) losziehen (ugs.)
(f) get a ~ on (coll.) einen Zahn zulegen (ugs.); **get a ~ on!** (coll.) [mach] Tempo! (ugs.)
[2] *v.t.* **(a)** (change position of) bewegen; wegräumen ‹*Hindernis, Schutt*›; (transport) befördern; **~ sth. to a new position** etw. an einen neuen Platz bringen; **~ house** umziehen
(b) (in game) ziehen
(c) (affect) bewegen; **~ sb. to tears** jmdn. zu Tränen rühren; **be ~d by sth.** über etw. (*Akk.*) gerührt sein
(d) (prompt) **~ sb. to do sth.** jmdn. dazu bewegen, etw. zu tun
(e) (propose) beantragen
[3] *v.i.* **(a)** sich bewegen; (in vehicle) fahren
(b) (in games) ziehen
(c) (do sth.) handeln
(d) (change home) umziehen **(to** nach); **~ into a flat** in eine Wohnung einziehen; **~ out of a flat** aus einer Wohnung ausziehen; **~ to London** nach London ziehen
(e) (change posture or state) sich bewegen; **don't ~!** keine Bewegung!

■ **move a'bout** [1] *v.i.* zugange sein; (travel) unterwegs sein
[2] *v.t.* herumräumen

■ **move a'long** [1] *v.i.* **(a)** gehen/fahren
(b) ~ along, please! gehen/fahren Sie bitte weiter!
[2] *v.t.* zum Weitergehen/-fahren auffordern

■ **move 'in** [1] *v.i.* **(a)** (to home etc.) einziehen
(b) ~ in on ‹*Truppen, Polizeikräfte:*› vorrücken gegen
[2] *v.t.* hineinbringen

■ **move 'off** *v.i.* sich in Bewegung setzen

■ **move 'on** [1] *v.i.* weitergehen/-fahren; **~ on to another question** (fig.) zu einer anderen Frage übergehen
[2] *v.t.* zum Weitergehen/-fahren auffordern

■ **move 'out** *v.t.* ausziehen **(of** aus)

■ **move 'over** *v.i.* rücken

■ **move 'up** *v.i.* **(a)** rücken
(b) (in queue, hierarchy) aufrücken

'movement *n.* **(a)** Bewegung, *die;* (trend, tendency) Tendenz, *die* **(towards** zu)
(b) *in pl.* Aktivitäten *Pl.*
(c) (Mus.) Satz, *der*

movie /'mu:vɪ/ *n.* (Amer. coll.) Film, *der;* **the ~s** der Film; **go to the ~s** ins Kino gehen

moving /'mu:vɪŋ/ *adj.* **(a)** beweglich
(b) (affecting) ergreifend

mow /məʊ/ *v.t., p.p.* **mown** /məʊn/ *or* **mowed** /məʊd/ mähen

■ **mow 'down** *v.t.* (shoot) niedermähen ‹*Menschen*›

'mower *n.* Rasenmäher, *der*

mown ▶ MOW

MP *abbr.* = **Member of Parliament**

m.p.g. *abbr.* = **miles per gallon**

m.p.h. *abbr.* = **miles per hour**

MPV *abbr.* = **multi-purpose vehicle**

Mr /'mɪstə(r)/ *n.* Herr; (in an address) Herrn

Mrs /'mɪsɪz/ *n.* Frau

Ms /mɪz/ *n.* Frau

MS *abbr.* (Med.) = **multiple sclerosis** MS

Mt. *abbr.* = **Mount**

much /mʌtʃ/ [1] *adj.,* **more** /mɔ:(r)/, **most** /məʊst/ viel; **too ~:** zu viel *indekl*
[2] *n.* vieles; **~ of the day** der Großteil des Tages; **not be ~ to look at** nicht sehr ansehnlich sein
[3] *adv.,* **more, most (a)** viel ‹*besser, schöner usw.*›; **~ more lively/attractive** viel lebhafter/attraktiver
(b) mit Abstand ‹*der/die/das Beste, Klügste usw.*›
(c) (greatly) sehr ‹*lieben, genießen usw.*›; (for ~ of the time) viel ‹*lesen, spielen usw.*›; (often) oft ‹*sehen, besuchen usw.*›
(d) [pretty *or* **very] ~ the same** fast [genau] der-/die-/dasselbe

muck /mʌk/ *n.* **(a)** (coll.: something disgusting) Dreck, *der* (ugs.)
(b) (coll.: nonsense) Mist, *der* (ugs.)

■ **muck a'bout, muck a'round** (Brit. coll.) *v.i.* **(a)** herumalbern (ugs.)
(b) (tinker) herumfummeln **(with** an + *Dat.*)

■ **muck 'in** *v.i.* (coll.) mit anpacken **(with** bei)

■ **muck 'up** *v.t.* **(a)** (Brit. coll.: bungle) vermurksen (ugs.)
(b) (make dirty) dreckig machen (ugs.)
(c) (coll.: spoil) vermasseln (salopp)

'mucky *adj.* dreckig (ugs.)

mucus /'mju:kəs/ *n.* Schleim, *der*

mud /mʌd/ *n.* Schlamm, *der*

muddle /'mʌdl/ [1] *n.* Durcheinander, *das*
[2] *v.t.* **~ [up]** durcheinander bringen; **~ up** (mix up) verwechseln **(with** mit)

■ **muddle a'long, muddle 'on** *v.i.* vor sich (*Akk.*) hin wursteln (ugs.)

■ **muddle 'through** *v.i.* sich durchwursteln (ugs.)

muddy /'mʌdɪ/ *adj.* schlammig; **get** *or* **become ~:** verschlammen

'mudguard *n.* Schutzblech, *das;* (of car) Kotflügel, *der*

muesli /'mju:zlɪ/ *n.* Müsli, *das*

muff¹ /mʌf/ *n.* Muff, *der*

muff² *v.t.* verpatzen (ugs.)

muffin /'mʌfɪn/ *n.* Muffin, *der*

muffle /'mʌfl/ *v.t.* **(a)** (envelop) **~ [up]** einhüllen
(b) dämpfen ‹*Geräusch*›

'muffler *n.* **(a)** (wrap, scarf) Schal, *der*
(b) (Amer. Motor Veh.) Schalldämpfer, *der*

mug /mʌg/ [1] *n.* **(a)** Becher, *der* (*meist mit Henkel*); (for beer etc.) Krug, *der*
(b) (coll.: face, mouth) Visage, *die* (salopp) ⋯›

(c) (Brit. coll.: gullible person) Trottel, *der* (ugs.) **2** *v.t.*, **-gg-** (rob) überfallen und berauben

'mugger *n.* Straßenräuber, *der*/-räuberin, *die*

'mugging *n.* Straßenraub, *der*

muggy /'mʌgɪ/ *adj.* schwül

mule /mju:l/ *n.* Maultier, *das*

multi: ~coloured (Brit.; Amer.: **~colored**) *adj.* mehrfarbig; bunt ‹*Stoff, Kleid*›; **~'cultural** *adj.* multikulturell; **~function button** *n.* Multifunktionstaste, *die;* **~media** *n. sing.* Multimedia, *das;* **~millio'naire** *n.* Multimillionär, *der*/-millionärin, *die;* **~national** /mʌltɪ'næʃənl/ **1** *adj.* multinational; **2** *n.* multinationaler Konzern, *der;* Multi, *der* (ugs.)

multiple /'mʌltɪpl/ *adj.* mehrfach

multiple: ~-'choice *adj.* Multiplechoice‹*test, -frage*›; **~ 'store** *n.* (Brit.) Kettenladen, *der*

multiplication /mʌltɪplɪ'keɪʃn/ *n.* Multiplikation, *die*

multiply /'mʌltɪplaɪ/ **1** *v.t.* multiplizieren, malnehmen (**by** mit)
2 *v.i.* sich vermehren

m

multi: ~-purpose *adj.* Mehrzweck-; **~-purpose 'vehicle** *n.* Großraumlimousine, *die;* **'~-storey** *adj.* mehrstöckig; mehrgeschossig; **~-storey car park/block of flats** Parkhaus/Wohnhochhaus, *das;* **~track** *adj.* mehrspurig; Mehrspur‹*aufnahme, -ton, -tonbandgerät*›

multitude /'mʌltɪtju:d/ *n.* (crowd) Menge, *die;* (great number) Vielzahl, *die*

mum¹ /mʌm/ (coll.) **1** *int.* **~'s the word** nicht weitersagen!
2 *adj.* **keep ~:** den Mund halten (ugs.)

mum² *n.* (Brit. coll.: mother) Mama, *die* (fam.)

mumble /'mʌmbl/ *v.i. & t.* nuscheln (ugs.)

mummy¹ *n.* (Brit. coll.: mother) Mutti, *die* (fam.)

mummy² /'mʌmɪ/ *n.* Mumie, *die*

mumps /mʌmps/ *n.* Mumps, *der*

munch /mʌntʃ/ *v.t. & i.* **~ [one's food]** mampfen (salopp)

mundane /mʌn'deɪn/ *adj.* **(a)** (dull) banal **(b)** (worldly) weltlich

Munich /'mju:nɪk/ *pr. n.* München (*das*)

municipal /mjʊ'nɪsɪpl/ *adj.* kommunal; Kommunal‹*politik, -verwaltung*›

munition /mju:'nɪʃn/ *n., usu. in pl.* Kriegsmaterial, *das;* **~[s] factory** Rüstungsbetrieb, *der*

mural /'mjʊərl/ *n.* Wandbild, *das*

murder /'mɜ:də(r)/ **1** *n.* Mord, *der* (**of** an + *Dat.*)
2 *v.t.* ermorden

'murderer *n.* Mörder, *der*/Mörderin, *die*

murderess /'mɜ:dərɪs/ *n.* Mörderin, *die*

murderous /'mɜ:dərəs/ *adj.* tödlich; Mord‹*absicht, -drohung*›; mörderisch (ugs.) ‹*Kampf*›

murk /mɜ:k/ *n.* Dunkelheit, *die*

'murky *adj.* **(a)** (dark) düster
(b) (dirty) schmutzig-trüb ‹*Wasser*›

murmur /'mɜ:mə(r)/ **1** *n.* **(a)** (subdued sound) Rauschen, *das*
(b) (expression of discontent) Murren, *das*
(c) (soft speech) Murmeln, *das*
2 *v.t.* murmeln
3 *v.i.* ‹*Person:*› murmeln; (complain) murren

muscle /'mʌsl/ *n.* Muskel, *der*

muscular /'mʌskjʊlə(r)/ *adj.* **(a)** (Anat.) Muskel-
(b) (strong) muskulös

muse /mju:z/ (literary) *v.i.* [nach]sinnen (geh.) (**on, over** über + *Akk.*)

museum /mju:'zi:əm/ *n.* Museum, *das*

mush /mʌʃ/ *n.* Brei, *der*

mushroom /'mʌʃrʊm, 'mʌʃru:m/ **1** *n.* Pilz, *der;* (cultivated) Champignon, *der*
2 *v.i.* wie Pilze aus dem Boden schießen

'mushroom cloud *n.* Rauchpilz, *der;* (after nuclear explosion) Atompilz, *der*

'mushy *adj.* breiig

music /'mju:zɪk/ *n.* **(a)** Musik, *die;* **piece of ~:** Musikstück, *das;* **set sth. to ~:** etw. vertonen
(b) (score) Noten *Pl.*

musical /'mju:zɪkl/ **1** *adj.* musikalisch; Musik‹*instrument, -verständnis, -notation, -abend*›
2 *n.* Musical, *das*

'musical box *n.* (Brit.) Spieldose, *die*

musician /mju:'zɪʃn/ *n.* Musiker, *der*/Musikerin, *die*

music: ~ lesson *n.* Musikstunde, *die;* **~ room** *n.* Musiksaal, *der;* **~ stand** *n.* Notenständer, *der;* **~ teacher** *n.* Musiklehrer, *der*/-lehrerin, *die;* **~ video** *n.* Musikvideo, *das*

Muslim /'mʊslɪm, 'mʌzlɪm/ **1** *adj.* moslemisch
2 *n.* Moslem, *der*/Moslime, *die*

muslin /'mʌzlɪn/ *n.* Musselin, *der*

mussel /'mʌsl/ *n.* Muschel, *die*

must /məst, *stressed* mʌst/ **1** *v. aux., only in pres., neg.* (coll.) **mustn't** /'mʌsnt/ müssen; *with neg.* dürfen
2 *n.* (coll.) Muss, *das*

mustache ▶ MOUSTACHE

mustard /'mʌstəd/ *n.* Senf, *der*

muster /'mʌstə(r)/ **1** *n.* **pass ~:** akzeptabel sein
2 *v.t.* versammeln; (Mil., Naut.) [zum Appell] antreten lassen; (fig.) zusammennehmen ‹*Kraft, Mut, Verstand*›
3 *v.i.* sich [ver]sammeln

▪ **muster 'up** *v.t.* aufbringen

mustn't /'mʌsnt/ (coll.) = **must not;** ▶ MUST 1

musty /'mʌstɪ/ *adj.* muffig

mutant /'mju:tənt/ 1 *adj.* mutiert 2 *n.* Mutante, *die*
mutation /mju:'teɪʃn/ *n.* Mutation, *die*
mute /mju:t/ 1 *adj.* stumm 2 *n.* Stumme, *der/die*
'muted *adj.* gedämpft
mutilate /'mju:tɪleɪt/ *v.t.* verstümmeln
mutilation /mju:tɪ'leɪʃn/ *n.* Verstümmelung, *die*
mutinous /'mju:tɪnəs/ *adj.* meuternd
mutiny /'mju:tɪnɪ/ 1 *n.* Meuterei, *die* 2 *v.i.* meutern
mutter /'mʌtə(r)/ *v.i. & t.* murmeln
'muttering *n.* Gemurmel, *das*
mutton /'mʌtn/ *n.* Hammelfleisch, *das*
mutual /'mju:tjʊəl/ *adj.* **(a)** gegenseitig **(b)** (coll.: shared) gemeinsam
'mutually *adv.* **(a)** gegenseitig; **be ~ exclusive** sich [gegenseitig] ausschließen **(b)** (in common) gemeinsam
muzak /'mju:zæk/ *n.* (often derog.) Hintergrundmusik, *die*
muzzle /'mʌzl/ 1 *n.* **(a)** (of dog) Schnauze, *die;* (of horse, cattle) Maul, *das* **(b)** (of gun) Mündung, *die* **(c)** (put over animal's mouth) Maulkorb, *der* 2 *v.t.* **(a)** einen Maulkorb anlegen (+ *Dat.*) ‹*Hund*› **(b)** (fig.) mundtot machen (ugs.) (+ *Dat.*)
muzzy /'mʌzɪ/ *adj.* verschwommen; **feel ~**: ein dumpfes Gefühl haben
MW *abbr.* (Radio) = **medium wave** MW
my /maɪ/ *poss. pron. attrib.* mein; **my[, my]!, [my] oh my!** [ach du] meine Güte! (ugs.)
myalgic encephalomyelitis /maɪæld͡ʒɪk ensefələʊmaɪə'laɪtɪs/ *n.* (Med.) myalgische Enzephalomyelitis
myopia /maɪ'ɒpɪə/ *n.* Kurzsichtigkeit, *die* (auch fig.)
myopic /maɪ'ɒpɪk/ *adj.* kurzsichtig (auch fig.)
myself /maɪ'self/ *pron.* **(a)** *emphat.* selbst; **I thought so ~**: das habe ich auch gedacht **(b)** *refl.* mich/mir. *See also* HERSELF
mysterious /mɪ'stɪərɪəs/ *adj.* rätselhaft; geheimnisvoll ‹*Fremder, Orient*›
my'steriously *adv.* auf rätselhafte Weise; geheimnisvoll ‹*lächeln usw.*›
mystery /'mɪstərɪ/ *n.* **(a)** Rätsel, *das* **(b)** (secrecy) Geheimnis, *das*
mystery: ~ tour *n.* Fahrt ins Blaue (ugs.); **~ writer** Kriminalschriftsteller, *der*/-schriftstellerin, *die*
mystic /'mɪstɪk/ 1 *adj.* mystisch 2 *n.* Mystiker, *der*/Mystikerin, *die*
mystical /'mɪstɪkl/ *adj.* mystisch
mysticism /'mɪstɪsɪzm/ *n.* Mystik, *die*
mystify /'mɪstɪfaɪ/ *v.t.* verwirren
myth /mɪθ/ *n.* Mythos, *der*
mythical /'mɪθɪkl/ *adj.* **(a)** (based on myth) mythisch **(b)** (invented) fiktiv
mythological /mɪθə'lɒd͡ʒɪkl/ *adj.* mythologisch
mythology /mɪ'θɒləd͡ʒɪ/ *n.* Mythologie, *die*

Nn

N, n /en/ *n.* N, n, *das*
N. *abbr.* **(a)** = **north** N **(b)** = **northern** n.
NAAFI /'næfɪ/ *abbr.* (Brit.) **Navy, Army and Air Force Institutes** *Kaufhaus für Angehörige der britischen Truppen*
nab /næb/ *v.t.*, **-bb-** (coll.) **(a)** (arrest) schnappen (ugs.) **(b)** (seize) sich (*Dat.*) schnappen
nag /næg/ *v.i. & t.* **-gg-: ~ [at] sb.** an jmdm. herumnörgeln; **~ [at] sb. to do sth.** jmdm. zusetzen (ugs.), dass er etw. tut
'nagging 1 *adj.* (persistent) quälend; bohrend ‹*Schmerz*› 2 *n.* Genörgel, *das*
nail /neɪl/ 1 *n.* Nagel, *der;* **hit the ~ on the head** (fig.) den Nagel auf den Kopf treffen (ugs.) 2 *v.t.* nageln (**to** an + *Akk.*)
▪ **nail 'down** *v.t.* festnageln; zunageln ‹*Kiste*›
nail: ~ brush *n.* Nagelbürste, *die;* **~ clippers** *n. pl.* **[pair of] ~ clippers** Nagelknipser, *der;* **~ file** *n.* Nagelfeile, *die;* **~ polish** *n.* Nagellack, *der;* **~ polish remover** Nagellackentferner, *der;* **~ scissors** *n. pl.* **[pair of] ~ scissors** Nagelschere, *die;* **~ varnish** (Brit.) ▶ **~** POLISH
naive, naïve /naɪ'i:v/ *adj.*, **na'ively, na'ïvely** *adv.* naiv
naked /'neɪkɪd/ *adj.* nackt; **visible to** *or* **with the ~ eye** mit bloßem Auge zu erkennen
'nakedness *n.* Nacktheit, *die*
name /neɪm/ 1 *n.* **(a)** Name, *der;* **what's your ~/the ~ of this place?** wie heißt du/dieser Ort?; **my ~ is Jack** ich heiße Jack; ⋯

last ~: Nachname, *der;* **by ~**: namentlich ‹*erwähnen, aufrufen usw.*›; **know sb. by ~**: jmdn. mit Namen kennen
(b) (reputation) Ruf, *der;* **make a ~ for oneself** sich (*Dat.*) einen Namen machen
(c) call sb. ~s jmdn. beschimpfen
2 *v.t.* **(a)** (give ~ to) einen Namen geben (+ *Dat.*); **~ sb. John** jmdn. John nennen; **~ sb./sth. after** *or* (Amer.) **for sb.** jmdn./etw. nach jmdm. benennen; **be ~d John** John heißen; **a man ~d Smith** ein Mann namens Smith
(b) (call by right ~) benennen
(c) (nominate) **~ sb. [as] sth.** jmdn. zu etw. ernennen

'name-drop *v.i.* [scheinbar beiläufig] bekannte Namen fallen lassen

'nameless *adj.* namenlos

'namely *adv.* nämlich

'namesake *n.* Namensvetter, *der*/ -schwester, *die*

nanny /'nænɪ/ *n.* (Brit.) Kindermädchen, *das*

nanny: ~ goat *n.* Ziege, *die;* **~ 'state** *n.* (derog.) Versorgungsstaat, *der*

nap /næp/ **1** *n.* Nickerchen, *das* (fam.); **have a ~**: ein Nickerchen halten
2 *v.i.*, **-pp-** dösen (ugs.); **catch sb. ~ping** (fig.) jmdn. überrumpeln

nape /neɪp/ *n.* **~ [of the neck]** Nacken, *der;* Genick, *das*

napkin /'næpkɪn/ *n.* Serviette, *die*

Naples /'neɪplz/ *pr. n.* Neapel (*das*)

nappy /'næpɪ/ *n.* (Brit.) Windel, *die*

narcissistic /nɑːsɪ'sɪstɪk/ *adj.* narzisstisch

narcissus /nɑː'sɪsəs/ *n., pl.* **narcissi** /nɑː'sɪsaɪ/ *or* **~es** Narzisse, *die*

narcotic /nɑː'kɒtɪk/ **1** *n.* **(a)** (drug) Rauschgift, *das*
(b) (active ingredient) Betäubungsmittel, *das*
2 *adj.* **(a)** narkotisch; **~ drug** Rauschgift, *das*
(b) (causing drowsiness) einschläfernd

narrate /nə'reɪt/ *v.t.* erzählen; kommentieren ‹*Film*›

narration /nə'reɪʃn/ *n.* Erzählung, *die*

narrative /'nærətɪv/ **1** *n.* Erzählung, *die*
2 *adj.* erzählend

narrator /nə'reɪtə(r)/ *n.* Erzähler, *der*/ Erzählerin, *die*

narrow /'nærəʊ/ **1** *adj.* **(a)** schmal; schmal geschnitten ‹*Rock, Hose, Ärmel usw.*›; eng ‹*Tal, Gasse*›
(b) (limited) eng; begrenzt ‹*Auswahl*›
(c) knapp ‹*Sieg, Mehrheit*›; **have a ~ escape** mit knapper Not entkommen (**from** *Dat.*)
(d) (not tolerant) engstirnig
2 *v.i.* sich verschmälern; ‹*Tal:*› sich verengen
3 *v.t.* verschmälern; (fig.) einengen

■ **narrow 'down** *v.t.* einengen (**to** auf + *Akk.*)

narrow-'minded *adj.* engstirnig

nasal /'neɪzl/ *adj.* **(a)** (Anat.) Nasen-
(b) näselnd; **speak in a ~ voice** näseln

nastily /'nɑːstɪlɪ/ *adv.* **(a)** (unpleasantly) scheußlich
(b) (ill-naturedly) gemein; **behave ~**: hässlich sein

nasty /'nɑːstɪ/ *adj.* **(a)** (unpleasant) scheußlich ‹*Geruch, Geschmack*›; gemein ‹*Trick, Person*›; hässlich ‹*Angewohnheit*›; **that was a ~ thing to say/do** das war gemein
(b) (ill-natured) böse; **be ~ to sb.** hässlich zu jmdm. sein
(c) (serious) übel; schlimm ‹*Krankheit, Husten, Verletzung*›; **she had a ~ fall** sie ist übel gefallen

nation /'neɪʃn/ *n.* Nation, *die;* (people) Volk, *das*

national /'næʃənl/ **1** *adj.* national; National‹*flagge, -held, -theater, -gericht, -charakter*›; Staats‹*sicherheit, -religion*›; überregional ‹*Rundfunkstation, Zeitung*›; landesweit ‹*Streik*›
2 *n.* (citizen) Staatsbürger, *der*/-bürgerin, *die;* **foreign ~**: Ausländer, *der*/Ausländerin, *die*

national: ~ 'anthem *n.* Nationalhymne, *die;* **~ call** *n.* (Brit. Teleph.) Inlandsgespräch, *das;* **~ 'costume** *n.* Nationaltracht, *die;* **N~ 'Health [Service]** *n.* (Brit.) staatlicher Gesundheitsdienst; **N~ Health doctor/patient/spectacles** ≈ Kassenarzt, *der*/ -patient, *der*/-brille, *die;* **N~ In'surance** *n.* (Brit.) Sozialversicherung, *die*

nationalism /'næʃənəlɪzm/ *n.* Nationalismus, *der*

nationalist /'næʃənəlɪst/ **1** *n.* Nationalist, *der*/Nationalistin, *die*
2 *adj.* nationalistisch

nationality /næʃə'nælɪtɪ/ *n.* Staatsangehörigkeit, *die;* **what's his ~?** welche Staatsangehörigkeit hat er?

nationalization /næʃənəlaɪ'zeɪʃn/ *n.* Verstaatlichung, *die*

nationalize /'næʃənəlaɪz/ *v.t.* verstaatlichen

'nationally *adv.* landesweit

National: n~ 'park *n.* Nationalpark, *der;* **~ 'Savings** *n. pl.* (Brit.) Staatsschuldverschreibungen *Pl.;* **~ Savings certificate** Sparkassengutschein, *der;* öffentlicher Sparbrief; **n~ 'service** *n.* (Brit.) Wehrdienst, *der;* **do n~ service** seinen Wehrdienst ableisten; **~ 'Socialist** *n.* Nationalsozialist, *der*/-sozialistin, *die; attrib.* nationalsozialistisch; **~ Vo'cational Qualification** *n.* (Brit.) *staatliches Berufsausbildungsprogramm*

native /'neɪtɪv/ **1** *n.* **(a)** (of specified place) **a ~ of Britain** ein gebürtiger Brite/eine gebürtige Britin
(b) (person born in a place) Eingeborene, *der*/ *die*
(c) (local inhabitant) Einheimische, *der*/*die*
2 *adj.* eingeboren; einheimisch ‹*Pflanze, Tier*›; **~ inhabitant** Eingeborene/

Einheimische, *der/die;* ~ **land** Geburts- *od.* Heimatland, *das;* ~ **language** Muttersprache, *die*

nativity /nəˈtɪvɪtɪ/ *n.* **the N~ [of Christ]** die Geburt Christi

naˈtivity play *n.* Krippenspiel, *das*

NATO, Nato /ˈneɪtəʊ/ *abbr.* = **North Atlantic Treaty Organization** NATO, *die*

natter /ˈnætə(r)/ (Brit. coll.) **1** *v.i.* quatschen (ugs.)
2 *n.* **have a ~:** quatschen (ugs.)

natural /ˈnætʃrəl/ *adj.* natürlich; Natur‹*zustand, -seide, -gewalt*›

natural: ~ **ˈchildbirth** *n.* natürliche Geburt; ~ **ˈgas** *n.* Erdgas, *das;* ~ **ˈhistory** *n.* Naturkunde, *die*

naturalism /ˈnætʃrəlɪzm/ *n.* Naturalismus, *der*

naturalist /ˈnætʃrəlɪst/ *n.* Naturforscher, *der*/-forscherin, *die*

naturalization /nætʃrəlaɪˈzeɪʃn/ *n.* Einbürgerung, *die*

naturalize /ˈnætʃrəlaɪz/ *v.t.* einbürgern

ˈnaturally *adv.* **(a)** (by nature) von Natur aus ‹*blass, fleißig usw.*›; (in a true-to-life way) naturgetreu
(b) (of course) natürlich

ˈnaturalness Natürlichkeit, *die*

nature /ˈneɪtʃə(r)/ *n.* **(a)** Natur, *die*
(b) (essential qualities) Beschaffenheit, *die;* **in the ~ of things** naturgemäß
(c) (kind) Art, *die;* **things of this ~:** derartiges
(d) (character) Wesen, *das;* **be proud/friendly** *etc.* **by ~:** ein stolzes/freundliches *usw.* Wesen haben

nature: ~ **conservation** *n.* Naturschutz, *der;* ~ **lover** *n.* Naturfreund, *der*/-freundin, *die;* ~ **reserve** *n.* Naturschutzgebiet, *das;* ~ **study** *n.* Naturkunde, *die;* ~ **trail** *n.* Naturlehrpfad, *der*

naturist /ˈneɪtʃərɪst/ *n.* (nudist) Naturist, *der*/Naturistin, *die;* FKK-Anhänger, *der*/FKK-Anhängerin, *die*

naught /nɔːt/ *n.* (arch./dial.) **come to ~:** zunichte werden

naughtily /ˈnɔːtɪlɪ/ *adv.* ungezogen

naughtiness /ˈnɔːtɪnɪs/ *n.* Ungezogenheit, *die*

naughty /ˈnɔːtɪ/ *adj.* ungezogen; **you ~ boy/dog** du böser Junge/Hund

nausea /ˈnɔːzɪə/ *n.* Übelkeit, *die*

nauseate /ˈnɔːzɪeɪt/ *v.t.* (disgust) anwidern

ˈnauseating *adj.* (disgusting) widerlich

nauseous /ˈnɔːzɪəs/ *adj.* **sb. is** *or* **feels ~:** jmdm. ist übel

nautical /ˈnɔːtɪkl/ *adj.* nautisch

nautical ˈmile *n.* Seemeile, *die*

naval /ˈneɪvl/ *adj.* Marine-; See‹*schlacht, -macht, -streitkräfte*›; ~ **ship** Kriegsschiff, *das*

naval: ~ **base** *n.* Flottenstützpunkt, *der;* ~ **officer** *n.* Marineoffizier, *der*

nave /neɪv/ *n.* [Mittel]schiff, *das*

navel /ˈneɪvl/ *n.* Nabel, *der*

navigate /ˈnævɪgeɪt/ *v.t.* **(a)** navigieren ‹*Schiff, Flugzeug*›
(b) befahren ‹*Fluss usw.*›

navigation /nævɪˈgeɪʃn/ *n.* Navigation, *die*

navigator /ˈnævɪgeɪtə(r)/ *n.* Navigator, *der*/Navigatorin, *die*

navy /ˈneɪvɪ/ **1** *n.* **(a)** [Kriegs]marine, *die*
(b) ▶ NAVY BLUE
2 *adj* ▶ NAVY-BLUE

navy: ~ **ˈblue** *n.* Marineblau, *das;* **~-blue** *adj.* marineblau

Nazi /ˈnɑːtsɪ/ **1** *n.* Nazi, *der*
2 *adj.* nazistisch; Nazi-

NB *abbr.* = **nota bene** NB

NCO *abbr.* = **non-commissioned officer** Uffz.

NE *abbr.* = **north-east** NO

near /nɪə(r)/ **1** *adv.* nah[e]; **stand/live [quite] ~:** [ganz] in der Nähe stehen/wohnen; **come** *or* **draw ~/~er** ‹*Tag, Zeitpunkt:*› nahen/näher rücken; **get ~er together** näher zusammenrücken; ~ **at hand** in Reichweite (*Dat.*); ‹*Ort*› ganz in der Nähe; ~ **to** = 2
2 *prep.* **(a)** (position) nahe an/bei (+ *Dat.*); (fig.) in der Nähe (+ *Gen.*); **keep ~ me** halte dich in meiner Nähe; **it's ~ here** es ist hier in der Nähe
(b) (motion) nahe an (+ *Akk.*); (fig.) in der Nähe (+ *Gen.*); **don't come ~ me** komm mir nicht zu nahe
3 *adj.* **(a)** (in space or time) nahe; **in the ~ future** in nächster Zukunft; **the ~est man** der am nächsten stehende Mann
(b) (in nature) **£30 or ~/~est offer** 30 Pfund oder nächstbestes Angebot; ~ **escape** Entkommen mit knapper Not; **that was a ~ miss/thing!** das war knapp!
4 *v.t.* sich nähern (+ *Dat.*); **the building is ~ing completion** das Gebäude steht kurz vor seiner Vollendung
5 *v.i.* ‹*Zeitpunkt:*› näher rücken

ˈnearby *adj.* nahe gelegen

ˈnearly *adv.* fast; **be ~ in tears** den Tränen nahe sein; **it is ~ six o'clock** es ist kurz vor sechs Uhr; **are you ~ ready?** bist du bald fertig?

ˈnearness *n.* Nähe, *die*

ˈnear-sighted *adj.* (Amer.) kurzsichtig

neat /niːt/ *adj.* **(a)** (tidy) ordentlich
(b) (undiluted) pur
(c) (smart) gepflegt ‹*Erscheinung, Kleidung*›
(d) (deft) geschickt

ˈneatly *adv.* ▶ NEAT A, C, D: ordentlich; gepflegt; geschickt

'neatness *n.* ▶ NEAT A, C, D: Ordentlichkeit, *die;* Gepflegtheit, *die;* Geschicktheit, *die*

necessarily /nesɪ'serɪlɪ/ *adv.* zwangsläufig; **it is not ~ true** es muss nicht [unbedingt] stimmen

necessary /'nesɪsərɪ/ [1] *adj.* nötig; notwendig; **do everything ~**: das Nötige *od.* Notwendige tun
[2] *n.* **the necessaries of life** das Lebensnotwendige

necessitate /nɪ'sesɪteɪt/ *v.t.* erforderlich machen

necessity /nɪ'sesɪtɪ/ *n.* Notwendigkeit, *die;* **do sth. out of** *or* **from ~**: etw. notgedrungen tun; **of ~**: notwendigerweise

neck /nek/ *n.* **(a)** Hals, *der;* **be a pain in the ~** (coll.) jmdm. auf die Nerven gehen (ugs.); **break one's ~** (fig. coll.) sich den Hals brechen; **~ and ~**: Kopf an Kopf
(b) (of garment) Kragen, *der*

neck: ~lace /'neklɪs/ *n.* [Hals]kette, *die;* (with jewels) Kollier, *das;* **~line** *n.* [Hals]ausschnitt, *der;* **~tie** *n.* Krawatte, *die*

nectar /'nektə(r)/ *n.* Nektar, *der*

née (*Amer.:* **nee**) /neɪ/ *adj.* geborene

need /ni:d/ [1] *n.* **(a)** Notwendigkeit, *die* (**for,** **of** *Gen.*); (demand) Bedarf, *der* (**for, of** an + *Dat.*); **as the ~ arises** nach Bedarf; **if ~ be** nötigenfalls; **there's no ~ for that** [das ist] nicht nötig; **there's no ~ to do sth.** es ist nicht nötig, etw. zu tun; **be in ~ of sth.** etw. brauchen; **there's no ~ for you to come** du brauchst nicht zu kommen
(b) *no pl.* (emergency) Not, *die;* **in case of ~**: im Notfall
(c) (thing) Bedürfnis, *das*
[2] *v.t.* **(a)** (require) brauchen; **sth. that urgently ~s doing** etw., was dringend gemacht werden muss; **it ~s a coat of paint** es muss gestrichen werden
(b) (expr. necessity) müssen; **I ~ to do it** ich muss es tun; **it ~s/doesn't ~ to be done** es muss getan werden/es braucht nicht getan zu werden
(c) *pres.* **he ~,** *neg.* **~ not** *or* (coll.) **~n't** /'ni:dnt/ (expr. desirability) müssen; *with neg.* brauchen zu

needle /'ni:dl/ [1] *n.* Nadel, *die*
[2] *v.t.* (coll.) nerven (ugs.)

needless /'ni:dlɪs/ *adj.* unnötig; **~ to add** *or* **say, ...**: überflüssig zu sagen, dass ...

'needlessly *adv.* unnötig

'needlework *n.* Handarbeit, *die;* **do ~**: handarbeiten

needn't /'ni:dnt/ (coll.) = **need not;** ▶ NEED 2C

'needy *adj.* notleidend; bedürftig

negation /nɪ'geɪʃn/ *n.* Verneinung, *die*

negative /'negətɪv/ [1] *adj.* negativ
[2] *n.* **(a)** (Photog.) Negativ, *das*
(b) (~ statement) negative Aussage; (answer) Nein, *das*

negative 'equity *n.* Negativwert, *der*

'negatively *adv.* negativ

neglect /nɪ'glekt/ [1] *v.t.* vernachlässigen; **she ~ed to write** sie hat es versäumt zu schreiben
[2] *n.* Vernachlässigung, *die;* **be in a state of ~** ‹*Gebäude:*› verwahrlost sein

neglectful /nɪ'glektfl/ *adj.* gleichgültig (**of** gegenüber); **be ~ of** sich nicht kümmern um

negligence /'neglɪdʒəns/ *n.* Nachlässigkeit, *die;* (Law, Insurance, etc.) Fahrlässigkeit, *die*

negligent /'neglɪdʒənt/ *adj.* nachlässig; **be ~ about sth.** sich um etw. nicht kümmern

negligible /'neglɪdʒɪbl/ *adj.* unerheblich

negotiable /nɪ'gəʊʃəbl/ *adj.* **(a)** verhandlungsfähig ‹*Forderung, Bedingungen*›
(b) passierbar ‹*Straße, Fluss*›

negotiate /nɪ'gəʊʃɪeɪt/ [1] *v.i.* verhandeln (**for, on, about** über + *Akk.*)
[2] *v.t.* **(a)** (arrange) aushandeln
(b) überwinden ‹*Hindernis*›; passieren ‹*Straße, Fluss*›; nehmen ‹*Kurve*›

negotiation /nɪgəʊʃɪ'eɪʃn/ *n.* Verhandlung, *die*

negotiator /nɪ'gəʊʃɪeɪtə(r)/ *n.* Unterhändler, *der*/-händlerin, *die*

Negress /'ni:grɪs/ *n.* (dated/offensive) Negerin, *die*

Negro /'ni:grəʊ/ [1] *n., pl.* **~es** (dated/offensive) Neger, *der*
[2] *adj.* Neger-

neigh /neɪ/ [1] *v.i.* wiehern
[2] *n.* Wiehern, *das*

neighbor *etc.* (*Amer.*) ▶ NEIGHBOUR *etc.*

neighbour /'neɪbə(r)/ [1] *n.* Nachbar, *der*/ Nachbarin, *die;* **my next-door ~s** meine Nachbarn von nebenan
[2] *v.t. & i.* **~ [upon]** grenzen an (+ *Akk.*)

'neighbourhood *n.* (district) Gegend, *die;* (neighbours) Nachbarschaft, *die;* **[somewhere] in the ~ of £100** [so] um [die] 100 Pfund

'neighbourhood watch *n.*: *Programm fur Verhütung von Straftaten, bes. von Wohnungseinbrüchen, durch erhöhte Wachsamheit aller in einem Wohngebiet lebenden Menschen*

'neighbouring *adj.* Nachbar-; angrenzend ‹*Felder*›

neighbourly /'neɪbəlɪ/ *adj.* [gut]nachbarlich

neither /'naɪðə(r), ni:ðə(r)/ [1] *adj.* keiner/ keine/keins der beiden
[2] *pron.* keiner/keine/keins von *od.* der beiden
[3] *adv.* (also not) auch nicht; **~ am I,** (coll.) **me ~**: ich auch nicht
[4] *conj.* (not either) weder; **~ ... nor ...**: weder ... noch ...

neo'classical *adj.* klassizistisch

neo'conservative [1] *adj.* neokonservativ
[2] *n.* Neokonservative, *der/die*

neo'fascist *adj.* neofaszistisch
neon /'ni:ɒn/ *n.* Neon, *das*
neo-'nazi 1 *n.* Neonazi, *der*
2 *adj.* neonazistisch; **a ~ group** eine Neonazigruppe
neon: ~ 'lamp, ~ 'light *ns.* Neonlampe, *die;* **~ 'sign** *n.* Neonreklame, *die*
nephew /'nevju:, 'nefju:/ *n.* Neffe, *der*
nepotism /'nepətɪzm/ *n.* Vetternwirtschaft, *die*
Neptune /'neptju:n/ *pr. n.* (Astron.) Neptun, *der*
nerve /nɜ:v/ *n.* Nerv, *der;* **get on sb.'s ~s** jmdm. auf die Nerven gehen (ugs.); **lose one's ~:** die Nerven verlieren; **what [a] ~!** [so eine] Frechheit!
nerve: ~ cell *n.* Nervenzelle, *die;* **~ centre** *n.* (fig.) Schaltzentrale, *die;* **~ gas** *n.* Nervengas, *das;* **~-racking** *adj.* nervenaufreibend
nervous /'nɜ:vəs/ *adj.* **(a)** (Anat., Med.) Nerven-; **~ breakdown** Nervenzusammenbruch, *der*
(b) (having delicate nerves) nervös; **be a ~ wreck** mit den Nerven völlig am Ende sein
(c) (Brit.: timid) **be ~ of** *or* **about** Angst haben vor (+ *Dat.*); **be a ~ person** ängstlich sein
'nervously *adv.* nervös
'nervousness *n.* Ängstlichkeit, *die*
nervy /'nɜ:vɪ/ *adj.* **(a)** nervös
(b) (Amer. coll.: impudent) unverschämt
nest 1 *n.* Nest, *das*
2 *v.i.* nisten
'nest egg *n.* (fig.) Notgroschen, *der*
nestle /'nesl/ *v.i.* **(a)** sich schmiegen (**to, up against** an + *Akk.*)
(b) (lie half hidden) eingebettet sein
net¹ /net/ 1 *n.* **(a)** Netz, *das*
(b) the Net (Comp.) das Netz
2 *v.t.*, **-tt-** [mit einem Netz] fangen
net² *adj.* **(a)** netto; Netto‹*einkommen, -[verkaufs]preis usw.*›; **~ weight** Nettogewicht, *das*
(b) (ultimate) End‹*ergebnis, -effekt*›
net: ~ball *n.* Netzball, *der;* **~ 'curtain** *n.* Store, *der*
Netherlands /'neðələndz/ *pr. n. sing. or pl.* Niederlande *Pl.*
net 'profit *n.* Reingewinn, *der*
'netspeak *n.* Internetjargon, *der*
nett ▶ NET² A
'netting *n.* ([piece of] net) Netz, *das;* **wire ~:** Maschendraht, *der*
nettle /'netl/ *n.* Nessel, *die*
'network *n.* Netz, *das;* (Comp.) Netzwerk, *das*
'network provider *n.* (Comp) Netzanbieter, *der*
neuralgia /njʊə'rældʒə/ *n.* Neuralgie, *die*
neurological /njʊərə'lɒdʒɪkl/ *adj.* neurologisch
neurologist /njʊə'rɒlədʒɪst/ *n.* Neurologe, *der*/Neurologin, *die*
neurology /njʊə'rɒlədʒɪ/ *n.* Neurologie, *die*
neurosis /njʊə'rəʊsɪs/ *n., pl.* **neuroses** /njʊə'rəʊsi:z/ Neurose, *die*
neurotic /njʊə'rɒtɪk/ *adj.* **(a)** nervenkrank
(b) (coll.) neurotisch
neuter /'nju:tə(r)/ *adj.* sächlich
neutral /'nju:trl/ 1 *adj.* neutral
2 *n.* (**~** gear) Leerlauf, *der*
neutrality /nju:'trælɪtɪ/ *n.* Neutralität, *die*
neutralize /'nju:trəlaɪz/ *v.t.* neutralisieren
neutron /'nju:trɒn/ *n.* Neutron, *das*
never /'nevə(r)/ *adv.* **(a)** nie; **~-ending** endlos
(b) (coll.) **you ~ believed that, did you?** du hast das doch wohl nicht geglaubt?; **well, I ~ [did]!** [na] so was!
neverthe'less *adv.* trotzdem
new /nju:/ *adj.* neu
new: New Age *n.* Newage, *das; attrib.* Newage-; **~-born** *adj.* neugeboren; **~comer** /'nju:kʌmə(r)/ *n.* Neuankömmling, *der;* **~fangled** /'nju:fæŋgld/ *adj.* neumodisch; **~-found** *adj.* neu; **~-laid** *adj.* frisch [gelegt]; **New 'Left** *n.* neue Linke; **~ 'look** *n.* (coll.) neuer Stil
'newly *adv.* (recently) neu; **~ married** seit kurzem verheiratet
'newly-wed *n.* Jungverheiratete, *der/die*
new: New 'Man *n.* der neue Mann; **~ 'moon** *n.* Neumond, *der*
'newness *n.* Neuheit, *die*
news /nju:z/ *n.* **(a)** Nachricht, *die;* **be in the ~:** Schlagzeilen machen; **good/bad ~:** schlechte/gute Nachrichten *Pl.*
(b) (Radio, Telev.) Nachrichten *Pl.*
news: ~ agency *n.* Nachrichtenagentur, *die;* **~agent** *n.* Zeitungshändler, *der*/-händlerin, *die;* **~ bulletin** *n.* Nachrichten *Pl.;* **~cast** *n.* Nachrichtensendung, *die;* **~caster** *n.* Nachrichtensprecher, *der*/-sprecherin, *die;* **~ desk** *n.* Nachrichtenredaktion, *die;* **this is Joe Smith at the ~ desk** (Radio) hier ist Joe Smith mit den Nachrichten; **~flash** *n.* Kurzmeldung, *die;* **~group** *n.* (Comp.) Newsgroup, *die;* **~ 'headline** *n.* Schlagzeile, *die;* **~letter** *n.* Rundschreiben, *das;* **~paper** *n.* **(a)** Zeitung, *die;* **~paper boy/girl** Zeitungsausträger, *der*/-austrägerin, *die;* **(b)** (material) Zeitungspapier, *das;* **~reader** *n.* Nachrichtensprecher, *der*/-sprecherin, *die;* **~reel** *n.* Wochenschau, *die;* **~room** *n.* Nachrichtenredaktion, *die;* **~-sheet** *n.* Informationsblatt, *das;* **~stand** *n.* Zeitungskiosk, *der;* Zeitungsstand, *der;* **~ summary** *n.* Kurznachrichten *Pl.;* **~ vendor** *n.* Zeitungsverkäufer, *der*/-verkäuferin, *die;* **~worthy** *adj.* [für die Medien] interessant
newt /nju:t/ *n.* [Wasser]molch, *der*

New: new town *n.*: *mit Unterstützung der Regierung völlig neu entstandene Ansiedlung;* **new 'year** *n.* Neujahr, *das;* **over the new year** über Neujahr; **a Happy New Year** ein glückliches *od.* gutes neues Jahr; **~ 'Year's** (Amer.), **~ Year's 'Day** *ns.* Neujahrstag, *der;* **~ Year's 'Eve** *n.* Silvester, *der od. das;* **~ Zealand** /- 'zi:lənd/ *pr. n.* Neuseeland (*das*); **~ 'Zealander** *n.* Neuseeländer, *der* /-länderin, *die*

next /nekst/ **1** *adj.* nächst...; **the ~ but one** der/die/das Übernächste; **~ to** (fig.: almost) fast; nahezu; **[the] ~ time** das nächste Mal; **the ~ best** der/die/das Nächstbeste; **am I ~?** komme ich jetzt dran?
2 *adv.* (in the ~ place) als Nächstes; (on the ~ occasion) das nächste Mal; **it's my turn ~:** ich komme als Nächster dran; **sit/stand ~ to sb.** neben jmdm. stehen/sitzen; **place sth. ~ to sb./sth.** etw. neben jmdn./etw. stellen
3 *n.* **(a) the week after ~:** [die] übernächste Woche
(b) (person) **~ of kin** nächster/nächste Angehörige; **~, please!** der Nächste, bitte!

'next-door *adj.* gleich nebenan *nachgestellt*

NHS *abbr.* (Brit.) = **National Health Service**

nib /nɪb/ *n.* Feder, *die*

nibble /'nɪbl/ *v.t. & i.* knabbern (**at, on** an + *Dat.*)

nice /naɪs/ *adj.* nett; angenehm ‹*Stimme*›; schön ‹*Wetter*›; (iron.: disgraceful, difficult) schön; **~ [and] warm/fast** schön warm/schnell; **~-looking** gut aussehend

'nicely *adv.* (coll.) **(a)** (well) nett; gut ‹*arbeiten, sich benehmen, platziert sein*›
(b) (all right) gut; **that will do ~:** das reicht völlig

niceties /'naɪsɪtɪz/ *n. pl.* Feinheiten *Pl.*

niche /nɪtʃ, ni:ʃ/ *n.* **(a)** (in wall) Nische, *die*
(b) (fig.: suitable place) Platz, *der*

nick **1** *n.* **(a)** (notch) Kerbe, *die*
(b) (sl. prison) Knast, *der* (salopp)
(c) (Brit.: police station) Wache, *die*
(d) in good/poor ~ (coll.) gut/nicht gut im Schuss (ugs.)
(e) in the ~ of time gerade noch rechtzeitig
2 *v.t.* **(a)** einkerben
(b) (Brit. coll.: arrest) einlochen (salopp)
(c) (Brit. coll.: steal) klauen (salopp)

nickel /'nɪkl/ *n.* **(a)** Nickel, *das*
(b) (Amer. coll.: coin) Fünfcentstück, *das*

nickname /'nɪkneɪm/ *n.* Spitzname, *der;* (affectionate) Koseform, *die*

nicotine /'nɪkəti:n/ *n.* Nikotin, *das*

'nicotine patch *n.* Nikotinpflaster, *das*

niece /ni:s/ *n.* Nichte, *die*

Nigeria /naɪ'dʒɪərɪə/ *pr. n.* Nigeria (*das*)

niggardly /'nɪgədlɪ/ *adj.* knaus[e]rig (ugs.)

niggling /'nɪglɪŋ/ *adj.* **(a)** (petty) belanglos
(b) (trivial) nichts sagend
(c) (nagging) nagend

night /naɪt/ *n.* Nacht, *die;* (evening) Abend, *der;* **the following ~:** die Nacht/der Abend darauf; **the previous ~:** die vorausgegangene Nacht/der vorausgegangene Abend; **on Sunday ~:** Sonntagnacht/[am] Sonntagabend; **for the ~:** über Nacht; **at ~:** nachts/abends; **late at ~:** spätabends

night: ~bird *n.* (person) Nachteule, *die* (ugs. scherzh.); **~ blindness** *n.* Nachtblindheit, *die;* **~cap** *n.* (drink) Schlaftrunk, *der;* **~clothes** *n. pl.* Nachtwäsche, *die;* **~club** *n.* Nachtklub, *der;* **~dress** *n.* Nachthemd, *das;* **~ duty** *n.* Nachtdienst, *der;* **be on ~ duty** Nachtdienst haben; **~fall** *n.* Einbruch der Dunkelheit

nightie /'naɪtɪ/ *n.* (coll.) Nachthemd, *das*

nightingale /'naɪtɪŋgeɪl/ *n.* Nachtigall, *die*

'nightlife *n.* Nachtleben, *das*

nightly /'naɪtlɪ/ **1** *adj.* (happening every night/evening) allnächtlich/allabendlich
2 *adv.* (every night) jede Nacht; (every evening) jeden Abend

night: ~mare *n.* Albtraum, *der;* **~marish** /'naɪtmeərɪʃ/ *adj.* albtraumhaft; **~ owl** *n.* **(a)** (Ornith.) Eule, *die;* **(b)** (coll.: person) Nachteule, *die* (ugs. scherzh.); **~ porter** *n.* Nachtportier, *der;* **~ safe** *n.* Nachttresor, *der;* **~ school** *n.* Abendschule, *die;* **~ shelter** *n.* Nachtasyl, *das;* **~ shift** *n.* Nachtschicht, *die;* **~ 'sky** *n.* Nachthimmel, *der;* **~ 'storage heater** *n.* Nachtspeicherofen, *der;* **~-time** *n.* Nacht, *die;* **in the** *or* **at ~-time** nachts; **~'watchman** *n.* Nachtwächter, *der;* **~wear** *n. sing.* ▶ NIGHTCLOTHES

nihilistic /naɪɪ'lɪstɪk, nɪhɪ'lɪstɪk/ *adj.* nihilistisch

nil /nɪl/ *n.* null

Nile /naɪl/ *pr. n.* Nil, *der*

nimble /'nɪmbl/ *adj.*, **nimbly** /'nɪmblɪ/ *adv.* flink

nine /naɪn/ **1** *adj.* neun
2 *n.* Neun, *die. See also* EIGHT

nineteen /naɪn'ti:n/ **1** *adj.* neunzehn
2 *n.* Neunzehn, *die. See also* EIGHT

nineteenth /naɪn'ti:nθ/ **1** *adj.* neunzehnt...
2 *n.* (fraction) Neunzehntel, *das. See also* EIGHTH

ninetieth /'naɪntɪɪθ/ *adj.* neunzigst...

ninety /'naɪntɪ/ **1** *adj.* neunzig
2 *n.* Neunzig, *die. See also* EIGHT; EIGHTY 2

ninth /naɪnθ/ **1** *adj.* neunt...
2 *n.* (in sequence, rank) Neunte, *der/die/das;* (fraction) Neuntel, *das. See also* EIGHTH

nip **1** *v.t.*, **-pp-** zwicken
2 *v.i.*, **-pp-** (Brit. coll.) **~ in** hinein-/hereinflitzen (ugs.); **~ out** hinaus-/herausflitzen (ugs.)
3 *n.* (pinch, squeeze) Kniff, *der;* (bite) Biss, *der*

'nipper *n.* (Brit. coll.: child) Balg, *das* (ugs.)

nipple /'nɪpl/ *n.* **(a)** Brustwarze, *die*
(b) (of feeding bottle) Sauger, *der*

nitrate /'naɪtreɪt/ *n.* **(a)** (salt) Nitrat, *das* **(b)** (fertilizer) Nitratdünger, *der*

nitric acid /'naɪtrɪk æsɪd/ *n.* Salpetersäure, *die*

nitrogen /'naɪtrədʒən/ *n.* Stickstoff, *der*

'nitrogen cycle *n.* Stickstoffkreislauf, *der*

nitwit /'nɪtwɪt/ *n.* (coll.) Trottel, *der* (ugs.)

no /nəʊ/ 1 *adj.* kein
2 *adv.* **(a)** (by no amount) nicht; **no less [than]** nicht weniger [als]; **no more wine?** keinen Wein mehr?
(b) (as answer) nein
3 *n., pl.* **noes** /nəʊz/ Nein, *das*

No. *abbr.* = **number** Nr.

Noah's ark /nəʊəz 'ɑ:k/ *n.* die Arche Noah

Nobel prize /nəʊbel 'praɪz/ *n.* Nobelpreis, *der*

nobility /nə'bɪlɪtɪ/ *n.* Adel, *der*; **many of the ~:** viele Adlige

noble /'nəʊbl/ 1 *adj.* ad[e]lig; edel ‹*Gedanken, Gefühle*›
2 *n.* Adlige, *der/die*

nobleman /'nəʊblmən/ *n., pl.* **noblemen** /'nəʊblmən/ Adlige, *der*

nobly /'nəʊblɪ/ *adv.* **(a)** edel [gesinnt] **(b)** (generously) edelmütig (geh.)

nobody /'nəʊbədɪ/ *n. & pron.* niemand; keiner; (person of no importance) Niemand, *der*

no-'claim[s] bonus *n.* (Insurance) Schadenfreiheitsrabatt, *der*

nocturnal /nɒk'tɜ:nl/ *adj.* nächtlich; **~ animal/bird** Nachttier, *das*/-vogel, *der*

nod /nɒd/ 1 *v.i.*, **-dd-** nicken
2 *v.t.*, **-dd-: ~ one's head [in greeting]** [zum Gruß] mit dem Kopf nicken
3 *n.* [Kopf]nicken, *das*
■ **nod 'off** *v.i.* einnicken (ugs.)

nodule /'nɒdju:l/ *n.* **(a)** Klümpchen, *das* **(b)** (Bot.) Knötchen, *das*

no-'fly zone *n.* Flugverbotszone, *die*

no-'go *adj.* Sperr‹*gebiet, -zone*›

'no-good *adj.* (coll.) nichtsnutzig (abwertend)

no-hoper /nəʊ'həʊpə(r)/ *n.* absoluter Außenseiter; **be a ~:** keine Chance haben

nohow /'nəʊhaʊ/ *adv.* (Amer. coll.) in keiner Weise

noise /nɔɪz/ *n.* Geräusch, *das;* (loud, harsh, unwanted) Lärm, *der*

'noise abatement *n.* Lärmbekämpfung, *die*

'noiseless *adj.*, **'noiselessly** *adv.* lautlos

noise: ~ level *n.* Geräuschpegel, *der;* (of unpleasant noise) Lärmpegel, *der;*
~ pollution *n.* Lärmbelästigung, *die*

noisily /'nɔɪzɪlɪ/ *adv.*, **noisy** /'nɔɪzɪ/ *adj.* laut

nomad /'nəʊmæd/ *n.* Nomade, *der*

nomadic /nəʊ'mædɪk/ *adj.* nomadisch; **~ tribe** Nomadenstamm, *der*

'no man's land *n.* Niemandsland, *das*

nominal /'nɒmɪnl/ *adj.* **(a)** (in name only) nominell
(b) (virtually nothing) äußerst gering

nominally /'nɒmɪnəlɪ/ *adv.* namentlich

nominate /'nɒmɪneɪt/ *v.t.* **(a)** (propose) nominieren
(b) (appoint) ernennen

nomination /nɒmɪ'neɪʃn/ *n.* ▶ NOMINATE: Nominierung, *die;* Ernennung, *die*

nominative /'nɒmɪnətɪv/ *adj. & n.* **~ [case]** Nominativ, *der*

nominee /nɒmɪ'ni:/ *n.* (candidate) Kandidat, *der*/Kandidatin, *die*

non- /nɒn/ *pref.* nicht-

non-alco'holic *adj.* alkoholfrei

nonchalant /'nɒnʃələnt/ *adj.* unbekümmert

non-commissioned 'officer *n.* Unteroffizier, *der*

non-committal /nɒnkə'mɪtl/ *adj.* unverbindlich; **he was ~:** er hat sich nicht klar geäußert

noncon'formist *n.* Nonkonformist, *der*/ Nonkonformistin, *die*

non-con'tributory *adj.* beitragsfrei

nondescript /'nɒndɪskrɪpt/ *adj.* unscheinbar; undefinierbar ‹*Farbe*›

'non-drip *adj.* nicht tropfend ‹*Farbe*›

non-'driver *n.* Nicht[auto]fahrer, *der*

none /nʌn/ 1 *pron.* kein...; **~ of them** keiner/keine/keines von ihnen; **~ of this** nichts davon
2 *adv.* keineswegs; **I'm ~ the wiser now** jetzt bin ich um nichts klüger; **~ the less** nichtsdestoweniger

nonentity /nɒ'nentɪtɪ/ *n.* Nichts, *das*

non-existent /nɒnɪg'zɪstənt/ *adj.* nicht vorhanden

non-'fiction *n.* Sachliteratur, *die*

non-'iron *adj.* bügelfrei

non-'member *n.* Nichtmitglied, *das*

'no-no *n., pl.* **~es** (coll.) **be a ~:** nicht infrage kommen (ugs.)

non-'payment *n.* Nichtzahlung, *die*

nonplus /nɒn'plʌs/ *v.t.*, **-ss-** verblüffen

non-'profit[-making] *adj.* nicht auf Gewinn ausgerichtet

non-prolife'ration *n.* Nichtverbreitung von Atomwaffen; **~ treaty** Atom[waffen]sperrvertrag, *der*

non-re'cyclable *adj.* nicht recycelbar

non-'resident *n.* (outside a country) Nichtansässige, *der/die;* **the bar is open to ~s** die Bar ist auch für Gäste geöffnet, die nicht im Hotel wohnen

nonsense /'nɒnsəns/ 1 *n.* Unsinn, *der*
2 *int.* Unsinn

nonsensical /nɒn'sensɪkl/ *adj.* unsinnig

non sequitur /nɒn 'sekwɪtə(r)/ *n.* unlogische Folgerung

non-'smoker *n.* **(a)** (person) Nichtraucher, *der*/-raucherin, *die*
(b) (train compartment) Nichtraucherabteil, *das*
non-'starter *n.* (fig. coll.) Reinfall, *der* (ugs.)
non-'stick *adj.* **~ frying pan** *etc.* Bratpfanne *usw.* mit Antihaftbeschichtung
non-stop [1] /'--/ *adj.* durchgehend ‹*Zug, Busverbindung*›; Nonstop‹*flug, -revue*›
[2] /-'-/ *adv.* ohne Unterbrechung ‹*tanzen, reden, reisen, senden*›; nonstop ‹*fliegen, tanzen, fahren*›
'non-toxic *adj.* ungiftig
noodle /'nu:dl/ *n., usu. pl.* Nudel, *die*
nook /nʊk/ *n.* Winkel, *der;* Ecke, *die*
noon /nu:n/ *n.* Mittag, *der;* zwölf Uhr [mittags]; **at/before ~**: um/vor zwölf [Uhr mittags]
'no one *pron.* ▶ NOBODY
noose /nu:s/ *n.* Schlinge, *die*
nor /nə(r), *stressed* nɔ:(r)/ *conj.* noch; **neither/not ... ~ ...**: weder ... noch ...
norm /nɔ:m/ *n.* Norm, *die*
normal /'nɔ:ml/ [1] *adj.* normal
[2] *n.* **(a)** (~ value) Normalwert, *der*
(b) (usual state) normaler Stand; **everything is back to** *or* **has returned to ~**: es hat sich wieder alles normalisiert
normality /nɔ:'mælɪtɪ/ Normalität, *die*
'normally *adv.* **(a)** (in normal way) normal
(b) (ordinarily) normalerweise
north /nɔ:θ/ [1] *n.* **(a)** Norden, *der;* **in/to[wards]/from the ~**: im/nach/von Norden; **to the ~ of** nördlich von
(b) *usu.* **N~** (Geog., Polit.) Norden, *der*
[2] *adj.* nördlich; Nord‹*wind, -küste, -grenze*›
[3] *adv.* nach Norden; **~ of** nördlich von
north: N~ 'Africa *pr. n.* Nordafrika (*das*); **N~ A'merica** *pr. n.* Nordamerika (*das*); **N~ A'merican** [1] *adj.* nordamerikanisch; [2] *n.* Nordamerikaner, *der*/-amerikanerin, *die;* **~bound** *adj.* ‹*Zug, Verkehr usw.*› in Richtung Norden; **~-'east** [1] *n.* Nordosten, *der;* [2] *adj.* nordöstlich; Nordost‹*wind, -küste*›; [3] *adv.* nordostwärts; nach Nordosten; **~-'eastern** *adj.* nordöstlich
northerly /'nɔ:ðəlɪ/ *adj.* nördlich; ‹*Wind*› aus nördlichen Richtungen
northern /'nɔ:ðən/ *adj.* nördlich; Nord‹*grenze, -hälfte, -seite*›
northern: N~ 'Ireland *pr. n.* Nordirland (*das*); **~ 'lights** *n. pl.* Nordlicht, *das*
North: ~ 'Germany *pr. n.* Norddeutschland (*das*); **~ 'Pole** *pr. n.* Nordpol, *der;* **~ 'Sea** *pr. n.* Nordsee, *die*
northward[s] /'nɔ:θwəd(z)/ *adv.* nordwärts
north: ~-'west [1] *n.* Nordwesten, *der;* [2] *adj.* nordwestlich; Nordwest‹*wind, -küste*›; [3] *adv.* nordwestwärts; nach Nordwesten; **~-'western** *adj.* nordwestlich
Norway /'nɔ:weɪ/ *pr. n.* Norwegen (*das*)
Norwegian /nɔ:'wi:dʒn/ [1] *adj.* norwegisch; **sb. is ~**: jmd. ist Norweger/Norwegerin
[2] *n.* **(a)** (person) Norweger, *der*/Norwegerin, *die*
(b) (language) Norwegisch, *das; see also* ENGLISH 2A
Nos. *abbr.* = **numbers** Nrn.
nose /nəʊz/ [1] *n.* Nase, *die*
[2] *v.t.* **~ one's way** sich (*Dat.*) vorsichtig seinen Weg bahnen
[3] *v.i.* sich vorsichtig bewegen
■ **nose a'bout, nose a'round** *v.i.* (coll.) herumschnüffeln (ugs.)
nose: ~bleed *n.* Nasenbluten, *das;* **~dive** [1] *n.* Sturzflug, *der;* [2] *v.i.* im Sturzflug hinuntergehen
nosey ▶ NOSY
nostalgia /nɒ'stældʒə/ *n.* Nostalgie, *die;* **~ for sth.** Sehnsucht nach etw.
nostalgic /nɒ'stældʒɪk/ *adj.* nostalgisch
nostril /'nɒstrɪl/ *n.* Nasenloch, *das;* (of horse) Nüster, *die*
nosy /'nəʊzɪ/ *adj.* (coll.) neugierig
not /nɒt/ *adv.* nicht; **he is ~ a doctor** er ist kein Arzt; **~ at all** überhaupt nicht; **~ ... but ...**: nicht ..., sondern ...; **~ a thing** gar nichts
notable /'nəʊtəbl/ *adj.* bemerkenswert; **be ~ for sth.** für etw. bekannt sein
notably /'nəʊtəblɪ/ *adv.* besonders
notation /nəʊ'teɪʃn/ *n.* Notierung, *die*
notch /nɒtʃ/ [1] *n.* Kerbe, *die*
[2] *v.t.* kerben
■ **notch 'up** *v.t.* erreichen
note /nəʊt/ [1] *n.* **(a)** (Mus.) (sign) Note, *die;* (key of piano) Taste, *die;* (sound) Ton, *der*
(b) (jotting) Notiz, *die;* **take** *or* **make ~s** sich (*Dat.*) Notizen machen; **take** *or* **make a ~ of sth.** sich (*Dat.*) etw. notieren
(c) (comment, footnote) Anmerkung, *die*
(d) (short letter) [kurzer] Brief
(e) (importance) **a person/something of ~**: eine bedeutende Persönlichkeit/etwas Bedeutendes; **be of ~**: bedeutend sein
[2] *v.t.* **(a)** (pay attention to) beachten
(b) (notice) bemerken
(c) (write) **~ [down]** [sich (*Dat.*)] notieren
'notebook *n.* **(a)** Notizbuch, *das;* (for lecture notes) Kollegheft, *das*
(b) **~book [computer]** Notebook, *das*
'noted *adj.* bekannt (**for** für, wegen)
note: ~pad *n.* Notizblock, *der;* **~paper** *n.* Briefpapier, *das;* **~worthy** *adj.* bemerkenswert
nothing /'nʌθɪŋ/ *n.* nichts; **~ interesting** nichts Interessantes; **~ much** nichts Besonderes; **~ more than** nur; **~ more, ~ less** nicht mehr, nicht weniger; **next to ~**: so gut wie nichts; **have [got]** *or* **be ~ to do with sb./sth.** (not concern) nichts zu tun haben mit jmdm./etw.; **have ~ to do with sb.** (avoid) jmdm. aus dem Weg gehen
notice /'nəʊtɪs/ [1] *n.* **(a)** Anschlag, *der;* (in newspaper) Anzeige, *die*

(b) (warning) **at short/a moment's ~:** kurzfristig/von einem Augenblick zum andern
(c) (formal notification) Ankündigung, *die;* **until further ~:** bis auf weiteres
(d) (ending an agreement) Kündigung, *die;* **give sb. a month's ~:** jmdm. mit einer Frist von einem Monat kündigen; **hand in one's ~, give ~** (Brit.), **give one's ~** (Amer.) kündigen
(e) (attention) **bring sb./sth. to sb.'s ~:** jmdn. auf jmdn./etw. aufmerksam machen; **take no ~ of sb./sth.** (disregard) keine Notiz von jmdm./etw. nehmen; **take no ~:** sich nicht darum kümmern
[2] *v.t.* bemerken

noticeable /'nəʊtɪsəbl/ *adj.* wahrnehmbar ‹*Fleck, Schaden, Geruch*›; merklich ‹*Verbesserung*›; spürbar ‹*Mangel*›

noticeably /'nəʊtɪsəblɪ/ *adv.* sichtlich ‹*größer, kleiner*›; merklich ‹*verändern*›; spürbar ‹*kälter*›

'noticeboard *n.* (Brit.) Anschlagbrett, *das;* schwarzes Brett

notifiable /'nəʊtɪfaɪəbl/ *adj.* meldepflichtig ‹*Krankheit*›

notification /nəʊtɪfɪ'keɪʃn/ *n.* Mitteilung, *die* (**of sth.** über etw. [*Akk.*])

notify /'nəʊtɪfaɪ/ *v.t.* **(a)** (make known) ankündigen
(b) (inform) benachrichtigen (**of** über + *Akk.*)

notion /'nəʊʃn/ *n.* Vorstellung, *die;* **not have the faintest/least ~ of how/what** *etc.* nicht die blasseste/geringste Ahnung haben, wie/was *usw.*

notoriety /nəʊtə'raɪətɪ/ *n.* traurige Berühmtheit

notorious /nə'tɔːrɪəs/ *adj.* berüchtigt (**for** wegen); notorisch ‹*Lügner*›

nougat /'nuːgɑː/ *n.* Nougat, *das od. der*

nought /nɔːt/ *n.* Null, *die*

noun /naʊn/ *n.* (Ling.) Substantiv, *das*

nourish /'nʌrɪʃ/ *v.t.* ernähren (**on** mit)

'nourishing *adj.* nahrhaft

'nourishment *n.* Nahrung, *die*

Nov. *abbr.* = **November** Nov.

novel /'nɒvl/ [1] *n.* Roman, *der*
[2] *adj.* neuartig

novelist /'nɒvəlɪst/ *n.* Romanautor, *der*/-autorin, *die*

novella /nə'velə/ *n.* Novelle, *die*

novelty /'nɒvltɪ/ *n.* **(a) be a/no ~:** etwas/nichts Neues sein
(b) (newness) Neuheit, *die*
(c) (gadget) Überraschung, *die*

November /nə'vembə(r)/ *n.* November, *der; see also* AUGUST

novice /'nɒvɪs/ *n.* Anfänger, *der*/Anfängerin, *die*

now /naʊ/ [1] *adv.* jetzt; (nowadays) heutzutage; (immediately) [jetzt] sofort; **just ~** (very recently) gerade eben; **[every] ~ and then** *or* **again** hin und wieder; **well ~:** also; **~, ~:** na, na; **~ then** na (ugs.)
[2] *conj.* **~ [that]** ...: jetzt, wo ...
[3] *n.* **before ~:** früher; **by ~:** inzwischen; **a week from ~:** [heute] in einer Woche

nowadays /'naʊədeɪz/ *adv.* heutzutage

nowhere /'nəʊweə(r)/ *adv.* nirgends; nirgendwo; (to no place) nirgendwohin

no-'win *attrib. adj.* Verlierer-

noxious /'nɒkʃəs/ *adj.* giftig

nozzle /'nɒzl/ *n.* Düse, *die*

nuance /'njuːɑ̃s/ *n.* Nuance, *die*

nuclear /'njuːklɪə(r)/ *adj.* Atom-; Kern‹*explosion*›; atomar ‹*Antrieb, Gefechtskopf, Wettrüsten, Abrüstung*›; nuklear ‹*Sprengkörper*›; atomgetrieben ‹*Unterseeboot*›

nuclear: ~ 'bomb *n.* Atombombe, *die;* **~ capa'bility** *n.* nukleares Potenzial; **a missile with ~ capability** eine nuklearfähige Rakete; **have ~ capability** nuklearfähig sein; **~ de'terrent** *n.* atomare *od.* nukleare Abschreckung; **~ 'energy** *n.* Atom- *od.* Kernenergie, *die;* **~ 'family** *n.* Kernfamilie, *die;* **~-free** *adj.* atomwaffenfrei ‹*Zone*›; **~ 'fuel** *n.* Kernbrennstoff, *der;* **~ 'physics** *n.* Kernphysik, *die;* **~ 'power** *n.* **(a)** Atom- *od.* Kernkraft, *die;* **(b)** (country) Atom- *od.* Nuklearmacht, *die;* **~-'powered** *adj.* atomgetrieben; **~ 'power station** *n.* Atom- *od.* Kernkraftwerk, *das;* **~ 'test** *n.* Atom[waffen]test, *der;* **~ 'testing** *n.* Atomversuche *Pl.;* **~ 'warfare** *n.* Atomkrieg, *der;* **~ 'waste** *n.* Atommüll, *der*

nucleus /'njuːklɪəs/ *n., pl.* **nuclei** /'njuːklɪaɪ/ Kern, *der*

nude /njuːd/ [1] *adj.* nackt
[2] *n.* **(a)** (figure) Akt, *der*
(b) in the ~: nackt

nudge /nʌdʒ/ [1] *v.t.* anstoßen
[2] *n.* Stoß, *der*

nudism /'njuːdɪzm/ *n.* Nudismus, *der;* Freikörperkultur, *die*

nudist /'njuːdɪst/ *n.* Nudist, *der*/Nudistin, *die; attrib.* Nudisten-

nudity /'njuːdɪtɪ/ *n.* Nacktheit, *die*

nugget /'nʌgɪt/ *n.* Klumpen, *der;* (of gold) Goldklumpen, *der;* (fig.) **~s of wisdom** goldene Weisheiten

nuisance /'njuːsəns/ *n.* Ärgernis, *das;* **what a ~!** so etwas Dummes!

null /nʌl/ *adj.* **~ and void** null und nichtig

numb /nʌm/ [1] *adj.* gefühllos, taub (**with** vor + *Dat.*); (without emotion) benommen
[2] *v.t.* betäuben

number /'nʌmbə(r)/ [1] *n.* **(a)** (in series) Nummer, *die;* **you've got the wrong ~** (Teleph.) Sie sind falsch verbunden; **dial a wrong ~:** sich verwählen (ugs.)
(b) (esp. Math.: numeral) Zahl, *die*
(c) (sum, total, quantity) [An]zahl, *die;* **a ~ of people/things** einige Leute/Dinge; **a ~ of times** mehrmals ⋯

2 *v.t.* **(a)** (assign ~ to) nummerieren **(b)** (amount to, comprise) zählen **(c)** (include) zählen (**among, with** zu) **(d) sb.'s days are ~ed** jmds. Tage sind gezählt

'numbering *n.* Nummerierung, *die*

'numberless *adj.* unzählig; zahllos

'number plate *n.* Nummernschild, *das*

numeracy /'nju:mərəsɪ/ *n.* rechnerische Fähigkeiten *Pl.*

numeral /'nju:mərl/ *n.* Ziffer, *die*

numerate /nju:mərət/ *adj.* **be ~**: rechnen können

numerical /nju:'merɪkl/ *adj.* numerisch; Zahlen‹*wert, -folge*›; zahlenmäßig ‹*Stärke, Überlegenheit*›

numerically /nju:'merɪkəlɪ/ *adv.* numerisch

numerous /'nju:mərəs/ *adj.* zahlreich

nun /nʌn/ *n.* Nonne, *die*

nurse /nɜ:s/ **1** *n.* Krankenschwester, *die;* [**male**] ~: Krankenpfleger, *der* **2** *v.t.* **(a)** pflegen ‹*Kranke*› **(b)** (fig.) hegen (geh.) ‹*Gefühl, Groll*›

'nursemaid *n.* (lit. or fig.) Kindermädchen, *das*

nursery /'nɜ:sərɪ/ *n.* **(a)** (room) Kinderzimmer, *das* **(b)** (crèche) Kindertagesstätte, *die* **(c)** ▶ NURSERY SCHOOL **(d)** (for plants) Gärtnerei, *die*

nursery: ~ rhyme *n.* Kinderreim, *der;* **~ school** *n.* Kindergarten, *der;* **~-school teacher** *n.* (female) Kindergärtnerin, *die;* Erzieherin, *die;* (male) Erzieher, *der;* **~ slopes** *n. pl.* (Skiing) Idiotenhügel, *der* (ugs. scherzh.)

nursing /'nɜ:sɪŋ/ *n.* Krankenpflege, *die; attrib.* Pflege‹*personal, -beruf*›

'nursing home *n.* Pflegeheim, *das*

nurture /'nɜ:tʃə(r)/ *v.t.* (rear) aufziehen; (fig.) nähren

nut /nʌt/ *n.* **(a)** Nuss, *die* **(b)** (Mech. Engin.) [Schrauben]mutter, *die* **(c)** (crazy person) Verrückte, *der/die* (ugs.)

nut: ~ case *n.* (coll.) Verrückte, *der/die* (ugs.); **~ crackers** *n. pl.* Nussknacker, *der*

nutmeg /'nʌtmeg/ *n.* Muskat, *der*

nutrient /'nju:trɪənt/ *n.* Nährstoff, *der*

nutrition /nju:'trɪʃn/ *n.* Ernährung, *die;* (food) Nahrung, *die*

nutritional /nju:'trɪʃənl/ *adj.* nahrhaft; **~ value** Nährwert, *der*

nutritionist /nju:'trɪʃənɪst/ *n.* Ernährungswissenschaftler, *der*/ -wissenschaftlerin, *die*

nutritious /nju:'trɪʃəs/ *adj.* nahrhaft

'nutshell *n.* Nussschale, *die;* **in a ~** (fig.) hurz [gesagt]

nutty /'nʌtɪ/ *adj.* **(a)** (in taste) nussig **(b)** (coll.: crazy) verrückt (ugs.)

nuzzle /'nʌzl/ *v.i.* sich kuscheln (**up to, against** an + *Akk.*)

NVQ *abbr.* (Brit.) = **National Vocational Qualification**

NW *abbr.* = **north-west** NW

nylon /'naɪlɒn/ *n.* **(a)** Nylon, *das; attrib.* Nylon- **(b)** *in pl.* (stockings) Nylonstrümpfe *Pl.*

nymph /nɪmf/ *n.* Nymphe, *die*

nymphomaniac /nɪmfə'meɪnɪæk/ *n.* Nymphomanin, *die*

NZ *abbr.* = **New Zealand**

Oo

O, o /əʊ/ *n.* O, o, *das*

oaf /əʊf/ *n.* Stoffel, *der* (ugs.)

oak /əʊk/ *n.* Eiche, *die*

'oak tree *n.* Eiche, *die*

OAP *abbr.* (Brit.) = **old-age pensioner** Rentner, *der*/Rentnerin, *die*

oar /ɔ:(r)/ *n.* Ruder, *das*

oarsman /'ɔ:zmən/ *n., pl.* **oarsmen** /'ɔ:zmən/ Ruderer, *der*

oasis /əʊ'eɪsɪs/ *n., pl.* **oases** /əʊ'eɪsi:z/ Oase, *die*

oat /əʊt/ *n.* **~s** Hafer, *der*

'oatcake *n.* [flacher] Haferkuchen

oath /əʊθ/ *n.* **(a)** Eid, *der;* Schwur, *der;* **take** *or* **swear an ~**: einen Eid schwören **(b)** (swear word) Fluch, *der*

'oatmeal *n.* Hafermehl, *das*

obedience /ə'bi:dɪəns/ *n.* Gehorsam, *der*

obedient /ə'bi:dɪənt/ *adj.* gehorsam; **be ~ to sb./sth.** jmdm./einer Sache gehorchen

o'bediently *adv.* gehorsam

obelisk /'ɒbəlɪsk/ *n.* Obelisk, *der*

obese /əʊ'bi:s/ *adj.* fettleibig

obesity /əʊ'bi:sɪtɪ/ *n.* Fettleibigkeit, *die*

obey /əʊ'beɪ/ **1** *v.t.* gehorchen (+ *Dat.*); sich halten an (+ *Akk.*) ‹*Vorschrift, Regel*›; befolgen ‹*Befehl*› **2** *v.i.* gehorchen

obituary /ə'bɪtjʊərɪ/ *n.* Nachruf, *der* (**to, of** auf + *Akk.*)

object [1] /'ɒbdʒɪkt/ *n.* **(a)** (thing) Gegenstand, *der*
(b) (purpose) Ziel, *das*
(c) (obstacle) **money/time** *etc.* **is no ~:** Geld/ Zeit *usw.* spielt keine Rolle
(d) (Ling.) Objekt, *das*
[2] /əb'dʒekt/ *v.i.* **(a)** Einwände/einen Einwand erheben (**to** gegen)
(b) (have objection or dislike) etwas dagegen haben; **~ to sb./sth.** etwas gegen jmdn./etw. haben
[3] /əb'dʒekt/ *v.t.* einwenden

objection /əb'dʒekʃn/ *n.* **(a)** Einwand, *der;* **raise** *or* **make an ~ [to sth.]** einen Einwand [gegen etw.] erheben
(b) (dislike) Abneigung, *die;* **have an/no ~ to sb./sth.** etw./nichts gegen jmdn./etw. haben; **have no ~s** nichts dagegen haben

objectionable /əb'dʒekʃənəbl/ *adj.* unangenehm ‹*Anblick, Geruch*›; anstößig ‹*Bemerkung, Wort, Benehmen*›

objective /əb'dʒektɪv/ [1] *adj.* objektiv
[2] *n.* (goal) Ziel, *das*

ob'jectively *adv.* objektiv

objectivity /ɒbdʒek'tɪvɪtɪ/ *n.* Objektivität, *die*

obligation /ɒblɪ'geɪʃn/ *n.* Verpflichtung, *die;* **be under an ~ to sb.** jmdm. verpflichtet sein; **without ~:** unverbindlich

obligatory /ə'blɪgətərɪ/ *adj.* obligatorisch; **it has become ~ to ...:** es ist jetzt Pflicht, zu ...

oblige /ə'blaɪdʒ/ *v.t.* **(a)** (be binding on) **~ sb. to do sth.** jmdm. vorschreiben, etw. zu tun
(b) (compel) zwingen; **be ~d to do sth.** gezwungen sein, etw. zu tun; **feel ~d to do sth.** sich verpflichtet fühlen, etw. zu tun
(c) (be kind to) **~ sb. by doing sth.** jmdm. den Gefallen tun und etw. tun
(d) (grateful) **be much/greatly ~d to sb. [for sth.]** jmdm. [für etw.] sehr verbunden sein; **much ~d!** besten Dank!

obliging /ə'blaɪdʒɪŋ/ *adj.* entgegenkommend

oblique /ə'bli:k/ *adj.* schief ‹*Gerade, Winkel*›; (fig.) indirekt

obliterate /ə'blɪtəreɪt/ *v.t.* auslöschen

oblivion /ə'blɪvɪən/ *n.* Vergessenheit, *die;* **sink** *or* **fall into ~:** in Vergessenheit geraten

oblivious /ə'blɪvɪəs/ *adj.* **be ~ to** *or* **of sth.** sich (*Dat.*) einer Sache (*Gen.*) nicht bewusst sein

oblong /'ɒblɒŋ/ [1] *adj.* rechteckig
[2] *n.* Rechteck, *das*

obnoxious /əb'nɒkʃəs/ *adj.* widerlich

oboe /'əʊbəʊ/ *n.* Oboe, *die*

obscene /əb'si:n/ *adj.* obszön

obscenity /əb'senɪtɪ/ *n.* Obszönität, *die*

obscure /əb'skjʊə(r)/ [1] *adj.* **(a)** (unexplained) dunkel
(b) (hard to understand) schwer verständlich ‹*Argument, Dichtung, Autor, Stil*›
(c) (unknown) unbekannt
[2] *v.t.* **(a)** (make indistinct) verdunkeln; versperren ‹*Aussicht*›
(b) (make unintelligible) unverständlich machen

obsequious /əb'si:kwɪəs/ *adj.* unterwürfig

observance /əb'zɜ:vəns/ *n.* Einhaltung, *die*

observant /əb'zɜ:vənt/ *adj.* aufmerksam

observation /ɒbzə'veɪʃn/ *n.* **(a)** Beobachtung, *die;* **be [kept] under ~:** beobachtet werden; (by police) überwacht werden
(b) (remark) Bemerkung, *die* (**on** über + *Akk.*)

obser'vation post *n.* Beobachtungsposten, *der*

observatory /əb'zɜ:vətərɪ/ *n.* (Astron.) Sternwarte, *die*

observe /əb'zɜ:v/ *v.t.* **(a)** (watch) beobachten; (perceive) bemerken
(b) (abide by, keep) einhalten
(c) (say) bemerken

ob'server *n.* Beobachter, *der*/Beobachterin, *die*

obsess /əb'ses/ *v.t.* **~ sb.** von jmdm. Besitz ergreifen (fig.); **be/become ~ed with** *or* **by sb./sth.** von jmdm./etw. besessen sein/ werden

obsession /əb'seʃn/ *n.* Zwangsvorstellung, *die*

obsessive /əb'sesɪv/ *adj.* zwanghaft; **be ~ about sth.** von etw. besessen sein

obsolescent /ɒbsə'lesənt/ *adj.* veraltend

obsolete /'ɒbsəli:t/ *adj.* veraltet

obstacle /'ɒbstəkl/ *n.* Hindernis, *das* (**to** für)

obstacle: ~ course *n.* Hindernisparcours, *der;* **~ race** *n.* Hindernisrennen, *das*

obstetrics /ɒb'stetrɪks/ *n.* (Med.) Obstetrik, *die* (fachspr.)

obstinacy /'ɒbstɪnəsɪ/ *n.* ▶ OBSTINATE: Starrsinn, *der;* Hartnäckigkeit, *die*

obstinate /'ɒbstɪnət/ *adj.* starrsinnig; (adhering to particular course of action) hartnäckig

obstruct /əb'strʌkt/ *v.t.* **(a)** (block) blockieren; behindern ‹*Verkehr*›; **~ sb.'s view** jmdm. die Sicht versperren
(b) (fig.: impede; also Sport) behindern

obstruction /əb'strʌkʃn/ *n.* Blockierung, *die;* (of progress; also Sport) Behinderung, *die*

obstructive /əb'strʌktɪv/ *adj.* hinderlich; obstruktiv ‹*Politik, Taktik*›; **be ~** ‹*Person:*› sich quer legen (ugs.)

obtain /əb'teɪn/ *v.t.* bekommen; erzielen ‹*Resultat, Wirkung*›

obtainable /əb'teɪnəbl/ *adj.* erhältlich

obtrusive /əb'tru:sɪv/ *adj.* aufdringlich; (conspicuous) auffällig

obtuse /əb'tju:s/ *adj.* **(a)** stumpf ‹*Winkel*›
(b) (stupid) begriffsstutzig

obvious /'ɒbvɪəs/ *adj.* offenkundig; (easily seen) augenfällig; **be ~ [to sb.] that ...:** [jmdm.] klar sein, dass ...

'obviously *adv.* offenkundig; sichtlich ‹*enttäuschen, überraschen usw.*›

occasion /ə'keɪʒn/ [1] *n.* **(a)** Gelegenheit, *die;* **rise to the ~:** sich der Situation gewachsen zeigen; **on several ~s** bei mehreren Gelegenheiten; **on ~[s]** gelegentlich
(b) (special occurrence) Anlass, *der;* **it was quite an ~:** es war ein Ereignis
(c) (reason) Grund, *der* (**for** zu)
[2] *v.t.* verursachen

occasional /ə'keɪʒənl/ *adj.* gelegentlich; vereinzelt ‹*Regenschauer*›

oc'casionally *adv.* gelegentlich; **[only] very ~:** gelegentlich einmal

occult /ɒ'kʌlt, 'ɒkʌlt/ *adj.* okkult; **the ~:** das Okkulte

occupant /'ɒkjʊpənt/ *n.* Bewohner, *der*/Bewohnerin, *die;* (of car, bus, etc.) Insasse, *der*/Insassin, *die*

occupation /ɒkjʊ'peɪʃn/ *n.* **(a)** (Mil.) Besetzung, *die;* (period) Besatzungszeit, *die*
(b) (activity) Beschäftigung, *die*
(c) (profession) Beruf, *der*

occupational /ɒkjʊ'peɪʃənl/ *adj.* Berufs‹*beratung, -risiko*›; **~ therapy** Beschäftigungstherapie, *die;* **~ therapist** Beschäftigungstherapeut, *der*/-therapeutin, *die*

occupier /'ɒkjʊpaɪə(r)/ *n.* (Brit.) Besitzer, *der*/Besitzerin, *die;* (tenant) Bewohner, *der*/Bewohnerin, *die*

occupy /'ɒkjʊpaɪ/ *v.t.* **(a)** (Mil.; as demonstration) besetzen
(b) (live in) bewohnen
(c) (take up, fill) einnehmen; belegen ‹*Zimmer*›; in Anspruch nehmen ‹*Zeit, Aufmerksamkeit*›
(d) (busy, employ) beschäftigen

occur /ə'kɜ:(r)/ *v.i.*, **-rr-: (a)** (be met with) vorkommen; ‹*Gelegenheit:*› sich bieten; ‹*Problem:*› auftreten
(b) (happen) ‹*Veränderung:*› eintreten; ‹*Unfall, Vorfall:*› sich ereignen
(c) ~ to sb. (be thought of) jmdm. in den Sinn kommen; ‹*Idee:*› jmdm. kommen

occurrence /ə'kʌrəns/ *n.* **(a)** (incident) Ereignis, *das;* Begebenheit, *die*
(b) (occurring) Vorkommen, *das*

ocean /'əʊʃn/ *n.* Ozean, *der;* Meer, *das*

o'clock /ə'klɒk/ *adv.* **it is two/six ~:** es ist zwei/sechs Uhr; **at two/six ~:** um zwei/sechs Uhr; **six ~** *attrib.* Sechsuhr‹*zug, -maschine, -nachrichten*›

Oct. *abbr.* = **October** Okt.

octagon /'ɒktəgən/ *n.* Achteck, *das*

octane /'ɒkteɪn/ *n.* Oktan, *das*

octave /'ɒktɪv/ *n.* Oktave, *die*

October /ɒk'təʊbə(r)/ *n.* Oktober, *der; see also* AUGUST

octopus /'ɒktəpəs/ *n.* Tintenfisch, *der*

odd /ɒd/ *adj.* **(a)** (surplus, spare) übrig ‹*Stück, Silbergeld*›; **£25 and a few ~ pence** 25 Pfund und ein paar Pence
(b) (occasional) gelegentlich; **~ job/~-job man** Gelegenheitsarbeit, *die*/-arbeiter, *der*
(c) (one of pair or group) einzeln; **~ socks** nicht zusammengehörende Socken; **be the ~ man out** ‹*Gegenstand:*› nicht dazu passen
(d) (uneven) ungerade ‹*Zahl, Seite, Hausnummer*›
(e) (plus something) **forty ~:** über vierzig; **twelve pounds ~:** etwas mehr als zwölf Pfund
(f) (strange, eccentric) seltsam

oddity /'ɒdɪtɪ/ *n.* (object, event) Kuriosität, *die*

'oddly *adv.* seltsam; **~ enough** seltsamerweise

odd 'man *n.* **~ out** Außenseiter, *der*/Außenseiterin, *die;* **be the ~ out** (extra person) überzählig sein

'odd-numbered *adj.* ungerade

odds /ɒdz/ *n. pl.* **(a)** (Betting) Odds *Pl.*
(b) [the] ~ are that she did it wahrscheinlich hat sie es getan; **the ~ are against/in favour of sb./sth.** jmds. Aussichten/die Aussichten für etw. sind gering/gut
(c) ~ and ends Kleinigkeiten; (of food) Reste
(d) be at ~ with sb. over sth. mit jmdm. in etw. (*Dat.*) uneinig sein
(e) it makes no/little ~ [whether ...] es ist völlig/ziemlich gleichgültig[, ob ...]

'odds-on [1] *adj.* gut ‹*Chance, Aussicht*›; hoch, klar ‹*Favorit*›
[2] *adv.* wahrscheinlich

odious /'əʊdɪəs/ *adj.* widerwärtig

odor *etc.* (*Amer.*) ▶ ODOUR *etc.*

odour /'əʊdə(r)/ *n.* Geruch, *der*

'odourless *adj.* geruchlos

oedema /ɪ'di:mə/ *n.* Ödem, *das*

oestrogen /'i:strədʒən/ *n.* Östrogen, *das*

œuvre /ɜ:vr/ *n.* Œuvre, *das* (geh.); Werk, *das*

of /əv, *stressed* ɒv/ *prep.* von; (indicating material, substance) aus; **articles of clothing** Kleidungsstücke; **a friend of mine** ein Freund von mir; **where's that pencil of mine?** wo ist mein Bleistift?; **it was clever of you to do that** es war klug von dir, das zu tun; **the approval of sb.** jmds. Zustimmung; **the works of Shakespeare** Shakespeares Werke; **be made of ...:** aus ... [hergestellt] sein; **the fifth of January** der fünfte Januar; **his love of his father** seine Liebe zu seinem Vater; **person of extreme views** Mensch mit extremen Ansichten; **a boy of 14 years** ein vierzehnjähriger Junge; **the five of us** wir fünf

off /ɒf/ [1] *adv.* **(a)** (away) **be a few miles ~:** wenige Meilen entfernt sein; **the lake is not far ~:** der See ist nicht weit [weg]; **I'm ~ now** ich gehe jetzt; **~ we go!** los gehts!
(b) (not on or attached or supported) ab; **get the lid ~:** den Deckel abbekommen

(c) be ~ (switched or turned ~) ‹*Wasser, Gas, Strom:*› abgestellt sein; **the light/radio** *etc.* **is ~**: das Licht/Radio *usw.* ist aus
(d) the meat *etc.* **is ~**: das Fleisch *usw.* ist schlecht [geworden]
(e) be ~ (cancelled) abgesagt sein; ‹*Verlobung:*› [auf]gelöst sein; **~ and on** immer mal wieder (ugs.)
(f) (not at work) frei; **on my day ~**: an meinem freien Tag; **have a week ~**: eine Woche Urlaub bekommen
(g) (no longer available) **[the] soup** *etc.* **is ~**: es gibt keine Suppe *usw.* mehr
(h) (situated as regards money etc.) **he is badly** *etc.* **~**: er ist schlecht *usw.* gestellt
2 *prep.* von; **be ~ school/work** in der Schule/am Arbeitsplatz fehlen; **be ~ one's food** keinen Appetit haben; **just ~ the square** ganz in der Nähe des Platzes

offal /'ɒfl/ *n.* Innereien *Pl.*

off: ~beat *adj.* (fig.: eccentric) unkonventionell; **~-'centre** *adv.* nicht [genau] in der Mitte; **~ 'colour** *adj.* unwohl; **~cut** *n.* Rest, *der;* **~-duty** *attrib. adj.* Freizeit-; ‹*Polizist usw.*›, der dienstfrei hat

offence /ə'fens/ *n.* (Brit.) **(a)** (hurting of sb.'s feelings) Kränkung, *die;* **I meant no ~**: ich wollte Sie/ihn *usw.* nicht kränken
(b) (annoyance) **give ~**: Missfallen erregen; **take ~**: verärgert sein
(c) (crime) Straftat, *die;* **criminal ~**: strafbare Handlung

offend /ə'fend/ **1** *v.i.* verstoßen **(against** gegen)
2 *v.t.* **~ sb.** bei jmdm. Anstoß erregen; (hurt feelings of) jmdn. kränken

of'fender *n.* Straffällige, *der/die*

offense (Amer.) ▶ OFFENCE

offensive /ə'fensɪv/ **1** *adj.* **(a)** (aggressive) offensiv; Angriffs‹*waffe*›
(b) (giving offence) ungehörig; (indecent) anstößig
2 *n.* Offensive, *die;* **take the** *or* **go on the ~**: in die *od.* zur Offensive übergehen

offer /'ɒfə(r)/ **1** *v.t.* anbieten; vorbringen ‹*Entschuldigung*›; bieten ‹*Chance*›; aussprechen ‹*Beileid*›; **~ to help** seine Hilfe anbieten; **~ resistance** Widerstand leisten
2 *n.* Angebot, *das;* **[have/be] on ~**: im Angebot [haben/sein]

'offering *n.* (thing) Angebot, *das;* (to a deity) Opfer, *das*

off'hand **1** *adv.* **(a)** (without preparation) auf Anhieb ‹*sagen, wissen*›; spontan ‹*beschließen, entscheiden*›
(b) (casually) leichthin
2 *adj.* **(a)** (without preparation) spontan
(b) (casual) beiläufig; **be ~ with sb.** zu jmdm. kurz angebunden sein

office /'ɒfɪs/ *n.* **(a)** Büro, *das*
(b) (branch) Zweigstelle, *die*
(c) (position) Amt, *das;* **hold ~**: amtieren

office: ~ block *n.* Bürogebäude, *das;* **~ hours** *n. pl.* Dienststunden *Pl.;* **~ job** *n.* Bürotätigkeit, *die*

officer /'ɒfɪsə(r)/ *n.* **(a)** (Army etc.) Offizier, *der*
(b) (official) Beamte, *der*/Beamtin, *die*
(c) (constable) Polizeibeamte, *der*/-beamtin, *die*

office: ~ technology *n.* Bürotechnik, *die;* **~ worker** *n.* Büroangestellte, *der/die*

official /ə'fɪʃl/ **1** *adj.* offiziell; amtlich ‹*Verlautbarung*›; regulär ‹*Streik*›
2 *n.* Beamte, *der*/Beamtin, *die;* (party, union, or sports ~) Funktionär, *der*/Funktionärin, *die*

officialdom /ə'fɪʃldəm/ *n., no art.* Beamtentum, *das;* Bürokratie, *die*

of'ficially *adv.* offiziell

officious /ə'fɪʃəs/ *adj.* übereifrig

offing /'ɒfɪŋ/ *n.* **be in the ~**: bevorstehen; ‹*Gewitter:*› aufziehen

off: ~-licence *n.* (Brit.) ≈ Wein- und Spirituosenladen, *der;* **~-line** (Comp.) **1** /'--/ *adj.* Offline-; **2** /-'-/ *adv.* offline; **~-load** *v.t.* abladen; **~-peak** *attrib. adj.* **during ~-peak hours** außerhalb der Spitzenlastzeiten; **~-peak power** *or* **electricity** Nachtstrom, *der;* **~-putting** /'ɒfpʊtɪŋ/ *adj.* (Brit.) abstoßend; **~print** *n.* Sonderdruck, *der;* **~-road** *attrib. adj.* Gelände-, Offroad‹*fahrzeug, -fahrrad, -wagen, -fahrt, -einsatz*›; **~-road driving** Fahren im Gelände; **~set** /'--, -'-/ *v.t., forms as* SET: ausgleichen; **~ season** *n.* Nebensaison, *die;* **~shore** *adj.* küstennah; **~'side** *adj.* Abseits-; **be ~-side** abseits sein; **~spring** *n., pl. same* Nachkommenschaft, *die;* (of animal) Junge *Pl.;* **~-the-peg** *attrib. adj.* Konfektions-; **~-the-shoulder** *attrib. adj.* schulterfrei ‹*Kleid*›; **~-the-wall** *attrib. adj.* (esp. Amer. coll.) ausgeflippt (ugs.); **~-'white** *adj.* gebrochen weiß

Oftel /'ɒftel/ *abbr.* (Brit.) = **Office of Telecommunications** *Regulierungsbehörde für Telekommunikation*

often /'ɒfn, 'ɒftn/ *adv.* oft; **every so ~**: gelegentlich

Ofwat /'ɒfwɒt/ *abbr.* (Brit.) = **Office of Water Services** *Regulierungsbehörde für Wasserwirtschaft*

oh /əʊ/ *int.* oh; *expr. pain* au

OHP *abbr.* (Brit.) = **overhead projector** OHP

oil /ɔɪl/ **1** *n.* Öl, *das*
2 *v.t.* ölen

oil: ~-burner *n.* Ölbrenner, *der;* **~can** *n.* Ölkanne, *die;* **~ change** *n.* (Motor Veh.) Ölwechsel, *der;* **~ drum** *n.* Ölfass, *das;* **~field** *n.* Ölfeld, *das;* **~ lamp** *n.* Öllampe, *die;* **~ painting** *n.* Ölgemälde, *das;* **~-producing** *adj.* [Erd]öl fördernd ‹*Land*›; **~ refinery** *n.* [Erd]ölraffinerie, ···›

O

die; ~ **rig** ▶ RIG[1] 1; ~**skins** *n. pl.* Ölzeug, *das;* ~ **slick** *n.* Ölteppich, *der;* ~ **tanker** *n.* Öltanker, *der;* ~ **well** *n.* Ölquelle, *die*

oily /ˈɔɪlɪ/ *adj.* ölig; ölverschmiert ‹*Gesicht, Hände*›

ointment /ˈɔɪntmənt/ *n.* Salbe, *die*

OK /əʊˈkeɪ/ (coll.) **1** *adj.* in Ordnung; okay (ugs.)
2 *adv.* gut
3 *int.* okay (ugs.)
4 *v.t.* (approve) zustimmen (+ *Dat.*); **be OK'd by sb.** von jmdm. das Okay bekommen (ugs.)

okay /əʊˈkeɪ/ ▶ OK

old /əʊld/ *adj.* alt; **be [more than] 30 years** ~: [über] 30 Jahre alt sein

old: ~ **'age** *n.* [fortgeschrittenes] Alter; ~**-age** *attrib. adj.* Alters‹*rente, -ruhegeld*›; ~**-age pensioner** Rentner, *der*/Rentnerin, *die;* ~**-fashioned** /əʊldˈfæʃnd/ *adj.* altmodisch; ~ **'people's home** *n.* Altenheim, *das;* Altersheim, *das;* ~ **'wives' tale** *n.* Ammenmärchen, *das*

olive /ˈɒlɪv/ *n.* Olive, *die*

olive 'oil *n.* Olivenöl, *das*

Olympic /əˈlɪmpɪk/ *adj.* olympisch; ~ **Games** Olympische Spiele

Olympics /əˈlɪmpɪks/ *n. pl.* Olympiade, *die;* **Winter** ~: Winterolympiade, *die*

omelette (**omelet**) /ˈɒmlɪt/ *n.* Omelett, *das*

omen /ˈəʊmən/ *n.* Vorzeichen, *das*

ominous /ˈɒmɪnəs/ *adj.* (of evil omen) ominös; (worrying) beunruhigend

omission /əˈmɪʃn/ *n.* Auslassung, *die;* (failure to act) Unterlassung, *die*

omit /əˈmɪt/ *v.t.*, **-tt-** weglassen; ~ **to do sth.** es versäumen, etw. zu tun

omnipotence /ɒmˈnɪpətəns/ *n.* Allmacht, *die* (geh.)

omnipotent /ɒmˈnɪpətənt/ *adj.* allmächtig

on /ɒn/ **1** *prep.* auf (*position:* + *Dat.; direction:* + *Akk.*); (attached to) an (+ *Dat.*/*Akk.*); (concerning, about) über (+ *Akk.*); (in expressions of time) an ‹*einem Abend, Tag usw.*›; **write sth. on the wall** etw. an die Wand schreiben; **be hanging on the wall** an der Wand hängen; **have sth. on one** etw. bei sich haben; **on the bus/train** im Bus/Zug; (by bus/train) mit dem Bus/Zug; **on Oxford 556767** unter der Nummer Oxford 556767; **on Sundays** sonntags; **on [his] arrival** bei seiner Ankunft; **on entering the room ...:** beim Betreten des Zimmers ...; **it's just on 9** es ist fast 9 Uhr; **the drinks are on me** (coll.) die Getränke gehen auf mich
2 *adv.* **with/without a hat/coat on** mit/ohne Hut/Mantel; **have a hat on** einen Hut aufhaben; **on and on** immer weiter; **speak/wait/work** *etc.* **on** weiterreden/-warten/-arbeiten *usw.;* **from now on** von jetzt an; **the light/radio** *etc.* **is on** das Licht/Radio *usw.* ist an; **is Sunday's picnic on?** findet das Picknick am Sonntag statt?; **what's on at the cinema?** was läuft im Kino?; **on and off** immer mal wieder (ugs.); **on to, onto** auf (+ *Akk.*)

once /wʌns/ **1** *adv.* **(a)** einmal; ~ **a week/month/year** einmal die Woche/im Monat/im Jahr; ~ **again** *or* **more** noch einmal; ~ **[and] for all** ein für alle Mal; **never/not** ~: nicht ein einziges Mal
(b) (multiplied by one) ein mal
(c) (formerly) früher einmal; ~ **upon a time there lived a king** es war einmal ein König
(d) at ~ (immediately) sofort; (at the same time) gleichzeitig; **all at** ~ (suddenly) plötzlich; (simultaneously) alle[s] zugleich
2 *conj.* wenn; (with past tense) als
3 *n.* **[just** *or* **only] this** ~: [nur] dieses eine Mal

'oncoming *adj.* entgegenkommend ‹*Fahrzeug, Verkehr*›

one /wʌn/ **1** *adj.* ein; *see also* EIGHT 1; (single, only) einzig; **no/not** ~: kein; **the** ~ **thing** das Einzige; **at** ~ **time** einmal; ~ **morning/night** eines Morgens/Nachts
2 *n.* **(a)** eins
(b) (number, symbol) Eins, *die*
(c) (unit) **in** ~**s** einzeln
3 *pron.* **(a)** ein... (**of** + *Gen.*); **big** ~**s and little** ~**s** Große und Kleine; **the older/younger** ~: der/die/das Ältere/Jüngere; **this** ~: dieser/diese/dieses [da]; **that** ~: der/die/das [da]; **which** ~**?** welcher/welche/welches?; **which** ~**s?** welche?; ~ **by** ~: einzeln; **love/hate** ~ **another** sich lieben/hassen; **be kind to** ~ **another** nett zueinander sein
(b) (people in general; coll.: I, we) man; *as indirect object* einem; *as direct object* einen; ~**'s** sein

one: ~**-night 'stand** *n.* (coll.) [sexuelles] Abenteuer für eine Nacht; ~**-off** (Brit.) **1** *n.* (article) Einzelstück, *das;* **2** *adj.* einmalig; ~**-parent family** *n.* Einelternfamilie, *die*

onerous /ˈəʊnərəs/ *adj.* schwer

one: ~**'self** *pron.* **(a)** *emphat.* selbst; **be** ~**self** man selbst sein; **(b)** *refl.* sich; *see also* HERSELF; ~**-sided** *adj.* einseitig; ~**-stop shopping** *n.* Einkaufen in einem Einkaufszentrum [mit Komplettangebot]; ~**-storey** *adj.* eingeschossig; ~**-touch** *adj.* ~**-touch dialling** Zielwahl, *die;* ~**-track** *adj.* eingleisig; **have a** ~**-track mind** (be obsessed) nur eins im Kopf haben; ~**-upmanship** /wʌnˈʌpmənʃɪp/ *n., no indef. art.* die Kunst, den anderen immer um eine Nasenlänge voraus zu sein; ~**-way** *adj.* **(a)** in einer Richtung *nachgestellt;* Einbahn‹*straße, -verkehr*›; **(b)** einfach ‹*Fahrpreis, Flug*›

'ongoing *adj.* aktuell ‹*Problem, Debatte*›; andauernd ‹*Situation*›

onion /ˈʌnjən/ *n.* Zwiebel, *die*

onion: ~ **skin** *n.* Zwiebelschale, *die;* ~ **'soup** *n.* Zwiebelsuppe, *die*

online (Comp.) **1** /ˈ--/ *adj.* Online-
2 /-ˈ-/ *adv.* online

'onlooker *n.* Zuschauer, *der*/Zuschauerin, *die*

only /'əʊnlɪ/ [1] *attrib. adj.* einzig...; **the ~ person** der/die Einzige; **an ~ child** ein Einzelkind
[2] *adv.* nur; **we had been waiting ~ 5 minutes when ...:** wir hatten erst 5 Minuten gewartet, als ...; **it's ~/~ just 6 o'clock** es ist erst 6 Uhr/gerade erst 6 Uhr vorbei; **he ~ just made it** er hat es gerade noch geschafft; **~ if** nur [dann] ..., wenn; **~ the other day/week** erst neulich

on-screen *adj.* (Comp., TV) Bildschirm-

'onset *n.* (of winter) Einbruch, *der;* (of disease) Ausbruch, *der*

onslaught /'ɒnslɔːt/ *n.* [heftige] Attacke (fig.)

'on-target *attrib. adj.* **~ earnings £50,000** Verdienst bei erfolgreicher Tätigkeit 50 000 Pfund

onto ▶ ON 2

onus /'əʊnəs/ *n.* **the ~ is on him to do it** es ist seine Sache, es zu tun

onward[s] /'ɒnwədz/ *adv.* (in space) vorwärts; **from X ~:** von X an; **from that day ~:** von diesem Tag an

onyx /'ɒnɪks/ *n.* Onyx, *der*

ooze /uːz/ [1] *v.i.* sickern (**from** aus)
[2] *v.t.* triefen von *od.* vor (+ *Dat.*); (fig.) ausstrahlen

op /ɒp/ *n.* (coll.) Operation, *die*

opaque /əʊ'peɪk/ *adj.* lichtundurchlässig; opak (fachspr.)

open /'əʊpn/ [1] *adj.* **(a)** offen; (not blocked or obstructed) frei; (available) frei ‹*Stelle*›; **in the ~ air** im Freien; **be ~** ‹*Laden, Museum, Bank usw.:*› geöffnet sein; **have an ~ mind about** *or* **on sth.** einer Sache gegenüber aufgeschlossen sein
(b) unverhohlen ‹*Bewunderung, Hass, Verachtung*›
(c) (frank, communicative) offen ‹*Wesen, Streit, Abstimmung, Regierungsstil*›; (not secret) öffentlich ‹*Wahl*›
(d) geöffnet ‹*Regenschirm*›; aufgeblüht ‹*Blume, Knospe*›; aufgeschlagen ‹*Zeitung, Landkarte*›
[2] *n.* **in the ~** (outdoors) unter freiem Himmel; **[out] in the ~** (fig.) öffentlich bekannt
[3] *v.t.* **(a)** öffnen
(b) eröffnen ‹*Konferenz, Diskussion, Laden*›; beginnen ‹*Verhandlungen, Spiel*›
(c) (unfold, spread out) aufschlagen ‹*Zeitung, Buch, Landkarte*›; öffnen ‹*Schirm*›
[4] *v.i.* **(a)** sich öffnen; **~ into/on to sth.** zu etw. führen
(b) (become ~ to customers) öffnen; (start trading etc.) eröffnet werden
(c) (start) beginnen; ‹*Ausstellung:*› eröffnet werden; ‹*Theaterstück:*› Premiere haben

■ **open 'up** [1] *v.t.* öffnen; (establish) eröffnen
[2] *v.i.* sich öffnen; ‹*Filiale:*› eröffnet werden; ‹*Firma:*› sich niederlassen

open: ~-air *attrib. adj.* Openair‹*konzert*›; **~-air [swimming] pool** Freibad, *das;* **~-and-'shut case** *n.* (coll.) klarer Fall; **~ day** *n.* Tag der offenen Tür

'opener *n.* Öffner, *der*

'opening [1] *n.* **(a)** Öffnen, *das;* (becoming open) Sichöffnen, *das;* (of exhibition, new centre) Eröffnen, *das*
(b) (establishment, ceremony) Eröffnung, die
(c) (initial part) Anfang, *der*
(d) (gap, aperture) Öffnung, *die*
(e) (opportunity) Möglichkeit, *die;* (vacancy) freie Stelle
[2] *adj.* einleitend

opening: ~ hours *n. pl.* Öffnungszeiten *Pl.;* **~ time** *n.* Öffnungszeit, *die*

'openly *adv.* **(a)** (publicly) in der Öffentlichkeit, öffentlich ‹*zugeben, verurteilen*›
(b) (frankly) offen

open: ~ 'market *n.* offener *od.* freier Markt; **~-'minded** *adj.* aufgeschlossen

openness /'əʊpnnɪs/ *n.* (frankness) Offenheit, *die*

open: ~-'plan *adj.* **~-plan office** Großraumbüro, *das;* **~ 'prison** *n.* offene Anstalt; **~ 'sandwich** *n.* belegtes Brot

opera /'ɒpərə/ *n.* Oper, *die*

opera: ~ glasses *n. pl.* Opernglas, *das;* **~ house** *n.* Opernhaus, *das;* **~ singer** *n.* Opernsänger, *der*/-sängerin, *die*

operate /'ɒpəreɪt/ [1] *v.i.* **(a)** (be in action) in Betrieb sein; ‹*Bus, Zug usw.:*› verkehren
(b) (function) arbeiten; **the torch ~s on batteries** die Taschenlampe arbeitet mit Batterien
(c) **~ [on sb.]** (Med.) [jmdn.] operieren
[2] *v.t.* bedienen ‹*Maschine*›; unterhalten ‹*Busverbindung, Telefondienst*›; betätigen ‹*Hebel, Bremse*›

operating: ~ system *n.* (Comp.) Betriebssystem, *das;* **~ theatre** *n.* (Brit. Med.) Operationssaal, *der*

operation /ɒpə'reɪʃn/ *n.* **(a)** (causing to work) (of machine) Bedienung, *die;* (of bus service, telephone service, etc.) Unterhaltung, *die;* (of lever, brake) Betätigung, *die*
(b) **come into ~** ‹*Gesetz, Gebühr usw.:*› in Kraft treten; **be in/out of ~** ‹*Maschine, Gerät usw.:*› in/außer Betrieb sein
(c) (Med.) Operation, *die;* **have an ~:** operiert werden

operational /ɒpə'reɪʃənl/ *adj.* (esp. Mil.: ready to function) einsatzbereit

operative /'ɒpərətɪv/ *adj.* **become ~** ‹*Gesetz:*› in Kraft treten; **the scheme is ~:** das Programm läuft

operator /'ɒpəreɪtə(r)/ *n.* [Maschinen]bediener, *der*/-bedienerin, *die;* (Teleph.) (at exchange) Vermittlung, *die;* (at switchboard) Telefonist, *der*/Telefonistin, *die*

ophthalmic op'tician /ɒf'θælmɪk/ *n.* (Brit.) Augenoptiker, *der*/-optikerin, *die*

opinion /ə'pɪnjən/ *n.* Meinung, *die* (**on** über ···>

+ *Akk.*, zu); **have a high/low ~ of sb.** eine/ keine hohe Meinung von jmdm. haben; **in my ~**: meiner Meinung nach

opinionated /ə'pɪnjəneɪtɪd/ *adj.* rechthaberisch

o'pinion poll *n.* Meinungsumfrage, *die*

opium /'əʊpɪəm/ *n.* Opium, *das*

opponent /ə'pəʊnənt/ *n.* Gegner, *der*/ Gegnerin, *die*

opportune /'ɒpətju:n/ *adj.* **(a)** (favourable) günstig
(b) (well-timed) zur rechten Zeit *nachgestellt*

opportunism /ɒpə'tju:nɪzm/ *n.* Opportunismus, *der*

opportunist /ɒpə'tju:nɪst/ *n.* Opportunist, *der*/Opportunistin, *die*

opportunity /ɒpə'tju:nɪtɪ/ *n.* Gelegenheit, *die*

oppose /ə'pəʊz/ [1] *v.t.* sich wenden gegen
[2] *v.i.* **the opposing team** die gegnerische Mannschaft

opposed /ə'pəʊzd/ *adj.* **as ~ to** im Gegensatz zu; **be ~ to sth.** ‹*Person:*› gegen etw. sein

opposite /'ɒpəzɪt/ [1] *adj.* gegenüberliegend ‹*Straßenseite, Ufer*›; entgegengesetzt ‹*Ende, Weg, Richtung*›; **the ~ sex** das andere Geschlecht
[2] *n.* Gegenteil, *das* (**of** von)
[3] *adv.* gegenüber
[4] *prep.* gegenüber

opposite 'number *n.* (fig.) Pendant, *das*

opposition /ɒpə'zɪʃn/ *n.* **(a)** Opposition, *die;* (resistance) Widerstand, *der* (**to** gegen); **in ~ to** entgegen
(b) (Brit. Polit.) **the O~**: die Opposition

oppress /ə'pres/ *v.t.* unterdrücken; (fig.) ‹*Gefühl:*› bedrücken

oppression /ə'preʃn/ *n.* Unterdrückung, *die*

oppressive /ə'presɪv/ *adj.* repressiv; (fig.) bedrückend ‹*Ängste, Atmosphäre*›; (hot and close) drückend ‹*Wetter, Klima, Tag*›

opt /ɒpt/ *v.i.* sich entscheiden (**for** für); **~ to do sth.** sich dafür entscheiden, etw. zu tun; **~ out** nicht mitmachen/(stop taking part) nicht länger mitmachen (**of** bei)

optic /'ɒptɪk/ [1] *adj.* (Anat.) Seh‹*nerv, -bahn*›
[2] *n. or* **O~** ® (Brit.: for spirits) Portionierer, *der*

optical /'ɒptɪkl/ *adj.* optisch

optical 'character reader *n.* (Comp.) Klarschriftleser, *der*

optician /ɒp'tɪʃn/ *n.* Optiker, *der*/ Optikerin, *die*

optics /'ɒptɪks/ *n.* Optik, *die*

optima *pl. of* OPTIMUM

optimise ▶ OPTIMIZE

optimism /'ɒptɪmɪzm/ *n.* Optimismus, *der*

optimist /'ɒptɪmɪst/ *n.* Optimist, *der*/ Optimistin, *die*

optimistic /ɒptɪ'mɪstɪk/ *adj.* optimistisch

optimize /'ɒptɪmaɪz/ *v.t.* (make the most of) das Beste machen aus

optimum /'ɒptɪməm/ [1] *n., pl.* **optima** /'ɒptɪmə/ Optimum, *das*
[2] *adj.* optimal

option /'ɒpʃn/ *n.* (choice) Wahl, *die;* (thing) Wahlmöglichkeit, *die*

optional /'ɒpʃənl/ *adj.* nicht zwingend; **~ subject** Wahlfach, *das*

opulence /'ɒpjʊləns/ *n.* Wohlstand, *der*

opulent /'ɒpjʊlənt/ *adj.* wohlhabend; feudal ‹*Auto, Haus usw.*›

or /ə(r), *stressed* ɔ:(r)/ *conj.* **(a)** oder; **he cannot read or write** er kann weder lesen noch schreiben; **without food or water** ohne Essen und Wasser; **15 or 20 minutes** 15 bis 20 Minuten; **in a day or two** in ein, zwei Tagen
(b) (introducing explanation) das heißt; **or rather** beziehungsweise

oracle /'ɒrəkl/ *n.* Orakel, *das*

oral /'ɔ:rəl/ *adj.* mündlich; (Med.) oral

orally /'ɔ:rəlɪ/ *adv.* **take ~**: einnehmen

orange /'ɒrɪndʒ/ [1] *n.* **(a)** (fruit) Orange, *die;* Apfelsine, *die*
(b) (colour) Orange, *das*
[2] *adj.* orange[farben]

orange: ~ juice *n.* Orangensaft, *der;* **~ peel** *n.* Orangenschale, *die;* **~ 'squash** *n.* Orangensaftgetränk, *das*

orator /'ɒrətə(r)/ *n.* Redner, *der*/Rednerin, *die*

oratory /'ɒrətərɪ/ *n.* Redekunst, *die*

orb /ɔ:b/ *n.* Kugel, *die*

orbit /'ɔ:bɪt/ [1] *n.* (Astron.) [Umlauf]bahn, *die*
[2] *v.i.* kreisen
[3] *v.t.* umkreisen

orbital /'ɔ:bɪtl/ *adj.* **~ road** Ringstraße, *die*

orchard /'ɔ:tʃəd/ *n.* Obstgarten, *der;* (commercial) Obstplantage, *die*

orchestra /'ɔ:kɪstrə/ *n.* Orchester, *das*

orchestral /ɔ:'kestrl/ *adj.* Orchester-

orchestrate /'ɔ:kɪstreɪt/ *v.t.* orchestrieren

orchid /'ɔ:kɪd/ *n.* Orchidee, *die*

ordain /ɔ:'deɪn/ *v.t.* **(a)** (Eccl.) ordinieren
(b) (decree) verfügen

ordeal /ɔ:'di:l/ *n.* Qual, *die*

order /'ɔ:də(r)/ [1] *n.* **(a)** (sequence) Reihenfolge, *die;* **out of ~**: durcheinander
(b) (regular arrangement, normal state) Ordnung, *die;* **be/not be in ~**: in Ordnung/nicht in Ordnung sein (ugs.); **be out of/in ~** (not in/in working condition) nicht funktionieren/ funktionieren; **'out of ~'** „außer Betrieb"; **in good/bad ~**: in gutem/schlechtem Zustand
(c) (command) Anweisung, *die;* (Mil.) Befehl, *der*
(d) in ~ to do sth. um etw. zu tun
(e) (Commerc.) Auftrag, *der* (**for** über + *Akk.*); (to waiter, **~ed goods**) Bestellung, *die*
(f) keep ~: Ordnung [be]wahren; *see also* LAW B
(g) (religious **~**) Orden, *der*

2 *v.t.* **(a)** (command) befehlen; ‹*Richter:*› verfügen; **~ sb. to do sth.** jmdn. anweisen/ (Milit.) jmdm. befehlen, etw. zu tun **(b)** (Commerc.) bestellen (**from** bei) **(c)** (arrange) ordnen

■ **order a'bout, order a'round** *v.t.* herumkommandieren

'order form *n.* Bestellformular, *das*

orderly /'ɔːdəlɪ/ **1** *adj.* friedlich; diszipliniert ‹*Menge*›; (methodical) methodisch; (tidy) ordentlich **2** *n.* **(a)** (Mil.) [Offiziers]bursche, *der* **(b) medical ~:** ≈ Krankenpflegehelfer, *der*

ordinal /'ɔːdɪnl/ *adj. & n.* **~ [number]** Ordinalzahl, *die*

ordinarily /'ɔːdɪnərɪlɪ/ *adv.* normalerweise; gewöhnlich

ordinary /'ɔːdɪnərɪ/ *adj.* (normal) normal ‹*Gebrauch*›; üblich ‹*Verfahren*›; (not exceptional) gewöhnlich

ordination /ɔːdɪ'neɪʃn/ *n.* (Eccl.) Ordination, *die;* Ordinierung, *die*

ordnance 'survey /'ɔːdnəns/ *n.* (Brit.) amtliche Landesvermessung; **~ survey map** amtliche topographische Karte

ore /ɔː(r)/ *n.* Erz, *das*

organ /'ɔːgən/ *n.* **(a)** (Mus.) Orgel, *die* **(b)** (Biol.) Organ, *das*

'organ donor *n.* Organspender, *der*/ -spenderin, *die;* **~ card** Organspende[r]ausweis, *der*

organic /ɔː'gænɪk/ *adj.* organisch; biologisch-dynamisch ‹*Ackerbau*›; biodynamisch ‹*Nahrungsmittel*›

organically /ɔː'gænɪkəlɪ/ *adv.* **(a)** (also Med.) organisch **(b)** (without chemicals) biologisch

organism /'ɔːgənɪzm/ *n.* Organismus, *der*

organist /'ɔːgənɪst/ *n.* Organist, *der*/ Organistin, *die*

organization /ɔːgənaɪ'zeɪʃn/ *n.* Organisation, *die;* **~ of time/work** Zeit-/ Arbeitseinteilung, *die*

organize /'ɔːgənaɪz/ *v.t.* organisieren; einteilen ‹*Arbeit, Zeit*›; veranstalten ‹*Konferenz, Festival*›; **~ into groups** in Gruppen einteilen

organized /'ɔːgənaɪzd/ *adj.* organisiert

'organizer *n.* Organisator, *der*/ Organisatorin, *die;* (of event, festival) Veranstalter, *der*/Veranstalterin, *die*

'organ transplant *n.* Organverpflanzung, *die*

orgasm /'ɔːgæzm/ *n.* Orgasmus, *der*

orgy /'ɔːdʒɪ/ *n.* Orgie, *die*

orient **1** /'ɔːrɪənt/ *n.* **the O~:** der Orient **2** /'ɒrɪent/ *v.t.* ausrichten (**towards** nach); **~ oneself** sich orientieren

oriental /ɒrɪ'entl/ **1** *adj.* orientalisch **2** *n.* Asiat, *der*/Asiatin, *die*

orientate /'ɒrɪənteɪt/ ▶ ORIENT 2

orientation /ɒrɪən'teɪʃn/ *n.* Orientierung, *die*

orienteering /ɒrɪən'tɪərɪŋ/ *n.* (Brit.) Orientierungslauf, *der*

orifice /'ɒrɪfɪs/ *n.* Öffnung, *die*

origin /'ɒrɪdʒɪn/ *n.* (derivation) Herkunft, *die;* (beginnings) Anfänge *Pl.;* (source) Ursprung, *der;* **country of ~:** Herkunftsland, *das;* **have its ~ in sth.** seinen Ursprung in etw. (*Dat.*) haben

original /ə'rɪdʒɪnl/ **1** *adj.* ursprünglich; Ur‹*text, -fassung*›; eigenständig ‹*Forschung*›; (inventive) originell; **an ~ painting** ein Original **2** *n.* Original, *das*

original 'gravity *n.* Stammwürze, *die*

originality /ərɪdʒɪ'nælɪtɪ/ *n.* Originalität, *die*

originally /ə'rɪdʒɪnəlɪ/ *adv.* **(a)** ursprünglich **(b)** originell ‹*schreiben usw.*›

originate /ə'rɪdʒɪneɪt/ *v.i.* **~ from** entstehen aus; **~ in** seinen Ursprung haben in (+ *Dat.*)

ornament /'ɔːnəmənt/ *n.* Ziergegenstand, *der*

ornamental /ɔːnə'mentl/ *adj.* dekorativ; Zier‹*pflanze, -naht usw.*›

ornate /ɔː'neɪt/ *adj.* reich verziert; prunkvoll ‹*Dekoration*›

ornithologist /ɔːnɪ'θɒlədʒɪst/ *n.*. Ornithologe, *der*/Ornithologin, *die*

ornithology /ɔːnɪ'θɒlədʒɪ/ *n.* Ornithologie, *die*

orphan /'ɔːfn/ **1** *n.* Waise, *die* **2** *v.t.* **be ~ed** [zur] Waise werden

orphanage /'ɔːfənɪdʒ/ *n.* Waisenhaus, *das*

orthodox /'ɔːθədɒks/ *adj.* orthodox

orthopaedic /ɔːθə'piːdɪk/ *adj.* orthopädisch

orthopaedics /ɔːθə'piːdɪks/ *n.* Orthopädie, *die*

oscillate /'ɒsɪleɪt/ *v.i.* schwingen

oscillation /ɒsɪ'leɪʃn/ *n.* Schwingen, *das;* (single **~**) Schwingung, *die*

osmosis /ɒz'məʊsɪs/ *n., pl.* **osmoses** /ɒz'məʊsiːz/ Osmose, *die*

ostensible /ɒ'stensɪbl/ *adj.* vorgeschoben

ostensibly /ɒ'stensɪblɪ/ *adv.* vorgeblich

ostentatious /ɒsten'teɪʃəs/ *adj.* prunkhaft ‹*Kleidung, Schmuck*›; prahlerisch ‹*Art*›

osteopath /'ɒstɪəpæθ/ *n.* Osteopath, *der*/ Osteopathin, *die*

osteoporosis /ɒstɪəʊpə'rəʊsɪs/ *n.* Osteoporose, *die*

ostrich /'ɒstrɪtʃ/ *n.* Strauß, *der*

other /'ʌðə(r)/ **1** *adj.* **(a)** (not the same) ander...; **the ~ two/three** *etc.* (the remaining) die beiden/drei *usw.* anderen; **the ~ one** der/die/das andere; **some ~ time** ein andermal

···›

(b) (further) **one ~ thing** noch eins; **some/six ~ people** noch ein paar/noch sechs [andere *od.* weitere] Leute; **no ~ questions** keine weiteren Fragen
(c) ~ than (different from) anders als; (except) außer
(d) the ~ day/evening neulich/neulich abends
2 *n.* anderer/andere/anderes; **there are six ~s** es sind noch sechs andere da; **any ~**: irgendein anderer/-eine andere/-ein anderes; **not any ~**: kein anderer/keine andere/kein anderes; **one after the ~**: einer/eine/eins nach dem/der/dem anderen
3 *adv.* anders; **~ than that, ...**: abgesehen davon, ...

otherwise /ˈʌðəwaɪz/ **1** *adv.* **(a)** (in a different way) anders
(b) (or else) anderenfalls
(c) (in other respects) im Übrigen
2 *pred. adj.* anders

otter /ˈɒtə(r)/ *n.* [Fisch]otter, *der*

ouch /aʊtʃ/ *int.* autsch

ought /ɔːt/ *v. aux. only in pres. and past* **ought**, *neg.* (coll.) **oughtn't** /ˈɔːtnt/ **I ~ to do/have done it** (expr. moral duty) ich müsste es tun/hätte es tun müssen; (expr. desirability) ich sollte es tun/hätte es tun sollen; **~ not** *or* **~n't you to have left by now?** müsstest du nicht schon weg sein?; **one ~ not to do it** man sollte es nicht tun; **he ~ to be hanged/in hospital** er gehört an den Galgen/ins Krankenhaus; **that ~ to be enough** das dürfte reichen; **he ~ to win** er müsste [eigentlich] gewinnen

oughtn't /ˈɔːtnt/ (coll.) = **ought not**

ounce /aʊns/ *n.* (measure) Unze, *die*

our /ˈaʊə(r)/ *poss. pron. attrib.* unser

ours /ˈaʊəz/ *poss. pron. pred.* unserer/unsere/unseres; *see also* HERS

ourselves /aʊəˈselvz/ *pron.* **(a)** *emphat.* selbst
(b) *refl.* uns. *See also* HERSELF

oust /aʊst/ *v.t.* verdrängen; **~ sb. from his job/from power** jmdn. von seinem Arbeitsplatz vertreiben/jmdn. entmachten

out /aʊt/ *adv.* **(a)** (away from place) **~ here/there** hier/da draußen; **be ~ in the garden** draußen im Garten sein; **what's it like ~?** wie ist es draußen?; **go ~ shopping** *etc.* einkaufen *usw.* gehen; **be ~** (not at home, not in one's office, etc.) nicht da sein; **she was ~ all night** sie war eine/die ganze Nacht weg; **have a day ~ in London** einen Tag in London verbringen; **row ~ to ...**: hinaus-/herausrudern zu ...; **be ~ at sea** auf See sein
(b) (Sport, Games) **be ~** ‹*Ball:*› aus *od.* im Aus sein; ‹*Mitspieler:*› ausscheiden; ‹*Schlagmann:*› aus[geschlagen] sein; **not ~**: nicht aus
(c) be ~ (asleep) weg sein (ugs.); (unconscious) bewusstlos sein
(d) (no longer burning) aus[gegangen]
(e) (in error) **be 3% ~ in one's calculations** sich um 3% verrechnet haben; **this is £5 ~**: das stimmt um 5 Pfund nicht
(f) (not in fashion) passee (ugs.); out (ugs.)
(g) say it ~ loud es laut sagen; **~ with it!** heraus mit der Sprache; **their secret is ~**: ihr Geheimnis ist bekannt geworden; **[the] truth will ~**: die Wahrheit wird an den Tag kommen; **the sun/moon is ~**: die Sonne/der Mond scheint; **the third volume is just ~**: der dritte Band ist soeben erschienen; **the roses are ~**: die Rosen blühen
(h) be ~ for sth./to do sth. auf etw. (*Akk.*) aus sein/darauf aus sein, etw. zu tun; **be ~ for trouble** Streit suchen
(i) (to or at an end) **before the day/month was ~**: am selben Tag/vor Ende des Monats. *See also* OUT OF

out: ~back *n.* (esp. Austral.) Hinterland, *das;* **~ˈbid** *v.t.*, **~bid** überbieten; **~board** *adj.* **~board motor** Außenbordmotor, *der;* **~break** *n.* Ausbruch, *der;* **at the ~break of war** bei Kriegsausbruch; **an ~break of flu** eine Grippeepidemie; **~building** *n.* Nebengebäude, *das;* **~burst** *n.* Ausbruch, *der;* **an ~burst of weeping/laughter** ein Weinkrampf/Lachanfall; **an ~burst of temper** ein Wutanfall; **~cast** *n.* Ausgestoßene, *der/die;* **a social ~cast** ein Geächteter/eine Geächtete; **~come** *n.* Ergebnis, *das;* Resultat, *das;* **~cry** *n.* [Aufschrei der] Empörung; **~ˈdated** *adj.* überholt; **~ˈdo** *v.t., forms as* DO: überbieten (**in** an + *Dat.*); **~door** *adj.* **~door shoes/things** Straßenschuhe/-kleidung, *die;* **~door games/pursuits** Spiele/Beschäftigungen im Freien; **~door swimming pool** Freibad, *das;* **~ˈdoors** **1** *adv.* draußen; **go ~doors** nach draußen gehen; **2** *n.* **the [great] ~doors** die freie Natur

outer /ˈaʊtə(r)/ *adj.* äußer...; Außen‹*fläche, -seite, -wand, -tür*›

outer ˈspace *n.* Weltraum, *der*

out: ~fit *n.* **(a)** (clothes) Kleider *Pl.;* **(b)** (equipment) Ausrüstung, *die;* **(c)** (coll.: organization) Laden, *der* (ugs.); **~going** **1** *adj.* **(a)** [aus dem Amt] scheidend ‹*Regierung, Präsident*›; **(b)** (friendly) kontaktfreudig ‹*Person*›; **2** *n., in pl.* **~s** (expenditure) Ausgaben *Pl.;* **~ˈgrow** *v.t., forms as* GROW: herauswachsen aus ‹*Kleider*›; (leave behind) entwachsen (+ *Dat.*); **~growth** *n.* Auswuchs, *der;* **~house** *n.* Nebengebäude, *das*

ˈouting *n.* Ausflug, *der*

out: ~landish /aʊtˈlændɪʃ/ *adj.* ausgefallen; **~ˈlast** *v.t.* überdauern; überleben ‹*Person, Jahrhundert*›; **~law** **1** *n.* Bandit, *der*/Banditin, *die;* **2** *v.t.* verbieten; **~lay** *n.* Ausgaben *Pl.* (**on** für); **~let** /ˈaʊtlet, ˈaʊtlɪt/ *n.* **(a)** Ablauf, Abfluss, *der;* Auslauf, Auslass, *der;* **(b)** (fig.) Ventil, *das;* **(c)** (market) Absatzmarkt, *der;* (shop) Verkaufsstelle, *die;* **~line** **1** *n.* **(a)** *in sing. or pl.* Umriss, *der;* **(b)** (short account)

Grundriss, *der;* (of topic) Übersicht, die (**of** über + *Akk.*); **2** *v.t.* (describe) umreißen; **~live** /aʊt'lɪv/ *v.t.* überleben; **~look** *n.* **(a)** (view) Aussicht, *die* (**over** über + *Akk.*, **on to** auf + *Akk.*); (fig.; Meteorol.) Aussichten *Pl.;* **(b)** (mental attitude) Einstellung, *die* (**on** zu); **~lying** *adj.* entlegen; **~ma'nœuvre** *v.t.* überlisten ‹*Truppen*›; **~moded** /aʊt'məʊdɪd/ *adj.* antiquiert; **~'number** *v.t.* zahlenmäßig überlegen sein (+ *Dat.*)

'out of *prep.* **(a)** (from within) aus; **go ~ the door** zur Tür hinausgehen
(b) (not within) **be ~ the country** im Ausland sein; **be ~ town/the room** nicht in der Stadt/im Zimmer sein; **feel ~ it** *or* **things** sich ausgeschlossen fühlen
(c) (from among) **one ~ every three smokers** jeder dritte Raucher; **58 ~ every 100** 58 von hundert
(d) (beyond range of) außer ‹*Reich-/Hörweite, Sicht, Kontrolle*›
(e) (from) aus; **get money ~ sb.** Geld aus jmdm. herausholen; **do well ~ sb./sth.** von jmdm./etw. profitieren
(f) aus ‹*Mitleid, Furcht, Neugier usw.*›
(g) (without) **~ money** ohne Geld; **we're ~ tea** wir haben keinen Tee mehr
(h) (away from) von ... entfernt; **ten miles ~ London** 10 Meilen außerhalb von London

out: ~-of-court settlement *n.* (Law) (agreement) außergerichtlicher Vergleich; (payment) Vergleichssumme, *die;* **~-of-'date** *attrib. adj.* veraltet; (expired) ungültig ‹*Karte*›; **~-of-'pocket** *attrib. adj.* Bar‹*auslagen*›; **~-of-print** *attrib. adj.* vergriffen; **~-of-work** *attrib. adj.* arbeitslos; **~patient** *n.* ambulanter Patient/ambulante Patientin; **~patients[' department]** Poliklinik, *die;* **~'play** *v.t.* (Sport) besser spielen als; **~post** *n.* Außenposten, *der;* (of civilization etc.; also Mil.) Vorposten, *der;* **~put** *n.* **(a)** Produktion, *die;* (of liquid, electricity, etc.) Leistung, *die;* **(b)** (Comp.) Ausgabe, *die*

outrage **1** /'aʊtreɪdʒ/ *n.* **(a)** (deed) Verbrechen, *das;* (during war) Gräueltat, *die;* (against decency) grober Verstoß
(b) (strong resentment) Empörung, *die* (**at** gegen)
2 /aʊt'reɪdʒ/ *v.t.* empören

outrageous /aʊt'reɪdʒəs/ *adj.* unverschämt; unverschämt hoch ‹*Preis*›; unerhört ‹*Frechheit, Skandal*›

out: ~right **1** /-'-/ *adv.* **(a)** ganz, komplett ‹*kaufen, verkaufen*›; **(b)** (openly) freiheraus ‹*erzählen, sagen, lachen*›; **2** /'--/ *adj.* ausgemacht ‹*Unehrlichkeit*›; glatt (ugs.) ‹*Ablehnung, Absage, Lüge*›; klar ‹*Sieg, Niederlage, Sieger*›; **~set** *n.* Anfang, *der;* **at the ~set** zu Anfang; **from the ~set** von Anfang an; **~'shine** *v.t.*, **~shone** /aʊt'ʃɒn/ (fig.) in den Schatten stellen

outside **1** /-'-, '--/ *n.* **(a)** Außenseite, *die;* **on the ~:** außen; **to/from the ~:** nach/von außen; **~ lane** Überholspur, *die*
(b) (external appearance) Äußere, *das*
(c) at the [very] ~ äußerstenfalls; höchstens
2 /'--/ *adj.* **(a)** äußer...; Außen‹*wand, -antenne, -kajüte, -toilette, -durchmesser*›; **~ lane** Überholspur, *die*
(b) have only an ~ chance nur eine sehr geringe Chance haben
3 /-'-/ *adv.* (on the ~) draußen; (to the ~) nach draußen
4 /-'-/ *prep.* **(a)** (position) außerhalb (+ *Gen.*); **~ the door** vor der Tür
(b) (to the ~ of) aus ... hinaus; **go ~ the house** nach draußen gehen

out'sider *n.* (Sport; also fig.) Außenseiter, *der*

out: ~size *adj.* überdimensional; **~size clothes** Kleidung in Übergröße; **~skirts** *n. pl.* Stadtrand, *der;* **the ~skirts of the town** die Außenbezirke der Stadt; **~'smart** *v.t.* (coll.) ausschmieren (ugs.); **~source** *v.t.* extern vergeben ‹*Arbeit, Aufträge*›; **~ sourcing** /'aʊtsɔːsɪŋ/ *n.* Outsourcing, *das* (fachspr.); Fremdbezug, *der* (fachspr.); **~'spoken** *adj.* freimütig; **be ~spoken about sth.** sich freimütig über etw. äußern; **~'standing** *adj.* **(a)** (exceptional) hervorragend; überragend ‹*Bedeutung*›; außergewöhnlich ‹*Person, Mut, Fähigkeit*›; **(b)** (not yet settled) ausstehend ‹*Schuld, Geldsumme*›; unbezahlt ‹*Rechnung*›; ungelöst ‹*Problem*›; **~stretched** *adj.* ausgestreckt; (spread out) ausgebreitet; **~'strip** *v.t.* (in competition) überflügeln; **~tray** *n.* Ablage für Ausgänge; **~'vote** *v.t.* überstimmen

outward /'aʊtwəd/ **1** *adj.* **(a)** (external, apparent) [rein] äußerlich; äußer... ‹*Erscheinung, Bedingung*›
(b) Hin‹*reise, -fracht*›
2 *adv.* nach außen ‹*aufgehen, richten*›

'outwardly *adv.* nach außen hin ‹*Gefühle zeigen*›; öffentlich ‹*Loyalität erklären*›

'outwards ▶ OUTWARD 2

out: ~'weigh *v.t.* schwerer wiegen als; überwiegen ‹*Nachteile*›; **~'wit** *v.t.*, **-tt-** überlisten; **~'worn** *adj.* veraltet

oval /'əʊvl/ **1** *adj.* oval
2 *n.* Oval, *das*

ovary /'əʊvərɪ/ *n.* (Anat.) Eierstock, *der*

ovation /əʊ'veɪʃn/ *n.* Ovation, *die;* **a standing ~:** stehende Ovationen *Pl.*

oven /'ʌvn/ *n.* [Back]ofen, *der*

oven: ~ cloth *n.* Topflappen, *der;* **~ glove** *n.* Topfhandschuh, *der;* **~proof** *adj.* feuerfest; **~-ready** *adj.* backfertig ‹*Pommes frites, Pastete*›; bratfertig ‹*Geflügel*›; **~ware** *n.* feuerfestes Geschirr

over /'əʊvə(r)/ **1** *adv.* **(a)** (outward and downward) hinüber; **climb/look/jump ~:** hinüber- *od.* (ugs.) rüberklettern/-sehen/-springen
(b) (so as to cover surface) **board/cover ~:** zunageln/-decken
(c) (across a space) hinüber; (towards speaker) herüber; **he swam ~ to us/the other side** er schwamm zu uns herüber/hinüber zur ⇢

anderen Seite; ~ **here/there** (direction) hier herüber/dort hinüber; (location) hier/dort; **[come in, please,]** ~ (Radio) übernehmen Sie bitte; ~ **and out** (Radio) Ende
(d) (in excess etc.) **children of 12 and ~:** Kinder im Alter von zwölf Jahren und darüber; **be [left] ~:** übrig [geblieben] sein
(e) (from beginning to end) von Anfang bis Ende; **say sth. twice ~:** etw. zweimal sagen; **[all] ~ again,** (Amer.) **~:** noch einmal [ganz von vorn]; **~ and ~ [again]** immer wieder
(f) (at an end) vorbei; vorüber; **be ~:** vorbei sein; ‹*Aufführung:*› zu Ende sein; **get sth. ~ with** etw. hinter sich (*Akk.*) bringen; **be ~ and done with** erledigt sein
(g) all ~ (completely finished) aus [und vorbei]; **I ache all ~:** mir tut alles weh; **be shaking all ~:** am ganzen Körper zittern
2 *prep.* **(a)** (above, on, round about) über (*position: + Dat.; direction: + Akk.*); (across) über (+ *Akk.*); **look ~ a wall** über eine Mauer sehen; **fall ~ a cliff** von einem Felsen stürzen; **the pub ~ the road** die Wirtschaft gegenüber; **hit sb. ~ the head** jmdm. auf den Kopf schlagen; **~ the page** auf der nächsten Seite
(b) (in or across every part of) [überall] in (+ *Dat.*); (to and fro upon) über (+ *Akk.*); (all through) durch; **all ~** (in or on all parts of) überall in (+ *Dat.*); **travel all ~ the country** das ganze Land bereisen; **all ~ Spain** in ganz Spanien; **all ~ the world** in der ganzen Welt
(c) (on account of) wegen
(d) (engaged with) bei; **take trouble ~ sth.** sich (*Dat.*) mit etw. Mühe geben; **be a long time ~ sth.** lange für etw. brauchen; **~ work/dinner** bei der Arbeit/beim Essen
(e) (superior to, in charge of) über (+ *Akk.*); **have command/authority ~ sb.** Befehlsgewalt über jmdn./Weisungsbefugnis gegenüber jmdm. haben; **be ~ sb.** (in rank) über jmdm. stehen
(f) (beyond, more than) über (+ *Akk.*); **~ and above** zusätzlich zu
(g) (throughout, during) über (+ *Akk.*); **~ the weekend/summer** übers Wochenende/den Sommer über; **~ the past years** in den letzten Jahren

over: ~'active *adj.* hyperaktiv; **~all** **1** *n.* (Brit.: garment) Arbeitskittel, *der;* **2** *adj.* **(a)** Gesamt‹*breite, -einsparung, -abmessung*›; **have an ~all majority** die absolute Mehrheit haben; **(b)** (general) allgemein; **3** /'---, --'-/ *adv.* **(a)** (in all parts) insgesamt; **(b)** (taken as a whole) im Großen und Ganzen; **~'awe** *v.t.* Ehrfurcht einflößen (+ *Dat.*); **~'balance** *v.i.* das Gleichgewicht verlieren; **~'bearing** *adj.* herrisch; **~'blown** *adj.* (past its prime, lit. or fig.) verblühend; **~board** *adv.* über Bord; **fall ~board** über Bord gehen; **~cast** *adj.* trübe; bewölkt ‹*Himmel*›; **~'charge** *v.t.* **(a)** (beyond reasonable price) zu viel abverlangen (+ *Dat.*); **(b)** (beyond right price) zu viel berechnen (+ *Dat.*); **~coat** *n.* Mantel, *der;* **~'come** *v.t., forms as* COME: **(a)** überwinden; bezwingen ‹*Feind*›; ‹*Dämpfe:*› betäuben; **(b) he was ~come by grief/with emotion** Kummer/Rührung überwältigte ihn; **~'confidence** *n.* übersteigertes Selbstvertrauen; **~'confident** *adj.* übertrieben zuversichtlich; **~'cooked** *adj.* verkocht; **~'critical** *adj.* zu kritisch; **~'crowded** *adj.* überfüllt; **~'crowding** *n.* (of room, bus, train) Überfüllung, *die;* (of city) Übervölkerung, *die;* **~'do** *v.t., forms as* DO: (carry to excess) übertreiben; **~do it** *or* **things** (work too hard) sich übernehmen; **~'done** *adj.* **(a)** (exaggerated) übertrieben; **(b)** (~cooked) verkocht; verbraten ‹*Fleisch*›; **~dose** **1** *n.* Überdosis, *die;* **2** *v.i.* **~dose on heroin** eine Überdosis Heroin nehmen; **~draft** *n.* Kontoüberziehung, *die;* **have an ~draft of £50** sein Konto um 50 Pfund überzogen haben; **~'draw** *v.t., forms as* DRAW 1: überziehen ‹*Konto*›; **~'drawn** *adj.* überzogen ‹*Konto*›; **I am ~drawn [at the bank]** mein Konto ist überzogen; **~drive** *n.* Schongang, *der;* **~'due** *adj.* überfällig; **the train is 15 minutes ~due** der Zug hat schon 15 Minuten Verspätung; **~'eager** *adj.* übereifrig; **~'eat** *v.i., forms as* EAT: zu viel essen; **~estimate** **1** /-'estɪmeɪt/ *v.t.* überschätzen; **2** /-'estɪmət/ *n.* zu hohe Schätzung; **~ex'ert** *v. refl.* sich überanstrengen; **~ex'pose** *v.t.* (Photog.) überbelichten; **~'fill** *v.t.* zu voll machen; **~'fish** *v.t.* überfischen; **~flow** **1** /--'-/ *v.t.* laufen über (+ *Akk.*) ‹*Rand*›; (flow over brim of) überlaufen aus; **~flow its banks** ‹*Fluss:*› über die Ufer treten; **2** /--'-/ *v.i.* überlaufen; **3** /'---/ *n.* **~flow [pipe]** Überlauf, *der;* **~flow car park** Ausweichparkplatz, *der;* **~'full** *adj.* zu voll; übervoll; **~grown** *adj.* überwachsen (**with** von); **~hang** **1** /--'-/ *v.t.*, **~hung** /əʊvə'hʌŋ/ ‹*Felsen, Stockwerk:*› hinausragen über (+ *Akk.*); **2** /'---/ *n.* Überhang, *der;* **~'hanging** *adj.* überhängend; **~haul** **1** /--'-/ *v.t.* überholen; überprüfen ‹*System*›; **2** /'---/ *n.* Überholung, *die;* **~head** **1** /--'-/ *adv.* über mir/ihm/uns *usw.;* **2** /'---/ *adj.* **~head wires** Oberleitung, *die;* **~head lighting** Deckenbeleuchtung, *die;* **3** /'---/ *n.* **~heads,** (Amer.) **~head** (Commerc.) Gemeinkosten *Pl.;* **~'hear** *v.t., forms as* HEAR 1 (accidentally) zufällig [mit]hören; (intentionally) belauschen; **~'heat** *v.i.* zu heiß werden; ‹*Maschine, Lager:*› heißlaufen; **~-in'dulge** *v.i.* es übertreiben; **~-indulge in food and drink** sich an Essen und Trinken mehr als gütlich tun; **~-in'dulgence** *n.* übermäßiger Genuss (**in** von); (towards a person) zu große Nachgiebigkeit; **~-in'dulgent** *adj.* unmäßig; (towards a person) zu nachgiebig

overjoyed /əʊvə'dʒɔɪd/ *adj.* überglücklich (**at** über + *Akk.*)

over: ~land /--'-/ *adv.* auf dem Landweg; **~lap** **1** /--'-/ *v.t.* überlappen; **2** /--'-/ *v.i.* ‹*Flächen, Dachziegel:*› sich überlappen; ‹*Aufgaben:*› sich überschneiden; **3** *n.* Überlappung, *die;* **~'leaf** *adv.* auf der Rückseite; **~'load** *v.t.* überladen; **~'look** *v.t.* **(a)** ‹*Hotel, Zimmer, Haus:*› Aussicht bieten auf (+ *Akk.*); **(b)** (ignore, not see) übersehen; (allow to go unpunished) hinwegsehen über (+ *Akk.*)

'overly *adv.* allzu

over: ~'man *v.t.* überbesetzen; **~manning** *n.* [personelle] Überbesetzung; **~'modest** *adj.* zu bescheiden; **~'much** [1] *adj.* allzu viel; [2] *adv.* allzu sehr; **~night** [1] /--'-/ *adv.* (also fig.: suddenly) über Nacht; **stay ~ night** übernachten; [2] /'---/ *adj.* **~night stay** Übernachtung, *die;* **be an ~night success** (fig.) über Nacht Erfolg haben; **~'pay** *v.t., forms as* PAY 2: überbezahlen; **~'populated** *adj.* überbevölkert; **~popu'lation** *n.* Übervölkerung, *die;* **~'power** *v.t.* überwältigen; **~'powering** *adj.* überwältigend; durchdringend ‹*Geruch*›; **~'priced** *adj.* zu teuer; **~'qualified** *adj.* überqualifiziert; **~'rate** *v.t.* überschätzen; **~re'act** *v.i.* unangemessen heftig reagieren (**to** auf + *Akk.*); **~re'action** *n.* Überreaktion, *die* (**to** auf + *Akk.*); **~'ride** *v.t. forms as* RIDE 3: sich hinwegsetzen über (+ *Akk.*); **~'riding** *adj.* vorrangig; **be of ~riding importance** wichtiger als alles andere sein; **~ripe** *adj.* überreif; **~'rule** *v.t.* aufheben ‹*Entscheidung*›; zurückweisen ‹*Einwand, Argument*›; **~rule sb.** jmds. Vorschlag ablehnen; **~'run** *v.t., forms as* RUN 3: **be ~run with** überlaufen sein von ‹*Touristen*›; überwuchert sein von ‹*Unkraut*›; **~seas** [1] /--'-/ *adv.* in Übersee ‹*leben, sein*›; nach Übersee ‹*gehen*›; [2] /'---/ *adj.* Übersee-; **~'see** *v.t., forms as* SEE 1: überwachen; (manage) leiten ‹*Abteilung*›; **~'sensitive** *adj.* überempfindlich; **~-sexed** /əʊvə'sekst/ *adj.* sexbesessen; **~'shadow** *v.t.* überschatten; **~'shoot** *v.t., forms as* SHOOT 2: hinausschießen über (+ *Akk.*); **~shoot [the runway]** ‹*Pilot, Flugzeug:*› zu weit kommen; **~sight** *n.* Versehen, *das;* **~simplifi'cation** *n.* zu starke Vereinfachung; **~'simplify** *v.t.* zu stark vereinfachen; **~'sleep** *v.i., forms as* SLEEP 2: verschlafen; **~'spend** *v.i., forms as* SPEND: zu viel [Geld] ausgeben; **~statement** *n.* Übertreibung, *die;* **~'stay** *v.t.* überziehen ‹*Urlaub*›; **~'step** *v.t.* überschreiten; **~'stretch** *v.t.* überdehnen; (fig.) überfordern

overt /əʊ'vɜ:t/ *adj.* unverhohlen

over: ~'take *v.t., forms as* TAKE: überholen; **'no ~taking'** (Brit.) „Überholen verboten"; **~-the-top** *adj.* überzogen; **~throw** [1] /--'-/ *v.t., forms as* THROW 1: stürzen; [2] /'---/ *n.* Sturz, *der;* **~time** [1] *n.* Überstunden *Pl.*; [2] *adv.* **work ~time** Überstunden machen; **~'tire** *v.t.* übermüden; **~tire oneself** sich übernehmen *od.* überanstrengen

overtly /'əʊvətlɪ, əʊ'vɜ:tlɪ/ *adv.* unverhohlen

'overtone *n.* (fig.) Unterton, *der*

overture /'əʊvətjʊə(r)/ *n.* (Mus.) Ouvertüre, *die*

over: ~'turn [1] *v.t.* umstoßen; [2] *v.i.* ‹*Auto, Boot:*› umkippen; ‹*Boot:*› kentern; **~use** /əʊvə'ju:z/ *v.t.* zu oft verwenden

overweening /əʊvə'wi:nɪŋ/ *adj.* maßlos ‹*Ehrgeiz, Gier, Stolz*›

'overweight *adj.* übergewichtig ‹*Person*›; **be ~weight** Übergewicht haben

overwhelm /əʊvə'welm/ *v.t.* überwältigen

over'whelming *adj.* überwältigend

over: ~'work [1] *v.t.* mit Arbeit überlasten; [2] *v.i.* sich überarbeiten; **~'wrought** *adj.* überreizt

ovulate /'ɒvjʊleɪt/ *v.i.* (Physiol.) ovulieren

ovulation /ɒvjʊ'leɪʃn/ *n.* Ovulation, *die*

owe /əʊ/ *v.t.*, **owing** /'əʊɪŋ/ schulden; **~ sb. sth., ~ sth. to sb.** jmdm. etw. schulden; (fig.) jmdm. etw. verdanken

owing /'əʊɪŋ/ *pred. adj.* ausstehend; **be ~:** ausstehen

'owing to *prep.* wegen

owl /aʊl/ *n.* Eule, *die*

own /əʊn/ [1] *adj.* eigen; **be sb.'s ~ [property]** jmdm. selbst gehören; **a house/ideas of one's ~:** ein eigenes Haus/eigene Ideen; **on one's/its ~:** allein [2] *v.t.* besitzen; **be ~ed by sb.** jmdm. gehören

■ **own 'up** *v.i.* gestehen; **~ up to sth.** etw. zugeben

'own-brand, 'own-label [1] *attrib. adjs.* Eigenmarken- [2] *n.* Hausmarke, *die*

'owner *n.* Besitzer, *der*/Besitzerin, *die;* (of shop, hotel, firm, etc.) Inhaber, *der*/Inhaberin, *die*

owner-'occupier *n.* (Brit.) Eigenheimbesitzer, *der*/-besitzerin, *die*

'ownership *n.* Besitz, *der*

own 'goal *n.* (lit. or fig.) Eigentor, *das*

ox /ɒks/ *n., pl.* **oxen** /'ɒksn/ Ochse, *der*

oxidize (oxidise) /'ɒksɪdaɪz/ *v.t. & i.* (Chem.) oxidieren; oxydieren (fachspr.)

oxtail 'soup *n.* Ochsenschwanzsuppe, *die*

oxygen /'ɒksɪdʒən/ *n.* Sauerstoff, *der*

'oxygen mask *n.* Sauerstoffmaske, *die*

oyster /'ɔɪstə(r)/ *n.* Auster, *die*

oz. *abbr.* = **ounce[s]**

ozone /'əʊzəʊn/ *n.* Ozon, *das*

ozone: ~ depletion *n.* Ozonabbau, *der;* **~-friendly** *adj.* ozonsicher; (not using CFCs) FCKW-frei; **~ hole** *n.* Ozonloch, *das* (ugs.); **~ layer** *n.* Ozonschicht, *die*

Pp

P, p /piː/ *n.* P, p, *das*

p. *abbr.* **(a)** = **page** S.
(b) (Brit.) = **penny/pence** p

pace /peɪs/ [1] *n.* **(a)** (step) Schritt, *der*
(b) (speed) Tempo, *das;* **keep ~ with** Schritt halten mit
[2] *v.i.* **~ up and down** auf und ab gehen
[3] *v.t.* auf und ab gehen in (+ *Dat.*)

'pacemaker *n.* (Sport, Med.) Schrittmacher, *der*

Pacific /pəˈsɪfɪk/ [1] *adj.* (Geog.) **~ Ocean** Pazifischer *od.* Stiller Ozean
[2] *n.* **the ~**: der Pazifik

pacifier /ˈpæsɪfaɪə(r)/ *n.* (Amer.: dummy) Schnuller, *der*

pacifism /ˈpæsɪfɪzm/ *n.* Pazifismus, *der*

pacifist /ˈpæsɪfɪst/ [1] *n.* Pazifist, *der*/Pazifistin, *die*
[2] *adj.* pazifistisch

pacify /ˈpæsɪfaɪ/ *v.t.* besänftigen

pack /pæk/ [1] *n.* **(a)** (bundle) Bündel, *das;* (Mil.) Tornister, *der;* (rucksack) Rucksack, *der*
(b) (derog.: lot) (people) Bande, *die;* **a ~ of lies/nonsense** ein Sack voll Lügen/eine Menge Unsinn
(c) (Brit.) **~ [of cards]** [Karten]spiel, *das*
(d) (of wolves, wild dogs) Rudel, *das;* (of hounds) Meute, *die*
(e) (packet) Packung, *die*
[2] *v.t.* **(a)** einpacken; (fill) packen; **~ one's bags** seine Koffer packen
(b) (cram) voll stopfen (ugs.)
(c) (wrap) verpacken (**in** in + *Dat. od. Akk.*)
[3] *v.i.* packen; **send sb. ~ing** (fig.) jmdn. rausschmeißen (ugs.)

■ **pack 'up** [1] *v.t.* zusammenpacken ‹*Sachen, Werkzeug*›; packen ‹*Paket*›
[2] *v.i.* (coll.: stop) aufhören

package /ˈpækɪdʒ/ [1] *n.* Paket, *das*
[2] *v.t.* verpacken

package: ~ deal *n.* Paket, *das;* **~ holiday, ~ tour** *ns.* Pauschalreise, *die*

packaging /ˈpækɪdʒɪŋ/ *n.* (material) Verpackung, *die*

packed /pækt/ *adj.* **(a)** gepackt; **~ lunch** Lunchpaket, *das*
(b) (crowded) [über]voll; **~ out** gerammelt voll (ugs.)

packet /ˈpækɪt/ *n.* Päckchen, *das;* (box) Schachtel, *die;* **a ~ of cigarettes** ein Päckchen/eine Schachtel Zigaretten; **cost/earn a ~**: ein Heidengeld kosten (ugs.)/ein Schweinegeld verdienen (ugs.)

packet 'soup *n.* Instantsuppe, *die*

'packing *n.* (material) Verpackungsmaterial, *das;* **postage and ~**: Porto und Verpackung

'packing case *n.* [Pack]kiste, *die*

pact /pækt/ *n.* Pakt, *der*

pad¹ /pæd/ [1] *n.* Polster, *das;* (block of paper) Block, *der*
[2] *v.t.,* **-dd-** polstern ‹*Jacke, Schulter*›

■ **pad 'out** *v.t.* (fig.) auswalzen

pad² *v.i.,* **-dd-** tappen

padded /ˈpædɪd/ *adj.* gepolstert

padded 'envelope *n.* wattierter Umschlag

padding /ˈpædɪŋ/ *n., no indef. art.* Polsterung, *die;* (fig.) Füllsel, *das*

paddle¹ /ˈpædl/ [1] *n.* [Stech]paddel, *das*
[2] *v.t. & i.* paddeln

paddle² [1] *v.i.* (with feet) planschen
[2] *n.* **have a/go for a ~**: ein bisschen planschen/planschen gehen

paddling pool /ˈpædlɪŋpuːl/ *n.* Planschbecken, *das*

paddock /ˈpædək/ *n.* Koppel, *die*

'padlock [1] *n.* Vorhängeschloss, *das*
[2] *v.t.* [mit einem Vorhängeschloss] verschließen

paediatrician /piːdɪəˈtrɪʃn/ *n.* Kinderarzt, *der*/-ärztin, *die*

paediatrics /piːdɪˈætrɪks/ *n.* Pädiatrie, *die* (fachspr.); Kinderheilkunde, *die*

paedophile /ˈpiːdəfaɪl/ [1] *n.* Pädophile, *der*
[2] *adj.* pädophil

pagan /ˈpeɪgən/ [1] *n.* Heide, *der*/Heidin, *die*
[2] *adj.* heidnisch

page¹ /peɪdʒ/ *n.* (boy) Page, *der*

page² *n.* (of book etc.) Seite, *die*

pageant /ˈpædʒənt/ *n.* (spectacle) Schauspiel, *das*

pageantry /ˈpædʒəntrɪ/ *n.* Prunk, *der*

page: ~ break *n.* (Comp.) Seitenbruch, *der;* **~ number** *n.* Seitenzahl, *die*

pager /ˈpeɪdʒə(r)/ *n.* Piepser, *der* (ugs.)

paginate /ˈpædʒɪneɪt/ *v.t.* paginieren

pagination /pædʒɪˈneɪʃn/ *n.* Paginierung, *die*

'paging device ▸ PAGER

paid /peɪd/ [1] ▸ PAY 2, 3
[2] *adj.* **(a)** bezahlt ‹*Urlaub, Arbeit*›
(b) put ~ to (Brit. coll.) zunichte machen; kurzen Prozess machen mit (ugs.) ‹*Person*›

pail /peɪl/ *n.* Eimer, *der*

pain /peɪn/ *n.* **(a)** (suffering) Schmerzen *Pl.*; (mental ~) Qualen *Pl.*; **be in ~**: Schmerzen haben
(b) (instance) Schmerz, *der;* **I have a ~ in my knee/stomach** mein Knie/Magen tut weh

(c) *in pl.* (trouble taken) Mühe, *die;* **take ~s** sich (*Dat.*) Mühe geben (**over** mit, bei)

painful /ˈpeɪnfl/ *adj.* **(a)** schmerzhaft; **be ~** ‹*Körperteil:*› wehtun **(b)** (distressing) schmerzlich ‹*Gedanke, Erinnerung*›; traurig ‹*Pflicht*›

ˈpainkiller *n.* schmerzstillendes Mittel

ˈpainless *adj.* schmerzlos; (fig.) unproblematisch

painstaking /ˈpeɪnzteɪkɪŋ/ *adj.* gewissenhaft

paint /peɪnt/ **1** *n.* Farbe, *die;* (on car) Lack, *der* **2** *v.t.* (cover, colour) [an]streichen; (make picture of, make by ~ing) malen; bemalen ‹*Wand, Vase, Decke*›

paint: ~box *n.* Malkasten, *der;* **~brush** *n.* Pinsel, *der*

ˈpainter *n.* Maler, *der*/Malerin, *die*

ˈpainting *n.* (art) Malerei, *die;* (picture) Gemälde, *das;* Bild, *das*

ˈpainting book *n.* Malbuch, *das*

paint: ~ stripper *n.* Abbeizer, *der;* **~work** *n.* (on walls etc.) Anstrich, *der;* (of car) Lack, *der*

pair /peə(r)/ **1** *n.* Paar, *das;* **a ~ of gloves/socks/shoes** *etc.* ein Paar Handschuhe/Socken/Schuhe *usw.;* **in ~s** paarweise; **a ~ of trousers/jeans** eine Hose/Jeans **2** *v.t.* paaren

■ **pair ˈoff** *v.i.* Zweiergruppen bilden

pajamas /pəˈdʒɑːməz/ (Amer.) ▶ PYJAMAS

Pakistan /pɑːkɪˈstɑːn/ *pr. n.* Pakistan (*das*)

Pakistani /pɑːkɪˈstɑːnɪ/ **1** *adj.* pakistanisch; **sb. is ~**: jmd. ist Pakistani **2** *n.* Pakistani, *der/die*

pal /pæl/ *n.* (coll.) Kumpel, *der* (ugs.)

palace /ˈpælɪs/ *n.* Palast, *der*

palate /ˈpælət/ *n.* Gaumen, *der*

palatial /pəˈleɪʃl/ *adj.* palastartig

pale¹ /peɪl/ *adj.* blass, (nearly white) bleich ‹*Gesichtsfarbe, Haut, Gesicht*›; blass ‹*Farbe*›; fahl ‹*Licht*›; **go ~**: blass/bleich werden; (fig.) **~ imitation** schlechte Nachahmung

pale² *n.* **beyond the ~**: unmöglich

Palestine /ˈpælɪstaɪn/ *pr. n.* Palästina (*das*)

Palestinian /pælɪˈstɪnɪən/ **1** *adj.* palästinensisch; **sb. is ~** jmd. ist Palästinenser/Palästinenserin **2** *n.* Palästinenser, *der*/Palästinenserin, *die*

palette /ˈpælɪt/ *n.* Palette, *die*

pall¹ /pɔːl/ *n.* **(a)** (over coffin) Sargtuch, *das* **(b)** (fig.) Schleier, *der*

pall² *v.i.* **~ [on sb.]** [jmdm.] langweilig werden

pallor /ˈpælə(r)/ *n.* Blässe, *die*

palm¹ /pɑːm/ *n.* (tree) Palme, *die*

palm² *n.* Handteller, *der*

■ **palm ˈoff** *v.t.* **~ sth. off on sb., ~ sb. off with sth.** jmdm. etw. andrehen (ugs.)

palmistry /ˈpɑːmɪstrɪ/ *n.* Handlesekunst, *die*

palm: P~ ˈSunday *n.* Palmsonntag, *der;* **~top** *n.* **~top [computer]** Palmtop, *der;* **~ tree** *n.* Palme, *die*

palpitation /pælpɪˈteɪʃn/ *n. in pl.* (Med.: of heart) Palpitation, *die* (fachspr.); **suffer from ~s** Herzklopfen haben

paltry /ˈpɔːltrɪ, ˈpɒltrɪ/ *adj.* schäbig

pamper /ˈpæmpə(r)/ *v.t.* verhätscheln; **~ oneself** sich verwöhnen

pamphlet /ˈpæmflɪt/ *n.* (leaflet) Prospekt, *der;* (booklet) Broschüre, *die*

pan /pæn/ *n.* [Koch]topf, *der;* (for frying) Pfanne, *die*

panacea /pænəˈsɪə/ *n.* Allheilmittel, *das*

Panama /pænəˈmɑː/ *pr. n.* Panama (*das*); **~ Caˈnal** Panamakanal, *der*

ˈpancake *n.* Pfannkuchen, *der*

pancreas /ˈpæŋkrɪəs/ *n.* Bauchspeicheldrüse, *die*

panda /ˈpændə/ *n.* Panda, *der*

pandemonium /pændɪˈməʊnɪəm/ *n.* Chaos, *das;* (uproar) Tumult, *der*

pander /ˈpændə(r)/ *v.i.* **~ to** allzu sehr entgegenkommen (+ *Dat.*)

pane /peɪn/ *n.* Scheibe, *die*

panel /ˈpænl/ *n.* **(a)** Paneel, *das* **(b)** (esp. Telev., Radio, etc.) (quiz team) Rateteam, *das;* (in public discussion) Podium, *das*

panelling /ˈpænəlɪŋ/ *n.* Täfelung, *die*

panellist /ˈpænəlɪst/ *n.* (Telev., Radio) (on quiz programme) Mitglied des Rateteams; (on discussion panel) Diskussionsteilnehmer, *der*/-teilnehmerin, *die*

ˈpan-fry *v.t.* [in der Pfanne] braten

pang /pæŋ/ *n.* (of pain) Stich, *der;* **feel ~s of conscience/guilt** Gewissensbisse haben; **~[s] of hunger** quälender Hunger

panic /ˈpænɪk/ **1** *n.* Panik, *die;* **hit the ~ button** (fig. coll.) Alarm schlagen; (~) durchdrehen (ugs.) **2** *v.i.*, **-ck-** in Panik (*Akk.*) geraten; **don't ~!** nur keine Panik!

panic: ~ attack *n.* Angstanfall, *der;* **~-stricken, ~-struck** *adjs.* von Panik erfasst

panorama /pænəˈrɑːmə/ *n.* Panorama, *das*

pansy /ˈpænzɪ/ *n.* Stiefmütterchen, *das*

pant /pænt/ *v.i.* keuchen; ‹*Hund:*› hecheln

panther /ˈpænθə(r)/ *n.* Panther, *der*

panties /ˈpæntɪz/ *n. pl.* (coll.) **[pair of] ~**: Schlüpfer, *der*

pantomime /ˈpæntəmaɪm/ *n.* (Brit.) *Märchenspiel im Varieteestil, das um Weihnachten aufgeführt wird*

pantry /ˈpæntrɪ/ *n.* Speisekammer, *die*

pants /pænts/ *n. pl.* **(a)** (esp. Amer. coll.: trousers) **[pair of] ~**: Hose, *die* **(b)** (Brit. coll.: underpants) Unterhose, *die*

paparazzo /pæpæ'rɑ:tsəʊ/ *n., pl.* **paparazzi** /pæpæ'rɑ:tsi:/ Paparazzo, *der*

paper /'peɪpə(r)/ 1 *n.* **(a)** (material) Papier, *das*
(b) *in pl.* (documents) Unterlagen *Pl.;* (to prove identity etc.) Papiere *Pl.*
(c) (in examination) (Univ.) Klausur, *die;* (Sch.) Arbeit, *die*
(d) (newspaper) Zeitung, *die*
(e) (learned article) Referat, *das*
2 *adj.* aus Papier *nachgestellt;* Papier‹*mütze, -taschentuch*›
3 *v.t.* tapezieren

paper: ~back 1 *n.* Paperback, *das;* 2 *adj.* **~back book** Paperback, *das;* **~ 'bag** *n.* Papiertüte, *die;* **~ boy** *n.* Zeitungsjunge, *der;* **~ clip** *n.* Büroklammer, *die;* (larger) Aktenklammer, *die;* **~ 'handkerchief** *n.* Papiertaschentuch, *das;* **~ mill** *n.* Papierfabrik *od.* -mühle, *die;* **~ money** *n.* Papiergeld, *das;* **~ 'napkin** *n.* Papierserviette, *die;* **~ round** *n.* Zeitungenaustragen, *das;* **~ servi'ette** ▶ ~ NAPKIN; **~ 'towel** *n.* Papierhandtuch, *das;* **~weight** *n.* Briefbeschwerer, *der;* **~work** *n.* Schreibarbeit, *die*

par /pɑ:(r)/ *n.* **feel below ~:** nicht ganz auf dem Posten sein (ugs.); **be on a ~ with sb./sth.** jmdm./einer Sache gleichkommen

parable /'pærəbl/ *n.* Gleichnis, *das*

parachute /'pærəʃu:t/ 1 *n.* Fallschirm, *der*
2 *v.i.* ‹*Truppen:*› abspringen (**into** über + *Dat.*)

parade /pə'reɪd/ 1 *n.* **(a)** (display) Zurschaustellung, *die*
(b) (Mil.) Appell, *der*
(c) (procession) Umzug, *der;* (of troops) Parade, *die*
2 *v.t.* zur Schau stellen
3 *v.i.* paradieren

pa'rade ground *n.* Exerzierplatz, *der*

paradise /'pærədaɪs/ *n.* Paradies, *das*

paradox /'pærədɒks/ *n.* Paradox[on], *das*

paradoxical /pærə'dɒksɪkl/ *adj.* paradox

paraffin /'pærəfɪn/ *n.* Paraffin, *das;* (Brit.: fuel) Petroleum, *das*

paragliding /'pærəglaɪdɪŋ/ *n.* Paragliding, *das*

paragon /'pærəgən/ Muster, *das* (**of** an + *Dat.*); **~ of virtue** Tugendheld, *der*/-heldin, *die*

paragraph /'pærəgrɑ:f/ *n.* Absatz, *der*

parallel /'pærəlel/ 1 *adj.* parallel; (fig.: similar) vergleichbar; **~ bars** Barren, *der*
2 *n.* Parallele, *die;* **~ [of latitude]** Breitenkreis, *der*

Paralympics /pærə'lɪmpɪks/ *n. pl.* Paralympics *Pl.*

paralyse /'pærəlaɪz/ *v.t.* lähmen; (fig.) lahm legen ‹*Verkehr, Industrie*›

paralysis /pə'rælɪsɪs/ *n.* Lähmung, *die*

paralyze (Amer.) ▶ PARALYSE

paramedic /pærə'medɪk/ *n.* medizinische Hilfskraft; (ambulance worker) Sanitäter, *der*/Sanitäterin, *die*

parameter /pə'ræmɪtə(r)/ *n.* Faktor, *der*

paramilitary /pærə'mɪlɪtərɪ/ *adj.* paramilitärisch

paramount /'pærəmaʊnt/ *adj.* größt... ‹*Wichtigkeit*›; Haupt‹*überlegung*›; **be ~:** Vorrang haben

paranoia /pærə'nɔɪə/ *n.* Paranoia, *die* (*Med.*); (*tendency*) Verfolgungswahn, *der*

paranoid /'pærənɔɪd/ *adj.* **be ~** ‹*Person:*› an Verfolgungswahn leiden

parapet /'pærəpɪt/ *n.* Brüstung, *die*

paraphernalia /pærəfə'neɪlɪə/ *n. sing.* Apparat, *der*

paraphrase /'pærəfreɪz/ 1 *n.* Umschreibung, *die*
2 *v.t.* umschreiben

paraplegic /pærə'pli:dʒɪk/ 1 *adj.* doppelseitig gelähmt
2 *n.* doppelseitig Gelähmter/Gelähmte

parasite /'pærəsaɪt/ *n.* Schmarotzer, *der*

parasitic /pærə'sɪtɪk/ *adj.* **(a)** (Biol.) parasitisch
(b) (fig.) schmarotzerhaft

parasol /'pærəsɒl/ *n.* Sonnenschirm, *der*

paratroops /'pærətru:ps/ *n. pl.* Fallschirmjäger *Pl.*

parcel /'pɑ:sl/ *n.* Paket, *das*

parched /pɑ:tʃt/ *adj.* ausgedörrt; trocken ‹*Lippen*›

parchment /'pɑ:tʃmənt/ *n.* Pergament, *das*

pardon /'pɑ:dn/ 1 *n.* Verzeihung, *die;* **beg sb.'s ~:** jmdn. um Entschuldigung bitten; **I beg your ~:** entschuldigen Sie bitte
2 *v.t.* **(a) ~ sb. [for] sth.** jmdm. etw. verzeihen
(b) (excuse) entschuldigen

pardonable /'pɑ:dənəbl/ *adj.* verzeihlich

pare /peə(r)/ *v.t.* (trim) schneiden; (peel) schälen

parent /'peərənt/ *n.* Elternteil, *der;* **~s** Eltern *Pl.*

parental /pə'rentl/ *adj.* Eltern‹*pflicht, -haus, -liebe*›

parenthesis /pə'renθɪsɪs/ *n., pl.* **parentheses** /pə'renθɪsi:z/ (bracket) runde Klammer

'parents' evening *n.* Elternabend, *der*

'parents-in-law *pl.* Schwiegeeltern *Pl.*

Paris /'pærɪs/ *pr. n.* Paris (*das*)

parish /'pærɪʃ/ *n.* Gemeinde, *die*

parish: ~ 'church *n.* Pfarrkirche, *die;* **~ 'council** *n.* (Brit.) Gemeinderat, *der*

parishioner /pə'rɪʃənə(r)/ *n.* Gemeinde[mit]glied, *das*

parish 'priest *n.* Gemeindepfarrer, *der*

park /pɑ:k/ 1 *n.* Park, *der*
2 *v.i.* parken
3 *v.t.* abstellen; parken ‹*Kfz*›; **a ~ed car** ein parkendes Auto

park-and-'ride *n.* Park-and-ride-System, *das;* (place) Park-and-ride-Parkplatz, *der*

'parking *n.* Parken, *das;* **'no ~'** „Parken verboten"

parking: ~ fine *n.* Geldbuße für falsches Parken; **~ light** *n.* Parkleuchte, *die;* **~ lot** *n.* (Amer.) Parkplatz, *der;* **~ meter** *n.* Parkuhr, *die;* **~ offence** *n.* Verstoß gegen das Parkverbot; **~ space** *n.* **(a)** *no pl.* Parkraum, *der;* **(b)** (single space) Parkplatz, *der;* **~ ticket** *n.* Strafzettel [für falsches Parken]

'park-keeper *n.* Parkwächter, *der*/ -wächterin, *die*

parliament /'pɑ:ləmənt/ *n.* Parlament, *das;* **[Houses of] P~** (Brit.) Parlament, *das*

parliamentary /pɑ:lə'mentərɪ/ *adj.* parlamentarisch; Parlaments‹*geschäfte, -wahlen, -reform*›

parlour (*Brit.; Amer.:* **parlor**) /'pɑ:lə(r)/ *n.* (dated) Wohnzimmer, *das*

parochial /pə'rəʊkɪəl/ *adj.* krähwinklig

parody /'pærədɪ/ 1 *n.* Parodie, *die* (**of** auf + *Akk.*)
2 *v.t.* parodieren

parole /pə'rəʊl/ *n.* bedingter Straferlass (Rechtsw.); **on ~**: auf Bewährung

paroxysm /'pærəksɪzm/ *n.* Krampf, *der;* (fit, convulsion) Anfall, *der* (**of** von)

parquet /'pɑ:kɪ, 'pɑ:keɪ/ *n.* **~ [floor/ flooring]** Parkett, *das*

parrot /'pærət/ *n.* Papagei, *der*

parry /'pærɪ/ *v.t.* abwehren ‹*Faustschlag*›; (Fencing; also fig.) parieren

parsley /'pɑ:slɪ/ *n.* Petersilie, *die*

parsnip /'pɑ:snɪp/ *n.* Gemeiner Pastinak, *der*

parson /'pɑ:sn/ *n.* Pfarrer, *der*

part /pɑ:t/ 1 *n.* **(a)** Teil, *der;* **the greater ~**: der größte Teil; der Großteil; **for the most ~**: größtenteils; **in ~**: teilweise; **in large ~**: groß[en]teils; **in ~s** zum Teil
(b) (of machine) [Einzel]teil, *das*
(c) (share) Anteil, *der*
(d) (Theatre) Rolle, *die*
(e) (Mus.) Part, *der;* Stimme, *die*
(f) *usu. in pl.* (region) Gegend, *die;* (of continent, world) Teil, *der*
(g) (side) Partei, *die;* **take sb.'s ~**: jmds. *od.* für jmdn. Partei ergreifen
(h) **take [no] ~ [in sth.]** sich [an etw. (*Dat.*)] [nicht] beteiligen
(i) **take sth. in good ~**: etw. nicht übel nehmen
2 *adv.* teils
3 *v.t.* **(a)** (divide into ~s) teilen; scheiteln ‹*Haar*›
(b) (separate) trennen
4 *v.i.* ‹*Seil, Tau, Kette:*› reißen; ‹*Wege, Personen:*› sich trennen; **~ with** sich trennen von ‹*Besitz, Geld*›

part ex'change *n.* **accept sth. in ~ for sth.** etw. für etw. in Zahlung nehmen; **sell sth. in ~**: etw. in Zahlung geben

partial /'pɑ:ʃl/ *adj.* **(a)** (biased) voreingenommen
(b) **be/not be ~ to sth.** eine Schwäche/keine besondere Vorliebe für etw. haben
(c) partiell ‹*Lähmung, Sonnenfinsternis*›; **a ~ success** ein Teilerfolg

'partially *adv.* teilweise

participant /pɑ:'tɪsɪpənt/ *n.* Beteiligte, *der/die* (**in** an + *Dat.*)

participate /pɑ:'tɪsɪpeɪt/ *v.i.* sich beteiligen (**in** an + *Dat.*); (in arranged event) teilnehmen (**in** an + *Dat.*)

participation /pɑ:tɪsɪ'peɪʃn/ *n.* Beteiligung, *die* (**in** an + *Dat.*); (in arranged event) Teilnahme, *die* (**in** bei, an + *Dat.*)

participle /'pɑ:tɪsɪpl/ *n.* Partizip, *das*

particle /'pɑ:tɪkl/ *n.* Teilchen, *das*

particular /pə'tɪkjʊlə(r)/ 1 *adj.* **(a)** besonder...; **here in ~**: besonders hier; **nothing/anything [in] ~**: nichts/irgendetwas Besonderes
(b) (fastidious) genau; **I am not ~**: es ist mir gleich; **be ~ about sth.** es mit etw. genau nehmen
2 *n., in pl.* Einzelheiten *Pl.*; Details *Pl.*; (of person) Personalien *Pl.*

par'ticularly *adv.* besonders

'parting 1 *n.* **(a)** **[final] ~**: Abschied, *der*
(b) (Brit.: in hair) Scheitel, *der*
2 *attrib. adj.* Abschieds-

partisan /'pɑ:tɪzæn/ *n.* Partisan, *der*/ Partisanin, *die*

partition /pɑ:'tɪʃn/ 1 *n.* **(a)** (Polit.) Teilung, *die*
(b) (room divider) Trennwand, *die*
2 *v.t.* **(a)** (divide) aufteilen ‹*Land, Zimmer*›
(b) (Polit.) teilen ‹*Land*›

■ **partition 'off** *v.t.* abteilen

'partly *adv.* zum Teil; teilweise

partner /'pɑ:tnə(r)/ *n.* Partner, *der*/ Partnerin, *die*

'partnership *n.* Partnerschaft, *die;* **business ~**: [Personen]gesellschaft, *die*

'part-owner *n.* Mitbesitzer, *der*/ -besitzerin, *die*

partridge /'pɑ:trɪdʒ/ *n., pl. same or* **~s** Rebhuhn, *das*

part: ~-time 1 /'--/ *adj.* Teilzeit‹*arbeit, -arbeiter*›; 2 /-'-/ *adv.* stundenweise, halbtags ‹*arbeiten, studieren*›; **~-'timer** *n.* Teilzeitkraft, *die;* **study as a ~-timer** halbtags *od.* stundenweise studieren

party /'pɑ:tɪ/ *n.* **(a)** (Polit., Law) Partei, *die; attrib.* Partei-
(b) (group) Gruppe, *die*
(c) (social gathering) Party, *die*

party: ~ po'litical *adj.* parteipolitisch; **~ 'politics** *n.* Parteipolitik, *die;* **~ wall** *n.* Mauer zum Nachbargrundstück/-gebäude

pass /pɑ:s/ 1 *n.* **(a)** (passing of an ⋯

examination) bestandene Prüfung; '~' (mark) Ausreichend, *das*; **get a ~ in maths** die Mathematikprüfung bestehen
(b) (written permission) Ausweis, *der*
(c) (Footb.) Pass, *der* (fachspr.); Ballabgabe, *die*
(d) (in mountains) Pass, *der*
2 *v.i.* **(a)** (go by) ‹*Fußgänger:*› vorbeigehen; ‹*Fahrer, Fahrzeug:*› vorbeifahren; ‹*Zeit, Sekunde:*› vergehen; (by chance) ‹*Person, Fahrzeug:*› vorbeikommen
(b) (come to an end) vorbeigehen; ‹*Gewitter, Unwetter:*› vorüberziehen
(c) (be accepted) durchgehen (**as** als, **for** für)
(d) (in exam) bestehen
3 *v.t.* **(a)** ‹*Fußgänger:*› vorbeigehen an (+ *Dat.*); ‹*Fahrer, Fahrzeug:*› vorbeifahren an (+ *Dat.*); (by chance) ‹*Person, Fahrzeug:*› vorbeikommen an (+ *Dat.*)
(b) (overtake) vorbeifahren an (+ *Dat.*)
(c) bestehen ‹*Prüfung*›
(d) (approve) verabschieden ‹*Gesetzentwurf*›; annehmen ‹*Vorschlag*›; bestehen lassen ‹*Prüfungskandidaten*›
(e) (Footb. etc.) abgeben (**to** an + *Akk.*)
(f) (spend) verbringen ‹*Leben, Zeit, Tag*›
(g) (hand) **~ sb. sth.** jmdm. etw. reichen
(h) fällen ‹*Urteil*›; machen ‹*Bemerkung*›
(i) **~ water** Wasser lassen
■ **pass a'way** *v.i.* (euphem.) verscheiden (*geh.*)
■ **pass 'off** *v.t.* **~ sth. off as sth.** etw. als etw. ausgeben
■ **pass 'on** *v.t.* weitergeben (**to** an + *Akk.*)
■ **pass 'out** *v.i.* ohnmächtig werden
■ **pass 'up** *v.t.* entgehen lassen ‹*Gelegenheit*›; ablehnen ‹*Angebot*›

p

passable /'pɑːsəbl/ *adj.* **(a)** (acceptable) passabel
(b) befahrbar ‹*Straße*›

passage /'pæsɪdʒ/ *n.* **(a)** (voyage) Überfahrt, *die*
(b) (way) Durchgang, *der;* (corridor) Korridor, *der*
(c) (part of book etc.) Textstelle, *die*

'passageway *n.* Gang, *der;* (between houses) Durchgang, *der*

passenger /'pæsɪndʒə(r)/ *n.* Passagier, *der;* (on train) Reisende, *der/die;* (on bus, in taxi) Fahrgast, *der;* (in car, on motor cycle) Mitfahrer, *der*/Mitfahrerin, *die;* (in front seat of car) Beifahrer, *der*/Beifahrerin, *die*

passenger: ~ aircraft *n.* Passagierflugzeug, *das;* **~ door** *n.* Beifahrertür, *die;* **~ lounge** *n.* Warteraum, *der;* **~ plane** *n.* Passagierflugzeug, *das;* **~ seat** *n.* Beifahrersitz, *der;* **~ service** *n.* (train) Personenzugverbindung, *die;* (ferry) Personenfährverbindung, *die*

passer-by /pɑːsə'baɪ/ *n.* Passant, *der*/Passantin, *die*

'passing **1** *n.* (of time, years) Lauf, *der;* **in ~:** beiläufig ‹*bemerken usw.*›
2 *adj.* **(a)** vorbeifahrend ‹*Zug, Auto*›; vorbeikommend ‹*Person*›
(b) flüchtig ‹*Blick*›; vorübergehend ‹*Mode, Interesse*›; flüchtig ‹*Bekanntschaft*›

'passing place *n.* Ausweichstelle, *die*

passion /'pæʃn/ *n.* Leidenschaft, *die;* (enthusiasm) leidenschaftliche Begeisterung; **he has a ~ for steam engines** Dampfloks sind seine Leidenschaft

passionate /'pæʃənət/ *adj.* leidenschaftlich; heftig ‹*Verlangen*›

passive /'pæsɪv/ **1** *adj.* **(a)** passiv; **~ smoker** Passivraucher, *der*/-raucherin, *die;* **~ smoking** passives Rauchen
(b) (Ling.) Passiv-
2 *n.* (Ling.) Passiv, *das*

pass: ~ key *n.* (master key) Hauptschlüssel, *der;* **~ mark** *n.* Mindestpunktzahl, *die;* **~port** *n.* **(a)** [Reise]pass, *der; attrib.* Pass-; **~port control** Passkontrolle, *die;* **(b)** (fig.) Schlüssel, *der* (**to** zu); **~word** *n.* **(a)** Parole, *die;* Losung, *die;* **(b)** (Comp.) Passwort, *das* **~word-protected** passwortegeschützt

past /pɑːst/ **1** *adj.* **(a)** *pred.* (over) vorbei
(b) *attrib.* (previous) früher; vergangen; ehemalig ‹*Präsident, Vorsitzende usw.*›
(c) *attrib.* (just gone by) letzt...; vergangen; **in the ~ few days** während der letzten Tage
(d) (Ling.) **~ tense** Vergangenheit, *die*
2 *n.* Vergangenheit, *die;* **in the ~:** früher; in der Vergangenheit ‹*leben*›; **be a thing of the ~:** der Vergangenheit angehören
3 *prep.* (in time) nach; (in place) hinter (+ *Dat.*); **half ~ three** halb vier; **five [minutes] ~ two** fünf [Minuten] nach zwei; **gaze/walk ~ sb./sth.** an jmdm./etw. vorbeiblicken/vorbeigehen; **~ repair** nicht mehr zu reparieren
4 *adv.* vorbei; **hurry ~:** vorübereilen

pasta /'pæstə/ *n.* Teigwaren *Pl.*

paste /peɪst/ **1** *n.* **(a)** Brei, *der*
(b) (glue) Kleister, *der*
(c) (of meat, fish, etc.) Paste, *die*
2 *v.t.* **(a)** kleben; **~ sth. into sth.** etw. in etw. (*Akk.*) einkleben
(b) (Comp.) einfügen (**into** in + *Akk.*); *see also* CUT 1E

pastel /'pæstl/ **1** *n.* (crayon) Pastellstift, *der*
2 *adj.* pastellfarben; Pastell‹*farben, -töne, -zeichnung*›

pasteurize /'pɑːstʃəraɪz/ *v.t.* pasteurisieren

pastille /'pæstɪl/ *n.* Pastille, *die*

pastime /'pɑːstaɪm/ *n.* Zeitvertreib, *der;* (person's specific ~) Hobby, *das*

past 'master *n.* (fig.) Meister, *der*

pastor /'pɑːstə(r)/ *n.* Pfarrer, *der*/Pfarrerin, *die;* Pastor, *der*/Pastorin, *die*

pastoral /'pɑːstərl/ *adj.* Weide-; ländlich ‹*Reiz, Idylle, Umgebung*›

pastry /'peɪstrɪ/ *n.* Teig, *der;* (article of food) Gebäckstück, *das;* **pastries** *collect.* [Fein]gebäck, *das*

pasture /'pɑːstʃə(r)/ *n.* Weide, *die*

'pastureland *n.* Weideland, *das*

pasty /'pæstɪ/ *n.* Pastete, *die*

pat¹ /pæt/ [1] *n.* **(a)** (tap) Klaps, *der*
(b) (of butter) Stückchen, *das*
[2] *v.t.*, **-tt-** leicht klopfen auf (+ *Akk.*); tätscheln, (once) einen Klaps geben (+ *Dat.*) ‹*Person, Hund, Pferd*›; **~ sb. on the arm/head** jmdm. den Arm/Kopf tätscheln

pat² *adv.* **have sth. off ~:** etw. parat haben

patch /pætʃ/ [1] *n.* **(a)** Stelle, *die;* **fog ~es** Nebelfelder
(b) (on worn garment) Flicken, *der;* **be not a ~ on sth.** (fig. coll.) nichts gegen etw. sein
[2] *v.t.* flicken

■ **patch 'up** *v.t.* reparieren; (fig.) beilegen ‹*Streit*›

patchwork *n.* Patchwork, *das*

patchy /'pætʃɪ/ *adj.* uneinheitlich ‹*Qualität*›; ungleichmäßig ‹*Arbeit*›; sehr lückenhaft ‹*Wissen*›

pâté /'pæteɪ/ *n.* Pastete, *die*

patent /'peɪtənt, 'pætənt/ [1] *adj.* (obvious) offenkundig
[2] *n.* Patent, *das*
[3] *v.t.* patentieren lassen

patent 'leather *n.* Lackleder, *das;* **~ shoes** Lackschuhe *Pl.*

'patently *adv.* offenkundig; **~ obvious** ganz offenkundig

paternal /pə'tɜ:nl/ *adj.* väterlich

paternity /pə'tɜ:nɪtɪ/ *n.* (fatherhood) Vaterschaft, *die*

pa'ternity leave *n.* Vaterschaftsurlaub, *der*

path /pɑ:θ/ *n.* Weg, *der;* (line of motion) Bahn, *die*

pathetic /pə'θetɪk/ *adj.* **(a)** (pitiful) Mitleid erregend
(b) (contemptible) armselig ‹*Entschuldigung*›; erbärmlich ‹*Person, Leistung*›

pathogen /'pæθədʒən/ *n.* [Krankheits]erreger, *der*

pathological /pæθə'lɒdʒɪkl/ *adj.* **(a)** pathologisch
(b) (fig.: obsessive) krankhaft

pathologist /pə'θɒlədʒɪst/ *n.* Pathologe, *der*/Pathologin, *die*

pathology /pə'θɒlədʒɪ/ *n.* Pathologie, *die;* **the ~ of a disease** das Krankheitsbild

'pathway *n.* Weg, *der*

patience /'peɪʃəns/ *n.* Geduld, *die*

patient /'peɪʃənt/ [1] *adj.* geduldig
[2] *n.* Patient, *der*/Patientin, *die*

'patiently *adv.* geduldig

patio /'pætɪəʊ/ *n., pl.* **~s** Veranda, *die;* Terrasse, *die*

patio 'door *n.* große Glasschiebetür (*zum Garten*)

patriarch /'peɪtrɪɑ:k/ *n.* (of family) Familienoberhaupt, *das*

patriarchal /peɪtrɪ'ɑ:kl/ *adj.* patriarchalisch

patriot /'peɪtrɪət/ *n.* Patriot, *der*/Patriotin, *die*

patriotic /peɪtrɪ'ɒtɪk/ *adj.* patriotisch

patriotism /'peɪtrɪətɪzm/ *n.* Patriotismus, *der*

patrol /pə'trəʊl/ [1] *n.* (Police) Streife, *die;* (Mil.) Patrouille, *die;* **be on ~:** patrouillieren
[2] *v.i.*, **-ll-** patrouillieren; ‹*Polizei:*› Streife laufen/fahren
[3] *v.t.*, **-ll-** patrouillieren durch (+ *Akk.*); abpatrouillieren ‹*Straßen, Gegend, Lager*›; patrouillieren vor (+ *Dat.*) ‹*Küste, Grenze*›; ‹*Polizei:*› Streife laufen/fahren in (+ *Dat.*) ‹*Straßen, Stadtteil*›

patrol: ~ boat *n.* Patrouillenboot, *das;* **~ car** *n.* Streifenwagen, *der*

patron /'peɪtrən/ *n.* **(a)** Gönner, *der*/Gönnerin, *die;* (of institution, campaign) Schirmherr, *der*/Schirmherrin, *die*
(b) (customer) (of shop) Kunde, *der*/Kundin, *die;* (of restaurant, hotel) Gast, *der;* (of theatre, cinema) Besucher, *der*/Besucherin, *die*
(c) ~ [saint] Schutzheilige, *der/die*

patronage /'pætrənɪdʒ/ *n.* Gönnerschaft, *die;* (for campaign, institution) Schirmherrschaft, *die*

patronize /'pætrənaɪz/ *v.t.* **(a)** (frequent) besuchen
(b) (condescend to) **~ sb.** jmdn. herablassend behandeln

patronizing /'pætrənaɪzɪŋ/ *adj.* gönnerhaft; herablassend

patter /'pætə(r)/ [1] *n.* (of rain) Prasseln, *das;* (of feet) Trappeln, *das*
[2] *v.i.* ‹*Regen:*› prasseln

pattern /'pætən/ *n.* Muster, *das;* (model) Vorlage, *die;* (for sewing) Schnittmuster, *das;* (for knitting) Strickmuster, *das*

paunch /pɔ:ntʃ/ *n.* Bauch, *der*

pauper /'pɔ:pə(r)/ *n.* Arme, *der/die*

pause /pɔ:z/ [1] *n.* Pause, *die*
[2] *v.i.* eine Pause machen; ‹*Redner:*› innehalten; (hesitate) zögern

pave /peɪv/ *v.t.* befestigen; (with stones) pflastern; **~ the way for sth.** (fig.) einer Sache (*Dat.*) den Weg ebnen

'pavement *n.* **(a)** (Brit.: footway) Bürgersteig, *der*
(b) (Amer.: roadway) Fahrbahn, *die*

'pavement café *n.* Straßencafé, *das*

pavilion /pə'vɪljən/ *n.* Pavillon, *der;* (Brit. Sport) Klubhaus, *das*

'paving stone *n.* Platte, *die;* Pflasterstein, *der*

paw /pɔ:/ *n.* Pfote, *die;* (of bear, lion, tiger) Pranke, *die*

pawn¹ /pɔ:n/ *n.* (Chess) Bauer, *der;* (fig.) Schachfigur, *die*

pawn² [1] *n.* Pfand, *das;* **in ~:** verpfändet
[2] *v.t.* verpfänden

pawn: ~broker *n.* Pfandleiher, *der*/-leiherin, *die;* **~shop** *n.* Leihhaus, *das*

pay /peɪ/ [1] *n.* (wages) Lohn, *der;* (salary) Gehalt, *das;* **be in the ~ of sb./sth.** für jmdn./etw. arbeiten

P

2 *v.t.*, **paid** /peɪd/ bezahlen; zahlen ‹*Geld*›; **~ sb. to do sth.** jmdn. dafür bezahlen, dass er etw. tut; **~ sb. £10** jmdm. 10 Pfund zahlen 3 *v.i.*, **paid (a)** zahlen; **~ for sth./sb.** etw./für jmdn. bezahlen; **sth. ~s for itself** etw. macht sich bezahlt
(b) (be profitable) sich lohnen; ‹*Geschäft:*› rentabel sein; **it ~s to be careful** es lohnt sich, vorsichtig zu sein. *See also* PAID
■ **pay 'back** *v.t.* zurückzahlen; **I'll ~ you back later** ich gebe dir das Geld später zurück
■ **pay 'in** *v.t.* einzahlen
■ **pay 'off** *v.t.* auszahlen ‹*Arbeiter*›; abbezahlen ‹*Schulden*›; ablösen ‹*Hypothek*›; befriedigen ‹*Gläubiger*›
■ **pay 'out** *v.t.* auszahlen; (spend) ausgeben
■ **pay 'up** *v.i.* zahlen

payable /'peɪəbl/ *adj.* zahlbar; **be ~ to sb.** an jmdn. zu zahlen sein; **make a cheque ~ to the Post Office/to sb.** einen Scheck auf die Post/auf jmds. Namen ausstellen

pay: ~ and display 1 *n.* Parken mit Parkschein; *attrib.* Parkschein-; 2 *n.* **~ and display car park** Parkplatz mit Parkscheinautomat; **~ cheque** *n.* Lohn-/Gehaltsscheck, *der;* **~ claim** *n.* Lohn-/Gehaltsforderung, *die;* **~ day** *n.* Zahltag, *der;* **~ increase** ▶ PAY RISE

payee /peɪ'i:/ *n.* Zahlungsempfänger, *der*/-empfängerin, *die*

paying /'peɪɪŋ/**: ~ 'guest** *n.* zahlender Gast; **~-'in slip** *n.* (Brit. Banking) Einzahlungsschein, *der*

'payment *n.* **(a)** (of sum, bill, debt, fine) Bezahlung, *die;* (of interest, instalment, tax, fee) Zahlung, *die;* **in ~ [for sth.]** als Bezahlung [für etw.]
(b) (amount) Zahlung, *die*

pay: ~ packet *n.* (Brit.) Lohntüte, *die;* **~phone** *n.* Münzfernsprecher, *der;* **~ rise** *n.* Lohn-/Gehaltserhöhung, *die;* **~roll** *n.* Lohnliste, *die;* **be on sb.'s ~roll** für jmdn. arbeiten; **~slip** *n.* Lohnstreifen, *der*/Gehaltszettel, *der;* **~ station** *n.* (Amer.) ▶ ~PHONE

p.c. *abbr.* = **per cent** v. H.

PC *abbr.* **(a)** (Brit.) = **police constable** Wachtm.
(b) = **personal computer** PC
(c) = **politically correct** politisch korrekt

PE *abbr.* = **physical education**

pea /pi:/ *n.* Erbse, *die*

peace /pi:s/ *n.* Frieden, *der;* (tranquillity) Ruhe, *die;* **~ of mind** Seelenfrieden, *der*

peaceable /'pi:səbl/ *adj.* friedfertig; (calm) friedlich

peaceful /'pi:sfl/ *adj.* friedlich; friedfertig ‹*Person, Volk*›

'peacefully *adv.* friedlich; **die ~**: sanft entschlafen

peace: ~keeper *n.* Friedenswächter, *der;* **~keeping force** Friedenstruppe, *die;* **~maker** *n.* Friedensstifter, *der*/-stifterin, *die;* **~ movement** *n.* Friedensbewegung, *die;* **~ process** *n.* Friedensprozess, *der* **~ treaty** *n.* Friedensvertrag, *der*

peach /pi:tʃ/ *n.* Pfirsich, *der*

'peacock *n.* Pfau, *der*

'pea-green *adj.* erbsengrün; maigrün

peak /pi:k/ 1 *n.* **(a)** (of cap) Schirm, *der*
(b) (of mountain) Gipfel, *der;* (fig.) Höhepunkt, *der*
2 *attrib. adj.* Höchst-, Spitzen‹*preise, -werte*›; **~-hour traffic** Stoßverkehr, *der*

peaked /pi:kt/ *adj.* **~ cap** Schirmmütze, *die*

'peak season *n.* Hochsaison, *die*

peal /pi:l/ *n.* Läuten, *das;* **~ of bells** Glockenläuten, *das;* **a ~/~s of laughter** schallendes Gelächter

peanut /'pi:nʌt/ *n.* Erdnuss, *die;* **~ butter** Erdnussbutter, *die;* **~s** (coll.: little money) ein paar Kröten (salopp)

pear /peə(r)/ *n.* Birne, *die*

pearl /pɜ:l/ *n.* Perle, *die*

pear: ~-shaped *adj.* birnenförmig: **~tree** *n.* Birnbaum, *der*

peasant /'pezənt/ *n.* [armer] Bauer, *der;* Landarbeiter, *der*

pea 'soup Erbsensuppe, *die*

peat /pi:t/ *n.* Torf, *der*

pebble /'pebl/ *n.* Kiesel[stein], *der*

peck /pek/ 1 *v.t.* hacken; picken ‹*Körner*›
2 *v.i.* picken **(at** nach); **~ at one's food** im Essen herumstochern
3 *n.* (kiss) flüchtiger Kuss

'pecking order *n.* Hackordnung, *die*

peckish /'pekɪʃ/ *adj.* (coll.) **feel/get ~**: Hunger haben/bekommen

peculiar /pɪ'kju:lɪə(r)/ *adj.* **(a)** (strange) seltsam; **I feel [slightly] ~**: mir ist [etwas] komisch
(b) (especial) besonder...
(c) (belonging exclusively) eigentümlich **(to** *Dat.*)

peculiarity /pɪkju:lɪ'ærɪtɪ/ *n.* **(a)** (odd trait) Eigentümlichkeit, *die*
(b) (distinguishing characteristic) [charakteristisches] Merkmal

pe'culiarly *adv.* **(a)** (strangely) seltsam
(b) (especially) besonders

pedal /'pedl/ 1 *n.* Pedal, *das*
2 *v.i.*, (Brit.) **-ll-** in die Pedale treten

'pedal bin *n.* Treteimer, *der*

pedalo /'pedələʊ/ *n., pl.* **~s** Tretboot, *das*

pedant /'pedənt/ *n.* Pedant, *der*/Pedantin, *die*

pedantic /pɪ'dæntɪk/ *adj.* pedantisch

peddle /'pedl/ *v.t.* auf der Straße verkaufen; (door to door) hausieren mit

pedestal /'pedɪstl/ *n.* Sockel, *der*

pedestrian /pɪ'destrɪən/ 1 *adj.* (uninspired) trocken; langweilig
2 *n.* Fußgänger, *der*/-gängerin, *die*

pedestrian 'crossing *n.* Fußgängerüberweg, *der*

pedestrianize (**pedestrianise**) /pɪˈdestrɪənaɪz/ *v.t.* zur Fußgängerzone machen; **~d zone** Fußgängerzone, *die*

pedestrian 'precinct ▶ PRECINCT A

pediatrician *etc.* ▶ PAEDIATRICIAN *etc.*

pedicure /ˈpedɪkjʊə(r)/ *n., no art.* Pediküre, *die*

pedigree /ˈpedɪgriː/ 1 *n.* Stammbaum, *der* 2 *adj.* mit Stammbaum *nachgestellt*

pedlar /ˈpedlə(r)/ *n.* Straßenhändler, *der*/-händlerin, *die;* (door to door) Hausierer, *der*/Hausiererin, *die*

pee /piː/ (coll.) 1 *v.i.* pinkeln (salopp); Pipi machen (Kinderspr.)
2 *n.* **(a)** **have a ~:** pinkeln (salopp)
(b) (urine) Pipi, *das* (Kinderspr.)

peek /piːk/ ▶ PEEP[2]

peel /piːl/ 1 *v.t.* schälen
2 *v.i.* ‹*Person, Haut:*› sich schälen; ‹*Farbe:*› abblättern
3 *n.* Schale, *die*

'peelings *n. pl.* Schalen *Pl.*

peep[1] /piːp/ 1 *v.i.* ‹*Maus, Vogel:*› piep[s]en
2 *n.* Piepsen, *das;* (coll.: remark etc.) Piep[s], *der*

peep[2] 1 *v.i.* gucken (ugs.); (furtively) verstohlen gucken (ugs.)
2 *n.* kurzer/verstohlener Blick

peep: ~hole *n.* Guckloch, *das;* **~ing 'Tom** *n.* Spanner, *der* (ugs.)

peer[1] /pɪə(r)/ *n.* Peer, *der;* (equal) Gleichgestellte, *der/die*

peer[2] *v.i.* forschend schauen; (with difficulty) angestrengt schauen; **~ at sth./sb.** [sich (*Dat.*)] etw. genau ansehen/jmdn. forschend ansehen; (with difficulty) [sich (*Dat.*)] etw./jmdn. angestrengt ansehen

peerage /ˈpɪərɪdʒ/ *n.* Peerswürde, *die*

'peer pressure *n.* Gruppenzwang, *der*

peevish /ˈpiːvɪʃ/ *adj.* nörgelig

peg /peg/ *n.* (for holding together) Stift, *der;* (for tying things to) Pflock, *der;* (for hanging things on) Haken, *der;* (clothes ~) Wäscheklammer, *die;* (tent ~) Hering, *der;* **off the ~** (Brit.: ready-made) von der Stange (ugs.)

pejorative /pɪˈdʒɒrətɪv/ *adj.*, **pe'joratively** *adv.* abwertend

pelican /ˈpelɪkən/ *n.* Pelikan, *der*

'pelican crossing *n.* (Brit.) Ampelübergang, *der*

pellet /ˈpelɪt/ *n.* Kügelchen, *das*

pelmet /ˈpelmɪt/ *n.* Blende, *die*

pelt[1] /pelt/ *n.* Fell, *das*

pelt[2] 1 *v.t.* **~ sb. with sth.** jmdn. mit etw. bewerfen
2 *v.i.* **(a)** **it was ~ing down [with rain]** es goss wie aus Kübeln (ugs.)
(b) (run fast) rasen (ugs.)

pelvic /ˈpelvɪk/ *adj.* Becken-

pelvis /ˈpelvɪs/ *n., pl.* **pelves** /ˈpelviːz/ *or* **~es** (Anat.) Becken, *das*

pen[1] /pen/ 1 *n.* (enclosure) Pferch, *der*
2 *v.t.*, **-nn-:** **~ sb. in a corner** jmdn. in eine Ecke drängen
■ **pen 'in** *v.t.* einpferchen

pen[2] 1 *n.* Federhalter, *der;* (fountain ~) Füller, *der;* (ball ~) Kugelschreiber, *der;* (felt-tip ~) Filzstift, *der*
2 *v.t.*, **-nn-** schreiben

penal /ˈpiːnl/ *adj.* Straf-

penalize /ˈpiːnəlaɪz/ *v.t.* bestrafen; (Sport) eine Strafe verhängen gegen

penalty /ˈpenltɪ/ *n.* **(a)** Strafe, *die;* **pay the ~/the ~ for** *or* **of sth.** dafür/für etw. büßen [müssen]
(b) (Footb.) Elfmeter, *der*

penalty: ~ box *n.* (Footb.) Strafraum, *der;* (Ice Hockey) Strafbank, *die;* **~ kick** *n.* (Footb.) Strafstoß, *der*

penance /ˈpenəns/ *n.* Buße, *die;* **act of ~:** Bußwerk, *das;* **do ~:** Buße tun

pence ▶ PENNY

pencil /ˈpensɪl/ 1 *n.* Bleistift, *der;* **red/coloured ~:** Rot-/Buntstift, *der*
2 *v.t.*, (Brit.) **-ll-** mit einem Bleistift/Farbstift schreiben

pencil: ~ case *n.* Griffelkasten, *der;* (of soft material) Federmäppchen, *das;* **~ sharpener** *n.* Bleistiftspitzer, *der*

pendant /ˈpendənt/ *n.* Anhänger, *der*

pending /ˈpendɪŋ/ 1 *adj.* unentschieden ‹*Angelegenheit, Sache*›; schwebend ‹*Verfahren*›
2 *prep.* **~ his return** bis zu seiner Rückkehr

pendulum /ˈpendjʊləm/ *n.* Pendel, *das*

penetrate /ˈpenɪtreɪt/ *v.t.* eindringen in (+ *Akk.*); (pass through) durchdringen

penetrating /ˈpenɪtreɪtɪŋ/ *adj.* durchdringend

penetration /penɪˈtreɪʃn/ *n.* Eindringen, *das* (of in + *Akk.*); (passing through) Durchdringen, *das*

'penfriend *n.* Brieffreund, *der*/-freundin, *die*

penguin /ˈpeŋgwɪn/ *n.* Pinguin, *der*

penicillin /penɪˈsɪlɪn/ *n.* Penizillin, *das*

peninsula /pɪˈnɪnsjʊlə/ *n.* Halbinsel, *die*

penis /ˈpiːnɪs/ *n.* Penis, *der*

penitence /ˈpenɪtəns/ *n.* Reue, *die*

penitent /ˈpenɪtənt/ *adj.* reuevoll (geh.); reuig (geh.) ‹*Sünder*›

penitentiary /penɪˈtenʃərɪ/ *n.* (Amer.) Straf[vollzugs]anstalt, *die*

pen: ~knife *n.* Taschenmesser, *das;* **~ light** *n.* [Mini]stablampe, *die*

pennant /ˈpenənt/ *n.* Wimpel, *der;* (on official car etc.) Stander, *der*

penniless /ˈpenɪlɪs/ *adj.* mittellos

penny /ˈpenɪ/ *n., pl. usu.* **pennies** /ˈpenɪz/ (for separate coins), **pence** /pens/ (for sum of money) Penny, *der;* **fifty pence** fünfzig Pence; **two/fifty pence [piece]** Zwei-/Fünfzigpencestück, *das*

pension /ˈpenʃn/ *n.* Rente, *die;* (payment to retired civil servant) Pension, *die;* **widow's ~:** Witwenrente, *die* /-pension, *die*; **be on a ~:** eine Rente beziehen

■ **pension 'off** *v.t.* berenten (Amtsspr.); auf Rente setzen (ugs.); pensionieren ‹*Lehrer, Beamten*›

'pensioner *n.* Rentner, *der*/Rentnerin, *die;* (retired civil servant) Pensionär, *der*/Pensionärin, *die*

pensive /ˈpensɪv/ *adj.* nachdenklich

pentagon /ˈpentəgən/ *n.* Fünfeck, *das*; **the P~** (Amer. Polit.) das Pentagon

Pentecost /ˈpentɪkɒst/ *n.* Pfingsten, *das*

pent: ~house *n.* Penthaus, *das;* **~-up** *adj.* angestaut ‹*Ärger, Wut*›; unterdrückt ‹*Sehnsucht, Gefühle*›

penultimate /peˈnʌltɪmət/ *adj.* vorletzt...

people /ˈpiːpl/ *n.* **(a)** *constr. as pl.* Leute *Pl.;* Menschen *Pl.*; (as opposed to animals) Menschen *Pl.;* **city/country ~** (inhabitants) Stadt-/Landbewohner *Pl.*; **local ~:** Einheimische *Pl.*; **working ~:** arbeitende Menschen; **coloured/white ~:** Farbige/Weiße *Pl.*; **~ say ...:** man sagt ...; **a crowd of ~:** eine Menschenmenge
(b) (nation) Volk, *das*

pepper /ˈpepə(r)/ **1** *n.* **(a)** Pfeffer, *der*
(b) (vegetable) Paprikaschote, *die;* **red/green ~:** roter/grüner Paprika
2 *v.t.* **(a)** pfeffern
(b) (pelt) bombardieren (ugs.)

pepper: ~corn *n.* Pfefferkorn, *das;* **~ mill** *n.* Pfeffermühle, *die;* **~mint** *n.* (sweet) Pfefferminz, *das;* **~ pot** *n.* Pfefferstreuer, *der*

peppery /ˈpepərɪ/ *adj.* pfeff[e]rig; (spicy) scharf

per /pə(r), *stressed* pɜː(r)/ *prep.* pro

perceive /pəˈsiːv/ *v.t.* wahrnehmen; (with the mind) spüren; **~d** vermeintlich ‹*Bedrohung, Gefahr, Wert*›

per cent (*Brit.; Amer.:* **percent**) /pəˈsent/ **1** *adv.* **ninety ~ effective** zu 90 Prozent wirksam
2 *adj.* **a 5 ~ increase** ein Zuwachs von 5 Prozent
3 *n.* **(a)** Prozent, *das*
(b) ▶ PERCENTAGE

percentage /pəˈsentɪdʒ/ *n.* Prozentsatz, *der*

per'centage sign *n.* Prozentzeichen, *das*

perceptible /pəˈseptɪbl/ *adj.* wahrnehmbar

perception /pəˈsepʃn/ *n.* (act) Wahrnehmung, *die;* (result) Erkenntnis, *die;* (faculty) Wahrnehmungsvermögen, *das*

perceptive /pəˈseptɪv/ *adj.* einfühlsam ‹*Person, Bemerkung*›

perch /pɜːtʃ/ **1** *n.* Sitzstange, *die*
2 *v.i.* **(a)** sich niederlassen
(b) (be supported) sitzen
3 *v.t.* setzen/stellen/legen

percolate /ˈpɜːkəleɪt/ *v.i.* [durch]sickern

percolator /ˈpɜːkəleɪtə(r)/ *n.* Kaffeemaschine, *die*

percussion /pəˈkʌʃn/ *n.* (Mus.) Schlagzeug, *das;* **~ instrument** Schlaginstrument, *das*

perennial /pəˈrenjəl/ **1** *adj.* **(a)** (Bot.) ausdauernd
(b) immer wieder auftretend ‹*Problem*›
2 *n.* (Bot.) ausdauernde Pflanze

perfect **1** /ˈpɜːfɪkt/ *adj.* vollkommen; perfekt ‹*Englisch, Timing*›; tadellos ‹*Zustand*›; (coll.: unmitigated) absolut; **a ~ stranger** ein völlig Fremder
2 /pəˈfekt/ *v.t.* vervollkommnen

perfection /pəˈfekʃn/ *n.* Perfektion, *die;* **to ~:** perfekt

perfectionism /pəˈfekʃənɪzm/ *n.* Perfektionismus, *der*

perfectionist /pəˈfekʃənɪst/ *n.* Perfektionist, *der*/Perfektionistin, *die*

'perfectly *adv.* **(a)** (completely) vollkommen; **be ~ entitled to do sth.** durchaus berechtigt sein, etw. zu tun
(b) (faultlessly) perfekt; tadellos ‹*sich verhalten*›

perfect 'pitch *n.* (Mus.) absolutes Gehör

perforate /ˈpɜːfəreɪt/ *v.t.* perforieren; (make opening into) durchlöchern

perforation /pɜːfəˈreɪʃn/ *n.* **(a)** (hole) Loch, *das*
(b) *in pl.* **~s** Perforation, *die;* (in sheets of stamps) Zähnung, *die*

perform /pəˈfɔːm/ **1** *v.t.* ausführen ‹*Arbeit, Operation*›; erfüllen ‹*Pflicht, Aufgabe*›; vollbringen ‹*[Helden]tat, Leistung*›; ausfüllen ‹*Funktion*›; vollbringen ‹*Wunder*›; anstellen ‹*Berechnungen*›; durchführen ‹*Experiment, Sektion*›; vorführen ‹*Trick*›; aufführen ‹*Theaterstück, Scharade*›; vortragen ‹*Lied, Sonate usw.*›
2 *v.i.* eine Vorführung geben; (sing) singen; (play) spielen

performance /pəˈfɔːməns/ *n.* **(a)** (of duty, task) Erfüllung, *die*
(b) ([notable] achievement; Motor Veh.) Leistung, *die*
(c) (at theatre, cinema, etc.) Vorstellung, *die;* **her ~ as Desdemona** ihre Darstellung der Desdemona; **the ~ of a play/opera** die Aufführung eines Theaterstücks/einer Oper

performance: ~ art *n.* Performance-Art, *die;* **~ artist** *n.* Performancekünstler, *der*/-künstlerin, *die* **~-enhancing** *adj.* **~-enhancing drug/substance** leistungsfördernde *od.* -steigernde Droge/Substanz

per'former *n.* Künstler, *der*/Künstlerin, *die*

per'forming *attrib. adj.* dressiert ‹*Tier*›

performing 'arts *n. pl.* darstellende Künste

perfume /ˈpɜːfjuːm/ *n.* Duft, *der;* (fluid) Parfüm, *das*

perfunctory /pəˈfʌŋktərɪ/ *adj.* oberflächlich ‹*Arbeit, Überprüfung*›; flüchtig ‹*Erkundigung, Bemerkung*›

perhaps /pəˈhæps/ *adv.* vielleicht

peril /ˈperl/ *n.* Gefahr, *die*

perilous /ˈperələs/ *adj.* gefahrvoll; **be ~:** gefährlich sein

perimeter /pəˈrɪmɪtə(r)/ *n.* [äußere] Begrenzung; Grenze, *die*

period /ˈpɪərɪəd/ [1] *n.* **(a)** (of history or life) Periode, *die;* Zeit, *die;* (any portion of time) Zeitraum, *der;* **the Classical/Romantic ~:** die Klassik/Romantik
(b) (Sch.) Stunde, *die;* **chemistry/English ~:** Chemie-/Englischstunde, *die*
(c) (menstruation) Periode, *die*
(d) (punctuation mark) Punkt, *der*
[2] *adj.* zeitgenössisch ‹*Tracht, Kostüm*›; antik ‹*Möbel*›

periodic /pɪərɪˈɒdɪk/ *adj.* regelmäßig; (intermittent) gelegentlich

periodical /pɪərɪˈɒdɪkl/ [1] *adj.* ▶ PERIODIC
[2] *n.* Zeitschrift, *die;* **weekly/monthly ~:** Wochenzeitschrift/Monatsschrift, *die*

periˈodically *adv.* regelmäßig; (intermittently) gelegentlich

peripheral /pəˈrɪfərl/ [1] *adj.* peripher (geh.); Rand‹*problem, -erscheinung*›
[2] *n.* (Comp.) Peripheriegerät, *das*

periphery /pəˈrɪfərɪ/ *n.* Peripherie, *die*

periscope /ˈperɪskəʊp/ *n.* Periskop, *das*

perish /ˈperɪʃ/ *v.i.* **(a)** (die) umkommen
(b) (rot) verderben; ‹*Gummi:*› altern

perishable /ˈperɪʃəbl/ *adj.* [leicht] verderblich

ˈperishing (coll.) [1] *adj.* mörderisch ‹*Kälte*›; **it's/I'm ~:** es ist bitterkalt/ich komme um vor Kälte (ugs.)
[2] *adv.* mörderisch ‹*kalt*›

perjury /ˈpɜːdʒərɪ/ *n.* Meineid, *der;* **commit ~:** einen Meineid leisten

perk¹ /pɜːk/ (coll.) [1] *v.i.* **~ up** munter werden
[2] *v.t.* **~ up** aufmuntern

perk² *n.* (Brit. coll.) [Sonder]vergünstigung, *die*

perky /ˈpɜːkɪ/ *adj.* lebhaft; munter

perm /pɜːm/ [1] *n.* Dauerwelle, *die*
[2] *v.t.* **have one's hair ~ed** sich (*Dat.*) eine Dauerwelle machen lassen

permanence /ˈpɜːmənəns/ *n.* Dauerhaftigkeit, *die*

permanent /ˈpɜːmənənt/ *adj.* fest ‹*Sitz, Bestandteil, Mitglied*›; ständig ‹*Wohnsitz, Adresse, Kampf*›; Dauer‹*stellung, -visum*›; bleibend ‹*Schaden*›

ˈpermanently *adv.* dauernd; auf Dauer ‹*verhindern, bleiben*›

permanent ˈwave *n.* Dauerwelle, *die*

permeable /ˈpɜːmɪəbl/ *adj.* durchlässig; **be ~ to sth.** etw. durchlassen

permeate /ˈpɜːmɪeɪt/ [1] *v.t.* dringen durch; **be ~d with** *or* **by sth.** (fig.) von etw. durchdrungen sein
[2] *v.i.* **~ through sth.** etw. durchdringen

permissible /pəˈmɪsɪbl/ *adj.* zulässig; **be ~ to** *or* **for sb.** jmdm. erlaubt sein

permission /pəˈmɪʃn/ *n.* Erlaubnis, *die;* (given by official body) Genehmigung, *die;* **give sb. ~ to do sth.** jmdm. erlauben, etw. zu tun

permissive /pəˈmɪsɪv/ *adj.* **the ~ society** die permissive Gesellschaft

permit [1] /pəˈmɪt/ *v.t.,* **-tt-** zulassen ‹*Berufung, Einspruch usw.*›; **~ sb. sth.** jmdm. etw. erlauben; **sb. is ~ted to do sth.** es ist jmdm. erlaubt, etw. zu tun
[2] *v.i.,* **-tt-** es zulassen
[3] /ˈpɜːmɪt/ *n.* Genehmigung, *die*

pernicious /pəˈnɪʃəs/ *adj.* verderblich; bösartig ‹*Krankheit*›

peroxide /pəˈrɒksaɪd/ *n.* Peroxid, *das;* **~ blonde** Wasserstoffblondine, *die*

perpendicular /pɜːpənˈdɪkjʊlə(r)/ *adj.* senkrecht

perpetrate /ˈpɜːpɪtreɪt/ *v.t.* begehen; verüben ‹*Gräuel*›

perpetual /pəˈpetjʊəl/ *adj.* **(a)** (eternal) ewig
(b) (continuous; coll.: repeated) ständig

perˈpetually *adv.* **(a)** (eternally) ewig
(b) (continuously; coll.: repeatedly) ständig

perpetuate /pəˈpetjʊeɪt/ *v.t.* aufrechterhalten

perplex /pəˈpleks/ *v.t.* verwirren

perplexed /pəˈplekst/ *adj.* verwirrt; (puzzled) ratlos

perplexity /pəˈpleksɪtɪ/ *n.* Verwirrung, *die;* (puzzlement) Ratlosigkeit, *die*

persecute /ˈpɜːsɪkjuːt/ *v.t.* verfolgen

persecution /pɜːsɪˈkjuːʃn/ *n.* Verfolgung, *die*

persecutor /ˈpɜːsɪkjuːtə(r)/ *n.* Verfolger, *der*/Verfolgerin, *die*

perseverance /pɜːsɪˈvɪərəns/ *n.* Beharrlichkeit, *die;* Ausdauer, *die*

persevere /pɜːsɪˈvɪə(r)/ *v.i.* ausharren; **~ with** *or* **at** *or* **in sth.** bei etw. dabeibleiben

Persian /ˈpɜːʃn/ *adj.* persisch; Perser‹*katze, -teppich*›

persist /pəˈsɪst/ *v.i.* **(a)** nicht nachgeben; **~ in doing sth.** etw. weiterhin [beharrlich] tun
(b) (continue to exist) anhalten

persistence /pəˈsɪstəns/ Hartnäckigkeit, *die*

persistent /pəˈsɪstənt/ *adj.* **(a)** hartnäckig
(b) (constantly repeated) dauernd; hartnäckig ‹*Gerüchte*›

perˈsistently *adv.* hartnäckig

person /ˈpɜːsn/ *n.* Mensch, *der;* **in ~:** persönlich; selbst

personal /ˈpɜːsənl/ *adj.* persönlich; ···

Privat‹*angelegenheit, -leben*›; ~ **computer** Personalcomputer, *der;* ~ **stereo** Walkman, *der;* ~ **hygiene** Körperpflege, *die*

personal: ~ **ad** *n.* Privatanzeige, *die;* (seeking friendship, romance) Kontaktanzeige, *die;* ~ **as'sistant** *n.* persönlicher Referent/ persönliche Referentin; ~ **'best** *n.* (Sport) persönliche Bestleistung; ~ **call** *n.* (Brit. Teleph.) Anruf mit Voranmeldung; ~ **column** *n.* Rubrik für private [Klein]anzeigen; ~ **identifi'cation number** *n.* persönliche Identifikationsnummer; Geheimnummer, *die*

personality /pɜ:sə'nælɪtɪ/ *n.* Persönlichkeit, *die*

'personal loan *n.* Personal- *od.* Privatdarlehen, *das;* Personal- *od.* Privatkredit, *der*

'personally *adv.* persönlich

personal: ~ **'organizer** *n.* Terminplaner, *der;* ~ **'pension plan** *n.* persönlicher Renten[vorsorge]plan; ~ **'property** *n.* persönliches Eigentum

personification /pəsɒnɪfɪ'keɪʃn/ *n.* Verkörperung, *die*

personify /pə'sɒnɪfaɪ/ *v.t.* verkörpern; **be kindness personified** die Freundlichkeit in Person sein

personnel /pɜ:sə'nel/ *n.* Belegschaft, *die;* (of shop, restaurant, etc.) Personal, *das; attrib.* Personal-; ~ **department** Personalabteilung, *die*

person-to-'person *adj.* (Amer. Teleph.) ~ **call** Anruf mit Voranmeldung

perspective /pə'spektɪv/ *n.* Perspektive, *die;* (fig.) Blickwinkel, *der*

perspiration /pɜ:spɪ'reɪʃn/ *n.* Schweiß, *der*

perspire /pə'spaɪə(r)/ *v.i.* schwitzen

persuade /pə'sweɪd/ *v.t.* **(a)** (convince) überzeugen (**of** von); ~ **oneself [that]** ...: sich (*Dat.*) einreden, dass ...
(b) (induce) überreden

persuasion /pə'sweɪʒn/ *n.* Überzeugung, *die;* **it didn't take much** ~: es brauchte nicht viel Überredungskunst

persuasive /pə'sweɪsɪv/ *adj.*, **per'suasively** *adv.* überzeugend

pert /pɜ:t/ *adj.* keck

pertinent /'pɜ:tɪnənt/ *adj.* relevant (**to** für)

perturb /pə'tɜ:b/ *v.t.* beunruhigen

Peru /pə'ru:/ *pr. n.* Peru (*das*)

Peruvian /pə'ru:vɪən/ [1] *adj.* peruanisch; **sb. is** ~: jmd. ist Peruaner/Peruanerin
[2] *n.* Peruaner, *der*/Peruanerin, *die*

peruse /pə'ru:z/ *v.t.* genau durchlesen; (fig.: examine) untersuchen

pervade /pə'veɪd/ *v.t.* durchdringen

pervasive /pə'veɪsɪv/ *adj.* durchdringend ‹*Geruch, Kälte*›; weit verbreitet ‹*Ansicht*›; sich ausbreitend ‹*Gefühl*›

perverse /pə'vɜ:s/ *adj.* starrköpfig

perversion /pə'vɜ:ʃn/ *n.* **(a)** (sexual) Perversion, *die*
(b) ~ **of justice** Rechtsbeugung, *die*

pervert [1] /pə'vɜ:t/ *v.t.* (morally) verderben
[2] /'pɜ:vɜ:t/ *n.* perverser Mensch

perverted /pə'vɜ:tɪd/ *adj.* (sexually) pervers

pessimism /'pesɪmɪzm/ *n.* Pessimismus, *der*

pessimist /'pesɪmɪst/ *n.* Pessimist, *der*/ Pessimistin, *die*

pessimistic /pesɪ'mɪstɪk/ *adj.* pessimistisch

pest /pest/ *n.* (thing) Ärgernis, *das;* (person) Nervensäge, *die* (ugs.); (animal) Schädling, *der*

pester /'pestə(r)/ *v.t.* belästigen; nerven (ugs.); ~ **sb. for sth.** jmdm. wegen etw. in den Ohren liegen

pesticide /'pestɪsaɪd/ *n.* Pestizid, *das*

pestle /'pesl/ *n.* Stößel, *der*

pet /pet/ [1] *n.* **(a)** (animal) Haustier, *das*
(b) (as term of endearment) Schatz, *der*
[2] *adj.* (favourite) Lieblings-
[3] *v.i.*, **-tt-** knutschen (ugs.)

petal /'petl/ *n.* Blütenblatt, *das*

peter /'pi:tə(r)/ *v.i.* ~ **out** [allmählich] zu Ende gehen; ‹*Weg:*› sich verlieren

'pet food *n.* Tierfutter, *das*

petite /pə'ti:t/ *adj.* zierlich

petition /pə'tɪʃn/ [1] *n.* Petition, *die;* Eingabe, *die*
[2] *v.t.* eine Eingabe richten an (+ *Akk.*)

petitioner /pə'tɪʃənə(r)/ *n.* Antragsteller, *der*/Antragstellerin, *die*

petrify /'petrɪfaɪ/ *v.t.* **be petrified with fear/ shock** starr vor Angst/Schrecken sein

petrol /'petrl/ *n.* (Brit.) Benzin, *das*

petrol: ~ **bomb** *n.* Benzinbombe, *die;* ~ **can** *n.* (Brit.) Benzinkanister, *der;* ~ **cap** *n.* (Brit.) Tankverschluss, *der*

petroleum /pɪ'trəʊlɪəm/ *n.* Erdöl, *das*

petroleum 'jelly *n.* Vaseline, *die*

petrol: ~ **pump** *n.* (Brit.) Zapfsäule, *die;* ~ **station** *n.* (Brit.) Tankstelle, *die;* ~ **tank** *n.* (Brit.) Benzintank, *der;* ~ **tanker** *n.* (Brit.) Benzintankwagen, *der*

'pet shop *n.* Tierhandlung, *die*

petticoat /'petɪkəʊt/ *n.* Unterrock, *der*

petty /'petɪ/ *adj.* kleinlich ‹*Vorschrift, Einwand*›; belanglos ‹*Detail, Sorgen*›; ~ **criminal** Kleinkriminelle, *der/die;* ~ **theft** Bagatelldiebstahl, *der;* ~ **thief** kleiner Dieb/ kleine Diebin

petty 'cash *n.* kleine Kasse; Portokasse, *die*

petulance /'petjʊləns/ *n.* Bockigkeit, *die*

petulant /'petjʊlənt/ *adj.* bockig

pew /pju:/ *n.* Kirchenbank, *die*

pewter /'pju:tə(r)/ *n.* Zinn, *das*

phallic /'fælɪk/ *adj.* phallisch; ~ **symbol** Phallussymbol, *das*

phantom /'fæntəm/ *n.* Phantom, *das*

pharmacist /ˈfɑːməsɪst/ *n.* Apotheker, *der*/Apothekerin, *die*

pharmacy /ˈfɑːməsɪ/ *n.* (dispensary) Apotheke, *die*

phase /feɪz/ *n.* Phase, *die*

▪ **phase 'in** *v.t.* stufenweise einführen

▪ **phase 'out** *v.t.* allmählich abschaffen ‹*Verfahrensweise, Methode*›; (stop producing) [langsam] auslaufen lassen

Ph.D. /piːeɪtʃˈdiː/ *abbr.* = **Doctor of Philosophy** Dr. phil.

pheasant /ˈfezənt/ *n.* Fasan, *der*

phenomenal /fɪˈnɒmɪnl/ *adj.*, **phenomenally** /fɪˈnɒmɪnəlɪ/ *adv.* phänomenal

phenomenon /fɪˈnɒmɪnən/ *n., pl.* **phenomena** /fɪˈnɒmɪnə/ Phänomen, *das*

phew /fjuː/ *int.* puh

philanderer /fɪˈlændərə(r)/ *n.* Schürzenjäger, *der* (spött.)

philanthropist /fɪˈlænθrəpɪst/ *n.* Philanthrop, *der*/Philanthropin, *die* (geh.)

philanthropy /fɪˈlænθrəpɪ/ *n.* Philanthropie, *die* (geh.)

Philippines /ˈfɪlɪpiːnz/ *pr. n. pl.* Philippinen *Pl.*

philistine /ˈfɪlɪstaɪn/ *n.* Banause, *der*/Banausin, *die*

Phillips /ˈfɪlɪps/ *n.* **~ screw** ® Kreuz[schlitz]schraube, *die;* **~ screwdriver** ® Kreuz[schlitz]schraubenzieher, *der*

philosopher /fɪˈlɒsəfə(r)/ *n.* Philosoph, *der*/Philosophin, *die*

philosophical /fɪləˈsɒfɪkl/ *adj.* **(a)** philosophisch
(b) (resigned) abgeklärt

philosophize (**philosophise**) /fɪˈlɒsəfaɪz/ *v.i.* philosophieren (**about, on** über + *Akk.*)

philosophy /fɪˈlɒsəfɪ/ *n.* Philosophie, *die*

phlegm /flem/ *n.* Schleim, *der*

phobia /ˈfəʊbɪə/ *n.* Phobie, *die*

phobic /ˈfəʊbik/ *adj.* phobisch

phone /fəʊn/ (coll.) **1** *n.* Telefon, *das;* **by ~:** telefonisch; **be on the ~:** Telefon haben; (be phoning) telefonieren
2 *v.t. & i.* anrufen

▪ **phone 'back** *v.t. & i.* zurückrufen; (make further call) wieder anrufen

▪ **phone 'up** *v.t. & i.* anrufen

phone: ~ book *n.* Telefonbuch, *das;* **~ booth, ~ box** *ns.* Telefonzelle, *die;* **~ call** *n.* Anruf, *der;* **~ card** *n.* Telefonkarte, *die;* **~-in** *n.* **~-in [programme]** (Radio) Hörersendung, *die;* (Telev.) Phone-in-Sendung, *die* (Jargon); **~ number** *n.* Telefonnummer, *die*

phonetic /fəˈnetɪk/ *adj.* phonetisch

phonetics /fəˈnetɪks/ *n.* Phonetik, *die*

phoney /ˈfəʊnɪ/ *adj.* (coll.) (sham) falsch; gefälscht ‹*Brief, Dokument*›

phonograph /ˈfəʊnəgrɑːf/ *n.* (Amer.) Plattenspieler, *der*

phony ▶ PHONEY

phosphate /ˈfɒsfeɪt/ *n.* Phosphat, *das*

phosphorus /ˈfɒsfərəs/ *n.* Phosphor, *der*

photo /ˈfəʊtəʊ/ *n., pl.* **~s** Foto, *das*

photo: ~ album *n.* Fotoalbum, *das;* **~call** *n.* Fototermin, *der;* **~copier** *n.* Fotokopiergerät, *das;* **~copy** **1** *n.* Fotokopie, *die;* **2** *v.t.* fotokopieren

photogenic /fəʊtəˈdʒiːnɪk/ *adj.* fotogen

photograph /ˈfəʊtəgrɑːf/ **1** *n.* Fotografie, *die;* Foto, *das;* **take a ~ [of sb./sth.]** [jmdn./etw.] fotografieren
2 *v.t. & i.* fotografieren

'photograph album *n.* Fotoalbum, *das*

photographer /fəˈtɒgrəfə(r)/ *n.* Fotograf, *der*/Fotografin, *die*

photographic /fəʊtəˈgræfɪk/ *adj.* fotografisch; Foto‹*ausrüstung, -apparat, -ausstellung*›

photography /fəˈtɒgrəfɪ/ *n.* Fotografie, *die*

photo: ~ session, ~ shoot *ns.* Shooting, *das;* **~'synthesis** *n.* Photosynthese, *die*

phrase /freɪz/ **1** *n.* [Rede]wendung, *die*
2 *v.t.* formulieren

'phrase book *n.* Sprachführer, *der*

physical /ˈfɪzɪkl/ *adj.* **(a)** physisch ‹*Gewalt*›; dinglich ‹*Welt, Universum*›
(b) (of physics) physikalisch
(c) (bodily) körperlich

physical edu'cation *n.* (Sch.) Sport, *der*

'physically *adv.* (relating to the body) körperlich

physical 'training *n.* Sport, *der;* (Sch.) Sport[unterricht], *der*

physician /fɪˈzɪʃn/ *n.* Arzt, *der*/Ärztin, *die*

physicist /ˈfɪzɪsɪst/ *n.* Physiker, *der*/Physikerin, *die*

physics /ˈfɪzɪks/ *n.* Physik, *die*

physiology /fɪzɪˈɒlədʒɪ/ *n.* Physiologie, *die*

physiotherapist /fɪzɪəʊˈθerəpɪst/ *n.* Physiotherapeut, *der*/-therapeutin, *die*

physiotherapy /fɪzɪəʊˈθerəpɪ/ *n.* Physiotherapie, *die*

physique /fɪˈziːk/ *n.* Körperbau, *der*

pianist /ˈpiːənɪst/ *n.* Pianist, *der*/Pianistin, *die*

piano /pɪˈænəʊ/ *n., pl.* **~s** (upright) Klavier, *das;* (grand) Flügel, *der*

piano: ~ ac'cordion *n.* Akkordeon, *das;* **~ music** *n.* Klaviermusik, *die;* **~ player** *n.* Klavierspieler, *der*/-spielerin, *die;* **~ stool** *n.* Klavierschemel, *der;* **~ tuner** *n.* Klavierstimmer, *der*/-stimmerin, *die*

pick[1] /pɪk/ *n.* (tool) Spitzhacke, *die*

pick[2] **1** *n.* **(a)** (choice) Wahl, *die;* **take your ~:** du hast die Wahl
(b) (best part) Elite, *die;* **the ~ of the fruit** die besten Früchte

···›

2 *v.t.* **(a)** pflücken ‹*Blumen, Äpfel usw.*›; lesen ‹*Trauben*›
(b) (select) auswählen; **~ one's way** sich (*Dat.*) vorsichtig [s]einen Weg suchen
(c) ~ one's nose in der Nase bohren
(d) ~ sb.'s pocket jmdn. bestehlen; **he had his pocket ~ed** er wurde von einem Taschendieb bestohlen
(e) ~ a lock ein Schloss knacken (salopp)
3 *v.i.* **~ and choose** wählerisch sein
▪ **'pick at** *v.t.* herumstochern in (+ *Dat.*) ‹*Essen*›
▪ **'pick on** *v.t.* (victimize) es abgesehen haben auf (+ *Akk.*)
▪ **pick 'out** *v.t.* **(a)** (choose) auswählen; (for oneself) sich (*Dat.*) aussuchen
(b) (distinguish) entdecken ‹*Detail, jmds. Gesicht in der Menge*›
▪ **pick up** **1** /'--/ *v.t.* **(a)** [in die Hand] nehmen; hochnehmen ‹*Baby*›; (after dropping) aufheben; aufnehmen ‹*Masche*›; **~ up the telephone** den [Telefon]hörer abnehmen
(b) (collect) mitnehmen; (by arrangement) abholen (**at, from** von); (obtain) holen
(c) (become infected by) sich (*Dat.*) holen (ugs.) ‹*Virus, Grippe*›
(d) ‹*Bus, Autofahrer:*› mitnehmen
(e) (rescue from the sea) [aus Seenot] bergen
(f) empfangen ‹*Signal, Funkspruch usw.*›
(g) (coll.: make acquaintance of) aufreißen (ugs.)
2 /-'-/ *v.i.* **(a)** sich bessern
(b) ‹*Wind:*› auffrischen

'pickaxe (*Amer.:* **'pickax**) ▶ PICK[1]

picket /'pɪkɪt/ **1** *n.* Streikposten, *der*
2 *v.i.* Streikposten stehen
3 *v.t.* Streikposten stellen vor (+ *Dat.*)

'picket fence *n.* Palisadenzaun, *der*

'picketing /'pɪkɪtɪŋ/ *n.* Aufstellen von Streikposten

'picket line *n.* Streikpostenkette, *die*

pickle /'pɪkl/ **1** *n., usu. in pl.* (food) Mixedpickles *Pl.*
2 *v.t.* einlegen ‹*Gurken, Zwiebeln, Eier*›; marinieren ‹*Hering*›

pick: ~-me-up *n.* Stärkungsmittel, *das;* **~pocket** *n.* Taschendieb, *der*/-diebin, *die;* **~up** *n.* **(a) ~up [truck]** Kleinlastwagen, *der;* **(b)** (of record player, guitar) Tonabnehmer, *der*

picnic /'pɪknɪk/ **1** *n.* Picknick, *das;* **go for** *or* **on/have a ~:** ein Picknick machen
2 *v.i.,* **-ck-** picknicken; Picknick machen

picnic: ~ basket *n.* Picknickkorb, *der;* **~ site** *n.* Picknickplatz, *der*

pictorial /pɪk'tɔːrɪəl/ *adj.* illustriert ‹*Bericht, Zeitschrift*›; bildlich ‹*Darstellung*›

picture /'pɪktʃə(r)/ **1** *n.* **(a)** Bild, *das;* **get the ~** (coll.) verstehen[, worum es geht]; **put sb. in the ~:** jmdn. ins Bild setzen
(b) (film) Film, *der*
(c) *in pl.* (Brit.: cinema) Kino, *das;* **go to the ~s** ins Kino gehen; **what's on at the ~s?** was läuft im Kino?
2 *v.t.* **~ [to oneself]** sich (*Dat.*) vorstellen

picture: ~ book *n.* Bilderbuch, *das;* **~ frame** *n.* Bilderrahmen, *der;* **~ 'postcard** *n.* Ansichtskarte, *die*

picturesque /pɪktʃə'resk/ *adj.* malerisch

pidgin /'pɪdʒɪn/ *n.* Pidgin, *das*

pidgin 'English *n.* Pidginenglisch, *das*

pie /paɪ/ *n.* (of meat, fish, etc.) Pastete, *die;* (of fruit etc.) ≈ Obstkuchen, *der*

piece /piːs/ **1** *n.* **(a)** Stück, *das;* (of broken glass or pottery) Scherbe, *die;* (of jigsaw puzzle, crashed aircraft, etc.) Teil, *der;* (Amer.: distance) [kleines] Stück; **a ~ of meat/cake** ein Stück Fleisch/Kuchen; **~ of furniture/luggage** Möbel-/Gepäckstück, *das;* **a three-~ suite** eine dreiteilige Sitzgarnitur; **~ of luck** Glücksfall, *der;* **~ of news/gossip/information** Nachricht, *die*/Klatsch, *der*/Information, *die*
(b) (Chess) Figur, *die*
(c) (coin) **gold ~:** Goldstück, *das;* **a 10p ~:** ein 10-Pence-Stück
(d) (literary or musical composition) Stück, *das;* **~ of music** Musikstück, *das*
2 *v.t.* **~ to'gether** zusammenfügen (**from** aus)

piece: ~meal *adv., adj.* stückweise; **~work** *n.* Akkordarbeit, *die*

pie: ~ chart *n.* Kreisdiagramm, *das;* **~crust** *n.* Teigmantel, *der*

pier /pɪə(r)/ *n.* (at seaside) Pier, *der*

pierce /pɪəs/ *v.t.* (prick) durchstechen; (penetrate) [ein]dringen in (+ *Akk.*) ‹*Körper, Fleisch, Herz*›; **~ a hole in sth.** ein Loch in etw. (*Akk.*) stechen

piercing /'pɪəsɪŋ/ *adj.* durchdringend ‹*Stimme, Schrei, Blick*›

piety /'paɪətɪ/ *n.* Frömmigkeit, *die*

pig /pɪg/ *n.* **(a)** Schwein, *das;* **~s might fly** (iron.) da müsste schon ein Wunder geschehen
(b) (coll.: greedy person) Vielfraß, *der* (ugs.)

pigeon /'pɪdʒɪn/ *n.* Taube, *die*

'pigeonhole *n.* [Ablage]fach, *das;* (for letters) Postfach, *das*

piggy /'pɪgɪ/**: ~back** *n.* **give sb. a ~back** jmdn. huckepack nehmen; **~ bank** *n.* Sparschwein[chen], *das*

pig'headed *adj.* dickschädelig (ugs.)

piglet /'pɪglɪt/ *n.* Ferkel, *das*

pigment /'pɪgmənt/ *n.* Pigment, *das*

pigmentation /pɪgmən'teɪʃn/ *n.* Pigmentierung, *die*

pig's 'ear *n.* (Brit. coll.) **make a ~'s ear of sth.** etw. verpfuschen *od.* (ugs.) vermurksen

pig: ~sty *n.* (lit. or fig.) Schweinestall, *der;* **~tail** *n.* (plaited) Zopf, *der;* **~tails** (at either side of head) Rattenschwänzchen *Pl.* (ugs.)

pike /paɪk/ *n., pl. same* Hecht, *der*

pilchard /'pɪltʃəd/ *n.* Sardine, *die*

pile[1] /paɪl/ **1** *n.* **(a)** (of dishes, plates) Stapel, *der;* (of paper, books, letters) Stoß, *der;* (of clothes) Haufen, *der*
(b) (coll.: large quantity) Haufen, *der* (ugs.)

2 *v.t.* **(a)** (load) [voll] beladen
(b) (heap up) aufstapeln ‹*Holz, Steine*›; aufhäufen ‹*Abfall, Schnee*›
▪ **pile 'in** *v.i.* (seen from outside) hineindrängen; (seen from inside) hereindrängen
▪ **'pile into** *v.t.* sich zwängen in (+ *Akk.*) ‹*Auto, Zimmer, Zugabteil*›
▪ **pile 'on** **1** *v.i.* ▶ PILE IN
2 *v.t.* (fig.) **~ on the pressure** Druck machen
▪ **'pile on to** *v.t.* drängen in (+ *Akk.*) ‹*Bus usw.*›
▪ **pile 'out** *v.i.* nach draußen drängen
▪ **pile 'up** **1** *v.i.* **(a)** ‹*Waren, Post, Arbeit, Schnee:*› sich auftürmen; ‹*Verkehr:*› sich stauen
(b) (crash) aufeinander auffahren
2 *v.t.* aufstapeln ‹*Steine, Bücher usw.*›; aufhäufen ‹*Abfall, Schnee*›
pile² *n.* (of fabric etc.) Flor, *der*
pile³ *n.* (stake) Pfahl, *der*
'piledriver *n.* [Pfahl]ramme, *die*
piles /paɪlz/ *n. pl.* (Med.) Hämorrhoiden *Pl.*
'pile-up *n.* Massenkarambolage, *die*
pilfer /'pɪlfə(r)/ *v.t.* stehlen
pilgrim /'pɪlgrɪm/ *n.* Pilger, *der*/Pilgerin, *die*
pilgrimage /'pɪlgrɪmɪdʒ/ *n.* Pilgerfahrt, *die*
pill /pɪl/ *n.* **(a)** Tablette, *die;* Pille, *die* (ugs.)
(b) (coll.: contraceptive) **the ~** *or* **P~:** die Pille (ugs.); **be on the ~:** die Pille nehmen (ugs.)
pillage /'pɪlɪdʒ/ *v.t.* [aus]plündern
pillar /'pɪlə(r)/ *n.* Säule, *die*
'pillar box *n.* (Brit.) Briefkasten, *der*
'pillbox *n.* Pillenschachtel, *die*
pillion /'pɪljən/ *n.* Beifahrersitz, *der;* **ride ~:** als Beifahrer/Beifahrerin mitfahren
pillow /'pɪləʊ/ *n.* [Kopf]kissen, *das*
'pillowcase, 'pillowslip *ns.* [Kopf]kissenbezug, *der*
'pill-popping *n.* (coll.) Pillenschluckerei, *die* (ugs.)
pilot /'paɪlət/ **1** *n.* **(a)** (Aeronaut.) Pilot, *der*/Pilotin, *die*
(b) (Naut.) Lotse, *der*
2 *adj.* Pilot‹*programm, -studie, -projekt usw.*›
3 *v.t.* **(a)** (Aeronaut.) fliegen
(b) (Naut.; fig.) lotsen
'pilot light *n.* Zündflamme, *die*
pimp /pɪmp/ *n.* Zuhälter, *der*
pimple /'pɪmpl/ *n.* Pickel, *der*
pimply /'pɪmplɪ/ *adj.* pick[e]lig
pin **1** *n.* **(a)** Stecknadel, *die;* **~s and needles** (fig.) Kribbeln, *das*
(b) (peg) Stift, *der*
(c) (Electr.) **a two-/three-~ plug** ein zwei-/dreipoliger Stecker
2 *v.t.*, **-nn-: (a)** nageln ‹*Knochen, Bein*›; **~ a badge to one's lapel** sich (*Dat.*) ein Abzeichen ans Revers stecken
(b) (fig.) **~ one's hopes on sb./sth.** seine [ganze] Hoffnung auf jmdn./etw. setzen; **~ the blame for sth. on sb.** jmdm. die Schuld an etw. (*Dat.*) zuschieben
(c) ~ sb. against the wall jmdn. an die Wand drängen
▪ **pin 'down** *v.t.* **(a)** (fig.) festnageln (**to** *or* **on** auf + *Akk.*)
(b) (trap) festhalten
▪ **pin 'up** *v.t.* aufhängen ‹*Bild, Foto*›; anschlagen ‹*Bekanntmachung, Liste*›; aufstecken ‹*Haar*›; abstecken ‹*Saum*›
PIN /pɪn/ *abbr.* = **PIN [number]**
▶ PERSONAL IDENTIFICATION NUMBER
pinafore /'pɪnəfɔː(r)/ *n.* Schürze, *die* (mit Oberteil)
pincers /'pɪnsəz/ *n. pl.* **(a) [pair of] ~:** Beißzange, *die*
(b) (of crab etc.) Schere, *die*
pinch /pɪntʃ/ **1** *n.* **(a)** (squeezing) Kniff, *der;* **give sb. a ~ on the arm/cheek** jmdn. *od.* jmdm. in den Arm/die Backe kneifen
(b) (fig.) **feel the ~:** knapp bei Kasse sein (ugs.); **at a ~:** zur Not
(c) (small amount) Prise, *die*
2 *v.t.* **(a)** kneifen; **~ sb.'s cheek/bottom** jmdn. in die Wange/den Hintern (ugs.) kneifen
(b) (coll.: steal) klauen (salopp)
'pincushion *n.* Nadelkissen, *das*
pine¹ /paɪn/ *n.* (tree) Kiefer, *die*
pine² *v.i.* sich [vor Kummer] verzehren (geh.)
▪ **pine a'way** *v.i.* dahinkümmern
pineapple /'paɪnæpl/ *n.* Ananas, *die*
'pine tree *n.* Kiefer, *die*
ping-pong (*Amer.:* **Ping-Pong**®) /'pɪŋpɒŋ/ *n.* Tischtennis, *das*
pinhole 'camera *n.* Lochkamera, *die;* Camera obscura, *die*
pink /pɪŋk/ **1** *n.* Rosa, *das*
2 *adj.* rosa
pinkie /'pɪŋkɪ/ *n.* (Amer., Scot.) kleiner Finger
'pin money *n.* Taschengeld, *das*
pinnacle /'pɪnəkl/ *n.* Gipfel, *der;* (fig.) Höhepunkt, *der*
pin: ~point *v.t.* genau festlegen; **~prick** *n.* Nadelstich, *der;* **~stripe** *n.* Nadelstreifen, *der;* **~stripe suit** Nadelstreifenanzug, *der*
pint /paɪnt/ *n.* Pint, *das;* ≈ halber Liter
pint 'mug *n.* ≈ Halbliterglas, *das od.* -humpen, *der*
'pin-up (coll.) *n.* Pin-up-Girl, *das;* (picture) (of beautiful girl) Pin-up[-Foto], *das;* (of sports, film or pop star) Starfoto, *das*
pioneer /paɪə'nɪə(r)/ **1** *n.* Pionier, *der*
2 *v.t.* Pionierarbeit leisten für
pious /'paɪəs/ *adj.* fromm
pip /pɪp/ *n.* (seed) Kern, *der*
pipe /paɪp/ **1** *n.* **(a)** (tube) Rohr, *das*
(b) (Mus.) Pfeife, *die*
(c) [tobacco] ~: [Tabaks]pfeife, *die* ⋯

2 *v.t.* [durch ein Rohr/durch Rohre] leiten
■ **pipe 'down** *v.i.* (coll.) ruhig sein
■ **pipe 'up** *v.i.* (coll.) etwas sagen
pipe: ~ dream *n.* Wunschtraum, *der;* Hirngespinst, *das* (abwertend); **~line** *n.* Pipeline, *die;* **in the ~line** (fig.) in Vorbereitung
piper /'paɪpə(r)/ *n.* Pfeifer, *der*/Pfeiferin, *die;* (bagpiper) Dudelsackspieler, *der*/-spielerin, *die*
piping hot /'paɪpɪŋ hɒt/ *adj.* kochend heiß
piquant /'pi:kənt/ *adj.* pikant
pique /pi:k/ *n.* **in a [fit of] ~:** verstimmt
piracy /'paɪrəsɪ/ *n.* Seeräuberei, *die*
piranha /pɪ'rɑ:nə, pɪ'rɑ:njə/ *n.* Piranha, *der*
pirate /'paɪrət/ *n.* **(a)** Pirat, *der;* Seeräuber, *der*
(b) (Radio) **~ radio station** Piratensender, *der*
Pisces /'paɪsi:z/ *n.* (Astrol, Astron.) Fische *Pl.*
piss /pɪs/ (coarse) 1 *n.* **(a)** (urine) Pisse, *die* (derb)
(b) have a/go for a ~: pissen/pissen gehen (derb)
2 *v.i.* pissen (derb)
■ **'piss down** *v.i.* (sl.) **~ down [with rain]** schiffen (salopp)
■ **piss 'off** (Brit. sl.) 1 *v.i.* sich verpissen (salopp)
2 *v.t.* ankotzen (derb)
pissed /pɪst/ *adj.* (sl.) **(a)** (drunk) voll (salopp)
(b) (Amer.: angry) [stock]sauer (**with** auf + *Akk.*) (salopp)
pissed 'off *adj.* (sl.) stocksauer (**with** auf + *Akk.*) (salopp)
'piss-up *n.* (sl.) Sauferei, *die* (salopp)
pistol /'pɪstl/ *n.* Pistole, *die*
piston /'pɪstən/ *n.* Kolben, *der*
pit /pɪt/ 1 *n.* (hole, mine) Grube, *die;* (natural) Vertiefung, *die*
2 *v.t.*, **-tt-: ~ one's wits/skill** *etc.* **against sth.** seinen Verstand/sein Können *usw.* an etw. (*Dat.*) messen
'pit bull terrier *n.* Pitbullterrier, *der*
pitch¹ /pɪtʃ/ 1 *n.* **(a)** (Brit.: usual place) [Stand]platz, *der;* (Sport: playing area) Feld, *das;* Platz, *der*
(b) (Mus.) Tonhöhe, *die*
(c) (slope) Neigung, *die*
2 *v.t.* **(a)** (erect) aufschlagen; **~ camp** ein/das Lager aufschlagen
(b) (throw) werfen
3 *v.i.* stürzen; ‹*Schiff:*› stampfen; **~ forward** vornüberstürzen
pitch² *n.* (substance) Pech, *das*
pitch: ~-'black *adj.* pechschwarz; stockdunkel (ugs.) ‹*Nacht*›; **~-'dark** *adj.* stockdunkel (ugs.)
pitcher /'pɪtʃə(r)/ *n.* [Henkel]krug, *der*
'pitchfork *n.* Heugabel, *die*
'pitfall *n.* Fallstrick, *der*
pith /pɪθ/ *n.* **(a)** (of orange etc.) weiße Haut
(b) (fig.) Kern, *der*
'pith helmet *n.* Tropenhelm, *der*
'pithy *adj.* (fig.) prägnant
pitiable /'pɪtɪəbl/, **pitiful** /'pɪtɪfl/ *adjs.* **(a)** Mitleid erregend
(b) (contemptible) jämmerlich
pitifully /'pɪtɪfəlɪ/ *adv.* erbärmlich; jämmerlich
'pitiless *adj.* unbarmherzig
'pit stop *n.* (Motor racing) Boxenstopp, *der*
pittance /'pɪtəns/ *n.* Hungerlohn, *der*
pity /'pɪtɪ/ 1 *n.* Mitleid, *das;* **feel ~ for sb.** Mitgefühl für jmdn. empfinden; **have/take ~ on sb.** Erbarmen mit jmdm. haben; **[what a] ~!** [wie] schade!
2 *v.t.* bemitleiden; **I ~ you** du tust mir leid
pivot /'pɪvət/ 1 *n.* [Dreh]zapfen, *der*
2 *v.i.* sich drehen
pivotal /'pɪvətl/ *adj.* (fig.: crucial) zentral
pixel /'pɪksel/ *n.* (Comp. etc.) Bildpunkt, *der;* Pixel, *das*
pixie /'pɪksɪ/ *n.* Kobold, *der*
pizza /'pi:tsə/ *n.* Pizza, *die*
pizzeria /pi:tsə'ri:ə/ *n.* Pizzeria, *die*
placard /'plækɑ:d/ *n.* Plakat, *das*
placate /plə'keɪt/ *v.t.* beschwichtigen
place /pleɪs/ 1 *n.* **(a)** Ort, *der;* (spot) Stelle, *die;* **a [good] ~ to park/to stop** ein [guter] Platz zum Parken/eine [gute] Stelle zum Halten; **do you know a good/cheap ~ to eat?** weißt du, wo man gut/billig essen kann?; **~ of worship** Andachtsort, *der;* **all over the ~:** überall; (coll.: in a mess) ganz durcheinander (ugs.)
(b) (rank, position) Stellung, *die;* **put sb. in his ~:** jmdn. in seine Schranken weisen
(c) (country, town) Ort, *der;* **~ of birth** Geburtsort, *der;* **~ of residence** Wohnort, *der;* **'go ~s** (coll.: fig.) es [im Leben] zu was bringen (ugs.)
(d) (coll.: premises) Bude, *die* (ugs.); **she is at his ~:** sie ist bei ihm
(e) (seat etc.) [Sitz]platz, *der;* **change ~s [with sb.]** [mit jmdm.] die Plätze tauschen; (fig.) [mit jmdm.] tauschen
(f) (step, stage) **in the first ~:** zuerst; **why didn't you say so in the first ~?** warum hast du das nicht gleich gesagt?
(g) (proper ~) Platz, *der;* **everything fell into ~** (fig.) alles wurde klar; **out of ~:** nicht am richtigen Platz; (several things) in Unordnung
(h) (position in competition) Platz, *der*
2 *v.t.* **(a)** (vertically) stellen; (horizontally) legen
(b) *in p.p.* (situated) gelegen
(c) (find situation or home for) unterbringen (**with** bei)
(d) (class) einordnen; einstufen; **be ~d second in the race** im Rennen den zweiten Platz belegen
placebo /plə'si:bəʊ/ *n.*, *pl.* **~s** Placebo, *das*
'place mat *n.* Set, *der od. das*
placement /'pleɪsmənt/ *n.* Platzierung, *die*
'place name *n.* Ortsname, *der*
placenta /plə'sentə/ *n.*, *pl.* **~e** /plə'senti:/ *or* **~s** Plazenta, *die*

'place setting *n.* Gedeck, *das*
placid /'plæsɪd/ *adj.* ruhig
plagiarism /'pleɪdʒərɪzm/ *n.* Plagiat, *das*
plagiarize /'pleɪdʒəraɪz/ *v.t.* plagiieren
plague /pleɪg/ [1] *n.* **(a)** (esp. Hist.: epidemic) Seuche, *die;* **the ~** (bubonic) die Pest
(b) (infestation) **~ of rats** Rattenplage, *die*
[2] *v.t.* plagen; **~d with** *or* **by sth.** von etw. geplagt
plaice /pleɪs/ *n., pl. same* Scholle, *die*
plain /pleɪn/ [1] *adj.* **(a)** (clear) klar; (obvious) offensichtlich
(b) (frank) offen; schlicht ‹*Wahrheit*›; **be ~ sailing** (fig.) [ganz] einfach sein
(c) (unsophisticated) einfach; schlicht ‹*Kleidung*›; unliniert ‹*Papier*›; ‹*Stoff*› ohne Muster
(d) wenig attraktiv ‹*Mädchen*›
[2] *adv.* **(a)** (clearly) deutlich
(b) (simply) einfach
[3] *n.* Ebene, *die*
plain: ~ 'chocolate *n.* halbbittere Schokolade; **~ 'clothes** *n. pl.* **in ~ clothes** in Zivil
'plainly *adv.* **(a)** (clearly) deutlich
(b) (obviously) offensichtlich; (undoubtedly) eindeutig
(c) (frankly) offen
(d) (simply) schlicht
plaintiff /'pleɪntɪf/ *n.* Kläger, *der*/Klägerin, *die*
plaintive /'pleɪntɪv/ *adj.* klagend
plait /plæt/ [1] *n.* Zopf, *der*
[2] *v.t.* flechten
plan /plæn/ [1] *n.* Plan, *der;* **[go] according to ~:** nach Plan [gehen]; planmäßig [verlaufen]
[2] *v.t.*, **-nn-** planen; (design) entwerfen
[3] *v.i.*, **-nn-** planen
plane¹ /pleɪn/ *n.* **~ [tree]** Platane, *die*
plane² [1] *n.* (tool) Hobel, *der*
[2] *v.t.* hobeln
plane³ *n.* **(a)** (Geom.: fig.) Ebene, *die*
(b) (aircraft) Flugzeug, *das;* Maschine, *die* (ugs.)
'planeload *n.* Flugzeugladung, *die*
planet /'plænɪt/ *n.* Planet, *der*
planetarium /plænɪ'teərɪəm/ *n., pl.* **~s** *or* **planetaria** /plænɪ'teərɪə/ Planetarium, *das*
planetary /'plænɪtərɪ/ *adj.* planetarisch
plank /plæŋk/ *n.* Brett, *das;* (thicker) Bohle, *die;* (on ship) Planke, *die*
plankton /'plæŋktən/ *n.* Plankton, *das*
planned e'conomy *n.* Planwirtschaft, *die*
'planner *n.* Planer, *der*/Planerin, *die*
'planning *n.* Planen, *das;* Planung, *die*
plant /plɑːnt/ [1] *n.* **(a)** (Bot.) Pflanze, *die*
(b) *no indef. art.* (machinery) Maschinen *Pl.*
(c) (factory) Fabrik, *die;* Werk, *das*
[2] *v.t.* **(a)** pflanzen
(b) (coll.: conceal) anbringen ‹*Wanze*›; legen ‹*Bombe*›; **~ sth. on sb.** jmdm. etw. unterschieben
plantation /plɑːn'teɪʃn/ *n.* Plantage, *die*
planter /'plɑːntə(r)/ *n.* (container) Pflanzgefäß, *das*
'plant food *n.* Pflanzennahrung, *die*
plaque /plɑːk, plæk/ *n.* **(a)** Platte, *die;* (commemorating sb.) [Gedenk]tafel, *die*
(b) (Dent.) Zahnbelag, *der*
plasma /'plæzmə/ *n.* Plasma, *das*
plaster /'plɑːstə(r)/ [1] *n.* **(a)** (for walls etc.) [Ver]putz, *der*
(b) ~ [of Paris] Gips, *der;* **have one's leg in ~:** ein Gipsbein haben
(c) ▶ STICKING PLASTER
[2] *v.t.* **(a)** verputzen ‹*Wand*›
(b) (daub) **~ sth. on sth.** etw. dick auf etw. (*Akk.*) auftragen
plaster: ~board *n.* Gipsplatte, *die;* **~ cast** *n.* (Med.) Gipsverband, *der*
plastered /'plɑːstəd/ *adj.* (sl.: drunk) voll (salopp); **get ~:** sich voll laufen lassen (salopp)
'plasterer *n.* Gipser, *der*
plastic /'plæstɪk/ [1] *n.* **(a)** Plastik, *das;* Kunststoff, *der*
(b) (coll.: credit cards etc.) Plastikgeld, *das*
[2] *adj.* aus Plastik *od.* Kunststoff *nachgestellt;* **~ bag** Plastiktüte, *die;* **~ money** (joc.) Kreditkarten *Pl.*
plastic 'bullet *n.* Plastikgeschoss, *das*
Plasticine ® /'plæstɪsiːn/ *n.* Plastilin, *das*
plastic: ~ 'surgeon *n.* Facharzt für plastische Chirurgie; **~ 'surgery** *n.* plastische Chirurgie
plate /pleɪt/ [1] *n.* **(a)** Teller, *der;* (serving **~**) Platte, *die*
(b) (metal **~** with name etc.) Schild, *das*
(c) (for printing) Platte, *die;* (illustration) [Bild]tafel, *die*
[2] *v.t.* **~ sth. [with gold/silver]** etw. vergolden/versilbern
plateau /'plætəʊ/ *n., pl.* **~x** /'plætəʊz/ *or* **~s** Hochebene, *die;* Plateau, *das*
plate: ~ 'glass *n.* Flachglas, *das;* **~ rack** *n.* (Brit.) Abtropfständer, *der;* Geschirrablage, *die*
platform /'plætfɔːm/ *n.* **(a)** (Brit. Railw.) Bahnsteig, *der;* **~ 4** Gleis 4
(b) (stage) Podium, *das*
platinum /'plætɪnəm/ *n.* Platin, *das*
platitude /'plætɪtjuːd/ *n.* Plattitüde, *die* (geh.); Gemeinplatz, *der*
platonic /plə'tɒnɪk/ *adj.* platonisch ‹*Liebe, Freundschaft*›
platoon /plə'tuːn/ *n.* (Mil.) Zug, *der*
plausible /'plɔːzɪbl/ *adj.* plausibel; einleuchtend
play /pleɪ/ [1] *n.* **(a)** (Theatre) [Theater]stück, *das;* **television ~:** Fernsehspiel, *das*
(b) (recreation) Spielen, *das;* Spiel, *das;* **~ on words** Wortspiel, *das*
(c) (Sport) Spiel, *das*

···>

(d) come into ~, be brought *or* **called into ~**: ins Spiel kommen
2 *v.i.* **(a)** spielen; **~ safe** sichergehen; **~ for time** Zeit gewinnen wollen
(b) (Mus.) spielen (**on** auf + *Dat.*)
3 *v.t.* (also Sport, Theatre, Cards, Mus.) spielen; abspielen ‹*Schallplatte, Tonband*›; schlagen ‹*Ball*›; spielen gegen ‹*Mannschaft, Gegner*›; **~ the violin** *etc.* Geige *usw.* spielen; **~ a trick/joke on sb.** jmdn. hereinlegen (ugs.)/ jmdm. einen Streich spielen; **~ one's cards right** (fig.) es richtig anfassen (fig.)

■ **play a'bout, play a'round** *v.i.* spielen; **stop ~ing about** *or* **around** hör doch auf mit dem Unsinn!

■ **play a'long** *v.i.* mitspielen

■ **play 'back** *v.t.* abspielen ‹*Tonband*›

■ **play 'down** *v.t.* herunterspielen

■ **play 'up** 1 *v.i.* (coll.) ‹*Kinder:*› nichts als Ärger machen
2 *v.t.* (coll.: annoy) ärgern

play: ~-acting *n.* Theater, *das* (ugs.); **~ area** *n.* Spielplatz, *der;* **~back** *n.* Wiedergabe, *die;* **listen to the ~back** die Aufnahme anhören; **~boy** *n.* Playboy, *der*

'player *n.* Spieler, *der*/Spielerin, *die*

playful /'pleɪfl/ *adj.* spielerisch; (frolicsome) verspielt

play: ~ground *n.* Spielplatz, *der;* (Sch.) Schulhof, *der;* **~ group** *n.* Spielgruppe, *die*

playing: ~ area *n.* (Sport) Spielfeld, *das;* **~ card** *n.* Spielkarte, *die;* **~ field** *n.* Sportplatz, *der*

play: ~mate *n.* Spielkamerad, *der*/ -kameradin, *die;* **~off** *n.* Entscheidungsspiel, *das;* **~pen** Laufgitter, *das;* **~ school** *n.* Kindergarten, *der;* **~thing** *n.* Spielzeug, *das;* **~wright** /'pleɪraɪt/ *n.* Dramatiker, *der*/Dramatikerin, *die*

PLC, plc *abbr.* (Brit.) = **public limited company** ≈ GmbH

plea /pli:/ *n.* Bitte, *die;* (public appeal) Appell, *der* (**for** zu)

plead /pli:d/ 1 *v.i.* **(a)** inständig bitten (**for** um); (imploringly) flehen (**for** um); **~ with sb. for sth.** jmdn. inständig um etw. bitten
(b) (Law; also fig.) plädieren
2 *v.t.* **(a)** inständig bitten; (imploringly) flehen
(b) (Law) **~ guilty/not guilty** sich schuldig/ nicht schuldig bekennen

'pleading *adj.* flehend

pleasant /'plezənt/ *adj.* angenehm

pleasantry /'plezəntrɪ/ *n.* Nettigkeit, *die*

please /pli:z/ 1 *v.t.* gefallen (+ *Dat.*); **~ oneself** tun, was man will; **~ yourself** ganz wie du willst
2 *v.i.* **I come and go as I ~**: ich komme und gehe, wie es mir gefällt; **if you ~**: bitte schön
3 *int.* bitte; **~ do!** aber bitte *od.* gern!

pleased /pli:zd/ *adj.* (satisfied) zufrieden (**by** mit); (happy) erfreut (**by** über + *Akk.*); **be ~ at** *or* **about sth.** sich über etw. (*Akk.*) freuen

pleasing /'pli:zɪŋ/ *adj.* gefällig

pleasure /'pleʒə(r)/ *n.* (joy) Freude, *die;* (enjoyment) Vergnügen, *das;* **have the ~ of doing sth.** das Vergnügen haben, etw. zu tun; **with ~**: mit Vergnügen

'pleasure cruise *n.* Vergnügungsfahrt, *die*

pleat /pli:t/ *n.* Falte, *die*

'pleated *adj.* gefältelt; Falten‹*rock*›

plebiscite /'plebɪsɪt, 'plebɪsaɪt/ *n.* Plebiszit, *das*

pledge /pledʒ/ 1 *n.* Versprechen, *das*
2 *v.t.* versprechen; geloben ‹*Treue*›

plentiful /'plentɪfl/ *adj.* reichlich; **be ~**: reichlich vorhanden sein

plenty /'plentɪ/ *n.* **~ of** viel; eine Menge; (coll.: enough) genug

pleurisy /'plʊərɪsɪ/ *n.* Pleuritis, *die;* Brustfellentzündung, *die*

pliable /'plaɪəbl/ *adj.* biegsam

plied ▶ PLY

pliers /'plaɪəz/ *n. pl.* **[pair of] ~**: Zange, *die*

plight /plaɪt/ *n.* Notlage, *die*

plimsoll /'plɪmsl/ *n.* (Brit.) Turnschuh, *der*

plinth /plɪnθ/ *n.* Sockel, *der*

plod /plɒd/ *v.i.*, **-dd-** trotten

■ **plod 'on** *v.i.* (fig.) sich weiterkämpfen

plonk /plɒŋk/ *n.* (coll.) [billiger] Wein

plot /plɒt/ 1 *n.* **(a)** (conspiracy) Verschwörung, *die*
(b) (of play, novel) Handlung, *die*
(c) (of ground) Stück Land
2 *v.t.*, **-tt-**: **(a)** [heimlich] planen
(b) (mark on map) einzeichnen
3 *v.i.*, **-tt-**: **~ against sb.** sich gegen jmdn. verschwören

'plotter *n.* Verschwörer, *der*/Verschwörerin, *die*

plough /plaʊ/ 1 *n.* Pflug, *der*
2 *v.t.* pflügen

■ **plough 'back** *v.t.* (Finance) reinvestieren

plow (Amer./arch.) ▶ PLOUGH

ploy /plɔɪ/ *n.* Trick, *der*

pluck /plʌk/ 1 *v.t.* **(a)** pflücken ‹*Obst*›; **~ [out]** auszupfen ‹*Federn, Haare*›
(b) (pull at) zupfen an (+ *Dat.*)
(c) (strip of feathers) rupfen
2 *v.i.* **~ at sth.** an etw. (*Dat.*) zupfen
3 *n.* Mut, *der*

■ **pluck 'up** *v.t.* **~ up [one's] courage** all seinen Mut zusammennehmen

pluckily /'plʌkɪlɪ/ *adv.*, **'plucky** *adj.* tapfer

plug /plʌg/ 1 *n.* **(a)** (filling hole) Pfropfen, *der;* (in cask) Spund, *der;* (for basin etc.) Stöpsel, *der*
(b) (Electr.) Stecker, *der*
2 *v.t.*, **-gg-**: **(a)** **~ [up]** zustopfen ‹*Loch usw.*›
(b) (coll.: advertise) Schleichwerbung machen für

■ **plug 'in** *v.t.* anschließen

'plughole *n.* Abfluss, *der*

plum /plʌm/ *n.* **(a)** Pflaume, *die*

(b) (fig.) Leckerbissen, *der;* **a ~ job** ein Traumjob (ugs.)

plumage /'plu:mɪdʒ/ *n.* Gefieder, *das*

plumb¹ /plʌm/ **1** *v.t.* [aus]loten **2** *adv.* **(a)** lotrecht **(b)** (fig.) genau

plumb² *v.t.* **~ in** fest anschließen

plumber /'plʌmə(r)/ *n.* Klempner, *der*

plumbing /'plʌmɪŋ/ *n.* **(a)** Klempnerarbeiten *Pl.* **(b)** (waterpipes) Wasserleitungen *Pl.*

'plumb line *n.* Lot, *das*

plume /plu:m/ *n.* Feder, *die;* (ornamental bunch) Federbusch, *der*

plummet /'plʌmɪt/ *v.i.* stürzen

plump /plʌmp/ *adj.* mollig; rundlich

■ **'plump for** *v.t.* sich entscheiden für

plunder /'plʌndə(r)/ **1** *v.t.* [aus]plündern ‹*Gebäude, Gebiet*› **2** *n.* Plünderung, *die;* (booty) Beute, *die*

plunge /plʌndʒ/ **1** *v.t.* stecken; (into liquid) tauchen **2** *v.i.* **(a) ~ into sth.** in etw. (*Akk.*) stürzen **(b)** ‹*Straße usw.:*› steil abfallen **3** *n.* Sprung, *der;* **take the ~** (fig. coll.) den Sprung wagen

plunger /'plʌndʒə(r)/ *n.* (suction cup) Stampfer, *der*

plural /'plʊərl/ **1** *adj.* pluralisch; Plural-; **~ noun** Substantiv im Plural **2** *n.* Mehrzahl, *die;* Plural, *der*

pluralism /'plʊərəlɪzm/ *n.* Pluralismus, *der*

plus /plʌs/ **1** *prep.* plus (+ *Dat.*) **2** *n.* (advantage) Pluspunkt, *der*

plush /plʌʃ/ **1** *n.* Plüsch, *der* **2** *adj.* (coll.) feudal (ugs.)

Pluto /'plu:təʊ/ *pr. n.* (Astron.) Pluto, *der*

plutonium /plu:'təʊnɪəm/ *n.* Plutonium, *das*

ply /plaɪ/ **1** *v.t.* **(a)** (use) gebrauchen **(b)** nachgehen (+ *Dat.*) ‹*Handwerk, Arbeit*› **(c)** (supply) **~ sb. with sth.** jmdn. mit etw. versorgen **(d)** (assail) überhäufen **2** *v.i.* **~ between** zwischen ‹*Orten*› [hin- und her]pendeln

'plywood *n.* Sperrholz, *das*

PM *abbr.* = **Prime Minister**

p.m. /pi:'em/ *adv.* nachmittags; **one ~:** ein Uhr mittags

PMT *abbr.* = **premenstrual tension** PMS

pneumatic /nju:'mætɪk/ *adj.* pneumatisch

pneumatic 'drill *n.* Pressluftbohrer, *der*

pneumonia /nju:'məʊnɪə/ *n.* Lungenentzündung, *die*

PO *abbr.* **(a)** = **postal order** PA **(b)** = **Post Office** PA

poach¹ /pəʊtʃ/ *v.t.* **(a)** (catch illegally) wildern; illegal fangen ‹*Fische*› **(b)** stehlen, (ugs.) klauen ‹*Idee*›

poach² *v.t.* (Cookery) pochieren ‹*Ei*›; dünsten ‹*Fisch, Fleisch, Gemüse*›; **~ed eggs** verlorene Eier

'poacher *n.* Wilderer, *der*

PO box ▶ POST OFFICE BOX

pocket /'pɒkɪt/ **1** *n.* **(a)** Tasche, *die* **(b)** (fig.) **be in ~:** Geld verdient haben; **be out of ~:** draufgelegt haben **2** *adj.* Taschen‹*rechner, -uhr, -ausgabe*› **3** *v.t.* **(a)** einstecken **(b)** (steal) in die eigene Tasche stecken (ugs.)

pocket: ~book *n.* (wallet) Brieftasche, *die;* (notebook) Notizbuch, *das;* **~ 'handkerchief** *n.* Taschentuch, *das;* **~ knife** *n.* Taschenmesser, *das;* **~ money** *n.* Taschengeld, *das;* **~-size[d]** *adj.* im Taschenformat *nachgestellt*

'pockmarked *adj.* **(a)** pockennarbig ‹*Gesicht, Haut*› **(b) a wall ~ with bullets** eine mit Einschüssen übersäte Wand

pod /pɒd/ *n.* Hülse, *die;* (of pea) Schote, *die*

podgy /'pɒdʒɪ/ *adj.* dicklich

poem /'pəʊɪm/ *n.* Gedicht, *das*

poet /'pəʊɪt/ *n.* Dichter, *der*/Dichterin, *die*

poetic /pəʊ'etɪk/ *adj.* dichterisch

poetry /'pəʊɪtrɪ/ *n.* [Vers]dichtung, *die*; Lyrik, *die*

pogrom /'pɒgrəm/ *n.* Pogrom, *das od. der*

poignant /'pɔɪnjənt/ *adj.* tief ‹*Bedauern, Trauer*›; ergreifend ‹*Anblick*›

point /pɔɪnt/ **1** *n.* **(a)** (tiny mark, dot) Punkt, *der* **(b)** (of tool, pencil, etc.) Spitze, *die* **(c)** (single item; unit of scoring) Punkt, *der* **(d)** (stage, degree) **up to a ~:** bis zu einem gewissen Grad; **he gave up at this ~:** an diesem Punkt gab er auf **(e)** (moment) Zeitpunkt, *der;* **be on the ~ of doing sth.** etw. gerade tun wollen **(f)** (distinctive trait) Seite, *die;* **best/strong ~:** starke Seite; Stärke, *die* **(g)** (thing to be discussed) **come to** *or* **get to the ~:** zum Thema kommen; **be beside the ~:** keine Rolle spielen; **make a ~ of doing sth.** [großen] Wert darauf legen, etw. zu tun **(h)** (of story, joke, remark) Pointe, *die* **(i)** (purpose) Zweck, *der;* Sinn, *der;* **there's no ~ in protesting** es hat keinen Sinn *od.* Zweck zu protestieren **(j)** (precise place, spot) Punkt, *der;* Stelle, *die;* **~ of view** (fig.) Standpunkt, *der* **(k)** (Brit.) **[power** *or* **electric] ~:** Steckdose, *die* **(l)** *usu in pl.* (Brit. Railw.) Weiche, *die* **2** *v.i.* **(a)** zeigen, weisen (**to, at** auf + *Akk.*) **(b) ~ towards** *or* **to** (fig.) [hin]deuten auf (+ *Akk.*) **3** *v.t.* richten ‹*Waffe, Kamera*› (**at** auf + *Akk.*); **~ one's finger at sth./sb.** mit dem Finger auf etw./jmdn. zeigen

■ **point 'out** *v.t.* hinweisen auf (+ *Akk.*); **~ sth./sb. out to sb.** jmdn. auf etw./jmdn. hinweisen

point-'blank [1] *adj.* (lit. or fig.) direkt; glatt ‹*Weigerung*›; ~ **range** kürzeste Entfernung [2] *adv.* (at very close range) aus kürzester Entfernung

'pointed *adj.* **(a)** spitz **(b)** (fig.) unmissverständlich

'pointer *n.* **(a)** Zeiger, *der;* (rod) Zeigestock, *der* **(b)** (coll.: indication) Hinweis, *der* (**to** auf + *Akk.*)

'pointless *adj.* sinnlos; belanglos ‹*Bemerkung, Geschichte*›

poise /pɔɪz/ *n.* (composure) Haltung, *die;* (self-confidence) Selbstvertrauen, *das*

poised /pɔɪzd/ *adj.* selbstsicher

poison /'pɔɪzn/ [1] *n.* Gift, *das* [2] *v.t.* vergiften

'poisoning *n.* Vergiftung, *die*

poisonous /'pɔɪzənəs/ *adj.* giftig

poke [1] *v.t.* **(a)** ~ **sth. [with sth.]** [mit etw.] gegen etw. stoßen; ~ **sth. into sth.** etw. in etw. (*Akk.*) stoßen; ~ **the fire** das Feuer schüren **(b)** stecken ‹*Kopf*› [2] *v.i.* **(a)** [herum]stochern (**at, in, among** in + *Dat.*) **(b)** (pry) schnüffeln (ugs.) [3] *n.* (thrust) Stoß, *der;* **give sb. a ~ [in the ribs]** jmdm. einen [Rippen]stoß versetzen; **give the fire a ~:** das Feuer [an]schüren

■ **poke a'bout, poke a'round** *v.i.* herumschnüffeln (ugs.)

'poker¹ *n.* Schüreisen, *das*

'poker² *n.* (Cards) Poker, *das od. der*

'poker-faced *adj.* mit unbewegter Miene *nachgestellt*

poky /'pəʊkɪ/ *adj.* winzig

Poland /'pəʊlənd/ *pr. n.* Polen (*das*)

polar /'pəʊlə(r)/ *adj.* polar ‹*Kaltluft, Gewässer*›; Polar‹*eis, -gebiet, -fuchs*›

polar: ~ **'bear** *n.* Eisbär, *der;* ~ **'cap** *n.* Polkappe, *die*

pole¹ *n.* (support) Stange, *die;* **drive sb. up the ~** (Brit. coll.) jmdn. zum Wahnsinn treiben (ugs.)

pole² *n.* (Astron., Geog., Magn., Electr., fig.) Pol, *der*

Pole /pəʊl/ *n.* Pole, *der*/Polin, *die*

pole: ~ **star** *n.* Polarstern, *der;* **~-vault** *n.* Stabhochsprung, *der;* ~ **vaulter** *n.* Stabhochspringer, *der*/-springerin, *die*

police /pə'li:s/ [1] *n. pl.* Polizei, *die;* (members) Polizisten *Pl.; attrib.* Polizei- [2] *v.t.* [polizeilich] überwachen ‹*Fußballspiel*›; kontrollieren ‹*Gebiet*›

police: ~ **force** *n.* **the ~ force** die Polizei; **~man** /pə'li:smən/ *n., pl.* **-men** /pə'li:smən/ Polizist, *der;* ~ **officer** *n.* Polizeibeamte, *der*/-beamtin, *die;* ~ **state** *n.* Polizeistaat, *der;* ~ **station** *n.* Polizeirevier, *das;* **~woman** *n.* Polizistin, *die*

policy¹ /'pɒlɪsɪ/ *n.* Politik, *die*

policy² *n.* (Insurance) Police, *die*

'policy holder *n.* Versicherte, *der/die*

polio /'pəʊlɪəʊ/ *n., no art.* Polio, *die;* [spinale] Kinderlähmung

polish /'pɒlɪʃ/ [1] *v.t.* **(a)** polieren; bohnern ‹*Fußboden*›; putzen ‹*Schuhe*› **(b)** (fig.) ausfeilen ‹*Text, Theorie, Stil*› [2] *n.* **(a)** (smoothness) Glanz, *der* **(b)** (substance) Politur, *die* **(c)** (fig.) Schliff, *der*

■ **polish 'off** *v.t.* (coll.) **(a)** (consume) verdrücken (ugs.) **(b)** (complete quickly) durchziehen (ugs.)

■ **polish 'up** *v.t.* **(a)** polieren **(b)** ausfeilen ‹*Stil*›; aufpolieren ‹*Kenntnisse*›

Polish /'pəʊlɪʃ/ [1] *adj.* polnisch; **sb. is ~:** jmd. ist Pole/Polin [2] *n.* Polnisch, *das; see also* ENGLISH 2A

polite /pə'laɪt/ *adj.,* **~r** /pə'laɪtə(r)/, **~st** /pə'laɪtɪst/ höflich

po'liteness *n.* Höflichkeit, *die*

political /pə'lɪtɪkl/ *adj.* politisch

politically /pə'lɪtɪkəlɪ/ *adv.* politisch; ~ **correct** politisch korrekt

political 'prisoner *n.* politischer Gefangener/politische Gefangene

politician /pɒlɪ'tɪʃn/ *n.* Politiker, *der*/ Politikerin, *die*

politicize (politicise) /pə'lɪtɪsaɪz/ *v.t.* politisieren

politics /'pɒlɪtɪks/ *n.* Politik, *die;* (of individual) politische Einstellung

polka /'pɒlkə, 'pəʊlkə/ *n.* Polka, *die*

'polka dot *n.* [großer] Tupfen

poll /pəʊl/ [1] *n.* **(a)** (voting) Abstimmung, *die;* (to elect sb.) Wahl, *die;* **go to the ~s** zur Wahl gehen **(b)** (opinion ~) Umfrage, *die* [2] *v.t.* **(a)** (take vote[s] of) abstimmen/wählen lassen **(b)** (take opinion of) befragen

pollen /'pɒlən/ *n.* Pollen, *der;* Blütenstaub, *der*

'pollen count *n.* Pollenmenge, *die*

pollinate /'pɒlɪneɪt/ *v.t.* bestäuben

pollination /pɒlɪ'neɪʃn/ *n.* Bestäubung, *die*

polling /'pəʊlɪŋ/: ~ **booth** *n.* Wahlkabine, *die;* ~ **station** *n.* (Brit.) Wahllokal, *das*

'poll tax *n.* Kopfsteuer, *die*

pollutant /pə'lu:tənt/ *n.* [Umwelt]schadstoff, *der*

pollute /pə'lu:t/ *v.t.* verschmutzen ‹*Luft, Boden, Wasser*›

pollution /pə'lu:ʃn/ *n.* **[environmental] ~:** [Umwelt]verschmutzung, *die;* **noise ~:** Lärmbelästigung, *die*

polo /'pəʊləʊ/ *n.* Polo, *das*

polo: ~ **neck** *n.* Rollkragen, *der;* ~ **shirt** *n.* Polohemd, *das*

poly /'pɒlɪ/ *n., pl.* **~s** (coll.) Polytechnikum, *das;* ≈ TH, *die*

polyester /pɒlɪ'estə(r)/ *n.* Polyester, *der*

polygamy /pə'lɪgəmɪ/ *n.* Polygamie, *die*

polystyrene /pɒlɪ'staɪri:n/ *n.* Polystyrol, *das;* ~ **foam** Styropor ⓦ, *das*

polytechnic /pɒlɪ'teknɪk/ *n.* (Brit.) ≈ technische Hochschule

polythene /'pɒlɪθi:n/ *n.* Polyäthylen, *das;* ~ **bag** Plastikbeutel, *der*

polyunsaturated /pɒlɪʌn'sætʃəreɪtɪd/ *adj.* mehrfach ungesättigt

polyunsaturates /pɒlɪʌn'sætjʊrəts/ *n. pl.* mehrfach ungestättigte Fettsäuren *Pl.*

pomegranate /'pɒmɪgrænɪt/ *n.* Granatapfel, *der*

'pommel horse *n.* Seitpferd, *das*

pomp /pɒmp/ *n.* Pomp, *der*

pompom /'pɒmpɒm/ *n.* Pompon, *der;* ~ **hat** Pudelmütze, *die*

pompous /'pɒmpəs/ *adj.* großspurig; gespreizt ‹*Sprache*›

pond /pɒnd/ *n.* Teich, *der*

ponder /'pɒndə(r)/ [1] *v.t.* nachdenken über (+ *Akk.*) ‹*Frage, Ereignis*›; abwägen ‹*Vorteile, Worte*›
[2] *v.i.* nachdenken (**over, on** über + *Akk.*)

ponderous /'pɒndərəs/ *adj.* schwer

pong /pɒŋ/ (Brit. coll.) [1] *n.* Mief, *der* (ugs.)
[2] *v.i.* miefen (ugs.)

pony /'pəʊnɪ/ *n.* Pony, *das*

pony: ~**tail** *n.* Pferdeschwanz, *der;* ~**-trekking** /'pəʊnɪtrekɪŋ/ *n.* (Brit.) Ponyreiten, *das*

poodle /'pu:dl/ *n.* Pudel, *der*

pool¹ /pu:l/ *n.* **(a)** Tümpel, *der*
(b) (temporary) Lache, *die;* ~ **of blood** Blutlache, *die*
(c) (swimming ~) Schwimmbecken, *das;* (public) Schwimmbad, *das;* (in house or garden) Pool, *der*

pool² [1] *n.* **(a)** (Gambling) [gemeinsame Spiel]kasse; **the** ~**s** (Brit.) das Toto
(b) (common supply) Topf, *der;* **a** ~ **of experience** ein Erfahrungsschatz
(c) (game) Pool[billard], *das*
[2] *v.t.* zusammenlegen ‹*Geld, Ersparnisse*›; bündeln ‹*Anstrengungen*›

'pool table *n.* Pool[billard]tisch, *der*

poor /pʊə(r)/ [1] *adj.* **(a)** arm
(b) (inadequate) schlecht; schwach ‹*Spiel, Gesundheit, Leistung, Rede*›; dürftig ‹*Kleidung, Essen, Unterkunft*›; **of** ~ **quality** minderer Qualität
(c) (paltry) schwach ‹*Trost*›; schlecht ‹*Aussichten*›
(d) (unfortunate) arm (auch iron.)
(e) karg ‹*Boden*›
(f) (deficient) arm (**in** an + *Dat.*); ~ **in vitamins** vitaminarm
[2] *n. pl.* **the** ~: die Armen *Pl.*

poorly /'pʊəlɪ/ *adv., pred. adj.* schlecht

pop¹ /pɒp/ [1] *v.i.*, **-pp-: (a)** (make sound) knallen
(b) (coll.: go quickly) **let's** ~ **round to Fred's** komm, wir gehen kurz bei Fred vorbei (ugs.)
[2] *v.t.*, **-pp-: (a)** (coll.: put) ~ **the meat in the fridge** das Fleisch in den Kühlschrank tun
(b) platzen ‹*Luftballon*›
[3] *n.* **(a)** Knall, *der;* Knallen, *das*
(b) (coll.: drink) Brause, *die* (ugs.)
[4] *adv.* **go** ~: knallen
■ **pop 'out** *v.i.* hervorschießen; ~ **out to the shops** schnell einkaufen gehen

pop² (coll.) [1] *n.* Popmusik, *die;* Pop, *der*
[2] *adj.* Pop‹*star, -musik usw.*›

'popcorn *n.* Popcorn, *das*

pope /pəʊp/ *n.* Papst, *der*/Päpstin, *die*

poplar /'pɒplə(r)/ *n.* Pappel, *die*

'pop music *n.* Popmusik, *die*

popper /'pɒpə(r)/ *n.* (Brit. coll.) Druckknopf, *der*

poppy /'pɒpɪ/ *n.* Mohn, *der*

popular /'pɒpjʊlə(r)/ *adj.* **(a)** (well liked) beliebt; populär ‹*Entscheidung, Maßnahme*›; ~ **music** Unterhaltungsmusik, *die*
(b) verbreitet ‹*Aberglaube, Irrtum, Meinung*›; allgemein ‹*Wahl, Unterstützung*›

popularity /pɒpjʊ'lærɪtɪ/ *n.* Beliebtheit, *die;* (of decision, measure) Popularität, *die*

popularize /'pɒpjʊləraɪz/ *v.t.* **(a)** (make popular) populär machen
(b) (make understandable) breiteren Kreisen zugänglich machen

'popularly *adv.* allgemein

populate /'pɒpjʊleɪt/ *v.t.* bevölkern; bewohnen ‹*Insel*›

population /pɒpjʊ'leɪʃn/ *n.* Bevölkerung, *die;* **Britain has a** ~ **of 56 million** Großbritannien hat 56 Millionen Einwohner; ~ **density** Bevölkerungsdichte, *die*

popu'lation explosion *n.* Bevölkerungsexplosion, *die*

'pop-up *adj.* Stehauf‹*buch, -illustration*›; ~ **toaster** Toaster mit Auswerfmechanismus; ~ **menu** (Comp.) Pop-up-Menü, *das;* ~ **window** (Comp.) Pop-up-Fenster, *das*

porcelain /'pɔ:slɪn/ *n.* Porzellan, *das*

porch /pɔ:tʃ/ *n.* Vordach, *das;* (with side walls) Vorbau, *der;* (enclosed) Windfang, *der*

porcupine /'pɔ:kjʊpaɪn/ *n.* Stachelschwein, *das*

pore¹ /pɔ:(r)/ *n.* Pore, *die*

pore² *v.i.* ~ **over sth.** etw. [genau] studieren

pork /pɔ:k/ *n.* Schweinefleisch, *das; attrib.* Schweine-

pork: ~ **'chop** *n.* Schweinekotelett, *das;* ~ **'pie** *n.* Schweinepastete, *die*

porn /pɔ:n/ *n.* (coll.) Pornographie, *die;* Pornos *Pl.* (ugs.)

pornographic /pɔ:nə'græfɪk/ *adj.* pornographisch; Porno- (ugs.)

pornography /pɔ:'nɒgrəfɪ/ *n.* Pornographie, *die*

porous /'pɔ:rəs/ *adj.* porös

porridge /'pɒrɪdʒ/ *n.* [Hafer]brei, *der*

port¹ /pɔːt/ [1] *n.* **(a)** Hafen, *der*
(b) (Naut., Aeronaut.: left side) Backbord, *das*
[2] *adj.* (Naut., Aeronaut.: left) Backbord-; backbordseitig

port² *n.* (wine) Portwein, *der*

portable /'pɔːtəbl/ *adj.* tragbar

port au'thority *n.* Hafenbehörde, *die*

porter¹ /'pɔːtə(r)/ *n.* (Brit.: doorman) Pförtner, *der;* (of hotel) Portier, *der*

porter² *n.* [Gepäck]träger, *der*/-trägerin, *die;* (in hotel) Hausdiener, *der*

portfolio /pɔːt'fəʊlɪəʊ/ *n. pl.* **~s (a)** (Polit.) Geschäftsbereich, *der*
(b) (case, contents) Mappe, *die*

porthole /'pɔːthəʊl/ *n.* (Naut.) Seitenfenster, *das;* (round) Bullauge, *das*

portion /'pɔːʃn/ *n.* **(a)** (part) Teil, *der;* (of ticket) Abschnitt, *der*
(b) (of food) Portion, *die*

portly /'pɔːtlɪ/ *adj.* beleibt

portrait /'pɔːtrɪt/ *n.* Porträt, *das*

portray /pɔː'treɪ/ *v.t.* darstellen; (make likeness of) porträtieren

Portugal /'pɔːtjʊgl/ *pr. n.* Portugal (*das*)

Portuguese /pɔːtjʊ'giːz/ [1] *adj.* portugiesisch; **sb. is ~:** jmd. ist Portugiese/ Portugiesin
[2] *n., pl. same* **(a)** (person) Portugiese, *der*/ Portugiesin, *die*
(b) (language) Portugiesisch, *das; see also* ENGLISH 2A

pose /pəʊz/ [1] *v.t.* aufwerfen ‹*Frage, Problem*›; darstellen ‹*Bedrohung*›; mit sich bringen ‹*Schwierigkeiten*›
[2] *v.i.* **(a)** (assume attitude) posieren; (fig.) sich geziert benehmen
(b) ~ as sich geben als
[3] *n.* Pose, *die;* **strike a ~:** eine Pose einnehmen

poser /'pəʊzə(r)/ *n.* (question) knifflige Frage

posh /pɒʃ/ *adj.* (coll.) vornehm; nobel (spött.); stinkvornehm (salopp)

position /pə'zɪʃn/ [1] *n.* **(a)** (place occupied) Platz, *der;* (of player in team, of plane, ship, etc.) Position, *die;* (of hands of clock, words, stars) Stellung, *die;* (of building) Lage, *die;* **be in/out of ~:** an seinem Platz/nicht an seinem Platz sein
(b) (Mil.) Stellung, *die*
(c) (fig.: mental attitude) Standpunkt, *der*
(d) (fig.: situation) **be in a good ~ [financially]** [finanziell] gut gestellt sein; **be in a ~ of strength** eine starke Position haben
(e) (rank) Stellung, *die*
(f) (job) Stelle, *die*
(g) (posture) Haltung, *die*
[2] *v.t.* platzieren; postieren ‹*Polizisten, Wachen*›; **~ oneself** sich stellen/(sit) setzen

positive /'pɒzɪtɪv/ *adj.* **(a)** (also Math.) positiv; konstruktiv ‹*Vorschlag*›; (definite) eindeutig; (convinced) sicher; **I'm ~ of it** ich bin [mir] [dessen] ganz sicher
(b) (Electr.) positiv ‹*Elektrode, Ladung*›; Plus‹*platte, -leiter*›
(c) *as intensifier* (coll.) echt

positive: ~ discrimi'nation *n.* positive Diskriminierung; **~ vetting** *n., no indef. art.* (Brit.) Sicherheitsüberprüfung, *die*

possess /pə'zes/ *v.t.* besitzen; (as faculty or quality) haben; ‹*Furcht usw.:*› ergreifen; **what ~ed you?** was ist in dich gefahren?

possessed /pə'zest/ *adj.* besessen

possession /pə'zeʃn/ *n.* **(a)** (thing possessed) Besitz, *der;* **some of my ~s** einige meiner Sachen
(b) *in pl.* (property) Besitz, *der*
(c) (possessing) Besitz, *der;* **be in ~ of sth.** im Besitz einer Sache (*Gen.*) sein; **take ~ of** in Besitz nehmen; beziehen ‹*Haus, Wohnung*›

possessive /pə'zesɪv/ *adj.* **(a) be ~ about sth./sb.** etw. eifersüchtig hüten/an jmdn. Besitzansprüche stellen
(b) (Ling.) possessiv; Possessiv‹*pronomen*›

possessor /pə'zesə(r)/ *n.* Besitzer, *der*/ Besitzerin, *die*

possibility /pɒsɪ'bɪlɪtɪ/ *n.* Möglichkeit, *die*

possible /'pɒsɪbl/ *adj.* möglich; (likely) [gut] möglich; **if ~:** wenn möglich; **as ... as ~:** so ... wie möglich; möglichst ...

possibly /'pɒsɪblɪ/ *adv.* **(a) as often as I ~ can** sooft ich irgend kann; **I cannot ~ commit myself** ich kann mich unmöglich festlegen
(b) (perhaps) möglicherweise

post¹ /pəʊst/ *n.* **(a)** (as support) Pfosten, *der*
(b) (stake) Pfahl, *der*
(c) (starting/finishing ~) Start-/Zielpfosten, *der*

post² [1] *n.* **(a)** (Brit.: one dispatch/delivery of letters) Postausgang, *der*/Post[zustellung], *die;* **by return of ~:** postwendend
(b) *no indef. art.* (Brit.: official conveying) Post, *die;* **by ~:** mit der Post; per Post
(c) (~ office) Post, *die*
[2] *v.t.* **(a)** abschicken
(b) (fig. coll.) **keep sb. ~ed** jmdn. auf dem Laufenden halten

post³ [1] *n.* **(a)** (job) Stelle, *die;* Posten, *der*
(b) (Mil.; also fig.) Posten, *der*
[2] *v.t.* postieren; aufstellen

postage /'pəʊstɪdʒ/ *n.* Porto, *das;* **~ paid** freigemacht; frankiert; Frei‹*umschlag*›

'postage stamp *n.* Briefmarke, *die*

postal /'pəʊstl/ *adj.* Post-; postalisch ‹*Aufgabe, Einrichtung*›; (by post) per Post *nachgestellt*

'postal order *n.* ≈ Postanweisung, *die*

post: ~box *n.* (Brit.) Briefkasten, *der;* **~card** *n.* Postkarte, *die;* **~code** *n.* (Brit.) Postleitzahl, *die;* **~'date** *v.t.* (give later date to) vordatieren

poster /'pəʊstə(r)/ *n.* Plakat, *das*

poste restante /pəʊst re'stɑ̃t/ *n.* Abteilung/Schalter für postlagernde Sendungen; **write to sb. [at the] ~ in Rome** jmdm. postlagernd nach Rom schreiben

posterior /pɒˈstɪərɪə(r)/ *n.* (joc.) Hinterteil, *das* (ugs.)

posterity /pɒˈsterɪtɪ/ *n., no art.* Nachwelt, *die*

postgrad /pəʊstˈgræd/ (coll.), **postˈgraduate** 1 *adj.* Graduierten- 2 *n.* Graduierte, *der/die*

posthumous /ˈpɒstjʊməs/ *adj.* postum

post: ~man /ˈpəʊstmən/, *pl.* **~men** /ˈpəʊstmən/ *n.* Briefträger, *der;* **~mark** 1 *n.* Poststempel, *der;* 2 *v.t.* abstempeln; **~ˈmodern** ▸ ~MODERNIST 1; **~ˈmodernist** 1 *adj.* postmodernistisch; 2 *n.* Postmodernist, *der*/Postmodernistin, *die*

postmortem /pəʊstˈmɔːtəm/ *n.* Obduktion, *die*

post: ~ office *n.* **(a)** (organization) **the P~ Office** die Post; **(b)** (place) Postamt, *das;* Post, *die;* **~ office box** *n.* Postfach, *das*

postpone /pəˈspəʊn/ *v.t.* verschieben; (for an indefinite period) aufschieben

postˈponement *n.* Verschiebung, *die*/ Aufschub, *der*

ˈpost room *n.* Poststelle, *die*

postscript /ˈpəʊskrɪpt/ *n.* Nachschrift, *die;* (fig.) Nachtrag, *der*

posture /ˈpɒstʃə(r)/ *n.* [Körper]haltung, *die*

ˈpost-war *adj.* Nachkriegs-; der Nachkriegszeit *nachgestellt*

posy /ˈpəʊzɪ/ *n.* Sträußchen, *das*

pot¹ /pɒt/ 1 *n.* **(a)** [Koch]topf, *der;* **go to ~** (coll.) den Bach runtergehen (ugs.) **(b)** (container, contents) Topf, *der;* (teapot, coffee pot) Kanne, *die* **(c)** (coll.: large sum) **a ~ of/~s of** massenweise 2 *v.t.* **~ [up]** eintopfen ‹*Pflanze*›

pot² *n.* (sl.: marijuana) Pot, *das* (Jargon)

potassium /pəˈtæsɪəm/ *n.* Kalium, *das*

potato /pəˈteɪtəʊ/ *n., pl.* **~es** Kartoffel, *die*

potato ˈsalad *n.* Kartoffelsalat, *der*

pot: ~belly *n.* Schmerbauch, *der* (ugs.); **~boiler** *n.* (derog.) Fließbandprodukt, *das*

potent /ˈpəʊtənt/ *adj.* [hoch]wirksam ‹*Droge*›; stark ‹*Schnaps usw.*›; schlagkräftig ‹*Waffe*›

potential /pəˈtenʃl/ 1 *adj.* potenziell (geh.); möglich 2 *n.* Potenzial, *das* (geh.); Möglichkeiten *Pl.*

potentially /pəˈtenʃəlɪ/ *adv.* potenziell (geh.); **he's ~ dangerous** er kann gefährlich werden; **a ~ rich country** ein Land, das reich sein könnte

pot: ~hole *n.* **(a)** Schlagloch, *das;* **(b)** (cave) [tiefe] Höhle; **~holer** *n.* Höhlenforscher, *der*/-forscherin, *die;* **~ plant** *n.* Topfpflanze, *die*

potpourri /pəʊpʊəˈriː/ *n.* Duftmischung, *die*

pot: ~ roast *n.* Schmorbraten, *der;* **~shot** *n.* **take a ~shot [at sb./sth.]** aufs Geratewohl [auf jmdn./etw.] schießen

ˈpotted *adj.* **(a)** (planted) Topf- **(b)** (abridged) kurz [gefasst]

ˈpotter¹ *n.* Töpfer, *der*/Töpferin, *die*

ˈpotter² *v.i.* **~ [about]** [he]rumwerkeln (ugs.)

pottery /ˈpɒtərɪ/ *n.* **(a)** Töpferware, *die* **(b)** (workshop, craft) Töpferei, *die*

potty¹ /ˈpɒtɪ/ *adj.* (Brit. coll.) verrückt (ugs.) **(about, on** nach)

potty² *n.* (Brit. coll.) Töpfchen, *das*

pouch /paʊtʃ/ *n.* Beutel, *der*

pouffe /puːf/ *n.* Sitzpolster, *das*

poultry /ˈpəʊltrɪ/ *n.* Geflügel, *das*

pounce /paʊns/ *v.i.* **(a)** sich auf sein Opfer stürzen; ‹*Raubvogel:*› herabstoßen auf (+ *Akk.*) **(b)** (fig.) **~ [up]on/at** sich stürzen auf (+ *Akk.*)

pound¹ /paʊnd/ *n.* **(a)** (unit of weight) [britisches] Pfund (*453,6 Gramm*); **two ~[s] of apples** 2 Pfund Äpfel **(b)** (unit of currency) Pfund, *das*

pound² *n.* (enclosure) Pferch, *der;* (for stray dogs) Zwinger, *der;* (for cars) Abstellplatz, *der*

pound³ 1 *v.t.* (crush) zerstoßen 2 *v.i.* **(a)** (make one's way heavily) stampfen **(b)** ‹*Herz:*› heftig schlagen

ˈpound[s] sign *n.* Pfundzeichen, *das*

pour /pɔː(r)/ 1 *v.t.* gießen; (into cup, glass) einschenken 2 *v.i.* **(a)** (flow) strömen; ‹*Rauch:*› hervorquellen (**from** aus); **~ [with rain]** in Strömen regnen **(b)** (fig.) strömen; **~ in** herein-/hineinströmen; **~ out** heraus-/hinausströmen

■ **pour ˈdown** *v.i.* **it's ~ing down** es gießt [in Strömen] (ugs.)

pout /paʊt/ 1 *v.i.* einen Schmollmund machen 2 *v.t.* aufwerfen ‹*Lippen*›

poverty /ˈpɒvətɪ/ *n.* Armut, *die*

poverty: ~ line *n.* Armutsgrenze, *die;* **be on the ~ line** an der Armutsgrenze liegen; **live below the ~ line** unterhalb der Armutsgrenze leben; **~-stricken** *adj.* Not leidend

powder /ˈpaʊdə(r)/ 1 *n.* **(a)** Pulver, *das* **(b)** (cosmetic) Puder, *der* 2 *v.t.* **(a)** pudern **(b)** (reduce to ~) pulverisieren; **~ed milk** Milchpulver, *das*

ˈpowdery *adj.* pulv[e]rig

power /ˈpaʊə(r)/ 1 *n.* **(a)** (ability) Kraft, *die;* **do all in one's ~ to help sb.** alles in seiner Macht Stehende tun, um jmdm. zu helfen **(b)** (faculty) Fähigkeit, *die* **(c)** (strength, intensity) Kraft, *die;* (of blow) Wucht, *die*

⇢

(d) (authority, political ~) Macht, *die* (**over** über + *Akk.*); **come into ~**: an die Macht kommen
(e) (authorization) Vollmacht, *die*
(f) (State) Macht, *die*
(g) (Math.) Potenz, *die*
(h) (Mech., Electr.) Kraft, *die;* (electric current) Strom, *der*
2 *v.t.* ‹*Treibstoff, Strom:*› antreiben; ‹*Batterie:*› mit Energie versorgen

power: ~-assisted *adj.* **~-assisted steering/brakes** Servolenkung, *die*/-bremsen *Pl.;* **~ brakes** *n. pl.* Servobremsen *Pl.;* **~ cable** *n.* Hochspannungsleitung, *die;* **~ cut** *n.* Stromsperre, *die;* **~ dressing** *n.: das Tragen betont streng wirkender Kleidung;* **~ failure** *n.* Stromausfall, *der*

powerful /'paʊəfl/ *adj.* **(a)** (strong) stark; kräftig ‹*Tritt, Schlag, Tier*›; heftig ‹*Gefühl, Empfindung*›; hell, strahlend ‹*Licht*›
(b) mächtig ‹*Clique, Person, Herrscher*›

'powerless *adj.* machtlos

power: ~ plant ▶ ~ STATION; **~ point** *n.* (Brit.) Steckdose, *die;* **~ station** *n.* Kraftwerk, *das;* **~ steering** *n.* Servolenkung, *die;* **~ supply** *n.* Energieversorgung, *die* (**to** *Gen.*)

pp. *abbr.* = **pages**

p.p. /piː'piː/ *abbr.* = **by proxy** pp[a].

practicable /'præktɪkəbl/ *adj.* durchführbar ‹*Projekt, Plan*›

practical /'præktɪkl/ *adj.* **(a)** praktisch; praktisch veranlagt ‹*Person*›
(b) (virtual) tatsächlich
(c) (feasible) möglich

practical 'joke *n.* Streich, *der*

'practically *adv.* praktisch; (almost) so gut wie; praktisch (ugs.)

practice¹ /'præktɪs/ *n.* **(a)** (repeated exercise) Übung, *die;* **be out of ~**: außer Übung sein
(b) (session) Übungen *Pl.;* **piano ~**: Klavierüben, *das*
(c) (of doctor, lawyer, etc.) Praxis, *die*
(d) (action) **put sth. into ~**: etw. in die Praxis umsetzen
(e) (custom) Gewohnheit, *die;* **regular ~**: Brauch, *der*

practice², practiced, practicing (Amer.) ▶ PRACTIS-

practise /'præktɪs/ **1** *v.t.* **(a)** (apply) anwenden; praktizieren
(b) ausüben ‹*Beruf, Religion*›
(c) trainieren in (+ *Dat.*) ‹*Sportart*›; **~ the piano/flute** Klavier/Flöte üben
2 *v.i.* üben

practised /'præktɪst/ *adj.* geübt

practising /'præktɪsɪŋ/ *adj.* praktizierend ‹*Arzt, Katholik usw.*›

practitioner /præk'tɪʃənə(r)/ *n.* Fachmann, *der; see also* GENERAL PRACTITIONER

pragmatic /præg'mætɪk/ *adj.* pragmatisch

Prague /prɑːg/ *pr. n.* Prag (*das*)

prairie /'preərɪ/ *n.* Grassteppe, *die;* (in North America) Prärie, *die*

praise /preɪz/ **1** *v.t.* loben; (more strongly) rühmen
2 *n.* Lob, *das*

'praiseworthy *adj.* lobenswert

pram /præm/ *n.* (Brit.) Kinderwagen, *der*

prance /prɑːns/ *v.i.* **(a)** ‹*Pferd:*› tänzeln
(b) (fig.) stolzieren; **~ about** *or* **around** herumhüpfen

prank /præŋk/ *n.* Streich, *der*

prattle /'prætl/ **1** *v.i.* plappern (ugs.)
2 *n.* Geplapper, *das* (ugs.)

prawn /prɔːn/ *n.* Garnele, *die*

prawn 'cocktail *n.* Krabbencocktail, *der*

pray /preɪ/ *v.i.* beten (**for** um)

prayer /preə(r)/ *n.* **(a)** Gebet, *das*
(b) *no art.* (praying) Beten, *das*

'prayer book *n.* Gebetbuch, *das*

preach /priːtʃ/ **1** *v.i.* predigen (**to** zu, vor + *Dat.;* **on** über + *Akk.*)
2 *v.t.* halten ‹*Predigt*›; predigen ‹*Evangelium, Botschaft*›

'preacher *n.* Prediger, *der*/Predigerin, *die*

pre-arrange /priːə'reɪndʒ/ *v.t.* vorher absprechen; vorher ausmachen ‹*Treffpunkt, Zeichen*›

precarious /prɪ'keərɪəs/ *adj.* **(a)** (uncertain) labil; prekär; **make a ~ living** eine unsichere Existenz haben
(b) (insecure, dangerous) gefährlich

precaution /prɪ'kɔːʃn/ *n.* Vorsichts-, Schutzmaßnahme, *die;* **as a ~**: vorsichtshalber

precede /prɪ'siːd/ *v.t.* (in order or time) vorangehen (+ *Dat.*)

precedence /'presɪdəns/ *n.* Priorität, *die* (geh.), Vorrang, *der* (**over** vor + *Dat.*)

precedent /'presɪdənt/ *n.* Präzedenzfall, *der*

precinct /'priːsɪŋkt/ *n.* **(a)** [**pedestrian**] **~**: Fußgängerzone, *die*
(b) (Amer.: district) Bezirk, *der*

precious /'preʃəs/ **1** *adj.* **(a)** kostbar ‹*Schmuckstück, Zeit*›; Edel‹*metall, -stein*›
(b) (beloved) lieb
(c) (affected) affektiert
2 *adv.* (coll.) herzlich ‹*wenig, wenige*›

precipice /'presɪpɪs/ *n.* Abgrund, *der*

precipitate **1** /prɪ'sɪpɪtət/ *adj.* eilig ‹*Flucht*›; übereilt ‹*Entschluss*›
2 /prɪ'sɪpɪteɪt/ *v.t.* (hasten) beschleunigen; (trigger) auslösen

precipitation /prɪsɪpɪ'teɪʃn/ *n.* (Meteorol.) Niederschlag, *der*

precipitous /prɪ'sɪpɪtəs/ *adj.* **(a)** (steep) sehr steil
(b) ▶ PRECIPITATE 1

précis /'preɪsiː/ *n., pl. same* /'preɪsiːz/ Zusammenfassung, *die*

precise /prɪˈsaɪs/ *adj.* genau; präzise; fein ‹*Instrument*›; förmlich ‹*Art*›; **be [more] ~:** sich präzise[r] ausdrücken

pre'cisely *adv.* genau

precision /prɪˈsɪʒn/ *n.* Genauigkeit, *die*

precision 'instrument *n.* Präzisions[mess]gerät, *das*

preclude /prɪˈkluːd/ *v.t.* ausschließen

precocious /prɪˈkəʊʃəs/ *adj.* frühreif ‹*Kind*›; altklug ‹*Äußerung*›

preconceived /priːkənˈsiːvd/ *adj.* vorgefasst ‹*Ansicht, Vorstellung*›

preconception /prɪːkənˈsepʃn/ *n.* vorgefasste Meinung (**of** über + *Akk.*)

precondition /priːkənˈdɪʃn/ *n.* Vorbedingung, *die* (**of** für)

pre-cooked /priːˈkʊkt/ *adj.* vorgekocht

precursor /priːˈkɜːsə(r)/ *n.* Wegbereiter, *der*/-bereiterin, *die*

predator /ˈpredətə(r)/ *n.* Raubtier, *das;* (fish) Raubfisch, *der*

'predatory *adj.* räuberisch; **~ animal** Raubtier, *das*

predecessor /ˈpriːdɪsesə(r)/ *n.* Vorgänger, *der*/-gängerin, *die*

predestine /priːˈdestɪn/ *v.t.* von vornherein bestimmen (**to** zu)

predicament /prɪˈdɪkəmənt/ *n.* Dilemma, *das*

predicate /ˈpredɪkət/ *n.* (Ling.) Prädikat, *das*

predicative /prɪˈdɪkətɪv/ *adj.* (Ling.) prädikativ

predict /prɪˈdɪkt/ *v.t.* voraus-, vorhersagen; vorhersehen ‹*Folgen*›

predictable /prɪˈdɪktəbl/ *adj.* voraussagbar; vorhersehbar ‹*Ereignis, Reaktion*›; berechenbar ‹*Person*›

prediction /prɪˈdɪkʃn/ *n.* Vorhersage, *die*

predominance /prɪˈdɒmɪnəns/ *n.* **(a)** (control) Vorherrschaft, *die* (**over** über + *Akk.*) **(b)** (majority) Überzahl, *die* (**of** von)

predominant /prɪˈdɒmɪnənt/ *adj.* (having more power) dominierend; (prevailing) vorherrschend

pre'dominantly *adv.* überwiegend

predominate /prɪˈdɒmɪneɪt/ *v.i.* (be more powerful) dominierend sein; (be more important) vorherrschen

pre-eminent /priːˈemɪnənt/ *adj.* herausragend

pre-empt /priːˈempt/ *v.t.* zuvorkommen (+ *Dat.*)

preen /priːn/ *v.t.* putzen ‹*Federn*›

prefab /ˈpriːfæb/ *n.* (coll.) Fertighaus, *das*

prefabricated /priːˈfæbrɪkeɪtɪd/ *adj.* vorgefertigt

preface /ˈprefəs/ **1** *n.* Vorwort, *das* (**to** *Gen.*) **2** *v.t.* (introduce) einleiten

prefect /ˈpriːfekt/ *n.* (Sch.) *die Aufsicht führender älterer Schüler/führende ältere Schülerin*

prefer /prɪˈfɜː(r)/ *v.t.*, **-rr-** vorziehen; **~ to do sth.** etw. lieber tun; **~ sth. to sth.** etw. einer Sache (*Dat.*) vorziehen

preferable /ˈprefərəbl/ *adj.* vorzuziehen *präd.;* vorzuziehend *attr.;* besser (**to** als)

preferably /ˈprefərəblɪ/ *adv.* am besten; (as best liked) am liebsten; **Wine or beer? – Wine, ~!** Wein oder Bier? – Lieber Wein!

preference /ˈprefərəns/ *n.* **(a)** (greater liking) Vorliebe, *die;* **for ~** ▶ PREFERABLY; **have a ~ for sth. [over sth.]** etw. [einer Sache (*Dat.*)] vorziehen; **do sth. in ~ to sth. else** etw. lieber als etw. anderes tun
(b) (thing preferred) **what are your ~s?** was wäre dir am liebsten?
(c) give ~ to sb. jmdn. bevorzugen

preferential /prefəˈrenʃl/ *adj.* bevorzugt ‹*Behandlung*›

preferred /prɪˈfɜːd/ *adj.* bevorzugt; **my ~ solution** *etc.* die Lösung *usw.*, der ich den Vorzug gebe

prefix /ˈpriːfɪks/ *n.* Präfix, *das*

pregnancy /ˈpregnənsɪ/ *n.* (of woman) Schwangerschaft, *die;* (of animal) Trächtigkeit, *die*

'pregnancy test *n.* Schwangerschaftstest, *der*

pregnant /ˈpregnənt/ *adj.* schwanger ‹*Frau*›; trächtig ‹*Tier*›

preheat /priːˈhiːt/ *v.t.* vorheizen ‹*Backofen*›; vorwärmen ‹*Geschirr, Essen*›

prehistoric /priːhɪˈstɒrɪk/ *adj.* prähistorisch

prehistory /priːˈhɪstərɪ/ Vorgeschichte, *die*

prejudge /priːˈdʒʌdʒ/ *v.t.* vorschnell urteilen über (+ *Akk.*)

prejudice /ˈpredʒʊdɪs/ **1** *n.* Vorurteil, *das* **2** *v.t.* beeinflussen

prejudiced /ˈpredʒʊdɪst/ *adj.* voreingenommen (**about** gegenüber, **against** gegen)

preliminary /prɪˈlɪmɪnərɪ/ **1** *adj.* Vor-; vorbereitend ‹*Forschung, Maßnahme*› **2** *n., usu. in pl.* **preliminaries** Präliminarien *Pl.;* **as a ~ to sth.** als Vorbereitung auf etw. (*Akk.*)

prelude /ˈpreljuːd/ *n.* **(a)** (introduction) Anfang, *der* (**to** *Gen.*)
(b) (Theatre, Mus.) Vorspiel, *das*

premature /ˈpremətjʊə(r)/ *adj.* **(a)** (hasty) übereilt
(b) (early) vorzeitig ‹*Altern, Ankunft*›; verfrüht ‹*Bericht, Eile*›; **~ baby** Frühgeburt, *die*

prema'turely *adv.* (early) vorzeitig; zu früh ‹*geboren werden*›; (hastily) übereilt

premeditated /priːˈmedɪteɪtɪd/ *adj.* vorsätzlich

premeditation /priːmedɪˈteɪʃn/ *n.* Vorsatz, *der*

premenstrual /priː'menstrʊəl/ *adj.* prämenstruell; ~ **tension** prämenstruelles Syndrom

premier /'premɪə(r)/ *n.* Premier[minister], *der*/Premierministerin, *die*

première /'premjeə(r)/ *n.* Premiere, *die;* Erstaufführung, *die*

premise /'premɪs/ *n.* **(a)** ~**s** *pl.* (building) Gebäude, *das;* (buildings and land) Gelände, *das;* (rooms) Räumlichkeiten *Pl.*
(b) ▶ PREMISS

premiss /'premɪs/ *n.* Prämisse, *die*

premium /'priːmɪəm/ *n.* Prämie, *die;* **be at a** ~ (fig.) sehr gefragt sein

'Premium Bond *n.* (Brit.) Prämienanleihe, *die;* Losanleihe, *die*

premonition /premə'nɪʃn/ *n.* Vorahnung, *die*

pre-natal /priː'neɪtl/ *adj.* pränatal (fachspr.); ~ **care** Schwangerschaftsfürsorge, *die*

preoccupation /prɪɒkjʊ'peɪʃn/ *n.* Sorge, *die* (**with** um)

preoccupied /prɪ'ɒkjʊpaɪd/ *adj.* (lost in thought) gedankenverloren; (concerned) besorgt (**with** um)

pre-'packed *adj.* abgepackt

prepaid /priː'peɪd/ *adj.* ~ **envelope** frankierter Umschlag

preparation /prepə'reɪʃn/ *n.* Vorbereitung, *die;* ~**s** *pl.* Vorbereitungen *Pl.* (**for** für)

preparatory /prɪ'pærətərɪ/ [1] *adj.* vorbereitend ‹*Maßnahme, Schritt*›; ~ **work** Vorarbeiten *Pl.*
[2] *adv.* ~ **to sth.** vor etw. (*Dat.*)

prepare /prɪ'peə(r)/ [1] *v.t.* **(a)** vorbereiten; ausarbeiten ‹*Plan, Rede*›; vorbereiten ‹*Person*› (**for** auf + *Akk.*); **be** ~**d to do sth.** (be willing) bereit sein, etw. zu tun
(b) herstellen ‹*Chemikalie usw.*›; zubereiten ‹*Essen*›
[2] *v.i.* sich vorbereiten (**for** auf + *Akk.*)

preponderance /prɪ'pɒndərəns/ *n.* Überlegenheit, *die* (**over** über + *Akk.*)

preposition /prepə'zɪʃn/ *n.* (Ling.) Präposition, *die*

prepossessing /priːpə'zesɪŋ/ *adj.* einnehmend

preposterous /prɪ'pɒstərəs/ *adj.* absurd; grotesk ‹*Äußeres, Kleidung*›

'pre-program *v.t.,* **-mm-** [vor]programmieren

prerequisite /priː'rekwɪzɪt/ [1] *n.* [Grund]voraussetzung, *die*
[2] *adj.* unbedingt erforderlich

prerogative /prɪ'rɒgətɪv/ *n.* Privileg, *das;* Vorrecht, *das*

Presbyterian /prezbɪ'tɪərɪən/ [1] *adj.* presbyterianisch
[2] *n.* Presbyterianer, *der*/Presbyterianerin, *die*

prescribe /prɪ'skraɪb/ *v.t.* **(a)** (impose) vorschreiben
(b) (Med.; also fig.) verschreiben

prescription /prɪ'skrɪpʃn/ *n.* **(a)** Vorschreiben, *das*
(b) (Med.) Rezept, *das*

pre'scription charge *n.* Rezeptgebühr, *die*

presence /'prezəns/ *n.* **(a)** (of person) Anwesenheit, *die;* (of things) Vorhandensein, *das;* **in the** ~ **of** in Anwesenheit (+ *Gen.*)
(b) ~ **of mind** Geistesgegenwart, *die*

present¹ /'prezənt/ [1] *adj.* **(a)** anwesend (**at** bei); **all those** ~: alle Anwesenden
(b) (existing now) gegenwärtig; jetzig ‹*Bischof, Chef usw.*›
(c) (Ling.) ~ **tense** Präsens, *das;* Gegenwart, *die*
[2] *n.* **(a) the** ~: die Gegenwart; **at** ~: zurzeit; **for the** ~: vorläufig
(b) (Ling.) Präsens, *das;* Gegenwart, *die*

present² [1] /'prezənt/ *n.* (gift) Geschenk, *das*
[2] /prɪ'zent/ *v.t.* **(a)** schenken; überreichen ‹*Preis, Medaille, Geschenk*›; ~ **sth. to sb.** *or* **sb. with sth.** jmdm. etw. schenken/überreichen; ~ **sb. with difficulties/a problem** jmdn. vor Schwierigkeiten/ein Problem stellen
(b) überreichen ‹*Gesuch*› (**to** bei); vorlegen ‹*Scheck, Bericht, Rechnung*› (**to** *Dat.*); ~ **one's case** seinen Fall darlegen
(c) (exhibit) zeigen; bereiten ‹*Schwierigkeit*›
(d) (introduce) vorstellen (**to** *Dat.*); vorlegen ‹*Abhandlung*›; moderieren ‹*Sendung*›
[3] *v. refl.* ‹*Problem:*› auftreten; ‹*Möglichkeit:*› sich ergeben; ~ **oneself for an interview** zu einem Gespräch erscheinen

presentable /prɪ'zentəbl/ *adj.* ansehnlich; **I'm not** ~: ich kann mich nicht so zeigen

presentation /prezən'teɪʃn/ *n.* **(a)** (giving) Schenkung, *die;* (of prize, medal) Überreichung, *die*
(b) (ceremony) Verleihung, *die*
(c) (of petition) Überreichung, *die;* (of cheque, report, account) Vorlage, *die;* (of case) Darlegung, *die*

present-day /prəzənt'deɪ/ *adj.* heutig

presenter /prɪ'zentə(r)/ *n.* (Radio, Telev.) Moderator, *der*/Moderatorin, *die*

presentiment /prɪ'zentɪmənt/ *n.* Vorahnung, *die*

presently /'prezəntlɪ/ *adv.* bald; (Amer., Scot.: now) zurzeit

preservation /prezə'veɪʃn/ *n.* Erhaltung, *die;* (of leather, wood, etc.) Konservierung, *die*

preservative /prɪ'zɜːvətɪv/ *n.* Konservierungsmittel, *das*

preserve /prɪ'zɜːv/ [1] *n.* **(a)** *in sing. or pl.* (fruit) Eingemachte, *das*
(b) (fig.: special sphere) Domäne, *die* (geh.)
(c) wildlife/game ~: Tierschutzgebiet, *das*/Wildpark, *der*
[2] *v.t.* **(a)** (keep safe) schützen (**from** vor + *Dat.*)
(b) bewahren ‹*Brauch*›; wahren ‹*Anschein, Reputation*›

(c) (keep from decay) konservieren; einmachen ‹*Obst, Gemüse*›
(d) (protect) hegen ‹*Tierart, Wald*›

preside /prɪˈzaɪd/ *v.i.* präsidieren, vorsitzen (**over** *Dat.*); (at meeting etc.) den Vorsitz haben (**at** bei)

presidency /ˈprezɪdənsɪ/ *n.* **(a)** Präsidentschaft, *die*
(b) (of society) Vorsitz, *der*

president /ˈprezɪdənt/ *n.* **(a)** Präsident, *der*/Präsidentin, *die*
(b) (of society) Vorsitzende, *der/die*

presidential /prezɪˈdenʃl/ *adj.* Präsidenten-

press¹ /pres/ **1** *n.* **(a)** (newspapers etc.) Presse, *die; attrib.* Presse-
(b) ▶ PRINTING PRESS
(c) (for flattening, compressing, etc.) Presse, *die*
2 *v.t.* **(a)** drücken; drücken auf (+ *Akk.*) ‹*Klingel, Knopf*›; treten auf (+ *Akk.*) ‹*Gas-, Brems-, Kupplungspedal usw.*›
(b) (urge) drängen ‹*Person*›; (force) aufdrängen ([**up**]**on** *Dat.*); nachdrücklich vorbringen ‹*Forderung, Argument*›; **he did not ~ the point** er ließ die Sache auf sich beruhen
(c) (compress) pressen; auspressen ‹*Orangen, Saft*›; keltern ‹*Trauben, Äpfel*›
(d) (iron) bügeln
(e) be ~ed for time/money zu wenig Zeit/Geld haben
3 *v.i.* **(a)** (exert pressure) drücken
(b) (be urgent) drängen
(c) (make demand) **~ for sth.** auf etw. (*Akk.*) drängen

■ **press aˈhead, press ˈon** *v.i.* (continue) [zügig] weitermachen; (continue travelling) [zügig] weitergehen/-fahren; **~ on with one's work** sich mit der Arbeit ranhalten (ugs.)

press² *v.t.* **~ into service/use** in Dienst nehmen; einsetzen

press: ~ agent *n.* Presseagent, *der*/-agentin, *die;* **~ conference** *n.* Pressekonferenz, *die;* **~ coverage** *n.* Berichterstattung in der Presse; **~ cutting** *n.* (Brit.) Zeitungsausschnitt, *der*

ˈpressing *adj.* (urgent) dringend

press: ~man *n.* (Brit.: journalist) Journalist, *der;* **~ release** *n.* Presseinformation, *die;* **~ stud** *n.* (Brit.) Druckknopf, *der;* **~-up** *n.* Liegestütz, *der*

pressure /ˈpreʃə(r)/ **1** *n.* Druck, *der;* **put ~ on sb.** jmdn. unter Druck setzen; **atmospheric ~**: Luftdruck, *der*
2 *v.t.* unter Druck setzen ‹*Person*›; **~ sb. into doing sth.** jmdn. [dazu] drängen, etw. zu tun

pressure: ~ cooker *n.* Schnellkochtopf, *der;* **~ group** *n.* Pressuregroup, *die*

pressurize /ˈpreʃəraɪz/ *v.t.* **(a)** ▶ PRESSURE 2
(b) ~d cabin Druckkabine, *die*

prestige /preˈstiːʒ/ *n.* Prestige, *das*

prestigious /preˈstɪdʒəs/ *adj.* angesehen

presumably /prɪˈzjuːməblɪ/ *adv.* vermutlich

presume /prɪˈzjuːm/ **1** *v.t.* **(a) ~ to do sth.** sich (*Dat.*) anmaßen, etw. zu tun; (take the liberty) sich (*Dat.*) erlauben, etw. zu tun
(b) (suppose) annehmen
2 *v.i.* [**up**]**on sth.** etw. ausnützen

presumption /prɪˈzʌmpʃn/ *n.* **(a)** (arrogance) Anmaßung, *die*
(b) (assumption) Annahme, *die*

presumptuous /prɪˈzʌmptjʊəs/ *adj.* anmaßend

presuppose /priːsəˈpəʊz/ *v.t.* voraussetzen

pre-teen /ˈpriːtiːn/ *adj.* ≈ zehn- bis zwölfjährig

pretence /prɪˈtens/ *n.* (Brit.) **(a)** (pretext) Vorwand, *der*
(b) *no art.* (make-believe, insincere behaviour) Verstellung, *die;* **it is all** *or* **just a ~**: das ist alles nicht echt

pretend /prɪˈtend/ **1** *v.t.* **(a)** vorgeben; **she ~ed to be asleep** sie tat, als ob sie schlief[e]
(b) (imagine in play) **~ to be sth.** so tun, als ob man etw. sei
2 *v.i.* sich verstellen; **she's only ~ing** sie tut nur so

pretense (Amer.) ▶ PRETENCE

pretension /prɪˈtenʃn/ *n.* **(a)** Anspruch, *der* (**to** auf + *Akk.*)
(b) (pretentiousness) Überheblichkeit, *die*

pretentious /prɪˈtenʃəs/ *adj.* hochgestochen; wichtigtuerisch ‹*Person*›; (ostentatious) großspurig

pretext /ˈpriːtekst/ *n.* Vorwand, *der;* [**up**]**on** *or* **under the ~ of doing sth.** unter dem Vorwand, etw. tun zu wollen

prettily /ˈprɪtɪlɪ/ *adv.* hübsch; sehr schön ‹*singen, tanzen*›

pretty /ˈprɪtɪ/ **1** *adj.* (also iron.) hübsch
2 *adv.* ziemlich; **I am ~ well** es geht mir ganz gut

prevail /prɪˈveɪl/ *v.i.* **(a)** die Oberhand gewinnen (**against, over** über + *Akk.*); **~ [up]on sb. to do sth.** jmdn. dazu bewegen, etw. zu tun
(b) (predominate) ‹*Zustand, Bedingung:*› vorherrschen
(c) (be current) herrschen

prevalence /ˈprevələns/ *n.* Vorherrschen, *das*

prevalent /ˈprevələnt/ *adj.* **(a)** (existing) herrschend; weit verbreitet ‹*Krankheit*›
(b) (predominant) vorherrschend

prevent /prɪˈvent/ *v.t.* (hinder) verhindern; (forestall) vorbeugen; **~ sb. from doing sth., ~ sb.'s doing sth.,** (coll.) **~ sb. doing sth.** jmdn. daran hindern, etw. zu tun

preventable /prɪˈventəbl/ *adj.* vermeidbar

prevention /prɪˈvenʃn/ *n.* Verhinderung, *die;* (forestalling) Vorbeugung, *die*

preventive /prɪ'ventɪv/ *adj.* vorbeugend; Präventiv‹*maßnahme*›
preventive 'medicine *n.* Präventivmedizin, *die*
preview /'pri:vju:/ *n.* (of film, play) Voraufführung, *die;* (of exhibition) Vernissage, *die* (geh.)
previous /'pri:vɪəs/ [1] *adj.* **(a)** früher ‹*Anstellung, Gelegenheit*›; vorherig ‹*Abend*›; vorig ‹*Besitzer, Wohnsitz*›; **the ~ page** die Seite davor
(b) (prior) **~ to** vor (+ *Dat.*)
[2] *adv.* **~ to** vor (+ *Dat.*)
'previously *adv.* vorher
pre-war /'pri:wɔ:(r)/ *adj.* Vorkriegs-
prey /preɪ/ [1] *n., pl. same* **(a)** (animal[s]) Beute, *die;* **beast/bird of ~**: Raubtier, *das*/ -vogel, *der*
(b) (victim) Opfer, *das*
[2] *v.i.* **~ [up]on** ‹*Raubtier, Raubvogel:*› schlagen; (plunder) ausplündern ‹*Person*›; Jagd machen auf (+ *Akk.*); **~ [up]on sb.'s mind** jmdm. keine Ruhe lassen
price /praɪs/ *n.* (lit. or fig.) Preis, *der;* **at a ~ of** zum Preis von; **what is the ~ of this?** was kostet das?; **at/not at any ~**: um jeden/ keinen Preis
price: ~ bracket ▶ **~** RANGE; **~ cut** *n.* Preissenkung, *die;* **~-cutting** *n.* Preisschleuderei, *die;* **~ increase** *n.* Preiserhöhung, *die*
'priceless *adj.* **(a)** (invaluable) unbezahlbar; **(b)** (coll.: amusing) köstlich
price: ~ list *n.* Preisliste, *die;* **~ range** *n.* Preisspanne, *die;* **~ rise** *n.* Preisanstieg, *der;* **~ tag** *n.* Preisschild, *das;* **~ war** *n.* Preiskrieg, *der*
pricey /'praɪsɪ/ *adj.* (Brit. coll.) teuer
prick /prɪk/ [1] *v.t.* stechen; stechen in ‹*Ballon*›; aufstechen ‹*Blase*›
[2] *v.i.* stechen
[3] *n.* Stich, *der*
■ **'prick up** *v.t.* aufrichten ‹*Ohren*›; **~ up one's/its ears** die Ohren spitzen
prickle /'prɪkl/ [1] *n.* **(a)** Dorn, *der*
(b) (Zool., Bot.) Stachel, *der*
[2] *v.i.* kratzen
prickly /'prɪklɪ/ *adj.* dornig; stachelig; (fig.) empfindlich
pride /praɪd/ [1] *n.* **(a)** Stolz, *der;* (arrogance) Hochmut, *der;* **take [a] ~ in sb./sth.** auf jmdn./etw. stolz sein; **sb's ~ and joy** jmds. ganzer Stolz
(b) (of lions) Rudel, *das*
[2] *v. refl.* **~ oneself [up]on sth.** auf etw. (*Akk.*) stolz sein
pried ▶ PRY
priest /pri:st/ *n.* Priester, *der*
'priesthood *n.* geistliches Amt
prig /prɪg/ *n.* Tugendbold, *der* (ugs., iron.)
priggish /'prɪgɪʃ/ *adj.* übertrieben tugendhaft
prim /prɪm/ *adj.* spröde; (prudish) zimperlich
primarily /'praɪmərɪlɪ/ *adv.* in erster Linie
primary /'praɪmərɪ/ [1] *adj.* **(a)** (first) primär (geh.); grundlegend
(b) (chief) Haupt‹*rolle, -ziel, -zweck*›
[2] *n.* (Amer.: election) Vorwahl, *die*
'primary school *n.* Grundschule, *die*
primate /'praɪmeɪt/ *n.* **(a)** (Eccl.) Primas, *der*
(b) (Zool.) Primat, *der*
prime¹ /praɪm/ [1] *n.* Höhepunkt, *der;* **be in one's ~**: in den besten Jahren sein
[2] *adj.* **(a)** Haupt-; hauptsächlich
(b) (excellent) erstklassig; vortrefflich ‹*Beispiel*›
prime² *v.t.* **(a)** (equip) vorbereiten; **~ sb. with information/advice** jmdn. instruieren/ jmdm. Ratschläge erteilen
(b) grundieren ‹*Wand, Decke*›
(c) schärfen ‹*Sprengkörper*›
prime: ~ 'minister *n.* Premierminister, *der*/-ministerin, *die;* **~ 'number** *n.* (Math.) Primzahl, *die*
'primer *n.* **(a)** (explosive) Zündvorrichtung, *die*
(b) (paint) Grundierlack, *der*
'prime time *n.* Hauptsendezeit, *die;* **~-time TV** Hauptsendezeit im Fernsehen
primeval /praɪ'mi:vl/ *adj.* urzeitlich; Ur‹*zeiten, -wälder*›
primitive /'prɪmɪtɪv/ *adj.* primitiv; (prehistoric) urzeitlich ‹*Mensch*›
primrose /'prɪmrəʊz/ *n.* gelbe Schlüsselblume
Primus ® /'praɪməs/ *n.* **~ [stove]** Primuskocher, *der*
prince /prɪns/ *n.* Prinz, *der*
'princely *adj.* fürstlich
princess /prɪn'ses/ *n.* Prinzessin, *die*
principal /'prɪnsɪpl/ [1] *adj.* Haupt-; (most important) wichtigst...
[2] *n.* (of college) Rektor, *der*/Rektorin, *die*
principality /prɪnsɪ'pælɪtɪ/ *n.* Fürstentum, *das*
'principally *adv.* in erster Linie
principle /'prɪnsɪpl/ *n.* Prinzip, *das;* **on the ~ that ...**: nach dem Grundsatz, dass ...; **in ~**: im Prinzip; **do sth. on ~** *or* **as a matter of ~**: etw. prinzipiell *od.* aus Prinzip tun
print /prɪnt/ [1] *n.* **(a)** (impression) Abdruck, *der;* (finger~) Fingerabdruck, *der*
(b) (~ed lettering) Gedruckte, *das;* (typeface) Druck, *der*
(c) be in/out of ~ ‹*Buch:*› erhältlich/ vergriffen sein
(d) (~ed picture or design) Druck, *der*
(e) (Photog.) Abzug, *der*
[2] *v.t.* **(a)** drucken ‹*Buch, Zeitschrift usw.*›
(b) (write) in Druckschrift schreiben
■ **print 'out** *v.t.* (Comp.) ausdrucken
'printed *adj.* **(a)** gedruckt
(b) (published) veröffentlicht
'printed matter *n.* (Post) Drucksachen *Pl.*
'printer *n.* **(a)** (worker) Drucker, *der*/ Druckerin, *die;* (firm) Druckerei, *die*

(b) (Comp.) Drucker, *der*

'printing *n.* **(a)** Drucken, *das*
(b) (writing like print) Druckschrift, *die*
(c) (edition) Auflage, *die*

'printing press *n.* Druckerpresse, *die*

print: ~out *n.* (Comp.) Ausdruck, *der;* **~ run** *n.* (Publishing) Auflage, die; **what is the ~ run?** wie hoch ist die Auflage?

prion /'pri:ɒn/ *n.* (Biol.) Prion, *das*

prior /'praɪə(r)/ **1** *adj.* vorherig ‹*Warnung, Zustimmung usw.*›; früher ‹*Verabredung*›; Vor‹*geschichte, -kenntnis*›
2 *adv.* **~ to** vor (+ *Dat.*); **~ to doing sth.** bevor man etw. tut/tat; **~ to that** vorher

priority /praɪ'ɒrɪtɪ/ *n.* **(a)** (precedence) Vorrang, *der; attrib.* vorrangig; **have** *or* **take ~:** Vorrang haben (**over** vor + *Dat.*); **have ~** (on road) Vorfahrt haben; **give ~ to sb./sth.** jmdm./einer Sache den Vorrang geben; **give top ~ to sth.** einer Sache (*Dat.*) höchste Priorität einräumen
(b) (matter) vordringliche Angelegenheit

prioritize (**prioritise**) /praɪ'ɒrɪtaɪz/ *v.t.* nach Vordringlichkeit ordnen

prism /'prɪzm/ *n.* Prisma, *das*

prison /'prɪzn/ *n.* **(a)** Gefängnis, *das; attrib.* Gefängnis-
(b) (custody) Haft, *die;* **in ~:** im Gefängnis; **go to ~:** ins Gefängnis gehen

'prison camp *n.* Gefangenenlager, *das*

'prisoner *n.* Gefangene, *der/die;* **take sb. ~:** jmdn. gefangen nehmen

prisoner of 'war *n.* Kriegsgefangene, *der/die*

prison: ~ sentence *n.* Gefängnisstrafe, *die;* **~ service** *n.* Strafvollzugsbehörde, *die*

pristine /'prɪsti:n/ *adj.* unberührt; **in ~ condition** in tadellosem Zustand

privacy /'prɪvəsɪ/ *n.* Privatsphäre, *die;* (being undisturbed) Ungestörtheit, *die;* **invasion of ~:** Eindringen in die Privatsphäre; **in the strictest ~:** unter strengster Geheimhaltung

private /'praɪvət/ **1** *adj.* **(a)** (outside State system) privat; Privat‹*schule, -industrie, -klinik usw.*›
(b) persönlich ‹*Dinge, Meinung, Interesse*›; nichtöffentlich ‹*Versammlung, Sitzung*›; privat ‹*Telefongespräch, Vereinbarung*›; Privat‹*strand, -parkplatz, -leben*›; geheim ‹*Verhandlung, Geschäft*›; persönlich ‹*Gründe*›; (confidential) vertraulich
2 *n.* **(a)** (Brit. Mil.) einfacher Soldat
(b) in ~: privat; in kleinem Kreis ‹*feiern*›; (confidentially) ganz im Vertrauen

private: ~ de'tective *n.* [Privat]detektiv, *der*/-detektivin, *die;* **~ 'enterprise** *n.* das freie Unternehmertum; **[spirit of] ~ enterprise** (fig.) Unternehmungsgeist, *der;* **~ 'income** *n.* private Einkünfte *Pl.*; **~ investigator** *n.* Privatdetektiv, *der*/-detektivin, *die*

'privately *adv.* privat ‹*erziehen, zugeben*›; vertraulich ‹*jmdn. sprechen*›; insgeheim ‹*denken, glauben*›; **~ owned** in Privatbesitz

private: ~ 'parts *n. pl.* Geschlechtsteile *Pl.;* **~ 'practice** *n.* (Med.) Privatpraxis, *die;* **~ 'property** *n.* Privateigentum, *das;* **~ 'view[ing]** *n.* (Art) Vernissage, *die*

privation /praɪ'veɪʃn/ *n.* Not, *die;* **suffer many ~s** viele Entbehrungen erleiden

privatize /'praɪvətaɪz/ *v.t.* privatisieren

privet /'prɪvɪt/ *n.* Liguster, *der*

privilege /'prɪvɪlɪdʒ/ *n.* (right, immunity) Privileg, *das;* (special benefit) Sonderrecht, *das;* (honour) Ehre, *die*

'privileged *adj.* privilegiert

privy /'prɪvɪ/ *adj.* **be ~ to sth.** in etw. (*Akk.*) eingeweiht sein

prize¹ /praɪz/ **1** *n.* **(a)** (reward, money) Preis, *der;* **win** *or* **take first ~:** den ersten Preis gewinnen
(b) (in lottery) Gewinn, *der*
2 *v.t.* **~ sth. [highly]** etw. hoch schätzen

prize² *v.t.* **~ [open]** aufstemmen

prize: ~-giving *n.* Preisverleihung, *die;* **~ money** *n.* Geldpreis, *der;* (Sport) Preisgeld, *das;* **~winner** *n.* Preisträger, *der*/-trägerin, *die;* (in lottery) Gewinner, *der*/Gewinnerin, *die*

pro /prəʊ/ *n. in pl.* **the ~s and cons** das Pro und Kontra

proactive /prəʊ'æktɪv/ *adj.* aktiv ‹*Haltung, Rolle*›; **be ~** ‹*Person:*› [selbst] die Initiative ergreifen

probability /prɒbə'bɪlɪtɪ/ *n.* Wahrscheinlichkeit, *die;* **in all ~:** aller Wahrscheinlichkeit nach

probable /'prɒbəbl/ *adj.* wahrscheinlich; **highly ~:** höchstwahrscheinlich

probably /'prɒbəblɪ/ *adv.* wahrscheinlich

probation /prə'beɪʃn/ *n.* **(a)** Probezeit, *die*
(b) (Law) Bewährung, *die;* **on ~:** auf Bewährung

probationary /prə'beɪʃənərɪ/ *adj.* Probe-; **~ period** Probezeit, *die*

pro'bation officer *n.* Bewährungshelfer, *der*/-helferin, *die*

probe /prəʊb/ **1** *n.* **(a)** Untersuchung, *die* (into *Gen.*)
(b) (Med., Astron.) Sonde, *die*
2 *v.t.* untersuchen

problem /'prɒbləm/ *n.* Problem, *das;* (puzzle) Rätsel, *das;* **what's the ~?** (coll.) wo fehlts denn?; **the ~ about** *or* **with sb./sth.** das Problem mit jmdm./bei etw.

problematic /prɒblə'mætɪk/, **problematical** /prɒblə'mætɪkl/ *adj.* problematisch

procedure /prə'si:djə(r)/ *n.* Verfahren, *das*

proceed /prə'si:d/ *v.i.* (formal) **(a)** (on foot) gehen; (as or by vehicle) fahren; (after interruption) weitergehen/-fahren ···›

(b) (begin and carry on) beginnen; (after interruption) fortfahren; **~ in** *or* **with sth.** (begin) [mit] etw. beginnen; (continue) etw. fortsetzen
(c) (be under way) ‹*Verfahren:*› laufen; (be continued after interruption) fortgesetzt werden

pro'ceedings *n. pl.* **(a)** (events) Vorgänge *Pl.*
(b) (Law) Verfahren, *das;* **legal ~:** Gerichtsverfahren, *das;* **start/take [legal] ~:** gerichtlich vorgehen (**against** gegen)

proceeds /'prəʊsi:dz/ *n. pl.* Erlös, *der* (**from** aus)

process¹ /'prəʊses/ **1** *n.* **(a)** (of time or history) Lauf, *der;* **he learnt a lot in the ~:** er lernte eine Menge dabei; **be in the ~ of doing sth.** gerade etw. tun
(b) (proceeding, natural operation) Vorgang, *der*
(c) (method) Verfahren, *das*
2 *v.t.* verarbeiten ‹*Rohstoff, Signal, Daten*›; bearbeiten ‹*Antrag, Akte*›; (Photog.) entwickeln ‹*Film*›

process² /prəʊ'ses/ *v.i.* ziehen

'process cheese (Amer.), **'processed cheese** *ns.* Schmelzkäse, *der*

procession /prə'seʃn/ *n.* Zug, *der;* (religious) Prozession, *die;* (festive) Umzug, *der;* **go/march in ~:** ziehen

proclaim /prə'kleɪm/ *v.t.* erklären ‹*Absicht*›; geltend machen ‹*Recht, Anspruch*›; verkünden ‹*Amnestie*›; ausrufen ‹*Republik*›

proclamation /prɒklə'meɪʃn/ *n.* **(a)** (proclaiming) Verkündung, *die*
(b) (notice) Bekanntmachung, *die;* (decree) Erlass, *der*

procreation /prəʊkrɪ'eɪʃn/ *n.* Fortpflanzung, *die*

procure /prə'kjʊə(r)/ *v.t.* beschaffen

prod /prɒd/ **1** *v.t.*, **-dd-** (poke) stupsen (ugs.); stoßen mit ‹*Stock, Finger usw.*›; **~ sb. gently** jmdn. anstupsen
2 *n.* Stupser, *der;* **give sb. a ~:** jmdm. einen Stupser geben

prodigal /'prɒdɪgl/ *adj.* verschwenderisch; **~ son** verlorener Sohn

prodigious /prə'dɪdʒəs/ *adj.* ungeheuer

prodigy /'prɒdɪdʒɪ/ *n.* [außergewöhnliches] Talent; **child ~:** Wunderkind, *das*

produce **1** /'prɒdju:s/ *n.* Produkte *Pl.;* Erzeugnisse *Pl.*
2 /prə'dju:s/ *v.t.* **(a)** vorzeigen ‹*Pass, Fahrkarte*›
(b) produzieren ‹*Show, Film*›; inszenieren ‹*Theaterstück, Hörspiel*›; herausgeben ‹*Schallplatte, Buch*›
(c) (manufacture) herstellen; (in nature; Agric.) produzieren
(d) (cause) hervorrufen; bewirken ‹*Änderung*›
(e) (bring into being) erzeugen; führen zu ‹*Situation*›
(f) (yield) geben ‹*Milch*›; legen ‹*Eier*›
(g) ‹*Baum, Blume:*› tragen ‹*Früchte, Blüten*›; entwickeln ‹*Triebe*›; bilden ‹*Keime*›

producer /prə'dju:sə(r)/ *n.* **(a)** (Cinemat., Theatre, Radio, Telev.) Produzent, *der*/Produzentin, *die*
(b) (Brit. Theatre/Radio/Telev.) Regisseur, *der*/Regisseurin, *die*

product /'prɒdʌkt/ *n.* **(a)** Produkt, *das;* (of industrial process) Erzeugnis, *das;* (of art or intellect) Werk, *das*
(b) (result) Folge, *die*
(c) (Math.) Produkt, *das* (**of** aus)

production /prə'dʌkʃn/ *n.* **(a)** (Cinemat.) Produktion, *die;* (Theatre) Inszenierung, *die;* (of record, book) Herausgabe, *die*
(b) (making) Produktion, *die;* (manufacturing) Herstellung, *die;* (thing produced) Produkt, *das;* (thing created) Werk, *das*
(c) (yielding) Produktion, *die;* (yield) Ertrag, *der*

production: ~ line *n.* Fertigungsstraße, *die;* **~ manager** *n.* Produktionsleiter, *der*/-leiterin, *die*

productive /prə'dʌktɪv/ *adj.* leistungsfähig ‹*Betrieb, Bauernhof*›; fruchtbar ‹*Gespräch, Verhandlungen*›

productivity /prɒdʌk'tɪvɪtɪ/ *n.* Produktivität, *die*

'product range *n.* Produktpalette, *die*

Prof. /prɒf/ *abbr.* = **Professor** Prof.

profane /prə'feɪn/ *adj.* **(a)** (irreligious) gotteslästerlich
(b) (secular) weltlich
(c) (irreverent) respektlos ‹*Bemerkung*›; profan ‹*Sprache*›

profess /prə'fes/ *v.t.* **(a)** (declare openly) bekunden ‹*Vorliebe, Abneigung*›; **~ to be/do sth.** erklären, etw. zu sein/tun
(b) (claim) vorgeben; **~ to be/do sth.** behaupten, etw. zu sein/tun

profession /prə'feʃn/ *n.* **(a)** Beruf, *der;* **be a pilot by ~:** von Beruf Pilot sein
(b) (body of people) Berufsstand, *der*

professional /prə'feʃənl/ **1** *adj.* **(a)** Berufs‹*ausbildung, -leben*›; beruflich ‹*Qualifikation*›
(b) (worthy of profession) (in technical expertise) fachmännisch; (in attitude) professionell; (in experience) routiniert
(c) ~ people Angehörige *Pl.* hoch qualifizierter Berufe
(d) (by profession) gelernt; (not amateur) Berufs‹*musiker, -sportler*›; Profi‹*sportler*›
(e) (paid) Profi‹*sport, -boxen*›
2 *n.* (trained person) Fachmann, *der*/Fachfrau, *die;* (non-amateur; also Sport) Profi, *der*

professor /prə'fesə(r)/ *n.* **(a)** (Univ.) Professor, *der*/Professorin, *die* (**of** für)
(b) (Amer.: teacher at university) Dozent, *der*/Dozentin, *die*

proficiency /prə'fɪʃənsɪ/ *n.* Können, *das*

proficient /prə'fɪʃənt/ *adj.* fähig; gut ‹*Pianist, Reiter usw.*›; geschickt ‹*Radfahrer, Handwerker*›; **be ~ at** *or* **in maths** viel von Mathematik verstehen

profile /'prəʊfaɪl/ *n.* **(a)** (side aspect) Profil, *das*

(b) (biographical sketch) Porträt, *das*
(c) (fig.) **keep a low ~:** sich zurückhalten

profit /'prɒfɪt/ *n.* Gewinn, *der;* Profit, *der;* **make a ~ from** *or* **out of sth.** mit etw. Geld verdienen; **make [a few pence] ~ on sth.** [ein paar Pfennige] an etw. (*Dat.*) verdienen; **~ and loss** Gewinn und Verlust; **~-and-loss account** Gewinn-und-Verlust-Rechnung, *die*

■ **'profit by** *v.t.* profitieren von; Nutzen ziehen aus ‹*Fehler, Erfahrung*›

■ **'profit from** *v.t.* profitieren von

profitable /'prɒfɪtəbl/ *adj.* rentabel; einträglich; (fruitful) nützlich

profiteer /prɒfɪ'tɪə(r)/ 1 *n.* Profitmacher, *der*/-macherin, *die*
2 *v.i.* sich bereichern

profi'teering *n.* Wucher, *der*

profit: ~ margin *n.* Gewinnspanne, *die;* **~-sharing** *n.* Gewinnbeteiligung, *die*

profligate /'prɒflɪgət/ *adj.* verschwenderisch; **be ~ of** *or* **with sth.** verschwenderisch umgehen mit etw.

profound /prə'faʊnd/ *adj.* tief; nachhaltig ‹*Wirkung, Einfluss*›; tief greifend ‹*Wandel, Veränderung*›; tief empfunden ‹*Beileid, Mitgefühl*›; tief sitzend ‹*Misstrauen*›

prognosis /prɒg'nəʊsɪs/ *n., pl.* **prognoses** /prɒg'nəʊsi:z/ Prognose, *die*

program /'prəʊgræm/ 1 *n.* **(a)** (Amer.) ▶ PROGRAMME 1
(b) (Comp.) Programm, *das;* **~ file** Programmdata, *die*
2 *v.t.,* **-mm-** (Comp.) programmieren

programme /'prəʊgræm/ *n.* **(a)** ([notice of] events) Programm, *das*
(b) (Radio, Telev.) Sendung, *die*
(c) (plan, instructions for machine) Programm, *das*

programmer /'prəʊgræmə(r)/ *n.* (Comp.) Programmierer, *der*/Programmiererin, *die*

progress 1 /'prəʊgres/ *n.* **(a)** *no pl., no indef. art.* (onward movement) [Vorwärts]bewegung, *die*
(b) (advance) Fortschritt, *der;* **make ~:** vorankommen; ‹*Student, Patient:*› Fortschritte machen; **in ~:** im Gange
2 /prə'gres/ *v.i.* **(a)** (move forward) vorankommen
(b) (be carried on, develop) Fortschritte machen

progression /prə'greʃn/ *n.* **(a)** (development) Fortschritt, *der*
(b) (succession) Folge, *die*

progressive /prə'gresɪv/ *adj.* **(a)** fortschreitend ‹*Verbesserung, Verschlechterung*›; schrittweise ‹*Reform*›; allmählich ‹*Veränderung*›
(b) (favouring reform; in culture) fortschrittlich; progressiv

pro'gressively *adv.* immer ‹*schlechter, weiter*›

prohibit /prə'hɪbɪt/ *v.t.* (forbid) verbieten; **~ sb.'s doing sth., ~ sb. from doing sth.** jmdm. verbieten, etw. zu tun

prohibition /prəʊhɪ'bɪʃn, prəʊɪ'bɪʃn/ *n.* Verbot, *das*

prohibitive /prə'hɪbɪtɪv/ *adj.* unerschwinglich ‹*Preis, Miete*›; untragbar ‹*Kosten*›

project 1 /prə'dʒekt/ *v.t.* werfen ‹*Schein*›; senden ‹*Strahl*›; (Cinemat.) projizieren
2 /prə'dʒekt/ *v.i.* (jut out) ‹*Felsen:*› vorspringen; ‹*Zähne, Brauen:*› vorstehen
3 /'prɒdʒekt/ *n.* Projekt, *das*

projectile /prə'dʒektaɪl/ *n.* Geschoss, *das*

projection /prə'dʒekʃn/ *n.* **(a)** (protruding thing) Vorsprung, *der*
(b) (estimate) Hochrechnung, *die;* (forecast) Voraussage, *die*

projectionist /prə'dʒekʃənɪst/ *n.* (Cinemat.) Filmvorführer, *der*/-vorführerin, *die*

pro'jection room *n.* (Cinemat.) Vorführraum, *der*

projector /prə'dʒektə(r)/ *n.* Projektor, *der*

proletarian /prəʊlɪ'teərɪən/ 1 *adj.* proletarisch
2 *n.* Proletarier, *der*/Proletarierin, *die*

'pro-life *adj.* Lebensschutz-

'pro-lifer *n.* Verfechter, *der*/Verfechterin, *die* des Rechts auf Leben

proliferate /prə'lɪfəreɪt/ *v.i.* (increase) sich ausbreiten

proliferation /prəlɪfə'reɪʃn/ *n.* starke Zunahme

prolific /prə'lɪfɪk/ *adj.* **(a)** (fertile) fruchtbar
(b) (productive) produktiv

prologue (*Amer.:* **prolog**) /'prəʊlɒg/ *n.* Prolog, *der* (**to** zu)

prolong /prə'lɒŋ/ *v.t.* verlängern

prolonged /prə'lɒŋd/ *adj.* lang; lang anhaltend ‹*Beifall*›

promenade /prɒmə'nɑ:d/ *n.* Promenade, *die*

prominence /'prɒmɪnəns/ *n.* **(a)** (conspicuousness) Auffälligkeit, *die*
(b) (distinction) Bekanntheit, *die*

prominent /'prɒmɪnənt/ *adj.* **(a)** (conspicuous) auffallend
(b) (foremost) herausragend; **he was ~ in politics** er war ein prominenter Politiker
(c) (projecting) vorspringend; vorstehend ‹*Backenknochen, Brauen*›

promiscuity /prɒmɪ'skju:ɪtɪ/ *n.* Promiskuität, *die* (geh.)

promiscuous /prə'mɪskjʊəs/ *adj.* promiskuitiv (geh.); **a ~ man** ein Mann, der häufig die Partnerin wechselt

promise /'prɒmɪs/ 1 *n.* **(a)** Versprechen, *das;* **sb.'s ~s** jmds. Versprechungen; **give** *or* **make a ~ [to sb.]** [jmdm.] ein Versprechen geben; **give** *or* **make a ~ [to sb.] to do sth.** [jmdm.] versprechen, etw. zu tun
(b) (fig.: reason for expectation) Hoffnung, *die;* **a painter of** *or* **with ~:** ein viel versprechender Maler
2 *v.t.* **(a)** versprechen; **~ sth. to sb., ~ sb. sth.** jmdm. etw. versprechen

···

(b) (fig.: give reason for expectation of) verheißen (geh.); **~ sb. sth.** jmdm. etw. in Aussicht stellen
3 *v.i.* **~ well** *or* **favourably** viel versprechend sein; **I can't ~:** ich kann es nicht versprechen

promising /'prɒmɪsɪŋ/ *adj.* viel versprechend

promote /prə'məʊt/ *v.t.* **(a)** (to more senior job) befördern
(b) (encourage) fördern
(c) (publicize) Werbung machen für
(d) (Footb.) **be ~d** aufsteigen

pro'moter *n.* Veranstalter, *der*/ Veranstalterin, *die*

promotion /prə'məʊʃn/ *n.* **(a)** Beförderung, *die;* **win** *or* **gain ~:** befördert werden
(b) (furtherance) Förderung, *die*
(c) (publicization) Werbung, *die;* (instance) Werbekampagne, *die*
(d) (Footb.) Aufstieg, *der*

promotional /prə'məʊʃənl/ *adj.* Werbe‹*kampagne, -broschüre usw.*›

prompt /prɒmpt/ **1** *adj.* **(a)** (ready to act) bereitwillig; **be ~ in doing sth.** *or* **to do sth.** etw. unverzüglich tun
(b) (done readily) sofortig; **her ~ answer** ihre prompte Antwort; **take ~ action** sofort handeln
(c) (punctual) pünktlich
2 *adv.* pünktlich; **at 6 o'clock ~:** Punkt 6 Uhr
3 *v.t.* **(a)** (incite) veranlassen
(b) (supply with words) souffliren (+ *Dat.*); (give suggestion to) weiterhelfen (+ *Dat.*)
(c) hervorrufen ‹*Kritik*›; provozieren ‹*Antwort*›

'promptly *adv.* **(a)** (quickly) prompt
(b) (punctually) pünktlich

prone /prəʊn/ *adj.* (liable) **be ~ to** anfällig sein für ‹*Krankheiten*›; **be ~ to do sth.** dazu neigen, etw. zu tun

prong /prɒŋ/ *n.* (of fork) Zinke, *die*

pronoun /'prəʊnaʊn/ *n.* (Ling.) Pronomen, *das;* Fürwort, *das*

pronounce /prə'naʊns/ **1** *v.t.* **(a)** (declare) verkünden; **~ sb./sth. [to be] sth.** jmdn./etw. für etw. erklären; **~ sb. fit for work** jmdn. für arbeitsfähig erklären
(b) aussprechen ‹*Wort, Buchstaben usw.*›
2 *v.i.* **~ on sth.** zu etw. Stellung nehmen; **~ for** *or* **in favour of/against sth.** sich für/ gegen etw. aussprechen

pronounced /prə'naʊnst/ *adj.* (marked) ausgeprägt

pro'nouncement *n.* Erklärung, *die;* **make a ~ [about sth.]** eine Erklärung [zu etw.] abgeben

pronunciation /prənʌnsɪ'eɪʃn/ *n.* Aussprache, *die;* **what is the ~ of this word?** wie wird dieses Wort ausgesprochen?

proof /pru:f/ **1** *n.* **(a)** (fact, evidence) Beweis, *der*
(b) *no indef. art.* (Law) Beweismaterial, *das*
(c) (proving) **in ~ of** zum Beweis (+ *Gen.*)
(d) *no art.* (standard of strength) Proof *o. Art.;* **100° ~** (Brit.), **128° ~** (Amer.) 64 Vol.-% Alkohol
(e) (Printing) [Korrektur]abzug, *der*
2 *adj.* **(a) be ~ against sth.** unempfindlich gegen etw. sein; (fig.) gegen etw. immun sein
(b) *in comb.* ‹*kugel-, einbruch-, idioten*›sicher; ‹*schall-, wasser*›dicht; **flame-~:** nicht brennbar

proof ~-read *v.t.* Korrektur lesen; **~-reader** *n.* Korrektor, *der*/Korrektorin, *die*

prop¹ /prɒp/ **1** *n.* Stütze, *die;* (Mining) Strebe, *die*
2 *v.t.*, **-pp-** stützen; **the ladder was ~ped against the house** die Leiter war gegen das Haus gelehnt
■ **prop 'up** *v.t.* stützen; (fig.) vor dem Konkurs bewahren ‹*Firma*›; stützen ‹*Regierung*›

prop² *n.* (Theatre, Cinemat.: also fig.) Requisit, *das*

propaganda /prɒpə'gændə/ *n.* Propaganda, *die*

propagate /'prɒpəgeɪt/ **1** *v.t.* **(a)** (Hort., Agric.) vermehren (**from, by** durch)
(b) (spread) verbreiten
2 *v.i.* **(a)** (Bot.) sich vermehren
(b) (spread) sich ausbreiten

propagation /prɒpə'geɪʃn/ *n.* **(a)** (Hort., Agric.) Züchtung, *die*
(b) (Bot.) Vermehrung, *die*
(c) (spreading) Verbreitung, *die*

propel /prə'pel/ *v.t.*, **-ll-** antreiben

propellant /prə'pelənt/ *n.* **(a)** Treibstoff, *der*
(b) (of aerosol spray) Treibgas, *das*

pro'peller *n.* Propeller, *der*

propelling 'pencil *n.* (Brit.) Drehbleistift, *der*

propensity /prə'pensɪtɪ/ *n.* **have a ~ to do sth.** *or* **for doing sth.** dazu neigen, etw. zu tun

proper /'prɒpə(r)/ *adj.* **(a)** (accurate) richtig; zutreffend ‹*Beschreibung*›; eigentlich ‹*Wortbedeutung*›
(b) *postpos.* (strictly so called) im engeren Sinn *nachgestellt;* **in London ~:** in London selbst
(c) (genuine) echt; richtig ‹*Wirbelsturm, Schauspieler*›
(d) (satisfactory) richtig; zufrieden stellend ‹*Antwort*›
(e) (suitable) angemessen; (morally fitting) gebührend; **do sth. the ~ way** etw. richtig machen
(f) *attrib.* (coll.: thorough) richtig

'properly *adv.* richtig; (rightly) zu Recht; **~ speaking** genau genommen

proper 'name, proper 'noun *ns.* (Ling.) Eigenname, *der*

property /'prɒpətɪ/ *n.* **(a)** (possession[s]) Eigentum, *das;* **lost ~ [department** *or* **office]** Fundbüro, *das*

(b) (estate) Besitz, *der;* Immobilie, *die* (fachspr.)
(c) (attribute) Eigenschaft, *die;* (effect, special power) Wirkung, *die*

'property developer *n.* ≈ Bauunternehmer, *der*/-unternehmerin, *die*

prophecy /'prɒfɪsɪ/ *n.* (prediction) Vorhersage, *die;* (prophetic utterance) Prophezeiung, *die*

prophesy /'prɒfɪsaɪ/ *v.t.* (predict) vorhersagen; (fig.) prophezeien ‹*Unglück*›; (as fortune teller) weissagen

prophet /'prɒfɪt/ *n.* Prophet, *der*

prophetic /prə'fetɪk/ *adj.* prophetisch

proportion /prə'pɔːʃn/ **1** *n.* **(a)** (portion) Teil, *der*
(b) (ratio) Verhältnis, *das;* **the ~ of sth. to sth.** das Verhältnis von etw. zu etw.
(c) (correct relation; Math.) Proportion, *die;* **be in ~ [to** *or* **with sth.]** im richtigen Verhältnis [zu *od.* mit etw.] stehen; **keep things in ~** (fig.) die Dinge im richtigen Licht sehen; **be out of ~/all** *or* **any ~ [to** *or* **with sth.]** in keinem/keinerlei Verhältnis zu etw. stehen
(d) *in pl.* (size) Dimensionen *Pl.*
2 *v.t.* proportionieren

proportional /prə'pɔːʃənl/ *adj.* **(a)** (in proportion) entsprechend; **be ~ to sth.** einer Sache (*Dat.*) entsprechen
(b) (Math.) **be directly/indirectly ~ to sth.** einer Sache (*Dat.*) direkt/umgekehrt proportional sein

proportionate /prə'pɔːʃənət/ ▶ PROPORTIONAL A

proposal /prə'pəʊzl/ *n.* Vorschlag, *der;* (offer) Angebot, *das;* **~ [of marriage]** [Heirats]antrag, *der*

propose /prə'pəʊz/ **1** *v.t.* **(a)** vorschlagen; **~ sth. to sb.** jmdm. etw. vorschlagen; **~ marriage [to sb.]** [jmdm.] einen Heiratsantrag machen
(b) (nominate) **~ sb. as/for sth.** jmdn. als/für etw. vorschlagen
(c) (intend) **~ doing** *or* **to do sth.** beabsichtigen, etw. zu tun
2 *v.i.* (offer marriage) **~ [to sb.]** jmdm. einen Heiratsantrag machen

proposition /prɒpə'zɪʃn/ *n.* **(a)** (proposal) Vorschlag, *der;* **make** *or* **put a ~ to sb.** jmdm. einen Vorschlag machen
(b) (statement; Logic) Aussage, *die*

propound /prə'paʊnd/ *v.t.* darlegen

proprietary /prə'praɪətərɪ/ *adj.* **~ name** *or* **term** Markenname, *der*

proprietor /prə'praɪətə(r)/ *n.* Inhaber, *der*/Inhaberin, *die*

propriety /prə'praɪətɪ/ *n.* Anstand, *der;* **breach of ~:** Verstoß gegen die guten Sitten

propulsion /prə'pʌlʃn/ *n.* Antrieb, *der*

prosaic /prə'zeɪɪk/ *adj.* prosaisch (geh.); nüchtern

proscribe /prə'skraɪb/ *v.t.* verbieten

prose /prəʊz/ *n.* Prosa, *die; attrib.* Prosa‹*werk, -stil*›

prosecute /'prɒsɪkjuːt/ **1** *v.t.* strafrechtlich verfolgen; **~ sb. for sth./doing sth.** jmdn. wegen etw. strafrechtlich verfolgen/jmdn. strafrechtlich verfolgen, weil er etw. tut/getan hat
2 *v.i.* Anzeige erstatten

prosecution /prɒsɪ'kjuːʃn/ *n.* (bringing to trial) [strafrechtliche] Verfolgung; (court procedure) Anklage, *die;* (prosecuting party) Anklage[vertretung], *die;* **the ~:** die Anklage

prosecutor /'prɒsɪkjuːtə(r)/ *n.* Ankläger, *der*/Anklägerin, *die;* **public ~** ≈ Generalstaatsanwalt, *der*/-anwältin, *die*

prospect **1** /'prɒspekt/ *n.* **(a)** (expectation) Erwartung, *die* (**of** hinsichtlich); **[at the] ~ of sth./doing sth.** [bei der] Aussicht auf etw. (*Akk.*)/[darauf], etw. zu tun
(b) *in pl.* (hope of success) Zukunftsaussichten *Pl.*; **a man with [good] ~s** ein Mann mit Zukunft; **sb.'s ~s of sth./doing sth.** jmds. Chancen auf etw. (*Akk.*)/darauf, etw. zu tun; **the ~s for sb./sth.** die Aussichten für jmdn./etw.
2 /prə'spekt/ *v.i.* nach Bodenschätzen suchen

prospective /prə'spektɪv/ *adj.* voraussichtlich; zukünftig ‹*Erbe, Braut*›; potenziell ‹*Käufer, Kandidat*›

prospector /prə'spektə(r)/ *n.* Prospektor, *der;* (for gold) Goldsucher, *der*

prospectus /prə'spektəs/ *n.* Prospekt, *der;* (Brit. Univ.) Studienführer, *der*

prosper /'prɒspə(r)/ *v.i.* gedeihen; ‹*Geschäft:*› florieren; ‹*Berufstätiger:*› Erfolg haben

prosperity /prɒ'sperɪtɪ/ *n.* Wohlstand, *der*

prosperous /'prɒspərəs/ *adj.* wohlhabend; florierend ‹*Unternehmen*›

prostitute /'prɒstɪtjuːt/ *n.* Prostituierte, *die*

prostitution /prɒstɪ'tjuːʃn/ *n.* Prostitution, *die*

prostrate **1** /'prɒstreɪt/ *adj.* [auf dem Bauch] ausgestreckt
2 /prə'streɪt/ *v. refl.* **~ oneself [at sth./before sb.]** sich [vor etw./jmdm.] niederwerfen

protagonist /prəʊ'tægənɪst/ *n.* (Lit.) Protagonist, *der*/Protagonistin, *die*

protect /prə'tekt/ *v.t.* **(a)** schützen (**from** vor + *Dat.*, **against** gegen)
(b) (preserve) unter [Natur]schutz stellen ‹*Pflanze, Tier*›

protection /prə'tekʃn/ *n.* Schutz, *der* (**from** vor + *Dat.*, **against** gegen)

protective /prə'tektɪv/ *adj.* schützend; Schutz‹*hülle, -anstrich, -vorrichtung, -maske*›; **be ~ towards sb.** fürsorglich gegenüber jmdm. sein

protein /'prəʊtiːn/ *n.* Protein, *das* (fachspr.); Eiweiß, *das*

protest 1 /'prəʊtest/ *n.* **(a)** Beschwerde, *die;* **make** *or* **lodge a ~ [against sb./sth.]** eine Beschwerde [gegen jmdn./etw.] einreichen **(b)** (gesture of disapproval) **~[s]** Protest, *der;* **under ~:** unter Protest; **in ~ [against sth.]** aus Protest [gegen etw.] **(c)** *no art.* (dissent) Protest, *der* 2 /prə'test/ *v.t.* (affirm) beteuern 3 /prə'test/ *v.i.* protestieren (**about** gegen); (make written or formal **~**) Protest einlegen (**to** bei)

Protestant /'prɒtɪstənt/ 1 *n.* Protestant, *der*/Protestantin, *die* 2 *adj.* protestantisch; evangelisch

Protestantism /'prɒtɪstəntɪzm/ *n., no art.* Protestantismus, *der*

pro'tester *n.* Protestierende, *der/die;* (at demonstration) Demonstrant, *der*/Demonstrantin, *die*

protocol /'prəʊtəkɒl/ *n.* Protokoll, *das*

proton /'prəʊtən/ *n.* Proton, *das*

prototype /'prəʊtətaɪp/ *n.* Prototyp, *der*

protract /prə'trækt/ *v.t.* verlängern

protractor /prə'træktə(r)/ *n.* (Geom.) Winkelmesser, *der*

protrude /prə'tru:d/ *v.i.* herausragen (**from** aus); ‹*Zähne*› vorstehen

protuberance /prə'tju:bərəns/ *n.* Auswuchs, *der*

proud /praʊd/ 1 *adj.* **(a)** stolz; **~ to do sth.** *or* **to be doing sth.** stolz darauf, etw. zu tun; **~ of sb./sth./doing sth.** stolz auf jmdn./etw./darauf, etw. zu tun **(b)** (arrogant) hochmütig 2 *adv.* (Brit. coll.) **do sb. ~:** jmdn. verwöhnen

'proudly *adv.* **(a)** stolz **(b)** (arrogantly) hochmütig

provable /'pru:vəbl/ *adj.* beweisbar

prove /pru:v/ 1 *v.t., p.p.* **~d** *or* **proven** /'pru:vn/ beweisen; nachweisen ‹*Identität*›; **~ one's ability** sein Können unter Beweis stellen; **~ sb. right/wrong** ‹*Ereignis:*› jmdm. recht/unrecht geben; **be ~d wrong** *or* **to be false** ‹*Theorie:*› widerlegt werden; **~ one's/sb.'s case** *or* **point** beweisen, dass man recht hat/jmdm. recht geben 2 *v. refl., p. p.* **proved** *or* **proven: ~ oneself** sich bewähren 3 *v.i., p. p.* **proved** *or* **proven: ~ [to be]** sich erweisen als

proven ▸ PROVE

proverb /'prɒvɜ:b/ *n.* Sprichwort, *das*

proverbial /prə'vɜ:bɪəl/ *adj.* sprichwörtlich

provide /prə'vaɪd/ *v.t.* **(a)** besorgen; liefern ‹*Beweis*›; bereitstellen ‹*Dienst, Geld*›; **~ a home/a car for sb.** jmdm. Unterkunft/ein Auto [zur Verfügung] stellen **(b)** ‹*Vertrag, Gesetz:*› vorsehen

■ **pro'vide for** *v.t.* **(a)** (make provision for) vorsorgen für; ‹*Plan, Gesetz:*› vorsehen **(b)** (maintain) sorgen für, versorgen ‹*Familie, Kind*›

pro'vided *conj.* **~ [that] ...:** vorausgesetzt, [dass] ...

providence /'prɒvɪdəns/ *n.* **(a) [divine] ~:** die [göttliche] Vorsehung **(b) P~** (God) der Himmel

province /'prɒvɪns/ *n.* **(a)** Provinz, *die* **(b) the ~s** (regions outside capital) die Provinz **(c)** (sphere of action) [Tätigkeits]bereich, *der;* (area of responsibility) Zuständigkeitsbereich, *der*

provincial /prə'vɪnʃl/ *adj.* Provinz-

provision /prə'vɪʒn/ *n.* **(a)** (providing) Bereitstellung, *die;* **make ~ for** vorsorgen *od.* Vorsorge treffen für ‹*Notfall*› **(b) ~s** *pl.* (food) Lebensmittel *Pl.*

provisional /prə'vɪʒənl/ *adj.*, **provisionally** /prə'vɪʒənəlɪ/ *adv.* vorläufig; provisorisch

proviso /prə'vaɪzəʊ/ *n., pl.* **~s** Vorbehalt, *der*

provocation /prɒvə'keɪʃn/ *n.* Provokation, *die*

provocative /prə'vɒkətɪv/ *adj.* provozierend; (sexually) aufreizend

provoke /prə'vəʊk/ *v.t.* **(a)** provozieren ‹*Person*›; reizen ‹*Person, Tier*›; **~ sb. into doing sth.** jmdn. so sehr provozieren, dass er etw. tut **(b)** (give rise to) hervorrufen; erregen

prow /praʊ/ *n.* (Naut.) Bug, *der*

prowl /praʊl/ 1 *v.i.* streifen 2 *v.t.* durchstreifen 3 *n.* **be on the ~:** auf einem Streifzug sein

proximity /prɒk'sɪmɪtɪ/ *n.* Nähe, *die*

proxy /'prɒksɪ/ *n.* **by ~:** durch einen Bevollmächtigten/eine Bevollmächtigte

prude /pru:d/ *n.* prüder Mensch

prudence /'pru:dəns/ *n.* Besonnenheit, *die*

prudent /'pru:dənt/ *adj.* **(a)** (careful) besonnen **(b)** (circumspect) vorsichtig

prudish /'pru:dɪʃ/ *adj.* prüde

prune¹ /pru:n/ *n.* Backpflaume, *die*

prune² *v.t.* **(a)** (trim) [be]schneiden **(b)** (fig.) reduzieren

pry /praɪ/ *v.i.* neugierig sein

■ **'pry into** *v.t.* seine Nase stecken in (+ *Akk.*) (ugs.) ‹*Angelegenheit*›

PS *abbr.* = **postscript** PS

psalm /sɑ:m/ *n.* Psalm, *der*

pseudo /'sju:dəʊ/ 1 *adj.* **(a)** (sham) unecht **(b)** (insincere) verlogen 2 *n., pl.* **~s** (pretentious person) Möchtegern, *der* (ugs. spött.)

pseudonym /'sju:dənɪm/ *n.* Pseudonym, *das*

psychiatric /saɪkɪ'ætrɪk/ *adj.* psychiatrisch

psychiatrist /saɪ'kaɪətrɪst/ *n.* Psychiater, *der*/Psychiaterin, *die*

psychiatry /saɪ'kaɪətrɪ/ *n.* Psychiatrie, *die*

psychic /'saɪkɪk/ *adj.* **be ~:** übernatürliche Fähigkeiten haben
psychoanalyse /saɪkəʊ'ænəlaɪz/ *v.t.* psychoanalysieren
psychoa'nalysis *n.* Psychoanalyse, *die*
psycho'analyst *n.* Psychoanalytiker, *der*/-analytikerin, *die*
psychological /saɪkə'lɒdʒɪkl/ *adj.* psychologisch; psychisch ‹*Problem*›
psychologist /saɪ'kɒlədʒɪst/ *n.* Psychologe, *der*/Psychologin, *die*
psychology /saɪ'kɒlədʒɪ/ *n.* Psychologie, *die*
psychopath /'saɪkəpæθ/ *n.* Psychopath, *der*/Psychopathin, *die*
psychopathic /saɪkə'pæθɪk/ *adj.* psychopathisch
psychosis /saɪ'kəʊsɪs/ *n., pl.* **psychoses** /saɪ'kəʊsi:z/ Psychose, *die*
psychotherapist /saɪkəʊ'θerəpɪst/ *n.* Psychotherapeut, *der*/-therapeutin, *die*
psycho'therapy *n.* Psychotherapie, *die*
psychotic /saɪ'kɒtɪk/ *adj.* psychotisch
PTO *abbr.* = **please turn over** b.w.
pub /ʌb/ *n.* (Brit. coll.) Kneipe, *die* (ugs.)
'pub crawl *n.* (Brit. coll.) Zechtour, *die* (ugs.)
puberty /'pju:bətɪ/ *n., no art.* Pubertät, *die*
'pub grub *n.* (Brit. coll.) Kneipenessen, *das* (ugs.)
pubic /'pju:bɪk/ *adj.* Scham-
public /'pʌblɪk/ **1** *adj.* öffentlich; **make sth. ~:** etw. bekannt machen
2 *n., sing. or pl.* **(a)** (the people) Öffentlichkeit, *die*
(b) (section of community) Publikum, *das*
(c) in ~: öffentlich
publican /'pʌblɪkən/ *n.* (Brit.) [Gast]wirt, *der*/-wirtin, *die*
publication /pʌblɪ'keɪʃn/ *n.* Veröffentlichung, *die*
public: ~ 'building *n.* öffentliches Gebäude; **~ con'venience** *n.* öffentliche Toilette; **~ 'figure** *n.* Persönlichkeit des öffentlichen Lebens; **~ 'footpath** *n.* öffentlicher Fußweg; **~ 'holiday** *n.* gesetzlicher Feiertag; **~ 'house** *n.* (Brit.) Gastwirtschaft, *die;* Gaststätte, *die*
publicity /pʌb'lɪsɪtɪ/ *n.* Publicity, *die;* (advertising) Werbung, *die;* **~ campaign** Werbekampagne, *die*
pub'licity agent *n.* Publicitymanager, *der*/-managerin, *die*
publicize /'pʌblɪsaɪz/ *v.t.* publik machen ‹*Ungerechtigkeit*›; werben für, Reklame machen für ‹*Produkt*›
public: ~ 'library *n.* öffentliche Bücherei; **~ limited company** *n.* (Brit.) ≈ Aktiengesellschaft, *die*
'publicly *adv.* öffentlich; **~ owned** staatseigen
public: ~ property *n.* Staatsbesitz, *der;* **~ re'lations** *n., sing. or pl.* Publicrelations *Pl.;* **~ school** *n.* **(a)** (Brit.) Privatschule, *die;* **(b)** (Scot., Amer.) staatliche *od.* öffentliche Schule; **~ 'servant** *n.* Inhaber/Inhaberin eines öffentlichen Amtes; **~ 'transport** *n.* öffentlicher Personenverkehr
publish /'pʌblɪʃ/ *v.t.* ‹*Verlag:*› verlegen ‹*Buch, Zeitschrift, Musik usw.*›; ‹*Autor:*› veröffentlichen ‹*Text*›
'publisher *n.* Verleger, *der*/Verlegerin, *die;* **~[s]** (company) Verlag, *der*
'publishing *n., no art.* Verlagswesen, *das*
puck /pʌk/ *n.* (Ice Hockey) Puck, *der*
pucker /'pʌkə(r)/ **1** *v.t.* **~ [up]** runzeln ‹*Brauen, Stirn*›; kräuseln ‹*Lippen*›
2 *v.i.* **~ [up]** ‹*Stoff:*› sich kräuseln
pudding /'pʊdɪŋ/ *n.* **(a)** Pudding, *der*
(b) (dessert) süße Nachspeise
puddle /'pʌdl/ *n.* Pfütze, *die*
puerile /'pjʊəraɪl/ *adj.* kindisch
puff /pʌf/ **1** *n.* **(a)** Stoß, *der;* **~ of breath/wind** Atem-/Windstoß, *der*
(b) ~ of smoke Rauchstoß, *der*
(c) (pastry) Blätterteigteilchen, *das*
2 *v.i.* **(a) ~ [and blow]** schnaufen [und keuchen]
(b) (~ cigarette smoke etc.) paffen (ugs.) (**at** an + *Dat.*)
(c) ‹*Person:*› keuchen; ‹*Zug, Lokomotive*› schnaufend fahren
3 *v.t.* blasen ‹*Rauch*›; stäuben ‹*Puder*›
■ **puff 'out** *v.t.* **(a)** bauschen ‹*Segel*›
(b) (put out of breath) außer Atem bringen ‹*Person*›; **be ~ed [out]** außer Atem sein
puff 'pastry *n.* Blätterteig, *der*
puffy /'pʌfɪ/ *adj.* verschwollen
pugnacious /pʌg'neɪʃəs/ *adj.* kampflustig
puke /pju:k/ (coarse) **1** *v.i.* kotzen (salopp)
2 *n.* Kotze, *die* (salopp)
pull /pʊl/ **1** *v.t.* **(a)** (draw, tug) ziehen an (+ *Dat.*); ziehen ‹*Hebel*›; **~ sb.'s** *or* **sb. by the hair/ears/sleeve** jmdn. an den Haaren/Ohren/am Ärmel ziehen; **~ sth. over one's ears/head** sich (*Dat.*) etw. über die Ohren/den Kopf ziehen; **~ to pieces** in Stücke reißen; (fig.) zerpflücken ‹*Argument usw.*›
(b) (extract) [her]ausziehen; [heraus]ziehen ‹*Zahn*›
(c) (strain) sich (*Dat.*) zerren ‹*Muskel*›
2 *v.i.* **(a)** ziehen; **'P~'** „Ziehen"
(b) ~ [to the left/right] ‹*Auto, Boot:*› [nach links/rechts] ziehen
(c) (pluck) **~ at** ziehen an (+ *Dat.*); **~ at sb.'s sleeve** jmdn. am Ärmel ziehen
3 *n.* **(a)** Zug, *der*
(b) (influence) Einfluss, *der* (**with** auf + *Akk.*, bei)
■ **pull a'part** *v.t.* **(a)** (take to pieces) auseinander nehmen
(b) (fig.: criticize) zerpflücken; verreißen ‹*Buch,* [*literarisches*] *Werk*›
■ **pull 'down** *v.t.* **(a)** herunterziehen
(b) (demolish) abreißen
■ **pull 'in** **1** *v.t.* hereinziehen

···›

[2] *v.i.* **(a)** ‹*Zug:*› einfahren
(b) (move to side of road) an die Seite fahren; (stop) anhalten
■ **pull 'off** *v.t.* **(a)** (remove) abziehen; (violently) abreißen
(b) (accomplish) an Land ziehen (ugs.)
■ **pull 'out** [1] *v.t.* herausziehen
[2] *v.i.* **(a)** (depart) abfahren
(b) (away from roadside) ausscheren
■ **pull 'through** *v.i.* ‹*Patient:*› durchkommen
■ **pull to'gether** *v. refl.* sich zusammennehmen
■ **pull 'up** [1] *v.t.* **(a)** hochziehen
(b) [he]rausziehen ‹*Unkraut, Pflanze*›
(c) (reprimand) zurechtweisen
[2] *v.i.* (stop) anhalten

'pull-down menu *n.* (Comp.) Pull-down-Menü, *das*

pulley /'pʊlɪ/ *n.* Rolle, *die*

pullover /'pʊləʊvə(r)/ *n.* Pullover, *der*

pulp /pʌlp/ [1] *n.* Brei, *der*
[2] *v.t.* zerdrücken ‹*Rübe*›; einstampfen ‹*Druckerzeugnis*›

pulpit /'pʊlpɪt/ *n.* Kanzel, *die*

pulsate /pʌl'seɪt/ *v.i.* pulsieren

pulse[1] /pʌls/ *n.* Puls, *der;* (single beat) Pulsschlag, *der*

pulse[2] *n.* (Cookery) Hülsenfrucht, *die*

'pulse rate *n.* Pulsfrequenz, *die*

pulverize /'pʌlvəraɪz/ *v.t.* pulverisieren

puma /'pju:mə/ *n.* Puma, *der*

pumice /'pʌmɪs/ *n.* ~ **[stone]** Bimsstein, *der*

pummel /'pʌml/ *v.t.*, (Brit) **-ll-** einschlagen auf (+ *Akk.*)

pump /pʌmp/ [1] *n.* Pumpe, *die*
[2] *v.i.* pumpen
[3] *v.t.* pumpen; ~ **sth. dry** etw. leer pumpen; ~ **sb. for information** Auskünfte aus jmdm. herausholen; ~ **up** aufpumpen

'pump-action *adj.* ~ **spray** Pumpspray, *das od. der*

pumpkin /'pʌmpkɪn/ *n.* Kürbis, *der*

pun /pʌn/ *n.* Wortspiel, *das*

punch[1] [1] *v.t.* **(a)** (with fist) boxen
(b) (pierce) lochen; ~ **a hole** ein Loch stanzen; ~ **a hole/holes in sth.** etw. lochen
[2] *n.* **(a)** (blow) Faustschlag, *der*
(b) (for making holes) (in leather, tickets) Lochzange, *die;* (in paper) Locher, *der*

punch[2] *n.* (drink) Punsch, *der*

punch: ~ **line** *n.* Pointe, *die;* **~-up** *n.* (Brit. coll.) Prügelei, *die*

punctual /'pʌŋktjʊəl/ *adj.* pünktlich

punctuality /pʌŋktjʊ'ælɪtɪ/ *n.* Pünktlichkeit, *die*

'punctually *adv.* pünktlich

punctuate /'pʌŋktjʊeɪt/ *v.t.* mit Satzzeichen versehen

punctuation /pʌŋktjʊ'eɪʃn/ *n.* Zeichensetzung, *die*

punctu'ation mark *n.* Satzzeichen, *das*

puncture /'pʌŋktʃə(r)/ [1] *n.* **(a)** (flat tyre) Reifenpanne, *die*
(b) (hole) Loch, *das*
[2] *v.t.* durchstechen; **be ~d** ‹*Reifen:*› platt sein

pundit /'pʌndɪt/ *n.* Experte, *der*/Expertin, *die*

pungent /'pʌndʒənt/ *adj.* beißend, ätzend ‹*Rauch*›; scharf ‹*Soße*›; stechend riechend ‹*Gas*›

punish /'pʌnɪʃ/ *v.t.* bestrafen

punishable /'pʌnɪʃəbl/ *adj.* strafbar

'punishment *n.* **(a)** (punishing) Bestrafung, *die*
(b) (penalty) Strafe, *die*

punitive /'pju:nɪtɪv/ *adj.* **(a)** (penal) Straf-
(b) (severe) [allzu] rigoros

punk /pʌŋk/ *n.* **(a)** (Amer. sl.: worthless person) Dreckskerl, *der* (salopp)
(b) (admirer of ~ rock) Punk, *der;* (performer) Punk[rock]er, *der*/-[rock]erin, *die*
(c) (music) Punkrock, *der*

punnet /'pʌnɪt/ *n.* (Brit.) Körbchen, *das*

punt /pʌnt/ *n.* Stechkahn, *der*

punter *n.* (coll.) **the ~s** (customers) die Leutchen (ugs.)

puny /'pju:nɪ/ *adj.* **(a)** (undersized) zu klein ‹*Baby, Junge*›
(b) (feeble) gering ‹*Kraft*›; schwach ‹*Waffe, Person*›

pup /pʌp/ *n.* Welpe, *der*

pupa /'pju:pə/ *n., pl.* **~e** /'pju:pi:/ Puppe, *die*

pupate /pju:'peɪt/ *v.i.* sich verpuppen

pupil /'pju:pɪl/ *n.* **(a)** Schüler, *der*/Schülerin, *die*
(b) (Anat.) Pupille, *die*

puppet /'pʌpɪt/ *n.* Puppe, *die;* (marionette; also fig.) Marionette, *die*

puppy /'pʌpɪ/ *n.* Hundejunge, *das;* Welpe, *der*

puppy: ~ **fat** *n.* (Brit.) Babyspeck, *der;*
~ **love** *n.* Jugendschwärmerei, *die*

purchase /'pɜ:tʃəs/ [1] *n.* **(a)** Kauf, *der;* **make a ~**: etwas kaufen
(b) (hold) Halt, *der;* (leverage) Hebelwirkung, *die*
[2] *v.t.* kaufen

'purchase price *n.* Kaufpreis, *der*

'purchaser *n.* Käufer, *der*/Käuferin, *die*

'purchasing power *n.* Kaufkraft, *die*

pure /pjʊə(r)/ *adj.* rein

purée /'pjʊəreɪ/ *n.* Püree, *das*

'purely *adv.* **(a)** (solely) rein
(b) (merely) lediglich

purgatory /'pɜ:gətərɪ/ *n.* **it was ~** (fig.) es war eine Strafe

purge /pɜ:dʒ/ [1] *v.t.* **(a)** (cleanse) reinigen **(of** von)
(b) (remove) entfernen
(c) (rid) säubern ‹*Partei*› **(of** von)
[2] *n.* Säuberung[saktion], *die*

purification /pjʊərɪfɪ'keɪʃn/ *n.* Reinigung, *die*

purify /'pjʊərɪfaɪ/ *v.t.* reinigen

purist /'pjʊərɪst/ *n.* Purist, *der*/Puristin, *die*

puritan, (Hist.) **Puritan** /'pjʊərɪtn/ *n.* Puritaner, *der*/Puritanerin, *die*

puritanical /pjʊərɪ'tænɪkl/ *adj.* puritanisch

purity /'pjʊərɪtɪ/ *n.* Reinheit, *die*

purl /pɜ:l/ [1] *n.* linke Masche
[2] *v.t.* links stricken; **~ three [stitches]** drei linke Maschen stricken

purple /'pɜ:pl/ [1] *adj.* lila; violett
[2] *n.* Lila, *das;* Violett, *das*

purport /pə'pɔ:t/ *v.t.* **~ to do sth.** (profess) [von sich] behaupten, etw. zu tun; (be intended to seem) den Anschein erwecken sollen, etw. zu tun

purpose /'pɜ:pəs/ *n.* **(a)** (object) Zweck, *der;* (intention) Absicht, *die;* **what is the ~ of doing that?** was hat es für einen Zweck, das zu tun?; **on ~:** mit Absicht; absichtlich
(b) (effect) **to no ~:** ohne Erfolg; **to some/good ~:** mit einigem/gutem Erfolg
(c) (determination) Entschlossenheit, *die*

'purpose-built *adj.* [eigens] zu diesem Zweck errichtet ‹*Gebäude*›

purposeful /'pɜ:pəsfl/ *adj.* zielstrebig; (with specific aim) entschlossen

'purposely *adv.* absichtlich

'purpose-made *adj.* spezialgefertigt

purr /pɜ:(r)/ [1] *v.i.* schnurren
[2] *n.* Schnurren, *das*

purse /pɜ:s/ [1] *n.* Portemonnaie, *das*
[2] *v.t.* kräuseln ‹*Lippen*›

purser /'pɜ:sə(r)/ *n.* Zahlmeister, *der*/-meisterin, *die*

pursue /pə'sju:/ *v.t.* **(a)** (chase) verfolgen
(b) (look into) nachgehen (+ *Dat.*)
(c) (engage in) betreiben

pursuer /pə'sju:ə(r)/ *n.* Verfolger, *der*/Verfolgerin, *die*

pursuit /pə'sju:t/ *n.* **(a)** Verfolgung, *die;* (of knowledge, truth, etc.) Streben, *das* (**of** nach); **in ~ of** auf der Jagd nach ‹*Wild, Dieb usw.*›; in Ausführung (+ *Gen.*) ‹*Beschäftigung*›; **with the police in [full] ~:** mit der Polizei [dicht] auf den Fersen
(b) (pastime) Beschäftigung, *die*

pus /pʌs/ *n.* Eiter, *der*

push /pʊʃ/ [1] *v.t.* **(a)** schieben; (make fall) stoßen; drücken gegen ‹*Tür*›; **~ one's way through/into/on to** *etc.* **sth.** sich (*Dat.*) einen Weg durch/in/auf *usw.* etw. (*Akk.*) bahnen
(b) (fig.: impel) drängen
(c) (tax) **~ sb. [hard]** jmdn. [stark] fordern; **be ~ed for sth.** (coll.: find it difficult to provide sth.) mit etw. knapp sein; **be ~ed for money** *or* **cash** knapp bei Kasse sein (ugs.)
(d) (sell illegally, esp. drugs) pushen (Drogenjargon)
[2] *v.i.* **(a)** schieben; (in queue) drängeln; (at door) drücken; **~ and shove** schubsen und drängeln
(b) (make demands) **~ for sth.** etw. fordern
(c) (make one's way) **he ~ed between us** er drängte sich zwischen uns; **~ through the crowd** sich durch die Menge drängeln
[3] *n.* **(a)** Stoß, *der;* **give sth. a ~:** etw. schieben
(b) (effort) Anstrengungen *Pl.;* (Mil.: attack) Vorstoß, *der*
(c) (crisis) **when it comes to the ~,** (Amer. coll.) **when ~ comes to shove** wenn es ernst wird
(d) (Brit. coll.: dismissal) **get the ~:** rausfliegen (ugs.)

■ **push a'head** *v.i.* **~ ahead with sth.** etw. vorantreiben

■ **push 'in** *v.i.* sich hineindrängen

■ **push 'off** *v.i.* **(a)** (Boating) abstoßen
(b) (coll.: leave) abhauen (salopp)

■ **push 'on** [1] *v.i.* (with plans etc.) weitermachen
[2] *v.t.* draufdrücken ‹*Deckel usw.*›

■ **push 'up** *v.t.* hochschieben; (fig.) hochtreiben

push: ~bike *n.* (Brit. coll.) Fahrrad, *das;* **~-button** *n.* [Druck]knopf, *der;* Drucktaste, *die;* **~chair** *n.* (Brit.) Sportwagen, *der*

pusher /'pʊʃə(r)/ *n.* (seller of drugs) Dealer, *der*/Dealerin, *die*

'pushover *n.* (coll.) Kinderspiel, *das*

pushy /'pʊʃɪ/ *adj.* (coll.) [übermäßig] ehrgeizig ‹*Person*›

pussy /'pʊsɪ/ *n.* (child lang.: cat) Miezekatze, *die* (fam.)

put /pʊt/ [1] *v.t.*, **-tt-, put (a)** (place) tun; (vertically) stellen; (horizontally) legen; **~ plates on the table** Teller auf den Tisch stellen; **~ a stamp on the letter** eine Briefmarke auf den Brief kleben; **~ the letter in an envelope/the letter box** den Brief in einen Umschlag/in den Briefkasten stecken; **~ sth. in one's pocket** etw. in die Tasche stecken; **~ petrol in the tank** Benzin in den Tank füllen; **~ the car in[to] the garage** das Auto in die Garage stellen; **~ the plug in the socket** den Stecker in die Steckdose stecken; **~ one's hands over one's eyes** sich (*Dat.*) die Hände auf die Augen legen; **where shall I ~ it?** wo soll ich es hintun (ugs.)/-stellen/-legen *usw.*?; (fig.) **be ~ in a difficult position** in eine schwierige Lage geraten; **~ sb. on to sth.** jmdn. auf etw. (*Akk.*) hinweisen; **~ sb. to work** jmdn. arbeiten lassen; **~ sb. on antibiotics** jmdn. auf Antibiotika setzen; **~ oneself in sb.'s place** *or* **situation** sich in jmds. Lage (*Akk.*) versetzen
(b) (submit) unterbreiten ‹*Vorschlag, Plan*› (**to** *Dat.*)
(c) (express) ausdrücken; **let's ~ it like this: ...:** sagen wir so: ...; **~ sth. into English** *etc.* etw. ins Englische *usw.* übertragen; **~ sth. into words** etw. in Worte fassen
(d) (write) schreiben; **~ one's name on the** ···›

list seinen Namen auf die Liste setzen; **~ sth. on the bill** etw. auf die Rechnung setzen
(e) (stake) setzen (**on** auf + *Akk.*)
(f) (estimate) **~ sb./sth. at** jmdn./etw. schätzen auf (+ *Akk.*)
2 *v.i.* **-tt-, put** (Naut.) **~** [out] to sea in See stechen

▪ **put a'cross** *v.t.* **(a)** (communicate) vermitteln (**to** *Dat.*)
(b) (make acceptable) ankommen mit

▪ **put a'way** *v.t.* **(a)** wegräumen; reinstellen ‹*Auto*›; (in file) abheften
(b) (save) beiseite legen
(c) (coll.) (eat) verdrücken (ugs.); (drink) runterkippen (ugs.)
(d) (coll.: confine) einsperren (ugs.)

▪ **put 'back** *v.t.* **(a)** **~ the book back** das Buch zurücktun
(b) **~ the clock back** die Uhr zurückstellen
(c) (postpone) verschieben

▪ **put 'down** *v.t.* **(a)** (set down) (vertically) hinstellen; (horizontally) hinlegen; auflegen ‹*Hörer*›
(b) (suppress) niederwerfen
(c) (humiliate) herabsetzen
(d) (kill) töten
(e) (write) notieren
(f) (attribute) **~ sth. down to sth.** etw. auf etw. (*Akk.*) zurückführen

▪ **put 'forward** *v.t.* **(a)** (propose) aufwarten mit
(b) (nominate) vorschlagen
(c) **~ the clock forward** die Uhr vorstellen

▪ **put 'in** **1** *v.t.* **(a)** (install) einbauen
(b) (submit) stellen ‹*Forderung*›; einreichen ‹*Bewerbung*›
(c) (devote) aufwenden ‹*Mühe*›; (perform) einlegen ‹*Sonderschicht, Überstunden*›
2 *v.i.* **~ in for** sich bewerben um ‹*Stellung*›; beantragen ‹*Urlaub*›

▪ **put 'off** *v.t.* **(a)** (postpone) verschieben (**until** auf + *Akk.*); (postpone engagement with) vertrösten (**until** auf + *Akk.*)
(b) (switch off) ausmachen
(c) (repel) abstoßen; **~ sb. off sth.** jmdm. etw. verleiden
(d) (distract) stören
(e) (dissuade) **~ sb. off doing sth.** jmdn. davon abbringen, etw. zu tun

▪ **put 'on** *v.t.* **(a)** anziehen ‹*Kleidung, Hose usw.*›; aufsetzen ‹*Hut, Brille*›; draufsetzen ‹*Deckel*›; **~ it on** (coll.) [nur] Schau machen (ugs.)
(b) anmachen ‹*Radio, Licht*›; aufsetzen ‹*Wasser, Kessel*›
(c) (gain) **~ on weight** zunehmen
(d) (stage) spielen ‹*Stück*›; zeigen ‹*Film*›

▪ **put 'out** *v.t.* **(a)** rausbringen
(b) ausmachen ‹*Licht*›; löschen ‹*Feuer*›
(c) (inconvenience) in Verlegenheit bringen

▪ **put 'through** *v.t.* **(a)** (carry out) durchführen ‹*Plan, Programm*›
(b) (Teleph.) verbinden (**to** mit)

▪ **put 'up** **1** *v.t.* **(a)** heben ‹*Hand*›; errichten ‹*Gebäude, Denkmal*›; aufstellen ‹*Gerüst*›
(b) (display) aushängen
(c) hochnehmen ‹*Fäuste*›; leisten ‹*Widerstand, Gegenwehr*›
(d) (propose) vorschlagen; (nominate) aufstellen
(e) (incite) **~ sb. up to sth.** jmdn. zu etw. anstiften
(f) (accommodate) unterbringen
(g) (increase) [he]raufsetzen ‹*Preis, Miete*›
2 *v.i.* (lodge) übernachten

▪ **put 'up with** *v.t.* sich (*Dat.*) bieten lassen ‹*Beleidigung, Benehmen*›; sich abfinden mit ‹*Lärm, Elend*›; sich abgeben mit ‹*Person*›

'put-down *n.* Herabsetzung, *die;* (snub) Abfuhr, *die*

putrefaction /pju:trɪ'fækʃn/ *n., no indef. art.* Zersetzung, *die*

putrefy /'pju:trɪfaɪ/ *v.i.* sich zersetzen

putrid /'pju:trɪd/ *adj.* (rotten) faul; **~ smell** Fäulnisgeruch, *der*

putt /pʌt/ (Golf) **1** *v.i. & t.* putten **2** *n.* Putt, *der*

'putter *n.* Putter, *der*

putty /'pʌtɪ/ *n.* Kitt, *der*

'put-up *adj.* **a ~ job** ein abgekartetes Spiel (ugs.)

puzzle /'pʌzl/ **1** *n.* (problem, enigma) Rätsel, *das;* (toy) Geduldsspiel, *das* **2** *v.t.* rätselhaft *od.* ein Rätsel sein (+ *Dat.*) **3** *v.i.* **~ over** *or* **about sth.** sich (*Dat.*) über etw. den Kopf zerbrechen

puzzled /'pʌzld/ *adj.* ratlos

puzzling /'pʌzlɪŋ/ *adj.* rätselhaft

PVC *abbr.* = **polyvinyl chloride** PVC, *das*

pygmy /'pɪgmɪ/ *n.* Pygmäe, *der*

pyjamas /pɪ'dʒɑ:məz/ *n. pl.* **[pair of] ~:** Schlafanzug, *der*

pylon /'paɪlən/ *n.* Mast, *der*

pyramid /'pɪrəmɪd/ *n.* Pyramide, *die*

Pyrenees /pɪrə'ni:z/ *pr. n. pl.* **the ~:** die Pyrenäen

python /'paɪθən/ *n.* Python, *der*

Qq

Q, q /kjuː/ *n.* Q, q, *das*

quack /kwæk/ 1 *v.i.* ‹*Ente:*› quaken
2 *n.* Quaken, *das*

quadrangle /ˈkwɒdræŋgl/ *n.* [viereckiger] Innenhof

quadruped /ˈkwɒdrʊped/ *n.* Vierfüßler, *der*

quadruple /ˈkwɒdrʊpl/ 1 *adj.* vierfach
2 *v.t.* vervierfachen
3 *v.i.* sich vervierfachen

quagmire /ˈkwægmaɪə(r)/ *n.* Sumpf, *der;* Morast, *der*

quail¹ /kweɪl/ *n.* (Ornith.) Wachtel, *die*

quail² *v.i.* ‹*Person:*› [ver]zagen

quaint /kweɪnt/ *adj.* drollig ‹*Häuschen, Einrichtung*›; malerisch ‹*Ort*›; (odd) kurios ‹*Bräuche, Anblick*›

quake /kweɪk/ 1 *n.* (coll.) [Erd]beben, *das*
2 *v.i.* beben; **~ with fear** vor Angst zittern

Quaker /ˈkweɪkə(r)/ *n.* Quäker, *der*/ Quäkerin, *die*

qualification /kwɒlɪfɪˈkeɪʃn/ *n.* **(a)** Qualifikation, *die;* (condition) Voraussetzung, *die*
(b) (limitation) Vorbehalt, *der;* **without ~:** vorbehaltlos

qualified /ˈkwɒlɪfaɪd/ *adj.* **(a)** qualifiziert; (by training) ausgebildet
(b) (restricted) nicht uneingeschränkt; **a ~ success** kein voller Erfolg; **~ acceptance** bedingte Annahme

qualify /ˈkwɒlɪfaɪ/ 1 *v.t.* **(a)** (make competent) berechtigen (**for** zu)
(b) (modify) einschränken
2 *v.i.* **(a) ~ in law/medicine** seinen [Studien]abschluss in Jura/Medizin machen; **~ as a doctor/lawyer** sein Examen als Arzt/ Anwalt machen
(b) (fulfil a condition) in Frage kommen (**for** für)
(c) (Sport) sich qualifizieren

qualifying /ˈkwɒlɪfaɪɪŋ/ *adj.* (Sport) **~ match** Qualifikationsspiel, *das*

quality /ˈkwɒlɪtɪ/ 1 *n.* **(a)** Qualität, *die*
(b) (characteristic) Eigenschaft, *die*
2 *adj.* Qualitäts-

quality: ~ control *n.* Qualitätskontrolle, *die;* **~ time** *n.: ganz dem Miteinander gewidmete Zeit*

qualm /kwɑːm/ *n.* Bedenken, *das* (**over, about** gegen)

quandary /ˈkwɒndərɪ/ *n.* Dilemma, *das*

quantify /ˈkwɒntɪfaɪ/ *v.t.* quantifizieren

quantity /ˈkwɒntɪtɪ/ *n.* **(a)** Quantität, *die*
(b) (amount, sum) Menge, *die*

ˈquantity surveyor *n.* Baukostenkalkulator, *der*/-kalkulatorin, *die*

quantum: ~ jump, ~ leap *ns.* (Phys.; also fig.) Quantensprung, *der;*
~ meˈchanics *n.* Quantenmechanik, *die*

quarantine /ˈkwɒrəntiːn/ *n.* Quarantäne, *die;* **be in ~:** unter Quarantäne stehen

quarrel /ˈkwɒrl/ 1 *n.* **(a)** Streit, *der;* **have/ pick a ~ with sb. [about/over sth.]** sich mit jmdm. [über etw. (*Akk.*)] streiten/mit jmdm. [wegen etw.] Streit anfangen
(b) (cause of complaint) Einwand, *der* (**with** gegen)
2 *v.i.,* (Brit.) **-ll-** [sich] streiten (**over** um, **about** über + *Akk.*); **~ with each other** [sich] [miteinander] streiten; (fall out) sich [zer]streiten (**over** um, **about** über + *Akk.*)

quarrelsome /ˈkwɒrlsəm/ *adj.* streitsüchtig

quarry¹ /ˈkwɒrɪ/ *n.* Steinbruch, *der*

quarry² *n.* (prey) Beute, *die*

quart /kwɔːt/ *n.* Quart, *das*

quarter /ˈkwɔːtə(r)/ 1 *n.* **(a)** Viertel, *das;* **a** *or* **one ~ of** ein Viertel (+ *Gen.*); **a ~ of a mile/an hour** eine Viertelmeile/-stunde
(b) (of year) Quartal, *das;* Vierteljahr, *das*
(c) [a] **~ to/past six** Viertel vor/nach sechs
(d) (direction) Richtung, *die*
(e) (area of town) [Stadt]viertel, *das*
(f) ~s *pl.* (lodgings) Quartier, *das* (bes. Milit.); Unterkunft, *die*
(g) (Amer. coin) Vierteldollar, *der*
2 *v.t.* **(a)** (divide) vierteln
(b) (lodge) einquartieren ‹*Soldaten*›

quarter-ˈfinal *n.* Viertelfinale, *das*

ˈquarterly 1 *adj.* vierteljährlich
2 *n.* Vierteljahr[e]sschrift, *die*

quarter-ˈpounder *n.* Viertelpfünder, *der*

quartet /kwɔːˈtet/ *n.* Quartett, *das*

quartz /kwɔːts/ *n.* Quarz, *der*

quash /kwɒʃ/ *v.t.* **(a)** (annul) aufheben
(b) (suppress) niederschlagen

quaver /ˈkweɪvə(r)/ 1 *n.* (Brit. Mus.) Achtelnote, *die*
2 *v.i.* (vibrate) zittern

quay /kiː/, **ˈquayside** *ns.* Kai, *der*

queasy /ˈkwiːzɪ/ *adj.* unwohl

queen /kwiːn/ *n.* **(a)** Königin, *die*
(b) (Chess, Cards) Dame, *die*

queen: ~ ˈbee *n.* Bienenkönigin, *die;*
~ ˈmother *n.* Königinmutter, *die*

queer /kwɪə(r)/ 1 *adj.* **(a)** (strange) sonderbar; (eccentric) verschroben
(b) (shady) merkwürdig
(c) (Brit. coll. dated: out of sorts) unwohl

⋯▸

(d) (sl. derog.: homosexual) schwul (ugs.)
2 *n.* (sl. derog.: homosexual) Schwule, *der* (ugs.)

quell /kwel/ *v.t.* (literary) niederschlagen ‹*Aufstand*›; zügeln ‹*Furcht*›

quench /kwentʃ/ *v.t.* löschen

query /ˈkwɪərɪ/ **1** *n.* Frage, *die*
2 *v.t.* in Frage stellen ‹*Anweisung, Glaubwürdigkeit*›; beanstanden ‹*Rechnung*›

quest /kwest/ *n.* Suche, *die* (**for** nach)

question /ˈkwestʃn/ **1** *n.* **(a)** Frage, *die;* **ask sb. a ~:** jmdm. eine Frage stellen
(b) (doubt, objection) Zweifel, *der* (**about** an + *Dat.*); **there is no ~ about sth.** es besteht kein Zweifel an etw. (*Dat.*); **beyond all** *or* **without ~:** ohne Frage
(c) (problem, concern) Frage, *die;* **sth./it is only a ~ of time** etw./es ist [nur] eine Frage der Zeit; **it is [only] a ~ of doing sth.** es geht [nur] darum, etw. zu tun; **the person/thing in ~:** die fragliche Person/Sache; **sth./it is out of the ~:** etw./es ist ausgeschlossen
2 *v.t.* **(a)** befragen; ‹*Polizei, Gericht usw.:*› vernehmen
(b) (throw doubt upon, raise objections to) bezweifeln

questionable /ˈkwestʃənəbl/ *adj.* fragwürdig

ˈ**question mark** *n.* Fragezeichen, *das*

questionnaire /kwestʃəˈneə(r)/ *n.* Fragebogen, *der*

queue /kju:/ **1** *n.* Schlange, *die;* **join the ~:** sich anstellen
2 *v.i.* **~ [up]** Schlange stehen

ˈ**queue-jumping** *n.* (Brit.) Vordrängen, *das*

quibble /ˈkwɪbl/ **1** *n.* Spitzfindigkeit, *die*
2 *v.i.* streiten

quibbling /ˈkwɪblɪŋ/ *adj.* spitzfindig

quiche /ki:ʃ/ *n.* Quiche, *die*

quick /kwɪk/ **1** *adj.* schnell; kurz ‹*Rede, Pause*›; flüchtig ‹*Kuss, Blick*›; **be ~!** mach schnell! (ugs.); **be ~ to do sth.** etw. schnell tun; **a ~ temper** ein aufbrausendes Wesen
2 *adv.* schnell
3 *n.* empfindliches Fleisch; **be cut to the ~** (fig.) tief getroffen sein

quicken /ˈkwɪkn/ **1** *v.t.* beschleunigen
2 *v.i.* sich beschleunigen

ˈ**quickly** *adv.* schnell

ˈ**quickness** *n.* **(a)** (speed) Schnelligkeit, *die*
(b) (~ of perception) Schärfe, *die*

quick: ~sand *n.* Treibsand, *der;* **~-tempered** /-ˈtempəd/ *adj.* hitzig; **be ~-tempered** leicht aufbrausen; **~-witted** *adj.* geistesgegenwärtig

quid /kwɪd/ *n., pl. same* (Brit. coll.) Pfund, *das*

quiet /ˈkwaɪət/ **1** *adj.*, **~er** /ˈkwaɪətə(r)/, **~est** /ˈkwaɪətɪst/ **(a)** (silent) still; (not loud) leise; **keep ~ about sth.** (fig.) etw. geheim halten
(b) (peaceful, not busy) ruhig
(c) (not overt) versteckt; **on the ~:** still und heimlich
2 *n.* Ruhe, *die;* (silence, stillness) Stille, *die*

quieten /ˈkwaɪətn/ *v.t.* beruhigen
■ **quieten ˈdown** *v.i.* sich beruhigen

ˈ**quietly** *adv.* **(a)** (silently) still; (not loudly) leise
(b) (peacefully) ruhig

ˈ**quietness** *n.* (absence of noise) Stille, *die;* (peacefulness) Ruhe, *die*

quill /kwɪl/ *n.* (feather) Kielfeder, *die;* (of porcupine) Stachel, *der*

quilt /kwɪlt/ **1** *n.* Schlafdecke, *die*
2 *v.t.* wattieren

quince /kwɪns/ *n.* Quitte, *die*

quintessential /kwɪntɪˈsenʃl/ *adj.* typisch; wesentlich

quintet /kwɪnˈtet/ *n.* Quintett, *das*

quip /kwɪp/ **1** *n.* Witzelei, *die*
2 *v.i.*, **-pp-** witzeln (**at** über + *Akk.*)

quirk /kwɜ:k/ *n.* Marotte, *die;* **a ~ of fate** eine Laune des Schicksals

quirky /ˈkwɜ:kɪ/ *adj.* schrullig (ugs.)

quit /kwɪt/ *v.t.*, **-tt-**, (Amer.) **quit (a)** (give up) aufgeben; (stop) aufhören mit; **~ doing sth.** aufhören, etw. zu tun; **they were given notice to ~ [the flat]** ihnen wurde [die Wohnung] gekündigt
(b) (Comp.) beenden

quite /kwaɪt/ *adv.* **(a)** (entirely) ganz; völlig; fest ‹*entschlossen*›; **~ [so]!** [ja,] genau!
(b) (to some extent) ziemlich; ganz ‹*gern*›; **~ a few** ziemlich viele

quits /kwɪts/ *pred. adj.* **be ~ [with sb.]** [mit jmdm.] quitt sein (ugs.)

quiver[1] /ˈkwɪvə(r)/ *v.i.* zittern (**with** vor + *Dat.*); ‹*Stimme, Lippen:*› beben (geh.); ‹*Lid:*› zucken

quiver[2] *n.* (for arrows) Köcher, *der*

quiz /kwɪz/ **1** *n., pl.* **~zes** Quiz, *das*
2 *v.t.*, **-zz-** ausfragen (**about sth.** nach etw., **about sb.** über jmdn.)

quizzical /ˈkwɪzɪkl/ *adj.* fragend

ˈ**quiz programme,** ˈ**quiz show** *ns.* (Radio, Telev.) Quizsendung, *die*

quoit /kɔɪt/ *n.* [Gummi]ring, *der*

quorum /ˈkwɔ:rəm/ *n.* Quorum, *das*

quota /ˈkwəʊtə/ *n.* **(a)** (share) Anteil, *der*
(b) (goods to be produced) Produktionsmindestquote, *die*
(c) (maximum number) Höchstquote, *die*

quotation /kwəʊˈteɪʃn/ *n.* **(a)** Zitieren, *das;* (passage) Zitat, *das*
(b) (estimate) Kosten[vor]anschlag, *der*

quoˈtation marks *n. pl.* Anführungszeichen *Pl.*

quote /kwəʊt/ **1** *v.t. also abs.* zitieren (**from** aus); zitieren aus ‹*Buch, Text*›; (mention) anführen; nennen ‹*Preis*›
2 *n.* (coll.) **(a)** (passage) Zitat, *das*
(b) (estimate) Kosten[vor]anschlag, *der*
(c) *usu. in pl.* (quotation mark) Anführungszeichen, *das*

quotient /ˈkwəʊʃnt/ *n.* (Math.) Quotient, *der;* *see also* INTELLIGENCE QUOTIENT

Rr

R, r /ɑ:(r)/ *n.* R, r, *das*

R. *abbr.* = **River** Fl.

rabbi /'ræbaɪ/ *n.* Rabbi[ner], *der;* (as title) Rabbi, *der*

rabbit /'ræbɪt/ *n.* Kaninchen, *das*

rabbit: ~ burrow *n.* Kaninchenbau, *der;* **~ hutch** *n.* (also fig.) Kaninchenstall, *der;* **~ warren** *n.* Kaninchengehege, *das;* (fig.) Labyrinth, *das*

rabble /'ræbl/ *n.* Mob, *der*

rabid /'ræbɪd/ *adj.* **(a)** tollwütig **(b)** (extreme) fanatisch

rabies /'reɪbi:z/ *n.* Tollwut, *die*

race¹ /reɪs/ **1** *n.* Rennen, *das;* (fig.) **a ~ against time** ein Wettlauf mit der Zeit **2** *v.i.* **(a)** (in swimming, running, etc.) um die Wette schwimmen/laufen *usw.* **(with, against** mit) **(b)** ‹*Motor:*› durchdrehen; ‹*Puls:*› jagen **(c)** (rush) sich sehr beeilen; **~ after sb.** jmdn. hinterherhetzen **3** *v.t.* um die Wette schwimmen/laufen *usw.* mit

race² *n.* (Anthrop., Biol.) Rasse, *die;* **the human ~**: die Menschheit

race: ~course *n.* Rennbahn, *die;* **~ hatred** *n.* Rassenhass, *der;* **~horse** *n.* Rennpferd, *das;* **~ meeting** *n.* Renntag, *der;* (on successive days) Renntage *Pl.* **~ relations** *n. pl.* Beziehung zwischen den Rassen; **~ riot** *n.* Rassenkrawall, *der;* **~track** *n.* Rennbahn, *die*

racial /'reɪʃl/ *adj.* Rassen‹*diskriminierung, -konflikt, -gleichheit, -spannung, -vorurteil*›; rassisch ‹*Gruppe, Minderheit*›

racialism /'reɪʃəlɪzm/ *n.* Rassismus, *der*

racialist /'reɪʃəlɪst/ **1** *n.* Rassist, *der*/Rassistin, *die* **2** *adj.* rassistisch

racially /'reɪʃəlɪ/ *adv.* rassisch; **be ~ prejudiced** Rassenvorurteile haben

racing /'reɪsɪŋ/ *n.* Rennsport, *der;* (with horses) Pferdesport, *der*

racing: ~ bicycle *n.* Rennrad, *das;* Rennmaschine, *die;* **~ car** *n.* Rennwagen, *der;* **~ driver** *n.* Rennfahrer, *der*/-fahrerin, *die*

racism /'reɪsɪzm/ *n.* Rassismus, *der*

racist /'reɪsɪst/ **1** *n.* Rassist, *der*/Rassistin, *die* **2** *adj.* rassistisch

rack /ræk/ **1** *n.* (for luggage) Ablage, *die;* (for toast, plates) Ständer, *der;* (on bicycle, motor cycle) Gepäckträger, *der* **2** *v.t.* **~ one's brain[s]** (fig.) sich (*Dat.*) den Kopf zerbrechen (ugs.)

racket¹ /'rækɪt/ *n.* Schläger, *der*

racket² *n.* **(a)** (disturbance) Lärm, *der;* Krach, *der* **(b)** (scheme) Schwindelgeschäft, *das* (ugs.)

racketeer /rækɪ'tɪə(r)/ *n.* Ganove, *der;* (profiteer) Wucherer, *der*

racketeering /rækɪ'tɪərɪŋ/ *n.* kriminelle Geschäfte *Pl.*

racoon /rə'ku:n/ *n.* Waschbär, *der*

racy /'reɪsɪ/ *adj.* flott (ugs.) ‹*Stil*›

radar /'reɪdɑ:(r)/ *n.* Radar, *das od. der*

'radar screen *n.* Radarschirm, *der*

radiant /'reɪdɪənt/ *adj.* strahlend; fröhlich ‹*Stimmung*›; **be ~**: strahlen (**with** vor + *Dat.*)

radiate /'reɪdɪeɪt/ **1** *v.i.* **(a)** ‹*Hitze, Wärme:*› ausstrahlen; ‹*Schein, Wellen:*› ausgehen (**from** von) **(b)** (from central point) strahlenförmig ausgehen (**from** von) **2** *v.t.* ausstrahlen ‹*Licht, Wärme; Glück, Liebe*›; aussenden ‹*Strahlen, Wellen*›

radiation /reɪdɪ'eɪʃn/ *n.* (of energy) Emission, *die;* (of signals) Ausstrahlung, *die;* (energy transmitted) Strahlung, *die*

radiator /'reɪdɪeɪtə(r)/ *n.* **(a)** (for heating) Heizkörper, *der* **(b)** (Motor Veh.) Kühler, *der*

'radiator cap *n.* Kühlverschraubung, *die*

radical /'rædɪkl/ *adj.* **1** **(a)** (thorough; also Polit.) radikal; drastisch ‹*Maßnahme*› **(b)** (progressive) radikal **(c)** (fundamental) grundlegend **2** *n.* (Polit.) Radikale, *der/die*

radio /'reɪdɪəʊ/ **1** *n., pl.* **~s** **(a)** *no indef. art.* Funk, *der;* (for private communication) Sprechfunk, *der* **(b)** *no indef. art.* (Broadcasting) Rundfunk, *der;* **on the ~**: im Radio **(c)** (apparatus) Radio, *das* **2** *attrib. adj.* (Broadcasting) Rundfunk-; Radio‹*welle, -teleskop*›; Funk‹*mast, -turm, -taxi*› **3** *v.t.* funken

radio: ~'active *adj.* radioaktiv; **~ac'tivity** *n.* Radioaktivität, *die;* **~ cas'sette player** *n.* Kassettenradio, *das;* Radio mit Kassettenteil; **~con'trolled** *adj.* funkgesteuert; **~ frequency** *n.* Hochfrequenz, *die; attrib.* **~-frequency** Hochfrequenz-; **~ play** *n.* Hörspiel, *das;* **~ station** *n.* Rundfunkstation, *die;* Rundfunk- *od.*

Radiosender, *der;* ~ '**telescope** *n.* Radioteleskop, *das;* ~'**therapy** *n.* Strahlentherapie, *die*

radish /'rædɪʃ/ *n.* Rettich, *der;* (small, red) Radieschen, *das*

radius /'reɪdɪəs/ *n., pl.* **radii** /'reɪdɪaɪ/ *or* ~**es** (Math.) Radius, *der;* (fig.) Umkreis, *der*

RAF /ɑ:reɪ'ef, (coll.) ræf/ *abbr.* = **Royal Air Force**

raffle /'ræfl/ [1] *n.* Tombola, *die;* ~ **ticket** Los, *das*
[2] *v.t.* ~ **[off]** verlosen

raft /rɑ:ft/ *n.* Floß, *das*

rafter /'rɑ:ftə(r)/ *n.* Sparren, *der*

rag¹ /ræg/ *n.* **(a)** [Stoff]fetzen, *der*
(b) *in pl.* (old and torn clothes) Lumpen *Pl.*
(c) (derog.: newspaper) Käseblatt, *das* (salopp)

rag² *v.t.,* **-gg-** (tease) aufziehen

rag: ~**bag** *n.* (fig.) Sammelsurium, *das;* ~ **doll** *n.* Stoffpuppe, *die*

rage /reɪdʒ/ [1] *n.* **(a)** (violent anger) Wut, *die;* (fit of anger) Wutausbruch, *der*
(b) sth. is [all] the ~: etw. ist [ganz] groß in Mode
[2] *v.i.* **(a)** (rave) toben; ~ **at** *or* **against sth./sb.** gegen etw./jmdn. wüten
(b) (be violent, unchecked) toben; ‹*Krankheit:*› wüten

ragged /'rægɪd/ *adj.* zerrissen

'**rag trade** *n.* (coll.) Modebranche, *die* (ugs.)

raid /reɪd/ [1] *n.* Einfall, *der;* Überfall, *der;* (Mil.) Überraschungsangriff, *der;* (by police) Razzia, *die* (**on** in + *Dat.*)
[2] *v.t.* ‹*Polizei:*› eine Razzia machen auf (+ *Akk.*); ‹*Räuber, Soldaten:*› überfallen

'**raider** *n.* Räuber, *der*/Räuberin, *die*

rail /reɪl/ *n.* **(a)** Stange, *die;* (on ship) Reling, *die;* (as protection against contact) Barriere, *die*
(b) (Railw.: of track) Schiene, *die*
(c) (~way) [Eisen]bahn, *die; attrib.* Bahn-; **by** ~: mit der Bahn

'**rail card** *n.* Bahnkarte, *die*

railing /'reɪlɪŋ/ *n.* (round park) Zaun, *der;* (on staircase) Geländer, *das*

rail: ~**road** (Amer.) ▶ ~WAY; **R**~**track** *n., no art.* (Brit.) *Betreibergesellschaft des britischen Schienennetzes;* ~**way** *n.* **(a)** (track) Bahnlinie, *die;* Bahnstrecke, *die;* **(b)** (system) [Eisen]bahn, *die*

railway: ~ **carriage** *n.* Eisenbahnwagen, *der;* ~ **crossing** *n.* Bahnübergang, *der;* ~ **engine** *n.* Lokomotive, *die;* ~ **line** *n.* [Eisen]bahnlinie, *die;* ~ **station** *n.* Bahnhof, *der;* ~ **worker** *n.* Bahnarbeiter, *der*/-arbeiterin, *die*

rain /reɪn/ [1] *n.* **(a)** Regen, *der*
(b) (fig.: of arrows, blows, etc.) Hagel, *der*
[2] *v.i. impers.* **it is** ~**ing** es regnet
[3] *v.t.* hageln lassen ‹*Schläge, Hiebe*›

rain: ~**bow** /'reɪnbəʊ/ *n.* Regenbogen, *der;* ~ **check** *n.* (Amer. fig.) **take a** ~ **check on sth.** auf etw. (*Akk.*) später wieder zurückkommen; ~ **cloud** *n.* Regenwolke, *die;* ~**coat** *n.* Regenmantel, *der;* ~**fall** *n.* Niederschlag, *der;* ~**forest** *n.* Regenwald, *der;* ~**proof** *adj.* regendicht; ~**water** *n.* Regenwasser, *das;* ~**wear** *n.* Regenkleidung, *die*

'**rainy** *adj.* regnerisch ‹*Tag, Wetter*›; regenreich ‹*Gebiet, Sommer*›; ~ **season** Regenzeit, *die;* **keep sth. for a** ~ **day** (fig.) sich (*Dat.*) etw. für schlechte Zeiten aufheben

raise /reɪz/ *v.t.* **(a)** (lift up) heben; erhöhen ‹*Temperatur, Miete, Gehalt*›; hochziehen ‹*Fahne*›; aufziehen ‹*Vorhang*›; hochheben ‹*Arm*›; ~ **one's glass to sb.** das Glas auf jmdn. erheben
(b) (set upright) aufrichten; erheben ‹*Banner*›; ~ **sb.'s spirits** jmds. Stimmung heben
(c) erheben ‹*Forderungen, Einwände*›; aufwerfen ‹*Frage*›; zur Sprache bringen ‹*Thema, Problem*›
(d) aufziehen ‹*Vieh, [Haus]tiere*›; großziehen ‹*Familie, Kinder*›
(e) aufbringen ‹*Geld, Betrag*›
(f) aufheben ‹*Belagerung, Blockade, Embargo, Verbot*›

raisin /'reɪzn/ *n.* Rosine, *die*

rake /reɪk/ [1] *n.* Rechen, *der;* Harke, *die*
[2] *v.t.* **(a)** harken
(b) ~ **the fire** die Asche entfernen
(c) (with eyes, shots) bestreichen

■ **rake 'in** *v.t.* (coll.) scheffeln (ugs.).

■ **rake 'up** *v.t.* zusammenharken; (fig.) wieder ausgraben

'**rake-off** *n.* (coll.) [Gewinn]anteil, *der*

rakish /'reɪkɪʃ/ *adj.* flott; kess

rally /'rælɪ/ [1] *v.i.* (regain health) sich wieder [ein wenig] erholen
[2] *v.t.* **(a)** (reassemble) wieder zusammenrufen
(b) einigen ‹*Partei, Kräfte*›; sammeln ‹*Anhänger*›
[3] *n.* **(a)** (mass meeting) Versammlung, *die*
(b) [motor] ~: Rallye, *die*
(c) (Tennis) Ballwechsel, *der*

ram /ræm/ [1] *n.* (Zool.) Schafbock, *der;* Widder, *der*
[2] *v.t.,* **-mm-: (a)** (force) stopfen; ~ **a post into the ground** einen Pfosten in die Erde rammen; ~ **sth. home to sb.** jmdm. etw. deutlich vor Augen führen
(b) (collide with) rammen

RAM /ræm/ *abbr.* (Comp.) = **random access memory** RAM

ramble /'ræmbl/ [1] *n.* **[nature]** ~: Wanderung, *die*
[2] *v.i.* **(a)** (walk) umherstreifen (**through, in** in + *Dat.*)
(b) (in talk) zusammenhangloses Zeug reden; **keep rambling on about sth.** sich endlos über etw. (*Akk.*) auslassen

rambler /'ræmblə(r)/ *n.* Wanderer, *der*/ Wanderin, *die*

rambling /'ræmblɪŋ/ [1] *n.* Wandern, *das*
[2] *adj.* **(a)** (irregularly arranged) verschachtelt; verwinkelt ‹*Straßen*›

(b) (incoherent) unzusammenhängend ‹*Erklärung*›
(c) ~ **rose** Kletterrose, *die*

ramp /ræmp/ *n.* Rampe, *die*

rampage 1 /'ræmpeɪdʒ/ *n.* Randale, *die* (ugs.); **be/go on the** ~ (coll.) randalieren
2 /ræm'peɪdʒ/ *v.i.* randalieren

rampant /'ræmpənt/ *adj.* zügellos ‹*Gewalt, Rassismus*›; steil ansteigend ‹*Inflation*›; üppig ‹*Wachstum*›

rampart /'ræmpɑːt/ *n.* Wehrgang, *der*

ram: ~ raid 1 *v.t.* [durch Rammen mit einem Fahrzeug] einbrechen in (+ *Akk.*);
2 *n.* [durch Rammen eines Gebäudes verübter] Einbruch; **~-raider** *n.: Einbrecher, der sich durch Einrammen bes. eines Schaufensters mit einem Fahrzeug Zutritt verschafft*

'ramshackle *adj.* klapprig ‹*Auto*›; verkommen ‹*Gebäude*›

ran ▶ RUN 2, 3

ranch /rɑːntʃ/ *n.* Ranch, *die*

'ranch hand *n.* Farmarbeiter, *der*/-arbeiterin, *die*

rancid /'rænsɪd/ *adj.* ranzig

rancour (*Brit.; Amer.:* **rancor**) /'ræŋkə(r)/ *n.* [tiefe] Verbitterung

R&B *abbr.* = **rhythm and blues** R&B

R&D *abbr.* = **research and development** F&E

random /'rændəm/ 1 *n.* **at** ~: wahllos; willkürlich; (aimlessly) ziellos; **choose at** ~: aufs Geratewohl wählen
2 *adj.* willkürlich

random 'access memory *n.* (Comp.) Schreib-Lese-Speicher, *der*

randy /'rændɪ/ *adj.* geil; scharf (ugs.)

rang ▶ RING[2] 2, 3

range /reɪndʒ/ 1 *n.* **(a)** ~ **of mountains** Bergkette, *die*
(b) (of subjects) Palette, *die;* (of knowledge, voice) Umfang, *der*
(c) (of missile etc.) Reichweite, *die;* **at a** ~ **of 200 metres** auf eine Entfernung von 200 Metern
(d) (series, selection) Kollektion, *die*
(e) (stove) Herd, *der*
2 *v.i.* ‹*Preise, Temperaturen:*› schwanken, sich bewegen (**from ... to** zwischen [+ *Dat.*] ... und)

'ranger *n.* Förster, *der*/Försterin, *die*

rank[1] /ræŋk/ 1 *n.* **(a)** (position in hierarchy) Rang, *der;* (Mil. also) Dienstgrad, *der*
(b) (social position) [soziale] Stellung
(c) (row) Reihe, *die;* **the** ~ **and file** (fig.) die breite Masse; **the ~s** (enlisted men) die Mannschaften und Unteroffiziere
2 *v.t.* ~ **among** zählen zu
3 *v.i.* ~ **among** zählen zu

rank[2] *adj.* **(a)** krass ‹*Außenseiter*›
(b) ~ **weeds** [wild]wucherndes Unkraut

rankings /'ræŋkɪŋz/ *n. pl.* (Sport) Rangliste, *die;* **the team has fallen in the** ~: die Mannschaft ist in der Tabelle nach unten gerutscht

ransack /'rænsæk/ *v.t.* **(a)** (search) durchsuchen (**for** nach)
(b) (pillage) plündern

ransom /'rænsəm/ *n.* ~ [**money**] Lösegeld, *das;* **hold to** ~: als Geisel festhalten

rant /rænt/ *v.i.* ~ [**and rave**] wettern (ugs.) (**about** über + *Akk.*)

rap /ræp/ 1 *n.* [energisches] Klopfen
2 *v.t.*, **-pp-** klopfen
3 *v.i.*, **-pp-** klopfen (**on** an + *Akk.*)

rape[1] /reɪp/ 1 *n.* Vergewaltigung, *die*
2 *v.t.* vergewaltigen

rape[2] *n.* (Bot., Agric.) Raps, *der*

rape: ~seed *n.* Rapssamen, *der;* **~seed oil** *n.* Rapsöl, *das*

rapid /'ræpɪd/ 1 *adj.* schnell ‹*Bewegung, Wachstum, Puls*›; rasch ‹*Fortschritt, Ausbreitung*›
2 *n. in pl.* Stromschnellen *Pl.*

rapid-'fire *adj.* Schnellfeuer‹*waffe, -schießen*›; (fig.) schnell aufeinander folgend ‹*Wiederholung*›; Schnellfeuer‹*witze, -fragen*›

rapidity /rə'pɪdɪtɪ/ *n.* Schnelligkeit, *die*

'rapidly *adv.* schnell

rapist /'reɪpɪst/ *n.* Vergewaltiger, *der*

rapport /rə'pɔː(r)/ *n.* [harmonisches] Verhältnis

rapt /ræpt/ *adj.* gespannt ‹*Miene*›

rapture /'ræptʃə(r)/ *n.* [**state of**] ~: Verzückung, *die*

rapturous /'ræptʃərəs/ *adj.* begeistert

rare[1] /reə(r)/ *adj.*, **'rarely** *adv.* selten

rare[2] *adj.* (Cookery) englisch gebraten

rarefied /'reərɪfaɪd/ *adj.* dünn ‹*Luft*›; (fig.) exklusiv

rarity /'reərɪtɪ/ *n.* Seltenheit, *die*

rash[1] /ræʃ/ *n.* [Haut]ausschlag, *der*

rash[2] *adj.* voreilig ‹*Urteil, Entscheidung*›; überstürzt ‹*Versprechung*›

rasher /'ræʃə(r)/ *n.* Speckscheibe, *die*

'rashly *adv.* voreilig

rasp /rɑːsp/ 1 *n.* (tool) Raspel, *die*
2 *v.t.* (say gratingly) schnarren

raspberry /'rɑːzbərɪ/ *n.* Himbeere, *die*

rat /ræt/ *n.* **(a)** Ratte, *die;* **smell a** ~ (fig.) Lunte riechen (ugs.)
(b) (coll. derog.: person) Ratte, *die* (derb)

ratchet /'rætʃɪt/ *n.* **(a)** (Mech. Engin.) (set of teeth) Zahnkranz, *der*
(b) ~ [**wheel**] Klinkenrad, *das*

'ratchet screwdriver *n.* Drillschraubenzieher, *der*

rate /reɪt/ 1 *n.* **(a)** (proportion) Rate, *die;* ~ **of inflation** Inflationsrate, *die*
(b) (tariff) Satz, *der;* ~ [**of pay**] Lohnsatz, *der*
(c) (speed) Geschwindigkeit, *die;* Tempo, *das*
(d) (Brit.: levy) [**local** *or* **council**] **~s** Gemeindeabgaben *Pl.*
(e) (coll.) **at any** ~ (at least) zumindest; ··➤

wenigstens; (whatever happens) auf jeden Fall; **at this ~ we won't get any work done** so kriegen wir gar nichts fertig (ugs.)
2 *v.t.* **(a)** einschätzen ‹*Intelligenz, Leistung*›
(b) (consider) betrachten; rechnen (**among** zu)
3 *v.i.* **~ as** gelten als

'ratepayer *n.* (Brit.) Realsteuerpflichtige, *der/die*

rather /'rɑːðə(r)/ *adv.* **(a)** (by preference) lieber
(b) (somewhat) ziemlich; **I ~ think that ...:** ich bin ziemlich sicher, dass ...
(c) (more truly) vielmehr; **or ~:** beziehungsweise

ratification /rætɪfɪ'keɪʃn/ *n.* Ratifizierung, *die*

ratify /'rætɪfaɪ/ *v.t.* ratifizieren

rating /'reɪtɪŋ/ *n.* **(a)** (estimated standing) Einschätzung, *die*
(b) (Radio, Telev.) [**popularity**] **~:** Einschaltquote, *die*
(c) (Brit. Navy) Matrose, *der*

ratio /'reɪʃɪəʊ/ *n., pl.* **~s** Verhältnis, *das*

ration /'ræʃn/ 1 *n.* **~[s]** Ration, *die* (**of** an + *Dat.*)
2 *v.t.* rationieren ‹*Benzin, Zucker usw.*›

rational /'ræʃənl/ *adj.* (having reason) rational ‹*Wesen*›; (sensible) vernünftig ‹*Person, Art usw.*›

rationalist /'ræʃənəlɪst/ *n.* Rationalist, *der*/Rationalistin, *die*

rationalize /'ræʃənəlaɪz/ *v.t.* rationalisieren

rationing /'ræʃənɪŋ/ *n.* Rationierung, *die*

rat: ~ poison *n.* Rattengift, *das;* **~ race** *n.* erbarmungsloser Konkurrenzkampf; **~ run** *n.* (Brit. coll.) Schleichweg, *der*

rattle /'rætl/ 1 *v.i.* **(a)** ‹*Fenster:*› klappern; ‹*Flaschen:*› klirren; ‹*Kette:*› rasseln
(b) ‹*Zug, Bus:*› rattern
2 *v.t.* **(a)** klappern mit ‹*Würfel, Geschirr*›; klirren lassen ‹*Fenster*[*scheiben*]›; rasseln mit ‹*Kette*›
(b) (coll.: disconcert) **~ sb., get sb. ~d** jmdn. durcheinander bringen
3 *n.* **(a)** (of baby) Rassel, *die*
(b) (sound) Klappern, *das*

■ **rattle 'off** *v.t.* (coll.) herunterrasseln (ugs.)

'rattlesnake *n.* Klapperschlange, *die*

raucous /'rɔːkəs/ *adj.* rau

raunchy /'rɔːntʃɪ/ *adj.* (lewd) vulgär; (suggestive) scharf (salopp)

ravage /'rævɪdʒ/ 1 *v.t.* heimsuchen ‹*Gebiet, Stadt*›
2 *n. in pl.* verheerende Wirkung

rave /reɪv/ 1 *v.i.* **(a)** (talk wildly) irrereden
(b) (speak admiringly) schwärmen (**about** von)
2 *attrib. adj.* (coll.) begeistert ‹*Kritik*›
3 *n.* (coll.: dancing party) Rave, *der od. das*

raven /'reɪvn/ *n.* Rabe, *der*

ravenous /'rævənəs/ *adj.* **I'm ~:** ich habe einen Bärenhunger (ugs.)

'rave-up *n.* (Brit. coll.) [wilde] Fete (ugs.)

ravine /rə'viːn/ *n.* Schlucht, *die*

raving /'reɪvɪŋ/ 1 *adj.* irreredend ‹*Idiot*›
2 *adv.* **be ~ mad** völlig verrückt sein (ugs.)

ravish /'rævɪʃ/ *v.t.* (charm) entzücken

'ravishing *adj.* bildschön ‹*Anblick, Person*›; hinreißend ‹*Schönheit*›

raw /rɔː/ *adj.* **(a)** (uncooked) roh
(b) (inexperienced) unerfahren
(c) (stripped of skin) blutig ‹*Fleisch*›; offen ‹*Wunde*›
(d) (chilly) nasskalt

raw ma'terial *n.* Rohstoff, *der*

Rawlplug ® /'rɔːlplʌg/ *n.* Dübel, *der*

ray /reɪ/ *n.* Strahl, *der;* **~ of sunshine/light** Sonnen-/Lichtstrahl, *der*

raze /reɪz/ *v.t.* **~ to the ground** dem Erdboden gleichmachen

razor /'reɪzə(r)/ *n.* Rasiermesser, *das;* [**electric**] **~:** [elektrischer] Rasierapparat

razor: ~ blade *n.* Rasierklinge, *die;* **~-sharp** *adj.* sehr scharf ‹*Messer*›; (fig.) messerscharf ‹*Verstand, Intellekt*›; scharfsinnig ‹*Person*›

RC *abbr.* = **Roman Catholic** r.-k.; röm.-kath.

Rd. *abbr.* = **Road** Str.

re /riː/ *prep.* (Commerc.) betreffs

RE *abbr.* (Brit.) = **Religious Education** Religionslehre, *die*

reach /riːtʃ/ 1 *v.t.* **(a)** (arrive at) erreichen; ankommen in (+ *Dat.*) ‹*Stadt, Land*›; erzielen ‹*Übereinstimmung*›; kommen zu ‹*Entscheidung; Ausgang, Eingang*›; **you can ~ her at this number** du kannst sie unter dieser Nummer erreichen
(b) (extend to) ‹*Straße:*› führen bis zu; ‹*Leiter, Haar:*› reichen bis zu
2 *v.i.* **(a)** (stretch out hand) **~ for sth.** nach etw. greifen; **~ across the table** über den Tisch langen
(b) (be long/tall enough) **sth. will/won't ~:** etw. ist/ist nicht lang genug; **I can't ~:** ich komme nicht daran
(c) (go as far as) ‹*Wasser, Gebäude, Besitz:*› reichen ([**up**] **to** bis [hinauf] zu)
3 *n.* Reichweite, *die;* **be within easy ~** ‹*Ort:*› leicht erreichbar sein; **be out of ~** ‹*Ort:*› nicht erreichbar sein; ‹*Gegenstand:*› außer Reichweite sein

■ **reach 'out** *v.i.* die Hand ausstrecken (**for** nach)

react /rɪ'ækt/ *v.i.* reagieren (**to** auf + *Akk.*)

reaction /rɪ'ækʃn/ *n.* Reaktion, *die* (**to** auf + *Akk.*)

reactionary /rɪ'ækʃənərɪ/ (Polit.) 1 *adj.* reaktionär
2 *n.* Reaktionär, *der*/Reaktionärin, *die*

reactor /rɪ'æktə(r)/ *n.* [**nuclear**] **~:** Kernreaktor, *der*

read /riːd/ 1 *v.t.,* **read** /red/ **(a)** lesen; **~ sb. sth., ~ sth. to sb.** jmdm. etwas vorlesen; **~ the gas meter** das Gas ablesen

(b) (interpret) deuten; **~ between the lines** zwischen den Zeilen lesen
(c) (study) studieren
[2] *v.i.*, **read (a)** lesen; **~ to sb.** jmdm. vorlesen
(b) (convey meaning) lauten; **the contract ~s as follows** der Vertrag hat folgenden Wortlaut
▪ **read 'out** *v.t.* laut vorlesen
▪ **read 'over, read 'through** *v.t.* durchlesen
▪ **read 'up** *v.t.* sich informieren (**on** über + *Akk.*)

readable /'ri:dəbl/ *adj.* **(a)** (pleasant to read) lesenswert
(b) (legible) leserlich

'reader *n.* **(a)** Leser, *der*/Leserin, *die*
(b) (book) Lesebuch, *das*

'readership *n.* Leserschaft, *die*

readily /'redɪlɪ/ *adv.* **(a)** (willingly) bereitwillig
(b) (easily) ohne weiteres

readiness /'redɪnɪs/ *n.* Bereitschaft, *die;* **be in ~:** bereit sein (**for** für)

'reading *n.* **(a)** Lesen, *das*
(b) (figure shown) Anzeige, *die*
(c) (recital) Lesung, *die* (**from** aus)
(d) (Parl.) Lesung, *die*

reading: ~ glasses *n. pl.* Lesebrille, *die;* **~ lamp, ~ light** *ns.* Leselampe, *die;* **~ matter** *n.* Lesestoff, *der;* Lektüre, *die*

readjust /ri:ə'dʒʌst/ [1] *v.t.* neu einstellen; neu anpassen ‹*Gehalt, Zinssatz*›
[2] *v. refl. & i.* **~ [oneself] to** sich wieder gewöhnen an (+ *Akk.*)

read /ri:d/: **~-'only memory** *n.* (Comp.) Fest[wert]speicher, *der;* **~-out** *n.* (Comp.) Ausgabe, *die;* **~-write** *n. attrib.* (Comp.) Schreib-Lese-; **~-write head** Schreib-Lese-Kopf, *der*

ready /'redɪ/ [1] *adj.* **(a)** (prepared) fertig; **be ~ to do sth.** bereit sein, etw. zu tun; **get ~:** sich fertig machen
(b) (willing) bereit
(c) (within reach) griffbereit
[2] *adv.* fertig
[3] *n.* **at the ~** ‹*Schusswaffe*› im Anschlag

ready: ~ 'cash ▸ **~** MONEY; **~-cooked** *adj.* vorgekocht; **~-cooked meal** Fertiggericht, *das;* Fertigmahlzeit, *die;* **~-'made** *adj.* **(a)** Konfektions‹*anzug, -kleidung*›; **(b)** (fig.) vorgefertigt; **~ 'money** *n.* Bargeld, *das;* **~-to-eat** *adj.* Fertig‹*mahlzeit, -dessert*›; **~-to-serve** *adj.* tischfertig; **~-to-wear** *adj.* Konfektions‹*anzug, -kleidung*›

real /rɪəl/ *adj.* **(a)** (actually existing) real ‹*Ereignis, Lebewesen*›; wirklich ‹*Macht*›
(b) (genuine) echt ‹*Interesse, Gold, Seide*›
(c) (complete) total (ugs.) ‹*Desaster, Enttäuschung*›
(d) (true) wahr ‹*Grund, Name, Glück*›; echt ‹*Mitleid, Sieg*›; **the ~ thing** der/die/das Echte
(e) be for ~ (coll.) echt sein

'real estate *n.* (Amer.) Immobilien *Pl.*

realism /'rɪəlɪzm/ *n.* Realismus, *der*

'realist *n.* Realist, *der*/Realistin, *die*

realistic /rɪə'lɪstɪk/ *adj.* realistisch

reality /rɪ'ælɪtɪ/ *n.* Realität, *die;* **in ~:** in Wirklichkeit

reality T'V *n.* Reality-TV, *das*

realization /rɪəlaɪ'zeɪʃn/ *n.* Erkenntnis, *die*

realize /'rɪəlaɪz/ *v.t.* **(a)** (be aware of) bemerken; erkennen ‹*Fehler*›; **I didn't ~** *abs.* ich habe es nicht gewusst; **~ [that] ...:** merken, dass ...
(b) (make happen) verwirklichen
(c) erbringen ‹*Summe, Preis*›

real-life *attrib. adj.* real

really /'rɪəlɪ/ *adv.* wirklich; **not ~:** eigentlich nicht; **[well,] ~!** [also] so was!

realm /relm/ *n.* Reich, *das*

realtor /'ri:əltə(r)/ (Amer.) Grundstücksmakler, *der*

reap /ri:p/ *v.t.* (cut) schneiden ‹*Getreide*›; (gather in) einfahren ‹*Getreide, Ernte*›

reappear /ri:ə'pɪə(r)/ *v.i.* wieder auftauchen; (come back) [wieder] zurückkommen

rear[1] /rɪə(r)/ [1] *n.* **(a)** (back part) hinterer Teil
(b) (back) Rückseite, *die*
(c) (Mil.) Rücken, *der*
[2] *adj.* hinter...; **~ axle** Hinterachse, *die*

rear[2] [1] *v.t.* großziehen ‹*Kind, Familie*›; halten ‹*Vieh*›
[2] *v.i.* ‹*Pferd:*› sich aufbäumen

rear: ~guard *n.* (Mil.) Nachhut, *die;* **~ light** *n.* Rücklicht, *das;* **~-wheel drive** [1] *n.* Hinterradantrieb, *der;* [2] *adj.* **a ~-wheel drive vehicle** ein Fahrzeug mit Hinterradantrieb

rearm /ri:'ɑ:m/ *v.i. & t.* wieder aufrüsten

rearrange /ri:ə'reɪndʒ/ *v.t.* umräumen ‹*Möbel*›; verlegen ‹*Spiel*› (**for** auf + *Akk.*); ändern ‹*Programm*›

rear-view 'mirror *n.* Rückspiegel, *der*

reason /'ri:zn/ [1] *n.* **(a)** (cause) Grund, *der;* **have no ~ to complain** sich nicht beklagen können; **for that [very] ~:** aus [eben] diesem Grund
(b) (power to understand; sense) Vernunft, *die;* (power to think) Verstand, *der;* **in** *or* **within ~:** innerhalb eines vernünftigen Rahmens; **it stands to ~ that ...:** es ist unzweifelhaft, dass ...
[2] *v.i.* **(a)** schlussfolgern (**from** aus)
(b) ~ with diskutieren mit (**about, on** über + *Akk.*); **you can't ~ with her** mit ihr kann man nicht vernünftig reden
[3] *v.t.* schlussfolgern

reasonable /'ri:zənəbl/ *adj.* **(a)** vernünftig
(b) (inexpensive) günstig

reasonably /'ri:zənəblɪ/ *adv.* **(a)** (within reason) vernünftig
(b) (fairly) ganz ‹*gut*›; ziemlich ‹*gesund*›

reasoned /'ri:znd/ *adj.* durchdacht

reasoning /'ri:zənɪŋ/ *n.* logisches Denken

reassurance /ri:ə'ʃʊərəns/ *n.* **(a)** (calming) **give sb. ~:** jmdn. beruhigen
(b) (confirmation) Bestätigung, *die*

reassure /ri:ə'ʃʊə(r)/ *v.t.* beruhigen; **~ sb. about his health.** jmdm. versichern, dass er gesund ist

reassuring /ri:ə'ʃʊərɪŋ/ *adj.* beruhigend

rebate /'ri:beɪt/ *n.* **(a)** (refund) Rückzahlung, *die*
(b) (discount) Preisnachlass, *der* (**on** auf + *Akk.*)

rebel 1 /'rebl/ *n.* Rebell, *der*/Rebellin, *die*
2 *attrib. adj.* Rebellen-
3 /rɪ'bel/ *v.i.*, **-ll-** rebellieren

rebellion /rɪ'beljən/ *n.* Rebellion, *die*

rebellious /rɪ'beljəs/ *adj.* rebellisch

rebirth /ri:'bɜ:θ/ *n.* (revival) Wiederaufleben, *das*

reboot /ri:'bu:t/ (Comp.) *v.t. & i.* neu booten

rebound 1 /rɪ'baʊnd/ *v.i.* **(a)** (spring back) abprallen (**from** von)
(b) (fig.) zurückfallen (**upon** auf + *Akk.*)
2 /'ri:baʊnd/ *n.* Abprall, *der*

rebuff /rɪ'bʌf/ 1 *n.* [schroffe] Abweisung
2 *v.t.* [schroff] zurückweisen

rebuild /ri:'bɪld/ *v.t.*, **rebuilt** /ri:'bɪlt/ wieder aufbauen

rebuke /rɪ'bju:k/ 1 *v.t.* tadeln, rügen (**for** wegen)
2 *n.* Rüge, *die*

recall 1 /rɪ'kɔ:l/ *v.t.* **(a)** (remember) sich erinnern an (+ *Akk.*)
(b) (serve as reminder of) erinnern an (+ *Akk.*)
(c) abberufen ‹*Botschafter*›
2 /rɪ'kɔ:l, 'ri:kɔ:l/ *n.* **(a)** [**powers of**] **~:** Gedächtnis, *das*
(b) beyond ~: unwiderruflich

recant /rɪ'kænt/ *v.i.* [öffentlich] widerrufen

recap /'rɪ:kæp/ *v.t. & i.*, **-pp-** (coll.) rekapitulieren

recapitulate /ri:kə'pɪtjʊleɪt/ *v.t. & i.* rekapitulieren

recapture /rɪ:'kæptʃə(r)/ *v.t.* wieder ergreifen ‹*Gefangenen*›; wieder einfangen ‹*Tier*›

recede /ri'si:d/ *v.i.* ‹*Hochwasser, Flut:*› zurückgehen; **~** [**into the distance**] in der Ferne verschwinden

receding /rɪ'si:dɪŋ/ *adj.* fliehend ‹*Kinn, Stirn*›

receipt /rɪ'si:t/ *n.* **(a)** (receiving) Empfang, *der*
(b) (written acknowledgement) Quittung, *die*
(c) *in pl.* (amount received) Einnahmen *Pl.* (**from** aus)

receive /rɪ'si:v/ *v.t.* **(a)** (get) erhalten; beziehen ‹*Gehalt, Rente*›
(b) (accept) entgegennehmen ‹*Strauß, Lieferung*›
(c) (entertain) empfangen ‹*Gast*›

re'ceiver *n.* **(a)** Empfänger, *der*/Empfängerin, *die*
(b) (Teleph.) [Telefon]hörer, *der*
(c) (of stolen goods) Hehler, *der*/Hehlerin, *die*

recent /'ri:sənt/ *adj.* jüngst... ‹*Ereignisse, Vergangenheit usw.*›; **the ~ closure of the factory** die kürzlich erfolgte Schließung der Fabrik

'recently *adv.* (a short time ago) vor kurzem; (in the recent past) in der letzten Zeit

receptacle /rɪ'septəkl/ *n.* Behälter, *der;* Gefäß, *das*

reception /rɪ'sepʃn/ *n.* **(a)** (welcome) Aufnahme, *die*
(b) (party) Empfang, *der*
(c) (Brit.: foyer) die Rezeption

reception: ~ com'mittee *n.* Empfangskomittee, *das;* **~ desk** *n.* Rezeption, *die*

re'ceptionist *n.* (in hotel) Empfangschef, *der*/-dame, *die;* (at doctor's) Sprechstundenhilfe, *die*

receptive /rɪ'septɪv/ *adj.* aufgeschlossen, empfänglich (**to** für)

recess /rɪ'ses, 'ri:ses/ *n.* **(a)** (alcove) Nische, *die*
(b) (Brit. Parl.; Amer.: short vacation) Ferien *Pl.;* (Amer. Sch.; between classes) Pause, *die*

recession /rɪ'seʃn/ *n.* (Econ.) Rezession, *die* (fachspr.); Konjunkturrückgang, *der*

recharge /ri:'tʃɑ:dʒ/ *v.t.* aufladen ‹*Batterie*›

rechargeable /ri:'tʃɑ:dʒəbl/ *adj.* wieder aufladbar

recipe /'resɪpɪ/ *n.* Rezept, *das*

recipient /rɪ'sɪpɪənt/ *n.* Empfänger, *der*/Empfängerin, *die*

reciprocal /rɪ'sɪprəkl/ *adj.* gegenseitig ‹*Abkommen, Zuneigung*›

reciprocate /rɪ'siprəkeɪt/ *v.t.* erwidern

recital /rɪ'saɪtl/ *n.* (performance) [Solisten]konzert, *das;* (of literature also) Rezitation, *die*

recitation /resɪ'teɪʃn/ *n.* Rezitation, *die*

recite /rɪ'saɪt/ *v.t.* **(a)** rezitieren ‹*Gedicht*›
(b) (list) aufzählen

reckless /'reklɪs/ *adj.* unbesonnen; rücksichtslos ‹*Fahrweise*›; **~ of the dangers/consequences** ungeachtet der Gefahren/Folgen

reckon /'rekn/ *v.t.* **(a)** (work out) ausrechnen ‹*Kosten*›; bestimmen ‹*Position*›
(b) (consider) halten (**as** für)
(c) (estimate) schätzen

■ **'reckon on** *v.t.* **(a)** (rely on) zählen auf (+ *Akk.*)
(b) (expect) rechnen mit

■ **'reckon with** *v.i.* rechnen mit

'reckoning *n.* Berechnung, *die;* **by my ~:** nach meiner Rechnung

reclaim /rɪ'kleɪm/ *v.t.* **(a)** zurückbekommen ‹*Steuern*›
(b) urbar machen ‹*Land*›

recline /rɪ'klaɪn/ *v.i.* liegen; **reclining seat** Liegesitz, *der*

recluse /rɪ'klu:s/ *n.* Einsiedler, *der*/ Einsiedlerin, *die*

recognition /rekəg'nɪʃn/ *n.* **(a)** Wiedererkennen, *das;* **be beyond all ~:** nicht wieder zu erkennen sein
(b) (acknowledgement) Anerkennung, *die;* **in ~ of** als Anerkennung für

recognize /'rekəgnaɪz/ *v.t.* **(a)** (know again) wieder erkennen (**by** an + *Dat.*, **from** durch)
(b) (acknowledge) erkennen; anerkennen ‹*Gültigkeit, Land*›; **be ~d as** gelten als

recoil **1** /rɪ'kɔɪl/ *v.i.* zurückfahren
2 /'ri:kɔɪl, rɪ'kɔɪl/ *n.* Rückstoß, *der*

recollect /rekə'lekt/ **1** *v.t.* sich erinnern an (+ *Akk.*)
2 *v.i.* sich erinnern

recollection /rekə'lekʃn/ *n.* Erinnerung, *die*

recommend /rekə'mend/ *v.t.* empfehlen

recommendation /rekəmen'deɪʃn/ *n.* Empfehlung, *die;* **on sb.'s ~:** auf jmds. Empfehlung (*Akk.*)

recompense /'rekəmpens/ **1** *v.t.* entschädigen
2 *n.* Entschädigung, *die*

reconcile /'rekənsaɪl/ *v.t.* **(a)** (restore to friendship) versöhnen
(b) **~ oneself to sth.** sich mit etw. versöhnen

reconciliation /rekənsɪlɪ'eɪʃn/ *n.* Versöhnung, *die*

recondition /ri:kən'dɪʃn/ *v.t.* [general]überholen; **~ed engine** Austauschmotor, *der*

reconnaissance /rɪ'kɒnɪsəns/ *n.* (Mil.) Aufklärung, *die*

reconnoitre (*Brit.; Amer.:* **reconnoiter**) /rekə'nɔɪtə(r)/ *v.i.* auf Erkundung [aus]gehen

reconsider /ri:kən'sɪdə(r)/ *v.t.* [noch einmal] überdenken

reconstruct /ri:kən'strʌkt/ *v.t.* wieder aufbauen; (fig.) rekonstruieren

reconstruction /ri:kən'strʌkʃn/ *n.* Wiederaufbau, *der;* (thing reconstructed) Rekonstruktion, *die*

record **1** /rɪ'kɔ:d/ *v.t.* **(a)** aufzeichnen; **~ a new CD** eine neue CD aufnehmen
(b) (register officially) dokumentieren; protokollieren ‹*Verhandlung*›
2 /'rekɔ:d/ *n.* **(a)** **be on ~** ‹*Prozess, Verhandlung, Besprechung:*› protokolliert sein; **have sth. on ~:** etw. dokumentiert haben
(b) (report) Protokoll, *das*
(c) (document) Dokument, *das;* **[strictly] off the ~:** [ganz] inoffiziell
(d) (for ~ player) [Schall]platte, *die*
(e) **have a [criminal/police] ~:** vorbestraft sein
(f) (Sport) Rekord, *der*

record /'rekɔ:d/**: ~-breaking** *adj.* Rekord-; **~ deck** *n.* Plattenspieler, *der*

recorded /rɪ'kɔ:dɪd/ *adj.* aufgezeichnet ‹*Konzert, Rede*›; **~ music** Musikaufnahmen *Pl.*

recorded de'livery *n.* (Brit. Post.) eingeschriebene Sendung (ohne Versicherung)

recorder /rɪ'kɔ:də(r)/ *n.* (Mus.) Blockflöte, *die*

'record holder *n.* (Sport) Rekordhalter, *der*/-halterin, *die*

recording /rɪ'kɔ:dɪŋ/ *n.* **(a)** (process) Aufzeichnung, *die*
(b) (what is recorded) Aufnahme, *die*

recording: ~ head *n.* Aufnahmekopf, *der;* **~ studio** *n.* Tonstudio, *das*

record /'rekɔ:d/**: ~ player** *n.* Plattenspieler, *der;* **~ sleeve** *n.* Plattenhülle, *die;* **~ token** *n.* [Schall]plattengutschein, *der*

re-count **1** /ri:'kaʊnt/ *v.t.* [noch einmal] nachzählen
2 /'ri:kaʊnt/ *n.* Nachzählung, *die*

recoup /rɪ'ku:p/ *v.t.* [wieder] hereinbekommen ‹[*Geld*]*einsatz*›

recourse /rɪ'kɔ:s/ *n.* **have ~ to sb./sth.** bei jmdm./zu etw. Zuflucht nehmen

recover /rɪ'kʌvə(r)/ **1** *v.t.* zurückbekommen
2 *v.i.* **~ from sth.** sich von etw. [wieder] erholen; **be [fully] ~ed** [völlig] wiederhergestellt sein

recovery /rɪ'kʌvərɪ/ *n.* Erholung, *die;* **make a quick/good ~:** sich schnell/gut erholen

recovery: ~ position *n.* (Med.) stabile Seitenlage; **~ vehicle** *n.* Bergungsfahrzeug, *das*

recreation /rekrɪ'eɪʃn/ *n.* Freizeitbeschäftigung, *die;* Hobby, *das*

recreational /rekrɪ'eɪʃənl/ *adj.* Freizeit-

recreational: ~ 'drug *n.* Freizeitdroge, *die;* **~ 'vehicle** *n.* (Amer.) Wohnmobil, *das*

recre'ation centre *n.* Freizeitzentrum, *das*

recrimination /rɪkrɪmɪ'neɪʃn/ *n.* Gegenbeschuldigung, *die*

recruit /rɪ'kru:t/ **1** *n.* **(a)** (Mil.) Rekrut, *der*
(b) (new member) neues Mitglied
2 *v.t.* (Mil.: enlist) anwerben; (into party etc.) werben ‹*Mitglied*›; einstellen ‹*neuen Mitarbeiter*›

re'cruitment *n.* (Mil.) Anwerbung, *die;* (of new staff) Neueinstellung, *die;* **~ of members** Mitgliederwerbung, *die*

rectangle /'rektæŋgl/ *n.* Rechteck, *das*

rectangular /rek'tæŋgjʊlə(r)/ *adj.* rechteckig

rector /'rektə(r)/ *n.* **(a)** Pfarrer, *der*
(b) (Univ.) Rektor, *der*/Rektorin, *die*

r

rectory /'rektərɪ/ *n.* Pfarrhaus, *das*

recuperate /rɪ'kju:pəreɪt/ *v.i.* sich erholen

recuperation /rɪkju:pə'reɪʃn/ *n.* Erholung, *die*

recur /rɪ'kɜ:(r)/ *v.i.*, **-rr-** sich wiederholen; ‹*Krankheit:*› wiederkehren; ‹*Symptom:*› wieder auftreten

recurrence /rɪ'kʌrəns/ *n.* Wiederholung, *die;* (of illness, thought, feeling) Wiederkehr, *die;* (of symptom) Wiederauftreten, *das*

recurrent /rɪ'kʌrənt/ *adj.* immer wiederkehrend

recycle /ri:'saɪkl/ *v.t.* wieder verwerten; **~d paper** Recyclingpapier, *das*

recyclable /rɪ:'saɪkləbl/ *adj.* recycelbar

recycling /rɪ:'saɪklɪŋ/ *n.* Recycling, *das*

red /red/ **1** *adj.* rot
2 *n.* **(a)** Rot, *das*
(b) (debt) **[be] in the ~:** in den roten Zahlen [sein]

red: ~ 'card *n.* (Footb.) rote Karte, *die;* **Red 'Crescent** *n.* Roter Halbmond; **Red 'Cross** *n.* Rotes Kreuz; **~'currant** *n.* [rote] Johannisbeere

redden /'redn/ *v.i.* ‹*Gesicht, Himmel:*› sich röten; ‹*Person:*› rot werden

reddish /'redɪʃ/ *adj.* rötlich

redecorate /ri:'dekəreɪt/ *v.t.* renovieren; (with wallpaper) neu tapezieren; (with paint) neu streichen

redeem /rɪ'di:m/ *v.t.* **(a)** [wieder] einlösen ‹*Pfand*›; einlösen ‹*Gutschein, Coupon*›
(b) (save) retten

redemption /rɪ'dempʃn/ *n.* (from sin) Erlösung, *die*

r

redeploy /ri:dɪ'plɔɪ/ *v.t.* woanders einsetzen ‹*Arbeitskräfte*›

red: ~-'handed *adj.* **catch sb. ~-handed** jmdn. auf frischer Tat ertappen; **~ 'herring** *n.* (fig.) Ablenkungsmanöver, *das;* **~-hot** *adj.* [rot] glühend

redial **1** /ri:'daɪəl/ *v.t.* noch einmal wählen ‹*Telefonnummer*›
2 /'ri:daɪəl/ *n.* Wahlwiederholung, *die;* **~ button** Wahlwiederholungstaste, *die*

Red 'Indian (Brit. dated) **1** *n.* Indianer, *der*/Indianerin, *die*
2 *adj.* Indianer-

redirect /ri:daɪ'rekt/ *v.t.* nachsenden ‹*Post, Brief usw.*›; umleiten ‹*Verkehr*›

rediscover /ri:dɪ'skʌvə(r)/ *v.t.* wieder entdecken

redistribute /ri:dɪ'strɪbju:t/ *v.t.* umverteilen ‹*Besitz, Einkommen*›

redistribution /ri:dɪstrɪ'bju:ʃn/ *n.* (of land, wealth) Umverteilung, *die*

red: ~-'letter day *n.* großer Tag; **~ 'light** *n.* rotes Warnlicht; (traffic light) rote Ampel; **drive through a ~ light** bei Rot über die Ampel fahren; **~-'light district** *n.* Strich, *der* (salopp); **~ meat** *n.* dunkles Fleisch (*z.B. vom Rind*)

redo /ri:'du:/ *v.t. forms as* DO: noch einmal machen ‹*Bett, Hausaufgabe*›; neu frisieren ‹*Haare*›

redouble /ri:'dʌbl/ *v.t.* verdoppeln

red 'pepper *n.* rote Paprika[schote]

redress /rɪ'dres/ **1** *n.* Entschädigung, *die*
2 *v.t.* wieder gutmachen; **~ the balance** das Gleichgewicht wiederherstellen

red 'tape *n.* (fig.) [unnötige] Bürokratie

reduce /rɪ'dju:s/ *v.t.* **(a)** senken ‹*Preis, Gebühr, Fieber, Aufwendungen, Blutdruck usw.*›; reduzieren ‹*Geschwindigkeit, Gewicht*›; **at ~d prices** zu herabgesetzten Preisen
(b) ~ to silence/tears verstummen lassen/zum Weinen bringen

reduction /rɪ'dʌkʃn/ *n.* (in price, costs, speed, etc.) Senkung, *die* **(in** *Gen.*); **~ in wages/weight** Lohnsenkung, *die*/Gewichtsabnahme, *die*

redundancy /rɪ'dʌndənsɪ/ *n.* (Brit.) Arbeitslosigkeit, *die;* **redundancies** Entlassungen *Pl.*; **take** *or* **accept voluntary ~:** seiner betriebsbedingten Kündigung zustimmen; **~ payment** Abfindung, *die*

redundant /rɪ'dʌndənt/ *adj.* (Brit.) arbeitslos; **be made ~:** den Arbeitsplatz verlieren; **make ~:** entlassen

red 'wine *n.* Rotwein, *der*

reed /ri:d/ *n.* Schilf[rohr], *das*

re-educate /ri:'edjʊkeɪt/ *v.t.* umerziehen

reef /ri:f/ *n.* Riff, *das*

'reef knot *n.* Kreuzknoten, *der*

reek /ri:k/ *v.i.* stinken **(of** nach)

reel /ri:l/ **1** *n.* ‹*Garn-, Angel*›rolle, *die;* ‹*Film-, Tonband*›spule, *die*
2 *v.i.* **(a)** (be in a whirl) sich drehen
(b) (sway) torkeln

re-establish /ri:ɪ'stæblɪʃ/ *v.t.* wiederherstellen

re-examine /ri:ɪg'zæmɪn/ *v.t.* (scrutinize) erneut überprüfen

ref /ref/ *n.* (Sport coll.) Schiri, *der* (Sportjargon)

ref. *abbr.* = **reference** Verw.; **your/our ref.** Ihr/unser Zeichen

refashion /ri:'fæʃn/ *v.t.* umgestalten

refectory /rɪ'fektərɪ/ *n.* Mensa, *die*

refer /rɪ'fɜ:(r)/ **1** *v.i.*, **-rr-: (a) ~ to** (allude to) sich beziehen auf (+ *Akk.*) ‹*Buch, Person usw.*›; (speak of) sprechen von ‹*Person, Problem usw.*›
(b) ~ to (apply to, relate to) betreffen
(c) ~ to (consult, cite as proof) nachsehen in (+ *Dat.*)
2 *v.t.*, **-rr-: ~ sb./sth. to sb./sth.** jmdn./etw. an jmdn./auf etw. (*Akk.*) verweisen

referee /refə'ri:/ (Sport) **1** *n.* (umpire) Schiedsrichter, *der*/-richterin, *die;* (Boxing) Ringrichter, *der*
2 *v.t.* als Schiedsrichter/-richterin leiten

reference /'refrəns/ *n.* **(a)** (allusion) Hinweis, *der* (**to** auf + *Akk.*); **make no ~ to sth.** etw. nicht ansprechen
(b) (testimonial) Zeugnis, *das*

reference: ~ book *n.* Nachschlagewerk, *das;* **~ number** *n.* [Kenn]nummer, *die;* **~ point** *n.* Bezugspunkt, *der*

referendum /refə'rendəm/ *n.* Volksentscheid, *der*

refill [1] /ri:'fɪl/ *v.t.* nachfüllen; **~ the glasses** nachschenken
[2] /'ri:fɪl/ *n.* (for ball pen) Ersatzmine, *die*

refine /rɪ'faɪn/ *v.t.* **(a)** (purify) raffinieren
(b) (make cultured) kultivieren
(c) (improve) verbessern; verfeinern ‹*Stil, Technik*›

refined /rɪ'faɪnd/ *adj.* kultiviert

re'finement *n.* Kultiviertheit, *die;* (improvement) Verbesserung, *die*

refinery /rɪ'faɪnərɪ/ *n.* Raffinerie, *die*

reflate /ri:'fleɪt/ *v.t.* (Econ.) ankurbeln

reflation /ri:'fleɪʃn/ *n.* (Econ.) Reflation, *die*

reflect /rɪ'flekt/ *v.t.* **(a)** reflektieren
(b) (fig.) widerspiegeln ‹*Ansichten*›
(c) (contemplate) nachdenken über (+ *Akk.*); **~ what/how ...**: überlegen, was/wie ...

■ **re'flect [up]on** *v.t.* **(a)** (consider) nachdenken über (+ *Akk.*)
(b) ~ badly [up]on sb./sth. auf jmdn./etw. ein schlechtes Licht werfen

reflection /rɪ'flekʃn/ *n.* **(a)** Reflexion, *die;* (by surface of water) Spiegelung, *die*
(b) (image) Spiegelbild, *das*
(c) (consideration) Nachdenken, *das* (**upon** über + *Akk.*); **on ~**: bei weiterem Nachdenken

reflective /rɪ'flektɪv/ *adj.* **(a)** reflektierend
(b) (thoughtful) nachdenklich

reflector /rɪ'flektə(r)/ *n.* Rückstrahler, *der*

reflex /'ri:fleks/ [1] *n.* Reflex, *der*
[2] *adj.* **~ action** Reflexhandlung, *die*

reflexive /rɪ'fleksɪv/ *adj.* (Ling.) reflexiv

reforestation /ri:fɒrɪ'steɪʃn/ *n.* Wiederaufforstung, *die*

reform /rɪ'fɔ:m/ [1] *v.t.* (make better) bessern ‹*Person*›; reformieren ‹*Institution*›
[2] *n.* Reform, *die* (**in** *Gen.*)

reformation /refə'meɪʃn/ *n.* (of character) Wandlung, *die;* **the R~** (Hist.) die Reformation

re'former *n.* **[political] ~**: Reformpolitiker, *der*/-politikerin, *die*

refract /rɪ'frækt/ *v.t.* (Phys.) brechen

refrain¹ /rɪ'freɪn/ *n.* Refrain, *der*

refrain² *v.i.* **~ from doing sth.** es unterlassen, etw. zu tun

refresh /rɪ'freʃ/ *v.t.* erfrischen

re'fresher course *n.* Auffrischungskurs, *der*

re'freshing *adj.* erfrischend; wohltuend ‹*Abwechslung*›

re'freshment *n.* Erfrischung, *die*

refrigerate /rɪ'frɪdʒəreɪt/ *v.t.* **(a)** kühl lagern ‹*Lebensmittel*›
(b) (chill) kühlen; (freeze) einfrieren

refrigeration /rɪfrɪdʒə'reɪʃn/ *n.* kühle Lagerung; (chilling) Kühlung, *die;* (freezing) Einfrieren, *das*

refrigerator /rɪ'frɪdʒəreɪtə(r)/ *n.* Kühlschrank, *der*

refuel /ri:'fju:əl/, (Brit.) **-ll-**: [1] *v.t.* auftanken
[2] *v.i.* [auf]tanken

refuge /'refju:dʒ/ *n.* Zuflucht, *die;* **take ~ in** Schutz *od.* Zuflucht suchen in (+ *Dat.*) (**from** vor + *Dat.*); **women's ~**: Frauenhaus, *das*

refugee /refjʊ'dʒi:/ *n.* Flüchtling, *der*

refu'gee camp *n.* Flüchtlingslager, *das*

refund [1] /ri:'fʌnd/ *v.t.* (pay back) zurückzahlen ‹*Geld*›; erstatten ‹*Kosten*›
[2] /'ri:fʌnd/ *n.* Rückzahlung, *die;* (of expenses) [Rück]erstattung, *die*

refundable /ri:'fʌndəbl/ *adj.* **be ~**: zurückerstattet werden

refurbish /ri:'fɜ:bɪʃ/ *v.t.* renovieren ‹*Haus*›

refurnish /ri:'fɜ:nɪʃ/ *v.t.* neu einrichten

refusal /rɪ'fju:zl/ *n.* Ablehnung, *die;* (after a period of time) Absage, *die;* **~ to do sth.** Weigerung, etw. zu tun

refuse¹ /rɪ'fju:z/ [1] *v.t.* ablehnen; verweigern ‹*Zutritt, Einreise, Erlaubnis*›; **~ sb. admittance/entry/permission** jmdm. den Zutritt/die Einreise/die Erlaubnis verweigern; **~ to do sth.** sich weigern, etw. zu tun
[2] *v.i.* ablehnen; (after request) sich weigern

refuse² /'refju:s/ *n.* Abfall, *der*

refuse /'refju:s/**: ~ collection** *n.* Müllabfuhr, *die;* **~ collector** *n.* Müllwerker, *der;* **~ disposal** *n.* Abfallbeseitigung, *die*

refute /rɪ'fju:t/ *v.t.* widerlegen

regain /rɪ'geɪn/ *v.t.* zurückgewinnen ‹*Zuversicht, Vertrauen, Augenlicht*›; **~ one's strength** wieder zu Kräften kommen

regal /'ri:gl/ *adj.* majestätisch

regalia /rɪ'geɪlɪə/ *n. pl.* (of royalty) Krönungsinsignien *Pl.*

regard /rɪ'gɑ:d/ [1] *v.t.* **(a)** (look at) betrachten
(b) (give heed to) beachten
(c) (fig.: look upon, contemplate) betrachten; **~ sb. as a friend/fool/genius** jmdn. als Freund betrachten/für einen Dummkopf/ein Genie halten; **be ~ed as** gelten als
(d) (concern, have relation to) betreffen; **as ~s sb./sth., ~ing sb./sth.** was jmdn./etw. angeht *od.* betrifft
[2] *n.* **(a)** (attention) **pay** *or* **have ~ to sb./sth.** jmdm./etw. Beachtung schenken; **without ~ to** ohne Rücksicht auf (+ *Akk.*)
(b) (esteem) Achtung, *die;* **hold sb./sth. in high ~**: jmdn./etw. sehr schätzen
(c) *in pl.* Grüße *Pl.*; **give her my ~s** grüße sie von mir; **with kind[est] ~s** mit herzlich[st]en Grüßen

r

re'gardless *adj.* ohne Rücksicht (**of** auf + *Akk.*)
regatta /rɪ'gætə/ *n.* Regatta, *die*
regenerate /rɪ'dʒenəreɪt/ *v.t.* erneuern
reggae /'regeɪ/ *n.* Reggae, *der*
regime, régime /reɪ'ʒi:m/ *n.* [Regierungs]system, *das*
regiment /'redʒɪmənt/ *n.* Regiment, *das*
regimental /redʒɪ'mentl/ *adj.* Regiments-
region /'ri:dʒn/ *n.* **(a)** (area) Gebiet, *das* **(b)** (administrative division) Bezirk, *der;* **in the ~ of** (fig.) ungefähr
regional /'ri:dʒənl/ *adj.* regional
regionalism /'ri:dʒənəlɪzm/ *n.* (Polit., Ling.) Regionalismus, *der*
regionalize /'ri:dʒənəlaɪz/ *v.t.* regionalisieren
register /'redʒɪstə(r)/ **1** *n.* Register, *das;* (at school) Klassenbuch, *das*
2 *v.t.* **(a)** (enter) registrieren; (cause to be entered) registrieren lassen; anmelden ‹*Auto, Patent*›; (at airport) einchecken ‹*Gepäck*›; *abs.* (at hotel) sich ins Fremdenbuch eintragen; **~ with the police** sich polizeilich anmelden
(b) (enrol) anmelden; (Univ.) sich einschreiben
(c) zum Ausdruck bringen ‹*Überraschung*›; **~ a protest** Protest anmelden
registered /'redʒɪstəd/ *adj.* eingetragen ‹*Firma*›; eingeschrieben ‹*Student, Brief*›; **~ trade mark** eingetragenes Warenzeichen; **by ~ post** per Einschreiben
registrar /'redʒɪstrɑ:(r)/ *n.* Standesbeamte, *der*/-beamtin, *die*
registration /redʒɪ'streɪʃn/ *n.* Registrierung, *die;* (enrolment) Anmeldung, *die;* (of students) Einschreibung, *die*
registration: ~ document *n.* (Brit.) Kraftfahrzeugbrief, *der;* **~ form** *n.* Anmeldeformular, *das;* **~ number** *n.* amtliches Kennzeichen; **~ plate** *n.* (Motor Veh.) Nummernschild, *das*
registry /'redʒɪstrɪ/ *n.* **~ [office]** Standesamt, *das*
regret /rɪ'gret/ **1** *v.t.*, **-tt-** bedauern; **I ~ to say that ...:** ich muss leider sagen, dass ...
2 *n.* Bedauern, *das;* **have no ~s** nichts bereuen
regretfully /rɪ'gretfəlɪ/ *adv.* mit Bedauern
regrettable /rɪ'gretəbl/ *adj.* bedauerlich
regrettably /rɪ'gretəblɪ/ *adv.* bedauerlicherweise
regroup /ri:'gru:p/ **1** *v.t.* umgruppieren
2 *v.i.* **(a)** (form new group) sich neu gruppieren
(b) (Mil.) sich neu formieren
regular /'regjʊlə(r)/ **1** *adj.* regelmäßig; geregelt ‹*Arbeit*›; fest ‹*Anstellung*›; **~ customer** Stammkunde, *der*/-kundin, *die;* **~ army** reguläre Armee
2 *n.* (coll.: ~ customer) Stammkunde, *der*/-kundin, *die;* (in pub) Stammgast, *der*
regularity /regjʊ'lærɪtɪ/ *n.* Regelmäßigkeit, *die*
'regularly *adv.* regelmäßig
regulate /'regjʊleɪt/ *v.t.* (control) regeln; (restrict) begrenzen; (adjust) regulieren
regulation /regjʊ'leɪʃn/ *n.* **(a)** ▶ REGULATE: Regelung, *die;* Begrenzung, *die;* Regulierung, *die*
(b) (rule) Vorschrift, *die*
rehabilitate /ri:hə'bɪlɪteɪt/ *v.t.* rehabilitieren; **~ [back into society]** wieder [in die Gesellschaft] eingliedern
rehabilitation /ri:həbɪlɪ'teɪʃn/ *n.* **~ [in society]** Wiedereingliederung, *die* [in die Gesellschaft]
rehash **1** /ri:'hæʃ/ *v.t.* aufwärmen
2 /'ri:hæʃ/ *n.* Aufguss, *der*
rehearsal /rɪ'hɜ:sl/ *n.* Probe, *die*
rehearse /rɪ'hɜ:s/ *v.t.* proben
reheat /ri:'hi:t/ *v.t.* wieder erwärmen; aufwärmen ‹*Essen*›
rehouse /ri:'haʊz/ *v.t.* umquartieren
reign /reɪn/ **1** *n.* Herrschaft, *die*
2 *v.i.* herrschen (**over** über + *Akk.*)
reimburse /ri:ɪm'bɜ:s/ *v.t.* [zurück]erstatten ‹[*Un*]*kosten, Spesen*›; entschädigen ‹*Person*›
rein /reɪn/ *n.* Zügel, *der*
reincarnation /ri:ɪnkɑ:'neɪʃn/ *n.* (Relig.) Reinkarnation, *die*
reindeer /'reɪndɪə(r)/ *n., pl. same* Ren[tier], *das*
reinforce /ri:ɪn'fɔ:s/ *v.t.* verstärken; **~d concrete** Stahlbeton, *der*
rein'forcement *n.* Verstärkung, *die;* **~[s]** (additional men etc.) Verstärkung, *die*
reinstate /ri:ɪn'steɪt/ *v.t.* (in job) wieder einstellen
reintegrate /ri:'ɪntɪgreɪt/ **1** *v.t.* wieder eingliedern (**into** in + *Akk.*)
2 *v. refl.* sich wieder eingliedern (**into** in + *Akk.*)
reintegration /ri:ɪntɪ'greɪʃn/ *n.* Wiedereingliederung, *die* (**into** in + *Akk.*)
reinvigorate /ri:ɪn'vɪgəreɪt/ *v.t.* neu beleben; **feel ~d** sich gestärkt fühlen
reissue /ri:'ɪʃu:/ *v.t.* neu herausbringen
reiterate /ri:'ɪtəreɪt/ *v.t.* wiederholen
reject **1** /rɪ'dʒekt/ *v.t.* ablehnen; zurückweisen ‹*Bitte, Annäherungsversuch*›
2 /'ri:dʒekt/ (thing) Ausschuss, *der*
rejection /rɪ'dʒekʃn/ *n.* Ablehnung, *die*/Zurückweisung, *die*
re'jection slip *n.* Absage, *die*
rejoice /rɪ'dʒɔɪs/ *v.i.* sich freuen (**over, at** über + *Akk.*)
rejoin[1] /rɪ'dʒɔɪn/ *v.t.* (reply) erwidern (**to** auf + *Akk.*)
rejoin[2] /ri:'dʒɔɪn/ *v.t.* wieder eintreten in (+ *Akk.*) ‹*Partei, Verein*›
rejoinder /rɪ'dʒɔɪndə(r)/ *n.* Erwiderung, *die* (**to** auf + *Akk.*)
rejuvenate /rɪ'dʒu:vəneɪt/ *v.t.* verjüngen

rekindle /ri:kɪndl/ *v.t.* wieder anfachen; wieder aufleben lassen ‹*Verlangen, Hoffnungen*›

relapse /rɪ'læps/ [1] *v.i.* ‹*Kranker:*› einen Rückfall bekommen
[2] *n.* Rückfall, *der*

relate /rɪ'leɪt/ [1] *v.t.* **(a)** erzählen ‹*Geschichte*›; erzählen von ‹*Abenteuer*›
(b) (bring into relation) in Zusammenhang bringen (**to, with** mit)
[2] *v.i.* **(a)** ~ **to** (have reference) in Zusammenhang stehen mit; betreffen ‹*Person*›
(b) ~ **to** (feel involved with) eine Beziehung haben zu

re'lated *adj.* verwandt (**to** mit)

relation /rɪ'leɪʃn/ *n.* **(a)** (connection) Beziehung, *die*, Zusammenhang, *der* (**of ... and** zwischen ... und); **in** *or* **with** ~ **to** in Bezug auf (+ *Akk.*)
(b) *in pl.* (dealings) Verhältnis, *das* (**with** zu)
(c) (relative) Verwandte, *der/die*

re'lationship *n.* **(a)** (mutual tie) Beziehung, *die* (**with** zu)
(b) (kinship) Verwandtschaftsverhältnis, *das*
(c) (connection) Beziehung, *die;* (between cause and effect) Zusammenhang, *der*
(d) (sexual) Verhältnis, *das*

relative /'relətɪv/ [1] *n.* Verwandte, *der/die*
[2] *adj.* relativ; Relativ‹*satz, -pronomen*›

'relatively *adv.* relativ; verhältnismäßig

relative 'pronoun *n.* (Ling.) Relativpronomen, *das*

relax /rɪ'læks/ [1] *v.t.* **(a)** entspannen ‹*Muskel, Körper*[*teil*]›; lockern ‹*Griff*›
(b) (make less strict) lockern ‹*Gesetz, Disziplin*›
[2] *v.i.* sich entspannen

relaxation /ri:læk'seɪʃn/ *n.* Entspannung, *die;* **for** ~: zur Entspannung

relaxed /rɪ'lækst/ *adj.* entspannt, gelöst ‹*Atmosphäre, Person*›

re'laxing *adj.* entspannend

relay [1] /'ri:leɪ/ *n.* **(a)** (race) Staffel, *die*
(b) (gang) Schicht, *die;* **work in** ~**s** schichtweise arbeiten
(c) (Electr.) Relais, *das*
[2] /ri:'leɪ/ *v.t.* **(a)** weiterleiten
(b) (Radio, Telev.) übertragen

'relay race *n.* Staffellauf, *der;* (Swimming) Staffelschwimmen, *das*

release /rɪ'li:s/ [1] *v.t.* **(a)** (free) freilassen ‹*Tier, Häftling, Sklaven*›; (from jail) entlassen (**from** aus)
(b) (let go) loslassen; lösen ‹*Handbremse*›
(c) (make known) veröffentlichen ‹*Erklärung, Nachricht*›; (issue) herausbringen ‹*Film, Schallplatte*›
[2] *n.* **(a)** ▶ 1A: Freilassung, *die;* Entlassung, *die*
(b) (of published item) Veröffentlichung, *die*
(c) (handle, lever, button) Auslöser, *der*

relegate /'relɪgeɪt/ *v.t.* **(a)** ~ **sb. to the position of ...:** jmdn. zu ... degradieren
(b) (Sport) absteigen lassen; **be** ~**d** absteigen (**to** in + *Akk.*)

relegation /relɪ'geɪʃn/ *n.* (Sport) Abstieg, *der*

relent /rɪ'lent/ *v.i.* nachgeben

re'lentless *adj.*, **re'lentlessly** *adv.* unerbittlich

relevance /'relɪvəns/ *n.* Relevanz, *die* (**to** für)

relevant /'relɪvənt/ *adj.* relevant (**to** für); wichtig ‹*Information*›

reliability /rɪlaɪə'bɪlɪtɪ/ *n.* Zuverlässigkeit, *die*

reliable /rɪ'laɪəbl/ *adj.*, **reliably** /rɪ'laɪəblɪ/ *adv.* zuverlässig

reliance /rɪ'laɪəns/ *n.* Abhängigkeit, *die* (**on** von)

reliant /rɪ'laɪənt/ *adj.* **be** ~ **on sb./sth.** auf jmdn./etw. angewiesen sein

relief[1] /rɪ'li:f/ *n.* **(a)** Erleichterung, *die;* **give** [**sb.**] ~ [**from pain**] [jmdm.] [Schmerz]linderung verschaffen; **what a** ~**!, that's a** ~**!** da bin ich aber erleichtert!
(b) (assistance) Hilfe, *die*

relief[2] *n.* (Art) Relief, *das*

relief: ~ **bus** *n.* Entlastungsbus, *der;* (as replacement) Ersatzbus, *der;* ~ **map** *n.* Reliefkarte, *die;* ~ **road** *n.* Entlastungsstraße, *die;* ~ **worker** *n.* Helfer, *der*

relieve /rɪ'li:v/ *v.t.* **(a)** erleichtern; unterbrechen ‹*Eintönigkeit*›; abbauen ‹*Anspannung*›; stillen ‹*Schmerzen*›; **I am** *or* **feel** ~**d to hear that ...:** es erleichtert mich zu hören, dass ...
(b) ablösen ‹*Wache, Truppen*›

religion /rɪ'lɪdʒn/ *n.* Religion, *die*

religious /rɪ'lɪdʒəs/ *adj.* religiös; Religions‹*freiheit, -unterricht*›

re'ligiously *adv.* (conscientiously) gewissenhaft

relinquish /rɪ'lɪŋkwɪʃ/ *v.t.* **(a)** (give up) aufgeben
(b) ~ **one's hold** *or* **grip on sb./sth.** jmdn./etw. loslassen

relish /'relɪʃ/ [1] *n.* **(a)** (liking) Vorliebe, *die;* **do sth. with** [**great**] ~**:** etw. mit [großem] Genuss tun
(b) (condiment) Relish, *das*
[2] *v.t.* genießen

relive /ri:'lɪv/ *n.* noch einmal durchleben

reload /ri:'ləʊd/ *v.t.* nachladen ‹*Schusswaffe*›

relocate /ri:lə'keɪt/ [1] *v.t.* verlegen ‹*Fabrik, Büro*›; versetzen ‹*Angestellten*›
[2] *v.i.* (settle) sich niederlassen

relocation /ri:lə'keɪʃn/ *n.* (of factory, office) Verlegung, *die;* (of employee) Versetzung, *die;* ~ **expenses** Umzugskosten *Pl.*

reluctance /rɪ'lʌktəns/ *n.* Widerwille, *der;* **have a** [**great**] ~ **to do sth.** etw. nur mit Widerwillen tun

reluctant /rɪ'lʌktənt/ *adj.* unwillig; **be ~ to do sth.** etw. nur ungern tun
re'luctantly *adv.* nur ungern
rely /rɪ'laɪ/ *v.i.* (have trust) sich verlassen/(be dependent) angewiesen sein (**[up]on** auf + *Akk.*)
remain /rɪ'meɪn/ *v.i.* **(a)** (be left over) übrigbleiben
(b) (stay) bleiben; **~ behind** noch dableiben
(c) (continue to be) bleiben; **it ~s to be seen** es wird sich zeigen
remainder /rɪ'meɪndə(r)/ *n.* Rest, *der*
re'maining *adj.* restlich
re'mains *n. pl.* **(a)** Reste *Pl.*
(b) (human) sterbliche [Über]reste *Pl.* (verhüll.)
remand /rɪ'mɑ:nd/ **1** *v.t.* **~ sb. [in custody]** jmdn. in Untersuchungshaft behalten
2 *n.* **on ~:** in Untersuchungshaft
remark /rɪ'mɑ:k/ **1** *v.t.* bemerken (**to** gegenüber)
2 *v.i.* eine Bemerkung machen (**[up]on** zu, über + *Akk.*)
3 *n.* Bemerkung, *die* (**on** über + *Akk.*)
remarkable /rɪ'mɑ:kəbl/ *adj.* **(a)** (notable) bemerkenswert
(b) (extraordinary) außergewöhnlich
remarkably /rɪ'mɑ:kəblɪ/ *adv.* **(a)** (notably) bemerkenswert
(b) (exceptionally) außergewöhnlich
remarry /ri:'mærɪ/ *v.i. & t.* wieder heiraten
remedy /'remɪdɪ/ **1** *n.* [Heil]mittel, *das* (**for** gegen)
2 *v.t.* beheben ‹*Problem*›; retten ‹*Situation*›
remember /rɪ'membə(r)/ *v.t.* **(a)** sich erinnern an (+ *Akk.*); **I ~ed to bring the book** ich habe daran gedacht, das Buch mitzubringen; **an evening to ~:** ein unvergesslicher Abend
(b) (convey greetings) **~ me to them** grüße sie von mir
remembrance /rɪ'membrəns/ *n.* Gedenken, *das;* **in ~ of sb.** zu jmds. Gedächtnis
Remembrance Day, Remembrance Sunday *ns.* (Brit.) ≈ Volkstrauertag, *der*
remind /rɪ'maɪnd/ *v.t.* erinnern (**of** an + *Akk.*); **~ sb. to do sth.** jmdn. daran erinnern, etw. zu tun; **that ~s me, ...:** dabei fällt mir ein, ...
re'minder *n.* Erinnerung, *die* (**of** an + *Akk.*); (letter) Mahnung, *die;* Mahnbrief, *der*
reminisce /remɪ'nɪs/ *v.i.* sich in Erinnerungen (*Dat.*) ergehen (**about** an + *Akk.*)
reminiscences /remɪ'nɪsənsɪz/ *n. pl.* Erinnerungen *Pl.*; (memoirs) [Lebens]erinnerungen *Pl.*
reminiscent /remɪ'nɪsənt/ *adj.* **be ~ of sth.** an etw. (*Akk.*) erinnern
remiss /rɪ'mɪs/ *adj.* nachlässig (**of** von)
remission /rɪ'mɪʃn/ *n.* **(a)** (of debt, punishment) Erlass, *der*
(b) (of prison sentence) Straferlass, *der*
remit /rɪ'mɪt/ *v.t.*, **-tt-** (send) überweisen ‹*Geld*›
remittance /rɪ'mɪtəns/ *n.* Überweisung, *die*
remnant /'remnənt/ *n.* Rest, *der*
remonstrate /'remənstreɪt/ *v.i.* protestieren (**against** gegen); **~ with sb.** jmdm. Vorhaltungen machen (**about, on** wegen)
remorse /rɪ'mɔ:s/ *n.* Reue, *die* (**for, about** über + *Akk.*)
re'morseful /rɪ'mɔ:sfl/ *adj.* reumütig
re'morseless *adj.* unerbittlich
remote /rɪ'məʊt/ *adj.*, **~r** /rɪ'məʊtə(r)/, **~st** /rɪ'məʊtɪst/ **(a)** fern ‹*Vergangenheit, Zukunft, Zeit*›; abgelegen ‹*Ort, Gebiet*›; **~ from** weit entfernt von
(b) (slight) gering ‹*Chance*›
remote: ~ con'trol *n.* (of vehicle) Fernlenkung, *die;* (for TV set) Fernbedienung, *die;* **~-con'trol[led]** *adj.* ferngelenkt; fernbedient ‹*Anlage*›
re'motely *adv.* entfernt ‹*verwandt*›; **they are not ~ alike** sie haben nicht die entfernteste Ähnlichkeit miteinander
removable /rɪ'mu:vəbl/ *adj.* abnehmbar; entfernbar ‹*Trennwand*›; herausnehmbar ‹*Futter*›
removal /rɪ'mu:vl/ *n.* **(a)** Entfernung, *die;* (of obstacle, problem) Beseitigung, *die*
(b) (transfer of furniture) Umzug, *der*
removal: ~ expenses *n. pl.* Umzugskosten *Pl.;* **~ firm** *n.* Spedition, *die;* **~ man** *n.* Möbelpacker, *der;* **~ van** *n.* Möbelwagen, *der*
remove /rɪ'mu:v/ *v.t.* entfernen; beseitigen ‹*Spur, Hindernis*›; (take off) abnehmen; ausziehen ‹*Kleidungsstück*›; **~ a book from the shelf** ein Buch vom Regal nehmen
re'mover *n.* **(a)** (of paint/varnish/hair/rust) Farb-/Lack-/Haar-/Rostentferner, *der*
(b) (man) Möbelpacker, *der;* **[firm of] ~s** Spedition[sfirma], *die*
remunerate /rɪ'mju:nəreit/ *v.t.* bezahlen
remuneration /rɪmju:nə'reɪʃn/ *n.* Bezahlung, *die*
Renaissance /rə'neɪsəns, rɪ'neɪsəns/ *n.* (Hist.) Renaissance, *die*
rename /ri:'neɪm/ *v.t.* umbenennen
render /'rendə(r)/ *v.t.* **(a)** (make) machen
(b) erweisen ‹*Dienst*›
(c) (translate) übersetzen (**by** mit)
'rendering *n.* (translation) Übersetzung, *die*
rendezvous /'rɒndeɪvu:/ *n., pl. same* /'rɒndeɪvu:z/ **(a)** (meeting place) Treffpunkt, *der*
(b) (meeting) Verabredung, *die*
renegade /'renɪgeɪd/ **1** *n.* Abtrünnige, *der/die*
2 *adj.* abtrünnig
renegotiate /ri:nɪ'gəʊʃɪeɪt/ *v.t.* neu aushandeln

renew /rɪ'nju:/ *v.t.* erneuern; fortsetzen ‹*Angriff, Bemühungen*›; (extend) erneuern ‹*Vertrag, Ausweis usw.*›; ~ **a library book** ‹*Bibliothekar/Benutzer:*› ein Buch [aus der Bücherei] verlängern/verlängern lassen

re'newable /rɪ'nju:əbl/ *adj.* regenerationsfähig ‹*Energiequelle*›; verlängerbar ‹*Vertrag, Genehmigung, Ausweis*›

renewal /rɪ'nju:əl/ *n.* Erneuerung, *die*

renounce /rɪ'naʊns/ *v.t.* verzichten auf (+ *Akk.*); verstoßen ‹*Person*›; ~ **the devil/one's faith** dem Teufel/seinem Glauben abschwören

renovate /'renəveɪt/ *v.t.* renovieren ‹*Gebäude*›; restaurieren ‹*Möbel usw.*›

renovation /renə'veɪʃn/ *n.* ▶ RENOVATE: Renovierung, *die;* Restaurierung, *die*

renown /rɪ'naʊn/ *n.* Renommee, *das*

renowned /rɪ'naʊnd/ *adj.* berühmt (**for** wegen, für)

rent /rent/ **1** *n.* (for house etc.) Miete, *die;* (for land) Pacht, *die*
2 *v.t.* **(a)** (use) mieten ‹*Haus, Wohnung usw.*›; pachten ‹*Land*›; mieten ‹*Auto*›
(b) (let) vermieten ‹*Haus, Auto usw.*› (**to** *Dat.*, an + *Akk.*); verpachten ‹*Land*› (**to** *Dat.*, an + *Akk.*)

■ **rent 'out** *v.t.* ▶ RENT 2B

rental /'rentl/ *n.* Miete, *die*

rent: ~ **boy** *n.* (coll.) Strichjunge, *der* (salopp); ~ **rebate** *n.* Mietermäßigung, *die;* ~ **tribunal** *n.* Mietgericht, *das*

renunciation /rɪnʌnsɪ'eɪʃn/ *n.* ▶ RENOUNCE: Verzicht, *der;* Verstoßung, *die*

reopen /rɪ'əʊpn/ **1** *v.t.* wieder öffnen; wieder aufmachen; wieder eröffnen ‹*Geschäft, Lokal usw.*›; wieder aufnehmen ‹*Diskussion, Verhandlung*›
2 *v.i.* ‹*Geschäft, Lokal usw.:*› wieder öffnen

reorder /ri:'ɔ:də(r)/ *v.t.* **(a)** (Commerc.) nachbestellen ‹*Ware*›
(b) (rearrange) umordnen

reorganization /ri:ɔ:gənaɪ'zeɪʃn/ *n.* Umorganisation, *die;* (of time, work) Neueinteilung, *die*

reorganize /ri:'ɔ:gənaɪz/ *v.t.* umorganisieren; neu einteilen ‹*Zeit, Arbeit*›

rep /rep/ *n.* (coll.: representative) Vertreter, *der*/Vertreterin, *die*

repaid ▶ REPAY

repair /rɪ'peə(r)/ **1** *v.t.* (mend) reparieren; ausbessern ‹*Kleidung, Straße*›
2 *n.* Reparatur, *die;* **be in good/bad** ~: in gutem/schlechtem Zustand sein

repair: ~ **man** *n.* Mechaniker, *der;* (in house) Handwerker, *der;* ~ **shop** *n.* Reparaturwerkstatt, *die*

repaper /ri:'peɪpə(r)/ *v.t.* neu tapezieren

repatriate /ri:'pætrɪeɪt/ *v.t.* repatriieren

repatriation /ri:pætrɪ'eɪʃn/ *n.* Repatriierung, *die*

repay /ri:'peɪ/ *v.t.*, **repaid** /ri:'peɪd/ zurückzahlen ‹*Schulden usw.*›; erwidern ‹*Besuch, Gruß, Freundlichkeit*›; ~ **sb. for sth.** jmdm. etw. vergelten

re'payment *n.* Rückzahlung, *die*

re'payment mortgage *n.* Tilgungshypothek, *die*

repeal /rɪ'pi:l/ **1** *v.t.* aufheben ‹*Gesetz, Erlass usw.*›
2 *n.* Aufhebung, *die*

repeat /rɪ'pi:t/ **1** *n.* Wiederholung, *die*
2 *v.t.* wiederholen; **please ~ after me: ...:** sprich/sprecht/sprechen Sie mir bitte nach: ...

re'peated *adj.* wiederholt; (several) mehrere; **make ~ efforts to ...:** wiederholt *od.* mehrfach versuchen, ...zu...

re'peatedly *adv.* mehrmals

repel /rɪ'pel/ *v.t.*, **-ll-: (a)** (drive back) abwehren
(b) (be repulsive to) abstoßen

repellent /rɪ'pelənt/ **1** *adj.* abstoßend
2 *n.* **[insect]** ~: Insektenschutzmittel, *das*

repent /rɪ'pent/ *v.i.* bereuen (**of** *Akk.*)

repentance /rɪ'pentəns/ *n.* Reue, *die*

repentant /rɪ'pentənt/ *adj.* reuig

repercussion /ri:pə'kʌʃn/ *n., usu. in pl.* Auswirkung, *die* (**[up]on** auf + *Akk.*)

repertoire /'repətwɑ:(r)/ *n.* Repertoire, *das*

repertory /'repətərɪ/ *n.* (Theatre) Repertoiretheater, *das*

'repertory company *n.* Repertoiretheater, *das*

repetition /repɪ'tɪʃn/ *n.* Wiederholung, *die*

repetitious /repɪ'tɪʃəs/ *adj.* sich immer wiederholend *attr.*

repetitive /rɪ'petɪtɪv/ *adj.* eintönig

repetitive 'strain injury *n.* chronisches Überlastungssyndrom

rephrase /ri:'freɪz/ *v.t.* umformulieren; **I'll ~ that** ich will es anders ausdrücken

replace /rɪ'pleɪs/ *v.t.* **(a)** (vertically) zurückstellen; (horizontally) zurücklegen
(b) (take place of) ersetzen; ~ **A with** *or* **by B** A durch B ersetzen
(c) (exchange) austauschen, auswechseln ‹*Maschinen[teile] usw.*›

re'placement *n.* **(a)** ▶ REPLACE A: Zurückstellen, *das;* Zurücklegen, *das*
(b) (provision of substitute for) Ersatz, *der; attrib.* Ersatz-
(c) (substitute) Ersatz, *der;* ~ **[part]** Ersatzteil, *das*

replay **1** /ri:'pleɪ/ *v.t.* wiederholen ‹*Spiel*›; nochmals abspielen ‹*Tonband usw.*›
2 /'ri:pleɪ/ *n.* Wiederholung, *die;* (match) Wiederholungsspiel, *das*

replenish /rɪ'plenɪʃ/ *v.t.* auffüllen

replica /'replɪkə/ *n.* Nachbildung, *die*

reply /rɪ'plaɪ/ **1** *v.i.* ~ **[to sb./sth.]** [jmdm./auf etw. (*Akk.*)] antworten
2 *v.t.* ~ **that ...:** antworten, dass ...
3 *n.* Antwort, *die* (**to** auf + *Akk.*)

re'ply-paid *adj.* **~-paid telegram** RP-Telegramm, *das;* **~-paid envelope** Freiumschlag, *der*

repopulate /riːˈpɒpjʊleɪt/ *v.t.* neu besiedeln

report /rɪˈpɔːt/ 1 *v.t.* **(a)** (relate) berichten/ (in writing) einen Bericht schreiben über (+ *Akk.*); (state formally also) melden
(b) (name to authorities) melden (**to** *Dat.*); (for prosecution) anzeigen (**to** bei)
2 *v.i.* **(a)** Bericht erstatten (**on** über + *Akk.*); berichten (**on** über + *Akk.*)
(b) (present oneself) sich melden (**to** bei)
3 *n.* **(a)** (account) Bericht, *der* (**on, about** über + *Akk.*)
(b) (Sch.) Zeugnis, *das*
(c) (of gun) Knall, *der*

reportedly /rɪˈpɔːtɪdlɪ/ *adv.* wie verlautet

reported 'speech *n.* indirekte Rede

re'porter *n.* Reporter, *der*/Reporterin, *die*

repossess /riːpəˈzes/ *v.t.* wieder in Besitz nehmen

reprehensible /reprɪˈhensɪbl/ *adj.* tadelnswert

represent /reprɪˈzent/ *v.t.* **(a)** darstellen (**as** als)
(b) (act for) vertreten

representation /reprɪzenˈteɪʃn/ *n.* **(a)** (depicting, image) Darstellung, *die*
(b) (acting for sb.) Vertretung, *die*
(c) make ~s to sb. bei jmdm. Protest einlegen

representative /reprɪˈzentətɪv/ 1 *n.* **(a)** (Commerc.) Vertreter, *der*/Vertreterin, *die*
(b) R~ (Amer. Polit.) Abgeordnete, *der/die*
2 *adj.* (typical) repräsentativ (**of** für)

repress /rɪˈpres/ *v.t.* **(a)** unterdrücken ‹*Aufruhr, Gefühle, Lachen usw.*›
(b) (Psych.) verdrängen ‹*Gefühle*› (**from** aus)

repressed /rɪˈprest/ *adj.* unterdrückt; (Psych.) verdrängt

repression /rɪˈpreʃn/ *n.* Unterdrückung, *die*

repressive /rɪˈpresɪv/ *adj.* repressiv

reprieve /rɪˈpriːv/ 1 *v.t.* **~ sb.** (postpone execution) jmdm. Strafaufschub gewähren; (remit execution) jmdn. begnadigen
2 *n.* Strafaufschub, *der* (**of** für)/ Begnadigung, *die;* (fig.) Gnadenfrist, *die*

reprimand /ˈreprɪmɑːnd/ 1 *n.* Tadel, *der*
2 *v.t.* tadeln

reprint 1 /riːˈprɪnt/ *v.t.* wieder abdrucken
2 /ˈriːprɪnt/ *n.* Nachdruck, *der*

reprisal /rɪˈpraɪzl/ *n.* Vergeltungsakt, *der* (**for** gegen)

reproach /rɪˈprəʊtʃ/ 1 *v.t.* **~ sb.** jmdm. Vorwürfe machen
2 *n.* Vorwurf, *der*

reproachful /rɪˈprəʊtʃfl/ *adv.* vorwurfsvoll

reproduce /riːprəˈdjuːs/ 1 *v.t.* wiedergeben
2 *v.i.* (multiply) sich fortpflanzen

reproduction /riːprəˈdʌkʃn/ *n.* **(a)** Wiedergabe, *die*
(b) (producing offspring) Fortpflanzung, *die*
(c) (copy) Reproduktion, *die*

reproductive /riːprəˈdʌktɪv/ *adj.* Fortpflanzungs-

reprove /rɪˈpruːv/ *v.t.* tadeln

reptile /ˈreptaɪl/ *n.* Reptil, *das*

republic /rɪˈpʌblɪk/ *n.* Republik, *die*

republican /rɪˈpʌblɪkən/ 1 *adj.* republikanisch
2 *n.* **R~** (Amer. Polit.) Republikaner, *der*/ Republikanerin, *die*

repudiate /rɪˈpjuːdɪeɪt/ *v.t.* zurückweisen

repugnance /rɪˈpʌgnəns/ *n.* Abscheu, *der* (**to[wards]** vor + Dat.)

repugnant /rɪˈpʌgnənt/ *adj.* widerlich (**to** *Dat.*)

repulse /rɪˈpʌls/ *v.t.* abwehren

repulsion /rɪˈpʌlʃn/ *n.* (disgust) Widerwille, *der* (**towards** gegen)

repulsive /rɪˈpʌlsɪv/ *adj.* abstoßend

reputable /ˈrepjʊtəbl/ *adj.* angesehen ‹*Person, Beruf, Zeitung usw.*›; anständig ‹*Verhalten*›; seriös ‹*Firma*›

reputably /ˈrepjʊtəblɪ/ *adv.* anständig

reputation /repjʊˈteɪʃn/ *n.* **(a)** Ruf, *der;* **have a ~ for** *or* **of doing/being sth.** in dem Ruf stehen, etw. zu tun/sein
(b) (good name) Name, *der*

repute /rɪˈpjuːt/ 1 *v.t. in pass.* **be ~d [to be] sth.** als etw. gelten; **she is ~d to have/ make ...:** man sagt, dass sie ... hat/macht
2 *n.* Ruf, *der*

reputed /rɪˈpjuːtɪd/ *adj.*, **re'putedly** *adv.* angeblich

request /rɪˈkwest/ 1 *v.t.* bitten; **~ sth. of** *or* **from sb.** jmdn. um etw. bitten
2 *n.* Bitte, *die* (**for** um); **at sb.'s ~:** auf jmds. Bitte (*Akk.*) [hin]

re'quest stop *n.* (Brit.) Bedarfshaltestelle, *die*

require /rɪˈkwaɪə(r)/ *v.t.* **(a)** (need) brauchen
(b) (order, demand) verlangen (**of** von); **be ~d to do sth.** etw. tun müssen

re'quirement *n.* **(a)** (need) Bedarf, *der*
(b) (condition) Erfordernis, *das*

requisite /ˈrekwɪzɪt/ 1 *adj.* notwendig (**to, for** für)
2 *n. in pl.* **toilet/travel ~s** Toiletten-/ Reiseartikel *Pl.*

requisition /rekwɪˈzɪʃn/ 1 *n.* (order for sth.) Anforderung, *die* (**for** *Gen.*)
2 *v.t.* anfordern

rescind /rɪˈsɪnd/ *v.t.* für ungültig erklären

rescue /ˈreskjuː/ 1 *v.t.* retten (**from** aus)
2 *n.* Rettung, *die; attrib.* Rettungs‹*dienst, -mannschaft*›; **go/come to the/sb.'s ~:** jmdm. zu Hilfe kommen

rescuer /ˈreskjuːə(r)/ *n.* Retter, *der*/ Retterin, *die*

'rescue worker *n.* [Einsatz]helfer, *der*/ -helferin, *die*

research /rɪ'sɜːtʃ, 'riːsɜːtʃ/ **1** *n.* Forschung, *die* (**into, on** über + *Akk.*)
2 *v.i.* forschen; ~ **into sth.** etw. erforschen

research as'sistant *n.* wissenschaftlicher Assistent/ wissenschaftliche Assistentin

researcher /-'--, '---/ *n.* Forscher, *der*/ Forscherin, *die*

research: ~ student *n.* ≈ Doktorand, *der*/Doktorandin, *die;* **~ work** *n.* Recherchen *Pl.;* (medical, scientific) Forschungsarbeit, *die;* **~ worker** *n.* ≈ Rechercheur, *der*/Rechercheurin, *die;* (medical, scientific) Forscher, *der*/Forscherin, *die*

resell /riː'sel/ *v.t.*, **resold** /riː'səʊld/ weiter verkaufen (**to** an + *Akk.*)

resemblance /rɪ'zembləns/ *n.* Ähnlichkeit, *die* (**to** mit)

resemble /rɪ'zembl/ *v.t.* ähneln, gleichen (+ *Dat.*)

resent /rɪ'zent/ *v.t.* übel nehmen

resentful /rɪ'zentfl/ *adj.* übelnehmerisch, nachtragend ‹*Person, Art*›; **be ~ of** *or* **feel ~ about sth.** etw. übel nehmen

re'sentment *n.* Groll, *der* (geh.); **feel ~ towards** *or* **against sb.** einen Groll auf jmdn. haben

reservation /rezə'veɪʃn/ *n.* **(a)** Reservierung, *die;* **have a ~ [for a room]** ein Zimmer reserviert haben
(b) (doubt) Vorbehalt, *der* (**about** gegen); Bedenken (**about** bezüglich + *Gen.*); **without ~**: ohne Vorbehalt

reserve /rɪ'zɜːv/ **1** *v.t.* reservieren lassen ‹*Zimmer, Tisch, Platz*›; (set aside) reservieren; **~ the right to do sth.** sich (*Dat.*) [das Recht] vorbehalten, etw. zu tun
2 *n.* **(a)** (extra amount) Reserve, *die* (**of** an + *Dat.*) **have/hold** *or* **keep sth. in ~**: etw. in Reserve haben/halten
(b) (place set apart) Reservat, *das*
(c) (Sport) Reservespieler, *der*/-spielerin, *die;* **the R~s** die Reserve
(d) (reticence) Zurückhaltung, *die*

reserved /rɪ'zɜːvd/ *adj.* (reticent) reserviert

reservoir /'rezəvwɑː(r)/ *n.* ([artificial] lake) Reservoir, *das*

reshape /riː'ʃeɪp/ *v.t.* umgestalten

reshuffle /riː'ʃʌfl/ **1** *v.t.* **(a)** umbilden ‹*Kabinett*›
(b) (Cards) neu mischen
2 *n.* Umbildung, *die*

reside /rɪ'zaɪd/ *v.i.* (formal) wohnen; wohnhaft sein (Amtsspr.)

residence /'rezɪdəns/ *n.* **(a)** (abode) Wohnsitz, *der;* (of ambassador etc.) Residenz, *die*
(b) (stay) Aufenthalt, *der*

'residence permit *n.* Aufenthaltsgenehmigung, *die*

resident /'rezɪdənt/ **1** *adj.* wohnhaft; **be ~ in England** seinen Wohnsitz in England haben
2 *n.* (inhabitant) Bewohner, *der*/Bewohnerin, *die;* (at hotel) Hotelgast, *der*

residential /rezɪ'denʃl/ *adj.* Wohn‹*gebiet, -siedlung, -straße*›; **~ hotel** Hotel für Dauergäste

residential 'care *n.* stationäre Pflege

resident's 'parking *n.* Parken nur für Anlieger

residual /rɪ'zɪdjʊəl/ *adj.* zurückgeblieben

residue /'rezɪdjuː/ *n.* **(a)** Rest, *der*
(b) (Chem.) Rückstand, *der*

resign /rɪ'zaɪn/ **1** *v.t.* zurücktreten von ‹*Amt*›
2 *v. refl.* **~ oneself to sth./to doing sth.** sich mit etw. abfinden/sich damit abfinden, etw. zu tun
3 *v.i.* ‹*Arbeitnehmer:*› kündigen; ‹*Regierungsbeamter:*› zurücktreten (**from** von)

resignation /rezɪg'neɪʃn/ *n.* **(a)** ▶ RESIGN 3: Kündigung, *die;* Rücktritt, *der;* **tender one's ~**: seine Kündigung/seinen Rücktritt einreichen
(b) (being resigned) Resignation, *die;* **with ~**: resigniert

resigned /rɪ'zaɪnd/ *adj.* resigniert; **be ~ to sth.** sich mit etw. abgefunden haben

resilience /rɪ'zɪlɪəns/ *n.* **(a)** Elastizität, *die*
(b) (fig.) Unverwüstlichkeit, *die*

resilient /rɪ'zɪlɪənt/ *adj.* elastisch; (fig.) unverwüstlich

resin /'rezɪn/ *n.* Harz, *das*

resist /rɪ'zɪst/ **1** *v.t.* **(a)** standhalten (+ *Dat.*) ‹*Frost, Hitze, Feuchtigkeit usw.*›
(b) (oppose) sich widersetzen (+ *Dat.*); widerstehen (+ *Dat.*) ‹*Versuchung*›
2 *v.i.* ▶ 1B: sich widersetzen; widerstehen

resistance /rɪ'zɪstəns/ *n.* Widerstand, *der* (**to** gegen)

re'sistance movement *n.* Widerstandsbewegung, *die*

resistant /rɪ'zɪstənt/ *adj.* **(a)** (opposed) **be ~ to** sich widersetzen (+ *Dat.*)
(b) (having power to resist) widerstandsfähig (**to** gegen)

reskill /riː'skɪl/ *v.t.* fort- *od.* weiterbilden; umschulen ‹*Arbeitslose*›

resold ▶ RESELL

resolute /'rezəluːt/ *adj.* resolut, energisch ‹*Person*›; entschlossen ‹*Tat*›

resolution /rezə'luːʃn/ *n.* **(a)** (firmness) Entschlossenheit, *die*
(b) (decision) Entschließung, *die;* (Polit. also) Resolution, *die*
(c) (resolve) Vorsatz, *der;* **make a ~**: einen Vorsatz fassen

resolve /rɪ'zɒlv/ **1** *v.t.* **(a)** lösen ‹*Problem, Rätsel*›; ausräumen ‹*Schwierigkeit*›
(b) (decide) beschließen

(c) (settle) beilegen ‹*Streit*›; regeln ‹*Angelegenheit*›
2 *n.* **(a)** Vorsatz, *der*
(b) (resoluteness) Entschlossenheit, *die*

resolved /rɪ'zɒlvd/ *adj.* **~ [to do sth.]** entschlossen[, etw. zu tun]

resonant /'rezənənt/ *adj.* hallend ‹*Ton, Klang*›

resort /rɪ'zɔ:t/ **1** *n.* **(a)** (place) Aufenthalt[sort], *der;* **[holiday] ~:** Ferienort, *der;* **ski ~:** Skiurlaubsort, *der;* **seaside ~:** Seebad, *das*
(b) (recourse) **as a last ~:** als letzter Ausweg
2 *v.i.* **~ to sth./sb.** zu etw. greifen/sich an jmdn. wenden **(for** um)

resound /rɪ'zaʊnd/ *v.i.* widerhallen

re'sounding *adj.* hallend ‹*Lärm*›; überwältigend ‹*Sieg, Erfolg*›

resource /rɪ'sɔ:s, rɪ'zɔ:s/ *n. usu. in pl.* (stock) Mittel *Pl.;* Ressource, *die*

resourceful /rɪ'sɔ:sfl, rɪ'zɔ:sfl/ *adj.* findig ‹*Person*›

respect /rɪ'spekt/ **1** *n.* **(a)** (esteem) Respekt, *der,* Achtung, *die* **(for** vor + *Dat.*); **show ~ for sb./sth.** Respekt vor jmdm./etw. zeigen
(b) (aspect) Hinsicht, *die;* **in some ~s** in mancher Hinsicht
(c) with ~ to ...: in Bezug auf ... (*Akk.*); was ... [an]betrifft
2 *v.t.* respektieren; achten

respectable /rɪ'spektəbl/ *adj.* angesehen ‹*Bürger usw.*›; ehrenwert ‹*Motive*›; (decent) ehrbar (geh.) ‹*Leute, Kaufmann*›; anständig, respektabel ‹*Beschäftigung usw.*›

respectful /rɪ'spektfl/ *adj.* respektvoll **(to[wards]** gegenüber)

re'spectfully *adv.* respektvoll

respective /rɪ'spektɪv/ *adj.* jeweilig

re'spectively *adv.* beziehungsweise

respiration /respɪ'reɪʃn/ *n.* Atmung, *die*

respiratory /'respərətərɪ/ *adj.* Atmungs‹*system, -organ, -funktion*›

respite /'respaɪt/ *n.* Ruhepause, *die;* (delay) Aufschub, *der;* **without ~:** ohne Pause

resplendent /rɪ'splendənt/ *adj.* prächtig

respond /rɪ'spɒnd/ **1** *v.i.* **(a)** (answer) antworten **(to** auf + *Akk.*)
(b) (react) reagieren **(to** auf + *Akk.*); ‹*Patient, Bremsen:*› ansprechen **(to** auf + *Akk.*)
2 *v.t.* antworten; erwidern

response /rɪ'spɒns/ *n.* **(a)** (answer) Antwort, *die* **(to** auf + *Akk.*); **in ~ [to]** als Antwort [auf (+ *Akk.*)]
(b) (reaction) Reaktion, *die*

responsibility /rɪspɒnsɪ'bɪlɪtɪ/ *n.* **(a)** (being responsible) Verantwortung, *die*
(b) (duty) Verpflichtung, *die*

responsible /rɪ'spɒnsɪbl/ *adj.* **(a)** verantwortlich; **be ~ to sb.** jmdm. gegenüber verantwortlich sein **(for** für)
(b) (trustworthy) verantwortungsvoll

responsibly /rɪ'spɒnsɪblɪ/ *adv.* verantwortungsbewusst

responsive /rɪ'spɒnsɪv/ *adj.* aufgeschlossen ‹*Person*›; **be ~ to sth.** auf etw. (*Akk.*) reagieren

rest¹ /rest/ **1** *v.i.* ruhen; **~ on** ruhen auf (+ *Dat.*); **~ from sth.** sich von etw. ausruhen; **~ assured that ...:** seien Sie versichert, dass ...; **~ with sb.** ‹*Verantwortung:*› bei jmdm. liegen
2 *v.t.* **(a) ~ sth. against sth.** etw. an etw. (*Akk.*) lehnen
(b) ausruhen ‹*Augen*›
3 *n.* **(a)** (repose) Ruhe, *die*
(b) (break, relaxation) Ruhe[pause], *die;* Erholung, *die* **(from** von); **take a ~:** sich ausruhen **(from** von); **give it a ~!** (coll.) hör jetzt mal auf damit!
(c) (pause) **have a ~:** [eine] Pause machen; **~ period** [Ruhe]pause, *die*

rest² *n.* **the ~:** der Rest; **we'll do the ~:** alles Übrige erledigen wir

restaurant /'restərɒnt/ *n.* Restaurant, *das*

'restaurant car *n.* (Brit. Railw.) Speisewagen, *der*

rest: ~ cure *n.* Erholungskur, *die;* **~ day** *n.* Ruhetag, *der*

'rested *adj.* ausgeruht

restful /'restfl/ *adj.* ruhig ‹*Tag, Woche*›

'rest home *n.* Pflegeheim, *das*

restive /'restɪv/ *adj.* unruhig

'restless *adj.* unruhig ‹*Nacht, Schlaf, Bewegung*›; ruhelos ‹*Person*›

restoration /restə'reɪʃn/ *n.* **(a)** (of peace, health) Wiederherstellung, *die;* (of work of art, building) Restaurierung, *die*
(b) the R~ (Brit. Hist.) die Restauration

restore /rɪ'stɔ:(r)/ *v.t.* **(a)** (give back) zurückgeben
(b) restaurieren ‹*Bauwerk, Kunstwerk usw.*›; **~ sb. to health** jmdn. wiederherstellen
(c) wiederherstellen ‹*Ordnung, Ruhe*›

restrain /rɪ'streɪn/ *v.t.* zurückhalten ‹*Gefühl, Lachen, Person*›; bändigen ‹*unartiges Kind, Tier*›; **~ sb./oneself from doing sth.** jmdn. davon abhalten/sich zurückhalten, etw. zu tun

restrained /rɪ'streɪnd/ *adj.* zurückhaltend ‹*Wesen, Kritik*›; beherrscht ‹*Reaktion, Worte*›

restraint /rɪ'streɪnt/ *n.* **(a)** (restriction) Einschränkung, *die*
(b) (reserve) Zurückhaltung, *die*
(c) (self-control) Selbstbeherrschung, *die*

restrict /rɪ'strɪkt/ *v.t.* beschränken **(to** auf + *Akk.*)

re'stricted *adj.* beschränkt

restriction /rɪ'strɪkʃn/ *n.* Beschränkung, *die* **(on** *Gen.*)

restrictive /rɪ'strɪktɪv/ *adj.* restriktiv

'rest room *n.* (esp. Amer.) Toilette, *die*

restyle /ri:'staɪl/ *v.t.* neu stylen; **~ sb.'s hair** jmdm. eine neue Frisur machen

result /rɪˈzʌlt/ 1 *v.i.* **(a)** (follow) **~ from sth.** die Folge einer Sache (*Gen.*) sein
(b) (end) **~ in sth.** in etw. (*Dat.*) resultieren
2 *n.* Ergebnis, *das;* **be the ~ of sth.** die Folge einer Sache (*Gen.*) sein; **as a ~ [of this]** infolgedessen

re'sultant /rɪˈzʌltənt/ *attrib. adj.* daraus resultierend

resume /rɪˈzjuːm/ *v.t.* wieder aufnehmen; fortsetzen ‹*Reise*›

résumé /ˈrezʊmeɪ/ *n.* **(a)** (summary) Zusammenfassung, *die*
(b) (Amer.: curriculum vitae) Lebenslauf, *der*

resumption /rɪˈzʌmpʃn/ *n.* Wiederaufnahme, *die*

resurface /riːˈsɜːfɪs/ 1 *v.t.* **~ a road** den Belag einer Straße erneuern
2 *v.i.* (lit. or fig.) wieder auftauchen

resurgence /rɪˈsɜːdʒəns/ *n.* Wiederaufleben, *das*

resurrection /rezəˈrekʃn/ *n.* Auferstehung, *die*

resuscitate /rɪˈsʌsɪteɪt/ *v.t.* wieder beleben

resuscitation /rɪsʌsɪˈteɪʃn/ *n.* Wiederbelebung, *die*

retail /ˈriːteɪl/ 1 *adj.* Einzel‹*handel*›; Einzelhandels‹*geschäft, -preis*›
2 *adv.* **buy/sell ~:** en détail kaufen/verkaufen

'retailer *n.* Einzelhändler, *der*/-händlerin, *die*

'retailing /ˈriːteɪlɪŋ/ *n., no art.* Einzelhandel, *der*

retail 'price index *n.* (Brit.) Preisindex des Einzelhandels

retain /rɪˈteɪn/ *v.t.* behalten; ein-, zurückbehalten ‹*Gelder*›

retaining: ~ fee *n.* Honorarvorschuss, *der;* **~ wall** *n.* Böschungsmauer, *die*

retaliate /rɪˈtælɪeɪt/ *v.i.* Vergeltung üben (**against** an + *Dat.*)

retaliation /rɪtælɪˈeɪʃn/ *n.* Vergeltung, *die;* **in ~ for** als Vergeltung für

retarded /rɪˈtɑːdɪd/ *adj.* **[mentally] ~:** [geistig] zurückgeblieben

retch /retʃ/ *v.i.* würgen

retentive /rɪˈtentɪv/ *adj.* gut ‹*Gedächtnis*›

rethink /riːˈθɪŋk/ *v.t.*, **rethought** /riːˈθɔːt/ noch einmal überdenken

reticence /ˈretɪsəns/ *n.* Zurückhaltung, *die*

reticent /ˈretɪsənt/ *adj.* zurückhaltend (**on, about** in Bezug auf + *Akk.*)

retina /ˈretɪnə/ *n.* Netzhaut, *die*

retinue /ˈretɪnjuː/ *n.* Gefolge, *das*

retire /rɪˈtaɪə(r)/ *v.i.* **(a)** ‹*Angestellter, Arbeiter:*› in Rente (*Akk.*) gehen; ‹*Beamter, Militär:*› in Pension *od.* den Ruhestand gehen
(b) (withdraw) sich zurückziehen (**to** in + *Akk.*)

retired /rɪˈtaɪəd/ *adj.* aus dem Berufsleben ausgeschieden; ‹*Beamter, Soldat*› im Ruhestand, pensioniert

re'tirement *n.* Ruhestand, *der;* **take early ~** ‹*Selbstständiger:*› sich vorzeitig zur Ruhe setzen; ‹*Angestellter, Arbeiter:*› vorzeitig in Rente (*Akk.*) gehen; ‹*Beamter, Militär:*› sich vorzeitig pensionieren lassen

retirement: ~ age *n.* Altersgrenze, *die;* **~ home** *n.* **(a)** (house, flat) Alters- *od.* Ruhesitz, *der;* **(b)** (institution) Alters- *od.* Altenheim, *das;* **~ pay, ~ pension** *ns.* [Alters]rente, *die*

retiring /rɪˈtaɪərɪŋ/ *adj.* (shy) zurückhaltend

retort /rɪˈtɔːt/ 1 *n.* Entgegnung, *die* (**to** auf + *Akk.*)
2 *v.t.* entgegnen

retrace /rɪˈtreɪs/ *v.t.* zurückverfolgen; **~ one's steps** denselben Weg noch einmal zurückgehen

retract /rɪˈtrækt/ *v.t.* zurücknehmen

retrain /riːˈtreɪn/ 1 *v.i.* [sich] umschulen [lassen]
2 *v.t.* umschulen

re'training *n.* Umschulung, *die*

retreat /rɪˈtriːt/ 1 *n.* **(a)** (withdrawal) Rückzug, *der;* **beat a ~** (fig.) das Feld räumen
(b) (place) Zufluchtsort, *der*
2 *v.i.* sich zurückziehen

retribution /retrɪˈbjuːʃn/ *n.* Vergeltung, *die*

retrieval /rɪˈtriːvl/ *n.* **(a)** (of situation) Rettung, *die;* **beyond** *or* **past ~:** hoffnungslos
(b) (rescue) Rettung, *die;* (from wreckage) Bergung, *die*

retrieve /rɪˈtriːv/ *v.t.* **(a)** (rescue) retten (**from** aus); (from wreckage) bergen (**from** aus)
(b) (recover) zurückholen ‹*Brief*›; wiederholen ‹*Ball*›; wiederbekommen ‹*Geld*›
(c) (Comp.) wieder auffinden ‹*Informationen*›
(d) ‹*Hund:*› apportieren
(e) retten ‹*Situation*›

re'triever *n.* Apportierhund, *der;* (breed) Retriever, *der*

retrospect /ˈretrəspekt/ *n.* **in ~:** im Nachhinein

retrospective /retrəˈspektɪv/
1 *adj.* retrospektiv (geh.)
2 *n.* (Art) Retrospektive, *die* (geh.)

retrovirus /ˈretrəʊvaɪrəs/ *n.* Retrovirus, *das od. der*

returf /riːˈtɜːf/ *v.t.* neuen Rasen verlegen auf (+ *Dat.*)

return /rɪˈtɜːn/ 1 *v.i.* (come back) zurückkommen; (go back) zurückgehen; (by vehicle) zurückfahren
2 *v.t.* **(a)** (bring back) zurückbringen; zurückgeben ‹*geliehenen/gestohlenen Gegenstand*›; **~ed with thanks** mit Dank zurück

··>

(b) erwidern ‹*Besuch, Gruß, Liebe*›; sich revanchieren für (ugs.) ‹*Freundlichkeit, Gefallen*›
(c) (elect) wählen ‹*Kandidaten*›
(d) **~ a verdict of guilty/not guilty** ‹*Geschworene:*› auf „schuldig"/„nicht schuldig" erkennen
[3] *n.* **(a)** Rückkehr, *die;* **many happy ~s [of the day]!** herzlichen Glückwunsch [zum Geburtstag]!
(b) **by ~ [of post]** postwendend
(c) (ticket) Rückfahrkarte, *die;* (for flight) Rückflugschein, *der*
(d) **~[s]** (proceeds) Gewinn, *der* (**on, from** aus)
(e) (bringing back) Zurückbringen, *das;* (of property, goods, book) Rückgabe, *die* (**to** an + *Akk.*); **receive/get sth. in ~ [for sth.]** etw. [für etw.] bekommen

returnable /rɪ'tɜːnəbl/ *adj.* Mehrweg‹*behälter, -flasche usw.*›; rückzahlbar ‹*Gebühr, Kaution*›; **~ bottle** Pfandflasche, *die;* **~ deposit** Pfand, *der*

return: ~ 'fare *n.* Preis für eine Rückfahrkarte/(for flight) einen Rückflugschein; **~ 'flight** *n.* Rückflug, *der;* **~ 'journey** *n.* Rückreise, *die;* Rückfahrt, *die;* **~ 'match** *n.* Rückspiel, *das;* **~ 'ticket** *n.* (Brit.) Rückfahrkarte, *die;* (for flight) Rückflugschein, *der;* **~ 'trip** *n.* **(a)** (trip back) Rückweg, *der;* Rückfahrt, *die;* **(b)** (trip out and back) Hin- und Rückfahrt, *die;* Hin- und Rückreise, *die*

retype /riː'taɪp/ *v.t.* neu tippen

reunification /riːjuːnɪfɪ'keɪʃn/ *n.* Wiedervereinigung, *die*

reunify /riːjuːnɪfaɪ/ *v.t.* wieder vereinigen

reunion /riː'juːnjən/ *n.* (gathering) Treffen, *das*

reunite /riːjʊ'naɪt/ *v.t.* wieder zusammenführen

reusable /riː'juːzəbl/ *adj.* wieder verwendbar

reuse [1] /riː'juːz/ *v.t.* wieder verwenden
[2] /riː'juːs/ *n.* Wiederverwendung, *die*

rev /rev/ (coll.) [1] *n., usu. in pl.* Umdrehung, *die*
[2] *v.i.,* **-vv-** hochtourig laufen
[3] *v.t.,* **-vv-** aufheulen lassen
■ **rev 'up** *v.t.* aufheulen lassen

Rev. /'revərənd, (coll.) rev/ *abbr.* = **Reverend** Rev.

reveal /rɪ'viːl/ *v.t.* enthüllen (geh.); **be ~ed** ‹*Wahrheit:*› ans Licht kommen

re'vealing *adj.* aufschlussreich

revel /'revl/ *v.i.,* (Brit.) **-ll-** genießen (**in** *Akk.*); **~ in doing sth.** es [richtig] genießen, etw. zu tun

revelation /revə'leɪʃn/ *n.* **(a)** Enthüllung, *die* (geh.); **be a ~:** einem die Augen öffnen
(b) (Relig.) Offenbarung, *die*

reveller /'revələ(r)/ *n.* Feiernde, *der/die*

revelry /'revəlrɪ/ *n.* Feiern, *das*

revenge /rɪ'vendʒ/ [1] *v.t.* rächen ‹*Person, Tat*›
[2] *n.* (action) Rache, *die;* **take ~ *or* have one's ~ [on sb.] [for sth.]** Rache [an jmdm.] [für etw.] nehmen; **in ~ for sth.** als Rache für etw

revengeful /rɪ'vendʒfl/ *adj.* rachsüchtig (geh.)

revenue /'revənjuː/ *n.* **~[s]** Einnahmen *Pl.*

revere /rɪ'vɪə(r)/ *v.t.* verehren

reverence /'revərəns/ *n.* Ehrfurcht, *die*

Reverend /'revərənd/ *adj.* **the ~ John Wilson** Hochwürden John Wilson

reverent /'revərənt/ *adj.* ehrfürchtig

reverie /'revərɪ/ *n.* Träumerei, *die*

reversal /rɪ'vɜːsl/ *n.* Umkehrung, *die*

reverse /rɪ'vɜːs/ [1] *adj.* entgegengesetzt ‹*Richtung*›; Rück‹*seite*›; umgekehrt ‹*Reihenfolge*›
[2] *n.* **(a)** (contrary) Gegenteil, *das*
(b) (Motor Veh.) Rückwärtsgang, *der;* **put the car into ~, go into ~:** den Rückwärtsgang einlegen
[3] *v.t.* **(a)** umkehren ‹*Reihenfolge*›; **~ the charge[s]** (Brit.) ein R-Gespräch anmelden
(b) zurücksetzen ‹*Fahrzeug*›
[4] *v.i.* zurücksetzen; rückwärts fahren

reverse: ~-'charge *adj.* (Brit.) **make a ~-charge call** ein R-Gespräch führen; **~ 'gear** *n.* (Motor Veh.) Rückwärtsgang, *der;* *see also* GEAR 1A

reversible /rɪ'vɜːsɪbl/ *adj.* beidseitig tragbar ‹*Kleidungsstück*›; Wende‹*mantel, -jacke*›

re'versing light *n.* Rückfahrscheinwerfer, *der*

revert /rɪ'vɜːt/ *v.i.* **~ to** zurückkommen auf (+ *Akk.*) ‹*Thema, Frage*›; **~ to savagery** in den Zustand der Wildheit zurückfallen

review /rɪ'vjuː/ [1] *n.* **(a)** (survey) Überblick, *der* (**of** über + *Akk.*)
(b) (re-examination) [nochmalige] Überprüfung
(c) (of book, play, etc.) Kritik, *die;* Rezension, *die*
[2] *v.t.* **(a)** (survey) untersuchen; prüfen
(b) (re-examine) überprüfen
(c) (Mil.) inspizieren
(d) (write a criticism of) rezensieren

re'viewer *n.* Rezensent, *der*/Rezensentin, *die*

revile /rɪ'vaɪl/ *v.t.* schmähen (geh.)

revise /rɪ'vaɪz/ *v.t.* **(a)** (check over) durchsehen ‹*Manuskript*›
(b) (for exam) wiederholen; *abs.* lernen

revision /rɪ'vɪʒn/ *n.* **(a)** (checking over) Durchsicht, *die*
(b) (amended version) revidierte Fassung
(c) (for exam) Wiederholung, *die*

revisit /riː'vɪzɪt/ *v.t.* wieder besuchen

revitalize /riː'vaɪtəlaɪz/ *v.t.* neu beleben

revival /rɪ'vaɪvl/ *n.* Neubelebung, *die*

revive /rɪ'vaɪv/ [1] *v.i.* (come back to consciousness) wieder zu sich kommen; (be reinvigorated) zu neuem Leben erwachen

[2] *v.t.* **(a)** (restore to consciousness) wieder beleben; (reinvigorate) wieder zu Kräften kommen lassen
(b) wieder wecken ‹*Lebensgeister, Interesse*›

revoke /rɪ'vəʊk/ *v.t.* aufheben ‹*Entscheidung*›; widerrufen ‹*Befehl, Erlaubnis, Genehmigung*›

revolt /rɪ'vəʊlt/ [1] *v.i.* revoltieren (**against** gegen)
[2] *v.t.* mit Abscheu erfüllen
[3] *n.* Revolte, *die* (auch fig.); Aufstand, *der*

re'volting *adj.* abscheulich; (unpleasant) widerlich

revolution /revə'lu:ʃn/ *n.* Revolution, *die*

revolutionary /revə'lu:ʃənərɪ/ [1] *adj.* revolutionär
[2] *n.* Revolutionär, *der*/Revolutionärin, *die*

revolve /rɪ'vɒlv/ [1] *v.t.* drehen
[2] *v.i.* sich drehen (**round, about, on** um)

revolver /rɪ'vɒlvə(r)/ *n.* [Trommel]revolver, *der*

revolving /rɪ'vɒlvɪŋ/ *attrib. adj.* Dreh‹*bühne, -tür*›

revue /rɪ'vju:/ *n.* Kabarett, *das;* (musical show) Revue, *die*

revulsion /rɪ'vʌlʃn/ *n.* Abscheu, *der* (**at** vor + *Dat.*, gegen)

reward /rɪ'wɔ:d/ [1] *n.* Belohnung, *die*
[2] *v.t.* belohnen

re'warding *adj.* lohnend; **be ~/financially ~**: sich lohnen/einträglich sein

rewind /ri:'waɪnd/ *v.t.*, **rewound** /ri:'waʊnd/
(a) wieder aufziehen ‹*Uhr*›
(b) zurückspulen ‹*Film, Band*›

'rewind button *n.* (on camera) Rückspulknopf, *der;* (on cassette recorder etc.) Rücklauftaste, *die*

reword /ri:'wɜ:d/ *v.t.* umformulieren

rewrite /ri:'raɪt/ *v.t.*, **rewrote** /ri:'rəʊt/, **rewritten** /ri:'rɪtn/ noch einmal [neu] schreiben; (write differently) umschreiben

rhetoric /'retərɪk/ *n.* **[art of] ~**: Redekunst, *die;* Rhetorik, *die*

rhetorical /rɪ'tɒrɪkl/ *adj.* rhetorisch

rheumatic /ru:'mætɪk/ *adj.* rheumatisch

rheumatism /'ru:mətɪzm/ *n.* Rheumatismus, *der;* Rheuma, *das* (ugs.)

Rhine /raɪn/ *pr. n.* Rhein, *der*

rhino /'raɪnəʊ/ *n., pl.* **same** *or* **~s** (coll.), **rhinoceros** /raɪ'nɒsərəs/ *n., pl. same or* **~es** Nashorn, *das;* Rhinozeros, *das*

rhododendron /rəʊdə'dendrən/ *n.* Rhododendron, *der*

rhubarb /'ru:bɑ:b/ *n.* Rhabarber, *der*

rhyme /raɪm/ [1] *n.* Reim, *der;* **without ~ or reason** ohne Sinn und Verstand
[2] *v.i.* sich reimen (**with** auf + *Akk.*)

rhythm /'rɪðm/ *n.* Rhythmus, *der*

rhythmic /'rɪðmɪk/, **rhythmical** /'rɪðmɪkl/ *adj.* rhythmisch

rib /rɪb/ [1] *n.* Rippe, *die*
[2] *v.t.*, **-bb-** (coll.) aufziehen (ugs.)

ribald /'rɪbəld/ *adj.* zotig

ribbon /'rɪbn/ *n.* Band, *das;* (on typewriter) [Farb]band, *das*

'ribcage *n.* Brustkorb, *der*

rice /raɪs/ *n.* Reis, *der*

rice: ~ 'pudding *n.* Milchreis, *der;* **~ wine** *n.* Reiswein, *der*

rich /rɪtʃ/ [1] *adj.* **(a)** reich (**in** an + *Dat.*); (fertile) fruchtbar ‹*Land, Boden*›
(b) (splendid) prachtvoll
(c) (containing much fat, oil, eggs, etc.) gehaltvoll
(d) (deep, full) voll[tönend] ‹*Stimme*›; voll ‹*Ton*›; satt ‹*Farbe, Farbton*›
[2] *n. pl.* **the ~**: die Reichen *Pl.*; **~ and poor** Arm und Reich

riches /'rɪtʃɪz/ *n. pl.* Reichtum, *der*

'richly *adv.* **(a)** (splendidly) reich; üppig ‹*ausgestattet*›; prächtig ‹*gekleidet*›
(b) (fully) voll und ganz; **~ deserved** wohlverdient

'richness *n.* **(a)** (of food) Reichhaltigkeit, *die*
(b) (of voice) voller Klang; (of colour) Sattheit, *die*

rickets /'rɪkɪts/ *n.* Rachitis, *die*

rickety /'rɪkɪtɪ/ *adj.* wack[e]lig

ricochet /'rɪkəʃeɪ/ [1] *n.* **(a)** Abprallen, *das*
(b) (hit) Abpraller, *der*
[2] *v.i.*, **~ed** /'rɪkəʃeɪd/ abprallen (**off** von)

rid /rɪd/ *v.t.*, **-dd-, rid: ~ sth. of sth.** etw. von etw. befreien; **~ oneself of sb./sth.** sich von jmdm./etw. befreien; **be ~ of sb./sth.** jmdn./etw. los sein (ugs.); **get ~ of sb./sth.** jmdn./etw. loswerden

riddance /'rɪdəns/ *n.* **good ~!** Gott sei Dank ist er/es *usw.* weg!

ridden ▶ RIDE 2, 3

riddle¹ /'rɪdl/ *n.* Rätsel, *das*

riddle² *v.t.* durchlöchern; **~d with bullets** von Kugeln durchsiebt

ride /raɪd/ [1] *n.* (on horseback) [Aus]ritt, *der;* (in vehicle, at fair) Fahrt, die; **~ in a train/coach** Zug-/Busfahrt, *die;* **go for a ~**: ausreiten; **go for a [bi]cycle ~**: Rad fahren; **go for a ~ [in the car]** [mit dem Auto] wegfahren; **take sb. for a ~** (fig. coll.: deceive) jmdn. reinlegen (ugs.)
[2] *v.i.*, **rode** /rəʊd/, **ridden** /'rɪdn/ (on horse) reiten; (on bicycle, in vehicle) fahren; **~ to town on one's bike/in one's car/on the train** mit dem Rad/Auto/Zug in die Stadt fahren
[3] *v.t.*, **rode, ridden** reiten ‹*Pferd usw.*›; fahren mit ‹*Fahrrad*›

■ **ride a'way, ride 'off** *v.i.* wegreiten/-fahren

'rider *n.* **(a)** Reiter, *der*/Reiterin, *die;* (of cycle) Fahrer, *der*/Fahrerin, *die*
(b) (addition) Zusatz, *der*

ridge /rɪdʒ/ *n.* **(a)** (of roof) First, *der*
(b) (long hilltop) Grat, *der;* Kamm, *der*
(c) (Meteorol.) **~ [of high pressure]** lang gestrecktes Hoch

ridicule /'rɪdɪkju:l/ [1] *n.* Spott, *der* ···›

2 *v.t.* verspotten

ridiculous /rɪˈdɪkjʊləs/ *adj.* lächerlich

riding /ˈraɪdɪŋ/ *n.* Reiten, *das*

riding: ~ **lesson** *n.* Reitstunde, *die;* ~ **school** *n.* Reitschule, *die*

rife /raɪf/ *pred. adj.* weit verbreitet

riff-raff /ˈrɪfræf/ *n.* Gesindel, *das*

rifle /ˈraɪfl/ 1 *n.* Gewehr, *das*
2 *v.t.* durchwühlen
3 *v.i.* ~ **through sth.** etw. durchwühlen

rift /rɪft/ *n.* Unstimmigkeit, *die*

rig[1] /rɪg/ *n.* (for oil well) [Öl]förderturm, *der;* (off shore) Förderinsel, *die*

■ **rig 'out** *v.t.* ausstaffieren

■ **rig 'up** *v.t.* aufbauen

rig[2] *v.t.*, **-gg-** manipulieren ‹[*Wahl*]*ergebnis*›; fälschen ‹*Wahl*›

rigging /ˈrɪgɪŋ/ *n.* Takelung, *die*

right /raɪt/ 1 *adj.* **(a)** (just, morally good, sound) richtig
(b) (correct, true) richtig; **you're [quite]** ~: du hast [völlig] recht; **be** ~ **in sth.** Recht mit etw. haben; **is that clock** ~**?** geht die Uhr da richtig?; **put** *or* **set** ~: richtig stellen ‹*Irrtum, Behauptung*›; wieder gutmachen ‹*Unrecht*›; berichtigen ‹*Fehler*›; richtig stellen ‹*Uhr*›; **put** *or* **set sb.** ~: jmdn. berichtigen; **that's** ~: ja[wohl]; so ist es; **is that** ~**?** stimmt das?; (indeed?) aha!; **[am I]** ~**?** nicht [wahr]?
(c) (preferable, most suitable) richtig; recht; **do sth. the** ~ **way** etw. richtig machen
(d) (opposite of left) recht...; **on the** ~ **side** rechts
(e) R~ (Polit.) recht...
2 *v.t.* aus der Welt schaffen ‹*Unrecht*›
3 *n.* **(a)** (fair claim, authority) Recht, *das;* **have a/no** ~ **to sth.** ein/kein Anrecht *od.* Recht auf etw. (*Akk.*) haben; **in one's own** ~: aus eigenem Recht; ~ **of way** Vorfahrtsrecht, *das;* **have** ~ **of way** Vorfahrt haben
(b) (what is just) Recht, *das;* **by** ~**[s]** von Rechts wegen; **in the** ~: im Recht
(c) (~-hand side) rechte Seite; **on** *or* **to the** ~ **[of sb./sth.]** rechts [von jmdm./etw.]
(d) (Polit.) **the R**~: die Rechte
4 *adv.* **(a)** (correctly) richtig
(b) (to the ~-hand side) nach rechts
(c) (completely) ganz
(d) (exactly) genau; ~ **'now** im Moment; jetzt sofort ‹*handeln*›
(e) (straight) direkt

'right angle *n.* rechter Winkel; **at** ~**s to sth.** rechtwinklig zu etw.

righteous /ˈraɪtʃəs/ *adj.* rechtschaffen

rightful /ˈraɪtfl/ *adj.* rechtmäßig ‹*Besitzer, Herrscher*›

right: ~**-hand** *adj.* recht...; ~**-'handed** 1 *adj.* rechtshändig; ‹*Werkzeug*› für Rechtshänder; **be** ~**-handed** ‹*Person:*› Rechtshänder/Rechtshänderin sein; 2 *adv.* rechtshändig; ~**-hand 'man** *n.* rechte Hand

'rightly *adv.* zu Recht

right: ~**-'minded** *adj.* gerecht denkend; ~**-to-'life** *attrib. adj.* Recht-auf-Leben-; ~ **'wing** *n.* rechter Flügel; ~**-wing** *adj.* (Polit.) rechtsgerichtet; Rechts‹*extremist, -intellektueller*›; ~**-winger** *n.* **(a)** (Sport) Rechtsaußen, *der;* **(b)** (Polit.) Rechte, *der/die*

rigid /ˈrɪdʒɪd/ *adj.* **(a)** starr; (stiff) steif **(b)** (strict) streng; unbeugsam ‹*System*›

rigidity /rɪˈdʒɪtɪ/ *n.* ▶ RIGID: Starrheit, *die;* Steifheit, *die;* Strenge, *die*

rigmarole /ˈrɪgmərəʊl/ *n.* **(a)** (talk) langatmiges Geschwafel (ugs.)
(b) (procedure) Zirkus, *der*

rigor /ˈrɪgə(r)/ (Amer.) ▶ RIGOUR

rigor mortis /rɪgə ˈmɔːtɪs/ *n.* Totenstarre, *die*

rigorous /ˈrɪgərəs/ *adj.* streng

rigour /ˈrɪgə(r)/ *n.* (Brit.) Strenge, *die*

rile /raɪl/ *v.t.* (coll.) ärgern

rim /rɪm/ *n.* Rand, *der;* (of wheel) Felge, *die*

rind /raɪnd/ *n.* (of fruit) Schale, *die;* (of cheese) Rinde, *die;* (of bacon) Schwarte, *die*

ring[1] /rɪŋ/ 1 *n.* **(a)** Ring, *der*
(b) (Boxing) Ring, *der;* (in circus) Manege, *die*
2 *v.t.* (surround) umringen; einkreisen ‹*Wort*›

ring[2] 1 *n.* **(a)** (act of sounding bell) Läuten, *das;* Klingeln, *das*
(b) (Brit. coll.: telephone call) Anruf, *der;* **give sb. a** ~: jmdn. anrufen
(c) (fig.: impression) **have the** ~ **of truth [about it]** glaubhaft klingen
2 *v.i.*, **rang** /ræŋ/, **rung** /rʌŋ/ **(a)** (sound clearly) [er]schallen; ‹*Hammer:*› [er]dröhnen
(b) (be sounded) ‹*Glocke, Klingel, Telefon:*› läuten; ‹*Wecker, Telefon, Kasse:*› klingeln; **the doorbell rang** es klingelte
(c) (~ bell) läuten (**for** nach)
(d) (Brit.: make telephone call) anrufen
3 *v.t.*, **rang, rung (a)** läuten ‹*Glocke*›; ~ **the [door]bell** läuten; klingeln; **it** ~**s a bell** (fig. coll.) es kommt mir [irgendwie] bekannt vor
(b) (Brit.: telephone) anrufen

■ **ring 'back** (Brit.) *v.t. & i.* **(a)** (again) wieder anrufen
(b) (in return) zurückrufen

■ **ring 'off** *v.i.* (Brit.) auflegen

■ **ring 'out** *v.i.* ertönen

■ **ring 'up** *v.t.* (Brit.: telephone) anrufen

ring: ~ **binder** *n.* Ringbuch, *das;* ~ **finger** *n.* Ringfinger, *der*

ringing /ˈrɪŋɪŋ/ *n.* Läuten, *das;* (Brit. Teleph.) ~ **tone** Freiton, *der*

'ringleader *n.* Anführer, *der*/Anführerin, *die*

ringlet /ˈrɪŋlɪt/ *n.* [Ringel]löckchen, *das*

ring: ~ **road** *n.* Ringstraße, *die;* ~**tone** *n.* Klingelton *der*

rink /rɪŋk/ *n.* (for ice skating) Eisbahn, *die;* (for roller skating) Rollschuhbahn, *die*

rinse /rɪns/ 1 *v.t.* **(a)** (wash out) ausspülen ‹*Mund, Gefäß usw.*›
(b) [aus]spülen ‹*Wäsche usw.*›; abspülen ‹*Hände, Geschirr*›

[2] *n.* Spülen, *das;* **give sth. a [good/quick] ~:** etw. [gut/schnell] ausspülen/abspülen/spülen
■ **rinse 'out** *v.t.* ausspülen
riot /ˈraɪət/ [1] *n.* Aufruhr, *der;* **~s** Unruhen *Pl.;* **run ~:** randalieren
[2] *v.i.* randalieren
'rioter *n.* Randalierer, *der*
'riot gear *n.* Schutzkleidung *od.* -ausrüstung
riotous /ˈraɪətəs/ *adj.* **(a)** gewalttätig
(b) (unrestrained) wild
rip /rɪp/ [1] *n.* Riss, *der*
[2] *v.t.*, **-pp-** zerreißen; **~ open** aufreißen
■ **rip 'off** *v.t.* **(a)** (remove from) reißen von; (remove) abreißen
(b) (coll.: defraud) übers Ohr hauen (ugs.)
■ **rip 'out** *v.t.* herausreißen (of aus)
RIP *abbr.* = **rest in peace** R.I.P.
'ripcord *n.* Reißleine, *die*
ripe /raɪp/ *adj.* reif (**for** zu)
ripen /ˈraɪpn/ [1] *v.t.* zur Reife bringen
[2] *v.i.* reifen
'ripeness *n.* Reife, *die*
'rip-off *n.* (coll.) Nepp, *der* (ugs.)
riposte /rɪˈpɒst/ [1] *n.* (retort) [rasche] Entgegnung
[2] *v.i.* [rasch] antworten
ripple /ˈrɪpl/ [1] *n.* kleine Welle
[2] *v.i.* ‹*See:*› sich kräuseln; ‹*Welle:*› plätschern
[3] *v.t.* kräuseln
rise /raɪz/ [1] *n.* **(a)** (advancement) Aufstieg, *der*
(b) (in value, price, cost) Steigerung, *die;* (in population, temperature) Zunahme, *die*
(c) (Brit.) **[pay] ~** (in wages) Lohnerhöhung, *die;* (in salary) Gehaltserhöhung, *die*
(d) (hill) Anhöhe, *die*
(e) give ~ to führen zu; Anlass geben zu ‹*Spekulation*›
[2] *v.i.*, **rose** /rəʊz/, **risen** /ˈrɪzn/ **(a)** (go up) aufsteigen
(b) ‹*Sonne, Mond:*› aufgehen
(c) (increase, reach higher level) steigen
(d) (advance) ‹*Person:*› aufsteigen
(e) ‹*Teig, Kuchen:*› aufgehen
(f) (Theatre) ‹*Vorhang:*› aufgehen
(g) ‹*Fluss:*› entspringen
■ **rise 'up** *v.i.* **(a) ~ up [in revolt]** aufbegehren (geh.)
(b) ‹*Berg:*› aufragen
risen ▸ RISE 2
'riser *n.* **early ~:** Frühaufsteher, *der*/Frühaufsteherin, *die*
rising /ˈraɪzɪŋ/ [1] *n.* (of sun, moon, etc.) Aufgang, *der*
[2] *adj.* **(a)** aufgehend ‹*Sonne, Mond usw.*›
(b) steigend ‹*Kosten, Temperatur, Wasser, Flut*›
(c) (sloping upwards) ansteigend
risk /rɪsk/ [1] *n.* Gefahr, *die;* (chance taken) Risiko, *das;* **at one's own ~:** auf eigene Gefahr *od.* eigenes Risiko; **take the ~ of doing sth.** es riskieren, etw. zu tun; **be at ~** ‹*Zukunft, Plan:*› gefährdet sein
[2] *v.t.* riskieren; **I'll ~ it** ich lasse es darauf ankommen
'risky *adj.* gefährlich; gewagt ‹*Experiment, Projekt*›
risotto /rɪˈzɒtəʊ/ *n., pl.* **~s** Risotto, *der od. das*
risqué /ˈrɪskeɪ/ *adj.* gewagt
rissole /ˈrɪsəʊl/ *n.* Frikadelle, *die*
rite /raɪt/ *n.* Ritus, *der*
ritual /ˈrɪtʃʊəl/ [1] *adj.* rituell; Ritual‹*mord, -tötung*›
[2] *n.* Ritual, *das*
rival /ˈraɪvl/ [1] *n.* (competitor) Rivale, *der*/Rivalin, *die;* **business ~s** Konkurrenten *Pl.*
[2] *v.t.*, (Brit.) **-ll-** nicht nachstehen (+ *Dat.*)
rivalry /ˈraɪvlrɪ/ *n.* Rivalität, *die* (geh.)
river /ˈrɪvə(r)/ *n.* Fluss, *das*
river: ~ bank Flussufer, *der;* **~ basin** *n.* Stromgebiet, *das;* **~ bed** *n.* Flussbett, *das* **~side** [1] *n.* Flussufer, *das;* [2] *attrib. adj.* am Fluss gelegen; am Fluss *nachgestellt*
rivet /ˈrɪvɪt/ [1] *n.* Niete, *die*
[2] *v.t.* **(a)** [ver]nieten
(b) (fig.) fesseln
'riveting *adj.* fesselnd
rivulet /ˈrɪvjʊlɪt/ *n.* Bach, *der*
RN *abbr.* (Brit.) = **Royal Navy** Königl. Mar.
road /rəʊd/ *n.* Straße, *die;* **across** *or* **over the ~ [from us]** [bei uns] gegenüber; **by ~** (by car/bus/lorry) per Auto/Bus/Lkw; **be on the ~:** auf Reisen *od.* unterwegs sein; ‹*Theaterensemble usw.:*› auf Tournee *od.* Tour sein
road: ~ accident *n.* Verkehrsunfall, *der;* **~ atlas** *n.* Autoatlas, *der;* **~block** *n.* Straßensperre, *die;* **~ bridge** *n.* Straßenbrücke, *die;* **~ haulage** *n.* Gütertransport auf der Straße; **~ hog** *n.* Verkehrsrowdy, *der;* **~ hump** ▸ SPEED BUMP
roadie /ˈrəʊdɪ/ *n.* (coll.) Roadie, *der*
road: ~ manager *n.* Roadmanager, *der;* **~ map** *n.* Straßenkarte, *die;* **~mender** *n.* Straßen[bau]arbeiter, *der*/-arbeiterin, *die;* **~ rage** *n.: häufig zu gewalttätigen Ausbrüchen führende Wut eines Autofahrers;* **~ safety** *n.* Verkehrssicherheit, *die;* **~ sense** *n.* Gespür für Verkehrssituationen; **~side** *n.* Straßenrand, *der;* **at** *or* **by/along the ~side** am Straßenrand; **~ sign** *n.* Verkehrszeichen, *das;* Straßenschild, *das* (ugs.); **~ sweeper** *n.* Straßenkehrer, *der*/-kehrerin, *die;* **~ tax** *n.* (Brit.) Kraftfahrzeugsteuer, *die;* Kfz-Steuer, *die;* **~ transport** *n.* Personen- und Güterbeförderung auf der Straße; **form of ~ transport** Verkehrsmittel der Straße; **~ user** *n.* Verkehrsteilnehmer, *der*/

⋯

-teilnehmerin, *die;* **~way** *n.* Fahrbahn, *die;* **~works** *n. pl.* Straßenbauarbeiten *Pl.;* **~worthy** *adj.* fahrtüchtig

roam /rəʊm/ [1] *v.i.* umherstreifen [2] *v.t.* streifen durch

roaming /'rəʊmɪŋ/ *n.* (Teleph.) Roaming, *das*

roar /rɔː(r)/ [1] *n.* (of wild beast) Gebrüll, *das;* (of applause) Tosen, *das;* (of engine, traffic) Dröhnen, *das;* **~s/a ~ [of laughter]** dröhnendes Gelächter [2] *v.i.* brüllen (**with** vor + *Dat.*); ‹*Motor:*› dröhnen

'roaring *adj.* **(a)** bullernd (ugs.) ‹*Feuer*› **(b) a ~ success** ein Bombenerfolg; **do a ~ trade** ein Bombengeschäft machen

roast /rəʊst/ [1] *v.t.* braten; rösten ‹*Kaffeebohnen, Kastanien*› [2] *attrib. adj.* gebraten ‹*Fleisch, Ente usw.*›; Brat‹*hähnchen, -kartoffeln*›; Röst‹*kastanien*›; **~ beef** (sirloin) Roastbeef, *das* [3] *n.* Braten, *der*

rob /rɒb/ *v.t.,* **-bb-** ausrauben ‹*Bank, Safe, Kasse*›; berauben ‹*Person*›

robber /'rɒbə(r)/ *n.* Räuber, *der*/Räuberin, *die*

robbery /'rɒbərɪ/ *n.* Raub, *der;* **robberies** Raubüberfälle *Pl.*

robe /rəʊb/ *n.* Gewand, *das* (*geh.*); (*of judge, vicar*) Talar, *der*

robin /'rɒbɪn/ *n.* **~ [redbreast]** Rotkehlchen, *das*

robot /'rəʊbɒt/ *n.* Roboter, *der*

robotics /rəʊ'bɒtɪks/ *n.* Robotertechnik, *die;* Robotik, *die*

robust /rəʊ'bʌst/ *adj.* robust

rock¹ /rɒk/ *n.* **(a)** (piece of **~**) Fels, *der* **(b)** (large **~**, hill) Felsen, *der* **(c)** (substance) Fels, *der;* (esp. Geol.) Gestein, *das* **(d)** (boulder) Felsbrocken, *der;* (Amer.: stone) Stein, *der* **(e) stick of ~:** Zuckerstange, *die* **(f) be on the ~s** (fig. coll.) ‹*Ehe, Firma:*› kaputt sein (ugs.)

rock² [1] *v.t.* wiegen; (in cradle) schaukeln [2] *v.i.* **(a)** schaukeln **(b)** (sway) schwanken [3] *n.* (Mus.) Rock, *der; attrib.* Rock-; **~ and** *or* **'n' roll [music]** Rock and Roll, *der*

rock: ~-'bottom (coll.) [1] *adj.* **~-bottom prices** Schleuderpreise *Pl.* (ugs.); [2] *n.* **reach** *or* **touch ~-bottom** ‹*Handel, Preis:*› in den Keller fallen (ugs.); **her spirits reached ~-bottom** ihre Stimmung war auf dem Tiefpunkt; **~ climber** *n.* Kletterer, *der*/Kletterin, *die;* **~ climbing** *n.* [Fels]klettern, *das*

rocker /'rɒkə(r)/ *n.* **be off one's ~** (fig. coll.) übergeschnappt *od.* durchgedreht sein (ugs.)

rockery /'rɒkərɪ/ *n.* Steingarten, *der*

rocket /'rɒkɪt/ [1] *n.* Rakete, *die* [2] *v.i.* ‹*Preise:*› in die Höhe schnellen

rocket: ~ base *n.* (Mil.) Raketen[abschuss]basis, *die;* **~ launcher** *n.* Raketenwerfer, *der;* **~-propelled** *adj.* raketengetrieben

rock: ~ face *n.* Felswand, *die;* **~fall** *n.* Steinschlag, *der;* **~ formation** *n.* Gesteinsformation, *die;* **~ garden** *n.* Steingarten, *der;* **~-hard** *adj.* steinhart

rocking: ~ chair *n.* Schaukelstuhl, *der;* **~ horse** *n.* Schaukelpferd, *das*

rock: ~ plant *n.* Felsenpflanze, *die;* (Hort.) Steingartengewächs, *das;* **~ salt** *n.* Steinsalz, *das*

'rocky *adj.* **(a)** felsig **(b)** (coll.: unsteady) wackelig (ugs.)

rod /rɒd/ *n.* Stange, *die;* (for punishing) Rute, *die;* (for fishing) [Angel]rute, *die*

rode ▶ RIDE 2, 3

rodent /'rəʊdənt/ *n.* Nagetier, *das*

rodeo /'rəʊdɪəʊ, rəʊ'deɪəʊ/ *n., pl.* **~s** Rodeo, *der od. das*

roe¹ /rəʊ/ *n.* (of fish) **[hard] ~:** Rogen, *der;* **[soft] ~:** Milch, *die*

roe² *n.* **~ [deer]** Reh, *das*

rogue /rəʊg/ *n.* Gauner, *der*

role, rôle /rəʊl/ *n.* Rolle, *die*

role: ~ model *n.* Leitbild, *das;* **~ playing** *n.* Rollenspiel, *das;* **~ reversal** *n.* Rollentausch, *der*

roll¹ /rəʊl/ *n.* **(a)** Rolle, *die;* (of cloth etc.) Ballen, *der;* **~ of film** Rolle Film **(b) [bread] ~:** Brötchen, *das* **(c) be on a ~** (coll.) eine Glückssträhne haben

roll² [1] *n.* (of drum) Wirbel, *der* [2] *v.t.* **(a)** rollen; (between surfaces) drehen **(b)** (shape by **~ing**) rollen; drehen ‹*Zigarette*› **(c)** walzen ‹*Rasen, Metall usw.*›; ausrollen ‹*Teig*› [3] *v.i.* **(a)** rollen **(b)** ‹*Maschine:*› laufen; **get sth. ~ing** (fig.) etw. ins Rollen bringen **(c) be ~ing in money** *or* **in it** (coll.) im Geld schwimmen (ugs.)

■ **roll a'bout** *v.i.* herumrollen; ‹*Schiff:*› schlingern; ‹*Kind, Hund:*› sich wälzen

■ **roll 'back** *v.t.* zurückrollen

■ **roll 'by** *v.i.* ‹*Zeit:*› vergehen

■ **roll 'in** *v.i.* (coll.) ‹*Briefe, Geldbeträge:*› eingehen

■ **roll 'over** *v.i.* ‹*Person:*› sich umdrehen, (to make room) sich zur Seite rollen

■ **roll 'up** [1] *v.t.* aufrollen ‹*Teppich*›; zusammenrollen ‹*Landkarte, Dokument usw.*›; hochkrempeln ‹*Ärmel*› [2] *v.i.* (coll.: arrive) aufkreuzen (salopp)

'roll-call *n.* Ausrufen aller Namen; (Mil.) Zählappell, *der*

rolled 'oats *n. pl.* Haferflocken *Pl.*

'roller *n.* **(a)** Rolle, *die;* (for lawn, road, etc.) Walze, *die* **(b)** (for hair) Lockenwickler, *der*

roller: R~blade ® *n.* Rollerblade, *der;*

Inliner, der; **~blade** *v.i.* Rollerblades fahren; **~ blind** *n.* Rouleau, *das;* **~ coaster** *n.* Achterbahn, *die;* **~ skate** *n.* Rollschuh, *der;* **~-skate** *v.i.* Rollschuh laufen; **~ skating** *n.* Rollschuhlaufen, *das*

'roll film *n.* Rollfilm, *der*

'rolling *adj.* wellig ‹*Gelände*›; **~ hills** sanfte Hügel *Pl.*

rolling: ~ pin *n.* Teigrolle, *die;* **~ stock** *n.* (Brit. Railw.) Fahrzeugbestand, *der*

roll: ~-neck [1] *n.* Rollkragen, *der;* [2] *adj.* Rollkragen-; **~-on ~-off** *adj.* **~-on ~-off ship/ferry** Roll-on-roll-off-Schiff, *das*/-Fähre, *die;* **~over** *n.* (*von Auslosung zu Auslosung*) aufgestockter Jackpot; **~-up** (Brit. coll.)**, ~-your-own** (esp. Amer. coll.) *ns.* Selbstgedrehte, *die*

ROM /rɒm/ *abbr.* (Comp.) = **read only memory** ROM

Roman /'rəʊmən/ [1] *n.* Römer, *der*/Römerin, *die*
[2] *adj.* römisch

Roman 'Catholic [1] *adj.* römisch-katholisch
[2] *n.* Katholik, *der*/Katholikin, *die;* **sb. is a ~:** jmd. ist römisch-katholisch

romance /rə'mæns/ *n.* **(a)** (love affair) Romanze, *die*
(b) (love story) [romantische] Liebesgeschichte

Romania /rəʊ'meɪnɪə/ *pr. n.* Rumänien (*das*)

Romanian /rəʊ'meɪnɪən/ [1] *adj.* rumänisch; **sb. is ~:** jmd. ist Romäne/Romänin
[2] *n.* **(a)** (person) Rumäne, *der*/Rumänin, *die*
(b) (language) Rumänisch, *das; see also* ENGLISH 2A

Roman 'numeral *n.* römische Ziffer

romantic /rəʊ'mæntɪk/ *adj.* romantisch

romanticism /rəʊ'mæntɪsɪzm/ *n.* (Lit., Art., Mus.) Romantik, *die*

romanticize /rəʊ'mæntɪsaɪz/ *v.t.* romantisieren

'roman type *n.* (Printing) Antiquaschrift, *die*

Romany /'rəʊmənɪ/ [1] **(a)** (person) Rom, *der*
(b) (language) Romani, *das*
[2] *adj.* Roma-; (Ling.) Romani-

Rome /rəʊm/ *pr. n.* Rom (*das*)

romp /rɒmp/ [1] *v.i.* **(a)** [herum]tollen
(b) ~ home *or* **in** (coll.: win easily) spielend gewinnen
[2] *n.* Tollerei, *die*

rompers /'rɒmpəz/ *n. pl.* Spielhöschen, *das*

roof /ru:f/ [1] *n.* **(a)** Dach, *das*
(b) ~ of the mouth Gaumen, *der*
[2] *v.t.* bedachen

'roof garden Dachgarten, *der*

'roofing *n.* (material) Deckung, *die*

'roof: ~ rack *n.* Dachgepäckträger, *der;* **~top** *n.* Dach, *das*

rook¹ /rʊk/ *n.* (Ornith.) Saatkrähe, *die*

rook² *n.* (Chess) Turm, *der*

rookery /'rʊkərɪ/ *n.* Saatkrähenkolonie, *die*

room /ru:m, rʊm/ *n.* **(a)** (in building) Zimmer, *das;* (for function) Saal, *der*
(b) (space) Platz, *der;* **make ~ [for sb./sth.]** [jmdm./einer Sache] Platz machen; **there is still ~ for improvement in his work** seine Arbeit ist noch verbesserungsfähig

room: ~-mate *n.* Zimmergenosse, *der*/-genossin, *die;* **~ service** *n.* Zimmerservice, *der;* **~ temperature** *n.* Zimmertemperatur, *die*

roomy /'ru:mɪ/ *adj.* geräumig

roost /ru:st/ [1] *n.* [Sitz]stange, *die*
[2] *v.i.* ‹*Vogel:*› sich [zum Schlafen] niederlassen

root¹ /ru:t/ [1] *n.* Wurzel, *die;* **put down ~s/take ~:** Wurzeln schlagen
[2] *v.i.* ‹*Pflanze:*› wurzeln
[3] *v.t.* **stand ~ed to the spot** wie angewurzelt dastehen

■ **root 'out** *v.t.* ausrotten

root² *v.i.* **(a)** (turn up ground) wühlen (**for** nach)
(b) (coll.) **~ for** (cheer) anfeuern

'root crop[s] *n.* [*pl.*] Hackfrüchte *Pl.*

'rooted *adj.* eingewurzelt

'rootless *adj.* wurzellos

'root vegetable *n.* Wurzelgemüse, *das*

rope /rəʊp/ [1] *n.* **(a)** (cord) Seil, *das*
(b) know the ~s sich auskennen
[2] *v.t.* festbinden

■ **rope 'in** *v.t.* (fig.) einspannen (ugs.)

rope 'ladder *n.* Strickleiter, *die*

ro-ro /'rəʊrəʊ/ *adj.* Ro-Ro-‹*Schiff, Fähre*›

rosary /'rəʊzərɪ/ *n.* Rosenkranz, *der*

rose¹ /rəʊz/ *n.* **(a)** (plant, flower) Rose, *die*
(b) (colour) Rosa, *das*

rose² ▶ RISE 2

rosé /rəʊ'zeɪ, 'rəʊzeɪ/ *n.* Rosé, *der*

rose: ~ bed *n.* Rosenbeet, *das;* **~bud** *n.* Rosenknospe, *die;* **~ bush** *n.* Rosenstrauch, *der;* **~ hip** *n.* Hagebutte, *die*

rosemary /'rəʊzmərɪ/ *n.* Rosmarin, *der*

'rose petal *n.* Rosen[blüten]blatt, *das*

rosette /rəʊ'zet/ *n.* Rosette, *die*

roster /'rɒstə(r)/ *n.* Dienstplan, *der*

rostrum /'rɒstrəm/ *n., pl.* **rostra** /'rɒstrə/ *or* **~s** Podium, *das*

rosy /'rəʊzɪ/ *adj.* rosig

rot /rɒt/ [1] *n.* **(a)** ▶ 2: Verrottung, *die;* Fäulnis, *die;* (fig.: deterioration) Verfall, *der;* **stop the ~** (fig.) dem Verfall Einhalt gebieten
(b) (coll.: nonsense) Quark, *der* (salopp)
[2] *v.i.*, **-tt-** verrotten; ‹*Fleisch, Gemüse, Obst:*› verfaulen
[3] *v.t.*, **-tt-** verrotten lassen; verfaulen lassen ‹*Fleisch, Gemüse, Obst*›; zerstören ‹*Zähne*›

rota /'rəʊtə/ *n.* (Brit.) (order of rotation) Turnus, *der;* (list) Arbeitsplan, *der*

rotary /'rəʊtərɪ/ *adj.* rotierend

r

rotate /rəʊ'teɪt/ 1 *v.i.* (revolve) rotieren; sich drehen
2 *v.t.* in Rotation versetzen
rotation /rəʊ'teɪʃn/ *n.* **(a)** Rotation, *die,* Drehung, *die* (**about** um)
(b) (succession) turnusmäßiger Wechsel; **in** *or* **by ~**: im Turnus
rote /rəʊt/ *n.* **by ~**: auswendig
rotten /'rɒtn/ *adj.*, **~er** /'rɒtənə(r)/, **~est** /'rɒtənɪst/ **(a)** (decayed) verrottet; verfault ‹*Obst, Gemüse*›; faul ‹*Ei, Holz, Zähne*›; **~ to the core** (fig.) verdorben bis ins Mark
(b) (corrupt) verdorben
(c) (coll.: bad) mies (ugs.)
rotund /rəʊ'tʌnd/ *adj.* **(a)** (round) rund
(b) (plump) rundlich
rouble /'ru:bl/ *n.* Rubel, *der*
rouge /ru:ʒ/ *n.* Rouge, *das*
rough /rʌf/ 1 *adj.* **(a)** (coarse, uneven) rau; holp[e]rig ‹*Straße usw.*›; uneben ‹*Gelände*›; unruhig ‹*Überfahrt*›
(b) (violent) grob ‹*Person, Worte, Behandlung*›
(c) (trying) hart; **this is ~ on him** das ist hart für ihn; **sth. is ~ going** etw. ist nicht einfach
(d) (approximate) grob ‹*Skizze, Schätzung*›; vag ‹*Vorstellung*›; **~ paper/notebook** Konzeptpapier, *das*/Kladde, *die*
(e) (coll.: ill) angeschlagen (ugs.)
2 *n.* **[be] in ~**: [sich] im Rohzustand [befinden]
3 *adv.* rau ‹*spielen*›; **sleep ~**: im Freien schlafen
4 *v.t.* **~ it** primitiv leben
■ **rough 'out** *v.t.* grob entwerfen
■ **rough 'up** *v.t.* (coll.) zusammenschlagen
roughage /'rʌfɪdʒ/ *n.* Ballaststoffe *Pl.*
rough: ~-and-ready *adj.* provisorisch; **~ and 'tumble** *n.* [milde] Rauferei; **~ copy, ~ draft** *ns.* grobe Skizze; grober Entwurf; **~ 'diamond** *n.* (fig.) ungehobelter, aber guter Mensch
roughen /'rʌfn/ *v.t.* aufrauen
rough: ~ 'justice *n.* ziemlich willkürliche Urteile *Pl.*; **~ 'luck** *n.* Pech, *das*
'roughly *adv.* **(a)** (violently) roh; grob
(b) (crudely) leidlich; grob ‹*skizzieren, bearbeiten, bauen*›
(c) (approximately) ungefähr; grob ‹*geschätzt*›
'roughness *n.* **(a)** Rauheit, *die;* (unevenness) Unebenheit, *die*
(b) (violence) Rohheit, *die*
'roughshod *adj.* **ride ~ over sb./sth.** jmdn./etw. mit Füßen treten
roulette /ru:'let/ *n.* Roulette, *das*
round /raʊnd/ 1 *adj.* rund; **in ~ figures** rund gerechnet
2 *n.* **(a)** (recurring series) Serie, *die;* **~ of talks/negotiations** Gesprächs-/Verhandlungsrunde, *die;* **the daily ~**: der Alltag
(b) (of ammunition) Ladung, *die;* **50 ~s [of ammunition]** 50 Schuss Munition
(c) (of game or contest) Runde, *die*
(d) (burst) **~ of applause** Beifallssturm, *der*
(e) ~ [of drinks] Runde, *die*
(f) (regular calls) Runde, *die;* Tour, *die;* **go [on]** *or* **make one's ~s** seine Runden machen
(g) a ~ of toast/sandwiches eine Scheibe Toast/eine Portion Sandwiches
3 *adv.* **(a) all the year ~**: das ganze Jahr hindurch; **the third time ~**: beim dritten Mal; **have a look ~**: sich umsehen; **ask sb. ~ [for a drink]** jmdn. [zu einem Gläschen zu sich] einladen
(b) (by indirect way) herum; **walk ~**: außen herum gehen
(c) (here) hier; (there) dort; **I'll go ~ tomorrow** ich gehe morgen hin
4 *prep.* **(a)** um [... herum]; **travel ~ England** durch England reisen; **run ~ the streets** durch die Straßen rennen; **walk ~ and ~ sth.** immer wieder um etw. herumgehen
(b) (in various directions from) um [... herum]; rund um ‹*einen Ort*›
5 *v.t.* **~ a bend** um eine Kurve fahren/gehen/kommen *usw*
■ **round 'off** *v.t.* abrunden
■ **round 'up** *v.t.* verhaften ‹*Verdächtige*›; zusammentreiben ‹*Vieh*›
round: ~ a'bout *adv.* (on all sides) ringsum; **~about** 1 *n.* **(a)** (Brit.: merry-go-round) Karussell, *das;* **(b)** (Brit.: road junction) Kreisverkehr, *der.* 2 *adj.* umständlich; **~ 'brackets** *n. pl.* runde Klammern *Pl.*
rounded /'raʊndɪd/ *adj.* **(a)** rund
(b) harmonisch ‹*Person*›
rounders /'raʊndəz/ *n. sing.* (Brit.) Rounders, *das;* ≈ Schlagball, *der*
round: ~ 'number *n.* runde Zahl; **~ 'robin** *n.* Petition, *die;* **~-shouldered** /raʊnd'ʃəʊldəd/ *adj.* ‹*Person*› mit einem Rundrücken; **~-the-'clock** *adj.* rund um die Uhr *nachgestellt;* **~ 'trip** *n.* Rundreise, *die;* **~-up** *n.* **(a)** (of animals) Zusammentreiben, *das;* **(b)** (summary) Zusammenfassung, *die*
rouse /raʊz/ *v.t.* wecken (**from** aus)
rousing /'raʊzɪŋ/ *adj.* mitreißend ‹*Lied*›; leidenschaftlich ‹*Rede*›
rout /raʊt/ 1 *n.* [wilde] Flucht; (defeat) verheerende Niederlage
2 *v.t.* aufreiben ‹*Feind, Truppen*›; vernichtend schlagen ‹*Gegner*›
route /ru:t/ *n.* Route, *die;* Weg, *der*
'route march *n.* (Mil.) Übungsmarsch, *der*
routine /ru:'ti:n/ 1 *n.* **(a)** Routine, *die*
(b) (coll.: set speech) Platte, *die* (ugs.)
(c) (Theatre) Nummer, *die;* (Dancing, Skating) Figur, *die*
2 *adj.* routinemäßig; Routine‹*arbeit*›
roux /ru:/ *n.* Mehlschwitze, *die*
row[1] /raʊ/ 1 (coll.) *n.* **(a)** (noise) Krach, *der;* **make a ~**: Krach machen
(b) (quarrel) Krach, *der* (ugs.); **have/start a ~**: Krach haben/anfangen (ugs.)
2 *v.i.* sich streiten
row[2] /rəʊ/ *n.* Reihe, *die;* **in a ~**: in einer Reihe
row[3] /rəʊ/ *v.i. & t.* (with oars) rudern

rowan /'rəʊən/ *n.* ~ [tree] Eberesche, *die*

rowboat /'rəʊbəʊt/ *n.* (Amer.) Ruderboot, *das*

rowdy /'raʊdɪ/ 1 *adj.* rowdyhaft; **the party was** ~: auf der Party ging es laut zu
2 *n.* Krawallmacher, *der*

rower /'rəʊə(r)/ *n.* Ruderer, *der*/Ruderin, *die*

rowing /'rəʊɪŋ/ *n.* Rudern, *das*

rowing: ~ **boat** *n.* (Brit.) Ruderboot, *das;* ~ **machine** *n.* Rudergerät, *das*

royal /'rɔɪəl/ *adj.* königlich

royal: R~ 'Air Force *n.* (Brit.) Königliche Luftwaffe; ~ **'blue** *n.* (Brit.) Königsblau, *das;* ~ **'family** *n.* königliche Familie; **R~ 'Navy** *n.* (Brit.) Königliche Kriegsmarine

royalty /'rɔɪəltɪ/ *n.* **(a)** (payment) Tantieme, *die* (**on** für)
(b) *collect.* (royal persons) Mitglieder *Pl.* des Königshauses

RSI *abbr.* = **repetitive strain injury**

RSPCA *abbr.* (Brit.) = **Royal Society for the Prevention of Cruelty to Animals** *britischer Tierschutzverein*

rub /rʌb/ 1 *v.t.*, **-bb-** reiben (**on, against** an + *Dat.*); (to remove dirt etc.) abreiben; (to dry) trockenreiben; ~ **sth. off sth.** etw. von etw. [ab]reiben
2 *v.i.*, **-bb-** reiben ([**up**]**on, against** an + *Dat.*)
3 *n.* **give it a** ~: reib es ab; **there's the** ~ (fig.) da liegt der Haken [dabei] (ugs.)

▪ **rub 'down** *v.t.* abreiben

▪ **rub 'in** *v.t.* einreiben; **there's no need to** *or* **don't** ~ **it in** (fig.) reib es mir nicht [dauernd] unter die Nase

▪ **rub 'off** *v.t.* wegreiben; wegwischen

▪ **rub 'out** 1 *v.t.* ausreiben; (using eraser) ausradieren
2 *v.i.* sich ausreiben/sich ausradieren lassen

rubber /'rʌbə(r)/ *n.* **(a)** Gummi, *das od. der*
(b) (eraser) Radiergummi, *der*

rubber: ~ **'band** *n.* Gummiband, *das;* ~ **'glove** *n.* Gummihandschuh, *der;* ~ **plant** *n.* Gummibaum, *der;* ~ **'stamp** *n.* Gummistempel, *der;* **~-stamp** *v.t.* (fig.) absegnen (ugs.)

rubbery /'rʌbərɪ/ *adj.* gummiartig; (tough) zäh

rubbish /'rʌbɪʃ/ 1 *n.* **(a)** (refuse) Abfall, *der;* (to be collected and dumped) Müll, *der*
(b) (worthless material) Plunder, *der* (ugs.); **be** ~: nichts taugen
(c) (nonsense) Quatsch, *der* (ugs.)
2 *int.* Quatsch (ugs.)

rubbish: ~ **bin** *n.* Abfall-/Mülleimer, *der;* (in factory) Abfall-/Mülltonne, *die;* ~ **chute** *n.* Müllschlucker, *der;* ~ **collection** *n.* Müllabfuhr, *die;* ~ **dump** *n.* Müllkippe, *die;* ~ **heap** *n.* Müllhaufen, *der;* ~ **tip** *n.* Müllabladeplatz, *der*

rubbishy /'rʌbɪʃɪ/ *adj.* mies (ugs.)

rubble /'rʌbl/ *n.* Trümmer *Pl.*

rubella /rʊ'belə/ *n.* (Med.) Röteln *Pl.*

ruby /'ru:bɪ/ *n.* Rubin, *der*

ruby 'wedding *n.* Rubinhochzeit, *die*

rucksack /'rʌksæk, 'rʊksæk/ *n.* Rucksack, *der*

rudder /'rʌdə(r)/ *n.* [Steuer]ruder, *das*

ruddy /'rʌdɪ/ *adj.* **(a)** (reddish) rötlich
(b) (Brit. coll.: bloody) verdammt (salopp)

rude /ru:d/ *adj.* **(a)** unhöflich; (stronger) rüde; **be** ~ **to sb.** zu jmdm. grob unhöflich sein/jmdn. rüde behandeln
(b) (abrupt) unsanft; ~ **awakening** böses Erwachen

'rudely *adv.* **(a)** (impolitely) unhöflich; rüde
(b) (abruptly) jäh (geh.)

'rudeness *n.* (bad manners) ungehöriges Benehmen

rudimentary /ru:dɪ'mentərɪ/ elementar; primitiv ‹*Gebäude*›

rudiments /'ru:dɪmənts/ *n. pl.* Grundlagen *Pl.*

rueful /'ru:fl/ *adj.* reumütig

ruffian /'rʌfɪən/ *n.* Rohling, *der*

ruffle /'rʌfl/ *v.t.* **(a)** kräuseln; ~ **sb.'s hair** jmdm. durch die Haare fahren
(b) (upset) aus der Fassung bringen

rug /rʌg/ *n.* [kleiner, dicker] Teppich; **Persian** ~: Perserbrücke, *die*

rugby /'rʌgbɪ/ *n.* Rugby, *das*

rugby: ~ **ball** *n.* Rugbyball, *der;* ~ **tackle** *n.* tiefes Fassen; **the policeman brought him down with a** ~ **tackle** der Polizist warf sich auf ihn und riss ihn zu Boden

rugged /'rʌgɪd/ *adj.* **(a)** (uneven) zerklüftet; unwegsam ‹*Land*›; zerfurcht ‹*Gesicht*›
(b) (sturdy) robust

ruin /'ru:ɪn/ 1 *n.* **(a)** *in sing. or pl.* (remains) Ruine, *die;* **in** ~**s** in Trümmern
(b) (downfall) Ruin, *der*
2 *v.t.* ruinieren; verderben ‹*Urlaub, Abend*›; ~**ed** (reduced to ruins) verfallen; **a** ~**ed castle/church** eine Burg-/Kirchenruine

ruinous /'ru:ɪnəs/ *adj.* ruinös

rule /ru:l/ 1 *n.* **(a)** Regel, *die;* **the** ~**s of the game** die Spielregeln; **be against the** ~**s** regelwidrig sein; (fig.) gegen die Spielregeln verstoßen; **as a** ~: in der Regel; ~ **of thumb** Faustregel, *die*
(b) *no pl.* (government) Herrschaft, *die* (**over** über + *Akk.*)
2 *v.t.* **(a)** (control) beherrschen
(b) (be the ruler of) regieren; ‹*Monarch, Diktator usw.:*› herrschen über (+ *Akk.*)
3 *v.i.* **(a)** (govern) herrschen
(b) (decide) entscheiden (**against** gegen; **in favour of** für)

▪ **rule 'out** *v.t.* ausschließen; (prevent) unmöglich machen

'rule book *n.* Regeln

ruled /ru:ld/ *adj.* liniert ‹*Papier*›

ruler /'ru:lə(r)/ *n.* **(a)** (person) Herrscher, *der*/Herrscherin, *die*
(b) (for measuring) Lineal, *das*

ruling /'ru:lɪŋ/ [1] *adj.* herrschend ‹*Klasse*›; regierend ‹*Partei*›
[2] *n.* Entscheidung, *die*

rum /rʌm/ *n.* Rum, *der*

Rumania *etc.* /ru:'meɪnɪə/ ▶ ROMANIA *etc.*

rumble /'rʌmbl/ [1] *n.* Grollen, *das*
[2] *v.i.* **(a)** grollen; ‹*Magen:*› knurren
(b) ‹*Fahrzeug:*› rumpeln (ugs.)

ruminate /'ru:mɪneɪt/ *v.i.* **~ on** *or* **over sth.** über etw. (*Akk.*) grübeln

rummage /'rʌmɪdʒ/ *v.i.* wühlen; **~ through sth.** etw. durchwühlen (ugs.)

rummy /'rʌmɪ/ *n.* Rommé, *das*

rumour (*Brit.; Amer.:* **rumor**) /'ru:mə(r)/
[1] *n.* Gerücht, *das;* **there is a ~ that ...:** es geht das Gerücht, dass ...
[2] *v.t.* **it is ~ed that ...:** es geht das Gerücht, dass ...

rump /rʌmp/ *n.* **(a)** (buttocks) Hinterteil, *das* (ugs.)
(b) (remmant) Rest, *der*

rumple /'rʌmpl/ *v.t.* **(a)** (crease) zerknittern
(b) (tousle) zerzausen

'rump steak *n.* Rumpsteak, *das*

rumpus /'rʌmpəs/ *n.* (coll.) Krach, *der* (ugs.); **kick up** *or* **make a ~:** einen Spektakel veranstalten (ugs.)

'rumpus room *n.* (Amer.) Spielzimmer, *das*

run /rʌn/ [1] *n.* **(a)** Lauf, *der;* **go for a ~:** laufen gehen; **on the ~** (fleeing) auf der Flucht
(b) (trip in vehicle) Fahrt, *die;* (for pleasure) Ausflug, *der*
(c) (continuous stretch) Länge, *die*
(d) (spell) **she has had a long ~ of success** sie war lange [Zeit] erfolgreich; **have a long ~** ‹*Stück, Show:*› viele Aufführungen erleben
(e) (succession) Serie, *die;* (Cards) Sequenz, *die;* **a ~ of victories** eine Siegesserie
(f) (use) **have the ~ of sth.** etw. zu seiner freien Verfügung haben
(g) (enclosure) Auslauf, *der*
(h) (in stocking etc.) Laufmasche, *die*
[2] *v.i.*, **-nn-, ran** /ræn/, **run (a)** laufen; **~ for the bus** laufen, um den Bus zu kriegen (ugs.); **~ to help sb.** jmdm. zu Hilfe eilen
(b) (roll, slide) laufen; ‹*Ball, Kugel:*› rollen, laufen; ‹*Schlitten,* [*Schiebe*]*tür:*› gleiten
(c) ‹*Rad, Maschine:*› laufen
(d) (operate on a schedule) fahren; **~ between two places** ‹*Zug, Bus:*› zwischen zwei Orten verkehren
(e) (flow) laufen; ‹*Fluss:*› fließen; ‹*Augen:*› tränen; **his nose was ~ning** ihm lief die Nase
(f) ‹*Vertrag, Theaterstück:*› laufen
(g) (have wording) lauten; ‹*Geschichte:*› gehen (fig.)
(h) ‹*Butter, Eis:*› zerlaufen; ‹*Farben:*› auslaufen
(i) (in election) kandidieren
[3] *v.t.*, **-nn-, ran, run (a)** laufen lassen; (drive) fahren; **~ one's hand/fingers through/along** *or* **over sth.** mit der Hand/den Fingern durch etw. fahren/über etw. (*Akk.*) streichen; **~ an** *or* **one's eye along** *or* **down** *or* **over sth.** (fig.) etw. überfliegen
(b) (cause to flow) [ein]laufen lassen; **~ a bath** ein Bad einlaufen lassen
(c) (organize, manage) führen, leiten ‹*Geschäft usw.*›; veranstalten ‹*Wettbewerb*›
(d) (operate) bedienen ‹*Maschine*›; verkehren lassen ‹*Verkehrsmittel*›; einsetzen ‹*Sonderbus, -zug*›; laufen lassen ‹*Motor*›
(e) (own and use) sich (*Dat.*) halten ‹*Auto*›
(f) **~ sb. into town** *etc.* jmdn. in die Stadt *usw.* fahren

■ **run a'cross** *v.t.* **~ across sb./sth.** jmdn. treffen/auf etw. (*Akk.*) stoßen

■ **run a'way** *v.i.* **(a)** (flee) weglaufen; fortlaufen
(b) (abscond) **~ away [from home]** [von zu Hause] weglaufen

■ **run 'down** [1] *v.t.* **(a)** (collide with) überfahren
(b) (criticize) heruntermachen (ugs.)
(c) (reduce) abbauen
[2] *v.i.* **(a)** hin-/herunterlaufen
(b) (decline) sich verringern
(c) ‹*Uhr, Spielzeug:*› ablaufen; ‹*Batterie*› leer werden

■ **'run into** *v.t.* **(a) ~ into a tree** gegen einen Baum fahren
(b) (meet) **~ into sb.** jmdm. in die Arme laufen (ugs.)
(c) stoßen auf (+ *Akk.*) ‹*Schwierigkeiten, Widerstand usw.*›
(d) (amount to) **~ into thousands** in die tausende gehen

■ **run 'off** [1] *v.i.* weglaufen
[2] *v.t.* abziehen ‹*Kopien*›

■ **run 'out** *v.i.* **(a)** hin-/herauslaufen
(b) ‹*Vorräte, Bestände:*› zu Ende gehen

■ **run 'out of** *v.t.* **sb. ~s out of sth.** jmdm. geht etw. aus; **I'm ~ning out of patience** meine Geduld geht zu Ende

■ **run 'over** [1] /'---/ *v.t.* (knock down) überfahren
[2] /-'--/ *v.i.* überlaufen

■ **'run through** *v.t.* durchspielen ‹*Theaterstück*›; durchgehen ‹*Plan*›

■ **'run to** *v.t.* **(a)** (amount to) sich belaufen auf (*Akk.*)
(b) (be sufficient for) **sth. will ~ to sth.** etw. reicht für etw.

■ **run 'up** [1] *v.i.* hinlaufen; **come ~ning up** hingelaufen kommen
[2] *v.t.* **(a)** rasch nähen ‹*Kleidungsstück*›
(b) zusammenkommen lassen ‹*Schulden, Rechnung*›

■ **run 'up against** *v.t.* stoßen auf (+ *Akk.*) ‹*Probleme, Widerstand usw.*›

run: ~about *n.* (coll.) **[little] ~about** Kleinwagen, *der;* **~around** *n.* (coll.) **give sb. the ~around** jmdn. an der Nase herumführen (ugs.); **~away** [1] *n.*

Ausreißer, *der*/Ausreißerin, *die* (ugs.); [2] *attrib. adj.* durchgegangen ‹*Pferd*›; außer Kontrolle geraten ‹*Fahrzeug, Preise*›; galoppierend ‹*Inflation*›; **~down** /'--/ *n.* (coll.: briefing) Übersicht, *die* (**on** über + *Akk.*); **~-down** /-'-/ *adj.* (tired) mitgenommen

rung¹ /rʌŋ/ *n.* Sprosse, *die*

rung² ▶ RING² 2, 3

'runner *n.* **(a)** Läufer, *der*/Läuferin, *die* **(b)** (Bot.) Ausläufer, *der* **(c)** (on sledge) Kufe, *die*

'runner bean *n.* (Brit.) Stangenbohne, *die*

runner-'up *n.* Zweite, *der/die;* **the runners-up** die Platzierten *Pl.*

'running [1] *n.* **(a)** (management) Leitung, *die* **(b)** (action) Laufen, *das;* **in/out of the ~:** im/aus dem Rennen [2] *adj.* (in succession) hintereinander; **win for the third year ~:** schon drei Jahre hintereinander gewinnen

running: ~ 'commentary *n.* (Broadcasting; also fig.) Livekommentar, *der;* **~ costs** *n. pl.* Betriebskosten *Pl.;* **~ shoe** *n.* Rennschuh, *der;* **~ 'total** *n.* fortlaufende Summe; **~ track** *n.* Aschenbahn, *die;* **~ 'water** *n.* **hot and cold ~ water** fließendes kaltes und warmes Wasser

runny /'rʌnɪ/ *adj.* **(a)** laufend ‹*Nase*› **(b)** zu dünn ‹*Farbe, Marmelade*›

run: ~-of-the-'mill *adj.* ganz gewöhnlich; **~-up** *n.* **(a) during** *or* **in the ~-up to an event** im Vorfeld eines Ereignisses; **(b)** (Sport) Anlauf, *der;* **~way** *n.* (for take-off) Startbahn, *die;* (for landing) Landebahn, *die*

rupture /'rʌptʃə(r)/ [1] *n.* Bruch, *der* [2] *v.t.* **~ oneself** sich (*Dat.*) einen Bruch zuziehen

rural /'rʊərl/ *adj.* ländlich

ruse /ru:z/ *n.* List, *die*

rush¹ /rʌʃ/ *n.* (Bot.) Binse, *die*

rush² [1] *n.* **(a)** (hurry) Eile, *die;* **what's all the ~?** wozu diese Hast?, **be in a [great] ~:** in [großer] Eile sein **(c)** (period of great activity) Hochbetrieb, *der;* (~ hour) Stoßzeit, *die* **(c) make a ~ for sth.** sich auf etw. (*Akk.*) stürzen [2] *v.t.* **(a) ~ sb./sth. somewhere** jmdn./etw. auf schnellstem Wege irgendwohin bringen; **be ~ed** (have to hurry) in Eile sein; **~ sb. into doing sth.** jmdn. dazu drängen, etw. zu tun **(b)** (perform quickly) auf die Schnelle erledigen; **~ it** zu schnell machen [3] *v.i.* **(a)** (move quickly) eilen; ‹*Hund, Pferd:*› laufen; **~ to help sb.** jmdm. zu Hilfe eilen **(b)** (hurry unduly) sich zu sehr beeilen; **don't ~!** nur keine Eile!

■ **rush a'bout, rush a'round** *v.i.* herumhetzen

rush: ~ hour *n.* Stoßzeit, *die;* **~ job** *n.* eilige Arbeit

rusk /rʌsk/ *n.* Zwieback, *der*

Russia /'rʌʃə/ *pr. n.* Russland (*das*)

Russian /'rʌʃn/ [1] *adj.* russisch; **sb. is ~:** jmd. ist Russe/Russin [2] *n.* **(a)** (person) Russe, *der*/Russin, *die* **(b)** (language) Russisch, *das; see also* ENGLISH 2A

rust /rʌst/ [1] *n.* Rost, *der* [2] *v.i.* rosten

rustic /'rʌstɪk/ *adj.* **(a)** ländlich **(b)** rustikal ‹*Mobiliar*›

rustle /'rʌsl/ [1] *n.* Rascheln, *das* [2] *v.i.* rascheln [3] *v.t.* **(a)** rascheln lassen **(b)** (Amer.: steal) stehlen

■ **rustle 'up** *v.t.* zusammenzaubern ‹*Mahlzeit*›

'rustproof *adj.* rostfrei

'rusty *adj.* rostig

rut /rʌt/ *n.* Spurrille, *die;* **be in a ~** (fig.) aus dem [Alltags]trott nicht mehr herauskommen

ruthless /'ru:θlɪs/ *adj.* rücksichtslos

RV *abbr.* (Amer.) = **recreational vehicle**

rye /raɪ/ *n.* Roggen, *der*

'rye bread *n.* Roggenbrot, *das*

Ss

S, s /es/ *n.* S, s, *das*

S. *abbr.* **(a)** = **south** S **(b)** = **southern** s.

sabbath /'sæbəθ/ *n.* Sabbat, *der*

sabbatical /sə'bætɪkl/ [1] *adj.* **~ term/year** Forschungssemester/-jahr, *das* [2] *n.* Forschungsurlaub, *der*

sabotage /'sæbətɑ:ʒ/ [1] *n.* Sabotage, *die* [2] *v.t.* einen Sabotageakt verüben auf (+ *Akk.*); (fig.) sabotieren

saboteur /sæbə'tɜ:(r)/ *n.* Saboteur, *der*

saccharin /'sækərɪn/ *n.* Saccharin, *das*

sachet /'sæʃeɪ/ *n.* Beutel, *der;* (cushion-shaped) Kissen, *das*

sack /sæk/ [1] *n.* **(a)** Sack, *der* ···›

(b) (coll.: dismissal) Rausschmiss, *der* (ugs.); **get the ~:** rausgeschmissen werden (ugs.); **give sb. the ~:** jmdn. rausschmeißen (ugs.)
2 *v.t.* (coll.) rausschmeißen (ugs.) (**for** wegen)

sacking /'sækɪŋ/ *n.* **(a)** (coll.: dismissal) Rausschmiss, *der* (ugs.)
(b) (coarse fabric) Sackleinen, *das*

sacrament /'sækrəmənt/ *n.* Sakrament, *das*

sacred /'seɪkrɪd/ *adj.* heilig

sacrifice /'sækrɪfaɪs/ **1** *n.* Opfer, *das*
2 *v.t.* opfern

sacrilege /'sækrɪlɪdʒ/ *n.* **[act of] ~:** Sakrileg, *das*

sad /sæd/ *adj.* traurig (**at, about** über + *Akk.*); schmerzlich ‹*Tod, Verlust*›; **feel ~:** traurig sein

sadden /'sædn/ *v.t.* traurig stimmen

SAD *abbr.* = **seasonal affective disorder**

saddle /'sædl/ **1** *n.* Sattel, *der*
2 *v.t.* **(a)** satteln ‹*Pferd usw.*›
(b) (fig.) **~ sb. with sth.** jmdm. etw. aufbürden (geh.)

'saddlebag *n.* Satteltasche, *die*

sadism /'seɪdɪzm/ *n.* Sadismus, *der*

sadist /'seɪdɪst/ *n.* Sadist, *der*/Sadistin, *die*

sadistic /sə'dɪstɪk/ *adj.*, **sa'distically** *adv.* sadistisch

'sadly *adv.* **(a)** (with sorrow) traurig
(b) (unfortunately) leider

'sadness *n.* Traurigkeit, *die*

sadomasochism /seɪdəʊ'mæsəkɪzm/ *n.* Sadomasochismus, *der*

s.a.e. /eseɪ'i:/ *abbr.* = **stamped addressed envelope** adressierter Freiumschlag

safari /sə'fɑ:rɪ/ *n.* Safari, *die;* **on ~:** auf Safari

safe /seɪf/ **1** *n.* Safe, *der;* Geldschrank, *der*
2 *adj.* **(a)** (out of danger) sicher (**from** vor + *Dat.*); **he's ~:** er ist in Sicherheit; **~ and sound** sicher und wohlbehalten
(b) (free from danger) ungefährlich; sicher ‹*Ort, Hafen*›; **wish sb. a ~ journey** jmdm. eine gute Reise wünschen; **to be on the ~ side** zur Sicherheit
(c) (reliable) sicher ‹*Methode, Investition*›

safe: ~guard **1** *n.* Schutz, *der;* **2** *v.t.* schützen; **~ 'haven** *n.* **(a)** (safe place) Zuflucht, *die;* **(b)** (Polit.) Schutzzone, *die*

safely /'seɪflɪ/ *adv.* sicher; **did the parcel arrive ~?** ist das Paket heil angekommen?

safe 'sex Safersex, *der*

safety: ~ belt *n.* Sicherheitsgurt, *der;* **~ catch** *n.* (of gun) Sicherungshebel, *der;* **~ helmet** *n.* Schutzhelm, *der;* **~ margin** *n.* Spielraum, *der;* **~ pin** *n.* Sicherheitsnadel, *die;* **~ valve** *n.* Sicherheitsventil, *das;* (fig.) Ventil, *das*

'safe zone *n.* (Polit.) Schutzzone, *die*

saffron /'sæfrən/ *n.* Safran, *der*

sag /sæg/ *v.i.*, **-gg-** durchhängen; (sink) sich senken

saga /'sɑ:gə/ *n.* **(a)** (story of adventure) Heldenepos, *das;* (medieval narrative) Saga, *die*
(b) (long involved story) [ganzer] Roman (fig.)

sage[1] /seɪdʒ/ *n.* (Bot.) Salbei, *der od. die*

sage[2] **1** *adj.* weise
2 *n.* Weise, *der*

Sagittarius /sædʒɪ'teərɪəs/ *n.* (Astrol; Astron.) der Schütze

Sahara /sə'hɑ:rə/ *pr. n.* **the ~ [Desert]** die [Wüste] Sahara

said ▶ SAY 1

sail /seɪl/ **1** *n.* **(a)** Segelfahrt, *die*
(b) (piece of canvas) Segel, *das*
2 *v.i.* **(a)** (travel on water) fahren; (in sailing boat) segeln
(b) (start voyage) auslaufen (**for** nach)
3 *v.t.* **(a)** steuern ‹*Boot, Schiff*›; segeln mit ‹*Segeljacht, -schiff*›
(b) durchfahren/‹*Segelschiff:*› durchsegeln ‹*Meer*›

sail: ~board *n.* Surfbrett, *das* (*zum Windsurfen*); **~boarding** *n.* Windsurfen, *das;* **~boat** *n.* (Amer.) Segelboot, *das*

'sailing *n.* Segeln, *das*

sailing: ~ boat *n.* Segelboot, *das;* **~ ship** *n.* Segelschiff, *das*

sailor /'seɪlə(r)/ *n.* Seemann, *der;* (in navy) Matrose, *der*

saint **1** /sənt/ *adj.* **S~ Michael** der heilige Michael; Sankt Michael
2 /seɪnt/ *n.* Heilige, *der/die*

'saintly /'seɪntlɪ/ *adj.* heilig

sake /seɪk/ *n.* **for the ~ of** um ... (*Gen.*) willen; **for my** *etc.* **~:** um meinetwillen *usw.;* mir *usw.* zuliebe

salad /'sæləd/ *n.* Salat, *der*

salad: ~ cream *n.* ≈ Mayonnaise, *die;* **~ dressing** *n.* Salatsoße, *die;* **~ servers** *n. pl.* Salatbesteck, *das*

salary /'sælərɪ/ *n.* Gehalt, *das*

sale /seɪl/ *n.* **(a)** Verkauf, *der;* (at reduced prices) Ausverkauf, *der;* (at end of season) Schlußverkauf, *der;* **[up] for ~:** zu verkaufen
(b) **~s** (amount sold) Verkaufszahlen *Pl.* (**of** für); Absatz, *der*
(c) **[jumble** *or* **rummage] ~:** [Wohltätigkeits]basar, *der*

'sale price *n.* **(a)** (retail price) Verkaufspreis, *der*
(b) (price in sale) Ausverkaufspreis, *der*

sales: ~ assistant (Brit.)**, ~ clerk** (Amer.) *ns.* Verkäufer, *der*/Verkäuferin, *die;* **~man** /'seɪlzmən/ *n.*, *pl.* **~men** /'seɪlzmən/ Verkäufer, *der*

'salesmanship *n.* Kunst des Verkaufens

sales: ~ rep (coll.)**, ~ representative** *ns.* [Handels]vertreter, *der*/-vertreterin, *die;* **~woman** *n.* Verkäuferin, *die*

salient /'seɪlɪənt/ *adj.* auffallend

saliva /sə'laɪvə/ *n.* Speichel, *der*

sallow /'sæləʊ/ *adj.* blassgelb

salmon /'sæmən/ *n.* Lachs, *der*

saloon /sə'lu:n/ *n.* **(a)** (Brit.) ~ **[bar]** *separater Teil eines Pubs mit mehr Komfort* **(b)** (Brit.) ~ **[car]** Limousine, *die*

salt /sɔ:lt, sɒlt/ **1** *n.* **[common]** ~: [Koch]salz, *das*
2 *adj.* (containing or tasting of ~) salzig; (preserved with ~) gepökelt ‹*Fleisch*›; gesalzen ‹*Butter*›
3 *v.t.* **(a)** salzen
(b) (cure) [ein]pökeln
(c) ~ **the roads** Salz auf die Straßen streuen

salt: ~ **cellar** *n.* Salzfässchen, *das*; ~ **'water** *n.* Salzwasser, *das*

'salty *adj.* salzig

salute /sə'lu:t/ **1** *v.t.* grüßen
2 *v.i.* (Mil., Navy) [militärisch] grüßen
3 *n.* Salut, *der;* militärischer Gruß

salvage /'sælvɪdʒ/ **1** *n.* Bergung, *die*
2 *v.t.* bergen

salvation /sæl'veɪʃn/ *n.* Erlösung, *die*

Salvation 'Army *n.* Heilsarmee, *die*

salvo /'sælvəʊ/ *n.* Salve, *die*

Samaritan /sə'mærɪtən/ *n.* **good** ~: [barmherziger] Samariter; **the** ~**s** (organization) ≈ die Telefonseelsorge

same /seɪm/ **1** *adj.* **the** ~: der/die/das gleiche; **the** ~ **[thing]** (identical) der-/die-/dasselbe
2 *adv.* **all** *or* **just the** ~: trotzdem

sample /'sɑ:mpl/ **1** *n.* (example) [Muster]beispiel, *das;* (specimen) Probe, *die;* **[commercial]** ~: Muster, *das*
2 *v.t.* probieren

'sample letter *n.* Musterbrief, *der*

sampler /'sɑ:mplə(r)/ *n.* (trial pack) Probe[packung], *die*

sanatorium /sænə'tɔ:rɪəm/ *n.* Sanatorium, *das*

sanctify /'sæŋktɪfaɪ/ *v.t.* heiligen

sanctimonious /sæŋktɪ'məʊnɪəs/ *adj.* scheinheilig

sanction /'sæŋkʃn/ **1** *n.* Sanktion, *die*
2 *v.t.* sanktionieren

sanctity /'sæŋktɪtɪ/ *n.* Heiligkeit, *die*

sanctuary /'sæŋktʃʊərɪ/ *n.* **(a)** (holy place) Heiligtum, *das*
(b) (refuge) Zufluchtsort, *der*
(c) (for animals) Naturschutzgebiet, *das*

sand /sænd/ **1** *n.* Sand, *der*
2 *v.t.* ~ **sth. [down]** etw. [ab]schmirgeln

sandal /'sændl/ *n.* Sandale, *die*

sand: ~**bag** **1** *n.* Sandsack, *der;* **2** *v.t.* mit Sandsäcken schützen; ~**bank** *n.* Sandbank, *die;* ~**castle** *n.* Sandburg, *die;* ~ **dune** *n.* Düne, *die;* ~**paper** **1** *n.* Sandpapier, *das;* **2** *v.t.* [mit Sandpapier] [ab]schmirgeln; ~**pit** *n.* Sandkasten, *der;* ~**stone** *n.* Sandstein, *der*

sandwich /'sænwɪdʒ/ **1** *n.* Sandwich, *der od. das;* ≈ [zusammengeklapptes] belegtes Brot; **cheese** ~: Käsebrot, *das*
2 *v.t.* einschieben (**between** zwischen + *Akk.;* **into** in + *Akk.*)

'sandy *adj.* **(a)** sandig; Sand‹*boden, -strand*›
(b) rotblond ‹*Haar*›

sane /seɪn/ *adj.* **(a)** geistig gesund
(b) (sensible) vernünftig

sang ▶ SING

sanitary /'sænɪtərɪ/ *adj.* sanitär ‹*Verhältnisse, Anlagen*›

'sanitary napkin (Amer.), **'sanitary towel** (Brit.) *ns.* Damenbinde, *die*

sanitation /sænɪ'teɪʃn/ *n.* Kanalisation und Abfallbeseitigung

sanitize (sanitise) /'sænɪtaɪz/ *v.t.* (fig.) entschärfen

sanity /'sænɪtɪ/ *n.* geistige Gesundheit; **lose one's** ~: den Verstand verlieren

sank ▶ SINK 2, 3

Santa Claus /'sæntə klɔ:z/ *n.* der Weihnachtsmann

sap /sæp/ **1** *n.* Saft, *der*
2 *v.t.,* **-pp-** zehren an (+ *Dat.*)

sapling /'sæplɪŋ/ *n.* junger Baum

sapphire /'sæfaɪə(r)/ *n.* Saphir, *der*

sarcasm /'sɑ:kæzm/ *n.* Sarkasmus, *der*

sarcastic /sɑ:'kæstɪk/ *adj.* sarkastisch

sardine /sɑ:'di:n/ *n.* Sardine, *die*

Sardinia /sɑ:'dɪnɪə/ *pr. n.* Sardinien (*das*)

sardonic /sɑ:'dɒnɪk/ *adj.* höhnisch; sardonisch ‹*Lächeln*›

SARS /sɑ:z/ *n.* SARS, *das*

sash /sæʃ/ *n.* Schärpe, *die*

sash 'window *n.* Schiebefenster, *das*

sat ▶ SIT

Sat. *abbr.* = **Saturday** Sa.

Satan /'seɪtən/ *pr. n.* Satan, *der*

satanic /sə'tænɪk/ *adj.* satanisch

satchel /'sætʃl/ *n.* [Schul]ranzen, *der*

satellite /'sætəlaɪt/ *n.* Satellit, *der*

satellite: ~ **'broadcasting** *n.* Satellitenfunk, *der;* ~ **dish** *n.* Satellitenschüssel, *die;* ~ **receiver** *n.* Satellitenempfänger, *der;* ~ **technology** *n.* Satellitentechnik, *die;* ~ **'television** *n.* Satellitenfernsehen, *das;* ~ **town** *n.* Satelliten- *od.* Trabantenstadt, *die*

satin /'sætɪn/ *n.* Satin, *der*

satire /'sætaɪə(r)/ *n.* Satire, *die* (**on** auf + *Akk.*)

satirical /sə'tɪrɪkl/ *adj.* satirisch

satisfaction /sætɪs'fækʃn/ *n.* Befriedigung, *die* (**at, with** über + *Akk.*); **meet with sb.'s [complete]** ~: jmdn. [in jeder Weise] zufrieden stellen

satisfactory /sætɪs'fæktərɪ/ *adj.* zufrieden stellend

satisfied /'sætɪsfaɪd/ *adj.* **(a)** (contented) zufrieden
(b) (convinced) überzeugt (**of** von)

S

satisfy /'sætɪsfaɪ/ *v.t.* **(a)** befriedigen; zufrieden stellen ‹*Kunden*›; stillen ‹*Hunger, Durst*›
(b) (convince) ~ **sb. [of sth.]** jmdn. [von etw.] überzeugen

'satisfying *adj.* befriedigend; sättigend ‹*Gericht, Speise*›

satphone /'sætfəʊn/ *n.* Satellitentelefon, *das*

saturate /'sætʃəreɪt/ *v.t.* durchnässen; [mit Feuchtigkeit durch]tränken ‹*Boden, Erde*›

saturated /'sætʃəreɪtɪd/ *adj.* durchnässt

Saturday /'sætədeɪ, 'sætədɪ/ *n.* Samstag, *der; see also* FRIDAY

'Saturday job *n.* Samstagsjob, *der* (ugs.)

Saturn /'sætən/ *pr. n.* (Astron.) Saturn, *der*

sauce /sɔːs/ *n.* **(a)** Soße, *die*
(b) (impudence) Frechheit, *die*

sauce: ~ **boat** *n.* Sauciere, *die;* ~**pan** /'sɔːspən/ *n.* Kochtopf, *der;* (with straight handle) [Stiel]kasserolle, *die*

saucer /'sɔːsə(r)/ *n.* Untertasse, *die*

saucy /'sɔːsɪ/ *adj.* **(a)** (rude) frech
(b) (pert, jaunty) keck

Saudi Arabia /saʊdɪ ə'reɪbɪə/ *pr. n.* Saudi-Arabien (*das*)

sauna /'sɔːnə, 'saʊnə/ *n.* Sauna, *die*

saunter /'sɔːntə(r)/ *v.i.* schlendern

sausage /'sɒsɪdʒ/ *n.* Wurst, *die*

sausage: ~ **meat** *n.* Wurstmasse, *die;* ~ **'roll** *n.*: *Blätterteig mit Wurstfüllung*

savage /'sævɪdʒ/ [1] *adj.* **(a)** (uncivilized) primitiv; wild ‹*Volksstamm*›; unzivilisiert ‹*Land*›
(b) (fierce) brutal; wild ‹*Tier*›
[2] *n.* Wilde, *der/die* (veralt.)

savagery /'sævɪdʒrɪ/ *n.* Brutalität, *die*

save /seɪv/ [1] *v.t.* **(a)** (rescue) retten **(from** vor + *Dat.*); ~ **oneself from falling** sich [beim Hinfallen] fangen
(b) (put aside) aufheben; sparen ‹*Geld*›; sammeln ‹*Briefmarken usw.*›; (conserve) sparsam umgehen mit
(c) (make unnecessary) sparen ‹*Geld, Zeit, Energie*›; ~ **sb./oneself sth.** jmdm./sich etw. ersparen
(d) (Sport) abwehren ‹*Schuss, Ball;*›
(e) (Comp.) speichern; sichern; ~ **sth. on [to] a disk** etw. auf Diskette abspeichern
[2] *v.i.* sparen **(on** *Akk.*)
[3] *n.* (Sport) Abwehr, *die*

■ **save 'up** [1] *v.t.* sparen
[2] *v.i.* sparen **(for** für, auf + *Akk.*)

'saver *n.* Sparer, *der*/Sparerin, *die*

saving /'seɪvɪŋ/ [1] *n. in pl.* Ersparnisse *Pl.*
[2] *adj.* ‹*kosten-, benzin*›sparend

savings: ~ **account** *n.* Sparkonto, *das;* ~ **bank** *n.* Sparkasse, *die*

saviour /'seɪvjə(r)/ *n.* **(a)** Retter, *der*/Retterin, *die*
(b) (Relig.) **the S~:** der Heiland

savor *etc.* (*Amer.*) ▶ SAVOUR *etc.*

savour /'seɪvə(r)/ (Brit.) [1] *n.* (flavour) Geschmack, *der*
[2] *v.t.* genießen

savoury /'seɪvərɪ/ (Brit.) [1] *adj.* **(a)** pikant; salzig
(b) (appetizing) appetitanregend
[2] *n.* [pikantes] Häppchen

saw[1] /sɔː/ [1] *n.* Säge, *die*
[2] *v.t., p.p.* **sawn** /sɔːn/ *or* **sawed** [zer]sägen; ~ **in half** in der Mitte durchsägen
[3] *v.i., p.p.* **sawn** *or* **sawed** sägen; ~ **through sth.** etw. durchsägen

saw[2] ▶ SEE

saw: ~**dust** *n.* Sägemehl, *das;* ~**mill** *n.* Sägemühle, *die*

sawn ▶ SAW[1] 2, 3

'sawn-off *adj.* (Brit.) ‹*Gewehr*› mit abgesägtem Lauf

saxophone /'sæksəfəʊn/ *n.* Saxophon, *das*

saxophonist /sæk'sɒfənɪst/ *n.* Saxophonist, *der*/Saxophonistin, *die*

say /seɪ/ [1] *v.t. pres. t.* **he says** /sez/, *p.t. & p.p.* **said** /sed/ **(a)** sagen; **that is to** ~: das heißt; **do as** *or* **what I** ~: tun Sie, was ich sage; **when all is said and done** letzten Endes; **go without** ~**ing** sich von selbst verstehen; **she is said to be clever/to have done it** man sagt, sie sei klug/habe es getan
(b) (recite) sprechen ‹*Gebet, Text*›
(c) (have specified wording or reading) sagen; ‹*Zeitung:*› schreiben; ‹*Uhr:*› zeigen ‹*Uhrzeit*›; **what does it** ~ **here?** was steht hier?
[2] *n.* **have a** *or* **some** ~: ein Mitspracherecht haben **(in** bei); **have no** ~: nichts zu sagen haben; **have one's** ~: seine Meinung sagen

'saying *n.* Redensart, *die*

scab /skæb/ *n.* [Wund]schorf, *der*

scaffold /'skæfəld/ *n.* Schafott, *das*

'scaffolding *n.* Gerüst, *das*

'scaffolding pole *n.* Gerüststange, *die*

scald /skɔːld, skɒld/ [1] *n.* Verbrühung, *die*
[2] *v.t.* verbrühen

scale[1] /skeɪl/ *n.* **(a)** (of fish, reptile, etc.) Schuppe, *die*
(b) (in kettle etc.) Kesselstein, *der;* (on teeth) Zahnstein, *der*

scale[2] *n.* **(a)** *in sing. or pl.* (weighing instrument) ~**[s]** Waage, *die*
(b) (dish of balance) Waagschale, *die*

scale[3] [1] *n.* **(a)** (series of degrees) Skala, *die*
(b) (Mus.) Tonleiter, *die*
(c) (dimensions) Ausmaß, *das;* **be on a small** ~: bescheidenen Umfang haben
(d) (ratio of reduction) Maßstab, *der;* **what is the** ~ **of the map?** welchen Maßstab hat diese Karte?
(e) (indication) (on map) Maßstab, *der;* (on thermometer) [Anzeige]skala, *die*
[2] *v.t.* ersteigen ‹*Mauer, Leiter, Gipfel*›

■ **scale 'down** *v.t.* [entsprechend] drosseln ‹*Produktion*›; Abstriche machen bei ‹*Planungen*›

scalp /skælp/ *n.* Kopfhaut, *die*

scalpel /'skælpl/ *n.* Skalpell, *das*

scam /skæm/ *n.* (coll.) Masche, *die* (ugs.)

scamper /'skæmpə(r)/ *v.i.* ‹*Person:*› flitzen; ‹*Tier:*› huschen

scampi /'skæmpɪ/ *n. pl.* Scampi *Pl.*

scan /skæn/ [1] *v.t.*, **-nn-**: **(a)** (search thoroughly) absuchen (**for** nach)
(b) (look over cursorily) flüchtig ansehen; überfliegen ‹*Zeitung, Liste usw.*› (**for** auf der Suche nach)
(c) (Med.) szintigraphisch untersuchen
(d) (Comp.) scannen
[2] *v.i.*, **-nn-** ‹*Vers*[*zeile*]*:*› das richtige Versmaß haben
[3] *n.* (Med.) szintigraphische Untersuchung, *die;* (image) Szintigramm, *das*

scandal /'skændl/ *n.* **(a)** Skandal, *der* (**about/of** um); (story) Skandalgeschichte, *die*
(b) (outrage) Empörung, *die*
(c) (gossip) Klatsch, *der* (ugs.)

scandalize /'skændəlaɪz/ *v.t.* schockieren

scandalous /'skændələs/ *adj.* skandalös; schockierend ‹*Bemerkung*›

Scandinavia /skændɪ'neɪvɪə/ *pr. n.* Skandinavien (*das*)

Scandinavian /skændɪ'neɪvɪən/ [1] *adj.* skandinavisch; **sb. is ~**: jmd. ist Skandinavier/Skandinavierin
[2] *n.***(a)** (person) Skandinavier, *der*/ Skandinavierin, *die*
(b) (Ling.) skandinavische Sprachen *Pl.*

scant /skænt/ *adj.* wenig

scanty /'skæntɪ/ *adj.* spärlich; knapp ‹*Bikini*›

scapegoat /'skeɪpgəʊt/ *n.* Sündenbock, *der;* **make sb. a ~**: jmdn. zum Sündenbock machen

scar /skɑ:(r)/ [1] *n.* Narbe, *die*
[2] *v.t.*, **-rr-**: **~ sb./sb.'s face** bei jmdm./in jmds. Gesicht (*Dat.*) Narben hinterlassen

scarce /skeəs/ *adj.* **(a)** (insufficient) knapp
(b) (rare) selten; **make oneself ~** (coll.) sich aus dem Staub machen (ugs.)

'scarcely *adv.* kaum

scarcity /'skeəsɪtɪ/ *n.* Knappheit, *die* (**of** an + *Dat.*)

scare /skeə(r)/ [1] *n.* **(a)** (sensation of fear) Schreck[en], *der;* **give sb. a ~**: jmdm. einen Schreck[en] einjagen
(b) (general alarm) [allgemeine] Hysterie; **bomb ~**: Bombendrohung, *die*
[2] *v.t.* (frighten) Angst machen (+ *Dat.*); (startle) erschrecken

■ **scare a'way, scare 'off** *v.t.* verscheuchen

'scarecrow *n.* Vogelscheuche, *die*

scared /skeəd/ *adj.* **be ~ of sb./sth.** vor jmdm./etw. Angst haben; **be ~ of doing/to do sth.** sich nicht [ge]trauen, etw. zu tun

scaremongering /'skeəmʌŋgərɪŋ/ *n.* Panikmache, *die*

scarf /skɑ:f/ *n., pl.* **~s** *or* **scarves** /skɑ:vz/ Schal, *der;* (square) Halstuch, *das;* (worn over hair) Kopftuch, *das*

scarlet /'skɑ:lɪt/ [1] *n.* Scharlach, *der*
[2] *adj.* scharlachrot

scarlet 'fever *n.* Scharlach, *der*

scarves ▶ SCARF

scary /'skeərɪ/ *adj.* Furcht erregend ‹*Anblick*›; schaurig ‹*Film, Geschichte*›

scathing /'skeɪðɪŋ/ *adj.* bissig ‹*Person, Humor, Bemerkung*›

scatter /'skætə(r)/ [1] *v.t.* **(a)** vertreiben; auseinander treiben ‹*Menge*›
(b) (distribute irregularly) verstreuen
[2] *v.i.* sich auflösen; ‹*Menge:*› sich zerstreuen; (in fear) auseinander stieben

scattered /'skætəd/ *adj.* verstreut; vereinzelt ‹*Regenschauer*›

scatty /'skætɪ/ *adj.* (Brit. coll.) dusslig (salopp)

scavenge /'skævɪndʒ/ *v.i.* **~ for sth.** nach etw. suchen

'scavenger *n.* (animal) Aasfresser, *der;* (fig. derog.: person) Aasgeier, *der* (ugs.)

scenario /sɪ'nɑ:rɪəʊ/ *n., pl.* **~s** Szenario, *das*

scene /si:n/ *n.* **(a)** (place of event) Schauplatz, *der;* **~ of the crime** Tatort, *der*
(b) (division of act) Auftritt, *der*
(c) (view) Anblick, *der*
(d) **behind the ~s** hinter den Kulissen
(e) **the political/drug/artistic ~**: die politische/Drogen-/Kunstszene

scenery /'si:nərɪ/ *n.* **(a)** Landschaft, *die*
(b) (Theatre) Bühnenbild, *das*

scenic /'si:nɪk/ *adj.* landschaftlich schön

scent /sent/ [1] *n.* **(a)** (smell) Duft, *der*
(b) (Hunting; also fig.: trail) Fährte, *die;* **be on the ~ of sb./sth.** (fig.) jmdm./einer Sache auf der Spur sein
(c) (Brit.: perfume) Parfüm, *das*
[2] *v.t.* wittern

scented /'sentɪd/ *adj.***(a)** (having smell) duftend
(b) (perfumed) parfümiert

sceptic /'skeptɪk/ *n.* Skeptiker, *der*/ Skeptikerin, *die*

sceptical /'skeptɪkl/ *adj.* skeptisch; **be ~ about** *or* **of sb./sth.** jmdm./einer Sache skeptisch gegenüberstehen

scepticism /'skeptɪsɪzm/ *n.* Skepsis, *die*

schedule /'ʃedju:l/ [1] *n.* **(a)** (list) Tabelle, *die;* (for event) Programm, *das*
(b) (of work) Zeitplan, *der*
(c) **on ~**: plangemäß
[2] *v.t.* zeitlich planen

'scheduled flight *n.* Linienflug, *der*

scheme /ski:m/ *n.* **(a)** (arrangement) Anordnung, *die*
(b) (plan) Programm, *das;* (project) Projekt, *das*
(c) (dishonest plan) Intrige, *die*

schizophrenia /skɪtsə'fri:nɪə/ *n.* Schizophrenie, *die*

S

schizophrenic /skɪtsə'frenɪk, skɪtsə'fri:nɪk/ *adj.* schizophren

scholar /'skɒlə(r)/ *n.* Gelehrte, *der/die*

'scholarly *adj.* wissenschaftlich; gelehrt ‹*Person*›

'scholarship *n.* **(a)** (award) Stipendium, *das* **(b)** (scholarly work) Gelehrsamkeit, *die*

school /sku:l/ *n.* Schule, *die;* (Amer.: college) Hochschule, *die;* **be at** *or* **in ~**: in der Schule sein; (attend ~) zur Schule gehen; **go to ~**: zur Schule gehen; **~ holidays/exchange** Schulferien *Pl.*/Schüleraustausch, *der*

school: ~ age *n.* Schulalter, *das;* **~bag** *n.* Schultasche, *die;* **~boy** *n.* Schüler, *der;* **~child** *n.* Schulkind, *das;* **~ friend** *n.* Schulfreund, *der*/-freundin, *die;* **~girl** *n.* Schülerin, *die;* **~ 'governor** *n.*: *Mitglied des Schulbeirats;* **~kid** *n.* (coll.) Schulkind, *das;* **~ leaver** *n.* (Brit.) Schulabgänger, *der*/-abgängerin, *die;* **~master** *n.* Lehrer, *der;* **~mistress** *n.* Lehrerin, *die;* **~ 'rule** *n.* Schulvorschrift, *die;* Schulregel, *die;* **it is a ~ rule that ...**: an der Schule ist es Vorschrift, dass ...; **~teacher** *n.* Lehrer, *der*/Lehrerin, *die;* **~ 'uniform** *n.* Schuluniform, *die;* **~ work** *n.* Schularbeiten *Pl.;* **~ 'year** *n.* Schuljahr, *das*

sciatica /saɪ'ætɪkə/ *n.* Ischias, *der od. das*

science /'saɪəns/ *n.* Wissenschaft, *die*

science 'fiction *n.* Sciencefiction, *die*

scientific /saɪən'tɪfɪk/ *adj.* wissenschaftlich

scientist /'saɪəntɪst/ *n.* Wissenschaftler, *der*/Wissenschaftlerin, *die*

sci-fi /'saɪfaɪ/ *n.* (coll.) Sciencefiction, *die*

scintillating /'sɪntɪleɪtɪŋ/ *adj.* (fig.) geistsprühend

scissors /'sɪzəz/ *n. pl.* **[pair of] ~**: Schere, *die*

scoff[1] /skɒf/ *v.i.* (mock) spotten; **~ at** sich lustig machen über (+ *Akk.*)

scoff[2] *v.t.* (coll.: eat greedily) verschlingen

scold /skəʊld/ *v.t.* ausschimpfen (**for** wegen); **she ~ed him for being late** sie schimpfte ihn aus, weil er zu spät kam

scone /skɒn, skəʊn/ *n.*: *weicher, oft zum Tee gegessener kleiner Kuchen*

scoop /sku:p/ [1] *n.* **(a)** Schaufel, *die;* (for ice cream etc.) Portionierer, *der* **(b)** (Journ.) Knüller, *der* (ugs.) [2] *v.t.* schaufeln ‹*Kohlen, Zucker*›; schöpfen ‹*Flüssigkeit*›

■ **scoop 'out** *v.t.* **(a)** (hollow out) aushöhlen; schaufeln ‹*Loch, Graben*› **(b)** [her]ausschöpfen ‹*Flüssigkeit*›; auslöffeln ‹*Fruchtfleisch*›; (with a knife) herausschneiden ‹*Gehäuse, Fruchtfleisch*›

■ **scoop 'up** *v.t.* schöpfen ‹*Flüssigkeit, Suppe*›; schaufeln ‹*Erde*›

scooter /'sku:tə(r)/ *n.* **(a)** (toy) Roller, *der* **(b)** **[motor] ~**: [Motor]roller, *der*

scope /skəʊp/ *n.* **(a)** Bereich, *der;* (of discussion etc.) Rahmen, *der* **(b)** (opportunity) Entfaltungsmöglichkeiten *Pl.*

scorch /skɔ:tʃ/ *v.t.* versengen

scorched 'earth policy *n.* Politik der verbrannten Erde

scorching /'skɔ:tʃɪŋ/ *adj.* glühend heiß

score /skɔ:(r)/ [1] *n.* **(a)** (points) [Spiel]stand, *der;* (made by one player) Punktzahl, *die;* **keep [the] ~**: zählen **(b)** (Mus.) Partitur, *die;* (Cinemat.) [Film]musik, *die* **(c)** *pl. same or* **~s** (group of 20) zwanzig **(d)** *in pl.* (great numbers) **~s [and ~s] of** zig (ugs.); Dutzende [von] **(e)** **on that ~**: was das betrifft **(f)** **pay off** *or* **settle an old ~** (fig.) eine alte Rechnung begleichen [2] *v.t.* erzielen ‹*Erfolg, Punkt usw.*›; **~ a goal** ein Tor schießen [3] *v.i.* **(a)** (make ~) Punkte/einen Punkt erzielen; (~ goal/goals) ein Tor/Tore schießen/werfen **(b)** (keep ~) aufschreiben

'scoreboard *n.* Anzeigetafel, *die*

'scorer *n.* **(a)** (recorder) Anschreiber, *der*/Anschreiberin, *die* **(b)** (Footb.) Torschütze, *der*/-schützin, *die*

'scoresheet *n.* Anschreibebogen, *der*

scorn /skɔ:n/ [1] *n.* Verachtung, *die* [2] *v.t.* verachten; in den Wind schlagen ‹*Rat*›; ausschlagen ‹*Angebot*›

scornful /'skɔ:nfl/ *adj.* verächtlich ‹*Lächeln, Blick*›; **be ~ of sth.** für etw. nur Verachtung haben

Scorpio /'skɔ:pɪəʊ/ *n.* (Astrol; Astron.) der Skorpion

scorpion /'skɔ:pɪən/ *n.* Skorpion, *der*

Scot /skɒt/ *n.* Schotte, *der*/Schottin, *die*

scotch *v.t.* den Boden entziehen (+ *Dat.*) ‹*Gerücht*›; zunichte machen ‹*Plan*›

Scotch /skɒtʃ/ [1] *adj.* ▶ SCOTTISH [2] *n.* Scotch, *der;* schottischer Whisky

Scotch: ~ 'egg *n.*: *hart gekochtes Ei in Wurstbrät;* **~ 'whisky** *n.* schottischer Whisky

scot-'free *adj.* **[get off/go] ~**: ungeschoren [davonkommen *od.* bleiben]

Scotland /'skɒtlənd/ *pr. n.* Schottland (*das*)

Scots /skɒts/ [1] *adj.* (esp. Scot.) schottisch; **sb. is ~**: jmd. ist Schotte/Schottin [2] *n.* (dialect) Schottisch, *das*

Scotsman /'skɒtsmən/ *n., pl.* **Scotsmen** /'skɒtsmən/ Schotte, *der*

'Scotswoman *n.* Schottin, *die*

Scottish /'skɒtɪʃ/ *adj.* schottisch; **sb. is ~**: jmd. ist Schotte/Schottin

scoundrel /'skaʊndrl/ *n.* Schuft, *der*

scour[1] /skaʊə(r)/ *v.t.* (search) durchkämmen (**for** nach)

scour[2] *v.t.* scheuern ‹*Topf, Metall*›

'scourer *n.* Topfreiniger, *der*

scourge /skɜ:dʒ/ *n.* Geißel, *die*

scout /skaʊt/ **1** *n.* **(a)** **[Boy] S~:** Pfadfinder, *der*
(b) (Mil.) Späher, *der*
2 *v.i.* **~ for** Ausschau halten nach

scowl /skaʊl/ **1** *v.i.* ein mürrisches Gesicht machen
2 *n.* mürrischer [Gesichts]ausdruck

scram /skræm/ *v.i.*, **-mm-** (coll.) abhauen (salopp)

scramble /'skræmbl/ **1** *v.i.* **(a)** (clamber) klettern; **~ through a hedge** sich durch eine Hecke zwängen
(b) (move hastily) rennen (ugs.); **~ for sth.** um etw. rangeln
2 *v.t.* (Teleph., Radio) verschlüsseln

scrambled 'egg *n.* Rührei, *das*

scrap¹ /skræp/ **1** *n.* **(a)** (of paper) Fetzen, *der;* (of food) Bissen, *der*
(b) *in pl.* (*odds and ends*) (*of food*) Reste *Pl.*
(c) (smallest amount) **not a ~ of** kein bisschen; (of sympathy, truth also) nicht ein Fünkchen; **not a ~ of evidence** nicht die Spur eines Beweises
(d) **~ [metal]** Schrott, *der;* **~ iron** Alteisen, *das*
2 *v.t.*, **-pp-** wegwerfen; (send for ~) verschrotten; (fig.) aufgeben

scrap² (coll.) **1** *n.* (fight) Rauferei, *die*
2 *v.i.*, **-pp-** sich raufen

'scrapbook *n.* [Sammel]album, *das*

scrape /skreɪp/ **1** *v.t.* **(a)** (make smooth) schaben ‹*Häute, Möhren, Kartoffeln usw.*›; abziehen ‹*Holz*›; (damage) verschrammen ‹*Fußboden, Auto*›
(b) (remove) [ab]kratzen ‹*Farbe, Schmutz, Rost*› **(off, from** von)
(c) (draw along) schleifen
(d) **~ together** (raise) zusammenkratzen (ugs.); (save up) zusammensparen
2 *v.i.* **(a)** (move with sound) schleifen
(b) (emit scraping noise) ein schabendes Geräusch machen
(c) (rub) streifen (**against, over** *Akk.*)
3 *n.* **(a)** (act, sound) Kratzen, *das* (**against** an + *Dat.*)
(b) (predicament) Schwulitäten *Pl.* (ugs.)

■ **scrape 'by** *v.i.* (fig.) sich über Wasser halten (**on** mit)

■ **scrape 'out** *v.t.* **(a)** (excavate) buddeln (ugs.); scharren
(b) (clean) auskratzen

■ **scrape through** **1** /'--/ *v.t.* sich zwängen durch; (fig.) mit Hängen und Würgen kommen durch ‹*Prüfung*›
2 /-'-/ *v.i.* sich durchzwängen; (fig.: in examination) mit Hängen und Würgen durchkommen

'scraper *n.* (for shoes) Kratzeisen, *das;* (grid) Abtreter, *der;* (tool, kitchen utensil) Schaber, *der;* (for removing ice from car windows) [Eis]kratzer, *der*

scrap: ~ heap *n.* Schrotthaufen, *der;* **~ merchant** *n.* Schrotthändler, *der*/-händlerin, *die;* **~ 'paper** *n.* Schmierpapier, *das*

scrappy /'skræpɪ/ *adj.* lückenhaft

'scrapyard *n.* Schrottplatz, *der*

scratch /skrætʃ/ **1** *v.t.* **(a)** (score surface of) zerkratzen; (score skin of) kratzen
(b) (get scratch[es] on) **~ oneself/one's hands** *etc.* sich schrammen/sich (*Dat.*) die Hände *usw.* zerkratzen
(c) (scrape without marking) kratzen; kratzen an (+ *Dat.*) ‹*Insektenstich usw.*›; **~ oneself/one's arm** sich kratzen/sich (*Dat.*) den Arm *od.* am Arm kratzen
2 *v.i.* kratzen; (~ oneself) sich kratzen
3 *n.* **(a)** (mark, wound) Kratzer, *der* (ugs.); Schramme, *die*
(b) (sound) Kratzen, *das*
(c) **have a [good] ~:** sich [ordentlich] kratzen
(d) **start from ~:** bei Null anfangen (ugs.); **be up to ~** ‹*Arbeit, Leistung:*› nichts zu wünschen übrig lassen; ‹*Person:*› den Anforderungen genügen

■ **scratch a'bout, scratch a'round** *v.i.* scharren; (fig.: search) suchen (**for** nach)

'scratch card *n.* Rubbellos, *das*

scrawl /skrɔ:l/ **1** *v.t.* hinkritzeln
2 *v.i.* kritzeln
3 *n.* Gekritzel, *das;* (handwriting) Klaue, *die* (salopp)

scrawny /'skrɔ:nɪ/ *adj.* hager; dürr

scream /skri:m/ **1** *v.i.* schreien (**with** vor + *Dat.*)
2 *v.t.* schreien
3 *n.* Schrei, *der;* (of jet engine) Heulen, *das;* **~s of pain** Schmerzensschreie *Pl.*

screech /skri:tʃ/ **1** *v.i.* & *t.* kreischen
2 *n.* Kreischen, *das*

screen /skri:n/ **1** *n.* **(a)** (partition) Trennwand, *die;* (piece of furniture) Wandschirm, *der*
(b) (of trees, persons, fog) Wand, *die*
(c) (Cinemat.) Leinwand, *die;* **[TV] ~:** Bildschirm, *der*
2 *v.t.* **(a)** (shelter) schützen (**from** vor + *Dat.*); (conceal) verdecken
(b) vorführen ‹*Film*›
(c) (for disease) untersuchen

screening /'skri:nɪŋ/ *n.* **(a)** (in cinema) Vorführung, *die;* (on TV) Sendung, *die*
(b) (Med.) Untersuchung, *die*

screen: ~play *n.* Drehbuch, *das;* **~ saver** *n.* (Comp.) Bildschirmschoner, *der;* **~writer** *n.* Filmautor, *der*/-autorin, *die*

screw /skru:/ **1** *n.* Schraube, *die;* **he has a ~ loose** (coll. joc.) bei ihm ist eine Schraube locker *od.* lose (salopp)
2 *v.t.* **(a)** schrauben (**to** an + *Akk.*); **~ together** zusammenschrauben; **~ down** festschrauben
(b) **~ you!** (coarse) leck mich am Arsch! (salopp)

S

▪ **screw 'up** *v.t.* **(a)** (crumple up) zusammenknüllen ‹*Blatt Papier*›
(b) verziehen ‹*Gesicht*›; zusammenkneifen ‹*Augen, Mund*›
(c) (sl.: bungle) vermurksen (salopp); **~ it/things up** Mist bauen (salopp)

screw: ~ cap *n.* Schraubverschluss, *der;* **~driver** *n.* Schraubenzieher, *der*

'screwed-up *adj.* (fig. coll.) neurotisch

'screw top ▸ ~ CAP

screwy /'skru:ɪ/ *adj.* (coll.) spinnig (ugs.)

scribble /'skrɪbl/ 1 *v.t.* hinkritzeln
2 *v.i.* kritzeln
3 *n.* Gekritzel, *das*

script /skrɪpt/ *n.* **(a)** (handwriting) Handschrift, *die*
(b) (of play) Regiebuch, *das;* (of film) [Dreh]buch, *das*
(c) (for broadcaster) Manuskript, *das*

scripture /'skrɪptʃə(r)/ *n.* **(a)** **[Holy] S~, the [Holy] S~s** die [Heilige] Schrift
(b) (Sch.) Religion, *die*

'scriptwriter *n.* (of film) Drehbuchautor, *der*/-autorin, *die*

scroll /skrəʊl/ 1 *n.* (roll) Rolle, *die*
2 *v.t.* (Comp.) scrollen

▪ **scroll 'down** *v.i.* (Comp.) runterscrollen

▪ **scroll 'up** *v.i.* (Comp.) hochscrollen

scrollable /'skrəʊləbl/ *adj.* (Comp.) scrollbar

'scroll bar *n.* (Comp.) Rollbalken, *der*

scrounge /'skraʊndʒ/ (coll.) 1 *v.t.* schnorren (ugs.) **(off, from** von)
2 *v.i.* schnorren (ugs.) **(from** bei)

'scrounger *n.* (coll.) Schnorrer, *der*/Schnorrerin, *die* (ugs.)

scrub¹ /skrʌb/ 1 *v.t.*, **-bb-: (a)** schrubben (ugs.); scheuern
(b) (coll.: cancel) zurücknehmen ‹*Befehl*›; sausen lassen (ugs.) ‹*Plan*›
2 *v.i.*, **-bb-** schrubben (ugs.); scheuern
3 *n.* **give sth. a ~:** etw. schrubben (ugs.) *od.* scheuern

scrub² *n.* (brushwood) Buschwerk, *das;* (area) Buschland, *das*

scruff¹ /skrʌf/ *n.* **by the ~ of the neck** beim Genick

scruff² *n.* (Brit. coll.) (man) vergammelter Typ (ugs.); (woman, girl) Schlampe, *die*

'scruffy *adj.* vergammelt (ugs.)

scrum /skrʌm/ *n.* Gedränge, *das*

scruple /'skru:pl/ *n.* Skrupel, *der;* **have no ~s about doing sth.** keine Skrupel haben, etw. zu tun

scrupulous /'skru:pjʊləs/ *adj.* gewissenhaft ‹*Person*›; unbedingt ‹*Ehrlichkeit*›; peinlich ‹*Sorgfalt*›

scrutinize /'skru:tɪnaɪz/ *v.t.* [genau] untersuchen ‹[*Forschungs*]*gegenstand*›; [über]prüfen ‹*Rechnung, Pass, Fahrkarte*›; mustern ‹*Person*›

scrutiny /'skru:tɪnɪ/ *n.* **(a)** (critical gaze) musternder Blick
(b) (examination) (of recruit) Musterung, *die;* (of bill, passport, ticket) [Über]prüfung, *die*

scuff /skʌf/ 1 *v.t.* streifen; verschrammen ‹*Schuhe, Fußboden*›
2 *n.* Schramme, *die*

scuffle /'skʌfl/ 1 *n.* Handgreiflichkeiten *Pl.*
2 *v.i.* handgreiflich werden (**with** gegen)

scullery /'skʌlərɪ/ *n.* Spülküche, *die*

sculptor /'skʌlptə(r)/ *n.* Bildhauer, *der*/-hauerin, *die*

sculpture /'skʌlptʃə(r)/ *n.* **(a)** (art) Bildhauerei, *die*
(b) (piece of work) Skulptur, *die;* Plastik, *die;* (pieces collectively) Skulpturen *Pl.*

scum /skʌm/ *n.* **(a)** Schmutzschicht, *die;* (film) Schmutzfilm, *der*
(b) (fig. derog.) Abschaum, *der*

'scumbag *n.* (sl. derog.) Schwein, *das* (salopp)

scurry /'skʌrɪ/ *v.i.* huschen

scuttle¹ /'skʌtl/ *n.* Kohlenfüller, *der*

scuttle² (Naut.) *v.t.* versenken

scuttle³ *v.i.* rennen; flitzen (ugs.); ‹*Maus, Krabbe:*› huschen

scythe /saɪð/ *n.* Sense, *die*

SE *abbr.* = **south-east** SO

sea /si:/ *n.* **(a)** Meer, *das;* **the ~:** das Meer; die See; **by ~:** mit dem Schiff; **by the ~:** am Meer; **at ~:** auf See (*Dat.*); **be all at ~** (fig.) nicht mehr weiter wissen; **put [out] to ~:** in See (*Akk.*) gehen
(b) (specific tract of water) Meer, *das*

sea: ~ 'air *n.* Seeluft, *die;* **~'bed** *n.* Meeresboden, *der;* **~bird** *n.* Seevogel, *der;* **~ breeze** *n.* Seewind, *der;* **~food** *n.* Meeresfrüchte *Pl.; attrib.* Fisch‹*restaurant*›; **~gull** *n.* [See]möwe, *die*

seal¹ /si:l/ *n.* (Zool.) Robbe, *die;* **[common] ~:** [Gemeiner] Seehund

seal² 1 *n.* (wax etc., stamp, impression) Siegel, *das*
2 *v.t.* **(a)** (stamp, affix ~ to) siegeln ‹*Dokument*›; (fasten with ~) verplomben ‹*Tür, Stromzähler*›
(b) (close securely) abdichten ‹*Behälter, Rohr usw.*›; zukleben ‹*Umschlag, Paket*›
(c) (stop up) verschließen; abdichten ‹*Leck*›; verschmieren ‹*Riss*›

▪ **seal 'off** *v.t.* abriegeln

sea: ~ lane *n.* See[schifffahrts]straße, *die;* **~ legs** *n. pl.* Seebeine *Pl.* (Seemannsspr.); **get** *or* **find one's ~ legs** sich (*Dat.*) Seebeine wachsen lassen; **~level** *n.* Meeresspiegel, *der*

'sealing wax *n.* Siegellack, *der*

'sea lion *n.* Seelöwe, *der*

seam /si:m/ *n.* **(a)** Naht, *die*
(b) (of coal) Flöz, *das*

sea: ~man /'si:mən/ *n., pl.* **~men** /'si:mən/ Matrose, *der;* **~ mist** *n.* Küstennebel, *der*

'seamless *adj.* nahtlos

seance /'seɪɒns/**, séance** /'seɪɑ̃s/ *n.* Séance, *die*

sea: ~plane *n.* Wasserflugzeug, *das;* **~port** *n.* Seehafen, *der;* **~ power** *n.* Seemacht, *die*

sear /'sɪə(r)/ *v.t.* versengen

search /sɜ:tʃ/ 1 *v.t.* durchsuchen (**for** nach); absuchen ‹*Gebiet, Fläche*› (**for** nach); (fig.: probe) erforschen ‹*Herz, Gewissen*›; suchen in (+ *Dat.*) ‹*Gedächtnis*› (**for** nach)
2 *v.i.* suchen (**for** nach)
3 *n.* Suche, *die* (**for** nach); (of building, room, etc.) Durchsuchung, *die;* **in ~ of sb./sth.** auf der Suche nach jmdm./etw

'search engine *n.* (Comp.) Suchmaschine, *die*

'searching *adj.* prüfend, forschend ‹*Blick*›; bohrend ‹*Frage*›

search: ~light *n.* Suchscheinwerfer, *der;* **~ party** *n.* Suchtrupp, *der;* **~ warrant** *n.* Durchsuchungsbefehl, *der*

sea: ~ salt *n.* Meersalz, *das;* Seesalz, das; **~shore** *n.* [Meeres]küste, *die;* (beach) Strand, *der;* **~sick** *adj.* seekrank; **~sickness** *n.* Seekrankheit, *die;* **~side** *n.* [Meeres]küste, *die;* **by/to/at the ~side** am/ans/am Meer; **~side town** Seestadt, *die*

season /'si:zn/ 1 *n.* **(a)** Jahreszeit, *die;* **nesting ~:** Nistzeit, *die*
(b) (period of social activity) **[opera/football] ~:** [Opern-/Fußball]saison, *die;* **holiday** *or* (Amer.) **vacation ~:** Urlaubszeit, *die;* **tourist ~:** Reisezeit, *die*
(c) raspberries are in/out of *or* **not in ~:** jetzt ist die/nicht die Saison *od.* Zeit für Himbeeren; **be in ~** (on heat) brünstig sein
(d) ▶ SEASON TICKET
2 *v.t.* würzen ‹*Fleisch, Rede*›

seasonable /'si:zənəbl/ *adj.* der Jahreszeit gemäß

seasonal /'si:zənl/ *adj.* Saison‹*arbeit, -geschäft*›; saisonabhängig ‹*Preise*›

seasonal af'fective disorder /si:zənl ə'fektɪv dɪsɔ:də(r)/ *n.* (Med.) saisonabhängige Depression

'seasoned *adj.* (fig.) erfahren

'seasoning *n.* Gewürze *Pl.;* Würze, *die*

'season ticket *n.* Dauerkarte, *die*

seat /si:t/ 1 *n.* **(a)** Sitzgelegenheit, *die;* (in vehicle, cinema, etc.) Sitz, *der;* (of toilet) [Klosett]brille, *die* (ugs.)
(b) (place) Platz, *der;* (in vehicle) [Sitz]platz, *der;* **have** *or* **take a ~:** sich [hin]setzen
(c) (part of chair) Sitzfläche, *die*
(d) (buttocks) Gesäß, *das;* (part of clothing) Gesäßpartie, *die;* (of trousers) Sitz, *der*
2 *v.t.* **(a)** (cause to sit) setzen; ‹*Platzanweiser:*› einen Platz anweisen (+ *Dat.*); **~ oneself** sich setzen
(b) (have **~s** for) Sitzplätze bieten (+ *Dat.*); **~ 500 people** 500 Sitzplätze haben

'seat belt *n.* Sicherheitsgurt, *der*

'seat-belt tensioner /'tenʃnə(r)/*n.* Gurtstraffer, *der*

'seated *adj.* sitzend; **remain ~:** sitzen bleiben

'seating *n.* Sitzplätze *Pl.*; *attrib.* Sitz‹*ordnung, -plan*›

sea: ~ urchin *n.* Seeigel, *der;* **~ wall** *n.* Strandmauer, *die;* **~ water** *n.* Meerwasser, *das;* **~weed** *n.* [See]tang, *der;* **~worthy** *adj.* seetüchtig

secateurs /sekə'tɜ:z/ *n. pl.* (Brit.) Gartenschere, *die*

secluded /sɪ'klu:dɪd/ *adj.* (hidden) versteckt; (isolated) abgelegen; zurückgezogen ‹*Leben*›

seclusion /sɪ'klu:ʒn/ *n.* (remoteness) Abgelegenheit, *die;* (privacy) Zurückgezogenheit, *die*

second¹ /'sekənd/ 1 *adj.* zweit...; **~ largest/highest** *etc.* zweitgrößt.../-höchst... *usw.;* **come/be ~:** Zweiter/Zweite werden/sein
2 *n.* **(a)** (unit of time or angle) Sekunde, *die*
(b) (coll.: moment) Sekunde, *die* (ugs.); **wait a few ~s** einen Moment warten; **in a ~** (immediately) sofort (ugs.); (very quickly) im Nu (ugs.); **just a ~!** (coll.) einen Moment!
(c) the ~ (in sequence, rank) der/die/das Zweite
(d) *in pl.* (helping of food) zweite Portion
3 *v.t.* (support) unterstützen

second² /sɪ'kɒnd/ *v.t.* (transfer) vorübergehend versetzen

secondary /'sekəndərɪ/ *adj.* (of less importance) zweitrangig; Neben‹*sache*›; **be ~ to sth.** einer Sache (*Dat.*) untergeordnet sein

'secondary school *n.* höhere Schule

second: ~-best 1 /'---/ *adj.* zweitbest...; 2 /--'-/ *n.* Zweitbeste, *der/die/das;* **~-class** 1 /'---/ *adj.* (of lower class) zweiter Klasse *nachgestellt;* Zweite[r]-Klasse-‹*Fahrkarte, Abteil, Post, Brief usw.*›; **~-class stamp** *Briefmarke für einen Zweiter-Klasse-Brief;* 2 /--'-/ *adv.* zweiter Klasse ‹*fahren*›; **~ 'floor** ▶ FLOOR 1B; **~ hand** *n.* Sekundenzeiger, *der;* **~-hand** 1 /'---/ *adj.* **(a)** gebraucht ‹*Kleidung, Auto usw.*›; antiquarisch ‹*Buch*›; **(b)** (selling used goods) Gebrauchtwaren-; Secondhand‹*laden*›; **(c)** ‹*Nachrichten, Bericht*› aus zweiter Hand; 2 /--'-/ *adv.* aus zweiter Hand; **~ 'home** *n.* Zweitwohnung, *die*

'secondly *adv.* zweitens

second: ~ name *n.* Nachname, *der;* **~-'rate** *adj.* zweitklassig; **~ 'thoughts** *n. pl.* **have ~ thoughts** es sich (*Dat.*) anders überlegen (**about** mit); **we've had ~ thoughts about buying it** wir wollen es nun doch nicht kaufen; **but on ~ thoughts ...:** wenn ich's mir [noch mal] überlege, ...

secrecy /'si:krɪsɪ/ *n.* **(a)** (keeping of secret) Geheimhaltung, *die*
(b) (secretiveness) Heimlichtuerei, *die*
(c) in ~: im Geheimen

secret /'si:krɪt/ 1 *adj.* geheim;

Geheim‹*fach, -tür, -abkommen, -kode*›; heimlich ‹*Trinker, Liebhaber*›; **keep sth. ~:** etw. geheim halten (**from** vor + *Dat.*)
2 *n.* **(a)** Geheimnis, *das;* **make no ~ of sth.** kein Geheimnis aus etw. machen; (fig.) keinen Hehl aus etw. machen; **keep ~s/ a ~:** schweigen (fig.)
(b) in ~: im Geheimen

secret 'agent *n.* Geheimagent, *der*/ -agentin, *die*

secretarial /sekrə'teərɪəl/ *adj.* Sekretärinnen‹*kursus, -tätigkeit*›; ‹*Arbeit*› als Sekretärin

secretary /'sekrətərɪ/ *n.* Sekretär, *der*/ Sekretärin, *die*

secret 'ballot *n.* geheime Abstimmung

secretive /'si:krɪtɪv/ *adj.* verschlossen ‹*Person*›: **be ~:** geheimnisvoll tun (**about** mit)

'secretly *adv.* heimlich; insgeheim ‹*etw. glauben*›

sect /sekt/ *n.* Sekte, *die*

section /'sekʃn/ *n.* **(a)** (part cut off) Abschnitt, *der;* Stück, *das;* (part of divided whole) Teil, *der*
(b) (of firm) Abteilung, *die;* (of organization) Sektion, *die*
(c) (of chapter, book) Abschnitt, *der;* (of statute etc.) Paragraph, *der*

sector /'sektə(r)/ *n.* Sektor, *der*

secular /'sekjʊlə(r)/ *adj.* weltlich

secure /sɪ'kjʊə(r)/ **1** *adj.* sicher; (firmly fastened) fest; **~ against burglars** gegen Einbruch geschützt
2 *v.t.* **(a)** sichern (**for** *Dat.*); beschaffen ‹*Auftrag*› (**for** *Dat.*); (for oneself) sich (*Dat.*) sichern
(b) (fasten) sichern

se'curely *adv.* (firmly) fest ‹*verriegeln, zumachen*›; sicher ‹*befestigen, untergebracht sein*›

security /sɪ'kjʊərɪtɪ/ *n.* **(a)** Sicherheit, *die;* **~ [measures]** Sicherheitsmaßnahmen *Pl.*
(b) (Finance) **securities** *pl.* Wertpapiere *Pl.*

security: ~ check *n.* Sicherheitskontrolle, *die;* **~ forces** *n. pl.* Sicherheitskräfte *Pl.;* **~ guard** *n.* Wächter, *der*/Wächterin, *die;* **~ risk** *n.* Sicherheitsrisiko, *das;* **~ van** *n.* gepanzerter Transporter; (for money) Geldtransporter, *der*

sedan /sɪ'dæn/ *n.* (Amer. Motor Veh.) Limousine, *die*

sedate /sɪ'deɪt/ **1** *adj.* bedächtig; gesetzt ‹*alte Dame*›; gemächlich ‹*Tempo, Leben*›
2 *v.t.* sedieren

sedation /sɪ'deɪʃn/ *n.* Sedation, *die;* **be under ~:** sediert sein

sedative /'sedətɪv/ **1** *n.* Beruhigungsmittel, *das*
2 *adj.* sedativ

sedentary /'sedəntərɪ/ *adj.* sitzend

sediment /'sedɪmənt/ *n.* Ablagerung, *die;* (of tea, coffee, etc.) Bodensatz, *der*

seduce /sɪ'dju:s/ *v.t.* verführen

seduction /sɪ'dʌkʃn/ *n.* Verführung, *die*

seductive /sɪ'dʌktɪv/ *adj.* verführerisch; verlockend ‹*Angebot*›

see /si:/ **1** *v.t.,* **saw** /sɔ:/, **seen** /si:n/ **(a)** sehen; **I can ~ it's hard for you** ich verstehe, dass es nicht leicht für dich ist; **I ~ what you mean** ich verstehe[, was du meinst]
(b) (meet [with]) sehen; treffen; (meet socially) sich treffen mit; **I'll ~ you there/at five** wir sehen uns dort/um fünf; **~ you!, [I'll] be ~ing you!** (coll.) bis bald! (ugs.)
(c) (speak to) sprechen ‹*Person*› (**about** wegen); (visit) gehen zu ‹*Arzt, Anwalt usw.*›; (receive) empfangen
(d) (find out) feststellen; (by looking) nachsehen
(e) (make sure) **~ [that] ...:** darauf achten, dass ...
(f) (imagine) sich (*Dat.*) vorstellen
(g) (escort) begleiten
2 *v.i.,* **saw, seen (a)** sehen
(b) (make sure) nachsehen
(c) I ~: ich verstehe; **you ~:** weißt du/wisst ihr/wissen Sie

■ **'see about** *v.t.* sich kümmern um

■ **see 'off** *v.t.* **(a)** (say goodbye to) verabschieden
(b) (chase away) vertreiben

■ **see 'out** *v.t.* (escort) hinausbegleiten (**of** aus); **~ oneself out** allein hinausfinden

■ **see through** *v.t.* **(a)** /'--/ hindurchsehen durch; (fig.) durchschauen
(b) /-'-/ (not abandon) zu Ende bringen

■ **'see to** *v.t.* sich kümmern um

seed /si:d/ **1** *n.* **(a)** Samen, *der;* (of grape etc.) Kern, *der*
(b) *no pl., no indef. art.* (**~s** collectively) Samen[körner] *Pl.;* (as collected for sowing) Saatgut, *das;* (for birds) Körner *Pl.;* **go** *or* **run to ~:** Samen bilden; (fig.) herunterkommen (ugs.)
(c) (Sport) gesetzter Spieler/gesetzte Spielerin
2 *v.t.* **(a)** (place **~s** in) besäen
(b) (Sport) setzen ‹*Spieler*›; **be ~ed number one** als Nummer eins gesetzt werden/sein

'seed bed *n.* [Saat]beet, *das*

'seedless *adj.* kernlos

seedling /'si:dlɪŋ/ *n.* Sämling, *der*

'seedy *adj.* **(a)** (coll.: unwell) **feel ~:** sich [leicht] angeschlagen fühlen
(b) (shabby) schäbig, (ugs.) vergammelt ‹*Aussehen*›; heruntergekommen ‹*Stadtteil*›
(c) (disreputable) zweifelhaft

'seeing *conj.* **~ [that] ...:** in Anbetracht dessen, dass ...

seek /si:k/ *v.t.,* **sought** /sɔ:t/ suchen; anstreben ‹*Posten, Amt*›; sich bemühen um ‹*Anerkennung, Interview, Einstellung*›; (try to reach) aufsuchen

seem /si:m/ *v.i.* scheinen; **you ~ tired** du wirkst müde; **she ~s nice** sie scheint nett zu sein

'seeming *adj.* scheinbar

'seemingly *adv.* **(a)** (evidently) offensichtlich **(b)** (to outward appearance) scheinbar

seemly /'si:mlɪ/ *adj.* schicklich

seen ▶ SEE

seep /si:p/ *v.i.* ~ **[away]** [ab]sickern

'see-saw *n.* Wippe, *die*

seethe /si:ð/ *v.i.* **(a)** ~ **[with anger/inwardly]** vor Wut/innerlich schäumen **(b)** ‹*Straßen usw.*:› wimmeln (**with** von)

'see-through *adj.* durchsichtig

segment /'segmənt/ *n.* (of orange, pineapple, etc.) Scheibe, *die*

segregate /'segrɪgeɪt/ *v.t.* trennen; (racially) absondern

segregation /segrɪ'geɪʃn/ *n.* Trennung, *die;* **[racial]** ~: Rassentrennung, *die*

seismic /'saɪzmɪk/ *adj.* seismisch

seize /si:z/ **1** *v.t.* **(a)** ergreifen; ~ **power** die Macht ergreifen; ~ **sb. by the arm/collar** jmdn. am Arm/Kragen packen; ~ **the opportunity [to do sth.]** die Gelegenheit ergreifen [und etw. tun]; ~ **any/a** *or* **the chance [to do sth.]** jede/die Gelegenheit nutzen[, um etw. zu tun]; **be ~d with remorse/panic** von Gewissensbissen geplagt/von Panik ergriffen werden **(b)** (capture) gefangen nehmen ‹*Person*›; kapern ‹*Schiff*›; mit Gewalt übernehmen ‹*Flugzeug, Gebäude*›; einnehmen ‹*Festung, Brücke*› **(c)** (confiscate) beschlagnahmen **2** *v.i.* ▶ ~ UP

■ **'seize on** *v.t.* sich (*Dat.*) vornehmen ‹*Einzelheit, Aspekt, Schwachpunkt*›; aufgreifen ‹*Idee, Vorschlag*›

■ **seize 'up** *v.i.* sich festfressen

seizure /'si:ʒə(r)/ *n.* **(a)** ▶ SEIZE 1B, C: Gefangennahme, *die;* Kapern, *das;* Übernahme, *die;* Einnahme, *die;* Beschlagnahme, *die* **(b)** (Med.) Anfall, *der*

seldom /'seldəm/ *adv.* selten

select /sɪ'lekt/ **1** *adj.* ausgewählt **2** *v.t.* auswählen

selection /sɪ'lekʃn/ *n.* **(a)** (what is selected [from]) Auswahl, *die* (**of** an + *Dat.*, **from** aus) **(b)** (act of choosing) [Aus]wahl, *die*

selective /sɪ'lektɪv/ *adj.* (using selection) selektiv; (careful in one's choice) wählerisch

self /self/ *n., pl.* **selves** [selvz] Selbst, *das* (geh.); Ich, *das*

self- *pref.* selbst-/Selbst-

self: **~-ab'sorbed** *adj.* mit sich selbst beschäftigt; **~-ad'dressed** *adj.* **~-addressed envelope** adressierter Rückumschlag; **~-ad'hesive** *adj.* selbstklebend; **~-ap'pointed** *adj.* selbst ernannt; **~-as'surance** *n.* Selbstsicherheit, *die;* **~-as'sured** *adj.* selbstsicher; **~-a'wareness** *n.* Selbsterkenntnis, *die;* **~-'catering** **1** *adj.* mit Selbstversorgung *nachgestellt;* **2** *n.* Selbstversorgung, *die;* **~-'centred** *adj.* egozentrisch; **~-con'fessed** *adj.* erklärt; **~-'confidence** *n.* Selbstbewusstsein, *das;* **~-'confident** *adj.* selbstbewusst; **~-'conscious** *adj.* unsicher; **~-'consciousness** *n.* Unsicherheit, *die;* **~-con'tained** *adj.* abgeschlossen ‹*Wohnung*›; **~-con'trol** *n.* Selbstbeherrschung, *die;* **~con'trolled** *adj.* voller Selbstbeherrschung *nachgestellt;* **~-'critical** *adj.* selbstkritisch; **~-de'ception** *n.* Selbsttäuschung, *die;* **~-de'feating** *adj.* unsinnig; **~-de'fence** *n.* Notwehr, *die;* **in ~-defence** aus Notwehr; **~-de'lusion** *n.* Selbsttäuschung, *die;* **~-de'nial** *n.* Selbstverleugnung, *die;* **~-de'structive** *adj.* selbstzerstörerisch; **~-'discipline** *n.* Selbstdisziplin, *die;* **~-drive** *adj.* **~-drive hire [company]** Autovermietung, *die;* **~-drive vehicle** Mietwagen, *der;* **~-em'ployed** *adj.* selbstständig; **~-e'steem** *n.* Selbstachtung, *die;* **~-'evident** *adj.* offenkundig; **~-ex'planatory** *adj.* ohne weiteres verständlich; **be ~-explanatory** für sich selbst sprechen; **~-ful'filling** *adj.* zur eigenen Bestätigung mit beitragend; **~-'help** *n.* Selbsthilfe, *die;* **~-im'portant** *adj.* eingebildet; **~-in'dulgent** *adj.* maßlos; **~-in'flicted** *adj.* selbst beigebracht ‹*Wunde*›; selbst auferlegt ‹*Strafe*›; **~-'interest** *n.* Eigeninteresse, *das*

'selfish *adj.*, **'selfishly** *adv.* selbstsüchtig

'selfishness *n.* Selbstsucht, *die*

self-'knowledge *n.* Selbsterkenntnis, *die*

selfless /'selflɪs/ *adj.* selbstlos

self: **~-'motivated** *adj.* von sich aus motiviert; **~-ob'sessed** *adj.* ichbesessen; **~-o'pinionated** *adj.* eingebildet; **~-'pity** *n.* Selbstmitleid, *das;* **~-'portrait** *n.* Selbstporträt, *das;* **~-pos'sessed** *adj.* selbstbeherrscht; **~-preser'vation** *n.* Selbsterhaltung, *die;* **~-'raising flour** *n.* (Brit.) mit Backpulver versetztes Mehl; **~-re'liant** *adj.* selbstbewusst; **~-re'spect** *n.* Selbstachtung, *die;* **~-re'specting** *adj.* **no ~-respecting person** ...: niemand, der etwas auf sich hält, ...; **~-'righteous** *adj.* selbstgerecht; **~-'sacrifice** *n.* Selbstaufopferung, *die;* **~-'satisfied** *adj.* selbstzufrieden; (smug) selbstgefällig; **~-'service** *n.* Selbstbedienung, *die; attrib.* Selbstbedienungs-; **~-suf'ficient** *adj.* unabhängig; selbstständig ‹*Person*›; **~-'taught** *adj.* autodidaktisch; **~-taught person** Autodidakt, *der*/Autodidaktin, *die;* **~-'willed** *adj.* eigenwillig

sell /sel/ **1** *v.t.*, **sold** /səʊld/ ~ **sth. to sb.**, ~ **sb. sth.** jmdm. etw. verkaufen; **be sold out** ausverkauft sein **2** *v.i.*, **sold** sich verkaufen; ‹*Person:*› verkaufen ⇢

■ **sell 'off** *v.t.* verkaufen
■ **sell 'out** [1] *v.t.* **(a)** ausverkaufen
(b) (coll.: betray) verraten
[2] *v.i.* **we have** *or* **are sold out** wir sind ausverkauft

'sell-by date *n.* ≈ Mindesthaltbarkeitsdatum, *das*

'seller *n.* **(a)** Verkäufer, *der*/Verkäuferin, *die*
(b) (product) **be a good/slow ~:** sich gut/nur langsam verkaufen

'selling point *n.* **a [good] ~ point** (fig.) ein Pluspunkt

'sellotape *v.t.* mit Tesafilm kleben

Sellotape ® /'seləteɪp/ *n.* ≈ Tesafilm, *der* (Wz)

'sell-out *n.* **be a ~:** ausverkauft sein; (coll.: betrayal) Verrat sein

selves *pl. of* SELF

semaphore /'seməfɔ:(r)/ [1] *n.* (system) Winken, *das*
[2] *v.i.* **~ to sb.** jmdm. ein Winksignal übermitteln

semblance /'sembləns/ *n.* Anschein, *der*

semen /'si:mən/ *n.* Samen, *der*

semester /sɪ'mestə(r)/ *n.* Semester, *das*

semi- /semɪ/ *pref.* halb-/Halb-

semi: ~bold *adj.* (Printing) halbfett; **~breve** *n.* (Brit. Mus.) ganze Note; **~circle** *n.* Halbkreis, *der;* **~'circular** *adj.* halbkreisförmig; **~'colon** *n.* Semikolon, *das;* **~-de'tached** *adj. & n.* **~-detached [house]** Doppelhaushälfte, *die;* **~-'final** *n.* Halbfinale, *das*

seminar /'semɪnɑ:(r)/ *n.* Seminar, *das*

semi: ~-'precious *adj.* **~-precious stone** Halbedelstein, *der;* **~-skimmed** [1] *adj.* teilentrahmt; [2] *n.* teilentrahmte Milch; **~tone** *n.* (Mus.) Halbton, *der*

semolina /semə'li:nə/ *n.* Grieß, *der*

senate /'senət/ *n.* Senat, *der*

senator /'senətə(r)/ *n.* Senator, *der*

send /send/ *v.t.,* **sent** [sent] schicken; senden (geh.)
■ **send a'way** [1] *v.t.* wegschicken
[2] *v.i.* **~ away [to sb.] for sth.** etw. [bei jmdm.] anfordern
■ **send 'back** *v.t.* zurückschicken
■ **'send for** *v.t.* **(a)** (tell to come) holen lassen; rufen ‹*Polizei, Arzt usw.*›
(b) (order from elsewhere) anfordern
■ **send 'off** *v.t.* [1] **(a)** (dispatch) abschicken ‹*Sache*›
(b) (Sport) vom Platz stellen
[2] *v.i.* ▶ SEND AWAY 2
■ **send 'up** *v.t.* (Brit. coll.: parody) parodieren

'sender *n.* Absender, *der*

'send-off *n.* Verabschiedung, *die*

senile /'si:naɪl/ *adj.* senil

senile de'mentia *n.* senile Demenz

senility /sɪ'nɪlɪtɪ/ *n.* Senilität, *die*

senior /'si:nɪə(r)/ [1] *adj.* **(a)** (older) älter
(b) höher ‹*Rang, Beamter, Stellung*›; leitend ‹*Angestellter, Stellung*›; **~ manager** obere Führungskraft; **~ management** oberer Führungskreis
[2] *n.* (older) Ältere, *der/die;* (of higher rank) Vorgesetzte, *der/die*

senior 'citizen *n.* Senior, *der*/Seniorin, *die*

seniority /si:nɪ'ɒrɪtɪ/ *n.* (greater length of service) höheres Dienstalter; (higher rank) höherer Rang

senior 'partner *n.* Seniorpartner, *der*/-partnerin, *die*

sensation /sen'seɪʃn/ *n.* **(a)** (feeling) Gefühl, *das*
(b) (person, event, etc.) Sensation, *die*

sensational /sen'seɪʃənl/ *adj.* sensationell

sensationalise ▶ SENSATIONALIZE

sensationalism /sen'seɪʃənəlɪzm/ *n.* Sensationshascherei, *die*

sensationalist /sen'seɪʃənəlɪst/ *adj.* sensationslüstern

sensationalize /sen'seɪʃənəlaɪz/ *v.t.* **~ sth.** etw. zur Sensation aufbauschen

sense /sens/ [1] *n.* **(a)** (faculty) Sinn, *der;* **~ of smell/touch/taste** Geruchs-/Tast-/Geschmackssinn, *der;* **come to one's ~s** das Bewusstsein wiedererlangen
(b) *in pl.* (normal state of mind) Verstand, *der;* **have taken leave of one's ~s** den Verstand verloren haben
(c) (consciousness) Gefühl, *das;* **~ of responsibility/guilt** Verantwortungs-/Schuldgefühl, *das*
(d) (practical wisdom) Verstand, *der;* **sound** *or* **good ~:** [gesunder Menschen]verstand; **not have the ~ to do sth.** nicht so schlau sein, etw. zu tun; **there is no ~ in doing that** es hat keinen Sinn, das zu tun
(e) (meaning) Sinn, *der;* (of word) Bedeutung, *die;* **make ~:** einen Sinn ergeben; **in a** *or* **one ~:** in gewisser Hinsicht; **make ~ of sth.** etw. verstehen
[2] *v.t.* spüren

'senseless *adj.* **(a)** (unconscious) bewusstlos
(b) (purposeless) sinnlos

sensible /'sensɪbl/ *adj.* **(a)** (reasonable) vernünftig
(b) (practical) zweckmäßig

sensibly /'sensɪblɪ/ *adv.* **(a)** (reasonably) vernünftig
(b) (practically) zweckmäßig

sensitive /'sensɪtɪv/ *adj.* empfindlich; **be ~ to sth.** empfindlich auf etw. (*Akk.*) reagieren

sensitivity /sensɪ'tɪvɪtɪ/ *n.* Empfindlichkeit, *die*

sensory /'sensərɪ/ *adj.* Sinnes-

sensual /'sensjʊəl/ *adj.* sinnlich

sensuous /'sensjʊəs/ *adj.* sinnlich

sent ▶ SEND

sentence /'sentəns/ [1] *n.* **(a)** (Law) [Straf]urteil, *das*

(b) (Ling.) Satz, *der*
2 *v.t.* verurteilen (**to** zu)
sentiment /'sentɪmənt/ *n.* **(a)** Gefühl, *das*
(b) (sentimentality) Sentimentalität, *die*
(c) (thought) Gedanke, *der*
sentimental /sentɪ'mentl/ *adj.* sentimental
sentimentality /sentɪmen'tælɪtɪ/ *n.* Sentimentalität, *die*
sentimentalize /sentɪ'mentəlaɪz/ *v.t.* sentimental darstellen
sentry /'sentrɪ/ *n.* Wache, *die*
separable /'sepərəbl/ *adj.* trennbar
separate **1** /'sepərət/ *adj.* verschieden ‹*Fragen, Probleme, Gelegenheiten*›; gesondert ‹*Teil*›; separat ‹*Eingang, Toilette, Blatt Papier, Abteil*›; (one's own, individual) eigen ‹*Zimmer, Identität, Organisation*›; **keep two things ~:** zwei Dinge auseinander halten
2 /'sepəreɪt/ *v.t.* trennen; **they are ~d** (no longer live together) sie leben getrennt
3 *v.i.* **(a)** (disperse) sich trennen
(b) ‹*Ehepaar:*› sich trennen
separately /'sepərətlɪ/ *adv.* getrennt
separation /sepə'reɪʃn/ *n.* Trennung, *die*
Sept. *abbr.* = **September** Sept.
September /sep'tembə(r)/ *n.* September, *der; see also* AUGUST
septic /'septɪk/ *adj.* septisch; **go ~:** eitrig werden
sequel /'si:kwl/ *n.* **(a)** (consequence, result) Folge, *die* (**to** von)
(b) (continuation) Fortsetzung, *die*
sequence /'si:kwəns/ *n.* **(a)** Reihenfolge, *die*
(b) (part of film) Sequenz, *die*
sequin /'si:kwɪn/ *n.* Paillette, *die*
Serbia /'sɜ:bɪə/ *pr. n.* Serbien, *das*
Serbian /'sɜ:bɪən/ **1** *adj.* serbisch; **sb. is ~:** jmd. ist Serbe/Serbin
2 *n.* **(a)** (Ling.) serbischer Dialekt
(b) (person) Serbe, *der*/Serbin, *die. See also* ENGLISH 2A
serenade /serə'neɪd/ **1** *n.* Ständchen, *das*
2 *v.t.* **~ sb.** jmdm. ein Ständchen bringen
serene /sɪ'ri:n/ *adj.* gelassen
serenity /sɪ'renɪtɪ/ *n.* Gelassenheit, *die*
sergeant /'sɑ:dʒənt/ *n.* (Mil.) Unteroffizier, *der;* (police officer) ≈ Polizeimeister, *der*
sergeant 'major *n.* ≈ [Ober]stabsfeldwebel, *der*
serial /'sɪərɪəl/ *n.* Fortsetzungsgeschichte, *die;* (Radio, Telev.) Serie, *die*
serialize /'sɪərɪəlaɪz/ *v.t.* in Fortsetzungen veröffentlichen; (Radio, Telev.) in Fortsetzungen senden
'serial killer *n.* Serienmörder, *der*
series /'sɪəri:z, 'sɪərɪz/ *n., pl. same* **(a)** (sequence) Reihe, *die;* (of events, misfortunes) Folge, *die*
(b) (set of successive issues) Serie, *die;* **radio/TV ~:** Hörfunkreihe/Fernsehserie, *die*
(c) (set of books) Reihe, *die*
serious /'sɪərɪəs/ *adj.* **(a)** (earnest) ernst
(b) (important, grave) ernst ‹*Angelegenheit, Lage, Problem, Zustand*›; ernsthaft ‹*Frage, Einwand, Kandidat*›; schwer ‹*Krankheit, Unfall, Fehler, Niederlage*›; ernst zu nehmend ‹*Rivale*›; ernstlich ‹*Gefahr, Bedrohung*›; bedenklich ‹*Mangel*›
'seriously *adv.* **(a)** (earnestly) ernst; **take sth./sb. ~:** etw./jmdn. ernst nehmen
(b) (severely) ernstlich; schwer ‹*verletzt*›
'seriousness *n.* Ernst, *der;* **in all ~:** ganz im Ernst
sermon /'sɜ:mən/ *n.* Predigt, *die*
serpent /'sɜ:pənt/ *n.* Schlange, *die*
serrated /se'reɪtɪd/ *adj.* gezackt; **~ knife** Sägemesser, *das*
serum /'sɪərəm/ *n.* Serum, *das*
servant /'sɜ:vənt/ *n.* Diener, *der*/Dienerin, *die*
serve /sɜ:v/ **1** *v.t.* **(a)** (work for) dienen (+ *Dat.*)
(b) (be useful to) dienlich sein (+ *Dat.*)
(c) (meet needs of) nutzen (+ *Dat.*); **~ a/no purpose** einen Zweck erfüllen/keinen Zweck haben
(d) durchlaufen ‹*Lehre*›; verbüßen ‹*Haftstrafe*›
(e) (dish up) servieren; (pour out) einschenken (**to** *Dat.*)
(f) **~[s]** *or* **it ~s him right!** [das] geschieht ihm recht!
2 *v.i.* **(a)** dienen; **~ as chairman** das Amt des Vorsitzenden innehaben; **~ as a Member of Parliament** Mitglied des Parlaments sein; **~ on a jury** Geschworener/Geschworene sein
(b) (be of use) **~ to do sth.** dazu dienen, etw. zu tun; **~ to show sth.** etw. zeigen; **~ for** *or* **as** dienen als
(c) (Sport) aufschlagen
3 *n.* ▶ SERVICE 1G
■ **serve 'up** *v.t.* **(a)** servieren
(b) (offer for consideration) auftischen (ugs.)
server /'sɜ:və(r)/ *n.* (Comp.) Server, *der*
service /'sɜ:vɪs/ **1** *n.* **(a)** Dienst, *der;* **do sb. a ~:** jmdm. einen guten Dienst erweisen
(b) (Eccl.) Gottesdienst, *der*
(c) (attending to customer) Service, *der;* (in shop, garage, etc.) Bedienung, *die*
(d) (system of transport) Verbindung, *die;* **there is no [bus] ~ on Sundays** sonntags verkehren keine Busse
(e) (provision of maintenance) **[after-sale] ~:** Kundendienst, *der;* **take one's car in for a ~:** sein Auto zur Inspektion bringen
(f) (operation) Betrieb, *der;* **out of ~:** außer Betrieb
(g) (Sport) Aufschlag, *der;* **whose ~ is it?** wer hat Aufschlag?
(h) (crockery set) Service, *das*
(i) (assistance) **can I be of ~ [to you]?** kann ich Ihnen behilflich sein?; **I'm at your ~:** ich stehe zu Ihren Diensten ··›

(j) (Mil.) **the [armed** *or* **fighting] ~s** die Streitkräfte *Pl.*; **in the ~s** beim Militär
(k) [motorway] ~s [Autobahn]raststätte, *die*
2 *v.t.* warten ‹*Wagen, Waschmaschine, Heizung*›

serviceable /'sɜːvɪsəbl/ *adj.* **(a)** (useful) nützlich
(b) (durable) haltbar

service: ~ area *n.* Raststätte, *die;* **~ charge** *n.* Bedienungsgeld, *das;* **~ hatch** *n.* Durchreiche, *die;* **~ industry** *n.* Dienstleistungsbetrieb, *der;* **~man** *n.* /'sɜːvɪsmən/ *n., Pl.* **~men** /'sɜːvɪsmən/ Militärangehörige, *der;* **~ provider** *n.* (Comp.) Provider, *der;* **Internet ~ provider** Internetanbieter, *der;* **~ station** *n.* Tankstelle, *die*

serviette /sɜːvɪ'et/ *n.* (Brit.) Serviette, *die*

servile /'sɜːvaɪl/ *adj.* unterwürfig

servility /sɜː'vɪlɪtɪ/ *n.* Unterwürfigkeit, *die*

serving /'sɜːvɪŋ/ *n.* Portion, *die*

'serving spoon *n.* Vorlegelöffel, *der*

servitude /'sɜːvɪtjuːd/ *n.* Knechtschaft, *die*

sesame /'sesəmɪ/ *n.* **~ [seed]** Sesamkorn, *das*

session /'seʃn/ *n.* (meeting) Sitzung, *die;* **be in ~:** tagen

set /set/ **1** *v.t.*, **-tt-, set (a)** (put) (horizontally) legen; (vertically) stellen; **~ sb. ashore** jmdn. an Land setzen; **~ sth./things right** *or* **in order** etw./die Dinge in Ordnung bringen
(b) (apply) setzen; **~ a match to sth.** ein Streichholz an etw. (*Akk.*) halten; *see also* FIRE 1A; LIGHT[1] 1D
(c) (adjust) einstellen (**at** auf + *Akk.*); aufstellen ‹*Falle*›; stellen ‹*Uhr*›; **~ the alarm for 5.30 a.m.** den Wecker auf 5.30 Uhr stellen
(d) be ~ ‹*Buch, Film:*› spielen (**in** in + *Dat.*)
(e) (specify) festlegen ‹*Bedingungen*›; festsetzen ‹*Termin, Ort usw.*› (**for** auf + *Akk.*); **~ limits** Grenzen setzen
(f) ~ sb. thinking that ...: jmdn. auf den Gedanken bringen, dass ...
(g) (put forward) stellen ‹*Frage, Aufgabe*›; aufgeben ‹*Hausaufgabe*›; aufstellen ‹*Rekord*›; (compose) zusammenstellen ‹*Rätsel, Fragen*›; **~ sb. an example, ~ an example to sb.** jmdm. ein Beispiel geben; **~ sb. a task/problem** jmdm. eine Aufgabe stellen/jmdn. vor ein Problem stellen; **~ [sb./oneself] a target** [jmdm./sich] ein Ziel setzen
(h) (Med.: put into place) [ein]richten; einrenken ‹*verrenktes Gelenk*›
(i) legen ‹*Haare*›
(j) decken ‹*Tisch*›; auflegen ‹*Gedeck*›
(k) fassen ‹*Edelstein*›
2 *v.i.*, **-tt-, set (a)** (solidify) fest werden
(b) (go down) ‹*Sonne, Mond:*› untergehen
3 *n.* **(a)** (group) Satz, *der;* **~ [of two]** Paar, *das;* **a ~ of chairs** eine Sitzgruppe
(b) (radio, TV) Gerät, *das*
(c) (Tennis) Satz, *der*
(d) (of hair) Legen, *das*
(e) (Theatre: scenery) Bühnenbild, *das;* (*area of performance*) (*of film*) Drehort, *der;* (of play) Bühne, *die*
(f) (of people) Kreis, *der*
(g) (Math.) Menge, *die*
4 *adj.* **(a)** (fixed) fest ‹*Absichten, Zielvorstellungen, Zeitpunkt*›; **be ~ in one's ways** *or* **habits** in seinen Gewohnheiten festgefahren sein; **~ meal** *or* **menu** Menü, *das*
(b) vorgeschrieben ‹*Buch, Lektüre*›
(c) (ready) **be [all] ~ for sth.** zu etw. bereit sein; **be [all] ~ to do sth.** bereit sein, etw. zu tun
(d) (determined) **be ~ on sth./doing sth.** zu etw. entschlossen sein/entschlossen sein, etw. zu tun

■ **'set about** *v.t.* **~ about sth.** sich an etw. (*Akk.*) machen; **~ about doing sth.** sich daranmachen, etw. zu tun

■ **set a'side** *v.t.* **(a)** beiseite legen
(b) aufheben ‹*Urteil, Entscheidung*›

■ **set 'back** *v.t.* **(a)** aufhalten ‹*Entwicklung*›; zurückwerfen ‹*Projekt, Programm*›
(b) (coll.: cost) kosten ‹*Person*›
(c) (place at a distance) zurücksetzen

■ **set 'down** *v.t.* **(a)** absetzen ‹*Fahrgast*›
(b) (record) niederschreiben

■ **set 'off** **1** *v.i.* (begin journey) aufbrechen; (start to move) loslaufen; ‹*Fahrzeug:*› losfahren
2 *v.t.* **(a)** (cause to explode) explodieren lassen; abbrennen ‹*Feuerwerk*›
(b) auslösen ‹*Reaktion, Alarmanlage*›

■ **set 'out** **1** *v.i.* **(a)** (begin journey) aufbrechen (**for** nach/zu)
(b) ~ out to do sth. sich (*Dat.*) vornehmen, etw. zu tun
2 *v.t.* darlegen

■ **set 'up** **1** *v.t.* **(a)** errichten ‹*Straßensperre, Denkmal*›; aufbauen ‹*Zelt, Klapptisch*›
(b) (establish) gründen ‹*Firma, Organisation*›; einrichten ‹*Büro*›
2 *v.i.* **~ up in business** ein Geschäft aufmachen

'setback *n.* Rückschlag, *der*

settee /se'tiː/ *n.* Sofa, *das*

'setting *n.* **(a)** (Mus.) Vertonung, *die*
(b) (surroundings) Rahmen, *der;* (of novel etc.) Schauplatz, *der*

'setting lotion *n.* Haarfestiger, *der*

settle /'setl/ **1** *v.t.* **(a)** (horizontally) [sorgfältig] legen; (vertically) [sorgfältig] stellen; (at an angle) [sorgfältig] lehnen
(b) (determine, resolve) sich einigen auf ‹*Preis*›; beilegen ‹*Streit, Konflikt, Meinungsverschiedenheit*›; ausräumen ‹*Zweifel*›; entscheiden ‹*Frage, Spiel*›
(c) bezahlen ‹*Rechnung, Betrag*›; erfüllen ‹*Forderung, Anspruch*›; ausgleichen ‹*Konto*›
2 *v.i.* **(a)** (become established) sich niederlassen; (as colonist) sich ansiedeln
(b) (pay) abrechnen
(c) (in chair, in front of fire, etc.) sich

niederlassen; (to work etc.) sich konzentrieren (**to** auf + *Akk.*); (into way of life, retirement, etc.) sich gewöhnen (**into** an + *Akk.*)
(d) (subside) ‹*Haus, Fundament, Boden:*› sich senken
(e) ‹*Schnee:*› liegen bleiben

■ **settle 'down** 1 *v.i.* **(a)** (make oneself comfortable) sich niederlassen (**in** in + *Dat.*)
(b) (in town or house) heimisch werden
2 *v.t.* **(a)** ~ **oneself down** sich [gemütlich] hinsetzen
(b) (calm down) beruhigen

■ **'settle for** *v.t.* (agree to) sich zufrieden geben mit

■ **settle 'in** *v.i.* (in new home) sich einleben

■ **'settle on** *v.t.* (decide on) sich entscheiden für

■ **settle 'up** *v.i.* abrechnen; ~ **up with the waiter** beim Kellner bezahlen

'settlement *n.* **(a)** (of argument, conflict, dispute, differences) Beilegung, *die;* (of question) Klärung, *die;* (of bill, account) Bezahlung, *die;* (of court case) Vergleich, *der*
(b) (colony) Siedlung, *die*

settler /'setlə(r)/ *n.* Siedler, *der*/Siedlerin, *die*

set: ~**-to** *n., pl.* ~**-tos: have a** ~**-to** Streit haben; (with fists) sich prügeln; ~**-up** *n.* System, *das*

seven /'sevn/ 1 *adj.* sieben
2 *n.* Sieben, *die. See also* EIGHT

seventeen /sevn'ti:n/ 1 *adj.* siebzehn
2 *n.* Siebzehn, *die. See also* EIGHT

seventeenth /sevn'ti:nθ/ 1 *adj.* siebzehnt...
2 *n.* (fraction) Siebzehntel, *das. See also* EIGHTH

seventh /'sevnθ/ 1 *adj.* sieb[en]t...
2 *n.* (in sequence, rank) Sieb[en]te, *der/die/das;* (fraction) Sieb[en]tel, *das. See also* EIGHTH

seventieth /'sevntɪɪθ/ *adj.* siebzigst...

seventy /'sevntɪ/ 1 *adj.* siebzig
2 *n.* Siebzig, *die. See also* EIGHT; EIGHTY 2

sever /'sevə(r)/ *v.t.* **(a)** (cut) durchtrennen; (fig.) abbrechen ‹*Beziehungen*›
(b) (separate) abtrennen; (with axe etc.) abhacken

several /'sevrl/ 1 *adv.* mehrere; einige; ~ **times** mehrmals
2 *pron.* einige; ~ **of us** einige von uns; ~ **of the buildings** einige *od.* mehrere [der] Gebäude

severe /sɪ'vɪə(r)/ *adj.,* ~**r** /sɪ'vɪərə(r)/, ~**st** /sɪ'vɪərɪst/ hart ‹*Urteil, Strafe, Kritik, Test, Prüfung*›; streng ‹*Frost, Stil, Schönheit*›; schwer ‹*Dürre, Verlust, Behinderung, Verletzung, Krankheit*›; rau ‹*Wetter*›; heftig ‹*Anfall, Schmerz*›; bedrohlich ‹*Mangel, Knappheit*›; stark ‹*Blutung*›

se'verely *adv.* hart; schwer ‹*verletzt, behindert*›

severity /sɪ'verɪtɪ/ *n.* Strenge, *die;* (of drought, shortage) großes Ausmaß; (of criticism) Schärfe, *die*

sew /səʊ/ *v.t. & i., p.p.* **sewn** /səʊn/ *or* **sewed** /səʊd/ nähen

■ **sew 'on** *v.t.* annähen ‹*Knopf*›; aufnähen ‹*Abzeichen, Band*›

■ **sew 'up** *v.t.* nähen ‹*Saum, Naht, Wunde*›

sewage /'sju:ɪdʒ/ *n.* Abwasser, *das*

'sewage disposal *n.* Abwasserbeseitigung, *die*

sewer /'sju:ə(r), 'su:ə(r)/ *n.* (tunnel) Abwasserkanal, *der;* (pipe) Abwasserleitung, *die*

'sewing *n.* Näharbeit, *die*

'sewing machine *n.* Nähmaschine, *die*

sewn ▸ SEW

sex /seks/ *n.* **(a)** Geschlecht, *das*
(b) (sexuality; coll.: intercourse) Sex, *der* (ugs.); **have** ~ **with sb.** (coll.) mit jmdm. schlafen; Sex mit jmdm. haben (salopp)

sex: ~ **appeal** *n.* Sexappeal, *der;* ~ **change** *n.* Geschlechtsumwandlung, *die;* ~ **discrimination** *n.* sexuelle Diskriminierung; ~ **education** *n.* Sexualerziehung, *die*

sexism /'seksɪzm/ *n.* Sexismus, *der*

sexist /'seksɪst/ *adj.* sexistisch

sex: ~ **life** *n.* Geschlechtsleben, *das;* Sexualleben, *das;* ~ **maniac** *n.* Triebverbrecher, *der;* **you** ~ **maniac!** (coll.) du geiler Bock! (ugs.); ~ **offender** *n.* Sexual[straf]täter, *der*/-täterin, *die*

sexploitation /seksplɔɪ'teɪʃn/ *n.* [kommerzielle] Ausbeutung der Sexualität

sex: ~ **shop** *n.* Sexshop, *der;* ~ **symbol** *n.* Sexidol, *das*

sexual /'sekʃʊəl/ *adj.* sexuell

sexual: ~ **a'buse** *n.* sexueller Missbrauch; ~ **'harassment** *n.* sexuelle Belästigung; ~ **'intercourse** *n.* Geschlechtsverkehr, *der*

sexuality /sekʃʊ'ælɪtɪ/ *n.* Sexualität, *die*

sexual: ~ **'organs** *n. pl.* Geschlechtsorgane *Pl.*; ~ **'partner** *n.* Sexualpartner, *der*/-partnerin, *die*

'sexy *adj.* sexy (ugs.)

sh /ʃ/ *int.* sch; pst

shabbily /'ʃæbɪlɪ/ *adv.,* **shabby** /'ʃæbɪ/ *adj.* schäbig

shack /ʃæk/ *n.* [armselige] Hütte

shackle /'ʃækl/ 1 *n., usu. in pl.* Fessel, *die*
2 *v.t.* anketten (**to** an + *Akk.*)

shade /ʃeɪd/ 1 *n.* **(a)** Schatten, *der*
(b) (colour) Ton, *der;* (fig.) Schattierung, *die*
(c) (lamp~) [Lampen]schirm, *der*
2 *v.t.* **(a)** (screen) beschatten
(b) (darken with lines) ~ **[in]** [ab]schattieren
3 *v.i.* übergehen (**into** in + *Akk.*)

shadow /'ʃædəʊ/ 1 *n.* Schatten, *der*
2 *v.t.* (follow) beschatten

S

'shadowy *adj.* (indistinct) schattenhaft
shady /'ʃeɪdɪ/ *adj.* **(a)** schattig
(b) (disreputable) zwielichtig
shaft /ʃɑːft/ *n.* **(a)** (of tool, golf club) Schaft, *der*
(b) (Mech. Engin.) Welle, *die*
(c) (of mine, lift) Schacht, *der*
(d) (of light, lightning) Strahl, *der*
shaggy /'ʃægɪ/ *adj.* zottelig
shake /ʃeɪk/ **1** *n.* Schütteln, *das;* **give sb./sth. a ~:** jmdn./etw. schütteln
2 *v.t.,* **shook** /ʃʊk/, **shaken** /'ʃeɪkn/ **(a)** (move violently) schütteln; **~ one's fist/a stick at sb.** jmdm. mit der Faust/einem Stock drohen; **~ hands** sich (*Dat.*) die Hand geben
(b) (cause to tremble) erschüttern ‹*Gebäude usw.*›; **~ one's head** den Kopf schütteln
(c) (shock) erschüttern
3 *v.i.,* **shook, shaken** wackeln; ‹*Boden, Stimme:*› beben; ‹*Hand:*› zittern
■ **shake 'off** *v.t.* abschütteln
■ **shake 'up** *v.t.* **(a)** (upset, shock) einen Schrecken einjagen (+ *Dat.*)
(b) (reorganize) umkrempeln (ugs.)
shaken ▶ SHAKE 2, 3
shaky /'ʃeɪkɪ/ *adj.* wack[e]lig ‹*Möbelstück, Leiter*›; zittrig ‹*Hand, Stimme, Greis*›; **feel ~:** sich zittrig fühlen
shall /ʃl, *stressed* ʃæl/ *v. aux. only in pres.* **shall,** *neg.* (coll.) **shan't** /ʃɑːnt/, *past* **should** /ʃəd, *stressed* ʃʊd/, *neg.* (coll.) **shouldn't** /'ʃʊdnt/ **(a)** (expr. simple future) werden
(b) should (expr. conditional) würde/würdest/würden/würdet; **I should have been killed if I had let go** ich wäre getötet worden, wenn ich losgelassen hätte; **if we should be defeated** falls wir unterliegen [sollten]
(c) (expr. will or intention) **what ~ we do?** was sollen wir tun?; **let's go in, ~ we?** gehen wir doch hinein, oder?; **we should be safe by now** jetzt dürften wir in Sicherheit sein; **he shouldn't do things like that!** er sollte so etwas nicht tun!
shallot /ʃə'lɒt/ *n.* Schalotte, *die*
shallow /'ʃæləʊ/ *adj.* seicht ‹*Wasser, Fluss*›; flach ‹*Schüssel, Teller, Wasser*›; (fig.) flach ‹*Person*›
sham /ʃæm/ **1** *adj.* unecht; imitiert ‹*Leder, Holz, Pelz*›
2 *n.* (pretence) Heuchelei, *die;* (person) Heuchler, *der*/Heuchlerin, *die*
3 *v.t.,* **-mm-** vortäuschen
4 *v.i.,* **-mm-** simulieren
shambles /'ʃæmblz/ *n.* (coll.) Chaos, *das;* **the room was a ~:** das Zimmer glich einem Schlachtfeld
shambolic /ʃæm'bɒlɪk/ *adj.* (coll.) chaotisch
shame /ʃeɪm/ *n.* **(a)** Scham, *die*
(b) (state of disgrace) Schande, *die;* **put sb./sth. to ~:** jmdn. beschämen/etw. in den Schatten stellen
(c) what a ~! wie schade!
'shamefaced *adj.* betreten
shameful /'ʃeɪmfl/ *adj.* beschämend
'shameless *adj.* schamlos
shampoo /ʃæm'puː/ **1** *v.t.* schamponieren
2 *n.* Shampoo[n], *das*
shamrock /'ʃæmrɒk/ *n.* Klee, *der*
shandy /'ʃændɪ/ *n.* Bier mit Limonade; Radlermaß, *die* (bes. südd.)
shan't /ʃɑːnt/ (coll.) = **shall not**
shanty¹ /'ʃæntɪ/ *n.* (hut) [armselige] Hütte
shanty² *n.* (song) Shanty, *das*
'shanty town *n.* Bidonville, *das*
shape /ʃeɪp/ **1** *v.t.* formen; bearbeiten ‹*Holz, Stein*› (**into** zu)
2 *n.* Form, *die;* **take ~:** Gestalt annehmen
■ **shape 'up** *v.i.* sich entwickeln
'shapeless *adj.* formlos; unförmig ‹*Kleid, Person*›
shapely /'ʃeɪplɪ/ *adj.* wohlgeformt ‹*Beine, Busen*›; gut ‹*Figur*›
share /ʃeə(r)/ **1** *n.* **(a)** (portion) Teil, *der od. das;* [**fair**] **~:** Anteil, *der;* **fair ~s** gerechte Teile; **do more than one's [fair] ~ of the work** mehr als seinen Teil zur Arbeit beitragen
(b) (Commerc.) Aktie, *die*
2 *v.t.* teilen; gemeinsam tragen ‹*Verantwortung*›
3 *v.i.* **~ in** teilnehmen an (+ *Dat.*); beteiligt sein an (+ *Dat.*) ‹*Gewinn*›; teilen ‹*Freude, Erfahrung*›
■ **share 'out** *v.t.* aufteilen (**among** unter + *Akk.*)
share: ~ certificate *n.* Aktienurkunde, *die;* **~holder** *n.* Aktionär, *der*/Aktionärin, *die;* **~ index** *n.* Aktienindex, *der;* **~-out** *n.* Aufteilung, *die;* **~ware** *n.* (Comp.) Shareware, *die*
shark /ʃɑːk/ *n.* Hai[fisch], *der*
sharp /ʃɑːp/ **1** *adj.* **(a)** scharf; spitz ‹*Nadel, Bleistift, Gipfel, Winkel*›; deutlich ‹*Unterscheidung*›; sauer ‹*Apfel*›; herb ‹*Wein*›; (shrill, piercing) schrill ‹*Schrei, Pfiff*›; heftig ‹*Schmerz, Krampf, Kampf*›; begabt ‹*Schüler, Student*›
(b) (derog.: dishonest) gerissen
(c) (Mus.) [um einen Halbton] erhöht ‹*Note*›
2 *adv.* **(a)** (punctually) **at six o'clock ~:** Punkt sechs Uhr
(b) turn ~ right/left scharf nach rechts/links abbiegen
(c) look ~! halt dich ran! (ugs.)
(d) (Mus.) zu hoch ‹*singen, spielen*›
sharpen /'ʃɑːpn/ *v.t.* schärfen; [an]spitzen ‹*Bleistift*›
'sharpener *n.* (for pencils) Spitzer, *der* (ugs.)
'sharp-eyed *adj.* scharfäugig; **be ~:** scharfe Augen haben
'sharpish *adv.* (coll.) (quickly) rasch; (promptly) unverzüglich; sofort
'sharply *adv.* scharf; in scharfem Ton ‹*antworten*›
'sharpness *n.* Schärfe, *die;* (fineness of point) Spitzheit, *die*
'sharp-witted *adj.* scharfsinnig

shatter /'ʃætə(r)/ [1] *v.t.* zertrümmern; zerbrechen ‹*Glas, Fenster*›; zerschlagen ‹*Hoffnungen*›
[2] *v.i.* zerbrechen

shattered /'ʃætəd/ *adj.* **(a)** zerbrochen ‹*Glas, Fenster*›; (fig.) zerstört ‹*Hoffnungen*›; zerrüttet ‹*Nerven*›
(b) (coll.: greatly upset) **she was ~ by the news** die Nachricht hat sie schwer mitgenommen; **I'm ~!** ich bin ganz erschüttert!; (Brit. coll.: exhausted) ich bin kaputt! (ugs.)

'shattering *adj.* verheerend ‹*Wirkung*›; vernichtend ‹*Schlag, Niederlage*›

shave /ʃeɪv/ [1] *v.t.* rasieren; abrasieren ‹*Haare*›
[2] *v.i.* sich rasieren
[3] *n.* Rasur, *die;* **have a ~**: sich rasieren

■ **shave 'off** *v.t.* abrasieren

'shaven /'ʃeɪvn/ *adj.* rasiert; [kahl] geschoren ‹*Kopf*›

'shaver *n.* Rasierapparat, *der*

'shaver point *n.* Anschluss, *der* für den Rasierapparat

shaving /'ʃeɪvɪŋ/ *n.* **(a)** Rasieren, *das*
(b) *in pl.* (of wood, metal, etc.) Späne *Pl.*

shaving: ~ brush *n.* Rasierpinsel, *der;* **~ cream** *n.* Rasiercreme, *die;* **~ foam** *n.* Rasierschaum, *der* **~ soap** *n.* Rasierseife, *die;* **~ stick** *n.* Stangenrasierseife, *die*

shawl /ʃɔ:l/ *n.* Schultertuch, *das*

she /ʃɪ, *stressed* ʃi:/ *pron.* sie

sheaf /ʃi:f/ *n., pl.* **sheaves** /ʃi:vz/ (of corn etc.) Garbe, *die;* (of paper, arrows, etc.) Bündel, *das*

shear /ʃɪə(r)/ *v.t., p.p.* **shorn** /ʃɔ:n/ *or* **sheared** (clip) scheren

shears /ʃɪəz/ *n. pl.* **[pair of] ~**: Schere, *die;* **garden ~**: Gartenschere, *die*

sheath /ʃi:θ/ *n., pl.* **~s** /ʃi:ðz, ʃi:θs/ **(a)** (for knife, sword, etc.) Scheide, *die*
(b) (condom) Gummischutz, *der*

sheaves *pl. of* SHEAF

shebang /ʃɪ'bæŋ/ *n.* (Amer. coll.) **the whole ~**: der ganze Kram (ugs.)

shed¹ /ʃed/ *v.t.*, **-dd-**, **shed (a)** verlieren; abwerfen ‹*Laub, Geweih*›
(b) vergießen ‹*Blut, Tränen*›
(c) verbreiten ‹*Licht*›

shed² *n.* Schuppen, *der*

she'd /ʃɪd, *stressed* ʃi:d/ **(a)** = **she had;**
(b) = **she would**

sheen /ʃi:n/ *n.* Glanz, *der*

sheep /ʃi:p/ *n., pl. same* Schaf, *das*

sheep: ~ dip *n.* Desinfektionsbad für Schafe; **~dog** *n.* Hütehund, *der;* Schäferhund, *der;* **Old English S~dog** Bobtail, *der*

sheepish /'ʃi:pɪʃ/ *adj.* verlegen

sheep: ~ shearer /'ʃi:p ʃɪərə(r)/ *n.* Schafscherer, *der;* **~-shearing** *n.* Schafschur, *die;* **~skin** *n.* Schaffell, *das*

sheer /ʃɪə(r)/ *adj.* **(a)** rein; blank ‹*Unsinn, Gewalt*›; **by ~ chance** rein zufällig
(b) schroff ‹*Felsen, Abfall*›

sheet /ʃi:t/ *n.* **(a)** Laken, *das*
(b) (of thin metal or plastic) Folie, *die;* (of iron, tin) Blech, *das;* (of glass) Platte, *die;* (of paper) Bogen, *der;* Blatt, *das*

sheet: ~ lightning *n.* Flächenblitz, *der;* **~ music** *n.* Notenblätter *Pl.*

sheik[h] /ʃeɪk, ʃi:k/ *n.* Scheich, *der*

shelf /ʃelf/ *n., pl.* **shelves** /ʃelvz/ Brett, *das;* Bord, *das;* **shelves** (set) Regal, *das*

'shelf life *n.* Lagerfähigkeit, *die*

shell /ʃel/ [1] *n.* **(a)** Schale, *die;* (of snail) Haus, *das;* (of turtle, tortoise) Panzer, *der;* (on beach) Muschel, *die*
(b) (Mil.) (bomb) Granate, *die*
[2] *v.t.* **(a)** (take out of ~) schälen
(b) (Mil.) [mit Artillerie] beschießen

■ **shell 'out** *v.t. & i.* (coll.) blechen (ugs.) (**on** für)

she'll /ʃɪl, *stressed* ʃi:l/ = **she will**

shell: ~fish *n., pl. same* **(a)** Schal[en]tier, *das;* (oyster, clam) Muschel, *die;* (crustacean) Krebstier, *das;* **(b)** *in pl.* (Gastr.) Meeresfrüchte *Pl.;* **~ shock** *n.* Kriegsneurose, *die;* **~ suit** *n.* Trilobalanzug, *der*

shelter /'ʃeltə(r)/ [1] *n.* **(a)** (shield) Schutz, *der* (**against** vor + *Dat.*, gegen); **bomb** *or* **air-raid ~**: Luftschutzraum, *der;* **get under ~**: sich unterstellen
(b) *no pl.* (place of safety) Zuflucht, *die*
[2] *v.t.* schützen (**from** vor + *Dat.*); Unterschlupf gewähren (+ *Dat.*) ‹*Flüchtling*›
[3] *v.i.* Schutz suchen (**from** vor + *Dat.*)

'sheltered /'ʃeltəd/ *adj.* geschützt; behütet ‹*Leben;*› **live in ~ housing** in einer Altenwohnung/in Altenwohnungen leben

shelve /ʃelv/ [1] *v.t.* (defer) auf Eis legen (ugs.)
[2] *v.i.* (slope) abfallen

shelves *pl. of* SHELF

'shelving *n.* Regale *Pl.*

shepherd /'ʃepəd/ [1] *n.* Schäfer, *der*
[2] *v.t.* führen

'shepherdess *n.* Schäferin, *die*

shepherd: ~'s 'crook *n.* Schäferstock, *der;* **~'s 'pie** *n.*: *Auflauf aus Hackfleisch mit einer Schicht Kartoffelbrei darüber*

sheriff /'ʃerɪf/ *n.* Sheriff, *der*

sherry /'ʃerɪ/ *n.* Sherry, *der*

she's /ʃɪz, *stressed* ʃi:z/ **(a)** = **she is;**
(b) = **she has**

Shia(h) /'ʃi:ə/ *n.* (Muslim Relig.) Schia, *die*

shield /ʃi:ld/ [1] *n.* Schild, *der*
[2] *v.t.* schützen (**from** vor + *Dat.*)

shift /ʃɪft/ [1] *v.t.* **(a)** (move) umstellen ‹*Möbel*›; wegnehmen ‹*Arm, Hand, Fuß*›; wegräumen ‹*Schutt*›; entfernen ‹*Schmutz, Fleck*›; **~ the responsibility/blame on to sb.** die Verantwortung/Schuld auf jmdn. schieben

(b) (Amer. Motor Veh.) ~ **gears** schalten
[2] *v.i.* **(a)** ‹*Wind:*› drehen (**to** nach); ‹*Ladung:*› verrutschen
(b) (coll.: move quickly) rasen
[3] *n.* **(a)** a ~ **in emphasis** eine Verlagerung des Akzents; a ~ **in public opinion** ein Umschwung der öffentlichen Meinung
(b) (for work) Schicht, *die;* **eight-hour/late** ~: Achtstunden-/Spätschicht, *die;* **do** *or* **work the late** ~: Spätschicht haben

'shift work *n.* Schichtarbeit, *die*

shifty /'ʃɪftɪ/ *adj.* verschlagen

Shiite /'ʃi:aɪt/ (Muslim Relig.) [1] *n.* Schiitt, *der*/Schiittin, *die*
[2] *adj.* schiitisch

shilling /'ʃɪlɪŋ/ *n.* (Hist.) Shilling, *der*

shilly-shally /'ʃɪlɪʃælɪ/ *v.i.* zaudern; **stop** ~**ing!** entschließ dich endlich!

shimmer /'ʃɪmə(r)/ [1] *v.i.* schimmern
[2] *n.* Schimmer, *der*

shin /ʃɪn/ [1] *n.* Schienbein, *das*
[2] *v.i.,* **-nn-:** ~ **up/down a tree** *etc.* einen Baum *usw.* hinauf-/hinunterklettern

'shin bone *n.* Schienbein, *das*

shine /ʃaɪn/ [1] *v.i.,* **shone** /ʃɒn/ ‹*Lampe, Licht, Stern:*› leuchten; ‹*Sonne, Mond:*› scheinen; (reflect light) glänzen
[2] *v.t.,* **shone:** ~ **a light on sth./in sb.'s eyes** etw. anleuchten/jmdm. in die Augen leuchten
[3] *n.* Glanz, *der*

shingle /'ʃɪŋgl/ *n.* (pebbles) Kies, *der*

'shingles *n.* (Med.) Gürtelrose, *die*

shin: ~ **guard,** ~ **pad** *ns.* Schienbeinschutz, *der*

shiny /'ʃaɪnɪ/ *adj.* glänzend

ship /ʃɪp/ [1] *n.* Schiff, *das*
[2] *v.t.,* **-pp-** (transport by sea) verschiffen; (send by road, train, or air) verschicken ‹*Waren*›

'shipbuilding *n.* Schiffbau, *der*

'shipment *n.* **(a)** Versand, *der;* (by sea) Verschiffung, *die*
(b) (amount) Sendung, *die*

'shipowner *n.* Schiffseigentümer, *der*/-eigentümerin, *die;* (of several ships) Reeder, *der*/Reederin, *die*

'shipper *n.* Spediteur, *der*/Spediteurin, *die;* (company) Spedition, *die*

'shipping *n.* **(a)** (ships) Schiffe *Pl.;* (traffic) Schifffahrt, *die*
(b) (transporting) Versand, *der*

shipping: ~ **agent** *n.* Schiffsagent, *der;* ~ **forecast** *n.* Seewetterbericht, *der;* ~ **lane** *n.* Schifffahrtsweg, *der*

ship: ~**shape** *adj.* in bester Ordnung; ~**wreck** [1] *n.* Schiffbruch, *der;* [2] *v.t.* **be** ~**wrecked** Schiffbruch erleiden; ~**yard** *n.* [Schiffs]werft, *die*

shirk /ʃɜ:k/ *v.t.* sich drücken vor (+ *Dat.*)

'shirker *n.* Drückeberger, *der*/Drückebergerin, *die* (ugs.)

shirt /ʃɜ:t/ *n.* **[man's]** ~: [Herren- *od.* Ober]hemd, *das*

'shirtsleeve *n.* Hemdsärmel, *der;* **in** ~**s** in Hemdsärmeln

shit /ʃɪt/ (coarse) [1] *v.i.,* **-tt-, shitted** *or* **shit** scheißen (derb)
[2] *n.* **(a)** Scheiße, *die* (derb); **have** (Brit.) *or* (Amer.) **take a** ~: scheißen (derb)
(b) (person) Scheißkerl, *der* (derb)
(c) (nonsense) Scheiß, *der* (salopp)

shiver /'ʃɪvə(r)/ [1] *v.i.* zittern (**with** vor + *Dat.*)
[2] *n.* Schau[d]er, *der* (geh.)

shoal /ʃəʊl/ *n.* (of fish) Schwarm, *der*

shock /ʃɒk/ [1] *n.* **(a)** Schock, *der;* **give sb. a** ~: jmdm. einen Schock versetzen
(b) (violent impact) Erschütterung, *die* (**of** durch)
(c) (Electr.) Schlag, *der*
(d) (Med.) Schock, *der*
[2] *v.t.* ~ **sb. [deeply]** ein [schwerer] Schock für jmdn. sein; (scandalize) jmdn. schockieren

'shock absorber *n.* Stoßdämpfer, *der*

'shocking *adj.* **(a)** schockierend
(b) (coll.: very bad) fürchterlich (ugs.)

shock: ~ **jock** *n.* (coll.) Skandal-DJ, *der;* ~**proof** *adj.* stoßfest; ~ **wave** *n.* Druckwelle, *die* (**from** *Gen.*); (of earthquake) Erschütterungswelle, *die* (**from** *Gen.*)

shod ▶ SHOE 2

shoddy /'ʃɒdɪ/ *adj.* schäbig; minderwertig ‹*Arbeit, Stoff, Artikel*›

shoe /ʃu:/ [1] *n.* Schuh, *der;* (of horse) [Huf]eisen, *das;* **put oneself into sb.'s** ~**s** (fig.) sich in jmds. Lage (*Akk.*) versetzen
[2] *v.t.,* ~**ing, shod** /ʃɒd/ beschlagen ‹*Pferd*›

shoe: ~**horn** *n.* Schuhlöffel, *der;* ~**lace** *n.* Schnürsenkel, *der;* ~**maker** *n.* Schuhmacher, *der;* ~ **polish** *n.* Schuhcreme, *die;* ~ **shop** *n.* Schuhgeschäft, *das;* ~**string** *n.* **on a** ~**string** (coll.) mit ganz wenig Geld

shone ▶ SHINE 1, 2

shoo /ʃu:/ [1] *int.* sch
[2] *v.t.* scheuchen; ~ **away** fortscheuchen

shook ▶ SHAKE 2, 3

shoot /ʃu:t/ [1] *v.i.,* **shot** /ʃɒt/ **(a)** schießen (**at** auf + *Akk.*)
(b) (move rapidly) schießen (ugs.)
[2] *v.t.,* **shot (a)** (wound) anschießen; (kill) erschießen; (hunt) schießen; ~ **sb. dead** jmdn. erschießen
(b) schießen mit ‹*Bogen, Munition, Pistole*›; abschießen ‹*Pfeil, Kugel*› (**at** auf + *Akk.*)
(c) (Cinemat.) drehen ‹*Film, Szene*›
[3] *n.* (Bot.) Trieb, *der*

■ **shoot 'down** *v.t.* niederschießen ‹*Person*›; abschießen ‹*Flugzeug*›

■ **shoot 'out** *v.i.* hervorschießen

■ **shoot 'up** *v.i.* in die Höhe schießen; ‹*Preise, Kosten, Temperatur:*› in die Höhe schnellen

shooting: ~ **range** *n.* Schießstand, *der;* ~ **'star** *n.* Sternschnuppe, *die*

'shoot-out *n.* Schießerei, *die*

shop /ʃɒp/ 1 *n.* Laden, *der;* Geschäft, *das;* **go to the ~s** einkaufen gehen; **talk ~:** fachsimpeln (ugs.)
2 *v.i.*, **-pp-** einkaufen; **go ~ping** einkaufen gehen

■ **shop a'round** *v.i.* sich umsehen (for nach)

shopaholic /'ʃɒpəhɒlɪk/ *n.* Kaufsüchtige, *der/die*

shop: ~ assistant *n.* (Brit.) Verkäufer, *der*/Verkäuferin, *die;* **~front** *n.* Schaufensterfront, *die;* **~keeper** *n.* Ladenbesitzer, *der*/-besitzerin, *die;* **~lifter** *n.* Ladendieb, *der*/-diebin, *die;* **~lifting** *n.* Ladendiebstahl, *der;* **~owner** ▶ ~KEEPER

'shopper *n.* Käufer, *der*/Käuferin, *die*

'shopping *n.* **(a)** Einkaufen, *das;* **do the/one's ~:** einkaufen/[seine] Einkäufe machen
(b) (items bought) Einkäufe *Pl.*

shopping: ~ bag *n.* Einkaufstasche, *die;* **~ basket** *n.* Einkaufskorb, *der;* **~ centre** *n.* Einkaufszentrum, *das;* **~ list** *n.* Einkaufszettel, *der;* **~ mall** /-mæl/ *n.* Einkaufszentrum, *das;* **~ precinct** *n.* Einkaufs- *od.* Geschäftsviertel, *das;* **~ street** *n.* Geschäftsstraße, *die;* **~ trolley** *n.* (in supermarket) Einkaufswagen, *der;* (personal) Einkaufsroller, *der*

shop: ~-soiled *adj.* (Brit.) (slightly damaged) leicht beschädigt; (slightly dirty) angeschmutzt; **~ steward** *n.* [gewerkschaftlicher] Vertrauensmann; **~ 'window** *n.* Schaufenster, *das*

shore /ʃɔ:(r)/ *n.* Ufer, *das;* (beach) Strand, *der*

■ **shore 'up** *v.t.* abstützen ‹*Mauer, Haus*›; (fig.) stützen

shorn ▶ SHEAR

short /ʃɔ:t/ 1 *adj.* **(a)** kurz; **in a ~ time** *or* **while** (soon) bald; in Kürze; **a ~ time** *or* **while ago/later** vor kurzem/kurze Zeit später; **in ~, ...:** kurz, ...
(b) klein ‹*Person, Wuchs*›
(c) (deficient, scanty) knapp; **go ~ [of sth.]** [an etw. (*Dat.*)] Mangel leiden; **sb. is ~ of sth.** jmdm. fehlt es an etw. (*Dat.*); **time is getting/is ~:** die Zeit wird/ist knapp; **be in ~ supply** knapp sein; **be ~ [of cash]** knapp [bei Kasse] sein (ugs.)
2 *adv.* **(a)** (abruptly) plötzlich; **stop ~:** plötzlich abbrechen; **stop sb. ~:** jmdm. ins Wort fallen
(b) stop ~ of doing sth. nicht so weit gehen, etw. zu tun

shortage /'ʃɔ:tɪdʒ/ *n.* Mangel, *der* (**of** an + *Dat.*); **~ of fruit/teachers** Obstknappheit, *die*/Lehrermangel, *der*

short: ~bread *n.* Shortbread, *das; Kekse aus Butterteig;* **~ 'circuit** *n.* (Electr.) Kurzschluss, *der;* **~coming** *n., usu. in pl.* Unzulänglichkeit, *die;* **~ 'cut** *n.* **(a)** Abkürzung, *die;* **take a ~ cut** den Weg abkürzen; **(b)** (Comp.) **[keyboard] ~cut** Shortcut, *der*

shorten /'ʃɔ:tn/ 1 *v.i.* kürzer werden
2 *v.t.* kürzen; verkürzen ‹*Besuch, Wartezeit*›

short: ~fall *n.* Fehlmenge, *die;* **~-haired** *adj.* kurzhaarig; Kurzhaar‹*dackel, -katze*›; **~hand** *n.* Stenografie, *die;* **~hand typist** Stenotypist, *der*/-typistin, *die;* **~ list** *n.* (Brit.) engere Auswahl; **be on/put sb. on the ~ list** in der engeren Auswahl sein/jmdn. in die engere Auswahl nehmen; **~-list** *v.t.* in die engere Auswahl nehmen; **~-lived** *adj.* kurzlebig

'shortly *adv.* in Kürze; demnächst; **~ before/after sth.** kurz vor/nach etw.

short: ~ 'pastry *n.* Mürbeteig, *der;* **~-range** *adj.* **(a)** Kurzstrecken‹*flugzeug, -rakete usw.*›; **(b)** (relating to time) kurzfristig

shorts /ʃɔ:ts/ *n. pl.* **(a)** (trousers) kurze Hose[n *Pl.*]; Shorts *Pl.*
(b) (Amer.: underpants) Unterhose, *die*

short: ~-'sighted *adj.* kurzsichtig; **~-sleeved** /'-sli:vd/ *adj.* kurzärm[e]lig; **~-staffed** /-'sta:ft/ *adj.* **be [very] ~-staffed** [viel] zu wenig Personal haben; **~ 'story** *n.* Kurzgeschichte, *die;* **~-'tempered** *adj.* aufbrausend; **~-term** *adj.* kurzfristig; (provisional) vorläufig ‹*Lösung*›; befristet ‹*Vertrag*›; **~ 'trousers** *n. pl.* kurze Hose[n *Pl.*]; **~ wave** *n.* (Radio) Kurzwelle, *die*

shot /ʃɒt/ 1 *n.* **(a)** Schuss, *der;* **fire a ~:** einen Schuss abgeben (**at** auf + *Akk.*); **like a ~** (fig.) wie der Blitz (ugs.); **I'd do it like a ~:** ich würde es auf der Stelle tun
(b) (Athletics) **put the ~:** die Kugel stoßen; **[putting] the ~:** Kugelstoßen, *das*
(c) (Sport: stroke, kick, throw) Schuss, *der*
(d) (Photog.) Aufnahme, *die;* (Cinemat.) Einstellung, *die*
2 ▶ SHOOT 1, 2
3 *adj.* **be/get ~ of** (coll.) los sein/loswerden

'shotgun *n.* [Schrot]flinte, *die*

should ▶ SHALL

shoulder /'ʃəʊldə(r)/ 1 *n.* Schulter, *die*
2 *v.t.* schultern; (fig.) übernehmen

shoulder: ~ bag *n.* Umhängetasche, *die;* **~ blade** *n.* Schulterblatt, *das;* **~ joint** *n.* Schultergelenk, *das;* **~-length** *adj.* schulterlang; **~ pad** *n.* Schulterpolster, *das;* **~ strap** *n.* (on garment) Schulterklappe, *die;* (on bag) Tragriemen, *der*

shouldn't /'ʃʊdnt/ (coll.) = **should not;** ▶ SHALL

shout /ʃaʊt/ 1 *n.* Ruf, *der;* (inarticulate) Schrei, *der*
2 *v.i. & t.* schreien

■ **shout 'down** *v.t.* niederschreien

■ **shout 'out** 1 *v.i.* aufschreien
2 *v.t.* [laut] rufen

'shouting *n.* Geschrei, *das*

shove /ʃʌv/ 1 *n.* Stoß, *der*
2 *v.t.* stoßen; schubsen (ugs.); (coll.: put) tun ···

■ **shove a'way** *v.t.* (coll.) wegschubsen (ugs.)
■ **shove 'off** *v.i.* (coll.: leave) abschieben (ugs.)

shovel /'ʃʌvl/ [1] *n.* Schaufel, *die*
[2] *v.t.*, (Brit.) **-ll-** schaufeln

show /ʃəʊ/ [1] *n.* **(a)** (entertainment, performance) Show, *die;* (Theatre) Vorstellung, *die;* (Radio, Telev.) [Unterhaltungs]sendung, *die*
(b) (exhibition) Ausstellung, *die;* Schau, *die;* **put sth. on ~:** etw. ausstellen; **be on ~:** ausgestellt sein
(c) (appearance) Anschein, *der;* **be for ~:** reine Angeberei sein (ugs.)
[2] *v.t.*, *p.p.* **shown** /ʃəʊn/ **(a)** zeigen; vorzeigen ‹*Pass, Fahrschein usw.*›; **~ sb. sth., ~ sth. to sb.** jmdm. etw. zeigen
(b) beweisen ‹*Mut, Urteilsvermögen usw.*›; **~ sb. that ...:** jmdm. beweisen, dass ...; **~ [sb.] kindness/mercy** freundlich [zu jmdm.] sein/Erbarmen [mit jmdm.] haben
(c) ‹*Thermometer, Uhr usw.:*› anzeigen
(d) (exhibit in a show) ausstellen; zeigen ‹*Film*›
[3] *v.i.*, *p.p.* **shown (a)** (be visible) sichtbar *od.* zu sehen sein; (come into sight) sich zeigen
(b) (be ~n) ‹*Film:*› laufen; ‹*Künstler:*› ausstellen
■ **show 'in** *v.t.* hinein-/hereinführen
■ **show 'off** *v.i.* angeben (ugs.); prahlen
■ **show 'out** *v.t.* hinausführen
■ **show 'round** *v.t.* herumführen
■ **show 'through** *v.i.* durchscheinen
■ **show 'up** [1] *v.t.* **(a)** (make visible) [deutlich] sichtbar machen
(b) (coll.: embarrass) blamieren
[2] *v.i.* **(a)** (be visible) [deutlich] zu sehen sein
(b) (coll.: arrive) sich blicken lassen (ugs.)

show: ~ biz (coll.)**, ~ business** *ns., no art.* Schaugeschäft, *das;* **~case** *n.* Vitrine, *die;* (fig.) Schaufenster, *das;* **'~down** *n.* (fig.) Kraftprobe, *die;* **have a ~down [with sb.]** sich [mit jmdm.] auseinander setzen

shower /'ʃaʊə(r)/ [1] *n.* **(a)** Schauer, *der;* **~ of rain/hail** Regen-/Hagelschauer, *der*
(b) (for washing) Dusche, *die;* **have** *or* **take a [cold/quick] ~:** [kalt/schnell] duschen
[2] *v.t.* (lavish) **~ sth. [up]on sb., ~ sb. with sth.** jmdn. mit etw. überhäufen
[3] *v.i.* (have a ~) duschen

shower: ~ cap *n.* Duschhaube, *die;* **~ curtain** *n.* Duschvorhang, *der;* **~ gel** *n.* Duschgel, *das;* **~proof** *adj.* [bedingt] regendicht

'showery *adj.* **it is ~:** es gibt immer wieder kurze Schauer; **a ~ day** ein Tag mit Schauerwetter

'showjumping *n.* Springreiten, *das*

shown ▶ SHOW 2, 3

show: ~-off *n.* (coll.) Angeber, *der*/Angeberin, *die;* **~piece** *n.* (of exhibition, collection) Schaustück, *das;* (highlight) Paradestück, *das;* **~room** *n.* Ausstellungsraum, *der;* **~ trial** *n.* Schauprozess, *der*

'showy *adj.* protzig (ugs.)

shrank ▶ SHRINK

shred /ʃred/ [1] *n.* Fetzen, *der;* (fig.) Spur, *die;* **tear sth. to ~s** etw. zerfetzen; (fig.) etw. zerpflücken
[2] *v.t.*, **-dd-** [im Reißwolf] zerkleinern

shredder /'ʃredə(r)/ *n.* (for paper) Reißwolf, *der*

shrew /ʃru:/ *n.* (Zool.) Spitzmaus, *die*

shrewd /ʃru:d/ *adj.* klug; genau ‹*[Ein]schätzung*›

shriek /ʃri:k/ [1] *n.* [Auf]schrei, *der*
[2] *v.i.* [auf]schreien
[3] *v.t.* schreien

shrift /ʃrɪft/ *n.* **give sb. short ~:** jmdn. kurz abfertigen (ugs.); **get short ~** kurz abgefertigt werden (ugs.)

shrill /ʃrɪl/ *adj.* schrill

shrimp /ʃrɪmp/ *n.* Garnele, *die*

shrine /ʃraɪn/ *n.* (tomb) Grab, *das*

shrink /ʃrɪŋk/ [1] *v.i.*, **shrank** /ʃræŋk/, **shrunk** /ʃrʌŋk/ **(a)** schrumpfen; ‹*Kleidung, Stoff:*› einlaufen; ‹*Metall, Holz:*› sich zusammenziehen
(b) (recoil) **~ from sb./sth.** vor jmdm. zurückweichen/vor etw. (*Dat.*) zurückschrecken; **~ from doing sth.** sich scheuen, etw. zu tun
[2] *v.t.*, **shrank, shrunk** einlaufen lassen ‹*Textilien*›

shrinkage /'ʃrɪŋkɪdʒ/ *n.* (of clothing) Einlaufen, *das*

shrink: ~-proof, ~-resistant *adjs.* schrumpffrei; **be ~-proof** nicht einlaufen; **~-wrap** *v.t.* in einer Schrumpffolie verpacken

shrivel /'ʃrɪvl/ *v.i.*, (Brit.) **-ll-: ~ [up]** verschrumpeln; ‹*Pflanze, Blume:*› welk werden

shroud /ʃraʊd/ [1] *n.* Leichentuch, *das*
[2] *v.t.* **~ sth. in sth.** etw. in etw. (*Akk.*) hüllen

Shrove 'Tuesday /ʃrəʊv/ *n.* Fastnachtsdienstag, *der*

shrub /ʃrʌb/ *n.* Strauch, *der*

shrubbery /'ʃrʌbərɪ/ *n.* Gesträuch, *das*

shrug /ʃrʌg/ [1] *v.t. & i.*, **-gg-: ~ [one's shoulders]** die Achseln zucken
[2] *n.* **~ [of one's** *or* **the shoulders]** Achselzucken, *das*
■ **shrug 'off** *v.t.* in den Wind schlagen

shrunk ▶ SHRINK

shrunken /'ʃrʌŋkn/ *adj.* verhutzelt (ugs.) ‹*Person*›; schrump[e]lig ‹*Apfel*›

shudder /'ʃʌdə(r)/ [1] *v.i.* zittern (**with** vor + *Dat.*)
[2] *n.* Zittern, *das*

shuffle /'ʃʌfl/ [1] *n.* **(a)** Schlurfen, *das;* **walk with a ~:** schlurfen
(b) (Cards) Mischen, *das;* **give the cards a [good] ~:** die Karten [gut] mischen
[2] *v.t.* **(a)** (Cards) mischen

(b) ~ **one's feet** von einem Fuß auf den anderen treten

shun /ʃʌn/ *v.t.*, **-nn-** meiden

shunt /ʃʌnt/ *v.t.* (Railw.) rangieren

shush /ʃʊʃ/ *int.* still

shut /ʃʌt/ [1] *v.t.*, **-tt-**, **shut** zumachen; schließen; zusammenklappen ‹*Klappmesser, Fächer*›; ~ **one's finger in the door** sich (*Dat.*) den Finger in der Tür einklemmen [2] *v.i.*, **-tt-**, **shut** schließen; ‹*Blüte:*› sich schließen

▪ **shut 'down** [1] *v.t.* **(a)** schließen, zumachen ‹*Deckel*› **(b)** stilllegen ‹*Fabrik*›; abschalten ‹*Kernreaktor*› [2] *v.i.* ‹*Laden, Fabrik:*› geschlossen werden

▪ **shut 'out** *v.t.* aussperren

▪ **shut 'up** [1] *v.t.* abschließen; einsperren ‹*Tier, Person*› [2] *v.i.* (coll.: be quiet) den Mund halten

shutter /'ʃʌtə(r)/ *n.* **(a)** [Fenster]laden, *der* **(b)** (Photog.) Verschluss, *der;* ~ **release** Auslöser, *der;* ~ **speed** Verschlusszeit, *die*

shuttle /'ʃʌtl/ [1] *n.* (in loom) Schiffchen, *das* [2] *v.i.* pendeln

shuttle: ~**cock** *n.* Federball, *der;* '~ **service** *n.* Pendelverkehr, *der*

shy /ʃaɪ/ *adj.*, ~**er** *or* **shier** /'ʃaɪə(r)/, ~**est** *or* **shiest** /'ʃaɪɪst/ scheu; (diffident) schüchtern

▪ **shy a'way** *v.i.* ~ **away from sth./doing sth.** etw. scheuen/sich scheuen, etw. zu tun

'shyness *n.* Scheuheit, *die;* (diffidence) Schüchternheit, *die*

Siamese /saɪə'mi:z/**:** ~ **'cat** *n.* Siamkatze, *die;* ~ **'twins** *n. pl.* siamesische Zwillinge *Pl.*

Siberia /saɪ'bɪərɪə/ *pr. n.* Sibirien (*das*)

sibling /'sɪblɪŋ/ *n.* (male) Bruder, *der;* (female) Schwester, *die; in pl.* Geschwister *Pl.*

Sicily /'sɪsɪlɪ/ *pr. n.* Sizilien (*das*)

sick /sɪk/ [1] *adj.* **(a)** (ill) krank; **be off** ~: krank [gemeldet] sein **(b)** (Brit.: vomiting or about to vomit) **be** ~: sich erbrechen; **I'm going to be** ~: ich muss mich erbrechen; **sb. gets/feels** ~: jmdm. wird/ist [es] übel *od.* schlecht; **be/get** ~ **of sb./sth.** (fig.) jmdn./etw. satt haben/ allmählich satt haben; **make sb.** ~ (disgust) jmdn. anekeln [2] *n. pl.* **the** ~: die Kranken *Pl.*

sick 'building syndrome *n.* Sickbuildingsyndrom, *das*

'sicken /'sɪkn/ [1] *v.i.* **be** ~**ing for sth.** (Brit.) krank werden; etw. ausbrüten (ugs.) [2] *v.t.* (disgust) anwidern

'sickening *adj.* Ekel erregend, widerlich ‹*Anblick, Geruch*›

sickle /'sɪkl/ *n.* Sichel, *die*

sick: ~ **leave** *n.* Urlaub wegen Krankheit; **be on** ~ ≈ krank geschrieben sein; ~ **list** *n.* Liste der Kranken, *die;* **on the** ~ **list:** krank [gemeldet/geschrieben]

'sickly *adj.* kränklich

'sickness *n.* Krankheit, *die;* (nausea) Übelkeit, *die*

sick: ~ **pay** *n.* Entgeltfortzahlung im Krankheitsfalle; (paid by insurance) Krankengeld, *das;* ~**room** *n.* Krankenzimmer, *das*

side /saɪd/ [1] *n.* **(a)** Seite, *die;* ~ **of beef** Rinderhälfte, *die;* ~ **of bacon** Speckseite, *die;* **walk/stand** ~ **by** ~: nebeneinander gehen/stehen; **work/fight** ~ **by** ~ **[with sb.]** Seite an Seite [mit jmdm.] arbeiten/ kämpfen; **live** ~ **by** ~ **[with sb.]** in [jmds.] unmittelbarer Nachbarschaft leben; **to one** ~: zur Seite; **on one** ~: an der Seite; **on the** ~ (as ~line) nebenbei; **take** ~**s [with/against sb.]** [für/gegen jmdn.] Partei ergreifen **(b)** (Sport: team) Mannschaft, *die* [2] *v.i.* ~ **with sb.** sich auf jmds. Seite (*Akk.*) stellen [3] *adj.* Seiten-

side: ~**board** *n.* Anrichte, *die;* ~**boards** (coll.)**,** ~**burns** *ns. pl.* (on cheeks) Backenbart, *der;* (in front of the ears) Koteletten *Pl.;* ~**car** *n.* Beiwagen, *der;* ~ **dish** *n.* Beilage, *die;* ~ **door** *n.* Seitentür, *die;* ~ **effect** *n.* Nebenwirkung, *die;* ~ **entrance** *n.* Seiteneingang, *der;* ~ **exit** *n.* Seitenausgang, *der;* ~ **issue** *n.* Randproblem, *das;* ~**kick** *n.* (coll.) Kumpan, *der;* ~**light** *n.* Begrenzungsleuchte, *die;* **drive on** ~**lights** mit Standlicht fahren; ~**line** *n.* (occupation) Nebenbeschäftigung, *die;* ~**long** *adj.* **a** ~**long look/glance** ein Seitenblick; ~ **plate** *n.* kleiner Teller (neben dem Teller für das Hauptgericht); ~ **road** *n.* Seitenstraße, *die;* ~**-saddle** *adv.* **ride** ~**-saddle** im Damensitz reiten; ~ **salad** *n.* Salat [als Beilage]; **steak with chips and a** ~ **salad** Steak mit Pommes frites und dazu ein Salat; ~**show** *n.* Nebenattraktion, *die;* ~**step** [1] *n.* Schritt zur Seite; [2] *v.t.* ausweichen (+ *Dat.*); ~ **street** *n.* Seitenstraße, *die;* ~ **table** *n.* Beistelltisch, *der;* ~**track** *v.t.* **get** ~**tracked** abgelenkt werden; ~**walk** *n.* (Amer.) Bürgersteig, *der;* ~**ways** /'saɪdweɪz/ [1] *adv.* **look at sb./sth.** ~**ways** jmdn./etw. von der Seite ansehen; [2] *adj.* seitlich; ~ **wind** *n.* Seitenwind, *der*

siding /'saɪdɪŋ/ *n.* Abstellgleis, *das*

sidle /'saɪdl/ *v.i.* schleichen **[up to** zu**]**

siege /si:dʒ/ *n.* Belagerung, *die;* (by police) Umstellung, *die;* **lay** ~ **to sth.** etw. belagern

siesta /sɪ'estə/ *n.* Siesta, *die*

sieve /sɪv/ [1] *n.* Sieb, *das* [2] *v.t.* sieben

sift /sɪft/ *v.t.* sieben; ~ **sth. from sth.** etw. von etw. trennen

▪ **sift 'out** *v.t.* aussieben

sigh /saɪ/ [1] *n.* Seufzer, *der;* **breathe** *or* **give** *or* **heave a** ~: einen Seufzer ausstoßen; ~ **of relief/contentment** Seufzer der Erleichterung/Zufriedenheit [2] *v.i.* seufzen; ~ **with relief/despair** erleichtert/verzweifelt seufzen

S

sight /saɪt/ [1] *n.* **(a)** (faculty) Sehvermögen, *das;* **know sb. by ~:** jmdn. vom Sehen kennen
(b) (act of seeing; spectacle) Anblick, *der;* **catch/lose ~ of sb./sth.** jmdn./etw. erblicken/aus dem Auge verlieren; **at first ~:** auf den ersten Blick
(c) *in pl.* **~s** (places of interest) Sehenswürdigkeiten *Pl.*; **see the ~s** die Sehenswürdigkeiten besichtigen
(d) (range) Sichtweite, *die;* **in ~:** in Sicht; **within** *or* **in ~ of sb./sth.** (able to see) in jmds. Sichtweite (*Dat.*)/in Sichtweite einer Sache; **out of ~:** außer Sicht
(e) (of gun) Visier, *das;* **set/have [set] one's ~s on sth.** (fig.) etw. anpeilen
[2] *v.t.* sichten ‹*Land, Schiff, Flugzeug*›; sehen ‹*Entflohenen, Vermissten*›

sighted /'saɪtɪd/ *adj.* sehend; **partially ~:** [hochgradig] sehbehindert

'sighting *n.* Beobachtung, *die*

sight-read (Mus.) *v.t. & i.* ‹*Pianist usw.:*› vom Blatt spielen; ‹*Sänger:*› vom Blatt singen

'sightseeing *n.* **go ~:** Besichtigungen machen

sightseer /'saɪtsi:ə(r)/ *n.* Tourist (*der die Sehenswürdigkeiten besichtigt*)

sign /saɪn/ [1] *n.* **(a)** (symbol, signal, indication) Zeichen, *das;* (of future event) Anzeichen, *das;* **as a ~ of** als Zeichen (+ *Gen.*)
(b) (Astrol.) **~ [of the zodiac]** Sternzeichen, *das*
(c) (notice; on shop etc.) Schild, *das*
[2] *v.t. & i.* unterschreiben; **~ one's name** [mit seinem Namen] unterschreiben

■ **sign 'on** *v.i.* (as unemployed) sich arbeitslos melden

■ **sign 'up** *v.i.* sich [vertraglich] verpflichten (**with** bei); (for course) sich einschreiben

signal /'sɪgnl/ [1] *n.* Signal, *das;* **a ~ for sth./to sb.** ein Zeichen zu etw./für jmdn
[2] *v.i.,* (Brit.) **-ll-** signalisieren; Signale geben; ‹*Kraftfahrer:*› blinken; (with hand) anzeigen; **~ to sb. [to do sth.]** jmdm. ein Zeichen geben[, etw. zu tun]

signal: ~ box *n.* Stellwerk, *das;* **~ man** /-mən/ *n.* Bahnwärter, *der*

signature /'sɪgnətʃə(r)/ *n.* Unterschrift, *die;* (on painting) Signatur, *die*

'signature tune *n.* Erkennungsmelodie, *die*

'signboard *n.* Schild, *das*

signet ring /'sɪgnɪt rɪŋ/ *n.* Siegelring, *der*

significance /sɪg'nɪfɪkəns/ *n.* Bedeutung, *die;* **be of [no] ~:** [nicht] von Bedeutung sein

significant /sɪg'nɪfɪkənt/ *adj.* **(a)** (noteworthy, important) bedeutend
(b) (full of meaning) bedeutsam

sig'nificantly *adv.* **(a)** (meaningfully) bedeutungsvoll; **~ [enough]** bedeutsamerweise
(b) (notably) bedeutend

signify /'sɪgnɪfaɪ/ *v.t.* bedeuten

sign: ~ language *n.* Zeichensprache, *die;* **~post** *n.* Wegweiser, *der;* **~writer** *n.* Schildermaler, *der*

Sikh /si:k, sɪk/ *n.* Sikh, *der*

silence /'saɪləns/ [1] *n.* Schweigen, *das;* (keeping a secret) Verschwiegenheit, *die;* (stillness) Stille, *die;* **there was ~:** es herrschte Schweigen/Stille; **in ~:** schweigend
[2] *v.t.* zum Schweigen bringen; (fig.) ersticken ‹*Proteste*›; mundtot machen ‹*Gegner*›

'silencer *n.* (on gun; Brit. Motor Veh.) Schalldämpfer, *der*

silent /'saɪlənt/ *adj.* stumm; (noiseless) unhörbar; (still) still; **be ~** (say nothing) schweigen; **~ film** Stummfilm, *der*

'silently *adv.* schweigend; stumm ‹*weinen, beten*›; (noiselessly) lautlos

silent ma'jority *n.* schweigende Mehrheit

silhouette /sɪlʊ'et/ [1] *n.* **(a)** (picture) Schattenriss, *der*
(b) (appearance against the light) Silhouette, *die*
[2] *v.t.* **be ~d against sth.** sich als Silhouette gegen etw. abheben

silicon /'sɪlɪkən/ *n.* Silicium, *das;* **~ chip** Siliciumchip, *der*

silicone /'sɪlɪkəʊn/ *n.* Silikon, *das;* **~ implant** Silikonimplantat, *das*

silk /sɪlk/ [1] *n.* Seide, *die*
[2] *attrib. adj.* seiden; Seiden-

'silkworm *n.* Seidenraupe, *die*

'silky *adj.* seidig

sill /sɪl/ *n.* (of door) [Tür]schwelle, *die;* (of window) Fensterbank, *die*

silly /'sɪlɪ/ *adj.* dumm; (imprudent, unwise) töricht; (childish) albern

silo /'saɪləʊ/ *n., pl.* **~s** Silo, *der*

silt /sɪlt/ *n.* Schlamm, *der;* Schlick, *der*

silver /'sɪlvə(r)/ [1] *n.* Silber, *das*
[2] *attrib. adj.* silbern; Silber‹*pokal, -münze*›

silver: ~ 'jubilee *n.* silbernes Jubiläum; **~ 'medal** *n.* Silbermedaille, *die;* **~ 'paper** *n.* Silberpapier, *das;* **~-plated** *adj.* versilbert; **~smith** *n.* Silberschmied, *der*/-schmiedin, *die;* **~ 'wedding** *n.* Silberhochzeit, *die*

SIM card /'sɪm kɑ:d/ *n.* SIM-Karte, *die*

similar /'sɪmɪlə(r)/ *adj.* ähnlich (**to** *Dat.*)

similarity /sɪmɪ'lærɪtɪ/ *n.* Ähnlichkeit, *die* (**to** mit)

'similarly *adv.* ähnlich; (in exactly the same way) ebenso

simile /'sɪmɪlɪ/ *n.* Vergleich, *der*

simmer /'sɪmə(r)/ [1] *v.i.* ‹*Flüssigkeit:*› sieden; ziehen
[2] *v.t.* köcheln *od.* ziehen lassen

■ **simmer 'down** *v.i.* sich abregen (ugs.)

simper /'sɪmpə(r)/ *v.i.* affektiert *od.* gekünstelt lächeln

simple /'sɪmpl/ *adj.* einfach; (unsophisticated, not elaborate) schlicht ‹*Mobiliar, Schönheit,*

Kunstwerk, Kleidung›; **it was a ~ misunderstanding** es war [ganz] einfach ein Missverständnis

'simple-minded *adj.* **(a)** (unsophisticated) schlicht
(b) (unintelligent) beschränkt

simpleton /'sɪmpltən/ *n.* Einfaltspinsel, *der* (ugs.)

simplicity /sɪm'plɪsɪtɪ/ *n.* Einfachheit, *die;* (unpretentiousness, lack of sophistication) Schlichtheit, *die*

simplification /sɪmplɪfɪ'keɪʃn/ *n.* Vereinfachung, *die*

simplify /'sɪmplɪfaɪ/ *v.t.* vereinfachen

simplistic /sɪm'plɪstɪk/ *adj.* [all]zu simpel

simply /'sɪmplɪ/ *adv.* einfach; (in an unsophisticated manner) schlicht; (merely) nur; **it ~ isn't true** es ist einfach nicht wahr; **I was ~ trying to help** ich wollte nur helfen

simulate /'sɪmjʊleɪt/ *v.t.* **(a)** (feign) vortäuschen
(b) simulieren ‹*Bedingungen, Wetter usw.*›

simulation /sɪmjʊ'leɪʃn/ *n.* **(a)** (feigning) Vortäuschung, *die*
(b) (imitation of conditions) Simulation, *die*
(c) (simulated object) Imitation, *die*

simulator /'sɪmjʊleɪtə(r)/ *n.* Simulator, *der*

simultaneous /sɪml'teɪnɪəs/ *adj.*, **simul'taneously** *adv.* gleichzeitig

sin /sɪn/ [1] *n.* Sünde, *die*
[2] *v.i.*, **-nn-** sündigen

since /sɪns/ [1] *adv.* seitdem
[2] *prep.* seit; **I have/had been waiting ~ 8 o'clock** ich warte/wartete [schon] seit 8 Uhr; **he has lived here ~ his childhood** er wohnt seit seiner Kindheit hier; **~ seeing you ...:** seit ich dich gesehen habe; **~ then/that time** inzwischen
[3] *conj.* **(a)** seit; **it is a long time/so long/not so long ~ ...:** es ist lange/so lange/gar nicht lange her, dass ...
(b) (seeing that, as) da

sincere /sɪn'sɪə(r)/ *adj.*, **~r** /sɪn'sɪərə(r)/, **~st** /sɪn'sɪərɪst/ aufrichtig; herzlich ‹*Grüße, Glückwünsche usw.*›

sin'cerely *adv.* aufrichtig; **yours ~:** mit freundlichen Grüßen

sincerity /sɪn'serɪtɪ/ *n.* Aufrichtigkeit, *die*

sinew /'sɪnju:/ *n.* Sehne, *die*

sinful /'sɪnfl/ *adj.* sündig; (reprehensible) sündhaft; **it is ~ to ...:** es ist eine Sünde, zu ...

sing /sɪŋ/ *v.i. & t.*, **sang** /sæŋ/, **sung** /sʌŋ/ singen

■ **sing 'up** *v.i.* lauter singen

singe /sɪndʒ/ *v.t. & i.*, **~ing** versengen

singer /'sɪŋə(r)/ *n.* Sänger, *der*/Sängerin, *die*

single /'sɪŋgl/ [1] *adj.* **(a)** einfach; (sole) einzig; (separate, individual, isolated) einzeln; **not a ~ one** kein Einziger/keine Einzige/kein Einziges; **every ~ one** jeder/jede/jedes Einzelne; **every ~ day** jeden Tag; **~ ticket** (Brit.) einfache Fahrkarte
(b) (for one person) Einzel‹*bett, -zimmer*›
(c) (unmarried) ledig; **a ~ man/woman** ein Lediger/eine Ledige; **~ people** Ledige *Pl.*; **~ parent** allein erziehender Elternteil; **~ mother** allein erziehende *od.* stehende Mutter
[2] *n.* **(a)** (Brit.: ticket) einfache Fahrkarte; [a] **~/two ~s to Manchester, please** einmal/zweimal einfach nach Manchester, bitte
(b) (record) Single, *die*
(c) *in pl.* (Tennis etc.) Einzel, *das*

■ **single 'out** *v.t.* **~ sb./sth. out as/for sth.** jmdn./etw. als/für etw. auswählen

single: ~ cream *n.* [einfache] Sahne; **~ 'currency** *n.* Einheitswährung, *die;* **~-decker** [1] *n.* Bus/Straßenbahn mit nur einem Deck; **be a ~-decker** ‹*Bus, Straßenbahn:*› nur ein Deck haben; [2] *adj.* **~-decker bus/tram** Bus/Straßenbahn mit [nur] einem Deck; **~ [European] market** *n.* [europäischer] Binnenmarkt; **~-'handed** *adv.* allein; **~-lens 'reflex camera** *n.* (Photog.) einäugige Spiegelreflexkamera; **~-minded** *adj.* zielstrebig; **~-mindedly** /sɪŋgl'maɪndɪdlɪ/ *adv.* zielstrebig; **~-sex** *adj.* **~ school** reine Mädchen-/Jungenschule

'singles bar *n.* Singlekneipe, *die*

'single-storey *adj.* eingeschossig

singlet /'sɪŋglɪt/ *n.* (Brit.) (vest) Unterhemd, *das;* (Sport) Trikot, *das*

singly /'sɪŋglɪ/ *adv.* einzeln

singular /'sɪŋgjʊlə(r)/ [1] *adj.* **(a)** (Ling.) singularisch; Singular-; **~ noun** Substantiv im Singular
(b) (extraordinary) einmalig
[2] *n.* (Ling.) Einzahl, *die;* Singular, *der*

'singularly *adv.* (extraordinarily) außerordentlich

sinister /'sɪnɪstə(r)/ *adj.* finster; (of evil omen) Unheil verkündend

sink /sɪŋk/ [1] *n.* Spülbecken, *das*
[2] *v.i.*, **sank** /sæŋk/ *or* **sunk** /sʌŋk/, **sunk** sinken
[3] *v.t.*, **sank** *or* **sunk, sunk (a)** versenken ‹*Schiff*›
(b) niederbringen ‹*Schacht*›

■ **sink 'in** *v.i.* (fig.) jmdm. ins Bewusstsein dringen; ‹*Warnung, Lektion:*› verstanden werden

'sink unit *n.* Spüle, *die*

'sinner *n.* Sünder, *der*/Sünderin, *die*

sinus /'saɪnəs/ *n.* Nebenhöhle, *die*

sinusitis /saɪnə'saɪtɪs/ *n.* Nebenhöhlenentzündung, *die*

sip /sɪp/ [1] *v.t.*, **-pp-: ~ [up]** schlürfen
[2] *v.i.*, **-pp-: ~ at/from sth.** an etw. (*Dat.*) nippen
[3] *n.* Schlückchen, *das*

siphon /'saɪfn/ [1] *n.* Siphon, *der* ⇢

2 v.t. [durch einen Saugheber] laufen lassen

sir /sɜː(r)/ *n.* **(a)** (formal address) der Herr; (to teacher) Herr Meier/Schmidt *usw.*
(b) (in letter) **Dear Sir** Sehr geehrter Herr; **Dear Sirs** Sehr geehrte [Damen und] Herren; **Dear Sir or Madam** Sehr geehrte Dame/Sehr geehrter Herr
(c) Sir /sə(r)/ (title of knight etc.) Sir

siren /'saɪrən/ *n.* Sirene, *die*

sirloin /'sɜːlɔɪn/ *n.* **(a)** (Brit.) Roastbeef, *das;* ~ **steak** Rumpsteak, *das*
(b) (Amer.) Rumpsteak, *das*

sissy /'sɪsɪ/ 1 *n.* Waschlappen, *der*
2 *adj.* feige

sister /'sɪstə(r)/ *n.* **(a)** Schwester, *die*
(b) (Brit.: nurse) Oberschwester, *die*

'sister-in-law *n., pl.* **sisters-in-law** Schwägerin, *die*

sisterly /'sɪstəlɪ/ *adj.* schwesterlich

sit /sɪt/ 1 *v.i.,* **-tt-, sat** /sæt/ **(a)** (become seated) sich setzen; ~ **on** *or* **in a chair/in an armchair** sich auf einen Stuhl/in einen Sessel setzen
(b) (be seated) sitzen
2 *v.t.,* **-tt-, sat (a)** setzen
(b) (Brit.) machen ‹*Prüfung*›

■ **sit 'back** *v.i.* sich zurücklehnen; (fig.) sich im Sessel zurücklehnen

■ **sit 'down** *v.i.* **(a)** (become seated) sich setzen (**on/in** auf/in + *Akk.*)
(b) (be seated) sitzen

■ **sit 'up** 1 *v.i.* **(a)** (rise) sich aufsetzen
(b) (be sitting erect) [aufrecht] sitzen
(c) (stay up) aufbleiben
2 *v.t.* aufsetzen

sitcom /'sɪtkɒm/ (coll.) ▶ SITUATION COMEDY

site /saɪt/ 1 *n.* **(a)** (land) Grundstück, *das*
(b) (location) Sitz, *der;* (of new factory etc.) Standort, *der*
2 *v.t.* stationieren ‹*Raketen*›; ~ **a factory in London** London als Standort einer Fabrik wählen; **be ~d** gelegen sein

siting /'saɪtɪŋ/ *n.* Standortwahl, *die* (**of** für); (position) Lage, *die*

sitter /'sɪtə(r)/ ▶ BABYSITTER

'sitting *n.* Sitzung, *die;* **the first ~ [for lunch]** der erste Schub [zum Mittagessen]

sitting: ~ 'duck *n.* (fig.) leichtes Ziel; ~ **room** *n.* Wohnzimmer, *das;* ~ **'target** ▶ ~ DUCK

situate /'sɪtjʊeɪt/ *v.t.* legen

'situated *adj.* gelegen; **be ~:** liegen

situation /sɪtjʊ'eɪʃn/ *n.* **(a)** (location) Lage, *die*
(b) (circumstances) Situation, *die*
(c) (job) Stelle, *die*

situation 'comedy *n.* Situationskomödie, *die*

six /sɪks/ 1 *adj.* sechs
2 *n.* Sechs, *die. See also* EIGHT

six: ~-'footer *n.* (person) Zweimetermann, *der*/-frau, *die;* **~-pack** *n.* Sechserpack, *der*

sixteen /sɪks'tiːn/ 1 *adj.* sechzehn
2 *n.* Sechzehn, *die. See also* EIGHT

sixteenth /sɪks'tiːnθ/ 1 *adj.* sechzehnt...
2 *n.* (fraction) Sechzehntel, *das. See also* EIGHTH

sixth /sɪksθ/ 1 *adj.* sechst...
2 *n.* (in sequence, rank) Sechste, *der/die/das;* (fraction) Sechstel, *das. See also* EIGHTH

sixth: ~ form *n.* (Brit. Sch.) ≈ zwölfte/dreizehnte Klasse; **~-form college** *n.* (Brit. Sch.) ≈ Oberstufenzentrum, *das; College, das nur Schüler der zwölften/dreizehnten Klasse aufnimmt;* **~-former** *n.* (Brit. Sch.) Schüler/Schülerin der zwölften/dreizehnten Klasse; ~ **'sense** *n.* sechster Sinn

sixtieth /'sɪkstɪɪθ/ *adj.* sechzigst...

sixty /'sɪkstɪ/ 1 *adj.* sechzig
2 *n.* Sechzig, *die. See also* EIGHT; EIGHTY 2

size /saɪz/ *n.* Größe, *die;* (of paper) Format, *das;* **be twice the ~ of sth.** zweimal so groß wie etw. sein; **a ~ 8 dress** ein Kleid [in] Größe 8; **be ~ 8** ‹*Person:*› Größe 8 haben

■ **size 'up** *v.t.* taxieren ‹*Lage*›

sizeable /'saɪzəbl/ *adj.* ziemlich groß; beträchtlich ‹*Summe, Einfluss*›

sizzle /'sɪzl/ *v.i.* zischen

skate 1 *n.* (ice ~) Schlittschuh, *der;* (roller ~) Rollschuh, *der*
2 *v.i.* (ice-~) Schlittschuh laufen; (roller-~) Rollschuh laufen

'skateboard 1 *n.* Skateboard, *das;* Rollerbrett, *das*
2 *v.i.* Skateboard fahren

'skateboarder *n.* Skateboardfahrer, *der*/-fahrerin, *die*

'skateboarding *n.* Skateboardfahren, *das*

'skater *n.* (ice ~) Eisläufer, *der*/-läuferin, *die;* (roller ~) Rollschuhläufer, *der*/-läuferin, *die*

skating /'skeɪtɪŋ/ *n.* (ice ~) Schlittschuhlaufen, *das;* (roller ~) Rollschuhlaufen, *das*

'skating rink *n.* (ice) Eisbahn, *die;* (for roller skating) Rollschuhbahn, *die*

skeleton /'skelɪtn/ *n.* Skelett, *das*

skeleton: ~ 'key *n.* Dietrich, *der;* ~ **'staff** *n.* Minimalbesetzung, *die*

skeptic *etc.* (Amer.) ▶ SCEPTIC *etc.*

sketch /sketʃ/ 1 *n.* **(a)** (drawing) Skizze, *die*
(b) (play) Sketch, *der*
2 *v.t.* skizzieren

sketch: ~book *n.* Skizzenbuch, *das;* ~ **map** *n.* Faustskizze, *die*

'sketchy *adj.* skizzenhaft; lückenhaft ‹*Informationen, Bericht*›

skew /skjuː/ 1 *adj.* schräg
2 *n.* **on the ~:** schief

skewer /'skjuːə(r)/ 1 *n.* Bratspieß, *der*
2 *v.t.* aufspießen

ski /skiː/ 1 *n.* **(a)** Ski, *der*
(b) (on vehicle) Kufe, *die*
2 *v.i.* Ski laufen *od.* fahren

'ski boot *n.* Skistiefel, *der*

skid /skɪd/ [1] *v.i.*, **-dd-** schlittern; (from one side to the other; spinning round) schleudern [2] *n.* Schlittern/Schleudern, *das*

'skid marks *n. pl.* Schleuderspur, *die*

skier /'ski:ə(r)/ *n.* Skiläufer, *der*/-läuferin, *die*

skiing /'ski:ɪŋ/ *n.* Skilaufen, *das;* (Sport) Skisport, *der*

'ski jumping *n.* Skispringen, *das*

skilful /'skɪlfl/ *adj.* geschickt; gewandt ‹*Redner*›; gut ‹*Beobachter, Lehrer*›

'ski lift *n.* Skilift, *der*

skill /skɪl/ *n.* **(a)** (expertness) Geschick, *das;* (of artist) Können, *das*
(b) (technique) Fertigkeit, *die;* (of weaving, bricklaying) Technik, *die*

skilled /'skɪld/ *adj.* **(a)** ▶ SKILFUL
(b) qualifiziert ‹*Arbeit, Tätigkeit*›; ~ **trade** Ausbildungsberuf, *der*
(c) (trained) ausgebildet

'skillful (Amer.) ▶ SKILFUL

skim /skɪm/ *v.t.*, **-mm-**: **(a)** (remove) abschöpfen
(b) abrahmen ‹*Milch*›
(c) ▶ ~ THROUGH

■ **skim 'off** *v.t.* abschöpfen

■ **'skim through** *v.t.* überfliegen ‹*Buch, Zeitung*›

skimmed 'milk *n.* entrahmte Milch

skimp /skɪmp/ [1] *v.t.* sparen an (+ *Dat.*) [2] *v.i.* sparen (**with, on** an + *Dat.*)

'skimpy *adj.* winzig ‹*Badeanzug*›; spärlich ‹*Wissen*›

skin /skɪn/ [1] *n.* **(a)** Haut, *die*
(b) (fur) Fell, *das*
(c) (peel) Schale, *die*
[2] *v.t.*, **-nn-** häuten; schälen ‹*Frucht*›

skin: ~ **cancer** *n.* Hautkrebs, *der;* ~ **colour** *n.* Hautfarbe, *die;* ~ **cream** *n.* Hautcreme, *die;* ~**-'deep** *adj.* (fig.) oberflächlich; ~ **disease** *n.* Hautkrankheit, *die;* ~ **diver** *n.* Taucher, *der*/Taucherin, *die;* ~ **diving** *n.* Tauchen, *das;* ~**flint** *n.* Geizhals, *der;* ~ **graft** *n.* Hauttransplantation, *die;* ~**head** *n.* Skinhead, *der*

skinny /'skɪnɪ/ *adj.* mager

skint /skɪnt/ *adj.* (Brit. coll.) **be** ~: blank *od.* pleite sein (ugs.)

'skin-tight *adj.* hauteng

skip¹ /skɪp/ [1] *v.i.*, **-pp-**: **(a)** hüpfen
(b) (with skipping rope) seilspringen
[2] *v.t.*, **-pp-** (omit) überspringen; ~ **breakfast/lunch** das Frühstück/Mittagessen auslassen
[3] *n.* Hüpfer, *der*

skip² *n.* (Building) Container, *der*

ski: ~ **pass** *n.* Skipass, *der;* ~ **pole** *n.* Skistock, *der*

skipper /'skɪpə(r)/ *n.* Kapitän, *der*

'skipping rope (Brit.), **'skip rope** (Amer.) *ns.* Sprungseil, *das*

'ski resort *n.* Skiurlaubsort, *der*

skirmish /'skɜ:mɪʃ/ *n.* (Mil.) Gefecht, *das*

skirt /skɜ:t/ [1] *n.* Rock, *der*
[2] *v.t.* herumgehen um

■ **skirt 'round** *v.t.* herumgehen um; (fig.) umgehen

'skirting *n.* ~ [**board**] (Brit.) Fußleiste, *die*

ski: ~ **run** *n.* Skihang, *der;* (prepared) [Ski]piste, *die;* ~**stick** *n.* Skistock, *der*

skittle /'skɪtl/ *n.* **(a)** Kegel, *der*
(b) ~**s** *sing.* (game) Kegeln, *das*

skive /skaɪv/ *v.i.* (Brit. coll.) sich drücken (ugs.)

■ **skive 'off** (Brit. coll.) [1] *v.i.* sich verdrücken (ugs.)
[2] *v.t.* schwänzen (ugs.)

skulk /skʌlk/ *v.i.* lauern

skull /skʌl/ *n.* Schädel, *der*

skunk /skʌŋk/ *n.* Stinktier, *das*

sky /skaɪ/ *n.* Himmel, *der;* **in the** ~: am Himmel

sky: ~**diving** *n.* Fallschirmspringen, *das* (als Sport); Fallschirmsport, *der;* ~**-high** [1] *adj.* himmelhoch; astronomisch (ugs.) ‹*Preise usw.*›; [2] *adv.* **go** ~**-high** ‹*Preise usw.*:› in astronomische Höhen klettern (ugs.); ~**light** *n.* Dachfenster, *das;* ~**line** *n.* Silhouette, *die;* (characteristic of certain town) Skyline, *die;* ~ **marshal** *n.* Skymarshal, *der;* ~**scraper** *n.* Wolkenkratzer, *der*

slab /slæb/ *n.* **(a)** (flat stone etc.) Platte, *die*
(b) (thick slice) [dicke] Scheibe; (of cake) [dickes] Stück; (of chocolate, toffee) Tafel, *die*

slack /slæk/ [1] *adj.* **(a)** (lax) nachlässig; schlampig (ugs.)
(b) (loose) schlaff; locker ‹*Verband*›
[2] *n.* **take in** *or* **up the** ~: das Seil/die Schnur *usw.* straffen
[3] *v.i.* (coll.) bummeln (ugs.)

slacken /'slækn/ [1] *v.i.* **(a)** (loosen) sich lockern
(b) (diminish) nachlassen; ‹*Geschwindigkeit*:› sich verringern
[2] *v.t.* **(a)** (loosen) lockern
(b) (diminish) verringern

slacker /'slækə(r)/ *n.* (derog.) Faulenzer, *der*/Faulenzerin, *die*

slacks /slæks/ *n. pl.* [**pair of**] ~: lange Hose; Slacks *Pl.*

slag /slæg/ *n.* Schlacke, *die*

slain ▶ SLAY

slake /sleɪk/ *v.t.* löschen, stillen ‹*Durst*›

slam /slæm/ [1] *v.t.*, **-mm-**: **(a)** (shut) zuschlagen
(b) (put violently) knallen (ugs.)
[2] *v.i.*, **-mm-** zuschlagen

slander /'slɑ:ndə(r)/ [1] *n.* Verleumdung, *die* (**on** *Gen.*)
[2] *v.t.* verleumden

slanderous /'slɑ:ndərəs/ *adj.* verleumderisch

S

slang /slæŋ/ *n.* Slang, *der;* ‹*Theater-, Soldaten-, Juristen*›jargon, *der; attrib.* Slang‹*wort, -ausdruck*›

'slanging match *n.* gegenseitige [lautstarke] Beschimpfung

slangy /'slæŋɪ/ *adj.* Slang‹*ausdruck, -wort*›; salopp ‹*Wortwahl, Redeweise*›

slant /slɑ:nt/ 1 *v.i.* ‹*Fläche:*› sich neigen; ‹*Linie:*› schräg verlaufen
2 *v.t.* **(a)** abschrägen
(b) (fig.: bias) [so] hinbiegen (ugs.) ‹*Meldung, Bemerkung*›
3 *n.* Schräge, *die;* **on the** *or* **a ~:** schräg

slanting /'slɑ:ntɪŋ/ *adj.* schräg

slap /slæp/ 1 *v.t.,* **-pp-: (a)** schlagen
(b) (put) knallen (ugs.)
2 *v.i.,* **-pp-** schlagen; klatschen
3 *n.* Schlag, *der*
4 *adv.* voll; **~ in the middle** genau in der Mitte

'slapdash *adj.* schludrig (ugs.)

'slap-up *attrib. adj.* (coll.) ‹*Essen*› mit allen Schikanen (ugs.)

slash /slæʃ/ 1 *v.t.* **(a)** aufschlitzen
(b) (fig.) [drastisch] reduzieren; [drastisch] kürzen ‹*Gehalt, Umfang*›
2 *n.* **(a)** (slit) Schlitz, *der*
(b) (~ing stroke) Hieb, *der*

slat /slæt/ *n.* Latte, *die*

slate /sleɪt/ 1 *n.* **(a)** (Geol.) Schiefer, *der*
(b) (Building) Schieferplatte, *die*
2 *v.t.* (Brit. coll.: criticize) in der Luft zerreißen (ugs.)

slaughter /'slɔ:tə(r)/ 1 *n.* Schlachten, *das;* (massacre) Gemetzel, *das*
2 *v.t.* schlachten; (massacre) abschlachten

slave /sleɪv/ 1 *n.* Sklave, *der*/Sklavin, *die*
2 *v.i.* **~ [away]** schuften (ugs.); sich abplagen (**at** mit)

'slave driver *n.* (fig.) Sklaventreiber, *der*/-treiberin, *die*

slavery /'sleɪvərɪ/ *n.* Sklaverei, *die*

slavish /'sleɪvɪʃ/ *adj.* sklavisch

slay /sleɪ/ *v.t.,* **slew** /slu:/, **slain** /sleɪn/ (literary) ermorden

sleaze /sli:z/ *n.* (derog.) Korruption, *die*

'sleazebag, 'sleazeball *ns.* (sl. derog.) Drecksack, *der* (derb abwertend)

sleazy /'sli:zɪ/ *adj.* schäbig; (disreputable) anrüchig

sled /sled/**, sledge** /sledʒ/ *ns.* Schlitten, *der*

'sledgehammer *n.* Vorschlaghammer, *der*

sleek /sli:k/ *adj.* (glossy) seidig

sleep /sli:p/ 1 *n.* Schlaf, *der;* **get/go to ~:** einschlafen; **put to ~:** einschläfern ‹*Tier*›
2 *v.i.,* **slept** /slept/ schlafen
3 *v.t.* **slept: the hotel ~s 80** das Hotel hat 80 Betten

■ **sleep a'round** *v.i.* (coll.) herumschlafen (ugs.)

■ **sleep 'in** *v.i.* im Bett bleiben

■ **sleep 'off** *v.t.* ausschlafen; **~ it off** seinen Rausch ausschlafen

■ **sleep 'over** *v.i.* [auswärts] übernachten; **our cousin was ~ing over** unser Cousin übernachtete bei uns

■ **sleep together** *v.i.* (also coll. euphem.) miteinander schlafen

■ **sleep with** *v.t.* **~ with sb.** (coll. euphem.) mit jmdm. schlafen

'sleeper *n.* **(a) be a heavy/light ~:** einen tiefen/leichten Schlaf haben
(b) (Brit. Railw.: support) Schwelle, *die*
(c) (Railw.) (coach) Schlafwagen, *der;* (train) **[night] ~:** Nachtzug mit Schlafwagen

sleeping: ~ accommodation *n.* Übernachtungsmöglichkeit, *die;* **~ bag** *n.* Schlafsack, *der;* **~ car** *n.* Schlafwagen, *der;* **~ 'partner** *n.* (Commerc.) stiller Teilhaber; **~ pill, ~ tablet** *ns.* Schlaftablette, *die*

sleep: ~less *adj.* schlaflos; **~walk** *v.i.* schlafwandeln; **~walker** *n.* Schlafwandler, *der*/-wandlerin, *die*

'sleepover *n.* Übernachtung außer Haus *od.* bei anderen Leuten

'sleepy *adj.* schläfrig

sleet /sli:t/ 1 *n.* Schneeregen, *der*
2 *v.i. impers.* **it is ~ing** es gibt Schneeregen

sleeve /sli:v/ *n.* **(a)** Ärmel, *der;* (fig.) **have sth. up one's ~:** etw. in petto haben (ugs.); **roll up one's ~s** die Ärmel hochkrempeln (ugs.)
(b) (for record) Hülle, *die*

'sleeveless *adj.* ärmellos

sleigh /sleɪ/ *n.* Schlitten, *der*

sleight of 'hand /slaɪt/ *n.* Fingerfertigkeit, *die*

slender /'slendə(r)/ *adj.* **(a)** (slim) schlank; schmal ‹*Buch, Band*›
(b) gering ‹*Chance, Mittel, Hoffnung*›

slept ▶ SLEEP 2, 3

sleuth /slu:θ/ *n.* Detektiv, *der*

slew[1] /slu:/ *v.i. & t.* schwenken

slew[2] ▶ SLAY

slice /slaɪs/ 1 *n.* Scheibe, *die;* (of apple, melon, peach, cake, pie) Stück, *das;* **a ~ of cake** ein Stück Kuchen
2 *v.t.* in Scheiben schneiden; in Stücke schneiden ‹*Bohnen, Apfel, Kuchen usw.*›; **~d bread** Schnittbrot, *das*

slick /slɪk/ 1 *adj.* **(a)** (dexterous) professionell
(b) (pretentiously dexterous) clever (ugs.)
2 *n.* **[oil] ~:** Ölteppich, *der*

slid ▶ SLIDE 1, 2

slide /slaɪd/ 1 *v.i.,* **slid** /slɪd/ rutschen; ‹*Kolben, Schublade, Feder:*› gleiten
2 *v.t.,* **slid** schieben
3 *n.* **(a)** (children's ~) Rutschbahn, *die*
(b) (Photog.) Dia[positiv], *das*

slide: ~ film *n.* Diafilm, *der;* **~ projector** *n.* Diaprojektor, *der;* **~ show** *n.* Diashow, *die*

sliding door /'slaɪdɪŋ/ *n.* Schiebetür, *die*

slight /slaɪt/ [1] *adj.* leicht; schwach ‹*Hoffnung, Aussichten, Wirkung*›; **not in the ~est** nicht im Geringsten
[2] *n.* Verunglimpfung, *die* (**on** *Gen.*); (lack of courtesy) Affront, *der* (**on** gegen)

'slightly *adv.* ein bisschen; leicht ‹*verletzen, riechen nach, gewürzt sein, ansteigen*›; flüchtig ‹*jmdn. kennen*›; oberflächlich ‹*etw. kennen*›

slim /slɪm/ [1] *adj.* schlank; schmal ‹*Band, Buch*›; schwach ‹*Aussicht, Hoffnung*›; gering ‹*Gewinn, Chancen*›
[2] *v.i.*, **-mm-** abnehmen

slime /slaɪm/ *n.* Schleim, *der*

slimmer /'slɪmə(r)/ *n.* (Brit.) *jmd., der etwas für die schlanke Linie tut;* **advice/a diet for ~s** Ratschläge *Pl.*/eine Diät zum Abnehmen

slimming /'slɪmɪŋ/ [1] *n.* Abnehmen, *das; attrib.* Schlankheits-
[2] *adj.* schlank machend

slimy /'slaɪmɪ/ *adj.* schleimig

sling /slɪŋ/ [1] *n.* (Med.) Schlinge, *die*
[2] *v.t.*, **slung** /slʌŋ/ (coll.: throw) schmeißen (ugs.)

sling 'out *v.t.* (coll.) wegschmeißen (ugs.); **~ sb. out** jmdn. rausschmeißen (ugs.)

slink /slɪŋk/ *v.i.*, **slunk** /slʌŋk/ schleichen

■ **slink a'way, slink 'off** *v.i.* davonschleichen

slip /slɪp/ [1] *v.i.*, **-pp-**: **(a)** (slide) rutschen; ‹*Messer:*› abrutschen; (and fall) ausrutschen
(b) (escape) schlüpfen
(c) (go) **~ to the butcher's** *etc.* [rasch] zum Fleischer *usw.* rüberspringen (ugs.)
[2] *v.t.*, **-pp-**: **(a)** stecken; **~ the dress over one's head** das Kleid über den Kopf streifen
(b) ~ sb.'s mind *or* **memory** jmdm. entfallen
[3] *n.* **(a)** (fall) **after his ~:** nachdem er ausgerutscht [und gestürzt] war
(b) (mistake) Versehen, *das;* **~ of the tongue** Versprecher, *der*
(c) (underwear) Unterrock, *der*
(d) (piece of paper) Zettel, *der*
(e) give sb. the ~: jmdm. entwischen (ugs.)

■ **slip a'way** *v.i.* **(a)** ‹*Person:*› sich fortschleichen
(b) ‹*Zeit:*› verfliegen

■ **slip 'down** *v.i.* runterrutschen (ugs.)

■ **slip 'in** *v.i.* ‹*Person:*› sich hineinschleichen

■ **'slip into** *v.t.* schlüpfen in (+ *Akk.*) ‹*Kleidungsstück*›

■ **slip 'off** [1] *v.i.* **(a)** runterrutschen (ugs.)
(b) ▶ SLIP AWAY A
[2] *v.t.* abstreifen ‹*Schmuck, Handschuh*›; schlüpfen aus ‹*Kleid, Schuh*›

■ **slip 'on** *v.t.* überstreifen ‹*Handschuh, Ring*›; schlüpfen in (+ *Akk.*) ‹*Kleid, Schuh*›

■ **slip 'out** *v.i.* ‹*Person:*› sich hinausschleichen

■ **slip 'over** *v.i.* (fall) ausrutschen

■ **slip 'up** *v.i.* (coll.) einen Schnitzer machen (ugs.)

slipped 'disc /slɪpt/ *n.* Bandscheibenvorfall, *der*

'slipper *n.* Hausschuh, *der*

slippery /'slɪpərɪ/ *adj.* schlüpfrig

slippy /'slɪpɪ/ (coll.) ▶ SLIPPERY

slip: ~ road *n.* (Brit.) (to motorway) Auffahrt, *die;* (from motorway) Ausfahrt, *die;* **~shod** *adj.* schludrig (ugs.); **~-up** *n.* (coll.) Schnitzer, *der*

slit /slɪt/ [1] *n.* Schlitz, *der*
[2] *v.t.*, **-tt-**, **slit** aufschlitzen; **~ sb.'s throat** jmdm. die Kehle durchschneiden

slither /'slɪðə(r)/ *v.i.* rutschen

sliver /'slɪvə(r)/ *n.* Splitter, *der*

slob /slɒb/ *n.* (coll.) Schwein, *das* (derb)

slobber /'slɒbə(r)/ *v.i.* sabbern (ugs.)

slog /slɒg/ [1] *v.t.*, **-gg-** (in boxing, fight) voll treffen
[2] *v.i.*, **-gg-** (work) schuften (ugs.)
[3] *n.* **(a)** (hit) wuchtiger Schlag
(b) (work) Plackerei, *die* (ugs.)

slogan /'sləʊgən/ *n.* Slogan, *der;* (advertising ~) Werbeslogan, *der*

slop /slɒp/ [1] *v.i.* schwappen (**out of, from** aus)
[2] *v.t.* schwappen; (intentionally) kippen

■ **slop 'over** *v.i.* überschwappen

slope /sləʊp/ [1] *n.* **(a)** (slant) Neigung, *die*
(b) (slanting ground) Hang, *der*
[2] *v.i.* (slant) sich neigen; ‹*Boden, Garten:*› abschüssig sein; **~ downwards/upwards** ‹*Straße:*› abfallen/ansteigen

■ **slope a'way** *v.i.* abfallen

■ **slope 'off** *v.i.* (coll.) sich verdrücken (ugs.)

sloppy /'slɒpɪ/ *adj.* schludrig (ugs.)

slosh /slɒʃ/ *adj.* [1] *v.i.* platschen (ugs.); ‹*Flüssigkeit:*› schwappen
[2] *v.t.* (coll.: pour clumsily) schwappen

sloshed /slɒʃt/ *adj.* (Brit. coll.) blau (ugs.)

slot /slɒt/ [1] *n.* **(a)** (hole) Schlitz, *der*
(b) (groove) Nut, *die*
[2] *v.t.*, **-tt-**: **~ sth. into place/sth.** etw. einfügen/in etw. (*Akk.*) einfügen

■ **slot 'in** [1] *v.t.* einfügen
[2] *v.i.* sich einfügen

■ **slot to'gether** [1] *v.t.* zusammenfügen
[2] *v.i.* (lit. or fig.) sich zusammenfügen

sloth /sləʊθ/ *n.* **(a)** (lethargy) Trägheit, *die*
(b) (Zool.) Faultier, *das*

'slot machine *n.* Automat, *der;* (for gambling) Spielautomat, *der*

slouch /slaʊtʃ/ *v.i.* sich schlecht halten

Slovak /'sləʊvæk/ [1] *adj.* slowakisch; **sb. is ~:** jmd. ist Slowake/Slowakin
[2] *n.* **(a)** (person) Slowake, *der*/Slowakin, *die*
(b) (language) Slowakisch, *das; see also* ENGLISH 2A

Slovakia /slə'vɑːkɪə/ *pr. n.* Slowakei, *die*

Slovene /'sləʊviːn/ [1] *adj.* slowenisch; **sb. is ~:** jmd. ist Slowene/Slowenin
[2] *n.* **(a)** (person) Slowene, *der*/Slowenin, *die*
(b) (language) Slowenisch, *das*

Slovenia /slə'viːnɪə/ *pr. n.* Slowenien (*das*)

S

Slovenian /slə'vi:nɪən/ ▶ SLOVENE

slovenly /'slʌvnlɪ/ *adj.* schlampig (ugs.)

slow /sləʊ/ 1 *adj.* langsam; langwierig ‹*Arbeit*›; **be [ten minutes] ~** ‹*Uhr:*› [zehn Minuten] nachgehen
2 *adv.* langsam
3 *v.i.* langsamer werden; **~ to a halt** anhalten

■ **slow 'down, slow 'up** *v.i.* langsamer werden

'slowcoach *n.* Trödler, *der*/Trödlerin, *die* (ugs.)

'slowly *adv.* langsam

slow 'motion *n.* **in ~:** in Zeitlupe

slowness *n.* Langsamkeit, *die*

slow: ~ 'puncture *n.* winziges Loch; **~ train** *n.* Bummelzug, *der* (ugs.); **~-witted** /sləʊ'wɪtɪd/ *adj.* [geistig] schwerfällig

sludge /slʌdʒ/ *n.* Schlamm, *der*

slug /slʌg/ *n.* Nacktschnecke, *die*

sluggish /'slʌgɪʃ/ *adj.* träge; schleppend ‹*Nachfrage*›

sluice /slu:s/ 1 *n.* Schütz, *das*
2 *v.t.* **~ [down]** abspritzen

'sluice gate *n.* Schütz, *das*

slum /slʌm/ *n.* Slum, *der;* (single house or apartment) Elendsquartier, *das*

slumber /'slʌmbə(r)/ (poet./rhet.) 1 *n.* **~[s]** Schlummer, *der* (geh.)
2 *v.i.* schlummern (geh.)

slump /slʌmp/ 1 *n.* Sturz, *der (fig.); (in demand, investment, sales)* starker Rückgang (in *Gen.*); (economic depression) Depression, *die*
2 *v.i.* **(a)** (Commerc.) stark zurückgehen; ‹*Preise, Kurse:*› stürzen
(b) (collapse) ‹*Person:*› fallen; **~ed in a chair** in einem Sessel zusammengesunken

slung ▶ SLING 2

slunk ▶ SLINK

slur /slɜ:(r)/ 1 *v.t.*, **-rr-: ~ one's words/speech** undeutlich sprechen
2 *n.* Beleidigung, *die* (**on** für)

slurp /slɜ:p/ (coll.) 1 *v.t.* **~ [up]** schlürfen
2 *n.* Schlürfen, *das*

slush /slʌʃ/ *n.* Schneematsch, *der*

'slush fund *n.* Fonds, *der* für Bestechungsgelder

'slushy *adj.* **(a)** matschig
(b) (sloppy) sentimental

slut /slʌt/ *n.* Schlampe, *die* (ugs.)

sly /slaɪ/ 1 *adj.* schlau; gerissen (ugs.) ‹*Geschäftsmann, Trick*›; verschlagen ‹*Blick*›
2 *n.* **on the ~:** heimlich

smack[1] /smæk/ 1 *n.* **(a)** (sound) Klatsch, *der*
(b) (blow) Schlag, *der;* (on child's bottom) Klaps, *der* (ugs.)
2 *v.t.* **(a)** [mit der flachen Hand] schlagen
(b) ~ one's lips [mit den Lippen] schmatzen
3 *adv.* (coll.) direkt

smack[2] *v.i.* **~ of** schmecken nach; (fig.) riechen nach (ugs.)

small /smɔ:l/ 1 *adj.* klein; gering ‹*Wirkung, Appetit, Fähigkeit*›; schmal ‹*Taille*›; dünn ‹*Stimme*›; **make sb. feel ~:** jmdn. beschämen
2 *n.* **~ of the back** Kreuz, *das*
3 *adv.* klein

small: ~ ad *n.* (coll.) Kleinanzeige, *die;* **~ 'change** *n.* Kleingeld, *das;* **~holding** *n.* landwirtschaftlicher Kleinbetrieb; **~-'minded** *adj.* kleinlich; **~pox** *n.* Pocken *Pl.;* **~ 'print** *n.* (lit. or fig.) Kleingedruckte, *das*

smalls /smɔ:lz/ *n. pl.* (Brit. coll.) Unterwäsche, *die*

small: ~ 'screen *n.* (Telev.) Bildschirm, *der;* **~ talk** *n.* leichte Unterhaltung; (at parties) Smalltalk, *der;* **make ~ talk [with sb.]** [mit jmdm.] Konversation machen

smarmy /'smɑ:mɪ/ *adj.* (coll.) kriecherisch

smart /smɑ:t/ 1 *adj.* **(a)** (clever) clever; (ingenious) raffiniert
(b) (neat) schick; schön ‹*Haus, Garten, Auto*›
(c) *attrib.* (fashionable) elegant; smart
2 *v.i.* schmerzen

smart: ~ alec[k] /smɑ:t 'ælɪk/ *n.* (coll.) Besserwisser, *der*/Besserwisserin, *die;* **~ bomb** *n.* intelligente Bombe; **~ card** *n.* Chipkarte, *die;* **~ drug** *n.* Nootropikum, *das*

smarten /'smɑ:tn/ *v.t.* herrichten; **~ oneself [up]** auf sein Äußeres achten

'smartly *adv.* **(a)** (cleverly) clever
(b) (neatly) schmuck ‹*[an]gestrichen*›; smart, flott ‹*gekleidet, geschnitten*›

'smart money *n.* **the ~ is on ...** Experten setzen auf ...

smash /smæʃ/ 1 *v.t.* **(a)** zerschlagen
(b) ~ sb. in the face/mouth jmdm. [hart] ins Gesicht/auf den Mund schlagen
(c) (Tennis etc.) schmettern
2 *v.i.* **(a)** zerbrechen
(b) (crash) krachen (**into** gegen)
3 *n.* **(a)** (sound) Krachen, *das*
(b) ▶ SMASH-UP
(c) (Tennis) Schmetterball, *der*

■ **smash 'in** *v.t.* zerschmettern; einschlagen ‹*Tür, Schädel*›

■ **smash 'up** *v.t.* zertrümmern

smash-and-'grab [raid] *n.* (coll.) Schaufenstereinbruch, *der*

smashed /smæʃt/ *adj.* (sl.) **(a)** (drunk) **get ~ on sth.** von etw. besoffen werden (derb); **be ~ out of one's head** *or* **mind** *or* **brains** sturzbetrunken (ugs.) *od.* (derb) sturzbesoffen sein
(b) (on drugs) stoned (Drogenjargon)

'smashing *adj.* (coll.) toll (ugs.)

'smash-up *n.* schwerer Zusammenstoß

smattering /'smætərɪŋ/ *n.* **[have] a ~ of German** *etc.* ein paar Brocken Deutsch *usw.* [können]

smear /smɪə(r)/ [1] *v.t.* **(a)** (daub) beschmieren; (put on or over) schmieren
(b) (smudge) verwischen
(c) (fig.) in den Schmutz ziehen
[2] *n.* **(a)** (blotch) [Schmutz]fleck, *der*
(b) (fig.) Beschmutzung, *die* **(on** *Gen.*)

smear: ~ campaign *n.* Schmutzkampagne, *die;* **~ tactics** *n. pl.* schmutzige Mittel *Pl.*; **~ test** *n.* (Med.) Abstrich, *der*

smell /smel/ [1] *n.* **(a) have a good/bad sense of ~:** einen guten/schlechten Geruchssinn haben
(b) (odour) Geruch, *der* **(of** nach); (pleasant also) Duft, *der* **(of** nach); **a ~ of burning/gas** ein Brand-/Gasgeruch
(c) (stink) Gestank, *der*
[2] *v.t.,* **smelt** /smelt/ *or* **smelled** /smeld/ **(a)** (perceive) riechen
(b) (inhale **~** of) riechen an (+ *Dat.*)
[3] *v.i.,* **smelt** *or* **smelled (a)** (emit **~**) riechen; (pleasantly also) duften
(b) ~ of sth. (lit. or fig.) nach etw. riechen
(c) (stink) riechen

'smelly *adj.* stinkend; **be ~:** stinken

smelt ▸ SMELL 2, 3

smile /smaɪl/ [1] *n.* Lächeln, *das;* **give sb. a ~:** jmdn. anlächeln
[2] *v.i.* lächeln; **~ at sb./sth.** jmdn. anlächeln/über etw. (*Akk.*) lächeln

smirk /smɜːk/ [1] *v.t.* grinsen
[2] *n.* Grinsen, *das*

smith /smɪθ/ *n.* Schmied, *der*

smithereens /smɪðəˈriːnz/ *n. pl.* **blow/smash sth. to ~:** etw. in tausend Stücke sprengen/schlagen

smock /smɒk/ *n.* Kittel, *der*

smog /smɒg/ *n.* Smog, *der*

smoke /sməʊk/ [1] *n.* Rauch, *der*
[2] *v.i. & t.* rauchen

smoked /sməʊkt/ *adj.* (Cookery) geräuchert

'smoke detector *n.* Rauchmelder, *der*

'smoke-free *adj.* rauchfrei

'smokeless *adj.* rauchlos; rauchfrei ‹*Zone*›

smoker/ˈsməukə(r)/ *n.* Raucher, *der*/Raucherin, *die;* **~'s cough** Raucherhusten, *der*

'smokescreen *n.* [künstliche] Nebelwand; (fig.) Vernebelung *die* **(for** *Gen.*)

smoking /ˈsməʊkɪŋ/ *n.* **(a)** Rauchen, *das;* **'no ~'** „Rauchen verboten"
(b) (seating area) **[do you want to sit in] ~ or non-~?** möchten Sie für Raucher oder Nichtraucher?

'smoking compartment *n.* (Railw.) Raucherabteil, *das*

smoky /ˈsməʊkɪ/ *adj.* (emitting smoke) rauchend; (smoke-filled) verräuchert

smooth /smuːð/ [1] *adj.* **(a)** (even) glatt; eben ‹*Straße, Weg*›
(b) (mild) weich
(d) (not jerky) geschmeidig ‹*Bewegung*›; ruhig ‹*Fahrt, Flug*›; weich ‹*Landung*›
(d) (without problems) reibungslos
[2] *v.t.* glätten

smoothie /ˈsmuːðɪ/ *n.* (coll. derog.) aalglatter Typ (ugs.)

'smoothly *adv.* **(a)** (evenly) glatt
(b) (not jerkily) geschmeidig ‹*sich bewegen*›; weich ‹*landen*›; reibungslos ‹*funktionieren*›

smother /ˈsmʌðə(r)/ *v.t.* ersticken; (fig.) unterdrücken ‹*Gähnen*›; ersticken ‹*Gelächter, Schreie*›

smoulder /ˈsməʊldə(r)/ *v.i.* schwelen; **she was ~ing with rage** Zorn schwelte in ihr

smudge /smʌdʒ/ [1] *v.t.* verwischen
[2] *v.i.* schmieren
[3] *n.* Fleck, *der*

smug /smʌg/ *adj.* selbstgefällig

smuggle /ˈsmʌgl/ *v.t.* schmuggeln

▪ **smuggle 'in** *v.t.* einschmuggeln; hinein-/hereinschmuggeln ‹*Person*›

▪ **smuggle 'out** *v.t.* hinaus-/herausschmuggeln

smuggler /ˈsmʌglə(r)/ *n.* Schmuggler, *der*/Schmugglerin, *die*

smuggling /ˈsmʌglɪŋ/ *n.* Schmuggel, *der*

smutty /ˈsmʌtɪ/ *adj.* (lewd) schmutzig

snack /snæk/ *n.* Imbiss, *der*

'snackbar *n.* Schnellimbiss, *der*

snag /snæg/ *n.* (problem) Haken, *der;* **what's the ~?** wo klemmt es? (ugs.)

snail /sneɪl/ *n.* Schnecke, *die;* **at [a] ~'s pace** im Schneckentempo (ugs.)

'snail mail *n.* (coll. joc.) Schneckenpost, *die*

snake /sneɪk/ *n.* Schlange, *die*

snap /snæp/ [1] *v.t.,* **-pp-: (a)** (break) zerbrechen; **~ sth. in two** *or* **in half** etw. in zwei Stücke brechen
(b) ~ one's fingers mit den Fingern schnalzen
(c) ~ sth. home *or* **into place** etw. einschnappen lassen; **~ shut** zuschnappen lassen ‹*Portemonnaie, Schloss*›; zuklappen ‹*Buch, Etui*›; **~ sth. open** etw. aufschnappen lassen
(d) (take photograph of) knipsen
(e) (say sharply) fauchen; (speak crisply or curtly) bellen
[2] *v.i.,* **-pp-: (a)** (break) brechen
(b) (fig.: give way under strain) ausrasten (ugs.); **my patience has finally ~ped** nun ist mir der Geduldsfaden aber gerissen
[3] *n.* (Photog.) Schnappschuss, *der*

▪ **'snap at** *v.t.* (speak sharply to) anfauchen (ugs.)

▪ **snap 'off** *v.t. & i.* abbrechen

▪ **snap 'up** *v.t.* (fig. coll.) [sich (*Dat.*)] schnappen (ugs.)

'snapshot *n.* Schnappschuss, *der*

snare /sneə(r)/ [1] *n.* Schlinge, *die*
[2] *v.t.* [in einer Schlinge] fangen

snarl[1] /snɑːl/ [1] *v.i.* knurren
[2] *n.* Knurren, *das*

snarl² *n.* (tangle) Knoten, *der*
▪ **snarl 'up** *v.t.* (bring to a halt) zum Erliegen bringen; **get ~ed up in the traffic** im Verkehr stecken bleiben
'snarl-up *n.* Stau, *der*
snatch /snætʃ/ [1] *v.t.* **(a)** (grab) schnappen; **~ sth. from sb.** jmdm. etw. wegreißen; **~ some sleep** ein bisschen schlafen
(b) (steal) klauen (ugs.)
[2] *v.i.* einfach zugreifen
[3] *n.* **~es of talk/conversation** Gesprächsfetzen *Pl.*
snazzy /'snæzɪ/ *adj.* (coll.) [super]schick (ugs.)
sneak /sni:k/ [1] *v.t.* schmuggeln; **~ a look at** schielen nach
[2] *v.i.* **(a)** schleichen
(b) (Brit. Sch. coll.: tell tales) petzen (Schülerspr.)
[3] *n.* (Brit. Sch. coll.) Petze, *die* (Schülerspr.)
▪ **sneak 'out** *v.i.* [sich] hinausschleichen
'sneaker (Amer.) Turnschuh, *der*
'sneaking *attrib. adj.* heimlich; leise ‹*Verdacht*›
'sneak thief *n.* Einschleichdieb, *der*
'sneaky *adj.* **(a)** (underhand) hinterhältig
'**(b) have a ~ feeling that ...:** so ein leises Gefühl haben, dass ...
sneer /snɪə(r)/ *v.i.* höhnisch lächeln/grinsen
▪ **'sneer at** *v.t.* höhnisch anlächeln/ angrinsen; (scorn) verhöhnen
sneeze /sni:z/ [1] *v.i.* niesen
[2] *n.* Niesen, *das*
snicker /'snɪkə(r)/ ▶ SNIGGER
snide /snaɪd/ *adj.* abfällig
sniff /snɪf/ [1] *n.* Schnuppern, *das;* (with running nose, while crying) Schniefen, *das*
[2] *v.i.* schniefen; (to detect a smell) schnuppern
[3] *v.t.* riechen *od.* schnuppern an (+ *Dat.*); **~ glue/cocaine** Klebstoff schnüffeln/Kokain sniffen (Drogenjargon)
▪ **'sniff at** *v.t.* **(a)** ▶ SNIFF 3
(b) (show contempt for) die Nase rümpfen über
sniffer dog /'snɪfə dɒg/ *n.* Spürhund, *der*
snigger /'snɪgə(r)/ [1] *v.i.* [boshaft] kichern
[2] *n.* [boshaftes] Kichern
snip /snɪp/ [1] *v.t.,* **-pp-** schnippeln (ugs.), schneiden ‹*Loch*›; schnippeln (ugs.) *od.* schneiden an (+ *Dat.*) ‹*Tuch, Haaren, Hecke*›; (cut off) abschnippeln (ugs.); abschneiden
[2] *n.* (cut) Schnitt, *der;* Schnipser, *der* (ugs.)
snipe /snaɪp/ *v.i.* **~ at** aus dem Hinterhalt beschießen
'sniper *n.* Heckenschütze, *der*
snippet /'snɪpɪt/ *n.* (of information in newspaper) Notiz, *die;* (of conversation) Gesprächsfetzen, *der;* **useful ~s of information** nützliche Hinweise
snivel /'snɪvl/ *v.i.,* (Brit.) **-ll-** schniefen
'snivelling (*Amer.:* **sniveling**) (fig.) *attrib. adj.* heulend
snob /snɒb/ *n.* Snob, *der*
snobbery /'snɒbərɪ/ *n.* Snobismus, *der*
snobbish /'snɒbɪʃ/ *adj.* snobistisch
snog /snɒg/ (Brit. coll.) [1] *v.i.,* **-gg-** knutschen (ugs.)
[2] *n.* Knutschen, *das* (ugs.)
snooker /'snu:kə(r)/ *n.* Snooker, *das*
snoop /snu:p/ *v.i.* schnüffeln (ugs.)
snooty /'snu:tɪ/ *adj.* (coll.) hochnäsig (ugs.)
snooze /snu:z/ (coll.) [1] *v.i.* dösen (ugs.)
[2] *n.* Nickerchen, *das* (fam.)
'snooze button *n.* Schlummertaste, *die*
snore /snɔ:(r)/ [1] *v.i.* schnarchen
[2] *n.* Schnarcher, *der* (ugs.); **~s** Schnarchen, *das*
snorkel /'snɔ:kl/ *n.* Schnorchel, *der*
snort /snɔ:t/ *v.i.* schnauben (**with, in** vor + *Dat.*); (sl.: take) **~ [coke]** [Koks] sniffen (Drogenjargon)
snot /snɒt/ *n.* (sl.) Rotz, *der* (derb)
snotty *adj.* rotznäsig (salopp); **~ child/nose** Rotznase, *die* (salopp)
snout /snaʊt/ *n.* Schnauze, *die;* (of pig) Rüssel, *der*
snow /snəʊ/ [1] *n.* Schnee, *der*
[2] *v.i. impers.* **it ~s/is ~ing** es schneit
▪ **snow 'in** *v.t.* **they are ~ed in** sie sind eingeschneit
▪ **snow 'under** *v.t.* **be ~ed under** (with work) erdrückt werden; (with gifts, mail) überschüttet werden
snow: ~ball [1] *n.* Schneeball, *der;* [2] *v.i.* (fig.) lawinenartig zunehmen; **~ blindness** *n.* Schneeblindheit, *die;* **~board** [1] *n.* Snowboard, *das;* [2] *v.i.* Snowboard fahren; **~boarder** *n.* Snowboarder, *der*/ Snowboarderin, *die;* **~boarding** *n.* Snowboardfahren, *das;* Snowboarden, *das;* **~bound** *adj.* eingeschneit; **~-capped** *adj.* schneebedeckt; **~ chains** *n. pl.* Schneeketten *Pl.;* **~drift** *n.* Schneewehe, *die;* **~drop** *n.* Schneeglöckchen, *das;* **~fall** *n.* Schneefall, *der;* **~flake** *n.* Schneeflocke, *die;* **~man** *n.* Schneemann, *der;* **~plough** *n.* Schneepflug, *der;* **~storm** *n.* Schneesturm, *der*
'snowy *adj.* schneereich ‹*Gegend*›; schneebedeckt ‹*Berge*›
snub /snʌb/ [1] *v.t.,* **-bb-: (a)** (rebuff) brüskieren
(b) (reject) ablehnen
[2] *n.* Abfuhr, *die*
snub-'nosed *adj.* stupsnasig
snuff¹ /snʌf/ *n.* Schnupftabak, *der;* **take a pinch of ~:** eine Prise schnupfen
snuff² *v.t.* **~ [out]** löschen ‹*Kerze*›
snuffle /'snʌfl/ *v.i.* schnüffeln
snug /snʌg/ *adj.* gemütlich; behaglich; **be a ~ fit** genau passen
snuggle /'snʌgl/ *v.i.* **~ up to sb.** sich an jmdn. kuscheln; **~ together** sich aneinander kuscheln; **~ up** *or* **down in bed** sich ins Bett kuscheln
so /səʊ/ [1] *adv.* **(a)** so; **as winter draws near, so it gets darker** je näher der Winter rückt, desto dunkler wird es; **so ... as** so ... wie; **so**

S

far bis hierher; (until now) bisher; (to such a distance) so weit; **so much the better** um so besser; **so long!** bis dann! (ugs.); **and so on [and so forth]** und so weiter [und so fort]; **so as to** um ... zu; **so [that]** damit; **I'm so glad/tired!** ich bin ja so froh/müde!; **It's a rainbow! – So it is!** Es ist ein Regenbogen! – Ja, wirklich!; **'You suggested it. – So I did** Du hast es vorgeschlagen. – Das stimmt; **is that so?** so? (ugs.); wirklich?; **so am/have/would/could/will/do I** ich auch
(b) *pron.* **he suggested that I take the train, and if I had done so, ...:** er riet mir, den Zug zu nehmen, und wenn ich es getan hätte, ...; **I'm afraid so** leider ja; **I told you so** ich habe es dir [ja] gesagt; **a week or so** etwa eine Woche; **very much so** in der Tat
2 *conj.* (therefore) daher; **so there you 'are!** ich habe also recht!; **so 'there!** [und] fertig!; **so?** na und?; **so you see ...:** du siehst also ...; **so where have you been?** wo warst du denn?

soak /səʊk/ 1 *v.t.* **(a)** einweichen ‹*Wäsche in Lauge*›; eintauchen ‹*Brot in Milch*›
(b) (wet) nass machen
2 *v.i.* **(a)** (steep) **put sth. in sth. to ~:** etw. in etw. (*Dat.*) einweichen
(b) (drain) ‹*Feuchtigkeit, Nässe:*› sickern

'soaking *adj. & adv.* **~ [wet]** völlig durchnässt

'so-and-so *n., pl.* **~'s (a)** (person not named) [Herr/Frau] Soundso
(b) (coll.: disliked person) Biest, *das* (ugs.)

soap /səʊp/ *n.* **(a)** Seife, *die;* **with ~ and water** mit Wasser und Seife
(b) (coll.) ▶ SOAP OPERA

soap: ~ flakes *n. pl.* Seifenflocken *Pl.;* **~ opera** *n.* Seifenoper, *die* (ugs.); **~ powder** *n.* Seifenpulver, *das;* **~suds** *n. pl.* Seifenschaum, *der*

'soapy *adj.* seifig; **~ water** Seifenlauge, *die*

soar /sɔ:(r)/ *v.i.* aufsteigen; (fig.) ‹*Preise, Kosten usw.:*› in die Höhe schießen (ugs.)

sob /sɒb/ 1 *v.i.,* **-bb-** schluchzen (**with** vor + *Dat.*)
2 *n.* Schluchzer, *der*

sober /'səʊbə(r)/ *adj.* **(a)** (not drunk) nüchtern
(b) (serious) ernst

■ **sober 'up** 1 *v.i.* nüchtern werden
2 *v.t.* ausnüchtern

'sobering *adj.* ernüchternd

so-called /'səʊkɔ:ld/ *adj.* so genannt; (alleged) angeblich

soccer /'sɒkə(r)/ *n.* Fußball, *der*

sociable /'səʊʃəbl/ *adj.* gesellig

social /'səʊʃl/ *adj.* **(a)** sozial; gesellschaftlich
(b) (of ~ life) gesellschaftlich; gesellig ‹*Abend, Beisammensein*›

'social club *n.* Klub für geselliges Beisammensein

socialism /'səʊʃəlɪzm/ *n.* Sozialismus, *der*

socialist /'səʊʃəlɪst/ 1 *n.* Sozialist, *der*/Sozialistin, *die*
2 *adj.* sozialistisch

socialize /'səʊʃəlaɪz/ *v.i.* geselligen Umgang pflegen; **~ with sb.** (chat) sich mit jmdm. unterhalten

'social life *n.* gesellschaftliches Leben; **not have much ~** ‹*Person:*› nicht viel ausgehen

'socially *adv.* **meet ~:** sich privat treffen; **~ deprived** sozial benachteiligt

social: ~ 'science *n.* Sozialwissenschaften *Pl.;* Gesellschaftswissenschaften *Pl.;* **~ se'curity** *n.* **(a)** (Brit.: benefit) Sozialhilfe, *die;* **(b)** (system) soziale Sicherheit; **~ 'service** *n.* staatliche Sozialleistung; **~ 'services** *n. pl.* Sozialdienste *Pl.;* **~ work** *n.* Sozialarbeit, *die;* **~ worker** *n.* Sozialarbeiter, *der*/-arbeiterin, *die*

society /sə'saɪətɪ/ *n.* **(a)** Gesellschaft, *die;* **high ~:** Highsociety, *die*
(b) (club, association) Verein, *der*

socio-eco'nomic *adj.* sozioökonomisch

sociological /səʊsɪə'lɒdʒɪkl/ *adj.* soziologisch

sociologist /səʊsɪ'ɒlədʒɪst/ *n.* Soziologe, *der*/Soziologin, *die*

sociology /səʊsɪ'ɒlədʒɪ/ *n.* Soziologie, *die*

sock[1] /sɒk/ *n.* Socke, *die*

sock[2] *v.t.* (coll.: hit) hauen (ugs.)

socket /'sɒkɪt/ *n.* **(a)** (Anat.) (of eye) Höhle, *die;* (of joint) Pfanne, *die*
(b) (Electr.) Steckdose, *die*

soda /'səʊdə/ *n.* Soda, *das*

'soda water *n.* Soda[wasser], *das*

sodden /'sɒdn/ *adj.* durchnässt (**with** von)

sodium /'səʊdɪəm/ *n.* Natrium, *das*

sodium: ~ bi'carbonate *n.* doppeltkohlensaures Natrium; Natriumhydrogenkarbonat, *das;* **~ 'chloride** *n.* Natriumchlorid, *das*

sofa /'səʊfə/ *n.* Sofa, *das*

soft /sɒft/ *adj.* weich; (quiet) leise; (gentle) sanft; **have a ~ spot for sb.** eine Vorliebe für jmdn. haben

soft: ~-boiled *adj.* weich gekocht ‹*Ei*›; **~-centred** *adj.* ‹*Praline usw.*› mit weicher Füllung; **~ copy** *n.* (Comp.) Softcopy, *die;* **~ cover** *n.* **book with a ~ cover** Buch mit einem Softcover (Verlagsw.) *od.* mit einem flexiblen Einband; **~ drink** *n.* alkoholfreies Getränk; **~ drug** *n.* weiche Droge

soften /'sɒfn/ 1 *v.i.* weicher werden
2 *v.t.* aufweichen ‹*Boden*›; enthärten ‹*Wasser*›; mildern ‹*Farbe*›

soft: ~ 'furnishings *n. pl.* (Brit.) Raumtextilien *Pl.;* **~-'hearted** /sɒft'hɑ:tɪd/ *adj.* weichherzig

'softly *adv.* (quietly) leise; (gently) sanft

soft: ~ option *n.* Weg des geringsten Widerstandes; **~ 'porn** (coll.), **~ por'nography** *ns.* Softpornographie, ···›

die; **~-spoken** *adj.* leise sprechend ‹*Person*›; **~ top** *n.* **(a)** (roof) Stoffverdeck, *das;* **(b)** (car) Cabrio, *das;* **~ 'toy** *n.* Stoffspielzeug, *das;* (toy animal) Stofftier, *das;* **~ verge** *n.* (Brit.) Grünstreifen, *der;* **~ware** *n.* (Comp.) Software, *die*

soggy /'sɒgɪ/ *adj.* aufgeweicht

soil¹ /sɔɪl/ *n.* Erde, *die;* Boden, *der*

soil² *v.t.* beschmutzen

solace /'sɒləs/ *n.* Trost, *der;* **take** *or* **find ~ in sth.** Trost in etw. (*Dat.*) finden

solar /'səʊlə(r)/ *adj.* Sonnen-

solar: ~ e'clipse *n.* Sonnenfinsternis, *die;* **~ 'energy** *n.* Sonnenenergie, *die;* **~ 'panel** *n.* Sonnenkollektor, *der;* (on satellite) Sonnensegel, *das;* **~-powered** *adj.* mit Sonnenenergie betrieben; **~ system** *n.* Sonnensystem, *das*

sold ▶ SELL

solder /'səʊldə(r)/ **1** *n.* Lot, *das*
2 *v.t.* löten

soldering iron /'səʊldərɪŋaɪən/ *n.* Lötkolben, *der*

soldier /'səʊldʒə(r)/ *n.* Soldat, *der*

sole¹ /səʊl/ *n.* (of foot/shoe) Sohle, *die*

sole² *adj.* einzig; alleinig ‹*Verantwortung, Recht*›; Allein‹*erbe, -eigentümer*›

'solely *adv.* einzig und allein

solemn /'sɒləm/ *adj.* feierlich; ernst ‹*Anlass, Gespräch*›

solicitor /sə'lɪsɪtə(r)/ *n.* (Brit.: lawyer) Rechtsanwalt, *der*/-anwältin, *die*

solid /'sɒlɪd/ **1** *adj.* **(a)** (rigid) fest
(b) (of the same substance all through) massiv
(c) (well-built) stabil; solide gebaut ‹*Haus, Mauer usw.*›
(d) (complete) ganz; **a good ~ meal** eine kräftige Mahlzeit
2 *n.* fester Körper

solidarity /sɒlɪ'dærɪtɪ/ *n.* Solidarität, *die*

solid: ~ 'fuel *n.* fester Brennstoff; **~-'fuel** *attrib. adj.* Festbrennstoff-; **~-fuel rocket** Feststoffrakete, *die*

solidify /sə'lɪdɪfaɪ/ *v.i.* fest werden

solitary /'sɒlɪtərɪ/ *adj.* **(a)** einsam; **~ confinement** Einzelhaft, *die*
(b) (sole) einzig

solitude /'sɒlɪtju:d/ *n.* Einsamkeit, *die*

solo /'səʊləʊ/ **1** *n., pl.* **~s** (Mus.) Solo, *das*
2 *adj.* **(a)** (Mus.) Solo-
(b) ~ flight Alleinflug, *der*
3 *adv.* **(a)** (Mus.) solo
(b) go/fly ~ (Aeronaut.) einen Alleinflug machen

soloist /'səʊləʊɪst/ *n.* (Mus.) Solist, *der*/Solistin, *die*

solstice /'sɒlstɪs/ *n.* Sonnenwende, *die*

soluble /'sɒljʊbl/ *adj.* **(a)** (esp. Chem.) löslich
(b) (solvable) lösbar

solution /sə'lu:ʃn/ *n.* **(a)** (esp. Chem.) Lösung, *die*
(b) ([result of] solving) Lösung, *die* (**to** *Gen.*); **find a ~ to sth.** eine Lösung für etw. finden; etw. lösen

solvable /'sɒlvəbl/ *adj.* lösbar

solve /sɒlv/ *v.t.* lösen

solvent /'sɒlvənt/ **1** *adj.* **(a)** (esp. Chem.) lösend
(b) (Finance) solvent
2 *n.* Lösungsmittel, *das*

sombre (*Amer.:* **somber**) /'sɒmbə(r)/ *adj.* dunkel; düster ‹*Stimmung, Atmosphäre*›

some /səm, *stressed* sʌm/ **1** *adj.* **(a)** (one or other) [irgend]ein; **~ day** eines Tages
(b) (a considerable quantity of) einig...
(c) (a small quantity of) ein bisschen; **would you like ~ wine/cherries?** möchten Sie [etwas] Wein/[ein paar] Kirschen?; **do ~ shopping/reading** einkaufen/lesen
(d) (to a certain extent) **~ guide** eine gewisse Orientierungshilfe
2 *pron.* einig...; **would you like ~?** möchtest du etwas/(plural) welche?; **~ ..., others ...:** manche ..., andere ...

somebody /'sʌmbədɪ/ *n. & pron.* jemand; **~ or other** irgendjemand

'somehow *adv.* **~** [**or other**] irgendwie

someone /'sʌmwʌn/ ▶ SOMEBODY

somersault /'sɒməsɔ:lt/ *n.* Purzelbaum, *der* (ugs.); Salto, *der* (Sport); **turn a ~:** einen Purzelbaum schlagen (ugs.)/einen Salto springen

'something *n. & pron.* etwas; **~ new** etwas Neues; **~ or other** irgendetwas; **see ~ of sb.** jmdn. sehen

'sometime **1** *adj.* ehemalig
2 *adv.* irgendwann

'sometimes *adv.* manchmal

'somewhat *adv.* ziemlich

'somewhere **1** *adv.* **(a)** (in a place) irgendwo
(b) (to a place) irgendwohin
2 *n.* **look for ~ to stay** sich nach einer Unterkunft umsehen

son /sʌn/ *n.* Sohn, *der*

sonata /sə'nɑ:tə/ *n.* Sonate, *die*

song /sɒŋ/ *n.* **(a)** Lied, *das*
(b) (bird cry) Gesang, *der*

song: ~bird *n.* Singvogel, *der;* **~book** *n.* Liederbuch, *das*

sonic /'sɒnɪk/ *attrib. adj.* Schall-; **~ bang** *or* **boom** Überschallknall, *der*

'son-in-law *n., pl.* **sons-in-law** Schwiegersohn, *der*

soon /su:n/ *adv.* **(a)** bald; (quickly) schnell
(b) (early) früh; **none too ~:** keinen Augenblick zu früh; **~er or later** früher oder später
(c) we'll set off as ~ as he arrives sobald er ankommt, machen wir uns auf den Weg; **as ~ as possible** so bald wie möglich
(d) (willingly) **just as ~** [**as ...**] genauso gern [wie ...]; **she would ~er die than ...:** sie würde lieber sterben, als ...

soot /sʊt/ *n.* Ruß, *der*
soothe /su:ð/ *v.t.* **(a)** (calm) beruhigen **(b)** lindern ‹*Schmerz*›
soothing /ˈsu:ðɪŋ/ *adj.* beruhigend; wohltuend ‹*Bad, Creme, Massage*›
ˈsooty *adj.* verrußt; rußig
sophisticated /səˈfɪstɪkeɪtɪd/ *adj.* **(a)** (cultured) kultiviert
(b) (elaborate, complex) hoch entwickelt; subtil ‹*Argument, System*›
soporific /sɒpəˈrɪfɪk/ *adj.* einschläfernd
sopping /ˈsɒpɪŋ/ *adj. & adv.* **~ [wet]** völlig durchnässt
soppy /ˈsɒpɪ/ *adj.* (Brit. coll.) rührselig; sentimental ‹*Person*›
soprano /səˈprɑ:nəʊ/ *n.* Sopran, *der;* (female also) Sopranistin, *die*
sorbet /ˈsɔ:bɪt, ˈsɔ:beɪ/ *n.* Sorbet, *das*
sorcerer /ˈsɔ:sərə(r)/ *n.* Zauberer, *der*
sorcery /ˈsɔ:sərɪ/ *n.* Zauberei, *die*
sordid /ˈsɔ:dɪd/ *adj.* dreckig; unerfreulich ‹*Detail, Geschichte*›
sore /sɔ:(r)/ **1** *adj.* weh; (inflamed or injured) wund; **a ~ throat** Halsschmerzen *Pl.;* **sb. has a ~ back/foot** *etc.* jmdm. tut der Rücken/Fuß *usw.* weh
2 *n.* wunde Stelle
ˈsorely *adv.* sehr; dringend ‹*nötig*›; **~ tempted** stark versucht
sorrow /ˈsɒrəʊ/ *n.* Kummer, *der*
sorry /ˈsɒrɪ/ *adj.* **(a) sb. is ~ that ...:** es tut jmdm. Leid, dass ...; **sb. is ~ about sth.** jmdm. tut etwas Leid; **I am** *or* **feel ~ for him** er tut mir Leid; **sb. is** *or* **feels ~ for sth.** jmd. bedauert etw.; **~!** Entschuldigung!; **~?** wie bitte?; **I'm ~ to say** leider; **you'll be ~!** das wird dir noch Leid tun
(b) (wretched) traurig
sort /sɔ:t/ **1** *n.* **(a)** Art, *die;* (type) Sorte, *die;* **a new ~ of bicycle** ein neuartiges Fahrrad; **all ~s of ...:** alle möglichen ...; **there are all ~s of things to do** es gibt alles Mögliche *od.* allerlei zu tun; **~ of** (coll.: more or less) mehr oder weniger; **nothing of the ~:** nichts dergleichen
(b) be out of ~s nicht in Form sein
2 *v.t.* sortieren
■ **sort ˈout** *v.t.* **(a)** (settle) klären; schlichten ‹*Streit*›; beenden ‹*Verwirrung*›
(b) (select) aussuchen
ˈsort code *n.* Bankleitzahl, *die*
sortie /ˈsɔ:tɪ/ *n.* Ausfall, *der;* (flight) Einsatz, *der*
ˈsorting office *n.* Postverteilstelle, *die*
SOS *n.* SOS, *das*
ˈso so, ˈso-so *adj., adv.* so lala (ugs.)
soufflé /ˈsu:fleɪ/ *n.* Soufflé, *das*
sought ▸ SEEK
soul /səʊl/ *n.* Seele, *die;* **not a ~:** keine Menschenseele
ˈsoul-destroying *adj.* **(a)** (boring) nervtötend
(b) (depressing) deprimierend
soulful /ˈsəʊlfl/ *adj.* gefühlvoll; (sad) schwermütig
soul: ~ mate *n.* Seelenverwandte, *der/die;* **~-searching** *n.* Gewissenskampf, *der*
sound¹ /saʊnd/ **1** *adj.* **(a)** (healthy) gesund; intakt ‹*Gebäude, Mauerwerk*›; **of ~ mind** im Vollbesitz seiner geistigen Kräfte
(b) (well-founded) vernünftig ‹*Argument, Rat*›; klug ‹*Wahl*›; **it makes ~ sense** es ist sehr vernünftig
(c) (Finance: secure) gesund, solide ‹*Basis*›; klug ‹*Investition*›
2 *adv.* fest, tief ‹*schlafen*›
sound² **1** *n.* **(a)** (Phys.) Schall, der
(b) (noise) Laut, *der;* (of wind, sea, car, footsteps, breaking glass or twigs) Geräusch, *das;* (of voices, laughter, bell) Klang, *der;* **do sth. without a ~:** etw. lautlos tun
(c) (Radio, Telev., Cinemat.) Ton, *der*
(d) (fig.: impression) **I like the ~ of your plan** ich finde, Ihr Plan hört sich gut an; **I don't like the ~ of this** das hört sich nicht gut an
2 *v.i.* klingen; **it ~s as if .../like ...:** es klingt, als .../wie ...; **that ~s a good idea to me** ich finde, die Idee hört sich gut an; **that ~s odd to me** das hört sich seltsam an, finde ich; **~s good to me!** klingt gut! (ugs.)
3 *v.t.* **(a)** ertönen lassen
(b) (utter) **~ a note of caution** zur Vorsicht mahnen
■ **sound ˈoff** *v.i.* tönen (ugs.), schwadronieren (**on, about,** von)
■ **sound ˈout** *v.i.* ausfragen ‹*Person*›; **~ sb. out on sth.** bei jmdm. wegen etw. vorfühlen
sound: ~ barrier *n.* Schallmauer, *die;* **~ bite** *n.* kurzes, prägnantes Zitat; **~ card** *n.* (Comp.) Soundkarte, *die;* **~ effect** *n.* Geräuscheffekt, *der;* **~ engineer** *n.* Toningenieur, *der/*-ingenieurin, *die*
ˈsounding board *n.* **(a)** (Mus.) Decke, *die*
(b) (fig.: trial audience) ≈ Testgruppe, *die*
ˈsoundless *adj.* lautlos
ˈsoundly *adv.* **(a)** (solidly) stabil, solide ‹*bauen*›
(b) (deeply) tief, fest ‹*schlafen*›
(c) (thoroughly) ordentlich (ugs.) ‹*verhauen*›; vernichtend ‹*schlagen, besiegen*›
sound: ~proof **1** *adj.* schalldicht; **2** *v.t.* schalldicht machen; **~ system** *n.* Tonanlage, *die;* **~track** *n.* Soundtrack, *der;* **~ wave** *n.* Schallwelle, *die*
soup /su:p/ *n.* Suppe, *die;* **be/land in the ~** (fig. coll.) in der Patsche sitzen/landen (ugs.)
souped-up /ˈsu:ptʌp/ *attrib. adj.* (Motor Veh. coll.) frisiert (ugs.)
soup: ~ plate *n.* Suppenteller, *der;* **~ spoon** *n.* Suppenlöffel, *der*
sour /ˈsaʊə(r)/ *adj.* **(a)** sauer
(b) (morose) griesgrämig; säuerlich ‹*Blick*›
(c) (unpleasant) bitter

source /sɔ:s/ *n.* Quelle, *die;* **~ of income/ infection** Einkommensquelle, *die*/ Infektionsherd, *der;* **at ~:** an der Quelle

sour 'cream *n.* saure Sahne; Sauerrahm, *der*

south /saʊθ/ [1] *n.* **(a)** Süden, *der;* **in/ to[wards]/from the ~:** im/nach/von Süden; **to the ~ of** südlich von
(b) *usu.* **S~** (Geog., Polit.) Süden, *der*
[2] *adj.* südlich; Süd‹*küste, -wind, -grenze*›
[3] *adv.* nach Süden; **~ of** südlich von

South: ~ 'Africa *pr. n.* Südafrika (*das*); **~ 'African** *adj.* südafrikanisch; **~ A'merica** *pr. n.* Südamerika (*das*); **~ A'merican** *adj.* südamerikanisch; **s~bound** *adj.* ‹*Zug, Verkehr usw.*› in Richtung Süden; **s~-'east** [1] *n.* Südosten, *der;* [2] *adj.* südöstlich; Südost‹*wind, -küste*›; [3] *adv.* südostwärts; nach Südosten; **s~-'eastern** *adj.* südöstlich

southerly /'sʌðəlɪ/ *adj.* südlich; ‹*Wind*› aus südlichen Richtungen

southern /'sʌðən/ *adj.* südlich; Süd‹*grenze, -hälfte, -seite*›

Southern Europe *pr. n.* Südeuropa (*das*)

South: ~ 'Germany *pr. n.* Süddeutschland (*das*); **~ 'Pole** *pr. n.* Südpol, *der*

southward[s] /'saʊθwəd(s)/ *adv.* südwärts

south: ~-'west [1] *n.* Südwesten, *der;* [2] *adj.* südwestlich; Südwest‹*wind, -küste*›; [3] *adv.* südwestwärts; nach Südwesten; **~-'western** *adj.* südwestlich

souvenir /su:və'nɪə(r)/ *n.* Souvenir, *das* (**of** aus); Andenken, *das*

sovereign /'sɒvrɪn/ *n.* (ruler) Souverän, *der*

sovereignty /'sɒvrɪntɪ/ *n.* Souveränität, *die*

Soviet /'səʊvɪət, 'sɒvɪət/ *adj.* (Hist.) sowjetisch; Sowjet‹*bürger, -literatur*›

Soviet 'Union *pr. n.* (Hist.) Sowjetunion, *die*

sow[1] /səʊ/ *v.t., p.p.* **sown** /səʊn/ *or* **sowed** /səʊd/ **(a)** (plant) [aus]säen
(b) einsäen ‹*Feld, Boden*›

sow[2] /saʊ/ *n.* (female pig) Sau, *die*

sown ▶ sow[1]

soya [bean] /'sɔɪə (bi:n)/ *n.* Sojabohne, *die*

soy sauce /'sɔɪ sɔ:s/ *n.* Sojasoße, *die*

sozzled /'sɒzld/ *adj.* (coll.) voll (ugs.)

spa /spɑ:/ *n.* **(a)** (place) Bad, *das;* Badeort, *der*
(b) (spring) Mineralquelle, *die*

space /speɪs/ *n.* **(a)** Raum, *der*
(b) (interval between points) Platz, *der;* **clear a ~:** Platz schaffen
(c) the wide open ~s das weite, flache Land
(d) (Astron.) Weltraum, *der*
(e) (blank between words) Zwischenraum, *der*
(f) (interval of time) Zeitraum, *der;* **in the ~ of a minute/an hour** innerhalb einer Minute/ Stunde; **in a short ~ of time he was back** nach kurzer Zeit war er zurück

■ **space 'out** *v.t.* verteilen

space: ~ age *n.* [Welt]raumzeitalter, *das;* **~ bar** *n.* Leertaste, *die;* **~craft** *n.* Raumfahrzeug, *das;* **~-saving** *adj.* Platz sparend; **~ship** *n.* Raumschiff, *das;* **~suit** *n.* Raumanzug, *der;* **~ travel** *n.* Raumfahrt, *die*

spacious /'speɪʃəs/ *adj.* geräumig

spade /speɪd/ *n.* **(a)** Spaten, *der*
(b) (Cards) Pik, *das; see also* CLUB 1C

spaghetti /spə'getɪ/ *n.* Spaghetti *Pl.*

Spain /speɪn/ *pr. n.* Spanien (*das*)

spam /spæm/ *n.* (Comput.) Spam, *der*

span /spæn/ [1] *n.* **(a)** Spanne, *die;* Zeitspanne, *die*
(b) (of bridge) Spannweite, *die*
[2] *v.t.,* **-nn-** überspannen ‹*Fluss*›; umfassen ‹*Zeitraum*›

Spaniard /'spænjəd/ *n.* Spanier, *der*/ Spanierin, *die*

Spanish /'spænɪʃ/ [1] *adj.* spanisch; **sb. is ~:** jmd. ist Spanier/Spanierin
[2] *n.* **(a)** (language) Spanisch, *das; see also* ENGLISH 2A
(b) the ~ *pl.* die Spanier *Pl.*

spank /spæŋk/ [1] *n.* ≈ Klaps, *der* (ugs.)
[2] *v.t.* **~ sb.** jmdm. einen Klaps geben (ugs.)

spanner /'spænə(r)/ *n.* (Brit.) Schraubenschlüssel, *der*

spar /spɑ:(r)/ *v.i.,* **-rr-: (a)** (Boxing) sparren
(b) (fig.: argue) [sich] zanken

spare /speə(r)/ [1] *adj.* **(a)** (not in use) übrig; **~ time/moment** Freizeit, *die*/freier Augenblick; **there is one ~ seat** ein Platz ist noch frei
(b) (for use when needed) zusätzlich, Extra‹*bett, -tasse*›; **~ room** Gästezimmer, *das*
[2] *n.* Ersatzteil, *das*/-reifen, *der usw*
[3] *v.t.* **(a)** entbehren; **we arrived with ten minutes to ~:** wir kamen zehn Minuten früher an
(b) (not inflict on) **~ sb. sth.** jmdm. etw. ersparen
(c) (not hurt) [ver]schonen
(d) (fail to use) **not ~ any expense/pains** *or* **efforts** keine Kosten/Mühe scheuen; **no expense ~d** an nichts gespart

spare: ~ 'part *n.* Ersatzteil, *das;* **~ 'tyre** *n.* Reserve-, Ersatzreifen, *der;* **~ 'wheel** *n.* Ersatzrad, *das*

sparing /'speərɪŋ/ *adj.*, **'sparingly** adv. sparsam

spark /spɑ:k/ [1] *n.* **(a)** Funke, *der;* (fig.) **a ~ of generosity/decency** ein Funke[n] Großzügigkeit/Anstand
(b) a bright ~ (coll.: person, also iron.) ein schlauer Kopf
[2] *v.t.* **~ [off]** zünden; (fig.) auslösen

sparkle /'spɑ:kl/ [1] *v.i.* **(a)** ‹*Diamant:*› glitzern; ‹*Augen:*› funkeln
(b) (be lively) sprühen (**with** vor + *Dat.*)
[2] *n.* Funkeln, *das*

S

sparkling /ˈspɑːklɪŋ/ *adj.* glitzernd ‹*Diamant*›; funkelnd ‹*Augen*›
sparkling ˈwine *n.* Schaumwein, *der*
ˈspark plug *n.* Zündkerze, *die*
sparrow /ˈspærəʊ/ *n.* Spatz, *der*
sparse /spɑːs/ *adj.* spärlich; dünn ‹*Besiedlung*›
spasm /ˈspæzm/ *n.* Krampf, *der*
spasmodic /spæzˈmɒdɪk/ *adj.* **(a)** (marked by spasms) krampfartig
(b) (intermittent) sporadisch
spastic /ˈspæstɪk/ **1** *n.* Spastiker, *der*/Spastikerin, *die*
2 *adj.* spastisch
spat ▶ SPIT 1, 2
spate /speɪt/ *n.* **(a) the river is in [full] ~:** der Fluss führt Hochwasser
(b) (fig.) **a ~ of sth.** eine Flut von etw.; **a ~ of burglaries** eine Einbruchsserie
spatial /ˈspeɪʃl/ *adj.* räumlich
spatter /ˈspætə(r)/ *v.t.* spritzen; **~ sb./sth. with sth.** jmdn./etw. mit etw. bespritzen
spatula /ˈspætjʊlə/ *n.* Spachtel, *der od. die*
spawn /spɔːn/ **1** *v.t.* (fig.) hervorbringen
2 *v.i.* (Zool.) laichen
3 *n.* (Zool.) Laich, *der*
speak /spiːk/ **1** *v.i.*, **spoke** /spəʊk/, **spoken** /ˈspəʊkn/ **(a)** sprechen; **~ [with sb.] on** *or* **about sth.** [mit jmdm.] über etw. (*Akk.*) sprechen; **~ for/against sth.** sich für/gegen etw. aussprechen
(b) (on telephone) **Is Mr Grant there? – S~ing!** Ist Mister Grant da? – Am Apparat!; **who is ~ing, please?** wer ist am Apparat, bitte?
2 *v.t.*, **spoke, spoken** sprechen ‹*Satz, Wort, Sprache*›; sagen ‹*Wahrheit*›; **~ one's mind** sagen, was man denkt
■ **ˈspeak for** *v.t.* sprechen für; **sth. is spoken for** (reserved) etw. ist schon vergeben
■ **ˈspeak of** *v.t.* sprechen von; **~ing of Mary** da wir gerade von Mary sprechen; **nothing to ~ of** nichts Besonderes
■ **ˈspeak to** *v.t.* sprechen *od.* reden mit
■ **speak ˈup** *v.i.* lauter sprechen
ˈspeaker *n.* **(a)** (in public) Redner, *der*/Rednerin, *die*
(b) (of a language) Sprecher *der*/Sprecherin, *die;* **be a ˈFrench ~:** Französisch sprechen
(c) (loudspeaker) Lautsprecher, *der*
ˈspeaking **1** *n.* Sprechen, *das;* **~ clock** (Brit.) telefonische Zeitansage
2 *adv.* **strictly/generally ~:** genau genommen/im Allgemeinen
spear /spɪə(r)/ *n.* Speer, *der*
ˈspearhead **1** *n.* (fig.) Speerspitze, *die*
2 *v.t.* (fig.) anführen
ˈspearmint *n.* Grüne Minze; **~ chewing gum** Pfefferminzkaugummi, *der od. das*
spec[1] /spek/ (coll.) ▶ SPECIFICATION
spec[2] /spek/ *n.* (coll.: speculation) **on ~:** auf gut Glück; auf Verdacht (ugs.)
special /ˈspeʃl/ *adj.* speziell; besonder...; **nobody ~:** niemand Besonderes
special deˈlivery *n.* (Post) Eilzustellung, *die*
special efˈfects *n. pl.* (Cinemat.) Special effects *Pl.*
specialist /ˈspeʃəlɪst/ *n.* **(a)** Spezialist, *der*/Spezialistin, *die* (**in** für)
(b) (Med.) Facharzt, *der*/-ärztin, *die*
speciality /speʃɪˈælɪtɪ/ *n.* Spezialität, *die*
specialization /speʃəlaɪˈzeɪʃn/ *n.* Spezialisierung, *die*
specialize /ˈspeʃəlaɪz/ *v.i.* sich spezialisieren (**in** auf + *Akk.*)
specialized /ˈspeʃəlaɪzd/ *adj.* **(a)** (requiring detailed knowledge) speziell; Spezial‹*kenntnisse, -gebiet*›
(b) (concentrating on small area) spezialisiert
ˈspecially *adv.* **(a)** speziell; **make sth. ~:** etw. speziell *od.* extra anfertigen
(b) (especially) besonders
special: ~ ˈneeds *n.* **children with ~ needs** Kinder, die besonders betreut werden müssen; **~ needs teacher** Förderlehrer, *der*/-lehrerin, *die;* **~ ˈoffer** *n.* Sonderangebot, *das;* **on ~ offer** im Sonderangebot; **~ school** *n.* Sonderschule, *die*
specialty /ˈspeʃltɪ/ (esp. Amer.) ▶ SPECIALITY
species /ˈspiːʃiːz/ *n., pl. same* Art, *die;* **~ barrier** Artenbarriere, *die;* Artengrenze, *die*
specific /spɪˈsɪfɪk/ *adj.* bestimmt; **could you be more ~?** kannst du dich genauer ausdrücken?
specifically /spɪˈsɪfɪkəli/ *adv.* ausdrücklich; eigens; extra (ugs.)
specification /spesɪfɪˈkeɪʃn/ *n., often pl.* (details) technische Daten *Pl.*; (for building) Baubeschreibung, *die*
specify /ˈspesɪfaɪ/ *v.t.* ausdrücklich sagen; **unless otherwise specified** wenn nicht anders angegeben
specimen /ˈspesɪmən/ *n.* **(a)** (example) Exemplar, *das*
(b) (sample) Probe, *die*
speck /spek/ *n.* **(a)** (spot) Fleck, *der*
(b) (particle) Teilchen, *das;* **~ of soot/dust** Rußflocke, *die*/Staubkörnchen, *das*
specs /speks/ *n. pl.* (coll.: spectacles) Brille, *die*
spectacle /ˈspektəkl/ *n.* **(a)** *in pl.* **[pair of] ~s** Brille, *die*
(b) (public show) Spektakel, *das*
ˈspectacle case *n.* Brillenetui, *das*
spectacular /spekˈtækjʊlə(r)/ *adj.* spektakulär
spectator /spekˈteɪtə(r)/ *n.* Zuschauer, *der*/Zuschauerin, *die*
specˈtator sport *n.* Publikumssport, *der*
specter (Amer.) ▶ SPECTRE
spectra *pl. of* SPECTRUM
spectre /ˈspektə(r)/ *n.* (Brit.) **(a)** (ghost) Gespenst, *das*
(b) (fig.) Schreckgespenst, *das*

S

spectrum /'spektrəm/ *n., pl.* **spectra** /'spektrə/ Spektrum, *das*

speculate /'spekjʊleɪt/ *v.i.* spekulieren (**about, on** über + *Akk.*)

speculation /spekjʊ'leɪʃn/ *n.* Spekulation, *die* (**over** über + *Akk.*)

speculative /'spekjʊlətɪv/ *adj.* spekulativ

speculator /'spekjʊleɪtə(r)/ *n.* Spekulant, *der*/Spekulantin, *die*

sped ▸ SPEED 2

speech /spi:tʃ/ *n.* **(a)** (public address) Rede, *die;* **make** *or* **deliver** *or* **give a ~**: eine Rede halten
(b) (faculty or manner of speaking) Sprache, *die*

'speechless *adj.* sprachlos (**with** vor + *Dat.*)

speed /spi:d/ [1] *n.* Geschwindigkeit, *die;* Schnelligkeit, *die;* **at a ~ of ...**: mit einer Geschwindigkeit von ...
[2] *v.i.* **(a)** *p.t. & p.p.* **sped** /sped/ *or* **speeded** schnell fahren; rasen (ugs.)
(b) *p.t.&p.p.* **speeded** (go too fast) zu schnell fahren; rasen (ugs.)

speed: ~boat *n.* Rennboot, *das;* **~ bump** *n.* Bodenschwelle, *die;* **~ camera** *n.* Geschwindigkeitsüberwachungskamera, *die;* **~ dating** *n.* Speeddating, *das*

'speeding *n.* Geschwindigkeitsüberschreitung, *die*

'speed limit *n.* Geschwindigkeitsbeschränkung, *die*

speedo /'spi:dəʊ/ *n., pl.* **~s** (Brit. coll.) Tacho, *der* (ugs.)

speedometer /spi:'dɒmɪtə(r)/ *n.* Tachometer, *der od. das*

speed: ~ ramp *n.* Bodenschwelle, *die;* **~way** *n.* Speedwayrennen, *das*

'speedy *adj.* schnell; umgehend, prompt ‹*Antwort*›

spell¹ /spel/ [1] *v.t.,* **spelt** /spelt/ (Brit.) *or* **spelled** **(a)** schreiben; (aloud) buchstabieren
(b) (fig.: mean) bedeuten
[2] *v.i.,* **spelt** (Brit.) *or* **spelled** (say) buchstabieren; (write) richtig schreiben

spell² *n.* (period) Weile, *die;* **a cold ~**: eine Kälteperiode

spell³ *n.* **(a)** (magic charm) Zauberspruch, *der;* **cast a ~ on sb.** jmdn. verzaubern
(b) (fascination) Zauber, *der;* **break the ~**: den Bann brechen

'spellbound *adj.* verzaubert

'spell checker ▸ SPELLING CHECKER

'spelling *n.* Rechtschreibung, *die*

spelling: ~ checker *n.* Rechtschreibprogramm, *das;* **~ mistake** *n.* Rechtschreibfehler, *der*

spelt ▸ SPELL¹

spend /spend/ *v.t.,* **spent** /spent/ **(a)** (pay out) ausgeben; **~ a penny** (fig. coll.) mal verschwinden (ugs.)
(b) verbringen ‹*Zeit*›

'spendthrift *n.* Verschwender, *der*/Verschwenderin, *die*

spent [1] ▸ SPEND
[2] *adj.* **(a)** (used up) verbraucht
(b) (drained of energy) erschöpft

sperm /spɜ:m/ *n. pl* **~s** *or same* Sperma, *der*

sperm: ~ bank *n.* Samenbank, *die;* **~ count** *n.* Spermienzahl, *die;* **~ donor** *n.* Samenspender, *der;* Spermaspender, *der*

spew /spju:/ *v.t.* spucken

sphere /sfɪə(r)/ *n.* **(a)** (field of action) Bereich, *der;* Sphäre, *die* (geh.)
(b) (Geom.) Kugel, *die*

spherical /'sferɪkl/ *adj.* kugelförmig

spice /spaɪs/ [1] *n.* Gewürz, *das;* (fig.) Würze, *die*
[2] *v.t.* würzen

'spice rack *n.* Gewürzregal, *das*

spicy /'spaɪsɪ/ *adj.* pikant; würzig

spider /'spaɪdə(r)/ *n.* Spinne, *die*

spider: ~ plant *n.* Grünlilie, *die;* **~'s web** (*Amer.:* **~ web**) Spinnennetz, *das*

spike /spaɪk/ *n.* Stachel, *der*

spiky /'spaɪkɪ/ *adj.* stachelig

spill /spɪl/ [1] *v.t.,* **spilt** /spɪlt/ *or* **spilled** verschütten ‹*Flüssigkeit*›; **~ sth. on sth.** etw. auf etw. (*Akk.*) schütten; **~ the beans** aus der Schule plaudern
[2] *v.i.,* **spilt** *or* **spilled** überlaufen

spilt ▸ SPILL

spin /spɪn/ [1] *v.t.,* **-nn-, spun** /spʌn/ **(a)** spinnen; **~ yarn** Garn spinnen
(b) (in washing machine etc.) schleudern
[2] *v.i.,* **-nn-, spun** sich drehen; **my head is ~ning** (fig.) mir schwirrt der Kopf

▪ **spin 'out** *v.t.* (prolong) in die Länge ziehen

spinach /'spɪnɪdʒ/ *n.* Spinat, *der*

spinal /'spaɪnl/ *adj.* Wirbelsäulen-; Rückgrat[s]-

spinal: ~ 'column *n.* Wirbelsäule, *die;* **~ 'cord** *n.* Rückenmark, *das*

spindle /'spɪndl/ *n.* Spindel, *die*

spindly /'spɪndlɪ/ *adj.* spindeldürr

spin: ~ doctor *n.* (coll.) Spin-Doktor, *der;* **~ 'drier** *n.* Wäscheschleuder, *die;* **~-'dry** *v.t.* schleudern

spine /spaɪn/ *n.* **(a)** (backbone) Wirbelsäule, die
(b) (Bot., Zool.) Stachel, *der*

'spineless *adj.* (fig.) rückgratlos

'spin-off *n.* Nebenprodukt, *das*

spinster /'spɪnstə(r)/ *n.* ledige Frau

spiny /'spaɪnɪ/ *adj.* stachelig

spiral /'spaɪrl/ [1] *adj.* spiralförmig
[2] *n.* Spirale, *die*
[3] *v.i.,* (Brit.) **-ll-** ‹*Weg:*› sich hochwinden; ‹*Kosten:*› in die Höhe klettern; ‹*Rauch:*› in einer Spirale aufsteigen

spiral 'staircase *n.* Wendeltreppe, *die*

spire /'spaɪə(r)/ *n.* Turmspitze, *die*

spirit /'spɪrɪt/ *n.* **(a)** *in pl.* (distilled liquor) Spirituosen *Pl.*
(b) (mental attitude) Geisteshaltung, *die;* **in the right/wrong ~**: mit der richtigen/falschen Einstellung; **take sth. in the wrong ~**: etw. falsch auffassen
(c) (courage) Mut, *der*
(d) (mental tendency) Geist, *der;* **high ~s** gehobene Stimmung; **in poor** *or* **low ~s** niedergedrückt

'spirited *adj.* beherzt

'spirit level *n.* Wasserwaage, *die*

spiritual /'spɪrɪtʃʊəl/ *adj.* spirituell (geh.)

spit /spɪt/ 1 *v.i.*, **-tt-**, **spat** /spæt/ *or* **spit** spucken
2 *v.t.*, **-tt-**, **spat** *or* **spit** spucken
3 *n.* Spucke, *die*

■ **spit 'out** *v.t.* ausspucken

spite /spaɪt/ 1 *n.* **(a)** Boshaftigkeit, *die*
(b) in ~ of trotz; **in ~ of oneself** obwohl man es eigentlich nicht will
2 *v.t.* ärgern

spiteful /'spaɪtfl/ *adj.* gehässig

spitting 'image *n.* **be the ~ of sb.** jmdm. wie aus dem Gesicht geschnitten sein

spittle /'spɪtl/ *n.* Spucke, *die*

splash /splæʃ/ 1 *v.t.* spritzen; **~ sth. on [to]** *or* **over sb./sth.** jmdn./etw. mit etw. bespritzen
2 *v.i.* **(a)** spritzen
(b) (in water) platschen (ugs.)
3 *n.* **(a)** (liquid) Spritzer, *der*
(b) (noise) Plätschern, *das*

■ **splash 'out** *vi.* (coll.) **~ out on sth.** für etw. unbekümmert Geld ausgeben

splendid /'splendɪd/ *adj.* (excellent) großartig; (magnificent) prächtig

splendour (*Brit.; Amer.:* **splendor**) /'splendə(r)/ *n.* Pracht, *die*

splint /splɪnt/ *n.* Schiene, *die*

splinter /'splɪntə(r)/ *n.* Splitter, *der*

split /splɪt/ 1 *n.* **(a)** (tear) Riss, *der*
(b) (division into parts) [Auf]teilung, *die;* (fig.) Spaltung, *die*
2 *adj.* gespalten; **be ~ on a question** [sich (*Dat.*)] in einer Frage uneins sein
3 *v.t.*, **-tt-**, **split (a)** (tear) zerreißen
(b) (divide) teilen
4 *v.i.*, **-tt-**, **split (a)** ‹*Holz:*› splittern; ‹*Stoff, Seil:*› reißen; **~ apart** zersplittern
(b) (divide into parts) sich teilen

■ **split 'up** 1 *v.t.* aufteilen
2 *v.i.* (coll.) sich trennen; **~ up with sb.** sich von jmdm. trennen

split: ~-level *adj.* mit Zwischengeschoss *nachgestellt;* auf zwei Ebenen *nachgestellt;* **a ~-level lounge** ein Wohnraum auf zwei Ebenen; **~-level cooker** *Einbauherd, bei dem Kochplatten und Backofen getrennt sind;* **~ 'pea** *n.* getrocknete [halbe] Erbse; **~ perso'nality** *n.* gespaltene Persönlichkeit; **~ 'second** *n.* **in a ~ second** im Bruchteil einer Sekunde; **~-second timing** [zeitliche] Abstimmung auf die Sekunde genau

splitting /'splɪtɪŋ/ *adj.* **a ~ headache** rasende Kopfschmerzen *Pl.*

splutter /'splʌtə(r)/ *v.i.* ‹*Person:*› prusten; ‹*Motor:*› stottern

spoil /spɔɪl/ 1 *v.t.*, **spoilt** /spɔɪlt/ *or* **spoiled**
(a) (impair) verderben
(b) (pamper) verwöhnen; **be ~t for choice** die Qual der Wahl haben
2 *v.i.*, **spoilt** *or* **spoiled (a)** verderben
(b) be ~ing for a fight Streit suchen
3 *n.* **~[s** *pl.*] Beute, *die*

'spoiler *n.* (of car, aircraft) Spoiler, *der*

'spoilsport *n.* Spielverderber, *der*/-verderberin, *die*

spoilt ▸ SPOIL 1, 2

spoke¹ /spəʊk/ *n.* Speiche, *die*

spoke², spoken ▸ SPEAK

spokesman /'spəʊksmən/ *n.*, *pl.* **spokesmen** /'spəʊksmən/ Sprecher, *der*

sponge /spʌndʒ/ 1 *n.* Schwamm, *der*
2 *v.t.* mit einem Schwamm waschen

■ **'sponge on** *v.t.* **~ on sb.** bei *od.* von jmdm. schnorren (ugs.)

sponge: ~ bag *n.* (Brit.) Kulturbeutel, *der;* **~ cake** *n.* Biskuitkuchen, *der*

sponger /'spʌndʒə(r)/ *n.* Schmarotzer, *der*/Schmarotzerin, *die*

spongy /'spʌndʒɪ/ *adj.* schwammig

sponsor /'spɒnsə(r)/ 1 *n.* Sponsor, *der*
2 *v.t.* **(a)** sponsern
(b) (Polit.) **~ sb.** jmds. Kandidatur unterstützen

spontaneity /spɒntə'ni:ɪtɪ/ *n.* Spontaneität, *die*

spontaneous /spɒn'teɪnɪəs/ *adj.* spontan

spooky /'spu:kɪ/ *adj.* gespenstisch

spool /spu:l/ *n.* Spule, *die*

spoon /spu:n/ *n.* **(a)** Löffel, *der*
(b) (amount) ▸ SPOONFUL

'spoon-feed *v.t.* (*fig.*) **~ sb.** jmdm. alles vorkauen (ugs.)

spoonful /'spu:nfʊl/ *n.* **a ~ of sugar** ein Löffel [voll] Zucker

sporadic /spə'rædɪk/ *adj.* sporadisch

sporadically /spə'rædɪkəlɪ/ *adv.* hin und wieder

spore /spɔ:(r)/ *n.* Spore, *die*

sport /spɔ:t/ 1 *n.* **(a)** Sport, *der;* **~s** Sportarten *Pl.*; **water/indoor ~**: Wasser-/Hallensport, *der*
(b) (fun) Spaß, *der*
(c) be a [real] ~ (coll.) ein prima Kerl sein (ugs.); **be a ~!** sei kein Spielverderber!
2 *v.t.* stolz tragen

'sporting *adj.* **(a)** sportlich
(b) give sb. a ~ chance jmdm. eine [faire] Chance geben

sports: ~ bra *n.* Sport-BH, *der;* **~ car** *n.* Sportwagen, *der;* **~ centre** *n.*

⋯›

Sportzentrum, *das;* ~ **channel** *n.* Sportkanal, *der;* ~ **commentator** *n.* Sportberichterstatter, *der*/-berichterstatterin, *die;* ~ **complex** *n.* Sportzentrum, *das;* ~ **field** *n.* Sportplatz, *der;* ~ **hall** *n.* Sporthalle, *die;* ~ **jacket** *n.* sportlicher Sakko; ~**man** /'spɔːtsmən/ *n., pl.* ~**men** /'spɔːtsmən/ Sportler, *der;* ~**manship** /'spɔːtsmənʃɪp/ *n.* (fairness) [sportliche] Fairness; ~ **page** *n.* (Journ.) Sportseite, *die;* ~ **section** *n.* (Journ.) Sportteil, *der;* ~**wear** *n.* Sport[be]kleidung, *die;* ~**woman** *n.* Sportlerin, *die*

'sporty *adj.* sportlich

spot /spɒt/ [1] *n.* **(a)** (precise place) Stelle, *die;* **on this ~**: an dieser Stelle; **be in a tight ~** (fig. coll.) in der Klemme sitzen (ugs.); **put sb. on the ~** (fig. coll.) jmdn. in Verlegenheit bringen
(b) (suitable area) Platz, *der*
(c) (dot) Tupfen, *der*
(d) (stain) ~ **[of blood/grease/ink]** [Blut-/Fett-/Tinten]fleck, *der*
(e) (Brit. coll.: small amount) **do a ~ of work/sewing** ein bisschen arbeiten/nähen
(f) (drop) **a ~** *or* **a few ~s of rain** ein paar Regentropfen
(g) (Med.) Pickel, *der*
[2] *v.t.*, **-tt-** (detect) entdecken; erkennen ‹*Gefahr*›

spot: ~ **'check** *n.* Stichprobe, *die;* ~**less** *adj.* fleckenlos; **her house is absolutely ~less** (fig.) ihr Haus ist makellos sauber; ~**light** *n.* Scheinwerfer, *der;* **be in the ~light** (fig.) im Rampenlicht stehen

spotted /'spɒtɪd/ *adj.* gepunktet

'spotty *adj.* (pimply) picklig

spouse /spaʊs/ *n.* [Ehe]gatte, *der*/-gattin, *die*

spout /spaʊt/ [1] *n.* Schnabel, *der;* (of tap) Ausflussrohr, *das*
[2] *v.i.* (gush) schießen (**from** aus)

sprain /spreɪn/ [1] *v.t.* verstauchen
[2] *n.* Verstauchung, *die*

sprang ▶ SPRING 2, 3

sprawl /sprɔːl/ *v.i.* **(a)** sich ausstrecken; (fall) der Länge nach hinfallen
(b) (straggle) sich ausbreiten

'sprawling *attrib. adj.* wuchernd ‹*Großstadt*›

spray[1] /spreɪ/ (bouquet) Strauß, *der*

spray[2] [1] *v.t.* spritzen; sprühen ‹*Parfüm*›; besprühen ‹*Haar, Pflanze*›
[2] *n.* **(a)** (drops) Sprühnebel, *der*
(b) (liquid) Spray, *der od. das*

spray: ~ **can** ▶ AEROSOL A; ~ **gun** *n.* Spritzpistole, *die*

spread /spred/ [1] *v.t.*, **spread (a)** ausbreiten ‹*Tuch, Landkarte*› (**on** auf + *Dat.*); streichen ‹*Butter, Farbe, Marmelade*›
(b) (extend range of) verbreiten
(c) (distribute) verteilen
[2] *v.i.*, **spread** sich ausbreiten
[3] *n.* **(a)** Verbreitung, *die;* (of city, poverty) Ausbreitung, *die*
(b) (coll.: meal) Festessen, *das*
(c) (paste) Brotaufstrich, *der*
(d) (Printing) **the advertisement was a full-page/double-page ~**: die Anzeige war ganzseitig/doppelseitig

▪ **spread 'out** [1] *v.t.* ausbreiten
[2] *v.i.* sich verteilen

'spreadsheet *n.* (Comp.) Arbeitsblatt, *das*

spree /spriː/ *n.* **go on a shopping ~**: ganz groß einkaufen gehen

'spree killer *n.* Amokläufer, *der*

sprig /sprɪg/ *n.* Zweig, *der*

sprightly /'spraɪtlɪ/ *adj.* munter

spring /sprɪŋ/ [1] *n.* **(a)** (season) Frühling, *der;* **in [the] ~**: im Frühling *od.* Frühjahr
(b) (water) Quelle, *die*
(c) (Mech.) Feder, *die*
(d) (jump) Sprung, *der*
[2] *v.i.*, **sprang** /spræŋ/ *or* (Amer.) **sprung** /sprʌŋ/, **sprung (a)** (jump) springen; **~ to life** (fig.) [plötzlich] zum Leben erwachen
(b) (arise) entspringen (**from** *Dat.*)
[3] *v.t.*, **sprang** *or* (Amer.) **sprung, sprung: ~ sth. on sb.** jmdn. mit etw. überfallen

spring: ~**board** *n.* Sprungbrett, *das;* ~ **'chicken** *n.* **be no ~ chicken** nicht mehr der/die Jüngste sein (ugs.); ~**-'clean** [1] *n.* Frühjahrsputz, *der;* [2] *v.t.* Frühjahrsputz machen in (+ *Dat.*): ~**-loaded** *adj.* mit Sprungfeder nachgestellt; ~ **'onion** *n.* Frühlingszwiebel, *die;* ~**time** *n.* Frühling, *der*

springy /'sprɪŋɪ/ *adj.* elastisch; federnd ‹*Schritt, Brett, Boden*›

sprinkle /'sprɪŋkl/ *v.t.* streuen; sprengen ‹*Flüssigkeit*›

sprinkler /'sprɪŋklə(r)/ *n.* (Hort.) Sprinkler, *der*

sprinkling /'sprɪŋklɪŋ/ *n.* **a ~ of snow/sugar/dust** eine dünne Schneedecke/Zucker-/Staubschicht

sprint /sprɪnt/ [1] *v.t. & i.* rennen; sprinten (bes. Sport)
[2] *n.* Sprint, *der*

sprout /spraʊt/ [1] *n.* **(a) Brussels ~s** Rosenkohl, *der*
(b) (Bot.) Trieb, *der*
[2] *v.i.* sprießen (geh.)

spruce /spruːs/ [1] *adj.* gepflegt
[2] *n.* Fichte, *die*

sprung /sprʌŋ/ [1] ▶ SPRING 2, 3
[2] *attrib. adj.* gefedert

spry /spraɪ/ *adj.* rege

spud /spʌd/ *n.* (coll.) Kartoffel, *die*

spun ▶ SPIN

spunk /spʌŋk/ *n.* (coll.: courage) Mumm, *der* (ugs.)

spur /spɜː(r)/ [1] *n.* Sporn, *der;* (fig.) Ansporn, *der;* **on the ~ of the moment** ganz spontan
[2] *v.t.*, **-rr-** (fig.) anspornen

spurious /'spjʊərɪəs/ *adj.* gespielt ‹*Interesse*›; unberechtigt ‹*Anspruch, Anklage*›

spurn /spɜ:n/ *v.t.* zurückweisen

spurt[1] /spɜ:t/ *n.* Spurt, *der;* **put on a ~:** einen Spurt einlegen

spurt[2] [1] *v.i.* **~ out [from** *or* **of]** herausspritzen [aus]
[2] *n.* Strahl, *der*

spy /spaɪ/ [1] *n.* Spion, *der*/Spionin, *die*
[2] *v.i.* spionieren; **~ on sb.** jmdm. nachspionieren

spy: ~master *n.* Chef, *der* eines Spionagerings; **~ ring** *n.* Spionagering, *der;* **~ story** *n.* Spionagegeschichte, *die*

squabble /'skwɒbl/ [1] *n.* Streit, *der*
[2] *v.i.* sich zanken (**over, about** wegen)

squad /skwɒd/ *n.* **(a)** (Mil.) Gruppe, *die*
(b) (group) Mannschaft, *die*

squadron /'skwɒdrən/ *n.* **(a)** (Navy) Geschwader, *das*
(b) (Air Force) Staffel, *die*

squalid /'skwɒlɪd/ *adj.* **(a)** (dirty) schmutzig
(b) (poor) schäbig

squall /skwɔ:l/ *n.* (gust) Bö, *die*

squalor /'skwɒlə(r)/ *n.* Schmutz, *der*

squander /'skwɒndə(r)/ *v.t.* vergeuden

square /skweə(r)/ [1] *n.* **(a)** (Geom.) Quadrat, *das*
(b) (open area) Platz, *der*
[2] *adj.* **(a)** quadratisch
(b) a ~ metre/mile ein Quadratmeter/eine Quadratmeile
(c) be all ~: [völlig] quitt sein (*ugs.*)
[3] *v.t.* **(a)** (Math.) quadrieren
(b) ~ it with sb. es mit jmdm. klären
[4] *v.i.* (agree) übereinstimmen

■ **square 'up** *v.i.* (settle up) abrechnen

square: ~ 'brackets *n. pl.* eckige Klammern *Pl.*; **~ 'meal** *n.* anständige Mahlzeit (ugs.); **~ 'root** *n.* Quadratwurzel, *die*

squash /skwɒʃ/ [1] *v.t.* (crush) zerquetschen; **~ sth. flat** etw. platt drücken
[2] *n.* **(a)** Fruchtsaftgetränk, *das*
(b) (Sport) Squash, *das*

squash: ~ court *n.* Squashfeld, *das;* **~ racket** *n.* Squashschläger, *der*

squat /skwɒt/ *v.i.*, **-tt-: (a)** (crouch) hocken
(b) ~ in a house ein Haus besetzen

'squatter *n.* Hausbesetzer, *der*/-besetzerin, *die*

squawk /skwɔ:k/ *v.i.* ‹*Krähe:*› krähen; ‹*Huhn:*› kreischen

squeak /skwi:k/ [1] *n.* **(a)** (of animal) Quieken, *das*
(b) (of brakes, hinge, etc.) Quietschen, *das*
[2] *v.i.* **(a)** ‹*Tier:*› quieken
(b) ‹*Scharnier, Tür, Bremse, Schuh usw.:*› quietschen

squeaky /'skwi:kɪ/ *adj.* quietschend

squeal /skwi:l/ [1] *v.i.* **(a) ~ with pain/in fear** ‹*Person:*› vor Schmerz/Angst aufschreien; ‹*Tier:*› vor Schmerz/Angst laut quieken
(b) ‹*Bremsen, Räder:*› kreischen; ‹*Reifen:*› quietschen
[2] *n.* Kreischen, *das;* (of tyres) Quietschen, *das;* (of animal) Quieken, *das*

squeamish /'skwi:mɪʃ/ *adj.* **be ~:** zart besaitet sein

squeeze /skwi:z/ [1] *n.* Druck, *der;* **give sth. a small ~:** etw. [leicht] drücken
[2] *v.t.* **(a)** (press) drücken; drücken auf (+ *Akk.*) ‹*Tube, Plastikflasche*›; (to get juice) auspressen
(b) (extract) drücken (**out of** aus); **~ out sth.** etw. herausdrücken
(c) (force) zwängen

squelch /skweltʃ/ *v.i.* quatschen (ugs.)

squid /skwɪd/ *n.* Kalmar, *der*

squiggle /'skwɪgl/ *n.* Schnörkel, *der*

squint /skwɪnt/ [1] *n.* Schielen, *das*
[2] *v.i.* **(a)** (Med.) schielen
(b) (with half-closed eyes) blinzeln

squire /'skwaɪə(r)/ *n.* ≈ Gutsherr, *der*

squirm /skwɜ:m/ *v.i.* sich winden (**with** vor + *Dat.*)

squirrel /'skwɪrl/ *n.* Eichhörnchen, *das*

squirt /skwɜ:t/ [1] *v.t.* spritzen; sprühen ‹*Spray, Puder*›; **~ sth. at sb.** jmdn. mit etw. bespritzen/besprühen
[2] *v.i.* spritzen
[3] *n.* Spritzer, *der*

st. *abbr.* (Brit.: unit of weight) = **stone**

St *abbr.* = **Saint** St.

St. *abbr.* = **Street** Str.

stab /stæb/ [1] *v.t.*, **-bb-** stechen; **~ sb. in the chest** jmdm. in die Brust stechen
[2] *v.i.*, **-bb-** stechen
[3] *n.* **(a)** Stich, *der*
(b) (coll.: attempt) **make** *or* **have a ~ [at it]** [es] probieren

stability /stə'bɪlɪtɪ/ *n.* Stabilität, *die*

stabilize /'steɪbɪlaɪz/ [1] *v.t.* stabilisieren
[2] *v.i.* sich stabilisieren

stable[1] /'steɪbl/ *adj.* stabil; gefestigt ‹*Person*›

stable[2] *n.* Stall, *der*

stack /stæk/ [1] *n.* **(a)** (pile) Stoß, *der;* Stapel, *der*
(b) (coll.: large amount) Haufen, *der* (ugs.)
(c) [chimney] ~: Schornstein, *der*
[2] *v.t.* **~ [up]** [auf]stapeln

stadium /'steɪdɪəm/ *n.* Stadion, *das*

staff /stɑ:f/ [1] *n.* **(a)** (stick) Stock, *der*
(b) (personnel) Personal, *das;* (of school) Lehrerkollegium, *das*
[2] *v.t.* mit Personal ausstatten

staff: ~ meeting *n.* [Lehrer]konferenz, *die;* **~room** *n.* Lehrerzimmer, *das*

stag /stæg/ *n.* Hirsch, *der*

stage /steɪdʒ/ [1] *n.* **(a)** (Theatre) Bühne, *die*
(b) (part of process) Stadium, *das;* **at this ~:** ⋯›

in diesem Stadium; **do sth. by ~s** etw. abschnittsweise tun; **in the final ~s** in der Schlussphase
(c) (distance) Etappe, *die*
2 *v.t.* **(a)** (present) inszenieren
(b) (arrange) veranstalten

stage: ~coach *n.* Postkutsche, *die;* **~ door** *n.* Bühneneingang, *der;* **~ effect** *n.* Bühneneffekt, *der;* **~ fright** *n.* Lampenfieber, *das;* **~hand** *n.* Bühnenarbeiter, *der*/-arbeiterin, *die;* **~-manage** *v.t.* (fig.) veranstalten; **~ name** *n.* Künstlername, *der*

stagger /'stægə(r)/ 1 *v.i.* schwanken
2 *v.t.* (astonish) die Sprache verschlagen (+ *Dat.*)

stagnant /'stægnənt/ *adj.* **(a)** stehend ‹*Gewässer*›
(b) (Econ.) stagnierend

stagnate /stæg'neɪt/ *v.i.* **(a)** ‹*Wasser:*› abstehen
(b) ‹*Wirtschaft, Geschäft:*› stagnieren; ‹*Person:*› abstumpfen

stagnation /stæg'neɪʃn/ *n.* **(a)** (of water) Stehen, *das*
(b) (Econ.) Stagnation, *die*

stag: ~ night *n.*: *Zechabend des Bräutigams mit seinen Freunden kurz vor seiner Hochzeit;* **~ party** *n.* Herrenabend, *der*

staid /steɪd/ *adj.* gesetzt

stain /steɪn/ 1 *v.t.* **(a)** verfärben; (make ~s on) Flecken hinterlassen auf (+ *Dat.*)
(b) (colour) beizen ‹*Holz*›
2 *n.* Fleck, *der*

stained 'glass *n.* farbiges Glas; **~ 'window** Fenster mit Glasmalerei

'stainless *adj.* fleckenlos

stainless 'steel *n.* Edelstahl, *der*

'stain remover *n.* Fleck[en]entferner, *der*

stair /steə(r)/ *n.* (step) [Treppen]stufe, *die;* **~s** Treppe, *die*

stair: ~case *n.* Treppenhaus, *das;* **~way** *n.* Treppe, *die*

stake /steɪk/ *n.* **(a)** (pointed stick) Pfahl, *der*
(b) (wager) Einsatz, *der;* **be at ~:** auf dem Spiel stehen

stale /steɪl/ *adj.* alt; muffig; abgestanden ‹*Luft*›; alt[backen] ‹*Brot*›; schal ‹*Bier, Wein usw.*›

'stalemate *n.* Patt, *das*

stalk¹ /stɔːk/ *v.t.* **(a)** sich heranpirschen an (+ *Akk.*)
(b) (follow obsessively) **~ sb.** jmdm. nachstellen

stalk² *n.* (Bot.) (main stem) Stängel, *der;* (of leaf, flower, fruit) Stiel, *der*

stalker /'stɔːkə(r)/ *n.* (obsessive pursuer) [lästiger] Verfolger

stall /stɔːl/ 1 *n.* **(a)** Stand, *der*
(b) (Brit. Theatre) **~s** Parkett, *das*
2 *v.t.* abwürgen (ugs.) ‹*Motor*›
3 *v.i.* ‹*Motor:*› stehen bleiben

'stallholder *n.* Standinhaber, *der*/-inhaberin, *die*

stallion /'stæljən/ *n.* Hengst, *der*

stalwart /'stɔːlwət/ *adj.* (determined) entschieden; (loyal) treu

stamen /'steɪmen/ *n.* Staubblatt, *das*

stamina /'stæmɪnə/ *n.* Ausdauer, *die*

stammer /'stæmə(r)/ 1 *v.i.* stottern
2 *v.t.* stammeln
3 *n.* Stottern, *das*

stamp /stæmp/ 1 *v.t.* **(a)** (impress, imprint sth. on) [ab]stempeln
(b) ~ one's foot mit dem Fuß stampfen
(c) (put postage ~ on) frankieren; **~ed addressed envelope** frankierter Rückumschlag
(d) become *or* **be ~ed on sb.'s memory** *or* **mind** sich jmdm. fest einprägen
2 *v.i.* aufstampfen
3 *n.* Marke, *die;* (postage ~) Briefmarke, *die;* (instrument for ~ing) Stempel, *der*

■ **'stamp on** *v.t.* **(a)** zertreten ‹*Insekt*›; **~ on sb's foot** jmdm. auf den Fuß treten
(b) (suppress) durchgreifen gegen

■ **stamp 'out** *v.t.* [aus]stanzen; (fig.) ausmerzen

stamp: ~ album *n.* Briefmarkenalbum, *das;* **~ collecting** *n.* Briefmarkensammeln, *das;* **~ collection** *n.* Briefmarkensammlung, *die;* **~ duty** *n.* Stempelsteuer, *die*

stampede /stæm'piːd/ *n.* Stampede, *die*

stance /stɑːns/ *n.* (posture; fig.: attitude) Haltung, *die*

stanch /stɑːnʃ/ *v.t.* stillen ‹*Blut*›; abbinden ‹*Wunde*›

stand /stænd/ 1 *v.i.*, **stood** /stʊd/ **(a)** stehen
(b) my offer/promise still ~s mein Angebot/Versprechen gilt nach wie vor; **as it ~s, as things ~:** wie die Dinge [jetzt] liegen; **I'd like to know where I ~** (fig.) ich möchte wissen, wo ich dran bin
(c) (be candidate) kandidieren
(d) [not] **~ in sb.'s way** (fig.) jmdm. [keine] Steine in den Weg legen
(e) (be likely) **~ to win** *or* **gain/lose sth.** etw. gewinnen/verlieren können
2 *v.t.*, **stood (a)** (set in position) stellen
(b) (endure) ertragen; **I cannot ~ [the sight of] him/her** ich kann ihn/sie nicht ausstehen; **he can't ~ the pressure/strain** er ist dem Druck/den Strapazen nicht gewachsen; **I can't ~ it any longer!** ich halte es nicht mehr aus!
(c) (buy) **~ sb. sth.** jmdm. etw. spendieren
3 *n.* **(a)** (support) Ständer, *der*
(b) (stall; at exhibition) Stand, *der*
(c) (raised structure) Tribüne, *die*

■ **stand a'bout, stand a'round** *v.i.* herumstehen

■ **stand a'side** *v.i.* zur Seite treten

■ **stand 'back** *v.i.* **(a) ~ [well] back [from sth.]** [ein gutes Stück] [von etw.] entfernt stehen

(b) (fig.: distance oneself) zurücktreten

■ **'stand between** *v.t.* **sth. ~s between sb. and sth.** (fig.) etw. steht jmdm. bei etw. im Wege

■ **stand by** [1] /-'-/ *v.i.* **(a)** (be near) daneben stehen
(b) (be ready) sich zur Verfügung halten
[2] /'--/ *v.t.* **(a)** (support) **~ by sb./one another** jmdm./sich [gegenseitig] beistehen
(b) (adhere to) **~ by sth.** zu etw. stehen

■ **stand 'down** *v.i.* verzichten

■ **'stand for** *v.t.* **(a)** (signify) bedeuten
(b) (coll.: tolerate) sich (*Dat.*) bieten lassen

■ **stand 'in** *v.i.* aushelfen; **~ in for sb.** für jmdn. einspringen

■ **stand 'out** *v.i.* (be prominent) herausragen; **~ out a mile** (fig.) nicht zu übersehen sein

■ **'stand over** *v.t.* beaufsichtigen

■ **stand 'up** *v.i.* **(a)** aufstehen; **~ up straight** sich aufrecht hinstellen
(b) ~ up well [in comparison with sb./sth.] [im Vergleich zu jmdm./etw.] gut abschneiden; **~ up for sb./sth.** für jmdn./etw. Partei ergreifen; **~ up to sb.** sich jmdm. entgegenstellen

stand-alone /stændə'ləʊn/ *adj.* (Comp.) selbstständig

standard /'stændəd/ [1] *n.* **(a)** Maßstab, *der;* **safety ~s** Sicherheitsnormen *Pl.*; **above/below/up to ~:** überdurchschnittlich [gut]/unter dem Durchschnitt/der Norm entsprechend
(b) (degree) Niveau, *das;* **~ of living** Lebensstandard, *der*
(c) ~s (morals) Prinzipien *Pl.*
(d) (flag) Standarte, *die*
[2] *adj.* Standard-; **be ~ practice** allgemein üblich sein

standardize /'stændədaɪz/ *v.t.* standardisieren

'standard lamp *n.* Stehlampe, *die*

stand: ~-by [1] *n.* **be on ~-by** einsatzbereit sein; [2] *adj.* Ersatz-; **~-in** [1] *n.* Ersatz, *der;* [2] *adj.* Ersatz-

'standing [1] *n.* **(a)** (repute) Ansehen, *das*
(b) (duration) **of long/short ~:** von langer/kurzer Dauer
[2] *adj.* **(a)** (erect) stehend
(b) fest ‹*Regel, Brauch*›

standing: ~ 'order *n.* Dauerauftrag, *der;* **~ o'vation** *n.* stürmischer Beifall; **~ room** *n.* Stehplätze *Pl.*

stand-offish /stænd'ɒfɪʃ/ *adj.* reserviert

stand: ~pipe *n.* Standrohr, *das;* **~point** *n.* (fig.) Standpunkt, *der;* **~still** *n.* Stillstand, *der;* **be at a ~still** stillstehen; **come to a ~still** zum Stehen kommen

stank ▸ STINK 1

staple¹ /'steɪpl/ [1] *n.* [Heft]klammer, *die*
[2] *v.t.* heften (**on to** an + *Akk.*)

staple² [1] *attrib. adj.* **(a)** Grund-; **a ~ diet** ein Grundnahrungsmittel
(b) (Commerc.) grundlegend; **~ goods** Haupthandelsartikel *Pl.*
[2] *n.* (Commerc.: major item) Haupterzeugnis, *das*

stapler /'steɪplə(r)/ *n.* [Draht]hefter, *der*

star /stɑ:(r)/ [1] *n.* **(a)** Stern, *der*
(b) (prominent person) Star, *der*
[2] *v.i.* **~ in a film** in einem Film die Hauptrolle spielen

starboard /'stɑ:bəd/ *n.* Steuerbord, *das*

starch /stɑ:tʃ/ *n.* Stärke, *die*

starchy /'stɑ:tʃɪ/ *adj.* stärkehaltig ‹*Nahrungsmittel*›; (fig.: prim) steif

stardom /'stɑ:dəm/ *n.* Starruhm, *der*

stare /steə(r)/ *v.i.* starren; **~ at sb./sth.** jmdn./etw. anstarren

'starfish *n.* Seestern, *der*

stark /stɑ:k/ [1] *adj.* scharf ‹*Kontrast, Umriss*›
[2] *adv.* völlig; **~ naked** splitternackt (ugs.)

'starless *adj.* stern[en]los

starlet /'stɑ:lɪt/ *n.* Starlet[t], *das*

starling /'stɑ:lɪŋ/ *n.* Star, *der*

'starlit *adj.* sternhell

starry /'stɑ:rɪ/ *adj.* sternklar

star: ~ sign *n.* Sternzeichen, *das;* **~-studded** *adj.* ‹*Show, Film, Besetzung*› mit großem Staraufgebot

start /stɑ:t/ [1] *v.i.* **(a)** (begin) anfangen; **~ on sth.** etw. beginnen
(b) (set out) aufbrechen
(c) (begin to function) anlaufen; ‹*Auto, Motor usw.*:› anspringen
[2] *v.t.* **(a)** (begin) beginnen [mit]; **~ doing** *or* **to do sth.** [damit] anfangen, etw. zu tun
(b) (cause) auslösen; anfangen ‹*Streit, Schlägerei*›; legen/(accidentally) verursachen ‹*Brand*›
(c) (set up) ins Leben rufen ‹*Organisation, Projekt*›
(d) (switch on) einschalten; anlassen ‹*Motor, Auto*›
[3] *n.* **(a)** Anfang, *der;* Beginn, *der;* (of race) Start, *der;* **from the ~:** von Anfang an; **from ~ to finish** von Anfang bis Ende; **make a ~:** anfangen (**on** mit); (on journey) aufbrechen
(b) (Sport: **~ing** place) Start, *der*

'starter *n.* **(a)** (food) Vorspeise, *die*
(b) (Sport) Starter, *der*

starting /'stɑ:tɪŋ/**: ~ point** *n.* (lit. or fig.) Ausgangspunkt, *der;* **~ post** *n.* (Sport) Startpfosten, *der;* **~ salary** *n.* Anfangsgehalt, *das*

startle /'stɑ:tl/ *v.t.* erschrecken; **be ~d by sth.** über etw. (*Akk.*) erschrecken

startling /'stɑ:tlɪŋ/ *adj.* erstaunlich

starvation /stɑ:'veɪʃn/ *n.* Verhungern, *das*

starve /stɑ:v/ *v.i.* **~ [to death]** verhungern

stash /stæʃ/ (coll.) [1] *v.t.* **~ [away]** verstecken
[2] *n.* [geheimes] Lager

state /steɪt/ [1] *n.* **(a)** (condition) Zustand, *der*
(b) (nation) Staat, *der*
(c) be in a ~: aufgeregt sein
(d) lie in ~: aufgebahrt sein

2 *v.t.* (express) erklären; angeben ‹*Alter usw.*›

stately /'steɪtlɪ/ *adj.* majestätisch; stattlich ‹*Körperbau, Gebäude*›

stately 'home *n.* Herrensitz, *der*

'statement *n.* **(a)** (stating, account) Aussage, *die;* (declaration) Erklärung, *die*
(b) **[bank] ~:** Kontoauszug, *der*

state: ~-of-the-'art *adj.* auf dem neuesten Stand der Technik *nachgestellt;* **~ school** *n.* (Brit.) staatliche Schule; **~-owned** *adj.* staatlich

statesman /'steɪtsmən/ *n., pl.* **statesmen** /'steɪtsmən/ Staatsmann, *der*

static /'stætɪk/ *adj.* statisch

static elec'tricity *n.* statische Elektrizität

station /'steɪʃn/ 1 *n.* **(a)** ▶ RAILWAY STATION
(b) (status) Rang, *der*
2 *v.t.* aufstellen ‹*Wache*›

stationary /'steɪʃənərɪ/ *adj.* stehend; **be ~:** stehen

stationer /'steɪʃənə(r)/ *n.* **~'s [shop]** Schreibwarengeschäft, *das*

stationery /'steɪʃənərɪ/ *n.* **(a)** (writing materials) Schreibwaren *Pl.*
(b) (writing paper) Briefpapier, *das*

'station wagon *n.* (Amer.) Kombiwagen, *der*

statistic /stə'tɪstɪk/ *n.* statistische Tatsache

statistical /stə'tɪstɪkl/ *attrib. adj.*, **statistically** /stə'tɪstɪkəlɪ/ *adv.* statistisch

statistics /stə'tɪstɪks/ *n.* Statistik, *die*

statue /'stætʃu:, 'stætju:/ *n.* Statue, *die*

statuesque /stætjʊ'esk/ *adj.* statuenhaft; (imposing) stattlich

stature /'stætʃə(r)/ *n.* Statur, *die;* (fig.) Format, *das*

status /'steɪtəs/ *n.* Rang, *der;* **social ~:** [gesellschaftlicher] Status

'status symbol *n.* Statussymbol, *das*

statute /'stætju:t/ *n.* Gesetz, *das*

statutory /'stætjʊtərɪ/ *adj.* gesetzlich

staunch /stɔ:ntʃ/ *adj.* treu ‹*Freund*›; überzeugt ‹*Katholik usw.*›

stave /steɪv/ *v.t.* **~ 'off** abwenden; stillen ‹*Hunger*›

stay /steɪ/ 1 *n.* Aufenthalt, *der;* (visit) Besuch, *der;* **come/go for a short ~ with sb.** jmdn. kurz besuchen
2 *v.i.* bleiben; **~ put** (coll.) ‹*Person:*› bleiben[, wo man ist]; **~ the night in a hotel** die Nacht in einem Hotel verbringen
3 *v.t.* **~ the course** (fig.) durchhalten

▪ **stay a'head** *v.i.* die Führung halten

▪ **stay a'way** *v.i.* wegbleiben

▪ **stay be'hind** *v.i.* zurückbleiben

▪ **stay 'in** *v.i.* zu Hause bleiben

▪ **stay 'out** *v.i.* **(a)** (not go home) wegbleiben (ugs.)
(b) (remain outside) draußen bleiben

▪ **stay 'over** *v.i.* (coll.) über Nacht bleiben

▪ **stay 'up** *v.i.* aufbleiben

'staying power *n.* Durchhaltevermögen, *das*

stead /sted/ *n.* **(a) in sb.'s ~:** an jmds. Stelle (*Dat.*)
(b) stand sb. in good ~: jmdm. zustatten kommen

steadfast /'stedfɑ:st/ *adj.* standhaft; zuverlässig ‹*Freund*›

steadily /'stedɪlɪ/ *adv.* **(a)** (stably) fest
(b) (continuously) stetig

steady /'stedɪ/ 1 *adj.* **(a)** (stable) stabil; (not wobbling) standfest
(b) (still) ruhig
(c) (regular, constant) stetig; gleichmäßig ‹*Arbeit, Tempo*›; stabil ‹*Preis, Lohn*›; gleich bleibend ‹*Temperatur*›; **we had ~ rain/drizzle** wir hatten Dauerregen/es nieselte [bei uns] ständig
(d) a ~ job eine feste Stelle; **a ~ boyfriend** ein fester Freund
2 *v.t.* festhalten ‹*Leiter*›; beruhigen ‹*Nerven*›

steak /steɪk/ *n.* Steak, *das*

'steak knife *n.* Messer mit Sägezahnung

steal /sti:l/ 1 *v.t.*, **stole** /stəʊl/, **stolen** /'stəʊln/ stehlen **(from** *Dat.***)**
2 *v.i.*, **stole, stolen (a)** stehlen; **~ from sb.** jmdn. bestehlen
(b) ~ in/out sich hinein-/hinausstehlen

stealth /stelθ/ *n.* Heimlichkeit, *die;* **by ~:** heimlich

stealthy /'stelθɪ/ *adj.* heimlich

steam /sti:m/ 1 *n.* Dampf, *der;* **let off ~** (fig.) Dampf ablassen (ugs.); **run out of ~** (fig.) den Schwung verlieren; **under one's own ~** (fig.) aus eigener Kraft
2 *v.t.* (Cookery) dämpfen; dünsten
3 *v.i.* dämpfen; **~ing hot** dampfend heiß

▪ **steam a'head** *v.i.* (fig. coll.) rasche Fortschritte machen

▪ **steam 'up** *v.i.* beschlagen

steam: ~boat *n.* Dampfschiff, *das;* (small) Dampfboot, *das;* **~ engine** *n.* Dampflok[omotive], *die;* (stationary) Dampfmaschine, *die*

'steamer *n.* Dämpfer, *der*

steam: ~ iron *n.* Dampfbügeleisen, *das;* **~roller** *n.* Dampfwalze, *die;* **~ train** *n.* Dampfzug, *der*

'steamy *adj.* dunstig; beschlagen ‹*Glas*›

steel /sti:l/ 1 *n.* Stahl, *der*
2 *attrib. adj.* stählern; Stahl‹*helm, -block, -platte*›
3 *v.t.* **~ oneself for/against sth.** sich für/gegen etw. wappnen (geh.); **~ oneself to do sth.** allen Mut zusammennehmen, um etw. zu tun

steel: ~ 'band *n.* (Mus.) Steelband, *die;* **~ 'drum** *n.* (Mus.) Steeldrum, *die;* **~ industry** *n.* Stahlindustrie, *die;* **~ 'wool** *n.* Stahlwolle, *die;* **~works** *n. sing. or pl.* Stahlwerk, *das*

steep¹ /stiːp/ *adj.* **(a)** steil
(b) (coll.: excessive) happig (ugs.); **the bill is [a bit]** ~: die Rechnung ist [ziemlich] gesalzen (ugs.)
steep² *v.t.* (soak) einweichen
steeped /stiːpt/ *adj.* durchdrungen (**in** von)
steeple /ˈstiːpl/ *n.* Kirchturm, *der*
steer /stɪə(r)/ **1** *v.t.* steuern; lenken
2 *v.i.* steuern; ~ **clear of sb./sth.** (fig. coll.) jmdm./einer Sache aus dem Weg[e] gehen
ˈsteering *n.* (Motor Veh.) Lenkung, *die*
steering: ~ **column** *n.* Lenksäule, *die;* ~ **lock** *n.* Lenkradschloss, *das;* ~ **wheel** *n.* Lenkrad, *das*
stem¹ /stem/ **1** *n.* **(a)** (Bot.) Stiel, *der*
(b) (Ling.) Stamm, *der*
2 *v.i.*, **-mm-:** ~ **from sth.** auf etw (*Akk.*) zurückzuführen sein
stem² *v.t.*, **-mm-** (check, dam up) aufhalten; eindämmen ‹*Flut*›; stillen ‹*Blutung*›
stench /stentʃ/ *n.* Gestank, *der*
stencil /ˈstensl/ *n.* Schablone, *die;* (for duplicating) Matrize, *die*
step /step/ **1** *n.* **(a)** Schritt, *der;* **take a** ~ **back/forwards** einen Schritt zurücktreten/ nach vorn treten
(b) (stair) Stufe, *die;* **a flight of** ~**s** eine Treppe; **[pair of]** ~**s** (ladder) Stehleiter, *die*
(c) be in ~: im Schritt sein; (with music) im Takt sein
(d) take ~**s to do sth.** Schritte unternehmen, um etw. zu tun
(e) (stage) ~ **by** ~: Schritt für Schritt; **what is the next** ~? wie geht es weiter?
(f) (grade) Stufe, *die*
2 *v.i.*, **-pp-** treten; ~ **inside** eintreten; ~ **into sb's shoes** (fig.) an jmds. Stelle treten; ~ **over sb./sth.** über jmdn./etw. steigen
■ **step ˈback** *v.i.* zurücktreten
■ **step ˈin** *v.i.* **(a)** eintreten
(b) (fig.) (take sb.'s place) einspringen; (intervene) eingreifen
■ **step ˈup** **1** *v.i.* (ascend) hinaufsteigen
2 *v.t.* erhöhen; verstärken ‹*Anstrengungen*›
step: ~ **aerobics** *n.* Stepaerobic, *das;* ~**child** *n.* Stiefkind, *das;* ~**daughter** *n.* Stieftochter, *die;* ~**father** *n.* Stiefvater, *der;* ~**ladder** *n.* Stehleiter, *die;* ~**mother** *n.* Stiefmutter, *die*
ˈstepping stone *n.* Trittstein, *der;* (fig.) Sprungbrett, das (**to** für)
stereo /ˈsterɪəʊ/ **1** *n.* Stereo, *das;* (equipment) Stereoanlage, *die*
2 *adj.* stereo; Stereo‹*aufnahme, -platte*›
stereophonic /sterɪəˈfɒnɪk/ *adj.* stereophon
stereotype /ˈsterɪətaɪp/ **1** *n.* Stereotyp, *das*
2 *v.t.* in ein Klischee zwängen; ~**d** stereotyp
sterile /ˈsteraɪl/ *adj.* steril
sterility /stəˈrɪlɪtɪ/ *n.* Sterilität, *die*
sterilization /sterɪlaɪˈzeɪʃn/ *n.* Sterilisation, *die*
sterilize /ˈsterɪlaɪz/ *v.t.* sterilisieren
sterling /ˈstɜːlɪŋ/ **1** *n.* Sterling, *der;* **in** ~: in Pfund [Sterling]
2 *attrib. adj.* **(a)** ~ **silver** Sterlingsilber, *das*
(b) (fig.) gediegen
stern¹ /stɜːn/ *adj.* streng; ernst ‹*Warnung*›
stern² *n.* (Naut.) Heck, *das*
ˈsternly *adv.* streng
steroid /ˈsterɔɪd/ *n.* Steroid, *das*
stethoscope /ˈsteθəskəʊp/ *n.* Stethoskop, *das*
stew /stjuː/ **1** *n.* Eintopf, *der*
2 *v.t.* schmoren [lassen]
steward /ˈstjuːəd/ *n.* **(a)** (on ship, plane) Steward, *der*
(b) (at public meeting etc.) Ordner, *der*
ˈstewardess *n.* Stewardess, *die*
stewed /stjuːd/ *adj.* (Cookery) geschmort
ˈstewing steak *n.* [Rinder]schmorfleisch, *das*
stick /stɪk/ **1** *v.t.*, **stuck** /stʌk/ **(a)** (thrust point of) stecken; ~ **sth. in[to] sth.** mit etw. in etw. (*Akk.*) stechen
(b) (coll.: put) stecken; ~ **a picture on the wall/a vase on the shelf** ein Bild an die Wand hängen/eine Vase aufs Regal stellen; ~ **sth. in the kitchen** etw. in die Küche tun (ugs.)
(c) (with glue etc.) kleben
(d) the car is stuck in the mud das Auto ist im Schlamm stecken geblieben; **the door is stuck** die Tür klemmt [fest]
2 *v.i.*, **stuck** **(a)** (be fixed by point) stecken
(b) (adhere) kleben; ~ **to sth.** an etw. (*Dat.*) kleben
(c) (become immobile) ‹*Auto, Räder:*› stecken bleiben; ‹*Schublade, Tür, Griff, Bremse:*› klemmen; ‹*Schlüssel:*› feststecken
3 *n.* Stock, *der;* **a** ~ **of chalk** ein Stück Kreide; **a** ~ **of celery/rhubarb** eine Stange Sellerie/Rhabarber
■ **stick aˈbout, stick aˈround** *v.i.* (coll.) dableiben; (wait) warten
■ **ˈstick by** *v.t.* (fig.) stehen zu
■ **stick ˈon** *v.t.* (glue on) aufkleben
■ **stick ˈout** **1** *v.t.* **(a)** herausstrecken ‹*Zunge*›
(b) ~ **it out** (coll.) durchhalten
2 *v.i.* **(a)** ‹*Bauch:*› vorstehen; **his ears** ~ **out** er hat abstehende Ohren
(b) (fig.: be obvious) sich abheben; ~ **out a mile** (coll.) [klar] auf der Hand liegen; ~ **out like a sore thumb** (coll.) ins Auge springen
■ **ˈstick to** *v.t.* **(a)** (be faithful to) halten ‹*Versprechen*›; bleiben bei ‹*Entscheidung*›
(b) ~ **to the point** beim Thema bleiben
■ **stick toˈgether** *v.t.* zusammenkleben; (fig.) zusammenhalten
■ **stick ˈup** **1** *v.t.* **(a)** (coll.) anschlagen ‹*Poster*›; ~ **up one's hand** die Hand heben

(b) (seal) zukleben
2 *v.i.* **~ up for sb./sth.** für jmdn./etw. eintreten; **~ up for yourself!** setz dich zur Wehr!

stick de'odorant *n.* Deo[dorant]stift, *der*

'sticker *n.* Aufkleber, *der*

'sticking plaster *n.* Heftpflaster, *das*

stickler /'stɪklə(r)/ *n.* **be a ~ for tidiness/authority** es mit der Sauberkeit sehr genau nehmen/in puncto Autorität keinen Spaß verstehen

'stick-up *n.* (coll.) bewaffneter Raubüberfall

'sticky *adj.* **(a)** klebrig; **~ label** Aufkleber, *der*
(b) (humid) schwül ‹*Klima, Luft*›

stiff /stɪf/ *adj.* **(a)** (rigid) steif; hart ‹*Bürste, Stock*›; **be frozen ~:** steif vor Kälte sein
(b) (intense, severe) hartnäckig
(c) (formal) steif
(d) (difficult) hart ‹*Test*›; schwer ‹*Frage, Prüfung*›
(e) (coll.) **be bored/scared ~:** sich zu Tode langweilen/eine wahnsinnige Angst haben (ugs.)

stiffen /'stɪfn/ **1** *v.t.* steif machen
2 *v.i.* steifer werden; ‹*Person:*› erstarren

'stiffness *n.* Steifheit, *die*

stifle /'staɪfl/ **1** *v.t.* ersticken; (fig.) unterdrücken
2 *v.i.* ersticken

stifling /'staɪflɪŋ/ *adj.* stickig; drückend ‹*Hitze*›

stigma /'stɪgmə/ *n.* Stigma, *das* (geh.)

stile /staɪl/ *n.* Zauntritt, *der*

stiletto /stɪ'letəʊ/ *n.* **~ [heel]** Stöckelabsatz, *der*

still¹ /stɪl/ **1** *pred. adj.* still; **be ~:** [still] stehen; **hold sth. ~:** etw. ruhig halten; **keep** *or* **stay ~:** stillhalten; **stand ~:** stillstehen
2 *adv.* **(a)** (without change) noch; *expr. surprise or annoyance* immer noch
(b) (nevertheless) trotzdem
(c) *with comparative* (even) noch

still² *n.* Destillierapparat, *der*

still: ~ birth *n.* Totgeburt, *die;* **~born** *adj.* tot geboren; **~ 'life** *n.* (Art) Stillleben, *das*

stilt /stɪlt/ *n.* Stelze, *die*

'stilted *adj.* gestelzt

stimulant /'stɪmjʊlənt/ *n.* Stimulans, *das*

stimulate /'stɪmjʊleɪt/ *v.t.* anregen

stimulation /stɪmjʊ'leɪʃn/ *n.* Anregung, *die*

stimulus /'stɪmjʊləs/ *n., pl.* **stimuli** /'stɪmjʊlaɪ/ Ansporn, *der*

sting /stɪŋ/ **1** *n.* **(a)** (wounding) Stich, *der;* (by jellyfish, nettles) Verbrennung, *die*
(b) (from ointment, wind) Brennen, *das*
2 *v.t.,* **stung** /stʌŋ/ stechen
3 *v.i.,* **stung** brennen

'stinging nettle *n.* Brennnessel, *die*

stingy /'stɪndʒɪ/ *adj.* geizig; knaus[e]rig (ugs.)

stink /stɪŋk/ **1** *v.i.,* **stank** /stæŋk/ *or* **stunk** /stʌŋk/, **stunk** stinken (**of** nach)
2 *n.* Gestank, *der*

'stink bomb *n.* Stinkbombe, *die*

stint /stɪnt/ **1** *v.i.* **~ on sth.** an etw. (*Dat.*) sparen
2 *n.* [Arbeits]pensum, *das*

stipulate /'stɪpjʊleɪt/ *v.t.* (demand) fordern; (lay down) festlegen

stipulation /stɪpjʊ'leɪʃn/ *n.* (condition) Bedingung, *die*

stir /stɜː(r)/ **1** *v.t.,* **-rr-: (a)** (mix) rühren; umrühren ‹*Tee, Kaffee*›
(b) (move) bewegen
2 *v.i.,* **-rr-** (move) sich rühren
3 *n.* Aufregung, *die*

▪ **stir 'in** *v.t.* einrühren

▪ **stir 'up** *v.t.* **(a)** (disturb) aufrühren
(b) (fig.: arouse) wecken ‹*Interesse, Leidenschaft*›

stirring /'stɜːrɪŋ/ *adj.* bewegend ‹*Musik, Poesie*›; mitreißend ‹*Rede*›

stirrup /'stɪrəp/ *n.* Steigbügel, *der*

stitch /stɪtʃ/ **1** *n.* **(a)** (Sewing) Stich, *der;* (Knitting) Masche, *die*
(b) (pain) **have a ~:** Seitenstechen haben
2 *v.t.* nähen

▪ **stitch 'up** *v.t.* **(a)** nähen; vernähen ‹*Loch, Riss, Wunde*›
(b) (Brit. fig. coll.: betray, cheat) reinlegen (ugs.); linken (salopp)

'stitching *n.* **(a)** Naht, *die*
(b) (ornamental stitches) Stickerei, *die*

stoat /stəʊt/ *n.* Hermelin, *das*

stock /stɒk/ **1** *n.* **(a)** (origin, family, breed) Abstammung, *die*
(b) (supply, store) Vorrat, *der;* (in shop etc.) Warenbestand, *der;* **be in/out of ~** ‹*Ware:*› vorrätig/nicht vorrätig sein; **have sth. in ~:** etw. auf Lager haben; **take ~ of sth.** (fig.) über etw. (*Akk.*) Bilanz ziehen
(c) (Cookery) Brühe, *die*
2 *v.t.* **(a)** (supply with ~) beliefern
(b) (Commerc.: keep in ~) auf Lager haben
3 *attrib. adj.* Standard-

stock: ~broker Effektenmakler, *der*/-maklerin, *die;* **~ cube** *n.* Brühwürfel, *der;* **~ exchange** *n.* Börse, *die*

stocking /'stɒkɪŋ/ *n.* Strumpf, *der*

'stockist *n.* Fachhändler, *der*/-händlerin, *die*

stock: ~ market *n.* **(a)** Börse, *die;* **(b)** (trading) Börsengeschäft, *das;* **~ market crash** Börsenkrach, *der;* **~pile 1** *n.* Vorrat, *der;* (weapons) Arsenal, *das;* **2** *v.t.* horten; anhäufen ‹*Waffen*›; **~pot** *n.* Suppentopf, *der;* **~room** *n.* Lager, *das;* **~-'still** *pred. adj.* bewegungslos; **~taking** *n.* Inventur, *die*

stocky /'stɒkɪ/ *adj.* stämmig

stodgy /'stɒdʒɪ/ *adj.* pappig

stoical /ˈstəʊɪkl/ *adj.* stoisch
stoicism /ˈstəʊɪsɪzm/ *n.* Stoizismus, *der*
stoke /stəʊk/ *v.t.* heizen ‹*Ofen, Kessel*›; unterhalten ‹*Feuer*›
stole ▶ STEAL
stolen /ˈstəʊln/ [1] ▶ STEAL
[2] *attrib. adj.* heimlich ‹*Vergnügen, Kuss*›
stolid /ˈstɒlɪd/ *adj.* stur (ugs.)
stomach /ˈstʌmək/ [1] *n.* **(a)** Magen, *der*
(b) (abdomen) Bauch, *der*
[2] *v.t.* (fig.: tolerate) ausstehen
stomach: ~ ache *n.* Magenschmerzen *Pl.*; **have a ~ ache** Magenschmerzen haben; **~ upset** *n.* Magenverstimmung, *die*
stone /stəʊn/ [1] *n.* **(a)** Stein, *der;* **a ~'s throw [away]** (fig.) nur einen Steinwurf weit entfernt; **be written** *or* **carved** *or* **set in ~** (fig.) unverrückbar sein
(b) (Brit.: weight unit) *Gewicht von 6,35 kg*
[2] *adj.* steinern; Stein‹*mauer, -brücke*›
[3] *v.t.* mit Steinen bewerfen
stone: S~ Age *n.* Steinzeit, *die;* **~-cold** *adj.* eiskalt
stoned /stəʊnd/ *adj.* (sl.) stoned (Drogenjargon); (drunk) voll zu (salopp)
stone: ~-'dead *pred. adj.* mausetot (fam.); **kill sth. ~-dead** (fig.) etw. völlig zunichte machen; **~-'deaf** *adj.* stocktaub (ugs.); **~mason** *n.* Steinmetz, *der;* **~'wall** (Brit.) *v.i.* mauern (fig.); **~ware** *n., no pl.* Steingut, *das; attrib.* ‹*Krug, Vase*› aus Steingut; **~washed** *adj.* mit Steinen ausgewaschen; **~work** *n.* Mauerwerk, *das*
stony /ˈstəʊnɪ/ *adj.* steinig
stood ▶ STAND 1, 2
stool /stuːl/ *n.* Hocker, *der*
stoop /stuːp/ [1] *v.i.* **~ [down]** sich bücken
[2] *n.* **walk with a ~:** gebeugt gehen
stop /stɒp/ [1] *v.t.*, **-pp-: (a)** anhalten ‹*Person, Fahrzeug*›; aufhalten ‹*Fortschritt, Verkehr, Feind*›
(b) (not let continue) unterbrechen ‹*Redner, Spiel, Gespräch*›; beenden ‹*Krieg, Arbeit*›; stoppen ‹*Produktion, Uhr*›; einstellen ‹*Zahlung, Lieferung*›; **~ that!** hör damit auf!; **~ smoking/crying** aufhören zu rauchen/weinen
(c) (not let happen) verhindern ‹*Verbrechen, Unfall*›; **~ sth. [from] happening** verhindern, dass etw. geschieht
(d) (switch off) abstellen ‹*Maschine*›
(e) (block up) zustopfen ‹*Loch*›; verschließen ‹*Wasserhahn, Flasche*›
(f) ~ a cheque einen Scheck sperren lassen
[2] *v.i.*, **-pp-: (a)** (not extend further) aufhören; ‹*Zahlungen, Lieferungen:*› eingestellt werden
(b) (not move further) ‹*Fahrzeug, Fahrer:*› halten; ‹*Maschine, Motor:*› stillstehen; ‹*Uhr, Fußgänger, Herz:*› stehen bleiben
[3] *n.* **(a)** (halt) Halt, *der;* **bring to a ~:** zum Stehen bringen ‹*Fahrzeug*›; zum Erliegen bringen ‹*Verkehr*›; unterbrechen ‹*Arbeit*›; **come to a ~:** stehen bleiben; ‹*Fahrzeug:*› zum Stehen kommen; ‹*Arbeit, Verkehr:*› zum Erliegen kommen; **put a ~ to** abstellen ‹*Missstände, Unsinn*›
(b) (place) Haltestelle, *die*
■ **stop 'by** *v.i.* (Amer.) vorbeischauen (ugs.)
■ **stop 'out** *v.i.* (coll.) draußen bleiben
■ **stop 'over** *v.i.* (coll.) übernachten (**at** bei)
■ **stop 'up** [1] *v.t.* zustopfen ‹*Loch, Öffnung*›
[2] *v.i.* (coll.) ▶ STAY UP
stop: ~ button *n.* Stopptaste, *die;* **~cock** *n.* Abstellhahn, *der;* **~gap** *n.* Notlösung, *die;* **~ light** *n.* (traffic light) rotes Licht; **~over** *n.* Stopover, *der*
stoppage /ˈstɒpɪdz/ *n.* **(a)** (halt) Stillstand, *der;* (strike) Streik, *der*
(b) (deduction) Abzug, *der*
stopper /ˈstɒpə(r)/ *n.* Stöpsel, *der*
stopping /ˈstɒpɪŋ/: **~ distance** *n.* Anhalteweg, *der*; **~ place, ~ point** *ns.* Station, *die*
stop: ~press *n.* letzte Meldung/Meldungen *Pl.*; **~ sign** *n.* Stoppschild, *das;* **~ signal** *n.* Haltesignal, *das;* **~watch** *n.* Stoppuhr, *die*
storage /ˈstɔːrɪdʒ/ *n.* Lagerung, *die;* (of films, books, documents) Aufbewahrung, *die;* (of data, water, electricity) Speicherung, *die*
storage: ~ capacity *n.* (Comp.) Speicherkapazität, *die;* **~ device** *n.* (Comp.) Speichermedium, *das;* **~ heater** *n.* [Nacht]speicherofen, *der;* **~ space** *n.* Lagerraum, *der;* (in house) Platz [zum Aufbewahren]; **~ tank** *n.* Sammelbehälter, *der*
store /stɔː(r)/ [1] *n.* **(a)** (Amer.: shop) Laden, *der*
(b) (Brit.: large general shop) Kaufhaus, *das*
(c) (warehouse) Lager, *das;* **put sth. in ~:** etw. einlagern
(d) (stock) Vorrat, *der* (**of** an + *Dat.*); **be** *or* **lie in ~ for sb.** jmdn. erwarten
(e) set [great] ~ by *or* **on sth.** [großen] Wert auf etw. (*Akk.*) legen
[2] *v.t.* einlagern; speichern ‹*Getreide, Energie, Wissen, Daten*›
■ **store 'up** *v.t.* speichern; **~ up provisions** sich (*Dat.*) Vorräte anlegen
store: ~ detective *n.* Kaufhausdetektiv, *der;* **~house** *n.* Lager[haus], *das;* **~keeper** *n.* (Amer.: shopkeeper) Besitzer eines Einzelhandelsgeschäftes; **~room** *n.* Lagerraum, *der*
storey /ˈstɔːrɪ/ *n.* Stockwerk, *das*
stork /stɔːk/ *n.* Storch, *der*
storm /stɔːm/ [1] *n.* Unwetter, *das;* (thunder~) Gewitter, *das*
[2] *v.t. & i.* stürmen
'storm damage *n.* Sturmschaden, *der* (*meist Pl.*)
'stormy *adj.* stürmisch
story[1] /ˈstɔːrɪ/ *n.* **(a)** Geschichte, *die*
(b) (news item) Bericht, *der*
(c) (coll.: lie) Märchen, *das*
story[2] (Amer.) ▶ STOREY

S

'story book *n.* Geschichtenbuch, *das;* (with fairy tales) Märchenbuch, *das*

stout /staʊt/ *adj.* **(a)** (strong) fest **(b)** (fat) beleibt

stove /stəʊv/ *n.* Ofen, *der;* (for cooking) Herd, *der*

stow /stəʊ/ *v.t.* verstauen (**into** in + *Dat.*)
■ **stow a'way** 1 *v.t.* verwahren
2 *v.i.* als blinder Passagier reisen

straddle /'strædl/ *v.t.* **~ a fence/chair** rittlings auf einem Zaun/Stuhl sitzen

straggle /'strægl/ *v.i.* **~ [along] behind the others** den anderen hinterherzockeln (ugs.)

straggler /'stræglə(r)/ *n.* Nachzügler, *der*

straggly /'stræglı/ zottig ‹*Haar, Bart*›

straight /streıt/ 1 *adj.* **(a)** gerade; glatt ‹*Haar*›; **in a ~ line** in gerader Linie
(b) (undiluted) **drink whisky ~:** Whisky pur trinken
(c) (direct) direkt ‹*Blick, Schuss, Weg*›; **be ~ with sb.** zu jmdm. offen sein; **get sth. ~** (fig.) etw. genau verstehen; **put** *or* **set the record ~:** die Sache richtig stellen
2 *adv.* **(a)** gerade
(b) (directly) geradewegs; **~ after** sofort nach; **come ~ to the point** direkt zur Sache kommen; **look sb. ~ in the eye** jmdm. direkt in die Augen blicken; **~ ahead** *or* **on** immer geradeaus
(c) (frankly) aufrichtig
(d) (clearly) klar ‹*sehen, denken*›

straight a'way *adv.* sofort

straighten /'streıtn/ 1 *v.t.* **(a)** gerade ziehen ‹*Teppich*›; glätten ‹*Kleidung, Haare*›
(b) (put in order) aufräumen
2 *v.i.* gerade werden
■ **straighten 'out** 1 *v.t.* **(a)** gerade biegen; glätten ‹*Decke, Teppich*›
(b) (clear up) klären
2 *v.i.* gerade werden
■ **straighten 'up** 1 *v.t.* ▶ TIDY UP
2 *v.i.* sich aufrichten

straight: ~ 'face *n.* **with a ~ face** ohne eine Miene zu verziehen; **keep a ~ face** keine Miene verziehen; **~-faced** *adj.* mit unbewegter Miene *nachgestellt;* **~'forward** *adj.* **(a)** (frank) freimütig; schlicht ‹*Stil, Sprache, Bericht*›; klar ‹*Anweisung, Vorstellungen*›; **(b)** (simple) einfach

strain /streın/ 1 *n.* **(a)** (pull) Belastung, *die;* (on rope) Spannung, *die*
(b) (tension) Stress, *der;* **be under [a great deal of] ~:** unter großem Stress stehen
(c) (person, thing) **be a ~ on sb./sth.** jmdn./ etw. belasten
(d) (muscular injury) Zerrung, *die*
2 *v.t.* **(a)** (overexert) überanstrengen; zerren ‹*Muskel*›
(b) (stretch tightly) [fest] spannen
(c) (filter) durchseihen; seihen (**through** durch)
3 *v.i.* (strive intensely) sich anstrengen

strained /streınd/ *adj.* gezwungen ‹*Lächeln*›; **~ relations** gespannte Beziehungen *Pl.*

'strainer *n.* Sieb, *das*

strait /streıt/ *n.* **(a)** *in sing. or pl.* (Geog.) Meerenge, *die*
(b) *usu. in pl.* (distress, difficulty) Schwierigkeiten *Pl.*

strait: ~jacket *n.* Zwangsjacke, *die;* **~-laced** /streıt'leıst/ *adj.* puritanisch

strand¹ /strænd/ *n.* (thread) Faden, *der;* (of beads) Kette, *die;* (of hair) Strähne, *die;* (of rope) Strang, *der*

strand² *v.t.* (leave behind) trockensetzen; **be [left] ~ed** festsitzen; (fig.) seinem Schicksal überlassen sein

strange /streındʒ/ *adj.* (peculiar) seltsam; sonderbar; **~ to say** seltsamerweise; **feel ~:** sich komisch fühlen

strangely /'streındʒlı/ *adv.* seltsam

stranger /'streındʒə(r)/ *n.* Fremde, *der/die;* **he is a ~ here/to the town** er ist hier/in der Stadt fremd; **be a/no ~ to sth.** etw. nicht gewöhnt/etw. gewöhnt sein

strangle /'stræŋgl/ *v.t.* erwürgen

'stranglehold *n.* Würgegriff, *der*

strangulation /stræŋgjʊ'leıʃn/ *n.* Erwürgen, *das*

strap /stræp/ 1 *n.* **(a)** (leather) Riemen, *der;* (textile) Band, *das;* (shoulder ~) Träger, *der;* (for watch) Armband, *das*
(b) (to grasp in vehicle) Halteriemen, *der*
2 *v.t.*, **-pp-: ~ [into position]/down** festschnallen; **~ oneself in** sich anschnallen

'strapless *adj.* trägerlos

strapping /'stræpıŋ/ *adj.* stramm

strata *pl. of* STRATUM

strategic /strə'ti:dʒık/ *adj.* strategisch

strategically /strə'ti:dʒıkəlı/ *adv.* strategisch

strategist /'strætıdʒıst/ *n.* Stratege, *der/* Strategin, *die*

strategy /'strætıdʒı/ *n.* Strategie, *die*

stratosphere /'strætəsfıə(r)/ *n.* Stratosphäre, *die*

stratum /'strɑ:təm/ *n., pl.* **strata** /'strɑ:tə/ Schicht, *die*

straw /strɔ:/ *n.* **(a)** *no pl.* Stroh, *das*
(b) (single stalk) Strohhalm, *der;* **that's the last** *or* **final ~:** jetzt reichts aber
(c) [**drinking**] **~:** Strohhalm, *der*

strawberry /'strɔ:bərı/ *n.* Erdbeere, *die*

stray /streı/ 1 *v.i.* **(a)** (wander) streunen
(b) (deviate) abweichen (**from** von)
2 *n.* (animal) streunendes Tier
3 *adj.* **(a)** streunend
(b) (occasional) vereinzelt

streak /stri:k/ *n.* Streifen, *der;* (in hair) Strähne, *die;* **have a jealous/cruel ~:** zur Eifersucht/Grausamkeit neigen

'streaky *adj.* streifig; **~ bacon** durchwachsener Speck

stream /stri:m/ [1] *n.* (of water) Wasserlauf, *der;* (brook) Bach, *der*
[2] *v.i.* strömen; ‹*Sonnenlicht:*› fluten; **have a ~ing cold** einen schlimmen Schnupfen haben

streamer /'stri:mə(r)/ *n.* (ribbon) Band, *das;* (of paper) Luftschlange, *die*

'streamline *v.t.* [eine] Stromlinienform geben (+ *Dat.*); **be ~lined** eine Stromlinienform haben

street /stri:t/ *n.* Straße, *die;* **in the ~:** auf der Straße; **in** (Brit.) *or* **on ... Street** in der ...straße

street: ~car *n.* (Amer.) Straßenbahn, *die;* **~ cred** /'stri:t kred/ (coll.), **~ credibility** *ns.* [glaubwürdiges] Image; **~ crime** *n., no indef. art.* Straßenkriminalität, *die;* **~ lamp** *n.* Straßenlaterne, *die;* **~ lighting** *n.* Straßenbeleuchtung, *die;* **~ map** *n.* Stadtplan, *der;* **~ market** *n.* Straßenmarkt, *der;* **~ plan** *n.* Stadtplan, *der;* **~ sweeper** *n.* **(a)** (person) Straßenfeger, *der*/-fegerin, *die* (bes. nordd.); Straßenkehrer, *der*/-kehrerin, *die* (bes. südd.); **(b)** (vehicle) Straßenkehrmaschine, *die;* **~ vendor** *n.* Straßenhändler, *der*/-händlerin, *die;* **~-wise** *adj.* (coll.) **be ~-wise** wissen, wo es langgeht

strength /streŋθ/ *n.* (power) Kraft, *die;* (strong point, force, intensity, amount of ingredient) Stärke, *die;* (of poison, medicine) Wirksamkeit, *die;* **not know one's own ~:** nicht wissen, wie stark man ist; **give sb. ~:** jmdn. stärken; **go from ~ to ~:** immer erfolgreicher werden; **on the ~ of sth./that** aufgrund einer Sache (*Gen.*)/dessen; **in full ~:** in voller Stärke; **the police were there in ~:** ein starkes Polizeiaufgebot war da

strengthen /'streŋθən/ *v.t.* stärken; (reinforce, intensify) verstärken

strenuous /'strenjʊəs/ *adj.* **(a)** (energetic) energisch; gewaltig ‹*Anstrengung*›
(b) (requiring exertion) anstrengend

stress /stres/ [1] *n.* **(a)** (strain) Stress, *der;* **be under ~:** unter Stress (*Dat.*) stehen
(b) (emphasis) Betonung, *die*
[2] *v.t.* (emphasize) betonen

'stressed out *adj.* (coll.) [völlig] gestresst

stressful /'stresfl/ *adj.* anstrengend

stress: ~ mark *n.* Betonungszeichen, *das;* **~-related** *adj.* stressbedingt

stretch /stretʃ/ [1] *v.t.* **(a)** (lengthen) strecken ‹*Arm, Hand*›; recken ‹*Hals*›; dehnen ‹*Gummiband*›; (tighten) spannen
(b) (widen) dehnen
[2] **(a)** *v.i.* (extend in length) sich dehnen
(b) ~ to sth. (be sufficient for) für etw. reichen
[3] *v. refl.* sich strecken
[4] *n.* **(a) have a ~:** sich strecken
(b) at a ~ (fig.) wenn es sein muss
(c) (expanse) Abschnitt, *der;* **a ~ of road** ein Stück Straße
(d) (period) **a four-hour ~:** eine [Zeit]spanne von vier Stunden; **at a ~:** ohne Unterbrechung
[5] *adj.* Stretch‹*hose, -gewebe*›

stretcher /'stretʃə(r)/ *n.* [Trag]bahre, *die*

stretch: ~ marks *n. pl.* Schwangerschaftsstreifen *Pl.;* **~ pants** *n. pl.* Stretchhose, *die*

stretchy /'stretʃɪ/ *adj.* (coll.) dehnbar

strew /stru:/ *v.t., p.p.* **strewed** /stru:d/ *or* **strewn** /stru:n/ streuen

stricken /'strɪkn/ *adj.* (afflicted) heimgesucht; havariert ‹*Schiff*›; **be ~ with fear/grief** angsterfüllt/gramgebeugt

strict /strɪkt/ *adj.* **(a)** (firm) streng; **in ~ confidence** streng vertraulich
(b) (precise) streng

'strictly *adv.* streng; **~ [speaking]** streng genommen

stride /straɪd/ [1] *n.* Schritt, *der;* **put sb. off his ~** (fig.) jmdn. aus dem Konzept bringen; **take sth. in one's ~** (fig). mit etw. gut fertig werden
[2] *v.i.,* **strode** /strəʊd/, **stridden** /'strɪdn/ [mit großen Schritten] gehen

strident /'straɪdənt/ *adj.* schrill

strife /straɪf/ *n.* Streit, *der*

strike /straɪk/ [1] *n.* (Industry) Streik, *der;* Ausstand, *der;* **be on/go [out]** *or* **come out on ~:** in den Streik getreten sein/in den Streik treten
[2] *v.t.,* **struck** /strʌk/ **(a)** (hit) schlagen; ‹*Schlag, Geschoss:*› treffen; ‹*Blitz:*› [ein]schlagen in (+ *Akk.*)
(b) (delete) streichen **(from, off** aus)
(c) (ignite) anzünden ‹*Streichholz*›
(d) (chime) schlagen
(e) (impress) beeindrucken; **~ sb. as [being] silly** jmdm. dumm erscheinen; **it ~s sb. that ...:** es scheint jmdm., dass ...
(f) (occur to) einfallen (+ *Dat.*)
[3] *v.i.,* **struck (a)** (deliver a blow) zuschlagen; ‹*Blitz:*› einschlagen; ‹*Unheil, Katastrophe:*› hereinbrechen (geh.); (hit) schlagen **(against** gegen, **[up]on** auf + *Akk.*)
(b) (ignite) zünden
(c) (chime) schlagen
(d) (Industry) streiken

▪ **strike 'back** *v.i.* zurückschlagen

▪ **strike 'off** *v.t.* (~ off list) streichen ‹*Namen*›; (from professional body) die Zulassung entziehen (+ *Dat.*)

▪ **'strike through** *v.t.* durchstreichen ‹*Wort*›; (on list also) ausstreichen

▪ **'strike up** *v.t.* beginnen ‹*Unterhaltung*›; schließen ‹*Freundschaft*›

strike: ~ action *n.* Streikaktionen *Pl.;* **~ pay** *n.* Streikgeld, *das*

'striker *n.* **(a)** (worker on strike) Streikende, *der/die*
(b) (Footb.) Stürmer, der/Stürmerin, *die*

striking /'straɪkɪŋ/ *adj.* auffallend; erstaunlich ‹*Ähnlichkeit*›; schlagend ‹*Beispiel*›

S

'striking distance *n.* Reichweite, *die*

string /strɪŋ/ [1] *n.* **(a)** (thin cord) Schnur, *die;* (to tie up parcels etc. also) Bindfaden, *der;* **pull [a few** *or* **some] ~s** (fig.) seine Beziehungen spielen lassen; **with no ~s attached** ohne Bedingung[en]
(b) (of bow) Sehne, *die;* (of racket, musical instrument) Saite, *die*
[2] *v.t.,* **strung** /strʌŋ/ (thread) auffädeln

■ **string a'long** *v.t.* (deceive) an der Nase herumführen (ugs.)

■ **string to'gether** *v.t.* auffädeln; miteinander verknüpfen ‹*Wörter*›

■ **string 'up** *v.t.* aufhängen

string: ~ bag *n.* [Einkaufs]netz, *das;* **~ 'bean** *n.* (Amer.) Stangenbohne, *die*

stringed /strɪŋd/ *attrib. adj.* (Mus.) Saiten-

stringent /'strɪndʒənt/ *adj.* streng

string 'vest *n.* Netzhemd, *das*

strip¹ /strɪp/ [1] *v.t.,* **-pp-** ausziehen ‹*Person*›
[2] *v.i.,* **-pp-** sich ausziehen

strip² *n.* (narrow piece) Streifen, *der*

strip: ~ cartoon *n.* Comic[strip], *der;* **~ club** *n.* Stripteaselokal, *das*

stripe /straɪp/ *n.* Streifen, *der*

striped /straɪpt/ *adj.* gestreift

strip: ~ light *n.* Neonröhre, *die;* **~ lighting** *n.* Neonbeleuchtung, *die*

stripped pine /strɪpt 'paɪn/ *n.* abgebeizte Kiefer

stripper /'strɪpə(r)/ *n.* Stripper, *der*/Stripperin, *die* (ugs.)

strip'tease *n.* Striptease, *der*

stripy /'straɪpɪ/ *adj.* gestreift; Streifen‹*muster*›

strive /straɪv/ *v.i.,* **strove** /strəʊv/, **striven** /'strɪvn/ sich bemühen; **~ after** *or* **for sth.** nach etw. streben

strode ▶ STRIDE 2

stroke¹ /strəʊk/ *n.* **(a)** (act of striking) Schlag, *der*
(b) (Med.) Schlaganfall, *der*
(c) (sudden impact) **~ of lightning** Blitzschlag, *der;* **~ of [good] luck** Glücksfall, *der*
(d) at a *or* **one ~:** auf einen Schlag; **not do a ~ [of work]** keinen [Hand]schlag tun; **~ of genius** genialer Einfall
(e) (in swimming) Zug, *der*
(f) (of clock) Schlag, *der;* **on the ~ of nine** Punkt neun [Uhr]

stroke² [1] *v.t.* streicheln
[2] *n.* **give sb./sth. a ~:** jmdn./etw. streicheln

stroll /strəʊl/ [1] *v.i.* spazieren gehen
[2] *n.* **go for a ~:** einen Spaziergang machen

strong /strɒŋ/ *adj.,* **~er** /'strɒŋgə(r)/, **~est** /'strɒŋgɪst/ stark; fest ‹*Fundament, Schuhe*›; robust ‹*Konstitution, Magen*›; kräftig ‹*Arme, Muskeln, Tritt, Zähne*›; leistungsfähig ‹*Wirtschaft*›; gut, handfest ‹*Grund, Beispiel, Argument*›; glühend ‹*Anhänger*›; kräftig ‹*Geruch, Geschmack, Stimme*›; **there is a ~ possibility that ...:** es ist sehr wahrscheinlich, dass ...; **take ~ measures/action** energisch vorgehen

strong: ~hold *n.* Festung, *die;* (fig.) Hochburg, *die;* **~ 'language** *n.* derbe Ausdrucksweise

'strongly *adv.* stark; solide ‹*gearbeitet*›; energisch ‹*protestieren, bestreiten*›; nachdrücklich ‹*unterstützen*›; dringend ‹*raten*›; fest ‹*glauben*›

strong: ~man *n.* Muskelmann, *der* (ugs.); **~-'minded** *adj.* willensstark; **~room** *n.* Tresorraum, *der;* **~-'willed** *adj.* willensstark

stroppy /'strɒpɪ/ *adj.* (Brit. coll.) pampig (salopp)

strove ▶ STRIVE

struck ▶ STRIKE 2, 3

structural /'strʌktʃərl/ *adj.* baulich

structure /'strʌktʃə(r)/ *n.* **(a)** Struktur, *die*
(b) (something constructed) Konstruktion, *die;* (building) Bauwerk, *das*

structured /'strʌktʃəd/ *adj.* strukturiert; geregelt ‹*Leben*›

struggle /'strʌgl/ [1] *v.i.* kämpfen; **~ to do sth.** sich abmühen, etw. zu tun; **~ against** *or* **with sb./sth.** mit jmdm./etw. *od.* gegen jmdn./etw. kämpfen; **~ with sth.** (try to cope) mit etw. kämpfen
[2] *n.* Kampf, *der*

strum /strʌm/ [1] *v.i.,* **-mm-** klimpern (ugs.) (**on** auf + *Dat.*)
[2] *v.t.,* **-mm-** klimpern (ugs.) auf (+ *Dat.*)

strung ▶ STRING 2

strut¹ /strʌt/ [1] *v.i.,* **-tt-** stolzieren
[2] *n.* stolzierender Gang

strut² *n.* (support) Strebe, *die*

stub /stʌb/ [1] *n.* **(a)** (remaining portion) Stummel, *der;* (of cigarette) Kippe, *die*
(b) (counterfoil) Abschnitt, *der*
[2] *v.t.,* **-bb-: (a) ~ one's toe [against** *or* **on sth.]** sich (*Dat.*) den Zeh [an etw. (*Dat.*)] stoßen
(b) ausdrücken ‹*Zigarette*›

■ **stub 'out** *v.t.* ausdrücken

stubble /'stʌbl/ *n.* Stoppeln *Pl.*

stubbly /'stʌblɪ/ *adj.* stopp[e]lig

stubborn /'stʌbən/ *adj.* **(a)** (obstinate) starrköpfig; störrisch ‹*Tier, Gesicht, Haltung*›
(b) (resolute) hartnäckig

'stubbornness *n.* ▶ STUBBORN: Starrköpfigkeit, *die;* Hartnäckigkeit, *die*

stuck ▶ STICK 1, 2

'stuck up *adj.* (conceited) eingebildet

student /'stju:dənt/ *n.* Student, *der*/Studentin, *die;* (in school or training establishment) Schüler, *der*/Schülerin, *die;* **be a ~ of sth.** etw. studieren

studio /'stju:dɪəʊ/ *n., pl.* **~s (a)** (workroom) Atelier, *das*
(b) (Cinemat., Radio, Telev.) Studio, *das*

studio: ~ apartment (Amer.) ▶ **~** FLAT;

~ '**audience** *n.* (Radio, Telev.) Publikum im Studio; ~ **flat** *n.* (Brit.) **(a)** Atelier, *das;* **(b)** (one-room flat) Einzimmerwohnung, *die*

studious /'stju:dɪəs/ *adj.* lerneifrig

study /'stʌdɪ/ **1** *n.* **(a)** Studium, *das* **(b)** (room) Arbeitszimmer, *das* **2** *v.t.* studieren; sich (*Dat.*) [sorgfältig] durchlesen ‹*Prüfungsfragen, Bericht*›

'**study group** *n.* Arbeitsgruppe, *die*

stuff /stʌf/ **1** *n.* (material[s]) Zeug, *das* (ugs.) **2** *v.t.* **(a)** stopfen; zustopfen ‹*Loch, Ohren*›; (Cookery) füllen; ~ **sth. with** *or* **full of sth.** etw. mit etw. voll stopfen (ugs.) **(b)** (sl.) ~ **him!** zum Teufel mit ihm!

stuffed 'shirt *n.* (coll. derog.) Spießer, *der* (ugs. abwertend)

'**stuffing** *n.* **(a)** (material) Füllmaterial, *das* **(b)** (Cookery) Füllung, *die*

stuffy /'stʌfɪ/ *adj.* stickig

stumble /'stʌmbl/ *v.i.* stolpern (**over** über + *Akk.*)

stumbling block /'stʌmblɪŋblɒk/ *n.* Stolperstein, *der*

stump /stʌmp/ **1** *n.* (of tree, branch, tooth) Stumpf, *der;* (of cigar, pencil) Stummel, *der* **2** *v.t.* verwirren; **be ~ed** ratlos sein

'**stumpy** *adj.* gedrungen; ~ **tail** Stummelschwanz, *der*

stun /stʌn/ *v.t.*, **-nn-** (knock senseless) betäuben; **be ~ned at** *or* **by sth.** (fig.) von etw. wie betäubt sein

stung ▶ STING 2, 3

stunk ▶ STINK 1

stunner /'stʌnə(r)/ *n.* (coll.) **be a ~**: Spitze sein (ugs.)

stunning /'stʌnɪŋ/ *adj.* (coll.) **(a)** (splendid) hinreißend **(b)** (shocking) bestürzend ‹*Nachricht*›; (amazing) sensationell

stunt[1] /stʌnt/ *v.t.* hemmen

stunt[2] *n.* halsbrecherisches Kunststück; (Cinemat.) Stunt, *der*

'**stunt man** *n.* Stuntman, *der*

stupefying /'stju:pɪfaɪɪŋ/ *adj.* die Sinne betäubend ‹*Hitze*›; (fig.: astonishing) unfassbar

stupendous /stju:'pendəs/ *adj.* gewaltig

stupid /'stju:pɪd/ *adj.* dumm; (ridiculous) lächerlich; **it would be ~ to do sth.** es wäre töricht, etw. zu tun

stupidity /stju:'pɪdɪtɪ/ *n.* Dummheit, *die*

'**stupidly** *adv.* dumm

stupor /'stju:pə(r)/ *n.* Benommenheit, *die;* **in a drunken ~**: sinnlos betrunken

sturdy /'stɜ:dɪ/ *adj.* kräftig; stämmig ‹*Beine, Arme*›

stutter /'stʌtə(r)/ **1** *v.i.* stottern **2** *n.* Stottern, *das*

sty[1] /staɪ/ ▶ PIGSTY

sty[2], **stye** /staɪ/ *n.* (Med.) Gerstenkorn, *das*

style /staɪl/ *n.* Stil, *der;* **[hair]~**: Frisur, *die;* **dress in the latest ~**: sich nach der neuesten Mode kleiden

styli *pl. of* STYLUS

stylish /'staɪlɪʃ/ *adj.* stilvoll; elegant ‹*Kleidung, Auto, Person*›

stylist /'staɪlɪst/ *n.* (hair~) Haarstilist, *der*/-stilistin, *die*

stylus /'staɪləs/ *n., pl.* **styli** /'staɪlaɪ/ *or* **~es** [Abtast]nadel, *die*

suave /swɑ:v/ *adj.* gewandt

sub- /sʌb/ *pref.* unter-; sub-

sub'conscious **1** *adj.* unterbewusst **2** *n.* Unterbewusstsein, *das*

sub'continent *n.* Subkontinent, *der*

'**subcontract** *v.t.* an einen Subunternehmer vergeben

subcon'tractor *n.* Subunternehmer, *der*/-unternehmerin, *die*

'**subculture** *n.* Subkultur, *die*

subdivide /'---, --'-/ *v.t.* unterteilen

subdue /səb'dju:/ *v.t.* bändigen ‹*Kind, Tier*›; dämpfen ‹*Zorn, Lärm, Licht*›

subdued /səb'dju:d/ *adj.* gedämpft

'**subgroup** *n.* Untergruppe, *die*

'**subheading** *n.* Untertitel, *der*

sub'human *adj.* unmenschlich

subject **1** /'sʌbdʒɪkt/ *n.* **(a)** Staatsbürger, *der*/-bürgerin, *die;* (to monarch) Untertan, *der*/Untertanin, *die* **(b)** (topic) Thema, *das;* (of study) Fach, *das;* **change the ~**: das Thema wechseln **2** /'sʌbdʒɪkt/ *adj.* **be ~ to sth.** von etw. abhängen **3** /səb'dʒekt/ *v.t.* unterwerfen (**to** *Dat.*); (expose) ~ **sb./sth. to sth.** jmdn./etw. einer Sache (*Dat.*) aussetzen

subjective /səb'dʒektɪv/ *adj.*, **sub'jectively** *adv.* subjektiv

'**subject matter** *n., no indef. art.* Gegenstand, *der*

subjugate /'sʌbdʒʊgeɪt/ *v.t.* unterjochen (**to** unter + *Akk.*)

subjugation /sʌbdʒʊ'geɪʃn/ *n.* Unterjochung, *die*

subjunctive /səb'dʒʌŋktɪv/ *n.* Konjunktiv, *der*

sub'let *v.t.*, **-tt-**, **sublet** untervermieten

sublime /sə'blaɪm/ *adj.* erhaben

submarine /sʌbmə'ri:n/ *n.* Unterseeboot, *das;* U-Boot, *das*

submerge /səb'mɜ:dʒ/ *v.t.* **(a)** ~ **sth. [in the water]** etw. eintauchen **(b)** (flood) ‹*Wasser:*› überschwemmen; **be ~d in water** unter Wasser stehen

submerged /səb'mɜ:dʒd/ *adj.* versunken

submission /səb'mɪʃn/ *n.* **(a)** (surrender, meekness) Unterwerfung, *die* **(b)** (presentation) Einreichung, *die* (**to** bei)

submissive /səb'mɪsɪv/ *adj.* gehorsam

submit /səb'mɪt/ *v.t.*, **-tt-** (present) einreichen; vorbringen ‹*Vorschlag*›; ~ **sth. to sb.** jmdm. etw. vorlegen

S

subordinate [1] /sə'bɔːdɪnət/ *adj.* untergeordnet
[2] /sə'bɔːdɪnət/ *n.* Untergebene, *der/die*
[3] /sə'bɔːdɪneɪt/ *v.t.* unterordnen (**to** *Dat.*)

subscribe /səb'skraɪb/ *v.i.* **(a)** (support) **~ to sth.** sich einer Sache anschließen
(b) (make contribution) **~ to sth.** eine Spende für etw. zusichern
(c) ~ to a newspaper eine Zeitung abonnieren

sub'scriber *n.* (to newspaper etc.) Abonnent, *der*/Abonnentin, *die* (**to** *Gen.*)

subscription /səb'skrɪpʃn/ *n.* (membership fee) Mitgliedsbeitrag, *der* (**to** für); (to newspaper etc.) Abonnement, *das*

subsequent /'sʌbsɪkwənt/ *adj.* folgend; später ‹*Gelegenheit*›

'subsequently *adv.* später; danach

subservient /səb'sɜːvɪənt/ *adj.* untergeordnet (**to** *Dat.*); (servile) unterwürfig

subside /səb'saɪd/ *v.i.* **(a)** (sink lower) ‹*Flut, Fluss:*› sinken; ‹*Boden, Haus:*› sich senken
(b) (abate) nachlassen

subsidence /səb'saɪdəns/ *n.* (of ground, structure) Senkung, *die*

subsidiary /səb'sɪdɪərɪ/ [1] *adj.* untergeordnet ‹*Funktion, Stellung*›; Neben‹*fach, -aspekt*›
[2] *n.* (Commerc.) Tochtergesellschaft, *die*

subsidize /'sʌbsɪdaɪz/ *v.t.* subventionieren

subsidy /'sʌbsɪdɪ/ *n.* Subvention, *die*

subsist /səb'sɪst/ *v.i.* **~ on sth.** von etw. leben

subsistence /səb'sɪstəns/ *n.* [Über]leben, *das*

'subsoil *n.* Untergrund, *der*

substance /'sʌbstəns/ *n.* **(a)** Stoff, *der*
(b) (solidity) Substanz, *die*
(c) (content) Inhalt, *der*

'substance abuse *n.* Drogen- und Genussmittelmissbrauch, *der*

sub'standard *adj.* unzulänglich

substantial /səb'stænʃl/ *adj.* **(a)** (considerable) beträchtlich
(b) gehaltvoll ‹*Essen*›
(c) (solid) solide ‹*Möbel, Haus*›; wesentlich ‹*Unterschied*›

sub'stantially *adv.* **(a)** (considerably) wesentlich
(b) (solidly) solide
(c) (essentially) im Wesentlichen

substitute /'sʌbstɪtjuːt/ [1] *n.* **(a)** **~[s** *pl.*] Ersatz, *der*
(b) (Sport) Ersatzspieler, der/-spielerin, *die*
[2] *v.t.* **~ A for B** B durch A ersetzen

substitution /sʌbstɪ'tjuːʃn/ *n.* Ersetzung, *die;* **make a ~** (Sport) [einen Spieler] auswechseln

subterfuge /'sʌbtəfjuːdʒ/ *n.* Täuschungsmanöver *Pl.*

'subtitle *n.* Untertitel, *der*

subtle /'sʌtl/ *adj.* subtil (geh.); zart ‹*Duft, Parfüm, Hinweis*›; fein ‹*Geschmack, Unterschied, Humor*›

'subtotal *n.* Zwischensumme, *die*

subtract /səb'trækt/ *v.t.* abziehen

subtraction /səb'trækʃn/ *n.* Subtraktion, *die*

sub'tropical *adj.* subtropisch

suburb /'sʌbɜːb/ *n.* Vorort, *der*

suburban /sə'bɜːbən/ *adj.* Vorort-; ‹*Leben, Haus*› am Stadtrand

suburbia /sə'bɜːbɪə/ *n.* (derog.) die [eintönigen] Vororte *Pl.*

subversive /səb'vɜːsɪv/ *adj.* subversiv

'subway *n.* **(a)** (passage) Unterführung, *die*
(b) (Amer.: railway) Untergrundbahn, *die;* U-Bahn, *die*

sub-'zero *adj.* **~ temperatures/conditions** Temperaturen unter Null

succeed /sək'siːd/ [1] *v.i.* **(a)** Erfolg haben; **sb. ~s in sth.** jmdm. gelingt etw.; jmd. schafft etw.; **sb. ~s in doing sth.** es gelingt jmdm., etw. zu tun; jmd. schafft es, etw. zu tun; **~ in business/college** geschäftlich/im Studium erfolgreich sein; **I did not ~ in doing it** ich habe es nicht geschafft
(b) (come next) die Nachfolge antreten
[2] *v.t.* (take place of) ablösen

success /sək'ses/ *n.* Erfolg, *der;* **make a ~ of sth.** bei etw. Erfolg haben

successful /sək'sesfl/ *adj.* erfolgreich; **be ~ in sth./doing sth.** Erfolg bei etw. haben/dabei haben, etw. zu tun

suc'cessfully *adv.* erfolgreich

succession /sək'seʃn/ *n.* **(a)** Folge, *die;* **in ~:** hintereinander
(b) (series) Serie, *die*
(c) (to throne) Erbfolge, *die*

successive /sək'sesɪv/ *adj.* aufeinander folgend

suc'cessively *adv.* hintereinander

successor /sək'sesə(r)/ *n.* Nachfolger, *der*/Nachfolgerin, *die*

suc'cess story *n.* Erfolgsstory, *die* (ugs.)

succinct /sək'sɪŋkt/ *adj.* **(a)** (terse) knapp
(b) (clear) prägnant

succulent /'sʌkjʊlənt/ *adj.* saftig

succumb /sə'kʌm/ *v.i.* unterliegen; **~ to sth.** einer Sache (*Dat.*) erliegen

such /sʌtʃ/ [1] *adj.* **(a)** (of that kind) solch...; **~ a person** ein solcher Mensch; **~ a book** ein solches Buch; **~ people** solche Leute; **~ things** so etwas; **I said no ~ thing** ich habe nichts dergleichen gesagt; **there is no ~ bird** einen solchen Vogel gibt es nicht; **or some ~ thing** oder so etwas; **you'll do no ~ thing** das wirst du nicht tun; **experiences ~ as these** solche Erfahrungen
(b) (so great) solch...; derartig; **I got ~ a fright that ...:** ich bekam einen derartigen *od.* (ugs.) so einen Schrecken, dass ...; **~ was the force of the explosion that ...:** die Explosion war so stark, dass ...; **to ~ an extent** dermaßen

(c) *with adj.* so; **~ a big house** ein so großes Haus; **~ a long time** so lange
2 *pron.* **as ~:** als solcher/solche/solches; (strictly speaking) im Grunde genommen; an sich; **~ as** wie [zum Beispiel]; **~ is life** so ist das Leben

such-and-such /'sʌtʃənsʌtʃ/ *adj.* **at ~ a time** um die und die Zeit

'suchlike *pron.* derlei

suck /sʌk/ **1** *v.t.* saugen (**out of** aus); lutschen ‹*Bonbon*›
2 sth. ~s (esp. Amer. sl.) etw. ist Scheiße (derb)

■ **suck 'up 1** *v.t.* aufsaugen
2 *v.i.* **~ up to sb.** (coll.) jmdm. in den Hintern kriechen (salopp)

'sucker *n.* **(a)** (suction pad) Saugfuß, *der;* (Zool.) Saugnapf, *der*
(b) (coll.: dupe) Dumme, *der/die*

suckle /'sʌkl/ *v.t.* säugen

suction /'sʌkʃn/ *n.* Saugwirkung, *die*

Sudan /suː'dɑːn/ *pr. n.* **[the] ~:** [der] Sudan

sudden /'sʌdn/ **1** *adj.* **(a)** (unexpected) plötzlich
(b) (abrupt) jäh ‹*Abgrund, Übergang, Ruck*›; **there was a ~ bend in the road** plötzlich machte die Straße eine Biegung
2 *n.* **all of a ~:** plötzlich

'suddenly *adv.* plötzlich

'suddenness *n.* Plötzlichkeit, *die*

suds /sʌdz/ *n. pl.* **[soap]~:** [Seifen]lauge, *die;* (froth) Schaum, *der*

sue /suː/ **1** *v.t.* verklagen (**for** auf + *Akk.*)
2 *v.i.* klagen (**for** auf + *Akk.*)

suede /sweɪd/ *n.* Wildleder, *das*

suet /'suːɪt/ *n.* Talg, *der*

Suez /'sʊɪz, 'sjuːɪz/ *pr. n.* Suez (*das*); **~ Canal** Suez-Kanal, *der*

suffer /'sʌfə(r)/ **1** *v.t.* erleiden; durchmachen ‹*Schweres, Kummer*›; dulden ‹*Unverschämtheit*›
2 *v.i.* leiden

■ **'suffer from** *v.t.* leiden unter (+ *Dat.*); leiden an (+ *Dat.*) ‹*Krankheit*›

sufferance /'sʌfərəns/ *n.* Duldung, *die;* **he remains here on ~ only** er ist hier bloß geduldet

'suffering *n.* Leiden, *das*

suffice /sə'faɪs/ **1** *v.i.* genügen; **~ it to say ...:** nur so viel sei gesagt: ...
2 *v.t.* genügen (+ *Dat.*)

sufficiency /sə'fɪʃənsɪ/ *n.* Zulänglichkeit, *die*

sufficient /sə'fɪʃənt/ *adj.* genug; **~ money/food** genug Geld/genug zu essen; **be ~:** genügen; **~ reason** Grund genug; **have you had ~?** (food, drink) haben Sie schon genug?

suf'ficiently *adv.* genug; (adequately) ausreichend; **~ large** groß genug; **a ~ large number** eine genügend große Zahl

suffix /'sʌfɪks/ *n.* Nachsilbe, *die*

suffocate /'sʌfəkeɪt/ **1** *v.t.* ersticken; **he was ~d by the smoke** der Rauch erstickte ihn
2 *v.i.* ersticken

suffocation /sʌfə'keɪʃn/ *n.* Erstickung, *die;* **a feeling of ~:** das Gefühl, zu ersticken

sugar /'ʃʊgə(r)/ **1** *n.* Zucker, *der;* **two ~s, please** (lumps) zwei Stück Zucker, bitte; (spoonfuls) zwei Löffel Zucker, bitte
2 *v.t.* zuckern

sugar: ~ basin ▶ **~** BOWL; **~ beet** *n.* Zuckerrübe, *die;* **~ bowl** *n.* Zuckerschale, *die;* (covered) Zuckerdose, *die;* **~ cane** *n.* Zuckerrohr, *das;* **~-coated** *adj.* gezuckert; mit Zucker überzogen ‹*Dragee usw.*›; **~ daddy** *n.* (coll.) *spendabler älterer Mann, der ein junges Mädchen aushält;* **~ lump** *n.* Zuckerstück, *das;* (when counted) Stück Zucker; **~ tongs** *n. pl.* Zuckerzange, *die*

'sugary *adj.* süß; (fig.) süßlich

suggest /sə'dʒest/ *v.t.* **(a)** (propose) vorschlagen; **~ sth. to sb.** jmdm. etw. vorschlagen; **he ~ed going to the cinema** er schlug vor, ins Kino zu gehen
(b) (assert) **are you trying to ~ that he is lying** wollen Sie damit sagen, dass er lügt?
(c) (make one think of) suggerieren; ‹*Symptome, Tatsachen:*› schließen lassen auf (+ *Akk.*)

suggestion /sə'dʒestʃn/ *n.* **(a)** Vorschlag, *der;* **at** *or* **on sb.'s ~:** auf jmds. Vorschlag (*Akk.*)
(b) (insinuation) Andeutungen *Pl.*
(c) (fig.: trace) Spur, *die*

suggestive /sə'dʒestɪv/ *adj.* **(a) be ~ of sth.** auf etw. (*Akk.*) schließen lassen
(b) (indecent) anzüglich

suicidal /suːɪ'saɪdl/ *adj.* selbstmörderisch; **I felt** *or* **was quite ~:** ich hätte mich am liebsten gleich umgebracht

suicide /'suːɪsaɪd/ *n.* Selbstmord, *der*

'suicide attempt *n.* Selbstmordversuch, *der*

suit /suːt/ **1** *n.* **(a)** (for men) Anzug, *der;* (for women) Kostüm, *das*
(b) (Law) **~ [at law]** Prozess, *der*
(c) (Cards) Farbe, *die;* **follow ~** (fig.) das Gleiche tun
2 *v.t.* **(a)** anpassen (**to** *Dat.*)
(b) be ~ed [to sth./one another] [zu etw./zueinander] passen
(c) (satisfy needs of) passen (+ *Dat.*); **will Monday ~ you?** passt Ihnen Montag?; **does the climate ~ you?** bekommt Ihnen das Klima?
(d) (go well with) passen zu; **does this hat ~ me?** steht mir dieser Hut?; **black ~s her** Schwarz steht ihr gut
3 *v. refl.* **~ oneself** tun, was man will; **~ yourself!** [ganz] wie du willst!

suitability /suːtə'bɪlɪtɪ/ *n.* Eignung, *die* (**for** für)

suitable /'suːtəbl/ *adj.* geeignet; angemessen ‹*Kleidung*›; (convenient) passend; ⋯

~ **for children** für Kinder geeignet; **Monday is the most ~ day [for me]** Montag passt [mir] am besten
suitably /'su:təblɪ/ *adv.* angemessen; entsprechend ‹*gekleidet*›
'suitcase *n.* Koffer, *der*
suite /swi:t/ *n.* **(a)** (of furniture) Garnitur, *die;* **three-piece ~:** Polstergarnitur, *die* **(b)** (of rooms) Suite, *die*
suitor /'su:tə(r)/ *n.* Freier, *der*
sulfur, sulfuric (Amer.) ▶ SULPH-
sulk /sʌlk/ *v.i.* schmollen
'sulky *adj.* schmollend; eingeschnappt (ugs.)
sullen /'sʌlən/ *adj.* mürrisch
sulphur /'sʌlfə(r)/ *n.* Schwefel, *der*
sulphuric /sʌl'fjʊərɪk/ *adj.* **~ acid** Schwefelsäure, *die*
sultan /'sʌltən/ *n.* Sultan, *der*
sultana /sʌl'tɑ:nə/ *n.* Sultanine, *die*
sultry /'sʌltrɪ/ *adj.* schwül
sum /sʌm/ *n.* **(a)** Summe, *die* **(of** aus); **~ [total]** Ergebnis, *das* **(b)** (Arithmetic) Rechenaufgabe, *die;* **do ~s** rechnen; **she is good at ~s** sie kann gut rechnen
▪ **sum 'up** 1 *v.t.* **(a)** zusammenfassen **(b)** (Brit.: assess) einschätzen 2 *v.i.* ein Fazit ziehen
summarily /'sʌmərɪlɪ/ *adv.* summarisch; **~ dismissed** fristlos entlassen
summarize /'sʌməraɪz/ *v.t.* zusammenfassen
summary /'sʌmərɪ/ 1 *adj.* summarisch; fristlos ‹*Entlassung*› 2 *n.* Zusammenfassung, *die*
summer /'sʌmə(r)/ *n.* Sommer, *der;* **in [the] ~:** im Sommer
summer: ~ house *n.* [Garten]laube, *die;* **~ school** *n.* Sommerkurs, *der;* **~ term** *n.* Sommerhalbjahr, *das;* **~time** *n.* Sommer, *der*
'summery *adj.* sommerlich
summing 'up *n.* Zusammenfassung, *die*
summit /'sʌmɪt/ *n.* Gipfel, *der;* **~ conference/meeting** Gipfelkonferenz, *die*/ -treffen, *das*
summon /'sʌmən/ *v.t.* **(a)** rufen **(to** zu); holen ‹*Hilfe*› **(b)** (Law) vorladen
▪ **summon 'up** *v.t.* aufbringen
summons /'sʌmənz/ *n.* Vorladung, *die*
sump /sʌmp/ *n.* Ölwanne, *die*
sumptuous /'sʌmptjʊəs/ *adj.* üppig; luxuriös ‹*Möbel, Kleidung*›
sun /sʌn/ 1 *n.* Sonne, *die;* **catch the ~** (be in sunny position) viel Sonne abbekommen; (get ~burnt) einen Sonnenbrand bekommen 2 *v. refl.*, **-nn-** sich sonnen
Sun. *abbr.* = **Sunday** So.
sun: ~baked *adj.* an der Sonne getrocknet ‹*Ziegel*›; ausgedörrt ‹*Landschaft, Prärie usw.*›; **~bathe** *v.i.* sonnenbaden; **~bathing** *n.* Sonnenbaden, *das;* **~beam** *n.* Sonnenstrahl, *der;* **~bed** *n.* (with UV lamp) Sonnenbank, *die;* (in garden) Gartenliege, *die;* **~block** *n.* Sonnenschutzcreme, *die* [mit hohem Lichtschutzfaktor]; **~burn** *n.* Sonnenbrand, *der;* **~burnt** *adj.* **be/get ~burnt** einen Sonnenbrand haben/ bekommen; **~cream** *n.* Sonnencreme, *die*
sundae /'sʌndeɪ/ *n.* **[ice cream] ~:** Eisbecher, *der*
Sunday /'sʌndeɪ, 'sʌndɪ/ *n.* Sonntag, *der;* **~ opening** die sonntägliche Öffnung; **~ trading** sonntägliche Ladenöffnung; *see also* FRIDAY
sun: ~deck *n.* Sonnendeck, *das;* **~dial** *n.* Sonnenuhr, *die;* **~-dried** *adj.* an der Sonne getrocknet
sundry /'sʌndrɪ/ 1 *adj.* verschieden 2 *n. in pl.* Verschiedenes
'sunflower *n.* Sonnenblume, *die*
sung ▶ SING
sun: ~glasses *n. pl.* Sonnenbrille, *die;* **~hat** *n.* Sonnenhut, *der*
sunk ▶ SINK 2, 3
sun: ~lamp *n.* Höhensonne, *die;* **~lit** *adj.* sonnenbeschienen; **~light** *n.* Sonnenlicht, *das*
Sunni /'sʌnɪ/ *n.* (Muslim Relig.) Sunnit, *der*/Sunnitin, *die; attrib.* sunnitisch
sunny /'sʌnɪ/ *adj.* sonnig; **~ intervals** Aufheiterungen
sun: ~ protection factor *n.* Lichtschutzfaktor, *der;* **~ray** *n.* Sonnenstrahl, *der;* **~rise** *n.* Sonnenaufgang, *der;* **~roof** *n.* (Motor Veh.) Schiebedach, *das;* **~set** *n.* Sonnenuntergang, *der;* **~shade** *n.* Sonnenschirm, *der;* **~shine** *n.* Sonnenschein, *der;* **~stroke** *n.* Sonnenstich, *der;* **~tan** *n.* [Sonnen]bräune, *die;* **get a ~tan** braun werden; **~tan lotion** *n.* Sonnencreme, *die;* **~tanned** *adj.* braun [gebrannt]; **~tan oil** *n.* Sonnenöl, *das;* **~trap** *n.* sonniges Plätzchen; **~ worshipper** *n.* (lit./joc.) Sonnenanbeter, *der*/-anbeterin, *die*
super /'su:pə(r)/ *adj.* (coll.) super (ugs.)
superb /su:'pɜ:b/ *adj.* einzigartig; erstklassig ‹*Essen*›
superbug /'sʊ:pəbʌg/ *n.* multiresistenter Erreger
supercilious /su:pə'sɪlɪəs/ *adj.* hochnäsig
supercomputer /'su:pəkəmpju:tə(r)/ *n.* Supercomputer, *der*
superficial /su:pə'fɪʃl/ *adj.* oberflächlich
superficiality /su:pəfɪʃɪ'ælɪtɪ/ *n.* Oberflächlichkeit, *die*
superfluous /sʊ'pɜ:flʊəs/ *adj.* überflüssig
super: ~glue *n.* Sekundenkleber, *der;* **~human** *adj.* übermenschlich; **~highway** *n.* **(a)** (Amer.) Autobahn, *die;* **(b)** (Comp.) Datenautobahn, *die*
superintendent /su:pərɪn'tendənt/ *n.* (Brit. Police) Kommissar, *der*/Kommissarin, *die*

superior /suːˈpɪərɪə(r)/ 1 *adj.* **(a)** (of higher quality) besonders gut ‹*Restaurant, Qualität, Stoff*›; überlegen ‹*Technik, Intelligenz*›; **he thinks he is ~ to us** er hält sich für besser als wir
(b) (having higher rank) höher…; **be ~ to sb.** einen höheren Rang als jmd. haben
2 *n.* Vorgesetzte, *der/die*

superiority /suːpɪərɪˈɒrɪtɪ/ *n.* Überlegenheit, *die* (**to** über + *Akk.*)

superlative /suːˈpɜːlətɪv/ 1 *adj.* **(a)** unübertrefflich
(b) (Ling.) **a ~ adjective/adverb** ein Adjektiv/Adverb im Superlativ
2 *n.* (Ling.) Superlativ, *der*

super: ~market *n.* Supermarkt, *der;* **~model** *n.* Supermodel, *das;* **~'natural** *adj.* übernatürlich; **~power** *n.* (Polit.) Supermacht, *die*

supersede /suːpəˈsiːd/ *v.t.* ablösen (**by** durch)

supersonic /suːpəˈsɒnɪk/ *adj.* Überschall-

superstar /ˈsuːpəstɑː(r)/ *n.* Superstar, *der*

superstition /suːpəˈstɪʃn/ *n.* Aberglaube, *der*

superstitious /suːpəˈstɪʃəs/ *adj.* abergläubisch

superstore /ˈsuːpəstɔː(r)/ *n.* Großmarkt, *der*

supervise /ˈsuːpəvaɪz/ *v.t.* beaufsichtigen

supervision /suːpəˈvɪʒn/ *n.* Aufsicht, *die*

supervisor /ˈsuːpəvaɪzə(r)/ *n.* Aufseher, *der*/Aufseherin, *die*

supper /ˈsʌpə(r)/ *n.* Abendessen, *das;* **have [one's] ~:** zu Abend essen

'suppertime *n.* Abendbrotzeit, *die;* **it's ~:** es ist Zeit zum Abendessen

supplant /səˈplɑːnt/ *v.t.* ablösen, ersetzen (**by** durch)

supple /ˈsʌpl/ *adj.* geschmeidig

supplement /ˈsʌplɪmənt/ 1 *n.* **(a)** Ergänzung, *die* (**to** + *Gen.*); (addition) Zusatz, *der*
(b) (of book) Nachtrag, *der;* (of newspaper) Beilage, *die*
(c) (to fare) Zuschlag, *der*
2 *v.t.* ergänzen

supplementary /sʌplɪˈmentərɪ/ *adj.* zusätzlich; **~ fare/charge** Zuschlag, *der*

supplier /səˈplaɪə(r)/ *n.* (Commerc.) Lieferant, *der*/Lieferantin, *die*

supply /səˈplaɪ/ 1 *v.t.* liefern ‹*Waren usw.*›; beliefern ‹*Kunden, Geschäft*›; **~ sth. to sb., ~ sb. with sth.** jmdn. mit etw. versorgen/(Commerc.) beliefern
2 *n.* Vorräte *Pl.;* **military/medical supplies** militärischer/medizinischer Nachschub; **~ and demand** (Econ.) Angebot und Nachfrage

sup'ply teacher *n.* Vertretung, *die*

support /səˈpɔːt/ 1 *v.t.* **(a)** (hold up) stützen ‹*Mauer, Verletzten*›; (bear weight of) tragen
(b) unterstützen ‹*Politik, Verein*›; (Footb.) **~ Spurs** Spurs-Fan sein
(c) (provide for) ernähren ‹*Familie, sich selbst*›
(d) (speak in favour of) befürworten
2 *n.* **(a)** Unterstützung, *die;* **in ~:** zur Unterstützung; **speak in ~ of sb./sth.** jmdn. unterstützen/etw. befürworten
(b) (money) Unterhalt, *der*
(c) (sb./sth. that ~s) Stütze, *die*

sup'porter *n.* Anhänger, *der*/Anhängerin, *die;* **football ~:** Fußballfan, *der*

sup'porting *adj.* (Cinemat., Theatre) **~ role** Nebenrolle, *die;* **~ actor/actress** Schauspieler/-spielerin in einer Nebenrolle; **~ film** Vorfilm, *der*

supportive /səˈpɔːtɪv/ *adj.* hilfreich; **be very ~ [to sb.]** [jmdm.] eine große Hilfe *od.* Stütze sein

suppose /səˈpəʊz/ *v.t.* **(a)** (assume) annehmen; **~** *or* **supposing [that] he ...:** angenommen, [dass] er ...
(b) (presume) vermuten; **I ~ so** (doubtfully) ja, vermutlich; (more confidently) ich glaube schon
(c) be ~d to do/be sth. (be generally believed to do/be sth.) etw. tun/sein sollen
(d) (allow) **you are not ~d to do that** das darfst du eigentlich nicht; **I'm not ~d to be here** ich dürfte eigentlich gar nicht hier sein

supposed /səˈpəʊzd/ *attrib. adj.* mutmaßlich

supposedly /səˈpəʊzɪdlɪ/ *adv.* angeblich

supposition /sʌpəˈzɪʃn/ *n.* Annahme, *die;* Vermutung, *die*

suppress /səˈpres/ *v.t.* unterdrücken

suppression /səˈpreʃn/ *n.* Unterdrückung, *die*

supremacy /suːˈpreməsɪ/ *n.* **(a)** (supreme authority) Souveränität, *die*
(b) (superiority) Überlegenheit, *die*

supreme /suːˈpriːm/ *adj.* höchst...

Supt. *abbr.* = **Superintendent**

surcharge /ˈsɜːtʃɑːdʒ/ *n.* Zuschlag, *der*

sure /ʃʊə(r)/ 1 *adj.* sicher; **be ~ of sth.** sich (*Dat.*) einer Sache (*Gen.*) sicher sein; **~ of oneself** selbstsicher; **don't be too ~:** da wäre ich mir nicht so sicher; **there is ~ to be a petrol station** es gibt bestimmt eine Tankstelle; **don't worry, it's ~ to turn out well** keine Sorge, es wird schon alles gut gehen; **for ~** (coll.) auf jeden Fall; **make ~ [of sth.]** sich [einer Sache] vergewissern; **make** *or* **be ~ you do it, be ~ to do it** (do not fail to do it) sieh zu, dass du es tust; (do not forget) vergiss nicht, es zu tun; **a ~ winner** ein todsicherer Tipp (ugs.)
2 *adv.* **~ enough** tatsächlich
3 *int.* **~!, ~ thing!** (Amer.) na klar! (ugs.)

sure: ~-fire *attrib. adj.* (Amer. coll.) todsicher; **~-footed** *adj.* trittsicher

'surely 1 *adv.* **(a)** *as sentence-modifier* doch; **~ we've met before?** wir kennen uns doch, oder?

(b) (steadily) sicher; **slowly but ~:** langsam, aber sicher
(c) (certainly) sicherlich
2 *int.* (Amer.) natürlich

surf /sɜːf/ *n.* **1** Brandung, *die*
2 *v.i.* **(a)** surfen
(b) (Comp.) surfen; (TV) zappen (ugs.)
3 *v.t.* (Comp., TV) **~ the Internet** im Internet surfen; **~ the channels** sich durch die Kanäle zappen (ugs.)

surface /ˈsɜːfɪs/ **1** *n.* Oberfläche, *die;* **outer ~:** Außenfläche, *die;* **the earth's ~:** die Erdoberfläche; **on the ~:** an der Oberfläche; (fig.) oberflächlich betrachtet
2 *v.i.* auftauchen; (fig.) hochkommen

surface: ~ area *n.* Oberfläche, *die;* **~ mail** *n.* gewöhnliche Post

ˈsurfboard *n.* Surfbrett, *das*

surfeit /ˈsɜːfɪt/ *n.* Übermaß, *das*

ˈsurfer *n.* Surfer, *der*/Surferin, *die*

ˈsurfing *n.* Surfen, *das*

surge /sɜːdʒ/ *v.i.* ‹*Wellen:*› branden; **the crowd ~d forward** die Menschenmenge drängte nach vorn

surgeon /ˈsɜːdʒən/ *n.* Chirurg, *der*/ Chirurgin, *die*

surgery /ˈsɜːdʒərɪ/ *n.* **(a)** Chirurgie, *die;* **undergo ~:** sich einer Operation (*Dat.*) unterziehen
(b) (Brit.: place) Praxis, *die;* **doctor's/dental ~:** Arzt-/Zahnarztpraxis, *die*
(c) (Brit.: time) Sprechstunde, *die*

surgical /ˈsɜːdʒɪkl/ *adj.* chirurgisch; **~ treatment** Operation, *die*/Operationen *Pl.*

surly /ˈsɜːlɪ/ *adj.* mürrisch

surmise /səˈmaɪz/ **1** *n.* Vermutung, *die*
2 *v.t.* mutmaßen

surmount /səˈmaʊnt/ *v.t.* überwinden

surmountable /səˈmaʊntəbl/ *adj.* überwindbar

surname /ˈsɜːneɪm/ *n.* Nachname, *der;* Zuname, *der*

surpass /səˈpɑːs/ *v.t.* übertreffen; **~ oneself** sich selbst übertreffen

surplus /ˈsɜːpləs/ **1** *n.* Überschuss, *der* (**of** an + *Dat.*)
2 *adj.* überschüssig; **be ~ to sb.'s requirements** von jmdm. nicht benötigt werden

surprise /səˈpraɪz/ **1** *n.* **(a)** Überraschung, *die;* **take sb. by ~:** jmdn. überrumpeln; **to my great ~, much to my ~:** zu meiner großen Überraschung; **it came as a ~ to us** es war für uns eine Überraschung
(b) *attrib.* überraschend, unerwartet ‹*Besuch*›; **a ~ attack** ein Überraschungsangriff
2 *v.t.* überraschen; überrumpeln ‹*Feind*›; **I shouldn't be ~d if ...:** es würde mich nicht wundern, wenn ...; **be ~d at sb./sth.** sich über jmdn./etw. wundern

surprising /səˈpraɪzɪŋ/ *adj.* überraschend

surprisingly *adv.* überraschend; **~ [enough], he was ...:** überraschenderweise war er ...

surreal /səˈriːəl/ *adj.* surrealistisch

surrealism /səˈriːəlɪzm/ *n.* Surrealismus, *der*

surrender /səˈrendə(r)/ **1** *n.* (to enemy) Kapitulation, *die;* (of possession) Aufgabe, *die*
2 *v.i.* kapitulieren
3 *v.t.* aufgeben

surreptitious /sʌrəpˈtɪʃəs/ *adj.* heimlich; verstohlen ‹*Blick*›

surrogate /ˈsʌrəgət/ *n.* Ersatz, *der*

surrogate ˈmother *n.* Leihmutter, *die*

surround /səˈraʊnd/ *v.t.* **(a)** (come or be all round) umringen; ‹*Truppen, Heer:*› umzingeln ‹*Stadt, Feind*›
(b) (encircle) umgeben; **be ~ed by** *or* **with sth.** von etw. umgeben sein

surˈrounding *adj.* umliegend; **the ~ countryside** die [Landschaft in der] Umgebung

surˈroundings *n. pl.* Umgebung, *die*

surveillance /səˈveɪləns/ *n.* Überwachung, *die;* **be under ~:** überwacht werden

survey **1** /səˈveɪ/ *v.t.* betrachten; überblicken ‹*Landschaft*›; inspizieren ‹*Gebäude*›; bewerten ‹*Situation*›
2 /ˈsɜːveɪ/ *n.* Überblick, *der* (**of** über + *Akk.*); (poll) Umfrage, *die;* (Surv.) Vermessung, *die*

surveyor /səˈveɪə(r)/ *n.* (of building) Gutachter, *der*/Gutachterin, *die;* (of land) Landvermesser, *der*/-vermesserin, *die*

survival /səˈvaɪvl/ *n.* Überleben, *das;* **fight for ~:** Existenzkampf, *der*

surˈvival kit *n.* Notausrüstung, *die*

survive /səˈvaɪv/ **1** *v.t.* überleben
2 *v.i.* ‹*Person:*› überleben; ‹*Schriften, Traditionen:*› erhalten bleiben

survivor /səˈvaɪvə(r)/ *n.* Überlebende, *der*/ *die*

sus /sʌs/ (Brit. coll.) *v.t.*, **-ss-** spitzkriegen (ugs.); **get sb. ~sed** jmdn. durchschauen

▪ **sus ˈout** *v.t.* (coll.) checken (ugs.); spannen (ugs.)

susceptible /səˈseptɪbl/ *adj.* empfänglich (**to** für); (to illness) anfällig (**to** für)

suspect **1** /səˈspekt/ *v.t.* **(a)** (imagine to be likely) vermuten; **~ the worst** das Schlimmste befürchten; **~ sb. to be sth., ~ that sb. is sth.** glauben *od.* vermuten, dass jmd. etw. ist
(b) (mentally accuse) verdächtigen; **~ sb. of sth./of doing sth.** jmdn. einer Sache verdächtigen/jmdn. verdächtigen, etw. zu tun
2 /ˈsʌspekt/ *adj.* fragwürdig; verdächtig ‹*Stoff, Paket*›
3 /ˈsʌspekt/ *n.* Verdächtige, *der/die*

suspend /səˈspend/ *v.t.* **(a)** (hang up) [auf]hängen
(b) (stop) suspendieren

(c) (from work) ausschließen (**from** von); sperren ‹*Sportler*›

suspended 'sentence *n.* (Law) Strafe mit Bewährung

suspender belt /sə'spendə belt/ *n.* (Brit.) Strumpfbandgürtel, *der*

suspenders /sə'spendəz/ *n. pl.* **(a)** (Brit.: for stockings) Strumpfbänder *Pl.*
(b) (Amer.: for trousers) Hosenträger *Pl.*

suspense /sə'spens/ *n.* Spannung, *die;* **keep sb. in ~:** jmdn. auf die Folter spannen

suspension /sə'spenʃn/ *n.* (Motor Veh.) Federung, *die*

su'spension bridge *n.* Hängebrücke, *die*

suspicion /sə'spɪʃn/ *n.* **(a)** (uneasy feeling) Misstrauen, *das* (**of** gegenüber); (unconfirmed belief) Verdacht, *der;* **have a ~ that ...:** den Verdacht haben, dass ...
(b) (suspecting) Verdacht, *der* (**of** auf + *Akk.*); **on ~ of murder** wegen Mordverdachts; **be under ~:** verdächtigt werden

suspicious /sə'spɪʃəs/ *adj.* **(a)** (tending to suspect) misstrauisch (**of** gegenüber); **be ~ of sb./sth.** jmdm./einer Sache misstrauen
(b) (arousing suspicion) verdächtig

sustain /sə'steɪn/ *v.t.* **(a)** (support) tragen ‹*Gewicht*›; (fig.) aufrechterhalten
(b) erleiden ‹*Verlust, Verletzung*›

sustainable /sʌ'steɪnəbl/ *adj.* (Ecology) nachhaltig

sustenance /'sʌstɪnəns/ *n.* Nahrung, *die*

SW *abbr.* **(a)** = **south-west** SW
(b) (Radio) = **short wave** KW

swab /swɒb/ *n.* (Med.: pad) Tupfer, *der*

swagger /'swægə(r)/ *v.i.* großspurig stolzieren

swallow¹ /'swɒləʊ/ **1** *v.t.* schlucken; (by mistake) verschlucken
2 *v.i.* schlucken
3 *n.* Schluck, *der*

■ **swallow 'up** *v.t.* verschlucken

swallow² *n.* Schwalbe, *die*

swam ▸ SWIM 1

swamp /swɒmp/ **1** *n.* Sumpf, *der*
2 *v.t.* überschwemmen

'swampy *adj.* sumpfig

swan /swɒn/ *n.* Schwan, *der*

'swansong *n.* (fig.) Schwanengesang, *der*

swap /swɒp/ **1** *v.t.*, **-pp-** tauschen (**for** gegen)
2 *v.i.*, **-pp-** tauschen
3 *n.* Tausch, *der*

swarm /swɔ:m/ **1** *n.* Schwarm, *der*
2 *v.i.* schwärmen; (teem) wimmeln (**with** von)

swarthy /'swɔ:ðɪ/ *adj.* dunkel

swastika /'swɒstɪkə/ *n.* Hakenkreuz, *das*

swat /swɒt/ *v.t.*, **-tt-** totschlagen

sway /sweɪ/ **1** *v.i.* [hin und her] schwanken; (gently) sich wiegen
2 *v.t.* **(a)** wiegen
(b) (influence) beeinflussen
3 *n.* (fig.) Herrschaft, *die;* **hold ~ over sb.** über jmdn. herrschen

swear /sweə(r)/ **1** *v.t.*, **swore** /swɔ:(r)/, **sworn** /swɔ:n/ schwören ‹*Eid usw.*›
2 *v.i.*, **swore, sworn (a)** fluchen
(b) ~ to sth. etw. beschwören

■ **'swear at** *v.t.* beschimpfen

■ **'swear by** *v.t.* (coll.) schwören auf (+ *Akk.*)

'swear word *n.* Kraftausdruck, *der*

sweat /swet/ **1** *n.* Schweiß, *der*
2 *v.i.* schwitzen

'sweatband *n.* Schweißband, *das*

sweater /'swetə(r)/ *n.* Pullover, *der*

sweat: ~shirt *n.* Sweatshirt, *das;* **~shop** *n.* ausbeuterische [kleine] Klitsche (ugs.)

'sweaty *adj.* schweißig

swede *n.* Kohlrübe, *die*

Swede /swi:d/ *n.* Schwede, *der*/Schwedin, *die*

Sweden /'swi:dn/ *pr. n.* Schweden (*das*)

Swedish /'swi:dɪʃ/ **1** *adj.* schwedisch; **sb. is ~:** jmd. ist Schwede/Schwedin
2 *n.* Schwedisch, *das; see also* ENGLISH 2A

sweep /swi:p/ **1** *v.t.*, **swept** /swept/ **(a)** fegen; kehren
(b) ~ the country ‹*Epidemie, Mode:*› das Land überrollen
2 *v.i.*, **swept (a)** fegen; kehren
(b) (go fast) ‹*Person, Auto:*› rauschen; ‹*Wind usw.:*› fegen
3 *n.* **(a) give sth. a ~:** etw. fegen *od.* kehren
(b) (curve) Bogen, *der*

■ **sweep 'up** *v.t.* zusammenfegen; zusammenkehren

'sweeping *adj.* pauschal; weit reichend ‹*Einsparung*›; umwälzend ‹*Veränderung*›

sweet /swi:t/ **1** *adj.* süß; reizend ‹*Wesen, Gesicht, Mädchen*›; **have a ~ tooth** gern Süßes mögen; **how ~ of you!** wie nett *od.* lieb von dir!
2 *n.* (Brit.) **(a)** (candy) Bonbon, *das od. der*
(b) (dessert) Nachtisch, *der*

sweet: ~-and-'sour *attrib. adj.* süßsauer; **~ corn** *n.* Zuckermais, *der*

sweeten /'swi:tn/ *v.t.* süßen

'sweetener *n.* Süßstoff, *der*

'sweetheart *n.* Schatz, *der*

'sweetness *n.* Süße, *die*

sweet: ~ 'pea *n.* Wicke, *die;* **~ po'tato** *n.* Batate, *die;* **~shop** *n.* (Brit.) Süßwarengeschäft, *das;* **~ talk** (Amer.) *n.* Süßholzgeraspel, *das* (ugs.); **~-talk** *v.t.* **~-talk sb. [into doing sth.]** jmdn. beschwatzen[, etw. zu tun]

swell /swel/ **1** *v.t.*, **swelled, swollen** /'swəʊlən/ *or* **swelled** anschwellen lassen
2 *v.i.*, **swelled, swollen** *or* **swelled (a)** (expand) ‹*Körperteil:*› anschwellen; ‹*Segel:*› sich blähen; ‹*Material:*› aufquellen
(b) ‹*Anzahl:*› zunehmen

'swelling *n.* Schwellung, *die*
swelter /'sweltə(r)/ *v.i.* ~ **in the heat** in der Hitze schmoren (ugs.) ~**ing** glühend heiß ‹*Tag, Wetter*›; ~**ing heat** Bruthitze, *die*
swept ▶ SWEEP 1, 2
swerve /swɜːv/ [1] *v.i.* einen Bogen machen; ~ **to the right/left** nach rechts/links [aus]schwenken
[2] *n.* Bogen, *der*
swift /swɪft/ [1] *adj.* schnell
[2] *n.* Mauersegler, *der*
'swiftly *adv.* schnell
swig /swɪg/ (coll.) Schluck, *der*
swill /swɪl/ *v.t.* ~ **[out]** [aus]spülen
swim /swɪm/ [1] *v.i.*, **-mm-, swam** /swæm/, **swum** /swʌm/ schwimmen; **my head was** ~**ming** mir war schwindelig
[2] *n.* **have a/go for a** ~: schwimmen/ schwimmen gehen
'swimmer *n.* Schwimmer, *der*/ Schwimmerin, *die;* **be a good/poor** ~: gut/ schlecht schwimmen können
'swimming *n.* Schwimmen, *das*
swimming: ~ **baths** *n. pl.* Schwimmbad, *das;* ~ **costume** *n.* Badeanzug, *der;* ~ **lesson** *n.* Schwimmstunde, *die;* ~ **lessons** Schwimmunterricht, *der;* ~ **pool** *n.* Schwimmbecken, *das;* (building) Schwimmbad, *das;* ~ **trunks** *n. pl.* Badehose, *die*
'swimsuit *n.* Badeanzug, *der*
swindle /'swɪndl/ [1] *v.t.* betrügen; ~ **sb. out of sth.** jmdn. um etw. betrügen
[2] *n.* Schwindel, *der;* Betrug, *der*
swindler /'swɪndlə(r)/ *n.* Schwindler, *der*/ Schwindlerin, *die*
swine /swaɪn/ *n.* Schwein, *das*
swing /swɪŋ/ [1] *n.* **(a)** Schaukel, *die*
(b) (~ing) Schaukeln, *das;* **in full** ~ (fig.) in vollem Gang[e]
[2] *v.i.*, **swung** /swʌŋ/ **(a)** schwingen; (in wind) schaukeln
(b) (go in sweeping curve) schwenken
[3] *v.t.*, **swung** schwingen
swing: ~**bin** *n.* Schwingdeckel[müll]eimer, *der;* ~ **'door** *n.* Pendeltür, *die*
swipe /swaɪp/ (coll.) [1] *v.t.* **(a)** (hit) knallen (ugs.)
(b) (coll.: steal) klauen (ugs.)
(c) ~ **the card through the swipe reader** die Karte durch das [Karten]lesegerät ziehen
[2] *n.* (device) ~ **[reader]** [Karten]lesegerät, *das*
'swipe card *n.* Magnetkarte, *die*
swirl /swɜːl/ [1] *v.i.* wirbeln
[2] *v.t.* umherwirbeln
[3] *n.* Spirale, *die*
swish /swɪʃ/ [1] *v.i.* zischen
[2] *n.* Zischen, *das*
[3] *adj.* (coll.) schick (ugs.)
Swiss /swɪs/ [1] *adj.* Schweizer; schweizerisch; **sb. is** ~: jmd. ist Schweizer/ Schweizerin
[2] *n.* Schweizer, *der*/Schweizerin, *die;* **the** ~ *pl.* die Schweizer *Pl.*
Swiss 'roll *n.* Biskuitrolle, *die*
switch /swɪtʃ/ [1] *n.* **(a)** (esp. Electr.) Schalter, *der*
(b) (change) Wechsel, *der*
[2] *v.t.* **(a)** (change) ~ **sth. [over] to sth.** etw. auf etw. (*Akk.*) umstellen *od.* (Electr.) umschalten
(b) (exchange) tauschen
[3] *v.i.* wechseln; ~ **[over] to sth.** auf etw. (*Akk.*) umstellen *od.* (Electr.) umschalten
■ **switch 'off** *v.t. & i.* ausschalten; (also fig. coll.) abschalten
■ **switch 'on** [1] *v.t.* einschalten; anschalten
[2] *v.i.* sich anschalten
switch: ~**back** *n.* Achterbahn, *die;* ~**blade** *n.* Springmesser, *das;* ~**board** *n.* [Telefon]zentrale, *die*
Switzerland /'swɪtsələnd/ *pr. n.* die Schweiz
swivel /'swɪvl/ [1] *v.i.*, **-ll-** sich drehen
[2] *v.t.*, **-ll-** drehen
'swivel chair *n.* Drehstuhl, *der*
swollen /'swəʊlən/ [1] ▶ SWELL
[2] *adj.* geschwollen; angeschwollen ‹*Fluss*›
swoon /swuːn/ (literary) *v.i.* ohnmächtig werden
swoop /swuːp/ [1] *n.* **(a)** Sturzflug, *der*
(b) (coll.: raid) Razzia, *die*
[2] *v.i.* herabstoßen; ~ **on sb.** sich auf jmdn. stürzen
swop ▶ SWAP
sword /sɔːd/ *n.* Schwert, *das*
'swordfish *n.* Schwertfisch, *der*
swore, sworn ▶ SWEAR
swot /swɒt/ (Brit. coll.) [1] *n.* Streber, *der*/ Streberin, *die*
[2] *v.i.*, **-tt-** büffeln (ugs.)
swum ▶ SWIM 1
swung ▶ SWING 2, 3
'swung dash *n.* Tilde, *die*
sycamore /'sɪkəmɔː(r)/ *n.* Bergahorn, *der*
sycophant /'sɪkəfænt/ *n.* Kriecher, *der*
syllable /'sɪləbl/ *n.* Silbe, *die*
syllabus /'sɪləbəs/ *n.* Lehrplan, *der;* (for exam) Studienplan, *der*
symbol /'sɪmbl/ *n.* Symbol, *das* (**of** für)
symbolic /sɪm'bɒlɪk/, **symbolical** /sɪm'bɒlɪkl/ *adj.* symbolisch
symbolism /'sɪmbəlɪzm/ *n.* Symbolik, *die*
symbolize /'sɪmbəlaɪz/ *v.t.* symbolisieren
symmetrical /sɪ'metrɪkl/ *adj.* symmetrisch
symmetry /'sɪmɪtrɪ/ *n.* Symmetrie, *die*
sympathetic /sɪmpə'θetɪk/ *adj.* mitfühlend
sympathize /'sɪmpəθaɪz/ *v.i.* **(a)** ~ **with sb.** mit jmdm. [mit]fühlen
(b) ~ **with** (understand) Verständnis haben für

sympathy /ˈsɪmpəθɪ/ *n.* Mitgefühl, *das;* **in deepest ~**: mit aufrichtigem Beileid
symphonic /sɪmˈfɒnɪk/ *adj.* sinfonisch
symphony /ˈsɪmfənɪ/ *n.* Sinfonie, *die*
ˈsymphony orchestra *n.* Sinfonieorchester, *das*
symposium /sɪmˈpəʊzɪəm/ *n., pl.* **symposia** /sɪmˈpəʊzɪə/ Symposion, *das*
symptom /ˈsɪmptəm/ *n.* Symptom, *das*
symptomatic /sɪmptəˈmætɪk/ *adj.* symptomatisch (**of** für)
synagogue (*Amer.*: **synagog**) /ˈsɪnəgɒg/ *n.* Synagoge, *die*
sync /sɪŋk/ (coll.) *n.* **be in ~/out of ~**: harmonieren/nicht harmonieren (**with** mit)
synchromesh /ˈsɪŋkrəmeʃ/ *n.* (Motor Veh.) Synchrongetriebe, *das*
synchronize /ˈsɪŋkrənaɪz/ *v.t.* synchronisieren; gleichstellen ‹*Uhren*›
syndicate /ˈsɪndɪkət/ *n.* Syndikat, *das*
syndrome /ˈsɪndrəʊm/ *n.* Syndrom, *das*
synonym /ˈsɪnənɪm/ *n.* Synonym, *das*
synonymous /sɪˈnɒnɪməs/ *adj.* **(a)** (Ling.) synonym (**with** mit)
(b) ~ **with** (fig.) gleichbedeutend mit
synopsis /sɪˈnɒpsɪs/ *n., pl.* **synopses** /sɪˈnɒpsi:z/ Inhaltsangabe, *die*
syntactic /sɪnˈtæktɪk/ *adj.* syntaktisch
syntax /ˈsɪntæks/ *n.* Syntax, *die*
synthesis /ˈsɪnθɪsɪs/ *n., pl.* **syntheses** /ˈsɪnθɪsi:z/ Synthese, *die*
synthesize /ˈsɪnθɪsaɪz/ *v.t.* zur Synthese bringen; (Chem.) synthetisieren
synthesizer /ˈsɪnθɪsaɪzə(r)/ *n.* (Mus.) Synthesizer, *der*
synthetic /sɪnˈθetɪk/ *adj.* synthetisch
syphilis /ˈsɪfɪlɪs/ *n.* Syphilis, *die*
syphon ▶ SIPHON
Syria /ˈsɪrɪə/ *pr. n.* Syrien (*das*)
syringe /sɪˈrɪndʒ/ **1** *n.* Spritze, *die*
2 *v.t.* spritzen; ausspritzen ‹*Ohr*›
syrup /ˈsɪrəp/ *n.* Sirup, *der*
system /ˈsɪstəm/ *n.* System, *das*
systematic /sɪstəˈmætɪk/ *adj.*, **systematically** /sɪstəˈmætɪkəlɪ/ *adv.* systematisch
systematize /ˈsɪstəmətaɪz/ *v.t.* systematisieren
system: ~ disk *n.* (Comp.) Systemdiskette, *die;* **~ error** *n.* (Comp.) Systemfehler, *der;* **~s analyst** *n.* Systemanalytiker, *der*/-analytikerin, *die*; **~ software** *n.* (Comp.) Systemsoftware, *die*

Tt

T, t /ti:/ *n.* T, t, *das;* **to a T** ganz genau; **T-junction** Einmündung, *die;* **T-bone steak** T-Bone-Steak, *das;* **T-shirt** T-Shirt, *das*
ta /tɑ:/ *int.* (Brit. coll.) danke
tab /tæb/ **1** *n.* **(a)** (projecting flap) Zunge, *die;* (on clothing) Etikett, *das;* (with name) Namensschild, *das*
(b) pick up the ~ (Amer. coll.) die Zeche bezahlen
(c) keep ~s *or* **a ~ on** (watch) [genau] beobachten
(d) (Comp.) Tabulator, *der*
2 *v.t.* (Comp.) tabellarisieren
tabby /ˈtæbɪ/ *n.* **~ [cat]** Tigerkatze, *die*
ˈtab key *n.* (Comp.) Tabulatortaste, *die*
table /ˈteɪbl/ **1** *n.* **(a)** Tisch, *der*
(b) (list) Tabelle, *die;* **~ of contents** Inhaltsverzeichnis, *das*
2 *v.t.* einbringen
tableau /ˈtæbləʊ/ *n., pl.* **~x** /ˈtæbləʊz/ Tableau, *das*
table: ~cloth *n.* Tischdecke, *die;* **~ leg** *n.* Tischbein, *das;* **~ linen** *n.* Tischwäsche, *die;* **~ manners** *n. pl.* Tischmanieren *Pl.;* **~ mat** *n.* Set, *das;* **~ salt** *n.* Tafelsalz, *das;* **~spoon** *n.* Servierlöffel, *der;* **~spoonful** *n.* Servierlöffel [voll]
tablet /ˈtæblɪt/ *n.* **(a)** Tablette, *die*
(b) (of soap) Stück, *das*
table: ~ tennis *n.* Tischtennis, *das;* **~ tennis bat** Tischtennisschläger, *der;* **~ wine** *n.* Tischwein, *der*
tabloid /ˈtæblɔɪd/ *n.* Boulevardzeitung, *die;* **the ~s** (derog.) die Boulevardpresse; **~ journalism** Sensationsjournalismus, *der*
taboo, tabu /təˈbu:/ **1** *n.* Tabu, *das*
2 *adj.* Tabu‹*wort*›; **be ~**: tabu sein
tabulate /ˈtæbjʊleɪt/ *v.t.* tabellarisch darstellen
tabulator /ˈtæbjʊleɪtə(r)/ *n.* Tabulator, *der*
tacit /ˈtæsɪt/ *adj.*, **ˈtacitly** *adv.* stillschweigend
taciturn /ˈtæsɪtɜ:n/ *adj.* schweigsam; wortkarg
tack /tæk/ **1** *n.* **(a)** (nail) kleiner Nagel
(b) (stitch) Heftstich, *der*
(c) (Naut., also fig.) Kurs, *der*
2 *v.t.* **(a)** (nail) festnageln
(b) (stitch) heften

[3] *v.i.* (Naut.) kreuzen

tackle /'tækl/ [1] *v.t.* **(a)** angehen ‹*Problem usw.*›; **~ sb. about/on/over sth.** jmdn. auf etw. (*Akk.*) ansprechen; (ask for sth.) jmdn. um etw. angehen
(b) (Sport) angreifen ‹*Spieler*›; (Amer. Footb.; Rugby) fassen
[2] *n.* **(a)** (equipment) Ausrüstung, *die*
(b) (Sport) Angriff, *der;* (sliding **~**) Tackling, *das;* (Amer. Footb.; Rugby) Fassen und Halten

tacky /'tækɪ/ *adj.* **(a)** (sticky) klebrig
(b) (coll. derog.: tasteless) geschmacklos

tact /tækt/ *n.* Takt, *der;* **he has no ~:** er hat kein Taktgefühl

tactful /'tæktfl/ *adj.*, **'tactfully** *adv.* taktvoll

tactical /'tæktɪkl/ *adj.* taktisch

tactics /'tæktɪks/ *n. pl.* Taktik, *die*

'tactless *adj.*, **'tactlessly** *adv.* taktlos

tadpole /'tædpəʊl/ *n.* Kaulquappe, *die*

tag¹ /tæg/ [1] *n.* **(a)** Schild, *das*
(b) (electronic device) (on person) elektronische Fessel; (on goods) Sicherungsetikett, *das*
(c) (Comp.) Tag, *das;* Markierung, *die*
[2] *v.t.*, **-gg-:** (Comp.) taggen; markieren

■ **tag a'long** *v.i.* mitkommen

tag² *n.* (game) Fangen, *das*

tail /teɪl/ [1] *n.* **(a)** Schwanz, *der*
(b) *in pl.* (on coin) **~s [it is]** Zahl
[2] *v.t.* (coll.: follow) beschatten

■ **tail 'back** *v.i.* sich stauen

■ **tail 'off** *v.i.* **(a)** zurückgehen
(b) (into silence) verstummen

tail: ~back *n.* (Brit.) Rückstau, *der;* **~ end** *n.* Ende, *das;* **~gate** [1] *n.* (Motor Veh.) Heckklappe, *die;* [2] *v.i.* zu dicht auffahren; **~ light** *n.* Rücklicht, *das*

tailor /'teɪlə(r)/ *n.* Schneider, *der*/ Schneiderin, *die*

tailored /'teɪləd/, **'tailor-made** *adjs.* maßgeschneidert

'tail wind *n.* Rückenwind, *der*

taint /teɪnt/ *v.t.* verderben; **be ~ed with sth.** mit etw. behaftet sein (geh.)

Taiwan /taɪ'wɑːn/ *pr. n.* Taiwan (*das*)

take /teɪk/ [1] *v.t.*, **took** /tʊk/, **taken** /'teɪkn/
(a) (get hold of, grasp, seize) nehmen
(b) (capture) einnehmen ‹*Stadt, Festung*›; machen ‹*Gefangenen*›
(c) (gain, earn) ‹*Laden:*› einbringen; ‹*Person:*› einnehmen; ‹*Film, Stück:*› einspielen; (win) gewinnen ‹*Satz, Spiel, Preis, Titel*›
(d) (~ away with one) mitnehmen; (steal) mitnehmen (verhüll.); **~ place** stattfinden; (spontaneously) sich ereignen; ‹*Wandlung:*› sich vollziehen
(e) (avail oneself of, use) nehmen; machen ‹*Pause, Ferien, Nickerchen*›; **~ the opportunity to do/of doing sth.** die Gelegenheit dazu benutzen, etw. zu tun
(f) (carry, guide, convey) bringen; **~ sb. to visit sb.** jmdn. zu Besuch bei jmdm. mitnehmen; **~ home** mit nach Hause nehmen; (earn) nach Hause bringen ‹*Geld*›; (accompany) nach Hause bringen
(g) (remove) nehmen; (deduct) abziehen; **~ sth./sb. from sb.** jmdm. etw./jmdm. wegnehmen
(h) (make) machen ‹*Foto, Kopie*›; (photograph) aufnehmen; aufnehmen ‹*Brief, Diktat*›; machen ‹*Prüfung, Sprung, Spaziergang, Reise*›; ablegen ‹*Gelübde, Eid*›; treffen ‹*Entscheidung*›
(i) (conduct) halten ‹*Gottesdienst, Unterricht*›; **Ms X ~s us for maths** in Mathe haben wir Frau X
(j) (eat, drink) nehmen ‹*Zucker, Milch, Tabletten, Überdosis*›; trinken ‹*Tee, Kaffee, Kognak usw.*›
(k) (need, require) brauchen ‹*Platz, Zeit*›; haben ‹*Objekt, Plural-s*›; gebraucht werden mit ‹*Kasus*›; **sth. ~s an hour/a year/all day** etw. dauert eine Stunde/ein Jahr/einen ganzen Tag
(l) (ascertain and record) notieren ‹*Namen, Adresse, Autonummer usw.*›; fühlen ‹*Puls*›; messen ‹*Temperatur, Größe usw.*›
(m) (assume) **~ it [that] ...:** annehmen, dass ...; **~ sb./sth. for/to be sth.** jmdn./etw. für etw. halten
(n) (react to) aufnehmen; **~ sth. well/badly** etw. gut/nur schwer verkraften; **~ sth. calmly** *or* **coolly** etw. gelassen [auf]nehmen
(o) (accept) annehmen
(p) (adopt, choose) ergreifen ‹*Maßnahmen*›; unternehmen ‹*Schritte*›; **~ the wrong road** die falsche Straße fahren/gehen
(q) **be ~n ill** krank werden
(r) **~ sth. to bits** *or* **pieces** etw. auseinander nehmen
[2] *v.i.*, **took, taken (a)** ‹*Transplantat:*› vom Körper angenommen werden; ‹*Sämling, Pflanze:*› angehen
(b) (detract) **~ from sth.** etw. schmälern

■ **'take after** *v.t.* **~ after sb.** (resemble) jmdm. ähnlich sein; (~ as one's example) es jmdm. gleichtun

■ **take a'way** *v.t.* **(a)** (remove) wegnehmen; (to a distance) mitnehmen; **~ sth. away from sb.** jmdm. etw. abnehmen; **to ~ away** ‹*Pizza, Snack usw.*› zum Mitnehmen
(b) (Math.: deduct) abziehen

■ **take a'way from** *v.t.* schmälern

■ **take 'back** *v.t.* zurücknehmen; (return) zurückbringen

■ **take 'down** *v.t.* **(a)** (carry or lead down) hinunterbringen
(b) abnehmen ‹*Bild, Ankündigung, Weihnachtsschmuck*›; herunterziehen ‹*Hose*›; **~ sth. down from a shelf** etw. von einem Regal herunternehmen
(c) (write down) aufnehmen

■ **take 'in** *v.t.* **(a)** hineinbringen; (bring indoors) hereinholen
(b) enger machen ‹*Kleidungsstück*›
(c) (understand) begreifen
(d) (cheat) hereinlegen (ugs.); (deceive) täuschen

■ **take 'off** [1] *v.t.* **(a)** abnehmen ‹*Deckel, Hut, Tischtuch, Verband*›; abziehen ‹*Kissenbezug*›; ausziehen ‹*Schuhe, Handschuhe*›; ablegen ‹*Mantel, Schmuck*›
(b) (deduct) abziehen; **~ sth. off sth.** etw. von etw. abziehen
(c) ~ a day *etc.* **off** sich (*Dat.*) einen Tag *usw.* frei nehmen (ugs.)
(d) (mimic) nachahmen
[2] *v.i.* (Aeronaut.) starten
■ **take 'on** *v.t.* **(a)** (undertake) übernehmen; auf sich (*Akk.*) nehmen ‹*Bürde*›
(b) (employ) einstellen
(c) (as opponent) es aufnehmen mit; (Sport: meet) antreten gegen
■ **take 'out** *v.t.* **(a)** (remove) herausnehmen; ziehen ‹*Zahn*›; **~ sth. out of sth.** etw. aus etw. [heraus]nehmen
(b) (withdraw) abheben ‹*Geld*›
(c) (go out with) **~ sb. out** mit jmdm. ausgehen; **~ sb. out to** *or* **for lunch** jmdn. zum Mittagessen einladen
(d) (get issued) abschließen ‹*Versicherung*›; ausleihen ‹*Bücher*›; **~ out a subscription to sth.** etw. abonnieren
(e) ~ it out on sb. seine Wut an jmdm. auslassen
■ **take 'over** [1] *v.t.* übernehmen
[2] *v.i.* übernehmen; ‹*Manager, Firmenleiter:*› die Geschäfte übernehmen; ‹*Regierung, Präsident:*› die Amtsgeschäfte übernehmen; **~ over from sb.** jmdn. ersetzen; (temporarily) jmdn. vertreten
■ **'take to** *v.t.* **(a)** (get into habit of) **~ to doing sth.** es sich (*Dat.*) angewöhnen, etw. zu tun
(b) (like) sich hingezogen fühlen zu ‹*Person*›; sich erwärmen für ‹*Sache*›
■ **take 'up** [1] *v.t.* **(a)** (lift up) hochheben; (pick up) aufheben; herausreißen ‹*Dielen*›; aufreißen ‹*Straße*›
(b) (carry or lead up) hinaufbringen
(c) in Anspruch nehmen ‹*Zeit*›; brauchen/ (undesirably) wegnehmen ‹*Platz*›
(d) (start) ergreifen ‹*Beruf*›; anfangen ‹*Tennis, Schach, Gitarre usw.*›; aufnehmen ‹*Arbeit, Kampf*›; antreten ‹*Stelle*›; **~ up a hobby** sich (*Dat.*) ein Hobby zulegen
(e) (pursue further) **~ sth. up with sb.** sich in einer Sache an jmdn. wenden
[2] *v.i.* **~ up with sb.** (coll.) sich mit jmdm. einlassen

'takeaway *n.* (meal) Essen zum Mitnehmen; (restaurant) Restaurant mit Straßenverkauf

taken ▸ TAKE

take: ~-off *n.* **(a)** (Aeronaut.) Start, *der;* **(b)** (coll.: caricature) Parodie, *die;* **~over** *n.* Übernahme, *die*

takings /'teɪkɪŋz/ *n. pl.* Einnahmen *Pl.*

talc /tælk/ *n.* Talkum, *das*

talcum /'tælkəm/ *n.* **~ [powder]** Körperpuder, *der*

tale /teɪl/ *n.* Erzählung, *die;* Geschichte, *die* (of von, **about** über + *Akk.*)

talent /'tælənt/ *n.* Talent, *das;* **have [great/ no** *etc.*] **~ [for sth.]** [viel/kein *usw.*] Talent [zu *od.* für etw.] haben

'talented *adj.* talentiert

'talent-spotting *n.* Talentsuche, *die*

talk /tɔːk/ [1] *n.* **(a)** (discussion) Gespräch, *das;* **have a ~ [with sb.] [about sth.]** [mit jmdm.] [über etw. (*Akk.*)] sprechen; **have** *or* **hold ~s [with sb.]** [mit jmdm.] Gespräche führen; **there is [much/some] ~ of ...:** man hört [häufig/öfter] von ...
(b) (speech, lecture) Vortrag, *der*
[2] *v.i.* sprechen (**with, to** mit); (lecture) sprechen; (converse) sich unterhalten; (have ~s) Gespräche führen; (gossip) reden; **~ on the phone** telefonieren
[3] *v.t.* reden; **~ sb. into/out of sth.** jmdn. zu etw. überreden/jmdm. etw. ausreden
■ **talk 'over** *v.t.* besprechen
■ **talk 'round** *v.t.* **~ sb. round** jmdn. überreden

talkative /'tɔːkətɪv/ *adj.* gesprächig

talking: ~ point *n.* Gesprächsthema, *das;* **~-to** *n.* (coll.) Standpauke, *die* (ugs.)

'talk show *n.* Talkshow, *die*

tall /tɔːl/ *adj.* hoch; groß ‹*Person, Tier*›; **that's a ~ order** das ist ziemlich viel verlangt; **~ story** unglaubliche Geschichte

tally /'tælɪ/ [1] *n.* **keep a ~ of sth.** über etw. (*Akk.*) Buch führen
[2] *v.i.* übereinstimmen

talon /'tælən/ *n.* Klaue, *die*

tambourine /tæmbə'riːn/ *n.* Tamburin, *das*

tame /teɪm/ [1] *adj.* zahm; (fig.: spiritless) lahm (ugs.)
[2] *v.t.* zähmen

tamper /'tæmpə(r)/ *v.i.* **~ with** sich (*Dat.*) zu schaffen machen an (+ *Dat.*)

tampon /'tæmpɒn/ *n.* Tampon, *der*

tan /tæn/ [1] *v.t.*, **-nn-** gerben ‹*Tierhaut, Fell*›
[2] *v.i.*, **-nn-** braun werden
[3] *n.* **(a)** (colour) Gelbbraun, *das*
(b) (sun-~) Bräune, *die;* **have/get a ~:** braun sein/werden
[4] *adj.* gelbbraun

tandem /'tændəm/ *n.* **~ [bicycle]** Tandem, *das*

tang /tæŋ/ *n.* (taste) Geschmack, *der;* (smell) Geruch, *der*

tangent /'tændʒənt/ *n.* Tangente, *die;* **go off at a ~** (fig.) plötzlich vom Thema abschweifen

tangerine /tændʒə'riːn/ *n.* (fruit) **~ [orange]** Tangerine, *die*

tangible /'tændʒɪbl/ *adj.* greifbar; spürbar ‹*Unterschied, Verbesserung*›; handfest ‹*Beweis*›

tangle /'tæŋgl/ [1] *n.* Gewirr, *das;* (in hair) Verfilzung, *die*
[2] *v.t.* verheddern (ugs.); verfilzen ‹*Haar*›
■ **tangle 'up** *v.t.* verheddern (ugs.)

tango /ˈtæŋgəʊ/ *n., pl.* **~s** Tango, *der*
tank /tæŋk/ *n.* **(a)** Tank, *der*
(b) (Mil.) Panzer, *der*
tankard /ˈtæŋkəd/ *n.* Krug, *der*
tanker /ˈtæŋkə(r)/ *n.* (ship) Tanker, *der;* (vehicle) Tank[last]wagen, *der*
tanned /tænd/ *adj.* braun gebrannt
tantalize /ˈtæntəlaɪz/ *v.t.* reizen
tantalizing /ˈtæntəlaɪzɪŋ/ *adj.* verlockend
tantamount /ˈtæntəmaʊnt/ *adj.* **be ~ to sth.** gleichbedeutend mit etw. sein
tantrum /ˈtæntrəm/ *n.* Wutanfall, *der;* (of child) Trotzanfall, *der;* **throw a ~:** einen Wutanfall/Trotzanfall bekommen
tap[1] /tæp/ 1 *n.* Hahn, *der;* **hot/cold[-water] ~:** Warm-/Kaltwasserhahn, *der;* **be on ~** (fig.) zur Verfügung stehen
2 *v.t.,* **-pp-: (a)** erschließen ‹*Reserven, Markt*›
(b) (Teleph.) abhören; anzapfen (ugs.)
tap[2] 1 *v.t.,* **-pp-** klopfen an (+ *Akk.*); (on upper surface) klopfen auf (+ *Akk.*)
2 *v.i.,* **-pp-: ~ at/on sth.** an etw. (*Akk.*) klopfen; (on upper surface) auf etw. (*Akk.*) klopfen
3 *n.* Klopfen, *das*
ˈtap dance 1 *n.* Stepp[tanz], *der*
2 *v.i.* Stepp tanzen; steppen
tape /teɪp/ 1 *n.* **(a)** Band, *das;* **adhesive** *or* (coll.) sticky **~:** Klebeband, *das*
(b) (for recording) [Ton]band, *das* (**of** mit); **make a ~ of sth.** etw. auf Band aufnehmen
2 *v.t.* **(a)** (record on ~) [auf Band] aufnehmen
(b) (bind with ~) [mit Klebeband] zukleben
(c) have got sb./sth. ~d (coll.) jmdn. durchschaut haben/etw. im Griff haben
tape: ~ cassette *n.* Tonbandkassette, *die;* **~ deck** *n.* Tapedeck, *das;* **~ measure** *n.* Bandmaß, *das*
taper /ˈteɪpə(r)/ 1 *v.i.* sich verjüngen; **~ [to a point]** spitz zulaufen
2 *n.* **[wax] ~:** Wachsstock, *der*
tape: ~ recorder *n.* Tonbandgerät, *das;* **~ recording** *n.* Tonbandaufnahme, *die*
tapestry /ˈtæpɪstrɪ/ *n.* Gobelingewebe, *das;* (wall-hanging) Bildteppich, *der*
ˈtapeworm *n.* Bandwurm, *der*
ˈtap water *n.* Leitungswasser, *das*
tar /tɑ:(r)/ 1 *n.* Teer, *der;* **high-~/low-~ cigarette** Zigarette mit hohem/niedrigem Teergehalt
2 *v.t.,* **-rr-** teeren
target /ˈtɑ:gɪt/ 1 *n.* **(a)** Ziel, *das;* **hit/miss the/its ~:** [das Ziel] treffen/das Ziel verfehlen; **production/export/savings ~:** Produktions-/Export-/Sparziel, *das;* **be above/below ~** (fig.) das Ziel über-/unterschritten haben
(b) (Sport) Zielscheibe, *die*
2 *v.t.* (fig.) zielen auf ‹*Käufergruppe*›
target: ~ date *n.* vorgesehener Termin; **~ figure** *n.* (esp. Commerc.) Ziel, *das*
tariff /ˈtærɪf/ *n.* **(a)** (tax) Zoll, *der*
(b) (list of charges) Tarif, *der*
tarnish /ˈtɑ:nɪʃ/ 1 *v.t.* stumpf werden lassen ‹*Metall*›; (fig.) beflecken ‹*Ruf*›
2 *v.i.* stumpf werden
tarpaulin /tɑ:ˈpɔ:lɪn/ *n.* Plane, *die*
tart[1] /tɑ:t/ *adj.* herb; sauer ‹*Obst*›; (fig.) scharfzüngig
tart[2] *n.* **(a)** (Brit.) (filled pie) ≈ Obstkuchen, *der;* (small pastry) Obsttörtchen, *das*
(b) (sl.: prostitute) Nutte, *die* (salopp)
■ **tart ˈup** *v.t.* (Brit. coll.) **~ oneself up, get ~ed up** sich auftakeln (ugs.)
tartan /ˈtɑ:tən/ 1 *n.* Schotten[stoff], *der*
2 *adj.* Schotten‹*rock, -jacke*›
tartar /ˈtɑ:tə(r)/ *n.* Zahnstein, *der*
tartar sauce /ˈtɑ:tə ˈsɔ:s/ *n.* Remoulade[nsoße], *die*
task /tɑ:sk/ *n.* Aufgabe, *die;* **take sb. to ~:** jmdm. eine Lektion erteilen
task: ~bar *n.* (Comp.) Taskleiste, *die;* **~ force** *n.* Sonderkommando, *das*
tassel /ˈtæsl/ *n.* Quaste, *die*
taste /teɪst/ 1 *v.t.* **(a)** schmecken; (try a little) probieren
(b) (recognize flavour of) [heraus]schmecken
2 *v.i.* schmecken (**of** nach); **not ~ of anything** nach nichts schmecken
3 *n.* **(a)** (flavour) Geschmack, *der;* **[sense of] ~:** Geschmack[ssinn], *der*
(b) (discernment) Geschmack, *der*
(c) (sample) Kostprobe, *die*
tasteful /ˈteɪstfl/ *adj.,* **ˈtastefully** *adv.* geschmackvoll
ˈtasteless *adj.* geschmacklos
tasty /ˈteɪstɪ/ *adj.* lecker
tat /tæt/ *n.* ▶ TIT[2]
tattered /ˈtætəd/ *adj.* zerlumpt ‹*Kleidung*›; zerfleddert ‹*Buch*›
tatters /ˈtætəz/ *n. pl.* Fetzen *Pl.*; **be in ~:** in Fetzen sein; (fig.) ruiniert sein
tattoo /təˈtu:/ 1 *v.t.* tätowieren
2 *n.* Tätowierung, *die*
tattooer /təˈtu:ə(r)/**, tattooist** /təˈtu:ɪst/ *ns.* Tätowierer, *der*/Tätowiererin, *die*
tatty /ˈtætɪ/ *adj.* (coll.) schäbig
taught ▶ TEACH
taunt /tɔ:nt/ 1 *v.t.* verspotten (**about** wegen)
2 *n.* spöttische Bemerkung
Taurus /ˈtɔ:rəs/ *n.* (Astrol., Astron.) der Stier
taut /tɔ:t/ *adj.* straff ‹*Seil, Kabel*›; gespannt ‹*Muskel*›
tavern /ˈtævən/ *n.* Schenke, *die*
tawny /ˈtɔ:nɪ/ *adj.* gelbbraun
tax /tæks/ 1 *n.* Steuer, *die;* **before/after ~:** vor Steuern/nach Abzug der Steuern; **for ~ reasons** aus steuerlichen Gründen
2 *v.t.* **(a)** besteuern; versteuern ‹*Einkommen*›
(b) (fig.) strapazieren ‹*Kräfte, Geduld*›
taxable /ˈtæksəbl/ *adj.* steuerpflichtig

tax: ~ allowance *n.* Steuerfreibetrag, *der;* **~ assessment** *n.* Steuerbescheid, *der*

taxation /tæk'seɪʃn/ *n.* Besteuerung, *die;* (taxes payable) Steuern *Pl.*

tax: ~ avoidance *n.* Steuerumgehung, *die;* **~ bill** *n.* Steuerbescheid, *der;* (amount) Steuerschuld, *die;* **~ bracket** *n.* Stufe im Steuertarif; **~-deductible** *adj.* steuerabzugsfähig; [steuerlich] absetzbar; **~ demand** *n.* Steuerforderung, *die;* **~ disc** *n.* (Motor Veh.) Steuerplakette, *die;* **~ evasion** *n.* Steuerhinterziehung, *die;* **~ exile** *n.* (person) Steuerflüchtling, *der;* **~ form** *n.* Steuerformular, *das;* **~-free** *adj.* steuerfrei; **~ haven** *n.* Steueroase, *die* (ugs.)

taxi /'tæksɪ/ [1] *n.* Taxi, *das*
[2] *v.i.,* **~ing** *or* **taxying** ‹*Flugzeug:*› rollen

'taxi driver *n.* Taxifahrer, *der*/-fahrerin, *die*

tax: ~ incentive *n.* steuerlicher Anreiz; **~ inspector** *n.* Steuerinspektor, *der*/-inspektorin, *die*

taxi: ~ rank (Brit.), **~ stand** (Amer.) *ns.* Taxistand, *der*

tax: ~man *n.* (coll.) Finanzbeamte, *der*/-beamtin, *die;* **~ office** *n.* Finanzamt, *das* **~payer** *n.* Steuerzahler, *der*/-zahlerin, *die;* **~ return** *n.* Steuererklärung, *die;* **~ relief** *n.* Steuererleichterung, *die;* **~ year** *n.* Steuerjahr, *das*

TB *abbr.* = **tuberculosis** Tb, *die*

tbsp. *abbr., pl. same or* **~s: tablespoon**

tea /ti:/ *n.* **(a)** Tee, *der*
(b) (meal) [**high**] **~**: Abendessen, *das*

tea: ~ bag *n.* Teebeutel, *der;* **~ break** *n.* (Brit.) Teepause, *die;* **~ caddy** *n.* Teebüchse, *die*

teach /ti:tʃ/ [1] *v.t.,* **taught** /tɔ:t/ unterrichten; (at university) lehren; **~ sb./oneself/an animal sth.** jmdm./sich/einem Tier etw. beibringen; **~ sb. to ride** jmdm. das Reiten beibringen
[2] *v.i.,* **taught** unterrichten

'teacher *n.* Lehrer, *der*/Lehrerin, *die*

teacher: ~ training *n.* Lehrerausbildung, *die;* **~-training college** *n.* ≈ pädagogische Hochschule

'teaching profession *n.* Lehrberuf, *der*

tea: ~ cloth *n.* Geschirrtuch, *das;* **~ cosy** *n.* Teewärmer, *der;* **~cup** *n.* Teetasse, *die*

teak /ti:k/ *n.* Teak[holz], *das*

'tea leaf *n.* Teeblatt, *das*

team /ti:m/ *n.* Team, *das;* (Sport also) Mannschaft, *die*

▪ **team 'up** *v.i.* sich zusammentun (ugs.)

team: ~ effort *n.* Team- *od.* Gemeinschaftsarbeit, *die;* **~ game** *n.* Mannschaftsspiel, *das;* **~ leader** *n.* Gruppenleiter, *der*/-leiterin, *die;* **~mate** *n.* Mannschaftskamerad, *der*/-kameradin, *die;* **~ 'spirit** *n.* Teamgeist, *der;* (Sport also) Mannschaftsgeist, *der;* **~work** *n.* Teamarbeit, *die*

'teapot *n.* Teekanne, *die*

tear¹ /teə(r)/ [1] *n.* Riss, *der*
[2] *v.t.,* **tore** /tɔ:(r)/, **torn** /tɔ:n/ **(a)** (rip) zerreißen; (pull apart) auseinander reißen; (damage) aufreißen; **~ open** aufreißen ‹*Brief, Paket*›
(b) ~ sth. out of sb.'s hands jmdm. etw. aus der Hand reißen
[3] *v.i.,* **tore, torn (a)** (rip) [zer]reißen
(b) (move hurriedly) rasen (ugs.)

▪ **tear a'way** *v.t.* wegreißen; **~ oneself away** (fig.) sich losreißen

▪ **tear 'up** *v.t.* zerreißen

tear² /tɪə(r)/ *n.* Träne, *die*

tearful /'tɪəfl/ *adj.* weinend

tear /tɪə(r)/**: ~drop** *n.* Träne, *die;* **~ gas** *n.* Tränengas, *das*

tease /ti:z/ [1] *v.t.* necken (**about** wegen); aufziehen (ugs.) (**about** mit)
[2] *v.i.* seine Späße machen

tea: ~ service, ~set *ns.* Teeservice, *das;* **~ shop** *n.* (Brit.) ≈ Café, *das;* **~spoon** *n.* Teelöffel, *der;* **~ strainer** *n.* Teesieb, *das*

teat /ti:t/ *n.* **(a)** Zitze, *die*
(b) (of rubber or plastic) Sauger, *der*

tea: ~time *n.* Teezeit, *die;* **~ towel** *n.* Geschirrtuch, *das;* **~ trolley** *n.* Teewagen, *der;* **~ urn** *n.* Teebehälter, *der*

techie /'tekɪ/ *n.* (coll.) Technikfreak, *der;* (computer expert) Computerfreak, *der*

technical /'teknɪkl/ *adj.* technisch ‹*Problem, Daten, Fortschritt*›; Fach‹*kenntnis, -sprache, -begriff, -wörterbuch*›; **~ college** Fachhochschule, *die;* **~ term** Fachbegriff, *der;* Fachausdruck, *der*

technicality /teknɪ'kælɪtɪ/ *n.* technisches Detail

technician /tek'nɪʃn/ *n.* Techniker, *der*/Technikerin, *die*

technique /tek'ni:k/ *n.* Technik, *die;* (procedure) Methode, *die*

techno [1] *adj.* Techno-
[2] *n.* Techno, *der od. das*

technological /teknə'lɒdʒɪkl/ *adj.* technisch; technologisch

technology /tek'nɒlədʒɪ/ *n.* Technik, *die;* (application of science) Technologie, *die*

technophobe /'teknəʊfəʊb/ *n.* Mensch mit einer Technikphobie

teddy /'tedɪ/ *n.* **~ [bear]** Teddy[bär], *der*

tedious /'ti:dɪəs/ *adj.* langwierig ‹*Reise, Arbeit*›; (uninteresting) langweilig

tee /ti:/ (Golf) Tee, *das*

teem /ti:m/ *v.i.* wimmeln (**with** von)

teen /ti:n/ *adj.* Teenager-

teenage[d] /'tɪ:neɪdʒ(d)/ *attrib. adj.* im Teenageralter *nachgestellt*

teenager /'ti:neɪdʒə(r)/ *n.* Teenager, *der;* (loosely) Jugendliche, *der/die*
teens /ti:nz/ *n. pl.* Teenagerjahre *Pl.*
'tee shirt *n.* T-Shirt, *das*
teeter /'ti:tə(r)/ *v.i.* wanken; **~ on the edge of sth.** schwankend am Rande einer Sache (*Gen.*) stehen
teeth *pl. of* TOOTH
teething troubles /'ti:ðɪŋ trʌblz/ *n. pl.* **have ~** (fig.) Anfangsschwierigkeiten haben
teetotal /ti:'təʊtl/ *adj.* abstinent lebend
teetotaller /ti:'təʊtələ(r)/ *n.* Abstinenzler, *der*/Abstinenzlerin, *die*
TEFL /'tefl/ *abbr.* = **teaching of English as a foreign language**
Teflon ® /'teflɒn/ *n.* Teflon (Wz), *das*
Tel., tel. *abbr.* = **telephone** Tel.
telebanking /'telɪbæŋkɪŋ/ *n.* Telebanking, *das*
telecommunications /telɪkəmju:nɪ'keɪʃnz/ *n. pl.* Fernmelde- *od.* Nachrichtentechnik, *die*
telecommute /'telɪkəmju:t/ *v.i.* Telearbeit verrichten
telecommuting /'telɪkəmju:tɪŋ/ *n.* Telearbeit, *die*
teleconference /'telɪkɒnfərəns/ *n.* Telekonferenz, *die*
telecottage /'telɪkɒtɪdʒ/ *n.: jedermann zugängliche Einrichtung, die bes. Telearbeitern Zugang zu einem ans Internet angeschlossenen Computer bietet*
telegram /'telɪgræm/ *n.* Telegramm, *das*
telegraph /'telɪgrɑ:f/ *n.* Telegraf, *der;* **~ pole** Telegrafenmast, *der*
telemarketing /'telɪmɑ:kɪtɪŋ/ *n.* Telefonmarketing, *das*
telepathy /tɪ'lepəθɪ/ *n.* Telepathie, *die*
telephone /'telɪfəʊn/ **1** *n.* Telefon, *das; attrib.* Telefon-; **answer the ~**: Anrufe entgegennehmen; (on one occasion) ans Telefon gehen; (speak) sich melden; **be on the ~**: Telefon haben; (be speaking) telefonieren (**to** mit)
2 *v.t.* anrufen
3 *v.i.* anrufen; **~ for a taxi** nach einem Taxi telefonieren
telephone: ~ 'answering machine *n.* Anrufbeantworter, *der;* **~ 'banking** *n.* Telefonbanking, *das;* **~ book** *n.* Telefonbuch, *das;* **~ booth,** (Brit.) **~ box** *ns.* Telefonzelle, *die;* **~ call** *n.* Telefongespräch, *das;* **~ connection** *n.* Telefonverbindung, *die;* **~ directory** *n.* Telefonverzeichnis, *das;* **~ exchange** *n.* Fernmeldeamt, *das;* **~ number** *n.* Telefonnummer, *die;* **~ operator** *n.* Telefonist, *der*/Telefonistin, *die*
telephonist /tɪ'lefənɪst/ *n.* Telefonist, *der*/Telefonistin, *die*
telephoto /telɪ'fəʊtəʊ/ *adj.* **~ lens** Teleobjektiv, *das*

teleprinter /'telɪprɪntə(r)/ *n.* Fernschreiber, *der*
'telesales *n. pl.* Telefonverkauf, *der;* Verkauf per Telefon
telescope /'telɪskəʊp/ *n.* Teleskop, *das;* Fernrohr, *das*
telescopic /telɪ'skɒpɪk/ *adj.* (collapsible) ausziehbar; Teleskop‹*antenne*›
Teletex ® /'telɪteks/ *n.* Teletex, *das*
teletext /'telɪtekst/ *n.* Teletext, *der*
televise /'telɪvaɪz/ *v.t.* im Fernsehen senden *od.* übertragen
television /'telɪvɪʒn, telɪ'vɪʒn/ *n.* **(a)** *no art.* das Fernsehen; **on ~**: im Fernsehen; **watch ~**: fernsehen
(b) (**~ set**) Fernsehapparat, *der;* Fernseher, *der* (ugs.)
television: ~ aerial *n.* Fernsehantenne, *die;* **~ channel** *n.* [Fernseh]kanal, *der;* **~ coverage** *n.* Fernsehberichterstattung, *die;* **~ licence** *n.* (Brit.) Fernsehgenehmigung, *die* (*die jährlich gegen Zahlen der Gebühren erneuert wird*); **~ licence fee** Fernsehgebühren *Pl.;* **~ lounge** *n.* Fernsehraum, *der;* **~ personality** *n.* Fernsehgröße, *die* (ugs.); **~ picture** *n.* Fernsehbild, *das;* **~ programme** *n.* Fernsehsendung, *die;* **~ screen** *n.* Bildschirm, *der;* **~ serial** *n.* Fernsehserie, *die;* **~ set** *n.* Fernsehgerät, *das;* **~ studio** *n.* Fernsehstudio, *das;* **~ viewer** *n.* Fernsehzuschauer, *der*/-zuschauerin, *die*
teleworking /'telɪwɜ:kɪŋ/ *n.* Telearbeit, *die*
telex /'teleks/ **1** *n.* Telex, *das*
2 *v.t.* ein Telex schicken (+ *Dat.*); telexen ‹*Nachricht*›
tell /tel/ **1** *v.t.*, **told** /təʊld/ **(a)** (relate) erzählen; (make known) sagen ‹*Name, Adresse*›; anvertrauen ‹*Geheimnis*›; **~ sb. sth.** *or* **sth. to sb.** jmdm. etw. erzählen/sagen/anvertrauen; **~ sb. the way to the station** jmdm. den Weg zum Bahnhof beschreiben; **~ sb. the time** jmdm. die Uhrzeit sagen; **~ tales** (lie) Lügengeschichten erzählen; (gossip) tratschen (ugs.)
(b) (instruct) sagen; **~ sb. [not] to do sth.** jmdm. sagen, er soll[e] etw. [nicht] tun
(c) (determine) feststellen; (see, recognize) erkennen (**by** an + *Dat.*); (with reference to the future) [vorher]sagen
(d) (distinguish) unterscheiden
(e) all told insgesamt
2 *v.i.*, **told (a)** (determine) **how can you ~?** wie kann man das feststellen *od.* wissen?; **you never can ~**: man kann nie wissen
(b) (give information) erzählen (**of, about** von)
(c) (reveal secret) es verraten; **time will ~**: das wird sich zeigen
(d) (produce an effect) sich auswirken
■ **tell a'part** *v.t.* auseinander halten
■ **tell 'off** *v.t.* (coll.) **~ sb. off [for sth.]** jmdn. [für *od.* wegen etw.] ausschimpfen
teller /'telə(r)/ *n.* **(a)** (in bank) ▶ CASHIER

(b) (counting votes) Stimmenzähler, *der*/-zählerin, *die*

telly /'telɪ/ *n.* (Brit. coll.) Fernseher, *der* (ugs.); **on ~**: im Fernsehen; **watch ~** : Fernsehen gucken (ugs.)

temp /temp/ *n.* (Brit. coll.) Zeitarbeitskraft, *die*

temper /'tempə(r)/ [1] *n.* **(a)** Naturell, *das;* **be in a good/bad ~**: gute/schlechte Laune haben; **keep/lose one's ~**: sich beherrschen/die Beherrschung verlieren **(b)** (anger) **fit of ~**: Wutanfall, *der;* **have a ~**: jähzornig sein [2] *v.t.* mäßigen; mildern ‹*Kritik*›

temperament /'temprəmənt/ *n.* (nature) Veranlagung, *die;* Natur, *die;* (disposition) Temperament, *das*

temperamental /temprə'mentl/ *adj.* launenhaft

temperate /'tempərət/ *adj.* gemäßigt

temperature /'temprɪtʃə(r)/ *n.* Temperatur, *die;* **have** *or* **run a ~** (coll.) Temperatur *od.* Fieber haben

template /'templɪt/ *n.* **(a)** Schablone, *die* **(b)** (Comp.) Schablone, *die;* Template, *das*

temple¹ /'templ/ *n.* Tempel, *der*

temple² *n.* (Anat.) Schläfe, *die*

tempo /'tempəʊ/ *n., pl.* **~s** *or* **tempi** /'tempi:/ Tempo, *das*

temporarily /'tempərərɪlɪ/ *adv.* vorübergehend

temporary /'tempərərɪ/ [1] *adj.* vorübergehend; provisorisch ‹*Gebäude, Büro;*› **~ job** Aushilfstätigkeit, *die* [2] *n.* Aushilfe, *die;* Aushilfskraft, *die*

tempt /tempt/ *v.t.* **(a) ~ sb. to do sth.** jmdn. geneigt machen, etw. zu tun; **be ~ed to do sth.** versucht sein, etw. zu tun; **~ sb. out** jmdn. hinauslocken **(b)** (provoke) herausfordern; **~ fate** das Schicksal herausfordern

temptation /temp'teɪʃn/ *n.* **(a)** *no pl.* (attracting) Verlockung, *die;* (being attracted) Versuchung, *die* **(b)** (thing) Verlockung, *die*

'tempting *adj.* verlockend

ten /ten/ [1] *adj.* zehn [2] *n.* Zehn, *die. See also* EIGHT

tenable /'tenəbl/ *adj.* haltbar ‹*Theorie*›; vertretbar ‹*Standpunkt*›

tenacious /tɪ'neɪʃəs/ *adj.* hartnäckig

tenacity /tɪ'næsɪtɪ/ *n.* Hartnäckigkeit, *die*

tenant /'tenənt/ *n.* (of flat, residential building) Mieter, *der*/Mieterin, *die;* (of farm, shop) Pächter, *der*/Pächterin, *die*

tend¹ /tend/ *v.i.* **~ to do sth.** dazu neigen *od.* tendieren, etw. zu tun; **~ to sth.** zu etw. neigen; **he ~s to get upset if ...**: er regt sich leicht auf, wenn ...

tend² *v.t.* sich kümmern um; hüten ‹*Schafe*›; bedienen ‹*Maschine*›

tendency /'tendənsɪ/ *n.* (inclination) Tendenz, *die;* **have a ~ to do sth.** dazu neigen, etw. zu tun

tender¹ /'tendə(r)/ *adj.* **(a)** (not tough) zart **(b)** (loving) zärtlich **(c)** (sensitive) empfindlich

tender² [1] *v.t.* **(a)** (present) einreichen ‹*Rücktritt*›; vorbringen ‹*Entschuldigung*› **(b)** (offer as payment) anbieten [2] *n.* Angebot, *das*

'tenderly *adv.* (gently) behutsam; (lovingly) zärtlich

'tenderness *n.* ▶ TENDER¹: Zartheit, *die;* Zärtlichkeit, *die;* Empfindlichkeit, *die*

tendon /'tendən/ *n.* (Anat.) Sehne, *die*

tenement /'tenɪmənt/ *n.* Mietshaus, *das*

tenet /'tenɪt/ *n.* Grundsatz, *der*

tenner /'tenə(r)/ *n.* (Brit. coll.) Zehnpfundschein, *der*

tennis /'tenɪs/ *n.* Tennis, *das*

tennis: ~ ball *n.* Tennisball, *der;* **~ club** *n.* Tennisverein, *der;* **~ court** *n.* (for lawn ~) Tennisplatz, *der;* (indoor) Tennishalle, *die;* **~ 'elbow** *n., no art.* (Med.) Tennisell[en]bogen, *der;* **~ match** *n.* Tennismatch, *das;* Tennisspiel, *das;* **~ racket** *n.* Tennisschläger, *der;* **~ shoe** *n.* Tennisschuh, *der*

tenor /'tenə(r)/ *n.* (Mus.) Tenor, *der*

tense¹ /tens/ *n.* (Ling.) Zeit, *die;* **in the present/future** *etc.* **~**: im Präsens/Futur *usw.*

tense² [1] *adj.* gespannt [2] *v.i.* **sb. ~s** jmds. Muskeln spannen sich an [3] *v.t.* anspannen

tension /'tenʃn/ *n.* **(a)** Spannung, *die* **(b)** (mental strain) Anspannung, *die*

tent /tent/ *n.* Zelt, *das*

tentacle /'tentəkl/ *n.* Tentakel, *der od. das*

tentative /'tentətiv/ *adj.* **(a)** (not definite) vorläufig **(b)** (hesitant) zaghaft

tenterhooks /'tentəhʊks/ *n. pl.* **be on ~**: [wie] auf glühenden Kohlen sitzen

tenth /tenθ/ [1] *adj.* zehnt... [2] *n.* (in sequence, rank) Zehnte, *der/die/das;* (fraction) Zehntel, *das. See also* EIGHTH

tent: ~ peg *n.* Zeltpflock, *der;* **~ pole** *n.* Zeltstange, *die*

tenuous /'tenjʊəs/ *adj.* dünn ‹*Atmosphäre*›; dürftig ‹*Argument*›; unbegründet ‹*Anspruch*›

tepid /'tepɪd/ *adj.* lauwarm

term /tɜ:m/ *n.* **(a)** [Fach]begriff, *der* **(b)** *in pl.* (conditions) Bedingungen *Pl.*; **come to ~s with sth.** mit etw. zurechtkommen; (resign oneself to sth.) sich mit etw. abfinden **(c)** *in pl.* (charges) Konditionen *Pl.* **(d) in the short/long/medium ~**: kurz-/lang-/mittelfristig **(e)** (Sch.) Halbjahr, *das;* (Univ.: one of two/three divisions per year) Semester, *das*/Trimester, *das* ···›

(f) (limited period) Zeitraum, *der;* **~ [of office]** Amtszeit, *die*
(g) *in pl.* (mode of expression) Worte *Pl.*
(h) *in pl.* (relations) **be on good/bad ~s with sb.** mit jmdm. auf gutem/schlechtem Fuß stehen

terminal /'tɜːmɪnl/ **1** *n.* **(a)** (for train or bus) Bahnhof, *der;* (for airline passengers) Terminal, *der od. das*
(b) (Teleph., Comp.) Terminal, *das*
2 *adj.* (Med.) unheilbar

terminally /'tɜːmɪnəlɪ/ *adv.* **~ ill** unheilbar krank

terminate /'tɜːmɪneɪt/ *v.t.* **(a)** beenden; lösen ‹*Vertrag*›
(b) (Med.) unterbrechen ‹*Schwangerschaft*›

termini *pl. of* TERMINUS

terminology /tɜːmɪ'nɒlədʒɪ/ *n.* Terminologie, *die*

terminus /'tɜːmɪnəs/ *n., pl.* **~es** *or* **termini** /'tɜːmɪnaɪ/ Endstation, *die*

terrace /'terəs, 'terɪs/ *n.* Terrasse, *die; (row of houses)* Häuserreihe, *die*

terraced house /'terəst haʊs, 'terɪst haʊs/ *n.* Reihenhaus, *das*

terracotta /terə'kɒtə/ *n., no indef. art.* Terrakotta, *die*

terrain /te'reɪn/ *n.* Gelände, *das*

terrestrial /tə'restrɪəl/ *adj.* terrestrisch ‹*Raumschiff, Fernsehen, Bevölkerung*›; Erd‹*satellit, -bevölkerung*›

terrible /'terɪbl/ *adj.* **(a)** (coll.: very great or bad) schrecklich (ugs.)
(b) (coll.: incompetent) schlecht
(c) (causing terror) furchtbar

terribly /'terɪblɪ/ *adv.* **(a)** (coll.: very) unheimlich (ugs.)
(b) (coll.: appallingly) furchtbar (ugs.)
(c) (coll.: incompetently) schlecht
(d) (fearfully) auf erschreckende Weise

terrier /'terɪə(r)/ *n.* Terrier, *der*

terrific /tə'rɪfɪk/ *adj.* (coll.) **(a)** (great, intense) irrsinnig (ugs.)
(b) (magnificent) sagenhaft (ugs.)
(c) (highly expert) klasse (ugs.)

terrify /'terɪfaɪ/ *v.t.* **(a)** Angst machen (+ *Dat.*); **be terrified that ...:** Angst haben, dass ...
(b) (scare) Angst einjagen (+ *Dat.*)

'terrifying *adj.* entsetzlich ‹*Erlebnis, Buch*›; Furcht erregend ‹*Anblick*›; beängstigend ‹*Geschwindigkeit*›

territorial /terɪ'tɔːrɪəl/ *adj.* territorial; Gebiets‹*anspruch usw.*›

territory /'terɪtrɪ/ *n.* Gebiet, *das*

terror /'terə(r)/ *n.* [panische] Angst; Schrecken, *der*

terrorism /'terərɪzm/ *n.* Terrorismus, *der;* (terrorist acts) Terror, *der*

'terrorist *n.* Terrorist, *der*/Terroristin, *die; attrib.* Terror‹*gruppe, -organisation, -angriff, -netzwerk, -zelle*›

terrorize /'terəraɪz/ *v.t.* **(a)** (frighten) in [Angst und] Schrecken versetzen
(b) (coerce) terrorisieren

terse /tɜːs/ *adj.* **(a)** (concise) kurz und bündig
(b) (curt) knapp

test /test/ **1** *n.* **(a)** (Sch.) Klassenarbeit, *die;* (Univ.) Klausur, *die;* **put sb./sth. to the ~:** jmdn./etw. erproben
(b) (analysis) Test, *der*
2 *v.t.* untersuchen ‹*Wasser, Augen*›; testen ‹*Gehör, Augen*›; prüfen ‹*Schüler*›; **~ sb. for Aids** jmdn. auf Aids untersuchen
■ **'test out** *v.t.* ausprobieren ‹*Produkte*› **(on** an + *Dat.*); erproben ‹*Theorie, Idee*›

Testament /'testəmənt/ *n.* **Old/New ~** (Bibl.) Altes/Neues Testament

test: ~ ban *n.* Atom[waffen]teststopp, *der;* **~ ban treaty** *n.* [Atom]teststopp-Abkommen, *das;* **~ drive** *n.* Probefahrt, *die;* **~-drive** *v.t.* Probe fahren

testicle /'testɪkl/ *n.* Testikel, *der* (fachspr.); Hoden, *der*

testify /'testɪfaɪ/ **1** *v.i.* **(a) ~ to sth.** etw. bezeugen
(b) (Law) **~ against sb.** gegen jmdn. aussagen
2 *v.t.* bestätigen

testimonial /testɪ'məʊnɪəl/ *n.* Zeugnis, *das;* Referenz, *die*

testimony /'testɪmənɪ/ *n.* Aussage, *die*

test: ~ pilot *n.* Testpilot, *der*/-pilotin, *die;* **~ tube** *n.* Reagenzglas, *das;* **~-tube baby** *n.* (coll.) Retortenbaby, *das* (ugs.)

testy /'testɪ/ *adj.* leicht reizbar ‹*Person*›; gereizt ‹*Antwort*›

tetanus /'tetənəs/ *n.* Tetanus, *der*

tetchy /'tetʃɪ/ *adj.* leicht reizbar; gereizt

tether /'teðə(r)/ **1** *n.* **be at the end of one's ~:** am Ende [seiner Kraft] sein
2 *v.t.* anbinden **(to** an + *Dat. od. Akk.*)

text /tekst/ **1** *n.* Text, *der*
2 *v.t.* **~ sb.** jmdm. eine [Text]nachricht schicken
3 *v.i.* eine Textnachricht [ver]schicken; (to mobile phone) eine SMS [ver]schicken; simsen (ugs.)

text: ~book *n.* Lehrbuch, *das;* **~book case** Paradefall, *der;* **~ file** *n.* (Comp.) Textdatei, *die*

textile /'tekstaɪl/ *n.* Stoff, *der;* **~s** Textilien *Pl.*

'textphone *n.* Texttelefon, *das*

'text processing *n.* (Comp.) Textverarbeitung, *die*

texture /'tekstʃə(r)/ *n.* Beschaffenheit, *die;* (of fabric) Struktur, *die*

Thai /taɪ/ **1** *adj.* thailändisch; **sb. is ~:** jmd. ist Thai
2 *n.* **(a)** *pl. same or* **~s** Thai, *der*/*die*
(b) (language) Thai, *das*

Thailand /'taɪlænd/ *pr. n.* Thailand (*das*)

Thames /temz/ *pr. n.* Themse, *die*

than /ðən, *stressed* ðæn/ *conj.* als; **I know you better ~ [I do] him** ich kenne dich besser als ihn

thank /θæŋk/ *v.t.* **~ sb. [for sth.]** jmdm. [für etw.] danken; **~ God** *or* **goodness** *or* **heaven[s]** Gott sei Dank; **[I] ~ you** danke; **no, ~ you** nein, danke; **yes, ~ you** ja, bitte; **~ you very much** vielen herzlichen Dank

thankful /ˈθæŋkfl/ *adj.* dankbar

thankfully /ˈθæŋkfəlɪ/ *adv.* **(a)** (gratefully) dankbar
(b) (as sentence-modifier: fortunately) glücklicherweise

ˈthankless *adj.* undankbar

thanks /θæŋks/ *n. pl.* **(a)** (gratitude) Dank, *der;* **~ to** (with the help of) dank; (on account of the bad influence of) wegen
(b) (formula expr. gratitude) danke; **no, ~:** nein, danke; **yes, ~:** ja, bitte; **many ~** (coll.) vielen Dank

thanksgiving /ˈθæŋksgɪvɪŋ/ *n.* **T~ [Day]** (Amer.) [amerikanisches] Erntedankfest; Thanksgiving Day, *der*

ˈthank-you *n.* (coll.) Dankeschön, *das*

that 1 /ðæt/ *adj., pl.* **those** /ðəʊz/ **(a)** dieser/diese/dieses
(b) (coupled or contrasted with 'this') der/die/das
2 /ðæt/ *pron., pl.* **those (a)** der/die/das; **what bird is ~?** was für ein Vogel ist das?; **like ~:** so; **[just] like ~** (without effort, thought) einfach so; **~'s right!** gut *od.* recht so; (iron.) nur so weiter!; **~ will do** das reicht
(b) (Brit.) **who is ~?** wer ist da?; (on telephone) wer ist am Apparat?
3 /ðət/ *rel. pron., pl. same* der/die/das; **everyone ~ I know** jeder, den ich kenne; **this is all [the money] ~ I have** das ist alles [Geld], was ich habe
4 /ðæt/ *adv.* (coll.) so
5 /ðət/ *rel. adv.* der/die/das; **the day ~ I first met her** der Tag, an dem ich sie zum ersten Mal sah
6 /ðət, *stressed* ðæt/ *conj.* dass; **[in order] ~:** damit

thatch /θætʃ/ *n.* (of straw) Strohdach, *das;* (of reeds) Schilfdach, *das;* (roofing) Dachbedeckung, *die*

thatched /θætʃt/ *adj.* stroh-/schilfgedeckt

thaw /θɔ:/ 1 *n.* Tauwetter, *das*
2 *v.i.* **(a)** tauen
(b) (melt) auftauen
3 *v.t.* auftauen

■ **thaw ˈout** ▶ THAW 2, 3

the /*before vowel* ðɪ, *before consonant* ðə, *when stressed* ði:/ 1 *def. art.* der/die/das
2 *adv.* **~ more I practise ~ better I play** je mehr ich übe, desto *od.* umso besser spiele ich; **so much ~ worse for sb./sth.** umso schlimmer für jmdn./etw

theatre (*Amer.:* **theater**) /ˈθɪətə(r)/ *n.* **(a)** Theater, *das*
(b) (lecture **~**) Hörsaal, *der*
(c) (Brit. Med.) ▶ OPERATING THEATRE

theatrical /θɪˈætrɪkl/ *adj.* **(a)** schauspielerisch
(b) (showy) theatralisch

theft /θeft/ *n.* Diebstahl, *der*

their /ðeə(r)/ *poss. pron. attrib.* ihr

theirs /ðeəz/ *poss. pron. pred.* ihrer/ihre/ihres

them /ðəm, *stressed* ðem/ *pron.* sie; (as indirect object) ihnen; *see also* HER[1]

theme /θi:m/ *n.* Thema, *das*

theme: ~ music *n.* Titelmelodie, *die;* **~ park** *n.: Freizeitpark, dessen Attraktionen und Einrichtungen auf ein bestimmtes Thema bezogen sind;* **~ song** *n.* Erkennungssong, *der;* **~ tune** Erkennungsmelodie, *die*

themselves /ðəmˈselvz/ *pron.* **(a)** *emphat.* selbst
(b) *refl.* sich ‹*waschen usw.*›; sich selbst ‹*die Schuld geben, regieren*›. *See also* HERSELF

then /ðen/ 1 *adv.* **(a)** (at that time) damals; **~ and there** auf der Stelle
(b) (after that) dann; **~ [again]** (and also) außerdem; **but ~** (after all) aber schließlich
(c) (in that case) dann; **but ~ again** aber andererseits
2 *n.* **before ~:** vorher; davor; **from ~ on** von da an; **since ~:** seitdem
3 *adj.* damalig

theological /θi:əˈlɒdʒɪkl/ *adj.* theologisch; Theologie‹*student*›

theology /θɪˈɒlədʒɪ/ *n.* Theologie, *die*

theoretical /θɪəˈretɪkl/ *adj.* theoretisch

theory /ˈθɪərɪ/ *n.* Theorie, *die;* **in ~:** theoretisch

therapeutic /θerəˈpju:tɪk/ *adj.* therapeutisch

therapist /ˈθerəpɪst/ *n.* Therapeut, *der*/Therapeutin, *die*

therapy /ˈθerəpɪ/ *n.* Therapie, *die*

there /ðeə(r)/ 1 *adv.* **(a)** (in/at that place) da; dort; (fairly close) da; **be down/in/up ~:** da unten/drin/oben sein
(b) (calling attention) **hello** *or* **hi ~!** hallo!; **you ~!** Sie da!
(c) (in that respect) da; **so ~:** und damit basta (ugs.)
(d) (to that place) dahin, dorthin ‹*gehen, fahren, rücken*›; **down/up ~:** dort hinunter/hinauf
(e) /ðə(r), *stressed* ðeə(r)/ **was ~ anything in it?** war da irgendwas drin?; **~ was once** es war einmal; **~ is enough food** es gibt genug zu essen
2 *int.* **~, ~:** na, na (ugs.); **~ [you are]!** da, siehst du!
3 *n.* da; dort; **near ~:** da *od.* dort in der Nähe

thereabouts /ˈðeərəbaʊts/ *adv.* **(a)** da [in der Nähe]
(b) (near that number) ungefähr

therefore /ˈðeəfɔ:(r)/ *adv.* deshalb; also

thermal /ˈθɜ:ml/ *adj.* thermisch; **~ underwear** kälteisolierende Unterwäsche

thermal imaging /θɜ:ml ˈɪmɪdʒɪŋ/ *n.* Thermographie, *die*

thermometer /θə'mɒmɪtə(r)/ *n.* Thermometer, *das*

Thermos, thermos ® /'θɜːməs/ *n.* ~ **[flask/jug/bottle]** Thermosflasche, *die* (Wz)

thermostat /'θɜːməstæt/ *n.* Thermostat, *der*

these *pl. of* THIS

thesis /'θiːsɪs/ *n., pl.* **theses** /'θiːsiːz/ **(a)** (proposition) These, *die*
(b) (dissertation) Dissertation, *die* (**on** über + *Akk.*)

they /ðeɪ/ *pron.* **(a)** sie
(b) (people in general) man

they'd /ðeɪd/ **(a)** = **they would**
(b) = **they had**

they'll /ðeɪl/ = **they will**

they're /ðeə(r)/ = **they are**

they've /ðeɪv/ = **they have**

thick /θɪk/ [1] *adj.* **(a)** dick; **a rope two inches ~, a two-inch ~ rope** ein zwei Zoll starkes *od.* dickes Seil
(b) (dense) dicht ‹*Haar, Nebel, Wolken usw.*›
(c) (filled) ~ **with** voll von
(d) dickflüssig ‹*Sahne*›; dick ‹*Suppe, Schlamm, Kleister*›
(e) (stupid) dumm
[2] *n.* **in the ~ of** mitten in (+ *Dat.*)

thick 'ear *n.* **give sb. a ~** (Brit. coll.) jmdm. ein paar hinter die Ohren geben (ugs.)

thicken /'θɪkn/ [1] *v.t.* dicker machen; eindicken ‹*Sauce*›
[2] *v.i.* **(a)** dicker werden
(b) ‹*Nebel:*› dichter werden
(c) the plot ~s die Sache wird kompliziert

'thickly *adv.* **(a)** (in a thick layer) dick
(b) (densely) dicht

'thickness *n.* **(a)** Dicke, *die;* **be two metres in ~:** zwei Meter dick sein
(b) (denseness) Dichte, *die*

thick: ~set *adj.* gedrungen; **~-skinned** *adj.* (fig.) dickfellig (ugs.)

thief /θiːf/ *n., pl.* **thieves** /θiːvz/ Dieb, *der*/ Diebin, *die*

thieve /θiːv/ *v.i.* stehlen

thieves *pl. of* THIEF

thigh /θaɪ/ *n.* Oberschenkel, *der*

thimble /'θɪmbl/ *n.* Fingerhut, *der*

thin /θɪn/ [1] *adj.* **(a)** dünn; **a tall, ~ man** ein großer, hagerer Mann
(b) (sparse) dünn, schütter ‹*Haar*›
[2] *adv.* dünn
[3] *v.t.,* **-nn-: (a)** dünner machen
(b) (dilute) verdünnen

■ **thin 'out** *v.i.* ‹*Menschenmenge:*› sich verlaufen; ‹*Verkehr:*› abnehmen

thing /θɪŋ/ *n.* **(a)** Sache, *die;* Ding, *das;* **what's that ~ in your hand?** was hast du da in der Hand?; **be a rare ~:** etwas Seltenes sein
(b) (action) **it was the right ~ to do** es war das einzig Richtige; **that was a foolish/friendly ~ to do** das war eine große Dummheit/das war sehr freundlich
(c) (fact) [Tat]sache, *die;* **it's a strange ~ that ...:** es ist seltsam, dass ...; **the best/worst ~ about her** das Beste/Schlimmste an ihr
(d) (idea) **say the first ~ that comes into one's head** das sagen, was einem gerade so einfällt; **what a ~ to say!** wie kann man nur so etwas sagen!
(e) (task) **she has a reputation for getting ~s done** sie ist für ihre Tatkraft bekannt; **a big ~ to undertake** ein großes Unterfangen
(f) (affair) Sache, *die;* Angelegenheit, *die*
(g) (circumstance) **take ~s too seriously** alles zu ernst nehmen; **how are ~s?** wie gehts [dir]?
(h) (individual, creature) Ding, *das*
(i) *in pl.* (personal belongings, clothes) Sachen *Pl.*
(j) (product of work) Sache, *die;* **the latest ~:** der letzte Schrei
(k) (what is important or proper) das Richtige; **the ~ is ...** (question) die Frage ist ...

thingamy /'θɪŋəmɪ/**, thingumabob** /'θɪŋəməbɒb/**, thingumajig** /'θɪŋəmədʒɪg/**, thingummy** /'θɪŋəmɪ/**, thingy** /'θɪŋɪ/ *ns.* (coll.) Dings, *der/die/das* (salopp); Dingsbums, *der/die/das* (ugs.)

think /θɪŋk/ [1] *v.t.,* **thought** /θɔːt/ **(a)** (consider) meinen; **we ~ [that] he will come** wir denken *od.* glauben, dass er kommt; **what do you ~?** was meinst du? **do you really ~ so?** findest du wirklich?; **what do you ~ of him/it?** was hältst du von ihm/ davon?; **..., don't you ~?** ... , findest *od.* meinst du nicht auch?; **I ~ so/not** ich glaube schon/nicht; **I ~ I'll try** ich glaube, ich werde es versuchen
(b) (imagine) sich (*Dat.*) vorstellen
[2] *v.i.,* **thought** [nach]denken; **I need time to ~:** ich muss es mir erst überlegen; **I've been ~ing** ich habe nachgedacht; **~ twice** es sich (*Dat.*) zweimal überlegen

■ **'think of** *v.t.* **(a)** denken an (+ *Akk.*); **he ~s of everything** er denkt einfach an alles
(b) (have as idea) **we'll ~ of something** wir werden uns etwas einfallen lassen; **can you ~ of anyone who ...?** fällt dir jemand ein, der ...?
(c) (remember) sich erinnern an (+ *Akk.*); **I just can't ~ of her name** ich komme einfach nicht auf ihren Namen
(d) ~ little/nothing of sb./sth. (consider contemptible) wenig/nichts von jmdm./etw. halten; **not ~ much of sb./sth.** nicht viel von jmdm./etw. halten

■ **think 'over** *v.t.* sich (*Dat.*) überlegen

■ **think 'through** *v.t.* [gründlich] durchdenken

■ **think 'up** *v.t.* (coll.) sich (*Dat.*) ausdenken

'thinker *n.* Denker, *der*/Denkerin, *die*

'think tank *n.* Beraterstab, *der*

'thin-skinned *adj.* (fig.) empfindlich; dünnhäutig (geh.)

third /θɜːd/ [1] *adj.* dritt...
[2] *n.* (in sequence, rank) Dritte, *der/die/das;* (fraction) Drittel, *das. See also* EIGHTH

'thirdly *adv.* drittens

third: ~ **'party** *n. attrib.* **~-party insurance** Haftpflichtversicherung, *die;* **~-rate** *adj.* drittklassig; **T~ 'World** *n.* Dritte Welt; **countries of the T~ World, T~ World countries** Länder der Dritten Welt

thirst /θɜːst/ **1** *n.* Durst, *der;* **die of ~:** verdursten
2 *v.i.* **~ for revenge/knowledge** nach Rache/Wissen dürsten (geh.)

'thirsty *adj.* durstig; **be ~:** Durst haben

thirteen /θɜːˈtiːn/ **1** *adj.* dreizehn
2 *n.* Dreizehn, *die. See also* EIGHT

thirteenth /θɜːˈtiːnθ/ *adj.* dreizehnt... *See also* EIGHTH

thirtieth /ˈθɜːtɪɪθ/ **1** *adj.* dreißigst...
2 *n.* (fraction) Dreißigstel, *das. See also* EIGHTH

thirty /ˈθɜːtɪ/ **1** *adj.* dreißig
2 *n.* Dreißig, *die. See also* EIGHT; EIGHTY 2

'thirty-something **1** *adj.* **be ~:** in den Dreißigern sein
2 *n.* Dreißiger, *der*/-in, *die*

this /ðɪs/ **1** *adj., pl.* **these** /ðiːz/ dieser/diese/dieses; (with less emphasis) der/die/das; **at ~ time** zu dieser Zeit; **by ~ time** inzwischen; mittlerweile; **these days** heut[zutag]e; **before ~ time** vorher; zuvor; **all ~ week** die[se] ganze Woche; **~ morning/evening** *etc.* heute Morgen/Abend *usw.;* **these last three weeks** die letzten drei Wochen; **~ Monday** (to come) nächsten Montag
2 *pron., pl.* **these (a) what's ~?** was ist [denn] das?; **fold it like ~:** falte es so!
(b) (the present) **before ~:** bis jetzt
(c) (Brit. Teleph.: person speaking) **~ is Andy** hier [spricht *od.* ist] Andy; (Amer. Teleph.) **who did you say ~ was?** wer ist am Apparat?
(d) ~ and that dies und das

thistle /ˈθɪsl/ *n.* Distel, *die*

thorn /θɔːn/ *n.* **(a)** (part of plant) Dorn, *der*
(b) (plant) Dornenstrauch, *der*

'thorny *adj.* **(a)** dornig
(b) (fig.) heikel

thorough /ˈθʌrə/ *adj.* gründlich

thorough: ~bred *n.* reinrassiges Tier; (horse) Rassepferd, *das;* **~fare** *n.* Durchfahrtsstraße, *die;* **'no ~fare'** „Durchfahrt verboten"; (on foot) „kein Durchgang"

'thoroughly *adv.* gründlich ‹*untersuchen*›; gehörig ‹*erschöpft*›; so richtig ‹*genießen*›; zutiefst ‹*beschämt*›; total ‹*verdorben, verwöhnt*›; **be ~ fed up with sth.** (coll.) von etw. die Nase gestrichen voll haben (ugs.)

'thoroughness *n.* Gründlichkeit, *die*

those ▶ THAT 1, 2

though /ðəʊ/ **1** *conj.* **(a)** (despite the fact that) obwohl; **late ~ it was** obwohl es so spät war; **the car, ~ powerful, is also economical** der Wagen ist zwar stark, aber [zugleich] auch wirtschaftlich
(b) (but nevertheless) aber; **a slow ~ certain method** eine langsame, aber *od.* wenn auch sichere Methode
(c) (even if) **[even] ~:** auch wenn
(d) (and yet) **~ you never know** obwohl man nie weiß
2 *adv.* (coll.) trotzdem

thought /θɔːt/ **1** ▶ THINK
2 *n.* **(a)** *no pl.* Denken, *das*
(b) *no pl., no art.* (reflection) Überlegung, *die;* Nachdenken, *das*
(c) (consideration) Rücksicht, *die* (**for** auf + *Akk.*)
(d) (idea, conception) Gedanke, *der;* **it's the ~ that counts** der gute Wille zählt; **give up all ~[s] of sth.** sich (*Dat.*) etw. aus dem Kopf schlagen

thoughtful /ˈθɔːtfl/ *adj.* **(a)** nachdenklich
(b) (considerate) rücksichtsvoll; (helpful) aufmerksam

'thoughtfully *adv.* **(a)** nachdenklich
(b) (considerately) rücksichtsvollerweise

'thoughtless *adj.* **(a)** gedankenlos
(b) (inconsiderate) rücksichtslos

'thoughtlessly *adv.* **(a)** gedankenlos
(b) (inconsiderately) aus Rücksichtslosigkeit

thought: ~ process *n.* Denkprozess, *der;* **~-provoking** *adj.* nachdenklich stimmend; **be ~-provoking** nachdenklich stimmen

thousand /ˈθaʊznd/ **1** *adj.* **(a)** tausend; **a** *or* **one ~:** eintausend; **two/several ~:** zweitausend/mehrere tausend; **a** *or* **one ~ and one** [ein]tausend[und]eins
(b) a ~ [and one] (fig.: innumerable) tausend (ugs.)
2 *n.* **(a)** (number) tausend; **a** *or* **one/two ~:** ein-/zweitausend
(b) (written figure; group) Tausend, *das*
(c) (indefinite amount) **~s** tausende

thousandth /ˈθaʊzndθ/ **1** *adj.* tausendst...
2 *n.* (fraction) Tausendstel, *das;* (in sequence) Tausendste, *der/die/das*

thrash /θræʃ/ *v.t.* **(a)** verprügeln
(b) (defeat) vernichtend schlagen

■ **thrash 'out** *v.t.* ausdiskutieren

thrashing /ˈθræʃɪŋ/ *n.* (beating) Prügel *Pl.;* **give sb. a ~:** jmdm. eine Tracht Prügel verpassen (ugs.)

thread /θred/ **1** *n.* **(a)** Faden, *der*
(b) (of screw) Gewinde, *das*
2 *v.t.* **(a)** einfädeln; auffädeln ‹*Perlen*›
(b) ~ one's way through sth. sich durch etw. schlängeln

'threadbare *adj.* abgenutzt; abgetragen ‹*Kleidung*›; (fig.) abgedroschen ‹*Argument*›

threat /θret/ *n.* Drohung, *die*

threaten /ˈθretn/ *v.t.* **(a)** bedrohen; **~ sb. with sth.** jmdm. etw. androhen
(b) ~ to do sth. damit drohen, etw. zu tun
(c) drohen mit ‹*Gewalt, Rache usw.*›

threatening /ˈθretnɪŋ/ *adj.* drohend
three /θriː/ [1] *adj.* drei
[2] *n.* Drei, *die. See also* EIGHT
three: ~-dimensional /θriːdɪˈmenʃənl/ *adj.* dreidimensional; **~fold** *adj., adv.* dreifach; **a ~fold increase** ein Anstieg auf das Dreifache; **~-lane** *adj.* dreispurig; **~-pin** ▶ PIN 1 C; **~-quarters** [1] *n.* drei Viertel *pl.* (**of** + *Gen.*); **~-quarters of an hour** eine Dreiviertelstunde; [2] *adv.* drei viertel ‹*voll*›; **~some** /ˈθriːsəm/ *n.* Dreigespann, *das;* Trio, *das*
thresh /θreʃ/ *v.t.* dreschen
threshold /ˈθreʃəʊld/ *n.* Schwelle, *die*
threw ▶ THROW 1
thrift /θrɪft/ *n.* Sparsamkeit, *die*
ˈthrifty *adj.* sparsam
thrill /θrɪl/ [1] *v.t.* **(a)** (excite) faszinieren
(b) (delight) begeistern
[2] *n.* **(a)** Erregung, *die*
(b) (exciting experience) aufregendes Erlebnis
ˈthriller *n.* Thriller, *der*
ˈthrilling *adj.* aufregend; spannend ‹*Buch, Film*›
thrive /θraɪv/ *v.i.,* **thrived** *or* **throve** /θrəʊv/, **thrived** *or* **thriven** /ˈθrɪvn/ **(a)** ‹*Pflanze:*› wachsen und gedeihen
(b) (prosper) aufblühen (**on** bei)
throat /θrəʊt/ *n.* Hals, *der;* (esp. inside) Kehle, *die;* **a [sore] ~:** Halsschmerzen *Pl.*
throb /θrɒb/ [1] *v.i.,* **-bb-** pochen; ‹*Motor:*› dröhnen
[2] *n.* Pochen, *das;* (of engine) Dröhnen, *das*
throes /θrəʊz/ *n. pl.* Qual, *die;* **be in the ~ of sth.** (fig.) mitten in etw. (*Dat.*) stecken (ugs.)
thrombosis /θrɒmˈbəʊsɪs/ *n., pl.* **thromboses** /θrɒmˈbəʊsiːz/ Thrombose, *die*
throne /θrəʊn/ *n.* Thron, *der*
throng /θrɒŋ/ *n.* [Menschen]menge, *die*
throttle /ˈθrɒtl/ *v.t.* erdrosseln
through /θruː/ [1] *prep.* **(a)** durch
(b) (Amer.: up to and including) bis [einschließlich]
(c) (by reason of) durch; infolge von ‹*Vernachlässigung, Einflüssen*›
[2] *adv.* **(a) let sb. ~:** jmdn. durchlassen
(b) (Teleph.) **be ~:** durch sein (ugs.); **be ~ to sb.** mit jmdm. verbunden sein
[3] *attrib. adj.* durchgehend ‹*Zug*›
throughˈout [1] *prep.* **~ the war/period** den ganzen Krieg/die ganze Zeit hindurch; **~ the country** im ganzen Land
[2] *adv.* (entirely) ganz; (always) stets; die ganze Zeit [hindurch]
throve ▶ THRIVE
throw /θrəʊ/ [1] *v.t.,* **threw** /θruː/, **thrown** /θrəʊn/ **(a)** werfen; **~ sth. to sb.** jmdm. etw. zuwerfen; **~ sth. at sb.** etw. nach jmdm. werfen
(b) (bring to the ground) zu Boden werfen; abwerfen ‹*Reiter*›
(c) (coll.: disconcert) ‹*Frage:*› aus der Fassung bringen
[2] *n.* Wurf, *der*
■ **throw aˈway** *v.t.* **(a)** wegwerfen
(b) (lose by neglect) verschenken ‹*Vorteil, Spiel usw.*›
■ **throw ˈup** [1] *v.t.* **(a)** hochwerfen ‹*Arme, Hände*›
(b) (produce) hervorbringen ‹*Ideen usw.*›
[2] *v.i.* (coll.) brechen (ugs.)
ˈthrowaway *adj.* **(a)** Wegwerf-; Einweg-
(b) beiläufig ‹*Bemerkung*›
thrown ▶ THROW 1
thrush /θrʌʃ/ *n.* (Ornith.) Drossel, *die*
thrust /θrʌst/ [1] *v.t.,* **thrust** stoßen; **~ aside** (fig.) beiseite schieben
[2] *n.* Stoß, *der*
thud /θʌd/ *n.* dumpfer Schlag
thug /θʌg/ *n.* Schläger, *der;* **football ~s** Fußballrowdys *Pl.*
thuggish /ˈθʌgɪʃ/ *adj.* aggressiv ‹*Verhalten, Fußballfan*›
thumb /θʌm/ [1] *n.* Daumen, *der;* **get the ~s up** ‹*Person, Projekt:*› akzeptiert werden; **be under sb.'s ~:** unter jmds. Fuchtel stehen
[2] *v.t.* **~ a lift** per Anhalter fahren
■ **ˈthumb through** *v.t.* durchblättern
thumb: ~ index *n.* Daumenregister, *das;* **~nail** *n.* Daumennagel, *der;* **~tack** *n.* (Amer.) Reißzwecke, *die*
thump /θʌmp/ [1] *v.t.* [mit Wucht] schlagen
[2] *v.i.* **(a)** hämmern (**at, on** gegen)
(b) ‹*Herz:*› heftig pochen
[3] *n.* (blow) Schlag, *der;* (sound) Bums, *der* (ugs.); dumpfer Schlag
thunder /ˈθʌndə(r)/ [1] *n.* Donner, *der*
[2] *v.i.* donnern
thunder: ~clap *n.* Donnerschlag, *der;* **~storm** *n.* Gewitter, *das*
thundery /ˈθʌndərɪ/ *adj.* gewittrig
Thurs. *abbr.* = **Thursday** Do.
Thursday /ˈθɜːzdeɪ, ˈθɜːzdɪ/ *n.* Donnerstag, *der; see also* FRIDAY
thus /ðʌs/ *adv.* so
thwart /θwɔːt/ *v.t.* durchkreuzen ‹*Pläne*›; vereiteln ‹*Versuch*›; **~ sb.** jmdm. einen Strich durch die Rechnung machen
thyme /taɪm/ *n.* Thymian, *der*
thyroid /ˈθaɪrɔɪd/ *n.* Schilddrüse, *die*
tiara /tɪˈɑːrə/ *n.* Diadem, *das*
tick /tɪk/ [1] *v.i.* ticken
[2] *v.t.* **(a)** mit einem Häkchen versehen
(b) ▶ **~** OFF A
[3] *n.* **(a)** (of clock etc.) Ticken, *das*
(b) (mark) Häkchen, *das*
■ **tick ˈoff** *v.t.* **(a)** (cross off) abhaken
(b) (coll.: reprimand) rüffeln (ugs.)
ticket /ˈtɪkɪt/ *n.* Karte, *die;* (for bus, train) Fahrschein, *der;* (for aeroplane) Flugschein, *der;* (for lottery, raffle) Los, *das;* (for library) Ausweis, *der;* **price ~:** Preisschild, *das*
ticket: ~ agency *n.* Kartenvorverkaufsstelle, *die;* **~ agent** *n.*

Inhaber/Inhaberin einer Kartenvorverkaufsstelle; ~ **collector** *n.* (on train) Schaffner, *der*/Schaffnerin, *die;* (on station) Fahrkartenkontrolleur, *der*/-kontrolleurin, *die;* ~ **dispenser** *n.* Kartenautomat, *der;* (for train etc.) Fahrschein- *od.* Fahrkartenautomat, *der;* ~ **holder** *n.* Besitzer/Besitzerin einer Eintrittskarte; ~ **machine** ▶ ~ DISPENSER; ~ **office** *n.* Fahrkartenschalter, *der;* (for advance booking) Kartenvorverkaufsstelle, *die*

tickle /'tɪkl/ *v.t. & i.* kitzeln

ticklish /'tɪklɪʃ/ *adj.* kitzlig

tidal /'taɪdl/ *adj.* Gezeiten

'tidal wave *n.* Flutwelle, *die*

tiddlywinks /'tɪdlɪwɪŋks/ *n. sing.* (game) Flohhüpfen, *das*

tide /taɪd/ 1 *n.* Tide, *die* (nordd.); **high** ~: Flut, *die;* **low** ~: Ebbe, *die;* **the** ~**s** die Gezeiten; **the** ~ **is in/out** es ist Flut/Ebbe
2 *v.t.* ~ **sb. over** jmdm. über die Runden helfen (ugs.)

tidiness /'taɪdɪnɪs/ *n.* Ordentlichkeit, *die*

tidy /'taɪdɪ/ 1 *adj.* ordentlich; aufgeräumt ‹*Zimmer, Schreibtisch*›
2 *v.t.* aufräumen; ~ **oneself** sich zurechtmachen

▪ **tidy 'up** *v.i.* aufräumen

tie /taɪ/ 1 *v.t.*, **tying** /'taɪɪŋ/ binden (**to** an + *Akk.*, **into** zu); ~ **a knot** einen Knoten machen; (Sport) ~ **the match** unentschieden spielen
2 *v.i.*, **tying (a)** (be fastened) **it** ~**s at the back** es wird hinten gebunden
(b) (have equal scores) ~ **for second place** mit gleicher Punktzahl den zweiten Platz erreichen
3 *n.* **(a)** Krawatte, *die*
(b) (bond) Band, *das;* (restriction) Bindung, *die*
(c) (equality of scores) Punktgleichheit, *die*
(d) (Sport: match) Begegnung, *die*

▪ **tie 'in** *v.i.* ~ **in with sth.** zu etw. passen

▪ **tie 'up** *v.t.* **(a)** festbinden; ~ **up a parcel** ein Paket verschnüren
(b) (keep busy) beschäftigen

tier /tɪə(r)/ *n.* **(a)** Rang, *der*
(b) (unit) Stufe, *die*

tiger /'taɪgə(r)/ *n.* Tiger, *der*

tiger e'conomy *n.* Tigerstaat, *der*

tight /taɪt/ 1 *adj.* **(a)** (firm) fest; fest angezogen ‹*Schraube, Mutter*›; fest sitzend ‹*Deckel*›
(b) (close-fitting) eng ‹*Kleid, Schuh usw.*›
(c) (impermeable) ~ **seal/joint** dichter Verschluss/dichte Fuge
(d) (taut) straff
(e) (difficult to negotiate) **a** ~ **corner** eine enge Kurve; **be in a** ~ **corner** (fig.) in der Klemme sein (ugs.)
(f) (strict) streng ‹*Kontrolle, Disziplin*›
(g) (coll.: stingy) knauserig (ugs.)
(h) (coll.: drunk) voll (salopp)
2 *adv.* fest; **hold** ~! halt dich fest!
3 *n. in pl.* **(a)** (Brit.) **[pair of]** ~**s** Strumpfhose, *die*
(b) (of dancer etc.) Trikothose, *die*

tighten /'taɪtn/ 1 *v.t.* **(a)** [fest] anziehen ‹*Knoten, Schraube*›; straff ziehen ‹*Seil*›
(b) verschärfen ‹*Kontrolle*›
2 *v.i.* sich spannen

tight-fisted /taɪt'fɪstɪd/ *adj.* geizig

'tightrope *n.* Drahtseil, *das*

tile /taɪl/ 1 *n.* (on roof) Ziegel, *der;* (on floor) Fliese, *die;* (on wall) Kachel, *die*
2 *v.t.* [mit Ziegeln] decken ‹*Dach*›; fliesen ‹*Fußboden*›; kacheln ‹*Wand*›

till[1] /tɪl/ 1 *prep.* bis; (followed by article + noun) bis zu; **not [...]** ~: erst
2 *conj.* bis

till[2] *n.* Kasse, *die*

'till receipt *n.* Kassenzettel, *der*

tilt /tɪlt/ 1 *v.i.* kippen
2 *v.t.* kippen; neigen ‹*Kopf*›
3 *n.* **(a)** Schräglage, *die;* **a 45°** ~: eine Neigung von 45°
(b) [at] full ~: mit voller Wucht

timber /'tɪmbə(r)/ *n.* [Bau]holz, *das*

time /taɪm/ 1 *n.* **(a)** Zeit, *die;* **in [the course of]** ~, **as** ~ **goes on/went on** mit der Zeit; im Laufe der Zeit; **in** ~, **with** ~ (sooner or later) mit der Zeit; **in [good]** ~ (not late) rechtzeitig; **all the** *or* **this** ~: die ganze Zeit; (without ceasing) ständig; **a short** ~ **ago** vor kurzem; ~ **off** *or* **out** freie Zeit; **in 'no** ~: im Handumdrehen; **in a week's/year's** ~: in einer Woche/in einem Jahr; **harvest/Christmas** ~: Ernte-/Weihnachtszeit, *die;* **on** ~ (punctually) pünktlich; **ahead of** ~: zu früh ‹*ankommen*›; vorzeitig ‹*fertig werden*›; **have a good** ~: sich amüsieren; Spaß haben (ugs.); **have no** ~ **for sb./sth.** (fig.) für jmdn./etw. ist einem seine Zeit zu schade
(b) (occasion) Mal, *das;* **for the first** ~: zum ersten Mal; **at** ~**s** gelegentlich; ~ **and again,** ~ **after** ~: immer [und immer] wieder; **at one** ~, **at [one and] the same** ~ (simultaneously) gleichzeitig; **one at a** ~: einzeln; **two at a** ~: jeweils zwei
(c) (point in day etc.) [Uhr]zeit, *die;* **tell the** ~: die Uhr lesen; **what** ~ **is it?, what is the** ~? wie spät ist es?; **by this/that** ~: inzwischen; **by the** ~ **[that] we arrived** bis wir hinkamen; **T**~! (Brit.: in pub) Feierabend!; ~, **[ladies and] gentlemen, please!** wir machen Feierabend, meine [Damen und] Herren!
(d) (multiplication) mal; **three** ~**s four** drei mal vier
(e) (Mus.) Takt, *der;* **in** ~: im Takt
2 *v.t.* **(a)** zeitlich abstimmen; **be well** ~**d** zur richtigen Zeit kommen
(b) (set to operate at correct ~) einstellen
(c) (measure ~ taken by) stoppen

time: ~ **bomb** *n.* Zeitbombe, *die;* ~**-consuming** *adj.* **(a)** (taking ~) zeitaufwendig; **(b)** (wasteful of ~) zeitraubend; ~ **lag** *n.* zeitliche Verzögerung

timeless /'taɪmlɪs/ *adj.* zeitlos
'time limit *n.* Frist, *die*
timely /'taɪmlɪ/ *adj.* rechtzeitig
time: ~scale *n.* Zeitskala, *die;* **~ sheet** *n.* Stundenzettel, *der;* **~ switch** *n.* Zeitschalter, *der;* **~table** *n.* **(a)** (scheme of work) Zeitplan, *der;* (Educ.) Stundenplan, *der;* **(b)** (Transport) Fahrplan, *der;* **~ warp** *n.* Verwerfung im Raum-Zeit-Kontinuum; **~ zone** *n.* Zeitzone, *die*
timid /'tɪmɪd/ *adj.* **(a)** scheu ‹*Tier*› **(b)** zaghaft ‹*Mensch*›; (shy) schüchtern
timing /'taɪmɪŋ/ *n.* **(a)** **that was perfect ~!** du kommst gerade im richtigen Augenblick! **(b)** (Theatre, Sport) Timing, *das*
tin /tɪn/ **1** *n.* **(a)** (metal) Zinn, *das;* **~[plate]** Weißblech, *das* **(b)** (Brit.: for preserving) [Konserven]dose, *die* **2** *v.t.*, **-nn-** (Brit.) zu Konserven verarbeiten
tin 'foil *n.* Stanniol, *das;* Alufolie, *die*
tinge /tɪndʒ/ **1** *v.t.*, **~ing** /'tɪndʒɪŋ/ tönen **2** *n.* [leichte] Färbung; (fig.) Hauch, *der*
tingle /'tɪŋgl/ *v.i.* kribbeln
tinker /'tɪŋkə(r)/ **1** *n.* Kesselflicker, *der* **2** *v.i.* **~ with sth.** an etw. (*Dat.*) herumbasteln (ugs.)
tinkle /'tɪŋkl/ **1** *n.* Klingeln, *das* **2** *v.i.* klingeln
tinned /tɪnd/ *adj.* (Brit.) Dosen-
tin: ~-opener *n.* (Brit.) Dosenöffner, *der;* **~pot** *attrib. adj.* (derog.) schäbig
tinsel /'tɪnsl/ *n.* Lametta, *das*
tint /tɪnt/ **1** *n.* Farbton, *der* **2** *v.t.* tönen; kolorieren ‹*Zeichnung*›
tiny /'taɪnɪ/ *adj.* winzig
tip¹ /tɪp/ *n.* (end, point) Spitze, *die*
tip² **1** *v.i.*, **-pp-** (lean, fall) kippen; **~ over** umkippen **2** *v.t.*, **-pp-**: **(a)** (make tilt) kippen **(b)** (make overturn) umkippen; (Brit.: discharge) kippen **(c)** voraussagen ‹*Sieger*›; **~ sb. to win** auf jmds. Sieg tippen **(d)** (reward) **~ sb.** jmdm. Trinkgeld geben **3** *n.* **(a)** (money) Trinkgeld, *das* **(b)** (special information) Hinweis, *der;* Tipp, *der* (ugs.) **(c)** (Brit.) Müllkippe, *die*
■ **tip 'off** *v.t.* **~ sb. off** jmdm. einen Hinweis *od.* (ugs.) Tipp geben
'tip-off *n.* Hinweis, *der*
tipsy /'tɪpsɪ/ *adj.* (coll.) angeheitert; beschwipst (ugs.)
tip: ~toe **1** *v.i.* auf Zehenspitzen gehen; **2** *n.* **on ~toe[s]** auf Zehenspitzen; **~top** *adj.* tipptopp (ugs.)
tire¹ /'taɪə(r)/ (Amer.) ▶ TYRE
tire² **1** *v.t.* ermüden **2** *v.i.* müde werden; ermüden; **~ of sth./doing sth.** einer Sache (*Gen.*) überdrüssig werden
■ **tire 'out** *v.t.* erschöpfen; **~ oneself out doing sth.** etw. bis zur Erschöpfung tun

tired /'taɪəd/ *adj.* **(a)** (weary) müde **(b)** (fed up) **be ~ of sth./doing sth.** etw. satt haben/es satt haben, etw. zu tun
tiredness /'taɪədnɪs/ *n.* Müdigkeit, *die*
'tireless *adj.* unermüdlich
tiresome /'taɪəsəm/ *adj.* **(a)** (wearisome) mühsam **(b)** (annoying) lästig
tiring /'taɪərɪŋ/ *adj.* ermüdend
tissue /'tɪʃu:, 'tɪsju:/ *n.* **(a)** Gewebe, *das* **(b)** **[paper] ~:** Papiertuch, *das;* (handkerchief) Papiertaschentuch, *das* **(c)** **~ [paper]** Seidenpapier, *das*
tit¹ /tɪt/ *n.* (Ornith.) Meise, *die*
tit² *n.* **it's ~ for tat** wie du mir, so ich dir
'titbit *n.* **(a)** (food) Häppchen, *das* (ugs.) **(b)** (piece of news) Neuigkeit, *die*
titchy /'tɪtʃɪ/ *adj.* (coll.) klitzeklein (ugs.)
titillate /'tɪtɪleɪt/ *v.t.* erregen
titillation /tɪtɪ'leɪʃn/ *n.* Kitzel, *der*
title /'taɪtl/ *n.* Titel, *der*
title: ~ deed *n.* (Law) Eigentumsurkunde, *die;* **~-holder** *n.* (Sport) Titelhalter, *der*/-halterin, *die;* **~ page** *n.* Titelseite, *die;* **~ role** *n.* Titelrolle, *die*
tittle-tattle /'tɪtltætl/ *n.* Klatsch, *der* (ugs.)
'T-junction *n.* Einmündung, *die*
to **1** /*before vowel* tʊ, *before consonant* tə, *stressed* tu:/ *prep.* **(a)** (in the direction of and reaching) zu; (with name of place) nach; **go to work/to the theatre** zur Arbeit/ins Theater gehen; **to France** nach Frankreich **(b)** (as far as) bis zu; **from London to Edinburgh** von London [bis] nach Edinburgh; **increase from 10% to 20%** von 10% auf 20% steigen **(c)** (introducing relationship or indirect object) **to sb./sth.** jmdm./einer Sache (*Dat.*); **lend/explain** *etc.* **sth. to sb.** jmdm. etw. leihen/erklären *usw.*; **speak to sb.** mit jmdm. sprechen; **that's all there is to it** mehr ist dazu nicht zu sagen; **what's that to you?** was geht das dich an?; **to me** (in my opinion) meiner Meinung nach; **14 miles to the gallon** 14 Meilen auf eine Gallone **(d)** (until) bis; **to the end** bis zum Ende; **to this day** bis heute; **five [minutes] to eight** fünf [Minuten] vor acht **(e)** (with infinitive of a verb) zu; (expr. purpose, or after) **too** um [...] zu; **want to know** wissen wollen; **do sth. to annoy sb.** etw. tun, um jmdn. zu ärgern; **too hot to drink** zu heiß zum Trinken; **he would have phoned but forgot to** er hätte angerufen, aber er vergaß es **2** *adv.* /tu:/ **to and fro** hin und her
toad /təʊd/ *n.* (also fig. derog.) Kröte, *die*
'toadstool *n.* Giftpilz, *der*
toast /təʊst/ **1** *n.* **(a)** *no pl.* Toast, *der;* **a piece of ~:** eine Scheibe Toast **(b)** (call to drink) Toast, *der;* **drink a ~ to sb./sth.** auf jmdn./etw. trinken **2** *v.t.* **(a)** rösten; toasten ‹*Brot*›

(b) (drink to) trinken auf (+ *Akk.*)
'toaster *n.* Toaster, *der*
'toast rack *n.* Toastständer, *der*
tobacco /tə'bækəʊ/ *n., pl.* **~s** Tabak, *der*
tobacconist /tə'bækənɪst/ *n.* Tabak[waren]händler, *der*/-händlerin, *die*
toboggan /tə'bɒgən/ **1** *n.* Schlitten, *der*
2 *v.i.* Schlitten fahren
tod /tɒd/ *n.* (Brit. coll.) **on one's ~:** [ganz] allein
today /tə'deɪ/ **1** *n.* heute; **~'s newspaper** die Zeitung von heute
2 *adv.* heute
toddler /'tɒdlə(r)/ *n.* ≈ Kleinkind, *das*
to-do /tə'du:/ *n.* Getue, *das* (ugs.)
toe /təʊ/ **1** *n.* Zeh, *der;* Zehe, *die;* (of footwear) Spitze, *die*
2 *v.t.,* **~ing** (fig.) **~ the line** *or* (Amer.) **mark** sich einordnen
'toenail *n.* Zeh[en]nagel, *der*
toffee /'tɒfɪ/ *n.* Karamell, *der;* (Brit.: piece) Toffee, *das;* Sahnebonbon, *das*
'toffee apple *n.* mit Karamell überzogener Apfel am Stiel
tofu /'təʊfu:/ *n., no indef. art.* Tofu, *der*
together /tə'geðə(r)/ *adv.* **(a)** (in or into company) zusammen
(b) (simultaneously) gleichzeitig
(c) (one with another) miteinander
toggle /'tɒgl/ **1** *n.* **(a)** (button) Knebelknopf, *der*
(b) (Comp.) [Kipp]schalter, *der;* Umschalttaste, *die*
2 *v.i.* (Comp.) [hin und her] schalten
toil /tɔɪl/ **1** *v.i.* schwer arbeiten
2 *n.* [harte] Arbeit
toilet /'tɔɪlɪt/ *n.* Toilette, *die;* **go to the ~:** auf die Toilette gehen
toilet: ~ bag *n.* Kulturbeutel, *der;* **~ brush** *n.* Klosettbürste, *die;* **~ paper** *n.* Toilettenpapier, *das*
toiletries /'tɔɪlɪtrɪz/ *n. pl.* Körperpflegemittel *Pl.;* Toilettenartikel *Pl.*
toilet: ~ roll *n.* Rolle Toilettenpapier; **~ seat** *n.* Klosettbrille, *die* (ugs.); Toilettensitz, *der;* **~ tissue** ▶ **~** PAPER; **~ water** *n.* Toilettenwasser, *das;* Eau de Toilette, *das*
token /'təʊkn/ **1** *n.* **(a)** (voucher) Gutschein, *der*
(b) (counter, disc) Marke, *die*
(c) (sign) Zeichen, *das*
2 *attrib. adj.* symbolisch ‹*Preis*›
Tokyo /'təʊkjəʊ/ *pr. n.* Tokio (*das*)
told ▶ TELL
tolerable /'tɒlərəbl/ *adj.* **(a)** (endurable) erträglich (**to, for** für)
(b) (fairly good) leidlich; annehmbar
tolerance /'tɒlərəns/ *n.* Toleranz, *die*
tolerant /'tɒlərənt/ *adj.* tolerant (**of, towards** gegen[über])
tolerate /'tɒləreɪt/ *v.t.* dulden; (bear) ertragen ‹*Schmerzen*›
toleration /tɒlə'reɪʃn/ *n.* Tolerierung, *die* (geh.)
toll¹ /təʊl/ *n.* **(a)** (tax, duty) Gebühr, *die*
(b) (damage etc.) Aufwand, *der;* **take its ~ of sth.** einen Tribut an etw. (*Dat.*) fordern (fig.)
toll² *v.i.* ‹*Glocke:*› läuten
toll: ~ bridge *n.* gebührenpflichtige Brücke; **~road** *n.* gebührenpflichtige Straße; Mautstraße, *die* (bes. österr.)
tom /tɒm/ *n.* (cat) Kater, *der*
tomato /tə'mɑ:təʊ/ *n., pl.* **~es** Tomate, *die*
tomato: ~ juice *n.* Tomatensaft, *der;* **~ 'ketchup** *n.* Tomatenketschup, *der od. das;* **~ 'purée** *n.* Tomatenmark, *das*
tomb /tu:m/ *n.* Grab, *das;* (monument) Grabmal, *das*
'tomboy *n.* Wildfang, *der*
'tombstone *n.* Grabstein, *der*
'tomcat *n.* Kater, *der*
tome /təʊm/ *n.* dicker Band; Wälzer, *der* (ugs.)
tomfoolery /tɒm'fu:lərɪ/ *n.* Blödsinn, *der* (ugs.)
tomorrow /tə'mɒrəʊ/ **1** *n.* morgen; **~ morning/afternoon/evening/night** morgen früh *od.* Vormittag/Nachmittag/Abend/Nacht; **~'s newspaper** die morgige Zeitung
2 *adv.* morgen; **see you ~!** (coll.) bis morgen!; **the day after ~:** übermorgen
ton /tʌn/ *n.* Tonne, *die*
tone /təʊn/ **1** *n.* **(a)** (sound) Klang, *der;* (Teleph.) Ton, *der*
(b) (style of speaking) Ton, *der*
(c) (tint, shade) [Farb]ton, *der*
(d) (fig.: character) **lower/raise the ~ of sth.** das Niveau einer Sache (*Gen.*) senken/erhöhen; **set the ~:** den Ton angeben
2 *v.t.* tönen; abtönen ‹*Farbe*›
■ **tone 'down** *v.t.* [ab]dämpfen ‹*Farbe*›; (fig.) mäßigen ‹*Sprache*›
tone: ~-'deaf *adj.* ohne musikalisches Gehör; **~ dialling** (Teleph.) *n.* Tonwahl, *die*
tongs /tɒŋz/ *n. pl.* **[pair of] ~:** Zange, *die*
tongue /tʌŋ/ *n.* Zunge, *die;* **bite one's ~** (lit. or fig.) sich auf die Zunge beißen; **find one's ~:** seine Sprache wieder finden; **hold one's ~:** stillschweigen; **he made the remark ~ in cheek** (fig.) er meinte die Bemerkung nicht ernst
tongue: ~-tied *adj.* schüchtern; **~-twister** *n.* Zungenbrecher, *der* (ugs.)
tonic /'tɒnɪk/ **1** *n.* **(a)** (Med.) Tonikum, *das*
(b) (fig.: invigorating influence) Wohltat, *die* (geh.)
(c) (~ water) Tonic, *das*
2 *attrib. adj.* kräftigend; (fig.) wohltuend ‹*Wirkung*›
'tonic water *n.* Tonic[wasser], *das*
tonight /tə'naɪt/ **1** *n.* **(a)** (this evening) heute Abend; **~'s performance** die heutige [Abend]vorstellung
(b) (this or the coming night) heute Nacht

[2] *adv.* **(a)** (this evening) heute Abend
(b) (during this or the coming night) heute Nacht; **[I'll] see you ~!** bis heute Abend!

tonne /tʌn/ *n.* [metrische] Tonne

tonsil /'tɒnsl/ *n.* [Gaumen]mandel, *die;* **have one's ~s out** sich (*Dat.*) die Mandeln herausnehmen lassen

tonsillitis /tɒnsə'laɪtɪs/ *n.* Mandelentzündung, *die*

too /tu:/ *adv.* **(a)** (excessively) zu; **~ difficult a task** eine zu schwierige Aufgabe
(b) (also) auch
(c) (coll.: very) besonders; **not ~ pleased** nicht gerade erfreut

took ▶ TAKE

tool /tu:l/ *n.* **(a)** Werkzeug, *das;* (garden ~) Gerät, *das;* **[set of] ~s** Werkzeug, *das*
(b) (Comp.) Tool, *das;* Werkzeug, *das*
(c) (fig.: means) [Hilfs]mittel, *das*

tool: ~bar *n.* (Comp.) Werkzeugleiste, *die;* **~box** *n.* Werkzeugkasten, *der;* **~ kit** *n.* Werkzeug, *das*

toot /tu:t/ [1] *v.i.* (on car etc. horn) hupen
[2] *n.* Tuten, *das*

tooth /tu:θ/ *n., pl.* **teeth** /ti:θ/ **(a)** Zahn, *der*
(b) (of rake, fork, comb) Zinke, *die;* (of cogwheel, saw) Zahn, *der*

tooth: ~ache *n.* Zahnschmerzen *Pl.;* **~brush** *n.* Zahnbürste, *die;* **~ decay** *n.* Zahnverfall, *der;* **~glass** *n.* Zahnputzglas, *das;* **~ mug** *n.* Zahnputzbecher, *der;* **~paste** *n.* Zahnpasta, *die;* **~pick** *n.* Zahnstocher, *der;* **~ powder** *n.* Zahnpulver, *das*

top[1] /tɒp/ [1] *n.* **(a)** (highest part) Spitze, *die;* (of table) Platte, *die;* (~ end) oberes Ende; (of tree) Wipfel, *der;* (~ floor) oberstes Stockwerk; (rim of glass) Rand, *der;* **on ~ of one another** aufeinander; **on ~ of sth.** (fig.: in addition) zusätzlich zu etw.; **from ~ to bottom** von oben bis unten; **at the ~:** oben; **at the ~ of the building/hill/pile/stairs** oben im Gebäude/[oben] auf dem Hügel/[oben] auf dem Stapel/oben an der Treppe
(b) (highest rank) Spitze, *die;* **~ of the table** (Sport) Tabellenspitze, *die;* **be [at the] ~ of the class** der/die Klassenbeste sein
(c) (upper surface) Oberfläche, *die;* (of cupboard, chest) Oberseite, *die;* **on ~ of sth.** [oben] auf etw. (*position: Dat.; direction: Akk.*)
(d) (folding roof) Verdeck, *das*
(e) (upper deck of bus) Oberdeck, *das*
(f) (cap of pen) [Verschluss]kappe, *die*
(g) (upper garment) Oberteil, *das*
(h) (lid) Deckel, *der;* (of bottle) Stöpsel, *der*
[2] *adj.* oberst...; höchst... ‹*Ton, Preis*›; **~ end** oberes Ende; **the ~ pupil** der beste Schüler; **~ speed** Spitzen- *od.* Höchstgeschwindigkeit, *die*
[3] *v.t.* **(a)** (be taller than) überragen
(b) (surpass) übertreffen

■ **top 'up** (Brit. coll.) *v.t.* auffüllen ‹*Tank, Flasche, Glas*›

top[2] *n.* (toy) Kreisel, *der*

top: ~-flight *attrib. adj.* erstrangig; Spitzen‹*sportler, -politiker*›; **~ 'hat** *n.* Zylinder[hut], *der;* **~-heavy** *adj.* oberlastig

topic /'tɒpɪk/ *n.* Thema, *das*

topical /'tɒpɪkl/ *adj.* aktuell

'topless *adj.* **a ~ dress/swimsuit** ein busenfreies Kleid/ein Oben-ohne-Badeanzug; **go/bathe ~:** oben ohne gehen/baden

top-level *attrib. adj.* Gipfel‹*treffen, -konferenz*›; **~-level negotiations/deals** Verhandlungen/Vereinbarungen auf höchster Ebene

topmost /'tɒpməʊst, 'tɒpməst/ *adj.* oberst...; höchst... ‹*Gipfel, Note*›

top-'notch *adj.* (coll.) fantastisch (ugs.)

topple /'tɒpl/ [1] *v.i.* fallen
[2] *v.t.* stürzen

■ **topple 'down** *v.i.* hinab-/herabfallen

■ **topple 'over** *v.i.* umfallen

top: ~-quality *adj.* [qualitativ] hochwertig; **~-ranking** *attrib. adj.* Spitzen‹*funktionär, -beamter, -politiker, -sportler*›; hochrangig ‹*Offizier*›; **~ 'secret** *adj.* streng geheim; **~soil** *n.* Mutterboden, *der*

topsy-turvy /tɒpsɪ'tɜ:vɪ/ *adv.* verkehrtrum (ugs.)

'top-up *n.* (coll.) Auffüllung, *die;* **I need a ~:** ich muss mir noch mal nachgießen/nachgießen lassen; **~ card** (for mobile phone) Aufladekarte, *die*

torch /tɔ:tʃ/ *n.* (Brit.) Taschenlampe, *die*

'torchlight *n.* Licht der/einer Taschenlampe; **by ~light** im Schein einer Taschenlampe

tore, torn ▶ TEAR[1] 2, 3

torment [1] /'tɔ:ment/ *n.* Qual, *die*
[2] /tɔ:'ment/ *v.t.* quälen

tornado /tɔ:'neɪdəʊ/ *n., pl.* **~es** Wirbelsturm, *der;* (in North America) Tornado, *der*

torpedo /tɔ:'pi:dəʊ/ [1] *n., pl.* **~es** Torpedo, *der*
[2] *v.t.* torpedieren

torrent /'tɒrənt/ *n.* reißender Bach; (fig.) Flut, *die*

torrential /tə'renʃl/ *adj.* wolkenbruchartig ‹*Regen*›

torso /'tɔ:səʊ/ *n., pl.* **~s** Rumpf, *der;* **bare ~:** nackter Oberkörper

tortoise /'tɔ:təs/ *n.* Schildkröte, *die*

tortoiseshell /'tɔ:təsʃel/ *n.* Schildpatt, *das*

tortuous /'tɔ:tjʊəs/ *adj.* verschlungen; (fig.) umständlich

torture /'tɔ:tʃə(r)/ [1] *n.* Folter, *die*
[2] *v.t.* foltern; (fig.) quälen

Tory /'tɔ:rɪ/ (Brit. Polit. coll.) *n.* Tory, *der*

toss /tɒs/ [1] *v.t.* **(a)** (throw upwards) hochwerfen; **~ a pancake** einen Pfannkuchen [durch Hochwerfen] wenden
(b) (throw casually) werfen; schmeißen (ugs.)
(c) ~ a coin eine Münze werfen

(d) (Cookery: mix) wenden; mischen ‹*Salat*›
[2] *v.i.* **(a)** ~ **and turn** sich [schlaflos] im Bett wälzen
(b) ‹*Schiff:*› hin und her geworfen werden
(c) (~ coin) eine Münze werfen; ~ **for sth.** mit einer Münze um etw. losen
[3] *n.* **(a)** ~ **of a coin** Hochwerfen einer Münze
(b) (throw) Wurf, *der*
(c) **I couldn't give a** ~ (fig. Brit. sl.) es ist mir scheißegal (salopp)

■ **toss 'up** *v.i.* eine Münze werfen; ~ **up for sth.** mit einer Münze um etw. losen

tot¹ /tɒt/ *n.* (coll.) **(a)** kleines Kind
(b) (of liquor) Gläschen, *das*

tot² (coll.) *v.t.*, **-tt-**: ~ **'up** zusammenziehen (ugs.)

total /'təʊtl/ [1] *adj.* **(a)** gesamt; Gesamt‹*gewicht, -wert, usw.*›
(b) (absolute) völlig *nicht präd.*; **a** ~ **beginner** ein absoluter Anfänger
[2] *n.* (number) Gesamtzahl, *die;* (amount) Gesamtbetrag, *der;* (result of addition) Summe, *die;* **a** ~ **of 200** insgesamt 200; **in** ~: insgesamt
[3] *v.t.*, (Brit.) **-ll-**: **(a)** addieren, zusammenzählen ‹*Zahlen*›
(b) (amount to) [insgesamt] betragen

total e'clipse *n.* (Astron.) totale Finsternis

totalitarian /təʊtælɪ'teərɪən/ *adj.* totalitär

'totally *adv.* völlig

totter /'tɒtə(r)/ *v.i.* wanken; taumeln

touch /tʌtʃ/ [1] *v.t.* **(a)** berühren
(b) (harm) anrühren
(c) (fig.: rival) ~ **sth.** an etw. (*Akk.*) heranreichen
(d) (affect emotionally) rühren
[2] *v.i.* sich berühren; **don't** ~! nicht anfassen!
[3] *n.* **(a)** Berührung, *die*
(b) *no art.* (faculty) [**sense of**] ~: Tastsinn, *der*
(c) (small amount) **a** ~ **of salt/pepper** *etc.* eine Spur Salz/Pfeffer *usw.*; **a** ~ **of irony** *etc.* ein Anflug von Ironie *usw.*
(d) (fig.) Detail, *das*
(e) (communication) **be in/out of** ~ [**with sb.**] [mit jmdm.] Kontakt/keinen Kontakt haben; **get in** ~: mit jmdm. Kontakt aufnehmen

■ **touch 'down** *v.i.* ‹*Flugzeug:*› landen

■ **'touch on** *v.t.* (mention) ansprechen

■ **touch 'up** *v.t.* (improve) ausbessern

'touch: **~-and-go** *adj.* **it is ~-and-go** [**whether…**] es steht auf des Messers Schneide [, ob…]; **~down** *n.* (Aeronaut.) Landung, *die*

'touching *adj.* rührend

touch: **~line** *n.* (Footb., Rugby) Seitenlinie, *die;* **~paper** *n.* Zündpapier, *das;* (on firework) Papierlunte, *die;* **~-tone** *adj.* **a ~-tone telephone** ein Telefon mit Mehrfrequenzwahl; **~-type** *v.i.* blind schreiben; **~-typing** *n.* Blindschreiben, *das*

touchy /'tʌtʃɪ/ *adj.* empfindlich; heikel ‹*Thema*›

tough /tʌf/ *adj.* **(a)** fest ‹*Material, Stoff*›; zäh ‹*Fleisch; fachspr.: Werkstoff, Metall*›; widerstandsfähig ‹*Belag, Glas, Haut*›; strapazierfähig ‹*Kleidung*›
(b) (hardy) zäh ‹*Person*›
(c) (difficult) schwierig
(d) (severe, harsh) hart
(e) (coll.) ~ **luck** Pech, *das*

toughen /'tʌfn/ *v.t.* ~ [**up**] abhärten ‹*Person*›; verschärfen ‹*Gesetz*›

toupee, toupet /'tu:peɪ/ *n.* Toupet, *das*

tour /tʊə(r)/ [1] *n.* **(a)** [Rund]reise, *die;* Tour, *die* (ugs.)
(b) (Theatre, Sport) Tournee, *die*
(c) (of house etc.) Besichtigung, *die*
(d) ~ [**of duty**] Dienstzeit, *die*
[2] *v.i.* **(a)** ~/**go ~ing in** *or* **through a country** eine Reise *od.* (ugs.) Tour durch ein Land machen
(b) (Theatre, Sport) eine Tournee machen
[3] *v.t.* **(a)** besichtigen ‹*Stadt, Gebäude*›; ~ **a country/region** eine Reise *od.* (ugs.) Tour durch ein Land/Gebiet machen
(b) (Theatre, Sport) ~ **a country/the provinces** eine Tournee durch das Land/die Provinz machen

tour de force /tʊə də 'fɔ:s/ *n.*, *pl.* **tours de force** /tʊə də 'fɔ:s/ Glanzleistung, *die*

'tour guide *n.* Reiseführer, *der*/Reiseführerin, *die;* (book) Reiseführer, *der* (**to, of** von)

'touring holiday *n.* **have a** ~ **in a country** in den Ferien/im Urlaub durch ein Land fahren

tourism /'tʊərɪzm/ *n.* **(a)** Tourismus, *der*
(b) (operation of tours) Touristik, *die*

tourist /'tʊərɪst/ [1] *n.* Tourist, *der*/Touristin, *die*
[2] *attrib. adj.* Touristen-

tourist: ~ **agency** *n.* Reisebüro, *das;* ~ **attraction** *n.* Touristenattraktion, *die;* ~ **board** *n.* (Brit.) Amt für Fremdenverkehrswesen; ~ **class** *n.* Touristenklasse, *die;* ~ **hotel** *n.* Touristenhotel, *das;* ~ **industry** *n.* Tourismusindustrie, *die;* ~ **infor'mation centre,** ~ **office** *ns.* Fremdenverkehrsbüro, *das;* Touristeninformation, *die* (ugs.); ~ **season** *n.* Touristensaison, *die;* ~ **trade** ▸ ~ INDUSTRY

touristy /'tʊərɪstɪ/ *adj.* (derog.) auf Tourismus getrimmt (ugs.); Touristen‹*stadt, -nest, -gegend*› (ugs. abwertend)

'tour leader *n.* Reiseleiter, *der*/-leiterin, *die*

tournament /'tʊənəmənt/ *n.* (Hist.; Sport) Turnier, *das*

tourniquet /'tʊənɪkeɪ/ *n.* (Med.) Tourniquet, *das*

'tour operator *n.* Reiseveranstalter, *der*/-veranstalterin, *die*

tousle /'taʊzl/ *v.t.* zerzausen

tout /taʊt/ 1 *v.i.* **~ for customers** Kunden anreißen (ugs.) *od.* werben
2 *n.* Anreißer, *der*/Anreißerin, *die* (ugs.); **ticket ~**: Kartenschwarzhändler, *der*/ -händlerin, *die*

tow /təʊ/ 1 *v.t.* schleppen; ziehen ‹*Anhänger, Wasserskiläufer*›
2 *n.* Schleppen, *das;* **give a car a ~**: einen Wagen schleppen; **on ~**: im Schlepp[tau]
■ **tow a'way** *v.t.* abschleppen

toward /tə'wɔ:d/, **towards** /tə'wɔ:dz/ *prep.* **(a)** (in direction of) **~ sb./sth.** auf jmdn./ etw. zu; **turn ~ sb.** sich zu jmdm. umdrehen
(b) (in relation to) gegenüber; **feel sth. ~ sb.** jmdm. gegenüber etw. empfinden
(c) (for) **a contribution ~ sth.** ein Beitrag zu etw.; **proposals ~ solving a problem** Vorschläge zur Lösung eines Problems
(d) (near) gegen; **~ the end of May** [gegen] Ende Mai

'tow bar *n.* (Motor Veh.) Anhängerkupplung, *die*

towel /'taʊəl/ *n.* Handtuch, *das*

towelling (*Amer.*: **toweling**) /'taʊəlɪŋ/ *n., no indef. art.* Frottierware, *die*

'towel rail *n.* Handtuchhalter, *der*

tower /'taʊə(r)/ 1 *n.* Turm, *der*
2 *v.i.* in die Höhe ragen
■ **'tower above** *v.t.* **~ above sb./sth.** jmdn./etw. überragen

'tower block *n.* Hochhaus, *das*

'towering *attrib. adj.* hoch aufragend; (fig.) herausragend ‹*Leistung*›

town /taʊn/ *n.* Stadt, *die;* **the ~ of Cambridge** die Stadt Cambridge; **in [the] ~**: in der Stadt; **the ~** (people) die Stadt; **be in/ out of ~**: in der Stadt/nicht in der Stadt sein

town: ~ 'centre *n.* Stadtmitte, *die;* Stadtzentrum, *das;* **~ 'council** *n.* (Brit.) Stadtrat, *der;* **~ 'councillor** *n.* (Brit.) Stadtrat, *der*/-rätin, *die;* **~ 'hall** *n.* Rathaus, *das;* **~ house** *n.* (residence in ~) Stadthaus, *das;* (terrace house) Reihenhaus, *das*

townie /'taʊni:/ *n.* Stadtmensch, *der*

town: ~ 'planner *n.* Stadtplaner, *der*/ -planerin, *die;* **~ 'planning** *n.* Stadtplanung, *die*

tow: ~path *n.* Leinpfad, *der;* **~ rope** *n.* Abschleppseil, *das*

toxic /'tɒksɪk/ *adj.* giftig

toxicity /tɒk'sɪsɪtɪ/ *n.* Giftigkeit, *die*

toxic 'waste *n.* Giftmüll *der;* **~ tip** *or* **dump** Giftmülldeponie, *die*

toxin /'tɒksɪn/ *n.* Toxin, *das*

toy /tɔɪ/ 1 *n.* Spielzeug, *das;* **~s** Spielzeug, *das*
2 *adj.* Spielzeug-
3 *v.i.* **~ with the idea of doing sth.** mit dem Gedanken spielen, etw. zu tun

toy: ~ boy *n.* (coll.) Gespiele, *der* (scherzh.); **~shop** *n.* Spielwarengeschäft, *das*

trace /treɪs/ 1 *v.t.* **(a)** (copy) durchpausen; abpausen
(b) zeichnen ‹*Linie*›
(c) (follow track of) folgen (+ *Dat.*); verfolgen
(d) (find) finden
2 *n.* Spur, *die*

'trace element *n.* (Chem.) Spurenelement, *das*

'tracing paper /'treɪsɪŋ peɪpə(r)/ *n.* Pauspapier, *das*

track /træk/ 1 *n.* **(a)** Spur, *die;* (of wild animal) Fährte, *die;* **~s** (footprints) [Fuß]spuren; (of animal also) Fährte, *die;* **keep ~ of sb./sth.** jmdn./etw. im Auge behalten
(b) (path) Weg, *der;* (footpath) Pfad, *der*
(c) (Sport) Bahn, *die;* **cycling/greyhound ~**: Radrennbahn, *die*/Windhundrennbahn, *die*
(d) (Railw.) Gleis, *das*
(e) (course taken) Route, *die;* (of rocket, satellite) Bahn, *die*
2 *v.t.* **~ an animal** die Spur/Fährte eines Tieres verfolgen; **the police ~ed him [to Paris]** die Polizei folgte seiner Spur [bis nach Paris]
■ **track 'down** *v.t.* aufspüren

'trackball, 'tracker ball *ns.* (Comp.) Rollball, *der*

'track events *n. pl.* Laufwettbewerbe *Pl.*

'tracking station *n.* (Astronaut.) Bahnverfolgungsstation, *die*

'track: ~shoe *n.* Rennschuh, *der;* **~suit** *n.* Trainingsanzug, *der*

tract[1] /trækt/ *n.* (area) Gebiet, *das*

tract[2] *n.* (pamphlet) [Flug]schrift, *die*

tractor /'træktə(r)/ *n.* Traktor, *der*

trad /træd/ (Mus. coll.) *adj.* traditional (Jargon); **~ jazz** Traditional Jazz, *der*

trade /treɪd/ 1 *n.* **(a)** (line of business) Gewerbe, *das;* **he's a butcher/lawyer** *etc.* **by ~**: er ist von Beruf Metzger/Rechtsanwalt *usw.*
(b) *no indef. art* (commerce) Handel, *der*
(c) (craft) Handwerk, *das*
2 *v.i.* (buy and sell) Handel treiben
3 *v.t.* tauschen; austauschen ‹*Waren, Grüße*›; sich (*Dat.*) sagen ‹*Beleidigungen*›; **~ sth. for sth.** etw. gegen etw. tauschen
■ **trade 'in** *v.t.* in Zahlung geben
■ **trade 'up** *v.i.* sich verbessern

trade: ~ balance *n.* Handelsbilanz, *die;* **~ deficit** *n.* passive Handelsbilanz; Handelsbilanzdefizit, *das;* **~ 'discount** *n.* Branchenrabatt, *der;* **~ fair** *n.* [Fach]messe, *die;* **~ journal** *n.* Fachzeitschrift, *die;* **~ mark** *n.* Warenzeichen, *das;* **leave one's ~ mark on sth.** (fig.) einer Sache (*Dat.*) seinen Stempel aufdrücken; **~ name** *n.* Fachbezeichnung, *die;* (proprietary name) Markenname, *der;* **~ price** *n.* Einkaufspreis, *der*

'trader *n.* Händler, *der*/Händlerin, *die*

trade: ~ 'secret *n.* Geschäftsgeheimnis, *das;* **~sman** /'treɪdzmən/ *n., pl.* **~smen** /'treɪdzmən/ (shopkeeper) [Einzel]händler, *der;*

(craftsman) Handwerker, *der;* ~ **'union** *n.* Gewerkschaft, *die; attrib.* Gewerkschafts-; ~ **'unionist** *n.* Gewerkschaft[l]er, *der*/ Gewerkschaft[l]erin, *die*

trading /'treɪdɪŋ/ *n.* Handel, *der*

trading: ~ **estate** *n.* (Brit.) Gewerbegebiet, *das;* ~ **hours** *n. pl.* Geschäftszeit, *die;* **during/outside** ~ **hours** während/außerhalb der Geschäftszeit; **'Trading hours: ...'** „Geschäftszeiten: ...“; ~ **partner** *n.* Handelspartner, *der*

tradition /trə'dɪʃn/ *n.* Tradition, *die*

traditional /trə'dɪʃənl/ *adj.* traditionell; herkömmlich ‹*Erziehung, Methode*›

tra'ditionally *adv.* traditionell

traffic /'træfɪk/ [1] *n.* **(a)** *no indef. art.* Verkehr, *der*
(b) (trade) Handel, *der*
[2] *v.i.*, **-ck-**: ~ **in sth.** mit etw. handeln

traffic: ~ **calming** *n.* Verkehrsberuhigung, *die;* ~ **circle** *n.* (Amer.) Kreisverkehr, *der;* ~ **cone** *n.* Pylon, *der;* Leitkegel, *der;* ~ **island** *n.* Verkehrsinsel, *die;* ~ **jam** *n.* [Verkehrs]stau, *der*

trafficker /'træfɪkə(r)/ *n.* Händler, *der*/ Händlerin, *die;* ~ **in drugs:** Drogenhändler, *der*/-händlerin, *die*

traffic: ~ **lights** *n. pl.* [Verkehrs]ampel, *die;* ~ **police** *n.* Verkehrspolizei, *die;* ~ **report** *n.* Verkehrsübersicht, *die;* (on radio) Verkehrsservice, *der;* ~ **sign** *n.* Verkehrszeichen, *das;* ~ **signals** ▶ ~ LIGHTS; ~ **warden** *n.* (Brit.) Hilfspolizist, *der;* (woman) Hilfspolizistin, *die;* Politesse, *die*

tragedy /'trædʒɪdɪ/ *n.* Tragödie, *die*

tragic /'trædʒɪk/ *adj.* tragisch

trail /treɪl/ [1] *n.* **(a)** Spur, *die;* ~ **of smoke/dust** Rauch-/Staubfahne, *die*
(b) (Hunting) Spur, *die;* Fährte, *die*
(c) (path) Pfad, *der;* Weg, *der*
[2] *v.t.* **(a)** (pursue) verfolgen
(b) (drag) ~ **sth. [after** *or* **behind one]** etw. hinter sich (*Dat.*) herziehen
[3] *v.i.* **(a)** (be dragged) schleifen
(b) (lag) hinterhertrotten
(c) ‹*Pflanze:*› kriechen

trailer /'treɪlə(r)/ *n.* **(a)** Anhänger, *der;* (Amer.: caravan) Wohnanhänger, *der*
(b) (Cinemat., Telev.) Trailer, *der*

train /treɪn/ [1] *v.t.* **(a)** ausbilden (**in** in + *Dat.*); erziehen ‹*Kind*›; abrichten ‹*Hund*›; dressieren ‹*Tier*›
(b) (Sport) trainieren
(c) (Hort.) ziehen
[2] *v.i.* **(a)** eine Ausbildung machen; **he is ~ing as** *or* **to be a doctor/engineer** er macht eine Arzt-/Ingenieursausbildung
(b) (Sport) trainieren
[3] *n.* **(a)** (Railw.) Zug, *der;* **on the** ~: im Zug
(b) (of skirt etc.) Schleppe, *die*
(c) ~ **of thought** Gedankengang, *der*

'train driver *n.* Lokomotivführer, *der*/ -führerin, *die*

trained /treɪnd/ *adj.* ausgebildet ‹*Arbeiter, Lehrer, Arzt, Stimme*›; abgerichtet ‹*Hund*›; dressiert ‹*Tier*›; geschult ‹*Geist, Auge, Ohr*›

trainee /treɪ'ni:/ *n.* Auszubildende, *der/die*

'trainer *n.* [Konditions]trainer, *der*/ -trainerin, *die*

'train fare *n.* Fahrpreis, *der*

'training *n.* **(a)** Ausbildung, *die*
(b) (Sport) Training, *das*

training: ~ **camp** *n.* (Sport) Trainingslager, *das;* ~ **college** *n.* berufsbildende Schule; ~ **course** *n.* Lehrgang, *der;* ~ **scheme** *n.* Ausbildungsprogramm, *das;* ~ **shoes** *n. pl.* Trainingsschuhe *Pl.*

train: ~ **journey** *n.* Bahnfahrt, *die;* (long) Bahnreise, *die;* ~ **service** *n.* Zugverbindung, *die;* ~ **set** *n.* [Modell]eisenbahn, *die;* ~**spotting** *n.*: *das Aufschreiben von Lokomotivnummern als Hobby;* ~ **station** *n.* (Amer.) Bahnhof, *der*

traipse /treɪps/ *v.i.* (coll.) latschen (salopp)

■ **traipse about, traipse around** *v.i.* rumlatschen (salopp)

trait /treɪt/ *n.* Eigenschaft, *die*

traitor /'treɪtə(r)/ *n.* Verräter, *der*/ Verräterin, *die*

traitorous /'treɪtərəs/ *adj.* verräterisch

trajectory /trə'dʒektərɪ/ *n.* [Flug]bahn, *die*

tram /træm/ *n.* (Brit.) Straßenbahn, *die;* ~**lines** Straßenbahnschienen *Pl.*

tramp /træmp/ [1] *n.* Landstreicher, *der*/ -streicherin, *die;* (in city) Stadtstreicher, *der*/ -streicherin, *die*
[2] *v.i.* **(a)** (tread heavily) trampeln
(b) (walk) marschieren

trample /'træmpl/ [1] *v.t.* zertrampeln
[2] *v.i.* trampeln

■ **'trample on** *v.t.* herumtrampeln auf (+ *Dat.*)

trampoline /'træmpəli:n/ *n.* Trampolin, *das*

'tram stop *n.* Straßenbahnhaltestelle, *die*

trance /trɑ:ns/ *n.* Trance, *die;* **be in a** ~: in Trance sein

tranquil /'træŋkwɪl/ *adj.* ruhig

tranquillity /træŋ'kwɪlɪtɪ/ Ruhe, *die*

tranquillizer /'træŋkwɪlaɪzə(r)/ *n.* Beruhigungsmittel, *das*

transact /træn'zækt/ *v.t.* ~ **business** Geschäfte tätigen

transaction /træn'zækʃn/ *n.* Geschäft, *das;* (financial) Transaktion, *die*

transatlantic /trænsət'læntɪk/ *adj.* transatlantisch

transcend /træn'send/ *v.t.* übersteigen

transcript /'trænskrɪpt/ *n.* Abschrift, *die;* (of trial) Protokoll, *das*

transfer [1] /træns'fɜ:(r)/ *v.t.*, **-rr-**: ⇢

(a) (move) verlegen (**to** nach); überweisen ‹*Geld*› (**to** auf + *Akk.*); übertragen ‹*Befugnis, Macht*› (**to** *Dat.*)
(b) übereignen ‹*Gegenstand, Grundbesitz*› (**to** *Dat.*)
(c) versetzen ‹*Arbeiter, Angestellte*›; (Footb.) transferieren
2 /træns'fɜ:(r)/ *v.i.*, **-rr-**: **(a)** (when travelling) umsteigen
(b) (change job etc.) wechseln
3 /'trænsfɜ:(r)/ *n.* **(a)** (moving) Verlegung, *die;* (of powers) Übertragung, *die* (**to** an + *Akk.*); (of money) Überweisung, *die*
(b) (of employee etc.) Versetzung, *die;* (Footb.) Transfer, *der*
(c) (picture) Abziehbild, *das*

transferable /træns'fɜ:rəbl/ *adj.* übertragbar

'transfer: ~ fee *n.* (Footb.) Ablösesumme, *die;* Transfersumme, *die* (fachspr.); **~ list** *n.* (Footb.) Transferliste, *die*

transform /træns'fɔ:m/ *v.t.* verwandeln

transformation /trænsfə'meɪʃn/ *n.* Verwandlung, *die*

trans'former *n.* (Electr.) Transformator, *der*

transfusion /træns'fju:ʒn/ *n.* (Med.) Transfusion, *die*

transient /'trænzɪənt/ *adj.* kurzlebig; vergänglich

transistor /træn'zɪstə(r)/ *n.* Transistor, *der*

transit /'trænsɪt/ *n.* **in ~**: auf der Durchreise; ‹*Waren*› auf dem Transport; **passengers in ~**: Transitreisende *Pl.*

transition /træn'sɪʒn, træn'zɪʃn/ *n.* Übergang, *der;* Wechsel, *der*

transitional /træn'zɪʃənl/ *adj.* Übergangs-

transitive /'trænsɪtɪv/ *adj.* (Ling.) transitiv

'transit lounge *n.* Transithalle, *die*

transitory /'trænsɪtərɪ/ *adj.* vergänglich; (fleeting) flüchtig

'transit passenger *n.* Transitpassagier, *der*

translate /træns'leɪt/ *v.t.* übersetzen

translation /træns'leɪʃn/ *n.* Übersetzung, *die*

translator /træns'leɪtə(r)/ *n.* Übersetzer, *der*/Übersetzerin, *die*

translucent /træns'lu:sənt/ *adj.* durchscheinend

transmission /træns'mɪʃn/ *n.* **(a)** Übertragung, *die*
(b) (Motor Veh.) Antrieb, *der;* (gearbox) Getriebe, *das*

transmit /træns'mɪt/ *v.t.*, **-tt-**: **(a)** (pass on) übersenden; übertragen
(b) durchlassen ‹*Licht*›; leiten ‹*Wärme*›

trans'mitter *n.* Sender, *der*

transparency /træns'pærənsɪ/ *n.* **(a)** Durchsichtigkeit, *die*
(b) (Photog.) Transparent, *das;* (slide) Dia, *das*

transparent /træns'pærənt/ *adj.* durchsichtig

transparently /træns'pærəntlɪ/ *adv.* offenkundig; **~ obvious** ganz offenkundig

transpire /træn'spaɪə(r)/ *v.i.* sich herausstellen; (coll.: happen) passieren

transplant **1** /træns'plɑ:nt/ *v.t.* **(a)** verpflanzen ‹*Organ*›
(b) (plant in another place) umpflanzen
2 /'trænsplɑ:nt/ *n.* (Med.) Transplantation, *die;* Verpflanzung, *die*

transport **1** /træns'pɔ:t/ *v.t.* transportieren; befördern
2 /'trænspɔ:t/ *n.* **(a)** Transport, *der;* Beförderung, *die; attrib.* Beförderungs-
(b) (means of conveyance) Verkehrsmittel, *das;* **be without ~**: kein [eigenes] Fahrzeug haben

'transport café *n.* (Brit.) Fernfahrerlokal, *das*

transpose /træns'pəʊz/ *v.t.* vertauschen; umstellen

transsexual /træns'seksjʊəl/ **1** *adj.* transsexuell
2 *n.* Transsexuelle, *der/die*

transvestite /træns'vestaɪt/ *n.* Transvestit, *der*

trap /træp/ **1** *n.* **(a)** Falle, *die;* **set** *or* **lay a ~ for an animal** eine Falle für ein Tier legen *od.* aufstellen; **set** *or* **lay a ~ for sb.** (fig.) jmdm. eine Falle stellen; **fall into a/sb.'s ~** (fig.) in die/jmdm. in die Falle gehen
(b) (sl.: mouth) Klappe, *die* (salopp)
2 *v.t.*, **-pp-**: **(a)** [in *od.* mit einer Falle] fangen ‹*Tier*›; (fig.) in eine Falle locken ‹*Person*›; **be ~ped** (fig.) in eine Falle gehen/in der Falle sitzen; **be ~ped in a cave/by the tide** in einer Höhle festsitzen/von der Flut abgeschnitten sein
(b) (confine) einschließen; einklemmen ‹*Körperteil*›

trap'door *n.* Falltür, *die*

trapeze /trə'pi:z/ *n.* Trapez, *das*

tra'peze artist *n.* Trapezkünstler, *der*/-künstlerin, *die*

trash /træʃ/ *n.* **(a)** (rubbish) Abfall, *der*
(b) (badly made thing) Mist, *der* (ugs.); (bad literature) Schund, *der* (ugs.)

trauma /'trɔ:mə/ *n., pl.* **~ta** /'trɔ:mətə/ *or* **~s** Trauma, *das*

traumatic /trɔ:'mætɪk/ *adj.* traumatisch

traumatize /'trɔ:mətaɪz/ *v.t.* traumatisieren

travel /'trævl/ **1** *n.* Reisen, *das; attrib.* Reise-
2 *v.i.*, (Brit.) **-ll-** reisen; (go in vehicle) fahren
3 *v.t.*, (Brit.) **-ll-** zurücklegen ‹*Strecke, Entfernung*›; benutzen ‹*Weg, Straße*›; **we had ~led 10 miles** wir waren 10 Meilen gefahren

■ **travel a'bout, travel a'round** *v.i.* umherreisen

travel: ~ agency *n.* Reisebüro, *das;* **~ agent** *n.* Reisebürokaufmann, *der*/-kauffrau, *die;* **~ brochure** *n.* Reiseprospekt, *der;* **~ bureau** *n.* Reisebüro, *das*

traveler, traveling (Amer.) ▶ TRAVELL-
'travel insurance *n.* Reiseversicherung, *die*
traveller /'trævlə(r)/ *n.* (Brit.) **(a)** Reisende, *der/die*
(b) *in pl.* (gypsies etc.) fahrendes Volk
'traveller's cheque *n.* Reisescheck, *der*
travelling /'trævlɪŋ/ *attrib. adj.* (Brit.) Wander‹*zirkus, -ausstellung*›
travelling: ~ clock *n.* Reisewecker, *der;* **~ 'salesman** *n.* Vertreter, *der*
travel: ~-sick *adj.* reisekrank; **~-sickness** *n.* Reisekrankheit, *die;* **~-sickness pill** *n.* Tablette gegen Reisekrankheit
trawler /'trɔːlə(r)/ *n.* [Fisch]trawler, *der*
tray /treɪ/ *n.* Tablett, *das;* (for correspondence) Ablagekorb, *der*
treacherous /'tretʃərəs/ *adj.* **(a)** treulos ‹*Person*›
(b) (deceptive) tückisch
treachery /'tretʃərɪ/ *n.* Verrat, *der*
treacle /'triːkl/ *n.* (Brit.) Sirup, *der*
tread /tred/ **1** *n.* **(a)** (of tyre, boot, etc.) Lauffläche, *die;* **2 millimetres of ~ on a tyre** 2 Millimeter Profil auf einem Reifen
(b) (sound of walking) Schritt, *der*
2 *v.i.,* **trod** /trɒd/, **trodden** /'trɒdn/ *or* **trod** treten (**in/on** in/auf + *Akk.*); (walk) gehen
3 *v.t.* **trod, trodden** *or* **trod** treten auf (+ *Akk.*); stampfen ‹*Weintrauben*›
'treadmill *n.* (lit. or fig.) Tretmühle, *die*
treason /'triːzn/ *n.* **[high] ~:** Hochverrat, *der*
treasure /'treʒə(r)/ **1** *n.* Schatz, *der;* Kostbarkeit, *die;* **art ~s** Kunstschätze *Pl.*
2 *v.t.* in Ehren halten
treasure: ~ house *n.* [wahre] Fundgrube; **~ hunt** *n.* Schatzsuche, *die*
treasurer /'treʒərə(r)/ *n.* Kassenwart, *der/* -wartin, *die*
treasury /'treʒərɪ/ *n.* **the T~:** das Finanzministerium
treat /triːt/ **1** *n.* **(a)** [besonderes] Vergnügen
(b) (entertainment) *Vergnügen, für dessen Kosten jmd. anderes aufkommt;* **lay on a special ~ for sb.** jmdm. etwas Besonderes bieten; **it's my ~:** ich lade ein
2 *v.t.* **(a)** behandeln; **~ sth. as a joke** etw. als Witz nehmen; **~ sth. with contempt** für etw. nur Verachtung haben
(b) (Med.) behandeln; **~ sb. for sth.** jmdn. wegen etw. behandeln; (before confirmation of diagnosis) jmdn. auf etw. (*Akk.*) behandeln
(c) klären ‹*Abwässer*›
(d) (provide with at own expense) einladen; **~ sb. to sth.** jmdm. etw. spendieren; **~ oneself to a new hat** sich (*Dat.*) einen neuen Hut leisten
treatise /'triːtɪs, 'triːtɪz/ *n.* Abhandlung, *die*
'treatment *n.* Behandlung, *die*
treaty /'triːtɪ/ *n.* [Staats]vertrag, *der*
treble /'trebl/ **1** *adj.* **(a)** dreifach
(b) (Brit. Mus.) **~ voice** Sopranstimme, *die*
2 *n.* **(a)** (~ quantity) Dreifache, *das*
(b) (Mus.) **he is a ~:** er singt Sopran
3 *v.t.* verdreifachen
4 *v.i.* sich verdreifachen
'treble clef *n.* (Mus.) Violinschlüssel, *der*
tree /triː/ *n.* Baum, *der*
'tree house *n.* Baumhaus, *das*
'treeless *adj.* baumlos
tree: ~-lined *adj.* von Bäumen gesäumt; **~ surgeon** *n.* Baumchirurg, *der;* **~ surgery** *n.* Baumchirurgie, *die;* **~top** *n.* [Baum]wipfel, *der;* **~ trunk** *n.* Baumstamm, *der*
trek /trek/ **1** *v.i.,* **-kk-** ziehen (**across** durch)
2 *n.* [schwierige] Reise
trellis /'trelɪs/ *n.* Gitter, *das;* (for plants) Spalier, *das*
tremble /'trembl/ *v.i.* zittern (**with** vor + *Dat.*)
trembling /'tremblɪŋ/ **1** *adj.* zitternd
2 *n.* Zittern, *das*
tremendous /trɪ'mendəs/ *adj.* gewaltig; (coll.: wonderful) großartig
tremor /'tremə(r)/ *n.* **(a)** Zittern, *das*
(b) [earth] ~: leichtes Erdbeben
trench /trentʃ/ *n.* Graben, *der;* (Mil.) Schützengraben, *der*
trench 'warfare *n.* Grabenkrieg, *der*
trend /trend/ *n.* **(a)** Trend, *der;* **upward ~:** steigende Tendenz
(b) (fashion) Mode, *die;* [Mode]trend, *der*
trendiness *n.* (Brit. coll.) modische Art
'trendsetter *n.* Trendsetter, *der*
'trendy *adj.* (Brit. coll.) modisch; Schickimicki‹*kneipe*› (ugs.)
trepidation /trepɪ'deɪʃn/ *n.* Beklommenheit, *die*
trespass /'trespəs/ *v.i.* **~ on** unerlaubt betreten ‹*Grundstück*›
'trespasser *n.* Unbefugte, *der/die*
trial /'traɪəl/ *n.* **(a)** (Law) [Gerichts]verfahren, *das;* **be on ~ [for murder]** [wegen Mordes] vor Gericht stehen
(b) (testing) Test, *der;* **employ sb. on ~:** jmdn. probeweise einstellen; **[by] ~ and error** [durch] Ausprobieren
(c) (trouble) Problem, *das*
(d) (Sport) (competition) Prüfung, *die;* (for selection) Testspiel, *das*
trial 'run *n.* (of car) Testfahrt, *die;* (fig.) Probelauf, *der*
triangle /'traɪæŋgl/ *n.* **(a)** Dreieck, *das*
(b) (Mus.) Triangel, *der od. das*
triangular /traɪ'æŋgjʊlə(r)/ *adj.* dreieckig
tribal /'traɪbl/ *adj.* Stammes-
tribalism /'traɪbəlɪzm/ *n.* Tribalismus, *der* (fachspr.)

tribe /traɪb/ *n.* Stamm, *der*
tribulation /trɪbjʊ'leɪʃn/ *n.* Kummer, *der*
tribunal /traɪ'bju:nl/ *n.* Schiedsgericht, *das*
tributary /'trɪbjʊtərɪ/ *n.* Nebenfluss, *der*
tribute /'trɪbju:t/ *n.* Tribut, *der* (**to** an + *Akk.*); **pay ~ to sb./sth.** jmdm./einer Sache den schuldigen Tribut zollen (geh.)
trice /traɪs/ *n.* **in a ~:** im Handumdrehen
trick /trɪk/ 1 *n.* **(a)** Trick, *der;* **it was all a ~:** das war [alles] nur Bluff
(b) (feat of skill etc.) Kunststück, *das;* **that should do the ~** (coll.) damit dürfte es klappen (ugs.)
(c) (knack) **get** *or* **find the ~ [of doing sth.]** den Dreh finden[, wie man etw. tut]
(d) (prank) Streich, *der;* **play a ~ on sb.** jmdm. einen Streich spielen
(e) (Cards) Stich, *der*
2 *v.t.* täuschen; hereinlegen; **~ sb. out of/into sth.** jmdm. etw. ablisten
3 *adj.* **~ photograph** Trickaufnahme, *die;* **~ question** Fangfrage, *die*
trickery /'trɪkərɪ/ *n.* [Hinter]list, *die*
trickle /'trɪkl/ *v.i.* rinnen; (in drops) tröpfeln
trickster /'trɪkstə(r)/ *n.* Schwindler, *der*/Schwindlerin, *die*
'tricky *adj.* verzwickt (ugs.)
tricycle /'traɪsɪkl/ *n.* Dreirad, *das*
tried ▸ TRY 2, 3
trifle /'traɪfl/ *n.* **(a)** (Brit. Gastron.) Trifle, *das*
(b) (thing of slight value) Kleinigkeit, *die*
trifling /'traɪflɪŋ/ *adj.* unbedeutend ‹*Angelegenheit*›; gering ‹*Wert*›
trigger /'trɪgə(r)/ 1 *n.* **(a)** (of gun) Abzug, *der;* (of machine) Drücker, *der*
(b) (fig.) Auslöser, *der*
2 *v.t.* **~ [off]** auslösen
trigonometry /trɪgə'nɒmɪtrɪ/ *n.* Trigonometrie, *die*
trilingual /traɪ'lɪŋgwəl/ *adj.* dreisprachig
trill /trɪl/ 1 *n.* Trillern, *das;* (Mus.) Triller, *der*
2 *v.i.* trillern
trillion /'trɪljən/ *n.* (million million) Billion, *die*
trilogy /'trɪlədʒɪ/ *n.* Trilogie, *die*
trim /trɪm/ 1 *v.t.,* **-mm-: (a)** schneiden ‹*Hecke*›; [nach]schneiden ‹*Haar*›; beschneiden ‹*Papier, Hecke, Budget*›
(b) (ornament) besetzen (**with** mit)
2 *adj.* proper; gepflegt ‹*Garten*›
3 *n.* **(a) be in ~** (healthy) in Form *od.* fit sein
(b) (cut) Nachschneiden, *das*
'trimming *n.* **(a)** (decorations) Verzierung, *die*
(b) *in pl.* (coll.: accompaniments) Beilagen *Pl.*; **with all the ~s** mit allem Drum und Dran (ugs.)
Trinity /'trɪnɪtɪ/ *n.* (Theol.) **the [Holy] ~:** die Heilige Dreieinigkeit
trinket /'trɪŋkɪt/ *n.* kleines, billiges Schmuckstück
trio /'tri:əʊ/ *n., pl.* **~s** Trio, *das*

trip /trɪp/ 1 *n.* **(a)** Reise, *die;* (shorter) Ausflug, *der*
(b) (coll.: drug-induced hallucinations) Trip, *der*
2 *v.i.,* **-pp-** stolpern (**on** über + *Akk.*)
■ **trip 'over** *v.t.* stolpern über (+ *Akk.*)
■ **trip 'up** 1 *v.i.* **(a)** stolpern
(b) (fig.) einen Fehler machen
2 *v.t.* **(a)** stolpern lassen
(b) (fig.) aufs Glatteis führen (fig.)
tripe /traɪp/ *n.* **(a)** Kaldaunen *Pl.*
(b) (coll.: rubbish) Quatsch, *der* (ugs.)
triple /'trɪpl/ 1 *adj.* **(a)** (threefold) dreifach
(b) (three times greater than) **~ the ...:** der/die/das dreifache ...
2 *n.* Dreifache, *das*
3 *v.i.* sich verdreifachen
4 *v.t.* verdreifachen
'triple jump *n.* (Sport) Dreisprung, *der*
triplet /'trɪplɪt/ *n.* Drilling, *der*
triplicate /'trɪplɪkət/ *n.* **in ~:** in dreifacher Ausfertigung
trip 'mileage recorder *n.* (Motor Veh.) Tageskilometerzähler, *der*
tripod /'traɪpɒd/ *n.* Dreibein, *das*
'tripper *n.* (Brit.) Ausflügler, *der*/Ausflüglerin, *die*
'tripwire *n.* Stolperdraht, *der*
trite /traɪt/ *adj.* banal
triumph /'traɪəmf, 'traɪʌmf/ 1 *n.* Triumph, *der* (**over** über + *Akk.*)
2 *v.i.* triumphieren (**over** über + *Akk.*)
triumphant /traɪ'ʌmfənt/ *adj.* **(a)** siegreich
(b) triumphierend ‹*Blick*›
trivia /'trɪvɪə/ *n. pl.* Belanglosigkeiten *Pl.*
trivial /'trɪvɪəl/ *adj.* belanglos
triviality /trɪvɪ'ælɪtɪ/ *n.* Belanglosigkeit, *die*
trivialize /'trɪvɪəlaɪz/ *v.t.* auf eine belanglose Ebene bringen
trod, trodden ▸ TREAD 2, 3
trolley /'trɒlɪ/ *n.* **(a)** (for serving food) Servierwagen, *der*
(b) [supermarket] ~: Einkaufswagen, *der*
trombone /trɒm'bəʊn/ *n.* Posaune, *die*
troop /tru:p/ 1 *n.* **(a)** *in pl.* Truppen *Pl.*
(b) (fig.) Schar, *die*
2 *v.i.* **~ in/out** hinein-/hinausströmen
troop: ~ carrier *n.* Truppentransporter, *der;* **~ship** *n.* Truppentransporter, *der*
trophy /'trəʊfɪ/ *n.* Trophäe, *die*
tropic /'trɒpɪk/ *n.* **the T~s** (Geog.) die Tropen; **the ~ of Cancer/Capricorn** (Astron., Geog.) der Wendekreis des Krebses/Steinbocks
tropical /'trɒpɪkl/ *adj.* tropisch; Tropen‹*krankheit, -kleidung*›
tropical: ~ 'medicine *n.* Tropenmedizin, *die;* **~ 'rainforest** *n.* tropischer Regenwald
trot /trɒt/ 1 *n.* (coll.) **on the ~:** hintereinander; **be on the ~:** auf Trab sein (ugs.)
2 *v.i.,* **-tt-** traben

trouble /'trʌbl/ [1] *n.* **(a)** Ärger, *der;* Schwierigkeiten *Pl.;* **there'll be ~ [if ...]** es wird Ärger geben, [wenn ...]; **what's the ~?** was ist denn?
(b) engine/brake ~: Probleme mit dem Motor/der Bremse; **suffer from heart/liver ~:** herz-/leberkrank sein
(c) (inconvenience) Mühe, *die;* **take a lot of ~:** sich (*Dat.*) sehr viel Mühe geben; **it's more ~ than it's worth** es lohnt sich nicht
(d) *in sing. or pl.* (unrest) Unruhen *Pl.*
[2] *v.t.* **(a)** (agitate) beunruhigen; **don't let it ~ you** mach dir deswegen keine Sorgen
(b) (inconvenience) stören
[3] *v.i.* (make an effort) sich bemühen

troubled /'trʌbld/ *adj.* **(a)** (worried) besorgt
(b) (restless) unruhig

trouble: ~-free *adj.* problemlos; **~maker** *n.* Unruhestifter, *der*/-stifterin, *die*

troublesome /'trʌblsəm/ *adj.* schwierig; lästig ‹*Krankheit*›

trough /trɒf/ *n.* Trog, *der*

troupe /tru:p/ *n.* Truppe, *die*

trouser /'traʊzə/**: ~ leg** *n.* Hosenbein, *das;* **~ press** *n.* Bügelpresse, *die;* Hosenbügler, *der*

trousers /'traʊzəz/ *n. pl.* **[pair of] ~:** Hose, *die*

'trouser suit *n.* (Brit.) Hosenanzug, *der*

trousseau /'tru:səʊ/ *n., pl.* **~s** *or* **~x** /'tru:səʊz/ Aussteuer, *die*

trout /traʊt/ *n., pl. same* Forelle, *die*

trout: ~ farm *n.* Forellenzuchtbetrieb, *der;* **~-fishing** *n.* Forellenfang, *der*

trowel /'traʊəl/ *n.* Kelle, *die;* (Hort.) Pflanzkelle, *die*

truant /'tru:ənt/ *n.* **play ~:** [die Schule] schwänzen (ugs.)

truce /tru:s/ *n.* Waffenstillstand, *der*

truck /trʌk/ *n.* **(a)** Last[kraft]wagen, *der;* Lkw, *der*
(b) (Brit. Railw.) offener Güterwagen

'truck driver, trucker /'trʌkə(r)/ *ns.* Lastwagenfahrer, *der*/-fahrerin, *die;* (long-distance) Fernfahrer, *der*/-fahrerin, *die*

truculent /'trʌkjʊlənt/ *adj.* aufsässig

trudge /trʌdʒ/ *v.i.* trotten; (through snow etc.) stapfen

true /tru:/ *adj.*, **~r** /'tru:ə(r)/, **~st** /'tru:ɪst/
(a) wahr; wahrheitsgetreu ‹*Bericht*›; richtig ‹*Vorteil*›; (rightly so called) eigentlich; echt, wahr ‹*Freund*›; **is it ~ that ...?** stimmt es, dass ...?; **~ to life** lebensecht
(b) (loyal) treu

truffle /'trʌfl/ *n.* Trüffel, *die od.* (*ugs.*) *der*

truism /'tru:ɪzm/ *n.* Binsenweisheit, *die*

truly /'tru:lɪ/ *adv.* **(a)** wirklich
(b) (accurately) zutreffend; **yours ~:** mit freundlichen Grüßen

trump /trʌmp/ (Cards) [1] *n.* Trumpf, *der*
[2] *v.t.* übertrumpfen

'trump card *n.* (lit. or fig.) Trumpf, *der*

trumped up /'trʌmpt ʌp/ *adj.* falsch ‹*Beschuldigung usw.*›

trumpet /'trʌmpɪt/ *n.* Trompete, *die*

'trumpeter *n.* Trompeter, *der*/ Trompeterin, *die*

truncheon /'trʌntʃn/ *n.* Schlagstock, *der*

trundle /'trʌndl/ *v.t. & i.* rollen

trunk /trʌŋk/ *n.* **(a)** (of elephant etc.) Rüssel, *der*
(b) (large box) Schrankkoffer, *der*
(c) (of tree) Stamm, *der*
(d) (of body) Rumpf, *der*
(e) (Amer.: of car) Kofferraum, *der*
(f) *in pl.* (Brit.) **[swimming] ~s** Badehose, *die*

truss /trʌs/ *n.* (Med.) Bruchband, *das*

trust /trʌst/ [1] *n.* **(a)** Vertrauen, *das;* **place** *or* **put one's ~ in sb./sth.** sein Vertrauen auf *od.* in jmdn./etw. setzen; **take sth. on ~:** etw. einfach glauben
(b) (organization managed by trustees) Treuhandgesellschaft, *die;* **[charitable] ~:** Stiftung, *die;* (association of companies) Trust, *der*
(c) (Law) **hold in ~:** treuhänderisch verwalten
[2] *v.t.* (rely on) trauen (+ *Dat.*); vertrauen (+ *Dat.*) ‹*Person*›; **~ sb. with sth.** jmdm. etw. anvertrauen
[3] *v.i.* **(a) ~ to** sich verlassen auf (+ *Akk.*)
(b) (believe) **~ in sb./sth.** auf jmdn./etw. vertrauen

trustee /trʌ'sti:/ *n.* Treuhänder, *der*/ Treuhänderin, *die*

trustful /'trʌstfl/**, 'trusting** *adjs.* vertrauensvoll

trust: ~ fund *n.* Treuhandvermögen, *das;* **~worthy** *adj.* vertrauenswürdig

truth /tru:θ/ *n., pl.* **~s** /tru:ðz, tru:θs/ Wahrheit, *die;* **tell the [whole] ~:** die [ganze] Wahrheit sagen

truthful /'tru:θfl/ *adj.* ehrlich

try /traɪ/ [1] *n.* Versuch, *der;* **have a ~ at sth./doing sth.** etw. versuchen/versuchen, etw. zu tun; **give it a ~, have a ~:** es versuchen
[2] *v.t.* **(a)** (attempt) versuchen
(b) (test usefulness of) probieren
(c) (test) auf die Probe stellen ‹*Fähigkeit, Kraft, Geduld*›
(d) (Law.: take to trial) **~ a case** einen Fall verhandeln; **~ sb. [for sth.]** jmdn. [wegen einer Sache] vor Gericht stellen
[3] *v.i.* es versuchen; **~ hard/harder** sich (*Dat.*) viel/mehr Mühe geben

■ **try 'on** *v.t.* anprobieren ‹*Kleidungsstück*›

■ **try 'out** *v.t.* ausprobieren

'trying *adj.* **(a)** (testing) schwierig
(b) (difficult to endure) anstrengend

tsar /zɑ:(r)/ *n.* (Hist.) Zar, *der*

'T-shirt *n.* T-Shirt, *das*

tub /tʌb/ *n.* Kübel, *der;* (for ice cream etc.) Becher, *der*

tuba /'tju:bə/ *n.* (Mus.) Tuba, *die*

tubby /'tʌbɪ/ *adj.* rundlich

tube /tju:b/ *n.* **(a)** (for conveying liquids etc.) Rohr, *das*
(b) (small cylinder) Tube, *die;* (for sweets, tablets) Röhrchen, *das*
(c) (Anat., Zool.) Röhre, *die*
(d) (of TV etc.) Röhre, *die*
(e) (Brit. coll.: underground railway) U-Bahn, *die*

tuber /'tju:bə(r)/ *n.* (Bot.) Knolle, *die*

tuberculosis /tju:bɜ:kjʊ'ləʊsɪs/ *n.* Tuberkulose, *die*

tube: ~ station *n.* (Brit. coll.) U-Bahnhof, *der;* **~ train** *n.* (Brit. coll.) U-bahn-Zug, *der*

tubing /'tju:bɪŋ/ *n.* Rohre *Pl.*

tubular /'tju:bjʊlə(r)/ *adj.* röhrenförmig

tuck /tʌk/ [1] *v.t.* stecken
[2] *n.* (in fabric) (for decoration) Biese, *die;* (to tighten) Abnäher, *der*

▪ **tuck 'in** [1] *v.t.* hineinstecken
[2] *v.i.* (coll.) zulangen (ugs.)

▪ **tuck 'up** *v.t.* **(a)** hochkrempeln ‹*Ärmel, Hose*›; hochnehmen ‹*Rock*›
(b) (cover snugly) zudecken

Tue., Tues. *abbrs.* = **Tuesday** Di.

Tuesday /'tju:zdeɪ, 'tju:zdɪ/ *n.* Dienstag, *der; see also* FRIDAY

tuft /tʌft/ *n.* Büschel, *das*

tug /tʌg/ [1] *n.* **(a)** Ruck, *der;* **~ of war** Tauziehen, *das*
(b) ~ [boat] Schlepper, *der*
[2] *v.t.*, **-gg-** ziehen
[3] *v.i.*, **-gg-** zerren (**at** an + *Dat.*)

tuition /tju:'ɪʃn/ *n.* Unterricht, *der*

tulip /'tju:lɪp/ *n.* Tulpe, *die*

tumble /'tʌmbl/ [1] *v.i.* stürzen; fallen
[2] *n.* Sturz, *der*

tumble: ~down *adj.* verfallen; **~-drier** *n.* Wäschetrockner, *der;* **~-dry** *v.t.* im Automaten trocknen

tumbler /'tʌmblə(r)/ *n.* (short) Whiskyglas, *das;* (long) Wasserglas, *das*

tummy /'tʌmɪ/ *n.* (child lang./coll.) Bäuchlein, *das*

tummy: ~ ache *n.* (child lang./coll.) Bauchweh, *das;* **~ button** *n.* (child lang./coll.) Bauchnabel, *der;* **~ upset** *n.* (child lang./coll.) Magenverstimmung, *die*

tumour (*Brit.; Amer.:* **tumor**) /'tju:mə(r)/ *n.* Tumor, *der*

tumult /'tju:məlt/ *n.* Tumult, *der*

tuna /'tju:nə/ *n., pl. same or* **~s** Thunfisch, *der*

tune /tju:n/ [1] *n.* **(a)** (melody) Melodie, *die;* **change one's ~** (fig.) sein Verhalten ändern; **call the ~:** den Ton angeben
(b) (correct pitch) **sing in/out of ~:** richtig/falsch singen; **be in/out of ~** ‹*Instrument:*› richtig gestimmt/verstimmt sein
[2] *v.t.* **(a)** (Mus.: put in ~) stimmen
(b) (Radio, Telev.) einstellen (**to** auf + *Akk.*)
(c) einstellen ‹*Motor, Vergaser*›

tune 'in *v.i.* (Radio, Telev.) **~ to a station** einen Sender einstellen

tuneful /'tju:nfl/ *adj.* melodisch

tuner /'tju:nə(r)/ *n.* **(a)** (Mus.) Stimmer, *der*/Stimmerin, *die*
(b) (radio) Tuner, *der*

tunic /'tju:nɪk/ *n.* (of soldier) Uniformjacke, *die;* (of schoolgirl) Kittel, *der*

'tuning fork /'tju:nɪŋfɔ:k/ *n.* Stimmgabel, *die*

Tunisia /tju:'nɪzɪə/ *pr. n.* Tunesien (*das*)

tunnel /'tʌnl/ [1] *n.* Tunnel, *der;* (dug by animal) Gang, *der*
[2] *v.i.*, (Brit.) **-ll-** einen Tunnel graben

turban /'tɜ:bən/ *n.* Turban, *der*

turbine /'tɜ:baɪn/ *n.* Turbine, *die*

turbocharged /'tɜ:bəutʃɑ:dʒd/ *adj.* mit Turbolader *nachgestellt*

turbot /'tɜ:bət/ *n.* Steinbutt, *der*

turbulence /'tɜ:bjʊləns/ *n.* **(a)** Aufgewühltheit, *die;* (fig.) Aufruhr, *der*
(b) (Phys.) Turbulenz, *die*

turbulent /'tɜ:bjʊlənt/ *adj.* **(a)** aufgewühlt
(b) (Phys.) turbulent

turd /tɜ:d/ *n.* (coarse) Scheißhaufen, *der* (derb)

tureen /tjʊə'ri:n/ *n.* Terrine, *die*

turf /tɜ:f/ *n., pl.* **~s** *or* **turves** /tɜ:vz/ **(a)** *no pl.* Rasen, *der*
(b) (segment) Rasenstück, *das*

▪ **turf 'out** *v.t.* (coll.) rausschmeißen (ugs.)

Turk /tɜ:k/ *n.* Türke, *der*/Türkin, *die*

turkey *n.* Truthahn, *der*/Truthenne, *die;* (esp. as food) Puter, *der*/Pute, *die*

Turkey /'tɜ:kɪ/ *pr. n.* die Türkei

Turkish /'tɜ:kɪʃ/ [1] *adj.* türkisch; **sb. is ~:** jmd. ist Türke/Türkin
[2] *n.* Türkisch, *das; see also* ENGLISH 2A

turmoil /'tɜ:mɔɪl/ *n.* Aufruhr, *der*

turn /tɜ:n/ [1] *n.* **(a) it is sb.'s ~ to do sth.** jmd. ist an der Reihe, etw. zu tun; **it's your ~ [next]** du bist als Nächster/Nächste dran (ugs.) *od.* an der Reihe; **out of ~:** außer der Reihe; (fig.) an der falschen Stelle ‹*lachen*›; **take [it in] ~s** sich abwechseln
(b) (rotary motion) Drehung, *die*
(c) (change of direction) Wende, *die;* **take a ~ to the right/left, do** *or* **take a right/left ~:** nach rechts/links abbiegen; (fig.) **take a favourable ~** sich zum Guten wenden; **the ~ of the year/century** die Jahres-/Jahrhundertwende
(d) (bend) Kurve, *die;* (corner) Ecke, *die*
(e) (short performance) Nummer, *die*
(f) (service) **do sb. a good ~:** jmdm. einen guten Dienst erweisen
(g) (coll.: fright) **give sb. quite a ~:** jmdm. einen gehörigen Schrecken einjagen (ugs.)
[2] *v.t.* **(a)** (make revolve) drehen
(b) (reverse) umdrehen; wenden ‹*Pfannkuchen, Auto, Heu*›; **~ sth. upside down** *or* **on its head** (lit. or fig.) etw. auf den Kopf stellen; **~ the page** umblättern
(c) (give new direction to) drehen, wenden ‹*Kopf*›; **~ a hose/gun on sb./sth.** einen

Schlauch/ein Gewehr auf jmdn./etw. richten; ~ **one's attention/mind to sth.** sich/seine Gedanken einer Sache (*Dat.*) zuwenden
(d) ~ **sb. loose on sb./sth.** jmdn. auf jmdn./etw. loslassen
(e) (cause to become) verwandeln; ~ **the lights [down] low** das Licht dämpfen; ~ **a play/book into a film** ein Theaterstück/Buch verfilmen
(f) (shape in lathe) drechseln ‹*Holz*›; drehen ‹*Metall*›
(g) drehen ‹*Pirouette*›; schlagen ‹*Purzelbaum*›
3 *v.i.* **(a)** (revolve) sich drehen
(b) (reverse direction) ‹*Person:*› sich herumdrehen; ‹*Auto:*› wenden
(c) (take new direction) sich wenden; (~ round) sich umdrehen; ~ **to the left/right** nach links/rechts abbiegen
(d) (become) werden; ~ **[in]to sth.** zu etw. werden; (be transformed) sich in etw. (*Akk.*) verwandeln
(e) (become sour) ‹*Milch:*› sauer werden

■ **turn a'way** 1 *v.i.* sich abwenden
2 *v.t.* **(a)** (avert) abwenden
(b) (send away) wegschicken

■ **turn 'down** *v.t.* **(a)** herunterschlagen ‹*Kragen*›
(b) niedriger stellen ‹*Heizung*›; herunterdrehen ‹*Gas*›; leiser stellen ‹*Ton, Radio, Fernseher*›
(c) (reject) ablehnen; abweisen ‹*Kandidaten usw.*›

■ **turn 'in** 1 *v.t.* **(a)** nach innen drehen
(b) (hand in) abgeben
2 *v.i.* **(a)** (enter) einbiegen
(b) (coll.: go to bed) in die Falle gehen (salopp)

■ **turn 'off** 1 *v.t.* abschalten; abstellen ‹*Wasser, Gas*›; zudrehen ‹*Wasserhahn*›
2 *v.i.* abbiegen

■ **turn on** *v.t.* **(a)** /-'-/ anschalten; aufdrehen ‹*Wasserhahn, Gas*›
(b) /'--/ (attack) angreifen

■ **turn 'out** 1 *v.t.* **(a)** (expel) hinauswerfen (ugs.)
(b) (switch off) ausschalten; abdrehen ‹*Gas*›
(c) (produce) produzieren
(d) (Brit.) (empty) ausräumen; leeren; (get rid of) wegwerfen
2 *v.i.* **(a)** (prove to be) **sb./sth.** ~**s out to be sth.** jmd./etw. stellt sich als jmd./etw. heraus; **everything** ~**ed out well/all right in the end** alles endete gut
(b) (appear) ‹*Fans usw.:*› erscheinen

■ **turn 'over** 1 *v.t.* umdrehen
2 *v.i.* **(a)** (tip over) umkippen; ‹*Boot:*› kentern; ‹*Auto, Flugzeug:*› sich überschlagen
(b) (from one side to the other) sich umdrehen
(c) (~ a page) umblättern

■ **turn 'round** *v.i.* sich umdrehen

■ **'turn to** *v.t.* (fig.) ~ **to sb.** sich an jmdn. wenden; ~ **to sb. for help/advice** bei jmdm. Hilfe/Rat suchen; ~ **to drink** sich in den Alkohol flüchten

■ **turn 'up** 1 *v.i.* **(a)** ‹*Person:*› erscheinen
(b) (present itself) auftauchen; ‹*Gelegenheit:*› sich bieten
2 *v.t.* **(a)** hochschlagen ‹*Kragen*›
(b) lauter stellen ‹*Ton, Radio, Fernseher*›; aufdrehen ‹*Heizung, Gas*›; heller machen ‹*Licht*›

'turnaround *n.* **(a)** (change) [Kehrt]wende, *die*
(b) (of aircraft, ship, vehicle) Abfertigung, *die*

turned-up /'tɜ:ndʌp/ *adj.* ~ **nose** Stupsnase, *die* (ugs.)

'turning *n.* Abzweigung, *die*

'turning point *n.* Wendepunkt, *der*

turnip /'tɜ:nɪp/ *n.* [weiße] Rübe

turn: ~**out** *n.* (of people) Beteiligung, *die* (for an + *Dat.*); ~**over** *n.* **(a)** (Commerc.) Umsatz, *der;* (of stock) Umschlag, *der;* **(b)** (of staff) Fluktuation, *die;* ~**pike** *n.* (Amer.) gebührenpflichtige Autobahn; ~**stile** *n.* Drehkreuz, *das;* ~**table** *n.* Plattenteller, *der;* ~**-up** *n.* (Brit. Fashion) Aufschlag, *der*

turpentine /'tɜ:pntaɪn/ *n.* Terpentin, *das*

turps /tɜ:ps/ *n.* (coll.) Terpentin, *das* (ugs.)

turquoise /'tɜ:kwɔɪz/ 1 *n.* **(a)** Türkis, *der*
(b) (colour) Türkis, *das*
2 *adj.* türkis[farben]

turret /'tʌrɪt/ *n.* Türmchen, *das*

turreted /'tʌrɪtɪd/ *adj.* ‹*Schloss*› mit Mauertürmchen

turtle /'tɜ:tl/ *n.* **(a)** Meeresschildkröte, *die*
(b) (Amer.: freshwater reptile) Wasserschildkröte, *die*

'turtleneck *n.* ~**neck pullover** Pullover mit Stehbund

turves ▸ TURF B

tusk /tʌsk/ *n.* Stoßzahn, *der*

tussle /'tʌsl/ 1 *n.* Gerangel, *das* (ugs.)
2 *v.i.* sich balgen

tutor /'tju:tə(r)/ *n.* **[private]** ~: [Privat]lehrer, *der*/-lehrerin, *die*

tut[-tut] /tʌt('tʌt)/ 1 *int.* na[, na]
2 *v.i.*, **-tt-:** ~ **[with disapproval]** [missbilligend] „na, na!" sagen

tutu /'tu:tu:/ *n.* Tutu, *das*

tuxedo /tʌk'si:dəʊ/ *n., pl.* ~**s** *or* ~**es** (Amer.) Smoking, *der*

TV /ti:'vi:/ *n.* **(a)** Fernsehen, *das*
(b) (television set) Fernseher, *der* (ugs.)

twaddle /'twɒdl/ *n.* Gewäsch, *das* (ugs.)

twang /twæŋ/ 1 *v.t.* zupfen ‹*Saite*›
2 *n.* **[nasal]** ~: Näseln, *das*

tweed /twi:d/ *n.* Tweed, *der*

tweezers /'twi:zəz/ *n. pl.* **[pair of]** ~: Pinzette, *die*

twelfth /twelfθ/ 1 *adj.* zwölft...
2 *n.* (fraction) Zwölftel, *das. See also* EIGHTH

twelve /twelv/ 1 *adj.* zwölf
2 *n.* Zwölf, *die. See also* EIGHT

twentieth /'twentɪɪθ/ 1 *adj.* zwanzigst...
2 *n.* (fraction) Zwanzigstel, *das. See also* EIGHTH

twenty /ˈtwentɪ/ [1] *adj.* zwanzig
[2] *n.* Zwanzig, *die. See also* EIGHT; EIGHTY 2
twice /twaɪs/ *adv.* **(a)** zweimal
(b) (doubly) doppelt
twiddle /ˈtwɪdl/ *v.t.* herumdrehen an (+ *Dat.*) (ugs.); **~ one's thumbs** (lit. or fig.) Däumchen drehen
twig¹ /twɪg/ *n.* Zweig, *der*
twig² (coll.) [1] *v.t.*, **-gg-** kapieren (ugs.)
[2] *v.i.*, **-gg-** es kapieren (ugs.)
twilight /ˈtwaɪlaɪt/ *n.* **(a)** (evening light) Dämmerlicht, *das*
(b) (period of half-light) Dämmerung, *die*
twin /twɪn/ [1] *attrib. adj.* **(a)** Zwillings-
(b) (forming a pair) Doppel-
[2] *n.* Zwilling, *der*
[3] *v.t.* **Bottrop is ~ned with Blackpool** Bottrop und Blackpool sind Partnerstädte
twin ˈbeds *n. pl.* zwei Einzelbetten *Pl.*
twine /twaɪn/ [1] *n.* Bindfaden, *der*
[2] *v.i.* sich winden (**about, around** um)
twinge /twɪndʒ/ *n.* Stechen, *das;* **~[s] of conscience** (fig.) Gewissensbisse *Pl.*
twinkle /ˈtwɪŋkl/ [1] *v.i.* funkeln (**with** vor + *Dat.*)
[2] *n.* Funkeln, *das*
twinkling /ˈtwɪŋklɪŋ/ *n.* **in a ~, in the ~ of an eye** im Handumdrehen
ˈtwin town *n.* (Brit.) Partnerstadt, *die*
twirl /twɜːl/ [1] *v.t.* [schnell] drehen
[2] *v.i.* wirbeln (**around** über + *Akk.*)
twist /twɪst/ [1] *v.t.* **(a)** verdrehen ‹*Worte, Bedeutung*›; **~ one's ankle** sich (*Dat.*) den Knöchel verrenken; **~ sb.'s arm** jmdm. den Arm umdrehen; (fig.) jmdm. [die] Daumenschrauben anlegen
(b) (rotate) drehen
[2] *v.i.* sich winden
[3] *n.* **(a)** (motion) Drehung, *die*
(b) (unexpected occurrence) überraschende Wendung
ˈtwisted *adj.* verbogen; (fig.) verdreht (ugs. abwertend) ‹*Geist*›; verquer ‹*Humor*›
twit /twɪt/ *n.* (Brit. coll.) Trottel, *der* (ugs.)
twitch /twɪtʃ/ [1] *v.i.* ‹*Mund, Lippe:*› zucken
[2] *n.* Zucken, *das*
twitter /ˈtwɪtə(r)/ [1] *n.* Zwitschern, *das*
[2] *v.i.* zwitschern
two /tuː/ [1] *adj.* zwei
[2] *n.* Zwei, *die. See also* EIGHT
two: ~-bit *adj.* (Amer.) (of poor quality) mies (ugs.) **~-faced** /ˈtuːfeɪst/ *adj.* (fig.) falsch; **~fold** *adj., adv.* zweifach; **a ~fold increase** ein Anstieg auf das Doppelte; **~-lane** *adj.* zweispurig; **~-piece** [1] *n.* Zweiteiler, *der;* [2] *adj.* zweiteilig; **~-seater** /-ˈ--/ *n.* Zweisitzer, *der;* **~some** /ˈtuːsəm/ *n.* Paar, *das;* **~-storey** *adj.* zweigeschossig; **~-tone** *adj.* zweifarbig; **~-up ~-down** *n.* kleines [Reihen]haus; **~-way** *adj.* **(a)** zweibahnig (Verkehrsw.); **'~-way traffic ahead'** „Achtung Gegenverkehr"; **(b) ~-way mirror** Einwegspiegel, *der*
tycoon /taɪˈkuːn/ *n.* Magnat, *der*
tying ▶ TIE 1, 2
type /taɪp/ [1] *n.* **(a)** Art, *die;* (person) Typ, *der;* **what ~ of car ...?** was für ein Auto ...?
(b) (Printing) Drucktype, *die*
[2] *v.t.* [mit der Maschine] schreiben; tippen (ugs.)
[3] *v.i.* Maschine schreiben
■ **type ˈout** *v.t.* [mit der Schreibmaschine] abschreiben; abtippen (ugs.)
type: ~cast *v.t.* [auf eine bestimmte Rolle] festlegen; **~face** *n.* Schriftbild, *das;* **~script** *n.* maschine[n]geschriebene Fassung; **~setter** *n.* [Schrift]setzer, *der*/ -setzerin, *die;* **~setting** *n.* [Schrift]setzen, *das;* **~writer** *n.* Schreibmaschine, *die;* **~written** *adj.* maschine[n]geschrieben
typhoid /ˈtaɪfɔɪd/ *n.* **~ [fever]** Typhus, *der*
typhoon /taɪˈfuːn/ *n.* Taifun, *der*
typical /ˈtɪpɪkl/ *adj.* typisch (**of** für)
typify /ˈtɪpɪfaɪ/ *v.t.* **~ sth.** als typisches Beispiel für etw. dienen
typing /ˈtaɪpɪŋ/ *n.* Maschineschreiben, *das*
ˈtyping error *n.* Tippfehler, *der*
typist /ˈtaɪpɪst/ *n.* Schreibkraft, *die*
typography /taɪˈpɒgrəfɪ/ *n.* Typographie, *die*
tyrannical /tɪˈrænɪkl/ *adj.* tyrannisch
tyranny /ˈtɪrənɪ/ *n.* Tyrannei, *die*
tyrant /ˈtaɪərənt/ *n.* Tyrann, *der*
tyre /ˈtaɪə(r)/ *n.* Reifen, *der*
ˈtyre pressure *n.* Reifendruck, *der*
tzar *etc.* ▶ TSAR *etc.*

t

Uu

U, u /juː/ *n.* U, u, *das*
'U-bend *n.* U-Rohr, *das*
ubiquitous /juː'bɪkwɪtəs/ *adj.* allgegenwärtig
udder /'ʌdə(r)/ *n.* Euter, *das*
UFO /'juːfəʊ/ *n., pl.* **~s** Ufo, *das*
ugh /ʌh, ʊh, ɜːh/ *int.* bah
ugliness /'ʌglɪnɪs/ *n.* Hässlichkeit, *die*
ugly /'ʌglɪ/ *adj.* **(a)** hässlich **(b)** (nasty) übel ‹*Wunde, Laune usw.*›
UHF *abbr.* = **ultra-high frequency** UHF
UHT *abbr.* = **ultra heat-treated** ultrahoch erhitzt
UK *abbr.* = **United Kingdom**
Ukraine /juː'kreɪn/ *pr. n.* Ukraine, *die*
Ukrainian /juː'kreɪnɪən/ **1** *adj.* ukrainisch; **sb. is ~:** jmd. ist Ukrainer/Ukrainerin
2 *n.* **(a)** (person) Ukrainer, *der*/Ukrainerin, *die*
(b) (language) Ukrainisch, *das; see also* ENGLISH 2 A
ulcer /'ʌlsə(r)/ *n.* Geschwür, *das*
ulterior /ʌl'tɪərɪə(r)/ *adj.* hintergründig; **~ motive** Hintergedanke, *der*
ultimate /'ʌltɪmət/ **1** *attrib. adj.* **(a)** (final) letzt...; (eventual) endgültig ‹*Sieg*›
(b) (fundamental) tiefst...
2 *n.* **the ~ in comfort/luxury** der Gipfel an Bequemlichkeit/Luxus
'ultimately *adv.* **(a)** (in the end) schließlich **(b)** (in the last analysis) letzten Endes
ultimatum /ʌltɪ'meɪtəm/ *n., pl.* **~s** *or* **ultimata** /ʌltɪ'meɪtə/ Ultimatum, *das*
ultra'sound *n.* Ultraschall, *der*
ultra'violet *adj.* (Phys.) ultraviolett; UV- ‹*Lampe, Filter*›
umbilical cord /ʌm'bɪlɪkl kɔːd/ *n.* Nabelschnur, *die*
umbrage /'ʌmbrɪdʒ/ *n.* **take ~ [at sth.]** [an etw. (+ *Dat.*)] Anstoß nehmen
umbrella /ʌm'brelə/ *n.* [Regen]schirm, *der*
um'brella stand *n.* Schirmständer, *der*
umpire /'ʌmpaɪə(r)/ *n.* Schiedsrichter, *der*/-richterin, *die*
umpteen /ʌmp'tiːn/ *adj.* (coll.) zig (ugs.); x (ugs.)
unabashed /ʌnə'bæʃt/ *adj.* ungeniert
unable /ʌn'eɪbl/ *pred. adj.* **be ~ to do sth.** etw. nicht tun können
unabridged /ʌnə'brɪdʒd/ *adj.* ungekürzt
unac'ceptable *adj.* unannehmbar
unaccompanied /ʌnə'kʌmpənɪd/ *adj.* ohne Begleitung *nachgestellt*
unac'countable *adj.* unerklärlich
unaccountably /ʌnə'kaʊntəblɪ/ *adv.* unerklärlicherweise
unac'customed *adj.* ungewohnt; **be ~ to sth.** etw. (*Akk.*) nicht gewöhnt sein
unadulterated /ʌnə'dʌltəreɪtɪd/ *adj.* **(a)** (pure) unverfälscht
(b) (utter) völlig
unadventurous /ʌnəd'ventʃərəs/ *adj.* bieder ‹*Person*›; ereignislos ‹*Leben*›
unafraid /ʌnə'freɪd/ *adj.* **be ~ [of sb./sth.]** keine Angst [vor jmdm./etw.] haben
unaided /ʌn'eɪdɪd/ *adj.* ohne fremde Hilfe
unalike /ʌnə'laɪk/ *pred. adj.* unähnlich
unambiguous /ʌnæm'bɪgjʊəs/ *adj.* unzweideutig
unambitious /ʌnæm'bɪʃəs/ *adj.* ‹*Person*› ohne Ergeiz
unanimity /juːnə'nɪmɪtɪ/ *n.* Einmütigkeit, *die*
unanimous /juː'nænɪməs/ *adj.* einstimmig; **be ~ in doing sth.** etw. einmütig tun
u'nanimously *adv.* einstimmig
unannounced /ʌnə'naʊnst/ *adj.* unangemeldet
unappetizing /ʌn'æpɪtaɪzɪŋ/ *adj.* unappetitlich
unarmed /ʌn'ɑːmd/ *adj.* unbewaffnet; **~ combat** Kampf ohne Waffen
unassuming /ʌnə'sjuːmɪŋ/ *adj.* bescheiden
unattached /ʌnə'tætʃt/ *adj.* **(a)** nicht befestigt
(b) (without a partner) ungebunden
unat'tended *adj.* **(a) ~ to** (not dealt with) unerledigt; nicht bedient ‹*Kunde*›; nicht behandelt ‹*Patient*›
(b) (not supervised) unbewacht ‹*Parkplatz, Gepäck*›
unat'tractive *adj.* unattraktiv
unauthorized /ʌn'ɔːθəraɪzd/ *adj.* unbefugt; **no entry for ~ persons** Zutritt für Unbefugte verboten
una'vailable *adj.* nicht erhältlich ‹*Ware*›; **be ~ for comment** zur Stellungnahme nicht zur Verfügung stehen
una'voidable *adj.* unvermeidlich
unaware /ʌnə'weə(r)/ *adj.* **be ~ of sth.** sich (*Dat.*) einer Sache (*Gen.*) nicht bewusst sein
unawares /ʌnə'weəz/ *adv.* **catch sb. ~:** jmdn. überraschen

unbalanced /ʌn'bælənst/ *adj.* **(a)** unausgewogen
(b) (mentally ~) unausgeglichen

un'bearable *adj.*, **unbearably** /ʌn'beərəblɪ/ *adv.* unerträglich

unbeatable /ʌn'biː'təbl/ *adj.* unschlagbar (ugs.)

un'beaten *adj.* **(a)** ungeschlagen
(b) (not surpassed) unerreicht; ungebrochen ‹*Rekord*›

unbe'lievable *adj.* **(a)** unglaublich
(b) (tremendous) unwahrscheinlich

unbiased, unbiassed /ʌn'baɪəst/ *adj.* unvoreingenommen

unblemished /ʌn'blemɪʃt/ *adj.* makellos ‹*Haut, Ruf*›

un'block *v.t.* frei machen

un'bolt *v.t.* aufriegeln ‹*Tür*›

unborn /ʌn'bɔːn, *attrib.* 'ʌnbɔːn/ *adj.* ungeboren

un'breakable *adj.* unzerbrechlich

unburden /ʌn'bɜːdn/ *v.t.* **~ oneself** sein Herz ausschütten

un'button *v.t.* aufknöpfen

uncalled-for /ʌn'kɔːldfɔː(r)/ *adj.* unangebracht

uncanny /ʌn'kænɪ/ *adj.* unheimlich

uncared-for /ʌn'keədfɔː(r)/ *adj.* vernachlässigt

uncaring /ʌn'keərɪŋ/ *adj.* gleichgültig

unceasing /ʌn'siːsɪŋ/ *adj.* unaufhörlich

unceremonious /ʌnserɪ'məʊnɪəs/ *adj.* **(a)** (informal) formlos
(b) (abrupt) brüsk

uncere'moniously *adv.* ohne Umschweife

un'certain *adj.* **(a)** (not sure) **be ~ [whether ...]** sich (*Dat.*) nicht sicher sein[, ob ...]
(b) (not clear) ungewiss ‹*Ergebnis, Zukunft*›; **of ~ age/origin** unbestimmten Alters/ unbestimmter Herkunft
(c) (ambiguous) vage; **in no ~ terms** ganz eindeutig

uncertainty /ʌn'sɜːtntɪ/ *n.* **(a)** Ungewissheit, *die*
(b) (hesitation) Unsicherheit, *die*

unchanged /ʌn'tʃeɪndʒd/ *adj.* unverändert

uncharacteristic /ʌnkærɪktə'rɪstɪk/ *adj.* uncharakteristisch (**of** für)

un'charitable *adj.*, **uncharitably** /ʌn'tʃærɪtəblɪ/ *adv.* lieblos

un'civil *adj.* unhöflich

uncle /'ʌŋkl/ *n.* Onkel, *der*

un'comfortable *adj.* **(a)** unbequem
(b) (feeling discomfort) **be ~:** sich unbehaglich fühlen
(c) (uneasy, disconcerting) unangenehm; peinlich ‹*Stille*›

un'comfortably *adv.* unbequem; **be ~ aware of sth.** sich (*Dat.*) einer Sache peinlich bewusst sein

un'common *adj.* ungewöhnlich

uncompli'mentary *adj.* wenig schmeichelhaft

uncompromising /ʌn'kɒmprəmaɪzɪŋ/ *adj.* kompromisslos

uncon'ditional *adj.* bedingungslos ‹*Kapitulation*›; kategorisch ‹*Ablehnung*›; ‹*Versprechen*› ohne Vorbehalte

unconfirmed /ʌnkən'fɜːmd/ *adj.* unbestätigt

un'conscious [1] *adj.* **(a)** (Med.) bewusstlos
(b) (unaware) **be ~ of sth.** sich einer Sache (*Gen.*) nicht bewusst sein
(c) (not intended; Psych.) unbewusst
[2] *n.* Unbewusste, *das*

un'consciously *adv.* unbewusst

uncontrollable /ʌnkən'trəʊləbl/ *adj.* unkontrollierbar; **the child is ~:** das Kind ist nicht zu bändigen

uncon'ventional *adj.*, **uncon'ventionally** *adv.* unkonventionell

unconvinced /ʌnkən'vɪnst/ *adj.* nicht überzeugt; **remain ~:** sich nicht überzeugen lassen

uncooked /ʌn'kʊkt/ *adj.* roh

unco'operative *adj.* unkooperativ; (unhelpful) wenig hilfsbereit

uncoordinated /ʌnkəʊ'ɔːdɪneɪtɪd/ *adj.* unkoordiniert

un'cork *v.t.* entkorken

uncouth /ʌn'kuːθ/ *adj.* ungehobelt ‹*Person, Benehmen*›; grob ‹*Bemerkung*›

un'cover *v.t.* aufdecken

undaunted /ʌn'dɔːntɪd/ *adj.* unverzagt

undecided /ʌndɪ'saɪdɪd/ *adj.* **(a)** (not settled) nicht entschieden
(b) (hesitant) unentschlossen

undeclared /ʌndɪ'kleəd/ *adj.* **~ income** (for tax) nicht angegebenes Einkommen

'undelete *v.t.* (Comp.) wiederherstellen

undemanding /ʌndɪ'mɑːndɪŋ/ *adj.* anspruchslos

unde'niable *adj.*, **undeniably** /ʌndɪ'naɪəblɪ/ *adv.* unbestreitbar

under /'ʌndə(r)/ [1] *prep.* **(a)** (underneath, below) unter (*position: + Dat.; motion: + Akk.*); **from ~ the table/bed** unter dem Tisch/Bett hervor
(b) (undergoing) **~ treatment** in Behandlung; **~ repair** in Reparatur; **~ construction** im Bau
(c) (in conditions of) bei ‹*Stress, hohen Temperaturen usw.*›
(d) (subject to) unter (+ *Dat.*); **~ the terms of the contract** nach den Bestimmungen des Vertrags
(e) (with the use of) unter (+ *Dat.*); **~ an assumed name** unter falschem Namen
(f) (less than) unter (+ *Dat.*)
[2] *adv.* **(a)** (in or to a lower or subordinate position) darunter

(b) (in/into a state of unconsciousness) **be ~/put sb. ~**: in Narkose liegen/jmdn. in Narkose versetzen

under: ~a'chieve *v.i.* unter dem erreichbaren Leistungsniveau bleiben; **~-age** *adj.* minderjährig; **~carriage** *n.* Fahrwerk, *das;* **~clothes** *n. pl.*, **~clothing** *n.* ▶ UNDERWEAR; **~coat** *n.* (layer of paint) Grundierung, *die;* (paint) Grundierfarbe, *die;* **~'cover** *adj.* (disguised) getarnt; (secret) verdeckt; **~cover agent** Geheimagent, *der;* **~current** *n.* Unterströmung, *die;* (fig.) Unterton, *der;* **~'cut** *v.t.*, **~cut** unterbieten; **~dog** *n.* **(a)** (in fight) Unterlegene, *der/die;* **(b)** (fig.) Benachteiligte, *der/die;* **~'done** *adj.* halb gar; **~estimate** /ʌndər'estɪmeɪt/ **1** *v.t.* unterschätzen; **2** /ʌndər'estɪmət/ *n.* Unterschätzung, *die;* **~'fed** *adj.* unterernährt; **~'foot** *adv.* am Boden; **be trampled ~foot** mit Füßen zertrampelt werden; **~'go** *v.t.*, *forms as* GO 1: durchmachen; **~go treatment** sich einer Behandlung unterziehen; **~go a change** sich verändern; **~'graduate** *n.* **~graduate [student]** Student/Studentin vor der ersten Prüfung; **~ground** **1** /--'-/ *adv.* **(a)** unter der Erde; (Mining) unter Tage; **(b)** (fig.) (in hiding) im Untergrund; (into hiding) in den Untergrund; **2** /'---/ *adj.* unterirdisch ‹*Höhle, See*›; **~ground railway** Untergrundbahn, *die;* U-Bahn, *die;* **~ground car park** Tiefgarage, *die;* **3** /'---/ *n.* (railway) U-Bahn, *die;* **~ground station/train** U-Bahnhof, *der*/U-Bahn-Zug, *der;* **~growth** *n.* Unterholz, *das;* **~hand, ~'handed** *adj.* **(a)** (secret) heimlich; **(b)** (crafty) hinterhältig; **~lay** *n.* Unterlage, *die;* **~'lie** *v.t.*, *forms as* LIE[2]: **~lie sth.** (fig.) einer Sache (*Dat.*) zugrunde liegen; **~lying cause** eigentliche Ursache; **~'line** *v.t.* unterstreichen

underling /'ʌndəlɪŋ/ *n.* Untergebene, *der/die*

under: ~'lying ▶ UNDERLIE; **~'mine** *v.t.* **(a)** unterhöhlen; **(b)** (fig.) untergraben; unterminieren ‹*Autorität*›

underneath /ʌndə'ni:θ/ **1** *prep.* unter (*position:* + *Dat.; motion:* + *Akk.*)
2 *adv.* darunter

under: ~'nourished *adj.* unterernährt; **~'paid** *adj.* unterbezahlt; **~pants** *n. pl.* Unterhose, *die;* **~pass** *n.* Unterführung, *die;* **~'play** *v.t.* herunterspielen; **~'privileged** *adj.* unterprivilegiert; **~'rate** *v.t.* unterschätzen; **~seal** *n.* Unterbodenschutz, *der;* **~signed** /ʌndə'saɪnd/ *adj.* (esp. Law) **the ~signed** der/die Unterzeichnete/(pl.) die Unterzeichneten (Papierdt.); **~'staffed** *adj.* unterbesetzt; **be ~staffed** an Personalmangel leiden

understand /ʌndə'stænd/ **1** *v.t.*, **understood** /ʌndə'stʊd/ **(a)** verstehen; **make oneself understood** sich verständlich machen
(b) (have heard) gehört haben
(c) (take as implied) **it was understood that ...**: es wurde allgemein angenommen, dass ...
2 *v.i.*, **understood (a)** verstehen
(b) (gather, hear) **if I ~ correctly** wenn ich mich nicht irre; **he is, I ~, no longer here** er ist, wie ich höre, nicht mehr hier

understandable /ʌndə'stændəbl/ *adj.* verständlich

understandably /ʌndə'stændəblɪ/ *adv.* verständlicherweise

under'standing **1** *adj.* verständnisvoll
2 *n.* **(a)** (agreement) Verständigung, *die;* **reach an ~ with sb.** sich mit jmdm. verständigen; **on the ~ that ...**: unter der Voraussetzung, dass ...
(b) (intelligence) Verstand, *der*
(c) (insight) Verständnis, *das* (**of, for** für)

under: ~statement *n.* Untertreibung, *die;* **~study** *n.* Ersatzspieler, *der*/-spielerin, *die;* **~'take** *v.t.*, *forms as* TAKE 1: unternehmen; **~take a task** eine Aufgabe übernehmen; **~take to do sth.** sich verpflichten, etw. zu tun; **~taker** *n.* Leichenbestatter, *der*/-bestatterin, *die;* **~'taking** *n.* **(a)** (task) Aufgabe, *die;* **(b)** (pledge) Versprechen, *das;* **~tone** *n.* **in ~tones** *or* **an ~tone** mit gedämpfter Stimme; **~tone of criticism** kritischer Unterton; **~tow** *n.* Unterströmung, *die;* **~'value** *v.t.* unterbewerten; **~water** **1** /'----/ *attrib. adj.* Unterwasser-; **2** /--'--/ *adv.* unter Wasser; **~wear** *n.* Unterwäsche, *die;* **~'weight** *adj.* untergewichtig; **~world** *n.* Unterwelt, *die*

undeserved /ʌndɪ'zɜ:vd/ *adj.* unverdient

unde'sirable *adj.* unerwünscht; **it is ~ that ...**: es ist nicht wünschenswert, dass ...

undeveloped /ʌndɪ'veləpt/ *adj.* **(a)** (immature) nicht voll ausgebildet
(b) (not built on) nicht bebaut

undies /'ʌndɪz/ *n. pl.* (coll.) Unterwäsche, *die*

un'dignified *adj.* blamabel

undisciplined /ʌn'dɪsɪplɪnd/ *adj.* undiszipliniert

undiscovered /ʌndɪ'skʌvəd/ *adj.* unentdeckt

undisguised /ʌndɪs'gaɪzd/ *adj.* unverhohlen

undisturbed /ʌndɪ'stɜ:bd/ *adj.* (not interrupted) ungestört

undo /ʌn'du:/ *v.t.*, **undoes** /ʌn'dʌz/, **undoing** /ʌn'du:ɪŋ/, **undid** /ʌn'dɪd/, **undone** /ʌn'dʌn/ (unfasten) aufmachen

un'done *adj.* **(a)** (not accomplished) unerledigt
(b) (not fastened) offen

undoubted /ʌn'daʊtɪd/ *adj.* unzweifelhaft

un'doubtedly *adv.* zweifellos

un'dress **1** *v.t.* ausziehen; **get ~ed** sich ausziehen
2 *v.i.* sich ausziehen

undrinkable /ʌn'drɪŋkəbl/ *adj.* nicht trinkbar; ungenießbar
un'due *attrib. adj.* übertrieben; übermäßig
undulating /'ʌndjʊleɪtɪŋ/ *adj.* Wellen‹*linie*›; **~ country** sanfte Hügellandschaft
unduly /ʌn'dju:lɪ/ *adv.* übermäßig
undying /ʌn'daɪɪŋ/ *adj.* ewig; unsterblich ‹*Ruhm*›
unearth /ʌn'ɜ:θ/ *v.t.* **(a)** ausgraben **(b)** (fig.: discover) aufdecken
unearthly /ʌn'ɜ:θlɪ/ *adj.* unheimlich; **at an ~ hour** in aller Herrgottsfrühe
un'easy *adj.* **(a)** (anxious) besorgt; **he felt ~:** ihm war unbehaglich zumute **(b)** (restless) unruhig
uneatable /ʌn'i:təbl/ *adj.* ungenießbar
uneco'nomic *adj.* unrentabel
uneco'nomical *adj.* **~ [to run]** unwirtschaftlich
uneducated /ʌn'edjʊkeɪtɪd/ *adj.* ungebildet
unemotional /ʌnɪ'məʊʃənl/ *adj.* emotionslos; nüchtern
unemployed /ʌnɪm'plɔɪd/ **1** *adj.* arbeitslos **2** *n. pl.* **the ~:** die Arbeitslosen *Pl.*
unem'ployment *n.* Arbeitslosigkeit, *die*
unem'ployment benefit *n.* Arbeitslosengeld, *das*
un'ending *adj.* endlos
un'equal *adj.* unterschiedlich; ungleich ‹*Kampf*›; **be ~ to sth.** einer Sache (*Dat.*) nicht gewachsen sein
unequalled (*Amer.:* **unequaled**) /ʌn'i:kwld/ *adj.* unerreicht
une'quivocal *adj.* eindeutig
unerring /ʌn'ɜ:rɪŋ/ *adj.* unfehlbar
un'ethical *adj.* unmoralisch
un'even *adj.* **(a)** (not smooth) uneben **(b)** (not uniform) ungleichmäßig **(c)** (odd) ungerade ‹*Zahl*›
un'evenly *adv.* ungleichmäßig
uneventful /ʌnɪ'ventfl/ *adj.* ereignislos
unexciting /ʌnɪk'saɪtɪŋ/ *adj.* wenig aufregend; (boring) langweilig
unex'pected *adj.* unerwartet
unexplained /ʌnɪk'spleɪnd/ *adj.* ungeklärt
un'fair *adj.* unfair; ungerecht
un'fairly *adv.* **(a)** (unjustly) ungerecht; unfair ‹*spielen*› **(b)** (unreasonably) zu Unrecht
un'fairness *n.* Ungerechtigkeit, *die*
un'faithful *adj.* untreu
unfa'miliar *adj.* **(a)** (strange) unbekannt; ungewohnt ‹*Arbeit*› **(b) be ~ with sth.** sich mit etw. nicht auskennen
un'fasten *v.t.* **(a)** öffnen **(b)** (detach) lösen
un'favourable *adj.* ungünstig
un'favourably *adv.* ungünstig; **be ~ disposed towards sb./sth.** jmdm./etw. gegenüber ablehnend eingestellt sein
un'feeling *adj.* gefühllos
unfinished /ʌn'fɪnɪʃt/ *adj.* unvollendet ‹*Werk*›; unerledigt ‹*Arbeit*›
un'fit *adj.* **(a)** ungeeignet **(b)** (not physically fit) nicht fit (ugs.); **~ for military service** [wehrdienst]untauglich
un'flattering *adj.* wenig schmeichelhaft
un'flinching *adj.* unerschrocken
un'fold **1** *v.t.* entfalten; ausbreiten ‹*Zeitung, Landkarte*› **2** *v.i.* sich entfalten; (develop) sich entwickeln
unfore'seen *adj.* unvorhergesehen
unforgettable /ʌnfə'getəbl/ *adj.* unvergesslich
unforgivable /ʌnfə'gɪvəbl/ *adj.* unverzeihlich
un'fortunate *adj.* unglücklich
un'fortunately *adv.* leider
un'founded *adj.* (fig.) unbegründet
un'freeze *v.t. & i.,* **unfroze** /ʌn'frəʊz/, **unfrozen** /ʌn'frəʊzn/ auftauen
un'friendly *adj.* unfreundlich; feindlich ‹*Staat*›
unfulfilled /ʌnfʊl'fɪld/ *adj.* unerfüllt ‹*Person*›
un'furl **1** *v.t.* aufrollen; losmachen ‹*Segel*› **2** *v.i.* sich aufrollen
un'furnished *adj.* unmöbliert
ungainly /ʌn'geɪnlɪ/ *adj.* unbeholfen
ungram'matical *adj.* ungrammatisch
un'grateful *adj.* undankbar
un'happily *adv.* **(a)** unglücklich **(b)** (unfortunately) leider
un'happiness *n.* Bekümmertheit, *die*
un'happy *adj.* unglücklich; (not content) unzufrieden (**about** with); **be** *or* **feel ~ about doing sth.** Bedenken haben, etw. zu tun
un'harmed *adj.* unbeschädigt; (uninjured) unverletzt
un'healthy *adj.* ungesund
unheard-of /ʌn'hɜ:dɒv/ *adj.* (unknown) [gänzlich] unbekannt; (unprecedented) beispiellos; (outrageous) unerhört
un'helpful *adj.* wenig hilfsbereit ‹*Person*›; ‹*Bemerkung, Kritik*› die einem nicht weiterhilft
un'hook *v.t.* vom Haken nehmen; aufhaken ‹*Kleid*›
un'hurt *adj.* unverletzt
unhy'gienic *adj.* unhygienisch
unicorn /'ju:nɪkɔ:n/ *n.* Einhorn, *das*
uni'dentified *adj.* nicht identifiziert; **~ flying object** unbekanntes Flugobjekt
unification /ju:nɪfɪ'keɪʃn/ *n.* Einigung, *die*
uniform /'ju:nɪfɔ:m/ **1** *adj.* einheitlich; **be ~ in shape/size** die gleiche Form/Größe haben

[2] *n.* Uniform, *die;* **in/out of ~**: in/ohne Uniform

uniformity /juːnɪˈfɔːmɪtɪ/ *n.* Einheitlichkeit, *die*

'uniformly *adv.* einheitlich

unify /ˈjuːnɪfaɪ/ *v.t.* einigen

unilateral /juːnɪˈlætərl/ *adj.* einseitig

uni'maginable *adj.* unvorstellbar

uni'maginative *adj.* fantasielos

unim'portant *adj.* unwichtig; bedeutungslos

unimpressed /ʌnɪmˈprest/ *adj.* nicht beeindruckt

unin'habitable *adj.* unbewohnbar

unin'habited *adj.* unbewohnt

un'injured *adj.* unverletzt

uninspired /ʌnɪnˈspaɪəd/ *adj.* einfallslos; **I am/feel ~**: mir fehlt die Inspiration

uninspiring /ʌnɪnˈspaɪərɪŋ/ *adj.* langweilig

unin'telligent *adj.* nicht intelligent

unin'telligible *adj.* unverständlich

unin'tended *adj.* unbeabsichtigt

unin'tentional *adj.*, **unin'tentionally** *adv.* unabsichtlich

un'interested *adj.* desinteressiert (**in** an + *Dat.*)

un'interesting *adj.* uninteressant

uninterrupted /ʌnɪntəˈrʌptɪd/ *adj.* ununterbrochen

uninvited /ʌnɪnˈvaɪtɪd/ *adj.* ungeladen

union /ˈjuːnɪən/ *n.* **(a)** (trade ~) Gewerkschaft, *die*
(b) (Polit.) Union, *die*

Union 'Jack *n.* (Brit.) Union Jack, *der*

unique /juːˈniːk/ *adj.* einzigartig

unisex /ˈjuːnɪseks/ *adj.* Unisex‹*mantel, -kleidung*›; **~ hairdresser** Damen-und-Herren-Frisör, *der*

unison /ˈjuːnɪsən/ *n.* Unisono, *das;* **in ~**: einstimmig; **act in ~** (fig.) vereint handeln

unit /ˈjuːnɪt/ *n.* **(a)** (also Mil., Math.) Einheit, *die;* **~ of length/monetary ~**: Längen-/Währungseinheit, *die*
(b) (piece of furniture) Element, *das;* **kitchen ~**: Küchenelement, *das*

unite /juːˈnaɪt/ [1] *v.t.* vereinigen; einen, einigen ‹*Partei, Mitglieder*›
[2] *v.i.* sich vereinigen

u'nited *adj.* **(a)** (harmonious) einig
(b) (combined) gemeinsam

United: ~ 'Kingdom *pr. n.* Vereinigtes Königreich [Großbritannien und Nordirland]; **~ 'Nations** *pr. n. sing.* Vereinte Nationen *Pl.;* **~ States [of A'merica]** *pr. n. sing.* Vereinigte Staaten [von Amerika] *Pl.*

unit 'price *n.* Stückpreis, *der*

unity /ˈjuːnɪtɪ/ *n.* Einheit, *die*

universal /juːnɪˈvɜːsl/ *adj.*, **uni'versally** *adv.* allgemein

universe /ˈjuːnɪvɜːs/ *n.* Universum, *das*

university /juːnɪˈvɜːsɪtɪ/ *n.* Universität, *die; attrib.* Universitäts-

uni'versity place *n.* Studienplatz, *der*

un'just *adj.* ungerecht

unjustified /ʌnˈdʒʌstɪfaɪd/ *adj.* ungerechtfertigt

unkempt /ʌnˈkempt/ *adj.* ungepflegt

un'kind *adj.*, **un'kindly** *adv.* unfreundlich

un'kindness *n.* Unfreundlichkeit, *die*

un'known [1] *adj.* unbekannt
[2] *adv.* **~ to sb.** ohne dass jmd. davon weiß/wusste

un'lawful *adj.* ungesetzlich

unleaded /ʌnˈledɪd/ *adj.* bleifrei ‹*Benzin*›

unless /ənˈles/ *conj.* es sei denn; wenn ... nicht

un'like [1] *adj.* nicht ähnlich
[2] *prep.* **be ~ sb./sth.** jmdm./einer Sache nicht ähnlich sein; **~ him, ...**: im Gegensatz zu ihm ...

un'likely *adj.* unwahrscheinlich; **be ~ to do sth.** etw. wahrscheinlich nicht tun

un'limited *adj.* unbegrenzt

un'load *v.t.* entladen ‹*Lastwagen, Waggon*›; löschen ‹*Schiff, Schiffsladung*›; ausladen ‹*Gepäck*›

un'lock *v.t.* aufschließen

un'lucky *adj.* **(a)** unglücklich; (not successful) glücklos; **be [very] ~**: [großes] Pech haben
(b) (bringing bad luck) **an ~ number** eine Unglückszahl; **be ~**: Unglück bringen

unmanageable /ʌnˈmænɪdʒəbl/ *adj.* widerspenstig ‹*Kind, Pferd*›; unkontrollierbar ‹*Situation*›

un'manned *adj.* unbemannt

un'married *adj.* unverheiratet; ledig

un'mask *v.t.* (fig.) entlarven

unmi'stakable/ʌnmɪˈsteɪkəbl/ *adj.* deutlich; unverwechselbar ‹*Handschrift, Stimme*›

unmistakably /ʌnmɪˈsteɪkəblɪ/ *adv.* unverkennbar

un'mitigated *adj.* vollkommen; **be an ~ disaster** (coll.) eine einzige Katastrophe sein

unmotivated /ʌnˈməʊtɪveɪtɪd/ *adj.* unmotiviert

un'natural *adj.*, **un'naturally** *adv.* unnatürlich; (abnormal) nicht normal

un'necessarily *adv.*, **un'necessary** *adj.* unnötig

unnerve /ʌnˈnɜːv/ *v.t.* entnerven

unnerving /ʌnˈnɜːvɪŋ/ *adj.* entnervend

unnoticed /ʌnˈnəʊtɪst/ *adj.* unbemerkt

unobservant /ʌnəbˈzɜːvənt/ *adj.* unaufmerksam

unobserved /ʌnəbˈzɜːvd/ *adj.* unbeobachtet

unob'tainable *adj.* nicht erhältlich; **number ~** (Teleph.) kein Anschluss unter dieser Nummer

unof'ficial *adj.*, **unof'ficially** *adv.* inoffiziell

un'pack *v.t. & i.* auspacken

un'paid *adj.* unbezahlt; nicht bezahlt; **~ for** nicht bezahlt

unpalatable /ʌn'pælətəbl/ *adj.* ungenießbar

un'paralleled *adj.* beispiellos

un'pardonable *adj.* unverzeihlich

un'pleasant *adj.*, **un'pleasantly** *adv.* unangenehm

un'pleasantness *n.* (bad feeling) Verstimmung, *die*

un'plug *v.t.*, **-gg-**: **~ a lamp** den Stecker einer Lampe herausziehen

un'popular *adj.* unbeliebt ‹*Lehrer, Regierung usw.*›; unpopulär ‹*Maßnahme, Politik*› **(with** bei**)**

un'precedented *adj.* beispiellos

unpre'dictable *adj.* unberechenbar

unpre'pared *adj.* unvorbereitet

unprepos'sessing *adj.* wenig attraktiv

unpre'tentious *adj.* einfach ‹*Wein, Stil, Haus*›; bescheiden ‹*Person*›

unprincipled /ʌn'prɪnsɪpld/ *adj.* skrupellos

unprintable /ʌn'prɪntəbl/ *adj.* nicht druckreif

unpro'ductive *adj.* fruchtlos ‹*Diskussion, Nachforschung*›; unproduktiv ‹*Zeit, Arbeit*›

unpro'fessional *adj.* (contrary to standards) standeswidrig

un'profitable *adj.* unrentabel

un'promising *adj.* nicht sehr viel versprechend

unpublished /ʌn'pʌblɪʃt/ *adj.* unveröffentlicht

un'qualified *adj.* **(a)** unqualifiziert **(b)** (absolute) uneingeschränkt; voll ‹*Erfolg*›

un'questionable *adj.* unbezweifelbar ‹*Tatsache*›; unbestreitbar ‹*Recht, Ehrlichkeit*›

unquestionably /ʌn'kwestʃənəblɪ/ *adv.* ohne Frage

unquote /ʌn'kwəʊt/ *v.i.* **…, quote, …, ~:** …, Zitat, …, Ende des Zitats

unravel /ʌn'rævl/ **1** *v.t.*, (Brit.) **-ll-** entwirren; (undo) aufziehen; (fig.) **~ a mystery/the truth** ein Geheimnis enträtseln/die Wahrheit aufdecken **2** *v.i.*, (Brit.) **-ll-** sich aufziehen

un'real *adj.* unwirklich

unrea'listic *adj.* unrealistisch

un'reasonable *adj.* unvernünftig; übertrieben ‹*Ansprüche, Forderung, Preis, Kosten*›

unrecognizable /ʌn'rekəgnaɪzəbl/ *adj.* **be [absolutely** *or* **quite] ~:** [überhaupt] nicht wieder zu erkennen sein

unre'lated *adj.* **be ~:** nicht miteinander zusammenhängen; (by family) nicht verwandt sein

unrelenting /ʌnrɪ'lentɪŋ/ *adj.* unvermindert, nicht nachlassend ‹*Hitze, Kälte*›

unre'liable *adj.* unzuverlässig

unrequited /ʌnrɪ'kwaɪtɪd/ *adj.* unerwidert

unreservedly /ʌnrɪ'zɜ:vɪdlɪ/ *adv.* uneingeschränkt

unresolved /ʌnrɪ'zɒlvd/ *adj.* **(a)** (not solved) ungelöst **(b)** (undecided) **be ~:** sich [noch] nicht entschieden haben

un'rest *n.* Unruhen *Pl.*

unre'stricted *adj.* unbeschränkt; uneingeschränkt

un'ripe *adj.* unreif

un'rivalled (*Amer.:* **un'rivaled**) *adj.* unübertroffen

un'roll **1** *v.t.* aufrollen **2** *v.i.* sich aufrollen

unromantic /ʌnrə'mæntɪk/ *adj.* unromantisch

unruly /ʌn'ru:lɪ/ *adj.* ungebärdig

un'safe *adj.* nicht sicher; **feel ~:** sich unsicher fühlen

un'said *adj.* ungesagt

un'salted *adj.* ungesalzen

unsatis'factory *adj.* unbefriedigend

unsatisfying /ʌn'sætɪsfaɪɪŋ/ *adj.* unbefriedigend

un'savoury (*Amer.:* **un'savory**) *adj.* unangenehm; zweifelhaft ‹*Angelegenheit*›; unerfreulich ‹*Einzelheiten*›

unscathed /ʌn'skeɪðd/ *adj.* unversehrt

unscented /ʌn'sentɪd/ *adj.* nicht parfümiert ‹*Seife, Shampoo*›

un'screw **1** *v.t.* abschrauben **2** *v.i.* sich abschrauben lassen

un'scrupulous *adj.* skrupellos

unsecured /ʌnsɪ'kjʊəd/ *adj.* (Finance) ohne Sicherheit[en] *nachgestellt*

un'seemly *adj.* unschicklich

unself'conscious *adj.* unbefangen

un'selfish *adj.* selbstlos

un'selfishness *n.* Selbstlosigkeit, *die*

un'settled *adj.* (changeable) wechselhaft; (fig.) ruhelos ‹*Leben*›; unruhig ‹*Zeit, Land*›

un'settling *adj.* störend

unshak[e]able /ʌn'ʃeɪkəbl/ *adj.* unerschütterlich

un'shaven *adj.* unrasiert

un'sightly *adj.* unschön

un'skilled *adj.* ungelernt ‹*Arbeiter*›

un'skimmed *adj.* **~ milk** Vollmilch, *die*

un'sociable *adj.* ungesellig

unsolved /ʌn'sɒlvd/ *adj.* unaufgeklärt ‹*Verbrechen*›

unso'phisticated *adj.* einfach

un'sound *adj.* **(a)** (diseased) nicht gesund; krank
(b) baufällig ‹*Gebäude*›
(c) (ill-founded) wenig stichhaltig; nicht vertretbar ‹*Ansicht, Methode*›
(d) **of ~ mind** unzurechnungsfähig

unspeakable /ʌn'spi:kəbl/ *adj.* unbeschreiblich; (very bad) unsäglich

unspecified /ʌn'spesɪfaɪd/ *adj.* nicht näher bezeichnet

unspoken /ʌn'spəʊkn/ *adj.* ungesagt

un'stable *adj.* nicht stabil; **[mentally/emotionally] ~**: [psychisch] labil

un'steadily *adv.* unsicher

un'steady *adj.* unsicher; wackelig ‹*Leiter, Tisch*›

unstoppable /ʌn'stɒpəbl/ *adj.* unhaltbar ‹*Schuss aufs Fußballtor*›; (fig.) unaufhaltsam

un'stuck *adj.* **come ~**: sich lösen; (fig. coll.: fail) ‹*Person*:› baden gehen (ugs.) (**over** mit)

unsuc'cessful *adj.* erfolglos; **be ~**: keinen Erfolg haben

unsuc'cessfully *adv.* erfolglos

un'suitable *adj.* ungeeignet

unsu'specting *adj.* nichtsahnend

un'sweetened *adj.* ungesüßt

unsympa'thetic *adj.* wenig mitfühlend; **be ~**: kein Mitgefühl zeigen

untalented /ʌn'tæləntɪd/ *adj.* untalentiert

untenable /ʌn'tenəbl/ *adj.* unhaltbar

unthinkable /ʌn'θɪŋkəbl/ *adj.* unvorstellbar

unthinking /ʌn'θɪŋkɪŋ/ *adj.*, **un'thinkingly** *adv.* gedankenlos

un'tidily *adv.* unordentlich

un'tidiness *n.* ▶ UNTIDY: Ungepflegtheit, *die;* Unaufgeräumtheit, *die*

un'tidy *adj.* ungepflegt ‹*Äußeres, Person, Garten*›; unaufgeräumt ‹*Zimmer*›

un'tie *v.t.*, **untying** aufknüpfen ‹*Seil, Paket*›; aufbinden ‹*Knoten*›; losbinden ‹*Pferd, Boot*›

until /ən'tɪl/ **1** *prep.* bis; **~ [the] evening** bis zum Abend; **~ then** bis dahin; **not ~ [Christmas/the summer]** erst [Weihnachten/im Sommer]
2 *conj.* bis

un'timely *adj.* **(a)** ungelegen
(b) (premature) vorzeitig

un'tiring *adj.* unermüdlich

un'told *adj.* unbeschreiblich; unermesslich ‹*Reichtümer, Anzahl*›

untoward /ʌntə'wɔ:d, ʌn'təʊəd/ *adj.* ungünstig; **nothing ~ happened** es gab keine Schwierigkeiten

untranslatable /ʌntræns'leɪtəbl/ *adj.* unübersetzbar

untreated /ʌn'tri:tɪd/ *adj.* unbehandelt

un'true *adj.* unwahr; **that's ~**: das ist nicht wahr

un'trustworthy *adj.* unzuverlässig

un'truth *n.* Unwahrheit, *die*

un'truthful *adj.* verlogen

un'typical *adj.* untypisch (**of** für)

unusable /ʌn'ju:zəbl/ *adj.* unbrauchbar

unused¹ /ʌn'ju:zd/ *adj.* (new, fresh) unbenutzt; (not utilized) ungenutzt

unused² /ʌn'ju:st/ *adj.* (unaccustomed) **be ~ to sth./doing sth.** etw. (*Akk.*) nicht gewohnt sein/nicht gewohnt sein, etw. zu tun

un'usual *adj.*, **un'usually** *adv.* ungewöhnlich

unvarnished /ʌn'vɑ:nɪʃt/ *adj.* unlackiert; (fig.) ungeschminkt ‹*Wahrheit*›

un'veil *v.t.* enthüllen; (fig.) vorstellen ‹*Produkt*›; enthüllen ‹*Plan*›

un'versed *adj.* nicht bewandert (**in** in + *Dat.*)

un'wanted *adj.* unerwünscht

un'warranted *adj.* ungerechtfertigt

un'welcome *adj.* unwillkommen

un'well *adj.* unwohl; **look ~**: nicht wohl *od.* gut aussehen; **he feels ~** (poorly) er fühlt sich nicht wohl

un'wholesome *adj.* (lit. or fig.) ungesund

unwieldy /ʌn'wi:ldɪ/ *adj.* sperrig

un'willing *adj.* widerwillig; **be ~ to do sth.** etw. nicht tun wollen

un'willingly *adv.* widerwillig

unwind /ʌn'waɪnd/ **1** *v.t.*, **unwound** /ʌn'waʊnd/ abwickeln
2 *v.i.*, **unwound (a)** sich abwickeln
(b) (coll.: relax) sich entspannen

un'wise *adj.* unklug

unwitting /ʌn'wɪtɪŋ/ *adj.*, **un'wittingly** *adv.* unwissentlich

un'workable *adj.* undurchführbar ‹*Plan*›

un'worthy *adj.* unwürdig; **be ~ of sth.** einer Sache (*Gen.*) nicht würdig sein; **be ~ of sb./sth.** ‹*Verhalten*:› einer Person/Sache (*Gen.*) unwürdig sein

un'wrap *v.t.*, **-pp-** auswickeln

un'written *adj.* ungeschrieben

un'zip *v.t.*, **-pp-**: **(a) ~ a dress/bag** *etc.* den Reißverschluss eines Kleides/einer Tasche *usw.* öffnen
(b) (Comp.) entpacken ‹*Datei*›

up /ʌp/ **1** *adv.* **(a)** (to higher place) nach oben; (in lift) aufwärts; **the bird flew up to the roof** der Vogel flog aufs Dach [hinauf]; **up into the air** in die Luft [hinauf]; **up here/there** hier herauf/dort hinauf; **higher/a little way up** höher/ein kurzes Stück hinauf; **come on up!** komm [hier/weiter] herauf!
(b) (to upstairs) herauf/hinauf; nach oben
(c) (in higher place, upstairs) oben; **up here/there** hier/da oben; **the next floor up** ein Stockwerk höher
(d) (out of bed) **be up** auf sein
(e) (in price, value, amount) **prices have gone up/are up** die Preise sind gestiegen; **butter is up [by ...]** Butter ist [...] teurer ···>

(f) (as far as) **up to sth.** bis zu etw.; **up to here/there** bis hier[hin]/bis dorthin
(g) **[not] be/feel up to sth.** (capable of sth.) einer Sache (*Dat.*) [nicht] gewachsen sein/ sich einer Sache (*Dat.*) [nicht] gewachsen fühlen; **[not] be/feel up to doing sth.** [nicht] in der Lage sein/sich [nicht] in der Lage fühlen, etw. zu tun
(h) **be up to sth.** (doing) etw. anstellen (ugs.); **it is [not] up to sb. to do sth.** (sb.'s duty) es ist [nicht] jmds. Sache, etw. zu tun
(i) **be three points/games up** mit drei Punkten/Spielen vorn liegen
(j) **walk up and down** auf und ab gehen
(k) **time is up** die Zeit ist abgelaufen
2 *prep.* herauf/hinauf; **walk up the hill/road** den Berg/die Straße hinaufgehen; **walk up and down the platform** auf dem Bahnsteig auf und ab gehen; **further up the ladder/coast** weiter oben auf der Leiter/an der Küste; **live just up the road** ein Stück weiter oben in der Straße wohnen
3 *adj.* (coll.: amiss) **what's up?** was ist los? (ugs.); **something is up** irgendwas ist los (ugs.)
4 *v.t.*, **-pp-** (coll.: increase) erhöhen

'up-and-coming *adj.* (coll.) aufstrebend

'up-and-up *n.* (coll.) **be on the ~:** auf dem aufsteigenden Ast sein (ugs.)

'upbeat 1 *n.* (Mus.) Auftakt, *der*
2 *adj.* (coll.) (optimistic) optimistisch; (cheerful) fröhlich

'upbringing *n.* Erziehung, *die*

up'date *v.t.* auf den aktuellen Stand bringen

up 'front *adv.* (coll.: as down payment) im Voraus

upgrade 1 /-'-/ *v.t.* **(a)** aufwerten ‹*Stellung*›
(b) (improve) verbessern
(c) (Comp.) aufrüsten, nachrüsten ‹*Computer*›
2 /'--/ *n.* (Comp.) (act of upgrading) Nachrüsten, *die;* Erweiterung, *die;* (upgraded version) erweiterte Version; Upgrade, *der* (fachspr.)

upheaval /ʌp'hi:vl/ *n.* Aufruhr, *der;* (disturbance) Durcheinander, *das*

up'hill 1 *adj.* (fig.) **an ~ task/struggle** eine mühselige Aufgabe/ein harter Kampf
2 *adv.* bergauf

uphold *v.t.*, **upheld** unterstützen; wahren ‹*Tradition*›

upholster /ʌp'həʊlstə(r)/ *v.t.* polstern

up'holsterer *n.* Polsterer, *der*/Polsterin, *die*

up'holstery *n.* **(a)** (craft) Polster[er]handwerk, *das*
(b) (padding) Polsterung, *die*

'upkeep *n.* Unterhalt, *der*

up'lifting *adj.* erhebend

'uplighter *n.* Deckenfluter, *der*

up'load *v.t.* (Comp.) hinaufladen ‹*Datei, Daten*›

'upmarket *adj.* exklusiv

upon /ə'pɒn/ *prep.* auf (*direction:* + *Akk.; position:* + *Dat.*)

upper /'ʌpə(r)/ 1 *compar. adj.* ober...; Ober‹*grenze, -lippe, -arm usw.*›; **~ circle** oberer Rang; **~ class[es]** Oberschicht, *die;* **have/get/gain the ~ hand** die Oberhand haben/gewinnen/erhalten
2 *n.* Oberteil, *das*

upper 'deck *n.* Oberdeck, *das*

'uppermost 1 *adj.* oberst...
2 *adv.* ganz oben

'upright *adj.* aufrecht

'uprising *n.* Aufstand, *der*

'uproar *n.* Aufruhr, *der*

up'root *v.t.* [her]ausreißen; ‹*Sturm:*› entwurzeln

upset 1 /ʌp'set/ *v.t.*, **-tt-, upset (a)** (overturn) umkippen; (accidentally) umstoßen ‹*Tasse, Milch usw.*›
(b) (distress) erschüttern; (make angry) aufregen; **don't let it ~ you** nimm es nicht so schwer
(c) (make ill) **sth. ~s sb.** etw. bekommt jmdm. nicht
(d) durcheinander bringen ‹*Plan*›
2 *v.i.*, **-tt-, upset** umkippen
3 *adj.* (distressed) bestürzt; (agitated) aufgeregt; **get ~ [about/over sth.]** sich [über etw. (*Akk.*)] aufregen
4 /'ʌpset/ *n.* **(a)** (agitation) Aufregung, *die;* (annoyance) Verärgerung, *die*
(b) **stomach ~:** Magenverstimmung, *die*
(c) (upheaval) Aufruhr, *der*

up'setting *adj.* erschütternd; (sad) traurig; (annoying) ärgerlich

'upshot *n.* Ergebnis, *das*

upside 'down 1 *adv.* verkehrt herum; **turn sth. ~:** etw. auf den Kopf stellen
2 *adj.* auf dem Kopf stehend ‹*Bild*›; **be ~:** auf dem Kopf stehen

upstairs 1 /-'-/ *adv.* nach oben ‹*gehen, kommen*›; oben ‹*sein, wohnen*›
2 /'--/ *adj.* im Obergeschoss *nachgestellt*

'upstart *n.* Emporkömmling, *der*

up'stream *adv.* flussaufwärts

'uptake *n.* **be quick/slow on the ~** (coll.) schnell begreifen/schwer von Begriff sein (ugs.)

uptight /-'-, '--/ *adj.* (coll.: tense) nervös (**about** wegen)

up to 'date *adj.* **be/keep ~:** auf dem neuesten Stand sein/bleiben; **bring sth. ~:** etw. auf den neuesten Stand bringen

up-to-'date *attrib. adj.* (current) aktuell; (modern) modern

up-to-the-'minute *adj.* hochaktuell

'upturn *n.* Aufschwung, *der* (**in** *Gen.*)

upturned /'ʌptɜ:nd/ *adj.* umgedreht; **~ nose** Stupsnase, *die*

upward /'ʌpwəd/ 1 *adj.* nach oben gerichtet
2 *adv.* aufwärts ‹*sich bewegen*›; nach oben ‹*sehen, gehen*›

upwards /ˈʌpwədz/ *adv.* **(a)** ▶ UPWARD 2 **(b)** ~ **of** über (+ *Akk.*)

uranium /jʊəˈreɪnɪəm/ *n.* Uran, *das*

Uranus /ˈjʊərənəs, jʊəˈreɪnəs/ *pr. n.* (Astron.) Uranus, *der*

urban /ˈɜːbn/ *adj.* städtisch; Stadt‹*gebiet, -bevölkerung, -planung*›

urbane /ɜːˈbeɪn/ *adj.* weltmännisch

urchin /ˈɜːtʃɪn/ *n.* Strolch, *der*

urge /ɜːdʒ/ **1** *v.t.* ~ **sb. to do sth.** jmdn. drängen, etw. zu tun **2** *n.* Trieb, *der*

■ **urge ˈon** *v.t.* antreiben; (encourage) anfeuern

urgency /ˈɜːdʒənsɪ/ *n.* Dringlichkeit, *die*

urgent /ˈɜːdʒənt/ *adj.* dringend; (to be dealt with immediately) eilig; **be in ~ need of sth.** etw. dringend brauchen

ˈurgently *adv.* dringend; (immediately) eilig

urinal /jʊəˈraɪnl/ *n.* **[public]** ~: [öffentliche] Herrentoilette; Pissoir, *das*

urinary /ˈjʊərɪnərɪ/ *adj.* Harn-

urinate /ˈjʊərɪneɪt/ *v.i.* urinieren

urine /ˈjʊərɪn/ *n.* Urin, *der;* Harn, *der*

URL *abbr.* (Comp.) = **uniform resource locator** URL, *der*

urn /ɜːn/ *n.* **(a) tea/coffee** ~: Tee-/ Kaffeemaschine, *die* **(b)** (vessel) Urne, *die*

Uruguay /ˈjʊərəgwaɪ/ *pr. n.* Uruguay (*das*)

us /əs, *stressed* ʌs/ *pron.* uns; **it's us** wir sinds (ugs.)

US *abbr.* = **United States** USA

USA *abbr.* = **United States of America** USA

usage /ˈjuːzɪdʒ, ˈjuːsɪdʒ/ *n.* **(a)** Brauch, *der* **(b)** (Ling.) Sprachgebrauch, *der*

use **1** /juːs/ *n.* **(a)** Gebrauch, *der;* (of dictionary, calculator, room) Benutzung, *die;* (of word, pesticide, spice) Verwendung, *die;* **[not] be in ~:** [nicht] in Gebrauch sein; **be no longer in ~:** nicht mehr verwendet werden; **make ~ of sb./sth.** jmdn./etw. gebrauchen/(exploit) ausnutzen; **make good ~ of, turn** *or* **put to good ~:** gut nutzen ‹*Zeit, Talent, Geld*›; **put sth. to ~:** etw. verwenden **(b)** (usefulness) Nutzen, *der;* **is it of [any] ~?** ist das [irgendwie] von Nutzen?; **be [of] no ~ [to sb.]** [jmdm.] nicht nützen; **it's no ~ [doing that]** es hat keinen Sinn[, das zu tun] **(c)** (purpose) Verwendung, *die;* **have/find a ~ for sth./sb.** für etw./jmdn. Verwendung haben/finden; **have no/not much ~ for sth./sb.** etw./jmdn. nicht/kaum brauchen **2** /juːz/ *v.t.* **(a)** benutzen; nutzen ‹*Gelegenheit*›; anwenden ‹*Gewalt*›; in Anspruch nehmen ‹*Firma, Dienstleistung*›; nutzen ‹*Zeit, Gelegenheit*›; verwenden ‹*Kraftstoff, Butter, Wort*› **(b) ~d to** /ˈjuːst tə:/ **I ~d to live in London** früher habe ich in London gelebt

■ **use ˈup** *v.t.* aufbrauchen; verbrauchen ‹*Geld, Energie*›

use-by date /ˈjuːzbaɪ/ *n.* (esp. Brit.) [Mindest]haltbarkeitsdatum, *das*

used **1** *adj.* **(a)** /juːzd/ gebraucht; gestempelt ‹*Briefmarke*›; **~ car** Gebrauchtwagen, *der* **(b)** /juːst/ **~ to sth.** [an] etw. (*Akk.*) gewöhnt **2** /juːst/ ▶ USE 2B

useful /ˈjuːsfl/ *adj.* nützlich; praktisch ‹*Werkzeug*›; hilfreich ‹*Rat, Idee*›

ˈusefulness *n.* Nützlichkeit, *die*

useless /ˈjuːslɪs/ *adj.* unbrauchbar ‹*Werkzeug, Rat, Idee*›; nutzlos ‹*Wissen, Information, Protest, Anstrengung, Kampf*›; zwecklos ‹*Widerstand, Protest*›

user /ˈjuːzə(r)/ *n.* Benutzer, *der*/Benutzerin, *die*

user: ~-friendly *adj.* benutzerfreundlich; **~ group** *n.* Benutzergruppe, *die;* **~ interface** *n.* (Comp.) Benutzerschnittstelle, *die;* **~ name** *n.* (Comp.) Benutzername, *der*

usher /ˈʌʃə(r)/ **1** *n.* (in court) Gerichtsdiener, *der;* (at cinema, church) Platzanweiser, *der* **2** *v.t.* führen

■ **usher ˈin** *v.t.* hineinführen; (fig.) einläuten

usherette /ʌʃəˈret/ *n.* Platzanweiserin, *die*

USSR *abbr.* (Hist.) = **Union of Soviet Socialist Republics** UdSSR, *die*

usual /ˈjuːʒʊəl/ *adj.* üblich

usually /ˈjuːʒʊəlɪ/ *adv.* gewöhnlich

usurp /juːˈzɜːp/ *v.t.* sich (*Dat.*) widerrechtlich aneignen

utensil /juːˈtensɪl/ *n.* Utensil, *das;* **writing ~s** Schreibutensilien *Pl.*; **kitchen ~s** Küchengeräte *Pl.*

uterus /ˈjuːtərəs/ *n.* Gebärmutter, *die*

utilitarian /juːtɪlɪˈteərɪən/ *adj.* funktionell

utility /juːˈtɪlɪtɪ/ *n.* **(a)** Nutzen, *der* **(b) [public] ~:** öffentlicher Versorgungsbetrieb

uˈtility room *n.: Raum, in dem [größere] Haushaltsgeräte (z.B. Waschmaschine) installiert sind*

utilize /ˈjuːtɪlaɪz/ *v.t.* nutzen

utmost /ˈʌtməʊst/ **1** *adj.* äußerst...; größt... ‹*Höflichkeit, Eleganz, Einfachheit, Geschwindigkeit*› **2** *n.* Äußerste, *das;* **do** *or* **try one's ~ to do sth.** mit allen Mitteln versuchen, etw. zu tun

utter[1] /ˈʌtə(r)/ *adj.* völlig; vollkommen; **~ fool** Vollidiot, *der* (ugs.)

utter[2] *v.t.* **(a)** von sich geben ‹*Schrei, Seufzer*› **(b)** (say) sagen

utterance /ˈʌtərəns/ *n.* Worte *Pl.*

ˈutterly *adv.* völlig; vollkommen; äußerst ‹*dumm, lächerlich*›

'U-turn *n.* Wende [um 180°]; (fig.) Kehrtwendung, *die;* **make a ~:** wenden; **'No ~s'** „Wenden verboten"

UV *abbr.* = **ultraviolet** UV

Vv

V¹, v /viː/ *n.* V, v, *das*

V² *abbr.* = **volt[s]** V

v. *abbr.* = **versus** gg.

vacancy /'veɪkənsɪ/ *n.* **(a)** (job) freie Stelle **(b)** (room) freies Zimmer; **'vacancies'** „Zimmer frei"; **'no vacancies'** „belegt"

vacant /'veɪkənt/ *adj.* **(a)** frei; **'situations ~'** „Stellenangebote" **(b)** (mentally) leer

vacate /və'keɪt/ *v.t.* räumen

vacation /və'keɪʃn/ *n.* **(a)** (Brit. Univ.) Ferien *Pl.* **(b)** (Amer.) ▶ HOLIDAY B

vaccinate /'væksɪneɪt/ *v.t.* impfen

vaccination /væksɪ'neɪʃn/ *n.* Impfung, *die;* **have a ~:** geimpft werden

vaccine /'væksiːn/ *n.* Impfstoff, *der*

vacillate /'væsɪleɪt/ *v.i.* schwanken

vacuum /'vækjʊəm/ **1** *n.* **(a)** Vakuum, *das;* **live in a ~:** im luftleeren Raum leben **(b)** (coll.: ~ cleaner) Staubsauger, *der* (ugs.) **2** *v.t. & i.* [staub]saugen

vacuum: ~ cleaner *n.* Staubsauger, *der;* **~ flask** *n.* (Brit.) Thermosflasche, *die;* **~-packed** *adj.* vakuumverpackt

vagaries /'veɪgərɪz/ *n. pl.* Launen *Pl.*

vagina /və'dʒaɪnə/ *n.* Scheide, *die*

vagrant /'veɪgrənt/ *n.* Landstreicher, *der*/-streicherin, *die;* (in cities) Stadtstreicher, *der*/-streicherin, *die*

vague /veɪg/ *adj.* vage; verschwommen ‹*Form, Umriss*›; (absent-minded) geistesabwesend; **not have the ~st idea** *or* **notion** nicht die blasseste *od.* leiseste Ahnung haben

'vaguely *adv.* vage; entfernt ‹*bekannt sein, erinnern an*›; schwach ‹*sich erinnern*›

vain /veɪn/ *adj.* **(a)** (conceited) eitel **(b)** (useless) leer; vergeblich ‹*Hoffnung, Versuch*›; **in ~:** vergeblich

'vainly *adv.* vergebens

vale /veɪl/ *n.* (arch./poet.) Tal, *das*

valentine /'væləntaɪn/ *n.* **~ [card]** Grußkarte zum Valentinstag; **St. V~'s Day** Valentinstag, *der*

valet /'væleɪ/ *n.* Kammerdiener, *der*

valiant /'vælɪənt/ *adj.*, **'valiantly** *adv.* tapfer

valid /'vælɪd/ *adj.* **(a)** (legally acceptable) gültig; berechtigt ‹*Anspruch*› **(b)** (justifiable) stichhaltig ‹*Argument*›; triftig ‹*Grund*›; begründet ‹*Einwand, Entschuldigung*›

validate /'vælɪdeɪt/ *v.t.* rechtskräftig machen

validity /və'lɪdɪtɪ/ *n.* Gültigkeit, *die*

valley /'vælɪ/ *n.* Tal, *das*

valour (*Amer.:* **valor**) /'vælə(r)/ *n.* Tapferkeit, *die*

valuable /'væljʊəbl/ **1** *adj.* wertvoll; **be ~ to sb.** für jmdn. wertvoll sein **2** *n.* **~s** Wertsachen *Pl.*

valuation /væljʊ'eɪʃn/ *n.* Schätzung, *die*

value /'væljuː/ **1** *n.* Wert, *der;* **be of great/little/some/no ~ [to sb.]** [für jmdn.] von großem/geringem/einigem/keinerlei Nutzen sein; **know the ~ of sth.** wissen, was etw. wert ist; **something/nothing of ~:** etwas/nichts Wertvolles **2** *v.t.* schätzen

value added 'tax *n.* Mehrwertsteuer, *die*

valued /'væljuːd/ *adj.* geschätzt

'value judgement *n.* Werturteil, *das*

'valueless *adj.* wertlos

valuer /'væljʊə(r)/ *n.* Schätzer, *der;* Taxator, *der*

valve /vælv/ *n.* **(a)** Ventil, *das* **(b)** (Anat.) Klappe, *die*

vampire /'væmpaɪə(r)/ *n.* Vampir, *der*

van /væn/ *n.* **[delivery] ~:** Lieferwagen, *der*

vandal /'vændl/ *n.* Rowdy, *der*

vandalism /'vændəlɪzm/ *n.* Wandalismus, *der*

vandalize /'vændəlaɪz/ *v.t.* [mutwillig] beschädigen

vanilla /və'nɪlə/ **1** *n.* Vanille, *die* **2** *adj.* Vanille-

vanish /'vænɪʃ/ *v.i.* verschwinden

vanity /'vænɪtɪ/ *n.* Eitelkeit, *die*

'vanity bag *n.* Kosmetiktäschchen, *das*

vantage point /'vɑːntɪdʒ pɔɪnt/ *n.* Aussichtspunkt, *der*

vapour (*Brit.; Amer.:* **vapor**) /'veɪpə(r)/ *n.* Dampf, *der*

'vapour trail *n.* (Aeronaut.) Kondensstreifen, *der*

variable /ˈveərɪəbl/ *adj.* **(a)** (alterable) veränderbar; **be ~:** verändert werden können
(b) (inconsistent) unbeständig ‹*Wetter, Wind, Leistung*›; wechselhaft ‹*Wetter, Launen, Qualität*›

variance /ˈveərɪəns/ *n.* **be at ~ [with sth.]** [mit etw.] nicht übereinstimmen

variant /ˈveərɪənt/ *n.* Variante, *die*

variation /veərɪˈeɪʃn/ *n.* **(a)** (varying) Veränderung, *die;* (difference) Unterschied, *der*
(b) (variant) Variante, *die* **(of, on** *Gen.***)**

varicose vein /værɪkəʊs ˈveɪn/ *n.* Krampfader, *die*

varied /ˈveərɪd/ *adj.* unterschiedlich; abwechslungsreich ‹*Diät, Leben*›

variety /vəˈraɪətɪ/ *n.* **(a)** (diversity) Vielfältigkeit, *die;* (in diet, routine) Abwechslung, *die;* **add or give ~ to sth.** etw. abwechslungsreicher gestalten
(b) (assortment) Auswahl, *die* **(of** an + *Dat.*, von); **for a ~ of reasons** aus verschiedenen Gründen
(c) (Theatre) Varietee, *das*
(d) (form) Art, *die;* (of fruit, vegetable) Sorte, *die;* (cultivated) Züchtung, *die*

various /ˈveərɪəs/ *adj.* **(a)** *pred.* (different) verschieden; unterschiedlich
(b) *attrib.* (several) verschiedene; **at ~ times** mehrere Male

ˈvariously *adv.* unterschiedlich

varnish /ˈvɑːnɪʃ/ **1** *n.* Lasur, *die*
2 *v.t.* lasieren

vary /ˈveərɪ/ **1** *v.t.* verändern; ändern ‹*Bestimmungen, Programm, Methode, Route*›; (add variety to) abwechslungsreicher gestalten
2 *v.i.* (become different) sich ändern; ‹*Preis, Qualität:*› schwanken; (be different) unterschiedlich sein

ˈvarying *adj.* wechselnd; (different) unterschiedlich

vase /vɑːz/ *n.* Vase, *die*

vast /vɑːst/ *adj.* **(a)** (huge) riesig; weit ‹*Fläche, Meer*›
(b) (coll.: great) enorm; Riesen‹*menge, -summe*›

ˈvastly *adv.* (coll.) enorm; weitaus ‹*besser*›; weit ‹*überlegen, unterlegen*›

vat /væt/ *n.* Bottich, *der*

VAT /viːeɪˈtiː, væt/ *abbr.* = **value added tax** MwSt.

Vatican /ˈvætɪkən/ *pr. n.* Vatikan, *der*

vault¹ /vɔːlt, vɒlt/ *n.* **(a)** (Archit.) Gewölbe, *das*
(b) (in bank) Tresorraum, *der*
(c) (tomb) Gruft, *die*

vault² **1** *v.i.* sich schwingen
2 *v.t.* sich schwingen über (+ *Akk.*)
3 *n.* Sprung, *der*

VD *n.* Geschlechtskrankheit, *die*

VDU *abbr.* = **visual display unit**

veal /viːl/ *n.* Kalb[fleisch], *das; attrib.* Kalbs-

veer /vɪə(r)/ *v.i.* ‹*Auto:*› ausscheren
■ **veer aˈway, veer ˈoff** *v.i.* ‹*Auto:*› ausscheren; ‹*Fahrer, Straße:*› abbiegen

veg /vedʒ/ *n., pl. same* (coll.) Gemüse, *das*

vegan /ˈviːgən/ **1** *n.* Veganer, *der*/ Veganerin, *die*
2 *adj.* vegan

vegetable /ˈvedʒɪtəbl/ *n.* Gemüse, *das;* **fresh ~s** frisches Gemüse; *attrib.* Gemüse‹*suppe, -extrakt, -garten*›

ˈvegetable oil *n.* Pflanzenöl, *das*

vegetarian /vedʒɪˈteərɪən/ **1** *n.* Vegetarier, *der*/Vegetarierin, *die*
2 *adj.* vegetarisch; **sb. is ~:** jmd. ist Vegetarier/Vegetarierin; **eat ~ [food]** vegetarisch essen

vegetarianism /vedʒɪˈteərɪənɪzm/ *n.* Vegetarismus, *der*

vegetate /ˈvedʒɪteɪt/ *v.i.* nur noch [dahin]vegetieren

vegetation /vedʒɪˈteɪʃn/ *n.* Vegetation, *die*

veggie /ˈvedʒɪ/ (coll.) **1** *adj.* vegetarisch; **~ burger** Bratling, *der*
2 *n.* Vegetarier, *der*/Vegetarierin, *die*

vehement /ˈviːəmənt/ *adj.*, **ˈvehemently** *adv.* heftig

vehicle /ˈviːɪkl/ *n.* **(a)** Fahrzeug, *das*
(b) (fig.: medium) Vehikel, *das*

vehicular /vɪˈhɪkjʊlə(r)/ *adj.* Fahrzeug-

veil /veɪl/ **1** *n.* Schleier, *der*
2 *v.t.* verschleiern

veiled /veɪld/ *adj.* verschleiert; (fig.) versteckt

vein /veɪn/ *n.* **(a)** Vene, *die;* (any blood vessel) Ader, *die*
(b) (fig.: mood) Stimmung, *die;* **in a similar ~:** vergleichbarer Art

Velcro ® /ˈvelkrəʊ/ *n.* Klettverschluss, *der* (Wz)

velocity /vɪˈlɒsɪtɪ/ *n.* Geschwindigkeit, *die*

velvet /ˈvelvɪt/ **1** *n.* Samt, *der*
2 *adj.* aus Samt *nachgestellt;* Samt-

ˈvelvety *adj.* samtig

vendetta /venˈdetə/ *n.* Hetzkampagne, *die;* (feud) Fehde, *die*

vending machine /ˈvendɪŋ məʃiːn/ *n.* [Verkaufs]automat, *der*

vendor /ˈvendə(r)/ *n.* Verkäufer, *der*/ Verkäuferin, *die*

veneer /vɪˈnɪə(r)/ *n.* Furnier, *das*

venerable /ˈvenərəbl/ *adj.* ehrwürdig

venerate /ˈvenəreɪt/ *v.t.* verehren

veˈnereal disease *n.* (Med.) Geschlechtskrankheit, *die*

venetian blind /vɪˈniːʃn blaɪnd/ *n.* Jalousie, *die*

Venezuela /venɪˈzweɪlə/ *pr. n.* Venezuela (*das*)

vengeance /'vendʒəns/ *n.* **(a)** Rache, *die;* **take ~ [up]on sb. [for sth.]** sich an jmdm. [für etw.] rächen
(b) with a ~ (coll.) gewaltig (ugs.)

Venice /'venɪs/ *pr. n.* Venedig *(das)*

venison /'venɪsn, 'venɪzn/ *n.* Hirsch, *der;* Hirschfleisch, *das;* (roe deer) Reh[fleisch], *das*

venom /'venəm/ *n.* Gift, *das*

venomous /'venəməs/ *adj.* giftig

vent[1] /vent/ 1 *n.* **(a)** Öffnung, *die*
(b) (fig.) Ventil, *das* (fig.); **give ~ to** Luft machen (+ *Dat.*)
2 *v.t.* (fig.) Luft machen (+ *Dat.*)

vent[2] *n.* (in garment) Schlitz, *der*

ventilate /'ventɪleɪt/ *v.t.* belüften

ventilation /ventɪ'leɪʃn/ *n.* Belüftung, *die*

ventilator /'ventɪleɪtə(r)/ *n.* **(a)** Ventilator, *der*
(b) (Med.) Beatmungsgerät, *das*

ventriloquist /ven'trɪləkwɪst/ *n.* Bauchredner, *der*/-rednerin, *die*

venture /'ventʃə(r)/ 1 *n.* Unternehmung, *die*
2 *v.i.* **(a)** (dare) wagen
(b) (dare to go) sich wagen
3 *v.t.* wagen

■ **venture 'out** *v.i.* sich hinauswagen

venue /'venju:/ *n.* (Sport) [Austragungs]ort, *der;* (Mus., Theatre) [Veranstaltungs]ort, *der;* (meeting place) Treffpunkt, *der*

Venus /'vi:nəs/ *pr. n.* (Astron.) Venus, *die*

veranda[h] /və'rændə/ *n.* Veranda, *die*

verb /vɜ:b/ *n.* Verb, *das*

verbal /'vɜ:bl/ *adj.*, **verbally** /'vɜ:bəlɪ/ *adv.* **(a)** (relating to words) sprachlich
(b) (oral[ly]) mündlich

verbatim /və'beɪtɪm/ *adj., adv.* [wort]wörtlich

verbose /və'bəʊs/ *adj.* weitschweifig ‹*Roman, Autor*›; langatmig ‹*Rede, Redner*›

verdict /'vɜ:dɪkt/ *n.* Urteil, *das;* **~ of guilty/not guilty** Schuld-/Freispruch, *der;* **reach a ~**: zu einem Urteil kommen

verge /vɜ:dʒ/ *n.* **(a)** Rasensaum, *der;* (on road) Bankette, *die*
(b) (fig.) **be on the ~ of war/tears** am Rande des Krieges stehen/den Tränen nahe sein; **be on the ~ of doing sth.** kurz davor stehen, etw. zu tun

■ **'verge on** *v.t.* [an]grenzen an (+ *Akk.*)

verger /'vɜ:dʒə(r)/ *n.* Küster, *der*

verifiable /'verɪfaɪəbl/ *adj.* nachprüfbar

verification /verɪfɪ'keɪʃn/ *n.* **(a)** (check) Überprüfung, *die*
(b) (confirmation) Bestätigung, *die*

verify /'verɪfaɪ/ *v.t.* **(a)** (check) überprüfen
(b) (confirm) bestätigen

veritable /'verɪtəbl/ *adj.* richtig

vermin /'vɜ:mɪn/ *n.* Ungeziefer, *das*

vermouth /'vɜ:məθ/ *n.* Wermut[wein], *der*

vernacular /və'nækjʊlə(r)/ *n.* Landessprache, *die*

versatile /'vɜ:sətaɪl/ *adj.* vielseitig; (having many uses) vielseitig verwendbar

versatility /vɜ:sə'tɪlɪtɪ/ *n.* Vielseitigkeit, *die*

verse /vɜ:s/ *n.* **(a)** (stanza) Strophe, *die*
(b) (poetry) Lyrik, *die;* **write some ~**: einige Verse schreiben; **piece of ~**: Gedicht, *das;* **written in ~**: in Versform
(c) (in Bible) Vers, *der*

versed /vɜ:st/ *adj.* **be [well] ~ in sth.** sich in etw. (*Dat.*) [gut] auskennen

version /'vɜ:ʃn/ *n.* Version, *die;* (in another language) Übersetzung, *die;* (of vehicle, machine, tool) Modell, *das*

versus /'vɜ:səs/ *prep.* gegen

vertebra /'vɜ:tɪbrə/ *n., pl.* **~e** /'vɜ:tɪbri:/ Wirbel, *der*

vertebrate /'vɜ:tɪbrət/ *n.* Wirbeltier, *das*

vertical /'vɜ:tɪkl/ *adj.* senkrecht; **be ~**: senkrecht stehen

vertically /'vɜ:tɪkəlɪ/ *adv.* senkrecht

vertigo /'vɜ:tɪgəʊ/ *n.* Schwindel, *der*

verve /vɜ:v/ *n.* Schwung, *der*

very /'verɪ/ 1 *attrib. adj.* **(a)** (precise, exact) genau; **you're the ~ person I wanted to see** genau dich wollte ich sehen; **at the ~ moment when ...**: im selben Augenblick, als ...; **at the ~ centre** genau in der Mitte; **the ~ thing** genau das Richtige
(b) (extreme) **at the ~ back/front** ganz hinten/vorn; **at the ~ end/beginning** ganz am Ende/Anfang; **from the ~ beginning** von Anfang an; **only a ~ little** nur ein ganz kleines bisschen
(c) (mere) bloß ‹*Gedanke*›
(d) (absolute) absolut ‹*Minimum, Maximum*›; **the ~ most I can offer is ...**: ich kann allerhöchstens ... anbieten; **for the ~ last time** zum allerletzten Mal
(e) *emphat.* **before their ~ eyes** vor ihren Augen
2 *adv.* **(a)** (extremely) sehr; **it's ~ near** es ist ganz in der Nähe; **~ probably** höchstwahrscheinlich; **not ~ much** nicht sehr; **~ little** [nur] sehr wenig ‹*verstehen, essen*›; **thank you [~,] ~ much** [vielen,] vielen Dank
(b) (absolutely) aller‹*best..., -letzt..., -leichtest...*›; **at the ~ latest** allerspätestens
(c) (precisely) **the ~ same one** genau der-/die-/dasselbe

vessel /'vesl/ *n.* **(a)** (receptacle) Gefäß, *das;* **[drinking] ~**: Trinkgefäß, *das*
(b) (Naut.) Schiff, *das*

vest /vest/ 1 *n.* **(a)** (Brit.) Unterhemd, *das*
(b) (Amer.: waistcoat) Weste, *die*
2 *v.t.* **~ sb. with sth., ~ sth. in sb.** jmdm. etw. verleihen

'vested *adj.* **have a ~ interest in sth.** ein persönliches Interesse an etw. (*Dat.*) haben

vestige /'vestɪdʒ/ *n.* Spur, *die;* **not a ~ of truth** kein Fünkchen Wahrheit

vestment /'vestmənt/ *n.* [Priester]gewand, *das*
vestry /'vestrɪ/ *n.* Sakristei, *die*
vet /vet/ 1 *n.* Tierarzt, *der*/-ärztin, *die* 2 *v.t.*, **-tt-** überprüfen
veteran /'vetərən/ *n.* Veteran, *der*/ Veteranin, *die*
veteran 'car *n.* (Brit.) Veteran, *der*
veterinarian /vetərɪ'neərɪən/ *n.* (Amer.) Tierarzt, *der*/-ärztin, *die*
veterinary /'vetərɪnərɪ/ *adj.* tiermedizinisch
veterinary 'surgeon *n.* (Brit.) Tierarzt, *der*/-ärztin, *die*
veto /'vi:təʊ/ 1 *n., pl.* **~es** Veto, *das* 2 *v.t.* sein Veto einlegen gegen
vex /veks/ *v.t.* [ver]ärgern; (cause to worry) beunruhigen; **be ~ed with sb.** sich über jmdn. ärgern
vexation /vek'seɪʃn/ *n.* Verärgerung, *die*
vexed /vekst/ *adj.* **(a)** verärgert **(b) ~ question** viel diskutierte Frage
VHF *abbr.* = **Very High Frequency** UKW
via /'vaɪə/ *prep.* über (+ *Akk.*) ‹*Ort, Sender, Telefon*›; durch ‹*Eingang, Schornstein, Person*›; per ‹*Post*›
viability /vaɪə'bɪlɪtɪ/ *n.* (feasibility) Realisierbarkeit, *die*
viable /'vaɪəbl/ *adj.* (feasible) realisierbar
viaduct /'vaɪədʌkt/ *n.* Viadukt, *das od. der*
Viagra ® /vaɪ'ægrə/ *n.* Viagra, *das*
vibrant /'vaɪbrənt/ *adj.* lebensprühend ‹*Atmosphäre*›; lebhaft ‹*Farbe*›
vibrate /vaɪ'breɪt/ 1 *v.i.* vibrieren; (under strong impact) beben 2 *v.t.* vibrieren lassen
vibration /vaɪ'breɪʃn/ *n.* Vibrieren, *das;* (under strong import) Beben, *das*
vicar /'vɪkə(r)/ *n.* Pfarrer, *der*
vicarage /'vɪkərɪdʒ/ *n.* Pfarrhaus, *das*
vicarious /vɪ'keərɪəs/ *adj.* nachempfunden
vice¹ /vaɪs/ *n.* Laster, *das*
vice² *n.* (Brit.: tool) Schraubstock, *der*
vice: ~-'chairman *n.* stellvertretender Vorsitzender; **~-'president** *n.* Vizepräsident, *der*/-präsidentin, *die;* **~ squad** *n.* Sittenpolizei, *die*
vice versa /vaɪsɪ 'vɜ:sə/ *adv.* umgekehrt
vicinity /vɪ'sɪnɪtɪ/ *n.* Umgebung, *die;* **in the ~ [of a place]** in der Nähe [eines Ortes]
vicious /'vɪʃəs/ *adj.* **(a)** (malicious) böse; bösartig ‹*Tier*› **(b)** (violent) brutal
vicious 'circle *n.* Teufelskreis, *der*
'viciously *adv.* **(a)** (maliciously) boshaft **(b)** (violently) brutal
victim /'vɪktɪm/ *n.* Opfer, *das;* (of sarcasm, abuse) Zielscheibe, *die* (fig.).
victimization /vɪktɪmaɪ'zeɪʃn/ *n.* Schikanierung, *die*
victimize /'vɪktɪmaɪz/ *v.t.* schikanieren
victor /'vɪktə(r)/ *n.* Sieger, *der*/Siegerin, *die*
victorious /vɪk'tɔ:rɪəs/ *adj.* siegreich
victory /'vɪktərɪ/ *n.* Sieg, *der* (**over** über + *Akk.*); *attrib.* Sieges-
video /'vɪdɪəʊ/ 1 *adj.* Video- 2 *n., pl.* **~s** (~ recorder) Videorekorder, *der;* (~tape, ~ recording) Video, *das* (ugs.) 3 *v.t.* ▸ VIDEOTAPE 2
video: ~ camera *n.* Videokamera, *die;* **~ cas'sette** *n.* Videokassette, *die;* **~ cas'sette recorder** *n.* Videokassettenrekorder, *der;* **~ clip** *n.* Videoclip, *der;* **~ film** *n.* Videofilm, *der;* **~ game** *n.* Videospiel, *das;* **~ library** *n.* Videothek, *die;* **~ machine** *n.* Videogerät, *das;* **~ 'nasty** *n.* Horrorvideo, *das;* **~-on-demand** *n.* Video-on-Demand, *das;* **~ player** *n.* Video-Player, *der;* **~ recorder** *n.* Videorekorder, *der;* **~ recording** *n.* Videoaufnahme, *die;* **~tape** 1 *n.* Videoband, *das;* 2 *v.t.* [auf Videoband (*Akk.*)] aufnehmen
vie /vaɪ/ *v.i.*, **vying** /'vaɪɪŋ/ **~ [with sb.] for sth.** [mit jmdm.] um etw. wetteifern
Vienna /vɪ'enə/ 1 *pr. n.* Wien (*das*) 2 *attrib. adj.* Wiener
Viennese /vɪə'ni:z/ 1 *adj.* Wiener 2 *n., pl. same* Wiener, *der*/Wienerin, *die*
Vietnam /vɪet'næm/ *pr. n.* Vietnam (*das*)
Vietnamese /vɪetnə'mi:z/ 1 *adj.* vietnamesisch; **sb. is ~:** jmd. ist Vietnamese/Vietnamesin 2 *n., pl. same* **(a)** (person) Vietnamese, *der*/ Vietnamesin, *die* **(b)** (language) Vietnamesisch, *das*
view /vju:/ 1 *n.* **(a)** (range of vision) Sicht, *die;* **be out of/in ~:** nicht zu sehen/zu sehen sein **(b)** (what is seen) Aussicht, *die* **(c)** (picture) Ansicht, *die* **(d)** (opinion) Ansicht, *die;* **what is your ~** *or* **are your ~s on this?** was meinst du dazu?; **hold** *or* **take the ~ that ...:** der Ansicht sein, dass ...; **in my ~:** meiner Ansicht nach **(e) be on ~:** besichtigt werden können; **in ~ of sth.** (fig.) angesichts einer Sache; **with a ~ to doing sth.** in der Absicht, etw. zu tun 2 *v.t.* **(a)** (look at) sich (*Dat.*) ansehen **(b)** (consider) betrachten **(c)** (inspect) besichtigen 3 *v.i.* (Telev.) fernsehen
viewdata /'vju:deɪtə/ *n.* Bildschirmtextsystem, *das*
'viewer *n.* **(a)** (Telev.) [Fernseh]zuschauer, *der*/-zuschauerin, *die;* **(b)** (for slides) Diabetrachter, *der*
viewfinder *n.* Sucher, *der*
viewing /'vju:ɪŋ/ *n.* (Telev.) Fernsehen, *das;* **~ figures** Einschaltquoten *Pl.*; **at peak ~ time** zur besten Sendezeit
'viewpoint *n.* Standpunkt, *der*

vigil /ˈvɪdʒɪl/ *n.* Wachen, *das;* **keep ~:** wachen
vigilance /ˈvɪdʒɪləns/ *n.* Wachsamkeit, *die*
vigilant /ˈvɪdʒɪlənt/ *adj.* wachsam
vigilante /vɪdʒɪˈlæntɪ/ *n.* Mitglied einer/der Bürgerwehr
vigor (Amer.) ▶ VIGOUR
vigorous /ˈvɪgərəs/ *adj.* kräftig; heftig ‹*Attacke, Protest*›; energisch ‹*Versuch, Anstrengung, Leugnen, Maßnahme*›
ˈvigorously *adv.* heftig; kräftig ‹*schrubben, drücken*›
vigour /ˈvɪgə(r)/ *n.* (Brit.) (of person) Vitalität, *die;* (of body) Kraft, *die;* (of protest, attack) Heftigkeit, *die*
vile /vaɪl/ *adj.* gemein ‹*Verleumdung*›; vulgär ‹*Sprache*›; (repulsive) widerwärtig; (coll.: very unpleasant) scheußlich (ugs.)
villa /ˈvɪlə/ *n.* **(a)** **[holiday] ~:** Ferienhaus, *das*
(b) **[country] ~:** Landhaus, *das*
village /ˈvɪlɪdʒ/ *n.* Dorf, *das; attrib.* Dorf-
village: ~ ˈgreen *n.* Dorfwiese, *die;* **~ ˈhall** *n.* Dorfgemeinschaftshaus, *das*
villager /ˈvɪlɪdʒə(r)/ *n.* Dorfbewohner, *der*/-bewohnerin, *die*
villain /ˈvɪlən/ *n.* **(a)** Verbrecher, *der*
(b) (Theatre) Bösewicht, *der*
villainous /ˈvɪlənəs/ *adj.* gemein
vindicate /ˈvɪndɪkeɪt/ *v.t.* **(a)** (justify) rechtfertigen
(b) (clear) rehabilitieren
vindication /vɪndɪˈkeɪʃn/ *n.* **(a)** (justification) Rechtfertigung, *die*
(b) (clearing) Rehabilitierung, *die*
vindictive /vɪnˈdɪktɪv/ *adj.* nachtragend
vine /vaɪn/ *n.* Weinrebe, *die*
vinegar /ˈvɪnɪgə(r)/ *n.* Essig, *der*
vinegary /ˈvɪnɪgərɪ/ *adj.* sauer
vineyard /ˈvɪnjɑːd, ˈvɪnjəd/ *n.* Weinberg, *der*
vintage /ˈvɪntɪdʒ/ **1** *n.* Jahrgang, *der*
2 *adj.* erlesen ‹*Wein*›
vintage ˈcar *n.* (Brit.) Oldtimer, *der*
vintner /ˈvɪntnə(r)/ *n.* Weinhändler, *der*/-händlerin, *die*
vinyl /ˈvaɪnɪl/ *n.* Vinyl, *das*
viola /vɪˈəʊlə/ *n.* Bratsche, *die*
violate /ˈvaɪəleɪt/ *v.t.* **(a)** verletzen; brechen ‹*Vertrag, Versprechen, Gesetz*›
(b) (profane, rape) schänden
violation /vaɪəˈleɪʃn/ *n.* ▶ VIOLATE: Verletzung, *die;* Bruch, *der;* Schändung, *die*
violence /ˈvaɪələns/ *n.* **(a)** (force) Heftigkeit, *die;* (of blow) Wucht, *die*
(b) (brutality) Gewalt, *die;* (at public event) Gewalttätigkeiten *Pl.*; **resort to** *or* **use ~:** Gewalt anwenden
violent /ˈvaɪələnt/ *adj.* gewalttätig; (fig.) heftig; wuchtig ‹*Schlag, Stoß*›; Gewalt‹*verbrecher, -tat*›
ˈviolently *adv.* brutal; (fig.) heftig
violet /ˈvaɪələt/ **1** *n.* **(a)** Veilchen, *das*
(b) (colour) Violett, *das*
2 *adj.* violett
violin /vaɪəˈlɪn/ *n.* Violine, *die;* Geige, *die*
vioˈlinist *n.* Geiger, *der*/Geigerin, *die*
VIP /viːaɪˈpiː/ *n.* Prominente, *der/die;* **the ~s** die Prominenz
viper /ˈvaɪpə(r)/ *n.* Viper, *die*
virgin /ˈvɜːdʒɪn/ **1** *n.* **(a)** Jungfrau, *die*
(b) **the [Blessed] V~ [Mary]** die [Heilige] Jungfrau [Maria]
2 *adj.* (unspoiled) unberührt; **~ olive oil** natives Olivenöl
virginity /vəˈdʒɪnɪtɪ/ *n.* Unschuld, *die*
Virgo /ˈvɜːgəʊ/ *n., pl.* **~s** (Astrol., Astron.) die Jungfrau
virile /ˈvɪraɪl/ *adj.* männlich
virility /vɪˈrɪlɪtɪ/ *n.* Männlichkeit, *die*
virology /vaɪəˈrɒlədʒɪ/ *n.* Virologie, *die*
virtual /ˈvɜːtjʊəl/ *adj.* **a ~ ...:** so gut wie ein/eine ...; **the traffic came to a ~ standstill** der Verkehr kam praktisch zum Stillstand (ugs.)
ˈvirtually *adv.* so gut wie; praktisch (ugs.)
virtual reˈality *n.* (Comp.) virtuelle Realität
virtue /ˈvɜːtjuː/ *n.* **(a)** (moral excellence) Tugend, *die*
(b) (advantage) Vorteil, *der*
(c) **by ~ of** aufgrund (+ *Gen.*)
virtuoso /vɜːtjʊˈəʊzəʊ/ *n., pl.* **virtuosi** /vɜːtjʊˈəʊziː/ *or* **~s** Virtuose, *der*/Virtuosin, *die*
virtuous /ˈvɜːtjʊəs/ *adj.* rechtschaffen ‹*Person*›; tugendhaft ‹*Leben*›
virulent /ˈvɪrʊlənt/ *adj.* **(a)** (Med.) virulent; stark wirkend ‹*Gift*›
(b) (fig.) heftig; scharf ‹*Angriff*›
virus /ˈvaɪərəs/ *n.* **(a)** Virus, *das*
(b) (Comp.) [Computer]virus, *das od. der*
visa /ˈviːzə/ *n.* Visum, *das*
vis-à-vis /viːzɑːˈviː/ *prep.* (in relation to) bezüglich (+ *Gen.*)
viscosity /vɪsˈkɒsɪtɪ/ *n.* Dickflüssigkeit, *die*
viscount /ˈvaɪkaʊnt/ *n.* Viscount, *der*
viscous /ˈvɪskəs/ *adj.* dickflüssig
visibility /vɪzɪˈbɪlɪtɪ/ *n.* **(a)** Sichtbarkeit, *die*
(b) (range of vision) Sicht, *die;* (Meteorol.) Sichtweite, *die*
visible /ˈvɪzɪbl/ *adj.* sichtbar
ˈvisibly *adv.* sichtlich
vision /ˈvɪʒn/ *n.* **(a)** (sight) Sehkraft, *die*
(b) (dream) Vision, *die*
(c) *usu. pl.* (imaginings) Fantasien *Pl.*
(d) (insight, foresight) Weitblick, *der*
visit /ˈvɪzɪt/ **1** *v.t.* besuchen; aufsuchen ‹*Arzt*›
2 *v.i.* einen Besuch/Besuche machen
3 *n.* Besuch, *der;* **pay** *or* **make a ~ to sb., pay sb. a ~:** jmdm. einen Besuch abstatten (geh.)
ˈvisiting: ~ card *n.* Visitenkarte, *die;* **~ hours** *n. pl.* Besuchszeiten *Pl.*

visitor /ˈvɪzɪtə(r)/ *n.* Besucher, *der*/ Besucherin, *die;* (to hotel) Gast, *der;* **have ~s/ a ~**: Besuch haben

ˈvisitors' book *n.* Gästebuch, *das;* **sign the ~**: sich ins Gästebuch eintragen

visual /ˈvɪzjʊəl, ˈvɪʒjʊəl/ *adj.* visuell; optisch ‹*Eindruck, Darstellung*›

visual: ~ aids *n. pl.* Anschauungsmaterial, *das;* **~ disˈplay unit** *n.* Bildschirmgerät, *das*

visualization /vɪzjʊəlaɪˈzeɪʃn/ *n.* Veranschaulichung, *die;* (imagining) Sichvorstellen, *das*

visualize /ˈvɪzjʊəlaɪz, ˈvɪʒjʊəlaɪz/ *v.t.* **(a)** (imagine) sich (*Dat.*) vorstellen **(b)** (envisage) voraussehen

ˈvisually *adv.* bildlich

vital /ˈvaɪtl/ *adj.* **(a)** (essential to life) lebenswichtig **(b)** (essential) unbedingt notwendig **(c)** (crucial) entscheidend (**to** für); **it is ~ that you ...**: es ist von entscheidender Bedeutung, dass Sie ...

vitality /vaɪˈtælɪtɪ/ *n.* Vitalität, *die*

ˈvitally *adv.* **~ important** von allergrößter Wichtigkeit; (crucial) von entscheidender Bedeutung

vitamin /ˈvɪtəmɪn, ˈvaɪtəmɪn/ *n.* Vitamin, *das*

vitamin pill *n.* Vitamintablette, *die*

vitriolic /vɪtrɪˈɒlɪk/ *adj.* ätzend

vivacious /vɪˈveɪʃəs/ *adj.* lebhaft

vivacity /vɪˈvæsɪtɪ/ *n.* Lebhaftigkeit, *die*

vivid /ˈvɪvɪd/ *adj.* lebhaft ‹*Farbe, Erinnerung*›; lebendig ‹*Schilderung*›

ˈvividly *adv.* lebendig ‹*beschreiben*›; **remember sth. ~**: sich lebhaft an etw. (*Akk.*) erinnern

vixen /ˈvɪksn/ *n.* Füchsin, *die*

vocabulary /vəˈkæbjʊlərɪ/ *n.* **(a)** (list) Vokabelverzeichnis, *das;* **learn ~**: Vokabeln lernen **(b)** (range of language) Wortschatz, *der*

vocal /ˈvəʊkl/ *adj.* **(a)** (concerned with voice) stimmlich **(b)** lautstark ‹*Minderheit, Protest*›

ˈvocal cords *n. pl.* Stimmbänder *Pl.*

vocalist /ˈvəʊkəlɪst/ *n.* Sänger, *der*/ Sängerin, *die*

vocation /vəˈkeɪʃn/ *n.* Berufung, *die*

vocational /vəˈkeɪʃənl/ *adj.* berufsbezogen

vocational: ~ college *n.* Berufsschule, *die;* **~ guidance** *n.* Berufsberatung, *die;* **~ training** *n.* berufliche Bildung

vociferous /vəˈsɪfərəs/ *adj.* laut; lautstark ‹*Forderung, Protest*›

vodka /ˈvɒdkə/ *n.* Wodka, *der*

vogue /vəʊg/ *n.* Mode, *die;* **be in/come into ~**: in Mode sein/kommen

voice /vɔɪs/ [1] *n.* Stimme, *die;* **in a firm/ loud/soft ~**: mit fester/lauter/sanfter Stimme [2] *v.t.* zum Ausdruck bringen

voice: ~mail *n.* Voicemail, *die;* **~-over** *n.* Begleitkommentar, *der;* **~ recognition** *n.* (Comp.) Spracherkennung, *die*

void /vɔɪd/ [1] *adj.* **(a)** (empty) leer **(b)** (invalid) ungültig **(c) ~ of** ohne [jeden/jedes/jede] [2] *n.* Nichts, *das*

vol. *abbr.* = **volume** Bd.

volatile /ˈvɒlətaɪl/ *adj.* **(a)** (Chem.) flüchtig **(b)** (fig.) impulsiv; brisant ‹*Lage*›

volcanic /vɒlˈkænɪk/ *adj.* vulkanisch

volcano /vɒlˈkeɪnəʊ/ *n., pl.* **~es** Vulkan, *der*

vole /vəʊl/ *n.* Wühlmaus, *die*

volition /vəˈlɪʃn/ *n.* Wille, *der;* **of one's own ~**: aus eigenem Willen

volley /ˈvɒlɪ/ *n.* **(a)** (of missiles) Salve, *die;* **a ~ of arrows** ein Hagel von Pfeilen **(b)** (Tennis) Volley, *der*

ˈvolleyball *n.* Volleyball, *der*

volt /vəʊlt/ *n.* Volt, *das*

voltage /ˈvəʊltɪdʒ/ *n.* Spannung, *die*

voluble /ˈvɒljʊbl/ *adj.* redselig

volume /ˈvɒljuːm/ *n.* **(a)** (book) Band, *der* **(b)** (loudness) Lautstärke, *die;* (of voice) Volumen, *das* **(c)** (space) Rauminhalt, *der;* (amount of substance) Teil, *der*

ˈvolume control *n.* Lautstärkeregler, *der*

voluntarily /ˈvɒləntərɪlɪ/ *adv.*, **voluntary** /ˈvɒləntərɪ/ *adj.* freiwillig

volunteer /vɒlənˈtɪə(r)/ [1] *n.* Freiwillige, *der/die* [2] *v.t.* anbieten ‹*Hilfe, Dienste*›; herausrücken mit ‹*Informationen*› [3] *v.i.* sich [freiwillig] melden; **~ to do** *or* **~ for the shopping** sich zum Einkaufen bereit erklären

voluptuous /vəˈlʌptjʊəs/ *adj.* üppig

vomit /ˈvɒmɪt/ [1] *v.t.* erbrechen [2] *v.i.* sich übergeben [3] *n.* Erbrochene, *das*

voodoo /ˈvuːduː/ *n.* Wodu, *der*

voracious /vəˈreɪʃəs/ *adj.* gefräßig ‹*Person*›; unbändig ‹*Appetit*›

vote /vəʊt/ [1] *n.* **(a)** (individual ~) Stimme, *die* **(b)** (act of voting) Abstimmung, *die;* **take a ~ on sth.** über etw. (*Akk.*) abstimmen **(c)** (right to ~) Stimmrecht, *das* [2] *v.i.* abstimmen; (in election) wählen; **~ for/ against** stimmen für/gegen; **~ to do sth.** beschließen, etw. zu tun; **~ Labour/ Conservative** *etc.* Labour/die Konservativen *usw.* wählen [3] *v.t.* **~ sb. Chairman/President** *etc.* jmdn. zum Vorsitzenden/Präsidenten *usw.* wählen

■ **vote ˈin** *v.t.* wählen

ˈvoter *n.* Wähler, *der*/Wählerin, *die*

ˈvote-catching *n.* Stimmenfang, *der*

voting /ˈvəʊtɪŋ/ *n.* Abstimmen, *das;* (in election) Wählen, *das*
voting: ~ age *n.* Wahlalter, *das;* **~ slip** *n.* Wahlzettel, *der;* Stimmzettel, *der;* **~ system** *n.* Wahlsystem, *das*
vouch /vaʊtʃ/ [1] *v.t.* **~ that ...**: sich dafür verbürgen, dass ...
[2] *v.i.* **~ for sb./sth.** sich für jmdn./etw. verbürgen
ˈvoucher *n.* Gutschein, *der*
vow /vaʊ/ [1] *n.* Gelöbnis, *das;* (Relig.) Gelübde, *das*
[2] *v.t.* geloben
vowel /ˈvaʊəl/ *n.* Vokal, *der*
voyage /ˈvɔɪɪdʒ/ [1] *n.* Reise, *die;* (sea ~) Seereise, *die;* **outward/homeward ~, ~ out/home** Hin-/Rückreise, *die;* **a ~ to the moon** ein Mondflug
[2] *v.i.* (literary) reisen
voyeur /vwɑːˈjɜː(r)/ *n.* Voyeur, *der*
voyeurism /vwɑːˈjɜːrɪzm/ *n.* Voyeurismus, *der*
vulgar /ˈvʌlgə(r)/ *adj.* vulgär; ordinär ‹*Person, Benehmen, Witz*›
vulgarity /vʌlˈgærɪtɪ/ *n.* Vulgarität, *die*
vulnerable /ˈvʌlnərəbl/ *adj.* **(a)** (exposed to danger) angreifbar; **be ~ to sth.** für etw. anfällig sein; **be ~ to attack/in a ~ position** leicht angreifbar sein
(b) (without protection) schutzlos
vulture /ˈvʌltʃə(r)/ *n.* Geier, *der*
vying ▶ VIE

Ww

W¹, w /ˈdʌbljuː/ *n.* W, w, *das*
W² *abbr.* = **watt[s]** W
W. *abbr.* **(a)** = **west** W.
(b) = **western** w.
wad /wɒd/ *n.* **(a)** Knäuel, *das;* (smaller) Pfropfen, *der*
(b) (of papers) Bündel, *das*
wadding /ˈwɒdɪŋ/ *n.* Futter, *das*
waddle /ˈwɒdl/ [1] *v.i.* watscheln
[2] *n.* watschelnder Gang
wade /weɪd/ *v.i.* waten
■ **ˈwade through** *v.t.* (fig. coll.) durchackern (ugs.) ‹*Buch*›
wafer /ˈweɪfə(r)/ *n.* Waffel, *die*
ˈwafer-thin *adj.* hauchdünn
waffle¹ /ˈwɒfl/ *n.* (Gastr.) Waffel, *die*
waffle² (Brit. coll.: talk) [1] *v.i.* schwafeln (ugs.)
[2] *n.* Geschwafel, *das* (ugs.)
waft /wɒft, wɑːft/ [1] *v.t.* wehen
[2] *v.i.* ziehen
wag /wæg/ [1] *v.t.*, **-gg-** ‹*Hund:*› wedeln mit ‹*Schwanz*›; **~ one's finger at sb.** jmdm. mit dem Finger drohen
[2] *v.i.*, **-gg-** ‹*Schwanz:*› wedeln

wage /weɪdʒ/ [1] *n. in sing. or pl.* Lohn, *der*
[2] *v.t.* führen ‹*Krieg*›
wage: ~ claim *n.* Lohnforderung, *die;* **~ earner** *n.* Lohnempfänger, *der*/-empfängerin, *die;* **be the ~ earner of the family** der Ernährer/die Ernährerin der Familie sein; **~ freeze** *n.* Lohnstopp, *der;* **~ increase** *n.* Lohnerhöhung, *die;* **~ packet** *n.* Lohntüte, *die*
wager /ˈweɪdʒə(r)/ (dated/formal) [1] *n.* Wette, *die;* **lay a ~ on sth.** auf etw. (*Akk.*) wetten
[2] *v.t. & i.* wetten
wage: ~ rise *n.* Lohnerhöhung, *die;* **~ scale** *n.* Tarif, *der;* **~ slave** *n.* Lohnsklave, *der*
waggle /ˈwægl/ (coll.) [1] *v.t.* **~ its tail** ‹*Hund:*› mit dem Schwanz wedeln
[2] *v.i.* hin und her schlagen
waggon (Brit.), **wagon** /ˈwægən/ *n.* Wagen, *der*
waif /weɪf/ *n.* (child) verlassenes Kind
wail /weɪl/ [1] *v.i.* klagen (geh.) (**for** um); ‹*Kind:*› heulen
[2] *n.* klagender Schrei; **~s** Geheul, *das*
waist /weɪst/ *n.* Taille, *die;* **tight round the ~**: eng in der Taille
ˈwaistband *n.* Gürtelbund, *der;* (of trousers) [Hosen]bund, *der;* (of skirt) [Rock]bund, *der*
waistcoat /ˈweɪskəʊt/ *n.* (Brit.) Weste, *die*
ˈwaistline *n.* Taille, *die;* **be bad for the ~**: schlecht für die schlanke Linie sein
wait /weɪt/ [1] *v.i.* **(a)** warten; **~ [for] an hour** eine Stunde warten; **~ a moment** Moment mal; **keep sb. ~ing, make sb. ~**: jmdn. warten lassen
(b) ~ at table servieren
[2] *v.t.* (await) warten auf (+ *Akk.*); **~ one's turn** warten, bis man drankommt
[3] *n.* **(a) after a long/short ~**: nach langer/kurzer Wartezeit
(b) lie in ~ for sb./sth. jmdm./einer Sache auflauern
■ **wait beˈhind** *v.i.* noch dableiben
■ **ˈwait for** *v.t.* warten auf (+ *Akk.*); **~ for sb. to do sth.** darauf warten, dass jmd. etw. tut; **~ for the rain to stop** warten, bis der Regen aufhört
■ **ˈwait on** *v.t.* (serve) bedienen
■ **wait ˈup** *v.i.* aufbleiben (**for** wegen)

'waiter *n.* Kellner, *der;* **~!** Herr Ober!

'waiting: ~ list *n.* Warteliste, *die;* **~ room** *n.* Wartezimmer, *das;* (Railw.) Warteraum, *der*

waitress /'weɪtrɪs/ *n.* Servierererin, *die;* **~!** Fräulein! (veralt.)

waive /weɪv/ *v.t.* verzichten auf (+ *Akk.*)

wake¹ /weɪk/ [1] *v.i.*, **woke** /wəʊk/, **woken** /'wəʊkn/ aufwachen
[2] *v.t.*, **woke, woken** wecken
[3] *n.* (by corpse) Totenwache, *die*

■ **wake 'up** [1] *v.i.* aufwachen; **~ up to sth.** (fig.: realize) etw. erkennen
[2] *v.t.* **(a)** wecken
(b) (fig.: enliven) wachrütteln

wake² *n.* Kielwasser, *das;* **in the ~ of sth.** (fig.) im Gefolge von etw.

waken /'weɪkn/ [1] *v.t.* wecken
[2] *v.i.* aufwachen

'wake-up call (esp. Amer.) ▶ ALARM CALL

Wales /weɪlz/ *pr. n.* Wales (*das*)

walk /wɔːk/ [1] *v.i.* **(a)** laufen; (not run) gehen; (not drive) zu Fuß gehen; **learn to ~:** laufen lernen
(b) (exercise) gehen
[2] *v.t.* **(a)** (lead) führen; ausführen ‹*Hund*›
(b) (accompany) bringen
[3] *n.* **(a)** Spaziergang, *der;* **go [out] for** *or* **take** *or* **have a ~:** einen Spaziergang machen; **ten minutes' ~ from here** zehn Minuten zu Fuß von hier
(b) (gait) Gang, *der*
(c) (path) [Spazier]weg, *der*

■ **walk a'way with** *v.t.* (coll.: win easily) spielend leicht gewinnen

■ **'walk into** *v.t.* (hit by accident) laufen gegen ‹*Pfosten, Laternenpfahl*›; **~ into sb.** mit jmdm. zusammenstoßen; **~ into a trap** in eine Falle gehen

■ **walk 'off with** *v.t.* sich davonmachen mit

■ **walk 'out** *v.i.* **(a)** (leave in protest) aus Protest den Saal verlassen
(b) (go on strike) in den Streik treten

■ **walk 'out of** *v.t.* (leave in protest) aus Protest verlassen

■ **walk 'out on** *v.t.* verlassen

'walker *n.* **(a)** Spaziergänger, *der*/ -gängerin, *die;* (rambler) Wanderer, *der*/ Wanderin, *die*
(b) (baby-~) Laufstuhl, *der*

walkie-talkie /wɔːkɪ'tɔːkɪ/ *n.* Walkie-Talkie, *das*

'walking *n.* [Spazieren]gehen, *das;* **at ~ pace** im Schritttempo; **be within ~ distance** zu Fuß zu erreichen sein

walking: ~ frame *n.* Gehbock, *der;* Gehgestell, *das;* **~ holiday** *n.* Wanderurlaub, *der;* **~ shoe** *n.* Wanderschuh, *der;* **~ stick** *n.* Spazierstock, *der;* **~ tour** *n.* Wanderung, *die*

Walkman ® /'wɔːkmən/ *n.*, *pl.* **Walkmans** Walkman, *der* (Wz)

walk: ~out *n.* Arbeitsniederlegung, *die;* **~over** *n.* (fig.: easy victory) Spaziergang, *der* (ugs.); **~way** *n.* Fußweg, *der;* (over machinery etc.) Laufsteg, *der*

wall /wɔːl/ *n.* Wand, *die;* (freestanding) Mauer, *die;* **drive sb. up the ~** (fig. coll.) jmdn. auf die Palme bringen (ugs.); **go to the ~** (fig.) an die Wand gedrückt werden

■ **wall 'up** *v.t.* zumauern

wall: ~chart *n.* Schautafel, *die;* **~ cupboard** *n.* Hängeschrank, *der*

wallet /'wɒlɪt/ *n.* Brieftasche, *die*

wall: ~flower *n.* Goldlack, *der;* **~ hanging** *n.* Wandbehang, *der;* **~ light** *n.* Wandlampe, *die*

wallop /'wɒləp/ (coll.) [1] *v.t.* schlagen
[2] *n.* Schlag, *der*

wallow /'wɒləʊ/ *v.i.* **(a)** sich wälzen
(b) (fig.) schwelgen (**in** in + *Dat.*)

wall: ~ painting *n.* Wandgemälde, *das;* **~paper** [1] *n.* **(a)** Tapete, *die;* **(b)** (Comp.) Hintergrund, *der;* (pattern) Hintergrundmuster, *das;* [2] *v.t.* tapezieren; **~-to-~** *adj.* **~-to-~ carpeting** Teppichboden, *der;* **~ unit** *n.* Hängeelement, *das*

walnut /'wɔːlnʌt/ *n.* Walnuss, *die*

walrus /'wɔːlrəs/ *n.* Walross, *das*

waltz /wɔːlts, wɔːls/ [1] *n.* Walzer, *der*
[2] *v.i.* Walzer tanzen

wan /wɒn/ *adj.* bleich

wand /wɒnd/ *n.* Stab, *der*

wander /'wɒndə(r)/ [1] *v.i.* (go aimlessly) umherirren; (walk slowly) bummeln
[2] *v.t.* wandern durch
[3] *n.* (coll.) Spaziergang, *der*

■ **wander a'bout** *v.i.* sich herumtreiben

■ **wander 'off** *v.i.* (stray) weggehen

wane /weɪn/ *v.i.* abnehmen

wangle /'wæŋgl/ *v.t.* (coll.) organisieren (ugs.)

wannabe /'wɒnəbɪ/ *n.* (coll. derog.) Möchtegern, *der; attrib.* Möchtegern-

want /wɒnt/ [1] *v.t.* **(a)** (desire) wollen; **~ to do sth.** etw. tun wollen; **I ~ it done by tonight** ich will, dass es bis heute Abend fertig wird
(b) (require, need) brauchen; **'W~ed – cook'** „Koch/Köchin gesucht"; **you're ~ed on the phone** du wirst am Telefon verlangt; **the windows ~ painting** die Fenster müssten gestrichen werden; **you ~ to be [more] careful** du solltest vorsichtig[er] sein
(c) ~ed [by the police] [polizeilich] gesucht
[2] *n.* **(a)** (lack) Mangel, *der* (**of** an + *Dat.*); **for ~ of sth.** aus Mangel an etw. (*Dat.*)
(b) (need) Not, *der*
(c) (desire) Bedürfnis, *das*

■ **'want for** *v.t.* **sb. ~s for nothing** *or* **doesn't ~ for anything** jmdm. fehlt es an nichts

'wanting *adj.* **be ~:** fehlen; **sb./sth. is ~ in** ···>

sth. jmdm./einer Sache fehlt es an etw. (*Dat.*); **be found ~:** für unzureichend befunden werden

wanton /ˈwɒntən/ *adj.*, **ˈwantonly** *adv.* mutwillig

war /wɔ:(r)/ *n.* Krieg, *der;* **between the ~s** zwischen den Weltkriegen; **declare ~:** den Krieg erklären (**on** *Dat.*); **be at ~:** sich im Krieg befinden; **make ~:** Krieg führen (**on** gegen)

warble /ˈwɔ:bl/ *v.t. & i.* trällern

war: ~ correspondent *n.* Kriegsberichterstatter, *der*/-berichterstatterin, *die;* **~ crime** *n.* Kriegsverbrechen, *das;* **~ criminal** *n.* Kriegsverbrecher, *der*/-verbrecherin, *die*

ward /wɔ:d/ *n.* **(a)** (in hospital) Station, *die;* **she's in W~ 3** sie liegt auf Station 3
(b) (child) Mündel, *das od. die*
(c) (electoral division) Wahlbezirk, *der*

■ **ward ˈoff** *v.t.* abwehren

ˈwar damage *n.* Kriegsschäden *Pl.*

warden /ˈwɔ:dn/ *n.* **(a)** (of hostel) Heimleiter, *der*/-leiterin, *die;* (of youth hostel) Herbergsvater, *der*/-mutter, *die*
(b) (supervisor) Aufseher, *der*/Aufseherin, *die*

ˈwarder *n.* (Brit.) Wärter, *der*

wardrobe /ˈwɔ:drəʊb/ *n.* **(a)** Kleiderschrank, *der*
(b) (clothes) Garderobe, *die*

warehouse /ˈweəhaʊs/ *n.* Lagerhaus, *das;* (part of building) Lager, *das*

wares /weəz/ *n. pl.* Ware, *die*

warfare /ˈwɔ:feə(r)/ *n.* Krieg, *der*

war: ~ game *n.* Kriegsspiel, *das;* **~ grave** *n.* Kriegs- *od.* Soldatengrab, *das;* **~head** *n.* Sprengkopf, *der*

warily /ˈweərɪlɪ/ *adv.* vorsichtig; (suspiciously) misstrauisch

ˈwarlike *adj.* kriegerisch

warm /wɔ:m/ [1] *adj.* **(a)** warm; **I am [very] ~:** mir ist [sehr] warm
(b) (enthusiastic) herzlich ‹*Grüße, Dank*›
[2] *v.t.* wärmen; warm machen ‹*Flüssigkeit*›; **~ one's hands** sich (*Dat.*) die Hände wärmen
[3] *v.i.* **~ to sb./sth.** (come to like) sich für jmdn./etw. erwärmen

■ **warm ˈup** [1] *v.i.* warm werden; ‹*Sportler:*› sich aufwärmen
[2] *v.t.* aufwärmen ‹*Speisen*›; erwärmen ‹*Raum, Zimmer*›

warm-blooded /ˈwɔ:mblʌdɪd/ *adj.* warmblütig;

ˈwar memorial *n.* Kriegerdenkmal, *das*

warm-hearted /ˈwɔ:mhɑ:tɪd/ *adj.* warmherzig ‹*Person*›

ˈwarmly *adv.* **(a)** warm
(b) (fig.) herzlich ‹*willkommen heißen, gratulieren, begrüßen, grüßen, danken*›

warmonger /ˈwɔ:mʌŋgə(r)/ *n.* Kriegshetzer, *der*/-hetzerin, *die*

warmth /wɔ:mθ/ *n.* **(a)** Wärme, *die*
(b) (fig.) Herzlichkeit, *die*

ˈwarm-up *n.* **have a ~** (Sport) sich aufwärmen; **~ [lap]** (Motor Racing) Aufwärmrunde, *die*

warn /wɔ:n/ *v.t.* **(a)** (inform, give notice) warnen (**against, of, about** vor + *Dat.*); **~ sb. that …:** jmdn. darauf hinweisen, dass …; **~ sb. not to do sth.** jmdn. davor warnen, etw. zu tun
(b) (admonish) ermahnen; (officially) abmahnen

warning [1] *n.* **(a)** (advance notice) Vorwarnung, *die*
(b) (lesson) **let that be a ~ to you** lass dir das eine Warnung sein
(c) (caution) Verwarnung, *die;* (less official) Warnung, *die*
[2] *adj.* Warn‹*schild, -signal usw.*›

ˈwarning triangle *n.* Warndreieck, *das*

warp /wɔ:p/ [1] *v.i.* sich verbiegen; ‹*Holz, Schallplatte:*› sich verziehen
[2] *v.t.* **(a)** verbiegen
(b) (fig.) **a ~ed sense of humour** ein abartiger Humor

war: ~path *n.* **be on the ~path** (fig.) in Rage sein; **~plane** *n.* Kampfflugzeug, *das*

warrant /ˈwɒrənt/ [1] *n.* (for sb.'s arrest) Haftbefehl, *der;* **[search] ~:** Durchsuchungsbefehl, *der*
[2] *v.t.* **(a)** (justify) rechtfertigen
(b) (guarantee) garantieren

ˈwarranty *n.* Garantie, *die*

warrior /ˈwɒrɪə(r)/ *n.* (esp. literary) Krieger, *der* (geh.)

Warsaw /ˈwɔ:sɔ:/ [1] *pr. n.* Warschau (*das*)
[2] *attrib. adj.* Warschauer; **~ Pact** (Hist.) Warschauer Pakt

ˈwarship *n.* Kriegsschiff, *das*

wart /wɔ:t/ *n.* Warze, *die*

war: ~time *n.* **(a)** Kriegszeit, *die;* **in** *or* **during ~:** im Krieg; **(b)** *attrib.* Kriegs‹*rationierung, -evakuierung usw.*›
~-torn *adj.* kriegsgeschunden

wary /ˈweərɪ/ *adj.* vorsichtig; (suspicious) misstrauisch (**of** gegenüber); **be ~ of sb./sth.** sich vor jmdm./etw. in Acht nehmen

ˈwar zone *n.* Kriegsgebiet, *das*

was ▶ BE

wash /wɒʃ/ [1] *v.t.* **(a)** waschen; **~ oneself** sich waschen; **~ one's hands/face/hair** sich (*Dat.*) die Hände/das Gesicht/die Haare waschen; **~ the clothes** Wäsche waschen; **~ the dishes** [Geschirr] spülen; **~ the floor** den Fußboden aufwischen
(b) (remove) waschen ‹*Fleck*› (**out of** aus); abwaschen ‹*Schmutz*› (**off** von)
(c) (carry along) spülen
[2] *v.i.* **(a)** sich waschen
(b) ‹*Stoff, Kleidungsstück:*› sich waschen lassen
[3] *n.* **(a) give sb./sth. a [good] ~:** jmdn./etw. [gründlich] waschen
(b) (laundering) Wäsche, *die*
(c) (of ship) Sog, *der*

■ **wash 'down** *v.t.* abspritzen ‹*Auto, Deck, Hof*›
■ **wash 'off** 1 *v.t.* ~ **sth. off** etw. abwaschen
2 *v.i.* abgehen; (from fabric etc.) herausgehen
■ **wash 'out** *v.t.* ausscheuern ‹*Topf*›; ausspülen ‹*Mund*›; ~ **dirt/marks out of clothes** Schmutz/Flecken aus Kleidern [her]auswaschen
■ **wash 'up** 1 *v.t.* (Brit.) ~ **the dishes up** das Geschirr spülen
2 *v.i.* abwaschen; spülen
washable /ˈwɒʃəbl/ *adj.* waschbar
'washbasin *n.* Waschbecken, *das*
washed-'out *adj.* verwaschen (fig.: exhausted) abgespannt
washed-'up *adj.* (coll.) kaputt (ugs.)
washer /ˈwɒʃə(r)/ *n.* (of tap) Dichtungsring, *der*
'washing *n.* Wäsche, *die;* **do the** ~: waschen
washing: ~ **machine** *n.* Waschmaschine, *die;* ~ **powder** *n.* Waschpulver, *das;* **~-'up** *n.* (Brit.) Abwasch, *der;* **do the ~-up** abwaschen; spülen; **~-'up liquid** *n.* Spülmittel, *das*
'washtub *n.* Waschbottich, *der*
wasn't /ˈwɒznt/ (coll.) = **was not;** ▸ BE
wasp *n.* Wespe, *die*
waste /weɪst/ 1 *n.* **(a)** (useless remains) Abfall, *der;* **kitchen** ~: Küchenabfälle *Pl.*
(b) (extravagant use) Verschwendung, *die;* **it's a ~ of time/money/energy** das ist Zeit-/Geld-/Energieverschwendung
2 *v.t.* (squander) verschwenden; **all his efforts were ~d** all seine Mühe war umsonst; **don't ~ my time!** stehlen Sie mir nicht die Zeit!
3 *adj.* **(a)** ~ **material** Abfall, *der*
(b) lay sth. ~: etw. verwüsten
■ **waste a'way** *v.i.* immer mehr abmagern
waste: **~basket** ▸ WASTE-PAPER BASKET; ~ **disposal** *n.* Abfallbeseitigung, *die;* ~ **disposal site** *n.* [Müll]deponie *die;* ~ **disposal unit** *n.* Müllzerkleinerer, *der*
wasteful /ˈweɪstfl/ *adj.* **(a)** (extravagant) verschwenderisch
(b) (causing waste) unwirtschaftlich
waste: **~land** *n.* Ödland, *das;* ~ **management** *n.* Abfallmanagement, *das;* Müllmanagement, *das;* ~ **'paper** *n.* Papierabfall, *der;* **~-'paper basket** *n.* Papierkorb, *der;* ~ **pipe** *n.* Abflussrohr, *das;* ~ **reduction** *n.* Abfallverminderung, *die;* Müllreduzierung, *die*
watch /wɒtʃ/ 1 *n.* **(a) [wrist/pocket]** ~: [Armband-/Taschen]uhr, *die*
(b) keep ~: Wache halten; **keep [a]** ~ **for sb./sth.** auf jmdn./etw. achten
(c) (Naut.) Wache, *die*
2 *v.i.* ~ **for sb./sth.** auf jmdn./etw. warten
3 *v.t.* **(a)** (observe) sich (*Dat.*) ansehen ‹*Sportveranstaltung, Fernsehsendung*›; ~ **[the] television** *or* **TV** fernsehen; ~ **sb. do** *or* **doing sth.** zusehen, wie jmd. etw. tut; **we are being ~ed** wir werden beobachtet
(b) (be careful of, look after) achten auf (+ *Akk.*)
■ **watch 'out** *v.i.* **(a)** (be careful) aufpassen; ~ **out!** Vorsicht!
(b) (look out) ~ **out for sb./sth.** auf jmdn./etw. achten
'watchdog *n.* Wachhund, *der;* (fig.) **[public]** ~: [*Leiter/Leiterin einer*] *Aufsichtsbehörde*
watchful /ˈwɒtʃfl/ *adj.* wachsam
watch: **~maker** *n.* Uhrmacher, *der*/-macherin, *die;* **~man** /ˈwɒtʃmən/ *n., pl.* **~men** /ˈwɒtʃmən/ Wachmann, *der;* ~ **strap** *n.* [Uhr]armband, *das;* **~tower** *n.* Wachturm, *der*
water /ˈwɔːtə(r)/ 1 *n.* **(a)** Wasser, *das*
(b) *in pl.* (part of the sea etc.) Gewässer *Pl.*
2 *v.t.* **(a)** bewässern ‹*Land*›; wässern ‹*Pflanzen*›; ~ **the flowers** die Blumen [be]gießen
(b) verwässern ‹*Bier usw.*›
(c) tränken ‹*Tier*›
3 *v.i.* ‹*Augen:*› tränen; **my mouth was ~ing** mir lief das Wasser im Munde zusammen
■ **water 'down** *v.t.* verwässern
water: **~bed** *n.* Wasserbett, *das;* ~ **birth** *n.* Unterwassergeburt, *die;* ~ **biscuit** *n.* Cracker, *der;* ~ **bottle** *n.* Wasserflasche, *die;* ~ **butt** *n.* Regentonne, *die;* ~ **closet** *n.* Toilette, *die;* WC, *das;* Wasserklosett, *das* (veralt.); **~colour** *n.* **(a)** (paint) Wasserfarbe, *die;* **(b)** (picture) Aquarell, *das;* **~cress** *n.* Brunnenkresse, *die;* **~fall** *n.* Wasserfall, *der;* **~front** *n.* Ufer, *das;* **a ~front location** eine Gegend am Wasser; ~ **heater** *n.* Heißwassergerät, *das;* **~hole** *n.* Wasserloch, *das*
watering: ~ **can** *n.* Gießkanne, *die;* ~ **place** *n.* (for animals) Wasserstelle, *die*
water: ~ **level** *n.* Wasserstand, *der;* **~lily** *n.* Seerose, *die;* **~line** *n.* (Naut.) Wasserlinie, *die;* **~logged** /ˈwɔːtəlɒgd/ *adj.* nass ‹*Boden*›; aufgeweicht ‹*Sportplatz*›; ~ **main** *n.* Hauptwasserleitung, *die;* **~mark** *n.* Wasserzeichen, *das;* **~melon** *n.* Wassermelone, *die;* ~ **meter** *n.* Wasseruhr, *die;* ~ **pipe** *n.* Wasserrohr, *das;* ~ **pistol** *n.* Wasserpistole, *die;* ~ **polo** *n.* Wasserball, *der;* **~proof** 1 *adj.* wasserdicht; wasserfest ‹*Farbe*›; 2 *v.t.* wasserdicht machen; imprägnieren ‹*Stoff*›; ~ **rates** *n. pl.* **the ~ rates** die Wassergebühren *Pl.*; **~-repellent** *adj.* Wasser abstoßend; **~-resistant** *adj.* wasserundurchlässig; wasserfest ‹*Farbe*›; **~shed** *n.* (fig.) Wendepunkt, *der;* **~ski** 1 *n.* Wasserski, *der;* 2 *v.i.* Wasserski laufen; **~skiing** *n.* Wasserskilaufen, *das;* ~ **softener** /ˈsɒfənə(r)/ *n.* Wasserenthärter, *der;* **~-soluble** *adj.* wasserlöslich; ~ **supply** *n.* Wasserversorgung, *die;* ~ **table** *n.* Grundwasserspiegel, *der;* ~ **tap** *n.* Wasserhahn, *der;* **~tight** *adj.* wasserdicht;

~ tower *n.* Wasserturm, *der;* **~way** *n.* Wasserstraße, *die;* **~ vapour** *n.* Wasserdampf, *der;* **~works** *n. sing., pl. same* (establishment) Wasserwerk, *das;* (system) Wasserversorgungssystem, *das*

'watery *adj.* wässrig

watt /wɒt/ *n.* Watt, *das*

wattage /'wɒtɪdʒ/ *n.* Wattzahl, *die*

wave /weɪv/ [1] *n.* **(a)** Welle, *die*
(b) (gesture) **give sb. a ~:** jmdm. zuwinken; **with a ~ of one's hand** mit einem Winken
[2] *v.i.* **(a)** ‹*Fahne, Flagge, Wimpel:*› wehen; ‹*Baum, Gras, Korn:*› sich wiegen
(b) (with hand) winken; **~ at** *or* **to sb.** jmdm. zuwinken
[3] *v.t.* schwenken; schwingen ‹*Schwert*›; **~ one's hand at** *or* **to sb.** jmdm. zuwinken; **~ goodbye to sb.** jmdm. zum Abschied zuwinken

▪ **wave a'side** *v.t.* **(a)** abtun ‹*Zweifel, Einwand*›
(b) ~ sb. aside [jmdm.] abwinken

wave: ~band *n.* Wellenbereich, *der;* **~length** *n.* Wellenlänge, *die;* **be on the same ~length [as sb.]** (fig.) die gleiche Wellenlänge [wie jmd.] haben

waver /'weɪvə(r)/ *v.i.* schwanken

wavy /'weɪvɪ/ *adj.* wellig; **~ line** Schlangenlinie, *die*

wax¹ /wæks/ [1] *n.* **(a)** Wachs, *das*
(b) (in ear) Schmalz, *das*
[2] *v.t.* wachsen

wax² *v.i.* **(a)** ‹*Mond:*› zunehmen
(b) (become) werden

wax 'crayon *n.* Wachsmalstift, *der*

waxed /wækst/ *adj.* gewachst; **~ paper** Wachspapier, *das*

wax: ~work *n.* Wachsfigur, *die;* **~works** *n. sing., pl. same* Wachsfigurenkabinett, *das*

'waxy *adj.* wachsweich

way /weɪ/ [1] *n.* **(a)** Weg, *der;* **ask the** *or* **one's ~:** nach dem Weg fragen; **'W~ In/Out'** „Ein-/Ausgang"; **by ~ of Switzerland** über die Schweiz; **lead the ~:** vorausgehen; **go out of one's ~:** einen Umweg machen; (fig.) keine Mühe scheuen
(b) (method) Art und Weise, *die;* **do it this ~:** mach es so
(c) (distance) Stück, *das;* **it's a long ~ off** *or* **a long ~ from here** es ist weit weg von hier; **all the ~:** den ganzen Weg

(d) (direction) Richtung, *die;* **she went this/that/the other ~:** sie ist in diese/die/die andere Richtung gegangen; **stand sth. the right/wrong ~ up** etw. richtig/falsch herum stellen
(e) (respect) **in [exactly] the same ~:** [ganz] genauso; **in some ~s** in gewisser Hinsicht; **in one ~:** auf eine Art; **in every ~:** in jeder Hinsicht; **in a ~:** auf eine Art
(f) (custom) Art, *die*
(g) get *or* **have one's [own] ~, have it one's [own] ~:** seinen Willen kriegen; **be in sb.'s** *or* **the ~:** [jmdm.] im Weg sein; **make ~ for sth.** für etw. Platz machen; (fig.) einer Sache (*Dat.*) Platz machen; **in a bad ~:** schlecht; **either ~:** so oder so; **by the ~:** übrigens
[2] *adv.* weit; **~ back** (coll.) vor langer Zeit

way: ~bill *n.* Frachtbrief, *der;* **~'lay** *v.t., forms as* LAY² 1: **(a)** (ambush) überfallen; **(b)** (stop for conversation) abfangen; **~-'out** *adj.* (coll.) extrem; verrückt; **~side** *n.* Wegrand, *der;* **fall by the ~side** (fig.) auf der Strecke bleiben (ugs.)

wayward /'weɪwəd/ *adj.* eigenwillig

WC *abbr.* = **water closet** WC, *das*

we /wɪ, *stressed* wi:/ *pl. pron.* wir

weak /wi:k/ *adj.* **(a)** schwach; (easily led) labil ‹*Charakter, Person*›
(b) dünn ‹*Getränk*›

weaken /'wi:kn/ [1] *v.t.* schwächen; beeinträchtigen ‹*Augen*›
[2] *v.i.* ‹*Entschlossenheit, Kraft:*› nachlassen

weak-kneed /'wi:kni:d/ *adj.* (fig.) feige

weakling /'wi:klɪŋ/ *n.* Schwächling, *der*

'weakly *adv.* schwach

'weakness *n.* Schwäche, *die*

'weak-willed *adj.* willensschwach

wealth /welθ/ *n.* **(a)** (abundance) Fülle, *die*
(b) (riches, being rich) Reichtum, *der*

'wealthy [1] *adj.* reich
[2] *n. pl.* **the ~:** die Reichen *Pl.*

'wealth tax *n.* Vermögenssteuer, *die*

wean /wi:n/ *v.t.* abstillen; **~ sb. [away] from sth.** (fig.) jmdm. etw. abgewöhnen

weapon /'wepən/ *n.* Waffe, *die;* **~ of mass destruction** Massenvernichtungswaffe, *die*

weaponry /'wepənrɪ/ *n.* Waffen *Pl.*

wear /weə(r)/ [1] *n.* **(a) ~ [and tear]** Abnutzung, *die*
(b) (clothes) Kleidung, *die*
[2] *v.t.,* **wore** /wɔ:(r)/, **worn** /wɔ:n/ **(a)** (have on) tragen ‹*Schmuck, Brille, Kleidung, Perücke*›; **I haven't a thing to ~:** ich habe überhaupt nichts anzuziehen
(b) (rub) abtragen ‹*Kleidungsstück*›; abnutzen ‹*Teppich*›; **a [badly] worn tyre** ein [stark] abgefahrener Reifen
[3] *v.i.,* **wore, worn (a)** ‹*Kleider:*› sich durchscheuern; ‹*Absätze:*› sich ablaufen; ‹*Teppich:*› sich abnutzen
(b) (endure rubbing) halten; **~ well/badly** sich gut/schlecht tragen

▪ **wear a'way** [1] *v.t.* abschleifen
[2] *v.i.* sich abnutzen

▪ **wear 'down** *v.t.* (fig.) zermürben

▪ **wear 'off** *v.i.* ‹*Schicht:*› abgehen; ‹*Wirkung, Schmerz:*› nachlassen

▪ **wear 'out** [1] *v.t.* **(a)** aufbrauchen; auftragen ‹*Kleidungsstück*›
(b) (fig.: exhaust) kaputtmachen (ugs.); **be worn out** kaputt sein (ugs.)
[2] *v.i.* kaputtgehen (ugs.)

▪ **wear 'through** [1] *v.i.* sich durchscheuern
[2] *v.t.* durchscheuern

wearable /ˈweərəbl/ *adj.* **sth. is [not] ~:** man kann etw. [nicht] anziehen

wearer /ˈweərə(r)/ *n.* Träger, *der*/Trägerin, *die*

wearily /ˈwɪərɪlɪ/ *adv.* müde

wearing /ˈweərɪŋ/ *adj.* ermüdend

wearisome /ˈwɪərɪsəm/ *adj.* ermüdend

weary /ˈwɪərɪ/ [1] *adj.* **(a)** (tired) müde **(b) be ~ of sth.** einer Sache (*Gen.*) überdrüssig sein [2] *v.t.* **be wearied by sth.** durch etw. erschöpft sein [3] *v.i.* **~ of sth./sb.** einer Sache/jmds. überdrüssig werden

weasel /ˈwiːzl/ *n.* Wiesel, *das*

weather /ˈweðə(r)/ [1] *n.* Wetter, *das;* **what's the ~ like?** wie ist das Wetter?; **in all ~s** bei jedem Wetter; **he is feeling under the ~** (fig.) er ist [zur Zeit] nicht ganz auf dem Posten [2] *v.t.* abwettern ‹*Sturm*›; (fig.) durchstehen ‹*schwere Zeit*›

weather: ~-beaten *adj.* wettergegerbt ‹*Gesicht*›; verwittert ‹*Felsen, Gebäude*›; **~ chart** *n.* Wetterkarte, *die;* **~cock** *n.* Wetterhahn, *der;* **~ conditions** *n. pl.* Witterungsverhältnisse *Pl.;* **~ forecast** *n.* Wettervorhersage, *die;* **~ man** *n.* Meteorologe, *der;* **~ map** *n.* Wetterkarte, *die;* **~proof** *adj.* wetterfest; **~ report** *n.* Wetterbericht, *der;* **~ vane** *n.* Wetterfahne, *die*

weave¹ /wiːv/ [1] *n.* Bindung, *die* [2] *v.t.,* **wove** /wəʊv/, **woven** /ˈwəʊvn/ **(a)** weben; flechten ‹*Korb, Kranz*› **(b)** (fig.) einflechten ‹*Thema usw.*› **(into** in + *Akk.*)

weave² *v.i.* (take intricate course) sich schlängeln

ˈweaver *n.* Weber, *der*/Weberin, *die*

web /web/ *n.* **(a)** Netz, *das;* **spider's ~:** Spinnennetz, *das* **(b) the Web** (Comp.) das Web (fachspr.); das Netz

ˈweb authoring *n.* Webauthoring, *das* (fachspr.) *attrib.* Webauthoring-‹*Programm, Software, usw.*›

webbed feet /webd ˈfiːt/ *n. pl.* Schwimmfüße *Pl.*

Web: ~ browser *n.* (Comp.) Web-Browser, *der;* **~ designer** *n.* Webdesigner, *der*/-designerin, *die;* **~ page** *n.* (Comp.) Webseite, *die;* **~ site** *n.* (Comp.) Website, *die*

we'd /wɪd, *stressed* wiːd/ **(a)** = **we had; (b)** = **we would**

Wed. *abbr.* = **Wednesday** Mi.

wedding /ˈwedɪŋ/ *n.* Hochzeit, *die*

wedding: ~ anniversary *n.* Hochzeitstag, *der;* **~ cake** *n.* Hochzeitskuchen, *der;* **~ day** *n.* Hochzeitstag, *der;* **~ dress** *n.* Brautkleid, *das;* **~ present** *n.* Hochzeitsgeschenk, *das;* **~ ring** *n.* Ehering, *der*

wedge /wedʒ/ [1] *n.* Keil, *der* [2] *v.t.* verkeilen; **~ a door/window open** eine Tür/ein Fenster festklemmen, damit sie/es offen bleibt

ˈwedge-shaped *adj.* keilförmig

wedlock /ˈwedlɒk/ *n.* **born in/out of ~:** ehelich/unehelich geboren

Wednesday /ˈwenzdeɪ, ˈwenzdɪ/ *n.* Mittwoch, *der; see also* FRIDAY

wee¹ /wiː/ *adj.* (child lang./Scot.) klein

wee² ▶ WEE-WEE

weed /wiːd/ [1] *n.* **~[s]** Unkraut, *das* [2] *v.t.* jäten

■ **weed ˈout** *v.t.* (fig.) aussieben

ˈweedkiller *n.* Unkrautvertilgungsmittel, *das*

ˈweedy *adj.* spillerig (ugs.) ‹*Person*›

week /wiːk/ *n.* Woche, *die;* **for several ~s** mehrere Wochen lang; **once a ~, every ~:** einmal in der Woche; **three times a ~:** dreimal in der Woche; **a two-~ visit** ein zweiwöchiger Besuch; **a ~ today/tomorrow** heute/morgen in einer Woche; **a ~ on Monday, Monday ~:** Montag in einer Woche

ˈweekday *n.* Wochentag, *der*

weekend /-ˈ-, ˈ--/ *n.* Wochenende, *das;* **at the ~:** am Wochenende; **go away for the ~:** übers Wochenende wegfahren

weekly /ˈwiːklɪ/ [1] *adj.* wöchentlich; Wochen‹*zeitung, -zeitschrift, -lohn*› [2] *adv.* wöchentlich [3] *n.* (newspaper) Wochenzeitung, *die;* (magazine) Wochenzeitschrift, *die*

weep /wiːp/ *v.i. & t.,* **wept** /wept/ weinen

weepie /ˈwiːpɪ/ *n.* (coll.) Schmachtfetzen, *der* (salopp)

weeping ˈwillow *n.* Trauerweide, *die*

weepy /ˈwiːpɪ/ [1] *adj.* weinerlich [2] *n.* ▶ WEEPIE

ˈwee-wee (coll.) [1] *n.* Pipi, *das* (ugs.); **do a ~:** Pipi machen (ugs.) [2] *v.i.* Pipi machen (ugs.)

weigh /weɪ/ *v.t. & i.* wiegen

■ **weigh ˈdown** *v.t.* (fig.: depress) niederdrücken

■ **weigh ˈup** *v.t.* abwägen

ˈweighing machine *n.* Waage, *die*

weight /weɪt/ *n.* Gewicht, *das;* **what is your ~?** wie viel wiegen Sie?; **be under/over ~:** zu wenig/zu viel wiegen

ˈweighting *n.* Zulage, *die*

ˈweightlessness *n.* Schwerelosigkeit, *die*

weight: ~lifter *n.* Gewichtheber, *der*/-heberin, *die;* **~lifting** *n.* Gewichtheben, *das* **~-train** *v.i.* mit Hanteln trainieren; **~ training** *n.* Hanteltraining, *das;* **~-watcher** *n.* Schlankheitsbewusste, *der*/*die*

ˈweighty *adj.* **(a)** (heavy) schwer **(b)** (important) gewichtig

weir /wɪə(r)/ *n.* Wehr, *das*

weird /wɪəd/ *adj.* (coll.: odd) bizarr

weirdo /ˈwɪədəʊ/ *n., pl.* **~s** ▶ WEIRDIE

welcome /ˈwelkəm/ [1] *int.* willkommen; **~ home/to England!** willkommen zu Hause/in England!
[2] *n.* **(a)** Willkommen, *das*
(b) (reception) Empfang, *der*
[3] *v.t.* begrüßen
[4] *adj.* **(a)** willkommen; gefällig ‹*Anblick*›
(b) *pred.* **you are ~ to take it** du kannst es gern nehmen; **you're ~**: gern geschehen!

welcoming /ˈwelkəmɪŋ/ *adj.* einladend

weld /weld/ *v.t.* (join) verschweißen; (repair, make, attach) schweißen (**[on] to** an + *Akk.*)

ˈwelder *n.* Schweißer, *der*/Schweißerin, *die*

ˈwelding *n.* Schweißen, *das*

welfare /ˈwelfeə(r)/ *n.* **(a)** (health and prosperity) Wohl, *das*
(b) (social work; payments etc.) Sozialhilfe, *die;* **be on ~** (Amer.) Sozialhilfe bekommen

welfare: W~ ˈState *n.* Wohlfahrtsstaat, *der;* **~ work** *n.* Sozialarbeit, *die;* **~ worker** *n.* Sozialarbeiter, *der*/-arbeiterin, *die*

well[1] /wel/ *n.* **(a)** Brunnen, *der*
(b) ▶ OIL WELL
(c) (stair~) Treppenloch, *das*

well[2] [1] *int.* **~!** meine Güte!; **~, let's forget that** na ja, lassen wir das; **~, who was it?** nun *od.* und, wer war's?; **oh ~[, never mind]** na ja[, macht nichts]; **~?** na?
[2] *adv.*, **better** /ˈbetə(r)/, **best** /best/ gut; gründlich ‹*trocknen, schütteln*›; **the business/patient is doing ~**: das Geschäft geht gut/dem Patienten geht es gut; **~ done!** großartig!; **he is ~ over forty** er ist weit über vierzig; **as ~** (in addition) auch; **A as ~ as B** B und auch [noch] A
[3] *adj.* (in good health) **How are you feeling now? – Quite ~, thank you** Wie fühlen Sie sich jetzt? – Ganz gut, danke; **look ~**: gut aussehen; **feel ~**: sich wohl fühlen; **he isn't [very] ~**: es geht ihm nicht [sehr] gut; **get ~ soon!** gute Besserung!; **make sb. ~**: jmdn. gesund machen

we'll /wɪl, *stressed* wiːl/ = **we will**

well: ~-aimed *adj.* gezielt; **~-balanced** *adj.* ausgeglichen ‹*Person*›; **~-behaved** ▶ BEHAVE 1; **~-being** *n.* Wohl, *das;* **~-bred** *adj.* anständig; **~-built** *adj.* ‹*Person*› mit guter Figur; **be ~-built** eine gute Figur haben; **~-chosen** *adj.* wohlgesetzt ‹*Worte*›; **~-connected** *adj.* ‹*Person*› mit guten Beziehungen; **~ done** *adj.* (Cookery) durchgebraten; **~-dressed** *adj.* gut gekleidet; **~-educated** *adj.* gebildet; **~-fed** *adj.* wohlgenährt; **~-founded** *adj.* [wohl] fundiert; **~-heeled** *adj.* (coll.) gut betucht (ugs.)

wellington /ˈwelɪŋtən/ *n.* **~ [boot]** Gummistiefel, *der*

well: ~-intentioned /ˈwelɪntenʃənd/ *adj.* gut gemeint; **~-known** *adj.* bekannt; **~ made** *adj.* gut [gearbeitet]; **~-mannered** *adj.* ‹*Person*› mit guten Manieren; **be ~-mannered** gute Manieren haben; **~-meaning** *adj.* wohlmeinend; **be ~-meaning** es gut meinen; **~-meant** *adj.* gut gemeint; **~ off** *adj.* wohlhabend; **sb. is ~ off** jmdm. geht es [finanziell] gut; **~ paid** *adj.* gut bezahlt; **~-read** /ˈwelred/ *adj.* belesen; **~-spoken** *adj.* sprachlich gewandt; **~-timed** *adj.* zeitlich gut gewählt; **~-to-do** *adj.* wohlhabend; **~-tried** *adj.* bewährt; **~-wisher** *n.* Sympathisant, *der*/Sympathisantin, *die*

Welsh /welʃ/ [1] *adj.* walisisch; **sb. is ~**: jmd. ist Waliser/Waliserin
[2] *n.* **(a)** (language) Walisisch, *das; see also* ENGLISH 2A
(b) *pl.* **the ~**: die Waliser *Pl.*

Welsh: ~man /ˈwelʃmən/ *n., pl.* **~men** /ˈwelʃmən/ Waliser, *der;* **~ ˈrabbit, ~ rarebit** /ˈreəbɪt/ *ns.* Käsetoast, *der*

went ▶ GO 1

wept ▶ WEEP

were ▶ BE

we're /wɪə(r)/ = **we are;** ▶ BE

weren't (coll.) = **were not;** ▶ BE

west /west/ [1] *n.* **(a)** Westen, *der;* **in/to[wards]/from the ~**: im/nach/von Westen; **to the ~ of** westlich von
(b) *usu.* **W~** (Geog., Polit.) Westen, *der*
[2] *adj.* westlich; West‹*küste, -wind, -grenze, -tor*›
[3] *adv.* nach Westen; **~ of** westlich von

West: ~ Berˈlin *pr. n.* (Hist.) West-Berlin (*das*); **w~bound** *adj.* ‹*Zug, Verkehr usw.*› in Richtung Westen; **~ Country** *n.* (Brit.) Westengland, *das;* **~ ˈEnd** *n.* (Brit.) Westend, *das*

westerly /ˈwestəlɪ/ *adj.* westlich; ‹*Wind*› aus westlichen Richtungen

western /ˈwestən/ [1] *adj.* westlich; West‹*grenze, -hälfte, -seite*›; **~ Germany** Westdeutschland, *das*
[2] *n.* Western, *der*

Western ˈEurope *pr. n.* Westeuropa (*das*)

West: ~ ˈGerman (Hist.) [1] *adj.* westdeutsch; **he/she is ~ German** er ist Westdeutscher/sie ist Westdeutsche; [2] *n.* Westdeutsche, *der/die;* **~ ˈGermany** *pr. n.* (Hist.) Westdeutschland (*das*); **~ ˈIndian** [1] *adj.* westindisch; **sb. is ~ Indian** jmd. ist Westinder/-inderin; [2] *n.* Westinder, *der*/-inderin, *die;* **~ ˈIndies** *pr. n. pl.* Westindische Inseln *Pl.*

westward[s] /ˈwestwəd(z)/ *adv.* westwärts

wet /wet/ [1] *adj.* **(a)** nass
(b) (rainy) regnerisch; feucht ‹*Klima*›
(c) frisch ‹*Farbe*›; **'~ paint'** „frisch gestrichen"
(d) (coll.: feeble) schlapp (ugs.)
[2] *v.t.*, **wet** *or* **wetted** befeuchten
[3] *n.* **(a)** (moisture) Feuchtigkeit, *die*
(b) **in the ~**: im Regen

ˈwetness *n.* Nässe, *die*

ˈwet suit *n.* Tauchanzug, *der*

we've /wɪv, *stressed* wiːv/ = **we have**

whack /wæk/ (coll.) **1** *v.t.* hauen (ugs.) **2** *n.* Schlag, *der*

whacked /wækt/ *adj.* (Brit. coll.: tired out) erledigt (ugs.); kaputt (ugs.)

whale /weɪl/ *n.* **(a)** Wal, *der*
(b) (coll.) **we had a ~ of a [good] time** wir haben uns bombig (ugs.) amüsiert

'whalebone *n.* Fischbein, *das*

whaler /'weɪlə(r)/ *n.* Walfänger, *der*

whaling /'weɪlɪŋ/ *n.* Walfang, *die*

wharf /wɔːf/ *n., pl.* **wharves** /wɔːvz/ *or* **~s** Kai, *der*

what /wɒt/ **1** *adj.* welch...; **~ book?** welches Buch?; **~ time does it start?** um wie viel Uhr fängt es an?; **~ kind of man is he?** was für ein Mensch ist er?; **~ a fool you are!** was für ein Dummkopf du doch bist!; **~ cheek/luck!** was für eine Frechheit/ein Glück!; **I will give you ~ help I can** ich werde dir helfen, so gut ich kann
2 *adv.* **~ do I care?** was kümmerts mich?; **~ does it matter?** was machts?
3 *pron.* was; **~?** wie?; was? (ugs.); **~ is your name?** wie heißt du/heißen Sie?; **~ about ...?** (~ will become of ...?) was ist mit ...?; **~ about a game of chess?** wie wärs mit einer Partie Schach?; **~'s-his/-her/-its-name** wie heißt er/sie/es noch; **~ for?** wozu?; **~ is it like?** wie ist es?; **so ~?** na und?; **do ~ I tell you** tu, was ich dir sage

whatever /wɒt'evə(r)/ **1** *adj.* **~ problems you have** was für Probleme Sie auch haben; **nothing ~**: absolut nichts
2 *pron.* **do ~ you like** mach, was du willst; **~ happens, ...**: was auch geschieht, ...; **or ~**: oder was auch immer; **~ does he want?** (coll.) was will er nur?

whatsit /'wɒtsɪt/ *n.* (coll.) (thing) Dingsbums, *das* (ugs.); (person) Dingsda, *der* (ugs.)

wheat /wiːt/ *n.* Weizen, *der*

wheedle /'wiːdl/ *v.t.* **~ sb. into doing sth.** jmdm. so lange gut zureden, bis er etw. tut; **~ sth. out of sb.** jmdm. etw. abschwatzen (ugs.)

wheel /wiːl/ **1** *n.* **(a)** Rad, *das;* **[potter's] ~**: Töpferscheibe, *die*
(b) (steering ~) Lenkrad, *das;* (ship's ~) Steuerrad, *das;* **at** *or* **behind the ~** (of car) am Steuer
2 *v.t.* (push) schieben
3 *v.i.* **(a)** (turn round) kehrtmachen
(b) (circle) kreisen

wheel: ~barrow *n.* Schubkarre, *die;* **~ brace** *n.* Radschlüssel, *der;* **~chair** *n.* Rollstuhl, *der;* **~ clamp** *n.* Parkkralle, *die*

wheeler-dealer /wiːlə'diːlə(r)/ *n.* Mauschler, *der*/Mauschlerin, *die;* (financial) Geschäftemacher, *der*/-macherin, *die*

'wheelie bin *n.* (Brit. coll.) Müllcontainer, *der* auf Rollen

'wheel reflector *n.* (on bicycle) Speichenreflektor, *der*

wheeze /wiːz/ *v.t.* schnaufen

whelk /welk/ *n.* Wellhornschnecke, *die*

when /wen/ **1** *adv.* wann; **the time ~ ...**: die Zeit, zu der/(with past tense) als ...; **the day ~ ...**: der Tag, an dem/(with past tense) als ...
2 *conj.* **(a)** (at the time that) als; (with present or future tense) wenn; **~ reading [a newspaper]** beim Lesen [einer Zeitung]
(b) (whereas) **why do you go abroad ~ it's cheaper here?** warum fährst du ins Ausland, wo es doch hier billiger ist?
3 *pron.* **by/till ~ ...?**; bis wann ...?; **since ~ ...?** seit wann ...?

whence /wens/ *adv., conj.* (arch./literary) woher

whenever /wen'evə(r)/ **1** *adv.* wann immer; **or ~**: oder wann immer; **~ did he do it?** (coll.) wann hat er es nur getan?
2 *conj.* jedes Mal wenn

where /weə(r)/ **1** *adv.* **(a)** (position) wo; **~ shall we sit?** wohin wollen wir uns setzen?
(b) (to ~) wohin
2 *conj.* wo
3 *pron.* **near/not far from ~ it happened** nahe der Stelle/nicht weit von der Stelle, wo es passiert ist

whereabouts **1** /weərə'baʊts/ *adv.* (where) wo; (to where) wohin
2 /'weərəbaʊts/ *n., sing. or pl.* (of thing) Verbleib, *der;* (of person) Aufenthalt[sort], *der*

where: ~'as *conj.* während; **he is very quiet, ~as she is an extrovert** er ist sehr ruhig, sie dagegen ist eher extravertiert; **~'by** *adv.* mit dem/der/denen; **~upon** /weərə'pɒn/ *adv.* worauf

wherever /weər'evə(r)/ **1** *adv.* **(a)** (position) wo immer; **sit ~ you like** setz dich, wohin du magst; **or ~**: oder wo immer
(b) (direction) wohin immer; **or ~**: oder wohin immer
(c) ~ have you been? (coll.) wo hast du bloß gesteckt?
2 *conj.* **(a)** (position) überall [da], wo; **~ possible** wo *od.* wenn [irgend] möglich
(b) (direction) wohin auch; **~ he went** wohin er auch ging

wherewithal /'weəwɪðɔːl/ *n.* (coll.) **the ~**: das nötige Kleingeld (ugs.)

whet /wet/ *v.t.,* **-tt-**: **(a)** (sharpen) wetzen
(b) (fig.) anregen ‹*Appetit*›

whether /'weðə(r)/ *conj.* ob; **I don't know ~ to go [or not]** ich weiß nicht, ob ich gehen soll [oder nicht]

which /wɪtʃ/ **1** *adj.* welch...; **~ one** welcher/welche/welches; **~ ones** welche; **~ way** (how) wie; (in ~ direction) wohin
2 *pron.* **(a)** *interrog.* welcher/welche/welches; **~ of you?** wer von euch?
(b) *rel.* der/die/das; **of ~**: dessen/deren; **after ~**: worauf[hin]

whichever /wɪtʃ'evə(r)/ **1** *adj.* welcher/welche/welches ... auch

[2] *pron.* **(a)** welcher/welche/welches ... auch **(b)** (coll.) ~ **could it be?** welcher/welche/welches könnte das nur sein?

whiff /wɪf/ *n.* (puff; fig.: trace) Hauch, *der;* (smell) leichter Geruch

while /waɪl/ [1] *n.* Weile, *die;* **[for] a ~:** eine Weile; **a long ~:** lange; **for a little** *or* **short ~:** eine kleine Weile; **[only] a little** *or* **short ~ ago** [erst] kürzlich *od.* vor kurzem; **be worth sb.'s ~:** sich [für jmdn.] lohnen
[2] *conj.* **(a)** während; (as long as) solange
(b) (although) obgleich
(c) (whereas) während

■ **while a'way** *v.t.* ~ **away the time** sich (*Dat.*) die Zeit vertreiben (**by, with** mit)

whilst /waɪlst/ (Brit.) ▶ WHILE 2

whim /wɪm/ *n.* Laune, *die*

whimper /ˈwɪmpə(r)/ [1] *n.* ~**[s]** Wimmern, *das;* (of dog etc.) Winseln, *das*
[2] *v.i.* wimmern; ‹*Hund:*› winseln

whimsical /ˈwɪmzɪkl/ *adj.* launenhaft; (odd, fanciful) spleenig

whine /waɪn/ [1] *v.i.* **(a)** heulen; ‹*Hund:*› jaulen
(b) (complain) jammern
[2] *n.* **(a)** Heulen, *das;* (of dog) Jaulen, *das*
(b) (complaint) ~**[s]** Gejammer, *das*

whip /wɪp/ [1] *n.* **(a)** Peitsche, *die*
(b) (Brit. Parl.) Fraktionsgeschäftsführer, *der*/-führerin, *die*
[2] *v.t.*, **-pp-: (a)** peitschen
(b) (Cookery) schlagen
(c) (move quickly) reißen
(d) (coll.: steal) klauen (ugs.)

■ **whip 'out** *v.t.* [blitzschnell] herausziehen

■ **whip 'up** *v.t.* **(a)** (arouse) anheizen (ugs.)
(b) (coll.: make quickly) schnell hinzaubern ‹*Gericht, Essen*›

whiplash *n.* ~**lash [injury]** Peitschenschlagverletzung, *die*

whipped 'cream *n.* Schlagsahne, *die*

'whipping cream *n.* [flüssige] Schlagsahne

'whip-round *n.* (Brit. coll.) Sammlung, *die*

whirl /wɜːl/ [1] *v.t.* [im Kreis] herumwirbeln
[2] *v.i.* wirbeln
[3] *n.* **(a)** Wirbeln, *das;* **she was** *or* **her thoughts were in a ~** (fig.) ihr schwirrte der Kopf
(b) (bustle) Trubel, *der*

W

■ **whirl 'round** [1] *v.t.* [im Kreis] herumwirbeln
[2] *v.i.* [im Kreis] herumwirbeln; ‹*Rad, Rotor:*› wirbeln

whirl: ~pool *n.* Strudel, *der;* (bathing pool) Whirlpool, *der;* **~wind** *n.* Wirbelwind, *der*

whirr /wɜː(r)/ [1] *v.i.* surren
[2] *n.* Surren, *das*

whisk /wɪsk/ [1] *n.* (Cookery) Schneebesen, *der;* (part of mixer) Rührbesen, *der*
[2] *v.t.* **(a)** (Cookery) [mit dem Schnee-/Rührbesen] schlagen
(b) (convey rapidly) in Windeseile bringen

■ **whisk a'way** *v.t.* **(a)** (remove suddenly) ~ **sth. away [from sb.]** [jmdm.] etw. [plötzlich] wegreißen
(b) (convey rapidly) in Windeseile wegbringen

whisker /ˈwɪskə(r)/ *n.* **(a)** ~**s** (on man's cheek) Backenbart, *der*
(b) (of cat, mouse, rat) Schnurrhaar, *das*

whiskey (Amer., Ir.)**, whisky** /ˈwɪskɪ/ *n.* Whisky, *der;* (American or Irish) Whiskey, *der*

whisper /ˈwɪspə(r)/ [1] *v.i.* flüstern; ~ **to sb.** jmdm. etwas zuflüstern
[2] *v.t.* flüstern; ~ **sth. to sb.** jmdm. etw. zuflüstern
[3] *n.* **(a)** Flüstern, *das;* **in a ~, in ~s** im Flüsterton
(b) (rumour) Gerücht, *das*

whistle /ˈwɪsl/ [1] *v.i.* pfeifen; ~ **at sb.** (in disapproval) jmdn. auspfeifen
[2] *v.t.* pfeifen
[3] *n.* **(a)** (sound) Pfiff, *der;* (whistling) Pfeifen, *das*
(b) (instrument) Pfeife, *die;* **blow a/one's ~:** pfeifen

whistling 'kettle *n.* Pfeifkessel, *der*

white /waɪt/ [1] *adj.* weiß
[2] *n.* **(a)** (colour) Weiß, *das*
(b) (of egg) Eiweiß, *das*
(c) W~ (person) Weiße, *der/die*

white: ~ bread *n.* Weißbrot, *das;* **~ cell** *n.* weißes Blutkörperchen; **~ 'coffee** *n.* (Brit.) Kaffee mit Milch; **~-'collar worker** *n.* Angestellte, *der/die;* **~ corpuscle** ▶ ~ CELL; **~ 'elephant** ▶ ELEPHANT; **W~ House** *pr. n.* (Amer. Polit.) **the W~ House** das Weiße Haus; **~-knuckle ride** *n.* Fahrt mit äußerstem Nervenkitzel; **~ 'lie** ▶ LIE[1] 1; **~ 'meat** *n.* weißes Fleisch [und Geflügel]

whiten /ˈwaɪtn/ [1] *v.t.* weiß machen; weißen ‹*Wand, Schuhe*›
[2] *v.i.* weiß werden

'whiteness *n.* Weiß, *das*

white: W~ 'Paper *n.* (Brit.) *öffentliches Diskussionspapier über Vorhaben der Regierung;* **~ 'sauce** *n.* weiße *od.* helle Soße; **~wash** [1] *n.* [weiße] Tünche; (fig.) Schönfärberei, *die;* [2] *v.t.* [weiß] tünchen; **~ 'wedding** *n.* Hochzeit, *die* in Weiß; **~ 'wine** *n.* Weißwein, *der*

Whit 'Monday /wɪt/ *n.* Pfingstmontag, *der*

Whitsun /ˈwɪtsn/ *n.* Pfingsten, *das od. Pl.;* **at ~:** zu *od.* an Pfingsten

whittle /ˈwɪtl/**: ~ a'way** *v.t.* ~ **away sb.'s rights/power** jmdm. nach und nach alle Rechte/Macht nehmen; **~ 'down** *v.t.* allmählich reduzieren ‹*Anzahl, Gewinn*›; verkürzen ‹*Liste*›

whiz, whizz /wɪz/ [1] *v.i.*, **-zz-** zischen
[2] *n.* Zischen, *das*

'whiz[z]-kid *n.* (coll.) Senkrechtstarter, *der*

who /hʊ, *stressed* huː/ *pron.* **(a)** *interrog.* wer; (coll.: whom) wen; (coll.: to whom) wem
(b) *rel.* der/die/das; *pl.* die; (coll.: whom) den/

die/das; (coll.: to whom) dem/der/denen; **anyone/those ~ ...:** wer ...; **everybody ~ ...:** jeder, der ...

whoa /wəʊ/ *int.* brr

who'd /hʊd, *stressed* hu:d/ **(a)** = **who had;** **(b)** = **who would**

whoever /hu:'evə(r)/ *pron.* **(a)** wer [immer]
(b) (no matter who) wer ... auch
(c) (coll.) **~ could it be?** wer könnte das nur sein?

whole /həʊl/ **1** *adj.* ganz; **the ~ lot [of them]** [sie] alle
2 *n.* Ganze, *das;* **the ~:** das Ganze; **the ~ of my money/the village/London** mein ganzes Geld/das ganze Dorf/ganz London; **as a ~:** als Ganzes; **on the ~:** im Großen und Ganzen

whole: ~food *n.* Vollwertkost, *die;* **~hearted** /həʊl'hɑ:tɪd/ *adj.* herzlich ‹*Dank[barkeit]*›; rückhaltlos ‹*Unterstützung*›; **~meal** *adj.* Vollkorn-; **~ 'milk** *n.* Vollmilch, *die;* **~ note** *n.* (Amer. Mus.) ganze Note; **~ 'number** *n.* ganze Zahl; **~sale** **1** *adj.* **(a)** Großhandels-; **(b)** (fig.: on a large scale) massenhaft; Massen-; **2** *adv.* **(a)** en gros; **(b)** (fig.: on a large scale) massenweise; **~saler** /'həʊlseɪlə(r)/ *n.* Großhändler, *der*/-händlerin, *die*

wholesome /'həʊlsəm/ *adj.* gesund

who'll /hʊl, *stressed* hu:l/ = **who will**

wholly /'həʊllɪ/ *adv.* völlig

whom /hu:m/ *pron.* **(a)** *interrog.* wen; *as indirect object* wem
(b) *rel.* den/die/das; *pl.* die; *as indirect object* dem/der/dem; *pl.* denen

whooping cough /'hu:pɪŋ kɒf/ *n.* Keuchhusten, *der*

whopper /'wɒpə(r)/ *n.* (coll.) **(a)** Riese, *der*
(b) (lie) faustdicke Lüge

whopping /'wɒpɪŋ/ *adj.* (coll.) riesig; Riesen- (ugs.); faustdick ‹*Lüge*›

whore /hɔ:(r)/ *n.* Hure, *die*

who's /hu:z/ **(a)** = **who is**
(b) = **who has**

whose /hu:z/ *pron.* **(a)** *interrog.* wessen; **~ [book] is that?** wem gehört das [Buch]?
(b) *rel.* dessen/deren/dessen; *pl.* deren

who've /hʊv, *stressed* hu:v/ = **who have**

why /waɪ/ **1** *adv.* **(a)** (for what reason) warum; (for what purpose) wozu; **~ is that?** warum das?
(b) (on account of which) **the reason ~ he did it** der Grund, warum er es tat
2 *int.* **~, certainly/of course!** aber sicher!

wick /wɪk/ *n.* Docht, *der*

wicked /'wɪkɪd/ *adj.* böse

'wickedness *n.* Bosheit, *die*

wicker /'wɪkə(r)/ *n.* Korbgeflecht, *das; attrib.* Korb‹*waren, -stuhl*›

'wickerwork *n.* **(a)** (material) Korbgeflecht, *das*
(b) (articles) Korbwaren *Pl.*

wicket /'wɪkɪt/ *n.* (Cricket) Tor, *das*

'wicketkeeper *n.* (Cricket) Torwächter, *der*/-wächterin, *die*

wide /waɪd/ **1** *adj.* **(a)** (broad) breit; groß ‹*Abstand, Winkel*›; **three feet ~:** drei Fuß breit
(b) (extensive) weit; umfassend ‹*Lektüre, Wissen, Kenntnisse*›; reichhaltig ‹*Auswahl, Sortiment*›
(c) (off target) **be ~ of sth.** etw. verfehlen
2 *adv.* **(a) ~ awake** hellwach
(b) (off target) **shoot ~:** danebenschießen; **go ~:** das Ziel verfehlen

wide: ~-angle 'lens *n.* (Photog.) Weitwinkelobjektiv, *das;* **~-eyed** *adj.* (surprised) mit großen Augen *nachgestellt*

'widely *adv.* **(a)** (over a wide area) weit ‹*verbreitet, gestreut*›
(b) (by many people) weithin ‹*bekannt, akzeptiert*›; **a ~ held view** eine weit verbreitete Ansicht
(c) (greatly) erheblich ‹*sich unterscheiden*›

widen /'waɪdn/ **1** *v.t.* verbreitern
2 *v.i.* sich verbreitern

wide: ~-open *attrib. adj.*, **~ 'open** *pred. adj.* weit geöffnet ‹*Fenster, Tür*›; weit aufgerissen ‹*Mund, Augen*›; **be ~ open** ‹*Fenster, Tür:*› weit offen stehen; **~-ranging** /'waɪdreɪndʒɪŋ/ *adj.* weit gehend ‹*Maßnahme, Veränderung*›; ausführlich ‹*Diskussion, Gespräch*›; **~ 'screen** *n.* Breitwand, *die;* **~screen television, ~screen TV** *ns.* Breitwandfernsehen, *das;* **~spread** *adj.* weit verbreitet

widow /'wɪdəʊ/ *n.* Witwe, *die*

widowed /'wɪdəʊd/ *adj.* verwitwet

widower /'wɪdəʊə(r)/ *n.* Witwer, *der*

width /wɪdθ/ *n.* Breite, *die;* (of garment) Weite, *die*

wield /wi:ld/ *v.t.* schwingen; (fig.) ausüben ‹*Macht, Einfluss*›

wife /waɪf/ *n., pl.* **wives** /waɪvz/ Frau, *die*

'wife battering *n.* Misshandlung, *die* der [Ehe]frau

wig /wɪg/ *n.* Perücke, *die*

wiggle /'wɪgl/ (coll.) **1** *v.t.* hin und her bewegen
2 *v.i.* wackeln

wild /waɪld/ **1** *adj.* **(a)** wild lebend ‹*Tier*›; wild wachsend ‹*Pflanze*›
(b) wild ‹*Landschaft*›
(c) (unrestrained) wild ‹*Erregung*›; **run ~** ‹*Pferd, Hund:*› frei herumlaufen; ‹*Kind:*› herumtoben; **send** *or* **drive sb. ~:** jmdn. rasend vor Erregung machen
(d) (coll.: very keen) **be ~ about sb./sth.** wild auf jmdn./etw. sein
2 *n.* **the ~[s]** die Wildnis; **see an animal in the ~:** ein Tier in freier Wildbahn sehen

wild: ~ 'boar *n.* Wildschwein, *das;* **~ card** *n.* wilde Karte; **~cat** *n.* Wildkatze, *die*

wilderness /'wɪldənɪs/ *n.* Wildnis, *die;* (desert) Wüste, *die*

wild: ~ 'goose chase *n.* (fig.) aussichtslose Suche; **~life** *n.* die Tier- und Pflanzenwelt; **~life park/reserve/sanctuary** Naturpark, *der*/-reservat, *das*/-schutzgebiet, *das*

'wildly *adv.* wild; **be ~ excited about sth.** über etw. (*Akk.*) ganz aus dem Häuschen sein (ugs.); **~ inaccurate** völlig ungenau

wilful /'wɪlfl/ *adj.*, **wilfully** /'wɪlfəlɪ/ *adv.* **(a)** (deliberate[ly]) vorsätzlich **(b)** (obstinate[ly]) starrsinnig

will¹ /wɪl/ *v. aux., only in: pres.* **will,** *neg.* (coll.) **won't** /wəʊnt/, *past* **would** /wʊd/, *neg.* (coll.) **wouldn't** /'wʊdnt/ **He won't help me. W~/Would you?** Er will mir nicht helfen. Bist du bereit?; **the car won't start** das Auto springt nicht an; **~/would you pass the salt, please?** gibst du bitte mal das Salz rüber?/würdest du bitte mal das Salz rübergeben?; **~ you be quiet!** willst du wohl ruhig sein!; **he ~ sit there hour after hour** er pflegt dort stundenlang zu sitzen; **he '~ insist on doing it** er besteht unbedingt darauf, es zu tun; **~ you have some more cake?** möchtest *od.* willst du noch etwas Kuchen?; **the box ~ hold 5 lb. of tea** in die Kiste gehen 5 Pfund Tee; **tomorrow he ~ be in Oxford** morgen ist er in Oxford; **I promise I won't do it again** ich verspreche, ich mach's nicht noch mal; **if he tried, he would succeed** wenn er es versuchen würde, würde er es schaffen; **~ you please tidy up** würdest du bitte aufräumen?

will² *n.* **(a)** (faculty) Wille, *der* **(b)** (Law: testament) Testament, *das* **(c)** (desire) **at ~:** nach Belieben; **~ to live** Lebenswille, *der;* **against one's/sb.'s ~:** gegen seinen/jmds. Willen

'willing *adj.* willig; **ready and ~:** bereit; **be ~ to do sth.** bereit sein, etw. zu tun

'willingly *adv.* **(a)** (with pleasure) gern[e] **(b)** (voluntarily) freiwillig

'willingness *n.* Bereitschaft, *die*

willow /'wɪləʊ/ *n.* Weide, *die*

willowy /'wɪləʊɪ/ *adj.* gertenschlank

'will power *n.* Willenskraft, *die*

willy-nilly /wɪlɪ'nɪlɪ/ *adv.* wohl oder übel ‹*etw. tun müssen*›

wilt /wɪlt/ *v.i.* ‹*Pflanze, Blumen:*› welk werden, welken

wily /'waɪlɪ/ *adj.* listig; gewieft ‹*Person*›

wimp /wɪmp/ *n.* (coll.) Schlappschwanz, *der* (ugs.)

wimpish /'wɪmpɪʃ/ *adj.* (coll.) lahm (ugs.)

win /wɪn/ **1** *v.t.*, **-nn-, won** /wʌn/ gewinnen; bekommen ‹*Stipendium, Vertrag, Recht*›; **~ sb. sth.** jmdm. etw. einbringen **2** *v.i.*, **-nn-, won** gewinnen **3** *n.* Sieg, *der;* **have a ~:** gewinnen

■ **win 'over, win 'round** *v.t.* bekehren; (to one's side) auf seine Seite bringen; (convince) überzeugen

■ **win 'through** *v.i.* Erfolg haben

wince /wɪns/ *v.i.* zusammenzucken (**at** bei)

winch /wɪntʃ/ **1** *n.* Winde, *die* **2** *v.t.* winden; **~ up** hochwinden

wind¹ /wɪnd/ **1** *n.* Wind, *der;* (Med.) Blähungen *Pl.*; **get ~ of sth.** (fig.) Wind von etw. bekommen; **be in the ~** (fig.) in der Luft liegen; **get/have the ~ up** (coll.) Manschetten (ugs.) kriegen/haben **2** *v.t.* **the blow ~ed him** der Schlag nahm ihm den Atem

wind² /waɪnd/ **1** *v.i.*, **wound** /waʊnd/ **(a)** (curve) sich winden; (move) sich schlängeln **(b)** (coil) sich wickeln **2** *v.t.*, **wound (a)** (coil) wickeln; **~ sth. on [to] sth.** etw. auf etw. (*Akk.*) [auf]wickeln **(b)** aufziehen ‹*Uhr*›

■ **wind 'down** *v.t.* **(a)** herunterdrehen ‹*Autofenster*› **(b)** (fig.: reduce gradually) einschränken

■ **wind 'up** **1** *v.t.* **(a)** hochdrehen ‹*Autofenster*› **(b)** (coil) aufwickeln **(c)** aufziehen ‹*Uhr*› **(d)** (coll.: annoy deliberately) auf die Palme bringen (ugs.) **(e)** beschließen ‹*Debatte*› **(f)** (Finance, Law) auflösen **2** *v.i.* **(a)** (conclude) schließen **(b)** (coll.: end up) **~ up in prison/hospital** [zum Schluss] im Gefängnis/Krankenhaus landen (ugs.)

wind /wɪnd/**: ~-blown** *adj.* vom Wind zerzaust ‹*Haar*›; **~break** *n.* Windschutz, *der;* **~breaker** (Amer.), **~cheater** (Brit.) *ns.* Windjacke, *die;* **~ chill factor** *n.* Wind-chill-Index, *der*

winded /'wɪndɪd/ *adj.* **be ~:** außer Atem sein

winder /'waɪndə(r)/ *n.* (of watch) Krone, *die;* (of clock, toy) Aufziehschraube, *die*

wind /wɪnd/**: ~fall** *n.* **(a)** (fruit) **~falls** Fallobst, *das;* **(b)** (fig.) warmer Regen (ugs.); **~fall tax** (*einmalige*) *Sondersteuer auf Privatisierungsgewinne;* **~ farm** *n.* Windpark, *der;* **~ force** *n.* Windstärke, *die;* **~ instrument** *n.* Blasinstrument, *das;* **~mill** *n.* Windmühle, *die*

window /'wɪndəʊ/ *n.* (also Comp.) Fenster, *das;* (shop ~) [Schau]fenster, *das;* **break a ~:** eine Fensterscheibe zerbrechen

window: ~ box *n.* Blumenkasten, *der;* **~ cleaner** *n.* Fensterputzer, *der*/-putzerin, *die;* **~ cleaning** *n.* Fensterputzen, *das;* **~ display** *n.* Schaufensterauslage, *die;* **~ dresser** *n.* Schaufensterdekorateur, *der*/-dekorateurin, *die;* **~ dressing** *n.* (fig.) Schönfärberei, *die;* **~ frame** *n.* Fensterrahmen, *der;* **~ ledge** *n.* (inside) Fensterbank, *die;* (outside) Fenstersims, *der* *od. das;* ~ **pane** *n.* Fensterscheibe, *die;* ~ **shopping** *n.* Schaufensterbummeln, *das;* **go** ~ **shopping** einen Schaufensterbummel machen; ~ **sill** *n.* (inside) Fensterbank, *die;* (outside) Fenstersims, *der od. das*

wind /wɪnd/**:** ~**pipe** *n.* (Anat.) Luftröhre, *die;* ~ **power** *n.* Windkraft, *die;* ~**proof** *adj.* windabweisend; ~**proof jacket** Windjacke, *die;* ~**screen,** (Amer.) ~**shield** *ns.* Windschutzscheibe, *die;* ~**screen/**~**shield wiper** Scheibenwischer, *der;* ~**screen/**~**shield washer** Scheibenwaschanlage, *die;* ~**surfer** *n.* Windsurfer, *der;* ~**surfing** *n.* Windsurfen, *das;* ~**swept** *adj.* windgepeitscht; vom Wind zerzaust ‹*Person, Haare*›; ~ **tunnel** *n.* Windkanal, *der*

windward /ˈwɪndwəd/ *adj.* ~ **side** Windseite, *die*

ˈwindy *adj.* windig

wine /waɪn/ *n.* Wein, *der*

wine: ~ **bar** *n.* Weinstube, *die;* ~ **bottle** *n.* Weinflasche, *die;* ~ **cellar** *n.* [Wein]keller, *das;* ~ **cooler** *n.* Weinkühler, *der;* ~**glass** *n.* Weinglas, *das;* ~**grower** *n.* Winzer, *der*/Winzerin, *die;* ~**growing** **1** *n.* Weinbau, *der;* **2** *adj.* ~**-growing area** Weingegend, *die;* ~ **list** *n.* Weinkarte, *die;* ~ **merchant** *n.* Weinhändler, *der*/-händlerin, *die;* ~ **merchants** (business) Weinhandlung, *die;* ~ **tasting** /ˈwaɪnteɪstɪŋ/ *n.* Weinprobe, *die;* ~ **vault** *n.* Weinkeller, *der;* ~ **ˈvinegar** *n.* Weinessig, *der*

wing /wɪŋ/ *n.* **(a)** (Ornith., Archit., Sport) Flügel, *der*
(b) (Aeronaut.) Tragfläche, *die*
(c) (Brit. Motor. Veh.) Kotflügel, *der*

winged /wɪŋd/ *adj.* geflügelt

winger /ˈwɪŋə(r)/ *n.* (Sport) Außenstürmer, *der*/-stürmerin, *die*

wing: ~ **mirror** *n.* (Brit. Motor Veh.) Außenspiegel, *der;* ~**span** *n.* [Flügel]spannweite, *die;* ~ **tip** *n.* Flügelspitze, *die*

wink /wɪŋk/ **1** *v.i.* **(a)** blinzeln; (as signal) zwinkern; ~ **at sb.** jmdm. zuzwinkern
(b) (flash) blinken
2 *n.* **(a)** Blinzeln, *das;* (signal) Zwinkern, *das;* **give sb. a** ~: jmdm. zuzwinkern
(b) not sleep a ~: kein Auge zutun

ˈwinner *n.* Sieger, *der*/Siegerin, *die;* (of competition or prize) Gewinner, *der*/ Gewinnerin, *die*

ˈwinning *adj.* **(a)** *attrib.* siegreich; ~ **number** Gewinnzahl, *die*
(b) (charming) einnehmend; gewinnend ‹*Lächeln*›

ˈwinning post *n.* Zielpfosten, *der*

ˈwinnings *n. pl.* Gewinn, *der*

winter /ˈwɪntə(r)/ *n.* Winter, *der;* **in [the]** ~: im Winter

winter ˈsports *n. pl.* Wintersport, *der*

wintry /ˈwɪntrɪ/ *adj.* winterlich; ~ **shower** Schneegestöber, *das*

wipe /waɪp/ **1** *v.t.* **(a)** abwischen; [auf]wischen ‹*Fußboden*›; (dry) abtrocknen; ~ **one's mouth/eyes/nose** sich (*Dat.*) den Mund/die Tränen/die Nase abwischen; ~ **one's feet/shoes** [sich (*Dat.*)] die Füße/ Schuhe abtreten
(b) (get rid of) [ab]wischen; ~ **one's/sb.'s tears** sich/jmdm. die Tränen abwischen
2 *n.* **give sth. a** ~: etw. abwischen

▪ **wipe ˈdown** *v.t.* abwischen

▪ **wipe ˈoff** *v.t.* **(a)** (remove) wegwischen; löschen ‹*Bandaufnahme*›
(b) (pay off) zurückzahlen ‹*Schulden*›

▪ **wipe ˈout** *v.t.* **(a)** (remove) wegwischen; (erase) auslöschen
(b) (cancel) tilgen; zunichte machen ‹*Vorteil, Gewinn usw.*›
(c) (destroy) ausrotten ‹*Rasse, Tierart, Feinde*›; ausmerzen ‹*Seuche, Korruption*›

▪ **wipe ˈup** *v.t.* **(a)** aufwischen
(b) (dry) abtrocknen

ˈwiper *n.* (Motor Veh.) Wischer, *der*

wire /ˈwaɪə(r)/ **1** *n.* **(a)** Draht, *der*
(b) (Electr., Teleph.) Leitung, *die*
(c) (coll.: telegram) Telegramm, *das*
2 *v.t.* **(a)** (fasten) ~ **sth. together** etw. mit Draht verbinden
(b) (Electr.) ~ **sth. to sth.** etw. an etw. (*Akk.*) anschließen; ~ **a house** in einem Haus die Stromleitungen legen

wire: ~ **ˈbrush** *n.* Drahtbürste, *die;* ~ **cutters** *n. pl.* Drahtschneider, *der*

ˈwireless **1** *adj.* (Comp.) drahtlos
2 *n.* (Brit. dated) Radio, *das*

wire: ~ **ˈnetting** *n.* Maschendraht, *der;* ~ **strippers** *n. pl.* Abisolierzange, *die;* ~ **ˈwool** *n.* Stahlwolle, *die*

wiring /ˈwaɪərɪŋ/ *n.* [elektrische] Leitungen *Pl.*

wisdom /ˈwɪzdəm/ *n.* **(a)** Weisheit, *die*
(b) (prudence) Klugheit, *die*

ˈwisdom tooth *n.* Weisheitszahn, *der*

wise /waɪz/ *adj.* **(a)** weise; vernünftig ‹*Meinung*›
(b) (prudent) klug
(c) be none the ~**r** kein bisschen klüger als vorher sein

wise: ~**crack** (coll.) *n.* witzige Bemerkung; ~ **guy** *n.* (coll.) Klugscheißer, *der* (salopp)

ˈwisely *adv.* weise; (prudently) klug

wish /wɪʃ/ **1** *v.t.* wünschen; **I** ~ **I was** *or* **were rich** ich wollte, ich wäre reich; **I** ~ **to go** ich möchte gehen; ~ **sb. luck/success** *etc.* jmdm. Glück/Erfolg *usw.* wünschen; ~ **sb. well** jmdm. alles Gute wünschen
2 *v.i.* wünschen; ~ **for sth.** sich (*Dat.*) etw. wünschen
3 *n.* Wunsch, *der;* **make a** ~: sich (*Dat.*) etwas wünschen; **get** *or* **have one's** ~: seinen Wunsch erfüllt bekommen

wishful thinking /wɪʃfl 'θɪŋkɪŋ/ *n.* Wunschdenken, *das*

'wishing well *n.* Wunschbrunnen, *der*

wishy-washy /'wɪʃɪwɒʃɪ/ *adj.* labberig (ugs.); (fig.) lasch

wisp /wɪsp/ *n.* (of straw) Büschel, *das;* **~ of hair** Haarsträhne, *die;* **~ of cloud/smoke** Wolkenfetzen, *der*/Rauchfahne, *die*

wistful /'wɪstfl/ *adj.*, wehmütig

wit /wɪt/ *n.* **(a)** (humour) Witz, *der*
(b) (intelligence) Geist, *der;* **be at one's ~'s** *or* **~s' end** sich (*Dat.*) keinen Rat mehr wissen; **be frightened** *or* **scared out of one's ~s** Todesangst haben; **have/keep one's ~s about one** auf Draht (ugs.) sein/nicht den Kopf verlieren
(c) (person) geistreicher Mensch

witch /wɪtʃ/ *n.* Hexe, *die*

witch: ~craft *n.* Hexerei, *die;* **~ doctor** *n.* Medizinmann, *der;* **~-hunt** *n.* Hexenjagd, *die* (**for** auf + *Akk.*)

with /wɪð/ *prep.* mit; **put sth. ~ sth.** etw. zu etw. stellen/legen; **have nothing to write ~:** nichts zum Schreiben haben; **I'm not '~ you** (coll.) ich komme nicht mit; **tremble ~ fear** vor Angst zittern; **I have no money ~ me** ich habe kein Geld dabei *od.* bei mir; **sleep ~ the window open** bei offenem Fenster schlafen

with'draw [1] *v.t., forms as* DRAW 1: zurückziehen; abziehen ‹*Truppen*›; **~ sth. from an account** etw. von einem Konto abheben
[2] *v.i., forms as* DRAW 1: sich zurückziehen

withdrawal /wɪð'drɔ:əl/ *n.* **(a)** Zurücknahme, *die;* (of troops) Abzug, *der;* (of money) Abhebung, *die*
(b) (from drugs) Entzug, *der;* **~ symptoms** Entzugserscheinungen *Pl.*

with'drawn *adj.* (unsociable) verschlossen

wither /'wɪðə(r)/ [1] *v.t.* verdorren lassen
[2] *v.i.* [ver]welken

■ **wither a'way** *v.i.* dahinwelken (geh.)

withered /'wɪðəd/ *adj.* verwelkt ‹*Gras, Pflanze*›; verkrüppelt ‹*Gliedmaße*›

withering /'wɪðərɪŋ/ *adj.* vernichtend ‹*Blick*›

with'hold *v.t., forms as* HOLD²: **~ sth. from sb.** jmdm. etw. vorenthalten

W

within /wɪ'ðɪn/ *prep.* innerhalb; **stay/be ~ the law** den Boden des Gesetzes nicht verlassen; **~ eight miles of sth.** acht Meilen im Umkreis von etw.

without /wɪ'ðaʊt/ *prep.* ohne; **~ doing sth.** ohne etw. zu tun; **~ his knowing** ohne dass er davon weiß/wusste

with'stand *v.t.,* **withstood** /wɪθ'stʊd/ standhalten (+ *Dat.*); aushalten ‹*Beanspruchung, hohe Temperaturen*›

witness /'wɪtnɪs/ [1] *n.* Zeuge, *der*/Zeugin, *die* (**of, to** *Gen.*)
[2] *v.t.* **(a)** (see) **~ sth.** Zeuge/Zeugin einer Sache (*Gen.*) sein
(b) bestätigen ‹*Unterschrift*›

'witness box (Brit.)**, 'witness stand** (Amer.) *ns.* Zeugenstand, *der*

witticism /'wɪtɪsɪzm/ *n.* Witzelei, *die*

wittingly /'wɪtɪŋlɪ/ *adv.* wissentlich

witty /'wɪtɪ/ *adj.* witzig; geistreich ‹*Person*›

wives *pl. of* WIFE

wizard /'wɪzəd/ *n.* Zauberer, *der*

wizardry /'wɪzədrɪ/ *n.* Zauberei, *die*

wizened /'wɪzənd/ *adj.* runz[e]lig

WMD *abbr.* = **weapon of mass destruction** MVW

wobble /'wɒbl/ *v.i.* wackeln

wobbly /'wɒblɪ/ *adj.* wack[e]lig

woe /wəʊ/ *n.* (arch./literary/joc.) **~[s]** Jammer, *der;* **~ betide you!** wehe dir!

woebegone /'wəʊbɪgɒn/ *adj.* jammervoll

woeful /'wəʊfl/ *adj.* (deplorable) beklagenswert; (distressed) jammervoll

wok /wɒk/ *n.* (Cookery) Wok, *der*

woke, woken ▶ WAKE¹ 1, 2

wolf /wʊlf/ [1] *n., pl.* **wolves** /wʊlvz/ Wolf, *der*
[2] *v.t.* **~ [down]** verschlingen

woman /'wʊmən/ *n., pl.* **women** /'wɪmɪn/ Frau, *die;* **~ doctor** Ärztin, *die;* **~ friend** Freundin, *die*

womanize /'wʊmənaɪz/ *v.i.* den Frauen nachstellen

womanizer /'wʊmənaɪzə(r)/ *n.* Schürzenjäger, *der*

'womanly *adj.* fraulich

womb /wu:m/ *n.* Gebärmutter, *die*

women *pl. of* WOMAN

women: ~folk *n. pl.* Frauen *Pl.*; **W~'s 'Lib** (coll.)**, W~'s Libe'ration** *ns.* die Frauenbewegung; **~'s movement** *n.* Frauenbewegung, *die;* **~'s 'prison** *n.* Frauengefängnis, *das;* **~'s 'refuge** *n.* Frauenhaus, *das;* **~'s 'rights** *n. pl.* die Rechte der Frau

won ▶ WIN 1, 2

wonder /'wʌndə(r)/ [1] *n.* **(a)** (thing) Wunder, *das*
(b) (feeling) Staunen, *das*
[2] *adj.* Wunder-
[3] *v.i.* sich wundern; staunen (**at** über + *Akk.*)
[4] *v.t.* sich fragen; **I ~ what the time is** wie viel Uhr mag es wohl sein?; **I ~ whether I might open the window** dürfte ich vielleicht das Fenster öffnen?

wonderful /'wʌndəfl/ *adj.*, **wonderfully** /'wʌndəfəlɪ/ *adv.* wunderbar

wondering /'wʌndərɪŋ/ *adj.*, **wonderingly** /'wʌndərɪŋlɪ/ *adv.* staunend

won't /wəʊnt/ (coll.) = **will not;** ▶ WILL¹

woo /wu:/ *v.t.* **(a)** (literary: court) **~ sb.** um jmdn. werben (geh.)
(b) umwerben ‹*Kunden, Wähler*›

wood /wʊd/ *n.* **(a)** Holz, *das;* **touch ~** (Brit.), **knock on ~** (Amer.) unberufen!

(b) (trees) Wald, *der*

wood: ~ carving *n.* (object) Holzschnitzerei, *die;* **~craft** *n.* (~work) Holzschnitzerei, *die;* **~cut** *n.* Holzschnitt, *der;* **~cutter** *n.* Holzfäller, *der*

'wooded *adj.* bewaldet

wooden /'wʊdn/ *adj.* **(a)** hölzern; Holz-
(b) (fig.: stiff) hölzern

wood: ~land /'wʊdlənd/ *n.* Waldland, *das;* **~pecker** *n.* Specht, *der;* **~ pigeon** *n.* Ringeltaube, *die;* **~shed** *n.* Holzschuppen, *der;* **~wind** *n.* **the ~wind [section]** die Holzbläser *Pl.;* **~wind instrument** Holzblasinstrument, *das;* **~work** *n.* **(a)** (craft) Arbeiten mit Holz; **(b)** (things) Holzarbeit[en *Pl.*]; **~worm** *n.* Holzwurm, *der;* **it's got ~worm** da ist der Holzwurm drin (ugs.)

'woody *adj.* **(a)** (wooded) waldreich
(b) (consisting of wood) holzig

wool /wʊl/ *n.* Wolle, *die; attrib.* Woll

woollen (*Amer.:* **woolen**) /'wʊlən/
[1] *adj.* wollen
[2] *n.* **~s** Wollsachen *Pl.*

'woolly *adj.* **(a)** wollig; Woll‹*pullover, -mütze*›
(b) (confused) verschwommen

woozy /'wu:zɪ/ *adj.* (coll.) **(a)** (dizzy) duselig (ugs.)
(b) (drunk) angeduselt (salopp)

word /wɜ:d/ [1] *n.* Wort, *das;* **~s** (of song or actor) Text, *der;* **in other ~s** mit anderen Worten; **~ for ~:** Wort für Wort; **too funny** *etc.* **for ~s** unsagbar komisch *usw.;* **have ~s** einen Wortwechsel haben; **have a ~ [with sb.] about sth.** [mit jmdm.] über etw. (*Akk.*) sprechen; **could I have a ~ [with you]?** kann ich dich mal sprechen?; **say a few ~s** ein paar Worte sprechen; **keep/break one's ~:** sein Wort halten/brechen; **by ~ of mouth** durch mündliche Mitteilung; **send ~ that ...:** Nachricht geben, dass ...
[2] *v.t.* formulieren

'wording *n.* Formulierung, *die*

word: ~ order *n.* Wortstellung, *die;* **~play** *n.* Wortspiel, *das;* **~ processing** *n.* Textverarbeitung, *die;* **~ processor** *n.* Textverarbeitungssystem, *das*

wordy /'wɜ:dɪ/ *adj.* weitschweifig

wore ▶ WEAR 2, 3

work /wɜ:k/ [1] *n.* **(a)** Arbeit, *die;* **at ~** (engaged in ~ing) bei der Arbeit; (fig.: operating) am Werk; (at job) auf der Arbeit; **out of ~:** arbeitslos; **be in ~:** eine Stelle haben; **set to ~** ‹*Person:*› sich an die Arbeit machen; **go out to ~:** arbeiten gehen
(b) **~s** *sing. or pl.* (factory) Werk, *das*
(c) **~s** *pl.* (~ing parts) Werk, *das;* (operations) Arbeiten *Pl.*
(d) (thing made or achieved) Werk, *das;* **a ~ of art/literature** ein Kunstwerk/literarisches Werk
[2] *v.i.* **(a)** arbeiten
(c) (function effectively) funktionieren; **make the television ~:** den Fernsehapparat in Ordnung bringen
(c) (have an effect) wirken (**on** auf + *Akk.*)
(d) **~ loose** sich lockern
[3] *v.t.* **(a)** bedienen ‹*Maschine*›; betätigen ‹*Bremse*›
(b) (get labour from) arbeiten lassen
(c) ausbeuten ‹*Steinbruch, Grube*›
(d) (cause to go gradually) führen; **~ one's way up/into sth.** sich hocharbeiten/in etw. hineinarbeiten

■ **work 'off** *v.t.* **(a)** (get rid of) loswerden; abreagieren ‹*Wut*›
(b) abarbeiten ‹*Schuld*›

■ **'work on** *v.t.* **(a)** **~ on sth.** an etw. (*Dat.*) arbeiten
(b) (try to persuade) **~ on sb.** jmdn. bearbeiten (ugs.)

■ **work 'out** [1] *v.t.* **(a)** (calculate) ausrechnen
(b) (solve) lösen
(c) (devise) ausarbeiten
[2] *v.i.* **(a)** **sth. ~s out at £2** etw. ergibt 2 Pfund
(b) (have result) laufen; **things ~ed out [well] in the end** es ist schließlich doch alles gut gegangen

■ **work 'up** [1] *v.t.* (excite) aufpeitschen ‹*Menge*›; **get ~ed up** sich aufregen
[2] *v.i.* **~ up to sth.** ‹*Musik:*› sich zu etw. steigern; ‹*Geschichte, Film:*› auf etw. (*Akk.*) zusteuern

workable /'wɜ:kəbl/ *adj.* (feasible) durchführbar

workaholic /wɜ:kə'hɒlɪk/ *n.* (coll.) arbeitswütiger Mensch

work: ~bench *n.* Werkbank, *die;* **~day** *n.* Werktag, *der*

'worker *n.* Arbeiter, *der*/Arbeiterin, *die*

'worker bee *n.* Arbeiterbiene, *die*

work: ~ ethic *n.* Arbeitsethos, *das;* **~ experience** *n.* (for schoolchildren) Praktikum, *das;* **~force** *n.* Belegschaft, *die;*

'working *adj.* **(a)** (in work) werktätig
(b) **~ model** funktionsfähiges Modell

working: ~ 'capital *n.* Betriebskapital, *das;* **~ 'class** *n.* Arbeiterklasse, *die;* **~-class** *adj.* der Arbeiterklasse *nachgestellt;* **sb. is ~-class** jmd. gehört zur Arbeiterklasse; **~ clothes** *n. pl.* Arbeitskleidung, *die;* **~ 'day** *n.* **(a)** (portion of day) Arbeitstag, *der;* **(b)** (day when work is done) Werktag, *der;* **~ 'hours** *n. pl.* Arbeitszeit, *die;* **~ 'knowledge** *n.* ausreichende Kenntnisse (**of** in + *Dat.*); **~ 'mother** *n.* berufstätige Mutter; **~ 'order** *n.* **be in [good] ~ order** betriebsbereit sein; ‹*Auto:*› fahrbereit sein; **~-'over** *n.* (sl.) Abreibung, *die* (ugs.); **~ 'week** *n.* Arbeitswoche, *die;* **a 35-hour ~ week** eine 35-Stunden-Woche; **~ 'wife** *n.* berufstätige Ehefrau

work: ~load *n.* Arbeitslast, *die;* **~man** ···>

/'wɜ:kmən/ *n.*, *pl.* **~men** /'wɜ:kmən/ Arbeiter, *der;* **~manship** /'wɜ:kmənʃɪp/ *n.* (quality) Kunstfertigkeit, *die;* **~out** *n.* [Fitness]training, *das;* **~ permit** *n.* Arbeitserlaubnis, *die;* **~sheet** *n.* **(a)** (recording work done) Arbeitszettel, *der;* **(b)** (for student) Formular mit Prüfungsfragen; **~shop** *n.* **(a)** (room) Werkstatt, *die;* **(b)** (building) Werk, *das;* **~station** *n.* (Comp.) Workstation, *die;* **~ table** *n.* Arbeitstisch, *der;* **~-to-'rule** *n.* Dienst nach Vorschrift

world /wɜ:ld/ *n.* **(a)** Welt, *die;* **in the ~:** auf der Welt; **the tallest building in the ~:** das höchste Gebäude der Welt; **all over the ~:** in *od.* auf der ganzen Welt
(b) (vast amount) **it will do him a** *or* **the ~ of good** es wird ihm unendlich gut tun; **a ~ of difference** ein weltweiter Unterschied

world: W~ 'Bank *n.* Weltbank, *die;* **~ 'champion** *n.* Weltmeister, *der*/-meisterin, *die;* **W~ 'Cup** *n.* Worldcup, *der;* **~-famous** *adj.* weltberühmt; **W~ 'Heritage Site** *n.* Welterbestätte, *die*

'worldly *adj.* weltlich; weltlich eingestellt ‹*Person*›

worldly 'wise *adj.* weltklug

world: ~ 'music *n.* Weltmusik, *die;* **~ 'power** *n.* Weltmacht, *die;* **~ 'record** *n.* Weltrekord, *der;* **~-record holder** Weltrekordhalter, *der*/-halterin, *die;* **~-shaking** *adj.* welterschütternd; **World 'Trade Organization** *n.* Welthandelsorganisation, *die;* **~ view** *n.* Weltsicht, *die;* **~ 'war** *n.* Weltkrieg, *der;* **the First/Second W~ War, W~ War I/II** der Erste/Zweite Weltkrieg; der 1./2. Weltkrieg; **~wide** /'--/ *adj.* weltweit *nicht präd.;* **W~ Wide 'Web** *n.* (Comp.) World Wide Web, *das*

worm /wɜ:m/ 1 *n.* Wurm, *der*
2 *v.t.* **~ oneself into sb.'s favour** sich in jmds. Gunst (*Akk.*) schleichen

worn ▸ WEAR 2, 3

'worn-out *adj.* **(a)** abgetragen ‹*Kleidungsstück*›; abgenutzt ‹*Teppich*›
(b) erschöpft ‹*Person*›

worried /'wʌrɪd/ *adj.* besorgt

worry /'wʌrɪ/ 1 *v.t.* **(a)** beunruhigen
(b) (bother) stören
2 *v.i.* sich (*Dat.*) Sorgen machen
3 *n.* Sorge, *die;* **sth. is the least of sb.'s worries** etw. ist jmds. geringste Sorge

'worrying *adj.* **(a)** (causing worry) beunruhigend
(b) (full of worry) sorgenvoll ‹*Zeit, Woche*›

worse /wɜ:s/ 1 *adj.* schlechter; schlimmer ‹*Schmerz, Krankheit, Benehmen*›
2 *adv.* schlechter; schlimmer, schlechter ‹*sich benehmen*›
3 *n.* Schlimmeres

worsen /'wɜ:sn/ 1 *v.t.* verschlechtern
2 *v.i.* sich verschlechtern

worship /'wɜ:ʃɪp/ 1 *v.t.*, (Brit.) **-pp-: (a)** anbeten
(b) (idolize) abgöttisch verehren
2 *v.i.*, (Brit.) **-pp-** am Gottesdienst teilnehmen
3 *n.* **(a)** Anbetung, *die;* (service) Gottesdienst, *der*
(b) Your/His W~: ≈ Euer/seine Ehren

'worshipper (*Amer.*: **worshiper**) *n.* Gottesdienstbesucher, *der*/-besucherin, *die*

worst /wɜ:st/ 1 *adj.* schlechtest...; schlimmst... ‹*Schmerz, Krankheit, Benehmen*›
2 *adv.* am schlechtesten/schlimmsten
3 *n.* **(a) the ~:** der/die/das Schlimmste; **get** *or* **have the ~ of it** (suffer the most) am meisten zu leiden haben; **if the ~ comes to the ~:** wenn es zum Schlimmsten kommt
(b) (poorest in quality) Schlechteste, *der/die/das*

worsted /'wʊstɪd/ *n.* Kammgarn, *das*

worth /wɜ:θ/ 1 *adj.* wert; **it's ~ £80** es ist 80 Pfund wert; **is it ~ hearing/the effort?** ist es hörenswert/der Mühe wert?; **is it ~ doing?** lohnt es sich?; **it isn't ~ it** es lohnt sich nicht
2 *n.* Wert, *der;* **ten pounds' ~ of petrol** Benzin für zehn Pfund

'worthless *adj.* **(a)** (valueless) wertlos
(b) (having bad qualities) nichtswürdig

'worthwhile *adj.* lohnend

worthy /'wɜ:ðɪ/ *adj.* würdig

wouldn't /'wʊdnt/ (coll.) = **would not;** ▸ WILL[1]

wound[1] /wu:nd/ 1 *n.* Wunde, *die*
2 *v.t.* verwunden; (fig.) verletzen

wound[2] ▸ WIND[2]

wove, woven ▸ WEAVE[1] 2

wrangle /'ræŋgl/ 1 *v.i.* [sich] streiten
2 *n.* Streit, *der*

wrap /ræp/ 1 *v.t.*, **-pp-** einwickeln; (fig.) hüllen; **~ped** abgepackt ‹*Brot usw.*›; **~ sth. [a]round sth.** etw. um etw. wickeln
2 *n.* Umschlag[e]tuch, *das*

▪ **wrap 'up** *v.t.* **(a)** einwickeln
(b) (conclude) abschließen
(c) be ~ped up in one's work in seine Arbeit völlig versunken sein

'wrapper *n.* **(a) sweet/toffee ~[s]** Bonbonpapier, *das*
(b) (of book) Schutzumschlag, *der*

'wrapping *n.* Verpackung, *die*

'wrapping paper *n.* (strong) Packpapier, *das;* (decorative) Geschenkpapier, *das*

wrath /rɒθ/ *n.* Zorn, *der*

wreak /ri:k/ *v.t.* **(a)** (cause) anrichten
(b) ~ vengeance on sb. an jmdm. Rache nehmen

wreath /ri:θ/ *n.*, *pl.* **wreaths** /ri:ðz, ri:θs/ Kranz, *der*

wreck /rek/ 1 *n.* **(a)** Wrack, *das*
(b) (destruction of ship) Schiffbruch, *der*
2 *v.t.* **(a)** (destroy) ruinieren; zu Schrott fahren ‹*Auto*›; **be ~ed** (shipwrecked) Schiffbruch erleiden
(b) (fig.: ruin) zerstören; ruinieren ‹*Gesundheit, Urlaub*›

wreckage /'rekɪdʒ/ *n.* Wrackteile *Pl.;* (fig.) Trümmer *Pl.*
wren *n.* Zaunkönig, *der*
wrench /rentʃ/ [1] *n.* **(a)** (*esp. Amer.*: spanner) Schraubenschlüssel, *der*
(b) (violent twist) Verrenkung, *die*
(c) (fig.) **be a great ~ [for sb.]** sehr schmerzhaft für jmdn. sein
[2] *v.t.* **(a)** reißen; **~ sth. from sb.** jmdm. etw. entreißen
(b) ~ one's ankle sich (*Dat.*) den Knöchel verrenken
wrest /rest/ *v.t.* **~ sth. from sb.** jmdm. etw. entreißen
wrestle /'resl/ *v.i.* ringen
wrestler /'reslə(r)/ *n.* Ringer, *der*/Ringerin, *die*
wrestling /'reslɪŋ/ *n.* Ringen, *das*
wretch /retʃ/ *n.* Kreatur, *die*
wretched /'retʃɪd/ *adj.* **(a)** (miserable) unglücklich
(b) (coll.: damned) elend
(c) (very bad) erbärmlich
wriggle /'rɪgl/ [1] *v.i.* **(a)** sich winden; ‹*Fisch:*› zappeln
(b) (move) sich schlängeln
[2] *v.t.* **~ one's way** sich schlängeln
[3] *n.* Windung, *die*
wring /rɪŋ/ *v.t.*, **wrung** /rʌŋ/ **(a)** wringen; **~ out** auswringen
(b) ~ sb.'s hand jmdm. fest die Hand drücken; **~ the neck of an animal** einem Tier den Hals umdrehen
(c) ~ sth. from *or* **out of sb.** (fig.) jmdm. etw. abpressen
wringing 'wet *adj.* tropfnass
wrinkle /'rɪŋkl/ [1] *n.* Falte, *die;* (in paper) Knick, *der*
[2] *v.t.* falten
[3] *v.i.* sich in Falten legen
wrinkled /'rɪŋkld/ *adjs.* runz[e]lig
wrinkly /'rɪŋklɪ/ [1] *adj.* runz[e]lig
[2] *n.* (coll.) Grufti, *der* (ugs.)
wrist /rɪst/ *n.* Handgelenk, *das*
'wristwatch *n.* Armbanduhr, *die*
writ /rɪt/ *n.* (Law) Verfügung, *die*
write /raɪt/ [1] *v.i.*, **wrote** /rəʊt/, **written** /'rɪtn/ schreiben; **~ to sb./a firm** jmdm./an eine Firma schreiben
[2] *v.t.*, **wrote, written** schreiben; ausschreiben ‹*Scheck*›; **the written language** die Schriftsprache; **written applications** schriftliche Anträge *Pl.*
■ **write 'back** *v.i.* zurückschreiben
■ **write 'down** *v.t.* aufschreiben
■ **write 'off** [1] *v.t.* **(a)** abschreiben ‹*Schulden, Verlust*›
(b) (destroy) zu Schrott fahren
[2] *v.i.* **~ off for sth.** etw. [schriftlich] anfordern
'write-off *n.* Totalschaden, *der*
write-pro'tect *v.t.* (Comp.) shreibschützen; mit einem Shreibschutz versehen
writer /'raɪtə(r)/ *n.* Schriftsteller, *der*/Schriftstellerin, *die;* (of letter, article) Verfasser, *der*/Verfasserin, *die*
'write-up *n.* (by critic) Kritik, *die*
writhe /raɪð/ *v.i.* sich winden
writing /'raɪtɪŋ/ *n.* **(a)** Schreiben, *das;* **put sth. in ~:** etw. schriftlich machen (ugs.)
(b) (handwriting, something written) Schrift, *die*
'writing paper *n.* Schreibpapier, *das*
written ▶ WRITE
wrong /rɒŋ/ [1] *adj.* **(a)** (morally bad) unrecht (geh.); (unfair) ungerecht
(b) (mistaken) falsch; **be ~** ‹*Person:*› sich irren; **the clock is ~:** die Uhr geht falsch
(c) (not suitable) falsch; **give the ~ answer** eine falsche Antwort geben; **[the] ~ way round** verkehrt herum
(d) (out of order) nicht in Ordnung; **what's ~?** was ist los?
[2] *adv.* falsch
[3] *n.* Unrecht, *das;* **do ~:** Unrecht tun
[4] *v.t.* **~ sb.** jmdn. ungerecht behandeln
'wrongdoer *n.* Übeltäter, *der*/-täterin, *die;* Missetäter, *der*/-täterin, *die* (geh.)
'wrongdoing *n. no indef. art.* Missetaten *Pl.* (geh.)
wrongful /'rɒŋfl/ *adj.* **(a)** (unfair) unrecht (geh.)
(b) (unlawful) rechtswidrig
'wrongfully *adv.* **(a)** (unfairly) unrecht (geh.) ‹*handeln*›; zu Unrecht ‹*beschuldigen*›
(b) (unlawfully) rechtswidrig
'wrongly *adv.* **(a)** falsch
(b) (mistakenly) zu Unrecht
(c) ▶ WRONGFULLY A
wrote ▶ WRITE
wrought iron /rɔːt 'aɪən/ *n.* Schmiedeeisen, *das; attrib.* schmiedeeisern
wrung ▶ WRING
wry /raɪ/ *adj.*, **~er** *or* **wrier** /'raɪə(r)/, **~est** *or* **wriest** /'raɪɪst/ ironisch ‹*Blick*›; fein ‹*Humor, Witz*›
WTO *abbr.* = World Trade Organisation
WWW *abbr.* = **World Wide Web** WWW

Xx

X, x /eks/ *n.* X, x, *das*
xenophobia /zenəˈfəʊbɪə/ *n.* Fremdenfeindlichkeit, *die*
xenophobic /zenəˈfəʊbɪk/ *adj.* fremdenfeindlich
Xerox ®, **xerox** /ˈzɪərɒks/ 1 *n.* (copy) Xerokopie, *die*
2 **xerox** *v.t.* xerokopieren

Xmas /ˈkrɪsməs, ˈeksməs/ *n.* (coll.) Weihnachten, *das*

ˈX-ray 1 *n.* (picture) Röntgenaufnahme, *die*
2 *v.t.* röntgen; durchleuchten ‹*Gepäck*›

Yy

Y, y /waɪ/ *n.* Y, y, *das*
yacht /jɒt/ *n.* **(a)** (for racing) Segeljacht, *die*
(b) (for pleasure) Jacht, *die*
ˈyachting *n.* Segeln, *das*
yachtsman /ˈjɒtsmən/ *n.*, *pl.* **yachtsmen** /ˈjɒtsmən/ Segler, *der*
yank (coll.) 1 *v.t.* reißen an (+ *Dat.*)
2 *n.* Reißen, *das*
Yank /jæŋk/ *n.* (Brit. coll.: American) Ami, *der* (ugs.)
yap /jæp/ *v.i.*, **-pp-** kläffen
yard¹ /jɑːd/ *n.* (measure) Yard, *das*
yard² *n.* **(a)** (attached to building) Hof, *der;* **in the ~:** auf dem Hof
(b) (for storage) Lager, *das*
(c) (Amer: garden) Garten, *der*
ˈyardstick *n.* (fig.) Maßstab, *der*
yarn /jɑːn/ *n.* **(a)** (thread) Garn, *das*
(b) (coll.: story) Geschichte, *die*
yawn /jɔːn/ 1 *n.* Gähnen, *das*
2 *v.i.* gähnen
ˈyawning *adj.* gähnend
year /jɪə(r)/ *n.* **(a)** Jahr, *das;* **for [many] ~s** jahrelang; **once a ~, every ~:** einmal im Jahr; **a ten-~-old** ein Zehnjähriger/eine Zehnjährige
(b) (group of students, vintage of wine) Jahrgang, *der*
ˈyearbook *n.* Jahrbuch, *das*
ˈyearly 1 *adj.* jährlich; Einjahres‹*abonnement*›
2 *adv.* jährlich
yearn /jɜːn/ *v.i.* **~ for** *or* **after sth./for sb.** sich nach etw./jmdm. sehnen; **~ to do sth.** sich danach sehnen, etw. zu tun
ˈyearning *n.* Sehnsucht, *die*
yeast /jiːst/ *n.* Hefe, *die*
yell /jel/ 1 *n.* gellender Schrei
2 *v.t. & i.* [gellend] schreien
yellow /ˈjeləʊ/ 1 *adj.* gelb
2 *n.* Gelb, *das*
yellow: ~ ˈcard *n.* (Footb.) gelbe Karte; **~ ˈfever** *n.* Gelbfieber, *das*
yellowish /ˈjeləʊɪʃ/ *adj.* gelblich
Yellow ˈPages *n. pl.* ® gelbe Seiten *Pl.*
yelp /jelp/ 1 *v.i.* jaulen
2 *n.* Jaulen, *das*
yen /jen/ *n.* (coll.: longing) **sb. has a ~ to do sth.** es drängt jmdn. danach, etw. zu tun
yes /jes/ 1 *adv.* ja; (in contradiction) doch
2 *n.*, *pl.* **~es** Ja, *das*
ˈyes-man *n.* (coll. derog.) Jasager, *der* (abwertend)
yesterday /ˈjestədeɪ, ˈjestədɪ/ 1 *n.* gestern; **the day before ~:** vorgestern; **~'s paper** die gestrige Zeitung
2 *adv.* gestern; **the day before ~:** vorgestern
yet /jet/ 1 *adv.* **(a)** (still) noch; **~ again** noch einmal
(b) (hitherto) bisher; **his best ~:** sein bisher bestes
(c) *neg.* **not [just] ~:** [jetzt] noch nicht
(d) (before all is over) doch noch; **he could win ~:** er könnte noch gewinnen
(e) *with compar.* (even) noch
(f) (nevertheless) doch
2 *conj.* doch
yew /juː/ *n.* **~ [tree]** Eibe, *die*
Yiddish /ˈjɪdɪʃ/ 1 *adj.* jiddisch
2 *n.* Jiddisch, *das; see also* ENGLISH 2A
yield /jiːld/ 1 *v.t.* (give) bringen; hervorbringen ‹*Ernte*›; abwerfen ‹*Gewinn*›
2 *v.i.* **(a)** sich unterwerfen
(b) (give right of way) Vorfahrt gewähren
3 *n.* Ertrag, *der*

yob /jɒb/ *n.* (Brit. coll.) Rowdy, *der*
yobbish /ˈjɒbɪʃ/ *adj.* (Brit. coll.) rowdyhaft
yobbo /ˈjɒbəʊ/ *n. pl.* **~s** ▶ YOB
yodel /ˈjəʊdl/ *v.i. & t.,* (Brit.) **-ll-** jodeln
yoga /ˈjəʊgə/ *n.* Joga, *der od. das*
yoghurt, yogurt /ˈjɒgət/ *n.* Joghurt, *der od. das*
yoke /jəʊk/ *n.* Joch, *das*
yokel /ˈjəʊkl/ *n.* [Bauern]tölpel, *der*
yolk /jəʊk/ *n.* Dotter, *der od. das;* Eigelb, *das*
yonder /ˈjɒndə(r)/ (literary) **1** *adj.* **~ tree** jener Baum dort (geh.)
2 *adv.* dort drüben
Yorkshire ˈpudding *n.* Yorkshirepudding, *der*
you /jʊ, *stressed* juː/ *pron.* **(a)** *sing./pl.* du/ihr; (polite) *sing. or pl.* Sie; *as direct object* dich/euch/Sie; *as indirect object* dir/euch/Ihnen; *refl.* dich/dir/euch; (polite) sich; **it was ~:** du warst/ihr wart/Sie waren es
(b) (one) man
you'd /jʊd, *stressed* juːd/ **(a)** = **you had**
(b) = **you would**
you'll /jʊl, *stressed* juːl/ **(a)** = **you will**
(b) = **you shall**
young /jʌŋ/ **1** *adj.,* **~er** /ˈjʌŋgə(r)/, **~est** /ˈjʌŋgɪst/ jung
2 *n. pl.* (of animals) Junge *Pl.*; **the ~** (**~ people**) die jungen Leute
youngish *adj.* ziemlich jung
youngster /ˈjʌŋstə(r)/ *n.* **(a)** (child) Kleine, *der/die/das*
(b) (young person) Jugendliche, *der/die*
your /jə(r), *stressed* jʊə(r), jɔː(r)/ *poss. pron. attrib.: sing.* dein; *pl.* euer; (polite) *sing. or pl.* Ihr
you're /jə(r), *stressed* jʊə(r), jɔː(r)/ = **you are**
yours /jʊəz, jɔːz/ *poss. pron. pred.: sing.* deiner/deine/dein[e]s; *pl.* eurer/eure/eures; (polite) *sing. or pl.* Ihrer/Ihre/Ihr[e]s; *see also* HERS
yourself /jəˈself, jʊəˈself, jɔːˈself/ *pron.* **(a)** *emphat.* selbst
(b) *refl.* dich/dir/(polite) sich. *See also* HERSELF
yourselves /jəˈselvz, jʊəˈselvz, jɔːˈselvz/ *pron.* **(a)** *emphat.* selbst
(b) *refl.* euch/(polite) sich. *See also* HERSELF
youth /juːθ/ *n.* **(a)** Jugend, *die*
(b) *pl.* **~s** /juːðz/ (young man) Jugendliche, *der*
youth: ~ centre *n.* Jugendzentrum, *das;* **~ club** *n.* Jugendklub, *der*
youthful /ˈjuːθfl/ *adj.* jugendlich
ˈyouth hostel *n.* Jugendherberge, *die*
you've /jʊv, *stressed* juːv/ = **you have**
yo-yo ® /ˈjəʊjəʊ/ *n., pl.* **~s** Jo-Jo, *das*
Yugoslav /ˈjuːgəslɑːv/ ▶ YUGOSLAVIAN
Yugoslavia /juːgəˈslɑːvɪə/ *pr. n.* Jugoslawien (*das*); **ex-~**: Ex-Jugoslawien (*das*)
Yugoslavian /juːgəˈslɑːvɪən/ **1** *adj.* jugoslawisch; **sb. is ~**: jmd. ist Jugoslawe/Jugoslawin
2 *n.* Jugoslawe, *der*/Jugoslawin, *die*
yuk /jʌk/ *int.* (coll.) bäh
yummy /ˈjʌmɪ/ (coll.) *int.* lecker
yuppie /ˈjʌpɪ/ *n.* (coll.) Yuppie, *der*
yuppie ˈflu *n.* (coll.) Yuppie-Grippe, *die*

Zz

Z, z /zed, (Amer.) ziː/ *n.* Z, z, *das*
Zaire /zɑːˈɪə(r)/ *pr. n.* Zaire (*das*)
Zambia /ˈzæmbɪə/ *pr. n.* Sambia (*das*)
zany /ˈzeɪnɪ/ *adj.* irre komisch (ugs.); Wahnsinns‹*humor, -komiker*›
zap /zæp/ (coll.) *v.i.* **-pp-** (Telev. coll.) zappen (ugs.)
zapper /ˈzæpə(r)/ *n.* (Telev. coll.) Drücker, *der* (ugs.)
zeal /ziːl/ *n.* Eifer, *der*
zealous /ˈzeləs/ *adj.* eifrig
zebra /ˈzebrə, ˈziːbrə/ *n.* Zebra, *das*
zebra ˈcrossing *n.* (Brit.) Zebrastreifen, *der*
zenith /ˈzenɪθ/ *n.* Zenit, *der*
zero /ˈzɪərəʊ/ *n., pl.* **~s** Null, *die*
zero: ~-ˈrated *adj.* **~-rated goods** nicht mehrwertsteuerpflichtige Güter; **~ ˈtolerance** *n.* Nulltoleranz, *die* (**for, to, of** gegenüber)
zest /zest/ *n.* (enthusiasm) Begeisterung, *die;* **~ for living** Lebenslust, *die*
zigzag /ˈzɪgzæg/ **1** *adj.* zickzackförmig; Zickzack‹*muster, -anordnung*›
2 *n.* Zickzacklinie, *die*
Zimbabwe /zɪmˈbɑːbwɪ/ *pr. n.* Simbabwe (*das*)
zinc /zɪŋk/ *n.* Zink, *das*
zip /zɪp/ **1** *n.* Reißverschluss, *der* ⋯

2 *v.t.*, **-pp-: (a)** ~ **[up] sth.** den Reißverschluss an etw. (*Dat.*) zuziehen **(b)** (Comp.) ~ **[up]** packen ‹*Datei*›

'zip bag *n.* Tasche, *die* mit Reißverschluss

'Zip code *n.* (Amer.) Postleitzahl, *die*

zip fastener ▶ ZIP 1

zipper /'zɪpə(r)/ ▶ ZIP 1

zither /'zɪðə(r)/ *n.* Zither, *die*

zodiac /'zəʊdɪæk/ *n.* Tierkreis, *der;* **sign of the** ~: Tierkreiszeichen, *das*

zombie (*Amer.:* **zombi**) /'zɒmbɪ/ *n.* Zombie, *der*

zone /zəʊn/ *n.* Zone, *die*

zoo /zu:/ *n.* Zoo, *der*

'zookeeper *n.* Zoowärter, *der*/-wärterin, *die*

zoological /zu:ə'lɒdʒɪkl/ *adj.* zoologisch

zoologist /zu:'ɒlədʒɪst/ *n.* Zoologe, *der*/Zoologin, *die*

zoology /zu:'ɒlədʒɪ/ *n.* Zoologie, *die*

zoom /zu:m/ *v.i.* rauschen

■ **zoom 'in on** *v.t.* zoomen auf (+ *Akk.*)

'zoom lens *n.* Zoomobjektiv, *das*

zucchini /zʊ'ki:nɪ/ *n.*, *pl. same or* ~**s** (esp. Amer.) Zucchino, *der*

Contents

Grammar Reference

Glossary of grammatical terms

Abbreviation A shortened form of a word or phrase: **etc.** = **usw.**

Absolute use The use of a transitive verb without an expressed object, as in: **I didn't** ***realize***

Accusative The case of a direct object; some German prepositions take the accusative

Active In the active form the subject of the verb performs the action: **he asked** = **er hat gefragt**

Adjective A word describing a noun: **a *red* pencil** = **ein *roter* Stift**

Adverb A word that describes or changes the meaning of a verb, an adjective, or another adverb: **she sings *beautifully*** = **sie singt *schön***

Article The definite article, **the** = **der/die/das**, and indefinite article, **a/an** = **ein/eine/ein**, used in front of a noun

Attributive An adjective or noun is attributive when it is used directly before a noun: **the *black* dog** = **der *schwarze* Hund**; ***farewell* speech** = **Abschiedsrede**

Auxiliary verb One of the verbs – as German **haben, sein, werden** - used to form the perfect or future tense: **I *will* help** = **ich *werde* helfen**

Cardinal number A whole number representing a quantity: **one/two/three** = **eins/zwei/drei**

Case The form of a noun, pronoun, adjective, or article that shows the part it plays in a sentence; there are four cases in German - nominative, accusative, genitive, and dative

Clause A self-contained section of a sentence that contains a subject and a verb

Collective noun A noun that is singular in form but refers to a group of individual persons or things, e.g. **royalty, grain**

Collocate A word that regularly occurs with another; in German, **Buch** is a typical collocate of the verb **lesen**.

Comparative The form of an adjective or adverb that makes it "more": **smaller** = **kleiner**, **more clearly** = **klarer**

Compound adjective An adjective formed from two or more separate words: **selbstbewusst (selbst + bewusst)** = **self-confident**

Compound noun A noun formed from two or more separate words: **der Flughafen (Flug+ Hafen)** = **airport**

Compound verb A verb formed by adding a prefix to a simple verb; in German, some compound verbs are separable **(an|fangen)**, and some are inseparable **(verlassen)**

Conditional tense A tense of a verb that expresses what might happen if something else occurred: **he would go** = **er würde gehen**

Conjugation Variation of the form of a verb to show tense, person, mood, etc.

Conjunction A word used to join clauses together: **and** = **und**, **because** = **weil**

Consonant In German, all the letters of the alphabet other than **a, e, i, o, u, ä, ö, ü**

Copula A verb, such as **be** or **become**, which links a **subject** and **predicate**

Dative The case of an indirect object; many German prepositions take the dative

Declension The form of a noun, pronoun, or adjective that corresponds to a particular case, number, or gender; some German nouns decline like adjectives, e.g. **Beamte, Taube**

Definite article: **the** = **der/die/das**

Demonstrative adjective: an adjective indicating the person or thing referred to; ***this* table** = ***dieser* Tisch**

Demonstrative pronoun A pronoun indicating the person or thing referred to; ***this* is my bicycle** = ***das* ist mein Fahrrad**

Direct object The noun or pronoun directly affected by the verb: **he caught *the ball*** = **er fing *den Ball***

Direct speech A speaker's actual words or the use of these in writing

Elliptical Having a word or words omitted, especially where the sense can be guessed from the context

Ending Letters added to the stem of verbs, as well as to nouns and adjectives, according to tense, case, etc.

Feminine One of the three noun genders in German: **die Frau** = **the woman**

Future tense The tense of a verb that refers to something that will happen in the future: **I will go** = **ich werde gehen**

Gender One of the three groups of nouns, pronouns, and adjectives in German: masculine, feminine, or neuter

Genitive The case that shows possession; some prepositions in German take the genitive

Imperative A form of a verb that expresses a command: **go away!** = **geh weg!**

Imperfect tense The tense of a verb that refers to an uncompleted or a habitual action in the past: **I went there every Friday** = **ich ging jeden Freitag dorthin**

Impersonal verb A verb in English used only with **'it'**, and in German only with **'es'**: **it is raining** = **es regnet**

Indeclinable adjective An adjective that has no inflected forms, as German **klasse, Moskauer**

Indefinite article: a/an = **ein/eine/ein**

Indefinite pronoun A pronoun that does not identify a specific person or object: **one** = **man, something** = **etwas**

Indicative form The form of a verb used when making a statement of fact or asking questions of fact: **he is just coming** = **er kommt gleich**

Indirect object The noun or pronoun indirectly affected by the verb, at which the direct object is aimed: **I gave *him* the book** = **ich gab *ihm* das Buch**

Indirect speech A report of what someone has said which does not reproduce the exact words

Infinitive The basic part of a verb: **to play** = **spielen**

Inflect To change the ending or form of a word to show its tense or its grammatical relation to other words: **gehe** and **gehst** are inflected forms of the verb **gehen**

Inseparable verb A verb with a prefix that can never be separated from it: **verstehen, ich verstehe**

Interjection A sound, word, or remark expressing a strong feeling such as anger, fear, or joy: **oh!** = **ach!**

Interrogative pronoun A pronoun that asks a question: **who?** = **wer?**

Intransitive verb A verb that does not have a direct object: **he died suddenly** = **er ist plötzlich gestorben**

Irregular verb A verb that does not follow one of the set patterns and has its own individual forms

Masculine One of the three noun genders in German: **der Mann** = **the man, der Stuhl** = **the chair**

Modal verb A verb that is used with another verb (not a modal) to express permission, obligation, possibility, etc., as German **können, sollen**, English **might, should**

Negative expressing refusal or denial; **there aren't any** = **es gibt keine**

Neuter One of the three noun genders in German: **das Buch** = **the book, das Kind** = **the child**

Nominative The case of the subject of a sentence; in sentences with **sein** and **werden** the noun after the verb is in the nominative: **that is my car** = **das ist mein Auto**

Noun A word that names a person or a thing

Number The state of being either singular or plural

Object The word or words naming the person or thing acted upon by a verb or preposition, as **'Buch'** in **er las das Buch** or **'ihm'** in **ich traue ihm**

Ordinal number A number that shows a person's or thing's position in a series: **the *twenty-first* century** = **das *einundzwanzigste* Jahrhundert, the *second* door on the left** = **die *zweite* Tür links**

Part of speech A grammatical term for the function of a word; noun, verb, adjective, etc., are parts of speech.

Passive In the passive form the subject of the verb experiences the action rather than performs it: **he was asked** = **er wurde gefragt**

Past participle The part of a verb used to form past tenses: **she had gone, er hat gelogen**

Perfect tense The tense of a verb that refers to a completed action in the past or an action that started in the past and is still going on: **I have already eaten** = **ich habe schon gegessen; I have been reading all day** = **ich habe den ganzen Tag gelesen**

Person Any of the three groups of personal pronouns and forms taken by verbs; the **first person** (e.g. **I/ich**) refers to the person(s) speaking, the **second person** (e.g. **you/du**) refers to the person(s) spoken to; the **third person** (e.g. **he/er**) refers to the persons spoken about

Personal pronoun A pronoun that refers to a person or thing: **he/she/it** = **er/sie/es**

Phrasal verb A verb in English combined with a preposition or an adverb to have a particular meaning: **run away** = **weglaufen**

Phrase A self-contained section of a sentence that does not contain a full verb

Pluperfect tense The tense of a verb that refers to something that happened before a particular point in the past: **als ich ankam, *war* er schon *losgefahren*** = **when I arrived, he *had* already *left***

Plural Of nouns etc., referring to more than one: **the trees** = **die Bäume**

Possessive adjective An adjective that shows possession, belonging to someone or something; **my** = **mein/meine/mein**

Possessive pronoun A pronoun that shows possession, belonging to someone or something: **mine** = **meiner/meine/meins**

Postpositive Placed after the word to which it relates, as **in stock** in the phrase **items in stock**

Predicate The part of a sentence that says something about the **subject**, e.g. **went home** in **John went home**

Predicative An adjective is predicative when it comes after a verb such as **be** or **become** in English, or after **sein** or **werden** in German: **she is beautiful** = **sie ist schön**

Prefix A letter or group of letters added to the beginning of a word to change its meaning; in German, the prefix can move from separable verbs (**an|fangen**), but stays fixed to inseparable verbs (**verlassen**)

Preposition A word that stands in front of a noun or pronoun, relating it to the rest of the sentence; in German prepositions are always followed by a particular case, usually either the accusative or dative, but occasionally the genitive: **with** = **mit (+ dative)**, **for** = **für (+ accusative)**, **because of** = **wegen (+ genitive)**

Present participle The part of a verb that in English ends in **-ing**, and in German adds **-d** to the infinitive: **asking** = **fragend**

Present tense The tense of a verb that refers to something happening now: **I make** = **ich mache**

Pronoun A word that stands instead of a noun: **he** = **er**, **she** = **sie**, **mine** = **meiner/meine/meins**

Proper noun A name of a person, place, institution, etc., in English written with a capital letter at the start; **Germany**, the **Atlantic**, **Karl**, **Europa** are all proper nouns

Reflexive pronoun A pronoun that goes with a reflexive verb: in German **mich, dich, sich, uns, euch, sich**

Reflexive verb A verb whose object is the same as its subject; in German, it is used with a reflexive pronoun: **du sollst dich waschen** = **you should wash yourself**

Regular verb A verb that follows a set pattern in its different forms

Relative pronoun A pronoun that introduces a subordinate clause, relating to a person or thing mentioned in the main clause: **the man *who* visited us** = **der Mann, *der* uns besucht hat**

Reported Speech Another name for **Indirect speech**

Root The part of a word to which inflections are added; **fahr-** is the root of the verb **fahren**

Sentence A sequence of words, with a subject and a verb, that can stand on their own to make a statement, ask a question, or give a command

Separable verb A verb with a prefix that can be separated from it in some tenses: **anfangen, anzufangen, angefangen**, but **ich fange an, du fingst an**

Singular Of nouns etc., referring to just one: **the tree** = **der Baum**

Stem The part of a verb to which endings are added; **fahr-** is the stem of **fahren**

Subject In a clause or sentence, the noun or pronoun that causes the action of the verb: ***he* caught the ball** = ***er* fing den Ball**

Subjunctive A verb form that is used to express doubt or unlikelihood: **if I were to tell you that ...** = **wenn ich dir sagen würde, dass ...**

Subordinate clause A clause which adds information to the main clause of a sentence but cannot be used as a sentence by itself

Suffix A letter or group of letters joined to the end of a word to make another word, as **-heit** in **Schönheit**

Superlative The form of an adjective or adverb that makes it "most": **the *smallest* house** = **das *kleinste* Haus**, **most clearly** = **am klarsten**

Syllable A division of a word that contains a vowel sound that is pronounced as a single unit: **Helikopter** has four syllables, he-li-kop-ter

Tense The form of a verb that tells when the action takes place: present, future, imperfect, perfect, pluperfect

Transitive verb A verb that is used with a direct object: **she read the book** = **sie las das Buch**

Verb A word or group of words that describes an action: **the children *are playing*** = **die Kinder *spielen***

Vowel In German, one of the following letters: **a, e, i, o, u, ä, ö, ü**

Summary of German grammar

1 Verbs

1.1 Regular verbs

Most German verbs are regular and add the same endings to their stem. You find the stem by taking away the **-en** (or sometimes just **-n**) from the end of the infinitive. The infinitive of the verb, for example the regular verb **machen**, is the form you look up in the dictionary. The stem of **machen** is **mach-**. There are six endings for each tense, to go with the different pronouns:

ich = *I*	du = *you*	er/sie/es = *he/she/it*
wir = *we*	ihr = *you*	sie/Sie = *they/you* (*polite form*).

1.2 Irregular verbs

Some German verbs are irregular and change their stem or add different endings. All the irregular verbs that appear in the dictionary are given in the section *German irregular verbs* on pages 944–947.

1.3 Present tense

For example, *I make*, *I am making*, or *I do make*:

infinitive	**ich**	**du**	**er/sie/es**	**wir**	**ihr**	**sie/Sie**
machen	mache	machst	macht	machen	macht	machen

1.4 Imperfect tense

For example, *I made*, *I was making*, or *I used to make*:

infinitive	**ich**	**du**	**er/sie/es**	**wir**	**ihr**	**sie/Sie**
machen	machte	machtest	machte	machten	machtet	machten

1.5 Future tense

For example, *I will make* or *I shall make*. The future is formed by using the present tense of **werden**, which is the equivalent of *will* or *shall*, with the infinitive of the main verb: **ich werde machen**.

infinitive	**ich**	**du**	**er/sie/es**	**wir**	**ihr**	**sie/Sie**
werden	werde	wirst	wird	werden	werdet	werden

1.6 Perfect tense

For example, *I made* or *I have made*. Most German verbs form the perfect tense with the present tense of **haben**, which is the equivalent of *have*, plus the past participle: **ich habe gemacht**. Some verbs form the perfect tense with **sein** instead of **haben**, and these are all marked (*sein*) in the dictionary. They are either verbs expressing motion and involving a change of place:

er ist heute nach Berlin gefahren = *he drove to Berlin today*
he went out = er ist hinausgegangen

or, they express a change of state, and this includes verbs meaning to happen (**geschehen**, **passieren**, **vorkommen**):

er ist aufgewacht = *he woke up*
sie ist gestern gestorben = *she died yesterday*

infinitive	ich	du	er/sie/es	wir	ihr	sie/Sie
haben	habe	hast	hat	haben	habt	haben
sein	bin	bist	ist	sind	seid	sind

1.7 The subjunctive

This is a form of the verb that is used to express speculation, hope, and doubt, and in reported speech. (It is rarely used in English; one example is: *if I were you*, instead of *if I was you*.) The subjunctive is used in both written and spoken German.

es könnte wahr sein = *it could be true*
wenn ich du wäre, ... = *if I were you, ...*
er sagt, dass er selten in die Stadt gehe = *he says he seldom goes into town*

Present subjunctive

infinitive	ich	du	er/sie/es	wir	ihr	sie/Sie
machen	mache	machest	mache	machen	machet	machen
sein	sei	sei(e)st	sei	seien	seid	seien

Imperfect subjunctive

For regular verbs this is the same as the normal imperfect forms, but irregular verbs vary.

infinitive	ich	du	er/sie/es	wir	ihr	sie/Sie
machen	machte	machtest	machte	machten	machtet	machten
werden	würde	würdest	würde	würden	würdet	würden
sein	wäre	wär(e)st	wäre	wären	wär(e)t	wären

1.8 Conditional tense

The conditional tense expresses what would happen if something else occurred. The imperfect subjunctive of **werden** (**würde**, **würdest**, etc) is used with the infinitive to form the conditional tense.

er würde gehen = *he would go*
das würde ich nicht machen = *I wouldn't do that*

1.9 Reflexive verbs

The object of a reflexive verb is the same as its subject. In German, the object is a reflexive pronoun. This is usually in the accusative (**ich wasche mich** = *I wash myself*). The reflexive pronouns of some verbs are in the dative (**ich stelle mir vor** = *I imagine*), and these are marked in both halves of the dictionary with the label (*Dat*).

infinitive	**ich**	**du**	**er/sie/es**	**wir**	**ihr**	**sie/Sie**
sich waschen	wasche mich	wäschst dich	wäscht sich	waschen uns	wascht euch	waschen sich
sich vorstellen	stelle mir vor	stellst dir vor	stellt sich vor	stellen uns vor	stellt euch vor	stellen sich vor

1.10 The passive

In the passive, the subject of the verb experiences the action rather than performs it: **er wurde gefragt** = *he was asked*. In German, the passive is formed as follows:

PRESENT PASSIVE	es wird gemacht (present tense of **werden** + past participle)	*it is done*
IMPERFECT PASSIVE	es wurde gemacht (imperfect tense of **werden** + past participle)	*it was done*
FUTURE PASSIVE	es wird gemacht werden (present tense of **werden** + past participle + **werden**)	*it will be done*
PERFECT PASSIVE	es ist gemacht worden (present tense of **sein** + past participle + **worden**)	*it has been done*

When forming the perfect passive, note that the past participle of **werden** used is **worden** rather than **geworden**.

1.11 Separable verbs

Some German verbs have stressed separable prefixes, such as **ab-**, **an-**, **aus**, **her-**, **hin-**, **nach-**, **vor-**, **zu-**. These prefixes become detached from the main verb in the simple tenses: **hinausgehen: ich gehe hinaus**, **sie ging hinaus**. In compound tenses formed with the past participle, for example the perfect tense, the **ge-** of the past participle comes between the prefix and the verb:

er/sie/es hat angefangen = *he/she/it has begun*
er/sie/es ist angekommen = *he/she/it has arrived*

1.12 Inseparable verbs

The following unstressed prefixes are never separated from their verb in either simple or compound tenses and do not take **ge-** in the past participle:

be-, emp-, ent-, er-, ge-, ver-, zer-.
er begleitet seinen Bruder = *he is accompanying his brother*
er wurde nicht begleitet = *he was not accompanied*

2 Articles

The definite article (*the*) can be translated in the nominative case by **der**, **die** or **das** in German. Similarly the indefinite article (*a*) can be translated by **ein**, **eine**, or **ein**.

There are three genders of nouns in German: masculine (**der Mann** = *the man*), feminine (**die Frau** = *the woman*), and neuter (**das Buch** = *the book*). There are two forms of number: singular (**der Baum** = *the tree*) and plural (**die Bäume** = *the trees*). And there are four cases, which show the part a noun plays in a sentence: nominative (for the subject), accusative (for the object), genitive (to show possession), and dative (for the indirect object). The plural forms of the definite article are the same for all three genders. More information on gender is given below.

2.1 Definite article: der/die/das, (*plural*) die = *the*

	SINGULAR masculine	feminine	neuter	PLURAL all genders
NOMINATIVE	**der** Mann	**die** Frau	**das** Buch	**die** Bäume
ACCUSATIVE	**den** Mann	**die** Frau	**das** Buch	**die** Bäume
GENITIVE	**des** Mannes	**der** Frau	**des** Buches	**der** Bäume
DATIVE	**dem** Mann	**der** Frau	**dem** Buch	**den** Bäumen

2.2 Indefinite article

ein/eine/ein = *a* or *an*. This article can only be singular.

	masculine	feminine	neuter
NOMINATIVE	**ein** Mann	**eine** Frau	**ein** Buch
ACCUSATIVE	**einen** Mann	**eine** Frau	**ein** Buch
GENITIVE	**eines** Mannes	**einer** Frau	**eines** Buches
DATIVE	**einem** Mann	**einer** Frau	**einem** Buch

3 Nouns

In German, all nouns take an initial capital letter wherever they appear in a sentence: **der Baum**, **die Schule**, **das Buch**.

3.1 Gender

All German nouns belong to one of the three genders: masculine (**der Mann** = *the man*), feminine (**die Frau** = *the woman*), and neuter (**das Buch** = *the book*). These three examples are logical, with masculine for a male person, feminine for a female person, and neuter for an object. But genders of German nouns do not always follow logic. For example, **der Fluss** (= *the river*), **die Menge** (= *the quantity/crowd*), **das Haus** (= *the house*). **Das Mädchen** (= *the girl*) is neuter and not feminine, because the ending **-chen** is always neuter.

The gender of German nouns is given in both sides of the dictionary by adding **der**, **die**, or **das** after each noun. There are some general rules regarding the gender of groups of nouns, but these cover only a small proportion of them and in many cases a noun's gender can only be established by looking it up.

3.2 Masculine nouns

- male persons and animals: **der Arbeiter** = *worker*; **der Bär** = *bear*
- 'doers' and 'doing' instruments ending in **-er** in German: **der Gärtner** = *gardener*; **der Computer** = *computer*
- days, months, and seasons: **(der) Montag** = *Monday*; **(der) März** = *March*; **der Frühling** = *spring*
- words ending in **-ich**, **-ig**, and **-ling**: **der Strich** = line; **der Honig** = *honey*; **der Lehrling** = *apprentice*
- words ending in **-ismus**, **-ist**, and **-ant**: **der Kapitalismus** = *capitalism*; **der Kriminalist** = *detective*; **der Diamant** = *diamond*

3.3 Feminine nouns

- female persons and animals: **die Schauspielerin** = *actress*; **die Henne** = *hen*. The feminine form of professions and animals is made by adding **-in** to the masculine: **der Schauspieler/die Schauspielerin** = *actor/actress*
- nouns ending in **-ei**, **-ie**, **-ik**, **-in**, **-ion**, **-heit**, **-keit**, **-schaft**, **-tät**, **-ung**, **-ur**: **die Gärtnerei** = *gardening*; **die Energie** = *energy*; **die Million** = *million*; **die Freiheit** = *freedom*; **die Freundlichkeit** = *friendliness*; **die Feindschaft** = *enmity*; **die Universität** = *university*; **die Verwaltung** = *management*; **die Natur** = *nature*
- many nouns ending in **-e**: **die Blume** = *flower*. Note that there are many common exceptions, including **der Name** = *name*; **der Käse** = *cheese*; **das Ende** = *end*

3.4 Neuter nouns

- names of continents, most countries, and towns: **(das) Europa** = *Europe*; **(das) Deutschland** = *Germany*; **(das) Köln** = *Cologne*
- nouns ending in **-chen** and **-lein** (diminutive suffixes): **das Mädchen**, **das Fräulein** = *girl*
- most (but not all) nouns beginning with **Ge-** or ending in **-nis**, **-tel**, or **-um**: **das Geheimnis** = *secret*; **das Viertel** = *quarter*; **das Zentrum** = *centre*
- infinitives of verbs used as nouns: **das Lachen** = *laughter*; **das Essen** = *food*

3.5 Compound nouns

When two nouns combine to make a compound noun, the gender of the compound is that of the second noun:

der Brief + die Marke = die Briefmarke (= *stamp*).

3.6 Plural

There are no hard and fast rules for the the formation of plural nouns in German. An ending is generally added. Masculine nouns frequently add **-e** (**der Freund**, **die Freunde**). When the vowels **-a-** or **-u-** appear in the stem of a noun, they may add an umlaut to give: **-ä-**, **-ü-** as in: (**der Gast**, **die Gäste**; **das Haus**, **die Häuser**). Feminine words ending in **-heit**, **-keit**, and **-ung** always add **-en** to make the plural (**die Abbildung**, **die Abbildungen**).

The plurals of all nouns are shown in the German-English part of the dictionary.

3.7 Case

There are four cases, which show the part a noun plays in a sentence: nominative, accusative, genitive, and dative. The noun's article changes according to the case, and the ending of the noun changes in some cases:

	SINGULAR **masculine**	**feminine**	**neuter**
NOMINATIVE	der Mann	die Frau	das Buch
ACCUSATIVE	den Mann	die Frau	das Buch
GENITIVE	des **Mann(e)s**	der Frau	des **Buch(e)s**
DATIVE	dem Mann	der Frau	dem Buch

	PLURAL **masculine**	**feminine**	**neuter**
NOMINATIVE	die Männer	die Frauen	die Bücher
ACCUSATIVE	die Männer	die Frauen	die Bücher
GENITIVE	der Männer	der Frauen	der Bücher
DATIVE	den **Männern**	den Frauen	den **Büchern**

The nominative is used for the subject of a sentence. It is important to note that in sentences with **sein** (*to be*) and **werden** (*to become*), the noun after the verb is in the nominative.

der Hund bellte = *the dog barked*
das ist mein Wagen = *that is my car*

The accusative is used for the direct object and after some prepositions (listed on page 941):

sie hat einen Sohn = *she has a son*

The genitive shows possession, and is also used after some prepositions (listed on page 941):

der Hund meines Mannes = *my husband's dog*

The dative is used for the indirect object. Some German verbs, such as **helfen**, take the dative when you might have expected the accusative. This information is given in both halves of the dictionary. The dative is also used after some prepositions (listed on page 941):

sie gab den Kindern die Bücher = *she gave the books to the children*
er hilft der Frau = *he is helping the woman*

The following sentence combines all four cases:

der Mann gibt der Frau den Bleistift des Mädchens = *the man gives the woman the girl's pencil*

der Mann *is the subject* (*in the nominative*)
gibt *is the verb*
der Frau *is the indirect object* (*in the dative*)
den Bleistift *is the direct object* (*in the accusative*)
des Mädchens *is in the genitive* (*showing possession*).

4 Adjectives

An adjective is a word qualifying a noun. In German, an adjective in front of a noun adds endings that vary with the noun's gender, number, and case. Adjectives that come after a noun do not add endings.

4.1 Adjectives following the definite article **der**, **die**, **das** take the following endings:

	SINGULAR **masculine**	**feminine**	**neuter**	PLURAL **all genders**
NOMINATIVE	der rot**e** Hut	die rot**e** Lampe	das rot**e** Buch	die rot**en** Autos
ACCUSATIVE	den rot**en** Hut	die rot**e** Lampe	das rot**e** Buch	die rot**en** Autos
GENITIVE	des rot**en** Hutes	der rot**en** Lampe	des rot**en** Buches	der rot**en** Autos
DATIVE	dem rot**en** Hut	der rot**en** Lampe	dem rot**en** Buch	den rot**en** Autos

4.2 German demonstrative adjectives follow the pattern of the definite article, and adjectives after them change their endings in the same way as after **der/die/das**. For example, **dieser/diese/dieses** (= *this*):

	SINGULAR **masculine**	**feminine**	**neuter**	PLURAL **all genders**
NOMINATIVE	dieser	diese	dieses	diese
ACCUSATIVE	diesen	diese	dieses	diese
GENITIVE	dieses	dieser	dieses	dieser
DATIVE	diesem	dieser	diesem	diesen

Other adjectives of this type are:

jeder, jede, jedes = *every, each*
jener, jene, jenes = *that*
mancher, manche, manches = *many a, some*
solcher, solche, solches = *such*
welcher, welche, welches = *which*

4.3 Adjectives following the indefinite article **ein**, **eine**, **ein** take the following endings:

	SINGULAR masculine	feminine	neuter
NOMINATIVE	ein rot**er** Hut	eine rot**e** Lampe	ein rot**es** Buch
ACCUSATIVE	einen rot**en** Hut	eine rot**e** Lampe	ein rot**es** Buch
GENITIVE	eines rot**en** Hutes	einer rot**en** Lampe	eines rot**en** Buches
DATIVE	einem rot**en** Hut	einer rot**en** Lampe	einem rot**en** Buch

Other German adjectives that follow the pattern of the indefinite article, and take the same endings as **ein**, **eine**, **ein**, are:

dein = *your*	ihr = *her/their*	mein = *my*	kein = *no*
euer = *your*	sein = *his/its*	unser = *our*	
Ihr = *your*			

These adjectives can also be used in the plural: **keine Autos** = *no cars*; **deine Eltern** = *your parents*; **unsere Lehrer** = *our teachers*, etc. The endings of adjectives that follow them are the same in the plural regardless of gender:

	PLURAL all genders
NOMINATIVE	kein**e** roten Autos
ACCUSATIVE	kein**e** roten Autos
GENITIVE	kein**er** roten Autos
DATIVE	kein**en** roten Autos

4.4 Adjectives in front of a noun, without an article, take the following endings:

	SINGULAR masculine	feminine	neuter	PLURAL all genders
NOMINATIVE	gut**er** Wein	frisch**e** Milch	kalt**es** Bier	alt**e** Leute
ACCUSATIVE	gut**en** Wein	frisch**e** Milch	kalt**es** Bier	alt**e** Leute
GENITIVE	gut**en** Weins	frisch**er** Milch	kalt**en** Biers	alt**er** Leute
DATIVE	gut**em** Wein	frisch**er** Milch	kalt**em** Bier	alt**en** Leuten

4.5 Adjectives as nouns

In German, adjectives can be used as nouns, spelt with a capital letter: **alt** = *old*, **ein Alter** = *an old man*, **eine Alte** = *an old woman*.

With the definite article (**der**, **die**, **das**), these nouns take the following endings:

	SINGULAR masculine	feminine	neuter	PLURAL all genders
NOMINATIVE	der Alte	die Alte	das Alte	die Alten
ACCUSATIVE	den Alten	die Alte	das Alte	die Alten
GENITIVE	des Alten	der Alten	des Alten	der Alten
DATIVE	dem Alten	der Alten	dem Alten	den Alten

Adjectives can be used in this way in the neuter, usually to express an abstract concept: **das Gute** = *the good* (nominative and accusative), **des Guten** (genitive), **dem Guten** (dative).

With the indefinite article (**ein**, **eine**, **ein**), these nouns take the following endings:

	SINGULAR masculine	feminine	neuter	PLURAL all genders without an article
NOMINATIVE	ein Alter	eine Alte	ein Altes	Alte
ACCUSATIVE	einen Alten	eine Alte	ein Altes	Alte
GENITIVE	eines Alten	einer Alten	eines Alten	Alter
DATIVE	einem Alten	einer Alten	einem Alten	Alten

4.6 Comparatives and superlatives of adjectives

In English, the comparative of the adjective *small* is *smaller*, and of *difficult* is *more difficult*. The superlatives are *smallest* and *most difficult*. In German, there is just one way to form the comparative and superlative: by adding the endings **-er** and **-(e)st**:

klein, kleiner, der/die/das kleinste = *small, smaller, smallest*

Many adjectives whose stem vowel is **-a-**, **-o-**, or **-u-** take an umlaut to become **-ä-**, **-ö-** or **-ü-**, in the comparative and superlative:

kalt, kälter, der/die/das kälteste = *cold, colder, coldest*
grob, gröber, der/die/das gröbste = *rude, ruder, rudest*
jung, jünger, der/die/das jüngste = *young, younger, youngest*

Some important adjectives are irregular:

groß, größer, der/die/das größte = *big, bigger, biggest*
gut, besser, der/die/das beste = *good, better, best*
hoch, höher, der/die/das höchste = *high, higher, highest*
viel, mehr, der/die/das meiste = *much, more, most*
nah, näher, der/die/das nächste = *near, nearer, nearest*

Comparative and superlative adjectives take the same endings as basic adjectives:

ein kleineres Kind = *a smaller child*
ein billigerer Hut = *a cheaper hat*
der kälteste Monat = *the coldest month*
die nächste Bushaltestelle = *the nearest bus stop*

5 Adverbs

5.1 In German almost all adjectives can also be used as adverbs. Adverbs can modify a verb, an adjective, or another adverb.

sie singt schön (adverb: schön + verb: singt) = *she sings beautifully*
sie war schnell fertig (adverb: schnell + adjective: fertig) = *she was ready quickly*
er fährt sehr langsam (adverb: sehr + adverb: langsam) = *he drives very slowly*

The following important adverbs are invariable: **auch** = *also*, **fast** = *almost*, **immer** = *always*, **sehr** = *very*, **leider** = *unfortunately*

sie ist sehr klug = *she is very clever*

5.2 Comparatives and superlatives of adverbs

The comparative is formed by adding **-er** to the basic adverb, and the superlative by adding the ending **-(e)sten** to the basic adverb and putting **am** in front:

klar, klarer, am klarsten = *clearly, more clearly, most clearly*

Some important adverbs are irregular:

bald, früher, am frühesten = *soon, earlier, at the earliest*
gut, besser, am besten = *well, better, best*
gern, lieber, am liebsten = *willingly, more willingly, most willingly*

5.3 Adverbs of time

There are many adverbs and adverbial expressions of time. They are invariable. Some common ones are:

morgens – *in the morning*
nachmittags = *in the afternoon*
nachts = *in the night*
wochenlang, jahrelang *etc* = *for weeks, for years* etc
montags, dienstags *etc* = *on Mondays, Tuesdays* etc

bald = *soon*
endlich = *in the end*
immer, stets = *always*
jetzt = *now*
kürzlich = *recently*
wieder = *again*

5.4 Adverbs of order

The use of adverbs and adverbial expressions to convey order is frequent in German. Here are some common patterns of usage:

erstens = *firstly*
zweitens = *secondly*
drittens = *thirdly*
zum ersten Mal = *for the first time*
zum zweiten Mal = *for the second time*
zum dritten Mal = *for the third time*

6 Pronouns

Pronouns are words that can replace a noun. Examples in English are: *I, you, he, she, it, which, theirs, mine, yours.*

6.1 Personal pronouns

These pronouns, such as **er, sie, es** = *he/she/it*, refer to people or things.

	I	**you**	**he/it**	**she/it**	**it**	**we**	**you**	**they**	**you**
NOMINATIVE	ich	du	er	sie	es	wir	ihr	sie	Sie
	me	**you**	**him/it**	**her/it**	**it**	**us**	**you**	**them**	**you**
ACCUSATIVE	mich	dich	ihn	sie	es	uns	euch	sie	Sie
DATIVE	mir	dir	ihm	ihr	ihm	uns	euch	ihnen	Ihnen

The genitive form is not given, because it is so rarely used.

In German there are two forms for you, **du** and **Sie**. **Du** (plural **ihr**) is informal and is used when speaking to a child, a member of your family, or someone you know well. When speaking to a person or a group of people you do not know very well, use the polite form, **Sie**.

German pronouns agree in gender with the noun they refer to. In the nominative case, 'it' can be be translated by **er** or **sie**, as well as **es**:

er (der Bleistift) ist rot = *it* (*the pencil*) *is red*
sie (die Rose) ist schön = *it* (*the rose*) *is beautiful*
es (das Auto) ist teuer = *it* (*the car*) *is expensive*

6.2 Possessive pronouns

The possessive pronouns are:

meiner/meine/mein(e)s = *mine*
deiner/deine/dein(e)s = *yours* (informal singular)
seiner/seine/sein(e)s = *his*
ihrer/ihre/ihr(e)s = *hers*
seiner/seine/sein(e)s = *its*
unserer/unsere/unser(e)s = *ours*
eurer/eure/eures = *yours* (informal plural)
ihrer/ihre/ihr(e)s = *theirs*
Ihrer, Ihre, Ihr(e)s = *yours* (polite)

They all take endings like **meiner/meine/mein(e)s**, as follows:

	SINGULAR			PLURAL
	masculine	**feminine**	**neuter**	**all genders**
NOMINATIVE	meiner	meine	mein(e)s	meine
ACCUSATIVE	meinen	meine	mein(e)s	meine
GENITIVE	meines	meiner	meines	meine
DATIVE	meinem	meiner	meinem	meinen

As can be seen in the table, in the neuter form an **-e-** can be added (making **meines**). This applies to all the possessive pronouns, but the extra **-e-** is rare.

6.3 Relative pronouns

Relative pronouns link a main clause to a subordinate clause. In English they are *who*, *which*, *that*, and *what*. In German they are **der**, **die**, or **das**, depending on the noun referred to:

	SINGULAR			PLURAL
	masculine	**feminine**	**neuter**	**all genders**
NOMINATIVE	der	die	das	die
ACCUSATIVE	den	die	das	die
GENITIVE	dessen	deren	dessen	deren
DATIVE	dem	der	dem	denen

Relative pronouns can be left out in English, but never in German:

das Buch, das ich lese = *the book* (*that*) *I'm reading*

They agree in gender and number with the noun they refer back to:

der Mann, der uns besucht hat = *the man who visited us*

(**der** is masculine singular)

der Mann, dessen Frau den Wagen vermietet hatte, wusste es nicht = *the man, whose wife had rented the car, did not know about it*

The case of the pronoun depends on its function in the clause it introduces:

der Bleistift, den ich gestern gekauft habe = *the pencil I bought yesterday*

(**den** is masculine singular, and accusative, because it is the object of the clause it introduces)

6.4 Interrogative pronouns

These pronouns are used to ask questions:

wer? = *who?* was? = *what?* welcher/welche/welches? = *which?*

Wer changes as follows:

NOMINATIVE wer? ACCUSATIVE wen? GENITIVE wessen? DATIVE wem?

wer sprach? = *who was speaking?*
wen trafst du? = *who (whom) did you meet?*
wessen Buch ist das? = *whose book is that?*
mit wem spricht er? = *who is he talking to?*

Was? is invariable.

was ist das? = *what is that?*

Welcher: The forms are the same as those given for dieser on page 934.

welche Zeitung hast du gekauft? = *which newspaper have you bought?*

Was für ein ... ? This expression means 'what kind or sort of ...?' **Ein** takes the endings according to whether the noun qualified is the subject, object, or indirect object.

was für ein Mann/eine Frau ist das? (subject) = *what sort of a man/woman is that?*
was für ein Geschenk bekam er? (object) = *what sort of a present did he get?*
was für Zeitungen haben Sie? (plural object) = *what sort of newspapers do you have?*

6.5 Reflexive pronouns

The object of a reflexive verb is the same as its subject. In German, the object is a reflexive pronoun. This is usually in the accusative (**ich wasche mich** = *I wash myself*). The reflexive pronouns of some verbs are in the dative (**ich stelle mir vor** = *I imagine*).

The following table shows which accusative reflexive pronoun corresponds to the normal (nominative) personal pronoun.

ich	mich	wir	uns
du	dich	ihr	euch
er, sie, es, man	sich	sie, Sie	sich

sie erinneren sich daran = *they remember it*
es bewegt sich = *it's moving*

The dative forms are the same as the above, except for the **ich** and **du** forms: **ich**: **mir**; **du**: **dir**.

6.6 Indefinite pronouns

Some of these pronouns take endings according to whether they are the subject, object, or indirect object in the sentence. Among those that do are: **jemand** = *someone* or *somebody*, **niemand** = *no one* or *nobody*, **irgend jemand** = *anyone* or *anybody*.

	someone	no one	anyone
NOMINATIVE	jemand	niemand	irgend jemand
ACCUSATIVE	jemanden	niemanden	irgend jemanden
DATIVE	jemandem	niemandem	irgend jemandem

jemand hat mein Fahrrad genommen = *someone has taken my bicycle*
sie sah niemanden = *she saw no one*
er gab es jemandem = *he gave it to someone*

The genitive case is rarely used.

6.7 One

The pronoun *one* is translated by **einer**, **eine**, **eines** or **eins**, which take the endings already given on page 938 for singular possessive pronouns, according to their function in the sentence.

trinken wir ein(e)s? (ein Bier) = *shall we have one? (a beer)*
einer von uns muss es tun = *one of us must do it*

Similarly **keiner**, **keine**, **keines** or **keins** = *no one* or *nobody*, *nothing* (neuter) take the endings according to their function in the sentence.

keiner will ihn begleiten = *no one wants to go with him*

Indefinite pronouns which are invariable are:

something = etwas; *everything* = alles; *nothing* = nichts
gefällt noch etwas? = *would you like something else?*
sie nahm alles = *she took everything*
er weisst nichts = *he knows nothing*

Note that *something/everything/nothing good* is translated by **etwas/alles/nichts Gutes**

something good has happened = etwas Gutes ist geschehen

7 Prepositions

Prepositions are words like *above, in, under* that convey the idea of place and come in front of a noun or pronoun. In German, the noun following a preposition always has to be in one of three cases: dative, accusative, or genitive.

Prepositions can also be prefixes and form separable verbs:

die Straße entlanggehen = *to walk along the street*
er geht die Straße entlang = *he is walking along the street*

In the dictionary, the case governed by a preposition is given as follows:

mit 1 *Präp mit Dat.*

This means that **mit** always takes the dative case.

The following prepositions always take the dative:

aus bei mit nach seit von zu

The following prepositions always take the accusative:

bis durch entlang für gegen ohne um

The following prepositions always take the genitive:

anstatt während trotz wegen

There is a group of prepositions that can take the dative or the accusative, depending on the sense of the sentence.

They are:

an auf außer hinter in unter neben vor über zwischen

If the speaker wishes to convey the idea that someone or something is stationary, the dative case is used:

sie saß in der Küche = *she sat in the kitchen*
es liegt auf dem Tisch = *it's lying on the table*

But if the speaker wishes to convey the idea of movement the accusative case is used:

sie ging in die Küche = *she went into the kitchen*
er legte den Beutel auf den Tisch = *he put the bag on the table*

Note the expressions **nach Hause** and **zu Hause**: **nach Hause** = *home* (*homewards*), and **zu Hause** = *at home*.

Some forms of the definite article are usually shortened when used with certain prepositions:

am (an dem); **ans** (an das); **aufs** (auf das); **beim** (bei dem)
durchs (durch das); **fürs** (für das); **im** (in dem); **ins** (in das)
ums (um das); **vom** (von dem); **zum** (zu dem); **zur** (zu der)

8 Conjunctions

Conjunctions are words, such as **und** = *and*, **aber** = *but*, which link clauses in a sentence.

Some common conjunctions are:

aber = *but* denn = *for* oder = *or* sondern = *but* (*on the contrary*) und = *and*

These conjunctions do not change normal word order in the two clauses:

ich gehe und er kommt auch = *I am going and he is coming too*

This is because the clauses are of equal weight or importance.

Conjunctions which introduce a subordinate clause make the verb in the subordinate clause appear at the end:

als = *when*, = *as*	bevor = *before*	bis = *until*	da = *since*	dass = *that*
ob = *whether*	während = *while*	wenn = *when*, = *if*	weil = *because*	

als er das erfuhr, wollte er nicht mitkommen	=	*when he found out, he didn't want to come*
er konnte nicht in die Schule gehen, weil er krank war	=	*he couldn't go to school, because he was ill*
wenn sie in die Stadt geht, nimmt sie immer ihre Handtasche	=	*when she goes to town, she always takes her handbag*

9 Word order

The basic rule for German word order is that the verb comes second in a sentence. The subject of the sentence usually comes before the verb:

meine Mutter fährt am Freitag nach Köln = *my mother is going to Cologne on Friday*

When the verb used is in a compound tense, such as the perfect and the future tenses, the auxiliary verb comes second in the sentence, while the past participle (in the perfect) or infinitive (in the future tense) goes to the end:

wir haben sehr lang gewartet = *we waited a very long time*
sie wird sicher bald kommen = *she is sure to come soon*

Infinitives go to the end in other sentences too, as when used with modal verbs or the verb **lassen**:

ich kann dieses Lied nicht leiden = *I can't stand this song*
du musst hier bleiben = *you must stay here*
ich lasse mir die Haare schneiden = *I'm going to have my hair cut*

In questions the normal order of the subject and the verb is inverted, as in English:

kommst du heute Abend? = *are you coming this evening?*

In commands the verb is placed first:

komm schnell rein! = *come in quickly!*

Subordinate clauses

A speaker or writer may start a sentence with a subordinate clause in order to introduce variety or for effect. In this case the verb stays in second place, after the subordinate clause, and the subject of the main clause follows the verb; **blieb** in the example below:

da ich kein Geld hatte, blieb ich zu Hause = *since I had no money, I stayed at home*

In the subordinate clause itself, the verb goes to the end; *cf*. **hatte** in the previous example and **war** in the following one:

er konnte nicht in die Schule gehen, weil er krank war

The relative pronouns **der**, **die**, and **das**, as well as conjunctions such as **als** = *when*, **dass** = *that*, **weil** = *because*, introduce subordinate clauses and therefore cause the verb to go to the end of the subordinate clause.

(See the section on Conjunctions for more examples.)

der Junge, der hier wohnt, ist in der Schule	=	*the boy, who lives here, is at school*
die Soldaten, die gestern hier waren, haben nicht bezahlt	=	*the soldiers, who were here yesterday, did not pay*

When separable verbs separate, the prefix goes to the end:

der Film fängt um acht Uhr an	=	*the film starts at 8 o'clock*
wann kommt der Zug an?	=	*when does the train arrive?*

When there are a number of phrases in a sentence, the usual order for the different elements is: 1 time, 2 manner, 3 place:

wir fahren heute mit dem Auto nach München	=	*we are driving to Munich today*

(*time* = heute; *manner* = mit dem Auto; *place* = nach München)

German irregular verbs / Deutsche unregelmäßige Verben

Irregular and partly irregular verbs are listed alphabetically by infinitive. 1st, 2nd, and 3rd person present and imperative forms are given after the infinitive, and preterite subjunctive forms after the preterite indicative, where they take an umlaut, change *e* to *i*, etc.

Verbs with a raised number in the German-English section of the Dictionary have the same number in this list.

Compound verbs (including verbs with prefixes) are only given if a) they do not take the same forms as the corresponding simple verb, e.g. *befehlen*, or b) there is no corresponding simple verb, e.g. *bewegen*.

An asterisk (*) indicates a verb which is also conjugated regularly.

Infinitive *Infinitiv*	Preterite *Präteritum*	Past Participle *2. Partizip*
abwägen	wog (wöge) ab	abgewogen
backen (du bäckst, er bäckt; *auch:* du backst, er backt)	backte, *älter:* buk (büke)	gebacken
befehlen (du befiehlst, er befiehlt; befiehl!)	befahl (beföhle, befähle)	befohlen
beginnen	begann (begänne, *seltener:* begönne)	begonnen
beißen	biss	gebissen
bergen (du birgst, er birgt; birg!)	barg (bärge)	geborgen
bersten (du birst, er birst; birst!)	barst (bärste)	geborsten
besinnen	besann (besänne)	besonnen
bewegen[2]	bewog (bewöge)	bewogen
biegen	bog (böge)	gebogen
bieten	bot (böte)	geboten
binden	band (bände)	gebunden
bitten	bat (bäte)	gebeten
blasen (du bläst, er bläst)	blies	geblasen
bleiben	blieb	geblieben
bleichen*	blich	geblichen
braten (du brätst, er brät)	briet	gebraten
brechen (du brichst, er bricht; brich!)	brach (bräche)	gebrochen
brennen	brannte (brennte)	gebrannt
bringen	brachte (brächte)	gebracht
denken	dachte (dächte)	gedacht
dreschen (du drischst, er drischt; drisch!)	drosch (drösche)	gedroschen
dringen	drang (dränge)	gedrungen
dürfen (ich darf, du darfst, er darf)	durfte (dürfte)	gedurft
empfehlen (du empfiehlst, er empfiehlt, empfiehl!)	empfahl (empföhle, *seltener:* empfähle)	empfohlen
erklimmen	erklomm (erklömme)	erklommen
erlöschen (du erlischst, er erlischt; erlisch!)	erlosch (erlösche)	erloschen

German irregular verbs

Infinitive *Infinitiv*	Preterite *Präteritum*	Past Participle *2. Partizip*
erschallen*	erscholl (erschölle)	erschollen
erschrecken[1,3] (du erschrickst, er erschrickt; erschrick!)	erschrak (erschäke)	erschrocken
erwägen	erwog (erwöge)	erwogen
essen (du isst, er isst; iss!)	aß (äße)	gegessen
fahren (du fährst, er fährt)	fuhr (führe)	gefahren
fallen (du fällst, er fällt)	fiel	gefallen
fangen (du fängst, er fängt)	fing	gefangen
fechten (du fichtst, er ficht; ficht!)	focht (föchte)	gefochten
finden	fand (fände)	gefunden
flechten (du flichtst, er flicht; flicht!)	flocht (flöchte)	geflochten
fliegen	flog (flöge)	geflogen
fliehen	floh (flöhe)	geflohen
fließen	floss (flösse)	geflossen
fressen (du frisst, er frisst; friss!)	fraß (fräße)	gefressen
frieren	fror (fröre)	gefroren
gären*	gor (göre)	gegoren
gebären (*geh.*: du gebierst, sie gebiert; gebier!)	gebar (gebäre)	geboren
geben (du gibst, er gibt; gib!)	gab (gäbe)	gegeben
gedeihen	gedieh	gediehen
gehen	ging	gegangen
gelingen	gelang (gelänge)	gelungen
gelten (du giltst, er gilt; gilt!)	galt (gölte, gälte)	gegolten
genesen	genas (genäse)	genesen
genießen	genoss (genösse)	genossen
geschehen (es geschieht)	geschah (geschähe)	geschehen
gewinnen	gewann (gewönne, gewänne)	gewonnen
gießen	goss (gösse)	gegossen
gleichen	glich	geglichen
gleiten	glitt	geglitten
glimmen	glomm (glömme)	geglommen
graben (du gräbst, er gräbt)	grub (grübe)	gegraben
greifen	griff	gegriffen
haben (du hast, er hat)	hatte (hätte)	gehabt
halten (du hältst, er hält)	hielt	gehalten
hängen[1]	hing	gehangen
hauen	haute, *geh.*: hieb	gehauen
heben	hob (höbe)	gehoben
heißen	hieß	geheißen
helfen (du hilfst, er hilft; hilf!)	half (hülfe, *selten*: hälfe)	geholfen
kennen	kannte (kennte)	gekannt
klingen	klang (klänge)	geklungen
kneifen	kniff	gekniffen
kommen	kam (käme)	gekommen
können (ich kann, du kannst, er kann)	konnte (könnte)	gekonnt
kriechen	kroch (kröche)	gekrochen
laden[1,2] (du lädst, er lädt)	lud (lüde)	geladen
lassen (du lässt, er lässt)	ließ	gelassen
laufen (du läufst, er läuft)	lief	gelaufen
leiden	litt	gelitten
leihen	lieh	geliehen
lesen[1,2] (du liest, er liest; lies!)	las (läse)	gelesen
liegen	lag (läge)	gelegen
lügen	log (löge)	gelogen
mahlen	mahlte	gemahlen
meiden	mied	gemieden

Infinitive *Infinitiv*	Preterite *Präteritum*	Past Participle *2. Partizip*
melken* (du milkst, er milkt; milk!; du melkst, er melkt; melke!)	molk (mölke)	gemolken
messen (du misst, er misst; miss!)	maß (mäße)	gemessen
misslingen	misslang (misslänge)	misslungen
mögen (ich mag, du magst, er mag)	mochte (möchte)	gemocht
müssen (ich muss, du musst, er muss)	musste (müsste)	gemusst
nehmen (du nimmst, er nimmt; nimm!)	nahm (nähme)	genommen
nennen	nannte (nennte)	genannt
pfeifen	pfiff	gepfiffen
preisen	pries	gepriesen
quellen (du quillst, er quillt; quill!)	quoll (quölle)	gequollen
raten (du rätst, er rät)	riet	geraten
reiben	rieb	gerieben
reißen	riss	gerissen
reiten	ritt	geritten
rennen	rannte (rennte)	gerannt
riechen	roch (röche)	gerochen
ringen	rang (ränge)	gerungen
rinnen	rann (ränne, *seltener:* rönne)	geronnen
rufen	rief	gerufen
salzen*	salzte	gesalzen
saufen (du säufst, er säuft)	soff (söffe)	gesoffen
saugen*	sog (söge)	gesogen
schaffen*	schuf (schüfe)	geschaffen
schallen*	scholl (schölle)	geschallt
scheiden	schied	geschieden
scheinen	schien	geschienen
scheißen	schiss	geschissen
schelten (du schiltst, er schilt; schilt!)	schalt (schölte)	gescholten
scheren[1]	schor (schöre)	geschoren
schieben	schob (schöbe)	geschoben
schießen	schoss (schösse)	geschossen
schinden	schindete	geschunden
schlafen (du schläfst, er schläft)	schlief	geschlafen
schlagen (du schlägst, er schlägt)	schlug (schlüge)	geschlagen
schleichen	schlich	geschlichen
schleifen[1]	schliff	geschliffen
schließen	schloss (schlösse)	geschlossen
schlingen	schlang (schlänge)	geschlungen
schmeißen	schmiss	geschmissen
schmelzen (du schmilzt, er schmilzt; schmilz!)	schmolz	geschmolzen
schneiden	schnitt	geschnitten
schrecken* (du schrickst, er schrickt; schrick!)	schrak (schräke)	geschreckt
schreiben	schrieb	geschrieben
schreien	schrie	geschrie[e]n
schreiten	schritt	geschritten
schweigen	schwieg	geschwiegen
schwellen (du schwillst, er schwillt; schwill!)	schwoll (schwölle)	geschwollen
schwimmen	schwamm (schwömme, *seltener:* schwämme)	geschwommen
schwinden	schwand (schwände)	geschwunden

Infinitive *Infinitiv*	Preterite *Präteritum*	Past Participle *2. Partizip*
schwingen	schwang (schwänge)	geschwungen
schwören	schwor (schwüre)	geschworen
sehen (du siehst, er sieht; sieh[e]!)	sah (sähe)	gesehen
sein (ich bin, du bist, er ist, wir sind, ihr seid, sie sind; sei!)	war (wäre)	gewesen
senden*	sandte (sendete)	gesandt
sieden*	sott (sötte)	gesotten
singen	sang (sänge)	gesungen
sinken	sank (sänke)	gesunken
sitzen	saß (säße)	gesessen
sollen (ich soll, du sollst, er soll)	sollte	gesollt
spalten*	spaltete	gespalten
speien	spie	gespie[e]n
spinnen	spann (spönne, spänne)	gesponnen
sprechen (du sprichst, er spricht; sprich!)	sprach (spräche)	gesprochen
sprießen	spross (sprösse)	gesprossen
springen	sprang	gesprungen
stechen (du stichst, er sticht; stich!)	stach (stäche)	gestochen
stehen	stand (stünde, *auch:* stände)	gestanden
stehlen (du stiehlst, er stiehlt; stiehl!)	stahl (stähle, *seltener:* stöhle)	gestohlen
steigen	stieg	gestiegen
sterben (du stirbst, er stirbt; stirb!)	starb (stürbe)	gestorben
stinken	stank (stänke)	gestunken
stoßen (du stößt, er stößt)	stieß	gestoßen
streichen	strich	gestrichen
streiten	stritt	gestritten
tragen (du trägst, er trägt)	trug (trüge)	getragen
treffen (du triffst, er trifft; triff!)	traf (träfe)	getroffen
treiben	trieb	getrieben
treten (du trittst, er tritt; tritt!)	trat (träte)	getreten
triefen*	troff (tröffe)	getroffen
trinken	trank (tränke)	getrunken
trügen	trog (tröge)	getrogen
tun	tat (täte)	getan
verderben (du verdirbst, er verdirbt; verdirb!)	verdarb (verdürbe)	verdorben
verdrießen	verdross (verdrösse)	verdrossen
vergessen (du vergisst, er vergisst, vergiss!)	vergaß (vergäße)	vergessen
verlieren	verlor (verlöre)	verloren
verschleißen*	verschliss	verschlissen
verzeihen	verzieh	verziehen
wachsen[1] (du wächst, er wächst)	wuchs (wüchse)	gewachsen
waschen (du wäschst, er wäscht)	wusch (wüsche)	gewaschen
weichen	wich	gewichen
weisen	wies	gewiesen
wenden[2] *	wandte (wendete)	gewandt
werben (du wirbst, er wirbt; wirb!)	warb (würbe)	geworben
werden (du wirst, er wird; werde!)	wurde, *dichter.:* ward (würde)	geworden; *als Hilfsv.:* worden
werfen (du wirfst, er wirft; wirf!)	warf (würfe)	geworfen
wiegen[1]	wog (wöge)	gewogen
winden	wand (wände)	gewunden
wissen (ich weiß, du weißt, er weiß)	wusste (wüsste)	gewusst

Infinitive *Infinitiv*	Preterite *Präteritum*	Past Participle *2. Partizip*
wollen (ich will, du willst, er will)	wollte	gewollt
wringen	wrang (wränge)	gewrungen
ziehen	zog (zöge)	gezogen
zwingen	zwang (zwänge)	gezwungen

English irregular verbs / Englische unregelmäßige Verben

Ein Sternchen (*) weist darauf hin, dass die korrekte Form von der jeweiligen Bedeutung abhängt.

Infinitive *Infinitiv*	Past Tense *Präteritum*	Past Participle *2. Partizip*
arise	arose	arisen
awake	awoke	awoken
be	was *sing.*, were *pl.*	been
bear	bore	borne
beat	beat	beaten
become	became	become
begin	began	begun
bend	bent	bent
bet	bet, betted	bet, betted
bid	*bade, bid	*bidden, bid
bind	bound	bound
bite	bit	bitten
bleed	bled	bled
blow	blew	blown
break	broke	broken
breed	bred	bred
bring	brought	brought
broadcast	broadcast	broadcast
build	built	built
burn	burnt, burned	burnt, burned
burst	burst	burst
bust	bust, busted	bust, busted
buy	bought	bought
cast	cast	cast
catch	caught	caught
choose	chose	chosen
cling	clung	clung
come	came	come
cost	*cost, costed	*cost, costed
creep	crept	crept
cut	cut	cut
deal	dealt	dealt
dig	dug	dug
dive	dived, *(Amer.)* dove	dived
do	did	done
draw	drew	drawn
dream	dreamt, dreamed	dreamt, dreamed
drink	drank	drunk
drive	drove	driven
dwell	dwelt	dwelt
eat	ate	eaten
fall	fell	fallen
feed	fed	fed
feel	felt	felt
fight	fought	fought

Infinitive *Infinitiv*	Past Tense *Präteritum*	Past Participle *2. Partizip*
find	found	found
flee	fled	fled
fling	flung	flung
floodlight	floodlit	floodlit
fly	flew	flown
forbid	forbade, forbad	forbidden
forecast	forecast, forecasted	forecast, forecasted
foretell	foretold	foretold
forget	forgot	forgotten
forgive	forgave	forgiven
forsake	forsook	forsaken
freeze	froze	frozen
get	got	got, *(Amer.)* gotten
give	gave	given
go	went	gone
grind	ground	ground
grow	grew	grown
hang	*hung, hanged	*hung, hanged
have	had	had
hear	heard	heard
hew	hewed	hewn, hewed
hide	hid	hidden
hit	hit	hit
hold	held	held
hurt	hurt	hurt
keep	kept	kept
kneel	knelt, *(esp. Amer.)* kneeled	knelt, *(esp. Amer.)* kneeled
know	knew	known
lay	laid	laid
lead	led	led
lean	leaned, *(Brit.)* leant	leaned, *(Brit.)* leant
leap	leapt, leaped	leapt, leaped
learn	learnt, learned	learnt, learned
leave	left	left
lend	lent	lent
let	let	let
lie[3]	lay	lain
light	lit, lighted	lit, lighted
lose	lost	lost
make	made	made

English irregular verbs

Infinitive *Infinitiv*	Past Tense *Präteritum*	Past Participle *2. Partizip*
mean	meant	meant
meet	met	met
mow	mowed	mown, mowed
overhang	overhung	overhung
pay	paid	paid
prove	proved	proved, proven
put	put	put
quit	quitted, (*Amer.*) quit	quitted, (*Amer.*) quit
read /riːd/	read /red/	read /red/
rid	rid	rid
ride	rode	ridden
ring[3]	rang	rung
rise	rose	risen
run	ran	run
saw	sawed	sawn, sawed
say	said	said
see	saw	seen
seek	sought	sought
sell	sold	sold
send	sent	sent
set	set	set
sew	sewed	sewn, sewed
shake	shook	shaken
shear	sheared	shorn, sheared
shed	shed	shed
shine	shone	shone
shit	shitted, shit	shitted, shit
shoe	shod	shod
shoot	shot	shot
show	showed	shown
shrink	shrank	shrunk
shut	shut	shut
sing	sang	sung
sink	sank, sunk	sunk
sit	sat	sat
slay	slew	slain
sleep	slept	slept
slide	slid	slid
sling	slung	slung
slink	slunk	slunk
slit	slit	slit
smell	smelt, smelled	smelt, smelled
sow	sowed	sown, sowed
speak	spoke	spoken
speed	*sped, speeded	*sped, speeded
spell	spelled, (*Brit.*) spelt	spelled, (*Brit.*) spelt

Infinitive *Infinitiv*	Past Tense *Präteritum*	Past Participle *2. Partizip*
spend	spent	spent
spill	spilt, spilled	spilt, spilled
spin	spun	spun
spit	spat, spit	spat, spit
split	split	split
spoil	spoilt, spoiled	spoilt, spoiled
spread	spread	spread
spring	sprang, (*Amer.*) sprung	sprung
stand	stood	stood
steal	stole	stolen
stick	stuck	stuck
sting	stung	stung
stink	stank, stunk	stunk
strew	strewed	strewed, strewn
stride	strode	stridden
strike	struck	struck
string	strung	strung
strive	strove	striven
sublet	sublet	sublet
swear	swore	sworn
sweep	swept	swept
swell	swelled	swollen, swelled
swim	swam	swum
swing	swung	swung
take	took	taken
teach	taught	taught
tear	tore	torn
tell	told	told
think	thought	thought
thrive	thrived, throve	thrived, thriven
throw	threw	thrown
thrust	thrust	thrust
tread	trod	trodden, trod
understand	understood	understood
undo	undid	undone
wake	woke	woken
wear	wore	worn
weave[1]	wove	woven
weep	wept	wept
wet	wet, wetted	wet, wetted
win	won	won
wind[2] /waɪnd/	wound /waʊnd/	wound /waʊnd/
wring	wrung	wrung
write	wrote	written

Cubic measure / Raummaße

1 cubic centimetre (cc) .... = 0.06 cubic inches
1 Kubikzentimeter (cm³)

1,000,000 cubic centimetres .... = 1 cubic metre (cu. m) .... = 35.714 cubic feet/
1 000 000 Kubikzentimeter .... = *1 Kubikmeter (m³)* .... 1.307 cubic yards

1 cubic inch .... = 16.4 cm³

1,728 cubic inches...................... = 1 cubic foot .... = 0.028 m³

27 cubic feet .... = 1 cubic yard .... = 0.764 m³

Capacity / Hohlmaße

10 millilitres (ml)........................ = 1 centilitre (cl)
10 Milliliter (ml) .... = *1 Zentiliter (cl)*

100 centilitres .... = 1 litre (l) .... = 1.76 pints (2.1 US pints)/
100 Zentiliter.............................. = *1 Liter (l)* .... 0.22 gallons (0.264 US gallons)

4 gills.................................... = 1 pint (pt.) (1.201 US pints) ... = 0.568 l

2 pints .... = 1 quart (qt.) (1.201 US quarts) = 1.136 l

4 quarts.................................. = 1 gallon (gal) (1.201 US gallons) = 4.546 l

Numbers / Zahlen

Cardinal numbers	*Kardinalzahlen*	Ordinal numbers	*Ordinalzahlen*
1 one	1 eins, ein...	1st first	1. erst...
2 two	2 zwei	2nd second	2. zweit...
3 three	3 drei	3rd third	3. dritt...
4 four	4 vier	4th fourth	4. viert...
5 five	5 fünf	5th fifth	5. fünft...
6 six	6 sechs	6th sixth	6. sechst...
7 seven	7 sieben	7th seventh	7. siebt..., siebent...
8 eight	8 acht	8th eighth	8. acht...
9 nine	9 neun	9th ninth	9. neunt...
10 ten	10 zehn	10th tenth	10. zehnt...
11 eleven	11 elf	11th eleventh	11. elft...
12 twelve	12 zwölf	12th twelfth	12. zwölft...
13 thirteen	13 dreizehn	13th thirteenth	13. dreizehnt...
14 fourteen	14 vierzehn	14th fourteenth	14. vierzehnt...
15 fifteen	15 fünfzehn	15th fifteenth	15. fünfzehnt...
16 sixteen	16 sechzehn	16th sixteenth	16. sechzehnt...
17 seventeen	17 siebzehn	17th seventeenth	17. siebzehnt...
18 eighteen	18 achtzehn	18th eighteenth	18. achtzehnt...
19 nineteen	19 neunzehn	19th nineteenth	19. neunzehnt...
20 twenty	20 zwanzig	20th twentieth	20. zwanzigst...
21 twenty-one	21 einundzwanzig	21st twenty-first	21. einundzwanzigst...
30 thirty	30 dreißig	30th thirtieth	30. dreißigst...
40 forty	40 vierzig	40th fortieth	40. vierzigst...
50 fifty	50 fünfzig	50th fiftieth	50. fünfzigst...
60 sixty	60 sechzig	60th sixtieth	60. sechzigst...
70 seventy	70 siebzig	70th seventieth	70. siebzigst...
80 eighty	80 achtzig	80th eightieth	80. achtzigst...
90 ninety	90 neunzig	90th ninetieth	90. neunzigst...
100 one hundred	100 [ein]hundert	100th [one] hundredth	100. [ein]hundertst...
101 one hundred and one	101 [ein]hundert[und]eins	101st [one] hundred and first	101. [ein]hundert[und]erst...
1,000 one thousand	1 000 [ein]tausend	1,000th [one] thousandth	1 000. [ein]tausendst...
1,001 one thousand and one	1 001 [ein]tausend[und]eins	1,001st one thousand and first	1 001. [ein]tausend[und]erst...
10,000 ten thousand	10 000 zehntausend	10,000th ten thousandth	10 000. zehntausendst...
13,438 thirteen thousand, four hundred and thirty-eight	13 438 dreizehntausendvierhundert[und]achtunddreißig	13,438th thirteen thousand, four hundred and thirty-eighth	13 438. dreizehntausendvierhundert[und]achtunddreißigst...
100,000 one hundred thousand	100 000 [ein]hunderttausend	100,000th [one] hundred thousandth	100 000. [ein]hunderttausendst...
1,000,000 one million	1 000 000 eine Million	1,000,000th [one] millionth	1 000 000. millionst...
2,000,000 two million	2 000 000 zwei Millionen	2,000,000th two millionth	2 000 000. zweimillionst...
1,000,000,000 one billion	1 000 000 000 eine Milliarde	1,000,000,000th one billionth	1 000 000 000. milliardst...

Vulgar fractions and mixed numbers / Brüche (gemeine Brüche) und gemischte Zahlen

in figures *in Zahlen*	in words	*in Worten*
1/2	a/one half	*ein halb*
1/3	a/one third	*ein drittel*
1/4	a/one quarter	*ein viertel*
1/10	a/one tenth	*ein zehntel*
2/3	two-thirds	*zwei drittel*
1/1	one over one	*ein eintel*
4/1	four over one	*vier eintel*
m/n	m over n	*m n-tel*
x/6	x over six	*x sechstel*
1 1/2	one and a half	*ein[und]einhalb*

Decimal numbers / Dezimalzahlen

written as	*geschrieben*	spoken as	*gesprochen*
0.1	*0,1*	nought point one	*null Komma eins*
0.015	*0,015*	nought point nought one five	*null Komma null eins fünf*
1.40	*1,40*	one point four o [əʊ]	*eins Komma vier null*

Weights and Measures / Maße und Gewichte

Weight / Gewichte

1,000 milligrams (mg)	= 1 gram (g)	= 15.43 grains
1 000 Milligramm (mg)	= *1 Gramm (g)*	
1,000 grams	= 1 kilogram (kg)	= 2.205 pounds
1 000 Gramm	= *1 Kilogramm (kg)*	
1,000 kilograms	= 1 tonne (t)	= 19.684 hundredweight
1 000 Kilogramm	= *1 Tonne (t)*	
	1 ounce (oz.)	= 28.35 g
16 ounces	= 1 pound (lb.)	= 0.454 kg
14 pounds	= 1 stone (st.)	= 6.35 kg
112 pounds	= 1 hundredweight	= 50.8 kg
20 hundredweight	= 1 ton (t.)	= 1,016.05 kg

Length / Längenmaße

10 millimetres (mm)	= 1 centimetre (cm)	= 0.394 inch
10 Millimeter (mm)	= *1 Zentimeter (cm)*	
100 centimetres	= 1 metre (m)	= 39.4 inches/1.094 yards
100 Zentimeter	= *1 Meter (m)*	
1,000 metres	= 1 kilometre (km)	= 0.6214 mile/ 5/8 mile
1 000 Meter	= 1 Kilometer (km)	
	1 inch (in.)	= 25.4 mm
12 inches	= 1 foot (ft.)	= 30.48 cm
3 feet	= 1 yard (yd.)	= 0.914 m
220 yards	= 1 furlong	= 201.17 m
8 furlongs	= 1 mile (m.)	= 1.609 km
1,760 yards	= 1 mile	= 1.609 km

Square measure / Flächenmaße

100 square metres (sq. m)	= 1 are	= 0.025 acre
100 Quadratmeter (m^2)	= *1 Ar (a)*	
100 ares	= 1 hectare (ha)	= 2.471 acres
100 Ar	= *1 Hektar (ha)*	
100 hectares	= 1 square kilometre (sq.km)	= 0.386 square miles
100 hektar	= *1 Quadratkilometer (km^2)*	
	1 square inch	= 6.452cm^2
144 square inches	= 1 square foot	= 929.03 cm^2
9 square feet	= 1 square yard	= 0.836 m^2
4,840 square yards	= 1 acre	= 0.405 ha
640 acres	= 1 square mile	= 2.59k^2/259 ha

Numbers / Zahlen

Cardinal numbers	*Kardinalzahlen*	Ordinal numbers	*Ordinalzahlen*
1 one	1 eins, ein...	1st first	1. erst...
2 two	2 zwei	2nd second	2. zweit...
3 three	3 drei	3rd third	3. dritt...
4 four	4 vier	4th fourth	4. viert...
5 five	5 fünf	5th fifth	5. fünft...
6 six	6 sechs	6th sixth	6. sechst...
7 seven	7 sieben	7th seventh	7. siebt..., siebent...
8 eight	8 acht	8th eighth	8. acht...
9 nine	9 neun	9th ninth	9. neunt...
10 ten	10 zehn	10th tenth	10. zehnt...
11 eleven	11 elf	11th eleventh	11. elft...
12 twelve	12 zwölf	12th twelfth	12. zwölft...
13 thirteen	13 dreizehn	13th thirteenth	13. dreizehnt...
14 fourteen	14 vierzehn	14th fourteenth	14. vierzehnt...
15 fifteen	15 fünfzehn	15th fifteenth	15. fünfzehnt...
16 sixteen	16 sechzehn	16th sixteenth	16. sechzehnt...
17 seventeen	17 siebzehn	17th seventeenth	17. siebzehnt...
18 eighteen	18 achtzehn	18th eighteenth	18. achtzehnt...
19 nineteen	19 neunzehn	19th nineteenth	19. neunzehnt...
20 twenty	20 zwanzig	20th twentieth	20. zwanzigst...
21 twenty-one	21 einundzwanzig	21st twenty-first	21. einundzwanzigst...
30 thirty	30 dreißig	30th thirtieth	30. dreißigst...
40 forty	40 vierzig	40th fortieth	40. vierzigst...
50 fifty	50 fünfzig	50th fiftieth	50. fünfzigst...
60 sixty	60 sechzig	60th sixtieth	60. sechzigst...
70 seventy	70 siebzig	70th seventieth	70. siebzigst...
80 eighty	80 achtzig	80th eightieth	80. achtzigst...
90 ninety	90 neunzig	90th ninetieth	90. neunzigst...
100 one hundred	100 [ein]hundert	100th [one] hundredth	100. [ein]hundertst...
101 one hundred and one	101 [ein]hundert[und]eins	101st [one] hundred and first	101. [ein]hundert[und]erst...
1,000 one thousand	1 000 [ein]tausend	1,000th [one] thousandth	1 000. [ein]tausendst...
1,001 one thousand and one	1 001 [ein]tausend[und]eins	1,001st one thousand and first	1 001. [ein]tausend[und]erst...
10,000 ten thousand	10 000 zehntausend	10,000th ten thousandth	10 000. zehntausendst...
13,438 thirteen thousand, four hundred and thirty-eight	13 438 dreizehntausendvierhundert[und]achtunddreißig	13,438th thirteen thousand, four hundred and thirty-eighth	13 438. dreizehntausendvierhundert[und]achtunddreißigst...
100,000 one hundred thousand	100 000 [ein]hunderttausend	100,000th [one] hundred thousandth	100 000. [ein]hunderttausendst...
1,000,000 one million	1 000 000 eine Million	1,000,000th [one] millionth	1 000 000. millionst...
2,000,000 two million	2 000 000 zwei Millionen	2,000,000th two millionth	2 000 000. zweimillionst...
1,000,000,000 one billion	1 000 000 000 eine Milliarde	1,000,000,000th one billionth	1 000 000 000. milliardst...

Vulgar fractions and mixed numbers / Brüche (gemeine Brüche) und gemischte Zahlen

in figures *in Zahlen*	in words	*in Worten*
$^1/_2$	a/one half	*ein halb*
$^1/_3$	a/one third	*ein drittel*
$^1/_4$	a/one quarter	*ein viertel*
$^1/_{10}$	a/one tenth	*ein zehntel*
$^2/_3$	two-thirds	*zwei drittel*
$^1/_1$	one over one	*ein eintel*
$^4/_1$	four over one.	*vier eintel*
$^m/_n$	m over n.	*m n-tel*
$^x/_6$	x over six	*x sechstel*
$1\,^1/_2$	one and a half	*ein[und]einhalb*

Decimal numbers / Dezimalzahlen

written as	*geschrieben*	spoken as	*gesprochen*
0.1	*0,1*	nought point one	*null Komma eins*
0.015	*0,015*	nought point nought one five	*null Komma null eins fünf*
1.40	*1,40*	one point four o [əʊ]	*eins Komma vier null*

Weights and Measures / Maße und Gewichte

Weight / Gewichte

1,000 milligrams (mg)	= 1 gram (g)	= 15.43 grains
1 000 Milligramm (mg)	= *1 Gramm (g)*	
1,000 grams	= 1 kilogram (kg)	= 2.205 pounds
1 000 Gramm	= *1 Kilogramm (kg)*	
1,000 kilograms	= 1 tonne (t)	= 19.684 hundredweight
1 000 Kilogramm	= *1 Tonne (t)*	
	1 ounce (oz.)	= 28.35 g
16 ounces	= 1 pound (lb.)	= 0.454 kg
14 pounds	= 1 stone (st.)	= 6.35 kg
112 pounds	= 1 hundredweight	= 50.8 kg
20 hundredweight	= 1 ton (t.)	= 1,016.05 kg

Length / Längenmaße

10 millimetres (mm)	= 1 centimetre (cm)	= 0.394 inch
10 Millimeter (mm)	= *1 Zentimeter (cm)*	
100 centimetres	= 1 metre (m)	= 39.4 inches/1.094 yards
100 Zentimeter	= *1 Meter (m)*	
1,000 metres	= 1 kilometre (km)	= 0.6214 mile/ 5/8 mile
1 000 Meter	= 1 Kilometer (km)	
	1 inch (in.)	= 25.4 mm
12 inches	= 1 foot (ft.)	= 30.48 cm
3 feet	= 1 yard (yd.)	= 0.914 m
220 yards	= 1 furlong	= 201.17 m
8 furlongs	= 1 mile (m.)	= 1.609 km
1,760 yards	= 1 mile	= 1.609 km

Square measure / Flächenmaße

100 square metres (sq. m)	= 1 are	= 0.025 acre
100 Quadratmeter (m^2)	= *1 Ar (a)*	
100 ares	= 1 hectare (ha)	= 2.471 acres
100 Ar	= *1 Hektar (ha)*	
100 hectares	= 1 square kilometre (sq.km)	= 0.386 square miles
100 hektar	= *1 Quadratkilometer (km^2)*	
	1 square inch	= 6.452cm^2
144 square inches	= 1 square foot	= 929.03 cm^2
9 square feet	= 1 square yard	= 0.836 m^2
4,840 square yards	= 1 acre	= 0.405 ha
640 acres	= 1 square mile	= 2.59k^2/259 ha

Cubic measure / Raummaße

1 cubic centimetre (cc)		= 0.06 cubic inches
1 Kubikzentimeter (cm^3)		
1,000,000 cubic centimetres	= 1 cubic metre (cu. m)	= 35.714 cubic feet/
1 000 000 Kubikzentimeter	= *1 Kubikmeter (m^3)*	1.307 cubic yards
	1 cubic inch	= 16.4 cm^3
1,728 cubic inches	= 1 cubic foot	= 0.028 m^3
27 cubic feet	= 1 cubic yard	= 0.764 m^3

Capacity / Hohlmaße

10 millilitres (ml)	= 1 centilitre (cl)	
10 Milliliter (ml)	= *1 Zentiliter (cl)*	
100 centilitres	= 1 litre (l)	= 1.76 pints (2.1 US pints)/
100 Zentiliter	= *1 Liter (l)*	0.22 gallons (0.264 US gallons)
4 gills	= 1 pint (pt.) (1.201 US pints)	= 0.568 l
2 pints	= 1 quart (qt.) (1.201 US quarts)	= 1.136 l
4 quarts	= 1 gallon (gal) (1.201 US gallons)	= 4.546 l